PENGUIN BOOKS

## Roget's Thesaurus

George Davidson is a former s          Chambers Harrap. In
addition to writing dictionaries a        uses, he is the author of five
books on English grammar, usage,       ...ing and vocabulary. He lives in
Edinburgh.

# Roget's Thesaurus
## of English words and phrases

GEORGE DAVIDSON

PENGUIN BOOKS

PENGUIN BOOKS

Published by the Penguin Group
Penguin Books Ltd, 80 Strand, London WC2R 0RL, England
Penguin Putnam Inc., 375 Hudson Street, New York, New York 10014, USA
Penguin Books Australia Ltd, 250 Camberwell Road, Camberwell, Victoria 3124, Australia
Penguin Books Canada Ltd, 10 Alcorn Avenue, Toronto, Ontario, Canada M4V 3B2
Penguin Books India (P) Ltd, 11, Community Centre, Panchsheel Park, New Delhi – 110 017, India
Penguin Books (NZ) Ltd, Cnr Rosedale and Airborne Roads, Albany, Auckland, New Zealand
Penguin Books (South Africa) (Pty) Ltd, 24 Sturdee Avenue, Rosebank 2196, South Africa

Penguin Books Ltd, Registered Offices: 80 Strand, London WC2R 0RL, England

www.penguin.com

Roget, Roget's and Rogets are registered trademarks of Longman Group UK Limited

First edition by Peter Mark Roget 1852
New and enlarged edition by John Lewis Roget 1879
New edition prepared by Samuel Romilly Roget 1933
New edition revised and modernized by Robert A. Dutch OBE 1962
New edition prepared by Susan A. Lloyd 1982
New edition prepared by Betty Kirkpatrick 1987
New edition prepared by Betty Kirkpatrick 1998
150th anniversary edition edited by George Davidson 2002
Paperback edition edited by George Davidson 2003
1

This edition copyright © Longman Group UK Limited, 1962, 1982, 1987, 1998, 2002, 2003
New material in the 1998 and 2002 editions copyright © Penguin Books, 1998, 2002

Set in 7.5/9.5 pt PostScript ITC Stone
Typeset by Rowland Phototypesetting Ltd, Bury St Edmunds, Suffolk
Printed and Bound in England by Clays Ltd, St Ives plc

A CIP catalogue record for this book is available from the British Library

HARDBACK ISBN 0-141-00442-8
PAPERBACK ISBN 0-140-51502-X

# Contents

# Editor's Preface to the 150th Anniversary Edition

*Roget's Thesaurus* is now one hundred and fifty years old.

What was eventually to become the *Thesaurus* began life as a simple notebook of words and phrases that Peter Mark Roget collected for his own personal use, as an aid to expressing himself well as a writer and lecturer. Recognizing that others too might find such a book useful, and that it constituted a 'desideratum hitherto unsupplied' in English or any other language, Roget spent the first four years of his retirement expanding and systematizing the material in his notebook into the *Thesaurus of English Words and Phrases*, which was published in 1852 in a first edition of 1000 copies.

First reactions to the book were mixed. Not everyone recognized the purpose and value of the work, nor how it would be used. One reviewer, however, did perceive that Roget would one day 'rank with Samuel Johnson as a literary instrument-maker of the first class', a prophecy that time has certainly confirmed. In the past century and a half, the *Thesaurus* has sold over 30 million copies and has become a national and international institution, one of the best-known and best-loved reference books in English. Possession of a *Thesaurus* has even been taken as a mark of good character, as evidenced by Sir J. M. Barrie's description of Captain Hook, the pirate captain in *Peter Pan*:

The man is not wholly evil – he has a *Thesaurus* in his cabin.

The original purpose of the book was clearly stated on its title page: it was to 'facilitate the expression of ideas and assist in literary composition'. This is still the main purpose of the *Thesaurus* today. Given an idea or concept that we wish to express, the *Thesaurus* helps us to find the word or words with which to express it. Far more than a mere synonym dictionary, it is a truly creative reference work that allows its users to both clarify and embody their thoughts. Because of the way in which it is structured, it allows readers either to home in quickly on the exact word or phrase they want or else to browse at leisure in search of ideas and expressions.

However, helping people to write and speak with accuracy and elegance is no longer the sole function of the *Thesaurus*, and has not been for some eighty years now. Since Roget's death in 1869, a new market for his book, completely unknown in his day, has developed – the world of the crossword puzzle. *Roget* is now not only the speaker and writer's companion, it is also the crossword-solver's friend. Beginning in the United States in 1913 and reaching the United Kingdom in the 1920s, the crossword-puzzle craze created a new demand for dictionaries and other word-books, and especially for the *Thesaurus*. The *New York Times Magazine* in 1925 named Roget the 'Saint of

Crosswordia' and described the *Thesaurus* as an 'efficacious poultice for [the] aching brow' of the crossword-puzzler. And so it remains to this day.

What changes have been made to the text of the *Thesaurus* since it was first published? In its structure, very few. The classification system that Roget devised for the original book is still in use in this Anniversary Edition, although over the years some new units have been added to the text and a few others, no longer felt to be useful, have been removed. From the 1962 edition on, units expressing opposites, or 'correlative' terms, as Roget called them, have no longer been set in columns next to one another on the page, as they had been until then, but instead are set consecutively throughout the book. Readers may, therefore, still easily find opposites, not by looking across the page, as in the earlier editions of the *Thesaurus*, but by referring backwards or forwards through the text to preceding or following units.

The main change to the *Thesaurus* over the past hundred and fifty years has, of course, been the huge increase in vocabulary coverage. Few words have been deleted from the text – some extremely rare or archaic words have been dropped, along with a few Latin tags that, while doubtless familiar to Roget and his contemporaries, have since fallen into disuse – but of course much has been added to reflect the changes in both science and society since 1852. And while it is only four years since the last edition of *Roget* was published, many new words have come into common use in English in that time. The coverage of terms connected with computing and the Internet, for example, is twice as large in this edition as it was in 1998, and many other recent changes to our world find expression for the first time in this new edition of *Roget*: from biotechnology (for example, *genetically modified organisms, Frankenstein food, golden rice* and *terminator seeds*) to beauty treatments (*acid peel, Botox, bus-stop surgery, laser resurfacing* and *micro-dermabrasion*), from the problems and scourges of the modern world (*air rage, noise pollution, blast bombs, election fatigue, elder abuse, rolling roadblocks, sink estates, sudden wealth syndrome, white van man* and *reality TV*) to those who attempt to escape from them (*economic migrant, asylum-seeker* and *health tourist*) and some ways of doing so (*shopping therapy, decluttering, duvet days* and *lifestyle drugs*), *Roget* is now up to date with the vocabulary of the early twenty-first century. Americanisms, too, have not been neglected, and a number have been added in this edition, among which are *battlefield detainee, brown-nose, cockamamie, fess up, go ape-shit, gross out, Kwanzaa, lethal injection, mixologist, wake up and smell the coffee* and *way to go*.

Perhaps Peter Roget would have rejected some of the more recent additions to the *Thesaurus* as 'new-fangled' words, coined unnecessarily by modern writers 'in the illegal mint of their own fancy' and doing 'manifest injury to the purity of the language' (see page xxvii), but to serve its purpose the *Thesaurus* must always keep up with the latest developments in vocabulary, passing no judgements on the usefulness or otherwise of lexical innovations that are, of course, completely beyond its control, but seeking only to record them and to offer them to its readers for their consideration.

There are two innovations in this Anniversary Edition of the *Thesaurus*: the literary quotations and the text boxes. As regards the literary quotations, it is probably true that even the very well educated nowadays are less familiar with the Bible, Shakespeare and English literature in general than those of a similar level of education would have been in previous generations, and certainly much less so than Roget's contemporaries would have been. For this reason, it was felt that including quotations and their sources, and where necessary also translations, to show the origin of many of the expressions included in *Roget* would be both of interest and of benefit to present-day readers. The text boxes, on the other hand, have been introduced in order to allow greater coverage than was previously, possible of particular areas of vocabulary (such as group nouns and phobias), without thereby interrupting the flow of the main text.

Born of an idea that Peter Mark Roget first had some two hundred years ago, and first published a hundred and fifty years ago, *Roget's Thesaurus* has stood the test of time and has become an invaluable language resource in households, offices and libraries throughout the English-speaking world. While there may now be other thesauruses and word-finders on the market, for the twenty-first century, as for the nineteenth and twentieth centuries, 'the *Thesaurus*' is still *Roget*.

GWD
July 2002

# Dr Peter Mark Roget and his Thesaurus

The name of Roget has become synonymous with the *Thesaurus*, yet Dr Roget himself is a shadowy figure. This is rather surprising as he played an active part in the intellectual, scientific and social life of his time, besides achieving some eminence in his own profession of medicine. It is also ironic that one who made such an important contribution to the study and practice of the English language should have so little English blood in his veins. His father, Jean Roget, was a Genevan pastor only recently come to Britain, while his mother's grandfather was a French Huguenot who had fled to London after the revocation of the Edict of Nantes. Roget's early years were spent in the French Protestant community, where he absorbed liberal ideas and a belief in the perfectibility of man, which was soon shaken, however, by the aftermath of the French Revolution.

Jean Roget died when his son was only four, so the young Roget was brought up by his mother Catherine, with some financial and moral support from her brother, the famous law reformer Sir Samuel Romilly. Catherine was strongly influenced by the ideas on education of Jean Roget's countryman Jean Jacques Rousseau, and went to great lengths to try to find the ideal environment for her son, even moving to Edinburgh when he was fourteen so that he could complete his education at the university there, considered superior to Oxford and Cambridge, and especially so for mathematics and science. These were Roget's absorbing interests, and remained so throughout his life. However, science was not yet a safe or lucrative career for a young man, and Roget finally took his degree in medicine and became a doctor.

In later life, Roget appears to us as rather a staid, unimaginative figure, but as a young man he found himself in some far from staid situations. He spent some time at Bristol observing Dr Beddoes's and Humphrey Davy's experiments with laughing gas at the famous Clifton 'Pneumatic Institution'. He also worked for a while for Jeremy Bentham on a project for a 'Frigidarium'. The unconventionality of the Bentham household soon led him to leave, but he was influenced all his life by Bentham's ideas of Utilitarianism and the happiness of the greatest number. Perhaps his most exciting adventure was when he took two young boys from Manchester on their 'Grand Tour' of Europe. This was during 1802–3, and when the fragile entente between Britain and France broke with the collapse of the Peace of Amiens, Roget and his charges were trapped in Geneva. He showed great ingenuity and persistence in getting them safely away, and only just in time: his friend Edgeworth did not succeed in escaping, and was imprisoned for eleven years.

On his return to England, Roget began to practise as a doctor, gaining experience in Manchester before settling in London, where he had a house in Barnard Street, Bloomsbury. His lively mind, his eagerness to become part of the ferment of scientific life of the capital, and his willingness to work hard quickly made him acceptable in intellectual circles. Only five years after his arrival, he was elected a Fellow of the prestigious Royal Society, of which he was later Secretary for twenty years. This was just the beginning of a long and energetic working life, both as a doctor and a scientist. Roget's medical skills were soon being called upon by people he knew socially and he quickly built up a considerable practice. He was also instrumental in setting up a charity clinic, the Northern Dispensary, where he treated needy patients free of charge. He added to his medical reputation by giving lectures to medical students and writing papers for the Medical and Chirurgical Society, of which he soon became Secretary. This involved him in editing their Transactions and classifying the library. Roget's reputation as a doctor was such that in 1823 he was one of the doctors appointed to investigate the Millbank prison epidemic. Later, he was called in to head a Commission to investigate London's water supply. One of his recommendations, that of sand filtration, is still in use today.

The crowning point of Roget's medical career came in 1831, with his election as Fellow *speciali grata* to the Royal College of Physicians. For many men such a distinguished career would have been enough. But simultaneously with his work as a doctor, Roget was also strenuously pursuing his other love, science. Besides his work for the Royal Society, he was a member, and frequently an active member, of many of the learned societies then proliferating in London. It was an exciting time, a time of discoveries, experiments and inventions, a time when the flood of new knowledge was leading inevitably to the specialization that is even more marked today. Societies were therefore formed to deal with separate branches of science, the Zoological Society, the Royal Geographical Society, the Royal Astronomical Society and so on. Roget, a polymath, like many of his generation, belonged to a number of them, writing papers on every aspect of knowledge, from insects to electricity. He also conducted his own experiments, and enjoyed inventing mathematical and optical devices. This was not mere amateur tinkering: Roget's reputation as a scientist was as high as his reputation as a doctor. Some of Roget's inventions, indeed, still affect us today. It was Roget who invented the log-log scale still used on modern slide rules. It was this which secured his entry to the Royal Society. Always busy with new ideas, he left it to others to explore the possibilities of his inventions or observations. It was the same with his paper on the effects of seeing a moving object through slats – in this case a carriage wheel seen through the venetian blinds in his basement. Roget had noticed that an image appeared to be retained on the retina for a fraction of time after it had disappeared from sight. This discovery was taken up by other scientists, notably Faraday, and eventually led to the making of moving pictures and the cinema industry.

With all this activity, Roget still found time to read voraciously, including works in French, Latin, German and Italian, and to amuse himself by the setting and solving of chess problems. Moreover, he was no recluse. He enjoyed dining with friends, going to the theatre and, especially after his marriage in 1824, strolling or driving round the London parks and squares, noting the new buildings and other improvements. He was an affectionate father to his two children, Kate and John, and with his wife Mary took great pleasure in their education.

Writing and lecturing took up a good deal of Roget's time. He was eager to communicate knowledge to as wide a public as possible, and took a professional pride in his lectures, which were very popular, especially in an age of self-improvement. He lectured for thirty years at the Russell Institution, where he was appointed Fullerian Professor of Physiology, and also gave courses at the Royal Institution, a signal honour. But it was typical of Roget that he should also be one of the founders of the Society for the Diffusion of Useful Knowledge, which issued sixpenny treatises in simple English on such subjects as electricity and magnetism. Of Roget's involvement with this Society, its publisher wrote:

Amongst the founders of the Society, Dr Roget was, from his accepted high reputation, the most eminent of its men of science. . . . He was a diligent attendant on its committees; a vigilant corrector of its proofs. Of most winning manners, he was as beloved as he was respected . . .[1]

Less ephemeral than such treatises, but also with a lay audience in mind, were Roget's articles for the *Encyclopedia Britannica*. These included a major piece on his speciality, physiology, and shorter ones on subjects ranging from ants and bees to phrenology (on which he poured scorn), and from the education of the deaf and dumb to the kaleidoscope. These, with several brief biographies of European scientists, were first published in the Supplement to the 4th, 5th and 6th Editions, but were often reprinted in a shortened form in later editions, though without acknowledgment. Roget's other major publication (apart from the *Thesaurus*) was much praised by his contemporaries, who thought it would carry his name to posterity. This was *Animal and Vegetable Physiology considered with reference to Natural Theology*, one of eight similar works commissioned by the Earl of Bridgewater to propound 'the power, wisdom and goodness of God, as manifested in the creation'. The world view it expressed, however, was already being challenged when it was published in 1834, and though it went through several editions, Roget's monumental work is no longer remembered.

Ironically, the work which did make him known to later generations, the *Thesaurus of English Words and Phrases*, was a product of Roget's retirement. Ousted from his Secretaryship of the Royal Society by a younger and more adventurous group of scientists, he found himself with unwonted leisure, and promptly began to devote himself to the conclusion of a project he had nursed for many years: the classification and organization of the English language. This may seem a strange preoccupation for a scientist and mathematician, but it was in many ways a task which Roget was uniquely equipped to carry out. All his life he had been concerned with order, with marshalling a mass of facts or observations into a meaningful form which both expressed their special qualities and reaffirmed their unity. He had done this, in particular, in his Bridgewater Treatise, where he had set out Natural History in all its variety, while showing the close links between the parts, and claiming that the whole revealed the design of the Creator. His involvement with the classification of the libraries of the Medical and Chirurgical Society, and of the Royal Society, had also been valuable experience. As a doctor, his preference had been for anatomy and physiology, subjects which by their very nature involved dissection and classification. It was the organization of knowledge (rather than the making of profound discoveries, for which he

---

1 D. L. Emblen, *Peter Mark Roget* (London 1970), p. 187.

lacked the imagination), that was Roget's forte, and which he was able to put to good use in compiling the *Thesaurus*. Then again, his lifelong belief in progress and utilitarianism were served by the book, which he hoped would enable people to communicate with each other more easily and effectively. Roget had always been concerned with communicating knowledge and was more concerned with this aspect of language than with beauties of style. Though a Renaissance man in the variety of his interests, literature for its own sake seems to have held little attraction for him: he was more concerned with facts and ideas. Though the *Thesaurus* is often used nowadays to achieve a polished style, Roget's intention for it was chiefly utilitarian and philo-sophical, as he made plain in his Introduction.

The *Thesaurus* began as a notebook Roget had carried round with him from his earliest lecturing days. In it he made lists of related words and phrases in various orders to help him express himself in the best possible way. Now, in his seventies, he was able to draw on a lifetime's experience of lecturing, writing and editing to make these lists into a coherent system available for others to use. It took him four years, longer than he had thought, and required all his organizational skills and the meticulous attention to detail that had characterized his editing work. Not only did the *Thesaurus* utilize all Roget's competences, it also fulfilled a need for him: the need, in a society changing with frightening speed, where the old moral and religious order was increasingly in question, to reaffirm order, stability and unity, and through them the purpose of a universal, supernatural authority.

Even with the publication of his *Thesaurus* when he was seventy-one, Roget did not cease from his labours. He continued to note improvements and prepare new editions as well as pursuing many other projects. He died in his ninety-first year at West Malvern secure in the knowledge that the work which summed up all his achievements in a long and productive life had gained public acceptance and proved its worth.

## The Thesaurus

Roget's *Thesaurus of English Words and Phrases* was first published by Longman, Brown, Green, and Longmans in May 1852, selling at 14 shillings. It was a handsome volume, a generous octavo, printed on good quality paper, with the text well spaced-out. The Heads numbered exactly one thousand, and were printed in two columns, positive Heads facing their negatives or correlatives. This layout, which Roget explained in his *Introduction* (see pp. xxiii–xxv), was retained in the copyright edition until 1962. The text was divided into the six Classes, each Class beginning a new page, with double column headings. Within each Head, the words given were sorted into parts of speech, and grouped according to ideas. Roget made a point of including phrases and idioms (see his *Introduction*, pp. xxiii), though these were not included in the Index. The vocabulary reflected Roget's wide knowledge, and the many classical and literary allusions, with some examples from the theatre of the day, could be expected to be familiar to all educated men and women. The work still bears some signs of being adapted from a private compilation to one for public use; explanatory subtitles were subjoined to the Class and Section titles, and sometimes to the Head titles as well, while footnotes frequently drew the reader's attention to points of interest or usage.

The success of the first edition (of only one thousand copies) led to a second in March 1853 and a third, described as 'a cheaper edition, enlarged and improved'[1], which sold for half a guinea, in February 1855. This edition was stereotyped, and used as the basis for the frequent subsequent printings until the plates were worn out. For the 1855 edition, Roget rewrote parts of the text, added 'many thousand' new expressions, and introduced a number of subsidiary Heads, labelled (a), to fill gaps which he had noticed in his scheme. Though the new duodecimo volume necessitated smaller type and a less spacious-looking format, Roget welcomed it in his *Advertisement to the third edition* as 'more portable and convenient'. The fame of the *Thesaurus* appears to have crossed the Atlantic, as he notes with some asperity that 'in the course of last summer, an imperfect edition of this work was published at Boston, in the United States of America, in which the editor, among other mutilations, has altogether omitted the Phrases . . . and has removed from the body of the work all the words and expressions borrowed from a foreign language, throwing them into an Appendix, where . . . they are completely lost to the inquirer'. The American edition[2] was the first of many imitations of Roget's work, both at home and abroad.

Roget continued to collect new words and expressions for his *Thesaurus* until his death in 1869. He noted them in the margins of his copy, planning to use them in a new enlarged edition. This duly appeared ten years later, thanks to the labours of his son, John Lewis Roget, MA. A lawyer, who was active in art circles as a critic and watercolourist, and later wrote the history of the Old Water-Colour Society (1891), John Roget modestly disclaimed in his Preface any special qualifications for his task, claiming that it was 'almost entirely of a practical nature, demanding industry and attention, rather than philosophic culture or the learning of a philologist'. Without changing Roget's system of classification in any way, he nevertheless made a distinctive contribution of his own to the evolution of the *Thesaurus*. Discovering that the sheer number of additions, both his father's and his own, threatened to overload the different Heads and blur the distinctions made between them, he extended the system of cross-references already present in embryo, and gave this policy a sound linguistic basis by observing that 'the fabric of our language has become a texture woven into one by the interlacing of countless branches, springing from separate stems'. To place each word in only one of its possible locations would be to lose much of the richness of the language, but to insert it under every suitable Head would lead to ideas being lost in a welter of words. The system of cross-references was the ideal compromise between too much or too little repetition, and has been adopted and extended by successive editors.

John Roget's other major contribution to the development of the *Thesaurus* was his recognition of the importance of the Index. Roget himself had thought of it only as a last resort – his original notebook had not had one. John Roget, however, noted in his Preface to the 1879 edition: 'I believe that almost everyone who uses the book finds it more convenient to have recourse to the Index first.' He accordingly expanded it to include for the first time not only all the words in the text, but also most of the phrases. The index, now in four columns rather than three, took up very nearly half of the new edition, which had also expanded from the original 418 pages to 646 of smaller, close-set print, in a rather smaller octavo size.

Frequent reprints of the *Thesaurus*, revised by John Roget, continued to be issued by

---

1 Samuel R. Roget, in the Preface to the 1933 edition.
2 Probably that by Rev. B. Sears (Boston 1854)

the publishers, now known as Longmans & Co., until the former's death in 1908. New words added to the text were listed in a supplementary index, bringing the book up to 670 pages. These additions reflect the topics of the day – 'veldt', 'outspan' and 'Afrikander' from Southern Africa, weapons such as 'Lee-Metford rifle' and 'Gatling gun', with the appearance of 'electrolier', 'lorry' and 'motor car'.

Samuel Romilly Roget, John's son, now took on the editorship. He was an electrical engineer who had something of his grandfather's gift for popularizing, publishing among other works a *Dictionary of Electrical Terms*[1] which was still in print twenty years later. He greatly expanded the vocabulary of the book, and extended the system of cross-references, but made no changes to the layout. His energetic promotion of the *Thesaurus* in papers such as *The Times* kept it in the public eye and helped to consolidate it as an English institution. The great crossword-puzzle boom soon generated a new class of Roget-user, and editions followed each other with great rapidity. From a printing about every other year, between 1890 and 1908, there was at least one a year from 1911 to 1929, and five printings in 1925, when Samuel Roget brought out his own new enlarged version. A New York edition was published in 1933, containing many expressions 'in commoner use in America than in England'. This seems to have been the same edition to appear in 1936 at home. The importance of the Index was now well-established: Roget noted in his Preface that it had been checked line by line for the 1936 edition. New plates were made and used for frequent reprints, even during the war years. In 1953, a Penguin paperback *Thesaurus* appeared.

Samuel Roget sold the family rights to Longmans, Green & Co., in 1952, and with his death in 1953, the family connection with the *Thesaurus* came to an end. The publishers commissioned Robert A. Dutch OBE, sometime Senior Scholar of Christ's College, Cambridge, to prepare a new edition, bringing *Roget's Thesaurus*, still much in the form the author had left it, up to date.

The new editor had to adapt the *Thesaurus* to users whose needs and background were rather different to those of the first generation of Roget readers a hundred years or so earlier. The philosophical interest in classification and analysis of words and their relationships, which had played an important part in Roget's conception of his book, already relegated to second place by his son John's extension of the Index, was now thought to be of negligible interest to most modern readers, who looked on the work as a purely practical aid in communication. The system of classification, therefore, though still the basis of the book, became latent rather than apparent in the text. While keeping the two-column layout, Heads were now printed consecutively instead of opposite each other, without any visual reminder of their relationship other than their consecutiveness. Classes and Sections were not labelled or separated in any way, the Heads following each other without a break. The original titles and subtitles were listed in the Tabular Synopsis for reference and this too was printed consecutively, rather than in columns showing Roget's three categories of positive, negative and intermediate.

Robert Dutch's revision resulted in the *Thesaurus* familiar to us today. He rewrote the whole text, within Roget's Heads, aiming to make each group of related words follow each other in a logical sequence, so that 'the mind is led by easy transitions

---

1 London 1924.

from one nuance to another without distraction' (Preface, p. xii in the 1962 edition). Heads which had shown their superfluity by wasting away in successive revisions were absorbed elsewhere, thus reducing the number of Heads to 990. Other Heads whose titles had become obscure were renamed. But perhaps Robert Dutch's happiest idea was the invention of *keywords*. The *keyword*, the word in italics at the beginning of each paragraph, whose use is explained on page xxxix, showed readers where to begin their search for the right word within the Head. Its use to identify paragraphs in cross-references and in the Index at once standardized references and enabled readers to pick out the most suitable of several locations for the meaning they sought.

There can be little doubt that revisions will continue to be called for, as the never-ending task of inserting new vocabulary and reassessing the existing word-stock continues, so that *Roget's Thesaurus* may continue to serve future generations as well as it has done past ones. With the dawn of the electronic age, however, the possibilities become very exciting. All editors of *Roget* have had in the past to exclude many items for lack of space. The data bank of a computer knows no such limitations. Every new use of every word could be fed in, thus creating a thesaurus that was continually updated. When every home has its own computer terminal, the *Roget* user would have the resources of such a thesaurus at his or her fingertips. Every item, moreover, could be listed in the Index. Even this, however, does not exhaust the possibilities. Roget's original dream could be fulfilled: since a thesaurus consists of concepts first, then words, any language in the world can be analysed according to Roget's Classification and thus added to the data bank. Such a multilingual thesaurus would have more than merely practical appliances: it would greatly assist international understanding. It might even be the imperfect forerunner of that Universal Language to which Roget and his fellow reformists aspired, which would help to bring about a golden age of union and harmony.[1]

---

**1** See the Introduction to the first edition, p. xxx–xxxi.

## Preface to the first edition, 1852

It is now nearly fifty years since I first projected a system of verbal classification similar to that on which the present Work is founded. Conceiving that such a compilation might help to supply my own deficiencies, I had, in the year 1805, completed a classed catalogue of words on a small scale, but on the same principle, and nearly in the same form, as the Thesaurus now published. I had often during that long interval found this little collection, scanty and imperfect as it was, of much use to me in literary composition, and often contemplated its extension and improvement; but a sense of the magnitude of the task, amidst a multitude of other avocations, deterred me from the attempt. Since my retirement from the duties of Secretary of the Royal Society, however, finding myself possessed of more leisure, and believing that a repertory of which I had myself experienced the advantage might, when amplified, prove useful to others, I resolved to embark in an undertaking which, for the last three or four years, has given me incessant occupation, and has, indeed, imposed upon me an amount of labour very much greater than I had anticipated. Notwithstanding all the pains I have bestowed on its execution, I am fully aware of its numerous deficiencies and imperfections, and of its falling far short of the degree of excellence that might be attained. But, in a work of this nature, where perfection is placed at so great a distance; I have thought it best to limit my ambition to that moderate share of merit which it may claim in its present form; trusting to the indulgence of those for whose benefit it is intended, and to the candour of critics who, while they find it easy to detect faults, can at the same time duly appreciate difficulties.

P.M. Roget
29 April, 1852.

# Introduction to the first edition, 1852

*Unbracketed footnotes are by Peter Mark Roget. Footnotes within brackets are attributed as follows: [JLR] – John Lewis Roget; [SRR] – Samuel Romilly Roget; [RAD] – Robert A. Dutch; [SML] – Susan M. Lloyd. Not all later footnotes have been retained.*

The present Work is intended to supply, with respect to the English language, a desideratum hitherto unsupplied in any language; namely, a collection of the words it contains and of the idiomatic combinations peculiar to it, arranged, not in alphabetical order as they are in a Dictionary, but according to the *ideas* which they express. The purpose of an ordinary Dictionary is simply to explain the meaning of the words: and the problem of which it professes to furnish the solution may be stated thus: – The word being given, to find its signification, or the idea it is intended to convey. The object aimed at in the present undertaking is exactly the converse of this: namely, – The idea being given, to find the word, or words, by which that idea may be most fitly and aptly expressed. For this purpose, the words and phrases of the language are here classed, not according to their sound or their orthography, but strictly according to their *signification*.

The communication of our thoughts by means of language, whether spoken or written, like every other object of mental exertion, constitutes a peculiar art, which, like other arts, cannot be acquired in any perfection but by long and continued practice. Some, indeed, there are more highly gifted than others with a facility of expression, and naturally endowed with the power of eloquence; but to none is it at all times an easy process to embody, in exact and appropriate language, the various trains of ideas that are passing through the mind, or to depict in their true colours and proportions, the diversified and nicer shades of feeling which accompany them. To those who are unpractised in the art of composition, or unused to extempore speaking, these difficulties present themselves in their most formidable aspect. However distinct may be our views, however vivid our conceptions, or however fervent our emotions, we cannot but be often conscious that the phraseology we have at our command is inadequate to do them justice. We seek in vain the words we need, and strive ineffectually to devise forms of expression which shall faithfully portray our thoughts and sentiments. The appropriate terms, notwithstanding our utmost efforts, cannot be conjured up at will. Like 'spirits from the vasty deep', they come not when we call; and we are driven to the employment of a set of words and phrases either too general or too limited, too strong or too feeble, which suit not the occasion, which hit not the mark we aim at; and the result of our prolonged exertion is a style at once laboured and obscure, vapid and redundant, or vitiated by the still graver faults of affectation or ambiguity.

It is to those who are thus painfully groping their way and struggling with the difficulties of composition, that this Work professes to hold out a helping hand. The assistance it gives is that of furnishing on every topic a copious store of words and phrases, adapted to express all the recognizable shades and modifications of the general idea under which those words and phrases are arranged. The inquirer can readily select, out of the ample collection spread out before his eyes in the following pages, those expressions which are best suited to his purpose, and which might not have occurred to him without such assistance. In order to make this selection, he scarcely ever need engage in any critical or elaborate study of the subtle distinction existing between synonymous terms; for if the materials set before him be sufficiently abundant, an instinctive tact will rarely fail to lead him to the proper choice. Even while glancing over the columns of this Work, his eye may chance to light upon a particular term, which may save the cost of a clumsy paraphrase, or spare the labour of a tortuous circumlocution. Some felicitous turn of expression thus introduced will frequently open to the mind of the reader a whole vista of collateral ideas, which could not, without an extended and obtrusive episode, have been unfolded to his view; and often will the judicious insertion of a happy epithet, like a beam of sunshine in a landscape, illumine and adorn the subject which it touches, imparting new grace and giving life and spirit to the picture.

Every workman in the exercise of his art should be provided with proper implements. For the fabrication of complicated and curious pieces of mechanism, the artisan requires a corresponding assortment of various tools and instruments. For giving proper effect to the fictions of the drama, the actor should have at his disposal a well-furnished wardrobe, supplying the costumes best suited to the personages he is to represent. For the perfect delineation of the beauties of nature, the painter should have within reach of his pencil every variety and combination of hues and tints. Now, the writer, as well as the orator, employs for the accomplishment of his purposes the instrumentality of words; it is in words that he clothes his thoughts; it is by means of words that he depicts his feelings. It is therefore essential to his success that he be provided with a copious vocabulary, and that he possess an entire command of all the resources and appliances of his language. To the acquisition of this power no procedure appears more directly conducive than the study of a methodized system such as that now offered to his use.

The utility of the present Work will be appreciated more especially by those who are engaged in the arduous process of translating into English a Work written in another language. Simple as the operation may appear, on a superficial view, of rendering into English each of its sentences, the task of transfusing, with perfect exactness, the sense of the original, preserving at the same time the style and character of its composition, and reflecting with fidelity the mind and the spirit of the author, is a task of extreme difficulty. The cultivation of this useful department of literature was in ancient times strongly recommended both by Cicero and by Quintilian, as essential to the formation of a good writer and accomplished orator. Regarded simply as a mental exercise, the practice of translation is the best training for the attainment of that mastery of language and felicity of diction, which are the sources of the highest oratory, and are requisite for the possession of a graceful and persuasive eloquence. By rendering ourselves the faithful interpreters of the thoughts and feelings of others, we are rewarded with the acquisition of greater readiness and facility in correctly expressing our own; as he who has best learned to execute the orders of a commander, becomes himself best qualified to command.

In the earliest periods of civilization, translators have been the agents for propagating knowledge from nation to nation, and the value of their labours has been inestimable; but, in the present age, when so many different languages have become the depositories of the vast treasures of literature and of science which have been accumulating for centuries, the utility of accurate translations has greatly increased, and it has become a more important object to attain perfection in the art.

The use of language is not confined to its being the medium through which we communicate our ideas to one another; it fulfils a no less important function as an *instrument of thought*; not being merely its vehicle, but giving it wings for flight. Metaphysicians are agreed that scarcely any of our intellectual operations could be carried on to any considerable extent, without the agency of words. None but those who are conversant with the philosophy of mental phenomena, can be aware of the immense influence that is exercised by language in promoting the development of our ideas, in fixing them in the mind, and in detaining them for steady contemplation. Into every process of reasoning, language enters as an essential element. Words are the instruments by which we form all our abstractions, by which we fashion and embody our ideas, and by which we are enabled to glide along a series of premises and con- clusions with a rapidity so great as to leave in the memory no trace of the successive steps of the process; and we remain unconscious how much we owe to this potent auxiliary of the reasoning faculty. It is on this ground, also, that the present Work founds a claim to utility. The review of a catalogue of words of analogous signification, will often suggest by association other trains of thought, which, presenting the subject under new and varied aspects, will vastly expand the sphere of our mental vision. Amidst the many objects thus brought within the range of our contemplation, some striking similitude or appropriate image, some excursive flight or brilliant conception, may flash on the mind, giving point and force to our arguments, awakening a respon- sive chord in the imagination or sensibility of the reader, and procuring for our reasonings a more ready access both to his understanding and to his heart.

It is of the utmost consequence that strict accuracy should regulate our use of language, and that every one should acquire the power and the habit of expressing his thoughts with perspicuity and correctness. Few, indeed, can appreciate the real extent and importance of that influence which language has always exercised on human affairs, or can be aware how often these are determined by causes much slighter than are apparent to a superficial observer. False logic, disguised under specious phraseology, too often gains the assent of the unthinking multitude, disseminating far and wide the seeds of prejudice and error. Truisms pass current, and wear the semblance of profound wisdom, when dressed up in the tinsel garb of antithetical phrases, or set off by an imposing pomp of paradox. By a confused jargon of involved and mystical sentences, the imagination is easily inveigled into a transcendental region of clouds, and the understanding beguiled into the belief that it is acquiring knowledge and approach- ing truth. A misapplied or misapprehended term is sufficient to give rise to fierce and interminable disputes; a misnomer has turned the tide of popular opinion; a verbal sophism has decided a party question; an artful watchword, thrown among combustible materials, has kindled the flame of deadly warfare, and changed the destiny of an empire.

In constructing the following system of classification of the ideas which are express-ible by language, my chief aim has been to obtain the greatest amount of practical utility. I have accordingly adopted such principles of arrangement as appeared to me to be the simplest and most natural, and which would not require, either for their comprehension or application, any disciplined acumen, or depth of metaphysical or antiquarian lore. Eschewing all needless refinements and subtleties, I have taken as my guide the more obvious characters of the ideas for which expressions were to be tabulated, arranging them under such classes and categories as reflection and experi-ence had taught me would conduct the inquirer most readily and quickly to the object of his search. Commencing with the ideas expressing abstract relations, I proceeded to those which relate to space and to the phenomena of the material world, and lastly to those in which the mind is concerned, and which comprehend intellect, volition, and feeling; thus establishing six primary Classes or Categories.

1 The first of these classes comprehends ideas derived from the more general and ABSTRACT RELATIONS among things, such as *Existence, Resemblance, Quantity, Order, Number, Time, Power*.

2 The second class refers to SPACE, and its various relations including 'motion' or change of place.

3 The third class includes all ideas that relate to the MATERIAL WORLD; namely, the *Properties of Matter*, such as *Solidity, Fluidity, Heat, Sound, Light*, and the *Phenomena* they present, as well as the simple *Perceptions* to which they give rise.

4 The fourth class embraces all ideas of phenomena relating to the INTELLECT and its operations; comprising the *Acquisition*, the *Retention*, and the *Communication of Ideas*.

5 The fifth class includes the ideas derived from the exercise of VOLITION; embracing the phenomena and results of our *Voluntary and Active Powers*; such as *Choice, Intention, Utility, Action, Antagonism, Authority, Compact, Property*, &c.

6 The sixth and last comprehends all ideas derived from the operation of our SENTIENT AND MORAL POWERS; including our *Feelings, Emotions, Passions*, and *Moral and Religious Sentiments*.[1]

The further subdivisions and minuter details will be best understood from an inspec-tion of the Tabular Synopsis of Categories prefixed to the Work, in which are specified the several *Topics* or *heads of signification*, under which the words have been arranged. By the aid of this table the reader will, with a little practice, readily discover the place

---

1 It must necessarily happen in every system of classification framed with this view, that ideas and expressions arranged under one class must include also ideas relating to another class; for the operations of the *Intellect* generally involve also those of the *Will* and *vice versa*; and our *Affections* and *Emotions*, in like manner, generally imply the agency both of the *Intellect* and of the *Will*. All that can be effected, therefore, is to arrange the words according to the principal or dominant idea they convey. *Teaching*, for example, although a Voluntary act, relates primarily to the communication of Ideas, and is accordingly placed at No. 537, under Class IV Division (II). On the other hand *Choice, Conduct, Skill* &c., although implying the co-operation of Voluntary with Intellectual acts, relate principally to the former, and are therefore arranged under Class V.

which the particular topic he is in search of occupies in the series; and on turning to the page in the body of the Work which contains it, he will find the group of expressions he requires, out of which he may cull those that are most appropriate to his purpose. For the convenience of reference, I have designated each separate group or heading by a particular number; so that if, during the search, any doubt or difficulty should occur, recourse may be had to the copious alphabetical Index of Words at the end of the volume, which will at once indicate the number of the required group.[1]

The object I have proposed to myself in this Work would have been but imperfectly attained if I had confined myself to a mere catalogue of words, and had omitted the numerous phrases and forms of expression composed of several words, which are of such frequent use as to entitle them to rank among the constituent parts of the language.[2] Very few of these verbal combinations, so essential to the knowledge of our native tongue, and so profusely abounding in its daily use, are to be met within ordinary dictionaries. These phrases and forms of expression I have endeavoured diligently to collect and to insert in their proper places, under the general ideas that they are designed to convey. Some of these conventional forms, indeed, partake of the nature of proverbial expressions; but actual proverbs, as such, being wholly of a didactic character, do not come within the scope of the present Work; and the reader must therefore not expect to find them here inserted.[3]

For the purpose of exhibiting with greater distinctness the relations between words expressing opposite and correlative ideas, I have, whenever the subject admitted of such an arrangement, placed them in two parallel columns in the same page, so that each group of expressions may be readily contrasted with those which occupy the adjacent column, and constitute their antithesis.[4] By carrying the eye from the one to the other, the inquirer may often discover forms of expression, of which he may avail himself advantageously, to diversify and infuse vigour into his phraseology. Rhetoricians, indeed, are well aware of the power derived from the skilful introduction of antithesis in giving point to an argument, and imparting force and brilliancy to the diction. A too frequent and indiscreet employment of this figure of rhetoric may, it is true, give rise to a vicious and affected style; but it is unreasonable to condemn indiscriminately the occasional and moderate use of a practice on account of its possible abuse.

The study of correlative terms existing in a particular language, may often throw valuable light on the manners and customs of the nations using it. Thus, Hume has drawn important inferences with regard to the state of society among

---

1 It often happens that the same word admits of various applications, or may be used in different senses. In consulting the Index the reader will be guided to the number of the heading under which that word, in each particular acceptation, will be found, by means of *supplementary words* printed in Italics; which words, however, are not to be understood as explaining the meaning of the word to which they are annexed, but only as assisting in the required reference. I have also, for shortness' sake, generally omitted words immediately derived from the primary one inserted, which sufficiently represents the whole group of correlative words referable to the same heading. Thus the number affixed to *Beauty* applies to all its derivatives, such as *Beautiful, Beauteous, Beautifulness, Beautifully*, &c., the insertion of which was therefore needless.

2 For example:- To take time by the forelock;- to turn over a new leaf; – to show the white feather; – to have a finger in the pie; – to let the cat out of the bag; – to take care of number one:- to kill two birds with one stone, &c., &c.

3 See Trench, *On the Lessons In Proverbs*.

4 This arrangement has been modified.][RAD].

the ancient Romans, from certain deficiencies which he remarked in the Latin language.[1]

In many cases, two ideas which are completely opposed to each other, admit of an intermediate or neutral idea, equidistant from both; all these being expressible by corresponding definite terms. Thus, in the following examples, the words in the first and third columns, which express opposite ideas, admit of the intermediate terms contained in the middle column, having a neutral sense with reference to the former.

| | | |
|---|---|---|
| *Identity* | *Difference* | *Contrariety* |
| *Beginning* | *Middle* | *End* |
| *Past* | *Present* | *Future* |

In other cases, the intermediate word is simply the negative to each of two opposite positions; as, for example –

| | | |
|---|---|---|
| *Convexity* | *Flatness* | *Concavity* |
| *Desire* | *Indifference* | *Aversion* |

Sometimes the intermediate word is properly the standard with which each of the extremes is compared; as in the case of

| | | |
|---|---|---|
| *Insufficiency* | *Sufficiency* | *Redundance* |

for here the middle term, *Sufficiency*, is equally opposed, on the one hand to *Insufficiency*, and on the other to *Redundance*.[2]

These forms of correlative expressions would suggest the use of triple, instead of double, columns for tabulating this threefold order of words; but the practical inconvenience attending such an arrangement would probably overbalance its advantages.

It often happens that the same word has several correlative terms, according to the different relations in which it is considered. Thus, to the word *Giving* are opposed both

---

1 'It is an universal observation', he remarks, 'which we may form upon language, that where two related parts of a whole bear any proportion to each other, in numbers, ranks, or consideration, there are always correlative terms invented which answer to both the parts, and express their mutual relation. If they bear no proportion to each other, the term is only invented for the less, and marks its distinction from the whole. Thus, *man* and *woman*, *master* and *servant*, *father* and *son*, *prince* and *subject*, *stranger* and *citizen*, are correlative terms. But the words *seaman*, *carpenter*, *smith*, *tailor*, &c., have no correspondent terms, which express those who are no seamen, no carpenters, &c. Languages differ very much with regard to the particular words where this distinction obtains; and may thence afford very strong inferences concerning the manners and customs of different nations. The military government of the Roman emperors had exalted the soldiery so high that they balanced all the other orders of the state: hence *miles* and *paganus* became relative terms; a thing, till then, unknown to ancient, and still so to modern languages.' – 'The term for a slave, born and bred in the family, was *verna*. As *servus* was the name of the genus, and *verna* of the species without any correlative, this forms a strong presumption that the latter were by far the least numerous: and from the same principles I infer that if the number of slaves brought by the Romans from foreign countries had not extremely exceeded those which were bred at home, *verna* would have had a correlative, which would have expressed the former species of slaves. But these, it would seem, composed the main body of the ancient slaves, and the latter were but a few exceptions.' – HUME, *Essay on the Populousness of Ancient Nations.*

The warlike propensity of the same nation may, in like manner, be inferred from the use of the word *hostis* to denote both *a foreigner* and *an enemy*.

2 [In the following cases, the intermediate word signifies an imperfect degree of each of the qualities set in opposition -

| | | |
|---|---|---|
| *Light* | *Dimness* | *Darkness* |
| *Transparency* | *Semitransparency* | *Opacity* |
| *Vision* | *Dimsightedness* | *Blindness* ][JLR] |

*Receiving* and *Taking*; the former correlation having reference to the *persons* concerned in the transfer, while the latter relates to the *mode* of transfer. *Old* has for opposite both *New* and *Young*, according as it is applied to *things* or to *living things*. *Attack* and *Defence* are correlative terms; as are also *Attack* and *Resistance*. *Resistance*, again, has for its other correlative *Submission*. *Truth in the abstract* is opposed to *Error*; but the opposite of *Truth communicated* is *Falsehood*. *Acquisition* is contrasted both with *Deprivation* and with *Loss*. *Refusal* is the counterpart both of *Offer* and of *Consent*. *Disuse* and *Misuse* may either of them be considered as the correlative of *Use*. *Teaching* with reference to what is taught, is opposed to *Misteaching*; but with reference to the act itself, its proper reciprocal is *Learning*.

Words contrasted in form do not always bear the same contrast in their meaning. The word *Malefactor*, for example, would from its derivation, appear to be exactly the opposite of *Benefactor*: but the ideas attached to these two words are far from being directly opposed; for while the latter expresses one who confers a benefit, the former denotes one who has violated the laws.

Independently of the immediate practical uses derivable from the arrangement of words in double columns, many considerations, interesting in a philosophical point of view, are presented by the study of correlative expressions. It will be found, on strict examination, that there seldom exists an exact opposition between two words which may at first sight appear to be the counterparts of one another; for in general, the one will be found to possess in reality more force or extent of meaning than the other with which it is contrasted. The correlative term sometimes assumes the form of a mere negative, although it is really endowed with a considerable positive form. Thus *Disrespect* is not merely the absence of *Respect*: its signification trenches on the opposite idea, namely, *Contempt*. In like manner, *Untruth* is not merely the negative of *Truth*; it involves a degree of *Falsehood*. *Irreligion*, which is properly *the want of Religion*, is understood as being nearly synonymous with *Impiety*. For these reasons, the reader must not expect that all the words which stand side by side in the two columns shall be the precise correlatives of each other; for the nature of the subject, as well as the imperfections of language, renders it impossible always to preserve such an exactness of correlation.

There exist comparatively few words of a general character to which no correlative term, either of negation or of opposition, can be assigned, and which therefore require no corresponding second column. The correlative idea, especially that which constitutes a sense negative to the primary one, may, indeed, be formed or conceived; but from its occurring rarely, no word has been framed to represent it; for, in language, as in other matters, the supply fails when there is no probability of a demand. Occasionally we find this deficiency provided for by the contrivance of prefixing the syllable *non*; as, for instance, the negatives of *existence, performance, payment*, &c. are expressed by the compound words, *nonexistence, nonperformance, nonpayment*, &c. Functions of a similar kind are performed by the prefixes *dis-*,[1] *anti-, contra-, mis-, in-*, and *un-*.[2] With respect to all these, and especially the last, great latitude is allowed according to the

---

1 The words *disannul* and *dissever*, however, have the same meaning as *annul* and *sever*; to *unloose* is the same as to *loose*, and *inebriety* is synonymous with *ebriety*.

2 In the case of adjectives, the addition to a substantive of the terminal syllable *less*, gives it a negative meaning: as *taste, tasteless; care, careless; hope, hopeless; friend, friendless; fault, faultless*; &c.

necessities of the case; a latitude which is limited only by the taste and discretion of the writer.

On the other hand, it is hardly possible to find two words having in all respect the same meaning, and being therefore interchangeable; that is, admitting of being employed indiscriminately, the one or the other, in all their applications. The investigation of the distinctions to be drawn between words apparently synonymous, forms a separate branch of inquiry, which I have not presumed here to enter upon; for the subject has already occupied the attention of much abler critics than myself, and its complete exhaustion would require the devotion of a whole life. The purpose of this Work, it must be borne in mind, is, not to explain the signification of words, but simply to classify and arrange them according to the sense in which they are now used, and which I presume to be already known to the reader. I enter into no inquiry into the changes of meaning they may have undergone in the course of time.[13] I am content to accept them at the value of their present currency, and have no concern with their etymologies, or with the history of their transformations; far less do I venture to thrid the mazes of the vast labyrinth into which I should be led by any attempt at a general discrimination of synonyms. The difficulties I have had to contend with have already been sufficiently great, without this addition to my labours.

The most cursory glance over the pages of a Dictionary will show that a great number of words are used in various senses, sometimes distinguished by slight shades of difference, but often diverging widely from their primary signification, and even, in some cases, bearing to it no perceptible relation. It may even happen that the very same word has two significations quite opposite to one another. This is the case with the verb *to cleave*, which means *to adhere tenaciously*, and also *to separate by a blow*. *To propugn* sometimes expresses *to attack*; at other times *to defend*. *To let* is *to hinder*, as well as *to permit*. *To ravel* means both *to entangle* and *to disentangle*. *Shameful* and *shameless* are nearly synonymous. *Priceless* may either mean *invaluable* or *of no value*. *Nervous* is used sometimes for *strong*, at other times for *weak*. The alphabetical Index at the end of this Work sufficiently shows the multiplicity of uses to which, by the elasticity of language, the meaning of words has been stretched, so as to adapt them to a great variety of modified significations in subservience to the nicer shades of thought, which, under peculiarity of circumstances, require corresponding expression. Words thus admitting of different meanings have therefore to be arranged under each of the respective heads corresponding to these various acceptations. There are many words, again, which express ideas compounded of two elementary ideas belonging to different classes. It is therefore necessary to place these words respectively under each of the generic heads to which they relate. The necessity of these repetitions is increased by the circumstance, that ideas included under one class are often connected by relations of the same kind as the ideas which belong to another class. Thus we find the same relations of *order* and of *quantity* existing among the ideas of *Time* as well as those of *Space*. Sequence in the one is denoted by the same terms as sequence in the other; and

---

**1** Such changes are innumerable: for instance, the words *tyrant, parasite, sophist, churl, knave, villain*, anciently conveyed no opprobrious meaning. *Impertinent* merely expressed *irrelative*, and implied neither *rudeness* nor *intrusion*, as it does at present. *Indifferent* originally meant *impartial*; extravagant was simply *digressive*, and *to prevent* was properly *to precede* and *assist*. The old translations of the Scriptures furnish many striking examples of the alterations which time has brought in the signification of words. Much curious information on this subject is contained in Trench's *Lectures on the Study of Words*.

the measures of time also express the measures of space. The cause and the effect are often designated by the same word. The word *Sound*, for instance, denotes both the impression made upon the ear by sonorous vibrations, and also the vibrations themselves, which are the cause of source of that impression. *Mixture* is used for the act of mixing, as well as for the product of that operation. *Taste* and *Smell* express both the sensations and the qualities of material bodies giving rise to them. *Thought* is the act of thinking; but the same word denotes also the idea resulting from the act. *Judgement* is the act of deciding, and also the decision come to. *Purchase* is that acquisition of a thing by payment, as well as the thing itself so acquired. *Speech* is both the act of speaking and the words spoken; and so on with regard to an endless multiplicity of words. Mind is essentially distinct from Matter; and yet, in all languages, the attributes of the one are metaphorically transferred to those of the other. Matter, in all its forms, is endowed by the figurative genius of every language with the functions which pertain to intellect; and we perpetually talk of its phenomena and of its powers, as if they resulted from the voluntary influence of one body on another, acting and reacting, impelling and being impelled, controlling and being controlled, as if animated by spontaneous energies and guided by specific intentions. On the other hand, expressions, of which the primary signification refers exclusively to the properties and actions of matter, are metaphorically applied to the phenomena of thought and volition, and even to the feelings and passions of the soul; and in speaking of a *ray of hope*, a *shade of doubt*, a *flight of fancy*, a *flash of wit*, the *warmth of emotion*, or the *ebullitions of anger*, we are scarcely conscious that we are employing metaphors which have this material origin.

As a general rule, I have deemed it incumbent on me to place words and phrases which appertain more especially to one head, also under the other heads to which they have a relation, whenever it appeared to me that this repetition would suit the convenience of the inquirer, and spare him the trouble of turning to other parts of the work; for I have always preferred to subject myself to the imputation of redundance, rather than incur the reproach of insuffiency.[1] When, however, the divergence of the associated from the primary idea is sufficiently marked, I have contented myself with making a reference to the place where the modified signification will be found.[2] But in order to prevent needless extension, I have, in general, omitted *conjugate words*,[3] which are so obviously derivable from those that are given in the same place, that the reader may safely be left to form them for himself. This is the case with adverbs derived from adjectives by the simple addition of the terminal syllable *-ly*; such as *closely, carefully, safely*, &c., from *close, careful, safe*, &c., and also with adjectives or participles

---

1 Frequent repetitions of the same series of expressions, accordingly, will be met with under various headings. For example, the word *Relinquishment* with its synonyms, occurs as a heading at No. 624, where it applies to *intention*, and also at No. 782, where it refers to *property*. The word *Chance* has two significations, distinct from one another: the one implying the *absence of an assignable cause*; in which case it comes under the category of the relation of Causation, and occupies the No. 156: the other, the *absence of design*, in which latter sense it ranks under the operations of the Will, and has assigned to it the place No. 621. I have, in like manner, distinguished *Sensibility, Pleasure, Pain, Taste*, &c., according as they relate to *Physical*, or to *Moral Affections*; the former being found at Nos. 375, 377, 378, 390, &c., and the latter at Nos. 822, 827, 828, 850, &c.

2 [Successive editors have developed this system of cross-references.][SML]

3 By *'conjugate* or *paronymous'* words is meant, correctly speaking, different parts of speech from the same root, which exactly corresponds in point of meaning'. – *A Selection of English synonyms*, edited by Archbishop Whately.

immediately derived from the verbs which are already given. In all such cases, an '&c.' indicates that reference is understood to be made to these roots. I have observed the same rule in compiling the Index; retaining only the primary or more simple word, and omitting the conjugate words obviously derived from them. Thus I assume the word *short* as the representative of its immediate derivatives *shortness, shorten, shortening, shortened, shorter, shortly*, which would have had the same references, and which the reader can readily supply.

The same verb is frequently used indiscriminately either in the active or transitive, or in the neuter or intransitive sense. In these cases, I have generally not thought it worth while to increase the bulk of the Work by the needless repetition of the word; for the reader, whom I suppose to understand the use of the words, must also be presumed to be competent to apply them correctly.

There are a multitude of words of a specific character which, although they properly occupy places in the columns of a dictionary, yet, having no relation to general ideas, do not come within the scope of this compilation, and are consequently omitted.[1] The names of objects in Natural History, and technical terms belonging exclusively to Science or to Art, or relating to particular operations, and of which the signification is restricted to those specific objects, come under this category. Exceptions must, however, be made in favour of such words as admit of metaphorical application to general subjects, with which custom has associated them, and of which they may be cited as being typical or illustrative. Thus, the word *Lion* will find a place under the head of *Courage*, of which it is regarded as the type. *Anchor*, being emblematic of *Hope*, is introduced among the words expressing that emotion; and in like manner, *butterfly* and *weathercock*, which are suggestive of fickleness, are included in the category of *Irresolution*.

With regard to the admission of many words and expressions, which the classical reader might be disposed to condemn as vulgarisms, or which he, perhaps, might stigmatize as pertaining rather to slang than to the legitimate language of the day, I would beg to observe, that, having due regard to the uses to which this Work was to be adapted, I did not feel myself justified in excluding them solely on that ground, if they possessed an acknowledged currency in general intercourse. It is obvious that, with respect to degrees of conventionality, I could not have attempted to draw any strict lines of demarcation; and far less could I have presumed to erect any absolute standard of purity. My object, be it remembered, is not to regulate the use of words, but simply to supply and to suggest such as may be wanted on occasion, leaving the proper selection entirely to the discretion and taste of the employer.[2] If a novelist or a dramatist, for example, proposed to delineate some vulgar personage, he would wish to have the power of putting into the mouth of the speaker expressions that would accord with his character; just as the actor, to revert to a former comparison, who had

---

1 [The author did not in all cases rigidly adhere to this rule; and the editors have thought themselves justified both in retaining and in adding some words of the specific character here mentioned, which may be occasionally in request by general writers [JLR], although in categories of this nature no attempt at completeness has been made. [SRR]

2 [It may be added that the Thesaurus is an aid not only in the choice of appropriate forms of expression, but in the rejection of those which are unfit; and that a vulgar phrase may often furnish a convenient clue to the group of classic synonyms among which it is placed. Moreover, the slang expressions admitted into the work bear a small proportion to those in constant use by English writers and speakers.][JLR]

to personate a peasant, would choose for his attire the most homely garb, and would have just reason to complain if the theatrical wardrobe furnished him with no suitable costume.

Words which have in the process of time, become obsolete, are of course rejected from this collection.[1] On the other hand, I have admitted a considerable number of words and phrases borrowed from other languages, chiefly the French and Latin, some of which may be considered as already naturalized; while others, though avowedly foreign, are frequently employed in English composition, particularly in familiar style, on account of their being peculiarly expressive, and because we have no corresponding words of equal force in our own language.[2] The rapid advances which are being made in scientific knowledge, and consequent improvement in all the arts of life, and the extension of those arts and sciences to so many new purposes and objects, create a continual demand for the formation of new terms to express new agencies, new wants, and new combinations. Such terms, from being at first merely technical, are rendered, by more general use, familiar to the multitude, and having a well-defined acceptation, are eventually incorporated into the language, which they contribute to enlarge and to enrich. *Neologies* of this kind are perfectly legitimate, and highly advantageous; and they necessarily introduce those gradual and progressive changes which every language is destined to undergo.[3] Some modern writers, however, have indulged in a habit of arbitrarily fabricating new words and a new-fangled phraseology, without any necessity, and with manifest injury to the purity of the language. This vicious practice, the offspring of indolence or conceit, implies an ignorance or neglect of the riches in which the English language already abounds, and which would have supplied them with words of recognized legitimacy, conveying precisely the same meaning as those they so recklessly coin in the illegal mint of their own fancy.

A Work constructed on the plan of classification I have proposed might, if ably executed, be of great value, in tending to limit the fluctuations to which language has always been subject, by establishing an authoritative standard for its regulation. Future historians, philologists, and lexicographers, when investigating the period when new words were introduced, or discussing the import given at the present time to the old, might find their labours lightened by being enabled to appeal to such a standard, instead of having to search for data among the scattered writings of the age. Nor would its utility be confined to a single language; for the principles of its construction are universally applicable to all languages, whether living or dead. On the same plan of classification there might be formed a French, a German, a Latin, or a Greek Thesaurus, possessing, in their respective spheres, the same advantages as those of the English

---

1 [A few apparently obsolete words have nevertheless found their way into the Thesaurus. In justification of their admission, it may be contended that well-known words, though no longer current, give occasional point by an archaic form of expression, and are of value to the novelist or dramatist who has to depict a bygone age.][JLR]

2 All these words and phrases are printed in Italics. [A few of these expressions, although widely used by writers of English, are of a form which is really incorrect or unusual in their own language; in some more extreme cases of this kind, the more widely used or incorrect form has been given.][SRR]

3 Thus, in framing the present classification, I have frequently felt the want of substantive terms corresponding to abstract qualities or ideas denoted by certain adjectives, and have been often tempted to invent words that might express these abstractions; but I have yielded to this temptation only in the four following instances, having framed from the adjectives *irrelative, amorphous, sinistral* and *gaseous*, the abstract nouns *irrelation, amorphism, sinistrality* and *gaseity*. I have ventured also to introduce the adjective *intersocial* to express the active voluntary relations between man and man. [Not all these coinages have been retained.][SML]

model.[1] Still more useful would be a conjunction of these methodized compilations in two languages, the French and English, for instance; the columns of each being placed in parallel juxtaposition. No means yet devised would so greatly facilitate the acquisition of the one language, by those who are acquainted with the other; none would afford such ample assistance to the translator in either language; and none would supply such ready and effectual means of instituting an accurate comparison between them, and of fairly appreciating their respective merits and defects. In a still higher degree would all those advantages be combined and multiplied in a *Polyglot Lexicon* constructed on this system.

Metaphysicians engaged in the more profound investigation of the Philosophy of Language will be materially assisted by having the ground thus prepared for them, in a previous analysis and classification of our ideas; for such classification of ideas is the true basis on which words, which are their symbols, should be classified.[2] It is by such analysis alone that we can arrive at a clear perception of the relation which these symbols bear to their corresponding ideas, or can obtain a correct knowledge of the elements which enter into the formation of compound ideas, and of the exclusions by which we arrive at the abstractions so perpetually resorted to in the process of reasoning, and in the communication of our thoughts.

Lastly, such analysis alone can determine the principles on which the strictly *Philosophical Language* might be constructed. The probable result of the construction of such a language would be its eventual adoption by every civilized nation; thus realizing that splendid aspiration of philanthropists – the establishment of a Universal Language. However Utopian such a project may appear to the present generation, and however

---

1 [This suggestion has been followed, in French, in a *'Dictionnaire Idéologique'* by T. Robertson (Paris, 1859); and, in German, in a *'Deutscher Sprachschatz'* by D. Sanders (Hamburg, 1878), and *'Deutscher Wortschatz oder Der passende Ausdruck'* by A. Schelling (Stuttgart, 1892).][JLR]

2 The principle by which I have been guided in framing my verbal classification is the same as that which is employed in the various departments of Natural History. Thus the sectional divisions I have formed, correspond to Natural Families in Botany and Zoology, and the filiation of words presents a network analogous to the natural filiation of plants or animals.

The following are the only publications that have come to my knowledge in which any attempt has been made to construct a systematic arrangement of ideas with a view to their expression. The earliest of these, supposed to be at least nine hundred years old, is the AMERA CÓSHA, or *Vocabulary of the Sanscrit Language*, by Amera Sinha, of which an English translation, by the late Henry T. Colebrooke, was printed at Serampoor, in the year 1808. The classification of words is there, as might be expected, exceedingly imperfect and confused, especially in all that relates to abstract ideas or mental operations. This will be apparent from the very title of the first section, which comprehends *'Heaven, Gods, Demons, Fire, Air, Velocity, Eternity, Much'*: while *Sin, Virtue, Happiness, Destiny, Cause, Nature, Intellect, Reasoning, Knowledge, Senses, Tastes, Odours, Colours*, are all included and jumbled together in the fourth section. A more logical order, however, pervades the sections relating to natural objects, such as *Seas, Earth, Towns, Plants,* and *Animals*, which form separate classes; exhibiting a remarkable effort at analysis at so remote a period of Indian literature.

The well-known work of Bishop Wilkins entitled *'An Essay towards a Real Character and a Philosophical Language'*, published in 1668, had for its object the formation of a system of symbols which might serve as a universal language. It professed to be founded on a 'scheme of analysis of the things or notions to which names were to be assigned'; but notwithstanding the immense labour and ingenuity expended in the construction of this system, it was soon found to be far too abstruse and recondite for practical application.

In the year 1797, there appeared in Paris an anonymous work, entitled 'PASIGRAPHIE, *ou Premiers Eléments du nouvel Art-Science d'écrire et d'imprimer une langue de manière à être lu et entendu dans toute autre langue sans traduction'*, of which an edition in German was also published. It contains a great number of tabular schemes of categories; all of which appear to be excessively arbitrary and artificial, and extremely difficult of application, as well as of apprehension. [Systems of grouping with relation to ideas are also adopted in an *'Analytical Dictionary of the English Language'* by David Booth (London, 1835), a *'Dictionnaire Analogique de la Langue Française'* by P. Boissière (Paris), and a *'Dictionnaire Logique de la Langue Française'* by L'Abbé Elie Blanc (Paris, 1882).][JLR]

abortive may have been the former endeavours of Bishop Wilkins and others to realize it.[1] its accomplishment is surely not beset with greater difficulties than have impeded the progress to many other beneficial objects, which in former times appeared to be no less visionary, and which yet were successfully achieved, in later ages, by the continued and persevering exertions of the human intellect. Is there at the present day, then, any ground for despair, that at some future stage of that higher civilization to which we trust the world is gradually tending, some new and bolder effort of genius towards the solution of this great problem may be crowned with success, and compass an object of such vast and paramount utility? Nothing, indeed, would conduce more directly to bring about a golden age of union and harmony among the several nations and races of mankind than the removal of that barrier to the interchange of thought and mutual good understanding between man and man, which is now interposed by the diversity of their respective languages.

---

1 'The Languages', observes Horne Tooke, 'which are commonly used throughout the world, are much more simple and easy, convenient and philosophical, than Wilkins' scheme for a *real character*; or than any other scheme that has been at any other time imagined or proposed for the purpose.' – 'Επεα Πϊερόενια' p. 125.

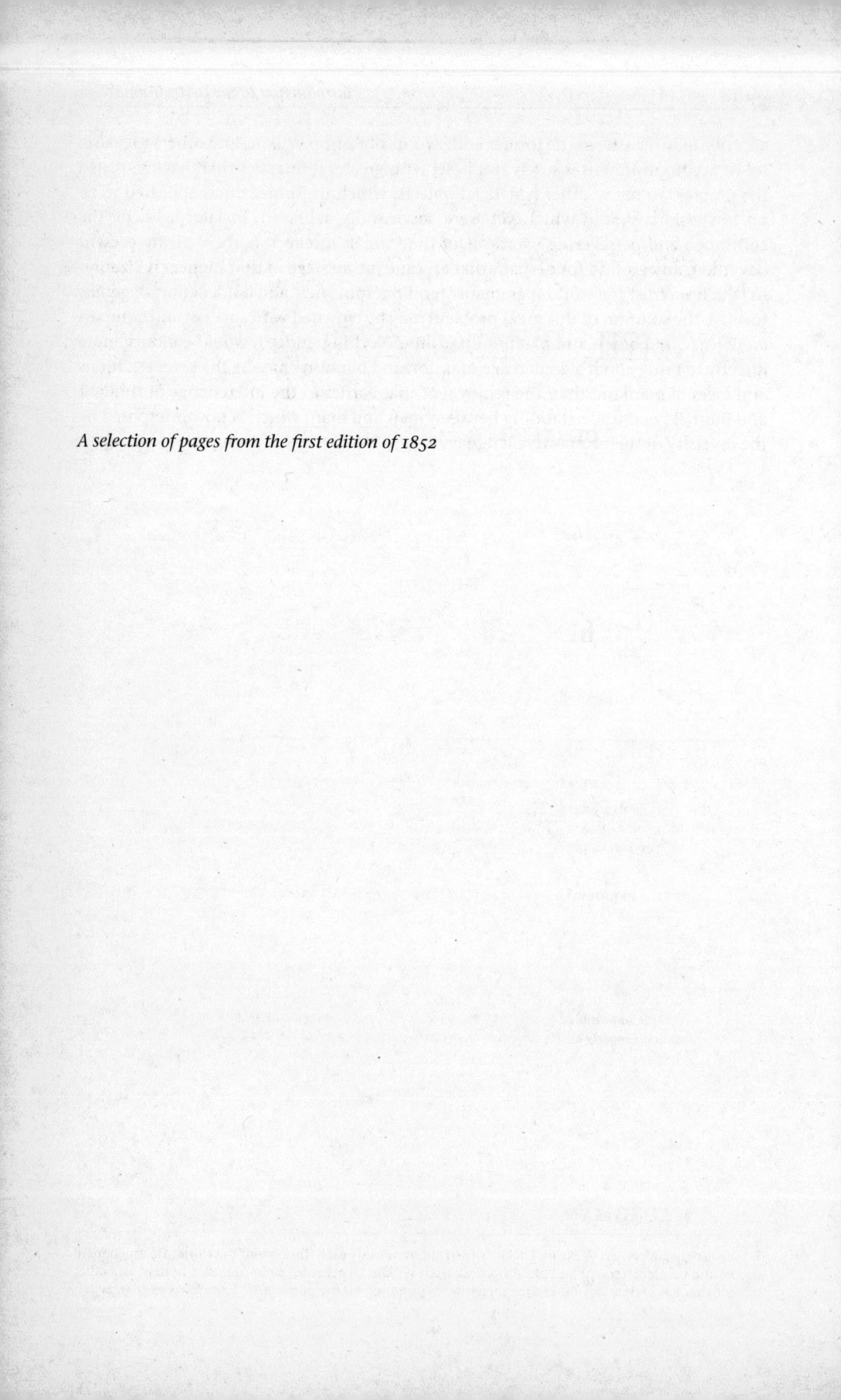

*A selection of pages from the first edition of 1852*

# THESAURUS

OF

# ENGLISH WORDS AND PHRASES,

## CLASSIFIED AND ARRANGED

SO AS

## TO FACILITATE THE EXPRESSION OF IDEAS

AND ASSIST IN

## LITERARY COMPOSITION.

BY PETER MARK ROGET, M.D., F.R.S., F.R.A.S., F.G.S.

FELLOW OF THE ROYAL COLLEGE OF PHYSICIANS;

MEMBER OF THE SENATE OF THE UNIVERSITY OF LONDON;
OF THE LITERARY AND PHILOSOPHICAL SOCIETIES ETC. OF MANCHESTER, LIVERPOOL,
BRISTOL, QUEBEC, NEW YORK, HAARLEM, TURIN, AND STOCKHOLM.

AUTHOR OF

THE "BRIDGEWATER TREATISE ON ANIMAL AND VEGETABLE PHYSIOLOGY,"
ETC.

_____

"It is impossible we should thoroughly understand the nature of the SIGNS, unless
we first properly consider and arrange the THINGS SIGNIFIED." — Ἔπεα Πτερόεντα.

_____

LONDON:
LONGMAN, BROWN, GREEN, AND LONGMANS.
1852.

# PLAN OF CLASSIFICATION.

*Adv.* Actually, really, absolutely, positively, &c., in fact, in reality, *ipso facto.*

Absence (187), removal (185).
*Adv.* Negatively, virtually, &c.

## 2°. BEING, IN THE CONCRETE.

(3) SUBSTANTIALITY, *hypostasis,* thing, something, a being, an existence, a body, substance, object, article, creature, matter, material, stuff (316), *substratum, plenum.*

Totality of existences, *see* World (318).

*Adj.* Substantive, substantial, bodily, material, objective, hypostatic.

*Adv.* Substantially, &c., essentially.

(4) UNSUBSTANTIALITY, nothingness, nihility, nothing, naught, *nil,* zero, nothing at all; nothing whatever, nothing on earth; — Nobody, *see* (187); a desert.

A shadow, phantom, phantasm, dream, air, thin air.

Void, vacuum, vacuity, vacancy, voidness, vacuousness, inanity, emptiness, hollowness, blank, chasm, gap, hiatus, &c. (198).

*Adj.* Unsubstantial, void, vacuous, blank, null, inane, vacant, hollow.

## 3°. FORMAL EXISTENCE.

*Internal conditions.*

(5) INTRINSICALITY, inbeing, inherence, inhesion, essence, essentialness, essential part, quintessence, quiddity, gist, pith, marrow, incarnation.

Nature, constitution, character, quality (157), crasis, temperament, temper, spirit, humour, grain, endowment, capacity, capability, moods, declensions, features, aspects, specialities, particularities, peculiarities (79), idiosyncrasy, idiocrasy, diagnostics.

*External conditions.*

(6) EXTRINSICALITY, extraneousness, accident.

*Adj.* Derived from without; extrinsic, extrinsical, extraneous, modal, adventitious, adscititious, (or ascititious), incidental, accidental, non-essential, objective.

Implanted, ingrafted.

*Adv.* Extrinsically, &c.

*Adj.* Derived from within; intrinsic, intrinsical, inherent, essential, natural, internal, innate, inborn, inbred, instinctive, ingrained, inherited, immanent, congenital, congenite, in the grain, bred in the bone.

Characteristic, peculiar, special, diagnostic (79).

*Adv.* Intrinsically, &c.

## 4°. MODAL EXISTENCE.

*Absolute.*

(7) STATE, condition, category, estate, case, constitution, diathesis.

Frame, fabric, structure, texture, contexture (329), conformation.

Mode, modality, schesis, form, shape, figure, cut, cast, mould, stamp, set, fit, tone, tenor, turn, trim, guise, fashion, aspect, complexion, character.

*V.* To be in a state, condition, &c.,

*Relative.*

(8) CIRCUMSTANCE, situation, phase, position, posture, attitude, place, point, terms, fare, *régime,* footing, standing, *status,* predicament, contingency, occasion, juncture, conjuncture, emergence, emergency, exigency, crisis, pass, push, pinch, pickle, plight.

*Adj.* Circumstantial, — given, conditional, provisional, critical, contingent, incidental (6, 151).

2

(363) INTERMENT, burial, sepulture, inhumation, obsequies, exequies, funeral, wake, pyre, funeral pile, cremation, obit, catafalque, *memento mori*, epitaph, *hic jacet.*

Knell, passing bell, tolling, dirge, requiem, epicedium.

A shroud, grave clothes, winding-sheet, pall, cerement, hearse, urn, coffin, bier.

Grave, pit, vault, sepulchre, sarcophagus, tomb, shrine, crypt, cenotaph, mausoleum, house of death, mortuary, cemetery, churchyard, grave-yard, burial-ground, burial-place, cromlech, barrow, tumulus, cairn, catacomb, ossuary, charnel-house, *la morgue.*

Exhumation, disinterment.

*V.* To inter, bury, lay in the grave, consign to the grave or tomb, entomb, intomb, inhume, lay out.

*Phr.* To be put to bed with a shovel.

To exhume, disinter.

*Adj.* Buried, &c., funereal, funebrial, mortuary, sepulchral.

## 2. *Special Vitality.*

(364) ANIMALITY, animal life, animation, breath, animalization.

(366) ANIMAL, the animal kingdom.

A beast, brute, creature; creeping or living thing; dumb creature; the beasts of the field; fowls of the air; denizens of the deep; flock, herd, flight.

Mammal, quadruped, bird, reptile, fish, mollusk, worm, insect, zoophyte, animalcule, &c., menagery, fossil remains.

*Adj.* Animal, zoological, piscatory, molluscous, vermicular, &c.

(368) The science of animals;
ZOOLOGY, Zoography, Anatomy, Zootomy, Comparative Anatomy, Animal or Comparative Physiology.
Oryctology, Palæontology.

(370) The economy or management of animals.
CICURATION, Zohygiastics.*

(365) VEGETABILITY, vegetable life, vegetation.

(367) PLANT, vegetable, the vegetable kingdom, fauna, herb, grass, creeper, shrub, bush.

Clump of trees, grove, glade, brake, thicket, underwood, copse, brushwood, jungle, weald, chase, frith, holt, hurst, park.

Tree, wood, forest, *parterre*, plantation, *arboretum*, foliage, &c.

*Hortus siccus, herbarium*, herbal.

*Adj.* Vegetable, vegetous, herbaceous, herbal, botanic, sylvan, woody, rural, verdant.

(369) The science of plants;
BOTANY, Phytography, Phytology, Vegetable Physiology.

(371) The economy or management of plants;
AGRICULTURE, cultivation, husbandry, Geoponics, georgics, tillage, gardening, horticulture, vintage, &c., arboriculture.

Vineyard, garden, nursery, *arboretum.*

A husbandman, horticulturalist, gardener, florist, agriculturalist, agricultor, farmer.

*Adj.* Agricultural, agrarian, arable, pastoral, bucolic.

# Instructions

## The Text

The *Thesaurus* is divided into six *Classes*. The first three Classes cover the external world: Class One, *Abstract relations*, deals with such ideas as number, order and time; Class Two, *Space*, is concerned with movement, shapes and sizes, while Class Three, *Matter*, covers the physical world and humankind's perception of it by means of the five senses. The last three Classes deal with the internal world of human beings: the human mind (Class Four, *Intellect*), the human will (Class Five, *Volition*), and the human heart and soul (Class Six, *Emotion, religion and morality*). There is a logical progression from abstract concepts, through the material universe, to mankind itself, culminating in what Roget saw as mankind's highest achievements: morality and religion.

Roget borrowed his scheme from natural history, with its hierarchy of Phyla, Classes, Orders and Families. His system has also been compared to a tree, with ever smaller ramifications diverging from the main branches. This is a workable way of dividing up human experience, as can be seen from the way Roget's system has survived intact through numerous revisions. But life, as Roget himself points out (see his *Introduction*, p.xxii), is not easily compartmentalized. 'Choice', for example, involves both the will (Class Five) and the intellect (Class Four). The language which reflects our experience is equally complex, more like a web than a tree, for it interconnects at all points. Also one word may have many meanings depending on its context. Roget was aware of this problem. His solution was to use copious cross-references to link related groups of words, a method which succeeded in both reflecting the complexity of language and coming to terms with it.

To see at a glance how Roget's system works, look up the *Plan of classification* on pp. lvii–xliii. This shows the Six Classes, further subdivided into *Sections*. Each Section deals with a particular aspect of the Class within which it is found. So under Class One, *Abstract relations*, we find Sections for *Quantity*, *Order*, *Time* and so on. The Sections themselves are further subdivided into *Heads*. Within Class One Section Six, *Time*, for instance, there are 35 Heads dealing with, among others, the ideas of *Present time*, *Past time*, *Transience*, and *Age*. Each Head is numbered. There are 990 in the present edition, a slight reduction from Roget's original 1,000. It is the Heads which form the basic units of the book, and they follow each other in a logical progression, as can be seen in the *Tabular synopsis of categories* which follows the *Plan of classification*. It is a sign of Roget's skill in compiling the *Thesaurus* that this basic framework has remained virtually intact through edition after edition of the copyright version, of which this is the most recent.

The Heads themselves are divided into paragraphs, grouped together according to their part of speech. Head **852**, *Hope*, for example, has three paragraphs of nouns (marked **N**.), two of adjectives (**Adj**.), two of verbs (**Vb**.), one of adverbs (**Adv**.) and one of interjections (**Int**.). Not all Heads have a full complement of parts of speech, nor are the labels themselves applied too strictly, words and phrases being allocated to the part of speech which most closely describes their function. Each paragraph begins with a word in italics known as the *keyword*. This is both a clue to the kind of words found in that paragraph, and also itself part of the vocabulary. It is *not* a synonym of the words which follow: it was Roget's intention to offer words which express every aspect of an idea, rather than to list the synonyms. It is called the *keyword* because it is both the 'key' to the rest of the paragraph, and the 'open sesame' to the whole book, being used to identify the position of other words in the index and cross-references.

Within the paragraphs, words are grouped between semicolons according to their meaning, context or level of usage (i.e. colloquial, formal, etc.). These groups follow one another in a logical sequence, exploring every aspect of the idea under consideration. By comparing, whether consciously or not, the words and phrases offered, you can now select the most appropriate. It was Roget's expectation that his readers would 'recognize' the word they wanted, guided by 'an instinctive tact'.[1] On this assumption, words having more than one meaning or context are not usually repeated within paragraphs, nor are transitive and intransitive verbs listed separately. Where the right word is not immediately apparent, but an unfamiliar one seems from the context as if it might answer, it is advisable, especially for non-English speakers, to check with a dictionary. Yet more ideas can be obtained by looking up the cross-references. These are found at the end of some groups of words and consist of a Head number and a word in italics. The latter, besides being an item of vocabulary in its own right, is also the *keyword* of a paragraph in the given Head. It is also worth consulting the Heads before and after the one originally looked up. Most Heads are in pairs, representing the positive and negative aspects of an idea, e.g. **852** *Hope*, **853** *Hopelessness*. Sometimes several Heads between them cover an idea – 'education' is dealt with in **534** *Teaching*, **545** *Misteaching*, **546** *Learning*, **537** *Teacher*, **538** *Learner* and **539** *School*. The *Tabular synopsis of categories* shows how the Heads are related to one another.

A few conventions should be explained. These have mainly been designed to avoid repetition and save space. Conjugate forms are often indicated by the use of 'etc.' For instance, 'be content, – satisfied etc. adj.' suggests that readers can form further verbs for themselves on the same pattern. In the same way, 'darkness etc. adj.' suggests how more nouns may be formed from the adjectives already given. Where consecutive expressions use the same word, two means are used to avoid repeating it. The phrases may be linked by '*or*', as in 'drop a brick *or* a clanger', 'countryman *or* -woman'. Alternatively, the repeated word is simply indicated by its first letter, followed by a full stop: 'weasel word, loan w., nonce w.,' and so on. Brackets within the text are occasionally used to clarify the context of a word, as in 'dissolve (a marriage)'. 'Tdmk' in brackets

---

1 Introduction to the 1852 edition, p. xx.

following a noun indicates a registered trade mark. An 'e' in brackets added to the end of a word means that it is of French origin and requires a final 'e' if applied to a woman. '**See** . . .' is used to refer the reader to another paragraph within the same Head, where the idea under consideration is dealt with more thoroughly. This often happens where a general paragraph, such as '*killing*' in Head **362**, is followed by more specific paragraphs, in this case '*homicide*' and '*slaughter*'.

Spelling and hyphenation are uniform with Longman dictionaries. It should be borne in mind, however, that a living language takes many shapes, and these are not the only correct or permitted orthographies. For the benefit of crossword puzzle enthusiasts and others, alternative current spellings are given in the Index.

## The Index

Once familiar with Roget's *Plan of classification*, readers will be able to find their own way round the book, and this is certainly the most rewarding method of using the *Thesaurus*. However, new readers, and those in a hurry, will probably prefer to use the Index at the back of this book.

The Index is based on a complete computer-listing of all the items in the book. It is intended as a guide to the text rather than as a catalogue of its contents, and the reader should not assume that a word is missing from the book simply because it is not in the Index. Nor is the list of references at each entry intended to be exhaustive. The reader should bear in mind that the Heads offer words to express a given idea or ideas; it really does not matter whether you look up a noun, a verb or an adjective, as once you have found the right Head, all the parts of speech conveying that idea will be available to you.

The Index consists of a list of items, each of which is followed by one or more references to the text. These references consist of: a Head number; a *keyword* in italics, and a part of speech label (n. for nouns, adj. for adjectives, vb. for verbs, adv. for adverbs and int. for interjections). The *keyword* is given to identify the paragraph which contains the word you have looked up; it also gives an indication of the ideas contained in that paragraph, so it can be used as a clue where a word has several meanings and therefore several references. To use the Index, look up your word, turn to the Head number given in your chosen reference, and under the relevant part of speech you will find a paragraph beginning with the keyword given in the Index.

Where several references are given choose the most appropriate *keyword*. For instance, suppose you need another expression for 'feeling happy'. Look up 'happy' in the Index, and you will find a list of references. The *keywords* given include 'apt', 'willing' and 'drunk', which refer to other uses of the word 'happy'. But the *keywords* 'cheerful' and 'happy' are obviously relevant, and looking up **833** *cheerful* and **824** *happy* will offer you an abundance of suitable terms.

# Some points to note

1) *Items are listed in alphabetical order*, whether they are words or phrases. For example: 'hall, halleluja, halliard, hallmark, hall of residence, halloo, hallow, hallowed, hallowed by custom, Hallowe'en'. 'The', 'a', and 'be' are disregarded for this purpose. The only exception to this rule is (2).

2) *Phrases beginning with a verb* are listed immediately under that verb, which is replaced by a dash. For example: 'hang, – about, – back, – by a thread' etc. A glance at this list will often help the reader to find the most apposite reference more quickly.

3) *References to the same Head* are not usually repeated under different grammatical forms of the same words. For example: 'abundance' has references to Heads **32**, **171**, **632**, **625** and **637**, while 'abundant' has reference to none of these, but lists **104**, **800** and **813**. This means that the adjective is found in three Heads which do not list the noun form: the idea of 'abundance', however, is present in all the Heads listed. It is a good idea to check other forms of the word you are looking up, to obtain the fullest list of references to suitable Heads. Forms that do not follow each other immediately are linked by the direction '*See . . .*'.

Obvious derivatives of words, such as nouns ending in '-ness', adjectives in '-ing' or '-ed' and adverbs in '-ly', are not usually given an entry of their own unless they have a different meaning from the parent word.

4) *Objects* should be looked up in their simplest form, e.g. 'ship' rather than 'clipper', 'dog' rather than 'wolfhound' and 'flag' rather than 'banneret'. An object with a compound name, such as 'money box' may be dealt with under either or both of its constituent parts.

5) *Phrases* are listed in alphabetical order as noted above. In idioms where the first word is variable, such as 'have (*or* know) by heart', the phrase will be indexed under both, or under the next word in the phrase.

6) *General expressions* such as 'good example', 'bad health', 'no meaning' and 'not mind' have been retained in the Index as useful guides for the reader.

7) *(s) after a word* indicates that references may apply to either the singular or the plural form.

8) *Alternative spellings* are given after the main form.

# Plan of classification

# Tabular synopsis of categories

## Class one: Abstract relations

### 1 Existence

| | | |
|---|---|---|
| Abstract: | 1 Existence | 2 Nonexistence |
| Concrete: | 3 Substantiality | 4 Insubstantiality |
| Formal: (internal/external) | 5 Intrinsicality | 6 Extrinsicality |
| Modal: (absolute/relative) | 7 State | 8 Circumstance |

### 2 Relation

| | | |
|---|---|---|
| Absolute: | 9 Relation | 10 Unrelatedness |
| | 11 Consanguinity | |
| | 12 Correlation | |
| | 13 Identity | 14 Contrariety |
| | 15 Difference | |
| Continuous: | 16 Uniformity | 17 Nonuniformity |
| Partial: | 18 Similarity | 19 Dissimilarity |
| | 20 Imitation | 21 Originality |
| | 22 Copy | 23 Prototype |
| General: | 24 Agreement | 25 Disagreement |

### 3 Quantity

| | | |
|---|---|---|
| Simple: (absolute/relative) | 26 Quantity | 27 Degree |
| | 28 Equality | 29 Inequality |
| Comparative: | 30 Mean | |
| | 31 Compensation | |
| (by comparison with a standard) | 32 Greatness | 33 Smallness |
| (by comparison with an object) | 34 Superiority | 35 Inferiority |
| (changes in quantity) | 36 Increase | 37 Decrease |
| Conjunctive: | 38 Addition | 39 Subtraction |
| | 40 Adjunct | 41 Remainder |
| | | 42 Decrement |
| | 43 Mixture | 44 Simpleness |
| | 45 Union | 46 Disunion |
| | 47 Bond | |
| | 48 Coherence | 49 Noncoherence |
| | 50 Combination | 51 Decomposition |
| | 52 Whole | 53 Part |
| Concrete: | 54 Completeness | 55 Incompleteness |

|  | 56 Composition | 57 Exclusion |
|---|---|---|
|  | 58 Component | 59 Extraneousness |

# 4 *Order*

| General: | 60 Order | 61 Disorder |
|---|---|---|
|  | 62 Arrangement | 63 Derangement |
| Consecutive: | 64 Precedence | 65 Sequence |
|  | 66 Precursor | 67 Sequel |
|  | 68 Beginning | 69 End |
|  | 70 Middle |  |
|  | 71 Continuity | 72 Discontinuity |
|  | 73 Term |  |
| Collective: | 74 Assemblage | 75 Nonassembly |
|  | 76 Focus |  |
| Distributive: | 77 Class |  |
|  | 78 Inclusion |  |
|  | 79 Generality | 80 Speciality |
| Categorical: | 81 Rule | 82 Multiformity |
|  | 83 Conformity | 84 Nonconformity |

# 5 *Number*

| Abstract: | 85 Number |  |
|---|---|---|
|  | 86 Numeration |  |
|  | 87 List |  |
| Determinate: | 88 Unity | 89 Accompaniment |
|  | 90 Duality |  |
|  | 91 Duplication | 92 Bisection |
|  | 93 Triality |  |
|  | 94 Triplication | 95 Trisection |
|  | 96 Quaternity |  |
|  | 97 Quadruplication | 98 Quadrisection |
|  | 99 Five and over | 100 Multisection |
| Indeterminate: | 101 Plurality | 102 Fraction |
|  |  | 103 Zero |
|  | 104 Multitude | 105 Fewness |
|  | 106 Repetition |  |
|  | 107 Infinity |  |

# 6 *Time*

| Absolute: (definite/indefinite) | 108 Time | 109 Neverness |
|---|---|---|
|  | 110 Period | 111 Course |
|  | 112 Contingent duration |  |
|  | 113 Long duration | 114 Transience |
|  | 115 Perpetuity | 116 Instantaneousness |
|  | 117 Chronometry | 118 Anachronism |
| Relative: (to succession) | 119 Priority | 120 Posterity |
|  | 121 Present time | 122 Different time |
|  | 123 Synchronism |  |
| (to a period) | 124 Futurity | 125 Past time |
|  | 126 Newness | 127 Oldness |
|  | 128 Morning | 129 Evening |
|  | 130 Youth | 131 Age |
|  | 132 Young person | 133 Old person |

| | | |
|---|---|---|
| | 134 Adultness | |
| (to an effect or purpose) | 135 Earliness | 136 Lateness |
| | 137 Occasion | 138 Untimeliness |
| Recurrent: | 139 Frequency | 140 Infrequency |
| | 141 Periodicity | 142 Fitfulness |

## 7 *Change*

| | | |
|---|---|---|
| Simple: | 143 Change | 144 Permanence |
| | 145 Cessation | 146 Continuance |
| | 147 Conversion | 148 Reversion |
| | 149 Revolution | |
| | 150 Substitution | 151 Interchange |
| Complex: | 152 Changeableness | 153 Stability |
| (present/future) | 154 Present events | 155 Destiny |

## 8 *Causation*

| | | |
|---|---|---|
| Constancy of sequence: | 156 Cause | 157 Effect |
| | 158 Attribution | 159 Chance |
| Connection between cause and effect: | 160 Power | 161 Impotence |
| | 162 Strength | 163 Weakness |
| Power in operation: | 164 Production | 165 Destruction |
| | 166 Reproduction | |
| | 167 Propagation | 168 Destroyer |
| | 169 Parentage | 170 Posterity |
| | 171 Productiveness | 172 Unproductiveness |
| | 173 Agency | |
| | 174 Vigour | 175 Inertness |
| | 176 Violence | 177 Moderation |
| Indirect power: | 178 Influence | |
| | 179 Tendency | |
| | 180 Liability | |
| Combination of causes: | 181 Concurrence | 182 Counteraction |

# Class two: Space

## 1 *Space in General*

| | | |
|---|---|---|
| Abstract space: (indefinite) | 183 Space | |
| (definite) | | 184 Region |
| (limited) | | 185 Place |
| Relative space: | 186 Situation | |
| | 187 Location | 188 Displacement |
| Existence in space: | 189 Presence | 190 Absence |
| | 191 Inhabitant | 192 Abode |
| | 193 Contents | 194 Receptacle |

## 2 *Dimensions*

| | | |
|---|---|---|
| General: | 195 Size | 196 Littleness |
| | 197 Expansion | 198 Contraction |
| | 199 Distance | 200 Nearness |
| | 201 Interval | 202 Contiguity |

| Linear: | 203 Length | 204 Shortness |
|---|---|---|
| | 205 Breadth | 206 Narrowness |
| | 207 Layer | 208 Filament |
| | 209 Height | 210 Lowness |
| | 211 Depth | 212 Shallowness |
| | 213 Summit | 214 Base |
| | 215 Verticality | 216 Horizontality |
| | 217 Pendency | 218 Support |
| | 219 Parallelism | 220 Obliquity |
| | 221 Inversion | |
| | 222 Crossing | |
| Centrical: (general) | 223 Exteriority | 224 Interiority |
| | | 225 Centrality |
| | 226 Covering | 227 Lining |
| | 228 Dressing | 229 Uncovering |
| | 230 Surroundings | 231 Interjacency |
| | 232 Circumscription | |
| | 233 Outline | |
| | 234 Edge | |
| | 235 Enclosure | |
| | 236 Limit | |
| (special) | 237 Front | 238 Rear |
| | 239 Laterality | 240 Contraposition |
| | 241 Dextrality | 242 Sinistrality |

## 3 Form

| General: | 243 Form | 244 Amorphism |
|---|---|---|
| | 245 Symmetry | 246 Distortion |
| Special: | 247 Angularity | |
| | 248 Curvature | 249 Straightness |
| | 250 Circularity | 251 Convolution |
| | 252 Rotundity | |
| Superficial: | 253 Convexity | |
| | 254 Prominence | 255 Concavity |
| | 256 Sharpness | 257 Bluntness |
| | 258 Smoothness | 259 Roughness |
| | 260 Notch | 261 Fold |
| | 262 Furrow | |
| | 263 Opening | 264 Closure |

## 4 Motion

| General: | 265 Motion | 266 Quiescence |
|---|---|---|
| | 267 Land travel | 268 Traveller |
| | 269 Water travel | 270 Mariner |
| | 271 Aeronautics | |
| | 272 Transference | 273 Carrier |
| | 274 Vehicle | 275 Ship |
| | | 276 Aircraft |
| Degrees of motion: | 277 Velocity | 278 Slowness |
| Conjoined with force: | 279 Impulse | 280 Recoil |
| With reference to direction: | 281 Direction | 282 Deviation |
| | 283 Preceding | 284 Following |
| | 285 Progression | 286 Regression |
| | 287 Propulsion | 288 Traction |
| | 289 Approach | 290 Recession |

## Class three: Matter

### 1 *Matter in general*

### 2 *Inorganic matter*

### 3 *Organic matter*

# Class four: Intellect: the exercise of the mind

## DIVISION ONE: FORMATION OF IDEAS

### 1 Intellectual operations in general

| | |
|---|---|
| 447 Intellect | 448 Absence of intellect |
| 449 Thought | 450 Absence of thought |
| 451 Idea | |
| 452 Topic | |

### 2 Precursory conditions and operations

| | |
|---|---|
| 453 Curiosity | 454 Incuriosity |
| 455 Attention | 456 Inattention |
| 457 Carefulness | 458 Negligence |
| 459 Enquiry | 460 Answer |
| 461 Experiment | |
| 462 Comparison | |
| 463 Discrimination | 464 Indiscrimination |
| 465 Measurement | |

### 3 Materials for reasoning

| | |
|---|---|
| 466 Evidence | 467 Counterevidence |
| 468 Qualification | |

(degrees of evidence)

| | |
|---|---|
| 469 Possibility | 470 Impossibility |
| 471 Probability | 472 Improbability |
| 473 Certainty | 474 Uncertainty |

### 4 Reasoning processes

| | |
|---|---|
| 475 Reasoning | 476 Intuition |
| | 477 Sophistry |
| 478 Demonstration | 479 Confutation |

### 5 Results of reasoning

| | |
|---|---|
| 480 Judgment | 481 Misjudgment |
| 482 Overestimation | 483 Underestimation |
| 484 Discovery | |
| 485 Belief | 486 Unbelief |
| 487 Credulity | |
| 488 Assent | 489 Dissent |
| 490 Knowledge | 491 Ignorance |
| 492 Scholar | 493 Ignoramus |
| 494 Truth | 495 Error |
| 496 Maxim | 497 Absurdity |

(faculties)

| | |
|---|---|
| 498 Intelligence | 499 Unintelligence |
| 500 Sage | 501 Fool |
| 502 Sanity | 503 Insanity |
| | 504 Madman |

## 6 Extension of thought

| | | |
|---|---|---|
| (to the past) | 505 Memory | 506 Oblivion |
| (to the future) | 507 Expectation | 508 Lack of expectation |
| | | 509 Disappointment |
| | 510 Foresight | |
| | 511 Prediction | |

## 7 Creative thought

512 Supposition
513 Imagination

DIVISION TWO: COMMUNICATION OF IDEAS

## 1 Nature of ideas communicated

| | |
|---|---|
| 514 Meaning | 515 Lack of meaning |
| 516 Intelligibility | 517 Unintelligibility |
| 518 Equivocalness | |
| 519 Metaphor | |
| 520 Interpretation | 521 Misinterpretation |

## 2 Modes of communication

| | |
|---|---|
| 522 Manifestation | 523 Latency |
| 524 Information | 525 Concealment |
| 526 Disclosure | 527 Hiding |
| 528 Publication | |
| 529 News | 530 Secret |
| 531 Communications | |
| 532 Affirmation | 533 Negation |
| 534 Teaching | 535 Misteaching |
| | 536 Learning |
| 537 Teacher | 538 Learner |
| 539 School | |
| 540 Veracity | 541 Falsehood |
| | 542 Deception |
| | 543 Untruth |
| 544 Dupe | 545 Deceiver |
| | 546 Exaggeration |

## 3 Means of communicating ideas

| | | |
|---|---|---|
| (natural means) | 547 Indication | |
| | 548 Record | |
| | 549 Recorder | 550 Obliteration |
| | 551 Representation | 552 Misrepresentation |
| | 553 Painting | |
| | 554 Sculpture | |
| | 555 Engraving | |
| | 556 Artist | |
| (conventional means: language) | 557 Language | |
| | 558 Letter | |
| | 559 Word | 560 Neology |

# Class five: Volition: the exercise of the will

## DIVISION ONE: INDIVIDUAL VOLITION

### 1 Volition in general

### 2 Prospective volition

711 Defiance
712 Attack
714 Retaliation
716 Contention
718 War
720 Mediation
721 Submission
722 Combatant
723 Arms
724 Arena

713 Defence
715 Resistance
717 Peace
719 Pacification

## 5 *Results of action*

725 Completion
727 Success
729 Trophy
730 Prosperity

726 Noncompletion
728 Failure

731 Adversity

732 Averageness

## DIVISION TWO: SOCIAL VOLITION

## 1 *General social volition*

733 Authority
735 Severity
737 Command
738 Disobedience
740 Compulsion
741 Master
743 Badge of rule
744 Freedom
746 Liberation

749 Keeper
751 Commission

754 Consignee
755 Deputy

734 Laxity
736 Leniency

739 Obedience

742 Servant

745 Subjection
747 Restraint
748 Prison
750 Prisoner
752 Abrogation
753 Resignation

## 2 *Special social volition*

756 Permission
758 Consent
759 Offer
761 Request
763 Petitioner

757 Prohibition

760 Refusal
762 Deprecation

## 3 *Conditional social volition*

764 Promise
765 Compact
766 Conditions
767 Security
768 Observance

769 Nonobservance

770 Compromise

## 4 *Possessive relations*

| | | |
|---|---|---|
| Property in general: | 771 Acquisition | 772 Loss |
| | 773 Possession | 774 Nonownership |
| | 775 Joint possession | |
| | 776 Possessor | |
| | 777 Property | |
| | 778 Retention | 779 Nonretention |
| Transfer of property: | 780 Transfer | |
| | 781 Giving | 782 Receiving |
| | 783 Apportionment | |
| | 784 Lending | 785 Borrowing |
| | 786 Taking | 787 Restitution |
| | 788 Stealing | |
| | 789 Thief | |
| | 790 Booty | |
| Interchange of property: | 791 Barter | |
| | 792 Purchase | 793 Sale |
| | 794 Merchant | |
| | 795 Merchandise | |
| | 796 Market | |
| Monetary relations: | 797 Money | |
| | 798 Treasurer | |
| | 799 Treasury | |
| | 800 Wealth | 801 Poverty |
| | 802 Credit | 803 Debt |
| | 804 Payment | 805 Nonpayment |
| | 806 Expenditure | 807 Receipt |
| | 808 Accounts | |
| | 809 Price | 810 Discount |
| | 811 Dearness | 812 Cheapness |
| | 813 Liberality | 814 Economy |
| | 815 Prodigality | 816 Parsimony |

# Class six: *Emotion, religion and morality*

## 1 *General*

| | |
|---|---|
| 817 Affections | |
| 818 Feeling | |
| 819 Sensibility | 820 Insensibility |
| 821 Excitation | |
| 822 Excitability | 823 Inexcitability |

## 2 *Personal emotion*

| | | |
|---|---|---|
| Passive: | 824 Joy | 825 Suffering |
| | 826 Pleasurableness | 827 Painfulness |
| | 828 Content | 829 Discontent |
| | | 830 Regret |
| | 831 Relief | 832 Aggravation |
| | 833 Cheerfulness | 834 Dejection |
| | 835 Rejoicing | 836 Lamentation |
| | 837 Amusement | 838 Tedium |

| | | |
|---|---|---|
| | 839 Wit | 840 Dullness |
| Discriminative: | 841 Beauty | 842 Ugliness |
| | 843 Beautification | |
| | 844 Ornamentation | 845 Blemish |
| | 846 Good taste | 847 Bad taste |
| | 848 Fashion | 849 Ridiculousness |
| | | 850 Affectation |
| | | 851 Ridicule |
| Prospective: | 852 Hope | 853 Hopelessness |
| | | 854 Fear |
| | 855 Courage | 856 Cowardice |
| | 857 Rashness | 858 Caution |
| | 859 Desire | 860 Indifference |
| | | 861 Dislike |
| | | 862 Fastidiousness |
| | 863 Satiety | |
| Contemplative: | 864 Wonder | 865 Lack of wonder |
| Extrinsic: | 866 Repute | 867 Disrepute |
| | 868 Nobility | 869 Commonalty |
| | 870 Title | |
| | 871 Pride | 872 Humility |
| | 873 Vanity | 874 Modesty |
| | 875 Ostentation | |
| | 876 Celebration | |
| | 877 Boasting | |
| | 878 Insolence | 879 Servility |

## 3 *Interpersonal emotion*

| | | |
|---|---|---|
| Social: | 880 Friendship | 881 Enmity |
| | 882 Sociality | 883 Unsociability |
| | 884 Courtesy | 885 Discourtesy |
| | 886 Congratulation | |
| | 887 Love | 888 Hatred |
| | 889 Endearment | |
| | 890 Darling | 891 Resentment |
| | | 892 Irascibility |
| | 893 Sullenness | |
| | 894 Marriage | 895 Celibacy |
| | | 896 Divorce |
| Diffusive: | 897 Benevolence | 898 Malevolence |
| | | 899 Malediction |
| | | 900 Threat |
| | 901 Philanthropy | 902 Misanthropy |
| | 903 Benefactor | 904 Evildoer |
| Special: | 905 Pity | 906 Pitilessness |
| | 907 Gratitude | 908 Ingratitude |
| | 909 Forgiveness | 910 Revenge |
| | | 911 Jealousy |
| | | 912 Envy |

## 4 Morality

| | | |
|---|---|---|
| Obligation: | 913 Right | 914 Wrong |
| | 915 Dueness | 916 Undueness |
| | 917 Duty | 918 Undutifulness |
| | | 919 Nonliability |

| | | |
|---|---|---|
| Sentiments: | 920 Respect | 921 Disrespect |
| | | 922 Contempt |
| | 923 Approbation | 924 Disapprobation |
| | 925 Flattery | 926 Detraction |
| | 927 Vindication | 928 Accusation |
| Conditions: | 929 Probity | 930 Improbity |
| | 931 Disinterestedness | 932 Selfishness |
| | 933 Virtue | 934 Wickedness |
| | 935 Innocence | 936 Guilt |
| | 937 Good person | 938 Bad person |
| | 939 Penitence | 940 Impenitence |
| | 941 Atonement | |
| Practice: | 942 Temperance | 943 Intemperance |
| | | 944 Sensualism |
| | 945 Asceticism | |
| | 946 Fasting | 947 Gluttony |
| | 948 Sobriety | 949 Drunkenness |
| | 950 Purity | 951 Impurity |
| | | 952 Libertine |
| Institutions: | 953 Legality | 954 Illegality |
| | 955 Jurisdiction | |
| | 956 Tribunal | |
| | 957 Judge | |
| | 958 Lawyer | |
| | 959 Litigation | |
| | 960 Acquittal | 961 Condemnation |
| | 962 Reward | 963 Punishment |
| | | 964 Means of punishment |

## 5 *Religion*

| | | |
|---|---|---|
| Superhuman beings and religions | 965 Divineness | |
| | 966 Deities in general | |
| | 967 Pantheon | |
| | 968 Angel | 969 Devil |
| | 970 Fairy | |
| | 971 Heaven | 972 Hell |
| Doctrines: | 973 Religion | 974 Irreligion |
| | 975 Revelation | |
| | 976 Orthodoxy | 977 Heterodoxy |
| | | 978 Sectarianism |
| Sentiments: | 979 Piety | 980 Impiety |
| Acts: | 981 Worship | 982 Idolatry |
| | | 983 Sorcery |
| | | 984 Occultism |
| Institutions: | 985 The church | |
| | 986 Clergy | 987 Laity |
| | 988 Ritual | |
| | 989 Canonicals | |
| | 990 Temple | |

# Abstract relations

## Existence

### 1 Existence

**N.** *existence*, being, entity; absolute being, the absolute 965 *divineness*; aseity, self-origination, self-existence, uncreatedness; monad, a being, an entity, ens, essence, quiddity; Platonic idea, universal; subsistence 360 *life*; survival, eternity 115 *perpetuity*; pre-existence 119 *priority*; this life 121 *present time*; existence in space, prevalence 189 *presence*; entelechy, realization, becoming, evolution 147 *conversion*; creation 164 *production*; potentiality 469 *possibility*; ontology, metaphysics; philosophy of existence, existentialism, Existenzphilosophie; idealism, materialism, realism 449 *philosophy*.

*reality*, realness, actuality, entelechy, Dasein, Existenz, Vorhandenheit; actual existence, material e. 319 *materiality*; positiveness; historicity, factuality, factualness 494 *truth*; fact, fact of life, brute f., matter of f., positive f., stubborn f., undeniable f., factoid; fait accompli 154 *event*; real thing, not a dream, no joke; realities, nitty-gritty, basics, fundamentals, bedrock, nuts and bolts, brass tacks 638 *important matter*.

*essence*, nature, very n., essential n., thatness, thisness, thusness, individuality, haecceity, quiddity, hypostasis 80 *speciality*; constitutive principle, inner being, sum and substance 5 *essential part*; prime constituent, soul, heart, core, centre 224 *interiority*.

**Adj.** *existing*, existent, in esse, ontic; existential; essential 5 *intrinsic*; absolute, given, self-existent, uncreated; being, in existence, under the sun, living 360 *alive*; pre-existent 119 *prior*; coexistent 121 *present*; undying, immortal, eternal, enduring 115 *perpetual*; extant, standing, surviving, indestructible 113 *lasting*; rife, prevalent, abroad, afloat, afoot 189 *ubiquitous*; ontological, metaphysical.

*real*, essential, substantive 3 *substantial*; not imagined, uninvented, actual, positive, factual, genuine, documented, well-d., historical, grounded, well-g. 494 *true*; natural, of nature, physical, flesh and blood 319 *material*; concrete, solid, tangible 324 *dense*.

**Vb.** *be*, exist, have being; be so and not otherwise; be the case 494 *be true*; consist in, inhere in, reside in 5 *be intrinsic*; pre-exist 119 *be before*; coexist, coincide, subsist 121 *be now*; abide, continue 146 *go on*; endure 113 *last*; vegetate, pass the time, live out one's life, drag out one's l. *or* existence; be alive, breathe, live, move, have one's being, draw breath 360 *live*; exist in space, be found, be met with, stand, lie 186 *be situated*; be here, be there, meet one 189 *be present*; obtain, prevail, reign, be rife 189 *pervade*; take place, come about, occur 154 *happen*; hold, hold good, stand 494 *be true*; represent, stand for, stand as 13 *be identical*.

*become*, come to be, come into being, come into existence, first see the light of day, take flesh 360 *be born*; arise, spring up 68 *begin*; unfold, develop, grow, take form, take shape 316 *evolve*; turn out, change into, metamorphose 147 *be turned to*.

**Adv.** *actually*, really, substantively; essentially, substantially, inherently, intrinsically; ipso facto; positively, factually, in actual fact, in f., in point of f. 494 *truly*; in essence, virtually, to all intents and purposes; potentially 469 *possibly*.

### 2 Nonexistence

**N.** *nonexistence*, inexistence, non-being, nonentity, nothingness, nihility, nullity; nonexistence in time 109 *neverness*; nonexistence in space 190 *absence*; blank, vacuum 190 *emptiness*; nothing, nil, cipher, zilch 103 *zero*; a nothing, nonentity 4 *insubstantial thing*; no such thing, no one, nonperson 190 *nobody*; nihilism, negativeness, negativity, negativism.

*extinction*, oblivion, nirvana; no life 361

*death*; dying out, obsolescence 51 *decay*; annihilation, nihilism 165 *destruction*; abeyance, suspension 752 *abrogation*; amnesty 506 *oblivion*; cancellation, erasure, clean slate 550 *obliteration*.

**Adj.** *nonexistent*, inexistent, unexisting, without being; null, minus; nowhere, missing, omitted 190 *absent*; negatived, nullified, null and void 752 *abrogated*; cancelled, wiped out 550 *obliterated*.

*unreal*, without reality, baseless, groundless, unfounded, without foundation, false 495 *erroneous*; fictitious, fabulous, visionary 513 *imaginary*; without substance, intangible 4 *insubstantial*; unrealized, undeveloped 670 *immature*; potential, in posse, only possible 469 *possible*; only supposed 512 *suppositional*.

*unborn*, uncreated, unmade; unbegotten, unconceived; undiscovered, uninvented, unimagined; as yet unborn, yet to come, in the womb of time 124 *future*.

*extinct*, died out, vanished, lost and gone forever; no more, dead and gone, defunct 361 *dead*; obsolescent, vanishing 361 *dying*; obsolete, dead as the dodo; finished, over and done with 125 *past*.

**Vb.** *not be*, have no existence, have no life; lack reality, exist only in the imagination; be null and void; not happen, never happen, fail to materialize, not come off, abort; be yet unborn.

*pass away*, cease to exist, become extinct, become obsolete, die out, vanish from the face of the earth; be no more 361 *die*; lose one's life 361 *perish*; come to nothing, abort 728 *miscarry*; sink into oblivion 506 *be forgotten*; go, vanish, be lost to sight, leave no trace; dematerialize, 'melt into thin air', go up in a puff of smoke, sink into the earth 446 *disappear*;

> Our revels now are ended. These our actors,
> As I foretold you, were all spirits and
> Are melted into air, into thin air
> William Shakespeare, *The Tempest*

evaporate 338 *vaporize*; melt, dissolve 337 *liquefy*.

*nullify*, reduce to nothing, annul, annihilate, extinguish, snuff out, blow o.; render null and void, suspend 752 *abrogate*; neutralize, negative 533 *negate*; cancel 550 *obliterate*; abolish, wipe out 165 *destroy*.

**Adv.** negatively; not really, by courtesy only.

## 3 Substantiality

**N.** *substantiality*, essentiality 1 *reality*; personality, personal existence; substantivity, objectivity; corporeality, corporeity; visibility; tangibility, palpability, concreteness, solidity 319 *materiality*; ponderability, weight 322 *gravity*; pithiness, meatiness; stuff, material 319 *matter*; totality of existence, plenum, world, world of nature 321 *universe*.

*substance*, hypostasis; substratum, core, nub, nitty-gritty 5 *essential part*; entity, thing, something, somebody 319 *object*; person, creature, Dasein; body, flesh and blood, living matter 360 *life*; solid, concretion 324 *solid body*; pith, marrow, meat 224 *interiority*; gist, drift 514 *meaning*.

**Adj.** *substantial*, hypostatic, personal 5 *intrinsic*; real, actual, objective, natural, corporeal, phenomenal, physical 319 *material*; concrete, solid, tangible, palpable 324 *dense*; considerable 638 *important*; bulky 195 *large*; heavy 322 *weighty*; pithy, meaty, meaningful, full of substance.

**Adv.** *substantially*, corporeally, bodily, physically; personally, in person; really 1 *actually*; essentially 5 *intrinsically*; largely, mainly, in the main 32 *greatly*.

## 4 Insubstantiality

**N.** *insubstantiality*, unsubstantiality, nothingness 2 *nonexistence*; naught, nothing, nothing at all, zilch, not a whit, not a jot, not a scrap 103 *zero*; no one, not a soul 190 *nobody*; abstraction, incorporeity, incorporeality 320 *immateriality*; lack of substance, imponderability 323 *lightness*; flimsiness, meagreness, tenuity 206 *thinness*; sparseness 325 *rarity*; lack of depth, superficiality 212 *shallowness*; intangibility, impalpability, invisibility; vacuity, vacancy, void, hollowness 190 *emptiness*; inanity, vanity, fatuity 497 *absurdity*; pointlessness 10 *irrelevance*; hallucination 440 *visual fallacy*; self-delusion 542 *deception*; dream world, fantasy 513 *ideality*; maya, unreality.

*insubstantial thing*, emblem, token, symbol 547 *indication*; mind, soul 447 *spirit*; abstraction, shadow without substance, shadow, shade, ghost, phantom, spectre, vision, dream, hallucination, mirage, optical illusion 440 *visual fallacy*; air, thin a., wind, breath, vapour, mist; bubble, gossamer, snowflake, snowman 163 *weak thing*; wisp, straw 639 *trifle*; vain thing, bauble, vanity, 'vanity of vanities', inanity, fatuity, fool's paradise 499 *folly*;

> Vanity of vanities, saith the Preacher, vanity of vanities; all is vanity.
> Bible, Ecclesiastes

flight of fancy, figment of the imagination, pipe dream, vapourware, castle in the air, castle in Spain 513 *fantasy*; all talk, moonshine, cock and bull story; hot air, idle talk, gossip, speculation, rumour 515 *empty talk*; tall talk 546 *exaggeration*; cry of 'wolf' 665 *false alarm*; mockery, pretence 875 *ostentation*; chimera, figment, courtesy title; nine days' wonder, flash in the pan; cipher, figurehead, man of straw 639 *non-entity*; pompous ass, stuffed shirt 873 *vain person*; fictitious person, invented character; Queen Dick, Pope Joan; pseudonym, stage name 562 *no name*.

**Adj.** *insubstantial*, unsubstantial, abstract, metaphysical, ideal, noumenal; inessential, not intrinsic; nonphysical, nonmaterial 320 *immaterial*; bodiless, bloodless, incorporeal; lightweight, light as air, airy, ethereal 323 *light*; thin, tenuous, gauzy, gossamer 422 *transparent*; pale 426 *colourless*; vaporous, misty 336 *gaseous*; fragile, delicate, brittle, unsound 163 *flimsy*; ghostly, spectral 970 *spooky*; fleeting, shadowy, vague 419 *dim*, 446 *disappearing*; vacuous, vacant, hollow, void 190 *empty*; vain, inane; honorary, nominal, paper, fictitious; emblematic, symbolic, token 547 *indicating*; without substance, groundless, without foundation, unfounded; visionary, dreamy, chimerical, fantastical 513 *imaginary*; pointless, senseless 515 *meaningless*; blank, characterless, featureless, null; without depth, superficial 212 *shallow*.

**Vb.** *not be*, not exist, die; die away, fade away, pass away; make null, annul, nullify.

**Adv.** *unsubstantially*, unreally; nominally, in name only, by courtesy; in a vacuum; 'sic transit gloria mundi'.

> Sic transit gloria mundi.
> *(Thus passes the glory of the world.)*
> Words spoken at the coronation of a pope.

## 5 Intrinsicality

**N.** *intrinsicality*, inherence, inhesion, immanence; essentialness, essentiality; virtuality, potentiality 160 *ability*; inwardness, introversion, autism, schizothymia; subjectiveness, subjectivity; ego, personality 80 *self*; subjectivism.

*essential part*, important part, sine qua non; prime ingredient, prime constituent 1 *essence*; principle, property, mark, attribute 89 *concomitant*; virtue, capacity; quintessence, flower, distillation, inscape; stuff, quiddity 3 *substance*; incarnation, embodiment; life, lifeblood, heart's blood, sap; jugular vein, artery; heart, soul, inner man 447 *spirit*; gumption, backbone, marrow, pith, fibre; core, kernel 225 *centre*; focus, gist, nub, nitty-gritty, nucleus 638 *chief thing*.

*character*, nature, quality; make-up, personality, type, make, stamp, breed 77 *sort*; constitution, characteristics, traits, ethos, cast,

colour, hue, complexion; aspects, features; diagnosis, diagnostics.

*temperament*, temper, frame of mind, humour, disposition, mood, spirit 817 *affections*; grain, vein, streak, strain, trait 179 *tendency*; idiosyncrasy, foible, habit, peculiarity 80 *speciality*.

*heredity*, endowment; DNA, chromosome, gene, allelomorph, inherited characteristic; inborn capacity *or* tendency, original sin; ancestry 169 *genealogy*; telegony, atavism 106 *recurrence*; hereditariness, heritability; Galton's law, Mendel's law, Mendelism; genetics, genetic counselling, genetic engineering, genetic modification, gene technology, biotechnology, biotech, cloning, transgenics 358 *biology*.

**Adj.** *intrinsic*, immanent, deep down, deep-seated, deep-set, deep-rooted, ingrained; inherent, integral 58 *component*; inward, internal, indwelling 224 *interior*; inwrought, inwoven, implicit, part and parcel of, built-in 78 *included*; indispensable, unalienable, inseparable 13 *identical*; autistic, subjective, introversive, reflexive, inward-looking, introspective, introverted; characteristic, personal; indigenous, native; natural, instinctive, automatic; basic, structural, radical, central, organic 156 *fundamental*; a priori, original, primary, elemental, cardinal, normal; essential, constitutional; virtual, potential, capable.

*genetic*, inherited, hereditary, familial, atavistic, heritable; native, inborn, innate, connate, congenital, connatural; inbred, bred in the bone; genetically modified, GM, transgenic.

*characteristic*, typical, representative, 80 *special*; characterizing, qualitative; diagnostic, indicative, idiomorphic, proper; ineradicable, incurable, invariable; constant, unchanging 153 *established*.

**Vb.** *be intrinsic*, – immanent etc. adj.; inhere, indwell 773 *belong*; be born like it; inherit, take after, run in the blood, run in the family; be marked with, bear the mark of, be stamped with, be characterized by; involve, mean, boil down to 523 *imply*.

**Adv.** *intrinsically*, implicitly etc. adj.; at bottom, fundamentally, essentially, substantially, virtually; per se, as such; in effect, in the main.

## 6 Extrinsicality

**N.** *extrinsicality*, objectiveness, objectivity; transcendence 34 *superiority*; otherness, the other, non-ego, not-self 59 *extraneousness*; externality, outwardness, outer darkness, outer space 223 *exteriority*; objectification, externalization; projection, extrapolation, extroversion, extrovert; accidence 7 *modality*; accident, contingency 159 *chance*; accrual, accessory, acquired characteristic 40 *adjunct*.

**Adj.** *extrinsic*, alien, foreign 59 *extraneous*; transcendent 34 *superior*; outward, external, extramural 223 *exterior*; outward-looking, extroverted; derived from without, environmental, acquired, engrafted, implanted, inbred, instilled, inculcated; supervenient, accessory, adventitious, adscititious; superadded, annexed, appended 38 *additional*; incidental, accidental, contingent, fortuitous 159 *casual*; nonessential, inessential; subsidiary, subordinate 35 *inferior*.

**Vb.** *be extrinsic*, lie without, be outwith, not belong; transcend 34 *be superior*; come from without, supervene 38 *accrue*.

*make extrinsic*, objectify, realize, project 223 *externalize*; body forth 551 *represent*.

**Adv.** *extrinsically*, superficially, on the surface, outwardly; from outside.

**7 State: absolute condition**
**N.** *state*, modal existence, state of being, condition; estate, lot, walk, walk of life, station in l., lifestyle; case, way, plight, pickle 8 *circumstance*; position, place, echelon, category, status, footing, standing, rank; habitude, habit, disposition, complexion 5 *temperament*; attitude, frame of mind, vein, temper, disposition, humour, mood 817 *affections*; state of mind, spirits, morale; state of health, physical condition; trim, kilter, fettle, fig.

*modality*, mode, manner, way, fashion, trend, style; stamp, set, fit, mould 243 *form*; shape, frame, fabric 331 *structure*; aspect, phase, light, complexion, character, guise 445 *appearance*; tenor, tone 179 *tendency*.

**Adj.** *such*, modal, conditional, formal 243 *formative*; organic 331 *structural*; in a state of; in condition 162 *athletic*; in form, in good f. 694 *skilful*; in bad shape, in a bad way 651 *sick*; in bad form 695 *clumsy*.

**Vb.** *be in a state of*, be such, be so; be on a footing; stand, lie, labour under; do, fare.

**Adv.** *conditionally*, it being so, as it is, as things are, such being the case, as the matter stands, provisionally.

**8 Circumstance: relative condition**
**N.** *circumstance*, situation, circumstances, conditions, factors, the times; total situation, personal world, life space; environment, milieu 230 *surroundings*; context 9 *relation*; status quo, state of affairs, how things stand; régime, set-up 7 *state*; posture, attitude; aspect, look of things, appearances 445 *appearance*; lie of the land, how the land lies 186 *situation*; sphere,

background, footing, standing, status, relative position 73 *serial place*, 9 *relativeness*; awkward situation, 'catch-22 s.' (see quotation at 663 *pitfall*), plight, pickle, pass, pretty pass, pinch, corner, fix, hole, jam, quandary, dilemma 700 *predicament*.

*juncture*, conjuncture, stage, point 154 *event*; contingency, eventuality; crossroads, turning point, match point, point of no return; moment, hour, right time, opportunity 137 *occasion*; critical moment, crucial m., defining m., when the chips are down, hour of decision, emergency, exigency 137 *crisis*.

**Adj.** *circumstantial*, given, modal 7 *such*; situated, placed, circumstanced; surrounding, environmental, situational, contextual 230 *circumjacent*; circumscribing, limiting 232 *circumscribed*; modifying 468 *qualifying*; provisional, temporary 114 *transient*; variable 152 *changeful*; dependent on circumstances, relative, contingent, incidental, adventitious 154 *eventual*; emergent, critical, crucial, key; auspicious, favourable 137 *opportune*; fitting the circumstances, suitable, seemly 24 *agreeing*; appropriate, convenient 642 *advisable*.

**Adv.** *thus*, so; like this, in this way; from that angle.

*accordingly*, and so, according as, depending on; according to circumstances, as the wind blows, as it turns out, as the case may be.

*if*, if so be, should it so happen, should it be that; in the event of, in the case of, in case; provisionally, provided that 7 *conditionally*; given that, supposing, assuming, granting, allowing, taking it that; if not, unless, except, without.

SECTION TWO

# Relation

**9 Relation**
**N.** *relation*, relatedness, connectedness, rapport, reference, respect, regard; bearing, direction; concern, concernment, interest, import 638 *importance*; involvement, implication 5 *intrinsicality*; appetency 291 *attraction*; relationship, homogeneity, affinity; filiation, kinship 11 *consanguinity*; classification, classifiability 62 *arrangement*; affiliation, alliance 706 *association*; relations, amicable r., friendly terms, intimacy 880 *friendship*; liaison, linkage, connection, merger, link, tie-up 47 *bond*; commercial relations 622 *business*; something in common, common interest, common reference, common source, common denominator; interdependence, ecology 358 *biology*; context, milieu, environment 8 *circumstance*; import, intention 514 *meaning*.

*relativeness*, relativity, interconnection, mutual relation 12 *correlation*; same relation, homology, correspondence 13 *identity*, 28 *equality*; similar relation, analogy 18 *similarity*; comparability 462 *comparison*; close relation, apposition, approximation 289 *approach*, 200 *nearness*, 202 *contiguity*, 89 *accompaniment*; parallel relation, collaterality 219 *parallelism*, 245 *symmetry*; proportionality, perspective, proportion, ratio, scale; causal relation, causality, cause and effect 156 *cause*; dependence 157 *effect*; governing relation 178 *influence*; subordinate relation 35 *inferiority*; logical relation (see also *relevance*); relative position, stage, status, rank, echelon 27 *degree*; serial order 65 *sequence*; relativism, relationism; relativist, relationist.

*relevance*, logical relation, logicality, logical argument 475 *reasoning*; chain of reasoning, thread 475 *argumentation*; just relation, due proportion 24 *conformance*; suitability, point, application, applicability, appositeness, pertinence, propriety, comparability 24 *fitness*; case in point, good example, classic e., poor e., palmary instance 83 *example*.

*referral*, making reference, reference, cross-r.; application, allusion, mention; citation, quotation; frame of reference, object of reference, referent; referee.

**Adj.** *relative*, not absolute 8 *circumstantial*; relational, referential, respective; relativist, relativistic; referable; related, connected, associated, en rapport, linked, entwined; bearing upon, concerning, in aid of; of concern, of interest, of import 638 *important*; belonging, appertaining, appurtenant 78 *included*; in common 775 *sharing*; mutual, reciprocal, corresponding, answering to 12 *correlative*; classifiable, in the same category 62 *arranged*; serial, consecutive 65 *sequential*; affinitive, congenial, affiliated, filiated, cognate, kindred 11 *akin*; homologous, analogous, like 18 *similar*; comparative, comparable 462 *compared*; approximative, approximating, approaching 200 *near*; collateral 219 *parallel*; proportional, proportionate, varying as, in ratio, to scale; in due proportion, proportionable, commensurate 245 *symmetrical*; perspectival, in perspective; contextual, environmental, ecological.

*relevant*, logical, in context; apposite, pertinent, applicable; pointed, to the point, to the purpose, well-directed 475 *rational*; proper, appropriate, suitable, fitting 24 *apt*; alluding, allusive; quotable, worth mentioning.

**Vb.** *be related*, have a relationship, stand in relation to; have reference to, refer to, regard, respect, have to do with; bear upon, have a bearing on, be a factor 178 *influence*; touch,

concern, deal with, interest, affect; be a relation 11 *be akin*; belong, pertain, appertain; approximate to 289 *approach*; answer to, correspond, reciprocate 12 *correlate*; have a connection, tie in with; be congruent 24 *accord*; be proportionate, vary as; be relevant, have some point, support an analogy, serve as an example; come to the point, get down to brass tacks, get down to the nitty-gritty.

*relate*, bring into relation, put in perspective, get into proportion; connect with, gear to, gear with; apply, bring to bear upon; link, connect, bracket together, treat as one, entwine, tie up with 45 *tie*; put in its context, provide a background, sketch in the b.; compare 18 *liken*; proportion, symmetrize, parallel; balance 28 *equalize*; establish a connection, draw a parallel, find an example 475 *reason*; make a reference to, refer to, touch on, allude to, mention, mention in passing, refer to en passant; index, supply or furnish with references 547 *indicate*.

**Adv.** *relatively*, not absolutely, in a context, in certain contexts; in relation to, contextually; in some degree, to some extent, comparatively, in comparison; proportionally, in ratio, to scale, in perspective; conditionally, depending on circumstance, circumstantially; appropriately 24 *pertinently*.

*concerning*, touching, regarding; as to, as regards, with regard to, with respect to; relative to, relating to, vis-à-vis, with reference to, about, re, anent (Scots), on, under; in connection with; in relation to, bearing on; speaking of, apropos, apropos of, by the way, by the bye, on the subject of; on the point of, as far as concerns; in the matter of, in re; under the head of; on the part of, on the score of; whereas; forasmuch, inasmuch; concerning which, whereto, whereunder; thereto, thereunder; hereto, hereunder; whereof, thereof, hereof.

## 10 Unrelatedness: absence of relation

**N.** *unrelatedness*, absoluteness; noninvolvement, independence 744 *freedom*; arbitrariness; unilaterality, unilateralism; separateness, insularity, isolation 46 *separation*; singularity, individuality 80 *speciality*; rootlessness, homelessness, no fixed abode; lack of connection, unconnectedness, no context; unclassifiability; randomness 61 *disorder*; inconsequence (see also *irrelevance*); disconnection, disconnectedness, dissociation 46 *disunion*, 72 *discontinuity*; misconnection, wrong association 495 *error*; disproportion, asymmetry 246 *distortion*; incommensurability, disparity 29 *inequality*; diversity, heterogeneity, multifariousness 15 *difference*, 17 *nonuniformity*, 19 *dissimilarity*, 82 *multiformity*; incongruence 84 *nonconformity*; irreconcilability 14 *contrariety*; intrusion, intrusiveness 138 *untimeliness*; no concern of, no business of, nobody's b.; square peg in a round hole, fish out of water 25 *misfit*; exotic, alien element, intruder, cuckoo in the nest 59 *extraneousness*.

*irrelevance*, irrelevancy; illogicality 477 *sophism*; pointlessness, inapplicability, bad example; ineptitude, inconsequence, non sequitur; parenthesis, obiter dictum 231 *interjection*; diversion, red herring, dust in the eyes 282 *deviation*; episode, incidental 154 *event*; inessential, non-essential 639 *unimportance*.

**Adj.** *unrelated*, irrelative, absolute, self-existent; independent 744 *unconfined*; owing nothing to 21 *original*; irrespective, regardless, unilateral, arbitrary; unclassified, unidentified; unclassifiable, rootless, homeless, of no fixed abode; adrift, wandering, astray 282 *deviating*; kinless, isolated, insular 88 *alone*; unconcerned, uninvolved 860 *indifferent*; floating, detached, unconnected, without context, disconnected, unallied 46 *disunited*; digressive, parenthetic, anecdotal; episodic, incidental 72 *discontinuous*; separate, singular, individual 80 *special*; private, of no concern, without interest, nothing to do with; inessential 6 *extrinsic*; exotic, foreign, alien, strange, outlandish, extraterrestrial 59 *extraneous*; intrusive, untimely 138 *ill-timed*; uncongenial, ungermane, inappropriate, incompatible 25 *disagreeing*; not comparable, incommensurable, disparate 29 *unequal*; disproportionate, out of proportion, asymmetrical 246 *distorted*; incongruent, discordant 84 *unconformable*; irreconcilable 14 *contrary*; heterogeneous 17 *nonuniform*; multifarious 82 *multiform*.

*irrelevant*, illogical; inapposite, inapplicable, pointless; impertinent, inept 25 *unapt*; out of order, misapplied 188 *misplaced*; misdirected 495 *erroneous*; off-target, off the beam, off-centre, peripheral; rambling, wandering 570 *diffuse*; adrift, beside the point, beside the mark, beside the purpose, off the point, neither here nor there; trivial, inessential 639 *unimportant*; inconsequent, inconsequential, six and half a dozen; incidental 159 *casual*; remote, far-fetched, forced, strained, laboured; academic, impractical, immaterial.

**Vb.** *be unrelated*, have no concern with, have nothing to do w., have no bearing on; owe nothing to, disown; have no right to be there, have no place in; not be one's business, be nobody's b.; not concern, not touch, not interest; be irrelevant, be off the point, be beside the p., avoid the issue, cloud the i., draw a red herring, throw dust in one's eyes; force,

strain, labour; drag in by the heels, drag in screaming; ramble, wander, lose the thread, stray from the point 570 *be diffuse*.

**Adv.** *unrelatedly*, irrespective, regardless; without regard, without respect, without reference, without relation to; irrelevantly, illogically, inappropriately; parenthetically, incidentally, episodically, coincidentally, by the way.

## 11 Consanguinity: kinship

**N.** *consanguinity*, kinship, kindred, blood 169 *parentage*; filiation, affiliation, relationship, affinity, propinquity; blood relationship, agnation, cognation; ancestry, lineage, descent 169 *genealogy*; connection, alliance, family, family connection; ties of family, ties of blood, ties of race, clanship, clannishness, tribalism, nationality 371 *nation*; nepotism; atavism 5 *heredity*.

*kinsman*, kinswoman, sib; kin, kindred, kith and kin, kinsfolk, ain folk (Scots), relations; near relative, next of kin; distant relation, blood r., kissing cousin; one of the family, relation by marriage, in-law, step-relation; grandparents, father, mother 169 *parentage*; children, offspring, issue, one's flesh and blood 170 *posterity*; agnate, cognate, collateral; twin, identical t., fraternal t.; sibling, sib; sister, brother, uterine b. *or* s., blood b. *or* s., brother *or* sister german, half-b. *or* -s.; stepbrother; cousin, cousin german, first c., second c., cousin once removed; uncle, aunt, auntie, great-uncle, great-great-u., great-aunt, great-great-a.; nephew, niece, grand-nephew, grand-niece; clansman, tribesman, compatriot.

*family*, matriarchy, patriarchy; motherhood, fatherhood, brotherhood, sisterhood, cousinhood; fraternity, sorority; adopted son *or* daughter, foster child, godchild, stepchild, adopted c.; adoptive mother *or* father, biological mother *or* father, natural mother, birth m., surrogate m., commissioning m.; relations by marriage, in-laws; one's people, one's folks; family circle, home c. 882 *sociality*; the old folks at home, household, hearth and home 192 *home*; nuclear family, extended f.; tribe, clan, horde.

*race*, stock, stem, stirps, breed, strain, line, side, spear s., distaff s.; house, tribe, clan, moiety, phratry, sept; geographical race, local r., ethnic group, nation, people; racialism, race hate, hate crime, ethnic cleansing, nationalism 481 *prejudice*; racial equality 915 *dueness*; inbreeding, interbreeding; crossbreeding.

**Adj.** *akin*, sib, kindred, kin, consanguineous, twin-born; matrilineal, out of; patrilineal, by; maternal, paternal 169 *parental*; sibling, fraternal, brotherly, sisterly, cousinly; avuncular; novercal; related, family, collateral, allied, affined; connatural, congenerous; agnate, cognate, german, uterine; near, related, intimately r. 9 *relative;* once removed, twice r.; next-of-kin; half-, step-.

*ethnic*, racial, tribal, clannish 371 *national;* interracial, intertribal; interbred, inbred 43 *mixed;* Australoid, Caucasoid, Mongoloid, Negroid.

**Vb.** *be akin*, share the blood of; claim relationship etc. n.; own a connection 9 *be related;* marry into 894 *wed;* father, sire 167 *generate;* be brother *or* sister to, brother, sister; affiliate, adopt, foster, bring into the family.

## 12 Correlation: double or reciprocal relation

**N.** *correlation*, correlativity, mutual relation, functionality 9 *relation;* proportionment, proportionality, proportion 245 *symmetry;* texture, design, pattern 62 *arrangement;* grid 222 *network;* correspondence 18 *similarity;* contingency table; opposite number 13 *identity;* mutuality, interrelation, interconnection; interdependence, mutual dependence; mutualism, mutualist; interaction, interplay, mutual influence; alternation, turn and turn about, swings and roundabouts, seesaw 317 *oscillation;* reciprocity, reciprocation 151 *interchange;* each, each other, one another; give and take 770 *compromise;* exchange, change, payment in kind 791 *barter*, trade-off, tit for tat 714 *retaliation.*

**Adj.** *correlative*, reciprocal, functional 9 *relative;* corresponding, opposite, answering to, analogous, parallel 18 *similar;* proportioned, proportional, proportionate 245 *symmetrical;* complementary, complemental, interdependent; interconnecting, interlocking; mutual, requited; reciprocating 714 *retaliatory;* reacting 280 *recoiling;* alternating, alternate, seesaw 317 *oscillating;* balancing 28 *equivalent;* interlocking, geared, interacting; patterned, woven; interchangeable, exchangeable 151 *interchanged;* inter-, intertribal, interracial, international, interstate; two-way, bilateral.

**Vb.** *correlate*, interrelate, interconnect, interlock, interplay, interact; interdepend; vary as, be a function of; proportion, symmetrize; correspond, be analogous to, answer to, reflect 18 *resemble;* react 280 *recoil;* alternate 317 *oscillate;* counterchange 151 *interchange;* reciprocate 714 *retaliate;* exchange, swap, barter, trade off 791 *trade;* balance 28 *equalize;* set off, act as a foil to 31 *compensate.*

**Adv.** *correlatively*, proportionately, as . . . so . . . ; mutually, reciprocally, each to each,

each other, one another; equivalently 28 *equally;* interchangeably, in mutual exchange 151 *in exchange;* in kind 791 *in trade;* alternately, by turns, turn and turn about, first one and then the other; contrariwise, vice versa 14 *contrarily;* inter, between, shuttlewise 317 *to and fro.*

## 13 Identity

**N.** *identity*, identicalness, sameness, oneness 88 *unity;* the same, no other, the very same, the very one; genuineness 494 *authenticity;* the real thing, it, absolutely it 21 *no imitation;* the very words, ipsissima verba, ditto, tautology, redundancy 106 *repetition;* other self, alter ego, ka, ba, genius, double; oneness with, identification, coincidence, congruence 24 *agreement;* coalescence, mergence, absorption 299 *reception;* convertibility, interchangeability, equivalence 28 *equality;* no difference, distinction without a difference, indistinguishability; synonymity, synonymy 514 *meaning;* same kind, homogeneity, consubstantiality 16 *uniformity;* no change, invariability, invariant, constant 153 *fixture;* counterpart, duplicate 22 *copy;* look-alike, dead ringer, spitting image; fellow, pair, match, twin 18 *analogue;* homonym, homograph, homophone, synonym 559 *word.*

**Adj.** *identical*, same, self, selfsame, of that ilk; one and the same, one and only 88 *one;* coalescent, merging, absorbed; identified with, indistinguishable, look-alike, interchangeable, confusable, unisex, convertible, equivalent 28 *equal;* homonymous, homographic, homophonic, synonymous, synonymic; coincident, congruent 24 *agreeing;* always the same, invariable, invariant, constant, unchanging, unaltered 153 *unchangeable;* monotonous 838 *tedious;* homogeneous, monolithic 16 *uniform;* tautologous, redundant, repetitive, repetitional 106 *repeated.*

**Vb.** *be identical*, show no difference, look the same, be as like as two peas in a pod, be look-alikes, be a dead ringer for, be the spitting image of, ditto 106 *repeat;* coincide, coalesce, merge, be one with, sink one's identity; be congruent, register, agree in all respects, be unanimous 24 *accord;* phase 123 *synchronize.*

*identify*, make as one, treat as o., unify, consubstantiate; make no difference, treat as the same, not distinguish, recognize no distinction 464 *not discriminate;* equate, tar with the same brush 28 *equalize;* assimilate, match, pair 18 *liken.*

**Adv.** *identically*, interchangeably, without distinction; in phase, on all fours; ibidem; ditto; in like case, same here.

## 14 Contrariety

**N.** *contrariety*, nonidentity, absolute difference, world of d. 15 *difference*; exclusiveness, mutual e., irreconcilability 10 *unrelatedness*; antipathy, repugnance, hostility 888 *hatred*; adverseness, contrariness, antagonism 704 *opposition*; antidote 182 *counteraction*; conflict, confrontation, clash 279 *collision*; discord 25 *disagreement*; contradistinction, contrast, relief, light r., variation, undertone, counterpoint 15 *differentiation*; contradiction, flat c. 533 *negation*; contraindication 467 *counterevidence*; countersense, antonym 514 *meaning*; antinomy, antilogy; inconsistency, two voices 17 *nonuniformity*; paradox, ambivalence 518 *equivocalness*; oppositeness, antithesis, direct opposite, antipodes, antipole, opposite pole, poles apart; other extreme, opposite e., quite the contrary, quite the reverse; other side, opposite s. 240 *contraposition*; reverse, wrong side 238 *rear*; inverse 221 *inversion*; converse, reverse image, mirror i., mirror, mirror symmetry 417 *reflection*; opposite direction, contraflow; headwind, undertow, counter-current 182 *counteraction*.

*polarity*, contraries 704 *opposites*, positive and negative; north and south; east and west; day and night; light and darkness; hot and cold; fire and water; chalk and cheese; black and white; good and evil; yin and yang, male and female; 'Hyperion to a satyr' 19 *dissimilarity*.

> So excellent a king; that was, to this,
> Hyperion to a satyr
> William Shakespeare, *Hamlet*

**Adj.** *contrary*, nonidentical, as different as chalk from cheese, anything but 15 *different*; contrasting, contrasted, incompatible, clashing, conflicting, discordant 25 *disagreeing*; inconsistent, not uniform 17 *nonuniform*; ambivalent, bittersweet, love-hate, sweet and sour; contradictory, antithetic, adversative 533 *negative*; antithetical, antonymous; diametrically opposite, poles asunder, poles apart, antipodal, antipodean 240 *opposite*; reverse, converse, inverse; antipathetic, inimical, hostile 888 *hating*; adverse, untoward, antagonistic 704 *opposing*; counteractive, antidotal 182 *counteracting*, counter-, contra-, anti-.

**Vb.** *be contrary*, have nothing in common, be poles apart 10 *be unrelated*, 15 *differ*; contrast, stand out 25 *disagree*; clash, conflict with; run counter to 240 *be opposite*, speak with two voices 518 *be equivocal*; contravene, fly in the face of 704 *oppose*, 738 *disobey*; exclude, deny, contradict, contraindicate 533 *negate*; cancel out 182 *counteract*; turn the tables 221 *invert*.

**Adv.** *contrarily*, per contra, on the other hand, conversely, contrariwise; vice versa, topsy-turvy, upside down; invertedly, inversely; on the contrary; otherwise, quite the other way, the other way round; in contrast, in opposition to; by contraries, by opposites.

## 15 Difference

**N.** *difference*, unlikeness 19 *dissimilarity*; disparity, odds 29 *inequality*; margin, differential, minus, plus 41 *remainder*; wide margin, clear blue water 199 *distance*; narrow margin 200 *nearness*; heterogeneity, variety, diverseness, diversity 17 *nonuniformity*; divergence, departure from 282 *deviation*; otherness, differentia, distinctness 10 *unrelatedness*, 21 *originality*; discrepancy, incongruity 25 *disagreement*; incompatibility, antipathy 861 *dislike*; disharmony, discord, variance 709 *dissension*; contrast 14 *contrariety*; opposite, antithesis 240 *contraposition*; variation, modification, alteration 143 *change*, 147 *conversion*.

*differentiation* 463 *discrimination*; bias, 481 *prejudice*, specification 80 *speciality*; distinction, contradistinction, delicate d., nice d., subtle d.; nuance, nicety, shade of difference, fine shade of meaning 514 *meaning*; distinction without a difference 13 *identity*; conjugation, declension 564 *grammar*.

*variant*, different thing, another t., something else, something else again; this, that or the other; quite another matter, a different kettle of fish, a different ball game, a whole new b. g.; another story, another version, horse of another colour, another light on, the other side of the coin; special case 80 *speciality*; freak, mutation; sport 84 *nonconformist*; edition, new e. version, new v. 589 *edition*; cut, director's cut, rough cut.

**Adj.** *different*, differing, unlike, like chalk and cheese 19 *dissimilar*, original, fresh 126 *new*; various, variform, diverse, diversified, heterogeneous 17 *nonuniform*; multifarious 82 *multiform*; assorted, of all sorts, all manner of, divers 43 *mixed*; distinct, distinguished, differentiated, discriminated, divided 46 *separate*; divergent, departing from 282 *deviating*; odd 84 *unusual*; discrepant, discordant, clashing, incongruent, incongruous 25 *disagreeing*; disparate 29 *unequal*; contrasting, contradistinctive; contrasted, far from it, poles apart, poles asunder, wide apart; anything but 14 *contrary*; other, another, not the same, peculiar 80 *special*; in a different class 34 *superior*, 35 *inferior*; somehow different, the same yet not the same, changed, altered, modified, genetically modified, GM, transgenic 147 *converted*.

*distinctive*, diagnostic, indicative 5 *characteristic*; differentiating, distinguishing, marking out; comparative, superlative, augmentative.

**Vb.** *differ*, be different etc. adj.; show variety; vary from, diverge f., depart f. 282 *deviate*; contrast, clash, jar, conflict 25 *disagree*, be at variance 709 *quarrel*; change one's tune, modify, vary, make alterations; suffer a sea change 143 *change*.

*differentiate*, distinguish, mark out, pick o., single o., severalize 463 *discriminate*; shade, refine, make a distinction, sharpen a d.; particularize 80 *specify*; widen the gap 46 *set apart*.

**Adv.** *differently*, variously, as modified, after alteration; otherwise, not so, some other way, in a different fashion, with a difference; in different ways, in many w., multifariously.

## 16 Uniformity

**N.** *uniformity*, uniformness, consistency, constancy, steadiness 153 *stability*; persistence 71 *continuity*, 146 *continuance*; unfailing regularity, conveyor belt 141 *periodicity*; order, regularity, method, centralization 60 *order*; homogeneity, homology 18 *similarity*; monolithic quality; unity, unison, correspondence, accordance 24 *agreement*; evenness, levelness, flushness 258 *smoothness*; roundness 245 *symmetry*; sameness 13 *identity*; invariableness, invariability, monotony, even tenor; mixture as before, same old story; even pace, jog trot, rhythm; round, daily r., routine, drill, treadmill 610 *habit*; monotone, greyness; men in grey suits, faceless people; droning, drone, sing-song, monologue; monolith; pattern, same p., mould; type, stereotype 22 *copy*; stamp, common s., same s., same mint; set, assortment; suit, flush; standard dress 228 *uniform*; assimilation, standardization, mass production, automation, computerization 83 *conformity*; cliché 106 *repetition*; regimentation, totalitarianism, intolerance, closed shop 740 *compulsion*.

*uniformist*, regimenter, sergeant major; egalitarian, equalitarian, leveller.

**Adj.** *uniform*, all of a piece, one-piece; same all through, solid, monolithic; of one kind, connatural, homogenetic; homogeneous, of a piece, of a pattern 18 *similar*; same, consistent, self-c., constant, steady, stable 153 *fixed*; undeviating, unchanging, unvarying, invariable 144 *permanent*; equable 823 *inexcitable*; rhythmic, measured, even-paced 258 *smooth*; undiversified, undifferentiated, unrelieved, unbroken 573 *plain*; uncontrasting, without contrast, lacking variety, in uniform, uniformed, liveried; characterless, featureless, faceless, blank; monotonous, droning, sing-song, monotone; monochrome, drab, grey; repetitive, running through 106 *repeated*; standard,

normal 83 *typical*; patterned, standardized, stereotyped, mass-produced, conveyor belt, unisex; sorted, assorted, sized; drilled, aligned, in line; orderly, regular 245 *symmetrical*; straight, even, flush, level, dead 1. 216 *flat*.

**Vb.** *be uniform*, – homogeneous etc. adj.; follow routine 610 *be wont*; sing in unison, sing the same song, chorus, harmonize 24 *accord*; typify 83 *conform*; toe the line, follow the crowd, fall in, dress; wear uniform, be in u.

*make uniform*, homogenize; stamp, characterize, run through 547 *mark*; level, level up *or* down, abolish differentials 28 *equalize*; assimilate, harmonize 18 *liken*; size, assort, grade; drill, align; regiment, institutionalize; standardize, stereotype, pattern; mass-produce; put into uniform; normalize, regularize, conventionalize 83 *make conform*.

**Adv.** *uniformly*, solidly etc. adj.; like clockwork, methodically, habitually, invariably, eternally, endlessly; without exception, in a rut, in a groove.

## 17 Nonuniformity

**N.** *nonuniformity*, variability, patchiness 72 *discontinuity*; unpredictability 152 *changeableness*; inconstancy, inconsistency, capriciousness, whimsy 604 *caprice*; irregularity, haphazardness, no system, no pattern 61 *disorder*; asymmetry 244 *amorphism*; ruggedness, raggedness, unevenness, jerkiness 259 *roughness*; heterogeneity, heteromorphism 15 *difference*; contrast 14 *contrariety*, 19 *dissimilarity*; decentralization, divarication, divergence 282 *deviation*; diversity, variety, variousness, multifariousness 82 *multiformity*; all sorts and conditions, all shapes and sizes, mixed bag, ragbag, lucky dip, hotchpotch, smorgasbord, odds and ends 43 *medley*; patchwork, motley, crazy paving, mosaic 437 *variegation*; abnormality, exception, special case, sport, mutation, freak 84 *nonconformity*; odd man out, lone wolf, rogue elephant 59 *extraneousness*; uniqueness, individuality 80 *speciality*; every man in his humour; 'quot homines tot sententiae'.

> Quot homines tot sententiae: suo' quoique mos.
> *(There are as many different opinions as there are people: everyone has their own way.)*
> Terence, *Phormio*

**Adj.** *nonuniform*, variable, unpredictable, changeable, never the same 152 *changeful*; spasmodic, sporadic 142 *fitful*; inconstant, inconsistent 604 *capricious*; temperamental 822 *excitable*; patchy 29 *unequal*; random, haphazard, irregular, unsystematic; asymmetrical 244 *amorphous*; untidy, out of order 61 *orderless*; uneven, bumpy, lumpy, choppy, jerky 259 *rough*; erratic, out of step, out of time, gaining, losing; contrasting, contrasted 14 *contrary*; heterogeneous, various, diverse 15 *different*, 19 *dissimilar*; multifarious, miscellaneous, of many kinds, of all sorts 82 *multiform*; multicoloured, decorated 844 *ornamental*; divergent, diversified 282 *deviating*; dissenting 25 *disagreeing*; aberrant, atypical 84 *unconformable*; exceptional, unusual, unconventional 84 *abnormal*; unique, lone 80 *special*; individual, hand-made; out of uniform, in civvies, in mufti, in plain clothes.

**Adv.** *nonuniformly*, irregularly, haphazardly, erratically, unsystematically; unevenly, bumpily, jerkily; confusedly, chaotically; all anyhow, all over the place; here, there and everywhere.

**18 Similarity**
**N.** *similarity*, resemblance, likeness, similitude; semblance, seeming, look 445 *appearance*; fashion, trend, style 243 *form*; common feature, point in common, point of resemblance 9 *relation*; congruity 24 *agreement*; affinity, kinship 11 *consanguinity*; homogeneity, homomorphism, connaturality; comparability, analogousness, analogy, correspondence, homology, parallelism 12 *correlation*; equivalence, parity 28 *equality*; proportionality 245 *symmetry*; no difference 13 *identity*; general resemblance, family likeness; close resemblance, good likeness, perfect l.; striking likeness, faithful l., photographic l. 551 *representation*; lifelikeness 494 *accuracy*; approximation 200 *nearness*; partial likeness, distant l., faint resemblance, simulacrum; adumbration, suggestion, hint; fair comparison, sufficient resemblance, about the size of it.

*assimilation*, likening 462 *comparison*; reduction to, identification 13 *identity*; simulation, camouflage, mimicry 20 *imitation*; parable, allegory, metaphor; portrayal 590 *description*; portraiture 553 *picture*; alliteration, assonance, rhyme 593 *prosody*; pun, play on words 518 *equivocalness*.

*analogue*, congener, the like, suchlike, the likes of; type, good example, perfect e., classic e. 83 *example*; correlate, correlative 12 *correlation*; simile, parallel, metaphor, allegory, parable; equivalent 150 *substitute*; brother, sister, twin; match, pair, fellow, mate, companion, pendant; complement, counterpart, other half, better half 89 *concomitant*; alter ego, other self, genius, ka, ba; fetch, doppelgänger; double, ringer, dead r., look-alike; likeness, reflection, shadow, the picture of 551 *image*; another edition of, dead spit of, spitting image, living image, chip off the old block; twins, two

peas, couple, pair 90 *duality*; two of a kind, 'Arcades ambo', Roland and Oliver, birds of a feather;

> **Ambo florentes aetatibus, Arcades ambo,**
> **Et cantare pares et respondere parati.**
> *(Both in the flower of youth, both Arcadians,*
> *matched and ready both to sing and to respond.)*
> Virgil, *Eclogues*

reproduction, copy, clone 22 *duplicate*.
**Adj.** *similar*, resembling, like, much l.; alike, ridiculously a., twin, matching, like as two peas (in a pod), cast in the same mould, out of the same m.; much of a muchness, nothing to choose between, virtually identical 13 *identical*; of a piece 16 *uniform*; analogical; analogous, parallel 28 *equivalent*; corresponding, bracketed with; consubstantial, homogeneous, connatural, congeneric 11 *akin*; close, approximate 200 *near*; typical, representative 551 *representing*; reproducing, reflecting; after the fashion of, after, après, in the style of, à la; much the same, something like, such as, quasi; rhyming, alliterative, assonant 106 *repeated*; punning 518 *equivocal*.

*lifelike*, realistic, photographic, exact, faithful, natural, typical; good of one, just one, true to life, true to nature, true to type; graphic, vivid, eidetic 443 *visible*.

*simulating* 20 *imitative*; seeming, deceptive, camouflaged 542 *deceiving*; mock, quasi, pseudo 542 *spurious*; making a show of 875 *ostentatious*; synthetic, artificial, simulated, ersatz 150 *substituted*.

**Vb.** *resemble*, be similar to, pass for, bear a resemblance; mirror, reflect 20 *imitate*; seem, seem like, sound l., look as if; look like, take after, favour, put one in mind of, have the look of; savour of, smack of; compare with, approximate to, come near to 289 *approach*; match, correspond to, answer to 24 *accord*; assonate, rhyme; run in pairs; typify 551 *represent*.

*liken*, assimilate to, approximate 462 *compare*; reduce to 13 *identify*; pair, twin, bracket with 28 *equalize*; allegorize, use a simile; portray 20 *imitate*; alliterate, rhyme 106 *repeat*; pun 518 *be equivocal*.

**Adv.** *similarly*, as, like, as if, quasi, so to speak, as it were; allegorically 519 *metaphorically*; likewise, so, correspondingly, in the same category, by the same token; just as, in a way; as in a mirror; like father like son, like mother like daughter.

**Int.** same difference (inf).

**19 Dissimilarity**
**N.** *dissimilarity*, dissimilitude, unlikeness; incomparability 10 *unrelatedness*; disparity 29 *inequality*; diversity, divergence 15 *difference*;

variation, variance, variety 17 *nonuniformity*, 82 *multiformity*; contrast 14 *contrariety*; little in common, nothing in c., no common ground, no match, not a pair 25 *disagreement*; novelty, uniqueness 21 *originality*; dissemblance, dissimilation, camouflage, make-up, cosmetic surgery 525 *concealment*, 527 *disguise*; caricature, bad likeness, poor l. 552 *misrepresentation*; foreign body, alien element 59 *extraneousness*; odd man out 25 *misfit*.

**Adj.** *dissimilar*, unlike, distinct, diverse 15 *different*; various 82 *multiform*; disparate 29 *unequal*; unalike, not comparable 10 *unrelated*; far above 34 *superior*; far below 35 *inferior*; unrelated, unmatched, unpaired 17 *nonuniform*; unique, peerless, matchless, nonpareil, one and only, original 21 *inimitable*; incongruent 25 *disagreeing*; untypical, atypical, exotic 84 *unconformable*; unprecedented, new and strange, novel 126 *new*; a far cry from 199 *distant*; bad of, not true to life, unrealistic.

**Vb.** *be unlike*, – dissimilar etc. adj.; bear no resemblance, have nothing in common 15 *differ*; stand out 34 *be superior*, 35 *be inferior*.

*make unlike*, discriminate, distinguish 15 *differentiate*; innovate, modify, modulate 143 *change*, 147 *convert*; caricature 552 *misrepresent*, 246 *distort*; dissemble 542 *deceive*; disguise 525 *conceal*; camouflage 18 *liken*, 541 *fake*.

**Adv.** *dissimilarly*, discordantly, contrastingly, variously 15 *differently*.

## 20 Imitation

**N.** *imitation*, copying etc. vb.; sincerest form of flattery; rivalry, emulation 716 *contention*; conventionality, doing as Rome does 83 *conformity*; lack of originality, following, literalism, slavishness, slavish imitation; imitativeness, parrotry (see also *mimicry*); affectedness 850 *affectation*; mimesis 551 *representation*; reflection, mirror, echo, shadow 18 *assimilation*; paraphrase, translation 520 *interpretation*; borrowing, cribbing, literary theft, piracy, pirating, plagiarism, plagiary 788 *stealing*; forgery, falsification, counterfeit, fake 541 *falsehood*; copying, transcribing, transcription, transliteration, tracing 22 *copy*; duplication, reduplication, multiplication 166 *reproduction*, 551 *photography*; reverse engineering.

*mimicry*, mimesis 551 *representation*; onomatopoeia; noises off 594 *dramaturgy*; mime, pantomime, sign language, gesticulation 547 *gesture*; ventriloquism 579 *speech*; portrayal, portraiture 553 *painting*, 590 *description*; realism 494 *accuracy*; mockery, caricature, parody, spoof, burlesque 851 *satire*; travesty 552 *misrepresentation*, 246 *distortion*; imitat-

iveness, mimicking, apery, apishness, parrotry 106 *repetition*, 850 *affectation*; conjuring, illusionism; simulator, simulation exercise 534 *teaching*; simulation, semblance, disguise, cosmetics, make-up, protective colouring, camouflage, dissimulation 18 *similarity*, 19 *dissimilarity*; pretence, mockery, simulacrum, pale shadow 542 *sham*, 4 *insubstantiality*.

*imitator*, copycat, ape, monkey; mockingbird, mynah bird, parrot, 'sedulous ape';

> I have thus played the sedulous ape to Hazlitt, to Lamb, to Wordsworth, to Sir Thomas Browne, to Defoe, to Hawthorne, to Montaigne, to Baudelaire and to Obermann.
> Robert Louis Stevenson

echo; sheep 83 *conformist*, 284 *follower*; follower of fashion, fashion victim 848 *beau monde*; poseur 850 *affecter*; echoer, yes-man 925 *flatterer*; mocker, burlesquer, parodist, caricaturist 839 *humorist*, 926 *detractor*; mimic, impersonator, female i., drag artiste, illusionist, ventriloquist, tribute band 594 *entertainer*; actor, portrayer, portraitist 556 *artist*; copyist, printer, tracer 586 *calligrapher*; translator, paraphraser 520 *interpreter*, transcriber of life, realist, naturalist; simulator, shammer, hypocrite 545 *impostor*; borrower, pasticheur, plagiarist, pirate; counterfeiter, forger, faker; duplicator, spirit d., copier, photocopier, Xerox (tdmk), mimeograph, pantograph, stencil.

**Adj.** *imitative*, mimetic; emulating; onomatopoeic, echoic; apish, aping, parroting, parrotlike; following; echoing, flattering; posing 850 *affected*; disguised, camouflaged; mock, mimic; simulating, shamming 541 *hypocritical*; pseudo, quasi, sham, imitation, phony, counterfeit 541 *false*; artificial, ersatz, synthetic, man-made 150 *substituted*; unoriginal, uninventive, derivative, imitated, second-hand, handed down 106 *repeated*; conventional 83 *conformable*; paraphrastic, modelled, moulded on; taken from nature, copied, slavish, literal; caricatured, parodied, travestied, burlesque; transcribed, transliterated; easy to copy, imitable.

**Vb.** *imitate*, emulate, ape, parrot, flatter, echo, mirror, reflect 18 *resemble*; make a show of, pose 850 *be affected*; pretend, masquerade, make-believe, make as if, make like; act, mimic, mime, portray, paint 551 *represent*; parody, take off, spoof, lampoon, caricature, burlesque, travesty 851 *ridicule*; sham, simulate, put on, feign, play the hypocrite 541 *dissemble*; disguise, camouflage 525 *conceal*; ventriloquize 542 *deceive*.

*copy*, draw, trace; copy faithfully, catch; set

up 587 *print*; reprint, duplicate, mimeograph, cyclostyle, photocopy, xerox, photostat; make copies, reduplicate, multiply, reel off 166 *reproduce*; copy out, transcribe, transliterate, type, type out; paraphrase, translate 520 *interpret*; copy from, crib, plagiarize, pirate, lift, borrow 788 *steal*; counterfeit, forge 541 *fake*.

*do likewise*, do as the Romans do, mould oneself on, pattern oneself on, take as a model; take a leaf out of another's book; follow, follow suit, tread in the steps of, follow my leader 284 *follow*; echo, ditto, re-echo, chorus 106 *repeat*; follow precedent, follow another's example, join in the cry, hunt with the hounds, jump on the bandwagon 83 *conform*; emulate, rival 716 *contend*.

**Adv.** *imitatively*, emulously, in rivalry; parrot-fashion; en travesti in drag; literally, to the letter, word for word, verbatim, literatim 494 *truly*.

## 21 Originality

**N.** *originality*, creativeness, inventiveness 513 *imagination*; creation, invention, all my own work, 'a poor thing but mine own' 164 *production*;

> A poor virgin, sir, an ill-favoured thing, sir, but mine own: a poor humour of mine, sir, to take that that no man else will.
>
> William Shakespeare, *As You Like It*

original thought, originality 119 *priority*, 10 *unrelatedness*; uniqueness, the one and only 88 *unity*; inimitability, transcendence 34 *superiority*; independence, defiance of precedent, line of one's own 744 *freedom*; precedent, example 23 *prototype*; new departure 68 *beginning*; something new, novelty, innovation, freshness 126 *newness*; eccentricity, idiosyncrasy, individuality 84 *nonconformity*; unlikeness 19 *dissimilarity*.

*no imitation*, genuineness, sincerity 494 *authenticity*; real thing, the very thing, the real McCoy, the genuine article; it, absolutely it 13 *identity*, 80 *self*; autograph, holograph, manuscript, one's own hand, usual signature.

**Adj.** *original*, creative, inventive 513 *imaginative*; unimitated, underived, not derivative; prototypical, archetypal; primordial, primary; first, first-hand, first in the field, pioneering 119 *prior*; unprecedented, fresh, novel 126 *new*; individual, personal 80 *special*; independent 744 *free*; eccentric, idiosyncratic 84 *unconformable*.

*inimitable*, transcendent, unmatched, incomparable, out of reach 34 *superior*; not imitated, not emulated, uncopied, unhackneyed; atypical 15 *different*; unique, one and only 88 *one*; authentic, real, true 494 *genuine*; natural 5

intrinsic; sincere, unadulterated 44 *unmixed*.

## 22 Copy

**N.** *copy*, exact c.; clone 166 *reproduction*; replica, replication, facsimile, tracing; fair copy, transcript, transcription, counterpart 18 *analogue*; cast, death mask; ectype, stamp, seal, impress, impression, imprint; mechanical copy, stereotype, electrotype, collotype, lithograph, print, offprint, printed matter 587 *letterpress*, 555 *engraving*; photocopy, Xerox (tdmk), photograph, photogravure, Photostat (tdmk), positive, negative, contact print 551 *photography*; microfilm, microfiche 548 *record*; dummy, imitation, pastiche; counterfeit, fake, forgery 542 *sham*; plagiarism, piracy, crib 20˙ *imitation*; likeness, resemblance, semblance 18 *similarity*; study, portrait, drawing 553 *picture*; icon, image 551 *representation*; model, effigy, statue 554 *sculpture*; echo, faithful copy, reflex, mirror, servile imitation 106 *repetition*, 417 *reflection*; bad copy, poor likeness, apology for – , mockery of – 552 *misrepresentation*; malicious copy, distorted image, caricature, cartoon, travesty, take-off, spoof, lampoon, parody 851 *ridicule*; hint, adumbration, shadow; silhouette, outline, sketch, diagram, first copy, draft, aperçu; metaphrase, paraphrase 520 *translation*.

*duplicate*, flimsy, carbon copy, carbon; stencil, master copy; transfer, rubbing; photograph 551 *photography*; reprint, reissue 589 *edition*; model, specimen, inspection copy 83 *example*.

## 23 Prototype

**N.** *prototype*, archetype, antitype; type, biotype, common type, norm, everyman 30 *average*; primitive form, protoplasm 358 *organism*; original, protoplast 68 *origin*; first occurrence, precedent, test case 119 *priority*; guide, rule, maxim 693 *precept*; standard, criterion, touchstone, standard of comparison, yardstick, bench mark, barometer, frame of reference 9 *referral*; ideal, beau idéal 646 *perfection*; cynosure 646 *paragon*; keynote, tuning fork, metronome 465 *gauge*; module, unit; specimen, sample 83 *example*; model, subject; exemplar, pattern, template, paradigm; dummy, mock-up; copybook, copy, printer's c., text, manuscript; blueprint, design, master plan, scheme 623 *plan*; rough plan, outline, draft, sketch, aperçu.

*living model*, model, artist's m., poser, sitter, subject; fashion model, mannequin; stroke, pacer, pacemaker; role model, trendsetter; bandleader, conductor, fugleman, drum major, cheerleader 690 *leader*.

*mould*, matrix, mint; plate, shell; stencil, negative; frame 243 *form*; wax figure, lay f., tailor's dummy; last; die, stamp, punch, seal, intaglio 555 *printing*.

**Adj.** *prototypical*, paradigmatic, exemplary, model, standard, classic, copybook.

**Vb.** *be an example*, set an e., serve as e., stand as e.; act as a pattern; serve as a model, model, sit for, pose.

## 24 Agreement

**N.** *agreement*, consentaneity 181 *concurrence*; consentience, consent 488 *assent*; accord, accordance, chorus, unison 16 *uniformity*; harmony 410 *melody*; consonance, concinnity, concordance; concert, understanding, mutual understanding, rapport, entente, entente cordiale; concordat, convention, pact 765 *compact*; unity, solidarity, unanimity 488 *consensus*; consortium 706 *cooperation*; union 50 *combination*; peace 710 *concord*.

*conformance* 83 *conformity*; congruence, coincidence 13 *identity*; consistency, congruity 16 *uniformity*; coherence, consequentiality, consequence, logic, logical conclusion 475 *reasoning*; correspondence, parallelism 18 *similarity*.

*fitness*, aptness, qualification, capability 694 *aptitude*; suitability, propriety 642 *good policy*; the right man in the right place, perfect candidate, the very thing, dream team, horses for courses 13 *identity*; relevancy, pertinence, admissibility, appositeness, case in point, good example 9 *relevance*; commensurability, proportion 9 *relation*; timeliness, right moment, fit occasion 137 *occasion*; mot juste.

*adaptation*, conformation, harmonization, synchronization, matching 18 *assimilation*; reconciliation, reconcilement 719 *pacification*; accommodation, negotiation 770 *compromise*; attunement, adjustment 62 *arrangement*; compatibility, congeniality, naturalness; fitting, suiting, good fit, perfect f., close f., tight f.

**Adj.** *agreeing*, right, accordant, in accord, in accordance with, in keeping with; corresponding, correspondent, answering; proportional, proportionate, commensurate, according to 12 *correlative*; coincident, coinciding, congruent, congruous 28 *equal*; squared with, consistent w., conforming 83 *comformable*; in conformity, in step, in phase, in tune, synchronized 123 *synchronous*; of a piece with, consistent, self-c. 16 *uniform*; consonant, concordant, harmonized 410 *harmonious*; combining, mixing; suiting, matching 18 *similar*; becoming 846 *tasteful*; natural, congenial, sympathetic; reconcilable, compatible, coexistent, coexisting, symbiotic;

consentaneous, consensual, consentient, agreeable, acquiescent, cool (inf) 488 *assenting*; concurrent, agreed, all a., at one, in unison, in chorus, unanimous; united, concerted; in rapport with, like-minded, of like mind, bipartisan 706 *cooperative*; treating, treaty-making, in treaty, negotiating 765 *contractual*.

*apt*, applicable, admissible, germane, appropriate, pertinent, in point, to the point, pointed, well-aimed 9 *relevant*; bearing upon; in loco, pat, in place, apropos; right, happy, felicitous, idiomatic 575 *elegant*; at home, in one's element; seasonable, opportune 137 *timely*.

*fit*, fitting, befitting, seemly, decorous; suited, well-adapted, adaptable; capable, qualified, groomed for, cut out for 694 *skilful*; suitable, up one's street 642 *advisable*; meet, proper 913 *right*.

*adjusted*, well-a. 60 *orderly*, 494 *accurate*; timed, synchronized; focused, tuned, fine-t.; strung, pitched, attuned 412 *musical*; trimmed, balanced 28 *equal*; well-cut, fitting, well-fitting, close-fitting, tight-fitting, tight; bespoke, made to measure, tailored, tailor-made, snug, comfortable.

**Vb.** *accord*, be accordant etc. adj.; agree, concur 488 *assent*, 758 *consent*; respond, echo, chorus, chime in, ditto 106 *repeat*; coincide, square with, quadrate w., mesh w., gear w., dovetail 45 *join*; fit, fit like a glove, fit like a second skin, fit to a T; tally, correspond, match 18 *resemble*; go with, comport with, tone in w., harmonize; come naturally to; take to like a duck to water; fit in, belong, feel at home, be in one's element; answer, do, meet, suit, suit down to the ground 642 *be expedient*; fall pat, come apropos, prove timely, fit the occasion; beseem, befit; keep together, pull t. 706 *cooperate*; be consistent, be logical, hang together, hold t. 475 *be reasonable*; seek accord, treat, negotiate, come to terms 766 *make terms*; get on with, be of one mind, be on the same wavelength, hit it off, fraternize, make friends 880 *befriend*; be natural, behave naturally, be oneself.

*adjust*, make adjustments 654 *rectify*; render accordant etc. adj.; readjust, repair 656 *restore*; fit, suit, adapt, accommodate, conform; attune, tune, tune up, pitch, string 410 *harmonize*; modulate, tune in; regulate 60 *order*; graduate, proportion 12 *correlate*; dress, align 62 *arrange*; balance 28 *equalize*; cut, trim 31 *compensate*; tailor, make to measure; concert; focus, synchronize.

**Adv.** *pertinently*, aptly etc. adj.; apropos of; in the right context.

## 25 Disagreement

**N.** *disagreement*, disaccord; nonagreement, failure to agree, agreement to disagree 489 *dissent*; divergent opinions, conflict of opinion, controversy, argumentation 475 *argument*; confrontation, wrangle, wrangling, bickering 709 *quarrel*; disunion, disunity, faction 709 *dissension*; dissidence 978 *schism*; jarring, clash 279 *collision*; challenge, defiance, rupture, breach 718 *war*; variance, divergence, discrepancy 15 *difference*; two voices, ambiguity, ambivalence 518 *equivocalness*; inconsistency, credibility gap; variety, inconsistency 17 *nonuniformity*; opposition, contradiction, conflict 14 *contrariety*; dissonance, discordance, disharmony, inharmoniousness 411 *discord*; noncoincidence, incongruence, incongruity 10 *unrelatedness*; disparity 29 *inequality*; disproportion, asymmetry 246 *distortion*; incompatibility, irreconcilability, hostility 881 *enmity*.

*inaptitude*, unfitness, incapacity, incompetence 695 *unskilfulness*; unfittingness, unsuitability, undecorousness; impropriety 643 *inexpedience*, 847 *bad taste*; inconcinnity 576 *inelegance*; inapplicability, inadmissibility, irrelevancy 10 *irrelevance*; intrusiveness, intrusion, interruption 138 *untimeliness*; maladjustment, incompatibility, unconformability 84 *nonconformity*.

*misfit*, maladjustment, bad fit; bad match, misalliance, mésalliance, mismarriage 894 *marriage*; oxymoron; paradox; incongruity, false note, jar 411 *discord*; fish out of water, square peg in a round hole; outsider, alien, foreigner, foreign body 59 *intruder*; dissident, dissenter 84 *nonconformist*; joker, odd man out, freak, mutation, sport 84 *variance*; eccentric, oddity 851 *laughingstock*; ass in a lion's skin, mutton dressed (up) as lamb 501 *fool*; wolf in sheep's clothing 542 *sham*.

**Adj.** *disagreeing*, dissenting, unagreed, not unanimous 489 *dissenting*; challenging 711 *defiant*; in opposition, confronting, at odds, at cross purposes, at variance; at one another's throats, at loggerheads, at war 718 *warring*; bickering, snapping 709 *quarrelling*; hostile, antagonistic 881 *inimical*; uncongenial, antipathetic 861 *disliked*; conflicting, clashing, contradictory 14 *contrary*; unnatural, against one's nature, against the grain, out of character; inconsistent 17 *nonuniform*; inconsonant, incompatible; unadaptable 84 *unconformable*; odd, alien, foreign 59 *extraneous*; not combining, not mixing; incommensurable 10 *unrelated*; disproportionate, disproportional, out of proportion, unsymmetrical 246 *distorted*; inharmonious, grating 411 *discordant*; mismatched, misallied; ill-matching, badly matched, ill-

assorted, discrepant 15 *different*; incongruous 497 *absurd*.

*unapt*, unfitted, unsuited, incapable, incompetent 695 *unskilful*; inept, maladjusted 695 *clumsy*; wrong, unfitting, unsuitable, unfortunate, unbecoming, not for one, improper, undue, inappropriate 643 *inexpedient*; impracticable 470 *impossible*; unfit for, ineligible 607 *rejected*; intrusive, ill-timed, unseasonable 138 *inopportune*; malapropos, inapplicable, inadmissible 10 *irrelevant*; unidiomatic 576 *inelegant*; out of character, out of keeping; misplaced, out of one's element, like a fish out of water, like a square peg in a round hole; out of place, out of joint, out of tune, out of time, out of step, out of phase.

**Vb.** *disagree* 489 *dissent*; differ, dispute 475 *argue*; fall out 709 *quarrel*, *bicker*; clash, conflict, confront, collide, contradict 14 *be contrary*; be discrepant, – unapt etc. adj.; vary, diverge 15 *differ*; not play, not play ball, noncooperate 702 *be obstructive*; have nothing to do with 10 *be unrelated*; come amiss, interfere, intrude; be incongruous, stick out like a sore thumb, strike a false note, jar.

*mismatch*, misalign, misfit, fit badly; miscast, misplace, mistime.

**Adv.** *in defiance of*, in contempt of, despite, in spite of; discordantly etc. adj.

SECTION THREE

## Quantity

## 26 Quantity

**N.** *quantity*, amount, sum 38 *addition*; total 52 *whole*; magnitude, amplitude, extent 465 *measurement*; mass, substance, body, bulk 195 *size*; dimension, dimensions, longitude 203 *length*; width, thickness 205 *breadth*; altitude 209 *height*; deepness 211 *depth*; area, volume, extension 183 *space*; weight 322 *gravity*, 323 *lightness*; strength, force, flow, potential, pressure, tension, stress, strain, torque 160 *energy*; numbers 104 *multitude*; quotient, fraction, multiple, function, quantic, vector 85 *number*, 86 *mathematics*, 101 *plurality*, 102 *fraction*, 103 *zero*, 107 *infinity*; mean, median 30 *average*.

*finite quantity*, matter of, limited amount, definite figure; lower limit, upper l., ceiling 236 *limit*; definite amount, quantum, quota, quorum; measured quantity, measure, dose, dosage 465 *measurement*; avoirdupois 322 *weighing*; ration, whack 783 *portion*; pittance, tad, driblet; bagful, capful, cupful, glassful, handful, mouthful, plateful, sackful, spoonful, dessertspoonful, tablespoonful, teaspoonful, thimbleful; whole amount, lot, batch; load, lorryload, containerful 193 *contents*; lock stock and barrel 52 *whole*; large amount, masses, heaps, mountains 32 *great quantity*; small amount, bit 33 *small quantity*; greater amount, more, most, majority 36 *increase*, 104 *greater number*; smaller amount, less, not so much 37 *decrease*, 39 *subtraction*, 105 *fewness*; stint, piece, task 682 *labour*.

**Adj.** *quantitative*, some, certain, any, more or less; so many, so much; quantified, measured.

**Vb.** *quantify*, express the quantity; allot, rate, ration 783 *apportion*.

**Adv.** *to the amount of*, to the sum of, to the tune of; to such an extent.

## 27 Degree: relative quantity

**N.** *degree*, relative quantity, proportion, ratio, scale 9 *relativeness*, 462 *comparison*; ration, stint 783 *portion*, 53 *part*; amplitude, extent, intensity, frequency, magnitude, size 26 *quantity*; level, pitch, altitude 209 *height*, 211 *depth*; key, register 410 *musical note*; reach, compass, scope 183 *range*; rate, tenor, way, speed 265 *motion*; gradation, graduation, calibration 15 *differentiation*; differential, shade, nuance; grade, remove, stepping stone; step, rung, tread, stair 308 *ascent*; point, stage, milestone, turning point, crisis 8 *juncture*; mark, peg, notch, score 547 *indicator*; bar, line, interval 410 *notation*; valuation, value 465 *measurement*; ranking, grading, league table 77 *classification*; class, kind 77 *sort*; standard, rank, grade 73 *serial place*; military rank, lieutenancy, captaincy, majority, colonelcy; ecclesiastical rank 985 *church office*; hierarchy 733 *authority*; sphere, station, status, social class, caste, standing, footing 8 *circumstance*; gradualism, gradualness 278 *slowness*.

**Adj.** *gradational*, hierarchical, graduated, scalar, calibrated, graded, scaled; gradual, shading off, tapering; fading, fading out.

*comparative*, relative, proportional, in scale 9 *relative*; within the bounds of 236 *limited*; measured by.

**Vb.** *graduate*, rate, class, rank 73 *grade*; scale, calibrate; compare, measure.

*shade off*, taper, die away, pass into, melt into, change gradually, dissolve, fade, fade out; raise by degrees 36 *augment*; lower by degrees 37 *abate*; whittle down, pare, trim 204 *shorten*; cut back.

**Adv.** *by degrees*, gradually, imperceptibly, slowly, steadily, little by little, step by step, drop by drop, bit by bit, inch by inch, by inches, slowly but surely, by slow degrees; in some degree, in slight measure; to some

extent, just a bit; however little, however much.

## 28 Equality: sameness of quantity or degree

**N.** *equality*, same quantity, same degree; parity, equal opportunity, equal status, 'a man's a man for a' that', sexual equality, gender e., level playing field, coequality, coextension, coincidence 24 *agreement*;

> What tho' on hamely fare we dine,
> Wear hoddin grey and a' that;
> Gie fools their silks, and knaves their wine,
> A man's a man for a' that!
>
> Robert Burns, *Is There for Honest Poverty*

symmetry, balance, poise; evenness, level 258 *smoothness*, 216 *horizontality*; equability, monotony 16 *uniformity*; roundness 250 *circularity*; impartiality 913 *justice*.

*equivalence*, likeness 18 *similarity*; sameness 13 *identity*, 219 *parallelism*; equation; interchangeability 151 *interchange*; equipollence, isotropy; synonymity, synonym; reciprocation, exchange, fair e., trade-off 791 *barter*; par, quits; equivalent, value, fair v., just price 809 *price*; not a pin to choose, six of one and half a dozen of the other, nothing to choose between, nothing in it, level-pegging, neck and neck, nip and tuck; level bet, even money.

*equilibrium*, equipoise, equiponderance, stable equilibrium, balance, poise; even keel, steadiness, uprightness; state of equilibrium, balance of forces, balance of nature, balance of power, balance of trade, balance of payments; deadlock, stalemate, logjam 145 *stop*; status quo, stable state, equilibrium, homoeostasis; road-holding ability 153 *stability*; sea legs, seat; fin, aileron, spoiler 153 *stabilizer*; balance, equilibrant; equilibrist, tightrope walker, acrobat 162 *athlete*.

*equalization*, equation, equilibration; balancing 322 *weighing*; coordination, adjustment, readjustment, levelling up *or* down 656 *restoration*, 31 *compensation*; positive discrimination, affirmative action, equal opportunities legislation, equal division, going halves 92 *bisection*, 775 *participation*; reciprocity 12 *correlation*; tit for tat 714 *retaliation*, 151 *interchange*; equalizer, counterpoise 31 *offset*; equator 92 *dividing line*; equalization fund; standardizer, bed of Procrustes; return match, second chance.

*draw*, drawn game, no result, drawn battle; level-pegging; tie, dead heat; no decision, stalemate, deadlock; neck-and-neck race, photo finish; love all, deuce; near thing, narrow margin 200 *short distance*.

*compeer*, peer, equal, coequal, match, mate,

twin; fellow, brother 18 *analogue*; equivalent, parallel, opposite number, pair, counterpart, shadow; rival, corrival, competitor 716 *contender*.

**Adj.** *equal*, equi-, iso-, co-; same 13 *identical*; like 18 *similar*; neither more nor less, coequal, coordinate, coextensive, coincident, congruent, homologous 24 *agreeing*; equiponderant; equipollent; equidistant; isotropic; balanced, poised, in equilibrium; homoeostatic, steady, stable 153 *fixed*; even, level, round, square, flush 258 *smooth*; even-sided, equilateral, regular 16 *uniform*, 245 *symmetrical*; equable, unvarying, monotonous 153 *unchangeable*; competitive, rival 716 *contending*; dingdong, Greek meeting Greek, matched, well-matched, drawn, tied; parallel, level-pegging, running level, keeping pace, abreast, neck-and-neck, nip and tuck; equalized, bracketed; sharing, cosharing; equally divided, half-and-half, fifty-fifty; impartial, democratic, equitable, even-stevens (inf) 913 *just*; on equal terms, on the same footing, on a par, on a level; par, quits, upsides with.

*equivalent*, comparable, parallel, interchangeable, synonymous, virtual, convertible; corresponding, reciprocal 12 *correlative*; as good as, no better, no worse; tantamount, virtually the same, more or less identical, indistinguishable; much the same, all the s., all one, as broad as it is long, pot calling the kettle black (see also *equivalence*) 18 *similar*; worth, valued at, quoted at, priced at, standing at 809 *priced*.

**Vb.** *be equal*, equal, countervail, counterbalance, counterpoise, compensate 31 *set off*; add nothing, detract n., make no difference, come to the same thing, coincide with, agree w. 24 *accord*; be equal to, measure up to, reach, touch; cope with 160 *be able*; come up to scratch, cut the mustard (inf), make the grade, measure up, pass muster 635 *suffice*; hold one's own, keep up with, keep pace w., run abreast, be level; parallel 219 *be parallel*; match, twin 18 *resemble*; tie, draw, halve the match; break even; make it all square; leave no remainder; go halves, go shares 775 *participate*.

*equalize*, equate; bracket, match; parallel 462 *compare*; balance, strike a b., poise; trim, dress, square, round off, make flush, level 258 *smooth*, 16 *make uniform*; fit, accommodate, readjust 24 *adjust*; add a makeweight, counterpoise, even up 31 *set off*; redress the balance, give points to, handicap 31 *compensate*; set on an even keel, equilibrate, restore to equilibrium 153 *stabilize*; right oneself, keep one's balance, hold the road.

**Adv.** *equally*, evenly etc. adj., even-stevens

(inf); pari passu, ceteris paribus; at the same rate; to all intents and purposes, as good as; on equal terms; in equilibrium; on an even keel.

## 29 Inequality: difference of quantity or degree

**N.** *inequality*, difference of degree 34 *superiority*, 35 *inferiority*; irregularity, variability, patchiness 17 *nonuniformity*; unevenness 259 *roughness*; disproportion, asymmetry 246 *distortion*, 25 *disagreement*; oddness, skewness, lopsidedness 220 *obliquity*; imparity, disparity 15 *difference*; unlikeness 19 *dissimilarity*; disequilibrium, unstable equilibrium, imbalance, unbalance; dizziness, the staggers; tilting of the scales, preponderance, overweight, top-hamper 322 *gravity*; underweight, short weight 323 *lightness*; defect, shortcoming, inadequacy 636 *insufficiency*; odds 15 *difference*; makeweight, counterpoise 31 *offset*; bonus 40 *extra*; casting vote; partiality, discrimination 481 *bias*, 914 *injustice*.

**Adj.** *unequal*, disparate, incongruent 15 *different*, 25 *disagreeing*, 19 *dissimilar*; unique, unequalled, at an advantage 34 *superior*, 644 *excellent*; at a disadvantage, below par 35 *inferior*; disproportionate, disproportioned, asymmetrical 246 *distorted*; irregular, scalene, lopsided 17 *nonuniform*; askew, awry 220 *oblique*; odd, uneven; unequable, variable, patchy 437 *variegated*; deficient, defective, falling short, inadequate 636 *insufficient*; underweight 323 *light*; overweight 322 *weighty*; in disequilibrium, unbalanced, swinging, swaying, rocking 152 *unstable*; untrimmed, unballasted, uncompensated; overloaded, top-heavy, unwieldy 695 *clumsy*; listing, leaning, canting, heeling 220 *oblique*; off balance, overbalanced, losing balance, dizzy, giddy, toppling, falling 309 *descending*; unequitable, partial, unfair, undemocratic 914 *unjust*, 481 *biased*.

**Vb.** *be unequal*, be mismatched 25 *disagree*; not balance, not equate, leave a remainder 15 *differ*; fall short 35 *be inferior*; preponderate, have the advantage, give points to, overtop, outclass, outrank 34 *be superior*; outstrip 306 *outdo*; be deficient 636 *not suffice*; overcompensate, overweight, tip the scales 322 *weigh*; be underweight, need a makeweight 323 *be light*; throw the casting vote; unbalance, throw off balance; overbalance, capsize; list, tilt, lean 220 *be oblique*; rock, swing, sway 317 *fluctuate*; vary 143 *change*.

**Adv.** *unevenly*, unequally etc. adj.

## 30 Mean

**N.** *average*, medium, mean, median; intermedium, middle term 73 *serial place*; balance;

happy medium, golden mean 177 *moderation*; standard product 79 *generality*; ruck, ordinary run 732 *averageness*; norm, par; the normal 610 *habit*.

*middle point*, midpoint, middle distance, half way 70 *middle*; middle years, middle youth 131 *middle age*; middle class 869 *middle classes*; middle of the road, midway, middle course, middle ground 625 *middle way*; splitting the difference 770 *compromise*; neutrality 606 *no choice*; central position 225 *centre*.

*common man* 869 *commoner*; everyman *or* -woman, man *or* woman in the street, man on the Clapham omnibus, ordinary m. *or* w., plain m. *or* w., Joe Bloggs, Joe Public, Joe Soap 79 *everyman*; typical individual, average specimen 732 *averageness*.

**Adj.** *median*, mean, average, medial 70 *middle*, 225 *central*; neither hot nor cold, luke-warm; intermediate, grey; normal, standard, par, ordinary, commonplace, run-of-the-mill, mediocre 732 *middling*; moderate, middle-of-the-road 625 *neutral*; middle class, middle brow.

**Vb.** *average out*, average, take the mean; split the difference, go halfway 770 *compromise*; strike a balance 28 *equalize*.

**Adv.** *on an average*, in the long run 79 *generally*; on the whole, overall, all in all; taking one thing with another, taking all things together; in round numbers.

## 31 Compensation

**N.** *compensation*, weighting 28 *equalization*; rectification 654 *amendment*; reaction, neutralization, antidote, nullification 182 *counteraction*; commutation 151 *interchange*, 150 *substitution*; redemption, recoupment, recovery; retrieval 771 *acquisition*; indemnification, reparation, redress 787 *restitution*, 656 *restoration*; amends, expiation 941 *atonement*; recompense, repayment 962 *reward*, 910 *revenge*, 714 *retaliation*; reciprocity, measure for measure 12 *correlation*.

*offset*, set-off, allowance, makeweight, balance, weighting, counterweight, counterpoise, counterbalance, ballast 28 *equalization*; indemnity, reparations, compensation, costs, damages 787 *restitution*; reimbursement, refund, one's money back; amends, penance 941 *atonement*; equivalent, quid pro quo 150 *substitute*; swings and roundabouts 151 *interchange*; cover, collateral, hostage 767 *security*; counter-claim 627 *requirement*; counterblow 713 *defence*; counterattraction 291 *attraction*; concession, cession 770 *compromise*; bribe, sweetener, graft, payola, hush money, tribute 804 *payment*, 962 *reward*.

**Adj.** *compensatory*, compensating, redeeming, countervailing, balancing 28 *equivalent*; self-correcting, self-cancelling; indemnificatory, reimbursing, in damages, restitutory 787 *restoring*; amendatory, expiatory 941 *atoning*; in the opposite scale, weighed against 462 *compared*.

**Vb.** *compensate*, offer compensation, make amends, make compensation etc. n.; do penance 941 *atone*; indemnify, restore, pay back 787 *restitute*; make good, make up, make up for, do instead 150 *substitute*; add a make-weight, ballast; pay, repay 714 *retaliate*; bribe, square 962 *reward*; reimburse, pay overtime 804 *pay*; redeem, outweigh; overcompensate, bend over backwards, lean over b.

*set off*, offset, allow for; counterpoise, countervail, balance 28 *equalize*; neutralize, cancel, nullify 182 *counteract*; cover, hedge 858 *be cautious*; give and take, concede, cede 770 *compromise*.

*recoup*, recover 656 *retrieve*; make up leeway, take up the slack; indemnify oneself, take back, get back 786 *take*; make a comeback 656 *be restored*.

**Adv.** *in return*, in consideration, in compensation, in lieu; though, although; at the same time, on the other hand; nevertheless, regardless of; despite, for all that, notwithstanding; but, still, even so, be that as it may; after all, allowing for; when all is said and done, taking one thing with another; at least, at all events, at any rate.

## 32 Greatness

**N.** *greatness*, largeness, bigness, girth 195 *size*; large scale, generous proportions, ample p., outsize dimensions, vastness, enormousness, gigantism 195 *hugeness*; muchness, abundance 635 *plenty*; amplitude, ampleness, fullness, maximum 54 *completeness, plenitude*; superabundance, superfluity, embarras de richesses, arm and a leg, more than enough 637 *redundance*; immoderation 815 *prodigality*; exorbitance, excessiveness, excess 546 *exaggeration*; enormity, immensity, boundlessness 107 *infinity*; numerousness, countlessness 104 *multitude*; dimensions, magnitude 26 *quantity*, 27 *degree*; extension, extent 203 *length*, 205 *breadth*, 209 *height*, 211 *depth*; expanse, area, volume, capacity 183 *space*; spaciousness, roominess 183 *room*; mightiness, might, strength, intensity 160 *power*, 178 *influence*; intensification, magnification, multiplication 197 *expansion*; aggrandizement 36 *increase*; seriousness, significance 638 *importance*; eminence 34 *superiority*; grandeur, grandness 868 *nobility*, 871 *pride*; majesty 733 *authority*; fame, renown 866 *repute, prestige*; noise, din 400 *loudness*.

*great quantity*, muchness, galore 635 *plenty*; crop, harvest, profusion, abundance, productivity 171 *productiveness*; superfluity, superabundance, shower, flood, spate, torrent 637 *redundance*, 350 *stream*; expanse, sheet, lake, sea, ocean, world, universe, sight of, world of, mort of, power of; much, lot, whole l., fat l., deal, good d., great d.; not a little, not peanuts, not chickenfeed, not to be sneezed at; too much, more than one bargained for; stock, mint, mine 632 *store*; quantity, peck, bushel, pints, gallons; lump, heap, mass, stack, mountain 74 *accumulation*; packet (of), pack (of), load (of), full l., cargo, shipload, boatload, trainload, carload, lorryload, truckload, sackload, sackful, containerful 193 *contents*; large quantities, bags, gobs (sl), heaps, lashings, loads, lots, masses, oodles, pots, quantities, scads (inf), shedloads, stacks, tons, wads; pots of money, a bomb, a packet, telephone numbers; oceans, seas, floods, streams; volumes, reams, sheets, pages and pages, screeds; large numbers, crowds, hordes, hosts, masses, millions, multitudes, not a few, numbers, quite a few, swarms 104 *multitude*; all, entirety, corpus, caboodle 52 *whole*.

*main part*, almost all, principal part, best p., essential p. 52 *chief part*; greater part, major p., majority 104 *greater number*; body, bulk, mass, substance; soul 1 *essence*.

**Adj.** *great*, greater, main, most, major 34 *superior*; maximum, greatest 34 *supreme*; grand, big, mickle or muckle (Scots) 195 *large*; fairsized, largish, biggish, pretty big; substantial, considerable, respectable; sizable, of size, economy-size, full-s., large-s., king-s., life-s., mansize; bulky, massive, massy, heavy 322 *weighty*; prolonged, lengthy 203 *long*; wide, thick 205 *broad*; puffed up, swollen 197 *expanded*; ample, generous, voluminous, capacious 183 *spacious*; profound 211 *deep*; great in stature, tall, lofty 209 *high*; great in strength, Herculean, gorilla-like 162 *strong*; mighty 160 *powerful*, 178 *influential*; intense, violent 174 *vigorous*; noisy 400 *loud*; soaring, mounting, climbing 308 *ascending*; culminating, at the maximum, at the peak, at the top, at its height, through the ceiling, in the zenith, at the limit, at the summit 213 *topmost*; great in quantity, plentiful, abundant, overflowing 635 *plenteous*; superabundant 637 *redundant*; great in number, many, swarming, teeming, hotching, alive with 104 *multitudinous*; great in age, antique, ancient, venerable, immemorial 127 *olden*, 131 *ageing*; great in honour, imperial, august, goodly, precious, of value

644 *valuable*, 868 *noble*; sublime, exalted 821 *impressive*; glorious, famed, famous 866 *renowned, worshipful*; grave, solemn, serious 638 *important*; excelling, excellent, awesome (inf), cool (inf), wicked (sl) 306 *surpassing*, 644 *best*.

*extensive*, ranging, wide-ranging, far-flying, far-flung, far-reaching, far-stretching 183 *spacious*; widespread, prevalent, epidemic; worldwide, global, universal, cosmic; mass, indiscriminate, wholesale, whole-hogging, full-scale, all-embracing, across-the-board, sweeping, comprehensive 78 *inclusive*.

*enormous*, immense, vast, colossal, giant, gigantic, humongous or humungous, monumental 195 *huge*; towering, sky-high 209 *high*; record, record-breaking, record-smashing, chart-buster, blockbuster, excelling 306 *surpassing*.

*prodigious*, marvellous, astounding, amazing, astonishing 864 *wonderful*; fantastic, fabulous, beyond description, incredible, unbelievable, passing belief 486 *unbelieved*, 472 *improbable*, 470 *impossible*; arrant, – on stilts; stupendous, tremendous, terrific; dreadful, frightful 854 *frightening*; breathtaking, overwhelming, out of this world 821 *impressive*.

*remarkable*, signal, noticeable, worth looking at 866 *noteworthy*; outstanding, extraordinary, exceptional, singular, uncommon, über- 84 *unusual*; eminent, distinguished, marked, of mark 638 *notable*.

*whopping*, walloping, whacking, spanking, thumping, thundering, socking, rattling, howling, father and mother of –; hefty, husky, hulking, strapping, overgrown, clumsy 195 *unwieldy*.

*flagrant*, blatant, in-your-face (inf), flaring, glaring, stark, staring, staring one in the face; signal, shocking 867 *discreditable*.

*unspeakable*, unutterable, indescribable, beyond description, indefinable, ineffable; beyond expression, past speaking 517 *inexpressible*.

*exorbitant*, extortionate, harsh, stringent, severe, Draconian 735 *oppressive*; excessive, exceeding, passing, extreme, utmost 306 *surpassing*; monstrous, outrageous, swingeing, unconscionable; unbearable 827 *intolerable*; inordinate, unwarranted, preposterous, extravagant, astronomical 546 *exaggerated*; beyond the limit, beyond the pale, going too far.

*consummate* 54 *complete*; finished, flawless 646 *perfect*; entire, sound 52 *whole*; thorough, thoroughpaced, thoroughgoing; utter, total, out and out, dyed in the wool, double-dyed, arch, crass, gross, arrant, rank, regular, downright, desperate, unmitigated, – on stilts; far gone.

*absolute*, the veriest; essential, positive, unequivocal; stark, pure, sheer, mere 44 *unmixed*; unlimited, unrestricted 107 *infinite*; undiminished, unabated, unreduced.

**Vb.** *be great* – large etc. adj.; bulk, bulk large, loom, loom up; stretch 183 *extend*; rear, tower, soar, mount 308 *ascend*; scale, transcend 34 *be superior*; clear, overtop; exceed, know no bounds, run to extremes, go off the deep end 306 *overstep*; enlarge 36 *augment*, 197 *expand*; swamp, overwhelm 54 *fill*.

**Adv.** *positively*, verily, veritably, actually, indeed, in fact 494 *truly*; seriously, indubitably, without doubt, in all conscience 473 *certainly*; decidedly, absolutely, definitely, finally, unequivocally, without equivocation; directly, specifically, unreservedly, unashamedly; essentially, fundamentally, radically; downright, plumb.

*greatly*, much, well, big time (inf), – for Britain or for England, etc; very, right, seriously, so; very much, mighty, ever so; fully, quite, entirely, utterly, without reservation 52 *wholly*, 54 *completely*; thoroughly, wholesale; widely, extensively, universally 79 *generally*; largely, mainly, mostly, to a great extent, to a large e.; something, considerably, fairly, pretty, pretty well; a sight, a deal, a great d., ever so much, in spades; materially, substantially; increasingly, more than ever, doubly, trebly; specially, particularly; dearly, deeply; vitally; exceptionally; on a large scale, in a big way; vastly, hugely, enormously, gigantically, colossally; heavily, strongly, powerfully, mightily 178 *influentially*; actively, strenuously, vigorously, heartily, intensely; closely, narrowly, intensively, zealously, fanatically, hotly, bitterly, fiercely; acutely, sharply, shrewdly, exquisitely; enough, more than e., abundantly, profusely, prodigiously; generously, richly, worthily, magnificently, splendidly, nobly; supremely, pre-eminently, superlatively; rarely, unusually, wonderfully, incomparably, strangely; indefinitely, immeasurably, incalculably, infinitely, unspeakably, ineffably.

*extremely*, ultra, to extremes, to the highest degree, to the limit, to the max (inf), to the nth degree; no end of, no limit to; beyond measure, beyond all bounds; beyond comparison, beyond compare, incomparably, drop dead (inf); overly, unduly, improperly, to a fault; out of all proportion; bitterly, harshly, drastically, rigorously, unconscionably, with a vengeance 735 *severely*; immoderately, uncontrollably, desperately, madly, frantically, frenziedly, furiously, fanatically, bitterly 176

*violently*; exceedingly, excessively, exorbitantly, inordinately, outrageously, prohibitively, preposterously; foully, abominably, grossly, beastly, monstrously, horribly; confoundedly, deucedly, devilishly, damnably, hellishly; tremendously, terribly, fearfully, dreadfully, awfully, frightfully; finally, irretrievably, for always; unforgivably, mortally.

*remarkably*, noticeably, sensibly, markedly, pointedly; notably, strikingly, conspicuously, signally, emphatically, prominently, glaringly, flagrantly, blatantly, unashamedly; publicly 400 *loudly*; pre-eminently 34 *eminently*; outstandingly, unco; singularly, peculiarly, curiously, oddly, queerly, strangely, strangely enough, uncommonly, unusually 84 *unconformably*; surprisingly, astonishingly, amazingly, astoundingly, impressively, incredibly, marvellously, magically 864 *wonderfully*.

*painfully*, unsparingly, till it hurts, till it bites; badly, bitterly, hard; seriously, sorely, grievously; sadly, miserably, wretchedly; distressingly, pitiably, piteously, woefully, lamentably; shrewdly, cruelly; savagely; unbearably, intolerably; exquisitely, excruciatingly, shockingly, frighteningly, terrifyingly; balefully, mortally.

## 33 Smallness

**N.** *smallness*, small size, diminutiveness, minuteness 196 *littleness*; brevity 204 *shortness*; leanness, meagreness 206 *thinness*; rarefaction 325 *rarity*; briefness, momentariness 114 *transience*; paucity 105 *fewness*; rareness, sparseness, sparsity 140 *infrequency*; scarceness, scarcity, inadequacy 636 *insufficiency*, 307 *shortfall*; exiguousness, exiguity, scantiness; moderateness, moderation; small means 801 *poverty*; pettiness, insignificance, meanness 639 *unimportance*, 35 *inferiority*; mediocrity 30 *average*, 732 *averageness*; no depth 212 *shallowness*; tenuity 4 *insubstantiality*; compression, abbreviation, abridgment 198 *contraction*; diminution 37 *decrease*; miniaturization; vanishing point, nothingness 2 *nonexistence*, 103 *zero*, 444 *invisibility*.

*small quantity*, fraction, modicum, minimum 26 *finite quantity*; minutiae, trivia; peanuts, chickenfeed 639 *trifle*; detail, petty detail 80 *particulars*; nutshell 592 *compendium*; drop in the bucket, drop in the ocean; homoeopathic dose, trifling amount, infinitesimal a., driblet, tad, dribs and drabs; cupful, handful, mouthful, spoonful, thimbleful; trickle, dribble, sprinkling, sprinkle, dash, splash, squirt, squeeze; tinge, tincture, trace, smidgen, spice, smack, lick, smell, breath, whisper, suspicion, vestige, soupçon, thought, suggestion, hint, nuance, shade, shadow, touch; cast, vein, strain, streak; spark, scintilla, gleam, flash, flicker, ray; pinch, snatch, handful; snack, sip, bite, mite, scrap, morsel, sop; dole, pittance, iron ration; fragment 53 *piece*; whit, bit, mite; iota, jot, tittle, fig, toss; ounce, gram, pennyweight, scruple, minim 322 *weighing*; inch, micron, millimetre 200 *short distance*; second, moment, nanosecond 116 *instant*; vanishing point, next to nothing, hardly anything; the shadow of a shade 4 *insubstantial thing*.

*small thing* 196 *miniature*; microcosm; particle, atom; dot, point, pinpoint; dab, spot, fleck, speck, mote, smut; grain, granule, seed, mustard s., crumb 332 *powder*; drop, droplet, driblet; thread, wisp, shred, rag, tatter, fragment 53 *piece*; flinders, smithereens, little pieces, confetti; flake, snip, snippet, gobbet, small slice, finger; confetti; splinter, chip, clipping, paring, shaving; shiver, sliver, slip; pinprick, snick, prick, nick; hair 208 *filament*.

*small coin*, farthing, groat, halfpenny, half p, mite, widow's m.; cent, dime, nickel; centime, sou, stiver; bean, small change 797 *coinage*.

*small animal*, amoeba, microbe 196 *microorganism*; gnat, flea, ant, tick; minnow, shrimp, sprat; sparrow, tit, wren; mouse, shrew, bantam, toy dog; homunculus, manikin, midget, Tom Thumb 196 *dwarf*.

**Adj.** *small*, not much, exiguous, minimal, moderate, modest, infinitesimal; microscopic, ultramicroscopic, homoeopathic 444 *invisible*; tiny, teeny, teeny-weeny, teensy, weeny, wee, minute, diminutive, miniature 196 *little*; smaller 35 *lesser*; least, minimum; petite, small-sized, small-framed, small-built, small-boned, undersized 196 *dwarfish*; slim, slender, slimline, lean, meagre, thin, anorexic 206 *narrow*; slight, feeble, puny, frail 163 *weak*; delicate, dainty, minikin, fragile 330 *brittle*; flimsy, weightless 323 *light*; fine, subtle, rarefied 325 *rare*; quiet, not loud, soft, low, faint, hushed 401 *muted*; not tall, squat 210 *low*; not long, brief, minute, skimpy, abbreviated 204 *short*; shortened, abridged, cut, concise, compact, compendious, thumbnail 198 *contracted*; scanty, scant, scarce 307 *deficient*; dribbling, trickling 636 *insufficient*; reduced, limited, restricted 747 *restrained*; declining, ebbing, at low ebb, less 37 *decreasing*.

*inconsiderable*, minor, lightweight, trifling, trivial, petty, paltry, not to be taken seriously, insignificant 639 *unimportant*; not many, soon counted 105 *few*; inappreciable, imperceptible, unnoticeable 444 *invisible*; shadowy, tenuous, evanescent 446 *disappearing*, 114 *transient*; marginal, negligible, laughable, remote, slight; superficial, cursory 4 *insubstantial*; skin-deep

212 *shallow*; average, middling, fair, fairish, so-so 30 *median*; moderate, modest, humble, tolerable, passable 732 *middling*; not much of a, no great shakes, second-rate 35 *inferior*; no more than, just, only, mere, bare; plain, simple 44 *unmixed*.

**Vb.** *be small*, fit into a nutshell, be put onto a thumbnail; stay small, not grow 196 *be little*; have no height 210 *be low*; have no depth; have no weight 323 *be light*; make no sound 401 *sound faint*; be less 307 *fall short*; get less 37 *decrease*; shrink 198 *become small*.

**Adv.** *slightly*, exiguously, to a small degree, little; lightly, softly, faintly, feebly; superficially, cursorily, grazingly; gradually, little by little, imperceptibly, insensibly, invisibly; on a small scale, in a small way, modestly, humbly; fairly, moderately, tolerably, quite; comparatively, relatively, rather, enough, well e.; indifferently, poorly, badly, miserably, wretchedly, dismally; hardly, scarcely, barely, only just, just and no more; narrowly, by the skin of one's teeth, by one's fingernails; hardly at all, no more than; only, merely, purely, simply; at least, at the very least.

*partially*, to some degree, in some measure, to a certain extent, to some e.; somehow, after a fashion, sort of, in a kind of way, in a manner of speaking; some, somewhat, a little, a bit, just a bit, ever so little, as little as maybe; not fully, restrictedly, limitedly, within bounds 55 *incompletely*; not wholly, in part, partly; not perfectly 647 *imperfectly*.

*almost*, all but, within an ace of, within an inch of, on the brink of, on the verge of, within sight of, in a fair way to 200 *near*; near upon, close u., approximately 200 *nearly*; pretty near, just short of, not quite, virtually.

*about*, somewhere, somewhere about, thereabouts; on an average, more or less; near enough, a little more, a little less; at a guess, say.

*in no way*, no ways, no wise, by no means, not by any manner of means, in no respect, not at all, not in the least, not a bit, not the least bit, not in the slightest; not a whit, not a jot, not by a long chalk.

## 34 Superiority

**N.** *superiority*, superior elevation, higher position; altitude, loftiness, sublimity 209 *height*; transcendence 32 *greatness*, 306 *overstepping*; top 213 *summit*; quality, quality time, excellence 644 *goodness*; ne plus ultra 646 *perfection*; preferability 605 *oice*; primacy, pride of place, seniority 64 *precedence*, 119 *priority*; eminence, pre-eminence 866 *prestige*; higher rank, higher degree 27 *degree*, 868 *nobility*, *aristocracy*; overlordship, paramountcy, supremacy, sovereignty, majesty, imperium 733 *authority*; ascendancy, domination, predominance, hegemony 178 *influence*; directorship, leadership 689 *management*; preponderance, prevalence 29 *inequality*; win, championship 727 *victory*-ominence 638 *importance*; one-upmanship 698 *cunning*, 727 *success*; excess, surplus 637 *superfluity*; climax, zenith, culmination 725 *completion*; maximum, top, ceiling, peak, pinnacle, crest, crest of the wave; record, high, new h. 213 *summit*.

*advantage*, privilege, prerogative, handicap, favour 615 *benefit*; head start, flying s., lead, commanding l., winning position, pole p., inside track; odds, points, vantage, pull, edge; seeded position; command, upper hand, whip h.; one up, something in hand, reserves; trump card, card up one's sleeve, ace up one's sleeve, ace in the hole; majority, the big battalions 104 *greater number*; lion's share; leverage, clout, scope 183 *room*; vantage ground, coign of vantage.

*superior*, superior person 644 *exceller*; superman *or* -woman, wonderwoman 864 *prodigy*; better man *or* woman, first choice 890 *favourite*; select few 644 *elite*; high-ups, one's betters, top people, best p. 638 *notable*; nobility, aristocracy 868 *upper class*; overlord, lord, sovereign 741 *master*; commander, chief, prophet, guide 690 *leader*; boss, foreman 690 *manager*; primate, primus inter pares; president, prime minister, premier, first minister 690 *director*; model 646 *paragon*; star, virtuoso 696 *proficient person*; specialist 696 *expert*; mastermind 500 *sage*; world-beater, record-breaker; chart-topper; winner, prizewinner, champion, cup-holder, record-h. 727 *victor*; prima donna, first lady, head boy *or* girl; first-born, elder, senior; 'Triton among the minnows', big fish in a small pool *or* pond.

> Sicinius: It is a mind
> That shall remain a poison where it is,
> Not poison any further.
> Coriolanus: Shall remain!
> Hear you this Triton of the minnows? mark
> you
> His absolute 'shall'?
> William Shakespeare, *Coriolanus*

**Adj.** *superior*, more so; comparative, superlative; major, greater, awesome (inf) 32 *great*; upper, higher, senior, over-, super-, supra-, hyper-; supernormal, above average, in a different class, in a class by himself *or* herself 15 *different*; better, a cut above, head and shoulders above 644 *excellent*; competitive, more than a match for; one up, ahead, always one step a., far a., streets a. 64 *preceding*; prior, preferable, preferred, favourite 605 *chosen*; record,

a record for, exceeding, overtopping, vaulting, outclassing 306 *surpassing*; in the lead, on top, winning, victorious 727 *successful*; outstanding, marked, distinguished 866 *noteworthy*; rare, not like the rest, not as others are 84 *unusual*; top-level, high-l., high-powered 689 *directing*, 638 *important*; commanding, in authority 733 *ruling*; revised, reformed, bettered, all the better for 654 *improved*; enlarged, the better for 654 *improved*; enlarged, enhanced 197 *expanded*.

*supreme*, arch-, greatest 32 *great*; highest, above all others, uppermost 213 *topmost*; first, chief, foremost 64 *preceding*; main, principal, leading, overruling, overriding, cardinal, capital 638 *important*; excellent, classic, superlative, super, champion, tip-top, top-notch, first-rate, first-class, A1, 5-star, front-rank, world-beating 644 *best*; facile princeps, in the lead, on top, top of the class, nulli secundus, second to none, none such, nonpareil; dominant, paramount, pre-eminent, sovereign, royal, every inch a king *or* queen; incomparable, unrivalled, unparagoned, matchless, peerless, unparalleled, unequalled, unsurpassable, unapproached, unapproachable 21 *inimitable*; unsurpassed, ultimate, the last word in 306 *surpassing*; without comparison, beyond compare, beyond criticism 646 *perfect*; transcendent, transcendental, out of this world.

*crowning*, capping, culminating 725 *completive*; climactic, maximal, maximum; record, record-breaking, chart-topping, chart-busting, best ever 644 *best*.

**Vb.** *be superior*, transcend, rise above, surmount, overtop, tower over, overlook, command 209 *be high*; go beyond, outrange, outreach 306 *overstep*; exceed, 'out-Herod Herod' (see quotation at 546 *exaggerate*), beat the limit, take the cake, take the biscuit; carry off the laurels, bear the palm, wear the crown; pass, surpass, beat the record, reach a new high; improve on, better, go one b., cap, trump, overtrump; show quality, shine, excel 644 *be good*; assert one's superiority, be too much for; steal the show, outshine, eclipse, overshadow, throw into the shade; put another's nose out of joint, take the shine out of; score off, have the laugh on 851 *ridicule*; best, outrival, outclass, outrank 306 *outdo*; outplay, outpoint, outmanoeuvre, outwit 542 *befool*; overtake, leave behind, lap 277 *outstrip*; get the better of, worst, trounce, sit on, beat, beat hollow, knock into a cocked hat, beat all comers 727 *defeat*; rise to the occasion.

*predominate*, preponderate, overbalance, overweigh, tip the scale, turn the s.; change the balance 29 *be unequal*; override, sit on 178 *prevail*; have the advantage, have the start of, have the whip hand, have the upper h., have the edge on; hold all the cards, hold all the aces; lead, hold the l., be up on, be one up.

*come first*, stand f., head the list 64 *come before*; take precedence, play first fiddle 638 *be important*; take the lead, lead the dance, be in the van 237 *be in front*; lead, play the l., star; head, captain 689 *direct*.

*culminate*, come to a head; cap, cap it all, crown all 213 *crown*; rise to a peak; set a new record, reach new heights, reach a new high 725 *climax*.

**Adv.** *beyond*, more, over; over the mark, above the m., above par, over the average; above the limit, upwards of, in advance of; over and above; at the top of the scale, on the crest, at its height, at the peak, at the zenith, at an advantage.

*eminently*, pre-eminently, outstandingly, surpassingly, prominently, superlatively, supremely; above all, of all things; the most, to crown it all, to cap it all; par excellence; principally, especially, particularly, peculiarly, singularly; a fortiori, even more, all the m.; still more, ever more, far and away, by far 32 *extremely*.

## 35 Inferiority

**N.** *inferiority*, minority, inferior numbers 105 *fewness*; littleness 33 *smallness*; subordinacy, subordination, dependence 745 *subjection*; secondariness, supporting role, second fiddle 639 *unimportance*; lowliness, humbleness 872 *humility*; second rank, third class; back seat, obscurity, commonness 869 *commonalty*; disadvantage, handicap 702 *hindrance*; faultiness, blemish, defect 647 *imperfection*; deficiency, inadequateness 307 *shortfall*, 636 *insufficiency*; failure 728 *defeat*; poor quality, second best 645 *badness*, 812 *cheapness*; vulgarity, kitsch 847 *bad taste*; beggarliness, shabbiness 801 *poverty*; worsening, decline, dumbing-down (inf) 655 *deterioration*; record low, low, all-time l., minimum, lowest point, nadir, the bottom, rock b. 214 *base*; depression, trough 210 *lowness*; flatness, level, plain 216 *horizontality*; mediocrity 732 *averageness*.

*inferior*, subordinate, subaltern, sub, underling, assistant, sidekick, subsidiary 707 *auxiliary*; agent 755 *deputy*, 150 *substitute*; tool, pawn 628 *instrument*; follower, retainer 742 *dependant*; menial, hireling 742 *servant*; poor relation, small fry 639 *nonentity*; subject, underdog 742 *slave*; backbencher, private, other ranks, lower classes 869 *commonalty*; second, second best, second string, second fiddle, second-rater; bad second, poor s., also-ran; failure, dregs, reject, turkey 607 *rejec-*

*tion*; canaille 869 *rabble*; lesser creation, beast, worm; younger, junior, minor.

**Adj.** *lesser*, less, minor, small-time, one-horse, hick, small-beer 639 *unimportant*; small 33 *inconsiderable*; smaller, diminished 37 *decreasing*; reduced 198 *contracted*; least, smallest, minimal, minimum; lowest, bottom-most 214 *undermost*; minus 307 *deficient*.

*inferior*, lower, B-list; junior, under-, sub-; subordinate, subaltern 742 *serving*; unfree, dependent, parasitical 745 *subjected*, *subject*; secondary, tributary, ancillary, subsidiary, auxiliary 703 *aiding*, 639 *unimportant*; second, second-best, second-class, second-rate, mediocre; third-class, third-rate 922 *contemptible*; humble, lowly, low-level, below the salt, menial; low-ranking, unclassified; subnormal, substandard, low-grade, not up to snuff, not up to the mark, not up to scratch 607 *rejected*; slight, underweight 307 *deficient*; spoilt, marred, shop-soiled 655 *deteriorated*; unsound, defective, patchy, unequal 647 *imperfect*; failing 636 *insufficient*; shoddy, jerry-built, crummy (inf) 645 *bad*, 812 *cheap*, 847 *vulgar*; low, common, low-caste 869 *plebeian*; scratch, makeshift 670 *unprepared*; temporary, provisional 114 *ephemeral*; feeble 163 *weak*; in a lower class, outclassed, outshone, thrown into the shade, worsted, trounced, beaten 728 *defeated*; humiliated 872 *humbled*; unworthy, not fit, not fit to hold a candle to, not in the same league, not a patch on; nothing special, nothing to shout about, nothing to write home about.

**Vb.** *be inferior*, fall short, come short of, not come up to, fall below 307 *fall short*; lag, fall behind; trail 284 *follow*; want, lack 636 *not suffice*; not make the grade, not come up to scratch, not pass 728 *fail*; bow to 739 *obey*; concede the victory; yield, give in, cede, yield the palm, hand it to, knuckle under 721 *submit*; play second fiddle, play a supporting role 742 *serve*; take a back seat, retire into the shade; sink into obscurity; lose face, lose caste 867 *lose repute*; get worse 655 *deteriorate*; slump, sink, sink low, sink without trace, touch rock bottom, reach one's nadir 309 *descend*, 313 *plunge*.

**Adv.** *less*, minus, short of; beneath 210 *under*; below average, below par, below the mark; at the bottom, in the lowest place, at low ebb, at one's lowest e.; inferiorly, poorly, basely.

## 36 Increase

**N.** *increase*, increment, augmentation, waxing, crescendo; advance, progress 285 *progression*; growth, growth area, development a., boom town; buildup, development 164 *production*; growing pains 68 *beginning*; extension, prolongation, protraction 203 *lengthening*; widening, broadening; spread, escalation, amplification, inflation, dilation 197 *expansion*; proliferation, baby boom, population explosion, swarming 171 *productiveness*, *abundance*; multiplication, squaring, cubing 86 *numerical operation*; adding 38 *addition*; enlargement, magnification, aggrandizement 32 *greatness*; overenlargement, excess 546 *exaggeration*; enhancement, appreciation, heightening, raising 310 *elevation*; concentration 324 *condensation*; recruitment 162 *strengthening*; intensification, stepping up, doubling, redoubling, trebling 91 *duplication*, 94 *triplication*; acceleration, speeding 277 *spurt*; hotting up 381 *heating*; excitation 174 *stimulation*; exacerbation 832 *aggravation*; advancement, boost 654 *improvement*; rise, spiral, upward curve, upward trend, upswing, upturn 308 *ascent*; uprush, upsurge, flood, tide, rising t., swell, surge 350 *wave*; progressiveness, cumulativeness, cumulative effect, synergistic e., snowball 74 *accumulation*; ascending order 71 *series*.

*increment*, augmentation, bulge; accretion, accrual, accession, contribution 38 *addition*; supplement, salary increase, pay rise 40 *extra*; padding, stuffing 303 *insertion*; percentage, commission, expenses, rake-off 771 *earnings*; interest, profit 771 *gain*; plunder, prey 790 *booty*; prize 962 *reward*; produce, harvest 164 *product*; takings, receipts, proceeds 782 *receiving*.

**Adj.** *increasing*, spreading, progressive, escalating; greater than ever 32 *great*; growing, waxing, filling, crescent, on the increase, on the up and up; supplementary 38 *additional*; ever-increasing, snowballing, cumulative 71 *continuous*; augmentative, intensive; productive, fruitful 171 *prolific*; increased, stretched, enlarged, swollen, bloated 197 *expanded*.

**Vb.** *grow*, increase, gain, develop, escalate; dilate, swell, bulge, wax, fill 197 *expand*; fill out, fatten, thicken 205 *be broad*; become larger, put on weight 322 *weigh*; sprout, bud, burgeon, flower, blossom 167 *reproduce itself*; breed, spread, swarm, proliferate, mushroom, multiply 104 *be many*, 171 *be fruitful*; grow up 669 *mature*; spring up, shoot up, grow taller, grow by leaps and bounds 209 *be high*; spiral, climb, mount, rise, go through the ceiling, rocket, skyrocket, take off 308 *ascend*; flare up, shine out 379 *be hot*, 417 *shine*; gain strength 656 *be restored*, 162 *be strong*; improve 654 *get better*; flourish, thrive, prosper; gain ground,

advance, snowball, accumulate 285 *progress*; earn interest 771 *be profitable*; gain in value, appreciate, rise in price 811 *be dear*; boom, break all records, surge, exceed, overflow 637 *superabound*, 32 *be great*; rise to a maximum 34 *culminate*.

*augment*, increase, bump up, double, triple 94 *treble*, 97 *quadruple*; redouble, square, cube; duplicate 106 *repeat*; multiply 166 *reproduce*; propagate, grow, breed, raise, rear 369 *breed stock*, 370 *cultivate*, 669 *mature*; enlarge, magnify, distend, inflate, blow up 197 *expand*; amplify, develop, build up, fill out, fill in, pad out 54 *make complete*; condense, concentrate 324 *be dense*; supplement, enrich, superadd, repay with interest; bring to, contribute to; increase the numbers, accrue 38 *add*; extend, prolong, stretch 203 *lengthen*; broaden, widen, thicken, deepen; heighten, enhance, send up 209 *make higher*; raise, exalt 310 *elevate*; advance, aggrandize 285 *promote*; aim higher, set one's sights higher, raise the sights; speed up 277 *accelerate*; intensify, redouble, step up, stimulate, energize 174 *invigorate*; recruit, reinforce, give a boost to, boost 685 *refresh*, 656 *restore*, 162 *strengthen*; glorify 546 *exaggerate*, 482 *overrate*; stoke, add fuel to the flame, exacerbate 832 *aggravate*; maximize, bring to the boil, bring to a head 725 *climax*.

**Adv.** *crescendo*, increasingly etc. adj.; more so, even more so, with a vengeance, with knobs on; on the increase, on the up and up, more and more, all the m.

## 37 Decrease: no increase

**N.** *decrease*, getting less, lessening, dwindling, falling off, de-escalation; waning, fading; fadeout, dimming 419 *dimness*; wane 198 *contraction*; shrinking 206 *narrowing*; ebb, reflux, retreat, withdrawal 286 *regression*; ebb tide, neap 210 *lowness*; descending order 71 *series*; subsidence, sinking, decline, declension, downward curve, downward spiral, downward trend, downturn, fall, drop, plunge 309 *descent*, 165 *ruin*; deflation, recession, slump 655 *deterioration*; retrenchment, cutback, cut, cutting back 814 *economy*; loss of value, depreciation 812 *cheapness*; loss of reputation 867 *disrepute*; weakening, enfeeblement 163 *weakness*; impoverishment 801 *poverty*; shortage 636 *scarcity*; diminishing returns, exhaustion 190 *emptiness*; shrinkage, evaporation, deliquescence, erosion, attrition, decay, crumbling 655 *dilapidation*; spoilage, leakage, wastage, damage, loss, wear and tear 42 *decrement*; using up, consumption 634 *waste*; limits to growth; no increase, anticlimax 14 *contrariety*; underproduction 175 *inertness*;

slackness, slackening 679 *inactivity*; forfeit, levy 963 *penalty*, 772 *loss*.

*diminution*, making less; deduction 39 *subtraction*; exception 57 *exclusion*; abatement, reduction, de-escalation, restriction 747 *restraint*; slowing down, deceleration 278 *slowness*; retrenchment, cut, economization 814 *economy*; cutting back, pruning, paring, shaving, clipping, docking, curtailment, abridgment, abbreviation 204 *shortening*; compression, squeeze 198 *contraction*; abrasion, erosion 333 *friction*; melting, dissolution 337 *liquefaction*; scattering, dispersal 75 *dispersion*; weeding out, elimination 62 *sorting*, 300 *ejection*; extenuation, alleviation, mitigation, minimization 177 *moderation*; belittlement, undervaluation 483 *underestimation*, 926 *detraction*; demotion, degradation 872 *humiliation*.

**Adj.** *decreasing*, dwindling; decrescent, waning, fading, deliquescent, melting, evaporating 337 *liquefied*; abated, decreased, diminished etc. vb.; unexpanded, unincreased, unstretched; de-escalating; declining, going down, sinking, ebbing; decaying, ruinous 655 *dilapidated*.

**Vb.** *abate*, make less, diminish, decrease, de-escalate, lessen, minify; take away, detract from, deduct 39 *subtract*; except 57 *exclude*; reduce, attenuate, scale down, downsize, whittle, pare, scrape 206 *make thin*; clip, trim, slash 46 *cut*; shrink, abridge, abbreviate, boil down 204 *shorten*; squeeze, compress, contract 198 *make smaller*; limit, restrict, curtail 747 *restrain*; cut down, cut back, retrench 814 *economize*; reduce speed, slow down, decelerate 278 *retard*; depress, send down 311 *lower*; tone down, minimize, mitigate, extenuate 177 *moderate*; allay, alleviate 831 *relieve*; deflate, puncture; disparage, decry, belittle, depreciate, undervalue 483 *underestimate*, 812 *cheapen*, 926 *detract*; dwarf, overshadow 34 *be superior*; steal one's thunder, put in the shade, obscure 419 *bedim*; degrade, demote 872 *humiliate*; loosen, ease, relax 701 *disencumber*; remit, pardon 909 *forgive*; unload, throw overboard 323 *lighten*; run down, drain, exhaust 300 *empty*; use up, consume, squander, fritter away 634 *waste*; let escape, let evaporate, boil away 338 *vaporize*; melt down 337 *liquefy*; grind, crumble 332 *pulverize*; rub away, abrade, file 333 *rub*; gnaw, nibble at, eat away 301 *eat*; erode, rust 655 *impair*; strip, peel, denude 229 *uncover*; pillage, plunder, dispossess 786 *deprive*, 801 *impoverish*; emasculate, unman 161 *disable*; dilute, water down 163 *weaken*, 43 *mix*; thin, thin out, weed o., depopulate 105 *render few*; eliminate, expel 300 *eject*; decimate, slaughter, kill off, wipe out 165 *destroy*, 362 *kill*; reduce to

nothing, annihilate 2 *nullify*; hush, quiet 399 *silence*, 578 *make mute*; damp down, cool 382 *extinguish*; crack down on, quell, subdue, tame 745 *subjugate*.

*decrease*, grow less, lessen, de-escalate, suffer loss; abate, slacken, ease, moderate, subside, die down; dwindle, shrink, shrivel up, contract 198 *become small*; wane, waste, decay, wear away, wither away, degenerate 655 *deteriorate*; fade, die away, grow dim 419 *be dim*; retreat, withdraw, ebb 286 *regress*, 290 *recede*; run low, run down, ebb away, drain away, dry up, fail 636 *not suffice*; tail off, taper off, fade away, peter out 206 *be narrow*, 293 *converge*; subside, sink 313 *plunge*; come down, decline, fall, drop, spiral, slump, collapse 309 *descend*; not grow, level off, bottom out, lag 278 *decelerate*; melt away 446 *disappear*; evaporate 338 *vaporize*; thin, thin out, become scarce 105 *be few*, 75 *disperse*; become endangered, die out, become extinct 2 *pass away*; reduce, lose weight, become anorexic 323 *be light*, 946 *starve*; lose one's voice, stop one's noise, pipe down, shut up, dry up 578 *be mute*; lose, shed, rid oneself of; cast off 229 *doff*; forfeit, sacrifice 772 *lose*.

**Adv.** *diminuendo*, decrescendo, decreasingly; less and less, ever l.; in decline, on the wane, at low ebb.

## 38 Addition

**N.** *addition*, adding to, annexation, fixture, agglutination 45 *union*; superimposing, superposition 187 *location*; prefixion 64 *precedence*; suffixion, affixture 65 *sequence*; supplementation, suppletion 725 *completion*; contribution 703 *aid*; superaddition, imposition, load 702 *encumbrance*; accession, accretion, accrual, supervention; interposition, interjection, epenthesis 303 *insertion*, 78 *inclusion*; reinforcement 36 *increase*; increment, supplement, additive; rollover; addendum, appendage, tailpiece, appendix 40 *adjunct*; extra time, overtime 113 *protraction*; appurtenance 89 *accompaniment*; summation, adding up, counting up, totalling, total, toll 86 *numeration*.

**Adj.** *additional*, additive; added, included etc. vb.; adjunctive, adventitious, supervenient, adopted, adscititious, occasional 59 *extraneous*, 6 *extrinsic*; supplementary, supplemental, suppletory 725 *completive*; conjunctive 45 *joined*; subsidiary, auxiliary, contributory 703 *aiding*; supernumerary, supererogatory; another, further, more; extra, spare 637 *superfluous*; interjected, interposed, epenthetic 303 *inserted*, 231 *interjacent*; prefixed 64 *preceding*.

**Vb.** *add*, add up, sum, total, do the addition

86 *do sums*; carry over 272 *transfer*; add to, annex, append, subjoin; attach, pin to, clip to, tag on, tack on; conjoin, hitch to, yoke to, unite to 45 *join, tie*; stick on, glue on 48 *agglutinate*; add on, insert an addendum, preface, prefix, affix, suffix; infix, introduce 231 *put between*; interpose, interject; engraft, let in 303 *insert*; bring to, contribute to, make one's contribution, add one's share 36 *augment*; swell, extend, expand 197 *enlarge*; supplement, crown 54 *make complete*; lay on, place on, impose, clap on, saddle with, burden w., load w. 187 *stow*, 702 *hinder*; superadd, superimpose, pile on, heap on 74 *bring together*; ornament, add frills, embellish 844 *decorate*; plaster, paint over, coat 226 *overlay*; mix with, mix in 43 *mix*; take to oneself, annex 786 *take*; encompass 78 *number with*; absorb, take in, include, receive 299 *admit*.

*accrue*, be added 78 *be included*; supervene 295 *arrive*, 189 *be present*; adhere, join 708 *join a party*; mix with, combine w. 50 *combine*; make an extra, make an addition to, make one more; reinforce, recruit 162 *strengthen*; swell the ranks, fill the gap.

**Adv.** *in addition*, additionally, more, plus, extra; with interest, with a vengeance, with knobs on; and, too, also, item, furthermore, further, likewise, and also, to boot, else, besides; et cetera, and so on, and so forth; moreover, into the bargain, over and above; including, inclusive of, with, cum, as well as, apart from, not to mention, let alone, not forgetting; together with, along w., coupled w., in conjunction w.; conjointly, jointly; even with, despite, for all that.

## 39 Subtraction
**N.** *subtraction*, deduction, taking away 86 *numerical operation*; diminution 37 *decrease*; abstraction, removal 786 *taking*; withdrawal, cash back; elimination 62 *sorting*; expulsion, clearance 300 *ejection*; unloading, unpacking 188 *displacement*, 304 *extraction*; precipitation, sedimentation, ablation, abrasion, erosion, detrition 333 *friction*; retrenchment, cutting back, curtailment 204 *shortening*; severance, detruncation, amputation, excision, abscission, circumcision 46 *scission*; castration, mutilation 655 *impairment*; expurgation, bowdlerization 648 *cleansing*; deletion 550 *obliteration*; minuend 85 *numerical element*; subtrahend, discount 42 *decrement*.

**Adj.** *subtracted*, subtractive, deducted; mutilated etc. vb.; curtailed, cut back, docked, tailless; beheaded, headless, decapitated; minus, without 307 *deficient*.

**Vb.** *subtract*, take away, deduct, do subtraction; detract from, diminish, decrease 37 *abate*, cut 810 *discount*; take off, knock o., allow 31 *set off*; except, take out, keep o., leave o. 57 *exclude*; expel 300 *eject*; abstract 786 *take*, 788 *steal*; withdraw, remove; unload, unpack 188 *displace*; shift 272 *transfer*; draw off 300 *empty*; abrade, scrape away, file down, erode 333 *rub*; eradicate, uproot, pull up, pull out 304 *extract*; pick, pick out, put on one side 605 *select*; cross out, blot o., delete, erase, blue-pencil, censor 550 *obliterate*; expurgate, bowdlerize, garble, mutilate 655 *impair*; sever, separate, amputate, excise; shear, shave off, clip 46 *cut*; retrench, cut back, cut down, whittle, lop, prune, pare, decapitate, behead, dock, curtail, abridge, abbreviate 204 *shorten*; geld, castrate, caponize, spay, emasculate 161 *unman*; peel, skin, fleece, strip, divest, denude 229 *uncover*.

**Adv.** *in deduction*, by subtraction etc. n.; at a discount; less; short of; minus, without, except, excepting, with the exception of, barring, bar, save, exclusive of, save and except, with reservations.

## 40 Adjunct: thing added
**N.** *adjunct*, addition, additive, something added, add-on, contribution 38 *addition*; additament, addendum, carry-over, rollover; supplement, annex; attachment, fixture; inflection, affix, suffix, prefix, infix; adjective, adverb 564 *part of speech*; ticket, tab, tag 547 *label*; appendage, tail, tail-piece, train, following 67 *sequel*; wake, trail 65 *sequence*; appendix, postscript, P.S., P.P.S., envoi, coda, ending 69 *extremity*; codicil, rider 468 *qualification*; marginalia, annotation, footnotes; corollary, complement 725 *completion*; appurtenance, appanage, accessory 89 *concomitant*; pendant, companion piece, fellow, pair 18 *analogue*; extension, prolongation, continuation, second part; annexe, wing, offices, outhouse 164 *building*; offshoot 53 *branch*; arm, extremity 53 *limb*; accretion 59 *extraneousness*; increment 36 *increase*; patch, reinforcement 656 *repair*; padding, stuffing 227 *lining*; interpolation, interlineation 303 *insertion*; interlude, intermezzo 231 *interjacency*; insertion, gusset, gore 228 *garment*; flap, lappet, lapel; admixture, ingredient 58 *component*; fringe, border, frill, edging 234 *edge*; embroidery 844 *ornamentation*; garnish, garnishing, seasoning 389 *sauce*; frills, trimmings, bells and whistles, all that goes with it; trappings, accoutrements 228 *dressing*, 226 *covering*; equipment, furnishing 633 *provision*.

*extra*, additive, addendum, increment, superaddition, something over and above, by-product; percentage, interest 771 *gain*; bonus, tip, perk, perquisite, graft, something on the side 962 *reward*; free gift, freebie (inf), giveaway, gratuity, golden handshake 781 *gift*; windfall, find, lucky f.; allowance 31 *offset*; oddment, item, odd i., odds and ends; supernumerary, extra; reserves, spare parts, spares 633 *provision*; extra help, reinforcement 707 *auxiliary*; surplus 637 *superfluity*; extra time, injury time, overtime 113 *protraction*.

## 41 Remainder: thing remaining

**N.** *remainder*, residue, residuum; residual, result, resultant 157 *effect*, 164 *product*; margin 15 *difference*; amount or sum outstanding, balance, net b. 31 *offset*; surplus, carry-over 36 *increment*; excess 637 *superfluity*; relic, rest, remains, remnant 105 *fewness*; rump, stump, stub, scrag end, fag e., butt e. 69 *extremity*; frustum, torso, trunk 53 *piece*; fossil, skeleton, bones 363 *corpse*; husk, empty h., shell, empty s.; wreck, wreckage, debris 165 *ruin*; ashes 332 *powder*; track, spoor, fingerprint 548 *record*, *trace*; wake, afterglow 67 *sequel*; all that is left, memorabilia, memories 505 *remembrance*; survival 113 *durability*; vestige, remains.

*leavings*, leftovers, doggy-bag; precipitate, deposit, sediment; alluvium, silt 344 *soil*; drift, loess, moraine, detritus 272 *thing transferred*; grounds, lees, heeltaps, dregs; scum, skimmings, dross, scoria, slag, sludge; bilge, dottle; scrapings, shavings, filings, sawdust, crumbs 332 *powder*; husks, bran, chaff, stubble; peel, peelings; skin, slough, scurf; combings, trimmings, clippings, remnants, offcuts; scraps, candle-ends, odds and ends, bin-ends, lumber 641 *rubbish*; rejects 779 *derelict*; sweepings, scourings, offscourings; waste, sewage 302 *excrement*; refuse, litter 649 *dirt*.

*survivor*, finisher; inheritor, heir, successor 776 *beneficiary*; widower, widow 896 *widowhood*; orphan 779 *derelict*; descendant 170 *posterity*.

**Adj.** *remaining*, surviving, left, vestigial, resting, resultant; residual, residuary; left behind, deposited, sedimentary, precipitated 187 *located*; abandoned, discarded 779 *not retained*; on the shelf 860 *unwanted*; over, left over, odd; net, surplus; unspent, unexpended, unexpired, unconsumed, unused; outstanding, carried over; spare, to s., superfluous 637 *redundant*; cast-off, outcast 607 *rejected*; orphaned, orphan, widowed.

**Vb.** *be left*, remain, rest, result, survive.

*leave over*, leave out 57 *exclude*; leave, leave behind, discard, abandon 607 *reject*.

## 42 Decrement: thing deducted

**N.** *decrement*, deduction, depreciation, cut 37 diminution; allowance; remission; tare, drawback, clawback, rebate 810 *discount*; refund, shortage, slippage, defect 307 *shortfall*, 636 *insufficiency*; loss, sacrifice, forfeit 963 *penalty*; leak, leakage, escape 298 *outflow*; shrinkage 204 *shortening*; spoilage, wastage, consumption 634 *waste*; subtrahend, rake-off 786 *taking*; toll 809 *tax*.

## 43 Mixture

**N.** *mixture*, mingling, mixing, stirring; blending, harmonization; admixture 38 *addition*; commixture 45 *union*; immixture 303 *insertion*; intermixture, interlarding, interpolation 231 *interjacency*; interweaving, interlacing 222 *crossing*; amalgamation, integration 50 *combination*; merger 706 *association*; syncretism, eclecticism; fusion, interfusion, infusion, suffusion, transfusion, instillation, impregnation 341 *moistening*; adulteration, watering down, sophistication 655 *impairment*; contamination, infection 653 *insalubrity*; infiltration, penetration, pervasion, permeation 297 *ingress*; cross-breeding; interbreeding, miscegenation, intermarriage 894 *marriage*; syngamy, allogamy 167 *propagation*; cross-fertilization, hybridism, hybridization, mongrelism; miscibility, solubility 337 *liquefaction*; crucible, melting pot; mixer, beater, shaker, blender, food processor, whisk; churn 315 *rotator*.

*tincture*, admixture; ingredient 58 *component*; strain, streak, element, vein; sprinkling, infusion; tinge, touch, drop, dash, soupçon 33 *small quantity*; smack, hint, suspicion, flavour 386 *taste*; seasoning, bouquet garni, herb, spice 389 *condiment*; colour, dye 425 *hue*; stain, blot 845 *blemish*.

*a mixture*, mélange; blend, harmony 710 *concord*; composition 331 *structure*; amalgam, fusion, compound, confection, potpourri, concoction 50 *combination*; cento, pastiche, pasticcio; alloy, bronze, brass, billon, electrum, pewter, steel; magma, paste; soup, stew, hash, goulash, ragout, blanquette, olla podrida, salmagundi 301 *dish*; cocktail, punch, brew, witches' b.; solution, infusion; medicinal compound, the mixture 658 *remedy*.

*medley*, heterogeneity, complexity, variety 17 *nonuniformity*, 82 *multiformity*; motley, patchwork, mosaic 437 *variegation*; arrangement, array, assortment, choice, collection, diversity, miscellany, miscellanea, raft, ragbag, range, selection, salmagundi, smorgasbord, a variety; job lot, lucky dip, mixed bag; farrago, gallimaufry, hotchpotch, hodgepodge, mishmash, linsey-woolsey, potpourri; jumble, hash, mess; conglomeration 74 *accumulation*;

tangle, entanglement, imbroglio 61 *confusion*; phantasmagoria, kaleidoscope; bear garden, Babel, clatter 411 *discord*; omnium gatherum, motley crew 74 *crowd*; menagerie, circus 369 *zoo*; variety show 594 *stage show*; all sorts, odds and ends, bits and pieces, paraphernalia, oddments, snippets.

*hybrid*, cross, cross-breed, mongrel; mule, hinny, tigon; half-blood, half-breed, half-caste; mestizo, métis; Eurasian, Cape Coloured, Creole, mulatto; quadroon, octaroon.

**Adj.** *mixed*, in the melting pot, mixed up, stirred; mixed up in, involved in; well-integrated, blended, harmonized, joined up; syncretic, eclectic; fused, alloyed 50 *combined*; tempered, qualified, adulterated, sophisticated, watered down 163 *weakened*; merged, amalgamated 45 *joined*; composite, half-and-half, fifty-fifty; complex, complicated, involved 251 *intricate*; tangled, confused, jumbled; unclassified, unsorted, out of order 61 *orderless*; heterogeneous 17 *nonuniform*; kaleidoscopic, phantasmagoric 82 *multiform*; patched, patchy, dappled, motley 437 *variegated*; shot 437 *iridescent*; miscellaneous, random 464 *indiscriminate*; miscible, soluble 337 *liquefied*; pervasive, spreading, contagious 653 *infectious*; hybrid, mongrel; cross-bred, crossed; half-blooded, half-caste; of mixed blood, interbred; intermixed, multiracial.

**Vb.** *mix*, make a mixture, mix up, stir, shake; shuffle, scramble 63 *jumble*; knead, pound together, mash 332 *pulverize*; brew, compound 56 *compose*; fuse, alloy, merge, amalgamate 45 *join*; interfuse, blend, harmonize 50 *combine*; mingle, intermingle, commingle, intersperse 437 *variegate*; immix, intermix, interlard, interleave 303 *insert*; intertwine, interlace, interweave 222 *weave*; tinge, dye 425 *colour*; imbue, instil, impregnate 303 *infuse*; dash, sprinkle, besprinkle 341 *moisten*; water, water down, adulterate, sophisticate 163 *weaken*; temper, doctor, tamper with 143 *modify*; season, spice, fortify, lace, spike; contaminate, hybridize, mongrelize, cross, cross-fertilize, cross-breed 167 *generate*.

*be mixed*, be entangled with, be involved, be mixed up in; pervade, permeate, run through 297 *infiltrate*; infect, contaminate; be shot with; stain 425 *colour*; intermarry, interbreed, cross with 167 *reproduce itself*.

**Adv.** *among*, amongst, amid, amidst, with; in the midst of, in the crowd; amongst many, inter alia.

## 44 Simpleness: freedom from mixture

**N.** *simpleness*, homogeneity 16 *uniformity*; purity 648 *cleanness*; oneness 88 *unity*; absoluteness, sheerness; fundamentality, bedrock 1 *essence*; indivisibility, insolubility, asexuality; lack of complication, simplicity 516 *intelligibility*, 573 *plainness*, 699 *artlessness*; freedom from mixture, not a trace of, not a hint of, not a suspicion of 190 *absence*.

*simplification*, purification, distillation 648 *cleansing*; reduction, reductio ad absurdum 51 *decomposition*; unification, assimilation 13 *identity*.

*elimination*, riddance, jettisoning, clearance 300 *ejection*; sifting, straining 62 *sorting*; expulsion 57 *exclusion*.

**Adj.** *simple*, homogeneous, monolithic, all of a piece 16 *uniform*; sheer, mere, utter, nothing but; undifferentiated, asexual; single, unified 88 *one*; elemental, indivisible, entire 52 *whole*; primary, irreducible, fundamental, nuts and bolts, basic, bog-standard, no-frills, without bells and whistles 5 *intrinsic*; elementary, disentangled, simplified, uncomplicated, unravelled, user-friendly 516 *intelligible*; direct, unmediated 249 *straight*; unadulterated, unalloyed; unsophisticated, homespun 573 *plain*, 699 *artless*; single-minded, whole-hearted, sincere, downright, unaffected 540 *veracious*, 929 *honourable*; bare, naked 522 *undisguised*.

*unmixed*, pure and simple, without alloy; clear, pure, undefiled, unpolluted, clarified, purified, cleansed 648 *clean*; purebred, thoroughbred 868 *noble*; free from, exempt f., excluding; unblemished, untarnished 646 *perfect*; unmingled, unblended, unalloyed, uncompounded, uncombined; undiluted, unadulterated, neat 162 *strong*; unqualified, unmodified; unmedicated, unfortified, unstrengthened; unflavoured, unspiced, unseasoned 387 *tasteless*; untinged, undyed, uncoloured 427 *white*.

**Vb.** *simplify*, render simple 16 *make uniform*; narrow down, break d., factorize, reduce, reduce to its elements 51 *decompose*; disentangle, unscramble 62 *unravel*; unify, make one, unite.

*eliminate*, sift 62 *class*; winnow, sieve, strain, pan; purge 648 *purify*; clear, clarify, cleanse, distil; get rid of, jettison, weed out 57 *exclude*; expel 300 *eject*.

**Adv.** *simply*, purely etc. adj.; without frills, au naturel; simply and solely; only, merely, exclusively.

## 45 Union

**N.** *union*, junction, joining etc. vb.; coming together, meeting, concurrence, conjunction 293 *convergence*; clash 279 *collision*; contact 202 *contiguity*, 378 *touch*; congress, concourse, forgathering, reunion 74 *assembly*; confluence, meeting-point, rendezvous, meeting-place 76 *focus*; concrescence, coalescence, fusion, merger 43 *mixture*; unification, synthesis 50 *combination*; cohesion, tenacity, inextricability, agglutination 48 *coherence*; concretion, consolidation, solidification, coagulation 324 *condensation*; closeness, tightness, compactness, impaction; coalition, alliance, symbiosis 706 *association*; connection, linkage, tie-up, hook-up, link-up, network 47 *bond*; syngamy, wedlock 894 *marriage*; interconnection, cross-connection, anastomosis, inosculation; interlocking 222 *crossing*; communication 305 *passage*; network, intercommunication, intercourse 882 *sociability*; trade, traffic, exchange 151 *interchange*, 791 *trade*; involvement 9 *relation*; arrival, latecomer 297 *incomer*; partner, sharer 775 *participator*; companion 89 *concomitant*.

*joining together*, bringing together 74 *assemblage*; unification 50 *combination*; jointing, articulation 56 *composition*, 331 *structure*; joining, stringing together, threading t., linking t., concatenation; suture, stitching, knitting, sewing, weaving 222 *crossing*; tightening, astriction, drawing together, contraction 198 *compression*, 264 *closure*; knotting, tying, binding, bandaging, ligation; fastening, pinning, infibulation; attaching, attachment, annexing, annexation 38 *addition*; connecting, earthing; affixture, suffixation, prefixion; grafting, planting; inoculation, injection 303 *insertion*; sticking on, fixture 48 *coherence*; coupling, yoking, pairing, matching 18 *assimilation*, 462 *comparison*; bracketing bracketing together, lumping t. 28 *equalization*; hyphenization 547 *punctuation*; joiner, coupler, riveter, welder; go-between, pander 231 *intermediary*, 894 *matchmaker*.

*joint*, joining, juncture, commissure; crease 261 *fold*; suture, seam, stitching 47 *bond*; bonding, English bond, Flemish b., rat-trap b.; weld, welded joint; splice, spliced joint; mitre, mitre joint; dovetail, dovetail and mortise joint; ball and socket j.; hasp, latch, sneck, catch 218 *pivot*; hinge-joint, ginglymus 247 *angularity*; finger, thumb, wrist, ankle, knuckle, knee, hip, elbow; node; junction, point of j., meeting-point, intersection, crossroads 222 *crossing*; decussation, figure X 222 *cross*.

*sexual intercourse*, lovemaking, making love, sex, bonk (sl), bonking (sl), fuck (sl), fucking (sl), ride (sl), rumpy-pumpy (inf), screw (sl), screwing (sl), shag (sl), carnal knowledge, coition, coitus, copulation, intimacy 376 *sexual pleasure*; foreplay; generation 167 *propagation*; pairing, mating, coupling; anal inter-

course 951 *illicit love*; union 894 *marriage*; enjoyment, consummation; violation, ravishment, sexual assault 951 *rape*; unprotected sex, casual s.; safe sex, barrier contraception 172 *contraception*; prostitution, survival sex; fellatio, blowjob (sl), cunnilingus; dildo, vibrator; Viagra (tdmk); sex addiction *or* sexual a.; cybersex.

*sexual partner*, lover 887 *lover*; husband, wife; mistress 887 *loved one*, 952 *kept woman*; prostitute, sex worker, hooker (inf), tart (inf), whore, male prostitute, rent-boy 952 *libertine*, *prostitute*; lay (sl), ride (sl), screw (sl); sex addict.

**Adj.** *joined*, united etc. vb.; connected, earthed; coupled, matched, paired 28 *equal*; conjoined, conjoint, partnered, participant 775 *sharing*; rolled into one, merged; conjunct, joint, allied, incorporated, associated, symbiotic 706 *cooperative*, 708 *corporate*; betrothed, engaged, wedded 894 *married*; holding hands, hand in hand, arm in arm; intimate, involved 5 *intrinsic*; coalescent, concretive, adhesive 48 *cohesive*; composite 50 *combined*; put together 74 *assembled*; articulated, jointed 331 *structural, textural*; stitched, seamed, patched; stitched up.

*conjunctive*, adjunctive, connective, copulative, adhesive 48 *cohesive*; coagulating, astringent 324 *solidifying*; coincident 181 *concurrent*; copulatory, coital, venereal, intimate.

*firm*, close, fast, secure, sound 153 *fixed*; solid, set, solidified 324 *dense*; glued, cemented, stuck 48 *cohesive*; put, pat; planted, rooted, deep-set; ingrown, impacted; close-set, crowded, tight, tight-fitting, wedged, jammed, stuck; inextricable, inseparable, immovable, unshakable; packed, jam-p. 54 *full*.

*tied*, bound, knotted, roped, lashed, secured, belayed, spliced; stitched, sewn, gathered; attached, fastened, adhering 48 *cohesive*; well-tied, tight, taut, tense, fast, secure; intricate, involved, tangled, inextricable, indissoluble.

**Vb.** *join*, conjoin, couple, yoke, hyphenate, harness together; pair, match 18 *liken*, 462 *compare*, 894 *marry*; bracket, bracket together 28 *equalize*; put together, lay t., throw t., clap t., fit t., piece t., assemble, unite 50 *combine*; collect, gather, lump together, bracket t., mobilize, mass 74 *bring together*; add to, amass, accumulate 38 *add*, 632 *store*; associate, ally, twin (town); merge 43 *mix*; incorporate, consolidate, make one, unify 88 *be one*, 16 *make uniform*; lump together, roll into one 464 *not discriminate*; include, embrace 78 *comprise*; grip, grapple 778 *retain*; make a joint, hinge, articulate, dovetail, mortise, mitre, rabbet; fit, set, interlock, engage, gear to; wedge, jam 303 *insert*; weld, solder, braze, fuse, cement, glue 48 *agglutinate*; draw together, lace, knit, sew, seam, stitch; pin, buckle; infibulate; do up, fasten, button up, zip up 264 *close*; lock, latch; close a gap, seal up; darn, patch, mend, heal over, scab over 656 *repair*.

*connect*, attach, annex (see also *affix*); staple, clip, pin together; put t., thread t., string t., rope t., link t., chain t., concatenate; contact 378 *touch*; make contact, plug in, earth 202 *juxtapose*; network, interconnect, inosculate, open into; link, bridge, span, straddle, bestride 305 *pass*; communicate, intercommunicate, establish communication; put through to, put in touch; hook up with, link up w., tie up w. 9 *relate*; link closely, entwine.

*affix*, attach, fix, fasten; fix on, yoke, leash, harness, saddle, bridle; tie up, moor, anchor; tie to, tether, picket; pin on, hang on, hook on, screw on, nail on; stick on, cement on, sellotape on, gum on 48 *agglutinate*; suffix, prefix 38 *add*; infix, splice, engraft, implant 303 *insert*; impact, set, frame 235 *enclose*; drive in, knock in, hammer in 279 *strike*; wedge, jam; screw, nail, rivet, bolt, clamp, clinch; thread, pass through, weave t.

*tie*, knot, hitch, lash, belay; knit, sew, seam, stitch, suture; tack, baste; braid, plait, crochet, twine, twist, intertwine, lace, interlace, interweave 222 *weave*; truss, string, rope, strap; do up, lace up, lash up; tether, picket, moor; pinion, manacle, handcuff; hobble, shackle 747 *fetter*; bind, splice, gird, girdle; bandage, swathe, swaddle, wrap; enfold, embrace, grip, grapple 235 *enclose*, 778 *retain*.

*tighten*, jam, impact; constrict, compress, narrow; fasten, screw up, make firm, make fast, secure; tauten, draw tight, pull t., lace t.; frap, brace, trice up, brail.

*unite with*, be joined, linked etc. vb.; join, meet 293 *converge*; fit tight, hold t., fit closely, adhere, hang together, hold t., stick t., be cemented t. 48 *cohere*; mesh, interlock, engage, grip, grapple, clinch; embrace, entwine; link up with, hold hands; associate with, partner, mix w. 882 *be sociable*; league together 708 *join a party*; marry, get hitched 894 *wed*; live with, cohabit.

*have sexual intercourse with*, have intercourse w., have sex w., make love to, go to bed with, sleep w., sleep together, bed (inf) bonk (sl) do (inf), frig (sl), fuck (sl), give someone one (sl), have (sl), have it off *or* away with (inf), knock off (sl), lay (sl), make (sl), ride (sl), roger (sl), screw (sl), shaft (sl), shag (sl), tumble (inf), enjoy, know, lie with, possess; have carnal knowledge of; consummate a marriage *or* a union; deflower, rape, ravish, take by force, violate 951 *debauch*; copulate, couple, mate,

pair 167 *generate*; cover, mount, serve, tup; cross with, breed w.

**Adv.** *conjointly*, jointly, with, in conjunction, in partnership 708 *in league*; all together, as one.

*inseparably*, inextricably, intimately; securely, firmly, fast, tight.

## 46 Disunion

**N.** *disunion*, disjunction, being separated; disconnection, disconnectedness, incoherence, break 72 *discontinuity*; looseness, separability, fissility 49 *noncoherence*; dissilience, diffusion, dispersal, scattering 75 *dispersion*; breakup, disintegration, dissolution, decay 51 *decomposition*, 655 *dilapidation*; abstraction, absent-mindedness 456 *abstractedness*; dissociation, withdrawal, disengagement, retirement 621 *relinquishment*, 753 *resignation*; surrender, sacrifice 779 *nonretention*, 37 *decrease*; moving apart, growing a., broadening, widening 294 *divergence*, 282 *deviation*; split, schism (see also *separation*); detachment, nonattachment, neutrality 860 *indifference*; isolation, loneliness, quarantine, segregation 883 *seclusion*; zone, compartment, box, cage 748 *prison*; insularity 620 *avoidance*; lack of unity 709 *dissension*; immiscibility, separateness, severalty 80 *speciality*; isolationism, separatism 80 *particularism*; no connection, no common ground 10 *unrelatedness*; distance apart 199 *farness*; dichotomy 15 *difference*; interval, breathing space, space, opening, hole, breach, break, rent, rift, tear, split; fissure, crack, cleft, chasm; cleavage, slit, slot, cut, gash, incision 201 *gap*.

*separation*, disjoining, severance, parting; uncoupling, divorcement, breaking up, splitting up 896 *divorce*; untying, undoing, unfastening, unzipping, unlacing, unbuttoning, unthreading, unravelling, laddering; loosening, loosing, freeing 746 *liberation*; setting apart, discrimination, segregation, ghettoization, apartheid 883 *seclusion*; exception, exemption 57 *exclusion*; boycott 620 *avoidance*; expulsion 300 *ejection*; picking out, selection 605 *choice*; putting aside, setting a., keeping a. 632 *storage*; conservation 666 *preservation*; taking away 39 *subtraction*; abstraction, deprivation, expropriation 786 *taking*; detaching, detachment, withdrawal, removal, transfer 188 *displacement*, 272 *transference*; denudation, stripping, peeling, plucking, fleecing, clipping, shearing 229 *uncovering*; disjointing, dislocation, luxation; scattering, dispersal 75 *dispersion*; dissolution, resolution, disintegration 51 *decomposition*; dissection, analysis, breakdown; disruption, shattering, fragmentation 165 *destruction*; splitting, fission, nuclear f. 160 *nuc-*

leonics; breaking, cracking, rupture, fracture 330 *brittleness*; dividing line, caesura; wall, fence, hedge, ha-ha, ring fence 231 *partition*; curtain 421 *screen*; boundary 236 *limit*; Styx.

*scission*, section, cleavage, cutting, tearing; division, dichotomy 92 *bisection*; subdivision, segmentation; partition 783 *apportionment*; abscission, cutting off, decapitation, curtailment, retrenchment 204 *shortening*, 37 *diminution*; cutting away, resection, circumcision; cutting open, incision, opening 658 *surgery*; dissection; rending, clawing, laceration, dilaceration, divulsion; tearing off, avulsion; nipping, pinching, biting etc. vb.

**Adj.** *disunited*, disjunct, disjoined, divorced, broken up, split up; separated, disconnected, unplugged, unstuck; unseated, dismounted; broken, interrupted 72 *discontinuous*; divided, subdivided, partitioned, bipartite, multipartite; in pieces, quartered, dismembered; severed, cut; torn, rent, riven, cleft, cloven; digitate 201 *spaced*; radiating, divergent 282 *deviating*; scattered, dispersed, fugitive, uncollected 75 *unassembled*; untied, unfastened, undone, unzipped, loosened, loose, free 746 *liberated*.

*separate*, apart, asunder; adrift, lost; unjoined, unfixed, unfastened; unattached, unannexed, unassociated; distinct, discrete, differentiated, separable, distinguishable 15 *different*; exempt, excepted 57 *excluded*; hived off, abstracted 304 *extracted*; immiscible, unassimilable, unassimilated 44 *unmixed*; alien, foreign 59 *extraneous*; external 6 *extrinsic*, 223 *exterior*; insular, self-sufficient, lonely, isolated 88 *alone*, 883 *friendless*; shunned, dropped, avoided, boycotted, sent to Coventry 620 *avoiding*; cast-off 607 *rejected*; picked out, set apart 605 *chosen*; abandoned, left 41 *remaining*; hostile, opposed, antipathetic 881 *inimical*, 14 *contrary*, 240 *opposite*; disjunctive, separative; dichotomous, dividing; selective, diagnostic 15 *distinctive*.

*severable*, separable, detachable; partible, divisible, fissionable, fissile, scissile, tearable; dissoluble, dissolvable; biodegradable 51 *decomposable*; distinguishable, not belonging 10 *unrelated*.

**Vb.** *separate*, stand apart, not mix 620 *avoid*; go, go away 296 *depart*; go apart, go different ways, radiate 294 *diverge*; go another way 282 *deviate*; part, part company, cut adrift, cut loose, divorce, split up; split off, hive off; get away, get free, get loose 667 *escape*; disengage, unclinch, free oneself, break away 746 *achieve liberty*; cast off, unmoor, let go 779 *not retain*; leave, quit, fall away 621 *relinquish*; scatter, break up 75 *disperse*; spring apart 280 *recoil*; come apart, fall a., break, come to bits, disinte-

grate 51 *decompose*; come undone, unravel, ladder, run; fall off 49 *come unstuck*; split, crack 263 *open*.

*disunite*, disjoin, dissociate, divorce; split up, break up, part, separate, sunder, sever, dissever; uncouple, unhitch, disconnect, unplug; disengage, throw out of gear; disjoint, displace, dislocate, wrench; detach, unseat, dismount 49 *unstick*; remove, detract, deduct 39 *subtract*, 272 *transfer*; skin, denude, strip, flay, peel, fleece, shear, pluck 229 *uncover*; unfasten, undo, unbutton, unhook, unlace, unzip, unclasp, unlock, unlatch 263 *open*; untie, cut the knot, sever the tie, disentangle 62 *unravel*; unstitch, unpick; loosen, relax, slacken, unstring 177 *moderate*; unbind, unchain, unfetter, unloose, loose, free, set f., release 746 *liberate*; expel 300 *eject*; dispel, scatter, break up, disband, demobilize 75 *disperse*; disintegrate, break down 51 *decompose*, 332 *pulverize*, 165 *destroy*.

*set apart*, put aside, set a., ring-fence 632 *store*; conserve 666 *preserve*; mark out, tick off, distinguish 15 *differentiate*, 463 *discriminate*; single out, pick o. 605 *select*; except, exempt, leave out 57 *exclude*; boycott, send to Coventry 620 *avoid*; taboo, black, blacklist 757 *prohibit*; insulate, isolate, cut off 235 *enclose*; zone, compartmentalize, screen off, declare a no-go area 232 *circumscribe*; segregate, ghettoize, sequester, quarantine, maroon 883 *seclude*; keep apart, hold a., drive a.; drive a wedge between, estrange, alienate, set against 881 *make enemies*, 888 *excite hate*.

*sunder* (see also *disunite*); divide, keep apart, flow between, stand b.; subdivide, fragment, fractionate, segment, sectionalize, fractionalize, fractionize; reduce, factorize, analyse; cut up, dissect, anatomize 51 *decompose*; dichotomize, halve 92 *bisect*; divide up, split, partition, parcel out 783 *apportion*; dismember, disbranch, quarter, carve (see also *cut*); behead, decapitate, curtail, dock, amputate 204 *shorten*; take apart, take to pieces, cannibalize, dismantle, break up, dismount; force open, force apart, wedge a. 263 *open*; slit, split, rive; cleave 263 *pierce*. (See also *break*.)

*cut*, hew, hack, slash, gash 655 *wound*; prick, stab, knife 263 *pierce*; cut through, cleave, rive, saw, chop; cut open, slit 263 *open*; cut into, make an incision, incise 555 *engrave*; cut deep, cut to the bone, carve, slice; cut round, pare, whittle, chisel, chip, trim, bevel, skive; clip, snick, snip; cut short, shave 204 *shorten*; cut down, fell, scythe, mow; cut off, lop, prune, dock, curtail (see also *sunder*); cut up, chop up, quarter, dismember; dice, shred, mince, make mincemeat of, pound 332 *pulverize*; bite, bite into, bite through 301 *chew*; scratch, scarify, score, plough 262 *groove*; nick 260 *notch*.

*rend*, rive (see also *sunder*); tear, scratch, claw; gnaw, fret, fray, make ragged; rip, slash, slit (see also *cut*); lacerate, dilacerate, dismember; tear limb from limb, tear to pieces, tear to shreds, tear to tatters 165 *destroy*; pluck to pieces; mince, grind, crunch, scrunch, pound 301 *chew*, 332 *pulverize*; explode, blow up, blow to pieces, burst.

*break*, fracture, rupture, bust; split, burst, blow up, explode; break in pieces, smash, smash to smithereens, shatter, splinter, shiver 165 *demolish*; fragment, comminute, crumble, grind, triturate 332 *pulverize*; disintegrate, cave in 51 *decompose*; break up, dismantle (see also *sunder*); chip, crack, damage 655 *impair*; bend, buckle, warp 246 *distort*; break in two, snap, knap; cleave, force apart, wedge a. 263 *open*.

**Adv.** *separately*, severally, singly, one by one, bit by bit, piecemeal, in bits, in pieces, in halves, in twain; discontinuously, unconnectedly, disjointedly, interruptedly.

*apart*, open, asunder, adrift; to pieces, to bits, to smithereens, to tatters, to shreds; limb from limb.

## 47 Bond: connecting medium

**N.** *bond*, connecting medium, vinculum, chain, shackle, fetter, handcuff, tie, band, hoop, yoke; bond of union, sympathy, empathy, fellow feeling 905 *pity*; obligation 917 *duty*; nexus, connection, link, liaison 9 *relation*; junction, hinge 45 *joint*; ramification, network 53 *branch*; connective, copula; hyphen, dash, bracket 547 *punctuation*; intermedium, cement (see also *adhesive*); bondstone, binder; tie-beam, stretcher, girder 218 *beam*; strut, stay 218 *prop*; interconnection, intercommunication, channel, passage, corridor 624 *access*; stepping-stone, causeway 624 *bridge*; span, arch; isthmus, neck; col, ridge; stair, steps, stepladder, ladder 308 *ascent*; lifeline; umbilical cord.

*cable*, line, guy, hawser, painter, moorings; guest-rope, towline, towrope, ripcord, lanyard, communication cord; rope, cord, whipcord, string, tape, twine 208 *fibre*; chain, wire, earth.

*tackling*, tackle, cordage; rig, rigging, running r., standing r., shroud, ratline; sheets, guy, stay; clewline, garnet, halliard, bowline, lanyard; harness.

*ligature*, ligament, tendon, muscle, abdominal muscle, abdominals, abs (inf), six-pack, biceps, deltoid, gastrocnemius, gluteus, masseter, pectoral muscle, pectorals, pecs (inf), trapezius, triceps; tendril, withe, withy, osier, bast, bass, raffia 208 *fibre*; lashing, binding;

string, cord, thread, tape, sticky tape, Sellotape (tdmk), Scotch tape (tdmk), Velcro (tdmk), band, fillet, ribbon, ribband; bandage, roller b., roller, tourniquet 198 *compressor*; drawstring, thong, lace, bootlace, tag; braid, plait 222 *network*; tie, stock, cravat 228 *neckwear*; knot, hitch, clinch, bend; running knot, slip k., granny k., reef k.; half hitch, clove h.; sheepshank, Turk's head; true-love knot, Gordian k.

*fastening* 45 *joining together*; fastener, snap f., press-stud, pop-fastener, popper, zip fastener, zip; drawstring, ripcord; stitch, basting; button, buttonhole, eyelet, loop, frog; hook and eye; Velcro (tdmk); stud, cufflink; garter, suspender, braces; tiepin, brooch 844 *jewellery*; clip, grip, slide, clasp, curlers; hairpin, hatpin; skewer, spit, brochette; pin, drawing p., safety p., toggle p., cotter p., linch p., king p.; peg, dowel, treenail, trenail, nail, brad, tack, tintack 256 *sharp point*; Blu-tack (tdmk), Sellotape (tdmk), Scotch tape (tdmk); holdfast, staple, clamp, brace, batten, cramp 778 *nippers*; nut, bolt, screw, rivet; buckle, clasp, morse; hasp, hinge 45 *joint*; catch, safety c., spring c., pawl, click, detent; latch, bolt; lock, lock and key 264 *closure*; combination lock, yale l., mortise l.; padlock, handcuffs, bracelets 748 *fetter*; ring, cleat; hold, bar, post, pile, pale, stake, bollard.

*coupling*, yoke; coupler, drawbar, traces; grappling iron, hook, claw; anchor, sheet a. 662 *safeguard*.

*girdle*, band, strap 228 *belt*; waistband, bellyband, cummerbund, girth, cinch, surcingle; money belt, belt-bag, bum-bag, sash, shoulder belt, bandolier, Sam Browne; collar, neckband 228 *neckwear*; bandeau, hairband, fillet.

*halter*, collar, noose; tether, lead, leash, jess, reins, ribbons; lasso, lariat 250 *loop*; shackle 748 *fetter*.

*adhesive*, glue, fish glue, lime, birdlime, gum, epoxy resin; fixative, hair lacquer, hair spray, brilliantine, grease; solder; paste, size, lute, clay, cement, putty, mortar, stucco, plaster, grout 226 *facing*; wafer, sealing wax; sticker, stamp, adhesive tape, sticky t., Sellotape (tdmk), Scotch tape (tdmk), Blu-tack (tdmk); fly-paper 542 *trap*; sticking plaster, Elastoplast (tdmk), Band-Aid (tdmk) 48 *coherence*.

## 48 Coherence

**N.** *coherence*, connection, connectedness 71 *continuity*; chain 71 *series*; holding together, cohesion, cohesiveness; holding on, tenacity, tenaciousness 778 *retention*; adherence, adhesion, adhesiveness; stickiness 354 *viscidity*; cementation, cementing, sticking, soldering, agglutination, conglutination 45 *union;* compaction, conglomeration, agglomeration, consolidation, congealment, set 324 *condensation;* inseparability, indivisibility, union 88 *unity;* indigestibility 329 *toughness;* phalanx, serried ranks, unbroken front, united f.; birds of a feather; monolith, agglomerate, concrete 324 *solid body;* bur, leech, remora, limpet, barnacle, parasite, epizoon, clinging vine; gum, plaster, sticking p. 47 *adhesive;* chewing gum; toffee.

**Adj.** *cohesive*, coherent, adhesive, adherent; sessile, clinging, tenacious; indigestible 329 *tough;* sticky, tacky, gummy, gluey, viscous 354 *viscid;* compact, well-knit, solid, coagulated, concrete, frozen 324 *dense;* shoulder to shoulder, side by side, phalanxed, serried; monolithic 16 *uniform;* united, infrangible, indivisible, inseparable, inextricable; close, tight, close-fitting, skintight, figure-hugging, clinging, moulding.

**Vb.** *cohere*, hang together, grow together 50 *combine;* hold, stick close, hold fast; bunch, close the ranks, stand shoulder to shoulder, rally 74 *congregate;* grip, take hold of 778 *retain;* hug, clasp, embrace, twine round; close with, clinch; fit, fit like a glove, fit tight, be skin tight, mould the figure; adhere, cling, stick; stick to, cleave to, come off on, rub off on; stick on to, freeze on to; stick like a leech, stick like a bur, stick like a limpet, cling like a shadow, cling like ivy; cake, coagulate, agglomerate, conglomerate, solidify, consolidate, freeze 324 *be dense.*

*agglutinate*, conglutinate, glue, gum, paste, lute, cement, weld, braze 45 *join;* stick to, affix 38 *add.*

**Adv.** *cohesively*, indivisibly, unitedly, solidly, compactly.

## 49 Noncoherence

**N.** *noncoherence*, incoherence 72 *discontinuity;* uncombined state, noncombination, lack of order, chaos 51 *decomposition;* scattering 75 *dispersion;* separability, immiscibility; looseness, bagginess; loosening, relaxation, laxity, freedom 46 *separation;* wateriness, runniness 335 *fluidity;* slipperiness 258 *smoothness;* frangibility, friability, rope of sand 330 *brittleness;* nonadhesion, aloofness; individualist, lone wolf, loner, separatist 84 *noncomformist.*

**Adj.** *nonadhesive*, nonadhering, slippery 258 *smooth;* not sticky, dry; detached, semi-detached 46 *separate;* noncohesive, incoherent, unconsolidated, loose, like grains of sand; unconfined, ranging, free, free-range, at large 746 *liberated;* relaxed, lax, slack, baggy, loose-fitting, flopping, floppy, flapping, flying,

streaming; watery, liquid, runny 335 *fluid;* pendulous, dangling 217 *hanging;* uncombined 51 *decomposed;* immiscible, unassimilated 59 *extraneous;* aloof 620 *avoiding.*

**Vb.** *unstick*, unglue, peel off; detach, unpin, unfasten, undo; free, loosen, loose, slacken 46 *disunite;* shake off, unseat, dismount; shed, slough 229 *doff.*

*come unstuck*, peel off, melt, thaw, run 337 *liquefy;* totter, slip 309 *tumble;* dangle, flap 217 *hang;* rattle, shake, flap.

## 50 Combination

**N.** *combination*, composition 45 *joining together;* growing together, coalescence, symphysis 45 *union;* fusion, blending, conflation, synthesis, syncretism 43 *mixture;* amalgamation, merger, assimilation, digestion, absorption 299 *reception;* uniting, unification, integration, centralization 88 *unity;* incorporation, embodiment; synchronization 706 *cooperation;* coagency 181 *concurrence;* marriage, union, league, alliance, federation, confederation 706 *association;* conspiracy, cabal 623 *plot;* chord, counterpoint 412 *music;* chorus 24 *agreement;* harmony, orchestration 710 *concord;* aggregation, assembly 74 *assemblage;* synopsis, conspectus, bird's-eye view 592 *compendium;* mosaic, jigsaw, collage.

*compound*, alloy, amalgam, blend, composite, chemical, chemical compound 43 *a mixture;* portmanteau word; make-up 56 *composition.*

**Adj.** *combined*, united, unified 88 *one;* integrated, joined up, centralized; incorporate, embodied; inbred, bred in the bone, ingrained, absorbed 5 *intrinsic;* fused, impregnated 43 *mixed;* blended, harmonized, adapted 24 *adjusted;* connected, yoked, linked, networked, conjugate, conjoint 45 *joined;* aggregated, congregated 74 *assembled;* coalescent, symphystic; synchronized 123 *synchronous;* in harmony, on the same wavelength, in partnership, in league; associated, leagued, allied 706 *cooperative;* conspiratorial; coagent 181 *concurrent.*

**Vb.** *combine*, put together, fit t.; make up 56 *compose;* intertwine, interweave 222 *weave;* harmonize, synchronize 24 *accord;* bind, tie 45 *join;* unite, unify, centralize; incorporate, embody, integrate, absorb, take in, soak up, assimilate, merge, amalgamate, pool; blend, fuse, compound 43 *mix;* impregnate, imbue, instil, inoculate 303 *infuse;* bracket together; lump together 38 *add;* group, regroup, rally 74 *bring together;* band together, brigade, associate; federate, ally, league with; partner, go into partnership with, join hands, join forces with, team up with 706 *cooperate*; fraternize, make friends 880 *be friendly*; cement a union, marry 894 *wed*; mate, couple 90 *pair*; put heads together, conspire 623 *plot*; coalesce, grow together, run t.; have an affinity, combine with; combine with water, hydrate 339 *add water*.

## 51 Decomposition

**N.** *decomposition* 46 *disunion*; division, partition, compartmentation 46 *separation*; dissection, dismemberment; anatomization, analysis, breakdown; factorization 44 *simplification*; syllabification, parsing 564 *grammar*; catalysis, electrolysis, hydrolysis, photolysis, resolution; atomization; dissolving, dissolution 337 *liquefaction*; fission 160 *nucleonics*; hiving off, demerging, decentralization, devolution, delegation; regionalism; collapse, breakup, disintegration, entropy 165 *destruction*; chaos 17 *nonuniformity*; composting, vermicomposting, worm composting.

*decay* 655 *dilapidation*; erosion, wear and tear 37 *diminution*; disintegration 361 *death*; corruption, mouldering, rotting, putridness, putrefaction, adipocere, mortification, necrosis, gangrene, caries 649 *uncleanness*; rot, rust, mould 659 *blight*; carrion 363 *corpse*.

**Adj.** *decomposed*, resolved, reduced, disintegrated, uncombined, chaotic 46 *disunited*; corrupted, mouldering 655 *dilapidated*; putrid, gangrenous, rotten, bad, off, high, rancid, sour, overripe.

*decomposable*, disposable, biodegradable, compostable, recyclable 656 *restored*.

**Vb.** *decompose*, decompound, unscramble; resolve, reduce, factorize 44 *simplify*; separate, separate out, parse, dissect; break down, analyse, take to pieces 46 *sunder*; electrolyse, catalyse; split, fission 46 *disunite*; atomize 165 *demolish*; disband, break up, hive off 75 *disperse*; decentralize, regionalize 783 *apportion*; unsettle, disorder, disturb, cause chaos 63 *derange*; dissolve, melt 337 *liquefy*; erode 37 *abate*; rot, rust, moulder, decay, consume, waste away, crumble, wear, perish 655 *deteriorate*; corrupt, putrefy, mortify, gangrene 649 *be unclean*; disintegrate, go to pieces 165 *be destroyed*.

**Adv.** *analytically*, partitively; on analysis, by a.

## 52 Whole. Principal part

**N.** *whole*, wholeness, integrality, omneity, fullness 54 *completeness*; integration, indivisibility, indiscerptibility, integrity, oneness 88 *unity*; a whole, whole number, integer, entity 88 *unit*; entirety, ensemble, corpus, complex, four

corners of – ; totality, summation, sum 38 *addition*; holism, holistic approach, global a., universalization, generalization 79 *generality*; comprehensiveness, inclusiveness 78 *inclusion*; collectivity, system, world, globe, cosmos 321 *universe*; microcosm; idioverse, life space, Lebensraum, total situation 7 *state*; grand view, bird's-eye v., panorama, overview, conspectus, synopsis 438 *view*; whole course, round, circuit 314 *circuition*.

*all*, no omissions, no exceptions, everybody, everyone, one and all, 'the quick and the dead' 79 *everyman*;

> . . . The third day he rose again from the dead; He ascended into heaven, And sitteth on the right hand of God the Father Almighty; From thence he shall come to judge the quick and the dead.
> Apostles' Creed

the world, all the w. 74 *crowd*; everything, all, the whole, total, aggregate, gross amount, sum, sum total, ensemble, tout e., lot, whole 1., the whole caboodle, the whole kit and caboodle, the whole bang shoot (inf), the works (inf), the full monty (inf); length and breadth, the rough with the smooth; 'be-all and end-all' (see quotation at 638 *important matter*), 'Alpha and Omega', lock, stock and barrel;

> I am Alpha and Omega, the beginning and the ending, saith the Lord . . .
> . . . I am Alpha and Omega, the first and the last . . .
> Bible, Revelation

hook, line and sinker; unit, family; set, complete s. 71 *series*; outfit, pack, kit; complete list, inventory 87 *list*.

*chief part*, best part, principal p., major p., essential p., nitty-gritty, nuts and bolts 638 *chief thing*; ninety-nine per cent, bulk, mass, substance; heap, lump 32 *great quantity*; tissue, staple, stuff; body, torso, trunk, bole, stem, stalk; hull, hulk, skeleton; lion's share, biggest slice of the cake; gist, sum and substance, the long and the short of it; almost all, nearly all, everything but the kitchen sink; all but a few, majority 104 *greater number*.

**Adj.** *whole*, total, universal, holistic; integral, pure, unadulterated 44 *unmixed*; entire, sound 646 *perfect*; grand, gross, full 54 *complete*; individual, single, integrated 88 *one*; in one piece, of a piece, seamless; fully restored 656 *restored*.

*intact*, untouched, unaffected; uncontaminated, unspoiled, virgin 126 *new*; undivided, unsevered, undiminished, unclipped, uncut, uncropped, unshorn; undissolved, unabolished, still there; unbroken, undestroyed, unbruised, unmangled, unimpaired, sound, without a scratch 646 *undamaged*; uncut, unabridged, unedited, uncensored, unexpurgated.

*indivisible*, impartible 324 *indissoluble*; undissolvable, indiscerptible; inseparable, 45 *joined*; monolithic 16 *uniform*.

*comprehensive*, omnibus, all-embracing, all-encompassing, across-the-board, full-length 78 *inclusive*; wholesale, all singing all dancing, sweeping 32 *extensive*, widespread, epidemic 79 *general*; international, world, world-wide, global, cosmic 79 *universal*, 189 *ubiquitous*.

**Adv.** *wholly*, integrally, body and soul, as a whole; entirely, totally, fully, every inch, in toto 54 *completely*; without deduction, one hundred per cent.

*on the whole*, by and large, altogether, all in all, all things considered, in the long run; substantially, essentially, in substance, in essence; virtually, to all intents and purposes, as far as one can tell, effectually, in effect; as good as; mainly, in the main 32 *greatly*; almost, all but 200 *nearly*.

*collectively*, one and all, all together, as a team, corporately; comprehensively, and all; in bulk, in the mass; in sum, in the aggregate; bodily, en masse, en bloc.

## 53 Part

**N.** *part*, not the whole, portion; proportion, certain p.; majority 32 *main part*, 104 *greater number*; minority 105 *fewness*, 33 *small quantity*; fraction, half, moiety, quarter, tithe, percentage; factor, aliquot, aliquant 85 *number*; balance, surplus 41 *remainder*; quota, contingent; dividend, share, whack 783 *portion*; item, article, particular, detail 80 *particulars*; clause, sentence, paragraph 563 *phrase*; ingredient, member, constituent, element 58 *component*; dissident element, schism, cabal, faction 708 *party*; heat, leg, lap, round 110 *period*; side 239 *laterality*; group, species (see also *subdivision*); detachment 42 *decrement*; attachment, fixture, wing 40 *adjunct*; page, leaf, folio, sheet 589 *book*; excerpt, extract, gobbet, passage, quotation, quote 605 *choice*; text, pericope; segment, sector, section 46 *scission*; arc 248 *curve*; hemisphere 252 *sphere*; part payment, instalment, advance, down payment, deposit, earnest 804 *payment*; sample, appetizer, foretaste 83 *example*; fragment (see also *piece*).

*limb*, member, organ, appendage; hind limb 267 *leg*; forelimb 271 *wing*; flipper, fin 269 *propeller*; arm, forearm, hand 378 *feeler*; elbow, funny bone 247 *angularity*.

*subdivision*, segment, sector, section 46 *scission*; division, compartment; group, subgroup, species, subspecies, family 74 *group*; classification 62 *arrangement*; ward, community,

parish, department, region 184 *district*; chapter, paragraph, clause, subordinate clause, phrase, verse; part, number, issue, instalment, volume 589 *edition, reading matter*; canto 593 *poem*.

*branch*, sub-b., ramification, offshoot 40 *adjunct*; bough, limb, spur, twig, tendril, leaf, leaflet; switch, shoot, scion, sucker, slip, sprig, spray 366 *foliage*.

*piece*, torso, trunk, stump 41 *remainder*; limb, segment, section (see also *part*); patch, insertion 40 *adjunct*; length, roll 222 *textile*; strip, swatch; fragment, unfinished symphony 55 *incompleteness*; bit, scrap, offcut, shred, wisp, rag 33 *small thing*; morsel, bite, crust, crumb 33 *small quantity*; splinter, skelf, sliver, chip, snip, snippet; cut, wedge, finger, slice, rasher; collop, cutlet, chop, gigot c., steak; hunk, chunk, wad, wodge, portion, slab, lump, mass 195 *bulk*; clod, turf, divot, sod 344 *soil*; sherd, shard, potsherd, flake, scale 207 *lamina*; dollop, dose 783 *portion*; bits and pieces, odds and ends, oddments, miscellanea, disjecta membra, flotsam and jetsam 43 *medley*; bin ends; clippings, shavings, parings, brash, rubble, scree, detritus, moraine, debris 41 *leavings*, 641 *rubbish*; rags, tatters 801 *poverty*; piece of land, parcel, plot, allotment.

**Adj.** *fragmentary*, broken, brashy, crumbly 330 *brittle*; in bits, in pieces, in smithereens 46 *disunited*; not whole, limbless, armless, legless 647 *imperfect*; partial, bitty, scrappy 636 *insufficient*; half-finished 55 *unfinished*; fractional, half, semi-, hemi-, aliquot; segmental, sectional, divided, multifid; departmentalized, compartmentalized, in compartments 46 *separate*; shredded, wispy, sliced, minced, ground 33 *small*.

*brachial*, cubital; membered, brachiate; with branches, branched, branchy.

**Vb.** *part*, divide, partition, segment; compartmentalize 46 *sunder*; share out, job-share 783 *apportion*; fragment 46 *disunite*.

**Adv.** *partly*, in part, scrappily, partially; in a sense 55 *incompletely*.

*piecemeal*, part by part, limb from limb; by instalments, by snatches, by inches, in dribs and drabs; bit by bit, inch by inch, centimetre by centimetre, foot by foot, drop by drop, a little at a time, little by little, by degrees; in detail, in lots.

## 54 Completeness

**N.** *completeness*, nothing lacking, nothing to add, entireness, wholeness 52 *whole*; integration, integrality 88 *unity*; solidity, solidarity 706 *cooperation*; harmony, balance 710 *concord*; self-sufficiency 635 *sufficiency*; entirety, totality

52 *all*; universality, comprehensiveness 79 *generality*; the ideal 646 *perfection*; ne plus ultra, the limit 236 *limit*; peak, culmination, zenith, crown 213 *summit*; finish 69 *end*; last touch, finishing t. 725 *completion*; fulfilment, consummation 69 *finality*; the whole hog, the full monty (inf), all the way; nothing less than, the utmost 69 *extremity*.

*plenitude*, fullness, amplitude, capacity, maximum, one's fill, saturation 635 *sufficiency*; saturation point 863 *satiety*; completion, filling, replenishment, refill; filling up, brimming, overfilling, overrunning, overwhelming, swamping, drowning; overfulfilment 637 *redundance*; full house, complement, full c., full crew, full load; requisite number, quorum; full measure, brimmer, bumper; bellyful, skinful, repletion; full size, full length, full extent, full volume; complement, supplement, makeweight 31 *compensation*.

**Adj.** complete, plenary, full; utter, total; integral, integrated 52 *whole*; entire, with all its parts, with nothing missing, with no exceptions, with supplement 52 *intact*, 646 *perfect*; full-blown, full-grown, full-fledged, fully-f. 669 *matured*; unbroken, undivided, solid 324 *dense*; self-contained, self-sufficient, self-sufficing 635 *sufficient*; fully furnished 633 *provisioning*; all-in, comprehensive, full-scale 78 *inclusive*; exhaustive, circumstantial, detailed 570 *diffuse*; absolute, extreme, radical; thorough, thoroughgoing, whole-hogging, sweeping, wholesale, regular 32 *consummate*; unmitigated, downright, plumb, plain 44 *unmixed*; crowning, completing, culminating, consummating; supplementary, complementary 725 *completive*, 38 *additional*; unconfined, unqualified 744 *unconditional*.

*full*, replete 635 *filled*; replenished, refilled, topped up 633 *provisioning*; well-filled, well-lined, bulging; brimful, brimming, level with, flush; overwhelmed; overfull, overflowing, running over, slopping, swamped, drowned; saturated, oozing, leaking 637 *redundant*; coming out at the ears, bursting at the seams; crop-full, gorged, fit to burst, full to bursting, sickened with 863 *sated*; chock-full, chock-a-block, not an inch to spare; cram-full, crammed, stuffed, packed, full-p., jam-p., packed like sardines, jammed, tight 45 *firm*; laden, heavy-l., freighted, fraught, fully charged, full to the hatches; all seats taken, standing room only; infested, overrun, crawling with, hotching w., alive w., seething w., jumping w., lousy w., stiff w.; full of, rolling in; soaked in, dripping with 341 *drenched*; ever-full, inexhaustible 146 *unceasing*.

**Vb.** *be complete*, be integrated, make a whole; reach *or* touch perfection, have everything; culminate, come to a head 725 *climax*; reach an end, come to a close, be all over 69 *end*; be self-sufficient 635 *have enough*; want nothing, lack n. 828 *be content*; become complete, fill out, attain full growth, become a man *or* woman, reach maturity 669 *mature*, be filled, fill, fill up, brim, hold no more, run over, slop o., overflow 637 *superabound*; gorge, eat *or* drink one's fill 947 *gluttonize*, 949 *get drunk*.

*make complete*, complete, complement, integrate, make into a whole 45 *join*; make whole 656 *restore*; build up, construct, make up, piece together 56 *compose*; eke out, supplement, supply, fill a gap 38 *add*; make good 31 *compensate*; do thoroughly, leave nothing undone, leave nothing to add, carry out 725 *carry through*; overfulfil 637 *be superfluous*; put the finishing touch, put the icing on the cake, round off 69 *terminate*.

*fill*, fill up, brim, top; soak, saturate 341 *drench*; overfill, swamp, drown, overwhelm; top up, replenish 633 *provide*; satisfy 635 *suffice*, 828 *content*, 863 *sate*; fill to capacity, cram, pack, stuff, line, bulge out, pack in, pile in, squeeze in, ram in, jam in 303 *insert*; load, charge, ram down; lade, freight 187 *stow*; fill space, occupy 226 *cover*; reach to, extend to 183 *extend*; spread over, sprawl o., overrun 189 *pervade*; leave no corner, fit tight, be full to overflowing, be chock-a-block 45 *tighten*; fill in, put in, write in, enter 38 *add*.

**Adv.** *completely*, fully, wholly, totally, entirely, utterly, extremely 32 *greatly*; all told, in all, in toto; effectually, virtually, as good as; to all intents, to all intents and purposes; on all counts, in all respects, in every way; quite, all of, altogether; outright, downright; to the heart, to the quick, to the core, to the marrow, through and through; thoroughly, clean, stark, hollow; to one's fill, to the top of one's bent, to the utmost, to the end, to the full; out and out, all out, heart and soul, through thick and thin; head and shoulders, head over heels, neck and crop; to the brim, up to the hilt, up to the neck, up to the ears, up to the eyes; hook, line and sinker; root and branch; down to the ground; with a vengeance, with knobs on, with all the trimmings, and then some; to the last man, to the last breath; every whit, every inch; at full length, full out, in full; as . . . as can be; as far as possible; to capacity, not an inch to spare.

*throughout*, all the way, all round, from first to last, from beginning to end, from end to end, from one end to the other, the length and breadth of, from coast to coast, from sea to sea, from Land's End to John o' Groats 183 *widely*;

from north and south and east and west; fore and aft; high and low; from top to bottom, de fond en comble; from top to toe, from head to foot, cap-à-pie; to the bitter end, à outrance, to the end of the road, to the end of the chapter, for good and all.

## 55 Incompleteness

**N.** *incompleteness*, defectiveness; unfinished state 647 *imperfection*; unreadiness 670 *nonpreparation*; underdevelopment, immaturity 670 *undevelopment*; first beginnings 68 *debut*; sketch, outline, first draft, rough d., aperçu 623 *plan*; skeleton, torso, trunk 53 *piece*; half measures, sketchiness, scrappiness, a lick and a promise 726 *noncompletion*; perfunctoriness, superficiality, hollowness 4 *insubstantiality*, 458 *negligence*; nonfulfilment, deficiency, slippage, falling short 307 *shortfall*, 636 *insufficiency*; nonsatisfaction, dissatisfaction 829 *discontent*; mutilation, impairment 655 *deterioration*; omission, break, gap, lacuna, missing link 72 *discontinuity*, 201 *interval*; semi-, half, quarter; instalment, part payment 53 *part*.

*deficit*, part wanting, screw loose, missing link, omission 647 *defect*; shortfall, slippage, ullage 42 *decrement*, 772 *loss*; default, defalcation 930 *improbity*; want, lack, need 627 *requirement*.

**Adj.** *incomplete*, inadequate, defective 307 *deficient*; short, scant, unsatisfactory 636 *insufficient*; like Hamlet without the Prince 641 *useless*; omitting, wanting, lacking, needing, requiring 627 *demanding*; short of, shy of; halting, maimed, lame, limping, mangled, marred, mutilated; without, -less, -free; limbless, armless, legless, one-armed, one-legged, one-eyed 163 *disabled*; garbled, impaired 655 *deteriorated*; cropped, lopped, docked, truncated, abbreviated, shortened 204 *short*; blemished, flawed 647 *imperfect*; half, semi-, partial 53 *fragmentary*; left unfinished, half-finished, neglected 726 *uncompleted*; not ready, unready 670 *unprepared*; undeveloped, underdeveloped, unripe 670 *immature*; raw, crude, rough-hewn 244 *amorphous*; sketchy, scrappy, bitty, hollow, superficial, meagre, thin, poor 4 *insubstantial*; perfunctory, half-hearted, half-done, undone 458 *neglected*; left in the air, left hanging; omitted, missing, lost 190 *absent*; interrupted 72 *discontinuous*; in default, in arrears, not up to date, defaulting.

*unfinished*, in progress, in hand, going on; in embryo, begun 68 *beginning*; in preparation, on the stocks.

**Vb.** *be incomplete*, miss, lack, need 627 *require*, 307 *fall short*; be wanting 190 *be absent*;

default, leave undone 458 *neglect*; omit, miss out 57 *exclude*; break off, interrupt 72 *discontinue*; leave in the air, leave dangling, leave hanging 726 *not complete*.

**Adv.** *incompletely*, partially, by halves, in instalments; inadequately, insufficiently; in arrears, in default.

## 56 Composition

**N.** *composition*, constitution, setup, make-up; make, conformation, formation, construction, build-up, build 331 *structure*; organization 62 *arrangement*; temper, habit, nature, humour, character, condition 5 *temperament*; embodiment, incorporation 78 *inclusion*; compound 43 *mixture*, 50 *combination*, 358 *organism*; syntax, sentence, period 563 *phrase*; artistic composition 412 *music*, 551 *art*, 553 *painting*, 554 *sculpture*; architecture 164 *building*; authorship 586 *writing*, 593 *poetry*; dramatic art 594 *drama*; composing, setting-up, printing, typography 587 *print*; compilation 74 *assemblage*; work, construction 164 *production*; choreography 594 *ballet*; orchestration, instrumentation, score 412 *musical piece*; work of art, picture, portrait, sculpture, piece of s., model; literary work 589 *book*, 593 *poem*, 591 *dissertation*, 592 *anthology*; play 594 *stage play*; 837 *dance*; pattern, design 12 *correlation*.

**Adj.** *composing*, constituting, making; composed of, made of; containing, having 78 *inclusive*.

**Vb.** *constitute*, compose, be the whole of, form, make; make up, build up to; inhere, belong to, go to the making of, enter into 58 *be one of*.

*contain*, subsume, include, consist of 78 *comprise*; hold, have, take in, absorb 299 *admit*; comprehend, embrace, embody 235 *enclose*; involve, imply 5 *be intrinsic*; hide 525 *conceal*.

*compose*, compound 43 *mix*, 50 *combine*; organize, set in order, put in o. 62 *arrange*; synthesize, put together, make up 45 *join*; compile, assemble 74 *bring together*; compose, set up, computer-set 587 *print*; draft, draw up, indite 586 *write*; orchestrate, score 413 *compose music*; draw 553 *paint*; sculpt, construct, build, make, fabricate 164 *produce*; knit, interweave 222 *weave*; pattern, design 12 *correlate*.

## 57 Exclusion

**N.** *exclusion*, preclusion, preoccupation, pre-emption; anticipation, forestalling 702 *hindrance*; exclusiveness, monopoly, closed shop, dog-in-the-manger policy; possessiveness 932 *selfishness*; noninclusion, exception; an exception, special case; exception in favour of, exemption, dispensation 746 *liberation*; leaving out, including o., omission, deliberate o. 607 *rejection*; nonadmission, blackball; no entry, no admission, no-go area, no-man's land, exclusion order, closed door, lockout; picket line; embargo, ban, bar, taboo 757 *prohibition*; ostracism, boycott 620 *avoidance*; social exclusion, segregation, quarantine, caste system, colour bar, apartheid 883 *seclusion*; intolerance, repression, suppression, discrimination 481 *prejudice*; expulsion, eviction; disbarment, dismissal, suspension, excommunication; deportation, exile, expatriation; removal, elimination, eradication 188 *displacement*; cancellation, blotting out 550 *obliteration*; dam, coffer d., wall, barricade, screen, partition, pale, curtain, 'Iron C.', Bamboo C. 235 *barrier*;

> From Stettin in the Baltic to Trieste in the Adriatic, an iron curtain has descended across the Continent.
>
> Winston Churchill (The term 'iron curtain' had been in use in this sense since the 1920s.)

Great Wall of China, Hadrian's wall, Antonine wall 713 *defence*; customs barrier, economic zone, tariff, tariff wall 809 *tax*; place of exile, place of voluntary e., place of segregation, ghetto, outer darkness 223 *exteriority*.

**Adj.** *excluding*, exclusive, exclusory, exclusionary, exemptive; restrictive, clannish, cliquish 708 *sectional*; preventive, interdictory, prohibitive 757 *prohibiting*; preclusive, preemptive; silent about 582 *taciturn*.

*excluded*, barred, excepted etc. vb.; extra-, not included, not admitted; peripheral, hardly in, half in, half out; included out, counted o.; not told, unrecounted, suppressed, stifled; not allowed, disallowed, banned 757 *prohibited*; disbarred, struck off 550 *obliterated*; shut out, outcast 607 *rejected*; inadmissible, beyond the pale 470 *impossible*; foreign 59 *extraneous*, 84 *unconformable*; removable, exemptile.

**Vb.** *be excluded*, not belong, stay outside, not gain admission; suffer exile, go into e., go into voluntary e. 296 *depart*, 190 *be absent*.

*exclude*, preclude 470 *make impossible*, preempt, forestall 64 *come before*; keep out, warn off 747 *restrain*; blackball, vote against, deny entry, shut out, debar, shut the door on, spurn 607 *reject*; bar, ban, place an embargo on, taboo, black, disallow 757 *prohibit*; ostracize, cold-shoulder, boycott, send to Coventry 620 *avoid*, 883 *make unwelcome*; not include, leave out, count o.; exempt, dispense, excuse 746 *liberate*; except, make an exception, treat as a special case 19 *make unlike*; omit, miss out, pass over, disregard 458 *neglect*; lay aside, put a., relegate 46 *set apart*, take out, strike o., cross o., cancel 550 *obliterate*; disbar, strike off,

remove, disqualify 188 *displace*, 963 *punish*; rule out, draw the line; wall off, fence off, screen off, curtain off, quarantine 232 *circumscribe*, 235 *enclose*; excommunicate, segregate, sequester 883 *seclude*; thrust out, dismiss, sack, declare redundant; deport, extradite, exile, banish, outlaw, expatriate; weed, sift, sieve, sort out 44 *eliminate*; eradicate, uproot 300 *eject*; expurgate, bowdlerize, censor 648 *purify*; deny 760 *refuse*; abandon 779 *not retain*.

**Adv.** *exclusive of*, excepting, barring, bar, not counting, including out, except, with the exception of, save; outside of, short of; let alone, apart from; outside of, extra-.

## 58 Component

**N.** *component*, component part, integral p., integrant p., element, item; piece, bit, segment; link, stitch; word, letter; constituent, part and parcel 53 *part*; factor, leaven 178 *influence*; additive, appurtenance, feature 40 *adjunct*; one of, member, one of us; staff, workforce, crew, men, company, complement 686 *personnel*; ingredient 193 *contents*, 43 *tincture*; works, inner workings, insides, interior 224 *interiority*; nuts and bolts, machinery 630 *machine*; spare part 40 *extra*; components, set, outfit 88 *unit*.

**Adj.** *component*, constituent, ingredient, integrant 56 *composing*; entering into, belonging, proper, native, inherent 5 *intrinsic*; built-in, appurtenant 45 *joined*; admitted, entered, made a member, part of, one of, on the staff; involved, implicated, mixed up in 43 *mixed*.

**Vb.** *be one of,* make part of, be a member etc. n.; inhere, belong 5 *be intrinsic*; enter into, enter into the composition of 56 *constitute*; become involved with, be mixed up in, be implicated in, share 775 *participate*; merge in, be merged in 43 *be mixed*; belong to, appertain to 9 *be related*.

## 59 Extraneousness

**N.** *extraneousness*, foreignness 6 *extrinsicality*, 223 *exteriority*; foreign parts 199 *farness*; foreign body, foreign substance, accretion 38 *addition*; alien element 84 *nonconformity*; exotica.

*foreigner*, person from foreign parts 268 *traveller*; alien, stranger, unco, emmet, Uitlander, outlander; continental, tramontane, ultramontane; Southerner, Northerner, Easterner, Westerner; Martian, Venusian, extraterrestrial being, little green man; Celtic fringe; Sassenach, jock, taffy, pommie (derog), limey (derog), rooineck (derog); Yank, Yankee, Aussie, Kiwi; wog (offensive), wop (offensive), dago (offensive); gringo (derog), whitey (derog), honkie (offensive), paleface; colonial,

Creole 191 *settler*; resident alien, expatriate; migrant, economic m., migrant worker, guest w., Gastarbeiter, emigrant, émigré, exile; immigrant, declarant 297 *incomer*; refugee, asylum-seeker, déraciné/déracinée 268 *wanderer*; diaspora, ten lost tribes.

*intruder*, interloper, alien, trespasser, cuckoo in the nest, squatter; uninvited guest, gatecrasher, stowaway; outsider, novus homo 126 *upstart*; not one of us, stranger in our midst; arrival, new a., nouveau arrivé, new face, newcomer, new boy, new kid on the block, tenderfoot 297 *incomer*; invader 712 *attacker*.

**Adj.** *extraneous*, of external origin, ulterior, outside 223 *exterior*, 6 *extrinsic*; ultramundane, extragalactic 199 *distant*; not indigenous, imported, foreign-made; foreign, alien, unearthly; strange, outlandish, barbarian; overseas, ultramarine, transatlantic; continental, tramontane, ultramontane; extraterrestrial; exotic, hothouse, unacclimatized; gypsy, nomad, wandering 267 *travelling*; unassimilated, undigested, unintegrated 46 *separate*; immigrant 297 *incoming*; intrusive, interloping, trespassing, gatecrashing; infringing, invading 712 *attacking*; exceptional 84 *unusual*; un-British, un-American 15 *different*; not of this world, unnatural, paranormal, supernatural 983 *magical*; inadmissible 57 *excluded*.

**Adv.** *abroad*, in foreign parts, in foreign lands; beyond seas, overseas; from outer space.

SECTION FOUR

*Order*

**60 Order**

**N.** *order*, state of order, orderliness, tidiness, neatness 648 *cleanness*, 258 *smoothness*; proportion 245 *symmetry*; peace, quiet 266 *quietude*; harmony, music of the spheres 710 *concord*; good order, economy, system, method, methodicalness, punctiliousness, methodology, systematization, prioritization; fixed order, pattern, set p., rule 81 *regularity*, 16 *uniformity*; custom, routine 610 *habit*; rite 988 *ritual*; strict order, discipline 739 *obedience*; due order, hierarchy, gradation, subordination, rank, place, position 73 *serial place*; unbroken order, course, even tenor, progression, series 71 *continuity*; logical order, serial o., alphabetical o. 65 *sequence*, 12 *correlation*; organization, putting in order, disposition, array 62 *arrangement*, 56 *composition*; a place for everything and e. in its place.

**Adj.** *orderly*, harmonious 710 *concordant*, 245 *symmetrical*; well-behaved, decorous 848

*well-bred*; well-drilled, disciplined 739 *obedient*; well-regulated, under control, according to rule 81 *regular*; ordered, classified, schematic 62 *arranged*; methodical, punctilious, systematic, businesslike; strict, invariable 16 *uniform*; routine, steady 610 *habitual*; correct, shipshape, Bristol fashion, just so, trim, neat, tidy, dinky, neat and tidy, neat as a pin, out of a bandbox; spick and span, spruce, dapper, well-groomed 648 *clean*; in good trim, well-kept, uncluttered, in apple-pie order, in perfect o., in its proper place, unconfused 62 *arranged*; unruffled, unrumpled 258 *smooth*; direct 249 *straigh*t; clear, lucid 516 *intelligible*.

**Vb.** *order*, reduce to order, dispose, prioritize 62 *arrange*; schematize, systematize, organize 62 *regularize*; harmonize, synchronize, regulate 24 *adjust*; normalize, standardize 16 *make uniform*; keep order, call to order, police, control, govern 733 *rule*, 737 *command*.

*be in order*, be shipshape, harmonize, synchronize 24 *accord*; fall in, range oneself, draw up, line up; fall into place, find one's level; take one's place, station oneself, take up one's station; take up one's position 187 *place oneself*; keep one's place; rally, rally round 74 *congregate*; follow routine 610 *be wont*.

**Adv.** *in order*, strictly, just so, verbatim, by the book, according to the rule book, by the card 81 *to rule*; by order, as directed; in turn, in its t., seriatim; step by step, by regular steps, by regular gradations, by regular stages, at regular intervals 141 *periodically*; orderly, in orderly fashion, in Bristol fashion, methodically, systematically, schematically; all correct, all right, OK.

**61 Disorder**

**N.** *disorder*, random order, nonarrangement, nonclassification; incoordination, muddle, no plan, no order, no method, no system, alphabet soup (see also *confusion*); bedlam, chaotic state, chaos, mayhem 734 *anarchy*; irregularity, anomalousness, anomaly 17 *nonuniformity*; disunion, disaccord 25 *disagreement*; disharmony 411 *discord*; disorderliness, unruliness, no discipline, lack of d. 738 *disobedience*; violent behaviour, outbreak (see also *turmoil*); nihilism 738 *sedition*; untidiness, clutter, littering, sluttishness, slovenliness 649 *uncleanness*; neglect 458 *negligence*; discomposure, disarray, dishevelment 63 *derangement*; dissolution, scattering 75 *dispersion*, 51 *decomposition*; upheaval, convulsion 149 *revolution*; subversion 221 *overturning*; destruction 165 *havoc*.

*confusion* (see also *disorder*); welter, jumble, shambles, hugger-mugger, mix-up, medley, embroilment, imbroglio 43 *mixture*; wilderness, jungle; chaos, 'fortuitous concurrence of atoms';

> You may call it coalition, you may call it the accidental and fortuitous concurrence of atoms.
> Lord Palmerston

swarm, seething mass, scramble 74 *crowd*; muddle, litter, clutter, lumber 641 *rubbish*; farrago, mess, mishmash, hash, hotchpotch, ragbag, witch's brew, jumble sale, lucky dip 43 *medley*; Babel, bedlam, madhouse (see also *turmoil*).

*complexity*, complication, problem, snarl-up 700 *difficulty*, 702 *hindrance*; implication, involvement, imbroglio, embroilment; intricacy, interlocking, involution, kink 251 *convolution*; maze, labyrinth, warren; web, spider's w. 222 *network*; coil, tangle, twist, tangled skein, snarl, ravel; knot, Gordian k. 47 *ligature*; wheels within wheels, clockwork, machinery; puzzle 517 *unintelligibility*; awkward situation, how d'ye do, how-do-you-do, pretty kettle of fish, pickle 700 *predicament*.

*turmoil*, turbulence, tumult, frenzy, ferment, storm, convulsion 176 *violence*; pandemonium, inferno; hullabaloo, hubbub, racket, row, riot, uproar 400 *loudness*; affray, fracas, dustup, stramash, brawl, mêlée 716 *fight*; hurly-burly, to-do, rumpus, ruction, shemozzle, spot of bother, pother, trouble, disturbance 318 *commotion*; whirlwind, tornado, hurricane 352 *gale*; beargarden, shambles, madhouse, Bedlam, Saturnalia, Bacchanalia; shindig, Donnybrook Fair, breach of the peace; roughhouse, rough and tumble, free for all, fisticuffs, all hell broken loose, bull in a china shop; street fighting, gang warfare 709 *quarrel*; fat in the fire, devil to pay, hell to p.

*slut*, sloven, slag, slattern, draggletail, litterer, litterlout 649 *dirty person*; ragamuffin, tatterdemalion 801 *poor person*.

*anarchist*, nihilist; lord of misrule, sons of Belial 738 *rioter*.

**Adj.** *orderless*, in disorder, in disarray, disordered, deranged, disorganized, jumbled, shuffled 63 *disarranged*; unclassified, ungraded, unsorted; out of order, not in working order, not working, not in operation 641 *useless*; out of joint, out of gear, dislocated 46 *disunited*; out of sorts 651 *sick*; out of place, misplaced 188 *displaced*; askew, awry, snafu; topsyturvy, upside down 221 *inverted*; wandering, straggling, dispersed 75 *unassembled*; random, unarranged, unorganized, uncoordinated, unschematic, planless 244 *amorphous*; incoherent, rambling, irregular, anomalous 17 *nonuniform*; unsystematic, unmethodical, desultory, aimless, without purpose, casual;

confused, muddled, chaotic, shambolic (inf), in chaos, in a mess, messy, all anyhow, haywire; unkempt, uncombed, dishevelled, tumbled, windswept, windblown, tousled, discomposed, pulled through a hedge backwards; littering, untidy, slovenly, sluttish, slatternly, bedraggled, messy 649 *dirty*; sloppy, slipshod, slack, careless 456 *inattentive*.

*complex*, intricate, involved, elaborate, sophisticated, complicated, over-c., over-involved 251 *coiled*; problematic 517 *puzzling*; mazy, winding, inextricable 251 *labyrinthine*; entangled, enmeshed, balled up, snarled 702 *hindered*; knotted 45 *tied*.

*disorderly*, undisciplined, unruly; out of control, out of step, out of line, not toeing the line; tumultuous, rumbustious 738 *riotous*; frantic 503 *frenzied*; orgiastic, Saturnalian, Bacchic, Dionysiac 949 *drunken*; rough, tempestuous, turbulent 176 *violent*, 318 *agitated*; anarchical, nihilistic, lawless 954 *lawbreaking*; wild, harum-scarum, rantipole, tomboyish, boisterous; scatterbrained 456 *lightminded*.

**Vb.** *be disordered*, fall into disarray, scatter, break up 75 *disperse*; get in a mess, fall into confusion, lose cohesion 49 *come unstuck*; get out of hand, throw off discipline, riot, undo the reins 738 *disobey*; not keep one's place, jump the queue 64 *come before*; disorder 63 *derange*.

*rampage*, go on the r., storm 176 *be violent*; rush, mob, break the cordon; roister, riot 738 *revolt*; romp 837 *amuse oneself*; play the fool 497 *be absurd*; fete, give a riotous welcome 876 *celebrate*.

**Adv.** *confusedly*, in confusion, in disorder, without regard to order, without order, anyhow, all a., all over the place, all over the shop; irregularly, without rhyme or reason; by fits and snatches, by fits and starts; chaotically, pell-mell, higgledy-piggledy, helter-skelter, harum-scarum; in turmoil, in a ferment; on the rampage; at sixes and sevens, at cross purposes; topsy-turvy, upside down 221 *inversely*; inextricably.

## 62 Arrangement: reduction to order
**N.** *arrangement*, reduction to order; ordering, disposal, disposition, marshalling, arraying, placing 187 *location*; relocation; collocation, grouping 45 *joining together*, 74 *assemblage*; division, distribution, allocation, allotment 783 *apportionment*; method, systematization, organization, reorganization, restructuring; rationalization 44 *simplification*; streamlining 654 *improvement*; centralization 48 *coherence*; decentralization, hiving off 49 *noncoherence*; administration, paperwork, staff-work 689 *management*; planning, making arrangements 623

*contrivance*, 669 *preparation*; taxonomy, categorization, classification 561 *nomenclature*; analysis 51 *decomposition*; codification, digestion, consolidation; syntax, conjugation 564 *grammar*; grading, gradation, subordination, graduation, calibration 465 *measurement*, 71 *series*; continuation, serialization 71 *continuity*; timing, synchronization 123 *synchronism*; formulation, construction 56 *composition*; result of arrangement, array, system, form 60 *order*; cosmos 321 *universe*; organic creature 358 *organism*; orchestration, score 412 *music*; layout, pattern, architecture 331 *structure*; weave 222 *crossing*; choreography 837 *dance*; collection, assortment 74 *accumulation*; schematic arrangement, schematism; computer program; spreadsheet; register, file 548 *record*; inventory, catalogue, table 87 *list*; syntagma, code, digest, synopsis 592 *compendium*; treatise, essay, composition, article 591 *dissertation*, 589 *book*; atlas 551 *map*; scheme 623 *plan*; composition 770 *compromise*, 765 *compact*, 766 *conditions*; class, group, sub-g. 77 *classification*.

*sorting*, grading, seeding, league table; reference system, cross-reference 12 *correlation*; file, computer f., folder, filing system, card index, Filofax (tdmk), personal organizer, pigeonhole, slot; sieve, strainer 263 *porosity*.

**Adj.** *arranged*, disposed, marshalled, arrayed etc. vb.; ordered, schematic, tabulated, tabular; methodical, systematic, organizational; precise, definite, cut and dried; analysed, classified, assorted; unravelled, disentangled, unscrambled, straightened out; regulated 81 *regular*; unconfused 60 *orderly*; sorted, seeded, graded, streamed, banded.

**Vb.** *arrange*, set, dispose, set up, set out, lay out; formulate, form, put into shape, knock into s., orchestrate, score 56 *compose*; range, rank, align, line up, form up; position 187 *place*; marshal, array; bring back to order, rally 74 *bring together*; place in order, put in order, set in order; grade, size, group, space; collocate, thread together 45 *connect*; settle, fix, determine, define; allot, allocate, assign, distribute, deal, dole out, parcel out 783 *apportion*; rearrange, trim, neaten, tidy, tidy up (see also *unravel*); arrange for, make arrangements 669 *prepare*, 623 *plan*, 689 *manage*.

*regularize*, reduce to order, bring order into, straighten out, set the record straight, put to rights 654 *rectify*, 24 *adjust*; regulate, coordinate, phase; organize, systematize, methodize, schematize; standardize, normalize, centralize 16 *make uniform*.

*class*, classify, subsume, group; specify 561 *name*; process, process the data; analyse, ana-

tomize, divide; dissect 51 *decompose*; rate, rank, grade, evaluate 480 *estimate*; sort, sift, sieve, seed; sift out 44 *eliminate*; docket, tag, label 547 *mark*; file, pigeonhole; index, reference, cross-r.; tabulate, alphabetize; catalogue, inventory 87 *list*; register 548 *record*; codify, program, digest.

*unravel*, untangle, disentangle, tease, disembroil, ravel, card, comb out, unweave, uncoil, unsnarl, untwist, untwine 316 *evolve*; iron, press, uncrease, iron out 258 *smooth*; debug 654 *make better*; unscramble; straighten out, tidy up, smarten up, clean up, neaten 648 *clean*; declutter; clear the air, remove misunderstanding, explain 520 *interpret*.

## 63 Derangement

**N.** *derangement*, subversion of order; shuffling 151 *interchange*; translocation, displacement 272 *transference*; sabotage, Luddism, obstruction 702 *hindrance*; disarrangement, disorganization, discomposure, dishevelment; dislocation 46 *separation*; disturbance, interruption 138 *untimeliness*; timeslip 108 *time*; creasing, corrugation 261 *fold*; madness 503 *mental disorder*; upsetting 221 *inversion*; convulsion 176 *violence*, 318 *agitation*; state of disorder 61 *disorder*.

**Adj.** *disarranged*, deranged, disordered 61 *orderless*; demented 503 *mentally disordered*; sabotaged 702 *hindered*.

**Vb.** *derange*, disarrange, disorder, throw into d., put out of gear, get out of order; disturb, touch 265 *move*; meddle, interfere 702 *hinder*; mislay, lose 188 *misplace*; disorganize, muddle, confound, confuse, convulse, throw into confusion, make havoc, scramble; tamper, spoil, mar, damage, sabotage, shaft (sl) 655 *impair*; strain, bend, twist 176 *force*; unhinge, dislocate, sprain, rick 188 *displace*; unseat, dislodge, derail, throw off the rails; throw off balance, unbalance, upset, overturn, capsize 221 *invert*, 149 *revolutionize*; declassify, detribalize, denationalize; shake, jiggle, toss 318 *agitate*; trouble, perturb, unsettle, discompose, disconcert, ruffle, rattle, flurry, fluster 456 *distract*; interrupt, break in on 138 *mistime*; misdirect, disorientate, throw one off his bearings 495 *mislead*, 655 *pervert*; unhinge, dement, drive mad 503 *make mad*, 891 *enrage*.

*jumble*, shuffle, get out of order 151 *interchange*, 272 *transpose*; mix up 43 *mix*; toss, tumble 318 *agitate*; ruffle, dishevel, tousle, fluff up; rumple, crumple, crease, wrinkle, crush 261 *fold*; untidy, mess, muck up; muddle, mess up, litter, clutter; scatter, fling about 75 *disperse*; play havoc with, play merry hell with 702 *hinder*.

*bedevil*, confuse, throw into confusion, make a mess *or* hash of; confound, complicate, perplex, involve, ravel, ball up, entangle, tangle, embroil; turn topsy-turvy, turn upside down 221 *invert*; send haywire.

## 64 Precedence

**N.** *precedence*, antecedence, antecedency, taking precedence, going before, coming b., queue-jumping 283 *preceding*; anteriority 119 *priority*; front position, anteposition, prefixion, prosthesis 237 *front*; higher position, pride of place 34 *superiority*; preference 605 *choice*; preeminence, excellence 638 *importance*; captaincy, leadership, hegemony 733 *authority*; the lead, the pas; leading, guiding, pioneering; precedent 66 *precursor*; past history 125 *past time*.

**Adj.** *preceding*, going first etc. vb.; precedent, antecedent, foregoing, outgoing; anterior, former, ex-, previous 119 *prior*; beforementioned, above-m.; aforesaid, said; precursory, precursive, prevenient, anticipatory; leading, guiding, pioneering, avant-garde; forewarning, premonitory, prodromal; preliminary, prelusive, proemial, prefatory, preparatory, introductory; prepositive, prosthetic, prefixed, prepositional 237 *frontal*; first come, first served.

**Vb.** *come before*, be first to arrive 283 *precede*; go first, run ahead, jump the queue; lead, guide, conduct, show the way, point the way 547 *indicate*; forerun, be the forerunner of, pioneer, clear the way, blaze the trail 484 *discover*; head, take the lead 237 *be in front*; have precedence, take p., outrank 34 *be superior*; lead the dance, set the fashion, be a trendsetter, set the example 178 *influence*; open, lead off, kick off, bully off 68 *begin*; preamble, prelude, preface, prologize; introduce, usher in, herald, ring in 68 *auspicate*; have the start, get ahead 119 *be before*; antedate 125 *be past*.

*put in front*, lead with, head w.; send a reconnaissance party, advance, send ahead, station before 187 *place*; prefix 38 *add*; front, face, tip, top 237 *be in front*; presuppose 512 *suppose*, 475 *premise*; trail; preface, prelude 68 *initiate*.

**Adv.** *before*, in advance 283 *ahead*; preparatory to, as a prelude to, as a preliminary; earlier 119 *before* (in time); ante, supra, above 237 *in front*.

## 65 Sequence

**N.** *sequence*, coming after, subsequence, descent, line, lineage 120 *posteriority*; going after 284 *following*; consecution, inference 475 *reasoning*; postposition, suffixion 38 *addition*,

45 *joining together*; sonship 170 *posterity*; succession, successorship, mantle, Elijah's m. 780 *transfer*; rota, Buggins' turn; series 71 *continuity*; successiveness, alternation, serialization; continuation, prolongation 113 *protraction*, 146 *continuance*; pursuance 619 *pursuit*; overtaking 306 *overstepping*, 727 *success*; subordination, second place, proxime accessit 35 *inferiority*; last place 238 *rear*; no priority 639 *unimportance*; consequence 67 *sequel*, 157 *effect*; conclusion 69 *end*.

**Adj.** *sequential*, sequent, following, succeeding, successional; incoming, ensuing; proximate, next 200 *near*; posterior, latter, later 120 *subsequent*; another, second, third 38 *additional*; successive, consecutive 71 *continuous*; alternating, antiphonal 12 *correlative*; alternate, every second, every other; postpositive, postpositional 238 *back*; consequent, resulting 157 *caused*.

**Vb.** *come after*, have one's turn, come next, ensue 284 *follow*; follow close, sit on one's tail, drive bumper to bumper, breathe down one's neck, tread on the heels 200 *be near*; succeed, inherit, step into the shoes of, supplant 150 *substitute*; alternate, take turn and turn about 141 *be periodic*; relieve, take over.

*place after*, suffix, append; subscribe, subjoin 38 *add*.

**Adv.** *after*, following; afterwards 120 *subsequently*, 238 *rearward*; at the end; in relays, in waves, successively; as follows, consequentially 157 *consequently*; in the end 69 *finally*; next, later; infra, below.

## 66 Precursor

**N.** *precursor*, predecessor, ancestor, forebear, patriarch 169 *parentage*; Adam and Eve, early man 371 *humankind*; the ancients, Deucalion and Pyrrha 125 *antiquity*; eldest, firstborn; protomartyr; discoverer, inventor 461 *experimenter*; pioneer, Voortrekker, pathfinder, explorer 268 *traveller*; guide, pilot, bell-wether 690 *leader*; scout, reconnaissance party, skirmisher; vanguard, avant-garde, innovator, trailblazer; trendsetter; forerunner, outrider; herald, harbinger, announcer 529 *messenger*; dawn, false d.; anticipation, prefigurement, foretaste, prognostic, preview, premonition, forewarning 664 *warning*, 511 *omen*; prodrome, trailer; prequel; precedent 83 *example*; antecedent, prefix, preposition 40 *adjunct*; eve, vigil, day before 119 *priority*.

*prelude*, preliminary, prolusion, preamble, preface, front matter, prologue, foreword, avant-propos; proem, opening, exordium, prolegomenon, introduction 68 *beginning*; lead, heading, frontispiece 237 *front*; groundwork, foundation 218 *basis*, 669 *preparation*; aperitif, appetizer, hors d'oeuvre, starter; overture, voluntary 412 *musical piece*; premises, presupposition 512 *supposition*, 475 *premise*.

**Adj.** *precursory*, preliminary, reconnoitring, exploratory 669 *preparatory*; prelusory, proemial, introductory, prefatory 68 *beginning*; inaugural, foundational; precedent 64 *preceding*.

## 67 Sequel
**N.** *sequel*, consequence, result, aftermath, by-product, spin-off 157 *effect*; conclusion 69 *end*; sequela, aftereffect; hangover, morning after 949 *crapulence*; aftertaste; afterglow, fallout; afterbirth, placenta, afterpains 167 *obstetrics*; inheritance, legacy 777 *dower*; surprise, afterclap 508 *lack of expectation*; afterthought, second thoughts, better t., esprit de l'escalier; double take, second try, second bite at the cherry; afterword, end matter, postlude, epilogue, postscript; peroration, envoi, last words; follow-through, follow-up 725 *completion*; continuation, sequel 589 *book*; tag, tailpiece, colophon, coda 238 *rear*; appendage, appendix, codicil, supplement 40 *adjunct*; suffix, affix, inflection 564 *grammar*; afterpart, tail; queue, pigtail, plait, ponytail 259 *hair*; afters, pudding, dessert 301 *dish*; survival, afterlife, afterworld, hereafter 124 *future state*.

*retinue*, following, followers, camp f., groupies 284 *follower*; queue 71 *series*; suite, train, cortège 71 *procession*; tail, tailback, wake 89 *concomitant*; trailer 274 *vehicle*.

*successor*, descendant, later generations, future g., generations as yet unborn, the unborn 170 *posterity*; heir, inheritor 776 *beneficiary*; next man in; replacement, supplanter 150 *substitute*; fresh blood, new broom 126 *modernist*, *upstart*; latecomer, newcomer, nouveau arrivé 297 *incomer*; gleaner 370 *farmer*; satellite, hanger-on 742 *dependant*; last man in, finalist, finisher 41 *survivor*.

## 68 Beginning
**N.** *beginning*, birth, rise (see also *origin*); infancy, babyhood 130 *youth*, 126 *newness*; primitiveness 127 *oldness*; commencement; onset 295 *arrival*; emergence 445 *appearance*; incipience, inception, inchoation, institution, constitution, foundation, establishment 156 *causation*; origination, invention 484 *discovery*; creation 164 *production*; innovation 21 *originality*; initiative, démarche; exordium, introduction, curtain-raiser 66 *prelude*; alpha, first letter, initial; head, heading, headline, caption 547 *label*; title page, prelims, front matter; van, front, forefront 237 *front*; dawn 128 *morning*;

running in, teething troubles, growing pains; first blush, first glance, first sight, first impression, first lap, first round, first stage; early stages, early days, incunabula; primer, outline; rudiments, elements, first principles, alphabet, ABC; leading up to 289 *approach*; outbreak, onset 712 *attack*; debutante, starter 538 *beginner*; precedent 66 *precursor*; preliminaries 669 *preparation*.

*debut*, coming out, presentation, initiation, launching; inauguration, opening, unveiling; first night, premiere, first appearance, first offence; premier pas, first step, first move, move, gambit; maiden battle, maiden voyage, maiden speech; baptism of fire.

*start*, outset; starting point, starting post, point of departure, zero hour, D-day; send-off, setting out, embarkation, countdown 296 *departure*; rising of the curtain; starting pistol, kick-off, bully-off; house-warming, honeymoon; fresh start, new beginning, pastures new; resumption, reopening 148 *reversion*; new departure, thin end of the wedge, precedent; standing start, flying s.; start-up; starter, self-s.

*origin*, origination, derivation, conception, genesis, birth, nativity; provenance, ancestry 169 *parentage*; fount, fons et origo; rise 156 *source*; nest, womb 156 *seedbed*; bud, germ, seed, egg, embryo, pre-embryo, protoplasm, primeval soup 358 *organism*; Big Bang; first beginnings, cradle 192 *home*.

*entrance* 297 *way in*; inlet 345 *gulf*; mouth, opening 263 *orifice*; threshold 624 *access*; porch 194 *lobby*; gateway 263 *doorway*; frontier, border 236 *limit*; outskirts, skirts, environs, suburbs 230 *surroundings*; foothills, outlier; pass, corridor 289 *approach*, 305 *passage*.

**Adj.** *beginning*, initiatory, initiative, inceptive; introductory, prefatory, proemial 66 *precursory*; inaugural, foundational; elemental, rudimental 156 *fundamental*; aboriginal, primeval, primordial 127 *primal*; rudimentary, elementary, crude 670 *immature*; embryonic, germinal, nascent, budding, incipient, inchoate, raw, begun, in preparation 726 *uncompleted*; early, infant 126 *new*; just begun, newly opened, launched.

*first*, initial, primary, maiden, starting, natal; pioneering 21 *original*; unprecedented 126 *new*; foremost, front 237 *frontal*; leading, principal, major, head, chief 34 *supreme*.

**Vb.** *begin*, make a beginning, make a start, commence, inchoate; set in, open, dawn, break out, burst forth, spring up, crop up; arise, emerge, appear; rise, take one's r., take one's birth; spring from; sprout, germinate; come into existence, come into the world, see the light of day 360 *be born*; make one's debut, come out; start, enter upon, embark on 296 *start out*; fire away, kick off, strike up; start work, clock in; roll up one's sleeves, limber up 669 *prepare*; run in; begin at the beginning, start from scratch, begin ab ovo; resume, begin again, go back to square one, make a fresh start 148 *revert*; start afresh, shuffle the cards, reshuffle, resume, recommence, reopen; put one's hand to the plough, put one's shoulder to the wheel, set to, set about, set to work, get cracking, get moving, get weaving; attack, wade into, tackle, face, address oneself; go to it 672 *undertake*.

*initiate*, found, launch; originate, invent, think of 484 *discover*; call into being 167 *generate*; usher in, herald, ring in, open the door to, introduce; start, start up, kick-start, switch on, ring up the curtain; prompt, promote, set going, set in motion, get under way; raise, set on foot; put to work 622 *employ*; handsel, run in; take the initiative, lead, lead off, lead the way, take the lead, pioneer, open up, break new ground 64 *come before*; broach, open, raise the subject, ventilate, air; open the ball, break the ice, kick off, set the ball rolling; throw the first stone, open fire; take the first step, take the plunge, cross the Rubicon, burn one's boats; apply the match, trigger off, touch off, spark off, set off.

*auspicate*, inaugurate, open; institute, install, induct 751 *commission*; found, set up, establish 156 *cause*; be a founder member, be in on the ground floor, be in with the bricks; baptize, christen, launch 561 *name*; initiate, blood, flesh; lay the foundations, lay the foundation stone, cut the first turf 669 *prepare*.

**Adv.** *initially*, originally, at the beginning, in the b., at the very start, in the bud, in embryo, in its infancy; from its birth, from its inception, from the beginning, from the word go; ab initio, ab ovo; de novo, de nouveau; first, firstly, in the first place, imprimis, primo; primarily, first of all, before everything, first and foremost; as a start, for starters, for a kick-off, for a beginning; from scratch; back to basics.

## 69 End

**N.** *end*, close, conclusion, consummation 725 *completion*; payoff, result, end r. 157 *effect*; end use; expiration, lapse; termination, determination, closure, guillotine; finishing stroke, death blow, quietus, coup de grâce; knockout, finisher, clincher 279 *knock*; catastrophe, denouement; ending, finish, finale, curtain; term, period, stop, halt 145 *cessation*; final

stage, latter end 129 *evening*; beginning of the end, peroration, last words, swansong, envoi, coda 67 *sequel*; last stage, last round, last lap, home stretch; last ball, last over; last breath, last gasp, extremities, terminal illness 361 *decease*; final examination, finals 459 *exam*. (See also *finality*.)

*extremity*, final point, omega; ultimate point, extreme, pole, antipodes; extreme case, ne plus ultra; farthest point, world's end, ultima Thule, where the rainbow ends 199 *farness*; fringe, verge, brink 234 *edge*; frontier, boundary 236 *limit*; end of the road, end of the line, terminal point, terminus, terminal 295 *goal*, 617 *objective*; dregs, last d.; foot, toe, bottom, nadir 214 *base*; bottom dollar, last cent, last penny 801 *poverty*; tip, cusp, point 256 *sharp point*; vertex, peak, head, top, zenith 213 *summit*; tail, tail end 67 *sequel*; arm, stump 53 *limb*; shirt-tail, coat-t. 217 *hanging object*; end, butt end, gable e., fag e. 238 *rear*; tag, epilogue, post-script, end matter, appendix 40 *adjunct*; desinence, inflection, suffix 564 *grammar*.

*finality*, bitter end; time, time up, deadline; conclusion, ending, end of the matter, closure 54 *completeness*; drop of the curtain, break-up, wind-up 145 *cessation*; dissolution 165 *destruction*; eschatology, last things, doom, destiny 596 *fate*; end of the world, end of time, end of all things, end of everything, Big Crunch, crack of doom, Götterdämmerung, last trump, resurrection day, Day of Judgment 124 *future state*.

**Adj.** *ending*, final, terminal, last, ultimate, supreme, closing; extreme, polar; definitive, conclusive, crowning, completing 725 *completive*; conterminal, conterminous, coterminous; ended, at an end; settled, terminated, finalized, decided, set at rest; over, over and done with; off, all off, cancelled; played out, finished; eschatological; penultimate, last but one; antepenultimate, last but two; hindmost, rear 238 *back*; caudal.

**Vb.** *end*, come to an end, expire, run out, become invalid 111 *elapse*; close, finish, conclude, be all over; become extinct, die out 361 *die*, 2 *pass away*; come to a close, draw to a c., have run its course; fade away, peter out, tail off; stop, clock out, go home 145 *cease*.

*terminate*, conclude, close, determine, decide, settle; apply the closure, bring to an end, put an end to, put a term to, put a stop to, make an end of, put paid to, pull the plug on; discontinue, drop, pursue no further; finish, achieve, consummate, get through, play out, act o., see it o. 725 *carry through*; ring down the curtain, draw stumps, put up the shutters, shut up shop, wind up, close down, call it a day;

switch off, ring off, hang up, cut off, stop 145 *halt*.

**Adv.** *finally*, in conclusion, in fine; at last, at long last; once for all, for good, for good and all; never again, nevermore; to the bitter end, à outrance, to the utterance, to the last gasp, to the end of the chapter, to the end of the line; in the end, in the long run, in the final analysis, when all's said and done, all things considered.

## 70 Middle

**N.** *middle*, midst, midpoint; mean 30 *average*; medium, middle term; thick, thick of things; heart, heart of the matter, body, kernel; nave, hub, navel 225 *centre*; nucleus, nucleolus 224 *interiority*; midweek, midwinter, half tide; midstream 625 *middle way*; bisection, midline, equator, the Line 28 *equalization*; midrib, midriff, diaphragm 231 *partition*; half distance, middle d., equidistance, halfway house; intermediate technology; mixed economy 43 *mixture*.

**Adj.** *middle*, medial, mesial, mean, mezzo, mid 30 *median*; mediate, middlemost, midmost 225 *central*; intermediate, betwixt and between 231 *interjacent*; equidistant; mediterranean, equatorial.

**Adv.** *midway*, in the middle, in the thick, in medias res; at the midpoint, halfway; midstream; midships.

## 71 Continuity: uninterrupted sequence

**N.** *continuity*, continuousness, uninterruptedness, unbrokenness, monotony 16 *uniformity*; continuation, consecution, overlap; immediacy, directness; consecutiveness, successiveness, succession; line, lineage, descent, dynasty; one thing after another, serialization 65 *sequence*; natural sequence, sere; continuous time, continuum 115 *perpetuity*; continuous motion, assembly line, conveyor belt 146 *continuance*; endless band 315 *rotation*; repetitiveness, alternation, recurrence, cycle 106 *repetition*, 141 *periodicity*, 139 *frequency*; cumulativeness, snowball 36 *increase*; gradualism 278 *slowness*; course, run, career, flow, steady f., steady stream, trend, steady t. 179 *tendency*; progressiveness 285 *progression*; circuit, round 314 *circuition*; daily round, routine, rut, practice, custom 610 *habit*; track, trail, wake 67 *sequel*; catenation, concatenation, catena, chain, food c., chain reaction, knock-on effect, domino e., domino theory; round robin, chain letter; Möbius strip, circle, vicious c. 250 *circularity*.

*series*, seriation, gradation 27 *degree*; succession, run, rally, break; progression,

arithmetical p., geometrical p.; ascending order 36 *increase*; descending order 37 *decrease*; pedigree, family tree, lineage 169 *genealogy*; chain, line, string, thread; train, parade; unbroken line, line of battle, line ahead, line abreast; rank, file, echelon; array 62 *arrangement*; row, windrow; range, ridge; colonnade, peristyle, portico; ladder, steps, stairs, staircase 308 *ascent*; range, tier, storey 207 *layer*; keyboard, manual; set, suite, suit (of cards); assortment 77 *classification*; spectrum, rainbow; gamut, scale 410 *musical note*; stepping stones 624 *bridge*; hierarchy, pyramid.

*procession* 267 *marching*; crocodile, queue, line-up, steady stream, traffic jam, gridlock, tailback; tail, train, suite 67 *retinue*; caravan, file, single f., Indian f.; cortège, funeral procession 364 *obsequies*; parade, triumph, Lord Mayor's Show 876 *celebration*; cavalcade 875 *pageant*.

**Adj.** *continuous*, continued, run-on 45 *joined*; consecutive, running, successive 65 *sequential*; serial, serialized; seriate, catenary; progressive, gradual 179 *tending*; overlapping, unbroken, solid, smooth, uninterrupted, circular; direct, immediate, unmediated; continuing, ongoing; continual, incessant, ceaseless, unremitting, unintermitted, nonstop, constant 115 *perpetual*; cyclical, rhythmic 110 *periodic*; repetitive, recurrent, monotonous 106 *repeated*, 16 *uniform*; linear, lineal, rectilinear 249 *straight*.

**Vb.** *run on*, continue, follow in a series; line up, fall in, queue up, join the queue, join the line-up; succeed, overlap 65 *come after*; file, defile, keep in single file, walk in a crocodile; circle 626 *circuit*.

*continue*, run on, extend, prolong 113 *spin out*, 203 *lengthen*; serialize, arrange in succession, catenate, thread, string 45 *connect*; size, grade 27 *graduate*; file, tabulate 87 *list*; maintain continuity, keep the kettle boiling 600 *persevere*; keep the succession, provide an heir.

**Adv.** *continuously*, consecutively etc. adj.; serially, seriatim; successively, in succession, in turn; one after another; at a stretch, together, running; at one go, without stopping, on the trot; around the clock, 24/7, night and day 115 *for ever*; cumulatively, progressively; gradually, step by step, hand over hand 27 *by degrees*; in procession, in file, in single f., in Indian f., in a crocodile, in column, in line ahead, nose to tail, bumper to bumper.

## 72 Discontinuity: interrupted sequence

**N.** *discontinuity*, lack of continuity, intermittence; discontinuation, discontinuance 145 *cessation*; interval, hiatus, pause, time lag 145 *lull*; disconnection, disconnectedness, randomness 61 *disorder*; unevenness, joltiness, jerkiness 17 *nonuniformity*, 259 *roughness*; dotted line; broken ranks; ladder, run 46 *disunion*; disruption, interruption, intervention, interposition; parenthesis, episode 231 *interjection*; caesura, division 46 *separation*, 547 *punctuation*; break, fracture, flaw, fault, split, crack, cut 201 *gap*; lacuna; missing link, lost connection; broken thread, broken train, anacoluthon, non sequitur; illogicality, sophism 477 *sophistry*; patchwork, crazy paving 437 *variegation*; incoherence, purple patch 568 *imperspicuity*, 25 *misfit*; alternation 141 *periodicity*; irregularity, ragged volley 142 *fitfulness*.

**Adj.** *discontinuous*, unsuccessive, nonrecurrent, unrepeated; discontinued; interrupted, broken, stopping; disconnected 46 *disunited*; discrete 46 *separate*; few and far between 140 *infrequent*; patchy, bitty 437 *variegated*; desultory, irregular, intermittent, intermitting 142 *fitful*; alternate, alternating, stop-go, on-off 141 *periodical*; spasmodic, snatchy 17 *nonuniform*; jerky, jolty, bumpy, uneven 259 *rough*; incoherent, anacoluthic 477 *illogical*; parenthetic, episodic, not belonging 303 *inserted*, 59 *extraneous*.

**Vb.** *be discontinuous*, halt, rest 145 *pause*; alternate, intermit.

*discontinue*, suspend, break off, refrain from, desist; interrupt, intervene, chip in, butt in, break, break in upon 231 *interfere*; interpose, interject, punctuate 231 *put between*; disconnect, break the connection, break *or* interrupt one's train of thought, snap the thread 46 *disunite*.

**Adv.** *discontinuously*, at intervals, occasionally, infrequently, irregularly, in jerks and snatches, in fits and starts; skippingly, desultorily; now and then, once in a while, here and there, passim.

## 73 Term: serial position

**N.** *serial place*, term, order, remove 27 *degree*; echelon, rank, ranking, grade, gradation; station, place, position, slot; status, standing, footing, social class, caste; point, mark, pitch, level, storey; step, tread, round, rung; stage, milestone, watershed, climacteric, climax, zenith 213 *summit*; bottom rung, nadir 214 *base*.

**Vb.** *grade*, rank, rate, place, classify; class; put someone in their place; bring down a peg; stagger, space out 201 *space*, 27 *graduate*.

*have rank*, hold r., hold a place, occupy a position 186 *be situated*; fall into place, drop into p., find one's *or* its own level, find a niche 187 *place oneself*.

## 74 Assemblage

**N.** *assemblage*, bringing together, collection 50 *combination*, 62 *arrangement*; collocation, juxtaposition 202 *contiguity*; colligation 45 *joining together*; compilation, corpus, anthology 56 *composition*; gathering, ingathering, reaping, harvest, vintage 370 *agriculture*, 771 *acquisition*; harvest home 632 *storage*, 876 *celebration*; consolidation, concentration; centring, focusing, zeroing in on; rallying point 76 *focus*; mobilization, muster, levy, call-up 718 *war measures*; review, parade 875 *pageant*; march, demonstration, rally; whipping in, roundup, lineup; herding, shepherding 369 *animal husbandry*; collectivization, collective, kolkhoz 740 *compulsion*, 370 *farm*; conspiracy, caucus 708 *party*; collective noun, syntax 564 *grammar*.

*assembly*, mutual attraction 291 *attraction*; getting together, ganging up; forgathering, congregation, concourse, conflux, concurrence 293 *convergence*; gathering, meeting, mass m., protest m., sit-in, meet; coven; conventicle; business meeting, board m.; convention, convocation 985 *synod*; gemot, shire moot, legislature, conclave 692 *council*; eisteddfod, mod, festival 876 *celebration*; reunion, get-together, gathering of the clans, ceilidh 882 *social gathering*; company, at home, party 882 *sociality*; circle, sewing-bee, knit-in; encounter group 658 *therapy*; discussion group, focus g., quality circle, symposium 584 *conference*.

*group*, constellation, galaxy, cluster 321 *star*; troop, bevy, swarm, flock, flight, herd, drove, team; pack, kennel; stable, string; nest, eyrie; brood, hatch, litter, shoal, school; unit, brigade 722 *formation*;

---

**Some Less Common Group Nouns**

bask (crocodiles), bevy (quail, swans), building (rooks), cast (hawks), cete (badgers), charm *or* chirm (goldfinches), chattering (choughs), clamour (rooks), clowder (cats), company (wigeon), congregation (crocodiles, plovers), covert (coots), covey (grouse, partridges), crash (rhinoceroses), down (hares), drift (pigs), dule (doves), exaltation (larks), fall (woodcock), fesnyng (ferrets), fluther (jellyfish), gaggle (geese on the ground), gam (whales), gang (elk), grist (bees), herd (cranes, curlews, seals, swans), husk (hares), kindle (kittens), leap (leopards), murder (crows), murmuration (starlings), muster (peacocks), mute (hounds), nye *or* nide (pheasant), pace (asses), parliament (owls), pod (seals, whales), pride (lions), sedge *or* siege (bitterns, cranes, herons), skein (geese in flight), skulk (foxes), sleuth *or* sloth (bears), smack (jellyfish), sord (mallard), sounder (pigs), spring (teal), stand (plovers), team (ducks in flight), tok (capercailzies), unkindness (ravens), walk (snipe), watch (nightingales), wing (plovers).

---

batch, lot, clutch; brace, pair, span 90 *duality*; leash, four-in-hand 96 *quaternity*; set, class, genus, species, sub-s. 77 *sort*; breed, tribe, clan, household 11 *family*; brotherhood, sisterhood, fellowship, guild, union 706 *association*; club 708 *society*; sphere, quarter, circle 524 *informant*; charmed circle, coterie 644 *elite*; social group, the caste system, the classes 868 *nobility*, 869 *commonalty*; in-group, out-group, us and them, they 80 *self*; age group, peer g., year g., stream 538 *class*; hand (at cards), set 71 *series*; rope (of onions, pearls), string (of pearls).

*band*, company, troupe; cast 594 *actor*; brass band, dance b., pop group, rock g., boy-band, tribute b., 413 *orchestra*; team, string, fifteen, eleven, eight; knot, bunch; set, coterie, dream team; clique, ring; gang, squad, party, work p., fatigue p.; ship's company, crew, complement, manpower, workforce, staff 686 *personnel*; following 67 *retinue*; squadron, troop, platoon, unit, regiment, corps 722 *formation*; squad, posse, force, body, host 722 *armed force*, 104 *multitude*; (Boy) Scouts, Girl Guides 708 *society*; band of brothers, sisters, merry men 880 *friendship*; committee, commission 754 *consignee*; panel 87 *list*; establishment, cadre 331 *structure*.

*crowd*, throng 104 *multitude*; huddle, cluster, swarm, colony; small crowd, knot, bunch; the masses, the hoi polloi, mass, mob, ruck 869 *rabble*; sea of faces, full house, houseful 54 *completeness*; congestion, press, squash, squeeze, jam, scrum, rush, crush; rush hour, crush h. 680 *haste*; flood, spate, deluge, stream, streams of 32 *great quantity*; volley, shower, hail, storm; populousness, over-population 36 *increase*; infestation, invasion 297 *ingress*; herd instinct, crowd psychology, mass hysteria 818 *feeling*.

*bunch*, assortment, lot, mixed l. 43 *medley*; clump, tuft, wisp, handful, hand (of bananas); pencil (of rays), fan; bag 194 *receptacle*; hand (of tobacco), bundle, packet, wad; batch, pack, package, parcel; portfolio, file, dossier 548 *record*; bale, roll, bolt; load, pack 193 *contents*; fascine, faggot; fascicle; tussock, shock, sheaf, stook, truss, heap; swathe, rick, stack 632 *storage*; thicket, copse 366 *wood*; bouquet, nosegay, posy, spray, floral tribute; skein, hank.

*accumulation*, heaping up, cumulation; agglomeration, conglomeration, conglobation, aggregation; massing, amassment; concentration, collectivization, centralization; pileup 279 *collision*; masonry, mass, pile, pyramid 164 *building*, 209 *high structure*; congeries, heap; drift, snowdrift; snowball 36 *increment*; debris, detritus 41 *leavings*; dustheap, dump 641 *rubbish*; cumulus, storm cloud 355 *cloud*; store, storage 633 *provision*, 799 *treasury*; magazine, battery, armoury, quiver 723 *arsenal*; bus garage, car park, parking lot; set, lot 71 *series*;

mixed lot, mixed bag 43 *medley*; kit, gear, stock; range, selection, assortment 795 *merchandise*; shop window, display 522 *exhibit*; museum 632 *collection*; menagerie, aquarium 369 *zoo*; literary collection 589 *library*; miscellanea, miscellany, collectanea, compilation 56 *composition*; symposium, festschrift 591 *dissertation*.

*accumulator*, hoarder, squirrel, miser 816 *niggard*, 798 *treasurer*; connoisseur 492 *collector*; beachcomber, gatherer, reaper, harvester, picker, gleaner 370 *farmer*; convener, assembler; whip, whipper-in; shepherd, sheep dog 369 *herdsman*.

**Adj.** *assembled*, met, well-met, ill-m.; convened, summoned; mobilized, called-up; banded 62 *arranged*; collectivized; crowded, packed, huddled, serried, high-density 324 *dense*; close-printed, tight; populated, over-p., overcrowded, humming with, lousy with, alive with, hotching with, stiff with 54 *full*; populous, teeming, swarming, thick on the ground, thick as flies 104 *multitudinous*; in a crowd, seething, milling; in formation, ranked, in order 62 *arranged*.

**Vb.** *congregate*, meet, forgather, rendezvous; assemble, reassemble, rejoin; associate, come together, get t., join t., flock t., make a crowd, gather, gather round, collect, troop, rally, roll up, swell the ranks; resort to, centre on, focus on, zero in on, make for 293 *converge*; band together, gang up; mass, concentrate, mobilize; conglomerate, huddle, cluster, bunch, crowd; throng, swarm, seethe, mill around; surge, stream, flood 36 *grow*; swarm in, infest, invade 297 *burst in*.

*bring together*, assemble, put together, draw t. 45 *join*; draw, pack them in 291 *attract*; gather, collect, rally, muster, call up, mobilize; concentrate, consolidate; collocate, lump together, group, brigade, unite; compile 56 *compose*; bring into focus, focus, centre; convene, convoke, convocate, summon, hold a meeting; herd, shepherd, get in, whip in, call in, round up, corral 235 *enclose*; mass, aggregate, rake up, dredge up; accumulate, conglomerate, heap, pile, amass; catch, take, rake in, net 771 *acquire*; scrape together, garner 632 *store*; truss, bundle, parcel, package; bunch, bind, colligate 45 *tie*; pack, cram, stuff 54 *fill*; build up, pile up, stack 310 *elevate*.

**Adv.** *together*, unitedly, as one, in a oner (inf); collectively, all together, en masse, in a mass, in a body.

## 75 Nonassembly. Dispersion

**N.** *dispersion*, scattering, diffraction, breakup 46 *separation*; branching out, fanning o., spread, scatter, radiation 294 *divergence*; sprawl, suburbia; distribution 783 *apportionment*; delegation, decentralization, regionalization; disintegration 51 *decomposition*; evaporation, boiling away 338 *vaporization*, 337 *liquefaction*; dissipation 634 *waste*; circulation, diffusion; dissemination, broadcasting; interspersion; spraying, sprinkling, circumfusion 341 *moistening*; dispersal, going home; disbandment, demobilization; flotsam and jetsam, sea drift, driftwood 272 *thing transferred*; disjecta membra; waifs and strays, dispersed population, diaspora.

**Adj.** *unassembled*, dispersed, disbanded, demobilized etc. vb.; scattered, dotted about, strung out, sporadic, sparse, few and far between 140 *infrequent*; broadcast, diffused; spreading, widespread, far-flung 183 *spacious*; epidemic 79 *universal*; spread, separated, in open order 46 *separate*; dishevelled, streaming, trailing, sprawling 61 *orderless*; decentralized, regionalized; branching, radiating, centrifugal 294 *divergent*; off-centre, askew, agley (dial), adrift, astray; straggling, wandering 267 *travelling*.

**Vb.** *be dispersed*, disperse, scatter, spread, spread out, fan o., thin o. 325 *rarefy*; spread fast, spread like wildfire, be rampant, flood; radiate, branch, branch out 294 *diverge*; break up, break ranks, fall out 46 *separate*; lose coherence, break away 49 *come unstuck*; hive off, go off on one's own, go each his *or* her own way 267 *wander*; drift away, drift apart; straggle, trail, fall behind 282 *stray*; spread over, sprawl over, cover, litter 226 *overlie*; explode, blow up, burst, fly apart, fly in all directions 176 *be violent*; evaporate, melt 338 *vaporize*, 337 *liquefy*; disintegrate, dissolve, decay 51 *decompose*.

*disperse*, scatter, diffract; spread out, splay 294 *diverge*; separate 46 *sunder*; thin out, string o.; disseminate, diffuse, broadcast, sow, strew, bestrew, spread; dissipate, dispel, disintegrate 51 *decompose*; scatter to the winds 634 *waste*; dispense, deal, deal out, dole out, allot 783 *apportion*; decentralize, regionalize; break up, disband, disembody, demobilize, dismiss, send home 46 *disunite*; draft, draft off, hive off, detach 272 *send*; sprinkle, besprinkle, splash, spray, spatter, bespatter 341 *moisten*; circulate, put into circulation; throw into confusion, disorder 63 *derange*; rout 727 *defeat*.

**Adv.** *sporadically*, here and there, sparsely, in twos and threes; passim, everywhere, in all quarters.

## 76 Focus: place of meeting

**N.** *focus*, focal point, point of convergence, junction, town centre, city c. 293 *convergence*, 225 *centre*; focus group; crossways, crossroads; switchboard, exchange, nerve centre; hub, nub, core, heart, kernel 70 *middle*; hall, civic centre, community c., village hall, village green, town square; campus, quad; market place 796 *market*; resort, retreat, haunt, stamping ground; club, pub, local 192 *pub*; headquarters, HQ, depot; rallying point, standard; venue, rendezvous, trysting place 192 *meeting place*; nest, home ground 192 *home*; fireside, campfire; cynosure, centre of attraction, honeypot 291 *attraction*; place of pilgrimage, Mecca, Lourdes, Rome, Zion, promised land 295 *goal*, 617 *objective*.

**Vb.** *focus*, centre on 293 *converge*; centralize, concentrate, focus upon, zero in on; bring to a point, point to, focus attention on.

## 77 Class

**N.** *classification*, categorization 62 *arrangement*; biosystematics, taxonomy; diagnosis, specification, designation; category, class, bracket; set, subset; head, heading, subhead, section, subsection 53 *subdivision*; division, branch, department, faculty; pocket, pigeonhole, slot 194 *compartment*; tier, rank, caste, status, social class, standing 27 *degree*; province, domain, field, sphere, range; sex, gender; blood group, age g., stream 74 *group*; coterie, clique 74 *band*; persuasion, school of thought, denomination 978 *sect*.

*sort*, order, type, version, variety, kind, species; manner, genre, style; nature, quality, grade, calibre 5 *character*; mark, brand 547 *label*; ilk, stripe, kidney, feather, colour; stamp, mould, shape, frame, make 243 *form*; assortment, kit, gear, set, suit, lot 71 *series*.

*breed*, strain, blood, family, kin, tribe, clan, sept, caste, line 11 *race*, 169 *genealogy*; kingdom, phylum, class, order, genus, species, subspecies; genotype, monotype.

**Adj.** *generic*, typical; sexual, masculine, feminine, neuter.

*classifactory*, taxonomic; sectional, denominational 978 *sectarian*.

## 78 Inclusion

**N.** *inclusion*, comprising; incorporation, embodiment, assimilation, encapsulation; comprehension, admission, integration 299 *reception*; admissibility, eligibility; membership 775 *participation*; inclusiveness, coverage, full c., blanket c. 79 *generality*; all-roundness, versatility 694 *skill*; comprehensiveness, no exception, no omission, nothing omitted; set, complete s., unbroken s., complement, package 52 *whole*; package deal 765 *compact*;

constitution 56 *composition*; capacity, volume, measure 183 *space*, 465 *measurement*; accommodation 183 *room*.

**Adj.** *inclusive*, including, comprising, counting, containing, having; holding, consisting of 56 *composing*; incorporative, incorporating; fully-furnished, all-inclusive, all-in; nonexclusive, nondiscriminatory, accommodating; overall, all-embracing 52 *comprehensive*; wholesale, blanket, sweeping 32 *extensive*; without omission, without exception, total, across-the-board, global, worldwide, universal 52 *whole*; encyclopedic, expansive, broad-based 79 *general*.

*included*, admitted, counted; admissible, eligible; integrated, unsegregated; constituent, making up 56 *composing*; inherent 58 *component*, 5 *intrinsic*; belonging, pertinent 9 *relative*; classified with, of the same class, in the same league 18 *similar*; congenerous, congeneric 11 *akin*; entered, noted, recorded, on the list 87 *listed*; merged 38 *additional*, 45 *joined*; inner 224 *interior*.

**Vb.** *be included*, be contained, be comprised, make one of 58 *be one of*; enlist, enrol oneself, swell the ranks, join, obtain membership 708 *join a party*; come under, go u., fall u. 58 *be one of*; merge in 43 *be mixed*; appertain to, pertain, refer to 9 *be related*; come in, go in, enter into 297 *enter*; constitute 56 *compose*; overlap; inhere, belong 5 *be intrinsic*.

*comprise*, include, involve, mean, imply, consist of, hold, have, count, boast 56 *contain*; take, measure 28 *be equal*; receive, take in 299 *admit*; accommodate, find room for; comprehend, encapsulate, cover; embody, incorporate; encompass, embrace, encircle, envelop 235 *enclose*; have everything, exhaust the possibilities 54 *be complete*.

*number with*, count w., reckon among, enumerate with; subsume, place under, classify as; put in, arrange in 62 *class*; not omit, take into account, take cognizance of.

**Adv.** *including*, inclusively; from A to Z; et cetera.

## 79 Generality

**N.** *generality*, universality, general applicability; catholicity, catholicism; ecumenicity, ecumenicalism 976 *orthodoxy*; universalism; generalization, universal; macrocosm 321 *universe*; globalization, global view, world-view; panorama, synopsis, conspectus, bird's eye view 52 *whole*; inclusiveness, comprehensivity, something for everybody, open house, dragnet 78 *inclusion*; currency, prevalence, custom 610 *habit*, 848 *fashion*; pervasiveness, rifeness, ubiquity 189 *presence*; pandemic, epidemic 651

*disease*; broadness, looseness, imprecision 495 *inexactness*, 464 *indiscrimination*; open letter, circular 528 *publicity*; commonness, ruck, run, general r., run of the mill 30 *average*; ordinariness 732 *averageness*; internationalism, cosmopolitanism 901 *philanthropy*; impersonality; categorization 77 *classification*.

*everyman*, everywoman; man or woman in the street, Mr or Mrs Average, man on the Clapham omnibus, Joe Bloggs, Joe Public, Joe Soap, little man; common type 30 *common man*; everybody, every one, each one, one and all, the long and the short and the tall, all and sundry, every mother's son, every man Jack, all hands 52 *all*; all the world and his wife, Tom, Dick and Harry, Uncle Tom Cobbley and all, the masses, the hoi polloi, the rabble 869 *commonalty*; all sorts, anyone, whosoever, N or M; anything, whatsoever, what have you, what you will 562 *no name*.

**Adj.** *general*, generic, typical, representative, standard; encyclopedic, broad-based; collective, all-embracing, pan-, blanket, across-the-board 52 *comprehensive*; broad, sweeping, panoramic, synoptic; current, prevalent 189 *ubiquitous*; usual, normal, unexceptional, run-of-the-mill, customary 610 *habitual*; vague, loose, indefinite 495 *inexact*; undetermined, unspecified, undenominational, unsectarian, impersonal 10 *unrelated*; common, ordinary, average 30 *median*; commonplace 83 *typical*; popular, mass, vulgar 869 *plebeian*; for everybody, for every occasion, multipurpose.

*universal*, catholic, ecumenical; national, international, cosmopolitan, global, worldwide, nationwide, widespread 32 *extensive*; pervasive, penetrating, besetting, prevalent, epidemic, pandemic 189 *ubiquitous*; every, each, any, all, all without exception 52 *whole*.

**Vb.** *be general*, cover all cases 78 *comprise*; prevail, obtain, be the rule, have currency 610 *be wont*; penetrate 189 *pervade*.

*generalize*, render general etc. adj.; broaden, widen, universalize, globalize; spread, broadcast, diffuse 75 *disperse*.

**Adv.** *generally*, without exception, universally etc. adj.; mainly 52 *wholly*; to a man, to the last m.; always, for better for worse; generally speaking, in the long run, by and large 30 *on an average*; loosely, vaguely.

## 80 Speciality

**N.** *speciality*, specific quality, specificity, personality, uniqueness; singularity 88 *unity*; originality, individuality, particularity 1 *essence*; personality, make-up 5 *character*; characteristic, personal c., recessive c., dominant c., one's middle name; distinctive feature, trademark, signature dish, signature tune; idiosyncrasy, eccentricity, peculiarity, mannerism, quirk, foible; trait, mark, feature, attribute; sine qua non 89 *accompaniment*; distinction, point of difference, differentia 15 *difference*; idiom, peculiar i.; slang, jargon, brogue, patois 560 *dialect*; technical language, private l., idiolect 557 *language*; variant reading, alternative r., version, lection 15 *variant*; exception, isolated instance, nonce word, special case 84 *nonconformity*; specialty, special skill, gift, rare g., special study, specialization 694 *skill*.

*particulars*, details, the nitty gritty, minutiae, items, counts, special points, specification; circumstances; the ins and outs of.

*particularism*, chosen race, chosen few, God's chosen, the elect, 'a peculiar people';

> **For thou art an holy people unto the Lord thy God, and the Lord hath chosen thee to be a peculiar people unto himself, above all the nations that are upon the earth.**
> Bible, Deuteronomy

> **But ye are a chosen generation, a royal priesthood, an holy nation, a peculiar people . . .**
> Bible, First Epistle of Peter

exclusiveness, class consciousness, classism, caste; chauvinism, nationality, nationalism, individualism, egoism.

*self*, ego, id, identity, selfhood, personality 320 *subjectivity*; atman, psyche, soul 447 *spirit*; I, myself, number one, numero uno; we, ourselves; yourself, himself, herself, itself, themselves; us, in-group 74 *group*; real self, inner s., inner being; outward self; a person, a character, individual, being, idioverse 371 *person*.

**Adj.** *special*, specific, respective, particular; sui generis, peculiar, singular, unique 88 *one*; individual, idiosyncratic, characteristic, idiomatic, original 21 *inimitable*; native, proper, personal, private, one-to-one, one-on-one (see also *private*); appropriate 24 *apt*; typical, diagnostic 5 *characteristic*; distinctive, uncommon, marked, noteworthy, out of the ordinary 84 *unusual*; several 15 *different*.

*definite*, definitive, defining; determinate, quantified, specified; distinct, concrete, express, explicit, clear-cut, clean-c., cut and dried; certain, exact, precise 494 *accurate*; itemized, detailed, circumstantial; bespoke, made to order, made to measure, custom-built, one-off, personalized.

*private*, intimate, esoteric, personal, personalized, exclusive; patented; extra-professional; off the record, for one's private ear, confidential, secret 523 *latent*.

**Vb.** *specify*, be specific, express in figures, enumerate, quantify 86 *number*; particularize,

itemize, detail, inventorize 87 *list*; cite, reel off, mention, name names 561 *name*; descend to particulars, enter into detail, spell out 570 *be diffuse*; define, determine 236 *limit*, 463 *discriminate*; pinpoint, locate 187 *place*; come to the point, explain 520 *interpret*; signify, denote 514 *mean*; designate, point out 547 *indicate*; realize, translate into fact, substantiate 156 *cause*; individualize, personalize 15 *differentiate*; specialize 455 *be attentive*, 536 *study*.

**Adv.** *specially*, especially, in particular; personally, for one's own part; specifically, ad hoc, ad hominem, to order; with respect to.

*severally*, each, apiece, one by one; respectively, in turn, seriatim; in detail, bit by bit.

*namely*, i.e., that is to say, to wit, videlicet, viz.; e.g., for example.

## 81 Rule

**N.** *rule*, norm, formula, canon, code; maxim, principle 693 *precept*; law, law of nature, universal principle; firm principle, hard and fast rule; strict law, 'law of the Medes and Persians';

> **Now, O king, establish the decree, and sign the writing, that it be not changed, according to the law of the Medes and Persians, which altereth not.**
> Bible, Daniel

law of the jungle, sod's law, Murphy's law, Parkinson's law; unwritten rule *or* law, rule of thumb; statute, by-law 953 *law*; regulation, order, standing o., party line; guide, precedent, model, pattern 23 *prototype*; form, standard, keynote 83 *example*.

*regularity*, consistency, constancy 16 *uniformity*; order, natural o., established o. 60 *order*; normality, normalcy, normal state, natural condition; form, set f., routine, drill, practice, custom 610 *habit*; fixed ways, rut, groove, tramlines; treadmill; methodicalness, method, system 62 *arrangement*; convention 83 *conformity*.

**Adj.** *regular*, constant, steady 141 *periodical*; even 258 *smooth*; circular, square 245 *symmetrical*; standardized 16 *uniform*; regulated, according to rule, according to the rule-book, methodical, systematic 60 *orderly*; regulative, normative; normal, unexceptional 83 *typical*; customary 610 *usual*; conforming, conventional, right-on (inf) 83 *conformable*.

**Adv.** *to rule*, by the book, by the clock; regularly.

## 82 Multiformity

**N.** *multiformity*, multiplicity, omnifariousness; heterogeneity, variety, diversity 17 *nonuniformity*; multifariousness, many-sidedness, many-headedness, polymorphism 101 *plurality*; schizophrenia, split personality, dual p., multiple p. 503 *personality disorder*; metamorphism, metamorphosis, sea change; variability, changeability 152 *changeableness*, 437 *variegation*; capriciousness 604 *caprice*; all-rounder; Proteus, Jekyll and Hyde; kaleidoscope.

**Adj.** *multiform*, multifarious, polymorphous, polymorphic; multifid; multiple, multiplex, multiplicate, manifold, many-headed, many-sided, many-faceted, hydra-headed, omnigenous, omnifarious; metamorphic; protean, versatile, all-round; variform, heterogeneous, diverse 17 *nonuniform*; motley, mosaic, kaleidoscopic 43 *mixed*; epicene, indiscriminate, irregular, diversified, many-coloured, polychrome 437 *variegated*; divers, sundry; all manner of, of every description, of all sorts and kinds 15 *different*; variable, changeable 152 *changeful*; whimsical 604 *capricious*; polypsychical; schizophrenic, schizoid.

## 83 Conformity

**N.** *conformity*, conformation 24 *conformance*; faithfulness 768 *observance*; accommodation, adjustment, reconcilement, reconciliation, conciliation 24 *agreement*, *adaptation*; self-adaptation, pliancy, malleability 327 *softness*; acquiescence 721 *submission*; assimilation, acclimatization, naturalization 147 *conversion*, 18 *similarity*; conventionality, conventionalism, bourgeois ethic 848 *etiquette*; political correctness, PC; traditionalism; orthodoxness 976 *orthodoxy*; formalism, strictness 735 *severity*; convention, form 848 *fashion*, 610 *practice*; Babbitry 850 *affectation*; parrotry, echoing, emulation 106 *repetition*, 925 *flattery*, 20 *imitation*; ordinariness 79 *generality*.

*example*, exemplar, type, pattern, model 23 *prototype*; exemplification, stock example, classic e., locus classicus; case, case in point, instance, palmary i.; illustration, practical demonstration, object lesson; sample, random s., cross-section; representative, specimen, specimen page, representative selection; trailer, foretaste 66 *precursor*; precedent.

*conformist*, conventionalist, traditionalist, belonger; follower of fashion, fashion victim 848 *beau monde*; Philistine, Babbitt; organization man, company m.; formalist, pedant, precisian; copycat, yes-man 20 *imitator*, 925 *flatterer*; follower, loyalist 976 *the orthodox*.

**Adj.** *conformable*, adaptable, adjustable, consistent with; malleable, pliant 327 *flexible*; agreeable, complaisant, accommodating 24 *agreeing*; conforming, following, faithful, loyal, true-blue 768 *observant*; conventional, current, traditional, right-on (inf) 976 *orthodox*; slavish, servile 20 *imitative*, 925 *flattering*; adjusted,

adapted, acclimatized 610 *habituated*; absorbed, digested, assimilated, naturalized 78 *included*.

*typical*, normal, natural, of daily occurrence, everyday, ordinary, common, common or garden 79 *general*; average 30 *median*, 732 *middling*; true to type; commonplace, prosaic; conventional; heterosexual, straight; habitual 610 *usual*; representative, stock, standard; normative, exemplary, illustrative; in point 9 *relevant*.

*regulated*, according to the book, by the b., according to rule, regular; politically correct, PC, on message; shipshape, Bristol fashion, copybook 60 *orderly*; correct, sound, proper, canonical 976 *orthodox*; precise, scrupulous, punctilious, meticulous 875 *formal*; rigid, strict, unbending, uncompromising, Procrustean 735 *severe*.

**Vb.** *conform*, correspond, conform to 24 *accord*; adapt oneself, accommodate o., adjust o., mould o.; fit in, know one's place; pass, pass muster 635 *suffice*; bend, yield, take the shape of 327 *soften*; fall into line, toe the l., fall in with 721 *submit*; comply with 768 *observe*; tally with, fit in with 24 *accord*; rubberstamp, echo 106 *repeat*; stick to the rules, obey regulations, follow precedent 739 *obey*; keep in step, follow the fashion, follow the trend, follow the crowd, do as others do, do as the Romans do; join in the cry, jump on the bandwagon, keep up with the Joneses 848 *be in fashion*; emulate, follow suit 20 *imitate*, *copy*; have no will of one's own, drift with the tide, swim with the stream 601 *be irresolute*; follow in the steps of, keep to the beaten track, run on tramlines, run in a groove, stick in a rut 610 *be wont*.

*make conform*, conform, assimilate, naturalize 18 *liken*; acclimatize 610 *habituate*; bring under rule, systematize 62 *regularize*; normalize, conventionalize, standardize; put in uniform, drill 16 *make uniform*; shape, press 243 *form*; stamp, imprint 547 *mark*; train, lead 689 *direct*; bend, twist, force 740 *compel*; accommodate, fit, fit in, square, trim, cut down to size, knock or lick into shape 24 *adjust*; rub off the corners 258 *smooth*.

*exemplify*, illustrate, cite, quote, instance; produce an example, give an instance.

**Adv.** *conformably*, conventionally etc. adj.; to rule; by the book; in conformity, in line with, in accordance, in keeping; according to; according to plan; consistently with; as usual, of course, as a matter of c.; for form's sake; for the look of it; for example, for instance.

## 84 Nonconformity

**N.** *nonconformity*, nonconformance, unconformity, inconsistency 25 *disagreement*, 17 *non-uniformity*; contrast, oasis 14 *contrariety*; exceptionality, strangeness 59 *extraneousness*; nonconformism, unorthodoxy 977 *heterodoxy*; alternative lifestyle, New Age philosophy; disconformity, dissidence 489 *dissent*, 769 *nonobservance*; deviationism, Titoism 744 *independence*; anomalousness, eccentricity, irregularity 282 *deviation*; informality, unconventionality, angularity, awkwardness 893 *sullenness*; bizarrerie, piquancy, freakishness, oddity; rarity 140 *infrequency*; infringement, infraction, infraction of the rules, violation of the law 954 *illegality*; breach of practice, defiance of custom, departure from usage; wonder, miracle 864 *prodigy*; anomaly, exception 57 *exclusion*; exemption, escape clause 919 *nonliability*; special case, isolated instance 80 *speciality*; individuality, trait, idiosyncrasy, quirk, kink, peculiarity, singularity, mannerism; uniqueness 21 *originality*.

variance, aberration, abnormality 282 *deviation*; mutation 15 *variant*; abortion, monstrous birth, terata, teratogenesis, monstrosity, monster; sexual abnormality, bisexuality; sexual inversion, homosexuality, 'the love that dare not speak its name', lesbianism, Sapphism;

> I am the Love that dare not speak its name.
> Lord Alfred Douglas, *Two Loves*

fetishism, necrophilia, sadism, masochism, sadomasochism, algolagnia; transvestism, gender-bending, gender identity disorder; virilism, gynandry 372 *male*; androgyny 373 *female*; hermaphroditism 161 *impotence*.

nonconformist, dissident, deviationist, dissenter, maverick, contrarian 489 *dissentient*, 977 *heretic*, 978 *sectarian*; nonstriker; blackleg, scab 938 *cad*; unconventionalist, Bohemian, hippie *or* hippy, beatnik, dropout, longhaired weirdie (inf); New Age traveller; rebel, angry young man, punk, handful, recalcitrant 738 *revolter*; fanatic 504 *crank*; outsider, outlaw, criminal 904 *offender*; pariah 883 *outcast*; hermit, lone wolf, loner 883 *solitary*; gypsy, nomad, tramp, bag lady 268 *wanderer*; odd man out, joker, ugly duckling; square peg in a round hole, fish out of water 25 *misfit*; heteroclite, deviant, mutant, odd type, albino, sport, freak, f. of nature, monster, teras, lusus naturae; oddity, original, character, card, caution, odd customer, queer c., oddball, weirdo (inf) 504 *crank*; queer fish 851 *laughingstock*; curiosity, rarity, rare example, a gem, one in a million; neither fish, flesh, fowl nor good red herring, neither one thing nor the other; 143 *transformation*,hermaphrodite, gynander, and-

rogyne 161 *eunuch*; invert; pervert, perv (sl); sadist, masochist, sadomasochist; mongrel, cur, half-breed, half-blood 43 *hybrid*.

transvestite, cross-dresser, gender-bender (sl); drag artist, female impersonator; transsexual, ladyboy.

non-heterosexual, homosexual, gay; friend of Dorothy (sl), batty-boy, fairy, fruit, homo, nancy, nancy boy, pansy, poof, poofter, queen, queer, shirtlifter (all derog or offensive, sl or inf); lesbian, les *or* lez (sl, often offensive), dyke *or* dike (sl, often offensive), tribade; pink economy; pink publishing.

**Adj.** unconformable, inadjustable 25 *unapt*; antipathetic 14 *contrary*; unmalleable, stiff 326 *rigid*, 602 *obstinate*; recalcitrant 711 *defiant*; crotchety, prickly, awkward, eccentric, whimsical 604 *capricious*, 893 *sullen*; arbitrary, a law to oneself 744 *independent*; freakish, outlandish; original, sui generis, unique 80 *special*; solitary, standoffish 883 *unsociable*; blacklegging 603 *tergiversating*; nonconformist, dissident 489 *dissenting*, 978 *sectarian*; unorthodox, heretical 977 *heterodox*; unconverted, nonpractising 769 *nonobservant*; unconventional, weird, off-beat, Bohemian, hippie *or* hippy, beatnik, informal, unfashionable; irregular, against the rules, not done 924 *disapproved*; infringing, lawless, criminal 954 *illegal*; aberrant, astray, agley, askew, off the beam, off the rails 282 *deviating*; misplaced, out of one's element, out of place, ectopic, out of order 188 *displaced*, 61 *orderless*; incongruous, out of step, out of line, off-message, out of tune, out of keeping 25 *disagreeing*; alien, exotic 59 *extraneous*; unidentifiable, unclassifiable, hard to place, nondescript, nameless 491 *unknown*; stray, nomadic, wandering 267 *travelling*; amphibious, ambiguous 518 *equivocal*; exempted, exempt 919 *nonliable*.

unusual, uncustomary, unwonted 611 *unhabituated*; unfamiliar 491 *unknown*; newfangled 126 *new*; out of the way, exotic 59 *extraneous*; out of the ordinary, extraordinary, way-out; phenomenal, supernormal; unparalleled, unexampled; singular, unique 80 *special*, 140 *infrequent*; rare, choice, recherché 644 *excellent*; strange, bizarre, curious, odd, queer, rum, unco; funny, peculiar, fantastic, grotesque 849 *ridiculous*; noteworthy, remarkable, surprising, astonishing, miraculous 864 *wonderful*; mysterious, inexplicable, unaccountable 523 *occult*; unimaginable, incredible 470 *impossible*, 472 *improbable*; monstrous, teratoid, teratological, miscreated; unnatural, preternatural, supernatural; outsize 32 *enormous*; outré 546 *exaggerated*; shocking, scandalizing 924 *dis-*

*approved*; mind-boggling, mind-blowing, inde-scribable 517 *inexpressible*.

*abnormal*, unnatural, supernatural, preter-natural (see also *unusual*); aberrant, terato-logical, teratoid, freakish; uncharacteristic, untypical, atypical, unrepresentative, excep-tional; anomalous, anomalistic 17 *nonuniform*; kinky, deviant; homosexual, gay, lesbian, bent (derog sl), lez *or* les (sl, often offensive), queer (derog sl), as queer as a coot; bisexual, AC/DC; epicene, androgynous, gynandrous; mongrel, hybrid 43 *mixed*; irregular, heteroclite; unidio-matic, solecistic 565 *ungrammatical*; nonstan-dard, substandard, below par, subnormal; supernormal 32 *great*; asymmetrical, deformed, amorphous, shapeless 246 *distorted*.

**Vb.** *be unconformable,* – unconventional etc. adj.; not fit in, be a fish out of water, be a square peg, be out of one's element, have no business there; be the exception that proves the rule; infringe a law, infringe usage, infringe custom; break a law, break an unwritten l., break a code, commit a breach of etiquette, break a habit, break with custom; violate a law, violate custom; drop out, freak o., do one's own thing 744 *be free*; come out, come out of the closet; be ahead of one's time 135 *be early*; put the clock back, turn back time 125 *look back*; get round, drive a coach and six *or* coach and horses through; stretch a point, make an exception; leave the beaten track; baffle all description, beggar all d.

**Adv.** *unconformably*, unusually etc. adj.; except, unless, save, but for, barring, beside, without, save and except, let alone; however, yet, but.

SECTION FIVE

## Number

### 85 Number

**N.** *number*, any n., real n., imaginary n.; natural n., cardinal n., ordinal n.; round n., complex n.; prime n., odd n., even n., whole n., integer; irrational n., transcendental n.; numeral, cipher, digit, figure, character; numerals, Arabic n., Roman n., algorithm; decimal system, binary s.; quantity, unknown q., unknown, X, symbol, constant; mapping; operator, sign; function, variable, argument; vector, matrix, tensor, quaternion; surd; expression, equation, quadratics; for-mula, chemical f., empirical f., molecular f., structural f.; series, set.

*numerical element*, minuend, subtrahend; multiplicand, multiplier; coefficient, multiple, dividend, divisor, aliquant, aliquot; quotient,

factor, submultiple, fraction, proper f., improper f., vulgar f.; mixed number; numer-ator, denominator; decimal, recurring d., rep-etend; common factor, common denominator; reciprocal, complement; parameter; power, root, square r., cube r.; exponent, index, logar-ithm, natural l., mantissa, antilogarithm; modulus, differential, derivative, integral, inte-grand, determinant, fluxion.

*ratio*, proportion; progression, arithmetical progression, geometrical p., harmonic p.; trig-onometrical ratio, sine, tangent, secant; cosine, cotangent, cosecant; percentage, per cent, percentile.

*numerical result*, answer, product, equation; sum, total, aggregate 52 *whole*; difference, residual 41 *remainder*; bill, score, tally 38 *addition*.

**Adj.** *numerical*, numerary, numeral, digital; arithmetical; cardinal, ordinal; round, whole; even, odd; prime; figurate; positive, negative, surd, radical; divisible, aliquot; multiple; reciprocal, complementary; fractional, decimal; incommensurable; commensurable, proportional; exponential, logarithmic, differ-ential, fluxional, integral; algebraic, transcen-dental; rational, irrational.

### 86 Numeration

**N.** *numeration*, numbering, enumeration, census, counting, ciphering, figuring, reck-oning, dead r.; calculating, computing; sum, tally, score, runs, points; count, recount, countdown; figure-work, summation, calcu-lation, computation, number-crunching 465 *measurement*; page-numbering, pagination; algorithm, decimal system; accountancy 808 *accounts*; counting heads, poll, capitation; head-count, hand-c.; numeracy; computer literacy.

*numerical operation*, figure-work, notation; addition, subtraction, multiplication, division, proportion, rule of three, practice, equations, analysis, extraction of roots, reduction, invol-ution, evolution, convolution, approximation, extrapolation, interpolation; differentiation, integration, permutation, combination, variation.

*mathematics*, pure m., applied m., arith-metic, algebra; quadratic equations; set theory, modern maths; differential calculus, integral c., infinitesimal c., vector c.; fluxions; calculus of variations; topology; geometry, trig-onometry; graphs, logarithms; algorithm, systems analysis (see also *computing*); oper-ational research, critical path analysis, linear programming 623 *policy*; axiomatics 475 *reasoning*.

*statistics*, figures, tables, 'lies, damned lies, and statistics';

**There are three kinds of lies: lies, damned lies and statistics.**
Benjamin Disraeli

averages, mode, mean 30 *average*; significance, deviation, normal d., standard d., standard error; distribution curve, skew; regression; correlation, rank c. test, chi-square t.; statistical enquiry, market research, poll, Gallup p. (tdmk) 605 *vote*; census, capitation; roll call, muster, muster roll, account 87 *list*; demography, birth rate, death r.; vital statistics; price index, retail p. i., cost of living, cost-of-living index 809 *price*; bar graph, histogram, scatter diagram, pie chart, flow c. 623 *plan*; cartogram 551 *map*.

*counting instrument*, abacus, suanpan, quipu; ready reckoner, multiplication table; tape measure, yardstick 465 *gauge*; sliding rule, slide r.; tallies, counters, Cuisenaire rods, Napier's bones *or* rods; comptometer, adding machine, calculating m., calculator, pocket c.; cash register, till, totalizator, tote; computer.

*enumerator*, numberer, computer, census-taker; calculator, counter, teller, pollster; mathematician, wrangler; arithmetician, geometrician, geometer, algebraist; knowledge engineer, systems analyst 623 *planner*; statistician, actuary, bookkeeper 808 *accountant*; statistics freak, quantoid; geodesist 465 *surveyor*.

*computer*, digital computer, analogue c., hybrid c., super c., parallel c., mainframe c., minicomputer, microcomputer, micro, personal computer, PC, desktop computer, laptop c., palmtop, notebook, games computer 196 *microelectronics*.

*computing*, artificial intelligence, AI, computer science, computer technology, cybernetics, informatics, information science, information technology, IT, software engineering 630 *mechanics*; computer literacy; computation, data capture, data-processing, DP, electronic data processing, EDP, information retrieval, database management system; computer-aided design, CAD, computer-aided diagnosis, computer-aided engineering, CAE, computer-aided instruction, computer-assisted i., CAI, computer-aided learning, computer-assisted l., CAL, computer-assisted language learning, CALL, computer-aided manufacture *or* manufacturing, CAM, computer-aided design and manufacture, CADCAM; viewdata, Prestel (tdmk), Ceefax (tdmk), Oracle (tdmk), teletext 524 *information*; program, computer p., software, firmware, shareware, DOS, MS-DOS (tdmk), protocol, application, applet, interface,

graphical user interface, GUI; machine code, computer language, programming l., authoring l. *or* author l., Ada, Algol, BASIC, C, C++, Cobol, Delphi, Fortran, PASCAL, Perl; virus, computer virus, e-mail v., macro v., micro v., computer bug, malicious code, malicious mobile c., Trojan horse, worm, millennium bug; antivirus software, virus detection, virus protection program, quarantine; spyware; firewall; agent, software a.; input, output, throughput, feedback; storage, retrieval; telematics; batch processing, real-time processing, time-sharing, multiprogramming, downtime; hardware (see also *counting instrument*); card punch, keypunch; keyboard, keypad, screen, visual display unit, VDU, visual display terminal 445 *appearance;* cursor, mouse, mouse pad; icon, earcon; data, bit, byte; punched cards, magnetic tape, floppy disk, diskette, hard disk, rigid d., Winchester d., compact d., optical d., video d., digital video d., digital versatile d., DVD; disk drive; add-on, processor, word processor (see also *computer*); central processing unit; database, data bank, memory, random-access memory, RAM, read-only memory, ROM 32 *store*; file, computer f., batch f., folder, defragmentation; window, spreadsheet; menu, drop-down m., pop-up m., pull-down m.; spell-check, spelling checker; hard copy, printout; peripheral, peripheral device, printer, dot-matrix p., daisy-wheel p., barrel p., drum p., ink-jet p., bubble-jet p., laser p., line p., scanner; benchmark; data transfer, multiplexing, modem, packet switching; desk-top publishing, DP, Windows (tdmk), QuarkXPress (tdmk), Pagemaker (tdmk); computer programmer, computer buff, computernik, geek (inf), hacker, techie (inf); computational linguistics, machine translation; computer game, video g. 837 *indoor game*; computer dating 894 *matchmaker*; Internet, World Wide Web 531 *Internet*.

**Adj.** *numerable*, numberable, countable; calculable, computable, measurable, mensurable 465 *metrical*; commensurable, commensurate 28 *equal*; proportionate 9 *relative*; incommensurable, incommensurate 29 *unequal*, 10 *unrelated*; eligible, admissible 78 *included*.

*statistical*, expressed in numbers, digital, ciphered, numbered, figured out; mathematical, arithmetical, algebraical; geometrical, trigonometrical; in ratio, in proportion, percentile, quartile.

*computerized*, automatic, e-, electronic, cyber-, robotic, on-line, off-line; programmable, processable; real-time, random-access, on-screen, user-friendly; bootable; analogue, digital, binary, alphanumeric; virtual, cybernetic.

**Vb.** *number*, cast, count, reckon, calculate, compute, tell; score, keep the s., keep a count, notch up; tell off, tick off, count down; affix numbers, foliate, paginate; enumerate, poll, count heads, count hands; take the number, take a poll, take a census; muster, call over, call the roll, take roll call; take stock, inventory 87 *list*; recount, go over 106 *repeat*; check, audit, balance, keep accounts 808 *account*; aggregate, amount to, add up to, total, tot up to, come to.

*do sums*, cast up, count up, carry over, totalize, tot up 38 *add*; take away 39 *subtract*; multiply 36 *augment*; divide 46 *sunder*; square, cube, extract roots; integrate, differentiate; figure, cipher; work out, reduce; map; compute, calculate, reckon, reckon up 465 *measure*; estimate 465 *appraise*.

*computerize*, automate 160 *empower*; digitize, digitalize; program, process; debug; compute, format, access, log on, boot, reboot, key in, keyboard, drag and drop, dump, download, upload, log off, scroll, browse 173 *operate*; hack; benchmark; surf the net, surf, flame (inf).

## 87 List

**N.** *list*, enumeration, items; list of items, inventory, stock list; chart, table, catalogue, listing; portfolio 767 *security*; statement, tabular s., schedule, manifest, bill of lading; checklist; invoice; numerical list, score; price list, tariff, bill, account, itemized a. 809 *price*; registry, cartulary; cadastre, terrier, Domesday Book; file, register, death r., birth r. 548 *record*; ticket, docket, tag, tally 547 *label*; ledger, books 808 *account book*; table of contents, index, card i. 547 *indication*; menu, window, spreadsheet 86 *computing*; bill of fare, menu, calorie table 301 *eating*; playbill, programme, prospectus, synopsis, syllabus 592 *compendium*; roll, electoral r., voting list, constituency l., top-up l. 605 *electorate*; muster roll, payroll; Army List, Navy L., active l., retired l. 686 *personnel*; statistical list, census 86 *numeration*; book list, bibliography, catalogue raisonnée 589 *reading matter*; discography, filmography; list of names, rota, roster, panel; waiting list, short l., short leet; string of names, visitors' book; dramatis personae; family tree, pedigree 169 *genealogy*; scroll, roll of honour, honours' board, martyrology, beadroll, diptych; blacklist 928 *accused person*, 924 *censure*; sick list 651 *sick person*; list of dates, book of days, calendar, Advent calendar, engagement book, diary 505 *reminder*; question paper, questionnaire; alphabetical list, A-Z, alphabet 60 *order*, 558 *letter*; repertory, repertoire.

*word list*, vocabulary, glossary, lexicon, thesaurus, gradus 559 *dictionary*.

*directory*, gazetteer, atlas; almanac, calendar, timetable 117 *chronology*; Bradshaw, ABC 524 *guidebook*; Army List, Navy L., Crockford, Burke's Peerage, Debrett, Almanac *or* Almanach de Gotha, Who's Who 589 *reference book*; telephone directory, phone book, Yellow Pages.

**Adj.** *listed*, entered, catalogued, tabulated, indexed; cadastral.

**Vb.** *list*, make a l., enumerate; itemize, reel off, inventory, catalogue, calendar, index, tabulate; file, docket, schedule, enter, book, post 548 *register*; enlist, matriculate, enrol, empanel, inscribe; score, keep the s., keep count 86 *number*.

## 88 Unity

**N.** *unity*, oneness, absoluteness 44 *simpleness*; consubstantiality 13 *identity*; integrality, integration, wholeness 52 *whole*; uniqueness, singularity, individuality 80 *speciality*; monotheism; monism; singleness 895 *celibacy*; isolation, solitude, loneliness 883 *seclusion*; isolability 46 *separation*; union, undividedness, indivisibility, solidarity 48 *coherence*, 706 *association*; unification 50 *combination*.

*unit*, integer, one, ace, item, article, piece; individual, atom, monad, entity 371 *person*; single piece, monolith; singleton, nonce word; none else, no other, naught beside; single instance, isolated i., isolated case, only exception; solo, monologue; single person, single, bachelor, bachelor girl, singleton 895 *celibate*, single parent 896 *divorce*, widowhood; hermit, lone wolf, loner 883 *solitary*; set, kit, outfit, package 78 *inclusion*; all-in-one, package deal.

**Adj.** *one*, not plural, singular, sole, single, solitary; unique, only, lone, one and only; one and the same 13 *identical*; unrepeated, only-begotten; without a second, first and last; once only, one-off, custom-built; a, an, a certain 562 *anonymous*; individual 80 *special*; absolute, universal 79 *general*; unitary, unific, univocal, unicameral, unilateral, unicellular; unisex; mono-; all of a piece, monolithic 16 *uniform*; unified, rolled into one, compact, solid 45 *joined*; 324 *dense*, 48 *cohesive*; indivisible, indissoluble.

*alone*, lonely, homeless, orphaned, deserted, abandoned, forsaken 883 *friendless*; lonesome, solitary, lone 883 *unsociable*; isolable, isolated 46 *disunited*; insular, enisled 199 *distant*, single-handed, on one's own; by oneself, on one's tod; unaccompanied, unescorted, unchaperoned; unpaired, fellowless, azygous; monadic, monatomic; celibate 895 *unwedded*.

**Vb.** *be one*, stand alone, stand on one's own

(two) feet, stew in one's own juice; unite 50 *combine*; isolate 46 *set apart*.

**Adv.** *singly*, one by one, one at a time; once, once only, once and for all, for the nonce, just this once, never again, only, solely, simply; alone, on one's own, by oneself, per se; in the singular.

## 89 Accompaniment

**N.** *accompaniment*, concomitance 71 *continuity*, 45 *union*, 5 *intrinsicality*; inseparability, permanent attribute; society 882 *sociability*; companionship, togetherness 880 *friendship*; partnership, marriage 706 *association*; coexistence, coagency 181 *concurrence*; coincidence, contemporaneity, simultaneity 123 *synchronism*; attendance, company; parallel course 219 *parallelism*.

*concomitant*, attribute, sine qua non 5 *essential part*; complement 54 *completeness*; accessory, appendage, appurtenance, fixture 40 *adjunct*; by-product, corollary; epiphenomenon, symptom, syndrome 547 *indication*; coincidence 159 *chance*; context, circumstance 7 *state*; background, noises off; accompaniment, obbligato; accompanist 413 *musician*; entourage, court 742 *retainer*; attendant, following, suite 67 *retinue*; groupie, camp follower; convoy, escort, guide 690 *leader*; chaperon, bodyguard 660 *protector*, 749 *keeper*; suitor, wooer 887 *lover*; tracker 619 *hunter*; inseparable, shadow, tail, Mary's little lamb 284 *follower*; consort, cohabitee, lover 894 *spouse*; comrade, companion, boon c., best friend 880 *friend*; stable companion, yokefellow, mate, co-worker, partner, associate 707 *colleague*; accomplice 707 *collaborator*; twin, pair, fellow 18 *analogue*; hanger-on, parasite, satellite 742 *dependant*.

**Adj.** *accompanying*, with, concomitant, attendant, background; always with, inseparable, built-in 45 *joined*; partnering, associated, coupled, paired; hand-in-glove 706 *cooperative*, 181 *concurrent*; obbligato 410 *harmonious*; accessory, belonging 78 *included*, 58 *component*; satellite, satellitic 745 *subject*; parallel, collateral; incidental, coincidental 159 *casual*; coexistent, contemporaneous, contemporary, simultaneous.

**Vb.** *accompany*, be found with, be seen w.; coexist; cohabit, live with, walk w., keep company w., consort w., walk out w.; string along with; attend, wait on, come to heel, dance attendance on 284 *follow*; bear one company, squire, chaperon, protect 660 *safeguard*; convoy, escort, guide, conduct, lead, usher, bring in tow 64 *come before*; track, dog, tail, shadow 619 *pursue*; associate with, partner 706

*cooperate*; gang up with, chum up w. 880 *befriend*; coincide, keep time with 123 *synchronize*, 181 *concur*; imply 5 *be intrinsic*; carry with, bring in its train, bring in its wake 156 *cause*; be inseparable, go hand in hand with, follow as night follows day 157 *depend*; belong, go with, go together 9 *be related*.

**Adv.** *with*, herewith 38 *in addition*; together with, cum, along with, in company w.; in the same boat; in convoy, in a crocodile, hand in hand, arm in arm, side by side; cheek by jowl; jointly, all together, in a body, collectively, inseparably, unitedly.

## 90 Duality

**N.** *duality*, dualism; double-sidedness; double life, dual personality, split p., Jekyll and Hyde; positive and negative, yin and yang 14 *polarity*; dyad, two, deuce, duo, twain, partnership, couple, item (inf), Darby and Joan, Jack and Jill, Romeo and Juliet; brace, pair, couple; doublets, twins, Castor and Pollux, Gemini, Siamese twins, identical t., Tweedledum and Tweedledee 18 *analogue*; yoke, span, double file; couplet, distich; double harness, twosome, two-hander; duel; duet; tandem, two-seater; biped; bivalve; Janus; double whammy.

**Adj.** *dual*, dualistic; dyadic, binary, binomial; bilateral, bicameral; twin, biparous; bisexual, double-barrelled, duplex 91 *double*; paired, coupled etc. vb.; conjugate, binate; two abreast, two by two; in twos, both; in pairs, tête-à-tête, à deux; double-sided, double-edged, bipartisan; amphibious; ambidextrous 91 *double*; bifocal; biform, two-dimensional, two-faced; dihedral; di-, bi-.

**Vb.** *pair*, couple, match, bracket, yoke; mate, pair off.

**Adv.** *and*, cum, with 38 *in addition*, 89 *with*.

## 91 Duplication

**N.** *duplication*, doubleness; doubling 261 *fold*; gemination, reduplication, encore, repeat, repeat performance; iteration, echo, parrotry 106 *repetition*; renewal 656 *restoration*; copy, carbon c., photocopy, Xerox (tdmk) 22 *duplicate*; double exposure; living image, look-alike 18 *analogue*.

**Adj.** *double*, doubled, twice; duplex, bifarious; biform; twofold, two-sided, two-headed, two-edged; bifacial, double-faced, two-faced; amphibious, ambidextrous; dual-purpose, two-way; of double meaning, ambiguous 518 *equivocal*; ambivalent; bisexual, AC/DC, hermaphrodite; twin, duplicate, geminate; second; dualistic 90 *dual*.

**Vb.** *double*, multiply by two; redouble, square; geminate, encore, echo, second 106 *repeat*; renew 656 *restore*; duplicate, twin; reduplicate, stencil, xerox, photocopy 20 *copy*.

**Adv.** *twice*, two times, once more; over again 106 *again*; as much again, twofold; secondly, in the second place, again; twice as much, twice over; doubly.

**92 Bisection**

**N.** *bisection*, bipartition, dichotomy; dividing by two, halving etc. vb.; hendiadys; half, moiety, fifty per cent 53 *part*; hemistich; hemisphere 252 *sphere*.

*bifurcation*, forking, branching, furcation 294 *divergence*; swallowtail, fork, prong 222 *cross*.

*dividing line*, diameter, diagonal, equator; parting, seam; date line; party wall, garden fence 231 *partition*.

**Adj.** *bisected*, halved etc. vb.; dimidiate, bifid, bipartite; bicuspid; bifurcate, bifurcated, forked; dichotomic, dichotomous; semi-, demi-, hemi-; split, cloven, cleft 46 *disunited*.

**Vb.** *bisect*, transect; divide, split, cleave 46 *sunder*; cut in two, dimidiate, dichotomize; share, go halves, go fifty-fifty 783 *apportion*; halve, divide by two; job-share.

*bifurcate*, separate, fork; branch off, ramify 294 *diverge*.

**93 Triality**

**N.** *triality*, trinity, trimurti; triunity; trimorphism; triplicity 94 *triplication*.

*three*, triad, trine; Fates, Furies, Graces; Faith, Hope and Charity; threesome, triumvirate, leash (of animals); troika; triplet, trey, trio, tern, trigon; trimester, triennium; trefoil, shamrock, triangle, trident, tripod, trivet, triskelion; three-wheeler, tricycle; three-decker, threehander; three-headed monster, Cerberus; triphthong, triptych, trilogy, triolet, trimeter; third power, cube; third person, gooseberry; tertium quid; Third World.

**Adj.** *three*, trinal, triadic, triform, trinomial; three in one, triune, tripartite; triphibious; tricolour; three-dimensional, tridimensional; three-sided, triangular, deltoid, trigonal, trilateral; three-pointed; trifoliate, three-leaved *or* -leafed; three-pronged, three-cornered; tricorn, tricuspid, tridentate; three-monthly, trimestrial; quarterly; tri-.

**Adv.** *in threes*, three by three; three times, thrice.

**94 Triplication**

**N.** *triplication*, triplicity; trebleness; hat trick; tercentenary.

**Adj.** *treble*, triple; trine, trinal, ternary; triplex, triplicate, threefold, three-ply; third, tertiary; trihedral; trilateral.

**Vb.** *treble*, triple, triplicate, cube.

**Adv.** *trebly*, triply, threefold; three times, thrice; in the third place, thirdly, in trine.

**95 Trisection**

**N.** *trisection*, tripartition, trichotomy; third, third part; tierce.

**Adj.** *trifid*, trisected; tripartite, trichotomous, trifurcate, trifoliate.

**Vb.** *trisect*, divide into three parts, divide by three; trifurcate.

**96 Quaternity**

**N.** *quaternity*, four, tetrad, tetrarchy; square, tetragon, quadrilateral, quadrangle, quad; tetrahedron; quadrature, quarter; fylfot, swastika 222 *cross*; tetrapod; tetrameter, quatrain; tetragram, Tetragrammaton; tetramorph; quaternion, quartet, foursome; four winds, four evangelists; four-in-hand, quadriga; quatrefoil; quadruplet, quad; quadruped, tetrapod; quadrennium; four corners of 52 *whole*.

**Adj.** *four*, quaternary, quadratic; quadrate, square, quadrilateral, tetrahedral, foursquare; four-footed, quadrupedal; quadrennial; quadri-, tetra-.

**97 Quadruplication**

**N.** *quadruplication*, quadruplicity; squaring; quatercentenary.

**Adj.** *fourfold*, quadruple, quadruplicate, quadruplex; squared; quadrable.

**Vb.** *quadruple*, quadruplicate, multiply by four; square, quadrate.

**Adv.** *four times*; fourthly, in the fourth place; in square.

**98 Quadrisection**

**N.** *quadrisection*, quadripartition; quartering, fourth, fourth part; quarterly; quart, quarter; farthing, quarto.

**Adj.** *quartered*; quadrifid, quadripartite.

**Vb.** *quadrisect*, quarter, divide into four parts, divide by four.

**99 Five and over**

**N.** *five*, cinque, quint, quintuplet, quin; quintet; lustrum; pentad; quincunx; pentagon, pentacle, pentagram, pentahedron; pentameter; Pentateuch; pentarchy; pentathlon; cinquefoil; quinquereme; five senses, Five Towns, Cinque Ports; five-a-side; a bunch of fives.

*over five*, six, half-a-dozen, sextet, hexad, sixer; hexagon, hexagram; Hexateuch; hexameter; seven, heptad, week, sabbatical year; septennium; septenary, septet; pleiad; Heptateuch; Seven Deadly Sins, Seven Wonders of the World, Seven Seas; eight, octave, octet, octad; octagon; one over the eight, piece of eight, figure of eight; nine, three times three; ennead, nonary; novena; nine Muses, nine days' wonder; ten, tenner, decade; decagon, decahedron, Decalogue; decury, decemvirate; Ten Commandments; eleven, hendecasyllable; twelve, dozen; dodecahedron; twelve apostles, the Twelve, twelve tribes; thirteen, baker's dozen, long d.; double figures, teens.

*twenty and over*, twenty, a score; icosahedron; four and twenty, two dozen; twenty-five, pony; forty, two score; fifty, half a hundred, jubilee; sixty, three score; sexagenarian; seventy, three score and ten, septuagenarian; eighty, four score, octogenarian; ninety, nonagenarian.

*hundred*, century, ton, centenary, centennial; hundredweight; centurion; centenarian; centipede; the hundred days; Old Hundredth; hundred per cent; treble figures.

*over one hundred*, a gross; hundreds and hundreds; thousand, chiliad, grand; millennium; ten thousand, myriad; hundred thousand, lakh; million; ten million, crore; thousand million, milliard; billion; million million; trillion; quadrillion, centillion, multimillion; zillion; millionaire, billionaire, milliardaire.

**Adj.** *fifth and over*, five, fifth; quinquennial, quinary, quintuple, fivefold; sixfold etc. n.; senary, sextuple; sixth; septuple; seventh; octuple; eighth; nonary; ninth; tenfold, decimal, denary, decuple, tenth; eleventh; twelfth; duodenary, duodecimal; thirteenth etc. n., in one's teens; vigesimal, vicenary, twentieth; vicennial; centesimal, centuple, centuplicate, centennial, centenary, centenarian, centurial; secular, hundredth; sesquicentenary, bicentenary, quincentenary; thousandth, millenary; bimillenary; millionth, billionth.

## 100 Multisection

**N.** *multisection*, decimation.

**Adj.** *multifid*, multifoil, multipartite, quinquepartite; octifid; decimal, tenth, tithe; duodecimal, twelfth; sexagesimal, sexagenary; hundredth, centesimal; millesimal.

**Vb.** *multisect*, decimate, decimalize.

## 101 Plurality

**N.** *plurality*, the plural; multiplicity 104 *multitude*; many-sidedness 82 *multiformity*; polygon, polyhedron; polytheism; a number, a certain number; some, one or two, two or three; a few, several; majority 104 *greater number*.

**Adj.** *plural*, in the p., not singular; composite, multiple; polydactyl, polypod; multiparous; polymorphic, multiform; many-sided;

multilateral, multipurpose, multirole; multi-, poly-; more than one, some, certain; not alone, accompanied, in company 45 *joined*; upwards of, more, in the majority 104 *many*.

**Adv.** *et cetera*.

## 102 Fraction: less than one

**N.** *fraction*, decimal f., vulgar f. 85 *numerical element*; fractional part, fragment 53 *part*, 783 *portion*; shred 33 *small quantity*.

**Adj.** *fractional*, partial 53 *fragmentary*, 33 *small*.

## 103 Zero

**N.** *zero*, nil, nothing, absolutely n., simply n., sweet n., damn all (inf), bugger a. (inf), fuck a. (inf), nada (inf), Fanny Adams (inf), sweet Fanny Adams (inf), sweet fuck all (inf), SFA (inf), zilch, zip; next to nothing, infinitely little; naught, nought, nix; no score, love, duck, goose egg; blank; figure nought, cipher; nothingness, nihility, nullity 2 *nonexistence*, 4 *insubstantiality*; none, nobody, not a soul 190 *absence*; zero level, nadir, rock bottom.

**Adj.** *not one*, not any, zero; invisible, infinitely little, null 4 *insubstantial*, 2 *nonexistent*.

## 104 Multitude

**N.** *multitude*, numerousness, multiplicity; large number, round n., enormous n., million 99 *over one hundred*; a quantity, lots, loads, heaps, masses, shedloads 32 *great quantity*; numbers, scores, myriads, millions, billions, trillions, squillions, zillions; a sea of, a mass of, a world of, a sight of; forest, thicket; host, array, fleet, battalions 722 *army*; throng, mob, high or large turnout, all the world and his wife 74 *crowd*; tribe, horde.

*certain quantity*, peck, bushel, pinch; galaxy, bevy, cloud, flock, flight, covey; shoal, school; flock, herd, drove; coachload, trainload; swarm, hive, colony 74 *group*; nest, clutch, litter, brood 132 *young creature*.

*greater number*, weight of numbers, majority, great m., mass, bulk, mainstream 32 *main part*; multiplication, multiple 101 *plurality*.

**Adj.** *many*, myriad, several, sundry, divers, various, a thousand and one; quite a few, not a f., a good f.; considerable, numerous, very many, a good many, ever so m., many more, no end of, umpteen, n; untold, unnumbered, innumerable, uncounted 107 *infinite*; multifarious, manifold 82 *multiform*; ever-recurring 139 *frequent*, 106 *repeated*; much, ample, multiple, multiplied; profuse, in profusion, abundant, superabundant, generous, lavish, overflowing, galore 635 *plenteous*, 32 *great*.

*multitudinous*, massed, crowded, thronged,

studded with 54 *full*; populous, peopled, populated, over-p., high-density 324 *dense*; teeming, crawling, humming, lousy with, hotching w., alive w., bristling w. 171 *prolific*; thick, thick on the ground, thick as hail, thick as flies; coming thick and fast 139 *frequent*; incalculable, innumerable, inexhaustible, countless, endless 107 *infinite*; countless as the stars, as the sands on the seashore, as the hairs on one's head; heaven knows how many.

**Vb.** *be many*, – various etc. adj.; swarm with, crawl w., hum w., bristle w., teem w., be hotching w., be lousy w., be alive w. 54 *fill*; pullulate, multiply 171 *be fruitful*; clutter, crowd, throng, swarm, mass, flock, troop 74 *congregate*; swarm like ants, swarm like locusts, swarm like bees round a honey-pot; flood, overflow, snow under, swamp, overwhelm 637 *superabound*; infest, overrun 297 *burst in*; add to the number, swell the ranks 36 *augment*; overweigh, outnumber, make a majority 32 *be great*.

## 105 Fewness

**N.** *fewness*, paucity, underpopulation; exiguity, thinness, sparsity, sparseness, rarity 140 *infrequency*; scantiness 636 *scarcity*; a few, a handful; wisps, tuft; thin audience, poor turnout; small number, trickle, mere t., soupçon, smidgen 33 *small quantity*; almost none; limited number, too few, no quorum; minority, one or two, two or three, half a dozen, not enough to matter, a minimal number, a derisory amount; remnant, sole survivor 41 *remainder*.

**Adj.** *few*, precious few, weak in numbers, scant, scanty, light, little 636 *scarce*; thin, thin on the ground, sparse, rare, scattered, low-density, few and far between 140 *infrequent*; not many, hardly any; soon counted, to be counted on one's fingers, to be counted on the fingers of one hand; fewer, reduced, diminishing 37 *decreasing*; too few, in a minority, without a quorum.

**Vb.** *be few*, be few in number, be weak in numbers, be underpopulated; straggle; seldom occur.

*render few*, reduce, diminish, pare 198 *make smaller*; scale down, slim down, cut back, decimate, thin the ranks; eliminate, weed, thin, sort out 300 *eject*; defect, desert; underman, understaff.

**Adv.** *here and there*, in dribs and drabs, in twos and threes, in a trickle; sparsely, rarely, infrequently.

## 106 Repetition

**N.** *repetition*, doing again, iteration, reiteration; doubling, ditto, reduplication 20 *imitation*, 91 *duplication*; going over, recital, recapitulation; practice, practising, rehearsal; beginning again, renewal, resumption, reprise 68 *beginning*; saying again, repeating, anaphora, epizeuxis 574 *ornament*; harping, tautology, redundancy 570 *diffuseness*; stammering, stuttering 580 *speech defect*; repetition, repeat, repeat performance, encore; second helping, seconds; playback, replay, action replay; return match, replay, revenge; chorus, refrain, ritornello 412 *vocal music*; echo, repercussion, reverberation 404 *resonance*; cliché, quotation, citation, plagiarism; hardy annual (see also *recurrence*); ancient history, chestnut, old news, old story, twice-told tale, Queen Anne's dead 838 *bore*; parrot-cry, gramophone record; new edition, reprint, reissue 589 *edition*; rifacimento, remake, rehash, recast, revival 656 *restoration*; repeater, cuckoo, parrot; creature of habit.

*recurrence*, repetitiveness, repetitive strain injury, RSI 139 *frequency*; cycle, round, return, rebirth, renaissance, reincarnation 141 *regular return*; succession, run, series, serial; serial killing, spree killing, serial monogamy 71 *continuity*; recurring decimal, repetend; throwback, atavism 5 *heredity*; reappearance, comeback, curtain call; rhythm, drumming, hammering 141 *periodicity*; alliteration, assonance, rhyme 18 *assimilation*, 593 *prosody*; stale repetition, monotony 16 *uniformity*, 838 *tedium*; same old round, mixture as before, rehash, busman's holiday, routine 610 *habit*.

**Adj.** *repeated*, repetitional; recurrent, recurring, ever-r. 141 *periodical*; haunting 505 *remembered*; tautological, redundant, repetitive, repetitious, harping, iterative; stuck in a groove; stale, cliché-ridden 572 *feeble*; echoing, rhyming, chiming, alliterative, assonant 18 *similar*; monotonous, singsong, dingdong 16 *uniform*, 838 *tedious*; rhythmical, drumming, hammering; incessant, habitual 139 *frequent*; retold, twice-told, said before, quoted, cited; above-mentioned, aforesaid 66 *precursory*; plagiarized 20 *imitative*; reheated, rehashed, recycled.

**Vb.** *repeat*, do again, iterate, cut and come again; duplicate, reduplicate, redouble 91 *double*; multiply 166 *reproduce*; reiterate, ingeminate, say again, recapitulate, go over, ring the changes on; retell, restate, reword, rephrase; always say, trot out; say one's piece, recite, reel off, say over, say after; echo, ditto, parrot, plagiarize 20 *copy*, 925 *flatter*; quote, cite 505 *remember*; go over the same ground, retrace one's footsteps; practise, rehearse; play back, rerun, rewind; recycle, reprocess; begin again, restart, resume 68 *begin*; replay, give an encore; reprint, reissue, republish; rehash, remake, renew, revive 656 *restore*; reheat.

*repeat oneself*, give an encore; reverberate, re-echo 404 *resound*; chant, chorus 16 *be uniform*; quote oneself, tautologize 570 *be diffuse*; stutter 580 *stammer*; trot out, plug, labour, harp on, harp on the same string; din into one's ears, go on at, hammer away at; recur to, revert to, return to 505 *remember*; go over the same ground, go back, retrace one's steps 286 *regress*; stick in a groove, be a creature of habit 610 *be wont*.

*reoccur*, recur, return, revert, happen again; reappear, pop up, show up again; never hear the last of; turn up like a bad penny; haunt, obsess 505 *be remembered*.

**Adv.** *repeatedly*, recurrently, frequently 139 *often*; by rote, parrot fashion; again and again, over and over, over and over again, many times o., times without number, time and again; time after time, day after day, year after year; day by day, day in day out, year in year out; morning, noon and night; ad nauseam.

*again*, afresh, anew, over again, for the second time, once more; ditto; encore, bis; de novo, da capo; re-.

## 107 Infinity

**N.** *infinity*, infinitude, infiniteness, boundlessness, limitlessness, illimitability; infinite space, outer s. 183 *space*; eternity 115 *perpetuity*.

**Adj.** *infinite*, indefinite; immense, measureless; eternal 115 *perpetual*; numberless, countless, innumerable, immeasurable, illimitable, interminable; incalculable, unfathomable, incomprehensible, unapproachable, beyond reckoning, beyond comprehension; inexhaustible, without number, without limit, without end, no end of; without measure, limitless, endless, boundless, termless; untold, unnumbered 104 *many*; unmeasured, unbounded, unlimited.

**Adv.** *infinitely*, to infinity, ad infinitum; without end, indefinitely; boundlessly, illimitably; immeasurably 32 *greatly*.

SECTION SIX

# Time

## 108 Time

**N.** *time*, tide; tense 564 *grammar*; duration, extent 113 *long duration*; quality time, limited t.; season, term, semester, tenancy, tenure; tour, shift, spell, stint; span, space 110 *period*; a bit, a while; the whole time, the entire period,

life, lifetime; eternity 115 *perpetuity*; passage of time, lapse of time, lapse, course 111 *course of time*; years, days; Time, Father Time, Time's scythe, Time's hourglass, sands of time, ravages of t., whirligig of t., t. the enemy, t. the healer; fourth dimension, space-time; time zone; timeslip, timewarp; aorist, indefinite time; past time, past tense, retrospective time 125 *past time*, 119 *priority*; prospective time 124 *futurity*; contemporaneity 121 *present time*; recent time 126 *newness*; antiquity, distant time 127 *oldness*.

*interim*, intermediate time, meantime, pendency, while; interval, interlude, break, breather, pause 145 *lull*; vacation 681 *leisure*; timelag, intermittence, interregnum, interlude, episode 72 *discontinuity*; close season, respite, adjournment 136 *delay*; midweek 70 *middle*.

*date*, day, age, day and a., reign 110 *era*; vintage, year, regnal y., time of life 117 *chronology*; birthday, Saint's day 141 *anniversary*; day of the week, calends, ides, nones; time of day 117 *clock time*; moment 116 *instant*; target date, zero hour, D-day; term, fixed day, quarter day, payday.

**Adj.** *continuing*, permanent 115 *perpetual*, 146 *unceasing*; on foot, in process of, pending; repetitive, recurrent 106 *repeated*; temporal 141 *periodical*.

*intermediate*, interglacial, interlunar, interwar; midweek; intercalary, intercalated, inter-.

*dated*, calendared; pre-Christian 119 *prior*; post-Christian, postwar 120 *subsequent*.

**Vb.** *continue*, endure, drag on 113 *last*; roll on, intervene, pass 111 *elapse*; take time, take up t., fill t., occupy t. 183 *extend*; live through, sustain; stay, remain, abide, outlive, survive 113 *outlast*; take its time, wait 136 *be pending*.

*pass time*, vegetate, breathe, subsist, exist 360 *live*; age 131 *grow old*; spend time, consume t., use t., employ t. 678 *be busy*; while away time, kill t., summer, winter, weekend 681 *have leisure*; waste time, fritter away t. 679 *be inactive*; mark time, tide over 136 *wait*; choose the right time, choose one's moment, take time by the forelock, grab the chance, seize an opportunity 137 *profit by*; enjoy a spell of, have one's day.

*fix the time*, calendar, date, pencil in, put a date to, settle on a date for 117 *time*.

**Adv.** *while*, whilst, during, pending; day by day 113 *all along*; in the course of, so long as; for the time being, for now, meantime, meanwhile; between whiles, in the meantime, in the interim; from day to day, from hour to hour; hourly 139 *often*; for a time, for a season; till, until, up to, yet; always, the whole time, all the time 139 *perpetually*; all along 54 *throughout*; for good 113 *for a long time.*

*when*, what time; one day, once upon a time, one fine morning; in the days of, in the time of, in the year of.

*anno domini*, AD; ante Christum, AC; before Christ, BC; anno urbis conditae, ab urbe condita, AUC; anno hegirae, AH; common era, CE; anno regni, AR, in the year of his *or* her reign.

## 109 Neverness

**N.** *neverness*, Greek Calends; month of Sundays, blue moon, when pigs fly; jam tomorrow (see quotation at 122 *different time*), mañana; dies non; no time, datelessness, eternity 115 *perpetuity.*

**Adv.** *never*, not ever, at no time, at no period, on no occasion; not in donkey's years; nevermore, never again; over one's dead body; never before, never in one's born days; without date, sine die; before the beginning of time; out of time.

## 110 Period

**N.** *period*, matter of time; long period, long run 113 *long duration*; short period, short run 114 *transience*; season; close season 145 *lull*; time of day, morning, evening 128 *morning*, 129 *evening*; time of year, spring, summer, autumn, fall, winter; one's time, fixed t., term; notice, warning, ultimatum 766 *conditions*; time up, full time 69 *finality*; measured time, spell, go, tour, stint, shift, span, stretch, sentence; innings, turn; round, bout, lap; quality time; vigil, watch, nightwatch, dogwatch; length of time, second, minute, hour; particular time, rush hour; pause, interval 108 *interim*; day, weekday, working day; week, working w., five-day w., sennight, octave, novena; fortnight, month, calendar m., lunar m., moon, lunation; quarter, trimester; half year, semester; twelvemonth, year, solar y., sidereal y., light y., leap y.; fiscal y.; Olympiad, lustrum, quinquennium; decade, decennium, Gay Nineties, Hungry Thirties, Swinging Sixties; golden wedding, jubilee 141 *anniversary*; century, millennium; annus mirabilis; time up to now, one's born days; life, lifetime, life sentence.

*era*, time, period, generation, age, days; epoch; aeon; cycle, Sothic c., Metonic c.; Platonic year, Great Year, Yuga, Kalpa; geological period, Ice Age; Stone A., Iron A., Dark Ages, Middle A. 125 *antiquity*; Renaissance, Age of Enlightenment, A. of Reason, belle époque, fin de siècle; modern times, Machine Age, Computer A., Space A.; Golden A., A. of Aquarius.

**Adj.** *periodic* 141 *seasonal*; hourly, horary; annual, biennial, quinquennial, decennial, centennial; period 127 *olden.*

*secular*, epochal, millennial; Pre-Cambrian, Palaeozoic, Mesozoic, Cainozoic, Quaternary; Pleistocene, Holocene; neolithic 127 *primal.*

**Adv.** *man and boy*, in a lifetime; periodically, seasonally; for a term, for the term of one's natural life, for the whole of one's life, for a lifetime.

## 111 Course: indefinite duration

**N.** *course of time*, matter of t., progress of t., process of t., lapse of t., flow of t., flux of t., stream of t., tide of t., march of t., heavy tread of t., flight of t.; duration 108 *time*, 146 *continuance*; continuous tense, imperfect t. 564 *grammar*; indefinite time, infinite t. 113 *long duration.*

**Adj.** *elapsing*, wearing, passing, rolling 285 *progressive*, 146 *unceasing*; consuming 114 *transient*; getting older 131 *ageing.*

**Vb.** *elapse*, pass, lapse, flow, run, roll, proceed, advance, press on 285 *progress*; wear on, drag on, crawl 278 *move slowly*; flit, fly, fleet, slip, slide, glide 277 *move fast*; run its course, run out, expire 69 *end*; go by, pass by, slip by, fly past 125 *be past*; have one's day, spend time 108 *pass time.*

**Adv.** *in time*, in due time, in due season; in the course of time, in the process of t., in the fullness of t., with the years.

## 112 Contingent duration

**Adv.** *provisionally*, precariously, by favour; at the pleasure of; for the present, for the time being; so long as it lasts; as *or* so long as.

## 113 Long duration

**N.** *long duration*, length of time, a long t., unconscionable t.; a month of Sundays, years, donkey's years, years on end, yonks; a lifetime, life sentence; generations, a century, an age, ages, aeons 115 *perpetuity*; length of days, cat's nine lives, longevity 131 *old age*; distance of time, corridor of t., antiquity 125 *past time.*

*durability*, lasting quality, endurance, will to live, defiance of time; stamina, staying power 162 *strength*; survival 146 *continuance*; permanence 153 *stability*; inveteracy, long standing, good age, ripe old a. 127 *oldness*; long run, long innings.

*protraction*, prolongation, extension 203 *lengthening*; dragging out, spinning o.; padding o., filibustering, stonewalling 702 *hindrance*, 715 *resistance*; interminability, wait, long w., long haul 136 *delay*, 278 *slowness*; extra time, injury t., overtime 38 *addition.*

**Adj.** *lasting*, abiding 146 *unceasing*; secular,

agelong, lifelong, livelong; long-time, long-
standing, inveterate, deep-seated, deep-rooted;
of long duration, long-term, long-service, marathon 203 *long*; too long, unconscionable; durable, perdurable, enduring 162 *strong*;
longeval, long-lived 127 *immemorial*; evergreen, unfading, fresh 126 *new*; eternal, perennial 115 *perpetual*; persistent, chronic 602
*obstinate*; nonbiodegradable, indestructible
162 *unyielding*; constant, stable, permanent
153 *unchangeable*.

*protracted*, prolonged, lengthened, extended,
stretched, spun out, drawn o., dragged o. 197
*expanded*; lingering, delayed, tarrying 278 *slow*;
long-pending, long-awaited 136 *late*; interminable, long-winded, verbose, time-wasting 570
*prolix*.

**Vb.** *last*, endure, stand, stay, remain, abide,
continue 146 *go on*; brave the years, defy time,
stand the test of time, never, end 115 *be
eternal*; carry one's years 131 *grow old*; wear,
wear well 162 *be strong*.

*outlast*, outlive, outwear, outstay, survive;
remain 41 *be left*; live to fight another day;
have nine lives.

*spin out*, draw o., drag o.; protract, prolong
203 *lengthen*; temporize, gain time, play for
time, procrastinate 136 *put off*; talk out, stonewall, filibuster 702 *obstruct*.

*drag on*, be interminable, never end; inch,
creep, linger, dawdle 278 *move slowly*; tarry,
delay, waste time, wait 136 *be late*.

**Adv.** *for a long time*, long, for long, for ages,
for years, since time immemorial, many a long
day; for good, for ever, for all time, for better
for worse; all one's life, from the cradle to the
grave; till blue in the face; till the cows come
home.

*all along*, all day, all day long, the live-long
day, as the day is long; all the year round,
round the clock, hour by hour, day by day; day
in day out, year in year out; before and since;
ever since.

*long ago*, long since, in the distant past, long
long ago, when the world was young; in the
past, in ancient days, in bygone times 125
*formerly*.

*at last*, at long last, in the end, in the long
run, after many days, not before it was time,
not before time.

## 114 Transience

**N.** *transience*, transientness, transitoriness 4
*insubstantiality*; ephemerality, impermanence;
evanescence 446 *disappearance*; volatility 338
*vaporization*; fugacity 277 *velocity*; caducity, fragility 330 *brittleness*; mortality, perishability
361 *death*; frailty, fragility 163 *weakness*; muta-

bility 152 *changeableness*; capriciousness,
fickleness 604 *caprice*; suddenness 116
*instantaneity*; temporariness, provisionality;
temporary arrangement, makeshift 150 *substitute*; interregnum 106 *interim*.

*brief span*, short space of time, a minute or
two, short while; briefness, momentariness,
brevity 204 *shortness*; mortal span, short life
and a merry one; summer lightning, shooting
star, meteor, flash in the pan, nine days'
wonder; ephemera, bubble, mayfly, snow on a
dyke, snows of yesteryear, smoke in the wind;
April shower, summer cloud 4 *insubstantial
thing*; bird of passage, ship that passes in the
night; brief encounter; short run 110 *period*,
277 *spurt*; spasm, moment 116 *instant*.

**Adj.** *transient*, time-bound, temporal, impermanent, transitory, fading, passing 4 *insubstantial*; fair-weather, summer; cursory, flying,
fleeting, flitting, fugitive, fugacious 277 *speedy*;
shifting, slipping; precarious, volatile, written
in water; evanescent 446 *disappearing*;
unsettled, restless, footloose, rootless; flickering, mutable, changeable 152 *changeful*;
fickle, flighty 604 *capricious*.

*ephemeral*, of a day, short-lived, fleeting, non-
durable; throwaway, disposable, nonreturn-
able, single-use, biodegradable 51
*decomposable*; perishable, mortal 361 *dying*;
annual, deciduous, frail, fragile 163 *weak*, 330
*brittle*; impermanent, temporary, acting, provisional, for the time being, for the nonce;
doomed, under sentence.

*brief*, short-term, short-service 204 *short*; summary, short and sweet, to the point 569 *concise*; quick, fleet, brisk 277 *speedy*; sudden,
momentary, meteoric, like a flash 116 *instantaneous*; hurried, pressed for time, in a hurry
680 *hasty*; at short notice, impromptu, off the
cuff, extemporaneous, offhand 609 *spontaneous*.

**Vb.** *be transient*, – transitory etc. adj.; not
stay, not last; flit, fleet, fly, gallop 277 *move
fast*; fade, flicker, vanish, evanesce, melt, evaporate 446 *disappear*; fade like a dream, flit like a
shadow, pass like a summer cloud, burst like a
bubble, have no roots 2 *pass away*.

**Adv.** *transiently*, briefly, momentarily;
awhile, in passing, en passant; temporarily,
provisionally; for the present, for the moment,
for a time, for the time being, for the nonce,
not for long; instantly 116 *instantaneously*; easy
come, easy go; here today and gone tomorrow.

## 115 Perpetuity: endless duration

**N.** *perpetuity*, endless time, infinite duration
107 *infinity*; sempiternity, everlastingness; eternity, timelessness; never-endingness, intermin-

ability 113 *long duration*; endurance 144
*permanence*, 71 *continuity*; immortality, atha-
nasia, deathlessness, incorruption 146 *continuance*; perpetuation, immortalization;
memorial, lasting monument 505 *reminder*.

**Adj.** *perpetual*, perennial, longlasting,
enduring, durable, perdurable 113 *lasting*;
aeonian, agelong 127 *immemorial*; nonstop,
constant, continual, ceaseless, incessant 146
*unceasing*; flowing, everflowing, uninterrupted
71 *continuous*; dateless, ageless, unageing,
unchanging, immutable 144 *permanent*; evergreen, unfading, amaranthine, everlasting,
incorruptible; imperishable, undying, deathless, immortal; unending, neverending,
interminable; endless, without end, timeless,
eternal, coeternal.

**Vb.** *perpetuate*, make permanent, continue,
establish; immortalize, eternalize.

*be eternal*, – perpetual etc. adj.; last for ever,
endure for e., live for e.; go on for e., have no
end, never cease.

**Adv.** *for ever*, in perpetuity, on and on; ever
and always, for always and always, for aye,
evermore, for ever and ever, for ever and a day;
time without end, world without e.; for keeps,
for good and all, for better for worse; to the
end of time, till doomsday, to the crack of
doom; to infinity 107 *infinitely*; from age to
age, from generation to generation;
unchangeably, constantly, 24/7, nonstop 71
*continuously*.

**116 Instantaneousness: point of time**
**N.** *instantaneousness*, instantaneity, immedi-
ateness, immediacy; simultaneity 121 *present
time*; suddenness, abruptness 508 *lack of expectation*; precise time 135 *punctuality*; momentariness 114 *transience*.

*instant*, moment, precise m., point, point of
time; second, split s., half a s., tick, trice, jiffy,
half a j., mo, half a mo; breath; burst, crack;
stroke, coup; flash, lightning f.; twinkle, twinkling, the twinkling of an eye; two shakes, two
shakes of a lamb's tail; the very moment, the
very hour, the stroke of.

**Adj.** *instantaneous*, simultaneous,
immediate, instant, sudden, abrupt, snap;
flickering, flashing; as quick as thought, as
quick as lightning, with the speed of light,
quick as a flash, like a flash 277 *speedy*; on
time, dead on t., punctual 135 *early*.

**Adv.** *instantaneously*, instantly, instanter, on
the instant, at once, immediately, at the
double, directly; punctually, without delay,
forthwith; in half a mo, soon; in no time at all,
in less than no time; promptly, readily, presto,
pronto; without warning, without notice,

abruptly; overnight, all at once, all of a sudden
135 *suddenly*; plump, slap, slap-bang, in one's
tracks; in the same breath, at the same instant,
at a stroke, at one jump, at one fell swoop; in a
trice, in a moment, in a wink, in the twinkling
of an eye; in two ticks, in a brace of shakes, in
two shakes of a lamb's tail; at the drop of a hat,
on the spot, on the dot; extempore,
impromptu, on the spur of the moment, off
the cuff; before you could say Jack Robinson,
before you could say knife; like a flash, like a
shot, like greased lightning 277 *swiftly*; no
sooner said than done.

**117 Chronometry**
**N.** *chronometry*, chronoscopy, horometry, horology; watch-making; calendar-making, timeta-
bling; timing, dating; timekeeping 108 *time*.

*clock time*, right time, exact t., correct t.,
BBC t., true t., astronomer's t., solar t.,
sidereal t., Greenwich Mean T., G.M.T., British
Standard T., British Summer T., B.S.T., local t.,
Central European T., continental t.; time zone;
date, date line; the time now, the hour, time of
day, time of night; bedtime; summer time,
double summer t., daylight saving t.

*timekeeper*, chronometer, timepiece, hor-
ologe; clock, dial, face; hand, minute h.; bob,
pendulum 317 *oscillation*; electric clock,
digital c., quartz c., long-case c., grandfather c.,
grandmother c., calendar c., carriage c.,
cuckoo c., alarm c., travelling alarm, travel
clock, clock radio, alarum; Big Ben; water-
clock, clepsydra; watch, ticker; turnip, fob-
watch, hunter, repeater; wristwatch, digital
watch, analogue w., dial w.; sundial, gnomon;
hour-glass, sand-glass, egg timer; chronograph,
chronoscope, chronopher; time signal, pip,
siren, hooter; gong, bell, five-minute b.,
minute-gun, time-ball; time-clock, timer, stopwatch; Tim, speaking clock; parking meter,
traffic light 305 *traffic control*; time fuse, time
switch, time bomb; metronome, conductor,
band-leader; watchmaker, clockmaker, hor-
ologist.

*chronology*, dendrochronology, glottochronology; radio-carbon dating, thermoluminescence; dating, chronogram; date, age, epoch,
style 110 *era*; old style, O.S., new style, N.S.;
almanac, calendar, perpetual c., fixed c.,
Gregorian c., Julian c.; ephemeris, astronomical almanac; menology, chronicle,
annals, fasti, book of days, diary, journal, logbook 548 *record*; date list, time-chart 87 *list*;
tide-table, timetable, schedule 87 *directory*.

*chronologist*, chronographer, chronologer,
calendar-maker, calendarist; chronicler,
annalist, diarist 549 *recorder*.

**Adj.** *chronological*, chronometrical, horological, timekeeping; chronographic; annalistic, diaristic 548 *recording*; calendrical, chronogrammatic, datal, temporal; isochronous, isochronal 123 *synchronous*; in time 137 *timely*.

**Vb.** *time*, clock; fix the time, fix the date; timetable, schedule; match times 123 *synchronize*; phase 24 *adjust*; adjust the hands, put the clock forward 135 *be early*; put the clock back 136 *be late*; wind the clock, set the alarm 669 *make ready*; calendar, chronologize, chronicle, diarize 548 *record*; date, be dated, bear a date; measure time, mark t., beat t., keep t.; count the minutes, watch the clock; clock in 68 *begin*; clock out 145 *cease*; ring in 68 *initiate*; ring out 69 *terminate*.

**Adv.** *o'clock*, a.m., p.m.

## 118 Anachronism

**N.** *anachronism*, parachronism, prochronism; wrong date, wrong day, chronological error; mistiming, previousness, prolepsis 135 *anticipation*; disregard of time, unpunctuality 136 *lateness*; neglect of time, oblivion of t. 506 *oblivion*; wrong moment, unfortunate m. 138 *untimeliness*.

**Adj.** *anachronistic*, misdated, undated; antedated, foredated, previous, before time, too early 135 *early*; parachronistic, postdated 136 *late*; too late, overdue, unpunctual, behind time; slow, losing; fast, gaining; out of due time, out of season, out of date, out of fashion, behind the times, old-fashioned 127 *antiquated*.

**Vb.** *misdate*, mistake the date, mistake the day 138 *mistime*; antedate, foredate, anticipate 135 *be early*; be overdue, be behind time, postdate 136 *be late*; be fast, gain; be slow, lose; be unpunctual, take no note of time.

## 119 Priority

**N.** *priority*, antecedence, anteriority, previousness, pre-existence; primogeniture, birthright; eldest, firstborn, son and heir; flying start 64 *precedence*; leading 283 *preceding*; the past, yesteryear, yesterday 125 *past time*; eve, vigil, day before; precedent, antecedent; foretaste, trailer, preview, prerelease; premonition, presentiment 510 *foresight*; herald 66 *precursor*; prequel.

**Adj.** *prior*, pre-, fore-; earliest, first, first in the field, precedent 64 *preceding*; previous, earlier, anterior, antecedent; antediluvian, prehistoric; pre-Christian, BC; prewar, antebellum; pre-existing, pre-existent; prenatal, antenatal; elder, eldest, firstborn; former, cidevant, one-time, whilom, erstwhile, sometime, ex-, retired, emeritus; foregoing,

aforementioned, above-mentioned; aforesaid, said; introductory, prefatory, preliminary, preluding 66 *precursory*; premised, given, presupposed 512 *supposed*.

**Vb.** *be before* 135 *be early*; come before, go b. 283 *precede*; anticipate, forerun, foreshadow, antecede; pre-exist.

*do before*, premise, presuppose 512 *suppose*; predecease, prefabricate, prearrange, precontract, pre-empt, prejudge, precondemn, prenotify, preview; be previous, anticipate, forestall, be beforehand with, jump the gun, jump the queue; steal a march on, have a start on 277 *outstrip*; lead 283 *precede*, 64 *come before*.

**Adv.** *before*, pre-, prior to, beforehand, by; just before, on the eve of; earlier, previously, formerly; ultimo, ult.; afore, ere; aforetime, ere now, before n.; ere then, before t., already, yet; in anticipation; until now, up to now, hitherto, heretofore.

## 120 Posteriority

**N.** *posteriority*, subsequence, supervention; ultimogeniture, succession 65 *sequence*, 284 *following*; days to come, time to come 124 *futurity*; line, lineage, family tree, ancestry, descent, successor, descendant 170 *posterity*; cadet; latecomer, new arrival; remainder, inheritance; aftermath 67 *sequel*.

**Adj.** *subsequent*, post-, posterior, following, ensuing, next, to come, after, later; last in date, junior, cadet, younger, youngest 130 *young*; successive, consecutive, consequent; succeeding, designate, to be 124 *future*; postnatal; postdiluvian, postglacial; posthumous, postobit; postindustrial, postwar; after Christ, AD; postprandial, after-dinner 65 *sequential*.

**Vb.** *ensue* supervene, follow after 65 *come after*; go after 284 *follow*, 157 *result*; succeed, follow in the footsteps of, step into the shoes of 771 *inherit*.

**Adv.** *subsequently*, later, in the process of time; after, afterwards; at a later date; next, next time; thereafter, thereupon; since, from that time, from that moment; from the start, from the word 'go'; after a while, after a time; soon after, close upon; next month, proximo.

## 121 Present time

**N.** *present time*, contemporaneity, contemporaneousness, topicality 126 *modernism*; time being, the present, present time, present day, present moment; this hour, this moment, this moment in time, this instant 116 *instantaneousness*; juncture, opportunity, crisis 137 *occasion*; ongoing situation 146 *continuance*; this time, the nonce; the times, modern t., current t., these days, this day and age; today, twentieth century, nowadays; this date, current d.; one's age, one's present a., mental a., physical a.; present generation, one's contemporaries 123 *contemporary*.

**Adj.** *present*, actual, instant, current, extant 1 *existing*; of this date, of today's d.; topical, contemporary, contemporaneous; present-day, latter-day, latest, up-to-the-minute, up-to-date, bang up-to-date 126 *modern*; for the occasion, occasional; latest, breaking.

**Vb.** *be now*, exist 1 *be*; live in the present, live for the day, live for today, live from hand to mouth; be modern 126 *modernize*; be one's age, act one's a., admit one's a. 123 *synchronize*.

**Adv.** *at present*, now, right now, at this time, at this moment, at this moment in time; live; at the present time, contemporaneously, contemporarily; today, nowadays; at this time of day, at this stage, even now; already, but now, just now; this time, on the present occasion; for the time being, for now, for the nonce; on the nail, on the spot 116 *instantaneously*; on the spur of the moment 609 *extempore*; now or never; now as always.

*until now*, to this day, to the present day, up to now, to date; including today, through; from the start, from the word 'go' 113 *all along*.

## 122 Different time

**N.** *different time*, other times, better t. 124 *futurity*, 125 *past time*; another time, some other t., not now, not today, any time but this; 'jam yesterday, and jam tomorrow, but never jam today' 109 *neverness*;

> The rule is, jam to-morrow and jam yesterday – but never jam to-day.
>
> Lewis Carroll, *Through the Looking-Glass*

parachronism 118 *anachronism*.

**Adj.** *not contemporary*, unmodern 84 *unconformable*; behind the times 127 *antiquated*; before the times 126 *new*; misdated 118 *anachronistic*.

**Adv.** *not now*, ago, earlier, later, then; sometimes; once, once upon a time; one day, one fine morning, one of these days; someday, some other time *or* day, sometime, some time or other, sooner or later; any time, any old t.; any time now; soon; whenever you will, as soon as you like.

## 123 Synchronism

**N.** *synchronism*, synchrony; coexistence, coincidence, concurrence, concomitance 89 *accompaniment*; simultaneity, simultaneousness, same time 116 *instantaneousness*; contemporaneity, contemporaneousness, same date, same day 121 *present time*; coevality, same age, twin

birth 28 *equality*; level-pegging, neck-and-neck, nip and tuck, level time, dead heat 28 *draw*; synchronization, sync, phasing, isochronism.

*contemporary*, coeval, twin 28 *compeer*; one's contemporaries, one's own generation; age group, peer g., class, year 74 *group*.

**Adj.** *synchronous*, synchronal; synchronic; contemporary, contemporaneous 121 *present*, 126 *modern*; simultaneous, coinstantaneous, coincident, coexistent, coeternal, contermi-nous, concomitant 24 *agreeing*, 89 *accompanying*; level, neck and neck 28 *equal*; matched in age, coeval, coetaneous, twin; of the same age, of the same year, of the same generation, of the same vintage; synchronized, timed, phased, isochronous, on the beat, punctual.

**Vb.** *synchronize*, sync, contemporize; concur, coexist 89 *accompany*; encounter, coincide 295 *meet*; keep time 410 *harmonize*; say together, say in unison, chorus; tune, phase 24 *adjust*; be level-pegging, run neck and neck, run a dead heat 28 *be equal*; pace, keep in step with; isochronize.

**Adv.** *synchronously*, concurrently, at the same time, isochronously, for the same time, along with, pari passu; in time, on the beat, simultaneously; in concert, in chorus, in unison, with one voice; as soon as, just as, at the moment of, in the same breath 116 *instantaneously*; while, whilst, concomitantly 89 *with*.

## 124 Futurity: prospective time

**N.** *futurity*, future tense; womb of time, time to come, days and years to come; morrow 120 *posteriority*; future, time ahead, prospect, outlook 507 *expectation*; coming events, fate 154 *event*, 155 *destiny*; near future, tomorrow, mañana, the day after tomorrow, next week, next year 121 *present time*, 200 *nearness*; advent 289 *approach*; long run, distant future, remote f., after ages 199 *distance*; future generations, descendants, heirs, heritage 170 *posterity*; successorship 65 *sequence*, 669 *preparation*.

*future state*, what fate holds in store 155 *destiny*, 596 *fate*; latter days, postindustrial age; doomsday, crack of doom 69 *finality*; post-existence, afterlife, life after death, life to come, hereafter, kingdom come 971 *heaven*; damnation 972 *hell*; good time coming, millennium 730 *prosperity*; rebirth, reincarnation 106 *repetition*.

*looking ahead*, anticipation 669 *preparation*; procrastination 136 *delay*; prospect, prospects, outlook 507 *expectation*; great expectations, expectancy 852 *hope*; horoscope, crystal gazing, forecast 511 *prediction*.

**Adj.** *future*, to be, to come; coming, nearing 289 *approaching*; nigh, just round the corner, close at hand 200 *near*; on the horizon, in the wind; due, destined, fated, threatening, imminent, overhanging 155 *impending*; in the future, ahead, yet to come, waiting, millennial 154 *eventual*; in embryo, on the stocks 669 *preparatory*; prospective, designate, earmarked 605 *chosen*; promised, looked for, anticipated 507 *expected*, 471 *probable*; predicted, predictable, foreseeable, sure 473 *certain*; ready to, rising, getting on for; potential, promising 469 *possible*; later, ulterior, posterior 120 *subsequent*.

**Vb.** *be to come*, lie ahead, lie in the future, be for tomorrow; have in store, be destined, threaten, overhang 155 *impend*; near, draw nigh 289 *approach*; be imminent, be just round the corner, cast its shadow before, stare one in the face 200 *be near*; shall, will.

*look ahead*, look forward, see it coming, await 507 *expect*, 852 *hope*; foresee 511 *predict*; anticipate, forestall 135 *be early*; take the long view, take the long-term view, think of the future 669 *prepare oneself*.

**Adv.** *prospectively*, eventually, ultimately, later; in the fullness of time, when the time is ripe, in due course, in the long run, by and by; tomorrow, soon, some day 122 *not now*; hereafter; on the eve of, on the point of, about to; in the wings, in the offing.

*henceforth*, in future, from this time forth, from now on.

## 125 Past time: retrospective time

**N.** *past time* 119 *priority*; retrospection, looking back 505 *remembrance*; past tense, historic t., preterite, perfect, pluperfect 564 *grammar*; the past, recent p., only yesterday 126 *newness*; distant past, history, antiquity; old story, matter of history 127 *oldness*; past times, days of yore, days of old, olden days, good old d., bygone d.; auld lang syne, yesterday, yesteryear, former times; ancien régime; Victorian Age, Elizabethan A., Golden A., Renaissance 110 *era*.

*antiquity*, high a., rust of a., eld; creation, when time began, when the world was young, time immemorial, distance of time, remote ages; prehistory, protohistory, ancient world; medieval times; geological times, Stone Age, prehistoric a., Classical A.; Dark Ages, Middle A. 110 *era*; the ancients, cavemen, Neanderthal man 371 *humankind*; antiquities, relics, eolith, neolith, microlith 41 *remainder*, 127 *archaism*; ruin, ancient monument, megalith, Stonehenge 548 *monument*, 253 *earthwork*; excavation, dig, archaeology 484 *discovery*; museum 632 *collection*; ancient lineage 169 *genealogy*.

*fossil*, fossilized remains *or* relics, petrified forest, trilobite, ammonite; trace fossil, fossil footprint 548 *record*; coal forest 385 *fuel*; sponge, coral 358 *organism*; Neanderthal man 371 *humankind*; mammoth, dinosaur 365 *animal*; fossilization, petrification.

*palaeology*, palaeontology, palaeozoology, palaeobotany, palaeoethnobotany, palaeogeography, palaeobiogeography, palaeobiology, palaeooceanography, palaeoecology, palaeography; palaeoanthropology 371 *humankind*; archaeology, digging up the past; antiquarianism; medievalism; industrial archaeology.

*antiquarian*, palaeontologist, archaeologist; palaeologist, palaeographer; antiquary, Dryasdust 492 *scholar*; historian, prehistorian; medievalist 549 *chronicler*; Egyptologist, Assyriologist, Hebraist, Arabist, Sanskritist, classicist 557 *linguist*; revivalist; archaist, Pre-Raphaelite.

**Adj.** *past*, in the p., historical, of historical interest only; ancient, prehistoric 127 *olden*; early, primitive, proto- 127 *primal*; recently past 126 *new*; wholly past, gone, gone for good, bygone, lost, irrecoverable, dead and buried 506 *forgotten*; passed away, no more, died out, dead as the Dodo 2 *extinct*, 361 *dead*; passé, has been, obsolete 674 *disused*, 127 *antiquated*; fossilized 326 *hard*; over, blown o., done, over and done with, behind one; elapsed, lapsed, expired, run out, ended, finished 69 *ending*; unrenewed, unrevived.

*former*, late, quondam, sometime, ex-119 *prior*; retired, emeritus, outgoing 753 *resigning*; ancestral, ancient, prehistoric 127 *immemorial*; not within living memory.

*preterite*, grammatically past, in the past tense; simple past, past continuous, perfect, imperfect, pluperfect.

*foregoing*, last, latter 64 *preceding*; recent, overnight 126 *new*.

*retrospective*, looking back, backward-looking; archaizing, reminiscing 505 *remembering*; diachronic, historical; retroactive, going back; with hindsight, from experience.

**Vb.** *be past*, have elapsed, have expired; have run its course, have had its day, be burnt out; pass, die, elapse, blow over, be o., be at an end 69 *end*; be a dead letter.

*look back*, trace back, cast the eyes b.; antiquarianize, archaeologize, dig up the past, exhume; put the clock back, turn back time, go back to the past, archaize, hark back 505 *retrospect*.

**Adv.** *formerly*, aforetime, of old, of yore; time was, ago, in olden times; long ago, long since; a long while, a long time ago; once upon a time; years ago, ages a. 127 *anciently*; lately, some time ago, some time back; yesterday, the day before yesterday; yestreen, yestereve, yesteryear; last year, last season, last month, last week; in old money.

*retrospectively*, retroactively; historically speaking; before now, up to now, hitherto; no longer; from time immemorial, time out of mind; already, yet; till now, up to this time 121 *until now*; ex post facto.

## 126 Newness

**N.** *newness*, recency, recentness; recent date, recent occurrence, recent past 125 *past time*, 121 *present time*; innovation, neoterism 560 *neology*, 21 *originality*; novelty, gloss of n.; freshness, dewiness 648 *cleanness*; greenness, immaturity, callowness, rawness 130 *youth*; renovation, restoration, renewal, resurrection 656 *revival*; clean slate, new leaf, new broom.

*modernism*, modernity, modernness, modernization; up-to-dateness, topicality, contemporaneity 121 *present time*; the latest, the latest thing, the in-thing, latest fashion; the last word, dernier cri; new look, contemporary style, trendiness 848 *fashion*.

*modernist*, neologist, neologian, neoteric, neophiliac, futurist; advanced thinker, avant-garde; bright young thing, trendy, yuppy, baby-boomer; modern generation, younger g.

*upstart*, novus homo, parvenu, nouveau arrivé, nouveau riche 847 *vulgarian*; Johnny-come-lately 297 *incomer*.

**Adj.** *new*, newish, recent, of recent date, of recent occurrence, overnight; upstart, nouveau arrivé, mushroom; novel, inventive, innovative, unhackneyed, unprecedented, unheard of 21 *original*; brand-new, spick and span, like new, in mint condition 648 *clean*; green, evergreen, dewy, juicy, sappy 128 *vernal*; fresh, fresh as a daisy, fresh as paint; maiden, virgin, virginal; newborn 130 *young*; raw, unfledged, callow 670 *immature*; just out, just published, hot from the press; new-made, new-laid; straight from the oven, factory-fresh; untouched by human hand; unused, first-hand; untried, untrodden, unbeaten, unexplored 491 *unknown*; untested 461 *experimental*; not broken in, not yet run in; budding, fledgeling, aspiring, wannabe (inf) 68 *beginning*.

*modern*, late, latter-day; contemporary, topical 121 *present*; up-to-the-minute, up-to-date, bang up-to-date, with it; à la mode, in the latest fashion, trendy 848 *fashionable*; ultramodern, modernistic, advanced, avant-garde, futuristic, untraditional, nontraditional, revolutionary; innovating, innovative, neo-

teric, newfangled, new-fashioned, state-of-the-art, cutting-edge, leading-edge 560 *neological*.

*modernized*, renewed, renovated, rejuvenated, refurbished, repainted 656 *restored*; given a new look, given a new lease of life, brought up to date, revised; looking like new, freshened up 648 *clean*.

**Vb.** *modernize*, do up; update, bring up to date, give a new lease of life; have the new look, go modern, go contemporary, get with it; move with the times 285 *progress*.

**Adv.** *newly*, freshly, afresh, anew, like new; fresh-, new-; recently, overnight, just now, only yesterday; not long ago, a short time a.; lately, latterly, of late.

## 127 Oldness

**N.** *oldness*, primitiveness 68 *beginning*; olden times 110 *era*; age, hoary a.; eld; cobwebs of antiquity, dust of ages, ruins 125 *antiquity*; maturity, mellowness 129 *autumn*; decline, rust 51 *decay*; senility 131 *old age*; eldership 131 *seniority*.

*archaism*, antiquities 125 *antiquity*; ancien régime; thing of the past, relic of the p.; listed building, ancient monument; museum piece, antique, heirloom, bygone, Victoriana; dodo, dinosaur 125 *fossil*; oldie, golden o.; old fogy, old fossil, fuddy-duddy, crumbly; archaist, square, old-timer, has-been, back number.

*tradition*, lore, folklore, mythology; inveteracy, custom, prescription, immemorial usage 610 *habit*; common law, smriti, Sunna, Hadith; ancient wisdom, the way of our forefathers; word of mouth 579 *speech*.

**Adj.** *olden*, old, ancient, antique, antiquarian, of historical interest; veteran, vintage; venerable, patriarchal; archaic, ancient; time-worn, ruined; prehistoric, mythological, heroic, classic, Hellenic, Byzantine, feudal, medieval, Saxon, Norman, Romanesque, Gothic, Tudor, Elizabethan, Jacobean, Georgian, Regency, Victorian; historical 125 *past*, 866 *renowned*.

*primal*, prime, primitive, primeval, primordial, aboriginal 68 *beginning*; geological, preglacial, fossil, palaeozoic 110 *secular*; eolithic, palaeolithic, mesolithic, neolithic; early, proto-, dawn-, eo-; antemundane, pre-adamite, antediluvian, before the Flood.

*immemorial*, ancestral, traditional, time-honoured 610 *habitual*; venerable 866 *worshipful*; inveterate, rooted, established, long-standing 153 *fixed*; Ogygian, old as the hills, old as Adam, old as Methuselah, old as history, old as time, age-old 113 *lasting*.

*antiquated*, of other times, of another age,

archaic, in old money; old-world, old-time; olde worlde, ye olde –; prewar, interwar 119 *prior*; anachronistic, archaistic, archaizing 125 *retrospective*; fossilized, ossified, static 144 *permanent*; behind the times, out of date, out of fashion, dated, antediluvian, before the Flood, out of the ark, horse-and-buggy, silent-screen, black-and-white; conservative, Victorian, old-fashioned, old-school, square, not with it; outworn, outdated, outmoded; passé, démodé, vieux jeu, old hat; gone by 125 *past*; decayed, perished 655 *dilapidated*; rusty, moth-eaten, crumbling; mildewed, moss-grown, mouldering 51 *decomposed*; fusty, stale, secondhand; obsolete, obsolescent; superseded, superannuated 674 *disused*; old 131 *ageing*.

**Vb.** *be old*, – antiquated etc. adj.; go back in time, belong to the past, have had its day, be burnt out 69 *end*; age 131 *grow old*; decline, fade, wither 655 *deteriorate*; fossilize; moulder, rot, rust, decay 51 *decompose*.

**Adv.** *anciently*, since the world was made *or* was young, since the year dot, since the days of Methuselah, before the Flood 125 *formerly*.

## 128 Morning. Spring. Summer

**N.** *morning*, morn, forenoon, a.m.; small hours, wee sma' hours (Scots) 135 *earliness*; breakfast-time, drive-time; matins, prime, tierce; dawn, false d., dawning, morning twilight, cockcrow, dawn chorus 66 *precursor*; sunrise, sun-up, daybreak, dayspring 417 *light*; peep of day, break of d.; first blush of day; daylight, daytime; full day, full light of day, prime of the morning; Aurora, Eos, 'rosy-fingered Dawn';

> Now when the child of morning, rosy-fingered Dawn, appeared, Telemachus rose and dressed himself.
>
> Homer, *The Odyssey*

daystar, orb of day 321 *sun*.

*noon*, high noon, meridian, midday, noonday, noontide; eight bells, twelve o'clock, twelve noon.

*spring*, springtime, springtide, Eastertide, vernal season, spring s., seed-time, blossom-time, maying; first cuckoo; vernal equinox, first point of Aries.

*summer* 379 *heat*; summertime, summertide, Whitsuntide; midsummer, summer solstice, longest day, Midsummer's Day, high summer, dog days; haymaking; aestivation; Indian summer, St Luke's s., St Martin's s.

**Adj.** *matinal*, matutinal, morning, forenoon; diurnal, daytime; auroral, dawning, fresh, dewy 135 *early*; antemeridian; noon, meridian.

*vernal*, equinoctial, spring; springlike, sappy, juicy, flowering, florescent 130 *young*.

*summery*, summer, aestival 379 *warm*.

**Adv.** *at sunrise*, at dawn of day, at daybreak, at first light, at crack of dawn; with the lark; past midnight, in the small hours, in the wee sma' hours (Scots); a.m.

## 129 Evening. Autumn. Winter

**N.** *evening*, eventide, even, eve, dewy e.; evensong, vespers, afternoon, p.m.; teatime, drive-time; matinée; afternoon tea, five o'clock; sundowner, soirée; dog-watches; sunset, sundown, setting sun, going down of the sun; evening star, Hesperus, Vesper; dusk, crepuscule, twilight, gloaming 419 *half-light*; candle-light, cockshut, dewfall; moonrise, moonset 321 *moon*; close of day, nightfall, darkfall, dark, blind man's holiday, nighttime, night-owl 418 *darkness*; bedtime 679 *sleep*; curfew, last post 136 *lateness*, 69 *finality*.

*midnight*, dead of night, witching hour, witching time; night-watch, small hours, wee sma' hours (Scots).

*autumn*, back-end, fall, fall of the leaf; harvest, harvest-time; harvest moon, hunter's m.; Michaelmas; Indian summer; autumnal equinox; 'season of mists and mellow fruitfulness'.

> Season of mists and mellow fruitfulness,
>   Close bosom-friend of the maturing sun;
> Conspiring with him how to load and bless
>   With fruit the vines that round the thatch-eaves run.
>
> John Keats, *To Autumn*

*winter* 380 *wintriness*; wintertime, wintertide; Advent; Christmas, Yule, Yuletide; Kwanzaa; midwinter, winter solstice, shortest day; hibernation; Advent calendar, Christmas cake, Christmas card, Christmas cracker, Christmas lights, Christmas party, Christmas present, Christmas tree, Father Christmas, Santa Claus, Yule log.

**Adj.** *vespertine*, afternoon, postmeridian; vesperal, evening; twilight, dusky, crepuscular 418 *dark*, 419 *dim*; nightly, nocturnal, noctivagant; benighted, late; bedtime.

*autumnal*, equinoctial.

*wintry*, winter, brumal, brumous, snowbound 380 *cold*; leafless, stark, bleak.

**Adv.** *post meridiem*, late, late at night; at night, by n.; all through the night.

## 130 Youth

**N.** *youth*, freshness, juiciness, sappiness 126 *newness*, 174 *vigorousness*; young blood, youthfulness, youngness, juvenility, juvenescence; juniority 35 *inferiority*; babyhood, infancy, childhood, childish years, tender age 68 *beginning*; puppyhood, puppy fat; boyhood, girlhood; one's teens, adolescence, pubescence, age of puberty, boyishness, girlishness, awkward age, growing pains; younger generation, rising g., yoof (inf), middle youth, young idea 132 *youngster*; growing boy *or* girl, minor, ward; Peter Pan.

*nonage*, tender age, immaturity, minority, infancy, pupillage, wardship, leading strings; cradle, nursery, kindergarten.

*salad days*, school d., student d., college d., happiest days of one's life; heyday, heyday of the blood, springtime of youth; prime of life, flower of l., bloom, bloom of youth, florescence.

**Adj.** *young*, youthful, childlike, boyish, girlish; virginal, maidenly, sweet-sixteen; adolescent, pubescent; teenage, preteen, subteenage, juvenile; maturing, developing, growing; budding, burgeoning, blooming, flowering 128 *vernal*; beardless, unripe, green, callow, awkward, raw, unfledged 670 *immature*; school-age, under-age, minor, infant, preschool; younger, minor, junior, puis-né, cadet; youngest; childish 132 *infantine*; juvenescent; young at heart, ever-young, evergreen, ageless.

## 131 Age

**N.** *age*, one's age, time of life, years, lifespan 113 *long duration*.

*middle age*, middle years, middle life, middle youth, adultescent, sandwich generation; riper years, years of discretion 134 *adultness*; maturity, prime of life; a certain age, climacteric, change of life, the change, menopause, male m., andropause, mid-life crisis; middle-aged spread.

*old age*, anno domini; pensionable age, retirement age; advanced years, three-score years and ten, allotted span, grey hairs, white hairs 133 *old person*; senescence, declining years, vale of years, evening of one's days, autumn *or* winter of life; infirmity, debility 163 *weakness*; second childhood, dotage, anecdotage, caducity, anility, senility 655 *deterioration*; longevity, green old age, ripe old age.

*seniority*, old man's privilege 64 *precedence*; primogeniture 119 *priority*; higher rank 34 *superiority*; eldership, deanship; doyen; gerontocracy, elders, presbytery, senate 692 *council*; ageism.

*gerontology*, nostology, geriatrics, care of the aged 658 *therapy*; old people's home, sheltered housing, eventide home.

**Adj.** *ageing*, aged, old, elderly, matronly; middle-aged, ripe, mature, mellow 669 *matured*; overblown, overripe, run *or* gone to seed; of a certain age, not so young as one was, no chicken, past one's prime; adultescent; get-

ting on, getting old, going grey, greying; white-haired, grey-h., hoary, hoary-headed, long in the tooth; senescent, waning, declining, moribund 361 *dying*; wrinkled, lined, marked with crow's feet, rheumy-eyed, toothless, shrivelled, wizened, decrepit, rickety 655 *deteriorated*; drivelling, doddering, gaga 499 *foolish*; senile, anile, failing, with softening of the brain; full of years, advanced in y., stricken in y., living on borrowed time, with one foot in the grave; longeval, old as the hills, old as Methuselah, old as Adam; well-preserved 650 *healthy*; venerable, patriarchal 920 *respected*; so many years old, turned, rising; too old, past it; retired 681 *leisurely*; superannuated, passé(e) 127 *antiquated*; gerontologic, geriatric.

*older*, major; elder, senior 34 *superior*; firstborn, eldest, primogenital 119 *prior*; eldest, maximus.

**Vb.** *grow old*, age; show one's years, have seen better days, be past one's prime, be getting on, go grey, turn white; pass three-score years and ten, pass the allotted span, have one foot in the grave.

## 132 Young person. Young animal. Young plant

**N.** *child*; embryo, pre-embryo, foetus 156 *source*; babe, baby, bundle of joy; infant, nursling, suckling, weanling, fosterling; bairn, little one, tiny tot, little chap, mite, moppet, toddler; brat, kid, kiddie; papoose, bambino; little darling, little angel, little monkey, little imp, imp of mischief; cherub, young innocent; changeling; children, small fry.

*youngster*, juvenile, young person, young adult, young hopeful, young'un; young people, yoof (inf) 130 *youth*; boy, schoolboy, stripling, adolescent; youth, young man, lad, laddie, sonny; urchin, nipper, cub, young shaver, whippersnapper; toyboy, hobbledehoy, yob, yobbo; Ted, mod, rocker, punk, skinhead; girl, young woman; schoolgirl, lass, lassie, missie, wench, maid, maiden, virgin; chit, slip, chick, miss; teenager, tweenager, sub-teen, teenybopper, weenybopper; groupie; tomboy, hoyden, ladette; little minx, baggage; colleen, mademoiselle, damsel, nymph, nymphet.

*young creature* (see also *child*); young animal 365 *animal*, *bird*; yearling; puppy, pup, whelp; cub (badger, bear, fox, leopard, lion, otter, tiger); kitten (beaver, cat, rabbit); foal (horse, zebra), colt, filly; piglet, pigling; lamb, lambkin; calf, heifer; kid; fawn; calf (camel, elephant, elk, giraffe, hippopotamus, moose, reindeer, rhinoceros, seal, whale); pup (rat, seal, walrus); joey (kangaroo, possum, wallaby); kit (ferret, fox, weasel); leveret (hare); fledgling, nestling; chick, chicken, pullet; duckling, gosling, cygnet; eyas, squab; tadpole, polliwog; elver (eel); alevin, fingerling, fry, grilse, parr, smolt (salmon); brood, clutch, farrow, fry, litter, spawn; larva, pupa, nymph; caterpillar, grub; chrysalis, cocoon; spiderling.

*young plant*, seedling, set; sucker, runner, spur, shoot, offshoot, sprout, slip; twig, sprig, scion, sapling 366 *plant*.

**Adj.** *infantine*, baby, infantile, babyish, childish, childlike; juvenile, boyish, girlish 130 *young*; kittenish, coltish, hoydenish; newborn, new-fledged, unfledged 126 *new*; in the cradle, in arms, in nappies, at the breast; small, knee-high, half-grown 196 *little*.

## 133 Old person

**N.** *old person*, elderly p., retired p., pensioner, old-age p., O.A.P., senior citizen; old dear, old body; sexagenarian, septuagenarian, octogenarian, nonagenarian, centenarian; Methuselah.

*old man*, old gentleman, elderly g., patriarch, elder statesman, Nestor 500 *sage*; grandsire, grandfather, grandad 169 *paternity*; veteran, old soldier, old hand, old stager, old trouper, old-timer 696 *expert*; oldster, old'un, old boy, gaffer, greybeard; old geezer, o. codger, o. buffer, dotard; old fogy, fossil 127 *archaism*.

*old woman*, old lady, elderly l., dowager; grandmother, grandma, gran, granny; old girl, old trout, old duck, old bag; old dutch 894 *spouse*; no spring chicken, mutton dressed as lamb; gammer, crone, hag, beldam, witch.

*old couple*, Darby and Joan, Philemon and Baucis, the old folks.

## 134 Adultness

**N.** *adultness*, adulthood, grown-upness, maturation, development 669 *preparedness*; riper years, years of discretion, matureness; age of consent, legal age, age of reason, voting age, majority, full age, man's *or* woman's estate; manhood, womanhood, virility, nubility 372 *male*, 373 *female*; badge of manhood, beard, toga virilis, key of the door; maturity, prime, prime of life 131 *middle age*; bloom, florescence; meridian of life, floruit.

*adult*, grown-up, big boy, big girl; man, gentleman 372 *male*; woman, lady, matron 373 *female*; youth, stripling.

**Adj.** *grown-up*, adult, post-pubescent, out of one's teens; major, of age, at the age of consent, responsible, old enough to know better; mature, fully-developed, full-grown 669 *matured*; nubile 894 *marriageable*; virile, manly 372 *male*; womanly, matronly 373 *female*;

blooming, florescent, full-blown, in full bloom, full-fledged; in one's prime, at one's peak 130 *young*; adult, X-rated, 18.

**Vb.** *come of age*, grow up, mature 36 *grow*; be grown up, reach man's *or* woman's estate, attain one's majority, have a vote, have the key of the door; reach the age of consent; grow a beard, put one's hair up; leave home, fly the nest; fend for oneself, earn one's living.

## 135 Earliness

**N.** *earliness*, early hour, unearthly h., prime 128 *morning*; beginnings, early stage, primitiveness 68 *beginning*; early riser, early bird; early comer, first arrival 66 *precursor*; primitive, aborigine, original settler, earliest inhabitant 191 *native*.

*punctuality*, timeliness 137 *occasion*; dispatch, promptitude 678 *activity*; immediacy 116 *instantaneousness*.

*anticipation*, prevenience, a stitch in time 510 *foresight*, 669 *preparation*; prematurity, early maturity, precocity; forestalling 64 *precedence*.

**Adj.** *early*, bright and e., good and e., in the small hours, in the wee sma' hours; prevenient, previous 119 *prior*, timely, in time, on t., in good t., punctual, prompt; forward, advance, in advance; advanced, precocious, ahead of its time 126 *new*; summary, sudden, immediate 116 *instantaneous*, 508 *unexpected*; expected soon, coming shortly, next on the list, forthcoming, ready 669 *prepared*; impending, imminent, at hand 200 *near*; too early, premature 670 *immature*.

**Vb.** *be early*, – premature etc. adj.; be betimes, be beforehand etc. adv.; anticipate, nip in the bud; forestall, pre-empt, get there first 64 *come before*; seize the occasion, take the opportunity, take time by the forelock; gain the start, corner the market, steal a march on, catch napping 306 *outdo*; engage, book, pre-empt, reserve, pay in advance; secure, order, bespeak; expedite 277 *accelerate*; lose no time 680 *hasten*; be precocious, ripen early; start too soon, jump the gun; put the clock forward, gain time, gain, go fast.

**Adv.** *betimes*, early, soon, anon; before long; first thing, at the first opportunity; with time to spare; punctually, to the minute, in time, in good time, in due time; time enough.

*beforehand*, in advance, in anticipation; without waiting, precipitately 680 *hastily*; precociously, prematurely, untimely, too soon, before one's time.

*suddenly*, without notice 508 *unexpectedly*; without delay 116 *instantaneously*; at the sight of; before the ink was dry; forthwith, shortly, right away, directly; at short notice, at the drop of a hat.

## 136 Lateness

**N.** *lateness*, late hour, small hours, wee sma' hours (Scots) 129 *midnight*; high time, eleventh hour, last minute; unreadiness, backwardness, slow development 670 *nonpreparation*, 499 *unintelligence*; tardiness, lagging, dragging one's feet 278 *slowness*; afterthought, delayed reaction, esprit de l'escalier 67 *sequel*; late-comer, last arrival; late developer 538 *learner*; slow starter, late riser 278 *slowcoach*; lie-abed, laggard 679 *idler*; Fabius Cunctator.

*delay*, cunctation, Fabian policy, 'wait and see' 858 *caution*; delaying tactics, prolongation, gaining time, dragging out, obstruction, stone-walling, filibustering, filibuster 113 *protraction*, 702 *hindrance*; deceleration, retardation, check 278 *slowness*; detention, holdup 747 *restraint*; postponement, adjournment, cooling-off period; prorogation, remand, pause; truce, time lag, jet lag 145 *lull*; deferment, mora-torium, respite, days of grace; suspension, stay, stay of execution; suspension of penalty, reprieve 752 *abrogation*; putting off, procrasti-nation, mañana 679 *sluggishness*; dilatoriness, law's delays, bureaucracy, red tape, form-filling 678 *overactivity*; shelving, pigeonholing, put-ting on ice, putting on hold, cold storage 679 *inactivity*.

**Adj.** *late*, late in the day, eleventh-hour, last-minute, deathbed; too late, time up; overdue, delayed, belated, benighted; held up, bogged down 702 *hindered*; behindhand, lagging, after time, behind t., behind schedule; sluggish, tardy; backward 278 *slow*; Fabian 858 *cautious*; unready, unpunctual, never on time; procrasti-nating, dilatory 679 *inactive*; delayed-action; deferred etc. vb.; on ice, on hold, in cold storage, posthumous 120 *subsequent*.

**Vb.** *be late*, sit up late, rise late, keep late hours, burn the midnight oil, burn the candle at both ends; lag, lag behind 284 *follow*; stay, tarry, take one's time, drag one's feet, be long about it, linger, dawdle, saunter, loiter 278 *move slowly*; hang about, hang around, hang back 679 *be inactive*; dally, dilly-dally, kick one's heels; miss a chance, miss the boat, lose an opportunity, let the moment pass, over-sleep 138 *lose a chance*; be behindhand, have leeway to make up, have a backlog; put the clock back, turn back time, not move with the times 125 *look back*; be losing, lose, stop (clock).

*wait* 507 *await*; bide, stay, bide one's time, hold one's horses, take one's time, wait and see 145 *pause*; sleep on it, consult one's pillow 677

*not act*; hang on, hold on, hold the line; stand about, sit a., hang a.; be kept waiting, wait impatiently, cool one's heels; count to ten.

*be pending*, drag 113 *drag on*; hang fire, hang in the balance, tremble in the b. 474 *be uncer-tain*; stand, stand over, stay put 266 *be quies-cent*; play a waiting game.

*put off*, defer, postpone, adjourn; keep, reserve, hold over; keep pending, file, pigeon-hole; table, lay on the t.; shelve, put in cold storage, keep on ice; remand, send back; sus-pend, hold in abeyance, hold in reserve; grant respite, reprieve 909 *forgive*; procrastinate, pro-tract, delay, retard, set back, hold up, gain time, stonewall, filibuster 113 *spin out*; temp-orize, tide over; stall, keep one waiting, with-hold 760 *refuse*.

**Adv.** *late*, after time, behind t.; late in the day, at sunset, at the eleventh hour, at the last minute, last thing; at length, at last, at long l., ultimately; till all hours; too late, too late for 138 *inopportunely*.

*tardily*, slowly, leisurely, deliberately, at one's leisure.

## 137 Occasion: timeliness

**N.** *occasion*, happy chance 154 *event*; meeting of events, juncture, conjuncture 181 *concur-rence*; timeliness, opportuneness, readiness, ripeness; fittingness 24 *fitness*, 642 *good policy*; just the time, just the moment; right time, proper t., suitable season; auspicious hour, moment, well-chosen m., well-timed initiative; high time, nick of t., eleventh hour 136 *lateness*.

*opportunity*, given time, borrowed t. 759 *offer*; favourable opportunity, fine o., golden o. 469 *possibility*; one's chance, break, lucky moment, piece of luck 159 *chance*; best chance 605 *choice*; only chance 606 *no choice*; opening, look-in, room, elbow r., field 744 *scope*; liberty, independence, freedom of choice 744 *freedom*; convenience, spare time 681 *leisure*; no obstacle, clear field, clear stage 159 *fair chance*; handle, lever, instrument 630 *tool*, 629 *means*; stepping-stone 624 *bridge*.

*crisis*, critical time, key point, key moment, defining m.; turning point, psychological moment, crucial m, crux, emergency, extremity, pressure, pinch, push 700 *predica-ment*; eleventh hour, last minute 136 *lateness*.

**Adj.** *timely*, in time, within the time limit; on time, to the minute, on the dot, punctual 135 *early*; seasonable, welcome, well-timed; just in time, not before time, in the nick of t., at the eleventh hour.

*opportune*, favourable, providential, heaven-sent, auspicious, propitious; fortunate, lucky, happy 730 *prosperous*; for the occasion, fitting 24 *apt*, 642 *advisable*; as occasion requires, occasional 140 *infrequent*.

*crucial*, critical, key, momentous, climactic, pivotal, gut, decisive 638 *important*.

**Vb.** *profit by*, improve the occasion; seize the chance, grab the c., take the opportunity, make an opening, create an o.; take time by the forelock, carpe diem, strike while the iron is hot, make hay while the sun shines; spare the time for; cash in on, capitalize, exploit, turn to good account 673 *use*.

**Adv.** *opportunely*, seasonably, in proper time, in due time, timely, in proper course, in due c., in the fullness *or* ripeness of time; in due season; at the right time, all in good time; in the nick of time, just in time, at the eleventh hour, at the last minute, now or never.

*incidentally*, by the way, by the by; en passant, apropos; parenthetically, by way of parenthesis; while speaking of, while on this subject, talking of, that reminds me; on the spur of the moment, for this occasion.

**138 Untimeliness**
**N.** *untimeliness*, wrong time, unsuitable t., improper t., inopportuneness, unseasonableness 643 *inexpedience*; mishap, contretemps; evil hour 731 *misfortune*; off day, time of the month; intrusion, interruption, disturbance 72 *discontinuity*; mistiming 118 *anachronism*.

**Adj.** *ill-timed*, mistimed, misjudged, ill-judged, ill-advised 481 *misjudging*; out-of-turn, untimely, untoward; interrupting, intrusive; malapropos, inconvenient, unsuited 25 *unapt*, 643 *inexpedient*; unseasonable, off-season; unpunctual, not in time 136 *late*; premature, too soon for 135 *early*; wise after the event 118 *anachronistic*.

*inopportune*, untoward, inauspicious, unpropitious, unfavourable, ill-omened, ill-starred, unlucky, unhappy, unfortunate 731 *adverse*.

**Vb.** *mistime*, time it *or* things badly 481 *misjudge*; intrude, disturb, break in upon, burst in on, find engaged.

*be engaged*, be too busy, be occupied, be not at home; be otherwise engaged, have a previous engagement, have other fish to fry 678 *be busy*.

*lose a chance*, waste time, miss the bus, miss the boat, miss the train 728 *fail*; drop a sitter, bungle 695 *be unskilful*; oversleep, lose the opportunity, lose one's chance, let the opportunity slip, let the occasion pass 136 *be late*; allow to lapse, let slip through one's fingers 458 *neglect*; spoil a good chance, stand in one's

own light, shut the stable door after the horse has bolted 695 *act foolishly*.

**Adv.** *inopportunely*, amiss; as ill luck would have it, in an evil hour; a day after the fair.

**139 Frequency**
**N.** *frequency*, rapid succession, rapid fire 71 *continuity*; oftenness, unfailing regularity 141 *periodicity*; doubling, redoubling 106 *repetition*; frequenting, haunting, regular visits, assiduous attendance.

**Adj.** *frequent*, recurrent 106 *repeated*; common, of common occurrence, not rare 104 *many*; thick on the ground 104 *multitudinous*; incessant, perpetual, continual, nonstop, constant, sustained, steady 146 *unceasing*; regular, hourly 141 *periodical*; haunting, frequenting, assiduous 610 *habitual*.

**Vb.** *recur* 106 *reoccur*; do nothing but; keep, keep on, fire away 146 *go on*, 106 *repeat oneself*; frequent, haunt 882 *visit*; preoccupy, obsess; plague, pester 827 *trouble*.

**Adv.** *often*, oft, many a time, time after t., time and time again, times out of number, times without n.; a thousand t.; frequently, commonly, generally; more often than not; not seldom, not infrequently, again and again 106 *repeatedly*; in quick succession, in rapid succession; thick and fast; regularly, daily, hourly, every hour, every minute; in innumerable cases, in the majority of c., in many instances; as often as you like, ad libitum.

*perpetually*, continually, constantly, incessantly, steadily, without ceasing, without respite 71 *continuously*; at all times, daily and hourly, night and day, day and night, day after day, day in, day out, morning, noon and night, 24/7; ever and anon.

*sometimes*, occasionally, every so often, once in a while; at times, now and then, now and again, every now and again; from time to time, often enough, more often than not.

**140 Infrequency**
**N.** *infrequency*, rareness, rarity 105 *fewness*; seldomness, uncommonness; intermittence 72 *discontinuity*; phoenix 365 *mythical beast*.

**Adj.** *infrequent*, uncommon, sporadic, occasional; intermittent, few and far between 72 *discontinuous*; scarce, rare, scarce *or* rare as hen's teeth, rare as a blue diamond 105 *few*; almost unobtainable, like gold dust 811 *of price*; almost unheard of, unprecedented 84 *unusual*; not to be repeated; single 88 *one*.

**Adv.** *seldom*, little, once in a while, once in a way; rarely, scarcely, hardly, only sometimes, only occasionally; not often, infrequently; scarcely ever, hardly e., once in a blue moon,

once in a month of Sundays; once, once for all,
just this once, once only; like angel's visits, few
and far between.

### 141 Periodicity: regularity of recurrence

**N.** *periodicity*, regularity, punctuality, regularity
of recurrence, rhythm, steadiness, evenness 16
*uniformity*; timing, phasing, serialization 71 *continuity*; alternation, turn and turn about, shot
about; reciprocity 12 *correlation*; tidal flow, ebb
and f., alternating current, AC, wave movement, tidal m. 317 *fluctuation*; to-and-fro movement, pendulum m., piston m., shuttle m.;
shuttle service; shuttle diplomacy; pulsation,
pulse, tick, beat, throb, rhythm, swing 317
*oscillation*; chorus, refrain 106 *recurrence*;
drumbeat, tattoo 403 *roll*; tide 350 *wave*; rate
of pulsation, frequency, wave f.; turn, go,
round, circuit, lap; shift, relay 110 *period*;
cycle.

*regular return*, rota, cycle, circuit, revolution,
life cycle, wheel of life 314 *circuition*, 315
*rotation*; biorhythm; menstrual cycle, menses;
yearly cycle, seasons 128 *morning*, 129 *evening*;
fixed interval, stated time 110 *period*; routine,
daily round 60 *order*, 610 *habit*; days of the
week, months of the year; leap year.

*anniversary*, birthday, saint's day, jubilee,
silver j., diamond j., wedding anniversary,
silver wedding, ruby w., golden w., diamond
w.; centenary, sesquicentenary, bicentenary,
tercentenary, quatercentenary, quincentenary,
millennium; St George's Day, St Andrew's D.,
St Patrick's D., St David's D., St Valentine's Day
988 *holy day*; Sovereign's Birthday, Fourth of
July, Independence Day, 14 Juillet, Bastille Day
876 *special day*.

**Adj.** *periodical*, periodic, cyclic, circling,
revolving 315 *rotary*; tidal, fluctuating 317 *oscillating*; measured, rhythmical, isochronal, isochronous, steady, even, regular, constant,
punctual, clocklike, like clockwork 81 *regular*;
breathing, pulsating, pulsatory, pulsatile;
throbbing, beating 318 *agitated*; recurrent,
recurring, intermittent, sporadic, spasmodic,
on-again-off-again, remittent 106 *repeated*;
reciprocal, alternate, alternating 12 *correlative*;
serial, successive, serialized 65 *sequential*, 71
*continuous*.

*seasonal*, anniversary; paschal, lenten; at
fixed intervals, hourly, daily, nightly, diurnal,
semi-diurnal, quotidian, tertian, biweekly,
weekly, hebdomadal, hebdomadary, fort-
nightly, monthly; menstrual; yearly, annual,
biennial, triennial, quadrennial, quinquennial,
sextennial, septennial, octennial, decennial;
bissextile; centennial, sesquicentennial, bicen-

tennial, tercentennial, quadricentennial,
quincentennial, millennial; secular.

**Vb.** *be periodic*, recur 106 *reoccur*; serialize,
recur in regular order, recur in constant succession 60 *be in order*, 71 *run on*, 65 *come after*;
turn, revolve, circle 315 *rotate*; return, come
round again; take its turn, alternate; be intermittent, intermit; reciprocate 12 *correlate*; fluctuate, undulate 317 *oscillate*; beat, pulse,
pulsate, throb 318 be agitated; heave, pant 352
*breathe*; swing, sway 217 *hang*; ply, go and
return, shuttle, commute 610 *be wont*.

**Adv.** *periodically*, rhythmically etc. adj.; regularly, at regular intervals, at stated times; at
fixed periods, at established p.; punctually etc.
adj.; seasonally, hourly, daily, on a daily basis,
weekly, monthly, yearly; per diem, per annum;
at intervals, intermittently, sporadically, spasmodically, fitfully, every now and then, every
so often, every once in a while, ever and anon.

*by turns*, in turn, in rotation, turn and turn
about, shot about, spell a., alternately, every
other day, off and on; round and round, to
and fro, up and down, from side to side.

### 142 Fitfulness: irregularity of recurrence

**N.** *fitfulness*, irregularity, randomness of recurrence 61 *disorder*; jerkiness, fits and starts 17
*nonuniformity*, 318 *spasm*; remission 114 *transience*, 72 *discontinuity*; unsteadiness, inconstancy, variability 152 *changeableness*, 143
*change*; whimsicality, capriciousness, April
weather, unpredictability 604 *caprice*; eccentricity; wobbling, staggering, lurching 317 *oscillation*.

**Adj.** *fitful*, periodic, remittent, intermittent,
on-off, on-again-off-again, stop-go 72 *discontinuous*; irregular 84 *unconformable*; uneven 29
*unequal*; occasional 140 *infrequent*; unrhythmical, unsteady, unstable, fluttering 17 *nonuniform*; inconstant, uncertain, unpunctual;
variable, vicissitudinous, veering 152
*changeful*; spasmodic, jerky, restless 318 *agitated*; wobbling, halting, wavering, flickering,
guttering, desultory, unsystematic 61 *orderless*;
erratic, eccentric, moody 604 *capricious*.

**Adv.** *fitfully*, irregularly etc. adj.; unevenly,
by fits and starts, every once in a while, now
and then 72 *discontinuously*.

SECTION SEVEN

## Change

### 143 Change: difference at different times

**N.** *change*, alteration, variation 12 *correlation*,

15 *difference*; mutation, permutation, modulation, inflexion, declension; frequent change, mutability, variability 152 *changeableness*; partial change, adjustment, modification, process, repackaging, treatment 468 *qualification*; total change, sea change 147 *conversion*; sudden change, violent c. 149 *revolution*; break, break with the past, innovation, new look, makeover 126 *newness*; 'winds of change';

> The wind of change is blowing through this continent [Africa].
> Harold Macmillan

change for the better, reformation 654 *improvement*; change for the worse, dumbing-down (inf) 655 *deterioration*; change of direction, U-turn, diversion, shift, turn 282 *deviation*, 286 *regression*; change of position, relocation, transition 305 *passage*; change of staff, turnover, staff t., churn; rate of change, churn rate; translation, transposition 151 *interchange*, 272 *transference*; alternation 141 *periodicity*; eversion, overthrow 221 *inversion*; catalysis, leavening; change of mind, c. of heart 603 *tergiversation*; change of status, mutualization, demutualization.

*transformation*, transfiguration, transfigurement; unrecognizability, transmogrification; sea change, metamorphosis, geological m., metasomatism; metabolism, anabolism, catabolism; transmutation, transubstantiation 147 *conversion*; metempsychosis, transmigration of souls; reincarnation, avatar; version, adaptation, transcription, translation 520 *interpretation*, 521 *misinterpretation*.

*alterer*, alterant, alterative; activator, converter, transformer; catalytic agent, catalyst, enzyme, ferment, leaven; adapter, modifier, reviser, editor; censor, bowdlerizer; alchemist, chemist; tailor, dressmaker, decorator, dyer; changer; magician 983 *sorcerer*; kaleidoscope 437 variegation; weathercock, renegade 603 *tergiversator*; improver, new broom 654 *reformer*; bad influence, bad apple 612 *motivator*.

**Adj.** *changeable*, variable, mutable; fickle 604 *capricious*; affected, changed etc. vb.; newfangled 126 *new*; transitional, provisional, modifiable, qualifiable; alternative, transmutative; chequered, kaleidoscopic 437 *variegated*.

**Vb.** *change*, be changed, alter 152 *vary*; wax and wane 36 *grow*, 37 *decrease*; change one's clothes; change colour, change countenance 426 *lose colour*; change one's tune 603 *change one's mind*; vacillate, wobble 474 *be uncertain*; blow hot and cold, chop and change, channel-hop, channel-graze 604 *be capricious*; turn, shift, veer, change course, do a U-turn 282 *deviate*; change the rules, move the goalposts; relocate, change jobs, change careers,

seek pastures new, downshift, make a transition, pass to 305 *pass*; take a turn, turn the corner 656 *be restored*; turn over a new leaf, be converted 654 *get better*; submit to change 83 *conform*; move with the times 126 *modernize*.

*modify*, alter, vary, modulate, diversify, shift the scene 437 *variegate*; superimpose 38 *add*; make a change, introduce changes, innovate, bring in new blood 126 *modernize*; computerize, automate; turn upside down, subvert, evert 149 *revolutionize*, 221 *invert*; reverse, turn back 148 *revert*; make changes, rearrange, reorder, reset 62 *arrange*; adapt 24 *adjust*; conform 83 *make conform*; recast, remould, reshape 243 *form*; process, treat; revise, edit, correct 654 *rectify*; reform 654 *make better*; vamp up, revamp, patch, darn 656 *restore*; change for the worse 655 *pervert*; tamper with, meddle w., fiddle w., mar, spoil 655 *impair*; warp, bend, strain, twist, deform 246 *distort*; stain, dye, discolour 425 *colour*, 426 *decolorize*; adulterate, denature, doctor, qualify 43 *mix*, 163 *weaken*; cover, mask, disguise 525 *conceal*; change round, ring the changes, shuffle the cards 151 *interchange*, 272 *transpose*; try a change, spin the wheel 461 *experiment*; effect a change, work a c., leaven 156 *cause*; affect, turn the scale 178 *influence*; transform, transfigure, metamorphose, transmute, transubstantiate, alchemize 147 *convert*; metabolize, digest; conjure, juggle 542 *deceive*.

**Adv.** *mutatis mutandis*.

## 144 Permanence: absence of change

**N.** *permanence*, permanency, no change, status quo; invariability, unchangeability, immutability 153 *stability*; lasting quality, persistence 600 *perseverance*; endurance, duration 113 *durability*, 115 *perpetuity*; fixity, fixity of purpose, immobility, immovableness, intransigence 602 *obstinacy*; firmness, rock, bedrock, foundation, solidity 324 *density*; sustenance, maintenance, conservation 666 *preservation*, 146 *continuance*; law, bylaw, rule 81 *regularity*; fixed law, entrenched clause 153 *fixture*; standing, long s., inveteracy 127 *oldness*; tradition, custom, practice 610 *habit*; fixed attitude, conservatism; routine, fixed r., rut 60 *order*; unprogressiveness, static condition 266 *quiescence*; traditionalist, conservative, reactionary, true-blue, stick-in-the-mud, die-hard 602 *obstinate person*.

**Adj.** *permanent*, enduring, durable 113 *lasting*; persisting, persistent, continuing, unfailing, sustained, maintained 146 *unceasing*, 115 *perpetual*; inveterate, rocklike, long-standing 127 *immemorial*; perpetuated, standing, well-established, entrenched, in with the bricks, fixed, unchangeable, immutable, unmodifiable, unrepealable, written on tablets of stone 153 *established*; intact, inviolate, undestroyed, unchanged, unsuppressed; living, well-preserved 666 *preserved*; unchanging, conservative, reactionary, dyed in the wool, true-blue, diehard 602 *obstinate*; unprogressive, stationary, static, immobile 266 *quiescent*; unaltered, unchanged, uninfluenced, unaffected, still the same, always the s. 13 *identical*.

**Vb.** *stay*, come to stay, be here for good, set in, take root 153 *be stable*; abide, endure, subsist, outlive, survive, outlast 113 *last*; persist, hold, hold good; hold on, hold it, maintain, sustain, keep up, keep on 146 *go on*; rest, remain, tarry, live 192 *dwell*; stand fast, refuse to budge, dig one's toes in, dig one's heels in 600 *persevere*; stand pat, stand one's ground, hold one's ground, keep one's footing 599 *stand firm*; stand still, resist change 266 *be quiescent*; grow moss 127 *be old*; remain the same, not change one's spots; allow to stand, let be, let alone, live and let live, let sleeping dogs lie 756 *permit*.

**Adv.** *as before*, still the same, in statu quo; at a standstill; permanently, for good.

## 145 Cessation: change from action to rest

**N.** *cessation*, ceasing; desistance, discontinuance, discontinuation 72 *discontinuity*; arrest 747 *restraint*; withdrawal 753 *resignation*, 621 *relinquishment*.

*stop*, halt, dead stop; logjam, impasse, standstill, deadlock, stalemate, gridlock 28 *draw*; checkmate 728 *defeat*; breakdown 728 *failure*; discontinuance, stoppage, stall; shutdown, closing down, nonresumption 69 *end*; hitch, check 702 *hindrance*; stopping-up, blockage 264 *closure*; interruption 72 *discontinuity*; breaking-off, walkout 709 *dissension*; closure of debate, guillotine 399 *silence*.

*strike*, stopping work 679 *inactivity*, 715 *resistance*; industrial action, general strike, 'national holiday', hartal; slow-down, work to rule; stoppage, walkout, sit-in, work-in, sit-down strike, lightning s.; unofficial strike, wildcat s., mutiny 738 *disobedience*; lockout 57 *exclusion*.

*lull*, interval, pause, remission, letup; break, breather, rest 685 *refreshment*; holiday, day off, time o., duvet day, leisure time 681 *leisure*; interlude, cooling-off period, breathing space, gap year 108 *interim*; abeyance, suspension; close season, respite, moratorium, truce, armistice, cease-fire, standstill 136 *delay*.

*stopping place*, port of call, port, harbour; stop, halt, pull-up, whistle-stop, station; bus stop, request s.; terminus, terminal, air t. 271 *air travel*; dead end, blind alley, cul-de-sac;

billet, destination, the grave 266 *resting place*, 295 *goal*.

**Vb.** *cease*, stay, desist, refrain, hold, hold one's hand, stay one's h.; stop, halt, pull up, draw up; stand, rest, rest on one's oars, repose on one's laurels 683 *repose*; have done with, see the last of, end, finish 69 *terminate*; interrupt, leave off, knock o.; break o., let up 72 *discontinue*; ring off, hang up 578 *be mute*; withhold one's labour, cease work, stop w., down tools, strike, come out, walk out, vote with one's feet 715 *resist*; lock out 57 *exclude*; pipe down 399 *be silent*; come to an end, dry up, peter out, run o., run down 636 *not suffice*; slacken off, fade out, fade away 446 *disappear*; come off, end its run, be taken off; fold up, collapse 728 *fail*; die away, blow over, clear up 125 *be past*; stand down, withdraw, retire 753 *resign*; leave, leave off; give up, give over 621 *relinquish*; shut up, shut down, close; shut up shop, put up the shutters, go out of business, wind up; shut off steam, switch off; cease fire 719 *make peace*; sound the last post, ring down the curtain, call it a day 266 *be quiescent*, 679 *sleep*.

*halt*, stop, put a stop to; arrest, check, stem 702 *obstruct*; hold up, call off; pull up, cut short, call a halt, interrupt 747 *restrain*; cause a stoppage, call out, stage a strike; bring to a standstill, cause a logjam, freeze; checkmate, stalemate, thwart 702 *hinder*; check oneself, stop short, stop in one's tracks, stop dead; grind to a halt, seize, seize up, stall, jam, stick, catch; brake, put on the b. 278 *retard*.

*pause*, halt for a moment, stop for breath, take a breather; hold back, hang fire 278 *move slowly*; stay one's hand, hold one's horses, hesitate 679 *be inactive*; wait awhile, suspend, adjourn, intermit, remit, shelve, put on ice, mothball, put on the back-burner 136 *wait*; rest 683 *repose*.

**Int.** halt!, hold!, stop!, enough!, whoa!, belay there!, avast!, refrain!, leave off!, shut up!, give over!, cut it out!, pack it in!, chuck it!, drop it!, knock it off!, come off it!, stow it!

## 146 Continuance in action

**N.** *continuance*, continuation, nonfinality, 'it ain't over till the fat lady sings' 71 *continuity*, 144 *permanence*;

The opera ain't over till the fat lady sings.
Dan Cook

flow 179 *tendency*; extension, prolongation 113 *protraction*; maintenance, perpetuation 115 *perpetuity*; sustained action, persistence 600 *perseverance*; progress 285 *progression*; uninterrupted course, break, run, rally 71 *series*; recurrence 106 *repetition*.

**Adj.** *unceasing*, continuing etc. vb.; continual, steady, sustained; nonstop, uninterrupted, unremitting, without respite, incessant 71 *continuous*; unvarying, rocklike, unshifting 81 *regular*; standing, unreversed, unrevoked, unvaried 153 *fixed*; undying 115 *perpetual*; unfailing, ever-running, inexhaustible 635 *plenteous*; invariable, inconvertible 153 *unchangeable*; not out, still in, in play 113 *lasting*; unstoppable, relentless, persistent, persisting 600 *persevering*; haunting, obsessive, recurrent, ongoing 106 *repeated*.

**Vb.** *go on*, wag; keep going, march on, drive on, proceed, advance 285 *progress*; run on, never end 115 *be eternal*; – and – (e.g. rain and rain, pour and pour); roll on, pursue its course, take its c., trend 179 *tend*; endure, stick, hold, abide, rest, remain, linger 144 *stay*; obsess, haunt, frequent 139 *recur*; keep at it, persist, hold on, carry on, jog on, plod on, peg away 600 *persevere*; stick it out to the bitter end, sit it out, wait, wait till the end, see the end of, hang on 725 *carry through*; be not out, carry one's bat; survive, see one's days out, live out one's time 69 *end*.

*sustain*, maintain, uphold, keep on foot 218 *support*; follow up, follow through 71 *continue*; keep up, keep alive 666 *preserve*; keep on, harp on 106 *repeat*; keep it up, prolong, protract 113 *spin out*, 115 *perpetuate*; keep things moving, keep the pot boiling, keep the ball rolling; not interfere, let be, let sleeping dogs lie, let alone, let things take their course, laisser faire 744 *give scope*, 734 *be lax*.

**Int.** carry on!, drive on!, keep going!, keep it up!, never say die!, not out!

## 147 Conversion: change to something different

**N.** *conversion*, converting, turning into, making i.; processing 164 *production*; reduction, resolution, crystallization; fermentation, ferment, leaven 143 *alterer*; chemistry, alchemy; mutation, transmutation, transfiguration 143 *transformation*; bewitchment, enchantment 983 *sorcery*; progress 285 *progression*, 157 *growth*; course, lapse, flux 111 *course of time*; development 36 *increase*; evolution 358 *biology*; degeneration, perversion 655 *deterioration*; regeneration, reformation 654 *improvement*; rebirth 656 *restoration*; assimilation, naturalization 78 *inclusion*; alienization, denaturalization 916 *loss of right*; brainwashing 178 *influence*; evangelization, proselytization 534 *teaching*, 612 *inducement*; convertibility 469 *possibility*.

*transition*, transit 305 *passage*; movement, shift, relocation, translation, transfer 272 *transference*; alteration 143 *change*; life cycle.

*crucible*, melting pot, alembic, cauldron, retort, test tube 461 *testing agent*; laboratory, foundry 687 *workshop*.

*changed person*, new man or woman; convert, neophyte, catechumen, proselyte 538 *learner*; renegade, deserter, apostate, turncoat 603 *tergiversator*; pervert, degenerate 938 *bad person*.

**Adj.** *converted*, influenced, affected; turned into, made i. etc. vb.; assimilated, naturalized; reborn, born again, regenerate 656 *restored*; proselytized, brainwashed; becoming, transitional; evolving, embryonic, developing, growing into; altered, changed, modified, genetically modified, transgenic, metamorphosed, transfigured, transformed, unrecognizable 15 *different*; bewitched; convertible, impressionable 143 *changeable*.

**Vb.** *be turned to*, be converted into, become, get; come to, turn to, ferment, develop into, evolve i., ripen i. 316 *evolve*; fall into, pass i., slide i., shift i. 305 *pass*; melt into, merge i. 43 *be mixed*; settle into, sink i.; mellow 669 *mature*; wax 36 *grow*; degenerate 655 *deteriorate*; take the shape of, take the nature of, assume the character of; be transformed, not know oneself; undergo a personality change, suffer a sea change, turn over a new leaf 143 *change*; metamorphose, enter a phase, enter a stage.

*convert*, reduce, process, ferment, leaven; make into, reduce to, resolve into, turn i., conjure i., enchant 983 *bewitch*; metamorphose; transmute, alchemize; render, make, mould, shape, hew into shape, knock or lick into s. 243 *form*; brainwash 178 *influence*; proselytize, evangelize 534 *teach*; win over 485 *convince*; regenerate 656 *revive*; paganize 655 *pervert*.

*transform*, transfigure; landscape 844 *decorate*; camouflage, disguise, paper over the cracks 525 *conceal*; render 520 *translate*; traduce 521 *misinterpret*; reshape, deform 246 *distort*; change the face of, change out of recognition 149 *revolutionize*; metamorphose 143 *modify*; reform, make something of 654 *make better*; remodel, reorganize, restructure, rationalize, redress 656 *restore*; assimilate, naturalize, Americanize, Anglicize, Frenchify, Europeanize, Africanize, westernize, orientalize; internationalize; detribalize, denaturalize, alienize 916 *disentitle*, 57 *exclude*.

**Adv.** *convertibly*, evolvingly; on the way to, in transit.

## 148 Reversion

**N.** *reversion*, reverting, going back, return, regress, retrogression, retreat, withdrawal, ebb

286 *regression*; tracing back, derivation 156 *source*; return to the past, turning the clock back, harking back 127 *archaism*; atavism, throwback 5 *heredity*; looking back, retrospection 505 *remembrance*; retrospective action, retroaction; reaction 182 *counteraction*, 31 *compensation*; repercussion, boomerang effect, backlash, backfire, ricochet 280 *recoil*; revulsion, revulsion of feeling, disenchantment 830 *regret*; counter-revolution, reversal 149 *revolution*; retraction, backdown 603 *tergiversation*; volte face, about-turn, U-t., right-about t. 240 *contra-position*; backsliding, recidivism 657 *relapse*; reconversion 656 *restoration*; retroversion, retroflexion, retortion 248 *curvature*, 246 *distortion*; giving back, cession, replacement, reinstatement 787 *restitution*; getting back, recovery, retrieval 771 *acquisition*; taking back, escheat 786 *taking*; reply, feedback 460 *answer*; retort, tu quoque 479 *confutation*; turn, turning point, watershed, crucial point, turn of the tide, calm before the storm 137 *crisis*; alternation, swing, swings and roundabouts, give-and-take, swing of the pendulum 141 *periodicity*, 106 *recurrence*, 317 *oscillation*; recycling; to-and-fro movement, coming and going, shuttling, commuting; round trip, there and back, out and home; return journey, return ticket, day return; back where one started, status quo; resumption, recommencement 68 *start*.

**Adj.** *reverted*, reversed, reversionary, retrograde, retrogressive, recessive, reflexive 286 *regressive*; reactive 280 *recoiling*; reactionary, retroactive 125 *retrospective*; atavistic 5 *genetic*; recycled, returned; recovered, disenchanted 656 *restored*.

**Vb.** *revert*, go back, turn b., turn, return, retrace 286 *regress*; reverse, face about, turn a., do a U-turn 221 *invert*; ebb, retreat, withdraw 290 *recede*; kick back, rebound, backfire, ricochet, boomerang 280 *recoil*; slip back, slide b., backslide 657 *relapse*; back down, retract 603 *recant*; hark back, archaize; start again, turn the clock back, restart, go back to the beginning, undo, unmake 68 *begin*; restore the status quo, revive 656 *restore*; derestrict, decontrol, deregulate, decriminalize, deration 746 *liberate*; reconvert, disenchant, open one's eyes, remove the spell 613 *dissuade*; take back, recover 656 *retrieve*; resume 771 *acquire*; get one's own back 714 *retaliate*; give back, make restitution, reinstate, replace 787 *restitute*.

**Adv.** *reversibly*, invertedly, wrong side out, back-to-front; back to the beginning, as you were.

## 149 Revolution: sudden or violent change

**N.** *revolution*, full circle, circuit 315 *rotation*; radical change, organic c.; tabula rasa, clean slate, clean sweep 550 *obliteration*; sudden change, catastrophe, peripeteia, surprise, coup d'état, velvet revolution 508 *lack of expectation*; transilience, leap, plunge, jerk, start, throe 318 *spasm*; shift, swing, switch, switch over, landslide; violent change, bouleversement, upset, overthrow, subversion, inversion 221 *overturning*; convulsion, shake-up, upheaval, reorganization, eruption, explosion, cataclysm 176 *outbreak*; avalanche, landslip, crash, debacle 309 *descent*, 165 *havoc*; revulsion, rebellion, counter-revolution 148 *reversion*, 738 *revolt*; total change, sea c., metamorphosis, abolition, nullification 752 *abrogation*, *deposal*.

*revolutionist*, abolitionist, radical, revolutionary, Marxist, Red 738 *revolter*; seditionist 738 *agitator*; anarchist 168 *destroyer*; idealist 654 *reformer*.

**Adj.** *revolutionary* 126 *new*; innovating, radical, thoroughgoing, out-and-out, root and branch 54 *complete*; cataclysmic, catastrophic, seismic, earth-shaking, world-shaking 176 *violent*; seditious, subversive, Marxist, red 738 *disobedient*; anarchistic 165 *destructive*.

**Vb.** *revolutionize*, subvert, overturn 221 *invert*; switch over 603 *change one's mind*; uproot, eradicate, make a clean sweep 550 *obliterate*, 165 *demolish*; break with the past, remodel, restructure, reorganize, refashion 126 *modernize*; change the face of, change beyond recognition, metamorphose 147 *transform*.

## 150 Substitution: change of one thing for another

**N.** *substitution*, subrogation, surrogation; by-election 605 *vote*; commutation, exchange, switch, shuffle 151 *interchange*; supplanting, supersession, replacement, transfer 272 *transference*; vicariousness, self-sacrifice 931 *disinterestedness*; expiation, compensation 941 *atonement*.

*substitute*, sub, succedaneum; proxy, alternate, agent, representative 755 *deputy*; surrogate; dual representative, twofer; understudy, stand-in, body double 594 *actor*; ghost, ghost-writer 589 *author*; locum tenens, locum 658 *doctor*; reserve, reservist, twelfth man 707 *auxiliary*; supply, replacement, remount; relief, supplanter 67 *successor*; double, ringer, look-alike, changeling 545 *impostor*; mother figure, father f., foster parent; synonym, doublet 559 *word*; metaphor, symbol 551 *representation*; prosthesis, artificial limb, pace-maker; transplant, xenotransplant; alternative, second best, pis aller, ersatz 35 *inferiority*; whipping boy, chopping block, scapegoat, guilt-offering, sacrifice 981 *oblation*; makeshift, temporary measure, stopgap; sticking plaster, Band-Aid (tdmk) 177 *moderator*; expedient, temporary e., modus vivendi 770 *compromise*, 642 *good policy*.

quid pro quo, equivalent 28 *compeer*; consideration, purchase money; value, worth 809 *price*; redemption, compensation 31 *offset*; something in exchange, new lamps for old, replacement; change 797 *money*.

**Adj.** *substituted*, substitutive, substitutionary, substitutional; vicarious 931 *disinterested*; substitutable, interchangeable, commutable 28 *equivalent*; dummy, imitation, plastic, mock, ersatz, counterfeit, false 542 *spurious*; makeshift, stopgap, Band-Aid (tdmk), provisional, acting, temporary 114 *ephemeral*.

**Vb.** *substitute*, change for, commute; exchange, switch 151 *interchange*; take *or* offer in exchange, swap, compound 770 *compromise*; palm off with, fob off w. 542 *deceive*; make do with, put up w., make shift w.; put in the place of, replace with; count as, treat as, regard as; replace, step into the shoes of, succeed 65 *come after*; supersede, supplant, displace, oust 300 *eject*; replace, take the place of, be substitute for, do duty f., count f., stand in f., act f., understudy f. 755 *deputize*; act the part of, ghost for; hold the fort; shoulder the blame for, accept responsibility for, take the rap f., cover up f.; rob Peter to pay Paul.

**Adv.** *instead*, in place, in lieu; in favour of; in loco parentis; by proxy; alternatively, as an alternative; in default of, for want of better, faute de mieux.

## 151 Interchange: double or mutual change

**N.** *interchange*, interchangeability, reciprocality; swap, exchange, trade-off 791 *barter*; commutation, permutation, anagram; transposal, transposition, metathesis, mutual transfer; all change, general post; castling (chess), shuffle, shuffling 272 *transference*; reciprocity, mutuality; cross-fire, interplay, two-way traffic, reciprocation 12 *correlation*; quid pro quo, rally (tennis), give and take; retort, repartee 460 *rejoinder*, 'an eye for an eye and a tooth for a tooth' (see quotation at 714 *retaliation*), measure for measure, tit for tat 714 *retaliation*; logrolling 706 *cooperation*.

**Adj.** *interchanged*, switched, exchanged, counter-changed etc. vb.; bartered, traded, swapped; in exchange, au pair; reciprocating, mutual, two-way 12 *correlative*; reciprocal,

requited 714 *retaliatory*; inter-, intercontinental, interdepartmental; interchangeable, substitutable, convertible, commutable 28 *equivalent*.

**Vb.** *interchange*, exchange, counterchange; change money, convert; swap, barter, trade off 791 *trade*; permute, commute, shuttle; change places; switch, shuffle, castle (chess) 272 *transpose*; give and take 770 *compromise*; reciprocate 12 *correlate*; requite, give as good as one gets 714 *retaliate*; bandy words, answer back, return the compliment, rejoin, retort 460 *answer*; take in each other's washing, scratch each other's back 706 *cooperate*.

**Adv.** *in exchange*, in return; vice versa, mutatis mutandis; backwards and forwards, to and fro, by turns, turn and turn about; each in his turn; in kind; au pair; interchangeably, conversely.

## 152 Changeableness

**N.** *changeableness*, changeability, mutability, modifiability, changefulness 143 *change*; variability, variety 17 *nonuniformity*, 437 *variegation*; inconsistency, inconstancy, irregularity; instability, imbalance, disequilibrium, unstable equilibrium 29 *inequality*; weak foundation, unsteadiness, rockiness, wobbliness; plasticity, pliancy 327 *softness*; fluidness 335 *fluidity*; lubricity, slipperiness 258 *smoothness*; mobility, restlessness, darting, starting, fidgeting, inquietude, disquiet 318 *agitation*; fluctuation, alternation 317 *oscillation*; turning, veering, chopping and changing 142 *fitfulness*; impermanence, flicker, flash 114 *transience*; vacillation, hesitation, wavering 601 *irresolution*; yea and nay 603 *tergiversation*; fickleness, capriciousness 604 *caprice*; flightiness, light-mindedness 456 *inattention*; versatility 694 *aptitude*.

changeable thing, moon, Proteus, chameleon; changing scene, kaleidoscope; shifting sands; man of straw; wax, clay; mercury, quicksilver 335 *fluid*; wind, weathercock, weathervane; eddy; April showers; wheel, whirligig; mobile 265 *motion*; fortune, wheel of Fortune; vicissitude, luck 159 *chance*; variable, variable quantity 85 *numerical element*; play of expression, mobile features 445 *appearance*; grasshopper mind 456 *inattention*; floating voter, don't know 603 *tergiversator*.

**Adj.** *changeful*, changing, mutable, alterable, phased 143 *changeable*; shifting, vicissitudinous; varying, variant, variable 17 *nonuniform*; kaleidoscopic 437 *iridescent*; protean 82 *multiform*; quick-change, versatile 694 *skilful*; uncertain, unreliable, vacillating, wavering 601 *irresolute*; moody, unpredictable, unaccountable 508 *unexpected*; never the same, ever-changing, volatile, mercurial 15 *different*; wayward, fickle, whimsical 604 *capricious*; giddy, dizzy, flighty, wanton, irresponsible, frivolous 456 *light-minded*; shifty, inconstant, unfaithful, disloyal, traitorous 603 *tergiversating*.

*unstable*, unsteady, unsound, labile, astatic, built on sand; wavering, wobbling, rocky, tottering, teetering, staggering, faltering, staggery, reeling, rolling 317 *oscillating*; mobile, unquiet, restless, tossing and turning, fidgety 318 *agitated*; desultory, spasmodic, flickering 142 *fitful*; touch and go 114 *transient*; shifting, veering, turning, chopping and changing 282 *deviating*; whiffling, gusty 352 *windy*; precarious, unsettled, unfixed, loose, unattached, floating; erratic, mercurial; rootless, homeless, of no fixed abode 59 *extraneous*; vagrant, rambling, roving, wandering 267 *travelling*; vibrating, vibratory, alternating, fluctuating, tidal 141 *periodical*; yielding, impressionable, malleable, alterable, puttylike, plastic 327 *soft*; flowing, running, melting 335 *fluid*.

**Vb.** *vary*, be changeful, be off with the old and on with the new, show variety 437 *variegate*; ring the changes, go through phases, show p., have as many phases as the moon 143 *change*; chop and change, change and change about; dodge, double 620 *avoid*; shuffle, be shifty 518 *be equivocal*; writhe 251 *wriggle*; dart, flit, flitter 265 *be in motion*; leap, dance, flicker, gutter 417 *shine*; twinkle, flash; wave, wave in the wind, flutter, flap 217 *hang*; shake, tremble 318 *be agitated*; wobble, stagger, teeter, totter, rock, reel, sway, swing, vibrate 317 *oscillate*; shuttle, alternate, ebb and flow, wax and wane 317 *fluctuate*; veer, tack, yaw 282 *deviate*, 269 *navigate*; whiffle, puff 352 *blow*; vacillate, waver, shilly-shally, hesitate, float, drift, change one's mind 601 *be irresolute*; hover, hover between two extremes, blow hot and cold, play fast and loose 603 *change one's mind*; be inconstant, change one's fancy 604 *be capricious*.

**Adv.** *changeably*, variably; fitfully, spasmodically, off and on, now this now that.

## 153 Stability

**N.** *stability*, immutability; unchangeableness, unchangeability; irreversibility, invariability, constancy 16 *uniformity*; firmness, fixity, rootedness 144 *permanence*; rest, immobility, immovability 266 *quiescence*; stableness, stabilization, steadiness, steady state, stable equilibrium, homoeostasis, balance 28 *equality*; nerve, unshaken n., iron n., aplomb 599 *resolution*; stiffness, inflexibility 326 *hardness*, 602

*obstinacy*; solidarity, solidity 324 *density*; stiffening, ankylosis 326 *hardening*.

*fixture*, establishment, firm foundation; foundations, cornerstone, rock, bedrock, pillar, tower, pyramid; invariant, constant; fast colour, indelible ink; leopard's spots; law, 'law of the Medes and Persians' (see quotation at 81 *rule*), the Twelve Tables, the Ten Commandments, written constitution, entrenched clause, prescriptive right, droit du seigneur 953 *legality*.

*stabilizer*, fin, spoiler, centreboard, keel; counterweight, ballast 31 *offset*; buttress 218 *prop*.

**Adj.** *unchangeable*, unsusceptible of change; stiff, inflexible 602 *obstinate*; unwavering, rocklike 599 *resolute*; predictable, reliable 473 *certain*; immutable, intransmutable, incommutable; unalterable, written on tablets of stone, inconvertible; irreducible, indissoluble; changeless, unchanging, unchanged, unaltered, inalterable, irreversible; unshrinkable, shrinkproof; indeclinable; stereotyped, unvarying, invariable, constant 16 *uniform*; steady, undeviating 81 *regular*; durable, as the hills 113 *lasting*, 144 *permanent*; undying, perennial, evergreen 115 *perpetual*; imperishable, indestructible, inextinguishable 660 *invulnerable*. (See also *fixed*.)

*established*, well-e., entrenched, in with the bricks, vested, settled; inveterate, prescriptive 113 *lasting*; irrevocable, irreversible; incontrovertible, indefeasible, of right; valid, confirmed, ratified 473 *undisputed*, 488 *assented*.

*fixed*, steadfast, firm, secure, immovable, irremovable; unassailable, unshakable, rocklike, steady as a rock; steady, stable, balanced, homoeostatic; fast, ingrained, indelible; engraved; ineradicable, rooted, well-r., deep-r.; deep-seated, foursquare, well-founded, built on a rock; standing, pat; tethered, moored, anchored 45 *tied*; at rest, at anchor, riding at a.; run aground, stuck fast, stranded, grounded, high and dry; pinned down, transfixed; immobile, frozen, rooted to the ground *or* spot, like a statue, still as a stone 266 *still*.

**Vb.** *be stable*, – fixed etc. adj.; stand, stick fast, hold 599 *stand firm*; show aplomb, show self-assurance, not bat an eyelid; stick it out to the bitter end, weather the storm 113 *outlast*; set in, come to stay 144 *stay*; settle, settle down 192 *dwell*; strike root, take r., strike deep, have long roots.

*stabilize*, root, entrench, found, establish, build on a rock 115 *perpetuate*; erect, set up, set on its feet 218 *support*; float, set afloat; fix, set, stereotype, grave on granite; make valid, validate, confirm, ratify 488 *endorse*; retain, stet;

bind, make sure, make fast 45 *tie*; keep steady, hold the road, retain equilibrium, balance 28 *equalize*.

## 154 Present events

**N.** *event*, phenomenon; fact, matter of f., actual f. 1 *reality*; case, circumstance, situation, state of affairs 7 *state*; occurrence, eventuality, incidence, realization, happening, turn of events; incident, episode, adventure 137 *occasion*; milestone, watershed 8 *juncture*; fortune, accident, casualty, contingency 159 *chance*; misadventure, mishap 731 *misfortune*; emergency, pass 137 *crisis*; coincidence 181 *concurrence*, advent 289 *approach*; encounter, meeting; transaction, proceeding, affairs 676 *action*; result, product, consequence, issue, outcome, upshot 157 *effect*; denouement, solution, unravelling 316 *evolution*; peripeteia, catastrophe 69 *end*.

*affairs*, matters, doings, transactions 676 *deed*; agenda, order of the day; involvement, concern, concerns, interests, business i., irons in the fire, axes to grind 622 *business*; world, life, situation 8 *circumstance*; current affairs, affairs in general, state of affairs; course of events, march of e., stream of e., tide of e. 111 *course of time*; run of affairs, chapter of accidents, ups and downs of life, vicissitudes 730 *prosperity*, 731 *adversity*.

**Adj.** *eventual*, consequential, resulting, resultant, eventuating, issuing in 157 *caused*; circumstantial, contingent.

*happening*, incidental, accidental, occasional; doing, current, on foot, afoot, afloat, in the wind, on the agenda; on the stocks, in preparation.

*eventful*, stirring, bustling, busy, full of incident, crowded with i. 678 *active*; momentous, critical 638 *important*.

**Vb.** *happen*, become, come into existence 360 *be born*; materialize, appear, be realized, come off 727 *succeed*; take place, occur, come about, come to pass, fulfil expectations; befall, betide 159 *chance*; turn up, pop up, crop up, start up, spring up, arise 295 *arrive*; present itself, announce i. 189 *be present*; supervene 284 *follow*; eventuate, issue, transpire, emanate 157 *result*; turn out, fall o., work o., pan o.; be on foot, be afoot, take its course, hold its c., advance 285 *progress*; continue 146 *go on*; go off, pass o. 125 *be past*; fall to one's lot, be one's good fortune *or* misfortune, be one's great chance; be the case, be so, prove, prove to be; bring about, occasion 156 *cause*.

*meet with*, incur, encounter 295 *meet*; realize, happen on, chance upon, stumble u., find 484 *discover*; experience, pass through, go t.; have been through 490 *know*, 818 *feel*; have adventures, endure, undergo 825 *suffer*.

**Adv.** *eventually*, ultimately, in the event of, in case; in due course, in the course of things, in the natural course of t., in the ordinary course of t.; as things go, as times go; as the world goes, as the world wags; as the cookie crumbles; as the cat jumps; as it may turn out, as it may happen.

## 155 Destiny: future events

**N.** *destiny*, what's to come, one's stars 596 *fate*; horoscope, forecast 511 *prediction*; prospect, outlook 507 *expectation*; coming events, future plans, intentions 124 *futurity*, 617 *intention*; trouble in store, danger 900 *threat*; imminence, impendence, proximity 200 *nearness*, 289 *approach*; post-existence, future existence, hereafter 124 *future state*; next world, Hades, afterworld, world to come, life after death 971 *heaven*; foredoom, predestination 596 *necessity*, 473 *certainty*.

**Adj.** *impending*, overhanging, hanging over, louring, hovering, imminent 900 *threatening*; preparing, brewing, cooking 669 *preparatory*; destined, predestined, in the stars, in the lap of the gods 596 *fated*; predicted, forthcoming, forecast 511 *predicting*; inescapable, inevitable, going to be, bound to happen 473 *certain*; due, owing 596 *necessary*; in the wind, on the cards 471 *probable*; on the agenda, intended, decided on 608 *predetermined*; in prospect, in view, in the offing, on the horizon, looming on the h., in the distance 443 *visible*; in the future, to come, in the womb of time 124 *future*; at hand, close 200 *near*, 289 *approaching*; instant, immediate, about to be, on the point of 116 *instantaneous*; pregnant with, heavy w. 511 *presageful*; in store, in reserve, in pickle, ready, kept r., on the stocks 669 *prepared*; in embryo, embryonic 68 *beginning*.

**Vb.** *impend* 124 *be to come*; hang over, lie o., hover, lour, loom, be on the horizon 900 *threaten*; come on, draw nigh 289 *approach*; front, face, stare one in the f. 237 *be in front*; breathe down one's neck 200 *be near*; ripen 669 *mature*.

*predestine*, destine, doom, foredoom, preordain, foreordain 596 *necessitate*; foreshadow, adumbrate, presage 511 *predict*; have ready, get r., have in store, have in pickle 669 *make ready*; plan, intend 608 *predetermine*.

**Adv.** *in the future*, in time, in the long run; all in good time; in the event 154 *eventually*; whatever may happen; expectedly 471 *probably*; soon, shortly, at any moment.

SECTION EIGHT

# *Causation*

## 156 Cause: constant antecedent

**N.** *causation*, causality, cause and effect, ground and consequent; aetiology 158 *attribution*; authorship; origination, creation 21 *originality*; invention 484 *discovery*; inspiration 178 *influence*; generation, evocation, provocation 164 *production*; impulsion, stimulation, fomentation, encouragement, motivation 612 *motive*; planting, watering, cultivation 370 *agriculture*; abetment 706 *cooperation*; temptation 612 *inducement*; opportunity 137 *occasion*.

*cause*, formal c., efficient c., material c., first c., final c.; prime mover, primum mobile, God 965 *the Deity*; sui causa 1 *existence*; creator, maker 164 *producer*; begetter, father 169 *parentage*; causer, effecter, occasioner; author, inventor, originator, founder; agent, leaven; stimulus 174 *stimulant*; contributor, factor, contributory f., decisive f., moment, determinant; inspirer, tempter, mainspring, McGuffin 612 *motivator*; fomenter, aider, abettor; hidden hand, hidden cause, power behind the throne, undercurrents 178 *influence*; planetary influence, astrological i., stars 155 *destiny*; fate 596 *necessity*; force 740 *compulsion*.

*source*, fountain, fount, fons et origo 68 *origin*; headwaters, spring, wellhead, fountainhead, wellspring; mine, quarry 632 *store*; birthplace 192 *home*; genesis, ancestry, lineage, descent 169 *parentage*; parent, ancestor, progenitor; loins 167 *genitalia*; rudiment, element, principle, first p., first thing; nucleus, germ, seed, sperm, spore; egg, foetus, embryo, pre-embryo; chrysalis, cocoon 132 *young creature*; bud, stem, stock, rootstock; taproot, root, bulb 366 *plant*; radix, radical, etymon, derivation, etymology 557 *linguistics*; foundation, fundamentals, the nitty gritty, bedrock 214 *base*; groundwork, spadework, beginnings 68 *beginning*; nuts and bolts, raw material, ore 631 *materials*.

*seedbed*, hotbed, nidus 192 *nest*; cradle, nursery 68 *origin*; breeding place, incubator, womb, fertile soil 167 *propagation*; grow bag, growing bag, hothouse, greenhouse, conservatory, propagator, cold frame, cloche 370 *garden*.

*instrument*, appliance 629 *means*; pivot, hinge, lever, instrument 630 *tool*; dynamo, generator, battery, spark 160 *energy*; motor, engine, turbine 630 *machine*; last straw that breaks the camel's back.

*reason why*, reason, cause, the why and wherefore; explanation, key 460 *answer*, 520

*interpretation*; excuse 614 *pretext*; ground, basis, rationale, motive, idea, occasion, causa causans, raison d'être; conspiracy theory.

**Adj.** *causal*, causative, formative, effective, effectual 727 *successful*; pivotal, determinant, decisive, final 69 *ending*; seminal, germinal 164 *productive*, inceptive, embryonic 68 *beginning*; suggestive, inspiring 178 *influential*; impelling 740 *compelling*; answerable, responsible, blameworthy; at the bottom of, original; aetiological, explanatory 158 *attributed*; creative, inventive 21 *inimitable*.

*fundamental*, primary, elemental, ultimate; foundational, radical, basic 5 *intrinsic*, crucial, central 638 *important*; original, aboriginal 68 *first*; primitive, primordial 127 *primal*.

**Vb.** *cause*, originate, bring into being, create, make 164 *produce*; beget, be the author of 167 *generate*; invent 484 *discover*; be the reason 158 *account for*; underlie, be *or* lie at the bottom of, be at the root of; sow the seeds of, be answerable, be responsible, have a hand in, be to blame; institute, found, lay the foundations, inaugurate 68 *auspicate*; set up, erect 310 *elevate*; launch, set afloat, set afoot, set going, trigger off, spark off, touch o. 68 *begin*; open, open up, broach 68 *initiate*; seed, sow, plant, water 370 *cultivate*; contrive, effect, effectuate, bring about, bring off, bring to pass 727 *succeed*; procure, provide the means, put up the wherewithal 629 *find means*; stage-manage, engineer 623 *plan*; bring on, induce, precipitate 680 *hasten*; bring out, draw o., evoke, elicit 291 *attract*; provoke, arouse, awaken 821 *excite*; stimulate 174 *invigorate*; kindle, inspire, incite, tempt 612 *induce*; occasion, give occasion for 612 *motivate*; have an effect, be a factor, show its result, make or mar 178 *influence*; be the agent, do the deed 676 *do*; determine, decide, give the decision 480 *judge*; decide the result, turn the scale, come down on one side or the other, give the casting vote 178 *prevail*, 34 *predominate*.

*conduce*, tend to 179 *tend*; lead to 64 *come before*; contribute to, operate to 628 *be instrumental*; involve, imply 5 *be intrinsic*; have the effect, entail, draw down, give rise to, open the door to, act as an open sesame to 68 *initiate*; promote, advance, encourage, foster, foment, abet 703 *aid*.

**Adv.** *causally*, because, by reason of, behind the scenes 178 *influentially*.

## 157 Effect: constant sequel

**N.** *effect*, consequent, consequence, corollary 65 *sequence*; result, resultance; derivation, derivative, precipitate 41 *remainder*; upshot, outcome, issue, denouement 154 *event*; final result, end r., termination 725 *completion*; visible effect, mark, print, impress 548 *trace*; by-product, side-effect, spin-off; aftermath, legacy, backwash, wake, repercussion 67 *sequel*; resultant action, response 460 *answer*, performance 676 *deed*; reaction, backlash, boomerang effect 182 *counteraction*; offspring 170 *posterity*; handiwork 164 *product*; karma 596 *fate*; moral effect 178 *influence*.

*growth*, outgrowth, development, expansion 36 *increase*; carcinoma 651 *cancer*; bud, blossom, florescence, fruit; ear, spike; produce, crop, harvest; profit 771 *gain*; growth industry.

**Adj.** *caused*, owing to, due to, attributed to; consequential, resulting from, consequent upon 65 *sequential*; contingent, depending, dependent on 745 *subject*; resultant, derivable, derivative, descended; monocausal; unoriginal, secondary 20 *imitative*; arising, emergent, emanating, developed from, evolved f.; born of, out of, by; ending in, issuing in 154 *eventual*; effected, done.

*inherited*, heritable, hereditary, Mendelian 5 *genetic*.

**Vb.** *result*, be the r., come of; follow on, ensue, wait on, accrue 284 *follow*; be owing to, be due to; owe everything to, borrow from 785 *borrow*; have a common origin 9 *be related*; take its source, have its roots in, derive from, descend f., originate f. *or* in, come from *or* out of; issue, proceed, emanate 298 *emerge*; begin from, grow f., spring f., arise f., flow f.; develop, unfold 316 *evolve*; bud, sprout, germinate 36 *grow*; show a trace, show an effect, receive an impression, bear the stamp 522 *be plain*; bear the consequences 154 *meet with*, 963 *be punished*; turn out, fall o., pan o., work o., eventuate 154 *happen*; result in 164 *produce*.

*depend*, hang upon, hinge on, pivot on, turn on, centre on 12 *correlate*, 745 *be subject*.

**Adv.** *consequently*, as a consequence, in consequence; because of, as a result; of course, naturally, necessarily; following upon, it follows that, and so 158 *hence*.

## 158 Attribution: assignment of cause

**N.** *attribution*, assignment of cause; reference to, imputation, ascription; theory, hypothesis, model, assumption, conjecture 512 *supposition*; explanation 520 *interpretation*; finding reasons, accounting for; aetiology, palaetiology 459 *enquiry*; rationale 156 *reason why*; filiation, affiliation 169 *parentage*; derivation, etymology 156 *source*; attribute 89 *concomitant*; credit, credit title, acknowledgment 915 *dueness*.

**Adj.** *attributed*, assigned etc. vb.; attributable, assignable, imputable, referable, referrible; assigned to, referred to 9 *relative*;

credited, imputed, putative 512 *supposed*; inferred, inferable, derivable, traceable; owing to, explained by 157 *caused*.

**Vb.** *attribute*, ascribe, impute: say of, assert of, predicate 532 *affirm*; accord, grant, allow 781 *give*; put down to, set down to; assign to, refer to, point to, trace to, connect with, derive from 9 *relate*; lay at the door of, affiliate, father upon; charge with, charge on, saddle with *or* on; found upon, ground u.; make responsible, make a scapegoat, scapegoat, blame for 928 *accuse*; bring home to 478 *demonstrate*; credit, credit with, acknowledge 915 *grant claims*.

*account for*, explain, say how it happens 520 *interpret*; theorize, hypothesize, assume 512 *suppose*; infer the cause, derive the reason.

**Adv.** *hence*, thence, therefore; whence, wherefore; for, since, on account of, because, owing to, thanks to, on that account, from this cause, from that cause, propter hoc, ergo, thus, so; that's why.

*why?*, wherefore?, whence?, how?, how come?, cui bono?

*somehow*, in some way, in some such way; by some means or other, somehow or other.

## 159 Chance: no assignable cause

**N.** *chance*, blind c., fortuity, indeterminacy; randomness; indetermination, fortuitousness; uncertainty principle, unpredictability 474 *uncertainty*; unaccountability, inexplicability 517 *unintelligibility*; lot, fortune, wheel of f., lady luck 596 *fate*; lottery, luck of the draw, postcode lottery, potluck, whatever comes; good fortune, luck, good l., run of good l. 730 *prosperity*; bad luck, run of bad l., rotten l. 731 *misfortune*; hap, hazard, accident, misadventure, casualty, contingency, coincidence, chapter of accidents 154 *event*; nonintention, chance hit, lucky shot, lucky strike, fluke 618 *nondesign*; rare chance, chance in a million 140 *infrequency*; chance meeting, chance encounter 508 *lack of expectation*; chance discovery, serendipity 484 *discovery*.

*equal chance*, even c., fifty-fifty 28 *equality*; toss-up, spin of the coin, heads or tails, throw of the dice, turn of the card, spin of the wheel; lucky dip, random sample; lottery, National Lottery, scratch card, raffle, tombola, sweepstake, premium bond 618 *gambling*, sortes Biblicae 511 *divination*.

*fair chance*, sporting c., fighting c., gambling c. 469 *possibility*; half a chance, small c. 472 *improbability*; good chance, main c., best c., favourable c. 137 *opportunity*; long odds, odds on, odds 34 *advantage*; small risk, safe bet, sure thing, the probabilities 471 *probability*.

*calculation of chance*, theory of probabilities, doctrine of chance, actuarial calculation, mathematical probability; risk-taking, assurance, insurance, life assurance, bancassurance *or* bankassurance, underwriting 672 *undertaking*; speculation 461 *experiment*; bookmaking 618 *gambling*.

**Adj.** *casual*, fortuitous, serendipitous, aleatory, chance, haphazard, hit-or-miss, random, stray, out of a hat 618 *designless*; adventitious, accidental, unexpected, incidental, contingent 154 *happening*; noncausal, epiphenomenal, coincidental 89 *accompanying*, 10 *unrelated*; chancy, fluky, dicey, incalculable, stochastic 474 *uncertain*.

*causeless*, groundless, uncaused, unforeseeable, unpredictable, undetermined, indeterminate 474 *uncertain*; unmotivated, unintended, undesigned, unplanned, unmeant 618 *unintentional*; unaccountable, inexplicable 517 *puzzling*.

**Vb.** *chance*, hap, turn up, crop up, fall to one's lot, so happen 154 *happen*; chance upon, come u., light u., hit u., stumble u., blunder u., bump into, run across 154 *meet with*, 484 *discover*; go out on a limb, risk it, try one's luck, chance it, leave it to chance 618 *gamble*; have small chance 472 *be unlikely*.

**Adv.** *by chance*, by accident; accidentally, casually, unintentionally, fortuitously, serendipitously, randomly 618 *at random*; perchance, perhaps; for all one knows 469 *possibly*; luckily, as good luck would have it; unluckily, as ill luck would have it; according to chance, as it may be, as it may chance, as it may turn up, as it may happen, as the case may be, whatever happens, in any event; unpredictably 508 *unexpectedly*; unaccountably, inexplicably.

## 160 Power

**N.** *power*, potency, mightiness 32 *greatness*; prepotency, prevalence, predominance 34 *superiority*; omnipotence, almightiness 733 *authority*; control, sway 733 *governance*; moral power, ascendancy 178 *influence*; spiritual power, charisma, mana; witchcraft 983 *sorcery*; staying power, endurance 153 *stability*; driving force 612 *motive*; physical power, might, muscle, brute force *or* strength, right arm, right hand 162 *strength*; dint, might and main, effort, endeavour, 'blood, sweat and tears' 682 *exertion*;

> I have nothing to offer but but blood, toil, tears and sweat.
> Winston Churchill

force 740 *compulsion*; stress, strain, shear; weight 322 *gravity*; weight of numbers 104 *greater number*; manpower, human resources

686 *personnel*; position of power, position of strength, vantage ground 34 *advantage*; validity 494 *truth*; cogency, emphasis 532 *affirmation*; extra power, overdrive.

*ability*, ableness, capability, potentiality, virtuality 469 *possibility*; competence, efficiency, efficacy, effectuality 694 *skill*; capacity, faculty, virtue, property 5 *intrinsicality*; qualification 24 *fitness*; attribute 89 *concomitant*; native wit, endowment, gift, flair, what it takes 694 *aptitude*; compass, reach, grasp 183 *range*; susceptibility, affectibility 180 *liability*; trend 179 *tendency*; empowering, enablement, authorization 756 *permission*.

*energy*, liveliness, vigour, drive, pep, zip, dynamism 174 *vigorousness*; internal energy, thermal e., chemical e., potential e.; work, binding energy, kinetic e., mass *or* rest e., radiant e., electrical e., atomic e., nuclear e.; mechanical energy, pedal power, engine power, horsepower; life-force, qi *or* ch'i; inertia, vis inertiae 175 *inertness*; resistance 333 *friction*; force, field of f. 162 *science of forces*; force of gravity 322 *gravity*; buoyancy 323 *lightness*; compression, spring 328 *elasticity*; pressure, head, charge, steam; full pressure, steam up; tension, high t.; motive power, electromotive force; pulling power 288 *traction*; pushing power, thrust, jet, jet propulsion 287 *propulsion*; momentum, impetus 279 *impulse*; magnetism, magnetic field 291 *attraction*; negative magnetism 292 *repulsion*; suction 299 *reception*; expulsion 300 *ejection*; potential function, potential; unit of work, erg, joule; foot-pound, poundal; calorie; energy-saving, energy audit.

*sources of energy*, coal, gas, oil 385 *fuel*; nuclear power (see also *nucleonics*); renewable energy sources, wind power, wave p., geothermal p., solar energy, alternative energy, hydroelectricity; powerhouse, power station, generating s., pumped storage scheme, hydro-electric station 350 *waterfall*; tidal barrage, tide mill 317 *fluctuation*; windmill, wind farm, windmill f. 315 *rotator*; solar panel, solar battery, heat exchanger 383 *heater*; generator, turbine, motor 630 *machine*.

*electricity*, induced electricity, thermoelectricity, photoelectricity, piezoelectricity; voltaic electricity, galvanic e.; static e.; lightning; electrodynamics, electrostatics, electromagnetism; induction, inductance, capacitance; resistance, conduction; oscillation, pulsation, frequency; electric charge, pulse, shock; electric current, direct c., alternating c.; circuit, short c., closed c.; electrode, anode, cathode; positive, negative; conductor, semiconductor, nonconductor, insulator; lightning conductor, earth 662 *safeguard*; electrification, live wire 661 *danger*.

*electronics*, electron physics, optics 417 *optics*; lasers 417 *radiation*; integrated circuit, microprocessor 196 *microelectronics*; computer electronics 86 *computing*, 531 *Internet*; automation 630 *machine*; telegraph, telephone, television, radio 531 *telecommunication*; electrical engineering, electricity supply; power line, lead, flex 47 *cable*; distributor; pylon, grid, national g.; generator, magneto, dynamo; oscillator, alternator; transformer, commutator, power pack; battery, dry b., rechargeable b., storage b., wet b., accumulator; cell, wet c., dry c., fuel c., photo c., photoelectric c.; valve, tube, transistor; voltage, volt, watt, kilowatt, megawatt; ohm; amperage, ampere, amp.

*nucleonics*, nuclear physics; fission, fusion, thermonuclear reaction; atom-smasher, particle accelerator, linear a., cyclotron, synchrotron; Zeta, Jet, Tokamek; atomic pile, nuclear reactor, fast breeder r., waste-reprocessing plant; Magnox reactor, AGR, LWR, PWR, SGHWR; fuel rods, moderator, coolant; radioactivity, fallout 417 *radiation*; radioactive waste 659 *poison*; nuclear warhead, nuclear missile, atomic bomb 723 *bomb*.

**Adj.** *powerful*, potent 162 *strong*; puissant, powerful, mighty 32 *great*; ascendant, rising, in the ascendant 36 *increasing*; prepotent, prevalent, prevailing, predominant 178 *influential*; almighty, omnipotent, irresistible 34 *supreme*; with full powers, empowered, plenipotentiary 733 *authoritative*; virtual, potential 469 *possible*; competent, capable, able, adequate, equal to, up to 635 *sufficient*; with resources 800 *rich*; omnicompetent 694 *expert*; more than a match for, efficacious, effectual, effective 727 *successful*; of power, of might, operative, workable, having teeth; in force, valid, unrepealed, unrepealable 153 *established*; cogent, compulsive 740 *compelling*; forcible 176 *violent*; bellicose 718 *warlike*.

*dynamic*, energetic, peppy 174 *vigorous*; high-potential, high-tension, super-charged, souped-up; magnetic 291 *attracting*; tractive 288 *drawing*; propelling 287 *propulsive*, 279 *impelling*; locomotive, kinetic 265 *moving*; powered, engined, driven; mechanized, automated 630 *mechanical*; electric, electrical, electromagnetic, electronic; computerized, solid-state; live, charged; on stream; atomic, nuclear, thermonuclear; hydroelectric, geothermal, wave-powered, solar-p., wind-driven, water-d., steam-operated.

**Vb.** *be able*, – powerful etc. adj.; can, have it in one's power, have it in one; be capable of, have the talent for, have the virtue, have the property; compass, manage 676 *do*; measure up to 635 *suffice*; have power, exercise p., control 733 *dominate*; force 740 *compel*; gain power, come to p. 178 *prevail*.

*empower*, enable, endow, authorize; endow with power, invest with p.; put teeth into, arm 162 *strengthen*; electrify, charge, magnetize; plug in, switch on, transistorize, automate; power, drive.

**Adv.** *powerfully*, mightily etc. adj.; by virtue of, by dint of; with might and main.

## 161 Impotence

**N.** *impotence*, lack of power, no authority, power vacuum; invalidity, impuissance 163 *weakness*; inability, incapacity; incapability, incompetence, inefficiency 728 *failure*, 695 *unskilfulness*; ineptitude, unfitness 25 *inaptitude*; decrepitude 131 *age*; frailness 114 *transience*; invalidation, disqualification 752 *abrogation*; sterility, sterilization, barrenness, impotence 172 *unproductiveness*, *contraception*; disarmament, decommissioning, demilitarization 719 *pacification*; demobilization 75 *dispersion*.

*helplessness*, defencelessness 661 *vulnerability*; harmlessness 935 *innocence*, powerlessness 745 *subjection*, 747 *restraint*; impotent fury, stamping of feet, gnashing of teeth 891 *anger*, prostration, exhaustion, inanition 684 *fatigue*; collapse, breakdown 728 *failure*; unconsciousness, faint, swoon, coma, catatonia; numbness, narcosis 375 *insensibility*; stroke, cerebrovascular accident, CVA, apoplexy, paralysis, hemiplegia, paraplegia 651 *disease*, torpor 677 *inaction*; atrophy 655 *deterioration*; senility, old age 131 *age*; ataxia, locomotor a.; loss of control, incontinence; mental decay, softening of the brain, dementia, Alzheimer's disease 503 *mental disorder*; mental weakness, imbecility 499 *unintelligence*; mutism, deaf mutism 578 *voicelessness*; legal incapacity, pupillage, minority 130 *nonage*; babyhood, infancy 130 *youth*; invalid 651 *sick person*, 163 *weakling*.

*eunuch*, castrato; gelding, capon, bullock, steer, neuter; freemartin, hermaphrodite.

*ineffectuality*, ineffectiveness, futility, labour of Sisyphus 497 *absurdity*; vanity 4 *insubstantiality*; uselessness 641 *inutility*; flash in the pan 114 *transience*; dead letter, scrap of paper 752 *abrogation*; figurehead, dummy, man of straw, broken reed 4 *insubstantial thing*; empty threats, bluster 515 *empty talk*.

**Adj.** *powerless*, impotent, not able, unable; not enabled, unempowered, unauthorized, without authority; nominal, figurehead, constitutional 4 *insubstantial*; nugatory, invalid, null and void; unconstitutional 954 *illegal*; without a leg to stand on 163 *weak*; inoperative, not working, unexercised, unemployed, disemployed 677 *nonactive*; suspended, in abeyance, cancelled, withdrawn 752 *abrogated*; abolished, swept away, gone by the board 165 *destroyed*; obsolete, on the shelf 674 *disused*; mothballed, laid up, out of circulation, kaput; disqualified, deposed; unqualified, unfit, unfitted, inept 25 *unapt*; unworkable, dud, good for nothing 641 *useless*; inadequate 636 *insufficient*; ineffective, inefficacious, ineffectual, feeble 728 *unsuccessful*; incapable, incompetent, inefficient 695 *unskilful*; mechanically powerless, unpowered, unengined; unequipped 670 *unprepared*.

*defenceless*, helpless, without resource; bereaved, bereft 772 *losing*; kithless, kinless, orphan, unfriended 883 *friendless*; weak, harmless 935 *innocent*; powerless, weaponless, unarmed, disarmed 670 *unequipped*; unprotected, unguarded, unfortified, exposed, indefensible, untenable, pregnable 661 *vulnerable*.

*impotent*, powerless, feeble 163 *weak*; emasculated, castrated, caponized, gelded, neutered, unsexed, unmanned, spayed, sterilized; sexless, neuter; sterile, barren, infertile 172 *unproductive*; worn out, exhausted, used up, effete; senile, gaga 131 *ageing*; paralytic, arthritic, stiff 326 *rigid*; unconscious, comatose, drugged, hypnotized, catatonic 375 *insensible*; incapacitated, disabled, paralysed 163 *disabled*; without self-control, incontinent; done up, all in, deadbeat, clapped out 684 *fatigued*; prostrated 216 *supine*; nerveless, spineless, boneless 601 *irresolute*; shattered, unhinged, unnerved, mindblown, demoralized, shell-shocked 854 *nervous*; hors de combat, out of the running 728 *defeated*; helpless, rudderless, drifting 282 *deviating*; waterlogged, swamped; on one's beam ends, laid on one's back 728 *grounded*; baffled, thwarted, gnashing one's teeth, stamping one's feet 702 *hindered*.

**Vb.** *be impotent*, – defenceless etc. adj.; be unable, cannot, not work, not do, not alter things; not help, have no help to offer 641 *be useless*; strive in vain, avail nothing 728 *fail*; not make the grade 307 *fall short*; have no power 745 *be subject*; get nowhere, have no say, cut no ice 639 *be unimportant*; lose the power of resistance 721 *submit*; feel helpless, shrug, wring one's hands; gnash one's teeth, stamp one's feet 830 *regret*; do nothing, look on, stand by 441 *watch*; have a hopeless case, not have a leg to stand on; go by the board 446 *disappear*; lose consciousness, faint, swoon, pass out 375 *be insensible*; drop, collapse 163 *be weak*.

*disable*, incapacitate, unfit 641 *make useless*;

disqualify 916 *disentitle*; deprive of power, invalidate 752 *abrogate*; disarm, decommission, demilitarize 163 *weaken*; neutralize 182 *counteract*; undermine, sap 255 *make concave*; exhaust, use up, consume 634 *waste*; wind, prostrate, bowl over, knock out 279 *strike*; double up, benumb, paralyse 679 *make inactive*; sprain, rick, wrench, twist, dislocate, break, fracture; cripple, lame, maim, hobble, nobble, hamstring 702 *hinder*, 655 *impair*; stifle, smother, throttle, suffocate, strangle, garrotte 362 *kill*; muzzle, deaden 399 *silence*; spike the guns, draw the teeth, clip the wings, tie one's hands, cramp one's style; sabotage, put a spoke into one's wheel, throw a spanner in the works; deflate, take the wind out of one's sails; put out of gear, unhinge, unstring 46 *disunite*; put out of action, put out of commission 674 *stop using*.

*unman*, unnerve, enervate, paralyse 854 *frighten*; devitalize 163 *weaken*; emasculate, castrate, neuter, spay, geld, caponize, effeminize, unsex 172 *make sterile*.

## 162 Strength

**N.** *strength*, might, potency, horsepower, HP 160 *power*; energy 160 *energy*, 174 *vigorousness*; force, physical f., main f. 735 *brute force*; resilience, spring 328 *elasticity*; tone, tonicity, temper; load-bearing capacity, tensile strength; iron, steel 326 *hardness*; oak, heart of oak 329 *toughness*; staying power, survivability, endurance, grit 600 *stamina*; life-force, qi *or* ch'i.

*vitality*, healthiness, fitness 650 *health*; vim, vigour, liveliness 360 *life*; animal spirits 833 *cheerfulness*; virility, redbloodedness 855 *manliness*; guts, nerve, spunk, pluck, backbone 599 *resolution*; aggressiveness 718 *bellicosity*; physique, muscularity, muscle, biceps, sinews, thews and sinews; beefiness, burliness, brawn 195 *size*; grip, iron g., vicelike g. 778 *retention*; Titanic strength, strength of Hercules.

*athletics* 837 *sport*, 716 *contest*; athleticism; gymnastics, acrobatics, body-building, weight-training, pumping iron, feats of strength, callisthenics, aerobics 682 *exercise*; stadium, gymnasium, astrodome 724 *arena*.

*athlete*, gymnast, tumbler, acrobat, funambulist, contortionist, trapeze artist, circus rider, bareback r., stunt man, escapologist 594 *entertainer*; marathon runner; Blue, all-rounder 716 *contender*; wrestler 716 *wrestling*; heavyweight 722 *pugilist*; weight-lifter, body-builder, strong man; champion 644 *exceller*; he-man, muscle man 372 *male*; strongarm man, bully, bruiser, tough guy 857 *desperado*; chucker-out, bouncer 300 *ejector*; amazon, virago 373 *woman*; bullfighter, matador, picador, toreador 362 *killer*;

Mr Universe, Tarzan, Hercules; Samson, Goliath, Atlas, Titan 195 *giant*; tower of strength 707 *auxiliary*.

*strengthening*, fortifying etc. vb.; reinforcement 703 *aid*; stiffening, toughening, tempering 326 *hardening*; invigoration, tonic effect 174 *stimulation*; reanimation 685 *refreshment*; revival, convalescence 656 *restoration*; emphasis, stress 532 *affirmation*.

*science of forces*, dynamics, statics, hydrodynamics, hydrostatics, electrodynamics, electrostatics; thermodynamics; triangle of forces.

**Adj. strong**, lusty, vigorous, youthful 130 *young*; mighty, puissant, potent, armed 160 *powerful*; high-powered, high-geared, high-tension; all-powerful, omnipotent, overpowering, overwhelming 34 *superior*; incontestable, irresistible, more than a match for, victorious 727 *unbeaten*; sovereign, supreme 733 *ruling*; valid, in full force; in full swing 146 *unceasing*; in the plenitude of power, undiminished 32 *great*; like a giant refreshed 685 *refreshed*; in high feather, in fine fettle, in tip-top condition, at one's peak, in top form, in good nick, fit as a fiddle, sound as a bell 650 *healthy*; heavy 322 *weighty*; strongarm, forceful, forcible 735 *severe*; urgent, pressing, compulsive 740 *compelling*; emphatic, emphasized 532 *assertive*; tempered, iron-hard, hard as iron, steely, adamantine 326 *hard*; case-hardened, reinforced, toughened 329 *tough*; deep-rooted 45 *firm*; solid, substantial, stable 153 *fixed*; thick-ribbed, well-built, stout; strong as a horse, strong as a lion, strong as an ox; strong as brandy, heady, alcoholic 949 *intoxicating*; undiluted, neat, undiminished 52 *whole*; strengthened, fortified, double-strength; entrenched, defended, inviolable, unassailable 660 *invulnerable*.

*unyielding*, staunch 599 *resolute*; stubborn, intransigent 602 *obstinate*; persistent 600 *persevering*; unstretchable, inelastic 326 *rigid*; shatterproof, unbreakable, infrangible, solid 324 *dense*; impregnable 660 *invulnerable*; of iron nerve, indomitable, unconquerable, invincible, unbeatable 727 *unbeaten*; inextinguishable, unquenchable, unallayed 146 *unceasing*; unflagging, tireless, unexhausted 678 *industrious*; unweakened, unwithered, unworn; indestructible, nonbiodegradable 113 *lasting*; proof, sound; waterproof, showerproof, weatherproof, rustproof, damp-proof, impermeable, gasproof, leakproof, hermetic 264 *sealed off*; fireproof, bulletproof, bombproof.

*stalwart*, stout, sturdy, hardy, rugged, robust, doughty 174 *vigorous*; of good physique, able-bodied, abled, muscular, brawny; sinewy, wiry 678 *active*; strapping, well-knit, well set-up,

broad-shouldered, barrel-chested, thickset, stocky, mesomorphic, burly, beefy, husky, hulking, hefty 195 *large*; gigantic, colossal, titanic, Herculean, Atlantean 195 *huge*.

*athletic*, gymnastic, acrobatic 837 *amusing*, 716 *contending*; exercised, fit, fighting f., in training, in condition, in top form, in good nick, in tip-top condition 650 *healthy*; amazonian.

*manly*, masculine, macho 372 *male*; amazonian; virile, red-blooded, manful 855 *courageous*; in the prime of manhood 134 *grown-up*.

**Vb.** *be strong*, – mighty etc. adj.; have what it takes; pack a punch; gird up one's loins 669 *prepare*; come in force; be stronger, overpower, overmatch, overwhelm, be more than a match for 727 *overmaster*; get stronger, rally, recover, convalesce, revive 656 *be restored*, 685 *be refreshed*; get up, freshen (wind), blow hard, blow great guns 352 *blow*.

*strengthen*, confirm, give strength to, lend force to 36 *augment*; underline, stress 532 *emphasize*; reinforce, fortify, entrench; stuff, pad 227 *line*; buttress, prop, sustain 218 *support*; nerve, brace, steel, screw up one's courage 855 *give courage*; stiffen, stiffen one's resolve, stiffen one's upper lip, toughen, temper, case-harden 326 *harden*; energize, act like a tonic, put body into, put beef into 174 *invigorate*; beef up, tone up, animate, enliven, quicken 821 *excite*; vivify, revivify 656 *revive*; reinvigorate 685 *refresh*; set one on his legs 656 *cure*; set up, build up 310 *elevate*; screw up 45 *tighten*; power, engine, motor 160 *empower*.

**Adv. strongly**, powerfully etc. adj.; by force etc. n.; by main force, by sheer f., by compulsion, with might and main; in force.

## 163 Weakness

**N. weakness**, lack of strength, feebleness, puniness; vulnerability, helplessness 161 *impotence*; slightness 323 *lightness*; flimsiness, wispiness, fragility, frailness 330 *brittleness*; delicacy, tenderness 374 *sensibility*; effeminacy, womanishness; unfirmness, unsteadiness, shakiness, wobbliness, giddiness, vertigo, disequilibrium 29 *inequality*; weak foundation, feet of clay, instability 152 *changeableness*; ineffectiveness 161 *ineffectuality*; moral weakness, frailty, infirmity of purpose 601 *irresolution*; bodily weakness, weakliness, debility, infirmity, decrepitude, caducity, senility 131 *old age*; invalidism, delicate health 651 *ill health*; atony, no tone, no toughness, flaccidity, flabbiness, floppiness 327 *softness*; fleshiness, corpulence 195 *bulk*; weak state, asthenia, cachexia; spasticity; lameness, claudication; anaemia, bloodlessness; loss of strength, enervation, inanition, faintness, languor, torpor, inactivity 679 *sluggishness*; exhaustion, prostration, collapse 684 *fatigue*; unconsciousness, swoon, coma 375 *insensibility*; decline, declension 655 *deterioration*; weakening, softening, mitigation 177 *moderation*; relaxation 734 *laxity*; loosening 46 *disunion*; adulteration, watering, watering down, dilution 43 *mixture*; enfeeblement, debilitation, devitalization 655 *impairment*; emasculation, evisceration; invalidation 752 *abrogation*; effect of weakness, crack, fault 201 *gap*; flaw 845 *blemish*; strain, sprain, dislocation, break, fracture 63 *derangement*; inadequacy 636 *insufficiency*; weak point, fatal flaw, Achilles heel 647 *defect*.

*weakling*, effeminate, pansy, patsy; lightweight, small fry 639 *nonentity*; softy, sissy, milksop, mollycoddle, namby-pamby; old woman, invalid, hypochondriac 651 *sick person*; lame dog, lame duck, basket case, weakest link 731 *unlucky person*; infant, babe-in-arms, kitten 132 *young creature*; baby, big baby, crybaby, chicken 856 *coward*; mummy's boy, mother's darling, teacher's pet 890 *favourite*; doormat, pushover, jellyfish, drip, weed, wimp, nerd, wet; victim 825 *sufferer*; gull 544 *dupe*.

*weak thing*, flimsy article, reed, broken r., thread, rope of sand; sandcastle, mud pie, house built on sand, house of cards, cobweb, gossamer 4 *insubstantial thing*; matchwood, matchstick, eggshell, paper, tissue p.; glass, china 330 *brittleness*; water, dishwater, slops, milk and water, thin gruel.

**Adj.** *weak*, powerless, strengthless, 161 *impotent*; without force, invalid, unconfirmed 161 *powerless*; understrength, underproof; unfortified, unstrengthened, unaided, helpless, vulnerable 161 *defenceless*; harmless 935 *innocent*; namby-pamby, sissy, babyish 132 *infantine*; effeminate, limp-wristed, pansy, womanish 373 *female*; poor, feeble, frail, delicate, slight, puny 33 *small*; lightweight 323 *light*; slightly built, made of skin and bone, anorexic, skeletal, of poor physique 196 *little*; thin 206 *lean*; feeble-minded, weak *or* soft in the head, dim-witted, imbecile 499 *foolish*; sheepish, gutless, weak-willed, mealy-mouthed, shilly-shallying, half-hearted 601 *irresolute*; nerveless, unnerved 854 *nervous*; spineless, weak-kneed, lily-livered, chicken-hearted, submissive, yielding 721 *submitting*; marrowless, pithless 4 *insubstantial*; sapless 342 *dry*; bloodless, anaemic, pallid, pale 426 *colourless*; untempered, unhardened, limp, flaccid, flabby, floppy 327 *soft*; drooping, sagging, giving 217 *hanging*; untaut, unstrung, slack, loose, relaxed 734 *lax*, 46 *disunited*; watery, washy, wishy-washy, milk-and-water,

insipid, wersh (Scots) 387 *tasteless*; low, quiet, faint, hardly heard 401 *muted*; palsied, doddering, tottering, decrepit, old 131 *ageing*; too weak, past it, good-for-nothing, weak as a child, weak as a baby, weak as a kitten; wavering, unreliable 604 *capricious*; rickety, tottery, teetering, shaky, wobbly 152 *unstable*; torpid 679 *inactive*, 266 *quiescent*; in its beginnings, in its infancy, only beginning, infant 68 *beginning*, 126 *new*, 130 *young*. (See also *flimsy*.)

*weakened*, debilitated, enfeebled, enervated, devitalized, diminished, deflated 37 *decreasing*; tapped, depleted, impoverished, drained, wasted, dissipated, spent, effete, used up, burnt out 673 *used*; misused, abused; sapped, undermined, disarmed, disabled, laid low 161 *defenceless*; stripped, denuded, exposed, laid bare, bare 229 *uncovered*; flagging, failing, waning, drooping, exhausted, wearied, weary 684 *fatigued*; strained, overstrained 246 *distorted*; weatherbeaten, worn, broken, crumbling, tumbledown 655 *dilapidated*; the worse for wear, not what it was, on its last legs, tottering; rotten, rusting, withered, decaying, in decay 51 *decomposed*; deactivated, neutralized 175 *inert*; diluted, adulterated, watered, watered down 43 *mixed*. (See also *crippled*.)

*weakly*, infirm, asthenic, delicate, sickly 651 *unhealthy*; groggy, rocky; run down, seedy, under the weather, coming apart at the seams, below par, one degree under, logy, poorly; underweight, anorexic, skinny 206 *lean*; languid, languishing, listless; faint, fainting, faintish; sallow, wan, pallid, lacklustre 426 *colourless*.

*disabled*, impaired, incapacitated, differently abled, physically challenged, handicapped 161 *impotent*; crippled, halt, lame, game, gammy, limping, hobbling; hamstrung, hobbled; knock-kneed 246 *deformed*; stiff in the joints, arthritic, rheumatic, gouty; limbless, legless, armless, handless, eyeless 647 *imperfect*.

*flimsy*, gossamer, wispy, tenuous 4 *insubstantial*; delicate, dainty 331 *textural*; frail, gracile, tearable, fragile, frangible, friable 330 *brittle*; gimcrack, jerry-built, makeshift, shoddy 641 *useless*; rickety, ramshackle, tumbledown, on its last legs, shaky, tottery, teetering, wobbly, wonky, creaky, crazy, tumble-down 655 *dilapidated*.

**Vb.** *be weak*, grow w., grow feeble, weaken; sicken, be in poor health 651 *be ill*; faint, fail, languish, flag 684 *be fatigued*; drop, fall 309 *tumble*; dwindle 37 *decrease*; decline 655 *deteriorate*; droop, wilt, fade 131 *grow old*; wear thin, crumble; yield, give way, sag 327 *soften*; split 263 *open*; dodder, totter, teeter, sway, stagger, reel 317 *oscillate*; tremble, shake 318 *be agitated*; halt, limp, go lame 278 *move slowly*; have one foot in the grave, not have long to go, be on the way out 127 *be old*.

*weaken*, enfeeble, debilitate, enervate; unnerve, rattle 854 *frighten*; relax, slacken, unbrace, loosen 46 *disunite*; shake, soften up 327 *soften*; strain, sprain, fracture, cripple, lame 161 *disable*; hurt, injure 655 *wound*; cramp 702 *obstruct*; effeminate 161 *unman*; disarm, take the edge off, cushion 257 *blunt*; impoverish, starve; deprive, rob 786 *take away*; reduce, degrade, extenuate, thin, lessen 37 *abate*; dilute, water, water down, adulterate 43 *mix*; denature, devitalize, eviscerate; deactivate, neutralize 182 *counteract*; reduce in number, decimate 105 *render few*; muffle 401 *mute*; invalidate 752 *abrogate*; damage, spoil 655 *impair*; sap, deplete, undermine; dismantle 165 *demolish*.

## 164 Production

**N.** *production*, producing, creation; mental creation, cerebration 449 *thought*; origination, invention, innovation, original work 21 *originality*, 484 *discovery*; creative urge, productivity 171 *productiveness*; effort, endeavour 671 *attempt*, 672 *undertaking*; artistic effort, composition, authorship 551 *art*, 553 *painting*, 554 *sculpture*, 586 *writing*; musicianship 413 *musical skill*; doing, performance, output, throughput, turnout 676 *action*; execution, accomplishment, achievement 725 *effectuation*; concoction, brewing 669 *preparation*; shaping, forming, moulding, conformation, workmanship, craftsmanship 243 *formation*; planning, design, computer-aided d., CAD 623 *plan*; organization 331 *structure*, 62 *arrangement*; engineering, civil e., computer-aided engineering, CAE, building, architecture, tectonics; construction; building design, geomancy, feng shui; establishment, erection 310 *elevation*; making, fabrication, manufacture, computer-aided manufacture *or* manufacturing, CAM, computer-aided design and manufacture, CADCAM; industry, sunrise i. 622 *business*; processing, process 147 *conversion*; machining, assembly; assembly line, production l. 71 *continuity*, 630 *machine*; factory 687 *workshop*; technology, intermediate t., new t., high-tech, third wave; ecodevelopment; industrialization, industrial revolution, increased output, kaizen, mass production, automation, computerization, robotics, new technology; nanotechnology; productivity deal, performance-related pay 706 *cooperation*; development, growth 36 *increase*, 171 *abundance*; limits to growth 636 *scarcity*; farming, growing, factory farming 370

*agriculture*; breeding 369 *animal husbandry*; procreation 167 *propagation*.

*product*, creature, creation, result 157 *effect*; output, turnout; printout; end-product, by-p.; waste, slag 41 *leavings*; extract, essence; confection, compound 43 *a mixture*; work of one's hands, handiwork, artifact; manufacture, article, finished a., thing 319 *object*; goods, wares 795 *merchandise*; goods and services, gross national product, GNP; earthenware 381 *pottery*; stoneware, hardware, ironware; fabric, cloth 222 *textile*; production, work, opus, oeuvre, piece 56 *composition*; chef d'oeuvre, magnum opus, crowning achievement 694 *masterpiece*; fruit, flower, blossom, berry; produce, yield, harvest, crop, vintage 157 *growth*; interest, increase, return 771 *gain*; mental product, brainwave, brainchild, conception 451 *idea*; figment, fiction 513 *ideality*; offspring, young, egg, spawn, seed 132 *young creature*.

*building*, piece of architecture, edifice, structure, erection, pile, dome, tower, high-rise building, block of flats, skyscraper 209 *high structure*; pyramid, ancient monument 548 *monument*; church 990 *temple*; mausoleum 364 *tomb*; habitation, mansion, hall 192 *house*; college 539 *school*; fortress 713 *fort*; stonework, timbering, brickwork, bricks and mortar 631 *building material*; sick building.

*producer*, creator, maker, Nature; the Creator 965 *the Deity*; originator, inventor, discoverer, mover, prime m., instigator 612 *motivator*; founding father, founder, founder member, establisher 156 *cause*; begetter 169 *parentage*; creative worker, poet, writer 589 *author*; composer 413 *musician*; painter, sculptor 556 *artist*; deviser, designer 623 *planner*; developer, constructor, builder, architect, engineer; manufacturer, industrialist, technocrat 686 *agent*; executive 676 *doer*; labourer 686 *worker*; artificer, craftsman *or* -woman 686 artisan; grower, planter, cultivator, agriculturalist, gardener 370 *farmer*, stock farmer, stock breeder, sheep farmer, rancher 369 *breeder*; miner, extractor; play-producer 594 *stage manager*, film producer, film director 445 *cinema*.

**Adj.** *productive*, creative, inventive, innovative 513 *imaginative*; shaping, constructive, architectonic 331 *structural*; manufacturing, industrial 243 *formative*; developed, industrialized; mechanized, automated, computerized, robotic; paying 640 *profitable*; fruitful 171 *prolific*; life-giving 167 *generative*.

*produced*, made, made-up, cobbled together; created, creaturely; artificial, man-made, synthetic, cultivated; manufactured, processed; handmade, done by hand; tailor-made; homemade, home-spun; architect-designed, craftsman-built; custom-built; ready-made 243 *formed*; untouched by hand, machine-made, mass-produced; multiplied 166 *reproduced*; begotten 360 *born*; bred, hatched; sown, grown; thought of, invented.

**Vb.** *produce*, create, originate, make; invent 484 *discover*; think up, conceive 513 *imagine*; write, design 56 *compose*; operate 676 *do*; frame, fashion, shape, mould 243 *form*; knit, spin 222 *weave*; sew, run up 45 *tie*; forge, chisel, carve, sculpture, cast; coin 797 *mint*; manufacture, fabricate, prefabricate, process, turn out, mill, machine; mass-produce, churn out, multiply 166 *reproduce*; construct, build, raise, rear, erect, set up, run up 310 *elevate*; put together, make up, assemble, compose, cobble together 45 *join*; synthesize, blend 50 *combine*; mine, quarry 304 *extract*; establish, found, constitute, institute 68 *initiate*; organize, get up 62 *arrange*; develop, exploit; industrialize, mechanize, automate, computerize; engineer, contrive 623 *plan*; perform, implement, execute, achieve, accomplish 725 *carry out*; bring about, yield results, effect 156 *cause*; unfold, develop 316 *evolve*; breed, hatch, rear 369 *breed stock*; sow, grow, farm 370 *cultivate*, bear young 167 *reproduce itself*; bring up, educate 534 *train*.

## 165 Destruction

**N.** *destruction*, unmaking, undoing 148 *reversion*; blotting out 550 *obliteration*; blowing out, snuffing o., annihilation, nullification 2 *extinction*; abolition, suppression, supersession 752 *abrogation*; suffocation, smothering, stifling, silencing 399 *silence*; subversion 221 *overturning*, 149 *revolution*; prostration, precipitation, overthrow 311 *lowering*; felling, levelling, razing, flattening 216 *horizontality*; dissolving, dissolution 51 *decomposition*; breaking up, tearing down, knocking d., demolition, demolishment 655 *dilapidation*, 46 *disunion*; disruption 46 *separation*; crushing, grinding, pulverization 332 *powderiness*; incineration 381 *burning*; liquidation, elimination, extermination; extirpation, eradication, deracination, rooting out, uprooting 300 *ejection*; wiping out, mopping up 725 *completion*; decimation, mass murder, massacre, genocide 362 *slaughter*; abortion 172 *contraception*; hatchet job; destructiveness, wanton d., mischief, vandalism, iconoclasm 176 *violence*; sabotage 702 *hindrance*; fire-raising, arson 381 *incendiarism*.

*havoc*, scene of destruction, scene of devastation, disaster area, chaos 61 *confusion, turmoil*; desolation, wilderness, scorched earth 172 *desert*; nuclear winter; carnage, shambles 362 *place of slaughter*; upheaval, cataclysm,

inundation, storm 176 *outbreak*; devastation, laying waste, ravages; depredation, raid 788 *spoliation*; blitz, explosion, nuclear blast 712 *bombardment*; holocaust, hecatomb 981 *oblation*.

*ruin*, downfall, ruination, perdition, one's undoing; crushing blow 731 *adversity*; catastrophe, disaster, act of God 731 *misfortune*; collapse, débâcle, landslide 149 *revolution*; breakdown, meltdown, break-up, crack-up 728 *failure*; crash, smash, smash-up 279 *collision*; wreck, shipwreck, wreckage, wrack, rack and ruin; sinking, loss, total l.; Waterloo 728 *defeat*; knockout blow, KO 279 *knock*; beginning of the end, slippery slope, road to ruin 655 *deterioration*; coup de grâce 725 *completion*; apocalypse, doom, crack of doom, knell, end 69 *finality*, 961 *condemnation*; ruins 127 *oldness*.

**Adj.** *destructive*, destroying, internecine, annihilating etc. vb.; root and branch 54 *complete*; consuming, ruinous 634 *wasteful*; sacrificial, costly 811 *dear*; exhausting, crushing 684 *fatiguing*; apocalyptic, cataclysmic, overwhelming 176 *violent*; raging 176 *furious*; merciless 906 *pitiless*; mortal, suicidal, cut-throat, life-threatening 362 *deadly*; subversive, subversionary 149 *revolutionary*; incendiary, mischievous, pernicious 645 *harmful*; poisonous 653 *toxic*.

*destroyed*, undone, ruined, fallen; wiped out etc. vb.; crushed, ground; pulverized, pulped, broken up; suppressed, squashed, quashed 752 *abrogated*; lost, foundered, torpedoed, sunk, sunk without trace; dished, done for, had it, kaput; falling, crumbling, in ruins 655 *dilapidated*; doomed, for the chop, marked out for destruction; in course of demolition, in the breaker's hands, on the scrapheap 69 *ending*.

**Vb.** *destroy*, undo, unmake, dismantle, take apart 148 *revert*; destruct, self-d.; annihilate, exterminate, liquidate, nuke (inf); abolish, axe, invalidate 2 *nullify*; devour, consume 634 *waste*; swallow up, engulf 299 *absorb*; swamp, overwhelm, drown 341 *drench*; incinerate, burn up, gut 381 *burn*; wreck, shipwreck, sink (see also *suppress*); end, exterminate, put an end to 69 *terminate*; do for, do in, put down, put away, do away with, make away w., get rid of 362 *kill*; poison 362 *murder*; decimate 105 *render few*; exterminate, spare none, leave no survivor 362 *slaughter*, 906 *be pitiless*; remove, extirpate, eradicate, deracinate, uproot, root up 300 *eject*; wipe out, wipe off the map, expunge, efface, erase, delete, rub out, blot out, strike out, scratch out, cross out, cancel 550 *obliterate*; annul, revoke, tear up 752 *abrogate*; dispel, scatter, dissipate 75 *disperse*; dissolve 337 *liquefy*; evaporate 338 *vaporize*; mutilate, deface 244 *deform*; knock out, flatten out; put the kibosh on, nip in the bud, put the skids under, make short work of, seal the doom of, make mincemeat of, mop up; spifflicate, trounce 726 *defeat*; dish, cook one's goose, sabotage 702 *obstruct*; play hell with, play the deuce with 63 *bedevil*, 634 *waste*; ruin, bring to ruin, be the ruin of, be one's undoing, put the mockers on (inf).

*demolish*, unbuild, dismantle, break down, knock d., pull d., tear d. 46 *disunite*; level, raze, raze to the ground, lay in the dust 216 *flatten*; throw down, steamroller, bulldoze 311 *fell*; blow down, blow away, carry a.; cut down, mow d. 362 *slaughter*; knock over, kick o.; subvert, overthrow, overturn, topple, cause the downfall of, overset, upset 221 *invert*; sap, sap the foundations 163 *weaken*; undermine, mine, dynamite, explode, blast, blow up, blow sky-high; bombard, bomb, blitz, blow to bits 712 *fire at*; wreck, break up, smash up; smash, shatter, shiver, smash to smithereens 46 *break*; pulp, crush, grind 332 *pulverize*; crush to pieces, atomize, grind to bits, make mincemeat of; rend, tear up, rend to pieces, tear to bits, tear to shreds, tear to rags, pull to pieces, pluck to p., pick to p. 46 *sunder*; shake to pieces 318 *agitate*; beat down, batter, ram 279 *strike*; gut, strip bare 229 *uncover*.

*suppress*, quench, blow out, put o., snuff o. 382 *extinguish*; put the kibosh on, nip in the bud, cut short, cut off, abort 72 *discontinue*; quell, put down, stamp out, trample out, trample under foot, stamp on, sit on, clamp down on 735 *oppress*; squelch, squash 216 *flatten*; quash, revoke 752 *abrogate*; blanket, stifle, smother, suffocate, strangle 161 *disable*; keep down, repress 745 *subjugate*; cover 525 *conceal*; drown, submerge, sink, scuttle, scupper, torpedo, sink without trace 313 *plunge*, 311 *lower*.

*lay waste*, desolate, devastate, depopulate 300 *empty*; despoil, depredate, raid, pillage, ransack 788 *rob*; damage, spoil, mar, vandalize, ruin 655 *impair*; ravage, deal destruction, run amok, make havoc, make a shambles 176 *be violent*; lay waste with fire and the sword 634 *waste*; lay in ruins 311 *abase*; lay in ashes 381 *burn*; deforest, defoliate 172 *make sterile*; make a wilderness and call it peace.

*consume*, devour, eat up, lick up, gobble up; swallow up, engulf, envelop 299 *absorb*; squander, run through, fling to the winds, play ducks and drakes with 634 *waste*; throw to the dogs, cast before swine 675 *misuse*.

*be destroyed*, go west, go under, be lost 361 *perish*; sink, go down 313 *plunge*; have had it, be all over with, be all up with 69 *end*; cop it,

fall, fall to the ground, bite the dust 309 *tumble*; founder, go on the rocks, break up, split, go to pieces, crumple up; fall into ruin, go to rack and ruin, crumble, crumble to dust 655 *deteriorate*; go to the wall, succumb; go downhill, go to pot, go to the dogs, go to hell, go to blazes, be history.

**Adv.** *destructively*, crushingly, with crushing effect, with a sledge hammer.

## 166 Reproduction

**N.** *reproduction*, procreation 167 *propagation*; remaking, refashioning, reshaping, remoulding, reconstruction 164 *production*; rediscovery 484 *discovery*; redoing 106 *repetition*; reduplication, mass production 171 *productiveness*; multiplication, duplication, printing 587 *print*; renovation, renewal 656 *restoration*; regeneration, resuscitation, reanimation 656 *revival*; resurrection, resurgence; reappearance 106 *recurrence*; atavism 5 *heredity*; reincarnation, palingenesis 124 *future state*; new edition, reprint 589 *edition*; copy 22 *duplicate*; Phoenix.

**Adj.** *reproduced*, renewed, renewing; reproductive 167 *generative*; resurrectional, resurrectionary; renascent, resurgent, reappearing; Hydra-headed, Phoenix-like.

**Vb.** *reproduce*, remake, refashion, remould, recoin, reconstruct; rebuild, refound, reestablish, rediscover; duplicate, clone 20 *copy*, 106 *repeat*; take after, inherit 18 *resemble*, 148 *revert*; renovate, renew 656 *restore*; regenerate, revivify, resuscitate, reanimate 656 *revive*; reappear 106 *reoccur*; resurrect, stir up the embers; mass-produce, multiply; print off, reel o. 587 *print*; crop up, spring up like mushrooms, burgeon, breed 167 *reproduce itself*, 104 *be many*.

## 167 Propagation

**N.** *propagation* 166 *reproduction*; fertility, fecundity 171 *productiveness*; proliferation, multiplication 36 *increase*; breeding, hatching, incubation 369 *animal husbandry*; eugenics 358 *biology*; sex, facts of life, birds and the bees; copulation 45 *sexual intercourse*; generation, procreation, genesis 156 *source*; biogenesis; parthenogenesis, virgin birth; abiogenesis, autogenesis, spontaneous generation; fertilization, pollination, fecundation, super-f., superfetation, impregnation, insemination, artificial i., AID, AIH; assisted reproduction, reproductive medicine, fertility treatment, fertility drug, test-tube baby, gamete intra-fallopian transfer, Gift, intra-cytoplasmic sperm injection, invitro fertilization, IVF; egg donation 171 *fertilizer*; conception, pregnancy, germination, gestation (see also *obstetrics*); birth, nativity, happy event 68 *origin*; abortion, miscarriage, stillbirth 728 *failure*; birth rate, natality; development 157 *growth*; fructification, fruition, florescence, efflorescence, flowering 669 *maturation*; puberty 134 *adultness*; parenthood, maternity, paternity 169 *parentage*; procreator, begetter; inseminator, donor; fertilizer, pollinator; propagator, cultivator 370 *gardener*.

*obstetrics*, midwifery; parturition, birth, childbirth, natural c., active birth, alternative b., water b., childbed, confinement, lying in, accouchement, birthing pool; epidural 375 *anaesthetic*; labour, labour pains, contractions; travail, birth-throes, birth pangs; delivery, breech d., forceps d., Caesarian section, Caesarian; amniotics fluid, waters, bag of w., caul, umbilical cord; placenta, afterbirth; amniocentesis, amnio, alphafetoprotein test 658 *diagnosis*; gynaecologist, obstetrician, maternity specialist, midwife 658 *nurse*; stork, gooseberry bush.

*genitalia*, loins, womb 156 *source*; genitals, reproductive organs, sex organs; pudenda, private parts, privates; intromittent organ, male member, penis, phallus, John Thomas (inf), cock (inf), prick (sl), dick (sl), willy (inf), pecker (sl), tool, weapon; testicles, scrotum, balls (inf), bollocks (sl), goolies (sl), nuts (sl), rocks (sl), dangly bits (inf), lunch-box (inf), crown jewels (inf), the last turkey in the shop (sl); erection, boner (sl), hard-on (sl), stiffy (sl); brewer's droop (inf); prostate, p. gland; vas deferens; female sex organ, vulva, clitoris, vagina, cunt (sl), fanny (inf), pussy (sl), twat (sl), slit (sl), quim (sl); uterus, cervix, ovary, Fallopian tubes; ovum, egg; seed, semen, seminal fluid, sperm, spermatozoa, spunk (sl).

**Adj.** *generative*, potent, virile; productive, reproductive, procreative, procreant; philoprogenitive, multiparous, fertile, fecund 171 *prolific*; life-giving, originative, germinal, seminal, spermatic, genetic 156 *fundamental*; sexual, bisexual, unisexual; genital, vulvar, clitoral, vaginal, penile, phallic.

*fertilized*, fecundated, impregnated; breeding, broody, pregnant, enceinte, gravid; in an interesting *or* delicate condition; heavy with, big with; expecting, expecting a happy event, expectant, carrying, with child, in the family way; up the spout, up the pole, in the club, having a bun in the oven, fallen, preggers; parturient, brought to bed of, in labour; obstetric, obstetrical 658 *medical*; puerperal, childbed, maternity; antenatal, perinatal, postnatal; viviparous, oviparous; parthenogenetic.

**Vb.** *reproduce itself*, yield, give increase 171

*be fruitful*; hatch, breed, spawn, multiply, teem, breed like rabbits 104 *be many*; germinate, sprout, burgeon 36 *grow*; bloom, flower, fruit, bear fruit, fructify 669 *mature*; seed, seed itself; conceive, get pregnant, fall; carry, bear; be brought to bed of, bring forth, give birth, have a baby; abort, lose the baby 728 *miscarry*; have children, have young, have offspring, have progeny; lay (eggs), drop, farrow, lamb, foal, calve, cub, pup, whelp, kitten, litter; have one's birth 360 *be born*.

*generate*, evolve 164 *produce*; bring into being, bring into the world, usher into the world; give life to, bring into existence, call into being; beget, get, engender, spawn, father, sire; copulate 45 *unite with*; fecundate, impregnate, inseminate, pollinate; procreate, propagate; breed, hatch, incubate, raise, bring up, rear 369 *breed stock*; raise from seed, take cuttings, bud, graft, layer 370 *cultivate*.

## 168 Destroyer

**N.** *destroyer*, demolisher, leveller; Luddite, iconoclast, destructionist, annihilationist, nihilist, anarchist 149 *revolutionist*; wrecker, vandal, arsonist, pyromaniac 381 *incendiarism*; spoiler, despoiler, ravager, pillager, raider 712 *attacker*, 789 *robber*; saboteur 702 *hinderer*; defacer, eraser, extinguisher 550 *obliteration*; hatchet man, hitman, killer, assassin 362 *murderer*; executioner, hangman 963 *punisher*; barbarian, Vandal, Hun; time, hand of t., time's scythe 111 *course of time*; angel of death 361 *death*; destructive agency, locust 947 *glutton*; moth, woodworm, dry rot, rust, erosion 51 *decay*; corrosive, acid, mildew, blight, poison 659 *bane*; earthquake, fire, flood 165 *havoc*; 'grim-visaged war' (see quotation at 718 *war*) 718 *war*; instrument of destruction, sword 723 *weapon*; gunpowder, dynamite, blasting powder 723 *explosive*; blockbuster 723 *bomb*; nuclear warhead; juggernaut, bulldozer 216 *flattener*; Four Horsemen of the Apocalypse, Exterminating Angel.

## 169 Parentage

**N.** *parentage*, paternity, maternity; parenthood, fatherhood, motherhood; loins, womb 156 *source*; kinship 11 *family*; adoption, fostering, guardianship, surrogateship, surrogacy 660 *protection*; parent, first parents, Adam and Eve 371 *humankind*; single parent 896 *divorce, widowhood*; godparent, guardian, appropriate person 660 *protection*; parenting skills.

*genealogy*, family tree, lineage, kin 11 *consanguinity*; race history, pedigree, heredity; line, blood-l., blood, strain; blue blood 868 *nobility*; stock, stem, tribe, house, clan 11 *race*;

descent, extraction, birth, ancestry 68 *origin*.

*paternity*, fatherhood; father, dad, daddy, pop, papa, pater, governor, the old man (inf); single dad, lone parent; head of the family, paterfamilias; procreator, begetter, author of one's existence; grandfather, grandsire, grandad, grandpa, great-grandfather 133 *old man*; founder of the family, ancestor, progenitor, forefather, forebear, patriarch, predecessor 66 *precursor*; father figure; adoptive father, foster-f., natural f., biological f., stepfather, father-in-law; fatherland.

*maternity*, motherhood; maternal instinct 887 *love*; expectant mother, mother-to-be 167 *propagation*; mother, mum, mummy, mama, mater, the old lady (inf); unmarried m., single m., lone parent, dam; mamma, mummy, mum, mater; biological mother, birth m., adoptive m., surrogate m.; grandmother, grandma, granny, gran, nan; materfamilias, matron, matriarch; ancestress, progenitrix; grandam 133 *old woman*; mother substitute; fostermother, stepmother, natural m.; mother-in-law; Mother Church, mother country, motherland.

**Adj.** *parental*, paternal; maternal, matronly; fatherly, fatherlike; motherly, stepmotherly; family, lineal, patrilineal, matrilineal; ancestral; hereditary 5 *genetic*; patriarchal 127 *immemorial*; racial, phyletic 11 *ethnic*.

## 170 Posterity

**N.** *posterity*, progeny, issue, offspring, young, little ones 132 *child*; breed 11 *race*; brood, seed, litter, farrow, spawn 132 *young creature*; fruit of the womb, children, grandchildren 11 *family*; aftercomers, succession, heirs; inheritance, heritage 120 *posteriority*; rising generation 130 *youth*.

*descendant*, son, daughter; chip off the old block, infant 132 *child*; scion, shoot, sprout 132 *young plant*; heir, heiress, heir of the body 776 *beneficiary*; love child 954 *bastardy*; branch, ramification, daughter-house, daughter-nation, colony; graft, offshoot, offset.

*sonship*, filiation, line, direct l., lineage, descent, male d.; agnation 11 *consanguinity*; indirect descent, collaterality, ramification; irregular descent, illegitimacy 954 *bastardy*; succession, heredity, heirship; primogeniture 119 *priority*.

**Adj.** *filial*, daughterly; descended, lineal; collateral; primogenital 119 *prior*; adopted, adoptive; step-; hereditary, inherited, Mendelian 5 *genetic*.

## 171 Productiveness

**N.** *productiveness*, productivity, mass pro-

duction 164 *production*; boom, booming economy 730 *prosperity*; overproductivity, superabundance, glut, butter mountain, wine lake 637 *redundance*; menarche, fecundity, fertility, luxuriance, lushness, exuberance, richness, embarras de richesses, Green Revolution 635 *plenty*; high birthrate, baby boom, population explosion; productive capacity, biotic potential; procreation, multiplication 167 *propagation*; fructification 669 *maturation*; fecundation, fertilization, pollination; inventiveness, resourcefulness 513 *imagination*.

*fertilizer*, organic f., manure, farmyard m., dung, guano, compost, bonemeal; artificial fertilizer, chemical f.; phosphates, nitrates, potash, lime; top-dressing, mulch 370 *agriculture*; semen, sperm, seed; fertility drug, gonadotrophin 167 *propagation*; fertility cult, f. rite, f. symbol, phallic s., phallus; linga, yoni; Earth Mother, Ceres, Demeter.

*abundance*, wealth, riot, profusion, harvest 32 *great quantity*; teeming womb, mother earth, rich soil; hotbed, nursery, propagator 156 *seedbed*; cornucopia, horn of plenty, 'land flowing with milk and honey' (see quotation at 730 *prosperity*); milch cow; second crop, aftergrowth, aftermath 67 *sequel*; rabbit warren, ant heap 104 *multitude*.

**Adj.** *prolific*, fertile, productive, fecund; teeming, multiparous, spawning 167 *generative*; fruitful, fruitbearing, fructiferous; pregnant, heavy with, parturient; exuberant, rife, lush, leafy, verdant, luxuriant, rich, fat 635 *plenteous*; copious, streaming, pouring; paying 640 *profitable*; propagatory, regenerative, creative, inventive, resourceful; scribacious.

**Vb.** *make fruitful*, make productive etc. adj.; make the desert bloom; plant, fertilize, water, irrigate, manure, compost, top-dress 370 *cultivate*; impregnate, fecundate, inseminate; procreate, produce, propagate 167 *generate*.

*be fruitful*, – prolific etc. adj.; fructify, flourish; burgeon, bloom, blossom; germinate; conceive, bear, give birth, have children 167 *reproduce itself*; teem, proliferate, pullulate, swarm, multiply, mushroom 104 *be many*; boom; send up the birthrate 36 *augment*; populate.

## 172 Unproductiveness

**N.** *unproductiveness*, unproductivity, dearth, famine 636 *scarcity*; sterility, barrenness, infertility, infecundity, impotence 161 *impotence*, 728 *failure*; overfishing, overgrazing; deforestation, erosion; defoliation; scorched earth policy, desertification, desertization; dying race, falling birthrate, zero population growth 37 *decrease*; virginity 895 *celibacy*; change of life, the change, menopause; abortion; unprofitableness, poor return, losing business 772 *loss*; unprofitability, fruitlessness 641 *inutility*; aridity, aridness, fallowness, stagnation, waste of time 641 *lost labour*; slump, slack market, idleness 679 *inactivity*.

*contraception*, birth control, planned parenthood, family planning; contraceptive; pill, minipill, morning-after p., abortion p., abortifacient, aborticide; coil, loop, diaphragm, Dutch cap, French letter, condom, sheath, barrier contraceptive; spermicide, C-film; rhythm method, Billing's m.; chastity 747 *restraint*; sterilization, vasectomy, hysterectomy.

*desert*, dryness, aridity, aridness 342 *dryness*; desolation, waste, barren w., wastelands, lunar landscape; heath, moor, bush, wild, wilderness, howling w.; desert sands, sand dunes, Gobi, Kalahari, Sahara; dustbowl 634 *waste*; desert island; salt flat 347 *marsh*; Arctic wastes 380 *ice*; waste of waters 343 *ocean*.

**Adj.** *unproductive*, dried up, exhausted, spent 634 *wasted*; sparse, scarce 636 *insufficient*; waste, desert, desolate; treeless, bleak, gaunt, bare 190 *empty*; poor, stony, shallow, eroded; barren, infertile, sour, sterile; withered, shrivelled, blasted; unprolific, unfruitful, infecund; rootless, seedless, ungerminating; arid, unwatered, unirrigated 342 *dry*; fallow, stagnating 674 *disused*; unsown, unmanured, unploughed, untilled, uncultivated, unharvested; impotent, sterilized, sterile, on the pill; childless, issueless, without issue; celibate 895 *unwedded*; otiose 679 *inactive*; fruitless, unprofitable 641 *profitless*; inoperative, out of action, null and void, of no effect 161 *impotent*; ineffective 728 *unsuccessful*; addled, abortive 670 *unprepared*.

**Vb.** *be unproductive* – unprolific etc. adj.; rust, stagnate, lie fallow 679 *be inactive*; cease work 145 *cease*; bury one's talent, hide one's light under a bushel 674 *not use*; hang fire, come to nothing, be of no avail, come to naught, flatline (sl) 728 *fail*; abort 728 *miscarry*; take precautions, practise birth control, contracept; have no issue, lower the birthrate.

*make sterile*, make unproductive 634 *waste*; sterilize, vasectomize, castrate, geld 161 *unman*; deforest, overgraze 165 *lay waste*; addle 51 *decompose*; pasteurize, disinfect 648 *purify*.

## 173 Agency

**N.** *agency*, operation, work, working, doing 676 *action*; job, position, office 622 *function*; exercise 673 *use*; force, strain, stress, play, swing 160 *power*; interaction, interworking 178 *influence*; procuration, procurement 689 *manage-ment*; service 628 *instrumentality*; effectiveness, effectualness, effectuality, efficiency 156 *causation*; quickening power 174 *stimulation*; maintenance, aliment, alimony, palimony, support 703 *aid*; co-agency 706 *cooperation*; implementation, execution 725 *effectuation*; process, processing, treatment, handling.

**Adj.** *operative*, effectual, efficient, efficacious 727 *successful*; drastic 735 *severe*; executive, operational, functional; acting, working, in action, in operation, in force, in play, up and running, being exercised, at work 676 *doing*, 673 *used*; on foot, afoot, on the active list, up and doing 678 *active*; live, potent 160 *dynamic*, 174 *vigorous*; practical, practicable, workable, applicable 642 *advisable*; serviceable 640 *useful*; worked upon, acted u., wrought u.

**Vb.** *operate*, be in action, be operative, be in play, play; act, work, go, run 676 *do*; start up, rev up, tick over, idle; serve, execute, perform 622 *function*; do its job, do its stuff, do one's thing 727 *be successful*; take effect 156 *cause*; have effect, act upon, bear u., work u., play u. 178 *influence*; take action, take industrial a., strike 678 *be active*; maintain, sustain 218 *support*; crew, man; make operate, bring into play, bring into action, wind up, turn on, plug in, switch on, flick *or* flip the switch, press the button; actuate, power, drive 265 *move*; process, treat; manipulate, handle, wield 378 *touch*, 673 *use*; stimulate, excite 174 *invigorate*.

## 174 Vigour: physical energy

**N.** *vigorousness*, lustiness, energy, vigour, life 678 *activity*; dynamism, physical energy, dynamic e., pressure, force, impetus 160 *energy*; intensity, high pressure 162 *strength*; dash, élan, pizzazz, impetuosity 680 *haste*; exertion, effort 682 *labour*; fervour, enthusiasm 571 *vigour*; gusto, relish, zest, zestfulness 824 *joy*; liveliness, spirit, vim, zing, zip, éclat; fire, mettle, pluck, smeddum, blood 855 *courage*; ginger, fizz, verve, snap, pep, drive, go, get up and go; enterprise, initiative 672 *undertaking*; movers and shakers; vehemence 176 *violence*; aggressiveness, oomph, thrust, push, kick, punch 712 *attack*; grip, bite, teeth, backbone, spunk 599 *resolution*; guts, grit 600 *stamina*; virility 162 *vitality*; live wire, spark, dynamo, dynamite, quicksilver; rocket, jet; display of energy 277 *spurt*; show of force, demonstration 854 *intimidation*.

*stimulation*, activation, tonic effect, turning on, galvanizing, whipping up; intensification, boost, stepping up, bumping up, hiking up 36 *increase*; excitement 821 *excitation*; stir, bustle 678 *activity*; perturbation 318 *agitation*; ferment, fermentation, leavening; ebullience, ebullition 318 *commotion*; froth, effervescence 355 *bubble*; steam 381 *heating*.

*keenness*, acridity, acrimony, mordancy, causticity, virulence 388 *pungency*; poignancy, point, edge 256 *sharpness*; zeal 597 *willingness*.

*stimulant*, energizer, activator, booster; yeast, leaven, catalyst; stimulus, fillip, shot, shot in the arm; crack of the whip, spur, prick, prod, jolt, goad, lash 612 *incentive*; restorative, tonic, pep pill 658 *tonic*; bracer, pick-me-up, aperitif, appetizer 390 *savouriness*; seasoning, spice 389 *sauce*; liquor, alcohol 301 *alcoholic drink*; aphrodisiac, philtre, love p., love potion; Viagra (tdmk); cantharides, Spanish fly; pep talk, rousing cheer, egging on 821 *excitant*.

**Adj.** *vigorous*, energetic, proactive 678 *active*; radioactive 362 *deadly*; forcible, forceful, robust, vehement 176 *violent*; drastic, stringent, harsh, punishing 735 *severe*; vivid, vibrant 160 *dynamic*; high-pressure, intense, strenuous 678 *industrious*; enterprising, go-getting, go-ahead 285 *progressive*; aggressive, pushful, thrustful 712 *attacking*; keen, alacritous 597 *willing*; double-edged, double-distilled, potent 160 *powerful*; hearty, virile, full-blooded 162 *strong*; full of beans, full of punch, full of pep, peppy, full of zip, zippy, zingy, zestful, lusty, mettlesome 819 *lively*; blooming, bouncing 650 *healthy*; spry, brisk, nippy, snappy; fizzy, effervescent, heady, racy; tonic, bracing, rousing, invigorating, stimulating 821 *exciting*; intensified, stepped up, hiked up, boosted; gingered up, souped up 160 *powerful*; revived 685 *refreshed*, 656 *restored*; thriving, lush 171 *prolific*.

*keen*, acute, sharp, incisive, trenchant 571 *forceful*; mordant, biting, poignant, pointed, sarcastic 851 *derisive*; virulent, corrosive, caustic 388 *pungent*; acrimonious, acrid, acid 393 *sour*.

**Vb.** *be vigorous*, thrive, have zest, be full of zip *or* zing, enjoy life 650 *be healthy*; burst with energy, overflow with e. 162 *be strong*; show energy 678 *be active*; steam away, be always on the go, be up and doing 682 *exert oneself*; exert energy, drive, push 279 *impel*; bang, slam, wrench, cut right through 176 *force*; raise the pressure, get up steam, put on a spurt, get psyched up, pull out all the stops 277 *accelerate*; be thorough, strike home 725 *carry through*; strike hard, hammer, dint, dent 279 *strike*; show one's power, tell upon, make an impression 178 *influence*, 821 *impress*; throw one's weight about 678 *meddle*; show fight, take the offensive 712 *attack*.

*invigorate*, energize, activate; galvanize, electrify, intensify, double, redouble; wind up, step up, bump up, hike up, pep up, ginger up,

boost, soup up 162 *strengthen*; rouse, kindle, inflame, stimulate, psych up, enliven, quicken, hothouse 821 *excite*; act like a tonic, hearten, animate, egg on 833 *cheer*; go to one's head, intoxicate 949 *inebriate*; freshen, revive 685 *refresh*; give an edge to 256 *sharpen*; fertilize, irrigate 370 *cultivate*.

**Adv.** *vigorously*, forcibly, hard, straight from the shoulder, with telling effect; zestfully, lustily, con brio, with a will; at full tilt, full steam ahead.

## 175 Inertness

**N.** *inertness*, inertia, accidie 677 *inaction*; lifelessness, languor, paralysis, torpor, torpidity 375 *insensibility*; rest, vegetation, stagnation, passivity 266 *quiescence*; dormancy 523 *latency*; mental inertness, apathy, dullness, sloth 679 *sluggishness*; immobility, passive resistance 602 *obstinacy*; impassiveness, stolidity 823 *inexcitability*; gutlessness 601 *irresolution*; vegetable, cabbage; extinct volcano.

**Adj.** *inert*, unactivated, unaroused, passive, dead 677 *nonactive*; lifeless, languid, torpid, numb 375 *insensible*; heavy, lumpish, sluggish 278 *slow*, 679 *inactive*; hibernating 679 *sleepy*; quiet, vegetating, stagnant 266 *quiescent*; fallow 172 *unproductive*; slack, low-pressure, untensed 734 *lax*; limp, flaccid 163 *weak*; apathetic, neutral 860 *indifferent*, 820 *impassive*; pacific, unwarlike, unaggressive 717 *peaceful*, 823 *inexcitable*; uninfluential 161 *powerless*; deactivated, unexerted, suspended, in abeyance 752 *abrogated*; smouldering, dormant 523 *latent*.

**Vb.** *be inert*, be inactive etc. adj.; slumber 679 *sleep*; hang fire, not catch; smoulder 523 *lurk*; lie, stagnate, vegetate 266 *be quiescent*; just sit there 677 *not act*.

**Adv.** *inactively*, passively etc. adj.; at rest; in suspense, in abeyance, in reserve.

## 176 Violence

**N.** *violence*, vehemence, frenzy, fury, ferment, impetuosity 174 *vigorousness*; destructiveness, vandalism 165 *destruction*; boisterousness, turbulence, storminess 318 *commotion*; bluster, uproar, riot, row, roughhouse, rumpus, ruckus, brouhaha, stramash, furore 61 *turmoil*; roughness, ungentleness, rough handling 735 *severity*; force, fisticuffs, hammer blows; domestic violence, wife-beating, child abuse; high hand, coup de main, strong-arm tactics, thuggery, terrorism 735 *brute force*; atrocity, outrage, torture 898 *cruel act*; barbarity, brutality, savagery, blood lust 898 *inhumanity*; fierceness, ferocity, malignity, mercilessness 906 *pitilessness*; rage, air r., desk r., golf r., hedge r., office r., parking r., road r., shop r. *or* shopping r., trolley r., hysterics 822 *excitable state*; fit, throes, paroxysm 318 *spasm*; shock, clash 279 *collision*; wrench, twist, dislocation 63 *derangement*, 246 *distortion*.

*outbreak*, outburst, ebullition, effervescence 318 *agitation*; flood, tidal wave 350 *wave*; cataclysm, convulsion, earthquake, quake, tremor 149 *revolution*; eruption, volcano 383 *furnace*; explosion, blow-up, flare-up, burst, blast 165 *destruction*; bursting open, dissilience 46 *disunion*; detonation 400 *loudness*; rush, onrush, assault, sortie 712 *attack*; gush, spurt, jet, torrent 350 *stream*.

*storm*, turmoil, turbulence, war of the elements; weather, dirty w., rough w., inclement w., inclemency; squall, tempest, typhoon, hurricane, tornado, cyclone 352 *gale*; thunder, thunder and lightning, fulguration; rainstorm, downpour, cloudburst 350 *rain*; hailstorm, snowstorm, blizzard 380 *wintriness*; sandstorm, duststorm, sirocco 352 *gale*; magnetic storm.

*violent creature*, brute, beast, wild b., savage b.; dragon, tiger, wolf, she w., mad dog; demon, devil, hellcat, hellhound, 'the Hound of the Baskervilles' 938 *monster*;

> **The Hound of the Baskervilles**
> Title of novel by Sir Arthur Conan Doyle.

savage, barbarian, vandal, iconoclast 168 *destroyer*, he-man, cave m., Neanderthal m. 372 *male*; man of blood, assassin, butcher, executioner, hangman, Herod 362 *murderer*; homicidal maniac, berserker, psychopath, headcase (sl) 504 *madman*; rough, tough, rowdy, thug, mugger 904 *ruffian*; hooligan, bully, bully boy, bovver b., boot b., football hooligan, lager lout, terror, holy t. 735 *tyrant*; thunderer, fire-eater, bravo 877 *boaster*; firebrand, incendiary, pyromaniac 738 *agitator*; revolutionary, anarchist, militant, nihilist, terrorist 149 *revolutionist*; hotspur, madcap 857 *desperado*; virago, termagant, Amazon; spitfire, fury, scold 892 *shrew*.

**Adj.** *violent*, vehement, forcible 162 *strong*; acute 256 *sharp*; unmitigated; excessive, outrageous, extravagant 32 *exorbitant*; rude, ungentle, abrupt, brusque, bluff 885 *discourteous*; extreme, severe, tyrannical, heavy-handed 735 *oppressive*; primitive, barbarous, savage, brutal, bloody 898 *cruel*; hot-blooded 892 *irascible*; aggressive, bellicose 718 *warlike*; rampant, charging 712 *attacking*; struggling, kicking, thrashing about 61 *disorderly*; rough, wild, furious, raging, blustery, tempestuous, stormy, gale force 352 *windy*; drenching, torrential 350 *rainy*; uproarious, obstreperous 400

loud; rowdy, turbulent, tumultuous, boisterous 738 *riotous*; incendiary, anarchistic, nihilistic 149 *revolutionary*; intemperate, immoderate, unbridled, unrestrained; ungovernable, unruly, uncontrollable 738 *disobedient*; irrepressible, inextinguishable 174 *vigorous*; ebullient, hot, red-hot, inflamed 381 *heated*; inflammatory, scorching, flaming 379 *fiery*; eruptive, cataclysmic, overwhelming, volcanic, seismic 165 *destructive*; detonating, explosive, bursting; convulsive, spasmodic 318 *agitated*; full of violence, disturbed, troublous 61 *orderless*.

*furious*, fuming, boiling, towering; infuriated, mad, like a mad bull, mad with rage, maddened 891 *angry*; impetuous, rampant, gnashing; roaring, howling; headstrong 680 *hasty*; desperate 857 *rash*; savage, tameless, wild; blustering, threatening 899 *cursing*; vicious, fierce, ferocious 898 *cruel*; bloodthirsty, ravening, rabid, berserk, out of control 362 *murderous*; waspish, tigerish; frantic, frenetic, hysterical, in hysterics 503 *frenzied*.

**Vb.** *be violent*, break bounds, run wild, run riot, run amok 165 *lay waste*; tear, rush, dash, hurtle, hurl oneself, rush headlong 277 *move fast*; crash in 297 *burst in*; surge forward, stampede, mob 712 *charge*; break the peace, raise a storm, riot, roughhouse, kick up a row, kick up a shindig, raise the dust, go on the rampage 61 *rampage*; resort to violence, resort to fisticuffs, take to arms 718 *go to war*, 738 *revolt*; see red, go berserk 891 *be angry*; storm, rage, roar, bluster, come in like a lion 352 *blow*; ferment, foam, fume, run high, boil over 318 *effervesce*; burst its banks, flood, overwhelm 350 *flow*; go up in flames, explode, go off, blow up, detonate, burst, fly, flash, flare; let fly, let off, fulminate; erupt, break out, fly o., burst o.; struggle, strain, scratch, bite, kick, lash out 715 *resist*; beat up, mug, savage, maul, knock *or* beat six *or* seven *or* ten bells out of 655 *wound*; bear down, bear hard on, ride roughshod, trample on, tyrannize, 'out-Herod Herod' (see quotation at 546 *exaggerate*) 735 *oppress*.

*force*, use f., smash 46 *break*; tear, rend 46 *sunder*; bruise, crush 332 *pulverize*; blow up 165 *demolish*; strain, wrench, pull, dislocate, fracture, sprain; twist, warp, deform 246 *distort*; force open, prize o., pry o., lever o., jimmy 263 *open*; blow open, burst o.; shock, shake 318 *agitate*; do violence to, mug, beat up, abuse 675 *misuse*; violate, ravish, rape 951 *debauch*; torture 645 *ill-treat*; bully, coerce, drag kicking and screaming, drive, pressgang, railroad 740 *compel*.

*make violent*, stir, quicken, stimulate 821 *excite*; urge, jolt, goad, lash, whip 612 *incite*;

stir up, inflame 381 *kindle*; add fuel to the flames, blow on the embers 381 *heat*; foment, exacerbate, exasperate 832 *aggravate*; whet 256 *sharpen*; irritate, infuriate, lash into fury 891 *enrage*; madden 503 *make mad*.

**Adv.** *violently*, forcibly, by storm, by force, by main force, amain; with might and main; tooth and nail, hammer and tongs, vi et armis, at the point of a sword, at knife-point, at the end of a gun; tyrannously, high-handedly; bodily, neck and crop; at one fell swoop; with a vengeance, like mad; precipitately, headlong, slap bang, wham; head foremost, head first; like a bull at a gate, like a battering ram, like Gadarene swine.

## 177 Moderation

**N.** *moderation*, nonviolence; mildness, gentleness 736 *leniency*; harmlessness, innocuousness 935 *innocence*; moderateness, reasonableness 502 *sanity*; measure, golden mean 732 *averageness*; temperateness, restraint, self-control 942 *temperance*; soberness 948 *sobriety*, 874 *modesty*; impassivity, mental calmness, ataraxy *or* ataraxia 823 *inexcitability*; impartiality, neutrality 625 *middle way*; correction, adjustment, modulation; mutual concession, trade-off 770 *compromise*; mitigation 831 *relief*; relaxation, remission, letup 734 *laxity*; easing, alleviation; mollification, appeasement, assuagement, détente 719 *pacification*; tranquillization, sedation; quiet, calm, dead c. 266 *quietude*; control, check 747 *restraint*.

*moderator*, palliative 658 *remedy*; lenitive, alleviative, demulcent 658 *balm*; rose water, soothing syrup, milk, oil on troubled waters; calmative, sedative, tranquillizer, Valium (tdmk), lullaby; nightcap, bromide, barbiturate, sleeping pill, Mogadon (tdmk) 679 *soporific*; anodyne, opiate, opium, laudanum 375 *anaesthetic*; dummy, pacifier 264 *stopper*; wet blanket, damper, killjoy 613 *dissuasion*; cooler, cold water, cold shower 382 *extinguisher*; clamp, brake 747 *restraint*; neutralizer; anaphrodisiac 658 *antidote*; cushion, shock absorber 327 *softness*; third force, mollifier, peacemaker 720 *mediator*; controller, restraining hand, rein.

**Adj.** *moderate*, unextreme, nonviolent, reasonable, within reason, judicious 913 *just*; tame, gentle, gentle as a lamb, harmless, mild, mild as milk 736 *lenient*; milk and water, innocuous 935 *innocent*, 163 *weak*; measured, restricted, limited, low-key, understated 747 *restrained*; chastened, subdued, self-controlled, tempered 942 *temperate*, 948 *sober*; cool, calm, composed 823 *inexcitable*; still, quiet, untroubled 266 *tranquil*; peaceable, pacific 717

*peaceful*; leftish, pink, nonextreme, nonreactionary, middle-American, middle-of-the-road 625 *neutral*, 860 *indifferent*.

*alleviative*, unexciting, unirritating, lenitive, nonirritant 658 *remedial*; alleviative, assuaging, pain-killing, anodyne, calmative, sedative, tranquillizing, hypnotic, narcotic 679 *soporific*; smooth 327 *soft*; soothing, bland, demulcent; emollient; oily 334 *lubricated*; comforting 685 *refreshing*; disarming 719 *pacificatory*.

**Vb.** *be moderate*, – gentle etc. adj.; not go to extremes 625 *be halfway*; go easy, keep within bounds, keep on an even keel, keep within reason 942 *be temperate*; sober down, settle 266 *be quiescent*; disarm, decommission, keep the peace 717 *be at peace*; remit, relent 905 *show mercy*; show consideration, not press 736 *be lenient*; not resist, go quietly, go out like a lamb; ease off 278 *decelerate*.

*moderate*, mitigate, temper; correct 24 *adjust*; tame, check, curb, control, chasten, govern, limit, keep within limits 747 *restrain*; lessen, diminish, slacken 37 *abate*; palliate, extenuate, qualify 163 *weaken*; obtund, take the edge off 257 *blunt*; break the fall, cushion 218 *support*; play down, soft-pedal, moderate language, tone down, blue-pencil, euphemize 648 *purify*; sober, sober down, dampen, damp, cool, chill, throw cold water on 382 *refrigerate*, 613 *dissuade*; put a damper on, reduce the temperature, bank down the fires; blanket, muffle, smother, subdue, quell 382 *extinguish*.

*assuage*, ease, pour balm, mollify 327 *soften*; alleviate, lighten 831 *relieve*; deactivate, neutralize, act as an antidote, take the sting out 182 *counteract*; allay, dull, deaden 375 *render insensible*; soothe, calm, tranquillize, comfort, still, quiet, hush, lull, rock, cradle, rock to sleep 266 *bring to rest*; dulcify 392 *sweeten*; disarm, appease, smooth over, bring round, pour oil on troubled waters 719 *pacify*; assuage one's thirst, quench one's t., slake 301 *drink*.

**Adv.** *moderately*, in moderation, within bounds, within limits, within compass, within reason; at half speed, gingerly, half-heartedly, nervously, softly softly 278 *gradatim*.

## 178 Influence

**N.** *influence*, capability, power, potency, potentiality 160 *ability*; prevalence, predominance 34 *superiority*; mightiness, magnitude 32 *greatness*, 638 *importance*; upper hand, whip h., casting vote, final say; vantage ground, footing, hold, grip, pou sto; leverage, play 744 *scope*; purchase 218 *pivot*; clout, weight, pressure; pull, drag, magnetism 291 *attraction*; counterattraction 292 *repulsion*, 182 *counteraction*; thrust, drive, get-up-and-go 287 *propul-*

*sion*; impact 279 *impulse*; leaven, contagion, infection; atmosphere, climate 8 *circumstance*; atavism, telegony 5 *heredity*; occult influence, mana, magic, spell 983 *sorcery*; stars, astrology, horoscope, heavens, destiny 596 *fate*; fascination, hypnotism, mesmerism; malign influence, curse, ruin 659 *bane*; emotion, impulse, impression, feeling 817 *affections*; suasion, persuasion, insinuation, suggestion, impulsion, inspiration 612 *motive*; personality, je ne sais quoi, charisma, leadership, credit, repute 866 *prestige*; hegemony, ascendancy, domination, tyranny 733 *authority*; sway, control, dominance, reign 733 *governance*; sphere of influence, orbit; factor, contributing f., vital role, leading part 156 *cause*; power dressing; indirect influence, patronage, interest, favour, pull, friend at court, wire-pulling 703 *aid*; strings, lever 630 *tool*; secret influence, hidden hand, hand that rocks the cradle, woman behind the great man, power behind the throne, kingmaker, power broker, Grey Eminence 523 *latency*; force, f. to be reckoned with; lobby, pressure group, vested interest, 612 *inducement*; manipulator, mover, manoeuvrer 612 *motivator*; person of influence, uncrowned king *or* queen, a host in oneself, big noise, big shot 638 *notable*; girl power; multinational company, transnational corporation, superpower; Big Brother, powers that be, the Establishment 733 *government*.

**Adj.** *influential*, dominant, predominant, prevalent, prevailing, monopolistic 34 *supreme*; in power, ruling, regnant, reigning, commanding, in the driving seat, listened to, obeyed; recognized, with authority, of a., in a. 733 *authoritative*; rising, ascendant, in the ascendant 36 *increasing*; strong, potent, mighty, multinational 32 *great*, 160 *powerful*; leading, guiding, hegemonic 689 *directing*; activating, inspiring, encouraging; active in, busy, meddling 678 *active*; contributing, effective 156 *causal*; weighty, key, momentous, decisive, world-shattering, earth-shaking 638 *important*; telling, moving, emotional 821 *impressive*; appealing, attractive 291 *attracting*; gripping, fascinating, charismatic; irresistible, hypnotic, mesmeric 740 *compelling*; persuasive, suggestive, insinuating, tempting 612 *inducing*; habit-forming, addictive; educative, instructive 534 *educational*; spreading, catching, contagious 653 *infectious*; pervasive 189 *ubiquitous*.

**Vb.** *influence*, have i., command i., have a pull, carry weight, cut ice 638 *be important*; be well connected, know the right people, have friends at court, have friends in high places; have a hold on, have in one's power; have the ear of, be listened to, be recognized, be obeyed

737 *command*; dominate, tower over, bestride; lead by the nose, have under one's thumb, wind round one's little finger, wear the trousers 34 *be superior*; exert influence, make oneself felt, assert oneself; pull one's weight, throw one's weight into the scale, weigh in; put pressure on, lobby, pull strings, pull the s. 612 *motivate*; make one's voice heard, gain a hearing 455 *attract notice*; have a voice, have a say in; affect, be a factor in, tell, turn the scale; bear upon, work u., tell u. 821 *impress*; soften up, work on 925 *flatter*; urge, prompt, tempt, incite, inspire, dispose, persuade, prevail upon, convince, carry with one 612 *induce*; force 740 *compel*; sway, tyrannize; predispose, brainwash, prejudice 481 *bias*; appeal, allure, fascinate, hypnotize, mesmerize 291 *attract*; disgust, put off 292 *repel*; militate against, counterbalance 182 *counteract*; make, be the making of 654 *make better*; make or mar, change 147 *transform*; infect, leaven, colour 143 *modify*; contaminate, adulterate, mar 655 *impair*; actuate, work 173 *operate*; have a rôle, play a part, play a leading p., guide 689 *direct*; lead the dance, set the fashion, establish a trend, be the model for 23 *be an example*.

*prevail*, establish one's influence, outweigh, overweigh, override, overbear, turn the scale 34 *predominate*; overawe, overcome, subdue, subjugate; hold the whip hand, gain the upper hand, hold all the cards, gain full play, master 727 *overmaster*; control, rule, monopolize 733 *dominate*; take a hold on, take a grip on, hold 778 *retain*; gain a footing, get a foothold, take root, take hold, strike in, settle 144 *stay*; permeate, run through, colour 189 *pervade*; catch on, spread, rage, be rife, spread like wildfire.

**Adv.** *influentially*, to good effect, with telling e.; within one's orbit.

## 179 Tendency

**N.** *tendency*, trend, tenor; tempo, rhythm, set, drift 281 *direction*; course, stream, main current, mainstream, Zeitgeist, spirit of the times, spirit of the age; climate 178 *influence*; gravitation, affinity 291 *attraction*; polarity 240 *contraposition*; aptness 24 *fitness*; gift, talent, instinct for 694 *aptitude*; proneness, proclivity, propensity, predisposition, readiness, inclination, penchant, predilection, liking, leaning, bias, prejudice; weakness 180 *liability*; cast, cast of mind, bent, turn, grain; a strain of 43 *tincture*; vein, humour, mood; tone, quality, nature, characteristic 5 *temperament*; special gift, genius, idiosyncrasy 80 *speciality*.

**Adj.** *tending*, trending, conducive, leading to, pointing to; tendentious, working towards, aiming at 617 *intending*; in a fair way to, calculated to 471 *probable*; centrifugal 620 *avoiding*; subservient 180 *liable*; apt to, prone to; ready to, about to 669 *prepared*.

**Vb.** *tend*, trend, verge, lean, incline; set in, set, set towards, gravitate t. 289 *approach*; affect, dispose, carry, bias, bend to, warp, turn 178 *influence*; point to, lead to 156 *conduce*; bid fair to, be calculated to 471 *be likely*; redound to, contribute to 285 *promote*.

## 180 Liability

**N.** *liability*, liableness, weakness 179 *tendency*; exposure 661 *vulnerability*; susceptibility, susceptivity, impressibility 374 *sensibility*; potentiality 469 *possibility*; likelihood 471 *probability*; obligation, responsibility, accountability, amenability 917 *duty*.

**Adj.** *liable*, apt to 179 *tending*; subject to, given to, prey to, at the mercy of 745 *subject*; open to, exposed to, in danger of 661 *vulnerable;* dependent on, contingent 157 *caused*; incident to, incidental; possible, within the realms of possibility, on the cards, within the range of 469 *possible*; incurring, unexempt from; susceptible 819 *impressible*; answerable, reportable, responsible, amenable, accountable 917 *obliged*.

**Vb.** *be liable*, – subject to etc. adj.; be responsible, 'the buck stops here', answer for 917 *incur a duty*;

> **The buck stops here.**
> Sign on the desk of former US president Harry S Truman.

incur, lay oneself open to, run the chance of, stand the chance of; stand to gain, stand to lose; run the risk of 661 *be in danger*; lie under 745 *be subject*; open a door to 156 *conduce*.

## 181 Concurrence: combination of causes

**N.** *concurrence*, combined operation, joint effort, collaboration, coagency, synergy, synergism 706 *cooperation*; coincidence 24 *conformance*, 83 *conformity*; concord, harmony 24 *agreement*; compliance 758 *consent*; concurrent opinion, consensus 488 *assent*; acquiescence, nonresistance 721 *submission*; concert, pooling of resources, two heads are better than one, two minds with but a single thought, joint planning, collusion, conspiracy 623 *plot*; league, alliance, partnership 706 *association*; conjunction, liaison 45 *union*; think tank.

**Adj.** *concurrent*, concurring etc. vb.; coactive, synergic 706 *cooperative*; coincident, concomitant, parallel 89 *accompanying*; in alliance, banded together 708 *corporate*; of one mind, at

one with 488 *assenting*; joint, combined 45 *joined*; conforming 24 *agreeing*; colluding, conniving, abetting, contributing, involved 703 *aiding*.

**Vb.** *concur*, acquiesce 488 *assent*; collude, connive, conspire 623 *plot*; agree, harmonize 24 *accord*; hang together, stick t., pull t. 706 *cooperate*; contribute, help, aid, abet, aid and abet, serve 703 *minister to*; promote, subserve 156 *conduce*; go with, go along w., go hand in hand w., keep pace w., keep abreast of, run parallel to 89 *accompany*; unite, stand together 48 *cohere*.

**Adv.** *concurrently*, with one consent, with one accord, with one voice, in harmony, in unison, hand in hand, hand in glove.

## 182 Counteraction

**N.** *counteraction*, opposing causes, action and reaction; polarity 240 *contraposition*; antagonism, antipathy, clash, aggro, conflict, mutual c. 14 *contrariety*, 279 *collision*; return action, reaction, retroaction, repercussion, backfire, backlash, boomerang effect 280 *recoil*; renitency, recalcitrance, kicking back 715 *resistance*, 704 *opposition*; inertia, vis inertiae, friction, drag, check 702 *hindrance*; interference, counterpressure, repression, suppression 747 *restraint*; intolerance, persecution 735 *severity*; neutralization, deactivation 177 *moderation*; nullification, cancellation 165 *destruction*; crosscurrent, headwind 702 *obstacle*; counterspell, countercharm, counterirritant, neutralizer, antibiotic, anticoagulant, anticonvulsant, antidepressant, anti-emetic, antiseptic, prophylactic 658 *antidote*; counterbalance, counterweight 31 *offset*; counterblast, countermove 688 *tactics*; defensive measures, deterrent 713 *defence*; prevention, preventive, preventative, inhibitor 757 *prohibition*.

**Adj.** *counteracting*, counter, counteractive; conflicting 14 *contrary*; antipathetic, antagonistic, hostile 881 *inimical*; resistant, recalcitrant, renitent 715 *resisting*; reactionary, reactive 280 *recoiling*; frictional, retarding, checking 747 *restraining*; preventive, preventative, contraceptive; antidotal, corrective; antibiotic, anticoagulant, anticonvulsant, antidepressant, antidiuretic, anti-emetic, antiinflammatory, antipsychotic, antispasmodic, antitussive, antiviral, antipyretic, antiseptic, prophylactic 658 *remedial*; balancing, offsetting 31 *compensatory*.

**Vb.** *counteract*, counter, run c., cross, traverse, work against, go a., militate a.; not conduce to 702 *hinder*; react 280 *recoil*; agitate against, persecute 881 *be inimical*; fight against, resist, withstand, defend oneself 704 *oppose*; antagonize, conflict with 14 *be contrary*; clash 279 *collide*; interfere 678 *meddle*; countervail, cancel out, counterpoise, counterbalance 31 *set off*; repress 165 *suppress*; undo, cancel 752 *abrogate*; neutralize, act as an antidote, deactivate, demagnetize, degauss; find a remedy, cure 658 *remedy*; recover 656 *retrieve*; obviate, be a way round, prevent, inhibit 757 *prohibit*.

**Adv.** *although*, in spite of, despite, notwithstanding; against, contrary to 704 *in opposition*.

# Space

## Space in general

### 183 Space: indefinite space

**N.** *space*, expanse, expansion; extension, spatial e., extent, superficial e., surface, area; volume, cubic content; continuum, stretch 71 *continuity*; space-time 108 *time*; empty space 190 *emptiness*; depth of space, abyss 211 *depth*; roominess; unlimited space, infinite s. 107 *infinity*; sky, aerospace, airspace, outer space, interstellar s. 321 *heavens*; world, wide w., length and breadth of the land; vastness, immensity, vastitude; geographical space, terrain, open space, open country; lung, green belt, wide horizons, wide open spaces 348 *plain*; upland, moorland, campagna, veld, prairie, steppe 348 *grassland*; outback, hinterland 184 *region*; wild, wilderness, waste 172 *desert*; everywhere, ubiquity 189 *presence*.

*measure*, proportions, dimension 203 *length*, 205 *breadth*, 209 *height*, 211 *depth*; area, surface a.; square measure, acreage, acres, rods, poles and perches; square inch, square yard, square metre, hectare, hide; volume, cubic content 195 *size*.

*range*, reach, carry, compass, coverage; stretch, grasp, span; radius, latitude, amplitude; sweep, spread, ramification; play, swing, margin 744 *scope*; sphere, field, arena 184 *region*; purview, prospect 438 *view*; perspective, focal distance 199 *distance*; aim, telescopic range, light-grasp; magnifying power 417 *optics*.

*room*, space, accommodation; capacity, internal c., stowage, storage space 632 *storage*; seating capacity, seating; standing room; margin, clearance, windage; room to spare, r. to manoeuvre, elbow room, legroom, room to swing a cat; room overhead, headroom, headway; sea room, seaway, leeway, latitude;

opening, way 263 *open space*; living space, Lebensraum, personal space.

**Adj.** *spatial*, space; spatio-temporal, space-time, fourth-dimensional; volumetric, cubic, three-dimensional; flat, superficial, two-dimensional.

*spacious* 32 *extensive*; expansive, roomy, commodious; ample, vast, vasty, cavernous, capacious, broad, deep, wide; voluminous, baggy, loose-fitting 195 *large*; broad-based 79 *general*; far-reaching, far-flung, widespread, wide-ranging, comprehensive, worldwide, global, world 52 *whole*; uncircumscribed, boundless, spaceless 107 *infinite*; shoreless, trackless, pathless; extending, spreading, branching, ramified.

**Vb.** *extend*, spread, outspread, spread out, range, cover, encompass; span, straddle, bestride 226 *overlie*; extend to, reach to 202 *be contiguous*; branch, ramify.

**Adv.** *widely*, extensively, everywhere, with no stone unturned, wherever; far and near, far and wide, all over, globally, universally, the whole world over, throughout the world; under the sun, on the face of the earth, in every quarter, in all quarters, in all lands; from end to end, from pole to pole, from coast to coast, from China to Peru, from Dan to Beersheba, from Land's End to John o' Groats 54 *throughout*; from all the points of the compass, from the furthest corners of the earth; to the four winds, to the uttermost parts of the earth; from here to the back of beyond; at every turn, here, there and everywhere, right and left, high and low, inside and out.

### 184 Region: definite space

**N.** *region*, locality, locale, parts 185 *place*; sphere, orb, hemisphere; zone, section, belt; latitude, parallel, meridian; clime, climate; tract, terrain, country, ground, soil 344 *land*; geographical unit, island, peninsula, continent, landmass; sea 343 *ocean*; Old World, New

W.; East and West, North and South; Third World, Fourth World 733 *political organization*; compass, circumference, circle, circuit 233 *outline*, boundaries, bounds, shore, confines, marches 236 *limit*; pale, precincts, close, enclave, exclave, salient 235 *enclosure*; corridor 624 *access*; area, field, theatre 724 *arena*; economic zone, exclusive area, charmed circle.

*territory*, sphere, zone; catchment area; beat, pitch, ground; plot, lot, holding, claim 235 *enclosure*; grounds, park 777 *estate*; national boundaries, domain, territorial waters, economic zone, three-mile limit; continental shelf, airspace, defensible space; possession, dependency, protectorate, dominion; colony, settlement; motherland, fatherland, homeland 192 *home*; commonwealth, republic, kingdom, realm, state, empire 733 *political organization*; debatable territory, no-man's-land, Tom Tiddler's ground 774 *nonownership*; no-go area.

*district*, purlieus, neighbourhood, haunt 187 *locality*; subregion, quarter, division 53 *subdivision*; state, province, county, shire, bailiwick, riding, lathe, wapentake, hundred, soke, rape, tithing; diocese, bishopric, archbishopric; parish, ward, constituency; borough, community, township, municipality; county, district, metropolitan area; canton, department, arrondissement, commune; hamlet, village, town, market t., county t. 192 *abode*; built-up area 192 *housing*; garden city, new town; suburb, burb (inf), suburbs, burbs (inf), suburbia, subtopia, dormitory suburb, stockbroker belt; green belt 183 *space*; Home Counties, golden circle; north of Watford, provinces, back of beyond, the sticks, Marches, Borders; Highlands, Lowlands, Wild West; outback, backwoods, bush, brush, bundu; woods and fields, countryside 344 *land*; hinterland, heartland.

*city*, capital c., cathedral c., metropolis, megalopolis, conurbation; Greater London, the Big City, the big smoke, the great wen, Cockaigne; Gotham, the Big Apple; West End, W. Side, East End, E. side, City, Wall Street, Manhattan; uptown, downtown.

**Adj.** *regional*, territorial, continental, peninsular, insular; national, state; subdivisional, local, municipal, parochial, redbrick 192 *provincial*; suburban, urban, rural, up-country; district, town, country.

**185 Place: limited space**
**N.** *place*, emplacement, site, location, position 186 *situation*; station, substation; quarter, locality 184 *district*; assigned place, pitch, beat, billet, socket, groove; centre, meeting place, rendezvous 76 *focus*; birthplace, dwelling

place, fireside 192 *home*; place of residence, address, habitat 187 *locality*, 192 *quarters*; premises, building, mansion 192 *house*; spot, plot; point, dot, pinpoint; niche, nook, corner, cranny, hole, pigeonhole, pocket, slot 194 *compartment*; confines, bounds, baseline, crease (cricket) 236 *limit*; confined place, prison, coffin, grave; precinct, bailey, garth, paddock, compound, pen 235 *enclosure*; close, quadrangle, quad, square, town s.; yard, area, backyard, courtyard, court 263 *open space*; farmyard, field 370 *farm*; sheepwalk, sheeprun 369 *stock farm*; highways and byways, ins and outs, every nook and corner, every nook and cranny.

**Adv.** *somewhere*, some place, wherever it may be, here and there, in various places, passim; locally 200 *near*.

**186 Situation**
**N.** *situation*, position, setting; scene, locale; time and place, when and where; location, address, whereabouts; Global Positioning System, GPS, satnav; point, stage, milestone 27 *degree*; site, seat, emplacement, base 185 *place*; habitat, ecosphere, ecosystem, biotype, range 184 *region*; post, station; standpoint, standing, ground, footing, pou sto 7 *state*; side, aspect, attitude, posture, asana; feng shui; frontage, orientation 239 *laterality*, 240 *contraposition*; geography, topography, chorography, cosmography, ecology 321 *earth sciences*; chart 551 *map*.

*bearings*, compass direction, latitude and longitude, declination, right ascension, easting, westing, northing, southing 281 *direction*; radiolocation 187 *location*; orienteering.

**Adj.** *situated*, situate, located at, sited at, living at, to be found at; settled, set; stationed, posted; occupying 187 *located*; local, topical; topographical, geographical.

**Vb.** *be situated*, be located, be sited, be situate, centre on; be found at, have one's address at, have one's seat in; have its centre in; be, lie, stand; be stationed, be posted; live, live at 192 *dwell*; touch 200 *be near*.

**Adv.** *in place*, in situ, in loco, here, there; in, on, over, under; hereabouts, thereabouts; whereabouts; here and there, passim; at the sign of.

**187 Location**
**N.** *location*, placing, siting, placement, emplacement, collocation, disposition; posting, stationing, relocation; finding the place, locating, pinpointing; radiolocation, radar; centring, localization 200 *nearness*; domestication, naturalization; settling, colonization,

population; settlement, resettlement, lodgment, establishment, fixation, installation; putting down, deposition, putting back, reposition 62 *arrangement*; putting in 303 *insertion*; packing, packaging, stowage, loading, lading 632 *storage*.

*locality*, quarters, purlieus, environs, environment, surroundings, milieu, neighbourhood, parts, neck of the woods 184 *district*; ecological community, biome; vicinity 200 *near place*; address, postal district, street, place of residence, habitat 192 *abode*; seat, site 185 *place*; meeting place, venue, haunt 76 *focus*; genius loci, spirit of place.

*site*, seat, emplacement, position, station 186 *situation*; depot, base, military b., barracks, naval base, air b.; colony, settlement; anchorage, roadstead, mooring 662 *shelter*; cantonment, lines, police l., civil l.; camp, encampment, laager, bivouac, campsite, caravan site, temporary abode; hostel 192 *abode*; halting place, lay-by, car park, parking bay, parking lot, parking place, park-and-ride 145 *stopping place*.

**Adj.** *located*, placed etc. vb.; positioned, stationed, posted 186 *situated*; ensconced, embedded, cradled, nestled 232 *circumscribed*; relocated, rooted, settled, domesticated 153 *fixed*; encamped, camping, lodged 192 *residing*; moored, anchored, at anchor 266 *quiescent*; vested in, in the hands of, in the possession of 773 *possessed*; reposed in, transferred to 780 *transferred*; well-placed, favourably situated.

**Vb.** *place*, collocate, assign a place 62 *arrange*; situate, position, site, locate, relocate; base, centre, localize; narrow down, pinpoint, pin down; find the place, put one's finger on; place right, aim well, hit, hit the nail on the head, hit the mark 281 *aim*; put, lay, set, seat; station, post, park; install, ensconce, set up, establish, fix 153 *stabilize*; fix in, root, plant, implant, embed, graft, slot in 303 *insert*; bed, bed down, put to bed, tuck in, tuck up, cradle; accommodate, find a place for, find room for, put one up, lodge, house, quarter, billet; quarter upon, billet on; impose, saddle on; moor, tether, picket, anchor 45 *tie*; dock, berth 266 *bring to rest*; deposit, lay down, put d., set d.; stand, put up, erect 310 *elevate*; place with, transfer, bestow, invest 780 *assign*; array, deploy.

*replace*, put back, sheathe, put up (a sword), bring back, reinstate 656 *restore*; repatriate, resettle, relocate 272 *transpose*; redeposit, reinvest, replant, reset.

*stow*, put away, put by; imburse, pocket, pouch, pack, package, bale, store, lade, freight, put on board 193 *load*; squeeze in, cram in 54 *fill*.

*place oneself*, stand, take one's place, take one's stand, anchor, drop a., cast a. 266 *come to rest*; settle, strike root, take r., gain a footing, get a foothold, entrench oneself, dig in 144 *stay*; perch, alight, sit on, sit, squat, park; pitch on, pitch one's tent, encamp, camp, bivouac; stop at, lodge, put up; hive, burrow; ensconce oneself, locate oneself, establish o., find a home, move in, put down roots; settle, colonize, populate, people 192 *dwell*; get naturalized, become a citizen, get citizenship.

## 188 Displacement

**N.** *displacement*, dislocation, derailment 63 *derangement*; misplacement, wrong place, ectopia 84 *variance*; shift, move 265 *motion*; red shift, Doppler effect; parallax; aberration, perturbation (astronomy) 282 *deviation*; translocation, transposition, transhipment, transfer 272 *transference*; mutual transfer 151 *interchange*; relief, replacement 150 *substitution*; uprooting, removal, taking away 304 *extraction*; unloading, unpacking, unshipping; expulsion 300 *ejection*; weeding, eradication 300 *voidance*; exile, banishment 883 *seclusion*; refugee, asylum-seeker 268 *wanderer*; fish out of water, square peg in a round hole 25 *misfit*; docker, stevedore, removal man.

*displaced person*, homeless person, the homeless, bag lady, bag people, rough sleeper, skell (sl); fish out of water, square peg in a round hole.

**Adj.** *displaced*, disturbed etc. vb.; removed, transported 272 *transferable*; aberrant 282 *deviating*; unplaced, unhoused, unharboured; unestablished, rootless, unsettled, déraciné(e); roofless, houseless, homeless, of no fixed abode, of no fixed address; out of a job, out of the picture, out of the running, out of touch, out in the cold 57 *excluded*.

*misplaced*, ectopic 84 *abnormal*; out of one's element, like a fish out of water, like a square peg in a round hole; out of place, inappropriate 10 *irrelevant*; mislaid, lost, gone missing, missing 190 *absent*.

**Vb.** *displace*, disturb, disarrange, disorientate, derail, dislocate; dislodge, disestablish, unseat, unfix, unstick 46 *disunite*; dispel, scatter, send flying 75 *disperse*; shift, remove 265 *move*; cart away, transport 272 *transfer*; alter the position, change round; transpose 151 *interchange*; dispatch, post 272 *send*; relegate, banish, exile, kick upstairs 300 *dismiss*; set aside, supersede 150 *substitute*, 752 *depose*; turn out, evict, unhouse 300 *eject*; wipe out, eradicate, uproot 165 *destroy*; discharge, unload, off-load, unship, tranship; clear away, rake, sweep, sweep up 648 *clean*; take away, take off, cart off; lift, raise, uplift 310 *elevate*; draw, draw out, pull o. 304 *extract*.

*misplace*, mislay, lose, lose touch with, lose track of.

## 189 Presence

**N.** *presence*, being there, existence, whereness; whereabouts 186 *situation*; being somewhere, ubiety; being everywhere, ubiquity, ubiquitousness, omnipresence; permeation, pervasion, diffusion; availability, bird in the hand; physical presence, bodily p., personal p.; attendance, personal a.; presenteeism; residence, occupancy, occupation, sit-in 773 *possession*; visit, descent, stay; nowness, present moment 121 *present time*; man on the spot; spectator, attendee, bystander 441 *onlookers*.

**Adj.** *on the spot*, present, existent, in being 1 *existing*; occupying, in occupation; inhabiting, resident, residentiary, domiciled 192 *residing*; attendant, waiting, still there, not gone, hanging on; ready, on tap, available, on the menu, on 669 *prepared*; at home, at hand, within reach, on call; under one's nose, before one's eyes 443 *obvious*; observing, looking on, standing by.

*ubiquitous*, omnipresent, permeating, pervading, pervasive 79 *universal*.

**Vb.** *be present*, exist, be; take up space, occupy; colonize, inhabit 192 *dwell*; hold 773 *possess*; stand, lie 186 *be situated*; look on, stand by, observe, witness 441 *watch*; resort to, frequent, haunt, meet one at every turn; occur 154 *happen*; stay, sojourn, summer, winter, revisit 882 *visit*; attend, assist at, grace the occasion, honour with one's presence; take part, make one at, make one of; show up, turn up, present oneself, announce o. 295 *arrive*; be in evidence, show one's face, put in an appearance, look in on; face, confront 711 *defy*.

*pervade*, permeate, fill 54 *make complete*; be diffused through, be disseminated, imbue, impregnate, soak, saturate, run through; overrun, swarm over, spread, filter through, meet one at every turn 297 *infiltrate*; make one's presence felt 178 *influence*.

**Adv.** *here*, there, where, everywhere, all over the place; in situ, in place; on location; aboard, on board, at home; on the spot; in the presence of, before, under the eyes of, under the nose of, in the face of; personally, in person, in propria persona.

## 190 Absence

**N.** *absence*, nonpresence, disappearing trick 446 *disappearance*; lack 636 *scarcity*; depri-

vation 772 *loss*; being nowhere, Utopia 513 *fantasy*; inexistence 2 *nonexistence*; being elsewhere, alibi; nonresidence, living out; leave of absence, sick leave, compassionate leave, vacation, holiday, sabbatical, furlough; nonattendance, nonappearance, truancy, skiving, bunking off, absenteeism, French leave 620 *avoidance*; absentee, truant 620 *avoider*; absentee landlord; backwoodsman, nonvoter, postal voter.

*emptiness*, bareness, empty space, void, vacuity, inanity, vacancy; blank 201 *gap*; nothing inside, hollowness, shell; vacuum, air pocket; empties, dead men (empty bottles); blank cartridge, blank paper, clean sheet, tabula rasa; virgin territory, no-man's-land; waste, desolation, wilderness 172 *desert*; vacant lot, bomb site 183 *room*.

*nobody*, no one, nobody present, nobody on earth; not a soul, not a single person, not a living thing; empty seats, nonexistent audience.

**Adj.** *absent*, not present, not found, unrepresented; away, not resident; gone from home, on tour, on location; out, not at home; gone, flown, disappeared 446 *disappearing*; lacking, wanting, missing, wanted; absent without leave, AWOL; truant, absentee 667 *escaped*; unavailable, unobtainable, unprocurable, off the menu, off 636 *unprovided*; lost, mislaid, missing, nowhere to be found; inexistent 2 *nonexistent*; exempt from, spared, exempted; on leave, on holiday, on vacation, on sabbatical, on furlough; omitted, left out 57 *excluded*.

*empty*, vacant, vacuous, inane; void, devoid, bare; blank, clean; characterless, featureless; without content, hollow; vacant, unoccupied, unlived-in, uninhabited, untenanted, tenantless; unstaffed, crewless; depopulated; desert, deserted 621 *relinquished*; unpeopled, unsettled, uncolonized; godforsaken, lonely; bleak, desolate 172 *unproductive*; uninhabitable.

**Vb.** *be absent*, have no place in, take no part in; absent oneself, not show up, stay away, keep away, keep out of the way, cut, skip, skive, play truant *or* hookey, bunk off, take French leave 620 *avoid*; be missed, leave a gap, be conspicuous by one's absence; leave empty, evacuate, vacate; exhaust 300 *empty*.

*go away*, withdraw, leave 296 *depart*; make oneself scarce, slip out, slip away, be off, naff off, retreat 296 *decamp*, 667 *escape*; vanish 446 *disappear*; move over, make room, vacate.

**Adv.** *without*, minus, sans; in default of, for want of; in vacuo.

*not here*, not there; neither here nor there;

elsewhere, somewhere else; nowhere, no place; in one's absence, behind one's back, in absentia.

## 191 Inhabitant

**N.** *dweller*, inhabitant, habitant, denizen, indweller; sojourner, transient, visitant; migrant, expatriate 59 *foreigner*; mainlander, Continental; insular, islander; boat-dweller, water gipsy; landsman *or* -woman, hill-dweller, dalesman, daleswoman, highlander, low-lander, plains-dweller, fenman, fenwoman, forest-dweller, bush-d.; frontiersman *or* -woman, borderer; city-dweller, town-d., urbanite, suburbanite, commuter; metro-politan, provincial; country-dweller, countryman *or* -woman, ruralist, villager, par-ishioner; peasant 370 *farmer*, desert-dweller, tent-d., bedouin; cave-dweller, troglodyte; slum-dweller 801 *poor person*. (See also *native*.)

*resident*, householder, ratepayer; housewife, hausfrau, chatelaine, housekeeper; cottager, crofter; addressee, owner-occupier, occupier, occupant, incumbent, residentiary 776 *possessor*; locum tenens 150 *substitute*; tenant, sitting t., protected t., renter, lessee, lease-holder; inmate, in-patient; house surgeon, house physician, house officer 658 *doctor*; gar-rison, crew 686 *personnel*; lodger, boarder, au pair, paying guest, p.g.; guest, visitor, inqui-line, commensal; uninvited guest, gatecrasher, cuckoo, squatter 59 *intruder*; parasite 659 *bane*.

*native*, aboriginal, abo (derog), autochthon 66 *precursor*; aborigines, autochthones, indi-genes, earliest inhabitants, first-comers; people, tribe, clan 371 *nation*; local, local inhabitant; parishioner, villager, townsperson, townee, city person, urbanite, city slicker, cockney, suburbanite, weekender, holiday-homer; yokel, rustic 869 *country-dweller*; fellow countryman *or* -woman, fellow citizen; national, patrial, citizen, burgher, burgess, voter; John Bull, Uncle Sam; Briton, Britisher, Brit; Celt, Gael, Scot, North Briton, Cale-donian, Welshman *or* -woman, Irishman *or* -woman, Hibernian; Jock, Jimmy, Taffy, Paddy; Englishman *or* -woman, Northerner, Southerner, Midlander, East Anglian, Westcountryman *or* -woman; Londoner, Brummie, Bristolian, Mancunian, Liverpud-lian, Scouse, Geordie, Glaswegian, Aberdonian; New Yorker, Parisian, Muscovite 59 *foreigner*; earth-dweller, earthman *or* -woman, earthling, terrestrial, tellurian; extraterrestrial, ET, space-dweller, Martian, Venusian, little green men, bug-eyed men.

*settler*, pioneer, Pilgrim Fathers 66 *precursor*; immigrant, colonist, colonial, creole; planter

370 *farmer*; economic migrant, resident alien 59 *foreigner*.

*inhabitants*, population, urban p., rural p., townspeople, country folk; populace, people, people at large, citizenry, tenantry, yeomanry; villadom, suburbia 192 *housing*; city-full, house-full; household, menage 11 *family*; settle-ment, stronghold; colony, neighbourhood, commune, community, village c.

**Adj.** *native*, vernacular, popular, national, ethnic; indigenous, autochthonous, aborig-inal; enchorial; earthbound, terrestrial, tel-lurian; home, home-made; domestic, domiciliary, domesticated; settled, domiciled, naturalized; resident 192 *residing*.

*occupied*, occupied by, indwelt; inhabited, lived in, tenanted, populated; garrisoned by, taken over by, manned, staffed.

## 192 Abode: place of habitation or resort

**N.** *abode*, habitat, haunt, station 186 *situation*; place of residence 187 *locality*; habitation, street, house, home, second h.; address, house number, number; accommodation address; domicile, residence, residency; town, city, postal district 184 *district*; headquarters, base, seat 76 *focus*; temporary abode, hangout, camp, pad, pied-à-terre; weekend cottage, country seat, holiday home, timeshare flat *or* apartment, seaside resort, watering place, hill station 837 *pleasure ground*; spa, sanatorium 658 *hospital*; cantonment, lines 187 *station*; biv-ouac, encampment; camp, refugee c.; campsite, caravan park; 'rus in urbe' (see quota-tion at 883 *seclusion*); home from home.

*quarters*, living q., married q., accommoda-tion, lodging, billet, berth, squat; barrack, casern; lodgings, rooms, chambers, digs; resi-dential hotel, guest house, boarding h., lodging h., pension; hostel, youth hostel, hostel for the homeless, foyer; boarding school, dormitory, dorm; hall of residence; con-vent 986 *monastery*; cardboard city.

*dwelling*, roof over one's head 226 *roof*; pre-historic dwelling, lake d., pile d., crannog; tower, keep, broch; cave, hut, kraal, igloo; hogan, wickiup, wigwam, tepee, tent 226 *canopy*; burrow, den, earth, form, hole, lair, sett, warren 662 *shelter*.

*nest*, nidus; drey; branch 366 *tree*; aerie, eyrie, perch, roost; covert, heronry, rookery, swannery, hatchery, aviary, apiary, beehive, skep; bike (dial); wasp's nest, antheap, anthill.

*home*, home-sweet-home, hearth and home, place where one hangs one's hat, hearth, fire-side, fireplace, chimney corner, inglenook, rooftree, roof, paternal r., ancestral halls; home-stead, toft, household; bosom of one's family,

family circle, cradle, birthplace, 'the house where I was born' 68 *origin*;

> I remember, I remember,
> The house where I was born,
> The little window where the sun
> Came peeping in at morn
>
> Thomas Hood, *I Remember*

native land, 'land of our birth', la patrie, motherland, fatherland, homeland, one's country, God's own country, the Old Country, Blighty, Albion;

> Land of our birth, we pledge to thee
> Our love and toil in the years to be;
> When we are grown and take our place,
> As men and women with our race.
>
> Rudyard Kipling, *The Children's Song*

native soil, native sod, native ground, native heath; home ground, home town, own backyard; haunt, stamping ground; familiar territory, second home; household gods, Lares and Penates; Hestia, Vesta.

*house* 164 *building*, *edifice*, house of God 990 *temple*; abode, home, residence, dwelling, dwelling house, messuage; country house, town h.; villa, detached house, semidetached h., semi, terraced house; Queen Anne house, Georgian h., Regency h.; council h., council flat, high-rise f., prefab; ranch house, chalet, bungalow, chalet-b.; seat, place, mansion, hall, stately home; palace, dome, alcazar; chateau, castle, keep, tower, peel, broch, crannog; manor house, dower h., manor, grange, lodge, priory, abbey; vicarage 986 *parsonage*; farmhouse, farmstead, croft, toft and croft, hacienda 370 *farm*; official residence, Buckingham Palace, Holyrood P., Chequers, Mansion House, White House; embassy, consulate.

*small house*, bijou residence; two-up two-down, back-to-back; chalet, lodge, cottage, cruck c., thatched c., cot, but and ben; cabin, log c., hut, Nissen h., shanty, bothy; hovel, dump, hole, slum dwelling; box, hunting-box *or* -lodge; shed, shack, lean-to, outhouse, outbuilding; shelter, tent 226 *canopy*; kiosk, booth, stall, shieling; houseboat 275 *boat*; mobile home, Dormobile (tdmk), caravan, trailer 274 *vehicle*. (See also *flat*.)

*housing*, high-density h.; bricks and mortar 631 *building material*; built-up area, urban sprawl; asphalt jungle, concrete j., urban blight; urbanization, conurbation; town, satellite t., new t., commuter t., dormitory t., burgh, suburb, garden city 184 *city*; housing estate, housing scheme, overspill estate, residential area, sink estate 184 *district*; villadom, suburbia, subtopia; crescent, close, terrace, circus, square, avenue, street 624 *road*; block,

court, row, mansions, villas, buildings; houses, tenements, high-rise flats; inner city, ghetto, slum, condemned building; shanty town, hutments, bustee, barrio; hamlet, village, community, thorp, dorp; scattered settlement, isolated s.

*flat*, flatlet, granny flat, tenement f., high-rise f., council f., furnished f., service f., mews f., penthouse; apartment, suite, chambers; bedsitting room, bed-sitter, bed-sit 194 *room*; maisonette, duplex, walkup; block of flats, apartment block, tower b.; mews, tenements; shell.

*shed*, byre, cowshed, shippen; stable; kennel, doghouse; sty, pigpen, fold, sheepfold 235 *enclosure*; dovecote, pigeon loft; stall, cage, coop, hencoop, hutch, battery; stabling, mews, coach-house, garage, car-port, hangar; boathouse; marina, dock, dry d., graving d., floating d.; basin, wharf, roads, roadstead, port 662 *shelter*; berth, quay, jetty, pier 266 *resting place*.

*inn*, hotel, boarding house, guesthouse, bed and breakfast (see also *quarters*), hostelry, roadhouse, motel, aparthotel *or* apartotel, boatel *or* botel; doss-house, bunk-h., kip, flophouse; hospice, night shelter, hostel, foyer; youth hostel; auberge, trattoria, posada, caravanserai, khan; dak bungalow, rest house.

*pub*, tavern, alehouse, beerhouse, pothouse, boozer (sl); public house, local; free house, tied h.; gin palace, saloon; speak-easy, dive, joint, honky-tonk; shebeen; wine cellar, wine bar, tapas bar, bodega; beer cellar, beer hall, beer garden; bar, public b., spit-and-sawdust b., lounge b., saloon b., snug; taproom; theme bar, theme pub.

*restaurant*, self-service r., cafeteria, café, greasy spoon (inf), eating-house, eatery, theme restaurant; steakhouse, diner, brasserie, bistro, pizzeria, kebab house, creperie, spaghetti house, trattoria, taqueria; grill room, rotisserie; coffee bar, milk b., juice b., ice-cream parlour, soda fountain; lunch counter, fast-food c., snack bar, sandwich bar; teahouse, teashop, tearoom; refreshment room, buffet, canteen, Naafi; fish and chip shop, fish and chicken bar, chippie (inf), baked potato shop, pancake house, take-away; coffee stall, pull-in, transport café, motorway services; cybercafé, Internet café.

*meeting place*, conventicle, meeting house 990 *church*; day centre, community c., village hall; assembly rooms, pump r.; club, clubhouse, night club, working men's c.; holiday camp 837 *place of amusement*; football ground, racecourse, dog track 724 *arena*; theatre, concert hall, opera house, stadium, stand 441 *onlookers*; astrodome, sports centre, gymnasium, drill hall, parade ground; piazza, quadrangle, quad, campus, village green, town square 76 *focus*; shopping centre, shopping mall 796 *market*.

*pleasance*, park, grounds, pleasure g., gardens, green; walk, mall, avenue, parade, promenade, boulevard; national park, theme p., adventure p., safari p.; parkland, chase 837 *pleasure ground*.

*pavilion*, kiosk, stand, bandstand, rotunda, folly, bower, grotto 194 *arbour*; stoa, colonnade, arcade, peristyle; tent, marquee 226 *canopy*.

*retreat*, sanctuary, sanctum sanctorum, refuge, asylum, haven, ark 662 *shelter*; priesthole, hidey-hole 527 *hiding-place*; cubbyhole, den, snuggery, snug, sanctum, study 194 *chamber*; cell, hermitage 883 *seclusion*; cloister 986 *monastery*; ashram; almshouse, grace and favour house; workhouse, poorhouse; orphanage, home, old people's h., rest h., hostel, foyer, hospice, halfway house, sheltered housing, safe haven.

*homeless person*, bag lady, bag people, bum (sl), down-and-out, rough sleeper, skell (sl), tramp, vagrant.

**Adj.** *residing*, abiding, dwelling, living, domiciled; at home, in residence; residential, fit for habitation; parasitical; inquiline, commensal

*homeless*, of no fixed abode, of no fixed address, roofless, sleeping rough 188 *displaced*.

*urban*, towny, metropolitan, cosmopolitan, inner-city, suburban; built-up, citified, urbanized, suburbanized; bungaloid.

*provincial*, parochial, parish-pump, local, domestic, vernacular; up-country, countrified, rural, rustic 184 *regional*.

*architectural*, architectonic, edificial; designed, architect-d., designer 243 *formed*; Gothic 990 *churchlike*; classical, Byzantine, Romanesque, Norman, Tudor, Renaissance, Elizabethan, Jacobean, baroque, neo-classical, Palladian, Queen Anne, rococo, Georgian, Victorian, neo-gothic, Bauhaus 127 *olden*; brick, concrete, granite, stone, cob, timber-framed; half-timbered; thatched, tiled 226 *covered*; modest, substantial, palatial, grand; detached, semi-d.; bijou; back-to-back, jerry-built; single-storey, multistorey, high-rise; double-fronted.

**Vb.** *dwell*, dwell in, inhabit, populate, people 189 *be present*; settle, colonize 786 *appropriate*; frequent, haunt 882 *visit*; take up one's abode, take up residence, hang up one's hat, move in; reside, remain, abide, sojourn, live 186 *be situated*; take rooms, put up at, stay, keep, lodge, lie, sleep at; live in, board out, be in digs; have an address, hang out at; tenant,

occupy, squat 773 *possess*; nestle, perch, roost, nest, hive, burrow, stable; camp, encamp, bivouac, squat, doss down, pitch one's tent, make one's quarters 187 *place oneself*; tent, shelter 662 *seek refuge*; berth, dock, anchor 266 *come to rest*.

*urbanize*, citify, suburbanize, develop, build up.

## 193 Contents: things contained

**N.** *contents*, ingredients, items, components, constituents, parts 58 *component*; inventory 87 *list*; furnishings, equipment 633 *provision*; load, payload, cargo, lading, freight, shipment, cartload, shipload, containerful 272 *thing transferred*; enclosure, inside 224 *insides*; stuffing, filling, stopping, wadding 227 *lining*; fistful, handful, cupful, quiverful 33 *small quantity*, 32 *great quantity*.

**Vb.** *load*, lade, freight, charge, burden 187 *stow*; palletize, containerize; take in, take on board, ship; overload, overburden, break one's back 322 *weigh*; pack, package, pack in, fit in, tuck in 303 *insert*; pack tight, squeeze in, cram, stuff 54 *fill*; pad, wad 227 *line*; hide, conceal 226 *cover*.

## 194 Receptacle

**N.** *receptacle*, container, holder; frame 218 *prop*; hutch, cage 748 *prison*; folder, wrapper, envelope, cover, file 235 *enclosure*; net, safety n., fishing n. 222 *network*; sheath, chrysalis, cocoon; packaging 226 *wrapping*; capsule, ampoule; pod, calyx, boll; mould 243 *form*; socket, mortise 255 *cavity*; groove, slot 262 *furrow*; pigeonhole, hole, cave, cavity 263 *opening*; bosom, lap 261 *fold*; pincushion; catch-all, trap; well, reservoir, hold, repository 632 *store*; drain, cesspit, sump 649 *sink*; crockery, chinaware, glassware 381 *pottery*.

*bladder*, airbladder, inflatable; inner tube; football; balloon, envelope, gasbag; sac, cyst, vesicle, utricle, blister, bubble 253 *swelling*; udder, teat 253 *bosom*.

*maw*, stomach, tummy, tum, breadbasket, little Mary; abdomen, belly, corporation, pot belly, venter, paunch 253 *swelling*; gizzard, gullet, crop, craw, jaws, mouth, oesophagus 263 *orifice*.

*compartment*, cell, cellule, loculus, follicle, ventricle; tray, in t., out t.; cage, iron lung; cubicle, carrel, booth, stall; sentry box; box 594 *theatre*; pew, choir-stall 990 *church interior*; niche, nook, cranny, recess, bay, oriel, mihrab; pigeonhole, cubbyhole; drawer, locker; shelving, rack 218 *shelf*; storey, floor, deck 207 *layer*.

*cabinet*, closet, commode, wardrobe, press,

chest of drawers, chiffonier, tallboy; cupboard, corner c., built-in c., unit; whatnot, dresser, Welsh d., china cabinet; buffet, sideboard 218 *stand*; freezer, fridge-freezer 384 *refrigerator*; cellaret, cocktail cabinet, dumbwaiter, lazy Susan, tea trolley; secretaire, escritoire, davenport, bureau, desk, writing d.; console; bookcase.

*basket*, creel; hamper, picnic basket; pannier; trug, punnet, pottle, skep, rush basket, frail; crib, cradle, bassinet; clothes basket, laundry basket; workbasket, workbox; wastepaper basket; wickerwork, basketwork; framework, crate 218 *frame*; gabion 713 *fortification*.

*box*, chest, ark; coffer, locker; case, canteen; safe, till, moneybox 799 *treasury*; coffin, sarcophagus 364 *tomb*; packing case, tea chest; tuckbox; attaché case, briefcase, dispatch box; suitcase, expanding s., overnight case, vanity c.; trunk, valise, portmanteau; sea chest, ditty-box; bandbox, hat box; ammunition chest, canister, caisson 723 *ammunition*; boxes, luggage, baggage, impedimenta, paraphernalia, bits and pieces, gear; boot, trunk, luggage van.

*small box*, pill b., snuff b., cigar b., pencil b., matchbox; cardboard box, carton, packet; airtight container, plastic box, lunch b.; metal box, can, tin, caddy, tea-caddy, canister; casket, pyx 988 *ritual object*; salt cellar, pepper mill, coffee mill; castor; nest of boxes.

*bag*, sack, poke; handbag, vanity case, reticule, clutch bag, dorothy b., shoulder b., tote b.; shopping bag, carrier b., polythene b., poly b., plastic b., paper b.; cornet, twist, sachet; Gladstone bag, carpet b., travelling b., overnight b., flight b., sponge b.; sleeping bag, survival b.; bedding-roll; holdall, grip; haversack, knapsack, rucksack, backpack; kitbag, ditty bag, duffle b.; pouch, sling; pannier, saddlebag, nosebag; school bag, satchel, sports bag, sabretache, bundle, swag; animal's pouch, marsupium.

*case*, étui, housewife; wallet, pocket book, notecase, billfold; spectacle case, cigarette c., compact; vasculum; attaché case, briefcase, portfolio; file, box f.; scabbard, sheath; pistol case, holster; arrow case, quiver 632 *store*.

*pocket*, waistcoat p., side p., hip p., trouser p., breast p., patch p., cargo p.; fob, pouch; purse, sporran.

*vat*, butt, water b., cask, barrel, tun, tub, keg, breaker; drum 252 *cylinder*; wine cask, puncheon, pipe, hogshead, firkin, kilderkin 465 *metrology*; hopper, cistern, tank 632 *store*.

*vessel*, vase, urn, jar, amphora, ampulla, cruse, crock, pot, water p.; pipkin, pitcher, ewer, jug, toby jug; gourd, calabash 366 *plant*; carafe, decanter, bottle; leather bottle, chagal

*or* chagul, blackjack, wineskin; wine bottle, demijohn, magnum, jeroboam, rehoboam, methuselah, balthazar; flask, hip f., flagon, vial, phial; honeypot, jamjar; gallipot, carboy, crucible, retort, pipette, test tube, cupel 461 *testing agent*; chamber pot, bedpan, toilet bowl 649 *latrine*; pail, bucket, wooden b., piggin; churn, can, watering c.; flowerpot, planter, jardinière; bin, litter b., rubbish b., dustbin 649 *sink*; scuttle, coal s., hod; skip, kibble; bath, tin b., tub.

*cooking pot* 383 *heater*; boiler, copper, cauldron, kettle, cooking pot, pot; double boiler, bain marie, steamer; pan, saucepan, stewpan, steamer, double-boiler; frying pan, skillet, wok, omelette pan, grill p., girdle; casserole, Dutch oven, tandoor; mess tin, dixie, billycan; tea urn, teapot, samovar, coffeepot, cafetière, percolator; vacuum flask, thermos f.; hot-water bottle, warming pan.

*cup*, eggcup, coffee cup, teacup, breakfast cup; tea service, tea set; chalice, goblet, beaker; drinking cup, loving c.; quaich; horn, drinking h., tankard, stoup, can, cannikin, pannikin, mug, stein, toby, noggin, rummer, schooner, tassie; tumbler, glass, liqueur g., wine-glass, brandy balloon, pony.

*bowl*, basin, hand b., wash b., finger b.; toilet b.; pudding basin, mixing bowl, punch b., drinking b., jorum; porringer, ramekin; manger, trough; colander, strainer, vegetable dish, tureen, terrine, gravy boat; rose bowl, vase 844 *ornamentation*.

*plate*, salver, silver s., tray, paten; platter, ashet, trencher, charger, dish; palette; saucer; pan, scale 322 *scales*; pallet; mortarboard, hod.

*ladle*, skimmer, dipper, baler, scoop, cupped hands; spoon, tablespoon, dessertspoon, teaspoon, eggspoon, soupspoon, apostle spoon; spade, trowel, spatula, slice, shovel.

*room*, room, chamber, apartment 192 *flat*; cockpit, cubicle, cab; cabin, stateroom; audience chamber, presence c., throne room; cabinet, closet, study, den, snug, snuggery, sanctum, adytum 192 *retreat*; library, studio, atelier, workroom, office 687 *workshop*; playroom, rumpus room, nursery; reception room, drawing room, front r., sitting r., living r., lounge, parlour, salon, boudoir; bedroom, bed deck, dormitory; dressing room; bathroom, washroom, toilet, shower room, sauna; dining room, breakfast r., dinette; messroom, mess, hall, refectory, canteen 192 *restaurant*; gunroom, wardrobe; smoking room, billiard r.; bar, snug 192 *pub*; cookhouse, galley, kitchen, kitchenette; scullery, pantry, larder, stillroom; dairy, laundry, utility room, offices, outhouse; coachhouse, garage 192 *shed*; storeroom, box room, lumber r., glory hole 632 *storage*; cloak-room, smallest room, lavatory 649 *latrine*. (See also *compartment*.)

*lobby*, vestibule, foyer, anteroom, ante-chamber, waiting room; corridor, passage, hall, entrance h.; gallery, verandah, stoop, patio, piazza, loggia, balcony, portico, porch 263 *doorway*; extension, lean-to.

*cellar*, cellarage, vault, crypt, basement, garden flat 214 *base*; coalhole, bunker 632 *storage*; hold, dungeon 748 *prison*.

*attic*, loft, hayloft; penthouse, garret 213 *summit*.

*arbour*, alcove, bower, grotto, grot, summer-house, gazebo, folly, pergola 192 *pavilion*; sun lounge, solarium, conservatory, orangery, greenhouse, glasshouse, hothouse 370 *garden*.

**Adj.** *recipient*, capacious, voluminous 183 *spacious*; containing, hiding, framing, enclosing; pouchy, baggy.

*cellular*, multicellular, honeycombed 255 *concave*; camerate, compartmentalized; multi-locular, locular; marsupial, polygastric, ventricular; abdominal, gastral, ventral, stomachic, ventricose, bellied 253 *convex*.

*capsular*, sacculate, cystic; vascular, vesicular.

SECTION TWO

# Dimensions

## 195 Size

**N.** *size*, magnitude, order of m.; proportions, dimensions, measurements 183 *measure*; extent, expanse, area 183 *space*; extension 203 *length*, 209 *height*, 211 *depth*; width, amplitude 205 *breadth*; volume, cubature; girth, circumference 233 *outline*; bulk, mass, weight 322 *gravity*; capacity, intake, tonnage; measured size, scantling, calibre 465 *measurement*; real size, true dimensions 494 *accuracy*; greatest size, maximum 32 *greatness*; full size, life size 54 *plenitude*; large size, king s., queen s., magnum; largest portion 52 *chief part*; excessive size, hypertrophy, giantism, gigantism.

*hugeness*, largeness, bigness, grandiosity 32 *greatness*; enormity, enormousness, immensity, vastness; towering proportions, monstrosity, gigantism 209 *height*.

*bulk*, mass, weight, heaviness, avoirdupois 322 *gravity*; lump, daud, dod, block, clod, boulder 324 *solid body*; hunk, chunk 53 *piece*; mound, heap 32 *great quantity*; mountain, pyramid 209 *high structure*; massiveness, bulki-ness; turgidity 197 *dilation*; obesity, corpulence, fatness, stoutness, chubbiness, plumpness, embonpoint, chunkiness, fleshi-ness, meatiness, beefiness; flesh and blood, folds of flesh, double chin, rotund figure, spare tyre, corporation 253 *swelling*; muscle man 162 *athlete*; fat person, fatty, tub, dumpling, mound of flesh, tub of lard, lard-lump, hulk; Billy Bunter, Bessie B., Falstaff, Teletubby Generation.

*giant*, giantess, colossus 209 *tall creature*; mountain of a man *or* woman, young giant, strapper; ogre, monster, King Kong; leviathan, behemoth, 'Triton among the minnows' (see quotation at 34 *superior*); whale, hippo-potamus, elephant, jumbo; mammoth, dino-saur; giantry, Titan, Titaness, Gargantua, Pantagruel, Brobdingnagian, Gog and Magog, Typhon, Antaeus, Atlas, Cyclops, Polyphemus, Og, Goliath.

*whopper*, spanker, walloper, whacker, humd-inger; a mountain of a, a father and mother of a –, a – and a half.

**Adj.** *large*, of size, big 32 *great*; large size, economy s., king s., queen s., jumbo; maxi-, mega-; pretty large, fair-sized, considerable, siz-able, good-sized; bulky, massive, massy 322 *weighty*; ample, capacious, voluminous, baggy; amplitudinous, comprehensive 205 *broad*; vast, extensive 183 *spacious*; monumental, towering, mountainous 209 *tall*; fine, magnifi-cent, spanking, thumping, thundering, whacking 32 *whopping*; man-size, life-s., large as life; well-grown, well-built, large-limbed, elephantine; macroscopic, large-scale, mega-lithic; big for one's age, lusty, healthy 162 *strong*; so big, of that order.

*huge*, immense, enormous, vast, stonking (sl), mega (inf), mighty, grandiose, stupen-dous, monstrous 32 *prodigious*; biggest ever, record size; colossal, mammoth, dinosaurian, gigantic, gigantean, gigantesque, giant, giant-like, mountainous; Brobdingnagian, titanic, Herculean, gargantuan; Cyclopean, mega-lithic; outsize, oversize, overlarge, overweight 32 *exorbitant*; limitless 107 *infinite*.

*fleshy*, meaty, fat, stout, obese, overweight; well-covered, well-upholstered, Falstaffian; plump, ample, plumpish, chubby, cuddly, fubsy, podgy, pudgy 205 *thick*; squat, squab, square, dumpy, chunky, stocky 205 *broad*; tubby, portly, corpulent, paunchy, pot-bellied 253 *convex*; puffy, pursy, bloated, bosomy, busty 197 *expanded*; round, rotund, roly-poly, full, full-faced, chubby-f.; double-chinned, dimpled, dimply, buxom, jolly, on the plump side; in condition, in good c., well-fed, well-grown, strapping, hunky, lusty, burly, beefy, brawny 162 *stalwart*; plump as a dumpling, plump as a partridge, fat as butter, fat as bacon, fat as a pig.

*unwieldy*, cumbersome, hulking, lumbering, gangling, lolloping; hulky, lumpy, lumpish, lubberly; too big, elephantine, whale-like, overweight; awkward, muscle-bound 695 *clumsy*.

**Vb.** *be large*, – big etc. adj.; become large 197 *expand*; have size, loom large, bulk l., bulk, fill space 183 *extend*; tower; soar 209 *be high*.

## 196 Littleness

**N.** *littleness*, daintiness etc. adj.; small size, miniature quality 33 *smallness*; lack of height 204 *shortness*; diminutiveness, dwarfishness, stuntedness; scantiness, paucity, exiguity 105 *fewness*; meagreness 206 *thinness*; -kin, -let.

*minuteness*, point, mathematical p., vanishing p.; pinpoint, pinhead; crystal; atom, molecule, particle, electron, neutron, proton, quark 319 *element*; nucleus, cell; corpuscle; drop, droplet, dust, grain, g. of sand; seed, mustard s. 33 *small thing*; bubble, button, molehill 639 *trifle*.

*miniature* 553 *picture*; microphotograph, microdot, microfilm, microfiche, thumbnail 551 *photography*; pocket edition, Elzevir e., duodecimo 589 *edition*; thumbnail sketch, epitome 592 *compendium*; model, microcosm; bubble car, minicar 274 *car*.

*dwarf*; midget, minikin, pigmy, Lilliputian, halfling, hobbit; little people 970 *elf*; chit, slip, titch; teeny, mite, tot, tiddler 132 *child*; dapperling, dandiprat, cock-sparrow, bantam 33 *small animal*; pipsqueak, squit, squirt 639 *nonentity*; manikin, doll, puppet, Pinocchio; Tom Thumb, Thumbelina, Hop-o'-my-thumb, homunculus; shrimp, runt, weakling, miserable specimen.

*microorganism*, protozoan, plankton, microfauna, animalcule, amoeba; bacillus, bacteria, bacterium, microbe, germ, virus, microvirus, retrovirus; microphyte, zoophyte; alga 366 *plant*.

*microscopy*, micrography, microphotography; microscope, electron m., microspectroscope, micrometer, vernier scale; microtechnique.

*microelectronics*, microminiaturization 160 *electronics*; integrated circuit, microcircuit; chip, microchip, silicon chip, transputer; microprocessor 86 *computing*.

**Adj.** *little* 33 *small*; petite, dainty, dinky, dolly, elfin; diminutive, mini, pigmy, Lilliputian; no bigger than; wee, titchy, tiny, teeny, teeny-weeny, itsy-witsy; toy, baby, pocket, pocket-size, pocket-handkerchief, pintsize, duodecimo, mini-, miniature, model; portable, handy, compact, bijou; snug, cosy, poky,

cramped, no room to swing a cat 206 *narrow*; runty, puny 163 *weak*; petty 33 *inconsiderable*; one-horse 639 *unimportant*.

*dwarfish*, dwarf, dwarfed, Lilliputian, pigmy, undersized, stunted, weazen, wizened, shrunk 198 *contracted*; squat, dumpy 204 *short*; knee-high, knee-high to a grasshopper.

*exiguous*, minimal, slight, scant, scanty, homoeopathic 33 *small*; thin, skinny, scraggy 206 *lean*; rudimentary, embryonic 68 *beginning*; bitty, itsy-bitsy 53 *fragmentary*.

*minute*, micro-, microscopic, ultramicroscopic, infinitesimal; atomic, molecular, corpuscular; granular 332 *powdery*; inappreciable, imperceptible, intangible, impalpable 444 *invisible*.

**Vb.** *be little*, – petite etc. adj.; contract 198 *become small*; dwindle 37 *decrease*; require little space, take up no room, lie in a nutshell, roll up into a ball, fit in a small compass, fit on the head of a pin.

**Adv.** *in small compass*, in a nutshell; on a small scale, in miniature.

## 197 Expansion

**N.** *expansion*, increase of size, ascending order, crescendo; enlargement, augmentation, aggrandizement 36 *increase*; amplification, supplementation, reinforcement 38 *addition*; hypertrophy, giantism, gigantism; overenlargement, hyperbole 546 *exaggeration*; stretching, extension, spread, deployment, fanning out 75 *dispersion*; ribbon development, urban sprawl 192 *housing*; increment, accretion 40 *adjunct*; upgrowth, overgrowth, pullulation, development 157 *growth*, 171 *productiveness*; overstaffing, Parkinson's law 637 *superfluity*; extensibility, expansibility, dilatability 328 *elasticity*.

*dilation*, dilatation, distension, diastole; inflation, reflation, puffing, puff 352 *blowing*; swelling up, turgescence, turgidity, tumescence, intumescence, tumefaction; puffiness, dropsy, tumour 253 *swelling*.

**Adj.** *expanded*, blown up etc. vb.; larger, bigger, bigger than before, bigger than ever; expanding 36 *increasing*; stuffed, padded out, eked out, supplemented; spreading, widespread, deployed; expansive 183 *spacious*; fan-shaped, flabellate, flabelliform, flared 205 *broad*; wide open, patulous, gaping 263 *open*; tumescent, budding, burgeoning, bursting, florescent, flowering, out; full-blown, full-grown, fully-formed 669 *matured*; overblown, overgrown, hypertrophied 546 *exaggerated*; obese, puffy, flabby, pot-bellied, bloated, fat 195 *fleshy*; swollen, turgescent, turgid; distended, stretched, tight; tumid, dropsical, varicose, bulbous 253 *convex*; bladder-like; ampullaceous, pouchy.

**Vb.** *expand*, wax, grow larger, increase, snowball 36 *grow*; widen, broaden, flare, splay 205 *be broad*; spread, extend, sprawl; fan out, deploy, take open order 75 *be dispersed*; spread over, spread like wildfire, overrun, mantle, straddle 226 *cover*; rise, prove (e.g. dough); gather, swell, distend, dilate, fill out; mushroom, balloon, belly 253 *be convex*; get fat, gain flesh, put on weight, put on the flab; burst at the seams; grow up, spring up, bud, burgeon, shoot, sprout, open, put forth, burst f., blossom, flower, blow, bloom, be out 171 *be fruitful*.

*enlarge*, aggrandize; make larger, expand; rarefy (by expansion); leaven 310 *elevate*; bore, ream; widen, broaden, let out; open, pull out; stretch, extend 203 *lengthen*; intensify, heighten, deepen, draw out; amplify, supplement, reinforce 38 *add*; double, redouble; develop, build up 36 *augment*; distend, inflate, reflate, pump up, blow up, puff, puff up, puff out 352 *blow*; bulk, thicken; stuff, pad 227 *line*; cram, fill to bursting 54 *fill*; feed up, fatten, plump up, bloat 301 *feed*; enlarge, blow up 551 *photograph*; magnify, overenlarge, overdevelop 546 *exaggerate*.

## 198 Contraction

**N.** *contraction*, reduction, abatement, lessening, deflation 37 *diminution*; decrease, shrinkage, descending order, diminuendo 42 *decrement*; curtailment, abbreviation, syncope, elision 204 *shortening*; consolidation 324 *condensation*; freezing 382 *refrigeration*; pulling together, drawing t. 45 *joining together*, 264 *closure*; contracting, systole; contractions, labour pains 167 *obstetrics*; attenuation, emaciation, consumption, marasmus, withering, atrophy; decline, retreat, recession, slump 655 *deterioration*; neck, isthmus, bottleneck, hourglass, wasp-waist 206 *narrowness*; epitome 592 *compendium*.

*compression*, pressure, compressure, compaction, squeeze, squeezing, stenosis, strangulation; constriction, constringency, astriction, astringency; contractility, contractibility, compressibility.

*compressor*, squeezer, liquidizer, mangle, roller 258 *smoother*; tightener, constrictor, astringent, styptic; bandage, binder, tourniquet 658 *surgical dressing*; belt, band, garter 47 *girdle*; whalebone, stays, corset 228 *underwear*; straitjacket, iron boot, thumbscrew 964 *instrument of torture*; bear, python, boa constrictor.

**Adj.** *contracted*, shrunk, shrunken, smaller 33 *small*; waning 37 *decreasing*; constricted,

strangled, strangulated; unexpanded, deflated, condensed 324 *dense*; compact, compacted, compressed; pinched, nipped, tightened, drawn tight 206 *narrow*, 264 *closed*; compressible, contractile, systaltic; stunted, shrivelled, wizened 196 *dwarfish*; tabid, tabescent, marasmic, wasting, consumptive 655 *deteriorated*.

*compressive*, contractional, astringent, binding, constipating.

**Vb.** *become small*, grow less, lessen, dwindle, wane, ebb, fall away 37 *decrease*; shrivel, wither, waste away 51 *decompose*; lose weight, lose flesh 323 *be light*; stop growing, level off, bottom out; contract, shrink, narrow, taper, taper off, draw in 206 *be narrow*; condense 324 *be dense*; evaporate 338 *vaporize*; draw together, close up 264 *close*; pucker, purse, corrugate, wrinkle 261 *fold*.

*make smaller*, lessen, reduce, scale down, downsize 37 *abate*; contract, shrink, abridge, take in, cut down to life size, dwarf, stunt 204 *shorten*; diet, slim, take off weight 323 *lighten*; taper, narrow, attenuate, thin, emaciate 206 *make thin*; puncture, deflate, rarefy, pump out, exhaust, drain 300 *empty*; boil down, evaporate 338 *vaporize*; dehydrate 342 *dry*; cramp, constrict, constringe, pinch, nip, squeeze, bind, bandage, corset; draw in, draw tight, strain, tauten 45 *tighten*; draw together, clench 264 *close*, 45 *join*; hug, crush, strangle, strangulate; compress, compact, constipate, condense, nucleate 324 *be dense*; huddle, crowd together; squeeze in, pack tight, pack like sardines, cram, jam 54 *fill*; squash 216 *flatten*; cramp, restrict 747 *restrain*; limit 232 *circumscribe*; chip away, whittle away, shave, shear, clip, trim, prune, pollard 46 *cut*; scrape, file, grind 332 *pulverize*; fold up, crumple 261 *fold*; roll, press, flatten 258 *smooth*.

## 199 Distance

**N.** *distance*, astronomical d., light years, depths of space 183 *space*; measured distance, mileage, food miles, footage 203 *length*; focal distance; elongation, greatest e., aphelion, apogee; far distance, horizon, false h., skyline, offing; background 238 *rear*; periphery, circumference 233 *outline*; drift, dispersion 282 *deviation*; reach, grasp, compass, span, stride, giant's s. 183 *range*; far cry, long way, fair w., tidy step, day's march, long long trail, marathon.

*farness*, far distance, remoteness, aloofness; removal 46 *separation*; antipodes, pole 240 *contraposition*; world's end, ends of the earth, ultima Thule, Pillars of Hercules; ne plus ultra, back of beyond; Far West, Far East; foreign parts 59 *extraneousness*; outpost 883 *seclusion*;

purlieus, outskirts 223 *exteriority*; outer edge, frontier 236 *limit*; unavailability 190 *absence*.

**Adj.** *distant*, distal, peripheral, terminal; far, farther; ulterior; ultimate, farthest, furthest, furthermost; long-distance, long-range; yon, yonder; not local, away, far away; outlying, peripheral; offshore, on the horizon; remote, aloof, far-flung, godforsaken; hyperborean, antipodean; out of range, telescopic; lost to sight, lost to view, out of sight 444 *invisible*; off-centre, wide, wide of the mark.

*removed*, separated, inaccessible, unapproachable, ungetatable, out of touch, out of the way; beyond, over the horizon; overseas, transmarine, transpontine, transoceanic, transatlantic, trans-Pacific, transpolar, transalpine, ultramontane; ultramundane, out of this world.

**Vb.** *be distant*, stretch to, reach to, extend to, spread to, go to, get to, stretch away to, carry to, carry on to 183 *extend*; carry, range; outdistance, outrange, outreach 306 *outdo*; keep one's distance, remain at a d., stay at arm's length, keep off, hold off, stand off, lie off; keep clear of, stand aloof, stand clear of, keep a safe distance, give a wide berth 620 *avoid*.

**Adv.** *afar*, away, not locally; far, far away, far afield, far off, way o., way behind, way in front; uptown, downtown; yonder, in the distance, in the offing, on the horizon, on the far h., beyond the blue h., as far as the eye can see; at a distance, a great way off, a long way away, a far cry from; out of sight; nobody knows where, out of the way; to the ends of the earth, to the back of beyond, to the uttermost end; east of the sun and west of the moon; far and wide 183 *widely*; asunder, apart, far a., abroad, afield; at arm's length.

*beyond*, further, farther; further on, ahead, in front; clear of, wide of, wide of the mark; below the horizon, hull down; up over, down under, over the border, over the hills and far away.

*too far*, out of reach, out of range, out of sight, out of hearing, out of earshot, out of the sphere of, out of bounds.

## 200 Nearness

**N.** *nearness*, proximity, propinquity, closeness, near distance, foreground 237 *front*; vicinage, vicinity, neighbourhood 230 *surroundings*; brink, verge 234 *edge*; adjacency 202 *contiguity*; collision course 293 *convergence*; approximation 289 *approach*; localization 187 *location*.

*short distance*, no d., shortest d., beeline, short cut; step, short s., no distance, walking d.; striking distance, close quarters, close grips; close range, earshot, gunshot, pistolshot, bowshot, arrowshot, stone's throw, spitting distance; short span, inch, millimetre, finger's breadth, hair's breadth 201 *gap*; close-up, near approach; nearest approach, perigee, perihelion; close finish, photo f., near thing 716 *contest*.

*near place*, vicinage, vicinity, neighbourhood, purlieu, environs, suburbs, confines 187 *locality*; approaches, marches, borderlands; ringside seat, next door 202 *contiguity*; second place, proxime accessit 65 *sequence*.

**Adj.** *near*, proximate, proximal; very near, approximate; approximating, close, getting warm, warm 289 *approaching*; about to meet 293 *convergent*; nearby, wayside, roadside 289 *accessible*; not far, hard by, inshore; near at hand, close at hand, at hand, handy, at one's fingertips, present 189 *on the spot*; near the surface 212 *shallow*; home, local, vicinal, in the neighbourhood; close to, next to, next-door to, neighbouring, limitrophe, bordering on, verging on, adjacent, adjoining, jostling, rubbing shoulders 202 *contiguous*; fronting, facing 237 *frontal*; close, intimate, inseparable 45 *joined*; bumper-to-bumper; at close quarters, at close grips; close-run, neck-and-neck, nip and tuck, with nothing between, level, level-pegging 716 *contending*; near in blood, related 11 *akin*.

**Vb.** *be near*, be around, be about 189 *be present*; hang around, hang about; approximate, draw near, get close, get warm 289 *approach*; meet 293 *converge*; neighbour, stand next to, abut, adjoin, border, verge upon 202 *be contiguous*; trench upon 306 *encroach*; hug the shore; come close, skirt, graze, shave, brush, skim, hedge-hop, hover over; jostle, buzz, get in the way 702 *obstruct*; sit on one's tail, tail, follow close, shadow; come to heel, tread on the heels of, breathe down one's neck 284 *follow*; clasp, cling to, hug, embrace, cuddle 889 *caress*; huddle, crowd, close up, close the ranks 74 *congregate*.

*bring near*, approach, approximate; move up, place side by side 202 *juxtapose*.

**Adv.** *near*, not far, locally, in the neighbourhood, in the vicinity; nigh, hard by, fast by, close to, close up to, close upon, in the way, at close range, at close quarters; close behind, right b.; within call, within hearing, within earshot, within a stone's throw, only a step, at no great distance, not far from; on one's doorstep, in one's own backyard; at one's door, at one's feet, at one's elbow, at one's side, under one's nose, at one's fingertips, within reach, close at hand; in the presence of, face to face, eyeball to eyeball, man to man; in juxtaposition, next door, side by side, cheek by jowl, tête-à-tête, arm in arm, beside, alongside; on the circumference, on the periphery, on *or* in the confines of, on the skirts of, on the outskirts, at the threshold; brinking on, verging on, on the brink of, on the verge of, on the tip of one's tongue.

*nearly*, practically, almost, all but; more or less, near enough, roughly, around, somewhere around; in the region of, in round figures, in round numbers; about, much a., hereabouts, thereabouts, nearabouts, there or thereabouts, circa; closely, approximately, hard on, close on; well-nigh, as good as, on the way to; within an ace of, just about to; pushing.

## 201 Interval

**N.** *interval*, distance between, space; narrow interval, half-space, hairspace 200 *short distance*; interspace, daylight, head, length; clearance, margin, freeboard 183 *room*; interval of time, timelag 108 *interim*; pause, break, intermission, breather, time out, gap year, truce 145 *lull*; hiatus 72 *discontinuity*; interruption, incompleteness, jump, leap; musical interval, tone, semitone, third, fourth, fifth 410 *musical note*.

*gap*, interstice, mesh 222 *network*; lacuna, cavity, hole, opening, aperture 263 *orifice*; pass, defile, ghat, wind-gap 305 *passage*; firebreak 662 *safeguard*; ditch, dike, trench 351 *drain*; water jump, haha, sunk fence 231 *partition*; ravine, gorge, gully, couloir, chimney, crevasse, canyon 255 *valley*; cleft, crevice, chink, crack, rift, cut, gash, tear, rent, slit 46 *scission*; flaw, fault, breach, break, split, fracture, rupture, fissure, chap 46 *separation*; slot, groove 262 *furrow*; indentation 260 *notch*; seam, join 45 *joint*; leak 298 *outlet*; abyss, chasm 211 *depth*; yawning gulf, void 190 *emptiness*; inlet, creek, gulch 345 *gulf*.

**Adj.** *spaced*, spaced out, intervallic, with an interval; gappy, gapped; split, cloven, cleft, cracked, rimous, rimose 46 *disunited*; dehiscent, gaping 263 *open*; sporadic, far between; latticed, meshed, reticulated.

**Vb.** *space*, interval, space out, place at intervals 46 *set apart*; crack, split, start, gape, dehisce 263 *open*; win by a head, win by a length; clear, show daylight between; lattice, mesh, reticulate.

**Adv.** *at intervals* 72 *discontinuously*; now and then, now and again, every so often, every now and then, off and on; with an interval, by a head, by a length.

## 202 Contiguity

**N.** *contiguity*, juxtaposition, apposition, proximity, close p. 200 *nearness*; touching 378 *touch*; no interval 71 *continuity*; contact, tangency; abuttal, abutment; intercommunication, osculation; meeting, encounter, confrontation, interface 293 *convergence*; conjunction, syzygy (astronomy) 45 *union*; close contact, adhesion, cohesion 48 *coherence*; coexistence, coincidence, concomitance 89 *accompaniment*; grazing contact, tangent; border, fringe 234 *edge*; borderland, frontier 236 *limit*; buffer state 231 *interjacency*.

**Adj.** *contiguous*, touching, in contact; osculatory, intercommunicating; tangential, grazing, skirting, brushing, abutting, end to end, bumper-to-bumper; conterminous, adjacent, with no interval 71 *continuous*; adjoining, close to, jostling, elbow to elbow, rubbing shoulders 200 *near*.

**Vb.** *be contiguous*, overlap 378 *touch*; make contact, come in c., brush, rub, skim, scrape, graze, kiss; join, meet 293 *converge*; stick, adhere 48 *cohere*; lie end to end, abut on, adjoin, reach to, extend to 183 *extend*; sit next to, rub shoulders with, crowd, jostle, elbow 200 *be near*; border with, march w., skirt 234 *hem*; coexist, coincide 89 *accompany*; osculate, intercommunicate 45 *connect*; get in touch, contact.

*juxtapose*, set side by side, range together, bring into contact, knock persons' heads together.

**Adv.** *contiguously*, tangentially; in contact, in close c.; next, close; end to end; cheek by jowl, elbow to elbow; hand in hand, arm in arm; from hand to hand.

## 203 Length

**N.** *length*, longitude; extent, extension; reach, long arm; full length, overall l.; stretch, span, mileage, footage 199 *distance*; perspective 211 *depth*.

*lengthening*, extending etc. vb.; prolongation, extension, production, spinning out 113 *protraction*; stretching, tension; spreading out, stringing o.

*line*, bar, rule, tape, measuring tape, strip, stripe, streak; spoke, radius; single file, line ahead, crocodile, queue 65 *sequence*; straight line, right l. 249 *straightness*; bent line, fractal 248 *curvature*.

*long measure*, linear m., measurement of length, micrometry 465 *measurement*; unit of length, finger, hand, hand's breadth, palm, span, cubit; arm's length, fathom; head, length; pace, step; inch, foot, yard; rod, pole, perch; chain, furlong; mile, statute m., geographical m., nautical m., knot, league; millimetre, centimetre, metre, kilometre; degree of latitude, degree of longitude; micro-inch, micron, wavelength; astronomical unit, light year, parsec.

**Adj.** *long*, lengthy, extensive, a mile long, measured in miles; long-drawn out 113 *protracted*; lengthened, elongated, outstretched, extended, strung out 75 *unassembled*; shoulder-length, ankle-length, down to . . . ; wire-drawn, lank 206 *lean*; lanky, leggy, long-legged 209 *tall*; as long as my arm, long as a wet week; interminable, no end to 838 *tedious*; polysyllabic, sesquipedalian 570 *diffuse*; unshortened, unabridged, uncut, full-length 54 *complete*.

*longitudinal*, oblong, linear; one-dimensional.

**Vb.** *be long*, – lengthy etc. adj.; stretch, outstretch, stretch out, reach out; make a long arm; reach, stretch to 183 *extend*; drag, trail, drag its slow length along 113 *drag on*.

*lengthen*, stretch, elongate, draw out, wire-draw 206 *make thin*; pull out, stretch o., spread-eagle 197 *expand*; spread oneself out, sprawl 216 *be horizontal*; spread out, string o., deploy 75 *disperse*; extend, pay out, uncoil, unfurl, unroll, unfold 316 *evolve*; let down, drop the hem; produce, continue; prolong, protract 113 *spin out*; drawl 580 *stammer*.

*look along*, view in perspective; have a clear view, see from end to end 438 *scan*; enfilade.

**Adv.** *longwise*, longways, lengthwise; along, longitudinally, radially, in line ahead, in single file, in Indian f.; one in front and one behind, in tandem; in a crocodile; in a line, in perspective; at full length, end to end, overall; fore and aft; head to foot, head to tail, stem to stern, top to toe, head to heels, from the crown of the head to the sole of the foot.

## 204 Shortness

**N.** *shortness*, squatness etc. adj.; brevity, briefness; transience 114 *brief span*; inch, centimetre 200 *short distance*; low stature, dwarfishness, short legs, duck's disease 196 *littleness*; lack of inches, no height 210 *lowness*; shrinkage 42 *decrement*; scantiness, exiguity; scarceness 636 *insufficiency*; slippage; concision 569 *conciseness*; short hair, short back and sides, bob, crew cut; shorts, miniskirt.

*shortening*, abridgment, abbreviation; précis, summary 592 *compendium*; curtailment, cutback, cut, reduction 37 *diminution*; contraction 198 *compression*; aphaeresis, apocope, syncope.

*shortener*, cutter, abridger, abstracter 592 *epitomizer*.

**Adj.** *short*, brief 114 *transient*; not big, dwarfish, stunted 196 *little*; knee-high to a grasshopper, not tall, squab, squabby, squat, dumpy, fubsy, stumpy, stocky, thickset, stubby

195 *fleshy*, 205 *thick*; not high 210 *low*; pug-nosed, snub-n.; snub, retroussé, blunt 257 *unsharpened*; not long, inch-long; skimpy, scanty 636 *insufficient*; foreshortened 246 *distorted*; abbreviated, abridged; shortened, sawn-off; cut, curtailed, docked, beheaded, decapitated, truncated, topless, headless; shaven, shorn, mown; sparing of words, terse 569 *concise*; elliptical (of style); half-finished 55 *unfinished*; epitomized, potted, compact 592 *compendious*; compacted, compressed 198 *contracted*.

**Vb.** *be short*, – brief etc. adj.; not reach 307 *fall short*.

*shorten*, abbreviate, abridge, cut; summarize, boil down, epitomize, pot, précis 592 *abstract*; sum up, recapitulate 569 *be concise*; compress, contract, ellipt, telescope 198 *make smaller*; reduce, diminish 37 *abate*; foreshorten 246 *distort*; take up, put a tuck in, raise the hem, turn up, tuck up, kilt; behead, decapitate, obtruncate, guillotine, axe, chop up 46 *sunder*; cut short, dock, curtail, truncate; cut back, cut down, slash, lop, prune; shear, shave, trim, crop, clip, bob, shingle 46 *cut*; mow, scythe; nip in the bud, stunt, check the growth of 278 *retard*; scrimp, skimp 636 *make insufficient*.

**Adv.** *shortly*, briefly etc. adj.; in brief, in short, to summarize 592 *in sum*.

## 205 Breadth. Thickness

**N.** *breadth*, width, latitude; width across, span, fingerspan, wingspan, wingspread; diameter, radius, semidiameter; gauge, broad g., bore, calibre; broadness, expanse, superficial extent, amplitude 183 *range*; wideness, fullness, bagginess.

*thickness*, crassitude, stoutness, corpulence 195 *bulk*; widening, dilatation 197 *dilation*.

**Adj.** *broad*, wide, expansive, unspanned 183 *spacious*; wide-cut, full, flared, ample, baggy; fan-like, flabelliform, patulous, umbelliferous; outspread, outstretched, splayed out 197 *expanded*; bell-bottomed, broad-b., broad-based; callipygian, steatopygous, wide-hipped; broad in the beam, beamy, wide-bodied; wide as a church door; broad-brimmed, wide-awake (hat); wide-angle (lens); wide-mouthed 263 *open*; broad-shouldered, broad-chested 162 *stalwart*; wide-ranging, global 79 *general*.

*thick*, stout, dumpy, squat 204 *short*; thickset, tubby, beefy, stubby 195 *fleshy*; thick-lipped, blubber-l., full-l.; thick-necked, bull-n.; thick-skinned, pachydermatous; thick-ribbed, barrel-chested, broad-shouldered, stout-timbered 162 *strong*; thick as a rope; pyknic, endomorphic; solidly built 324 *dense*; semiliquid, ropy, lumpy, to be cut with a knife 354 *viscid*.

**Vb.** *be broad,* – thick etc. adj.; get broad, get wide, broaden, widen, fatten, thicken; fan out, flare, splay 197 *expand*; straddle, bestride, span 226 *overlie*.

**Adv.** *broadways,* broadwise, breadthways, breadthwise; widthways, widthwise; broadways on 239 *sideways*.

## 206 Narrowness. Thinness

**N.** *narrowness,* tightness etc. adj.; narrow interval, closeness, tight squeeze, crack, chink, hair's breadth, finger's b. 200 *short distance*; lack of breadth, length without b., line, strip, stripe, streak; vein, capillary 208 *filament*; knife-edge, razor's edge, tightrope, wire; narrow gauge; bottleneck, narrows, strait 345 *gulf*; ridge, col, saddle 209 *high land*; ravine, gully 255 *valley*; pass, defile 305 *passage*; neck, isthmus, land-bridge 624 *bridge*.

*thinness,* tenuity, fineness 325 *rarity*; slenderness, gracility; skinniness, emaciation, anorexia (nervosa), consumption; scrag, skin and bone, skeleton; miserable specimen, scarecrow, rake, beanpole, broomstick, shadow, spindleshanks, barebones; haggardness, lantern jaws, hatchet face, sunken cheeks; thread, paper, tissue 422 *transparency*; shaving, splinter 33 *small thing*; slip, wisp 208 *filament*.

*narrowing,* compression 198 *contraction*; taper, tapering 293 *convergence*; neck, isthmus; stricture, constriction; waistline, waist, wasp-w., hourglass.

**Adj.** *narrow,* not wide, single track; strait, tight, close; compressed, coarctate, pinched, unexpanded 198 *contracted*; not thick, fine, slimline, thin, wafer-thin 422 *transparent*; tight-drawn, attenuated, spun, fine-s., wiredrawn 203 *long*; thread-like, capillary 208 *fibrous*; tapering 293 *convergent*; slight, slightly-built, wispy, delicate 163 *weak*; gracile, attenuate, slender, slim, slimline, svelte, slinky, sylphlike; willowy, rangy, skinny; long-legged, leggy, lanky, gangling; narrow-waisted, wasp-w.; isthmian; bottlenecked.

*lean,* thin, ectomorphic, spare, rangy, wiry; meagre, skinny, bony; cadaverous, fleshless, skin-and-bone, skeletal, rawboned, haggard, gaunt, drawn, lantern-jawed, sunken-eyed, hatchet-faced; twiggy, spindly, spindle-shanked, spidery; undersized, weedy, scrawny, scrubby, scraggy 196 *exiguous*; consumptive, emaciated, anorexic, wasted, withered, wizened, pinched, peaky 651 *sick*; sere, shrivelled 131 *ageing*; starved, starveling 636 *underfed*; wraith-like, scarecrow-like, worn to a shadow, thin as a rake, thin as a lath, thin as a pencil, without an ounce of flesh to spare.

**Vb.** *be narrow,* – thin etc. adj.; narrow,

taper 293 *converge*; taper off 198 *become small*.

*make thin,* contract, compress, pinch, nip 198 *make smaller*; make oneself thin, starve, underfeed, diet, reduce, lose weight; improve one's figure, slenderize, slim; draw, wiredraw, spin, spin fine 203 *lengthen*; attenuate 325 *rarefy*.

## 207 Layer

**N.** *layer,* stratum, substratum, underlay, floor 214 *base*; outcrop, basset 254 *projection*; bed, course, string c., range, row; zone, vein, seam, lode; thickness, ply; storey, tier, floor, mezzanine f., entresol, landing; stage, planking, platform 218 *frame*; deck, top d., lower d., upper d., orlop d., quarterdeck, bridge 275 *ship*; film 423 *opacity*; bloom, dross, scum; patina, coating, coat, undercoat, veneer, top layer, top-dressing, topcoat 226 *covering*; scale, scab, membrane, peel, pellicle, sheathe, bark, integument 226 *skin*; level, water l., water table 216 *horizontality*; atmospheric layer 340 *atmosphere*.

*lamina,* sheet, slab, foil, strip; plate glass, plate, tinplate, latten, sheet iron, sheet steel; plank, board, weatherboard, fascia; laminate, Formica (tdmk), plywood; slat, lath, leaf, tabletop; tablet, plaque, panel, pane; slab, flag, flagstone, slate; shingle, tile; lamella, slide, wafer, shaving, flake, slice, rasher; cardboard, sheet of paper 631 *paper*; card, playing c.; platter, disc 250 *circle*.

*stratification,* stratigraphy; bedding, layering, lamination; laminability, flakiness, schistosity, scaliness, squamation; overlapping, overlap; nest of boxes, Chinese b., nest of tables, Russian doll; onion skin, exfoliation dome; layer cake, sandwich, double-decker; layer on layer, coat on coat, level upon level 231 *interjacency*.

**Adj.** *layered,* lamellar, lamelliform, lamellate; laminated, laminar, laminose; laminable, flaky; schistose, micaceous, slaty, shaly; foliated, foliaceous; foliate, leaf-like; bedded, stratified, stratiform; zoned, seamed; overlapping, clinker-built 226 *overlying*; tabular, decked, storeyed, in storeys, in layers; scaly, squamose, squamous; membranous, filmy 226 *covered*.

**Vb.** *laminate,* lay, deck, layer, shingle, overlap 226 *overlay*; zone, stratify, sandwich; plate, veneer 226 *coat*; exfoliate, delaminate, split; flake off, whittle, skive, pare, peel, strip 229 *uncover*; shave, slice 206 *make thin*.

## 208 Filament

**N.** *filament,* flagellum, cilium, lash, eyelash, beard, down 259 *hair*; barb, feather, harl 259 *plumage*; flock, lock, shred of wool, thread, lock of hair, strand, wisp, curl; fringe 234 *edging*; fibre, fibril, fibrilla, rootlet, stalk, tendril 366 *plant*, whisker, antenna, antennule 378 *feeler*; gossamer, cobweb, web 222 *network*; capillary, vein, venule, veinlet 351 *conduit*; ramification, branch; wire, element, wick 420 *torch*.

*fibre*, natural f., animal f., hair, camel h., rabbit h.; Angora, goat's hair, mohair, cashmere; llama hair, alpaca, vicuna; wool, Shetland w., botany w., merino, fingering; mungo, shoddy; silk, real s., wild silk, tussore, floss; vegetable fibre, cotton, cotton wool, silk cotton, kapok; linen, flax; manila, hemp; jute, sisal, coir; hards; tow, oakum; bast, raffia; worsted, yarn; spun yarn, continuous filament y.; thread, twine, twist, strand, cord, string, line, rope 47 *cable*; artificial fibre, man-made f., acrylic f., microfibre; rayon, nylon 222 *textile*, staple, denier 331 *texture*.

*strip*, fascia, band, bandage; belt, cord, thong, braid, tape, strap, ribbon, ribband; fillet 47 *girdle*; lath, slat, batten, stave, spline 207 *lamina*; shaving, wafer; splinter, shiver, shred 53 *piece*; streak, stripe, strake 203 *line*.

**Adj.** *fibrous*, fibroid, fibrillose, fibrillar, fibrilliform; woolly, cottony, silky; filamentous, filamentary, filiform; whiskery, downy, fleecy 259 *hairy*; wiry, threadlike; capillary, capillaceous; fine-spun, wire-drawn 206 *narrow*; stringy, cordlike, ropy 205 *thick*; flagelliform, lashlike; ligulate, strap-shaped; antenniform, antennary, antennal.

## 209 Height

**N.** *height*, perpendicular length, vertical range, long way to fall; altitude, elevation, ceiling, pitch 213 *summit*; loftiness, steepness, dizzy height; tallness, stature; eminence, sublimity; sky, stratosphere 340 *atmosphere*; zenith.

*high land*, height, highlands, heights, steeps, uplands, wold, moor, moorland, downs, rolling country; rising ground, rise, bank, brae, slope, climb 220 *incline*; knap, hill, eminence, mountain, Munro, mount, ben, Ben Nevis, Snowdon, Everest, K2, Kangchenjunga, Fuji, Kilimanjaro; fell, scar, tor; alp, Mont Blanc; mountain range, chain, sierra, cordillera, massif, Alps, Andes, Himalayas, Pyrenees, Rockies, Urals; ridge, hog's back, col, saddle spur, headland, foothill 254 *projection*; crest, peak, pike, hilltop 213 *summit*; steepness, precipice, cliff, white cliffs of Dover; crag, scar, bluff, steep, escarpment; gorge, canyon, ravine 255 *valley*; summit level, mesa; plateau, tableland 216 *horizontality*.

*small hill*, hillock, monticle, knoll, kopje, butte; roche moutonée, drumlin, hummock, hump, tump, dune, sand d., esker, moraine;

barrow, long b., round b. 364 *tomb*; mound, heap 253 *earthwork*; cairn, tell 548 *monument*; anthill, molehill, tussock 253 *swelling*.

*high structure*, column, pillar, turret, tower, 'cloud-capped towers';

> Our revels now are ended. These our actors,
> As I foretold you, were all spirits and
> Are melted into air, into thin air:
> And, like the baseless fabric of this vision,
> The cloud-capp'd towers, the gorgeous palaces,
> The solemn temples, the great globe itself,
> Yea, all which it inherit, shall dissolve
> And, like this insubstantial pageant faded,
> Leave not a rack behind.
>
> William Shakespeare, *The Tempest*

pile, noble p., skyscraper, high-rise flats, tower block 164 *building*; chimney stack, steeple, spire, flèche, belfry, campanile 990 *church exterior*; minaret, muezzin's tower; obelisk, Cleopatra's Needle; dome, cupola 226 *roof*; colossus 554 *sculpture*; mausoleum, pyramid 364 *tomb*; pagoda 990 *temple*; ziggurat, Tower of Babel; Eiffel Tower; mast, topmast, topgallant mast; flagstaff, pikestaff; pole, maypole; lamppost, standard; pylon, radio mast, telecommunication mast, telemast; masthead 213 *summit*; watchtower, lookout, crow's nest, eyrie 438 *view*; column of smoke, mushroom cloud.

*tall creature*, giraffe, elephant, mammoth, ostrich, daddy longlegs, lamppost, beanpole, six-footer, seven-f., grenadier, colossus 195 *giant*; poplar, pine, sequoia, big tree, Californian redwood 366 *tree*.

*high water*, high tide, flood t., spring t. 350 *current*; billow, tidal wave, white horses 350 *wave*; cataract 350 *waterfall*; flood, flash f., flood level.

*altimetry*, altimeter, height-finder, hypsometer, barograph 465 *meter*, *gauge*.

**Adj.** *high*, high-up, sky-high; eminent, uplifted, exalted, lofty, sublime, supernal 310 *elevated*; highest 213 *topmost*; perching, hanging (gardens); aerial, midair, airborne, flying; soaring, aspiring 308 *ascending*; spiry, towering, cloud-capp'd, cloud-topped, skyscraping; steep, dizzy, giddy, vertiginous; knee-high, thigh-h., breast-h., shoulder-h.; altitudinal.

*tall*, lanky, leggy, rangy, slab-sided 206 *narrow*; long-legged, long-necked, ostrich-necked, giraffe-like, beanpole-like; statuesque, Junoesque, Amazon-like; colossal, gigantic, monumental 195 *huge*; tall as a maypole, high as a steeple.

*alpine*, subalpine, alpestrine, Himalayan; mountainous, hilly, moorland, upland, highland; not flat, rolling, hillocky, hummocky; orogenetic, orological.

*overhanging*, beetling, superimposed, over-lying; towering over, overshadowing, domin-ating; incumbent, superincumbent; hovering, floating over; over one's head, aloft; jettied, prominent 254 *projecting*.

**Vb.** be high, – tall etc. adj.; tower, rear, soar; surmount, clear, overtop, overlook, dominate, command 34 *be superior*; overhang, over-shadow 226 *cover*; beetle, impend 254 *jut*; hover, hang over 217 *hang*; culminate, peak, be at the zenith 725 *climax*; mount, bestride, bestraddle; grow taller, shoot up, add to one's inches; rise 308 *ascend*; stand on tiptoe, stand on another's shoulders 310 *lift oneself*.

*make higher*, heighten, build up, raise, hold aloft 310 *elevate*.

**Adv.** *aloft*, up, on high, high up, in the clouds, on the rooftops; atop, on top, on the crest; above, overhead, up over; above stairs, upstairs; upwards, skyward, heavenward; straight up, steeply 215 *vertically*; on tiptoe, on stilts, on the shoulders of; breast high, up to the neck, up to the eyes, over head and ears; from top to bottom 54 *throughout*.

## 210 Lowness

**N.** *lowness*, debasement 311 *lowering*; pros-tration 216 *recumbency*; nonelevation, no height, sea level, flatness 216 *horizontality*; flats, levels 347 *marsh*; levelness, steppe 348 *plain*; low elevation, lowlands, molehill, pimple 196 *littleness*; gentle slope, nursery s., slight gradient 220 *incline*; subjacency, lower level, foothill 35 *inferiority*; bottom, hollow, depression 255 *valley*; sea-bottom, sea-floor 343 *ocean*; subterraneity, depths, cellar, nether regions, basement, well, mine 211 *depth*; floor, foot 214 *base*; underside, under-surface, underbelly 240 *contraposition*; nadir, lowest point, the pits; low water, low ebb, low tide, ebb t., neap t. 350 *current*; low ball, grubber, shooter, daisy-cutter.

**Adj.** *low*, not high, squat 204 *short*; unerect, not upright, crouched, crouching, stooping, slouching, bending 220 *oblique*; recumbent, laid low, prostrate 216 *supine*; low-lying, flat, level with the ground, at sea level 216 *flat*; low-level, single-storey; subjacent, lower, under, nether 35 *inferior*; sunken, lowered 255 *concave*; flattened, rounded, blunt 257 *unsharpened*; subterranean, subterraneous, underground, below the surface, submarine 523 *latent*, 211 *deep*; underfoot 745 *subjected*.

**Vb.** *be low*, – flat etc. adj.; lie low, lie flat 216 *be horizontal*; be beneath, underlie 523 *lurk*; slouch, crouch 311 *stoop*; crawl, wallow, grovel 721 *knuckle under*; depress 311 *lower*.

**Adv.** *under*, beneath, underneath, neath; below, at the foot of; downwards; adown, down, face-down; underfoot, underground, downstairs, below stairs; at a low ebb; below par.

## 211 Depth

**N.** *depth*, drop, fall; deepness etc. adj.; perspec-tive 203 *length*; vertical range, profundity, lowest depth, lowest point, nadir; deeps, deep water 343 *ocean*; unknown depths, unfathomable d. 663 *pitfall*; depression, bottom 255 *valley*; hollow, pit, shaft, mine, well 255 *cavity*; abyss, abysm, chasm, yawning depths 201 *gap*; vault, crypt, dungeon 194 *cellar*; cave, pothole, catacomb, hypogeum, bowels of the earth 210 *lowness*; pot-holing, deep-sea diving 309 *descent*; caisson disease, the bends; underworld, bottomless pit 972 *hell*; fathoming, soundings, sounding line, sound, probe, plummet, lead, lead line; sonar 484 *detector*; diving bell, bathysphere, bathyscaphe; submarine, submariner, frogman 313 *diver*; depth required, draught, displacement, sinkage; bathometer, bathometry 465 *measurement*.

**Adj.** *deep*, steep, plunging, profound; abysmal, yawning, cavernous; abyssal, deep-sea; deep-seated, deep-rooted 153 *fixed*; unplumbed, bottomless, soundless, fathom-less; unsounded, unfathomed, unsoundable, unfathomable; subjacent, subterranean, under-ground, hypogeal; underwater, undersea, subaqueous, submarine; buried, deep in, immersed, submerged 311 *lowered*; sunk, foun-dered, drowned; navigable; knee-deep, ankle-d.; deep as a well; infernal, deep as hell; depth-haunting, bathypelagic, benthic; depth-measuring, bathymetric.

**Vb.** *be deep*, – profound etc. adj.; gape, yawn; deepen, hollow, dig 255 *make concave*; fathom, sound, take soundings, plumb, heave the lead; drop, lower 311 *let fall*; go deep, plumb the depths, touch bottom, reach rock bottom, be on one's knees, reach one's nadir; sink to the bottom, plunge 313 *founder*.

**Adv.** *deeply*, profoundly; deep down, beyond one's depth, out of one's depth, deep in, over one's head, over head and ears, up to the eyes.

## 212 Shallowness

**N.** *shallowness*, no depth, superficiality 4 *insub-stantiality*; thin surface, film 223 *exteriority*; veneer, thin coat 226 *skin*; surface injury, super-ficial wound, scratch, mere s., pinprick, graze 639 *trifle*; shoal water, shoals, shallows; ford 305 *passage*; pond, puddle 346 *lake*; ripple, catspaw 350 *wave*; light soil, stony ground 344 *soil*.

**Adj.** *shallow*, slight, superficial 4 *insubstantial*; surface, skin-deep; near the surface, not deep; ankle-deep, knee-d.; shoal, shoaly, unnavigable; just enough to wet one's feet; light, thin, thinly spread 206 *narrow*.

## 213 Summit

**N.** *summit*, sky, heaven, seventh h., cloud nine; pole, north p., south p.; highest point, top, peak, crest, apex, pinnacle, crown; maximum height, utmost h., pitch; zenith, meridian, high noon, culmination, apogee; culminating point, crowning p.; acme, ne plus ultra, peak of perfection 646 *perfection*; crest of the wave, top of the tree 730 *prosperity*; top of the curve, highwater mark 236 *limit*; climax, turning point, turn of the tide 137 *crisis*; dividing line, divide, watershed, water-parting, Great Divide 231 *partition*; coping, copingstone, capstone, keystone; lintel, pediment, entablature, architrave, epistyle; tympanum, capital, cornice; battlements, parapet 713 *fortification*.

*vertex*, apex, crown, top, cap, brow, head; tip, cusp, spike, point, nib, end 69 *extremity*; spire, finial 990 *church exterior*; stairhead, landing 308 *ascent*; acropolis 713 *fort*; summit level, hilltop, mountaintop, plateau, tableland 209 *high land*; treetop, housetop, rooftop; gable, gable-end; leads, ceiling 226 *roof*; upper chamber, garret, loft 194 *attic*; top storey; topside, upper deck, quarterdeck, hurricane deck, boat d., bridge 275 *ship*; top-mast, topgallant mast; masthead, crow's nest 209 *high structure*.

*head*, headpiece, pate, poll, sconce; noddle, nob, nut, noggin, coco, conk, bonce, crumpet, bean, block, chump; upper storey, belfry; brow, dome, temple, forehead; loaf, brain, grey matter 498 *intelligence*; epicranium, pericranium; scalp, crown, double c.; skull, cranium, brainpan 255 *cavity*; occiput, sinciput; fontanelle; craniology, craniometry, cranioscopy, craniotomy; phrenology; brain scanning, brain scan, neuroradiology, brain surgery, neurosurgery.

**Adj.** *topmost*, top, highest 209 *high*; uppermost, upmost 34 *supreme*; polar, apical, crowning; capital, head; cephalic, dolichocephalic, brachycephalic, orthocephalic; cranial, occipital, sincipital; culminating, zenithal, meridian, meridional; tiptop, super 644 *best*.

**Vb.** *crown*, cap, head, top, pinnacle, tip, surmount, crest, overtop 209 *be high*; culminate, consummate 725 *climax*; go up top, take top place, go into the lead 34 *be superior*; top out, put the finishing touches to 54 *make complete*.

**Adv.** *atop*, on top, at the top, at the top of the tree, at the top of the ladder, at the peak of one's career; on the crest, on the crest of the wave; tiptoe, on tiptoe.

## 214 Base

**N.** *base*, foot, toe, skirt 210 *lowness*; bottom, fundus, root; lowest point, the depths, rock bottom, nadir, low water; footing, foundation, pou sto 218 *basis*; the nitty gritty; fundamental 68 *origin*; groundwork, substructure, infrastructure, chassis 218 *frame*; baseboard, plinth, pedestal 218 *stand*; substratum, floor, underlayer, bed, bedrock; subsoil, pan, hardpan; ground, earth, foundations; footing, sill; damp course, damp-proof course; basement, ground floor 194 *cellar*; flooring, pavement, pavingstone, flagstone, hard standing 226 *paving*; carpet 226 *floor-cover*; skirting board, wainscot, plinth, dado; keel, keelson; hold, bilge; sump, drain 649 *sink*.

*foot*, feet, tootsies (inf), dogs, plates (sl); beetle-crusher; forefoot, hindfoot, sole, heel, Achilles tendon, instep, arch; toe, toenail, big toe, hallux; trotter, hoof, cloven h.; paw, pad; claw, talon 778 *nippers*; ankle, ankle-bone, tarsus, metatarsus, fetlock, pastern.

**Adj.** *undermost*, lowermost, nethermost, bottom, rock-b. 210 *low*; basic, basal, fundamental; grounded, on the bottom, touching b.; based on, founded on, grounded on, built on, underlying 218 *supporting*.

*footed*, pedal; plantigrade, digitigrade; hoofed, cloven-h., ungulate, clawed, taloned; web-footed, soled, heeled, shod, shoed; toed, five-t.; club-footed, flat-f., hammer-toed 845 *blemished*.

**Adv.** *in the trough*, at the bottom 210 *under*; basically, fundamentally.

## 215 Verticality

**N.** *verticality*, the vertical, erectness, erect stance, uprightness, upright carriage; steepness, sheerness, precipitousness 209 *height*; perpendicularity, right angle, square; elevation, azimuth circle; vertical line, plumbline, plummet; vertical structure, hoist, upright, pole, stalagmite 218 *pillar*; sheer face, precipice, cliff, bluff, scarp, steep 209 *high land*; perpendicular drop, straight d., vertical height, rise.

**Adj.** *vertical*, upright, erect, standing; perpendicular, rectangular, orthogonal; sheer, abrupt, steep, precipitous 209 *high*; straight, plumb; straight up, straight down; upstanding, standing up, on one's feet, on one's legs, on one's hindlegs; bolt upright, stiff as a ramrod, unbowed, head-up; rampant, rearing; on end.

**Vb.** *be vertical,* stick up, cock up, bristle, stand on end; stand erect, stand upright, hold oneself straight; sit up, stand up, straighten up; rise, stand, be upstanding, rise to one's feet, get to one's feet, ramp, rear; keep standing, have no seat, sit on one's thumb.

*make vertical,* erect, rear, raise, pitch 310 *elevate;* raise on its legs, up-end; stand, set up, stick up, raise up, cock up.

**Adv.** *vertically,* abruptly etc. adj.; palewise (heraldry); upright, bolt upright, head-up; on end, up on end, endwise, up; on one's legs, on one's hind legs, standing, all standing; at right angles, perpendicularly; down, straight-d., plumb.

### 216 Horizontality

**N.** *horizontality,* horizontalness; horizontal angle, azimuth; horizontal line, ruled line, ruler, rule; horizontal course, strike; flatness 258 *smoothness;* level, plane, dead level, dead flat, level plane; sea level, water l., water table; stratum; slab, tablet, table 207 *layer;* level stretch, steppe 348 *plain;* flats 347 *marsh;* platform, ledge 254 *projection;* terrace, esplanade; plateau, tableland 209 *high land;* billiard table, bowling green, cricket ground, croquet lawn 724 *arena;* gridiron, platter 194 *plate;* spirit level, T square 465 *gauge;* skyline, horizon, false h., horizon line 236 *limit.*

*recumbency,* lying down etc. vb.; supination; prostration; proneness, supineness.

*flattener,* iron, flatiron, steam iron, mangle, press, trouser p.; rolling pin, roller, garden r., steamroller 258 *smoother;* bulldozer, juggernaut 168 *destroyer.*

**Adj.** *flat,* horizontal, two-dimensional, level, plane, even, flush 258 *smooth;* trodden, trodden flat, beaten f.; flat as a pancake, flat as a board, flat as my hand; unwrinkled, smooth, smooth as a baby's bottom, smooth as glass, calm, calm as a millpond.

*supine,* resupine, flat on one's back, flat out; prone, face down, prostrate; recumbent, decumbent, procumbent; lying down, couchant; abed, laid up, laid out; stretched out, sprawling, spread-eagled, lolling.

**Vb.** *be horizontal,* lie, lie down, lie flat, lie prostrate, lie on one's back; measure one's length, recline, couch, sprawl, spread-eagle, loll 311 *sit down;* grovel 311 *stoop;* become horizontal, straighten out, level out.

*flatten,* lay out, roll o., lay down, spread; lay flat, beat f., tread f., stamp down, trample d., squash; make flush, align, level, even, grade, plane 28 *equalize;* iron, iron out, roll out 258 *smooth;* pat down, smooth d., plaster d.; prostrate, knock down, floor, ground 311 *fell.*

**Adv.** *horizontally,* flat, flat out, on one's back; fesse-wise, fesse-ways (heraldry); at full length.

### 217 Pendency

**N.** *pendency,* pensility, pensileness; suspension, hanging, dangle; set, hang, drape; droop.

*hanging object,* hanging ornament, mobile, pendant, dangler, drop, eardrop, earring, dangling e. 844 *jewellery;* tassel, bobble, tag 844 *trimming;* hangings, draperies, drapes, curtains, arras, tapestry 226 *covering;* train, skirt, coattails; flap, lappet, tippet 228 *headgear;* pigtail, tail 67 *sequel,* 259 *hair;* dewlap, lobe, appendix 40 *adjunct;* pendulum, bob, swing, hammock 317 *oscillation;* chandelier 420 *lamp;* icicle, stalactite.

*hanger,* coat h., curtain rod, curtain ring, runner, rack; hook, coathook, peg, knob, nail, hatstand 218 *prop;* suspender, braces, suspender belt 228 *underwear;* clothesline 47 *cable;* clotheshorse, airer, Scotch a. 218 *frame;* davit, crane 310 *lifter;* spar, mast 218 *pillar;* gallows, gibbet 964 *pillory.*

**Adj.** *hanging,* pendent, pendulous, pensile; hanging from, dependent, suspended, penduline, dangling etc. vb.; hanging the head, nodding, drooping, weeping; lowering, overhanging; beetling 254 *projecting;* open-ended, loose 46 *disunited;* baggy, flowing; floating (in the wind), waving, streaming, rippling; pedunculate, tailed, caudate; lop-eared.

**Vb.** *hang,* be pendent, drape, set; hang down, draggle, trail, flow; hang on to, swing from; swing, sway, dangle, bob; hang the head, nod, weep, loll, droop, sag, swag; hang in the wind, stream, wave, float, ripple, flap; hang over, hover; overhang, lour 226 *overlie;* suspend, hang up, sling, hook up, hitch, kilt, fasten to, append 45 *join;* curtain 226 *cover.*

### 218 Support

**N.** *support,* underpinning 703 *aid;* leg to stand on, point d'appui, footing, ground, pou sto; terra firma; hold, foothold, handhold, toe-hold 778 *retention;* life jacket, lifebelt 662 *safeguard;* life-support machine *or* system.

*prop,* support, mounting, bearing; carriage, undercarriage, carrier, underframe, chassis; buttress, flying b., arc boutant; abutment, bulwark, embankment, wall, retaining w.; underpinning, shore, jack; flagstaff, jackstaff, stanchion, rod, bar, transom, steadier, brace, strut; stay, mainstay, guy, shrouds, rigging 47 *tackling;* sprit, boom, spar, mast, yard, yardarm, crosstree 254 *projection;* trunk, stem, stalk, caudex, pedicle, pedicel, peduncle 366 *plant;* arch, Gothic a., Romanesque a.,

Moorish a., ogive 248 *curve*; keystone, headstone, cornerstone, springer; cantilever; pier (see also *pillar*); strapping, bandage, elastic b., jockstrap, truss, splint; stiffener, whalebone; corset 228 *underwear*; yoke 217 *hanger*; rest, headrest, backrest, footrest, stirrup; banisters, handrail (see also *handle*); skid, chock, sprag, wedge 702 *obstacle*; staff, baton, stick, shooting s., walking s., cane, alpenstock, crutch, crook, shepherd's c.; leg support, splint, calliper, irons; bracket (see also *shelf*); trivet, hob (see also *stand*); arm, back, shoulder; broad shoulders; shoulder blade, clavicle, collarbone, backbone (see also *pillar*); worldbearer, Atlas; supporter, helper, patron, charity organizer, fund-raiser 707 *auxiliary*.

*handle*, holder, pen h., cigarette h. 194 *receptacle*; hold, grip, hilt, pommel, haft; knob, doorhandle; lug, ear, loop; railing, handrail, rail, poop r., taffrail, banisters, balustrade; shaft, spear s., oar s., loom; handlebar, tiller; winder, crank, crankhandle; lever, trigger 630 *tool*.

*basis*, foundation, solid f., concrete f., footings, deck; raft, pallet, sleeper; stereobate, substratum 207 *layer*; ground, groundwork, floor, bed, bedrock, rock bottom 214 *base*; sill *or* cill; flooring, pavement 226 *paving*; terra firma 344 *land*; perch, footing, foothold.

*stand*, tripod, trivet, hob; table mat, coaster; anvil, block, bench; teapoy, trolley, tea trolley; table, console t., coffee t., card t., gateleg t., drop-leaf t., refectory t., board; sideboard, dresser, Welsh d. 194 *cabinet*; work table, desk, counter; pedestal, plinth, socle; stylobate, podium; platform, launching pad, launchpad, staddle, gantry; emplacement, banquette; footplate; landing, half l.; landing stage, pier; dais, pulpit, stage 539 *rostrum*; doorstep, threshold; altar step, predella 990 *altar*; step, stair, tread, rung, round 308 *ascent*; stilt 310 *lifter*; shank 267 *leg*.

*seat*, throne, woolsack; bank, bench, form, settle; bucket seat, box s., rumble s., dicky; front seat, back s., booster s.; pew, choirstall, misericord 990 *church interior*; stall, fauteuil 594 *theatre*; chair, armchair; easy chair, wing c., club c., rocking c., revolving c., basket c., Windsor c., high c., deck c., lounger; chaise longue; sofa, settee, divan, couch, studio c., ottoman, chesterfield, sociable, loveseat, windowseat; tabouret, pouffe, stool, footstool, kitchen stool, campstool, faldstool; priedieu, hassock; saddle, side s., pillion, pad, howdah; stocks, ducking-stool 964 *pillory*; electric chair, hot seat; lap, knees; mat 226 *floorcover*.

*bed*, cot, crib, cradle, bassinet; marriage bed, bridal b., double b., single b., king-size b., bunk b., bunk; bed settee, daybed, couch; tester, four-poster; charpoy, truckle bed, trundle b., camp b., pallet, airbed, futon, bedroll, shakedown; hammock 217 *hanging object*; sick bed, litter, hurdle, stretcher 658 *hospital*; bier 364 *funeral*; bedding, duvet 226 *coverlet*; bedstead, divan; headboard.

*cushion*, pillow; bolster, Dutch wife; mattress, palliasse; squab, hassock, kneeler.

*beam*, balk, joist, RSJ, girder, box g., rafter, purlin, tie beam, truss 47 *bond*; summer, bressummer; wall-plate 226 *roof*; cross-beam, transom, crossbar, traverse; architrave, lintel.

*pillar*, shaft, pier, pile, pole, stake, stud 331 *structure*; post, king post, queen p., crown p.; jamb, door j., doorpost; stanchion, puncheon; newelpost, banister, baluster; mullion; pilaster, column, Doric c., Ionic c., Corinthian c., Tuscan c.; caryatid, telamon, atlantes; spinal column, spine, backbone, vertebral column, vertebrae; neck, cervix.

*pivot*, fulcrum, lever, purchase; hinge 45 *joint*; pole, axis; gimbals; axle, swivel, spindle, arbor, pintle 315 *rotator*; bearing, gudgeon, trunnion; rowlock, tholepin; centreboard, keel.

*shelf*, bookshelf, ledge, offset 254 *projection*; corbel, bracket, console, ancon; retable, niche 194 *compartment*; sill, windowsill, mantelpiece, mantelshelf; rack, dresser 194 *cabinet*; desktop, counter, worktop, plank, board, table, leaf, slab 207 *lamina*.

*frame*, bony f., skeleton, ribs; framework, infrastructure, staging, scaffolding 331 *structure*; trellis, espalier; chassis, fuselage, body (of a car), undercarriage; trestle, easel, clotheshorse; housing 235 *enclosure*; picture frame, window f., sash 233 *outline*.

**Adj.** *supporting*, sustaining, maintaining; fundamental, basal; columnar; cervical, spinal, vertebral; structural, skeletal; framing, holding.

**Vb.** *support*, sustain, bear, carry, hold, shoulder; uphold, hold up, bear up, buoy up; prop, shore up, underprop, underpin, jack up 310 *elevate*; buttress, bolster, bolster up, cushion; reinforce, underset 162 *strengthen*; bandage, brace, truss 45 *tighten*; steady, stay; cradle, pillow, cup, cup one's chin; maintain, give aliment, give alimony 633 *provide*; give one a hand, back up, give support, lend s., furnish s., afford s., supply s. 703 *aid*; frame, set, mount 235 *enclose*; give foundations, be the infrastructure, bottom, ground, found, base, embed 153 *stabilize*; stand, endure, survive, stand up to, stand the strain, take the s. 635 *suffice*.

*be supported*, stand on, recline on, lie on, sit

on, loll on, lounge on, repose on, rest on; bear on, press, press on, step on, lean on, abut on; rely on, ground oneself on, be based on; command support, have at one's back, have behind one, receive aliment *or* alimony.

**Adv.** *astride*, astraddle, pick-a-back, piggyback.

## 219 Parallelism

**N.** *parallelism*, nonconvergence, nondivergence, equidistance, coextension, collimation, concentricity; parallel, correspondence 28 *equality*; parallel lines, lines of latitude; tramlines, rails, railway lines; parallel bars; parallelogram, parallelepiped.

**Adj.** *parallel*, coextensive, collateral, concurrent, concentric; equidistant 28 *equal*; corresponding, correspondent 18 *similar*.

**Vb.** *be parallel*, run together, run abreast, lie parallel; correspond, concur; collimate, parallel, draw a p.

**Adv.** *in parallel*, alongside, collaterally; side by side, abreast.

## 220 Obliquity

**N.** *obliquity*, obliqueness, skewness; oblique line, diagonal; oblique figure, rhomboid 247 *angular figure*; oblique angle, inclination 247 *angularity*; indirection, indirectness, squint; curvature, camber, bend, z-bend, chicane, humpback 248 *curve*; changing direction, crookedness, zigzag, chevron; switchback 251 *meandering*; oblique motion, circumlocution, divagation, digression, swerve, lurch, stagger 282 *deviation*; splay, bias, twist, warp 246 *distortion*; leaning, list, tip, cant; slope, slant, tilt, pitch, rake, rakish angle; sloping face, batter; sloping edge, bevel, bezel; inclined plane, ramp, chute, slide; Tower of Pisa, leaning tower; measurement of inclination 247 *angular measure*.

*incline*, rise, ascent; ramp, acclivity, gradient; hill, rising ground, hillock 209 *small hill*; hillside, versant 239 *laterality*; declivity, fall, dip, downhill 309 *descent*; easy ascent easy descent, gentle slope, nursery s., dip s.; scarp s., escarpment, steepness, cliff, precipice 215 *verticality*; scarp, counterscarp, glacis 713 *fortification*; talus, bank, scree, landslip, landslide.

**Adj.** *oblique*, inclined, bevel; tipsy, tilted, rakish; biased, askew, skew, slant, aslant, out of true, off the straight; out of the perpendicular, battered, leaning; recumbent, stooping; catercornered, rhomboidal 247 *angular*; wry, awry, agley, wonky, skew-whiff, crooked, squinting, cock-eyed, knock-kneed 246 *distorted*; diagonal, transverse, transversal; athwart, across 222 *crossed*; indirect, zigzag, herringbone, bent

248 *curved*; stepped, terraced, in echelon; divergent, nonparallel 282 *deviating*.

*sloping*, acclivous, uphill, rising 308 *ascending*; downhill, falling, declining, dipping 309 *descending*; anticlinal, synclinal; declivitous, steep, abrupt, sheer, precipitous, vertiginous, breakneck 215 *vertical*; easy, gentle, shelving, rounded.

**Vb.** *be oblique*, – tilted etc. adj.; incline, lean, tilt; pitch, slope, slant, shelve, dip, decline 309 *descend*; rise, climb 308 *ascend*; cut, cut across, transect 222 *cross*; lean, list, tip, lean over, bank, heel, careen, cant; bend, sag, give; bend over 311 *stoop*; walk sideways, edge, sidle, sidestep; look sideways, squint; zigzag; jink, jouk, dodge, duck, swerve; diverge, converge.

*make oblique*, incline, lean, slant, slope, cant, tilt, tip, rake; splay 282 *deviate*; bend, crook, twist, warp, skew 246 *distort*; chamfer, bevel; sway, bias, divert 282 *deflect*; curve, camber 248 *make curved*.

**Adv.** *obliquely*, diagonally, crosswise 222 *across*; catercorner, cornerwise; on the cross, on the bias; askew, rakishly, tipsily; aslant, slantwise, on the slant; askance, askant, asquint; edgewise, crabwise, sidelong, sideways; aslope, off the vertical, off the straight, off plumb, out of true, at an angle, at a rakish a.; on one side, all on one s.

## 221 Inversion

**N.** *inversion*, turning back to front, palindrome, hysteron proteron; turning inside out, eversion, evagination; turning backwards, retroversion, reversal 148 *reversion*; turning inward, introversion, invagination; turning over, capsizal (see also *overturning*); turn of the tide, return 286 *regression*; oppositeness 14 *contrariety*, 240 *contraposition*; transposition, metathesis 151 *interchange*; inverted order, chiasmus, anastrophe, hyperbaton 519 *trope*; confused order, spoonerism.

*overturning*, capsizal, upset, purler, spill; somersault, summerset, cartwheel, handspring; subversion, undermining, overthrowing 149 *revolution*; pronation 216 *recumbency*.

**Adj.** *inverted*, invaginated etc. vb.; inverse, back-to-front; upside down, inside out, wrong side out; capsized, bottom up, keel upwards; capsizing, topheavy; topsy-turvy, arsy-versy, head over heels, on one's head; flat, prone 216 *supine*; reverse, reversed 14 *contrary*; antipodean, antipodal 240 *opposite*; chiastic, palindromic.

**Vb.** *be inverted*, turn round, go r., wheel r., swing r., turn about, face a., right about turn 286 *turn back*; turn over, heel o., keel o., capsize, turn turtle, turn topsy-turvy; tilt over 220 *be oblique*; go over, topple o. 309 *tumble*; do a handstand, stand on one's head; loop the loop; reverse, back, back away, go backwards 286 *regress*.

*invert*, transpose, put the cart before the horse 151 *interchange*; reverse, turn the tables; retrovert, turn back; turn down 261 *fold*; introvert, invaginate; turn inside out, evaginate; upend, upturn, overturn, tip over, spill, upset, overset, capsize; turn topsy-turvy.

**Adv.** *inversely*, vice versa; contrariwise, quite the reverse, just the opposite, on the contrary, other way round; back to front, upside down; arsy-versy, topsy-turvy, head over heels, heels in the air; face down, face downwards, bottom side up.

## 222 Crossing: intertexture
**N.** *crossing*, crossing over and under, plain weaving; crisscross, transection, intersection; decussation, X-shape; quincunx; intertexture, interlacement, interdigitation, intertwinement, interweaving, arabesque 844 *pattern*; anastomosis, inosculation; braid, wreath, plait, pigtail 251 *convolution*; entanglement, intricacy, skein, cat's cradle 61 *complexity*; crossroads, intersection, roundabout, interchange, road junction 624 *road*; level crossing 624 *railway*; viaduct, flyover, overpass, underpass, subway 624 *bridge*, 305 *traffic control*.

*cross*, crux, rood, crucifix 988 *ritual object*; pectoral 989 *vestments*; ankh, ansate cross, tau c., Latin c., c. of Lorraine, Greek c., Maltese c., Celtic C., St Anthony's C., St Andrew's C.; saltire, crosslet 547 *heraldry*; gammadion, swastika, fylfot; crossbones, skull and c. 547 *flag*; crossbar, transom 218 *beam*; scissors, shears, secateurs, nutcrackers 778 *nippers*.

*network*, reticulation, meshwork, netting, wire n., chicken wire; webbing, matting, wickerwork, basketwork, trellis, wattle; honeycomb, lattice, grating, grid, grille, gridiron; craquelure; tracery, fretwork, filigree 844 *ornamental art*; lace, crochet, knitting, darning, tatting, macramé 844 *needlework*; web, cobweb; net, fishnet, seine, purse-s., drag-net, trawl, beam t. 235 *enclosure*; plexus, mesh, reticle; chain, group, interconnection.

*textile*, weave, web, loom; woven stuff, piece goods, dry g.; bolt, roll, length, piece, cloth, stuff, material; broadcloth, fabric, tissue; suiting; batik 844 *ornamental art*; jute, hessian, gunny, sacking, hopsack, canvas, sailcloth, duck; ticking, crash, huckaback, towelling, terry t., candlewick; chintz, cretonne, damask, brocade, brocatelle, grosgrain, rep, chenille,

tapestry 226 *covering*; mohair, cashmere; alpaca, vicuna, angora 208 *fibre*; wool, worsted, grogram; frieze, felt, baize; homespun, khadar, duffel, kersey, tweed, serge, shalloon, bombazine, gabardine, doeskin; flannel, swanskin, swansdown; paisley, jacquard 844 *pattern*; stockinette, jersey, tricot, nainsook, flannelette, winceyette; velvet, velveteen, velour; corduroy, needlecord; cotton, chino, denim, drill, nankeen, cavalry twill, khaki; fustian, moleskin, sharkskin; poplin, calico, dimity, gingham, madras, seersucker, piqué; batiste, organdie, organza; silesia, cheesecloth, muslin, mull, voile, percale; cambric, lawn, toile, holland, linen; silk, surah, foulard, georgette, crêpe de chine, chiffon, mousseline; satin, sateen, taffeta, moire; tussore *or* tussah, shantung, pongee; ninon; tulle, net, gauze; lace, guipure; rayon, nylon, Terylene (tdmk), Crimplene (tdmk), polyester, Courtelle (tdmk), Acrilan (tdmk), fibreglass 208 *fibre*.

*weaving*, texture; web, warp, weft, woof, selvedge; nap, pile 259 *hair*; frame, loom, shuttle; weaver, knitter; knitting machine, sewing m.; spinning wheel, distaff, whorl; spinner, spider, weaverbird; Arachne, Penelope.

**Adj.** *crossed*, crossing, cross, crisscross; quadrivial; diagonal, transverse, cross-eyed, squinting 220 *oblique*; decussate, X-shaped, quincunxial; cross-legged, cruciform, crucial, cruciate, forked, furcate 247 *angular*; plexiform; knotted, matted, tangled, balled-up, ravelled 61 *complex*; pleached, plashed, plaited, braided, interlaced, interfretted, interwoven; textile, loomed, woven, handwoven, tweedy; twill, herringbone; trellised, latticed, honeycombed, mullioned, barred; corded, ribbed, streaked, striped 437 *variegated*.

*reticular*, reticulated, retiform, webbed, webby; netted, meshed, micromesh 201 *spaced*.

**Vb.** *cross*, cross over, cross under 305 *pass*; intersect, cut 220 *be oblique*; decussate, inosculate, interdigitate; splice, dovetail, link 45 *join*; reticulate, mesh, net, knot; fork, bifurcate 247 *make angular*.

*weave*, loom; pleach, plash, plait, braid; felt, twill, knit, crochet, darn; spin, slub.

*enlace*, interlace, interlink, interlock, interdigitate, intertwine, intertwist, interweave, enmesh, engage gear; twine, entwine, wattle; twist, raddle, wreathe, pleach; mat, ravel, snarl, tangle, entangle, dishevel 63 *derange*.

**Adv.** *across*, athwart, transversely; crosswise, saltire-wise; with folded arms, arm in arm.

## 223 Exteriority
**N.** *exteriority*, the external; outwardness, exter-

nality 230 *surroundings*; periphery, circumference, sidelines 233 *outline*; exterior, outward appearance 445 *appearance*; superficiality, surface, superficies, superstratum, crust, cortex, shell, integument 226 *skin*; outer side, face, facet, facade 237 *front*; other side 240 *contraposition*; externalism, regard for externals 982 *idolatry*; externalization, extroversion, extrovert 6 *extrinsicality*; outside, out of doors, open air; outer space 199 *distance*; extraterritoriality 57 *exclusion*; foreignness 59 *extraneousness*; eccentricity 84 *nonconformity*; outsider 84 *nonconformist*.

**Adj.** *exterior*, exoteric, outward, extra-; external 10 *unrelated*; roundabout, peripheral 230 *circumjacent*; outer, outermost, outlying, extraterrestrial 199 *distant*; outside, outboard; outdoor, extramural; foreign 59 *extraneous*; extraterrestrial, extraterritorial 57 *excluding*; extrovert, outward-looking 6 *extrinsic*; centrifugal 620 *avoiding*; exogenous; eccentric 282 *deviating*; surface, superficial, epidermal, cortical; skin-deep 212 *shallow*; facial 237 *frontal*.

**Vb.** *be exterior*, lie beyond, lie outside etc. adv.; frame, enclose 230 *surround*; look outward 6 *be extrinsic*.

*externalize*, body forth, objectify 6 *make extrinsic*; project, extrapolate; expel 300 *eject*.

**Adv.** *externally*, outwardly, outwards, superficially, on the surface; on the face of it, to the outsider; outside, extra muros; out, out of doors, in the cold, in the sun, in the open, in the open air, al fresco.

**224 Interiority**
**N.** *interiority*, interior, inside, indoors; inner surface, undersurface; endoderm 226 *skin*; sapwood, heartwood 366 *wood*; inmost being, heart's blood, soul; heart, centre, breast, bosom 225 *centrality*; inland, Midlands, heartland, hinterland, up-country; the nitty gritty, pith, marrow 3 *substance*; subsoil, substratum 214 *base*; permeation, pervasion 189 *presence*, 231 *interjacency*; interspace 201 *interval*; deepness, cave, pit, pothole, penetralia, recesses, innermost r. 211 *depth*; endogamy 894 *marriage*; introversion 5 *intrinsicality*; self-absorption, egoism, egotism, egocentrism, egocentricity, egomania 932 *selfishness*; introvert, egoist 932 *egotist*; inmate, indweller 191 *dweller*; internee 750 *prisoner*.

*insides* 193 *contents*; inner man *or* woman, interior man; internal organs, viscera, vitals; heart, ticker; lungs, lights; liver, kidneys, spleen; offal 301 *meat*; bowels, entrails, innards, guts, pluck, tripe; intestines, colon, rectum, back passage; abdomen, belly, paunch, underbelly; womb, uterus; stomach, tummy

194 *maw*; chest, breast, bosom, solar plexus; gland; endocrine; cell 358 *organism*.

**Adj.** *interior*, internal, inward 5 *intrinsic*; inside, inner, innermost, midmost 225 *central*; inland, up-country 199 *removed*; domestic, home, vernacular; intimate, familiar 490 *known*; indoor, intramural, shut in, enclosed; inboard, built-in, inwrought; endemic 192 *residing*; deep-seated, deep-rooted, ingrown 153 *fixed*; intestinal, visceral; intravenous, subcutaneous; interstitial 231 *interjacent*; inward-looking, introvert 5 *intrinsic*; endo-, endogamous; endogenous.

**Vb.** *be inside*, – internal etc. adj.; be within etc. adv.; lie within, lie beneath, be at the bottom of; show through 443 *be visible*.

*hold within*, hold 78 *comprise*; place within, embed 303 *insert*; keep inside, intern 747 *imprison*; enfold, embay 235 *enclose*; internalize 299 *absorb*.

**Adv.** *inside*, within, in, deep in, deep down; inly, inwardly, intimately; deeply, profoundly, at heart; withinside, within doors, indoors, at home, en famille, chez, at the sign of.

**225 Centrality**
**N.** *centrality*, centricity, centralness; concentricity; centralization, focalization, concentration 324 *condensation*; central position, mid p. 231 *interjacency*; midriff, waistline, centreline, parting 231 *partition*; Ptolemaic system, Copernican s.

*centre*, dead c.; centroid, centre of mass, centre of gravity, centre of pressure, centre of percussion, centre of buoyancy, metacentre; nerve centre, ganglion; centre of activity, focal point 76 *focus*; epicentre; storm centre, hotbed; heart, core, kernel 5 *essential part*; omphalos, nub, hub; nucleus, nucleolus; navel, umbilicus; spine, backbone, vertebrae, chine, midrib; marrow, pith 224 *interiority*; pole, axis, fulcrum, centreboard 218 *pivot*; centre point, mid p. 70 *middle*; fess-point 547 *heraldry*; eye, pupil; bull's-eye, target 617 *objective*.

**Adj.** *central*, centro-, centric, centrical; nuclear, nucleolar; centremost, midmost 70 *middle*; axial, focal, pivotal, important; umbilical; homocentric, concentric; geocentric; heliocentric; spinal, vertebral; centripetal; metropolitan, chief, head 34 *supreme*.

**Vb.** *centralize*, centre, focus, bring to a f., zero in on, centre upon; concentrate, nucleate, consolidate 324 *be dense*.

**Adv.** *centrally*, at the heart of, at the core, middle, midst, amongst; in the midst, in the middle.

## 226 Covering

**N.** *covering*, capping etc. vb.; superposition, superimposition, overlaying; overlap, overlapping, imbrication; coating, stratification 207 *layer*; veneer, top layer, top dressing, mulch, topsoil 344 *soil*; topping, icing, frosting 844 *ornamentation*; cover, lid; gravestone, ledger 364 *tomb*; hatch, trapdoor; flap, shutter, operculum; film 423 *opacity*; glass, glass front, watch glass, crystal 422 *transparency*; cap, top, plug, bung, cork 264 *stopper*; pledget, plaster, Elastoplast (tdmk), Band-Aid (tdmk) 658 *surgical dressing*; carapace, shell, snail s., tortoiseshell 326 *hardness*; mail, plate, armour p. 713 *armour*; shield, cowl, cowling, bonnet, hood (of a car); scab 207 *lamina*; crust, fur 649 *dirt*; capsule, ferrule, sheath, involucre, envelope 194 *receptacle*; pillowcase, pillowslip, cushion cover; table cloth, tray c.; chair cover, antimacassar; soft furnishings, loose covers; hangings, curtains, drapes 217 *hanging object*; wallpaper 227 *lining*; mask, domino 527 *disguise*.

*roof*, cupola 253 *dome*; mansard roof, hipped r., pitched r., gable r., flat r., catslide; housetop, rooftop, rooftree 213 *vertex*; leads, slates, slating, tiles, tiling, pantile, shingle, thatch, thatching, corrugated iron 631 *building material*; eaves 234 *edge*; ceiling, deck; vaulting, vault, barrel v., groin v.; rafters, hammerbeam roof 218 *beam*.

*canopy*, ciborium, baldachin; velarium, tilt, awning, sunblind 421 *screen*; marquee, pavilion, big top; tent, bell tent, ridge t., frame t.; tepee 192 *dwelling*; tent-cloth, canvas, tarpaulin, fly sheet; mosquito net 222 *network*.

*shade*, hood, eyelid, eyelash; blind, venetian b., roller b., festoon b., jalousie, persiennes, shutters, slats; curtain, veil; umbrella, gamp, brolly; parasol, sunshade; sun hat, sun helmet, topee 228 *headgear*; visor, eye shade 421 *screen*; peak (of a cap); dark glasses, sunglasses, shades 442 *eyeglass*.

*wrapping*, wrapper, paper, tissue p., cellophane, polythene; polystyrene 227 *lining*; packaging, blister pack, bubble p., gift box, shrinkpack 194 *receptacle*; bandage, roller 47 *girdle*; plaster cast 658 *surgical dressing*; book cover, binding, boards, dust jacket *or* cover 589 *book-binding*; tunic, coat 228 *jacket*; mantle 228 *cloak*; comforter, scarf 228 *neckwear*; life belt, life jacket 662 *safeguard*; lagging; cocoon, chrysalis; shroud, winding sheet 364 *grave clothes*.

*skin*, epithelium; outer skin, scarf s., epidermis, cuticle; true skin, cutis, dermis, derma, corium; tegument 223 *exteriority*; integument, peel, bark, crust, rind, coat, cortex; pericarp,

husk, hull, shell, pod, jacket; pellicle, membrane, film; scalp 213 *head*; scale 207 *lamina*; pelt, peltry, fleece, fell, fur; leather, hide, rawhide, imitation leather, leatheroid; shagreen, patent leather; crocodile, alligator; pigskin, morocco, calf, kid, chamois, suede, buff, buckskin, doeskin; rabbitskin, moleskin, sealskin; sheepskin, lamb, Persian 1., astrakhan; mink, sable, ermine, vair, miniver, cony; chinchilla 208 *fibre*; feathers, coverts 259 *plumage*.

*paving*, flooring, floor, parquet, quarry tiles; deck, floorboards, duckboards; pavement, sidewalk (US), pavé; flags, paving stone, crazy paving; sett, cobble, cobblestone; gravel, chippings, asphalt, tarmac 624 *road*.

*coverlet*, bedspread, counterpane, bedding, bedclothes, bed linen; sheet, quilt, eiderdown, duvet, continental quilt, Downie (tdmk); blanket, rug, caparison, housings, trappings; saddlecloth, horsecloth; pall.

*floor-cover*, carpeting, carpet, fitted c.; broadloom, pile carpet, Persian c.; mat, doormat, bath mat, prayer m.; rug, hearth r.; drugget, numdah; linoleum, lino, vinyl, tiles; matting, coconut m.; red carpet 875 *formality*.

*facing*, revetment, cladding 162 *strengthening*; veneer, coating, varnish, japan, lacquer, enamel, glaze; incrustation, roughcast, pebbledash; ashlar, weatherboarding 631 *building material*; stucco, compo, plaster, pargeting, rendering, screed; wash, whitewash, distemper, emulsion, paint; stain, polish, smearing, anointment; coat of paint 425 *pigment*.

**Adj.** *overlying*, overlaying, overarching; overlapping, tegular, imbricated; cloaking etc. vb.

*covered*, roofed, roofed in, vaulted, ceiled, wallpapered, carpeted; tented, garaged, under cover, under canvas; under shelter 660 *safe*; cloaked, cowled, veiled, hooded 525 *concealed*; loricated, armourplated, iron-clad; metalled, paved; built over; snow-capped, ice-covered, mist-covered, inundated, flooded; smothered, plastered, coated etc. vb.

*dermal*, cutaneous, cortical, cuticular; tegumentary; scaly, squamous; epidermic, epidermal, epidermoid.

**Vb.** *cover*, superpose, superimpose; roof, roof in, put the lid on, cork, cap, tip; ice, frost, decorate (a cake); spread, lay (a table); overlay, smother; insulate, lag 227 *line*; lap, enwrap, wrap up, enfold, envelope 235 *enclose*; blanket, shroud, mantle, muffle; hood, veil 525 *conceal*; case, bind, cover (books); box, pack, vacuumpack; wrap, shrink-w.; bandage, swathe, wrap round, dress 658 *doctor*; sheathe, encapsulate, encase 303 *insert*; wall in, wall up; cover up, keep under cover, garage.

*overlie*, overarch, overhang, overlap; overshadow 419 *bedim*; span, bestride, straddle, bestraddle 205 *be broad*; flood, inundate 341 *drench*; skin over, crust, scab.

*overlay*, pave, floor, cement, carpet; ceil, roof, dome, vault, overarch, deck; tile, thatch; paper, wallpaper 227 *line*; overspread, topdress, mulch; spread, smear, besmear; lard, butter, anoint; powder, dust, sprinkle, sand; gravel, tarmac, metal.

*coat*, revet, face, front, do over; grout, roughcast, encrust, shingle; stucco, plaster, pebbledash, render, parget 844 *decorate*; veneer, varnish, lacquer, japan, enamel, glaze, size; paint, whitewash, colourwash, distemper, emulsion, stain 425 *colour*; creosote; tar, pitch, pay; daub, bedaub, scumble, overpaint, grease, lard, lay it on thick; gild, plate, silver, besilver; electroplate, silverplate; waterproof, fireproof, damp-proof 660 *safeguard*.

**227 Lining**

**N.** *lining*, liner, interlining 231 *interjacency*; coating, inner c.; stuffing, wadding, padding, batting, quilting; kapok, foam, polystyrene 631 *materials*; lagging, insulation, double-glazing, damp-proofing, soundproofing; backing, facing; doublure 589 *bookbinding*; upholstery; papering, wallpaper; wainscotting, panelling, wainscot, skirting board, dado, brattice; metal lining, bush; brake lining; packing, dunnage; packaging 226 *wrapping*; filling, stopping (dentistry); washer, shim.

**Vb.** *line*, encrust 226 *coat*; insulate 226 *cover*; interlard, inlay; back, face, paper, wallpaper; upholster, cushion; stuff, pad, wad; fill, pack; bush 303 *insert*.

**228 Dressing**

**N.** *dressing*, investment, investiture; clothing, covering, dressing up, toilet, toilette; overdressing, foppishness; power dressing; underdressing, casualness 848 *fashion*; vesture, dress, garb, attire, rig, gear, clobber; panoply, array; garniture, trim, accoutrements, caparison, harness, housing, trappings; traps, paraphernalia, accessories; rig-out, turn-out; tailoring, dressmaking, millinery; haute couture; the rag trade, the fashion world; power dressing.

*clothing*, wear, apparel, raiment, linen; clothes, garments, vestments, habiliments; togs, gear, kit, clobber; outfit, wardrobe, trousseau; maternity wear; layette, baby clothes, swaddling c., Babygro (tdmk); old clothes, duds, reach-me-downs, cast-offs, rags, tatters; uniform, school uniform, strip, team strip, working clothes, slops; hand-me-downs, second-hand clothes; leisure wear, sportswear, tracksuit, casual clothes; best c., fine raiment;

Sunday best, Sunday-go-to-meeting clothes, best bib and tucker; party dress, glad rags; pearlies, ostrich feathers, frippery 844 *finery*; fancy dress, masquerade; motley; silks, colours; national costume; intelligent wear, I-wear.

*garment*, article of clothing; neck, collar (see also *neckwear*, *neckline*); top, bodice, bosom; corsage, bib, stomacher; shirt-front, dickey; waistline (see also *belt*); peplum, bustle, train; crutch, codpiece; arms (see also *sleeve*); flaps, coat tails 217 *hanging object*; placket, fly 263 *opening*; cargo pocket, patch pocket 194 *pocket*; flap, gusset, gore; pleat, kick pleat; lapel, turn-up 261 *fold*; cuff, hemline 234 *edging*.

*formal dress*, correct d., court d., full d. 875 *formality*; grande toilette, evening dress, tails, white tie and tails; dinner jacket, black tie, tuxedo; morning dress; academic dress, academicals, cap and gown, subfusc; mourning, black, widow's weeds.

*uniform*, regimentals 547 *livery*; dress uniform, undress, mess kit; battledress, fatigues, khaki; school uniform, academic dress; robes, vestments, clerical dress 989 *canonicals*.

*informal dress*, undress, mufti, civvies; casual clothes, leisure wear, slacks, jeans, dress-down Friday; déshabillé, dishabille; dressing gown, loungewear, peignoir, bathrobe, robe, wrapper, housecoat; smoking jacket, slippers.

*robe*, gown, robes, drapery; sari; kimono, caftan; jubbah, djellaba, burka; chiton, himation; toga, t. virilis; peplos, pallium (see also *cloak*); cassock 989 *canonicals*; winding sheet, shroud 364 *grave clothes*.

*dress*, frock, gown; creation, number, ballgown, cocktail dress; sheath d., tube d., cheongsam, chemise, shift, sack; shirtwaister, coatdress, overdress, pinafore dress, jumper, gymslip; sundress.

*suit*, outfit, ensemble; coordinates, separates; lounge suit, zoot s., drape s., pin-stripe s.; costume, tweeds, trouser suit, pantsuit; jumpsuit, catsuit, leotard, body-suit, body stocking; overalls, dungarees, boiler suit, siren s., tracksuit, leisure suit, skinsuit, wetsuit; G-suit, spacesuit.

*jacket*, coat, tail c., dinner jacket, tuxedo; monkey jacket, mess j., pea j., Eton j.; blazer, reefer, sports jacket, Barbour j. (tdmk), Barbour (tdmk), waxed jacket, Norfolk j.; hacking jacket, riding habit, hunting pink; donkey jacket, lumber j. (see also *overcoat*); parka, windcheater, anorak, kagoule; bomber jacket, blouson, body-warmer; Mao jacket, Nehru j., jerkin, tunic, tabard, surcoat, waistcoat, vest, gilet, spencer; bolero, coatee, matinee jacket.

*jersey*, pullover, woolly, knit, homeknit, handknit, jumper, sweater, V-neck, polo neck, turtle neck, crew neck, sloppy joe, sweatshirt, guernsey, Fair Isle, cardigan, cardi, shrug, tank, tank top, twin set.

*trousers*, pants, trews, breeks; cords, flannels, pinstripes; hipsters, drainpipes, bell-bottoms, flares; slacks, bags, Oxford b., plus fours; galligaskins, breeches, britches, jodhpurs, knickerbockers, pedal-pushers, leggings, tights; chaps, dungarees, denims, jeans, blue j., Levi's (tdmk), cargo pants, cargos, chinos, combat trousers *or* combats; cigarette pants, palazzo p.; shorts, Bermuda s., hot pants, lederhosen; bloomers, pantaloons, rompers.

*skirt*, maxi s., midi s., miniskirt; pleated s., flared s., A-line s., gored s., full s., dirndl, kilt, kirtle, filibeg; sarong; straight skirt, slit s., hobble s.; sports s., divided s., culottes; ballet skirt, tutu; crinoline, farthingale, hoop, panier.

*loincloth*, lungi, dhoti, sarong; fig leaf, G-string, jockstrap; nappy, diaper (US).

*apron*, bib, pinafore, pinny, overall.

*shirt*, smock, angel top; dashiki, caftan, aloha shirt; polo neck, tee shirt, T-shirt, tee, tank, sweatshirt; blouse, choli, camisole, top, sun top.

*underwear*, underclothes, undies, linen; lingerie, smalls, unmentionables; underpants, shorts, pants, Y-fronts, boxer shorts; briefs, panties, scanties, French knickers, camiknickers, teddy, knickers, bloomers, drawers, pantalets; combinations, long johns, thermal underwear; singlet, vest, string v., undershirt, semmit; camisole, chemise, slip, half-slip, underskirt, petticoat; foundation garment, body stocking, corset, stays, girdle, pantie-g., roll-on; brassiere, bra; suspender belt, braces.

*nightwear*, nightclothes, sleeping suit; nightgown, nightdress, nightie, negligee; nightshirt, pyjamas; bedsocks, bed jacket, nightcap.

*beachwear*, sunsuit, sundress; bikini, bankini, monokini, tankini, bandeau; swimming costume, swimsuit, one-piece s., bathing suit, trunks, bathers; beach robe; aloha shirt.

*overcoat*, coat (see also *jacket*); fur coat, mink c. 226 *skin*; topcoat, greatcoat, frock coat; redingote, raglan, ulster; car coat, duffel c.; waterproof, oilskins; mac, mackintosh, raincoat, gabardine; Burberry (tdmk), trench coat; light coat, duster; fitted coat.

*cloak*, mantle; cape, cycling c.; pelisse, pelerine, dolman; domino 527 *disguise*; djellaba, burnous (see also *robe*); shawl, pashmina, shatoosh, plaid, poncho, Afghan.

*neckwear*, scarf, fichu; stole, boa, tippet; comforter, muffler; neckerchief, stock, jabot, cravat, necktie, tie, bow t.; necklace 844 *jewellery*; ruff, collar, dog c. 989 *canonicals*; Eton collar, mandarin c., Peter Pan c., Vandyke c., Bertha, sailor c., shawl c.; button-down c., stand-up c. (See also *neckline*.)

*headgear*, millinery; hat, cap, lid, titfer, tile; headdress, mantilla; plumes, ribbons 844 *finery*; crown, coronet, tiara 743 *regalia*; fillet, snood; juliet cap, skull c., coif; headscarf, kerchief, bandanna, headband, sweatband, Alice band; turban, pugree; hood, cowl, wimple; veil, yashmak 421 *screen*; fez, tarboosh; shako, kepi, busby, bearskin, helmet 713 *armour*; tin hat, hard h., crash helmet, safety h., skid lid 662 *safeguard*; woolly hat, bobble h., ski h.; rainhat, sou'wester; cap, cloth c., beret, tam-o'-shanter, tammy; Balmoral, glengarry, deerstalker; Homburg, trilby, pork-pie hat, billycock, fedora, beaver, bowler, derby; slouch hat, stetson, ten-gallon hat, sombrero, shovel hat, picture h., Dolly Varden, straw h., boater, panama, coolie hat, bush h., sunhat, pith helmet 226 *shade*; bonnet, Easter b., poke b., mob cap, toque, cloche, pillbox; top hat, topper, silk hat, stovepipe h.; cocked h., tricorne, mortarboard; biretta 989 *canonicals*; witch's hat, wizard's h., dunce's cap.

*wig*, peruke, periwig; full-bottomed wig, bagwig, tie-wig; false hair, hairpiece, toupee; coiffure 259 *hair*.

*neckline*, boat neck, crew n., cowl n., turtle n., roll n., polo n., halter n., V-n., round n.; low n. 229 *bareness*.

*belt*, waistband; cummerbund, sash, obi; money belt, belt-bag, bum bag; armlet, armband; shoulder belt, bandolier, baldric 47 *girdle*.

*sleeve*, arm, armhole; leg-of-mutton sleeve, raglan s., dolman s., batwing s., magyar s., puff s., cap s., short s., long s.; wristband, cuff.

*glove*, gauntlet, driving gloves, long g., evening g.; mitten, mitt, muff.

*legwear*, hosiery; stockings, nylons, tights, fleshings; trunks, hose; half-hose, socks, knee-length s., over-the-knee s., ankle s., bootees; leggings, gaiters, spats, puttees; greaves 713 *armour*; garter, suspender 47 *fastening*.

*footwear*, footgear; buskin, cothurnus, sock; slipper, carpet s., mule; patten, clog, sabot; flipflops, jelly sandals, jellies (inf), sandals, Jesus boots, chappals; rope-soled shoes, espadrilles, rubber-soled shoes, crepe-soled s., creepers, brothel creepers, sneakers, plimsolls, gym shoes, tennis shoes, trainers, high-tops; pumps, ballet shoes; moccasins, slip-ons, casuals; winklepickers, beetle-crushers, clodhoppers; shoe, court s., high heels, stiletto h., platform h., Cuban h., wedge h.; square-toed shoes, peeptoed s., slingbacks, flat shoes, driving s., lace-ups, buckled shoes; Oxfords, brogues; boots, fashion b., high b., cowboy b.; thigh b., waders, wellingtons, wellies, gumboots; Doc Martens (tdmk), Dr Martens (tdmk), DMs; skiboots 274 *sled*; running shoes, spikes.

*clothier*, outfitter, costumier; tailor, couturier, couturière; fashion designer 848 *fashion*; dressmaker, sempstress, seamstress, modiste; shoemaker, bootmaker; cobbler, cordwainer, souter 686 *artisan*; hosier, hatter, milliner, draper, haberdasher; Savile Row, Carnaby Street; boutique; valet, batman 742 *domestic*; dresser, mistress of the wardrobe 594 *stagehand*.

**Adj.** *dressed*, clothed, clad, garbed, dight, bedight; attired etc. adj.; rigged out, turned o., decked o., got up like a dog's dinner 844 *bedecked*; uniformed, liveried; shod, gloved, hatted; well dressed, soignée, en grande toilette, en grande tenue.

*tailored*, tailor-made, bespoke, made-to-measure, custom-made; designer, ready-to-wear, off-the-peg, mass-produced; single-breasted, double-b.; one-piece, two-p.; unisex; well-cut, fully fashioned; classic, princess-line, Empire-line, A-line; ballerina-length; step-in, pull-on, button-through, zip-up; skintight, slinky 24 *adjusted*; gathered 261 *folded*; bloused, bouffant 205 *broad*; sartorial.

**Vb.** *dress*, clothe, array, apparel, garment, dight, garb, attire; robe, enrobe, drape, sheet, mantle; invest, accoutre, uniform, put in u., equip, rig out, fit o., harness, caparison 669 *make ready*; dress up, bedizen, deck, prink 843 *primp*; envelop, wrap, lap, enfold, wrap up, fold up, muffle up, roll up in, swaddle, swathe, shroud, sheathe 226 *cover*.

*wear*, put on, try on, assume, don, slip on, slip into, get i., huddle i.; clothe oneself, attire o., get dressed, get one's clothes on; button up, do up, zip up, lace up 45 *tie*; change, change one's clothes, get changed; have on, dress in, carry, sport; dress up 875 *be ostentatious*.

## 229 Uncovering

**N.** *uncovering*, divestment, undressing etc. vb.; exposure, indecent e. 526 *disclosure*; nudism, naturism, striptease, stripping, dance of the seven veils, fan dance, burlesque (US), burlesque show (US), bump and grind (US) 594 *stage show*; undress, dishabille, déshabillé 228 *informal dress*; moult, moulting, ecdysis, shedding; decortication, exfoliation, abscission, excoriation, peeling, desquamation; depilation, shaving; denudation, devastation 165 *havoc*.

*bareness*, décolleté, décolletage, bare neck, low n., plunging neckline, revealing n.; nudity, nakedness, state of nature, birthday suit, nu intégral, the altogether, the buff, the raw, the full monty, starkers, not a stitch on, streaking; baldness, premature b., hairlessness, falling hair, alopecia, alopecia areata; tonsure; baldpate, baldhead, baldtop.

*uncovered person* nude, nudist, naturist; striptease artiste (see also *stripper*); bald-headed person, baldie (inf), slaphead (sl).

*stripper*, striptease artiste, burlesque dancer (US), ecdysiast, exotic dancer, fan dancer, lap-dancer, table-dancer; blue movie actor *or* actress; flasher, dirty old man in a raincoat, streaker; nudist, naturist; skinner, furrier, flayer, fleecer, shearer, peeler; hair-remover, depilatory, wax, electrolysis; nude figure, nude model, nude.

**Adj.** *uncovered*, bared; exposed, unveiled, showing 522 *manifest*; divested, forcibly d., debagged; stripped, peeled; without one's clothes, unclad, unclothed, undressed, unattired, unapparelled; décolleté(e), bare-necked, low-n., off-the-shoulder, topless; bare-backed, bare-armed, barelegged; barefoot, unshod, discalced; hatless, bareheaded; en déshabillé, in one's shirt-sleeves; miniskirted, bikini-clad, swimsuited; underclothed, underdressed, indecently dressed; bare, naked, nude, raw; in a state of nature, in nature's garb, mother naked, in a state of undress, in the buff (inf), au naturel, in one's birthday suit, with nothing on, without a stitch on; stark, stark naked, starkers (inf); leafless; plucked, moulting, unfeathered, unfledged; poorly dressed, tattered, threadbare, out-at-elbows, ragged 801 *poor*; drawn, unsheathed 304 *extracted*.

*hairless*, bald, baldheaded, smooth, beardless, shaved, shaven, clean-s., tonsured; as bald as a coot, as bald as an egg, as bald as a billiard ball, as bare as the back of one's hand; napless, threadbare; mangy 651 *diseased*; thin, thin on top.

**Vb.** *uncover*, unveil, undrape, unrobe, uncloak, undress, unclothe; divest, debag; strip, skin, scalp, flay, tear off; pluck, deplume, peel, pare, bark, decorticate, excoriate; hull, pod, shell, stone; bone, fillet 300 *empty*; denude, denudate 165 *lay waste*; expose, bare, lay open 526 *disclose*; unsheathe, draw (a sword) 304 *extract*; unwrap, unfold, unpack; unroof, uncap, uncork, take the lid off 263 *open*; scrape off, abrade 333 *rub*.

*doff*, uncap, uncover, raise one's hat; take off, strip off, peel off, slip off, slip out of, step out of, drop; change, change one's clothes; shed, cast, cast a clout; moult, slough, exuviate, cast its skin; desquamate, exfoliate;

flake off, scale; divest oneself, undress, disrobe, peel, strip; undo, unbutton, unzip, unhook, unlace, untie 46 *disunite*.

## 230 Surroundings

**N.** *surroundings* 223 *exteriority*; circumambience, circumjacence; ambience, atmosphere, mood, aura; ambient music, Muzak (tdmk) 412 *music*; medium, matrix; encompassment, containment, surrounding 235 *enclosure*; compass, circuit, circumference, periphery, perimeter 233 *outline*; circumjacencies, milieu, environment, entourage; background, setting, scene, scenario 186 *situation*; neighbourhood, vicinity 200 *near place*; outskirts, environs, boulevards, suburbs, faubourgs, banlieue; green belt; purlieus, precincts 192 *housing*; sticks, outpost, border 236 *limit*; wall, fortification 235 *fence*; cordon 47 *girdle*.

**Adj.** *circumjacent*, circum-; circumambient, circumfluent, circumfluous, ambient, atmospheric; surrounding etc. vb.; framing, circumferential, peripheral; shutting in, claustrophobic; roundabout 314 *circuitous*; suburban 200 *near*.

**Vb.** *surround*, lie around, compass, encompass, environ, lap; encircle 314 *circle*; girdle, begird, engird, cincture 235 *enclose*; wreathe around, twine a.; embrace, cuddle, hug 889 *caress*; contain, keep in, cloister, shut in, close round, hem in 232 *circumscribe*; beset, invest, blockade 712 *besiege*.

**Adv.** *around*, about, on every side, round about, all round; on all sides, right and left; without, outside, in the neighbourhood, in the outskirts.

## 231 Interjacency

**N.** *interjacency*, intermediacy, intervention, penetration, interpenetration, permeation, infiltration 189 *presence*; interdigitation 222 *crossing*; dovetailing 45 *union*; middle position 70 *middle*.

*partition*, curtain, 'Iron C.' (see quotation at 57 *exclusion*), Bamboo C. 421 *screen*; Great Wall of China 713 *defences*; Berlin Wall 57 *exclusion*; wall, party w., garden fence, brattice, bulkhead 235 *fence*; divide, watershed, parting 46 *separation*; Chinese wall; division, panel 53 *subdivision*; interface, septum, diaphragm, midriff 225 *centre*; field boundary, balk, hedge, ditch 201 *gap*; common frontier 236 *limit*.

*intermediary*, medium, intermedium, link 47 *bond*; negotiator, go-between, pander, broker, usual channels 720 *mediator*; marriage broker 894 *matchmaker*; agent 755 *deputy*; middleman, retailer 794 *merchant*; intercessor, pleader, advocate 707 *patron*; buffer, bumper, fender, crumple zone, airbag, cushion 662 *safeguard*;

air lock, buffer state, no-man's-land, halfway house 70 *middle*.

*interjection*, putting between, interposition, sandwiching; interpolation, intercalation, interlineation, interspersion 303 *insertion*; embolism 264 *closure*; interruption, intrusion, chipping in, butting in 72 *discontinuity*; interference, meddling 702 *hindrance*; thing inserted, episode, parenthesis, obiter dictum 40 *adjunct*; infix, insert, fly leaf; wedge, washer, shim 227 *lining*; thin end of the wedge.

*interjector*, interpolator; intruder, interloper 702 *hinderer*.

**Adj.** *interjacent*, interposed, sandwiched; episodic, parenthetical, in brackets, in parentheses; intercurrent, intermediary, intervenient, intervening etc. vb.; intercessory, mediating 720 *mediatory*; intercalary 303 *inserted*; intrusive 59 *extraneous*; inter-, interstitial, intercostal, intermural; interplanetary, interstellar; intermediate, thematic 303 *inserted*; median, medium, mean, mediterranean 70 *middle*; partitioning, dividing, septal.

**Vb.** *lie between*, come b., stand b.; mediate, intervene 625 *be halfway*; slide in, interpenetrate, permeate, soak in 189 *pervade*.

*introduce*, let in 299 *admit*; sheathe, invaginate; throw in, foist in, plough in, work in, wedge in, edge in, jam in, force in, thrust in 303 *insert*; ingrain 303 *infuse*; splice, dovetail, mortise 45 *join*; smuggle in, slide in, worm in, insinuate 297 *infiltrate*.

*put between*, sandwich; cushion 227 *line*; interpose, interject; spatchcock, interpolate, intercalate, interline; interleave, interlard, intersperse; interweave, interdigitate 222 *enlace*; bracket, put between brackets, parenthesize.

*interfere*, come between, get b., intercept 702 *hinder*; step in, intervene, intercede 720 *mediate*; interrupt, put in, chip in, get a word in; obtrude, thrust in, poke one's nose in, horn in, butt in 297 *intrude*; invade, trespass 306 *encroach*; put one's oar in; have a finger in the pie 678 *meddle*.

**Adv.** *between*, betwixt, twixt, betwixt and between; among, amongst, amid, amidst, mid, midst; in the middle of; in the thick of; parenthetically; in the meanwhile, in the meantime 108 *while*.

## 232 Circumscription

**N.** *circumscription*, enclosing 235 *enclosure*; drawing round, encircling, encompassing, circle, balloon; ringing round, hedging r., fencing r.; surrounding, framing, girdling, cincture; investment, siege, blockade 712 *attack*; envelopment, encirclement, containment, confinement, limitation 747 *restriction*; ring 235 *fence*.

**Adj.** *circumscribed*, encircled, encompassed, enveloped; surrounded, begirt; lapped, enfolded, embosomed, embayed, landlocked; framed 233 *outlined*; boxed, boxed up, encysted; walled in, mewed up, cloistered, immured 747 *imprisoned*; invested, beleaguered, besieged; held in, contained, confined 747 *restrained*; limited, restricted, finite.

**Vb.** *circumscribe*, describe a circle, ring round, circle, encircle, encompass; envelop, close in, cut off, cordon off, rope off, mark off, invest, beleaguer, blockade, picket 712 *besiege*; beset, hem in, pen in, corral; enclose, rail in, hedge in, fence in; box, cage, wall in, immure, cloister 747 *imprison*; frame 230 *surround*; encase, enfold, enshrine, embosom, embay; edge, border 236 *limit*; clasp, hug, embrace, cuddle 889 *caress*.

### 233 Outline

**N.** *outline*, circumference, perimeter, periphery; surround, frame, rim 234 *edge*; ambit, compass, circuit 250 *circle*; delineation, lines, lineaments, configuration, features 445 *feature*; profile, relief 239 *laterality*; silhouette, skyline, horizon 553 *picture*; sketch, rough s., draft 623 *plan*; figure, diagram, layout; trace, tracing; skeleton, framework 331 *structure*; contour, contour line, shape 243 *form*; isogonic line, coastline, bounds 236 *limit*; circlet, band 250 *loop*; balloon, circle 232 *circumscription*; ring, cordon 235 *barrier*.

**Adj.** *outlined*, framed etc. vb.; in outline, etched; peripheral, perimetric, circumferential.

**Vb.** *outline*, describe a circle, construct a figure 232 *circumscribe*; frame 230 *surround*; delineate, draw, silhouette, profile, skeletonize, trace 551 *represent*; etch 555 *engrave*; map, block out, rough o., sketch o., sketch; diagrammatize, not fill in.

### 234 Edge

**N.** *edge*, verge, brim; outer edge, fly (of a flag); tip, brink, skirt, fringe, margin 69 *extremity*; inner edge, hoist (of a flag); confines, bounds, boundary, bourn, frontier, border 236 *limit*; littoral, coast, coastline, beach, strand, seaside, seashore, waterline, waterside, water's edge, front, waterfront 344 *shore*; wharf, quay, dock 192 *stable*; sideline, side, brim, kerb *or* curb, kerbside, wayside, roadside, riverside, bank 239 *laterality*; hedge, railing 235 *fence*; felloe, felly, tyre 250 *wheel*; projecting edge, lip, ledge, eave, cornice, rim, welt, flange, gunwale 254 *projection*; raised edge, coaming; horizon, ends of the earth, skyline 199 *farness*; cutting edge,

knife e., razor e.; sharpness, acrimony; advantage, upper hand.

*threshold*, sill, doorstep, door, portal, porch 263 *doorway*; mouth, jaws, chops, chaps, fauces 194 *maw*.

*edging*, frame 233 *outline*; thrum, list, selvedge; hem, hemline, border; purfling 844 *pattern*; binding, piping; basque, fringe, frill, ruffle, flounce, furbelow, valance 844 *trimming*; crenation, milling 260 *notch*; deckle edge, wavy edge, scallop, picot, purl 251 *coil*.

**Adj.** *marginal*, border, skirting, marginated; riverine, riparian, coastal; riverside, roadside, wayside; labial, labiated; edged, trimmed, bordered; borderline, peripheral.

**Vb.** *hem*, edge, lower e., border, trim, piping, fringe, purl; mill, crenellate 260 *notch*; bound, confine 236 *limit*.

### 235 Enclosure

**N.** *enclosure*, envelope, case 194 *receptacle*; wrapper, packaging 226 *wrapping*; girdle, ring, perimeter, circumference, periphery 233 *outline*; surround, frame, picture-f., photograph frame; enceinte, precinct, close; cloister, courtyard 185 *place*; reserve 883 *seclusion*; lot, holding, claim 184 *territory*; fold, pen, pinfold, sheepfold, shippen, sty 369 *cattle pen*; stockyard, croft 370 *farm*; garth, park 370 *garden*; compound, yard, pound, paddock, field; car park, parking lot 192 *shed*; corral, kraal, stockade, zareba, boma, circumvallation, lines 713 *defences*; net, trawl 222 *network*; lobster pot 542 *trap*; cell, box, cage 748 *prison*.

*fence*, ring f., barbed-wire f., razor-wire fence, electric f., chain-link f. 222 *network*; hurdle, wooden fence, picket f., sunk f., ha-ha, hedge, privet h., quickset h., hedgerow, espalier; rails, balustrade, banisters, paling, railing, taffrail; pale, wall, boundary w.; moat, dike, ditch, fosse, trench, vallum, curtain wall 713 *defences*.

*barrier*, wall, cavity w., brick w., dry-stone w. 231 *partition*; fence, ring fence 46 *separation*; buffer zone, cordon sanitaire; soundproofing, double-glazing, damp-proofing 660 *protection*; barricade, cordon, pale; balustrade, parapet; turnstile 702 *obstacle*; palisade, stockade 713 *fort*; portcullis, gate, door, bolt, bar, padlock 264 *closure*.

**Vb.** *enclose*, fence in, cordon, cordon off, rope off, surround, wall; pen, hem, ring, corral, ring-fence 232 *circumscribe*; cloister, immure, wall up, confine, cage 747 *imprison*; wrap, lap, enwrap, enfold, fold up 261 *fold*; embosom, fold in one's arms, hug, embrace, cuddle 889 *caress*; frame, set, mount, box.

## 236 Limit

**N.** *limit*, limitation, constraint 747 *restriction*, 468 *qualification*; definition, delimitation, demarcation 783 *apportionment*; limiting factor, parameter, upper limit, ceiling, high-water mark 213 *summit*; lower limit, threshold, low-water mark 214 *base*; legal limit, Plimsoll line; saturation point 54 *completeness*; utmost, uttermost, extreme, furthest point, farthest reach, ne plus ultra, pole 69 *extremity*; ends of the earth, Ultima Thule, Pillars of Hercules 199 *farness*; terminus, terminal 69 *end*; goal, target, winning post, touch, touchline, home, base 617 *objective*; turning point, watershed 137 *crisis*; point of no return, Rubicon 599 *resolution*; limit of endurance, threshold of pain, tolerance, capacity, end of one's tether; physical limit, outside edge, perimeter, periphery, circumference 233 *outline*; tidemark, sea line 344 *shore*; landmark, boundary stone; milestone 27 *degree*; kerb *or* curb, kerbstone 624 *road*; metes and bounds, bourne, boundary, verge; frontier, border, marches 234 *edge*; national frontier, state boundary; three-mile limit; line, demarcation l., international date l., divide, parting 231 *partition*; skyline, horizon, equator, terminator; deadline, time limit, term 110 *period*; ultimatum 900 *threat*; speed limit 278 *slowness*; sound barrier.

**Adj.** *limited*, definite, conterminous, con-terminal; limitable, finite; limitative, limitary, terminal; frontier, border, borderline, bordering, boundary.

**Vb.** *limit*, bound, border, edge 234 *hem*; top 213 *crown*; define, confine, condition 468 *qualify*; restrict, stint 747 *restrain*; encompass, beat the bounds 232 *circumscribe*; draw the line, delimit, demarcate, stake out; rope off, mark out, chalk o. 547 *mark*.

**Adv.** *thus far*, so far, thus far and no further, up to now; between the tidemarks, on the borderline.

## 237 Front

**N.** *front*, fore, forefront 64 *precedence*; forepart; prefix, frontispiece, preface, foreword, front matter; forelock 259 *hair*; forecourt, anteroom, entrance, hall 263 *doorway*; foreground, proscenium 200 *nearness*; anteriority 119 *priority*; front rank, first line, front l.; leading edge; forward line, centre forward; avant-garde, van-guard, van, advance guard; spearhead, bridgehead 712 *attacker*; outpost, scout, reconnaissance party; forerunner, pioneer 66 *precursor*; prequel.

*face*, frontage, façade, fascia; face of a coin, obverse, head; right side, outer s., recto; front view, front elevation; sinciput 213 *head*; brow, forehead, glabella; chin, physiognomy, meto-poscopy, features, visage, countenance, phiz, phizog, mug, mush, kisser, boat, boat-race, dial, clock 445 *feature*; prominent feature, nose, aquiline n., Roman n., snout, conk 254 *protuberance*; lip, hare l., filtrum.

*prow*, nose, beak, rostrum, figurehead; bow, bows; bowsprit; jib, foremast, forecastle, fo'c'sle, forestay, forepeak 275 *ship*.

**Adj.** *frontal*, fore, forward, front, obverse; full frontal, head-on, oncoming, facing 240 *opposite*; anterior, prefixed 64 *preceding*.

**Vb.** *be in front*, stand in front etc. adv.; front, confront, face, eyeball, face up to 240 *be opposite*; breast, stem, brave; bend forwards, lean f. 220 *be oblique*; come to the front, come to the fore, forge ahead, take the lead, head 283 *precede*.

**Adv.** *in front*, before, in advance, in the lead, in the van, vanward; ahead, ahead of one's time, right a., infra, further on 199 *beyond*; far ahead, coastward, landward; before one's face, before one's eyes; face to face, eyeball to eye-ball, man to man, vis-à-vis; in the foreground, in the forefront, in the limelight; head first, head foremost; feet first, feet foremost.

## 238 Rear

**N.** *rear*, rearward, afterpart, back end, rear end, tail end, stern 69 *extremity*; tail-piece, heel, colophon; coda 412 *musical piece*; tail, brush, scut, pigtail 67 *sequel*; wake, train 67 *retinue*; last place, booby prize, wooden spoon, rear rank, back seat 35 *inferiority*; rearguard 67 *successor*; subsequence 120 *posteriority*; back-ground, backdrop 594 *stage set*; hinterland, depths, far corner 199 *distance*; behind, back-stage, back side; reverse side, wrong s., verso 240 *contraposition*; reverse, other side, flip side, B-side; back door, back entrance, tradesmen's e., postern 263 *doorway*; back (of the body), dorsum, chine; backbone, spine, rachis 218 *prop*; back of the neck, scruff of the n., nape, scruff, short hairs; back of the head, occiput 213 *head*.

*buttocks*, backside, behind, rear end, derrière, posterior, posteriors, cheeks; bottom, btm (inf), seat, sit-me-down, sit-upon; bum, arse (sl), ass (sl), butt (sl), fanny (sl), rear, stern, tail; hindquarters, croup, crupper; hips, haunches, hams, hunkers; rump, loin; dorsal region, lumbar r., small of the back, lower back, coccyx; fundament, anus.

*poop*, stern, stern-sheets, afterpart, quarter, counter, rudderpost, rudder, rearmast, mizzen-mast 275 *ship*.

**Adj.** *back*, rear, postern; posterior, after, hind, hinder, hindermost, rearmost, tail-end;

bent back, backswept 253 *convex*; reverse 240 *opposite*; placed last 35 *inferior*; spinal, vertebral, retral, dorsal, lumbar; anal; caudal, caudate.

**Vb.** *be behind*, stand b.; back on, back; back up 703 *aid*; follow, bring up the rear 65 *come after*; lag, trail, drop behind, fall astern 278 *move slowly*; trail, tail, shadow, dog 619 *pursue*; follow at heel 284 *follow*; bend backwards, lean b. 220 *be oblique*.

**Adv.** *rearward*, behind, back of; in the rear, at the end, in the ruck; at the back, in the background; behind one's back; behind the scenes, offstage; after, aftermost, sternmost; aft, abaft, astern, aback; to the rear, hindward, backward, retro-; supra, above; overleaf; on the heels of, hard on the heels of, at the tail of, at the back of, close behind; one behind the other, in tandem; back to back.

### 239 Laterality
**N.** *laterality*, sidedness; side movement 317 *oscillation*; sidestep 282 *deviation*; sideline, side, bank 234 *edge*; coast 344 *shore*; siding, side entrance, side door; gable, gable-end; broadside; beam; quarter 238 *poop*; flank, ribs, pleura; wing, fin, arm, hand; cheek, jowl, chops, chaps, gills; side whiskers 259 *hair*; temples, side-face, half-face; profile, side elevation; lee, lee side, leeward; weatherside, windward 281 *direction*; orientation, east, Orient, Levant; west, Occident 281 *compass point*; off side, on s., near s. 241 *dextrality*, 242 *sinistrality*.

**Adj.** *lateral*, laparo-; side 234 *marginal*; sidelong, glancing; parietal, buccal; costal, pleural, winglike, aliform; flanking, skirting; flanked, sided; manysided, multilateral, unilateral, bilateral, trilateral, quadrilateral; collateral 219 *parallel*; moving sideways, edging, sidling; eastern, eastward, easterly, orient, oriental, auroral, Levantine; west, western, westerly, westward, occidental, Hesperian 281 *directed*.

**Vb.** *flank*, side, edge, skirt, border 234 *hem*; coast, move sideways, passage, sidle; sideslip, sidestep 282 *deviate*; extend sideways, deploy, outflank 306 *overstep*.

**Adv.** *sideways*, crabwise, laterally; askance, asquint 220 *obliquely*; half-face, in profile, sideways on; sidelong, broadside on; on one side, abreast, abeam, alongside; aside, beside; by the side of, side by side, cheek by jowl 200 *near*; to windward, to leeward, alee; coastwise; right and left; on her beam ends.

### 240 Contraposition
**N.** *contraposition*, antithesis, opposition, antipodes 14 *contrariety*; frontage 281 *direction*;

opposite side, other s., other s. of the fence; reverse, back 238 *rear*; polarity, polarization; opposite poles, poles apart, North and South; crosscurrent, headwind 704 *opposition*; reversal, inverse 221 *inversion*.

**Adj.** *opposite*, contrapositive, reverse, inverse 221 *inverted*; contrary, subcontrary 14 *contrary*; facing, face to face, vis-à-vis, eyeball to eyeball, man to man, fronting, confronting, oncoming 237 *frontal*; diametrically opposite, diametrically opposed, antipodal, antipodean, antithetical; polarized, polar; antarctic, arctic, northern, septentrional, Boreal, southern, austral 281 *directed*.

**Vb.** *be opposite*, – facing etc. adj.; stand opposite, lie o.; subtend; face, confront 237 *be in front*; run counter 182 *counteract*; oppose, contrapose.

**Adv.** *against*, over the way, over against; poles asunder, poles apart; facing, face to face, eyeball to eyeball, man to man, vis-à-vis; back to back; on the other side, on the other side of the fence, overleaf; contrariwise, vice versa.

### 241 Dextrality
**N.** *dextrality*, right hand, right-handedness; ambidexterity, ambidextrousness 694 *skill*; right, offside, starboard; right-hand page, recto; right wing, right-winger; dextral, ambidexter.

**Adj.** *dextral*, dexter, dextro-; right-hand, starboard, offside; right-handed, dextrous, ambidextral, ambidextrous 694 *skilful*; dextrorse, dextrorsal; dextrorotatory; right-wing.

**Adv.** *dextrally*, on the right; right-handedly, ambidextrously; dextrorsely; to the right, astarboard.

### 242 Sinistrality
**N.** *sinistrality*, left hand, left-handedness, cackhandedness; left, near side, on s.; larboard, port; left-hand page, verso; left wing, left-winger; sinistral, south-paw.

**Adj.** *sinistral*, sinister, sinistrous, laevo-, left, left-handed, cack-handed; onside, nearside, sinistrorse, sinistrorsal; laevorotatory; left-wing.

**Adv.** *sinistrally*, on the left, aport, offside; leftwards; sinisterwise.

SECTION THREE

## Form

### 243 Form
**N.** *form*, substantial f., Platonic f., idea; Gestalt 52 *whole*; essence 3 *substance*; significant form, inner f., inscape 5 *character*; art form 551 *art*, 598 *verse form*; word form 557 *linguistics*;

shape, turn, lines, architecture; formation, conformation, configuration, fashion, style, trend, design 331 *structure*; contour, silhouette, relief, profile, frame, outline; figure, cut, set, trim, build, cut of one's jib, lineament 445 *feature*; physiognomy 237 *face*; look, expression, appearance 445 *mien*; posture, attitude, stance, asana; get-up, turnout, rig, gear; type, kind, pattern, stamp, cast, mould, blank 23 *prototype*; format, typeface, typography 587 *print*; morphology, isomorphism.

*formation*, forming, shaping, creation 164 *production*; expression, formulation 62 *arrangement*; designing, patterning 844 *ornamental art*; weaving, knitting 222 *network*; tailoring 844 *needlework*; throwing 381 *pottery*; moulding 554 *sculpture*; turning, joinery 694 *skill*; etymology, word-formation 557 *linguistics*.

**Adj.** *formed*, created etc. vb.; receiving form, plastic, fictile; sculptured, carved, moulded, thrown, turned, rounded, squared; shaped, fashioned, fully f., styled, stylized; designer, tailor-made, custom-built; ready-made, off the peg; matured, ready 669 *prepared*; solid, concrete 324 *dense*; dimensional, two-d., three-d.; isomorphous.

*formative*, giving form, formal; plastic, glyptic, architectural 331 *structural*.

**Vb.** *form*, create, bring into being, make 164 *produce*; formalize, shape, fashion, figure, pattern; throw (pots), blow (glass); turn, round, square; cut, tailor; cut out, silhouette 233 *outline*; sketch, draft, draw 551 *represent*; model, carve, whittle, chisel 554 *sculpt*; hew, rough-h. 46 *cut*; mould, cast; stamp, coin, mint; hammer out, block o., knock o., punch o.; carpenter, mason; forge, smith; knead, work, work up into; construct, build, frame 310 *elevate*; express, put into words, verbalize, formulate, put into shape, pull into s., lick into s., knock into s.

**244 Amorphism: absence of form**
**N.** *amorphism*, absence of form, formlessness; prime matter; confusion, chaos 61 *disorder*; amorphousness, lack of shape, shapelessness; lack of definition, vagueness, fuzziness; rawness, uncouthness 670 *undevelopment*; raw material 631 *materials*; rough diamond; disfigurement, defacement, mutilation, deformation, deformity 246 *distortion*.

**Adj.** *amorphous*, formless, unformed, unstructured, structureless, inchoate; liquid 335 *fluid*; shapeless, featureless, characterless; messy, chaotic 61 *orderless*; undefined, ill-defined, lacking definition, indistinct, nondescript, nebulous, vague, fuzzy, blurred 419 *shadowy*; unfashioned, unshapen, unformed,

unmade; embryonic 68 *beginning*; raw, callow, unlicked 670 *immature*; unhewn, in the rough 55 *incomplete*; rude, uncouth, barbaric 699 *artless*; rugged 259 *rough*; unshapely 842 *unsightly*; malformed, misshapen, gnarled 246 *deformed*.

**Vb.** *deform*, deprive of form, unmake, unshape 165 *destroy*; dissolve, melt 337 *liquefy*; knock out of shape, batter 46 *break*; grind, pulp 332 *pulverize*; warp, twist 246 *distort*; deface, disfigure 842 *make ugly*; mutilate, truncate 655 *impair*; jumble, disorder 63 *derange*.

**245 Symmetry: regularity of form**
**N.** *symmetry*, bilateral s., radial s., correspondence, proportion 12 *correlation*; balance 28 *equilibrium*; regularity, evenness 16 *uniformity*; arborescence, branching, ramification 219 *parallelism*; shapeliness, regular features, classic f. 841 *beauty*; harmony, concinnity, congruity, eurhythmy 24 *agreement*; rhythm 141 *periodicity*; finish 646 *perfection*.

**Adj.** *symmetrical*, balanced, well-balanced 28 *equal*; proportioned, well-p. 12 *correlative*; rhythmical, eurhythmic, harmonious, concinnous, congruous 24 *agreeing*; congruent, coextensive; corresponding 219 *parallel*; analogous 18 *similar*; smooth, even 16 *uniform*; squared, rounded, round, evensided, isosceles, equilateral 81 *regular*, crystalline; arborescent, dendriform, branching, ramose; formal, classic, comely 841 *shapely*; undeformed, undistorted, unwarped, well set up 249 *straight*; finished, complete in all its parts 54 *complete*.

**246 Distortion: irregularity of form**
**N.** *distortion*, asymmetry, disproportion, disproportionateness, misproportion, lack of symmetry 10 *unrelatedness*; fractal; imbalance, disequilibrium 29 *inequality*; lopsidedness, crookedness, skewness 220 *obliquity*; anamorphosis, projection, Mercator's p. 551 *map*; contortion, twisting; thrust, stress, strain, shear; bias, warp; buckle, bend, screw, twist 251 *convolution*; facial distortion, grimace, moue, snarl, rictus 547 *gesture*.

*deformity*, malformation, disfigurement, monstrosity, mutation, abortion 84 *variance*; curvature of the spine 248 *curvature*; teratogeny; clubfoot, talipes, knock knees, bow legs, rickets, valgus, hunchback, kyphosis 845 *blemish*; ugliness 842 *eyesore*; teratology.

**Adj.** *distorted*, contorted etc. vb.; irregular, asymmetric, scalene, unsymmetrical, disproportionate 17 *nonuniform*; weighted, biased; not true, not straight; anamorphous, grotesque; out of shape, warped, mutative 244 *amorphous*; mangled, buckled, twisted, wrinkled, gnarled 251 *convoluted*; wry, awry, askew, crazy, crooked, cock-eyed, on one side 220 *oblique*; slouched, slumped; grimacing, scowling, snarling.

*deformed*, ugly 842 *unsightly*; misproportioned, ill-proportioned; defective 647 *imperfect*; mutative, ill-made, malformed, misshapen, misbegotten; disabled, crippled, handicapped, hunchbacked, humpbacked, crook-backed, kyphotic, crooked as a ram's horn; bandy, bandy-legged, bow-legged, knock-kneed; pigeon-toed, splay-footed, clubfooted, taliped, web-footed, round-shouldered, pigeon-chested; snub-nosed, hare-lipped 845 *blemished*; stunted, stumpy 204 *short*; haggard, gaunt 206 *lean*; bloated 195 *fleshy*.

**Vb.** *distort*, disproportion, weight, bias; contort, screw, twist, knot 251 *twine*; bend, warp 251 *crinkle*; spring, buckle, crumple; strain, sprain, skew, wrest, torture, rack 63 *derange*; misshape, botch 244 *deform*; mangle, batter, knock out of shape 655 *impair*; pervert 552 *misrepresent*; misconstrue 521 *misinterpret*; slant, spin, twist; writhe 251 *wriggle*; wince, grimace, make faces, make a moue, mop and mow 547 *gesticulate*; snarl, scowl, frown 893 *be sullen*.

## 247 Angularity

**N.** *angularity*, angulation, aduncity, hookedness, crotchet, bracket, crook, hook; bend, scythe, sickle, scimitar 248 *curvature*; chevron, zigzag 220 *obliquity*; V-shape, elbow, knee, knee-joint; shoulder blade, withers 253 *camber*; knuckle, ankle, groin 45 *joint*; crutch, crotch, fluke 222 *cross*; fork, bifurcation, cross-ways, branching 222 *crossing*; quoin, corner, cranny, nook, niche, recess, oriel 194 *compartment*; nose, Roman n., hook n. 254 *protuberance*; wedge, arrowhead 256 *sharp point*; broad arrow, cusp; flexure 261 *fold*; indentation 260 *notch*.

*angle*, right a., acute a., obtuse a., salient a., reentrant a., spherical a., solid a., dihedral a.

*angular measure*, goniometry, trigonometry, altimetry; angular elevation, angular distance, angular velocity; zenith distance; second, degree, minute; radian; goniometer, altimeter, clinometer, level, theodolite; transit circle; sextant, quadrant; protractor, set square.

*angular figure*, triangle, isosceles t., equilateral t., scalene t., spherical t., trigon; parallelogram, rectangle, square, quadrangle, quadrature; quadrilateral, lozenge, diamond; rhomb, rhombus, rhomboid; trapezium, trapezoid; tetragon, polygon, pentagon, hexagon, heptagon, octagon, nonagon, decagon, dodecahedron, icosahedron; cube, pyramid, wedge; prism, parallelepiped; Platonic bodies.

**Adj.** *angular*, hooked, uncinate, hook-nosed,

Roman-nosed, aquiline, rostrate; unciform, falciform, falcate 248 *curved*; angled, sharp-a., cornered; staggered, crooked, zigzag 220 *oblique*; jagged, serrated, crinkled 260 *notched*; bony, jointed, geniculate, elbowed; akimbo; knockkneed; crotched, forked, bifurcate, furcate, furcular, V-shaped.

*angulated*, triangular, trigonal, trilateral; wedge-shaped, cuneate, cuneiform, fusiform; rectangular, right-angled, orthogonal; square, square-shaped, four-square, quadrangular, quadrilateral, four-sided, squared; diamond-shaped, lozenge-s.; trapezoid, trapezoidal; multilateral, polygonal, decahedral, polyhedral; cubical, rhomboidal, pyramidal.

**Vb.** *make angular*, angle, make corners, corner; hook, crook, bend 248 *make curved*; wrinkle, fold 251 *crinkle*; zigzag 220 *be oblique*; fork, bifurcate, divaricate, branch, ramify 294 *diverge*; go off at a tangent 282 *deviate*.

## 248 Curvature

**N.** *curvature*, curvation; incurvature, incurvation, inward curve 255 *concavity*; outward curve 253 *convexity*; flexure, flexion, inflexion, bending 261 *fold*; arcuation, sweep; bowing, stooping 311 *obeisance*; bending down, deflexion; turning away, swerve, detour 282 *deviation*; downward bend 309 *descent*; recurvature, retroflexion 221 *inversion*; curling, curliness, sinuosity 251 *convolution*; aduncity 247 *angularity*; curvature of the spine 246 *deformity*.

*curve*, slight c. 253 *camber*; elbow 247 *angularity*; turn, bend, Z-bend, sharp b., hairpin b., U-turn; horseshoe, oxbow; bay, bight 345 *gulf*; figure of eight 250 *loop*; ogee, S-shape; tracery, curl 251 *convolution*; festoon, swag 844 *pattern*; bow, Cupid's b., rainbow 250 *arc*; arch, ogee a., spring of an a., arcade, vault 253 *dome*; sickle, scimitar, crescent, lunula, half-moon, meniscus, lens; trajectory, catenary, parabola, hyperbola, conic section; cone biopsy; caustic, cardioid, conchoid; arch (of the foot), instep; swan neck.

**Adj.** *curved*, cambered etc. vb.; flexed, bent 220 *oblique*; bowed, stooping 311 *lowered*; curviform, bowlike, curvilineal, curvilinear; rounded, curvaceous, curvy, bosomy, busty, wavy, billowy 251 *undulatory*; aquiline, hook-nosed, parrot-beaked 247 *angular*; rostrate, beaked, beaklike, bill-shaped; bent back, recurved, recurvate, retroflex; retroussé, turned-up, tip-tilted 221 *inverted*; circumflex; ogival, vaulted 253 *arched*; bowlegged, bandy-legged 246 *deformed*; down-curving 309 *descending*; hooked, adunc, falciform, falcate; semicircular 250 *round*; crescent, lunular, lunate, lunar, semilunar, horned; meniscal, len-

ticular; reniform; cordiform, cordate, heart-
shaped, bell-s., pear-s., hour-glass.

**Vb.** *be curved*, – bent etc. adj.; curve, swerve,
bend, loop, camber, wind, arch, sweep, sag,
swag, give, give in the middle 217 *hang*;
reenter, recurve; intort 251 *twine*; curvet 312
*leap*.

*make curved*, bend, crook 247 *make angular*;
turn, round 250 *make round*; bend in, incurvate, inflect; bend back, recurve, retroflect 221
*invert*; bend over, bend down, bow, incline 311
*stoop*; turn over 261 *fold*; turn away 282 *deflect*;
arcuate, arch, arch over; coil 251 *twine*; loop,
curl, kink, wave, perm 251 *crinkle*; loop the
loop, make figures of eight.

**249 Straightness**
**N.** *straightness*, directness, rectilinearity; perpendicularity 215 *verticality*; inflexibility,
intransigence, rigidity 326 *hardness*; honesty;
chord, radius, tangent 203 *line*; straight line,
right l., direct l., beeline; Roman road; straight
stretch, straight, reach; short cut 200 *short
distance*.

**Adj.** *straight*, direct, even, right, true; in a
line, linear; straight-lined, rectilinear, recti-
lineal; perpendicular 215 *vertical*; unbent,
unwarped, undistorted; stiff, inflexible 326
*rigid*; uncurled, straightened, unfrizzed,
dekinked; dead straight, undeviating,
unswerving, undeflected, on the beam,
straight as an arrow; straight as a die 929
*honourable*; not bent, heterosexual 83 *typical*.

**Vb.** *be straight*, – direct etc. adj.; keep
straight on, steer straight, follow the great
circle; go straight, have no turning, not
incline, not bend, not turn, not deviate, not
deviate to either side, turn neither right nor
left, make a beeline for.

*straighten*, make straight, align; iron out 216
*flatten*; unbend (a bow); uncross (legs), unfold
(arms); dekink, uncurl 258 *smooth*; stretch
tight; unwrap 62 *unravel*; uncoil, unroll,
unfurl, unfold 316 *evolve*.

**Adv.** *straight on*, directly, as the crow flies
281 *towards*; straight, plumb.

**250 Circularity: simple circularity**
**N.** *circularity*, orbicularity, roundness, rondure
252 *rotundity*; annularity.

*circle*, full c., circumference 233 *outline*; great
circle, equator; orb, annulus; roundel,
roundlet; areola; plate, saucer; round, disc,
disk, discus; coin, button, sequin; washer,
hoop, ring, bracelet, quoit; eye, iris; eyelet,
loophole, keyhole 263 *orifice*; circular course,
circuit, circus, roundabout; zodiac; fairy ring;
smoke ring; crop circle.

*loop*, figure of eight 251 *convolution*; bow,
knot; ringlet, curl, kink 259 *hair*, circlet,
bracelet, armlet, torque 844 *finery*; crown, coronet 743 *regalia*; corona, aureole, halo; wreath,
garland 228 *headgear*; collar, neckband, necklace, choker 228 *neckwear*; band, cordon, sash,
girdle, cummerbund 228 *belt*; baldric, bandolier 47 *girdle*; lasso, lariat 47 *halter*.

*wheel*, pulley, castor 315 *rotator*; hub, felloe,
felly, tyre; rubber tyre, spare t., radial t.,
crossply t., tubeless t., inner tube, outer t.;
roller 252 *rotundity*.

*arc*, semicircle, half-circle, hemicycle,
lunette; half-moon, crescent, rainbow 248
*curve*; sector, quadrant, sextant; ellipse, oval,
ovule; ellipsoid, cycloid, epicycloid.

*orbit*, cycle, epicycle, circuit, ecliptic; circulation 314 *circuition*.

**Adj.** *round*, rounded, circular, cyclic, discoid;
orbicular, ringlike, ringed, annular, annulate,
annulose, semicircular, hemicyclic; oval,
ovate, elliptic, ovoid, egg-shaped, crescent-s.,
pear-s. 248 *curved*; cycloidal, spherical 252
*rotund*.

**Vb.** *make round*, – oval etc. adj.; round, turn.
*go round*, girdle, encircle 230 *surround*;
describe a circle 233 *outline*; move round, circulate, orbit, go into o. 314 *circle*.

**251 Convolution: complex circularity**
**N.** *convolution*, involution, circumvolution;
intricacy; flexuosity, anfractuosity, sinuosity,
sinuousness; tortuosity, tortuousness, torsion,
intorsion; reticulation 222 *network*; twine,
twist 208 *fibre*; ripple 350 *wave*; kink, wrinkle,
corrugation 261 *fold*; indentation, ragged edge,
scallop 260 *notch*; waviness, undulation, ogee
248 *curve*.

*coil*, roll, twist; turban, pugree 228 *headgear*;
Turk's head 47 *ligature*; spiral, helix; screw,
screw-thread, worm, corkscrew; spring,
wound s., coiled s.; intrauterine device 172 *contraception*; whorl, snailshell, ammonite; whirlpool 350 *eddy*, 315 *vortex*; verticil, tendril 366
*plant*; scollop, scallop, scalloped edge 234
*edging*; kink, curl; ringlet, lovelock 259 *hair*;
scroll, volute, fiddlehead, flourish, twirl,
curlicue, squiggle 844 *ornamentation*.

*meandering*, meander, winding course, crankiness; winding, windings and turnings, twists
and turns, circumbendibus 282 *deviation*; labyrinth, maze 61 *complexity*; switchback, zigzag
220 *obliquity*.

*serpent*, snake, eel, worm 365 *reptile*; wriggler,
looper, sidewinder.

**Adj.** *convoluted*, twisted, contorted, intorted
246 *distorted*; tortile, cranky, ambagious;
winding, looping, twining, anfractuous,

sinuous, tortuous, flexuous; indented, ragged 260 *notched*; crumpled, buckled 261 *folded*.

*labyrinthine*, mazy, Daedalian, meandering, serpentine; twisting, turning 314 *circuitous*.

*snaky*, serpentine, serpentiform, anguine, eel-like, anguilliform, wormlike, vermiform, vermicular; undulating, curvy, sinuous, squiggly, squirming, wriggling, peristaltic; S-shaped, sigmoid.

*undulatory*, undulating, rolling, heaving; up-and-down, switchback; crinkle-crankle (wall), wavy, curly, frizzy, kinky, crinkly; crimped, curled, permed; scolloped, wrinkled, corrugated, indented, ragged 260 *notched*; Flamboyant, Decorated.

*coiled*, spiral, helical, cochlear; convolute, involute, turbinate, whorled, scroll-like, verticillate; wound, wound up; coiling, spiralling.

*intricate*, involved, complicated, knotted 61 *complex*.

**Vb.** *twine*, twist, twirl, roll, coil, corkscrew, convolute, spiral 315 *rotate*; wreathe, entwine 222 *enlace*; be convuluted, – twisted etc. adj.; turn and twist, bend 248 *be curved*.

*crinkle*, crimp, frizz, perm, crisp, curl; wave, undulate, ripple, popple; wrinkle, corrugate 261 *fold*; indent, scallop, scollop 260 *notch*; crumple 246 *distort*.

*meander*, loop, snake, crankle, twist and turn, zigzag, corkscrew. (See also *twine*.)

*wriggle*, writhe, squirm, shimmy, shake; move sinuously, worm.

**Adv.** *in and out*, round about.

## 252 Rotundity

**N.** *rotundity*, rondure, roundness, orbicularity 250 *circularity*; sphericity, sphericality, spheroidicity; globularity, globosity, cylindricity, cylindricality, gibbosity, gibbousness 253 *convexity*.

*sphere*, globe, spheroid, prolate s., oblate s., ellipsoid, globoid, geoid; hollow sphere, bladder; balloon 276 *airship*; soap bubble 355 *bubble*; ball, football, pelota, wood (bowls), billiard ball, marble, ally, taw; crystal ball; cannonball, bullet, shot, pellet; bead, pearl, pill, pea, boll, oakapple, puffball, spherule, globule; drop, droplet, dewdrop, inkdrop, blot; vesicle, bulb, onion, knob, pommel 253 *swelling*; boulder, rolling stone; hemisphere, hump, mushroom 253 *dome*; round head, bullet h., turnip h.

*cylinder*, roll, rolypoly; roller, rolling pin; round, rung, rundle; round tower, martello t., column; bole, trunk, stalk, stem; pipe, drainpipe 263 *tube*; funnel, chimneypot; round box, hat b., pillbox; drum, barrel, cask.

*cone*, conoid; shadow cone, penumbra; sugar-

loaf 253 *dome*; cornet, horn 194 *cup*; top, spinning t., peg t.; pear shape, bell s., egg s.

**Adj.** *rotund*, orbicular 250 *round*; spherical, sphery, spherular; globular, global, globose, globoid; round-headed, bullet-headed, brachycephalic; beady, beadlike, moniliform; hemispherical; spheroidal, ovoid, oviform, egg-shaped; cylindrical, columnar, tubular; cigar-shaped 256 *tapering*; conic, conical; conoid, conoidal; bell-shaped, campanulate, napiform, turnip-shaped; pyriform, pear-shaped, heart-shaped; humped, gibbous; bulbous 253 *convex*; pot-bellied 195 *fleshy*; sphered, balled, rolled up.

**Vb.** *round*, make spherical; form into a sphere, form into a globe etc. n.; sphere, globe, ball, bead; balloon 253 *be convex*; coil up, roll, roll up 315 *rotate*.

## 253 Convexity

**N.** *convexity*, convexness; arcuation, arching 248 *curvature*; sphericity 252 *rotundity*; gibbosity, bulginess, lumpiness, humpiness, bulge, bump, lump; projection, protrusion, protuberance 254 *prominence*; excrescency, tumescence, tumidity, swelling 197 *dilation*; paunchiness, pot-belliedness 195 *bulk*; pimpliness, wartiness; double convexity, lenticular form; lens 442 *optical device*.

*swelling*, bump, lump, bulge, growth, excrescence, gall, knot, nodosity, node, nodule, nodulus; exostosis, apophysis, condyle, knuckle; oedema, emphysema; sarcoma, tumour, neoplasm, carcinoma 651 *cancer*; bubo, goitre; Adam's apple; bunion, corn, blain, wart, wen, verruca; cyst, boil, carbuncle, furuncle, stye, pimple, papula, blister, bleb, vesicle; polyp, adenoids, haemorrhoids, piles; proud flesh, weal, welt; cauliflower ear; drop 252 *sphere*; air bubble, soap b. 355 *bubble*; boss, torus, knob, nub, nubble; bulb, button, bud; belly, potbelly, corporation, paunch 195 *bulk*; billow, swell 350 *wave*.

*bosom*, bust, breast, breasts; boobs (sl), bristols (sl), knockers (sl), tits (sl); mamma, mamilla, papilla, nipple; pap, dug, teat, udder; thorax, chest; silicone implant, breast reduction, breast enlargement 843 *beautification*; mammography, mastectomy, lumpectomy; cuirass, breastplate.

*dome*, cupola, vault, Millennium Dome 226 *roof*; beehive, skep; brow, forehead 237 *face*; skull, cranium, bald head 213 *head*; hemisphere, arch of heaven; anticline, hog's back, mound; hummock, hillock, mamelon, sugarloaf 209 *small hill*; molehill, anthill, mushroom, umbrella.

*earthwork*, tumulus; tell 548 *monument*;

barrow, round b., long b.; hill fort, circumvallation 713 *defences*; cursus, embankment,
levee.

*camber*, gentle curve 248 *curve*; arch, bow,
rainbow; hump, humpback, hunchback
246 *deformity*; shoulders, calf, elbow 247
*angularity*.

**Adj.** *convex*, protruding 254 *projecting*; hemi-
spheric, domelike 252 *rotund*; lentiform, lenticular; biconvex, gibbous, humpy, lumpy,
bumpy; curvaceous, bosomy, busty, billowy
248 *curved*; billowing, bulging, bellying, ballooning, bouffant; swelling, swollen 197
*expanded*; bloated, potbellied, barrel-chested
195 *fleshy*; turgid, tumid, tumescent,
tumorous, tuberous; nubbly 259 *rough*; verru-
cose, warty, papulose, pimply, spotty, acned;
blistery, vesicular.

*arched*, arcuate, cambered, bowed 248 *curved*;
rounded; hillocky, hummocky, anticlinal;
mammiform.

**Vb.** *be convex*, camber, arch, bow; swell,
belly, bulge, bag, balloon, billow; make
convex, emboss, chase, beat out 254 *jut*.

**254 Prominence**
**N.** *prominence*, eminence 209 *high land*; conspicuousness 443 *visibility*; solar prominence,
solar flare, tongue, tongue of flame.

*projection*, salient, salient angle 247 *angle*; outstretched arm, forefinger, index f.; bowsprit,
cathead, outrigger; tongue of land, spit, point,
mull, promontory, foreland, headland, naze,
ness 344 *land*; peninsula 349 *island*; spur, foothill; jetty, mole, breakwater, groyne, pier 662
*shelter*; outwork 713 *fortification*; pilaster, buttress 218 *prop*; shelf, sill, ledge, soffit, balcony;
eaves 226 *roof*; overhang, rake 220 *obliquity*;
flange, lip 234 *edge*; nozzle, spout; tang,
tongue; tenon 45 *joint*; snag, stump, outcrop;
landmark 209 *high structure*.

*protuberance*, bump 253 *swelling*; prominent
feature; nose, snout, snoot, schnozz,
schnozzle, conk, hooter, neb, pecker, bill,
beak, rostrum; muzzle, proboscis, trunk;
antenna 378 *feeler*; chin, mentum, jaw, forehead, brow, beetle brow 237 *face*; figurehead
237 *prow*; horn, antler 256 *sharp point*.

*relievo*, relief, basso relievo, alto r., mezzo r.,
low relief, bas r., high r.; embossment 844 *ornamental art*; cameo 554 *sculpture*.

**Adj.** *projecting*, jutting, prominent, salient,
bold; protuberant, protruding, bulging, popping etc. vb.; bug-eyed, goggle-e., pop-e., with
eyes out on stalks; toothy; beetle-browed, over-
hung; underhung, undershot; repoussé, raised,
embossed, in relief, in high r., in low r.; ridged,
nobbly 259 *rough*.

**Vb.** *jut*, project, protrude, pout, pop, pop
out, start o.; stand out, stick o., stick out like a
sore thumb, poke o., hang o. 443 *be visible*;
bristle up, prick up, cock up 259 *roughen*; shoot
up, swell up 197 *expand*; overhang, hang over,
beetle over, impend 217 *hang*.

**255 Concavity**
**N.** *concavity*, concaveness, incurvation,
incurvity 248 *curvature*; hollowness 190 *emptiness*; depression, dint, dimple, dent, fossa;
impression, stamp, imprint, footprint 548
*trace*; intaglio 555 *engraving*; ploughing, fur-
rowing 262 *furrow*; indentation 260 *notch*; gap,
lacuna 201 *interval*.

*cavity*, hollow, niche, nook, cranny, recess,
corner 194 *compartment*; hole, den, burrow,
warren; chasm, abyss 211 *depth*; cave, cavern,
antre; grot, grotto, alcove 194 *arbour*; bowl,
cup, saucer, basin, trough 194 *vessel*; sump 649
*sink*; cell, follicle, alveolus, pore 263 *orifice*;
dimple, pockmark; saltcellar, armpit; honeycomb, sponge 263 *porosity*; funnel, tunnel 263
*tube*; groove, mortise, socket, pocket 262
*furrow*; antrum, sinus; bay, bight, cove, creek,
inlet 345 *gulf*; channel, river-bed, wadi, ditch,
qanat, moat, canal 351 *conduit*; hole in the
ground, excavation, shaft, dip, depression, pothole, swallowhole, punchbowl, crater, pit.

*valley*, vale, dell, dingle, combe, cwm, corrie,
cirque, U-shaped valley, river valley, strath;
glen, dip, depression, slade; ravine, chine, gill,
clough, gorge, canyon, gully 201 *gap*.

*excavation*, dugout, grave, gravepit 364 *tomb*;
opencast mining; vertical excavation, shaft,
borehole, well, mine, coal m., shale m.,
diamond m., pit, coal p., colliery, quarry 632
*store*; gallery, working g., adit, sap, trench,
burrow, warren; underground railway, tube
263 *tunnel*; archaeological excavation, dig; cutting, cut.

*excavator*, miner, coal-m., quarrier; archaeologist, digger; dredger, drag-line; sapper, burrower, tunneller; ditcher, grave-digger.

**Adj.** *concave*, hollow, cavernous; vaulted,
arched 248 *curved*; incurvate, incurved, hol-
lowed out, scooped o., dug o.; caved in, stove
in; depressed, sunk, sunken; biconcave; spoon-
like, saucer-shaped, cup-shaped, scyphate,
cyathiform, cupped; capsular, funnel-shaped,
infundibular; bell-shaped, campanulate;
cellular, socketed, alveolate, dented, dimpled,
pockmarked; full of holes, pincushion-like,
honeycombed; spongy, porous 263 *perforated*.

**Vb.** *be concave*, retreat, retire, cave in; cup,
incurve.

*make concave*, depress, press in, punch in,
stamp, impress; buckle, dent, dint, stave in;

crush, push in, beat in; excavate, hollow, dig, spade, delve, scrape, scratch, scrabble, trench, canalize 262 *groove*; mine, sap, undermine, burrow, tunnel, bore; honeycomb, perforate 263 *pierce*; scoop out, hollow o., dig o., gouge o., scratch o. 300 *eject*; hole, pit, pockmark; indent 260 *notch*; sink a shaft, make a hole; cut and cover.

## 256 Sharpness
**N.** *sharpness*, acuity, acuteness, acumination, pointedness, sting; serration, saw-edge 260 *notch*; spinosity, thorniness, prickliness; acridity 388 *pungency*.

*sharp point*, sting, thorn, prick, point, cusp 213 *vertex*; nail, tack, drawing pin, staple 47 *fastening*; nib, tag, pin, needle, knitting-needle, stylus, bodkin, skewer, spit, broach, brochette; lancet, lance, fleam, awl, gimlet, drill, borer, auger 263 *perforator*; arrow, shaft, bolt, quarrel, arrowhead; barb, fluke, swordpoint, rapier, lance, pike 723 *spear*; fishing spear, gaff, harpoon; dagger, dirk, stiletto 723 *side arms*; spike, caltrop, chevaux-de-frise, barbed wire, razor w. 713 *defences*; spur, rowel; goad, ankus 612 *incentive*; fork, prong, tine, pick, horn, antler; claw, talon, nails 778 *nippers*; spire, flèche, steeple; peak, crag, arête 213 *summit*.

*prickle*, thorn, brier, bramble, thistle, nettle, cactus; bristle 259 *hair*; beard, awn, spica, spicule; porcupine, hedgehog; spine, needle, quill.

*tooth*, tusk, tush, fang; first teeth, milktooth; canine tooth, eye tooth, incisor, grinder, molar, premolar teeth, wisdom t.; pearls, ivories; dentition, front teeth, back t., cheek t.; set of teeth, denture, false teeth, gold t., plate, bridge; comb, saw; cog, ratchet, sprocket, dentil, denticle, denticulation 260 *notch*.

*sharp edge*, cutting e., edge tool; jagged edge, broken glass; cutlery, steel, razor; blade, razor blade; share, ploughshare, coulter 370 *farm tool*; spade, mattock, trowel, shovel; scythe, sickle, hook, reaping h., billhook; cutter, grass c., lawn mower; scissors, barber's s., pinking s.; shears, clippers, secateurs, pruners; surgical knife, scalpel, bistoury; chisel, plane, spokeshave, scraper, draw-knife 258 *smoother*; knife, bread-k., kitchen-k., cook's k., carver, carving knife, fish k., slicer, skiver, hachinette; penknife, pocketknife, flick-knife, switchblade, sheath knife, clasp k., jack k., hunting k., bowie k.; flint knife, microlith; machete, kris, parang, panga; chopper, cleaver, wedge; hatchet, axe, adze; battleaxe 723 *axe*; sword, broadsword, cutlass, scimitar 723 *side arms*.

*sharpener*, knife s., pencil s., oilstone, whetstone, grindstone; hone, steel, carborundum, file, strop; emery, emery board, emery paper, sandpaper, glasspaper.

**Adj.** *sharp*, stinging, keen, acute; edged, cutting; swordlike, ensiform; pointed, unblunted; sharp-pointed, cusped, cuspidate, mucronate; barbed, spurred; sagittal, arrowy; spiked, spiky, spiny, spinose, spinous, thorny, brambly, briery, thistly; needle-like, needlesharp, acicular, aciculate; prickly, bristly, bristling, awned, bearded 259 *hairy*; hastate, spear-like, bayonet-like; studded, muricated, snaggy, craggy, jagged 259 *rough*; comb-like, pectinate, serrated 260 *notched*; sharp-edged, knife-e., razor-e.; sharp as a razor, keen as a r., sharp as a needle; sharpened, whetted etc. vb.; sharp-set, razor-sharp.

*toothed*, odontoid; toothy, brick-toothed; tusky, fanged, dental, denticulate, dentiform; cogged, serrated, saw-edged, emarginate 260 *notched*.

*tapering*, acuminate, fastigiate, conical, pyramidal 293 *convergent*; spired, spiry; horned, cornuted, corniculate; star-shaped, stellate, stellular; spindle-shaped, fusiform, lance-shaped, lanceolate.

**Vb.** *be sharp*, – stinging etc. adj.; have a point, prick, sting; bristle with; have an edge, bite, pierce 46 *cut*; taper, come to a point, end in a point 293 *converge*.

*sharpen*, edge, put an edge on, whet, hone, oilstone, grind, file, strop; barb, spur, point, acuminate, spiculate; stud.

## 257 Bluntness
**N.** *bluntness*, obtuseness, obtusion, flatness, bluffness; curves 258 *smoothness*; rustiness, dullness; toothlessness, toothless tiger, lack of bite; blunt instrument, foil; blunt edge, blade, flat.

**Adj.** *unsharpened*, unwhetted; blunt, blunted, obtunded, unpointed, obtuse; rusty, dull, dull-edged; edgeless, pointless; lacking bite, toothless, edentate; blunt-nosed, stubby, snub, square; round, rounded, curving 248 *curved*; flat, flattened, bluff.

**Vb.** *blunt*, make blunt, turn, turn the edge; take off the point, bate (a foil); obtund, dull, rust; draw the teeth 161 *disable*; be blunt, not cut, pull, scrape, tear.

## 258 Smoothness
**N.** *smoothness*, evenness etc. adj.; smooth texture, silkiness; silk, satin, velvet, velour; fleeciness, down, swansdown 327 *softness*; smooth hair, sleekness; smooth surface, baby's bottom; millpond; mahogany, marble, glass, ice; dance floor, ice rink; flatness, levelness, lawn, plumb wicket, bowling green, billiard table 216 *hori-*

*zontality*; tarmac, asphalt, flags 226 *paving*; levigation, polish, wax, varnish, gloss, glaze, shine, finish; slidderiness, slipperiness, slipway, slide, chute; lubricity, oiliness, greasiness 334 *lubrication*; smooth water, dead w., calm, dead c. 266 *quiescence*.

*smoother*, roller, garden r., road r., steamroller; bulldozer; rolling pin 216 *flattener*; iron, electric i., smoothing-i., flatiron, tailor's goose; mangle, wringer; press, hot p., trouser p.; plane, spokeshave, draw knife 256 *sharp edge*; rake, harrow; card, comb, brush, hairbrush; sandpaper, glasspaper, emery paper, emery board; file, nail f.; burnisher, turpentine and beeswax; polish, French p., varnish, enamel 226 *facing*; lubricator, grease, oil, grease gun, oilcan 334 *lubricant*.

**Adj.** *smooth*, nonfrictional, frictionless, nonadhesive, streamlined; without lumps 16 *uniform*; slithery, slippery, sliddery, skiddy; lubricious, oily, greasy, buttery, soapy; greased, oiled 334 *lubricated*; polished, shiny, gleaming, varnished, waxed, enamelled, lacquered, glazed; soft, suave, bland, soothing 177 *lenitive*; smooth-textured, silky, silken, satiny, velvety; peachlike, downy, woolly 259 *fleecy*; marble, glassy; bald, glabrous, clean-shaven 229 *hairless*; sleek, slick, brushed, well-brushed, unruffled; combed, carded, raked, harrowed; unwrinkled, uncrumpled; plane, rolled, even, unbroken, level, flush 216 *flat*; glassy, quiet, calm, c. as a millpond 266 *still*; rounded, waterworn 248 *curved*; edgeless, blunt 257 *unsharpened*; smooth-skinned; smooth-haired; smooth as marble, smooth as glass, smooth as ice, smooth as a baby's bottom, smooth as velvet, satin-smooth; slippery as an eel.

**Vb.** *smooth*, remove friction, streamline; oil, grease, butter 334 *lubricate*; smoothen, plane, planish, even, level; rake, comb; file, rub down 333 *rub*; roll, calender, press, hot-p., uncrease, iron 216 *flatten*; mow, shave, cut 204 *shorten*; smooth over, smooth down, smarm d., slick d., plaster d.; iron out 62 *unravel*; starch, launder 648 *clean*; shine, burnish 417 *make bright*; levigate, buff, polish, glaze, wax, varnish 226 *coat*; pave, tarmac 226 *overlay*.

*go smoothly*, glide, float, roll, bowl along, run on rails; slip, slide, skid 265 *be in motion*; skate, ski; feel no friction, coast, freewheel.

## 259 Roughness

**N.** *roughness*, asperity, harshness; salebrosity, broken ground; rough water, choppiness 350 *wave*; rough air, turbulence 352 *wind*; shattered surface, brokenness, jaggedness, broken glass, barbed wire, razor w. 256 *sharp edge*; serration, saw edge, deckle e., scalloped e. 260 *notch*; rug_

gedness, cragginess; sierra 209 *high land*; rough going, dirt road, dirt track, sheeptrack; unevenness, joltiness, bumpiness 17 *nonuniformity*; kink, corrugation, rugosity, ripple, ripple mark, corrugated iron 261 *fold*; rut 262 *furrow*; coarseness, coarse grain, knobbliness, nodosity 253 *convexity*; rough surface, washboard, grater, file, sandpaper, glasspaper, emery paper, emery board; rough texture, sackcloth, tweed, homespun 222 *textile*; creeping flesh, gooseflesh, goose pimples, horripilation; rough skin, chap, hack, crack; hispidity, scabrousness, bristliness, shagginess; hairiness, villosity; undergrowth, overgrowth 366 *wood*; stubble, five o'clock shadow, burr, bristle, scrubbing brush, nailbrush, awn 256 *prickle*.

*hair* 208 *filament*; head of h., shock of h., matted h., thatch, fuzz, wool; crop, mop, mane, fleece, shag; bristle, stubble, five o'clock shadow; locks, flowing 1.; crowning glory, tresses, curls, ringlet, tight curl; kiss curl; strand, plait, braid; pigtail, ponytail, bunches, rat's tails; topknot, forelock, elflock, lovelock, scalplock, dreadlocks; fringe, bangs, cowlick, quiff, widow's peak; roll, French pleat, bun, chignon 843 *hairdressing*; false hair, hairpiece, hair extension, switch, wig, toupee 228 *headgear*; thin hair, wisp; beard, full b., beaver, goatee, imperial, Van Dyke, Abe Lincoln; whiskers, face fungus, sideboards, sideburns, mutton-chops, dundrearies; moustache, moustachio, toothbrush, handlebars; facial hair; eyebrows, eyelashes, cilia; woolliness, fleeciness, downiness, fluffiness, flocculence; down, pubes, pubic hair, pubescence, pappus, wool, fur 226 *skin*; tuft, flock, floccule; mohair, cashmere, Angora 208 *fibre*, pile, nap; velvet, velour, plush 327 *softness*; floss, fluff, fuzz, thistledown 323 *lightness*; horsehair 227 *lining*.

*plumage*, pinion 271 *wing*; plumosity, feathering; quill, rachis, barb, web; feathers, coverts, wing c.; neck feathers, hackle f., hackle; ruff, frill, plume, panache, crest; peacock's feathers, ostrich f., osprey f. 844 *finery*.

**Adj.** *rough*, unsmooth, irregular, uneven, broken; rippling, choppy, stormtossed; stony, rocky, rutty, rutted, pitted, potholed, trampled, poached; bumpy, jolting, bonebreaking; chunky, crisp, roughcast; lumpy, stony, nodular, nodose, knobby, studded, roughened, frosted; muricate, nubbly, slubbed, bouclé; crinkled 251 *undulatory*; knotted, gnarled, knurled, cross-grained, coarse-g., coarse; cracked, hacked, chapped 845 *blemished*; lined, wrinkled, corrugated, ridged 262 *furrowed*; rough-edged, deckle-e. 260 *notched*; craggy, cragged, jagged; horripilant, creeping; scabrous, scabby, pockmarked, acned, warty, scaly, blistered, blebby; ruffled, unkempt, unpolished; unbolted, unsifted.

*hairy*, pilose, villous, crinite; napped, brushed; woolly, fleecy, furry; hirsute, shaggy, shagged, tufty, matted, shockheaded; hispid, bristly, bristling 256 *sharp*; setose, setaceous; wispy, straggly, filamentous, plumate, fimbriated, ciliated, fringed, befringed; bewhiskered, bearded, moustached; unshaven, unshorn; unplucked; curly, frizzy, fuzzy, permed, tight-curled, woolly.

*downy*, pubescent, tomentose, pappose; peachy, velvety, mossy 258 *smooth*; fluffy, feathery, plumose, feathered, fledged.

*fleecy*, woolly, fluffy, flocculent; lanate, lanuginose.

**Vb.** *be rough*, – hairy etc. adj.; bristle, bristle up 254 *jut*; creep (of flesh), horripilate; scratch, catch; jolt, bump, jerk 278 *move slowly*.

*roughen*, roughcast, rough-hew; mill, crenate, serrate, indent, engrail 260 *notch*; stud, boss; crisp, corrugate, wrinkle, ripple, kink, popple 251 *crinkle*; disorder, ruffle, tousle, tangle 63 *derange*; rumple, crumple, crease 261 *fold*; rub up the wrong way, set on edge; chap, crack, hack.

**Adv.** *on edge*, against the grain, against the nap; in the rough.

## 260 Notch

**N.** *notch*, serration, serrulation, saw edge, ragged e. 256 *sharpness*; indentation, deckle edge; machicolation, crenellation 713 *fortification*; nick, snip, cut, gash, kerf; crenation, crenulation; crenature 201 *gap*; indent, dent, dint, dimple 255 *concavity*; picot edge, Vandyke e., scollop, scallop, dogtooth 844 *pattern*; sprocket, cog, ratchet, cogwheel, ratchet w.; saw, hacksaw, chain saw, circular saw 256 *tooth*; battlement, embrasure, crenel.

**Adj.** *notched*, indented, scalloped, jagged, jaggy, barbed 256 *sharp*; crenate, crenulate, crenellated; toothed, saw-t., dentate, denticulated; serrated, palmate, emarginate; finely serrated, serrulate; serratodentate.

**Vb.** *notch*, serrate, tooth, cog; nick, blaze, score, scratch, scotch, scarify, bite, slice 46 *cut*; crenellate, machicolate; indent, scallop, Vandyke; jag, pink, slash; dent, mill, knurl 259 *roughen*; pinch, snip, crimp 261 *fold*.

## 261 Fold

**N.** *fold*, plication, flexure, flection, doubling; facing, revers, hem; lapel, cuff, turnup, dog's ear; plait, braid, ply, pleat, box p., accordion p., knife-edge p.; tuck, gather, pucker, ruche, ruffle; flounce, frill; crumple, crush, rumple, crease; wrinkle, ruck; frown, lines, wrinkles, age zones, crow's feet 131 *age*; crinkle, kink, crankle; joint, elbow 247 *angularity*; syncline, anticline.

**Adj.** *folded*, doubled; gathered etc. vb.; plicate, pleated; creasy, wrinkly, puckery; dog-eared; creased, crumpled, crushed 63 *disarranged*; turn-down, turn-over.

**Vb.** *fold*, double, turn over, bend over, roll; crease, pleat; corrugate, furrow, wrinkle 262 *groove*; rumple, crumple 63 *derange*; curl, kink, frizzle, frizz 251 *crinkle*; pucker, purse; ruffle, cockle up, gather, frill, ruck, shirr, smock; tuck, tuck up, kilt; hem, cuff; turn up, turn down, turn under, double down; enfold, enwrap, wrap, swathe 235 *enclose*; fold up, roll up, furl, reef.

## 262 Furrow

**N.** *furrow*, groove, sulcus, chase, slot, slit, rabbet, mortise; crack, split, chink, cranny 201 *gap*; trough, hollow 255 *cavity*; glyph, triglyph; flute, fluting, goffering, rifling; chamfer, bezel, incision, gash, slash, scratch, score 46 *scission*; streak, striation 437 *stripe*; wake, wheel-mark, rut 548 *trace*; gutter, runnel, ditch, dike, trench, qanat, dugout, moat, fosse, channel 351 *conduit*; ravine 255 *valley*; furrowed surface, wrinkle, sulcation, corrugation; corduroy, corrugated iron, washboard, ploughed field; ripple, cats-paw 350 *wave*.

**Adj.** *furrowed*, ploughed etc. vb.; fluted, rifled, goffered; striated, sulcate, bisulcate; canalled, canaliculated; gullied, channelled, rutty; wrinkled, lined 261 *folded*; rippling, wavy 350 *flowing*.

**Vb.** *groove*, slot, flute, chamfer, rifle; chase; gash, scratch, score, incise 46 *cut*; claw, tear 655 *wound*; striate, streak 437 *variegate*; grave, carve, enchase, bite in, etch, cross-hatch 555 *engrave*; furrow, plough, channel, rut, wrinkle, line; corrugate, goffer 261 *fold*.

## 263 Opening

**N.** *opening*, throwing open, flinging wide; unstopping, uncorking, uncapping 229 *uncovering*; pandiculation, stretching oneself 197 *expansion*; yawn, yawning, oscitation; dehiscence, bursting open, splitting; hiation, gaping; hiatus, lacuna, space, interval, gat 201 *gap*; aperture, split, crack, leak 46 *disunion*; hole, potato (inf); hollow 255 *cavity*; placket 194 *pocket*.

*perforation*, piercing, tattooing, body-piercing etc. vb. 843 *beautification*; impalement, puncture, acupuncture, venipuncture; trepanation, trephining; boring, borehole, bore, calibre; pinhole, eyelet.

*porosity*, porousness, sponge; sieve, sifter,

riddle, screen 62 *sorting*; strainer, tea s., colander; grater; holeyness, honeycomb, pincushion.

*orifice*, blind o., aperture, slot; oral cavity, mouth, gob, trap, kisser, mush, moosh, jaws, muzzle; throat, gullet 194 *maw*; sucker; vagina, anus; mouthpiece, flue pipe 353 *air pipe*; nozzle, spout, vent, vent-hole, vomitory 298 *outlet*; blower, blowhole, air-hole, spiracle; nasal cavity, nostril, nosehole; inlet, outlet; rivermouth, embouchure; small orifice, ostiole; foramen, pore; breathing pores, stomata; hole, crater, pothole 255 *cavity*; manhole, armhole, keyhole, buttonhole, punch hole, pin h.; pigeonhole 194 *compartment*; eye, eye of a needle, eyelet; deadeye, grummet, ring 250 *loop*.

*window*, fenestration; shop window, plate-glass w., glass front; embrasure, loophole 713 *fortification*; lattice, grille; fenestella, oeil de boeuf; casement window, leaded w., sash w., bay w., oriel w., dormer w., French w., picture w.; rose window, lancet w. 990 *church interior*; light, lightwell, fanlight, skylight, sunshine roof; companion, cabin window, port, porthole; peephole, keyhole; hagioscope, squint; car window, windscreen, windshield; window frame, casement, sash, mullion, transom; window pane 422 *transparency*.

*doorway*, archway; doorstep, threshold 68 *entrance*; approach, drive, drive-in, entry 297 *way in*; exit, way out; passage, corridor, gangway, drawbridge 624 *access*; gate, gateway, city gates; portal, porch, propylaeum; door, front d., Dutch d.; swing doors, revolving d., double d.; church d., lychgate; back door, tradesmen's d., postern 238 *rear*; small door, wicket; cat-flap; scuttle, hatch, hatchway; trapdoor, companionway; stairwell; door jamb, gatepost, lintel; concierge 264 *doorkeeper*, entryphone.

*open space* 183 *space*; yard, court 185 *place*; opening, clearing, glade; panorama, vista 438 *view*; rolling downs, landscape, open country 348 *plain*; alley, aisle, gangway, thoroughfare, carriageway 305 *passage*; estuary 345 *gulf*.

*tunnel*, boring; subway, underpass, underground railway, underground, tube, metro; Channel Tunnel, chunnel; mine, shaft, pit, gallery, adit 255 *excavation*; cave 255 *cavity*; bolthole, rabbit hole, fox h., mouse h. 192 *dwelling*; funnel 252 *cone*; sewer 351 *drain*; qanat.

*tube*, pipe, duct 351 *conduit*; efflux tube, adjutage; tubule, pipette, cannula; catheter, tubing, piping, pipeline, hose; artery, vein, capillary; colon, gut 224 *insides*; funnel, fistula.

*chimney*, factory c., chimneypot, chimney stack, smokestack, funnel; smokeduct, flue; volcano, fumarole, smokehole 383 *furnace*.

*opener*, key, master k., skeleton k., passepartout; doorknob, handle; corkscrew, tin opener, can o., bottle o.; aperient, purgative; password, open sesame; passport, safe conduct; pass, ticket 756 *permit*.

*perforator*, piercer, borer, corer; gimlet, wimble, corkscrew; auger, drill, pneumatic d., road d., dentist's d.; burr, bit, spike b., brace and b.; reamer; trepan, trephine; probe, lancet, lance, stylet, trocar; bodkin, needle, hypodermic n.; awl, bradawl 256 *sharp point*; pin, nail 47 *fastening*; skewer, spit, broach, stiletto 723 *weapon*; punch, card p., puncheon, stapler; dibble; digging stick; pickaxe, pick, ice p.

**Adj.** *open*, patent, exposed to view, on view 522 *manifest*; unclosed, unstopped, uncapped, uncorked, unshut, ajar; unbolted, unlocked, unbarred, unobstructed, admitting 289 *accessible*; open-plan; wide-open, agape, gaping, dehiscent; yawning, oscitant; open-mouthed, gaping, slack-jawed; opening, aperient; blooming, in bloom, out.

*perforated*, pierced etc. vb.; perforate, drilled, bored; honeycombed, riddled; peppered, shot through; cribriform, foraminous; holey, full of holes; windowed, fenestrated, fenestrate.

*porous*, permeable, pervious, spongy, percolating, leachy, leaky, leaking.

*tubular*, tubulous, tubulated, cannular, piped; cylindrical 252 *round*; funnel-shaped, infundibular; fistulous; vascular, capillary.

**Vb.** *open*, declare open, give the open sesame, give a passport to, unclose, unfold, unwrap, unpack, unpackage, undo, ope; unlock, unlatch, unbolt, open the door, fling wide the gates 299 *admit*; pull out (a drawer); uncover, bare 229 *doff*; unplug, unstop, uncap, uncork; unrip, unseam 46 *disunite*; lay open, throw o. 522 *show*; kick open, force open, steam o. 176 *force*; cut open, rip o., tear o., crack o.; enlarge a hole, ream; dehisce, fly open, split, gape, yawn; burst, explode; crack at the seams, start, leak; space out 201 *space*; open out, fan o., deploy 75 *be dispersed*; separate, part, hold apart; unclench, open one's hand; bloom, be out.

*pierce*, transpierce, transfix, impale; gore, run through, stick, pink, lance, bayonet, spear 655 *wound*; spike, skewer, spit; prick, puncture; tattoo, body-pierce; probe, stab, poke; inject; perforate, hole, riddle, pepper, honeycomb; nail, drive, hammer in 279 *strike*; knock holes in, punch, punch full of holes; hull (a ship), scuttle, stave in; tap, drain 304 *extract*; bore, drill, wimble; trephine, trepan; burrow, tunnel, mine 255 *make concave*; cut through, penetrate 297 *enter*.

**Adv.** *openly*, patently, frankly, unguardedly, without pretence *or* subterfuge; on the rooftops; out, out in the open.

## 264 Closure

**N.** *closure*, closing, closing down, shutting etc. vb.; door in one's face; occlusion, stoppage; contraction, strangulation 198 *compression*; sealing off, ring of steel, blockade 232 *circumscription*; encirclement 235 *enclosure*; embolism, obstruction, obturation; infarction, constipation, obstipation, strangury; dead end, cul-de-sac, impasse, blank wall, roadblock, rolling r. 702 *obstacle*; blind gut, caecum; imperforation, imperviousness, impermeability.

*stopper*, stopple, cork, plug, bung, peg, spill, spigot; ramrod, rammer, piston; valve, slide v.; wedge, wad, dossil, pledget, tampon; wadding, padding, stuffing, stopping 227 *lining*; dummy, gag, muzzle 748 *fetter*; shutter 421 *screen*; tight bandage, tourniquet 198 *compressor*; damper, choke, cut-out; ventpeg, tap, faucet, stopcock, bibcock; top, lid, cap, cover, seal 226 *covering*; lock, Yale (tdmk) lock, mortise l., deadlock, key, bolt, latch, bar 47 *fastening*; door, gate 263 *doorway*; cordon 235 *fence*.

*doorkeeper*, doorman, gatekeeper, porter, janitor, ostiary; commissionaire, concierge; sentry, sentinel, night watchman 660 *protector*; warden, guard, guard dog, vigilante, 749 *keeper*; jailer, prison warder, turnkey, Cerberus, Argus 749 *gaoler*.

**Adj.** *closed*, unopened, unopenable; shut etc. vb.; shuttered, bolted, barred, locked; stoppered, corked, obturated; unpierced, imperforate, unholed; nonporous, impervious, impermeable 324 *dense*; impenetrable, impassable, unpassable 470 *impracticable*; pathless, untrodden 883 *secluded*; dead-end, blank; clogged up, stuffed up, bunged up; strangulated 198 *contracted*; drawn tight, drawn together 45 *joined*.

*sealed off*, sealed, hermetically s., vacuum-packed, shrink-wrapped; cloistered, claustral; close, unventilated, airless, stuffy, muggy, fuggy, fusty 653 *insalubrious*; staunch, tight, airtight, watertight, proof, waterproof, dampproof, gasproof, airproof, soundproof, mouseproof 660 *invulnerable*.

**Vb.** *close*, shut, occlude, seal; clinch, fix, bind, make tight 45 *tighten*; put the lid on, cap 226 *cover*; batten down the hatches, make all tight; clap to, slam, bang (a door); lock, fasten, snap, snap to; plug, caulk, bung up, cork, stopper, obturate; button, zip up, do up 45 *join*; knit, furrow, draw the ends together; clench (fist); block, dam, staunch, choke, throttle, strangle, smother, asphyxiate 702 *obstruct*; blockade 712 *besiege*; enclose, surround, shut in, seal off 232 *circumscribe*; trap, bolt, latch, bar, lock in 747 *imprison*; shut down, clamp d., batten d., ram d., tamp d., cram d.; draw the curtains, put up the shutters; close down, go out of business, flop, go bust, fail.

SECTION FOUR

# Motion

## 265 Motion: successive change of place

**N.** *motion*, change of position 143 *change*; movement, going, move, march; speed rate, speed, acceleration, air speed, ground s.; pace, tempo; locomotion, motility, mobility, movableness; kinetic energy, motive power, motivity; forward motion, advance, progress, headway 285 *progression*; backward motion 286 *regression*, 290 *recession*; motion towards 289 *approach*, 293 *convergence*; motion away, shift 294 *divergence*, 282 *deviation*; motion into 297 *ingress*; motion out of 298 *egress*; upward motion, rising 308 *ascent*; downward motion, sinking, plummeting 309 *descent*, 313 *plunge*; motion round, circumnavigation 314 *circuition*; axial motion 315 *rotation*, 316 *evolution*; to and fro movement, fluctuation 317 *oscillation*; irregular motion 318 *agitation*; stir, bustle, unrest, restlessness 678 *activity*; rapid motion 277 *velocity*; slow motion 278 *slowness*; regular motion 16 *uniformity*, 71 *continuity*; recurring movement, cycle, rhythm 141 *periodicity*; motion in front 283 *preceding*; motion after 284 *following*, 619 *pursuit*; conduction, conductivity 272 *transference*; current, flow, flux, drift 350 *stream*; course, career, run; traffic, traffic movement, flow of traffic 305 *passing along*; transit 305 *passage*; transportation 272 *transport*; running, jogging, walking, foot-slogging, marathoning 267 *walking*; riding 267 *equitation*; travel 267 *land travel*, 269 *water travel*, 271 *air travel*; dancing, tangoing, gliding, sliding, skating, rolling, skipping; manoeuvre, manoeuvring, footwork; bodily movement, exercise, aerobics, step, gymnastics 162 *athletics*; gesticulation 547 *gesture*; cinematography, motion picture, film 445 *cinema*; laws of motion, kinematics, kinetics, dynamics; kinesiatrics 658 *therapy*.

*gait*, rolling g.; walk, port, carriage 688 *conduct*; tread, tramp, footfall, stamp; pace, step, stride; run, lope, jog, jog trot, dog t.; dance step, hop, skip, jump 312 *leap*; skid, slide, slip;

waddle, shuffle; undulation, swagger, proud step, stalk, strut, goosestep 875 *formality*; march, slow m., quick m., double; trot, piaffer, amble, canter, gallop, hand-g. 267 *equitation*.

**Adj.** *moving*, rolling etc. vb.; in motion, under way; motive, motory, motor; motile, movable, mobile; progressive, regressive; locomotive, automotive; transitional, shifting 305 *passing*; mercurial 152 *changeful*; unquiet, restless 678 *active*; nomadic 267 *travelling*; drifting, erratic, meandering, runaway 282 *deviating*; kinematic, kinematical; kinetic; cinematographic.

**Vb.** *be in motion*, move, go, hie, gang, wend, trail; gather way 269 *navigate*; budge, stir; stir in the wind, flutter, wave, flap 217 *hang*; march, tramp 267 *walk*; place one's feet, tread; trip, dance 312 *leap*; shuffle, waddle 278 *move slowly*; toddle, patter; run, jog 277 *move fast*; run on wheels, roll, taxi; stream, roll on, drift 350 *flow*; paddle 269 *row*; skitter, slide, slither, skate, ski, sledge, toboggan, glide, roller-skate, roller-blade 258 *go smoothly*; fly, volitate, frisk, flit, flitter, dart, hover; climb 308 *ascend*; sink, plunge, plummet 309 *descend*; coast, cruise, steam, chug, keep going, proceed 146 *go on*; make one's way, pick one's w., fight one's w., push one's w., elbow one's w., shoulder one's w. 285 *progress*; pass through, wade t., pass by 305 *pass*; make a move, shift, dodge, duck, shift about, jink, jouk, tack, manoeuvre 282 *deviate*; twist 251 *wriggle*; creep, crawl, worm one's way, go on all fours; hover about, hang a. 136 *wait*; move house, flit, change one's address, shift one's quarters, relocate; change places 151 *interchange*; move over, make room 190 *go away*; travel, stray 267 *wander*.

*move*, impart motion, put in m.; render movable, set going, power; put on wheels, put skates under; put a bomb under, galvanize, actuate, switch on, put into operation 173 *operate*; stir, stir up, jerk, pluck, twitch 318 *agitate*; budge, shift, manhandle, trundle, roll, wheel 188 *displace*; push, shove 279 *impel*; move on, drive, hustle 680 *hasten*; tug, pull 288 *draw*; fling, throw 287 *propel*; convey, transport 272 *transfer*; dispatch 272 *send*; mobilize 74 *bring together*; scatter 75 *disperse*; raise, uplift 310 *elevate*; throw down, drop 311 *let fall*; motion, gesture 547 *gesticulate*; transpose 151 *interchange*.

**Adv.** *on the move*, under way, on one's w., on the go, on the hop, on the run; in transit; on the march, on the tramp, on the wing.

## 266 Quiescence

**N.** *quiescence*, motionlessness; dying down, running down, subsidence 145 *cessation*; rest, stillness; deathliness, deadness; stagnation, stagnancy 679 *inactivity*; pause, truce, standstill 145 *lull*; stand, stoppage, halt, gridlock; fix, deadlock, lock; full stop, dead s. 145 *stop*; embargo, freeze 757 *prohibition*; immobility, fixity, rigidity, stiffness 326 *hardness*; steadiness, equilibrium 153 *stability*; numbness, trance, faint 375 *insensibility*.

*quietude*, quiet, quietness, stillness, hush 399 *silence*; tranquillity, peacefulness, no disturbance 717 *peace*; rest 683 *repose*; eternal rest 361 *death*; sleepiness, slumber 679 *sleep*; calm, dead c., flat c., millpond 258 *smoothness*; windlessness, not a breath of air; dead quiet, not a mouse stirring; armchair travel, staying at home; placidity, composure, cool 823 *inexcitability*; passivity, quietism; quietist 717 *pacifist*; tranquillizer, sedation 177 *moderator*.

*resting place*, bivouac 192 *quarters*, roof 192 *home*, inn; shelter, safe house, haven 662 *refuge*; place of rest, pillow 218 *bed*; journey's end 295 *goal*; last rest, grave 364 *tomb*.

**Adj.** *quiescent*, quiet, still; asleep 679 *sleepy*; resting, at rest, becalmed; at anchor, anchored, moored, docked; at a stand, at a standstill, stopped, idle 679 *inactive*; unemployed, disemployed, out of commission, inoperative 674 *unused*; dormant, unaroused, dying 361 *dead*; standing, stagnant, vegetating, unprogressive, static, stationary 175 *inert*; sitting, sedentary, chair-borne; on one's back 216 *supine*; disabled, housebound, confined to bed 747 *restrained*; settled, stay-at-home, home-loving, domesticated 828 *content*; untravelled, unadventurous 858 *cautious*; unmoved 860 *indifferent*.

*tranquil*, undisturbed, sequestered 883 *secluded*; peaceful, restful; unhurried, easygoing 681 *leisurely*; uneventful, without incident 16 *uniform*; calm, like a millpond, windless, airless; unbroken, glassy 258 *smooth*; sunny, halcyon 730 *palmy*; at ease, easeful, comfortable, relaxed 683 *reposeful*; tranquillized, sedated, under sedation; cool, unruffled, unwrinkled, unworried, serene 823 *inexcitable*.

*still*, unmoving, unstirring, unbudging; not fizzy, flat 387 *tasteless*; immobile, motionless, gestureless; expressionless, deadpan, pokerfaced 820 *impassive*; steady, unwinking, unblinking 153 *unchangeable*; standing still, rooted, rooted to the ground or spot 153 *fixed*; transfixed, spellbound; immovable, unable to move, becalmed, stuck; stiff, frozen 326 *rigid*; benumbed, numb, petrified, paralysed 375 *insensible*; quiet, so quiet you could hear a pin drop, hushed, soundless 399 *silent*; stock-still, stone-still, still as a statue, still as a post, still as death; quiet as a mouse.

**Vb.** *be quiescent*, – still etc. adj.; subside, die down 37 *decrease*; pipe down 399 *be silent*; stand still, lie s., keep quiet; stagnate, vegetate 175 *be inert*; stand, mark time 136 *wait*; stay put, sit tight, stand pat, remain in situ, not stir, not budge, remain, abide 144 *stay*; stand to, lie to, ride at anchor; tarry 145 *pause*; rest, sit down, take breath, take a breather, rest on one's laurels, rest on one's oars, rest and be thankful 683 *repose*; retire, go to bed, doss down, turn in 679 *sleep*; settle, settle down 187 *place oneself*; stay at home, not go out 883 *be unsociable*; ground, stick fast; catch, jam, lodge; stand fast, stand firm; not move a muscle, not stir a step, not stir an inch; be at a standstill 145 *cease*.

*come to rest*, stop, hold, stop short, stop in one's tracks, stop dead in one's tracks, freeze 145 *halt*; pull up, draw up; slow down 278 *decelerate*; anchor, cast a., alight 295 *land*; relax, calm down, cool it, rest, pause 683 *repose*.

*bring to rest*, quiet, make q., quieten, quell, hush 399 *silence*; lull, soothe, calm down, tranquillize, sedate 177 *assuage*; lull to sleep, cradle, rock; let alone, let well alone, let sleeping dogs lie 620 *avoid*; bring to a standstill, bring to, lay to, heave to; brake, put the brake on 278 *retard*; stay, immobilize 679 *make inactive*.

**Adv.** *at a stand*, at a halt; in repose, far from the madding crowd.

**Int.** stop!, stay!, halt!, whoa!, hold!, hold hard!, hold on!, hold it!, don't move!, freeze!

## 267 Land travel

**N.** *land travel*, travel, travelling, wayfaring; seeing the world, globe-trotting, country-hopping, tourism; walking, hiking, riding, driving, motoring, cycling, biking; journey, voyage, peregrination, odyssey; course, passage, sweep; pilgrimage, hajj; quest, expedition, safari, trek, field trip; reconnaissance, exploration, orienteering, youth hostelling, backpacking; visit, trip, business t., pleasure t., tour, grand t., coach t.; package t.; circuit, turn, round, patrol, commuting; round trip, day t. 314 *circuition*; jaunt, hop, spin; ride, bike r., joy r., drive, lift, free l.; excursion, outing, airing; ramble, constitutional, promenade. (See also *walking*.)

*wandering*, wanderlust, nomadism; vagrancy, vagabondage, vagabondism; no fixed address, no fixed abode; roving, rambling, walkabout, waltzing Matilda; tramping, traipsing, flitting, gadding, gallivanting; itchy feet, the travel

bug; migration, völkerwanderung, emigration 298 *egress*; immigration 297 *ingress*; transmigration 305 *passage*.

*walking*, going on foot, footing it, Shanks's pony, pedestrianism; foot-slogging, stumping, striding, tramping, marching, backpacking; ambulation, perambulation; circumambulation, walkabout 314 *circuition*; walk, promenade, constitutional; stroll, saunter, amble, ramble; hike, tramp, march, walking tour; run, cross-country run, jog, trot, jog t., lope 265 *gait*; paddle, paddling, wading; foot race, racewalking, heel-and-toe w.; marathon 716 *racing*; stalking, stalk 619 *chase*; prowling, loitering; sleepwalking, noctambulation, noctambulism, somnambulism.

*marching*, campaigning, campaign; manoeuvres, marching and counter-marching, advance, retreat; march, forced m., route m., quick march, slow m.; march past, parade, cavalcade, procession 875 *formality*; column, file, cortege, train, caravan.

*equitation*, equestrianism, horsemanship *or* horsewomanship, manège, dressage 694 *skill*; show jumping, eventing, gymkhana, steeplechasing, point-to-point racing 716 *contest*; horse racing; riding, bareback r. 162 *athletics*; haute école, caracol, piaffer, curvet 265 *gait*.

*conveyance*, lift, elevator, escalator, paternoster, travelator 274 *conveyor*; feet, own two f. 214 *foot*; legs, Shanks's pony; horseback, mount 273 *horse*; ambulance, bicycle, bus, car, coach, microscooter, moped, scooter, taxi, train 274 *vehicle*; traffic, wheeled t., motor t., road t. 305 *passing along*.

*leg*, limb, foreleg, hindleg; shank, shin, calf; thigh, ham, hamstrings; knee, kneecap 247 *angularity*; tibia, fibula, legs, pegs, pins 218 *prop*; stumps, stilts; stump, wooden leg, artificial l., prosthesis 150 *substitute*; bow legs, bandy l., knock-knees 845 *blemish*; thick legs, piano l., legs like tree stumps; long legs, spindle shanks.

*itinerary*, route 624 *way*; march, course 281 *direction*; route map, road m., plan, chart 551 *map*; guide, Baedeker, timetable, Bradshaw, A–Z 524 *guidebook*; milestone, fingerpost 547 *signpost*; halt, stop, stopover, terminus 145 *stopping place*.

**Adj.** *travelling*, journeying, itinerant, vagrant, wayfaring, on the road; travel-stained, dusty 649 *dirty*; travelled, much t.; touring, globe-trotting, country-hopping, rubbernecking; migratory, passing through, transient, transit, stopping over, visiting 305 *passing*; nomadic, nomad, floating, unsettled, restless; of no fixed address *or* abode, homeless, rootless, déraciné(e) 59 *extraneous*; footloose, errant, roving, roaming, rambling, hiking, wandering 282 *deviating*; ambulant, strolling, peripatetic; tramping, vagabond; walking, pedestrian, ambulatory, perambulatory; marching, foot-slogging; gadding, flitting, traipsing, gallivanting; automotive, locomotive, self-moving, self-driven 265 *moving*, noctivagant, somnambulant, sleepwalking.

*legged*, bow-l., bandy-l., knock-kneed 845 *blemished*; thighed, strong-t., heavy-t.; well-calved, well-hocked; long-legged, leggy 209 *tall*; spindly, spindle-shanked 206 *lean*; pianolegged, thick-ankled 205 *thick*.

**Vb.** *travel*, fare, journey, peregrinate; tour, see the world, go globe-trotting, go on a world cruise, visit, explore 484 *discover*; get around, knock about, go places, sightsee, rubberneck; pilgrimage, go on a pilgrimage; go on a trip, make a journey, go on a j.; go on safari, trek, hump bluey; hike, backpack; be always on the move, live out of a suitcase; set out, fare forth, take wing 296 *depart*; migrate, emigrate, immigrate, settle 187 *place oneself*; shuttle, commute; take oneself off, swan off, slope o.; go to, hie to, repair to, resort to, betake oneself to 295 *arrive*, 882 *visit*; go 265 *be in motion*; wend, wend one's way, stir one's stumps, bend one's steps, shape one's course, tread a path, follow the road; make one's way, pick one's way, thread one's w., elbow one's w., force a w., plough through; jog on, trudge on, shuffle on, pad on, plod on, tramp on, march on, chug on 146 *sustain*; course, race, post 277 *move fast*; proceed, advance 285 *progress*; coast, freewheel, glide, slide, skate, ski, skim, roll along, bowl a., fly a. 258 *go smoothly*.

*traverse*, cross, range, pass through, range t. 305 *pass*; go round, beat the bounds 314 *circle*; go the rounds, make one's rounds, patrol; scout, reconnoitre 438 *scan*; scour, sweep, sweep through 297 *burst in*.

*wander*, nomadize, migrate; rove, roam, bum around; ramble, amble, stroll, saunter, mosey along, potter, dawdle, walk about, trail around; gad, traipse, gallivant, gad about, hover, flit about, dart a. 265 *be in motion*; prowl, skulk 523 *lurk*; straggle, trail 75 *be dispersed*; lose the way, wander away 282 *stray*.

*walk*, step, tread, pace, stride; stride out 277 *move fast*; strut, stalk, prance, mince 871 *be proud*; tread lightly, tiptoe, trip, skip, dance, curvet 312 *leap*; tread heavily, lumber, clump, stamp, tramp, goosestep; toddle, patter, pad; totter, stagger, lurch, reel, stumble 317 *oscillate*; limp, hobble, waddle, shuffle, shamble, dawdle 278 *move slowly*; paddle, wade; go on foot, go by Shanks's pony, foot it, hoof it, hike, footslog, wear out shoe leather; plod, stump,

trudge, jog; go, go for a walk, ambulate, perambulate, circumambulate, pace up and down; go for a run *or* a jog, take the air, take one's constitutional; march, quick march, slow march, troop; file, file past, defile, march in procession 65 *come after*; walk behind 284 *follow*; walk in front 283 *precede*.

*ride*, mount, take horse, hack; trot, amble, tittup, canter, gallop; prance, caper, curvet, piaff, caracol, passage; cycle, bicycle, bike, motorcycle; freewheel, coast; drive, motor; go by bike, go by car, go by bus, bus it, go by coach, go by taxi, go by cab; go by road, go by tube, go by train; go by air 271 *fly*; take a lift, take a ride, cadge a lift, thumb a l., hitchhike.

**Adv.** *on foot*, on the beat; on hoof, on horseback, on Shanks's pony *or* mare; en route 272 *in transit*; by road, by rail, awheel.

**Int.** be off!, buzz off!, come along!, get along!, get going!, get out!, git!, go away!, hop it!, move along there!, move it!, scram!, skedaddle!

## 268 Traveller

**N.** *traveller*, itinerant, itinerant teacher, itinerant preacher, flying bishop; wayfarer, viator, peregrinator; explorer, adventurer, voyager 270 *mariner*; air traveller, spaceman *or* -woman, astronaut, astrotourist, space tourist 271 *aeronaut*; pioneer, pathfinder, explorer 66 *precursor*; alpinist, mountaineer, cragsman 308 *climber*; pilgrim, palmer, hajji; walker, hiker, rambler, trekker; backpacker, camper, caravanner, youth hosteller; tourist, country-hopper, globe-trotter, rubberneck, sightseer 441 *spectator*; tripper, day-t., excursionist; sunseeker, holidaymaker, visitor; health tourist; roundsman, hawker 794 *pedlar*; travelling salesman, commercial traveller, rep 793 *seller*; messenger, errandboy 529 *courier*; daily traveller, commuter, straphanger; Odysseus, Ulysses, Gulliver, Marco Polo.

*wanderer*, migrant, bird of passage, visitant 365 *bird*; floating population, nomad, bedouin; gypsy, didicoi, Romany, Bohemian, New Age traveller, zigane; rover, ranger, rambler, promenader, stroller; strolling player, wandering minstrel, touring company 594 *entertainer*; rolling stone, drifter, vagrant, vagabond, tramp, knight of the road, bag lady, bag people, swagman, sundowner, hobo, bum, bummer; loafer, beachcomber 679 *idler*; emigrant, émigré, refugee, asylum-seeker, deportee, exile 59 *foreigner*; runaway, fugitive, escapee 620 *avoider*; déraciné(e), homeless wanderer 883 *solitary*; waif, stray, destitute, street beggar, the homeless, rough sleeper 188 *displaced person*, 192 *homeless person*, 801 *poor person*; the Wandering Jew, the Flying Dutchman.

*pedestrian*, foot passenger, walker, tramper; jogger, sprinter, runner 716 *contender*; toddler; wader, paddler; skater, skier; skateboarder, roller-skater; hiker, hitch-h., foot-slogger; marcher 722 *infantry*; somnambulist, sleep-walker; prowler, loiterer; footpad 789 *robber*.

*rider*, horse-rider, camel-r., cameleer; elephant-rider, mahout; horseman, horsewoman, equestrian, equestrienne; postilion, postboy 529 *courier*; mounted police, Mounties; cavalier, knight, knight errant 722 *cavalry*; hunt, huntsman 619 *hunter*; jockey, jockette, steeplechaser, show jumper, eventer 716 *contender*; trainer, breaker 369 *breeder*; roughrider, bareback r., broncobuster, cowboy, cowgirl, cowpuncher, gaucho, rodeo rider; cyclist, bicyclist, pedal-pusher, rough-stuffer; circus rider, trick rider 162 *athlete*; motorcyclist, moped rider, scooterist; back-seat driver, passenger, pillion p.

*driver*, drover, teamster, muleteer; charioteer, coachman, whip, Jehu; carter, waggoner, drayman; car driver, chauffeur, motorist, roadhog 277 *speeder*; joy rider; L-driver 538 *beginner*; taxi driver, cab d., cabby; bus driver, coach d.; lorry d., truck d., van d., trucker, routier, teamster; tractor d.; bad driver, white van man; motorman, train driver, engine d.; stoker, footplateman, fireman; guard, conductor, ticket collector; pilot 271 *aeronaut*.

## 269 Water travel

**N.** *water travel*, ocean t., sea t., river t., canal t., inland navigation; seafaring, nautical life, life on the ocean wave; navigation, voyaging, sailing, cruising; coasting, longshore sailing; boating, yachting, rowing (see also *aquatics*); voyage, navigation, cruise, sail; course, run, passage, crossing, ferry c.; circumnavigation 314 *circuition*; marine exploration, submarine e. 484 *discovery*; sea adventures, naval exploits; sea trip, river t., breath of sea air 685 *refreshment*; way, headway, steerage way, sternway, seaway 265 *motion*; leeway, driftway 282 *deviation*; wake, track, wash, backwash 350 *eddy*; sea-path, ocean track, steamer route, sea lane, approaches 624 *route*; boat, sailing ship 275 *ship*; sailor 270 *mariner*.

*navigation*, piloting, steering, pilotage 689 *directorship*; astronavigation, celestial navigation; plane sailing, plain s., spherical s., great-circle s., parallel s.; compass reading, dead reckoning 465 *measurement*; pilotship, helmsmanship, seamanship 694 *skill*; nautical experience, weather eye, sea legs; naval exercises, naval manoeuvres, fleet operations, naval tactics 688 *tactics*.

*aquatics*, boating, sailing, yachting, cruising; rowing, sculling, canoeing; yacht racing, speedboat r., ocean r. 716 *racing*; water skiing, surf riding, skiboarding, wakeboarding, surfing, body-surfing, wind s., boardsailing; rafting, white-water r., jet-skiing, hydrospeeding, canyoning, watersports 837 *sport*; natation, swimming, floating; stroke, breast s., side s., back s., crawl, back c., front c., trudgen, butterfly, dogpaddle; diving, plunging 313 *plunge*; wading, paddling; swimsuit 228 *beachwear*.

*sailing aid*, navigational instrument, sextant, quadrant 247 *angular measure*; chronometer, ship's c. 117 *timekeeper*; log, line; lead, plummet 211 *depth*; anchor 662 *safeguard*; compass, astrocompass, magnetic c., ship's c.; needle, magnetic n.; card, compass c. *or* rose; binnacle; gyrocompass 689 *directorship*; radar 484 *detector*; helm, wheel, tiller, rudder, steering oar; sea mark, buoy, lighthouse, pharos, lightship 547 *signpost*; chart, Admiralty c., portolano 551 *map*; nautical almanac, ephemeris 524 *guidebook*.

*propeller*, screw, twin screw, blade, rotor 287 *propellant*; paddle wheel, stern w., floatboard; oar, sweep, paddle, scull; pole, punt p., barge p.; fin, flipper, fish's tail 53 *limb*; sails, canvas 275 *sail*.

**Adj.** *seafaring*, sea, salty, deep-sea, longshore; sailorlike, sailorly 270 *seamanlike*; nautical, naval 275 *marine*; navigational, navigating, sailing, steaming, plying, coasting, ferrying; sea-going, ocean-g.; at sea, on the high seas, afloat, waterborne, seaborne, on board; pitching, tossing, rolling, wallowing, yawing; seasick, green; seaworthy, tight, snug; navigable, deep.

*swimming*, natatory, floating, sailing; launched, afloat, buoyant; natatorial, aquatic, like a fish; amphibian.

**Vb.** *go to sea*, follow the s., join the navy; become a sailor, get one's sea legs; be in sail, sail before the mast; live on board, live afloat; go sailing, boat, yacht, cruise; launch, launch a ship, christen a s. 68 *auspicate*.

*voyage*, sail, go by sea, go by ship, go by boat, take the ferry, take the sea route; take ship, book one's berth, book a passage, work one's p.; embark, go on board, put to sea, set sail, up anchor 296 *start out*; cross the ocean, cross the channel 267 *traverse*; disembark, land 295 *arrive*; cruise, visit ports; navigate, steam, ply, run, tramp, ferry; coast, hug the shore; roll, pitch, toss, buffet the waves, tumble, wallow 317 *oscillate*.

*navigate*, man a ship, work a s., crew; put to sea, set sail; launch, push off, boom off; unmoor, cast off, weigh anchor; raise steam, get up s.; hoist sail, spread canvas; get under way, gather w., make w., carry sail 265 *be in motion*; drop the pilot; set a course, make for, head for 281 *steer for*; read the chart, go by the card 281 *orientate*; pilot, steer, hold the helm, captain 689 *direct*; stroke, cox, coxswain; trim the sails, square, square away; change course, veer, gybe, yaw 282 *deviate*; put about, wear ship 282 *turn round*; run before the wind, scud 277 *move fast*; put the helm up, fall to leeward, pay off; put the helm down, luff, bring into the wind; beat to windward, tack, weather; back and fill; round, double a point, circumnavigate 314 *circle*; be caught amidships 700 *be in difficulty*; careen, list, heel over 220 *be oblique*; turn turtle, capsize, overturn 221 *invert*; ride out the storm, weather the s., keep afloat 667 *escape*; run for port 662 *seek refuge*; lie to, lay to, heave to 266 *bring to rest*; take soundings, heave the lead 465 *measure*; tide over 507 *await*; tow, haul, warp, kedge, club-haul 288 *draw*; ground, run aground, wreck, be cast away 165 *destroy*; sight land, make a landfall, take on a pilot 289 *approach*; make port; cast anchor, drop a.; moor, tie up, dock, disembark 295 *land*; cross one's bows, take the wind out of one's sails, outmanoeuvre, gain the weather gauge 702 *obstruct*; foul 279 *collide*; back, go astern 286 *regress*; surface, break water 298 *emerge*; flood the tanks, dive 313 *plunge*; shoot, shoot a bridge, shoot the rapids 305 *pass*.

*row*, ply the oar, get the sweeps out; pull, stroke, scull; feather; catch a crab; ship oars; punt; paddle, canoe; boat; shoot the rapids.

*swim*, float, sail, ride, ride on an even keel; scud, skim, skitter; surf-ride, surf, water-ski, aquaplane; strike out, breast the current, stem the stream; tread water; dive 313 *plunge*; bathe, dip, duck; wade, paddle, splash about, get wet 341 *be wet*.

**Adv.** *under way*, under sail, under canvas, under steam; before the mast; on deck, on the bridge, on the quarterdeck; at the helm, at the wheel.

**Int.** ship ahoy!, avast!, belay there!, all aboard!, man overboard!, yo-heave-ho!, hard aport!, hard astarboard!, steady as she goes!, land ahoy!

## 270 Mariner

**N.** *mariner*, sailor, sailorman, seaman, seafarer, seafaring man; salt, old s., sea-dog, shellback; tar, Jack Tar, limey, matelot; no sailor, bad s., fairweather s., landlubber 697 *bungler*; skipper,

master mariner, master, ship m.; mate, boatswain, bosun; coxswain; able seaman, A.B. 696 *expert*; deckhand, swabbie; ship's steward, cabin boy 742 *servant*; shipmates, hearties; crew, complement, ship's c., men, watch 686 *personnel*; trawler, whaler, deep-sea fisherman; sea rover, privateer, buccaneer, sea king, Viking, pirate 789 *robber*; sea scout, sea cadet; argonaut, Jason; Ancient Mariner, Flying Dutchman, Captain Ahab, Sinbad the Sailor; Neptune, Poseidon 343 *sea god*.

*navigator*, pilot, sailing master, helmsman, steersman, wheelman, man at the wheel, quartermaster; coxswain, cox 690 *leader*; leadsman, lookout man; foretopman, reefer; boatswain, bosun's mate; circumnavigator 314 *circler*; compass, binnacle, gyrocompass 269 *sailing aid*.

*nautical personnel*, marine, submariner, naval cadet, bluejacket, rating 722 *naval person*; petty officer, midshipman, middy, lieutenant, sub-l., commander, captain, commodore, admiral 741 *naval officer*; Admiralty, Sea Lord; Trinity House, lighthouse keeper, coastguard 660 *protector*; lifeboatman 703 *aider*; river police, naval patrol, harbour p., harbourmaster.

*boatman*, waterman, rowing man, wet bob; gigsman; galley slave; oar, oarsman, sculler, rower, punter; paddler, canoeist; yachtsman *or* -woman; gondolier, ferryman, Charon; wherryman, bargeman, bargee, lighterman; stevedore, docker, longshoreman; lock keeper.

**Adj.** *seamanlike*, sailorly, like a sailor 694 *expert*; nautical, naval 275 *marine*.

## 271 Aeronautics

**N.** *aeronautics*, aeromechanics, aerodynamics, aerostatics; aerostation, ballooning; aerospace, astronautics; aeroballistics, rocketry 276 *rocket*; volitation, flight, vertical f., horizontal f.; subsonic f., supersonic f. 277 *velocity*; stratospheric flight, hypersonic f., space f.; aviation, flying, night f., blind f., instrument f.; shoran, teleran; microlighting, gliding, powered g., hang-g.; parachuting, skydiving, free fall; flypast, formation flying, stunt f., aerobatics 875 *ostentation*; skywriting, vapour trail; planing, volplaning, looping the loop; spin, roll, sideslip; volplane, nose dive, pull-out; crash dive, crash, prang 309 *descent*; pancake, landing, belly l., crash l., forced l.; talkdown, touchdown 295 *arrival*; takeoff, vertical t. 296 *departure*.

*air travel*, air transport, airlift 272 *transport*; air service, airline; shuttle service, scheduled flight, charter f.; air miles; airlane, airway, air route 624 *route*; flight path, glide p., line of flight 281 *direction*; airspace 184 *territory*;

takeoff, touchdown, landing, three-point l.; landing field, flying f., airbase; airstrip, runway, tarmac, airfield, aerodrome, airport, heliport, helipad; terminal, air t., check-in desk, luggage carousel, baggage reclaim, airside, landside 295 *goal*; hangar 192 *shed*; fear of flying, aerophobia; jetlag.

*space travel*, space flight, manned s.f., spacefaring 276 *spaceship*; lift-off, blast-off; orbit, flyby; docking, space walk; reentry, splashdown, soft landing; cosmodrome, spaceport, space station, space platform, space shuttle; launching pad, silo; spacesuit.

*aeronaut*, aerostat, balloonist; glider, hang g., sky diver, parachutist; paratrooper 722 *soldier*; aviator, aviatrix, airwoman, airman, birdman; astronaut, cosmonaut, spaceman, spacewoman, space traveller; air traveller, air passenger, jet set 268 *traveller*; air hostess, steward, stewardess, cabin personnel 742 *servant*; flier, pilot, test p., jet p., copilot; automatic pilot, autopilot; navigator, air crew; pilot officer, flying o. 741 *air officer*; aircraftman 722 *airforce*; air personnel, ground crew 686 *personnel*; Icarus, Daedalus, Mercury; Pegasus.

*wing*, pinion, feathers, flight f., wing feather, wing spread 259 *plumage*; sweptback wing, deltawing, swingwing, variable w.; aerofoil, aileron, flaps.

**Adj.** *flying*, on the wing; volitant, volant; fluttering, flitting, hovering 265 *moving*; winged, alar, pinnate, feathered; aerial 340 *airy*; airworthy, airborne; air-to-air; soaring, climbing 308 *ascending*; in-flight; airsick; losing height 309 *descending*; grounded 311 *lowered*; aeronautical, aerospace 276 *aviational*; aerodynamic, aerostatic; aerobatic; fly-drive.

**Vb.** *fly*, wing, take the w., be on the w.; wing one's way, take one's flight, be wafted, cross the sky, overfly; soar, rise 308 *ascend*; hover, hang over 217 *hang*; flutter, flit 265 *be in motion*; taxi, take off, clear, leave the ground, climb, circle 296 *depart*; be airborne, have lift-off; aviate, glide, plane 258 *go smoothly*; float, drift, drift like thistledown 323 *be light*; hit an air pocket, experience turbulence, stunt, spin, roll, side-slip, loop the loop, volplane; hedgehop, skim the rooftops, buzz 200 *be near*; stall, dive, power-dive, nose-d., spiral 313 *plunge*; crash, prang, force land, crash-land, pancake, ditch 309 *tumble*; pull out, flatten o.; touch down 295 *land*; bale out, jump, parachute, eject; blast off, lift o., take o.; orbit, go into o. 314 *circle*.

**Adv.** *in flight*, on the wing, in the air, on the beam, in orbit.

## 272 Transference

**N.** *transference*, change of place, translocation, relocation, transplantation, transhipment, transfer, bussing, commuting, shuttling; shifting, shift, drift, longshore d., continental d. 282 *deviation*; posting 751 *mandate*; transposition, metathesis 151 *interchange*; removal, moving house, flitting, remotion, relegation, deportation, expulsion 300 *ejection*; unpacking, unloading, airdrop 188 *displacement*; exportation, export 791 *trade*; trade-off, mutual transfer 791 *barter*; importation, import 299 *reception*; distribution, logistics 633 *provision*; transmittal, forwarding, sending, remittance, dispatch; recalling, recall, extradition 304 *extraction*; recovery, retrieval 771 *acquisition*; handing over, delivery; takeover 792 *purchase*; conveyance, transfer of property, donation 780 *transfer*; committal, trust 751 *commission*; gaol delivery, habeas corpus, release 746 *liberation*; transition, metastasis; passing over, ferry, ferriage 305 *passage*; transmigration 143 *transformation*; transmission, throughput; conduction, convection; transfusion; decantation; diffusion, dispersal 75 *dispersion*; communication, contact 378 *touch*; contagion, infection, contamination 178 *influence*; transcription, transumption, copying, transliteration 520 *translation*.

*transport*, transportation; conveyance, carriage, shipping, shipment; carrying, humping, portage, porterage, haulage, draught 288 *traction*; carting, cartage, waggonage, drayage, freightage, air freight, airlift; means of transport, rail, road 274 *vehicle*; sea, canal 275 *ship*; pipeline, conveyor belt 274 *conveyor*.

*thing transferred*, flotsam, jetsam, driftwood, drift, sea-d.; alluvium, detritus, scree, moraine, sediment, deposit; pledge, hostage, trust 767 *security*; legacy, bequest 781 *gift*; lease 777 *property*; cargo, load, payload, freight; black ivory 742 *slave*; consignment, shipment 193 *contents*; goods, mails; luggage, baggage, impedimenta; container, container-load, lorryload, trainload, coachload, busload; person transferred, passenger, rider, commuter 268 *traveller*.

*transferrer*, testator, conveyancer 781 *giver*; sender, remitter, dispatcher, dispatch clerk, consignor, addresser; shipper, shipping agent, transporter; exporter, importer 794 *merchant*; haulier, removal man, conveyor, ferryman 273 *carrier*; post office, post 531 *postal communications*; communicator, transmitter, diffuser; vector, carrier (of a disease) 651 *sick person*.

*astral projection*, astral travel, out-of-body t., out-of-body experience, OBE, near-death experience, NDE.

**Adj.** *transferable*, negotiable; transportable, movable, portable; roadworthy, airworthy, seaworthy; portative, transmissive, conductive; transmissible, communicable; contagious 653 *infectious*.

**Vb.** *transfer*, hand over, deliver 780 *assign*; devise, leave 780 *bequeath*; commit, entrust 751 *commission*; transmit, hand down, hand on, pass on; make over, turn over, hand to, pass to; transfer responsibility to, delegate, pass the buck; export, transport, convey, ship, airlift, fly, ferry 273 *carry*; infect, contaminate 178 *influence*; conduct, convect; carry over 38 *add*; transfer itself to, come off on, adhere, stick 48 *cohere*.

*transpose*, change round, shift, move, tranship 188 *displace*; transfer, relocate, switch, shunt, shuffle, castle (chess) 151 *interchange*; detach, detail, draft; relegate, deport, expel, sack 300 *eject*; drag, pull 288 *draw*; push, shove 279 *impel*; containerize 193 *load*; channel, funnel, pour in *or* out, transfuse, decant, strain off, siphon off 300 *empty*; unload, remove 188 *displace*; download, upload; shovel, ladle, spoon out, bail out, excavate 255 *make concave*; transliterate 520 *translate*.

*send*, have conveyed, remit, transmit, dispatch; direct, consign, address; post, mail; redirect, readdress, post on, forward; send by hand, deliver in person, send by post; send for, order, mail-order, tele-order 627 *require*; send away, detach, detail; send flying 287 *propel*.

**Adv.** *in transit*, en route, on the way; in the post; in the pipeline; by hand; from hand to hand, from pillar to post.

## 273 Carrier

**N.** *carrier*, common c., haulier, carter, waggoner, tranter; shipper, transporter, exporter, importer 272 *transferrer*; ferryman 270 *boatman*; lorry driver, truck d., van d., bus d. 268 *driver*; delivery boy; delivery van, lorry, truck, juggernaut, cart, goods train 274 *vehicle*; barge, cargo vessel, freighter, tramp 275 *ship*; chassis, undercarriage 218 *prop*; pallet, container; carrier bag, plastic b. 194 *bag*; conveyor belt, escalator 274 *conveyor*.

*bearer*, litter b., stretcher b.; caddy, golf c.; shieldbearer, cupbearer 742 *retainer*; porter, baggage handler, coolie, bummaree, stevedore; letter carrier, carrier pigeon, postman *or* -woman, special messenger, King's *or* Queen's m. 529 *courier*.

*beast of burden*, packhorse, pack-mule, pack train, sumpter-horse, sumpter-mule; ass, she-a., donkey, moke, Neddy, cuddy, burro; ox, oxen, bullock, draught animals 365 *cattle*;

sledge dog, husky; camel, dromedary, ship of the desert; elephant 365 *mammal*.

*horse*, equine species, quadruped, horseflesh; dobbin, gee-gee; nag, Rosinante; mount, steed, trusty s.; stallion, gelding, mare, colt, filly, foal; stud horse, brood mare, stud, stable; carthorse; circus horse, liberty h.; roan, strawberry r., grey, dapple g., bay, chestnut, sorrel, black, piebald, skewbald, pinto, dun, palomino; winged horse, Pegasus; legendary horse, Al Borak, Bayard, Black Bess; Houyhnhnm.

*thoroughbred*, purebred, blood-horse, bloodstock; Arab, Barbary horse, Barb; pacer, stepper, high-s., trotter; courser, racehorse, racer, goer, stayer; sprinter 277 *speeder*; steeplechaser, hurdler, fencer, jumper, hunter, foxhunter; Morgan, Tennessee walker, Hanoverian, Lipizzaner.

*draught horse*, carthorse, dray h.; shaft-horse, trace-h.; carriage-horse, coach-h., post-h.; plough-horse, shire-h., Clydesdale, punch, Suffolk P., Percheron, pit pony.

*warhorse*, cavalry h., remount; charger, destrier, courser, steed 722 *cavalry*; Bucephalus, Copenhagen, Marengo.

*saddle horse*, riding h., cow pony; cow-cutting horse, stock h.; mount, hack, roadster; jade, screw, nag; pad, pad-nag, ambler; mustang, bronco; palfrey, jennet.

*pony*, cob, galloway, garron, sheltie; Shetland pony, fell p., Welsh p., Dartmoor p., Exmoor p., New Forest p.

**Adj.** *bearing*, carrier, shouldering, burdened, freighted, loaded, overloaded, overburdened; pick-a-back.

*equine*, horsy, horse-faced; neighing; roan, grey etc. n.; asinine; mulish.

**Vb.** *carry*, bear 218 *support*; hump, humf, lug, heave, tote; caddy; stoop one's back to, shoulder, bear on one's back, carry on one's shoulders; fetch, bring, reach; fetch and carry; transport, cart, truck, rail, railroad; ship, waft, raft; lift, fly 272 *transfer*; carry through, carry over, pass o., carry across, traject, ferry; convey, conduct, convoy, escort 89 *accompany*; have a rider, be ridden, be mounted; be saddled with, be lumbered with, be burdened w.; be loaded with, be fraught 54 *be complete*.

## 274 Vehicle

**N.** *vehicle*, conveyance, public c.; public service vehicle, transport, public t.; vehicular traffic, motorized t., road t., wheeled t.; pedal power, horse p.; sedan chair, palanquin; litter, horse l.; brancard, stretcher, hurdle, crate; ambulance, bloodwagon, fire engine; Black Maria, paddy wagon; tumbril, hearse; snowplough, snowmobile, weasel; breakdown van, recovery vehicle; tractor, caterpillar t., tracked vehicle, bulldozer, JCB (tdmk); amphibian, moon buggy, space vehicle; all-terrain vehicle, ATV; rollercoaster, switchback, dodgem car; time machine.

*sled*, sledge, sleigh, dogsleigh, horse s., deer s., kibitzka, carriole; bobsleigh, bobsled, toboggan, luge, coaster, ice yacht; sand y., surfboard, sailboard; skateboard, skate, ice s., roller s., Roller Blade (tdmk), blade (inf); snowshoes, skis, snowboard, runner, skids, skibob.

*bicycle*, cycle, pedal c., bike, push b.; wheel, gridiron, crate; velocipede, hobby-horse, boneshaker, penny-farthing, Ordinary, Safety, sit-up-and-beg; folding bicycle, sports model, racer, tourist, roadster, mountain bicycle; ladies' bicycle, man's b.; five-speed, ten-s.; BMX (tdmk), Chopper (tdmk); stabilized bicycle; small-wheeler; tandem, randem; monocycle, unicycle, tricycle, fairy cycle, trike, quadricycle; motorized bicycle, moped; scooter, motor s., motorcycle, motorbike, trail bike, scrambler, quad bike, quad; motorcycle combination, sidecar; invalid carriage; cycle-rickshaw, trishaw.

*pushcart*, perambulator, pram, baby buggy, buggy, pushchair, stroller; bath chair, wheelchair, invalid c.; rickshaw; barrow, wheelbarrow, hand b., coster b.; handcart, go-cart; trolley, truck, float; shopping trolley.

*cart*, ox-c., bullock-c., horse-and-cart; dray, milk float; farm cart, haywain, hay waggon; wain, waggon, covered w., prairie schooner; caravan, mobile home, trailer, horse-box, loose-b.; dustcart, watercart. (See also *lorry*.)

*carriage*, horse-drawn c., equipage, turnout, rig; chariot, coach, state c., coach and four; barouche, landau, landaulet, berlin, victoria, brougham, phaeton, clarence; surrey, buckboard, buggy, wagonette; travelling carriage, chaise, shay, calèche, calash, britzka, droshky, troika; racing chariot, quadriga; four-in-hand, drag, brake, charabanc; two-wheeler, cabriolet, curricle, tilbury, whisky, jaunting car; trap, gig, ponycart, dogcart, governess cart; carriole, sulky; shandrydan, rattletrap.

*war chariot*, scythed c.; gun carriage, caisson, limber, ammunition waggon; tank, armoured car 722 *cavalry*; jeep, staff car.

*stagecoach*, stage, mail coach; diligence, post chaise, omnibus. (See also *bus*.)

*cab*, hackney carriage, horsecab, four-wheeler, growler, hansom, fly; fiacre, droshky; gharry, tonga; taxicab, taxi, minicab; rickshaw, jinricksha, pedicab, cycle-rickshaw.

*bus*, horsebus, motorbus, omnibus, double-decker, single-d.; articulated bus, bendibus; autobus, trolleybus, motor coach, coach, postbus, minibus, midibus; airbus; battle bus.

*tram*, horse t., tramcar, trolley, streetcar, cablecar.

*car*, horseless carriage, car, motor car, motor, automobile, auto; limousine, limo, gas guzzler (sl); saloon, two-door s., four-d. s.; tourer, roadster, runabout, buggy; hard-top, soft-t., convertible; coupé, sports car; racing car, stock c., dragster, hot-rod; go-kart *or* go-cart, kart; fastback, hatchback, estate car, station waggon, shooting brake; Land Rover (tdmk), jeep; police car, patrol c., panda c.; veteran car, vintage car, model T; tin Lizzie, banger, bus, jalopy, old crock, rattle-trap; beetle, bubble car, minicar; invalid car, three-wheeler; minibus, camper, Dormobile (tdmk); cannibalized car, Frankencar; automatic, gear-lever car; zero-emission vehicle; concept car; car theft, auto-theft, carjacking, twoc (sl), joy-riding, hotting (sl); car-surfing; drive-by crime, drive-by shooting; hit-and-run acccident.

*lorry*, truck, pickup t., dump t.; refuse lorry, dustcart; container lorry, articulated l., roadliner, juggernaut; tanker, bowser; car transporter, low-loader; van, delivery v., removal v., pantechnicon; breakdown van; electric van, float.

*train*, railway t., passenger t., special t., excursion t., boat t., motorail; express train, through t., intercity t., high-speed t., HST, advanced passenger train, APT, bullet train; slow train, stopping t.; goods train, freight t., freightliner; milk train, mail t., night mail; rolling stock, multiple unit; coach, carriage, compartment, first-class c., second-class c., smoker, nonsmoker; Pullman, wagon-lit, sleeping car, sleeper; restaurant car, dining c., buffet c., observation c.; guard's van, luggage v., brake v., caboose; truck, waggon, tank w., hopper w., trolley; bogie; steam train, diesel t., electric t., tube t., model t.; live rail, third r., overhead wires, pantograph; cable railway, electric r., underground r. 624 *railway*; Flying Scotsman, Golden Arrow, Orient Express, Le Shuttle, Eurostar.

*locomotive*, iron horse; diesel engine, diesel, steam engine, pony e., tank e., shunter, cab, tender; choo-choo, puff-puff, puffer, chuffer, Puffing Billy, Rocket; traction engine, steam roller; Thomas the Tank Engine.

*conveyor*; conveyor belt, escalator, moving staircase, moving pavement, moving walkway, travelator; shovel, hod 194 *ladle*; fork, trowel 370 *farm tool*; crane 310 *lifter*.

**Adj.** *vehicular*, wheeled, on wheels; on rails, on runners, on sleds, on skates; horse-drawn, pedal-driven, motorized, electrified;

automobile, automotive, locomotive; non-stop, high-speed, express, through; stopping, local.

## 275 Ship

**N.** *ship*, vessel, boat, craft, watercraft; bark, barque, barquentine; great ship, tall s.; little ship, cockleshell; bottom, keel; sail; hooker, tub, hull; hulk, prisonship; Argo, Golden Hind, Noah's Ark; steamer, screw s., steamship, steamboat, motor vessel; paddle steamer, paddleboat, stern-wheeler, riverboat, show-boat; passenger ship, liner, luxury l., cruise ship, ocean greyhound, floating palace; channel steamer, ferry; hovercraft, hydrofoil; rotor ship; mail-boat, packet, steam p.; dredger, hopper, icebreaker; transport, hospital ship; storeship, tender, escort vessel; pilot vessel; tug, launch; lightship, weather ship; underwater craft, submarine, U-boat 722 *warship*; aircraft carrier.

*galley*, war g., galleass, galliot; pirate ship, privateer, corsair; Viking ship, longship; bireme, trireme, quadrireme, quinquereme.

*merchant ship*, merchantman, trader; cog, galleon, argosy, dromond, carrack, polacre; caravel, galliot, Indiaman; banana boat, tea clipper; slave ship, slaver; cargo boat, freighter, tramp; coaster, chasse-marée; fly-boat, bilander, lugger, hoy; collier, tanker, oil t., supertanker; containership.

*fishing boat*, inshore f. b.; fishing smack, dogger, hooker, buss, coble; drifter, trawler, purse-seiner; factory ship; whaler, whale-catcher.

*sailing ship*, sailing boat, sailboat, sailer; windjammer, clipper, tall ship; square-rigged ship (see also *rig*); four-masted ship, three-masted s., threemaster; barque, barquentine; two-masted ship, brig, hermaphrodite b., brigantine, schooner, pinnace; frigate, corvette 722 *warship*; cutter, sloop, ketch, yawl; wherry; yacht, racing y.; sailing dinghy, catamaran, smack; xebec, felucca, caique, dhow, junk, sampan; theft of ship, yachtjacking.

*rig*, square rig, fore-and-aft rig, lateen r., schooner r., sloop r., cutter r., Bermuda r., gaff r.

*sail*, sailcloth, canvas; square sail, lug-sail, lug, lateen sail, fore-and-aft s., leg-of-mutton s., spanker; course, mainsail, foresail, topsail, topgallant sail, royal, skysail; jib, staysail, spinnaker, balloon sail, studding s.; rigging 47 *tackling*; mast, foremast, mainmast, mizzenmast 218 *prop*.

*boat*, skiff, foldboat, cockboat; lifeboat; ship's boat, tender, dinghy, pram; long-boat, jolly boat, whaleboat, dory; pinnace,

cutter, gig; bumboat, surf boat; barge, lighter, pontoon; ferry, ferryboat, canalboat, narrow-boat; houseboat; towboat, tugboat, tug; sailing boat, sailboat, sailing dinghy, yacht, catamaran; powerboat, motorboat, motor launch; pleasure-boat, cabin cruiser; speedboat.

*rowing boat*, galley; eight, racing e.; sculler, shell, randan; skiff, dinghy, rubber dinghy; coracle, currach; punt, gondola; canoe, outrigger, dugout; pirogue, proa, kayak, umiak.

*raft*, liferaft, balsa, catamaran, trimaran; float, pontoon.

*shipping*, craft, forest of masts; argosy, fleet, armada, flotilla, squadron 722 *navy*; marine, mercantile marine, merchant navy, shipping line; flag of convenience 547 *flag*.

**Adj.** *marine*, maritime, naval, nautical, sea-going, ocean-g. 269 *seafaring*; sea-worthy, water-w., weatherly; snug, tight, shipshape, shipshape and Bristol fashion; rigged, square-r. (see also *rig*); clinker-built, carvel-b.; flush-decked.

**Adv.** *afloat*, aboard, on board ship, on ship-board; under sail, under steam, under canvas; on the high seas, at sea.

## 276 Aircraft

**N.** *aircraft* 271 *aeronautics*; aerodyne, flying machine; aeroplane, airplane, crate; plane, monoplane, biplane, triplane; amphibian; hydroplane, seaplane, flying boat, floatplane; airliner, airbus, transport, freighter; warplane, fighter, bomber 722 *air force*; stratocruiser, jet plane, jet, jumbo j., jump j., supersonic j., tur-bojet, turboprop, turbofan, propfan; VTOL, STOL, HOTOL; microlight; helicopter, auto-gyro, whirlybird, chopper, copter; ornithopter; hovercraft 275 *ship*; glider, sailplane; flying instruments, controls, flight recorder, black box, autopilot, automatic pilot, joystick, rudder; aerofoil, fin, tail; flaps, aileron 271 *wing*; prop 269 *propeller*; cockpit, flight deck; undercarriage, landing gear; safety belt, life jacket, parachute, ejection seat 300 *ejector*; test bed, wind tunnel; flight simulator; aerodrome, airport 271 *air travel*.

*airship*, aerostat, balloon, Montgolfier b., hot-air b.; captive balloon, barrage b., observation b., weather b., blimp; dirigible, Zeppelin; kite, box-k.; parachute, chute; hang glider; magic carpet; balloon-basket, nacelle, car, gondola.

*rocket*, rocketry; step rocket, multistage r.; booster; nose cone, warhead; guided missile, intercontinental ballistic m., ICBM, Exocet (tdmk), nuclear missile, Cruise m. 723 *missile weapon*; V2; anti-missile defence system, Star

Wars, Strategic Defence Initiative, SDI, Son of Star Wars.

*spaceship*, spacecraft, space probe, space shot, space capsule, space shuttle, spaceplane, aerospaceplane; space lab; lunar module, command m.; space tug, orbital manoeuvring vehicle; space platform, space station, sputnik 321 *satellite*; flying saucer, UFO, unidentified flying object.

*squadron*, flight, group, wing; airborne division.

**Adj.** *aviational*, aeronautical, aerospace; aerodynamic, aerostatic; astronautical, space-travelling; airworthy 271 *flying*; heavier-than-air, lighter-than-air; supersonic; vertical take-off.

## 277 Velocity

**N.** *velocity*, celerity, rapidity, speed, swiftness, fleetness, quickness, liveliness, alacrity, agility; instantaneousness, speed of thought 116 *instantaneousness*; no loss of time, promptness, expedition, dispatch; speed, tempo, rate, pace, bat 265 *motion*; speed-rate, miles per hour, mph, knots; mach number; speed of light, speed of sound, supersonic speed; great speed, lightning s.; maximum speed, express s., full s., full steam; utmost speed, press of sail, full s.; precipitation, hurry, flurry 680 *haste*; reckless speed, breakneck s. 857 *rashness*; streak, blue s., streak of lightning, flash, lightning f.; flight, jet f., supersonic f.; gale, hurricane, tempest, torrent; electricity, telegraph, lightning, greased l.; speed measurement, tachometer, speedometer 465 *gauge*; wind gauge 340 *pneumatics*; log, logline; speed trap, radar t. 542 *trap*.

*spurt*, acceleration, speed-up, overtaking; burst, burst of speed, burst of energy; thrust, drive, impetus 279 *impulse*; jump, spring, bound, pounce 312 *leap*; whizz, swoop, swoosh, vroom, zip, zing, zap, uprush, zoom; down rush, dive, power d.; flying start, rush, dash, scamper, run, sprint, gallop, tantivy.

*speeding*, driving, hard d., scorching, racing, burn-up; bowling along, rattling a., batting a.; course, race, career, full c.; full speed, full lick; pace, smart p., rattling p., spanking rate, fair clip; quick march, double, forced march 680 *haste*; clean pair of heels, quick retreat 667 *escape*; race course, speed track 716 *racing*.

*speeder*, hustler, speed merchant, speed maniac, scorcher, racing driver 268 *driver*; runner, harrier; racer, sprinter; galloper; courser, racehorse 273 *thoroughbred*; greyhound, cheetah, hare, deer, doe, gazelle, antelope; ostrich, eagle, swallow; arrow, arrow from the bow, bullet, cannonball 287 *missile*;

jet, rocket; speedboat, clipper 275 *ship*; express, express train; express messenger, Ariel, Mercury 529 *courier*; magic carpet, seven-league boots.

**Adj.** *speedy*, swift, fast, quick, rapid, nimble, volant; darting, dashing, lively, brisk, smart, snappy, nifty, zippy 174 *vigorous*; wasting no time, expeditious, fast-track, hustling 680 *hasty*; double-quick, rapid-fire; prompt 135 *early*; immediate 116 *instantaneous*; high-geared, high-speed, adapted for speed, streamlined, souped-up, go-go; speeding, racing, ton-up; running, charging, runaway; flying, whizzing, hurtling, pelting; whirling, tempestuous; breakneck, headlong, precipitate 857 *rash*; fleet, fleet of foot, wing-footed, light-f., nimble-f.; quick-f.; darting, starting, flashing; swift-moving, agile, nimble, slippery, evasive; mercurial, like quicksilver 152 *changeful*; winged, eagle-w., like a bird; arrowy, like an arrow; like a shot; like a flash, like greased lightning, like the wind, quick as lightning, quick as thought, quick as a flash, quick as the wind, like a bat out of hell; meteoric, electric, telegraphic, transonic, supersonic, hypersonic, jet-propelled.

**Vb.** *move fast*, move, shift, travel, speed; drive, pelt, streak, flash, shoot; scorch, burn up the miles, scour the plain, tear up the road; scud, careen; skim, nip, cut; bowl along 258 *go smoothly*; sweep along, tear a., rattle a., thunder a., storm a.; tear, rip, vroom, zip, zing, zap, rush, dash; fly, wing, whizz, skirr; hurtle, zoom, dive; dash off, tear o., dart o., dash on, dash forward; plunge, lunge, swoop; run, trot, double, lope, spank, gallop; bolt, cut and run, hotfoot it, leg it, scoot, skedaddle, scamper, scurry, skelter, scuttle; show a clean pair of heels, be unable to be seen for dust 620 *run away*; hare, run like a h., run like the wind, run like mad, run like the clappers; start, dart, dartle, flit; frisk, whisk; spring, bound, leap, jump, pounce; ride hard, put one's best foot forward, stir one's stumps, get cracking, get a move on, get one's finger out; hie, hurry, post, haste 680 *hasten*; chase, charge, stampede, career, go full tilt, go full pelt, go full lick, go full bat, go full steam, go all out; break the speed limit, break the sound barrier.

*accelerate*, speed up, raise the tempo; gather momentum, impart m., gather speed, spurt, sprint, put on speed, pick up s., whip up s., step on it, step on the gas, put one's foot down, open the throttle, open up, let it rip; crowd on sail; quicken one's speed, mend one's pace, get a move on; put on one's running shoes, set off at a run, get off to a flying start; make up time, make up for lost time, make forced marches; quicken, step up, give one his head, drive, spur, urge forward, urge on; clap spurs to, lend wings to, put dynamite under, put a bomb under, hustle, expedite 680 *hasten*.

*outstrip*, overtake, overhaul, catch up, catch up with; lap, outpace, outrun, outmarch, outsail, outwalk, outdrive 306 *outdo*; gain on, distance, outdistance, leave behind, leave standing, leave at the starting post; lose, shake off; make the running, have the legs of, romp home, win the race, outclass 34 *be superior*.

**Adv.** *swiftly*, rapidly etc. adj.; trippingly, apace; posthaste, with speed, at express s., at full s., at full tilt; in full career, in full gallop, with whip and spur, all out, flat out, ventre à terre; helter-skelter, headlong, lickety-split, hell for leather; presto, pronto, smartish, p.d.q.; like greased lightning, like a shot, like the clappers, in a flash, before you could say Jack Robinson 116 *instantaneously*; in full sail, under press of sail *or* canvas, under full steam, full speed ahead; on eagle's wings, with giant strides; nineteen to the dozen, hand over fist; at a rate of knots, at the double, in double-quick time, as fast as one's legs would carry one; in high gear, at the top of one's speed, for all one is worth; by leaps and bounds, in geometrical progression, like wildfire.

**278 Slowness**
**N.** *slowness*, slackness, languor 679 *sluggishness*; inertia 175 *inertness*; refusal to be hurried, festina lente, deliberation 823 *inexcitability*; tentativeness, gradualism, Fabianism, Fabian tactics; hesitation 858 *caution*; reluctance 598 *unwillingness*; go-slow, working to rule 145 *strike*; slowing down, slowdown, deceleration, retardation 113 *protraction*; drag 333 *friction*; brake, curb 747 *restraint*; leisureliness, no hurry, time to spare, time on one's hands, all the time in the world, leisurely progress, easy stages 681 *leisure*; slow motion, low gear; slow march, dead m.; slow time, andante; slow pace, foot p., snail's p., crawl, creep, dawdle; dragging one's feet; mincing steps, walk, piaffer, amble, jog trot, dog t. 265 *gait*; limping, hobbling; standing start, slow s.; lagging, lag, time lag 136 *delay*.

*slowcoach*, snail, slug, tortoise, tardigrade; stopping train, slow t.; funeral procession, cortege; dawdler, loiterer, lingerer; slow starter, slow learner, late developer; laggard, sluggard, lie-abed, sleepyhead, Weary Willie; slouch, sloucher 598 *slacker*; drone 679 *idler*.

**Adj.** *slow*, painfully s.; slow-paced, low-geared, slow-motion, time-lapse; oozy, trickling, dripping; snail-like, tortoise-l., creeping,

crawling, dragging; tardigrade, slow-moving 695 *clumsy*; limping, halting; taking one's time, dragging one's feet, hanging fire, tardy, dilatory, lagging 136 *late*; long about it, unhurried 681 *leisurely*; sedate 875 *formal*; deliberate 823 *patient*; painstaking 457 *careful*; Fabian, cunctative 858 *cautious*; groping, tentative 461 *experimental*; languid, slack, sluggish 679 *lazy*; apathetic, phlegmatic 375 *insensible*; gradual, stealthy, imperceptible, unnoticeable, invisible.

**Vb.** *move slowly*, go slow, amble, crawl, creep, inch, inch along, ease a., glide a.; ooze, drip, trickle, dribble 350 *flow*; drift 282 *deviate*; hang over, hover; shamble, slouch, mooch, shuffle, scuff; toddle, waddle, take short steps, mince; plod, trudge, tramp, lumber, stump, stump along; wobble, totter, teeter, stagger, lurch; struggle, toil, labour, chug, jolt, bump, creak; limp, hobble, go lame; drag one's steps, flag, falter 684 *be fatigued*; trail, lag, fall behind 284 *follow*; not get started, not start, hang fire, drag one's feet, drag oneself 598 *be unwilling*; tarry, be long about it, not be hurried, take one's time 136 *be late*; laze, maunder, idle 679 *be inactive*; take it easy, not exert oneself, linger, stroll, saunter, dawdle 267 *walk*; march in slow time, march on the spot, barely move, hardly beat, tick over; grope, feel one's way 461 *be tentative*; soft-pedal, hesitate 858 *be cautious*; speak slowly, drawl, spin something out 580 *stammer*.

*decelerate*, slow down, slow up, ease up, let up, lose momentum; reduce speed, slacken s., slacken one's pace, slacken off; smell the ground (of ships); relax, slacken, ease off 145 *pause*; lose ground, flag, falter, waver 684 *be fatigued*.

*retard*, check, curb, rein in, throttle down 177 *moderate*; reef, shorten sail, take in s., strike s. 269 *navigate*; brake, put on the b., put on the drag 747 *restrain*; backpedal, backwater, backpaddle, put the engines astern, reverse 286 *regress*; handicap, impair, clip the wings 702 *hinder*.

**Adv.** *slowly*, deliberately etc. adj.; leisurely, lazily, sluggishly; creepingly, creakily, joltily; at half speed, at low s., in low gear, in bottom g.; with mincing steps, at a foot's pace, at a snail's p., at a funeral p.; with leaden step; on crutches; gingerly; in one's own good time; in slow time, adagio, largo, larghetto, lento, andante.

*gradatim*, gradually etc. adj.; by degrees, by slow d., by inches, little by little, bit by bit, inch by inch, step by step, one at a time, by easy stages.

## 279 Impulse

**N. impulse**, impulsion, pressure; impetus, momentum; boost, stir-up 174 *stimulant*; encouragement 612 *incentive*; thrust, push, shove, heave; batting, stroke; throw, fling 287 *propulsion*; lunge, kick 712 *attack*; percussion, beating, tapping, drumming; beat, drumbeat 403 *roll*; recoilless beat, dead b., thud; ramming, bulldozing, hammering; butting, butt (see also *collision*); concussion, shaking, rattling; shock, impact; slam, bang; flick, clip, tap 378 *touch*; shake, rattle, jolt, jerk, wrench 318 *agitation*; pulsation, pulse 318 *spasm*; science of forces, mechanics, dynamics.

*knock*, dint, dent 255 *concavity*; rap, tap, clap; dab, pat, fillip, flip, flick; nudge, dig 547 *gesture*; smack, slap; cuff, clip on *or* round the ear (sl), conk, clout, clump, buffet, box on the ears; blow, fourpenny one (sl); bunch of fives (sl), knuckle sandwich (sl); lash, stroke, hit, crack; cut, drive (cricket); thwack, thump, biff, bang, slug; punch, rabbit p., left, right, straight left, uppercut, jab, hook; body blow, wild b., haymaker, swipe; knockout blow, shrewd b.; stamp, kick; whop, swat; spanking, trouncing, dusting, pasting, licking, leathering, whipping, flogging, thrashing, beating, bashing, hammering, pummelling, rain of blows; hiding 963 *corporal punishment*; assault, assault and battery 712 *attack*; exchange of blows, fisticuffs, cut and thrust, hammer and tongs 61 *turmoil*.

*collision*, encounter, meeting, confrontation; head-on collision, frontal c.; bird strike; graze, scrape 333 *friction*; clash 14 *contrariety*; cannon, carom; impact, bump, shock, crash, smash, smashup, accident; brunt, charge, force 712 *attack*; collision course 293 *convergence*; multiple collision, pileup 74 *accumulation*; near miss, air miss, signal passed at danger, SPAD.

*hammer*, sledge h., steam h., trip h.; hammerhead, peen; punch, puncher; beetle, maul, mallet; flail; racquet, bat, hockey stick, golf club; tapper, knocker, door k.; cosh, blackjack, knuckle-duster, cudgel, club, mace, bicycle chain, sandbag 723 *weapon*; boxing glove; pestle, anvil; hammerer, cudgeller, pummeller, beater, carpet-b.

*ram*, battering r., bulldozer; JCB (tdmk); piledriver, monkey; ramrod; rammer, tamper; cue, billiard c., pusher 287 *propellant*.

**Adj. impelling**, pushing etc. vb.; impellent; dynamic, dynamical, thrusting; impelled etc. vb.

**Vb. impel**, fling, heave, throw 287 *propel*; give an impetus, impart momentum; slam, bang 264 *close*; press, press in, press up, press down; push, thrust, shove; ram down, tamp; shove off, push off, pole, punt; hustle, prod, urge, spur, railroad, pressurize 277 *accelerate*; fillip, flip, flick; jerk, shake, rattle, shock, jog, jolt, jostle 318 *agitate*; shoulder, elbow, push out of the way, push around 282 *deflect*; throw out, run out, expel 300 *eject*; frogmarch; drive forward, flog on, whip on; goad 612 *incite*; drive, start, run, set going, set moving 173 *operate*; raise 310 *elevate*; plunge, dip, douse 311 *lower*.

*collide*, make impact 378 *touch*; impinge 306 *encroach*; come into collision 293 *converge*; meet, encounter, confront, clash; cross swords, fence 712 *strike at*; ram, butt, bunt, batter, bash, dint, dent; batter at, bulldoze 165 *demolish*; cannon into, bump into, bump against; graze, graze against 333 *rub*; butt against, collide a.; drive into, crash i., smash i., run i., run down, run over; clash with, collide w., foul, fall foul of; run one's head against, run into a brick wall, run against, dash a. 712 *charge*; clash against, grate a., bark one's shins, stub one's toe; trip, trip over 309 *tumble*; knock together, knock heads t., clash the cymbals, clap one's hands.

*strike*, smite, hit, land a blow, plant a b., fetch one a b.; aim a blow, hit out at; lunge, lunge at, poke at, strike at; lash out at, lace into, let fly; hit wildly, swing, flail, beat the air; strike hard, slam, bang, knock; knock for six, knock into the middle of next week, send flying; knock down, floor 311 *fell*; pat, patter; flip, fillip, tickle; tap, rap, clap; slap, smack; bop, clock, clump, clout, bash, clobber, box the ears of, clip one's ear; box, spar, fisticuff 716 *fight*; buffet, punch, paste, thump, thwack, whack, wham, rain blows, pummel, trounce, belabour, beat up, sock it to, let one have it; give one a black eye *or* a bloody nose, make one see stars, knock *or* beat six *or* seven *or* ten bells out of; pound, batter, bludgeon 332 *pulverize*; biff, bash, dash, slosh, sock, slog, slug, cosh, cudgel, club, mug, spifflicate; blackjack, sandbag, hit over the head, conk, crown; concuss, stun, knock out, leave senseless; spank, wallop, thrash, lash, lam, lambast, beat, whip, cane 963 *flog*; leather, strap, belt, tan one's hide, give a hiding 963 *punish*; thresh, scutch, swingle, flail; hammer, drum; flap, squash, swat 216 *flatten*; paw, stroke 889 *caress*; scratch, maul 655 *wound*; run through, bayonet, pink 263 *pierce*; tear 46 *cut*; throw stones at, stone, pelt, snowball 712 *lapidate*; head (a football); bat, strike a ball, swipe, drive, turn, glance, cut, crack, lift, lob, smash, volley 287 *propel*.

*kick*, spurn, boot, knee, put the boot in; trample, tread on, stamp on, kneel on; ride over, ride roughshod; spur, dig in one's heels; heel, dribble, shoot (a football).

## 280 Recoil

**N.** *recoil*, revulsion, reaction, retroaction, reflux 148 *reversion*; repercussion, reverberation, echo 404 *resonance*; reflex 417 *reflection*; kick, kickback, backlash; ricochet, cannon, carom; rebound, bounce, spring, springboard, trampoline 328 *elasticity*; ducks and drakes; swingback, swing of the pendulum 317 *oscillation*; volley, return (at tennis), boomerang; rebuff, repulse 292 *repulsion*; riposte, return fire.

**Adj.** *recoiling*, rebounding etc. vb.; reactive, repercussive, refluent; retroactive 148 *reverted*.

**Vb.** *recoil*, react 182 *counteract*; shrink, wince, blench, quail, start, flinch, jib, shy, jump back, shy away, back off 620 *avoid*; kick back, hit b.; ricochet, cannon, cannon off; uncoil, spring back, fly b., bound b., rebound; return, swing back 148 *revert*; have repercussions; reverberate, echo 404 *resound*; be reflected, reflect 417 *shine*; return on one's head, boomerang 714 *retaliate*.

## 281 Direction

**N.** *direction*, bearing, compass reading 186 *bearings*; lie of the land 186 *situation*; orientation, collimation, alignment; set, drift 350 *current*; tenor, trend, bending 179 *tendency*; aim; course, beam; beeline, straight shot, line of sight, optical axis 249 *straightness*; course, tack; line, line of march, track, way, path, road 624 *route*; steering, steerage; aim, target 295 *goal*; compass, pelorus 269 *sailing aid*; collimator, sights 442 *optical device*; fingerpost 547 *signpost*; direction finder, range f. 465 *gauge*; orienteering, cross-country race, point-to-point.

*compass point*, cardinal points, half points, quarter points; quarter, north, east, south, west; north-east, north-west, etc; east-north-east, north-north-east, west-south-west, south-south-west, etc; north-north-east by north, south-south-west by south, etc; magnetic north; rhumb, azimuth.

**Adj.** *directed*, orientated, directed towards, pointing t., signposted; aimed, well-a., well-directed, well-placed 187 *located*; bound for 617 *intending*; aligned with 219 *parallel*; axial, diagonal 220 *oblique*; sideways 239 *lateral*; facing 240 *opposite*; direct, undeviating, unswerving, straightforward, one-way 249 *straight*; northbound, southbound; northern, northerly, southerly, meridional; western, occidental; eastern, oriental; directive, guiding; showing the way.

**Vb.** *orientate*, orientate oneself, box the compass, take one's bearings, shoot the sun, check one's course, plot one's c. 269 *navigate*; find which way the wind blows, see how the land lies; take a direction, have a d., bear; direct oneself, ask the way, ask for directions; signpost, direct, show the way, put on the right track 547 *indicate*; pinpoint, locate 187 *place*; keep on the beam 249 *be straight*; face, front 240 *be opposite*.

*steer for*, steer, shape a course for, set the helm f., be bound f., head f., run f., stand f., make f., aim f.; make towards, bend one's steps to, go to, go towards, go straight for, direct oneself towards, make a beeline for, march on, align one's march; go straight to the point, hold the line, keep on the beam, keep the nose down 249 *be straight*.

*point to*, point out, point, show, point towards, signpost 547 *indicate*; trend, trend towards, incline t., verge, dip, bend 179 *tend*.

*aim*, level, point; take aim, aim at; train one's sights, draw a bead on, level at; cover, have one covered; collimate, set one's sights; aim well, hit the mark, get a bull's-eye, land, plant 187 *place*.

**Adv.** *towards*, versus, facing; on the way, on the road to, through, via, en route for, by way of; straight, direct, straight forwards; point blank, straight as an arrow; in a direct line, in a straight line, in a line with, in a line for; directly, full tilt at, as the crow flies; upstream, downstream; upwind, downwind; before the wind, close to the w., near the w.; against the w., in the wind's eye, close hauled; seaward, landward, homeward; downtown; cross-country; up-country; in all directions 183 *widely*; from or to the four winds; hither, thither; clockwise, anticlockwise, counter-clockwise, widdershins; whither, which way?

## 282 Deviation

**N.** *deviation*, disorientation, misdirection, wrong course, wrong turning; aberration, aberrancy, deflection, refraction; diversion, digression; shift, veer, slew, swing; departure, declension 220 *obliquity*; flection, flexion, swerve, bend 248 *curvature*, branching off, divarication 294 *divergence*; deviousness, detour, bypath, circumbendibus, ambages, long way round, scenic route, tourist r. 626 *circuit*; vagrancy 267 *wandering*; fall, lapse 495 *error*; wandering mind, maundering 456 *abstractedness*; drift, leeway; oblique motion, passaging, crab-walk, sidestep, sideslip; break, leg b., off b., googly (cricket); knight's move (chess); yaw, tack; zigzag, slalom course.

**Adj.** *deviating*, aberrant, mutating, nonconformist, abnormal, bent, deviant 84 *unconform-*

*able*; eccentric, off-centre; out of orbit; errant, wandering, rambling, maundering, roving, vagrant, loose, footloose 267 *travelling*; undirected, directionless, unguided, random, erratic 495 *inexact*, desultory 72 *discontinuous*; abstracted 456 *inattentive*; excursive, digressing; discursive, off the subject 10 *irrelevant*; disorientated, confused, off-course, off-beam, lost, stray, astray; misdirected, misaimed, ill-aimed, off-target, off the mark, wide of the m., wide; off the fairway, in the rough (golf); devious, winding, roundabout 314 *circuitous*; indirect, crooked, zigzag, zigzagging 220 *oblique*; branching, divaricating 294 *divergent*.

**Vb.** *deviate*, leave the straight, digress, make a detour, go a roundabout way, go the long way round; branch out, divaricate 294 *diverge*; turn, filter, turn a corner, turn aside, swerve, slew; go out of one's way, depart from one's course; step aside, make way for; alter course, change direction, yaw, tack; veer, back (wind); trend, bend, curve 248 *be curved*; zigzag, twine, twist 251 *meander*; swing, wobble 317 *oscillate*; steer clear of, give a wide berth, sheer off; sidle, passage; slide, skid, sideslip; break (cricket); glance, fly off at a tangent 220 *be oblique*; shy, jib, sidestep 620 *avoid*.

*turn round*, turn about, about turn, wheel, wheel about, face a., face the other way, do a U-turn, change one's mind; reverse, reverse direction, return 148 *revert*; go back 286 *turn back*.

*stray*, err, ramble, maunder, rove, drift, divagate, straggle 267 *wander*; go astray, go adrift, miss one's way, lose the w., get lost; miss one's footing, lose one's bearings, lose one's sense of direction, take the wrong turning 495 *blunder*; lose track of, lose the thread 456 *be inattentive*.

*deflect*, bend, crook 220 *make oblique*, warp, skew; put off the scent, lead astray, draw a red herring, throw dust in one's eyes, set off on a wild-goose chase, misdirect, misaddress 495 *mislead*; avert 713 *parry*; divert, change the course of; sidetrack, draw aside, push a., pull a.; elbow a., edge off; bias, slice, pull, hook, glance, bowl a break, bowl wide (cricket); shuffle, shift, switch, shunt 151 *interchange*; wear ship 269 *navigate*.

**Adv.** *astray*, adrift, amiss; out; wide of the mark, off the mark; right about; round about; erratically, all manner of ways, every which way; indirectly, at a tangent, sideways, diagonally 220 *obliquely*; sidling, crabwise.

## 283 Preceding: going before

**N.** *preceding* 119 *priority*, 64 *precedence*; going before, going ahead of, leading, heading, flying start; pre-emption, queue-jumping; pride of place, head of the table, head of the river (bumping races); lead, leading role, star role 34 *superiority*; pioneer 66 *precursor*; van, vanguard, avant-garde 237 *front*; prequel, foreword, prelude.

**Vb.** *precede*, antecede, go before, go ahead of, forerun, herald, be the precursor of, be the prelude to; usher in, introduce; head, spearhead, lead, be in the van, head the queue; go in front, go in advance, clear the way, light the w., lead the w.; open the ball, lead the dance, guide, conduct 689 *direct*; take the lead, get the lead, have the start on, have a head start; steal a march on, pre-empt, steal one's thunder; get in front, jump the queue; get ahead of, lap 277 *outstrip*; be beforehand 135 *be early*; take precedence over, take priority over, have right of way 64 *come before*.

**Adv.** *ahead*, before, in advance, in the van, in the forefront, in front, foremost, headmost; primarily, first of all; elders first, women and children first; age before beauty.

## 284 Following: going after

**N.** *following* 65 *sequence*; run, suit 71 *series*; sub-sequence 120 *posteriority*; pursuit, pursuance, stalking 619 *chase*; succession, reversion 780 *transfer*; last place 238 *rear*.

*follower*, pursuer, tail, stalker; attendant, suitor, hanger-on, camp follower, groupie 742 *dependant*; train, tail, wake, cortège, suite, followers 67 *retinue*; following, party, adherent, supporter, fan 703 *aider*; satellite, moon, artificial satellite, space station 276 *spaceship*; trailer, caravan 274 *cart*; tender 275 *ship*.

**Adj.** *following*, subsequent, next 65 *sequential*.

**Vb.** *follow*, come behind, succeed, follow on, follow after, follow close upon, sit on one's tail, breathe down one's neck, be bumper to bumper, follow in the wake of, tread on the heels of, tread in the steps of, follow the footprints of, come to heel 65 *come after*; stick like a shadow, tag after, hang on the skirts of, beset; attend, wait on, dance attendance on 742 *serve*; tag along 89 *accompany*; dog, shadow, trail, tail, stalk, track, chase 619 *pursue*; drop behind, fall b., lag, trail, dawdle 278 *move slowly*; bring up the rear 238 *be behind*.

**Adv.** *behind*, in the rear 238 *rearward*; on the heels of; in the train of, in the wake of, in tow 65 *after*; one after another; later 120 *subsequently*.

## 285 Progression: motion forwards

**N.** *progression*, going forward; procession,

march, way, course, career; march of time 111 *course of time*; progress, steady p., forward march 265 *motion*; sudden progress, stride, giant strides, leap, quantum l., jump, leaps and bounds 277 *spurt*; irreversibility, irresistible progress, relentless p., majestic p., flood, tide 350 *current*; gain, ground gained, advance, headway 654 *improvement*; getting ahead, overtaking 283 *preceding*; encroachment 306 *overstepping*; next step, development, evolution 308 *ascent*, 71 *continuity*; mystic progress, purgation, illumination 979 *piety*, 981 *worship*; furtherance, promotion, step up the ladder, advancement, preferment; rise, raise, lift, leg-up 310 *elevation*; progressiveness 654 *reformism*; enterprise, go-getting, go-go 672 *undertaking*; achievement 727 *success*; economic progress 730 *prosperity*; progressive, improver 654 *reformer*; go-getter, coming man *or* woman, man *or* woman of the moment, whiz kid, upstart 730 *prosperous person*.

**Adj.** *progressive*, progressing, enterprising, resourceful, go-ahead, go-go, go-getting, forward-looking, reformist; advancing etc. vb.; profluent, flowing on 265 *moving*; unbroken, irreversible; advanced, up-to-date, abreast of the times, state-of-the-art, cutting-edge, leading-edge 126 *modern*.

**Vb.** *progress*, proceed 265 *be in motion*; advance, go forward, take a step forward, come on, develop 316 *evolve*; show promise, promise well 654 *get better*; get on, get ahead, do well 730 *prosper*; march on, run on, flow on, pass on, jog on, wag on, rub on, hold on, keep on, slog on 146 *go on*; move with the times 126 *modernize*; maintain progress, never look back, hold one's lead; press on, push on, drive on, push forward, press f., press onwards 680 *hasten*; make a good start, make initial progress, make good p., break the back of; gain, gain ground, make headway, make strides, make rapid s., cover the ground 277 *move fast*; get a move on, get ahead, shoot a., forge a., advance by leaps and bounds; gain on, distance, outdistance, overtake, leave behind 277 *outstrip*; gain height, rise, rise higher, climb the ladder 308 *climb*; reach towards, reach out to, raise the sights; make up leeway, recover lost ground 31 *recoup*; gain time, make up t.

*promote*, further, contribute to, advance 703 *aid*; prefer, upgrade, move up, raise, lift 310 *elevate*; bring forward, push, force, develop 174 *invigorate*; step up, speed up, hothouse 277 *accelerate*; put ahead, put forward 64 *put in front*; favour, make for, bring on, conduce 156 *cause*.

**Adv.** *forward*, forwards, onward, forth, on, ahead, forrard; progressively, by leaps and bounds, with giant strides; on the way, on one's way, under w., en route for, on the road to 272 *in transit*; in progress, in mid p., in sight of.

**Int.** Forward!, Forrard!, En avant!, Excelsior!

## 286 Regression: motion backwards

**N.** *regression*, regress; reverse direction, retroflexion, retrocession, retrogression, retrogradation, retroaction, backward step 148 *reversion*; motion from, retreat, withdrawal, retirement, disengagement 290 *recession*; regurgitation 300 *voidance*; sternway, reversing, backing, reining back; falling away, decline, drop, fall, downward trend, slump, dumbing-down (inf) 655 *deterioration*.

*return*, remigration, homeward journey; homecoming 295 *arrival*; reentrance, reentry 297 *ingress*; going back, turn of the tide, reflux, refluence, ebb, regurgitation 350 *current*; veering, backing; relapse, losing ground, backsliding, recidivation 603 *tergiversation*; U-turn, volte-face, about turn 148 *reversion*; countermarch, countermovement, countermotion 182 *counteraction*; turn, turning point 137 *crisis*; resilience 328 *elasticity*; reflex 280 *recoil*.

**Adj.** *regressive*, receding, declining, ebbing; refluent, reflex; retrogressive, retrograde, backward; backward-looking, reactionary 125 *retrospective*; retroactive 280 *recoiling*; backing, anticlockwise, counterclockwise; reverse, reversible 148 *reverted*; resilient 328 *elastic*; remigrating, returning, homing, homeward bound.

**Vb.** *regress*, recede, retrogress, retrograde, retrocede; retreat, sound a r., beat a r.; retire, withdraw, fall back, draw b.; turn away, turn tail 620 *run away*; disengage, back out, back down 753 *resign*; backtrack, backpedal; give way, give ground, lose g.; recede into the distance 446 *disappear*; fall behind, fall astern, drop a. 278 *move slowly*; reverse, back, back water, go backwards; run back, flow back, regurgitate; not hold, slip back; ebb, slump, fall, drop, decline 309 *descend*; bounce back 280 *recoil*.

*turn back*, put b., retrace one's steps; remigrate, go back, go home, return 148 *revert*; look back, look over one's shoulder, hark back 505 *retrospect*; turn one's back, turn on one's heel; veer round, wheel r., about face, execute a volte-face, do a U-turn 603 *change one's mind*; double, double back, countermarch; start back, jib, flinch, shrink 620 *avoid*; come back, come back again, come home; come back to where one started.

**Adv.** *backwards*, back, astern, in reverse; to the right about.

**Int.** back!, hard astern!, hands off!

## 287 Propulsion

**N.** *propulsion*, jet p., drive; impulsion, push, forward thrust 279 *impulse*; projection, throwing, tossing, hurling, pelting, slinging, stone-throwing; precipitation; cast, throw, chuck, toss, fling, sling, shy, cock-shy; pot shot, pot, shot, long s.; shooting, firing, discharge, volley 712 *bombardment*; bowling, pitching, throw-in, full toss, yorker, lob (cricket); kick, punt, dribble (football); stroke, drive, swipe 279 *knock*; pull, slice (golf); rally, volley, smash (tennis); ballistics, gunnery, musketry, sniping, pea-shooting; archery, toxophily; marksmanship 694 *skill*; gunshot, bowshot, stone's throw 199 *distance*.

*missile*, ball, bullet, cannonball, grapeshot, projectile, rocket, shell, shot, small s.; depleted uranium, DU; pellet, brickbat, stone, snowball; arrow, dart 723 *missile weapon*; ball, tennis b., golf b., cricket b., hockey b.; football, rugby ball; bowl, boule, wood, jack, puck, curling stone; quoit, discus; javelin; hammer, caber.

*propellant*, thrust, driving force, jet, steam 160 *energy*; spray, aerosol, CFC, chlorofluorocarbons; thruster, pusher, shover 279 *ram*; tail wind, following w. 352 *wind*; lever, treadle, pedal, bicycle p.; oar, sweep, paddle; screw, blade, paddlewheel 269 *propeller*; coal, petrol, diesel oil 385 *fuel*; gunpowder, dynamite 723 *explosive*; shotgun, rifle 723 *firearm*; revolver 723 *pistol*; airgun, pop gun, water pistol; blowpipe, pea-shooter; catapult, sling, bow 723 *missile weapon*.

*shooter*, gunman, rifleman, musketeer, pistoleer; gunner, artilleryman 722 *soldiery*; archer, bowman, toxophilite; marksman, markswoman, sharpshooter, sniper, shot, crack s. 696 *proficient person*.

*thrower*, hurler, caster, pelter, stoner, snowballer; knife-thrower, javelin-t., discus-t., stone-t., slinger; bowler, pitcher, curler, tosser, caber-t.

**Adj.** *propulsive*, propellant, propelling etc. vb.; expulsive, explosive, propelled etc. vb.; projectile, missile; ballistic.

**Vb.** *propel*, launch, project, set on its way; flight, throw, cast, deliver, heave, pitch, toss, cant, chuck, shy, bung; bowl, lob, york; hurl, fling, sling, catapult; dart, flick; pelt, stone, shower, snowball 712 *lapidate*; precipitate, get moving, send flying, send headlong; expel, pitchfork 300 *eject*; blow away, puff a.; blow up, explode, put dynamite under, put a bomb under; serve, return, volley, smash, kill (tennis); bat, slam, slog, wham; sky, loft; drive, cut, pull, hook, glance (cricket); slice 279 *strike*; kick, dribble, punt (football); putt, push, shove, shoulder, ease along 279 *impel*; wheel,

pedal, roll, bowl, trundle 315 *rotate*; move on, drive, hustle 265 *move*; sweep, sweep up, sweep before one, carry before one, drive like leaves; put to flight 727 *defeat*.

*shoot*, fire, open fire, fire off; volley, fire a v.; discharge, explode, let off, set off; let fly, shower with arrows, volley and thunder; draw a bead on, pull the trigger; cannonade, bombard 712 *fire at*; snipe, pot, pot at, take a potshot at, loose off at; pepper 263 *pierce*.

## 288 Traction

**N.** *traction*, drawing etc. vb.; pulling back, retraction; retractility, retractability; magnetism 291 *attraction*; towage, haulage; draught, pull, haul; tug, tow; towline, towrope; rake, harrow, draw-hoe; trawl, dragnet; drawer, puller, tugger, tower, hauler, haulier; retractor; lugsail, square sail 275 *sail*; windlass 310 *lifter*; tug, tugboat 275 *ship*; tractor, traction engine 274 *locomotive*; loadstone 291 *magnet*; rowing; strain, tug of war 716 *contest*; thing drawn, trailer, caravan 274 *cart*.

**Adj.** *drawing*, pulling etc. vb., tractional, tractive; pulling back, retractive, retractile, retractable; attractive, magnetic 291 *attracting*; tractile, ductile; drawn, horse-d.

**Vb.** *draw*, pull, haul, hale; trice, warp, kedge 269 *navigate*; tug, tow, take in tow; lug, drag, draggle, train, trail, trawl; rake, harrow; winch, reel in, wind in, wind up, lift, heave, hitch 310 *elevate*; drag down 311 *lower*; suck in 299 *absorb*; pluck, pull out 304 *extract*; wrench, twist 246 *distort*; yank, jerk, twitch, tweak, pluck at, snatch at 318 *agitate*; pull towards 291 *attract*; pull back, draw b., pull in, draw in, retract, sheathe (claws).

**Int.** yo-heave-ho!

## 289 Approach: motion towards

**N.** *approach*, coming towards, advance 285 *progression*; near approach, approximation 200 *nearness*; flowing towards, afflux 350 *stream*; meeting, confluence 293 *convergence*; access, accession, advent, coming 295 *arrival*, 189 *presence*; approach from behind, overtaking, overlapping 619 *pursuit*; onset 712 *attack*; advances, pass, overture 759 *offer*; way in, means of approach, accessibility, approaches 624 *access*.

**Adj.** *approaching*, nearing, getting warm etc. vb.; close, approximative 200 *near*; meeting 293 *convergent*; confluent, affluent, tributary; overhanging, hovering, closing in, imminent 155 *impending*; advancing, coming, oncoming, on the way 295 *arriving*.

*accessible*, approachable, get-at-able; within reach, within easy r., attainable 469 *possible*; available, obtainable, on tap 189 *on the spot*;

wayside, roadside, pavement, nearby 200 *near*; welcoming, inviting 291 *attracting*, 882 *sociable*; well-paved, made-up, metalled 624 *communicating*.

**Vb.** **approach**, draw near 200 *be near*; approximate 200 *bring near*; come within range 295 *arrive*; come into view 443 *be visible*; feel the attraction of, be drawn; come to close quarters, come closer, meet 293 *converge*; run down 279 *collide*; near, draw n., get n., go n., come n.; move near, walk up to, run up to, step up to, sidle up to; roll up 74 *congregate*; come in 297 *enter*; accede, adhere, join 38 *accrue*; get hold of, waylay, buttonhole; accost 884 *greet*; make up to, make overtures, make passes 889 *court*; nestle, snuggle up to 889 *caress*; lean towards, incline, trend 179 *tend*; move towards, walk t., make t., drift t. 265 *be in motion*; advance 285 *progress*; advance upon, bear down on 712 *attack*; close, close in, close in on 232 *circumscribe*; hover 155 *impend*; gain upon, catch up with, overtake 277 *outstrip*; follow hard, narrow the gap, breathe down one's neck, tread on one's heels, sit on one's tail, drive bumper to bumper, run one close; be in sight of, be within shouting distance of, make the land, make a landfall 295 *land*; hug the coast, hug the shore 269 *navigate*.

**Int.** this way!, come closer!, roll up!, land ahoy!

## 290 Recession: motion from

**N.** *recession*, retirement, withdrawal, retreat, stepping back, retrocession 286 *regression*; leak 298 *outflow*; emigration, evacuation 296 *departure*; resignation 621 *relinquishment*; flight 667 *escape*; shrinking, shying, flinching 620 *avoidance*; revulsion 280 *recoil*.

**Adj.** *receding*, ebbing etc. vb., retreating 286 *regressive*.

**Vb.** *recede*, retire, withdraw, fall back, draw b., retreat, back off 286 *regress*; ebb, subside, shrink, decline 37 *decrease*; fade from view 446 *disappear*; go, go away, leave, clear out, evacuate, emigrate 296 *depart*; go outside, go out, pour out 298 *emerge*; leak, leak out 298 *flow out*; move from, move away, move off, move further, stand off, put space between, widen the gap 199 *be distant*; stand aside, make way, veer away, sheer off 282 *deviate*; drift away 282 *stray*; back away, shrink a., flinch 620 *avoid*; flee 620 *run away*; get away 667 *escape*; go back 286 *turn back*; jump back 280 *recoil*; come off, come away, come unstuck 46 *separate*.

## 291 Attraction

**N.** *attraction*, pull, drag, draw, tug; suction, drawing to, pulling towards; magnetization,

magnetism, magnetic field; gravity, force of g.; itch, itch for 859 *desire*; affinity, sympathy, empathy; attractiveness, seductiveness, allure, appeal, sex a., it; allurement, seduction, temptation, lure, bait, decoy, charm, siren song 612 *inducement*; charmer, temptress, siren, Circe 612 *motivator*; centre of attraction, cynosure, honeypot 890 *favourite*.

*magnet*, bar m., horseshoe m.; coil magnet, solenoid; magnetite, magnetized iron, lodestone; lodestar 520 *guide*; magnetizer.

**Adj.** *attracting*, drawing etc. vb.; adductive, associative, attractive; magnetic, magnetized; charming, seductive, siren, tempting 612 *inducing*; addictive, sticky; centripetal.

**Vb.** *attract*, magnetize, pull, drag, tug 288 *draw*; adduct, exercise a pull, draw towards, pull t., drag t., tug t.; appeal, charm, move, pluck at one's heartstrings 821 *impress*; lure, allure, bait, seduce 612 *tempt*; decoy 542 *ensnare*.

## 292 Repulsion

**N.** *repulsion*, repellence; repulsive force, centrifugal f.; repellent quality, repulsiveness 842 *ugliness*; reflection 280 *recoil*; driving off, beating o. 713 *defence*; repulse, rebuff, snub, refusal, the cold shoulder, the bird 607 *rejection*; brush-off, dismissal 300 *ejection*.

**Adj.** *repellent*, repelling etc. vb.; repulsive, off-putting, antipathetic 861 *disliked*; abducent, abductive; centrifugal.

**Vb.** *repel*, put off, excite nausea, make sick 861 *cause dislike*; put away, push away, butt a., butt, head 279 *impel*; drive away, chase a., repulse, beat off, fend off, block, stonewall, talk out 713 *parry*; dispel 75 *disperse*; head off, turn away, reflect 282 *deflect*; be deaf to 760 *refuse*; rebuff, snub, brush off, reject one's advances 607 *reject*; give one the bird, cold-shoulder, keep at arm's length, make one keep his distance 883 *make unwelcome*; show the door to, shut the door in one's face, send one off with a flea in his ear, send packing, send one about his business, give one his marching orders; boot out, give the boot, kick out, sack 300 *dismiss*.

**Int.** be off!, away with you!, scram!, hop it!, leg it!, get lost!, vamoose!

## 293 Convergence

**N.** *convergence*, mutual approach 289 *approach*; narrowing gap; confrontation, collision course 279 *collision*; concourse, confluence, conflux, meeting 45 *union*; congress, concurrence, concentration, resort, assembly 74 *assemblage*; closing in, pincer movement 232 *circumscription*; centring, focalization, zeroing in 76 *focus*;

narrowing, coming to a point, tapering, taper 206 *narrowness*; converging line, asymptote, tangent; convergent view, perspective, vanishing point 438 *view*.

**Adj.** *convergent*, converging etc. vb.; focusing, zeroing in on, focused; centripetal, centring; confluent, concurrent 45 *conjunctive*; tangential; pointed, conical, pyramidal 256 *tapering*; knock-kneed.

**Vb.** *converge*, come closer, draw nearer, draw in, close in; narrow the gap; fall in with, come together 295 *meet*; unite, gather together, get t. 74 *congregate*; roll in, pour in, enter in 297 *enter*; close with, intercept, head off, close in upon 232 *circumscribe*; pinch, nip 198 *make smaller*; concentrate, focus, bring into f.; align convergently, toe in; centre, centre on, centre in, zero in on 225 *centralize*; taper, come to a point, narrow down 206 *be narrow*.

**294 Divergence**
**N.** *divergence*, divergency 15 *difference*; complete divergence, clear blue water; contradiction 14 *contrariety*; going apart, divarication; moving apart, drifting a., parting 46 *separation*; aberration, declination 282 *deviation*; spread, fanning out, deployment 75 *dispersion*; parting of the ways, fork, bifurcation, crossroads, watershed, points 222 *crossing*; radiation, ramification, branching out; Y-shape 247 *angularity*; star, rays, spokes.

**Adj.** *divergent*, diverging etc. vb.; divaricate, separated; radiating, radiant, palmate, stellate; centrifugal, centrifuge; aberrant 282 *deviating*.

**Vb.** *diverge* 15 *differ*; radiate; divaricate, ramify, branch off, branch out; split off, fork, bifurcate; part, part ways, part company, come to the parting of the ways 46 *separate*; file off, go one's own way; change direction, switch; glance off, fly off, fly off at a tangent 282 *deviate*; deploy, fan out, spread, scatter 75 *be dispersed*; straddle, spread-eagle; splay, splay apart.

**295 Arrival**
**N.** *arrival*, advent, accession, appearance, entrance 289 *approach*, 189 *presence*; onset 68 *beginning*; coming, reaching, making; landfall, landing, touch-down, docking, mooring 266 *quiescence*; debarkation, disembarkation 298 *egress*; rejoining, meeting, encounter 154 *event*; greeting, handshake, formalities 884 *courteous act*; homecoming 286 *return*; prodigal's return, reception, welcome 876 *celebration*; guest, visitor, visitant, new arrival, nouveau arrivé, recent arrival, homing pigeon 297 *incomer*; arrival at the winning post, finish, close f., neck-and-neck f., needle f., photo f. 716 *contest*; last lap, home stretch.

*goal* 617 *objective*; terra firma, native land 192 *home*; journey's end, final point, point of no return, terminus 69 *extremity*; stop, stop-over, transit stop, stage, halt 145 *stopping place*; billet, resting place, landing p., landing stage, pier; port, harbour, haven, anchorage, roadstead 662 *shelter*; dock, dry d., berth 192 *stable*; aerodrome, airport, airfield, heliport, terminal, air t. 271 *air travel*; terminus, railway t., railway station, bus s., depot, rendezvous 192 *meeting place*.

**Adj.** *arriving*, landing etc. vb.; home-seeking, homing, homeward-bound; terminal; nearing 289 *approaching*, 155 *impending*.

**Vb.** *arrive*, come, reach, fetch up at, end up at, get there 189 *be present*; reach one's destination, get there, make land, sight, raise; make a landfall, make port; dock, berth, tie up, moor, drop anchor 266 *come to rest* (see also *land*); unharness, unhitch, outspan; draw up, pull up, park; home, come h., get h., return h. 286 *regress*; hit, make, win to, gain, attain; finish the race, breast the tape; achieve one's aim, reach one's goal 725 *carry through*; stand at the door, be on the doorstep, look for a welcome 297 *enter*; make an entrance 297 *burst in*; appear, show up, pop up, turn up, roll up, drop in, blow in 882 *visit*; put in, pull in, stop at, stop over, stop off, break one's journey, stop 145 *pause*; clock in, time one's arrival 135 *be early*; arrive at, find 484 *discover*; arrive at the top 727 *be successful*, 730 *prosper*; be brought, be delivered, come to hand.

*land*, unload, discharge 188 *displace*; beach, ground, run aground, touch down, make a landing; step ashore, go a., disembark, debouch, pour out 298 *emerge*; detrain, debus; get off, get out, get down, alight, light on, perch 309 *descend*; dismount, quit the saddle, set foot to ground.

*meet*, join, rejoin, see again; receive, greet, welcome, shake hands 882 *be sociable*; go to meet, come to m., meet the train, be at the station; keep a date, rendezvous; come upon, encounter; come in contact, run into, meet by chance; hit, bump into, butt i., knock i., collide with 279 *collide*; burst upon, light u., pitch u.; gather, assemble 74 *congregate*.

**Int.** greetings!, hi!, how are you?, how do you do!, hullo! *or* hallo! *or* hello!, namaste!, pleased to meet you!, welcome!, welcome home!, what cheer?, wotcher!, aloha!, salaam!, shalom!

**296 Departure**
**N.** *departure*, leaving, parting, removal, going away; walk-out, exit 298 *egress*; pulling out, emigration 290 *recession*; remigration, going

back 286 *return*; migration, exodus, general e.,
Hegira; hop, flight, flit, moonlight f., decampment, elopement, getaway 667 *escape*; embarkation, going on board 297 *ingress*; mounting,
saddling 267 *equitation*; setting out, starting
out, outset 68 *start*; takeoff, blast-off 308
*ascent*; zero hour, time of departure, moment
of leave-taking; point of departure, port of
embarkation; starting point, starting post,
stake-boat.

*valediction*, farewell, valedictory, funeral
oration, epitaph, obituary 364 *obsequies*; leave-
taking, congé, dismissal; goodbyes, good-
nights, farewells, adieus; last handshake,
waving goodbye, wave of the handkerchief
884 *courteous act*; send-off, farewell address;
last post, last words, final goodbye, parting
shot; stirrup cup, doch-an-dorris, one for the
road, nightcap.

**Adj.** *departing*, going etc. vb.; valedictory,
farewell; parting, leaving, taking leave; outward bound; emigratory.

**Vb.** *depart*, quit, leave, abandon 621 *relinquish*; retire, withdraw, retreat 286 *turn back*;
remove, move house, flit, leave the neighbourhood, leave the country, leave home, emigrate,
expatriate oneself, absent o. 190 *go away*; leave
the nest, fly the n., take wing; take one's leave,
take one's departure, be going, be getting
along; bid farewell, say goodbye, say good
night, make one's adieus, tear oneself away,
part, part company; receive one's congé, get
one's marching orders; leave work, cease w.
145 *cease*; clock out, go home 298 *emerge*; quit
the scene, leave the stage, bow out, give one's
swan song, exit, make one's e. 753 *resign*;
depart this life 361 *die*.

*decamp*, up sticks, strike tents, break camp,
break up; walk out, march out, pack up, clear
off; clear out, pull out, evacuate; make tracks,
walk one's chalks; be off, beetle o., buzz o.,
slink o., slope o., swan o., push o., shove o.,
make oneself scarce; take wing 271 *fly*;
vamoose, skedaddle, beat it, hop it, scram,
bolt, scuttle, skip, slip away, cut and run 277
*move fast*; flee, take flight, make a break for it
620 *run away*; flit, make a moonlight f., make
one's getaway 446 *disappear*; elope, abscond,
give one the slip 667 *escape*.

*start out*, be off, get going, get on one's way,
set out 68 *begin*; set forth, sally f., take up one's
bed and walk, issue forth, strike out, light out,
march out 298 *emerge*; gird oneself, be ready to
start, warm up 669 *make ready*; take ship,
embark, go on board 297 *enter*; hoist the Blue
Peter, unmoor, cast off, weigh anchor, push
off, get under way, set sail, drop the pilot, put
out to sea, leave the land behind 269 *navigate*;

mount, set foot in the stirrup, bit, bridle, harness, saddle 267 *ride*; hitch up, inspan, pile in,
hop on; emplane, entrain; catch a train, catch
a plane, catch a bus; pull out, drive off, take
off, be on one's way, be in flight, be on the first
lap; see off, wish Godspeed, wave goodbye,
speed the parting guest.

**Int.** be seeing you!, bye-bye!, bye for now!,
cheerio!, farewell!, God be with you!,
goodbye!, see you later!, so long!, ta-ta!, adieu!,
adios!, aloha!, au revoir!, arrivederci!, auf Wied-
ersehen!, ciao!, sayonara!; have a good trip!,
pleasant journey!, bon voyage!

## 297 Ingress: motion into

**N.** *ingress*, incoming, entry, entrance; reentry
286 *return*; inflow, influx, flood 350 *stream*;
inpouring, inrush; intrusion, trespass 306 *overstepping*; invasion, forced entry, inroad, raid,
irruption, incursion 712 *attack*; immersion, diffusion, osmosis; penetration, interpenetration,
infiltration, insinuation 231 *interjacency*, 303
*insertion*; immigration, expansionism;
indraught, intake 299 *reception*; import, importation 272 *transference*; right of entry, nonre-
striction, admission, admittance, access, entrée
756 *permission*; free trade, free market, open-
door policy 791 *trade*, 744 *scope*; ticket, pass,
visa 756 *permit*; foot in the door 263 *opener*.

*way in*, way, path 624 *access*; entrance,
entrance hall, entry, door 263 *doorway*; mouth,
opening 263 *orifice*; intake, inlet 345 *gulf*;
channel 351 *conduit*; open door, free port 796
*market*.

*incomer*, newcomer, Johnny-come-lately;
new arrival, nouveau arrivé, new member, new
face; new boy, new girl 538 *beginner*; visitant,
visitor, caller 882 *sociable person*; immigrant,
migrant, economic m., colonist, settler 59
*foreigner*; stowaway, unwelcome guest 59
*intruder*; invader, raider 712 *attacker*; house-
breaker, burglar 789 *thief*; entrant, competitor
716 *contender*; person admitted, ticket holder,
visa h., card h.; audience, spectator, house,
gate 441 *onlookers*.

**Adj.** *incoming*, ingressive, ingoing, inward,
inward bound, homing; ingrowing; intrusive,
trespassing; irruptive, invasive 712 *attacking*;
penetrating, flooding; allowed in, imported.

**Vb.** *enter*, turn into, go in, come in, move in,
drive in, run in, breeze in, venture in, sidle in,
step in, walk in, file in; follow in 65 *come after*;
set foot in, cross the threshold, darken the
doors; let oneself in; unlock the door, turn the
key 263 *open*; gain admittance, have entrée to,
be invited; look in, drop in, pop in, blow in,
call 882 *visit*; mount, board, get aboard; get in,
hop in, jump in, pile in; squeeze into, wedge

oneself i., pack oneself i., jam oneself i.; creep in, slip in, edge in, slink in, sneak in, steal in; work one's way into, buy one's way into, insinuate oneself; worm into, bore i. 263 *pierce*; bite into, eat i., cut i. 260 *notch*; put one's foot in, tread in, fall into, drop i. 309 *tumble*; sink into, plunge i., dive i. 313 *plunge*; join, enlist in, enrol oneself 58 *be one of*; immigrate, settle in 187 *place oneself*; let in 299 *admit*; put in 303 *insert*; enter oneself, enter for 716 *contend*.

*infiltrate*, percolate, seep, soak through, go t., soak into, leak i., drip i.; sink in, penetrate, permeate, mix in, interpenetrate, interfuse 43 *mix*; taint, infect 655 *impair*, filter in, wriggle into, worm one's way i., find one's way in.

*burst in*, irrupt, rush in, charge in, crash in, smash in, break in, force one's way, storm in 176 *force*; flood, overflow, flow in, pour in, flood in 350 *flow*; crowd in, throng in, roll in, swarm in, press in 74 *congregate*; invade, raid, break through, board, storm, escalade 712 *attack*.

*intrude*, trespass, gatecrash, outstay one's welcome; horn in, barge in, push in, muscle in, break in upon, burst in u., interrupt 63 *derange*; pick the lock, break in, burgle 788 *steal*.

## 298 Egress: motion out of

**N.** *egress*, egression, going out; exit, walk-off; walkout, exodus, general e., evacuation 296 *departure*; emigration, expatriation, exile 883 *seclusion*; emergence, emerging, debouchment; emersion, surfacing; emanation, efflux, issue; evaporation, exhalation, effluvium 338 *vaporization*; eruption, outburst 176 *outbreak*; sortie, breakout 667 *escape*; export, exportation 272 *transference*; migrant, economic m., emigrant, émigré 59 *foreigner*; expatriate, colonist 191 *settler*; expellee, exile, remittance man.

*outflow*, effluence, efflux, effluxion, effusion; emission 300 *ejection*; issue, outpouring, gushing, streaming; exudation, oozing, dribbling, weeping; extravasation, bleeding 302 *haemorrhage*; transudation, perspiration, sweating, sweat; percolation, filtration; leak, escape, leakage, seepage 634 *waste*; drain, running sore 772 *loss*; defluxion, outfall, discharge, drainage, draining 300 *voidance*; overflow, spill, flood 350 *waterfall*; jet, fountain, spring 156 *source*; gush, squirt 350 *stream*; gusher, geyser 300 *ejector*; streaming eyes, runny nose, postnasal drip.

*outlet*, vent, chute; spout, nozzle, tap, faucet; pore, blowhole, spiracle 263 *orifice*, 352 *respiration*; sluice, floodgate 351 *conduit*; exhaust, exhaust pipe, adjutage; drainpipe, overflow, gargoyle; exit, way out, path 624 *access*;

sallyport 263 *doorway*; escape, loophole 667 *means of escape*.

**Adj.** *outgoing*, outward bound; emergent, issuing, emanating; oozy, weeping, runny, leaky; running, leaking, bleeding; effused, extravasated; erupting, eruptive, explosive, volcanic 300 *expulsive*; spent 806 *expended*.

**Vb.** *emerge*, pop out, stick out, project 254 *jut*; pop one's head out, peep out, peer out 443 *be visible*; surface, break water 308 *ascend*; emanate, transpire 526 *be disclosed*; egress, issue, debouch, sally, make a sortie; issue forth, sally f., come f., go f.; issue out of, go out, come o., creep o., sneak o., march o., flounce o., fling o. 267 *walk*; jump out, bale o. 312 *leap*; clear out, evacuate 296 *decamp*; emigrate 267 *travel*; exit, walk off 296 *depart*; erupt, break out, break through, burst the bonds 667 *escape*; get the boot, get the bird, get the push, get the heave-ho.

*flow out*, flood o., pour o., stream o. 350 *flow*; gush, spirt, spout, jet 300 *emit*; drain out, run, drip, dribble, trickle, ooze; rise, surge, well out, well up, well over, boil o.; overflow, spill, spill over, slop o.; run off, escape, leak, vent itself, discharge i., disembogue, debouch; bleed, weep, effuse, extravasate; flood, inundate 341 *drench*.

*exude*, transude, perspire, sweat, steam 379 *be hot*; ooze, seep, seep through, soak t., run t., leak t.; percolate, strain, strain out, filter, filtrate, distil; run, dribble, drip, drop, drivel, drool, slaver, slobber, salivate, water at the mouth 341 *be wet*; transpire, exhale 352 *breathe*.

## 299 Reception

**N.** *reception*, admission, admittance, entrance, entrée, access 297 *ingress*; invitation 759 *offer*; receptivity, acceptance; open arms, welcome, effusive w., liberty hall 876 *celebration*; enlistment, enrolment, naturalization 78 *inclusion*; initiation, baptism, baptismal fire 68 *debut*; asylum, sanctuary, shelter, refuge 660 *protection*; introduction; importation, import 272 *transference*; radio receiver, telephone r. 531 *telecommunication*; indraught; inbreathing, inhalation 352 *respiration*; sucking, suction; assimilation, digestion, absorption, resorption; engulfing, engulfment, swallowing, ingurgitation; ingestion (of food) 301 *eating*; imbibition, fluid intake 301 *drinking*; intake, consumption 634 *waste*; infusion 303 *insertion*; interjection 231 *interjacency*; admissibility.

**Adj.** *admitting*, receptive; freely admitting, inviting, welcoming 289 *accessible*; receivable, admissible, acceptable; absorptive, absorbent, hygroscopic; ingestive; consuming, imbibing;

digestive, assimilative; introductory, initiatory, baptismal.

**Vb.** *admit*, readmit; receive, accept, take in; naturalize; grant asylum, afford sanctuary, shelter, give refuge 660 *safeguard*; welcome, fling wide the gates; invite, call in 759 *offer*; enlist, enrol, take on 622 *employ*; give entrance *or* admittance to, pass in, allow in, allow access, give a ticket to, grant a visa to; throw open, open the door 263 *open*; bring in, import, land 272 *transfer*; let in, show in, usher in, introduce 64 *come before*; send in 272 *send*; initiate, baptize 534 *teach*; infiltrate 303 *insert*; take, be given, get 782 *receive*.

*absorb*, incorporate, engross, assimilate, digest; suck, suck in; soak up, sponge, mop up, blot 342 *dry*; resorb, reabsorb; internalize, take in, ingest, ingurgitate, imbibe; lap up, swallow, swallow up, engulf, engorge, gulp, gobble, devour 301 *eat*, *drink*; breathe in, inhale 352 *breathe*; sniff, snuff, snuff up, sniff up 394 *smell*; get the taste of 386 *taste*.

## 300 Ejection

**N.** *ejection*, ejaculation, extrusion, expulsion; precipitation 287 *propulsion*; disbarment, striking off, disqualification, excommunication 57 *exclusion*; throwing out, chucking o. (inf), bum's rush (sl); drumming out, marching orders; the heave ho (inf), dismissal, discharge, redundancy, golden handshake, decruitment, downsizing, outplacement, rightsizing, sack, boot, push, kick upstairs, garden leave *or* gardening l. 607 *rejection*; repatriation, resettlement; deportation, extradition; relegation, downgrading, exile, banishment 883 *seclusion*; eviction, dislodgment 188 *displacement*; dispossession, deprivation 786 *expropriation*; jettison, throwing overboard 779 *nonretention*; total ejection, clean sweep, elimination 165 *destruction*; emission, effusion, shedding, spilling 298 *outflow*; libation 981 *oblation*; secretion, salivation 302 *excretion*; emissivity, radioactivity 417 *radiation*; expellee, deportee, refugee 883 *outcast*.

*ejector*, evicter, dispossessor, bailiff; depriver 786 *taker*; displacer, supplanter, superseder 150 *substitute*; expeller, chucker-out (inf), bouncer; expellant, emetic, aperient, enema 658 *purgative*; propellant 723 *explosive*; volcano 383 *furnace*; emitter, radiator, radio transmitter 531 *telecommunication*; ejector seat 276 *aircraft*.

*voidance*, clearance, clearage, drainage, curettage, aspiration; eruption, eruptiveness 176 *outbreak*; egestion, regurgitation, disgorgement; vomiting, throwing up, nausea, vomit, puke; eructation, gas, wind, burp, belch, fart (sl); breaking wind, crepitation, belching; elimination, evacuation 302 *excretion*.

**Adj.** *expulsive*, expellant, extrusive, explosive, eruptive; radiating, emitting, emissive; secretory, salivary; sialogogue; vomitive, vomitory, sickening, emetic; cathartic 302 *excretory*.

*vomiting*, sick, sickened, nauseated, sick to one's stomach, throwing up, green, g. around the gills; belching, seasick, airsick, carsick; sick as a dog.

**Vb.** *eject*, expel, send down 963 *punish*; strike off, strike off the roll, strike off the register, disbar, excommunicate 57 *exclude*; export, send away 272 *transfer*; deport, expatriate, repatriate, resettle; exile, banish, transport 883 *seclude*; extrude, throw up, cast up, wash up, wash ashore; spit out, cough up, spew out; put out, push o., turf o. (inf), throw o., chuck o. (inf), fling o., bounce 287 *propel*; kick out, boot o., give the bum's rush (sl), throw out on one's ear, give the heave-ho (inf), bundle out, hustle o.; drum out; precipitate 287 *propel*; pull out 304 *extract*; unearth, root out, weed o., uproot, eradicate, deracinate 165 *destroy*; rub out, scratch o., eliminate 550 *obliterate*; exorcise, rid, get rid of, rid oneself, get shot of; shake off, brush o.; dispossess, expropriate 786 *deprive*; out, oust, evict, dislodge, unhouse, turn out, turn adrift, turn out of house and home 188 *displace*; hunt out, smoke o. 619 *hunt*; jettison, discard, throw away, throw overboard 779 *not retain*; blackball 607 *reject*; ostracize, cut, cut dead, send to Coventry, give the cold shoulder, keep at arm's length 883 *make unwelcome*; take the place of, supplant, supersede, replace 150 *substitute*.

*dismiss*, discharge, lay off, make redundant, drop 674 *stop using*; axe, sack, fire, give the sack, give the boot, give the push, give the heave-ho, give marching orders to 779 *not retain*; turn away, send one about his business, send one away with a flea in his ear, send packing, send to Jericho 292 *repel*; see off, shoo o., shoo away 854 *frighten*; show the door, show out, bow o.; bowl out, run o., catch o., take one's wicket; exorcize, tell to go, order off, order away 757 *prohibit*.

*empty*, drain, void; evacuate, eliminate 302 *excrete*; vent, disgorge, discharge; pour out, decant 272 *transpose*; drink up, drain to the dregs 301 *drink*; drain off, strain off, ladle out, bail o., pump o., suck o., aspirate; run off, siphon o., open the sluices, open the floodgates, turn on the tap 263 *open*; draw off, tap, broach 263 *pierce*; milk, bleed, let blood, catheterize 304 *extract*; clear, sweep away, clear a., clean up, mop up, make a clean sweep of, clear the decks 648 *clean*; clean out, clear out, curette; unload, unlade, unship, unpack 188 *displace*; disembowel, eviscerate, gut, clean, bone, fillet 229 *uncover*; disinfest 648 *purify*; desolate, depopulate, dispeople, unpeople 105 *render few*.

*emit*, let out, give vent to; send out 272 *send*; emit rays 417 *radiate*; emit a smell, give off, exhale, breathe out, perfume, scent 394 *smell*; vapour, fume, smoke, steam, puff 338 *vaporize*; spit, spatter, sputter, splutter; pour, spill, shed, sprinkle, spray; spurt, squirt, jet, gush 341 *moisten*; extravasate, bleed, weep 298 *flow out*; drip, drop, ooze; dribble, drool, slobber 298 *exude*; sweat, perspire 379 *be hot*; secrete 632 *store*; egest, pass 302 *excrete*; drop (a foal), lay (an egg) 167 *generate*.

*vomit*, be sick, be sick to one's stomach, bring up, throw up, cast up, regurgitate, disgorge, retch, keck, gag, upchuck (sl); spew (inf), puke (inf), cat (sl) honk (sl), poop (sl), chunder (sl), ralph (sl); be seasick, feed the fishes; feel nausea, heave, have a bilious attack.

*belch*, eructate, eruct, crepitate, burp, gurk; break wind, blow off (sl), fart (sl); hiccup, cough, hawk, clear the throat, expectorate, spit, gob (sl).

## 301 Food: eating and drinking

**N.** *eating*, munching etc. vb.; taking food, ingestion; alimentation, nutrition; feeding, drip-f., force-f., gavage; consumption, devouring; swallowing, downing, getting down, bolting; manducation, biting, chewing, mastication; rumination, digestion; chewing the cud; pasturing, cropping; eating meals, table, diet, dining, lunching, breakfasting, supping, having tea, snacking; communal feeding, messing; dining out 882 *sociability*; partaking; delicate feeding, tasting, nibbling, pecking, licking, playing with one's food, toying with one's f.; lack of appetite, eating disorder, anorexia, anorexia nervosa; ingurgitation, guzzling, gobbling; overeating, overindulgence, bingeing, bulimia nervosa, seesaw eating 944 *sensualism*, 947 *gluttony*; obesity 195 *bulk*; appetite, voracity, wolfishness 859 *hunger*; omnivorousness, omophagia 464 *indiscrimination*; eating habits, table manners 610 *practice*; flesh-eating, carnivorousness, creophagy, ichthyophagy; anthropophagy, man-eating, cannibalism; herbivorousness, vegetarianism, veganism 942 *abstainer*; edibility, digestibility; food chain, food web.

*feasting*, eating and drinking, gormandizing, guzzling, swilling; banqueting, eating out, dining out, having a meal out; regalement; orgy, bacchanalia, Lucullan banquet, state b., feast; reception, wedding breakfast, annual dinner, do 876 *celebration*; harvest supper, beanfeast, beano, bunfight, thrash; Christmas dinner, blowout, spread (see also *meal*); loaded table, festal cheer, festive board, groaning b.; fleshpots, 'land flowing with milk and honey' (see quotation at 730 *prosperity*) 635 *plenty*; banqueting hall, dining room, mess r., canteen, refectory 192 *restaurant*.

*dieting*, dietetics 658 *therapy*; slimming, losing weight, juice fasting, reducing, weight-watching, figure-watching 206 *thinness*, 946 *fasting*; diet, balanced d., crash d., macrobiotic d.; nouvelle cuisine, cuisine minceur, lean cuisine; regimen, regime, course, dietary, diet sheet, calorie counter; meagre diet, poor table 636 *insufficiency*; malnutrition 651 *disease*; calories, vitamins (see also *food content*); vitamin pill, food supplement, vitamin supplement, folic acid; dietitian, nutritionist, nutrition expert.

*gastronomy*, gastronomics, gastrology, palate-tickling, epicureanism, epicurism 944 *sensualism*; gourmandise, gourmandism, foodism, good living, high l. 947 *gluttony*; dainty palate, refined p. 463 *discrimination*; epicure, gourmet, foodie (inf), Lucullus (see also *eater*).

*cookery*, cooking, baking, cuisine, haute c., nouvelle c., lean c.; food preparation, dressing; domestic science, home economics, catering 633 *provision*; food processing (see also *provisions*); baker, cook, chef, sous c., commis c., cuisinier, cordon bleu 633 *caterer*; bakery, rotisserie, delicatessen, restaurant 192 *restaurant*; kitchen, cookhouse, galley; oven 383 *furnace*; cooking medium, butter, margarine, ghee, Olestra (tdmk), corn oil, olive o., rape seed o., sunflower o., vegetable o. 357 *oil*; dripping, lard 357 *fat*; yeast 323 *leaven*; flour, cornflour 332 *powder*; vinegar, balsamic v., malt v. 393 *sourness*; recipe, cookery magazine, cookery programme, cookery book, cookbook 589 *textbook*.

*eater*, feeder, consumer, partaker, taster etc. vb.; nibbler, picker, pecker; boarder, messer, messmate; diner, banqueter, feaster, picnicker; diner-out, dining club 882 *sociability*; dainty feeder, connoisseur, gourmet, epicure; gourmand, trencherman, trencherwoman, bon vivant, Lucullus, bacchanal, bacchant, belly-worshipper, foodie (inf) 947 *glutton*; flesh-eater, meat-e., carnivore; man-eater, cannibal, anthropophagite; vegetarian, vegan 942 *abstainer*; herbivore; omnivore, hearty eater, hungry e.; wolf, gannet, vulture, hyena, locust; teeth, jaws, mandibles 256 *tooth*; mouth, pecker, gullet, stomach, belly, paunch 194 *maw*.

*eating disorder*, anorexia, anorexia nervosa, bulimia, bulimia nervosa, bingeing, yo-yo dieting, seesaw eating.

*provisions*, stores, commissariat; provender, contents of the larder, freezer stock, foodstuff, groceries; tinned *or* canned food, frozen f., cook-chill f., dehydrated f., convenience f., junk f., fast f.; provisioning, keep, board, maintenance, aliment, entertainment, sustenance 633 *provision*; home-grown food, self-sufficiency; commons, rations, iron r.; helping 783 *portion*; buttery, pantry, larder, stillroom, cellar 632 *storage*; hay box, meat safe; freezer, fridge 384 *refrigerator*.

*provender*, animal food, fodder, feed, pasture, pasturage, forage; corn, oats, barley, grain, hay, grass, clover, lucerne, silage; beechmast, acorns; foodstuffs, dry feed, winter f.; chicken feed, pigswill, cattle cake; saltlick; meat and bonemeal, MBM.

*food*, meat, bread, staff of life; aliment, nutriment, liquid n.; alimentation, nutrition; nurture, sustenance, nourishment, food and drink, pabulum, pap; food for the body, food for the mind, food for the spirit; manna; food for the gods, nectar and ambrosia, amrita; daily bread, staple food, wheat, maize, rice, pulses, beans, potatoes; foodstuffs, comestibles, edibles, eatables, eats, victuals, viands, provender; grub (sl), tuck (sl), tucker (sl), nosh (sl), scoff (sl), chow (sl), chuck (sl), scran (sl); tack, hard t., biscuit, salt pork, pemmican; heavy food, stodge 391 *unsavouriness*; processed food, bad f., carrion, offal; wholefood, health food, functional f., organic foodstuff, high-fibre food, low-fat f.; genetically modified food, genetically altered f., GM f., Frankenstein f., Frankenfood; irradiated food; cheer, good c., good food, good table, regular meals, fleshpots, 'the fat of the land'(see quotation at 730 *prosperity*) 730 *prosperity*; creature comforts, 'cakes and ale' (see quotation at 824 *enjoyment*); delicatessen, delicacies; dainties, titbits, snacks, luxuries 637 *superfluity*; garnish, flavouring, herbs, sauce 389 *condiment*.

*food content*, vitamins; calories, roughage, bulk, fibre; minerals, salts; calcium, iron; protein, amino acid, folic a., antioxidants; fat, oil, cholesterol, saturated fats, polyunsaturates, essential fatty acid, trans-fatty acid 357 *fat*; carbohydrates, starch; sugar, glucose, sucrose, lactose, fructose 392 *sweet thing*; additive, preservative, antioxidant, artificial flavouring; E numbers; obsession with healthy food, orthorexia.

*mouthful*, bite, nibble, morsel 33 *small quantity*; sop, sip, swallow, bolus; gobbet, slice, titbit, bonne bouche; sandwich, open s., club s., submarine sandwich *or* submarine; tortilla, burrito, fajita, nacho, wrap; snack, savoury, crust; petit four, biscuit, chocolate,

sweet, toffee, chewing gum (see also *sweet-meat*); popcorn, crisps, nuts, Bombay mix; cud, quid, something to chew; tablet, pill 658 *drug*.

*meal*, refreshment, fare; light meal, snack, bite to eat; piece, butty, sandwich, open s., hamburger, hot dog, fish and chips, Buffalo wings; packed lunch, ploughman's l.; square meal, three-course m., full m., substantial m., heavy meal; sit-down meal, repast, collation, regalement, refection, spread, feed (inf), blowout (inf), beanfeast (inf), beano (inf) (see also *feasting*); thrash (inf), junket 837 *festivity*; picnic, fête champêtre, barbecue; austerity lunch, bread and cheese l., love-feast; chance meal, potluck; breakfast, elevenses, luncheon, lunch, brunch, tiffin; tea, afternoon t., five o'clock, high tea; dinner, supper, fork s., buffet s.; table d'hôte, à la carte; menu, bill of fare, diet sheet 87 *list*; dietary (see also *dieting*); cover, table, place; help, helping 783 *portion*; seconds; serving, serving up, dishing up; waitress service, self-service.

*dish*, course; main dish, entrée; salad, side dish, entremets; dessert, pudding, savoury; speciality, pièce de résistance, signature dish; dish of the day, plat du jour; meat and two veg (see also *meat*); casserole, stew, Irish s., hotpot, Lancashire h., ragout, blanquette 43 *a mixture*; meat loaf, hamburger; nut roast, nut loaf; goulash; moussaka; paella; noodles, chop suey, chow mein, stir-fry, spring roll, dim sum, egg fu yung; curry, dhal, bhaji, biryani, tandoori, tikka, pilau rice, Balti, samosa, pakora, raita; pasta, ravioli, lasagne, macaroni, spaghetti, tagliatelle, fettuccine, vermicelli, tortellini, penne, orzo, cannelloni, risotto, pizza; pancake, crepe; taco, tortilla, burrito, chimichanga, fajita; kebabs; pasty, pie, flan, quiche; fricassee, fritters, croquettes, fry-up, mixed grill, fritto misto; fondue, soufflé, omelette; egg dish, cheese d., Welsh rabbit *or* rarebit, buck r., scrambled eggs, poached e., boiled e., fried e.; bread and butter, bread and cheese, bread and dripping; réchauffé, rehash, leftovers.

*hors d'oeuvres*, antipasto, smorgasbord; starter, appetizer, canapé; angels on horseback, devils on h.; bruschetta, crostini; taramasalata, hummus, raita, mezze; vol-au-vent; blini, samosa, pakora; soup, cream s., clear s.; broth, brew, potage, consommé; stock, bouillon, julienne, bisque, chowder, purée; cock-a-leekie, mulligatawny, minestrone, borscht, gazpacho, bouillabaisse; cold meats, cooked m., cold cuts, salami, pâté, terrine, galantine; salad, side s., green s., mixed s., potato s., Russian s., Waldorf s., coleslaw, macedoine; mayonnaise, dressing, French d. 389 *sauce*.

*fish food*, fish 365 *marine life*; fish and chips, fish pie, fish cakes, gefilte fish, fish fingers, quenelles, kedgeree; white fish, oily f., fresh f., smoked f.; freshwater fish, trout, salmon, lox, gravlax, eel; seafish, cod, coley, rock salmon, dogfish, whiting, plaice, sole, skate, hake, halibut, haddock, smoked h., finnan haddie, turbot, mullet, mackerel, herring, rollmops, brisling, whitebait, sprats; sardine, pilchard, anchovies, tuna *or* tunny *or* tunny fish; kippers, bloaters, Arbroath smoky; Bombay duck; seafood, shellfish, oyster, lobster, crayfish, crab, shrimp, prawn, scampi; scallop, cockle, winkle, mussel, whelk, jellied eel; roe, soft r., hard r., caviar; sushi; frankenfish.

*meat*, flesh; red meat, white m.; beef, mutton, lamb, veal, pork, venison, game, bushmeat; pheasant, grouse, partridge, chicken 365 *table bird, poultry*; meat substitute, Quorn (tdmk), soya flour, textured vegetable protein, TVP 150 *substitute*; roast meat, Sunday roast, S. joint, roast beef and Yorkshire pudding; boiled beef and carrots; haggis, black pudding; shepherd's pie, cottage p.; minced meat, mince; meatballs, rissoles, hamburgers; mechanically recovered meat, MRM; sausage, banger, chipolata, frankfurter, knackwurst *or* knockwurst, smoked sausage, chorizo; toad in the hole, Cornish pasty, steak and kidney pudding; cut, joint, leg; baron of beef, sirloin; shoulder, hand of pork, skirt, scrag end, breast, brisket; shin, loin, flank, ribs, topside, silverside; cutlet, chop, loin c., chump c., gigot c., escalope; steak, fillet s., rump s., porterhouse s., entrecôte s., sirloin s.; pork pie, ham, bacon, bacon rasher, streaky b., back b., boiled b., gammon; tongue, knuckle, Bath chap, brawn, oxtail, cowheel, pig's trotters, sweetbreads, tripe, chitterlings, pig's fry; offal, kidney, liver, haslet 224 *insides*; suet, dripping, crackling; forcemeat, stuffing; human flesh, long pig.

*dessert*, pudding, sweet; milk pudding, rice p., semolina, tapioca, bread-and-butter pudding; steamed p., suet p., Christmas p., plum p., summer p., rolypoly, spotted dick; jam tart, mince pies (see also *pastries*); crumble, charlotte, strudel, sticky toffee pudding, baklava; stewed fruit, compôte, fool; fresh fruit, fruit salad; icecream, sorbet, mousse, tiramisu, soufflé, cheese cake, sundae, trifle, blancmange, jelly, custard 392 *sweet thing*; cheese board; yoghourt.

*sweets*, boiled s., confectionery; candy, chocolate, vegelate, caramel, toffee, fudge, Turkish delight, marshmallows, mints, liquorice; acid drops, pear d., barley sugar, humbugs, butterscotch, nougat; gob-stopper, aniseed ball,

chewing gum, bubble g.; lolly, lollipop 392 *sweet thing*; sweetmeat, comfit, bonbon; crystallized fruit; toffee apple, candy floss.

*fruit*, soft fruit, berry, gooseberry, strawberry, raspberry, loganberry, blackberry, tayberry, tummelberry, bilberry, mulberry; currant, redcurrant, blackcurrant, whitecurrant; stone fruit, apricot, peach, nectarine, plum, greengage, damson, cherry; apple, crab a., pippin, russet, pear; citrus fruit, orange, grapefruit, pomelo, lemon, lime, tangerine, clementine, mandarin; banana, pineapple, grape; rhubarb; date, fig; dried fruit, currant, raisin, sultana, prune; pomegranate, persimmon, Sharon fruit, passion fruit, guava, lichee, star fruit; mango, avocado; melon, water m., cantaloupe, honeydew; pawpaw, papaya; breadfruit; nut, coconut, Brazil nut, cashew n., pecan, peanut, groundnut, monkey nut; almond, walnut, chestnut, pine nut, hazel n., cob n., filbert; bottled fruit, tinned f., preserves 392 *sweet thing*.

*vegetable*, greens 366 *plant*; root vegetable, tuber, turnip, swede, parsnip, carrot, Jerusalem artichoke; potato, sweet p., yam; spud, baked potato, roast p., boiled p., mashed p., duchesse p., fried p., sauté p., French fries, chips; green vegetable, cabbage, Chinese c., red c., green c., white c., savoy, cauliflower, broccoli, calabrese, kohlrabi, kale, curly k., seakale; sprouts, Brussels s., spring greens; peas, petits pois, mangetout, beans, French b., broad b., runner b.; okra, lady's fingers, sorrel, spinach, chard, spinach beet, seakale b., asparagus, globe artichoke; leek, onion, shallots, garlic (see also *herb*); marrow, courgette, zucchini, cucumber, pumpkin, squash; aubergine, eggplant, capsicum, pepper, green p., red p., yellow p., chilli; sweetcorn; salads, lettuce, cos l., chicory, endive; spring onion, scallion, radish, celery, beetroot; tomato, beef t., cherry t., tomatoes on the vine, sun-dried tomatoes, love-apple; beansprouts, bamboo shoots; cress, watercress, mustard and cress; dried vegetables, pulses, lentils, split peas, chick p.; haricot beans, butter b., kidney b., soya b., adzuki b. *or* aduki b.; edible fungus, mushroom, boletus, truffle; edible seaweed, laver, laverbread, samphire; vegetarian cooking; tofu, bean curd, Quorn (tdmk); pease pudding, baked beans, bubble and squeak, sauerkraut, ratatouille, cauliflower cheese, nut cutlet.

*herb*, culinary h., sweet h., bouquet garni, fines herbes; marjoram, sweet m., oregano, rosemary, sage, mint, lemon mint, peppermint, parsley, chervil, chives, thyme, basil, balm, bergamot, savory, tarragon, bayleaf, dill, fennel, rue, hyssop, lovage, lemon balm, borage, camomile, hops, seasoning 389 *condiment*.

*spice*, spicery; coriander, cumin, cardamom, pepper, cayenne, paprika, chilli, curry powder, garam masala, turmeric, allspice, mace, cinnamon, ginger, nutmeg, clove, caraway, five spices, juniper berries, capers, vanilla pod 389 *condiment*.

*cereals*, grains, wheat, buckwheat, oats, rye, maize, mealies, corn; rice, brown r., unpolished r., wild r., long grain r., patna r., basmati r., short grain r., pudding r., golden r.; millet, sorghum; breakfast cereal, cornflakes, muesli, oatmeal, porridge, gruel, skilly, brose; flour, meal, wholemeal, wheat germ, bran; bread, dough, flour, yeast; crust, crumb; white bread, sliced b., soda b., brown b., wholemeal b., malt b., granary b., black b., rye b., pumpernickel, corn b., pitta b., ciabatta; toast, rusk, croûtons; loaf, pan l., cottage l., cob, tin, farmhouse, bloomer, baguette, French stick, bread s.; roll, breakfast r., bridge r., finger r., bap, bagel, croissant, brioche, bun, currant b.; crumpet, muffin, scone, drop s., pancake, crêpe, teacake; oatcake, bannock; pappadum, chapatti, nan, paratha, polenta, tortilla, taco, waffle, wafer, crispbread, cracker, cream c.

*pastries and cakes*, confectionery; patty, pasty, turnover, dumpling; tart, flan, quiche, puff, pie, piecrust; pastry, shortcrust p., flaky p., puff p., rough p. p., choux p.; onion tart, leek t.,; apple pie, banoffee pie, Mississippi mud pie; apple tart, patisserie, Danish pastry; gateau, cake, lardy c., fruit c., Dundee c., seed c., sponge c., Madeira c., angel c., battenburg c., layer c., galette, cheesecake; brownies, fairy cakes, cup cakes, meringue, eclair, macaroon; Chelsea bun, Bath b., doughnut, flapjack, brandysnap, gingerbread, shortbread, cookies, biscuits, crackers, digestive biscuit, Nice b., tea b., garibaldi b., custard cream, gingernut.

*dairy product* (see also *milk*); cream, clotted c., curds, whey, junket, yogurt *or* yoghurt *or* yoghourt, fruit y., acidophilus, probiotic; fromage frais; cheese, goat's c., cottage c., curd c., crowdie; cream cheese, full-fat c.; ripe cheese, blue c.; vegetarian cheese; grated c; mousetrap.

---

**Cheeses**

Bel Paese, Bleu d'Auvergne, blue Brie, Boursin, Brie, Caboc, Caerphilly, Cambozola, Camembert, Cashel Blue, Cheddar, Cheshire, Danish blue, Dolcelatte, Doolin, Dorset Blue Vinny, Double Gloucester, Dunlop, Edam, Emmental, Gouda, Gorgonzola, Gruyère, Halloumi, Havarti, Jarlsberg, Lancashire, Leerdammer, Leicestershire, Limburger, Lymeswold, mascarpone, mozzarrella, Munster, Parmesan, Pont-l'Éveque, Port Salut, Provolone, red Windsor, ricotta, Roquefort, sage Derby, Saint-Paulin, Stilton, Vacherin, Wensleydale.

---

*drinking*, imbibing, imbibition, fluid intake; potation; sipping, tasting, wine-tasting 463 *discrimination*; gulping, swilling, soaking, wine-bibbing; drinking to excess, alcoholism, binge-drinking 949 *drunkenness*; giving to drink, watering; libation 981 *oblation*; drinker, bibber, heavy drinker, swiller, quaffer; toper 949 *drunkard*.

*draught*, drink, beverage, dram, bevvy; gulp, swallow, sip, sup; bottle, bowl, glass 194 *cup*; cuppa, pinta; glassful, bumper; swig, nip, noggin, jigger, tot, slug; peg, double peg, snorter, snifter, chaser; long drink, thirst-quencher; short drink, short; quick one, quickie, snort; sundowner, nightcap; loving cup, stirrup c., doch-an-dorris, one for the road; health, toast; mixed drink, concoction, cocktail, punch, spritzer 43 *mixture*; potion, decoction, infusion 658 *medicine*; divine drink, amrita, nectar.

*soft drink*, teetotal d., nonalcoholic beverage; water, drinking w., filtered w., eau potable, spring water, fountain; soda water, soda, cream s., soda fountain, siphon; table water, carbonated w., mineral w., Perrier (tdmk), tonic water, barley w., squash, low calorie drink, mixer; energy drink; iced drink, frappé; milk, milk shake; ginger beer, ginger ale, Coca Cola *or* Coke (tdmk); fizz, pop, lemonade, orangeade, bitter lemon; cordial, fruit juice, orange j., apple j., tomato j., vegetable j.; juice box; coconut milk; tea, iced t., lemon t., herbal t., char, pekoe, orange p., Indian t., China t., green t., black t., Russian t., herb t., maté, redbush *or* rooibos, tisane 658 *tonic*; coffee, café au lait, café noir, black coffee, white coffee, decaffeinated coffee, decaf, Irish coffee, Turkish c., espresso, cappuccino, latte, cocoa (see also *milk*); sherbet, syrup, julep, hydromel.

*alcoholic drink*, strong d., booze, bevvy, wallop, tipple, poison; brew, fermented liquor, intoxicating l. (see also *wine*); alcohol, wood a.; malt liquor, John Barleycorn, beer, small b., swipes; draught beer, keg b., bottled b.; strong beer, stingo; heavy, export; ale, real ale; barley wine; stout, lager, bitter, porter, mild, home brew; low-alcohol beer, no-alcohol b., shandy; alcopop; cider, rough c., scrumpy; perry, mead, Athole brose; wheat wine, palm w., rice beer, toddy, sake, mescal, tequila; distilled liquor, spirituous l., spirits, ardent s., raw s., aqua vitae, firewater, hooch, moonshine, mountain dew, rotgut, hard stuff; brandy, cognac, eau-de-vie, armagnac, marc, applejack, Calvados, kirsch, slivovitz, jambava; gin, mother's ruin, geneva, sloe gin, schnapps, blue ruin; whisky, usquebaugh, Scotch whisky, scotch; rye, bourbon; Irish whiskey, poteen; vodka, aquavit, ouzo, raki, arrack; rum, white r., demon r., grog, hot g., hot toddy, punch, rum p.; egg flip, egg nog; cordial, spiced wine, mulled w., negus, posset, hippocras; flavoured wine, cup, claret c.; mixed drink, Pimms (tdmk), gin and tonic, pink gin, highball, brandy and soda, whisky and s.; cocktail; aperitif, Pernod (tdmk), absinthe; liqueur, cassis, Cointreau (tdmk), Drambuie (tdmk), curaçao, crème de menthe.

### Cocktails

Alaska, alexander, Algonquin, Americano, aviation, Bellini, between the sheets, black Russian, Black Watch, Bloody Mary, blue lagoon, Bronx, Clover Club, Collins, Combustible Edison, Cuba libre, daiquiri, death in the afternoon, Delilah, flaming Ferrari, Gibson, gimlet, gin rickey, godfather, golden dawn, grasshopper, Harvey Wallbanger, highball, hurricane, John Collins, maiden's prayer, mai tai, Manhattan, margarita, martini, mint julep, mojito, negroni, old-fashioned, piña colada, pink gin, pink lady, planter's punch, presbyterian, Rob Roy, rusty nail, sazerac, screwdriver, sea breeze, sidecar, Singapore sling, slow comfortable screw, snowball, stinger, tequila sunrise, Tom Collins, whiskey sour, white lady, white Russian, yellow bird, Yokohama, zombie.

*wine*, the grape, juice of the g., blood of the g.; ampelology, ampelography; red wine, white w., vin rosé, rosé wine, blush wine; vermouth; spumante, sparkling wine, still w., sweet w., dry w., light w., full-bodied w., vintage w.; vin ordinaire, vin de table, vin du pays; vino (inf), plonk (inf); table wine; house wine; dessert w.; fortified w., sherry, manzanilla, port, vintage p., ruby p., white p., tawny p.; champagne, champers, shampoo, fizz, bubbly, buck's fizz; alcohol-free wine, low-alcohol w.; vintage wine, first great growth, premier cru; sangria.

### Wines and Grapes

Auslese, Beerenauslese, Trockenbeerenauslese, Spätlese; Kabinett.

Asti, Asti Spumante, Beaujolais, Beaujolais nouveau, Beaune, Bordeaux, burgundy, Cabernet Franc, Cabernet Sauvignon, Chablis, Chambertin, champagne, Chardonnay, Châteauneuf-du-Pape, Chianti, claret, Côtes-du-Rhône, Frascati, Gewürztraminer, Graves, hock, Lambrusco, Liebfraumilch, Macon, madeira, marsala, Mateus rosé, Médoc, Merlot, Moselle, Muscadet, muscat, muscatel, Niersteiner, Pinot Blanc, Pinot Noir, port, retsina, Riesling, sack, Sauternes, Sauvignon, Sekt, Sémillon, Shiraz, Soave, Sylvaner, Tarragona, Tokay, Valpolicella, vinho verde.

*milk*, top of the m., cream; cow's milk, beestings; goat's milk, mare's m., koumiss; mother's milk, breast m.; buttermilk, dried m.,

skimmed m., semi-skimmed m., condensed m., evaporated m., pasteurized m.; soya milk, plant m.; milk drink, m. shake, malted m., cocoa, chocolate, hot c., Horlicks (tdmk), latte; curdled milk, curds, junket. (See also *dairy product*.)

**Adj.** *feeding*, eating, grazing etc. vb.; flesh-eating, meat-e.; carnivorous, creophagous, cannibalistic; omophagic, omophagous; insectivorous; herbivorous, graminivorous, frugivorous; vegetarian, vegan 942 *abstainer*; omnivorous 464 *indiscriminating*; greedy, wolfish, gannet-like 947 *gluttonous*; water-drinking, teetotal, on the wagon 942 *temperate*; swilling, tippling, drinking 949 *drunken*; well-fed, well-nourished, bloated; nursed, breast-fed; full up, crammed 863 *sated*.

*edible*, eatable; ritually pure, kosher; esculent, comestible; digestible, predigested; potable, drinkable; milky, lactic; worth eating, palatable, succulent, moreish, palate-tickling, dainty, delicious 386 *tasty*, 390 *savoury*; gluggable; cereal, wheaten; fermented, distilled, spirituous, alcoholic, hard 949 *intoxicating*; nonalcoholic, soft.

*nourishing*, feeding, sustaining, nutritious, nutritive, nutritional; alimental, alimentary; dietary, dietetic; fattening, rich, calorific, high in calories; protein-rich, body-building; non-fattening, wholesome 652 *salubrious*.

*culinary*, dressed, oven-ready, ready-to-cook, made-up, ready-to-serve; cooked, done to a turn, well-done; al dente; underdone, red, rare, raw; over-cooked, burnt, b. to a cinder; roasted etc. vb. (see also *cook*); à la meunière, au gratin, au naturel, mornay, au fromage, à la campagne, à la mode, à la maison; gastronomic, epicurean; mensal, prandial, post-p., after-dinner; mealtime.

**Vb.** *eat*, feed, fare, board, mess; partake 386 *taste*; take a meal, have a feed, break one's fast, break bread; breakfast, have brunch, snack, eat between meals, lunch, have tea, take tea, dine, sup; dine out, regale, feast, banquet, carouse 837 *revel*; eat well, have a good appetite, do justice to, be a good trencherman *or* -woman, ask for more; water at the mouth, drool, raven 859 *be hungry*; fall to, set to, tuck in, lay into; fork in, spoon in, shovel in; stuff oneself, binge, fill one's stomach 863 *sate*; guzzle, gormandize 947 *gluttonize*; put on weight 197 *expand*; work one's way through a meal, take every course, eat up, leave a clean plate, eat everything in sight; lick the platter clean 165 *consume*; swallow, gulp down, snap up, devour, dispatch, bolt, wolf, make short work of; feed on, live on, fatten on, batten on, prey on; nibble, peck, lick, play with one's food, toy with one's f., have a poor appetite, be anorexic; nibble at, peck at, sniff at; be a seesaw eater; ingest, digest 299 *absorb*.

*chew*, masticate, manducate, champ, chomp, munch, crunch, scrunch; mumble, mouth, worry, gnaw, grind 332 *pulverize*; bite, tear, rend, chew up 46 *cut*.

*graze*, browse, pasture, crop, feed; ruminate, chew the cud; nibble.

*drink*, imbibe, suck 299 *absorb*; quaff, drink up, drink one's fill, drain, drink like a fish, slake one's thirst, lap, sip, gulp; wet one's lips, wet one's whistle; draw the cork, crack a bottle; lap up, soak up, wash down; booze, swill, swig, tipple, tope 949 *get drunk*; toss off one's glass, drain one's g., knock it back; raise one's glass, pledge 876 *toast*; have another, take one for the road, have one over the eight; refill one's glass 633 *replenish*; give to drink, wine, water; prepare a drink *or* medicine *or* posset; lay in drink, lay down a cellar 633 *provide*.

*feed*, nourish, vitaminize; nurture, sustain, board; give to eat, victual, cater, purvey 633 *provide*; nurse, breast-feed, give suck; pasture, graze, put out to grass; fatten, fatten up 197 *enlarge*; dine, wine and dine, feast, fête, banquet, have to dinner, regale with 882 *be hospitable*.

*cook*, prepare a meal; pressure-cook; put in the oven, put in the microwave, microwave, bake, brown; roast, spit-roast, pot-r., braise; broil, grill, charcoal-grill, barbecue, spatchcock, griddle, devil, curry; sauté, fry, deep-f., shallow-f., stir-f.; fry sunny side up, double-fry (eggs); scramble, poach; boil, parboil; coddle, seethe, simmer, steam; casserole, stew; baste, lard, bard; whip, whisk, beat, blend, liquidize, stir; draw, gut, bone, fillet; stuff, dress, garnish, spice up, zap up (inf); dice, shred, mince, grate; sauce, flavour, herb, spice 388 *season*.

**Int.** bon appétit!, here's health!, here's to you!, here's mud in your eye!, bottoms up!, down the hatch!, slàinte!, prosit!, skol!, cheers!

## 302 Excretion

**N.** *excretion*, discharge, secretion 300 *ejection*; effusion, extravasation; emanation 298 *egress*; exhalation, breathing out 352 *respiration*; exudation, perspiration, sweating, diaphoresis 298 *outflow*; suppuration, maturation 651 *infection*; cold, common c., coryza, catarrh, hay fever, allergic rhinitis, allergy; salivation, expectoration, spitting; coughing, hawking, cough; urination, micturition, peeing, pissing (sl), slashing; waterworks, plumbing; enuresis, incontinence.

*haemorrhage*, bleeding, extravasation, haemophilia 335 *blood*; menses, menarche, cata-menia, period, time of the month, curse; dysmenorrhoea, menorrhagia; leucorrhoea.

*defecation*, evacuation, elimination, clearance 300 *voidance*; bowel movement, shit (sl), crap (sl), motion; one's natural functions, bodily f.; diarrhoea, the runs (sl), the trots (sl) 651 *digestive disorders*; constipation.

*excrement*, waste matter, meconium; faeces, stool, shit (sl), crap (sl), excreta, ordure, night soil; coprolite; dung, cowpat, manure, muck; droppings, guano; urine, piss (sl), water; ice-bomb; sweat, beads of s., lather; spittle, spit, gob (sl), sputum; saliva, slaver, slobber, froth, foam; rheum, phlegm; catarrh, mucus, snot; matter, pus; afterbirth, lochia; slough, cast, exuviae, pellet; feculence 649 *dirt*.

**Adj.** *excretory*, secretory; purgative, laxative, aperient; excretive, diuretic; menstrual; diaphoretic, sudorific; perspiratory; faecal, feculent; anal, urinary; emetic, rheumy, watery; mucous, phlegmy; cast-off, exuvial.

**Vb.** *excrete*, secrete; pass, move; defecate, move one's bowels, shit (sl), crap (sl); be taken short (sl), have the runs (sl), have the trots (sl), relieve oneself, ease o., answer the call of nature, go, go to the lavatory; urinate, micturate, piddle (inf), pee (inf); have a p., piss (sl), have a p. (sl), have a slash (sl), take a leak (sl), make water, pay a visit (inf), spend a penny (inf), wet oneself (inf); sweat, perspire, steam, glow 379 *be hot*; salivate, slobber, snivel; cough, hawk, spit, gob (sl) 300 *belch*, weep 298 *exude*; water at the mouth 859 *be hungry*; foam at the mouth 891 *be angry*; cast, slough, shed one's skin 229 *doff*.

## 303 Insertion: forcible ingress

**N.** *insertion*, intercalation, interpolation, parenthesis 231 *interjection*; adding 38 *addition*; introduction, insinuation 297 *ingress*; infixation, impaction; planting, transplantation 370 *agriculture*; inoculation, injection, jab, shot 263 *perforation*; infusion, enema, catheter; thing inserted, insert, inset; implant, silicone i.; stuffing 227 *lining*.

*immersion*, submersion, submergence 311 *lowering*; dip, bath 313 *plunge*; baptism 988 *Christian rite*; burial, burial at sea 364 *interment*.

**Adj.** *inserted*, introduced etc. vb.; added 38 *additional*; intermediate 231 *interjacent*; coffined 364 *buried*.

**Vb.** *insert*, introduce; weave into 222 *enlace*; put into, thrust i., intrude; poke into, jab i., stick i.; transfix, run through 263 *pierce*; ram into, jam i., stuff i., pack i., push i., shove i., tuck i., press i., pop i. 193 *load*; pocket 187 *stow*; ease into place, slide in, fit in; knock into, hammer i., drive i. 279 *impel*; put in, inlay, inset 227 *line*; mount, frame 232 *circumscribe*; subjoin 38 *add*; interpose 231 *put between*; drop in, put in the slot 311 *let fall*; putt, hole out; pot, hole; put in the ground, bury 364 *inter*; sheathe, encapsulate, encase 226 *cover*.

*infuse*, drop in, instil, pour in 43 *mix*; imbue, imbrue, impregnate 297 *infiltrate*; transfuse, decant 272 *transpose*; squirt in, inject 263 *pierce*.

*implant*, plant, transplant, plant out, prick o., bed o., dibble; graft, engraft, bud; inoculate, vaccinate; embed, bury; infix, wedge in, impact, dovetail 45 *join*.

*immerse*, bathe, steep, souse, marinate, soak 341 *drench*; baptize, duck, dip 311 *lower*; submerge, flood; immerse oneself 313 *plunge*.

## 304 Extraction: forcible egress

**N.** *extraction*, withdrawal, removal, pulling out 188 *displacement*; elimination, eradication 300 *ejection*; abortion, extermination, extirpation 165 *destruction*; extrication, unravelment, disengagement, liberation 668 *deliverance*; evulsion, avulsion, tearing out, ripping o.; cutting out, exsection, excision; Caesarian birth, forceps delivery; expression, squeezing out; suction, sucking out, aspiration; vacuuming, pumping; drawing out, pull, tug, wrench 288 *traction*; digging out 255 *excavation*; mining, quarrying; fishery; distillation 338 *vaporization*; drawing off, tapping, milking; thing extracted, essence, extract.

*extractor*, gouger; miner, quarrier; wrench, forceps, pincers, pliers, tweezers 778 *nippers*; mangle, squeezer 342 *dryer*; corkscrew, screwdriver 263 *opener*; lever 218 *pivot*; scoop, spoon, ladle, shovel; pick, pickaxe; rake; toothpick 648 *cleaning utensil*; vacuum cleaner, Hoover (tdmk); excavator, dredge, dredger, dragline; syringe, siphon; aspirator, suction pump; Archimedes' screw, shadoof 341 *irrigator*.

   **Adj.** *extracted*, removed etc. vb.; extractive.

   **Vb.** *extract*, remove, pull 288 *draw*; draw out, elicit, educe; unfold 316 *evolve*; pull out, take o., get o., pluck; withdraw, excise, cut out, rip o., tear o., whip o.; excavate, mine, quarry, dig out, unearth; dredge, dredge up; expel, lever out, winkle o., smoke o. 300 *eject*; extort, wring from; express, press out, squeeze o., gouge o.; force out, wring o., wrench o., drag o.; draw off, milk, tap; syphon off, aspirate, suck, void, pump; wring from, squeeze f., drag f.; pull up, dig up, grub up, rake up; eliminate, weed out, root up, uproot, pluck up by the roots, eradicate, deracinate, extirpate 165 *destroy*; prune, thin out 105 *render few*; distil 338 *vaporize*; extricate, unravel, free 746 *lib-*

*erate*; unpack, unload 188 *displace*; eviscerate, gut 300 *empty*; unwrap 229 *uncover*; pick out 605 *select*.

## 305 Passage: motion through

**N.** *passage*, transmission 272 *transference*; transportation 272 *transport*; passing, passing through, traversing; transilience 147 *transition*; trespass 306 *overstepping*; transit, traverse, crossing, journey, patrol 267 *land travel*; passage into, penetration, interpenetration, permeation, infiltration; transudation, osmosis, endosmosis 297 *ingress*; exosmosis 298 *egress*; intervention 231 *interjacency*; right of way 624 *access*; stepping-stone, flyover, underpass, subway 624 *bridge*; track, route, orbit 624 *path*; intersection, junction 222 *crossing*; waterway, channel 351 *conduit*.

*passing along*, passage, thoroughfare; traffic, pedestrian t., wheeled t., vehicular t.; road traffic, ocean t., air t.; traffic movement, flow of traffic, circulation; walking, crossing, cycling, driving, pulling, pushing, pram-p.; loading, unloading; waiting, parking, zone p., kerb-side p., off-street p.; traffic load, traffic density; traffic jam, procession, queue; road rage; road user 268 *pedestrian, driver*; passerby.

*traffic control*, traffic engineering; traffic calming, traffic c. measures, speed bump, sleeping policeman, road hump, chicane, road pricing, road tolling; traffic rules, highway code, Green Cross C., green man 693 *precept*; traffic lane, motorway l., bus l., cycle l., one-way street, carriageway, dual c., clearway 624 *road*; diversion, alternative route 282 *deviation*; contraflow, lane closure; white lines, yellow l., red l., red route, dedicated bus lane; cat's-eyes (tdmk); street furniture, traffic lights, lampposts, roundabout; pedestrian crossing, zebra c., pelican c., subway (see also *passage*); Belisha beacon, bollard, refuge, island; car park, parking lot, parking place, parking zone, park-and-ride; parking meter, lay-by; point duty, road patrol, speed trap, radar t., speed camera; traffic police, traffic cop; traffic engineer; traffic warden, meter maid; lollipop man *or* lady.

   **Adj.** *passing*, crossing etc. vb.; transitional, transilient; osmotic.

   **Vb.** *pass*, pass by, leave on one side, skirt, coast 200 *be near*; flash by 277 *move fast*, 114 *be transient*; go past, not stop 146 *go on*, 265 *be in motion*; pass along, join the traffic, circulate, weave; pass through, transit, traverse; shoot through, shoot a bridge, shoot the rapids 269 *navigate*; pass out, come out the other side 298 *emerge*; go through, soak t., seep t., percolate, permeate 189 *pervade*; pass and repass, patrol, walk up and down, work over, beat, scour, go over the ground; pass into, penetrate, infiltrate 297 *enter*; bore, perforate 263 *pierce*; thread, thread through, string 45 *connect*; enfilade, rake; open a way, force a passage 297 *burst in*; worm one's way, squeeze through, elbow t., clear the way 285 *progress*; cross, go across, cross over, make a crossing, reach the other side 295 *arrive*; wade across, ford; get through, get past, negotiate; pass beyond 306 *overstep*; repass 286 *turn back*; pass in front, cut across, cross one's bows 702 *obstruct*; step over, straddle, bestride 226 *overlie*; bridge, bridge over 226 *cover*; carry over, carry across, transmit 272 *send*; pass to, hand, reach, pass from hand to hand, hand over 272 *transfer*.

**Adv.** *en passant*, by the way; on the way, in transit, en route.

## 306 Overstepping: motion beyond

**N.** *overstepping*, going beyond, overstepping the mark, stretching a point 305 *passage*; transcendence 34 *superiority*; excursion, digression 282 *deviation*; violation, transgression, trespass 936 *guilty act*; usurpation, encroachment 916 *arrogation*; infringement, infraction, intrusion 916 *undueness*; expansionism, greediness 859 *desire*; overextension, ribbon development 197 *expansion*; overfulfilment, excessiveness 637 *redundance*; overrating 482 *overestimation*; overdoing it, going overboard 546 *exaggeration*; overindulgence 943 *intemperance*.

**Adj.** *surpassing*, transcending etc. vb.; one up on 34 *superior*; overextended, overlong, overhigh; too strong, overpowered; excessive 32 *exorbitant*; out of bounds, out of reach.

**Vb.** *overstep*, overstep the mark, overpass; pass, leave behind; go beyond, go too far, throw out the baby with the bathwater; exceed, exceed the limit; overrun, override, overshoot, overshoot the mark, aim too high; overlap 226 *overlie*; surmount, jump over, leap o., skip o., leapfrog 312 *leap*; step over, cross 305 *pass*; cross the Rubicon, pass the point of no return, burn one's boats; overfill, brim over, slop o., spill o. 54 *fill*; overgrow, overspread 637 *superabound*; overdo 546 *exaggerate*; strain, stretch, stretch a point; overbid, overcall one's hand, have one's bluff called, overestimate 482 *overrate*; overindulge 943 *be intemperate*; overstay, outstay one's welcome, oversleep 136 *be late*.

*encroach*, invade, make inroads on 712 *attack*; infringe, transgress, trespass 954 *be illegal*; poach 788 *steal*; squat, usurp 786 *appropriate*; barge in, horn in, butt in 297 *intrude*; overlap, impinge, trench on; entrench upon;

eat away, erode 655 *impair*; infest, overrun 297 *burst in*; overflow, flood 341 *drench*.

*outdo*, exceed, surpass, outclass; transcend, rise above, mount a., soar a., outsoar, outrange, outrival 34 *be superior*; go one better, overcall, overbid, outbid; outwit, overreach 542 *deceive*; outmanoeuvre, outflank, steal a march on, steal one's thunder; make the running 277 *move fast*; outgo, outpace, outwalk, outmarch, outrun, outride, outjump, outsail, outdistance, distance; overhaul, gain upon, overtake, come in front, shoot ahead; lap, leave standing, leave at the starting post 277 *outstrip*; leave behind, race, beat, beat hollow 727 *defeat*.

## 307 Shortfall

**N.** *shortfall*, falling short etc. vb.; inadequacy, negative equity 636 *insufficiency*; a minus, deficit, short measure, shortage, slippage, loss 42 *decrement*; leeway, drift 282 *deviation*; unfinished state 55 *incompleteness*; nonfulfilment, default, defalcation 726 *noncompletion*; half measures 641 *lost labour*; no go 728 *failure*; fault, defect, shortcoming 647 *imperfection*, 845 *blemish*; something missing, want, lack, need 627 *requirement*.

**Adj.** *deficient*, short, short of, minus, wanting, lacking, missing; catalectic; underpowered, substandard; undermanned, understaffed, short-staffed, below establishment; half-done, perfunctory 55 *incomplete*; out of one's depth, not up to scratch, inadequate 636 *insufficient*; failing, running short 636 *scarce*; below par 647 *imperfect*; unattained, unreached, tantalizing.

**Vb.** *fall short*, come s., run s. 636 *not suffice*; not stretch, not reach to; lack, want, be without 627 *require*; underachieve, not make the grade, not come up to scratch; miss, miss the mark; lag 136 *be late*; stop short, fall by the way, fall out, not stay the course; break down, get bogged down; fall behind, lose ground, slip back; slump, collapse 286 *regress*; fall through, fall to the ground, come to nothing, end in smoke, fizzle out, fail 728 *miscarry*; labour in vain 641 *waste effort*; tantalize, not come up to expectations 509 *disappoint*.

**Adv.** *behindhand*, in arrears; not enough; below par, below the mark, far from it; to no purpose, in vain.

## 308 Ascent: motion upwards

**N.** *ascent*, ascension, lift, upward motion, gaining height; defiance of gravity, levitation; taking off, leaving the ground, takeoff, lift-off, blast-off 296 *departure*; flying up, soaring, spiralling, spiral; zooming, zoom 271 *aeronautics*; culmination 213 *summit*; floating up, surfacing, breaking surface; going up, rising, uprising; rise, upgrowth, upturn, upward trend; uprush, upsurge, crescendo 36 *increase*; updraught, rising air, rising current, thermal; sunrise, sun-up, dawn 128 *morning*; moonrise, star-rise; mounting, climbing; hill-walking, Munro-bagging, hill-climbing, rock-c., mountaineering, alpinism; ladder-scaling, escalade 712 *attack*; jump, vault, pole v., pole jump 312 *leap*; bounce 280 *recoil*; rising ground, hill 209 *high land*; gradient, slope, ramp 220 *incline*; rising pitch 410 *musical note*; means of ascent, stairs, steps, stile, flight of stairs, staircase, spiral s., stairway, landing; ladder, step l., accommodation l., Jacob's l., companionway; rope ladder, ratlines; stair, step, tread, rung; lift, ski l., chair l., elevator, escalator 310 *lifter*; fire escape 667 *means of escape*.

*climber*, mountaineer, rock-climber, alpinist, cragsman *or* -woman, fell walker, hill-walker, Munro-bagger; steeplejack; rocket, sky r.; soarer, lark, skylark, laverock; gusher, geyser, fountain 350 *stream*.

**Adj.** *ascending*, rising etc. vb., climbing, scansorial; rearing, rampant; buoyant, floating 323 *light*; supernatant; airborne, gaining height; anabatic, in the ascendant; uphill, steep 215 *vertical*; ladderlike, scalariform; scalable, climbable.

**Vb.** *ascend*, rise, rise up, go up, leave the ground; defy gravity, levitate; take off, become airborne, have lift-off, fly up 271 *fly*; gain height, mount, soar, spiral, zoom, climb; reach the top, get to the top of the ladder, reach the zenith, culminate; float up, bob up, surface, break water; jump up, spring, vault 312 *leap*; bounce 280 *recoil*; push up, grow up, shoot up 36 *grow*; curl upwards; tower, aspire, spire 209 *be high*; gush, spirt, spout, jet, play 298 *flow out*; get up, start up, stand up, rear, rear up, ramp 215 *be vertical*; rise to one's feet, get up 310 *lift oneself*; trend upwards, wind u., slope u., steepen 220 *be oblique*.

*climb*, walk up, struggle up; mount, make one's way up, work one's way up; go climbing, go mountaineering, mountaineer; clamber, scramble, swarm up, shin up, climb like a monkey, go up hand over fist; surmount, top, breast, conquer, scale the heights 209 *be high*; go over the top, escalade 712 *attack*; go upstairs, climb a ladder; mount (a horse), climb into the saddle.

**Adv.** *up*, upstairs; upwards 209 *aloft*; excelsior, ever higher; per ardua ad astra.

## 309 Descent

**N.** *descent*, declension, declination 282 *devi-* *ation*; falling, dropping; cadence; landing; downward trend, spiral, decline, drop, slump 37 *decrease*; sunset, moonset; comedown, demotion 286 *regression*; downfall, débâcle, collapse, setback 165 *ruin*; trip, stumble; titubation, lurch, capsize 221 *overturning*; tumble, crash, spill, fall; cropper, purler; downrush, swoop, stoop, pounce; dive, header, bellyflop 313 *plunge*; nosedive, power-dive 271 *aeronautics*; landing, crash l., splashdown 295 *arrival*; sliding down, glissade; subsidence, landslide, avalanche; downdraught 352 *wind*; downpour, shower 350 *rain*; cascade 350 *waterfall*; downthrow (geology); declivity, slope, tilt, dip 220 *incline*; chute, slide, helter-skelter; precipice, sheer drop 215 *verticality*; submergence, sinkage, slippage 311 *lowering*; boring, tunnelling, burrowing, mining, sapping, undermining 255 *excavation*; speleology, potholing, caving; descender, faller, tumbler; plunger 313 *diver*; burrower, miner, sapper 255 *excavator*; parachutist 271 *aeronaut*; paratrooper 722 *soldier*; speleologist, pot-holer, caver.

**Adj.** *descending*, dropping etc. vb.; descendent, declining, declivitous 220 *sloping*; swooping, stooping; tumbledown, falling, tottering; tilting, sinking, foundering; burrowing, sapping; drooping 311 *lowered*; submersible, sinkable.

**Vb.** *descend*, come down, go d., dip d.; decline, abate, ebb 37 *decrease*; reach a lower level, slump, plummet, fall, drop, sink; sink like a lead balloon, sink without trace 322 *weigh*; soak in, seep down 297 *infiltrate*; get lower and lower, reach the depths, touch bottom 210 *be low*; bottom out, reach one's nadir 35 *be inferior*; sink to the bottom, gravitate, precipitate, settle, set; fall down, fall in, cave in, fall to the ground, collapse; sink in, subside, slip, give way; hang down, prolapse, droop, sag, swag 217 *hang*; go under water, draw, have draught; submerge, fill the tanks, dive 313 *plunge*; drown 313 *founder*; go underground, sink into the earth; dig down, burrow, bore, tunnel, mine, sap, undermine 255 *make concave*; drop from the sky, parachute; swoop, stoop, pounce; fly down, flutter d., float d.; lose height, drop down, swing low; touch down, alight, light, perch 295 *land*; lower oneself, abseil; get down, climb d., step d., get off, fall o., dismount; coast down, slide down, glissade, toboggan; fall like rain, shower, cascade, drip 350 *rain*; take a lower place, come down a peg 286 *regress*; bow down, dip, duck 311 *stoop*; flop, plop, splash down.

*tumble*, fall; tumble down, fall d.; topple, topple over, heel o., keel o., overbalance, capsize, tumble head over heels 221 *be inverted*; miss one's footing, slip, slip up, trip, stumble; lose one's balance, titubate, stagger, totter, teeter, lurch, tilt, droop 220 *be oblique*; rise and fall, pitch, toss, roll; take a header (inf), dive 313 *plunge*; take a running jump, precipitate oneself 312 *leap*; fall off, take a fall, be thrown, come a cropper, fall heavily, crash to the ground, fall flat on one's face, fall prostrate, bite the dust, measure one's length; plummet, plop, plump, plump down 311 *sit down*; slump, sprawl; fall through the air, spiral, spiral down, nosedive, crash, prang (sl).

**Adv.** *down*, downwards; downhill, downstairs, downstream.

## 310 Elevation

**N.** *elevation*, raising etc. vb.; erection, uplift, upheaval; picking up, lift; hoist, boost; leg-up 703 *aid*; levitation; exaltation, Assumption; uprising, uptrend, growth, upswing 308 *ascent*; an elevation, eminence 209 *high land*, 254 *prominence*; height above sea level 209 *height*.

*lifter*, erector, builder, spiderman; raiser, raising agent, yeast, baking powder 323 *leaven*; lever, jack 218 *pivot*; dredger 304 *extractor*; crane, derrick, hoist, windlass; winch, capstan; rope and pulley, block and tackle, parbuckle, jeers; forklift, elevator, dumb waiter, escalator, lift, ski l., cable railway 274 *conveyor*; hot air, gas, hydrogen, helium; spring, springboard, trampoline; stilts; scaffolding, platform 218 *stand*.

**Adj.** *elevated*, raised etc. vb.; exalted, uplifted; erectile, erective; erected, set up; upright, erect, upstanding, rampant 215 *vertical*; mounted, on high, soaring; towering over, head and shoulders above; lofty, sublime 209 *high*.

**Vb.** *elevate*, heighten 209 *make higher*; puff up, blow up, swell, leaven 197 *enlarge*; raise, erect, set up, put up, run up, rear up, build up, build; lift, lift up, raise up, heave up; uplift; upraise; jack up, lever up, hike up, prop 218 *support*; stand on end 215 *make vertical*; prevent from falling, hold up, bear up; prevent from sinking, buoy up; raise aloft, hold a., hold up, wave; hoist, haul up, brail, trice; raise from the ground, pick up, take up; pull up, wind up; weigh, trip (anchor); fish up, drag up, dredge up, pump up 304 *extract*; chair, shoulder, carry shoulder-high; exalt, put on a pedestal 866 *honour*; put on top, mount 213 *crown*; jump up, bounce up 285 *promote*; give a lift, give a leg-up 703 *aid*; throw in the air, throw up, cast up, toss up; sky, loft; send up, shoot up, lob 287 *propel*; perk up (one's head), prick up (one's ears); bristle, bristle up 215 *be vertical*.

*lift oneself*, arise, rise 308 *ascend*; stand up, get up, get to one's feet, pick oneself up, jump up, leap up, spring up, spring to one's feet; pull oneself up; hold oneself up, hold one's head up, draw oneself up to one's full height, stand on tiptoe 215 *be vertical*.

**Adv.** *on*, on stilts, on tiptoe; on one's legs, on one's hind legs; on the shoulders of, on the back of.

**Int.** upsy-daisy!, on your feet!, up you get!

## 311 Lowering

**N.** *lowering*, depression, hauling down etc. vb.; pushing down, detrusion 279 *impulse*; ducking, sousing 313 *plunge*; debasement, demotion, reduction 872 *humiliation*; subversion 149 *revolution*; overthrow, prostration; overturn, upset 221 *overturning*; precipitation, defenestration 287 *propulsion*; keeping under, suppression; a depression, dent, dip, dimple, hollow 255 *cavity*; low pressure 340 *weather*.

*obeisance*, bow, kowtow, namaskar, namaste, reverence, salaam 884 *courtesy*; curtsy, bob, duck, nod, salute 884 *courteous act*; kneeling, genuflexion 920 *respect*.

**Adj.** *lowered*, depressed etc. vb.; at a low ebb 210 *low*; prostrate 216 *supine*; sedentary, sitting, sit-down; depressive, depressing; submersible.

**Vb.** *lower*, depress, detrude, push down, thrust d. 279 *impel*; shut down (a lid) 264 *close*; hold down, keep d., hold under 165 *suppress*; lower, let down, take d.; lower a flag, dip, half-mast, haul down, strike; deflate, puncture, flatten, squash, crush 198 *make smaller*; let drop (see also *let fall*); sink, scuttle, send to the bottom, drown 309 *descend*; duck, souse, douse, dip 313 *plunge*; weigh on, press on 322 *weigh*; capsize, roll over, tip, tilt 221 *invert*; crush, stave in, bash in, dent, make a dint in, hollow 255 *make concave*.

*let fall*, drop, shed; let go 779 *not retain*; let slip *or* slide through one's fingers; pour, pour out, decant 300 *empty*; spill, slop 341 *moisten*; sprinkle, shower, scatter, dust, dredge; sow, broadcast 75 *disperse*; lay down, put d., set d., throw d., fling d. (see also *fell*); pitch *or* chuck overboard, jettison, drop over the side; precipitate, send headlong 287 *propel*.

*fell*, trip, topple, tumble, overthrow; prostrate, spread-eagle, lay low, lay one on his back 216 *flatten*; knock down, bowl over, skittle, floor, drop, down 279 *impel*; throw down, cast d., fling d. (see also *let fall*); pull down, tear d., dash d., raze, level, raze to the ground, pull about one's ears, trample in the dust 165 *demolish*; hew down, cut d., axe 46 *cut*; blow down 352 *blow*; bring down, undermine; shoot down, wing 287 *shoot*.

*abase*, debase, lower the standard; lower one's sights; demote, reduce to the ranks, cashier 752 *depose*; humble, deflate, puncture, debunk, take down a peg, cut down to size, take the wind out of one's sails 872 *humiliate*; crush, squash, grind down 165 *suppress*.

*sit down*, sit, sit oneself down, be seated, sit on the ground, squat, squat on one's hunkers, hunker; subside, sink, lower oneself; kneel, recline, stretch oneself out 216 *be horizontal*; roost, nest 683 *repose*; take a seat, seat oneself, take a pew, park oneself; perch, alight 309 *descend*.

*stoop*, bend, bend down, get d.; bend over, bend forward, bend backward; lean forward, lean over backwards; cringe, crouch, cower 721 *knuckle under*; slouch, hunch one's back 248 *make curved*; bow, scrape, duck, bob, curtsy, bob a c. 884 *pay one's respects*; nod, incline one's head, bow down, make obeisance, kiss hands, salaam, prostrate oneself, kowtow 920 *show respect*; kneel, kneel to, genuflect, kiss the ground.

### 312 Leap

**N.** *leap*, saltation, skipping, capering, leapfrogging; jump, hop, skip; spring, bound, vault, pole v.; high jump, long j., running j.; triple j., hop, skip and jump; bungee jump, barfly jump, base jumping 837 *sport*; caper, gambol, frolic; kick, high k., cancan; jeté, entrechat; prance, curvet, caracole, capriole, gambade; springy step, light tread 265 *gait*; dance step; dance, breakdance, reel, jig, Highland fling 837 *dancing*.

*jumper*, high-j., pole-vaulter, hurdler, steeplechaser; skipper, hopper, leapfrogger; caperer; prancer; dancer, jiver; twister, rock 'n roller 837 *dance*; tap dancer, clog d., morris d., breakdancer; ballet dancer; dancing girl, chorus girl 594 *entertainer*, kangaroo, goat, chamois, springbok; jerboa, frog, grasshopper, froghopper, flea; bucking horse, bucking bronco; jumping bean; jumping jack, Jack-in-the-box 837 *plaything*.

**Adj.** *leaping*, jumping etc. vb.; saltatory, saltatorial; skittish, frisky, fresh 819 *lively*; skipping, hopping; dancing, jiving; bobbing, bucking, bouncing; tossing 318 *agitated*.

**Vb.** *leap*, jump, take a running j.; spring, bound, vault, pole-v., hurdle, jump over the sticks, steeplechase, take one's fences; bungee jump, barfly jump; skip, hop, leapfrog, bob, bounce, rebound, buck, bob up and down 317 *oscillate*; trip, foot it, tread a measure, stamp 837 *dance*; caper, cut capers, gambol, frisk,

romp; prance, paw the ground, ramp, rear, plunge; cavort, curvet, caracole; start, give a jump; jump on, pounce; jump up, leap up, spring up 308 *ascend*; jump over, clear; flounce, flounder, jerk 318 *be agitated*; writhe 251 *wriggle*.

**Adv.** *by leaps and bounds*, on the light fantastic toe, trippingly; at a single bound.

### 313 Plunge

**N.** *plunge*, swoop, pounce, stoop, plummet 309 *descent*; nosedive, power dive 271 *aeronautics*; dive, header, bellyflop; swallow dive, duck d.; dip, ducking; immersion, submergence; crash dive; drowning, sinking.

*diver*, skin d., scuba d., deepsea d., frogman; underwater swimmer, aquanaut; the bends, caisson disease; diving bird, dipper 365 *bird*; submariner; submersible, submarine, bathyscaphe, bathysphere, diving-bell; plunger, sinker, lead, plummet; fathometer 465 *meter*.

**Vb.** *plunge*, dip, duck, bathe 341 *be wet*; walk the plank, fall in, jump in, plump, plop, plummet; dive, stage-dive, make a plunge, take a header, go headfirst; welter, wallow, pitch and toss; souse, douse, immerse, submerse, drown; submerge, flood the tanks, crash-dive 309 *descend*; sink, scuttle, send to the bottom, send to Davy Jones's locker 311 *lower*; sound, fathom, plumb the depths, heave the lead 465 *measure*.

*founder*, go down 309 *descend*; get out of one's depth; drown, settle down, go to the bottom, go down like a stone 211 *be deep*; plummet, sink, sink without trace, sink like lead, sink like a sack of potatoes 322 *weigh*.

### 314 Circuition: curvilinear motion

**N.** *circuition*, circulation, circumambulation, circumnavigation, circling, wheeling, gyre, spiral 315 *rotation*; turning, cornering, turn, U-turn 286 *return*; orbit; lap; circuit, milk round, tour, round trip, full circle; figure of eight 250 *loop*; helix 251 *coil*; unwinding 316 *evolution*; circuitousness, roundabout way, scenic route, tourist r. 626 *circuit*.

*circler*, circumambulator; circumnavigator 270 *mariner*; roundsman 794 *tradespeople*; patrol, patrolman *or* -woman, vigilante; moon, satellite 321 *planet*.

**Adj.** *circuitous*, turning etc. vb.; orbital, ecliptic; geostationary; circumforaneous, peripatetic 267 *travelling*; circumfluent, circumflex 248 *curved*; circumnavigable; devious 626 *roundabout*, 282 *deviating*.

**Vb.** *circle*, circulate, go the rounds, make the round of; compass, circuit, make a c., lap; tour, do the round trip; go round, skirt; circumambulate, circumnavigate, circumaviate; go round the world, put a girdle round the earth, go globetrotting; turn, round, double a point, weather a p.; round a corner, corner, turn a c.; revolve, orbit; wheel, spiral, come full circle, chase one's tail 315 *rotate*; do a U-turn, turn round, bend r.; put about, wheel a., face a., turn on one's heel 286 *turn back*; draw a circle, describe a circle 232 *circumscribe*; curve, wind, twist, wind one's way 251 *meander*; make a detour 626 *circuit*.

### 315 Rotation: motion in a continued circle

**N.** *rotation*, orbital motion, revolving, orbiting; revolution, full circle; gyration, circling, wheeling, spiralling; circulation, circumfluence; spinning motion, spin, circumrotation, circumvolution; rolling, volution 285 *progression*; spiral, roll, spin, flat s.; turn, twirl, pirouette, waltz 837 *dance*; whirlabout, whirl, whirr; dizzy round, rat race, milk round 678 *overactivity*; dizziness, vertigo; gyrostatics.

*vortex*, whirl; whirlwind, tornado, cyclone 352 *gale*; waterspout, whirlpool, swirl 350 *eddy*; whirlpool bath, Jacuzzi (tdmk); maelstrom, Charybdis; smoke ring 250 *loop*.

*rotator*, rotor, spinner; whirligig, teetotum, top, peg t., spinning t., humming t.; roundabout, merry-go-round; churn, whisk; potter's wheel, lathe, circular saw; spinning wheel, spinning jenny; girandole, catherine wheel; flywheel, prayer w., roulette w., wheel of Fortune 250 *wheel*; Hula Hoop (tdmk); gyroscope, turntable; gramophone record, disc, magnetic tape, cassette, compact disc; wind pump, windmill, fan, sail; propeller, prop, screw; turbine; winder, capstan 310 *lifter*; swivel, hinge; spit, jack; spindle, axle, axis, shaft 218 *pivot*; spool, reel, roller 252 *cylinder*; rolling stone, planet, satellite 268 *wanderer*; whirling dervish; dancer, figure skater; Ixion.

**Adj.** *rotary*, rotating, spinning etc. vb.; rotatory, circumrotatory; gyratory, gyroscopic, gyrostatic; geostationary; circling, cyclic; vortical, vorticose; cyclonic; vertiginous, dizzy.

**Vb.** *rotate*, revolve, orbit, go into orbit 314 *circle*; turn right round, chase one's own tail; spin, spin like a top, twirl, pirouette; corkscrew 251 *twine*; gyre, gyrate, waltz, wheel; whirl, whirr, hum 404 *resound*; mill around, swirl, eddy 350 *flow*; bowl, trundle; set rolling, roll, roll along; spin with one's fingers, twirl, twiddle, twizzle; churn, whisk 43 *mix*; turn, crank, wind, reel, spool, spin; slew, slew round, swing round, swivel r.; roll up, furl 261 *fold*; roll itself up, curl up, scroll.

**Adv.** *round and round*, in a circle, in circles,

clockwise, anticlockwise, counterclockwise, sunwise, widdershins; head over heels.

### 316 Evolution: motion in a reverse circle

**N.** *evolution*, unrolling, unfolding, unfurling; eversion 221 *inversion*; development 157 *growth*; evolutionism, Darwinism, Neo-D. 358 *biology*.

**Adj.** *evolving*, unwinding etc. vb.; evolved etc. vb.; evolutional 358 *biological*.

**Vb.** *evolve*, unfold, unfurl, unroll, unwind, uncoil, uncurl, untwist, untwine, explicate, disentangle 62 *unravel*; evolute, develop, grow into 147 *be turned to*, 1 *become*; roll back 263 *open*.

### 317 Oscillation: reciprocating motion

**N.** *oscillation*, libration, nutation; harmonic motion, pendular m., swing of the pendulum; vibration, tremor; vibrancy, resonance 141 *periodicity*; pulsation, rhythm; throbbing, drumming, pulse, beat, throb; pitter-patter, flutter, palpitation 318 *agitation*; breathing 352 *respiration*; undulation, wave motion, frequency, frequency band, wavelength 417 *radiation*; sound wave, radio w.; tidal w. 350 *wave*; seismic disturbance, earthquake, tremor 176 *violence*; seismology, seismograph; oscillator, vibrator; metronome; pendulum, bob, yoyo 217 *hanging object*. (See also *fluctuation*.)

*fluctuation*, wave motion (see also *oscillation*); alternation, reciprocation 12 *correction*; to and fro movement, coming and going, shuttling, shuttle service; ups and downs, boom and bust, ebb and flow, flux and reflux, systole and diastole; night and day 14 *contrariety*; reeling, lurching, rolling, pitching; roll, pitch, lurch, stagger, teeter, totter, reel; shake, nod, wag, dance; springboard 328 *elasticity*; swing, seesaw; rocker, rocking chair, rocking horse; shuttlecock, shuttle; mental fluctuation, wavering, vacillation 601 *irresolution*.

**Adj.** *oscillating*, undulating etc. vb.; oscillatory, undulatory; swaying, libratory; pulsatory, palpitating; vibrant, vibratory, vibratile; earthshaking, seismic; pendulous, dangling; reeling, staggery, tottery, wobbly, groggy; rhythmic, rhythmical 141 *periodical*.

**Vb.** *oscillate*, librate, nutate; emit waves 417 *radiate*; wave, undulate, vibrate, pulsate, pulse, beat, drum; tick, throb, palpitate; respire, pant, heave 352 *breathe*; play, sway, nod; swing, dangle 217 *hang*; seesaw, rock; shunt (trains), lurch, reel, stagger, totter, teeter, waddle, wobble, wamble, wiggle, waggle, wag; bob, bounce, bob up and down, dance 312 *leap*; toss, roll, pitch, tumble, wallow; rattle, chatter,

shake; flutter, quiver, shiver 318 *be agitated*;
flicker 417 *shine*; echo 404 *resound*. (See also
*fluctuate*.)

*fluctuate*, alternate, reciprocate 12 *correlate*;
ebb and flow, come and go, pass and repass,
shuttle; slosh about, slop a.

*brandish*, wave, wag, waggle, shake, flourish;
wave to and fro, shake up and down, pump;
flutter 318 *agitate*.

**Adv.** *to and fro*, backwards and forwards,
back and forth; in and out, up and down, side
to side, left to right and right to left; zigzag,
seesaw, wibble-wabble; like a yoyo;
shuttlewise.

## 318 Agitation: irregular motion

**N.** *agitation*, irregular motion, jerkiness, fits
and starts, unsteadiness, shakiness 152 *changeableness*; joltiness, bumpiness, broken water,
choppiness, pitching, rolling 259 *roughness*;
unsteady beam, flicker, twinkle 417 *flash*;
sudden motion, start, jump 508 *lack of expectation*; hop 312 *leap*; shake, jig, jiggle; toss 287
*propulsion*; shock, shake, jar, jolt, jerk, judder;
jounce, bounce, bump 279 *impulse*; nudge, dig,
jog 547 *gesture*; vibration, thrill, throb, pulse,
pit-a-pat, palpitation, flutter 317 *oscillation*;
shuddering, shudder, shiver, frisson; quiver,
quaver, tremor; tremulousness, trembling (see
also *spasm*); restlessness, ants in one's pants
(inf); feverishness, fever; tossing, turning, jacti-
tation; jiving, rock 'n' roll, breakdancing 678
*activity*, 837 *dancing*; itchiness, itch 378 *formication*; twitchiness, twitch, grimacing, grimace;
mental agitation, perturbation, disquiet 825
*worry*; trepidation, jumpiness, twitter, flap,
butterflies, collywobbles 854 *nervousness*;
delirium tremens, dt's, the shakes; Parkinson's
disease, Parkinsonism; shivers, jumps, jitters,
fidgets; aspen, aspen leaf.

*spasm*, ague, shivering, chattering; twitch,
tic, nervous t.; chorea, St Vitus' dance, taran-
tism; lockjaw, tetanus; cramp, the cramps;
throe 377 *pang*; convulsion, paroxysm, access,
orgasm 503 *frenzy*; fit, epilepsy, falling sickness
651 *nervous disorders*; pulse, throb 317 *oscillation*; attack, seizure, stroke.

*commotion*, turbulence, tumult 61 *turmoil*;
hurly-burly, hubbub, brouhaha, hassle; fever,
flurry, rush, bustle 680 *haste*; furore 503 *frenzy*;
fuss, to-do, bother, kerfuffle, shemozzle 678
*restlessness*; racket, din 400 *loudness*; stir, fer-

ment 821 *excitation*; boiling, fermentation,
ebullition, effervescence 355 *bubble*; ground
swell, heavy sea 350 *wave*; squall, tempest,
thunderstorm, magnetic storm 176 *storm*;
whirlpool 315 *vortex*; whirlwind 352 *gale*; disturbance, atmospherics.

**Adj.** *agitated*, shaken, fluttering, waving,
brandished; shaking etc. vb.; troubled, unquiet
678 *active*; feverish, fevered, restless; scratchy,
jittery, jumpy, twitchy, flustered, wound up
(inf), wired up (sl), all of a twitter, all of a
doodah, all of a dither, in a flap, in a flutter
854 *nervous*; hopping, leaping, jumping up and
down, like a cat on hot bricks; breathless,
panting; twitching, itchy; convulsive, spasmodic, spastic; saltatory; skittish 819 *lively*;
flighty 456 *light-minded*; doddering, tottering,
shaky, wavery, tremulous, atremble, wobbly;
thrilling, vibrating 317 *oscillating*.

**Vb.** *be agitated*, ripple, popple, boil 355
*bubble*; stir, move, dash; shake, tremble,
quiver, quaver, shiver; have a fever, throw a fit,
be all of a doodah, be all of a dither; writhe,
squirm, twitch 251 *wriggle*; toss, turn, toss
about, thresh a.; kick, plunge, rear 176 *be
violent*; flounder, flop, wallow, roll, reel, pitch
317 *fluctuate*; sway 220 *be oblique*; pulse, beat,
thrill, vibrate, judder, shudder; wag, waggle,
wobble, stagger, lurch, dodder, totter, teeter,
dither 317 *oscillate*; whirr, whirl 315 *rotate*; jig
around, jig up and down, jump about, hop,
bob, bounce, dance 312 *leap*; flicker, twinkle,
gutter, sputter 417 *shine*; flap, flutter, twitter,
start, jump; throb, pant, palpitate, miss a
beat, go pit-a-pat 821 *be excited*; bustle, rush,
mill around 61 *rampage*; ramp, roar 891 *be
angry*.

*agitate*, disturb, rumple, ruffle, untidy 63
*derange*; discompose, wind up (inf), perturb,
worry, hassle, throw into a panic 827 *trouble*;
ripple, puddle, muddy; stir, stir up 43 *mix*;
whisk, whip, beat, churn 315 *rotate*; shake up,
shake; wag, waggle, wave, flourish 317 *brandish*; flutter, fly (a flag); jog, joggle, jiggle, jolt,
jounce, nudge, dig; jerk, pluck, twitch.

*effervesce*, froth, spume, foam, foam at the
mouth, bubble up 355 *bubble*; boil, boil over,
seethe, simmer, sizzle, spit 379 *be hot*; ferment,
work.

**Adv.** *jerkily*, pit-a-pat; convulsively etc. adj.;
by fits and starts, with a hop, skip and a jump;
in fits, in spasms.

# Matter

## SECTION ONE

### Matter in general

#### 319 Materiality

**N.** *materiality*, materialness, empirical world, world of experience; corporeity, corporeality, corporality, bodiliness; material existence, world of nature 3 *substantiality*; physical being, physical condition 1 *existence*; plenum 321 *world*; concreteness, tangibility, palpability, solidity 324 *density*; weight 322 *gravity*; personality, individuality 80 *speciality*; embodiment, incarnation, reincarnation, metempsychosis; realization, materialization; positivism, materialism, dialectical m.; unspirituality, worldliness, sensuality 944 *sensualism*; materialist, realist, positivist.

*matter*, brute m., stuff; plenum; hyle, prime matter; body, fabric, frame, mass, material 331 *structure*; substance, solid s., corpus; organic matter, flesh, flesh and blood, plasma, protoplasm 358 *organism*; real world, world of nature, Nature.

*object*, tangible o., bird in the hand; inanimate object, still life; physical presence, body, flesh and blood, real person 371 *person*; thing, gadget, gizmo, something, commodity, article, item; stocks and stones 359 *mineral*; raw material 631 *materials*.

*element*, elementary unit, sense datum, sensibilia; principle, first p., nitty-gritty 68 *origin*; the four elements, earth, air, fire, water; unit of being, monad; factor, ingredient, nuts and bolts 58 *component*; chemical, chemical element, basic substance; isotope;

##### Chemical Elements

actinium, aluminium, americium, antimony, argon, arsenic, astatine, barium, berkelium, beryllium, bismuth, bohrium, boron, bromine, cadmium, caesium, calcium, californium, carbon, cerium, chlorine, chromium, cobalt, copper, curium, dubrium, dysprosium, einsteinium, erbium, europium, fermium, fluorine, francium, gadolinium, gallium, germanium, gold, hafnium, hassium, helium, holmium, hydrogen, indium, iodine, iridium, iron, krypton, lanthanum, lawrencium, lead, lithium, lutetium, magnesium, manganese, meitherium, mendelevium, mercury, molybdenum, neodymium, neon, neptunium, nickel, niobium, nitrogen, nobelium, osmium, oxygen, palladium, phosphorus, platinum, plutonium, polonium, potassium, praseodymium, promethium, protactinium, radium, radon, rhenium, rhodium, rubidium, ruthenium, rutherfordium, samarium, scandium, seaborgium, selenium, silicon, silver, sodium, strontium, sulphur, tantalum, technetium, tellurium, terbium, thallium, thorium, thulium, tin, titanium, tungsten, uranium, vanadium, xenon, ytterbium, yttrium, zinc, zirconium.

physical element, atom, molecule, nucleus, particle, free radical; ion; quantum 196 *minuteness*.

##### Terms used in Particle Physics

electron; positron; nucleon, neutron, proton; elementary particle, fundamental particle, subatomic particle; antiparticle; baryon, fermion, kaon, lepton, meson, muon, pi-meson, pion, neutrino, tau particle; boson, gluon, graviton, photon; tachyon; exciton; quark, antiquark; flavour, up, down, strange, charm, top *or* truth, bottom *or* beauty; colour; string theory, superstring; strong interaction, weak interaction; strangeness; quantum chromodynamics, quantum electrodynamics, quantum mechanics; grand unified theories; particle accelerator, cyclotron, synchrotron 160 *nucleonics*.

*physics*, physical science, natural s., science of matter; natural history 358 *biology*; chemistry, organic c., inorganic c., physical c.; mechanics, Newtonian m., quantum m., theory of relativity; thermodynamics; electromagnetism; atomic physics, nuclear physics 160 *nucleonics*; applied physics, technology 694 *skill*; natural philosophy, experimental p. 490 *science*; chemist, physicist, scientist.

**Adj.** *material*, hylic; real, natural; massy, solid, concrete, palpable, tangible, ponderable, sensible, weighty; physical, chemical, spatio-temporal; objective, impersonal, clinical, neuter; hypostatic 3 *substantial*; embodied, incarnate, personified, – on a stick (inf); corporal, somatic, corporeal, bodily, fleshly, of flesh and blood, in the flesh, carnal; reincarnated, realized, materialized; materialistic, worldly, unspiritual 944 *sensual*.

**Vb.** *materialize*, substantialize, substantiate, hypostatize, corporealize, reify; objectify 223 *externalize*; realize, make real, body forth; embody, incarnate, personify.

## 320 Immateriality

**N.** *immateriality*, unreality 4 *insubstantiality*; incorporeity, incorporeality, dematerialization, disembodiment, imponderability, intangibility, impalpability, ghostliness, shadowiness; immaterialism, idealism, Platonism; spirituality, otherworldliness; animism; spiritualism 984 *occultism*; other world, world of spirits, eternity 115 *perpetuity*; animist, spiritualist 984 *occultist*; idealist 449 *philosopher*; astral body 970 *ghost*.

*subjectivity*, personality, selfhood, myself, me, yours truly 80 *self*; ego, id, superego; Conscious, Unconscious; psyche, higher self, spiritual s. 447 *spirit*.

**Adj.** *immaterial*, without mass: incorporeal, incorporate; abstract 447 *mental*; aery, ethereal, ghostly, shadowy 4 *insubstantial*; imponderable, intangible; bodiless, unembodied, discarnate, disembodied; supernal, extramundane, unearthly, transcendent; supersensory, psychic, spiritistic, astral 984 *psychical*; spiritual, otherworldly 973 *religious*; personal, subjective; illusory 513 *imaginary*.

**Vb.** *disembody*, spiritualize, dematerialize, disincarnate.

## 321 Universe

**N.** *universe*, omneity 52 *whole*; world, globe, creation, all c.; sum of things, plenum, matter and antimatter, dark matter, mirror matter 319 *matter*; cosmos, macrocosm, microcosm; spacetime continuum; expanding universe, metagalaxy; outer space, deep s., intergalactic s.; void; cosmogony, nebular hypothesis, planetesimal h.; big bang theory, steady state t. 68 *start*.

*world*, wide w., four corners of the earth; home of man, sublunary sphere; earth, mother e., Gaea; middle earth, planet e., spaceship e.; globe, sphere, terrestrial s., terraqueous globe, geoid; geosphere, biosphere, ecosphere; terrestrial surface, crust; subcrust, moho; plate tectonics, continental drift 344 *land*; waters of the earth 343 *ocean*; atlas, world-map 551 *map*; Old World, New World 184 *region*; earthshine; geocentric system, Ptolemaic s.; personal world 8 *circumstance*.

*heavens*, sky, welkin, empyrean, ether, ethereal sphere, celestial s., hemisphere; firmament, vault of heaven; primum mobile, music of the spheres; night sky, starlit s., aurora borealis, merry dancers, northern lights, aurora australis; zodiacal light, gegenschein 417 *glow*.

*star*, fixed s., heavenly body, celestial b. 420 *luminary*; sidereal sphere, starry host, host of heaven; asterism, constellation, Great Bear, Little B., Plough, Big Dipper, Charles's Wain, Cassiopeia's Chair, Pleiades, Orion, Orion's belt, Southern Cross; starlight, starshine; main sequence, spectral type; blue star, white s., yellow s., red s.; double star, binary, spectroscopic b., eclipsing b., eclipsing variable; multiple star; variable star, cepheid; giant, supergiant, red giant; subgiant, dwarf, red d., white d.; X-ray star, radio s. 417 *radiation*; quasistellar object, quasar, pulsar, neutron star, black hole, white h.; collapsar; nova, supernova; Pole Star, North Star, Polaris; Pointers; Dog star, Sirius; Star of Bethlehem; Milky Way, Galaxy; star cluster, globular c., galaxy, radio g.; island universe; stellar motion, proper m., radial velocity; Star of David, Magen David.

*nebula*, galactic n., planetary n., protogalaxy, protostar; cosmic dust, interstellar matter; Magellanic cloud, nebula, spiral n.

*zodiac*, signs of the z., ecliptic; house, mansion, lunar m.; cusp; ascendant, rising sign.

---

**Signs of the Zodiac**
air sign, earth sign, fire sign, water sign.
 Aries (the Ram), Taurus (the Bull), Gemini (the Twins), Cancer (the Crab), Leo (the Lion), Virgo (the Virgin), Libra (the Balance), Scorpio (the Scorpion), Sagittarius (the Archer), Capricornus (the Goat), Aquarius (the Watercarrier), Pisces (the Fishes).

---

*planet*, major p., minor p., inferior p., superior p.; asteroid, planetoid; Mercury; Venus, morning star, evening s., Lucifer, Vesper, Hesperus; Mars, red planet; Earth, Jupiter, Saturn, Uranus, Neptune, Pluto; comet, wandering star, Halley's comet; planetary orbit, cometary o., parabolic o., hyperbolic o. 315 *rotation*.

*meteor*, falling star, shooting s., fireball, bolide; meteorite, aerolite, siderite, chondrite; chondrule; meteoroid; micrometeorite; meteor shower; radiant point.

*sun*, day-star, orb of day, eye of heaven; midnight sun; parhelion, sun dog, mock sun; sunlight, sunshine, photosphere, chromosphere; facula, flocculus, granule, sun spot, prominence, solar flare, corona; solar wind; Sol, Helios, Phoebus, Apollo; solar system, heliocentric s., Copernican s.

*moon*, satellite; new moon, waxing moon,

waning m., half-m., crescent m., horned m., gibbous m., full m., harvest m., hunter's m.; paraselene, mock moon; moonscape, crater, mare, rill; Queen of the night, Selene, Luna, Diana, Phoebe, Cynthia, Hecate, Astarte; man in the moon; parish lantern; moonlight, moonshine.

*satellite*, moon; earth satellite, artificial s., orbiter, sputnik, moonlet, biosatellite, weather satellite, communications s., comsat; space station, skylab, space lab; space shuttle 276 *spaceship*; astronaut 271 *aeronaut*; satellite country.

*astronomy*, star lore, stargazing, star watching; satellite tracking; radioastronomy; astrophysics, astrochemistry; exobiology; astrophotography; selenography, selenology; uranography; astrology, horoscope 511 *divination*; observatory, planetarium; tracking station; telescope, refracting t., reflecting t., Newtonian t., Cassegrainian t., Gregorian t. 442 *telescope*; astronomical telescope, altazimuth, equatorial; transit instrument; radio telescope, parabolic reflector, dish; spectroscope, spectrohelioscope, spectroheliograph 551 *photography*; orrery, celestial globe, astrolabe; planisphere; astronomer, radio a., astrophysicist; stargazer, star-watcher; astrologer.

*uranometry*, uranography; right ascension, declination, hour; hour circle, great c., ecliptic; celestial pole, galactic p., celestial equator, galactic e.; equinoctial line, equinoctial point; equinoctial colure, solstitial c.; equinox, vernal e., first point of Aries, autumnal equinox; solstice, summer s., winter s.; geocentric latitude *or* longitude, heliocentric latitude *or* longitude, galactic latitude *or* longitude; node, ascending n., descending n.; libration, nutation; precession, precession of the equinox.

*cosmography*, cosmology, cosmogony, cosmogonist, cosmographer.

*earth sciences*, geography, orography, oceanography, physiography, geomorphology, speleology; geology, geodesy, geodetics; geographer, geodesist, geologist, speleologist; hydrology, hydrography.

**Adj.** *cosmic*, universal, cosmical, cosmological, cosmogonic, cosmographical; interstellar, interplanetary, intermundane; galactic, intragalactic; extragalactic; ultramundane 59 *extraneous*; metagalactic.

*celestial*, heavenly, ethereal, empyreal; starry, star-spangled, star-studded; sidereal, astral, stellar; solar, heliacal, zodiacal; lunar, lunate, lunisolar; nebular, nebulous; heliocentric, geocentric; cometary, meteoric; meteoritic; equinoctial, solstitial.

*planetary*, planetoidal, asteroidal, satellitic;

Mercurian, Venusian, Martian, Jovian, Saturnian, Neptunian, Uranian, Plutonian.

*telluric*, tellurian, terrestrial, terrene, terraqueous; sublunary, subastral; Old-World, New-World; polar, circumpolar, equatorial; worldwide, world, global, international, universal 183 *spacious*; worldly, earthly.

*astronomic*, astronomical, astrophysical, stargazing, star-watching; astrological, telescopic, spectroscopic.

*geographic*, geographical, oceanographic, orographical; geological, geomorphic, speleological; geodesic, geodetic, physiographic; hydrographic, hydrological.

**Adv.** *under the sun*, on the face of the globe, here below, on earth.

## 322 Gravity

**N.** *gravity*, gravitation, force of gravity, gravitational pull; gravity feed; weight, weightiness, heaviness, ponderousness, ponderosity 195 *bulk*; specific gravity; pressure, displacement, sinkage, draught; encumbrance, load, lading, freight; burden, burthen; ballast, make-weight, counterpoise 31 *offset*; mass, lump 324 *solid body*; lump of, weight of, mass of; plummet 313 *diver*; weight, bob, sinker, lead, brick, stone, millstone; statics.

*weighing*, ponderation; balancing, equipoise 28 *equalization*; weights, avoirdupois weight, troy w., apothecaries' w.; grain, carat, scruple, pennyweight, drachm; ounce, pound, stone, quarter, quintal, hundredweight, ton; milligram, gram, kilogram, kilo; megaton, kiloton; axle load, laden weight.

*scales*, weighing machine; steelyard, weighbeam; balance, spring b.; bathroom scales, kitchen s., pan, scale, weight, calibrator; platform scale, weighbridge.

**Adj.** *weighty*, heavy, heavyweight, ponderous; leaden, heavy as lead; weighing etc. vb.; cumbersome, cumbrous 195 *unwieldy*; lumpish, massive 324 *dense*; heavy-handed, heavy-footed, pressing, incumbent, superincumbent, oppressive; ponderable, having weight, weighing, with a weight of; weighted, loaded, laden, charged, burdened; overweighted, overburdened, overloaded, top-heavy 29 *unequal*; gravitational, gravitative.

**Vb.** *weigh*, have weight, exert w.; weigh the same, balance 28 *be equal*; counterpoise, counterweigh 31 *compensate*; outweigh, overweigh, overbalance 34 *predominate*; tip the scales, turn the s., tip the balance, depress the scales; wallow, sink, gravitate, settle 313 *founder*, 309 *descend*; weigh heavy, be h., lie h.; press, weigh on, weigh one down, oppress, hang like a millstone 311 *lower*; load, cumber 702 *hinder*; try the weight of, take the w. of, find the w. of, put on the scales, lay in the scale 465 *measure*; weigh oneself, stand on the scales.

*make heavy*, weight, hang weights on; charge, burden, overweight, overburden, overload 193 *load*; gain weight, put on w. 195 *be large*.

**Adv.** *weightily*, heavily, leadenly; like a ton of bricks, like a lead balloon

### 323 Lightness

**N.** *lightness*, portability; thinness, air, ether 325 *rarity*; buoyancy; volatility 338 *vaporization*; weightlessness, imponderability, imponderableness; defiance of gravity, levitation 308 *ascent*; feather, thistledown, cobweb, gossamer; fluff, oose, dust, straw 4 *insubstantial thing*; cork, buoy, lifebelt, life jacket; balloon, bubble; hot air, helium 310 *lifter*.

*leaven*, raising agent, ferment, enzyme, barm, yeast, baking-powder, self-raising flour.

**Adj.** *light*, underweight 307 *deficient*; lightweight, featherweight; portable, handy 196 *little*; lightsome, light-footed; light on one's feet; light-handed, having a light touch; weightless, without weight, lighter than air; imponderable, unweighable; sublime, ethereal, airy, gaseous, volatile 325 *rare*; uncompressed, doughy, barmy, yeasty, fermenting, zymotic, enzymic; aerated, frothy, bubbly, sparkling, pétillant, foamy, whipped; floating, buoyed up, buoyant, unsinkable; feathery, cobwebby, gossamery, fluffy; light as air, light as a feather, light as thistledown, light as a fairy; lightening, unloading; raising, self-raising, leavening.

**Vb.** *be light*, buoyant etc. adj.; defy gravity, levitate, surface, float to the surface, float, swim; drift, waft, glide, be airborne 271 *fly*; soar, hover 308 *ascend*.

*lighten*, make light, make lighter, reduce weight, lose w.; ease 701 *disencumber*; lighten ship, throw overboard, jettison 300 *empty*; volatilize, gasify, vaporize 340 *aerate*; leaven, work; raise, levitate 310 *elevate*.

SECTION TWO

## Inorganic matter

### 324 Density

**N.** *density*, solidity, consistency; compactness, solidness, concreteness, thickness, concentration; incompressibility 326 *hardness*; impenetrability, impermeability; indissolubility, indiscerptibility, indivisibility; coalescence, cohesion, inseparability 48 *coherence*; relative density, specific gravity; densimeter, hydrometer, aerometer.

*condensation*, consolidation, concentration; constipation; thickening etc. vb.; concretion, nucleation; solidification, consolidation; coagulation, thrombosis; congealment, gelatinization; glaciation; ossification, petrifaction, fossilization 326 *hardening*; crystallization; sedimentation, precipitation; condenser, compressor, thickener, gelatine, rennet, pepsin 354 *thickening*.

*solid body*, solid; block, mass 319 *matter*; knot, nugget, lump, chunk, dod, burl; condensation, nucleus, hard core; aggregate, conglomerate, concretion; concrete, cement; stone, crystal, hardpan 344 *rock*; precipitate, deposit, sediment, silt, clay, cake, clod, clump; bone, ossicle; gristle, cartilage 329 *toughness*; coagulum, curd, clot, blood-c.; solid mass, phalanx, serried ranks; forest, thicket; wall, blank w. 702 *obstacle*.

**Adj.** *dense*, thick, crass; close, heavy, stuffy (air); foggy, murky, smoky, to be cut with a knife; lumpy, ropy, grumous, clotted, coagulated, curdled; caked, matted, knotted, tangled 48 *cohesive*; consistent, monolithic; firm, close-textured, knotty, gnarled; substantial, massy, massive 322 *weighty*; concrete, solid, set, gelled *or* jelled, frozen, solidified etc. vb.; crystalline, crystallized; condensed, nucleated; costive, constipated; compact, close-packed, firm-p. 54 *full*; thickset, thick-growing, thick, bushy, luxuriant 635 *plenteous*; serried, massed, densely arrayed 74 *assembled*; incompressible, inelastic 326 *rigid*; impenetrable, impermeable, impervious, without holes; indivisible, indiscerptible, infrangible, unbreakable 162 *strong*.

*indissoluble*, insoluble, infusible; undissolved, unliquefied, unmelted, unthawed, deep-frozen; precipitated, sedimentary.

*solidifying*, binding, constipating; setting, gelling *or* jelling, freezing, congealing; clotting, coagulating, styptic, astringent, haemostatic.

**Vb.** *be dense*, – solid etc. adj.; become solid, solidify, consolidate; conglomerate, cement 48 *cohere*; condense, nucleate, form a core *or* kernel; densify, thicken, inspissate; precipitate, deposit; freeze, glaciate 380 *be cold*; set, gelatinize, jellify, gell *or* jell; congeal, coagulate, clot, curdle; cake, crust; crystallize; fossilize, petrify, ossify 326 *harden*; compact, compress, firm down, contract, squeeze 198 *make smaller*; pack, squeeze in, cram, tamp, ram down 193 *load*; mass, crowd 74 *bring together*; bind, constipate; precipitate, deposit.

### 325 Rarity

**N.** *rarity*, low pressure, vacuum, near v. 190 *emptiness*; compressibility, sponginess 327 *softness*; tenuity, subtility, fineness 206 *thinness*;

lack of substance 4 *insubstantiality*, 323 *light-ness*; incorporeality, ethereality 320 *immateri-ality*; airiness, windiness, ether, gas 336 *gaseousness*, 340 *air*; rarefaction, expansion, dilatation, pressure reduction, attenuation; sub-tilization, etherealization.

**Adj.** *rare*, tenuous, thin, fine, subtile, subtle; flimsy, airy, airy-fairy, slight 4 *insubstantial*; low-pressure, uncompressed; compressible, spongy 328 *elastic*; rarefied, aerated 336 *gaseous*; void, hollow 190 *empty*; ethereal, aery 323 *light*; incorporeal 320 *immaterial*; wispy, straggly 75 *unassembled*.

**Vb.** *rarefy*, reduce the pressure, expand, dilate; make a vacuum, hermetically seal, pump out, exhaust 300 *empty*; subtilize, atten-uate, refine, thin; dilute, adulterate 163 *weaken*; gasify, volatilize 338 *vaporize*.

## 326 Hardness

**N.** *hardness*, unyielding quality, intractability, intransigence, renitency, resistance 329 *tough-ness*; starchiness, stiffness, rigour, rigidity, inflexibility; inextensibility, inelasticity; firm-ness, temper; callosity, callousness, lumpiness, nodosity, nodularity; grittiness, stoniness, rock-iness, cragginess; grit, stone, pebble, boulder; flint, silica, quartz, granite, marble, diamond 344 *rock*; adamant, metal, duralumin; steel, hard s., iron, wrought i., cast i.; nails, hard-ware, stoneware; cement, concrete, reinforced c., ferroconcrete; brick, baked b.; block, board, heartwood, duramen; hardwood, teak, oak, heart of o. 366 *wood*; bone, gristle, cartilage; spine, backbone; lump, nodule, a cal-losity, callus, corn, wart; horn, ivory; crust, shell, hard s.; hard core, hard centre, jaw-breaker; brick wall; stiffener, starch, wax; whalebone, corset, splint 218 *prop*.

*hardening*, induration; toughening, stiff-ening, backing; starching; steeling, tempering; vulcanization; petrifaction, lapidification, fos-silization; crystallization, vitrification, glaci-ation; ossification; sclerosis, hardening of the arteries.

**Adj.** *hard*, adamantine; indestructible, unbreakable, shatterproof 162 *strong*; fortified, armoured, armour-plated; steeled, proof; iron, cast-i.; steel, steely; hard as iron, hard as steel, hard as stone, rock-hard; sun-baked; stony, rocky, flinty; gritty, gravelly, pebbly; lithic, granitic; crystalline, vitreous, glassy; horny, corneous; callous, calloused; bony, osseous, oss-ific; cartilaginous, gristly 329 *tough*; hardened, indurate, indurated, tempered, case-hardened; vitrified, petrified, fossilized, ossified; icy, frozen, frozen solid, frozen over.

*rigid*, stubborn, resistant, intractable,

unmalleable, intransigent, unadaptable; firm, inflexible, unbending 162 *unyielding*; incom-pressible, inelastic, unsprung; starchy, starched; boned, reinforced; muscle-bound 695 *clumsy*; braced, tense, taut, tight, set, solid; crisp 330 *brittle*; stiff, stark, stiff as a poker, stiff as a ramrod, stiff as a board.

**Vb.** *harden*, render hard etc. adj.; steel 162 *strengthen*; indurate, temper, vulcanize, toughen; crisp, bake 381 *heat*; petrify, fossilize, ossify; calcify, vitrify, crystallize 324 *be dense*; set, gell *or* jell, glaciate, freeze 382 *refrigerate*; stiffen, back, bone, starch, wax (a moustache), tauten 45 *tighten*.

## 327 Softness

**N.** *softness*, tenderness; pliableness etc. adj.; compliance 739 *obedience*; pliancy, pliability, flexibility, plasticity, ductility, tractability; mal-leability, adaptability; suppleness, litheness; springiness, springing, suspension 328 *elas-ticity*; extendibility, extensibility; impressi-bility, doughiness 356 *pulpiness*; sponginess, flaccidity, flabbiness, floppiness, laxity, loose-ness 354 *semiliquidity*; sogginess, squelchiness, marshiness, bogginess 347 *marsh*; flocculence, downiness; velvetiness; butter, grease, oil, wax, putty, paste, Plasticine (tdmk), clay, dough, soap, plastic; padding, foam-filling, wadding, pad 227 *lining*; cushion, pillow, armchair, feather bed 376 *euphoria*; velvet, plush, down, thistledown, fluff, fleece 259 *hair*; feathers 259 *plumage*; snow, snowflake 323 *lightness*.

**Adj.** *soft*, not tough, tender 301 *edible*; melting 335 *fluid*; giving, yielding, compress-ible; springy, sprung 328 *elastic*; pneumatic, foam-filled, cushiony, pillowed, padded, podgy; impressible, as wax, waxy, doughy, argillaceous; spongy, soggy, mushy, squelchy, boggy 347 *marshy*; medullary, pithy; squashy, juicy, overripe 356 *pulpy*; fleecy, flocculent 259 *downy*; turfy, mossy, grassy; velvety, silky 258 *smooth*; unstiffened, unstarched, limp; flaccid, flabby, floppy; unstrung, relaxed, slack, loose; soft as butter, soft as wax, soft as soap, soft as down, soft as velvet, soft as silk; tender as a chicken; softening, emollient 177 *alleviative*.

*flexible*, whippy, bendable; pliant, pliable, putty-like; ductile, tractile, malleable, trac-table, mouldable, plastic, thermoplastic; exten-sile, stretchable 328 *elastic*; lithe, lithesome, willowy, supple, lissom, limber, loose-limbed, double-jointed; acrobatic 162 *athletic*.

**Vb.** *soften*, render soft, tenderize; mellow 669 *mature*; oil, grease 334 *lubricate*; knead, massage, mash, pulp, squash 332 *pulverize*; macerate, marinade, steep 341 *drench*; melt, thaw 337 *liquefy*; cushion, featherbed, pillow; relax, unstring 46 *disunite*; yield, give, give way, relax, loosen up, hang loose, bend, unbend 328 *be elastic*.

## 328 Elasticity

**N.** *elasticity*, give, stretch; spring, springiness; suspension; stretchability, tensibility, extensibility; resilience, bounce 280 *recoil*; buoyancy, rubber, india r., foam r., elastomer; caoutchouc, guttapercha, balata; whalebone, baleen; elastic; elastic band, rubber band, rubber ball; bouncy castle; stretch jeans; gum, chewing g., bubble g.

**Adj.** *elastic*, stretchy, stretchable, tensile, extensile, extensible; rubbery, springy, bouncy, resilient 280 *recoiling*; buoyant; flexible; sprung, well-s.; ductile 327 *soft*.

**Vb.** *be elastic* – tensile etc. adj.; bounce, spring, spring back 280 *recoil*; stretch, give.

## 329 Toughness

**N.** *toughness*, durability, survivability, infrangibility 162 *strength*; tenacity, cohesion 48 *coherence*; viscidity 354 *semiliquidity*; leatheriness, inedibility, indigestibility; leather, gristle, cartilage 326 *hardness*.

**Adj.** *tough*, durable, resisting; closewoven, strong-fibred 162 *strong*; tenacious, retentive, clinging, sticky 48 *cohesive*; viscid 354 *semiliquid*; infrangible, unbreakable, indestructible, untearable, shockproof, shatter-proof; vulcanized, toughened, strengthened; tanned, weatherbeaten; hardboiled, overdone; stringy, sinewy, woody, fibrous; gristly, cartilaginous; rubbery, leathery, coriaceous, tough as old boots *or* shoe leather; chewy, indigestible, inedible; nonelastic, inelastic, unsprung, unyielding, stubborn 326 *rigid*.

**Vb.** *be tough*, – durable etc. adj.; resist fracture, be indestructible, be unbreakable; be a survivor, have survivability; toughen, strengthen, tan, case-harden; mercerize, vulcanize, temper, anneal 162 *strengthen*.

## 330 Brittleness

**N.** *brittleness*, crispness etc. adj.; frangibility; friability, friableness, crumbliness 332 *powderiness*; fissility 46 *scission*; laminability, flakiness 207 *lamina*; fragility, frailty, flimsiness 163 *weakness*; bubble, eggshell, pie crust, pastry, matchwood, shale, slate; glass, porcelain 381 *pottery*; windowpane, glasshouse, greenhouse, house of cards, sandcastle 163 *weak thing*.

**Adj.** *brittle*, breakable, frangible; inelastic 326 *rigid*; fragile, brittle as glass; papery, like parchment; shattery, shivery, splintery; friable,

crumbly 332 *powdery*; crisp, crispy, short, flaky, laminable; fissile, splitting; scissile, lacerable, tearable 46 *severable*; frail, delicate, flimsy, eggshell 163 *weak*; gimcrack, crazy, jerry-built 4 *insubstantial*; tumbledown 655 *dilapidated*; ready to break, ready to burst, explosive.

**Vb.** *be brittle*, – fragile etc. adj.; fracture 46 *break*; crack, snap; star, craze; chip, split, shatter, shiver, fragment; splinter, break off, snap off; burst, fly, explode; give way, fall in, crash 309 *tumble*; fall to pieces 655 *deteriorate*; wear thin; crumble 332 *pulverize*, live in a glass house.

**Int.** fragile!, with care!

## 331 Structure. Texture

**N.** *structure*, organization, pattern, plan; complex, syndrome 52 *whole*; mould, shape, build 243 *form*; constitution, make-up, set-up, content, substance 56 *composition*; construction, make, works, workings, nuts and bolts; architecture, tectonics, architectonics; fabric, work, brickwork, stonework, woodwork, timberwork, studwork 631 *materials*; substructure, infrastructure, superstructure 164 *building*; scaffold, framework, chassis, shell 218 *frame*; nogging, infilling 303 *insertion*; lamination, cleavage 207 *stratification*; body, carcass, person, physique, anatomy 358 *organism*; bony structure, skeleton, bone, vertebra, horn; science of structure, organology, anatomy, morbid a., physiology, histology 358 *biology*.

*texture*, contexture, network 222 *crossing*; tissue, fabric, stuff 222 *textile*; staple, denier 208 *fibre*; web, weave, warp and woof, warp and weft 222 *weaving*; nap, pile 259 *hair*; granular texture, granulation, grain, grit; fineness of grain 258 *smoothness*; coarseness of grain 259 *roughness*; surface 223 *exteriority*; feel 378 *touch*.

**Adj.** *structural*, organic; skeletal; anatomical; organismal, organological; organizational, constructional; tectonic, architectural.

*textural*, textile, woven 222 *crossed*; finewoven, close-w.; ribbed, twilled; grained, granular; fine-grained, silky, satiny 258 *smooth*; coarse-grained, gritty 259 *rough*; fine, fine-spun, delicate, gossamery, cobwebby, filmy; coarse, rough, homespun, tweedy 259 *hairy*.

## 332 Powderiness

**N.** *powderiness*, friability, crumbliness 330 *brittleness*; dustiness 649 *dirt*; sandiness, grittiness; granulation; friability, crumbliness 330 *brittleness*; pulverization, levigation, trituration; attrition, detrition, attenuation, disintegration, erosion 51 *decomposition*; grinding, milling; abrasion, filing 333 *friction*; fragmentation, comminution 46 *disunion*; sprinkling, dusting, powdering, frosting.

*powder*, face p., foot p., talcum p.; talc, chalk; pollen, spore, microspore, sporule; dust, coaldust, soot, ash 649 *dirt*; icing sugar, flour, plain f., self-raising f., white f., wholemeal f., cornflour, farina, arrowroot, kuzu, starch; grist, meal, bran; sawdust, filings; powdery deposit, efflorescence, flowers; scurf, dandruff; debris, detritus 41 *leavings*; sand, grit, gravel, hoggin *or* hogging, shingle; grain, seed, crumb 53 *piece*; granule, grain of powder, speck 33 *small thing*; flake, snowflake; smut, smoke, column of s., smoke cloud, dust c.; fog, smog 355 *cloud*; sandstorm, dust storm, dust devil, fen blow 176 *storm*.

*pulverizer*, miller, grinder; roller, crusher, masher, atomizer; mill, millstone, muller, quern, quernstone; pestle, pestle and mortar; hand mill, coffee m., pepper m.; grater, grindstone, file; abrasive, sandpaper, emery paper, emery board; molar 256 *tooth*; chopper 256 *sharp edge*; sledgehammer 279 *hammer*; bulldozer 279 *ram*.

**Adj.** *powdery*, pulverulent; chalky, dusty, dust-covered, sooty, smoky 649 *dirty*; sandy, sabulous, arenaceous 342 *dry*; farinaceous, branny, floury, mealy; granulated, granular; gritty, gravelly; flaky, furfuraceous, efflorescent; grated, milled, ground, sifted, sieved; crumbling, crumbled; crumbly, friable 330 *brittle*.

**Vb.** *pulverize*, powder, reduce to p., grind to p.; triturate, levigate, granulate; crush, kibble, mash, smash, comminute, shatter, fragment, disintegrate 46 *break*; grind, mill, mince, beat, bruise, pound, bray; knead; crumble, crumb, rub in (pastry); crunch, scrunch 301 *chew*; chip, flake, grate, scrape, rasp, file, abrade, rub down 333 *rub*; weather, wear down, rust, erode 51 *decompose*.

### 333 Friction

**N.** *friction*, frictional force, drag 278 *slowness*; rubbing etc. vb.; attrition, rubbing against, rubbing together 279 *collision*; rubbing out, erasure 550 *obliteration*; abrasion, excoriation, scraping; filing 332 *powderiness*; wearing away, erosion 165 *destruction*; scrape, graze, scratch; brushing, rub; polish, levigation, elbow grease; shampoo, massage, facial m., cosmetic scrub, exfoliator, exfoliant, facial 843 *beautification*; pumice stone; eraser, rubber, rosin; whetstone 256 *sharpener*; masseur, masseuse, shampooer 843 *beautician*.

**Adj.** *rubbing*, frictional, fretting, grating; abrasive, excoriating; fricative.

**Vb.** *rub*, rub against, strike (a match); gnash,

grind; fret, fray, chafe, gall; graze, scratch, bark, take the skin off 655 *wound*; rub off, abrade, excoriate; skin, flay; scuff, scrape, scrub, scour, burnish; brush, rub down, towel, curry, curry-comb 648 *clean*; polish, buff, levigate 258 *smooth*; rub out, erase 550 *obliterate*; gnaw, erode, wear away 165 *consume*; rasp, file, grind 332 *pulverize*; knead, shampoo, massage; rub in; anoint 334 *lubricate*; wax, rosin, chalk (one's cue); grate, be rusty, catch, stick, snag; rub gently, stroke 889 *caress*; iron 258 *smooth*.

### 334 Lubrication

**N.** *lubrication*, greasing; anointment, unction, oiling etc. vb.; lubricity 357 *unctuousness*; nonfriction 258 *smoothness*.

*lubricant*, graphite, plumbago, black lead; glycerine, wax, grease, axle g. 357 *oil*; soap, lather 648 *cleanser*; saliva, spit, spittle, synovia; ointment, salve 658 *balm*; emollient, lenitive 357 *unguent*; lubricator, oil-can, grease-gun.

**Adj.** *lubricated*, greased etc. vb.; nonfrictional, smooth-running, well-oiled, well-greased; not rusty, silent.

**Vb.** *lubricate*, oil, grease, wax, soap, lather; butter 357 *grease*; anoint, pour balm.

### 335 Fluidity

**N.** *fluidity*, fluidness, liquidity, liquidness; wateriness, rheuminess 339 *water*; juiciness, sappiness 356 *pulpiness*; nonviscosity, noncoagulation, haemophilia; solubility, solubleness, liquescence 337 *liquefaction*; gaseous character 336 *gaseousness*; viscosity 354 *semiliquidity*; hydrology, hydrometry, hydrostatics, hydrodynamics; hydraulics, hydrokinetics; fluid mechanics.

*fluid*, elastic f. 336 *gas*; nonelastic fluid, liquid; water, running w. 339 *water*; drink 301 *draught*; milk, whey; juice, sap, latex; humour, chyle, rheum, mucus, saliva 302 *excrement*; serum, lymph, plasma; ichor, pus, matter, sanies; gore (see also *blood*); hydrocele, dropsy 651 *disease*.

*blood*, claret; lifeblood 360 *life*; bloodstream, circulation; red blood 162 *vitality*; blue blood 868 *nobility*; blood of the gods, ichor; gore, cruor, grume; clot, blood c., coagulation 324 *solid body*; corpuscle, red c., white c., platelet; lymph, plasma, serum, blood s.; haemoglobin, factor VIII, haematosis, sanguification; blood group, ABO system, Rhesus factor; blood count; haematics, haematology; blood transfusion; haemophilia, anaemia, leukaemia, AIDS.

**Adj.** *fluid*, fluidic, fluidal 244 *amorphous*; liquid, not solid, not gaseous; insuspension; not congealing, uncongealed; uncoagulated, unclotted, clear, clarified; soluble, liquescent, melting 337 *liquefied*; viscous 354 *viscid*; fluent, running 350 *flowing*; runny, rheumy, phlegmy 339 *watery*; succulent, juicy, sappy, squashy 354 *semiliquid*; serous, sanious, ichorous; pussy, mattery, suppurating 653 *toxic*.

*sanguineous*, haematic, haemic, haemal; serous, lymphatic, plasmatic; bloody, sanguinary 431 *bloodstained*; gory, bleeding; haemophilic, haemolytic.

## 336 Gaseousness

**N.** *gaseousness*, vaporousness etc. adj.; windiness, flatulence 352 *wind*; aeration, gasification; volatility 338 *vaporization*; aerostatics, aerodynamics 340 *pneumatics*.

*gas*, vapour, elastic fluid; ether 340 *air*; effluvium, exhalation, miasma 298 *egress*; flatus 352 *wind*; fumes, reek, smoke; steam, water vapour 355 *cloud*; laughing gas, coal g., natural g., North Sea g., methane 385 *fuel*; marsh gas, poison g. 659 *poison*; damp, after-d., black d., choke d., fire d.; gasbag 194 *bladder*; balloon 276 *airship*; gasworks, gas plant, gasification p. 687 *workshop*; gasholder, gasometer 632 *storage*; gaslight, neon light 420 *lamp*; gas stove, gas cooker 383 *furnace*; gas meter 465 *meter*.

**Adj.** *gaseous*, gasiform; vaporous, steamy, volatile, evaporable 338 *vaporific*; aerial, airy, aeriform, ethereal 340 *airy*; carbonated, effervescent, pétillant 355 *bubbly*; gassy, windy, flatulent; effluvial, miasmic 659 *baneful*; pneumatic, aerostatic, aerodynamic.

**Vb.** *gasify*, vapour, steam, emit vapour 338 *vaporize*; let off steam, blow off s. 300 *emit*; turn on the gas; oxygenate 340 *aerate*; carbonate; hydrogenate, hydrogenize.

## 337 Liquefaction

**N.** *liquefaction*, liquidization; fluidization; solubility, deliquescence 335 *fluidity*; fusion 43 *mixture*; lixiviation, dissolution; thaw, melting, unfreezing 381 *heating*; solvent, dissolvent, flux, diluent, menstruum, alkahest; liquefier, liquefacient; liquidizer; anticoagulant 658 *antidote*.

*solution*, decoction, infusion; aqua; suspension; flux, lixivium, lye.

**Adj.** *liquefied*, molten; runny, liquescent, uncongealed, uncoagulated, unclotted, deliquescent; liquefacient, solvent; soluble, dissoluble, liquefiable, fusible 335 *fluid*; in suspension.

**Vb.** *liquefy*, liquidize, render liquid, unclot, clarify 350 *make flow*; liquate, dissolve, deliquesce, run 350 *flow*; unfreeze, thaw, melt, smelt 381 *heat*; melt down, fuse, render, clarify; leach, lixiviate; hold in solution, fluidize; cast, found.

## 338 Vaporization

**N.** *vaporization*, gasification; exhalation 355 *cloud*; evaporation, volatilization, distillation, sublimation; steaming, fumigation, vapourability, volatility; atomization.

*vaporizer*, evaporator; atomizer, spray, aerosol; retort, still, distillery, vaporimeter.

**Adj.** *vaporific*, volatilized etc. vb.; reeking; vapouring, steaming etc. vb.; vaporous, vapoury, vapourish; steamy, gassy, smoky; evaporable, vaporable, vaporizable, volatile.

**Vb.** *vaporize*, evaporate; render vaporous, render gaseous; aerify 336 *gasify*; volatilize, distil, sublime, sublimate, exhale, transpire, emit vapour, blow off steam 300 *emit*; smoke, fume, reek, steam; fumigate, spray; make a spray, atomize.

## 339 Water

**N.** *water*, $H_2O$; heavy water $D_2O$; hard water, soft w.; drinking water, tap w., Adam's ale; mineral water, soda w. 301 *soft drink*; water vapour, steam 355 *cloud*; rain water 350 *rain*; spring water, running w., fresh w. 350 *stream*; holy water 988 *ritual object*; weeping, tears 836 *lamentation*; sweat, saliva 335 *fluid*; high water, high tide, spring t., neap t., low water 350 *wave*; standing water, still w., stagnant w. 346 *lake*; sea water, salt w., brine, briny 343 *ocean*; water cure, taking the waters, hydrotherapy, hydropathy 658 *therapy*; bath water, bath, tub, shower, douche, splash 648 *ablutions*; lotion, lavender water 843 *cosmetic*; diluent, adulteration, dilution 655 *impairment*; wateriness, damp, humidity, wet; watering, spargefaction 341 *moistening*; jug, ewer 194 *vessel*; tap, faucet, stand-pipe, hydrant 351 *conduit*; waterer, hose 341 *irrigator*; water supply, waterworks; hot spring, geyser; well, aquifer w., Artesian w., borehole 632 *store*; hydrometry 341 *hygrometry*.

**Adj.** *watery*, aqueous, aquatic, lymphatic 335 *fluid*; hydro-, hydrated, hydrous; hydrological, hydrographic 321 *geographic*; adulterated, diluted 163 *weak*; still, noneffervescent; fizzy, effervescent; wet, moist, drenching 341 *humid*; balneary 648 *cleansing*; hydrotherapeutic; sudorific 658 *medical*.

**Vb.** *add water*, water, water down, adulterate, dilute 163 *weaken*; steep, soak, liquor; irrigate, drench 341 *moisten*; combine with water, hydrate; slake 51 *decompose*.

## 340 Air

**N.** *air* 336 *gas*; thin air, ether 325 *rarity*; cushion of air, air pocket 190 *emptiness*; blast

352 *wind*; common air, oxygen, nitrogen, argon; welkin, blue, blue sky 355 *cloud*; open air, open, out of doors, exposure 183 *space*; sea air, ozone; fresh air, country a., smokeless zone 648 *cleanness*; airing 342 *desiccation*; aeration 338 *vaporization*; fanning 352 *ventilation*; air-conditioning, air-cooling 382 *refrigeration*; ventilator, blower, fan, air-conditioner 384 *refrigerator*; air-filter 648 *cleanser*; humidifier, vaporizer, atomizer, ionizer 341 *moisture*.

*atmosphere*, troposphere, tropopause, stratosphere, ionosphere; mesosphere, exosphere; aerosphere; Heaviside layer, Kennelly-Heaviside l., Appleton l.; ozone layer, hole in the ozone l., CFC, chlorofluorocarbons; isothermal l.; radiation layer, Van Allen belt; aeronomy, aerospace; greenhouse effect 381 *heating*;

*weather*, the elements; fair weather, fine w., balmy days, halcyon days; dry spell, heat wave, Indian summer 379 *heat*; windless weather, doldrums; atmospheric pressure, anticyclone, high pressure; cyclone, depression, low pressure; rough weather 176 *storm*, 352 *gale*; bad weather, foul w., wet w. 350 *rain*; cold weather 380 *wintriness*; changeable weather, rise and fall of the barometer; meteorology, micrometeorology; weather forecast 511 *prediction*; isobar, millibar; glass, mercury, barometer; vane, weathervane, weathercock; hygrometer 341 *hygrometry*; weather ship, weather station, rain gauge, Stevenson's Screen; weather-prophet, weatherman *or* -woman, meteorologist; clime, climate, microclimate; climatology, climatography; climatologist.

*pneumatics*, aerodynamics, aerography, aerology, barometry 352 *anemometry*; aerometer, barometer, aneroid b., barograph, barogram.

**Adj.** *airy*, ethereal 4 *insubstantial*; skyey, aerial, aeriform; pneumatic, containing air, aerated, oxygenated; inflated, blown up 197 *expanded*; flatulent 336 *gaseous*; breezy 352 *windy*; well-ventilated, fresh, air-conditioned 382 *cooled*; meteorological, weather-wise; atmospheric, barometric; cyclonic, anticyclonic; high-pressure 324 *dense*; low-pressure 325 *rare*; climatic, climatological.

**Vb.** *aerate*, oxygenate; air, expose 342 *dry*; ventilate, freshen 648 *clean*; fan, winnow, make a draught 352 *blow*; take the air 352 *breathe*.

**Adv.** *alfresco*, out of doors, in the open air, en plein air, in the open, under the open sky, à la belle étoile.

## 341 Moisture

**N.** *moisture*, humidity, sap, juice 335 *fluid*; dampness, wetness, moistness, dewiness; dew point; dankness, condensation, rising damp; sogginess, swampiness, marshiness, bogginess; saturation, saturation point 54 *plenitude*; leakiness 298 *outflow*; raininess, showeriness; rainfall, high r., wet weather 350 *rain*; damp, wet; spray, spindrift, froth, foam 355 *bubble*; mist, haar, fog, fog bank 355 *cloud*; Scotch mist, drizzle, drip, dew, night d., morning d.; drop, droplet, gobbet, raindrop, dewdrop, teardrop; wet eyes, tears 836 *lamentation*; saliva, salivation, slabber, slobber, spit, spittle 302 *excrement*; ooze, slime, mud, squelch, fen, bog 347 *marsh*; soaked object, sop.

*moistening*, humidification, bedewing, damping, wetting, drenching, soaking, saturation, deluge 350 *rain*; spargefaction, sprinkling, sprinkle, aspersion, ducking, submersion 303 *immersion*; overflow, flood, inundation 350 *waterfall*; wash, bath, douche, shower 648 *ablutions*; baptism 988 *Christian rite*; infiltration, percolation, leaching; irrigation, watering, spraying, hosing.

*irrigator*, sprinkler, waterer, watercart; watering can; spray, rose; hose, garden h., syringe, squirt; pump, fire engine; shadoof, noria, Archimedes' screw, swipe; water butt, dam, reservoir 632 *store*; catheter; sluice, water pipe, qanat 351 *conduit*.

*hygrometry*, hydrography, hydrology; hygrometer, udometer, rain gauge, pluviometer, Nilometer 465 *gauge*; hygroscope, weatherhouse.

**Adj.** *humid*, moistened, wet 339 *watery*; pluvious, pluvial; drizzling, drizzly 350 *rainy*; undried, damp, moist, dripping, dank, muggy, foggy, misty 355 *cloudy*; steaming, reeking; undrained, oozy, muddy, slimy, sloppy, slushy, squashy, squelchy, splashy, plashy, fenny, boggy 347 *marshy*; dewy, fresh, bedewed; juicy, sappy 335 *fluid*; dribbling, drip-dropping, seeping, percolating; wetted, steeped, soaked, sprinkled; dabbled; gory, bloody 335 *sanguineous*.

*drenched*, saturated; watered, irrigated; soaking, sopping, streaming, soggy, sodden, soaked, deluged; wet through, wet to the skin, wringing wet, dripping w., soaking w., sopping w.; wallowing, waterlogged, awash, swamped, drowned.

**Vb.** *be wet*, – moist etc. adj.; be soggy, squelch, suck; slobber, salivate, sweat, perspire 298 *exude*; steam, reek 300 *emit*; percolate, seep 297 *infiltrate*; weep, bleed, stream; ooze, drip, leak 298 *flow out*; trickle, drizzle, rain, pour, rain cats and dogs 350 *rain*; get wet, – drenched etc. adj.; not have a dry stitch; dip, duck, dive 313 *plunge*; bathe, wash, shower, douche; wallow; paddle, wade, ford.

*moisten*, humidify, wet, dampen; dilute, hydrate 339 *add water*; lick, lap, wash; plash, splosh, splash, splatter; spill, slop; flood, spray, shower, spatter, bespatter, sprinkle, besprinkle, sparge, syringe; bedew, bedabble, dabble; baste 303 *infuse*.

*drench*, saturate, imbrue, imbue; soak, deluge, wet through, make run with; leach, lixiviate; wash, lave, bathe, shower, douche; hose down, sluice, slosh, rinse 648 *clean*; baptize 988 *perform ritual*; plunge, dip, duck, submerge, drown 303 *immerse*; swamp, flood, inundate, flood out, waterlog; dunk, douse, souse, steep; macerate, marinate; pickle, brine 666 *preserve*.

*irrigate*, water, supply w., hose, pump; inundate, flood, overflow, submerge; percolate 297 *infiltrate*; squirt, inject, douche.

## 342 Dryness

**N.** *dryness*, aridity; need for water, thirst 859 *hunger*; drought, drouth, low rainfall, rainlessness, desert conditions; sandiness, sands, desertification, desertization 172 *desert*; dry climate, dry season; sun, sunniness 379 *heat*.

*desiccation*, exsiccation, drying, drying up; airing, evaporation 338 *vaporization*; draining, drainage, catheterization; dehydration, insolation, sunning 381 *heating*; bleaching, fading, withering, searing 426 *achromatism*; blotting, mopping 648 *cleansing*.

*dryer*, dehydrator, desiccator, evaporator; dehydrant, siccative, silica gel, sand, blotting paper, blotter, blotting; absorbent, absorbent material; mop, swab, sponge, towel, towelling; paper towel, kitchen t., tissue, toilet roll; hair drier, hand d., spin d., tumble d.; wringer, mangle; airer, clotheshorse 217 *hanger*; airing cupboard.

**Adj.** *dry*, needing water, thirsty 859 *hungry*; unirrigated, irrigable; arid, rainless, waterless, riverless; sandy, dusty, desertized 332 *powdery*; bare, brown, grassless; desert, Saharan; anhydrous, dehydrated, desiccated; shrivelled, withered, seared, sere, faded 426 *colourless*; dried up, sapless, juiceless, mummified, parchment-like; sunned, insolated; aired; sun-dried, wind-d., bleached; burnt, scorched, baked, parched 379 *hot*; free from rain, sunny, fine, cloudless, fair; dried out, drained, evaporated; squeezed dry, wrung out, mangled; protected from wet, waterproofed, waterproof, rainproof, showerproof, damp-proof; watertight, tight, snug, proof; unwetted, unmoistened, dry-footed, dry-shod; out of water, high and dry; dry as a bone, dry as a biscuit; adapted to drought, xerophilous; non-greasy, nonskid, skidproof.

**Vb.** *be dry*, – thirsty etc. adj.; keep dry, wear waterproof clothing; hold off the wet, keep watertight, keep the rain out; dry up, evaporate 338 *vaporize*; become dry, dry off, dry out.

*dry*, dehumidify, desiccate, exsiccate, freeze-dry; dehydrate; ditch, drain, catheterize, pump out, suck dry 300 *empty*; wring out, mangle; spin-dry, tumble-d., drip-d.; hang out, peg o., air, evaporate 338 *vaporize*; sun, expose to sunlight, solarize, insolate, sun-dry; smoke, kipper, cure; parch, scorch, bake, burn 381 *heat*; sere, sear, shrivel, wither, bleach; mummify 666 *preserve*; dry up, stop the flow, apply a tourniquet 350 *staunch*; blot, blot up, mop, mop up, soak up, sponge 299 *absorb*; swab, wipe, wipe up, wipe dry.

## 343 Ocean

**N.** *ocean*, sea, blue, salt water, brine, briny; waters, billows, waves, tide 350 *wave*; Davy Jones's locker; main, deep, deep sea; high seas, great waters; trackless deep, watery waste; herring pond, drink; sea lane, shipping lane; ocean floor, sea bed, sea bottom, ooze, benthos; the seven seas.

---

**Oceans and Seas**

Antarctic Ocean, Arctic Ocean, Atlantic Ocean, Indian Ocean, Pacific Ocean.

   Adriatic Sea, Aegean Sea, Andaman Sea, Arabian Sea, Aral Sea, Baltic Sea, Barents Sea, Beaufort Sea, Bering Sea, Black Sea, Caribbean Sea, Caspian Sea, Coral Sea, Dead Sea, East China Sea, Greenland Sea, Irish Sea, Mediterranean Sea, North Sea, Norwegian Sea, Red Sea, Sargasso Sea, Sea of Azov, Sea of Galilee, Sea of Japan, Sea of Okhotsk, South China Sea, Tasman Sea, Tyrrhenian Sea.

---

*sea god*, Oceanus, Neptune, Poseidon, Triton; Nereus, merman 970 *mythical being*.

*sea nymph*, Oceanid, Nereid, siren; Amphitrite, Thetis, Tethys; Calypso, Undine; mermaid; bathing beauty; water sprite 970 *fairy*.

*oceanography*, hydrography, bathymetry; sea survey, Admiralty chart; bathysphere, bathyscaphe; oceanographer, hydrographer.

**Adj.** *oceanic*, thalassic, pelagic, pelagian; sea, marine, maritime; ocean-going, sea-g., seaworthy 269 *seafaring*; deep-sea, submarine, subaqueous, subaquatic, subaqua, undersea, underwater; benthic; abyssal 211 *deep*; hydrographic, bathymetric.

**Adv.** *at sea*, on the sea, on the high seas; afloat.

## 344 Land

**N.** *land*, dry l., terra firma; earth, ground, crust, earth's c. 321 *world*; continent, mainland; heartland, hinterland; midland, inland, interior 224 *interiority*; peninsula, delta, promontory, tongue of land 254 *projection*; isthmus, neck of land, landbridge; terrain; heights, highlands 209 *high land*; lowlands 210 *lowness*; reclaimed land, polder; steppe, fields 348 *plain*; wilderness 172 *desert*; oasis, Fertile Crescent; isle 349 *island*; zone, clime; country, district, tract 184 *region*; territory, possessions, acres, estate, real e. 777 *lands*; physical features, landscape, scenery; topography, geography, stratigraphy, geology 321 *earth sciences*; landsman, landlubber, continental, mainlander, islander 191 *dweller*.

*shore*, coastline 233 *outline*; coast, rocky c., ironbound c. 234 *edge*; strand, beach, sands, shingle; seaboard, seashore, seaside; sea cliff, sea wall; plage, lido, riviera; marina; bank, river bank, riverside, lea, water meadow, washlands; submerged coast, continental shelf.

*soil*, glebe, farmland, arable land 370 *farm*; pasture 348 *grassland*; deposit, glacial d., aeolian d., moraine, loess, geest, silt, alluvium, alluvion; topsoil, sand, dust, subsoil; mould, leaf m., humus; loam, clay, bole, marl; Fuller's earth; argil, potter's clay, china clay, kaolin 381 *pottery*; flinty soil, gravel; stone, pebble, flint; turf, sod, clod 53 *piece*.

*rock*, cliff, scar, crag; stone, boulder; submerged rock, reef; stack, skerry; dyke, sill, batholith; igneous rock, plutonic r., granite, basalt, hypabyssal rock; volcanic r.; volcanic glass, obsidian; magma, lava, lapilli, tuff; sedimentary rock, sandstone, shale, limestone, chalk, conglomerate; metamorphic rock, schist, marble; massive rock, bedded r.; metal-bearing rock, ore 359 *mineralogy*; quartz; precious stone, semi-p. s. 844 *gem*.

**Adj.** *territorial*, terrestrial, farming, agricultural 370 *agrarian*; terrigenous, terrene 321 *telluric*; earthy, alluvial, silty, sandy, loamy; peaty; clayey, marly, chalky; flinty, pebbly, gravelly, stony, rocky; granitic, marble; slaty, shaly; Pre-Cambrian 141 *seasonal*; geological, morphological, orographical, topographical.

*coastal*, littoral, riparian, riverine, riverside, seaside, seashore; shore, onshore.

*inland*, continental, midland, mainland, heartland, hinterland, interior, central.

**Adv.** *on land*, on dry l., on terra firma, by land, overland, ashore, on shore, long-shore; between the tides.

### 345 Gulf: inlet

**N.** *gulf*, bay, bight, cove, creek, lagoon, reach; slough; natural harbour, road, roadstead; inlet, outlet, fleet, bayou; arm of the sea, fjord, sea loch; drowned valley, ria; mouth, estuary; firth, frith; kyle, sound, strait, belt, gut, channel.

### 346 Lake

**N.** *lake*, lagoon, land-locked water; loch, lough, llyn, linn; freshwater lake, salt l.; inland sea, Aral Sea, Caspian Sea, Dead Sea, Sea of Azov, Sea of Galilee; oxbow lake, bayou l., mortlake; broad, broads; sheet of water, standing w., stagnant w., backwater; mud flat, wash 347 *marsh*; pool, tarn, mere, pond, dewpond; fishpond, stew; swimming pool, swimming bath; Jacuzzi (tdmk) 648 *ablutions*; birthing pool; millpond, millpool; artificial lake, dam, reservoir 632 *storage*; well 339 *water*; basin, tank, cistern, sump 649 *sink*; ditch, irrigation d., sough, dike 351 *drain*; waterhole, puddle, splash, wallow; water garden.

**Adj.** *lacustrine*, lake-dwelling, land-locked.

### 347 Marsh

**N.** *marsh*, morass; marshland, slobland, wetlands; washlands, flat, mud f., salt f., salt marsh; fen, fenland, carr, moor; moss, bog, peat b., quaking b., quag, quagmire, quicksand; playa, salina, salt-pan; mudhole, wallow, slough, mire, mud, ooze; swamp, swampland, everglade, swamp-forest, mangrove swamp; sudd; 'the Slough of Despond' (see quotation at 731 *adversity*).

**Adj.** *marshy*, paludal; moorish, moory; mossy, swampy, boggy, fenny; oozy, quaggy, poached, trampled; squashy, squishy, squelchy, spongy 327 *soft*; slushy 354 *semi-liquid*; muddy, miry 649 *dirty*; undrained, water-logged 341 *drenched*.

### 348 Plain

**N.** *plain*, peneplain; dene, dale, flood plain, levels 216 *horizontality*; river basin, lowlands 255 *valley*; flats 347 *marsh*; delta, alluvial plain; sands, desert s., waste 172 *desert*; tundra; ice plain, ice field, ice floe 380 *ice*; grasslands, steppe, prairie, pampas, savanna, llanos, campos; heath, common, wold, downland, downs, moor, moorland, fell; upland, plateau, tableland, mesa 209 *high land*; bush, veld, range, open country, flat c., rolling c. 183 *space*; champaign, campagna; fields, green belt, parkland, national park, safari p. 263 *open space*; lowlands, low countries 210 *lowness*.

*grassland*, pasture, pasturage, grazing 369 *animal husbandry*; sheeprun, sheep track, sheep walk; field, meadow, water m., mead, lea; chase, park, grounds; green, greensward, sward, lawn, turf.

**Adj.** *campestral*, rural; flat, open, steppe-like, rolling.

### 349 Island

**N.** *island*, isle, islet, skerry; river island, eyot,

ait, inch, holm; lagoon island, atoll, reef, coral r.; cay, key; sandbank, bar; floating island, iceberg, ice floe, calf; peninsula, 'all but island';

> . . . – as we wander'd to and fro
> Gazing at the Lydian laughter of the Garda lake below
> Sweet Catullus' all-but-island, olive-silvery Sirmio!
> Alfred, Lord Tennyson, *Frater Ave atque Vale*

island continent; island universe, galaxy 321 *star*; archipelago; insularity 883 *seclusion*; islander, islesman 191 *dweller*.

**Adj.** *insular,* sea-girt; islanded, isolated, marooned; isleted, archipelagic.

## 350 Stream: water in motion
**N.** *stream,* running water, watercourse, river, Amazon, Ganges, Mississippi, Nile, Seine, Thames, Tiber; Rubicon, Styx; subterranean river; navigable river, waterway; tributary, branch, feeder, distributary; streamlet, rivulet, brook, brooklet, bourne, burn, rill, beck, gill, kill, runnel, runlet; freshet, torrent, mountain t., force; arroyo, wadi; spring, fountain, fountainhead, headwaters 156 *source*; jet, spout, gush; geyser, hot spring; well 632 *store*.

*current,* flow, set, flux 285 *progression*; effluence 298 *egress*; confluence 293 *convergence*; inflow 297 *ingress*; outflow, reflux 286 *regression*; undercurrent, undertow, crosscurrent, rip tide 182 *counteraction*; tide, spring t., neap t.; tidal flow, tidal current, ebb and flow, tidal rise and fall 317 *fluctuation*; tideway, bore, eagre; race, tidal r., millrace, millstream; tap, standpipe, hydrant 351 *conduit*; bloodstream, circulation 314 *circuition*.

*eddy,* whirlpool, swirl, maelstrom 315 *vortex*; whirlpool bath, Jacuzzi (tdmk); surge, reflux 290 *recession*; wash, backwash, wake 67 *sequel*.

*waterfall,* falls, cataract, Niagara, Victoria; linn, cascade, force, rapids, shoot, weir; water power 160 *sources of energy*; flush, chute, spillway, sluice; overflow, spill; fresh, freshet; flood, flash f., spate, inundation, deluge, cataclysm 341 *moistening*, 298 *outflow*.

*wave,* bow w.; wash, swash, backwash; ripple, cat's-paw 262 *furrow*; swell, ground s.; billow, roller, comber, beach c.; breaker, surf, spume, white horses, whitecap; tidal wave, tsunami, rogue wave; bore, eagre; rip, overfall; broken water, choppiness 259 *roughness*; sea, choppy s., long s., short s., heavy s., angry s.; waviness, undulation.

*rain,* rainfall 341 *moisture*; precipitation; drizzle, mizzle, Scotch mist, smirr; sleet, hail 380 *wintriness*; shower, downpour, deluge, drencher, soaker, cloudburst, thunderstorm 176 *storm*; flurry 352 *gale*; pouring rain, teeming r., drenching r., driving r.,

torrential r., sheets of rain; raininess, wet spell, foul weather; rainy season, the rains, monsoon; lovely weather for ducks; plash, patter; dropping, dripping etc. vb.; rain-making, cloud-seeding; hyetograph; rain gauge 341 *hygrometry*.

**Adj.** *flowing,* falling etc. vb.; runny 335 *fluid*; fluent, profluent, affluent; riverine, fluvial, fluviatile, tidal; making, running, coursing, racing; streaming; in flood, overflowing, in spate; flooding, inundatory, cataclysmic; surging; rolling, rippling, purling, eddying; popply, choppy 259 *rough*; winding, meandering 251 *labyrinthine*; oozy, sluggish 278 *slow*; pouring, sheeting, lashing, driving, dripping, dropping; gushing, spirting, spouting 298 *outgoing*; inflowing 297 *incoming*.

*rainy,* showery, drizzly, spitting, smirry, spotting; wet 341 *humid*.

**Vb.** *flow,* run, course, pour; ebb, regurgitate 286 *regress*; swirl, eddy 315 *rotate*; surge, break, dash, ripple, popple, wrinkle; roll, swell; buck, bounce 312 *leap*; gush, rush, spirt, spout, spew, effuse, jet, play, squirt, splutter; well, well up, bubble up, issue 298 *emerge*; pour, stream; trickle, dribble 298 *exude*; drip, drop 309 *descend*; plash, lap, wash, swash, slosh, splash 341 *moisten*; flow softly, purl, trill, murmur, babble, bubble, burble, gurgle, guggle; glide, slide; flow over, overflow, cascade, fall, flood, inundate, deluge 341 *drench*; flow into, fall i., drain i., empty i., spill i., leak i., distil i. 297 *enter*; run off, discharge itself 298 *flow out*; flow through, leak, ooze, percolate, pass through 305 *pass*; ooze, wind 251 *meander*.

*rain,* shower, stream, pour, pelt; snow, sleet, hail; fall, come down, bucket, bucket down, piss down, rain hard, pour with rain, rain in torrents, rain cats and dogs; sheet, come down in sheets, come down in stair-rods, rain pitchforks; patter, drizzle, mizzle, smirr, drip, drop, spit, sprinkle; be wet, rain and rain, set in.

*make flow,* cause to f., send out a stream 300 *emit*; make or pass water 302 *excrete*; broach, tap, turn on the t., open the cocks, open the sluice gates 263 *open*; pour, pour out, spill 311 *let fall*; transfuse, decant 272 *transpose*; pump out, drain out 300 *empty*; water 341 *irrigate*; unclot, clear, clarify, melt 337 *liquefy*.

*staunch,* stop the flow, stem the course 342 *dry*; apply a tourniquet; stop a leak, plug 264 *close*; obstruct the flow, stem, dam, dam up 702 *obstruct*.

## 351 Conduit
**N.** *conduit,* water channel, tideway, riverbed; arroyo, wadi; trough, basin, river b., drainage b.; canyon, ravine, gorge, gully 255 *valley*;

inland waterways, canal system; canal,
channel, watercourse, qanat; ditch, dike;
trench, moat, runnel; Irish bridge; gutter, leat,
mill race; duct, aqueduct; plumbing, water
pipe, main, water m.; pipe, hosepipe, hose,
garden h.; standpipe, hydrant, siphon, tap,
spout, funnel 263 *tube*; valve, penstock, flume,
sluice, weir, lock, floodgate, watergate,
spillway; chute 350 *waterfall*; oilpipe, pipeline
272 *transferrer*; gullet, throat; neck (of a bottle);
blood vessel, vein, artery, aorta, carotid,
jugular vein; veinlet, capillary.

*drain*, gully, gutter, gargoyle, waterspout;
scupper, overflow, wastepipe, drainpipe 298
*outlet*; covered drain, culvert; open drain,
ditch, sewer 649 *sink*; intestine, colon, alimentary canal; catheter 300 *voidance*.

## 352 Wind: air in motion

**N.** *wind* 340 *air*; draught, downdraught,
updraught, thermal; windiness etc. adj.; blowi-
ness, gustiness, breeziness, squalliness, storminess, weather; blast, blow (see also *breeze*, *gale*);
air stream, jet s.; current, air c., crosswind,
headwind 182 *counteraction*; tailwind, following wind 287 *propellant*; air flow, slip
stream; air pocket; windlessness, calm air 266
*quietude*; cold draught, cold wind, raw w., icy
blast; hot wind, sirocco, leveche, khamsin, har-
mattan; seasonal wind, monsoon, etesian
winds; regular wind, prevailing w., trade w.,
antitrades, Brave West Winds, Roaring Forties;
north wind, Boreas, bise, mistral, tramontano;
south wind, föhn, chinook; east wind, Eurus,
levanter; west wind, westerly, Zephyr,
Favonius; wind god, Aeolus, cave of Aeolus.

*anemometry*, aerodynamics 340 *pneumatics*;
wind rose; Beaufort scale; anemometer, wind
gauge, weathercock, weathervane, windsock,
windcone.

*breeze*, zephyr; breath, breath of air, waft,
whiff, puff, gust, capful of wind; light breeze,
sough, gentle b., fresh b., stiff b., spanking b.;
sea breeze, cooling b.

*gale*, half g., fresh g., strong wind, high w.,
howling w.; blow, hard b., blast, gust, flurry,
flaw; squall, black s., white s.; storm-wind,
nor'wester, sou'wester, hurricane, whirlwind,
cyclone, tornado, twister, baguio, typhoon, wil-
liwaw, simoom 315 *vortex*; thunderstorm, dust
storm, sandstorm, haboob, dust devil, blizzard
176 *storm*; wind shear, microburst; weather,
dirty w., ugly w., stormy w., windy w., gale
force.

*blowing*, insufflation, inflation 197 *dilation*;
blowing up, pumping, pumping up; pumping
out 300 *voidance*; pump, air p., stirrup p.,
bicycle p.; bellows, windbag, bagpipe; wood-

wind, brass 414 *musical instrument*; blowpipe;
exhaust pipe, exhaust 298 *outlet*.

*ventilation*, airing 340 *air*; crossventilation,
draught; fanning, cooling; ventilator 353 *air
pipe*; blower, fan, extractor f., electric f.,
punkah, air-conditioner, air-conditioning 384
*refrigerator*.

*respiration*, breathing, breathing in and out,
inhalation, exhalation, expiration, inspiration;
stomach wind, flatus, windiness, flatulence,
eructation, belch; gills, lungs, bellows; respirator, iron lung, oxygen tent; windpipe 353 *air
pipe*; sneezing, coughing, cough, whooping c.,
croup 651 *respiratory disease*; sigh, sob, gulp,
hiccup, catching of the breath, yawn; hard
breathing, panting, gasping, huffing and puffing; wheeze, rattle, death r.

**Adj.** *windy*, airy, exposed, draughty, breezy,
blowy; ventilated, fresh; blowing, gusty,
gusting, squally; blusterous, blustery, dirty,
foul, stormy, tempestuous, boisterous 176
*violent*; windswept, windblown; storm-tossed,
storm-bound; flatulent; fizzy, gassy 336
*gaseous*; aeolian, favonian, boreal, zephyrous;
cyclonic; gale-force, hurricane-f.

*puffing*, huffing, huffing and puffing;
snorting, wheezing, gasping; wheezy, asthmatic, stertorous, panting, heaving; breathless
318 *agitated*; sniffling, snuffly, sneezy; pulmonary, pulmonic, pulmonate; coughing,
chesty.

**Vb.** *blow*, puff, blast; freshen, insufflate,
blow up, get up, blow hard, blow great guns,
blow a hurricane, rage, storm 176 *be violent*;
wail, howl, roar 409 *ululate*; screech, scream,
whistle, pipe, sing in the shrouds 407 *shrill*;
hum, moan, mutter, sough, sigh 401 *sound
faint*; stream in the air, wave, flap, shake,
flutter, flourish 318 *agitate*; draw, make a
draught, ventilate, fan 382 *refrigerate*; blow
along, waft 287 *propel*; veer, back 282 *deviate*;
die down, subside, drop, abate.

*breathe*, respire, breathe in, inhale; draw *or*
take a deep breath, fill one's lungs; breathe out,
exhale; aspirate, puff, huff, huff and puff,
whiff, whiffle, sniff, sniffle, snuffle, snort;
breathe hard, breathe heavily, breathe noisily,
gasp, pant, heave; wheeze, sneeze, cough 407
*rasp*; sigh, sob, gulp, suck one's breath, catch
the b.; hiccup, get the hiccups; yawn; 300
*belch*, burp eruct.

*blow up*, pump up, inflate, dilate 197 *enlarge*;
pump out, exhaust 300 *empty*.

## 353 Air pipe

**N.** *air pipe*, airway, air-passage, windway, air
shaft, air well; wind tunnel, smoke tunnel;
blowpipe, peashooter 287 *propellant*; windpipe,

trachea, larynx; bronchia, bronchus; throat,
gullet, oesophagus; nose, nostril, spiracle, blowhole, nozzle, vent, mouthpiece 263 *orifice*; flue
pipe, mouth organ 414 *organ*; gas main, gas
pipe; tobacco pipe, pipe, briar, hookah 388
*tobacco*; funnel, flue, exhaust pipe 263 *chimney*;
airbrick, air duct, ventilator, grating, louvre, air
hole 263 *window*.

### 354 Semiliquidity

**N.** *semiliquidity*, mucosity, viscidity; clammi-
ness, ropiness; thickness, stodginess; semiliquid, colloid, emulsion, grume, gore,
albumen, mucus, mucilage, phlegm, clot 324
*solid body*; pus, matter; juice, sap 335 *fluidity*;
soup, slop, gruel, cream, curds 356 *pulpiness*;
molten lava; oil slick; mud, glaur, slush,
sludge, thaw, ooze, slime; sullage, silt 347
*marsh*.

*thickening*, inspissation, coagulation,
curding, clotting 324 *condensation*; gelation,
gelatinization; emulsification; thickener,
starch, arrowroot, flour, cornflour; gelatine,
isinglass, pectin.

*viscidity*, viscosity, glutinousness, glueyness,
gumminess, stickiness, treacliness,
adhesiveness 48 *coherence*; glue, gluten, gum
47 *adhesive*; emulsion, colloid; glair, size, paste,
glaze, slip; gel, jelly; treacle, jam, syrup, honey,
goo; wax, mastic 357 *resin*; flypaper.

**Adj.** *semiliquid*, semifluid; stodgy, starchy,
thick, soupy, curdy, lumpy, ropy 324 *dense*;
unclarified, curdled, clotted, coagulated,
jellied, gelatinous, pulpy, juicy, sappy, milky,
creamy, lactescent, lacteal; emulsive; colloidal;
thawing, half-frozen, half-melted, mushy,
slushy, sloppy, waterlogged, muddy, glaury,
squashy, squishy, squidgy, squelchy 347
*marshy*.

*viscid*, viscous, gummy, gooey 48 *cohesive*;
slimy, clammy, sticky, tacky; jammy, treacly,
syrupy, gluey; glairy, glaireous; mucilaginous,
mucous.

**Vb.** *thicken*, inspissate, congeal 324 *be dense*;
coagulate 48 *cohere*; emulsify; gelatinize, gel,
jelly, jell; starch 326 *harden*; curdle, clot;
churn, whip up, beat up, mash, pulp 332
*pulverize*; muddy, puddle 649 *make unclean*.

### 355 Bubble. Cloud: air and water mixed

**N.** *bubble*, bubbles, suds, soapsuds, lather,
foam, froth; head, top; sea foam, spume, surf,
spray, spindrift 341 *moisture*; mousse, soufflé,
meringue, candyfloss; yeast, barm 323 *leaven*;
scum 649 *dirt*; bubbling, boiling, seething, simmering, ebullition, effervescence; fizzy drink,
champagne, sparkling wine; fermentation,
yeastiness, fizziness, fizz.

*cloud*, cloudlet, scud, rack; cloudbank, cloudscape; rain cloud, storm c.; woolpack, cumulus,
altocumulus, cirrus, cirrocumulus, stratus,
cirrostratus, nimbostratus; mackerel sky,
mare's tail; vapour, steam 338 *vaporization*;
brume, haze, mist, haar, fog, smog, pea-souper;
cloudiness, film 419 *dimness*; nebulosity 321
*nebula*; nephology, nephoscope.

**Adj.** *bubbly*, bubbling etc. vb.; bubbling
over, effervescent, fizzy, sparkling, pétillant
336 *gaseous*; mousseux, foaming, foamy;
spumy, spumous; with a head on, frothy,
soapy, lathery; yeasty, aerated 323 *light*;
scummy 649 *dirty*.

*cloudy*, clouded, overcast, overclouded;
nubilous, nebulous; cirrose, thick, foggy, hazy,
misty, filmy, brumous 419 *dim*; vaporous,
steamy, steaming 338 *vaporific*.

**Vb.** *bubble*, spume, foam, froth, cream, form
a head; mantle, scum; boil, simmer, seethe,
fizzle, gurgle 318 *effervesce*; work, ferment,
fizz, sparkle; aerate, carbonate; steam 338
*vaporize*.

*cloud*, cloud over, overcast, overcloud; be
cloudy, – misty etc. adj.; becloud, befog, fog
over, mist up 419 *be dim*.

### 356 Pulpiness

**N.** *pulpiness*, doughiness, sponginess; fleshi-
ness, juiciness, sappiness 327 *softness*; mash,
mush, pap, paste, pith, porridge, poultice,
pulp, puree, putty, squash; batter, dough,
sponge; soft fruit, stewed f.; jam 354 *viscidity*;
mousse, puree 355 *bubble*; ooze, slush 354 *semiliquidity*; papier mâché, wood pulp; pulping,
mastication; steeping, maceration.

**Adj.** *pulpy*, pulped, pulpous, mashed,
crushed, pureed 354 *semiliquid*; mushy, pappy
327 *soft*; succulent, fleshy, juicy, sappy,
squashy, ripe, overripe 669 *matured*; flabby,
dimply 195 *fleshy*; doughy, pasty; macerated,
steeped 341 *drenched*; soggy, spongy 347
*marshy*.

### 357 Unctuousness

**N.** *unctuousness*, unctuosity, oiliness, greasiness, lubricity, soapiness 334 *lubrication*; fattiness, pinguidity; saponification; anointment,
unction.

*oil*, volatile o., essential o.; animal oil,
whale o., sperm o., train o., cod-liver o.; vegetable oil, corn o., sunflower o., olive o., virgin
olive o., extra virgin olive o., coconut o.,
almond o., linseed o., cotton-seed o., castor o.,
rape o., rape seed o., groundnut o., sesame o.,
palm o., jojoba o.; mineral oil, shale o., rock o.,
crude o., petroleum; refined oil, coal o.; fuel
oil, paraffin, kerosene, petrol, gasoline, gas 385

*fuel*; lubricating oil 334 *lubricant*; bath oil, suntan o.

*fat*, animal f., grease, adipocere, body fat, excess f.; liposuction 843 *beautification*; saturated fat, unsaturated f., polyunsaturated f., monounsaturated f., essential fatty acid, trans-fatty a., triglyceride; blubber, tallow, spermaceti; sebum, wax, beeswax, ceresin; suet, lard, dripping, bacon fat 301 *cookery*; glycerine, stearin, olein; butyrin; margarine, butter, clarified b., ghee, spread; milk fats, cream, Devonshire c., Cornish c.; top of the milk; buttermilk; soap, carbolic s., soft s., toilet s., liquid s., soap flakes, washcream 648 *cleanser*.

*unguent*, salve, unction, ointment, cerate; liniment, embrocation, lanolin; spikenard, nard; pomade, brilliantine; cream, cold cream 843 *cosmetic*.

*resin*, resinoid, rosin, colophony, gum, gum arabic, tragacanth, myrrh, frankincense, camphor, labdanum; lac, amber, ambergris; pitch, tar, bitumen, asphalt; varnish, copal, mastic, megilp, shellac, lacquer, japan; synthetic resin, epoxy r., polyurethane, plastics.

**Adj.** *fatty*, pinguid, fat, adipose, blubbery, flabby 195 *fleshy*; sebaceous, cereous, waxy, waxen; lardaceous, lardy; saponaceous, soapy; butyraceous, buttery, creamy, milky, rich 390 *savoury*.

*unctuous*, unguentary, unguineous, greasy, oily, oleaginous; anointed, dripping with oil, basted; slippery, greased, oiled 334 *lubricated*.

*resinous*, resiny, resinoid, resiniferous; bituminous, pitchy, tarry, asphaltic 354 *viscid*; myrrhic, gummous, gummy; varnished, japanned.

**Vb.** *grease*, oil, anoint 334 *lubricate*; baste, lard; butter, butter up; saponify; resinify, resin, rosin.

SECTION THREE

## Organic matter

### 358 Organisms: living matter
**N.** *organism*, organic matter, animate m.; organized world, organized nature, organic n., living n., living beings; animal and vegetable kingdom, flora and fauna, biota; ecosystem; ecotype, biotype 77 *breed*; living matter 360 *life*; microscopic life 196 *microorganism*; cell, protoplasm, cytoplasm, nucleoplasm; nucleus, nucleolus; nucleic acid, RNA, DNA; germ plasm; chromatin, chromosome, chromatid, gene 5 *heredity*; albumen, protein, antioxidants, interleukin, perforin, rogue protein, prion; enzyme, globulin; serotonin; organic remains 125 *fossil*.

*biology*, microbiology; natural history, nature study; biochemistry, biophysics, developmental biology, molecular b., cell b., cytology, cytogenetics; glycobiology; histology; morphology, embryology; anatomy, morbid a., physiology 331 *structure*; zoography 367 *zoology*; phytography 368 *botany*; ecology, human e., bionomics, biodiversity; ethology, biogeography; marine biology; genetics, biogenetics, eugenics, sociobiology; genetic engineering, genetic modification, gene technology, biotechnology, biotech, biomedicine; genetically modified organism, GMO, genetically modified food, golden rice, Frankenstein food 301 *food*; genetic use restriction technology, GURT, terminator technology, terminator seed, suicide s.; ontogeny, phylogeny; evolution, natural selection, 'the survival of the fittest' (see quotations at 716 *contention*); Darwinism, Neo-D., Lamarckism; biogenesis; vitalism; mechanism; naturalist, biologist, zoologist, ecologist; evolutionist, Darwinist.

**Adj.** *organic*, organized; biogenic; cellular, unicellular, multicellular; plasmic, protoplasmic, cytoplasmic.

*biological*, physiological, zoological, palaeontological; genetic, biogenetic; vitalistic; evolutionistic, evolutionary, Darwinian; ecological.

### 359 Mineral: inorganic matter
**N.** *mineral*, mineral world, mineral kingdom; inorganic matter, unorganized m., inanimate m., brute m.; earth's crust 344 *rock*; ore, metal, noble m., precious m., base m.; alloy 43 *a mixture*; mineralogical deposit, coal measures 632 *store*.

*mineralogy*, geology, lithology, petrography, petrology; metallurgy, metallography; speleology, glaciology 321 *earth sciences*.

**Adj.** *inorganic*, unorganized; inanimate, azoic; mineral, nonanimal, nonvegetable; mineralogical, petrological; metallurgical, metallic.

### 360 Life
**N.** *life*, living, being alive, animate existence, being 1 *existence*; the living, living and breathing world; living being, being, soul, spirit; plant life 366 *vegetable life*; animal life 365 *animality*; human life 371 *humankind*; gift of life, birth, nativity 68 *origin*; new birth, revivification, renaissance 656 *revival*; life to come, the hereafter 124 *future state*; immortal life 971 *heaven*; imparting life, vivification, vitalization, animation; vitality, vital force, vital principle, élan vital, life force; soul 447 *spirit*; beating heart, strong pulse; will to live,

hold on life, survival; cat's nine lives, longevity 113 *long duration*; animal spirits, liveliness, animation 819 *moral sensibility*; wind, breath, breathing 352 *respiration*; vital air, breath of life, breath of one's nostrils; lifeblood, heart's blood 5 *essential part*; vital spark, vital flame; seat of life, heart, artery; vital necessity, nourishment, staff of life 301 *food*; life-force, qi *or* ch'i 160 *energy*; biological function, parenthood, motherhood, fatherhood 167 *propagation*; sex, sexual activity 45 *sexual intercourse*; living matter, protoplasm, bioplasm, tissue, living t.; macromolecule, bioplast; cell, unicellular organism 358 *organism*; cooperative living, symbiosis 706 *association*; life-support system; lifetime, one's born days; life expectancy, life span, allotted s., life cycle; capacity for life, survivability, viability, viableness 469 *possibility*.

**Adj.** *alive*, living, quick, live, animate; breathing, respiring, alive and kicking; animated 819 *lively*; in life, incarnate, in the flesh, personified; not dead, surviving, in the land of the living, above ground, with us, on this side of the grave; long-lived, tenacious of life 113 *lasting*; survivable, capable of life, viable; vital, vivifying, Promethean; vivified, enlivened 656 *restored*; biotic, symbiotic, biological; protoplasmatic, protoplasmic, protoplastic, bioplasmic.

*born*, born alive; begotten, fathered, sired; mothered, dammed; foaled, dropped; out of, by 11 *akin*; spawned, littered; laid, new-l., hatched 164 *produced*.

**Vb.** *live*, be alive, have life, have being; respire, draw breath 352 *breathe*; exist, subsist 1 *be*; live one's life, walk the earth; come to life, come to, liven, liven up, quicken, revive 656 *be restored*; not die, be spared, survive 41 *be left*; cheat death, have nine lives; live in 192 *dwell*.

*be born*, come into the world, come into existence, first see the light 68 *begin*; have one's nativity, be incarnated; fetch breath, draw b.; be begotten, be conceived.

*vitalize*, give birth to, beget, conceive, support life 167 *generate*; vivify, liven, enliven, breathe life into, bring to life 174 *invigorate*; revitalize, give a new lease of life, put new life into, ginger, put zest into, reanimate 656 *revive*; support life, provide a living; maintain, provide for, keep alive, keep body and soul together, make ends meet, keep the wolf from the door 301 *feed*.

## 361 Death

**N.** *death*, no life, 'the end of woes' 2 *extinction*;

> Death is the end of woes.
> Edmund Spenser, *The Faerie Queen*

process of death, dying (see also *decease*); Dance of Death, mortality, perishability, ephemerality 114 *transience*; sentence of death, doom, crack of d., knell, death k.; execution, martyrdom; curtains, deathblow, quietus 362 *killing*; necrosis, mortification, autolysis 51 *decay*; the beyond, the great divide, the great adventure, crossing the bar, crossing the Styx *or* Lethe; deathliness, rest, eternal r.; long sleep, big s. 266 *quietude*; Abraham's bosom 971 *heaven*; the grave 364 *tomb*; hand of death, jaws of d., shadow of d., shades of d.; nether regions, Stygian darkness, Hades 972 *hell*; Death, the Grim Reaper, the Great Leveller; Angel of Death, Azrael; Lord of the Underworld, Pluto; post mortem, autopsy, necroscopy 364 *inquest*; mortuary, charnel house, morgue 364 *cemetery*; near-death experience, NDE, out-of-body experience, OBE.

*decease*, clinical death, brain d., cerebral d.; cot death, sudden infant death syndrome, sudden death s., SDS, sudden adult death syndrome, SADS; end of life, extinction, exit, demise, curtains 69 *end*; departure, passing, passing away, passing over; natural death, easy d., quiet end, euthanasia 376 *euphoria*; release, happy r., welcome end; loss of life, fatality, fatal casualty; sudden death, violent d., untimely end; death by drowning, watery grave; death on the roads; accidental death, death by misadventure; karoshi 362 *suicide*; fatal disease, mortal illness, terminal i. *or* disease 651 *disease*; dying day, last hour; valley of the shadow of death; deathbed, deathwatch, deathbed repentance, death scene; last agony, last gasp, last breath, dying b.; swan song, death rattle, rigor mortis 69 *finality*; extreme unction; passing bell 364 *obsequies*.

*the dead*, forefathers 66 *precursor*; loved ones, dear departed, saints, souls 968 *saint*; the shades, the spirits, ghosts, phantoms 970 *ghost*; dead body 363 *corpse*; next world 124 *future state*; world of spirits, underworld, netherworld, halls of death, Sheol; Jordan, Styx; Hades, Stygian shore 972 *mythic hell*; Elysian fields, meads of asphodel, happy hunting grounds, Davy Jones's locker 971 *mythic heaven*.

*death roll*, fatality, death toll, death rate, mortality, collateral damage; bill of mortality, casualty list; necrology, death register 87 *list*; death certificate 548 *record*; martyrology; obituary, obit, deaths column, death notice; the dead, the fallen, the lost; casualties, the dead and dying.

**Adj.** *dying*, expiring etc. vb.; mortal, ephemeral, perishable 114 *transient*; moribund, half-dead, with one foot in the grave, deathlike, deathly; deathly pale; given over, given up, despaired of, all over with, all up with, not long for this world, not long to go; done for, had it; slipping, going, slipping away, sinking, sinking fast; sick unto death 651 *sick*; on the danger list, in a critical condition, terminally ill, on one's deathbed, at death's door; in extremis; one's hour having come, one's number being up, sands of life running out, death knocking at the door, life hanging by a thread; at the last gasp, struggling for breath; on one's last legs, at the point of death; sentenced to death, under sentence of death, fated to die, fey, doomed.

*dead*, deceased, demised, no more; passed over, passed away, released, departed, gone, gone before; long gone, dead and gone, dead and buried, in the grave, six feet under 364 *buried*; born dead, stillborn; lifeless, breathless, still; extinct, inanimate, exanimate, bereft of life; stone dead, cold, stiff; dead as mutton, dead as a doornail, dead as a dodo; kaput, done for, under hatches, gone for a burton; off the hook, out of one's misery; departed this life, out of this world, called to one's eternal rest, gathered to one's fathers, in Abraham's bosom, asleep in Jesus, numbered with the dead; launched into eternity, behind the veil, on the other side, beyond the grave, beyond mortal ken; gone to join one's forefathers, gone to the majority, gone to Elysium, gone to the happy hunting-grounds; defunct, late, lamented, late-lamented, gone but not forgotten, regretted, sainted, of sainted memory; martyred, slaughtered, massacred, killed.

**Vb.** *die* (see also *perish*); be dead, lie in the grave, be gone, be no more, cease to be, cease to live, lose one's life 2 *pass away*; die young, not make old bones; die a natural death, die in one's sleep, die in bed; end one's life, decease, predecease; succumb, expire, stop breathing, give up the ghost, breathe one's last; close one's eyes, fall asleep, sleep one's last sleep; pass, pass over, be taken; depart this life 296 *depart*; ring down the curtain, end one's earthly career, 'shuffle off this mortal coil', pay the debt of nature, 'go the way of all flesh', go to one's reward, go to one's last home, go to one's long account;

> To die, to sleep;
> To sleep: perchance to dream: ay, there's the rub;
> For in that sleep of death what dreams may come
> When we have shuffled off this mortal coil,
> Must give us pause.
>
> William Shakespeare, *Hamlet*

> Alack he's gone the way of all flesh.
>
> William Congreve, *Squire Bickerstaff Detected*

(The phrase is based on a Biblical passage, in the Book of Joshua, 'And behold, this day I am going the way of all the earth: . . .')

cross the bar *or* the Styx *or* the River Jordan; enter the Celestial City, enter the Pearly Gates; join the majority, join the choir invisible, join the angels, meet one's Maker, go to glory, reach a better world, awake to life immortal; croak (sl), peg out, snuff it (sl); cop it (sl), have bought it (sl), have had one's chips (sl); cash in one's chips (sl), conk out, pop off, go west, go for a burton, pop one's clogs (sl), hop the twig, kick the bucket (inf), bite the dust (inf), turn up one's toes (sl), push up the daisies (sl), flatline (sl).

*perish*, die out, become extinct 2 *pass away*; go to the wall 165 *be destroyed*; wilt, wither, come to dust, turn to d. 51 *decompose*; meet one's death, meet one's end, meet one's fate; die in harness, die with one's boots on; die hard, die fighting; get killed, be killed, fall, fall in action, lose one's life, be lost; relinquish one's life, lay down one's l., surrender one's l.; become a martyr, give one's life for another, make the supreme sacrifice; catch one's death, die untimely, die young, snuff out like a candle, drop down dead; meet a sticky end, die a violent death, break one's neck; bleed to death; drown, go to Davy Jones's locker 313 *founder*; be put to death, suffer execution, die the death, walk the plank, receive one's death warrant; commit suicide 362 *kill oneself*.

**Adv.** *post-obit*, post mortem; in the event of death; posthumously.

## 362 Killing: destruction of life

**N.** *killing*, serial killing, slaying 165 *destruction*; destruction of life; taking life, dealing death; blood sports, hunting, shooting 619 *chase*; poaching 788 *stealing*; blood-shedding, blood-letting; vivisection; selective killing, cull; abortion; mercy killing, euthanasia, living will; murder (see also *homicide*); poisoning, drowning, suffocation, strangulation, hanging; ritual killing, immolation, sacrifice; martyrization, martyrdom; crucifixion, execution 963 *capital punishment*; judicial murder, auto da fé, burning alive, the stake; dispatch, deathblow, coup de grâce, final stroke, quietus; death by misadventure, violent death, fatal accident, fatal casualty, death on the roads, car crash, train c., plane c.

*homicide*, manslaughter; murder, premeditated m., capital m., first-degree m. (US), second-degree m. (US), third-degree m. (US), serial killing, contract k., contract, bumping-off (inf); assassination; thuggery; crime passionel 911 *jealousy*; abortion, exposure of infants; genocide, ethnocide (see also *slaughter*).

**Murders and Victims**
aborticide (= abortion), deicide (killing of a god), filicide (child), foeticide (foetus), fratricide (brother),
giganticide (giant), homicide (human being), infanticide (child), matricide (mother), parricide (parent or
relative), patricide (father), regicide (king), sororicide
(sister), tyrannicide (tyrant), uxoricide (wife), vaticide
(prophet).

*suicide*, self-slaughter, self-destruction, death
by one's own hand, felo de se; self-
immolation, suttee, seppuku, hara-kiri; assisted
suicide, doctor-assisted s., physician-assisted s.;
parasuicide, attempted suicide; mass suicide,
Gadarene swine, lemmings.

*slaughter*, bloodshed, high casualties,
butchery, carnage; wholesale murder, bloodbath, massacre, noyade, fusillade, battue, holocaust; pogrom, purge, liquidation, decimation,
extermination, annihilation 165 *destruction*;
genocide, ethnocide, ethnic cleansing, Final Solution; war, battle 718 *warfare*; Roman holiday,
gladiatorial combat 716 *duel*; Massacre of the
Innocents, Sicilian Vespers, St Bartholomew's
Day Massacre, Night of the Long Knives.

*place of slaughter*, slaughterhouse, abattoir,
knacker's yard, shambles; bullring 724 *arena*;
field of battle, battlefield 724 *battleground*; field
of blood, killing-fields, Aceldama; gas
chamber, Auschwitz, Belsen.

*killer*, slayer, man of blood; mercy killer 905
*pity*; abortionist; soldier, guerrilla, urban g. 722
*combatant*; slaughterer, butcher, knacker;
huntsman 619 *hunter*; trapper, mole-catcher,
rat-catcher, rodent officer, pest exterminator;
bullfighter, matador, picador, toreador 162 *athlete*; executioner, hangman 963 *punisher*; homicide (see also *murderer*); lynch mob; homicidal
maniac, pathological killer, psychopath; head-
hunter, cannibal; predator, bird of prey, beast
of prey, man-eater; block, gibbet, axe, guillotine, scaffold 964 *means of execution*; insecticide, fungicide, pesticide, organophosphates,
herbicide, weedkiller, poison 659 *bane*.

*murderer*, homicide, killer; mass murderer,
serial killer; Bluebeard, Cain, Doctor Crippen,
Jack the Ripper, Sweeney Todd; assassin; terrorist; poisoner, strangler, garrotter, thug; hatchet man, hitman, gangster, contract killer,
gunman; bravo, desperado, cutthroat 904 *ruffian*; parricide, patricide, matricide, fratricide,
sororicide, uxoricide, filicide, infanticide, regicide, tyrannicide; suicide, kamikaze.

**Adj.** *deadly*, killing, lethal; fell, mortal, fatal,
deathly; involving life, life-threatening,
capital; death-bringing, malignant, poisonous
653 *toxic*; asphyxiant, suffocating, stifling;
unhealthy, miasmic 653 *insalubrious*; inoperable, incurable, terminal.

*murderous*, slaughterous, homicidal, geno-
cidal; suicidal, self-destructive; internecine,
death-dealing, trigger-happy; sanguinary,
ensanguined, bloody, gory, bloodstained, red-
handed; bloodthirsty, thirsting for blood 898
*cruel*; head-hunting, man-eating, cannibalistic.

**Vb.** *kill*, slay, take life, end l., deprive of l.;
do in, do for, top (sl) 165 *destroy*; cut off, nip in
the bud, shorten one's life; put down, put to
sleep; hasten one's end, bring down to the
grave; drive to one's death, work to d., put
to d., send to the scaffold, hang, behead, guillotine, electrocute, send to the electric chair 963
*execute*; stone, stone to death 712 *lapidate*;
string up, lynch; make away with, do away w.,
dispatch, send out of the world, get rid of, send
one to his account, launch into eternity; deal a
deathblow, give the coup de grâce, put one out
of his misery, give one his quietus; shed blood,
knife, sabre, spear, put to the sword, lance, bayonet, stab, run through 263 *pierce*; shoot down,
pick off, pistol, blow the brains out 287 *shoot*;
strangle, wring the neck of, garrotte, choke, suffocate, smother, stifle, drown; wall up, bury
alive; smite, brain, spill the brains of, poleaxe,
sandbag 279 *strike*; send to the stake, burn alive,
roast a. 381 *burn*; immolate, sacrifice, offer up;
martyr, martyrize; condemn to death, sign the
death warrant, ring the knell 961 *condemn*.

*slaughter*, butcher, poleaxe, cut the throat of,
drain the lifeblood of; massacre, slay en masse,
smite hip and thigh, put to the sword; decimate, scupper, wipe out; cut to pieces, cut to
ribbons, cut down, shoot d., mow d.; steep
one's hands in blood, wade in b., give no
quarter, spare none 906 *be pitiless*; annihilate,
exterminate, liquidate, purge, send to the gas
chamber, commit genocide 165 *destroy*.

*murder*, commit m., commit homicide,
commit manslaughter, assassinate, finish off,
make away with, do in, do to death, do for, fix,
settle, bump off, wipe out, liquidate, rub out,
top (sl); make to walk the plank; smother, suffocate, strangle, poison, gas.

*kill oneself*, do oneself in, do away with oneself, make away with oneself, commit suicide,
suicide, put an end to one's life; commit hara-
kiri, commit suttee; hang oneself, shoot o.,
top o. (sl), blow out one's brains, cut one's
throat, slash one's wrists; fall on one's sword,
die Roman fashion; put one's head in the
oven, gas oneself; take poison, take an overdose; jump overboard, drown oneself; get oneself killed, have a fatal accident, die by
misadventure 361 *perish*.

**Adv.** *in at the death*, in at the kill.

**Int.** no quarter!, cry havoc!

## 363 Corpse

**N.** *corpse*, corse, dead body, body; dead man *or* woman, victim; deceased, defunct, goner, stiff; the dead; cadaver, carcass, skeleton, bones, dry b.; death's-head, skull, memento mori; embalmed corpse, mummy; reliquiae, mortal remains, relics, ashes; clay, dust, earth; tenement of clay; carrion, food for worms, food for fishes; long pig 301 *meat*; organic remains 125 *fossil*; shade, manes, zombie 970 *ghost*.

**Adj.** *cadaverous*, corpse-like; skeletal; death-like, deathly; stiff, carrion.

## 364 Interment

**N.** *interment*, burial, sepulture, entombment; urn burial; disposal of the dead, burial customs, inhumation, cremation, incineration; scattering of the ashes; embalming, mummification; embalmment, myrrh, spices, natron; coffin, cist, shell, casket, Canopic jar, urn, cinerary u., funeral u.; sarcophagus, mummy-case; pyre, funeral pile, burning-ghat, crematorium; mortuary, morgue, charnel house; bone-urn, ossuary; undertaker's, funeral parlour; sexton, gravedigger; undertaker, funeral director; mortician; embalmer.

*obsequies*, exequies; mourning, weeping and wailing, wake 836 *lamentation*; lying-in-state; last rites, burial service; funeral rites, funeral solemnity, funeral procession, cortège; knell, passing bell; dead march, muffled drum, last post, taps; memorial service, requiem, funeral hymn, Dies Irae, funeral oration; elegy, dirge 836 *lament*; inscription, epitaph, obituary, lapidary phrases; sepulchral monument, tombstone, gravestone, headstone, ledger; brass; hatchment; cross, war memorial; cenotaph 548 *monument*; necrologist, obituary-writer; monumental mason.

*funeral*, hearse, bier, pall, catafalque, coffin; mourner, weeper, keener; mute, pallbearer; lychgate (see also *obsequies*).

*grave clothes*, burial c., cerements, cerecloth, shroud, winding sheet, mummy wrapping.

*cemetery*, burial place, boneyard, Golgotha; churchyard, graveyard, God's Acre; catacombs, columbarium, cinerarium; tower of silence; necropolis, city of the dead; garden of remembrance, garden of rest.

*tomb*, vault, crypt; burial chamber, mummy c.; pyramid, mastaba; mausoleum, sepulchre; pantheon; grave, narrow house, long home; common grave, mass grave, plague pit; grave pit, cist, beehive tomb, shaft t.; barrow 253 *earthwork*; cromlech, dolmen, menhir 548 *monument*; shrine, aedicule, memorial, cenotaph.

*inquest* 459 *enquiry*; necropsy, autopsy, post-mortem; exhumation, disinterment, disentombment.

**Adj.** *buried*, interred, entombed, coffined, urned etc. vb.; laid to rest, in the grave, below ground, under g., six feet under, pushing up the daisies 361 *dead*.

*funereal*, funerary, funebrial; sombre, sad 428 *black*; mourning; elegiac, mortuary, cinerary, crematory, sepulchral; obsequial, obituary; lapidary, epitaphic; necrological, dirgelike 836 *lamenting*.

**Vb.** *inter*, inhume, bury; lay out, prepare for burial, close the eyes; embalm, mummify; coffin, encoffin; urn, entomb, ensepulchre; lay in the grave, consign to earth, lay to rest, put to bed with a shovel; burn on the pyre, cremate, incinerate 381 *burn*; pay one's last respects, go to a funeral, toll the knell, sound the last post; mourn, keen, hold a wake 836 *lament*.

*exhume*, disinter, unbury; disentomb; unearth, dig up.

**Adv.** *in memoriam*, post-obitum, post-mortem, beneath the sod; hic jacet, RIP.

## 365 Animality. Animal

**N.** *animality*, animal life, wild life; animal kingdom, fauna, brute creation; physique, flesh, flesh and blood; animalization, zoomorphism, Pan; animalism 944 *sensualism*; animal liberation movement, animal rights m.; antivivisectionist, animalist, animal liberationist.

*animal*, created being, living thing; birds, beasts and fishes; creature, brute, beast, dumb animal, creeping thing; protozoon, metazoon; zoophyte 196 *microorganism*; mammal, amphibian, fish, bird, reptile; worm, mollusc, arthropod; crustacean, insect, arachnid; invertebrate, vertebrate; biped, quadruped; carnivore, herbivore, insectivore, omnivore, ruminant, man-eater; wild animal, game, big game; prey, beast of prey; pack, flock, herd 74 *group*; stock, livestock 369 *stock farm*; tame animal, domestic a.; pet a., pet, household pet, animal companion, companion animal; cyberpet, virtual pet, Pokémon (tdmk), Tamagotchi (tdmk); goldfish, koi, shubunkin; hamster, gerbil, guinea pig, tortoise; male animal 372 *male animal*; female animal 373 *female animal*; young animal 132 *young creature*; draught animal 273 *horse, beast of burden*; endangered species, blue whale, oryx; extinct animal, dodo, auk, aurochs, prehistoric animal, dinosaur, megathere, mammoth, mastodon, sabre-toothed tiger;

---

**Dinosaurs and Related Animals**
archosaur, dinosaur, pterosaur *or* -saurus, pteran-

odon, pterodactyl; ichthyosaur *or* -saurus, plesiosaur *or* -saurus, thecodont.

bird-hipped dinosaur, ornithischian; lizard-hipped dinosaur, saurischian.

allosaur *or* -saurus, ankylosaur *or* -saurus, apatosaur *or* -saurus, argentinosaur *or* -saurus, brachiosaur *or* -saurus, brontosaur *or* -saurus, carnosaur, coelurosaur *or* -saurus, compsognathus, deinonychus, diplodocus, gigantosaur *or* -saurus, hadrosaur *or* -saurus, iguanodon, maiasaur *or* -saurus, megalosaur *or* -saurus, raptor, sauropod, stegosaur *or* -saurus, theropod, titanosaur *or* -saurus, triceratops, tyrannosaur *or* -saurus, tyrannosaurus rex, velociraptor.

fabulous beast, heraldic b., unicorn, griffin (see also *mythical beast*).

*mammal*, viviparous animal; man 371 *humankind*; primate, ape, anthropoid ape, gorilla, orang-outang, chimpanzee, bonobo, gibbon, siamang, baboon, drill, mandrill, monkey, howler m., marmoset; lemur, indris *or* indri; marsupial, kangaroo, wallaby, wombat, koala bear, opossum; rodent, rat, mouse, field m., dormouse, shrew, vole, porcupine, mongoose, chipmunk, skunk, polecat, squirrel; insectivorous mammal, aardvark, ant-eater, mole; nocturnal mammal, bat, bush baby, raccoon, badger, hedgehog; carnivorous mammal, stoat, weasel, ferret; fox, dog f., vixen, Reynard; jackal, hyena, lion (see also *cat*); herbivorous mammal (see also *sheep* etc.); hare, mountain h., rabbit, bunny; aquatic mammal, otter, beaver, water rat, water vole; marine mammal, walrus, seal, sea lion; cetacean, dolphin, porpoise, whale, sperm w., right w.; pachyderm, elephant, rhinoceros, hippopotamus; bear, polar b., black b., brown b., grizzly b., bruin; giant panda; ungulate, giraffe, zebra (see also *cattle*); deer, stag, hart, buck, doe, fawn, pricket; red deer, fallow d., roe d., muntjac; reindeer, caribou; elk, moose; gazelle, antelope, chamois, springbok, eland, hartebeest, wildebeest, gnu; horse, donkey, camel 273 *beast of burden*.

*bird*, winged thing, fowl, fowls of the air; fledgling, nestling, squab 132 *young creature*; avifauna, birdlife; cagebird, canary, finch, lovebird; talking bird, budgerigar, budgie (inf); parrot, polly (inf); cockatiel, cockatoo, macaw, parakeet, mynah *or* mynah bird; songbird, songster, warbler, nightingale, philomel, bulbul, lark, thrush, throstle, mavis, blackbird, linnet; curlew, plover, lapwing, peewit; dove, collared d., turtle d., pigeon, wood p. *or* ring dove; woodpecker, yaffle, jay, magpie, pie; jackdaw, rook, raven, crow; finch, bunting, bullfinch, chaffinch, goldfinch, greenfinch, yellowhammer; tit, blue t., great t., wren, robin, sparrow, house s., tree s., hedge sparrow *or* dunnock, wagtail, pied w.; exotic bird,

humming b., sunbird, weaver b., b. of paradise, lyrebird; hoopoe, golden oriole; bird of passage, summer visitor, migrant, cuckoo, martin, swallow, swift; winter visitor, fieldfare, goldeneye, redwing, snow bunting, waxwing; flightless bird, cassowary, emu, kiwi, ostrich, penguin, rhea; nightbird, owl, barn o., tawny o., screech o., nightjar; scavenging bird, vulture, marabou, carrion crow; bird of prey, raptor, eagle, golden e., bald e., bird of Jove, King of Birds; kite, kestrel, harrier, osprey, buzzard, hawk, sparrowhawk, falcon, peregrine f., hobby, merlin, shrike; fishing bird, pelican, kingfisher, gannet, cormorant, shag, skua, Arctic s.; gull, herring g., kittiwake, tern, oystercatcher, puffin, guillemot; ocean bird, albatross, shearwater, petrel, stormy p., Mother Carey's chicken; marsh bird, wader, stork, crane, demoiselle c., avocet, heron, bittern; spoonbill, ibis, flamingo; water bird, waterfowl, swan, mute s., cob, pen, cygnet; duck, drake, duckling; goose, gander, gosling; merganser, mallard, pintail, pochard, teal, widgeon; coot, moorhen, lilytrotter, diver, dipper, grebe, dabchick.

*table bird*, game b., woodcock, wood pigeon, squab; peafowl, peacock, peahen; grouse, ptarmigan, capercaillie, pheasant, partridge, quail; goose, duck, snipe; turkey, gobbler, bubblyjock; guinea fowl, guinea hen.

*poultry*, fowl, hen, biddy; cock, cockerel, rooster, Chanticleer; chicken, pullet; spring chicken, boiler, broiler, roaster, capon; Rhode Island Red, Leghorn, bantam.

*cattle*, kine, livestock 369 *stock farm*; bull, cow, calf, heifer, fatling, yearling; bullock, steer; beef cattle, highland c., Aberdeen Angus, Luing cattle, Hereford, Charolais; dairy cattle, milch cow, Guernsey, Jersey, Friesian; Simmental, dual-purpose cattle, Redpoll, shorthorn; zebu, brahmin, zho *or* zo *or* dzo *or* dzho; ox, oxen; buffalo, beefalo, bison; yak, musk ox; goat, billy g., nanny g., mountain g., ibex.

*sheep*, ram, tup, wether, bell w., ewe, lamb, baa-l., lambkin; teg; Southdown, Lincoln, Cheviot, Herdwick, Merino, blackface; mountain sheep, mouflon.

*pig*, swine, boar, tusker, warthog; hog, sow, piglet, pigling, sucking pig, shoat, porker; Berkshire, Large White, pot-bellied pig, Tamworth, Wessex Saddleback.

*dog*, canine, bow-wow, man's best friend; bitch, whelp, pup, puppy; cur, hound, tyke, pooch, mutt; mongrel, pariah dog, pye-d.; guide dog, hearing d., house d., watch d., police d., guard d., sniffer d., bloodhound, mastiff; sheepdog, Old English s., collie, Border c.;

Dobermann pinscher, black Russian, boxer, bulldog, bull terrier, Rottweiler; basset hound, wolfhound, borzoi, Afghan hound, Alsatian, Dalmatian; Great Dane; St Bernard; greyhound, courser, whippet; foxhound, staghound, beagle, basset *or* basset hound, dachshund; gun dog, retriever, golden r., Labrador r., Labrador, golden l., pointer, setter, Irish s., Gordon s.; terrier, smooth-haired t., wire-h. t., fox t., sealyham, Aberdeen terrier, Scottish t., Scottie, West Highland terrier, Yorkshire t.; spaniel, cocker s., springer s., King Charles s.; show dog, fancy d., toy d., chihuahua, Pomeranian, chow; lap dog, Pekinese, peke, pug; Welsh corgi; poodle, French p., miniature p., toy p.; schipperke, schnauzer; basenji, barkless dog ; husky, sledge dog; wild dog, dingo; wolf, coyote; dangerous dog; fighting d., bandog.

*cat*, feline; grimalkin, moggie, puss, pussy, kitten, kit, kitty-cat, pussycat; tom, tom cat, queen c., tabby; mouser; Cheshire Cat; Persian c., Siamese c., Manx c., calico c., tortoiseshell c., marmalade c., tabby c.; big cat, lion, lioness, King of Beasts; tiger, tigress, tigon, leopard, leopardess, cheetah, panther, black p., puma, jaguar, cougar, ocelot; wildcat, bobcat, lynx, catamount *or* catamountain.

*amphibian*, frog, bullfrog, tree frog, platanna f.; frogspawn, tadpole; paddock, puddock, toad, natterjack; newt, eft; salamander, axolotl.

*reptile*, ophidian, serpent, sea s.; snake, water s., harmless s., grass s., smooth s.; venomous s., viper, adder, asp; cobra, king c., hamadryad; puff adder, mamba, horned viper, rattlesnake; anaconda, boa constrictor, python; crocodile, alligator, cayman; lizard, legless l., slowworm, blindworm; chameleon, iguana, monitor, gecko; turtle, tortoise, terrapin.

*marine life*, denizens of the deep; marine organisms, nekton, benthos; cetacean (see also *mammal*); sea urchin, sea anemone, coral, coral reef, jellyfish, Portuguese man of war, starfish, brittle-star; shellfish, mollusc, bivalve, clam, oyster, mussel, cockle; whelk, winkle, limpet; cephalopod, cuttlefish, squid, octopus; crustacean, crab, lobster, crayfish, shrimp; barnacle.

*fish*, flying f., swordfish, angelfish, dogfish, moray eel, shark; piranha, barracuda; stingray, electric ray; marlin, tuna *or* tunny *or* tunny fish, turbot, bass, conger eel 301 *fish food*; coelacanth; pipefish, sea horse; blenny, goby, wrasse; pike, roach, perch, dace, bream, carp; lamprey; minnow, gudgeon, stickleback; trout, grayling; salmon, grilse, parr, smolt; eel, elver 132 *young creature*.

*insect*, larva, pupa, imago; winged insect, fly, house f., horse f., gadfly, cleg, bluebottle; mayfly, caddis fly; gnat, midge, tsetse fly, mosquito; thunder fly; ladybird, lacewing, hoverfly; firefly, glow-worm, dragonfly, crane fly, daddy longlegs; butterfly, cabbage white, Camberwell Beauty, fritillary, painted lady, peacock butterfly, red admiral, skipper, swallowtail, tortoiseshell; moth, hawk m., clothes m., codling *or* codlin m.; bee, bumble bee, humble b., honey b., queen b., worker b., drone; wasp, hornet; beetle, stag b., dung b., cockroach; insect pests, vermin, parasites, bug, bed bug, flea, louse, nit, mite, tick, jigger; woodworm, weevil, borer, cockchafer, deathwatch beetle, Colorado beetle, aphid, greenfly, blackfly, whitefly 659 *blight*; pismire, emmet, ant, soldier a., worker a., white a., termite; stick insect, praying mantis; locust, grasshopper, cicada, cricket.

*creepy-crawly*, bug, grub, maggot, caterpillar, looper, inchworm; worm, earthworm, lugworm, wireworm, roundworm, flatworm, tapeworm, fluke; myriapod, centipede, millipede; slug, snail; earwig, woodlouse, pill bug; spider, money s.; black widow s., tarantula; scorpion 904 *noxious animal*.

*mythical beast*, unicorn, phoenix, griffin, simurg, roc, rara avis; sphinx, hippogriff, manticore, chimera, centaur, Minotaur; foo dog *or* foo lion; dragon, wyvern, firedrake, cockatrice, basilisk, salamander, hydra; sea serpent, leviathan, kraken, Loch Ness monster, Nessie; the Abominable Snowman, Yeti, Bigfoot, Sasquatch, bunyip; Bandersnatch, Boojum, Jabberwocky, Snark 513 *fantasy*.

**Adj.** *animal*, animalcular; brutish, beastly, bestial; feral, domestic; human, manly, subhuman; therianthropic, theriomorphic, zoomorphic; zoological; vertebrate, invertebrate; mammalian, warm-blooded; primatial, anthropoid, simian; equine, asinine, mulish; deerlike, cervine; bovine, taurine, ruminant; ovine, sheepish; goatlike, goatish; porcine, piggy; bearish, ursine; elephantine; canine, doggy; lupine, wolfish; feline, catlike, cattish; tigerish, leonine; vulpine, foxy; avian, birdlike; aquiline, vulturine; passerine; owlish; dovelike; gallinaceous, anserine; cold-blooded, fishy, piscine, molluscan, molluscoid; amphibian, amphibious, salientian; reptilian, saurian, ophidian, snaky, serpentine, viperish; vermicular, wormy, weevilly; verminous; lepidopterous, entomological.

## 366 Vegetable life

**N.** *vegetable life*, vegetable kingdom; flora, vegetation; biomass; flowering, blooming, florescence; lushness, rankness, luxuriance 635 *plenty*, 171 *abundance*; Flora, Pan; faun, dryad, hamadryad, wood nymph 967 *nymph*.

*wood*, timber, lumber, softwood, hardwood, heartwood, sapwood; forest, virgin f., primeval f.; rain f., jungle; coniferous forest, taiga; bush, heath, scrub, maquis, chaparral; woods, timberland, greenwood, woodland, bocage, copse, coppice, spinney; thicket, bosk, brake, covert; park, chase, game preserve; hurst, holt; plantation, arboretum, pinetum, pinery; orchard, orangery 370 *garden*; grove, clump; clearing, glade; brushwood, underwood, undergrowth; bushiness, bushes, shrubbery, windbreak, hedge, hedgerow.

*forestry*, dendrology, silviculture, tree-planting, afforestation, conservation; woodman, forester, verderer; woodcutter, lumberman, lumberjack; dendrologist 370 *gardener*.

*tree*, shrub, bush, sapling, scion, stock; pollard; bonsai; shoot, sucker, trunk, bole; limb, branch, bough, twig; conifer, coniferous tree, greenwood t., evergreen t., deciduous t., softwood t., hardwood t., ironwood t.; fruit tree, nut t., timber t.; mahogany, ebony, teak, walnut, oak, elm, ash, beech, sycamore, maple, plane, lime, linden; horse chestnut, copper beech; cedar of Lebanon, redwood, larch, fir, Douglas fir, spruce, pine, Scots p., lodgepole p., Christmas tree; poplar, Lombardy p., aspen, alder, sallow, willow, weeping w., pussy w.; birch, silver b., rowan, mountain ash; crab apple, sweet chestnut; hazel, elder, spindle, hawthorn, may, blackthorn, sloe; privet, yew, holly, ivy, box, bay, laurel; rhododendron, camellia, azalea; magnolia, laburnum, lilac; wisteria, Virginia creeper; acacia, jacaranda; palm, date p., coconut p., oil p.; baobab, banyan, mangrove; gum tree, eucalyptus, rubber tree 370 *agriculture*.

*foliage*, foliation, frondescence; greenery, verdure; leafiness, leafage; herbage; umbrage; limb, branch, bough, twig, shoot; spray, sprig; treetop; leaf, simple l., compound l.; frond, flag, blade; leaflet, foliole; pine needle; seed-leaf, cotyledon; leaf-stalk, petiole, stipule, node, stalk, stem; tendril, prickle, thorn.

*plant*, growing thing, herb, superweed, weed, wort; root, bulb, corm, rhizome, tuber 156 *source*; stolon, rootstock, cutting 132 *young plant*; thallophyte, gametophyte, sporophyte; culinary herb 301 *herb*; medicinal herb 658 *remedy*; food plant, fodder 301 *vegetable*, *fruit*, *provender*; national plant, rose, leek, daffodil, thistle, shamrock, fleur-de-lis; garden plant, pansy, primula, marigold, lupin, iris, dahlia, gladiolus, hyacinth, chrysanthemum, snapdragon, sweet william, pink, carnation, lily; lavender, honeysuckle 396 *fragrance*; wild plant, daisy, dandelion, buttercup, poppy, primrose, snowdrop, bluebell, harebell, foxglove, cowslip, forget-me-not, clover, heather; water plant, water lily, marsh marigold, flag; desert plant, cactus, succulent; prickly plant, bramble, gorse, whin; insectivorous plant, Venus's flytrap, sundew; deadly nightshade 659 *poisonous plant*; trailing plant, creeper, climber, twiner, vine, bine, convolvulus, bindweed, liane; parasite, mistletoe; non-flowering plant, horsetail, fern, bracken; moss, clubmoss, bog m., sphagnum; liverwort; lichen, fungus, mushroom, toadstool, agaric, puffball; mould, penicillin; seaweed, wrack, bladderwrack, kelp, gulfweed; algae 196 *microorganism*.

*flower*, floweret, floret, blossom, bloom, bud, burgeon; inflorescence, head, corymb, panicle, cyme, umbel, spike, catkin; petal, sepal; corolla, calyx; ovary, ovule, receptacle; pistil, style, stigma, stamen, anther, pollen; nectary; fruit, berry, nut, drupe; seed vessel, pod, capsule, cone; pip, spore, seed 156 *source*; annual, biennial, perennial; house plant, indoor p., pot p.; hothouse p., exotic; garden flower, wild flower; flowerbed, seedbed, propagator; gardening, horticulture, floriculture 370 *garden*; bouquet of flowers, bunch of flowers, floral tribute, Interflora (tdmk); hanging basket.

*grass*, mowing g., hay; pasture, pasturage, herbage 348 *grassland*; verdure, turf, sod, lawn; meadow grass, rye g., couch g., bent g., fescue; sedge, rush, bulrush, reed, papyrus; marram grass, esparto g.; Pampas grass, elephant g., bamboo, sugar cane; grain plant, wheat, oats, barley, rye, millet, sorghum, rice 301 *cereals*; grain, husk, bran, chaff, stubble, straw.

**Adj.** *vegetal*, vegetative, vegetable, botanical; evergreen; deciduous; hardy, half-hardy; horticultural, floricultural; floral, flowery, blooming; rank, lush, luxuriant, overgrown; weedy, weed-ridden; leafy, verdant, verdurous 434 *green*; grassy, mossy; turfy; gramineous, graminiferous, herbaceous, herbal; leguminous, cruciferous, composite, umbelliferous; foliate, trifoliate, pinnate; fungous, fungoid, fungiform; exogenous, endogenous; dicotyledonous, monocotyledonous.

*arboreal*, arboreous, dendriform, dendritic, arborescent, treelike; forested, timbered; woodland, woody, wooded, sylvan, arboraceous; grovy, bosky; wild, jungly, scrubby; bushy, shrubby; afforested, planted; dendrologous, dendrological.

*wooden*, wood, treen, woody, ligneous, ligniform; hard-grained, soft-grained.

**Vb.** *vegetate*, germinate, sprout, shoot 36 *grow*; plant, garden, botanize 370 *cultivate*; forest, afforest, reforest, replant.

### 367 Zoology: the science of animals

**N.** *zoology*, zoography, zootomy; zoogeography; animal physiology, comparative p., morphology 331 *structure*; embryology 358 *biology*; anatomy, comparative a.; animal behaviour, ethology; anthropography 371 *anthropology*; ornithology, bird lore, bird watching, twitching; cryptozoology, Nessie-hunting; taxidermy.

*zoologist*, biologist, entomologist, ichthyologist, lepidopterist, ornithologist, etc n.; cryptozoologist, Nessie-hunter; anatomist, anthropologist etc. n.

**Adj.** *zoological*, entomological etc. n.

### 368 Botany: the science of plants

**N.** *botany*, phytography, phytogeography, phytotomy; taxonomy; plant physiology, plant pathology; plant ecology; dendrology 366 *forestry*; agrostology; mycology, fungology, bryology, algology, phycology; palaeobotany; botanical garden 370 *garden*; hortus siccus, herbarium, herbal; botanist, herbalist, taxonomist etc. n.

**Adj.** *botanical*, dendrological etc. n.

**Vb.** *botanize*, herbalize.

### 369 Animal husbandry

**N.** *animal husbandry*, animal management; training, manège; thremmatology, breeding, stock-b., rearing; domestication, taming etc. vb.; veterinary science; horse-breeding, cattle-raising; dairy farming, beef f. 365 *cattle*; sheep farming, hill f., pig-f., pig-keeping, goat-k., bee-k., poultry farming; stirpiculture, pisciculture, aviculture, apiculture, sericulture; veterinary surgeon, vet, veterinarian, animal doctor, horse d. 658 *doctor*; ostler, groom, stable boy 742 *servant*; farrier, blacksmith; keeper, gamekeeper, gillie *or* ghillie; game warden.

*stock farm*, stud f., stud; dairy farm, cattle f., rancho, hacienda, ranch; fish farm, trout f., hatchery; fish pond, fish tank; duck pond; pig farm, piggery; bee-hive, hive, apiary; pasture, grazing, horse(y)culture *or* horsiculture, sheep farm, hill f., sheeprun, sheepwalk 348 *grassland*; poultry farm, chicken run, hen r., free range; broiler house, battery, deep litter; factory farm; game preserve.

*cattle pen*, byre, cowshed, veal crate 192 *shed*; sheepfold 235 *enclosure*; hutch, coop, hencoop,

hen run, henhouse; cowshed, pigsty; swannery; bird cage, aviary.

*zoo*, zoological gardens, menagerie, circus; Noah's Ark; aviary, vivarium, terrarium, aquarium, dolphinarium; reptile house, monkey temple; bear pit; wild-life park, safari p.; game park, game reserve.

*breeder*, stock b., horse b., dog b.; cattle farmer, sheep f., pig f., pig-keeper, bee-k., apiarist; fancier, bird-f., pigeon-f.; trainer 537 *trainer*.

*herdsman*, herd; cowherd, stockman, cattleman, byreman, cowman, rancher; cowboy, cowgirl, cowpuncher; broncobuster, gaucho; shepherd, shepherdess; swineherd; goatherd; goosegirl; milkmaid, dairymaid; kennel maid.

**Adj.** *tamed*, broken, broken in; gentle, docile; domestic, domesticated; reared, raised, bred; purebred, thoroughbred, half-bred; stirpicultural.

**Vb.** *break in*, tame, domesticate, acclimatize 610 *habituate*; train 534 *teach*; back, mount, whip, spur 267 *ride*; yoke, harness, hitch, bridle, saddle; round up, herd, corral, cage 235 *enclose*.

*breed stock*, breed, rear, raise, grow, hatch, culture, incubate, nurture, fatten; ranch, farm 370 *cultivate*.

*groom*, currycomb, rub down, stable, bed down; tend, herd, shepherd; shear, fleece; milk; drench, water, fodder 301 *feed*.

### 370 Agriculture

**N.** *agriculture*, agronomy, agronomics, rural economy; Common Agricultural Policy, CAP, set-aside policy, coresponsibility levy, decerealization; butter mountain, grain m., wine lake; agribusiness, agro-industry, agrochemical i. 622 *business*; cultivation, ploughing, contour p., sowing, reaping; growth, harvest, produce, crop, vintage 632 *store*; cash crop, catch c., fodder c.; husbandry, farming, mixed f., contract f., factory f., intensive f., subsistence f., dry f., organic f.; monoculture; cattle farming, dairy f., horse(y)culture *or* horsiculture 369 *animal husbandry*; cereal farming, arable f.; hydroponics, tray agriculture, tank farming; biodynamic farming, biodynamics, permaculture; irrigation 341 *moistening*; geoponics, tillage, tilth, spadework; green fingers; floriculture, flower-growing; horticulture, gardening, market g.; indoor g., bonsai; vegetable growing, fruit g., soft-fruit g., mushroom g.; viticulture, viniculture, wine-growing, vinedressing; arboriculture, silviculture, afforestation 366 *forestry*; landscape gardening, landscape architecture; dung, manure, farmyard m. 171 *fertilizer*; agrochemical; pesticide, herbicide, weed killer 659 *poison*; fodder, winter feed 301 *provender*; silage, ensilage 632 *storage*.

*farm*, home f., grange; arable farm, dairy f., sheep f., hill f., cattle f. 369 *stock farm*; ranch, rancho, hacienda; model farm; farmstead, steading, farmhouse; farmyard, barnyard 235 *enclosure*; state farm, collective f., kolkhoz, kibbutz; farmland, arable l., ploughed l., fallow 344 *soil*; field, corn field, crop circle; rice paddy, paddyfield; herbage, pasturage, pasture, fields, meadows 348 *grassland*; demesne, manor farm, estate, holding, smallholding, croft 777 *lands*; allotment, kitchen garden; market garden, hop g., herb g.; nursery, garden centre, garden shop; vineyard, vinery; fruit farm, orchard; tea garden, tea estate, coffee e., coffee plantation, cotton p., rubber p., sugar p.

*garden*, alpine g., cottage g., Dutch g., flower g., herb g., knot g., rock g., rose g., water g.; botanical garden, indoor g., winter g.; vegetable garden, kitchen g., potager, cabbage patch, allotment; fruit garden, orchard; arboretum, pinery, pinetum 366 *wood*; patch, plot, grass p., grass, greensward, lawn, park 235 *enclosure*; shrubbery, border, herbaceous b., bed, flowerbed, parterre 844 *ornamental art*; seedbed, frame, cold f., cloche, propagator 167 *propagation*; conservatory, hothouse, stove, greenhouse, glasshouse, orangery; grow bag, growing-bag; flowerpot, cachepot, jardinière, planter; compost heap, compost bin, composter.

*farmer*, husbandman, farm manager, grieve, factor, farm agent, bailiff; cultivator, planter, tea p., coffee p.; agronomist, agriculturalist; tiller of the soil, peasant, kulak, moujik, paysan; serf; villein; sharecropper, metayer, tenant farmer; gentleman farmer, yeoman; hill farmer; sharefarmer; smallholder, crofter, allotment-holder; fruit grower, fruit farmer, orchardist; wine-grower, vigneron, vineyardist; farm hand, farm labourer, orraman, agricultural worker; land girl; ploughman, tractor driver, sower, reaper, harvester, gleaner; thresher; picker, potato p., hop p., fruit p., vintager; agricultural folk, farming community, peasantry; rustic, Giles 869 *country-dweller*.

*gardener*, horticulturist, flower grower; topiarist, landscape gardener; seedsman, nurseryman or -woman; market gardener; hop-grower, fruit-g., vine-grower, vigneron, vine-dresser; arborist, arboriculturalist, silviculturist 366 *forestry*; planter, digger, delver, Adam.

*farm tool*, plough, disc p., rotary p., ploughshare, coulter; harrow, chain h., spike h.; cultivator, rotary c., Rotovator (tdmk); spade, fork, farm f., graip, hoe, draw h., Dutch h., onion h., Canterbury h., rake, trowel; dibble, dibber, digging stick; drill; hayrake, hayfork, pitchfork; scythe, sickle, reaping hook, shears, loppers, pruners, secateurs 256 *sharp edge*; flail, winnowing fan; winepress, cider-press; mowing machine, mower, Flymo (tdmk), rotary m., cylinder m., hover m., trimmer, reaper, thresher, binder, baler, combine harvester, pea viner; silage cutter *or* forager; tractor; hay waggon, hay wain; haystack, hayrick, haycock, stook; elevator, barn, hayloft, silo 632 *storage*.

**Adj.** *agrarian*, peasant, farming; agrestic, georgic, bucolic, pastoral, rural, rustic, agricultural, agronomic, geoponic; predial, manorial, collective; arable, cultivable; ploughed, dug, planted etc. vb.

*horticultural*, garden, gardening, topiary; silvicultural; herbal; cultured, forced, hothouse, exotic.

**Vb.** *cultivate*, bring under cultivation 171 *make fruitful*; farm, ranch, garden, grow; till, till the soil, scratch the s.; dig, double-dig, trench, bastard t., delve, spade, dibble; seed, sow, broadcast, scatter the seed, set, plant, prick out, dibble in, puddle in, transplant, plant out, bed o.; plough, disc, harrow, rake, hoe; weed, prune, top and lop, thin out, deadhead 204 *shorten*; graft, engraft 303 *implant*; layer, take cuttings; force, vernalize; fertilize, topdress, mulch, dung, manure 174 *invigorate*; grass over, sod, rotate the crop; leave fallow 674 *not use*; harvest, gather in 632 *store*; glean, reap, mow, cut, scythe, cut a swathe; bind, bale, stook, sheaf; flail, thresh, winnow, sift, bolt 46 *separate*; crop, pluck, pick, gather; tread out the grapes; ensile, ensilage; improve one's land 654 *make better*; fence in 235 *enclose*; ditch, drain, reclaim; water 341 *irrigate*.

### 371 Humankind

**N.** *humankind*, mankind, homo sapiens, womankind; humanity, human nature; flesh, mortality, human frailty; generations of man, peoples of the earth; the world, everyone, everybody, every living soul, the living, ourselves; human race, human species, man; tellurian, earthling; human being, Adam, Eve, Adamite, lords of creation; civilized humanity, political animal, civilized world 654 *civilization*; uncivilized humanity, barbarians, savages; primitive humanity, bushmen, aborigines; early humanity, primeval h., Stone-Age h., Cro-Magnon man, Neanderthal man, cavemen and -women, troglodytes; apemen and -women, Pithecanthropus, Australopithecus, Peking man, Java man; bionic person, cyborg, android, robot; ethnic type 11 *race*.

*anthropology*, anthropography; anthropometrics, craniometry, craniology; anthropogenesis, somatology; ethnology, ethnography, folklore, mythology; social anthropology, demography; social science, humanitarianism 901 *sociology*; humanism; anthroposophy; anthropomorphism, pathetic fallacy; anthropologist, craniologist, ethnographer, demographer, folklorist, humanist.

*person*, individual, human being, mortal, body, bod (inf), a being, soul, living s.80 *self*; everyman, everywoman; creature, fellow c.; God's image; one, somebody, someone, so and so, such a one; party, customer, character, type, element; chap, fellow 372 *male*; girl, female, bird 373 *woman*; personage, figure, person of note, VIP 638 *notable*; celebrity, star 890 *favourite*; dramatis personae, all those concerned 686 *personnel*; unit, head, hand, nose.

*social group*, society, community, ethnic group, ghetto 74 *group*; kinship group 11 *family*; primitive society, tribalism; organized society, international s., comity of nations 706 *cooperation*; community at large, people, persons, folk; public, general p., man *or* woman in the street, Joe Bloggs, Joe Public, Joe Soap, the average punter, everyman, you and me, the 'me' generation 79 *generality*; population, populace, citizenry 191 *inhabitants*; the masses 869 *commonalty*; stratified society, social classes 869 *lower classes, middle c.*, 868 *upper class, aristocracy*.

*nation*, nationality, statehood, nationalism, national consciousness, race c.; Pan-Slavism, Pan-Africanism, Negritude; ultranationalism, chauvinism, jingoism, gung-ho nationalism, expansionism, imperialism, colonialism; Lebensraum; civil society, body politic, people, demos; state, city s., welfare s., civil s., nation s., multiracial s.; realm, commonwealth 733 *political organization*; democracy, republic 733 *government*.

**Adj.** *human*, creaturely, mortal, fleshly; earthborn, tellurian; anthropoid, hominoid; subhuman 35 *inferior*; anthropological, ethnographical, racial 11 *ethnic*; humanistic; anthropocentric, anthropomorphic; personal, individual.

*national*, state, civic, civil, public, general, communal, tribal, social, societal; cosmopolitan, international.

## 372 Male

**N.** *male*, male sex, man, he, him; Adam; manliness, masculinity, manhood; virility, machismo; male chauvinism, male exclusiveness;

male-dominated society, patriarchy; men's movement; mannishness, virilism; gentleman, sir, esquire, master; lord, my l., his lordship; Mr, mister, monsieur, Herr, señor, don, dom, senhor, signor, sahib; tovarich, comrade, citoyen; squire, guvnor, guv; buster, Mac, Jock, Jimmy; mate, buddy, butty, pal 880 *chum*; goodman, wight, swain; gaffer, buffer 133 *old man*; fellow, guy, scout, bloke, bugger (inf), chap, chappie, johnny, gent; codger, card, cove, joker; Jack the lad, blade, rake, gay dog 952 *libertine*; he-man, caveman, macho, Alpha Man, male chauvinist pig, MCP, New Lad, lad, laddism; New Man; sissy, mummy's boy 163 *weakling*; homosexual, homo (inf), queer(inf) 84 *non-heterosexual*; eunuch, castrato; escort, beau, boy friend, toyboy; bachelor, widower; bridegroom 894 *bridal party*; married man, husband, house h., man, live-in 894 *spouse*; family man, paterfamilias, patriarch; father 169 *paternity*; uncle, brother, nephew; lad, stripling, boy 132 *youngster*; blue-eyed boy, son 170 *sonship*; spear side; stag party, menfolk.

*male animal*, dog (coyote, dog, fox, otter, wolf), dog fox; tom cat; horse, stallion (horse, zebra), entire horse, stud h., colt; bull, bull-calf, bullock, ox, steer; boar, hog; ram, tup; he-goat, billy g.; buck (deer, reindeer), hart (red deer), roebuck, stag (caribou, deer, red deer); buck (antelope, goat, hare, kangaroo, rabbit); bull (buffalo, camel, elephant, elk, giraffe, hippopotamus, moose, rhinoceros, seal, walrus, whale); boar (badger, bear, beaver, hedgehog, raccoon); jack (donkey), jackass; hob, jack (ferret); cock, cockerel, rooster; drake, gander, cob (swan), tiercel *or* tercel (falcon); drone (bee); gelding, capon 161 *eunuch*.

**Adj.** *male*, masculine, manly, gentlemanly, chivalrous; virile, macho; laddish, mannish, manlike, butch, unfeminine, unwomanly.

## 373 Female

**N.** *female*, feminine gender, she, her, -ess; femineity, feminality, muliebrity; femininity, feminineness, the eternal feminine; womanhood 134 *adultness*; womanliness, girlishness; feminism, post-feminism, gynography, women's rights, Women's Lib *or* Liberation, Women's Movement, girl power; matriarchy, gynarchy, gynocracy, 'regiment of women';

> The First Blast of the Trumpet Against the Monstrous Regiment of Women
> Title of pamphlet by John Knox

womanishness, effeminacy, androgyny 163 *weakness*; gynaecology, gyniatrics; obstetrics 167 *propagation*.

*womankind*, second sex, female s., fair s., gentle s., weaker s.; the distaff side, womenfolk, women, matronage; hen party; women's quarters, zenana, purdah, seraglio, harem.

*woman*, Eve, she; girl, little g., young g. 132 *youngster*; virgin, maiden; nun, unmarried woman, old maid 895 *spinster*; bachelor girl, career woman; woman doctor, woman engineer, woman MP, Emily's list; feminist, sister, women's libber, bra burner; suffragette; bride, married woman; wife, 'trouble and strife', woman, live-in, squaw, widow, matron 894 *spouse*; dowager 133 *old woman*; mother, grandmother 169 *maternity*; unmarried mother, working wife *or* mother, superwoman, housewife; aunt, auntie, niece, sister, daughter; wench, lass, lassie, nymph; colleen, damsel; petticoat, skirt, doll, chick, bird; honey, hinny, baby, babe, totty (sl); grisette, midinette; brunette, blonde, platinum blonde; lesbian, lez *or* les (sl, usually offensive), dyke *or* dike (sl, usually offensive) 84 *non-heterosexual*; harpy, harridan, she-devil, virago, ballbreaker (sl) 892 *shrew*, 904 *hellbag*.

*lady*, gentlewoman; dame; milady, her ladyship, donna; madam, ma'am, marm, mistress, Mrs, missus (inf), Ms, miss, madame, mademoiselle, Frau, Fräulein; signora, signorina, señora, señorita, memsahib; goody, goodwife.

*female animal*, bitch (dog, fox, otter, wolf); tabby cat; mare (horse, zebra), filly; cow, heifer; sow, gilt; ewe, ewe-lamb; nanny goat, she-g.; hind, doe; jenny (ass, donkey), jenny-ass; she-wolf, vixen, lioness, leopardess, tigress; she-bear, sow; cow (buffalo, camel, elephant, elk, giraffe, hippopotamus, moose, rhinoceros, seal, walrus, whale); doe (antelope, ferret, hare, kangaroo, rabbit, rat); sow (badger, guinea pig, hedgehog, mink, raccoon); gill *or* jill (ferret); hen, pullet; duck, goose, pen (swan); pea-hen (peafowl).

**Adj.** *female*, she, feminine, petticoat, girlish, womanly, ladylike, maidenly, matronly; childbearing 167 *generative*; feminist, feministic, post-feminist; viraginous, Amazonian; lesbian, lez *or* les, dykey *or* dikey; womanish, effeminate, unmanly, pansy; feminized, androgynous.

## 374 Physical sensibility

**N.** *sensibility*, sensitivity, responsiveness; sensitiveness, soreness, tenderness, delicateness, threshold of pain; exposed nerve, unhealed wound; perceptivity, awareness, consciousness 819 *moral sensibility*; physical sensibility *or* susceptivity, susceptibility, passibility; hyperaesthesia, allergy; funny bone; sensuousness, aestheticism, aesthetics; aesthete 846 *people of taste*; touchy person, sensitive plant, thin skin 892 *irascibility*.

*sense*, sense-perception; sensory apparatus, sense organ, nerve system, nervous s., sensorium; five senses, touch, hearing, taste, smell, sight; sensation, impression 818 *feeling*; effect, response, reaction, reflex, synaesthesia; autosuggestion, autohypnosis; sixth sense, feyness, second sight, extrasensory perception, ESP; telepathy, thought-transference 984 *psychics*.

**Adj.** *sentient*, perceptive, sensitive, sensitized; sensible, susceptible, passible; sensory, perceptual; sensuous, aesthetic 818 *feeling*; percipient, aware, conscious 490 *knowing*; acute, sharp, keen 377 *painful*; ticklish, itchy; tender, raw, sore, exposed; impressionable, alive, alive to, warm, responsive; allergic, oversensitive, hypersensitive 819 *impressible*.

*striking*, keen, sharp, poignant, acute, vivid, clear, lively; electrifying 821 *exciting*; sudden, sensational 821 *impressive*.

**Vb.** *have feeling*, sense, become aware; come to one's senses, awaken, wake up; perceive, realize 490 *know*; be sensible of 818 *feel*; react, tingle 819 *be sensitive*; have all one's senses, hear, see, touch, taste, smell; be alert, have one's wits about one, be on the ball, be on the qui vive.

*cause feeling*, stir the senses, stir the blood; stir, disturb 318 *agitate*; arouse, awaken, excite, make *or* produce an impression 821 *impress*; arrest, astonish, cause a sensation 508 *surprise*; sharpen, cultivate 174 *invigorate*; refine, aestheticize; increase sensitivity, sensitize; hurt 377 *give pain*.

**Adv.** *to the quick*, to the heart, to one's very being, on the raw.

## 375 Physical insensibility

**N.** *insensibility*, physical i., impassibility, insensitiveness; mental insensibility, imperceptiveness, obtuseness 499 *unintelligence*; impassivity 820 *moral insensibility*; insentience, anaesthesia; analgesia; narcotization, hypnosis, hypnotism, autohypnosis; suspended animation; apoplexy, paralysis, palsy; numbness; catalepsy, stupor, coma, trance, drugged t., freak-out; faint, swoon, blackout, syncope, unconsciousness, senselessness; narcolepsy, narcotism, sleeping sickness 651 *disease*; narcosis, twilight sleep, drugged s. 679 *sleep*; Sleeping Beauty, Rip van Winkle.

*anaesthetic*, dope 658 *drug*; local anaesthetic, general a.; ether, chloroform, morphine, cocaine, novocaine, chloral; gas, nitrous oxide, laughing gas; gas and air, epidural, pethidine; narcotic, sleeping tablets, Mogadon (tdmk), knockout drops, draught 679 *soporific*; opium,

laudanum; painkiller, analgesic 177 *moderator*;
acupuncture. .

**Adj.** *insensible*, insensitive, insentient, insensate; obtuse, dull, imperceptive 499 *unintelligent*; unaware, oblivious; unhearing 416 *deaf*;
unseeing 439 *blind*; senseless, sense-bereft,
unconscious; inert 679 *inactive*; inanimate, out
cold, out for the count, dead 266 *quiescent*;
numb, benumbed, frozen; paralysed, paralytic,
palsied; doped, dopy, drugged; freaked out,
spaced o.; stoned 949 *dead drunk*; anaesthe-
tized, hypnotized; punch-drunk, dazed, stupefied; semiconscious, in a trance; catatonic,
cataleptic, comatose; anaesthetic, analgesic;
hypnotic, mesmeric 679 *soporific*.

*unfeeling*, cold, callous, insensitive, inured,
indurated, toughened, hardened, case-h.;
pachydermatous, thick-skinned; stony, impassible, proof, shockproof 820 *impassive*.

**Vb.** *be insensible*, – insentient etc. adj.; not
react 679 *be inactive*; have a thick skin *or* hide
820 *be insensitive*; harden oneself, indurate,
cease to feel; become insensible, lose consciousness, pass out, black o., faint, swoon; go into a
coma.

*render insensible*, make insensible; obtund,
blunt, deaden; paralyse, benumb; freeze 382
*refrigerate*; put to sleep, send to sleep, hypnotize, mesmerize 679 *make inactive*; anaesthetize, put under, gas, chloroform; narcotize,
drug, dope; dull, stupefy; stun, concuss, brain,
knock out, render unconscious 279 *strike*; pall,
cloy 863 *sate*.

**376 Physical pleasure**
**N.** *pleasure*, physical p., sensual p., sensuous p.;
enjoyment, gratification, sensuousness, sensuality; self-indulgence, animal gratification, luxuriousness, hedonism 944 *sensualism*;
dissipation, round of pleasure 943 *intemperance*; rest 685 *refreshment*; treat, diversion,
entertainment, divertissement 837 *amusement*;
feast, thrash 301 *feasting*; epicurism, epicureanism, good feeding, relish 386 *taste*;
gusto, zest, keen appreciation; mental *or* spiritual pleasure, delight, happiness, ecstasy 824
*joy*.

*sexual pleasure*, s. satisfaction; thrill 821 *excitation*; sexual intercourse, lovemaking, making
love, sex, casual sex, foreplay 45 *sexual intercourse*; free love, wife-swapping 951 *illicit love*;
masturbation, autoeroticism, autoerotism, frigging (sl), onanism, self-abuse, self-stimulation,
wank (sl), wanking (sl); dildo, vibrator;
frottage; tribadism; climax, orgasm; sex addiction *or* sexual a.; oral sex, fellatio, blowjob (sl),
cunnilingus; G-spot, Gräfenberg spot; Viagra
(tdmk); cybersex.

*euphoria*, well-being, contentment 828 *content*, 824 *happiness*; physical well-being 650
*health*; easeful living, gracious l.; ease, convenience, comfort, cosiness, snugness, creature
comforts; luxury, luxuries 637 *superfluity*; lap
of luxury 800 *wealth*; feather bed, bed of down,
bed of roses, velvet, cushion, pillow 327 *softness*; peace, quiet, rest 683 *repose*; quiet dreams
679 *sleep*; painlessness, euthanasia.

**Adj.** *pleasant*, pleasure-giving 826 *pleasurable*; pleasing, tickling, titillating, arousing;
delightful, delightsome; welcome, grateful,
gratifying, satisfying 685 *refreshing*; genial, congenial, friendly, matey, cordial, heart-
warming; nice, agreeable, enjoyable 837
*amusing*; palatable, delicious 386 *tasty*; sugary
392 *sweet*; perfumed 396 *fragrant*; tuneful 410
*melodious*; lovely 841 *beautiful*.

*comfortable*, affording comfort, comfy,
homely, snug, cosy, warm, comforting, restful
683 *reposeful*; painless, peaceful 266 *tranquil*;
convenient, easy, cushy; easeful, downy 327
*soft*; luxurious, de luxe; enjoying comfort,
euphoric, in comfort, at one's ease, slippered;
pampered, featherbedded, in clover, on a bed
of roses, on velvet; happy, gratified 828 *content*; relieved 685 *refreshed*.

*sensuous*, of the senses, appealing to the s.;
bodily, physical 319 *material*; voluptuous, pleasure-loving, luxuriating, enjoying, epicurean,
hedonistic 944 *sensual*.

**Vb.** *enjoy*, relish, like, quite l., love, adore;
feel pleasure, experience p., take p. in 824 *be
pleased*; thrill to 821 *be excited*; luxuriate in,
revel in, riot in, bask in, roll in, wallow in;
gloat on, gloat over, get a kick out of; lick one's
lips, smack one's l. 386 *taste*; 'live on the fat of
the land' (see quotation at 730 *prosperity*), live
comfortably, live in comfort, live in clover, rest
on a bed of roses 730 *prosper*; give pleasure 826
*please*.

*have or give sexual pleasure*, have sex with,
make love, sleep around, sleep together, sleep
with 45 *have sexual intercourse with*; masturbate, frig (sl), toss off (sl), wank (sl); climax,
have an orgasm, orgasm, come (sl); feel up (sl),
touch up (sl); arouse, excite, turn on (inf) 821
*excite*; fellate, go down on (sl); satisfy 826
*please*.

**Adv.** *in comfort*, at one's ease; in clover, on
velvet, on a bed of roses.

**377 Physical pain**
**N.** *pain*, physical p., bodily p., threshold of
pain; no pain no gain; discomfort, malaise,
inconvenience; distress, thin time, hell 731
*adversity*; exhaustion, weariness, strain, stress
684 *fatigue*; hurt, bruise, sprain, break, fracture;

cut, gash 655 *wound*; aching, smarting, throbbing; heartache, anguish, agony 825 *suffering*; slow death, painful d., death by inches, torment, torture; crucifixion, martyrdom, vivisection; rack, wheel, thumbscrew 964 *instrument of torture*; painfulness, soreness, tenderness; painful aftermath, post-operative pain, hangover 949 *crapulence.*

*pang*, thrill, throes; stab, labour pangs, hunger p., twinge, nip, pinch; pins and needles 378 *formication*; stitch, crick, cramp, convulsion 318 *spasm*; smart, sting, sharp pain, shooting p., darting p., gnawing p.; ache, headache, splitting head, migraine, megrim; toothache, earache; stomachache, bellyache, gripes, colic, collywobbles (inf); neuritis, neuralgia, angina; arthritis, rheumatoid a., rheumatism, fibrositis; repetitive strain injury, RSI; sciatica, lumbago, backache 651 *ill health.*

**Adj.** *painful*, paining, aching, agonizing, excruciating, exquisite, mind-blowing; harrowing, racking, tormenting; poignant 827 *distressing*; burning, biting, searing, stabbing, lancinating, shooting, tingling, smarting, throbbing; sore, raw, tender, exposed, grazed; bitter, bittersweet 393 *sour*; disagreeable, uncomfortable, inconvenient 827 *unpleasant.*

*pained*, hurt, tortured, martyred etc. vb.; suffering, aching, flinching, wincing, quivering, writhing.

**Vb.** *give pain*, ache, hurt, pain, sting, graze; inflict pain, excruciate, put to torture, lacerate, torment, twist the arm of 963 *torture*; flog, whip, crucify, martyr 963 *punish*; vivisect, tear, lacerate 46 *cut*; touch the quick; prick, stab 263 *pierce*; gripe, nip, pinch, tweak, twinge, shoot, throb; devour, bite, gnaw; grind, grate, jar, set on edge; fret, chafe, gall 333 *rub*; irritate 832 *aggravate*; put on the rack, break on the wheel; kill by inches, prolong the agony; grate on the ear 411 *discord*; inconvenience, annoy, distress 827 *trouble.*

*feel pain*, suffer p., feel the pangs 825 *suffer*; agonize, ache, smart, chafe; twitch, wince, flinch, writhe, squirm, creep, shiver, quiver 318 *be agitated*; tingle, get pins and needles; sit on thorns, have a thin time, be a martyr, go through it 731 *have trouble*; shriek, yell, scream, howl, groan 408 *cry*; weep 836 *lament*; lick one's wounds.

## 378 Touch: sensation of touch

**N.** *touch*, tactility, touchy-feeliness; palpability; handling, feeling, palpation, manipulation; massage, kneading, squeeze, pressure 333 *friction*; graze, contact 202 *contiguity*; light touch, lambency; stroke, pat, caress; flick, flip, tap 279

*knock*; sense of touch, fine t., precision 494 *accuracy*; delicacy, artistry 694 *skill.*

*formication*, tingle, tingling, pins-and-needles; titillation, tickling sensation; creeps, gooseflesh or -bumps or -pimples, someone walking over one's grave; scratchiness, itchiness, itch, urtication; urticaria, nettlerash, hives, allergic reaction; rash, dhobi's itch, prickly heat 651 *skin disease*; pediculosis 649 *uncleanness.*

*feeler*, organ of touch, palp, palpus, antenna, whisker, tentacle; proboscis, tongue; digit, forefinger, thumb (see also *finger*); green fingers; hand, paw, palm, flipper, mitt.

*finger*, forefinger, index, middle finger, ring f., little f., pinkie; thumb, pollex; hallux, big toe 214 *foot*; five fingers, bunch of fives, bone sandwich, knuckle s., dukes; hand, fist, 'pickers and stealers' 778 *nippers*; fingernail, talon, claw.

> Rosencrantz: My lord, you once did love me.
> Hamlet: And do still, by these pickers and stealers.
> William Shakespeare, *Hamlet*

**Adj.** *tactual*, tactile; touchy-feely (inf); palpal, tentacular; prehensile 778 *retentive*; touching, licking, grazing etc. vb.; touchable, tangible, palpable 319 *material*; light of touch, light-handed, heavy-h. 695 *clumsy.*

*handed*, with hands; right-handed 241 *dextral*; left-handed 242 *sinistral*; thumbed, fingered, polydactyl; digitate, digital, manual; five-finger.

**Vb.** *touch*, make contact, come into c.; graze, scrape, shave, brush, glance; kiss, osculate 202 *be contiguous*; impinge, overlap; hit, meet 279 *collide*; feel, palpate; finger, thumb, take between finger and thumb, pinch, nip, massage 333 *rub*; palm, run the hand over, pass the fingers o.; stroke, pat down 258 *smooth*; wipe, sweep 648 *clean*; touch lightly, tap, tip, pat, dab, flick, flip, tickle, scratch; lip, lap, lick, tongue; nuzzle, rub noses; paw, fondle 889 *caress*; handle, twiddle, fiddle with, play with; manipulate, wield, ply, manhandle 173 *operate*; touch roughly, jab, poke, goose, bruise, crush 377 *give pain*; fumble, grope, grabble, scrabble; put out a feeler 461 *be tentative.*

*itch*, tickle, tingle, creep, crawl, have gooseflesh, have the creeps; prick, prickle, titillate, urticate, scratch; thrill, excite, irritate, inflame 374 *cause feeling.*

## 379 Heat

**N.** *heat*, caloric; phlogiston; radiant heat; convected heat; incalescence, recalescence, decalescence; emission of heat, diathermancy; incandescence, flame, glow, flush, hot flush, blush; warmth, fervour, ardour; tepidity, lukewarmness; specific heat, blood h., body h.; sweat, perspiration, swelter; fever heat, pyrexia, fever, hectic, inflammation 651 *disease*; high temperature, white heat; ebullition, boiling point, flash p., melting p.; torrid heat, tropical h., sweltering h., summer h., high summer, flaming June, Indian summer; dog days, heat haze 128 *summer*; heat wave, scorcher, blisterer, roaster, sizzler; hot wind, simoom, sirocco; hot springs, thermal s., thermae, geyser, hot water, steam; tropics, torrid zone; sun, midday s., sunshine, solar heat, insolation 381 *heating*.

*fire*, devouring element, flames; bonfire, bale fire, watch f., beacon f.; St Elmo's f. 417 *glow*; hellfire; death fire, pyre 364 *obsequies*; coal fire, gas f., electric f., wood-burning stove 383 *furnace*; Greek fire, wild f. 723 *bomb*; deflagration, conflagration, holocaust; heath fire, forest f., bush f.; fireball, blaze, flame, tongue of f., sheet of f., wall of f.; spark, scintillation, flicker, arc 417 *flash*; flare 420 *torch*; eruption, volcano; pyrotechnics 420 *fireworks*; arson 381 *incendiarism*; fire worship 981 *worship*; salamander, phoenix.

*thermometry*, heat measurement, thermometer, differential t., clinical t., Fahrenheit t., centigrade *or* Celsius t., Réaumur t.; thermoscope, thermopile, thermostat, air-conditioner; pyrometer, calorimeter; thermal unit, British Thermal Unit, BTU, therm, calorie; solar constant; thermodynamics; thermography, thermograph.

**Adj.** *hot*, heated, superheated, overheated; inflamed, fervent, fervid; flaming, glowing, fiery, red-hot, white-h.; like an oven, like a furnace, hot as hell; piping hot, smoking h., steaming h.; hot as pepper 388 *pungent*; incalescent, recalescent; feverish, febrile, fevered; sweltering, sudorific, sweating, perspiring; steaming, smoking; running with sweat, dripping with s.; on the boil, boiling, seething, ebullient, scalding; tropical, torrid; scorching, grilling, broiling, searing, blistering, baking, toasting, roasting etc. vb.; scorched, scalded 381 *heated*; thirsty, burning, parched 342 *dry*; running a temperature, in a fever, in a lather, in a sweat, in a muck s.

*fiery*, ardent, burning, blazing, flaming, flaring; unquenched, unextinguished; smoking, smouldering; ablaze, afire, on fire, aflame, in flames; candescent, incandescent, molten, glowing, aglow 431 *red*; pyrogenic, igneous, pyrogenous; ignited, lit, alight, kindled, enkindled; volcanic, erupting, plutonic.

*warm*, tepid, lukewarm, unfrozen; temperate, mild, genial, balmy; fair, set f., sunny,

sunshiny 417 *undimmed*; summery, aestival; tropical, equatorial; torrid, sultry; stuffy, close, muggy; overheated, uncooled, unventilated; oppressive, suffocating, stifling, like a hothouse 653 *insalubrious*; warm as toast; snug 376 *comfortable*; at room temperature, at blood heat; caloric, calorific, calorimetric; thermic, thermal, isothermal.

**Vb.** *be hot*, be warm, get warm etc. adj.; recalesce, incandesce; burn, kindle, catch fire, take f., draw; blaze, flare, flame, flame up, burst into flame, go up in flames; glow, flush; smoke, smoulder, reek, fume, steam 300 *emit*; boil, seethe 318 *effervesce*; toast, grill, broil, roast, sizzle, crackle, frizzle, fry, bake 381 *burn*; get burnt, scorch, boil dry; bask, sun oneself, sunbathe; get sunburnt, tan; swelter, sweat, perspire, glow; melt, thaw 337 *liquefy*; thirst, parch 342 *be dry*; suffocate, stifle, pant, gasp for breath, fight for air; be in a fever, be feverish, have a fever, run a temperature; keep warm, wrap up, insulate, keep out the cold.

## 380 Cold

**N.** *coldness*, low temperature, drop in t.; cool, coolness, freshness; cold, freezing c., zero temperature, zero, absolute z.; freezing point; frigidity, gelidity; iciness, frostiness; sensation of cold, chilliness, chill factor, windchill factor, algidity, rigour, hypothermia, shivering, shivers, chattering of the teeth, chittering, gooseflesh, goose pimples, frostbite, chilblains, chap, hack; chill, catching cold, common cold, coryza, a cold in the head; cold climate, high latitudes, Frigid Zone, Siberia, North Pole, South P.; Arctic, Antarctica; snowline, permafrost; glacial epoch, Ice Age; polar bear, husky, Eskimo; igloo.

*wintriness*, winter, depth of w., hard w., severe w.; nip in the air, cold snap; cold weather, cold front; inclemency, wintry weather, arctic conditions, polar temperature, degrees of frost; snowstorm, hailstorm, blizzard; frost, touch of f., Jack Frost, frostwork, rime, hoarfrost, white frost, sharp f., hard f.; sleet, hail, hailstone, silver thaw, black ice, freeze.

*snow*, snowfall, snowflake, snow crystal; avalanche, snow slip, snowdrift, snowpack, snowfield; snowstorm, flurry of snow, the old woman plucking her geese; snow line, snowcap, snowfield; snowball, snowman; snowplough, snowshoe, snowmobile, snow tyre; winter sports 837 *sport*; snow blindness; snowbound.

*ice*, dry i., ice cube; hailstone, icicle; ice cap, ice field, ice sheet, ice shelf, floe, ice f., iceberg, tip of the iceberg, berg, ice front, glacier, icefall, sérac; shelf ice, pack i.; driven snow, frozen s., névé, frozen sea; icebreaker, ice yacht; ice house, icebox 384 *refrigerator*; ice action, glaciation 382 *refrigeration*; glaciology.

**Adj.** *cold*, without heat, impervious to heat, adiathermanous; cool, temperate; shady, chill, chilly, parky, nippy, perishing; unheated, unwarmed, unthawed; fresh, raw, keen, bitter, nipping, biting, piercing; inclement, freezing, gelid, ice-cold, bitterly c., below zero; frigid, brumal 129 *wintry*; winterbound, frosty, frostbound, snowy, snow-covered, mantled in snow, blanketed in s.; slushy, sleety, icy; glacial, ice-capped, glaciered, glaciated; boreal, polar, arctic, Siberian.

*chilly*, feeling cold, acold; shivering, chattering, chittering, shivery, algid, aguish; blue, blue with cold; shrammed, perished, perishing, starved with cold, chilled to the bone, hypothermic, frozen, frostbitten, frost-nipped; like ice, cold as charity, cold as a frog, cold as marble, stone-cold, cold as death.

**Vb.** *be cold*, – chilly etc. adj.; grow cold, lose heat, drop in temperature; feel cold, chatter, chitter, shiver, tremble, shake, quake, quiver, shudder; freeze, starve, perish with cold, suffer from hypothermia; catch cold, get a chill; chill 382 *refrigerate*.

**Adv.** *frostily*, frigidly, bitterly, coldly, nippily.

## 381 Heating

**N.** *heating*, superheating, increase of temperature, calefaction, torrefaction; diathermy; diathermancy; transcalency; calorific value, thermal efficiency; warming, keeping warm; space heating, central h., district heating system 383 *heater*; solar heating, insolation, sunning 342 *desiccation*; greenhouse effect; melting, thawing 337 *liquefaction*; smelting, scorification, cupellation; boiling, seething, simmering, ebullition; baking, cooking 301 *cookery*; decoction, distillation; antifreeze mixture.

*burning*, combustion; inflammation, kindling, ignition; reheat, afterburning; deflagration, conflagration 379 *fire*; incineration, calcination; roasting; cremation 364 *interment*; suttee, self-burning 362 *suicide*; auto-da-fé, holocaust 981 *oblation*; cauterization, cautery, branding; scorching, singeing, charring, carbonization; inflammability, combustibility; burner 383 *furnace*; cauterizer, caustic, moxa, vitriol; hot iron, branding i., brand; match, touchpaper 385 *lighter*; stoker, fireman; burn mark, burn, scorch mark, brand, singe, scald, sunburn, tan, sun-stroke.

*incendiarism*, arson, fire-raising, pyromania; incendiary, arsonist, fire-raiser, fire-bug; fire-brand, revolutionary 738 *agitator*.

*warm clothes*, furs, synthetic f., fun f., woollens, woollies, red flannel, thermal underwear; parka, anorak, windcheater, wrap, muffler, scarf, muff, earmuffs; winter coat 228 *overcoat*; blanket 226 *coverlet*; padding, wadding 227 *lining*.

*ash*, ashes, volcanic ash, lava, tuff; carbon, soot, smut, lamp-black, smoke; product of combustion, clinker, charcoal, ember, cinder, coke, slag, dross, scoria, oxide, bone-ash.

*pottery*, ceramics; earthenware, stoneware, lustre ware, glazed w.; majolica, faience, china-ware, porcelain; crockery, china, bone c., Wedgwood (tdmk) c., Spode c., Worcester c., Doulton c., Chelsea c., Staffordshire c., Derby c., Sèvres c., Dresden c.; delft, willow pattern, terracotta; tile, encaustic t., brick, sundried b., mud b., adobe; pot, urn 194 *vessel*; potter's wheel.

**Adj.** *heated*, superheated 379 *hot*, centrally-heated, winterized, insulated; lit, kindled, fired; incinerated, burnt, burnt out, burnt down, gutted; cooked, roasted, toasted, grilled, broiled, baked; réchauffé, hotted up, warmed up; melted, fused, molten; overheated; steamy, smoky; scorched, seared, charred, singed, branded; bronzed, tanned, sun-t., sunburnt.

*heating*, warming etc. vb.; calefactory, calefactive, calorific, caustic, burning; solid-fuel, coal-burning, oil-fired, gas-fired; incendiary, inflammatory; thermoplastic, thermosetting; diathermic, diathermanous; inflammable, flammable 385 *combustible*; antifreeze.

**Vb.** *heat*, raise the temperature, warm; provide heating, winterize, insulate; keep the cold out, take the chill off; hot up, warm up, stoke up; rub one's hands, stamp one's feet; thaw, thaw out; inflame, foment, poultice; overheat, stew, stifle, suffocate; insolate, sun, parch, shrivel, sear 342 *dry*; torrefy, toast, bake, grill, broil, fry, roast 301 *cook*; melt, defrost, deice 337 *liquefy*; smelt, cupel, scorify; fuse, weld, vulcanize, cast, found.

*kindle*, enkindle, ignite, light, strike a l.; apply the match, set fire to, light the touchpaper, light the fuse, touch off 385 *fire*; rekindle, relume; fuel, stoke, feed the flames, fan the fire, add fuel to the f., poke the f., stir the f., blow the f.; lay the fire, make the f., rub two sticks together.

*burn*, burn up, burn out, gut; commit to the flames, consign to the f., make a bonfire of, send to the stake; fire, set fire to, set on fire, set alight; cremate, incinerate, burn to ashes; boil dry 342 *dry*; carbonize, calcine, oxidize, corrode; coal, char, singe, sear, scorch, tan; cauterize, brand, burn in; scald.

### 382 Refrigeration

**N.** *refrigeration*, cooling, reduction of temperature; icing etc. vb.; freezing, freezing up, glaciation, gelation, congelation 380 *ice*; solidification 324 *condensation*; exposure; ventilation, air-conditioning; cold storage 384 *refrigerator*; cryonic suspension, cryonics 364 *interment*; cryogenics, cryobiology, cryosurgery, cryotherapy.

*incombustibility*, noninflammability, fire resistance; asbestos, amiantus, fire-bricks, fireclay.

*extinguisher*, fire e.; foam, powder, water; hose, hydrant, fire h., sprinkler, standpipe; fire blanket; fire engine, fire appliance, fire tender, fire truck, Green Goddess, fireboat, fire station; firefighter, fireman, firewoman; fire brigade; firebreak, fire line; fire door, fire wall.

**Adj.** *cooled*, chilled etc. vb.; ventilated, air-conditioned; iced up; frozen, deep-frozen, freeze-dried, lyophilized; ice-capped; glaciated; frosted, iced, glacé, frappé; with ice, on the rocks 380 *cold*; cooling etc. vb.; frigorific, refrigerative, refrigeratory.

*incombustible*, unburnable; uninflammable, noninflammable, nonflammable; fire-resistant, fireproof, flameproof; asbestive; damped, wetted 341 *drenched*.

**Vb.** *refrigerate*, cool, air-cool, water-c., fan, air-condition, freshen up 685 *refresh*; ventilate, air 340 *aerate*; reduce the temperature, turn off the heat; keep the heat out, keep the sun off, shade, shadow 421 *screen*; frost, freeze, congeal, glaciate; deep-freeze, freeze-dry, lyophilize; make ice, ice; ice up, ice over; chill, benumb, starve, nip, pinch, bite, pierce, chill to the marrow, make one's teeth chatter; expose to the cold, frost-bite.

*extinguish*, quench, snuff, put out, blow o., snuff o.; choke, suffocate, stifle, smother 165 *suppress*; damp, douse, damp down, bank d.; rake out, stamp o., stub o.; stop burning, go out, burn o., die down.

### 383 Furnace

**N.** *furnace*, fiery f.; the stake 964 *means of execution*; volcano, Etna, Krakatoa, Stromboli, Vesuvius, solfatara, fumarole; touchhole, gun barrel; forge, blast furnace, reverberatory f., kiln, lime k., brick k.; oast, oasthouse; incinerator, destructor; crematory, crematorium; brazier, stove, kitchen s., charcoal s., wood-burning s., gas s., electric s., primus s.; oil s.; oven, gas o., electric o., circotherm o., microwave o.; range, kitchen r., kitchener; cooker, oil c., gas c., electric c., split-level c., turbo-fan c., ceramic hob; gas ring, burner, bunsen b.; blowlamp, oxyacetylene lamp; fire, open f., coal f., log f. 379 *fire*; brand 385 *lighter*; firebox, fireplace, grate, hearth, ingle; fire-irons, andirons, firedog; poker, tongs, shovel; hob, trivet; fireguard, fender; flue 263 *chimney*.

*heater*, space h., paraffin h., radiator, solar panel; hot-air duct, hypocaust; hot-water pipe, hot-water heater, immersion h., boiler, back b., central-heating b., combi-b., geyser, copper, kettle, electric k. 194 *cooking pot*; hotplate; warming pan, hot-water bottle; electric blanket, foot-warmer; still, retort, alembic, crucible 461 *testing agent*; blowpipe, bellows, tuyère, damper; hot baths, thermae, Turkish bath, sauna, Jacuzzi (tdmk) 648 *ablutions*; hotbed, hothouse, greenhouse, conservatory 370 *garden*; sun trap, solarium; kitchen, galley, cook-house, caboose; gridiron, grill, frying pan, saucepan; toaster, electric t.; iron, flat i., electric i., steam i., soldering i., curling tongs; heating agent, flame, sunlight 381 *heating*; gas, electricity, solar energy, greenhouse effect 160 *sources of energy*; steam, hot air; wood, coal, peat 385 *fuel*.

### 384 Refrigerator

**N.** *refrigerator*, cooler; ventilator, fan, punkah, air-conditioner; cooling-room, frigidarium; refrigerating plant, fridge, chiller, cooler, wine c., ice bucket; coolant, freezing mixture, snow, ice; icehouse, icebox, ice pack, cold p., icebag; ice-cubes, rocks; cold storage, freezer, fridge-freezer, deep-freeze 382 *refrigeration*.

### 385 Fuel

**N.** *fuel*, inflammable material, flammable m., combustible, food for the flames; firing, kindling; wood, brushwood, firewood, faggot, log, Yule l.; biomass 366 *vegetable life*; turf, peat; cow dung, camel d.; lignite, brown coal, wood c., charcoal; fossil fuel, coal, natural gas, petroleum 357 *oil*, 336 *gas*; nuclear fuel, plutonium, uranium, depleted u., DU 160 *nucleonics*; petrol, high octane p., three-star, four-s., unleaded petrol, superunleaded p., lead-free p., lead replacement p., LRP, juice (inf), gasoline, gas; diesel oil, derv; biodiesel, alternative fuel; carbon tax; paraffin, kerosene; alcohol, spirit, methylated s.; North Sea gas, coal g., acetylene, propane, butane, methane, biogas.

*coal*, black diamond, sea coal, hard c., anthracite, cannel coal, bituminous c.; briquette; coal dust, culm, slack; coal seam, coal deposit, coal measure, coalfield 632 *store*; cinders, embers 381 *ash*; coke, gas c.; smokeless fuel.

*lighter*, fire-l., cigarette l., igniter, light, pilot l., illuminant, taper, spill, candle, tealight 420 *torch*; coal, ember, brand, firebrand; fire ship, incendiary bomb 723 *bomb*; wick, fuse, touchpaper, match, slow m.; linstock, portfire, percussion cap, detonator; safety match, friction m., lucifer, vesta, fusee; flint, steel, tinder, touchwood, punk, spunk, amadou; tinderbox, matchbox.

*fumigator*, incense, joss stick, sulphur, brimstone.

**Adj.** *combustible*, burnable, inflammable, flammable, incendiary, explosive; carboniferous, carbonaceous, coal-bearing, coaly.

**Vb.** *fire*, stoke, feed, fuel, coal, add fuel to the flames; mend the fire; put a match to, light the touchpaper 381 *kindle*.

## 386 Taste

**N.** *taste*, sapor, sapidity, savour; flavour, flavouring; smack, smatch, tang, twang, aftertaste; relish, gusto, zest, appetite 859 *liking*; tasting, gustation; palate, tongue, tastebuds; tooth, sweet t., stomach.

**Adj.** *tasty*, sapid, saporous, palatable, full of flavour, flavourful, mouth-watering, tempting, appetizing 390 *savoury*; well-seasoned, salty, peppery, tangy 388 *pungent*; flavoured, spiced, spicy, herbed, herby, racy, rich, strong, full-flavoured, full-bodied, fruity, hoppy, generous, well-matured, mellow, vintage; gustatory, gustative.

**Vb.** *taste*, find palatable, lick one's lips, smack one's lips, roll on the tongue, lick one's fingers 376 *enjoy*; savour, sample, try; sip, lick, sup, nibble 301 *eat*; have a taste, taste of, savour of, smack of 18 *resemble*; taste good, tickle the palate, tempt the appetite, stimulate the tastebuds 390 *make appetizing*.

## 387 Insipidity

**N.** *insipidity*, vapidity, vapidness, jejuneness, flatness, staleness, tastelessness, wershness etc. adj.; water, milk and water, gruel, pap, slops, catlap.

**Adj.** *tasteless*, without taste, devoid of taste, wersh; jejune, vapid, insipid, watery, milk-and-water; mild, underproof; with water, diluted, adulterated 163 *weakened*; wishy-washy, sloppy; unappetizing 391 *unsavoury*; flat, stale; savourless, zestless, flavourless, unflavoured, unspiced, unseasoned, unsalted, unherbed; unsavoured, untasted.

## 388 Pungency

**N.** *pungency*, piquancy, poignancy, sting, kick, bite, edge; burning taste, causticity; hot taste, spiciness; sharp taste, acridity, sharpness,

acerbity, acidity 393 *sourness*; roughness, harshness; strong taste, strength, tang, twang, raciness; bad taste 391 *unsavouriness*; salt, brine, pepper, pickle, spice 389 *condiment*; sal volatile, smelling salts 656 *revival*; cordial, pick-me-up, tonic, bracer 174 *stimulant*; dram, nip, tot, hot toddy 301 *draught*; hemp, marijuana 658 *drug*.

*tobacco*, baccy (inf), snout (sl), nicotine; the weed, fragrant w., Indian w., filthy w.; tobacco leaf; Virginia tobacco, Turkish t., latakia, perique; blend, smoking mixture; snuff, rappee, maccaboy; plug of tobacco, plug, quid, fid, twist; chewing tobacco, nicotine chew, tobacco sachet, tobacco teabag, pipe tobacco, flake, cavendish, shag; cigar, cigarillo, cheroot, panatella, perfecto, Havana, corona; smoke, cigarette, cig (inf), ciggie (inf), fag (sl), gasper (sl), stinker (sl), coffin-nail (sl); reefer, joint 949 *drug*; filter tip, cork tip, low-tar cigarette, high-tar c., menthol c., roll-up; butt, stub, fag-end (sl), dog-end; tobacco pipe, clay p., dudeen, churchwarden; briar, corncob; meerschaum; water pipe, hubble-bubble, hookah, narghile; pipe of peace, calumet; bowl, stem; dottle, tobacco juice; nicotine patch; smoker's cough; snuff taker, snuffer; snuff dipper, tobacco chewer; tobacco inhaler, smoker, pipe s., cigarette s., cigar s., chain s.; smoking, passive s.; tobacconist, cigarette machine; snuff box, cigarette case, cigar c., cigarette box, cigar b.; humidor; pipe rack; pipe cleaner, reamer; tobacco pouch, tobacco jar; smokeroom; smoker, smoking compartment, smoking zone; smoke-free zone *or* area.

**Adj.** *pungent*, penetrating, strong; stinging, mordant, biting 256 *sharp*; caustic, burning, smoky; harsh 259 *rough*; bitter, acrid, tart, astringent 393 *sour*; heady, overproof; full-flavoured, nutty 386 *tasty*; strong-flavoured, high, gamy, off; highly-seasoned, herby, herbed, spicy, spiced, curried; hot, gingery, peppery, fiery, hot as pepper; zesty, tangy, minty, piquant, aromatic 390 *savoury*.

*salty*, salt, brackish, briny, saline, pickled; salt as the sea, salt as Lot's wife.

**Vb.** *be pungent*, sting, bite the tongue, set the teeth on edge, make the eyes water.

*season*, salt, brine, marinade, souse, pickle; flavour, sauce; spice, herb, pepper, devil, curry; smoke, smoke-dry, kipper 666 *preserve*.

*smoke*, use tobacco, indulge, smoke a pipe, pull, draw, take a draw, suck, inhale; take a drag; puff, blow smoke rings; chain-smoke, smoke like a chimney; chew a quid, suck tobacco sachets; snuff, take snuff, take a pinch.

## 389 Condiment

**N.** *condiment*, seasoning, flavouring, dressing, relish, garnish; chaudfroid, aspic; salt, sea s., garlic s., celery s.; mustard, grain m., French m., Dijon m., German m., English m., American m.; pepper, black p., white p., peppercorn; onion, garlic 301 *herb*; vinegar, balsamic v., malt v. 393 *sourness*; curry powder 301 *spice*.

*sauce*, roux; gravy, stock; brown sauce, white s., béchamel; bolognaise sauce, pesto; parsley sauce, bread s., tartar s., mint s., horseradish s., sauce piquante; apple sauce, cranberry s. 392 *sweet thing*; tomato sauce, ketchup, barbecue sauce ; chilli sauce, Tabasco s. (tdmk), soy s., soya s., Worcester s.; chutney, sweet c., mango c., pickles, dill pickle, piccalilli, pickled onions, gherkins; dressing, salad dressing, French d., Thousand Island d., mayonnaise, vinaigrette.

**Vb.** *spice* salt, 388 *season*.

## 390 Savouriness

**N.** *savouriness*, right taste, tastiness, palatability; raciness, fine flavour, full f., richness; body, bouquet; savoury, relish, appetizer; delicacy, dainty, titbit, bonne bouche 301 *mouthful*; cocktail snacks, hors d'oeuvre, appetizer; game, venison, turtle, caviar; ambrosia, nectar; epicure's delight.

**Adj.** *savoury*, nice, good, good to eat, worth eating; seasoned, flavoured, spicy, herby 386 *tasty*; well-dressed, well-cooked, done to a turn; tempting, appetizing, aromatic, zestful, piquant 388 *pungent*; to one's taste, palatable, toothsome, sweet; dainty, delicate; delectable, delicious, exquisite, choice, epicurean; ambrosial, nectareous, fit for the gods, fit for a king; scrumptious, yummy, moreish; fresh, crisp, crunchy; mature, ripe, mellow, luscious, juicy, succulent; creamy, rich, velvety; gamy, racy, high; rare-flavoured, full-f., vintage.

**Vb.** *make appetizing*, garnish, spice, ginger, pep up 388 *season*; be savoury, tempt the appetite, tickle the palate, flatter the p., stimulate the tastebuds; smell good, taste good, taste sweet 392 *sweeten*; like, relish, savour, lap up, gobble up, smack the lips, roll on one's tongue, lick one's fingers, water at the mouth, salivate 386 *taste*.

**Int.** yum-yum!, mmm!

## 391 Unsavouriness

**N.** *unsavouriness*, unpalatability, nasty taste, wrong t., sour t.; rankness, rottenness, overripeness, unwholesomeness 653 *insalubrity*; roughness, coarseness, plain cooking 573 *plainness*; acerbity, acridity 393 *sourness*; austerity, prison fare, bread and water, nursery fare, iron rations; aloes, rue; bitter pill, 'gall and wormwood' (see quotation at 861 *dislike*); emetic, sickener 659 *poison*.

**Adj.** *unsavoury*, flat 387 *tasteless*; unpalatable, unappetizing, wersh, uninviting; coarse, raw, underdone, undressed 670 *uncooked*; badly cooked, overdone, burnt, burnt to a cinder; uneatable, inedible; stale, hard, leathery 329 *tough*; soggy 327 *soft*; sugarless, unsweetened; rough 388 *pungent*; bitter, acrid, acid 393 *sour*; undrinkable, corked; overripe, rank, rancid, putrid, rotten, gone off, high, stinking 397 *fetid*; nasty, repulsive, foul, revolting, disgusting, loathsome 827 *unpleasant*; sickly, cloying, mawkish; sickening, emetic, nauseous, nauseating 861 *disliked*; poisonous 653 *toxic*.

**Vb.** *be unpalatable*, – unappetizing etc. adj.; taste horrid; disgust, repel, sicken, nauseate, turn the stomach 861 *cause dislike*; poison; lose its savour, pall.

**Int.** Ugh!, yuk!

## 392 Sweetness

**N.** *sweetness*, sweetening, dulcification; sugariness, saccharinity; sweet tooth; saccharimeter.

*sweet thing*, sweetening, honey, honeycomb, honeypot, honeydew; honeysuckle 396 *fragrance*; saccharin, sucrose, glucose, dextrose, fructose, lactose, galactose; sugar, cane s., beet s., malt s., milk s., invert s.; granulated s., castor s., icing s., brown s., demerara, muscovado; molasses, syrup, golden syrup, maple s., treacle; artificial sweetener; sweet sauce, custard, condensed milk; sweet drink, julep, nectar, hydromel, mead, metheglin; conserve, preserve; candied peel, glacé cherries; jam, marmalade, jelly; marzipan, icing, fondant, sugar coating; fudge, candy, sugar c. 301 *sweets*; jujube, cachou, lozenge, pastille; lollipop, ice cream, candyfloss, rock; confectionery, confection, cake 301 *pastries, dessert*.

**Adj.** *sweet*, sweet to the taste, sweetened, honeyed, candied, crystallized; iced, glacé; sugared, sugary, saccharine, honey-bearing, melliferous; ambrosial, nectareous, luscious, delicious 376 *pleasant*; sweet as honey, sweet as sugar, sweet as a nut; cloying, oversweet; 390 *savoury*.

**Vb.** *sweeten*, sugar, add sugar, candy, crystallize, ice, glaze; sugar the pill, coat the p.; dulcify, saccharize; sweeten wine, mull.

## 393 Sourness

**N.** *sourness*, acerbity; astringency; tartness, bitterness, vinegariness; sharpness 388 *pungency*; acidity, acidosis; acid, argol, tartar;

lemon, lime; vinegar, balsamic v., cider v., malt v., raspberry v., red wine v., sherry v., tarragon v., white wine v.; sloe, crab apple; verjuice, alum, bitter aloes, bitters; gall, wormwood, absinth; sour milk, sour cream.

**Adj.** *sour*, sourish, acid, acidy, acidulous, acidulated, subacid, acescent, acetous, acetic, acid-forming, tartaric; acerbic, crabbed, tart, bitter, bitter as gall; sharp, astringent 388 *pungent*; vinegary, sour as vinegar 391 *unsavoury*; unripe, green, hard, rough 670 *immature*; sugarless, unsugared; unsweetened, dry.

**Vb.** *be sour*, – acid etc. adj.; sour, turn, turn sour; acetify, acidify, acidulate; ferment; set one's teeth on edge.

## 394 Odour

**N.** *odour*, smell, aroma, bouquet, nose; sweet smell, perfume, scent, essence 396 *fragrance*; bad smell, pong, niff, stink 397 *stench*; exhalation, effluvium, emanation; smoke, fume, reek; breath, whiff, waft; strong smell, odorousness, redolence; tang, scent, trail 548 *trace*; olfaction, sense of smell, act of smelling; olfactories, smeller, nostril, nosehole, nose, naris 254 *protuberance*; good nose, keen-scentedness, flair.

**Adj.** *odorous*, endowed with scent, odoriferous, smelling; scented, perfumed 396 *fragrant*; graveolent, strong, heady, heavy, full-bodied 388 *pungent*; smelly, redolent, nidorous, reeking; malodorous, whiffy, niffy, ponging 397 *fetid*; smelt, reaching one's nostrils; olfactory; keen-scented, sharp-nosed.

**Vb.** *smell*, have an odour, reach one's nostrils; smell of, breathe of, smell strongly of, reek of, reek, pong of, pong; give out a smell, exhale; smell a mile off; smell out, scent, nose, wind, get wind of 484 *detect*; get a whiff of, get a niff of; snuff, snuff up, sniff, breathe in, inhale 352 *breathe*; cause to smell, scent, perfume, incense, fumigate.

## 395 Inodorousness

**N.** *inodorousness*, odourlessness, scentlessness; absence of smell, lack of s.; loss of s.; inability to smell, anosmia; noselessness, lack of flair; deodorant, deodorizer; fumes, incense, pastille, mouthwash; deodorization, fumigation, ventilation, purification 648 *cleansing*.

**Adj.** *odourless*, inodorous, scentless, without smell, wanting s.; unscented, unperfumed; deodorized; deodorizing; noseless, without sense of smell, without flair.

**Vb.** *have no smell*, not smell; be inodorous, – scentless etc. adj.; deodorize, take away the

smell, defumigate; ventilate, clear the air 648 *purify*; lose the scent 495 *err*; hold one's nose.

## 396 Fragrance

**N.** *fragrance*, sweet smell, perfume, sweet savour, balminess; redolence, aroma, bouquet 394 *odour*; violet, rose; bank of violets, bed of roses; flower garden, rose g. 370 *garden*; buttonhole, boutonnière, carnation, nosegay; thurification, fumigation; perfumery, perfumer.

*scent*, perfume, aromatic p., aromatic gum; balm, myrrh, incense, frankincense, spikenard; spicery 389 *condiment*; breath-sweetener, cloves, cachou; musk, civet, ambergris, camphor; sandalwood, patchouli; essential oil, otto, attar; lavender, thyme, spearmint, chypre, vanilla, citronella oil; frangipani, bergamot, orris root, tonka bean; honeysuckle, woodruff, new-mown hay; toilet water, eau-de-toilette, lavender water, rose w., attar of roses, eau-de-cologne; pomade, hair oil; face powder, scented soap 843 *cosmetic*; mothball, lavender bag, sachet; pomander, potpourri, scent bottle, smelling b., vinaigrette; joss stick, censer, thurible.

**Adj.** *fragrant*, redolent, odorous, odoriferous, aromatic, scented, perfumed 376 *pleasant*; incense-breathing, balmy, ambrosial; sweet-scented, sweetly-perfumed; thuriferous, perfumatory; musky, spicy, fruity; rose-scented, fragrant as a rose; laid up in lavender.

**Vb.** *be fragrant*, smell sweet, smell like a rose, have a perfume, scent, perfume; fumigate, thurify, cense; embalm, lay up in lavender.

## 397 Stench

**N.** *stench*, fetor, fetidity, fetidness, offensiveness; offence to the nose, bad smell, bad odour, foul o., malodour; body odour, BO, armpits; foul breath, bad b., halitosis; fart (sl); stink, pong, niff, reek; noxious stench, mephitis; fumes, miasma 336 *gas*; smell of death, taint, corruption, rancidity, putrefaction 51 *decay*; foulness 649 *dirt*; mustiness, fustiness, staleness, stale air, frowst, fug; fungus, stinkhorn, garlic, asafoetida; hydrogen sulphide, ammonia; skunk, polecat; stinkard, stinker, stinkpot, stink bomb, bad egg; dung 302 *excrement*; latrine, sewer, septic tank 649 *sink*.

**Adj.** *fetid*, graveolent, strong-smelling, heavy, strong; reeking, nidorous, ill-smelling, malodorous, not smelling of roses; smelly, whiffy, niffy, pongy, humming; stinking, rank, hircine, foxy; fruity, gamy, high; bad, gone b., tainted, rancid; putrid, suppurating, gangrenous 51 *decomposed*; stale, airless, musty, fusty, frowsty, frowzy, fuggy, smoky, unventilated, stuffy, suffocating; foul, noisome, noxious, sulphurous, ammoniacal, mephitic, miasmic 653 *toxic*; acrid, burning 388 *pungent*; nasty, disagreeable, offensive 827 *unpleasant*.

**Vb.** *stink*, smell, reek, pong, niff, hum; make a smell, fart (sl), blow off; have bad breath, have halitosis; have a bad smell, smell strong, smell offensive; smell bad 51 *decompose*; stink in the nostrils, stink to high heaven, make one hold one's nose; smell like a bad egg, smell like a drain; stink like a goat, stink like a polecat; overpower with stink, stink out.

## 398 Sound

**N.** *sound*, auditory effect, distinctness; audibility, reception 415 *hearing*; sounding, sonancy, sound-making; audio, mono, monophonic sound, binaural s., stereophonic s., stereo, quadraphonic sound, surround-sound system; sound waves, vibrations 417 *radiation*; electronic sound, sound effect; sound track, voice-over; sonority, sonorousness 404 *resonance*; noise, loud sound 400 *loudness*; low sound, softness 401 *faintness*; quality of sound, tone, pitch, level, cadence; accent, intonation, twang, timbre 577 *voice*; tune, strain 410 *melody*, 412 *music*; types of sound 402 *bang*, 403 *roll*, 404 *resonance*, 405 *nonresonance*, 406 *sibilation*, 407 *stridor*, 408 *cry*, 409 *ululation*, 411 *discord*; transmission of sound, telephone, cellular t., radio 531 *telecommunication*; recorded sound, high fidelity, hi-fi; gramophone 414 *record-player*; ghetto blaster, personal stereo; loudspeaker 415 *hearing instrument*; unit of sound, decibel, phon, sone; sonic barrier, sound b.

*acoustics*, phonics; phonology, phonography; phonetics; acoustician, sound engineer; phonetician, phoneticist, phonographer; audiometer, sonometer.

*speech sound*, simple s., phone, syllable, disyllable, polysyllable; consonant, fricative, affricate, plosive, implosive, spirant, liquid, sibilant; dental, alveolar, labial, bilabial, labiodental, nasal, palatal, guttural, velar, labiovelar; aspiration, inspiration, expiration; rough breathing, smooth b.; stop, glottal s.; click; sonant, sonorant, mute, aspirate, surd; semivowel; glide, glide sound; voiced breath, vowel, front v., middle v., back v.; vocoid, contoid; diphthong, triphthong 577 *voice*; rising diphthong, falling d.; monophthongization, diphthongization; vowel gradation, ablaut; umlaut; assimilation, dissimilation; sandhi; vocable 559 *word*; sound symbol, phonogram, International Phonetic Alphabet, IPA 586 *script*.

**Adj.** *sounding*, soniferous, sonant; sonic; supersonic; plain, audible, distinct, heard; resounding, sonorous 404 *resonant*; stentorian 400 *loud*; auditory, acoustic; electrophonic, radiophonic; monaural, monophonic, mono; binaural, stereophonic, stereo, high fidelity, hi-fi; audio, audiovisual; phonic, phonetic; voiced 577 *vocal*; monophthongal, diphthongal; consonantal; vocalic, vowelled; surd, unvoiced, voiceless.

**Vb.** *sound*, produce s., give out s., emit s. 415 *be heard*; make audible, make a noise 400 *be loud*, 404 *resound*; phoneticize, phonate, vocalize 577 *voice*.

## 399 Silence

**N.** *silence*, soundlessness, inaudibility, total silence, not a sound, not a squeak; stillness, hush, lull, rest, peace, quiet 266 *quiescence*; taciturnity, muteness, speechlessness 578 *voicelessness*; solemn silence, awful s., pin-drop s., dead s., perfect s., uncanny s., deathly hush; enforced silence, gagging order 747 *prohibition*.

**Adj.** *silent*, still, stilly, hushed; calm, peaceful, quiet 266 *quiescent*; soft, faint 401 *muted*; noiseless, soundless, inaudible; soundproof; aphonic, speechless, taciturn, tongueless, mute 578 *voiceless*; unsounded, unuttered, unspoken; solemn, awful, deathlike, silent as the grave.

**Vb.** *be silent*, not open one's mouth, not say a word, hold one's tongue 582 *be taciturn*; not speak 578 *be mute*; be still, make no noise, make not a sound, not utter a squeak; become silent, relapse into silence, pipe down, be quiet, lose one's voice, fall silent.

*silence*, still, lull, hush, quiet, quieten, make silent; play down, soft-pedal; stifle, muffle, gag, stop, stop someone's mouth, muzzle, put the lid on, put to silence 578 *make mute*; drown, drown the noise.

**Int.** hush!, quiet!, sh!, silence!, peace!, soft!, whist!, cut the cackle!, dry up!, hold your tongue!, keep your mouth shut!, keep your trap shut!, mum's the word!, pipe down!, shut up!, stow it!

## 400 Loudness

**N.** *loudness*, distinctness, audibility 398 *sound*; noise, loud n., ear-splitting n.; high volume; broken silence, shattered s., knock, knocking; burst of sound, report, loud r., sonic boom, slam, clap, thunderclap, burst, shell b., explosion 402 *bang*; siren, alarm, honk, toot 665 *danger signal*; prolonged noise, reverberation, plangency, boom, rattle 403 *roll*; thunder, rattling t., war in heaven 176 *storm*; dashing, surging, hissing 406 *sibilation*; fire, gunfire, artillery, blitz 712 *bombardment*; stridency, brassiness, shrillness, blast, blare, bray, fanfare, flourish 407 *stridor*; trumpet blast, clarion call, view halloo 547 *call*; sonority, organ notes, clang, clangour 404 *resonance*; ringing tones; bells, peal, chimes 412 *campanology*; diapason, swell, crescendo, fortissimo, tutti, full blast, full chorus; vociferation, clamour, outcry, roaring, shouting, bawling, yelling, screaming, whoop, shout, howl, shriek, scream, roar 408 *cry*, 409 *ululation*; loud laughter, cachinnation 835 *laughter*; loud breathing, stertorousness 352 *respiration*; noisiness, din, row, deafening r., racket, crash, clash, clatter, hubbub, hullabaloo, ballyhoo, song and dance, slamming, banging, stamping, chanting, hooting, uproar, stramash, shemozzle, tumult, bedlam, pandemonium, all hell let loose 61 *turmoil*; noise pollution.

*megaphone*, amplifier, loud pedal; public address system, loudhailer, loudspeaker, speaker, microphone, mike; ear trumpet 415 *hearing instrument*; loud instrument, whistle, siren, hooter, horn, klaxon, gong; rattle, bullroarer; buzzer, bell, alarm, door knocker; trumpet, brass; ghetto blaster; stentorian voice, lungs, good l., good pair of l., lungs of brass, iron throat; Stentor, town crier.

**Adj.** *loud*, distinct, audible, heard; turned right up, at full volume, at full pitch, at the top of one's voice; noisy, full of noise, rackety, uproarious, rowdy, rumbustious 61 *disorderly*; multisonous, many-tongued 411 *discordant*; clamorous, clamant, shouting, yelling, whooping, screaming, bellowing 408 *crying*; big-mouthed, loud-m.; sonorous, booming, deep, full, powerful; lusty, full-throated, stentorian, brazen-mouthed, trumpet-tongued; ringing, carrying; deafening, dinning; piercing, ear-splitting, ear-rending; thundering, thunderous, rattling, crashing; pealing, clangorous, plangent; shrill, high-sounding 407 *strident*; blaring, brassy; echoing, resounding 404 *resonant*; swelling, crescendo; fortissimo, enough to waken the dead.

**Vb.** *be loud*, – noisy etc. adj.; break the silence; speak up, give tongue, raise the voice, strain one's v.; call, catcall, caterwaul; skirl, scream, whistle 407 *shrill*; vociferate, shout 408 *cry*; cachinnate 835 *laugh*; clap, stamp, raise the roof, raise the rafters; roar, bellow, howl 409 *ululate*; din, sound, boom, reverberate 404 *resound*; rattle, thunder, fulminate, storm, clash; ring, peal, clang, crash; bray, blare; slam 402 *bang*; burst, explode, detonate, go off; knock, knock hard, hammer, drill; deafen, stun; split the ears, rend the eardrums, shatter the e., ring in the ear; swell, fill the air; rend the skies, make the welkin ring, rattle the

windows, awake the echoes, waken the dead; raise Cain, kick up a shindy, make the devil of a row 61 *rampage*.

**Adv.** *loudly*, distinctly etc. adj.; noisily, dinningly; aloud, at the top of one's voice, lustily; in full cry, full blast, full chorus; fortissimo, crescendo.

## 401 Faintness

**N.** *faintness*, softness, indistinctness, inaudibility; less sound, low volume, reduction of sound, s.-proofing, noise abatement; dull sound, thud, thump, bump 405 *nonresonance*; whisper, susurration; breath, bated b., muffled tones 578 *voicelessness*; undertone, undercurrent of sound; murmur, hum, drone 403 *roll*; sigh, sough, moan; scratch, squeak, creak, pop; tick, click; tinkle, clink, chink; buzz, whirr; purr, purl, plash, swish; burble, gurgle; rustle, frou-frou; patter, pitter-p., pit-a-pat; soft footfall, pad; soft voice, quiet tone, hushed tones, conversation level.

*silencer*, noise queller, mute, damper, muffler, soft pedal 414 *mute*; cork, double-glazing; rubber soles; grease, oil 334 *lubricant*; ear plugs.

**Adj.** *muted*, distant, faint, inaudible, barely audible, just caught, sotto voce; just heard, half-h.; trembling in the air, dying away; weak, feeble, unemphatic, unstressed, unaccented; soft, low, gentle; purling, rippling; piano, subdued, hushed, stealthy, whispered; dull, dead 405 *nonresonant*; muffled, suppressed, stifled, bated 407 *hoarse*.

**Vb.** *sound faint*, drop one's voice, lower one's v., whisper, breathe, murmur, mutter 578 *speak low*; sing low, hum, croon, purr; buzz, drone; purl, babble, ripple, plash, lap, gurgle, guggle 350 *flow*; tinkle, chime; moan, sigh, sough 352 *blow*; rustle, swish; tremble, melt; float on the air, steal on the a., melt on the a., die on the ear, fade away, sink into silence; squeak, creak; plop, pop; tick, click; clink, chink; thud, thump 405 *sound dead*.

*mute*, soften, dull, deaden, dampen, softpedal; turn down the volume; hush, muffle, stifle 399 *silence*.

**Adv.** *faintly*, in a whisper, with bated breath, under one's breath, between the teeth; sotto voce, aside, in an undertone; piano, pianissimo; à la sourdine; inaudibly, distantly, out of earshot.

## 402 Bang: sudden and violent noise

**N.** *bang*, report, explosion, detonation, blast, blowout, backfire, sonic boom; peal, thunderclap, crash 400 *loudness*; crepitation, crackling, crackle; smack, crack, snap; slap, clap, tap, rap, rat-tat-tat; thump, knock, slam; pop, plop, plunk; burst, burst of fire, firing, crackle of musketry; volley, round, salvo; shot, pistol-s.; cracker, banger, squib; bomb, grenade; gun, rifle, shot gun, pop g., air g. 723 *firearm*.

**Adj.** *rapping*, banging, etc. vb.

**Vb.** *crackle*, crepitate; sizzle, fizzle, spit 318 *effervesce*; crack, split; click, rattle; snap, clap, rap, tap, slap, smack; plop, plonk, plunk.

*bang*, slam, wham, clash, crash, boom; explode, blast, detonate; pop, go p.; backfire; burst, burst on the ear 400 *be loud*.

### 403 Roll: repeated and protracted sounds

**N.** *roll*, rumbling, grumbling; mutter, witter, murmur, background m., rhubarb rhubarb, blahblah; din, rattle, racket, clack, clatter, chatter, clutter; booming, clang, ping, reverberation 404 *resonance*; chugging; knocking, drumming, tattoo, devil's t., rub-a-dub, rat-a-tat, pit-a-pat, pitter-patter; peal, carillon 412 *campanology*; dingdong, tick-tock, cuckoo 106 *repetition*; trill, tremolo, vibrato 410 *musical note*; quaver; hum, whirr, buzz, drone, bombination; humming top, bee in a bottle; ringing, singing; drumfire, barrage, cannonade, machine gun.

**Adj.** *rolling*, roaring etc. vb.; reverberant 404 *resonant*; dingdong, monotonous 106 *repeated*.

**Vb.** *roll*, drum, tattoo, beat a t.; tap, thrum; chug, rev up, vroom; drum in the ear; boom, roar, din in the ear; grumble, rumble, drone, hum, whirr, bombinate; trill, chime, peal, toll; tick, beat 317 *oscillate*; rattle, chatter, clatter, clack; reverberate, clang, ping, ring, sing, sing in the ear; quaver, shake, tremble, vibrate; patter 401 *sound faint*.

### 404 Resonance

**N.** *resonance*, sonorousness; vibration 317 *oscillation*; reverberation, reflection; lingering note, echo 106 *recurrence*; twang, twanging; ringing, ringing in the ear, singing, tinnitus; bell ringing, tintinnabulation 412 *campanology*; peal, carillon; sonority, boom; clang, clangour, plangency; brass 400 *loudness*; peal, blare, bray, flourish, tucket; sounding brass, tinkling cymbal; tinkle, jingle; chink, clink; ping, ring, ting-a-ling, chime; low note, deep n., grave n., bass n., pedal n. 410 *musical note*; low voice, basso, basso profondo, bass, baritone, bass b., contralto.

**Adj.** *resonant*, vibrant, reverberant, reverberative; fruity, carrying 400 *loud*; resounding etc. vb.; booming, echoing, lingering; sonorous, reboant, plangent; ringing, tintinnabulary;

basso, deep-toned, deep-sounding, deep-mouthed; booming, hollow, sepulchral.

**Vb.** *resound*, vibrate, reverberate, echo, re-echo 403 *roll*; whirr, buzz; hum, ring in the ear, sing; ping, ring, ding; jingle, jangle, chink, clink, clank, clunk; ting, tinkle; twang, thrum; gong, chime, tintinnabulate; tootle, toot, trumpet, blare, bray 400 *be loud*.

### 405 Nonresonance

**N.** *nonresonance*, nonvibration, dead sound, dull s.; thud, thump, bump; plump, plop, plonk, plunk; cracked bell 411 *discord*; muffled sound, muffled drums 401 *faintness*; mute, damper, sordino 401 *silencer*.

**Adj.** *nonresonant*, muffled, damped, soft-pedalled 401 *muted*; dead, dull, heavy; cracked 407 *hoarse*; soundproof 399 *silent*.

**Vb.** *sound dead*, be nonresonant, not vibrate, arouse no echoes, fall dead on the ear; tink, click, flap; thump, thud, bump, pound; stop the vibrations, damp the reverberations; soft-pedal, muffle, damp, stop, soften, deaden, stifle, silence 401 *mute*.

### 406 Sibilation: hissing sound

**N.** *sibilation*, sibilance, hissing, hiss; assibilation, sigma, sibilant; sputter, splutter; splash, plash; rustle, frou-frou 407 *stridor*; sucking noise, squelch, squish; swish, swoosh, escape of air; hisser, goose, serpent, snake.

**Adj.** *sibilant*, sibilation, hissing etc. vb.; wheezy, asthmatic.

**Vb.** *hiss*, sibilate, assibilate; snort, wheeze, snuffle, whistle; buzz, fizz, fizzle, sizzle, sputter, splutter, spit; splash, plash 318 *effervesce*; swish, swoosh, whizz; squelch, squish, suck; rustle 407 *rasp*.

### 407 Stridor: harsh sound

**N.** *stridor*, stridency, discordance, cacophony 411 *discord*; roughness, raucousness, hoarseness, huskiness, gruffness; harsh sound, aspirate, guttural; squeakiness, rustiness 333 *friction*; scrape, scratch, jarring, creak, squeak; stridulation, screechiness; shriek, screech, squawk, yawp, yelp, braying 409 *ululation*; high pitch, shrillness, piping, whistling, wolf whistle; bleep; piercing note, high n., acute n., sharp n. 410 *musical note*; high voice, soprano, treble, falsetto, tenor, countertenor; nasality, twang, drone; skirl, brassiness, brass, blare, tantara 400 *loudness*; pipe, fife, piccolo, penny whistle 414 *flute*.

**Adj.** *strident*, stridulous, stridulatory; unoiled, grating, rusty, creaky, creaking, jarring (see also *hoarse*); harsh, brassy, brazen, metallic; high, high-pitched, high-toned, acute, shrill, piping, bleeping; penetrating, piercing, tinny, ear-splitting 400 *loud*; blaring, braying; dry, reedy, squeaky, squawky, screechy, scratchy; cracked 405 *nonresonant*; sharp, flat, inharmonious, cacophonous 411 *discordant*.

*hoarse*, husky, throaty, guttural, raucous, rough, gruff; rasping, jarring, scraping, creaking; grunting, growling; hollow, deep, sepulchral; snoring, stertorous.

**Vb.** *rasp*, stridulate, grate, crunch, scrunch, grind, saw, scrape, scratch, squeak; snore, snort; cough, hawk, clear the throat, hem, choke, gasp, sob, catch the breath; bray, croak, caw, screech 409 *ululate*; grunt, speak in the throat, burr, aspirate, gutturalize; crack, break (of the voice); jar, grate on the ear, set the teeth on edge, clash, jangle, twang, clank, clink 411 *discord*.

*shrill*, stridulate, bleep; play the bagpipes, drone, skirl; trumpet, blare 400 *be loud*; pipe, flute, wind the horn 413 *play music*; whistle, catcall, caterwaul 408 *cry*; scream, squeal, yelp, yawl, screech, squawk; buzz, hum, whine 409 *ululate*; split the ears, go right through one, strain, crack one's voice, strain one's vocal cords.

**408 Human cry**

**N.** *cry*, animal cry 409 *ululation*; human cry, exclamation, ejaculation 577 *voice*; utterances 579 *speech*; talk, chat, chit-chat, conversation 584 *interlocution*; raised voice, vociferation, vociferousness, clamorousness, shouting, outcry, clamour, hullabaloo 400 *loudness*; yodel, song, chant, chorus 412 *vocal music*; shout, yell, whoop, bawl; howl, scream, shriek, screech 407 *stridor*, 377 *pain*; halloo, hail 547 *call*; view halloo, tallyho, hue and cry 619 *chase*; cheer, hurrah, hip-hip-hurrah, hooray, huzza 835 *rejoicing*; cachinnation, laugh, giggle, titter 835 *laughter*; hoot, boo, guffaw 924 *disapprobation*; plaint, complaint 762 *deprecation*; plaintiveness, sob, sigh 836 *lamentation*; caterwaul, yawl, squeal, wail, whine, boohoo; grunt, gasp 352 *respiration*; shouter, bawler, yeller; rooter, cheerer, cheerleader; crier, barker; town crier.

**Adj.** *crying*, bawling, clamant, clamorous; loud, vocal, vociferous; stentorian, full-throated, full-lunged, lusty; rousing, cheering; sobbing, blubbing 836 *lamenting*.

**Vb.** *cry*, cry out, exclaim, ejaculate, pipe up 579 *speak*; call, call out, hail 884 *greet*; raise a cry, whoop; hoot, boo, whistle 924 *disapprove*; cheer, hurrah (see also *vociferate*); scream, screech, yawl, yowl, howl, groan 377 *feel pain*; cachinnate, snigger, titter, giggle 835 *laugh*; caterwaul, squall, boohoo, whine, whimper,

wail, fret, mewl, pule 836 *weep*; yammer, moan, sob, sigh 836 *lament*; mutter, grumble 401 *sound faint*, 829 *be discontented*; gasp, grunt, snort, snore 352 *breathe*; squeak, squawk, yap, bark 409 *ululate*.

*vociferate*, clamour, start shouting, shout, bawl, yell, yawl, yowl, holler; chant, chorus 413 *sing*; cheer, give three cheers, hurrah, hooray, huzza, exult 835 *rejoice*; cheer for, root for, shout for; hiss, hoot, boo, bawl out, shout down 924 *disapprove*; roar, bellow 409 *ululate*; yell, cry out, sing o.; thunder o.; raise the voice, give v., strain one's lungs, strain one's voice, strain one's vocal cords, crack one's throat, make oneself hoarse, shout at the top of one's voice, shout at the top of one's lungs 400 *be loud*.

**409 Ululation: animal sounds**

**N.** *ululation*, animal noise, howling, belling, wailing, yowling, yawling; barking, baying; buzzing, humming, bombination, drone; chattering, twittering, chirping, chirruping; warble, call, cry, note, woodnote, birdsong; squeak, cheep, twitter, tweet-tweet; buzz, hum; croak, caw, coo, hiss, quack, cluck, squawk, screech, yawp; baa, moo, neigh, whinny, hee-haw; cock-a-doodle-doo, cuckoo, tu-whit tu-whoo; miaow, mew; bark, yelp, yap, snap, snarl, growl. (See also *ululate*.)

**Adj.** *ululant*, reboant; deep-mouthed, full-m.; full-throated 400 *loud*; roaring, lowing, cackling etc. vb.

**Vb.** *ululate*, cry, call, give tongue; squawk, screech, yawp; caterwaul, yowl, yawl, howl, wail; roar, bellow, bell; hum, drone, buzz, bombinate, bombilate; spit 406 *hiss*; woof, bark, bay, bay atthe moon; yelp, yap; snap, snarl, growl, whine; trumpet, bell, troat; bray, neigh, whinny, whicker; bleat, baa; low, moo; miaow, mew, mewl, purr; quack, cackle, gaggle; gobble, gabble, cluck, clack; grunt, gruntle, snort, squeal; pipe, pule; chatter, sing, chirp, chirrup, cheep, peep, tweet, twitter, chuckle, churr, whirr, coo; caw, croak; hoot, honk, boom; grate, stridulate, squeak 407 *rasp*; sing like a bird, warble, carol, whistle 413 *sing*.

**410 Melody: concord**

**N.** *melody*, musicality 412 *music*; musicalness, melodiousness, musical quality, tonality, euphony, euphoniousness; harmoniousness, chime, harmony, concord, concert 24 *agreement*; consonance, assonance, attunement; unison, homophony; resolution (of a discord), cadence, perfect c.; harmonics, harmonization, counterpoint, polyphony; faux-bourdon, faburden, thorough bass, continuo, figured bass, ground b.; part, second, chorus; orchestration, instrumentation; tone, tone colour; phrasing 413 *musical skill*; phrase, passage, theme, leitmotiv, cõda; movement 412 *musical piece*.

*musical note*, note, keys, keyboard, manual, pedal point; black notes, white n., sharp, flat, double f., double sharp, accidental, natural, tone, semitone; keynote, fundamental note; tonic, supertonic, mediant, subdominant, dominant, submediant, subtonic, leading note; interval, second, third, fourth, fifth, sixth, seventh, octave, ninth; diatesseron, diapason; gamut, scale (see also *key*); chord, common c., triad, tetrachord, arpeggio; grace note, grace, ornament, crush note, appoggiatura, acciaccatura, mordent, turn, shake, trill, tremolo, vibrato, cadenza; tone, tonality, register, pitch, concert p., high p., low p.; high note 407 *stridor*; low note 404 *resonance*; undertone, overtone, harmonic, upper partial; sustained note, monotone, drone; phrase, flourish 412 *tune*; bugle call 547 *call*.

*notation*, musical n., tonic solfa, solfège, solfeggio, solmization; written music, sheet m., score; signature, time s., key s., clef, treble c., bass c., tenor c., alto c.; bar, stave, staff; line, ledger l., space, brace; rest, pause, interval; breve, semibreve, minim, crotchet, quaver, semiquaver, demisemiquaver, hemidemisemiquaver.

*tempo*, time, beat; rhythm 593 *prosody*; measure, timing; syncopation; upbeat, downbeat; suspension, long note, short n., suspended n.; prolonged n.; tempo rubato; rallentando, andante, adagio; metronome.

*key*, signature, clef, modulation, transposition, major key, minor k.; scale, gamut, major scale, minor s., diatonic s., chromatic s., harmonic s., melodic s., enharmonic s., twelve-tone s.; series, tone row; mode, Lydian m., Phrygian m., Dorian m., mixolydian; Indian mode, raga.

**Adj.** *melodious*, melodic, musical, lyrical, canorous, lilting, tuneful, singable, catchy, tripping; tinkling, low, soft 401 *muted*; sweet, dulcet, velvet, mellifluous, sweet-sounding, Orphean; high-fidelity, clear, clear as a bell, ringing, chiming; silvery, silver-toned, silver-tongued, golden-toned; fine-toned, full-t. 404 *resonant*; euphonious, euphonic, true, well-pitched.

*harmonious*, harmonizing, concordant, consonant 24 *agreeing*; in pitch; in chorus; assonant, rhyming, matching 18 *similar*; symphonic, symphonious, polyphonic; unisonous, homophonic, monophonic; monotonous, droning, intoning.

*harmonic*, enharmonic, diatonic, chromatic;

tonal, atonal, polytonal, sharp, flat, twelve-toned, dodecaphonic; keyed, modal, minor, major, Dorian, Lydian.

**Vb.** *harmonize*, concert, have the right pitch, blend, chime 24 *accord*; chorus 413 *sing*; attune, tune, tune up, pitch, string 24 *adjust*; be in key, be in unison, be on the beat; compose, melodize, put to music, set to music, score, symphonize, orchestrate 413 *compose music*; modulate, transpose; resolve a discord, restore harmony.

## 411 Discord

**N.** *discord*, conflict of sounds, discordance, dissonance, disharmony, jangle 25 *disagreement*; atonality, twelve-tone scale, tone row; imperfect cadence; preparation (of a discord); harshness, hoarseness, jarring, cacophony 407 *stridor*; confused sounds, Babel, cat's concert, caterwauling, yowling 400 *loudness*; row, din, noise, pandemonium, bedlam, tumult, racket 61 *turmoil*; atmospherics, wow, flutter.

**Adj.** *discordant*, dissonant, jangling, discording 25 *disagreeing*; conflicting 14 *contrary*; jarring, grating, scraping, rasping, harsh, raucous, cacophonous 407 *strident*; inharmonious, unharmonized; unmelodious, unmusical, untuneful; untuned, cracked; off pitch, off key, out of tune, sharp, flat; atonal, toneless, tuneless, droning, singsong.

**Vb.** *discord*, lack harmony 25 *disagree*; jangle, jar, grate, clash, crash; saw, scrape 407 *rasp*; be harsh, be out of tune, be off key; play sharp, play flat; thrum, drone, whine; prepare a discord; render discordant.

## 412 Music

**N.** *music*, harmony; sweet music 410 *melody*; musicianship 413 *musical skill*; minstrelsy, music-making, playing; strumming, thrumming, vamping; improvisation; orchestration, instrumentation, writing music, composing, composition; instrumental music, pipe m.; military m.; counterpoint, contrapuntal music; classical music, chamber m., organ m., choral m., operatic m., ballet m., sacred m., soul m.; light music, popular m., pop m., pop, indie pop, Britpop; descriptive music, programme m.; musique concrète; live music, recorded music, canned m., piped m., musical wallpaper, wall-to-wall m., Muzak (tdmk); ambient music; disco music; baggy; dance m., waltztime; hot music, syncopation, jazz, progressive j., modern j., cool j., acid jazz, mainstream jazz, traditional j., trad, Dixieland, ragtime, swing, swingbeat, doowop, bebop, bop, stride piano, boogiewoogie, blue note; blues, soul, northern s.; skiffle, jive, rock 'n' roll, rock, rock music, hard rock, soft r., adult-oriented r., album-oriented r., AOR, glam rock, heavy metal, black m., agit-rock, drum'n'base, grunge, goth, jungle, jazz-funk, electronic m., electro, techno, trance, acid house, gabba, gangsta, garage, hip-hop, house, new wave, mod, punk; bangra *or* bhangra; reggae, ska; rhythm 'n blues, country and western, blue grass, folk, folk music; written music, sheet m., the music, score, full s.; performance, concert, orchestral c., choral c., promenade c., prom; singsong; music festival, eisteddfod, feis, mod; school of music, conservatoire; Tin Pan Alley, Nashville.

*campanology*, bell ringing, hand r.; ringing, chiming; carillon, chime, peal; full p., muffled p.; touch; method-ringing, change-r., hunting, dodging, making place; hunt, hunt forward, hunt backward, dodge; round; changes; method, Grandsire, Plain Bob, Treble Bob, Stedman; set of bells, doubles, triples, caters, cinques; minor, major, royal; maximus; bell, Great Tom, Great Paul, Tsar Kolokol; treble bell, tenor b. 414 *gong*; church bell 547 *call*; bell ringer, campanologist.

*tune*, melody, strain; theme song, signature tune; descant; reprise, refrain; melodic line; air, popular a., aria, solo; peal, chime, carillon; flourish, sennet, tucket; phrase, passage, measure; Siren strains.

*musical piece*, piece, composition, opus, work, piece of music; tape, cassette, recording, sampling 414 *record player*; orchestration, instrumentation; arrangement, adaptation, setting, transcription; accompaniment, obbligato; voluntary, prelude, overture, intermezzo, finale; incidental music, background m., wallpaper m., wall-to-wall m.; romance, rhapsody, extravaganza, impromptu, fantasia, caprice, capriccio, humoresque, divertissement, divertimento, variations, raga; medley, potpourri; étude, study; suite, fugue, canon, toccata; sonata, sonatina; concerto, symphony, sinfonietta; symphonic poem, tone p.; pastorale, scherzo, rondo, gigue, jig, reel, strathspey; passacaglia, chaconne, gavotte, minuet, tarantella, mazurka, polonaise, polka, waltz 837 *dance*; march, grand m., bridal m., wedding m., dead m., funeral m.; dirge, pibroch; nocturne, serenade, berceuse, lullaby; introductory phrase, anacrusis; statement, exposition, development, recapitulation, variation; theme, motive, leitmotiv; movement; passage, phrase; chord 410 *musical note*; cadenza, coda.

*vocal music*, singing, vocalism, lyricism; vocalization; scat singing; part, singing p.; opera, operetta, light opera, comic o., opéra bouffe, musical comedy, musical 594 *stage play*; choir-singing, oratorio, cantata, chorale; hymn-singing, psalmody, hymnology; descant, chant, plain c., Gregorian c., Ambrosian c., plainsong; cantus, c. firmus, cantillation, recitative; bel canto, coloratura, bravura; singing practice, choir p., solfège, solfa, solmization; introit, anthem, canticle, psalm 981 *hymn*; song, lay, roundelay, carol, lyric, lilt; canzonet, cavatina, lieder, lied, ballad; folk song, popular *or* pop s., rap, gangsta; top twenty, hit parade, the charts; karaoke; ditty, shanty, calypso; spiritual, blues; part song, glee, madrigal, round, catch, canon; chorus, refrain, burden; choral hymn, antiphony, dithyramb; boat song, barcarole; lullaby, cradle song, berceuse; serenade, aubade; bridal hymn, wedding h., epithalamium, prothalamium; love song, amorous ditty; song, birdsong, bird call, dawn chorus; requiem, dirge, threnody, coronach 836 *lament*; musical declamation, recitative; words to be sung, lyrics, libretto; songbook, hymnbook, psalter.

*duet*, duo, trio, quartet, quintet, sextet; septet, octet; concerto, concerto grosso, solo, monody; ensemble, tutti.

**Adj.** *musical* 410 *melodious*; philharmonic, symphonic; melodic, arioso, cantabile; vocal, singable, hummable; operatic, recitative; lyric, melic; choral, dithyrambic; hymnal, psalmodic; harmonized 410 *harmonious*; contrapuntal; orchestrated, scored; set, set to music, arranged; instrumental, orchestral, for strings; blue, cool; hot, jazzy, syncopated, swinging, swung, doo-wop.

**Adv.** adagio, lento, largo, larghetto, andante, andantino, maestoso, moderato; allegro, allegretto; spiritoso, vivace, accelerando, presto, prestissimo; piano, mezzo-p., pianissimo, forte, mezzo-f., fortissimo, sforzando, con brio, capriccioso, scherzando; glissando, legato, sostenuto; staccato; crescendo, diminuendo, rallentando; affettuoso, cantabile, parlante; tremolo, pizzicato, vibrato; rubato; da capo.

## 413 Musician

**N.** *musician*, artiste, virtuoso, soloist; bravura player 696 *proficient person*; player, executant, performer, concert artist; ripieno 40 *extra*; bard, minstrel, jongleur, troubadour, trovatore, minnesinger; street musician, busker; composer, symphonist, contrapuntist; scorer, arranger, harmonist; syncopator, jazzman, swinger, cat; music writer, librettist, song writer, lyrics w., lyricist, liederwriter, hymnwriter, hymnographer, psalmist; musical director, music teacher, répétiteur, music master, kapellmeister, master of the music, bandmaster, conductor (see also *orchestra*); the Muses, Apollo, Pan, Orpheus, Amphion; musicologist, musicotherapist, music lover, music critic, concertgoer, operagoer 504 *enthusiast.*

*instrumentalist*, player, piano p., pianist, accompanist; keyboard player, organist, cembalist, harpsichordist, accordionist, concertina player, harmonica p.; violinist, fiddler, scraper; violist, cellist; harper, harpist, lyre player, lute p., lutanist, sitarist, guitarist, bassist, mandolinist, banjoist; strummer, thrummer; piper, fifer, piccolo player, flautist, flutist, clarinettist, oboist, bassoonist; saxophonist, horn player, trumpeter, bugler; cornetist; bell ringer, carilloneur, campanologist; drummer, drummer boy, drum major; percussionist, timpanist; organ-grinder, hurdy-gurdy man.

*orchestra*, symphony o., chamber o., sinfonietta, quartet, quintet; ensemble, wind e.; strings, brass, woodwind, percussion, drums; band, string b., jazz b., ragtime b.; brass b., military b., pipe b.; skiffle group, steel band; rock b. *or* group, punk b. *or* g., pop g.; conductor, maestro, bandmaster; bandleader, leader, first violin; orchestra player, bandsman.

*vocalist*, singer, songster, warbler, caroller, chanter; chantress, chanteuse, songstress; Siren, mermaid, Lorelei; melodist, troubadour, madrigal singer, minstrel, wandering m., busker; ballad singer, folk s., pop s.; serenader, crooner, jazz singer, blues s., scat s.; opera singer, prima donna, diva; cantatrice, coloratura; aria singer, lieder s.; castrato, treble, soprano, mezzo-s., contralto, alto, tenor, countertenor, baritone, bass b., bass, basso, basso profondo; songbird, nightingale, philomel, lark, thrush, mavis, blackbird, canary 365 *bird.*

*choir*, chorus, waits, wassailers, carol singers, glee club, barbershop quartet; choir festival, massed choirs, eisteddfod; chorister, choirboy *or* -girl; precentor, cantor, choirmaster, choirleader.

*musical skill*, musical ability, musical talent, musical appreciation; musicianship, bardship, minstrelsy; performance, execution, fingering, touch, phrasing, expression; virtuosity, bravura 694 *skill.*

**Adj.** *musicianly*, fond of music, knowing music, musical; minstrel, Orphean, bardic; vocal, coloratura, lyric, choral; plainsong, Gregorian, melodic 410 *melodious*; instrumental, orchestral, symphonic, contrapuntal; songful, warbling, carolling etc. vb.; scored, arranged, composed, set to music; in music, to m.

**Vb.** *be musical*, learn music, teach m., like m., read m., sight-read; have a good ear, have perfect pitch.

*compose music*, compose, write music, put to music, set to m., score, arrange, transpose, orchestrate, arrange in parts, supply the counterpoint, harmonize, melodize, improvise, extemporize.

*play music*, play, perform, execute, render, interpret; pick out a tune; conduct, wield the baton, beat time, mark the time; syncopate; play the piano, accompany; pedal, vamp, strum; brush the ivories, tickle the i., thump the keyboard; harp, pluck, pick, sweep the strings, strike the lyre, pluck the guitar, bottleneck; thrum, twang; fiddle, bow, scrape, saw; play the concertina, squeeze the box, grind the organ; play the harmonica; wind, wind the horn, blow, bugle, blow the b., sound the horn, sound, trumpet, sound the t., toot, tootle; pipe, flute, whistle; clash the cymbals; drum, tattoo, beat, tap, ruffle, beat the drum 403 *roll*; ring, peal the bells, ring a change; toll, knell; tune, string, set to concert pitch; practise, do scales, improvise, jam, extemporize, play a voluntary, prelude; begin playing, strike up; give an encore.

*sing*, vocalize, chant, hymn; intone, cantillate, descant; warble, carol, lilt, trill, croon, hum, whistle, yodel; belt out; solfa; harmonize, sing seconds; chorus, choir; sing to, serenade; sing the praises, minstrel; chirp, chirrup, twitter, pipe 409 *ululate*; purr 401 *sound faint.*

## 414 Musical instruments

**N.** *musical instrument*, band, music, concert 413 *orchestra*; strings, brass, wind, woodwind, percussion; sounding board, diaphragm, sound box; synthesizer.

*stringed instrument*, harp, Aeolian h.; lyre, lute, sitar; theorbo; cithara, cithern, zither, gittern, autoharp, guitar, acoustic g., semi-acoustic g., electric g., bass g., rhythm g., lead g., mandolin, ukulele, banjo, balalaika, bouzouki, psaltery, vina; plectrum, fret, capo *or* capodastro *or* capotasto; air guitar.

*viol*, violin, Cremona, Stradivarius, fiddle, kit, crowd, rebec; viola *or* tenor violin, viola d'amore, viola da gamba *or* bass viol, cello *or* violoncello, double bass *or* contrabasso; musical saw; bow, fiddlestick; string, catgut; bridge; resin.

*piano*, pianoforte, grand piano, concert grand, baby g., upright piano, cottage p.; virginals, dulcimer, harpsichord, cembalo, spinet, clavichord, celesta; piano-organ, player piano, Pianola (tdmk); clavier, keyboard, manual, keys, ivories; loud pedal, soft p., celeste, damper.

*organ*, pipe o., church o., Hammond o., electric *or* electronic o., steam o., calliope; reed organ, harmonium, American organ, melodeon; mouth organ, harmonica; kazoo, comb; accordion, piano a., concertina; barrel organ, hurdy-gurdy; great organ, swell o., choir o.; organ pipe, flue p., organ stop, flue s.; manual, keyboard.

*flute*, fife, piccolo, flageolet, cornetto, recorder, fipple flute; woodwind, reed instrument, clarinet, bass c., basset horn; saxophone, sax, tenor s.; shawm, hautboy, oboe, tenor o., cor Anglais; bassoon, double b.; ocarina; pipe, oaten p., reed, straw; chanter, bagpipes, small p., uillean *or* uilleann p., musette; pan pipes, Pandean p., syrinx; nose flute; whistle, penny w., tin w.; pitch-pipe; bazooka; mouthpiece, embouchure.

*horn*, brass; bugle horn, post h., hunting h.; bugle, trumpet, clarion; alpenhorn, French horn, flugelhorn, saxhorn, althorn, helicon horn, bass h., sousaphone; euphonium, ophicleide, serpent, bombardon; cornet, trombone, sackbut, tuba, saxtuba, bass tuba; conch, shell.

*gong*, bell, tintinnabulum; treble bell, tenor b.; church bell, alarm bell, tocsin 665 *danger signal*; tintinnabulation, peal, carillon, chimes, bells; bones, rattle, clappers, castanets, maracas; cymbals; xylophone, marimba; vibraphone, vibes; musical glasses, harmonica; tubular bell, glockenspiel; triangle; tuning fork; Jew's harp; sounding board; percussion instrument.

*drum*, big d., bass d., tenor d., side d., snare d., kettle d., timpani, steel drum; war drum, tomtom, bongo; tabor, tambourine; bodhran; tabla.

*record player*, gramophone, phonograph, radiogram; tape recorder, cassette r., high-fidelity system, hi-fi, stereo set, stereo system, music centre, stack system, stereo tower, hi-fi t.; personal stereo, personal hi-fi, personal headset, Walkman (tdmk), ghetto blaster, compact disc player, CD player, digital music player, MP3 player; playback.

*recording*, tape r., tape, cassette; talking book; gramophone record, disc, vinyl, compact d., CD, laser d., platter, long-playing record, LP, EP, 33, 45, 78; album, single, track 548 *registration*; musical box, jukebox; head, needle, stylus, pickup, cartridge; deck, turntable; amplifier, speaker, tweeter, woofer.

*mute*, damper, sordine, pedal, soft p., celeste 401 *silencer*.

## 415 Hearing

**N.** *hearing*, audition 398 *acoustics*; sense of hearing, good h.; good ear, sharp e., acute e., quick e., sensitive e., musical e., ear for music; audibility, reception, good r.; earshot, carrying distance, range, reach; something to hear, earful.

*listening*, hearkening 455 *attention*; auscultation, aural examination 459 *enquiry*; listening-in, tuning-in; lip-reading 520 *interpretation*; eavesdropping, overhearing, wire-tapping, bugging 523 *latency*; sound recording 548 *record*; audition, voice testing 461 *experiment*; interview, audience, hearing 584 *conference*; legal hearing 959 *legal trial*.

*listener*, hearer, audience, auditorium; stalls, pit, gallery, the gods; bums on seats (inf) 441 *spectator*; radio listener, radio ham, CB user; hi-fi enthusiast, audiophile; disciple, lecture-goer 538 *learner*; monitor, auditor, examiner 459 *questioner*; eavesdropper, listener-in, little pitcher 453 *inquisitive person*.

*ear*, auditory apparatus, auditory nerve, acoustic organ; lug, lobe, auricle, pinna, earhole, lughole; external ear, middle e., internal e.; aural cavity, cochlea, eardrum, tympanum; auditory canal, labyrinth; otology; aurist, hearing specialist, otologist, otolaryngologist, otorhinolaryngologist, ENT specialist, ear, nose and throat s.; Ménière's disease.

*hearing instrument*, deaf-aid, ear trumpet; hearing instrument, stethoscope, otoscope, auriscope; loudspeaker, loudhailer, tannoy, public address system 528 *publication*; microphone, mike, amplifier 400 *megaphone*; speaking tube; telephone, phone, cellular telephone, cellular phone, car p., mobile p., mobile, Vodafone (tdmk), blower (inf); receiver, earpiece, extension, headphones, headset, earphones; walkie-talkie 531 *telecommunication*; sound recorder, asdic, sonar, magnetic tape, Dictaphone (tdmk), Dictograph (tdmk) 549 *recording instrument*; radiogram 414 *record player*, 531 *broadcasting*.

**Adj.** *auditory*, hearing, auricular, aural; audiovisual 398 *sounding*; otic, otological, stethoscopic; auditive, acoustic, audile, keen-eared, sharp-e., open-e.; listening, tuned in; prick-eared, ears flapping, all ears 455 *attentive*; within earshot, within hearing distance, audible, heard 398 *sounding*.

**Vb.** *hear*, catch; list, listen, examine by ear, auscultate, put one's ear to; lip-read 520 *interpret*; listen in, switch on, tune in, tune to, adjust the receiver, answer the phone; prepare to hear, lift the receiver, answer the phone; overhear, eavesdrop, listen at keyholes, keep one's ears open; intercept, bug, tap, tap the wires; hearken, give ear, lend an e., incline one's e.; give audience, interview, grant an interview 459 *interrogate*; hear confession 526 *confess*; listen with both ears, be all ears, hang on the lips of, lap up 455 *be attentive*; strain one's ears, prick up one's e.; catch a sound, pick up a message; be told, hear it said, hear it on *or* through the grapevine, come to one's ears 524 *be informed*.

*be heard*, become audible, reach the ear, fill the e., sound in the e., fall on the e. 398 *sound*; ring in the e. 400 *be loud*; gain a hearing, have an audience; go out on the air, be broadcast.

**Adv.** *in earshot*, in one's hearing, within hearing distance.

## 416 Deafness

**N.** *deafness*, defective hearing, imperfect h., hardness of hearing; deaf ears, deaf-mutism; deaf-and-dumb speech, dactylology; deaf-and-dumb person, deaf-mute, the deaf and dumb; inaudibility 399 *silence*.

**Adj.** *deaf*, earless, dull of ear, hard of hearing, hearing-impaired, profoundly deaf, stone-d., deaf as a post, deaf as mutton, deaf and dumb, deaf-mute; deafened, stunned, unable to hear, with ears bunged up; deaf to, unhearing, not listening 456 *inattentive*; deaf to music, tone-deaf, unmusical; hard to hear 401 *muted*; inaudible, out of earshot, out of hearing 399 *silent*.

**Vb.** *be deaf*, not hear, hear nothing, fail to catch; not listen, refuse to hear, shut one's ears, stop one's e., close one's e., plug one's e. 458 *disregard*; turn a deaf ear to 760 *refuse*; have hearing difficulties, have impaired hearing, be hard of hearing, use a hearing aid; lip-read, use lip-reading 520 *translate*; talk with one's fingers.

*deafen*, make deaf, stun, split the eardrum, drown one's voice 400 *be loud*.

## 417 Light

**N.** *light*, daylight, light of day, noonday, noontide, noon, high n., broad day, broad daylight 128 *morning*; sunbeam, sunlight, sun 420 *luminary*; starlight, moonlight, moonshine, earthshine; half-light, twilight, gloaming 419 *dimness*; artificial light, electric light, gaslight, candlelight, firelight 420 *lighting*; floodlight, son et lumière; illumination, irradiation, splendour, resplendence, effulgence, refulgence, intensity, brightness, vividness, brilliance; luminousness, luminosity, luminance, candle power, magnitude; incandescence, radiance (see also *glow*); sheen, shine, gloss, polish, lustre (see also *reflection*); blaze, blaze of light, sheet of l., flood of l.; glare, dazzle, dazzlement;

flare, flame 379 *fire*; halo, nimbus, glory, gloriole, aureole, corona; variegated light, spectrum, visible s., iridescence, rainbow 437 *variegation*; coloration, riot of colour, blaze of c. 425 *colour*; white 427 *whiteness*.

*flash*, fulguration, coruscation; lightning, lightning flash, forked lightning, sheet l.; beam, stream, shaft, bar, ray, pencil; streak, meteor flash; scintillation, sparkle, spark; glint, glitter, glisten, play, play of light; blink, twinkle, twinkling, flicker, flickering, glimmer, gleam, shimmer, shimmering; spangle, tinsel; strobe light, searchlight, torchlight 420 *lamp*; firefly 420 *glowing thing*.

*glow*, flush, sunset glow, afterglow, alpenglow, dawn, 'rosy-fingered Dawn' (see quotation at 128 *morning*), sunset; steady flame, steady beam; lambency, lambent light, soft l.; aurora, aurora borealis, aurora australis, northern lights; zodiacal light 321 *heavens*; radiance, incandescence 379 *heat*; luminescence, fluorescence, phosphorescence, thermoluminescence; ignis fatuus, will-o'-the-wisp, St Elmo's fire 420 *glow-worm*.

*radiation*, visible r., invisible r.; background r.; actinism, emission, absorption; radioactivity, irradiation 160 *nucleonics*; radioisotope; particle counter, Geiger c.; fallout, nuclear f., mushroom cloud 659 *poison*; radiation belt, Van Allen layer 340 *atmosphere*; radio wave, frequency w. 398 *sound*; sky wave, ground w.; long w., short w., medium w. 317 *oscillation*; wavelength, waveband; high frequency, VHF, UHF; interference, static 160 *electricity*; electromagnetic radiation, microwave; infrared radiation, radiant heat *or* energy; visible light; black l.; ultraviolet radiation; X-ray, gamma r., alpha r., beta r., cosmic radiation, cosmic noise; magnetic storm; photon; photoelectric cell; curie, millicurie, roentgen, rem, rad, becquerel, gray, sievert; half-life, radiology, industrial r., medical r., diagnostic r., radiotherapy; food irradiation.

*reflection*, refraction, double r.; diffraction, dispersion, scattering, interference, polarization; albedo, polish, gloss, sheen, shine, glisten, gleam, lustre; glare, dazzle, blink, ice b.; reflecting surface, reflector 442 *mirror*; mirror image, hologram 551 *image*.

*light contrast*, tonality, chiaroscuro; value, light and shade, black and white, half-tone, mezzotint; highlights.

*optics*, electro-optics, fibre optics; photics, photometry, actinometry; dioptrics, catoptrics, spectroscopy 442 *optical device*; holography 551 *photography*; radioscopy, radiometry, radiology; magnification, magnifying power 197 *expansion*.

**Adj.** *luminous*, luminiferous, lucid, lucent; light, lit, well-lit, floodlit, flooded with light; bright, gay, shining, nitid, fulgent, resplendent, splendent, splendid, brilliant, flamboyant, vivid; colourful 425 *coloured*; radiant, effulgent, refulgent; dazzling, blinding, glaring, lurid, garish; incandescent, flaring, flaming, aflame, aglow, afire, ablaze 379 *fiery*; glowing, blushing, auroral, rutilant 431 *red*; luminescent, fluorescent, phosphorescent, noctilucous; soft, lambent, playing; beaming; glittery, flashing, glinting etc. vb.; scintillant, scintillating, sparkling; lustrous, chatoyant, shimmering, shiny, sheeny, glossy, polished; reflecting, catoptric; refractive, dioptric; optical, photometric; photosensitive.

*undimmed*, clear, bright, fair, set f.; cloudless, shadowless, unclouded, unshaded; sunny, sunshiny; moonlit, starlit, starry; light as day, bright as noonday, bright as silver; burnished, polished, glassy, gleaming; lucent, lucid, pellucid, diaphanous, translucent 422 *transparent*.

*radiating*, radiant; cosmic, cosmogenic; radioactive, irradiated, hot; reflective, reflecting.

**Vb.** *shine*, be bright, burn, blaze, flame, flare 379 *be hot*; glow, incandesce, luminesce, phosphoresce; shine full, glare, dazzle, bedazzle, blind; play, dance; flash, fulgurate, coruscate; glisten, glister, blink; glimmer, flicker, twinkle; glitter, shimmer, glance; scintillate, sparkle, spark; shine again, reflect; take a shine, come up, gleam, glint.

*radiate*, beam, shoot, shoot out rays, send out r. 300 *emit*; reflect, refract; be radioactive, bombard; X-ray.

*make bright*, lighten, dispel the darkness, brighten the gloom, dawn, rise, wax (moon); clear, clear up, lift, brighten; light, strike a l., ignite 381 *kindle*; light up, switch on; show a light, hang out a l.; shed lustre, throw light on; shine upon, flood with light, irradiate, illuminate, illume, relume; shine within, shine through 443 *be visible*; transilluminate, pass light through, let light through; polish, burnish, gleam, rub up 648 *clean*.

**418 Darkness**
**N.** *darkness*, dark; black 428 *blackness*; night, dark n., night-time, nightfall; dead of night, witching time 129 *midnight*; pitch darkness, pitchy darkness, thick d., tangible d., total d.; Cimmerian darkness, Stygian gloom, Erebus; obscurity, murk, murkiness, gloom, dusk, gloaming, twilight, half-dark, semi-darkness 421 *obfuscation*; shadiness, shadows 419 *dimness*; shade, dense s., shadow, umbra, penumbra; silhouette, skiagraph, negative, radiograph, shadowgraph 551 *photography*; skia-graphy; dark place, darkroom; cavern, mine, dungeon, depths.

*obscuration*, obfuscation, darkening 419 *dimness*; blackout, dimout, fadeout, fade; occultation, eclipse, total e. 446 *disappearance*; extinction of light, lights out; Tenebrae 988 *ritual act*; sunset, sundown 129 *evening*; blackening, adumbration, shading, hatching, cross-h.; distribution of shade, chiaroscuro; dark lantern; snuffer, dimmer, dip switch, off s.

**Adj.** *dark*, subfusc, sombre, dark-coloured, swart, swarthy, dusky 428 *black*; darksome, poorly lit, obscure, pitch-dark, pitchy, sooty, inky, jet-black, black as night; cavernous, dark as a tunnel, black as ink, black as hell, black as pitch, black as the ace of spades, black as a pit; Cimmerian, Stygian, Tartarean; caliginous, murky; funereal, gloomy, dreary, bleak, dismal, sombre; louring, lurid 419 *dim*; tenebrous, shady, umbrageous 419 *shadowy*; all black, silhouetted; shaded, darkened 421 *screened*; darkling, benighted; nocturnal, noctivagant; hidden, veiled, secret 523 *occult*.

*unlit*, unlighted, unilluminated; not shining, lightless; sunless, moonless, starless; eclipsed, overshadowed, overcast 421 *screened*; misted, hazy, befogged, clouded, beclouded, cloudy 423 *opaque*; switched off, extinguished; dipped, dimmed, blacked out; obscured, obfuscated.

**Vb.** *be dark*, grow d., get d., darkle; lour, gather; fade out 419 *be dim*; lurk in the shadows 523 *lurk*; cloud over, look black, gloom.

*darken*, black, brown; black out, dim o.; lower the light, dim the l., put out the l., switch off the l., turn down the wick; occult, eclipse, mantle 226 *cover*; curtain, shutter, veil 421 *screen*; obscure, obfuscate; befog, cloud, dim, tone down 419 *bedim*; overcast, overcloud, overshadow, cast in the shade, spread gloom; spread a shade, cast a shadow; adumbrate, silhouette 551 *represent*; shade, hatch, cross-h., fill in; paint over 440 *blur*; underexpose 428 *blacken*.

*snuff out*, extinguish, quench, put out the light, switch off the l., pinch out, blow o., switch off, dip, douse.

**Adv.** *darkling*, in the dark, in the shade, in the shadows, in the gloom, in the murk; at night, by night.

**419 Dimness**
**N.** *dimness*, indistinctness, vagueness, fuzziness, blur, lack of definition, soft focus; loom; faintness, paleness 426 *achromatism*; grey 429 *greyness*; dullness, lacklustre, lack of sparkle; no

reflection, matt finish; leaden skies; cloudiness, smokiness, poor visibility, impaired v., white-out 423 *opacity*; mistiness, fogginess, nebulosity; murk, gloom 418 *darkness*; fog, mist, haar 355 *cloud*; shadowiness, shadow, shade, shadow of a shade; spectre 440 *visual fallacy*.

*half-light*, semidarkness, half-dark, bad light; waning light, gloaming 129 *evening*; shades of evening, twilight, dusk, crepuscule; owl-light; daybreak, break of day, demi-jour, grey dawn; penumbra, half-shadow, partial eclipse, annular e.

*glimmer*, flicker 417 *flash*; 'ineffectual fire', noctiluca, firefly 420 *glowing thing*;

> Fare thee well at once!
> The glow-worm shows the matin to be near,
> And 'gins to pale his uneffectual fire:
> Adieu, adieu! Hamlet, remember me.
> William Shakespeare, *Hamlet*

side lights, dipped l., dips; candlelight, firelight 417 *light*; ember, hot coal; smoky light, tallow candle, dip; dark lantern 420 *lamp*; moonbeam, moonlight, starlight, earthlight; earthshine.

**Adj.** *dim*, darkish, darksome; tenebrous, sombre, dusky, dusk, twilight, crepuscular; wan, dun, subfusc, grey, pale 426 *colourless*; faint, faded, waning; imperceptible, indistinct, blurred, blurry, bleary; glassy, dull, lustreless, lacklustre, leaden; flat, matt; filmy, hazy, fuzzy, foggy, fogbound, misty, obnubilated, nebulous 355 *cloudy*; thick, smoky, sooty, muddy 423 *opaque*; dingy, grimy, rusty, rusted, mildewed, lustreless, unpolished, unburnished 649 *dirty*.

*shadowy*, umbrageous, shady, shaded, overspread, overshadowed, overcast, overclouded 226 *covered*; vague, indistinct, undefined, ill-defined, obscure, confused, fuzzy, blurry, looming; deceptive; half-seen, half-glimpsed, withdrawn, half-hidden 444 *invisible*; half-lit, partially eclipsed 418 *unlit*; dreamlike, ghostly 4 *insubstantial*; coming and going 446 *disappearing*.

**Vb.** *be dim*, – faint etc. adj.; be indistinct, loom; grow grey, lose definition, fade, wane, fade out, pale, grow p. 426 *lose colour*; lour, gloom, darkle; glimmer, flicker, gutter, sputter; lurk in the shade, be hidden in the gloom, be lost in the shadows 523 *lurk*.

*dim*, dim, bedim, dip; lower *or* turn down the lights, fade out 418 *snuff out*; obscure, blur the outline, make fuzzy, blear 440 *blur*; smirch, smear, besmirch, besmear, sully; rust, mildew, begrime, muddy, dirty 649 *make unclean*; smoke, fog, mist, befog, becloud 423 *make opaque*; overshadow, overcast; shade, shadow,

veil, veil the brightness 226 *cover*; shade in, hatch 418 *darken*.

**Adv.** *dimly*, vaguely, indistinctly etc. adj.; in the half-light, in the gloaming, in the gloom.

## 420 Luminary: source of light

**N.** *luminary*, illuminant 417 *light*; naked light, flame 379 *fire*; flare, gas f. (see also *lamp*); source of light, orb of day 321 *sun*; orb of night 321 *moon*; starlight 321 *star*; bright star, first magnitude s., Sirius, Aldebaran, Betelgeuse, Canopus, Alpha Centauri; evening star, Hesperus, Vesper, Venus; morning star, Lucifer; shooting star, fireball 321 *meteor*; galaxy, Milky Way, northern lights 321 *heavens*; lightning, bolt of l., sheet l., forked l., ball l., summer l., lightning flash, levin; scintilla, spark, sparkle 417 *flash*.

*glowing thing* 417 *glow*; glow-worm, firefly, noctiluca, fata morgana, ignis fatuus, will-o'-the-wisp, friar's lantern, Jack-o'-lantern; fireball, St Elmo's fire, corposant; phosphorescent light, corpse-candle; firedrake, fiery dragon.

*torch*, brand, coal, ember; torchlight, link, flambeau, cresset, match 385 *lighter*; candle, bougie, tallow candle, wax c.; flower c., cake c., Christmas c; taper, wax t.; spill, wick, dip, rushlight, nightlight, naked light, flare, gas jet, burner, Bunsen b.; torchbearer, linkboy.

*lamp*, lamplight; lantern, lanthorn, bull's-eye; safety lamp, Davy l., miner's l., acetylene l.; oil lamp, hurricane l., paraffin l., spirit l.; gas lamp, Calor gas (tdmk) lamp, incandescent l., gas mantle, mantle; electric lamp, flash l., flash gun, torch, pocket t., penlight, flashlight, searchlight, arc light, floodlight; headlamp, headlight, side light; anti-dazzle l., foglamp; stop-light, tail light, brake l., reflector; bulb, flashbulb, flashcube, photoflood, electric bulb, light b., filament; strobe light, stroboscope, strobe; vapour light, neon l., strip l., fluorescent l.; street l., mercury vapour lamp, sodium l., Chinese lantern, fairy lights, Christmas tree l.; magic lantern, projector; light fitting, chandelier, gaselier, lustre, electrolier, candelabra, girandole; standard lamp, table l., desk l., reading l., Anglepoise (tdmk) l.; sun l., sunray l.; lamppost, standard; socket, bracket, pricket; sconce, candle holder, candle-stick; linkboy, lamplighter.

*lighting*, illumination, irradiation 417 *light*; artificial lighting, street l.; indirect lighting; gas lighting, electric l., neon l., daylight l., fluorescent l.; floodlighting, son et lumière, limelight, spotlight, footlight, houselights.

*signal light*, warning l. 665 *danger signal*; traffic light, red l., green l., amber l., stop-light,

trafficator, indicator, winker; Very light,
Bengal l., rocket, star shell, parachute flare,
flare; flare path, beacon, beacon fire, balefire
547 *signal*; lighthouse, lightship.

*fireworks*, illuminations, firework display,
pyrotechnics; sky rocket, Roman candle, Catherine wheel, sparkler; banger 723 *explosive*;
Bengal light.

**Adj.** *luminescent*, luminous, self-l., incandescent, shining; phosphoric, phosphorescent,
fluorescent, neon; radiant 417 *radiating*;
colourful 425 *coloured*; illuminated, well-lit;
bright, gay.

**Vb.** *illuminate*, light up, light 417 *shine*,
make bright.

**421 Screen**

**N.** *screen*, shield 660 *protection*; covert 662
*shelter*; bower 194 *arbour*; shady nook 418 *darkness*; sunshade, parasol; sun hat, sola topee 226
*shade*; awning 226 *canopy*; sunscreen, visor;
lampshade; eyeshade, blinkers; eyelid, eyelashes 438 *eye*; dark glasses, tinted g., sun g.,
shades 442 *eyeglass*; smoked glass, frosted g.,
reeded g., opaque g., polarized g. 424 *semitransparency*; stained glass 437 *variegation*; double
glazing, soundproofing, partition, wall, hedge
235 *fence*; filter 57 *exclusion*; mask 527 *disguise*;
hood, veil, mantle 228 *cloak*.

*curtain*, 226 *shade*; window curtain, net c.,
bead c.; drapes, shade, blind, sunblind; persi-
enne, jalousie, venetian blind, roller b., festoon b.; shutter, deadlight.

*obfuscation*, smoke screen; fog, mist, haze,
haar 341 *moisture*; pall, cloud, dust, film, scale
423 *opacity*.

**Adj.** *screened*, sheltered; sunproof, cool 380
*cold*; shaded, shady, umbrageous, bowery 419
*shadowy*; blindfolded, hooded, masked 439
*blind*; screening, impervious, impermeable.

**Vb.** *screen*, shield, shelter 660 *safeguard*; protect 713 *defend*; ward off, fend off, keep at bay
713 *parry*; blanket, keep off, keep out, filter out
57 *exclude*; cover up, veil, hood 226 *cover*;
mask, hide, shroud 525 *conceal*; intercept 702
*obstruct*; blinker, blindfold 439 *blind*; keep out
the light, shade, shadow, darken; curtain, curtain off, canopy, draw the curtains, pull down
the blind, spread the awning; put up the shutters, close the s. 264 *close*; cloud, fog, mist 419
*bedim*; smoke, frost, glaze, film 423 *make
opaque*.

**422 Transparency**

**N.** *transparency*, transmission of light, transil-
lumination; transparence, translucence,
lucency, diaphaneity, unobstructed vision;
thinness, gauziness; lucidity, pellucidity, lim-

pidity; clearness, clarity; glassiness; vitre-
ousness; transparent medium, hyaline, water,
ice, crystal, Perspex (tdmk), cellophane,
shrink-wrapping, bubble pack, blister p., glass,
crown g., flint g., sheet g., float g., plate g.,
optical g., magnifying g., lens, eyepiece 442 *eyeglass*; pane, window p.; sheer silk, gossamer,
gauze, lace, chiffon 4 *insubstantial thing*.

**Adj.** *transparent*, diaphanous, revealing,
sheer, see-through; thin, fine, filmy, gauzy, pellucid, translucid; translucent; lucent 424 *semitransparent*; liquid, limpid; crystal, crystalline,
hyaline, vitreous, glassy; clear, serene, lucid;
crystal-clear, clear as crystal, clear as glass.

**Vb.** *be transparent*, – translucent etc. adj.;
transmit light, show through; shine through,
transilluminate, pass light through 417 *make
bright*; render transparent, clarify.

**423 Opacity**

**N.** *opacity*, opaqueness; thickness, solidity 324
*density*; filminess, frost; turbidity, muddiness,
dirtiness 649 *dirt*; devitrification; fog, mist,
haar, dense fog, smog, pea-souper 355 *cloud*;
film, scale 421 *screen*; smoke-cloud, smoke
screen 421 *obfuscation*.

**Adj.** *opaque*, nontransparent, thick, impervious to light, blank, windowless; not clear,
unclarified, devitrified; cloudy, milky, filmy,
turbid, muddy, muddied, puddled; foggy,
hazy, misty, murky, smoky, sooty, fuliginous
419 *dim*; unwashed, uncleaned 649 *dirty*;
vaporous, fumy; coated, frosted, misted,
clouded.

**Vb.** *make opaque*, devitrify; cloud, cloud
over, thicken; frost, film, smoke 419 *bedim*;
obfuscate; scumble, overpaint 226 *coat*; be
opaque, keep out the light, obstruct the light
421 *screen*.

**424 Semitransparency**

**N.** *semitransparency*, milkiness, lactescence;
pearliness, opalescence; smoked glass,
ground g., frosted g., tinted spectacles, dark
glasses; gauze, muslin, net; pearl, opal 437 *variegation*; horn, mica; tissue, tissue paper.

**Adj.** *semitransparent*, semipellucid, semi-
opaque, semidiaphanous, gauzy, filmy; translucent, opalescent, opaline, milky, lactescent,
pearly; frosted, matt, misty, smoked 419 *dim*,
355 *cloudy*.

**425 Colour**

**N.** *colour*, natural c., pure c., positive c.,
neutral c., primitive c., primary c.; three pri-
maries, complementary colour, secondary c.,
tertiary c.; chromatism, chromatic aberration;
range of colour, chromatic scale; prism, spec-

trum, rainbow 437 *variegation*; mixture of colours, harmony, discord; colour scheme, palette; coloration 553 *painting*; colour photography, Technicolor (tdmk); riot of colour, splash 437 *variegation*; heraldic colour, tincture, metal, fur 547 *heraldry*.

*chromatics*, science of colour, colorimetry, chromatology, spectrum analysis, spectrometer; colorimeter, tintometer; spectroscope, prism.

*hue*, colour quality, chroma, chromaticity, saturation, tone, value; brilliance, intensity, warmth, loudness; softness, deadness, dullness; coloration, livery; pigmentation, colouring, complexion, natural colour; hue of health, flush, blush, glow; rosy cheek, ruddiness 431 *redness*; sickly hue, pallor 426 *achromatism*; faded hue, discoloration; tint, shade, nuance, cast, dye; tinge, patina; half-tone, half-light, mezzotint.

*pigment*, colouring matter, rouge, blusher, warpaint 843 *cosmetic*; dyestuff, dye, fast d.; natural d., vegetable d., madder, cochineal 431 *red pigment*; indigo 436 *purpleness*; woad 435 *blueness*; artificial dye, synthetic d., aniline d.; stain, fixative, mordant; wash, colourwash, whitewash, distemper; paint, emulsion p., gloss p., undercoat; oil paints, acrylic p., watercolours 553 *art equipment*.

**Adj.** *coloured*, in colour, painted, toned, tinct, tinged, dyed, double-d., tinted etc. vb.; colorific, tinctorial; fast, unfading, constant; colourful, chromatic, polychromatic; monochromatic 16 *uniform*; prismatic, spectroscopic; technicoloured, kaleidoscopic, many-coloured, parti-coloured 437 *variegated*.

*florid*, colourful, high-coloured, full-c., deep-c., bright-hued; ruddy 431 *red*; intense, deep, strong, emphatic; unfaded, vivid, brilliant 417 *luminous*; warm, glowing, rich, gorgeous; painted, gay, bright; gaudy, garish, showy, flashy; glaring, flaring, flaunting, spectacular; harsh, stark, raw, crude; lurid, loud, screaming, shrieking; clashing, discordant 25 *disagreeing*.

*soft-hued*, soft, quiet, understated, tender, delicate, refined, discreet; pearly, creamy 427 *whitish*; light, pale, pastel, muted; dull, flat, matt, dead; simple, sober, sad 573 *plain*; sombre, dark 428 *black*; drab, dingy, faded; patinated, weathered, mellow; matching, toning, harmonious 24 *agreeing*.

**Vb.** *colour*, lay on the c., colour in, colourize, block in, crayon, daub 553 *paint*; rouge 431 *redden*, 843 *primp*; pigment, tattoo; dye, tie-dye, dip, imbue, imbrue; woad 435 *blue*; tint, touch up; shade, shadow 428 *blacken*; tincture, tinge; wash, colourwash, distemper, lac-

quer 226 *coat*; stain, run, discolour; come off (e.g. on one's fingers); tan, weather, mellow; illuminate, miniate, emblazon; whitewash, silver 427 *whiten*; yellow 433 *gild*; enamel 437 *variegate*.

## 426 Achromatism: absence of colour

**N.** *achromatism*, achromaticity, colourlessness; decoloration, discoloration, etiolation, weathering, fading, bleaching 427 *whiteness*; overexposure 551 *photography*; pallor, pallidity, paleness; lightness, faintness etc. adj.; no colour, absence of c., anaemia, bloodlessness; pigment deficiency, albinism, albinoism; neutral tint; monochrome; black and white; albino, blond(e), platinum b., peroxide b., artificial b.

*bleacher*, decolorant, peroxide, bleaching powder, bleach, lime.

**Adj.** *colourless*, hueless, toneless, neutral; uncoloured, achromatic; decoloured, discoloured; bleached, etiolated, overexposed, weathered; faint, faded, fading; unpigmented, albino, lightskinned, fair-s., fair, blond(e) 433 *yellow*, 427 *whitish*; lustreless, glossless, mousy; bloodless, anaemic; without colour, drained of colour, drained of blood; washed out, washy, wishy-washy, peaky; pale, pallid 427 *white*; ashy, ashen, ashen-hued, livid, tallow-faced, whey-f.; pasty, doughy, mealy, sallow, sickly 651 *unhealthy*; dingy, dull, leaden 429 *grey*; blank, glassy, lacklustre; lurid, ghastly, wan 419 *dim*; deathly, deathly pale, cadaverous, white as a sheet, ghostlike, pale as death, pale as ashes 361 *dead*.

**Vb.** *lose colour* 419 *be dim*; pale, fade, bleach, blanch, turn pale, change countenance, go as white as a sheet 427 *whiten*; run, come out in the wash.

*decolorize*, achromatize, fade, etiolate; blanch, bleach, peroxide 427 *whiten*; deprive of colour, drain of c., wash out; tone down, deaden, weaken; pale, dim 419 *bedim*; dull, tarnish, discolour 649 *make unclean*.

## 427 Whiteness

**N.** *whiteness*, albescence, etiolation; lack of pigment, albinism, albinoism 426 *achromatism*; whitishness, lactescence, creaminess, off-whiteness, pearliness; hoariness, canescence; white light 417 *light*; white heat 379 *heat*; white man, white woman, white person, white, paleface; albino.

*white thing*, alabaster, marble; hoar frost, snow, driven s., new-fallen s.; chalk, paper, milk, flour, salt, ivory, lily, swan; albino; silver, white metal, white gold, pewter, platinum; pearl, teeth; white patch, blaze.

*whiting*, blanco, white lead, pipeclay; whitewash, white paint, Chinese white, Paris w., flake w., zinc w., titanium w.

**Adj.** *white*, candid, pure, albescent; dazzling, light, bright 417 *luminous*; silvered, silvery, silver, argent, argental, argentine; alabaster, marble; chalky, snowy, snow-capped, snow-covered; ice-c.; hoar, frosty, frosted; foaming, spumy, foam-flecked; soapy, lathery; white hot 379 *hot*; white as marble, white as alabaster, white like ivory, white as a lily, white as milk, white as a sheet, white as the driven snow; pure white, lily-white, milk-w., snow-w., white-skinned, Caucasian; lacking pigment, albinotic; whitened, whitewashed, bleached 648 *clean*.

*whitish*, pearly, milky, creamy 424 *semitransparent*; ivory, waxen, sallow, pale 426 *colourless*; off-white, half-w.; oyster-w., mushroom, magnolia; unbleached, ecru, beige 430 *brown*; canescent, hoary, grizzled 429 *grey*; pepper-and-salt 437 *mottled*; blond(e), fair, Nordic; ash-blond(e), platinum b., fair-haired, golden-h., flaxen-h., tow-headed; dusty, white with dust.

**Vb.** *whiten*, white, blanco, pipeclay, whitewash, *calcimine*, wash 648 *clean*; blanch, bleach; pale, fade 426 *decolorize*; frost, silver, grizzle.

## 428 Blackness

**N.** *blackness*, nigrescence, nigritude 418 *darkness*; inkiness, lividity, black, sable; melanism, swarthiness, swartness, duskiness, pigmentation, pigment, dark colouring, colour; depth, deep tone; black and white, chiaroscuro 437 *chequer*; blackening, darkening 418 *obscuration*; black man, black woman, black, Negro, Negress, Negrillo, Negrito; coloured man *or* woman, coloured; African-American, Afro-A., African Caribbean, Afro-C., West Indian; Ethiopian, blackamoor.

*black thing*, coal, charcoal, soot, pitch, tar; ebony, jet, ink, smut; sable; bruise, black eye; blackberry, sloe; crow, raven, blackbird; black clothes, crepe, mourning.

*black pigment*, blacking, lampblack, blacklead; ivory black, blue-b., nigrosine; ink, Indian i., printer's i., japan, niello; burnt cork; melanin.

**Adj.** *black*, sable; jetty, ebon; inky, pitchy, black as thunder 418 *dark*; sooty, fuliginous, smoky, smudgy, smutty 649 *dirty*; blackened, singed, charred; black-haired, black-locked, raven-haired, dark-headed; black-eyed, sloe-e.; dark, brunette; black-skinned, Negro, Negroid, coloured, African-American, Afro-A., African Caribbean, Afro-C., West Indian; Ethiopian;

pigmented, coloured; melanistic; sombre, gloomy, mourning 364 *funereal*; coal-black, jet-b., sloe-b., pitch-b.; blue-b.; deep, of the deepest dye; black as coal, black as jet, black as ink, black as pitch, black as my hat, black as the ace of spades, black as a tinker's pot, black as hell; nocturnal, black as night, black as midnight 129 *vespertine*; Afrocentric.

*blackish*, rather black, nigrescent; swarthy, swart, black-faced, dusky, dark, dark-skinned, tanned, sun-t.; coloured, pigmented; livid, black and blue; low-toned, low in tone 419 *dim*.

**Vb.** *blacken*, black, blacklead, japan, ink, ink in; dirty, blot, smudge, smirch 649 *make unclean*; deepen 418 *darken*; singe, char 381 *burn*.

## 429 Greyness

**N.** *greyness*, neutral tint, greige, grisaille; pepper and salt, grey hairs, hoary head; pewter, silver; gunmetal, ashes, slate; grey, Payne's g.; dove g. etc. adj.; oyster, taupe.

**Adj.** *grey*, neutral, dull, sombre, leaden, livid; cool, quiet; canescent, greying, grizzled, grizzly, hoary, hoar; silvery, silvered, pearly, frosted 427 *whitish*; greige; light-grey, pale-g., powder-g., ash-g., dove-g., pearl-g.; mouse-coloured, mousy, dun, drab, donkey-grey; steely, steel-grey, iron-g., charcoal-g.; bluish-grey, slate-coloured; greyish, ashen, ashy, smoky, fuliginous, cinereous; dapple-grey.

## 430 Brownness

**N.** *brownness*, brown, bronze, copper, amber; tobacco leaf, dead l., autumn colours; cinnamon, coffee, chocolate; butterscotch, caramel, toffee, burnt almond; walnut, mahogany; dark skin *or* complexion, suntan; brunette.

*brown pigment*, bistre, ochre, sepia, raw sienna, burnt s., raw umber, burnt u., Vandyke brown.

**Adj.** *brown*, bronze, mahogany etc. n.; browned, toasted; bronzed, tanned, sunburnt; dark, brunette; nut-brown, hazel; light brown, ecru, oatmeal, beige, buff, fawn, biscuit, mushroom, café-au-lait; brownish, greyish-brown, dun, drab, mud-coloured; yellowish-brown, snuff-coloured, feuillemort, khaki; tawny, tan, foxy; reddish-brown, bay, roan, sorrel, chestnut, auburn, copper-coloured; russet, rust-coloured, liver-c., maroon; purple-brown, puce; dark brown, peat-b., mocha, chocolate, coffee-coloured etc. n.; fuscous, subfusc; brown as a berry, brown as a nut, brown as mahogany.

**Vb.** *brown*, embrown, bronze, tan, sunburn; singe, char, toast 381 *burn*.

**431 Redness**
**N.** *redness*, rubescence, blush, flush, hectic f.; fireglow, sunset, dawn, 'rosy-fingered Dawn' (see quotation at 128 *morning*) 417 *glow*; rubefaction, reddening, warmth; rosiness, ruddiness, bloom, red cheeks, rosy c., apple c., cherry lips; high colour, floridness, rubicundity; red colour, crimson, scarlet, red etc. adj.; carnation, rose, geranium, poppy; cherry, tomato; burgundy, port, claret; gore 335 *blood*; ruby, garnet, cornelian; flame 379 *fire*; red ink, rubric; red planet, Mars; redbreast, robin r.; redskin, Red Indian, Indian, Native American, Native Canadian, First Nation; redhead, carrot-top, gingernob.

*red pigment*, red dye, murex, cochineal, carmine, kermes; dragon's blood; cinnabar, vermilion; ruddle, madder, rose m.; alizarin, crimson lake, Venetian red, rosaniline, solferino; red ochre, red lead, minium; rouge, blusher, lipstick 843 *cosmetic*.

**Adj.** *red*, reddish; ruddy, rubicund, sanguine, florid, blowzy; warm, hot, fiery, glowing, red-hot 379 *hot*; flushed, fevered; erubescent, rubescent, flushing, blushing; red-cheeked, rosy-c.; bright red, red as a lobster, red as a beetroot; red-haired, ginger-h.; carroty, sandy, auburn, titian-red, flame-coloured; rufous, rufescent; russet, rusty, rust-coloured, ferruginous, rubiginous 430 *brown*; pink, rose-p., roseate, rosy, rose-coloured, peach-c., flesh-c., flesh-pink, shell-p., salmon-p., shocking-p.; coral, carnation, damask, crushed strawberry; crimson, cherry-red, cerise, carmine, cramoisy; Tyrian purple, fuchsine, fuchsia, magenta, maroon 436 *purple*; wine-coloured, wine-dark; oxblood, sang-de-boeuf; sanguine, murrey, gules; scarlet, cardinal-red, vermilion, vermeil, pillarbox red, Turkey r.; dyed red, reddened, rouged, painted.

*bloodstained*, bloodshot; blood-red; sanguine; sanguinary, ensanguined, incarnadine, bloody, gory.

**Vb.** *redden*, rubefy, rubricate, miniate; rouge, apply blusher, raddle 843 *primp*; incarnadine, dye red, stain with blood; flush, blush, glow; mantle, colour, colour up, crimson, go red, go pink.

**432 Orange**
**N.** *orange*, red and yellow, gold, old gold; or, tenné; copper, amber; sunflower, marigold; apricot, tangerine; marmalade; ochre, Mars orange, cadmium o., henna.

**Adj.** *orange*, apricot etc. n.; ochreous,

luteous, cupreous, coppery, ginger, tan; orangeish, orangey, orange-coloured, flame-c., copper-c., brass-c., brassy.

**433 Yellowness**
**N.** *yellowness*, yellow, sunshine y. etc. adj.; brass, gold, old gold, topaz, amber, old ivory; sulphur, brimstone; buttercup, daffodil, primrose, dandelion; lemon, honey; saffron, mustard; biliousness, jaundice, yellow fever; sallow skin, fair hair, golden hair; blond(e), ash b., platinum b., strawberry b.; yellow rain.

*yellow pigment*, gamboge, cadmium yellow, chrome y., Indian y., Naples y., lemon y., orpiment; yellow ochre, massicot, weld, luteolin, xanthin.

**Adj.** *yellow*, gold, amber etc. n.; tawny, fulvous, sandy; fair-haired, golden-h., yellow-h. 427 *whitish*; creamy, cream-coloured, buff-c.; honey-c., straw-c., fallow; pale yellow, acid y., lemon y.; primrose y., jasmine, citrine, chartreuse, champagne; canary yellow, sunshine y., bright y.; sulphur y., mustard y.; golden, aureate, gilt, gilded; deep yellow, luteous, yellowy, yellowish, flavescent, xanthic; sallow, jaundiced, bilious; yellow as parchment, yellow as butter, yellow with age.

**Vb.** *gild*, yellow.

**434 Greenness**
**N.** *greenness*, green etc. adj.; verdancy, greenery, greenwood; verdure, viridity, viridescence; grass, moss, turf, green leaf 366 *foliage*; lime, greengage; jade, emerald, malachite, beryl, aquamarine, olivine, chrysoprase, verd antique; verdigris, patina; celadon, reseda, mignonette; Lincoln green; loden; vert.

*green pigment*, terre verte, viridian, verditer, bice, green bice, Paris green; chlorophyll.

**Adj.** *green*, viridescent, verdant; verdurous, grassy, leafy; bright green, deep g., dark g., pale g.; grass-green, leaf-g., moss-g.; emerald, sea-green 435 *blue*; jade-green, sap-g., bottle-g.; sage-g., willow-g.; pea-g., acid-g., apple-g., lime-g., chartreuse; eau-de-Nil, avocado, olive, olive-green, olivaceous; glaucous, greenish, virescent; vert.

**435 Blueness**
**N.** *blueness*, blue, cyan, azure; blue sky, blue sea; sapphire, aquamarine, turquoise, lapis lazuli; bluebell, cornflower, forget-me-not; gentian blue etc. adj.; bluishness, cyanosis; lividness, lividity.

*blue pigment*, blue dye, bice, indigo, woad; Prussian blue, French b., ultramarine, cobalt, cobalt blue, zaffre, smalt; bluebag.

**Adj.** *blue*, cyanic, azure, azury; cerulean, sky-blue; duck-egg blue, eggshell b., turquoise; light blue, pale blue, ice-b., powder-b., Cambridge-b.; air-force b., Saxe-b., slate-b., steel-b., electric-b.; sapphire, aquamarine, peacock-b., kingfisher-b., bright b., royal-b., ultramarine, deep blue, dark b., Oxford-b., midnight-b., navy-b., navy, French n.; indigo, perse; hyacinthine, blue-black, black and blue, livid; cold, steely, bluish, blue with cold.

**Vb.** *blue*, turn blue; dye blue, woad.

### 436 Purpleness
**N.** *purpleness*, purple, blue and red; imperial purple; amethyst; lavender, violet, heliotrope, heather, foxglove; plum, damson, aubergine; Tyrian purple, gentian violet; amaranth, lilac, mauve; purpure.

**Adj.** *purple*, plum etc. n.; purplish, purpled; violet, violaceous, mauve, pale purple, lavender, lilac; purple-red, bright purple, fuchsia, magenta, plum-coloured, damson-coloured, puce; hyacinthine, heliotrope; deep purple, dark purple, mulberry, murrey; livid, purple with rage; black and blue 435 *blue*.

**Vb.** *empurple*, purple.

### 437 Variegation
**N.** *variegation*, variety, diversification, diversity 15 *difference*; dancing light, glancing l. 417 *light*; play of colour, shot colours, iridescence, irisation, chatoyance; tiger's eye, opal, nacre, mother-of-pearl; shot silk, moiré, pigeon's neck, gorge-de-pigeon; dichromatism, trichromatism; dichroism, trichroism, tricolour, polychromy 425 *colour*; peacock, peacock's tail, peacock butterfly, tortoiseshell, chameleon; Joseph's coat, motley, harlequin, patchwork, patchwork quilt; mixture of colour, medley of c., riot of c.; enamelwork, enamelling; stained glass, kaleidoscope; rainbow, rainbow effect, band of colour, spectrum, prism; collage.

*chequer*, check, Prince of Wales c., hound's tooth, pepper-and-salt; plaid, tartan; chessboard, draughtboard; marquetry, parquetry, inlay, inlaid work 844 *ornamental art*; mosaic, tessellation, tesserae, crazy paving 43 *medley*.

*stripe*, stria, striation; line, streak, band, bar, bar code; agate; zebra, tiger; streakiness, mackerel sky; crack, craze, crackle; reticulation 222 *network*.

*mottling*, mottle, dappling, stippling, marbling, maculation; spottiness, patchiness 17 *nonuniformity*; patch, speck, speckle, macula, spots, pimples, pockmarks, freckle, foxing 845 *blemish*; fleck, dot, polka d.; blotch, splotch, splodge, splash; leopard, Dalmatian.

**Adj.** *variegated*, fretted etc. vb.; diversified,

daedal; patterned, embroidered, worked 844 *ornamental*; polychromatic, colourful 425 *florid*; bicolour, tricolour; dichroic, dichromatic, trichromatic, trichroic; many-hued, many-coloured, multi-c., parti-c., motley, patched, random, crazy, of all colours; tortoiseshell, chameleon, harlequin, kaleidoscopic 82 *multiform*; plaid, tartan; rainbow-coloured, rainbow, iridal, iridian; prismatic, spectral; mosaic, tessellated, parquet; paned, panelled.

*iridescent*, irisated, versicolour, chameleon; nacreous, mother-of-pearl; opalescent, opaline, pearly 424 *semitransparent*; shot, shot through with, gorge-de-pigeon, pavonine, moiré, watered, chatoyant, cymophanous.

*pied*, parti-coloured, black-and-white, pepper-and-salt, grizzled, piebald, skewbald, roan, pinto, chequered, check, dappled, patchy.

*mottled*, marbled, jaspered, veined, reticulated; studded, maculose, spotted, spotty, pimply, patchy; speckled, speckledy, freckled; streaky, streaked, striated, lined, barred, banded, striped 222 *crossed*; brindled, tabby; pocked, pockmarked 845 *blemished*; cloudy, hazy, powdered, dusted, dusty.

**Vb.** *variegate*, diversify, fret, pattern; punctuate; chequer, check, counterchange; patch 656 *repair*; embroider, work 844 *decorate*; braid, quilt; damascene, inlay, tessellate, tile; stud, pepper, dot with, mottle, speckle, freckle, spangle, spot; sprinkle, powder, dust; tattoo, stipple, dapple; streak, stripe, striate; craze, crack 330 *be brittle*; marble, vein, cloud 423 *make opaque*; stain, blot, discolour 649 *make unclean*; make iridescent, irisate; interchange colour, play.

### 438 Vision
**N.** *vision*, sight, power of s., light-grasp; eyesight; seeing, visualization, mind's eye 513 *imagination*; perception, recognition; acuity (of vision), good eyesight, good sight, keen s., sharp s., long s., far s., normal s.; defective vision, short sight 440 *dim sight*; second sight 984 *occultism*; type of vision, double vision, stereoscopic v., binocular v.; aided vision, magnification; tired vision, winking, blinking, tic, squint; eye-testing, sight-t.; oculist, optician, ophthalmologist, optometrist; optometer, ophthalmoscope 442 *optical device*; dream 440 *visual fallacy*.

*eye*, visual organ, organ of vision, eyeball, iris, pupil, white, cornea, retina, optic nerve; optics, orbs, sparklers, peepers, weepers; windows of the soul; saucer eyes, goggle e.; eyelashes, eyelid 421 *screen*; lashes, sweeping l.;

naked eye, unaided e.; clear eye, sharp e., piercing e., penetrating e., gimlet e., X-ray e.; weak eyes 440 *dim sight*; dull eye, glass e. 439 *blindness*; evil eye 983 *sorcery*; hawk, eagle, cat, lynx; Argus; basilisk, cockatrice, Gorgon.

*look*, regard, glance, side g., sideways look, squint; tail *or* corner of the eye; glint, blink, flash; penetrating glance, gaze, steady g.; observation, close o., contemplation, watch; stare, fixed s.; come-hither look, glad eye, sheep's eyes, ogle, leer 889 *wooing*; wink 524 *hint*; grimace, dirty look, scowl, evil eye; peep, peek, glimpse, rapid g., brief g., half an eye.

*inspection*, ocular i., ocular demonstration 443 *visibility*; examination, visual e., autopsy 459 *enquiry*; view, preview, sneak p. 522 *manifestation*; oversight, supervision 689 *management*; survey, overview, bird's-eye view; sweep, reconnaissance, reconnoitre, recce, tour of inspection, surveillance; sightseeing, rubbernecking, gawping; look, butcher's, lookaround, look-see, dekko, once-over, coup d'oeil, shufti, rapid survey, rapid glance; second glance, double take; review, revision; viewing, home v. 445 *cinema*, 531 *broadcasting*; discernment, catching sight, espial, view, first v., first sight; looking round, observation, prying, spying; espionage; peeping, scopophilia, voyeurism, Peeping Tom.

*view*, full v., eyeful; vista, prospect, outlook, perspective; aspect 445 *appearance*; panorama, bird's-eye view, commanding v., unimpeded v.; horizon, false h.; line of sight, line of vision; range of view, purview, ken; field of view, amphitheatre; scene, setting, stage 594 *theatre*; angle of vision, slant, point of view, viewpoint, standpoint; observation point, vantage p., lookout, crow's nest, watchtower 209 *high structure*; belvedere, gazebo; camera obscura; astrodome, conning tower; observatory, observation balloon; stand, grandstand, stall, ringside seat 441 *onlookers*; loophole, peephole, hagioscope 263 *window*.

**Adj.** *seeing*, glimpsing etc. vb.; visual, perceptible 443 *visible*; panoramic, perspectival; ocular, ophthalmic; optical, optometric; stereoscopic, binocular; orthoptic, perspicacious, clear-sighted, sharp-s., sharp-eyed, keen-e., gimlet-e., eagle-e., hawk-e., lynx-e.; vigilant, all eyes, with eyes in the back of one's head, Argus-eyed; second-sighted, visionary 513 *imaginative*.

**Vb.** *see*, behold, visualize, use one's eyes; see truly, keep in perspective; perceive, discern, distinguish, make out, pick o., recognize, ken 490 *know*; take in, see at a glance 498 *be wise*; descry, discover 484 *detect*; sight, espy, spy, spot, observe 455 *notice*; lay *or* set eyes on, clap

eyes on, catch sight of, sight, raise land; catch a glimpse of, glimpse; view, command a view of, hold in view, have in sight; see with one's own eyes, witness, look on, be a spectator 441 *watch*; dream, see visions, see things 513 *imagine*; see in the dark, have second sight 510 *foresee*; become visible 443 *be visible*.

*gaze*, regard, quiz, look quizzically at, gaze at, look, look at; look full in the face, look straight at, look in the eyes; look intently, eye, stare, peer; stare at, stare hard, goggle, gape, gawk, gawp; focus, rivet one's eyes, fix one's gaze; glare, glower, look daggers, give a black look, look black 891 *be angry*; glance, glance at; squint, look askance, look down one's nose; wink, blink 524 *hint*; make eyes at, give the glad eye, give a come-hither look, ogle, leer 889 *court*; feast one's eyes on, gloat over 824 *be pleased*; steal a glance, peep, peek, take a peep; direct one's gaze, cock one's eye, cast one's eyes on, bend one's looks on, turn one's eyes on; notice, take n., look upon 455 *be attentive*; lift up one's eyes, look up; look down, look round, look behind, look in front; look ahead 858 *be cautious*; look away, drop one's eyes, avert the e., avert one's gaze 439 *be blind*; look at each other, exchange glances, make eye contact.

*scan*, scrutinize, inspect, examine, take stock of, look one up and down; contemplate, pore, pore over, post-mortem 536 *study*; look over, look through, read t., riffle t., leaf t., skim t.; have *or* take a look at, have a dekko, have a butcher's, take a shufti at, take a gander *or* a squint at, run one's eye over, give the once-over; see, go and see, take in, sight-see, rubberneck, gawp; make a pilgrimage, go to see 882 *visit*; view, survey, sweep, reconnoitre; scout, spy out the land, take a recce; peep, peek 453 *be curious*; spy, pry, snoop; observe, keep under observation, keep under surveillance, watch 457 *invigilate*; hold in view, keep in sight; watch out for, look out f. 507 *await*; keep watch, look out, keep a lookout for, keep an eye out for, keep a weather eye open for, keep cave, keep looking, keep one's eyes skinned *or* peeled; strain one's eyes, peer; squint at, squinny; crane, crane one's neck, stand on tiptoe.

**Adv.** *at sight*, at first sight, at first glance, at the first blush, prima facie; in view 443 *visibly*; in sight of; with one's eyes open.

**Int.** look!, view halloo!, land ahoy!

## 439 Blindness

**N.** *blindness*, lack of vision; lack of light 418 *darkness*; sightlessness, eyelessness, anophthalmia, microphthalmia, small eye syndrome;

eye disease, amaurosis, amblyopia, glaucoma, river blindness, cataract; night blindness, snow b., colour b.; dim-sightedness 440 *dim sight*; tunnel vision; blind eye 456 *inattention*; glass eye, artificial e.; blind man *or* woman, the blind; aid for the blind, Braille, Moon, Moon type, talking book; white stick, guide dog; unawareness 491 *ignorance*; blind side, blind spot 444 *invisibility*; word blindness, alexia, dyslexia; sandman 679 *sleep*.

**Adj.** *blind*, sightless, unsighted, eyeless, visionless, visually challenged, dark; unseeing, undiscerning, unperceiving, unnoticing, unobserving 456 *inattentive*; blinded, blindfold, blinkered; in the dark, benighted; cataractous, glaucomatous, amaurotic 440 *dim-sighted*; gravel-blind, sand-blind, stone-blind; blind as a bat, blind as a beetle, blind as a mole, blind as an owl.

**Vb.** *be blind*, not use one's eyes; go blind, lose one's sight, lose one's eyes; not see; lose sight of; grope in the dark, feel one's way 461 *be tentative*; have the eyes bandaged, be blindfolded, wear blinkers; be blind to 491 *not know*; ignore, have a blind spot, not see for looking, not see what is under one's nose; not see the wood for the trees; not look, shut the eyes to, turn a blind eye, avert the eyes, avert one's gaze, turn away the eyes, look the other way 458 *disregard*; not bear the light, blink, wink, squint 440 *be dim-sighted*.

*blind*, render b., make b., deprive of sight; put one's eyes out, gouge one's eyes o.; dazzle, daze; darken, obscure, eclipse 419 *bedim*; screen from sight; blinker, blindfold, bandage 421 *screen*; hoodwink, bluff, throw dust in one's eyes 495 *mislead*.

## 440 Dim-sightedness: imperfect vision

**N.** *dim sight*, weak s., failing s., defective eyesight, dim-sightedness, dull-sightedness; near-blindness, purblindness 439 *blindness*; half-vision, partial v., blurred v., imperfect v., defective v., impaired v.; weak eyes, eyestrain, bleariness; amblyopia, half-sight, short s., near s., near-sightedness, myopia; hypermetropia, presbyopia, long sight, far s.; double sight, double vision, confusion of v.; astigmatism; cataract, film; glaucoma, iridization; scotoma, dizziness, swimming; colour-blindness, daltonism, dichromatism; snow-blindness, day-blindness; night-blindness, nyctalopia, moon-blindness; ophthalmia, ophthalmitis; conjunctivitis, pink eye; obliquity of vision, cast; convergent vision, strabismus, squint, cross-eye; wall-eye, cock-e., swivel e.; miosis; wink, blink, nictitation, nystagmus, nervous tic; obstructed vision, eyeshade,

blinker, veil, curtain 421 *screen*; tunnel vision, blind side, blind spot 444 *invisibility*.

*visual fallacy*, anamorphosis 246 *distortion*; refraction 417 *reflection*; aberration of light 282 *deviation*; false light 552 *misrepresentation*; illusion, optical i., trick of light, trick of the eyesight, phantasm, phantasmagoria, spectre of the Brocken *or* Brocken spectre, fata morgana, mirage 542 *deception*; ignis fatuus, will-o'-the-wisp 420 *glowing thing*; phantom, spectre, wraith, apparition 970 *ghost*; vision, dream 513 *fantasy*; distorting mirror, magic m., hall of mirrors, magic lantern 442 *optical device*.

**Adj.** *dim-sighted*, purblind, half-blind, semi-b., gravel-b., dark; visually impaired, weak-eyed, bespectacled; myopic, short-sighted, near-s.; hypermetropic, presbyopic, long-sighted, far-sighted, astigmatic; colour-blind, dichromatic; dim-eyed, one-e., monocular; wall-eyed, squinting; strabismal, strabismic, cross-eyed; boss-eyed, cock-e., swivel-e., goggle-e., bug-e. 845 *blemished*; miotic, nystagmic; bleary-eyed, blinking, winking, dazzled, dazed; blinded, temporarily b. 439 *blind*; swimming, dizzy; amaurotic, cataractous, glaucomatous.

**Vb.** *be dim-sighted*, – myopic etc. adj.; not see well, see imperfectly, need spectacles, change one's glasses; have a mist before the eyes, have a film over the e., get something in one's eye; grope, peer, screw up the eyes, squint; blink, bat an eyelid; wink, nictitate, have a nervous tic; see double, grow dazzled, be blinded by, dazzle, swim; grow blurred, dim, fail; see through a glass darkly.

*blur*, render indistinct, confuse; glare, dazzle, bedazzle, blind, daze 417 *shine*; darken, dim, mist, fog, smoke, smudge 419 *bedim*; be indistinct, be hazy, loom 419 *be dim*.

## 441 Spectator

**N.** *spectator*, beholder; seer, mystic 513 *visionary*; looker, viewer, observer, watcher, invigilator; inspector, examiner, scrutator, scrutinizer, overseer 690 *manager*; waiter, attendant 742 *servant*; witness, eyewitness; attendee; passerby, bystander, onlooker; looker-on, gazer, starer, gaper, gawper, goggler; eyer, ogler, voyeur, scopophiliac, peeping Tom; window shopper; tourist, globetrotter, rubberneck, sightseer, astrotourist, space tourist 268 *traveller*; stargazer, astronomer; bird watcher, twitcher, train spotter, lookout 484 *detector*; watchman, night-w., watch, security officer, security man, sentinel, sentry, 664 *warner*; patrolman, patrol 314 *circler*; scout, spy, mole, spook, snoop 459 *detective*; filmgoer, cinemagoer 445 *cinema*; theatregoer 594 *play-*

*goer*; televiewer, viewer, TV addict, square-eyes; captive audience.

*onlookers*, audience, auditorium, sea of faces; box office, gate; house, gallery, gods, circle, dress c., pit, stalls; stadium, grandstand, terraces, the Kop; crowd, supporters, followers, aficionados, fans 707 *patron*, 504 *enthusiast*; bums on seats (inf).

**Vb.** *watch*, spectate, look on, look at, look in, view, watch television, tune in, 438 *see*; witness 189 *be present*; follow, follow with the eyes, observe, attend 455 *be attentive*; eye, ogle, give the glad eye, quiz; gape, gawk, stare; spy, spy out, scout, scout out, reconnoitre 438 *scan*.

**442 Optical instrument**

**N.** *optical device*, optical instrument; glass, crystal 422 *transparency*; optic, lens, meniscus, achromatic lens, chromatic l., astigmatic l., anastigmatic l., bifocal l.; telephoto l., zoom l., wide-angle l., fisheye l.; eyepiece, ocular, objective; sunglass, burning glass; optometer, ophthalmoscope, skiascope, retinoscope 417 *optics*; helioscope, coronagraph; prism, spectroscope, spectrometer, diffraction grating, polariscope; kaleidoscope; stroboscope; thaumatrope; stereoscope, stereopticon; photometer, light meter, exposure m., actinometer, radiometer; visual display unit, VDU 86 *computing*; projector, slide *or* film p., overhead p., epidiascope, episcope, magic lantern 445 *cinema*; microfilm reader, slide viewer 551 *photography*.

*eyeglass*, spectacles, specs, goggles, giglamps; glasses, reading g., steel-rimmed g., horn-rimmed g., pince-nez, sunglasses, dark glasses, Polaroid (tdmk) g., photochromic g., bifocal g., bifocals; thick glasses, pebble g.; contact lens, hard c. l., soft c. l.; lorgnette, monocle; magnifying glass, hand lens, loupe.

*telescope*, refractor, reflector; terrestrial telescope, achromatic t., inverting t., condé t.; astronomical t. 321 *astronomy*; collimator; sight, finder, viewfinder, rangefinder; periscope; spyglass, night glass; binoculars, prism b., field glasses, opera g.

*microscope*, electron m., photomicroscope, ultramicroscope 196 *microscopy*.

*mirror*, reflector; metal mirror, distorting m., concave m., speculum; rear-view mirror, wing m.; glass, looking g., pier g., cheval g., full-length mirror, dressing-table m., hand m.

*camera*, camera lucida, camera obscura, spectrograph 321 *astronomy*; pin-hole camera, box c., single-lens reflex c., slr, twin-lens reflex camera; hand-held c., disc c.; instant c., Polaroid (tdmk) c., digital c., digicam; cinecamera, super-8 camera; television camera, videopack, ENG, camcorder; electric eye, closed-circuit

television 484 *detector*; webcam; shutter, aperture, stop; flashgun 420 *lamp*; film 551 *photography*.

**443 Visibility**

**N.** *visibility*, perceptibility, observability; visuality, presence to the eyes 445 *appearance*; apparency, sight, exposure; distinctness, clearness, clarity, definition, conspicuity, conspicuousness, prominence; eyewitness, ocular proof, visible evidence, object lesson 522 *manifestation*; visual aid 534 *teaching*; scene, field of view, field of vision 438 *view*; atmospheric visibility, seeing, high visibility, low v., impaired v., reduced v.; limit of visibility, ceiling, horizon, skyline, visible distance, eyeshot 183 *range*; landmark, seamark 547 *signpost*; symptom.

**Adj.** *visible*, seeable, viewable; perceptible, perceivable, discernible, observable, detectable; noticeable, remarkable; recognizable, unmistakable, palpable, tangible; symptomatic 547 *indicating*; apparent 445 *appearing*; evident, showing 522 *manifest*; exposed, open, naked, outcropping, exposed to view, open to v.; sighted, in view, in full v.; before one's eyes, under one's nose, for all to see 189 *on the spot*; visible to the naked eye, macroscopic; telescopic, just visible, at the limit of vision; panoramic, stereoscopic, periscopic.

*obvious*, showing, for all to see 522 *shown*; plain, clear, clear-cut, crystal-clear, as clear as day; definite, well-defined, well-marked; distinct, unblurred, in focus; unclouded, undisguised, uncovered, unhidden; spectacular, conspicuous, pointed, prominent, salient; eye-catching, striking, shining 417 *luminous*; glaring, staring; pronounced, in bold relief, in strong r., in high r., highlighted, spotlit; visualized, vivid, eidetic; under one's nose, before one's very eyes, staring one in the face, plain to see, plain as plain, plain as a pikestaff, plain as the nose on your face.

**Vb.** *be visible*, become visible, be seen, obvious etc. adj.; show, show through, shine t. 422 *be transparent*; speak for itself, attract attention, ask to be noticed, leap to the eye 455 *attract notice*; meet the eye; hit, strike, catch the eye, stand out, act as a landmark; come to light, dawn upon; loom, heave in sight, come into view, show its face 445 *appear*; pop up, crop up, turn up, show up 295 *arrive*; spring up, start up, arise 68 *begin*; surface, break s. 308 *ascend*; emanate, come out, creep out 298 *emerge*; stick out, project 254 *jut*; show, materialize, develop; manifest itself, expose i., betray i. 522 *be plain*; symptomize 547 *indicate*; come on the stage, make one's entry, make an

entrance 297 *enter*; come forward, stand f.,
step f., advance; fill the eyes, dazzle, glare;
shine forth, break through the clouds 417
*shine*; have no secrets, live in the public eye;
remain visible, stay in sight, float before one's
eyes; make visible, expose 522 *manifest*.

**Adv.** *visibly*, clearly etc. adj.; in sight of,
before one's eyes, within eyeshot; on show, on
view.

**444 Invisibility**

**N.** *invisibility*, nonappearance 190 *absence*; vanishing 446 *disappearance*; imperceptibility,
indistinctness, vagueness, indefiniteness, poor
definition, lack of d.; poor visibility,
reduced v., obscurity 419 *dimness*; remoteness,
distance 199 *farness*; littleness, smallness 196
*minuteness*; sequestration, privacy 883 *seclusion*; submergence 523 *latency*; disguisement,
hiding 525 *concealment*; mystification, mystery
525 *secrecy*; smoke screen, mist, fog, haar, veil,
curtain 421 *obfuscation*; blind spot, blind eye
439 *blindness*; blind corner 663 *pitfall*; hidden
menace 661 *danger*; impermeability, blank wall
423 *opacity*; black light 417 *radiation*.

**Adj.** *invisible*, imperceptible, unapparent,
unnoticeable, indiscernible; indistinguishable,
unrecognizable; unseen, unsighted; viewless,
sightless; unnoticed, unregarded 458 *neglected*;
out of sight, out of range of vision, out of eyeshot 446 *disappearing*; not in sight, remote 199
*distant*; sequestered 883 *secluded*; hidden,
lurking 523 *latent*; disguised, camouflaged 525
*concealed*; shadowy, dark, secret, mysterious
421 *screened*; obscured, eclipsed, darkened,
dark 418 *unlit*.

*indistinct*, partly-seen, half-s.; unclear, ill-
defined, poorly-defined, ill-marked, undefined,
indefinite, indistinct 419 *dim*; faint, incon-
spicuous, microscopic 196 *minute*; confused,
vague, blurred, blurry, filmy, out of focus;
fuzzy, misty, hazy 424 *semitransparent*.

**Vb.** *be unseen*, lie out of sight; hide, lie low,
go to earth, go to ground, lie in ambush 523
*lurk*; escape notice, blush unseen 872 *be
humble*; become invisible, pale, fade, die 419 *be
dim*; move out of sight, be lost to view, vanish
446 *disappear*; make invisible, hide away, submerge 525 *conceal*; veil 421 *screen*; darken,
eclipse 419 *bedim*.

**Adv.** *invisibly*, silently 525 *stealthily*; behind
the scenes; in the dark.

**445 Appearance**

**N.** *appearance*, phenomenon; apparency 443
*visibility*; first appearance, first sighting, rise,
arising 68 *beginning*; becoming, realization,
materialization, embodiment, bodying forth,

presence 1 *existence*; showing, exhibition, display, view, preview, demonstration 522 *manifestation*; shadowing forth 511 *prediction*, 471
*probability*; revelation 484 *discovery*; externals,
outside, superficies 223 *exteriority*; appearances,
look of things; visual impact, face value, first
blush; impression, first impressions, effect;
image, pose, front, public face, public persona,
corporate identity, façade 541 *duplicity*; veneer,
show, seeming, semblance; side, aspect, facet;
phase, guise, garb 228 *dressing*; colour, light,
outline, shape, dimension 243 *form*; set, hang,
look; respect, light, angle, slant, point or angle
of view, spin 438 *view*; a manifestation, emanation, theophany; vision 513 *fantasy*; false
appearance, mirage, hallucination, illusion
440 *visual fallacy*; apparition, phantasm,
spectre 970 *ghost*; reflection, image, mirror i.
18 *similarity*; mental image, afterimage; likeness 551 *representation*; visual 551 *image*.

*spectacle*, impressiveness, effectiveness,
impression, effect, something to write home
about; speciousness, meretriciousness; decoration 844 *ornamentation*; feast for the eyes,
eyeful, vision, sight, scene; scenery, landscape,
seascape, cloudscape, townscape, estatescape;
panorama, bird's-eye view 438 *view*; display,
lavish d., pageantry, pageant, parade, review
875 *ostentation*; revue, extravaganza, pantomime, floor show 594 *stage show*; television,
video 531 *broadcasting*; illuminations, son et
lumière; pyrotechnics 420 *fireworks*; presentation, show, demonstration, exhibition, exposition 522 *exhibit*; art exhibition 553 *picture*;
visual entertainment, in-flight e., peep show,
slide s., film s., picture s., home movies; phantasmagoria, kaleidoscope 437 *variegation*; panorama, diorama, cyclorama; staging, tableau,
transformation scene; set, decor, setting, backcloth, background, scenario 594 *stage set*.

*cinema*, cinematography; big screen, silver s.,
Hollywood, Bollywood, film industry; film
studio, film production, film-making, shooting
551 *photography*; direction, continuity, editing,
cutting, montage, projection; photoplay,
screenplay, scenario, script, shooting s.;
credits, titles; special effects, animation, claymation, animatronics, anime, hentai, H-anime;
voiceover, sound effects, soundtrack; cinemato-
graph, projector 442 *optical device*; cinema complex, multiplex or multiplex cinema, picture
house, picture palace, circuit cinema,
drive-in c., nickelodeon, bioscope,
cinematheque, flea pit 594 *theatre*; film
director, film star 594 *actor*; filmgoer, cineast
504 *enthusiast*.

*film*, films, pictures, motion p., moving p.,
movies, flicks, celluloid; cut, director's cut,

rough cut; Technicolor (tdmk), 3-D, Cinerama (tdmk), Cinemascope (tdmk); silent film, sound f., talkie; 15, 18, PG, U; big picture, B p., B movie, supporting film, short, newsreel, trailer; cartoon, animated c., toon, anime, hentai, H-anime; travelogue, documentary, docu-drama, feature film, cinéma vérité; art film, new wave, nouvelle vague; epic, blockbuster, extravaganza, musical, box-office movie, low-budget m.; weepie, creepie, bodice-ripper, thriller, spine-chiller, cliffhanger, war film, horror f., Hammer (tdmk) f., splatter movie, snuff m., snuff film, blue movie, skin-flick, chick f., biopic; Western, spaghetti w., horse opera, cop o., space o., space odyssey; oldie, remake; rush, preview; general release.

*mien*, look, face; play of feature, expression; brow, countenance, looks; complexion, colour, cast; air, demeanour, carriage, bearing, deportment; poise, presence; gesture, posture, behaviour 688 *conduct*.

*feature*, trait, mark, lineament; lines, cut, shape, fashion, figure 243 *form*; outline, contour, relief, elevation, profile, silhouette; visage, physiognomy, cut of one's jib 237 *face*.

**Adj.** *appearing*, apparent, phenomenal; seeming, specious, ostensible; deceptive 542 *deceiving*; outward, external, superficial 223 *exterior*; salient, outcropping, showing, on view 443 *visible*; visual, video-; showing, open to view, exhibited, hung 522 *shown*; impressive, effective, spectacular 875 *showy*; decorative, meretricious 844 *ornamental*; showing itself, revealed, theophanic 522 *manifest*; visionary, dreamlike 513 *imaginary*.

**Vb.** *appear*, show, show through 443 *be visible*; seem, look so 18 *resemble*; have the look of, have an air of, wear the look of, present the appearance of, exhibit the form of, assume the guise of, take the shape of; figure in, display oneself, cut a figure 875 *be ostentatious*; be on show, be on exhibition; be showing; appear on television, star in; exhibit 522 *manifest*; start,

rise, arise; dawn, break 68 *begin*; eventuate 154 *happen*; materialize, pop up 295 *arrive*; walk 970 *haunt*.

**Adv.** *apparently*, manifestly, distinctly 443 *visibly*; ostensibly, seemingly, to all appearances, as it seems, as far as the eye could tell, to the eye, at first sight, at first blush; on the face of it, at face value; to the view, in the eyes of; on view, on show, on exhibition.

## 446 Disappearance

**N.** *disappearance*, loss, vanishing; disappearing trick, vanishing t., escapology 542 *sleight*; flight 667 *escape*; exit 296 *departure*; evanescence, evaporation 338 *vaporization*; disembodiment, dematerialization, dissipation, dissolution 51 *decomposition*; extinction 2 *nonexistence*; occultation, eclipse 418 *obscuration*; dissolving views, fadeout; vanishing point, thin air (see quotation at 2 *pass away*) 444 *invisibility*.

**Adj.** *disappearing*, vanishing; evanescent 114 *transient*; dissipated, dispersed; missing, vanished 190 *absent*; lost, lost to sight, lost to view 444 *invisible*; gone to earth, gone to ground 525 *concealed*; gone 2 *extinct*.

**Vb.** *disappear*, vanish, do the vanishing trick; dematerialize, 'melt into thin air' (see quotation at 2 *pass away*); evanesce, evaporate 338 *vaporize*; dissolve, melt, melt away 337 *liquefy*; wear away, wear off, dwindle, dwindle to vanishing point 37 *decrease*; fade, fade out, pale 426 *lose colour*; fade away 114 *be transient*; be occulted, suffer an eclipse 419 *be dim*; disperse, dissipate, diffuse, scatter 75 *be dispersed*; absent oneself, fail to appear, play truant, take French leave, go AWOL 190 *be absent*; go, be gone, depart 296 *decamp*; run away, get a. 667 *escape*; hide, lie low, be in hiding 523 *lurk*; cover one's tracks, leave no trace 525 *conceal*; sink from view, be lost to sight 444 *be unseen*; retire from view, seclude oneself 883 *seclude*; become extinct 2 *pass away*; make disappear, erase, dispel 550 *obliterate*.

# Intellect: the exercise of the mind

## 4.1
## Formation of ideas

SECTION ONE

### General

**447 Intellect**
**N.** *intellect*, mind, psyche, mentality; affect 817
*affections*; conation 595 *will*; understanding,
intellection, conception; thinking principle,
powers of thought, intellectual faculty, cogitative f.; rationality, reasoning power; reason,
discursive r., association of ideas 475 *reasoning*;
philosophy 449 *thought*; awareness, sense, consciousness, self-c., stream of c. 455 *attention*;
cognition, perception, apperception, percipi-
ence, insight; extrasensory perception, ESP,
instinct, sixth sense 476 *intuition*; flair, judgment 463 *discrimination*; intellectualism, intel-
lectuality; mental capacity, brains, wits, senses,
sense, grey matter, IQ, intelligence quotient,
mind sorts 498 *intelligence*; great intellect,
genius; mental evolution, psychogenesis; seat
of thought, organ of t., brain, cerebrum, cer-
ebellum, cortex 213 *head*; electroencephalo-
graph, EEG, brain scan; alpha waves;
sensorium 818 *feeling*; healthy mind 502
*sanity*; diseased mind 503 *personality disorder*;
mind over matter 984 *occultism*.

*spirit*, soul, geist, mind, inner m., inner
sense, inner·being; heart, heart's core, breast,
bosom, inner man 5 *essential part*; double, ka,
ba, genius 80 *self*; psyche, pneuma, id, ego,
superego, animus, anima, self, subliminal s.,
the unconscious, the subconscious; personality, dual p., multiple p., split p. 503 *personality disorder*; spiritualism, spiritism,
psychomancy, psychical research 984
*occultism*; spiritualist, occultist.

*psychology*, science of mind, metapsych-
ology; parapsychology 984 *psychics*; abnormal
psychology; Freudian psychology, Jungian p.,
Adlerian p.; Gestalt psychology, configuration
theory; behaviourism; crowd psychology; personality testing, psychometry 459 *enquiry*; pro-
filing, psychological p.; psychopathology,
psychiatry, antipsychiatry, psychotherapy, psychodrama, psychoanalysis, cognitive therapy,
cognitive behaviour *or* behavioural t., neurolinguistic programming 658 *therapy*; self-analysis,
enneagram; psychosurgery 658 *surgery*; psycho-
physiology, psychobiology, psychophysics,
psycholinguistics.

*psychologist*, psychoanalyst, psychiatrist, psy-
chotherapist 658 *doctor*; analyst, head shrinker,
shrink, trick cyclist; profiler; sports psychologist.

**Adj.** *mental*, thinking, endowed with reason,
reasoning 475 *rational*; cerebral, intellective,
intellectual, conceptive, noological, noetic,
conceptual, abstract; theoretical 512 *suppositional*; unconcrete 320 *immaterial*; perceptual,
percipient, perceptive; cognitive, cognizant
490 *knowing*; conscious, self-c., subjective.

*psychic*, psychological; psychogenic, psychosomatic; subconscious, subliminal; spiritualistic, mediumistic, psychomantic 984
*psychical*; spiritual, otherworldly 320
*immaterial*.

**Vb.** *cognize*, perceive, apperceive 490 *know*;
realize, sense, become aware of, become conscious of; objectify 223 *externalize*; note 438
*see*; advert, mark 455 *notice*; ratiocinate 475
*reason*; use one's head, understand 498 *be wise*;
conceptualize, intellectualize 449 *think*; conceive, invent 484 *discover*; ideate 513 *imagine*;
appreciate 480 *estimate*.

**448 Absence of intellect**
**N.** *absence of intellect*, unintelligence; brute creation 365 *animality*; vegetation 366 *vegetable
life*; inanimate nature, stocks and stones;
instinct, brute i. 476 *intuition*; unreason 449
*thought*; vacuity, brainlessness, mindlessness
450 *absence of thought*; brain damage, dis-

ordered intellect, unsound mind, insanity 503 *mental disorder*.

**Adj.** *mindless*, unintelligent; animal, vegetable; mineral, inanimate 359 *inorganic*; unreasoning 450 *unthinking*; instinctive, brute 476 *intuitive*; unoriginal, uninventive, unidea'd 20 *imitative*; brainless, empty-headed, vacuous 499 *foolish*; moronic, wanting 503 *mentally disordered*.

## 449 Thought

**N.** *thought*, mental process, thinking, thought processes; mental act, ideation; intellectual exercise, mental e., mental action, mentation, cogitation 447 *intellect*; cerebration, lucubration, headwork, thinking cap; brainwork, brainfag; hard thinking, hard thought, concentrated t., concentration 455 *attention*; deep thought, profound t., depth of t., profundity 498 *wisdom*; abstract thought, imageless t.; conceptual thinking, thoughts, ideas 451 *idea*; conception, ideation, workings of the mind, inmost thoughts 513 *ideality*; flow of ideas, current of thought, train of t.; association of ideas, reason 475 *reasoning*; brown study, deep thought, reverie, musing, wandering thoughts 456 *abstractedness*; thinking out, excogitation (see also *meditation*); intellectual suicide, unreason, 'believing six impossible things before breakfast';

> There is no use trying, said Alice; one can't believe impossible things.
> I dare say you haven't had much practice, said the Queen. When I was your age, I always did it for half an hour a day. Why, sometimes I've believed as many as six impossible things before breakfast.
> Lewis Carroll, *Through the Looking-Glass*

invention, inventiveness 513 *imagination*; second thoughts, afterthought, reconsideration 67 *sequel*; retrospection, hindsight, wisdom after the event 505 *memory*; mature thought 669 *preparation*; forethought, forward planning, prudence 510 *foresight*; thought transference, telepathy 984 *psychics*.

*meditation*, thoughtfulness, speculation 459 *enquiry*; lateral thinking; reflection, deep r., deep thought, brooding, rumination, consideration, pondering; contemplation 438 *inspection*; absorption, pensiveness; introspection, self-absorption, self-communing, navel-gazing; transcendental meditation, TM, yogic flying; religious contemplation, retreat, mysticism 979 *piety*; deliberation, taking counsel 691 *advice*; excogitation, thinking out, thinking through 480 *judgment*; examination, close study, concentration, application 536 *study*.

*philosophy*, ontology, teleology, metaphysics, ethics; speculation, philosophical thought, abstract t., systematic t.; scientific thought, science, natural philosophy; philosophical doctrine, philosophical system, philosophical theory 512 *supposition*; school of philosophy 485 *opinion*; monism, dualism, pluralism; idealism, subjective i., objective i., conceptualism, transcendentalism; phenomenalism, phenomenology, realism, nominalism, positivism, logical p., analytic philosophy, linguistic philosophy 475 *reasoning*; epistemology, intuitionism 490 *knowledge*; philosophy of existence, Existenzphilosophie, existentialism; voluntarism; determinism, mechanism; vitalism; holism, organicism, structuralism, functionalism, reductionism, reductivism; rationalism, humanism, hedonism, eudaemonism; utilitarianism, materialism; empiricism, probabilism, pragmatism; relativism, relativity; agnosticism, scepticism, irrationalism 486 *doubt*; eclecticism; atheism 974 *irreligion*; nihilism, fatalism 596 *fate*; Pythagoreanism, Platonism, Aristotelianism; Pyrrhonism, Scepticism, Cynicism, Epicureanism, Stoicism; gnosticism, Neo-Platonism; scholasticism, Thomism, Neo-T.; Cartesianism, Hegelianism, Neo-H., Kantianism, Neo-K., Spinozism; dialectical materialism, Marxism; anthroposophy, theosophy; Buddhism, Confucianism, Hinduism, Sufism, yoga, Zen 973 *religion*, 973 *religious faith*.

*philosopher*, thinker, man *or* woman of thought 492 *intellectual*; metaphysician, existentialist etc. (see also *philosophy*); school of philosophers, Eleatics, Peripatetics, Academy, Garden, Porch, Lyceum; Diogenes 945 *ascetic*.

**Adj.** *thoughtful*, conceptive, speculative (see also *philosophic*); cogitative, deliberative; full of thought, pensive, meditative, ruminant, ruminative, contemplative, reflective; self-communing, introspective; wrapt in thought, lost in t., deep in t.; absorbed 455 *obsessed*; musing, dreaming, day-dreaming, dreamy 456 *abstracted*; concentrating, concentrated 455 *attentive*; studying 536 *studious*; thoughtful for others, considerate 901 *philanthropic*; prudent 510 *foreseeing*.

*philosophic*, metaphysical, ontological, speculative, abstract, conceptual, systematic, rational, logical.

**Vb.** *think*, ween, trow 512 *suppose*; conceive, form ideas, ideate; fancy 513 *imagine*; devote thought to, bestow thought upon, think about, ponder, cogitate (see also *meditate*); employ one's mind, use one's brain, put on one's thinking cap, use one's grey matter; concentrate, collect one's thoughts, pull one's wits together 455 *be attentive*; bend the mind, apply the m., trouble one's head about, lucubrate, cerebrate, mull, mull over, puzzle over, work over, hammer out 536 *study*; think hard, beat one's brains, cudgel one's b., rack one's b., worry at; think through, reason out 475 *reason*; think out, think up, excogitate, invent 484 *discover*; devise 623 *plan*; take into one's head, entertain a notion, harbour a n., have a sudden fancy, have an idea, toy with an i., kick an i. around; cherish an i. 485 *believe*; become obsessed, get a bee in one's bonnet, have a hang-up about 481 *be biased*; bear in mind, take account of, be mindful, think on 505 *remember*.

*meditate*, ruminate, chew the cud, chew over, digest; wonder about, debate, enquire into 459 *enquire*; reflect, contemplate, study; speculate, philosophize, theorize; intellectualize, cerebrate 447 *cognize*; think about, consider, take into account, take into consideration; take stock of, ponder, cogitate, weigh 480 *estimate*; think over, turn o., revolve, run over in the mind 505 *memorize*; bethink oneself, reconsider, review, reexamine, have second thoughts, have an afterthought, think better of; take counsel, advise with, consult one's pillow, sleep on it 691 *consult*; commune with oneself, introspect; brood, brood upon, muse, fall into a brown study; go into retreat.

*dawn upon*, occur to, flash on the mind, cross the m., come to m.; come into one's head, come to one in a blinding flash, strike one; suggest itself, present itself to the mind.

*cause thought*, provoke *or* challenge t., make one think, make one stop and think, make an impression 821 *impress*; penetrate, sink in, fasten on the mind, become an idée fixe, become a hang-up, obsess 481 *bias*.

*engross*, absorb, preoccupy, monopolize; engross one's thoughts, be never out of one's thoughts, run in one's head, go round and round in one's head, occupy the mind, fill the m., be uppermost in one's mind, come first in one's thoughts; prey on one's mind, haunt, obsess 481 *bias*; fascinate 983 *bewitch*.

**Adv.** *in mind*, on one's mind, on the brain; under consideration; taking into consideration, bearing in mind, all things considered, taking into account, all in all; on reflection, on consideration, on second thoughts, after due thought *or* consideration; come to think of it, now that you mention it.

**450 Absence of thought**
**N.** *absence of thought*, inability to think 448 *absence of intellect*; blank mind, fallow m. 491 *ignorance*; vacancy, abstraction 456 *abstractedness*; inanity, vacuity, blankness, fatuity,

empty head 499 *unintelligence*; lack of thought, thoughtlessness 456 *inattention*; conditioned reflex, automatism; knee-jerk response, gut reaction; instinctiveness, instinct 476 *intuition*; stocks and stones.

**Adj.** *unthinking*, unreflecting, unphilosophic, unintellectual 448 *mindless*; incapable of thought, idealess, unidea'd, unimaginative, uninventive 20 *imitative*; automatic, instinctive 476 *intuitive*; blank, vacant, vacuous, empty-headed 190 *empty*; incogitant, not thinking 456 *inattentive*; unoccupied, relaxed; thoughtless, inconsiderate 932 *selfish*; irrational 477 *illogical*; dull-witted, stolid, stupid, block-like, wanting 499 *unintelligent*; inanimate, animal, vegetable, mineral.

*unthought*, unthought of, inconceivable, incogitable, unconsidered, undreamt, not to be thought of, not to be dreamt of 470 *impossible*.

**Vb.** *not think*, not reflect; leave the mind fallow *or* unoccupied, leave one's mind uncultivated 491 *not know*; be blank, be vacant; not think of, put out of one's mind, dismiss from one's thoughts, laugh off 458 *disregard*; dream, daydream, indulge in reveries 456 *be inattentive*; go by instinct, play it by ear 476 *intuit*; think wrongly 481 *misjudge*.

**451 Idea**
**N.** *idea*, noumenon, notion, abstraction, a thought; object of thought, abstract idea, concept; mere idea, theory 512 *supposition*; percept, image, mental i.; Platonic idea, archetype 23 *prototype*; conception, perception, apprehension 447 *intellect*; reflection, observation 449 *thought*; impression, conceit, fancy 513 *imagination*; product of imagination, figment, fiction; associated ideas, complex; stream of consciousness, free association of ideas; invention, brain-child; brain wave, happy thought 484 *discovery*; wheeze, wrinkle, device 623 *contrivance*; what one thinks, view, point of v., slant, way of thinking, attitude 485 *opinion*; principle, leading idea, main idea; one idea, idée fixe, obsession, hang-up 481 *prejudgment*.

**Adj.** *ideational*, conceptual 449 *thoughtful*; theoretical 512 *suppositional*; notional, ideal 513 *imaginary*.

**452 Topic**
**N.** *topic*, subject of thought, food for t., mental pabulum; gossip, rumour 529 *news*; subject matter, subject; contents, chapter, section, head, main h. 53 *subdivision*; what it is about, argument, plot, theme, message; text, commonplace, burden, motif; musical topic, statement, leitmotiv 412 *musical piece*; concern,

interest, human i.; matter, affair, situation 8 *circumstance*; shop 622 *business*; topic for discussion, business on hand, agenda, any other business, AOB, order paper 623 *policy*; item on the agenda, motion 761 *request*; resolution 480 *judgment*; problem, problematics, headache 459 *question*; heart of the question, gist, drift, pith; theorem, proposition 512 *supposition*; thesis, case, point 475 *argument*; issue, moot point, debatable p., point at issue; field, field of enquiry, field of study 536 *study*.

**Adj.** *topical*, thematic; challenging, thought-provoking; mooted, debatable 474 *uncertain*; thought about, uppermost in the mind, fit for consideration, worthy of discussion.

**Adv.** *in question*, in the mind, on the brain, in one's thoughts; on foot, afoot, on the tapis, on the agenda, on the table; before the house, before the committee, under consideration, under discussion.

SECTION TWO

## Precursory conditions and operations

**453 Curiosity: desire for knowledge**

**N.** *curiosity*, intellectual c., speculativeness, enquiring mind, thirst *or* itch for knowledge 536 *study*; interest, itch, inquisitiveness, curiousness; zeal, meddlesomeness, officiousness, nosiness 678 *overactivity*; wanting to know; asking questions, quizzing 459 *question*; sightseeing, rubbernecking, thirst for travel 267 *land travel*; morbid curiosity, ghoulishness; voyeurism 951 *impurity*.

*inquisitive person*, examiner, cross-e., inquisitor, interrogator, questioner, enfant terrible 459 *enquirer*; nosy parker, stickybeak; busybody, gossip 678 *meddler*; newshound, gossip columnist, chequebook journalist 529 *news reporter*; seeker, searcher, explorer, experimentalist 461 *experimenter*; sightseer, globetrotter, rubberneck, gawper 441 *spectator*; snoop, snooper, spy, spoof, mole 459 *detective*; eavesdropper, interceptor, phonetapper 415 *listener*; Paul Pry, Peeping Tom; little pitchers, walls have ears.

**Adj.** *inquisitive*, curious, interested; speculating, searching, seeking, avid for knowledge, hungry for information 536 *studious*; morbidly curious, ghoulish, prurient; newsmongering, hungering for news, agog, all ears 455 *attentive*; wanting to know, burning with curiosity, consumed with c., eaten up with c.; itching, hungry for; overcurious, nosy, snoopy, prying, spying, peeping, peeking; questioning, inquisitorial 459 *enquiring*; meddlesome, interfering, officious 678 *meddling*.

**Vb.** *be curious*, want to know, only want to know; seek, look for 459 *search*; test, research 461 *experiment*; feel a concern, be interested, take an interest; show interest, show curiosity, prick up one's ears, be all agog 455 *be attentive*; mosey around, dip into; dig up, nose out, pick up news; peep, peek, spy 438 *scan*; snoop, pry, nose into 459 *enquire*; eavesdrop, tap the line, intercept, bug, listen, listen in, eavesdrop 415 *hear*; poke *or* stick one's nose in, be nosy, interfere, act the busybody 678 *meddle*; ask questions, quiz, question, bombard with questions 459 *interrogate*; look, stare, stand and stare, gape, gawk 438 *gaze*.

**Int.** well?, what news?, what's going on?, what's up?, who?, what?, where?, when?, how?, why?, why on earth?

**454 Incuriosity**

**N.** *incuriosity*, lack of interest, lack of curiosity, incuriousness, no questions, mental inertia; uninterest, unconcern, no interest, insouciance 860 *indifference*; apathy, phlegmatism 820 *moral insensibility*; adiaphorism, indifferentism; blunted curiosity 863 *satiety*.

**Adj.** *incurious*, uninquisitive, unreflecting 450 *unthinking*; without interest, uninterested; aloof, distant; blasé, unadmiring 865 *unastonished*; wearied, apathetic 838 *bored*; unconcerned, uninvolved 860 *indifferent*; listless, inert, apathetic 820 *impassive*.

**Vb.** *be incurious*, – indifferent etc. adj.; have no curiosity, not think about, take no interest 456 *be inattentive*; feel no concern, couldn't care less, not trouble oneself, not bother with 860 *be indifferent*; mind one's own business, go one's own way 820 *be insensitive*; see nothing, hear n., look the other way 458 *disregard*.

**455 Attention**

**N.** *attention*, notice, regard 438 *look*; consideration 449 *thought*; heed, alertness, readiness, attentiveness, solicitude, observance 457 *carefulness*; observation, watchfulness, vigilance, eyes on, watch, guard, invigilation 457 *surveillance*; wariness, circumspection 858 *caution*; contemplation, introspection 449 *meditation*; intentness, earnestness, seriousness 599 *resolution*; undivided attention, whole a.; whole mind, concentration, application, studiousness, close study 536 *study*; examination, scrutiny, checkup, review 438 *inspection*; close attention, minute a., meticulousness, attention to detail, particularity, minuteness, finicalness, pernicketiness, pedantry 494 *accuracy*; diligent attention, diligence, pains, trouble 678 *assiduity*; exclusive attention, rapt a.; single-mindedness; absorption, preoccupation, brown study, attention deficit disorder, attention-deficit hyperactive disorder, ADHD 456 *inattention*; interest, inquisitive attention 453 *curiosity*; one-track mind, fixation, obsession, hang-up, monomania 503 *personality disorder*.

**Adj.** *attentive*, intent, diligent, assiduous 678 *industrious*; considerate, caring, thoughtful 884 *courteous*; heedful, mindful, regardful 457 *careful*; alert, ready, ready for anything, on one's toes, on the qui vive, on the ball, with it; open-eyed, waking, wakeful, awake, wide-a.; awake to, alive to, sensing 819 *sensitive*; aware, conscious, thinking 449 *thoughtful*; observant, sharp-eyed, observing, watching, watchful 457 *vigilant*; attending, rapt, paying attention, missing nothing; all eyes, all agog 438 *seeing*; all ears, prick-eared; all attention, undistracted, concentrating, deep in; serious, earnest; eager to learn 536 *studious*; close, minute, nice, meticulous, particular, pernickety, punctilious 494 *accurate*; finical, pedantic 862 *fastidious*; on the watch, on the lookout 507 *expectant*.

*obsessed*, interested, overinterested, overcurious 453 *inquisitive*; single-minded, possessed, engrossed, preoccupied, wrapped up in, taken up with, into, hooked on, addicted to, hung up; rapt, enthralled, spellbound; haunted by 854 *fearing*; monomaniacal 503 *crazy*.

**Vb.** *be attentive*, attend, give attention, pay a.; look to, heed, pay h., take notice of, mind 457 *be careful*; trouble oneself, care, take trouble, take pains, put oneself out for, bother 682 *exert oneself*; listen, prick up one's ears, sit up, sit up and take notice; take seriously, fasten on 638 *make important*; devote or give one's attention to, give one's mind to, bend the mind to, direct one's thoughts to 449 *think*; think of nothing else, be obsessed with, be preoccupied with 481 *be biased*; keep one's eye on the ball, concentrate, miss nothing; watch, be all eyes, be all agog 438 *gaze*; be all ears, drink in, hang on the lips of 415 *hear*; focus one's mind on, rivet one's attention to, concentrate on, fix on; examine, inspect, scrutinize, vet, review, pass under review, post-mortem 438 *scan*; overhaul, revise 654 *make better*; study closely, pore, mull, read, reread, digest 536 *study*; pay some attention, browse through, dip into, flip through, flick t., flick over the leaves, glance at, leaf through, look into, skim, skim-read, turn the pages.

*be mindful*, keep in mind, bear in m., have in m., be thinking of 505 *remember*; not forget, think of, spare a thought for, regard, look on 438 *see*; lend an ear to 415 *hear*; take care of, see to 457 *look after*; have regard to, have an eye to, keep in sight, keep in view 617 *intend*; not lose sight of, keep track of 619 *pursue*.

*notice*, note, take n., register; mark, recognize, spot; take cognizance of, take into consideration, take into account, review, reconsider 449 *meditate*; take account of, consider, weigh 480 *judge*; comment upon, remark on, talk about 584 *converse*; mention, just m., mention in passing, refer to en passant, touch on 524 *hint*; recall, revert to, hark back 106 *repeat*; think worthy of attention, have time for, spare time f., find time f.; deign to notice, acknowledge, salute 884 *greet*.

*attract notice*, draw the attention, hold the a., engage the a., focus the a., rivet the a., be the cynosure of all eyes, draw the crowds, cut a figure 875 *be ostentatious*; stick out like a sore thumb, arouse notice, arrest one's n., strike one's n.; interest 821 *impress*; excite attention, invite a., claim a., demand a., meet with a.; catch the eye, fall under observation 443 *be visible*; make one see, bring to one's notice *or* attention 522 *show*; bring forward, call attention to, advertise, publicize 528 *publish*; lay the finger on, point the finger, point out, point to, show 547 *indicate*; stress, underline 532 *emphasize*; occupy, keep guessing 612 *tempt*; fascinate, haunt, monopolize, obsess 449 *engross*; alert, warn 665 *raise the alarm*; call to attention 737 *command*.

**Int.** see!, mark!, lo!, ecce!, behold!, lo and behold!, look!, look here!, look out!, look alive!, look to it!, hark!, oyez!, hey!, mind out!, nota bene, NB, take notice!, warning!, cave!, achtung!, take care!, watch out!, watch your step!

### 456 Inattention

**N.** *inattention*, inadvertence, forgetfulness 506 *oblivion*; oversight, aberration; lapse 495 *error*; lack of interest, lack of observation 454 *incuriosity*; aloofness, detachment, unconcern, apathy 860 *indifference*; nonobservance, disregard 458 *negligence*; thoughtlessness, heedlessness 857 *rashness*; lack of thought, carelessness, inconsiderateness 481 *misjudgment*, 932 *selfishness*; aimlessness, desultoriness 282 *deviation*; superficiality, flippancy 212 *shallowness*; étourderie, dizziness, giddiness, light-mindedness, levity, volatility 604 *caprice*; deaf ears 416 *deafness*; unseeing eyes, blind spot, blind side, tunnel vision 439 *blindness*; diversion, distraction, dust in the eyes, wild-goose chase, red herring 612 *inducement*; attention deficit disorder, attention-deficit hyperactive disorder, ADHD, absent-mindedness, wandering wits 450 *absence of thought*; stargazer, daydreamer, woolgatherer, head in the clouds, Johnny-head-in-air, Walter Mitty; scatterbrain, grasshopper mind, butterfly.

*abstractedness*, abstraction, absent-mindedness, wandering attention, absence of mind; woolgathering, daydreaming, stargazing, doodling; fit of abstraction, deep musing, deep thought, reverie, brown study; distraction, preoccupation, divided attention.

**Adj.** *inattentive*, careless 458 *negligent*; off one's guard, with one's trousers *or* pants down 508 *off guard*; unobservant, unnoticing 454 *incurious*; unseeing 439 *blind*; unhearing 416 *deaf*; undiscerning 464 *indiscriminating*; unmindful, unheeding, inadvertent, not thinking, unreflecting 450 *unthinking*; not concentrating, half asleep, only half awake; uninterested 860 *indifferent*; apathetic, unaware 820 *impassive*; oblivious 506 *forgetful*; inconsiderate, thoughtless, tactless, heedless, without consideration, regardless 857 *rash*; cavalier, offhand, cursory, superficial 212 *shallow*.

*abstracted*, distrait(e), absent-minded, absent, far away, not there, not with it, miles away; lost, lost in thought, wrapped in t., rapt, absorbed, in the clouds, with one's head in the c., stargazing; bemused, sunk in a brown study, deep in reverie, pensive, dreamy, dreaming, daydreaming, mooning, woolgathering; nodding, napping, cat-napping, half-awake 679 *sleepy*.

*distracted*, preoccupied, engrossed; otherwise engaged, with divided attention; diverted 282 *deviating*; dazed, dazzled, disconcerted, put out, put out of one's stride, put off, put off one's stroke; rattled, unnerved 854 *nervous*.

*light-minded*, unfixed, unconcentrated, wandering, desultory, trifling; frivolous, flippant, insouciant, light-headed; airy, volatile, mercurial, bird-witted, flighty, giddy, dizzy, écervelé(e); grasshopper-minded, scatty, scatterbrained, harebrained, featherbrained; wild, romping, harum-scarum, rantipole; addled, brain-sick 503 *crazy*; inconstant, to one thing constant never 604 *capricious*.

**Vb.** *be inattentive*, not attend, pay no attention, pay no heed, not listen, hear nothing, see n.; close one's eyes, turn a blind eye 439 *be blind*; stop one's ears 416 *be deaf*; not register, not notice, not use one's eyes; not hear the penny drop, not get the message, not click, not catch; overlook, commit an oversight 495 *blunder*; be off one's guard, be caught with one's trousers *or* pants down, let the cat out of the bag, let slip, be caught out, catch oneself o., catch oneself doing; lose track of, lose sight of; not remember 506 *forget*; dream, drowse, catnap, nod 679 *sleep*; not concentrate, trifle, play at, toy with; be abstracted, moider, moither, wander, let one's thoughts

wander, let one's mind w., let one's wits go bird-nesting, go woolgathering, indulge in reverie, build castles in Spain, build castles in the air 513 *imagine*; fall into a brown study, muse, be lost in thought, moon, stargaze, have one's head in the clouds; idle, doodle 679 *be inactive*; be distracted, digress, lose the thread, lose the train of thought, fluff one's lines 282 *stray*; be disconcerted, be rattled 854 *be nervous*; be put off, be put off one's stroke, be put out of one's stride 702 *hinder* (see also *distract*); disregard, ignore 458 *neglect*; have no time for, think nothing of, think little of 922 *hold cheap*.

*distract*, call away, divert, divert one's attention; make forget, put out one's head, drive out of one's mind; entice, throw a sop to Cerberus 612 *tempt*; confuse, muddle 63 *derange*; disturb, interrupt 72 *discontinue*; disconcert, upset, perplex, discompose, hassle, fluster, bother, flurry, rattle 318 *agitate*; put one off his stroke 702 *obstruct*; daze, dazzle 439 *blind*; bewilder, flummox, throw off the scent, draw a red herring 474 *puzzle*; fuddle, addle 503 *make mad*.

*escape notice*, escape attention, blush unseen, be overlooked 523 *lurk*; fall on deaf ears, pass over one's head, meet a blind spot, not click; not hold the attention, go in at one ear and out at the other, slip one's memory 506 *be forgotten*.

**Adv.** *inadvertently*, per incuriam, by oversight, by accident, accidentally; in an unguarded moment, inattentively, rashly, giddily, gaily, lightheartedly.

## 457 Carefulness

**N.** *carefulness*, mindfulness, attentiveness, diligence, pains 678 *assiduity*; heed, care, utmost c. 455 *attention*; anxiety, solicitude 825 *worry*; loving care 897 *benevolence*; tidiness, orderliness, neatness 60 *order*; attention to detail, thoroughness, meticulousness, minuteness, circumstantiality, particularity; nicety, exactness, exactitude 494 *accuracy*; overnicety, pedantry, perfectionism 862 *fastidiousness*; conscience, scruples, scrupulosity 929 *probity*; vigilance, wakefulness, watchfulness, alertness, readiness 669 *preparedness*; circumspection, prudence, wariness 858 *caution*; forethought 510 *foresight*.

*surveillance*, an eye on, eyes on, watching, guarding, watch and ward, neighbourhood watch, home w. 660 *protection*; houseminding, homesitting, caretaking; vigilance, invigilation, inspection; babysitting, childminding, chaperonage; lookout, weather eye, Hoolivan, electronic surveillance; vigil, watch, death-watch; doomwatch; guard, sentry-go; eyes of

Argus, taskmaster's eye, watchful e., unsleeping e., lidless e. 438 *eye*.

*carer*, nurse, district nurse 658 *nurse*; care assistant, home help, granny-sitter, buddy; baby-sitter, childminder; house-sitter, home-sitter; cat-sitter, dog-sitter, pet-sitter.

*guard*, sentry, sentinel 660 *protector*, 749 *keeper*.

**Adj.** *careful*, thoughtful, considerate, considered, mindful, regardful, heedful 455 *attentive*; taking care, painstaking; solicitous, anxious; cautious, afraid to touch; loving, tender; conscientious, scrupulous, honest 929 *honourable*; diligent, assiduous 678 *industrious*; thorough, thorough-going; meticulous, minute, particular, circumstantial; nice, exact 494 *accurate*; pedantic, overcareful, perfectionist 862 *fastidious*; tidy, neat, clean 60 *orderly*; minding the pence, balancing the books, penurious, miserly 816 *parsimonious*.

*vigilant*, alert, ready 669 *prepared*; on the alert, on guard, on the qui vive, on one's toes; keeping cave, watching, watchful, wakeful, wide-awake; observant, sharp-eyed; all eyes, open-eyed, Argus-e., eagle-e. 438 *seeing*; prudent, provident, far-sighted 510 *foreseeing*; sure-footed, picking one's steps; circumspect, guarded, wary, looking before and after 858 *cautious*.

**Vb.** *be careful*, reck, mind, heed, beware 455 *be attentive*; take precautions, think twice, think things through, check, recheck 858 *be cautious*; be on the qui vive, be on the alert, have one's eyes open, have one's wits about one, keep a lookout, keep cave, look before and after, look right then left, mind one's step, watch one's s., mind how one goes; pick one's steps, feel one's way 461 *be tentative*; be on one's guard, mind one's Ps and Qs; mind one's business; count one's money, balance the books, have regard to the bottom line, look after the pence 814 *economize*; tidy, keep t. 62 *arrange*; take a pride in, take pains, do with care, be meticulous, dot one's i's and cross one's t's; try, do one's best 682 *exert oneself*.

*look after*, look to, see to, take care of, caretake, act as houseminder, homesit 689 *manage*; take charge of, accept responsibility for; care for, mind, tend, keep 660 *safeguard*; sit up with, baby-sit, childmind; nurse, foster, take into care, cherish 889 *pet*; have regard for, treat gently 920 *respect*; keep an eye on, keep a sharp eye on, keep tabs on, monitor; escort, chaperon, play gooseberry; serve 703 *minister to*.

*invigilate*, stay awake, sit up; take part in a wake, keep vigil, watch; stand sentinel; keep watch, keep watch and ward; look out, keep a sharp lookout, watch out for; keep one's wits about one, keep one's eyes peeled, keep one's weather-eye open, sleep with one eye o., keep one's ear to the ground; mount guard, set watch, post sentries, stand to 660 *safeguard*.

**Adv.** *carefully*, attentively, diligently; studiously, thoroughly; lovingly, tenderly; painfully, anxiously; with care, gingerly, softly softly, with kid gloves.

**458 Negligence**
**N.** *negligence*, carelessness 456 *inattention*; neglectfulness, forgetfulness 506 *oblivion*; remissness, neglect, oversight, omission; nonobservance, pretermission, default, laches, culpable negligence 918 *undutifulness*; unwatchfulness, unwariness, unguarded hour *or* minute, unpreparedness 670 *nonpreparation*; disregard, noninterference, laissez-faire 620 *avoidance*; unconcern, insouciance, nonchalance, don't-care attitude, couldn't-care-less a. 860 *indifference*; recklessness, incautiousness 857 *rashness*; procrastination 136 *delay*; supineness, slackness, laziness 679 *inactivity*; slovenliness, sluttishness, untidiness 61 *disorder*; sloppiness, inaccuracy, inexactitude 495 *inexactness*; offhandedness, casualness, laxness 734 *laxity*; perfunctoriness, superficiality 212 *shallowness*; trifling, scamping, skipping, dodging, botching 695 *bungling*; scamped work, skimped w., botched job, loose ends 728 *failure*; trifler, slacker, waster 679 *idler*; procrastinator, shirker; sloven 61 *slut*.

**Adj.** *negligent*, neglectful, careless, unmindful 456 *inattentive*; remiss 918 *undutiful*; thoughtless 450 *unthinking*; oblivious 506 *forgetful*; uncaring, insouciant 860 *indifferent*; regardless, reckless 857 *rash*; heedless 769 *nonobservant*; casual, offhand, happy-go-lucky 734 *lax*; sloppy, slipshod, slaphappy, slapdash, couldn't care less, unthorough, perfunctory, superficial, with a lick and a promise; hit-and-miss, hurried 680 *hasty*; inaccurate 495 *inexact*; slack, supine 679 *lazy*; procrastinating 136 *late*; sluttish, untidy, slovenly 649 *dirty*; not looking, unwary, unwatchful, unheedful, unguarded, off guard 508 *off guard*; improvident 670 *unprepared*; disregarding, ignoring 620 *avoiding*; lapsed 974 *irreligious*.

*neglected*, uncared for, untended; ill-kept, unkempt 649 *dirty*; unprotected, unguarded, unchaperoned; deserted; unattended, left alone, home a. 621 *relinquished*; lost sight of, unthought of, unheeded, unmissed, unregarded 860 *unwanted*; disregarded, ignored, out in the cold; unconsidered, overlooked, omitted; unnoticed, unmarked, unremarked, unperceived, unobserved 444 *invisible*; in limbo; shelved, pigeonholed, put aside, mothballed, on the back-burner 136 *late*; unread, unstudied, unexamined, unsifted, unscanned, unweighed, unexplored; undone, half-done, skimped, perfunctory 726 *uncompleted*; buried, hid under a bushel 674 *unused*.

**Vb.** *neglect*, omit, pretermit; pass over; lose sight of, overlook 456 *be inattentive*; leave undone, not finish, leave half-done, leave loose ends, do by halves 726 *not complete*; botch, bungle 695 *be clumsy*; slur, skimp, scamp 204 *shorten*; skip, skim, skip over, jump, skim through, leaf over, riffle through; not mention, skate over, gloss over, slur over 525 *conceal*; not take seriously, dabble in, play with, toy w., trifle, fribble 837 *amuse oneself*.

*disregard*, ignore, pass over, give the go-by, dodge, shirk, blink 620 *avoid*; allow to pass, let pass, wink at, connive at, take no notice 734 *be lax*; refuse to see, pay no attention to, turn a blind eye to, pay no regard to, dismiss 439 *be blind*; forbear, forget it, excuse, overlook 909 *forgive*; leave out of one's calculations, discount 483 *underestimate*; pass by, pass by on the other side 282 *deviate*; turn one's back on, slight, cold-shoulder, cut, cut dead, send to Coventry 885 *be rude*; turn a deaf ear to 416 *be deaf*; take lightly, not take seriously, not trouble oneself with, not trouble one's head about 860 *be indifferent*; have no time for, laugh off, pooh-pooh, treat as of no account 922 *hold cheap*; leave out in the cold 57 *exclude*; leave to their own devices, leave in the lurch, desert, abandon 621 *relinquish*.

*be neglectful*, doze, drowse, nod 679 *sleep*; be off one's guard, omit precautions; be caught napping, oversleep; be caught with one's pants *or* trousers down 508 *not expect*; drift, freewheel, laisser faire, procrastinate, put off until tomorrow, let slide, let slip, let the grass grow under one's feet 677 *not act*; not bother, take it easy, coast, let things go 679 *be inactive*; shelve, pigeonhole, lay aside, mothball, put on the back-burner, push aside, put a., lay a. 136 *put off*; make neglectful, lull, throw off one's guard, put off one's guard, catch napping, catch bending 508 *surprise*.

**Adv.** *negligently*, per incuriam; anyhow; any old how; cursorily, carelessly, perfunctorily.

## 459 Enquiry

**N.** *enquiry*, asking, questioning (see also *interrogation*); challenge (see also *question*); asking after, asking about, directing oneself, taking information, getting i. 524 *information*; close enquiry, searching e., strict e., witch-hunt, McCarthyism, spy mania (see also *search*); inquisition, examination, investigation, visitation; check-up, medical; inquest, post mortem, autopsy, necropsy, audit, trial 959 *legal trial*; public enquiry, secret e.; commission of enquiry, work party, working party (see also *enquirer*); census, canvass, survey, market research; poll, public opinion poll, Gallup p. (tdmk), straw p. *or* vote 605 *vote*; probe, test, means t., check, spot c., trial run 461 *experiment*; review, scrutiny 438 *inspection*; IQ test; introspection, self-examination, navel-gazing; personality testing, Rorschach *or* inkblot test; research, fundamental r., applied r. 536 *study*; analysis, dissection; exploration, reconnaissance, recce, reconnoitre, survey 484 *discovery*; discussion, ventilation, airing, soundings, canvassing, consultation 584 *conference*; speculation, philosophical enquiry, metaphysical e., scientific e. 449 *philosophy*; enquiring mind 453 *curiosity*.

*interrogation*, questioning, interpellation, asking questions, putting q., formulating q.; forensic examination, examination-in-chief; leading question, cross-examination, cross-question; reexamination; quiz, brains trust; interrogatory; catechism; inquisition, third degree, grilling; dialogue, dialectic, question and answer, interlocution; Socratic method, Socratic elenchus; question time, Prime Minister's question t.

*question*, question mark, interrogation m. 547 *punctuation*; query, request for information; questions, questionnaire 87 *list*; question sheet, question paper, examination p., test p.; interrogatory, interpellation, Parliamentary question; challenge, fair question, plain q.; trick q., catch, cross-question, loaded q.; indirect question, feeler, leading question; rhetorical q.; moot point, knotty p., debating p.; quodlibet, question propounded, point at issue, subject of dispute 452 *topic*; crucial question, burning q., sixty-four-thousand-dollar q.; vexed question, controversy, field of c., contention, bone of c. 475 *argument*; problem, knotty p., 'three-pipe p.', hard nut to crack, brain-teaser, poser, stumper, floorer, mind-boggler, headache, unsolved mystery 530 *enigma*.

> It is quite a three-pipe problem.
> Sir Arthur Conan Doyle, *The Red-Headed League* (Sherlock Holmes)

*exam*, examination, oral e., viva voce e., viva; interview, audition 415 *hearing*; practical examination, written e., multiple choice e.; test, series of tests, battery; continuous assessment; intelligence test, IQ test; 11-plus, qualifying examination, entrance e., common entrance, matriculation; Certificate of Secondary Education, CSE, 16-plus, General Certificate of Education, GCE, General Certificate of Secondary Education, GCSE; 'O' level, 'A' level, 'S' level, 'A/S' level; 'O' grade, Standard g., Higher, SYS, baccalaureate; prelims, pre-Meds, Responsions; tripos, Moderations, Mods., Greats, finals, degree exams; doctorate examination, bar e.; degree level, pass l., honours l.; catechumen 460 *respondent*; examinee, entrant, candidate, sitter 461 *testee*.

*search*, probe, investigation, enquiry; quest, hunt, witch-h., treasure h. 619 *pursuit*; house-search, domiciliary visit, house-to-house search; search of one's person, frisking, skin-search, strip-search; rummaging, turning over; exploration, excavation, archaeological e., digging, dig; speleology, pot-holing; search party; searchlight; search warrant.

*police enquiry*, investigation, criminal i., detection 484 *discovery*; detective work, shadowing, tailing, house-watching; grilling, third degree; Criminal Investigation Department, CID, Federal Bureau of Investigation, FBI, Interpol; secret police, Gestapo.

*secret service*, espionage, counter-e., spying, intelligence, counter-i., MI5, Security Service, MI6, Secret Intelligence Service, SIS, CIA, KGB; informer, intelligence officer, spy, operative, mole, sleeper, spook, 007, undercover agent, secret a., cloak-and-dagger man; double agent, inside a.; counterspy; spy ring.

*detective*, investigator, criminologist; plain-clothes man; enquiry agent, private detective, private investigator, private eye; hotel detective, store d.; amateur detective; Federal agent, FBI a., G-man, CID man; tec, sleuth, blood-hound, gumshoe, dick, snooper, nose, spy 524 *informer*; graphologist, handwriting expert; Sherlock Holmes; forensic expert, profiler.

*enquirer*, investigator, prober; asker (see also *questioner*); journalist 529 *news reporter*; student, seeker, thinker, seeker for truth 449 *philosopher*; searcher, looker, rummager, search party; inventor, discoverer; dowser, water diviner 484 *detector*; prospector, gold-digger; talent scout; scout, spy, surveyor, reconnoitrer; inspector, visitor 438 *inspection*; checker, screener, scrutineer, censor, ombudsperson 480 *estimator*; scanner, examiner, examining board, board of examiners; tester, test pilot, researcher, research worker, analyst, analyser; dissector 461 *experimenter*; market researcher, sampler, pollster, canvasser; explorer 268 *traveller*.

*questioner*, cross-q., cross-examiner, catechizer; interrogator, inquisitor, Grand I.; querist, interpellator, interlocutor, interviewer; challenger, heckler; quizzer, enfant terrible 453 *inquisitive person*; question *or* quiz master;

riddler, enigmatist; examiner of conscience, confessor 986 *clergy*.

**Adj.** *enquiring*, curious, prying, nosy 453 *inquisitive*; quizzing, quizzical; interrogatory, interrogative; examining, catechetical, inquisitional, cross-questioning; elenctic, dialectic, maieutic, heuristic, zetetic; probing, poking, digging, investigative; testing, searching, fact-finding, exploratory, empirical, tentative 461 *experimental*; analytic, diagnostic.

*moot*, in question, open to q. *or* discussion, questionable, at issue, controversial, debatable; problematic, doubtful 474 *uncertain*; knotty, puzzling 700 *difficult*; fit for enquiry, proposed, propounded; undetermined, undecided, untried, left open; the jury is out.

**Vb.** *enquire*, ask, want to know, seek an answer 491 *not know*; demand 761 *request*; canvass, agitate, air, ventilate, discuss, query, bring in question, subject to examination 475 *argue*; ask for, look for, enquire for, seek (see also *search*); hunt for 619 *pursue*; enquire into, make enquiries, probe, delve into, dig i., dig down i., go deep i., sound, take a look at, look into, investigate, throw open to enquiry, hold *or* conduct an enquiry, appoint a commission of e., call in Scotland Yard; try, hear 959 *try a case*; review, overhaul, audit, scrutinize, monitor, screen; analyse, dissect, parse, sift, winnow, thrash out; research 536 *study*; consider, examine 449 *meditate*; check, check on; feel the pulse, take the temperature, put a toe in the water, take soundings; follow up an enquiry, pursue an e., get to the bottom of, fathom, see into, X-ray 438 *scan*; ferret out, nose out; peer, peep, peek, snoop, spy, pry, nose around 453 *be curious*; survey, reconnoitre, case, sus out; explore, feel one's way 461 *be tentative*; test, trial, try, sample, taste 461 *experiment*; post-mortem, hold a post-mortem.

*interrogate*, ask questions, put q.; interpellate, question; cross-question, cross-examine, reexamine; badger, challenge, heckle; interview, hold a viva; examine, subject to questioning, sound out, probe, quiz, catechize, grill, give the third degree; put to the question 963 *torture*; pump, pick one's brains, suck one dry; move the question, put the q., pop the q.; pose, propose a question, propound a q., frame a q., raise a q., moot a q., moot, postulate a question.

*search*, seek, look for; conduct a search, rummage, ransack, comb; scrabble, forage, fossick, root about; scour, clean out, turn over, rake o., pick o., turn out, turn inside out, rake through, rifle t., go t., search t., look into every nook and corner; look high and low; sift through, winnow, quarter the ground, explore every inch, go over with a fine-tooth comb; pry into, peer i., peep i., peek i.; overhaul, frisk, strip-search, skin-search, go over, search one's pockets, feel in one's p., search for, feel for, grope for, hunt for, drag for, fish, go fishing, fish for, dig for; leave no stone unturned, explore every avenue 682 *exert oneself*; cast about, seek a clue, follow the trail 619 *pursue*; probe, explore, go in quest of 461 *be tentative*; dig, excavate, archaeologize; prospect, dowse, treasure-hunt, embark on a t.-h.

*be questionable*, – debatable etc. adj.; be open to question, be a moot point, arouse suspicion, call for enquiry, challenge an answer, demand *or* require an explanation; be subject to examination, be open to enquiry, be under investigation.

**Adv.** *on trial*, under investigation, under enquiry, sub judice; up for enquiry.

*in search of*, on the track of, cui bono?

### 460 Answer

**N.** *answer*, reply, response; replication, reaction; answer by post, answer by return of post, acknowledgment, return 588 *correspondence*; official reply, rescript; returns, results 548 *record*; feedback 524 *information*; echo, antiphon, antiphony, respond 106 *repetition*; password, countersign 547 *identification*; keyword, open sesame; answering back, backchat, repartee; retort, counterblast, riposte 714 *retaliation*; give and take, question and answer, dialogue, discussion 584 *interlocution*; last word, final answer; Parthian shot; clue, key, right answer, explanation 520 *interpretation*; solution 658 *remedy*; enigmatic answer, oracle, Delphic Oracle 530 *enigma*.

*rejoinder*, counterstatement, reply, counterblast, rebuttal, rebutter, surrejoinder, surrebutter 479 *confutation*; defence, speech for the defence, reply; refutation, contradiction 533 *negation*, 467 *counterevidence*; countercharge, counterclaim, counteraccusation, tu quoque 928 *accusation*.

*respondent*, defendant; answerer, responder, replier, correspondent; examinee 461 *testee*; candidate, applicant, entrant, sitter, examinee 716 *contender*.

**Adj.** *answering*, replying etc. vb.; respondent, responsive, echo-like, parrotlike 106 *repeated*; counter 182 *counteracting*; corresponding 588 *epistolary*; antiphonic, antiphonal; corresponding to 12 *correlative*; contradicting 533 *negative*; refuting, rebutting; oracular; conclusive, final, Parthian.

**Vb.** *answer*, give a., make a., return an a.; reply, reply by return of post, reply to an invitation, RSVP, write back, acknowledge, respond, be responsive, echo, re-echo 106 *repeat*; react, answer back, talk back, flash back, come back at, retort, riposte 714 *retaliate*; say in reply, rejoin, rebut, counter 479 *confute*; field; parry, refuse to answer 620 *avoid*; contradict 533 *negate*; be respondent, defend, have the right of reply; provide the answer, have the a. 642 *be expedient*; answer the question, get the right answer, solve the riddle 520 *interpret*; settle, decide 480 *judge*; suit the requirements, suit one down to the ground 642 *be expedient*; answer to, correspond to 12 *correlate*.

**Adv.** *in reply*, by way of reply, by way of rejoinder; antiphonally.

### 461 Experiment

**N.** *experiment*, practical e., scientific e., controlled e.; experimentalism, experimentation, experimental method, verification, verification by experiment; exploration, probe; analysis, examination 459 *enquiry*; object lesson, proof 478 *demonstration*; assay 480 *estimate*; testability; check, test, crucial t., acid t., test case; probation; double-blind test; practical test, beta test, trial, trials, try-out, trial run, practice r., dry r., test flight 671 *attempt*; audition, voice test; ordeal, ordeal by fire, ordeal by water 959 *legal trial*; pilot scheme, rough sketch, first draft, sketchbook; first steps, teething troubles 68 *debut*.

*empiricism*, speculation, guesswork, guesstimation 512 *conjecture*; tentativeness, tentative method; experience, practice, rule of thumb, trial, trial and error, hit and miss; random shot, shot in the dark, leap in the d., gamble 618 *gambling*; instinct, light of nature 476 *intuition*; sampling, random sample, straw vote; feeler 459 *question*; straw to show which way the wind is blowing, kite-flying, toe in the water, trial balloon, ballon d'essai.

*experimenter*, experimentalist, empiricist, researcher, research worker, analyst, analyser, vivisector; assayer, chemist; tester; test driver, test pilot; speculator, prospector, sourdough, forty-niner; prober, explorer, adventurer 459 *enquirer*; 493 *dabbler*; gamester 618 *gambler*.

*testing agent*, criterion, touchstone; standard, yardstick 465 *gauge*; breathalyser, sniffer torch; control; indicator, reagent, litmus paper, methylene blue, cupel, retort, test tube 147 *crucible*; pyx, pyx chest; proving ground, wind tunnel; simulator, flight s., test track; laboratory.

*testee*, examinee 460 *respondent*; probationer 538 *beginner*; candidate, entrant, sitter, examinee 716 *contender*; subject of experiment, subject, patient; laboratory animal, guinea pig, rat, monkey.

**Adj.** *experimental*, analytic, analytical, verificatory, probative, probationary, probational; provisional, tentative 618 *speculative*; trial, exploratory 459 *enquiring*; empirical, experiential, guided by experience; venturesome 671 *attempting*; testable, verifiable, in the experimental stage 474 *uncertain*.

**Vb.** *experiment*, experimentalize, make experiments; check, check on, verify; prove, put to the proof; assay, analyse; research; dabble; experiment upon, vivisect, make a guinea pig of, practise upon; test, beta-test, put to the t., subject to a t., run a t. on, put through a battery of tests, try out, trial, give a trial to 459 *enquire*; try, give something a try, try a thing once 671 *attempt*; try one's strength, pit one's strength against, test one's muscles; give one a try; sample 386 *taste*; take a random sample, take a straw vote; put to the vote 605 *vote*; rehearse, practise 534 *train*; be tested, undergo a test, come to the t.

*be tentative*, be empirical, seek experience, feel one's way, proceed by trial and error, proceed by guess and by God; feel 378 *touch*; probe, grope, fumble; get the feel of 536 *learn*; put out a feeler, dip a toe in, put a toe in the water, fly a kite, feel the pulse, consult the barometer, take the temperature, see how the land lies, see how the wind blows; fish, fish for, angle for, bob for, cast one's net, trawl, put out a t.; wait and see, see what happens; try it on, see how far one can go; try one's fortune, try one's luck, speculate 618 *gamble*; venture, explore, prospect 672 *undertake*; probe, sound 459 *enquire*.

**Adv.** *experimentally*, on test, on trial, on approval, on probation; empirically, by rule of thumb, by trial and error, by the light of nature, by guess and by God; on spec.

## 462 Comparison

**N.** *comparison*, analogical procedure; comparing, likening; confrontation, collation, juxtaposition, setting side by side 202 *contiguity*; check 459 *enquiry*; comparability, points of comparison, analogy, parallel, likeness, similitude 18 *similarity*; identification 13 *identity*; antithesis 14 *contrariety*; contrast 15 *differentiation*; simile, allegory 519 *metaphor*; standard of comparison, criterion, pattern, model, check list, control 23 *prototype*; comparer, collator.

**Adj.** *compared*, collated etc. vb.; compared with, in comparison with, likened, set against, measured a., contrasted; comparative, comparable, analogical; relative, correlative; allegorical, metaphorical 519 *figurative*.

**Vb.** *compare*, collate, confront; set side by side, bring together 202 *juxtapose*; draw a comparison 18 *liken*, 13 *identify*; parallel; contrast 15 *differentiate*; compare and contrast 463 *discriminate*; match, pair, balance 28 *equalize*; view together, check with 12 *correlate*; institute a comparison, draw a parallel; compare to, compare with, criticize; compare notes, match ideas, exchange views.

**Adv.** *comparatively*, analogically; in comparison, as compared; relatively 12 *correlatively*.

## 463 Discrimination

**N.** *discrimination*, distinction 15 *differentiation*; discernment, discretion, ability to make distinctions, appreciation of differences, discriminating judgment, connoisseurship 480 *judgment*; insight, perception, acumen, flair 498 *intelligence*; appreciation, careful a., critique, critical appraisal 480 *estimate*; sensitivity 494 *accuracy*; sensibility 819 *moral sensibility*; tact, delicacy, kid gloves, refinement 846 *good taste*; timing, sense of t., sense of occasion; nicety, particularity 862 *fastidiousness*; fine palate 386 *taste*; logical nicety, subtlety, hair-splitting 475 *reasoning*; sifting, winnowing, separation, sorting out 62 *sorting*; selection 605 *choice*; nice difference, subtle d., shade of d., nuance, fine shade 15 *difference*; bias 481 *prejudice*.

*discriminating person*, connoisseur, oenophile.

**Adj.** *discriminating*, discriminative, selective, judicious, discerning, discreet; sensitive 494 *accurate*; fine, delicate, nice, particular 862 *fastidious*; thoughtful, tactful 513 *imaginative*; tasting, appraising, critical 480 *judicial*; distinguishing 15 *distinctive*.

**Vb.** *discriminate*, distinguish, contradistinguish 15 *differentiate*; compare and contrast 462 *compare*; sort, sort out, sieve, sift; severalize, separate, separate the sheep from the goats, winnow, sort the wheat from the chaff 46 *set apart*; pick out 605 *select*; exercise discretion, see the difference, make a distinction, make an exception, draw the line 468 *qualify*; refine, refine upon, split hairs 475 *reason*; criticize, appraise, taste 480 *estimate*; weigh, consider, make a judgment, make a value j. 480 *judge*; discern, be a good judge of, have insight; have a feel for, have an eye *or* an ear for; know what's what, know how many beans make five, know one's way about, know one's stuff, 'know a hawk from a handsaw' 490 *know*;

> I am but mad north-north-west; when the wind is southerly, I know a hawk from a handsaw.
> William Shakespeare, *Hamlet*

take into account, take cognizance of, give

weight to 638 *make important*; attribute just value to 913 *be just*.

## 464 Indiscrimination

**N.** *indiscrimination*, lack of discrimination, promiscuousness, promiscuity, universality 79 *generality*; lack of judgment, uncriticalness, simplicity, naiveté; obtuseness 499 *unintelligence*; indiscretion, lack of consideration 857 *rashness*; imperceptivity 439 *blindness*; unimaginativeness, tactlessness, insensitiveness, insensibility 820 *moral insensibility*; tastelessness, lack of refinement, coarseness, vulgarity 847 *bad taste*; inaccuracy 495 *inexactness*; vagueness, loose terms.

**Adj.** *indiscriminate*, unsorted 61 *orderless*; rolled into one, undistinguished, undifferentiated, same for everybody 16 *uniform*; random, unaimed, undirected; confused, undefined, unmeasured 474 *uncertain*; promiscuous, haphazard, wholesale, blanket, global 79 *general*.

*indiscriminating*, unselective, undiscerning, uncritical 499 *unintelligent*; imperceptive, obtuse; tactless, insensitive, unimaginative 820 *impassive*; unrefined, tasteless, coarse 847 *vulgar*; indiscreet, ill-judged 857 *rash*; tone-deaf 416 *deaf*; colour-blind 439 *blind*; inaccurate 495 *inexact*.

**Vb.** *not discriminate*, be indiscriminate, avoid precision, confound opposites, be unselective 606 *be neutral*; exercise no discretion 499 *be foolish*; make no distinction, see no difference, swallow whole; roll into one, lump everything together, heap t. 74 *bring together*; jumble, muddle, confuse, confound 63 *derange*; ignore distinctions, obliterate d., average, take an a., establish a mean, smooth out 30 *average out*.

## 465 Measurement

**N.** *measurement*, admeasurement, quantification; mensuration, surveying, triangulation; cadastral survey; geodetics, geodesy; metage 322 *weighing*; posology, dose, dosage 26 *finite quantity*; rating, valuation, evaluation; appraisal, appraisement, assessment, appreciation, estimation 480 *estimate*; calculation, computation, number-crunching, reckoning 86 *numeration*; dead reckoning, gauging; checking, check; reading, reading off; metrics, micrometry 203 *long measure*; trigonometry; second, degree, minute, quadrant 247 *angular measure*; quadrature, cubature.

*geometry*, plane g., planimetry; solid geometry, stereometry; altimetry, hypsometry; Euclidean geometry, non-Euclidean g.; geometer.

*metrology*, dimensions, length, breadth, height, depth, thickness 195 *size*; weights and measures, avoirdupois, metric system, unit of measurement; weights 322 *weighing*; axle load; linear measure 203 *long measure*; measure of capacity, volume, cubature, cubic contents 183 *measure*; liquid measure, gill, pint, imperial p., quart, gallon, imperial g.; barrel, pipe, hogshead 194 *vessel*; litre; apothecaries' fluid measure, minim, dram; dry measure, peck, bushel, quarter, chaldron; unit of energy, ohm, watt 160 *electricity*; horsepower 160 *energy*; candlepower 417 *light*; decibel, sone 398 *sound*.

*coordinate*, ordinate and abscissa, polar coordinates, latitude and longitude, right ascension and declination, altitude and azimuth; grid reference.

*gauge*, measure, scale, graduated s.; time scale 117 *chronometry*; balance 322 *scales*; nonius, vernier, micrometer; foot-rule, yardstick, metre bar; yard measure, tape m., measuring tape, metal rule; chain, link, pole, perch, rod; lead, log, log-line; fathometer, echo sounder; ruler, slide rule; straight-edge, T-square, try s., set s.; dividers, callipers, compass, protractor; sextant, quadrant 269 *sailing aid*; Jacob's staff, theodolite, planisphere, alidade; astrolabe 321 *astronomy*; index, Plimsoll line, Plimsoll mark, bench m. 547 *indication*; high-water mark, tidemark, floodmark, water line 236 *limit*; axis, coordinate; rule of thumb, standard, criterion, norm 23 *prototype*; milestone 547 *signpost*.

*meter*, measuring instrument; goniometer, planimeter; altimeter 209 *altimetry*; bathometer 211 *depth*; thermometer 379 *thermometry*; barometer, anemometer 352 *anemometry*; dynamometer; hygrometer, fluviometer 341 *hygrometry*; gas etc. meter; speed gauge, speedometer, tachometer, tachymeter, tachograph, spy-in-the-cab, odometer, milometer 277 *velocity*; cyclometer, pedometer 267 *land travel*; time gauge, metronome, time switch, parking meter 117 *timekeeper*; micrometer; Geiger counter; seismograph; geophone.

*surveyor*, land s., quantity s.; topographer, cartographer, oceanographer, hydrographer, geodesist; survey equipment, survey vehicle, autonomous underwater vehicle, AUV, remote operated vehicle, ROV.

*appraiser*, valuer, loss adjuster, assessor, measurer, surveyor 480 *estimator*.

**Adj.** *metrical*, mensural; imperial, metric; metrological, modular; dimensional, three-d.; cubic, volumetric, linear, micrometric; cadastral, topographical; geodetic.

*measured*, surveyed, mapped, plotted, taped; graduated, calibrated; mensurable, measurable, meterable, assessable, computable, calculable.

**Vb.** *measure*, mensurate, survey, triangulate;

compute, calculate, count, reckon 86 *number*; quantify, take the dimensions, take the measurements, measure the length and breadth, measure up; size up, calculate the s.; estimate the average 30 *average out*; beat the bounds, pace out, count one's steps; tape, span; calliper, use the dividers; probe, sound, fathom, plumb 313 *plunge*; take soundings, heave the lead; pace, check the speed 117 *time*; balance 322 *weigh*.

*gauge*, meter, take a reading, read, read off; standardize, fix the standard, set a standard 16 *make uniform*; grade, mark off, mark out, calibrate 27 *graduate*; reduce to scale, draw to s., map 551 *represent*.

*appraise*, gauge, value, cost, rate, set a value on, fix the price of 809 *price*; evaluate, estimate, make an e., form an e.; appreciate, assess, assay 480 *estimate*; form an opinion 480 *judge*; tape, have taped, have the measure of, size up.

*mete out*, mete, measure out, weigh, weigh out, dole o., allocate, divide, share, share out, portion out 775 *participate*, 783 *apportion*.

SECTION THREE

## Materials for reasoning

### 466 Evidence
**N.** *evidence*, facts, data, grounds 475 *reasons*; premises 475 *premise*; hearsay, hearsay evidence 524 *report*; indirect evidence, collateral e., secondary e.; circumstantial evidence 8 *circumstance*; constructive evidence 512 *supposition*; proof, conclusive evidence, direct e., demonstrative e., final e., incriminating e., internal e., substantive e., smoking gun 478 *demonstration*; presumptive evidence, prima facie e.; supporting evidence, corroboration; verification, confirmation 473 *certainty*; rebutting evidence 467 *counterevidence*; one-sided evidence, ex parte e.; piece of evidence, fact, relevant f.; document, exhibit, fingerprints, DNA fingerprinting, genetic f. 548 *record*; clue 524 *hint*; symptom, syndrome, sign, sure s. 547 *indication*; mention, reference, quotation, citation, chapter and verse; one's authorities, documentation; line of evidence, chain of authorities; authority, scripturality, canonicity; curriculum vitae, biodata, biopic, case history.

*testimony*, witness; statement, evidence in chief 524 *information*; admission, confession 526 *disclosure*; one's case, plea 614 *pretext*; word, assertion, allegation 532 *affirmation*; Bible evidence, evidence on oath; sworn evidence, legal e., deposition, affidavit, attest-ation 532 *oath*; State's evidence, Queen's e.; word of mouth, oral evidence, verbal e., verbal; documentary evidence, written e.; evidence to character, character reference, compurgation 927 *vindication*; copy of the evidence, case record, dossier 548 *record*; written contract, contract of employment 765 *compact*; deed, testament 767 *security*.

*credential*, compurgation 927 *vindication*; testimonial, chit, character, recommendation, references; seal, signature, countersignature, endorsement, docket, counterfoil; voucher, warranty, warrant, certificate, diploma 767 *security*; ticket, passport, visitor's p., visa, pet passport, animal p. 756 *permit*; authority, scripture.

*witness*, eye w. 441 *spectator*; ear witness 415 *listener*; indicator, informant, telltale, grass, supergrass 524 *informer*; deponent, testifier, swearer, attestor 765 *signatory*; witness to character, compurgator, referee; expert witness; sponsor 707 *patron*.

**Adj.** *evidential*, evidentiary, offering evidence; prima facie 445 *appearing*; suggesting, suggestive, significant 514 *meaningful*; showing, indicative, symptomatic, identifying, diagnostic 547 *indicating*; indirect, secondary, circumstantial; first-hand, direct, seen, heard; deducible, verifiable 471 *probable*; constructive 512 *suppositional*; cumulative, supporting, corroborative, confirmatory; telling, damning 928 *accusing*; presumptive, reliable 473 *certain*; probative, proving, demonstrative, conclusive, decisive, final 478 *demonstrating*; based on, grounded on; founded on fact, factual, documentary, documented, well-documented 473 *positive*; authentic, well-grounded, well-founded 494 *true*; weighty, authoritative 178 *influential*; biblical, scriptural, canonical 976 *orthodox*; testified, attested, witnessed; spoken to, sworn to; in evidence, on the record 548 *recorded*.

**Vb.** *evidence*, show, evince, furnish evidence; show signs of, betray symptoms of, have the makings of 852 *give hope*; betoken, bespeak 551 *represent*; breathe of, tell of, declare witness to 522 *manifest*; lend colour to 471 *make likely*; tell its own tale, speak for itself, speak volumes; have weight, carry w. 178 *influence*; suggest 547 *indicate*; argue, involve 523 *imply*.

*testify*, witness; take one's oath, swear, be sworn, speak on oath 532 *affirm*; bear witness, take the stand, give testimony, give evidence, witness for *or* against, speak to, depose, swear to, vouch for, give one's word; authenticate, validate, give credence, certify 473 *make certain*; attest, subscribe, countersign, endorse, sign; plead, state one's case 475 *argue*; admit, avow, acknowledge 526 *confess*; give a character reference, act as referee, testimonialize, compurgate.

*corroborate*, support, buttress 162 *strengthen*; sustain, uphold in evidence, substantiate 927 *vindicate*; bear out, circumstantiate, verify; validate, confirm, ratify, establish, make a case for, make out, make good 473 *make certain*; lead evidence, adduce e.; bring one's witnesses, produce one's w., confront w.; put the evidence, produce the e., document, give credence; collect evidence, rake up *or* scrape together e.; concoct evidence, fabricate e. 541 *fake*; countervail 467 *tell against*; adduce, cite the evidence, quote the e., quote the leading case, refer to a precedent, quote one's authorities, give the reference, give chapter and verse.

### 467 Counterevidence

**N.** *counterevidence*, contraindication 14 *contrariety*; answering evidence, opposite e., rebutting e.; evidence against, evidence on the other side, defence, rebuttal, rejoinder 460 *answer*; refutation, disproof 479 *confutation*; denial 533 *negation*; justification 927 *vindication*; oath against oath, one word against another; counteroath, counterprotest, counterclaim, tu quoque argument; conflicting evidence, contradictory e., negative e.; mitigating evidence 468 *qualification*; hostile witness, hostile evidence 603 *tergiversation*.

**Adj.** *countervailing*, rebutting 460 *answering*; cancelling out, counteractive 182 *counteracting*; cutting both ways, ambiguous 518 *equivocal*; converse, opposite, in the opposite scale 14 *contrary*; denying, negatory 533 *negative*; damaging, telling against, contraindicating; qualificatory 468 *qualifying*.

*unattested*, unsworn; lacking proof, unproven, not proved, lacking credence 474 *uncertain*; unsupported, uncorroborated; disproved 479 *confuted*; trumped-up, fabricated 541 *false*.

**Vb.** *tell against*, damage the case; weigh against, countervail; contravene, traverse, run counter, contradict, contraindicate; rebut 479 *confute*; oppose, point the other way 14 *be contrary*; cancel out 182 *counteract*; cut both ways 518 *be equivocal*; prove a negative 533 *negate*; lead counterevidence, lead for the other side; fail to confirm, tell another story, alter the case; not improve, weaken, damage, spoil; undermine, subvert 165 *destroy*; demolish the case, turn the tables, turn the scale, convict of perjury; contradict oneself, turn hostile 603 *change one's mind*.

**Adv.** *conversely*, per contra, on the other hand, on the other side, in rebuttal, in rejoinder.

### 468 Qualification

**N.** *qualification*, specification 80 *speciality*; prerequisite 627 *requirement*; assumption 512 *supposition*; leaven, colouring, tinge; modification 143 *change*; mitigation 177 *moderation*; stipulation, condition, sine qua non 766 *conditions*; limitation 747 *restriction*; proviso, reservation; exception, salvo, saving clause, escape c., letout c., escalator c., penalty c.; exemption 919 *nonliability*; demur, objection, but 704 *opposition*; consideration, concession, allowance; extenuating circumstances; redeeming feature 31 *offset*.

**Adj.** *qualifying*, qualificative, qualificatory; restricting, limiting; modifying, altering the case; mitigatory 177 *alleviative*; extenuating, palliative, excusing, weakening, colouring, leavening; contingent, provisional 766 *conditional*; discounting, allowing for, taking into account; saving, excepting, exempting; circumstanced, qualified, not absolute; exceptional, exempted, exempt 919 *nonliable*.

**Vb.** *qualify*, condition, limit, restrict 747 *restrain*; colour, shade; leaven, alter 143 *modify*; temper, season, palliate, mitigate 177 *moderate*; adulterate 163 *weaken*; excuse 927 *extenuate*; grant, concede, make allowance for, take into account, take cognizance of; lessen 37 *abate*; make exceptions 919 *exempt*; introduce new conditions, alter the case; insert a qualifying clause; insist on 627 *require*; relax, relax the rigour of 734 *be lax*; take exception, object, demur, raise an objection 762 *deprecate*.

**Adv.** *provided*, provided always, with the proviso that, according as, subject to, conditionally, with the understanding that, so *or* as long as; granting, admitting, supposing; allowing for; with a pinch of salt; not absolutely, not invariably; if, if not, unless 8 *if*; though, although, even if.

*nevertheless*, even so, all the same, for all that, after all; despite, in spite of; but, yet, still, at all events; whether, whether or no.

### 469 Possibility

**N.** *possibility*, potentiality; capacity, viability, viableness, workability 160 *ability*; what is possible, all that is p. 635 *sufficiency*; what may be 124 *futurity*; what might be, the might-have-been 125 *past time*; the possible, the feasible; what one can do, best one can do, all in one's power, limit of one's endeavour; contingency, eventuality, a possibility, chance, off-chance 159 *fair chance*; good chance 137 *opportunity*; bare possibility, ghost of a chance, outside c.;

likelihood 471 *probability*; thinkableness, credibility 485 *belief*; practicability, operability 642 *good policy*; practicableness, feasibility, easiness 701 *facility*; superableness, negotiability; availability, accessibility, approachability; compatibility 24 *agreement*; risk of.

**Adj.** *possible*, potential, hypothetical; able, capable, viable; arguable, reasonable; feasible, practicable, negotiable 701 *easy*; workable, performable, achievable; doable, operable; attainable, approachable, accessible, obtainable, realizable; superable, surmountable; not too difficult, not impossible, within the bounds *or* realms of possibility; available, still open, not excluded, not too late; conceivable, thinkable, credible, imaginable; practical, compatible with the circumstances 642 *advisable*; allowable, permissible, legal 756 *permitted*; contingent 124 *future*; on the cards 471 *probable*; only possible, not inevitable, evitable, revocable 620 *avoidable*; liable, tending.

**Vb.** *be possible*, – feasible etc. adj.; may, might, may be, might be; might have been, could have b., should have b.; admit of, allow 756 *permit*; bear, be open to, offer an opportunity for; be a possibility, depend, be contingent, lie within the bounds *or* realms of possibility; stand a chance 471 *be likely*.

*make possible*, enable 160 *empower*, allow 756 *permit*; give the green light, clear the path, smooth the way, remove the obstacles, put in the way of 701 *facilitate*.

**Adv.** *possibly*, potentially; conceivably, hypothetically, in posse; perhaps, perchance, for all one knows; within reach, within one's grasp; peradventure, haply, mayhap; maybe, could be; if possible, if humanly possible, if so be; wind and weather permitting, God willing, Deo volente, D.V.

## 470 Impossibility

**N.** *impossibility*, inconceivability etc. adj.; unthinkableness, no chance, no way, not a chance of, not a cat's chance, not a snowball's chance in hell, not a hope 853 *hopelessness*; what cannot be, what can never be; irrevocability, what might have been; impasse, deadlock, logjam, gridlock 702 *obstacle*; unfeasibility, impracticability 643 *inexpedience*; no permission 757 *prohibition*; unavailability, inaccessibility, unobtainability, sour grapes; insuperability, impossible task, no go 700 *hard task*.

**Adj.** *impossible*, not possible; not allowed, ruled out, excluded, against the rules 757 *prohibited*; not to be thought of, out of the question, hopeless; unnatural, against nature; unreasonable, contrary to reason, self-

contradictory 477 *illogical*; unscientific; untrue, incompatible with the facts 495 *erroneous*; too improbable, incredible, inconceivable, unthinkable, unimaginable, unheard of 486 *unbelieved*; miraculous 864 *wonderful*; visionary, idealistic, unrealistic 513 *imaginary*; irrevocable, beyond recall 830 *regretted*.

*impracticable*, unfeasible, not to be done; unworkable, unviable; out of the question, unachievable, unattainable, unrealizable, unsolvable, insoluble, inextricable, too hard, too much for, beyond one 700 *difficult*; incurable, inoperable; insuperable, insurmountable, impassable, unbridgable, unbridged; impenetrable, unnavigable, not motorable, unscalable; unapproachable, inaccessible, unobtainable, unavailable, not to be had, not to be had for love or money, out of reach, beyond one's reach, not within one's grasp; elusive 667 *escaped*.

**Vb.** *be impossible*, – impracticable etc. adj.; exceed possibility, defy nature, fly in the face of reason, have no chance whatever.

*make impossible*, rule out, exclude, disallow 757 *prohibit*; put out of reach, tantalize, set an impossible task; deny the possibility, eat one's hat if 533 *negate*.

*attempt the impossible*, labour in vain 641 *waste effort*; have nothing to go upon, grasp at shadows, clutch at straws; be in two places at once, square the circle, discover the secret of perpetual motion, discover the philosopher's stone, find the elixir of life, find a needle in a haystack; weave a rope of sand, skin a flint, gather grapes from thorns *or* figs from thistles, get blood from a stone, fetch water in a sieve; make bricks without straw, make a silk purse out of a sow's ear, change a leopard's spots; have one's cake and eat it; write on water, set the Thames on fire.

**Adv.** *impossibly*, nohow, no way.

## 471 Probability

**N.** *probability*, likelihood, likeliness 159 *chance*; good chance, favourable c., reasonable c., fair c., sporting c., odds-on c. 469 *possibility*; prospect, excellent p. 511 *prediction*; fair expectation 507 *expectation*; well-grounded hope 852 *hope*; safe bet, sure thing 473 *certainty*; real risk, real danger 661 *danger*; natural course 179 *tendency*; presumption, natural p.; presumptive evidence, circumstantial e. 466 *evidence*; credibility; likely belief 485 *belief*; plausibility, reasonableness, good reason 475 *reasons*; verisimilitude, colour, show of, semblance 445 *appearance*; theory of probability; probabilism, probabilist.

**Adj.** *probable*, likely 180 *liable*; on the cards,

in a fair way; natural, to be expected, foreseeable, foreseen; presumable, presumptive; reliable, to be acted on 473 *certain*; hopeful, promising 507 *expected*; looming, on the horizon, in the wind 155 *impending*; in danger of 661 *vulnerable*; highly possible 469 *possible*.

*plausible*, specious, colourable; apparent, ostensible, to all intents and purposes, to all appearances 445 *appearing*; logical, reasonable 475 *rational*; convincing, persuasive, believable, easy to believe 485 *credible*; well-grounded, well-founded 494 *true*; ben trovato 24 *apt*.

**Vb.** *be likely*, – probable etc. adj.; have a chance, be on the cards, stand a chance, be in with a c., run a good c. 469 *be possible*; bid fair to, be in danger of 179 *tend*; show signs, have the makings of, promise 852 *give hope*.

*make likely*, make probable, increase the chances; involve 523 *imply*; entail 156 *conduce*; put in the way to, promote 703 *aid*; lend colour to, point to 466 *evidence*.

*assume*, presume, take for granted, flatter oneself 485 *believe*; conjecture, guess, dare say 512 *suppose*; think likely, look for 507 *expect*; read the future, see ahead 510 *foresee*; rely, count upon 473 *be certain*; gather, deduce, infer 475 *reason*.

**Adv.** *probably*, presumably; in all probability, in all likelihood, doubtless, as is to be expected, all things considered; very likely, most l., ten to one, by all odds, Lombard Street to a China orange, a pound to a penny; seemingly, apparently, on the face of it, to all intents and purposes, prima facie; belike, like enough, as likely as not.

## 472 Improbability

**N.** *improbability*, unlikelihood, doubt, real d. 474 *uncertainty*; little chance, little or no c., chance in a million, off-chance, small c., poor c., slim c., outside c., long shot; scarcely any chance, not a ghost of a c., no c., not a hope 470 *impossibility*; long odds, bare possibility; pious hopes, forlorn hope, small h., poor prospect 508 *lack of expectation*; rare occurrence, rarity 140 *infrequency*; implausibility, traveller's tale, fisherman's yarn 541 *falsehood*.

**Adj.** *improbable*, unlikely, more than doubtful, dubious 474 *uncertain*; contrary to all reasonable expectations, unforeseeable, unforeseen 508 *unexpected*; hard to believe, fishy, unconvincing, implausible 474 *uncertified*; rare 140 *infrequent*; unheard of, unimaginable, inconceivable 470 *impossible*; stretching the imagination, incredible, too good to be true 486 *unbelieved*.

**Vb.** *be unlikely*, – improbable, look imposs-

ible etc. adj.; have a bare chance, show little hope, offer small chance; be implausible, not wash, be hard to believe, lend no colour to, strain one's credulity 486 *cause doubt*; think unlikely, whistle for 508 *not expect*.

**Int.** not likely!, no fear!, no way!, not on your life!, not on your nelly!, not a hope!, some hopes!

## 473 Certainty

**N.** *certainty*, objective c., certitude, certain knowledge 490 *knowledge*; certainness, assuredness, sureness; certain issue, inevitability, inexorability, irrevocability, necessity 596 *fate*; inerrancy, freedom from error, infallibilism, infallibility; indubitability, reliability, utter r., unimpeachability 494 *truth*; certainty of meaning, unambiguity, unequivocalness, univocity; no case to answer, incontrovertibility, irrefutability, indisputability, proof 478 *demonstration*; authentication, ratification, validation; certification, verification, confirmation, spell-check; attestation 466 *testimony*; making sure, check 459 *enquiry*; ascertainment 484 *discovery*; dead certainty, cert, dead c., sure thing, safe bet, cinch, open and shut case, foregone conclusion; fact, ascertained f., indubitable f., positive f. 3 *substantiality*; matter of fact, accomplished f., fait accompli 154 *event*; res judicata, settled decision 480 *judgment*; gospel, Bible 511 *oracle*; dogma 976 *orthodoxy*; dictum, ipse dixit, ex cathedra utterance, axiom 496 *maxim*; court of final appeal, judgment seat 956 *tribunal*; last word, ultimatum 766 *conditions*.

*positiveness*, subjective certainty, moral c.; assurance, confidence; conviction, persuasion 485 *belief*; unshakable opinion, doctrinaire o. 485 *opinion*; idée fixe, fixity, obsession 481 *bias*; dogmatism, orthodoxy, bigotry 602 *opinionatedness*; infallibility, air of i., self-confidence; confidence-building, assertiveness training; pontification, laying down the law.

*doctrinaire*, dogmatist, infallibilist; self-opinionated person 602 *obstinate person*; bigot, fanatic, zealot; oracle, Sir Oracle, knowall, smarty-pants 500 *wiseacre*.

**Adj.** *certain*, sure, solid, unshakable, well-founded, well-grounded 3 *substantial*; reliable 929 *trustworthy*; authoritative, official 494 *genuine*; factual, historical 494 *true*; authenticated, ascertained, certified, attested, guaranteed, warranted; tested, tried, foolproof 660 *safe*; infallible, unerring, inerrant 540 *veracious*; axiomatic, dogmatic, taken for granted 485 *creedal*; self-evident, axiomatic, evident, apparent; unequivocal, unambiguous, univocal; unmistakable, clear, clear as day 443 *obvious*; inevitable, unavoidable, ineluctable, irrevocable, inexorable 596 *fated*; bound, bound to be, in the bag; sure as fate, sure as death and taxes 124 *future*; inviolable, safe as houses, safe as the Bank of England 660 *invulnerable*; verifiable, testable, demonstrable 478 *demonstrated*.

*positive*, confident, assured, self-assured, self-confident, certain in one's mind, undoubting, convinced, persuaded, certified, sure 485 *believing*; opinionated, self-o.; dogmatizing, pontifical, pontificating, oracular 532 *assertive*; dogmatic, doctrinaire 976 *orthodox*; obsessed, bigoted, fanatical 481 *biased*; unshaken, set, set in one's ways, fixed, fixed in one's opinions 153 *unchangeable*; clean-cut, clear-c., definite, decisive, defined, unambiguous, unambivalent, unequivocal, univocal 516 *intelligible*; convincing 485 *credible*; classified, in its place 62 *arranged*; affirmative, categorical, absolute, unqualified, unreserved, final, ultimate, conclusive, settled, without appeal.

*undisputed*, beyond doubt, beyond all reasonable d., without a shadow of doubt, axiomatic, uncontroversial; unquestioned, undoubted, uncontested, unarguable, undebatable, indubitable, unquestionable, questionless, incontrovertible, incontestable, unchallengeable, unimpeachable, undeniable, irrefutable, irrefragable, indefeasible.

**Vb.** *be certain*, – sure etc. adj.; leave no doubt, be clear as day, be plain as the nose on your face, stand to reason, be axiomatic 475 *be reasonable*; be positive, be assured, satisfy oneself, convince o., feel sure, be clear in one's mind, have no doubts, make no doubt, hold for true 485 *believe*; understand, know for certain 490 *know*; hold to one's opinions, stick to one's guns, have made up one's mind, dismiss all doubt; depend on it, rely on, bank on, trust in, swear by; gamble on, bet on, go nap on, put one's shirt on, lay one's bottom dollar.

*dogmatize*, pontificate, lay down the law 532 *affirm*; play the oracle, know all the answers.

*make certain*, certify, authenticate, ratify, seal, sign 488 *endorse*; guarantee, warrant, assure; finalize, settle, decide 480 *judge*; remove doubt, persuade 485 *convince*; classify 62 *arrange*; make sure, ascertain, check, double-check, verify, confirm, confirm in writing, clinch 466 *corroborate*; reassure oneself, take a second look, do a double take; insure against 660 *safeguard*; reinsure 858 *be cautious*; ensure, make inevitable 596 *necessitate*.

**Adv.** *certainly*, definitely, certes, for sure, to be sure, no doubt, doubtless, indubitably, as sure as anything, as sure as eggs is eggs, as sure as God made little green apples, as night

follows day, of course, as a matter of c., no question; no two ways about it, no ifs or buts; without fail, sink or swim, rain or shine, come hell or high water, come what may, whatever happens.

## 474 Uncertainty

**N.** *uncertainty*, unverifiability, incertitude, doubtfulness, dubiousness; ambiguity, ambivalence 518 *equivocalness*; vagueness, haziness, obscurity 418 *darkness*; mist, haze, fog 423 *opacity*; grey area; yes and no, don't know, floating voter, vacillation, indeterminacy, indetermination, the jury is still out, borderline case; indefiniteness, roving commission; query, question mark 459 *question*; open question, anybody's guess, a matter of tossing a coin; nothing to go on, guesswork, guesstimate 512 *conjecture*; contingency, doubtful c., doubtful event 159 *chance*; gamble, toss-up, wager 618 *gambling*; leap *or* shot in the dark, bow at a venture, pig in a poke, blind date; something or other, this or that.

*dubiety*, dubitation 486 *doubt*; state of doubt, open mind, suspended judgment, open verdict, a verdict of not proven; suspense, waiting 507 *expectation*; doubt, indecision, hesitancy, shilly-shallying, vacillation 317 *fluctuation*; seesaw, floating vote 601 *irresolution*; embarrassment, perplexity, bewilderment, bafflement, nonplus, quandary; dilemma, cleft stick, Morton's fork 530 *enigma*.

*unreliability*, liability to error, fallibility 495 *error*; insecurity, precariousness, unstable condition, touch and go 661 *danger*; untrustworthiness, treacherousness; fluidity, unsteadiness, variability, changeability 152 *changeableness*; unpredictability, unexpectedness 508 *lack of expectation*; fickleness, capriciousness, whimsicality 604 *caprice*; slipperiness, suppleness 930 *improbity*; lack of security, no guarantee, no collateral, gentleman's agreement, handshake deal, bare word, dicer's oath, scrap of paper.

**Adj.** *uncertain*, unsure, doubtful, dubious, not axiomatic; unverifiable (see also *uncertified*); insecure, chancy, risky 661 *unsafe*; treacherous (see also *unreliable*); subject to chance, at the mercy of events; occasional, sporadic 140 *infrequent*; temporary, provisional 114 *transient*; fluid 152 *unstable*; contingent, depending on 766 *conditional*; unpredictable, unforeseeable 508 *unexpected*; aoristic, indeterminate, undefined, undetermined, unclassified; random 61 *orderless*; indecisive, undecided, vacillating, open, in suspense; in question, under enquiry; open to question, questionable, not decided, undecided, the jury is out 459 *moot*; arguable, debatable, disputable, controvertible, controversial; suspicious 472 *improbable*; problematical, hypothetical, speculative 512 *suppositional*; undefinable, borderline, grey-area, marginal; ambiguous 518 *equivocal*; paradoxical 477 *illogical*; oracular, enigmatic, cryptic, obscure 517 *puzzling*; vague, hazy, misty, cloudy 419 *shadowy*; mysterious, veiled 523 *occult*; unsolved, unresolved, unexplained 517 *unintelligible*; perplexing, bewildering, embarrassing, confusing 61 *complex*.

*unreliable*, undependable, untrustworthy; treacherous 930 *dishonest*; unsteady, unstable, variable, vacillating, changeable 152 *changeful*; unpredictable, unforeseeable; fickle 604 *capricious*; fallible, open to error 495 *erroneous*; precarious, ticklish, touch and go.

*doubting*, in doubt, doubtful, dubious, full of doubt, riddled with d., plagued by uncertainty; agnostic, sceptical 486 *unbelieving*; sitting on the fence, hedging one's bets, in two minds; in suspense, open-minded; distrustful, mistrustful 858 *cautious*; uncertain, unassured, unconfident, diffident; hesitant, undecided, wavering, vacillating, unsure which way to jump 601 *irresolute*; unable to say, afraid to say; moithered, moidered, mazed, dazed, baffled, perplexed, bewildered, mind-boggled, distracted, distraught 517 *puzzled*; nonplussed, stumped, brought to a standstill, at one's wits' end, in a cleft stick, on the horns of a dilemma; lost, disorientated, guessing, in the dark, abroad, all at sea, adrift, drifting, astray, at a loss, at fault, clueless 491 *ignorant*.

*uncertified*, unverified, unchecked; awaiting confirmation, unconfirmed, uncorroborated, unauthenticated, unratified, unsigned, unsealed, unwitnessed, unattested; unwarranted, unguaranteed; unauthoritative, unofficial, apocryphal, uncanonical, unauthentic; unproved, undemonstrated; unascertained, untold, uncounted; untried, untested, in the experimental stage, at the trial s.

**Vb.** *be uncertain*, be contingent, lie in the lap of the gods; hinge on, be dependent on 157 *depend*; be touch and go, hang by a thread, tremble in the balance; be open to question, be ambiguous 518 *be equivocal*; have one's doubts 486 *doubt*; wait and see, wait on events 507 *await*; have a suspicion, suspect, wonder, wonder whether; dither, be in two minds, hover, float, be a don't know, sit on the fence, sway, seesaw, waver, teeter, vacillate, shilly-shally, falter, pause, hesitate 601 *be irresolute*; avoid a decision, boggle, stickle, demur; be in a maze, flounder, drift, be at sea; be in the dark, have nothing to go on, grope, fumble, cast about, beat a., experiment 461 *be tentative*; lose the thread, miss one's way, get lost 282 *stray*; lose the scent, lose track of, come to a standstill; not know which way to turn, be at one's wits' end, be at a loss, not know what to make of, have no answer, be in a dilemma, be in a quandary; wouldn't swear, could be wrong.

*puzzle*, perplex, confuse, maze, daze, bewilder, baffle, boggle the mind, nonplus, flummox, stump, floor 727 *defeat*; mystify, keep one guessing; bamboozle 542 *befool*; fog, fox, throw off the scent 495 *mislead*; plunge in doubt, plague *or* riddle with d. 486 *cause doubt*; make one think, ask for thought, demand reflection.

**Adv.** *in suspense*, in a state of uncertainty, on the horns of a dilemma, in a maze, in a daze.

SECTION FOUR

## Reasoning processes

### 475 Reasoning

**N.** *reasoning*, ratiocination, force of argument; reason, discursive r.; intuitive reason, lateral thinking 476 *intuition*; sweet reason, reasonableness, rationality; dialectics, art of reasoning, logic; logical process, logical sequence, inference, general i., generalization; distinction 463 *discrimination*; apriorism, apriority, a priori reasoning, deductive r., deduction; induction, inductive reasoning, a posteriori r., empirical r.; rationalism, dialectic 449 *philosophy*; Boolean algebra, set theory, Venn diagram; modern maths 86 *mathematics*; plain reason, simple arithmetic.

*premise*, postulate, basis of reasoning; universals; principle, general p., first p.; lemma, starting point; assumption, stipulation 512 *supposition*; axiom, self-evident truth 496 *maxim*; datum, data; hypothesis, provisional hypothesis, one's position; Occam's razor.

*argumentation*, critical examination, analysis 459 *enquiry*; dialectic, Socratic elenchus, dialogue, logical disputation; formal logic, symbolic l.; logical scheme, synthesis; syllogization, sorites, elench, major premise, minor p.; quodlibet, proposition, statement, thesis, theorem, problem; predication, lemma, predicate; inference, corollary; dilemma, horns of a d. 474 *uncertainty*; conclusion, logical c., QED 478 *demonstration*; reductio ad absurdum; paradoxical conclusion, paradox, Zeno's paradoxes 497 *absurdity*.

*argument*, discussion, symposium, dialogue; swapping opinions, exchange of views, give and take, cut and thrust; opposing arguments, disputation, controversy, debate 489 *dissent*;

appeal to reason, set *or* formal argument, plea, pleading, special p., thesis, case; reasons, submission; defensive argument, apologetics, defence; aggressive argument, destructive a., polemics, polemic; conciliatory argument 719 *peace offering*; war of words, paper war 709 *quarrel*; propaganda, soundbite, pamphleteering 534 *teaching*; controversialism, argumentativeness; hairsplitting, logic-chopping; logomachy; contentiousness, wrangling, jangling 709 *dissension*; bad argument, sophism 477 *sophistry*; legal argument, pleadings 959 *litigation*; argumentum ad hominem, play on the feelings; argument by analogy, parity of reasoning; tu quoque argument, same to you.

*reasons*, basis of argument, grounds; real reasons 156 *cause*; alleged reason 614 *pretext*; arguments, pros and cons; case, good c., case to answer; sound argument, strong a., cogent a., conclusive a., unanswerable a. 478 *demonstration*; point, valid p., point well taken, clincher.

*reasoner*, theologian 449 *philosopher*; logician, dialectician, syllogizer; methodist, methodologist; rationalist, euhemerist, demythologizer; sophister 477 *sophist*; casuist; polemic, polemist, polemicist, apologist, controversialist, eristic, controverter; arguer, debater, disputant; proponent, mooter, canvasser; pleader 958 *lawyer*; wrangler 709 *quarreller*; heckler, argumentative person, sea lawyer, barrack-room l., logomachist, quibbler, pedant; scholastic, schoolman 492 *intellectual*; mathematician, pure m.

**Adj.** *rational*, clear-headed, reasoning, reasonable; rationalistic, euhemeristic; ratiocinative, logical; cogent, acceptable, admissible, to the point, pointed, well-grounded, well-argued 9 *relevant*; sensible, fair 913 *just*; dianoetic, discursory, analytic, synthetic; consistent, systematic, methodological; dialectic, discursive, deductive, inductive, epagogic, maieutic; inferential, a posteriori, a priori, a fortiori, universal; axiomatic 473 *certain*; tenable 469 *possible*.

*arguing*, appealing to reason; polemical, irenic, apologetic; controversial, disputatious, eristic, argumentative, logomachic; quibbling 477 *sophistical*; disputable, controvertible, debatable, arguable 474 *uncertain*.

**Vb.** *be reasonable* 471 *be likely*; stand to reason, follow, hang together, hold water; appeal to reason; listen to reason, be guided by r., bow to r.; accept the argument, yield to a.; admit, concede, grant, allow 488 *assent*; have a case, have a case to be answered, have logic on one's side, have right on one's s.

*reason*, philosophize 449 *think*; syllogize, ratiocinate; rationalize, explain away; apply reason, bring reason to bear, use one's grey matter, put two and two together; deduce, induct; explain 520 *interpret*.

*argue*, argufy, argy-bargy, bandy arguments, give and take, cut and thrust; hold an argument, hold a symposium; exchange opinions, have an exchange of views, discuss, canvass 584 *confer*; debate, dispute, controvert; discept; quibble, split hairs, chop logic; indulge in argument, argue the case, argue the point, take a p., stick to one's p., stick to one's guns, refuse to budge; stress, strain, work an argument to death 532 *emphasize*; put one's case, plead; propagandize, pamphleteer 534 *teach*; take up the case, defend; attack, polemicize; try conclusions with, cross swords, take up a point with, join issue, demur, cavil 489 *dissent*; analyse, pull to pieces; out-argue, overwhelm with argument, bludgeon 479 *confute*; prove one's case 478 *demonstrate*; have words, have a confrontation, wrangle 709 *bicker*; answer back, make a rejoinder 460 *answer*; start an argument, move a motion, open a discussion *or* debate; propose, bring up, moot; have the last word, wind up a meeting.

*premise*, posit, postulate, stipulate, lay down, assume, hypothesize 512 *suppose*; take for granted, regard as axiomatic, refer to first principles.

**Adv.** *reasonably*, fairly, in all fairness, rationally, logically; polemically; hypothetically; a priori, a posteriori, a fortiori, how much the more, much less; consequently; for reasons given; in argument, in one's submission

## 476 Intuition: absence of reason

**N.** *intuition*, instinct, association, Pavlovian response, automatic reaction, gut r., knee-jerk r. 450 *absence of thought*; light of nature, sixth sense, extrasensory perception, ESP, psi, psi faculty; telepathy; insight, second sight, clairvoyance 984 *psychics*; id, subconscious 447 *spirit*; intuitiveness, direct apprehension, unmediated perception, a priori knowledge; divination, dowsing; inspiration, presentiment, impulse 818 *feeling*; intuitionism; hunch, impression, sense, guesswork; value judgment 481 *bias*; rule of thumb; feminine logic; self-deception, wishful thinking; irrationality, illogicality, illogic; unreason 503 *mental disorder*.

**Adj.** *intuitive*, instinctive, impulsive; nondiscursive, devoid of logic 477 *illogical*; impressionistic, subjective; involuntary 609 *spontaneous*; subconscious 447 *psychic*; above reason, beyond r., noumenal, independent of reason, unknown to logic, inspirational, inspired, clairvoyant, ESP, telepathic, direct, unmediated.

**Vb.** *intuit*, know by instinct, have a sixth sense; sense, feel in one's bones, have a funny feeling, have a hunch; somehow feel, get the impression; react automatically, have a gut reaction, react instinctively; play it by ear, go by impressions, rely on intuition, dispense with reason, use feminine logic; guess, have a g., use guesswork, work on a hunch.

**Adv.** *intuitively*, instinctively, by instinct, by guess and by God, by the light of nature.

### 477 Sophistry: false reasoning

**N.** *sophistry*, illogicalness, illogic; feminine logic 476 *intuition*; sophistical reasoning, false r., fallacious r., specious r., evasive r.; rationalization; double think, self-deception; mental reservation, arrière pensée 525 *conceal-ment*; equivocation, mystification; blinding with science, word fencing, casuistry; subtlety, oversubtlety; special pleading, hair-splitting, logic-chopping; claptrap, mere words 515 *empty talk*; logomachy, quibbling, quibble; chicanery, chicane, subterfuge, shuffle, dodge; evasion 614 *pretext*.

*sophism*, a sophistry, specious argument, insincere a.; exploded argument, fallacious a.; illogicality, fallacy, paralogism; bad logic, loose thinking, sloppy t.; solecism, flaw, logical f., flaw in the argument; begging the question, petitio principii; circular reasoning; ignoratio elenchi; unwarranted conclusion, non sequitur, irrelevancy, post hoc ergo propter hoc; contradiction in terms, antilogy; ignotum per ignotius; weak case, bad c., false c.

*sophist*, sophister, sophistical reasoner, casuist, quibbler, equivocator; caviller, devil's advocate.

**Adj.** *sophistical*, sophistic, specious, plaus-ible, ad captandum; evasive, insincere; hollow, empty; deceptive, illusive, illusory; overre-fined, oversubtle, fine-spun; pettifogging, cap-tious, quibbling; sophisticated, tortuous; casuistical.

*illogical*, contrary to reason, irrational, unreasonable; unreasoned, arbitrary; paral-ogistic, fallacious, fallible; contradictory, self-c., inconsistent, incongruous; unwar-ranted, invalid, untenable, unsound; unfounded, ungrounded, groundless; irrel-evant, inconsequent, inconsequential; incor-rect, unscientific, false 495 *erroneous*.

*poorly reasoned*, unrigorous, inconclusive; unproved, unsustained; weak, feeble; frivolous, airy, flimsy; loose, woolly, muddled, confused; woolly-headed, muddle-h.

**Vb.** *reason badly*, paralogize, argue in a

circle, beg the question, fail to get to the point, not see the wood for the trees, 'strain at a gnat and swallow a camel' (see quotation at 695 *act foolishly*) ; not have a leg to stand on; talk at random, babble, burble 515 *mean nothing*.

*mislead*, delude, sophisticate 535 *misteach*; mystify, fetishize 542 *befool*; quibble, cavil, split hairs 475 *argue*; equivocate 518 *be equivocal*; dodge, shuffle, fence 713 *parry*; not come to the point, beat about the bush 570 *be diffuse*; evade 667 *elude*; draw a veil over, var-nish, gloss over, whitewash 541 *cant*; colour 552 *misrepresent*; pervert, misapply 675 *misuse*; pervert reason, twist the argument, torture logic; prove that white is black.

### 478 Demonstration

**N.** *demonstration*, logic of facts, docu-mentation, authentication 466 *evidence*; proven fact 494 *truth*; proof, rigorous p.; estab-lishment, conclusive proof, final p.; conclus-iveness, irrefragability 473 *certainty*; verification, ascertainment 461 *experiment*; deduction, inference, argument, triumph of a. 475 *reasoning*; exposition, clarification 522 *manifestation*; burden of proof, onus.

**Adj.** *demonstrating*, demonstrative, proba-tive 466 *evidential*; deducible, inferential, conse-quential, following 9 *relevant*; apodictic 532 *affirmative*; convincing, proving; conclusive, categorical, decisive, crucial; heuristic 534 *edu-cational*.

*demonstrated*, evident, in evidence 466 *eviden-tial*; taken as proved, established, granted, allowed; unconfuted, unrefuted, unanswered; open and shut, unanswerable, undeniable, irre-futable, irrefragable, irresistible, incontrovert-ible 473 *certain*; capable of proof, demonstrable, testable, discoverable.

**Vb.** *demonstrate*, prove; show, evince 522 *manifest*; justify 927 *vindicate*; bear out 466 *cor-roborate*; produce the evidence, document, pro-vide documentation, substantiate, establish, verify 466 *evidence*; infer, deduce, draw, draw a conclusion 475 *reason*; settle the question, satisfy 473 *make certain*; make out, make out a case, prove one's point, clinch an argument, have the best of an a., win an a. 485 *convince*.

*be proved*, be demonstrated, prove to be true, emerge, follow, follow of course, stand to reason 475 *be reasonable*; stand, stand up to investi-gation, hold water, hold good 494 *be true*.

**Adv.** *of course*, provedly, undeniably, without doubt; as already proved; QED.

### 479 Confutation

**N.** *confutation*, refutation, disproof, invalida-tion; successful cross-examination, elenchus, exposure; conviction 961 *condemnation*; rebuttal, rejoinder, crushing *or* effective r., complete answer 460 *answer*; clincher, finisher, knock-down argument, crowning a.; tu quoque argument, last word, retort, repartee 839 *witticism*; reductio ad absurdum 851 *ridicule*; contradiction, denial, denunciation 533 *negation*; exploded argument, proved fallacy 477 *sophism*.

**Adj.** *confuted*, disproved etc. vb.; silenced, reduced to silence, exposed, without a leg to stand on; convicted 961 *condemned*; convicted on one's own showing, condemned out of one's own mouth; disprovable, refutable, confutable; tending to refutation, refutatory, refutative.

**Vb.** *confute*, refute, disprove, invalidate; rebut, rejoin, retort, have an answer, explain away; negative, deny, contradict 533 *negate*; give the lie to, force to withdraw; prove the contrary, show the fallacy of; cut the ground from under, leave someone without a leg to stand on; confound, rout, silence, reduce to s., stop the mouth, shut up, floor, gravel, nonplus; condemn one out of his own mouth; show up, expose; convict 961 *condemn*; convict one of unreason, defeat one's logic; blow sky-high, shoot full of holes, puncture, riddle, destroy, explode, demolish one's arguments, drive a coach and horses through, knock the bottom out of 165 *demolish*; have, have in one's hand, have one on the hip; overthrow, squash, crush, overwhelm 727 *defeat*; riddle the defence, outargue, triumph in argument, have the better of the a., get the better of, score off; parry, avoid the trap; stand, stand up to argument; dismiss, override, sweep aside, brush a.; brook no denial, affirm the contrary 532 *affirm*.

*be confuted*, – refuted etc. adj.; fall to the ground, have not a leg to stand on; exhaust one's arguments; have nothing left to say, have no answer.

**Adv.** *in rebuttal*, in disproof; on the other hand, per contra.

SECTION FIVE

## Results of reasoning

### 480 Judgment: conclusion

**N.** *judgment*, judging (see also *estimate*); good judgment, discretion 463 *discrimination*; bad judgment, lack of discretion 464 *indiscrimination*; power of judgment, discretionary judgment, arbitrament 733 *authority*; arbitration, umpirage; judgment on facts, verdict, finding; penal judgment, sentence, tariff 963 *punish-*

*ment*; summing-up, spoken judgment, pronouncement; act of judgment, decision, adjudication, award; order, court order, legal ruling, ruling, fatwa, order of the court 737 *decree*; interlocutory decree, decree nisi; decree absolute; judgment in appeal, appellate judgment; irrevocable decision; settled decision, res judicata; final judgment, conclusion, conclusion of the matter, result, upshot; moral 496 *maxim*; value judgment 476 *intuition*; reasoned judgment, deduction, inference, corollary 475 *reasoning*; wise judgment, j. of Solomon 498 *wisdom*; fair judgment, unclouded eye 913 *justice*; vox populi, voting, referendum, plebiscite, poll 605 *vote*.

*estimate*, estimation, view 485 *opinion*; axiology 449 *philosophy*; assessment, valuation, evaluation, calculation 465 *measurement*; consideration, ponderation; comparing, contrasting 462 *comparison*; transvaluation 147 *conversion*; appreciation, appraisal, appraisement 520 *interpretation*; criticism, constructive c. 703 *aid*; destructive criticism 702 *hindrance*; critique, crit, review, notice, press n., comment, comments, observations, remarks, profile 591 *article*; summing-up, recapitulation; survey 438 *inspection*; inspection report 524 *report*; favourable report 923 *approbation*: unfavourable report, censure 924 *disapprobation*; legal opinion, counsel's o., second o., professional advice 691 *advice*.

*estimator*, judge, adjudicator; arbitrator; referee, assistant r., linesman *or* -woman, fourth official, umpire; surveyor, valuer, valuator 465 *appraiser*; inspector, inspecting officer, reporter, examiner, ombudsman, ACAS (= Advisory, Conciliation and Arbitration Service) 459 *enquirer*; counsellor 691 *adviser*; censor, critic, reviewer 591 *dissertator*; commentator, observer 520 *interpreter*; juror, assessor 957 *jury*; voter, elector 605 *electorate*.

**Adj.** *judicial*, judicious, judgmatic 463 *discriminating*; shrewd 498 *wise*; unbiased, dispassionate 913 *just*; juridical, juristic, arbitral; judicatory, decretal; determinative, conclusive; moralizing, moralistic, sententious; expressive of opinion, censorial; censorious 924 *disapproving*; critical, appreciative; advisory 691 *advising*.

**Vb.** *judge*, sit in judgment, hold the scales; arbitrate, referee, umpire; hear, try, hear the case, try the cause 955 *hold court*; uphold an objection, disallow an o.; rule, pronounce; find, find for, find against; decree, award, adjudge, adjudicate; decide, settle, conclude; confirm, make absolute; pass judgment, deliver j.; sentence, pass s., doom 961 *condemn*; agree on a verdict, return a v., bring in a v.;

consider one's vote 605 *vote*; judge well, see straight; deduce, infer 475 *reason*; gather, collect; sum up, recapitulate; moralize 534 *teach*.

*estimate*, form an e., make an e., measure, calculate, make 465 *gauge*; value, evaluate, appraise; rate, rank; sum up, size up; conjecture, guess 512 *suppose*; take stock 808 *account*; consider, weigh, ponder, weigh the pros and cons, take everything into consideration 449 *meditate*; examine, investigate, run a check on, vet, post-mortem 459 *enquire*; express an opinion, pass an o., report on; commentate, comment, criticize, review 591 *dissertate*; survey, pass under review 438 *scan*; censor, censure 924 *disapprove*.

**Adv.** *sub judice*, under investigation, under trial, under sentence.

## 481 Misjudgment. Prejudice

**N.** *misjudgment*, miscalculation, misreckoning, misconception, wrong impression 495 *error*; loose thinking, sloppy t. 495 *inexactness*; bad judgment, poor j. 464 *indiscrimination*; lack of vision, blindness, short-sightedness, short-termism; fallibility, gullibility 499 *unintelligence*; obliquity of judgment, misconstruction 521 *misinterpretation*; wrong verdict, miscarriage of justice 914 *injustice*; overvaluation 482 *overestimation*; undervaluation 483 *underestimation*; autosuggestion, self-deception, self-delusion, wishful thinking 542 *deception*; fool's paradise 513 *fantasy*; false dawn 509 *disappointment*.

*prejudgment*, foregone conclusion, prejudication 608 *predetermination*; preconception, prenotion; mind made up, parti pris; preconceived idea, fixation, hang-up, idée fixe, monomania, obsession, bee in the bonnet, emotional baggage, something on the brain 503 *personality disorder*.

*prejudice*, prepossession, predilection; partiality, favouritism 914 *injustice*; penchant, bias, biased judgment, warped j., jaundiced eye; blind spot, blind side, tunnel vision, mote in the eye, beam in the e. 439 *blindness*; onesidedness, party spirit 708 *party*; partisanship, clannishness, cliquishness, esprit de corps; sectionalism, parochialism, provincialism, insularity; odium theologicum 978 *sectarianism*; nationalism, chauvinism, xenophobia, gung-ho attitude, 'my country right or wrong';

> Our country! In her intercourse with foreign nations, may she always be in the right; but our country, right or wrong.
>
> Stephen Decatur

> Our country, right or wrong! When right, to be kept right; when wrong, to be put right!
>
> Carl Schurz

snobbishness, class war, class prejudice, classism, social discrimination; ageism, granny-bashing, queer-bashing (offensive); ableism; fattism; heightism; sizeism; sexism, sex prejudice, sex discrimination, gender discrimination, male chauvinism, glass ceiling; heterosexism, homophobia; xenophobia, race prejudice, racialism, racism, institutional r., race hate, race hatred, Paki-bashing (offensive), colour prejudice, colour bar, apartheid, segregation, differentiation, discrimination 57 *exclusion*; intolerance, persecution, anti-Semitism 888 *hatred*.

*narrow mind*, narrow-mindedness, small-m., narrow views, narrow sympathies, cramped ideas, confined i.; insularity, parochialism, provincialism; closed mind, one-track m., tunnel vision; one-sidedness, overspecialization; legalism, pedantry, donnishness, hypercriticism 735 *severity*; illiberality, intolerance, dogmatism 473 *positiveness*; bigotry, fanaticism 602 *opinionatedness*; legalist, pedant, stickler 862 *perfectionist*; faddist 504 *crank*; zealot, bigot, fanatic 473 *doctrinaire*; racialist, racist, white supremacist; chauvinist, sexist.

*bias*, unbalance, disequilibrium 29 *inequality*; warp, bent, slant, liability, penchant 179 *tendency*; angle, point of view, private opinion 485 *opinion*; parti pris, mind made up (see also *prejudgment*); infatuation, obsession 503 *eccentricity*; crankiness, whimsicality, fad, craze, bee in one's bonnet, hang-up, obsession, emotional baggage 604 *whim*; Afrocentrism, Anglocentrism, Eurocentrism.

**Adj.** *misjudging*, misconceiving, misinterpreting etc. vb.; miscalculating, in error, out 495 *mistaken*; fallible, gullible 499 *foolish*; wrong, wrong-headed; unseeing 439 *blind*; myopic, purblind, short-sighted 440 *dim-sighted*; misguided, superstitious 487 *credulous*; subjective, unrealistic, visionary, impractical; crankish, faddy, faddish, whimsical 503 *crazy*; besotted, infatuated 887 *enamoured*; haunted, obsessed, hung up, eaten up with, consumed by.

*narrow-minded*, petty-m., narrow, confined, cramped, hidebound; short-sighted, tunnel-visioned; parochial, provincial, insular; pedantic, donnish 735 *severe*; legalistic, literal, literal-minded, unimaginative, matter-of-fact; hypercritical, overscrupulous, fiky, fussy 862 *fastidious*; stiff, unbending 602 *obstinate*; dictatorial, dogmatic 473 *positive*; opinionated, opinionative; self-opinioned, self-conceited 871 *proud*.

*biased*, warped, twisted, swayed; jaundiced, embittered; prejudiced, closed; snobbish, clannish, cliquish 708 *sectional*; partisan, one-sided, party-minded 978 *sectarian*; Afrocentric, Anglocentric, Eurocentric; nationalistic, chauvinistic, gung-hoish, jingoistic, xenophobic; racist, racialist; sexist, ageist, classist; class-prejudiced, colour-p.; predisposed, prepossessed, preconceived; prejudging 608 *predetermined*; unreasoning, unreasonable 477 *illogical*; discriminatory 914 *unjust*; illiberal, intolerant, persecuting 735 *oppressive*; bigoted, fanatic 602 *obstinate*; blinded 439 *blind*.

**Vb.** *misjudge*, miscalculate, miscount, misestimate 495 *blunder*; not take into account, reckon without; undervalue, minimize 483 *underestimate*; overestimate, overvalue 482 *overrate*; guess wrong, come to the wrong conclusion, misconjecture, misconceive 521 *misinterpret*; overreach oneself, overplay one's hand; get the wrong end of the stick, get the wrong sow by the ear 695 *act foolishly*; overspecialize, not see the wood for the trees; not see beyond one's nose 499 *be foolish*; fly in the face of facts 477 *reason badly*.

*prejudge*, forejudge, judge beforehand, prejudicate, make up one's mind in advance 608 *predetermine*; prejudice the issue, precondemn; preconceive, presuppose, presume 475 *premise*; rush to conclusions, jump to c., run away with a notion 857 *be rash*.

*bias*, warp, twist, bend; jaundice, prejudice, fill with p.; prepossess, predispose 178 *influence*; infatuate, haunt, obsess 449 *engross*.

*be biased*, – prejudiced etc. adj.; be one-sided, see one side only, show favouritism, favour one side 914 *do wrong*; lean, favour, take sides, have a down on, have it in for, hold it against one, be unfair, discriminate against 735 *oppress*; pontificate 473 *dogmatize*; be obsessed with, lose one's sense of proportion; suffer from tunnel vision, blind oneself to, have a blind side, have a blind spot 439 *be blind*.

### 482 Overestimation

**N.** *overestimation*, overestimate, overenthusiasm, overvaluation 481 *misjudgment*; overstatement 546 *exaggeration*; boasting 877 *boast*; ballyhoo, hype, build-up, overkill 528 *publicity*; overpraise, panegyric, gush, hot air 515 *empty talk*; storm in a teacup, much ado about nothing; megalomania, vanity 871 *pride*; overconfidence 857 *rashness*; egotism 932 *selfishness*; overoptimism, optimistic forecast, optimism; unnecessary pessimism, defeatism 853 *hopelessness*; optimist 852 *hope*; pessimist, prophet of doom, doomwatcher, doomster, Jonah, defeatist; exaggerator, puffer, barker, advertiser, promoter 528 *publicizer*.

**Adj.** *optimistic*, can-do, upbeat, sanguine, oversanguine, overconfident; highpitched,

overpitched; enthusiastic, overenthusiastic, raving.

*overrated*, overestimated, overvalued, overpraised; puffed, puffed-up, cracked-up, hyped-up, overdone, over-promoted 546 *exaggerated*.

**Vb.** *overrate*, overestimate, count all one's geese swans; overvalue, overprice, set too high a value on 811 *overcharge*; rave, idealize, overprize, overpraise, think too much of; make too much of 546 *exaggerate*; strain, overemphasize, overstress, overdo, play up, overpitch, inflate, magnify 197 *enlarge*; boost, cry up, puff, panegyrize, hype 923 *praise*; attach too much importance to, make mountains out of molehills, catch at straws; maximize, make the most of; make the best of, whitewash, paper over the cracks.

### 483 Underestimation

**N.** *underestimation*, underestimate, undervaluation, minimization; conservative estimate, modest calculation 177 *moderation*; depreciation 926 *detraction*; understatement, litotes, meiosis; euphemism 950 *prudery*; self-depreciation, self-effacement, overmodesty 872 *humility*; false modesty, mock m., irony 850 *affectation*; pessimism 853 *hopelessness*; pessimist, minimizer, cynic 926 *detractor*.

**Adj.** *depreciating*, depreciative, depreciatory, derogatory, pejorative, slighting, belittling, pooh-poohing 926 *detracting*; underestimating, minimizing, conservative 177 *moderate*; modest 872 *humble*; pessimistic, despairing 853 *hopeless*; mock-modest 850 *affected*; euphemistic 541 *hypocritical*.

*undervalued*, underrated, underpriced, insufficiently appreciated, underpraised, unprized, unappreciated; slighted, pooh-poohed 458 *neglected*.

**Vb.** *underestimate*, underrate, undervalue, underprice; mark down, discount 812 *cheapen*; depreciate, underpraise, run down, cry d., disparage 926 *detract*; slight, pooh-pooh 922 *hold cheap*; misprize, not do justice to, do less than justice 481 *misjudge*; understate, spare one's blushes; euphemize; play down, soft-pedal, slur over; shrug off 458 *disregard*; make little of, minimize; deflate, cut down to size, make light of, belittle, make no account of, set no store by, think too little of 922 *despise*; set at naught, scorn 851 *ridicule*.

### 484 Discovery

**N.** *discovery*, finding, rediscovery; invention; exploration, archaeology, speleology, potholing; excavation 459 *search*; detective instinct, nose, flair 619 *pursuit*; detection, spotting, espial 438 *inspection*; radiolocation 187 *location*; dowsing, water divining, rhabdomancy; ascertainment 473 *certainty*; exposure, revelation 522 *manifestation*; realization, lightbulb moment, the penny drops; illumination, disenchantment; hitting upon, accidental discovery, serendipity; a discovery, an invention, an inspiration; strike, find, lucky f., trouvaille, trover, treasure trove; eye-opener 508 *lack of expectation*; solution, explanation 520 *interpretation*; key, open sesame 263 *opener*.

*detector*, probe; space p., spy satellite 276 *spaceship*; asdic, sonar; early warning system, Earlybird; radar, radar trap, speed trap, Vascar (tdmk); breathalyser, breath test, sniffer torch; finder, telescopic f. 442 *telescope*; lie detector, polygraph; sensor; Geiger counter 465 *meter*; metal detector; divining rod, dowsing r.; dowser, water diviner; spotter, scout, talent s.; discoverer, inventor; explorer 268 *traveller*; archaeologist, speleologist, potholer 459 *enquirer*; prospector 461 *experimenter*; gastroscope, auriscope, ophthalmoscope, colposcope 658 *diagnosis*.

**Adj.** *discovering*, exploratory 461 *experimental*; on the scent, on the track, on the trail, warm, getting w.; near discovery, ripe for detection.

**Vb.** *discover*, rediscover, invent, explore, find a way 461 *experiment*; find out, hit it, have it; strike, hit, hit upon; come upon, happen on, stumble on; meet, encounter 154 *meet with*; realize, tumble to, awake to, see the truth, see the light, see as it really is, see in its true colours 516 *understand*; find, locate 187 *place*; recognize, identify 490 *know*; verify, ascertain 473 *make certain*; fish up, dig up, unearth, uncover, disinter, bring to light 522 *manifest*; elicit, worm out, ferret o., nose o., sniff o., smell o. 459 *search*; get wind of 524 *be informed*.

*detect*, expose, show up 522 *show*; get at the facts, find a clue, be on the track, be near the truth, be getting warm, see daylight; put one's finger on the spot, hit the nail on the head, saddle the right horse; descry, discern, perceive, notice, spot, sight, catch sight of 438 *see*; sense, trace, pick up; see the cloven hoof, smell a rat; nose, scent, wind, scent out; follow, tail, trail, trace, track down 619 *hunt*; set a trap for, trap, catch out 542 *ensnare*.

**Int.** eureka!, got it!

**485 Belief**
**N.** *belief*, act of believing, suspension of disbelief; credence, credit; state of belief, assurance, conviction, persuasion; strong feeling, firm impression; confidence, reliance, depen-

dence on, trust, faith; religious belief 973 *religious faith*; full belief, full assurance; uncritical belief 487 *credulity*; implicit belief, firm b., unshakable b., fixed b. 473 *certainty*; obsession, blind belief 481 *prejudice*; instinctive belief 476 *intuition*; subjective belief, self-persuasion, self-conviction; hope and belief, expectation, sanguine e. 852 *hope*; traditional belief, folklore; public belief, popular b., common b., public opinion; credibility 471 *probability*; one's credit, one's word of honour 929 *probity*; token of credit, pledge.

*creed*, formulated belief, credo, what one holds, what one believes; dogma 976 *orthodoxy*; precepts, principles, tenets, articles; catechism, articles of faith; rubric, canon, rule 496 *maxim*; declaration of faith, professed belief, profession, confession, confession of faith 526 *disclosure*; doctrine, system, school, ism 449 *philosophy*; study of creeds, symbolics 973 *theology*.

*opinion*, one's opinions, one's views, one's conviction, one's persuasion; sentiment, mind, view; point of view, viewpoint, stand, position, attitude, angle 438 *view*; received wisdom 488 *consensus*; impression 818 *feeling*; conception, concept, thought 451 *idea*; thinking, way of thinking, way of thought, body of opinions, outlook on life, Weltanschauung 449 *philosophy*; assumption, presumption, principle 475 *premise*; theory, hypothesis 512 *supposition*; surmise, guess 512 *conjecture*; conclusion 480 *judgment*; thought police.

**Adj.** *believing*, holding, maintaining, declaring etc. vb.; confident, assured, reliant, unshaken, secure 473 *certain*; sure, cocksure 473 *positive*; convinced, persuaded, satisfied, converted, sold on; imbued with, penetrated w., obsessed w., hung up on, possessed; firm in, wedded to; confiding, trustful, trusting, unhesitating, undoubting, unquestioning, unsuspecting, unsuspicious 487 *credulous*; conforming, loyal, pious 976 *orthodox*; having opinions, opinionated 481 *biased*.

*credible*, plausible, believable, tenable, reasonable 469 *possible*; likely, to be expected 471 *probable*; reliable, trustworthy, trusty, fiducial; worthy of credence, deserving belief, commanding b., persuasive, convincing, impressive 178 *influential*; trusted, believed; held, maintained; accepted, credited, accredited; supposed, putative, hypothetical 512 *suppositional*.

*credal*, taught, doctrinal, dogmatic, confessional; canonical, orthodox, authoritative, accredited, ex cathedra; of faith, accepted on trust; sacrosanct, unquestioned, God-given;

undeniable, absolute, unshakable 473 *undisputed.*

**Vb.** *believe*, be a believer 976 *be orthodox*; credit, put faith in, give faith to; hold, hold to be true; maintain, declare 532 *affirm*; believe religiously, perceive as true, take for gospel, believe for certain, firmly believe; profess, confess, recite the creed; receive, accept, admit, agree 488 *assent*; take on trust, take on credit; buy, swallow, swallow whole 487 *be credulous*; take for granted, assume 475 *premise*; have no doubt, make no d., cast doubt away, know for certain, be convinced, be sold on, be obsessed with, be hung up on 473 *be certain*; rest assured, be easy in one's mind about, be secure in the belief, rest in the b., believe implicitly; have confidence in, confide, trust, rely on, depend on, take one at his *or* her word; give one credit for, pin one's faith on, pin one's hopes on; have faith in, believe in, swear by, reckon on, count on, calculate on, bank on, be told, understand, know 524 *be informed*; come to believe, be converted; realize 484 *discover*; take as proven, grant, allow.

*opine*, think, conceive, fancy, ween, trow; have a hunch, surmise, guess 512 *suppose*; suspect, rather s.; be under the impression, have the i. 818 *feel*; deem, esteem, apprehend, assume, presume, take it, hold; embrace an opinion, adopt an o., imbibe an o., get hold of an idea, get it into one's head; have views, have a point of view, view as, take as, regard as, consider as, look upon as, set down as, hold for, account; hold an opinion, cherish an o., foster an o.; express an opinion, hazard an o. 532 *affirm*; change one's opinion, change one's mind 603 *recant.*

*convince*, make believe, assure, persuade, satisfy; make realize, bring home to 478 *demonstrate*; make confident, restore one's faith; convert, win over, bring o., bring round, wean from; bring to the faith, evangelize, spread the gospel; propagate a belief, propagandize, indoctrinate, proselytize, din into 534 *teach*; cram down one's throat; sell an idea to, put over, put across; have the ear of, gain one's confidence, sway one's belief 178 *influence*; compel belief, exact b.; obsess, haunt, mesmerize, hypnotize; come round to, convince oneself, be sold on.

*be believed*, be widely b., be received, gain wide acceptance; go down, go down well, be swallowed; find ready listeners, find willing ears; carry conviction, find credence, pass current, pass for truth, take hold of the mind, possess the m., dominate the m., obsess the m.

**Adv.** *credibly*, believably, supposedly, to the best of one's knowledge and belief; faithfully, on faith, on trust, on authority; on the strength of, on the evidence of, in the light of.

## 486 Unbelief. Doubt

**N.** *unbelief*, nonbelief, disbelief, incredulity, discredit; disagreement 489 *dissent*; inability to believe, agnosticism; denial, denial of assent 533 *negation*; contrary belief, conviction to the contrary 704 *opposition*; blank unbelief, unfaith, lack of faith; infidelity, misbelief 977 *heresy*; atheism 974 *irreligion*; derision, scorn, mockery 851 *ridicule*; change of belief, loss of faith, lapse of f., crisis of conscience, reversal of opinion, retraction 603 *recantation*; incredibility, implausibility 472 *improbability.*

*doubt* 474 *dubiety*; half-belief, critical attitude, hesitation, wavering, vacillation, shilly-shallying, uncertainty; misgiving, distrust, mistrust; suspiciousness, scrupulosity; scepticism, agnosticism, pyrrhonism; reserve, reservation, second thoughts 468 *qualification*; demur, objection 704 *opposition*; scruple, qualm, suspicion 854 *nervousness*; jealousness 911 *jealousy.*

*unbeliever*, no believer, disbeliever; heathen, infidel 977 *heretic*; atheist 974 *irreligionist*; sceptic, pyrrhonist, agnostic; doubter, doubting Thomas; dissenter 489 *dissentient*; lapsed believer, retractor, recanter 603 *tergiversator*; denier 533 *negation*; absolute disbeliever, dissenter from all creeds, nullifidian; cynic, pessimist, nobody's fool; scoffer, mocker, scorner 926 *detractor.*

**Adj.** *unbelieving*, disbelieving, incredulous, sceptical; heathen, infidel; nullifidian, creedless; unfaithful, lapsed 603 *tergiversating*; doubtful, undecided, wavering 474 *doubting*; suspicious, shy, shy of 854 *nervous*; oversuspicious 911 *jealous*; slow to believe, wary, distrustful, mistrustful; inconvincible, impervious, hard to convince; cynical, hardboiled, pessimistic, not born yesterday, no flies on 498 *intelligent.*

*unbelieved*, disbelieved, discredited, exploded; distrusted, mistrusted etc. vb.; incredible, unbelievable 470 *impossible*; inconceivable, unthinkable, unimaginable, staggering 864 *wonderful*; hard to believe, hardly credible; untenable, undeserving of belief, unworthy of credit; open to suspicion, open to doubt, unreliable, suspect, suspicious, questionable, disputable, far-fetched 474 *uncertified*; so-called, pretended, self-styled.

**Vb.** *disbelieve*, be incredulous, find hard to believe, explain away, discredit, refuse credit, greet with scepticism, withhold assent, disagree 489 *dissent*; not fall for, not buy; mock, scoff at 851 *ridicule*; deny, deny outright 533 *negate*; refuse to admit, ignore; change one's belief, retract, lapse, relapse 603 *recant*.

*doubt*, half-believe 474 *be uncertain*; demur, object, cavil, question, scruple, boggle, stick at, have reservations 468 *qualify*; pause, stop and consider, hesitate, waver 601 *be irresolute*; treat with reserve, distrust, mistrust, suspect, have fears 854 *be nervous*; be shy of, shy at; be sceptical, doubt the truth of, take leave to doubt; not trust, set no store by; have questions, have one's doubts, take with a pinch of salt, harbour doubts, cherish d., cherish scruples; entertain suspicions, smell a rat, scent a fallacy; hold back, not go all the way with one 598 *be unwilling*.

*cause doubt*, cast d., raise questions; cast a shadow over, involve in suspicion, render suspect; call in question, discredit 926 *defame*; shake, shake one's faith, undermine one's belief; stagger, startle 508 *surprise*; pass belief 472 *be unlikely*; argue against, deter, tempt 613 *dissuade*; impugn, attack 479 *confute*; keep one guessing 517 *be unintelligible*.

**Adv.** *incredibly*, unbelievably; in utter disbelief.

*doubtfully*, hesitatingly, with a pinch of salt.

**487 Credulity**
**N.** *credulity*, credulousness; simplicity, gullibility, naiveté; rash belief, uncritical acceptance 485 *belief*; will to believe, blind faith, unquestioning belief 612 *persuadability*; infatuation, dotage; self-delusion, self-deception, wishful thinking 481 *misjudgment*; superstition, superstitiousness; one's blind side 439 *blindness*; bigotry, fanaticism 602 *opinionatedness*; uncritical orthodoxy 83 *conformity*; credulous person, simpleton, sucker, mug 544 *dupe*.

**Adj.** *credulous*, believing, persuasible, persuadable, amenable; easily taken in, easily deceived, easily duped 544 *gullible*; uncynical, unworldly; naive, simple, unsophisticated, green; childish, silly, soft, stupid 499 *foolish*; overcredulous, overtrustful, overconfiding; doting, infatuated; obsessed; superstitious 481 *misjudging*; confiding, trustful, unsuspecting.

**Vb.** *be credulous*, be easily persuaded; kid oneself, fool o.; suspend one's judgment 477 *reason badly*; follow implicitly, believe every word, fall for, buy it, take on trust, take for granted, take for gospel 485 *believe*; accept 299 *absorb*; take the bait, rise to the b., swallow, swallow anything, swallow whole, swallow hook, line and sinker 544 *be duped*; run away with an idea *or* a notion, rush *or* jump to a conclusion; be superstitious, touch wood, keep one's fingers crossed; think the moon is made of green cheese, take the shadow for the substance; catch *or* clutch at straws, hope eternally 482 *overrate*; not hear a word against, dote, worship 481 *be biased*.

**488 Assent**
**N.** *assent*, yes, aye, uh-huh, yea, amen; hearty assent; welcome; agreement, concurrence 758 *consent*; acceptance, agreement in principle 597 *willingness*; acquiescence 721 *submission*; acknowledgment, recognition, realization; admission, no denial, clean breast, plea of guilty, self-condemnation, plea bargain, plea-bargaining 939 *penitence*; confession, avowal 526 *disclosure*; declaration of faith, profession 532 *affirmation*; sanction, nod, OK, imprimatur, thumbs up, go-ahead, green light 756 *permission*; approval 923 *approbation*; concurrent testimony, accordance, corroboration 466 *evidence*; confirmation, verification 478 *demonstration*; validation, ratification; authentication, certification, endorsement, seal, signature, mark, cross; visa, passport, pass 756 *permit*; stamp, rubber s. 547 *label*; favour, sympathy 706 *cooperation*; support 703 *aid*; assentation 925 *flattery*.

*consensus*, consentience, same mind 24 *agreement*; concordance, harmony, unison 710 *concord*; unanimity, solid vote, general consent, common c., universal agreement, universal testimony; consentaneity, popular belief, public opinion, vox populi, general voice, received wisdom; chorus, single voice; likemindedness, thinking alike, same wavelength, mutual sympathy, two minds with but a single thought 18 *similarity*; bipartisanship, interparty agreement, global a.; understanding, mutual u., bargain 765 *compact*.

*assenter*, follower 83 *conformist*; fellow traveller, ally, cooperator 707 *collaborator*; assentator, yes-man 925 *flatterer*; the ayes, consentient voice, willing voter; cheerer, acclaimer 923 *commender*; upholder, supporter, active s., abettor 703 *aider*; seconder, assentor 707 *patron*; ratifier, authenticator; subscriber, endorser 765 *signatory*; party, consenting p., covenanter; confessor, professor, declarant.

**Adj.** *assenting*, assentient 758 *consenting*; consentient, concurring, party to 24 *agreeing*; fellow-travelling, aiding and abetting, supporting, collaborating 706 *cooperative*; likeminded, sympathetic, on the same wavelength, welcoming 880 *friendly*; consentaneous 710 *concordant*; unanimous, solid, with one voice, in chorus; acquiescent 597 *willing*; delighted 824 *pleased*; allowing, granting 756 *permitting*; sanctioning, ratificatory; not opposed, conceding.

*assented*, acquiesced in, voted, carried, carried by acclamation, carried nem. con., carried unanimously, agreed on all hands; unopposed, unanimous; uncontradicted, unquestioned, uncontested, unchallenged, uncontroverted 473 *undisputed*; admitted, granted, conceded 756 *permitted*; ratified, confirmed, signed, rubber-stamped, sealed; uncontroversial, nonparty, bipartisan.

**Vb.** *assent*, concur, agree with 24 *accord*; welcome, hail, cheer, acclaim 923 *applaud*; agree on all points, accept in toto, go all the way with, have no reservations 473 *be certain*; accept, agree in principle, like the idea, buy it; not deny, concede, admit, own, acknowledge, grant, allow 475 *be reasonable*; admit the charge, plead guilty, avow 526 *confess*; signify assent, nod a., nod, say aye, say yes, raise one's hand in assent, agree to, give one's assent, go along with 758 *consent*; sanction 756 *permit*; ratify (see also *endorse*); coincide in opinion, voice the same o., agree with, see eye to eye, be on the same wavelength; chime in with, echo, ditto, say amen, say hear hear; back up, say the same, chorus; defer to 920 *respect*; be a yes-man, rubberstamp 925 *flatter*; reciprocate, sympathize 880 *be friendly*; accede, adhere, side with 708 *join a party*; collaborate, go along with 706 *cooperate*; tolerate (see also *acquiesce*); covenant, agree upon, come to an understanding, have a mutual agreement 765 *contract*.

*acquiesce*, not oppose, accept, abide by 739 *obey*; tolerate, not mind, put up with, suffer, bear, endure, wear it; sign on the dotted line, toe the l., bite the bullet 721 *submit*; yield, defer to, withdraw one's objections; let the ayes have it, allow 756 *permit*; let it happen, look on 441 *watch*; go with the stream *or* crowd, swim with the s., float with the current, join in the chorus, follow the fashion *or* trend, run with the pack, jump on the bandwagon 83 *conform*.

*endorse*, second, support, back up, vote for, give one's vote to 703 *patronize*; subscribe to, attest 547 *sign*; seal, stamp, rubberstamp, confirm, ratify, sanction, authorize, homologate 758 *consent*; authenticate 473 *make certain*; countersign.

**Adv.** *consentingly*, willingly, with all one's heart, wholeheartedly; by consent, in full agreement, all the way, on all points.

*unanimously*, with one accord, with one voice, with one consent, one and all, in chorus, to a man, nem. con.; by show of hands, by acclamation; on the nod.

**Int.** amen!, amen to that!, hear hear!, aye, aye!, so be it!, well said!, as you say!, you said it!, you can say that again!, how right you are!, I couldn't agree more!, yes indeed!, yes!, absolutely!

## 489 Dissent

**N.** *dissent*, amicable dissent, agreement to disagree *or* differ; dissidence, difference, confirmed opposition 704 *opposition*; dissentience, no brief for; difference of opinion, diversity of o., dissentient voice, contrary vote, a vote against, disagreement, discordance, controversy 709 *dissension*; party feeling, party spirit, faction 708 *party*; popular clamour 891 *anger*; disaffection 829 *discontent*; dissatisfaction, disapproval 924 *disapprobation*; repudiation 607 *rejection*; protestantism, nonconformism, schism 978 *sectarianism*; counterculture, alternative life style, New Age philosophy, alternative medicine, alternative birth, alternative comedy 84 *nonconformity*; withdrawal, secession 621 *relinquishment*; walkout 145 *strike*; reluctance 598 *unwillingness*; recusancy 738 *disobedience*; noncompliance 769 *nonobservance*; denial, lack of consent 760 *refusal*; contradiction 533 *negation*; recantation, retraction 603 *tergiversation*; doubtfulness 486 *doubt*; cavil, demur, objection, demurrer, reservation 468 *qualification*; protest, expostulation, protestation, hostile demonstration 762 *deprecation*; challenge 711 *defiance*; passive resistance, noncooperation 738 *sedition*.

*dissentient*, objector, caviller, critic 926 *detractor*; interrupter, heckler, obstructor 702 *hinderer*; dissident, dissenter, protester, protestant; sectary 978 *sectarian*; separatist, seceder 978 *schismatic*; rebel 738 *revolter*; dropout 84 *nonconformist*; grouser 829 *malcontent*; odd man out, minority; splinter group, breakaway party, cave, faction 708 *party*; the noes, the opposition 704 *opposition*; noncooperator, conscientious objector, passive resister, peace women, CND, green party, ecowarrior, ecotage 705 *opponent*; challenger, agitator, firebrand, revolutionary 149 *revolutionist*; recanter, apostate 603 *tergiversator*.

**Adj.** *dissenting*, dissentient, differing, dissident 709 *quarrelling*; agnostic, sceptical, unconvinced, unconverted 486 *unbelieving*; separatist, schismatic 978 *sectarian*; nonconformist 84 *unconformable*; malcontent, dissatisfied 829 *discontented*; recanting, apostate 603 *tergiversating*; unassenting, unconsenting, not consenting 760 *refusing*; protesting 762 *deprecatory*; recusant, noncompliant 769 *nonobservant*; disinclined, loath, reluctant 598 *unwilling*; obstructive 702 *hindering*; challenging 711 *defiant*; resistant 704 *opposing*; intolerant, persecuting 735 *oppressive*.

*unadmitted*, unacknowledged, negatived, denied 533 *negative*; out of the question, disallowed 757 *prohibited*.

**Vb.** *dissent*, differ, agree to d. 25 *disagree*; beg to differ, make bold to d., combat an opinion, pick a bone with, take one up on 479 *confute*; demur, enter a demurrer, object, raise objections, have reservations, cavil, boggle, scruple 468 *qualify*; protest, raise one's voice against, demonstrate a. 762 *deprecate*; resist 704 *oppose*; challenge 711 *defy*; show reluctance 598 *be unwilling*; withhold assent, say no, shake one's head, not wear it 760 *refuse*; shrug one's shoulders, wash one's hands of it 860 *be indifferent*; disallow 757 *prohibit*; negative, contradict 533 *negate*; repudiate, hold no brief for, not defend; have no notion of, never intend to 607 *reject*; look askance at, not hold with, revolt at the idea 924 *disapprove*; go one's own way, secede, form a breakaway party, form a splinter group, withdraw 621 *relinquish*; recant, retract 603 *change one's allegiance*; argue, wrangle, bicker 709 *quarrel*.

**Adv.** *no*, on the contrary, no way; at issue with, at variance w.; under protest; in the negative 760 *denyingly*.

**Int.** God forbid!, not on your life!, not on your nelly!, over my dead body!, ask me another!, tell that to the marines!, never again!, not likely!

## 490 Knowledge

**N.** *knowledge*, ken; knowing, cognition, cognizance, recognition, realization; intellection, apprehension, comprehension, perception, understanding, grasp, mastery 447 *intellect*; conscience, consciousness, awareness; consciousness raising; insight 476 *intuition*; precognition 510 *foresight*; illumination 975 *revelation*; lights, enlightenment 498 *wisdom*; acquired knowledge, learning, lore (see also *erudition*); folk wisdom, folklore; occult lore 983 *sorcery*; education, background; experience, practical e., hands-on e., acquaintance, nodding a., acquaintanceship, familiarity, intimacy; private knowledge, privity, being in the know, sharing the secret 524 *information*; no secret, un secret de Polichinelle; public knowledge, notoriety, common knowledge, open secret 528 *publicity*; complete knowledge, omniscience; partial knowledge, intimation, sidelight, glimpse, glimmering, inkling, suggestion 524 *hint*; suspicion, scent; sensory knowledge, impression 818 *feeling*; self-knowledge, introspection, navel-gazing; detection, clue 484 *discovery*; specialism, specialization, expert knowledge, savoir faire, savvy, know-how, expertise 694 *skill*; half-knowledge, semi-

ignorance, smattering 491 *sciolism*; knowability, knowableness, recognizability 516 *intelligibility*; epistemics, science of knowledge; epistemology, theory of knowledge; cognitive science.

*erudition*, lore, wisdom, scholarship, letters, literature 536 *learning*; acquired knowledge, general k., practical k., empirical k., experimental k.; academic knowledge, professional k., encyclopedic k., universal k., polymathy, pansophy; solid learning, deep l., profound learning; small l., little l.; superficial l., smattering, dilettantism 491 *superficial knowledge*; reading, wide r., desultory r.; learning by rote, book-learning, bookishness, bibliomania; pedantry, donnishness; information, precise i., varied i., general i.; mine of information, store of knowledge, encyclopedia 589 *library*; department of learning, faculty 539 *academy*; scholar 492 *intellectual*.

*culture*, letters 557 *literature*; the humanities, the arts, the visual a.; education, instruction, computer-aided or -assisted i., CAI 534 *teaching*; literacy, numeracy; liberal education, scientific e.; autodidactism, self-education, self-instruction; civilization, cultivation, cultivation of the mind; sophistication, acquirements, acquisitions, attainments, accomplishments, proficiency, mastery.

*science*, exact s., natural s., metascience, the life sciences; natural philosophy, experimental p.; scientific knowledge, systematic k., progressive k., accurate k., verified k., body of k., organized k., applied science, technology, computer science; tree of knowledge, ologies and isms.

**Adj.** *knowing*, all-k., encyclopedic, comprehensive, omniscient 498 *wise*; cognizant, cognitive 447 *mental*; conscious, aware, mindful of 455 *attentive*; alive to, sensible of 819 *impressible*; experienced, competent, no stranger to, at home with, acquainted, familiar with, au fait with 610 *habituated*; intimate, privy to, sharing the secret, wise to, on to, in the know, in on, behind the scenes 524 *informed*; fly, canny, shrewd 498 *intelligent*; conversant, practised, versed in, proficient 694 *expert*; having hands-on experience.

*instructed*, briefed, primed, made acquainted, informed of, au courant 524 *informed*; taught, trained, bred to; lettered, literate; numerate; computerate; schooled, educated, well-e.; learned, book-l., bookish, literary; erudite, scholarly 536 *studious*; read in, well-read, widely-r., well-informed, knowledgeable; donnish, scholastic, pedantic; highbrow, intellectual, cultured, cultivated, sophisticated, Bloomsbury, bluestocking; strong in, well-qualified; professional, specialized 694 *expert*; given hands-on experience.

*known*, cognized, perceived, seen, heard; ascertained, verified 473 *certain*; realized, understood; discovered, explored; noted, celebrated, famous 866 *renowned*; no secret, open s., public, notorious 528 *well-known*; familiar, intimate, dear; too familiar, hackneyed, stale, trite; proverbial, household, commonplace, corny, clichéd 610 *usual*; current, prevalent 79 *general*; memorized, known by heart, learnt by rote, learnt off 505 *remembered*; knowable, cognizable, cognoscible; teachable, discoverable 516 *intelligible*.

**Vb.** *know*, savvy, ken, wot, wot of, ween; have knowledge, have a nodding acquaintance with, be acquainted; apprehend, conceive, catch, grasp, twig, click, have, take in, get 516 *understand*; know entirely, possess, comprehend, master; come to know, latch on, get the hang of, get into one's head, realize; get to know, acquaint oneself, familiarize o., become au fait with; know again, recognize; know the value, appreciate; be conscious of, be aware, have cognizance, be cognizant 447 *cognize*; discern 463 *discriminate*; perceive 438 *see*; examine, study 438 *scan*; go over, mull, con 455 *be attentive*; know well, know full w., be thoroughly acquainted with, see through, read one like a book, have one's measure, have one taped, have one sized up, know inside out; know down to the ground, know from A to Z, know like the back of one's hand; know for a fact 473 *be certain*; know of, have knowledge of, know something; be in the know, be in the secret, have the lowdown 524 *be informed*; know by heart, know by rote 505 *memorize*; know backwards, have it pat, have at one's fingertips, be master of, know one's stuff 694 *be expert*; have a little knowledge of 491 *not know*; experience, know by e., learn one's lesson 536 *learn*; get the picture, see the light; know all the answers; be omniscient; know what's what, see one's way, know one's way about 498 *be wise*.

*be known*, become k., come to one's knowledge, be brought to one's notice, come to one's ears; lie within one's cognizance, be knowable; be a well-known fact, be public knowledge, be an open secret, be no secret 528 *be published*.

**Adv.** *knowingly*, with knowledge; learnedly, scientifically; as every schoolchild knows.

**491 Ignorance**
**N.** *ignorance*, unknowing, nescience; lack of news, no news, no word of; unawareness, unconsciousness 375 *insensibility*; incogniz-

ance, nonrecognition, nonrealization; incomprehension, incapacity, backwardness 499 *unintelligence*; inappreciation, Philistinism 439 *blindness*; ecological ignorance, bioblindness; obstacle to knowledge, obscurantism; false knowledge, superstition 495 *error*; blind ignorance, abysmal i., crass i.; monumental i.; lack of knowledge, no science; lack of education, no schooling; untaught state, blankness, blank mind, tabula rasa; unacquaintance, unfamiliarity, inexperience, lack of experience, greenness, rawness; gaucherie, awkwardness, Asperger's syndrome; inexpertness, amateurishness 695 *unskilfulness*; innocence, simplicity, naivety 699 *artlessness*; nothing to go on, no lead, lack of information, general ignorance, anybody's guess, bewilderment 474 *uncertainty*; moral ignorance, unwisdom 499 *folly*; darkness, benightedness, unenlightenment; savagery, heathenism, paganism 982 *idolatry*; Age of Ignorance, Dark Ages; imperfect knowledge, semi-ignorance (see also *sciolism*); ignorant person, illiterate 493 *ignoramus*; layman, autodidact, amateur, no expert 697 *bungler*; obscurantist; Philistine.

*unknown thing*, obstacle to knowledge; unknown quantity, matter of ignorance; prehistory 125 *antiquity*; sealed book, closed b., Greek; Dark Continent, terra incognita, unknown country, unexplored ground, virgin soil, lion country; frontiers of knowledge; dark horse, wild card, enigma, mystery 530 *secret*; unidentified flying object, UFO; unidentified body; unknown person, mystery p., Mr *or* Miss X., anonymity 562 *no name*.

*superficial knowledge*, sciolism, smattering, smatter, a little learning; glimmering, glimpse, half-glimpse 524 *hint*; vagueness, half-knowledge 495 *inexactness*; unreal knowledge 495 *error*; superficiality 212 *shallowness*; dilettantism, dabbling; affectation of knowledge, pedantry, quackery, charlatanism, bluff 850 *affectation*; smatterer 493 *sciolist*.

**Adj.** *ignorant*, nescient, unknowing, blank; incognizant, unrealizing, uncomprehending; in ignorance, unwitting; unaware, unconscious, oblivious 375 *insensible*; unhearing, unseeing; unfamiliar with, not au fait with, unacquainted, a stranger to, not at home with; in the dark (see also *uninstructed*); reduced to guessing, mystified 474 *uncertain*; bewildered, confused, at one's wits' end; clueless, without a clue, with nothing to go on; blinkered, blindfolded 439 *blind*; groping, tentative 461 *experimental*; lay, amateurish, nonprofessional, unqualified, inexpert, ham 695 *unskilful*; unversed, not conversant, inexperienced, uninitiated, green, raw, wet behind the ears; innocent of, guiltless 935 *innocent*; naive, simple, unworldly 699 *artless*; knowing no better, gauche, awkward; unenlightened, benighted; savage, uncivilized; pagan, heathenish 982 *idolatrous*; backward, dull, dense, dumb 499 *unintelligent*; empty-headed, foolish 499 *unwise*; half-baked, obscurantist, unscientific; dark, superstitious, prescientific 481 *misjudging*; old-fashioned, out of touch, behind the times 125 *retrospective*; unretentive, forgetting 506 *forgetful*; regardless 456 *inattentive*; wilfully ignorant, indifferent 454 *incurious*.

*uninstructed*, unbriefed, uninformed, unapprised, not told, no wiser, kept in the dark; not rightly informed, misinformed, mistaught, misled, hoodwinked; not fully informed, ill-i., vague about 474 *uncertain*; unschooled, untaught, untutored, untrained; unlettered, illiterate, innumerate, uneducated; unlearned, uncultivated, uncultured, lowbrow; unscholarly, unbookish, unread, Philistine; simple, dull, dense, dumb (see also *ignorant*).

*unknown*, unbeknown, untold, unheard; unspoken, unsaid, unvoiced, unuttered; unseen, never seen 444 *invisible*; hidden, veiled 525 *concealed*; unrecognized 525 *disguised*; unapprehended, unrealized, unperceived; unexplained 517 *unintelligible*; dark, enigmatic, mysterious 523 *occult*; strange, new, newfangled, unfamiliar, unprecedented; unnamed 562 *anonymous*; unidentified, unclassified, uninvestigated 458 *neglected*; undiscovered, unexplored, uncharted, untravelled, unplumbed, unfathomed; untried, untested; virgin, novel 126 *new*; unknowable, undiscoverable; unforeseeable, unpredictable 124 *future*; unknown to fame, unheard of, obscure, humble 639 *unimportant*; lost, missing 190 *absent*; out of mind 506 *forgotten*.

*dabbling*, smattering, sciolistic; unqualified, quack, charlatanic, bluffing 850 *affected*; half-educated, semiliterate, semieducated; half-baked, shallow, superficial, dilettante.

**Vb.** *not know*, be ignorant, be in the dark, lack information, have nothing to go on, have no lead; be unacquainted, not know from Adam; be innocent of, be green, be wet behind the ears, know no better; know not, wist not, cannot say; not know the half of, have no conception, have no notion, have no clue, have no idea, have not the remotest i., not have the foggiest, not have an inkling, can only guess, be reduced to guessing 512 *suppose*; know nothing of, wallow in ignorance; not hear 416 *be deaf*; have a film over one's eyes, not see, suffer from tunnel vision 439 *be blind*; be at a loss, be stumped, not know what to make of 474 *be uncertain*; not know the first thing

about, have everything to learn, have to start at the bottom, not know one's arse from one's elbow (inf) 695 *be unskilful*; not know chalk from cheese 464 *not discriminate*; misunderstand 517 *not understand*; misconstrue 481 *misjudge*; half know, know a little, have a smattering, dabble in; half glimpse, guess, suspect, wonder 486 *doubt*; unlearn 506 *forget*; lack interest 454 *be incurious*; refuse to know, ignore 458 *disregard*; make ignorant, unteach 535 *misteach*; keep in the dark, mystify 525 *keep secret*; profess ignorance, shrug one's shoulders, not want to know 860 *be indifferent*; want to know, ask 459 *enquire*; grope, fumble 461 *be tentative*.

**Adv.** *ignorantly*, in ignorance, unawares; unconsciously; amateurishly, unscientifically; dimly, through a glass darkly; for all one knows.

## 492 Scholar

**N.** *scholar*, savant(e), learned person, erudite p., educated p., man *or* woman of learning, man *or* woman of letters, bookman, bookwoman, bibliophile; don, reader, professor, pedagogue 537 *teacher*; doctor, clerk, scribe, pedant, bookworm, bluestocking; classicist, humanist; polymath, polyhistor, pantologist, encyclopedist; prodigy of learning, mine of information, walking encyclopedia, talking dictionary; student, serious student 538 *learner*; degree-holder, graduate, diploma-holder, qualified person, professional, specialist 696 *proficient person*; world of learning, academic circles, academia, groves of academe, senior common room, professoriate.

*intellectual*, academic, scholastic, schoolman 449 *philosopher*; brain worker; mastermind, brain, genius, gifted child, prodigy 500 *sage*; know-all, brainbox; highbrow, egghead, bluestocking, bas bleu, brahmin, longhair; intelligentsia, literati, illuminati, intellectual snob; man *or* woman of science, scientist, technologist; boffin, backroom boy *or* girl; academician, Immortal; patron of learning, Maecenas.

*collector*, connoisseur, dilettante 846 *people of taste*; librarian, curator 749 *keeper*; antiquary 125 *antiquarian*; book-collector, coin-collector, egg-collector, stamp-collector 504 *enthusiast*; completist;

---

**Collectors and Collecting**

*collectors:* arctophile (teddy bears), bibliophile *or* bibliophilist *or* bibliomaniac *or* bibliomane (books), cartophilist (cigarette cards), deltiologist (postcards), discophile *or* discophil (gramophone records), lepidopterist (butterflies and moths), medallist (medals), notaphilist (banknotes and cheques), numismatist (coins and medals), philatelist (stamps), phillumenist (match-boxes), scripophilist (bonds and share certificates), tegestologist or tegetologist (beer mats).

*collecting:* arctophily (teddy bears), bibliophily or bibliomania (books), cartophily (cigarette cards), deltiology (postcards), notaphily (banknotes and cheques), numismatics (coins and medals), philately (stamps), phillumeny (match-boxes), scripophily (bonds and share certificates), tegestology or tegetology (beer mats).

collector of words, compiler, lexicographer, philologist 557 *linguist*.

### 493 Ignoramus

**N.** *ignoramus*, know-nothing, illiterate, analphabet, no scholar, lowbrow; philistine 847 *vulgarian*; duffer, wooden spoon, thickhead, numskull, bimbo, empty suit 501 *dunce*; bonehead, blockhead, goof, goose, bungler 501 *fool*; greenhorn, novice, raw recruit 538 *beginner*; simpleton, babe, innocent 544 *dupe*; bigot 481 *narrow mind*.

*dabbler*, sciolist, smatterer, half-scholar, pedant 500 *wiseacre*; dabbler, dilettante; quack, charlatan 545 *impostor*.

### 494 Truth

**N.** *truth*, the very t., verity, sooth, good s.; rightness, intrinsic truth; basic truth, primary premise; truism, platitude 496 *axiom*; consistency, self-c., accordance with fact; truth of the matter, honest truth, living t., plain t., simple t.; sober truth, stern t.; light, light of truth, revealed t., gospel t., gospel, Holy Writ, Bible 975 *revelation*; nature 321 *world*; facts, lowdown, the heart of the matter, facts of life 1 *existence*; actuality, historicity 1 *reality*; factualness, fact, matter of f., factoid 3 *substantiality*; home truth, candour, frankness 929 *probity*; naked truth, unvarnished t., unqualified t., unalloyed t.; the t., the whole t. and nothing but the t.; truth-speaking, truthfulness 540 *veracity*; appearance of truth, verisimilitude 471 *probability*.

*authenticity*, validity, realness, genuineness; the real Simon Pure, the real McCoy, the real thing, the very t., the genuine article, it 13 *identity*; no illusion, not a fake 21 *no imitation*.

*accuracy*, care for truth, attention to fact; verisimilitude, realism, naturalism, local colour, 'warts and all' (see quotation below) ; fine adjustment, sensitivity, fidelity, high f., exactitude, exactness, preciseness, precision, mathematical p., clockwork p.; micrometry 465 *measurement*; mot juste, hitting the nail on the head, aptness 24 *adaptation*; meticulousness, punctiliousness 455 *attention*; pedantry, rigidity, rigour, letter of the law, acting according to the book 735 *severity*; literality, literalness 514 *meaning*; spell-check; true report,

the very words, a verbatim account 540 *veracity*; chapter and verse, facts, statistics 466 *evidence*.

**Adj.** *true*, veritable; correct, right, so; real, tangible 3 *substantial*; actual, factual, historical; well-grounded, well-founded, well-thought-out; well-argued, well-taken 478 *demonstrated*; literal, truthful 540 *veracious*; true to the facts, true to scale, true to the letter, according to the book (see also *accurate*); categorically true, substantially t.; likely, very l. 471 *probable*; ascertained 473 *certain*; unquestionable 473 *undisputed*; consistent, self-c., logical, reasonable 475 *rational*; natural, true to life, true to nature, undistorted, faithful, verbatim; realistic, objective, unbiased; unromantic, unideal, down to earth; candid, honest, unflattering, 'warts and all' 522 *undisguised*.

> Mr Lely, I desire you would use all your skill to paint my picture truly like me, and not flatter me at all; but remark all these roughnesses, pimples, warts, and everything as you see me, otherwise I will never pay a farthing for it.
> Oliver Cromwell

*genuine*, no other, as represented; authentic, veritable, bona fide, valid, guaranteed, authenticated, official, pukka; sound, solid, reliable, honest 929 *trustworthy*; natural, pure, sterling, hallmarked, true as steel; dinkum, fair d., Simon Pure; true-born, by birth; rightful, legitimate; unadulterated, unsophisticated, unvarnished, uncoloured, straight from the shoulder, undisguised, undistorted, unexaggerated.

*accurate*, exact, precise, definite, defined; well-adjusted, well-pitched, high-fidelity, dead-on 24 *adjusted*; well-aimed, direct, straight, dead-centre 281 *directed*; unerring, undeviating; constant, regular 16 *uniform*; punctual; correct, right, true, bang on, bang to rights (inf), spot on, on the button, on the mark; never wrong, infallible; close, faithful, representative, photographic; fine, nice, delicate, sensitive; mathematical, scientific, electronic, micrometric; mathematically exact, scientifically e., religiously e.; scrupulous, punctilious, meticulous, strict, severe 455 *attentive*; word for word, verbatim, literal; literal-minded, rigid, pedantic, just so 862 *fastidious*.

**Vb.** *be true*, be so, be just so, be the case, happen, exist 1 *be*; hold, hold true, hold good, hold water, wash, stand, stand the test, ring true; conform to fact, prove true, hold together, be consistent; have truth, enshrine a t.; speak the truth, omit nothing 540 *be truthful*; look true, seem real, come alive, copy nature 551 *represent*; square, set, trim 24 *adjust*; substantiate 466 *corroborate*; prove 478 *demon-*

*strate*; be right, be correct, have the right answer; get at the truth, hit the nail on the head, hit the mark, be spot on 484 *detect*.

**Adv.** *truly*, verily, undeniably, indubitably, certainly, undoubtedly, really, veritably, genuinely, indeed; as a matter of fact 1 *actually*; to tell the truth 540 *truthfully*; strictly speaking, sensu stricto; sic, literally, to the letter, word for word, verbatim; exactly, accurately, precisely, plumb, right, to an inch, to a hair, to a nicety, to a turn, to a T, just right, spot on; in every detail, in all respects, tout à fait.

**495 Error**
**N.** *error*, erroneousness, wrongness, unsoundness; silliness 497 *absurdity*; untruth, unreality, nonobjectivity; falsity, unfactualness, nonhistoricity 2 *nonexistence*; errancy, straying from the truth, inexactitude 282 *deviation*; inaccuracy, logical error, fallacy, self-contradiction 477 *sophism*; credal error, misbelief, unorthodoxy 977 *heterodoxy*; mists of error, wrong ideas, old wives' tales, superstition, vulgar error, popular misconception, mumpsimus 491 *ignorance*; liability to error, fallibility 481 *misjudgment*; subjective error, subjectivity, unrealism, mistaken belief, wishful thinking, doublethink, self-deceit, self-deception; misunderstanding, misconception, misconstruction, cross-purposes 521 *misinterpretation*; misguidance 535 *misteaching*; bad memory, forgetfulness, senior moment 506 *oblivion*; falseness, untruthfulness 541 *falsehood*; illusion, hallucination, mirage 440 *visual fallacy*; false memory; false pregnancy, pseudocyesis; false light, false dawn 509 *disappointment*; mental error, delusion 503 *mental disorder*; flattering hope, dream 513 *fantasy*; false impression, wrong idea (see also *mistake*); warped notion, prejudice 481 *bias*.

*inexactness*, inexactitude, inaccuracy, imprecision, nonadjustment; faultiness, systematic error, probable e.; unrigorousness, looseness, laxity, broadness, generalization 79 *generality*; loose thinking, sloppy t. 477 *sophistry*; sloppiness, carelessness 458 *negligence*; mistiming 118 *anachronism*; misstatement, misreport, misinformation, bad reporting 552 *misrepresentation*; misquotation (see also *mistake*); misuse of language, malapropism 565 *solecism*.

*mistake*, bad idea (see also *error*); inappropriate move, miscalculation 481 *misjudgment*; blunder, botch-up 695 *bungling*; wrong impression, mistaken identity, wrong person, wrong address; glaring error, bloomer (inf), boner (sl), clanger, howler (inf), schoolboy h., gaffe, bull, Irish b. 497 *absurdity*; loose thread, oversight 456 *inattention*; mishit, bosh shot 728 *failure*;

own goal, friendly fire, fratricide; bungle, foul-up, louse-up (sl), screw-up (sl), balls-up (sl), cock-up (sl), boo-boo (sl), slip-up, boob (inf), goof (sl), blooper; fluff, muff; leak, slip, slip of the pen, slip of the tongue, spoonerism 565 *solecism*; clerical error, typist's e.; typographical error, printer's e., misprint, typo, literal, erratum, corrigendum; human error, computer e.; inadvertency, trip, stumble; bad tactics, wrong step, faux pas; solecism 847 *bad taste*; blot, flaw 845 *blemish*.

**Adj.** *erroneous*, erring, wrong; solecistic 565 *ungrammatical*; in error (see also *mistaken*); unfactual, unhistorical, mythical 2 *unreal*; aberrant 282 *deviating*; wide of the mark, wide of the truth, devoid of t. 543 *untrue*; unsound, unscientific, unreasoned, cock-eyed, ill-reasoned, self-contradictory 477 *illogical*; implausible 472 *improbable*; baseless, unsubstantiated, uncorroborated, unfounded, ungrounded, groundless, disproved 479 *confuted*; exploded, discredited 924 *disapproved*; fallacious, misleading 535 *misteaching*; unauthentic, apocryphal, unscriptural, unbiblical; perverted, unorthodox, heretical 977 *heterodox*; untruthful, lying 541 *false*; flawed, not genuine, fake, simulated, bogus 542 *spurious*; hallucinatory, illusive, illusory, delusive, deceptive 542 *deceiving*; subjective, unrealistic, fantastical 513 *imaginary*; wild, crackpot 497 *absurd*; fallible, liable to error, wrong-headed, perverse, prejudiced 481 *biased*; superstitious 491 *ignorant*.

*mistaken*, wrongly taken, misunderstood, misconceived; misrepresented, perverted; misinterpreted, misconstrued, misread, misprinted; miscalculated, misjudged 481 *misjudging*; in error, misled, misguided; misinformed, ill-informed, deluded 491 *uninstructed*; slipping, blundering 695 *clumsy*; straying, wandering 282 *deviating*; wide, misaimed, misdirected, off-target, off-beam, out to lunch 25 *unapt*; at fault, out, cold, off the scent, off the track, off the beam, wide of the mark, on the wrong tack, on the wrong scent, off the rails, at sea 474 *uncertain*.

*inexact*, inaccurate; approximate, ballpark, rough; not strict, unrigorous, not literal, free, loose; broad, generalized 79 *general*; not factual, incorrect, misstated, misreported, garbled; imprecise, erratic, wild, hit-or-miss; insensitive, clumsy; out, wildly o., maladjusted, badly adjusted; untuned, out of tune, out of gear; out of synch, unsynchronized, slow, losing, fast, gaining; uncorrected, unrevised; faulty, full of faults, full of holes, flawed, botched, mangled 695 *bungled*; misprinted, misread, mistranslated 521 *misinterpreted*.

**Vb.** *err*, commit an error, fall into e., go wrong, stray from the straight and narrow, mistake, make a m.; labour under a misapprehension, bark up the wrong tree, be on the wrong scent; be in the wrong, be mistaken; delude oneself, suffer hallucinations 481 *misjudge*; be misled, be misguided; receive a wrong impression, get hold of the wrong end of the stick, be at cross-purposes, misunderstand, misconceive, misapprehend, get it wrong 517 *not understand*; miscount, misreckon 482 *overrate*, 483 *underestimate*; go astray 282 *stray*; gain, be fast 135 *be early*; lose, be slow, stop 136 *be late*.

*blunder*, trip, stumble, miss, fault 695 *be clumsy*; slip, slip up, drop a brick, drop a clanger, boob, goof, foul up, screw up, mess up, make a hash of; commit a faux pas, put one's foot in it; betray oneself, give oneself away 526 *disclose*; blot one's copybook, blot, flaw; fluff, muff, botch, bungle; blow it 728 *fail*; play into one's hands 695 *act foolishly*; miscount, miscalculate 481 *misjudge*; misread, misquote, misprint, mistake the meaning, misapprehend, mistranslate 521 *misinterpret*.

*mislead*, misdirect, give the wrong address 282 *deflect*; misinform, lead into error, lead astray, pervert, cause to err, involve in error, steep in e. 535 *misteach*; beguile, befool, lead one a dance, lead one up the garden path 542 *deceive*; give a false impression, create a false i., falsify, garble, spin 541 *dissemble*; gloze over, gloss o., whitewash, cover up 525 *conceal*.

**Adv.** *approximately*, about, almost, around, nearly, roughly, in the region of; more or less, somewhere around 200 *nearly*; pushing; -plus, -something; broadly, broadly speaking, sensu lato.

## 496 Maxim

**N.** *maxim*, apophthegm, gnome, adage, saw, sentence, proverb, byword, aphorism; dictum, tag, saying, pithy s., stock s., sententious s., common s., received s., true s., truth; epigram, mot 839 *witticism*; wise maxim, sage reflection; truism, cliché, commonplace, platitude, banality, hackneyed saying, trite remark, statement of the obvious, bromide; motto, watchword, slogan, catchword; formula, mantra; text, canon, sutra, rule, golden r. 693 *precept*; gloss, comment, note, remark, observation, aperçu 520 *commentary*; moral, edifying story, fable, cautionary tale 590 *narrative*; phylactery, formulary; book of proverbs, collection of sayings; folklore.

*axiom*, self-evident truth, truism, tautology; principle, postulate, theorem, formula; Sod's Law, Murphy's Law.

**Adj.** *aphoristic*, gnomic, sententious, proverbial, moralizing, holier than thou 498 *wise*; epigrammatic, piquant, pithy 839 *witty*; terse, snappy 569 *concise*; enigmatic, oracular 517 *puzzling*; common, banal, trite, corny, hackneyed, platitudinous, clichéd, commonplace, stock 610 *usual*; axiomatic 693 *preceptive*.

**Adv.** *proverbially*, as the saying goes, as they say, as the old adage has it, to coin a phrase; pithily, in a nutshell; aphoristically, epigrammatically, wittily; by way of moral.

## 497 Absurdity

**N.** *absurdity*, height of a., height of nonsense, absurdness 849 *ridiculousness*; ineptitude, inconsequence 10 *irrelevance*; false logic 477 *sophistry*; foolishness, silliness, silly season 499 *folly*; senselessness, futility, fatuity 641 *lost labour*; nonsense verse, doggerel, amphigory; talking rot, talking through one's hat; rot, rubbish, nonsense, stuff and nonsense, gibberish, jargon, twaddle 515 *silly talk*; rhapsody, romance, romancing, fustian, bombast 546 *exaggeration*; Irish bull, Irishism, malapropism, howler 495 *mistake*; paradox, Zeno's paradoxes 508 *lack of expectation*; spoonerism, joke, limerick 839 *witticism*; pun, equivoque, play upon words 518 *equivocalness*; riddle, riddle-me-ree 530 *enigma*; quibble, verbal q. 477 *sophism*; anticlimax, bathos, descent from the sublime to the ridiculous; sell, catch 542 *trickery*.

*foolery*, antics, capers, fooling about, horsing around, silliness, asininity, tomfoolery, shenanigans, high jinks, sky-larking 837 *revel*; vagary, whimsy, whimsicality 604 *whim*; extravagance, extravaganza; escapade, scrape 700 *predicament*; practical joke, monkey trick, piece of nonsense; drollery, comicality 849 *ridiculousness*; clowning, buffoonery, burlesque, parody, caricature 851 *ridicule*; farce, mummery, pretence 850 *affectation*; showing off 875 *ostentation*.

**Adj.** *absurd*, inept 25 *unapt*; ludicrous, laughable, risible, farcical, comical, grotesque, Pythonesque 849 *ridiculous*; rash, silly, asinine, idiotic, cock-eyed, cockamamie (US), moronic, tomfool 499 *foolish*; nonsensical, senseless 515 *meaningless*; preposterous, without rhyme or reason 477 *illogical*; wild, overdone, extravagant 546 *exaggerated*; pretentious 850 *affected*; frantic 503 *frenzied*; mad, crazy, crackpot, harebrained 495 *erroneous*; fanciful, fantastic 513 *imaginative*; futile, fatuous 641 *useless*; paradoxical 508 *unexpected*; inconsistent 10 *irrelevant*; quibbling 477 *sophistical*; punning 518 *equivocal*; macaronic 43 *mixed*.

**Vb.** *be absurd*, play the fool, play the clown, act like a fool, behave like an idiot 499 *be foolish*; fool, fool about, lark about, muck a.,

horse a., monkey around, play practical jokes
837 *amuse oneself*; be a laughingstock 849 *be ridiculous*; clown, clown about, burlesque,
parody, caricature, mimic, guy, make a fool of
851 *ridicule*; talk like a fool, talk rot, talk nonsense, talk through one's hat, talk gibberish
515 *mean nothing*; talk wildly, rant, rave 503 *be
insane*; rhapsodize, romance 546 *exaggerate*.

## 498 Intelligence. Wisdom

**N.** *intelligence*, thinking power, powers of
thought, intellectualism 447 *intellect*; brains,
good b., brain, brainpan, grey matter, head,
headpiece, loaf, upper storey, upstairs, noddle;
nous, wit, mother-w., commonsense; lights,
understanding, sense, good s., horse s., savvy,
gumption, knowhow; wits, sharp w., ready w.,
quick thinking, quickness, readiness, esprit;
ability, capacity, mental c., mental grasp; calibre, mental c., intelligence quotient, IQ; high
IQ, Mensa, forwardness, brightness; braininess,
cleverness 694 *aptitude*; mental gifts, gift-
edness, brilliance, talent, genius; ideas, inspiration, sheer i. 476 *intuition*; brainwave, bright
idea 451 *idea*.

sagacity, judgment, good j., sound j., cool j.,
discretion, discernment 463 *discrimination*; perception, perspicacity, clear thought, clear
thinking, clearheadedness; acumen, sharpness,
acuteness, acuity, penetration; practicality,
practical mind, shrewdness, longheadedness;
level-headedness, balance 502 *sanity*; prudence, forethought, longsightedness, far-
sightedness 510 *foresight*; subtleness, subtlety,
craft, craftiness 698 *cunning*; worldly wisdom,
oneupmanship, gamesmanship 694 *skill*; vigilance, alertness, awareness 457 *carefulness*;
policy, good p., tact, statesmanship, strategy
688 *tactics*.

wisdom, ripe w., wise understanding,
mature u., sapience; grasp of intellect, profundity of thought 449 *thought*; depth, depth
of mind, breadth of m., reach of m., enlargement of m.; experience, life-long e.,
digested e., ripe e., fund of e., ripe knowledge
490 *knowledge*; tolerance, broadmindedness,
catholic outlook; right views, soundness;
mental poise, mental balance, sobriety, objectivity, enlightenment.

**Adj.** *intelligent*, endowed with brains,
brainy, clever, forward, bright, bright as a
button; brilliant, scintillating, talented, of
genius 694 *gifted*; capable, able, practical 694
*skilful*; apt, ready, quick, quick on the uptake,
receptive; acute, sharp, sharp as a needle,
sharp-witted, quick w., nimble-w.; alive, aware,
on one's toes, streetwise, with it 455 *attentive*;
astute, shrewd, fly, smart, canny, not born yes-

terday, up to snuff, all there, on the ball;
knowing, sophisticated, worldlywise; too
smart for one's own good, too clever by half,
overclever, clever clever; sagacious, provident,
prudent, watchful 457 *careful*; farseeing, far-
sighted, clear-sighted 510 *foreseeing*; discerning
463 *discriminating*; penetrating, perspicacious,
clear-headed, long-h., hard-h., calculating;
subtle, crafty, wily, foxy, artful 698 *cunning*;
politic, statesmanlike.

wise, sage, sagacious, sapient; thinking,
reflecting 449 *thoughtful*; reasoning 475
*rational*; knowledgeable 490 *instructed*; highbrow, intellectual, profound, deep, oracular;
sensible, grounded, reasonable, sound, well-
balanced 502 *sane*; staid, sober 834 *serious*;
reliable, responsible 929 *trustworthy*; not born
yesterday, experienced, cool, collected,
unflappable; unperplexed, unbaffled; proof
against flattery; balanced, level-headed,
realistic, objective; judicious, impartial 913
*just*; tolerant, fair-minded, enlightened,
unbiased, nonpartisan; unfanatical, unbigoted,
unprejudiced; broad, broad-minded, latitudinarian; prudent, tactful, politic 698 *cunning*;
wise as a serpent, wise as an owl, wise as
Solomon, 'like a Daniel come to judgment'
(see quotation at 957 *magistracy*); well-advised,
well-considered, well-judged, wisely decided
642 *advisable*.

**Vb.** *be wise*, – intelligent etc. adj.; use one's
wits, use one's head, use one's loaf *or* noddle,
use one's intelligence; accumulate experience,
have a fund of wisdom 490 *know*; have brains,
have plenty of grey matter; sparkle, scintillate,
shine 644 *be good*; have a head on one's shoulders, have one's wits about one, know how
many beans make five, see with half an eye,
see at a glance; have one's head screwed on the
right way, know a thing or two, know what's
what, know how to live, get around, know the
score; be up on, be in the know, be au courant;
be realistic, be one's age; show foresight 510
*foresee*; know which side one's bread is
buttered on, be prudent, take care 858 *be cautious*; grasp, fathom, take in 516 *understand*; discern, see through, penetrate 438 *see*;
distinguish 463 *discriminate*; have sense, listen
to reason 475 *be reasonable*; plan well, be
politic 623 *plan*; have tact, be wise in one's generation 698 *be cunning*; learn from one's mistakes, come to one's senses, repent 939 *be
penitent*.

## 499 Unintelligence. Folly

**N.** *unintelligence*, lack of intelligence, lack of
intellect 448 *absence of intellect*; poverty of intellect, clouded i. 503 *mental disorder*; weakness of

intellect, lack of brains, feeble-mindedness, low IQ, low mental age, immaturity, infantilism; brain damage, dementia, mental deficiency; mental handicap, learning disability, arrested development, retardation, backwardness; imbecility, idiocy; stupidity, slowness, dullness, obtuseness, thickheadedness, crassness, denseness; blockishness, sottishness, oafishness, owlishness, stolidity, hebetude 820 *moral insensibility*; one's weak side, poor head, no head for, no brain; incapacity, ineptitude, incompetence 695 *unskilfulness*; naivety, simplicity, fallibility, gullibility 481 *misjudgment*; inanity, vacuity, vacuousness, no depth, superficiality 212 *shallowness*; unreadiness, delayed reaction; impercipience, tactlessness, awkwardness, gaucherie, Asperger's syndrome 464 *indiscrimination*.

*folly*, foolishness, extravagance, eccentricity 849 *ridiculousness*; tomfool idea, tomfoolery, act of folly 497 *foolery*; trifling, levity, frivolity, giddiness 456 *inattention*; irrationality, unreason, illogic 477 *sophistry*; unwisdom, imprudence, indiscretion, tactlessness; fatuity, fatuousness, pointlessness; wild-goose chase 641 *lost labour*; silliness, asininity; brainlessness, idiocy, lunacy, sheer l., utter folly; recklessness, wildness, incaution 857 *rashness*; blind side, obsession, hang-up, infatuation 481 *misjudgment*; puerility, boyishness, girlishness, childishness 130 *nonage*; second childhood, senility, anility, dotage, senile dementia 131 *old age*; drivelling, babbling, maundering, wandering; conceit, empty-headedness 873 *vanity*.

**Adj.** *unintelligent*, unintellectual, low-brow; ungifted, untalented, talentless, no genius; incompetent 695 *clumsy*; not bright, dull; subnormal, ESN, mentally handicapped, having a learning disability, mentally disadvantaged, mentally deficient; undeveloped; immature; backward, retarded, feeble-minded, moronic, cretinous, imbecile 503 *mentally disordered*; deficient, wanting, not all there, vacant, not quite the full pound note, not right in the head; limited, weak, weak in the upper storey; impercipient, unperceptive, slow, slow on the uptake, slow to learn; stupid, obtuse, dense, thick, gormless, crass, gross, heavy, sottish, stolid, bovine, Boeotian, blockish, oafish, doltish, owlish; dumb, dopey, dim, dim-witted, dull-w., slow-w., thick-w., half-w.; pig thick *or* ignorant, dead from the neck up, thick as two short planks, thick as a brick; thick-skulled, addle-brained, clod-pated, bone-headed, muddle-h., muddy-h., puzzle-h.; cracked, barmy 503 *crazy*; nonunderstanding, impenetrable, unteachable, impervious; pro-

saic, literal, matter-of-fact, unimaginative; muddled, addled, wrong-headed, pig-h. 481 *misjudging*.

*foolish*, silly, idiotic, imbecile, asinine, apish; nonsensical, senseless, insensate, fatuous, futile, inane, cockamamie (US) 497 *absurd*; ludicrous, laughable, risible 849 *ridiculous*; like a fool, like an idiot, fallible 544 *gullible*; simple, naive 699 *artless*; inexperienced 491 *ignorant*; tactless, impolitic, gauche, awkward; soft, wet, soppy, sappy, sawney, goody-goody 935 *innocent*; gumptionless, gormless; goofy, gawky, dopey; childish, babyish, puerile, infantile 132 *infantine*; gaga, senile, away with the fairies, anile 131 *ageing*; besotted, fond, doting; amorous, sentimental, spoony 887 *enamoured*; dazed, fuddled, maudlin 949 *drunk*; vapouring, babbling, burbling, drivelling, maundering, wandering; mindless, witless, brainless (see also *unintelligent*); shallow, shallow-minded, shallow-headed, superficial, frivolous, anserine, bird-witted, feather-brained, crack-b., rattle-b., scatter-b., hare-b. 456 *light-minded*; fooling, playing the fool, acting the f., horsing around, larking about, misbehaving, boyish; eccentric, unstable, extravagant, wild, madcap, rantipole; scatty, nutty, dotty, daft 503 *crazy*.

*unwise*, unblessed with wisdom, unenlightened; obscurantist, unscientific 491 *ignorant*; unphilosophical, unintellectual; unreasoning, irrational 477 *illogical*; indiscreet 464 *indiscriminating*; injudicious 481 *misjudging*; undiscerning, unseeing, unforeseeing, short-sighted 439 *blind*; unteachable, insensate; thoughtless 450 *unthinking*; uncalculating, impatient 680 *hasty*; incautious, foolhardy, reckless 857 *rash*; prejudiced, intolerant 481 *narrow-minded*; inconsistent, unbalanced, penny-wise, pound-foolish; unreasonable, against reason; inept, incongruous, unseemly, improper 643 *inexpedient*; ill-considered, ill-advised, ill-judged 495 *mistaken*.

**Vb.** *be foolish*, maunder, dote, drivel, babble, burble, wander, talk through one's hat 515 *mean nothing*; go haywire, lose one's wits, take leave of one's senses, go off one's head, go off one's rocker 503 *be insane*; be unintelligent, have no brains, have no sense, not have the sense one was born with; not see farther than one's nose, not see the wood for the trees; never learn, stay bottom of the class; invite ridicule, look like a fool, look foolish 849 *be ridiculous*; make a fool of oneself, play the fool, act the f., act the giddy goat, play silly devils 497 *be absurd*; sow one's wild oats, misbehave 837 *amuse oneself*; burn one's fingers 695 *act foolishly*; go on a fool's errand 641 *waste effort*;

plunge into error 495 *err*; miscalculate 481 *misjudge*.

## 500 Sage

**N.** *sage*, nobody's fool; learned person 492 *scholar*; wise man, wise woman, statesman *or* -woman; elder statesman *or* -woman, counsellor, consultant, authority 691 *adviser*, expert 696 *proficient person*; genius, master mind; master, mentor, guide, guru, pundit 537 *teacher*; rishi, Buddha 973 *religious teacher*; seer, prophet 511 *oracle*; yogi, swami, sannyasi 945 *ascetic*; leading light, shining l., luminary; master spirit, great soul, mahatma; doctor, thinker 449 *philosopher*; egghead, boffin, highbrow, blue stocking 492 *intellectual*; wizard, shaman, witch doctor 983 *sorcerer*; magus, magian, Magi, wise men from the East; Solomon, Daniel, second D., 'Daniel come to judgment' (see quotation at 957 *magistracy*), learned judge; Nestor, Solon, Seven Sages; Grand Old Man, GOM.

*wiseacre*, wise guy, know-all, smarty-pants, smart ass 873 *vain person*; smart alec, clever dick; brains trust; witling, wise fool, wise men of Gotham; 'the wisest fool in Christendom'.

**The wisest fool in Christendom.**
Said of James VI (of Scotland) and I (of England), probably by Henry IV of France.

## 501 Fool

**N.** *fool*, silly f., tomfool, Tom o' Bedlam 504 *madman*; buffoon, clown, comic, jester, zany, merry andrew, harlequin 594 *entertainer*; perfect fool, complete idiot, big girl's blouse (inf), nincompoop, ninny, ass, jackass, donkey, goose, cuckoo; mooncalf, zombie, born fool, idiot, congenital i., cretin, imbecile, moron, natural; half-wit, dimwit, sot, stupid, silly, silly-billy, twerp; stooge, butt, turkey 851 *laughingstock*; madcap 857 *desperado*; addlehead, fathead, lunkhead (US), muddle-h., pinhead, nit, nitwit, empty suit (see also *dunce*); bampot (Scots), blunderer, clot, clown, dipstick, incompetent, nerd (sl), numpty (Scots), numskull, plonker (sl), twit, wally (sl) 697 *bungler*; scatterbrains, birdbrain, featherbrain, bimbo, dingbat (sl), rattle-head, giddy-h., flibbertigibbet; trifler 493 *dabbler*; witling 500 *wiseacre*; crackpot, eccentric, geek, odd fellow 504 *crank*; gaffer, old fogy; babbler, burbler, driveller; dotard 133 *old man*.

*ninny*, simpleton, Simple Simon; tom noddy, charley (inf); noodle, noddy, nincompoop, moonraker, juggins, muggins, booby, sap, saphead (sl), softhead, big stiff, stick, poor s., dizzy, dope, jerk (sl), gowk (dial), galoot, goof; greenhorn 538 *beginner*; wet, weed, drip,

milksop, mollycoddle, goody-goody, softy, wimp (inf) 163 *weakling*; child, babe 935 *innocent*; sucker, mug 544 *dupe*; gaper, gawker.

*dunce*, dullard; blockhead, woodenhead, numskull, duffer, dummkopf, dolt, dumb-bell, dumb blonde, dumb cluck (sl), bimbo, himbo, dim bulb (inf), dumdum (inf), goof (inf), bozo (sl) 493 *ignoramus*; fathead, thickhead, thicko (sl), bonehead, pinhead, blockhead, dunderhead, blunderhead, muttonhead, knucklehead, chucklehead, puddinghead, jobbernowl; nitwit, dimwit; chump, clot, clod, clodpoll, clodhopper, oaf, lout, booby, loon, bumpkin; block, stock, stone.

## 502 Sanity

**N.** *sanity*, saneness, soundness, soundness of mind; reasonableness; rationality, reason; balance, balance of the mind, mental balance; mental equilibrium; sobriety, common sense, mother wit; coherence 516 *intelligibility*; lucidity, lucid interval, lucid moment; normality, proper mind, right m., senses; sound mind, mens sana; mental hygiene, mental health.

**Adj.** *sane*, normal, not neurotic; of sound mind, sound-minded, mentally sound, all there; in one's senses, compos mentis, in one's right mind, in possession of one's faculties, with all one's wits about one; rational, reasonable 498 *intelligent*; showing good sense, commonsensical, grounded, sober, sober-minded, with both feet on the ground; fully conscious, in one's sober senses; coherent 516 *intelligible*; lucid, not wandering, clear-headed; undisturbed, balanced, well-b.; cool, calculating 480 *judicial*; sane enough, not certifiable.

**Vb.** *be sane*, have one's wits, keep one's senses, retain one's reason; be of sound mind, become sane, recover one's mind, come to one's senses, cool down, sober.

*make sane*, restore to sanity, bring to their senses *or* their right mind; sober, bring round.

**Adv.** *sanely*, soberly, lucidly; reasonably.

## 503 Insanity: mental disorder

**N.** *mental disorder*, insanity, unsoundness of mind, lunacy, madness, certifiability; mental sickness, mental illness; mental instability; abnormal psychology, mental derangement, mental aberration, loss of reason, sick mind, unsound m., darkened m., troubled brain, clouded b., disordered reason, delirium, brain damage, mental decay, Creutzfeldt-Jakob disease, CJD, new variant CJD, Creutzfeldt-Jakob disease nv, kuru, persistent vegetative state, PVS 651 *nervous disorders*; senile decay, Alzheimer's disease, softening of the brain, dotage

131 *age*; dementia, d. praecox, senile d., pre-senile d.; psychiatry, clinical psychology 447 *psychology*; psychotherapy 658 *therapy*; psycho-analyst, analyst, psychiatrist, shrink 658 *doctor*.

*psychosis*, paranoia, delusions, hallucina-tions, folie à deux; catatonia, schizophrenia; confusion; melancholia 834 *melancholy*; clinical depression, manic d., cyclothymia, mania, megalomania, persecution mania, religious mania, spy mania; self-mutilation, self-harm; body dysmorphic disorder.

### Manias

ablutomania (an obsession with washing and cleanli-ness), Anglomania (obsession with all things English), arithmomania (a compulsion to count people and things), bibliomania (a mania for collecting books), demonomania (belief that one is possessed by the Devil), dipsomania (a craving for alcoholic drinks), egomania (extreme egotism), eleutheromania (obsessive desire for freedom), erotomania (excessive sexual desire), Gallomania (obsession with all things French), graphomania (obsession with writing), hydro-mania (craving for water), hypomania (a mild form of mania), idolomania (idol-worship), kleptomania (obsessive impulse to steal), megalomania (delusions of power or importance), metromania (mania for writing verse), monomania (obsession with a single idea), mythomania (a tendency to lie or exaggerate), nostomania (a great desire to return to familiar places), nymphomania (excessive sexual desire in a woman), pyromania (obsessive desire to set fire to things), sitomania (an abnormal craving for food), theomania (belief that one is a god).

*learning disability*, special needs, amentia, mental deficiency, mental handicap, idiocy, congenital i., imbecility, cretinism, mongolism, Down's syndrome, feeble-mindedness; autism, Asperger's syndrome 84 *abnormality*.

*personality disorder*, psychopathology, psy-chopathy, sociopathy, maladjustment; iden-tity crisis, personal anomie; psychopathic condition, emotional disturbance; split person-ality, dual p., multiple p., multiple personality disorder, MPD, dissociative identity disorder, DID; persecution mania; kleptomania; nymphomania, satyriasis; – complex, inferiority c., Oedipus c., Electra c.; affluenza, squandermania; control-freakery.

*neurosis*, psychoneurosis, anxiety neurosis, nerves, nervous disorder, neurasthenia; hys-teria; attack of nerves, social phobia, perform-ance anxiety, shattered nerves, nervous breakdown, brainstorm; shellshock, combat fatigue, post-traumatic stress disorder; obses-sion, compulsion, phobia, orthorexia 854 *phobia*; hypochondria; depression, clinical d., manic d., depressed state, blues, cyclothymia.

*frenzy*, monomania, furore, frenetic con-dition; ecstasy, raving, hysteria; distraction

456 *abstractedness*; incoherence 517 *unintelligi-bility*; delirium tremens, DT's, jimjams; epi-lepsy, fit, epileptic f., epileptic frenzy, paroxysm 318 *spasm*.

*eccentricity*, craziness, crankiness, faddish-ness; queerness, oddness, weirdness, strange behaviour; oddity, twist, quirk, kink, craze, fad 84 *abnormality*; a screw loose, bats in the belfry; fixation, hang-up, inhibition, repression; obsession, infatuation, mono-mania, ruling passion, fixed idea 481 *bias*; hobbyhorse, bee in one's bonnet 604 *whim*; emotional baggage.

*mental hospital*, psychiatric h., psychiatric unit, mental institution; mental home, mad-house, lunatic asylum, Bedlam; booby-hatch, loony-bin, nuthouse, bughouse, funny farm; locked ward, padded cell 658 *hospital*.

*person with a learning disability* n. mentally handicapped person, idiot, congenital i., natural, cretin, moron 501 *fool*.

**Adj.** *mentally disordered*, insane, mad, lunatic, moon-struck; of unsound mind, not in one's right m., non compos mentis, out of one's mind, deprived of one's wits, deranged, demented; certifiable, mental; abnormal, psychologically a., sick, mentally disturbed, mentally ill, of diseased *or* disordered *or* distem-pered mind; unbalanced; brain-damaged; raving mad, stark staring mad, mad as a hatter, mad as a March hare, off one's rocker (sl), off one's trolley (sl) (see also *frenzied*); gaga (sl), loony (sl), declared insane, certified; locked up, put away.

*having a learning disability*, mentally handi-capped, imbecile, moronic, idiotic, cretinous, mongoloid, defective, feebleminded, sub-normal 499 *unintelligent*; autistic.

*psychotic*, paranoiac, paranoid, schizo-phrenic; manic, maniacal; catatonic, depressive, clinically depressed 834 *melan-cholic*; hyperactive; manic depressive, cyclo-thymic.

*neurotic*, hypochondriac; claustrophobic, ago-raphobic; hysterical, obsessional.

*maladjusted*, psychopathic, psychopatholog-ical; kleptomaniac, nymphomaniac; schizoid; dipsomaniac, alcoholic.

*crazy*, bewildered, wandering, bemused, pixi-lated, mazed, moidered 456 *abstracted*; not all there, not right in the head; off one's head *or* one's nut (sl), off one's trolley (sl), round the bend *or* the twist, up the pole; crazed, demented, driven mad, maddened (see also *frenzied*); unhinged, unbalanced, off one's rocker (sl); bedevilled, bewitched, deluded; infatuated, obsessed, hung up, eaten up with, possessed; fond, doting, besotted 887 *enamoured*; drivelling, gaga (sl), in one's second childhood, away with the fairies; touched in the head, touched, wanting; idiotic, scatter-brained, shatterbrained, crack-brained 499 *foolish*; bananas (inf), barmy (inf), bats (inf), batty (inf), bonkers (inf), cracked, crackers, cranky, cuckoo (inf), daft, daffy (inf), dappy (inf), dippy (inf), dotty, goofy, loco (sl), loony (inf), loopy (inf), meshuga (sl), nutty (inf), nuts (inf), potty (inf), scatty, screwy (inf), nutty as a fruit cake (inf); eccentric, erratic, flaky (sl), funny, odd, peculiar, queer, wacky (sl), out to lunch (inf) 84 *abnormal*; crotchety, whimsical 604 *capricious*; dizzy, giddy 456 *light-minded*.

*frenzied*, rabid, maddened, madding; horn-mad, furious, foaming at the mouth 891 *angry*; haggard, wild, distraught 825 *suffering*; possessed, possessed with a devil, bedevilled, bacchic, corybantic; frantic, frenetic, demented, like one possessed, out of one's mind, beside oneself, uncontrollable; berserk, seeing red, running amok, running wild 176 *violent*; epileptic, having fits; hysterical, delirious, hallucinating, seeing things, raving, rambling, wandering, incoherent, fevered, brain-sick 651 *sick*.

**Vb.** *be insane*, – mad, – crazy etc. adj.; have bats in the belfry, have a screw loose (sl); dote, drivel 499 *be foolish*; ramble, wander; babble, rave; foam at the mouth; be delirious, see things.

*go mad*, go off one's head, go off one's rocker *or* nut (sl), go crackers, become a lunatic, have to be certified; lose one's reason, lose one's wits, lose one's marbles (sl), go out of one's mind, crack up; go berserk, run amok, see red, foam at the mouth, lose one's head 891 *get angry*.

*make mad*, drive m., send m., drive insane, madden; craze, derange, dement; send one off his head *or* out of his mind; send round the bend *or* the twist, drive up the wall; overthrow one's reason, turn one's brain; blow one's mind 821 *excite*; unhinge, unbalance, send off one's rocker (sl); infuriate, make one see red 891 *enrage*; infatuate, possess, obsess; go to one's head, turn one's h. 542 *befool*.

### 504 Madman: maladjusted person

**N.** *madman*, madwoman, lunatic, mental case; bedlamite, Tom o' Bedlam, candidate for Bedlam; raving lunatic, maniac; screwball (sl), nut (sl), nutcase (sl), headcase (sl), loon (sl), loony (sl), kook (sl), meshuggenah.

*psychotic*, paranoiac, schizophrenic, manic depressive; megalomaniac; catatonic.

*neurotic*, hysteric; neuropath; hypochon-driac; obsessive; phobic, claustrophobic, agoraphobic; depressive, melancholic; kleptomaniac, pyromaniac, monomaniac; control freak.

*maladjusted people*, psychopath, psycho, psychopathic personality, sociopath, schizoid, unstable personality, aggressive p., antisocial p.; dipsomaniac, alcoholic 949 *drunkard*; dope addict, dope fiend, junkie; drug addict 949 *drug-taking*.

*crank*, crackpot, nut, nutter, crackbrain; eccentric, oddity, oddball 851 *laughingstock*; freak, deviationist 84 *nonconformist*; fad, faddist, fanatic, extremist, nympholept, 'lunatic fringe';

> **Every reform movement has a lunatic fringe.**
> Theodore Roosevelt

seer, dreamer 513 *visionary*; knight errant, Don Quixote.

*enthusiast*, energumen 678 *busy person*; zealot 602 *obstinate person*; devotee, aficionado, addict, fiend, nut, freak, anorak (sl), trainspotter (sl), geek, bug (sl), buff; fan, supporter 707 *patron*; Europhile; connoisseur, fancier 846 *people of taste*; computer buff, fitness freak, radio ham, discophile, balletomane, opera buff, film b., cineast; bibliophile 492 *collector*.

SECTION SIX

## Extension of thought

### 505 Memory

**N.** *memory*, good m., retentiveness, retention; tenacious memory, capacious m., trustworthy m., correct m., exact m., photographic m., eidetic m., ready m., prompt m.; collective memory, race m., tribal m., atavism; Mnemosyne; recovered memory, false memory.

*remembrance*, exercise of memory, recollection, recall, total r.; anamnesis; commemoration, evocation, mind's eye; rehearsal, recapitulation 106 *repetition*; memorization, remembering, learning by heart, committing to memory, learning by rote 536 *learning*; reminiscence, thoughts of the past, reminiscent vein, retrospection, review, retrospect, hindsight; flashback, recurrence, voice from the past; déjà vu 984 *psychics*; afterthought 67 *sequel*; nostalgia, regrets 830 *regret*; memorabilia, memoirs, reminiscences, recollections; history, narration 590 *narrative*; fame, notoriety, place in history 866 *famousness*; memoranda, things to be remembered.

*reminder*, memorial, testimonial, commemoration 876 *celebration*; token of remembrance,

souvenir, keepsake, relic, memento, autograph; trophy, bust, statue 548 *monument*;
remembrancer, keeper of one's conscience,
prompter; testifier 466 *witness*; memorandum,
memo, chit, note, notebook, memo pad, aide-
mémoire, diary, engagement d., personal
organizer, Filofax (tdmk); telephone book, telephone directory; album, autograph a.,
photograph a., scrapbook, commonplace
book, promptbook; leading question, prompt,
prompting, suggestion, cue 524 *hint*; mnemonic, aid to memory, knotted handkerchief.

*mnemonics*, mnemotechnics, mnemotechny,
art of memory, Pelmanism; mnemonic device,
memoria technica, artificial memory, electronic brain; data bank 632 *store*; mnemonist.

**Adj.** *remembered*, recollected etc. vb.;
retained, retained in the memory, not forgotten, unforgotten; green, fresh, fresh in
one's memory, of recent memory, as clear as if
it were yesterday; present to the mind, uppermost in one's thoughts; of lasting remembrance, of blessed memory, missed, regretted;
memorable, unforgettable, not to be forgotten;
haunting, persistent, undying; deep-rooted,
deep-seated, deep-set, indelible, ineffaceable,
inscribed upon the mind, lodged in one's m.,
kept in the dim recesses of one's mind,
stamped on one's memory, impressed on one's
recollection; embalmed in the memory, kept
alive in one's mind; got by heart, memorized
490 *known*.

*remembering*, mindful, faithful to the
memory, keeping in mind, holding in remembrance; evocative, memorial, commemorative
876 *celebratory*; reminiscent, recollecting, anec-
dotic, anecdotal; living in the past, dwelling
upon the past, nostalgic; unable to forget,
haunted, obsessed, plagued; recalling,
reminding, mnemonic, prompting, suggesting.

**Vb.** *remember*, mind, bring to m., call to m.;
recognize, know again 490 *know*; recollect,
bethink oneself; not forget, bottle up 778
*retain*; hold in mind, retain the memory of;
embalm *or* keep alive in one's thoughts, treasure in one's heart, enshrine in one's memory,
store in one's mind, cherish the memory;
never forget, be unable to f.; recall, call to
mind, return to thoughts of, think of; keep in
mind 455 *be mindful*; reminisce, write one's
memoirs; remind oneself, make a note of, tie a
knot in one's handkerchief, write it down. (See
also *memorize*.)

*retrospect*, recollect, recall, recapture; reflect,
review, think back, think back upon, muse
upon, trace back, retrace, hark back, carry
one's thoughts back, cast one's mind b.; bring
back to memory, summon up, conjure u., rake

up the past, dig up the p., delve into the p.,
dwell on the p., live in the p.; archaize 125 *look
back*; reopen old wounds, renew old days,
recapture old times; make an effort to
remember, rack one's brains, tax one's
memory.

*remind*, cause to remember, jog one's
memory, refresh one's m., renew one's m.; put
one in mind of, take one back; drop a hint,
cue, prompt, suggest 524 *hint*; not allow one to
forget, abide in the memory, haunt, obsess;
not let sleeping dogs lie, fan the embers, keep
the wounds open 821 *excite*; turn another's
mind back, make one think of, evoke the
memory of, awake memories of; commemorate, memorialize, raise a memorial, redeem
from oblivion, keep the memory green, toast
876 *celebrate*; relate, recount, recapitulate 106
*repeat*; petition 761 *request*; write history, narrate 590 *describe*.

*memorize*, commit to memory, get to know,
con 490 *know*; get by heart, learn by rote 536
*learn*; repeat one's lesson 106 *repeat*; fix in
one's memory, implant in one's m., rivet in
one's m., impress on one's m., grave on the m.,
engrave on the m., hammer into one's head,
din into one's h., drive into one's h.; burden
the memory with, stuff the mind w., cram the
mind w., load the mind w.

*be remembered*, stay in the memory, linger in
the m., stick in the mind, make a lasting
impression; recur, recur to one's thoughts 106
*reoccur*; flash across one's mind, ring a bell,
refresh one's memory, set one's memory
working; haunt, dwell in one's thoughts, abide
in one's memory, run in one's thoughts, haunt
one's t. *or* mind, not leave one's t., be at the
back of one's mind, lurk in one's mind, rise
from the subconscious, emerge into consciousness; make history, live in h., leave a name 866
*have a reputation*; live on 115 *be eternal*.

**Adv.** *in memory*, in memory of, to the
memory of, as a memorial to, in memoriam,
lest we forget; by heart, by rote, from memory.

## 506 Oblivion

**N.** *oblivion*, blankness, no recollection, no
memory; obliviousness, forgetfulness, absent-
mindedness, senior moment 456 *abstractedness*; loss of memory, amnesia, blackout,
total blank, mental block; hysterical amnesia,
fugue state 503 *neurosis*; misrecollection, par-
amnesia; insensibility, insensibility of the past,
no sense of history; forgetfulness of favours
908 *ingratitude*; dim memory, hazy recollection; short memory, poor m., defective m.,
failing m., faulty m., treacherous m., false
memory syndrome; decay of memory, lapse

of m., memory like a sieve; effacement 550 *obliteration*; Lethe, waters of L., waters of oblivion; nepenthe; good riddance.

*amnesty*, letting bygones be bygones, burial of grievances, burial of the hatchet, shaking of hands; pardon, free p., absolution 909 *forgiveness*.

**Adj.** *forgotten*, clean f., beyond recall; well forgotten, not missed; unremembered, left in limbo 458 *neglected*; disremembered, misremembered etc. vb.; almost remembered, on the tip of one's tongue; in the recesses of one's mind, gone out of one's head, passed out of recollection; buried, suppressed, repressed; out of mind, over and done with, dead and buried, sunk in oblivion, amnestied 909 *forgiven*.

*forgetful*, forgetting, oblivious; sunk in oblivion, steeped in Lethe; insensible, unconscious of the past; not historically minded; unable to remember, suffering from amnesia, amnesic; causing loss of memory, amnestic, Lethean; unmindful, heedless, mindless 458 *negligent*; absent-minded, inclined to forget 456 *abstracted*; willing to forget, unresentful 909 *forgiving*; unwilling to remember, conveniently forgetting 918 *undutiful*; unmindful of favours 908 *ungrateful*.

**Vb.** *forget*, clean f., not remember, disremember, have no recollection of; not give another thought to, think no more of; wean one's thoughts from, eliminate from one's mind, suppress the memory, consign to oblivion, be oblivious; amnesty, let bygones be bygones, bury the hatchet 909 *forgive*; break with the past, unlearn, efface 550 *obliterate*; suffer from amnesia, lose one's memory, remember nothing; remember wrongly, misremember, misrecollect; be forgetful, have a short memory, have a poor m., need reminding; lose sight of, leave behind, overlook; be absent-minded, fluff one's notes 456 *be inattentive*; forget one's lines, dry; have a memory like a sieve, go in one ear and out of the other, forget one's own name; almost remember, have on the tip of one's tongue, not quite recall, not call to mind, draw a blank.

*be forgotten*, slip one's memory, escape one's m., fade from one's mind; sink into oblivion, fall into o., be consigned to o., drop out of the news; become passé, be overlooked 456 *escape notice*.

## 507 Expectation

**N.** *expectation*, state of e., expectancy 455 *attention*; contemplation 617 *intention*; confident expectation, reliance, confidence, trust 473 *certainty*; presumption 475 *premise*; foretaste 135 *anticipation*; optimism, cheerful expectation

833 *cheerfulness*; eager expectation, anxious e., sanguine e. 859 *desire*; ardent expectation, breathless e. 852 *hope*; waiting, suspense 474 *uncertainty*; pessimism, dread, feelings of doom, doom watching, apprehension, apprehensiveness 854 *fear*; anxiety 825 *worry*; waiting for the end 853 *hopelessness*; expectance, one's expectations, one's prospects 471 *probability*; reckoning, calculation 480 *estimate*; prospect, lookout, outlook, forecast 511 *prediction*; contingency 469 *possibility*; destiny 596 *fate*; defeated expectation, unfulfilled e., frustrated e., tantalization, torment of Tantalus 509 *disappointment*; what is expected, the usual thing 610 *practice*.

**Adj.** *expectant*, expecting, in expectation, in hourly e.; in suspense, on the waiting list, on the short l., on the short leet; sure, confident 473 *certain*; anticipatory, anticipant of, anticipative, anticipating, banking on, putting all one's money on; presuming, taking for granted; predicting 510 *foreseeing*; unsurprised 865 *unastonished*; forewarned, forearmed, ready 669 *prepared*; waiting, waiting for, awaiting; on the lookout, keeping cave, on the watch for, standing by, on call 457 *vigilant*; tense, keyed up 821 *excited*; tantalized, on tenterhooks, on the rack, in agonies of expectation, agog 859 *desiring*; optimistic, hopeful, sanguine 852 *hoping*; apprehensive, dreading, worried, anxious 854 *nervous*; pessimistic, expecting the worst, doom-watching 853 *hopeless*; wondering, open-eyed, open-mouthed, curious 453 *inquisitive*; expecting a baby, expecting a happy event, parturient 167 *fertilized*.

*expected*, long e.; up to expectation, as one expected, not surprising 865 *unastonishing*; anticipated, presumed, predicted, on the cards, foreseen, foreseeable 471 *probable*; prospective, future, on the horizon 155 *impending*; promised, contemplated, intended, in view, in prospect 617 *intending*; hoped for, longed for 859 *desired*; apprehended, dreaded, feared 854 *frightening*.

**Vb.** *expect*, look for, have in prospect, face the prospect, face; contemplate, have in mind, hold in view, promise oneself 617 *intend*; reckon, calculate 480 *estimate*; predict, forecast 510 *foresee*; see it coming 865 *not wonder*; think likely, presume, dare say 471 *assume*; be confident, rely on, bank on, count upon, put one's money on 473 *be certain*; count one's chickens before they are hatched 509 *be disappointed*; anticipate, forestall 669 *prepare oneself*; look out for, watch out f., be waiting f., be ready f. 457 *be careful*; stand by, be on call; hang around (see also *await*); apprehend, dread, doomwatch 854 *fear*; look forward to, hope for 852 *hope*, 859 *desire*; hope and believe, flatter oneself 485 *believe*.

*await*, be on the waiting list; stand waiting, stand and wait, watch and pray 136 *wait*; queue up, line up, mark time, bide one's t.; stand to attention, stand by, hold oneself ready, be on call; hold one's breath, be in suspense; keep one waiting; have in store for, be in store for, be expected 155 *impend*; tantalize, make one's mouth water, lead one to expect 859 *cause desire*.

**Adv.** *expectantly*, in suspense, with bated breath, on edge, on the edge of one's chair; on the waiting list.

## 508 Lack of expectation
**N.** *lack of expectation*, no expectation 472 *improbability*; false expectation 509 *disappointment*; inexpectancy, resignation, no hope 853 *hopelessness*; lack of interest, apathy 454 *incuriosity*; unpreparedness 670 *nonpreparation*; unexpectedness, unforeseen contingency, unusual occurrence; unexpected result, miscalculation 495 *error*; lack of warning, surprise, surprisal, disconcertment; the unexpected, the unforeseen, surprise packet, Jack-in-the-box, afterclap; windfall, gift from the gods, something to one's advantage 615 *benefit*; shock, nasty s., start, jolt, turn; blow, sudden b., staggering b.; bolt from the blue, thunderbolt, thunderclap, bombshell; revelation, eye-opener; culture shock; paradox, reversal, peripeteia 221 *inversion*; astonishment, amazement 864 *wonder*; anticlimax, bathos, descent from the sublime to the ridiculous.

**Adj.** *unexpected*, unanticipated, unprepared for, unlooked for, unhoped for; unguessed, unpredicted, unforeseen; unforeseeable, unpredictable 472 *improbable*; unheralded, unannounced; without warning, surprising; arresting, astounding, mind-boggling, eye-opening, staggering, amazing 864 *wonderful*; shocking, startling 854 *frightening*; like a bombshell, like a thunderbolt, like a bolt from the blue, dropped from the clouds; uncovenanted, unbargained for, uncatered for 670 *unprepared*; contrary to expectation, against e.; paradoxical 518 *equivocal*; out of one's reckoning, out of one's ken, out of one's experience, beyond one's wildest dreams, unprecedented, unexampled 84 *unusual*; freakish 84 *abnormal*; whimsical 604 *capricious*; full of surprises, unaccountable 517 *puzzling*.

*off guard*, unexpecting, unguessing, unsuspecting, unguarded 456 *inattentive*; unaware, uninformed 491 *ignorant*; unwarned, not fore-warned; surprised, disconcerted, taken by surprise, taken aback, caught napping, caught bending, caught with one's pants *or* trousers down, caught on the hop, on the wrong foot 670 *unprepared*; astonished, amazed, thunderstruck, dumbfounded, gobsmacked (sl), dazed, stunned 864 *wondering*; startled, jolted, shocked; without expectations, unhopeful 853 *hopeless*; apathetic, incurious 860 *indifferent*.

**Vb.** *not expect*, not look for, not contemplate, think unlikely, not foresee 472 *be unlikely*; not hope for 853 *despair*; be caught out, walk into the trap, fall into the t.; be taken aback, be taken by surprise, be caught with one's pants *or* trousers down, not bargain for 670 *be unprepared*; get a shock, have a jolt, start, jump, jump out of one's skin; have one's eyes opened, receive a revelation; look surprised, goggle, stare, gawp.

*surprise*, take by s., spring something on one, spring a mine under; catch, trap, ambush 542 *ensnare*; catch unawares, catch napping, catch bending, catch off one's guard, catch with one's pants *or* trousers down; startle, jolt, make one jump, give one a turn, make one jump out of one's skin; take aback, leave speechless, stagger, stun; take one's breath away, gobsmack (sl); knock one down with a feather, bowl one over, strike one all of a heap; be one in the eye for 509 *disappoint*; give one a surprise, pull out of the hat; astonish, amaze, astound, dumbfound 864 *be wonderful*; shock, electrify 821 *impress*; flutter the dovecotes, set the cat among the pigeons, let all hell loose 63 *derange*; come like a thunderclap; drop from the clouds, come out of the blue; fall upon, burst u., bounce u., spring u., pounce on; steal upon, creep up on; come up from behind, take one on his blind side, appear from nowhere.

**Adv.** *unexpectedly*, suddenly, abruptly 116 *instantaneously*; all of a sudden, without warning, without notice, unawares; like a thief in the night.

## 509 Disappointment
**N.** *disappointment*, sad d., bitter d., cruel d.; regrets 830 *regret*; continued disappointment, tantalization, frustration, feeling of f., bafflement; frustrated expectations, blighted hopes, unsatisfied h., betrayed h., hopes unrealized 853 *hopelessness*; false expectation, vain e. 482 *overestimation*; bad news 529 *news*; not what one expected, disenchantment, disillusionment 829 *discontent*; miscalculation 481 *misjudgment*; mirage, trick of the light, false dawn, fool's paradise; shock, blow, setback, double whammy, own goal, balk 702 *hitch*; nonfulfilment, partial success, near failure 726 *noncom-*

*pletion*; bad luck, trick of fortune, slip 'twixt the cup and the lip 731 *misfortune*; anticlimax 508 *lack of expectation*; one in the eye for, comedown, letdown 872 *humiliation*; damp squib 728 *failure*.

**Adj.** *disappointed*, expecting otherwise 508 *off guard*; frustrated, thwarted, balked 702 *hindered*; baffled, foiled 728 *defeated*; disconcerted, crestfallen, chagrined, humiliated 872 *humbled*; disgruntled, dischuffed, soured 829 *discontented*; sick with disappointment 853 *hopeless*; heartbroken 834 *dejected*; badly served, let down, betrayed, jilted; refused, turned away 607 *rejected*.

*disappointing*, unsatisfying, unsatisfactory 636 *insufficient*; not up to expectation, less than one's hopes 829 *discontenting*; miscarried, abortive 728 *unsuccessful*; cheating, deceptive 542 *deceiving*.

**Vb.** *be disappointed*, – unsuccessful etc. adj.; try in vain 728 *fail*; have hoped for something better, not realize one's expectations 307 *fall short*; expect otherwise, be let down, be left in the lurch, be jilted, have hoped better of; find to one's cost 830 *regret*; listen to a false prophet 544 *be duped*; laugh on the wrong side of one's face, be crestfallen, look blue, look blank 872 *be humbled*; be sick with disappointment, be sick at heart, be without hope 853 *despair*.

*disappoint*, not come up to expectations 307 *fall short*; belie one's expectation; defeat one's hopes, dash one's h., crush one's h., blight one's h., deceive one's h., betray one's h.; burst the bubble, disillusion; serve badly, fail one, let one down, leave one in the lurch, not come up to scratch; balk, foil, thwart, frustrate 702 *hinder*; amaze, dumbfound, boggle one's mind 508 *surprise*; disconcert, humble 872 *humiliate*; betray, play one false 930 *be dishonest*; play one a trick, jilt, bilk 542 *befool*; dash the cup from one's lips, tantalize, leave unsatisfied, discontent, spoil one's pleasure, dissatisfy, sour, dischuff, embitter with disappointment 829 *cause discontent*; refuse, deny, turn away 607 *reject*.

**Adv.** *disappointingly*, tantalizingly, so near and yet so far.

## 510 Foresight

**N.** *foresight*, prevision; anticipation, foretaste; precognition, foreknowledge, prescience, second sight, clairvoyancy; premonition, presentiment, foreboding, forewarning 511 *omen*; prognosis, prognostication 511 *prediction*; foregone conclusion 473 *certainty*; programme, prospectus 623 *plan*; forward planning, forethought, vision, longsightedness 498 *sagacity*; premeditation 608 *predetermination*; prudence,

providence 858 *caution*; intelligent anticipation, readiness, provision 669 *preparation*.

**Adj.** *foreseeing*, foresighted, prospective, prognostic, predictive 511 *predicting*; clairvoyant, second-sighted, prophetic; prescient, farsighted, weatherwise, sagacious 498 *wise*; looking ahead, provident, prudent 858 *cautious*; anticipant, anticipatory 507 *expectant*.

**Vb.** *foresee*, divine, prophesy, forecast 511 *predict*; forewarn 664 *warn*; foreknow, see *or* peep *or* pry into the future, read the f., look into one's crystal ball, read one's palm, have second sight; have prior information, be forewarned, know in advance 524 *be informed*; see ahead, look a., see it coming, scent, scent from afar, feel in one's bones; look for 507 *expect*; be beforehand, be prepared, anticipate, forestall 135 *be early*; make provision 669 *prepare*; surmise, make a good guess 512 *suppose*; forejudge 608 *predetermine*; show prudence, plan ahead 623 *plan*; look to the future, have an eye to the f., see how the cat jumps, see how the wind blows 124 *look ahead*; have an eye on the main chance 498 *be wise*; feel one's way, keep a sharp lookout 455 *be attentive*; lay up for a rainy day 633 *provide*; take precautions, provide against 858 *be cautious*.

## 511 Prediction

**N.** *prediction*, foretelling, forewarning, prophecy; apocalypse 975 *revelation*; forecast, weather f.; prognostication, prognosis; presentiment, foreboding 510 *foresight*; presage, prefiguration, prefigurement, 1984; programme, prospectus, forward planning 623 *plan*; announcement, notice, advance n. 528 *publication*; warning, preliminary w., warning shot 665 *danger signal*; prospect 507 *expectation*; shape of things to come, horoscope, fortune, palm-reading, palmistry, crystal-gazing, tarot cards; futurology, scenario planning; type 23 *prototype*.

*divination*, clairvoyancy; augury, taking the auspices; haruspication; vaticination, soothsaying; astrology, horoscopy, Panchang, casting nativities; fortune-telling, palmistry; crystal-gazing, scrying; reading teacups *or* tea leaves; I Ching; casting lots, sortilege; necromancy 984 *occultism*; dowsing 484 *discovery*.

**Some Other Methods of Divination**
aeromancy (by atmospheric phenomena), ailuromancy (from the behaviour of cats), alectryomancy (from a cockerel eating grain placed on the letters of the alphabet, so spelling out something), alomancy (from random patterns of salt), anthropomancy (from human entrails), arithmancy *or* arithmomancy (by numbers), astromancy (= astrology), axinomancy (by means of an axe), belomancy (by means of arrows), bibliomancy (by opening a book, such as the Bible, at

random; 'rhapsodomancy' if it is a book of poetry), botanomancy (by means of plants, especially by burning leaves or branches), capnomancy (by means of smoke), cartomancy (by means of playing cards), ceromancy (by dropping melted wax into water), cheiromancy *or* chiromancy (= palmistry), cleromancy (by casting lots), coscinomancy (by means of a sieve, and sometimes shears), crithomancy (by scattering meal over sacrificial animals), crystallomancy (by looking into transparent bodies such as crystals or water), dactyliomancy (by means of a ring), geomancy (from the shapes formed when earth is thrown down onto a surface, or by shapes formed by joining dots on paper or points on the ground), gyromancy (by walking round and round in a circle until you fall down from giddiness), hieromancy (by observing objects offered in sacrifice), hydromancy (by means of water), lampadomancy (by means of a flame), lithomancy (by means of stones), molybdomancy (from the shape of molten lead dropped into water), myomancy (from the movements of mice), necromancy (by consulting spirits of the dead), oenomancy (from the appearance of wine poured out in libations), omphalomancy (from the form of a baby's umbilical cord), oneiromancy (from dreams), onychomancy (by means of fingernails), ornithomancy (from the flight of birds), pyromancy (by means of fire), rhabdomancy (by means of a rod, e.g. in water-divining), scapulimancy (from the cracks that form in a burning shoulder-blade), spodomancy (by means of ashes), tasseomancy (by the patterns formed by tea leaves in a cup), tephromancy (by means of the ashes from sacrificial pyres), theomancy (by means of divinely inspired oracles), theriomancy *and* zoomancy (from the appearance or behaviour of animals).

*omen,* portent, presage, writing on the wall; prognostic, symptom, syndrome, sign 547 *indication*; augury, auspice; forewarning, caution 664 *warning*; harbinger, herald 529 *messenger*; prefigurement, foretoken, type; ominousness, portentousness, gathering clouds, signs of the times 661 *danger*; luck-bringer, black cat, horseshoe 983 *talisman*; portent of bad luck, broken mirror, spilt salt, shooting star, walking under a ladder; bird of ill omen, owl, raven.

*oracle,* consultant 500 *sage*; meteorologist, weatherman *or* woman; calamity prophet, doom merchant, doomster, doomwatcher, Cassandra 664 *warner*; prophet, prophetess, seer, vaticinator; futurologist, prognosticator, forecaster; soothsayer 983 *sorcerer*; clairvoyant, medium 984 *occultist*; Delphic oracle, Pythian o., Pythoness, Pythia; Sibyl, Sibylline books; Old Moore, Nostradamus; Witch of Endor; cards, tarot c., dice, lot; tripod, crystal ball, mirror, tea leaves, palm; Bible, sortes Vergilianae.

*diviner,* water d., dowser; tipster 618 *gambler*; astrologer, stargazer, caster of nativities; fortune-teller, gipsy, palmist, crystal-gazer, interpreter of dreams; augur, haruspex.

**Adj.** *predicting,* predictive, foretelling; presentient, clairvoyant 510 *foreseeing*; fortune-telling; weather-wise, weather-forecasting;

prophetic, vatic, vaticinatory, mantic, fatidical, apocalyptic; oracular, sibylline; monitory, premonitory, foreboding 664 *cautionary*; heralding, prefiguring 66 *precursory*.

*presageful,* significant, ominous, portentous, big with fate, pregnant with doom; augural, auspicial, haruspical; auspicious, promising, fortunate, favourable 730 *prosperous*; inauspicious, sinister 731 *adverse*.

**Vb.** *predict,* forecast, make a prediction, prognosticate, make a prognosis; foretell, prophesy, vaticinate, forebode, bode, augur, spell; foretoken, presage, portend; foreshow, foreshadow, prefigure, shadow forth, forerun, herald, be harbinger, usher in 64 *come before*; point to, betoken, typify, signify 547 *indicate*; announce, give notice, notify 528 *advertise*; forewarn, give warning 664 *warn*; look black, look ominous, lour, menace 900 *threaten*; promise, augur well, bid fair to, give hopes of, hold out hopes, build up h., raise expectations, excite e. 852 *give hope*.

*divine,* auspicate, haruspicate; read the entrails, take the auspices, take the omens; soothsay, vaticinate; cast a horoscope, cast a nativity; cast lots 618 *gamble*; tell fortunes; read the future, read the signs, read the stars; read the cards, read one's hand, read one's palm.

SECTION SEVEN

## Creative thought

**512 Supposition**
**N.** *supposition,* supposal, notion, the idea of 451 *idea*; fancy, conceit 513 *ideality*; pretence, pretending 850 *affectation*; presumption, assumption, presupposition, postulation, postulate 475 *premise*; condition, stipulation, sine qua non 766 *conditions*; proposal, proposition 759 *offer*; submission 475 *argument*; hypothesis, working h., theory, model, theorem 452 *topic*; thesis, position, stand, attitude, orientation, point of view, standpoint 485 *opinion*; suggestion, casual s.; suggestiveness 524 *hint*; basis of supposition, clue, data, datum 466 *evidence*; suspicion, hunch, inkling (see also *conjecture*); instinct 476 *intuition*; association of ideas 449 *thought*; supposability, conjecturability 469 *possibility*.

*conjecture,* unverified supposition, guess, surmise, suspicion; mere notion, bare supposition, vague suspicion, rough guess, crude estimate, guesstimate; shrewd idea 476 *intuition*; construction, reconstruction; guesswork, guessing, speculation; gamble, shot, shot in the dark 618 *gambling*.

*theorist*, hypothesist, theorizer, theoretician, model builder, research worker; supposer, surmiser, guesser; academic, critic, armchair c., armchair detective; doctrinarian 473 *doctrinaire*; speculator, thinker 449 *philosopher*; boffin, ideas hamster *or* idea h. 623 *planner*; speculator 618 *gambler*.

**Adj.** *suppositional*, supposing etc. vb.; suppositive, notional, conjectural, guessing, guesstimating, propositional, hypothetical, theoretical, armchair, speculative, blue-sky, academic, of academic interest; gratuitous, unverified; suggestive, hinting, allusive, stimulating, thought-provoking.

*supposed*, conjectured etc. vb.; assumed, presumed, premised, taken, taken as read, postulated; proposed, mooted 452 *topical*; given, granted, granted for the sake of argument 488 *assented*; suppositive, putative, presumptive; pretended, so-called, quasi; not real 2 *unreal*; alleged, supposititious, fabled, fancied 543 *untrue*; supposable, surmisable, imaginable 513 *imaginary*.

**Vb.** *suppose*, just s., pretend, fancy, dream 513 *imagine*; think, conceive, take into one's head, get into one's head 485 *opine*; divine, have a hunch, have an inkling 476 *intuit*; surmise, conjecture, guess, hazard a g., make a g.; suppose so, dare say; persuade oneself 485 *believe*; presume, assume, presuppose, presurmise 475 *premise*; posit, lay down, assert 532 *affirm*; take for granted, take, take it, postulate 475 *reason*; speculate, have a theory, hypothesize, theorize 449 *meditate*; sketch, draft, outline 623 *plan*; rely on supposition 618 *gamble*.

*propound*, propose, mean seriously 759 *offer*; put on the agenda, moot, move, propose a motion, postulate 761 *request*; put a case, submit, make one's submission 475 *argue*; put forth, make a suggestion, venture to say, put forward a notion, throw out an idea, throw something into the melting-pot 691 *advise*; suggest, adumbrate, allude 524 *hint*; put an idea into one's head, urge 612 *motivate*.

**Adv.** *supposedly*, reputedly, seemingly; on the assumption that, ex hypothesi.

## 513 Imagination

**N.** *imagination*, power of i., visual i., vivid i., highly-coloured i., fertile i., bold i., wild i.; fervid i.; lively i.; imaginativeness, creativeness; inventiveness, creativity 21 *originality*; ingenuity, resourcefulness 694 *skill*; fancifulness, fantasy, fantasticalness, stretch of the imagination (see also *ideality*); understanding, insight, empathy, sympathy 819

*moral sensibility*; poetic imagination, frenzy, poetic f., ecstasy, inspiration, afflatus, divine a.; fancy, the mind's eye, recollection, recollection in tranquillity, visualization, objectification, image-building, imagery, word-painting; artistry, creative work.

*ideality*, conception 449 *thought*; idealization, ego ideal; mental image, projection 445 *appearance*; concept, image, conceit, fancy, coinage of the brain, brain-creation, notion 451 *idea*; whim, whimsy, whimwham, crinkum-crankum 497 *absurdity*; vagary 604 *caprice*; figment, f. of the imagination, fiction 541 *falsehood*; work of fiction, story 590 *novel*; science fiction, space odyssey, steam punk, cyberpunk; fairy tale; imaginative exercise, flight of fancy, play of f., uncontrolled imagination, romance, fantasy, extravaganza, rhapsody 546 *exaggeration*; poetic licence 593 *poetry*; quixotry, knight-errantry, skiamachy, shadow boxing.

*fantasy*, wildest dreams; vision, dream, bad d., nightmare, night terror; Jabberwocky 84 *rara avis*; bogey, phantom 970 *ghost*; shadow, vapour 419 *dimness*; mirage, fata Morgana 440 *visual fallacy*; delusion, hallucination, chimera 495 *error*; reverie, daydream, brown study 456 *abstractedness*; trance, somnambulism 375 *insensibility*; sick fancy, delirium 503 *frenzy*; subjectivity, autosuggestion; wishful thinking 477 *sophistry*; window-shopping, make-believe, vapourware, golden dream, pipe d. 859 *desire*; romance, stardust; romanticism, escapism, idealism, Utopianism; Utopia, Erewhon; promised land, El Dorado, the end of the rainbow; Happy Valley, Fortunate Isles, Isles of the Blest; land of Cockaigne, Ruritania, Shangri-la, Atlantis, Lyonesse, Middle Earth, Narnia; fairyland, wonderland; cloud-cuckoo-land, dream l., dream world, castles in the air, castles in Spain; 'pie in the sky', good time coming, millennium 124 *future state*;

> You will eat / Bye and bye
> In that glorious land above the sky.
> Work and pray / Live on hay,
> You'll get pie in the sky when you die.
>
> Joe Hill, *The Preacher and the Slave*

idle fancy, myth, fantasy fiction 543 *fable*; fantasy game, fantasy football, fantasy cricket.

*visionary*, seer 511 *diviner*; dreamer, day-d., somnambulist 456 *inattention*; fantast, fantasist; idealist, Utopian 901 *philanthropist*; escapist, ostrich 620 *avoider*; romantic, romancer, romanticist, rhapsodist, mythmaker; enthusiast, knight-errant, Don Quixote 504 *crank*; creative worker 556 *artist*; ideas hamster *or* idea h.

**Adj.** *imaginative*, creative, lively, original, idea'd, inventive, fertile, ingenious; resourceful 694 *skilful*; fancy-led, romancing, romantic; high-flown, rhapsodical, carried away 546 *exaggerated*; poetic, fictional; Utopian, idealistic; rhapsodic, enthusiastic; dreaming, day-dreaming, in a trance; extravagant, grotesque, bizarre, fantastical, unreal, whimsical, airy-fairy, preposterous, impractical, Heath Robinson 497 *absurd*; visionary, otherworldly, quixotic, Laputan; imaginal, visualizing, eidetic, eidotropic.

*imaginary*, unreal, unsubstantial 4 *insubstantial*; subjective, notional, chimerical, illusory 495 *erroneous*; dreamy, visionary, not of this world, of another world, ideal; cloudy, vaporous 419 *shadowy*; unhistorical, fictitious, fabulous, fabled, legendary, mythic, mytho-logical 543 *untrue*; fanciful, fancy-bred, fancied, imagined, fabricated, hatched; thought-up, dreamed-up; hypothetical 512 *suppositional*; pretended, make-believe.

**Vb.** *imagine*, ideate 449 *think*; fancy, dream; excogitate, think of, think up, conjure up, dream up; make up, devise, invent, originate, create, have an inspiration 609 *improvise*; coin, hatch, concoct, fabricate 164 *produce*; visualize, envisage, see in the mind's eye 438 *see*; conceive, form an image of; figure to oneself, picture to o., represent to o.; paint, p. in words, write a pen portrait of, conjure up a vision, objectify, realize, capture, recapture 551 *represent*; use one's imagination, give reins to one's i., run riot in imagination 546 *exaggerate*; play with one's thoughts, pretend, make-believe, daydream 456 *be inattentive*; build Utopias, build castles in the air, build castles in Spain; see visions, dream dreams; fantasize, idealize, romanticize, fictionalize, rhapsodize 546 *exaggerate*; enter into, empathize, sympathize 516 *understand*.

**Adv.** *imaginatively*, in imagination, in thought; with imagination; in the mind's eye; with one's head in the clouds.

**4.2**

# Communication of ideas

SECTION ONE

## Nature of ideas communicated

### 514 Meaning

**N.** *meaning*, idea conveyed, substance, essence, spirit, sum, sum and substance, gist, pith, nitty-gritty; contents, text, matter, subject m.

452 *topic*; semantic content, deep structure, sense, value, drift, tenor, purport, import, implication, colouring; force, effect; relevance, bearing, scope; meaningfulness, semantic flow, context (see also *connotation*); expression, mode of e., diction 566 *style*; semantics, semiology 557 *linguistics*.

*connotation*, denotation, signification, significance, reference, application; construction 520 *interpretation*; context; original meaning, derivation, etymology 156 *source*; range of meaning, semantic field, comprehension; extended meaning, extension; intention, main meaning, core m., leading sense; specialized meaning, peculiar m., idiom 80 *speciality*; received meaning, usage, acceptance, accepted meaning 610 *practice*; single meaning, univocity, unambiguity 516 *intelligibility*; double meaning, ambiguity 518 *equivocalness*; many meanings, polysemy, plurisignation; same meaning, equivalent meaning, convertible terms; synonym, synonymousness, synonymity, equivalence 13 *identity*; opposite meaning, antonym, antonymy 14 *contrariety*; contradictory meaning, countersense; changed meaning, semantic shift; level of meaning, literal meaning, literality 573 *plainness*; metaphorical meaning 519 *metaphor*; hidden meaning, esoteric sense 523 *latency*; constructive sense, implied s.; no sense 497 *absurdity*.

**Adj.** *meaningful*, significant, of moment 638 *important*; substantial, pithy, meaty, full of meaning, replete with m., packed with m., pregnant; meaning etc. vb.; importing, purporting, significative, indicative 547 *indicating*; telling 516 *expressive*; pointed, epigrammatic 839 *witty*; suggestive, evocative, allusive, implicit; express, explicit 573 *plain*; declaratory 532 *affirmative*; interpretative 520 *interpretive*.

*semantic*, semiological. philological, etymological 557 *linguistic*; connotational, connotative; denotational, denotative; literal, verbal 573 *plain*; metaphorical 519 *figurative*; univocal, unambiguous 516 *intelligible*; polysemous, ambiguous 518 *equivocal*; synonymous, homonymous 13 *identical*; tantamount, equivalent 18 *similar*; tautologous 106 *repeated*; antonymous 14 *contrary*; idiomatic 80 *special*; paraphrastic 520 *interpretive*; obscure 568 *unclear*; clear 567 *perspicuous*; implied, constructive 523 *tacit*; nonsensical 497 *absurd*; without meaning 515 *meaningless*.

**Vb.** *mean*, have a meaning, bear a sense, mean something; convey a meaning, get across 524 *communicate*; typify, symbolize 547 *indicate*; signify, denote, connote, stand for 551 *represent*; import, purport, intend; point to, add up to, boil down to, spell, involve 523 *imply*; convey, express, declare, assert 532 *affirm*; bespeak, tell of, speak of, breathe of, savour of, speak volumes 466 *evidence*; mean to say, be trying to s., be getting at, be driving at, really mean, have in mind, allude to, refer to, hint at; be synonymous, have the same meaning, co-refer 13 *be identical*; say it in other words, put it another way, tautologize 106 *repeat*; mean the same thing, be the same thing in the end, agree in meaning, coincide 24 *accord*; conflict in meaning, be opposed in m., contradictory 25 *disagree*; draw a meaning, infer, understand by 516 *understand*.

**Adv.** *significantly*, meaningly, meaningfully, with meaning, to the effect that 520 *in plain words*; in a sense, in some s.; as meant, as intended, as understood; in the sense that *or* of; according to the book, from the context; literally, verbally, word for word; so to speak 519 *metaphorically*.

## 515 Lack of meaning

**N.** *lack of meaning*, meaninglessness, unmeaningness, absence of meaning, no m., no context; no bearing 10 *irrelevance*; nonsignificance 639 *unimportance*; amphigouri 497 *absurdity*; inanity, emptiness, triteness; truism, platitude, cliché 496 *maxim*; mere words, empty w., verbalism; unreason, illogicality 477 *sophistry*; invalidity, dead letter, nullity 161 *ineffectuality*; illegibility, scribble, scribbling, scrawl 586 *script*; daub 552 *misrepresentation*; empty sound, meaningless noise, strumming; sounding brass, tinkling cymbal 400 *loudness*; jargon, rigmarole, gobbledygook, galimatias, psychobabble, bafflegab; abracadabra, hocus-pocus, mumbo jumbo; gibberish, gabble, double Dutch, Greek, Babel 517 *unintelligibility*; incoherence, raving, delirium 503 *frenzy*; double-talk, mystification 530 *enigma*; insincerity 925 *flattery*.

*silly talk*, senseless t., nonsense 497 *absurdity*; stuff, stuff and nonsense, balderdash, rubbish, load of r., rot, tommyrot; drivel, twaddle, fiddle-faddle, bosh, tosh, tripe, piffle, bilge, bull, bollocks (sl).

*empty talk*, idle speeches, sweet nothings, endearments, wind, gas, hot air, vapouring, verbiage 570 *diffuseness*; rant, bombast, fustian, rodomontade 877 *boasting*; blether, blather, blah-blah, flapdoodle, flimflam; gup, guff, pi-jaw, eyewash, claptrap, poppycock 543 *fable*; humbug 541 *falsehood*; moonshine, malarkey, hokum, bunkum, bunk, boloney, hooey; flannel, flummery, blarney 925 *flattery*; sales talk, patter, sales p., spiel; talk, chatter, prattle, prating, yammering, babble, gabble,

jabber, jabber jabber, jaw, yackety yack, yak yak, rhubarb rhubarb 581 *chatter*.

**Adj.** *meaningless*, unmeaning, without meaning, Pickwickian; amphigoric, nonsense, nonsensical 497 *absurd*; senseless, null; unexpressive, unidiomatic 25 *unapt*; nonsignificant, insignificant, inane, empty, trivial, trite 639 *unimportant*; fatuous, piffling, blithering; trashy, trumpery, rubbishy; twaddling, waffling, windy, ranting 546 *exaggerated*; incoherent, raving, gibbering 503 *frenzied*.

*unmeant*, unintentional, involuntary, unintended, unimplied, unalluded to; mistranslated 521 *misinterpreted*; insincere 925 *flattering*.

**Vb.** *mean nothing*, be unmeaning, have no meaning, make no sense, be irrelevant; scribble, scratch, daub, strum; talk bunkum, talk like an idiot 497 *be absurd*; talk, babble, prattle, prate, gabble, gibber, jabber, yak 581 *be loquacious*; talk double dutch, talk gibberish, double-talk 517 *be unintelligible*; rant 546 *exaggerate*; gush, rave, drivel, drool, blether, waffle, twaddle; vapour, talk hot air, gas 499 *be foolish*; not mean what one says, blarney 925 *flatter*; make nonsense of 521 *misinterpret*; have no meaning for, be Greek to, pass over one's head 474 *puzzle*.

**Int.** rubbish!, what rot!, nonsense!, fiddlesticks!, etc. n.

## 516 Intelligibility

**N.** *intelligibility*, knowability, cognizability; explicability, teachability, penetrability; apprehensibility, comprehensibility, adaptation to the understanding; readability, legibility, decipherability; clearness, clarity, coherence, limpidity, lucidity 567 *perspicuity*; precision, unambiguity 473 *certainty*; simplicity, straightforwardness, plain speaking, plain speech, downright utterance; plain words, plain English, no gobbledygook, mother tongue; simple eloquence, unadorned style 573 *plainness*; paraphrase, simplification 701 *facility*; amplification, popularization, haute vulgarisation 520 *interpretation*.

*moment of understanding*, lightbulb moment.

**Adj.** *intelligible*, apprehensible, comprehensible, penetrable, realizable, understandable; coherent 502 *sane*; audible, recognizable, distinguishable, unmistakable; discoverable, cognizable, knowable 490 *known*; explicable, teachable; unambiguous, unequivocal 514 *meaningful*; explicit, positive 473 *certain*; unblurred, distinct, clear-cut, precise 80 *definite*; well-spoken, articulate, eloquent; plainspoken, unevasive, unadorned, downright, forthright 573 *plain*; uninvolved, straightforward, simple 701 *easy*; obvious, self-explanatory, easy to understand, user-friendly, easy to grasp, made easy, adapted to the understanding, clear to the meanest capacity; explained, predigested, simplified, popularized, popular, for the million 520 *interpreted*; clear, limpid 422 *transparent*; pellucid, lucid 567 *perspicuous*; readable, decipherable, legible, well-written, printed, in print; luminous, crystal clear, clear as daylight, clear as noonday, plain as a pikestaff 443 *visible*.

*expressive*, telling, meaningful, informative, striking, vivid, graphic, highly coloured, emphatic, forceful, strong, strongly worded 590 *descriptive*; illustrative, explicatory 520 *interpretive*; amplifying, paraphrasing, popularizing.

**Vb.** *be intelligible*, – clear, – easy etc. adj.; be realized, come alive, take on depth; be readable, be an easy read, read easily; make sense, add up, speak to the understanding 475 *be reasonable*; tell its own tale, speak for itself, be self-explanatory 466 *evidence*; have no secrets, be on the surface 443 *be visible*; be understood, come over, get across, sink in, dawn on; make understood, clarify, clear up, open one's eyes, elucidate 520 *interpret*; make easy, simplify, popularize 701 *facilitate*; recapitulate 106 *repeat*; labour the obvious 532 *emphasize*.

*understand*, comprehend, apprehend 490 *know*; master 536 *learn*; have, hold, retain 505 *remember*; have understanding 498 *be wise*; see through, penetrate, fathom, get to the bottom of 484 *detect*; spot, descry, discern, distinguish, make out, see at a glance, see with half an eye 438 *see*; recognize, make no mistake 473 *be certain*; grasp, get hold of, seize, seize the meaning, be on to it, cotton on to, dig; get the hang of, take in, register; be with one, follow, savvy; collect, get, catch on, latch on to, twig; catch one's drift, get the idea, get the picture; realize, get wise to, tumble to, rumble; begin to understand, come to u., have one's eyes opened, see the light, see through, see it all; be undeceived, be disillusioned 830 *regret*; get to know, get the hang of, be told 524 *be informed*.

**Adv.** *intelligibly*, expressively, lucidly, plainly, simply, in words of one syllable; in plain terms, in clear terms, in plain English, for the layman.

## 517 Unintelligibility

**N.** *unintelligibility*, incomprehensibility, inapprehensibility, unaccountability, inconceivability; inexplicability, impenetrability; perplexity, difficulty 474 *uncertainty*; obscurity 568 *imperspicuity*; ambiguity 518 *equivocalness*; mystification 515 *lack of meaning*; incoherence 503 *mental disorder*; double dutch, gibberish; jargon, psychobabble, bafflegab;foreign tongue, private language, idiolect 560 *dialect*, *slang*; stammering 580 *speech defect*; undecipherability, illegibility, unreadability; scribble, scrawl 586 *lettering*; inaudibility 401 *faintness*; Greek, sealed book 530 *secret*; hard saying, paradox, koan, knotty point, obscure problem, pons asinorum, crux, riddle, oracular pronouncement 530 *enigma*; mysterious behaviour, Sphinx-like attitude, baffling demeanour.

**Adj.** *unintelligible*, incomprehensible, inapprehensible, inconceivable, not understandable, not to be understood, inexplicable, unaccountable, not to be accounted for; unknowable, unrecognizable, incognizable, undiscoverable, as Greek to one, like double Dutch 491 *unknown*; unfathomable, unbridgeable, unsearchable, inscrutable, impenetrable; blank, poker-faced, expressionless 820 *impassive*; inaudible 401 *muted*; unreadable, illegible, scrawly, scribbled, undecipherable, crabbed; undiscernible 444 *invisible*; hidden, arcane 523 *occult*; cryptic, obscure, shrouded in mystery; esoteric 80 *private*; Sphinx-like, enigmatic, oracular (see also *puzzling*).

*puzzling*, hard to understand, complex 700 *difficult*; hard, beyond one, over one's head, recondite, abstruse, elusive; sphinxian, enigmatic, mysterious 523 *occult*; half-understood, nebulous, misty, foggy, hazy, dim, obscure 419 *shadowy*; clear as mud, clear as ditch water 568 *unclear*; ambiguous 518 *equivocal*; of doubtful meaning, oracular; paradoxical 508 *unexpected*; fishy, strange, odd 84 *abnormal*; unexplained, without a solution, insoluble, unsolvable; unsolved, unresolved 474 *uncertain*.

*inexpressible*, unspeakable, untranslatable; unpronounceable, unutterable, ineffable; incommunicable, indefinable; profound, deep; mystic, mystical, transcendental.

*puzzled*, mystified, unable to understand, wondering, out of one's depth, flummoxed, stumped, baffled, perplexed, nonplussed 474 *uncertain*.

**Vb.** *be unintelligible*, – puzzling, – inexpressible etc. adj.; be hard, be difficult, present a puzzle, make one's head ache *or* swim 474 *puzzle*; talk in riddles, speak oracles 518 *be equivocal*; talk double dutch, talk gibberish 515 *mean nothing*; speak badly 580 *stammer*; write badly, scribble, scrawl; keep one guessing 486 *cause doubt*; perplex, complicate, entangle, confuse 63 *bedevil*; require explanation, have no answer, need an interpreter; be too deep, go over one's head, be beyond one's reach; elude one's grasp, escape one; pass comprehension, baffle understanding.

*not understand*, not penetrate, not get it, not grasp it; find unintelligible, not make out, not know what to make of, make nothing of, make neither head nor tail of, be unable to account for; puzzle over, rack one's brains over, find too difficult, be floored by, be stumped by, give up; be out of one's depth 491 *not know*; wonder, be at sea 474 *be uncertain*; not know what one is about, have no grasp of 695 *be unskilful*; have a blind spot 439 *be blind*; misunderstand one another, be on different wavelengths, be at cross-purposes 495 *blunder*; get it into one's head, get one wrong 481 *misjudge*; not register 456 *be inattentive*.

## 518 Equivocalness

**N.** *equivocalness*, two voices 14 *contrariety*; ambiguity, ambivalence 517 *unintelligibility*; indefiniteness, vagueness 474 *uncertainty*; double meaning, amphibology 514 *connotation*; newspeak, doubletalk, weasel word 515 *lack of meaning*; conundrum, riddle, oracle, oracular utterance 530 *enigma*; mental reservation 525 *concealment*; prevarication, balancing act; equivocation, white lie 543 *untruth*; quibble, quibbling 477 *sophistry*; word-play, play upon words, paronomasia 574 *ornament*; pun, calembour, equivoque, double entendre 839 *witticism*; faux ami, confusible; anagram, acrostic; synonymy, homonymy, polysemy; homonym, homograph, homophone 18 *analogue*.

**Adj.** *equivocal*, not univocal, ambiguous, ambivalent, epicene; double, double-tongued, two-edged; left-handed, back-h.; equivocating, prevaricating, facing both ways; vague, evasive, oracular; amphibolous, homonymous; anagrammatic.

**Vb.** *be equivocal*, cut both ways; play upon words, pun; have two meanings, have a second meaning 514 *mean*; speak oracles, speak with two voices 14 *be contrary*; fudge, waffle, stall, not give a straight answer, beat about the bush, sit on the fence 620 *avoid*; equivocate, prevaricate, weasel 541 *dissemble*.

## 519 Metaphor: figure of speech

**N.** *metaphor*, mixed m.; transference; allusion, application; misapplication, catachresis; extended metaphor, allegorization, allegory; mystical interpretation, anagoge 520 *interpretation*; fable, parable 534 *teaching*; objective correlative, symbol; symbolism, nonliterality, figurativeness, imagery 513 *imagination*; simile, likeness 462 *comparison*; personification, prosopopeia.

*trope*, figure, figure of speech, turn of s., flourish; manner of speech, façon de parler; irony, sarcasm 851 *satire*; rhetorical figure 574 *ornament*; metonymy, antonomasia, synecdoche, transferred epithet, enallage; zeugma, anaphora; litotes 483 *underestimation*; hyperbole 546 *exaggeration*; stress, emphasis, epizeuxis; circumlocution, euphuism, euphemism; dysphemism 850 *affectation*; anacoluthon, colloquialism 573 *plainness*; contrast, antithesis 462 *comparison*; metathesis 221 *inversion*; paradox, epigram, paronomasia, word-play 518 *equivocalness*; aposiopesis; apostrophe.

**Adj.** *figurative*, metaphorical, tropical, tralatitious; catachrestic; allusive, symbolical, allegorical, anagogic; parabolical; comparative 462 *compared*; euphuistic, tortured, euphemistic 850 *affected*; colloquial 573 *plain*; hyperbolic 546 *exaggerated*; satirical, sarcastic, ironical 851 *derisive*; flowery, florid 574 *ornate*; oratorical 574 *rhetorical*.

**Vb.** *figure*, image, embody, personify; typify, symbolize 551 *represent*; allegorize, parabolize, fable; prefigure, adumbrate; apply, allude; refer, liken, contrast 462 *compare*; employ metaphor, indulge in tropes 574 *ornament*.

**Adv.** *metaphorically*, not literally, tropically, figuratively, tralatitiously, by allusion; in a way, as it were, so to speak, in a manner of speaking.

## 520 Interpretation

**N.** *interpretation*, definition, explanation, explication, exposition, exegesis, epexegesis; elucidation, light, clarification, illumination; illustration, exemplification 83 *example*; resolution, solution, key, clue, the secret 460 *answer*; decipherment, decoding, decryption, cracking 484 *discovery*; emendation 654 *amendment*; application, particular interpretation, twist, turn, quirk; construction, construe, reading, lection 514 *meaning*; subaudition 514 *connotation*; euhemerism, circumlocution, demythologization; allegorization 519 *metaphor*; accepted reading, usual text, vulgate; alternative reading, variant r.; criticism, textual c., form c., the higher c., literary c., practical c., appreciation, deconstruction 557 *literature*; critique, review, notice 480 *estimate*; critical power, critic's gift 480 *judgment*; insight, feeling, sympathy 819 *moral sensibility*.

*commentary*, comment, editorial c., Targum; scholium, gloss, footnote; inscription, caption, legend 563 *phrase*; motto, moral 693 *precept*; annotation, notes, marginalia, adversaria; exposition 591 *dissertation*; apparatus criticus, critical edition, variorum; glossary, lexicon 559 *dictionary*.

*translation*, version, rendering, free translation, loose rendering; faithful translation, literal t., construe; key, crib; rewording, paraphrase, metaphrase; précis, abridgment, epitome 592 *compendium*; adaptation, simplification, amplification 516 *intelligibility*; transliteration, decoding, decryption, decipherment; lip-reading.

*hermeneutics*, exegetics, science of interpretation, translator's art; epigraphy, palaeography 557 *linguistics*; cryptanalysis, cryptology; diagnostics, symptomatology; semiology, semiotics; graphology; phrenology, palmistry; prophecy 511 *divination*.

*interpreter*, clarifier, explainer, exponent, expounder, expositor, exegete 537 *teacher*, 973 *religious teacher*; rationalist, rationalizer, euhemerist, demythologizer; editor, copy e. 528 *publicizer*; Masorete, textual critic; emender, emendator; commentator, annotator, notemaker, glossator, scholiast; glossarist, critic, reviewer, Leavisite 480 *estimator*; oneirocritic 511 *diviner*; medium 984 *spiritualism*; polyglot 557 *linguist*; translator, paraphraser, paraphrast; cipher clerk, cryptographer, encoder; solver, code-breaker; decoder; cryptanalyst, cryptologist; lip-reader; epigraphist, palaeographer 125 *antiquarian*; spokesman, mouthpiece, representative 754 *delegate*; public relations officer, PR consultant, press officer, spin-doctor 524 *informant*; executant, performer 413 *musician*; player 594 *actor*; poet, novelist, painter, sculptor 556 *artist*.

*guide*, precedent 83 *example*; lamp, light, star, guiding s.; dragoman, courier, cicerone 690 *director*; showman, demonstrator 522 *exhibitor*.

**Adj.** *interpretive*, interpretative, constructive; explanatory, explicatory, explicative, elucidatory; expositive, expository 557 *literary*; exegetical, hermeneutic; defining, definitive; illuminating, illustrative, exemplary; glossarial, annotative, scholiastic, editorial; lip-reading, translative, paraphrastic, metaphrastic; polyglot; mediumistic; synonymous, equivalent 28 *equal*; literal, strict, word-for-word, verbatim 494 *accurate*; faithful 551 *representing*; free 495 *inexact*.

*interpreted*, glossed etc. vb.; explained, defined, expounded, elucidated, clarified; annotated, commented, commentated, edited; translated, rendered, Englished; deciphered, decoded, cracked.

**Vb.** *interpret*, define, clarify, make clear, disambiguate; explain, unfold, expound, elucidate 516 *be intelligible*; illustrate 83 *exemplify*; demonstrate 522 *show*; act as guide, show

round; comment on, edit, write notes for, add footnotes to, annotate, compose a commentary, gloss; read, spell, spell out; adopt a reading, accept an interpretation, construe, put a construction on, understand by, give a sense to, make sense of, ascribe a meaning to 516 *understand*; illuminate, throw light on, enlighten 524 *inform*; account for, find the cause, deduce, infer 475 *reason*; act as interpreter, spin-doctor, put a spin on, be spokesman *or* -woman *or* -person 755 *deputize*; typify, symbolize, personify; popularize, simplify 701 *facilitate*.

*translate*, make a version, make a key, make a crib; render, do into, turn i., English; retranslate, rehash, reword, rephrase, paraphrase; abridge, précis, amplify, adapt; transliterate, transcribe; cipher, encode, encrypt, put into code; lip-read.

*decipher*, crack, crack the cipher, decode, decrypt; find the meaning, read hieroglyphics; read, spell out, puzzle o., make o., work o.; piece together, find the sense of, find the key to; solve, resolve, enucleate, unravel, unriddle, disentangle, read between the lines.

**Adv.** *in plain words*, plainly, in plain English; by way of explanation; that is, i.e.; in other words, to put it another way, to wit, namely, viz.; to make it plain, to explain.

## 521 Misinterpretation

**N.** *misinterpretation*, misunderstanding, malentendu, misconstruction, misapprehension, wrong end of the stick; crosspurposes, different wavelengths, crossed lines 495 *mistake*; wrong explanation 535 *misteaching*; mistranslation, misconstrue, translator's error; wrong interpretation, false construction; twist, turn, quirk, misapplication, perversion 246 *distortion*; strained sense, circumlocution; false reading; false colouring, dark glasses, rose-coloured spectacles; garbling, falsification 552 *misrepresentation*; overdoing it 546 *exaggeration*; depreciation 483 *underestimation*; parody, travesty 851 *ridicule*; abuse of language, misapplication 565 *solecism*.

**Adj.** *misinterpreted*, misconceived etc. vb., misconstrued, mistranslated 495 *mistaken*; misread, misquoted.

**Vb.** *misinterpret*, misunderstand, misapprehend, misconceive 481 *misjudge*; get wrong, get one wrong, get hold of the wrong end of the stick 495 *blunder*; misread, misspell 495 *err*; set in a false light 535 *misteach*; mistranslate, misconstrue, put a false sense *or* construction on; give a twist *or* turn, pervert, strain the sense, wrest the meaning, do violence to the m., wrench, twist, twist the words 246 *dis-*

*tort*; equivocate, weasel, play upon words 518 *be equivocal*; add a meaning, read into, write i. 38 *add*; leave out, omit, suppress 39 *subtract*; misrepeat, misquote; falsify, garble 552 *misrepresent*; travesty, parody, caricature, guy 851 *ridicule*; overpraise 482 *overrate*; underpraise 483 *underestimate*; inflate 546 *exaggerate*; traduce, misrepresent 926 *defame*.

SECTION TWO

## Modes of communication

### 522 Manifestation

**N.** *manifestation*, revelation, unfolding, discovery, daylight, exposure 526 *disclosure*; expression, formulation 532 *affirmation*; proof 466 *evidence*; confrontation 462 *comparison*; presentation, production, projection, enactment 551 *representation*; symbolization, typification, personification 547 *indication*; sign, token 547 *signal*; symptom, syndrome 511 *omen*; press conference, prerelease, preview 438 *view*; showing, demonstration, exhibition; display, showing off 875 *ostentation*; proclamation 528 *publication*; openness, flagrancy 528 *publicity*; candour, glasnost, plain speech, home truth, words of one syllable 573 *plainness*; prominence, conspicuousness 443 *visibility*; apparition, vision, materialization 445 *appearance*; séance 984 *occultism*; Shekinah, glory 965 *theophany*; incarnation, avatar.

*exhibit*, specimen, sample 83 *example*; piece of evidence, quotation, citation 466 *evidence*; model, mock-up 551 *image*; show piece, collector's p., museum p., antique, curio; display, show, dress s., mannequin parade 445 *spectacle*; scene 438 *view*; exhibition hall, exhibition centre, showplace, showroom, showcase, placard, hoarding, bill 528 *advertisement*; sign 547 *label*; shop window, museum, gallery 632 *collection*; retrospective, exhibition, exposition; fair 796 *market*.

*exhibitor*, advertiser, publicist, promotion manager 528 *publicizer*; displayer, demonstrator; showman; impresario 594 *stage manager*; exhibitionist, peacock 873 *vain person*; model, male m., mannequin; wearer, sporter, flaunter.

**Adj.** *manifest*, apparent, ostensible 445 *appearing*; plain, clear, defined 80 *definite*; explained, plain as a pikestaff, plain as the nose on one's face, clear as daylight 516 *intelligible*; unconcealed, showing 443 *visible*; conspicuous, noticeable, notable, prominent, pronounced, signal, marked, striking, in relief, in the foreground, in the limelight 443 *obvious*; open, patent, evident; gross, crass, palpable;

self-evident, written all over one, for all to see, unmistakable, recognizable, identifiable, incontestable, staring one in the face 473 *certain*; public, famous, notorious, infamous 528 *well-known*; catching the eye, eye-catching, gaudy 875 *showy*; arrant, glaring, stark staring, flagrant, loud, on the rooftops, shouting from the r., – on stilts.

*undisguised*, unconcealed, uncamouflaged, overt, explicit, express, emphatic 532 *affirmative*; in the open, public; exoteric; unreserved, open, candid, heart-to-heart, off the record 540 *veracious*; free, frank, downright, forthright, straightforward, outspoken, blunt, plainspoken, no-nonsense 573 *plain*; honest to goodness, honest to God; bold, daring 711 *defiant*; impudent, brazen, shameless, immodest, barefaced 951 *impure*; bare, naked, naked and unashamed 229 *uncovered*; flaunting, unconcealed, inconcealable (see also *manifest*).

*shown*, manifested etc. vb.; declared, divulged, made public 526 *disclosed*; showing, featured, on show, on display, on view, on 443 *visible*; exhibited, shown off; brought forth, produced; mentioned, brought to one's notice; adduced, cited, quoted; confronted, brought face to face; worn, sported; paraded; unfurled, flaunted, waved, brandished; advertised, publicized, promoted 528 *published*; expressible, producible, showable.

**Vb.** *manifest*, reveal, divulge, give away, betray 526 *disclose*; evince, betoken, show signs of 466 *evidence*; bring to light, unearth 484 *discover*; explain, make plain, make obvious 520 *interpret*; expose, lay bare, unroll, unfurl, unsheathe 229 *uncover*; open up, throw open, lay o. 263 *open*; elicit, draw forth, drag out 304 *extract*; invent, bring forth 164 *produce*; bring out, shadow forth, body f.; incorporate, incarnate, personify 223 *externalize*; typify, symbolize, exemplify 547 *indicate*; point up, accentuate, enhance, develop 36 *augment*; throw light on 420 *illuminate*; highlight, spotlight, throw into relief 532 *emphasize*; express, formulate 532 *affirm*; bring, bring up, make reference to, mention, adduce, cite, quote; bring to the fore, place in the foreground 638 *make important*; bring to notice, produce, trot out, come out with, proclaim, publicize, promote 528 *publish*; show for what it is, show up (see also *show*); solve, elucidate 520 *decipher*.

*show*, exhibit, display; set out, put on display, put on show, put on view, expose to v., offer to the v., set before one's eyes, dangle; wave, flourish 317 *brandish*; sport 228 *wear*; flaunt, parade 875 *be ostentatious*; make a show of, affect 850 *be affected*; present, feature, enact

551 *represent*; put on, stage, release 594 *dramatize*; put on television, televise, screen, film; stage an exhibition, put on show *or* display, hang (a picture); show off, set o., model (garments); put one through his paces; demonstrate 534 *teach*; show round, show over, give a guided tour, point out, draw attention to, bring to notice 547 *indicate*; confront, force a confrontation, bring face to face, bring eyeball to eyeball; reflect, image, mirror, hold up the mirror to 20 *imitate*; tear off the mask, show up, expose 526 *disclose*.

*be plain*, – explicit etc. adj.; show one's face, unveil, unmask 229 *doff*; show one's true colours, have no secrets, make no mystery, not try to hide, wear one's heart on one's sleeve; have no shame, wash one's dirty linen in public; show one's mind, speak out, tell to one's face, make no secret of, give straight from the shoulder, make no bones about 573 *speak plainly*; speak for itself, tell its own story, require no explanation 516 *be intelligible*; be obvious, stand to reason, go without saying 478 *be proved*; be conspicuous, be as plain as the nose on one's face, stand out, stand out a mile 443 *be visible*; show the flag, be seen, show up, show up well, hold the stage, be in the limelight, have the spotlight on one, stand in full view 455 *attract notice*; loom large, stare one in the face 200 *be near*; appear on the horizon, rear its head, show its face, transpire, emanate, come to light 445 *appear*.

**Adv.** *manifestly*, plainly, obviously, patently, palpably, grossly, crassly, openly, publicly, for all to see, notoriously, flagrantly, undisguisedly; at first blush, prima facie; externally, on the face of it, superficially; open and above-board, with cards on the table; frankly, honestly; before God, before all, under the eye of heaven; in full view, in broad daylight, in public, on the stage.

### 523 Latency

**N.** *latency*, no signs of 525 *concealment*; insidiousness, treachery 930 *perfidy*; dormancy, dormant condition, potentiality 469 *possibility*; esotericism, cabbala 984 *occultism*; occultness, mysticism; hidden meaning, occult m., veiled m. 517 *unintelligibility*; ambiguous advice 511 *oracle*; symbolism, allegory, anagoge 519 *metaphor*; implication, adumbration, symbolization; mystery 530 *secret*; inmost recesses 224 *interiority*; dark 418 *darkness*; shadowiness 419 *dimness*; imperceptibility 444 *invisibility*; more than meets the eye; deceptive appearance, hidden fires, hidden depths; iron hand in a velvet glove; slumbering volcano, sleeping dog, sleeping giant 661 *danger*; dark

horse, mystery man, anonymity 562 *no name*; red under the bed, nigger in the woodpile, snake in the grass, mole 663 *pitfall*; manipulator, puppeteer, hidden hand, wire-puller, strings, friends in high places, friend at court, power behind the throne, éminence grise 178 *influence*; old-boy network, networking, Freemasonry; subconscious; subliminal influence, subliminal advertising, secret influence, lurking disease; unsoundness, something rotten; innuendo, insinuation, suggestion 524 *hint*; half-spoken word, mutter, sealed lips 582 *taciturnity*; undercurrent, undertone; aside 401 *faintness*; clandestineness, secret society, cabal, intrigue 623 *plot*; ambushment 527 *ambush*; code, invisible writing, cryptography.

**Adj.** *latent*, lurking, skulking, delitescent 525 *concealed*; dormant, sleeping 679 *inactive*; passive 266 *quiescent*; in abeyance 175 *inert*; potential, undeveloped 469 *possible*; unguessed, unsuspected, crypto- 491 *unknown*; subconscious, subliminal, submerged, underlying, subterranean, below the surface 211 *deep*; in the background, behind the scenes, backroom, undercover 421 *screened*; unmanifested, unseen, unspied, undetected, unexposed 444 *invisible*; murky, obscure 418 *dark*; arcane, impenetrable, undiscoverable 517 *unintelligible*; tucked away, sequestered 883 *secluded*; awaiting discovery, undiscovered, unexplored, untracked, untraced, uninvented, unexplained, unsolved.

*tacit*, unsaid, unspoken, half-spoken, unpronounced, unexpressed, unvoiced, unmentioned, unarticulated, untold of, unsung; undivulged, unproclaimed, unprofessed, undeclared; unwritten, unpublished, unedited; unpromoted; understood, implied, inferred, implicit, between the lines; implicative, suggestive; inferential, allusive.

*occult*, mysterious, mystic; symbolic, allegorical, anagogical 519 *figurative*; cryptic, esoteric 984 *cabbalistic*; veiled, masked, muffled, covert; indirect, crooked 220 *oblique*; clandestine, secret, kept quiet; insidious, treacherous 930 *perfidious*; underhand 525 *stealthy*; undiscovered, hush-hush, top-secret; not public, off the record 80 *private*; coded, cryptographic 525 *disguised*.

**Vb.** *lurk*, hide, be latent, lie dormant, be a stowaway; burrow, stay underground; lie hidden, lie in ambush; lie low, lie low and say nothing, lie doggo, make no sign 266 *be quiescent*; avoid notice, escape observation 444 *be unseen*; evade detection, escape recognition; act behind the scenes, laugh in one's sleeve 541 *dissemble*; creep, slink, tiptoe, walk on tiptoe 525 *be stealthy*; pull the strings, act as puppet-master, stage-manage, underlie, be at the bottom of 156 *cause*; smoke, smoulder 175 *be inert*; be subliminal.

*imply*, insinuate, whisper, murmur, suggest 524 *hint*; understand, infer, leave an inference, allude, be allusive; symbolize, connote, carry a suggestion, involve, spell 514 *mean*.

## 524 Information

**N.** *information*, communication of knowledge, transmission of k., dissemination, diffusion, informatics; information technology, IT, computerized information, Internet, the Net, World Wide Web, website, information highway, information superhighway, telematics, data base, computer file, viewdata 86 *computing*, 531 *Internet*; mailing list, distribution l. 588 *correspondence*; chain of authorities, tradition, hearsay, word of mouth; enlightenment, instruction, briefing 534 *teaching*; thought-transference, intercommunication; sharing of information, communication; mass media 528 *the press*, 531 *broadcasting*; telling, narration 590 *narrative*; notification, announcement, annunciation, intimation, warning, advice, notice, mention, tip, tip-off (see also *hint*); newspaper announcement, hatches matches and dispatches, obit, small ad, advertisement, circular 528 *publicity*; common knowledge, general information, gen, info; factual information, background, facts, the goods; credit-rating, black information, white i., documentary 494 *truth*; material, literature 589 *reading matter*; instructions, directions for use, care label, user's manual; inside information, king's *or* queen's evidence, dope, lowdown, private source, undisclosed s., confidence 530 *secret*; earliest information, scoop; stock of information, acquaintance, the know 490 *knowledge*; recorded information, file, dossier 548 *record*; piece of information, word, report, intelligence, item of news 529 *news*; a communication, wire, telegram, telemessage, telex, cable, cablegram 529 *message*; flood of information, spate of news, outpouring; communicativeness, talking 581 *loquacity*; unauthorized communication, indiscretion, leak, disinformation 526 *disclosure*.

*report*, review, compte rendu, annual report; information called for 459 *enquiry*; paper, Green Paper, White P., Black P.; account, true a., eyewitness a. 590 *narrative*; statement, return, annual r., tax r. 86 *statistics*; specification, estimates 480 *estimate*; progress report, confidential r.; information offered, dispatch, bulletin, communiqué, handout, press release 529 *news*; representation, presentation, case; memorial, petition 761 *entreaty*; remonstrance,

round robin 762 *deprecation*; letters, letters to the editor, dispatches 588 *correspondence*.

*hint*, gentle h., whisper, aside 401 *faintness*; indirect hint, intimation; broad hint, signal, nod, a nod is as good as a wink to a blind horse, wink, look, nudge, kick, kick under the table, gesticulation 547 *gesture*; prompt, cue 505 *reminder*; suggestion, lead, leading question 547 *indication*; caution 664 *warning*; something to go on, tip, tip-off (see also *information*); word, passing w., word in the ear, word to the wise, verb. sap. 691 *advice*; insinuation, innuendo, insinuendo 926 *calumny*; clue, symptom 520 *interpretation*; sidelight, glimpse, inkling, adumbration 419 *glimmer*; suspicion, inference, guess 512 *conjecture*; good tip, wheeze, dodge, wrinkle 623 *contrivance*.

*informant*, teller 590 *narrator*; spokesman *or* -woman *or* -person 579 *speaker*; mouthpiece, representative 754 *delegate*; announcer, radio a., television a., weather-forecaster, weatherman *or* -woman 531 *broadcaster*; notifier, advertiser, promoter, annunciator 528 *publicizer*; harbinger, herald 529 *messenger*; testifier 466 *witness*; one in the know, authority, source; quarter, channel, circle, grapevine; pander, go-between, contact 231 *intermediary*; informed circles: information centre, information bureau, information desk, help d., call centre; news agency, wire service, Reuter, TASS 528 *the press*; communicator, intelligencer, correspondent, special c., reporter, newshound, chequebook journalist, commentator, columnist, gossip writer 529 *news reporter*; tipper, tipster 691 *adviser*; guide, topographer; bigmouth, blabbermouth; little bird; chattering classes.

*informer*, delator 928 *accuser*; spy, spook, snoop, sleuth 459 *detective*; undercover agent, inside a., mole; stool pigeon, nark, copper's n., snitch, sneak, nose, blabber, squealer, squeaker, whistle-blower, grass, supergrass; eavesdropper, telltale, talebearer, clype, tattler, tattle-tale, gossip 581 *chatterer*.

*guidebook*, Baedeker, Rough Guide; travelogue, topography; handbook, book of words, manual, vade mecum, ABC, A-Z; time-table, Bradshaw; roadbook, itinerary, route map, chart, plan 551 *map*; gazetteer 589 *reference book*; nautical almanac, ephemeris; telephone directory, phone book, Yellow Pages; index, catalogue 87 *directory*; courier 520 *guide*.

**Adj.** *informative*, communicative, newsy, chatty, gossipy; informatory, informational, instructive, instructional, documentary 534 *educational*; expressive 532 *affirmative*; expository 520 *interpretive*; in writing 586 *written*; oral, verbal, spoken, nuncupative 579 *speaking*; annunciatory 528 *publishing*; advisory 691 *advising*; monitory 664 *cautionary*; explicit, clear 80 *definite*; candid, plainspoken 573 *plain*; overcommunicative, talking, indiscreet 581 *loquacious*; hinting, insinuating, suggesting.

*informed*, well-i., kept i., au fait, au courant; posted, primed, briefed, instructed 490 *knowing*; told, au courant, genned-up, clued-up, wised-up; in the know, in on, in the picture, sussed (sl), brought up to date, up to speed (inf).

**Vb.** *inform*, certify, advise, beg to a.; intimate, impart, convey (see also *communicate*); apprise, acquaint, have one know, give to understand; give one the facts, brief, instruct 534 *teach*; let one know, put one in the picture, fill one in on; enlighten, open the mind, fill with information 534 *educate*; point out, direct one's attention 547 *indicate*; insinuate (see also *hint*); entrust with information, confide, get confidential, mention privately; put one wise, put right, correct, disabuse, undeceive, disillusion; be specific, state, name, signify 80 *specify*; mention, mention en passant, refer to, touch on, speak of 579 *speak*; gossip, spread rumours; be indiscreet, open one's mouth, let the cat out of the bag, blurt out, talk 581 *be loquacious*; leak information, give disinformation, break the news, reveal 526 *disclose*; tell, clype, blab, split, grass, snitch, peach, squeal, blow the gaff 526 *confess*; rat, turn Queen's evidence, turn State's e., implicate an accomplice 603 *change one's mind*; betray one, blow the whistle on, sell one down the river; tell tales, tell on, clype on, report against; inform against, lay an infor-mation against, shop, denounce 928 *accuse*.

*communicate*, transmit, pass on, pass on information; dispatch news 588 *correspond*; report, cover, make a report, submit a r.; report progress, post, keep posted; get through, get across, put it over; contact, get in touch; convey, bring word, send w., leave w., write 588 *correspond*; flash news, flash, beam; send a message, speak, semaphore 547 *signal*; wire, telegraph, send a telemessage, send a singing telegram, send a kissogram, etc., telex, radio; telephone, phone, call, dial, ring, ring up, give one a ring *or* a tinkle *or* a buzz; text, send a text-message; disseminate, broadcast, telecast, televise; announce, annunciate, notify, give notice, serve n. 528 *advertise*; give out, put out, carry a report, issue a press notice *or* release, publicize 528 *publish*; retail, recount, narrate 590 *describe*; commune 584 *converse*; swap news, exchange information, pool one's knowledge.

*hint*, drop a h., adumbrate, suggest, throw out a suggestion; put an idea in one's head;

prompt, give the cue 505 *remind*; caution 664 *warn*; tip off 691 *advise*; wink, tip the wink; nudge 547 *gesticulate*; insinuate, breathe, whisper, say in one's ear, touch upon, just mention, mention in passing, say by the way, let fall, imply, allude, leave one to gather, intimate.

*be informed*, be in possession of the facts 490 *know*; be told, receive information, have it from, have it on good authority; keep one's ears open, keep one's ear to the ground, get to hear of, hear it on the grapevine, use one's ears, be a fly on the wall, overhear 415 *hear*; be told by a little bird, get wind of, scent 484 *discover*; gather, infer, realize 516 *understand*; come to know, get a line on, get a report, get the facts, get the info 536 *learn*; open one's eyes, awaken to, become alive to 455 *be attentive*; ask for information, surf the net, call for a report 459 *enquire*; have information, have the dope, have the gen *or* info, have something to tell; claim to know 532 *affirm*.

**Adv.** *reportedly*, as stated, on information received, by report, straight from the horse's mouth; in the air, according to rumour, from what one can gather, if one can trust one's ears.

## 525 Concealment

**N.** *concealment*, confinement, purdah 883 *seclusion*; hiding 523 *latency*; covering up, burial 364 *interment*; occultation 446 *disappearance*; cache 527 *hiding-place*; disguisement, disguise, camouflage, steganography 542 *deception*; masquerade, bal masqué; anonymity, incognito 562 *no name*; smoke screen 421 *screen*; reticence, reserve, closeness, discretion, no word of 582 *taciturnity*; secret thought, unspoken t., mental reservation, arrière pensée, ulterior motive, hidden agenda; lack of candour, vagueness, evasion, evasiveness 518 *equivocalness*; mystification 421 *obfuscation*; misinformation, disinformation 535 *misteaching*; white lie 543 *mental dishonesty*; subterfuge 542 *trickery*; suppression, D notice, Official Secrets Act; suppression of the truth, cover-up 543 *untruth*; deceitfulness, dissimulation 541 *duplicity*.

*secrecy*, close s. 399 *silence*; secretness, mystery 530 *secret*; seal of secrecy, hearing in camera, auricular confession; secret society, Freemasonry; clandestineness, secretiveness, furtiveness, stealthiness, clandestine behaviour; low profile; underhand dealing 930 *improbity*; conspiracy 623 *plot*; cryptography, cryptogram, cipher, code, encoding, encryption 517 *unintelligibility*; invisible ink, sympathetic i.

**Adj.** *concealed*, crypto-, hidden, closet;

hiding, lost, perdu; ensconced, in ambush, lying in wait 523 *latent*; confined, incommunicado 747 *imprisoned*; mysterious, recondite, arcane 517 *unintelligible*; cryptic 523 *occult*; private 883 *secluded*; privy, confidential, off the record, unattributable; secret, top secret, restricted, hush-hush, inviolable; inviolate, unrevealed, ex-directory; undisclosed, untold; unsigned, unnamed 562 *anonymous*; covert, behind the scenes; covered 364 *buried*; hooded, masked, veiled, eclipsed 421 *screened*; smothered, stifled, suppressed, clandestine, undercover, underground, subterranean 211 *deep*.

*disguised*, camouflaged; incognito 562 *anonymous*; unrecognized, unrecognizable 491 *unknown*; disfigured, deformed 246 *distorted*; masked 421 *screened*; overpainted 226 *covered*; blotted out 550 *obliterated*; coded, codified, cryptographic 517 *unintelligible*.

*stealthy*, silent, furtive, sneaking, like a thief; treading softly, catlike, on tiptoe; prowling, skulking, loitering, lurking; clandestine, hugger-mugger, conspiratorial, cloak-and-dagger; hole-and-corner, backdoor, underhand, surreptitious 930 *dishonest*.

*reticent*, reserved, shy, self-contained, withdrawn; noncommittal, uncommunicative, uninformative, cagey, evasive; vague, studiously v.; not talking, keeping one's own counsel, discreet, silent 582 *taciturn*; tight-lipped, poker-faced; close, secretive, buttoned-up, close as an oyster, clamlike; in one's shell 883 *unsociable*.

**Vb.** *conceal*, hide, hide away, plank, secrete, ensconce, confine, keep in purdah 883 *seclude*; stow away, lock up, seal up, bottle up 632 *store*; hide underground, bury 364 *inter*, put out of sight, sweep under the carpet, cover up, paper over, whitewash 226 *cover*; varnish, gloss over 226 *overlay*; overpaint, blot out 550 *obliterate*; slur, slur over, not mention 458 *disregard*; smother, stifle 165 *suppress*; veil, muffle, mask, disguise, camouflage; shroud, becurtain, draw the curtain, draw a veil over 421 *screen*; shade, obscure, eclipse 418 *darken*; befog, becloud, obfuscate 419 *bedim*; hide one's identity, go incognito, assume a mask, masquerade 541 *dissemble*; code, encode, encrypt, use a cipher 517 *be unintelligible*.

*keep secret*, keep it dark, keep under wraps, keep close, keep under one's hat; look blank, look poker-faced, give nothing away, keep a straight face, keep mum, keep one's mouth shut, hold one's tongue, not breathe a word, not utter a syllable, not talk, keep one's counsel, make no sign 582 *be taciturn*; be discreet, neither confirm nor deny, make no comment; keep back, reserve, withhold, keep it to oneself, let it go no further; hush up, cover up, suppress; keep a low profile, keep in the background, stay in the shadows; let not one's right hand know what one's left hand does; blindfold, bamboozle, keep in the dark 542 *deceive*.

*be stealthy*, – furtive, – evasive etc. adj.; hugger-mugger, conspire 623 *plot*; snoop, sneak, slink, creep; glide, steal, steal along, steal by, steal past; tiptoe, go on t., pussyfoot; prowl, skulk, loiter; be anonymous, stay incognito, conceal one's identity; wear a mask, assume a disguise 541 *dissemble*; lie doggo 523 *lurk*; evade, shun, hide from, dodge 620 *avoid*; play hide-and-seek, play bo-peep, hide in holes and corners; leave no address, cover one's tracks, take cover, go to earth; go underground, hide out, take to the hills, vanish 446 *disappear*; hide from the light, retire from sight, withdraw into seclusion, bury oneself, stay in one's shell 883 *be unsociable*; lay an ambush 527 *ambush*.

**Adv.** *secretly*, hugger-mugger, conspiratorially; confidentially, sotto voce, with bated breath; entre nous, between ourselves, between you and me and the gatepost; aside, to oneself, in petto; in one's sleeve; sub rosa, without beat of drum; not for publication, privately, in private, in the privacy of one's own home, in camera, in closed court, à huis clos, behind closed doors, anonymously, incognito, with nobody any the wiser.

*stealthily*, furtively, by stealth, like a thief in the night; under cloak of darkness 444 *invisibly*; underhand, by the back door, in a hole-and-corner way, under-the-counter; on the sly, on the quiet, on the QT, by subterfuge.

## 526 Disclosure

**N.** *disclosure*, revealment, revelation, apocalypse; daylight, cold light of day; discovery, uncovering; unwelcome discovery, disillusionment 509 *disappointment*; last act, denouement, catastrophe, peripeteia 154 *event*; lid off, exposé, divulgation, divulgence 528 *publication*; exposure, showing up 522 *manifestation*; telling all, explanations, clearing the air, showdown; communication, leak, indiscretion 524 *hint*; betrayal, giveaway; cloven hoof, telltale sign, blush, self-betrayal; State's evidence, Queen's e. 603 *tergiversation*; acknowledgment, admission, avowal, confession, coming clean; auricular confession, confessional 939 *penitence*; clean breast, whole truth, cards on the table 494 *truth*.

**Adj.** *disclosed*, exposed, revealed 522 *shown*; showing 443 *visible*; confessed, admitted, avowed, acknowledged; with the lid off 263 *open*; laid bare 229 *uncovered*.

*disclosing,* uncovering, exposing, unclosing, opening; revelatory, apocalyptic, manifesting; epiphanic 975 *revelational;* revealing 422 *transparent;* expository, explicatory, explanatory 520 *interpretive;* divulging 528 *publishing;* communicative 524 *informative;* leaky, indiscreet, blabbing, garrulous 581 *loquacious;* tell-tale, indicative 547 *indicating;* tale-bearing, clyping, betraying; confessing, confessional, penitent 939 *repentant.*

**Vb.** *disclose,* reveal, expose, take the wraps off, disinter 522 *manifest;* bare, lay b., strip b., denude 229 *doff;* unfold, unroll, unfurl, unpack, unwrap 229 *uncover;* unscreen, uncurtain, unveil, lift the veil, draw the v., raise the curtain, let in daylight, let some light in; unseal, break the seal, unclose 263 *open;* lay open, open up 484 *discover;* catch out 484 *detect;* not hide 422 *be transparent;* make known, give away, betray, blow one's cover, out; uncloak, unmask, tear off the mask; expose oneself, betray o., give oneself away 495 *blunder;* declare oneself, lift the mask, drop the m., throw off the m., throw off all disguise; show oneself in one's true colours, show for what it is, cut down to life size, debunk; disabuse, correct, set right, undeceive, disillusion, open the eyes 524 *inform;* take the lid off, unkennel, unleash, let the cat out of the bag (see also *divulge*).

*divulge,* declare, be open about, bring into the open, express, vent, give vent to 579 *speak;* ventilate, air, canvass, publicize 528 *publish;* tell all, let on, blurt out, blow the gaff, talk out of turn, spill the beans, let the cat out of the bag, give the show *or* the game away; speak of, talk, must tell; utter, breathe; let out, leak 524 *communicate;* let drop, let fall 524 *hint;* come out with, spit it out 573 *speak plainly;* get it off one's chest, unbosom oneself, unburden o.; confide, let one into the secret, open one's mind *or* heart to, bare one's breast to; declare one's intentions, show one's hand, show one's cards, put one's cards on the table; report, tell, tell tales out of school, tell on, kiss and tell, clype (Scot), name names 928 *accuse;* betray the secret, split, peach, squeal, blab, grass 524 *inform;* rat 603 *change one's mind.*

*confess,* admit, acknowledge, avow; concede, grant, allow, own 488 *assent;* own up, cough up, fess up (US inf); implicate oneself, plead guilty; talk, sing, sing like a canary; come out with, come across with, come clean, tell all, admit everything, speak the truth 540 *be truthful;* make a clean breast of it, unburden one's conscience, go to confession, recount one's sins 939 *be penitent;* turn Queen's evidence 603 *tergiversate.*

*be disclosed,* come out, blow up, break 445 *appear;* come out in evidence, come to light 478 *be proved;* show the cloven hoof, show its face, show its true colours, stand revealed 522 *be plain;* transpire, become known, become public knowledge 490 *be known;* leak out, ooze o., creep o. 298 *emerge;* peep out, show 443 *be visible;* show through 422 *be transparent;* come as a revelation, break through the clouds, come with a blinding flash, flash on the mind 449 *dawn upon;* give oneself away, there speaks . . .

## 527 Hiding. Disguise

**N.** *hiding-place,* hide, hideout, hideaway, hole, hidey-h., priesthole, safe house 662 *refuge;* lair, den 192 *retreat;* cache, secret place, oubliette; crypt, vault 194 *cellar;* closet, secret drawer, hidden panel, safe place, safe, safe deposit 632 *storage;* recess, corner, nook, cranny, niche, holes and corners, secret passage, underground p.; cover, underground 662 *shelter;* backstairs, backroom, inmost recesses 224 *interiority.*

*ambush,* ambuscade, ambushment 525 *concealment;* lurking place, spider's web 542 *trap;* catch 663 *pitfall;* stalking horse, Trojan h., decoy, stool pigeon 545 *impostor;* agent provocateur 663 *troublemaker.*

*disguise,* blind, masquerade 542 *deception;* camouflage, protective colouring 20 *mimicry;* dummy 542 *sham;* veneer 226 *covering;* mask, visor, veil, domino 228 *cloak;* fancy dress; cloud, smoke screen, cover 421 *screen.*

*hider,* lurker, prowler, skulker, stowaway; dodger 620 *avoider;* masker, masquerader; wolf in sheep's clothing 545 *impostor.*

**Vb.** *ambush,* set an a., lie in a., lie in wait 523 *lurk;* set a trap for 542 *ensnare;* assume a disguise, wear a mask; throw out a smoke-screen, obfuscate; waylay.

## 528 Publication

**N.** *publication,* spreading abroad, dissemination, divulgation 526 *disclosure;* promulgation, proclamation; edict, ukase, ban 737 *decree;* call-up, summons; cry, rallying c., hue and c., bugle call 547 *call;* beat of drum, flourish of trumpets 400 *loudness;* press conference, press release, advance publicity (see also *advertisement*); notification, public notice, official bulletin; announcement, press a., pronouncement, pronunciamento, manifesto, programme, platform; the media, mass m.; publishing, book trade, bookselling 589 *book;* broadcasting, narrowcasting, televising 531 *telecommunication;* broadcast, telecast, webcast, newscast 529 *news;* kite-flying 529 *rumour;* circulation, circular; bull, encyclical.

*publicity*, limelight, spotlight, public eye; publicness, common knowledge 490 *knowledge*; open discussion, seminar, ventilation, canvassing, canvass; openness, flagrancy, blatancy 522 *manifestation*; open secret, open scandal; notoriety, fame 866 *famousness*; currency, wide c.; circulation, wide c., countrywide c.; sale, extensive sales; readership, audience, viewership; viewing figures, listening f., ratings; public relations, PR, promotion, sales p., propaganda, party political broadcast, PPB, soundbite, gesture politics; photocall, photo-opportunity; display, showmanship, salesmanship, window dressing 875 *ostentation*; sensationalism, ballyhoo, hype 546 *exaggeration*; publicization, advertising, skywriting; medium of publicity, television, radio 531 *broadcasting*; public address system, loudspeaker, loud hailer 415 *hearing instrument*; public comment, journalism, reporting, the media, rapportage, coverage, report, notice, write-up (see also *the press*); investigative journalism, chequebook j. 459 *enquiry*; newsreel, newsletter, news round-up 529 *news*; sounding board, correspondence column, open letter, letters to the editor; editorial 591 *article*; pulpit, platform, hustings, soapbox 539 *rostrum*; roadshow; printing press 587 *print*; blaze of publicity, letters of fire *or* of gold, letters a foot high; name in lights.

*advertisement*, notice, insertion, advert, ad, small a., classified a., advertorial; personal column; agony column; headline, banner h., streamer, screamer, spread; puff, blurb, buildup, hype, ballyhoo; promotional literature, unsolicited mail, handout, handbill; bill, affiche, poster, flyer 522 *exhibit*; billboard, hoarding, placard, sandwich board, display b., notice b., bulletin b.; yellow pages; advertising copy, slogan, jingle; plug, teaser, trailer, commercial, infomercial 531 *broadcasting*; ad-avoidance; hard sell, soft s., subliminal advertising; Madison Avenue; cold-calling.

*the press*, fourth estate, Fleet Street, newspaper world, news business, the papers; newspaper, newssheet, freesheet, sheet, paper, rag, tabloid, red-top, comic; serious press, underground p., gutter p., yellow p., tabloid p.; organ, journal, daily paper, daily, quality d., broadsheet, heavy; morning paper, evening p., Sunday p., local p., picture p.; issue, edition, late e., stop-press e., sports e., extra; magazine section, feuilleton, supplement, colour s., trade s.; insert, leaflet, handbill, pamphlet, brochure, open letter, newsletter.

*journal*, review, magazine, glossy m., specialist m., women's m., male-interest m., pulp m.; part-work, periodical, serial, daily, weekly, monthly, quarterly, annual; gazette, trade journal, house magazine, trade publication 589 *reading matter*; fanzine, zine; e-magazine, e-zine.

*publicizer*, notifier, announcer; herald, trumpet 529 *messenger*; proclaimer, crier, town crier; barker, tout; bill sticker, bill poster, sandwichman; demonstrator, promoter, publicist, publicity agent, press a., advertising a.; adman, advertiser, hidden persuader; copywriter, blurb writer, commercial artist, public relations officer, PRO, image-maker, propagandist, pamphleteer 537 *preacher*; printer, publisher 589 *bookperson*; reporter, journalist, investigative j., chequebook j. 529 *news reporter*.

**Adj.** *published*, in print 587 *printed*; in circulation, circulating, passing round, current; in the news, in the headlines, public 490 *known*; open, exoteric; distributed, circularized, disseminated, broadcast; ventilated, well-v.; on the air, on television; multimedia, mixed media.

*publishing*, declaratory, notificatory.

*well-known*, public, celebrated, famous, notorious 866 *noteworthy*; crying, flagrant, blatant, glaring, sensational 522 *manifest*.

**Vb.** *publish*, make public, carry a report 524 *communicate*; report, cover, write up; write an open letter, drag into the limelight, bring into the open, reveal 526 *divulge*; highlight, spotlight 532 *emphasize*; radio, broadcast, narrowcast, tape, telecast, televise, relay, diffuse 524 *inform*; spread, circulate, distribute, disseminate, circularize; canvass, ventilate, discuss 475 *argue*; pamphleteer, propagate, propagandize 534 *teach*; use the press 587 *print*; syndicate, serialize, edit, subedit, sub; issue, release, get out, put o., give o., send forth, give to the world, lay before the public; bring to public notice, let it be known; spread a rumour, fly a kite; rumour, bruit about, noise abroad, spread a.; talk about, retail, pass round, put about, bandy a., hawk a., buzz a. 581 *be loquacious*; voice, broach, talk of, speak of, utter, emit 579 *speak*.

*proclaim*, announce, herald, promulgate, notify; ban, denounce, raise a hue and cry 928 *accuse*; pronounce, declare, go on record 532 *affirm*; make one's views public, make a proclamation, issue a public statement, issue a pronouncement, publish a manifesto; celebrate, sound, noise, trumpet, blazon, blaze abroad, cry, shout, scream, thunder 400 *be loud*; declaim, shout from the rooftops 415 *be heard*; beat the big drum, announce with a flourish of trumpets.

*advertise*, publicize; insert a notice, place an ad, bill, placard, post, stick up a notice, put up a poster; tell the world, put on the map, put in headlines, headline, splash; make a cynosure of, put in lights, spotlight, build up, promote; make much of, feature; sell, boost, puff, promote, cry up, crack up, hype up, write up, extol, rave about 482 *overrate*; din, din into one's ears, plug 106 *repeat*.

*be published*, become public, come out; acquire notoriety, hit the headlines, make the front page; become the talk of the town, circulate, pass current, pass from mouth to mouth, pass round, go the rounds, get about, spread abroad, be bruited a., spread like wildfire, fly about, buzz a.; find a publisher, see oneself in print, get printed, get into the papers; have a circulation, sell well, go like a best-seller, become a blockbuster 793 *be sold*.

**Adv.** *publicly*, openly, in open court, with open doors; in the limelight, in the public eye, for all to see.

## 529 News

**N.** *news*, good n., no news is good n.; bad news 509 *disappointment*; tidings, glad t.; gospel, evangel 973 *religion*; dispatches, diplomatic bag; intelligence, report, dispatch, word, intimation, advice; piece of information, something to tell, titbit 524 *information*; bulletin, communiqué, handout, press release; newspaper report, press notice; news item, news flash, soundbite 531 *broadcast*; fresh news, breaking n., hot n., latest n., stirring n., stop-press n.; sensation, scoop, exclusive; old news, stale n., old story, ancient history, Queen Anne's dead; copy, filler; yarn, story, tall s.; newscast, newsreel 528 *publicity*; news value, news-worthiness.

*rumour*, unverified news, unconfirmed report; flying rumour, fame; on dit, hearsay, gossip, gup, talk, talk of the town, tittle-tattle 584 *chat*; scandal 926 *calumny*; whisper, buzz, noise, bruit; false report, hoax, canard; grapevine, bush telegraph; kite-flying.

*message*, oral m., word of mouth, word, advice, tip 524 *information*; communication 547 *signal*; wireless message, radiogram, cablegram, cable, telegram, telemessage, wire, fax, electronic mail, e-mail, attachment, text-message 531 *telecommunication*; postcard, pc, note, letters, Post-it Note (tdmk), sticky (inf); dispatches 588 *correspondence*, 531 *postal communications*; ring, phone call, buzz, tinkle; errand, embassy 751 *commission*.

*news reporter*, newspaperman *or* -woman, reporter, cub r., journalist, correspondent, legman, stringer 589 *author*; gentleman *or* lady of the press, pressman *or* -woman, press representative 524 *informant*; newsreader, newscaster 531 *broadcaster*; newsmonger, quidnunc, gossip, tittle-tattler, talker 584 *interlocutor*; tattler, chatterer; muckraker, scandalmonger 926 *defamer*; retailer of news 528 *publicizer*; newsagent, newsvendor, newspaper boy *or* girl.

*messenger*, forerunner 66 *precursor*; harbinger 511 *omen*; announcer, town crier 528 *publicizer*; ambassador, minister, nuncio, legate, spokesman *or* -woman *or* -person 754 *envoy*; apostle, emissary; flag-bearer, herald, trumpet; summoner, process-server 955 *law officer*; go-between, pander, contact, contact man *or* woman 231 *intermediary*.

*courier*, runner, Queen's Messenger, express m., express, dispatch-bearer, dispatch rider, mounted courier, deliveryman *or* -woman; postman *or* -woman 531 *postal communications*; telegraph boy *or* girl, messenger b. *or* girl, errand b. *or* girl, office b. *or* girl; call-boy, bellhop, page, buttons, commissionaire; carrier pigeon 273 *carrier*; Iris, Hermes, Mercury, Ariel.

**Adj.** *rumoured*, talked about, in the news, in the papers; reported, currently r., bruited abroad, going about, going the rounds, passing around, bandied about; rife, afloat, in circulation, on everyone's lips; full of news, newsy, gossipy, chatty 524 *informative*; newsworthy.

**Vb.** *rumour*, fly a kite; send *or* dispatch news 588 *correspond*. (See also 524 *inform*, 526 *disclose*, 528 *publish*.)

## 530 Secret

**N.** *secret*, profound s.; secret lore, esotery, esotericism, arcanum, mystery 984 *occultism*; confidential matter, confidential information, sealed orders, hush-hush subject, top-secret file, state secret, affairs of state; confidential communication, confidence; sphinx, man *or* woman of mystery, enigmatic personality, Gioconda smile, inscrutable s.; Mr X 562 *no name*; dark horse, unknown quantity; unknown warrior; unmentionable thing, skeleton in the cupboard; sealed book; unknown country, terra incognita 491 *unknown thing*.

*enigma*, mystery, 'a riddle wrapped in a mystery inside an enigma', puzzle, Chinese p., tangram, Rubik's cube (tdmk); problem, poser, brain-twister, teaser;

> I cannot forecast to you the action of Russia. It is a riddle wrapped in a mystery inside an enigma.
> Winston Churchill

hard nut to crack, hard saying, knotty point, vexed question, crux 700 *difficulty*; cipher, code, cryptogram, hieroglyphics 517 *unintelligibility*; word-puzzle, logograph, anagram, acrostic, crossword; riddle, riddlemeree, conundrum, rebus; charade, dumb c.; intricacy, labyrinth, maze 61 *complexity*.

**531 Communications**
**N.** *telecommunication*; teleinformatics; long-distance communication, telephony, cellular t., telegraphy, radio *or* wireless t., Comsat; signalling, semaphore, morse 547 *signal*; cable, cablegram, telegram, telemessage, wire, fax, electronic mail, e-mail, voicemail 529 *message*; bush telegraph, grapevine 529 *rumour*; radar 484 *discovery*; loran, Decca (tdmk); telex, teleprinter, tape machine, ticker; teleconferencing; videoconferencing; intercom, walkie-talkie; bleeper, bleep, pager; microphone 400 *megaphone*; headset 415 *hearing instrument*; telephone, radio t., cellular t., cellphone, cordless telephone, car phone, mobile p., mobile, Vodafone (tdmk), videophone; Wireless Application Protocol, WAP; line, land-l., trunk l., party l., hot l.; extension; telephone exchange, switchboard; call centre, telesales; tone dialling, pulse d.; telephonist, telephone receptionist, wireless operator, radio ham, telegrapher; broadband.

*postal communications*, postal services, Postal Union, GPO; post, first class p., second class p., letters, mail, snail mail 588 *correspondence*; surface mail, sea m., air m., parcel post, registered p., recorded delivery, express d., red star d.; stamp, postage s., first class s., second class s.; definitive stamp, commemorative s.; address, accommodation a., postcode; mailing list, mailshot, mail merge; mail order; air letter, aerogramme; pillarbox, postbox, letterbox; post office, sorting o., mailbag; postmaster *or* -mistress, postman *or* -woman 529 *messenger*; pigeon post; diplomatic bag, dispatch box; hate mail, poison-pen letter, letter bomb, parcel b.

*broadcasting*, the media 528 *publicity*; bimedia; broadcasting authority, BBC, Beeb, Auntie; IBA, ITA; ITV, independent television *or* radio; commercial t. *or* r., local t. *or* r., cable t. *or* r., satellite t., pirate r., Citizens' Band r., CB r.; transmitter, booster, communications satellite; aerial, antenna; radio waves, wave lengths, modulation, AM, FM 417 *radiation*; radio station, television channel, network; wireless, radio, cellular r., mobile r., steam r., cat's whisker, crystal set; radiopaging; portable, transistor, tranny *or* ghetto-blaster; personal stereo; television, telly, TV, the box, gogglebox, small screen, talking head; colour television, black-and-white t., monochrome t.; cable TV, digital TV, satellite TV, terrestrial TV; actuality TV, reality TV; closed-circuit t. 442 *camera*; net-top box, set-top box; video-

recorder, videocassette, videocassette recorder, VCR, video, videotape, video nasty, kidvid, video game 549 *recording instrument*; Teleprompter (tdmk), autocue; teletext, Ceefax (tdmk), Oracle (tdmk), Prestel (tdmk) 524 *information*; Open University; radio listener 415 *listener*; viewer, televiewer, TV addict 441 *spectator*.

*broadcast*, outside b., telecast, simulcast, transmission, relay, live r. 528 *publication*; recording, repeat, transcription 548 *record*; programme, request p., phone-in, telethon, quiz, chat show, music 837 *amusement*; news, newsflash, soundbite, news roundup 529 *news*; time signal, pips; talk, feature, documentary, infotainment 524 *report*; actuality TV, reality TV; series, soap opera, situation comedy, sitcom, saga, docudrama, faction 594 *drama*; cartoon, film 445 *cinema*; commercial, commercial break, infomercial 528 *advertisement*.

*broadcaster*, announcer, commentator, talking head, newsreader, newscaster 524 *informant*; presenter, frontman *or* -woman, anchorman *or* -woman, linkman *or* -woman, compere, question master; disc jockey, DJ, deejay, shock jock (inf); media personality 866 *person of repute*.

*Internet*, the Net, World Wide Web, the Web, information highway, information superhighway, portal, Usenet; website, web page, home page; webcast, webcam; FAQ, Frequently Asked Questions; HTML; e-mail, e-address, domain, domain name, URL, cybersquatter; Internet service provider, ISP, music service provider, MSP; net-top box, hypertext link, bookmark, search engine, browser, net-surfing, surfing, chatroom, emoticon *or* smiley; netiquette, flame, flaming, flame war, spam, spamming, smurfing; cyberspace, virtual reality; local area network, LAN, intranet; geek, hacker, web architect, internaut, netizen, silver surfer, telecommuter, e-lancer; cybercafé, Internet c.; dotcom, e-business, e-commerce, e-tailing, electronic shopping, cybershopping, e-shopping, virtual shopping, virtual storefront, virtual mall, clicks and mortar, shopping engine; mousetrapping, page-jacking; computer crime, computer fraud, cybercrime, cybercriminal, e-stalking, cyberterrorism, cyberterrorist, cyberwar, cyberwarfare, electronic civil disobedience, hacktivism, hacktivist, information warfare; cyber cop, cyber court, cyberlaw, cyber lawyer; electronic virtual assistant, EVA; cyberchondriac; cyberflirtation, cybersex; electronic book, e-book; MP3 414 *record player*; Wireless Application Protocol, WAP; intelligent wear, I-wear; digital divide; electronic publishing, e-magazine, e-zine.

## 532 Affirmation

**N.** *affirmation*, affirmance; proposition, subject and predicate; saying, dictum 496 *maxim*; predication, statement, mission s., submission, thesis 512 *supposition*; expressed opinion, conclusion 480 *judgment*; voice, choice, suffrage, ballot 605 *vote*; expression, formulation; written statement, prepared text; one's position, one's stand *or* stance; mission statement; declaration, profession; allegation 928 *accusation*; assertion, unsupported a., ipse dixit, say-so; asseveration, averment; admission, confession, avowal 526 *disclosure*; corroboration, confirmation, assurance, avouchment, one's word, warrant 466 *testimony*; insistence, vehemence, peremptoriness 571 *vigour*; stress, accent, accent on, emphasis, overstatement, protesting too much; reiteration 106 *repetition*; challenge, provocation 711 *defiance*; protest 762 *deprecation*; appeal, representation, adjuration 761 *entreaty*; observation, remark, aside, interjection 579 *speech*; comment, criticism, positive c., constructive c. 480 *estimate*; assertiveness, self-assertion, attitude, push, thrust, drive, oomph 174 *vigorousness*; assertiveness training; pontification, dogmatism 473 *positiveness*.

*oath*, Bible o., oath-taking, oath-giving, swearing, swearing on the Bible, assertory oath, adjuration, solemn affirmation, statement on oath, deposition, affidavit 466 *testimony*; promissory oath, word of a gentleman, word of honour, pledge, promise, mission statement, warrant, guarantee 764 *promise*.

**Adj.** *affirmative*, affirming, professing etc. vb.; not negative 473 *positive*; predicative; declaratory, declarative 526 *disclosing*; pronouncing, enunciative 528 *publishing*; valid, in force, unretracted, unretractable 473 *undisputed*; committed, pledged, guaranteed, promised 764 *promissory*; earnest, meaning 617 *intending*; solemn, sworn, on oath, formal; affirmable, predicable.

*assertive*, assertory, saying, telling; assured, dogmatic, pontificating, confident, self-assured 473 *positive*; pushing, thrustful, trenchant, incisive, pointed, decisive, decided 571 *forceful*; distinct 80 *definite*; express, peremptory, categorical, absolute, brooking no denial, emphatic, insistent; vehement, thundering 176 *violent*; making no bones, flat, broad, round, blunt, strong, outspoken, strongly-worded, straight from the shoulder 573 *plain*; pontifical, of faith, unquestionable, ex cathedra 485 *creedal*; challenging, provocative 711 *defiant*.

**Vb.** *affirm*, state, express, formulate, set down; declare, pronounce, deliver, enunciate 528 *proclaim*, 579 *orate*; give expression to, voice 579 *speak*; remark, comment, observe, say; state with conviction, be bound, dare swear 485 *opine*; mean what one says, vow, protest; make a statement, make a verbal, make an assertion, assert, predicate; maintain, hold, contend 475 *argue*; make one's point 478 *demonstrate*; advance, urge 512 *propound*; represent, put one's case, put forward, submit; appeal, adjure, claim 761 *request*; allege, asseverate, avouch, aver; bear witness 466 *testify*; certify, confirm, warrant, guarantee 466 *corroborate*; commit oneself, go as far as; pledge, engage 764 *promise*; hold out 759 *offer*; profess, avow; admit 526 *confess*; abide by, not retreat, not retract, stick to one's guns 599 *stand firm*; challenge 711 *defy*; repudiate 533 *negate*; speak up, speak out, say outright, assert roundly, put it bluntly, make no bones about 573 *speak plainly*; be assertive, brook no denial, shout, shout down; claim to know, say so, lay down the law, speak ex cathedra, pontificate 473 *dogmatize*; get on one's soapbox, hold the floor, have one's say, have the last word.

*swear*, be sworn, swear an oath, take one's o., take one's Bible o.; attest, confirm by oath 466 *corroborate*; outswear 533 *negate*; cross one's heart, solemnly affirm, make solemn affirmation 466 *testify*; kiss the book, swear on the Bible, swear by all that is holy.

*emphasize*, stress, lay stress on, accent, accentuate; underline, put in italics, italicize, dot the i's and cross the t's, put in bold letters; raise one's voice, speak up, shout, thunder, roar, bellow, fulminate 400 *be loud*; bang one's fist down, thump the table; be urgent, be insistent, be earnest, urge, enforce; insist, positively i. 737 *command*; say with emphasis, drive home, impress on, din in, rub in; plug, dwell on, say again and again, reaffirm, reassert, labour 106 *repeat*; single out, highlight, enhance, point up 638 *make important*.

**Adv.** *affirmatively*, positively, without fear of contradiction, ex cathedra; seriously, in all seriousness, joking apart, in sober earnest; on oath, on the Bible; in all conscience, upon one's word, upon one's honour 540 *truthfully*.

**Int.** As I stand here!, As God is my witness!, Cross my heart and hope to die!, Scout's honour!

## 533 Negation

**N.** *negation*, negative, nay, no; denial 760 *refusal*; refusal of belief, disbelief 486 *unbelief*; disagreement 489 *dissent*; contrary assertion, rebuttal, appeal, cross-a. 460 *rejoinder*; refutation, disproof 479 *confutation*; emphatic denial, contradiction, flat c., gainsaying; the lie, démenti; challenge 711 *defiance*; demurrer

468 *qualification*; protest 762 *deprecation*; repudiation, disclaimer, disavowal, disownment, dissociation, nonassociation 607 *rejection*; abnegation, renunciation 621 *relinquishment*; retractation, abjuration, swearing off 603 *recantation*; negativism, negative attitude, noncorroboration, inability to confirm; refusal of consent 757 *prohibition*; recusancy 769 *nonobservance*; contravention 738 *disobedience*; cancellation, invalidation, nullification, revocation, disallowance 752 *abrogation*.

**Adj.** *negative*, denying, negating, negatory; adversative, contradictory 14 *contrary*; contravening 738 *disobedient*; protesting 762 *deprecatory*; recusant 769 *nonobservant*; abrogative, revocatory; abnegating, renunciatory 753 *resigning*; denied, disowned, dissociated.

**Vb.** *negate*, negative; contravene 738 *disobey*; deny, gainsay, give the lie to, belie, contradict, deny flatly, contradict absolutely, issue a démenti; deny the possibility, eat one's hat if 470 *make impossible*; disaffirm, repudiate, disavow, disclaim, disown 607 *reject*; not confirm, refuse to corroborate; not maintain, hold no brief for 860 *be indifferent*; deny in part, demur, object 468 *qualify*; disagree 489 *dissent*; dissociate oneself 704 *oppose*; affirm the contrary, controvert, traverse, impugn, question, call in q., express doubts, refute, rebut, disprove 479 *confute*; refuse credence 486 *disbelieve*; protest, appeal against 762 *deprecate*; challenge, stand up to 711 *defy*; thwart 702 *obstruct*; say no, decline, shake one's head, disallow 760 *refuse*; not allow 757 *prohibit*; revoke, invalidate, nullify 752 *abrogate*; abnegate, renounce 621 *relinquish*; abjure, forswear, swear off 603 *recant*; go back on one's word, do a U-turn 603 *change one's mind*.

**Adv.** nay 489 *no*; negatively; not at all 33 *in no way*.

**Int.** never!, a thousand times no!, nothing of the kind!, quite the contrary!, far from it!, anything but!, no such thing!, no way!, not likely!

## 534 Teaching

**N.** *teaching*, pedagogy, pedagogics, private teaching, tutoring; education, schooling, upbringing; tutelage, leading strings *or* reins; direction, guidance, instruction, edification; spoon-feeding, dictation; chalk and talk; programmed instruction, direct method, immersion m., induction 475 *reasoning*; computer-aided *or* -assisted instruction, CAI; tuition, preparation, coaching, cramming; seminar, teach-in, clinic, workshop, tutorial; initiation, introduction; training, discipline,

drill 682 *exercise*; inculcation, catechization, indoctrination, preaching, pulpitry, homiletics; proselytism, propagandism, love-bombing, flirty-fishing; persuasion, conversion, conviction; conditioning, brainwashing; pamphleteering, propaganda, agit-prop 528 *publicity*; assertiveness training.

*education*, liberal e. 490 *culture*; classical education, scientific e., technical e.; religious e., denominational e., secular e.; moral education, moral training; technical training, technological t., edutainment, vocational training; coeducation, progressive education, Froebel system, Froebelism, kindergarten method, Montessori system; monitorial system; elementary education, grounding; nursery education, preschool e., primary e., secondary e., further e., higher e., tertiary e., university e., adult e., adult learning, lifelong l., community education; distance learning; day release, block r.; sandwich course, refresher c.; advanced studies, postgraduate s.; compensatory education, special e., remedial e.; home-schooling; physical education, PE, gymnastics, physical jerks, callisthenics, eurhythmics, aerobics.

*curriculum*, course of study 536 *learning*; National Curriculum, access c., core c., common core; first lessons, propaedeutics, ABC, the three R's 68 *beginning*; foundation course, access c.; set books, prescribed text 589 *textbook*; module, set task, project, exercise, simulation e., homework, prep; liberal arts, liberal studies; trivium, grammar, rhetoric, logic; quadrivium, arithmetic, geometry, astronomy, music; sixth-form studies, general s.; Greats, Finals 459 *exam*; Open University course, correspondence c., inservice c., course of lectures, university extension l., extramural l., classes, evening c., night school 539 *school*.

*lecture*, talk, illustrated t., radio t., documentary 531 *broadcasting*; reading, prelection, discourse, disquisition; sermon, preachment, homily 579 *oration*; lesson, apologue, parable; problem play 594 *stage play*; readership, lectureship, professorship, chair; lecturer 537 *teacher*.

**Adj.** *educational*, pedagogic, tutorial; scholastic, scholarly, academic; instructional, informational; audiovisual, instructive 524 *informative*; educative, didactic, hortative; doctrinal, normative; edifying, moralizing, homiletic, preachy; primary, secondary etc. n.; single-sex, coeducational, comprehensive, all-ability, all-in; set, streamed, creamed, mixed-ability; extramural, intramural; extracurricular;

redbrick, Oxbridge, Ivy League; cultural, humane, scientific, technological; practical, utilitarian; multidisciplinary.

**Vb.** *educate*, edify (see also *teach*); breed, rear, nurse, nurture, bring up, develop, form, mould, shape, lick into shape; put to school, send to s., have taught; tutor, teach, school; train, retrain, reskill; ground, coach, cram, prime 669 *prepare*; guide 689 *direct*; instruct 524 *inform*; enlighten, illumine, enlarge the mind, develop the m., open the m.; sharpen the wits, open the eyes; fill with new ideas, stuff with knowledge, cram with facts, spoonfeed with f.; impress on the memory, din in, knock into the head, inculcate, indoctrinate, imbue, impregnate, infuse, instil, infix, implant, engraft, sow the seeds of; disabuse, unteach; chasten, sober.

*teach*, be a teacher, give lessons, take a class, hold classes; lecture, deliver lectures; tutor, give tutorials, hold seminars, impart instruction; dictate, read out; preach, harangue, sermonize, pontificate; discourse, hold forth; moralize, point a moral; elucidate, expound 520 *interpret*; train the mind, indoctrinate, inoculate; pamphleteer, disseminate propaganda, propagandize, proselytize, condition, brainwash 178 *influence*.

*train*, coach 669 *prepare*; take on, take in hand, initiate, tame 369 *break in*; nurse, foster, cultivate; inure, put through the mill, keep one's nose to the grindstone; drill, exercise, practise, make second nature, familiarize, accustom, groom one for 610 *habituate*; show one the ropes; make fit, qualify; housetrain, teach manners, teach etiquette, teach how to behave.

## 535 Misteaching

**N.** *misteaching*, misinstruction, misguidance, misleading, misdirection; quackery, a case of the blind leading the blind; false intelligence, misinformation, disinformation 552 *misrepresentation*; mystification 421 *obfuscation*; false name 525 *concealment*; wrong attribution, wrong emendation, miscorrection 495 *mistake*; obscurantism 491 *ignorance*; false teaching, bad t., propaganda, brainwashing 541 *falsehood*; perversion, spin 246 *distortion*; false logic, illogic 477 *sophistry*.

**Adj.** *misteaching*, misguiding etc. vb.; unedifying, propagandist, brainwashing; obscurantist 491 *ignorant*; mistaught, misled, misdirected 495 *mistaken*.

**Vb.** *misteach*, miseducate, bring up badly; misinstruct, misinform, misname, misdirect, misguide 495 *mislead*; not edify, corrupt, abuse the mind 934 *make wicked*; pervert 246 *distort*;

misdescribe 552 *misrepresent*; cry wolf, put on a false scent, put off the track 542 *deceive*; lie 541 *be false*; preach to the converted, teach one's grandmother to suck eggs; leave no wiser, keep in ignorance, take advantage of one's ignorance; suppress knowledge, unteach; propagandize, brainwash; explain away.

## 536 Learning

**N.** *learning*, lore, wide reading, scholarship, attainments 490 *erudition*; acquisition of knowledge, acquisition of skills; computer-aided or -assisted learning, CAL, computer-assisted language learning, CALL; thirst for knowledge, intellectual curiosity 453 *curiosity*; pupillage, tutelage, apprenticeship, novitiate, initiation 669 *preparation*; basic training, basics, first steps, teething troubles 68 *beginning*; docility, teachability 694 *aptitude*; self-instruction, self-education, self-improvement; culture, cultivation, self-c.; late learning, opsimathy; learned person 492 *scholar*.

*study*, studying; application, studiousness; cramming, swotting, grind, mugging up, burning the midnight oil; studies, course of s., lessons, class, classwork, deskwork; homework, prep, preparation; revision, refresher course, further reading, further study; crash course; perusal, reading, close r., attentive r. 455 *attention*; research, research work, field w., investigation 459 *enquiry*; learning curve.

---

**Subjects of Study: -ics, -ologies and others**
acoustics (sound), aesthetics (beauty and fine arts), aetiology (causation), agrostology (grasses), algology (algae), ampelology or ampelography (vines), anatomy (structure of the body), anthropology (human beings), arachnology (spiders), archaeology (human antiquities), astrology (stars and planets as supposed indicators of character and events), astronomy (stars and planets), bacteriology (bacteria), ballistics (projectiles), biochemistry (chemistry of living organisms), biology (living things), botany (plants and flowers), bryology (mosses), cereology (crop circles), cetology (whales), chemistry (structure and properties of substances), chronology (measuring time), climatology (climate), conchology (molluscs and shells), cosmography and cosmology (the universe), craniology (skulls), criminology (crime and criminals), cryptozoology (undiscovered animals), cybernetics (control systems in the brain and computers, etc), cytology (cells), demography (population), dendrology (trees), deontology (duty), dermatology (skin), dialectology (dialects), ecology (the relationship between plants and animals and the environment), economics (the production and use of goods and services), electronics (conduction of electricity and its uses), embryology (embryos), entomology (insects), epidemiology (epidemics), epistemology (knowledge), eschatology (death, heaven and hell), ethics (morality and duty), ethnology (human culture), ethology (animal behaviour), etymology (word origins), genetics (biological heredity), geography (the earth), geology (rocks and

minerals), geometry (the measurement and relationships of points, lines, angles, etc), geriatrics *and* gerontology (ageing and old people), glaciology (ice), graphology (handwriting), gynaecology (diseases of women), hagiology (saints), helminthology (worms), herpetology (reptiles and amphibians), horology (measurement of time; clock-making), ichthyology (fish), immunology (immunity against disease), informatics (processing of information, especially by computer), lepidopterology (butterflies and moths), lexicology (words), linguistics (language), malacology (molluscs), mammalogy (mammals), mathematics (numbers and quantities), mechanics (the effect of energy and forces on bodies), metallurgy (metals and ores), metaphysics (the nature of things), meteorology (atmospheric phenomena, the weather), microbiology (bacteria and viruses), mineralogy (minerals), morphology (structure, e.g. of words or of bodies), mycology (fungi), myrmecology (ants), nematology (parasitic worms), nosology (classification of diseases), obstetrics (childbirth), oenology (wine), onomastics *or* onomasiology (proper names), ontology (being), ophiology (snakes), ophthalmology (eye), optics (light), orismology (definition of technical terms), ornithology (birds), otology (ear), otorhinolaryngology (ear, nose and throat), paediatrics (diseases of children), palaeography (ancient writing), palaeontology (fossils), parapsychology (psychic phenomena), parasitology (parasites), pathology (diseases), penology (punishment of crime), phaleristics (medals and decorations), pharmacology (drugs and their effects), philology (ancient texts, or the development of language), philosophy (the nature of existence, knowledge, morality, etc), phonetics *and* phonology (speech sounds), phrenology (the skull as a supposed indicator of character and aptitudes), phycology (algae), physics (matter and energy), physiology (functions of cells, organs, etc), posology (administration of drugs), primatology (primates), psephology (elections), psychology (the mind), radiology (use of radioactivity in diagnosing and treating disease), robotics (robots), seismology (earthquakes), semantics (meaning), semiotics *or* semiology (signs and symbols), taxonomy (classification), theology (God or gods), thermodynamics (heat and energy), toponymy (place names), toxicology (poisons), trichology (hair), trigonometry (triangles), virology (viruses), zoology (animals).

*learning difficulty*, dyscalculia, dysgraphia, dyslexia, dyspraxia; attention deficit disorder, attention-deficit hyperactive disorder, ADHD; mental retardation 503 *learning disability*.

*person with learning difficulties*, dyscalculic, dysgraphic, dyslexic, dyspraxic; person with learning disabilities 503 *person with a learning disability*.

**Adj.** *studious*, devoted to studies, academic; partial to reading, bookish, well-read, scholarly, erudite, learned, scholastic 490 *knowing*; sedulous, diligent 678 *industrious*; receptive, teachable, docile 597 *willing*; self-taught, self-instructed, autodidactic; immersed in one's books 455 *attentive*.

*having a learning difficulty*, dyscalculic, dysgraphic, dyslexic, dyspraxic; mentally retarded 503 *having a learning disability*.

**Vb.** *learn*, pursue one's education, get one-self taught, get tuition, go to school, attend college, read, take lessons, sit at the feet of, hear lectures, take a course; acquire knowledge, gain information, collect i., glean i., assimilate learning, imbibe, drink in, cram oneself with facts, know one's f. 490 *know*; apprentice oneself, learn one's trade, serve an apprenticeship, article oneself 669 *prepare oneself*; train, practise, exercise 610 *be wont*; learn the basics, get the feel of, get the hang of, master; get by heart, learn by rote 505 *memorize*; finish one's education, graduate.

*study*, prosecute one's studies, apply oneself, burn the midnight oil; do, take up; research into 459 *enquire*; study particularly, specialize, major in; swot, cram, grind, mug, get up; revise, go over, run over, brush up, take a refresher course; read, peruse, pore over, wade through; browse, dip into, flip through, skim, skim-read, skip, thumb, turn the leaves; be studious, be bookish, always have one's nose in a book; devote oneself to reading, bury oneself in one's books, become a polymath.

**Adv.** *studiously*, at one's books; under training, in articles.

## 537 Teacher

**N.** *teacher*, preceptor, mentor 520 *guide*; minister 986 *pastor*; guru 500 *sage*; instructor, educator; tutor, private t., crammer, coach; governor, governess, nursemaid 749 *keeper*; educationist, educationalist, pedagogue; pedant 500 *wiseacre*; dominie, beak, school-marm; master *or* mistress, school teacher, supply t., class t., form t., subject t.; year tutor; house master *or* mistress; assistant teacher, deputy head, head teacher, head, headmaster *or* -mistress, principal, rector; pupil teacher, trainee t., usher, monitor; prefect, proctor; dean, don, fellow; lecturer, demonstrator, expositor, exponent 520 *interpreter*; prelector, reader, professor, Regius p., professor emeritus; catechist, catechizer; initiator, mystagogue; confidant, consultant 691 *adviser*; teaching staff, faculty, professoriate, senior common room.

*trainer*, instructor, physical education i., swimming i., sensei; personal trainer; coach, athletics c., team c.; sports psychologist; choirmaster; dancing-master *or* mistress; life coach; animal trainer, dog t., sheepdog t., horse t., breaker-in, broncobuster, horse-breaker, horse-tamer, horse whisperer, lion-tamer, puppy-walker, falconer; disciplinarian, caner, martinet.

*preacher*, lay p. 986 *pastor*; pulpiteer, Boanerges, orator 579 *speaker*; hot gospeller, evangelist; apostle, missionary, pioneer 66 *pre-*

*cursor*; seer, prophet, major p., minor p. 511 *oracle*; pamphleteer, propagandist 528 *publicizer*.

**Adj.** *pedagogic* 534 *educational*.

**538 Learner**
**N.** *learner*, disciple, follower, chela; proselyte, convert, initiate, catechumen; late learner, opsimath, mature student; self-taught person, autodidact; do-it-yourself fan; empiricist 461 *experimenter*; swotter, swot, mugger, bookworm 492 *scholar*; pupil, scholar, schoolboy *or* -girl, student; day pupil, boarder; sixth-former; school-fellow, schoolmate, classmate, fellow student; gifted child, fast learner, high flier; slow learner, late developer, under-achiever, remedial pupil; school-leaver; old boy, old girl, former pupil.

*beginner*, young idea, novice, debutant; abecedarian; new boy *or* girl, tyro, greenhorn, tenderfoot, neophyte; rabbit, amateur 987 *lay person*; recruit, raw r., rookie; colt, cadet, trainee, apprentice, articled clerk, cub reporter; probationer, L-driver, examinee 461 *testee*.

*student*, university s., college s., collegian, seminarist; undergraduate, undergrad, freshman, fresher, sophomore; former student, alumnus, alumna; commoner, pensioner, foundationer, exhibitioner; scholarship-holder, bursary-h., Rhodes Scholar; prize boy *or* girl, prizeman; honours student; graduand, graduate, post-g., fellow; mature student, research worker, researcher, specialist.

*class*, reception c.; form, grade, remove, shell; set, band, stream; age group, tutor g., vertical grouping, house; lower form, upper f., sixth f.; art class, life c.; study group, workshop; colloquium 584 *conference*; seminar, discussion group 534 *teaching*.

**Adj.** *studentlike*, schoolboyish 130 *young*; undergraduate, collegiate; pupillary, discipular; scholarly 536 *studious*; preschool; elementary, rudimentary, abecedarian; probationary; in leading strings, in statu pupillari.

**539 School**
**N.** *academy*, institute, institution, educational i.; college, lycée, gymnasium, senior secondary school; conservatoire, school of music, school of dancing, ballet school, art s., academy of dramatic art; charm school, finishing school; correspondence college; university, university college, campus; Open University; redbrick university, Oxbridge, varsity; sixth-form college, college of further *or* higher education; polytechnic, poly; school of philosophy, Academy, Lyceum, Stoa; alma mater, old school, groves of academe.

*school*, nursery s., crèche, playgroup, kindergarten; infant school, dame s.; private school, independent s., public s., opt-out s., aided s., state-aided s., maintained s., state s., local-authority s., free s.; preparatory school, prep s., crammer; primary school, middle s., secondary s., high s., secondary modern s., grammar s., senior secondary s.; comprehensive s., sixth form college; Beacon school, city academy, specialist school, arts college, city technology c., languages c., sports c., technology c.; boarding school, day s.; night s., evening classes; convent school, denominational s.; Sunday s.; school for the blind, deaf-and-dumb school, special s., school for the educationally subnormal; community home, approved school, List D s.; reform s., Borstal; remand home, detention centre; catchment area, parents' charter; blackboard jungle.

*training school*, nursery, training ground, nursery slope 724 *arena*; training ship, training college, agricultural c., technical c., tech; college of commerce, secretarial college; c. of education; theological college, seminary; law school, medical school, medical college, teaching hospital; military college, staff college; Dartmouth, Sandhurst, Cranwell; West Point.

*classroom*, schoolroom, chalk-face; study; lecture room, lecture hall, auditorium, amphitheatre; resources area, library; workshop, laboratory, lab, language lab; gymnasium, playing fields; campus; desk, school d.; school-book, reader, primer, crib 589 *textbook*; slate, copybook, workbook, exercise book 548 *record*; visual aid, blackboard 445 *spectacle*.

*rostrum*, bema, tribune, dais, forum; platform, stage, podium, estrade; hustings, soapbox; chair 534 *lecture*; pulpit, lectern, ambo; microphone 531 *broadcasting*; leader page, column 528 *publicity*.

**Adj.** *scholastic* 534 *educational*.

**540 Veracity**
**N.** *veracity*, veraciousness, truthfulness, truth-telling, truth-speaking; truth, the whole truth and nothing but the truth, nothing but fact, fidelity, fidelity to fact, verisimilitude, realism, exactitude 494 *accuracy*; openness, frankness, candour 522 *manifestation*; bona fides, honour bright, scout's honour, no kidding; love of truth, honesty, sincerity 929 *probity*; simplicity, ingenuousness 699 *artlessness*; downrightness, plain speaking, plain dealing, speaking straight from the shoulder 573 *plainness*; baldness, plain words, words of one syllable, home truth, unvarnished tale, undisguised meaning, unambiguity, true state-

ment, honest truth, sober t. 494 *truth*; clean breast, true confession, unqualified admission 526 *disclosure*; circumstantiality, particularity, full details, nothing omitted 570 *diffuseness*; gate of horn; truth-speaker, no liar, true prophet.

**Adj.** *veracious*, truthful 494 *true*; telling the truth, veridical, not lying; as good as one's word, reliable 929 *trustworthy*; factual, sticking to fact, ungarbled, undistorted, bald, unembroidered, unvarnished, unexaggerated, scrupulous, exact, just 494 *accurate*; full, particular, circumstantial 570 *diffuse*; simple, ingenuous 699 *artless*; bona fide, meant, intended; unaffected, unpretentious, unfeigned, undissembling, open, above-board 522 *undisguised*; frank, candid, unreserved, forthcoming; blunt, free, downright, forthright, plain-speaking, outspoken, straightforward, straight from the shoulder, honest to goodness, honest to God 573 *plain*; unambiguous 516 *intelligible*; honest, sincere, true-hearted, on the up and up, on the level 929 *honourable*; truly spoken, fulfilled, proved, verified 478 *demonstrated*; infallible, prophetic 511 *presageful*.

**Vb.** *be truthful*, tell the truth, tell the truth and shame the devil, tell no lie, tell the whole truth and nothing but the truth, swear true 532 *swear*; stick to the facts, play it according to the letter 494 *be true*; speak in earnest, mean it, really mean, honestly m.; not joke, weigh one's words 834 *be serious*; speak one's mind, open one's heart, keep nothing back 522 *show*; come clean, make a clean breast of it, confess the truth 526 *confess*; drop the mask, appear in one's true colours 526 *disclose*; be prophetic 511 *predict*; verify one's words, say truly 478 *demonstrate*.

**Adv.** *truthfully*, really and truly, bona fide, sincerely, from the bottom of one's heart 494 *truly*; to tell the truth, the whole t., and nothing but the t.; frankly, candidly, without fear or favour; factually, exactly, to the letter, just as it happened.

**541 Falsehood**

**N.** *falsehood*, falseness, spuriousness, falsity; treachery, bad faith, Punic f. 930 *perfidy*; untruthfulness, unveracity, mendacity, deceitfulness, malingering; lie, 'terminological inexactitude' (see quotation at 543 *untruth*); lying, habitual l., pathological l., mythomania; oath-breaking, perjury, false swearing 543 *untruth*; invention of lies, fabrication, fiction; faking, forgery, falsification 542 *deception*; imaginativeness, invention 513 *imagination*; disingenuousness, prevarication, equivocation, ambivalence, evasion, double-talk, shuf-

fling, fencing 518 *equivocalness*; economy of truth, suppressio veri, suggestio falsi; whitewashing, cover-up; casuistry 477 *sophistry*; overstatement 546 *exaggeration*; perversion 246 *distortion*; false colouring, misrepresentation, spin, subreption 521 *misinterpretation*; meretriciousness 875 *ostentation*; humbug, bunkum, boloney, hooey (sl), rubbish, bull (sl), flimflam 515 *empty talk*; cant, eyewash, hogwash (see also *duplicity*); euphemism, mealy-mouthedness, blarney, soft soap 925 *flattery*; liar 545 *deceiver*.

*duplicity*, false conduct, double life, double-dealing 930 *improbity*; guile 542 *trickery*; hollowness, front, facade, outside, mask, show, false s., window-dressing, fanfaronade 875 *ostentation*; pretence, hollow p., bluff, act, fake, counterfeit, imposture 542 *sham*; hypocrisy, Tartuffery; acting, play-a., simulation, dissimulation, dissembling, insincerity, tongue in cheek, cant; lip service, cupboard love; pharisaism, false piety; outward show, crocodile tears, show of sympathy; Judas kiss; fraud, pious f., sting, legal fiction, diplomatic illness; cheat, cheating, sharp practice; collusion, nod and a wink; put-up job, frame-up 930 *foul play*; quackery, charlatanry, charlatanism 850 *pretension*; low cunning, artfulness 698 *cunning*.

**Adj.** *false*, not true, truthless, without truth; imagined, made-up; untruthful, lying, unveracious, mendacious 543 *untrue*; perfidious, treacherous, forsworn, perjured; sneaky, artful 698 *cunning*; disingenuous, dishonest, uncandid, unfair, ambiguous, evasive, ambivalent, shuffling 518 *equivocal*; falsified, garbled; meretricious, embellished, touched up, varnished, painted; overdone 546 *exaggerated*; ungenuine, imitated, imitation, simulated, counterfeit, fake, phoney, sham, pseudo, snide, quack, bogus, faux 542 *spurious*; cheating, deceptive, deceitful, fraudulent 542 *deceiving*; covinous, collusive; fiddled, fixed, engineered, rigged, packed; trumped up.

*hypocritical*, hollow, empty, insincere, diplomatic; put on, imitated, pretended, simulated, seeming, feigned; make-believe, acting, play-a.; all fur coat and nae knickers (Scots); double, two-faced, double-tongued, lying, shifty, sly, treacherous, double-dealing, designing, Machiavellian 930 *perfidious*; lying 542 *deceiving*; sanctimonious, Tartuffian, Pecksniffian, pharisaical; casuistical; plausible, smooth, smooth-tongued, smooth-spoken, oily; creepy, goody-goody; mealy-mouthed, euphemistic 850 *affected*; canting, gushing 925 *flattering*.

**Vb.** *be false*, – perjured, – forsworn etc. adj.; perjure oneself, bear false witness, swear falsely, swear that black is white; palter, palter *or* trifle with the truth; lie, tell lies, utter a falsehood, lie in one's teeth *or* one's throat; tell the tale, swing the lead, malinger; strain, stretch the truth, tell a tall story 546 *exaggerate*; tell a white lie, fib, tell a fib, tell a whopper, lie hard; invent, make believe, make up, romance 513 *imagine*; put a false construction on 521 *misinterpret*; garble, doctor, tamper with, falsify 246 *distort*; overstate, understate 552 *misrepresent*; misreport, misquote, miscite, misinform, cry wolf 535 *misteach*; lull, soothe 925 *flatter*; play false, play a double game 930 *be dishonest*; run with the hare and hunt with the hounds, have a foot in both camps; break faith, betray 603 *change one's mind*.

*dissemble*, dissimulate, disguise 525 *conceal*; simulate, counterfeit 20 *imitate*; put on, assume, affect, dress up, play-act, play a part, go through the motions, make a show of 594 *act*; feign, pass off for, sham, pretend, be under false pretences, sail under false colours; malinger, sham Abraham 542 *deceive*; lack candour, be less than honest, say one thing and mean another; hide the truth, say less than the t., keep something back, fail to declare; fudge the issue, obfuscate the facts, not give a straight answer, prevaricate, beat about the bush, shuffle, dodge, trim 518 *be equivocal*.

*cant*, gloze, euphemize, mince matters 850 *be affected*; colour, varnish, touch up, paint, embroider, dress up; gloss over, gloze o. 477 *sophisticate*; play the hypocrite, act a part, role-play, put on an act; say the grapes are sour.

*fake*, fudge, fabricate, coin, forge, plagiarize, counterfeit 20 *imitate*; get up, trump up, frame; manipulate, fiddle, fix, wangle, rig, pack (a jury); spin, weave, cook, cook up, concoct, hatch, invent 623 *plot*.

**Adv.** *falsely*, slyly, deceitfully, under false pretences; hypocritically, mendaciously.

## 542 Deception

**N.** *deception*, kidding, kidology, tongue in cheek; circumvention, outwitting; self-deception, wishful thinking 487 *credulity*; infatuation 499 *folly*; fallacy 477 *sophistry*; illusion, delusion, hallucination, imagination's artful aid 495 *error*; deceptiveness, speciousness 523 *latency* (see also *trap*); false appearance, mockery, mirage, will-o'-the-wisp 440 *visual fallacy*; show, false s., outward s., meretriciousness, paint (see also *sham*); false reputation, feet of clay; hollowness, bubble 4 *insubstantiality*; falseness, deceit, quackery, imposture, lie, 'terminological inexactitude' (see quotation at 543 *untruth*), pious fraud 541 *falsehood*; deceitfulness, guile, craft, artfulness

698 *cunning*; hypocrisy, insincerity 541 *duplicity*; treachery, betrayal 930 *perfidy*; machination, hanky-panky, jiggery-pokery, monkey business, wheeler-dealing, collusion 623 *plot*; fraudulence, cozenage, cheating, cheat, diddling; cheat 545 *deceiver*.

*trickery*, dupery, swindling, skulduggery, shenanigan; sharp practice, wheeler-dealing, chicane, chicanery, legal c., pettifoggery; swindle, ramp, racket, wangle, fix, fiddle, diddle, swizzle, swiz, sell, fraud, cheat; cardsharping 930 *foul play*; trick, dirty t., bag of tricks, tricks of the trade, confidence trick, con trick, fast one, wiles, ruse, shift, dodge, artful d., fetch, blind, feint 698 *stratagem*; wrinkle 623 *contrivance*; bait, gimmick, shtick; diversion, red herring, smoke screen, 'a tub to a whale';

> ... seamen have a custom when they meet a whale, to fling him out an empty tub by way of amusement, to divert him from laying violent hands upon the ship.
> Jonathan Swift, *A Tale of a Tub*

hoax, bluff, spoof, leg-pull; game, sport, joke, practical j., rag 839 *witticism*; April fooling.

*sleight*, pass, sleight of hand, legerdemain, prestidigitation, conjuring, hocuspocus, illusion, ventriloquism; juggling, jugglery, juggle, googly; thimblerig, three-card trick; magic 983 *sorcery*.

*trap*, deathtrap 527 *ambush*; catch 530 *enigma*; plant, frame-up 930 *foul play*; hook, noose, snare, springe, gin, spring gun, man trap; net, meshes, toils, web; diversion, blind, decoy, decoy duck, bait, lure, sprat to catch a mackerel; baited trap, mouse t., flypaper, limetwig, birdlime; booby trap, mine, tripwire, deadfall, pit 663 *pitfall*; car bomb, letter b., parcel b.; trapdoor, sliding panel, false bottom 530 *secret*; fatal gift, poisoned apple, Trojan horse, Greek gift; honey trap.

*sham*, false front, veneer 541 *duplicity*; lip service, tokenism; make-believe, pretence 850 *affectation*; paint, whitewash, varnish, gloss; 'whited sepulchre', man of straw, 'paper tiger';

> Woe unto you, scribes and Pharisees, hypocrites! For ye are like unto whited sepulchres, which indeed appear beautiful outward, but are within full of dead men's bones, and of all uncleanness.
> Bible, Jesus in St Matthew's Gospel

> The atomic bomb is a paper tiger which the US reactionaries use to scare people. It looks terrible, but in fact it isn't.
> All reactionaries are paper tigers. In appearance, the reactionaries are terrifying, but in reality they are not powerful.
> Mao Zedong

wolf in sheep's clothing 545 *impostor*; dummy, scarecrow, tattie bogle; imitation, simulacrum, facsimile 22 *copy*; trompe-l'oeil, film *or* stage

set 4 *insubstantial thing*; mockery, hollow m.;
counterfeit, forgery, fake; masquerade, mummery, mask, veil, cloak, disguise, borrowed
plumes, false colours 525 *concealment*; shoddy,
Brummagem, jerry-building 641 *rubbish*; imitation ware, tinsel, paste; ormolu, Mosaic gold;
German silver, Britannia metal.

**Adj.** *deceiving*, deceitful, lying, 'economical
with the truth' 543 *untrue*;

> A misleading impression; not a lie. It was being
> economical with the truth.
>
> Sir Robert Armstrong (The phrase was possibly first
> coined by Edmund Burke.)

deceptive 523 *latent*; hallucinatory, illusive,
delusive, illusory; specious 445 *appearing*; glib,
slick, oily, slippery, sleekit 258 *smooth*; fraudulent, humbugging, cheating; lulling, soothing
925 *flattering*; beguiling, treacherous, insidious
930 *perfidious*; trumped-up, framed, colourable
541 *false*; feigned, simulated, pretended 541
*hypocritical*; juggling, conjuring, prestigious;
tricky, crafty, wily, guileful, artful, on the
fiddle 698 *cunning*; collusive, plotting; painted,
whitewashed, veneered, varnished, sugared,
coated, plated (see also *spurious*).

*spurious*, ungenuine, false, faked, fake; sham,
counterfeit 541 *false*; make-believe, mock,
ersatz, bogus, phoney; pseudo-, so-called; cosmetic; not natural, artificial, simulated, man-
made, plastic, paste, cultured, imitation;
shoddy, rubbishy 641 *useless*; tinsel, meretricious, flash, gaudy, catchpenny, pinchbeck,
Brummagem 812 *cheap*; jerry-built, cardboard,
pasteboard 330 *brittle*; adulterated, sophisticated 43 *mixed*; underweight 323 *light*.

**Vb.** *deceive*, delude, dazzle; beguile, sugar the
pill, gild the p., give a false impression, belie;
let down 509 *disappoint*; pull the wool over
one's eyes, blinker, blindfold 439 *blind*; kid,
bluff, bamboozle, hoodwink, hoax, humbug,
hornswoggle; throw dust in the eyes, create a
smoke screen, lead up the garden path 495 *mislead*; spoof, mystify 535 *misteach*; play false,
leave in the lurch, betray, twotime, double-
cross 930 *be dishonest*; intrigue against 623 *plot*;
circumvent, overreach, outwit, outmanoeuvre
306 *outdo*; forestall, steal a march on 135 *be
early*; pull a fast one, take one for a ride, be too
smart for, outsmart 698 *be cunning*; trick, dupe
(see also *befool*); cheat, cozen, con, swindle,
sell, rook, do, do down; diddle, do out of, bilk,
gyp, fleece, pluck, rip off, shaft (sl) shortch-
ange, obtain money by false pretences 788
*defraud*; juggle, conjure, force a card, palm off,
foist o.; fob, fob off with; live on one's wits, try
it on, practise chicanery, pettifog; gerrymander, tinker with, fiddle, wangle, fix; load
the dice, mark the cards, pack the c., stack the

deck; play the hypocrite, impose upon 541
*dissemble*; brazen out, put a good face
upon, whitewash 541 *cant*; counterfeit 541
*fake*.

*befool*, fool, make a fool of, make an ass of,
make a wally of, make one look silly; mock,
make fun of 851 *ridicule*; rag, play tricks on,
play practical jokes on, pull one's leg, have one
on, make an April fool of, play a joke on 497 *be
absurd*; sport with, trifle w., throw over, jilt;
take in, have, dupe, bull, victimize, gull,
outwit, outsmart; trick, trap, catch out, take
advantage of, manipulate, twist round one's
little finger; kid, spoof, bamboozle, string
along, lead one on (see also *deceive*); cajole,
wheedle, get round, fawn on, lull, soothe 925
*flatter*, let down, let in for, play fast and loose
with, leave in the lurch, leave one holding the
baby 509 *disappoint*; send on a fool's errand,
send on a wild-goose chase 495 *mislead*; make
one an apple-pie bed.

*ensnare*, snare, trap, entrap, set a trap for, lay
a trap for, lime, lime the twig; enmesh,
entangle, net; trip, trip up, catch, catch out,
hook, sniggle; bait, bait the trap, bait the hook,
dangle a bait, lure, decoy, lead astray, entice,
inveigle 612 *tempt*; lie in wait, waylay 527
*ambush*; nab, nick, kidnap, shanghai, hijack,
take hostage 788 *steal*.

**Adv.** *deceptively*, deceitfully; under cover of,
in the garb of, disguisedly, under the guise of;
tongue in cheek.

## 543 Untruth

**N.** *untruth*, thing that is not, reverse of the
truth 541 *falsehood*; less than the truth, understatement 483 *underestimation*; more than the
truth, overstatement 546 *exaggeration*; lie,
downright l., shameless l., barefaced l.; tara-
diddle, white lie, fib, diplomatic excuse,
whopper; false statement, 'terminological
inexactitude';

> A labour contract into which men enter voluntarily
> for a limited and for a brief period, under which
> they are paid wages which they consider adequate
> . . . cannot in the opinion of His Majesty's Govern-
> ment be classified as slavery in the extreme accept-
> ance of the word without some risk of
> terminological inexactitude.
>
> Winston Churchill

broken word, dicer's oath, lover's o., breach of
promise 930 *perfidy*; perjury, false oath; false
evidence, pack of lies, tissue of l., trumped-up
story, frame-up 466 *evidence*; concoction, fiction, fabrication, invention 513 *ideality* (see
also *fable*); false excuse, Bunbury; misstatement, misinformation, disinformation 535 *misteaching*; misrepresentation, perversion 246
*distortion*; gloss, varnish, garbling, falsification

521 *misinterpretation*; lie factory, propaganda machine; gate of ivory.

*mental dishonesty*, disingenuousness, economy of truth, half-truth, partial t., near t., half-lie, white l., diplomatic excuse, trumped-up e., pious fraud, mental reservation 468 *qualification*; suggestio falsi, suppressio veri 525 *concealment*; show, false s., make-believe; tongue in cheek, pretence, profession, false plea, excuse 614 *pretext*; evasion, subterfuge, shift, shuffle, ambiguity, ambivalence, doublethink 518 *equivocalness*; self-deprecation, irony, backhanded compliment 850 *affectation*; artificiality, unnaturalness; sham, empty words, lip service, tokenism 541 *duplicity*; Judas kiss 930 *perfidy*; mask 527 *disguise*.

*fable*, invention, fiction, imaginative exercise 513 *ideality*; story, tale 590 *narrative*; tall story, shaggy dog story, fishy s., fisherman's yarn, traveller's tale 546 *exaggeration*; fairy tale, nursery t., romance, tale, yarn, story, cock-and-bull s., all my eye and Betty Martin 497 *absurdity*; claptrap, gossip, gup, guff, bull, canard 529 *rumour*; old wives' tale, urban myth, urban legend; myth, mythology; moonshine, farce, mare's nest, sell, swiz, hoax, humbug, flummery 515 *empty talk*.

**Adj.** *untrue*, lying, mendacious 541 *false*, 542 *deceiving*; trumped-up, framed, cooked, fixed, hatched, concocted; far from the truth, nothing less true; mythological, fabulous; unfounded, ungrounded, empty; fictitious, imagined, hallucinatory, make-believe, well-invented, ben trovato; faked, artificial, synthetic, simulated, factitious; phoney, bogus, soi-disant, so-called 542 *spurious*; overstated 546 *exaggerated*; boasting 877 *boastful*; perjured, forsworn 930 *perfidious*; evasive, shuffling, surreptitious 518 *equivocal*; ironical 850 *affected*; satirical, mocking 851 *derisive*.

**Vb.** *be untrue*, not hold water, not stand up in court, be wide of the mark; sound untrue, not ring true 472 *be unlikely*; lie, be a liar 541 *be false*; spin a yarn, tell a tall story, draw the long bow 546 *exaggerate*; make-believe, draw on one's imagination 513 *imagine*; be phoney, pretend, sham, counterfeit, forge, falsify 541 *dissemble*.

## 544 Dupe

**N.** *dupe*, fool, old f., April f. 851 *laughing-stock*; Simple Simon, Joe Soap 501 *ninny*; credulous fool, gobe-mouche, gudgeon; one easily taken in, easy prey, easy target, sitting duck, soft touch, soft mark, pushover, cinch; fair game, victim, schlemiel, fall guy, patsy (sl), stooge, mug (sl), sap (sl), sucker (sl), schmuck (sl), schnook (sl), gull, pigeon; dude, greenhorn,

innocent 538 *beginner*; puppet, cat's-paw, pawn 628 *instrument*; vulnerable public, admass.

**Adj.** *gullible* 487 *credulous*; duped, deceived, taken in, had, done, diddled, sold a pup, sold a pig in a poke 542 *deceiving*; innocent, green, silly 499 *foolish*.

**Vb.** *be duped*, be had, be done, be taken in; fall for, walk into the trap, rise, nibble, swallow the bait, swallow hook line and sinker; get taken for a ride; carry the can, catch a Tartar 508 *not expect*.

## 545 Deceiver

**N.** *deceiver*, kidder, ragger, leg-puller; practical joker, Puck, Loki, Till Eulenspiegel 839 *humorist*; dissembler, actor, shammer, hypocrite, canter, 'whited sepulchre' (see quotation at 542 *sham*), Pharisee, Pecksniff, Tartuffe, Uriah Heep, Joseph Surface; false friend, fair-weather f., jilt, jilter; shuffler, turncoat, trimmer, rat 603 *tergiversator*; two-timer, double-crosser, double agent; traitor, Judas 938 *knave*; seducer 952 *libertine*; serpent, snake in the grass, snake in one's bosom, joker in the pack 663 *troublemaker*; plotter, Guy Fawkes, intrigant, intriguer, conspirator 623 *planner*; counterfeiter, forger, faker, plagiariser 20 *imitator*; Holocaust denier.

*liar*, confirmed l., pathological l., mythomaniac; Ananias; fibster, fibber, story-teller; romancer, fabulist; imaginative person, yarner, yarn-spinner; angler, traveller 546 *exaggeration*; fabricator, equivocator, palterer; oathbreaker, perjurer, false witness 541 *falsehood*.

*impostor*, shammer, ringer, malingerer, adventurer, carpetbagger; usurper; cuckoo in the nest 59 *intruder*; ass in the lion's skin, wolf in sheep's clothing; boaster, bluffer, four-flusher; pretender, charlatan, quack, quacksalver, mountebank, saltimbanco 850 *affecter*; fake, fraud, con man, humbug; pseud, pseudo, phoney; masquerader, mummer; front man 525 *concealment*.

*trickster*, hoaxer, spoofer, hoodwinker, bamboozler; cheat, cheater, cozener; sharper, cardsharp, rook, thimblerigger 542 *trickery*; shyster, pettifogger; fraudster, fraudsman, swindler, bilker, diddler, shark 789 *defrauder*; slicker, spieler, twister, jobber, rogue 938 *knave*; confidence trickster, con man 477 *sophist*; decoy, stool pigeon, decoy-duck, agent provocateur; fiddler, manipulator, rigger, fixer; wily bird, fox 698 *slyboots*.

*conjuror*, illusionist, prestidigitator, juggler, ventriloquist; quick-change artist; magician, necromancer 983 *sorcerer*.

## 546 Exaggeration

**N.** *exaggeration*, overemphasis, inflation, magnification, enlargement 197 *expansion*; optimism 482 *overestimation*; stretch, strain, straining; extravagance, exaggerated lengths, gilding the lily, extremes, immoderation, extremism; overkill; excess, excessiveness, feeding frenzy, violence 943 *intemperance*; inordinacy, exorbitance, overdoing it, piling it on, 'piling Pelion on Ossa';

> They [Otus and Ephialtes] tried to pile Mount Ossa on top of Mount Olympus, and on top of Mount Ossa leafy Mount Pelion, so that there might be a pathway to the heavens.
>
> Homer, *The Odyssey*

overacting, histrionics 875 *ostentation*; sensationalism, ballyhoo, puffery, hype 528 *publicity*; overstatement, hyperbole 519 *trope*; adulation 925 *flattery*; colouring, high c. 574 *ornament*; embroidery 38 *addition*; disproportion 246 *distortion*; caricature, burlesque 851 *satire*; exacerbation 832 *aggravation*; big talk, fanfaronade, 877 *boasting*; rant, ranting, tirade, rodomontade, grandiloquence 574 *rhetoric*; overpraise, excessive loyalty, chauvinism 481 *prejudice*; tall story, yarn, traveller's tale 543 *fable*; teratology, miracle-mongering; flight of fancy, stretch of the imagination 513 *imagination*; fuss, pother, excitement, storm in a teacup, much ado about nothing 318 *commotion*; extremist, exaggerator; sensationalist, miracle-monger, teratologist; Baron Munchhausen 545 *liar*.

**Adj.** *exaggerated*, magnified, enlarged 197 *expanded*; blown up, out of all proportion, built up, puffed up, hyped, hyped up; added to, touched up, embroidered; strained, laboured, overemphasized, overweighted, overdone, overstated, overcoloured, inflated, hyperbolical 574 *rhetorical*; overacted, histrionic; melodramatic, blood-and-thunder; bombastic, swelling 877 *boastful*; tall, fanciful, high-flown, steep, egregious, preposterous, outrageous, farfetched 497 *absurd*; vaulting, lofty, extravagant, excessive, outré, extremist; violent, immoderate 32 *exorbitant*; fulsome, inordinate 637 *superfluous*.

**Vb.** *exaggerate*, maximize, magnify, expand, inflate, blow up 197 *enlarge*; overamplify, overelaborate; add to, pile up, pile it on 38 *add*; touch up, enhance, heighten, add a flourish, embroider, varnish 844 *decorate*; lay it on thick *or* with a trowel, depict in glowing terms, overvalue; overdo, overcolour, overdraw, overcharge, overload; overweight, overstress, overemphasize 638 *make important*; overpraise, puff, hype up, oversell, cry up 482 *overrate*; make much of, make too much of 925 *flatter*;

stretch, strain, labour 246 *distort*; caricature 851 *satirize*; go to all lengths, gild the lily, not know when to stop, protest too much, speak in superlatives, hyperbolize; overact, melodramatize, dramatize, 'out-Herod Herod';

> Speak the speech, I pray you, as I pronounced it to you, trippingly on the tongue; but if you mouth it, as many of your players do, I had as lief the town-crier spoke my lines. Nor do not saw the air too much with your hand, thus; but use all gently: for in the very torrent, tempest, and – as I may say – whirlwind of passion, you must acquire and beget a temperance, that may give it smoothness. O! it offends me to the soul to hear a robustious periwig-pated fellow tear a passion to tatters, to very rags, to split the ears of the groundlings, who for the most part are capable of nothing but inexplicable dumb-shows and noise: I would have such a fellow whipped for o'er-doing Termagant; it out-herods Herod: pray you, avoid it.
>
> William Shakespeare, *Hamlet*

rant, talk big, bull 877 *boast*; run riot, go to extremes, 'pile Pelion on Ossa' (see quotation above); draw the long bow, overshoot the mark, overstep the m., go too far 306 *overstep*; spin a yarn, tell a tall tale, draw on the imagination, deal in the marvellous, tell travellers' tales 541 *be false*; make mountains out of molehills, make a storm in a tea cup; intensify, exacerbate 832 *aggravate*; overcompensate, lean over backwards.

SECTION THREE

## Means of communicating ideas

## 547 Indication

**N.** *indication*, pointing out, drawing attention, showing 522 *manifestation*; signification, meaning 514 *connotation*; notification 524 *information*; symbolization, symbolism 551 *representation*; symbol, conventional s., x 558 *letter*; rune, secret symbol, hieroglyph 530 *enigma*; sacred symbol, cross, crescent, mandala; magic symbol, pentacle 983 *talisman*; natural symbol, image, type, figure; token, emblem, figurehead (see also *badge*); something to go by, symptom, syndrome, sign 466 *evidence*; tell-tale sign, blush 526 *disclosure*; nudge, wink, kick 524 *hint* (see also *gesture*); kite-flying, straw in the wind, sign of the times 511 *omen*; clue, scent, whiff, trace 484 *discovery*; noise, footfall 398 *sound*; interpretation of symptoms, symptomatology, semiology, semiotics 520 *hermeneutics*; pointer, finger, forefinger, index finger (see also *indicator*); guide, index, thumb i. 87 *directory*; key 520 *interpretation*; contour lines, hachures; marker, mark; blaze; nick, scratch 260 *notch*; stamp, print, impression; stigma, stigmata; prick, tattooing, tattoo mark 263 *perforation*;

scar 845 *blemish*; wrinkle, line, score, stroke; note, side n., catchword (see also *punctuation*); legend, caption 590 *description*; inscription, epitaph; motto, cipher, monogram; love token, favour. (See also *badge*.)

*identification*, naming 561 *nomenclature*, 77 *classification*; means of identification, brand, earmark, trademark, logo, marque, imprint (see also *label*); name and address; autograph, signature, hand 586 *script*; fingerprint, footprint, spoor, track, trail, scent 548 *trace*; dental record; genetic fingerprinting, DNA f.; secret sign, password, open sesame, watchword, countersign, shibboleth; diagnosis, markings, stripes, spots, colour, colouring; characteristic, trait, lineament, outline, form, shape 445 *feature*; personal characteristic, mannerism, trick, trick of speech, idiolect; mole, scar, birthmark, strawberry mark 845 *blemish*; divining rod 484 *detector*; litmus paper 461 *testing agent*; mark, note.

*symbology*, symbolization; semiotics, semiology; dactylology; cipher, code 525 *secrecy*; picture writing, hieroglyphics, runes 586 *script*; gypsy signs, scout s.

*gesture*, gesticulation, sign language, dactylology; deaf-and-dumb language; sign 524 *hint*; pantomime, dumb show, charade, mime, air guitar, air quotes; by-play, stage business; body language, kinesics; demeanour, look in one's eyes, tone of one's voice 445 *mien*; motion, move; tic, twitch 318 *spasm*; shrug, shrug of the shoulders; raising of the eyebrows, wag of the head, nod, beck, wink, flicker of the eyelash, batting of the eyelids *or* eyelashes, twinkle, glance, ogle, leer, grimace 438 *look*; smile, laugh 835 *laughter*; touch, kick, kick under the table, nudge, jog, dig in the ribs 279 *knock*; hug, clap on the shoulders; handpressure, squeeze of the hand, handshake, grip; push, shove 279 *impulse*; pointing, signal, waving, wave, hand-signal, wave of the hand, Mexican wave; raising one's hand, wagging one's forefinger; drumming one's fingers, tapping one's foot, stamp of the foot 822 *excitable state*; clenching one's teeth, gritting one's t. 599 *resolution*; gnashing *or* grinding one's teeth, snap, snapping one's jaws 892 *irascibility*; wringing one's hands, tearing one's hair 836 *lamentation*; clenched fist 711 *defiance*; V-sign, flagwaving, umbrella-w., hat-w. 876 *celebration*; clap, clapping, hand-c., cheer 923 *applause*; hiss, hissing, hooting, boo, booing, catcall, Bronx cheer, raspberry 924 *disapprobation*; two-finger gesture, Harvey Smith salute; stuck-out tongue 878 *sauciness*; frown, scowl 893 *sullenness*; pout, moue, pursing of the lips 829 *discontent*.

*signal* 529 *message*; sign, symptom, syndrome 522 *manifestation*; flash, rocket, Very light, maroon; signalling, railway signal, smoke s., heliograph, semaphore, tick-tack; telegraph, morse 531 *telecommunication*; flashlamp, signal lamp 420 *lamp*; warning light, beacon, beacon fire, bale-f., watch-f. 379 *fire*; warning signal, red flag, warning light, red l., Belisha beacon, green light, all clear 420 *signal light*; alarum, alarm, fire a., burglar a., warning signal, distress s., SOS 665 *danger signal*; whistle, police w.; siren, hooter; bleeper, bleep, pager; buzzer, knocker, doorknocker 414 *gong*; bell, doorbell, alarm bell, Lutine b.; church bells, angelus, carillon, sacring bell; time signal, pip, minute gun, dinner gong, dinner bell 117 *chronometry*; passing bell, knell, muffled drum 364 *obsequies*.

*indicator*, index, pointer, arrow, needle, compass n., magnetic n.; arm, finger, index-f.; hand, hour h., minute h. 117 *timekeeper*; Plimsoll line 465 *gauge*; traffic indicator, trafficator, winker; direction finder, radar; cursor; white line, cat's-eyes (tdmk) 305 *traffic control*; weathercock, wind sock 340 *weather*.

*signpost*, direction post, fingerpost, guidepost; milestone, milepost, milliary column, waymark; lighthouse, lightship, buoy 662 *safeguard*; compass 269 *sailing aid*; lodestar, cynosure, guiding star, pole s., Southern Cross 321 *star*; landmark, seamark, Pillars of Hercules; cairn 253 *earthwork*; monument, memorial, war m. 505 *reminder*; triangulation point, benchmark; tidemark 236 *limit*.

*call*, proclamation, ban, hue-and-cry 528 *publication*; shout, hail; invitation; call to prayer, church bell, muezzin's cry 981 *worship*; summons, word, word of command 737 *command*; call for help, cry of help, distress call, Mayday; bugle, trumpet, bugle-call, reveille, assemble, charge, advance, rally, retreat; lights out, last post; peal, sennet, flourish; drum, drumbeat, drum-roll, tattoo, taps 403 *roll*; call to arms, fiery cross; battle cry, war c., rallying c., slogan, catchword, watchword, shibboleth; challenge, countersign.

*badge*, token, emblem, symbol, sign, totem (see also *indication*); insignia (see also *heraldry*); markings, military m., roundel; badge of sovereignty, throne, sceptre, orb, crown 743 *regalia*; mark of authority, badge of office, robes of o., wand of o., Black Rod, mace, keys 743 *badge of rule*; baton, stars, pips, spurs, stripes, epaulette 743 *badge of rank*; medal, gong, cross, Victoria Cross, George C., Iron C., Croix de Guerre; order, star, garter, sash, ribbon 729 *decoration*; badge of merit, laurels, bays, wreath, fillet, chaplet, garland 729 *trophy*; colours, blue, half-b., cap, oar; badge of loyalty, favour, rosette, love knot; badge of mourning, black armband, black, crepe, widow's weeds 228 *clothing*.

*livery*, dress, national d. 228 *uniform*; tartan, tie, old school t., club t., blazer; regimental badge, brassard, epaulette, aiguillette, chevron, stripes, pips, wings; flash, hackle, cockade, rosette.

*heraldry*, armory, blazonry; heraldic register, Roll of Arms; armorial bearings, coat of arms, blazon; achievement, funereal a., hatchment; shield, escutcheon; crest, torse, wreath, helmet, crown, coronet, mantling, lambrequin; supporters, motto; field, quarter, dexter, sinister, chief, base; charge, device, bearing; ordinary, fess, bar, label, pale, bend, bend sinister, chevron, pile, saltire, cross; canton; inescutcheon, bordure, lozenge, fusil, gyron, flanches; marshalling, quartering, impaling, dimidiation; differencing; fess point, honour p., nombril p.; animal charge, lion, lion rampant, lion couchant, unicorn, griffin, cockatrice, eagle, falcon, martlet; floral charge, Tudor rose, cinquefoil, trefoil, planta genista; badge, rebus, antelope, bear and ragged staff, portcullis; national emblem, rose, thistle, leek, daffodil, shamrock, lilies, fleur-de-lis; device, national d., lion and unicorn, spread eagle, bear, hammer and sickle, triskelion; swastika, fylfot; skull and crossbones; heraldic tincture, colour, gules, azure, vert, sable, purpure, tenné, murrey; metal, or, argent; fur, ermine, ermines, erminois, pean, vair, potent; heraldic personnel, College of Arms, Earl Marshal, King of Arms, Lord Lyon K. of A.; herald, herald extraordinary, pursuivant, Bluemantle, Rouge Croix, Rouge Dragon, Portcullis.

*flag*, ensign, white e., blue e.; red ensign, Red Duster; jack, pilot j., merchant j.; flag of convenience; colours, ship's c., regimental c., King's Colour, Queen's C.; guidon, standard, vexillum, labarum, banner, gonfalon; bannerette, bannerol, banderole, oriflamme; pennon, streamer, pennant, swallowtail, triple tail; pendant, broad p., burgee; bunting; Blue Peter, yellow flag; white flag 721 *submission*; eagle, Roman e.; tricolour; Union Jack; Stars and Stripes, Old Glory, star-spangled banner; Red Flag; black flag, pirate f., Jolly Roger, skull and crossbones; parts of a flag, hoist, fly, canton; flagpole, flagstaff.

*label*, mark of identification, tattoo, caste mark (see also *identification*); ticket, bus t., raffle t., cloakroom t.; bill, docket, chit, counterfoil, stub, duplicate; tally, tessera, counter, chip; tick, letter, number, check, mark, countermark; luggage label, sticky l.,

sticker; tie-on label, tab, tag; name badge, name tape, nameplate, nameboard, signboard, fascia; number-plate, cherished n.; sign, inn s., bush, barber's pole, three balls 522 *exhibit*; plate, brass p., trade sign, trademark, logotype, logo, hallmark, cachet, rebus; earmark, brand, stigma, broad arrow; dunce's cap; seal, signet, sigil, stamp, impress, impression; letterhead, masthead, caption, heading, title, headline, superscription, rubric; imprint, colophon, watermark; bookplate, ex libris, name, name and address, personal details; card, visiting c.; birth certificate, marriage c., death c., identification papers, identity card, identification tag; tag, electronic t.; passport, pet p., animal p., pass, swipe card, PIN, PIN number 756 *permit*; endorsement, bank card, cheque card, smart card 466 *credential*; witness, signature, hand, sign manual, autograph, cipher, mark, cross, initials, monogram, paraph; fingerprint, thumbprint, footprint 548 *trace*; genetic fingerprint.

*punctuation*, punctuation mark, point, stop, full s., period; comma, colon, semicolon; inverted commas, quotation marks, quotes, air q., apostrophe; exclamation mark, question mark, interrobang, query; parentheses, brackets, square b., crotchet, crook, brace; solidus, virgule, hyphen, hyphenation; en rule, em r., dash, swung d., dot, caret, omission mark, ellipsis, blank; reference mark, asterisk, asterism, star; obelus, dagger, squiggle; hand, index; accent, grave a., acute a., circumflex a.; diaeresis, cedilla, tilde; diacritical mark, vowel point, macron, breve, umlaut; sigla, stroke, mark of abbreviation, paragraph, virgule; plus sign, minus s., multiplication s., division s., equals s., decimal point; underlining, sublineation; italics, bold type, heavy t. 587 *print-type*.

**Adj.** *indicating*, indicative, indicatory, pointing; significative, connotative, denotative; expressive, implicative, suggestive, suggesting 514 *meaningful*; figuring, typical, representative, token, symbolic, emblematic, totemistic, nominal, diagrammatic 551 *representing*; telltale, revealing, betraying, giving away 526 *disclosing*; signalizing, symptomatic 466 *evidential*; semiological, semiotic; diagnostic, symptomatological; characteristic, personal, individual 80 *special*; demonstrative, explanatory, exponential 520 *interpretive*; ominous, prophetic 511 *presageful*; gesticulatory, pantomimic; signalling, signing, thumbing etc. vb.

*heraldic*, emblematic; crested, armorial, blazoned, emblazoned etc. vb.; paly, barry; dexter, sinister; gules, azure, vert, purpure, sable, tenné, murrey, or, argent, ermine; fleury, semé, pommé; rampant, gardant, regardant, couchant, statant, sejant, passant.

*marked*, labelled etc. vb.; recognized, characterized, known by; tagged; scarred, branded, stigmatized, earmarked; patterned, sigillate; spotted 437 *mottled*; denoted, numbered, lettered; referenced, indexed, catalogued; denotable; indelible.

**Vb.** *indicate*, point 281 *point to*; point out, exhibit 522 *show*; describe heraldically, blazon; delineate, demarcate, mark out, blaze, waymark, signpost; register 548 *record*; name, give a name to, identify, classify 80 *specify*; index, make an i., reference, supply references, refer; point the way, show the w., guide 689 *direct*; signify, denote, connote, suggest, imply, involve, spell, bespeak, argue 514 *mean*; symbolize, typify, betoken, stand for, be the sign of 551 *represent*; declare 532 *affirm*; signalize, highlight 532 *emphasize*; evince, show signs of, bear the marks of, bear the stamp of, give evidence of, attest, testify, bear witness to, witness to 466 *evidence*; intimate, smack of, smell of, hints at 524 *hint*; betray, give away, reveal 526 *disclose*; inform against 524 *inform*; herald, prefigure, forebode, presage 511 *predict*.

*mark*, mark off, mark out, chalk o., flag o., lay o., demarcate, delineate, delimit 236 *limit*; label, ticket, docket, tab, tag, tag electronically, chip, microchip; keep tabs on; earmark, designate; note, annotate, put a mark on, trace upon, line, score, underline, underscore; number, letter, page, paginate, index; tick, tick off; nick, scribe 260 *notch*; chalk, chalk up; scratch, scribble, cover 586 *write*; blot, stain, blacken 649 *make unclean*; scar, disfigure 842 *make ugly*; punctuate, dot, dash, cross, cross out, obelize, asterisk; put one's mark on, leave fingerprints *or* footprints; blaze, brand, earmark, burn in; stigmatize, prick, tattoo 263 *pierce*; stamp, seal, punch, impress, emboss; imprint, overprint 587 *print*; etch 555 *engrave*; mark heraldically, emblazon, blazon; impale, dimidiate, quarter, difference; marshal, charge.

*sign*, ratify, countersign 488 *endorse*; autograph, write one's signature, write one's name, inscribe; put one's hand to, subscribe, undersign; initial, paraph; put one's mark, put one's cross.

*gesticulate*, pantomime, mime, mimic, suit the action to the word 20 *imitate*; wave one's hands, talk with one's h., saw the air; wave, wag, waggle 318 *agitate*; wave to, hold out one's hand 884 *greet*; wave one's hat, stamp 923 *applaud*; wave one's arms, gesture, motion, sign; point, point one's finger, thumb, beckon,

raise one's hand, bat one's eyelashes 455 *attract notice*; nod, beck, wink, shrug; jog, nudge, kick, poke, prod, dig in the ribs, clap on the back; look, look volumes, look daggers, glance, leer, ogle 438 *gaze*; twinkle, smile 835 *laugh*; raise one's eyebrows, wag one's finger, shake one's head, purse one's lips 924 *disapprove*; wring one's hands, tear one's hair 836 *lament*; grit one's teeth, clench one's t. 599 *be resolute*; gnash one's teeth 891 *be angry*; snap, bite 893 *be sullen*; grimace, pout, scowl, frown 829 *be discontented*; shrug one's shoulders, cock a snook, curl one's lip 922 *despise*; shuffle, scrape one's feet, paw the ground; pat, stroke 889 *caress*.

*signal*, make a s., hang out a s., send a s., exchange signals, send smoke s., speak 524 *communicate*; tap out a message, semaphore, wigwag, heliograph; flag down, thumb; wave on, wave by, wave through; unfurl the flag, break the f., fly the f., strike the f., dip the f., dip, half-mast, salute; alert, sound the alarm, send an SOS, dial 999, cry help 665 *raise the alarm*; beat the drum, sound the trumpets; fire a warning shot 664 *warn*.

**Adv.** *symbolically*, heraldically; by this token, in token of; in dumb show, in sign language, in pantomime.

**Int.** banzai!

## 548 Record

**N.** *record*, recording, documentation; historical record, memoir, chronicle, annals, history, official report 590 *narrative*; biographical record, case history, case notes, curriculum vitae 590 *biography*; photograph, portrait, sketch 551 *representation*; file, dossier, rogues' gallery; public record, gazette, official journal, Hansard; official publication, blue book, White Paper; recorded material, minutes, transactions, acta; notes, annotations, marginalia, adversaria, jottings, dottings, cuttings, press c.; memorabilia, memorandum, memo 505 *reminder*; reports, annual report, returns, tax r., statements 524 *report*; tally, scoresheet, scoreboard; evidentiary record, form, document, muniment; voucher, certificate, diploma, charter 466 *credential*; birth certificate, death c., marriage c., marriage lines 767 *title deed*; copy, spare c., carbon c., Xerox (tdmk) 22 *duplicate*; documentation, records, files, archives, papers, correspondence; record, book, roll, register, registry, cartulary; tablet, table, notebook, memo pad, minutebook, logbook, log, diary, journal, commonplace book, scrapbook, album; ledger, cashbook, chequebook 808 *account book*; catalogue, index, waiting list 87 *list*; card, index c., microcard, microfilm, microfiche 196 *miniature*; tape, computer t., disk 86 *computing*; magnetic tape, pressing 414 *record player*; inscription, legend, caption, heading 547 *indication*; wall writing, graffiti 586 *script*.

*registration*, registry, record-keeping; recording, sound r., sampling, tape r.; inscribing, engraving, epigraphy; enrolment, enlistment; booking, reservation; entering, entry, double e., book-keeping, accountancy 808 *accounts*; filing, indexing.

*monument*, memorial, war m. 505 *reminder*; mausoleum 364 *tomb*; statue, bust 551 *image*; brass, tablet, slab, stela, inscription 364 *obsequies*; hatchment, funerary achievement 547 *heraldry*; pillar, column, memorial arch, obelisk, monolith; national monument, ancient m., cromlech, dolmen, menhir, megalith 125 *antiquity*; cairn, barrow, tell 253 *earthwork*; testimonial, cup, ribbon, decoration 729 *trophy*.

*trace*, vestige, relic, remains 41 *leavings*; track, tracks, footstep, footprint, footmark, hoofmark, clawmark, pug, tread; spoor, slot; scent, smell, piste; wake, wash, trail, vapour t.; furrow, swathe, path; scuffmark, skidmark, tyremark, fingermark, thumb impression 547 *indication*; fingerprint, dabs 466 *evidence*; mark, tidemark, stain, scar, cicatrix, scratch, weal, wale, welt 845 *blemish*.

**Adj.** *recording*, logging etc. vb.; annalistic, record-making; self-recording; recordable; monumental, epigraphic, inscriptional 505 *remembering*.

*recorded*, on record, in the file, documented; filmed, taped; stored, canned, in the can, on wax; filed, indexed, entered, booked, registered; down, put d.; in writing 586 *written*; in print, in black and white 587 *printed*; traceable, vestigial, extant 41 *remaining*.

**Vb.** *record*, tape-record, telerecord, tape, videotape; store in a database, input, film 551 *photograph*; paint 551 *represent*; document, put *or* place on record; docket, file, index, catalogue, store in the archives; inscribe, cut, carve, grave, incise 555 *engrave*; take down, note down, set down in black and white, put in a book, commit to writing 586 *write*; capture on film, preserve for posterity; have printed 587 *print*; log, write down, jot d.; note, mark, make a note of; take minutes of, minute, calendar; chronicle 590 *describe*.

*register*, mark up, chalk up, tick off, cross o., tally, notch up, score; tabulate, table, enrol, enlist 87 *list*; fill in, fill up, enter, post, book 808 *account*; reserve, put on the list, put on the waiting l.; inscribe, blazon; log, diarize, journalize 505 *remember*.

**Adv.** *on record*, in the file, in the index, on the books, in the database.

## 549 Recorder

**N.** *recorder*, registrar, record-keeper, archivist, remembrancer; Master of the Rolls; protonotary 958 *notary*; amanuensis, stenographer, scribe; secretary, receptionist; writer, penpusher; clerk, babu; record clerk, tally c., filing c., bookkeeper 808 *accountant*; engraver 555 *engraving*; draughtsman 556 *artist*; photographer, cameraman 551 *photography*; sound recordist; filing cabinet, record room, muniment r., Record Office; Recording Angel.

*chronicler*, annalist, diarist, historian, historiographer, biographer, autobiographer 590 *narrator*; archaeologist 125 *antiquarian*; memorialist 763 *petitioner*; reporter, journalist, columnist, gossip-writer, newsman *or* -woman, newshound 529 *news reporter*; press photographer, paparazzo, candid camera.

*recording instrument*, recorder, tape r., videotape r., VTR, videocassette recorder, VCR, video disc, digital video d., digital versatile d., DVD; record, disc, compact d., laser d. 414 *record player*; dictaphone, telautograph, teleprinter, tape machine 531 *telecommunication*; cash register, till, checkout; turnstile; seismograph, speedometer, tachograph 465 *gauge*; flight recorder, black box; time-recorder, stopwatch 117 *timekeeper*; hygrometer 341 *hygrometry*; anemometer 340 *pneumatics*; camera, speed camera; photocopier, Xerox (tdmk); pen, pencil, Biro (tdmk) 586 *stationery*.

## 550 Obliteration

**N.** *obliteration*, wiping out etc. vb.; erasure, effacement; overprinting, defacement; deletion, blue pencil, censorship; crossing out, cancellation, cancel; annulment, cassation 752 *abrogation*; burial, oblivion 506 *amnesty*; blot, stain 649 *dirt*; tabula rasa, clean slate, clean sweep 149 *revolution*; rubber, eraser, duster, sponge; paint-stripper, abrasive 648 *cleaning utensil*.

**Adj.** *obliterated*, wiped out, effaced, erased; out of print, leaving no trace, printless, unrecorded, unregistered, unwritten; intestate.

**Vb.** *obliterate*, remove the traces, cover, cover up 525 *conceal*; overpaint, overprint, deface, make illegible; efface, eliminate, erase, scratch out, rub o.; abrade 333 *rub*; expunge, sponge out, wash o., wipe o.; blot, black out, blot o.; rub off, wipe o., wash o.; brush o., take out, cancel, delete, dele; strike out, cross o., score o., score through, censor, blue-pencil; raze 165 *demolish*; wipe off the map, bury, cover 364 *inter*; sink in oblivion 506 *forget*; submerge 311 *lower;* drown 399 *silence;* leave no trace, sink without t. 446 *disappear;* be effaced 506 *be forgotten.*

### 551 Representation

**N.** *representation,* personification, incarnation, embodiment, bodying forth; typifying, typification, figuration, symbolization 547 *indication;* conventional representation, diagram, picture-writing, hieroglyphics, runes 586 *writing;* presentment, presentation, realization, evocation 522 *manifestation;* assuming the part of, personation, impersonation; enactment, performance, doing 594 *acting;* role-playing, sociodrama, psychodrama 658 *therapy;* mimesis, mimicry, noises off, charade, mime, dumb show 20 *imitation;* depiction, characterization 590 *description;* delineation, drawing, technical d., mechanical d., free-hand d., illustration, book i., artwork, graphics, iconography 553 *painting;* creation, work of art 164 *product;* impression, likeness, identikit, Photofit (tdmk), E-fit, electronically generated picture 18 *similarity;* exact likeness, double, spitting image, lookalike, facsimile 22 *duplicate;* trace, tracing 233 *outline;* reflection (see also *image*); portraiture, portrayal; pictorial equivalent, true picture, striking likeness, speaking l., photographic l., realism 553 *picture;* bad likeness, indifferent l. 552 *misrepresentation;* reproduction, copy, Xerox (tdmk), lithograph, collotype 555 *printing;* etching 555 *engraving;* design, blueprint, draft, rough d., croquis, cartoon, sketch, outline 623 *plan;* projection, axonometric p., isometric p., isometric drawing.

*image,* very i., exact i., spitting i. 22 *duplicate;* eidetic image, clear i.; mental image, after-image 451 *idea;* projection, reflected image, hologram, silhouette, ombres chinoises 417 *reflection;* pixel; magic eye, autostereogram, stereogram; visual, visual aid 445 *spectacle;* idol, graven image 982 *idolatry;* painted image, icon; putto, cherub; statuary, statue, colossus; statuette, bust, torso, head 554 *sculpture;* effigy, figure, stick f., figurine, figure-head; gargoyle; wax figure, waxwork; dummy, tailor's d., lay figure, manikin; maquette, model, working m.; doll, china d., rag d., Sindy (tdmk) d., Barbie (tdmk), golliwog, teddy bear; marionette, fantoccini, puppet, finger p., glove p. 837 *plaything;* snowman, gingerbread man; scarecrow, tattie bogle, guy, Guy Fawkes; robot, Dalek, automaton; type, symbol.

*art,* architecture 243 *formation;* fine arts, beaux arts; graphic art 553 *painting;* plastic art 554 *sculpture;* classical art, oriental a., Byzantine a., Renaissance a., Trecento, Quattrocento, Cinquecento, Baroque, Rococo; art nouveau, Jugendstil, art deco, modern art, abstract art; correspondence art, mail a.; classicism, realism; Surrealism, Expressionism 553 *school of painting;* op art, pop a.; kitsch, camp, high c. 847 *bad taste;* aestheticism, functionalism, De Stijl, Bauhaus; functional art, commerical a.; decorative a. 844 *ornamental art;* the minor arts, illumination, calligraphy, weaving, tapestry, collage, embroidery, pottery.

*photography,* radiography, skiagraphy, scanning; time-lapse photography, aerial p., telephotography, microphotography, macrophotography; cinematography 445 *cinema;* telecine 531 *broadcasting;* photograph, photo, picture, snapshot, snap; plate, film, fast f., slow f., panchromatic f.; exposure, negative, print, contact p., enprint, sepia p., colour p., slide, diapositive, transparency, thumbnail; frame, still; reel, spool, cassette; filmstrip, microfilm, microfiche, movie, home m. 445 *film;* daguerrotype, heliotype; spectrogram, hologram; photogram, shadowgraph; skiagram, radiograph, X-ray, scan 417 *radiation;* photocopy, Xerox (tdmk) 22 *copy;* photogravure 555 *printing;* shot, take, close-up, mug shot, pan, zoom, cover shot, tracking s., dissolve, fade; lens 442 *camera;* cameraman, cinematographer, photographer, lensman, paparazzo, snapshotter; radiographer.

*map,* chart, plan, town p., outline, cartogram 86 *statistics;* sketch map, relief m., political m., survey m., Ordnance S. m., road m., star m., planisphere; Admiralty chart; ground plan, ichnography; elevation, side-e.; projection, Mercator's p., orthographic p., conic p.; atlas, world a.; globe; orrery 321 *astronomy;* mapmaking, cartography, computerized c.

**Adj.** *representing, reflecting etc. vb.; representative* 590 *descriptive;* iconic, pictorial, graphic, vivid; emblematic, symbolic, totemistic, hieroglyphic 547 *indicating;* figurative, illustrative, diagrammatic; representational, realistic, naturalistic, true-to-life; primitive, naive, impressionistic, surrealistic, surreal; abstract, nonfigurative, nonobjective, conceptual; artistic, painterly 694 *well-made;* Rembrandtesque, Turneresque, Daliesque; paintable, photogenic; photographic.

*represented,* drawn, delineated etc. vb.; fairly drawn, well represented; reflected, imaged; painted, pictured; being drawn, sitting for.

**Vb.** *represent,* stand for, denote, symbolize 514 *mean;* type, typify, incarnate, embody, body forth, personify; act the part of, assume the role of, role-play; personate, impersonate, pose as 542 *deceive;* pose, model, sit for 23 *be* *an example*; present, enact, perform, do 594 *dramatize*; project, shadow forth, adumbrate, suggest; reflect, image, hold the mirror up to nature; mimic, mime, copy 20 *imitate*; depict, characterize 590 *describe*; delineate, limn, draw, picture, portray, figure; illustrate, emblazon 553 *paint*; hit off, catch a likeness, catch, catch exactly, capture, realize, register 548 *record*; make an image, carve, cast 554 *sculpt*; cut 555 *engrave*; mould, shape 243 *form*; take the shape of, follow the s., mould upon, fashion u.; design, blue-print, draft, sketch out, rough o., chalk o., block o. 623 *plan*; diagrammatize, diagram, make a d., construct a figure, describe a circle 233 *outline*; sketch, scrawl, doodle, dash off 609 *improvise*; map, chart, survey, plot.

*photograph*, photo, take a p. *or* a picture; snapshot, snap, take a s.; take, shoot, film; X-ray, radiograph, scan; expose, develop, process, print, enlarge, blow up, reduce.

**552 Misrepresentation**
**N.** *misrepresentation*, not a true picture 19 *dissimilarity*; false light 541 *falsehood*; unfair picture, bad likeness, poor l. 914 *injustice*; travesty, parody 546 *exaggeration*; caricature, burlesque, guy 851 *ridicule*; flattering portrait 925 *flattery*; nonrealism, nonrepresentational art 551 *art*; bad art, daubing; daub, botch, scrawl; anamorphosis, deformation, distorted image, false i., distorting mirror 246 *distortion*; misinformation, disinformation 535 *misteaching*; misevaluation 521 *misinterpretation*.
**Adj.** *misrepresented*, travestied etc. vb; misrepresenting, unrepresentative, flat, cardboard.
**Vb.** *misrepresent*, misdescribe 535 *misteach*; deform 246 *distort*; give a twist *or* turn, miscolour, tone down 925 *flatter*; overdramatize 546 *exaggerate*; gild the lily, overembellish, overdraw, caricature, guy, burlesque, parody, travesty; daub, botch, splash; lie, spin 541 *be false*.

**553 Painting**
**N.** *painting*, graphic art, colouring, rubrication, illumination; daubing, finger painting; washing, colourwashing, tinting, touching up; depicting, drawing, sketching 551 *representation*; artistry, composition, rectilinear c., design, technique, draughtsmanship, brushwork; line, perspective, golden section; treatment, tone, values, atmosphere, ambience; highlight, local colour, shading, contrast; monotone, monochrome, polychrome 425 *colour*; black and white, chiaroscuro, grisaille.
*art style*, style of painting, grand style, grand manner 243 *form*; intimate style, genre

painting (see also *art subject*); pasticcio, pastiche; trompe l'oeil; iconography, portrait-painting, portraiture; scenography, scene painting, sign p., poster p., miniature p.; oil painting, watercolour, tempera, gouache; fresco painting, mural p., encaustic p., impasto, secco.

*school of painting*, the Primitives, Byzantine school, Renaissance s., Sienese s., Florentine s., Venetian s., Dutch s., Flemish s., French s., Spanish s.; Mannerism, Baroque, Rococo, Pre-Raphaelitism, Neo-Classicism, Realism, Romanticism, Impressionism, Post-Impressionism, Neo-I., Pointillism, Symbolism, Fauvism, Dada, Cubism, Expressionism, Die Brücke, Der Blaue Reiter, Vorticism, Futurism, Surrealism, Abstract Expressionism, Tachism, action painting; minimal art, Minimalism, Conceptualism; modernism 551 *art*.

*art subject*, landscape, seascape, skyscape, cloudscape; scene, prospect, diorama, panorama 438 *view*; interior, conversation piece, still life, pastoral, nocturne, nude; crucifixion, pietà, nativity.

*picture*, pictorial equivalent 551 *representation*; tableau, mosaic, tapestry; collage, montage, photomontage; frottage, brass rubbing; painting, pastiche; icon, triptych, diptych, panel; fresco, mural, wall painting, poster; canvas, daub; drawing, line d.; sketch, outline, cartoon; oil painting, oleograph, gouache, watercolour, aquarelle, pastel, wash drawing, pen-and-ink d., pencil d., charcoal d.; design, pattern, doodle; silhouette, cartoon, caricature, chad, toon, manga, hentai; miniature, vignette, thumbnail sketch, illuminated initial; old master, masterpiece; study, portrait, full-length p., half-l. p., kit-cat, head, profile, full-face portrait; studio portrait, snap, Polaroid (tdmk), pin-up 551 *photography*; rotogravure, photogravure, chromolithograph, reproduction, photographic r., halftone; aquatint, woodcut 555 *engraving*; print, plate; illustration, fashion plate, picture postcard, cigarette card, tea c., stamp, transfer, scrap, sticker; picture book, illustrated b., scrapbook, photograph album, illustrated work 589 *book*.

*art equipment*, palette, palette knife, spatula, paintbrush, paintbox, paint tube; paints, oils, oil paint, poster p., acrylic p.; watercolours, tempera, distemper, gouache, gesso, varnish 226 *facing*; ink, crayon, pastel, chalk, charcoal, heelball; pen, pencil; sketchbook 631 *paper*; canvas, easel, picture frame, mount; studio, atelier, art museum, picture gallery, art g.; model, sitter, poser, subject.
**Adj.** *painted*, daubed, scumbled, plastered

etc. vb.; graphic, pictorial, scenic, picturesque, decorative 844 *ornamental*; pastel, in paint, in oils, in watercolours, in tempera 425 *coloured*; linear, black-and-white, chiaroscuro, shaded, stippled, sfumato; grisaille 429 *grey*; painterly, paintable 551 *representing*.

**Vb.** *paint*, wash, lay *or* float a w. 425 *colour*; tint, touch up, retouch, daub; scumble, put on, paint on; lay on the colour, lay it on thick 226 *coat*; splash on the colour, slap on paint; paint a picture, do a portrait, portray, draw, sketch, limn, cartoon 551 *represent*; miniate, rubricate, illuminate; do in oils *or* watercolours *or* tempera, do in black-and-white; ink, chalk, crayon, pencil, stencil, shade, stipple; block in, rough in; pinxit, delineavit, fecit.

## 554 Sculpture

**N.** *sculpture*, plastic art 551 *representation*; modelling, figuring 243 *formation*; carving, stone cutting, wood carving; moulding, ceroplastics; paper modelling, origami; petroglyph, rock carving, bone c., shell c., scrimshaw; toreutics 844 *ornamental art*; constructivism 553 *school of painting*; construction, stabile, mobile; kinetic art; statuary; group; statue, colossus; statuette, figurine, bust, torso, head; model, maquette, cast, plaster c., death mask, waxwork 551 *image*; objet trouvé; ceramics 381 *pottery*; glyph, anaglyph, medallion, cameo, intaglio; repoussé, relief, bas-relief, mezzo-rilievo 254 *relievo*; stone, marble, Parian m.; bronze, clay, modelling c., wax, Plasticine (tdmk), papier-mâché; claymation; armature; modelling tool, chisel, burin.

**Adj.** *glyptic*, sculptured, carved; statuary, sculpturesque, statuesque, marmoreal; anaglyptic, in relief 254 *projecting*; plastic, ceroplastic; toreutic, glyphic.

**Vb.** *sculpt*, sculpture, sculp, block out, rough-hew 243 *form*; cut, carve, whittle, chisel, chip, scrimshaw; chase, engrave, emboss; model, mould, cast; sculpsit.

## 555 Engraving. Printing

**N.** *engraving*, etching, line engraving, plate e., steel e., copper e., chalcography; photogravure, photoengraving; zincography, cerography, glyptography, gem cutting, gem engraving; glass engraving; mezzotint, aquatint; wood engraving, xylography, lignography, woodcut; linoprinting, linocut; scraperboard; silverpoint; drypoint; steel plate, copper p.; stone, block, wood-b.; chisel, graver, burin, burr, needle, dry-point, etching-p., style.

*printing*, type-p., typography 587 *print*; laser printing; plate printing, copper-plate p.,

intaglio p.; lithography, photolithography, photogravure, chromolithography, colour printing; fabric printing, batik; silk-screen printing, serigraphy, stevengraph; stereotype, autotype, heliotype, collotype; stamping, impression; die, punch, stamp.

**Vb.** *engrave*, grave, incise, cut, undercut; etch, stipple, scrape; bite, bite in, eat in; sandblast; impress, stamp; lithograph 587 *print*; mezzotint, aquatint; incisit, sculpsit, imprimit.

## 556 Artist

**N.** *artist*, craftsman *or* -woman 686 *artisan*; architect 164 *producer*; art-master *or* mistress, designer, graphic d., draughtsman *or* -woman; fashion artist, dress-designer, couturier; drawer, sketcher, delineator, limner; copyist; caricaturist, cartoonist; illustrator, commercial artist; painter, colourist, luminist; dauber, amateur, Sunday painter; pavement artist, scene-painter, sign-p.; oil-painter, watercolourist, pastellist; illuminator, miniaturist; portrait painter, landscape p., marine p., genre p., still-life p.; Academician, RA, old master, modern m.; naive painter, primitive; Pre-Raphaelite, Impressionist, Fauve, Dadaist, Cubist, Vorticist, Surrealist, action painter, Minimalist 553 *school of painting*; art historian, iconographer; aesthetician.

*sculptor*, sculptress, carver, wood c., statuary, monumental mason, modeller, wax m., moulder, figurist; image-maker, idol-m.; whittler.

*engraver*, etcher, aquatinter; lapidary, chaser, gem-engraver, enameller, enamellist; typographer, type-cutter 587 *printer*.

## 557 Language

**N.** *language*, tongue, speech, idiom, parlance, talk, dialect; langue, parole, competence, performance; spoken language, living l.; patter, lingo 560 *dialect*; personal language, idiolect; mother tongue, native t.; vernacular, common speech, demotic s., vulgar tongue; colloquial speech, informal English, English as she is spoke (inf) 579 *speech*; Queen's English; correct speech, idiomatic s., slang, jargon, vulgarism; Estuary English; lingua franca, koine, creole, Gullah, Krio, Swahili; pidgin, pidgin English, bêche-de-mer *or* Beach-la-Mar, Chinook Jargon, Hiri Motu, Tok Pisin; sign language, semiology 547 *gesture*; diplomatic language, international l., International Scientific Vocabulary, Basic English; pasigraphy; artificial language, Esperanto, Ido, Interlingua, Novial, Volapük; official language, Mandarin, Hindi; Received Pronunciation, Standard English, BBC English; officialese, translatorese 560 *neology*; machine language 86 *computing*; learned language, dead l., Anglo-Saxon, Etruscan, Gothic, Greek, Latin, Pictish, Sanskrit; metalanguage; confusion of tongues, polyglot medley, Babel, babble 61 *confusion*.

*language type*, inflected language, analytic l., agglutinative l., polysynthetic l., monosyllabic l., tone l., tonal l.; language group, family of languages, Aryan, Indo-European, Indo-Germanic; Anatolian, Baltic, Celtic, Germanic, Indo-Iranian, Italic, Romance, Slavic *or* Slavonic, Tocharian; Altaic, Turanian, Uralic, Ural-Altaic, Finno-Ugric; Afro-Asiatic, Hamito-Semitic; Sino-Tibetan; Dravidian; Niger-Congo, Bantu; Nilo-Saharan; Khoisan; Austro-Asiatic, Austronesian, Indo-Pacific; Palaeosiberian.

*linguistics*, language study, linguistic science, descriptive linguistics, general l., synchronic l., theoretical l.; structuralism, transformational-generative grammar, stratificational g., systemic g.; dialectology, philology, comparative p.; comparative linguistics, comparative grammar, syntax 564 *grammar*; phonetics, phonology 577 *pronunciation*; historical linguistics, diachronic linguistics, Grassmann's law, Grimm's l., Verner's l., Wackernagel's l.; glottochronology; applied linguistics; clinical l., neurolinguistics, psycholinguistics; lexicography, lexicology 559 *etymology*; morphology; semasiology, semantics 514 *meaning*; onomasiology, onomastics 561 *nomenclature*; sociolinguistics; palaeography 125 *palaeology*; linguistic distribution, linguistic geography, isogloss, speech community; computational linguistics, mathematical linguistics.

*linguistic ability*, bilingualism, multilingualism, polyglottism; genius of a language, feel of a l., sprachgefühl, sense of idiom.

*literature*, written language, creative writing, belles lettres 589 *reading matter*; letters, polite l., classics, arts, humanities, literae humaniores 654 *civilization*; Muses, literary circles, republic of letters, PEN 589 *author*; literary genre, fiction, metafiction, faction, non-fiction 590 *narrative, description*; lyricism, poetry 593 *poem*; plays 594 *drama*; criticism 480 *estimate*; literary criticism 520 *interpretation*; literary style, l. convention 519 *metaphor*; literary movement, Classicism, Neoclassicism, Sturm und Drang, Romanticism, Symbolism, Idealism, Expressionism, Surrealism, Realism, Naturalism, structuralism, post-structuralism; deconstruction; literary history, history of literature; Golden Age, Silver A., Augustan A., Classical A. 110 *era*; compendium of literature 592 *anthology*; digest, chrestomathy, reader 589 *textbook*.

*linguist*, linguistician, language student, student of language, philologist; etymologist, lexicographer, lexicologist 559 *etymology*; onomasiologist, semanticist; grammarian, morphologist, syntactician 564 *grammar*; phonetician, phonologist 398 *acoustics*; dialectologist; clinical linguist, psycholinguist, neurolinguist; student of literature, man *or* woman of letters, belletrist 492 *scholar*; classical scholar, oriental s. 125 *antiquarian*; Anglicist *or* Anglist, Arabist, Germanist, Hebraist, Hellenist, Hispanicist *or* Hispanist, Indo-Europeanist, Latinist, Romanicist, Sanskritist, Sinologist, Slavist *or* Slavicist; polyglot, multilingual; diglot, bilingual.

**Adj.** *linguistic*, lingual, philological, etymological, grammatical, morphological; diachronic, synchronic; lexicographical, lexicological, onomasiological, semasiological, semantic; analytic; agglutinative; monosyllabic; tonal, inflected; holophrastic; correct, pure; written, literary, standard; spoken, living, idiomatic; vulgar, colloquial, vernacular, slangy, jargonistic 560 *dialectal*; local, enchorial, familial; current, common, demotic; bilingual, diglot; multilingual, polyglot.

*literary*, written, polished, polite, humanistic, belletristic; classical, romantic, naturalistic, surrealistic, futuristic, decadent; lettered, learned; formal; critical 520 *interpretive*.

## 558 Letter

**N.** *letter*, part of the alphabet; sign, symbol, character, written c. 586 *writing*; alphabet, ABC, abecedary, criss-cross row; initial teaching alphabet, i.t.a., International Phonetic Alphabet, IPA; syllabic alphabet, syllabary; phonogram 398 *speech sound*; Chinese character, ideogram, ideograph; pictogram, cuneiform, hieroglyph 586 *lettering*; ogham alphabet, runic a., futhorc; Greek alphabet, Roman a., Cyrillic a., Hebrew a., Arabic a.; Pinyin; Devanagari; runic letter, rune, wen; lettering, black letter, Gothic, italic; ampersand; big letter, capital l., cap, majuscule; small letter, minuscule; block letter, uncial; cursive; printed letter, letter-press, type, bold t. 587 *print-type*.

*initials*, first letter; monogram, cipher; anagram, acrostic, acronym.

*spoken letter*, phone, phoneme; consonant, vowel, syllable 577 *voice*; guttural, liquid, spirant, sonant 398 *speech sound*; polyphone; digraph.

*spelling*, misspelling; spell-check, spelling check; orthography, cacography; phonography, lexigraphy; anagrammatism;

spelling game, spelling bee; transliteration 520 *translation*.

**Adj.** *literal*, in letters, lettered; alphabetic, abecedarian; in syllables, syllabic; Cyrillic; runic, oghamic; cuneiform, hieroglyphic 586 *written*; Gothic, italic, roman, uncial; large, majuscule, capital, initial; small, minuscule; lexigraphical, spelt, orthographic; ciphered, monogrammatic; anacrostic, anagrammatic; phonetic, consonantal, vocalic, voiced 577 *vocal*.

**Vb.** *spell*, spell out, read, syllable, syllabify; alphabetize; transliterate; letter, form letters 586 *write*; initial 547 *sign*; anagrammatize.

**Adv.** *alphabetically*, by letters; literatim, letter-for-letter; syllabically, in syllables.

## 559 Word

**N.** *word*, term, vocable 561 *name*; expression, locution 563 *phrase*; synonym, tautonym 13 *identity*; homonym, homograph, homophone 13 *identity*; palindrome, pun, weasel word 518 *equivocalness*; antonym 14 *contrariety*; etymon, root, false r., back-formation; folk etymology; derivation, derivative, paronym, doublet; syllable, phoneme, allophone, phone 398 *speech sound*; sememe, semanteme 514 *meaning*; morphological unit, morpheme, morph, allomorph, formative, root, stem, inflexion, affix, prefix, suffix, infix; part of speech 564 *grammar*; diminutive, pejorative, intensive; enclitic, proclitic, contraction, abbreviation, acronym, portmanteau word 569 *conciseness*; cliché, catchword, vogue word, buzz w., trigger w., nonce w., new w., neologism, loan w. 560 *neology*; rhyming word, assonant 18 *similarity*; four-letter word 573 *plainness*; swearword, oath 899 *malediction*; hard word, jawbreaker, long word, polysyllable; short word, monosyllable, word of one syllable; many words, verbiage, wordiness, verbal diarrhoea, loquacity, verbosity, bafflegab 570 *pleonasm*; Verbum, Logos 965 *the Deity*.

*dictionary*, rhyming d., reverse word d., monolingual d., learners' d., school d., illustrated d., bilingual d., multilingual d., polyglot d.; lexicon, wordbook, wordstock, word list, glossary, vocabulary; gradus, thesaurus, wordhoard 632 *store*; compilation, concordance, index.

*etymology*, derivation of words, philology 557 *linguistics*; folk etymology; morphology; semasiology 514 *meaning*; phonology, orthoepy 577 *pronunciation*; onomasiology, terminology 561 *nomenclature*; lexicology, lexicography; logophile, philologist, etymologist, lexicologist, lexicographer, compiler.

**Adj.** *verbal*, literal; titular, nominal; etymo-

logical, lexical, vocabular; philological, lexicographical, glossarial; derivative, conjugate, cognate, paronymous; synonymous, autonymous 514 *semantic*; wordy, verbose 570 *pleonastic*.

**Adv.** *verbally*, lexically; verbatim, word for word.

## 560 Neology

**N.** *neology*, neologism, neoterism 126 *newness*; coinage, new word, nonce w., vogue w., buzz w., catch phrase, cliché; imported word, borrowing, loan word, loan translation, calque 559 *word*; unfamiliar word, jawbreaker, newfangled expression, slang e.; technical language, technical term, jargon, legalese, psychobabble, technospeak; barbarism, caconym, hybrid, hybrid expression; corruption, monkish Latin, dog L.; novelese, reporterese, journalese, officialese, telegraphese; baby talk; bafflegab, gobbledygook, newspeak, doubletalk 518 *equivocalness*; affected language, archaism, Wardour Street English 850 *affectation*; abuse of language, abuse of terms, malapropism 565 *solecism*; wordplay, spoonerism 839 *witticism*; idioglossia, idiolalia 580 *speech defect*.

*dialect*, idiom, lingo, patois, vernacular 557 *language*; idiolect, burr, brogue, accent 577 *pronunciation*; cockney, mockney, rockny, Geordie, Scots, broad Scots, Doric, Lallans; broken English, pidgin E., pidgin; lingua franca, hybrid language; Briticism, Strine, Franglais; Anglicism, Americanism, Hibernicism, Irishism, Scotticism, Gallicism, Teutonism; provincialism, localism, vernacularism; iotacism 580 *speech defect*; word-coiner, neologist; dialectology 557 *linguistics*.

*slang*, vulgarism, colloquialism; jargon, psychobabble, technospeak, technobabble, argot, cant, patter; gipsy lingo, Romany; thieves' Latin, pedlar's French, St Giles Greek, rhyming slang, back slang, pig Latin; backchat, Billingsgate 899 *scurrility*; gibberish, gobbledygook 515 *empty talk*.

**Adj.** *neological*, neoteric, newfangled, newly coined, not in the dictionary; barbaric, barbarous, unidiomatic, hybrid, corrupt, pidgin; loaned, borrowed, imported, foreign, revived, archaic, obsolete; irregular, solecistic 565 *ungrammatical*.

*dialectal*, vernacular; Doric, Cockney, broad; guttural, nasal, burred; provincial, local; homely, colloquial; unliterary, nonstandard, slangy, argotic, canting, cant; jargonistic, journalistic; technical, special.

**Vb.** *neologize*, coin words, invent vocabulary, use a nonce word; talk slang, jargonize, cant; talk cockney, speak with an accent, burr 577 *voice*.

## 561 Nomenclature

**N.** *nomenclature*, naming etc. vb.; eponymy; onomastics, onomatology, terminology, orismology; description, designation, appellation, denomination; antonomasia 519 *trope*; addressing, apostrophe, roll-call 583 *allocution*; christening, naming ceremony, baptism 988 *Christian rite*; study of place names, toponymy.

*name*, nomen, first name, forename, Christian name, praenomen; middle name(s), surname, family name, patronymic, matronymic, cognomen; maiden name, married n.; appellation, moniker; nickname, pet name, diminutive, byname, sobriquet, agnomen; epithet, description; handle, style 870 *title*; heading, caption 547 *indication*; designation, appellative; name and address, signature 547 *label*; domain name; term, cant t., special t., technical t., trade name 560 *neology*; namechild, same name, namesake, synonym, eponym, tautonym; pen name, pseudonym 562 *misnomer*; noun, proper n. 564 *part of speech*; list of names; place name, local n.

*nomenclator*, terminologist; namer, namegiver, eponym, christener, baptizer; roll-caller, announcer.

**Adj.** *named*, called etc. vb.; titled, entitled, christened; known as, alias, under the name of; so-called, soi-disant, self-styled; hight, yclept; nominal, titular; binominal; named after, eponymous; fitly named, what one may fairly call; namable.

*naming*, denominative, appellative, terminological, orismological, onomastic.

**Vb.** *name*, call, give a name, christen, baptize 988 *perform ritual*; give one's name to; give a handle to, call by the name of, surname, nickname, dub, clepe; address, give one his title, sir, bemadam; title, entitle, style, term 80 *specify*; distinguish 463 *discriminate*; define, characterize 547 *mark*; call by name, call the roll, call out the names, announce; blacklist 924 *reprobate*.

*be named*, own *or* bear *or* go by the name of; rejoice in the name of, answer to; sail under the flag of.

**Adv.** *by name*; namely; terminologically.

## 562 Misnomer

**N.** *misnomer*, misnaming, miscalling; malapropism 565 *solecism*; wrong name, false n., alias, assumed title; nom de guerre, nom de plume, pen name; stage name, pseudonym, allonym; nickname, pet name 561 *name*; pseudonymity.

*no name*, anonymity; anon, anonym, certain person, so-and-so, what's his name, what's his face; Richard Roe, Jane Doe, N or M, sir or madam; Miss X, Monsieur un Tel, A. N. Other; what d'you call it, thingummy, thingummyjig, thingamabob, whatsit, oojakapivvy; this or that; and co., etc.; some, any, what-have-you.

**Adj.** *misnamed*, miscalled, mistitled etc. vb.; self-christened, self-styled, soi-disant, would-be, so-called, quasi, pseudonymous.

*anonymous*, unknown, faceless, nameless, without a name; incognito, innominate, unnamed, unsigned; a certain, certain, such; some, any, this or that.

**Vb.** *misname*, mistake the name of, miscall, misterm, mistitle; nickname, dub 561 *name*; misname oneself, assume an alias, go under a false name; conceal one's name, be anonymous; write under an assumed name, usurp the name of, pass oneself off as 541 *dissemble*.

## 563 Phrase

**N.** *phrase*, form of words; subject and predicate; clause, sentence, period, paragraph; collocation, frozen c,, expression, locution; idiom, mannerism 80 *speciality*; fixed expression, formula, verbalism, façon de parler; set phrase, set terms; euphemism, metaphor 519 *trope*; catch phrase, slogan; hackneyed expression, well-worn phrase, cliché, commonplace 610 *habit*; saying, proverb, motto, moral, epigram, adage 496 *maxim*; lapidary phrase, epitaph 364 *obsequies*; inscription, legend, caption 548 *record*; phrases, empty p., words, empty w., compliments 515 *empty talk*; terminology 561 *nomenclature*; surface structure, deep s.; phraseology, phrasing, diction, wording, choice of words, choice of expression, turn of e., turn of phrase; well-turned phrase, rounded p. 575 *elegance*; roundabout phrase, periphrasis, circumlocution 570 *diffuseness*; paraphrase 520 *translation*; written phrase, phraseogram 586 *script*; phrasemonger, phrasemaker, epigraphist, epigrammatist, proverbialist 575 *stylist*.

**Adj.** *phraseological*, sentential, periodic, in phrases, in sentences; idiomatic; well-rounded, well-couched.

**Vb.** *phrase*, word, verbalize, voice, articulate, syllable; reword, rephrase 520 *translate*; express, formulate, put in words, clothe in w., find words for, state 532 *affirm*; sloganize, talk in clichés; put words together, turn a sentence, round a period 566 *show style*.

**Adv.** *in terms*, in good set t., in round t.; in a phrase.

## 564 Grammar

**N.** *grammar*, comparative g., philology 557 *linguistics*; grammatical studies, analysis, parsing, construing; paradigm; accidence, inflection *or* inflexion, declension, case, nominative, vocative, accusative, genitive, dative, ablative, locative, instrumental, ergative; conjugation; mood, indicative, imperative, infinitive, optative, subjunctive; voice, active, passive, middle; tense, present, future, past, perfect, imperfect, past perfect, pluperfect; number, singular, plural, dual; gender, masculine, feminine, neuter, agreement, concord; accentuation, pointing 547 *punctuation*; umlaut, ablaut, attraction, assimilation, dissimilation 559 *etymology*; syntax, word order, hypotaxis, parataxis, asyndeton, ellipsis, apposition; bad grammar 565 *solecism*; good grammar, grammaticalness, correct style, Standard English, Queen's E., good E.

*part of speech*, substantive, noun, common n., proper n., collective n., abstract n., concrete n., count n., mass n.; pronoun, demonstrative p., indefinite p., interrogative p., personal p., reflexive p., relative p.; adjective; verb, intransitive v., transitive v., reflexive v., deponent v., auxiliary v., modal v.; adverb, sentence a., preposition, conjunction, interjection; article, definite a., indefinite a., determiner; particle, affix, infix, prefix, suffix; inflection, declension, case-ending, conjugation, verb-ending; subject, object, direct o., indirect o.; predicate, copula, complement; formative, morpheme, sememe, semanteme; diminutive, intensive, augmentative.

**Adj.** *grammatical*, correct; syntactic, inflectional; heteroclite, irregular, anomalous; masculine, feminine, neuter; singular, dual, plural; substantival, adjectival, attributive, predicative; verbal, adverbial; participial; prepositional; denominative, deverbative; conjunctive, copulative; positive, comparative, superlative.

**Vb.** *parse*, analyse, inflect, conjugate, decline; punctuate; construe 520 *interpret*.

## 565 Solecism

**N.** *solecism*, bad grammar, incorrectness, misusage; faulty syntax, anacoluthon; antiphrasis 574 *ornament*; catachresis, cacology; irregularity 560 *dialect*; impropriety, barbarism 560 *neology*; malapropism, bull, slip, Freudian s., slip of the pen, lapsus calami, slip of the tongue, lapsus linguae 495 *mistake*; mispronunciation, dropping one's aitches 580 *speech defect*; misspelling, cacography; verbicide.

**Adj.** *ungrammatical*, solecistic; irregular, abnormal; faulty, improper, incongruous; misapplied, catachrestic.

**Vb.** *be ungrammatical*, violate grammar, commit a solecism; break Priscian's head, murder the Queen's English; mispronounce 580 *stammer*; drop one's aitches; misspell 495 *blunder*.

## 566 Style

**N.** *style*, fashion, mode, tone, manner, vein, strain, idiom; one's own style, personal s., idiosyncrasy, mannerism 80 *speciality*; mode of expression, diction, parlance, phrasing, phraseology 563 *phrase*; choice of words, idiolect, vocabulary, choice v.; literary style, command of language *or* idiom, raciness, power 571 *vigour*; feeling for words, sprachgefühl, sense of language; literary charm, grace 575 *elegance*; word magic, word power, word-spinning 579 *oratory*; weak style 572 *feebleness*; severe style, vernacular s. 573 *plainness*; elaborate style 574 *ornament*; clumsy style 576 *inelegance*.

**Adj.** *stylistic*, mannered, literary; elegant, ornate, rhetorical; expressive, eloquent, fluent; racy, idiomatic; plain, perspicuous, forceful.

**Vb.** *show style*, care for words, spin w.; style, express, measure one's words, choose one's words carefully 563 *phrase*.

## 567 Perspicuity

**N.** *perspicuity*, perspicuousness, clearness, clarity, lucidity, limpidity 422 *transparency*; limpid style, lucid prose 516 *intelligibility*; directness 573 *plainness*; definition, definiteness, exactness 494 *accuracy*.

**Adj.** *perspicuous*, lucid, limpid 422 *transparent*; clear, unambiguous 516 *intelligible*; explicit, clear-cut 80 *definite*; exact 494 *accurate*; uninvolved, direct 573 *plain*.

## 568 Imperspicuity: lack of clairty

**N.** *imperspicuity*, unclarity, lack of clarity, obscurity, obfuscation 517 *unintelligibility*; cloudiness, fogginess 423 *opacity*; abstraction, abstruseness; complexity, involved style 574 *ornament*; purple prose, hard words, Johnsonese 700 *difficulty*; imprecision, impreciseness, vagueness 474 *uncertainty*; inaccuracy 495 *inexactness*; ambiguity 518 *equivocalness*; mysteriousness, oracular style 530 *enigma*; profundity 211 *depth*; overcompression, ellipsis 569 *conciseness*; cloud of words, verbiage 570 *diffuseness*.

**Adj.** *unclear*, imperspicuous, not transparent, muddied, clear as mud, cloudy 423 *opaque*; cloudy, obscure 418 *dark*; oracular, mysterious, enigmatic 517 *unintelligible*; abstruse, profound 211 *deep*; allusive, indirect 523 *latent*;

vague, imprecise, indefinite 474 *uncertain*; ambiguous 518 *equivocal*; muddled, confused, tortuous, convoluted, involved 61 *complex*; harsh, crabbed, stiff 576 *inelegant*; hard, full of long words, Johnsonian 700 *difficult*.

### 569 Conciseness

**N.** *conciseness*, concision, succinctness, brevity, soul of wit; pithiness, pithy saying 496 *maxim*; aphorism, epigram, clerihew 839 *witticism*; economy of words, no words wasted, few words, terseness, words of one syllable, laconism, laconicism; compression, telegraphese; overconciseness, brachylogy; ellipsis, syncope, abbreviation, contraction 204 *shortening*; compendiousness, epitome, précis, outline, brief sketch 592 *compendium*; monostich, haiku; compactness, portmanteau word; clipped speech, monosyllabism 582 *taciturnity*; nutshell, the long and the short of it 204 *shortness*.

**Adj.** *concise*, brief, not long in telling, short and sweet 204 *short*; laconic, monosyllabic, sparing of words 582 *taciturn*; irreducible, succinct; crisp, brisk, to the point; trenchant, mordant, incisive; terse, curt, brusque 885 *ungracious*; compendious, condensed, tight-knit, compact; pithy, pregnant, sententious, neat, exact, pointed, aphoristic, epigrammatic; Taciturn; elliptic, telegraphic, contracted, compressed; summary, cut short, abbreviated, truncated.

**Vb.** *be concise*, – brief etc. adj.; need few words, not beat about the bush, pull no punches, come straight to the point, cut the cackle, cut a long story short, get down to brass tacks, talk turkey; telescope, compress, condense, contract, abridge, abbreviate, truncate 204 *shorten*; outline, sketch; summarize, sum up, resume 592 *abstract*; allow no words, be short with, be curt with, cut short, cut off; be sparing with words, waste no w., clip one's w. 582 *be taciturn*; express pithily, epigrammatize 839 *be witty*.

**Adv.** *concisely*, pithily, summarily, briefly; without wasting words, in brief, in short, in fine, in a word, in a nutshell; to put it succinctly, to cut a long story short; to sum up.

### 570 Diffuseness

**N.** *diffuseness*, verboseness etc. adj.; profuseness, copiousness, amplitude; amplification, dilation 197 *expansion*; expatiation, circumstantiality, minuteness, blow-by-blow account; fertility, output, productivity 171 *productiveness*; inspiration, vein, flow, outpouring; abundance, superabundance, overflowing words, exuberance, redundancy 637 *redundance*; richness, rich vocabulary, wealth of terms,

verbosity, wordiness, verbiage, flatulence; fluency, nonstop talking, verbal diarrhoea 581 *loquacity*; long-windedness, prolixity, epic length; repetitiveness, reiteration 106 *repetition*; twice-told tale 838 *tedium*; gush, rigmarole, waffle, blah 515 *empty talk*; effusion, tirade, harangue, sermon, speeches 579 *oration*; descant, disquisition 591 *dissertation*.

*pleonasm*, superfluity, redundancy 637 *redundance*; battology, tautology; circumlocution, roundabout phrases, periphrasis; ambages, beating about the bush 518 *equivocalness*; padding, expletive, filler 40 *extra*; episode, excursus, digression 10 *irrelevance*.

**Adj.** *diffuse*, verbose, nonstop, in love with one's own voice 581 *loquacious*; profuse, copious, ample, rich; fertile, abundant, superabundant, voluminous, scribacious 171 *prolific*; inspired, flowing, fluent; exuberant, overflowing 637 *redundant*; expatiating, circumstantial, detailed, minute; gushing, effusive; flatulent, windy, frothy; turgid, bombastic 574 *rhetorical*; polysyllabic, sesquipedalian, magniloquent 574 *ornate*.

*prolix*, of many words, long-winded, wordy, prosy, prosing; spun out, made to last, long-drawn-out 113 *protracted*; boring 838 *tedious*; lengthy, epic, never-ending, going on and on 203 *long*; spreading, diffusive, discursive, excursive, digressing, episodic; rambling, maundering, wandering 282 *deviating*; loose-knit, incoherent 61 *orderless*; desultory, waffling, pointless 10 *irrelevant*; indirect, circumlocutory, periphrastic, ambagious, roundabout.

*pleonastic*, redundant, excessive 637 *superfluous*; repetitious, repetitional, repetitive 106 *repeated*; tautologous, tautological; padded, padded out.

**Vb.** *be diffuse*, – prolix etc. adj.; dilate, expatiate, amplify, particularize, detail, go into detail, expand, enlarge upon; descant, discourse at length; repeat, tautologize 106 *repeat oneself*; pad, pad out, draw o., spin o., protract 203 *lengthen*; gush, be effusive, pour out 350 *flow*; let oneself go, rant, rant and rave, harangue, perorate 579 *orate*; use long words, have swallowed the dictionary; launch out on, spin a long yarn 838 *be tedious*; blether on, rabbit on, go on and on 581 *be loquacious*; wander, waffle, digress 282 *deviate*; ramble, maunder, drivel, yarn, never end; beat about the bush, not come to the point 518 *be equivocal*.

**Adv.** *diffusely*, in extenso, at great length, on and on, ad nauseam.

### 571 Vigour

**N.** *vigour* 174 *vigorousness*; power, strength, vitality, drive, force, forcefulness, oomph, go, get-up-and-go 160 *energy*; incisiveness, trenchancy, decision; vim, punch, pep, guts, smeddum; sparkle, verve, élan, panache, vivacity, liveliness, vividness, gusto, pizzazz, raciness; spirit, fire, ardour, glow, warmth, fervour, vehemence, enthusiasm, passion 818 *feeling*; bite, piquancy, poignancy, sharpness, mordancy 388 *pungency*; strong language, stress, underlining, emphasis 532 *affirmation*; iteration, reiteration, tautology 106 *repetition*; seriousness, solemnity, gravity, weight; impressiveness, loftiness, elevation, sublimity, grandeur, grandiloquence, declamation 574 *rhetoric*; rhetoric 579 *eloquence*.

**Adj.** *forceful*, powerful, strenuous 162 *strong*; energetic, peppy, zingy, punchy 174 *vigorous*; racy, idiomatic; bold, in-your-face (inf), dashing, spirited, sparkling, vivacious 819 *lively*; warm, glowing, fiery, ardent, enthusiastic, impassioned 818 *fervent*; vehement, emphatic, insistent, reiterative, positive 532 *affirmative*; slashing, cutting, incisive, trenchant 256 *sharp*; pointed, pungent, mordant, salty, pithy 839 *witty*; grave, sententious, strongly-worded, pulling no punches 834 *serious*; heavy, meaty, solid; weighty, forcible, cogent 740 *compelling*; vivid, graphic, effective 551 *representing*; flowing, inspired 579 *eloquent*; high-toned, lofty, grand, sublime 821 *impressive*.

**Adv.** *forcefully*, vigorously, energetically, strenuously, vehemently, with conviction; in glowing terms.

## 572 Feebleness

**N.** *feebleness* 163 *weakness*; weak style, enervated s.; prosiness, frigidity, ineffectiveness, flatness, staleness, vapidity 387 *insipidity*; jejuneness, poverty, thinness; enervation, flaccidity, lack of force, lack of sparkle, lack of conviction; lack of style, baldness 573 *plainness*; anticlimax.

**Adj.** *feeble*, weak, thin, flat, vapid, insipid 387 *tasteless*; wishy-washy, watery, wersh; cutesy, sloppy, sentimental, schmaltzy, novelettish; meagre, jejune, exhausted, spent; wan, colourless, bald 573 *plain*; languid, flaccid, nerveless, emasculated, tame, conventional; undramatic, unspirited, uninspired, unelevated, unimpassioned, unemphatic; ineffective, cold, frigid, prosaic, uninspiring, unexciting; monotonous, prosy, pedestrian, dull, dry, boring 838 *tedious*; cliché-ridden, hackneyed, platitudinous, stale, pretentious, flatulent, overambitious; forced, overemphatic, forcible-feeble; inane, empty, pointless; juvenile, childish; careless, slovenly, slipshod; limping, lame, unconvincing 477 *poorly*

*reasoned*; limp, loose, lax, inexact, disconnected, disjointed, garbled, rambling, vapouring 570 *prolix*; poor, trashy 847 *vulgar*.

## 573 Plainness

**N.** *plainness*, naturalness, simplicity, unadorned s. 699 *artlessness*; austerity, severity, baldness, spareness, bareness, starkness; matter-of-factness, plain prose 593 *prose*; plain words, plain English 516 *intelligibility*; home truths 540 *veracity*; homespun, household words; rustic flavour, vernacular, kaleyard school; common speech, vulgar parlance; idiom, natural i.; unaffectedness 874 *modesty*; bluntness, frankness, speaking straight from the shoulder, mincing no words, coarseness, four-letter word, Anglo-Saxon monosyllable.

**Adj.** *plain*, simple 699 *artless*; austere, severe, disciplined; bald, spare, stark, bare, bog-standard, no-frills, vanilla, without bells and whistles, unfussy, minimalist; neat 648 *clean*; pure, unadulterated 44 *unmixed*; unadorned, uncoloured, unpainted, unvarnished, unembellished 540 *veracious*; unemphatic, undramatic, unsensational, played down, understated; unassuming, unpretentious 874 *modest*; uninflated, chaste, restrained; unaffected, honest, natural, straightforward; homely, homey, homespun, vernacular; prosaic, sober 834 *serious*; dry, stodgy 838 *tedious*; humdrum, workaday, everyday, commonplace 610 *usual*; unimaginative, uninspired, unpoetical 593 *prosaic*.

**Vb.** *speak plainly*, call a spade a spade, use plain English 516 *be intelligible*; discipline one's style, moderate one's vocabulary; say outright, tell it like it is, spell it out, tell one straight *or* to his *or* her face; not mince words, speak straight from the shoulder, not beat about the bush, come to the point, come down to brass tacks, talk turkey.

**Adv.** *plainly*, simply 516 *intelligibly*; prosaically, in prose; in the vernacular, in plain words, in common parlance; directly, point-blank; not to put too fine a point upon it, in words of one syllable.

## 574 Ornament

**N.** *ornament*, embellishment, colour, decoration, embroidery, frills, flourish 844 *ornamentation*; floridness, floweriness, flowers of speech, arabesques 563 *phrase*; gongorism, euphuism; preciosity, preciousness, euphemism; rhetoric, flourish of r., purple patch *or* passage, dithyramb; figurativeness, figure of speech 519 *trope*; alliteration, assonance; paralipsis, aposiopesis; antiphrasis, catachresis; palillogy, anaphora, epistrophe;

anadiplosis; inversion, anastrophe, hyperbaton, chiasmus; zeugma; metaphor, simile, antithesis.

*rhetoric*, high tone, magniloquence 579 *eloquence*; grandiloquence, declamation, rhetoric, orotundity 571 *vigour*; overstatement, extravagance, hyperbole 546 *exaggeration*; turgidity, turgescence, flatulence, inflation; pretentiousness, affectation, pomposity 875 *ostentation*; talking big 877 *boasting*; highfalutin, highsounding words, bombast, rant, fustian, rodomontade 515 *empty talk*; Johnsonese, long words, sesquipedalian w. 570 *diffuseness*.

*phrasemonger*, fine writer, word-spinner, euphuist 575 *stylist*; rhetorician, orator 579 *speaker*.

**Adj.** *ornate*, aureate, beautified 844 *ornamented*; rich, luxuriant, florid, flowery; precious, euphuistic, euphemistic; pretentious 850 *affected*; meretricious, flashy, flamboyant, frothy 875 *showy*; brassy, sonorous, clanging 400 *loud*; tropical, alliterative 519 *figurative*; overloaded, stiff, stilted; pedantic, longworded, Latinate, sesquipedalian, Johnsonian.

*rhetorical*, declamatory, oratorical 579 *eloquent*; resonant, sonorous, ringing 400 *loud*; ranting, mouthy, orotund; high-pitched, highflown, high-flying, highfalutin; grandiose, stately; bombastic, pompous, fustian, Ossianic; grandiloquent, magniloquent; inflated, tumid, turgid, swollen, dithyrambic; antithetical, alliterative, metaphorical 519 *figurative*.

**Vb.** *ornament*, beautify, grace, adorn, enrich, gild 844 *decorate*; charge, overlay, overload; elaborate, load with ornament; euphuize, euphemize; smell of the lamp, overelaborate, gild the lily.

## 575 Elegance

**N.** *elegance*, style, perfect s.; grace, gracefulness 841 *beauty*; refinement, taste 846 *good taste*; propriety, restraint, distinction, dignity; clarity 567 *perspicuity*; purity, simplicity; naturalness 573 *plainness*; classicism, Atticism; harmony, euphony, concinnity, balance, proportion 245 *symmetry*; rhythm, ease, flow, fluidity, smoothness, fluency, readiness, felicity, the right word in the right place, the mot juste; neatness, polish, finish; well-turned period, rounded p., well-turned phrase; elaboration, flourish, artificiality 574 *ornament*.

*stylist*, stylish writer 574 *phrasemonger*; classical author, classic, purist.

**Adj.** *elegant*, majestic, stately 841 *beautiful*; graced, graceful; stylish, polite, refined 846 *tasteful*; uncommon, distinguished, dignified; chaste 950 *pure*; good, correct, idiomatic; sensitive, expressive, clear 567 *perspicuous*; simple,

natural, unaffected 573 *plain*; unlaboured, ready, easy, smooth, flowing, fluid, fluent, tripping, rhythmic, mellifluous, euphonious; harmonious, balanced, well-proportioned 245 *symmetrical*; concinnous, neat, felicitous, happy, right, neatly put, well-turned 694 *well-made*; artistic, wrought, elaborate, artificial; polished, finished, soigné, manicured; restrained, controlled; flawless 646 *perfect*; classic, classical, Attic, Ciceronian, Augustan.

**Vb.** *be elegant*, show taste 846 *have taste*; have a good style, write well, have a light touch; elaborate, polish, refine 646 *perfect*; grace one's style, turn a period, point an antithesis 566 *show style*.

## 576 Inelegance

**N.** *inelegance*, inconcinnity; clumsiness, awkwardness, roughness, uncouthness 699 *artlessness*; coarseness, lack of finish, lack of polish, lack of finesse 647 *imperfection*; harshness, cacophony 411 *discord*; lack of flow, stiffness, stiltedness 326 *hardness*; unwieldiness, cumbrousness, sesquipedality; impropriety; barbarism; incorrectness, bad grammar 565 *solecism*; mispronunciation 580 *speech defect*; vulgarism, vulgarity 847 *bad taste*; mannerism, unnaturalness, artificiality 850 *affectation*; exhibitionism 875 *ostentation*; meretriciousness 542 *sham*; lack of style; anti-chic; lack of restraint, excess 637 *superfluity*; turgidity, pomposity 574 *rhetoric*.

**Adj.** *inelegant*, ungraceful, graceless 842 *ugly*; faulty, incorrect; crabbed, tortuous 568 *unclear*; long-winded 570 *diffuse*; unfinished, unpolished, unrefined, unclassical 647 *imperfect*; bald 573 *plain*; coarse, crude, rude, doggerel, uncouth, barbarous 699 *artless*; impolite, tasteless 847 *vulgar*; unchaste, impure, meretricious; unrestrained, immoderate, excessive; turgid, pompous 574 *rhetorical*; forced, laboured, artificial, unnatural, mannered 850 *affected*; ludicrous, grotesque, bathetic 849 *ridiculous*; offensive, repulsive, jarring, grating 861 *disliked*; heavy, ponderous, insensitive; rough, harsh, uneasy, abrupt; halting, cramped, unready, unfluent; clumsy, awkward, gauche; wooden, stiff, stilted 875 *formal*.

## 577 Voice

**N.** *voice*, vocal sound 398 *sound*; speaking voice 579 *speech*; singing voice, musical v., fine v. 412 *vocal music*; powerful voice, vociferation, lung power 400 *loudness*; tongue, vocal organs, vocal cords; lungs, bellows; larynx, voice box; syrinx; vocalization, phoneme, vowel, broad v., pure v., diphthong, triphthong, open vowel, closed v., semivowel, voiced consonant, syllable 398 *speech sound*; articulation, clear a., distinctness; utterance, enunciation, delivery, articulation, attack; articulate sound 408 *cry*; exclamation, ejaculation, gasp; mutter, whisper, stage w., aside 401 *faintness*; tone of voice, accents, timbre, pitch, tone, intonation, modulation.

*pronunciation*, articulation, elocution, enunciation, inflection, accentuation, stress, emphasis; ictus, arsis, thesis; accent, tonic a.; pure accent, correct a., received pronunciation, RP, 557 *native accent*, broad a., foreign a.; burr, brogue, drawl, twang 560 *dialect*; trill; aspiration, rough breathing, glottal stop; nasality 407 *stridor*; lisping, stammer 580 *speech defect*; mispronunciation 565 *solecism*.

**Adj.** *vocal*, voiced, oral, aloud, out loud; vocalic, vowel-like, sonant 398 *sounding*; phonetic, enunciative; articulate, distinct, clear; well-spoken, well-sung, in good voice 410 *melodious*; pronounced, uttered, spoken, articulated, dictated, read out, read aloud, recited; aspirated 407 *hoarse*; accented, tonal, accentual, accentuated; guttural 407 *hoarse*; shrill 407 *strident*; wheezy 406 *sibilant*.

**Vb.** *voice*, pronounce, syllable, verbalize, put into words 579 *speak*; mouth, give tongue, give voice, express, utter, enunciate, articulate; vocalize; inflect, modulate; breathe, aspirate, sound one's aitches; trill, roll, burr, roll one's r's; accent, stress 532 *emphasize*; raise the voice, lower the v., whisper, stage-w., make an aside, speak sotto voce; exclaim, ejaculate, rap out 408 *cry*; drone, intone, chant, warble, carol, hum 413 *sing*; bellow, shout, roar, vociferate, use one's voice 400 *be loud*; mispronounce, lisp, drawl, swallow one's consonants, speak thickly 580 *stammer*.

## 578 Voicelessness

**N.** *voicelessness*, aphonia, no voice, loss of v.; difficulty in speaking, dysphonia, inarticulation; thick speech, hoarseness, huskiness, raucousness; muteness 399 *silence*; dumbness, mutism, deaf-m.; harsh voice, unmusical v., tuneless v. 407 *stridor*; childish treble, falsetto; changing voice, breaking v., cracked v.; sob, sobbing; undertone, aside, low voice, small v., muffled tones, whisper, bated breath 401 *faintness*; surd, unvoiced consonant; voiceless speech, sign language, deaf and dumb language 547 *gesture*; meaningful look; mute, deaf-mute.

**Adj.** *voiceless*, aphonic, dysphonic; unvoiced, surd; breathed, whispered, muffled, low-voiced, inaudible 401 *muted*; mute, dumb, deaf and dumb; incapable of utterance, speechless, tongueless, wordless, at a loss for words;

inarticulate, unvocal, tongue-tied; silent, not speaking, mum, mumchance, shtum 582 *taciturn*; silenced, gagged; dry, hollow, sepulchral, breaking, cracked, croaking, hoarse as a raven 407 *hoarse*; breathless, out of breath.

**Vb.** *be mute*, keep mum 582 *be taciturn*; be silent, keep quiet, hold one's tongue 525 *keep secret*; bridle one's tongue, check oneself, dry up, shut up, ring off, hang up; lose one's voice, be struck dumb, lose one's tongue, lose the power of speech; talk with one's hands, make sign language, exchange meaningful glances 547 *gesticulate*; have difficulty in speaking 580 *stammer*.

*make mute*, strike dumb, dumbfound, take one's breath away, rob one of words; stick in one's throat, choke on; muffle, hush, deaden 401 *mute*; shout down, make one inaudible, drown one's voice; muzzle, gag, stifle 165 *suppress*; stop one's mouth, cut out one's tongue; reduce one to silence, shut one up, cut one short, hang up on; still, hush, put to silence, put to sleep 399 *silence*.

*speak low*, speak softly, whisper, stage-w., speak sotto voce 401 *sound faint*; whisper in one's ear 524 *hint*; lower one's voice, drop one's v., speak in hushed tones.

**Adv.** *voicelessly*, in hushed tones, in a whisper, with bated breath; in an undertone, sotto voce, under one's breath, in an aside.

## 579 Speech

**N.** *speech*, faculty of s., gift of s., organ of s., tongue, lips 577 *voice*; parlance 557 *language*; oral communication, word of mouth, personal account 524 *report*; spoken word, accents, tones 559 *word*; verbal intercourse, discourse, colloquy, conversation, talk, chat, rap, palaver, prattle, chinwag 584 *interlocution*; address, apostrophe 583 *allocution*; ready speech, fluency, talkativeness, volubility 581 *loquacity*; prolixity, effusion 570 *diffuseness*; cultivated speech, elocution, voice production; mode of speech, articulation, utterance, delivery, enunciation 577 *pronunciation*; ventriloquism; speech without words, sign language, eye l., meaningful glance *or* look 547 *gesture*; thing said, speech, dictum, utterance, remark, observation, comment, interjection 532 *affirmation*; fine words 515 *empty talk*; spiel, patter 542 *trickery*.

*oration*, speech, effusion; one's say, one's piece, a word in edgeways; public speech, formal s., prepared s., discourse, disquisition, address, talk; salutatory, welcoming address 876 *celebration*; panegyric, eulogy; valedictory, farewell address, funeral oration 364 *obsequies*; after-dinner speech, toast, vote of thanks;

broadcast, commentary 534 *lecture*; recitation, recital, reading; set speech, declamation, display of oratory (see also *eloquence*); pulpit eloquence, sermon, preachment, homily, exhortation; platform eloquence, harangue, ranting, tubthumping, rodomontade, earful, mouthful; hostile eloquence, tirade, diatribe, philippic, invective; monologue 585 *soliloquy*; written speech, dictation, paper, screed 591 *dissertation*; proem, preamble, prologue, foreword, narration, account, digression, peroration.

*oratory*, art of speaking, rhetoric, public speaking, stump oratory, tub-thumping; speech-making, speechifying, speechification; declamation, rhetoric, elocution, vapouring, ranting, rant; vituperation, invective; soapbox 539 *rostrum*; Hyde Park Corner.

*eloquence*, eloquent tongue, gift of the gab, fluency, articulacy; blarney 925 *flattery*; glossolalia 821 *excitation*; command of words, way with w., word-spinning, word power 566 *style*; power of speech, power 571 *vigour*; grandiloquence, orotundity, sublimity 574 *rhetoric*; elocution, good delivery, impressive diction, rolling periods, burst of eloquence, torrent of words, peroration, purple passage.

*speaker*, sayer, utterer; talker, spieler, prattler, gossiper 581 *chatterer*; conversationalist, deipnosophist 584 *interlocutor*; speechifier, speechmaker, speech-writer, rhetorician, elocutionist; orator, Public O., oratress, oratrix, public speaker, after-dinner s., toastmaster *or* -mistress; improviser, adlibber; declaimer, ranter, soap-box orator, tub-thumper, haranguer, demagogue 738 *agitator*; word-spinner, spellbinder; lecturer, dissertator; pulpiteer, Boanerges 537 *preacher*; presenter, announcer 531 *broadcaster*; prologue, narrator, chorus 594 *actor*; mouthpiece, spokesman *or* -woman *or* -person 754 *delegate*; advocate, pleader, mediator 231 *intermediary*; patter merchant, salesman *or* -woman *or* -person, rep 793 *seller*; Demosthenes, Cicero; monologist, soliloquizer 585 *soliloquist*.

**Adj.** *speaking*, talking; able to speak, with a tongue in one's head, vocal; anglophone, francophone, bilingual, polyglot; articulate, fluent, outspoken, free-speaking, talkative 581 *loquacious*; oral 577 *vocal*; well-spoken, soft-s., loud-s.; audible, spoken, verbal; plummy, fruity 404 *resonant*; elocutionary.

*eloquent*, spellbinding, silver-tongued, trumpet-t. 925 *flattering*; elocutionary, oratorical 574 *rhetorical*; grandiloquent, declamatory 571 *forceful*; tub-thumping, fire-and-brimstone, ranting, word-spinning; rousing 821 *exciting*.

**Vb.** *speak*, mention, say; utter, articulate 577 *voice*; pronounce, declare 532 *affirm*; let out, blurt out, come clean, tell all 526 *divulge*; whisper, breathe 524 *hint*; confabulate, talk, put in a word 584 *converse*; emit, give utterance, deliver oneself of; break silence, open one's mouth *or* lips, find one's tongue; pipe up, speak up, raise one's voice; wag one's tongue, give t., rattle on, gossip, prattle, chatter, rap 581 *be loquacious*; patter, give a spiel, jabber, gabble; sound off, speak one's mind, tell a thing or two, have one's say, talk one's fill, expatiate 570 *be diffuse*; trot out, reel off, recite; read, read aloud, read out, dictate; speak a language, speak in tongues; have a tongue in one's head, speak for oneself; talk with one's hands, use sign language 547 *gesticulate*.

*orate*, make speeches, speechify; declaim, deliver a speech; hold forth, spout, be on one's legs; take the floor *or* the stand, rise to speak; preach, preachify, sermonize, harangue; lecture, address 534 *teach*; invoke, apostrophize 583 *speak to*; perorate, mouth, rant, rail, sound off, tub-thump; speak like an angel, spellbind, hold enthralled, be eloquent, have the gift of the gab, have kissed the Blarney Stone, blarney 925 *flatter*; talk to oneself, monologize 585 *soliloquize*; speak off the top of one's head, ad-lib 609 *improvise*.

## 580 Speech defect

**N.** *speech defect*, aphasia, loss of speech, aphonia 578 *voicelessness*; paraphasia, paralalia; idioglossia, idiolalia; stammering, stammer, stutter, lallation, lisp; sigmatism 406 *sibilation*; dysphonia, speech impediment, hesitation, drawl, slur; indistinctness, inarticulateness, thick speech, cleft palate; burr, brogue 560 *dialect*; accent, twang, nasal t. 577 *pronunciation*; affectation, plum in one's mouth, marble in one's m., Oxford accent, haw-haw 246 *distortion*; speech therapy.

**Adj.** *stammering*, stuttering etc. vb.; nasal, adenoidal; indistinct, thick, inarticulate; tongue-tied, aphasic; breathless 578 *voiceless*.

**Vb.** *stammer*, stutter, trip over one's tongue; drawl, hesitate, falter, quaver, hem and ha, hum and haw; um and ah, mumble, mutter; lisp; lallate; snuffle, snort, sputter, splutter, sibilate; nasalize, speak through the nose, drone; clip one's words, swallow one's w., gabble, slur; blubber, sob; mispronounce 565 *be ungrammatical*.

## 581 Loquacity

**N.** *loquacity*, loquaciousness, garrulity, talkativeness, communicativeness, yak, yackety-yack; volubility, runaway tongue, flow of words, fluency, cacoethes loquendi 570 *diffuseness*; verbosity, wordiness, prolixity; running on, spate of words, logorrhoea, verbal diarrhoea, inexhaustible vocabulary; patter, spiel, gab, gift of the g., bafflegab 579 *eloquence*; garrulous old age, anecdotage 505 *remembrance*.

*chatter*, chattering, gossiping, gabble, jabber, rap, palaver, jaw-jaw (sl), talkee-talkee, yackety-yack (sl); clack, quack, cackle, babble, prattle; small talk, gossip, idle g., tittle-tattle; waffle, blether, gush, guff (sl), gas (sl), hot air 515 *empty talk*.

*chatterer*, nonstop talker, rapid speaker; chinwag, rattle, chatterbox; gossip, blabber, tattler, tittle-tattler, tattletale 529 *news reporter*; magpie, parrot, jay; talker, gabber, driveller, haverer, ranter, quacker, blatherskite; preacher, sermonizer; proser, windbag, gas-bag (sl), gasser; conversationalist 584 *interlocutor*; the chattering classes.

**Adj.** *loquacious*, talkative, garrulous, tongue-wagging, gossiping, tattling, tittle-tattling, yakking (sl), communicative, rapping, chatty, gossipy, newsy 524 *informative*; gabbing (sl), babbling, gabbling, gabby (sl), gassy (sl), windy (sl), prosing, verbose, long-winded 570 *prolix*; nonstop, voluble, going on and on, running on, running at the mouth (sl), fluent, glib, ready, effusive, gushing; conversational 584 *conversing*.

**Vb.** *be loquacious*, – talkative etc. adj.; have a long tongue, chatter, rattle, go on and on, run on, bang on (sl), reel off, talk nineteen to the dozen; gossip, tattle 584 *converse*; clack, quack, gabble, jabber 515 *mean nothing*; talk, jaw (sl), yak (sl), go yackety-yack (sl), gab (sl), prate, prose, gas (sl), waffle, haver, blether, twitter, ramble on, rabbit on, witter on (inf); drone, maunder, wander, drivel; launch out, launch into speech, start talking, give tongue, shoot; be glib, oil one's tongue; have one's say, talk at length; expatiate, effuse, gush, spout 570 *be diffuse*; outtalk, talk down; talk out, filibuster, stonewall 113 *spin out*; talk oneself hoarse, talk one's head off, talk the hind leg off a donkey; talk shop, bore 838 *be tedious*; engage in conversation, buttonhole; monopolize the conversation, hold the floor, not let one get a word in edgeways, never stop talking.

**Adv.** *loquaciously*, fluently, glibly etc. adj.

**Int.** blah blah!, patati patata!, rhubarb rhubarb!, yak yak!

## 582 Taciturnity

**N.** *taciturnity*, silent habit 399 *silence*; incommunicativeness, reserve, reticence, guarded utterance 525 *secrecy*; few words, shortness, brusqueness, curtness, gruffness 885 *rudeness*; muteness 578 *voicelessness*; economy of words, laconism 569 *conciseness*; no speaker, no orator; no talker, not a gossip, person of few words; clam, oyster, statue; Trappist.

**Adj.** *taciturn*, mute, mum, shtum 399 *silent*; sparing of words, saying little, monosyllabic, short, curt, laconic, brusque, grunting, gruff 569 *concise*; not talking, vowed to silence; incommunicative; withdrawn, reserved, keeping oneself to oneself, guarded, with sealed lips 525 *reticent*; close, close-mouthed, tight-lipped; not to be drawn, keeping one's counsel, discreet 858 *cautious*; inarticulate, tongue-tied 578 *voiceless*; not hearing 416 *deaf*.

**Vb.** *be taciturn*, – laconic etc. adj.; spare one's words, use few w. 569 *be concise*; not talk, say nothing, have little to say; observe silence, make no answer; not be drawn, refuse comment, neither confirm nor deny; keep one's counsel 525 *keep secret*; hold one's peace, hold one's tongue, put a bridle on one's t., keep one's mouth *or* one's trap shut; fall silent, relapse into silence, pipe down, dry up, run out of words 145 *cease*; be speechless, lose one's tongue 578 *be mute*; waste no words on, save one's breath to cool one's porridge; not mention, leave out, pass over, omit 458 *disregard*.

**Int.** hush!, sh!, shut up!, mum's the word!, no comment!, verb. sap.!, a word to the wise!

## 583 Allocution

**N.** *allocution*, apostrophe; address, lecture, talk, speech, pep talk, sermon 579 *oration*; greeting, salutation, hail; invocation, appeal, interjection, interpellation; buttonholing, word in the ear, aside; hearers, audience 415 *listener*.

**Adj.** *vocative*, salutatory, invocatory.

**Vb.** *speak to*, speak at; address, talk to, lecture to; turn to, direct one's words at, apostrophize; appeal to, pray to, invoke; sir, bemadam; approach, accost; hail, call to; salute, say good morning 884 *greet*; pass the time of day, parley with 584 *converse*; take aside, buttonhole.

## 584 Interlocution

**N.** *interlocution*, parley, colloquy, converse, conversation, causerie, talk, chat, rap, cybertalk; dialogue, question and answer; exchange, repartee, banter, badinage; slanging match 709 *quarrel*; confabulation, confab, verbal intercourse, social i. 882 *sociality*; commerce, communion, intercommunion, communication, intercommunication 524 *information*; duologue, tête-à-tête.

*chat*, causerie, chinwag, natter; chitchat,

talk, small t., table t., idle t., rap, rapping prattle, prittle-prattle, gossip 529 *rumour*, tattle, tittle-tattle, tongue-wagging 581 *chatter*; fireside chat, cosy chat, tête-à-tête, heart-to-heart.

*conference*, colloquy, conversations, talks, pourparler, parley, pow-wow, palaver; discussion, debate, forum, focus group, quality circle, symposium, seminar, teach-in, talk-in; talkfest, gabfest; controversy, polemics, logomachy 475 *argument*; exchange of views, talks across the table, high-level talks, summit meeting, summit conference, summit; negotiations, bargaining, proximity talks, treaty-making 765 *treaty*; conclave, convention, meeting, gathering 74 *assembly*; working lunch; reception, conversazione, party 882 *social gathering*; audience, interview, audition 415 *listening*; consultation, putting heads together, huddle, council, war c., family c., round-table conference 691 *advice*.

*interlocutor*, collocutor, colloquist, dialogist, symposiast; examiner, interviewer, cross-examiner, interpellator 459 *enquirer*; answerer 460 *respondent*; partner, confabulator, conversationalist, talker 581 *chatterer*; gossip, tattler, informant 529 *news reporter*.

**Adj.** *conversing*, interlocutory, confabulatory; dialogistic, dialogic; conversable, conversational; chatty, gossipy 581 *loquacious*; newsy, communicative 524 *informative*; discussing, conferring, in conference, conferential; in committee; consultatory, consultative, advisory 691 *advising*.

**Vb.** *converse*, colloquize, parley, talk together (see also *confer*); confabulate, pass the time of day, exchange pleasantries; lead one on, draw one out; buttonhole, engage in conversation, carry on a c., join in a c., butt in, put in a word, bandy words, exchange w., question, answer; shine in conversation 839 *be witty*; chat, have a chat *or* a natter *or* a good talk; have a cosy chat, be drawn out 579 *speak*; buzz, natter, chinwag, chew the fat, rap, gossip, tattle 581 *be loquacious*; commune with, talk privately, get confidential with, be closeted with; whisper together, talk tête-à-tête, go into a huddle, indulge in pillow talk.

*confer*, talk it over, take counsel, sit in council *or* in conclave, sit in committee, hold a council of war, pow-wow, palaver; canvass, discuss, debate 475 *argue*; parley, negotiate, hold talks, hold a summit, get round the table; consult with 691 *consult*.

**585 Soliloquy**

**N.** *soliloquy*, monologue, monody; interior monologue, stream of consciousness; apos-trophe; aside; one-man *or* one-woman show, onehander.

*soliloquist*, soliloquizer, monologist, monodist.

**Adj.** *soliloquizing*, thinking aloud, talking to oneself; monological.

**Vb.** *soliloquize*, talk to oneself, say to oneself, say aside, make an aside, think aloud; apostrophize, pray aloud; talk to the four walls, talk to the wall, address an empty house, have an audience of one.

**586 Writing**

**N.** *writing*, creative w., creative prose, composition, literary c., authorship, journalism, itch to write, cacoethes scribendi 590 *description*; literary output 557 *literature*; script, copy, writings, works, books 589 *reading matter*; inkslinging, quill-driving, pen-pushing, hackwork, Grub Street; paperwork 548 *record*; copying, transcribing, transcription, rewriting, editing, overwriting; autography, holography; ways of writing, handwriting, chirography, stylography, cerography; micrography; longhand, longhand reporting; shorthand writing, shorthand, stenography, tachygraphy, lexigraphy, speedwriting, phonography, stenotypy; phonogram, phraseogram; logograph, logogram, stereotype; typewriting, typing 587 *print*; braille; secret writing, cipher, code, mirror writing, invisible ink 530 *secret*; picture writing, ideography, hieroglyphics; signwriting, skywriting 528 *advertisement*; inscribing, carving, cutting, graving, epigraphy 555 *engraving*; boustrophedon; study of handwriting, graphology.

*lettering*, formation of letters, stroke, stroke of the pen, up-stroke, down-s., pothook; line, dot, point; flourish, curlicue, squiggle, scroll 251 *convolution*; handwriting, hand, fist; calligraphy, penmanship; fair hand, law h.; cursive hand, flowing h., round h.; script, italic, copperplate; printing, block letters; clumsy hand, cacography, illegible writing, scribble, scrawl, hen tracks 517 *unintelligibility*; letters, characters, alphabet 558 *letter*; runes, pictogram, ideogram; hieroglyph; cuneiform, arrowhead; Linear A, Linear B, Rosetta stone; palaeography.

*script*, written matter, inscribed page, illuminated address; specimen, calligraph; writing, screed, scrawl, scribble; manuscript, MS, palimpsest, codex 589 *book*; original, one's own hand, autograph, holograph; signature, sign-manual 547 *indication*; copy, transcript, transcription, fair copy 22 *duplicate*; typescript, stencil; newsprint; printed matter 587 *letterpress*; letter, epistle, rescript, written reply 588 *correspondence*; inscription, epigraph, graffito 548 *record*; superscription, caption, heading; illuminated letters, letters of gold.

*stationery*, writing materials, pen and paper, pen and ink; stylus, reed, quill, pen, quill-p., fountain p., cartridge p., felt-tip p., ballpoint p., Biro (tdmk); nib, steel n.; stylograph, stylo; pencil, propelling p., lead p., coloured p.; crayon, chalk; papyrus, parchment, vellum; foolscap 631 *paper*; writing paper, notepaper, wove paper, laid p., scented p., recycled p; lined p., blank p., notebook, pad, jotter; slate, blackboard; inkstand, inkwell; pencil sharpener, penknife; blotting paper, blotter; typewriter, ribbon, daisy wheel; stencil.

*calligrapher*, calligraphist, penman *or* -woman; cacographer, scribbler, scrawler; writer, pen-pusher, scrivener, scribe, clerk 549 *recorder*; copyist, transcriber; sign-writer 528 *publicizer*; epigraphist, inscriber; subscriber, signer, initialler, signatory; creative writer, script w. 589 *author*; letter writer 588 *correspondent*; graphologist, handwriting expert 484 *detector*.

*stenographer*, shorthand writer, typist, shorthand t., stenotypist, audiotypist, secretary.

**Adj.** *written*, inscribed, inscriptional, epigraphic; in black and white 548 *recorded*; in writing, in longhand, in shorthand; logographic, stenographic; handwritten, manuscript, autograph, holograph; signed, countersigned, under one's hand; penned, pencilled, scrawled, scribbled etc. vb.; cursive, copybook, copperplate; italic, calligraphic; demotic, hieratic; ideographic, hieroglyphic, cuneiform; lettered, alphabetic; runic, Gothic, uncial, roman, italic 558 *literal*; perpendicular, upright, sloping, bold, spidery.

**Vb.** *write*, be literate; form characters, trace c., engrave, inscribe; letter, block, print; flourish, scroll; write well, write a clear hand; write badly, write illegibly, write like a hen scratching, scribble, scrawl, blot, erase, interline, overwrite; put in writing, confirm in writing, set down, set down in black and white, commit to paper, write down, jot d., scribble down, note 548 *record*; transcribe, copy, copy out, make a fair copy, rewrite, write out, engross; take down, take dictation, take down in shorthand, stenotype, typewrite, type, type out, key; take down longhand, write in full; throw on paper, draft, formulate, redact; compose, concoct, indite; pen, pencil, dash off; write letters 588 *correspond*; write one's name 547 *sign*; take up the pen, take pen in hand, put pen to paper, spill ink, cover

reams; be an author, write books 590 *describe*, 591 *dissertate*; write poetry 593 *poetize*.

**587 Print**
**N.** *print*, printing, laser p., typing, typewriting 586 *writing*; typography, printing from type, block printing, plate p., offset process, web offset; lithography, litho, photolithography, photolitho 555 *printing*; photocopying 551 *photography*; photocomposition, phototypesetting, computer typesetting, cold type; composition, cold c., hot c., typesetting, hand-setting, make-up; monotype, linotype, stereotype, electrotype; plate, shell; make-ready, printing off, running off.

*letterpress*, linage, printed matter, print, impression, presswork; pressrun; printout, run-off; copy, pull, proof, galley p., bromide, page proof, revise; colophon, imprint 589 *edition*; dummy, trial copy, proof c.; offprint.

*print-type*, type, stereotype, plate; flong, matrix; broken type, pie; upper case, lower c., capitals, small c., caps; fount, face, typeface, boldface, bold, clarendon, lightface, old face, bastard type; roman, italic, Gothic, black letter 558 *letter*; body, bevel, shoulder, shank, beard, ascender, descender, serif, sanserif; lead, rule, en, em; space, hairspace, quad; type bar, slug, logotype.

*type size*, point s., type measure, type scale; brilliant, diamond, pearl, ruby, nonpareil, minion, brevier, bourgeois, elite, long primer, small pica, pica, great primer.

*press*, printing p., printing works, printers; typefoundry; composing machine, c. room, press r., machining r.; handpress, flatbed, platen press, rotary press, Linotype (tdmk), Monotype (tdmk), offset press; galley, chase, forme, quoin, composing stick; roller, brayer, web.

*printer*, book p., jobbing p., typographer, compositor, typesetter, phototypesetter, computer typesetter; typefounder, printer's devil, pressman, printer's reader, proof r.

**Adj.** *printed*, in print 528 *published*; coldtype, hot-metal; set, composed, machined etc. vb.; in type, in italic, in bold, in roman; typographic; leaded, spaced, justified; solid, tight, crowded.

**Vb.** *print*, stamp; typeset, key, compose, photocompose; align, register, justify; set up in type, make ready, impose, machine, run off, pull off, print off; collate, foliate; lithograph, litho, offset, stereotype; get ready for the press, send to p., put to bed; see through the press, proofread, correct; have printed, bring out 528 *publish*.

## 588 Correspondence

**N.** *correspondence*, stream of c., barrage of c., exchange of letters, backlog of correspondence; communication 524 *information*; mailshot, mailing list, distribution l.; letters, mail, post, postbag 531 *postal communications*; letter, epistle, missive, dispatch, bulletin; love letter, billet doux, greetings card, Christmas c., Easter c., birthday c., Valentine 889 *endearment*; postcard, picture p., pc, card, letter c., notelet; air letter, aerogramme, air mail, sea m.; business letter, bill, account, enclosure; open letter 528 *publicity*; unsolicited mail, junk m., circular, round robin, chain letter, begging l.; note, line, chit; answer, acknowledgment; envelope, cover, stamp, seal; postcode.

*correspondent*, letter writer, penfriend, penpal, poison pen; recipient, addressee; foreign correspondent, contributor 529 *news reporter*; contact 524 *informant*.

**Adj.** *epistolary*, postal, by post; under cover of, enclosed.

**Vb.** *correspond*, correspond with, exchange letters, maintain *or* keep up a correspondence, keep in touch with 524 *communicate*; use the post, write to, send a letter to, drop a line; compose dispatches, report 524 *inform*; deal with one's correspondence, catch up on one's c., acknowledge, reply, write back, reply by return 460 *answer*; circularize 528 *publish*; write again, bombard with letters; post off, forward, mail, airmail; stamp, seal, frank, address.

**Adv.** *by letter*, by mail, by express m., by air m., through the post; in correspondence, in touch, in contact.

## 589 Book

**N.** *book*, title, volume, tome, roll, scroll, document; codex, manuscript, MS, palimpsest; script, typescript, unpublished work; published work, publication, bestseller, potboiler, blockbuster; unsold book, sleeper, remainder; work, standard w., classic, definitive work, collected works; major work, monumental w., magnum opus; opuscule, slim volume, chapbook, booklet, bouquin; illustrated work, picture book, coffee-table b. 553 *picture*; magazine, periodical, rag 528 *journal*; brochure, pamphlet, leaflet 528 *the press*; bound book, cased book, hardback, softback, limpback, paperback (see also *edition*); electronic book, e-book.

*reading matter*, printed word, written w. 586 *writing*; forms, papers, bumf, 548 *record*; circular, junk mail; script, copy; text, the words, libretto, lyrics, scenario, screenplay, book of words; proof, revise, pull 587 *letterpress*; writings, prose literature 593 *prose*; poetical literature 593 *poetry*; classical literature, serious l.,

light l. 557 *literature*; books for children, children's books, juveniles; history, biography, travel 590 *description*; work of fiction 590 *novel*; biographical work, memoirs, memorabilia 590 *biography*; addresses, speeches 579 *oration*; essay, tract, treatise 591 *dissertation*; piece, occasional pieces 591 *article*; miscellanea, marginalia, jottings, thoughts, pensées; poetical works 593 *poem*; selections, flowers 592 *anthology*; dedicatory volume, Festschrift; early works, juvenilia; posthumous works, literary remains; complete works, oeuvre, corpus; newspaper, magazine 528 *journal*; issue, number, back n.; fascicle, part, instalment, serial, sequel, prequel.

*textbook*, school book, reader 539 *classroom*; abecedary, hornbook; primer, grammar, gradus; text, annotated t., prescribed t., set t., required reading; selection 592 *anthology*; standard text, handbook, manual, enchiridion; pocket book (see also *reference book*).

*reference book*, work of reference, encyclopaedia, cyclopaedia 490 *erudition*; lexicon, thesaurus 559 *dictionary*; biographical dictionary, dictionary of quotations, rhyming dictionary, dictionary of reverse words, specialist dictionary, technical d., gazetteer, yearbook, annual 87 *directory*; calendar 117 *chronology*; guide 524 *guidebook*; notebook, diary, album 548 *record*; bibliography, publisher's catalogue, reading list.

*edition*, impression, issue, run; series, set, collection, library; bound edition, library e., de luxe e., school e., trade e., popular e., standard e., definitive e., omnibus e., complete e., collected e., complete works; incunabula, editio princeps, first edition, new e., revised e.; reissue, reprint, réchauffé, rehash, scissors-and-paste job; illustrated edition, special e., limited e., expurgated e.; critical e., annotated e., variorum e.; adaptation, abridgment 592 *compendium*; octodecimo, sextodecimo, duodecimo, octavo, quarto, folio; book production, layout, format; house style; front matter, prelims, preface, prefatory note; dedication, invocation, acknowledgments; title, bastard t., half-t.; flyleaf, title page, endpaper, colophon 547 *label*; table of contents, table of illustrations; errata, corrigenda, addenda; back matter, appendix, supplement, index, thumb i., bibliography; caption, heading, headline, running h., footnote; guide word, catchword; margin, head m., foot m., gutter; folio, page, leaf, recto, verso; sheet, forme, signature, gathering, quire; chapter, division, part, section; paragraph, clause, passage, excerpt, inset; plate, print, illustration, halftone, line drawing 553 *picture*.

*bookbinding*, binding, spiral b., perfect b., stitching, casing, rebinding, stripping; case, slip c., cover, jacket, dust j. 226 *wrapping*; boards, paper b., millboard 631 *paper*; cloth, limp c., linen, scrim, buckram, leather, pigskin, calf, morocco, vellum, parchment; spine, headband; tooling, blind t., gold t., gilding, marbling; bindery, bookbinder.

*library*, book collection; national library, public l., branch l., local l., reference l., mobile l., lending l., circulating l., book club; bookshelf, bookcase, bookrack, bookends; bookstall, bookshop, booksellers.

*bookperson*, man *or* woman of letters, littérateur, literary person, bluestocking; reader, bookworm 492 *scholar*; bibliophile, book lover, book collector, bibliomaniac; bibliographer; librarianship, librarian, chief l., library assistant; bookselling, bibliopole, stationer, bookseller, antiquarian b., book dealer, secondhand d., bouquinist; publisher, printer 528 *publicizer*; editor, redactor; reviewing, book reviewer, critic, reviewer 480 *estimator*.

*author*, authoress, writer, creative w., word-painter, wordsmith; literary person, man *or* woman of letters; fiction-writer, novelist, crime writer, historian, biographer 590 *narrator*; essayist, editorialist 591 *dissertator*; prose writer; verse writer 593 *poet*; playwright, librettist, script writer 594 *dramatist*; freelance; copywriter 528 *publicizer*; pressman *or* -woman, journalist 529 *news reporter*; editor, editor-in-chief, assistant editor, subeditor, copy editor, contributor, correspondent, special c., war c., sports c., columnist, paragraphist, gossip writer, diarist; agony aunt; astrologist; scribbler, penpusher, hack, Grub Street h., penny-a-liner, inkslinger, potboiler; ghost, ghost writer; reviser, translator, adapter.

**Adj.** *bibliographical*, in book form; bound, half-b., quarter-b., case-b., leather-b., cloth-b., buckram-b., hardback, paperback, limp, soft-cover; loose-leaf; tooled, marbled, gilt; bibliophilic, bookloving, antiquarian; in print, out of print.

## 590 Description

**N.** *description*, account, full a., detailed a.; statement, exposé, statement of facts, summary 524 *report*; brief, abstract, inscription, caption, subtitle, supertitle, surtitle, legend 592 *compendium*; narration, relation, rehearsal, recital, version (see also *narrative*); reportage, nonfiction, documentary account, actuality TV, reality TV; specification, characterization, details, particulars 87 *list*; portrayal, delineation, depiction; portrait, word p., sketch, character s., profile, psychological p., prosopog-

raphy 551 *representation*; psychic profile, case history 548 *record*; faction, documentary drama; evocation, word-painting, local colour; picture, true p., realism, naturalism; descriptive account, travelogue 524 *guidebook*; vignette, cameo, thumbnail sketch, outline; idyll, eclogue 593 *poem*; eulogy 923 *praise*; parody 851 *satire*; obituary, epitaph, lapidary inscription 364 *obsequies*.

*narrative*, storyline, plot, subplot, scenario 594 *stage play*; episode 154 *event*; complication 61 *complexity*; dénouement 725 *completion*; dramatic irony, comic relief; catharsis; stream of consciousness; fantasia 513 *fantasy*; imaginary account, fiction, faction, story, tale, conte, fabliau, romance, fairytale, folk tale; tradition, legend, legendry, mythology, myth, saga, river s., soap opera, serial, epic, epos; ballad 593 *poem*; allegory, parable, apologue, cautionary tale; yarn 543 *fable*; anecdote, reminiscence 505 *remembrance*; annals, chronicle, history, historiography 548 *record*.

*biography*, real-life story, human interest; life, curriculum vitae, cv, biodata, life story *or* history; experiences, adventures, fortunes; hagiology, hagiography, martyrology, Foxe's Book of Martyrs; obituary, obit, necrology; rogue's gallery, Newgate calendar; personal account, autobiography, confessions, memoirs 505 *remembrance*; diary, journals 548 *record*; personal correspondence, letters 588 *correspondence*.

*novel*, fiction, tale; roman à clef, Bildungsroman, roman fleuve; antinovel, nouveau roman, metafiction; historical novel, fictional biography, novelization; short story, novelette, novella, nouvelle; light reading, bedside r. 589 *reading matter*; romance, love story, fairy s., adventure s., Western, science fiction, sci-fi, cyberpunk; gothic novel, ghost story; novel of low life, picaresque novel; crime story, detective s., spy s., whodunit, whydunit; cliffhanger, thriller, horror story, shocker, bodice ripper, penny dreadful, horror comic; sex-and-shopping novel; Aga saga; paperback, pulp literature, airport fiction; potboiler, trash; popular novel, blockbuster, best-seller 589 *book*.

*narrator*, describer, delineator, descriptive writer; reporter, relater; raconteur, anecdotist; yarn-spinner, teller of tales, storyteller, fabler, fabulist, mythologist, allegorist; fiction writer 589 *author*; romancer, novelist, fictionist; biographer, Boswell, Plutarch; hagiographer, martyrologist, autobiographer, memoir writer, diarist; historian, historiographer, chronicler, annalist 549 *recorder*; Muse of History, Clio.

**Adj.** *descriptive*, representational; graphic,

colourful, vivid; well-drawn, sharp 551 *representing*; true-to-life, naturalistic, realistic, real-life, photographic, convincing; picturesque, striking; impressionistic, suggestive, evocative, emotive; moving, poignant, thrilling 821 *exciting*; traditional, legendary, storied, mythological 519 *figurative*; epic, heroic, romantic, cloak-and-dagger; picaresque, low-life, kitchen-sink; narrative, historical, biographical, autobiographical; full, detailed, circumstantial 570 *diffuse*; factual, documentary, nonfiction 494 *accurate*; fictitious, fictional, imaginative 513 *imaginary*; Dickensian, Jamesian, Lawrentian, Kafkaesque 557 *literary*.

**Vb.** *describe*, delineate, limn, draw, picture, depict, paint 551 *represent*; evoke, bring to life, capture, tell vividly, make one see; characterize, particularize, detail, enter into, descend to 80 *specify*; sketch, adumbrate 233 *outline*; relate, recount, rehearse, recite, report, give an account 524 *communicate*; write, write about 548 *record*; narrate, tell, tell a story, yarn, spin a y., unfold a tale; construct a plot, make a story out of; put into a novel, fictionalize, novelize, dramatize; romance, mythicize, mythologize 513 *imagine*; review, recapitulate 106 *repeat*; reminisce, relive the past 505 *retrospect*.

## 591 Dissertation

**N.** *dissertation*, treatise, tract, tractate; exposition, summary 592 *compendium*; theme, thesis 475 *argument*; disquisition, essay, examination, survey 459 *enquiry*; discourse, descant, discussion; excursus, memoir, paper, monograph, study, lucubration; introductory study, prolegomena; screed, harangue, homily, sermon 534 *lecture*; commentary, textbook, almagest.

*article*, signed a., syndicated a., news a., features a., column; leading article, leader, editorial; essay, causerie, feuilleton, belles-lettres; literary composition, set piece, companion p.; comment, review, rave r., notice, critique, criticism, write-up 480 *estimate*.

*dissertator*, essayist, expositor; pamphleteer, publicist 528 *publicizer*; editor, leader writer, editorialist; writer, belletrist, contributor 589 *author*; reviewer, critic, commentator, pundit 520 *interpreter*.

**Adj.** *discursive*, disquisitional 475 *arguing*; expository, critical 520 *interpretive*.

**Vb.** *dissertate*, treat, handle, write about, deal with, do justice to; descant, discourse upon 475 *argue*; pursue a theme, enlarge upon a t., develop a thesis; go into, go into in depth, enquire into, conduct an in-depth enquiry,

survey; set out, discuss, canvass, ventilate, air one's views; notice, criticize, comment on, write up; write an essay, write a treatise, do a paper, write an article, do a piece; annotate, commentate 520 *interpret*.

## 592 Compendium

**N.** *compendium*, epitome, resumé, summary, brief; contents, heads, analysis; abstract, sum and substance, gist, drift; consolidation, digest, pandect; multum in parvo, précis; aperçu, conspectus, synopsis, bird's-eye view, survey; review, recapitulation, recap; rundown, runthrough; draft, minute, note 548 *record*; sketch, thumbnail s., outline, brief o., skeleton; blueprint 623 *plan*; syllabus, prospectus, brochure 87 *list*; abridgment, abbreviation, concise version 204 *shortening*; contraction, compression 569 *conciseness*.

*anthology*, treasury, garland, florilegium, flowers, beauties, best pieces, gems; selections, extracts, chrestomathy 589 *textbook*; collection, compilation, cento, collectanea, miscellanea, miscellany; mythography; analects, fugitive pieces, ephemera; gleanings, leaves, pages; cuttings, album, scrapbook, notebook, sketchbook, commonplace book; anthologist.

*epitomizer*, epitomist, abridger, abbreviator; abstracter, summarizer, précis writer, shortener, cutter.

**Adj.** *compendious*, pithy 569 *concise*; analytical, synoptic; abstracted, abridged 204 *short*; potted, compacted, capsular; collected, excerpted etc. vb.

**Vb.** *abstract*, sum up, resume, summarize, run over; epitomize, make a synopsis of, reduce, abbreviate, abridge 204 *shorten*; capsulize, encapsulate; docket 548 *record*; condense, pot, give sum and substance, give an outline 569 *be concise*; consolidate, compile 87 *list*; collect 74 *bring together*; conflate 50 *combine*; excerpt, glean, select, anthologize; diagrammatize, sketch, sketch out 233 *outline*.

**Adv.** *in sum*, in substance, in brief, to sum up 569 *concisely*; at a glance.

## 593 Poetry. Prose

**N.** *poetry*, poesy, balladry, minstrelsy, song; versification (see also *prosody*); poetic art, poetics; verse, rhyme, numbers; poetic licence; poetic fire, poetic vein, poetic inspiration, muse, numen, afflatus, divine a.; Muses 967 *lesser god*; Apollo, Orpheus; Parnassus, Helicon, Castalian spring, Pierian s., Hippocrene.

*poem*, poetic composition; versification, piece of verse, lines, verses, stanzas, strains; narrative verse, heroic poem, epic, epos, Edda, chansons de geste; dramatic poem, dramatic

monologue, lyric drama, verse drama, Greek
tragedy, Greek comedy, satyric drama, trilogy,
tetralogy 594 *drama*; light verse, vers de soc-
iété, lyric verse, melic v.; comic verse,
nonsense v., limerick; ode, epode, choric ode,
Pindaric o., Sapphic o., Horatian o.; palinode;
dithyramb; monody, dirge, elegiac poem,
elegy; idyll, eclogue; georgic, bucolics;
occasional poem, prothalamion, epithalamium; song, hymn, psalm, shanty, lay,
ballad 412 *vocal music*; warsong, marching
song; love song, drinking s., anacreontic; collected poems 592 *anthology*; canto, fit; cycle,
sequence.

*doggerel*, lame verse, balladry; jingle, ditty,
runes, nursery rhyme, Mother Goose r.; nonsense verse, comic v.; clerihew, limerick; cento,
macaronic verse, macaronics, Leonine verse,
Fescennine v., Hudibrastic v.; mock epic, burlesque, satirical verse.

*verse form*, sonnet, sestet, Petrarchan *or*
Italian sonnet, Shakespearean *or* English s.; bal-
lade, rondeau, virelay, triolet, villanelle, bouts
rimés; burden, refrain, envoi; couplet, distich,
sloka; haiku, tanka; triplet, tercet, terza rima,
quatrain, ghazal; sestina, rhyme royal, ottava
rima, Spenserian stanza; accentual verse,
syllabic v., metrical v., blank v.; concrete
poetry; Sapphics, Alcaics; limping iambics,
scazon; free v., vers libre; verse, versicle,
stanza, stave, laisse, strophe, antistrophe; stich-
omythia; broken line, half l., hemistich.

*prosody*, versification, metrics, metre,
syllabic m., measure, numbers, scansion;
rhyme, masculine r., feminine r., internal r.,
eye r.; rhyme scheme; assonance, alliteration;
cadence, rhythm, sprung r.; metrical unit, foot;
iamb, trochee, spondee, pyrrhic; dactyl, ana-
paest, tribrach, amphibrach, choriamb; dim-
eter, trimeter, tetrameter, pentameter,
hexameter, heptameter, octameter; iambic pen-
tameters, blank verse; alexandrine, heroic
couplet, elegiac c.; anacrusis, arsis, thesis, ictus,
beat, stress, accent, accentuation; elision;
enjambment, caesura, diaeresis.

*poet*, major p., minor p., poet laureate; Lake
poet, Georgian p., Metaphysical p., beat p.,
modern p.; versemonger, poetaster; prosodist,
versifier, metrist, hexametrist, vers-librist;
rhymer, rhymester, rhymist, jingler; bard, minstrel, balladist, balladeer, skald, troubadour,
trouvère, jongleur, minnesinger, Meistersinger;
epic poet, lyric p., lyrist, bucolic poet,
dramatic p., dithyrambist, elegist, elegiac poet;
sonneteer, ballad-monger; songwriter, librettist; improviser, improvisatore, improvisatrice;
reciter, rhapsode, rhapsodist.

*prose*, not verse, prose rhythm; prose poem;

piece of prose, prose composition, prosaicness,
prosaism, prosiness, prose-writing, everyday
language 573 *plainness*; prosaist, prose writer
589 *author*.

**Adj.** *poetic*, poetical, bardic; songful, tuneful;
Parnassian, Pierian; heroic, Homeric,
Dantesque, Miltonic *or* Miltonian; mock-
heroic, satiric; elegiac, lyrical, dithyrambic,
rhapsodic; lyric, anacreontic, Pindaric,
Sapphic, Horatian; bucolic, eclogic, Virgilian;
Augustan 557 *literary*; rhyming, jingling, etc.
vb.; doggerel, macaronic; prosodic, accentual,
metrical, measured, rhythmic, scanning,
scanned; octosyllabic, hendecasyllabic, iambic,
trochaic, spondaic, dactylic, anapaestic; catalectic; Petrarchan, Shakespearean, Spenserian.

*prosaic*, pedestrian, uninspired, unpoetical,
unversified; in prose, matter-of-fact 573 *plain*.

**Vb.** *poetize*, sing, tune one's lyre, mount Pegasus; syllabize, scan; rhyme, chime, jingle; ver-
sify, put into verse, put into rhyme; make
verses, elegize, compose an epic, write a lyric,
write a sonnet; make up a limerick; celebrate in
verse; berhyme; lampoon 851 *satirize*.

*write prose*, stick to prose, prose, prosify.

## 594 Drama. Ballet

**N.** *drama*, the drama, the theatre, the stage, the
play, the boards, the footlights; theatreland,
Broadway, West End; silver screen, Hollywood
445 *cinema*; show business, show biz, dramatic
entertainment, straight drama, legitimate
theatre, live t.; intimate t., theatre in the
round, total theatre, alternative t., street t., the
Fringe, off-off-Broadway; repertory, rep; theatricals, amateur t., amateur dramatics,
dressing-up; masque, charade, dumb show,
puppetry, tableau, t. vivant 551 *representation*; tragic mask, comic m., sock, buskin,
cothurnus; Tragic Muse, Melpomene; Comic
Muse, Thalia; Thespis.

*dramaturgy*, play construction, dramatic
form 590 *narrative*; dramatic unities; dramatization, theatricals, dramatics; melodramatics,
histrionics; theatricality, staginess; bardolatry;
good theatre, bad t., good cinema, good television; play writing, scenario w., script w., libretto w.; stagecraft, theatrecraft, histrionic art,
Thespian a.; action, movement, plot, subplot
590 *narrative*; characterization 551 *representation*; production, new p., modern p., revival;
auditions, casting; walkthrough, rehearsal,
dress r.; direction, stage management; continuity; showmanship; staging, stage directions;
choreography; dialogue, soliloquy, stage
whisper, aside, cue; gagging, business, byplay;
entrance, exit (see also *acting*); rising of the curtain, prologue, chorus; act, scene, opening s.,

scène à faire, coup de théâtre, deus ex machina, alarums and excursions; curtain, drop of the c., blackout; finale, final curtain, epilogue; curtain call, encore; interval, intermission, break; enactment, performance, command p., first p., première, preview, first night, gala n.; matinée, first house, second h.; one-night stand, road show; successful production, sell-out, hit, smash h., box-office h., long run; flop.

*stage play*, play, drama, work; piece, show, vehicle; libretto, scenario, script, text, book of words, prompt book; part, lines 579 *speech*; dramatic representation 551 *representation*; five-act play, one-act p., playlet; sketch, skit; double bill; curtain-raiser, entr'acte, intermezzo, divertissement; monologue, dramatic m.; duologue, two-hander; masque, mystery play, miracle play, morality p., passion p., Oberammergau; commedia dell'arte; No, Kabuki; Greek drama, trilogy, tetralogy, cycle; poetic drama, verse d.; melodrama, gothic drama, blood and thunder; tragedy, high t., classical t.; tragicomedy, comédie larmoyante; comedy, high c., low c., light c., alternative c.; comedy of manners, Restoration comedy; situation comedy, sitcom; well-made play, problem p., slice-of-life drama, kitchen-sink d., theatre of the absurd, t. of cruelty; black comedy, Grand Guignol, farce, knockabout f., slapstick, burlesque, extravaganza 849 *ridiculousness*; pantomime, panto, harlequinade; musical comedy, musical, light opera, comic o., opera bouffe, grand opera 412 *vocal music*; radio drama, drama-documentary, television play 531 *broadcast*; photoplay, screenplay 445 *cinema*; mime, shadow play, puppet show, Punch and Judy show.

*stage show* 445 *spectacle*; live show; ice show, circus 837 *amusement*; variety, music hall, vaudeville; review, revue, intimate r., late-night r.; Follies, leg show, strip s.; floor show, cabaret; alternative comedy; song and dance, act, turn; star turn, transformation scene, set piece, tableau.

*ballet*, dance, ballet dancing 837 *dancing*; choreography; classical ballet, Russian b., romantic b., modern b., modern dance; toe dance 837 *dance*; solo, pas seul, pas de deux; chassé, glissade; arabesque; fouetté, plié, pirouette 315 *rotation*; pas de chat, entrechat, jeté 312 *leap*.

*stage set*, set, setting, décor, mise-en-scène, scenery, scene 445 *spectacle*; drop curtain, drop, backdrop, backcloth, cyclorama; screen, wings, flat; background, foreground, front stage, upstage, down stage, stage, boards; apron, proscenium, proscenium arch, apron

stage, picture frame stage; stage in the round, gauze, curtain, fire c., safety c.; trap, star t.; prompt box (see also *theatre*); properties, props, costume, theatrical c.; make-up, greasepaint.

*theatre*, amphitheatre, stadium 724 *arena*; circus, hippodrome; fleapit, picture house, movie theatre 445 *cinema*; Greek theatre, Elizabethan t., t. in the round, arena t., open-air t.; showboat, pier, pavilion; big top; playhouse, opera house, music hall, vaudeville theatre, variety t.; night club, boîte, cabaret; stage, boards, proscenium, wings, coulisses; flies (see also *stage set*); dressing room, green r.; footlights, floats, battens, spotlight, spot, limelight, floodlight, flood, houselights; auditorium, orchestra; seating, stalls, front s., back s., orchestra s., fauteuil, front rows; pit, parterre; box, loge, circle, dress c., upper c., mezzanine; gallery, balcony, gods; front of house, foyer, bar, box office, stage door.

*acting*, impersonation, mimesis 551 *representation*; interpretation, improvisation, impression, pantomime, miming, taking off 20 *mimicry*; histrionics, play-acting, character-a., the Method; ham-acting, hamming, barnstorming; over-acting, camping it up, staginess, theatricality; repertoire; character, personage, role, creating a r.; starring role, leading r.; part, good p., fat p.; vignette, cameo; supporting part, bit p., speaking p.; walk-on p.; stock part, stereotype, ingenue, soubrette, confidante, heavy father, injured husband, merry widow, stage villain, stage Irishman; principal boy *or* girl; Harlequin, Columbine, Pierrot, Pantaloon, Scaramouche; pantomime dame; chief part, name p.; hero, heroine, anti-hero; stage fever; stage fright, first-night nerves, performance anxiety.

*actor*, actress, Thespian, Roscius, luvvy (inf); mimic, mime, pantomimist 20 *imitator*; mummer, masker, guisard; play-actor, player, strolling p., trouper, cabotin(e); barn-stormer, ham; rep player, character actor; actor-manager, star, star actor *or* actress, star of stage and screen, film star, starlet, matinée idol 890 *favourite*; tragedian, tragedienne; comedian, comedienne, comedy actor *or* actress; opera singer, prima donna, diva; ballet dancer, ballerina, prima b., coryphée; danseur, danseuse, figurant(e); protagonist, lead, second l., leading man, leading lady, juvenile lead, jeune premier; understudy, stand-in, body double, stunt man *or* woman 150 *substitute*; lookalike 18 *analogue*; supernumerary, super, extra, bit player; chorus, gentlemen *or* ladies of the chorus; corps de ballet, troupe, company, repertory c., stock c.; dramatis personae, characters, cast; presenter, narrator; prologue 579 *speaker*.

*entertainer*, public e., performer, performance artist; artiste, artist, quick-change a., drag a.; striptease a., exotic dancer, fan dancer 229 *stripper*; diseur *or* diseuse, monologist; impressionist, impersonator, female i.; tribute band; troubadour, minstrel; street musician, busker; crooner, pop singer 413 *vocalist*; comic, stand-up c., comedian, alternative c., comedienne 839 *humorist*; ventriloquist, fire-eater, juggler 545 *conjuror*; ropewalker, acrobat 162 *athlete*; clown, buffoon, cap and bells 501 *fool*; pierrot, pierrette, Punch, Punchinello; hoofer, dancer, show girl, chorus g., cancan dancer, belly d., gogo d., pole dancer; dancing girl, nautch g., geisha g.

*stagehand*, scene shifter; prop man, stage carpenter, scene painter; electrician, machinist; sound recordist, special effects man, continuity girl; costumier, wardrobe mistress, wigmaker, make-up artist; prompter, call-boy, programme seller, usher, usherette, doorman.

*stage manager*, producer, director, regisseur; designer; manager, actor m., business m., press agent *or* officer, publicity manager; impresario, showman; backer, sponsor, angel.

*dramatist*, dramaturge; tragic poet, comic p. 593 *poet*; playwright, scenario writer, script w., lyric w., librettist; farceur, gag man, joke-writer 839 *humorist*; choreographer.

*playgoer*, theatregoer, operagoer; film fan, opera buff, balletomane 504 *enthusiast*; first-nighter; stage-door Johnny; audience, house, packed h., full h., sell-out; stalls, boxes, pit, circle, gods, gallery, balcony; groundling, pittite 441 *spectator*; claque, claqueur; dramatic critic, play *or* film reviewer.

**Adj.** *dramatic*, dramaturgical; scenic, theatrical, stagy 551 *representing*; operatic, balletic, Terpsichorean, choreographic; live, legitimate; Thespian, Roscian; histrionic, camp, mimetic

20 *imitative*; tragic, buskined; Thalian, comic, tragi-comic; farcical, burlesque, knockabout, slapstick 849 *funny*; cathartic, melodramatic, sensational, horrific, blood and thunder 821 *exciting*; Brechtian, Shavian, Pinteresque, avant-garde; produced, released, showing, running 522 *shown*; dramatized, acted; badly-acted, hammed up, camped up; hammy, barnstorming; on the stage, acting, play-a.; cast, cast as, typecast, miscast; featured, starred, billed, top of the bill; well-cast, all-star; stagestruck, film-struck, theatregoing.

**Vb.** *dramatize*, be a dramatist, write plays, write for the stage; make a play of, put in a play; adapt for the stage *or* for radio; do a play, put on the stage, stage, mount, produce, direct, stage-manage; rehearse, cut; cast, typecast, give a part, assign a role; star, feature, bill; present, put on, release 522 *show*; open, open for a season; raise *or* ring up the curtain.

*act*, go on the stage, tread the boards; face the cameras; perform, enact, play, playact, do a play 551 *represent*; personify, personate, impersonate; act the role, take the part; mime, pantomime, take off 20 *imitate*; create a role, play a part, play the lead; play opposite, support; star, co-star, get one's name in lights, steal the show, take the centre of the stage, upstage, take all the limelight; play to the gallery, ham, ham it up, camp it up, send up, barnstorm, overact, overdramatize 546 *exaggerate*; rant, roar, 'out-Herod Herod' (see quotation at 546 *exaggerate*); underact, throw away; walk on; understudy, stand in 150 *substitute*; con one's part, rehearse, say one's lines; cue in; fluff, forget one's lines, dry; ad-lib, gag; take a curtain call, do an encore, receive a standing ovation, dramatize oneself 875 *be ostentatious*.

**Adv.** *on stage*, offstage, upstage, downstage; backstage, behind the scenes; behind the footlights, in the limelight; dramatically.

# Volition: the exercise of the will

## 5.1
## Individual volition

### SECTION ONE

### Volition in general

**595 Will**
**N.** *will*, willing, volition; nonconative will, velleity; disposition, inclination, mind, cast of mind, fancy, preference 597 *willingness*; conative will, conation, act of will, effort of w. 682 *exertion*; strength of will, willpower, determination, firmness of purpose, 599 *resolution*; controlled will, self-control 942 *temperance*; intent, purpose, end use 617 *intention*; decision 608 *predetermination*; one's will and pleasure 737 *command*; appetence 859 *desire*; one's own sweet will 932 *selfishness*; self-will, iron will, wilfulness 602 *obstinacy*; whimsicality 604 *caprice*; acte gratuit; free will, self-determination 744 *independence*; free choice, option, discretion 605 *choice*; unprompted will, voluntariness, voluntaryism, spontaneousness, spontaneity 597 *voluntary work*; primacy of will, voluntarism.
   **Adj.** *volitional*, willing, volitive, conative; unprompted, unasked, unbidden, freewill, spontaneous, original 597 *voluntary*; discretional, discretionary, optional 605 *choosing*; minded, so m. 617 *intending*; self-willed, ironwilled, wayward, wilful 602 *obstinate*; arbitrary, autocratic, dictatorial 735 *authoritarian*; independent, self-determined 744 *free*; determined, hell-bent 599 *resolute*; decided, prepense, intentional, willed, intended 608 *predetermined*.
   **Vb.** *will*, exercise the will; impose one's will, have one's w., have one's way, have it all one's own w. 737 *command*; do what one chooses, do as one likes 744 *be free*; be so minded, have a mind to, see fit, think f., think best 605 *choose*; purpose, determine 617 *intend*; wish

859 *desire*; have a mind of one's own, have a will of one's own, be independent, go one's own way, do as one chooses, be one's own man *or* woman 734 *please oneself*; exercise one's discretion, judge for oneself 480 *judge*; act on one's own authority, take the responsibility, take it upon oneself; be self-willed, be hell-bent on, take the law into one's own hands, take the bit between one's teeth 602 *be obstinate*; know one's own mind 599 *be resolute*; volunteer, offer, do of one's own accord, do without prompting 597 *be willing*; originate 156 *cause*.
   **Adv.** *at will*, at pleasure, ad libitum, ad lib, at one's discretion, as one wishes, as one thinks best, as it seems good; voluntarily, of one's own free will, of one's own accord; spontaneously, for the heck of it.

**596 Necessity**
**N.** *necessity*, hard n., stern n., compelling n.; no alternative, no escape, no option, zero o., Hobson's choice, the only show in town 606 *no choice*; last shift, last resort 700 *predicament*; inevitability, the inevitable, inescapability, sure thing, what must be 155 *destiny*; necessitation, dictation, necessitarianism, determinism, fatalism 608 *predetermination*; pressure of events, pressure of work, force of circumstances, c. beyond one's control, act of God, fatality 154 *event*; no freedom 745 *subjection*; physical necessity, law of nature; force, superior f. 740 *compulsion*; logical necessity, logic, necessary conclusion, proof 478 *demonstration*; legal necessity, force of law 953 *law*; moral necessity, obligation, conscience 917 *duty*; necessitude, indispensability, sine qua non, a necessity, a necessary, a must, matter of life and death, must-do, must-have, must-see 627 *requirement*; necessitousness, want, lack 801 *poverty*; involuntariness, reflex action, reflex, conditioned r.; instinct, impulse, blind i. 476 *intuition*.

*fate*, inexorable f., lot, inescapable l., cup, portion; weird, karma, kismet; doom, die, foredoom, predestination, preordination, election 155 *destiny*; book of fate, God's will, will of Allah, will of heaven; fortune, wheel of f., 159 *chance*; stars, planets, astral influence; Dame Fortune, the Fates, Parcae, Norns; Destinies; Fatal Sisters, Weird S., S. Three, Lachesis, Clotho, Atropos.

*fatalist*, determinist, predeterminist, predestinarian, necessitarian; calvinist; stoic; pawn, tool, automaton, robot, machine.

**Adj.** *necessary*, indispensable, essential, vital, important, requisite, must-do, must-have, must-see 627 *required*; logically necessary, logical, dictated by reason, unanswerable; demonstrable 478 *demonstrated*; necessitating, imperative, compulsive 740 *compelling*; overriding, irresistible, resistless 34 *superior*; compulsory, mandatory, binding 917 *obligatory*; with force of law 953 *legal*; necessitated, inevitable, unavoidable, inescapable, inexorable, life-and-death 473 *certain*; sure thing, leaving no choice, dictated, imposed, necessitarian, deterministic 606 *choiceless*.

*involuntary*, instinctive 476 *intuitive*; unpremeditated, unwilled, unintended 618 *unintentional*; unconscious, subliminal, unthinking, gut, unwitting, blind, impulsive 609 *spontaneous*; unassenting 598 *unwilling*; under a spell 983 *bewitched*; conditioned, reflex, controlled, automatic, machinelike, mechanistic, mechanical.

*fated*, decided by fate, karmic, fatal; appointed, destined, predestined, ordained, preordained 608 *predetermined*; elect 605 *chosen*; doomed, foredoomed, prejudged, precondemned 961 *condemned*; bound, obliged 745 *subject*.

**Vb.** *be forced*, compelled etc. adj.; incur the necessity, lie under the n.; admit the necessity, submit to the n. 721 *submit*; be fated, bow to fate, dree one's weird; be cornered, be driven into a corner, be pushed to the wall 700 *be in difficulty*; be faced with a sine qua non, know no alternative, have no choice, have no option, have zero o., needs must; make a virtue of necessity; be unable to help it, be made that way; be subject to impulse, be guided by instinct 745 *be subject*.

*necessitate*, dictate, impose, oblige 740 *compel*; bind by fate, destine, doom, foredoom, predestinate, predetermine 155 *predestine*; insist, brook no denial, not take no for an answer, leave no choice, face with a sine qua non, impose the necessity, drive into a corner, bulldoze; demand 627 *require*.

**Adv.** *necessarily*, of necessity, of course, by

force of circumstances, perforce; nothing for it, no help for it, needs must, no two ways about it; willy-nilly, nolens volens, bon gré mal gré, coûte que coûte, when *or* if push comes to shove.

## 597 Willingness

**N.** *willingness*, voluntariness, volunteering; spontaneousness 609 *spontaneity*; free choice, option 605 *choice*; disposition, mind, animus; inclination, fancy, leaning, bent, bias, penchant, propensity 179 *tendency*; facility 694 *aptitude*; predisposition, readiness, right mood, favourable humour, receptive frame of mind; cordiality, good will 897 *benevolence*; acquiescence 488 *assent*; compliance 758 *consent*; ready acquiescence, cheerful consent, alacrity, gameness, promptness, zeal, earnestness, eagerness, zealousness, ardour, enthusiasm; initiative, forwardness; impatience, overeagerness, overzealousness, ardour of the chase 678 *overactivity*; devotion, self-d., dedication, sacrifice 931 *disinterestedness*; helpfulness 706 *cooperation*; loyalty 739 *obedience*; pliancy, putty in one's hands, docility, tractability 612 *persuadability*; submissiveness 721 *submission*; obsequiousness 879 *servility*.

*voluntary work*, voluntary service 901 *philanthropy*; honorary employment, unpaid labour, labour of love, self-appointed task; gratuitous effort, supererogation; freewill offering 781 *gift*.

*volunteer*, unpaid worker, ready w., willing horse; no shirker, no sloucher, no slouch 678 *busy person*; do-gooder 901 *philanthropist*.

**Adj.** *willing*, ungrudging, acquiescent 488 *assenting*; compliant, agreeable, content, game for, up for it 758 *consenting*; in the mood, in the right m., feeling like, receptive, favourable, favourably minded, inclined, disposed, well-d., predisposed, amenable; gracious, genial, cordial; happy, pleased, glad, charmed, delighted; ready 669 *prepared*; ready and willing, prompt, quick 678 *active*; forward, anticipating; alacritous, zealous, eager, enthusiastic, dedicated, keen as mustard; over-eager, impatient, spoiling for, raring to go; dependable, reliable 768 *observant*; earnest, trying, doing one's best 671 *attempting*; helpful 706 *cooperative*; docile, teachable, pliable, pliant, putty-like, biddable, easy-going 24 *agreeing*; loyal 739 *obedient*; submissive 721 *submitting*; obsequious 879 *servile*; fain, desirous, panting to, dying to 859 *desiring*; would-be 852 *hoping*; meaning, meaning to 617 *intending*.

*voluntary*, offered, unprompted, unforced, unsought, unasked, unbidden 609 *spontaneous*; unsolicited, uncalled for, self-imposed; supererogatory, beyond the call of duty; nonmandatory, discretionary, open to choice, optional 605 *chosen*; volunteering, on one's own initiative, without being told, off one's own bat, of one's own free will 759 *offering*; gratuitous, free, honorary, unpaid 812 *uncharged*.

**Vb.** *be willing*, – ready etc. adj.; not mind, have half a mind to; feel like, have a fancy to, have a good mind to 595 *will*; yearn to, pant to 859 *desire*; mean to 617 *intend*; agree, acquiesce 488 *assent*; show willing, be ready and waiting, find it in one's heart, comply 758 *consent*; hearken, lend a willing ear, be found willing 739 *obey*; try, do one's best 671 *attempt*; show zeal, go out of one's way to, lean over backwards, overcompensate; collaborate 706 *cooperate*; anticipate, meet halfway; swallow, jump at, leap at; can't wait, be burning to, be thrilled at the idea; stomach, make no bones about, make no scruple, not scruple, not hesitate, not hold back; choose freely 605 *choose*; volunteer, sacrifice oneself 759 *offer oneself*.

**Adv.** *willingly*, with a will, readily, with relish, with zest, cordially, heartily; voluntarily, spontaneously, without being asked 595 *at will*; readily, like a shot, at the drop of a hat; with open arms, with all one's heart, heart and soul, con amore, with a good grace, without demur, nothing loath; fain, as lief; gladly, with pleasure.

## 598 Unwillingness

**N.** *unwillingness*, disinclination, indisposition, reluctance; disagreement 489 *dissent*; demur, objection 468 *qualification*; protest 762 *deprecation*; renitency, recalcitrance 704 *opposition*; rejection 760 *refusal*; unhelpfuless, noncooperation 702 *hindrance*; dissociation, nonassociation, abstention 190 *absence*; unenthusiasm, lifelessness, faintheartedness, lack of alacrity, lack of zeal 860 *indifference*; backwardness 278 *slowness*; hesitation 858 *caution*; scruple, qualm of conscience 486 *doubt*; repugnance 861 *dislike*; recoil, aversion, averseness, no stomach for, shrinking 620 *avoidance*; bashfulness 874 *modesty*; nonobservance, noncompliance 738 *disobedience*; indocility, refractoriness, fractiousness; sulks, sulkiness 893 *sullenness*; perfunctoriness, grudging service; undependability, unreliability 474 *uncertainty*; shelving, postponement, procrastination, mañana 136 *delay*; laziness 679 *sluggishness*; neglect, remissness 458 *negligence*.

*slacker*, shirker, sloucher 679 *idler*; forced labour, unwilling servant 278 *slowcoach*.

**Adj.** *unwilling*, indisposed, loath, reluctant, averse; not prepared, not minded, not so m., not in the mood, not feeling like 760 *refusing*;

unconsenting, unreconciled 489 *dissenting*; renitent, adverse, opposed, unalterably o., vehemently o., irreconcilable 704 *opposing*; demurring, protesting 762 *deprecatory*; squeamish, with no stomach for 861 *disliking*; full of regrets, regretful, with regret 830 *regretting*; hesitant 858 *cautious*; shy, bashful 874 *modest*; shrinking, shirking 620 *avoiding*; unzealous, unenthusiastic, half-hearted, lukewarm; backward, dragging, dragging one's feet 278 *slow*; unhelpful, uncooperative 702 *hindering*; noncooperating, fractious, restive, recalcitrant, kicking 738 *disobedient*; not trying, perfunctory, unthorough, remiss 458 *negligent*; grudging, sulky 893 *sullen*; unspontaneous, forced, begrudged, with bad grace.

**Vb.** *be unwilling*, – reluctant etc. adj.; cannot be bothered, cannot be arsed (sl); not have the heart to, not stomach 861 *dislike*; disagree, stickle, stick, boggle, scruple 489 *dissent*; object, raise objections, demur, protest 762 *deprecate*; resist 704 *oppose*; reject, give the thumbs down, give the red light 760 *refuse*; recoil, turn away, back a., edge a., not face, blench, fight shy, duck, jib, shirk 620 *avoid*; skimp, scamp 458 *neglect*; drag one's feet, look over one's shoulder, hold back, hang back, hesitate, tread warily, hang fire, go slow 278 *move slowly*; slack, not try, not pull one's weight, be a passenger 679 *be inactive*; not play, not play ball, noncooperate, dissociate oneself, abstain 702 *obstruct*; grudge, begrudge, make faces, turn up one's nose, show one's distaste, grimace 893 *be sullen*; drag oneself, force o., make o.; do with regret, have regrets 830 *regret*; tear oneself away 296 *depart*.

**Adv.** *unwillingly*, reluctantly, under protest, under pressure, under threat, at gun point, with a bad grace, with an ill g., in spite of oneself, against one's will, against the grain; regretfully, with regret, with dragging feet, with a heavy heart; not for the world.

## 599 Resolution

**N.** *resolution*, sticking point, resoluteness, determination, grim d.; zeal, ardour, earnestness, seriousness; resolve, fixed r., mind made up, decision 608 *predetermination*; drive, vigour 174 *vigorousness*; energy, frantic e., desperate e., desperation 678 *activity*; thoroughness 725 *completion*; fixity of purpose, concentration, iron will, willpower 595 *will*; strength of character, self-control, self-restraint, self-mastery, self-conquest, self-command, self-possession; tenacity 600 *perseverance*; aplomb, mettle, daring, dash, élan 712 *attack*; guts, pluck, spunk, grit, backbone, spirit; fortitude, stiff upper lip, gritted teeth, moral fibre 855 *courage*; single-mindedness, commitment, total c., devotedness, devotion, utter d., self-d., dedication; firm principles, reliability, staunchness, steadiness, constancy, firmness 153 *stability*; insistence, pressure 740 *compulsion*; sternness, relentlessness, ruthlessness, inexorability, implacability 906 *pitilessness*; inflexibility, steeliness 326 *hardness*; iron, cast i., steel, rock; clenched teeth, hearts of oak, bulldog breed 600 *stamina*; Mr Standfast.

**Adj.** *resolute*, resolved, made up, determined 597 *willing*; desperate, stopping at nothing, all out; serious, earnest, concentrated; intent upon, set u., bent u. 617 *intending*; insistent, pressing, urgent, driving, forceful, energetic, heroic 174 *vigorous*; zealous, thorough, wholehogging 455 *attentive*; steady, firm, staunch, reliable, constant 153 *unchangeable*; ironwilled, strong-w., strong-minded, decisive, decided, unbending, immovable, unyielding, inflexible, uncompromising, intransigent 602 *obstinate*; stern, grim, inexorable, implacable, relentless, ruthless, merciless 906 *pitiless*; iron, cast-i., steely, tough as steel, hard as iron 326 *hard*; undaunted, nothing daunted 855 *unfearing*; steadfast, unwavering, unshaken, unshakable, unshrinking, unflinching, game, tenacious 600 *persevering*; indomitable 727 *unbeaten*; steeled, armoured, proof; self-controlled, self-restrained 942 *temperate*; self-possessed, self-reliant, self-confident; purposive, purposeful, single-minded, wholehearted, committed, devoted, dedicated, card-carrying.

**Vb.** *be resolute*, – determined etc. adj.; steel oneself, brace o., set one's face, clench one's teeth, grit one's t. (see also *stand firm*); make up one's mind, take a resolution, will, resolve, determine, purpose 617 *intend*; decide, fix, seal, conclude, finish with 69 *terminate*; take on oneself, accept responsibility 595 *will*; know one's own mind, insist, press, urge, not take no for an answer 532 *emphasize*; cut through, override, put one's foot down, stand no nonsense; mean business, stick at nothing, not stop at trifles, go to all lengths, go to any length, push to extremes; go the whole hog, see it through 725 *carry through*; face, face the odds, take on all comers, 661 *face danger*; bell the cat, outface, dare 711 *defy*; endure, go through fire and water 825 *suffer*; face the issue, bring to a head, take the bull by the horns; take the plunge, cross the Rubicon, burn one's boats, burn one's bridges, throw away the scabbard, throw down the gauntlet, nail one's colours to the mast; be singleminded, set one's heart on, take up, go in for, take up in earnest, devote *or* dedicate oneself, commit oneself, give oneself to,

give up everything for; set to, buckle to, go to it, put one's shoulder to the wheel, put one's heart into, grapple, strain 682 *exert oneself*.

*stand firm*, not be moved, dig in, dig one's toes *or* heels in, stand one's ground, stay put; not budge, not yield, not compromise, not give an inch; never despair, stand fast, hold f., stick f., hold out 600 *persevere*; be hell-bent on, bear the brunt, have what it takes, fight on, soldier on, stick it out, grin and bear it, endure 825 *suffer*; die hard, die game, die fighting, fight to the death, die with one's boots on; go down with colours flying.

**Adv.** *resolutely*, seriously, earnestly, in good earnest; at any price, at all costs; in spite of everything, quand même; manfully, like a man; come what may, come hell or high water 600 *persistently*; live or die, neck or nothing, once and for all.

**Int.** Here goes!, Alea jacta est!, We who are about to die salute you!, Once more unto the breach, dear friends!

## 600 Perseverance

**N.** *perseverance*, persistence, tenacity, pertinacity, pertinaciousness, stubbornness 602 *obstinacy*; staunchness, constancy, steadfastness 599 *resolution;* singlemindedness, commitment, singleness of purpose, concentration 455 *attention*; sedulousness, application, tirelessness, indefatigability, assiduousness, industriousness 678 *assiduity*; doggedness, plodding, hard work 682 *exertion*; endurance, patience, fortitude 825 *suffering*; maintenance 146 *continuance*; ceaselessness 144 *permanence*; iteration, repeated efforts, unflagging e. 106 *repetition*.

*stamina*, endurance, staying power, indefatigability, fortitude 162 *strength*; grit, true g., backbone, gameness, guts, gutsiness, pluck; bulldog courage 855 *courage*; hard core, diehard, last ditcher, old guard 602 *obstinate person*; trier, stayer, willing worker 686 *worker*.

**Adj.** *persevering*, persistent, tenacious, stubborn 602 *obstinate*; game, gutsy, plucky; patient, plodding, dogged, trying hard 678 *industrious*; strenuous 682 *laborious*; steady, unfaltering, unwavering, undrooping, enduring, unflagging, unwearied, untiring, indefatigable; unsleeping, sleepless 457 *vigilant*; unfailing, unremitting, unintermittent, constant 146 *unceasing*; renewed, iterated, reiterated 106 *repeated*; indomitable, unconquerable, unconquered 727 *unbeaten*; undaunted, nothing daunted, undiscouraged, game to the last, going down fighting, true to the end 599 *resolute*.

**Vb.** *persevere*, persist, keep at it, not take no

for an answer, hold out for; not despair, never d., never say die, never give up hope, hope on 852 *hope*; endure, have what it takes, come up for more 825 *suffer*; try, keep on trying, try and try again, renew one's efforts 671 *attempt*; maintain, keep up, follow up 146 *sustain*; plod, slog, slog away, peg a., plug a., hammer away at, work at 682 *work*; continue, go on, keep on, keep the pot boiling, keep the ball rolling, rally, keep going; not let go, cling, hold fast, maintain one's grip, hang on like grim death 778 *retain*; hang on, stick it out, sweat it out, stay the course, stick with it, see it through, stay till the end; be in at the death, see one buried first, survive 41 *be left*; maintain one's ground, not budge, not stir, dig in one's heels, grit one's teeth 602 *be obstinate*; stick to one's guns, hold out, hold out to the last, die in the last ditch, die at one's post 599 *stand firm*; work till one drops, die with one's boots on, die in harness; labour unceasingly, spare no pains, work miracles, move heaven and earth 682 *exert oneself*; bring to conclusion, see the end of, complete 725 *carry through*.

**Adv.** *persistently*, perseveringly, never say die; through thick and thin, through fire and water, sink or swim 599 *resolutely*; repeatedly, unendingly, ceaselessly; to the bitter end, à outrance.

### 601 Irresolution

**N.** *irresolution*, infirmity of purpose, faint-heartedness, squeamishness, loss of nerve, spinelessness, no backbone, no grit 856 *cowardice*; nonperseverance, broken resolve, broken promise 603 *tergiversation*; unsettlement, indecision, uncertainty, doubt, floating vote 474 *dubiety*; hesitation, overcaution 858 *caution*; inconstancy, fluctuation, vacillation, variability, blowing hot and cold 152 *changeableness*; levity, fickleness, whimsicality, irresponsibility 604 *caprice*; lack of willpower, lack of drive 175 *inertness*; passivity 679 *inactivity*; good nature, easygoingness, compromise 734 *laxity*; lack of thoroughness, half-heartedness, half measures 726 *noncompletion*; lukewarmness, wishy-washiness, listlessness, apathy 860 *indifference*; no will of one's own, weak will 163 *weakness*; impressibility, suggestibility 612 *persuadability*; pliancy, putty in one's hands, overpliancy 327 *softness*; obsequiousness 879 *servility*; submissiveness, slavishness 721 *submission*.

*waverer*, wobbler, dodderer, staller, shilly-shallyer; shuttlecock, butterfly, feather 152 *changeable thing*; floating voter; weathercock, chameleon, turn-coat 603 *tergiversator*; faintheart, compromiser.

**Adj.** *irresolute*, undecided, indecisive, of two minds, wavering, vacillating; unable to make up one's mind, stalling, undetermined, unresolved, uncertain 474 *doubting*; squeamish, boggling, hesitating 598 *unwilling*; gutless, timid, tremulous, faint-hearted, unheroic, faint, nerveless 856 *cowardly*; shaken, rattled 854 *nervous*; half-hearted, wishy-washy, lukewarm 860 *indifferent*; wobbling, unstaunch, unsteadfast, infirm, infirm of purpose 474 *unreliable*; characterless, featureless 175 *inert*; compromising, weak-willed, weak-minded, weak-kneed, spineless 163 *weak*; suggestible, flexible, pliant, putty-like 327 *soft*; easygoing, good-natured 734 *lax*; inconstant, variable, temperamental 152 *changeful*; whimsical, mercurial, not to be pinned down, grasshopper-like 604 *capricious*; emotional, restless, unsteady, without ballast 152 *unstable*; uncommitted, irresponsible, giddy, feather-brained, light 456 *lightminded*; fidgety, impatient, unpersevering; unthorough, superficial 456 *inattentive*; unfaithful 603 *tergiversating*.

**Vb.** *be irresolute*, – undecided etc. adj.; back away, blink, jib, shy, shirk 620 *avoid*; palter, shuffle, shilly-shally 518 *be equivocal*; fluctuate, vacillate, seesaw, wobble, waver, sway, hover, teeter, stall, dither 317 *oscillate*; not know one's own mind, blow hot and cold, back and fill, hum and haw, will and will not, be in two minds, go round in circles, not know what to do, be at one's wits' end 474 *be uncertain*; leave in suspense, keep undecided, delay, put off a decision, put off until tomorrow 136 *put off*; dally, dilly-dally 136 *wait*; debate, balance, weigh up the pros and cons, seesaw 475 *argue*; have second thoughts, hesitate 858 *be cautious*; falter, grow weary 684 *be fatigued*; not persevere, give up 621 *relinquish*; make a compromise, take half measures 770 *compromise*; yield, give way 721 *submit*; change sides, go over 603 *change one's allegiance*.

**Adv.** *irresolutely*, faint-heartedly, hesitantly; from pillar to post; seesaw; between the devil and the deep blue sea.

### 602 Obstinacy

**N.** *obstinacy*, mind of one's own; determination, will, single-mindedness 599 *resolution*; grimness, doggedness, tenacity, bulldog t., pertinacity 600 *perseverance*; stubbornness, obduracy, obdurateness; self-will, pigheadedness; inelasticity, inflexibility, immovability, woodenness, toughness 326 *hardness*; intransigence, hard line, hard core, no compromise; constancy, irreversibility, fixity 153 *stability*; stiff neck, contumacy 715 *resistance*; incorrigibility 940 *impenitence*; indocility, intractability, mulishness, dourness, sulkiness 893 *sullenness; perversity, wrongheadedness, cussedness, bloody-mindedness.*

*opinionatedness,* self-opinion, opiniativeness 473 *positiveness;* dogmatism, bigotry, zealotry; rigorism, intolerance, fanaticism 735 *severity;* ruling passion, obsession, idée fixe, mono-mania 481 *bias;* blind side 439 *blindness;* illiber-ality, obscurantism 491 *ignorance;* old school, ancien régime.

*obstinate person,* stubborn fellow, mule; stick-in-the-mud, Blimp; hard-liner, hard core, dry; fanatic, rigorist, stickler, pedant, dogma-tist, zealot, bigot, persecutor 481 *narrow mind;* sticker, stayer; last-ditcher, die-hard, bitter-ender 600 *stamina;* old fogy 504 *crank.*

**Adj.** *obstinate,* stubborn, obdurate; bull-headed, pig-headed, mulish, stubborn as a mule; pertinacious, unyielding, firm, deter-mined 599 *resolute;* dogged, bulldog-like, ten-acious 600 *persevering;* stiff, inelastic, wooden 326 *rigid;* adamant, inflexible, unbending; obdurate, hard-nosed, hardened, case-h.; uncompromising, hard-core, intransigent; unmoved, uninfluenced, unrelenting, immov-able 153 *unchangeable;* inexorable, unappeas-able, implacable, merciless 906 *pitiless;* set, wedded to, set in one's ways, hidebound, ultraconservative, blimpish 610 *habituated;* unteachable, obscurantist, impervious, blind, deaf; opinionated, dogmatic, pedantic 473 *posi-tive;* obsessed, bigoted, fanatical 481 *biased;* dour, grim 893 *sullen;* indocile, hard-mouthed, stiff-necked, contumacious 940 *impenitent* (see also *wilful*); perverse, incorrigible, bloody-minded, plain cussed; possessive, dog-in-the-manger; irremovable, irreversible; persistent, incurable, chronic 113 *lasting.*

*wilful,* self-willed, pig-headed, bullheaded, mulish, froward, wayward, arbitrary; entêté, headstrong, perverse; unruly, jibbing, restive, refractory; irrepressible, ungovernable, unman-ageable, intractable, uncontrollable 738 *dis-obedient;* unpersuadable, incorrigible, contumacious; cross-grained, crotchety 892 *irascible.*

**Vb.** *be obstinate,* – stubborn etc. adj.; persist 600 *persevere;* brazen it out 940 *be impenitent;* stick to one's guns, dig in one's heels, stand out, not budge, stay put 599 *stand firm;* insist, brook no denial, not take no for an answer; go one's own way, want one's own w., must have one's w. 734 *please oneself;* be wedded to one's own opinions, not change one's mind 473 *dog-matize;* stay in a rut, cling to custom 610 *be wont;* not listen, stop up one's ears, take no advice, take the bit between one's teeth, damn

the consequences 857 *be rash;* not yield to treat-ment, become chronic 113 *last.*

**Adv.** *obstinately,* obdurately, pigheadedly, mulishly, like a mule; over one's dead body.

## 603 Tergiversation: change of allegiance

**N.** *tergiversation,* change of mind, better thoughts; afterthought, second thoughts 67 *sequel;* change of allegiance, conversion; change of purpose, alteration of plan, mission creep; new resolve; good resolution, break with the past, repentance 939 *penitence;* revulsion 280 *recoil;* backsliding, recidivism 657 *relapse;* shifting ground, change of direction 282 *devi-ation;* reversal, backpedalling, veering round, about-face, about-turn, U-turn, volte-face, looking back 286 *return;* versatility, slipperi-ness, suppleness, unreliability, untrustworthi-ness 930 *improbity;* apostasy, turning renegade *or* traitor, recreancy (see also *recantation*); defec-tion, desertion 918 *undutifulness;* ratting, going over, treachery 930 *perfidy;* secession, with-drawal 978 *schism;* abandonment 621 *relin-quishment;* change of mood, temperament; coquetry 604 *caprice.*

*recantation,* palinode, eating one's words, retractation, retraction, withdrawal, apology; renunciation, abjuration, forswearing, swearing off 532 *oath;* disavowal, disclaimer, denial 533 *negation;* revocation, revoking, recall 752 *abrogation.*

*tergiversator,* turncoat, rat; weathercock 152 *changeable thing;* back-pedaller; opportunist, timeserver, trimmer, Vicar of Bray 518 *equivo-calness;* double-dealer, Janus, two-faced person 545 *deceiver;* jilt, flirt, coquette 604 *caprice;* recanter, recreant, apostate, renegade, for-swearer; traitor, Judas, betrayer 938 *knave;* quis-ling, fifth columnist, collaborationist 707 *collaborator;* lost leader, deserter, defector, quitter, ratter; tell-tale, squealer, grass 524 *informer;* strike-breaker, blackleg, scab; deviati-onist, secessionist, seceder 978 *schismatic;* run-away, bolter, flincher 620 *avoider;* recidivist, backslider 904 *offender;* convert, proselyte 147 *changed person.*

**Adj.** *tergiversating,* trimming etc. vb.; shuf-fling 518 *equivocal;* slippery, supple, versatile, treacherous 930 *perfidious;* double-dealing 541 *hypocritical;* reactionary, going back, back-pedalling 286 *regressive;* fickle 604 *capricious;* timeserving 925 *flattering;* vacillating 601 *irres-olute;* apostate, recanting, renegade; recidivist, relapsed; false, unfaithful, disloyal 918 *undutiful.*

**Vb.** *change one's mind,* tergiversate, think again, think better of it 601 *be irresolute;*

change one's tune, shift one's ground 152 *vary*; get cold feet, back out, scratch, withdraw 753 *resign*; back down, crawl 872 *be humbled*; apologize (see also *recant*); change front, change round, swerve, tack, veer round, do a U-turn, backpedal, wheel about 282 *turn round*; turn one's back on 286 *turn back*; turn over a new leaf, make good resolutions, repent 939 *be penitent*; reform, mend one's ways 654 *get better*; fall back, backslide 657 *relapse*; trim, shuffle, face both ways, run with the hare and hunt with the hounds 518 *be equivocal*; ditch, jilt, throw over, desert, walk out on 918 *fail in duty*; forsake, abandon, wash one's hands of 621 *relinquish*; turn against, play false.

*change one's allegiance*, turn one's coat, change sides, let the side down, change one's allegiance, apostatize, turn renegade *or* traitor; switch, switch over, join the opposition, cross over, cross the floor, go over, desert, defect, fall away; blackleg, rat; betray, collaborate 930 *be dishonest*; be off with the old love, jump on the band wagon, follow the rising star.

*recant*, unsay, eat one's words, eat one's hat; eat humble pie, apologize; take back, go back on, backpedal, backtrack, do a U-turn; recall one's words, resile, withdraw 769 *not observe*; retract, disavow, disclaim, repudiate, deny 533 *negate*; renounce, abjure, forswear, swear off; recall, revoke, rescind 752 *abrogate*.

## 604 Caprice

**N.** *caprice*, capriciousness, arbitrariness, motivelessness, purposelessness; whimsicality, freakishness, crankiness 497 *absurdity*; faddishness, faddism, fad-surfing 481 *bias*; inconsistency 25 *disagreement*; fitfulness, changeability, variability, fickleness, unreliability, levity, giddiness, light-mindedness, irresponsibility 152 *changeableness*; inconstancy, coquettishness, flirtatiousness, playfulness; fretfulness, pettishness 892 *irascibility*.

*whim*, whimsy, caprice, fancy, megrim, fantastic notion, weird idea 513 *ideality*; passing fancy, impulse 609 *spontaneity*; vagary, sweet will, humour, mood, fit, crotchet, bee in the bonnet, maggot, quirk, kink, fad, craze, freak, idiosyncrasy 503 *eccentricity*; escapade, prank, boutade, wild-goose chase 497 *foolery*; coquetry, flirtation, cyberflirtation 887 *love affair*.

**Adj.** *capricious*, motiveless, purposeless; whimsical, fanciful, fantastic; eccentric, humoursome, temperamental, crotchety, maggoty, freakish, fitful; hysterical, mad 503 *crazy*; prankish, mischievous, wanton, wayward, perverse; faddy, faddish, particular 862 *fastidious*; captious, arbitrary, unreasonable; fretful,

moody, contrary 892 *irascible*; undisciplined, refractory 602 *wilful*; erratic, uncertain, unpredictable 508 *unexpected*; volatile, mercurial, skittish, giddy, frivolous 456 *light-minded*; inconsistent, inconstant, variable 152 *unstable*; irresponsible, unreliable, fickle, feckless 603 *tergiversating*; flirtatious, coquettish, playful.

**Vb.** *be capricious*, – whimsical etc. adj.; submit to a whim, take it into one's head, have a sudden fancy for, pick and choose 862 *be fastidious*; chop and change, blow hot and cold 152 *vary*; have a bee in one's bonnet 481 *be biased*; be fickle, take up a thing and drop it; vacillate 601 *be irresolute*; play pranks, play tricks 497 *be absurd*; flirt, coquette 837 *amuse oneself*.

**Adv.** *capriciously*, fitfully, by fits and starts, now this, now that; as the mood takes one, as the fancy takes one, at one's own sweet will; on impulse.

## 605 Choice

**N.** *choice*, act of choosing, election 463 *discrimination*; picking and choosing, eclecticism, finickiness 862 *fastidiousness*; picking out, selection; co-option, co-optation, adoption; designation, nomination, appointment 751 *commission*; right of choice, option; freedom of choice, discretion, pick; deliberate choice, decision 480 *judgment*; third way; preference, predilection, partiality, inclination, leaning, bias 179 *tendency*; taste 859 *liking*; availability 759 *offer*; range of choice, assortment, list, short l., raft, range, selection 43 *medley*; possible choice, alternative, embarras de choix; alternative medicine, alternative energy; difficult choice, dilemma 474 *dubiety*; limited choice, no real alternative; only choice, Hobson's c., zero option; nothing for it but 606 *no choice*; blind choice 464 *indiscrimination*; better choice, preferability, desirability, greater good, lesser evil 642 *good policy*; one's preference, favour, fancy, first choice, top seed; thing chosen, selection, pickings, gleanings, excerpts; the best of; literary selection 592 *anthology*; unlucky choice, bad bargain; unfair choice, favouritism 914 *injustice*; deselection.

*vote*, voice 485 *opinion*; representation, proportional r., cumulative vote, transferable v., single transferable v., majority v., first past the post; one man one vote, one member one vote, OMOV, alternative voting; additional member system; casting v.; ballot, secret b., open vote, postal v.; card vote; vote of confidence; vote of no confidence, blackballing, vote-counting, show of hands, division, poll, straw p., plebiscite, referendum; suffrage, universal s., adult s., manhood s.; franchise, right of representation, votes for women, women's suffrage, suffragettism; Parliamentary system, electoral s., ballot box, vox populi; polling, counting heads, counting noses; straw vote, Gallup poll (tdmk), opinion p.; election, general e.; by-election; local election, local-government e.; indirect e., primary e., primary; polls, voting; election campaign, electioneering, whistle-stop tour, battle bus, canvassing, doorstepping, polling, hustings, candidature; successful election, return; election fatigue; psephology, psephologist; suffragette, suffragist.

*electorate*, voters, balloter, elector, electoral college; quorum; electoral roll, voting list 87 *list*; constituent, constituency, marginal c.; borough, pocket b., rotten b.; polling booth, ballot box, voting paper; slate, ticket, manifesto.

**Adj.** *choosing*, optional, discretional 595 *volitional*; exercising choice, choosy, picky 463 *discriminating*; involving choice, pick'n'mix; showing preference, preferential, favouring 923 *approving*; selective, eclectic; co-optative, elective, electoral; voting, enfranchised; vote-catching, electioneering, canvassing; psephological; pro-choice.

*chosen*, well-c.; worth choosing, to be jumped at, not to be sniffed at; preferable, better 642 *advisable*; select, choice, recherché, picked, hand-p. 644 *excellent*; sorted, assorted, seeded 62 *arranged*; elect, designate; elected, returned; adopted, selected; deselected; on approval, on appro; preferred, special, favourite, fancy, pet; God's own; by appointment; being considered, in the frame, on the short list.

*alternative* different, other, complementary 143 *changeable*.

**Vb.** *choose*, have a voice, have free will 595 *will*; eliminate the alternatives, make one's choice, make one's bed; shop around, be choosy, be picky; exercise one's discretion, accept, opt, opt for, take up an option; elect, co-opt, adopt, put on the list 923 *approve*; would like, favour, fancy, like best; incline, lean, have a bias 179 *tend*; prefer, have a preference, like better, would rather; might as well, might do worse; go in for, take up, be into; think fit, think it best to, decide, make up one's mind 480 *judge*; settle on, fix on, come out for, come down f., plump f., come down on one side, commit oneself; take the plunge, leap into, cross the Rubicon, burn one's boats 599 *be resolute*; range oneself, take sides, side, back, support, embrace, espouse, cast in one's lot with, throw in one's lot with 703 *patronize*; take for better or worse 894 *wed*.

*select*, pick, pick out, single o.; pass 923 *approve*; nominate, appoint 751 *commission*; designate, detail, mark out, mark down 547 *mark*; preselect, earmark, reserve 46 *set apart*; recommend, put up, propose, second 703 *patronize*; excerpt, cull, anthologize 592 *abstract*; glean, winnow, sift 463 *discriminate*; draw the line, separate; skim, skim off, cream, pick the best; indulge one's fancy, take one's pick, cherry-pick, pick and choose 862 *be fastidious*.

*vote*, have a v., have a voice, have a say; have the vote, be enfranchised, be on the electoral roll; poll, go to the polls; cast a vote, register one's v., raise one's hand, divide; vote for, vote in, elect, return; vote down, deselect, vote with one's feet 607 *reject*; electioneer, canvass; accept a candidature, stand 759 *offer oneself*; put to the vote, present the alternatives, take a poll, hold a referendum; count heads, count noses, count straws; hold an election, go to the country, appeal to the electorate, ask for a vote of confidence.

**Adv.** *optionally*, at pleasure; by ballot; alternatively, either . . . or; preferably, rather, sooner; by choice, à la carte.

## 606 Absence of choice

**N.** *no choice*, Hobson's c., no alternative, zero option, the only show in town 596 *necessity*; dictation 740 *compulsion*; any, the first that comes 464 *indiscrimination*; no favouritism, impartiality, first come first served 913 *justice*; no preference, noncommitment, nonalignment, neutrality, apathy 860 *indifference*; moral apathy, amoralism, amorality; no difference, six of one and half a dozen of the other, 'a plague on both your houses' 28 *equality*;

> A plague o' both your houses!
> They have made worms' meat of me.
> William Shakespeare, *Romeo and Juliet*

indecision, open mind, open-mindedness 474 *dubiety*; don't know, floating vote 601 *irresolution*; refusal to vote, abstention 598 *unwillingness*; no election, spoilt ballot paper; disfranchisement, disqualification, no vote, no voice.

**Adj.** *choiceless*, without alternative, necessitated 596 *necessary*; without a preference, unable to choose, happy either way 625 *neutral*; open-minded, open to conviction, unresolved, don't know, undecided, undetermined, vacillating 601 *irresolute*; uninterested, apathetic 860 *indifferent*; morally neutral, amoral; disinterested, motiveless; without favouritism, impartial 913 *just*; not voting, abstaining 598 *unwilling*; nonvoting, without a vote, voteless, unenfranchised, disfranchised, disqualified; nothing to offer, featureless, characterless 860 *unwanted*.

**Vb.** *be neutral*, take no sides, make no choice, not vote, refuse to v., withhold one's v., abstain; waive, waive one's choice, stand aside 621 *relinquish*; stand between 625 *be halfway*; sit on the fence 601 *be irresolute*; not know, not care 860 *be indifferent*.

*have no choice*, have no alternative, have Hobson's choice; have zero option; take it or leave it, make a virtue of necessity, make the best of a bad job 596 *be forced*; have no voice, have no say, have no vote.

**Adv.** *neither*, neither . . . nor.

### 607 Rejection

**N.** *rejection*, nonacceptance; nonapproval, disapproval 924 *disapprobation*; repudiation, denial 533 *negation*; apostasy 603 *recantation*; rebuff, repulse, frozen mitt, cold shoulder 760 *refusal*; spurn, kick, more kicks than ha'pence, more bricks than bouquets; rejection at the polls, electoral defeat, lost election, nonelection, forfeiture of deposit 728 *defeat*; elimination 300 *ejection*; nonconsideration, counting out, exception, exemption 57 *exclusion*; disuse, discarding, deselection, disemployment 674 *nonuse*; discard, reject, wallflower; no-hoper, unpopular cause, lost c.

**Adj.** *rejected*, thrown out etc. vb.; unsuitable, ineligible, unchosen 860 *unwanted*; unaccepted, returned, sent back, tried and found wanting, declined with thanks 924 *disapproved*; kept out, excluded, cast out, deselected 57 *excluded*; unfit for consideration, not be thought of, out of the question 643 *inexpedient*; discarded 674 *disused*.

**Vb.** *reject*, not accept, decline, say no to, draw the line at, rebuff, repulse, spurn, dismiss out of hand, opt out 760 *refuse*; not approve, not pass, return, send back, return with thanks 924 *disapprove*; not consider, pass over, ignore 458 *disregard*; vote against, not vote for, not choose, outvote 489 *dissent*; scrap, discard, deselect, ditch, junk, throw away, throw aside, lay a., give up 674 *stop using*; disallow, revoke 752 *abrogate*; set aside, supersede 752 *depose*; expel, cast out, throw o., chuck o., sling o., kick o., fling o. 300 *eject*; kick upstairs; sort out 44 *eliminate*; except, count out, exempt 57 *exclude*; blackball, cold-shoulder, hand the frozen mitt to, turn one's back on, give the brush-off 885 *be rude*; not want, not cater for 883 *make unwelcome*; disclaim, disavow, deny 533 *negate*; abnegate, repudiate, apostatize 603 *recant*; scout, scorn, disdain, laugh at, mock, deride 851 *ridicule*; turn up one's nose at, sniff

at, look a gift horse in the mouth 922 *hold cheap*.

**Int.** stick it where the sun don't shine (inf).

### 608 Predetermination

**N.** *predetermination*, predestination 596 *necessity*; foreordination, preordination 155 *destiny*; decree 595 *will*; premeditation, resolve, project 617 *intention*; prearrangement 669 *preparation*; order of the day, order paper, agenda 622 *business*; frame-up, put-up job, packed jury 623 *plot*; parti pris, closed mind 481 *prejudice*; foregone conclusion, agreed result.

**Adj.** *predetermined*, decreed, premeditated etc. vb.; appointed, predestined, foreordained 596 *fated*; deliberate, willed, aforethought, thought through, prepense 617 *intending*; with a motive, designed, studied, calculated, measured; weighed, considered, advised; devised, controlled, contrived 623 *planned*; put-up, framed, stacked, packed, prearranged 669 *prepared*.

**Vb.** *predetermine*, destine, appoint, foreordain, predestinate 155 *predestine*; premeditate, preconceive, resolve beforehand 617 *intend*; agree beforehand, preconcert; settle, fix; contrive a result 156 *cause*; contrive, arrange, prearrange 623 *plan*; frame, put up, pack a jury, stack the cards 541 *fake*.

### 609 Spontaneity

**N.** *spontaneity*, unpremeditation; ad hoc measures, improvisation; extemporization, ad-libbing, impromptu thinking on one's feet 670 *nonpreparation*; involuntariness, reflex, automatic r.; impulsiveness, impulse, blind i., instinct 476 *intuition*; inconsideration, spur of the moment; snap decision; spurt, burst of confidence 526 *disclosure*; inspiration, sudden thought, hunch, flash 451 *idea*.

*improviser*, extemporizer, ad-libber, improvisatore, improvisatrice; creature of impulse.

**Adj.** *spontaneous*, offhand, ad hoc, improvised, ad-libbing, extemporaneous, extemporary, sudden, snap; makeshift, catch-as-catch-can 670 *unprepared*; impromptu, unpremeditated, uncalculated, unmeditated, unrehearsed 618 *unintentional*; unprompted, unmotivated, unprovoked; unforced 597 *voluntary*; unguarded, incautious 857 *rash*; natural, instinctive, involuntary, automatic, knee-jerk 476 *intuitive*; untaught 699 *artless*; impulsive, emotional 818 *feeling*.

**Vb.** *improvise*, not prepare, extemporize, think on one's feet, vamp, ad-lib 670 *be unprepared*; obey an impulse, act on the spur of the moment 604 *be capricious*; blurt, come out with, say whatever comes into one's head, flash out with, have a sudden brainwave; rise to the occasion.

**Adv.** *extempore*, extemporaneously, impromptu, ad hoc, on the spur of the moment, offhand, off the cuff, off the top of one's head.

## 610 Habit

**N.** *habit*, disposition, habit of mind 5 *temperament*; habitude, assuetude, force of habit; familiarity, second nature; study, occupation; addiction, confirmed habit, daily h., constitutional; trait, idiosyncrasy; knack, trick, mannerism; instinct, leaning 179 *tendency*; bad habit, cacoethes; usage, standard u., long habit, consuetude, custom, standing c., old c., mores; use, wont 146 *continuance*; inveteracy, prescription 113 *long duration*; tradition, law, precedent; way, ways, the old w.; lifestyle, way of life; beaten track, tramlines, groove, rut; fixed ways, round, daily r., daily grind, métro, boulot, dodo 16 *uniformity*; regularity 141 *periodicity*; run, routine, drill, system 60 *order*; red tape, bureaucracy, beadledom, conventionalism, traditionalism, conservatism, old school 83 *conformity*; usual suspects.

*practice*, common p., usual custom, usual policy, matter of course; conformism, conventionalism, conventionality 83 *conformity*; mores, manners and customs, social usage, behaviour patterns; institution, ritual, observance 988 *rite*; religious observance, cultus 981 *cult*; mode, vogue, craze, in-thing, order of the day 848 *fashion*; usual suspects; convention, protocol, unwritten law, done thing, the usual thing; recognized procedure, drill, fire drill, fire practice; form, good f., netiquette 848 *etiquette*; manners, table m., eating habits; rules and regulations, house rules, standing order, rules of business, routine 688 *conduct*; spit and polish 60 *order*.

*habituation*, training, indoctrination 534 *teaching*; inurement, seasoning, hardening 669 *maturation*; naturalization, acclimatization; conditioning, association, reflex, conditioned r., fixation, complex; drill, routine, repetitive job 106 *repetition*.

*habitué*, creature of habit, addict, drug a., dope fiend 949 *drug-taking*; traditionalist, conventionalist 83 *conformist*; customer, patron, regular, client 792 *purchaser*; frequenter, devotee, fan, groupie, camp follower 504 *enthusiast*.

**Adj.** *habitual*, customary, familiar 490 *known*; routine, stereotyped, role-playing 81 *regular*; conventional, traditionary, traditional 976 *orthodox*; inveterate, prescriptive, time-honoured, permanent 113 *lasting*; resulting from habit, occupational; incorrigible, haunting, besetting, clinging, obsessive; habit-forming 612 *inducing*; ingrained, dyed-in-the-wool, bred in the bone 5 *intrinsic*; rooted, deep-r., deep-seated, implanted 153 *fixed*; imbued, dyed, soaked, permeated. (See also *usual*.)

*usual*, accustomed, wonted, consuetudinary, traditional; in character, natural; household, familiar, well-known 490 *known*; unoriginal, trite, trodden, beaten, well-worn, hackneyed; banal, commonplace, common, ordinary 79 *general*; set, stock, stereotyped 83 *typical*; prevalent, widespread, obtaining, current 79 *universal*; monthly, daily, everyday, of everyday occurrence 139 *frequent*; practised, done; admitted, acknowledged, received, accepted, accredited, recognized, understood; right, settled, established, professional, official, hallowed by custom 923 *approved*; de rigueur 740 *compelling*; invariable 153 *unchangeable*; in the fashion, in, in vogue 848 *fashionable*.

*habituated*, in the habit of, accustomed to, known to; given to, addicted to; dedicated, devoted to, wedded to; used to, familiar with, conversant w., au fait w., at home in 490 *knowing*; inveterate, confirmed; practised, inured, seasoned, incorrigible, hardened 669 *prepared*; broken in, trained, tame 369 *tamed*; naturalized, acclimatized.

**Vb.** *be wont*, love to, be known to, be used to, use to; have the habit of, be a creature of habit; go daily, haunt, frequent; make a habit of, take up, embrace, go in for; never vary, be set in one's ways, observe routine, move in a rut, stick in a groove, tread the beaten track, go on in the same old way, cling to custom; become a habit, catch on, grow on one, take hold of o., stick; settle, take root; be the rule, obtain, hold good 178 *prevail*; come into use, acquire the force of custom.

*habituate*, accustom oneself, get used to, get into the way of, get the knack of, get the feel of, get the hang of, play oneself in, warm up, get into one's stride; take to, acquire the habit, learn a h., cultivate a h.; fall into a habit; get into a habit, catch oneself doing; keep one's hand in, practise 106 *repeat*; accustom, inure, season, harden, case-harden 534 *train*; domesticate, tame 369 *break in*; radicate, naturalize, acclimatize; implant, ingraft, imbue 534 *teach*; condition, brainwash 178 *influence*.

**Adv.** *habitually*, regularly, with regularity 141 *periodically*; customarily, wontedly, occupationally, in the habit of; of course, as usual, as always, as is one's wont; mechanically, automatically, by force of habit; in one's stride.

## 611 Desuetude

**N.** *desuetude*, disusage, discontinuance, disuse 674 *nonuse*; rust, decay 655 *deterioration*; lost habit, lost skill, rustiness, lack of practice 695 *unskilfulness*; discarded custom, forgotten c. 506 *oblivion*, 550 *obliteration*; outgrown custom, outgrowing, weaning 134 *adultness*; new custom 21 *originality*; unwontedness, no such custom, nonprevalence; not the form, not the thing, not protocol, not etiquette, unconventionality 84 *nonconformity*; lack of habit, inexperience, unfamiliarity 491 *ignorance*.

**Adj.** *unwonted*, not customary, not current, nonprevalent; unpractised, not observed, not done; unnecessary, not de rigueur; unfashionable, bad form, non-U 847 *vulgar*; out of fashion, old-fashioned, old hat, defunct 125 *past*; outgrown, discarded 674 *disused*; against custom, unconventional 84 *unconformable*; unsanctified by custom, untraditional, unprecedented, unhackneyed 21 *original*.

*unhabituated*, unaccustomed, not used to, not in the habit of 769 *nonobservant*; untrained, unbroken, not broken in, untamed, undomesticated; unseasoned, unripe 670 *immature*; unfamiliar, inexperienced, new to, new, raw, fresh, callow, green 491 *uninstructed*; disaccustomed, weaned; dried out; out of the habit, rusty 695 *unskilful*.

**Vb.** *disaccustom*, wean from, cure of 656 *cure*; disaccustom oneself, break a habit, drop a h., lose a h., kick the h.; dry out; wean oneself from, outgrow; give up, throw off, slough, slough off, shed.

*be unpractised*, – unfashionable etc. adj.; not catch on; try a thing once, not do it again; not be done, offend custom, infringe protocol; lapse, fall into disuse, wear off 127 *be old*; rust 655 *deteriorate*.

## 612 Motive

**N.** *motive*, cause of action, what is behind it 156 *cause*; rationale, reasons, grounds 156 *reason why*; motivation, driving force, impetus, spring, mainspring, what makes one tick, what turns one on 156 *causation*; intention 617 *objective*; ideal, principle, guiding p., guiding star, lodestar, direction 689 *directorship*; aspiration 852 *hope*; ambition 859 *desire*; calling, call 622 *vocation*; conscience, dictate of c., honour 917 *duty*; shame 854 *fear*; personal reasons, ulterior motive, hidden agenda 932 *selfishness*; impulse, spur of the moment, inspiration, brainwave 609 *spontaneity*.

*inducement*, pressure, instancy, urgency, press, insistence, pester power; lobbying 178 *influence*; indirect influence, side pressure; provocation, urging, incitement, encouragement, incitation, instigation, prompting, inspiration 821 *excitation*; support, abetment 703 *aid*; solicitation, invitation 761 *request*; temptation, enticement, carrot, allurement, seduction, seductiveness, tantalization, witchery, bewitchment, fascination, charm, charm offensive; sex appeal, it; attractiveness, magnetism 291 *attraction*; cajolery, blandishment 925 *flattery*; coaxing, teasing, wheedling 889 *endearment*; persuasion, persuasiveness, salesmanship, sales talk, patter 579 *eloquence*; pep talk, trumpet call, rallying cry 547 *call*; exhortation 534 *lecture*; pleading, advocacy 691 *advice*; propaganda, agitprop; advertising, sales promotion, soft sell, hard s. 528 *advertisement*; promises, election p.; bribery, b. and corruption, graft, palm-greasing, back-scratching 962 *reward*; castigation, tongue-lashing; honeyed words, siren song, voice of the tempter, winning ways.

*persuadability*, docility, tractability, teachableness 597 *willingness*; pliancy, pliability, putty in one's hands 327 *softness*; susceptibility, susceptivity, suggestibility, impressibility, sensitivity, emotionalism 819 *moral sensibility*; credulousness 487 *credulity*.

*incentive*, inducement; stimulus, fillip, tickle, prod, spur, goad, lash, whip; rod, big stick, crack of the whip 900 *threat*; energizer, tonic, provocative, carrot, carrot and stick, 'jam tomorrow' (see quotation at 122 *different time*), sop, sop to Cerberus 174 *stimulant*; charm 983 *spell*; attraction, lodestone 291 *magnet*; will-o'-the-wisp 440 *visual fallacy*; lure, decoy, decoy duck, bait 542 *trap*; come-on, loss leader, special offer; profit 771 *gain*; cash, gold 797 *money*; pay, salary, perks, pay increase, increment, rise, raise, bonus 804 *payment*; donation, handout, freebie 781 *gift*; gratuity, tip, bribe, hush money, slush fund, backhander, brown envelope 962 *reward*; political favours, pork barrel; golden apple, forbidden fruit; tempting offer, offer one cannot refuse 759 *offer*.

*motivator*, mover, prime m. 156 *cause*; manipulator, manager, wire-puller 178 *influence*; manoeuvrer, tactician, strategist 623 *planner*; instigator, prompter, suggester, hinter; inspirer, counsellor 691 *adviser*; abettor, aider and abettor 703 *aider*; agent provocateur 545 *deceiver*; tantalizer, tempter, seducer; seductress, temptress, vamp, femme fatale, siren; Circe, Lorelei; hypnotizer, hypnotist; persuader, orator, rhetorician 579 *speaker*; advocate, pleader; coaxer, wheedler 925 *flatterer*; vote-catcher, vote-snatcher; salesman, advertiser, promotion manager, propagandist 528 *publicizer*; ringleader 690 *leader*; firebrand, rabble-rouser 738 *agitator*; lobbyist, lobby, pressure group, ginger g.

**Adj.** *inducing*, inciting; incentive, provocative, persuasive; hortatory, protreptic, directive; motivating, wire-pulling, lobbying 178 *influential*; energizing, stimulating, tonic, challenging, encouraging, rousing, inflaming 821 *exciting*; prompting, insinuating, hinting; teasing, tantalizing; turning-on, inviting, tempting, alluring, attractive 291 *attracting*; magnetic, fascinating, bewitching 983 *sorcerous*; irresistible, hypnotic, mesmeric; habit-forming 610 *habitual.* .

*induced*, brought on 157 *caused*; inspired, motivated, goal-oriented; incited, egged on, spurred on 821 *excited*; receptive, tractable, docile 597 *willing*; spellbound 983 *bewitched*; persuasible 487 *credulous*.

**Vb.** *motivate*, motive, move, actuate, manipulate 173 *operate*; work upon, play u., act u., operate u. 178 *influence*; weigh, count, be a consideration, sway 178 *prevail*; call the tune, override 34 *predominate*; work on the feelings, appeal, challenge, shame into (see also *incite*); infect, inject with, infuse into 534 *educate*; interest, intrigue 821 *impress*; charm, fascinate, captivate, hypnotize, spellbind 983 *bewitch*; turn on; pull 291 *attract*; push 279 *impel*; force, enforce 740 *compel*; bend, incline, dispose; predispose, prejudice 481 *bias*; predestine 608 *predetermine*; lead, direct 689 *manage*; lead astray 495 *mislead*; give a lead, set the fashion, be a trendsetter, set an example, set the pace 283 *precede*.

*incite*, energize, galvanize, stimulate 174 *invigorate*; sound the trumpet, encourage, cheer on, act as cheer-leader, root for 855 *give courage*; inspirit, inspire, animate, provoke, rouse, rally 821 *excite*; evoke, call forth, challenge; exhort, invite, urge, insist, press, exert pressure, bring pressure to bear on, lobby; nag, needle, goad, prod, jog, jolt; spur, prick, tickle; whip, lash, flog; spur on, set on, egg on; drive, hurry, hurry up 680 *hasten*; instigate, prompt, put up to; abet, aid and a. 703 *aid*; insinuate, suggest 524 *hint*; advocate, recommend, counsel 691 *advise*; start, kindle 68 *initiate*.

*induce*, instigate, bring about 156 *cause*; persuade, carry with one 485 *convince*; carry one's point, prevail upon, talk into, push i., drive i., nag i., bully i., browbeat (see also *motivate*); twist one's arm 740 *compel*; wear down, soften up; get round, bring r., talk r. 147 *convert*; bring to one's side, bring over, win o., procure, enlist, engage; talk over, sweet-talk into, coax into, cajole, blandish 925 *flatter*; conciliate,

appease 719 *pacify*; entice, seduce (see also *tempt*).

*tempt*, try, lead into temptation; entice, hold out a carrot to, dangle before one's eyes, make one's mouth water; tantalize, tease; allure, lure, inveigle 542 *ensnare*; coax, wheedle, pat on the back 889 *pet*; pander to, make things easy for, gild the pill, sugar the p. 701 *facilitate*.

*bribe*, offer an inducement, hold out a carrot 759 *offer*; suborn, seduce, corrupt; square, buy off; oil, grease the palm, give a sop to Cerberus; tip 962 *reward*.

*be induced*, yield, succumb 721 *submit*; fall for 487 *be credulous*; concede 758 *consent*; obey one's conscience, act on principle; come *or* fall under the influence; feel the urge, hear the call; be infected, catch the bug, get it bad, not be immune.

**Int.** encore!, hear hear!, more!, right on!, way to go! (inf) 488 int., 923 int.

## 613 Dissuasion

**N.** *dissuasion*, contrary advice; caution 664 *warning*; discouragement, setback 702 *hindrance*; deterrence 854 *intimidation*; objection, expostulation, remonstrance, reproof, admonition 762 *deprecation*; rebuff 715 *resistance*; no encouragement, disincentive; deterrent, red light 665 *danger signal*; contraindication, countersymptom 14 *contrariety*; cold water, damper, wet blanket; killjoy, spoilsport 702 *hinderer*.

**Adj.** *dissuasive*, discouraging, chilling; damping; reluctant 598 *unwilling*; expostulatory 762 *deprecatory*; monitory, warning against 664 *cautionary*.

**Vb.** *dissuade*, persuade against, advise a., argue a., convince to the contrary, talk out of 479 *confute*; caution 664 *warn*; remonstrate, castigate 924 *reprove*; expostulate, cry out against, protest a. 762 *deprecate*; shake, stagger, make one stop in one's tracks, give one pause 486 *cause doubt*; intimidate 900 *threaten*; terrorize, deter, frighten away, daunt, cow 854 *frighten*; choke off, head off, steer one away from, turn one aside 282 *deflect*; wean away from 611 *disaccustom*; hold one back, keep back, act as a drag 747 *restrain*; render averse, disenchant, disillusion, disincline, indispose, disaffect; set against, turn a., put off, repel, disgust, fill with distaste 861 *cause dislike*; dishearten, discourage, dispirit 834 *depress*; crush, squelch, throw cold water on, dampen, quench, cool, chill, damp the ardour, be a wet blanket; take the edge off 257 *blunt*; calm, quiet 177 *moderate*.

## 614 Pretext

**N.** *pretext*, ostensible motive, alleged m., reason given; statement, allegation, profession, claim 532 *affirmation*; plea, excuse, defence, apology, apologia, rationale, justification 927 *vindication*; let-out, loophole, alibi 667 *means of escape*; locus standi, leg to stand on, peg to hang something on 218 *prop*; shallow pretext, thin excuse, lame e., equivocation 518 *equivocalness*; special pleading, quibble 477 *sophism*; salvo, proviso 468 *qualification*; subterfuge 698 *stratagem*; false plea, pretence, Bunbury, previous engagement, diplomatic illness 543 *untruth*; blind, red herring, dust thrown in the eyes 421 *obfuscation*; stalking horse, smoke screen, cloak, cover 421 *screen*; apology for, pale imitation of, simulacrum, makeshift 150 *substitute*; colour, gloss, guise 445 *appearance*; bluff, sour grapes.

**Adj.** *ostensible*, alleged, pretended; specious, plausible; seeming.

*excusing*, self-e., exculpatory, apologetic, vindicatory, justificatory 927 *vindicating*.

**Vb.** *plead*, allege, claim, give as one's reason *or* rationale, profess 532 *affirm*; pretext, make one's pretext, make a plea of 475 *argue*; make excuses, offer an excuse, excuse oneself, defend o. 927 *justify*; gloss over, palliate 927 *extenuate*; shelter under, take shelter u., shelter behind, take hold as a handle for, use as a stalking horse; make capital out of, cash in on 137 *profit by*; find a loophole, wriggle out of 667 *escape*; bluff, say the grapes are sour; varnish, colour; blind, throw dust in the eyes, draw a red herring across 542 *befool*; pretend, affect 541 *dissemble*.

**Adv.** *ostensibly*, as an excuse, as alleged, as claimed; on the plea of, on the pretext of.

## 615 Good

**N.** *good*, one's g., what is good for one; advantage, benefit; the best, supreme good, summum bonum; public weal, common weal, common good; balance of interest, greater good, lesser evil, the greatest happiness of the greatest number, utilitarianism 642 *good policy*; weal, well-being, welfare 730 *prosperity*; riches 800 *wealth*; luck, good l., fortune, good f.; happy days, happy ending 824 *happiness*; blessing, benison, world of good (see also *benefit*); well-wishing, benediction 897 *benevolence*.

*benefit*, something to one's advantage, advantage, interest; service, convenience, behoof, behalf 640 *utility*; crop, harvest, return 771 *acquisition*; profit, increment, unearned i. 771 *gain*; edification, betterment 654 *improvement*; boon 781 *gift*; good turn 897 *kind act*; favour,

blessing, blessing in disguise; turn-up for the book, godsend, windfall, legacy, piece of luck, treasure trove, find, prize; good thing, desirable object, the very thing, just the t. 859 *desired object*;; peace dividend.

**Adj.** *good*, goodly, fine; blessed, beatific 824 *happy*; gainful 640 *profitable*; advantageous, heaven-sent 644 *beneficial*; worthwhile 644 *valuable*; helpful 706 *cooperative*; praiseworthy, commendable, recommended 923 *approved*; edifying, moral 933 *virtuous*; pleasure-giving 826 *pleasurable*.

**Vb.** *benefit*, favour, bless; do good, help, serve, avail, be of service 640 *be useful*; edify, advantage, profit; pay, repay 771 *be profitable*; do one a power of good 654 *make better*; turn out well, be all for the best, come right in the end.

*flourish*, thrive, do well, be on a roll (inf), be on top of the world, be on the crest of a wave; rise, rise in the world 730 *prosper*; arrive 727 *succeed*; benefit by, gain by, be the better for, improve 654 *get better*; turn to good account, cash in on 137 *profit by*; make a profit 771 *gain*; make money 800 *get rich*.

**Adv.** *well*, aright, satisfactorily, favourably, profitably, happily, healthily, not amiss, all to the good; to one's advantage, to one's benefit, for the best, in one's best interests; in fine style, on the up and up.

## 616 Evil

**N.** *evil*, evil conduct, wickedness, iniquity, mischievousness, injuriousness, disservice, injury, putting the boot in, dirty trick 930 *foul play*; wrong, injury, outrage 914 *injustice*; crying evil, crying shame, shame, abuse; curse, scourge, poison, pest, plague, sore, running s. 659 *bane*; ill, ills that flesh is heir to, Pandora's box; sad world, vale of tears; bale, trouble, troubles 731 *adversity*; affliction, bread of a., misery, distress 825 *suffering*; grief, woe 825 *sorrow*; unease, malaise, angst, discomfort 825 *worry*; nuisance 827 *annoyance*; hurt, bodily harm, wound, bruise, cut, gash 377 *pain*; blow, mortal b., death b., buffet, stroke 279 *knock*; calamity, bad luck, 'outrageous fortune', 'slings and arrows' 731 *misfortune*;

> To be, or not to be: that is the question:
> Whether 'tis nobler in the mind to suffer
> The slings and arrows of outrageous fortune,
> Or to take arms against a sea of troubles,
> And by opposing end them?
>
> William Shakespeare, *Hamlet*

casualty, accident 154 *event*; fatality 361 *death*; catastrophe 165 *ruin*; tragedy, sad ending 655 *deterioration*; mischief, devilry, harm, damage 772 *loss*; ill effect, bad result; disadvantage 35 *inferiority*; drawback, fly in the ointment 647 *defect*; set-back 702 *hitch*; evil plight 700 *predicament*; indigence 801 *poverty*; sense of injury, grievance 829 *discontent*; vindictiveness 910 *revengefulness*; cause of evil 898 *malevolence.*

**Adj.** *evil*, wicked, iniquitous 934 *vicious*; black, foul, shameful 914 *wrong*; bad, too bad 645 *damnable*; unlucky, inauspicious, sinister 731 *adverse*; insidious, injurious, prejudicial, disadvantageous 645 *harmful*; trouble-making 898 *maleficent*; troublous 827 *distressing*; fatal, fell, mortal, deathly 362 *deadly*; ruinous, disastrous 165 *destructive*; catastrophic, calamitous, tragic 731 *unfortunate*; all wrong, awry, out of joint, out of kilter.

**Adv.** *amiss*, wrong, all wrong, awry, sour, pear-shaped (inf); unfortunately, unhappily, unluckily; to one's cost, for one's sins; worse luck!

SECTION TWO

## Prospective volition

### 617 Intention
**N.** *intention*, intent, intendment, meaning; intentionality, deliberateness; calculation, calculated risk 480 *estimate*; purpose, set p., settled p., determination, predetermination, resolve 599 *resolution*; animus, mind 447 *intellect*; mens rea, criminal intent 936 *guilt*; good intentions 897 *benevolence*; view, prospect, purview; future intention, proposal 124 *looking ahead*; constant intention, study, pursuit, occupation 622 *business*; project, design 623 *plan*; enterprise 672 *undertaking*; ambition 859 *desire*; formulated intention, decision 480 *judgment*; final decision, ultimatum 766 *conditions*; bid, bid for 671 *attempt*; engagement 764 *promise*; solemn threat 900 *threat*; final intention, destination, end use 69 *end*; teleology, final cause 156 *causation*; 'be-all and end-all' (see quotation at 638 *important matter*), raison d'être 156 *reason why*; trend 179 *tendency*; tendentiousness 523 *latency*.

*objective*, destination, object, end, end in view, aim, mission statement; axe to grind; mark, butt, target, quintain; target area, bull's-eye 225 *centre*; tape, winning post 295 *goal*; place of pilgrimage, Mecca 76 *focus*; quarry, game, prey 619 *chase*; prize, crown, wreath, laurels 729 *trophy*; dream, aspiration, vision 513 *ideality*; heart's desire, Promised Land, El Dorado, 'land flowing with milk and honey' (see quotation at 730 *prosperity*), pot *or* crock of gold at the end of the rainbow, Holy Grail 859 *desired object.*

**Adj.** *intending*, intent on, hell-bent 599 *resolute*; intentional, deliberate, voluntary 595 *volitional*; out to, out for, all out f.; having in view, purposive, teleological; studying, serious, minded, so m., disposed, inclined 597 *willing*; prospective, would-be, aspiring, ambitious 859 *desiring.*

*intended*, for a purpose, tendentious; deliberate, intentional, studied, designed, planned, purposed, purposeful, aforethought 608 *predetermined.*

**Vb.** *intend*, purpose, propose; have in mind, have in view, have an eye to, contemplate, think of; study, meditate; reckon on, calculate, look for 507 *expect*; foresee the necessity of 510 *foresee*; have a mind to, mean to, really mean, have every intention 599 *be resolute*; have a purpose, harbour a design; resolve, determine, premeditate 608 *predetermine*; project, design, plan for 623 *plan*; take on oneself, shoulder 672 *undertake*; engage 764 *promise*; threaten to 900 *threaten*; intend for, destine f. 155 *predestine*; mark down for, earmark 547 *mark*; hold for, put aside for, keep f, reserve f.; intend for oneself (see also *aim at*); declare one's intention, set out one's stall.

*aim at*, make one's target, go for, go in for, take up; go after, go all out for, drive at, labour for, study f., work towards, strive after 619 *pursue*; try for, bid f., make a bid, endeavour 671 *attempt*; be after, have an eye on, have designs on, promise oneself, propose to oneself, nurse an ambition, aspire to, dream of, think of, talk of 859 *desire*; take aim, zero in on, focus on, point at, level at, train one's sights on, raise one's s., aim high, hitch one's wagon to a star 281 *aim.*

**Adv.** *purposely*, on purpose, seriously, with one's eyes open, in cold blood, deliberately, pointedly, intentionally; designedly, advisedly, knowingly, wittingly, voluntarily; premeditatedly, with forethought, with malice aforethought; for, for a purpose, in order to; with the intention of, with a view to, with an eye to, with the object of, in pursuance of, pursuant to; by design, as planned, according to plan, as arranged.

### 618 Nondesign. Gamble
**N.** *nondesign*, indetermination, indeterminacy, unpredictability 159 *chance*; involuntariness, instinct 609 *spontaneity*; coincidence, mere c. 89 *accompaniment*; accident, fluke, luck, mere l., lucky break 154 *event*; good luck, windfall, stroke of luck; bad luck, hard l. 616 *evil*; lottery, luck of the draw, postcode lottery; potluck; sortition, drawing lots, casting l. 159 *equal chance*; sortilege, sortes Biblicae 511 *divi-*

*nation*; lot, wheel of Fortune 596 *fate*; mascot, amulet, charm, lucky c. 983 *talisman*.

*gambling*, taking a chance, risk-taking; plunge, flier, risk, hazard, Russian roulette 661 *danger*; gamble, potluck 159 *chance*; venture, speculation, flutter 461 *experiment*; shot, random s., shot in the dark, leap in the d., pig in a poke, blind bargain 474 *uncertainty*; bid, throw; toss of a coin, turn of a card; wager, bet, stake, ante, psychic bid; last throw, desperate bid 857 *rashness*; dice, die, bones, ivories; element of risk, game of chance; bingo; fruit machine, gaming m., one-armed bandit; roulette, rouge et noir 837 *gambling game*; betting, turf, horse-racing, dog-r. 716 *racing*; football pool, treble chance, pools; draw, lottery, National Lottery, scratch card, raffle, tombola, sweepstake; premium bond; gambling on the market, futures, options.

*gaming-house*, hell, gambling den; betting shop, bookie's, bookmaker's, turf accountant's; casino, pool room, bingo hall, amusement arcade; racecourse, turf; totalizator, tote, pari mutuel.

*bourse*, exchange, stock e., share shop, bucket shop.

*gambler*, gamester, player, dicer; better, layer, backer, punter; turf accountant, bookmaker, bookie, tout, tipster; enterprising person, risk-taker; gentleman of fortune, venturer, merchant v., venture capitalist, adventurer, undertaker, entrepreneur 672 *undertaking*; speculator, piker, plunger, manipulator; bear, bull, stag; arbitrageur, arb; experimentalist 461 *experimenter*.

**Adj.** *unintentional*, nonintentional, inadvertent, unintended, unmeant, not meant 596 *involuntary*; unpurposed, undesigned, unpremeditated, unrehearsed 609 *spontaneous*; accidental, fortuitous, coincidental 159 *casual*.

*designless*, aimless, planless, purposeless; motiveless 159 *causeless*; happy-go-lucky, devil-may-care; unselective 464 *indiscriminate*; undirected, unguided, random, haphazard 282 *deviating*; wandering, footloose 267 *travelling*.

*speculative*, experimental 474 *uncertain*; hazardous, risky, chancy, dicey, aleatory; risk-taking, venturesome, adventurous, enterprising.

**Vb.** *gamble*, game, play, do the pools; throw, dice, bet, stake, wager, lay; call one's hand, overcall; play high, play for high stakes, double the s.; take bets, offer odds, make a book; back, punt; cover a bet, cover, hedge 660 *seek safety*; play the market, speculate, arbitrage, have a flutter 461 *experiment*; hazard, risk, run a r., take risks, push one's luck, tempt Providence; buy blind, buy a pig in a poke 857

be rash; venture, chance it, chance one's arm, tempt fortune, tempt fate, try one's luck, trust to chance; spin the wheel, raffle, draw, draw lots, cut straws, cut for aces, spin a coin, toss up.

**Adv.** *at random*, randomly, by the way, incidentally, haphazardly; unintentionally, unwittingly; chancily, riskily; at a venture, by guess and by God, on the off-chance, on spec.

## 619 Pursuit

**N.** *pursuit*, pursuing, pursuance, follow-up 65 *sequence*; hunting, seeking, looking for, quest 459 *search*; tracking, spooring, trailing, tailing, dogging, stalking, poaching, lamping 284 *following*; hounding, persecution, witch-hunt; persistence 600 *perseverance*; prosecution, execution 725 *effectuation*; activities, affairs 622 *business*.

*chase*, run, run for one's money; steeple-chase, paperchase 716 *racing*; hunt, hunting, hounding, hue and cry, tally-ho; beat, drive, battue, beating; shooting, gunning, hunting, shooting and fishing 837 *sport*; blood sport, fox hunt, stag h., big-game h., lion h., tiger h.; elephant h., boar h., pigsticking; stalking, deer s.; hawking, fowling, falconry; fishing, angling, fly fishing, coarse f., sea f.; inshore f., deep-sea f., whaling; beagling, coursing, ratting, trapping, ferreting, rabbiting, mole-catching; fishing tackle, rod and line, bait, fly, fly-tying; fowling-piece 723 *firearm*; fishtrap, rat-trap 542 *trap*; manhunt, dragnet; game, quarry, prey, victim 617 *objective*; catch 771 *acquisition*.

*hunter*, quester, seeker, searcher 459 *enquirer*; search party; pursuer, stalker, dogger, tracker, trailer, sleuth, tail, shadow; huntsman, huntress; whip, whipper-in; beater; Nimrod, Diana; sportsman, sportswoman, sportsperson 837 *player*; gun, shot, good s., marksman *or* -woman 287 *shooter*; headhunter 362 *killer*; big-game hunter, fox h., deer stalker; poacher, guddler, trout-tickler; trapper, rat-catcher, rodent officer, mole-catcher; bird catcher, fowler, falconer, hawker; fisherman, piscator, angler, compleat a.; shrimper; trawler, trawlerman, whaler; field, pack, hounds, cry of h.; hound, foxhound, otterhound, bloodhound 365 *dog*; hawk 365 *bird*; beast of prey, man-eater 365 *mammal*; mouser 365 *cat*.

**Adj.** *pursuing*, pursuant, seeking, questing 459 *enquiring*; in quest of, sent after; on one's tail, chasing, in pursuit, in hot p., in full cry, on the scent, on the trail, sleuthing 284 *following*; hunting, shooting, fishing, piscatorial.

**Vb.** *pursue*, seek, look for, cast about for; be gunning for, hunt for, fish for, dig for 459 *search*; send after, send for, send out a search party; stalk, prowl after, sneak a.; shadow, dog, track, trail, sleuth, tail, sit on one's t., dog one's footsteps, follow the scent 284 *follow*; scent out 484 *discover*; witch-hunt, harry, chivvy, chevy, persecute 735 *oppress*; chase, give c., hunt, whoop, halloo, hark, cry on; raise the hunt, raise the hue and cry; run down, ride d., rush at, tilt at, ride full tilt at, charge at 712 *charge*; leap at, jump at 312 *leap*; snatch at 786 *take*; mark as one's prey, make one's quarry 617 *aim at*; set one's course 281 *steer for*; run after, set one's cap at, throw oneself at, woo 889 *court*; mob, swarm over; be after, make it one's business 617 *intend*; pursue one's ends, pursue one's own interests 622 *busy oneself*; follow up, persist 600 *persevere*; press on 680 *hasten*; push one's way, elbow one's w., fight one's w. 285 *progress*.

*hunt*, go hunting, go big-game h., go shooting, follow the chase, ride to hounds; go fishing, cast one's net, fish, angle, fly-fish; trawl; whale; shrimp; net, catch 542 *ensnare*; mouse, play cat and m.; stalk, deer-s., fowl, hawk; course; start game, flush, beat, start, start up; set snares, poach, guddle.

**Adv.** *pursuant to*, in pursuance of, in quest of, in search of, on the lookout for, after; on the trail, on the track, on the scent; in hot pursuit, hot on the trail, in full cry.

**Int.** Halloo!, View halloo!, Yoicks!, Tally-ho!, There she blows!

## 620 Avoidance
**N.** *avoidance*, prevention 702 *hindrance*; abstinence, abstention 942 *temperance*; forbearance, refraining 177 *moderation*; refusal 607 *rejection*; inaction, cop-out, sitting on the fence 679 *inactivity*; passivity 266 *quiescence*; nonintervention, noninvolvement, neutrality 860 *indifference*; evasiveness 518 *equivocalness*; evasive action, dodge, duck, sidestep; delaying action, noncooperation 769 *nonobservance*; centrifugal force; retreat, withdrawal 286 *regression*; evasion, flight 667 *escape*; shy, jibbing, shrinking 854 *fear*, shunning, wide berth, safe distance 199 *distance*; shyness 598 *unwillingness*; shirking 458 *negligence*; skulking 523 *latency*; revulsion 280 *recoil*; defence mechanism, defensive reaction 713 *defence*; repression, suppression 757 *prohibition*; nonattendance 190 *absence*; escapism.

*avoider*, nondrinker 942 *abstainer*; dodger, sidestepper, evader, tax e., moonlighter, bilker, welsher 545 *trickster*; shrinker, quitter 856 *coward*; shirker, skiver, slacker, sloucher, scrimshanker, leadswinger 679 *idler*; skulker 527 *hider*; draft-dodger, truant, deserter 918 *unduti-*

*fulness*; apostate, renegade 603 *tergiversator*; runaway, fugitive, refugee, displaced person, asylum-seeker, escapee 667 *escaper*; escapist, dreamer 513 *visionary*; head in the sand, ostrich.

**Adj.** *avoiding*, shunning; evasive, elusive, slippery, hard to catch; untamed, wild; shy 874 *modest*; blinking, blenching, shrinking, cowering 854 *nervous*; backward, reluctant, noncooperative 598 *unwilling*; noncommittal, unforthcoming 582 *taciturn*; passive, inert 679 *inactive*; not involved, noncommitted, uncommitted 625 *neutral*; centrifugal; fugitive, hunted, runaway, fly-by-night 667 *escaped*; hiding, skulking 523 *latent*; repressive, suppressive; on the defensive.

*avoidable*, avertable, escapable, preventable; unsought, unattempted.

**Vb.** *avoid*, not go near, keep off, keep away; bypass, circumvent 282 *deviate*; turn aside, look the other way, turn a blind eye, cold-shoulder 883 *make unwelcome*; hold aloof, stand apart, have no hand in, play no part in, not soil one's fingers, keep one's hands clean, wash one's hands of, shun, eschew, leave, let alone, have nothing to do with, not touch with a bargepole; give a miss, give the go-by; fight shy, back away, back off, draw back 290 *recede*; hold off, stand aloof, keep one's distance, keep a respectful d., keep at arm's length, give a wide berth, sup with a long spoon 199 *be distant*; keep out of the way, keep clear, stand c., get out of the way, make way for; forbear, spare; refrain, abstain, forswear, deny oneself, do without, not touch 942 *be temperate*; pull one's punches, soften the blow 177 *moderate*; hold back, hang b., not push oneself forward, not try, not attempt, balk at 598 *be unwilling*; shelve, postpone 136 *put off*; pass the buck, get out of; cop out, funk, shirk 458 *neglect*; shrink, flinch, start aside, jib, refuse, shy, blink, blench 854 *be nervous*; take evasive action, shy away, lead one a dance, draw a red herring, throw dust in one's eyes, throw one off the scent, play hide-and-seek; sidestep, dodge, duck; deflect, ward off 713 *parry*; duck the issue, avoid the i., fudge the i., get round, obviate, skirt round, fence, hedge, pussyfoot 518 *be equivocal*; evade, escape, give one the slip 667 *elude*; skulk, cower, hide 523 *lurk*; bury one's head in the sand, be ostrich-like; disown, deny 533 *negate*; repress, suppress 757 *prohibit*; make excuses 614 *plead*; prevent, foil 702 *hinder*.

*run away*, desert, play truant, jump bail, take French leave, go AWOL 918 *fail in duty*; abscond, welsh, flit, elope 667 *escape*; absent oneself 190 *be absent*; withdraw, retire, retreat, beat a r., turn tail, turn one's back 282 *turn round*; flee, flit, fly, take to flight, run for one's life; be off, make o., slope o., scamper o., bolt, run, run for it, cut and run, show a clean pair of heels, take to one's h., beat it, make oneself scarce, scoot, scram, skedaddle 277 *move fast*; slip the cable, part company, break away 296 *decamp*; shake the dust from one's feet, steal away, sneak off, slink o., shuffle o., creep o.; scuttle, do a bunk.

**Int.** hands off!, keep off!, beware!, forbear!

#### 621 Relinquishment

**N.** *relinquishment*, abandonment; going, leaving, evacuation 296 *departure*; dereliction, desertion, truancy, defection 918 *undutifulness*; withdrawal, secession 978 *schism*; walk-out 145 *strike*; cop-out 620 *avoidance*; yielding, giving up, handing over, cession 780 *transfer*; forgoing, waiver, abnegation, renunciation 779 *nonretention*; abdication, retirement 753 *resignation*; disuse 674 *nonuse*; discontinuance 611 *desuetude*; cancellation, annulment 752 *abrogation*; world well lost 883 *seclusion*.

**Adj.** *relinquished*, forsaken, cast-off, castaway, marooned, abandoned etc. vb.; waived, forgone 779 *not retained*.

**Vb.** *relinquish*, drop, let go, leave hold of, unclench, quit one's hold, loosen one's grip 779 *not retain*; surrender, resign, give up, yield; waive, forgo; lower one's sights 872 *be humble*; cede, hand over, transfer 780 *assign*; forfeit 772 *lose*; renounce, swear off, abnegate, recant, 603 *change one's mind*; not proceed with, drop the idea, give up the idea, forget it 506 *forget*; wean oneself 611 *disaccustom*; forswear, deny oneself, abstain 620 *avoid*; shed, slough, cast off, divest 229 *doff*; drop, discard, get rid of, jettison, write off 674 *stop using*; lose interest, have other fish to fry 860 *be indifferent*; abdicate, back down, scratch, stand down, withdraw, retire, drop out 753 *resign*; jack it in, give in, throw in the sponge *or* the towel, throw up the game, throw in one's hand 721 *submit*; leave, quit, move out, vacate, evacuate 296 *depart*; forsake, abandon, run out on, leave stranded, quit one's post, desert 918 *fail in duty*; play truant 190 *be absent*; down tools, strike, come out 145 *cease*; walk out, secede 978 *schismatize*; go over, rat, sell out 603 *change one's allegiance*; throw over, ditch, jilt, break it off, go back on one's word 542 *deceive*; abandon discussion, waste no more time, pass on to the next, shelve, postpone 136 *put off*; annul, cancel 752 *abrogate*.

#### 622 Business

**N.** *business*, affairs, business a., interests, irons in the fire; main business, occupation, con-

cern, care; aim, ambition 617 *intention*; business on hand, case, agenda 154 *affairs*; enterprise, venture, undertaking, pursuit 678 *activity*; new business, new enterprise, start-up, spin-off company, spin-out c., venture capital; routine, business r., office r., round, daily r. 610 *practice*; business life, daily work; business circles, business world, City, world of commerce; art, technology, industry, light i., heavy i., smokestack i., sunrise i., sunset i., commerce, big business, e-business, e-commerce, retailing, e-tailing; multinational, business company, dotcom 708 *corporation*; agriculture, agribusiness; cottage industry, home-based i.; industrialism, industrialization, industrial arts, manufacture 164 *production*; trade, craft, handicraft, art and mystery 694 *skill*; guild, union, chamber of commerce, business association 706 *association*; employment, work, avocation (see also *vocation*); black economy, grey e.; sideline, hobby, pastime 837 *amusement*.

*vocation*, calling, life work, mission, apostolate 751 *commission*; life, lifestyle, walk of life, career, chosen career, labour of love, self-imposed task 597 *voluntary work*; living, livelihood, daily bread, one's bread and butter; profession, métier, craft, trade; line, line of country (see also *function*); exacting profession, high calling; religious profession, ministry; cloth, veil, habit 985 *the church*; military profession, arms 718 *war*; naval profession, sea; legal profession 953 *law*; teaching profession, education 534 *teaching*; medical profession, medicine, practice; business profession, industry, commerce 791 *trade*; government service, diplomatic s., civil s., administration 689 *management*; public service, public life; social service 901 *sociology*.

*job*, ploys, activities 678 *activity*; chores, odd jobs, work, task, set task, exercise 682 *labour*, duty, charge, commission, mission, errand, quest 751 *mandate*; employ, service, employment, full e., self-employment; hours of work, working day, workday, working week, man-hour; occupation, situation, position, berth, incumbency, appointment, post, office; regular employment, full-time job, permanency; temporary job, part-time j., freelance work, casual w.; casualization, contractorization, outsourcing, subcontracting; situation wanted; situation vacant, opening, vacancy; labour exchange, employment agency, Job Centre, Department of Employment; personnel management, human resource m.

*function*, what one has to do; capacity, office, duty; area, area of interest, realm, province, domain, orbit, sphere; scope, field, terms of reference 183 *range*; beat, round; department, line, line of country; role, part; business, job; responsibility, brief, concern, care, look-out, baby, pigeon.

**Adj.** *businesslike*, efficient 694 *skilful*; industrious, busy 678 *active*; vocational, professional, career; industrial, technological, commercial, financial, mercantile; labour-intensive, capital-i.; occupational, functional; official, governmental; routine, systematic 60 *orderly*; workaday 610 *habitual*; earning, in employment, employed, self-e., freelance; in hand, on h. 669 *preparatory*.

**Vb.** *employ*, busy, occupy, take up one's time, fill one's t., keep one engaged; give employment, engage, recruit, hire, enlist, appoint, post 751 *commission*; take on, take on the payroll 804 *pay*; give a situation to, offer a job to, fill a vacancy, staff with, staff; industrialize.

*busy oneself*, work, work for 742 *serve*; have a profession, have a career, be employed, be self-employed, be freelance, work from home, do a job, hold down a j., earn, earn one's living; earn an honest crust, turn an honest penny, keep the wolf from the door 771 *acquire*; take on a job, apply for a j., take a situation; be doing, be up and d., bustle 678 *be busy*; concern oneself with, make it one's business, take a hand in 678 *meddle*; work at, ply; engage in, turn to, turn one's hand to, take up, engage in, go in for; have to do, have on one's hands, have one's hands full, take on oneself, bear the burden, assume responsibility, bear the brunt, take on one's shoulders 917 *incur a duty*; work with one's hands, work with one's brains; pursue one's hobby 837 *amuse oneself*.

*function*, work, go 173 *operate*; fill a role, play one's part, carry on; officiate, act, do the offices, discharge the functions, exercise the f., discharge one's duties, serve as, do duty for, perform the duties, do the work of; substitute, stand in for 755 *deputize*; hold office, hold a portfolio, hold a place, hold down a job, have a job, have a brief, serve (see also *busy oneself*).

*do business*, transact, negotiate 766 *make terms*; ply a trade, ply a craft, exercise a profession, follow a calling, follow a career, work at a job; have a business, engage in, carry on, drive a trade, carry on a t., keep shop; do business with, deal w., enter into trade relations 791 *trade*; transact business, attend to one's b., go about one's b.; pursue one's vocation, earn one's living (see also *busy oneself*); be an employer, be an industrialist; be self-employed, work from home, run a cottage industry, freelance, set up in business, go into b., open a shop, put up one's sign.

**Adv.** *professionally*, in businesslike fashion; in the course of, all in the day's work; business as usual.

## 623 Plan

**N.** *plan*, scheme, design, planning; geomancy, feng shui; contrivance; organization, systematization, rationalization, centralization 60 *order*; programme, project, proposal 617 *intention*; proposition, suggestion, motion, resolution (see also *policy*); master plan, five-year p., detailed p., ground p., floor p., scale drawing, blueprint 551 *map*; diagram, flow chart 86 *statistics*; sketch, outline, draft, first d., schedule, memorandum; skeleton, roughcast; model, pattern, pilot scheme 23 *prototype*; proof, revise, proof copy 22 *copy*; drawing board, planning office, back room, operations r., headquarters, base.

*policy*, forethought 510 *foresight*; statesmanship 498 *wisdom*; course of action, plan of attack, procedure, strategy 688 *tactics*; operational research 459 *enquiry*; address, approach, attack 624 *way*; steps, measures 676 *action*; stroke of policy, coup, coup d'état 676 *deed*; proposed action, proposed line of a., scenario, forecast 511 *prediction*; programme, prospectus, platform, outline, plank, ticket, slate; line, party l.; formula 81 *rule*; schedule, agenda, order of the day, any other business, AOB 622 *business*.

*contrivance*, expedient, resource, recourse, resort, last r., card, trump c., card up one's sleeve 629 *means*; recipe, nostrum 658 *remedy*; loophole, way out, alternative, answer 667 *means of escape*; artifice, device, gimmick, dodge, ploy, shift, shtick, flag of convenience 698 *stratagem*; wangle, fiddle 930 *foul play*; knack, trick 694 *skill*; stunt, wheeze; inspiration, brainwave, brainstorm, happy thought, bright idea, right i. 451 *idea*; notion, invention; tool, weapon, contraption, gadget, gizmo 628 *instrument*; ad hoc measure, improvisation 609 *spontaneity*; makeshift, pis aller 150 *substitute*; feat, tour de force; bold move, stroke, master-stroke 676 *deed*.

*plot*, deep-laid p., intrigue; web, web of intrigue; cabal, conspiracy, inside job, insider trading *or* dealing; scheme, racket, game 698 *stratagem*; frame-up, put-up job, fit-up, machination; manipulation, wire-pulling 612 *motive*; secret influence 523 *latency*; counterplot, countermine 713 *defence*.

*planner*, contriver, framer, inventor, originator, deviser, hatcher; proposer, promoter, projector; founder, author, architect, designer; town-planner; backroom boy, boffin 696 *expert*; brains, mastermind; organizer, systematizer, systems analyst; strategist, tactician, manoeuvrer; statesman *or* -woman, politician, Machiavellian; wheeler-dealer, schemer, axegrinder; careerist, go-getter 678 *busy person*; plotter, intriguer, intrigant, spinner, spider; cabal; conspirator 545 *deceiver*; control freak.

**Adj.** *planned*, blueprinted, schematic, worked out, matured 669 *prepared*; organized, systematized 60 *orderly*; under consideration, at the planning stage, in draft, on the stocks, in proof; strategic, tactical; framed, plotted, engineered.

*planning*, contriving, resourceful, ingenious 698 *cunning*; purposeful, scheming, up to something; involved, deep in; intriguing, plotting, wheeler-dealing, conspiratorial; Machiavellian.

**Vb.** *plan*, form a p., resolve 617 *intend*; approach, approach a problem, attack a p.; make a plan, draw up, design, draft, blueprint; frame, shape 243 *form*; revise, recast 654 *rectify*; project, plan out, work o., sketch o., chalk o., map o., lay o., design a prototype; programme, draw up a p., lay the foundation; shape a course, mark out a c.; organize, systematize, rationalize, schematize, methodize 60 *order*; schedule, draw up a s., phase, adjust; invent, think up, hit on, fall on 484 *discover*; conceive a plan 513 *imagine*; find a way, make shift to; contrive, devise, engineer; hatch, concoct, mature 669 *prepare*; arrange, prearrange 608 *predetermine*; calculate, think ahead, look a. 498 *be wise*; have a policy, follow a plan, work to a schedule; do everything with a purpose, have an axe to grind, grind one's axe.

*plot*, scheme, have designs, be up to something, wheel and deal; manipulate, pull strings 178 *influence*; cabal, conspire, intrigue, machinate; concoct, cook up, brew; hatch a plot 698 *be cunning*; dig a pit for, undermine, countermine 542 *ensnare*; work against, manoeuvre a.; frame 541 *fake*.

**624 Way**
**N.** *way*, route 267 *itinerary*; manner, wise, guise; fashion, style 243 *form*; method, mode, line, approach, address, attack; procedure, process, way of, way of doing things, modus operandi 688 *tactics*; operation, treatment; modus vivendi, working arrangement 770 *compromise*; usual way, routine 610 *practice*; technique, know-how 694 *skill*; going, gait 265 *motion*; way forward, progress 285 *progression*; royal road, 'primrose path' (see quotation at 655 *deterioration*); way of life, lifestyle, behaviour 688 *conduct*. (See also *route*.)

*access*, means of a., right of way, communications; way to, direct approach 289 *approach*; entrance, door 263 *doorway*; side-entrance,

back-e., tradesman's e.; adit, drive, driveway, gangway; porch, hall, hallway, corridor, vestibule 194 *lobby*; way through, pass, defile, passageway 305 *passage*; intersection, junction, crossing; zebra crossing, pedestrian c., pelican c. 305 *traffic control*; strait, sound 345 *gulf*; channel, fairway, canal 351 *conduit*; lock, stile, turnstile, tollgate; way up, stairs, flight of s., stairway, ladder 308 *ascent*.

*bridge*, brig, way over; footbridge, flyover, road bridge, aqueduct; suspension bridge, swing b., bascule b., Bailey b., humpback b., packhorse b.; viaduct, span; railway bridge; pontoon bridge, floating b., transporter b.; drawbridge; causeway, stepping-stone, gangway, gangplank, catwalk, duckboards; ford, ferry 305 *passage*; way under, subway, underpass 263 *tunnel*; isthmus, neck.

*route*, direction, way to *or* from, way through *or* by, way up *or* over, way in *or* out; line, course, march, tack, track, beaten t., beat; trajectory, orbit; carriageway, lane, traffic l., bus l. 305 *traffic control*; air lane, sea-l., seaway, fairway, waterway, inland w. 351 *conduit*; trade route; short cut, bypass; detour, circumbendibus, roundabout way 626 *circuit*; line of communication, line of retreat, line of advance.

*path*, pathway, footway, footpath, pavement, sidewalk (US); towpath, bridlepath, bridleway, ride; byway, lane, green l., track, sheep t., rabbit run, trail, heritage t., mountain t.; right of way, public footpath; glade, walk, promenade, esplanade, parade, front, sea f., avenue, drive, boulevard, mall; pedestrian precinct, arcade, colonnade, aisle, cloister, ambulatory; racetrack, running track, speed t. 724 *arena*; fairway, runway.

*road*, high r., highway, Queen's h., highways and byways; main road, A road, minor r., B r., dirt r., cinder track; side road, access r., service r., private r.; corniche, switchback; toll road, turnpike, route nationale; thoroughfare, through road, trunk r., arterial r., artery, bypass, ring road; motorway, M-way, autoroute, autobahn, autostrada; expressway, throughway, clearway; sliproad, acceleration lane, fast lane; crossroads, junction, T-junction, turnoff; intersection, roundabout, cloverleaf; crossing, pedestrian c., zebra c, pelican c. 305 *traffic control*; roadway, carriageway, dual c.; central reservation, crash barrier; cycle track, cycleway; street, high s., one-way s., side s., back s., back doubles; alleyway, wynd, alley, blind a., cul de sac; close, avenue 192 *housing*; pavement, sidewalk (US), kerb, kerbstone; paving, cobbles, setts, paving stone, flagstones; hard shoulder, verge; macadam, tarmac, asphalt, road metal, laterite;

surface, road s., skidproof s.; road building, traffic engineering.

*railway*, railroad, line; permanent way, track, lines, railway l., electrified l., third rail; main line, branch l., loop l.; tramlines, tramway; monorail, maglev, cog railway, rack and pinion, funicular, cableway, ropeway, telpher line; overhead railway, elevated r., underground r., electric r., subway, tube, metro 274 *train*; light railway, narrow gauge, standard g.; junction, crossover, level crossing, tunnel, cutting, embankment; siding, marshalling yard, goods y., shunting y., turntable; station, halt, stop, whistle s., platform 145 *stopping place*; signal, gantry, signal box, cabin; rails, points, sleepers, frog, fishplate, ballast.

**Adj.** *communicating*, granting access, giving access 289 *accessible*; through, main, arterial, trunk; bridged, crossed, forded; paved, metalled, cobbled, tarmac; well-paved, well-laid, skid-proof; signposted, waymarked, lit, well-lit; well-used, busy; trodden, beaten.

**Adv.** *via*, by way of, in transit; on the way, chemin faisant.

*how*, in what manner?, by what means?, on what lines?

### 625 Middle way

**N.** *middle way*, middle course, middle of the road, via media; balance, golden mean, happy medium 30 *average*; central position, halfway, halfway house, midstream 30 *middle point*; slack water, half tide; direct course, nondeviation, straight line, short cut, beeline; short circuit 249 *straightness*; noncommittal, neutrality 177 *moderation*; lukewarmness, half measures 601 *irresolution*; mutual concession 770 *compromise*.

*moderate*, nonextremist, wet, Girondist, Minimalist, Menshevik; middle-of-the-roader, half-and-halfer; neutral, uncommitted person, uncommitted nation; don't know; Laodicean.

**Adj.** *neutral*, impartial 913 *just*; noncommittal, uncommitted, unattached, free-floating, don't-know; detached 860 *indifferent*; moderate, wet, nonextreme, unextreme, middle-of-the-road 225 *central*; sitting on the fence, lukewarm, half-and-half, shilly-shallying 601 *irresolute*; neither one thing nor the other, grey.

*undeviating*, unswerving, keeping to the middle 225 *central*; looking neither to right nor left, direct 249 *straight*; in between, halfway, midway, intermediate 231 *interjacent*.

**Vb.** *be midstream*, keep to the middle, steer a middle course, go straight, hold straight on, not deviate, not swerve, look neither to right nor to left.

*be halfway*, go halfway, meet h., go so far and no further 770 *compromise*; be in between, occupy the centre, hold the scales, balance 28 *equalize*; sit on the fence, shilly-shally, have a foot in both camps 474 *be uncertain*.

### 626 Circuit

**N.** *circuit*, roundabout way, longest w., circuitous route, bypass, detour, ring road, loop, loop line, divagation, digression 282 *deviation*; ambages 251 *convolution*; circulation, circumambulation, orbit, beat, ambit, round, lap 314 *circuition*; circumference 250 *circle*; full circle, looping the loop.

**Adj.** *roundabout*, circuitous, indirect, meandering, ambagious, out of the way 251 *convoluted*; circumlocutory 570 *diffuse*; circulatory, circumambulating; rounding, skirting; encompassing, surrounding 230 *circumjacent*.

**Vb.** *circuit*, round, lap, beat the bounds, go round, make a circuit, loop the loop 314 *circle*; make a detour, go a roundabout way, go out of one's way 282 *deviate*; turn, bypass, short-circuit 620 *avoid*; lead one a dance, beat about the bush; encircle, embrace, encompass 230 *surround*; keep to the circumference, skirt, edge round.

**Adv.** *round about*, round the world, in a roundabout way, circuitously, indirectly, from pillar to post.

### 627 Requirement

**N.** *requirement*, essential, sine qua non, a necessary, a must 596 *necessity*; needs, necessities, necessaries; indent, order, requisition, shopping list; stipulation, prerequisite, prior conditions 766 *conditions*; desideratum, want, lack, need 636 *insufficiency*; gap, lacuna 190 *absence*; demand, consumer d., call for, run on, seller's market, bearish m., bullish m. 792 *purchase*; consumption, input, intake; shortage 307 *shortfall*; slippage; balance due, what is owing 803 *debt*; claim 761 *request*; ultimatum, injunction 737 *command*.

*needfulness*, case of need, occasion; necessity for, essentiality, indispensability, desirability; necessitousness, want, pinch, breadline, poverty level 801 *poverty*; exigency, urgency, emergency 137 *crisis*; vitalness, matter of life and death 638 *important matter*; obligation 917 *duty*; bare minimum, the least one can do; face-saving measures.

**Adj.** *required*, requisite, prerequisite, needful, needed; necessary, essential, vital, indispensable, not to be spared; called for, in request, in demand 859 *desired*; reserved, earmarked, booked; wanted, lacking, missing 190 *absent*.

*necessitous*, in want, in need, pinched,

feeling the pinch, on the breadline, in the poverty trap, at poverty level; lacking, deprived of; needing badly, craving; destitute 801 *poor*; starving 636 *underfed*; disadvantaged.

*demanding*, crying, crying out for, calling for, imperative, urgent, instant, exigent, pressing, pinching; compulsory 740 *compelling*.

**Vb.** *require*, need, have need of, want, lack 636 *be unsatisfied*; not have, be without, stand in need of, feel the need for, have occasion for *or* to; have a vacancy for; miss, desiderate; need badly, crave 859 *desire*; call for, cry out f., clamour f.; claim, put in a claim for, apply for 761 *request*; find necessary, find indispensable, be unable to do without, must have; consume, take 634 *waste*, 673 *use*; create a need, render necessary, necessitate, oblige 740 *compel*; make demands 737 *demand*; stipulate 766 *give terms*; order, send an order for, tele-order, indent, requisition; reserve, book, earmark, set aside.

**Adv.** *in need*, in want; necessarily, sine qua non; of necessity, at a pinch.

## 628 Instrumentality

**N.** *instrumentality*, operation 173 *agency*; occasion 156 *cause*; result 157 *effect*; pressure 178 *influence*; efficacy 160 *power*; occult power, paranormal p., magic 983 *sorcery*; services, help, assistance, midwifery 703 *aid*; support 706 *cooperation*; intervention, intermediacy, interference 678 *activity*; subservience 739 *obedience*; medium 629 *means*; use, employment, application, serviceability, handiness 640 *utility*; use of machinery, instrumentation, mechanization, automation, computerization 630 *machine*.

*instrument*, hand, organ, sense o.; amanuensis, scribe, handmaid, lackey, slave, slave of the lamp 742 *servant*, agent, midwife, medium, help, assistant 703 *aider*; go-between, pander 720 *mediator*; catalyst; vehicle; pawn, piece on the board; robot 630 *machine*; cat's paw, stooge, puppet, creature 707 *auxiliary*; weapon, implement, appliance, lever 630 *tool*; magic ring, Aladdin's lamp 983 *spell*; key, skeleton k., master k., passkey 263 *opener*; open sesame, watchword, password, slogan, shibboleth, passport, safeconduct, warrant 756 *permit*; stepping-stone 624 *bridge*; channel, high road, highway 624 *road*; push button, switch, controls; device, expedient, makeshift, gadget, gizmo 623 *contrivance*; card, ace, trump.

**Adj.** *instrumental*, working 173 *operative*; hand-operated, manual; automatic, computerized, electronic, push-button 630 *mechanical*; effective, efficient, efficacious, effectual 160 *powerful*; telling, weighty 178 *influential*; paranormal, magic 983 *magical*; conducive 156

*causal*; practical, applied; serviceable, general-purpose, employable, handy 640 *useful*; ready, available 597 *willing*; forwarding, promoting, assisting, helpful 703 *aiding*; Socratic, maieutic; functional, agential, subservient, ministering; mediational, intermediate, intervening; mediated by.

**Vb.** *be instrumental*, work, act 173 *operate*; perform 676 *do*; serve, subserve, work for, lend oneself *or* itself to, pander to 703 *minister to*; help, assist 703 *aid*; advance, promote 703 *patronize*; have a hand in 775 *participate*; be to blame for 156 *cause*; be the instrument, be the creature of, be a cat's paw, pull another's chestnuts out of the fire 640 *be useful*; intermediate, interpose, intervene 720 *mediate*; use one's influence, pull strings 178 *influence*; effect 156 *cause*; tend 156 *conduce*; achieve 725 *carry through*.

**Adv.** *through*, per, by the hand of, by means of, with the help of, thanks to.

## 629 Means

**N.** *means*, ways and m., wherewithal; power, capacity 160 *ability*; strong hand, trumps, aces; conveniences, facilities; appliances, tools, tools of the trade, bag of tricks 630 *tool*; technology, new t., high t., high tech, third wave 490 *knowledge*; technique, know-how 694 *skill*; wherewithal, matériel, equipment, supplies, stock, munitions, ammunition 633 *provision*; resources, economic r., natural r., raw material 631 *materials*; nuts and bolts 630 *machine*; labour resources, pool of labour, workforce, manpower 686 *personnel*; financial resources 800 *wealth*; liquidity, cash flow 797 *money*; capital, working c. 628 *instrument*; assets, stock-in-trade 777 *property*; stocks and shares, investments, investment fund, investment portfolio, tracker fund, PEP, ISA, Tessa-only ISA, TOISA; mutualization, demutualization; revenue, income, receipts, credits 807 *receipt*; borrowing capacity, line of credit 802 *credit*; reserves, something in reserve, stand-by, shot in one's locker, card up one's sleeve, two strings to one's bow 662 *safeguard*; freedom of choice, alternative 605 *choice*; method, measures, steps 624 *way*; cure, specific 658 *remedy*; expedient, device, resort, recourse 623 *contrivance*; makeshift, ad-hoc measure 150 *substitute*; let-out 667 *means of escape*; desperate remedy, last resort, last hope, last gasp, last throw 618 *gambling*.

**Vb.** *find means*, provide the wherewithal, supply, find, furnish 633 *provide*; equip, fit out 669 *make ready*; finance, raise the money, promote, float; subsidize; have the means, be in a position to 160 *be able*; contrive, be resourceful, not be at a loss, find a way 623 *plan*; beg, borrow or steal, get by hook or by crook 771 *acquire*.

**Adv.** *by means of*, with, wherewith; by, using, through; with the aid of; by dint of; by fair means or foul.

### 630 Tool

**N.** *tool*, precision t., machine t., hand t, implement 628 *instrument*; apparatus, appliance, utensil; weapon, arm 723 *arms*; device, mechanical d., contraption, gadget, gizmo 623 *contrivance*; doodah, doohickey, thingummy, whatsit; screw, screwdriver, turnscrew, drill, electric d. 263 *perforator*; wrench, monkey w., pipe w., mole w., Stillson (tdmk), spanner; pliers, pincers, tweezers 778 *nippers*; chisel, wedge, edged tool, knife, Stanley (tdmk) k. 256 *sharp edge*; rope 47 *cable*; peg, nail 217 *hanger*, 218 *support*; leverage, lever, jemmy, crowbar, handspike, jack 218 *pivot*; grip, lug, helve, haft, shaft, tiller, helm, rudder 218 *handle*; pulley, sheave 250 *wheel*; switch, stopcock; gunlock, trigger; pedal, pole, punt-p. 287 *propulsion*; ram 279 *hammer*; prehistoric tool, celt, flint; tools of the trade, tool-kit, do-it-yourself k., bag of tricks.

*machine*, mechanical device; machinery, mechanism, works; clockwork, wheelwork, wheels within wheels; nuts and bolts 58 *component*; spring, mainspring, hairspring; gears, gearing, spur gears, bevel g., syncromesh, automatic gear change; motor, engine, internal combustion e., lean-burn e., Wankel e., diesel e., steam e.; turbine, dynamo 160 *sources of energy*; servomechanism, servomotor; robot, automaton; computer 86 *computing*.

*mechanics*, engineering, computer-aided e., CAE; civil e.; electrical e. 160 *electronics*; cybernetics; automatic control, automation, computerization, robotics; artificial intelligence, AI, expert system; mechanical power, mechanical advantage; technics, technology, advanced t., low t., high t., high tech, ultratech, third wave; nanotechnology; terotechnology.

*equipment*, furniture, appointments; gear, tackle, harness; fittings, fixture 40 *adjunct*; outfit, kit; upholstery, furnishing; trappings, accoutrement 228 *dress*; utensils, impedimenta, paraphernalia, chattels 777 *property*; wares, stock-in-trade 795 *merchandise*; plant 687 *workshop*.

*machinist*, operator, operative; driver, minder, machine-m. 686 *agent*; engineer, technician, mechanician, mechanic, fitter; tool-user, craftsman, skilled worker 686 *artisan*.

**Adj.** *mechanical*, mechanized, motorized, powered, power-driven; labour-saving, automatic 628 *instrumental*; robot-like, automated, computerized, electronic; machine-minded, tool-using.

### 631 Materials

**N.** *materials*, resources 629 *means*; material, stuff, staple, stock 3 *substance*; raw material, grist; meat, fodder 301 *food*; oil, yellowcake 385 *fuel*; chemical feedstock; ore, mineral, metal, pig-iron, ingot; clay, adobe, china clay, potter's c., gypsum 344 *soil*; glass 422 *transparency*; plastic, polythene, polyethylene, polypropylene, polystyrene, polyvinyl chloride, PVC, polytetrafluoroethylene, latex, celluloid, fibreglass; rope, yarn, wool 208 *fibre*; leather, hide 226 *skin*; timber, log, faggot, stick 366 *wood*; rafter, board 218 *beam*; plank, planking, plywood, lath, stave 207 *lamina*; stuffing 227 *lining*; cloth, fabric 222 *textile*.

*building material*, building block, breeze b., brick 381 *pottery*; bricks and mortar, lath and plaster, wattle and daub, cob; studwork 331 *structure*; thatch, slate, tile, shingle 226 *roof*; stone, marble, granite, flint, ashlar, masonry; rendering 226 *facing*; compo, composition, cement, concrete, reinforced c., ferroconcrete; paving material, flag, cobble 226 *paving*; hard core, gravel, hoggin *or* hogging, tarmac, asphalt 624 *road*.

*paper*, rag p., pulp, wood p., newsprint; card, Bristol board, calendered paper, art p., cartridge p., India p., carbon p., tissue p., crepe p., sugar p., tracing p., cellophane; papier mâché, cardboard, pasteboard, millboard, strawboard, fibreboard, chipboard, hardboard, plasterboard; sheet, foolscap, quarto, imperial, A1, A2, A3, A4, A5; quire, ream; notepaper 586 *stationery*.

### 632 Store

**N.** *store*, mass, heap, load, stack, stockpile, mountain, butter m., lake, wine l., buildup 74 *accumulation*; packet, bundle, bagful, bucketful etc. 26 *quantity*; harvest, crop, vintage, mow 771 *acquisition*; haystack, haycock, hayrick; stock, stock-in-trade 795 *merchandise*; assets, capital, holding, investment 777 *property*; fund, reserve f., reserves, something in reserve, something in hand, backlog; unexpended balance, savings, savings account, nest egg, baby bond; deposit, hoard, treasure; buried treasure, cache 527 *hiding-place*; bottom drawer, hope chest, trousseau 633 *provision*; pool, kitty; common fund, appeal f., community chest 775 *joint possession*; quarry, mine, gold-m.; natural resources, natural deposit, mineral d., coal d.; coalfield, coalbed, gasfield, oilfield; coal mine, colliery, working, shaft; coalface, seam, stringer, lode; pipe, pipe vein; vein, rich v.; bonanza, strike 484 *discovery*; well, oil w., gusher; fountain, fount 156 *source*; supply, constant s., stream; tap, pipeline, artesian well 341 *irrigator*; milch cow, the goose that lays the golden eggs, treacle well, cornucopia, abundance 635 *plenty*; repertoire, range (see also *collection*).

*storage*, stowage, gathering, garnering 74 *accumulation*; conservation, ensilage, bottling 666 *preservation*; safe deposit 660 *protection*; stabling, warehousing; mountain, butter m., lake, wine l.; storage, storage space, shelf-room, space, accommodation 183 *room*; boxroom, loft; hold, bunker 194 *cellar*; storeship, supply base, storehouse, storeroom, stockroom; warehouse, goods shed, godown; depository, depot, entrepôt; dock, wharf, garage 192 *shed*; magazine, arsenal, armoury, gunroom; treasure house 799 *treasury*; exchequer, strongroom, vault, coffer, moneybox, moneybag, till, safe, night s., bank; blood b., sperm b.; data b. 86 *computing*; store of memories 505 *memory*; hive, honeycomb; granary, garner, barn, silo; water tower, reservoir, cistern, tank, gasholder, gasometer; battery, storage b., dry b., wet b.; garage, petrol station, gas s., filling s., petrol pump; dump, sump, drain, cesspool, sewage farm 649 *sink*; pantry, larder, buttery, stillroom 194 *room*; cupboard, shelf 194 *cabinet*; refrigerator, fridge, deep freeze, freezer, fridge-freezer; portmanteau, holdall, packing case 194 *box*; container, holder, quiver 194 *receptacle*.

*collection*, set, complete s.; archives, file 548 *record*; folder, bundle, portfolio 74 *accumulation*; museum 125 *antiquity*; gallery, art g., art museum; book-collection, library, thesaurus 559 *dictionary*; menagerie, aquarium 369 *zoo*; waxworks, Madame Tussaud's; exhibition 522 *exhibit*; repertory, repertoire, bag of tricks.

**Adj.** *stored*, hoarded etc. vb.; in store, in deposit; in hand, held; put aside, put by; in reserve, unexpended; banked, funded, invested; available, in stock; spare, supernumerary.

**Vb.** *store*, stow, pack, bundle 193 *load*; roll up, fold up; lay up, stow away, put a., put in mothballs, mothball; dump, garage, stable, warehouse; garner, barn; gather, harvest, reap, mow, pick, glean 370 *cultivate*; stack, heap, pile, amass, accumulate 74 *bring together*; stock up, stock up one's cupboards *or* larder, lay in, bulk-buy, panic buy, stockpile, pile up, build up, build up one's stocks 36 *augment*; take on, take in, fuel, coal, bunker 633 *provide*; fill, fill

up, top up, refill, refuel 633 *replenish*; put by, save, keep, hold, file, hang on to, keep by one 778 *retain*; bottle, pickle, conserve 666 *preserve*; leave, set aside, put a., lay by, put b., keep back, keep in hand, reserve; fund, bank, deposit, invest; hoard, treasure, hive; bury, cache, squirrel away, stash a., secrete 525 *conceal*; husband, save up, salt away, make a nest egg, prepare for a rainy day 814 *economize*; equip oneself, put in the bottom drawer 669 *prepare oneself*; pool, put in the kitty 775 *communalize*.

## 633 Provision

**N.** *provision*, providing, furnishing, logistics, equipment 669 *fitting out*; purveyance, catering; service, delivery, distribution; self-service; procuring, pandering; feeding, entertainment, bed and breakfast, board and lodging, maintenance; assistance, lending 703 *economic aid*; supply, food s., water s., constant s., feed; pipeline 272 *transference*; commissariat, provisioning, supplies, stores, rations, iron r., starvation r., emergency r., reserves 632 *store*; reinforcement, replenishment, refill, filling-up 54 *plenitude*; food, provender 301 *provisions*; helping, portion 301 *meal*; grist to the mill, fuel to the flame; produce 164 *product*; increase, return 771 *gain*; conservation, resource management 814 *economy*; budgeting, budget, cash flow 808 *accounts*; possible need 669 *preparation*.

*provider*, donor 781 *giver*; creditor, moneylender 784 *lender*; wet nurse, feeder; purser 798 *treasurer*; steward, butler; commissary, quartermaster, storekeeper; supplier, victualler, sutler; provision merchant, ship's chandler, drysalter, grocer, greengrocer, baker, poulterer, fishmonger, butcher, vintner, wine merchant; retailer, middleman, shopkeeper 794 *tradespeople*; procurer, pander, pimp 952 *bawd*.

*caterer*, purveyor, hotelier, hotelkeeper, hotel manager, restaurateur, head waiter, maître d'hôtel; innkeeper, alewife, landlord, landlady, licensee, mine host, publican; housekeeper, housewife; cook, chef; pastrycook, confectioner.

**Adj.** *provisioning*, commissarial; self-service; sufficing, all-s. 635 *sufficient*; supplied, provided, all found, all-in; well-appointed, highly-rated, three star; available, available on request, on tap, on the menu.

**Vb.** *provide*, afford, offer, lend 781 *give*; provision, find; equip, furnish, arm, man, fit out, kit o. 669 *make ready*; supply, maintain s., keep supplied; yield 164 *produce*; bring in a supply, pump in; cater, purvey; procure, pander, pimp;

service, service an order, meet an o. 793 *sell*; distribute, deliver, make deliveries, deliver the goods; hand out, hand round, serve, serve up, dish up; victual, feed, cook for, do for, board, put up, maintain, keep, clothe; stock, keep a s.; budget, make provision, make due p.; provide for oneself, provision o., do for o.; take on supplies, stock up, lay in a stock 632 *store*; fuel, coal, bunker; gather food, forage, water, take on w.; tap, draw, draw on, milk 304 *extract*; export, import 791 *trade*.

*replenish*, reinforce, make good, make up; fill up, top up, refill 54 *fill*; revictual, restock, refuel, reload.

### 634 Waste

**N.** *waste*, wastage 42 *decrement*; leakage, ebb 298 *outflow*; inroads, consumption; intake 627 *requirement*; spending, outlay, expense 806 *expenditure*; using up, depletion, exhaustion, drainage 300 *voidance*; dissipation 75 *dispersion*; evaporation 338 *vaporization*; melting 337 *liquefaction*; damage 772 *loss*; wear and tear, built-in obsolescence 655 *deterioration*; wastefulness, improvidence, lack of economy, lavishness, extravagance, overspending, potlatch, squandering, unnecessary expenditure 815 *prodigality*; overproduction 637 *superfluity*; misapplication, useless expenditure, frittering away 675 *misuse*; vandalism, wilful destruction, destructiveness, sabotage 165 *destruction*; waste product, litter, refuse 641 *rubbish*.

**Adj.** *wasteful*, extravagant, unnecessary, uneconomic 815 *prodigal*; throwaway 637 *superfluous*; labour-consuming, time-c., energy-c.; damaging 165 *destructive*.

*wasted*, exhausted, depleted, consumed; gone to waste, gone down the drain; fruitless, bootless 641 *profitless*; ill-spent, squandered, misapplied; of no avail, futile, in vain.

**Vb.** *waste*, consume, make a dent in, make inroads on, wade into; swallow, devour, gobble up 301 *eat*; spend, lay out 806 *expend*; take, use up, exhaust, deplete, drain, suck dry 300 *empty*; dissipate, scatter, throw to the four winds 75 *disperse*; abuse, overwork, overcrop, overfish, overgraze, impoverish, milk dry 675 *misuse*; wear out, erode, damage 655 *impair*; put to the wrong use, misapply, fritter away, cast pearls before swine; make no use of 674 *not use*; labour in vain 641 *waste effort*; be extravagant, overspend, squander, run through, throw away, pour down the drain, burn the candle at both ends, throw out the baby with the bath water 815 *be prodigal*; be careless, slop, spill; be destructive, ruin, destroy, sabotage, vandalize 165 *lay waste*; be wasted, suffer loss, decay 37 *decrease*; leak, ebb

away, run low, dry up 298 *flow out*; melt, melt away 337 *liquefy*; evaporate 338 *vaporize*; run out, give o. 636 *not suffice*; burn out, burn away, gutter 381 *burn*; run to seed 655 *deteriorate*; run to waste, go down the drain.

### 635 Sufficiency

**N.** *sufficiency*, elegant s., sensible modicum, quantum sufficit, right amount; right qualities, qualification; right number, quorum; adequacy, enough, pass marks; assets, adequate income, competence, living wage; subsistence farming; self-sufficiency, autarky; exact requirement, no surplus; breadline; minimum, no less, bare minimum, least one can do; acceptability, the possible, all that is p. 469 *possibility*; full measure, satisfaction, ample s., contentment, all that could be desired 828 *content*; fulfilment 725 *completion*; repletion, one's fill, bellyful 863 *satiety*.

*plenty*, God's p., horn of p., cornucopia 171 *abundance*; outpouring, showers of, flood, spate, streams 350 *stream*; lots, lashings, oodles, galore 32 *great quantity*; fullness, copiousness, amplitude 54 *plenitude*; affluence, riches 800 *wealth*; 'the fat of the land' (see quotation at 730 *prosperity*), luxury, loaded table, groaning board, feast, banquet 301 *feasting*; orgy, riot, profusion 815 *prodigality*; richness, fat; fertility, productivity, luxuriance, lushness 171 *productiveness*; foison, harvest, rich h., vintage h., bumper crop; rich vein, bonanza, ample store, endless supply, more where it came from 632 *store*; more than enough, too much, superabundance, embarras de choix, embarras de richesses 637 *redundance*.

**Adj.** *sufficient*, sufficing, all-s. 633 *provisioning*; self-sufficient 54 *complete*; enough, adequate, competent; enough to go round; equal to, a match for 28 *equal*; satisfactory, satisfying 828 *contenting*; measured, commensurate, up to the mark; just right, not too much, not too little; barely sufficient, only just enough; makeshift, provisional 150 *substituted*.

*plenteous*, plentiful, ample, enough and to spare, more than enough 637 *superfluous*; openhanded, generous, lavish 813 *liberal*; extravagant 815 *prodigal*; wholesale, without stint, unsparing, unmeasured, exhaustless, inexhaustible 32 *great*; luxuriant, luxuriating, riotous, lush, rank, fertile, fat 171 *prolific*; profuse, abundant, copious, overflowing 637 *redundant*; rich, opulent, affluent 800 *moneyed*.

*filled*, well-f., flush 54 *full*; full up, chock-full, chock-a-block, replete, satiated, had it up to here, ready to burst 863 *sated*; satisfied, contented 828 *content*; well-provided, well-stocked, well-furnished 633 *provisioning*; rich in, teeming, overflowing with, crawling with 104 *multitudinous.*

**Vb.** *suffice*, be enough, do, answer 642 *be expedient*; just do, do and no more, work, serve, serve as a makeshift; fill the bill, make the grade, pass, pass muster, qualify, reach, wash, measure up, meet requirements, cut the mustard (inf) 727 *be successful*; do all that is possible, rise to the occasion; stand, stand up to, take the strain 218 *support*; do what is required 725 *carry out*; fill up, top up, saturate 54 *fill*; refill 633 *replenish*; prove acceptable, satisfy 828 *content*; more than satisfy, satiate, give one his *or* her bellyful 863 *sate*; provide for, make adequate provision 633 *provide.*

*abound*, be plentiful, proliferate, teem, swarm, bristle with, crawl w. 104 *be many*; exuberate, riot, luxuriate 171 *be fruitful*; flow, shower, snow, pour, stream, sheet 350 *rain*; brim, overflow, 'flow with milk and honey' (see quotation at 730 *prosperity*) 637 *superabound*; roll in, wallow in, swim in 800 *be rich.*

*have enough*, be satisfied 828 *be content*; eat one's fill 301 *eat*; drink one's fill 301 *drink*; be sated, be chock-full, have had enough, have had it up to here, have had one's bellyful, be fed up 829 *be discontented*; have the means 800 *afford.*

**Adv.** *enough*, sufficiently, tolerably, amply, to the full, to one's heart's content; ad libitum, ad lib, on tap, on demand; abundantly, inexhaustibly, interminably.

## 636 Insufficiency

**N.** *insufficiency*, not enough, drop in the bucket; nonsatisfaction 829 *discontent*; inadequacy, incompetence; mininess, little enough, nothing to spare, less than somewhat 33 *small quantity*; too few, no quorum 105 *fewness*; deficiency, imperfection 647 *defect*; deficit 55 *incompleteness*; nonfulfilment 726 *noncompletion*; half measures, tinkering, failure, weakness, slippage 307 *shortfall*; bankruptcy 805 *insolvency*; bare subsistence, subsistence level, breadline, poverty level, pittance, dole, mite; stinginess, meanness 816 *parsimony*; short allowance, short commons, iron rations, starvation r., half r.; austerity, Lenten fare, Spartan f., starvation diet, bread and water 945 *asceticism*; fast day 946 *fasting*; malnutrition, vitamin deficiency 651 *disease.*

*scarcity*, scarceness, paucity 105 *fewness*; dearth, leanness, seven lean years; drought, famine, starvation; infertility 172 *unproductiveness*; shortage 307 *shortfall*; slippage; power cut 37 *decrease*; none to spare, short supply, seller's market, bearish m.; scantiness, meagreness; deprivation 801 *poverty*; lack, want, need

627 *needfulness*; ebb, low water 212 *shallowness.*

**Adj.** *insufficient*, not satisfying, unsatisfactory, disappointing 829 *discontenting*; inadequate, not enough, too little; scant, scanty, skimpy, slender; too small, cramping 33 *small*; deficient, light on, low on, lacking 55 *incomplete*; wanting, found w., poor 35 *inferior*; incompetent, unequal to, not up to it 695 *unskilful*; weak, thin, watery, wersh, jejune, unnourishing 4 *insubstantial*; niggardly, miserly; stingy 816 *parsimonious.*

*unprovided*, unsupplied, unfurnished, ill-furnished, ill-supplied, ill-equipped, vacant, bare, unreplenished 190 *empty*; empty-handed 728 *unsuccessful*; unsatisfied, unfulfilled, unfilled, unsated 829 *discontented*; unprovided for, unaccommodated; insatiable 859 *greedy*; deficient in, lacking in, starved of; cramped 702 *hindered*; hard up 801 *poor*; undercapitalized, underfinanced, understaffed, undermanned, shorthanded, under establishment, under strength; stinted, rationed, skimped; not provided, unavailable, off the menu, off 190 *absent.*

*underfed*, undernourished; half-fed, half-starved, on short commons; unfed, famished, starved, famine-stricken, starving, ravening, ravenous 946 *fasting*; starveling, spare, scurvy, thin, skinny, skin and bone, anorexic, emaciated, macerated, stunted 206 *lean.*

*scarce*, rare 140 *infrequent*; sparse 105 *few*; short, in short supply, at a premium, hard to get, hard to come by, not to be had for love or money, not to be had at any price, unavailable, unprocurable, unobtainable, out of season, out of stock.

**Vb.** *not suffice*, be insufficient, – inadequate etc. adj.; not meet requirements 647 *be imperfect*; cramp one's style 747 *restrain*; want, lack, need, require, leave a gap, leave a lacuna 627 *require*; fail 509 *disappoint*; fall below 35 *be inferior*, come short, default 307 *fall short*; run out, dry up; take half measures, tinker, paper over the cracks 726 *not complete.*

*be unsatisfied*, ask for more, beg for m., come again, take a second helping, still feel hungry 859 *be hungry*; feel dissatisfied, increase one's demands 829 *be discontented*; spurn an offer, reject with contempt 607 *reject*; desiderate, miss, want, feel the lack, stand in need of, feel something is missing 627 *require*; be a glutton for, be unable to have enough of 947 *gluttonize.*

*make insufficient*, ask too much, expect too much; overwork, overcrop, impoverish, damage 655 *impair*; exhaust, deplete, run down, squander 634 *waste*; grudge, hold back, stint, skimp, ration, put on half rations, put on short commons 816 *be parsimonious*; disinherit, cut off without a penny, cut off with a shilling 786 *deprive*.

**Adv.** *insufficiently*, not enough; in default, failing, for want of; at a low ebb.

### 637 Redundance

**N.** *redundance*, redundancy, overspill, overflow, inundation, flood 298 *outflow*; abundance, superabundance, exuberance, luxuriance, riot, profusion 635 *plenty*; richness, embarras de richesses, bonanza 632 *store*; upsurge, uprush 36 *increase*; avalanche, spate 32 *great quantity*; too many, mob 74 *crowd*; saturation, saturation point 54 *plenitude*; excess 634 *waste*; excessiveness, nimiety, exorbitance, extremes, too much 546 *exaggeration*; overdoing it, overstretching oneself, overextension, overexpansion, too many irons in the fire 678 *overactivity*; overpoliteness, officiousness, red tape; overpraise, overoptimism 482 *overestimation*; overmeasure, overpayment, overweight; burden, load, overload, last straw 322 *gravity*; more than is fair, lion's share 32 *main part*; overindulgence 943 *intemperance*; overfeeding, feeding frenzy 947 *gluttony*; overdrinking 949 *drunkenness*; engorgement, plethora, congestion 863 *satiety*; more than enough, bellyful 635 *sufficiency*; glut (see also *superfluity*); fat, fattiness; obesity 651 *disease*.

*superfluity*, more than is needed, luxury, luxuriousness; frills, luxuries, nonessentials, luxury article; overfulfilment, overkill, duplication, supererogation; something over, bonus, cash crop, spare cash, money to burn 40 *extra*; margin, overlap, excess, overplus, surplusage, surplus, balance 41 *remainder*; superfluousness, excrescence, accessory, fifth wheel, parasite 641 *inutility*; padding, expletive, verse-filler 570 *pleonasm*; tautology 570 *diffuseness*; redundancy 300 *ejection*; underemployment, unemployment 679 *inactivity*; overemployment, overmanning 678 *activity*; too much of a good thing, embarras de richesses, glut, drug on the market; inflation; surfeit, overdose 863 *satiety*.

**Adj.** *redundant*, too many, one too m., one over the eight 104 *many*; overmuch, overabundant, excessive, immoderate 32 *exorbitant*; overdone, 546 *exaggerated*; overflowing, overfull, slopping, running over, brimming over, filled to overflowing 54 *full*; flooding, streaming 350 *flowing*; snowed under, overwhelmed, saturated, supersaturated 341 *drenched*; cloying, satiating 838 *tedious*; cloyed, satiated 863 *sated*; replete, gorged, crammed, stuffed, overfed, bursting; overstretched; over-

charged, overburdened, overloaded; congested, plethoric; bloated 197 *expanded*.

*superfluous*, supererogatory; redundant, supernumerary; adscititious, excrescent; needless, unnecessary, unrequired, uncalled for 641 *useless*; excessive, more than one asked for 634 *wasteful*; luxury, luxurious, with all the trimmings; surplus, extra, over and above 41 *remaining*; above one's needs, spare, to spare 38 *additional*; de trop, on one's hands, left over, going begging 860 *unwanted*; dispensable, expendable, replaceable.

**Vb.** *superabound*, riot, luxuriate 635 *abound*; run riot, overproduce, overpopulate 171 *be fruitful*; bristle with, burst w., swarm w., teem w., hotch w., crawl w., meet one at every turn, outnumber 104 *be many*; overflow, brim over, well o., ooze at every pore, burst at the seams 54 *be complete*; stream, flood, inundate, burst its banks, deluge, overwhelm 350 *flow*; engulf 299 *absorb*; know no bounds, spread far and wide 306 *overstep*; overlap 183 *extend*; soak, saturate 341 *drench*; stuff, gorge, cram 54 *fill*; congest, choke, suffocate; overdose, oversatisfy, glut, cloy, satiate, sicken 863 *sate*; overfeed, pamper oneself, overindulge o., overeat, overdrink 943 *be intemperate*; overfulfil, oversubscribe, do more than enough; oversell, flood the market; overstock, pile up; overdo, go over the top, overstep the mark, overegg the pudding, pile it on, lay it on thick, lay it on with a trowel 546 *exaggerate*; overload, overburden; overcharge, surcharge; lavish, lavish upon 813 *be liberal*; be lavish, make a splash 815 *be prodigal*; roll in, stink of 800 *be rich*.

*be superfluous*, – redundant etc. adj.; go begging, remain on one's hands 41 *be left*; have time on one's hands 679 *be inactive*; do twice over, duplicate; carry coals to Newcastle, gild the lily, teach one's grandmother to suck eggs; labour the obvious, take a sledgehammer to crack a nut, break a butterfly on a wheel, hold a candle to the sun 641 *waste effort*; exceed requirements, have no use 641 *be useless*; go in for luxuries.

**Adv.** *redundantly*, over and above, too much, overly, excessively, unnecessarily, beyond measure; enough and to spare; in excess of requirements.

### 638 Importance

**N.** *importance*, first i., primacy, priority, urgency 64 *precedence*; paramountcy, supremacy 34 *superiority*; essentiality, irreplaceability; import, consequence, significance, weight, weightiness, gravity, seriousness, solemnity; materiality, materialness, substance, pith, moment 3 *substantiality*; interest, consideration, concern 622 *business*; notability, memorability, mark, prominence, distinction, eminence 866 *repute*; influence 866 *prestige*; size, magnitude 32 *greatness*; rank, high standing 27 *degree*; value, excellence, merit 644 *goodness*; use, usefulness 640 *utility*; stress, emphasis, insistence 532 *affirmation*.

*important matter*, vital concern, hot-button issue, bottom line; crucial moment, turning point, defining moment 137 *crisis*; breath of life, 'the be-all and end-all';

> If it were done when 'tis done, then 'twere well
> It were done quickly: if the assassination
> Could trammel up the consequence, and catch
> With his surcease success; that but this blow
> Might be the be-all and the end-all here,
> But here, upon this bank and shoal of time,
> We'd jump the life to come.
>
> William Shakespeare, *Macbeth*

grave affair, not peanuts, not chickenfeed, no joke, no laughing matter, matter of life and death; notable point, memorandum 505 *reminder*; big news, great n. 529 *news*; great doings, exploit 676 *deed*; landmark, milestone; red-letter day, great d. 876 *special day*.

*chief thing*, what matters, the thing, great t., main t.; issue, supreme i., crux 452 *topic*; grass root, fundamentals, bedrock, nitty-gritty, fact 1 *reality*; nuts and bolts, essential, sine qua non 627 *requirement*; priority, first choice 605 *choice*; gist 514 *meaning*; substance 5 *essential part*; highlight, main feature; best part, cream, crème de la crème, salt, pick 644 *elite*; keynote, cornerstone, mainstay, linchpin, kingpin; head, spearhead; sum and substance, heart of the matter, heart, core, kernel, nucleus, nub 225 *centre*; hub 218 *pivot*; cardinal point, main p., half the battle 32 *main part*; chief hope, trump card, main chance; numero uno.

*notable*, personage, notability, personality, heavyweight, somebody 866 *person of repute*; local worthy, pillar of the community; great man *or* woman, VIP, bigwig, brass hat; his *or* her nibs (inf), big gun, big shot, big noise, big bug (sl), big wheel, big chief, big white c., big Daddy, Mr Big; high muck-a-muck, great panjandrum; numero uno; leading light, master spirit 500 *sage*; kingpin, key person 696 *expert*; first fiddle, prima donna, star, lion, catch, great c. 890 *favourite*; uncrowned king *or* queen, head, chief, godfather, Big Brother 34 *superior*; superior person, lord of creation, the greatest 644 *exceller*; grandee 868 *aristocrat*; magnate, mogul, mandarin; baron, tycoon 741 *autocrat*; captains of industry, big battalions, top brass, top people, establishment 733 *authority*; superpower 178 *influence*.

**Adj.** *important*, weighty, grave, solemn,

serious; pregnant, big; of consequence, of consideration, of importance, of concern; considerable, worth considering; world-shattering, earth-shaking, momentous, critical, fateful 137 *timely*; chief, capital, cardinal, staple, major, main, paramount 34 *supreme*; crucial, essential, material, to the point 9 *relevant*; pivotal, hot-button (inf) 225 *central*; basic, fundamental, bedrock, radical, going to the root, grassroots; primary, prime, foremost, leading; overriding, overruling, uppermost 34 *superior*; worthwhile, to be taken seriously, not to be despised, not to be overlooked, not to be sneezed at 644 *valuable*; necessary, vital, indispensable, irreplaceable, key 627 *required*; helpful 640 *useful*; significant, telling, trenchant 514 *meaningful*; imperative, urgent, taking precedence, high-priority; overdue 136 *late*; high-level, top-l., summit 213 *topmost*; top-secret, hush-hush 523 *latent*; high, grand, noble 32 *great*.

*notable*, of mark, egregious 32 *remarkable*; memorable, signal, unforgettable 505 *remembered*; first-rate, A1, outstanding, excelling 34 *superior*; ranking, top-rank, top-flight, A-list 644 *excellent*; conspicuous, prominent, eminent, distinguished, exalted, august 866 *noteworthy*; dignified, imposing, commanding 821 *impressive*; formidable, powerful 178 *influential*; newsworthy, front-page; eventful, stirring, breath-taking, shattering, world-s., earth-shaking, seismic, epoch-making.

**Vb.** *be important*, matter, be a consideration, bulk large 612 *motivate*; weigh, carry, carry weight, tell, count, cast a long shadow 178 *influence*; import, signify 514 *mean*; concern, interest, affect 9 *be related*; have priority, take precedence, come first 34 *predominate*; take the lead 64 *come before*; be something, be somebody 920 *command respect*; take the limelight, deserve notice, make a stir, create a sensation, cut a figure, cut a dash 455 *attract notice*.

*make important*, give weight to, attach *or* ascribe importance to; seize on, fasten on; bring to the fore, place in the foreground; enhance, highlight; rub in, stress, underline, labour 532 *emphasize*; put in capital letters, headline, splash 528 *advertise*; bring to notice, put on the map 528 *proclaim*; write in letters of gold 876 *celebrate*; magnify 197 *enlarge*; make much of 546 *exaggerate*; lionize, honour, glorify, exalt 920 *show respect*; take seriously, make a fuss about, make a stir, make much ado; value, esteem, make much of, set store by, think everything of 920 *respect*; overestimate 482 *overrate*.

**Adv.** *importantly*, primarily, significantly; materially, largely, in the main, above all, to crown all; par excellence.

## 639 Unimportance

**N.** *unimportance*, inconsequence, insignificance, secondariness 35 *inferiority*; immateriality, inessentiality, lack of substance 4 *insubstantiality*; nothingness, nullity, nihility 190 *emptiness*; pettiness 33 *smallness*; paltriness, meanness 922 *contemptibility*; triviality, superficiality 212 *shallowness*; flippancy, snap of the fingers, frivolity, floccinaucinihilipilification; worthlessness 812 *cheapness*; uselessness 641 *inutility*; irrelevance, red herring 10 *unrelatedness*.

*trifle*, inessential, triviality, technicality; nothing, mere n., no matter, no great m., parish-pump; accessory, secondary matter, side-show; nothing in particular, nothing of note, matter of indifference, not the end of the world; no great shakes, nothing to speak of, nothing to boast of, nothing to write home about, nothing to worry about, storm in a teacup 482 *overestimation*; tithe, fraction 53 *part*; bagatelle, tinker's cuss, fig, damn, toss, straw, chaff, pin, button, feather, dust; cobweb, gossamer 330 *brittleness*; small item, tuppence, small change, small beer, small potatoes; paltry sum, peanuts, chickenfeed, fleabite; pinprick, scratch; nothing to it, child's play 701 *easy thing*; jest, joke, practical j., farce 837 *amusement*; peccadillo, venial sin; trifles, trivia, minutiae, detail, petty d. 80 *particulars*; whit, jot, tittle, the least bit, trickle, drop in the ocean 33 *small quantity*; cent, brass farthing 33 *small coin*; whim-wham, nonsense, fiddle-faddle 497 *absurdity*; piffle, drivel 515 *empty talk*.

*bauble*, toy, rattle 837 *plaything*; gewgaw, geegaw, doodad, kickshaw, knick-knack, bric-a-brac; novelty, trinket, bibelot; tinsel, trumpery, frippery, trash, gimcrack; froth, foam 355 *bubble*.

*nonentity*, nobody, nonperson, obscurity; man of straw 4 *insubstantial thing*; figurehead, cipher, sleeping partner; fribble, trifler, smatterer, jack of all trades and master of none 697 *bungler*; mediocrity, lightweight, small beer; small fry, small game; banana republic; other ranks, lower orders 869 *commonalty*; second fiddle 35 *inferior*; underling, understrapper 742 *servant*; pawn, pawn in the game, piece on the board, cat's paw, stooge, puppet 628 *instrument*; Cinderella, poor relation 801 *poor person*; pipsqueak, whippersnapper, squirt, squit, punk, twerp, trash 867 *object of scorn*.

**Adj.** *unimportant*, immaterial 4 *insubstantial*; ineffectual, uninfluential, inconsequential, of no consequence, of no great weight; insignificant 515 *meaningless*; off the point 10 *irrelevant*; inessential, nonessential, not vital, fringe; unnecessary, dispensable, expendable; small, petty, trifling, nugatory, flimsy, paltry 33 *inconsiderable*; negligible, inappreciable, not worth considering, out of the running; weak, puny, powerless 161 *impotent*; wretched, measly, miserable, pitiful, pitiable, pathetic; mean, sorry, shabby 801 *poor*; obscure, disregarded, overlooked 458 *neglected*; overrated, beneath notice, beneath contempt 922 *contemptible*; jumped-up, no-account, tinpot, potty; low-level, of second rank, secondary, minor, by-, subsidiary, peripheral 35 *inferior*.

*trivial*, trifling, piffling, piddling, fiddling, niggling; pettifogging, pinpricking, nit-picking, technical; footling, frivolous, puerile, childish 499 *foolish*; windy, airy, frothy 4 *insubstantial*; superficial 212 *shallow*; slight 33 *small*; lightweight 323 *light*; not serious, forgivable, venial; parish-pump, small-time; twopenny-halfpenny, one-horse, second-rate, third-r.; potty, grotty, rubbishy, trumpery, trashy, tawdry, catchpenny, pinchbeck, pot-boiling, shoddy, gimcrack 645 *bad*; two-a-penny 812 *cheap*; worthless, valueless 641 *useless*; not worthwhile, not worth a thought, not worth a second t. 922 *contemptible*; toy, token, nominal, symbolic 547 *indicating*; mediocre, nondescript, forgettable, eminently f.; commonplace, ordinary, uneventful 610 *usual*.

**Vb.** *be unimportant*, – valueless etc. adj.; be of no importance, not matter, weigh light upon, carry no weight, not weigh, not count, get one nowhere, count for nothing, cut no ice, have no clout, signify little; think unimportant, attach no importance to, not overrate, shrug off 458 *disregard*; snap one's fingers at 922 *hold cheap*; reduce one's importance, cut down to size 872 *humiliate*.

**Int.** never mind!, no matter!, so what!, too bad!

## 640 Utility

**N.** *utility*, use, usefulness; employability, serviceability, handiness 628 *instrumentality*; efficacy, efficiency 160 *ability*; adequacy 635 *sufficiency*; adaptability, applicability, suitability 642 *good policy*; readiness, availability 189 *presence*; service, avail, help, great h., good stead 703 *aid*; value, worth, merit 644 *goodness*; virtue, function, capacity, potency, clout 160 *power*; advantage, commodity; profitability, bottom line, earning capacity, productivity 171 *productiveness*; profit, mileage 771 *gain*; convenience, benefit, general b., public utility, common weal, public good 615 *good*; utilitarianism, functionalism; employment, utilization 673 *use*.

**Adj.** *useful*, helpful, of service, of use, user-friendly, -friendly, utile 703 *aiding*; sensible, practical, applied, functional; versatile, multipurpose, all-purpose, of all work; practicable, commodious, convenient, expedient 642 *advisable*; handy, ready, rough and r.; at hand, available, on tap; serviceable, fit for, good for, disposable, adaptable, applicable; fit for use, ready for u., operative, on stream, usable, reusable, employable; good, valid, current; subsidiary, subservient 628 *instrumental*; able, competent, efficacious, effective, effectual, efficient 160 *powerful*; conducive 179 *tending*; adequate 635 *sufficient*; pragmatic, utilitarian.

*profitable*, paying, remunerative, bankable 771 *gainful*; prolific, fertile 164 *productive*; beneficial, advantageous, to one's advantage, edifying, worthwhile 615 *good*; worth one's salt, worth one's keep, worth one's weight in gold, invaluable, priceless 644 *valuable*.

**Vb.** *be useful*, – of use etc. adj.; avail, prove helpful, be of value, bestead, stand one in good stead; come in handy, have some use, perform a function; function, work 173 *operate*; perform 676 *do*; serve, subserve, serve one's turn, answer 635 *suffice*; suit one's purpose 642 *be expedient*; further one's purpose, help, advance, promote 703 *aid*; do service, do sterling s., do yeoman s. 742 *serve*; conduce 179 *tend*; benefit, profit, advantage, be to one's a. 644 *do good*; bear fruit 171 *be fruitful*; pay, pay off, make a profit, be worth one's while 771 *be profitable*.

*find useful*, have a use for, find a use for, employ, make use of, utilize 673 *use*; turn to good account, improve on, make capital out of 137 *profit by*; reap the benefit of 771 *gain*; be the better for 654 *get better*.

**Adv.** *usefully*, serviceably; advantageously; pro bono publico; cui bono?, to whose advantage?

## 641 Inutility

**N.** *inutility*, uselessness; no function, no purpose, superfluousness 637 *superfluity*; futility, inanity, vanity, 'vanity of vanities' (see quotation at 4 *insubstantial thing*) 497 *absurdity*; worthlessness, unemployability; inadequacy 636 *insufficiency*; inefficacy, ineffectualness, inability 161 *impotence*; inefficiency, incompetence, ineptitude 695 *unskilfulness*; unserviceableness, inconvenience, unsuitability, unfitness 643 *inexpedience*; inapplicability, unadaptability; unprofitability, no benefit 172 *unproductiveness*; disservice, mischief, damage, detriment 772 *loss*; unhelpfulness, recalcitrance 598 *unwillingness*.

*lost labour*, wasted l., wasted effort 728 *failure*; game not worth the candle; waste of breath, waste of time, dead loss, no-win situation; lost trouble, labour in vain, wild-goose chase, fool's errand; blind alley 702 *obstacle*; labour of Sisyphus, Penelope's web; half measures, tinkering; futilitarian.

*rubbish*, good riddance, trash, load of old rubbish, stuff; waste, refuse, lumber, junk, scrap, litter; spoilage, wastage, bilge, waste products, wastepaper, mullock; scourings, off-s., sweepings, shavings 41 *leavings*; chaff, husks, bran; scraps, bits; crumbs; offal, carrion; dust, muck, debris, slag, clinker, dross, scoria, scum 649 *dirt*; peel, orange p., banana skin, dead wood, stubble, weeds, tares; odds and ends, bits and pieces, rags and bones, old clothes, cast-offs; reject, throw-out; midden, rubbish heap, tip, dustheap, slag heap, dump.

**Adj.** *useless*, inutile, functionless, purposeless, pointless, Sisyphean; naff; futile 497 *absurd*; unpractical, impracticable, unworkable, effort-wasting, no go; nonfunctional 844 *ornamental*; redundant, nonreturnable 637 *superfluous*, expendable, dispensable, unnecessary, unneeded 860 *unwanted*; unfit, unapt, inapplicable 643 *inexpedient*; fit for nothing, unusable, unemployable, unadaptable; unqualified, inefficient, incompetent 695 *unskilful*; unable, ineffective, feckless, ineffectual 161 *impotent*; nonfunctioning, inoperative, dud, kaput; uncurrent, invalid 752 *abrogated*; unserviceable, out of order, not working 61 *orderless*; broken down, effete, worn out, past work, hors de combat, past it, obsolete, outmoded 127 *antiquated*; hopeless, vain, idle (see also *profitless*).

*profitless*, bootless, unavailing; loss-making, unprofitable, not worthwhile, wasteful, not paying, ill-spent 772 *losing*; vain, in vain, abortive 728 *unsuccessful*; nothing to show for 634 *wasted*; unrewarding, unrewarded, thankless; fruitless, barren, sterile 172 *unproductive*; idle 679 *lazy*; worthless, good for nothing, valueless, no earthly use; rubbishy, trashy, no good, not worth the effort, not worth powder and shot, not worth the paper it is written on 645 *bad*; unsalable, dear at any price 811 *dear*.

**Vb.** *be useless*, have no use, waste one's time, be on a hiding to nothing; achieve no purpose, end in futility; not help 702 *hinder*; not work, not function 728 *fail*; refuse to work 677 *not act*; fall by the wayside 172 *be unproductive*; go begging 637 *be superfluous*.

*make useless*, disqualify, unfit, decommission, disarm, render harmless, take the sting out of 161 *disable*; castrate, emasculate 161 *unman*; cripple, lame, clip the wings 655 *impair*; dismantle, unmount, dismast, unrig, put out of commission, lay up 679 *make inactive*; sabotage, throw a spanner in the works, put a spoke in one's wheel, cramp one's style 702 *obstruct*; disassemble, undo, take to pieces, break up 46 *disunite*; deface, withdraw from currency 752 *abrogate*; devalue 812 *cheapen*; pollute, contaminate, lay waste 172 *make sterile*.

*waste effort*, labour the obvious; waste one's breath, waste one's time, talk to a brick wall, beat one's head against a b. w.; preach to the converted 637 *be superfluous*; be on a hiding to nothing, get nowhere, lose one's labour, labour in vain, sweat for nothing, flog a dead horse, beat the air, tilt at windmills; cry for the moon 470 *attempt the impossible*; tinker, paper over the cracks, spoil the ship for a ha'porth of tar 726 *not complete*; rearrange the deckchairs on the Titanic 497 *be absurd*.

**Adv.** *uselessly*, to no purpose; helplessly, ineffectually, to no avail, until one is blue in the face.

## 642 Good policy

**N.** *good policy*, expediency, expedience; answer, right a., advisability, desirability, worthwhileness, suitability 640 *utility*; fitness, propriety 915 *dueness*; high time, due t., right t., proper t., opportunity 137 *occasion*; rule of expediency, convenience, pragmatism, utilitarianism, opportunism, timeserving; profit, advantage 615 *benefit*; facilities, conveniences 629 *means*; an expedient, pis aller 623 *contrivance*.

**Adj.** *advisable*, commendable; as well to, better to, desirable, worthwhile 644 *beneficial*; acceptable 923 *approved*; up one's street, suitable 24 *fit*; fitting, befitting, seemly, proper 913 *right*; owing 915 *due*; in loco, well-timed, auspicious, opportune 137 *timely*; prudent, politic, judicious 498 *wise*; expedient, expediential; advantageous, profitable 640 *useful*; convenient, workable, practical, pragmatic, practicable, negotiable; qualified, cut out for; to the purpose, adapted to, applicable; handy, effective, effectual.

**Vb.** *be expedient*, not come amiss, come in useful, serve the time, suit the occasion, befit; be to the purpose, expedite one's end, help 703 *aid*; forward, advance, promote 640 *be useful*; answer, have the desired effect, produce results 156 *conduce*; wash, work, do, serve, be better than nothing, deliver the goods, fill *or* fit the bill 635 *suffice*; achieve one's aim 727 *succeed*; qualify for, fit, be just the thing 24 *accord*; profit, advantage, benefit 644 *do good*.

**Adv.** *expediently*, conveniently, fittingly, opportunely 615 *well*; in the right place at the right time.

## 643 Inexpedience

**N.** *inexpedience*, inexpediency; no answer, not the a., lack of planning, bad policy, counsel of despair 495 *error*; inadvisability, undesirability; unsuitability, unfitness 25 *inaptitude*; impropriety, unfittingness, unseemliness 916 *undueness*; wrongness 914 *wrong*; inopportuneness 138 *untimeliness*; disqualification, disability, handicap 702 *obstacle*; incommodity, inconvenience, disadvantage, detriment; doubtful advantage, mixed blessing, two-edged weapon, pis aller; last resort 596 *necessity*.

**Adj.** *inexpedient*, better not, as well not to, inadvisable, undesirable, uncommendable, not recommended 924 *disapproved*; ill-advised, impolitic, imprudent, injudicious, off message 499 *unwise*; inappropriate, unfitting, malapropos, out of place, unseemly 916 *undue*; not right, improper, objectionable 914 *wrong*; beneath one's dignity, infra dig; unfit, ineligible, inadmissible, unsuitable, unhappy, infelicitous, inept 25 *unapt*; unseasonable, inopportune, untimely, wrongly timed 138 *ill-timed*; unsatisfactory 636 *insufficient*; discommodious, incommodious, inconvenient; detrimental, disadvantageous, hurtful 645 *harmful*; unhealthy, unwholesome 653 *insalubrious*; unprofitable 641 *useless*; unhelpful 702 *hindering*; untoward 731 *adverse*; ill-contrived, awkward 695 *clumsy*; incommodious, cumbersome, lumbering, hulking 195 *unwieldy*.

**Vb.** *be inexpedient*, – inadvisable etc. adj.; not fit, come amiss, won't do, won't wash, not answer; not help 641 *be useless*; bother, discommode, incommode, inconvenience, put to inconvenience 827 *trouble*; disadvantage, be to one's d., penalize, hurt 645 *harm*; work against, militate a. 702 *obstruct*; embarrass 700 *be difficult*.

## 644 Goodness

**N.** *goodness*, soundness 650 *health*; virtuosity 694 *skill*; quality, good q., classic q., vintage; long suit, good points, redeeming feature, likeable trait; merit, desert, title to fame, claim to f.; excellence, eminence, supereminence 34 *superiority*; virtue, worth, value 809 *price*; pricelessness, superexcellence 32 *greatness*; flawlessness 646 *perfection*; distilled essence, quintessence 1 *essence*; beneficence 897 *benevolence*; virtuous character 933 *virtue*.

*elite*, chosen few, chosen people, the saints; pick, prime, flower; cream, crème de la crème, salt of the earth, pick of the bunch, meritocracy; crack troops, corps d'élite; top people 638 *notable*; charmed circle, top drawer, upper crust, aristocracy, Sloane Rangers 868 *upper class*; choice bit, titbit, prime cut, pièce de résistance; plum, prize 729 *trophy*.

*exceller*, nonpareil, nonesuch; prodigy, gifted child, genius; superman, wonderwoman, wonder, wonder of the world 864 *prodigy*; Admirable Crichton 646 *paragon*; grand fellow, one of the best 937 *good person*; one in a thousand, one in a million, treasure, perfect t. 890 *favourite*; jewel, pearl, ruby, diamond 844 *gem*; gem of the first water, pearl of price, gold, pure g., refined g.; chef-d'oeuvre, pièce de résistance, collector's item, collector's piece, museum p. 694 *masterpiece*; record-breaker, best-seller, chart-topper, best ever, absolute end, last word in, ne plus ultra, best thing since sliced bread; bee's knees, cat's whiskers, cat's pyjamas; the goods, winner, corker, humdinger, wow, knockout, hit, smash h.; smasher, charmer 841 *a beauty*; star, idol 890 *favourite*; best of its kind, Rolls-Royce, the tops, the greatest, top of the pops; topnotcher, top seed, first-rater; cock of the walk, toast of the town, Queen of the May, pride of the north; champion, title-holder, world-beater, prize-winner 727 *victor*.

**Adj.** *excellent*, fine, braw (Scots); exemplary, worth imitating; good, good as gold 933 *virtuous*; above par, preferable, better 34 *superior*; very good, first-rate, ace, A1, superexcellent, alpha plus; prime, quality, good q., fine, super-fine, most desirable, to die for, TDF; God's own, superlative, in a class by itself; all-star, of the first water, rare, vintage, classic 646 *perfect*; choice, select, picked, handpicked, tested, exquisite, recherché 605 *chosen*; exclusive, pure 44 *unmixed*; worthy, meritorious 915 *deserving*; admired, admirable, estimable, praiseworthy, creditable 923 *approvable*; famous, great; couleur de rose, lovely 841 *beautiful*; glorious, dazzling, splendid, splendiferous, magnificent, marvellous, wonderful, cool (inf), wicked (sl), terrific, sensational, superb, awesome (inf), phat (sl).

*super*, superduper, fantastic, way-out, out of sight, fabulous, fab, groovy, brill, magic, wizard, wizzo; spot-on, bang-on; top-notch, top-flight, über- (see also *best*); lovely, glorious, gorgeous, heavenly, out of this world 32 *prodigious*; smashing, stunning, spiffing, ripping, topping, swell, great, grand, famous, capital, dandy, bully, hunky-dory; scrumptious, delicious, juicy, plummy, jammy 826 *pleasurable*.

*best*, very b., optimum, A1, champion, tiptop, top-notch, ace, nothing like it; first, first-rate, crack; a cut above, second to none 34 *supreme*; unequalled, unparalleled, unmatched,

peerless, matchless, unbeatable, unsurpassable 646 *perfect*; best-ever, record, record-breaking, best-selling, chart-topping 34 *crowning*; capital, cardinal 638 *important*.

*valuable*, of value, invaluable, inestimable, priceless, above price, beyond p., costly, rich 811 *of price*; irreplaceable, unique, rare, precious, golden, worth its weight in gold, worth a king's ransom; sterling, gilt-edged, blue-chip, sound, solid.

*beneficial*, wholesome, healthy, salutary, sound 652 *salubrious*; refreshing, edifying, worthwhile, advantageous, profitable 640 *useful*; favourable, kind, propitious 730 *prosperous*; harmless, hurtless, inoffensive, innocuous 935 *innocent*.

*not bad*, tolerable, so-so, passable, respectable, standard, up to the mark, in good condition, in fair c., fair, satisfactory 635 *sufficient*; nice, decent, pretty good, all right, okay, OK; sound, fresh, unspoiled; unexceptionable, unobjectionable; indifferent, middle-of-the-road, middling, mediocre, ordinary, fifty-fifty, average 30 *median*.

**Vb.** *be good*, – sound etc. adj.; have quality; have merit, deserve well 915 *deserve*; qualify, stand the test, pass, pass muster 635 *suffice*; stand comparison, challenge c., vie, rival, equal the best 28 *be equal*; excel, transcend, overtop, walk off with all the prizes, take the prize 34 *be superior*.

*do good*, have a good effect, improve, edify; do a world of good 652 *be salubrious*; be the making of, make a man of 654 *make better*; help 615 *benefit*; favour, smile on 730 *prosper*; do a favour, do a good turn, confer an obligation, put in one's debt 897 *be benevolent*; not hurt, do no harm, break no bones.

**Adv.** *aright*, well, rightly, properly, admirably, excellently, famously.

## 645 Badness

**N.** *badness*, bad qualities, obnoxiousness, nastiness, beastliness, foulness, grossness, rottenness; demerit, unworthiness, worthlessness; second-rateness, low quality, low standard 35 *inferiority*; faultiness, flaw 647 *imperfection*; poor make, shoddiness 641 *inutility*; clumsiness 695 *unskilfulness*; rankness, unsoundness, taint, decay, corruption 655 *deterioration*; disruption, confusion 61 *disorder*; peccancy, morbidity 651 *disease*; harmfulness, hurtfulness, balefulness, ill, hurt, harm, injury, detriment, damage, mischief 616 *evil*; noxiousness, poisonousness, deadliness, virulence 653 *insalubrity*; poison, blight, canker, cancer 659 *bane*; pestilence, sickness 651 *plague*; contamination, centre of infection, plague spot, trouble s., hotbed 651 *infection*; affair, scandal 867 *slur*; abomination, filth 649 *uncleanness*; sewer 649 *sink*; bitterness, gall, wormwood 393 *sourness*; painfulness, sting, ache, pang, thorn in the flesh 377 *pain*; molestation 827 *annoyance*; angst, anguish 825 *suffering*; harshness, tyranny, maltreatment, oppression, persecution, intolerance 735 *severity*; unkindness, cruelty, malignancy, malignity, spitefulness, spite 898 *malevolence*; depravity, vice 934 *wickedness*; sin 936 *guilt*; bad influence, evil genius; evil spirit 970 *demon*; ill wind, evil star 731 *misfortune*; black magic, evil eye, hoodoo, jinx, gremlin 983 *sorcery*; curse 899 *malediction*; snake in the grass 663 *troublemaker*, bad character 904 *evildoer*.

**Adj.** *bad*, arrant, vile, base, evil, ill-conditioned; gross, black; utterly bad, irredeemable, as bad as bad can be; bad of its kind, poor, mean, wretched, grotty, gungy, gruesome, measly, low-grade, second-rate, not good enough, execrable, awful, cringe-making, cringeworthy 35 *inferior*; no good, worthless, shoddy, tacky, naff, crummy, ropy, punk, pathetic 641 *useless*; unsatisfactory, faulty, flawed 647 *imperfect*; bad at, incompetent, inefficient, unskilled 695 *clumsy*; badly done, mangled, spoiled 695 *bungled*; scruffy, filthy, mangy, manky 649 *dirty*; foul, noisome 397 *fetid* (see also *not nice*); gone bad, rank, not fresh, unsound, affected, tainted 655 *deteriorated*; corrupt, decaying, decayed, rotten to the core 51 *decomposed*; peccant, disordered, infected, envenomed, poisoned, septic 651 *diseased*; irremediable, incurable; depraved, vicious, villainous, accursed 934 *wicked*; heinous, sinful 936 *guilty*; mean, shabby 930 *dishonest*; wrongful, unjust 914 *wrong*; sinister 616 *evil* (see also *harmful*); undeserving, unworthy, contemptible; shameful, scandalous, disgraceful 867 *discreditable*; sad, melancholy, lamentable, deplorable, pitiable, pitiful, woeful, grievous, sore 827 *distressing*; unendurable 827 *intolerable*; heavy, onerous, burdensome 684 *fatiguing*; too bad 827 *annoying*.

*harmful*, hurtful, injurious, damaging, detrimental, prejudicial, disadvantageous 643 *inexpedient*; deleterious, corrosive, wasting, consuming 165 *destructive*; pernicious, fatal 362 *deadly*; costly 811 *dear*; disastrous, ruinous, calamitous 731 *adverse*; degenerative, noxious, malign, malignant, unhealthy, unwholesome, noisome, miasmal, infectious 653 *insalubrious*; polluting, poisonous, radioactive 653 *toxic*; *unsafe*, risky 661 *dangerous*; sinister, ominous, dire, dreadful, baleful, baneful, accursed, devilish 616 *evil*; malefic, mischievous, spiteful, malicious, malevolent, ill-disposed;

mischief-making, puckish, impish 898 *unkind*; bloody, bloodthirsty, inhuman 898 *cruel*; outrageous, rough, furious 176 *violent*; harsh, intolerant, persecuting 735 *oppressive*; monstrous 32 *exorbitant*.

*not nice*, unlikable, obnoxious, nasty, beastly, horrid, horrific, horrible, terrible, gruesome, grim, ghastly, awful, dreadful, perfectly d., – from hell; scruffy 867 *disreputable*; foul, rotten, lousy, putrid, putrefying, stinking, stinky, sickening, revolting, nauseous, nauseating 861 *disliked*; loathsome, detestable, abominable 888 *hateful*; vulgar, sordid, low, indecent, improper, gross, filthy, pornographic, obscene 951 *impure*; shocking, disgusting, reprehensible, monstrous, horrendous 924 *disapproved*; plaguy, wretched, miserable 827 *annoying*.

*damnable*, damned, darned, blasted, bloody, confounded, blinking, dratted, bothersome, perishing, fucking (sl), effing, frigging (sl), blankety-blank; execrable, accursed, cursed, hellish, infernal, devilish, diabolic, diabolical.

**Vb.** *harm*, do h., do one a hurt, do one a mischief, scathe 827 *hurt*; cost one dear 811 *be dear*; disagree with, make one ill, make one sick; injure, damage, pollute 655 *impair*; corrupt 655 *pervert*; play havoc with 63 *derange*; do no good 641 *be useless*; make things worse, worsen, disimprove, have a deleterious effect on; do evil, work e. 914 *do wrong*; molest, pain 827 *torment*; plague, vex 827 *trouble*; land one in trouble, queer one's pitch, do for; spite, be unkind 898 *be malevolent*.

*ill-treat*, maltreat, mishandle, abuse 675 *misuse*; ill-use, burden, overburden, put upon, tyrannize, bear hard on, tread on, trample under foot, trample on, victimize, prey upon; persecute 735 *oppress*; wrong, aggrieve 914 *do wrong*; distress 827 *torment*; outrage, violate, force 176 *be violent*; savage, maul, bite, scratch, tear 655 *wound*; stab 263 *pierce*; batter, bruise, buffet 279 *strike*; agonize, rack, crucify 963 *torture*; spite, use despitefully, take one's spite out on, wreak one's malice on 898 *be malevolent*; crush 165 *destroy*.

**Adv.** *badly*, amiss, wrong, ill; to one's cost; cruelly 32 *painfully*.

## 646 Perfection

**N.** *perfection*, sheer p.; finish, classic quality; perfectness, the ideal; nothing wrong with, immaculacy, immaculateness, faultlessness, flawlessness, mint condition; correctness, correctitude, irreproachability; impeccancy, impeccability, infallibility, indefectibility; transcendence 34 *superiority*; quintessence, essence; peak, zenith, pinnacle 213 *summit*;

height *or* pitch of perfection, acme of p., pink of p., ne plus ultra, extreme, last word; chef d'oeuvre, flawless performance 694 *masterpiece*.

*paragon*, nonesuch, nonpareil, flower, a beauty, prince of 644 *exceller*; ideal, beau idéal, dream team, knight in shining armour, saint, plaster s.; classic, pattern, pattern of perfection, standard, norm, model, mirror, shining example 23 *prototype*; phoenix, rarity 365 *mythical beast*; superman, superwoman, wonderwoman, demigod 864 *prodigy*.

**Adj.** *perfect*, perfected, finished, brought to perfection, ripened; ripe, fully r. 669 *matured*; just right, just so, ideal, flawless, faultless, impeccable, infallible, indefectible; correct, irreproachable; immaculate, unblemished, unflawed, unstained; spotless, unspotted, unblemished, blemish-free, without blemish, without a stain; uncontaminated, pure 44 *unmixed*; guiltless 935 *innocent*; sound, uncracked, sound as a bell, right as rain, right as a trivet, in perfect condition; tight, watertight, seaworthy; whole, entire, one hundred per cent, A1; complete 52 *intact*; dazzling, beyond praise 644 *excellent*; consummate, unsurpassable 34 *supreme*; brilliant, masterly 694 *skilful*; pattern, standard, model, classic, classical, Augustan.

*undamaged*, safe and sound, with a whole skin, unhurt, unscathed, scatheless, no harm done; unscarred, unscratched, unmarked; without blemish, unmarred, untainted, unspoilt; unreduced, undiminished, without loss, whole, entire 52 *intact*; in the pink 650 *healthy*.

**Vb.** *perfect*, consummate, bring to perfection; ripen 669 *mature*; correct 654 *rectify*; put the finishing touch 213 *crown*; complete, leave nothing to be desired 725 *carry through*.

**Adv.** *perfectly*, flawlessly, impeccably, irreproachably, to perfection, to a turn, just as one would wish.

## 647 Imperfection

**N.** *imperfection*, imperfectness, not one hundred per cent; room for improvement, not one's best; possibility of perfection, perfectibility 654 *improvement*; faultiness, erroneousness, defectibility, fallibility 495 *error*; patchiness, unevenness, curate's egg 17 *nonuniformity*; immaturity, unripeness, underdevelopment, underachievement 670 *undevelopment*; defectiveness, bit missing 55 *incompleteness*; lack, want 627 *requirement*; deficiency, inadequacy 636 *insufficiency*; unsoundness 661 *vulnerability*; failure, failing, weakness 307 *shortfall*; low standard, third class, pass degree; inferior version, poor relation 35 *inferiority*;

second best, third rate, pis aller, consolation prize, makeshift 150 *substitute*; mediocrity, averageness 30 *average*; loss of fitness, staleness 684 *fatigue*; adulteration 43 *mixture*.

*defect*, fault 495 *error*; flaw, rift, leak, loophole, crack, lacuna 201 *gap*; deficiency, limitation 307 *shortfall*; kink, foible, screw loose 503 *eccentricity*; weak point, vulnerable point, soft spot, chink in one's armour, Achilles heel, 'soft underbelly' (see quotation at 661 *vulnerability*), tragic flaw 661 *vulnerability*; feet of clay, weak link in the chain, weakest link 163 *weakness*; scratch, taint, stain, blot, spot, smudge 845 *blemish*; drawback, catch, snag, fly in the ointment 702 *obstacle*.

**Adj.** *imperfect*, not quite right, not ideal, less than perfect, not classic; fallible, peccable; uneven, patchy, good in parts, like the curate's egg 17 *nonuniform*; faulty, botched 695 *bungled*; flawed, cracked; leaky, not waterproof; wobbly, rickety 163 *flimsy*; unsound 661 *vulnerable*; soiled, shop-s., tainted, stained, spotted, marked, scratched 845 *blemished*; overripe, underripe; past its best 655 *deteriorated*; below par, off form; unfit, stale 684 *fatigued*; off-colour, not in the pink 651 *unhealthy*; not good enough, not up to the mark, inadequate, deficient, wanting, lacking 636 *insufficient*; defective, not entire 55 *incomplete*; partial, broken 53 *fragmentary*; legless, armless 163 *disabled*; unfilled, half-filled, undermanned, short-staffed, short-handed, below strength 670 *unequipped*; half-finished 55 *unfinished*; unthorough, perfunctory 456 *inattentive*; overwrought, overelaborated, overdone 546 *exaggerated*; warped, twisted, distorted 246 *deformed*; mutilated, maimed, lame 163 *weakened*; undeveloped, raw, crude, untrained, scratch 670 *immature*; makeshift, makedo, jerry-built, rough and ready, provisional 150 *substituted*; secondary 639 *unimportant*; second-best, second-rate, third-rate 35 *inferior*; poor, unimpressive, negative, underwhelming 645 *bad*; ordinary, much of a muchness, so-so, middling, average 30 *median*; middle-of-the-road, moderate, wet, unheroic; no great shakes, nothing to boast of, nothing to write home about; only passable, tolerable, bearable, better than nothing 923 *approvable*.

**Vb.** *be imperfect*, fall short of perfection, have a fault; be flawed, be defective 307 *fall short*; lie open to criticism, not bear inspection, not pass muster, fail the test, dissatisfy 636 *not suffice*; barely pass, scrape through; fail to gain approval, not impress, not make the grade 924 *incur blame*; have feet of clay, show one's Achilles heel 163 *be weak*.

**Adv.** *imperfectly*, to a limited extent, barely,

scarcely, almost, not quite, all but; with all its faults.

## 648 Cleanness

**N.** *cleanness*, freedom from dirt, absence of dust, immaculateness 950 *purity*; freshness, dewiness, whiteness; shine, polish, spit and polish; cleanliness, kid gloves, daintiness 862 *fastidiousness*; lack of pollution, zero-emission vehicle.

*cleansing*, clean, spring-cleaning, dry-c.; washing, cleaning up, mopping up, washing up, wiping up, scrubbing; refining, clarification, purification, sprinkling, asperges, lustration, purgation; washing out, flushing, dialysis; purging, enema, defecation, colonic irrigation 302 *excretion*; airing, ventilation, fumigation 338 *vaporization*; deodorization 395 *inodorousness*; antisepsis, sterilization, disinfection, decontamination, disinfestation, delousing; sanitation, waterborne s., drainage, sewerage, plumbing 652 *hygiene*; water closet, flush 649 *latrine*.

*ablutions*, washing; hygiene, oral h.; lavage, lavation, douche, flush; wash, catslick, lick and a promise; soaking, bathing, dipping; soaping, lathering, scrubbing, sponging, rinsing, shampoo; dip 313 *plunge*; bath, tub; bathtub, hipbath, bidet; washbasin, wash-hand basin, washstand, basin and ewer; hot bath, cold b., steam b., vapour b., blanket b., Turkish b., sauna, Jacuzzi (tdmk), hot tub; shower, cold s.; bathroom, washroom, public baths, thermae; hammam, sudatorium; plunge bath, swimming bath, swimming pool; wash, laundry; washtub, washboard, dolly; copper, boiler, washing machine, washer, twin tub, launderette.

*cleanser*, purifier; disinfectant, carbolic, deodorant; soda, washing s., detergent, soap, scented s., toilet s., soap flakes; washing powder, soap p., washing-up liquid, water, hot w., soap and w., shampoo; mouth wash, gargle; lotion, hand l.; cleansing cream, cold c.; dentifrice, toothpaste; pumice stone, hearthstone, holystone; polish, furniture p., boot p., blacking; wax, varnish; whitewash, paint 427 *whiting*; blacklead 428 *black pigment*; aperient 658 *purgative*; sewer, drainpipe, wastepipe 351 *drain*; waterworks.

*cleaning utensil*, broom, besom, mop, sponge, swab, scourer; strigil; loofah; duster, feather d., whisk; brush, scrubbing b., nailbrush, toothbrush, toothpick, dental floss; comb, hair brush, clothes b.; dustpan and brush, waste bin, dustbin, wastepaper basket, litter bin, waste disposal unit, compactor; poopscoop; carpet sweeper, vacuum cleaner, Hoover (tdmk); doormat, foot-scraper; squeegee, squilgee; pipe cleaner, pullthrough, reamer; windscreen wiper; screen, sieve, riddle, strainer 263 *porosity*; filter, air-f., oil-f.; blotter, eraser 550 *obliteration*; rake, hoe; sprinkler 341 *irrigator*; dishwasher.

*cleaning cloth*, duster; dishcloth, tea towel; leather, wash-l.; chamois, shammy; flannel, face f., facecloth, towel, bath t., hand t.; handkerchief, paper h., tissue; toilet tissue, toilet paper, lavatory p., toilet roll; bib, apron, napkin, serviette, place mat, tablemat, doyley, tablecloth; mat 226 *floor-cover*; cover, chair-c., dustsheet 226 *coverlet*.

*cleaner*, refiner, distiller; dry cleaner, launderer, laundryman, laundress, washerwoman, dhobi; fuller; scrubber, swabber; washer-up, dish-washer, scullion; charwoman, char, charlady, cleaner, help, daily help, daily, home help; Mrs Mop; scavenger, sweeper, dustman, refuse collector; lavatory attendant, sanitary engineer; chimneysweep, window cleaner; shoeblack, bootblack; barber, hairdresser 843 *beautician*; gleaner, picker; scavenger bird, crow, vulture.

**Adj.** *clean*, dirt-free; snowy 427 *white*; polished, clean, bright, shining 417 *undimmed*; cleanly, dainty, nice 862 *fastidious*; dewy, fresh; bright as a new pin, fresh as a daisy; cleaned, scrubbed, polished etc. vb.; shaven, shorn, barbered, trimmed; cleaned up, laundered, starched; spruce, natty, spick and span, neat, tidy, well-groomed 60 *orderly*; deodorized, disinfected, aseptic, antiseptic, hygienic, sterilized, sterile 652 *salubrious*; pure, purified, refined, immaculate, spotless, speckless, stainless, unsoiled, unmuddied, untarnished, unsullied, clean as a whistle; unpolluted, environmentally-friendly 646 *perfect*; untouched, blank; ritually clean, kosher 301 *edible*.

*cleansing*, lustral, purificatory; disinfectant; hygienic, sanitary; purgative, purgatory; detergent, abstersive; ablutionary, balneary.

**Vb.** *clean*, spring-clean, clean up, clear up; remove the dirt, lay the dust; groom, valet, spruce, neaten, trim 62 *arrange*; wash, wipe, wash clean, wipe c., wash up, wipe up *or* down, dry, wring, wring out; sponge, mop, mop up, swab, wash down; scrub, scour; flush, flush out; sandblast, holystone, scrape 333 *rub*; do the washing, launder, starch, iron; drip-dry, tumble-dry; bleach, dry-clean; soap, lather, shampoo; bathe, dip, dunk, rinse, swill down, sluice, douche, shower 341 *drench*; dust, whisk, sweep, sweep up, beat, vacuum, hoover; brush, brush up; comb, rake; buff, polish; shine, black, blacklead 417 *make bright*; whitewash

427 *whiten*; erase 550 *obliterate*; strip, pick, pick clean, clean out, clear, clear out, rake o., make a clean sweep 300 *eject*.

*purify*, purge, clean up; bowdlerize, censor, blue-pencil, expurgate; sublimate, elevate 654 *make better*; cleanse, lave, lustrate, asperge; purify oneself, wash one's hands of; freshen, ventilate, fan, deodorize, fumigate; edulcorate, desalt, desalinate; decontaminate, disinfect, sterilize, antisepticize, chlorinate, pasteurize 652 *sanitate*; free from impurities, depurate, refine, distil, clarify, rack, skim, scum, despumate; decarbonize; elutriate, strain, filter, percolate, lixiviate, leach; sift, sieve 44 *eliminate*; sort out, weed o.; flush, dialyse, catheterize, clean out, wash o., drain 350 *make flow*.

## 649 Uncleanness

**N.** *uncleanness*, uncleanliness, dirty habits, wallowing, beastliness; soiling, dirtiness (see also *dirt*); muckiness, miriness 347 *marsh*; scruffiness, grottiness, filthiness; lousiness, pediculosis, phthiriasis; squalidity, squalidness, squalor, slumminess 801 *poverty*; untidiness, sluttishness, slovenliness 61 *disorder*; stink 397 *stench*; pollution, defilement; corruption, taint, putrescence, putrefaction 51 *decomposition*; contamination 651 *infection*; abomination, scatology, obscenity 645 *badness*; unwashed body, dirty linen.

*dirt*, filth, stain, patch, blot; crud, yuk, gunge, gunk, muck, mud, sludge, slime; quagmire, bog 347 *marsh*; night soil, dung, droppings, ordure, faeces 302 *excrement*; snot, mucus; dust, mote 332 *powder*; cobweb, grime, smut, smudge, soot, smoke; grounds, grouts, dregs, lees, draff; sweepings, scourings, offscourings 41 *leavings*; sediment, sedimentation, deposit, precipitate, residuum, fur; scum, dross, froth; scoriae, ashes, cinders, clinker, slag 381 *ash*; drainage, sewerage; castoffs, cast skin, exuviae, slough; scurf, dandruff; tartar, plaque; pus, matter, feculence; refuse, garbage, litter 641 *rubbish*; rot, dry r., wet r., rust, mildew, mould, fungus 51 *decay*; carrion, offal; vermin, flea, nit 365 *insect*.

*swill*, pig-s., hogwash; bilge, bilge-water; ditch-w., dish-w., slops; sewage, drainage; wallow, hog-w., slough.

*latrine*, privy, heads, jakes, bog, john, loo; closet, earth c., long drop, water closet, WC; cloakroom, powder room, rest r., washroom, lavatory, toilet; urinal, public convenience, comfort station, Ladies, Gents; toilet bowl, lavatory b., close-stool, commode, thunderbox, bedpan, chamber pot, potty, jerry 302 *defecation*.

*sink*, sink of corruption; kitchen sink,

draining board; cesspit, cesspool, sump, septic tank, soakaway; gutter, sewer, main, cloaca 351 *drain*; laystall, dunghill, midden, tip, rubbish heap, dust-h., compost h.; dustbin, trashcan 194 *vessel*; coalhole 194 *cellar*; Augean stables, pigsty, pigpen, den; slum, tenement 192 *housing*; shambles 362 *place of slaughter*; plaguespot 651 *infection*; spittoon, cuspidor.

*dirty person*, sloven, slattern, slammerkin, drab, draggletail, traipse 61 *slut*; litterbug, litter lout; mudlark, street arab; scavenger 648 *cleaner*; beast, pig, wallower; ratbag, fleabag.

**Adj.** *unclean*, unhallowed, unholy 980 *profane*; smutty, scatological, obscene, corrupt 951 *impure*; coarse, unrefined, unpurified; septic, festering, poisonous 653 *toxic*; unsterilized, nonsterile 653 *infectious*; sordid, squalid, slummy, insanitary, unhygienic 653 *insalubrious*; foul, offensive, nasty, grotty, manky, yukky; abominable, disgusting, repulsive 645 *not nice*; noisome, nauseous, nauseating, stinking, ponging, malodorous 397 *fetid*; uncleanly, unfastidious, beastly, hoggish; grubby, scruffy, scurfy; leprous, scabby, mangy; flea-ridden, lousy, pediculous, crawling; faecal, dungy, stercoraceous, excrementitious 302 *excretory*; carious, rotting, rotted, tainted, high; fly-blown, maggoty, carrion 51 *decomposed*.

*dirty*, filthy; dusty, grimy, sooty, smoky, fuggy; befouled, polluted, littered, rubbish-strewn; thick with dust, unswept; untidy, unkempt, slatternly, sleazy, slovenly, sluttish, bedraggled, frowzy 61 *orderless*; unsoaped, unwashed, unscoured, unrinsed, unwiped; black, dingy, uncleaned, unpolished, unburnished; tarnished, stained, soiled; greasy, oily; clotted, caked, matted, muddied, begrimed, dirt-encrusted; messy, mucky, muddy, slimy 347 *marshy*; thick, turbid; furred up, scummy; musty, fusty, cobwebby; mouldy, rotten 655 *dilapidated*.

**Vb.** *be unclean*, – dirty etc. adj.; get dirty, collect dust, foul up, clog; rust, mildew, moulder, fester, rot, go bad, go off, addle 51 *decompose*; grow rank, smell 397 *stink*; wallow, roll in the mud.

*make unclean*, foul, befoul; dirty, soil; grime, begrime, cover with dust; stain, blot, sully, tarnish; muck up, make a mess, untidy 61 *be disordered*; daub, smirch, besmirch, smut, smudge, blur, smoke 419 *bedim*; spot, patch, maculate 437 *variegate*; streak, smear, besmear, grease; cake, clog, bemire, beslime, muddy, roil, rile; draggle, drabble; spatter, bespatter, splash, slobber, slaver 341 *moisten*; poison, taint, infect, corrupt, pollute, contaminate 655 *impair*; defile, profane, desecrate, unhallow 980 *be impious*.

## 650 Health

**N.** *health*, rude h., robust h., glowing h., good h.; healthiness, good constitution, iron c., health and strength 162 *vitality*; fitness, condition, good c., pink of c.; bloom, rosiness, rosy cheeks, apple c., ruddy complexion; well-being, physical w.; eupepsia 376 *euphoria*; mens sana in corpore sano; whole skin, soundness; incorruptibility 644 *goodness*; long life, longevity, ripe old age 131 *age*; hygiene, healthy state, clean bill of health; goddess of h., Hygeia.

**Adj.** *healthy*, healthful, wholesome, hygienic, sanitary 652 *salubrious*; in health, in good h., bursting with h., eupeptic, euphoric; fresh, blooming, ruddy, rosy, rosy-cheeked, florid; lusty, bouncing, strapping, hale, hearty, hale and hearty, sound, fit, well, fine, bonny, full of beans 174 *vigorous*; of good constitution, never ill, robust, hardy, strong, vigorous 162 *stalwart*; fighting fit, in condition, in good c., in peak c., in tip-top c., in the pink, in good nick, in good shape, in good heart, in fine fettle, in fine form, in fine trim, in fine feather; feeling fine, feeling great; sound in wind and limb, sound as a bell, fit as a fiddle, fit as a flea, strong as a horse, A1; fresh as a daisy, fresh as April; a picture of health, feeling good; getting well, convalescent, on the mend, on the upgrade, on the up and up, up and about, on one's legs 656 *restored*; pretty well, no worse, as well as can be expected; safe and sound, unharmed 646 *undamaged*.

**Vb.** *be healthy*, – well etc. adj.; mind one's health, look after oneself, take care of o.; feel fine, bloom, thrive, flourish, enjoy good health; be in the pink, have never felt better; wear well, be well-preserved, look young; keep one's health, keep fit, keep well, keep body and soul together, keep on one's legs; have a clean bill of health.

*get healthy*, – fit etc. adj.; recuperate, be well again, return to health, recover one's h., put on weight, get the colour back in one's cheeks; mend, convalesce, become convalescent, get back on one's feet, take a fresh lease of life, become a new man *or* woman 656 *revive*.

## 651 Ill health. Disease

**N.** *ill health*, bad h., poor h., delicate h., failing h.; delicacy, weak constitution, diathesis; unhealthiness, weakliness, infirmity, debility 163 *weakness*; seediness, loss of condition, manginess; morbidity, indisposition, cachexia; chronic complaint, allergy, hay fever, catarrh;

chronic ill health, invalidism, valetudinarianism, hypochondria; nerves 503 *neurosis*.

*illness*, loss of health 655 *deterioration*; affliction, disability, handicap, infirmity, lameness, spasticity 163 *weakness*; dysfunction 728 *failure*; sickness, indisposition, ailment, complaint, virus, viral illness, post-viral illness, healthcare-associated infection, hospital-acquired i., HAI; retrovirus, HIV virus, AIDS, immune deficiency disorder; complication; condition, history of; bout of sickness, visitation, attack, acute a.; spasm, stroke, seizure, apoplexy, fit; shock; poisoning, metal p., food p.; nausea, waves of n., queasiness, heaving stomach, vomiting, airsickness, carsickness, seasickness, mal de mer; dizziness, vertigo; headache, migraine 377 *pain*; sign of illness, symptom, syndrome 547 *indication*; temperature, feverishness, fever, ague, shivers, shakes 318 *spasm*; hypothermia, hyperthermia; pyrexia, calenture; delirium 503 *frenzy*; stress-related illness, post-traumatic stress disorder, breakdown, collapse; fainting 375 *insensibility*; prostration, coma; terminal disease, fatal illness 361 *decease*; sickbed, deathbed.

*disease*, malady, distemper, disorder; epidemic disease, endemic d.; infectious d., contagious d., communicable d., notifiable d.; debilitating d., killer d.; congenital d.; occupational d., industrial d.; alcoholism, drug addiction; eating disorder, obesity, anorexia, bulimia, Prader-Willi syndrome; deficiency disease, malnutrition, avitaminosis, kwashiorkor, beri-beri, pellagra, rickets, scurvy; degenerative disease, wasting d., marasmus, atrophy; traumatic disease, trauma; organic disease, functional d., circulatory d., neurological d., nervous d., epilepsy, falling sickness; musculo-skeletal disease; cardio-vascular d.; heart d., cardiac d.; endocrine d., diabetes; urogenital disease; venereal d.; herpes virus; dermatological d.; cancer; respiratory disease; gastro-intestinal d.; synergistic triad; virus disease, lentivirus d., retrovirus d., bacterial d., water-borne d.; febrile d., sweating sickness; hydrocele, dropsy; fibrosis; chronic fatigue syndrome, ME, myalgic encephalomyelitis; Gulf War Syndrome, desert fever; post-traumatic stress disorder; brain disease 503 *mental disorder*.

*plague*, pest, scourge 659 *bane*; pestilence, infection, contagion; epidemic, pandemic; pneumonic plague, bubonic p., Black Death; epizootic.

*infection*, contagion, bug, super-bug (inf); miasma, pollution, taint; infectiousness, infectivity, contagiousness 653 *insalubrity*; suppuration, maturation, festering, purulence, gangrene; toxicity, sepsis, poisoning 659 *poison*; plague spot, trouble s., hotbed; vector, carrier, germ c., host; parasite, worm, toxocara canis 659 *bane*; virus, parvovirus, retrovirus, lentivirus, bacillus, bacteria, bacterium, germ, pathogen; Coxsackie virus; blood-poisoning, toxaemia, septicaemia, pyaemia; necrotizing fasciitis, flesh-eating bug; food-poisoning, E coli, E coli 0157, botulism, campylobacter, heliobacter pylorus, gastroenteritis, cholera (see also *digestive disorders*); parasitical disease, toxocariasis, toxoplasmosis, bilharzia (see also *tropical disease*); infectious disease, cold, common c., influenza, flu, Asian f., bird f.; diphtheria, pneumonia, viral p.; infective hepatitis; tuberculosis, consumption; measles, German measles, rubella; whooping-cough, pertussis, mumps; chickenpox, smallpox, variola; scarlet fever, scarlatina, roseola; fever, malarial f., malaria (see also *tropical disease*); typhus, jail fever; trench f.; typhoid, paratyphoid; glandular fever, infectious mononucleosis; poliomyelitis, polio; encephalitis, meningitis; encephalitis lethargica, sleepy sickness; tetanus, lockjaw; rabies, hydrophobia.

*tropical disease*, fever, malarial f., malaria, ague; cholera, Asiatic c.; yellow fever, blackwater f., breakbone f., Lassa f., dengue; green monkey disease; kalaazar, dumdum fever, leishmaniasis; trypanosomiasis, sleeping sickness; schistosomiasis, bilharzia; ascariasis, hook-worm; trachoma, glaucoma, river blindness 439 *blindness*; yaws; leprosy; beriberi, kwashiorkor.

*digestive disorders*, indigestion, dyspepsia, liverishness; biliousness, nausea, sickness, vomiting, retching; colic, gripes; stomach ache, tummy a., belly a., guts ache; stomach upset, tummy u., collywobbles, gippy tummy, holiday t., Spanish t., diarrhoea, travellers' d., gutrot, lurgy, Montezuma's revenge (sl) Aztec two-step (sl), the runs (sl), the trots (sl), galloping trots (sl) 302 *defecation*; diarrhoea and vomiting, D and V, gastroenteritis; dysentery, cholera, typhoid; food poisoning, botulism; flatulence, wind, belching 300 *voidance*; dysbiosis, acidosis, heartburn; hiatus hernia; ulcer, peptic u., gastric u., duodenal u.; gastritis, duodenitis, enteritis, colitis, peritonitis, appendicitis, perforated appendix, diverticulitis, diverticulosis; cancer of the stomach; jaundice, hepatitis, hepatitis B,. cirrhosis, cystitis, nephritis, kidney failure; gallstones, haemorrhoids, piles; constipation; bowel cancer.

*respiratory disease*, cough, cold, sore throat, catarrh, coryza; rhinitis, sinusitis, adenoids, tonsillitis, pharyngitis; laryngitis, tracheitis, croup, bronchitis; emphysema, asthma; pleurisy, pneumonia, bronchopneumonia, legionnaire's disease; sick building syndrome; pneumoconiosis, silicosis, asbestosis, farmer's lung; diphtheria; whooping cough; lung cancer; smoker's cough, graveyard c.; cystic fibrosis; pulmonary tuberculosis, phthisis, consumption.

*cardiovascular disease*, cardiac d.; carditis, endocarditis, myocarditis, pericarditis, angina pectoris, angina; breast-pang, chest-spasm, chest-pain; bradycardia, tachycardia; gallop rhythm, palpitation, dyspnoea; murmur, heart m.; valve disease, valvular lesion, mitral stenosis; cardiac hypertrophy, enlarged heart, athlete's heart; fatty degeneration of the heart; heart condition, bad heart, weak h., heart trouble; congenital heart disease, hole in the heart; rheumatic heart disease, coronary h. d.; myocardial infection; heart failure, cardiac arrest; heart attack, coronary thrombosis, coronary; cerebral thrombosis, brain haemorrhage, stroke; blood pressure, high b. p., hypertension; hypotension, low blood pressure; vascular disease, atheroma, aneurysm; hardened arteries, arteriosclerosis; arteritis, phlebitis, varicose veins; thrombosis, coronary t., clot, blood c., embolism, pulmonary e., infarction, myocardial I; deep vein thrombosis, DVT, economy-class syndrome.

*blood disease*, anaemia, aplastic a., haemolytic a., haemorrhagic a., pernicious a., sickle-cell a., thalassaemia; leukaemia, Hodgkin's disease, lymphoma; haemophilia, AIDS; bleeding, internal b., haemorrhage.

*cancer*, neoplasm, growth; primary g., secondary g., tumour, benign t., innocent t.; malignant t., cancerous growth; carcinoma, epithelioma, sarcoma, melanoma; rodent ulcer.

*skin disease*, cutaneous d., skin lesion; mange; lupus; yaws; leprosy; erythema, miliaria, prickly heat; erysipelas, St. Anthony's fire; impetigo, tetters, herpes, herpes zoster, shingles; dermatitis, eczema; serpigo, ringworm; prurigo, pruritus, itch, dhobi's i. 378 *formication*; hives, urticaria, nettlerash; thrush; athlete's foot; rash, eruption, breaking out, acne, rosacea, spots, blackheads; pustule, papula, pimple; goitre, cyst, blister, wart, verruca 253 *swelling*; macula, mole, freckle, birthmark, pockmark 845 *blemish*; skin cancer, melanoma.

*venereal disease*, VD, sexually-transmitted disease, social d., pox; syphilis, gonorrhoea, the clap; AIDS, herpes; venereal ulcer, chancre, syphilitic sore.

*ulcer*, ulceration, gathering, festering, purulence; lesion 655 *wound*; scald, burn, first-degree b.; sore, boil, abscess, fistula; cyst; blain, chilblain, kibe; gangrene, rot 51 *decay*; discharge, pus, matter.

*inflammation*, corn 253 *swelling*.

---

**Inflammation**
adenitis (inflammation of a gland), appendicitis (appendix), arteritis (artery), arthritis (joint), balanitis (glans penis), blepharitis (eyelid), bronchitis (bronchial tubes), bursitis (sac-like membrane in shoulder, foot, etc), carditis (heart), colitis (colon), conjunctivitis (membrane of the eye), cystitis (bladder), dermatitis (skin), diverticulitis (sacs in the wall of the intestine), duodenitis (duodenum), encephalitis (brain), endocarditis (lining of the heart), endometritis (lining of the uterus), enteritis (intestine), fasciitis (plantar fasciitis: inflammation of a ligament in the sole of the foot; necrotizing fasciitis: inflammation of the sheath of tissue around a muscle or organ accompanied by destruction of tissue), fibrositis (fibrous tissue), gastritis (lining of the stomach), gastroenteritis (lining of the stomach and the intestine), gingivitis (gums), hepatitis (liver), laryngitis (larynx), mastitis (breast), meningitis (membranes surrounding brain and spinal cord), myelitis (spinal cord or bone marrow), myocarditis (heart muscle), nephritis (kidney), neuritis (nerve), oöphoritis (ovary), ophthalmitis (eye, especially the membrane of the eye), orchitis (testicle), osteoarthritis (arthritis with damage to bone and cartilage), otitis (ear), pericarditis (sac around the heart), peritonitis (abdominal membrane), pharyngitis (pharynx), phlebitis (vein), pleuritis (inflammation of the membrane around the lungs; = pleurisy), poliomyelitis (nerve cells of the spinal cord), retinitis (retina of the eye), rhinitis (mucous membrane of the nose), salpingitis (Fallopian tube), sinusitis (sinus), spondylitis (joint in the backbone), tendonitis (tendon), tonsillitis (tonsils), tracheitis (windpipe), tympanitis (membrane of the ear), urethritis (urinary tract).

---

*rheumatism*, rheumatics; rheumatic fever; muscular rheumatism, myalgia; fibrositis; frozen shoulder, tennis elbow, housemaid's knee, pulled muscle; arthritis, rheumatoid a.; gout 377 *pang*; osteoarthritis; lumbago, sciatica; slipped disc.

*nervous disorders*, nervous breakdown 503 *psychopathy*; brain tumour; brain haemorrhage, cerebral h., stroke, seizure; hemiplegia, diplegia, paraplegia; general paralysis, atrophy 375 *insensibility*; partial paralysis, paresis; palsy, cerebral p., spasticity; involuntary movements, tremor, tic 318 *spasm*; petit mal, grand mal, epilepsy, falling sickness; infantile paralysis, poliomyelitis, polio; spina bifida; Parkinson's disease; Huntington's chorea, St Vitus's dance; multiple sclerosis, MS; muscular dystrophy; myasthenia gravis; motor neurone disease.

*animal disease*, veterinary d.; distemper, foot-and-mouth disease, swine fever, swine vesicular disease; BSE, bovine spongiform encephalopathy, mad cow disease; myxomatosis; rinderpest, murrain; anthrax, sheeprot, bloat, scrapie; liver fluke, worms; megrims, staggers; glanders, farcy, sweeny, spavin; thrush; Newcastle disease, fowl pest; psittacosis; hard pad, kennel cough; mange; rabies; parapox.

*sick person*, sufferer; patient, in-p., out-p.; case, stretcher c., hospital c.; mental case 504 *madman*; invalid, chronic i.; valetudinarian, hypochondriac, cyberchondriac, malingerer, leadswinger, martyr to ill health; consumptive, asthmatic, bronchitic, dyspeptic, diabetic; haemophiliac, bleeder; person with AIDS, PWA; insomniac; neuropath, addict, alcoholic; spastic, arthritic, paralytic; paraplegic, disabled person; crock, old c., cripple 163 *weakling*; sick list.

*pathology*, forensic p.; diagnosis, prognosis; aetiology, nosology, epidemiology, bacteriology, parasitology 658 *therapy*.

**Adj.** *unhealthy*, unsound, sickly; infirm, decrepit, weakly 163 *weak*; delicate, of weak constitution, liable to illness, always ill; in bad health, in poor h., out of kilter, in poor condition, mangy; undernourished, anorexic, malnourished 636 *underfed*; peaked, peaky, emaciated, skin and bones; sallow, pale, anaemic 426 *colourless*; bilious 434 *green*; jaundiced 433 *yellow*; invalid, valetudinarian, hypochondriac.

*sick*, ill, unwell, not well, indisposed, out of sorts, under the weather, off-colour, below par, one degree under, out of kilter; acidotic, nauseated, nauseous, queasy, green around the gills; in poor shape, in bad nick; in a bad way, poorly, seedy, squeamish, groggy, grotty, queer, ailing; sickening for, showing symptoms of; feverish, headachy, off one's food, off one's oats; confined, laid up, bedridden, on one's back, in bed, in hospital, on the sick list, invalided, hospitalized; run down, exhausted 684 *fatigued*; seized, taken ill, taken bad; prostrate, collapsed; in a coma 375 *insensible*; on the danger list, in intensive care, not allowed visitors; critical, serious, comfortable; chronic, incurable, inoperable; mortally ill, moribund 361 *dying*; peaky, drooping, flagging, pining, languishing, wasting away, in a decline.

*diseased*, pathological, disordered, distempered; affected, infected, plague-stricken; contaminated, tainted, vitiated, rotten, rotting, gangrenous 51 *decomposed*; peccant, morbid, morbific, pathogenic; iatrogenic; psychosomatic 447 *mental*; infectious, contagious; poisonous, festering, purulent 653 *toxic*; degenerative, consumptive, phthisic, phthisical, tuberculous, tubercular; diabetic, dropsical, hydrocephalic; anaemic; bloodless,

leukaemic, haemophilic; HIV positive, arthritic, rheumatic, rheumatoid, rheumaticky,
creaking; rickety, palsied, paralysed, paralytic,
spastic, epileptic; leprous; carcinomatous, cancerous, oncogenic, carcinogenic, cankered;
syphilitic, venereal; swollen, oedematous;
gouty; bronchial, throaty, bronchitic, croupy,
sniffly, full of cold, bunged up, choked up;
asthmatic; allergic; pyretic, febrile, fevered,
shivering, aguish, feverish, delirious; sore,
tender; ulcerous, ulcerated, inflamed; spotty,
pimply, erythematous, erysipelatous; spav-
ined, broken-winded; mangy.

**Vb.** *be ill,* – sick etc. adj.; enjoy poor health;
ail, suffer, labour under, undergo treatment;
have a complaint *or* an affliction, be a chronic
invalid; not feel well, complain of; feel queer
etc. adj., come over all queer; feel sick 300
*vomit*; lose one's health, sicken, fall sick, fall ill;
catch, catch an infection, catch a bug, contract
a disease; break out with, go down with; be
seized, be stricken, be taken, be taken bad, not
feel so good; have a stroke, collapse; be laid up,
take to one's bed; be invalided out; languish,
pine, peak, droop, waste away, go into a
decline, fall into a consumption; fail, flag, lose
strength, get worse, sink, fade away 655 *deteriorate*; grow weak 163 *be weak*.

**Adv.** *morbidly,* unhealthily 653 *unwholesomely*; in sickness; in hospital, under the
doctor, in the doctor's hands, under treatment,
on the sick list.

### 652 Salubrity

**N.** *healthiness,* salubrity, state of health; well-
being 650 *health*; salubriousness, healthful-
ness, wholesomeness; whole food, health food;
smokeless zone, ventilation, fresh air, open a.,
sea a., ozone 340 *air*; sunshine, outdoors, out
of doors; benign climate, genial c.; health
resort, health farm.

*hygiene,* sanitation, cleanliness 648 *cleanness*;
preventive medicine, prophylaxis 658 *prophylactic*; quarantine, cordon sanitaire, biosecurity
zone 660 *protection*; immunity, immunization,
inoculation, vaccination, pasteurization; antisepsis, sterilization, disinfection, chlorination;
sanatorium, spa 658 *hospital*; hot springs,
thermae 658 *therapy*; keeping fit, working-out,
jogging, cycling, constitutional 682 *exercise*;
hygienics.

*sanitarian,* hygienist, sanitationist, sanitary
inspector, public health i.; sanitary engineer;
medical officer; fresh-air fiend, sun-
worshipper, naturist, nudist.

**Adj.** *salubrious,* healthful, healthy, wholesome; pure, fresh 648 *clean*; ventilated, well-v.,
air-conditioned; tonic, bracing, invigorating,

refreshing 656 *restorative*; hygienic, sanitary,
disinfected, chlorinated, pasteurized, sterilized,
sterile, aseptic, antiseptic; sanative, sanatory;
prophylactic, immunizing, protective 658
*remedial*; good for, salutary, what the doctor
ordered 644 *beneficial*; nutritious, nourishing,
high-fibre, low-calory, low-fat, low-salt, non-
fattening, slimline, body-building, health-
giving, nutraceutical; noninjurious, harmless,
benign, nonmalignant; uninfectious, noninfec-
tious, innoxious, innocuous; immune, immunized, vaccinated, inoculated, protected 660
*invulnerable*.

**Vb.** *be salubrious,* – bracing etc. adj.; be good
for one's health, be good for one; agree with
one; have a good climate; prevent disease; keep
fit 650 *be healthy*.

*sanitate,* disinfect, boil, sterilize, antisepticize, chlorinate, pasteurize; immunize, inoculate, vaccinate; quarantine, put in q., isolate
883 *seclude*; ventilate 340 *aerate*; freshen,
decontaminate 648 *purify*; cleanse 648 *clean*;
drain 342 *dry*; conserve 666 *preserve*.

**Adv.** *healthily,* wholesomely, salubriously,
hygienically.

### 653 Insalubrity

**N.** *unhealthiness,* insalubrity, unwholesomeness; uncleanliness, lack of hygiene, lack
of sanitation; dirty habits, verminousness 649
*uncleanness*; unhealthy conditions, unwholesome surroundings; condemned housing,
slum; mephitis, bad air, bad climate; smoke
haze, fug, smog; infectiousness, infectivity,
contagiousness; bad drains, sewer 649 *sink*;
infectious person, carrier, germ-c., vector;
germ, microbe 196 *microorganism*; miasma, contagion 651 *infection*; pollution, radioactivity,
fallout; deadliness, poisonousness 659 *bane*.

**Adj.** *insalubrious,* unwholesome, unhealthy;
bad for one's health, insanitary, unhygienic
649 *unclean*; bad, nasty, noxious, miasmal,
injurious 645 *harmful*; radioactive, carcinogenic; verminous, rat-infested, flea-ridden, fly-
blown; undrained 347 *marshy*; stagnant, foul,
polluted, undrinkable, inedible; indigestible,
unnutritious; unsound, not fresh, stale, gone
bad, gone off 655 *deteriorated*; unventilated,
windowless, airless 264 *sealed off*; smoke-filled,
stuffy, fuggy; overheated, underheated.

*infectious,* morbific, pathogenic; infective,
germ-carrying; contagious, catching, taking,
communicable; pestiferous, pestilent, plague-
stricken; malarious, malarial, aguish; epidemic,
pandemic, endemic; epizootic, enzootic, sporadic; unsterilized, nonsterile, infected 649
*dirty*.

*toxic,* poisonous, mephitic, pestilential,

germ-laden; venomous, envenomed, poisoned, steeped in poison; gathering, festering, septic, pussy, purulent, suppurating; lethal 362 *deadly*.

**Adv.** *unwholesomely*, insalubriously, poisonously; unhealthily, unhygienically; morbidly.

## 654 Improvement

**N.** *improvement*, betterment, amelioration, melioration, kaizen; uplift, regeneration; good influence, the making of 178 *influence*; a turn for the better, change for the b., sea change, transfiguration 143 *transformation*; conversion, new leaf 939 *penitence*; revival, recovery, economic r., green shoots 656 *restoration*; evolution, development, perfectibility; elaboration, enrichment; decoration 844 *ornamentation*; advance, onward march, march of time, progress 285 *progression*; furtherance, advancement, preferment, promotion, uptitling, kick upstairs, rise, raise, lift, jump 308 *ascent*; upturn, upward mobility, upswing 310 *elevation*; revaluation, enhancement 36 *increase*; no pain no gain.

*amendment*, mending etc. vb.; renovation 656 *repair*; reorganization 62 *arrangement*; reformation, reform, radical r. (see also *reformism*); Borstal 539 *school*; purification, sublimation 648 *cleansing*; refining, rectification; castigation, correction, redaction, revision, red ink, blue pencil; emendation, recension, revised edition, new e., improved version 589 *edition*; revise, proof, corrected copy; second thoughts, better t., review, reconsideration, reexamination; further reflections 67 *sequel*; polish, finishing touch 725 *completion*; perfectionism 862 *fastidiousness*.

*civilization*, culture, kultur; Western civilization, Eastern c., ancient c., modern c.; black culture, Negritude; civility, refinement 846 *good taste*; training, proper upbringing 534 *education*; cultivation, polish, improvement of the mind 490 *culture*; eurhythmics, callisthenics, aerobics 682 *exercise*; telesis, euthenics, yoga.

*reformism*, meliorism, perfectionism, idealism; Moral Rearmament; liberalism, socialism, radicalism; extremism, revolution 738 *sedition*; masculinism, progressivism; gradualism, Fabianism; social engineering 901 *sociology*.

*reformer*, improver, repairer, restorer 656 *mender*; emender, corrector, editor, proofreader, reviser; progressive, progressist, progressionist; gradualist, Fabian 625 *moderate*; liberal, radical, feminist, masculinist; extremist, revolutionary 738 *agitator*; socialist, communist, Marxist, Red; reformist, New Dealer; idealist, Utopian 513 *visionary*; champagne socialist; sociologist, social worker 901 *philanthropist*.

**Adj.** *improved*, bettered, enhanced; touched up 843 *beautified*; reformed, revised 34 *superior*; better, better off, all the better for; looking up, on the mend; better advised, wiser 498 *wise*; improvable, corrigible, curable, reformable, perfectible.

*improving*, reformative, reformatory, remedial 656 *restorative*; reforming, reformist, progressive, radical; civilizing, cultural; idealistic, perfectionist, Utopian, millenarian, chiliastic; perfectionist 862 *fastidious*.

**Vb.** *get better*, grow b., improve, mend, take a turn for the better, turn the corner; pick up, rally, revive, recover 656 *be restored*; make progress, make headway, advance, develop, evolve 285 *progress*; mellow, ripen 669 *mature*; bear fruit 171 *be fruitful*; rise 308 *ascend*; graduate 727 *succeed*; rise in the world, better oneself, be upwardly mobile, make one's way 730 *prosper*; mend one's ways, reform, turn over a new leaf, go straight 939 *be penitent*; improve oneself, learn by experience 536 *learn*; take advantage of, make capital out of, cash in on 137 *profit by*.

*make better*, better, improve, ameliorate, meliorate, reform; make improvements, improve upon, refine u.; polish, elaborate, enrich, enhance; work a miracle in, do one a power of good 644 *do good*; improve out of all recognition, transfigure 147 *transform*; make, be the making of, have a good influence, leaven 178 *influence*; uplift, regenerate; refine, elevate, sublimate 648 *purify*; civilize, socialize, teach manners; mend 656 *repair*; restore 656 *cure*; recruit, revive, infuse fresh blood into 685 *refresh*; soften, lenify, mitigate, palliate 177 *moderate*; forward, advance, upgrade 285 *promote*; foster, encourage, hype, bring to fruition 669 *mature*; make the most of, get the best out of 673 *use*; develop, open up, reclaim; till, weed, dress, water 370 *cultivate*; tidy, tidy up, make shipshape, neaten 62 *arrange*; spruce up, freshen up 648 *clean*; do up, vamp up, tone up, rationalize; renovate, refurbish, renew, give a face lift; bring up to date 126 *modernize*; touch up 841 *beautify*; improve on nature, gild the lily, make up, titivate 843 *primp*; embellish, adorn, ornament 844 *decorate*.

*rectify*, put right, set right, straighten, straighten out 24 *adjust*; mend, patch 656 *repair*; correct, debug, decontaminate, make corrections, blue-pencil, proofread, remove errors; revise, redact, edit, subedit, amend, emend; rewrite, redraft, retell, recast, remould, refashion, remodel, recreate, reform; reorganize 62 *regularize*; make improvements, streamline, fine-tune, rationalize; review, reexamine, reconsider; correct one's mistakes, stop in time, think again, think better of, have second thoughts.

## 655 Deterioration

**N.** *deterioration*, debasement, coarsening; cheapening, devaluation; retrogradation, retrogression, slipping back, losing ground 286 *regression*; reversion to type, throwback 5 *heredity*; decline, ebb 37 *decrease*; twilight, fading 419 *dimness*; falling off, downtrend, downturn, slump, depression, recession; impoverishment 801 *poverty*; law of diminishing returns; Gresham's law; Malthusianism; exhaustion 634 *waste*; vitiation, corruption, perversion, prostitution, depravation, degeneration, loss of morale, degeneracy, degenerateness, decadence, depravity 934 *wickedness*; downward course, 'primrose path' (see quotation below) 309 *descent*; recidivism 603 *tergiversation*; setback 657 *relapse*; bad ending, tragedy 731 *misfortune*.

*dilapidation*, collapse, ruination 165 *destruction*; planning blight; inner city deprivation, sink estate; lack of maintenance, disrepair, neglect 458 *negligence*; slum, back street 801 *poverty*; ravages of time, wear and tear, erosion, corrosion, oxidization, rustiness, rust, moth and rust, rot, canker, corruption, putrefaction, rottenness, cancer, concrete cancer 51 *decay*; mouldiness, mildew 659 *blight*; decrepitude, senility 131 *old age*; atrophy 651 *disease*; ruin, wreck, mere w., perfect w., physical w., shadow of one's former self.

*impairment*, spoiling 675 *misuse*; detriment, damage, spoilage, waste 772 *loss*; discoloration, weathering, patina; pollution, contamination, defilement 649 *uncleanness*; ulceration, poisoning, autointoxication, contamination 651 *infection*; adulteration, sophistication, watering down 43 *mixture*; assault, insult, outrage 712 *attack*; ruination, demolition 165 *destruction*; injuriousness, injury, mischief, harm 165 *havoc*; disablement, crippling, laming, hobbling, nobbling, disabling, mutilation, weakening 163 *weakness*; sprain, strain, pulled muscle, dislocation; disorganization, bedevilment, sabotage, demoralization 63 *derangement*; exacerbation 832 *aggravation*.

*wound*, injury, trauma; repetitive strain injury, RSI; brain injury, brain damage, shaken baby syndrome; open wound, fresh w., bloody nose; sore, running s. 651 *ulcer*; laceration, lesion; cut, gash, incision, abrasion, nick, snick, scratch 46 *scission*; stab, prick, jab, puncture 263 *perforation*; contusion, bruise, bump, discoloration, black eye, shiner, thick ear, cauliflower ear 253 *swelling*; burn, scald; rupture,

hernia; broken head, broken bones, fracture; scar, mark, scab, cicatrice 845 *blemish*.

*wounded person*, casualty, fatality, victim, basket case (inf); the injured, wounded, walking wounded; collateral damage.

**Adj.** *deteriorated*, not improved, the worse for; exacerbated 832 *aggravated*; spoilt, impaired, damaged, hurt, ruined etc. vb.; worn out, effete, exhausted, worthless 641 *useless*; stale, gone bad, gone off, rotten 645 *bad*; corked, flat 387 *tasteless*; undermined, sapped, shaken 163 *weakened*; tired, overtired, done in, washed up 684 *fatigued*; no better, deteriorating, worse, getting w., worse and worse, in a bad way, far gone; going downhill, failing, past one's best, declining, in decline, on the d.; senile, senescent 131 *ageing*; on the way out, on the downgrade, on the downward path; falling, slipping, nodding, tottering 309 *descending*; faded, withered, sere, decaying 51 *decomposed*; wasting away, ebbing, at low ebb; slumping, falling off 37 *decreasing*; degenerative, retrogressive, retrograde, unprogressive, unimproved, backward 286 *regressive*; lapsed, recidivist 603 *tergiversating*; degenerate, depraved, corrupt 934 *vicious*; come down in the world, impoverished 801 *poor*.

*dilapidated*, the worse for wear, falling to pieces, in disrepair, in shreds, in ruins; broken, kaput, cracked, leaking; battered, weatherbeaten, storm-tossed; decrepit, ruinous, ramshackle, tottery, wonky, shaky, rickety, tumbledown, run-down, on its last legs 163 *weakened*; slummy, condemned; worn, well-w., frayed, shabby, tatty, dingy, holey, in holes, in tatters, in rags, out-at-elbows; worn out, worn to a frazzle, worn to a shadow, reduced to a skeleton, done for 641 *useless*; seedy, down at heel, down and out 801 *poor*; rusty, rotten, mildewed, mouldering, moss-grown, moth-eaten, worm-e., dog-eared 51 *decomposed*.

**Vb.** *deteriorate*, not improve, get no better; get worse, worsen, disimprove, go from bad to worse, take a turn for the worse; slip, slide, go downhill; have seen better days; not maintain improvement 657 *relapse*; fall off, slump, decline, wane, ebb, sink, fail 37 *decrease*; slip back, retrograde, revert 286 *regress*; lapse 603 *change one's mind*; degenerate, let oneself go, ruin oneself, go to pieces, run to seed, hit the skids 165 *be destroyed*; 'tread the primrose path', go to the bad 934 *be wicked*;

> Do not, as some ungracious pastors do,
> Show me the steep and thorny way to heaven,
> Whiles, like a puff'd and reckless libertine,
> Himself the primrose path of dalliance treads,
> And recks not his own rede.
> William Shakespeare, *Hamlet*

disintegrate, fall apart, collapse, break down, fall, totter, droop, stoop 309 *tumble*; contract, shrink 198 *become small*; wear out, age 131 *grow old*; fade, wither, wilt, shrivel, perish, crumble, moulder, mildew, grow moss; go to rack and ruin; weather, rust, rot, decay 51 *decompose*; spoil, stale, lose its taste, lose its flavour, go flat, go off, go sour, turn 391 *be unpalatable*; go bad, smell, pong 397 *stink*; corrupt, putrefy, rankle, fester, suppurate, maturate, gangrene 51 *decompose*; sicken 651 *be ill*; do worse, make things worse, go from bad to worse, jump from the frying pan into the fire, go farther and fare worse 832 *aggravate*.

*pervert*, deform, warp, twist 246 *distort*; abuse, prostitute 675 *misuse*; deprave 951 *debauch*; vitiate, corrupt 934 *make wicked*; lower, degrade, debase 311 *abase*; brutalize, dehumanize, barbarize; denature, denaturalize 147 *transform*; denationalize, detribalize; propagandize, brainwash 535 *misteach*.

*impair*, damage, make inoperative, damnify, hurt, injure, scathe 645 *harm*; mess up, muck up, untidy 63 *jumble*; play havoc with 63 *derange*; disorganize, dismantle, dismast; spoil, maul, mar, botch, cock up, make a balls-up of 695 *be clumsy*; touch, tinker, tamper, meddle with, fool w., monkey w. 678 *meddle*; not improve, worsen, deteriorate, disimprove, exacerbate, embitter 832 *aggravate*; do no good, kill with kindness 499 *be foolish*; degrade, lower, coarsen 847 *vulgarize*; devalue, debase 812 *cheapen*; blacken, blot, spot, stain, uglify 842 *make ugly*; scar, mark, wrinkle 845 *blemish*; deface, disfigure, deform, warp 246 *distort*; corrupt, vitiate (see also *pervert*); mutilate, maim, lame, cripple 161 *disable*; scotch, pinion, clip the wings, cramp, hamper 702 *hinder*; castrate 161 *unman*; expurgate, eviscerate, bowdlerize; curtail, dock 204 *shorten*; cream, skim, take the heart out of; adulterate, sophisticate, alloy 43 *mix*; denature, deactivate 679 *make inactive*; subvert, shake, sap, mine, undermine, demoralize 163 *weaken*; honeycomb, bore, gnaw, gnaw at the roots, eat away, fret, erode, corrode, rust, rot, mildew 51 *decompose*; blight, blast; ravage, rape, waste, scorch, overrun 165 *lay waste*; vandalize, wreck, ruin 165 *destroy*; crumble 332 *pulverize*; dilapidate, fray, wear out, reduce to rags; exhaust, deplete, drain, consume, use up 634 *waste*; infect, contaminate, poison, envenom, ulcerate; taint, canker, foul, pollute 649 *make unclean*; defile, desecrate, profane 980 *be impious*.

*wound*, scotch, draw blood, let b.; tear, rend, lacerate, slit, mangle, rip 46 *disunite*; maul, savage, traumatize 176 *be violent*, black one's eye, bloody one's nose; bite, scratch, claw; slash, gash, hack, incise 46 *cut*; scarify, score 262 *groove*; nick 260 *notch*; sting, prick, pink, stab, gore, run through, puncture 263 *pierce*; bruise, contuse, buffet 279 *strike*; crush, grind 332 *pulverize*; chafe 333 *rub*; smash 46 *break*; graze, pepper, wing.

## 656 Restoration

**N.** *restoration*, returning, giving back, retrocession 787 *restitution*; redress, amends, reparation, reparations 941 *atonement*; finding again, getting back, retrieval, recovery 786 *taking*; reestablishment, reinstallation, reinvestment, recall, replacement, reinstatement, reinstalment; rehabilitation; replanting, reafforestation, reclamation, gentrification, recycling; rescue, salvage, redemption, ransom, salvation 668 *deliverance*; reconstitution, reerection, rebuilding, reformation, reconstruction, reorganization; readjustment; remodelling 654 *amendment*; reconversion; reaction, counterreformation 182 *counteraction*; resumption, return to normal, derestriction; recruitment, reinforcement 162 *strengthening*; replenishment 633 *provision*.

*repair*, reparation, repairs, running r., service, servicing, renovation, renewal, reconditioning, redintegration, reassembling; overhauling, DIY; rectification, emendation; restoration, making like new; mending, invisible m., darning, patching, patching up; cobbling, soling, heeling, tinkering etc. vb.; clout, patch, darn, insertion, reinforcement; new look, facelift 843 *beautification*.

*revival*, recruitment, recovery 685 *refreshment*; renewal, reawakening, revivescence, resurgence, recovery, rally, comeback; fresh spurt, new energy; economic recovery, green shoots, economic miracle, boom 730 *prosperity*; reactivation, revivification, reanimation, resuscitation, artificial respiration; rejuvenation, rejuvenescence, second youth, Indian summer; face-lift, new look; rebirth, renaissance, new birth, second b.; palingenesis, regeneration, regeneracy; new life, resurrection, awaking from the dead, recall from the grave; resurrection day 124 *future state*.

*recuperation*, recovery, pulling through, rallying, perking up, taking a turn for the better, turning the corner, cure; healing, mending; cicatrization, closing, scabbing over, healing o.; convalescence, restoration to health 658 *remedy*; moderation, easing 831 *relief*; psychological cure, catharsis, abreaction; curability.

*mender*, repairer, renovator, painter, decorator, interior d., DIYer; mechanic; emendator, rectifier; rebuilder, restorer, refurbisher; patcher, darner, cobbler, shoe-repairer; knife grinder, tinker, plumber, fixer, handyman; salvor, salvager; curer, healer, bone-setter; osteopath 658 *doctor*; faith healer; psychiatrist; reformist 654 *reformer*.

**Adj.** *restored*, revived, refreshed etc. vb.; remade, rebuilt, refitted, reconstituted, re-equipped, reconditioned, reproofed; redone, rectified 654 *improved*; reinforced; like new, renewed; saved, born again 979 *sanctified*; resuscitated, reborn, redivivus, renascent, resurgent, like a phoenix from the ashes; alive and kicking 650 *healthy*; cured, as good as new, none the worse, better, convalescent, on the mend, pulling through; in one's right mind, back on one's feet, back to normal, oneself again; retrievable, restorable, recoverable; mendable, amendable; medicable, curable, sanable, operable; found, recovered, salvaged, reclaimed.

*restorative*, reparative, analeptic, reviving, recuperative, curative, sanative, healing, medicated, medicinal 658 *remedial*.

**Vb.** *be restored*, recover, come round, come to, revive, pick up, rally, regroup 685 *be refreshed*; pull through, get over, get up, get well, convalesce, recuperate; turn the corner 654 *get better*; weather the storm, survive, live through; reawake, live again, resurrect, come to life again, arise from the dead, return from the grave; reappear, make a comeback, take on a new lease of life; sleep off, be oneself again, bounce back, snap out of it, come up smiling; pick oneself up, find one's feet again; return to normal, get back to n., go on as before; resume, start again 68 *begin*; look like new, undergo repairs.

*restore*, give back, hand b., retrocede, yield up 787 *restitute*; make amends 941 *atone*; put back, bring b., replace; recall, reappoint, reinstall, reestablish, rehabilitate; reconstitute, reconstruct, reform, reorganize 654 *make better*; valet 648 *clean*; renovate, renew, rebuild, reerect, remake, redo; overhaul, service, refit, refurbish, make like new 126 *modernize*; make whole, reintegrate; reforest, reafforest, replant, reclaim; recycle, reprocess; revalidate, reinforce, build up one's strength 162 *strengthen*; fill up 633 *replenish*; rally, reassemble 74 *bring together*; redeem, ransom, rescue, salvage 668 *deliver*; release, derestrict 746 *liberate*.

*revive*, revivify, revitalize, resuscitate, regenerate, recall to life, resurrect, reanimate, rekindle; breathe fresh life into, give a new lease of life, rejuvenate; freshen, recruit 685 *refresh*.

*cure*, heal, make well, cure of, break of; nurse, physic, medicate 658 *doctor*; bandage, put a plaster on, bind up one's wounds; nurse through, work a cure, snatch from the grave, restore to health, set up, set on one's feet again; set (a bone); cicatrize, heal over, skin o., scab o., close, knit together; right itself, put itself right, work its own cure.

*repair*, do repairs; amend, emend, right, set to rights, put right, put back into operation, remedy 654 *rectify*; overhaul, DIY, mend, fix; cobble, resole, heel; reface, retread, recover, resurface, thatch 226 *cover*; reline 227 *line*; darn, patch, patch up; stop, fill (teeth); make over, do up, touch up, freshen up, retouch, revamp, plaster up, fill in the cracks, paper over; seal, stop a gap, plug a hole 350 *staunch*; caulk 264 *close*; splice, bind 45 *tie*; pick up the pieces, piece together, refit, reassemble, cannibalize 45 *join*; give a face-lift, upgrade, gentrify, refurbish, recondition, renovate, renew, remodel, reform.

*retrieve*, get back, recover, regain, retake, recapture; find again, reclaim, claim back, compensate oneself 31 *recoup*; make up for, make up time, make up leeway.

## 657 Relapse

**N.** *relapse*, lapse, falling back; throwback, return 148 *reversion*; retrogression, retrogradation 286 *regression*; sinking, falling off, fall 655 *deterioration*; backsliding, recidivism, apostasy 603 *tergiversation*; recrudescence, reinfection, recurrence, fresh outbreak.

**Vb.** *relapse*, slip back, slide b., sink b., fall b., lose ground; throw back, return, retrogress 286 *regress*; degenerate 655 *deteriorate*; backslide, recidivate, lapse, fall from grace 603 *change one's allegiance*; fall off again, revert to 148 *revert*; have a relapse, suffer a recurrence, not maintain an improvement.

## 658 Remedy

**N.** *remedy*, succour, help 703 *aid*; oil on troubled waters 177 *moderator*; remedial measure, corrective, correction 654 *amendment*; redress, amends 787 *restitution*; expiation 941 *atonement*; cure, certain c. 656 *recuperation*; medicinal value, healing gift, healing quality *or* property; sovereign remedy, specific r., specific, answer, right a., solution; prescribed remedy, prescription, recipe, formula, nostrum; quack remedy, patent medicine; sovereign remedy, panacea, heal-all, cure-all, catholicon; elixir, elixir vitae, philosopher's stone.

*medicine*, materia medica, pharmacopoeia; vegetable remedy, herbal r., galenical, herb, medicinal h., simple; balm, balsam; medication, medicament, patent medicine, proprietary drug, generic d., ethical d. (see also *drug*), pharmaceutical, nutraceutical; placebo; pill, bolus, tablet, tabloid, capsule, caplet, lozenge; physic, draught, potion, elixir; nosode; decoction, infusion; dose, booster d.; drench; drops, drip; injection, jab, shot; preparation, mixture, powder, electuary, linctus; plaster (see also *surgical dressing*); spray, inhaler; medicine chest, medicine cabinet, medicine bottle; inappropriate use of drugs, off-label use, off-labelling.

*diagnosis*, computer-aided d.; symptom, syndrome; sample, urine s., semen s.; battery of tests, test, laboratory t., lab t., blood t., serotest, sputum t., stool t., eye t., hearing t, breath t.; pregnancy t.; amniocentesis, alphafetoprotein test, chorionic villus sampling; cervical smear, smear test, Pap t., liquid-based cytology; radiology, radiodiagnosis; mammogram, angiogram, arteriogram, cardiogram, ECG, hysterogram, hysterosalpingogram, lymphogram, pyelogram, venogram; radiograph; chest X-ray, spirometry; barium meal, barium enema; ultrasound, screening, scanning, CAT s., body s., brain s., EEG; MRI, magnetic resonance imaging; biopsy, cone b.; stethoscope, bronchoscope, ophthalmoscope, auriscope; endoscope, colposcope, ureteroscope, bronchoscopy, colonoscopy, endoscopy, gastroscopy, laparoscopy; dowsing, kinesiology, applied kinesiology; forensic test; DNA fingerprinting, genetic f.

*prophylactic*, preventive; sanitation, sanitary precaution, cordon sanitaire, quarantine 652 *hygiene*; prophylaxis, immunization, inoculation, vaccination, chemoprevention; vaccine, triple v., BCG, TAB, MMR (= measles, mumps and rubella); antimalarial pill, quinine; antisepsis, disinfection, sterilization; antiseptic, disinfectant, iodine, carbolic, boric acid, boracic a.; bactericide, germicide, insecticide, acaricide 659 *poison*; fumigant, fumigator; dentifrice, toothpaste, tooth powder 648 *cleanser*; mouthwash, gargle; fluoridation, fluoride.

*antidote*, counterirritant, antihistamine; counterpoison, antiserum, antitoxin, mithridate, theriac; anti-emetic; antipyretic, febrifuge, quinine; vermifuge, anthelmintic; antigen, antibody, interferon; antibiosis, antibiotic; immunosuppressant; antispasmodic, anticonvulsant; sedative, muscle relaxant; anticoagulant; antacid, analgesic, painkiller; antidepressant. (See also *drug*.)

*purgative*, purge, cathartic, laxative, aperient; castor oil, Epsom salts, health s., senna pods; cascara, milk of magnesia; diuretic; expectorant, emetic, nauseant, ipecacuanha; carminative, digestive, liquorice, dill water; douche, enema.

*tonic*, restorative; cordial, tonic water, tonic wine; reviver, refresher, pick-me-up 174 *stimulant*; caffeine, nicotine, alcohol; spirits, smelling salts, sal volatile, hartshorn; infusion, tisane, herb tea; coca, betel nut; ginseng, royal jelly, adaptogen; vitamin tablet, vitamin supplement, iron pill, folic acid.

*drug*, medicinal d., miracle d., synthetic d., wonder d.; antibiotic, sulpha drug, sulphonamide; penicillin; aureomycin, streptomycin, insulin, cortisone; steroid; bronchodilator; AZT, azidothymidine, Zidovidine; Aricept; Ritalin; tamoxifen; hormone, HRT, progesterone, oestrogen; contraceptive pill 172 *contraception*; Viagra (tdmk); analgesic, aspirin, codeine, paracetamol, 375 *anaesthetic*; sedative, tranquillizer, diazepam, Valium (tdmk), temazepan; antidepressant, Prozac (tdmk); barbiturate, barb (sl); sleeping pill 679 *soporific*; narcotic, dope, morphia, morphine, opium, cocaine, heroin; intoxicant, stimulant 949 *drug-taking*; lotus, nepenthe, kef.

*balm*, balsam, oil, soothing syrup, emollient, antipruritic 177 *moderator*; salve, ointment; cream, face c. 843 *cosmetic*; lanolin, liniment, embrocation; lotion, wash; eyewash, collyrium; placebo.

*surgical dressing*, dressing, lint, gauze; swab; bandage, roller, sling, splint, cast, plaster of Paris; tourniquet; fingerstall; patch; application, external a., plaster, sticking p., Elastoplast (tdmk), Band-Aid (tdmk), corn plaster, court p., mustard p., sterile strip; cataplasm, fomentation, poultice, compress; tampon, tent, roll, pledget; pessary, suppository; traumatic.

*medical art*, leechcraft; therapeutics, art of healing, healing touch 656 *recuperation*; medical advice, practice, medical p., medical care, managed c., primary c., integrated c., triage; telemedicine; allopathy, homoeopathy, naturopathy, nature cure; medicine, clinical m., preventive m., fringe m., alternative m., complementary m., holistic m., unorthodox m., folk m., herbal medicine, ayurveda, ayurvedic medicine, iridology, reflexology, radiesthesia, acupuncture, acupressure (see also *alternative therapy*); radiography, radiology, tomography; diagnosis, prognosis 651 *pathology*; healing, gift of h., laying on of hands, faith healing, Christian Science; sexology, gynaecology, midwifery 167 *obstetrics*; gerontology, geriatrics, paediatrics; orthopaedics, orthotics, ophthalmology, orthoptics, neurology, dermatology, ear nose and throat,

ENT, cardiology, oncology; nuclear medicine; radiotherapy; psychodiagnostics, psychopathology, bacteriology, microbiology, virology, immunology; pharmaceutics, pharmacology, posology; veterinary medicine.

*surgery*, general surgery, keyhole s., telesurgery, laser s., brain s., heart s., cardiac s., angioplasty, balloon a., open-heart surgery, by-pass s., transplant s., xenotransplantation; plastic surgery, cosmetic s., bus-stop s., nip and tuck (inf), liposuction, rhinoplasty 843 *beautification*; prosthesis, prosthetics; manipulative surgery, chiropractic; operation, surgical o., op; phlebotomy, venesection; bleeding, bloodletting, cupping, tranfusion, perfusion; dialysis; D and C, dilatation and curettage; transplant, xenotransplant; cauterization; amputation; trephination, trepanning; colostomy.

---

**Surgical Operations: -ectomies and -otomies**
adenectomy (removal of a gland), appendectomy *or* appendicectomy (appendix), craniotomy (skull), cystectomy *and* cystotomy (bladder, or gall bladder), episiotomy (opening of the vagina), gastrectomy (stomach), hysterectomy (uterus), keratectomy *and* keratotomy (cornea), laparotomy (abdomen), laryngectomy *and* laryngotomy (larynx), leucotomy (nerve fibres in the brain), lithotomy (stone from the bladder, kidney or urinary tract), lobectomy (lobe of lung, brain, etc), lobotomy (lobe of brain), lumpectomy (lump in the breast), mastectomy (breast), radical m. (breast, pectoral muscles and lymph nodes), nephrectomy (kidney), neurotomy (nerve), oöphorectomy (ovary), orchidectomy (testicle), ovariectomy *or* ovariotomy (ovary), pharyngotomy (pharynx), phlebotomy (vein), pneumonectomy (lung), rhytidectomy (wrinkles; = a facelift), salpingectomy (Fallopian tube), splenectomy (spleen), sympathectomy (sympathetic nerve), tenotomy (tendon), thoracotomy (chest), tonsillectomy (tonsils), tracheotomy (windpipe), tubectomy (Fallopian tube), varicotomy (varicose vein), vasectomy (vas deferens).

---

*dentistry*, bridging, drawing, extracting, stopping, filling, crowning.

*massage*, chiropody, podiatry, pedicure, nail surgery.

*therapy*, therapeutics, medical care; treatment, medical t., clinical t.; nursing, bedside manner; first aid, aftercare; course, cure, faith c., nature c., cold-water c., hydrotherapy, thalassotherapy; regimen, diet, dietary; bonesetting, orthopaedics, osteopathy, osteotherapy; hypnotherapy; hormone therapy, HRT, HRT patch; immunotherapy; chemotherapy; gene therapy, germ-line therapy; combination therapy; physiotherapy, occupational therapy; radiotherapy, phototherapy; heat treatment; electrotherapy, shock treatment, ECT, EST; mental treatment, clinical psychology; child psychology; psychotherapy, psy-

chiatry, psychoanalysis, counselling, genetic c. 447 *psychology*; group therapy, behaviour t., cognitive behaviour *or* behavioural t., cognitive t., neurolinguistic programming, aversion t., Gestalt t., primal t.; self-analysis, enneagram; catheterization; intravenous injection, dripfeed; fomentation, poulticing; retail therapy, shopping t.

*alternative therapy*, complementary t., supplementary t., homoeopathy, holistic medicine, folk m., traditional m., traditional Chinese m., TCM, fringe medicine, herbal m., ayurveda, ayurvedic medicine; macrobiotics; naturopathy, urine therapy; acupuncture, acupressure, moxibustion, jin shin do, shiatsu, craniosacral therapy, reiki; osteopathy, chiropractic; faith healing, laying on of hands; self-healing; relaxation therapy, autogenic t., autogenics, autogenic training; meditation; aromatherapy; crystal healing, crystal therapy; Bach flower remedies; colonic irrigation; reflexology; iridology; kinesiology; cellular therapy *or* live-cell t.; bodywork, therapeutic massage, Alexander technique, Rolfing *or* structural integration, Hellerwork; breathwork, vivation, rebirthing; sensory deprivation, flotation tank.

*hospital*, infirmary, general hospital, hospital trust, hospital manager; maternity h., children's h.; 503 *mental hospital*; dispensary, clinic, antenatal c.; nursing home, convalescent h., rest h.; home for the dying, hospice; lazaret, lazaretto, lazar-house, leper asylum, leper colony; hospital ship, hospital train; stretcher, ambulance; ward, hospital w., casualty w., isolation w., sick bay, sickroom, sickbed; hospital bed, ripple b.; bed-blocking; tent, oxygen t., iron lung; respirator, life-support system, heart-lung machine, kidney m.; incubator, intensive care unit; X-ray machine, scanner, body s., brain s., head s., CAT s.; dressing station, first-aid s., casualty department, crash team, operating room, operating theatre, operating table; consulting room, surgery, clinic, community health centre; sanatorium, spa, hydro, watering place; pump room, baths, hot springs, thermae; solarium, sun lamp, sun bed.

*doctor*, physician; leech, quack, charlatan; veterinary surgeon, vet, horse-doctor; herbalist, herb doctor; faith healer, layer-on of hands, Christian Scientist; allopath, homoeopath, naturopath; acupuncturist, acupressurist; hakim, barefoot doctor, flying d.; witch doctor, medicine man 983 *sorcerer*; medic, medical student; houseman, house officer, intern, registrar; medical practitioner, general p., GP, family doctor, fundholder; locum tenens, locum; clinician, therapeutist, healer; surgeon, general s., plastic s., neurosurgeon; sawbones; health professional; medical officer, health o., sanitary inspector; medical adviser, consultant, specialist; diagnostician, pathologist, forensic p.; alienist, psychiatrist, psychoanalyst, shrink, neurologist; paramedic, anaesthetist, radiologist, radiographer; physiotherapist, occupational therapist, speech t.; paediatrician, geriatrician; obstetrician, midwife; gynaecologist; sexologist; dermatologist, haematologist; biochemist, microbiologist; radiotherapist; orthopaedist, orthotist, osteopath, bonesetter, chiropractor, masseur, masseuse; pedicurist, podiatrist, chiropodist, manicurist; ophthalmologist, optician, ophthalmic optician, oculist, orthoptist 438 *vision*; aurist, otologist, audiologist 415 *ear*; dentist, dental surgeon, orthodontist; nutritionist, dietician; medical profession, private medicine, Harley Street, National Health Service, hospital trust; Red Cross, St. John Ambulance, St Andrew's Ambulance Association; Aesculapius, Hippocrates, Galen; Hippocratic oath.

*druggist*, apothecary, chemist, pharmaceutical c., pharmacist; dispenser, posologist, pharmacologist; chemist's, pharmacy.

*nurse*, male n., probationer n., student n., staff n.; charge n., sister, night s., ward s., theatre s., nursing officer, senior n. o.; matron; state-enrolled nurse, SEN; state-registered nurse, SRN; registered sick children's nurse, RSCN; special nurse, day n., night n.; district nurse, community n., home n., Diana n., Macmillan n., Marie Curie n., palliative care n. 703 *aider*; health visitor; nursing auxiliary, ward orderly, dresser, medical attendant, stretcher-bearer, ambulanceman *or* -woman; almoner, hospital social worker, medical s. w. 901 *social care*; caring profession; Florence Nightingale, the Lady of the Lamp, ministering angel.

**Adj.** *remedial*, corrective, analeptic, curative, first-aid 656 *restorative*; helpful 644 *beneficial*; therapeutic, medicinal, healing, curing, hygienic, salutiferous 652 *salubrious*; specific, sovereign; panacean, all-healing; soothing, paregoric, balsamic, demulcent, emollient, palliative 177 *alleviate*; anodyne, analgesic, narcotic, hypnotic, anaesthetic 375 *insensible*; peptic, digestive; purging 648 *cleansing*; cathartic, emetic, vomitory, laxative; antidotal, antibiotic, anticoagulant, anticonvulsant, antidepressant, antidiuretic, anti-emetic, antiinflammatory, antipsychotic, antispasmodic, antitussive, antiviral, antipyretic, febrifugal, antiseptic, disinfectant, theriacal, prophylactic

182 *counteracting*; tonic, stimulative; dietetic, alimentary, nutritive, nutritional.

*medical*, pathological, physicianly, Aesculapian, Hippocratic, Galenic; allopathic, homoeopathic, herbal; surgical, anaplastic, rhinoplastic, orthopaedic, orthotic; vulnerary, traumatic; obstetric, obstetrical; clinical; medicable, operable, curable.

**Vb.** *remedy*, fix, put right, correct 656 *restore*; succour, help 703 *aid*; apply a remedy, treat, heal, work a cure 656 *cure*; palliate, soothe, neutralize 831 *relieve*.

*doctor*, be a d., practise, have a practice, practise medicine; treat, prescribe, advise; attend 703 *minister to*; tend, nurse; give first aid, give the kiss of life 656 *revive*; hospitalize, put on the sick list, put to bed; physic, medicate, drench, dose, purge; inject, give a jab, give a shot; dress, bind, swathe, bandage, put a plaster on; stop the bleeding, apply a tourniquet 350 *staunch*; poultice, plaster, foment; set, put in splints; drug, dope, anaesthetize; operate, use the knife, cut open, amputate; trepan, trephine, curette; cauterize; bleed, phlebotomize; transfuse, perfuse; massage, rub, manipulate; draw, extract, pull, stop, fill, crown; pedicure, manicure; immunize, vaccinate, inoculate; sterilize, pasteurize, antisepticize, disinfect 652 *sanitate*.

**659 Bane**
**N.** *bane*, cause of injury, malevolent influence; curse, plague, infestation, pest, scourge, ruin 616 *evil*; malady 651 *disease*; weakness, bad habit, besetting sin 934 *vice*; hell, cup, visitation, affliction 731 *adversity*; woe, funeral 825 *sorrow*; cross, cross to bear, trial; bore 838 *tedium*; bugbear, bête noire 827 *annoyance*; burden, imposition, white elephant; thorn in the flesh, stone round one's neck; stress, strain, perpetual worry, constant anxiety, angst, torment, nagging pain 825 *worry*; running sore 651 *ulcer*; bitterness, acid, gall, wormwood 393 *sourness*; sickener, emetic 391 *unsavouriness*; bite, sting, poison dart, serpent's tooth, fang, briar, nettle 256 *sharp point*; source of trouble, trouble spot, hornet's nest 663 *pitfall*; viper, adder, serpent 365 *reptile*; snake, snake in the grass 663 *troublemaker*; parasite, leech, threadworm, tapeworm 365 *insect, creepy-crawly*; mosquito, mozzie, wasp 904 *noxious animal*; locust 168 *destroyer*; oppressor, holy terror 735 *tyrant*.

*blight*, rot, dry r., wet r., dieback; mildew, mould, rust, fungus; moth, woodworm, cankerworm, canker, cancer 51 *decay*; nuclear winter; visitation 651 *plague*; frost, nip, cold 380 *coldness*; drought 342 *desiccation*.

*poison*, poisonousness, virulence, venomousness, toxicity; bad food, bad water, pollution; bacteria, bacterium, salmonella, bacillus, germ, virus 651 *infection*; teratogen, carcinogen, oncogene; chemical weapon, biological w.; venom, toxicant, toxin; deadly poison, snake p.; rat p., ratsbane, rodenticide, warfarin; germicide; slug pellets; insecticide, carburfuran, organo-phosphates; pesticide, sheep dip; fungicide, systemic f.; herbicide, weed-killer, agrochemicals, defoliant, dioxin, Agent Orange (tdmk), 2,4,5-T, paraquat, derris, DDT; acid, corrosive; hemlock, arsenic, strychnine, cyanide, prussic acid, vitriol; nicotine 388 *tobacco*; asphyxiant, poison gas, nerve g., Lewisite, mustard gas, tear g., CS gas; carbon monoxide, carbon dioxide, choke damp; CFC, chlorofluorocarbon; foul air, mephitis, miasma, effluvium, sewer gas 653 *insalubrity*; atmospheric pollution, acid rain, smog; lead pollution; plutonium, uranium, depleted u., DU; radioactivity, radioactive cloud, mushroom, fallout, nuclear f., strontium 90 417 *radiation*; dope, opium, heroin, 949 *drug*; intoxicant, depressant 949 *alcoholism*; lethal dose, overdose; toxicology.

*poisonous plant,* hemlock, deadly nightshade, belladonna, datura, henbane, monkshood, aconite, hellebore; nux vomica, upas tree.

*poisoning,* venenation 362 *homicide*; blood poisoning, toxaemia 651 *infection*; food poisoning, botulism; chemical poisoning; germ warfare 718 *warfare*; poisoner 362 *murderer.*

**Adj.** *baneful,* pestilent, noisome 645 *harmful*; blighting, withering, virulent, poisonous, venomous 653 *toxic*; cursed, accursed 616 *evil.*

## 660 Safety

**N.** *safety,* safeness, security; invulnerability, impregnability, immunity, charmed life; safety in numbers 104 *multitude*; secure position, permanent post, safe job; social security, welfare state 901 *sociology*; safe distance, wide berth 620 *avoidance*; all clear, coast c., danger past, storm blown over; guarantee, warrant 473 *certainty*; sense of security, assurance, confidence, false sense of security 855 *courage*; safety valve 667 *means of escape*; close shave, narrow escape 667 *escape*; rescue 668 *deliverance.*

*protection,* conservation 666 *preservation*; insurance, surety 858 *caution*; patronage, care, sponsorship, good offices, auspices, aegis, fatherly eye 703 *aid*; protectorate, guardianship, wardenship, wardship, tutelage, custody, protective c., care in the community, community care; surrogacy 747 *restraint*; custodianship, safekeeping, keeping, charge, safe hands, grasp, grip, embrace 778 *retention*; ward, watch and w., electronic surveillance, Big Brother, vetting, positive v. 457 *surveillance*; safeguard, precaution, security system, alarm s., preventive measure, ring of steel 713 *defence*; fire door; fire wall; safety cage; sanitary precaution, immunization, prophylaxis, quarantine, cordon sanitaire 652 *hygiene*; segregation 883 *seclusion*; cushion, buffer; screen, cover; sun screen, suntan cream, sun protection factor, protection f.; umbrella 662 *shelter*; means of protection, deterrent 723 *weapon*; safe-conduct, passport, pass 756 *permit*; escort, convoy, guard 722 *armed force*; defence, sure d., bastion, bulwark, tower of strength 713 *defences*; haven, sanctuary, asylum 662 *refuge*; anchor, sheet a. 662 *safeguard*; moat, ditch, palisade, stockade 235 *fence*; shield, breastplate, panoply, armour plate 713 *armour*; human shield.

*protector,* protectress, guardian, tutor; guardian angel, patron saint, tutelary god, liege lord, feudal l., patroness, fairy godmother 707 *patron*; defender, preserver, shepherd; bodyguard, minder, lifeguard, strongarm man, bouncer; vigilante 713 *defender*; conservator, custodian, curator, warden; warder, guard, security g., coastguard; chaperon, duenna, governess, nursemaid, nurse, nanny, babysitter, au pair 749 *keeper*; care assistant, buddy, carer 457 *watcher*; caring profession; lookout, watch, watchman, night w. 664 *warner*; firewatcher, fire fighter, fireman; policeman *or* -woman, police constable, community policeman *or* -woman, police sergeant, sheriff; copper, cop 955 *police*; private eye 459 *detective*; sentry, sentinel, garrison, security forces 722 *soldiery*; sky marshal, air m.; watchdog, guard dog, police d. 365 *dog*; Cerberus, Argus 457 *surveillance.*

**Adj.** *safe,* without risk, unhazardous; assured, secure, sure, snug; safe and sound, spared 666 *preserved*; with a whole skin, intact, unharmed 646 *undamaged*; garrisoned, well-defended; insured, covered; immunized, vaccinated, inoculated; disinfected, hygienic 652 *salubrious*; in safety, in security, on the safe side, on sure ground, home and dry, on home ground, on the home stretch, on terra firma; in harbour, in port, at anchor; above water, high and dry; out of the wood, out of danger, out of harm's way; clear, in the clear, unaccused, unthreatened, unmolested; unexposed, unhazarded; under shelter, sheltered, shielded, screened, protected etc. vb.; patronized, under the protection of, under the wing of; in safe hands, held, in custody, behind bars, under lock and key 747 *imprisoned*; reliable, guaranteed, warranted 929 *trustworthy*; benign, innocent, harmless, unthreatening 615 *good*.

*invulnerable*, immune, impregnable, sacrosanct; inexpugnable, unassailable, unattackable, unbreakable, unchallengeable; founded on a rock, defensible, tenable 162 *strong*; proof, foolproof; weatherproof, waterproof, showerproof, leakproof, gasproof, fireproof, bulletproof, bombproof, shatterproof; snug, tight, seaworthy, airworthy; shrinkwrapped, vacuum sealed, hermetically s.; armoured, steel-clad, panoplied.

*tutelary*, custodial, guardian, protective, surrogate, shepherdlike; ready to die for 931 *disinterested*; watchful 457 *vigilant*; fail-safe; doubly sure, belt and braces; keeping, protecting 666 *preserving*; antiseptic, disinfectant 652 *salubrious*.

**Vb.** *be safe*, – invulnerable etc. adj.; find safety, reach s., come through, save one's bacon 667 *escape*; land on one's feet, keep one's head above water, weather the storm, ride it out; keep a whole skin, bear a charmed life, have nine lives; be snug, nestle, stay at home, be under shelter, have a roof over one's head; be under cover 523 *lurk*; keep a safe distance, give a wide berth 620 *avoid*.

*safeguard*, keep safe, guard, protect; spare 905 *show mercy*; stand up for, stand surety for, go bail for 713 *defend*; cover up for, shield; champion 703 *patronize*; grant asylum, afford sanctuary; keep, conserve 666 *preserve*; treasure, hoard 632 *store*; keep in custody 747 *imprison*; ward, watch over, care for, mother, take under one's wing; nurse, foster, cherish; have charge of, take charge of, keep an eye on, chaperon 457 *look after*; hide, put in a safe place 525 *conceal*; cushion, cocoon 218 *support*; insulate, earth; cover, shroud, cloak, shade 421 *screen*; keep under cover, garage, lock up; take in, house, shelter; ensconce, enfold, embrace 235 *enclose*; make safe, secure, fortify 162 *strengthen*; entrench, fence in, fence round 232 *circumscribe*; arm, armour, armour-plate; shepherd, convoy, escort; flank, support; garrison, mount guard; immunize, inoculate, vaccinate; pasteurize, chlorinate, fluoridate, fluoridize, disinfect 652 *sanitate*; give assurances, warrant, guarantee 473 *make certain*; keep order, police, patrol.

*seek safety*, demand assurances, take precautions, hedge one's bets, play safe, take no chances, be on the safe side 858 *be cautious*; dig in, lie low 523 *lurk*; run away 667 *escape*; cut and run 277 *move fast*; live to fight another day, think better of it; shorten sail, run for port, take refuge 662 *seek refuge*.

**Adv.** *under shelter*, under cover, in the lee of; under the aegis of; out of harm's way, safely, with impunity.

## 661 Danger

**N.** *danger*, peril; dangerousness, perilousness, shadow of death, jaws of d., lion's mouth, dragon's lair; dangerous situation, unhealthy s., desperate s., parlous state, dire straits, forlorn hope 700 *predicament*; emergency 137 *crisis*; insecurity, jeopardy, risk, hazard, banana skin, ticklishness, precariousness, slipperiness, ticklish business, razor's edge 474 *uncertainty*; black spot, snag 663 *pitfall*; trap, death t. 527 *ambush*; endangerment, imperilment, hazarding, dangerous course; venturesomeness, daring, overdaring 857 *rashness*; venture, risky v. 672 *undertaking*; leap in the dark 618 *gambling*; slippery slope, road to ruin 655 *deterioration*; sword of Damocles, menace 900 *threat*; sense of danger, apprehension, fears 854 *nervousness*; cause for alarm, rocks ahead, breakers a., storm brewing, gathering clouds, gathering storm, cloud on the horizon 665 *danger signal*; narrow escape, hairbreadth e., close shave, near thing 667 *escape*.

*vulnerability*, nonimmunity, susceptibility, danger of 180 *liability*; security risk; exposure, nakedness, defencelessness, naivety 161 *helplessness*; instability, insecurity 152 *changeableness*; easy target, sitting duck; exposed part, vulnerable point, chink in the armour, Achilles heel, 'soft underbelly' 163 *weakness*;

> . . . the soft under-belly of the Axis . . .
> Winston Churchill

tender spot, soft s. 327 *softness*; unsoundness, feet of clay, human error, tragic flaw, fatal f. 647 *imperfection*; weaker brethren.

**Adj.** *dangerous*, perilous, fraught with danger, treacherous, beset with perils; unlit, unfrequented 854 *frightening*; risky, snaggy, hazardous, venturous, venturesome, dicey, dodgy, chancy 618 *speculative*; serious, ugly, nasty, critical, at flashpoint; at stake, in question; menacing, ominous, foreboding, alarming 900 *threatening*; toxic, poisonous 645 *harmful*; unhealthy, infectious 653 *insalubrious*; inflammable, flammable, explosive, radioactive.

*unsafe*, not safe, slippery, treacherous, untrustworthy 474 *unreliable*; insecure, unsecure, unsound, precarious, dicky; top-heavy, unsteady 152 *unstable*; shaky, tottering, crumbling, ramshackle, rickety, frail 655 *dilapidated*; jerry-built, gimcrack, crazy 163 *weak*; built on sand, on shaky foundations; leaky, waterlogged; critical, ticklish, touch and go, hanging by a thread, trembling in the balance, teetering on the edge, on the edge, on the brink, on the verge.

*vulnerable*, expugnable, in danger of, not immune 180 *liable*; open to, wide open, exposed, naked, bare 229 *uncovered*; unarmoured, unfortified, undefended, unprotected, at the mercy of 161 *defenceless*; unshielded, shelterless, helpless, guideless; unguarded, unescorted, unshepherded, unsupported, unflanked, isolated, out on a limb; unwarned, off one's guard 508 *off guard*.

*endangered*, in danger, in peril etc. n.; facing death, in a bad way; slipping, drifting; on the rocks, in shoal water; on slippery ground, on thin ice; in a tight corner, surrounded, trapped, under fire; in the lion's den, be thrown to the lions, on the razor's edge; between two fires, between the devil and the deep blue sea, between Scylla and Charybdis; on the run, not out of the wood; at bay, with one's back to the wall, at the last stand, reduced to the last extremity; under sentence, with a noose round one's neck, awaiting execution 961 *condemned*.

**Vb.** *be in danger*, run the risk of 180 *be liable*; run into danger, enter the lion's den, walk into a trap; tread on dangerous ground, skate on thin ice, get out of one's depth, sail too near the wind, ride the tiger, play with fire, sit on a powder barrel, sleep on a volcano; lean on a broken reed, feel the ground give way, be up against it, have to run for it; hang by a thread, tremble in the balance, hover on the brink, teeter on the edge 474 *be uncertain*; totter, slip, slide 309 *tumble*; get lost 282 *stray*.

*face danger*, face death, dice with death, have one's back to the wall; take one's life in one's hands 855 *be courageous*; expose oneself, lay oneself open to; stand in the breach 711 *defy*; bell the cat, look danger in the face, look down a gun barrel; face heavy odds, have the odds against one; engage in a forlorn hope, be on a hiding to nothing, challenge fate, tempt f., tempt providence, court disaster; take a tiger by the tail, put one's head in the lion's mouth 857 *be rash*; run the gauntlet, come under fire; venture, dare, risk it, take a chance, stick one's neck out 618 *gamble*.

*endanger*, be dangerous, spell danger, expose to d., put at risk, put in jeopardy, face with, confront w.; imperil, hazard, jeopardize, compromise; risk, stake, venture 618 *gamble*; drive headlong, run on the rocks, drive dangerously, drive without due care and attention, put one in fear of his *or* her life; be dangerous, threaten danger, loom, forebode, bode ill,

menace 900 *threaten*; warm up, hot up; run one hard, overtake 306 *outdo*.

## 662 Refuge. Safeguard

**N.** *refuge*, sanctuary, asylum, retreat, safe place; traffic island, zebra crossing, pedestrian crossing, pelican c., green man; last resort, funkhole, bolthole, foxhole, burrow; trench, dugout, airraid shelter, fallout s.; earth, hole, den, lair, covert, nest, lap, hearth 192 *home*; defensible space, privacy; sanctum 194 *room*; cloister, cell, hermitage, ivory tower 192 *retreat*; sanctum sanctorum, temple, ark, acropolis, citadel; wall, rampart, bulwark, bastion; stronghold, fastness 713 *fort*; keep, ward; secret place 527 *hiding-place*; dungeon 748 *prison*; rock, Rock of Ages, pillar, tower, tower of strength, mainstay 218 *prop*.

*shelter*, cover, roof, roof over one's head; covert, earth, hole; fold, sheepfold, pinfold; lee; lee wall, windbreak, hedge 235 *fence*; camp, stockade 235 *enclosure*; shield, wing; fireguard, fender, bumper, mudguard, windscreen 421 *screen*; umbrella, oilskins; sun helmet, sunglasses, goggles, ear muffs, ear plugs; shinguard, pads; protective clothing, overalls; haven, harbour, port; harbourage, anchorage, quay, jetty, ghat, marina, dock 192 *stable*; padded cell 503 *mental hospital*; halfway house, sheltered housing; almshouse, old people's home, children's home, dog's h., charitable institution, hospice, home for the dying; Welfare State.

*safeguard*, means of safety, protection 660 *safety*; precautions 702 *hindrance*; crush barrier, guardrail, railing; safety cage; mail 713 *armour*; arms, deterrent, anti-missile defence system, Star Wars, Strategic Defence Initiative, SDI, Son of Star Wars 723 *weapon*; respirator, gas mask; safety device, air-bag, dead man's handle, safety catch, safety valve, lightning conductor, fuse, earth; crash helmet, safety h. 228 *headgear*; seat belt, safety b., safety harness; ejector-seat, parachute; safety net; lifeboat, rubber dinghy, life raft 275 *raft*; life belt, life jacket, buoyancy j., Mae West, lifeline, breeches buoy; rope, plank 667 *means of escape*; anchor, kedge, grapnel, grappling iron, killick, drogue; lead, reins, brake 748 *fetter*; bolt, bar, lock, key 264 *stopper*; ballast 31 *offset*; mole, breakwater, groyne, sea wall, embankment; lighthouse, lightship 269 *sailing aid*; jury mast, spare parts 40 *extra*.

**Vb.** *seek refuge*, take refuge 660 *seek safety*; take to the woods, take to the hills; turn to, throw oneself in the arms of, shelter under the wing of, put up one's umbrella, pull the blankets over one's head; claim sanctuary, seek political asylum; clasp the knees of, nestle under one's wing, hide behind the skirts of; make port, reach safety, reach home, find shelter; lock oneself in, bolt the door, bar the entrance, let down the portcullis, raise the drawbridge, batten down the hatches.

## 663 Pitfall: source of danger

**N.** *pitfall*, pit, trap for the unwary, banana skin, catch, 'catch-22';

> There was only one catch and that was Catch-22, which specified that a concern for one's safety in the face of dangers that were real and immediate was the process of a rational mind. Orr was crazy and could be grounded. All he had to do was ask; and as soon as he did, he would no longer be crazy and would have to fly more missions. Orr would be crazy to fly more missions and sane if he didn't, but if he was sane he had to fly them. If he flew them he was crazy and didn't have to; but if he didn't want to he was sane and had to. Yossarian was moved very deeply by the absolute simplicity of this clause of Catch-22 and let out a respectful whistle.
>
> Joseph Heller, *Catch-22*

snag, pons asinorum 702 *obstacle*; booby trap, death t., firetrap, minefield 542 *trap*; surprise 508 *lack of expectation*; lying in wait 527 *ambush*; sleeping dog; thin ice; quagmire 347 *marsh*; quicksands, sandbar; shoal, shoal water, breakers, shallows 212 *shallowness*; reef, sunken r., coral r., rock; ironbound coast, lee shore; steep, chasm, abyss, crevasse, precipice 209 *high land*; rapids, crosscurrent, undertow 350 *current*; vortex, maelstrom, whirlpool 350 *eddy*; tidal wave, flash flood 350 *wave*; storm, squall, hurricane 352 *gale*; volcano 383 *furnace*; dynamite, time bomb, powder keg 723 *explosive*; trouble spot 661 *danger*; plague-spot, hotbed 651 *infection*; source of trouble, hornet's nest, hazard 659 *bane*.

  *troublemaker*, mischiefmaker, stirrer, wrecker; ill-wisher 881 *enemy*; firebrand, agent provocateur 738 *agitator*; dangerous person, ugly customer, undesirable, delinquent 904 *ruffian*; nigger in the woodpile, snake in the grass, viper in the bosom; hidden hand 178 *influence*; a wolf in sheep's clothing; yellow peril, red p.; Nemesis 910 *avenger*.

## 664 Warning

**N.** *warning*, caution, caveat; example, warning e., counsel, lesson, object l.; notice, advance n. 524 *information*; wake-up call; word, word in the ear, word to the wise, tip, tip-off, wink, nudge 524 *hint*; whistle-blowing 528 *publication*; final warning, final notice, ultimatum 737 *demand*; monition, admonition, admonishment 924 *reprimand*; deterrent 613 *dissuasion*; protest, expostulation 762 *dep-*

*recation*; warning shot, s. across the bows; foreboding, premonition 511 *prediction*; voice, voice of conscience, warning voice 917 *conscience*; alarm, siren, foghorn, fog signal, storm s., alert, red alert 665 *danger signal*; Mother Carey's chickens, stormy petrel, bird of ill omen 511 *omen*; gathering cloud, cloud on the horizon, war cloud 661 *danger*; signs of the times, writing on the wall, symptom, sign 547 *indication*; knell, death k. 364 *obsequies*; beacon, light 547 *signal*, *indicator*; menace 900 *threat*.

  *warner*, admonisher 691 *adviser*; prophet, Cassandra 511 *diviner*; flagman, signaller; lighthouse-keeper; watchman, lookout, security man *or* woman, watch 457 *surveillance*; scout, spy; picket, sentinel, sentry 660 *protector*; advanced guard, rearguard; watchdog.

  **Adj.** *cautionary*, hinting, warning, monitory, admonitory; protesting 762 *deprecatory*; exemplary, instructive 524 *informative*; symptomatic, prognostic 547 *indicating*; premonitory, boding, ill-omened, ominous 511 *presageful*; menacing, minatory 900 *threatening*; deterrent 854 *frightening*.

  *warned*, cautioned etc. vb.; once bitten 858 *cautious*; forewarned 507 *expectant*; forearmed 669 *prepared*.

  **Vb.** *warn*, caution; give fair warning, give notice, notify 524 *inform*; drop a hint, tip off, blow the whistle on 524 *hint*; counsel 691 *advise*; put one in mind 505 *remind*; admonish 924 *reprove*; spell danger, forewarn 511 *predict*; forearm, put someone on their guard, alert 669 *prepare*; lour, menace 900 *threaten*; issue a caveat, advise against 613 *dissuade*; remonstrate, protest 762 *deprecate*; sound the alarm 665 *raise the alarm*.

  *be warned*, receive notice; beware, take heed, watch one's step 457 *be careful*; be taught a lesson, learn one's l., profit by the example, profit by one's mistakes.

  **Int.** cave!, look out!, look where you are going!, mind your step!, wake up and smell the coffee!, watch out!

## 665 Danger signal

**N.** *danger signal*, note of warning 664 *warning*; murmur, muttering 829 *discontent*; writing on the wall, black cap, evil omen 511 *omen*; storm cone, gale warning; warning sound, alarum, alarm clock, alarm bell, burglar alarm, fire alarm, fire bell, foghorn, fog signal, bell buoy, motor horn, klaxon, bicycle bell, police whistle; blast, honk, toot 400 *loudness*; alarm, church bell, curfew, tocsin, siren, alert, red a.; tattoo, beat of drum, trumpet-call 547 *call*; war cry, battle c., rallying cry; fiery cross; warning light, red l., Very l., beacon; red flag, yellow f.; distress signal, SOS 547 *signal*; sign of alarm, start, tremor, blench, sweat, hair on end 854 *fear*.

*false alarm*, cry of 'wolf', scare, hoax; bugbear, bugaboo, bogey, nightmare, bad dream 854 *intimidation*; blank cartridge, flash in the pan 4 *insubstantiality*; canard 543 *untruth*; scaremonger 854 *alarmist*.

**Vb.** *raise the alarm*, sound the a., give the a., dial 999, alert, arouse, scare, startle 854 *frighten*; sound one's horn, honk, toot; turn out the guard, call the police, raise a hue and cry, cry blue murder 528 *proclaim*; give a false alarm, cry wolf, cry too soon; sound a warning, toll, knell.

## 666 Preservation

**N.** *preservation*, safekeeping, keeping alive; safe conduct 660 *protection*; saving, salvation 668 *deliverance*; conservation, conservancy, environmentalism, tree-hugging; energy-saving, energy audit; perpetuation, prolongation 144 *permanence*; upkeep, maintenance, support 633 *provision*; service, servicing, valeting 648 *cleansing*; insulation, heat retention; saving up 632 *storage*; reservation 814 *economy*; self-preservation 932 *selfishness*; game reserve, nature r., bird sanctuary, conservation area, listed building; protected species; conservation of the environment, ecotage, tree-hugging, tree-house, twigloo; taxidermy, mummification, embalmment, embalming 364 *interment*; cold storage, freezing, deep-freezing, freeze-drying 382 *refrigeration*; boiling, drying, sun-d., UHT, dehydration 342 *desiccation*; canning, tinning, processing, packing; sterilization 652 *hygiene*; preventive medicine, quarantine, cordon sanitaire.

*preserver*, life-saver, saviour, rescuer, deliverer 668 *deliverance*; amulet, charm, mascot 983 *talisman*; preservation order; preservative, ice, amber, formaldehyde; camphor, mothball, lavender; spice, pickle, marinade, brine, aspic 389 *condiment*; freezer 384 *refrigerator*; thermos flask (tdmk); silo; cannery, canning factory, bottling plant; safety device, seat belt, airbag, gas mask 662 *safeguard*; incubator, respirator, iron lung, life support system; embalmer, mummifier; canner, bottler; preservationist, conservationist, conservator, environmentalist, green, eco-activist, ecowarrior, tree-hugger; green peace movement, green m.

**Adj.** *preserving*, conserving etc. vb.; energy-saving; preservative, conservative; prophylactic, protective, preventive, hygienic 652 *salubrious*.

*preserved*, well-p., kept, well-k., long-life, fresh, undecayed, intact, whole 646 *perfect*; frozen, on ice, in the fridge; pickled, marinated, salted, corned, tinned, canned, potted, bottled; mummified, embalmed; laid up in lavender, mothballed, treasured 632 *stored*; conserved, protected 660 *safe*.

**Vb.** *preserve*, conserve, keep alive, keep fresh, freeze, freeze-dry, keep on ice 382 *refrigerate*; embalm, mummify, stuff; pickle, salt 388 *season*; souse, marinate; cure, smoke, kipper, dehydrate, sun-dry 342 *dry*; pot, bottle, tin, can, process; protect, paint, varnish, whitewash, creosote, waterproof; maintain, keep up, keep in good repair, service 656 *repair*; prop up, shore up 218 *support*; keep alive, feed, sustain, provision, supply 633 *provide*; keep safe, keep under cover, garage 660 *safeguard*; save up, bottle up 632 *store*; reserve, save 814 *economize*; nurse, tend 658 *doctor*; cherish, treasure 457 *look after*; not let go, hug, hold 778 *retain*; keep going, prolong; save, save alive, rescue 668 *deliver*.

## 667 Escape

**N.** *escape*, leak, leakage, loss 298 *egress*; extrication, delivery, rescue 668 *deliverance*; riddance, good r. 831 *relief*; get-away, breakout; decampment, flight, flit, moonlight f., French leave 296 *departure*; withdrawal, retreat, hasty r. 286 *regression*; disappearing trick 446 *disappearance*; elopement, runaway match; evasion, truancy, tax-dodging, black economy, moonlighting 620 *avoidance*; narrow escape, hairbreadth e., close shave, close call, narrow squeak, near thing 661 *danger*; let-off, discharge, reprieve 960 *acquittal*; setting free 746 *liberation*; immunity, impunity, exemption 919 *nonliability*; escapology, escapism.

*means of escape*, exit, emergency e., way out, back door, secret passage 298 *egress*; ladder, fire escape, escape hatch; drawbridge 624 *bridge*; vent, safety valve 662 *safeguard*; dodge, device, trick 623 *contrivance*; loophole, escape clause, technicality, let-out, get-out 468 *qualification*.

*escaper*, escapee, runaway; truant, escaped prisoner, prison-breaker; fugitive, refugee, asylum-seeker; survivor; escapist; escapologist, Houdini.

**Adj.** *escaped*, fled, flown, stolen away; eloping, truant; fugitive, runaway; slippery, elusive 620 *avoiding*; free, at large, scot free, acquitted; relieved, rid of, well out of, well rid of; exempt 919 *nonliable*.

**Vb.** *escape*, find or win freedom 746 *achieve liberty*; effect one's escape, make good one's e., make a getaway, vamoose, break gaol, break out of prison; abscond, jump bail, flit, elope, skip, take flight, take French leave, go AWOL 620 *run away*; steal away, sneak off, duck and run, make oneself scarce, beat a hasty retreat 296 *decamp*; slip through, break t., break out, break loose, break away, get free, break one's chains, go over the wall, slip one's lead, shake one's yoke; get out, bluff one's way o., sneak o. 298 *emerge*; get away, slip through one's fingers; get off, get off lightly, secure an acquittal, go scot-free, go unpunished; get off on a technicality, scrape through, save one's bacon, weather the storm, survive; get away with it, secure exemption, wriggle out of 919 *be exempt*; rid oneself, be well rid of, find relief 831 *be relieved*; leak, leak away 298 *flow out*.

*elude*, evade, welsh, abscond, dodge 620 *avoid*; lie low 523 *lurk*; give one the slip, shake off, throw off the scent, give one a run for one's money; escape notice, be found to be missing 190 *be absent*.

## 668 Deliverance

**N.** *deliverance*, delivery, extrication 304 *extraction*; disencumberment, riddance 831 *relief*; emancipation 746 *liberation*; rescue, life-saving; salvage, retrieval 656 *restoration*; salvation, redemption 965 *divine function*; ransom, buying off 792 *purchase*; release, let-off, amnesty; discharge, reprieve, reprieval 960 *acquittal*; day of grace, respite 136 *delay*; truce, standstill 145 *cessation*; way out, let-out 667 *escape*; dispensation, exemption 919 *nonliability*.

**Adj.** *extricable*, rescuable, deliverable, redeemable, fit for release.

**Vb.** *deliver*, save, rescue, come to the r., save by the bell, snatch from the jaws of death, throw a lifeline; get one out of 304 *extract*; extricate 62 *unravel*; unloose, untie, unbind 46 *disunite*; disburden 701 *disencumber*; rid, save from 831 *relieve*; release, unlock, unbar; emancipate, free, set free, set at large 746 *liberate*; let one off, get one off 960 *acquit*; deliver oneself 667 *escape*; save oneself, save one's skin, rid oneself, get rid of, be rid of; snatch a brand from the burning, be the salvation of; redeem, ransom, buy off 792 *purchase*; salvage, retrieve, recover, bring back 656 *restore*; spare, excuse, dispense from 919 *exempt*.

**Int.** to the rescue!, all hands to the pump!, help!

## 669 Preparation

**N.** *preparation*, preparing, making ready; premedication; clearance, clearing the decks; preliminaries, preliminary step, tuning, priming, loading; mobilization 718 *war measures*; preliminary course, trial run, trial, trials 461 *experi-*

*ment*; practice, rehearsal, dress r.; brief, briefing; training, inurement 534 *teaching*; novitiate 68 *beginning*; study, prep, homework 536 *learning*; spadework 682 *labour*; groundwork, foundation 218 *basis*; scaffold, scaffolding 218 *frame*; planning, rough sketch, first draft, outline, blueprint, prototype, scheme, pilot s. 623 *plan*; shadow cabinet, shadow factory, advance f.; arrangement, prearrangement, premeditation 608 *predetermination*; consultation, preconsultation 691 *advice*; forethought, anticipation, precautions 510 *foresight*; bottom drawer, nest egg 632 *store*.

*fitting out*, provisioning, furnishing, logistics 633 *provision*; appointment, commission, equipment, marshalling, array, armament; promotion, company-promoting; inauguration, flotation, launching 68 *debut*.

*maturation*, ripening, bringing to a head; seasoning, hardening, acclimatization; brewing, hatching, gestation, incubation, sitting 167 *propagation*; nursing, nurture; cultivation, tillage, sowing, planting 370 *agriculture*; bloom, florescence, efflorescence; fructification, fruition 725 *completion*.

*preparedness*, readiness, ripeness, mellowness, maturity; puberty, nubility 134 *adultness*; fitness, shipshape condition, height of training, peak, pitch of perfection 646 *perfection*.

*preparer*, coach, personal trainer 537 *trainer*; torch-bearer, trail-blazer, pioneer, bridge-builder 66 *precursor*; sappers and miners 722 soldiery; paver, paviour; loader, packer, stevedore; fitter, equipper, provisioner 633 *provider*; cultivator, agriculturalist, ploughman, sower, planter 370 *farmer*; brewer, cook 301 *cookery*.

**Adj.** *preparatory*, preparative; preparing etc. adj.; precautionary, preliminary 64 *preceding*; provisional, stopgap, Band-Aid (tdmk) 150 *substituted*; marinating, brewing, cooking, stewing; brooding, hatching, incubating, maturing; in embryo; in preparation, on foot, on the stocks, on the anvil; in store, in the offing, forthcoming 155 *impending*; under consideration, at the committee stage, agitated for, mooted 623 *planned*; under training, learning 536 *studious*.

*prepared*, ready, alert 457 *vigilant*; made ready, readied, in readiness, at the ready; mobilized, standing by, on call; all set, ready to go, raring to go; teed up, keyed up, psyched up, spoiling for; trained, fully t., qualified, well-prepared, practised, in practice, at concert pitch, word-perfect; primed, briefed, instructed 524 *informed*; forewarned, forearmed 664 *warned*; saddled, in the saddle; tight, snug, battened down; groomed, fully dressed, in one's best bib and tucker, in full feather, dressed to kill, got up to k., in full warpaint 228 *dressed*; accoutred, armed, in armour, in harness, fully armed, armed to the teeth, armed at all points; rigged, rigged out, equipped, furnished, fully f., well-appointed, provided 633 *provisioning*; in store, in hand 632 *stored*; in reserve, ready to hand, ready for use; ready for anything; fit for use, in working order, operational.

*matured*, ripened, cooked, digested, hatched etc. vb.; ripe, mellow, mature, seasoned, weathered, hardened; tried, experienced, veteran 694 *expert*; adult, grown, full-g., fledged, full-f. 134 *grown-up*; out, in flower, florescent, flowering, fruiting; overripe, overmature; well-cooked, well-done; elaborated, wrought, highly w., worked up, laboured, smelling of the lamp; deep-laid; perfected 725 *completed*.

*ready-made*, ready-mixed, cut and dried, ready to use, ready-to-wear, off the peg; ready-formed, ready-furnished; prefabricated; processed, oven-ready; predigested, precooked, instant.

**Vb.** *prepare*, take steps, take measures; make preparations, make ready, pave the way, show the w., bridge, build a b., lead up to, pioneer 64 *come before*; choose one's ground, lay the foundations, do the groundwork, provide the basis; predispose, incline, soften up; prepare the ground, sow the seed 370 *cultivate*; set to work, address oneself to 68 *begin*; rough-hew, cut out, block o.; sketch, outline, blueprint 623 *plan*; plot, concert, prearrange 608 *predetermine*; prepare for, forearm, guard against, insure, take precautions, prepare for a rainy day 660 *seek safety*; anticipate 507 *expect*.

*make ready*, ready, have r., finish one's preparations; set in order, put in readiness, make operational; stow, stow away, pack 632 *store*; batten down the hatches; commission, put in c.; put one's house in order, put in working order, bring up to scratch, wind up, screw up, tune, tune up, adjust 62 *arrange*; set the stage; settle preliminaries, clear the decks, close the ranks; array, mobilize 74 *bring together*; whet the knife, shuffle the cards, tee up; set, cock, prime, load; raise steam, warm up, crank, crank up, rev up, get into gear; equip, crew, man; fit, fit out, furnish, kit out, rig out, dress; arm, provide with arms, provide with teeth 633 *provide*; improvise, rustle up; edit; rehearse, drill, groom, exercise, lick into shape 534 *train*; inure, acclimatize 610 *habituate*; coach, brief, bring one up to date 524 *inform*.

*mature*, mellow, ripen, bring to fruition 646 *perfect*; force, bring on 174 *invigorate*; bring to a

head 725 *climax*; stew, brew 301 *cook*; gestate, hatch, incubate, breed 369 *breed stock*; grow, farm 370 *cultivate*; fledge, nurse, nurture; elaborate, work out 725 *carry through*; season, weather, smoke, dry, cure; temper, season 326 *harden*.

*prepare oneself*, brace o., compose o.; qualify oneself, serve an apprenticeship; study, brief oneself, do one's homework; train, exercise, go for the burn, rehearse, practise 536 *learn*; gird up one's loins, roll up one's sleeves; limber up, warm up, gear oneself up, psych oneself up, flex one's muscles; buckle on one's armour, take sword in hand, shoulder arms; be prepared, get ready for action, stand ready, stand by, hold oneself in readiness, keep one's powder dry.

**Adv.** *in preparation*, in anticipation, in readiness, just in case; in hand, in train, under way, under construction.

## 670 Nonpreparation

**N.** *nonpreparation*, lack of preparation; potluck; unpreparedness, unreadiness; lack of training, lack of practice, rustiness; disqualification, unfitness; rawness, immaturity, crudity, greenness, unripeness 126 *newness*; belatedness 136 *lateness*; improvidence, nonprovision, neglect 458 *negligence*; no deliberation 857 *rashness*; hastiness, precipitance, rush, hassle 680 *haste*; improvisation, impromptu, snap answer 609 *spontaneity*; surprise 508 *lack of expectation*; forwardness, precocity 135 *earliness*; imperfection 55 *incompleteness*.

*undevelopment*, delayed maturity, slow ripening; state of nature, native state, virgin soil; untilled ground 458 *negligence*; raw material, unlicked cub, rough diamond; late developer; rough copy, unfinished attempt; embryo, abortion.

**Adj.** *unprepared*, unready, not ready, backward, behindhand 136 *late*; unorganized, unarranged, makeshift; unpremeditated, without preparation, ad hoc, ad lib, extemporized, improvised, impromptu, snap, catch-as-catch-can, off the top of one's head, off the cuff 609 *spontaneous*; unstudied 699 *artless*; rash, careless 458 *negligent*; rush, precipitant, overhasty 680 *hasty*; unguarded, exposed, with one's trousers down 661 *vulnerable*; unwarned, caught unawares, taken off guard, caught napping, on the wrong foot, unexpecting 508 *off guard*; at sixes and sevens 61 *orderless*; shiftless, improvident, unthrifty, thoughtless, happy-go-lucky 456 *light-minded*; scratch, untrained, untaught, untutored 491 *uninstructed*; undrilled, unpractised, unexercised, unrehearsed 611 *unhabituated*; in a state of nature, uncultivated, unworked, untilled, fallow, virgin 674 *unused*.

*immature*, ungrown, half-grown, unripe, green, underripe, half-ripe, unripened, unmellowed, unseasoned; unblown, half-blown; unfledged, unlicked, callow, wet behind the ears; nonadult, adolescent, juvenile, childish, puerile, boyish, girlish 130 *young*; undeveloped, half-developed, half-baked, raw 647 *imperfect*; underdeveloped, backward, retarded 136 *late*; unhatched, unborn, embryonic, rudimentary 68 *beginning*; half-formed, unformed, unfashioned, unhewn, unwrought, unworked, roughhewn, uncut, unpolished, half-finished, unfinished; undigested, ill-digested; before time, premature, abortive, at half-cock 728 *unsuccessful*; untrained, apprentice, undergraduate 695 *unskilled*; crude, coarse, rude, savage, uncivilized 699 *artless*; early matured, forced, precocious.

*uncooked*, raw, red, rare, underdone; half-baked, cold, unwarmed; unprepared, undressed, ungarnished; indigestible, inedible 329 *tough*.

*unequipped*, untrimmed, unrigged, dismasted, dismantled, undressed 229 *uncovered*; unfurnished, half-furnished, ill-provided 307 *deficient*; unfitted, unqualified, disqualified.

**Vb.** *be unprepared*, – unready etc. adj.; lack preparation 55 *be incomplete*; lie fallow, rust 655 *deteriorate*; want practice, need training; not plan, make no preparations, offer potluck, extemporize 609 *improvise*; live from day to day, let tomorrow take care of itself; be premature, go off at half-cock 135 *be early*; take no precautions, drop one's guard 456 *be inattentive*; catch unawares 508 *surprise*.

**Adv.** *unreadily*, extempore, off the cuff, ad hoc, off-hand.

## 671 Attempt

**N.** *attempt*, essay, bid; step, move, gambit 676 *deed*; endeavour, struggle, strain, effort 682 *exertion*; tackle, try, some attempt; good try, stout t., brave t., valiant effort; best effort, one's level best, best one can do; random effort, catch-as-catch-can; determined effort, set, dead s. 712 *attack*; trial, probation 461 *experiment*; go at, shot at, stab at, jab at, crack at, whack at, bash at; first attempt, first go, first shot, first offence, first strike 68 *debut*; final attempt, swan song, last bid, last throw; venture, adventure, quest, speculation, operation, exercise 672 *undertaking*; aim, goal 617 *objective*; straining after, high endeavour, perfectionism 862 *fastidiousness*.

*trier*, bidder, tackler, essayer 852 *hoper*; tester 461 *experimenter*; searcher, quester 459 *enquirer*; struggler, striver, fighter 716 *contender*; idealist 862 *perfectionist*; lobbyist, activist 654 *reformer*; undertaker, contractor, entrepreneur, intrapreneur, jobber.

**Adj.** *attempting*, tackling, trying, striving, doing one's best 597 *willing*; game, nothing daunted 599 *resolute*; questing, searching 459 *enquiring*; tentative, catch-as-catch-can; testing, probationary, on approval, on appro 461 *experimental*; ambitious, venturesome, daring 672 *enterprising*.

**Vb.** *attempt*, essay, try; seek to, aim, make it one's a. 617 *intend*; angle for, fish for, seek 459 *search*; offer, bid, make a b.; make an attempt, make shift to, make the effort, do something about, not just stand there; endeavour, struggle, strive, try hard, try and try again 599 *be resolute*; do one's best, do one's damnedest, go all out, redouble one's efforts 682 *exert oneself*; pull hard, push h., strain, sweat 682 *work*; tackle, take on, try one's hand at, have a go, give it a try, give it a whirl, have a shot at, have a crack at, have a stab at 672 *undertake*; get down to, get to grips with, take the bull by the horns, make a go of; take a chance, chance one's arm, try one's luck, tempt providence, tempt fate, venture, speculate 618 *gamble*; test, make trial of 461 *experiment*; put out a feeler, dip in a toe, put a toe in the water, fly a kite 461 *be tentative*; be ambitious, attempt too much, bite off more than one can chew, die in the attempt 728 *fail*.

**Int.** Here goes!, nothing venture, nothing gain *or* nothing win!

## 672 Undertaking

**N.** *undertaking*, job, task, assignment; self-imposed task, labour of love, pilgrimage 597 *voluntary work*; contract, engagement, obligation, subcontract 764 *promise*; operation, exercise; programme, project, design 623 *plan*; tall order, big undertaking 700 *hard task*; enterprise, emprise; quest, search, adventure 459 *enquiry*; venture, speculation 618 *gambling*; occupation, matter in hand 622 *business*; struggle, effort, campaign 671 *attempt*.

**Adj.** *enterprising*, pioneering, adventurous, venturesome, daring; go-ahead, progressive, innovative; opportunist, alive to opportunity, with an eye to the main chance; ambitious 859 *desiring*; overambitious 857 *rash*; responsible, shouldering responsibility.

**Vb.** *undertake*, engage in, apply oneself to, address o. to, take up, go in for, devote oneself to; venture on, take on, tackle 671 *attempt*; go about, take in hand, turn *or* put *or* set one's hand to; set forward, set going 68 *initiate*; proceed to, embark on, launch into, plunge into, fall to, set to, get one's head down, buckle to, put one's best foot forward, set one's shoulder to the wheel, set one's hand to the plough 68 *begin*; grasp the nettle 855 *be courageous*; assume responsibility, take charge of 689 *manage*; execute 725 *carry out*; set up shop, have irons in the fire 622 *busy oneself*; shoulder, take on one's shoulders, take upon oneself, assume an obligation 917 *incur a duty*; engage to, commit oneself 764 *promise*; get involved, let oneself in for, volunteer 597 *be willing*; take on too much, bite off more than one can chew, have too many irons in the fire 678 *be busy*; show enterprise, pioneer; venture, dare 661 *face danger*; apprentice oneself 669 *prepare oneself*.

### 673 Use

**N.** *use*, usufruct, enjoyment, disposal 773 *possession*; conversion to use, conversion, utilization, exploitation; employment, application, appliance; exercise 610 *practice*; resort, recourse; mode of use, treatment, good usage, proper treatment 457 *carefulness*; ill-treatment, hard usage, wrong use 675 *misuse*; effect of use, wear, wear and tear 655 *dilapidation*; exhaustion, consumption 634 *waste*; reuse, palimpsest; usefulness, benefit, service 642 *good policy*; serviceability, practicality, convertibility, applicability 640 *utility*; office, purpose, point 622 *function*; long use, wont 610 *habit*.

**Adj.** *used*, applied, employed etc. vb.; in service, in use, in constant u., in practice; used up, consumed, worn, threadbare, down-at-heel; second-hand, pre-owned; well-used, well-thumbed, dog-eared, well-worn 655 *dilapidated*; beaten, well-trodden 490 *known*; hackneyed, stale; pragmatical, practical, utilitarian 642 *advisable*; makeshift, provisional 150 *substituted*; subservient, like wax or putty in one's hands 628 *instrumental*; available, usable, employable, utilizable, convertible 640 *useful*; at one's service, consumable, disposable.

**Vb.** *use*, employ, exercise, practise, put into practice, put into operation; apply, exert, bring to bear, administer; spend on, give to, devote to, consecrate to, dedicate to; assign to, allot (see also *dispose of*); utilize, make use of, convert, convert to use 640 *find useful*; reuse, recycle, exploit, get mileage out of, use to the full, get the best out of, make the most of, maximize, exhaust the possibilities; milk, drain 304 *extract*; put to good use, turn to account, capitalize on, make capital out of, use to advantage, make hay with 137 *profit by*; make play with, play on, trade on, cash in on; play off, play off against; make a tool or handle

of; make a pawn or cat's-paw of, take advantage of 542 *befool*; put to use, wear, wear out, use up, consume 634 *waste*; handle, thumb 378 *touch*; tread, follow, beat (a path); work, drive, manipulate 173 *operate*; wield, ply, brandish; overwork, tax, task 684 *fatigue*; prepare for use, work on, work up, mould 243 *form*.

*avail oneself of*, take up, adopt, try; resort to, run to, have recourse to, fall back on, turn to, draw on; impose on, presume on; press into service, enlist in one's s.; make do with, make shift w., do what one can w., make the best of.

*dispose of*, command; have at one's disposal, control, have at one's command, do what one likes with; allot, assign 783 *apportion*; spare, have to s.; requisition, call in; call into play, set in motion, set in action, set going, deploy 612 *motivate*; enjoy, have the usufruct 773 *possess*; consume, expend, absorb, use up 634 *waste*.

### 674 Nonuse

**N.** *nonuse*, abeyance, suspension 677 *inaction*; nonavailability 190 *absence*; stagnation, unemployment 679 *inactivity*; forbearance, abstinence 620 *avoidance*; savings 632 *store*; disuse, obsolescence, superannuation 611 *desuetude*; redundancy, dismissal 300 *ejection*; waiver, giving up, surrender, throwing in the towel 621 *relinquishment*; withdrawal, cancellation 752 *abrogation*; unsuitability 643 *inexpedience*; uselessness, write-off 641 *inutility*.

**Adj.** *unused*, not used; not available 190 *absent*; out of order, not in service, inoperational, unusable, unemployable 641 *useless*; unpracticable 643 *inexpedient*; unutilized, unapplied, unconverted; nonconvertible, non-returnable; undisposed of, in hand, reserved, saved 632 *stored*; on the spike, pigeonholed; spare, extra; unspent, unconsumed 666 *preserved*; untilled, unexploited, untapped, lying idle or fallow; unessayed, untried; unexercised, in abeyance, suspended; untrodden, unbeaten; untouched, unhandled, unopened 126 *new*; ungathered, unplucked, unharvested, unreaped, left to rot 634 *wasted*; unnecessary, not wanted, not required, redundant 860 *unwanted*; unrequired, free, vacant; dispensed with, waived; underused, not made use of, resting, unemployed, idle 679 *inactive*; jobless, out of work.

*disused*, derelict, discarded, cast-off, jettisoned, scrapped, written off; sacked, discharged, laid off etc. vb.; laid up, mothballed, out of commission, rusting; in limbo 458 *neglected*; done with, used up, run down, worn out; on the shelf, retired; out of use, superseded, superannuated, obsolete, discredited 127 *antiquated*.

**Vb.** *not use*, not utilize, hold in abeyance; not touch, have no use for; abstain, forbear, hold off, do without 620 *avoid*; dispense with, waive, not proceed with 621 *relinquish*; overlook, disregard 458 *neglect*; underuse, underutilize; spare, save, reserve, keep in hand 632 *store*; not accept, decline 607 *reject*.

*stop using*, disuse, leave off 145 *cease*; outgrow 611 *disaccustom*; leave to rust, lay up, put in mothballs, put out of commission, dismantle 641 *make useless*; have done with, lay aside, put on the shelf, hang up; pension off, put out to grass; discard, dump, ditch, scrap, write off; jettison, throw away, throw overboard 300 *eject*; slough, cast off 229 *doff*; give up, relinquish, resign 779 *not retain*; suspend, withdraw, cancel 752 *abrogate*; discharge, lay off, pay off, make redundant 300 *dismiss*; drop, supersede, replace 150 *substitute*; be unused, rust 655 *deteriorate*.

**675 Misuse**
**N.** *misuse*, abuse, wrong use, alcohol abuse, drug a., inhalant a., substance a., steroid a., solvent a., volatile substance a., VSA 949 *drug-taking*; misemployment, misapplication; misdirection, mismanagement, maladministration 695 *bungling*; misappropriation, malpractice 788 *peculation*; perversion 246 *distortion*; prostitution, violation; profanation, desecration 980 *impiety*; commercialization, commodification 847 *bad taste*; malapropism 565 *solecism*; pollution 649 *uncleanness*; overuse, overgrazing, overcropping, overfishing; extravagance 634 *waste*; misusage, mishandling, mistreatment, maltreatment, ill-treatment, force, domestic violence 176 *violence*; outrage, injury 616 *evil*.

**Vb.** *misuse*, abuse; use wrongly, misemploy, put to bad use, misdirect; divert, manipulate, misappropriate 788 *defraud*; commercialize, commodify 847 *vulgarize*; violate, desecrate, take in vain 980 *profane*; prostitute 655 *pervert*; pollute 649 *make unclean*; do violence to 176 *force*; strain 246 *distort*; take advantage of, exploit 673 *use*; manhandle, knock about 645 *ill-treat*; maltreat 735 *oppress*; misgovern, misrule, mishandle, mismanage 695 *be unskilful*; overwork, overtask, overtax 684 *fatigue*; work hard, wear out 655 *impair*; squander, fritter away 634 *waste*; misapply, use a sledgehammer to crack a nut 641 *waste effort*.

SECTION THREE

*Voluntary action*

**676 Action**
**N.** *action*, doing, performance; steps, measures,

move 623 *policy*; transaction, enactment, commission, perpetration; dispatch, execution, effectuation, accomplishment 725 *completion*; procedure, routine, praxis 610 *practice*; behaviour 688 *conduct*; movement, play, swing 265 *motion*; operation, working, interaction, evolution 173 *agency*; force, pressure 178 *influence*; work, labour 682 *exertion*; militancy, activism, activeness, drama 678 *activity*; occupation 622 *business*; manufacture 164 *production*; employment 673 *use*; effort, endeavour, campaign, crusade, battle, war on 671 *attempt*; implementation, administration, handling 689 *management*.

*deed*, act, overt a.; action, piece of the a., exploit, beau geste, feat, achievement 855 *prowess*; bad deed, crime 930 *foul play*; stunt, tour de force, stroke of genius 875 *ostentation*; gesture, measure, step, move 623 *policy*; manoeuvre, evolution 688 *tactics*; stroke, blow, coup, coup de main, coup d'état 623 *contrivance*; job, task, operation, exercise 672 *undertaking*; proceeding, transaction, deal, doings, dealings 154 *affairs*; work, handiwork, workmanship, craftsmanship 694 *skill*; pièce de résistance, chef d'oeuvre 694 *masterpiece*; drama, scene; acts 590 *narrative*.

*doer*, man *or* woman of action, go-getter, activist 678 *busy person*; practical person, realist; achiever, finisher; hero, heroine 855 *brave person*; practitioner 696 *expert*; stunt man *or* woman, player 594 *actor*; executant, performer; perpetrator, committer; offender, criminal 904 *evildoer*; mover, movers and shakers, controller, manipulator 612 *motivator*; operator 686 *agent*; contractor, undertaker, entrepreneur, intrapreneur; campaigner, canvasser; executor, executive, administrator, manager 690 *director*; hand, workman, operative 686 *worker*; craftsman, craftswoman 686 *artisan*; creative worker 556 *artist*.

**Adj.** *doing*, acting, operating, performing, committing etc. vb.; in the act, red-handed, bang to rights (inf); working, at work, in action, in operation, up and running, in harness; at the coal face 173 *operative*; up and doing, industrious, busy 678 *active*; occupational 610 *habitual*.

**Vb.** *do*, act, perform, get in on the act; be in action, come into operation 173 *operate*; militate, act upon 178 *influence*; manipulate 612 *motivate*; use tactics, twist, turn, manoeuvre 698 *be cunning*; do something, lift a finger; proceed, proceed with, get on with, get going, move, take action, take steps, lance the boil; try 671 *attempt*; tackle, take on 672 *undertake*; adopt a measure, enact, legislate 953 *make legal*; do the deed, perpetrate, commit, achieve, accomplish, complete, been there, done that 725 *carry through*; do the needful, take care of, dispatch, execute, implement, fulfil, put into practice 725 *carry out*; solemnize, observe; do great deeds, make history, win renown 866 *have a reputation*; practise, exercise, carry on, discharge, prosecute, pursue, wage, ply, ply one's trade, employ oneself 622 *busy oneself*; officiate, do one's stuff 622 *function*; transact, proceed 622 *do business*; administer, administrate, manage, control 689 *direct*; have to do with 688 *deal with*; sweat, labour, campaign, canvass 682 *work*; exploit, make the most of 673 *use*; intervene, strike a blow for 703 *aid*; have a hand in, be active in, play a part in 775 *participate*; deal in, have a finger in, get mixed up in 678 *meddle*; conduct oneself, indulge in 688 *behave*; play about, lark around, fool a. 497 *be absurd*; stunt, show off 875 *be ostentatious*.

**Adv.** *in the act*, in flagrante delicto, redhanded; in the midst of, in the thick of; while one's hand is in, while one is about it.

## 677 Inaction

**N.** *inaction*, nonaction, nothing doing, inertia 175 *inertness*; inability to act 161 *impotence*; failure to act, neglect 458 *negligence*; abstinence from action, abstention, refraining 620 *avoidance*; passive resistance 711 *defiance*; suspension, abeyance, dormancy 674 *nonuse*; deadlock, stalemate, logjam, gridlock 145 *stop*; immobility, paralysis, impassivity 375 *insensibility*; passivity, stagnation, vegetation, doldrums, stillness, quiet, calm 266 *quiescence*; time on one's hands, idle hours, dolce far niente 681 *leisure*; rest 683 *repose*; nonemployment, underemployment, unemployment, joblessness; no work, sinecure; loafing, idleness, indolence, twiddling one's thumbs 679 *inactivity*; Fabian policy, Fabian tactics, do-nothingism 136 *delay*; lack of progress 655 *deterioration*; noninterference, nonintervention 860 *indifference*; head in the sand, defeatism 856 *cowardice*.

**Adj.** *nonactive*, inoperative, idle, suspended, in abeyance 679 *inactive*; passive, dull, sluggish 175 *inert*; unoccupied, leisured 681 *leisurely*; do-nothing, unprogressive, ostrich-like; Fabian, cunctative, delaying, procrastinating; defeatist 853 *hopeless*; stationary, motionless, immobile, becalmed 266 *quiescent*; cold, extinct; not stirring, without a sign of life, dead-and-alive 361 *dead*; laid off, unemployed, jobless, out of work, on the dole, without employment 674 *unused*; incapable of action 161 *impotent*; benumbed, paralysed 375 *insensible*; apathetic, phlegmatic 820 *impassive*; neutral 860 *indifferent*; unhearing 416 *deaf*.

**Vb.** *not act*, fail to a., refuse to a., hang fire 598 *be unwilling*; refrain, abstain, pass the buck 620 *avoid*; look on, stand by 441 *watch*; let the world go by, watch and wait, wait and see, bide one's time 136 *wait*; procrastinate 136 *put off*; live and let live, let it rip, let things take their course, laisser aller, laisser faire, let sleeping dogs lie, let well alone; hold no brief for, stay neutral, sit on the fence 860 *be indifferent*; do nothing, tolerate, turn a blind eye 458 *disregard*; sit tight, not move, not budge, not stir, show no sign, not lift a finger, not even attempt 175 *be inert*; rest on one's oars, rest on one's laurels, relax one's efforts; drift, slide, coast, free-wheel; have no hope 853 *despair*; let pass, let go by, leave alone, let a., give it a miss 458 *neglect*; stay still, keep quiet 266 *be quiescent*; sit back, relax 683 *repose*; have no function 641 *be useless*; have nothing to do, kick one's heels, twiddle one's thumbs, sit on one's hands 681 *have leisure*; pause, desist 145 *cease*; rust, lie idle, stay on the shelf, lie fallow 674 *not use*; have no life, lie dead 361 *die*.

**Adv.** *without action*, without movement; nothing doing, hands in one's pockets, with folded arms; with the job half done.

## 678 Activity

**N.** *activity*, activeness, activism, militancy 676 *action*; scene; interest, active i. 775 *participation*; social activity, group a. 882 *sociability*; activation 612 *motive*; excitation 174 *stimulation*; agitation, movement, mass m. 738 *sedition*; life, stir 265 *motion*; nimbleness, briskness, smartness, alacrity, promptitude 597 *willingness*; readiness 135 *punctuality*; quickness, dispatch, expedition 277 *velocity*; spurt, burst, fit 318 *spasm*; hurry, flurry, hurry-skurry, hustle, bustle, overhaste, frantic haste 680 *haste*; hassle, fuss, bother, botheration, ado, to-do, racketing, tumult, frenzy 61 *turmoil*; whirl, scramble, mad s., rat race, maelstrom 315 *vortex*; drama, great doings, much ado, thick of things, thick of the action, the fray; plenty to do, a piece of the action, irons in the fire 622 *business*; call on one's time, press of business; pressure of work, no sinecure; high street, marketplace, heavy traffic; press, madding crowd, seething mob, hoi polloi; hum, hive, hive of industry 687 *workshop*.

*restlessness*, pottering, fiddling, aimless activity, desultoriness, no concentration 456 *inattention*; unquiet, fidgets, fidgetiness 318 *agitation*; jumpiness 822 *excitability*; fever, fret 503 *frenzy*; eagerness, enthusiasm, ardour, fervour, abandon, vehemence 818 *warm feeling*; vigour, energy, ceaseless e., dynamic e., dynamism, aggressiveness, militancy, enterprise, initiative, push, drive, go, get-up-and-go, pep 174 *vigorousness*; vivacity, spirit, animation, liveliness, vitality 360 *life*; watchfulness, wakefulness, vigilance 457 *carefulness*; sleeplessness, insomnia.

*assiduity*, application, concentration, intentness 455 *attention*; sedulity, industriousness, industry, laboriousness, legwork, drudgery 682 *labour*; determination, earnestness, empressement 599 *resolution*; tirelessness, indefatigability 600 *perseverance*; studiousness, painstaking, diligence; whole-heartedness, devotedness.

*overactivity*, overextension, overexpansion, excess 637 *redundance*; Parkinson's law; displacement activity, futile a., chasing one's own tail 641 *lost labour*; song and dance 318 *commotion*; hyperthyroidism, overexertion; officiousness, beadledom, meddlesomeness, interference, intrusiveness, interruption, meddling, interfering, finger in every pie; tampering, intrigue 623 *plot*.

*busy person*, new broom, enthusiast, bustler, hustler, someone in a hurry, jetsetter; zealot, fanatic 602 *obstinate person*; slogger, no slouch, hard worker, tireless w., high-pressure w., Stakhanovite, demon for work, glutton for w., workaholic 686 *worker*; factotum, jack-of-all-trades, maid-of-all-work, housewife, drudge, dogsbody, fag, slave, galley s., Trojan; horse, beaver, ant, bee; eager beaver, busy bee, workhorse, willing horse; person of active habits, man *or* woman of action, activist, militant 676 *doer*; participator; sharp fellow, live wire, dynamo, human d., powerhouse, whiz kid, go-getter, pusher, thruster; careerist.

*meddler*, dabbler, stirrer, interferer, intermeddler, troublemaker, officious person, spoilsport, nosy parker, ultracrepidarian, busybody 453 *inquisitive person*; tamperer, intriguer 623 *planner*; kibitzer, back-seat driver 691 *adviser*; fusspot, nuisance.

**Adj.** *active*, stirring, kicking (sl) 265 *moving*; going, working, incessant 146 *unceasing*; expeditious 622 *businesslike*; able, able-bodied, abled 162 *strong*; quick, brisk, nippy, spry, smart, gleg (dial) 277 *speedy*; nimble, light-footed, lightsome, tripping; energetic, forceful, thrustful, proactive 174 *vigorous*; pushing, go-getting, up-and-coming 672 *enterprising*; frisky, coltish, dashing, sprightly, spirited, mettlesome, live, alive and kicking, full of beans, animated, vivacious 819 *lively*; eager, ardent, perfervid 818 *fervent*; fierce, desperate 599 *resolute*; enthusiastic, zealous, prompt, instant, ready, on one's toes 597 *willing*; awake, alert, watchful, wakeful, on the qui vive 457 *vigilant*; sleepless, restless, feverish, fretful, tossing, dancing, fidgety, jumpy, fussy, nervy, like a cat on hot bricks, like a hen on a hot griddle 318 *agitated*; frantic, demonic 503 *frenzied*; hyperactive, overactive 822 *excitable*; involved, engagé; aggressive, militant, up in arms 718 *warlike*.

*busy*, bustling, hustling, humming, lively, eventful; coming and going, rushing to and fro, as though one's life depended on it; pottering, doing chores; up and doing, stirring, astir, afoot, on the move, on the go, on the trot, in full swing; slogging, rushed off one's feet, hard at work, hard at it, up to one's eyes, fully engaged; in harness, at work, at one's desk; occupied, fully o., employed, over-e.; fussing like a hen with one chicken, busy as a bee.

*industrious*, studious, sedulous, assiduous 600 *persevering*; labouring, hardworking, plodding, slogging 682 *laborious*; unflagging, unwearied, unsleeping, tireless, indefatigable, keeping long hours, burning the candle at both ends, never-tiring, never-resting, never-sleeping; efficient, workmanlike 622 *businesslike*.

*meddling*, overbusy, officious, pushy, interfering, meddlesome, intrusive, intriguing; dabbling; participating, in the business.

**Vb.** *be active*, show interest, interest oneself in, trouble oneself, be part of the scene, join in 775 *participate*; be stirring, stir, come and go, rush to and fro 265 *move*; run riot, have one's fling 61 *rampage*; not sleep, wake up, rouse oneself, bestir o., stir one's stumps, rub the sleep from one's eyes, be up and doing; hum, thrive 730 *prosper*; make progress 285 *progress*; keep moving, keep on the go, keep the pot boiling 146 *go on*; push, shove, thrust, drive 279 *impel*; elbow one's way, thrust oneself forward 174 *be vigorous*; rush, surge 350 *flow*; roar, rage, bluster 352 *blow*; explode, burst 176 *be violent*; dash, fly, run 277 *move fast*; make the effort, do one's best 671 *attempt*; take pains 455 *be attentive*; buckle to, put one's shoulder to the wheel, put one's hand to the tiller 682 *exert oneself*; persist, beaver away 600 *persevere*; polish off, dispatch, make short work of, not let the grass grow under one's feet; rise to the occasion, work wonders 727 *be successful*; jump to it, show willing, show zeal, make the sparks fly, make things hum 676 *do*; burn with zeal, be on fire 597 *be willing*; be on one's toes, anticipate, wake, watch 457 *be careful*; seize the opportunity, take one's chance, take the bull by the horns 137 *profit by*; assert oneself, not take it lying down, be up in arms, react, react sharply, show fight 711 *defy*; protest, agitate, demonstrate, kick up a shindy, raise the dust 762 *deprecate*.

*be busy*, keep b., have irons in the fire 622 *busy oneself*; be always on the go, bustle, hurry, hassle, scurry 680 *hasten*; live in a whirl, join the rat race, go all ways at once, run round in circles; chase one's own tail 641 *waste effort*; not know which way to turn 700 *be in difficulty*; have one's hands full, be rushed off one's feet, have not a moment to spare *or* to call one's own, have no time to lose, rise early, go to bed late, burn the midnight oil, burn the candle at both ends, strain oneself; fuss, fret, fume, drum one's fingers, stamp with impatience 822 *be excitable*; have other things to do, have other fish to fry 138 *be engaged*; slave, slog 682 *work*; overwork, overdo it, make work, make heavy weather of, never stop, improve the shining hour; affect zeal 850 *be affected*.

*meddle*, intermeddle, interpose, intervene, interfere, be officious, not mind one's own business, have a finger in every pie; pry into, poke one's nose in, shove one's oar in, butt in 297 *intrude*; pester, bother, dun, annoy 827 *trouble*; be bossy, boss, boss one around, tyrannize 735 *oppress*; tinker, tamper, touch 655 *impair*.

**Adv.** *actively*, on the go, on one's toes; full tilt, full belt, whole hog, like a bomb, on all cylinders; with might and main, for all one is worth, for dear life, as if one's life depended on it.

**Int.** get going!, rise and shine!, shake a leg!, up you get!, wakey wakey!

## 679 Inactivity

**N.** *inactivity*, inactiveness 677 *inaction*; inertia, heaviness, torpor 175 *inertness*; lull, suspension, suspended animation 145 *cessation*; immobility, stillness, slack period, doldrums, grave, morgue 266 *quiescence*; no progress, logjam, putting off till tomorrow, stagnation 655 *deterioration*; rust, rustiness 674 *nonuse*; slump, recession 37 *decrease*; unemployment, shutdown; absenteeism 598 *unwillingness*; procrastination, laissez-faire, mañana 136 *delay*; idleness, indolence, loafing; idle hours 681 *leisure*.

*sluggishness*, lethargy, laziness, indolence, sloth; remissness 458 *negligence*; dawdling, slow progress 278 *slowness*; stiffness, debility 163 *weakness*; inanimation, lifelessness; languor, lentor, dullness, listlessness 820 *moral insensibility*; stupor, torpor, torpidity, numbness 375 *insensibility*; apathy 860 *indifference*; phlegm, impassivity 823 *inexcitability*; supineness, no resistance, line of least r. 721 *submission*.

*sleepiness*, tiredness, weariness, lassitude 684 *fatigue*; somnolence, doziness, drowsiness,

heaviness, nodding; oscitation, oscitancy, yawning; tired eyes, heavy lids, sand in the eyes; dreaminess 513 *fantasy*.

*sleep*, slumber, kip, bye-byes; deep sleep, sound s., heavy s., beauty s.; untroubled sleep, sleep of the just; half-sleep, drowse; light sleep, nap, catnap, power-n., forty winks, shut-eye, snooze, doze, siesta 683 *repose*; winter sleep, summer s., hibernation, aestivation; unconsciousness, coma, oblivion, trance, catalepsy, hypnosis 375 *insensibility*; sleepwalking, somnambulism; sleepy sickness 651 *disease*; dreams, gate of ivory, g. of horn; Morpheus, sandman; dreamland, Land of Nod; cot, cradle, pillow, bed.

*soporific*, somnifacient, sleeping draught, nightcap; sleeping pill, sedative, barbiturate; opiate, poppy, opium, morphine 375 *anaesthetic*; lullaby, berceuse, cradlesong, bedtime story.

*idler*, drone, lazybones, lie-abed, loafer, lounger, flâneur, sloucher, sluggard; couch potato, slacker, skiver, clock-watcher; Weary Willie, moper, sleepyhead; dawdler 278 *slowcoach*; hobo, bum, tramp 268 *wanderer*; mendicant 763 *beggar*; spiv, parasite, cadger, sponger, scrounger, moocher, freeloader; layabout, good-for-nothing, ne'er-do-well, wastrel, slubberdegullion; floater, drifter, free-wheeler; opium-eater, lotus-e., waiter on Providence 596 *fatalist*; nonworker, sinecurist, rentier; fainéant, dummy, passenger, sleeping partner, absentee landlord; idle rich, jet set, Sloane Rangers, leisured classes; dreamer, sleeper, slumberer, dozer, drowser; hibernator, dormouse, hedgehog; Seven Sleepers, Rip van Winkle, Sleeping Beauty.

**Adj.** *inactive*, motionless, stationary, at a standstill, still, hushed, extinct 266 *quiescent*; suspended, discontinued, taken off, not working, not operating, not in use, laid up, out of commission 674 *disused*; inanimate, lifeless, exanimate 175 *inert*; torpid, benumbed, unconscious, dopey, drugged 375 *insensible*; sluggish, stiff, rusty 677 *nonactive*; lymphatic, listless, lackadaisical 834 *dejected*; tired, faint, languid, languorous 684 *fatigued*; dull, heavy, leaden, lumpish, stolid 820 *impassive*; unresisting, supine, submissive 721 *submitting*; uninterested 454 *incurious*; apathetic 860 *indifferent*; lethargic, unaroused, unawakened 823 *inexcitable*; nonparticipating, sleeping 190 *absent*; leisured, idle, empty, unoccupied, disengaged 681 *leisurely*; on strike, out, locked o.

*lazy*, bone-l., do-nothing, fainéant; slothful, sluggish, work-shy, indolent, idle, bone-idle, spivvish, parasitical; idling, lolling, loafing 681 *leisurely*; dawdling 278 *slow*; tardy, laggard, dilatory, procrastinating 136 *late*; slack, remiss, careless 458 *negligent*.

*sleepy*, ready for bed, tired 684 *fatigued*; half-awake, half-asleep; slumberous, somnolent, heavy-eyed, stupid with sleep; drowsy, dozy, dopey, groggy, nodding, yawning; napping, dozing; asleep, dreaming, snoring, fast asleep, sound a., dead to the world; unconscious, out, out cold; dormant, hibernating, comatose; in dreamland, in the land of Nod, in the arms of Morpheus, in bed.

*soporific*, somnific, somniferous, sleep-inducing, sedative, hypnotic.

**Vb.** *be inactive*, do nothing, relax, hang out, chill out (inf), rust, stagnate, vegetate, veg (inf), smoulder, hang fire 677 *not act*; let the grass grow under one's feet, let the world go by, delay 136 *put off*; not bother, take it easy, let things go, laisser faire 458 *be neglectful*; hang about, kick one's heels 136 *wait*; slouch, lag, loiter, dawdle 278 *move slowly*; dally, drag one's feet 136 *be late*; stand, sit, lie, lollop, loll, lounge, laze, rest, take it easy 683 *repose*; lie down on the job, slack, skive, shirk 620 *avoid*; not work, fold one's arms, sit around; have nothing to do, loaf, idle, mooch about, moon a., while away the time, kill t., sit on one's hands, twiddle one's thumbs; waste time, drone away, consume the golden hours, trifle, dabble, fribble, fiddle-faddle, fritter away the time, piddle, potter, putter 641 *waste effort*; slow down, come to a standstill 278 *decelerate*; dilly-dally, hesitate 474 *be uncertain*; droop, faint, fail, languish, slacken 266 *come to rest*; slump 37 *decrease*; be still, be hushed 266 *be quiescent*; discontinue, stop, come to an end 145 *cease*; strike, come out, take industrial action.

*sleep*, slumber, snooze, nap, catnap, power-n.; aestivate, hibernate; sleep soundly, sleep well, sleep like a log, sleep like a top, sleep like a little child, sleep the sleep of the just; dream; snore, drive pigs to market; go to sleep, nod off, drop off, fall asleep, take a nap, have a kip, have forty winks; close one's eyes, feel sleepy, yawn, nod, doze, drowse; go to bed, turn in, doss down, kip d., shake d., hit the hay; settle down, bed d., roost, perch.

*make inactive*, put to sleep, put to bed, seal up the eyelids; send to sleep, lull, rock, cradle; soothe 177 *assuage*; deaden, paralyse, benumb, anaesthetize, dope, drug, narcotize, put out 375 *render insensible*; stiffen, cramp, immobilize 747 *fetter*; lay up, put out of commission 674 *stop using*; dismantle 641 *make useless*; pay off, stand o., lay o. 300 *dismiss*.

## 680 Haste

**N.** *haste*, hurry, scurry, hurry-scurry, hustle, bustle, hassle, flurry, whirl, scramble 678 *activity*; flap, flutter, fidget, fuss 318 *agitation*; rush, rush job 670 *nonpreparation*; feverish haste, tearing hurry, race against time, no time to lose 136 *lateness*; immediacy, urgency 638 *importance*; push, drive, expedition, dispatch 277 *velocity*; hastening, acceleration, forced march, dash 277 *spurt*; overhaste, precipitance, precipitateness, impetuosity 857 *rashness*; inability to wait, hastiness, impatience 822 *excitability*; the more haste the less speed.

**Adj.** *hasty*, overhasty, impetuous, impulsive, hot-headed, precipitant 857 *rash*; feverish, impatient, all impatience, ardent 818 *fervent*; pushing, shoving, elbowing; uncontrolled, boisterous, furious 176 *violent*; precipitate, headlong, breathless, breakneck 277 *speedy*; expeditious, prompt, without delay; hasting, hastening, making speed; in haste, in all h., hotfoot, running, racing; in a hurry, unable to wait, pressed for time, hardpressed, driven; done in haste, hurried, scamped, slapdash, cursory 458 *negligent*; rough and ready, forced, rushed, rush, last-minute 670 *unprepared*; rushed into, railroaded; stampeded; allowing no time, brooking no delay, urgent, immediate 638 *important*.

**Vb.** *hasten*, expedite, dispatch 285 *promote*; urge, drive, stampede, spur, goad, whip, lash, flog 612 *incite*; bundle off, hustle away; rush, allow no time, railroad, brook no delay; be hasty, be precipitate, rush headlong 857 *be rash*; haste, make haste; post, race, run, dash off, tear off 277 *move fast*; catch up, make up for lost time, overtake 277 *outstrip*; spurt, dash, make a forced march 277 *accelerate*; hurry, scurry, hustle, bustle, fret, fume, fidget, rush to and fro, dart to and fro 678 *be active*; be in a hurry, have no time to spare, have no time to lose, act without ceremony, cut short the preliminaries, brush aside; cut corners, rush one's fences; rush through, dash through, make short work of; be pressed for time, work against time *or* to a deadline, work under pressure, think on one's feet; do at the last moment 136 *be late*; lose no time, lose not a moment, make every minute count; hasten away, cut and run, make oneself scarce, not be seen for dust 296 *decamp*.

**Adv.** *hastily*, hurriedly, precipitately, helter-skelter, pell-mell, feverishly, posthaste, hotfoot, apace 277 *swiftly*; with all haste, at short notice, on the spur of the moment; immediately, urgently, with urgency, under pressure, against the clock, by forced marches, with not a moment to lose.

**Int.** hurry up!, at the double!, be quick!, buck up!, get a move on!, get a wiggle on!, look lively!, look sharp!, quick march!, step on it!

## 681 Leisure

**N.** *leisure*, spare time, free t., convenience; spare hours, vacant moments, odd m., idle m.; time on one's hands, time to kill; not enough work, sinecure; no work, idleness, dolce far niente; breathing space, gap year, off duty, time off, day o., duvet day, holiday, half-h., break, vacation, leave, sabbatical, furlough 679 *inactivity*; time to spare, no hurry, ample time, all the time in the world; rest, ease, relaxation 683 *repose*; no more work, redundancy 300 *rejection*; retirement 753 *resignation*.

**Adj.** *leisurely*, deliberate, unhurried 278 *slow*; at one's convenience, in one's own time, at any odd moment; leisured, at leisure, disengaged, unoccupied 683 *reposeful*; at a loose end, at ease; off duty, on holiday, on vacation, on leave, on furlough, on sabbatical; retired, in retirement, redundant; affording leisure, labour-saving.

**Vb.** *have leisure*, have time enough, have plenty of time, have all the time in the world, have time to spare; be master of one's time, take one's ease, spend, pass, while away; see no cause for haste, be in no hurry, take one's time 278 *move slowly*; want something to do, find time hang heavy on one's hands 679 *be inactive*; take a holiday 683 *repose*; give up work, go into retirement, take early r., retire, be made redundant 753 *resign*; find time for, save labour.

## 682 Exertion

**N.** *exertion*, effort, struggle 671 *attempt*; straining, strain, stress, might and main; tug, pull, stretch, heave, lift, throw; drive, force, pressure, full p., maximum p., applied energy 160 *energy*; ergonomics; ado, hassle, trouble, toil and t., mighty efforts, the hard way; muscle, elbow grease, 'sweat of one's brow' (see quotation at 682 *labour*); pains, taking pains, operoseness 678 *assiduity*; elaboration, artificiality; overwork, overexertion 678 *overactivity*; extra work, overtime, busman's holiday; battle, campaign, fray.

*exercise*, practice, regular p., drill, training, resistance t., weight t.; work-out, working out; the bar (ballet) 669 *preparation*; physical education, PE, keeping fit, jogging, jarming, cycling, constitutional, daily dozen; gymnastics 162 *athletics*; weight-lifting, body-building; yoga, isometrics, eurhythmics, Medau, callisthenics, aerobics, step, qigong *or* qi gong *or* ch'i kung, tai ji *or* tai ji quan *or* t'ai chi *or* t'ai chi ch'uan, Tae Bo (tdmk); games, sports, races 837 *sport*.

*exercise equipment*, exercise bike, rowing machine, stepper, treadmill, multi-gym, weights; Indian clubs, medicine ball, skipping rope.

*labour*, industry, work, hard w., heavy w., uphill w., warm w., punishing w., back-breaking w., long haul; spadework, donkeywork; legwork; manual labour, 'sweat of one's brow';

> **In the sweat of thy face shalt thou eat bread.**
> Bible, Genesis

housework, chores, daily grind, toil, travail, swink, drudgery, slavery, sweat, fag, grind, strain, treadmill, grindstone, 'blood, sweat and tears' (see quotation at 160 *power*); work ethic, 'Protestant work ethic';

> **The Protestant Ethic and the Spirit of Capitalism**
> Title of book by Max Weber

hack work; bull; penal work, hard labour, picking oakum, breaking stones 963 *penalty*; forced labour, corvée 740 *compulsion*; fatigue, fatigue duty, spell of d. 917 *duty*; piecework, taskwork, homework, homeworking, outwork, telecommuting; journeywork; task, chore, job, operation, exercise 676 *deed*; shift, trick, stint, stretch, bout, spell of work 110 *period*; job of work, stroke of w., hand's turn; working life, working week, working day, man-hours, woman-h.

**Adj.** *labouring*, born to toil, horny-handed; working, drudging, sweating, grinding, etc. vb.; on the go, hard at it 678 *busy*; hardworking, laborious 678 *industrious*; slogging, plodding 600 *persevering*; strenuous, energetic 678 *active*; painstaking, thorough 455 *attentive*; exercising, taking exercise, practising; gymnastic, athletic.

*laborious*, full of labour, involving effort; crushing, killing, backbreaking; gruelling, punishing, unremitting, exhausting; toilsome, troublesome, weary, wearisome, painful, burdensome; heroic, Herculean; arduous, hard, warm, heavy, uphill 700 *difficult*; hard-fought, hard-won; thorough, painstaking, laboured; elaborate, artificial; detailed, fiddling; effort-wasting 641 *useless*.

**Vb.** *exert oneself*, apply oneself, put one's best foot forward, make an effort, try 671 *attempt*; struggle, strain, strive, sweat blood; trouble oneself, bestir oneself, put oneself out, bend over backwards; spare no effort, turn every stone, leave no stone unturned, do one's utmost, try one's best, use one's best endeavours, do all one can, go to any lengths, move heaven and earth; go all out, pull out all the stops, put one's heart and soul into it, put out one's whole strength, put one's back into it, strain every nerve, use every muscle 678 *be active*; love one's job, have one's heart in one's work 597 *be willing*; force one's way, elbow one's way, drive through, wade t.; hammer at, slog at 600 *persevere*; battle, campaign, take action 676 *do*.

*work*, labour, toil, moil, drudge, fag, grind, slog, sweat, work up a sweat, work up a lather; sweat blood; pull, haul, tug, shove, hump, heave, ply the oar; dig, spade, lumber; do the work, soil one's hands; spit on one's palms, get down to it, set about, set to, roll up one's sleeves, take one's coat off 68 *begin*; keep at it, plod 600 *persevere*; work hard, work overtime, moonlight, work double shift, work double tides, work all hours, work night and day, be firing on all cylinders, burn the midnight oil 678 *be busy*; work at home, be self-employed, telecommute; job-share; slave, slave away, beaver away, work one's fingers to the bone, work like a galley slave, work like a horse, work like a Trojan; work oneself to death; overdo it, make work; work for, serve 703 *minister to*; put to work, overwork, task, tax 684 *fatigue*.

*exercise*, drill, practise, train; do one's daily dozen, do physical jerks, go for the burn, pump iron; cycle, jog, power-walk, run, swim, walk, work out.

**Adv.** *laboriously*, the hard way' manually, by hand; 'by the sweat of one's brow' (see quotation at 682 *labour*); arduously, strenuously, energetically; lustily, heartily, heart and soul, with might and main, with all one's might, on all cylinders, tooth and nail, hammer and tongs, for all one is worth.

## 683 Repose

**N.** *repose*, rest, rest from one's labours 679 *inactivity*; restfulness, ease, comfort 376 *euphoria*; peace and quiet, tranquillity 266 *quiescence*; sweet sleep, happy dreams 679 *sleep*; relaxation, lack of stress, freedom from stress, relaxation therapy; breathing space, breather 685 *refreshment*; pause, respite, let-up, breather, recess, break 145 *lull*; interval 108 *interim*; holiday, vacation, leave, furlough, day off, sabbatical year 681 *leisure*; day of rest, Sabbath, Lord's day.

**Adj.** *reposeful*, restful, easeful, relaxing; slippered, unbuttoned, in one's shirtsleeves, carefree, casual, relaxed, laid-back, at ease 828 *content*; cushioned, pillowed, snug 376 *comfortable*; peaceful, quiet 266 *tranquil*; leisured, sabbatical, vacational, holiday 681 *leisurely*; postprandial, after-dinner.

**Vb.** *repose*, rest, take a rest, take it easy, take one's ease, sit back, put one's feet up; recline, lie down, loll, lounge, laze, sprawl 216 *be horizontal*; perch, roost 311 *sit down*; couch, go to bed, kip down, go to sleep 679 *sleep*; relax, unwind, unbend, forget work, put on one's slippers, rest and be thankful; breathe, take a breather 685 *be refreshed*; slack off, let up, slow down; rest on one's oars 266 *come to rest*; take time off *or* out, take a holiday, go on leave 681 *have leisure*.

**Adv.** *at rest*, reposefully, restfully, peacefully, on holiday, on vacation, on sabbatical.

## 684 Fatigue

**N.** *fatigue*, tiredness, weariness, lassitude, languor, lethargy; physical fatigue, aching muscles; shortness of breath, hard breathing, laboured b., panting, palpitations 352 *respiration*; mental fatigue, brainfag (inf); stress, distress, burn-out, karoshi; staleness, jadedness; limit of endurance, exhaustion, collapse, prostration; strain, overtiredness, overexertion, overwork 682 *exertion*; languishment, faintness, fainting, faint, swoon, blackout 375 *insensibility*; compassion fatigue, disaster f.

**Adj.** *fatigued*, tired, ready for bed 679 *sleepy*; asleep on one's feet, tired out, exhausted, spent; done, done up, done in, pooped, fagged, fagged out, knocked up, washed up, washed out, clapped o., tuckered o., worn to a frazzle; stupid with fatigue, dull, stale; strained, overworked, overtired, overfatigued, overstrained, burned out (inf), stressed, stressed out; dog-tired, dog-weary, bone-weary, tired to death, dropping, ready to drop, on one's last legs, all in, dead beat, beat, whacked, knackered, flaked out, flat o.; more dead than alive, swooning, fainting, prostrate; stiff, aching, sore, toilworn; way-worn, footsore, footweary, walked off one's feet; tired-eyed, heavy-e., hollow-e.; tired-looking, haggard, worn; faint, drooping, flagging, languid, languorous; still tired, unrefreshed; tired of, bored with 838 *bored*; jaded, satiated 863 *sated*.

*panting*, out of breath, short of b.; blown, breathless, gasping, puffing and blowing, snorting, winded, broken-w. 352 *puffing*.

*fatiguing*, gruelling, punishing 682 *laborious*; tiresome, wearisome; wearing, exacting, demanding, high maintenance; irksome, trying 838 *tedious*.

**Vb.** *be fatigued*, – fagged etc. adj.; tire oneself out, overdo it, overtax one's strength; get weary, ache in every muscle *or* limb, gasp, pant, puff, blow, grunt 352 *breathe*; languish, droop, drop, sink, flag, fail 163 *be weak*; stagger, faint, swoon, feel giddy; yawn, nod, drowse 679 *sleep*; succumb, drop, collapse,

flake out, crack up, crock up, pack up; cry out
for rest, have no strength left, be at the end of
one's strength, be at the end of one's tether;
can go no further, can do no more, must have
a rest, must sit down; overwork, get stale, need
a rest, need a break, need a change, need a
holiday, be burned out.

*fatigue*, tire, tire out, wear, wear out, exhaust,
do up, fag, whack, knock up, crock up, prostrate; double up, wind; demand too much,
task, tax, strain, work, drive, overdrive, flog,
overwork, overtax, overtask, overburden, over-
strain, burn out; enervate, drain, take it out of,
distress, harass, irk, jade 827 *trouble*; tire to
death, weary, bore, send to sleep 838 *be tedious*;
keep from sleep, deprive of s., allow no rest.

### 685 Refreshment

**N.** *refreshment*, breather, breath of air 683
*repose*; break, recess 145 *lull*; renewal, recreation, recruitment, recuperation 656 *restoration*; reanimation 656 *revival*; easing 831 *relief*;
stimulation, refresher, reviver, nineteenth hole
174 *stimulant*; refreshments, refection 301
*food*; wash, wash and brush up 648 *cleansing*.

**Adj.** *refreshing*, thirst-quenching; cooling,
cool 380 *cold*; comforting 831 *relieving*;
bracing, reviving, recreative, recreational,
recruiting 656 *restorative*; easy on, labour-
saving 683 *reposeful*.

*refreshed*, freshened up, breathed, recovered,
revived, enlivened 656 *restored*; like a giant
refreshed, like a new man *or* woman, twice the
man *or* woman one was; perked up, ready for
more.

**Vb.** *refresh*, freshen, freshen up 648 *clean*;
air, fan, ventilate 340 *aerate*; shade, cool, cool
off, cool one down 382 *refrigerate*; brace, stimulate 174 *invigorate*; recruit, recreate, revive,
reanimate, reinvigorate, recuperate 656 *restore*;
ease 831 *relieve*; allow rest, give a breather;
offer food 301 *feed*.

*be refreshed*, breathe, draw breath, get one's
breath back, regain *or* recover one's breath,
take a deep b., fill one's lungs; respire, clear
one's head; come to, perk up, get one's second
wind, feel like a giant refreshed, feel like a new
man *or* woman; revive 656 *be restored*; mop
one's brow, stretch one's legs, renew oneself,
refresh o., take a breather, sleep it off; have a
change, have a rest 683 *repose*.

### 686 Agent

**N.** *agent*, operator, actor, performer, player,
executant, practitioner; perpetrator 676 *doer*;
minister, tool 628 *instrument*; functionary 741
*officer*; representative 754 *delegate*; deputizer,
spokesman 755 *deputy*; proxy 150 *substitute*;

executor, executrix, executive, administrator,
dealer; middleman 794 *merchant*; employer,
manufacturer, industrialist, technocrat 164 *producer*; subcontractor.

*worker*, voluntary w. 597 *volunteer*; social
worker 901 *philanthropist*; independent worker,
freelance, freelancer, e-lancer, self-employed
person, homeworker, teleworker, telecommuter; organization man 83 *conformist*; trade
unionist 775 *participator*; toiler, moiler, drudge,
dogsbody, fag, erk, hack; flunkey, menial, factotum, wallah, maid-of-all-work, domestic servant 742 *servant*; hewer of wood and drawer of
water, beast of burden 742 *slave*; ant, beaver,
Stakhanovite 678 *busy person*; professional
person, business man, business woman,
career w., executive, breadwinner, earner,
salary e., wage e., wage slave, employee; subcontractor; brain worker, boffin; clerical
worker, desk w., white-collar w., black-coat w.;
office w., girl Friday, man Friday; shop assistant 793 *seller*; charwoman, dustman 648
*cleaner*; labourer, casual l., day l., agricultural l.,
farm worker 370 *farmer*; piece-worker,
manual w., blue-collar w.; working man *or*
woman, working girl, workman, hand, operative, factory worker, factory hand; navvy,
roadman; ganger, plate-layer; docker, stevedore, packer; porter, coolie.

*artisan*, artificer, tradesman, technician;
skilled worker, semi-skilled w., master 696 *proficient person*; journeyman, apprentice 538
*learner*; craftsman *or* -woman, potter, turner,
joiner, cabinet-maker, carpenter, chippie,
carver, woodworker, sawyer, cooper; wright,
wheelwright, wainwright, coach-builder; ship-
wright, boat-builder; builder, architect, master
mason, mason, housebuilder, bricklayer, plas-
terer, tiler, thatcher, painter, decorator;
cowboy, ladder gang; forger, metalworker,
smith, blacksmith, tinsmith, goldsmith, silver-
smith, gunsmith, locksmith; tinker, knife-
grinder; collier, miner, face-worker,
steelworker, foundryman; mechanic,
machinist, fitter; engineer, civil e., mining e.,
computer e., television e.; powerworker,
waterworker; plumber, welder, electrician, gas-
fitter; weaver, spinner, tailor, cutter, needle-
woman 228 *clothier*; watchmaker, clockmaker;
jeweller; glass-blower.

*personnel*, staff, force, company, team, gang,
squad, crew, complement, cadre 74 *band*; dramatis personae 594 *actor*; co-worker, fellow w.,
mate, colleague, associate, partner 707 *colleague*; workpeople, hands, men, payroll;
labour, casual l.; workforce, labour pool,
labour force, human resources, liveware,
peopleware, manpower; working classes, prolet-

ariat; personnel management, human resource management; staff turnover, churn, churn rate.

## 687 Workshop

**N.** *workshop*, studio, atelier; workroom, study, den, library; laboratory, research l.; plant, installation; business park, industrial estate, science park, technopole; works, factory, manufactory; workshop, yard; sweatshop; mill, cotton m., loom; sawmill, paper mill; foundry, metalworks; steelyard, steelworks, smelter; blast furnace, forge, smithy, stithy 383 *furnace*; powerhouse, power station, gasworks 160 *energy*; quarry, mine 632 *store*; colliery, coalmine, pit, coalface; tin mine, stannary; mint; arsenal, armoury; dockyard, shipyard, slips; wharf, dock 192 *shed*; construction site, building s.; refinery, distillery, brewery, maltings; shop, shopfloor, bench, production line; nursery 370 *farm*; dairy, creamery 369 *stock farm*; kitchen, laundry; office, bureau, call centre; business house, firm, company; offices, secretariat, Whitehall; manufacturing town, hive of industry 678 *activity*.

## 688 Conduct

**N.** *conduct*, behaviour, deportment; bearing, personal b., comportment, carriage, port; demeanour, attitude, posture 445 *mien*; aspect, look, look in one's eyes 445 *appearance*; tone, tone of voice, delivery 577 *voice*; motion, action, gesticulation 547 *gesture*; mode of behaviour, fashion, style; manner, guise, air; poise, savoir faire, dignity, presence; breeding, graciousness, good manners 884 *courtesy*; ungraciousness, boorishness, rudeness, bad manners 885 *discourtesy*; pose, roleplaying 850 *affectation*; mental attitude, outlook 485 *opinion*; mood 818 *feeling*; good behaviour 933 *virtue*; misbehaviour, misconduct 934 *wickedness*; democratic behaviour, common touch; past behaviour, record, track r., history; reward of conduct, deserts 915 *dueness*; way of life, ethos, morals, principles, ideals, customs, mores, manners, lifestyle 610 *habit*; proposed conduct, line of action 623 *policy*; career, course, race, walk, walk of life 622 *vocation*; observance, routine, rules of business 610 *practice*; procedure, process, method, modus operandi 624 *way*; organization, orchestration, treatment, handling, manipulation, direction, masterminding 689 *management*; gentle handling, kid gloves, velvet glove 736 *leniency*; rough handling, putting the boot in, jackboot, iron hand 735 *severity*; dealings, transactions 154 *affairs*; deeds 676 *deed*; behaviourism.

*tactics*, strategy, campaign, plan of c., logis-

tics; programme 623 *plan*; line, party l. 623 *policy*; political science, art of the possible, politics, realpolitik, diplomacy, statesmanship 733 *governance*; lifemanship, gamesmanship, one-upmanship 698 *cunning*; brinkmanship, generalship, seamanship 694 *skill*; manoeuvres, manoeuvring, marching and counter-marching, jockeying, jockeying for position; tactical advantage, vantage ground 34 *advantage*; playing for time 136 *delay*; manoeuvre, shift 623 *contrivance*; move, gambit 676 *deed*; game, little g. 698 *stratagem*.

**Adj.** *behaving*, behavioural, behaviouristic; psychological; tactical, strategical; political, statesmanlike 622 *businesslike*.

**Vb.** *behave*, act 676 *do*; behave well, mind one's p's and q's, play the game 933 *be virtuous*; behave badly, break all the rules, misbehave, try it on, carry on 934 *be wicked*; deserve well of, deserve ill of; keep out of mischief, be on one's best behaviour, keep a low profile; gesture 547 *gesticulate*; posture, pose, affect 850 *be affected*; conduct oneself, behave o., carry o., bear o., deport o., acquit o., comport o., demean o.; set an example, lead a good life, lead a bad l.; indulge in 678 *be active*; play one's part 775 *participate*; pursue, follow one's career, conduct one's affairs 622 *busy oneself*; follow a course, shape a c., steer a c. 281 *steer for*; paddle one's own canoe, be master of one's own ship, shift for oneself 744 *be free*; employ tactics, manoeuvre, manipulate, mastermind, jockey, twist, turn; behave towards, treat.

*deal with*, have on one's plate, have to do with 676 *do*; handle, manipulate 173 *operate*; conduct, carry on, run 689 *manage*; see to, cope with, do the needful; transact, enact, execute, dispatch, carry through, put into practice 725 *carry out*; work out 623 *plan*; work at, work through, wade t. 682 *work*; go through, read 536 *study*.

## 689 Management

**N.** *management*, conduct, conduct of affairs, manipulation, running, handling; managership, stewardship, proctorship, agency 751 *commission*; care, charge, control 733 *authority*; superintendence, oversight 457 *surveillance*; patronage 660 *protection*; art of management, tact, way with 694 *skill*; business management, work study, management s., time and motion s., operational research, cost-benefit analysis; organization, masterminding, decision-making, adhocracy 623 *policy*; housekeeping, housewifery, husbandry, economics, political economy; national economy, the economy, stakeholder e.; statecraft, statesmanship; government 733 *governance*; ménage, regimen, regime, dispensation; regulation, law-making 953 *legislation*; reins, reins of government, ministry, cabinet, inner c.; staff work, administration; bureaucracy, civil service; secretariat, government office 687 *workshop*.

*directorship*, direction, responsibility, control, supreme c. 737 *command*; dictatorship, leadership, premiership, chairmanship, captaincy 34 *superiority*; guidance, steering, steerage, pilotage, steersmanship; pole star, lodestar 520 *guide*; controls, helm, rudder, wheel, tiller, joystick; steering wheel, power steering; needle, magnetic n., compass, binnacle; gyrocompass, gyropilot, automatic pilot, autopilot 269 *sailing aid*; direction-finding, beam, radar 281 *direction*; remote control.

**Adj.** *directing*, directorial, leading, hegemonic; directional, guiding, steering, at the helm; governing, controlling, gubernatorial, holding the reins, in the chair, heading up, in charge, in the driving seat 733 *authoritative*; dictatorial 735 *authoritarian*; supervisory, managing, managerial; executive, administrative; legislative, nomothetic; high-level, top-l. 638 *important*; economic, political; official, bureaucratic 733 *governmental*.

**Vb.** *manage*, organize, manipulate, manoeuvre, pull the strings 178 *influence*; have taped, have the measure of 490 *know*; handle, conduct, run, carry on; minister, administer, prescribe; supervise, superintend, oversee, caretake 457 *invigilate*; nurse 457 *look after*; have charge of, have in one's charge, hold the portfolio, hold the purse strings, hold the reins 612 *motivate* (see also *direct*); keep order, police, regulate; legislate, pass laws 953 *make legal*; control, govern, sway 733 *rule*; know how to manage, have a way with.

*direct*, lead, pioneer, precede 64 *come before*; boss, dictate 737 *command*; be in charge, head up, wear the trousers; hold office, hold a responsible position, have responsibility; mastermind, have overall responsibility; assume r. 917 *incur a duty*; assume command; preside, take the chair, be in the chair; head, captain, skipper, stroke; pilot, cox, steer, take the helm, hold the tiller 269 *navigate*; point 281 *point to*; show the way 547 *indicate*; shepherd, guide, conduct, lead on; introduce, compère; escort 89 *accompany*; channel, canalize, funnel; route, train, lead, lead over, lead through 281 *steer for*.

**Adv.** *in control*, in charge, in command, at the helm, at the wheel, on the bridge, in the driving seat, in the saddle, in the chair, at the head; ex officio.

## 690 Director

**N.** *director*, governing body 741 *governor*; steering committee, quango, select committee; cabinet, inner c. 692 *council*; board of directors, board, chair; staff, brass, top b., VIPs, management; manager, controller; legislator, lawgiver, lawmaker; employer, capitalist, boss 741 *master*; headman, chief, head of the household, head of state 34 *superior*; principal, head, headmaster *or* -mistress, rector, moderator, dean, vice-chancellor, chancellor; president, vice-p.; chairperson, chairman, chairwoman, speaker, presiding officer; premier, prime minister, first minister; captain, skipper; stroke, cox, master 270 *mariner*; steersman, helmsman 270 *navigator*, pilot 520 *guide*; forerunner 66 *precursor*; drill sergeant 537 *trainer*; director of studies 537 *teacher*; backseat driver 691 *adviser*; king-maker, wire-puller, animator 612 *motivator*; hidden hand 178 *influence*; organizer, planner, control freak 623 *planner*.

*leader*, charismatic l., judge (Old Testament) 741 *governor*; messiah, mahdi; ayatollah, guru; leader of the House, leader of the opposition; spearhead, centre forward; shepherd, teamster, cowhand, drover 369 *herdsman*; bell-wether; fugleman, file-leader; pacemaker; pacesetter, symposiarch, toastmaster, master of ceremonies, MC; high priest, mystagogue; coryphaeus, chorus-leader, choragus, conductor, leader of the orchestra, first violin; precentor; drum major; Caudillo, Duce, Führer 741 *autocrat*; ringleader, demagogue, rabble-rouser 738 *agitator*; captain, condottiere; technocrat.

*manager*, person in responsibility, responsible person, VIP; man *or* woman in charge, key person, kingpin, tsar 638 *notable*; procurator, administrator, executive, executor 676 *doer*; statesman *or* -woman, politician; economist, political e.; housekeeper, chatelaine, housewife, house husband; steward, bailiff, farm manager, reeve, greeve; agent, factor 754 *consignee*; superintendent, supervisor, inspector, overseer, foreman *or* -woman, ganger, gaffer; warden, house master *or* mistress, matron, nurse, senior nursing officer, tutor 660 *protector*; proctor, disciplinarian; party manager, whip, chief whip; custodian, caretaker, curator, librarian 749 *keeper*; master of hounds, whipper-in, huntsman; circus manager, ringmaster; compère.

*official*, office-holder, office-bearer, Jack-in-office, tin god; marshal, steward; shop steward; MP, Member of Parliament, MEP, Euro-MP, AM (Wales), MLA (Northern Ireland), MSP (Scotland), constituency MSP, regional MSP, constituency member, additional m., list m., regional list m., TD (Eire), MHK (Isle of Man), government servant, public s., civil s., apparatchik 742 *servant*; officer of state, high official, vizier, grand v., minister, cabinet m., secretary of state, secretary-general, secretary, under-s.; permanent s., bureaucrat, Eurocrat, mandarin 741 *officer*; judicial officer, district o., magistrate 733 *position of authority*; commissioner, prefect, intendant; consul, proconsul, praetor, quaestor, aedile; first secretary, counsellor 754 *envoy*; alderman, mayor 692 *councillor*; functionary, party official, petty o., clerk; school prefect, monitor.

## 691 Advice

**N.** *advice*, word of a., piece of a., counsel; words of wisdom, rede 498 *wisdom*; impractical advice, counsel of perfection; counselling, marriage c., debt c. 658 *therapy*; criticism, constructive c. 480 *estimate*; didacticism, moralizing, moral injunction, prescription 693 *precept*; caution 664 *warning*; recommendation, proposition, proposal, motion 512 *supposition*; suggestion, submonition, submission; tip, word to the wise 524 *hint*; guidance, briefing, instruction 524 *information*; charge, charge to the jury 959 *legal trial*; taking counsel, deliberation, consultation, mutual c., huddle, heads together, tête-à-tête, powwow, parley 584 *conference*; seeking advice, reference, referment 692 *council*; advice against 762 *deprecation*.

 *adviser*, counsellor, consultant, troubleshooter; professional consultant, life coach 696 *expert*; personal trainer 537 *trainer*; referee, arbiter, arbitrator 480 *estimator*; prescriber, commender, advocate, recommender, mover, prompter 612 *motivator*; medical adviser, therapist 658 *doctor*; legal adviser, advocate, counsel 958 *lawyer*; expert witness, amicus curiae; guide, philosopher and friend, mentor, confidant(e) 537 *teacher*; monitor, admonisher, remembrancer 505 *reminder*; Nestor, Egeria, Dutch uncle; oracle, wise man 500 *sage*; backseat driver, busybody 678 *meddler*; committee of enquiry, public enquiry, consultative body 692 *council*; focus group; information bureau, information centre, information desk, help d., call centre.

**Adj.** *advising*, advisory, consultative, deliberative; hortative, recommendatory 612 *inducing*; advising against 613 *dissuasive*; admonitory, warning 664 *cautionary*; didactic; moral, moralizing.

**Vb.** *advise*, give advice, counsel, offer c.; think best, recommend, prescribe, advocate, commend; propose, move, put to, submit, suggest 512 *propound*; prompt 524 *hint*; press, urge, exhort 612 *incite*; advise against 613 *dissuade*; admonish 664 *warn*; enjoin, charge, dic-

tate 737 *command*; advise aptly 642 *be expedient*.

 *consult*, seek advice, refer; call in, call on; refer to arbitration, ask for a second opinion, hold a public enquiry; confide in, be closeted with, have at one's elbow; take advice, listen to, be advised; accept advice, take one's cue from, submit one's judgment to another's, follow advice; sit in council, sit in conclave, put heads together, advise with, hold a consultation, hold a council of war, have a powwow with, deliberate, parley, sit round a table, compare notes 584 *confer*.

## 692 Council

**N.** *council*, council board, round table; council chamber, board room; Star Chamber, court 956 *tribunal*; Privy Council, presidium; ecclesiastical council, Curia, consistory, Bench of Bishops; vestry; cabinet, kitchen c.; panel, quango, think tank, board, advisory b., consultative body, Royal Commission; assembly, conventicle, congregation 74 *assembly*; conclave, convocation 985 *synod*; convention, congress, meeting, top-level m., summit; durbar, diet; folkmoot, moot, comitia, ecclesia; federal council, League of Nations, UNO, Security Council; municipal council, county c., regional c., district c., town c., parish c.; community c; zemstvo, soviet; council of elders, genro, Sanhedrin; sitting, session, séance, audience, hearing 584 *conference*.

 *parliament*, Mother of Parliaments, Westminster, Upper House, House of Lords, House of Peers, 'another place'; Lower House, House of Commons; European P.; senate, senatus; legislature, legislative assembly, deliberative a., consultative a., witenagemot, Loya Jirga; quorum, division.

---

**Parliaments**
Althing *or* Althingi (Iceland); Assembly of the Republic (Portugal); Bundestag, Bundesrat, (Germany; *formerly* Reichstag, Reichsrat); Bundesrat, Nationalrat (Austria); Chamber of Deputies, Senate (Italy); Chief Pleas (Sark); Congress, House of Representatives, Senate (United States); Cortes, Congress of Deputies, Senate (Spain); Diet, House of Representatives, House of Councillors (Japan); Eduskunta, Riksdag (Finland); Federal Assembly, Federal Council, State Duma (Russia; Duma *also* pre-1917 parliament); Folketing (Denmark; *formerly* Rigsdag); Great Hural (Mongolia); House of Commons, Senate (Canada); House of Representatives (New Zealand); House of Representatives, Senate (Australia); Knesset (Israel); Lok Sabha, Rajya Sabha (India); Majlis (Iran); Majlis as-Shoora, Senate (Pakistan); National Assembly, National Council of Provinces (South Africa); National Assembly/Chambre des Députés, Senate (France); National Assembly, Sejm, Senate (Poland); Nationalrat, Ständerat (Switzerland); Oireachtas, Dáil Éireann, Seanad Éireann (Republic of Ireland); Riksdag (Sweden); Sabor

(Croatia); States (Alderney, Guernsey, Jersey); States-General (Netherlands); Storting (Norway); Supreme Rada (Ukraine); Supreme Soviet (parliament of the former USSR); Tynwald, House of Keys, Legislative Council (Isle of Man).

*councillor*, privy councillor; senator, conscript fathers, Areopagite, sanhedrist; peer, life peer; Lords Spiritual, L. Temporal; representative, deputy, congressman *or* -woman, Member of Parliament, MP, Euro-MP, MEP, MSP, AM, MLA, TD, MHK 690 *official*, 754 *delegate*; backbencher, lobby fodder; parliamentarian, legislator; municipal councillor, mayor, alderman 690 *official*.

**Adj.** *parliamentary*, senatorial, congressional; unicameral, bicameral; curule, conciliar; convocational, synodal.

## 693 Precept

**N.** *precept*, firm advice 691 *advice*; direction, instruction, general i.; instructions, directions for use, care label, user's manual; injunction, charge 737 *command*; commission 751 *mandate*; order, written o., writ 737 *warrant*; rescript, decretal 480 *judgment*; prescript, prescription, ordinance, regulation 737 *decree*; canon, form, norm, formula, formulary, rubric; guidelines 81 *rule*; principle, rule, golden r., moral 496 *maxim*; recipe, receipt 658 *remedy*; commandment, statute, enactment, act, code, penal c., corpus juris 953 *legislation*; tenet, article, set of rules, constitution; ticket, party line; Ten Commandments, Twelve Tables, laws of the Medes and the Persians (see quotation at 81 *rule*); canon law, common l., unwritten l. 953 *law*; rule of custom, habit and repute, convention 610 *practice*; technicality, nice point 530 *enigma*; precedent, leading case, text 83 *example*.

**Adj.** *preceptive*, prescriptive, decretal, mandatory, binding; canonical, rubrical, statutory 953 *legal*; moralizing 496 *aphoristic*; customary, conventional, current, right-on (inf) 610 *usual*.

## 694 Skill

**N.** *skill*, skilfulness, dexterity, dexterousness, handiness, ambidexterity; grace, style 575 *elegance*; neatness, deftness, adroitness, address; ease 701 *facility*; proficiency, competence, efficiency; faculty, capability, capacity 160 *ability*; many sidedness, all-round capacity, versatility, ambidextrousness, amphibiousness; adaptability, flexibility, suppleness; touch, grip, control; mastery, mastership, wizardry, virtuosity, excellence; prowess 644 *goodness*; strong point, métier, forte, major suit; acquirement, attainment, accomplishment, skills; seamanship, air-

manship, horsemanship, marksmanship; experience, expertise, professionalism; specialism; technology, science, know-how, technique, technical knowledge, practical k. 490 *knowledge*; practical ability, clever hands, deft fingers; craftsmanship, art, artistry, delicacy, fine workmanship, art that conceals art; finish, execution 646 *perfection*; ingenuity, resourcefulness, craft, craftiness 698 *cunning*; cleverness, sharpness, nous, worldly wisdom, sophistication, lifemanship 498 *sagacity*; savoir faire, finesse, tact, discretion 463 *discrimination*; feat of skill, trick, gimmick, dodge 623 *contrivance*; sleight of hand, conjuring 542 *sleight*; funambulism, rope-dancing, tightrope walking; stratagem, brinkmanship 688 *tactics*; skilful use, exploitation 673 *use*.

*aptitude*, inborn a., innate ability, inherent a., good head for; bent, natural b. 179 *tendency*; faculty, endowment, gift, flair; turn, knack, green fingers; talent, natural t., genius, genius for; aptness, fitness, qualification.

*masterpiece*, chef-d'oeuvre, a beauty, a creation; pièce de résistance, masterwork, magnum opus; workmanlike job, craftsman's j.; stroke of genius, masterstroke, coup-de-maître, coup, feat, exploit, hat trick 676 *deed*; smash hit; tour de force, bravura, fireworks; ace, trump, clincher 644 *exceller*; work of art, objet d'art, curio, collector's piece *or* item.

**Adj.** *skilful*, good, good at, top-flight, top-notch, first-rate, ace 644 *excellent*; skilled, crack; apt, handy, dexterous, ambidextrous, deft, slick, adroit, agile, nimble, neat; nimble-fingered, green-f.; sure-footed; cunning, clever, quick, quick-witted, shrewd, smart, ingenious 498 *intelligent*; politic, diplomatic, statesmanlike 498 *wise*; adaptable, flexible, resourceful, ready; many-sided, versatile; ready for anything, panurgic; sound, able, competent, efficient, competitive; wizard, masterful, masterly, like a master, magisterial, accomplished, finished 646 *perfect*.

*gifted*, naturally g.; of many parts, talented, endowed, well-e., born for, cut out for.

*expert*, experienced, veteran, seasoned, tried, versed in, up in, well up in, au fait 490 *instructed*; skilled, trained, practised, well-p. 669 *prepared*; computer-literate; finished, passed, specialized 669 *matured*; proficient, qualified, competent, up to the mark; efficient, professional 622 *businesslike*.

*well-made*, well-crafted; craftily contrived, deep-laid; professional; finished, felicitous, happy; artistic, artificial, sophisticated, stylish 575 *elegant*; daedalian, cunning; shipshape, workmanlike.

**Vb.** *be skilful*, – deft etc. adj.; be good at, do

well 644 *be good*; shine, excel 34 *be superior*; have a turn for, have a gift for, be born for, show aptitude, show a talent for; have the knack, have the trick of, have the right touch; be in practice, be on form, be in good f., have one's eye in, have one's hand in; play one's cards well, not put a foot wrong, know what one is all about, know just when to stop; use skilfully, exploit, squeeze the last ounce out of 673 *use*; take advantage of, make hay while the sun shines 137 *profit by*; live by one's wits, get around, know all the answers, know what's what, have one's wits about one 498 *be wise*; exercise discretion 463 *discriminate*.

*be expert*, turn professional; be at the top of one's profession, be master of one's profession, be good at one's job, be a top-notcher, know one's stuff *or* one's onions, have the know-how; acquire the technique, qualify oneself 536 *learn*; have experience, be an old hand, know the ropes, know all the ins and outs, know backwards, be up to every trick, take in one's stride 490 *know*; display one's skill, play with, demonstrate, stunt 875 *be ostentatious*.

**Adv.** *skilfully*, craftily, artfully etc. adj.; well, with skill, with aplomb, like a master; handily, neatly, featly; stylishly, artistically; knowledgeably, expertly, scientifically; faultlessly, like a machine; naturally, as to the manner born, in one's stride.

## 695 Unskilfulness

**N.** *unskilfulness*, lack of skill, no gift for; lack of practice, rustiness 674 *non-use*; rawness, unripeness, immaturity 670 *undevelopment*; inexperience, inexpertness 491 *ignorance*; incapacity, inability, incompetence, inefficiency 161 *ineffectuality*; disqualification, lack of proficiency; quackery, charlatanism 850 *pretension*; clumsiness, unhandiness, lubberliness, left-handedness, awkwardness, gaucherie (see also *bungling*); backwardness, slowness 499 *unintelligence*; booby prize, wooden spoon.

*bungling*, botching, tinkering, half-measures, pale imitation, travesty 726 *noncompletion*; bungle, botch, dog's breakfast, pig's ear, cock-up, balls-up, shambles; off day, poor performance, poor show, bad job, unsatisfactory work, flop 728 *failure*; missed chance 138 *untimeliness*; hamhandedness, dropped catch, butterfingers, fumble, foozle, muff, fluff, miss, mishit, slice, bosh shot, overthrow, misthrow, misfire, own goal, friendly fire 495 *mistake*; thoughtlessness 456 *inattention*; tactlessness, heavy-handedness; infelicity, indiscretion 464 *indiscrimination*; mishandling, misapplication 675 *misuse*; too many cooks; mismanagement, misrule, misgovernment, maladministration

481 *misjudgment*; misconduct, antics; much ado about nothing, wild-goose chase 641 *lost labour*.

**Adj.** *unskilful*, ungifted, untalented, talentless, unendowed, unaccomplished; stick-in-the-mud, unversatile 679 *inactive*; disqualified, unadapted, unadaptable, unfit, inept 25 *unapt*; unable, incapable 161 *impotent*; incompetent, inefficient, ineffectual; unpractical, unbusinesslike, unstatesmanlike, undiplomatic; impolitic, ill-considered, stupid, foolish 499 *unwise*; thoughtless 456 *inattentive*; wild, giddy, happy-go-lucky 456 *lightminded*; feckless, futile; not up to scratch, failed 728 *unsuccessful*; inadequate 636 *insufficient*.

*unskilled*, raw, green, unripe, undeveloped 670 *immature*; uninitiated, under training, untrained, apprentice, half-skilled, semi-s. 670 *unprepared*; unqualified, inexpert, scratch, inexperienced, ignorant, unversed, unconversant, untaught 491 *uninstructed*; nonprofessional, ham, lay, amateurish, amateur, self-taught; unscientific, unsound, charlatan, quack, quackish; specious, pretentious 850 *affected*.

*clumsy*, awkward, uneasy, gauche, gawky, gawkish, boorish, churlish, uncouth 885 *discourteous*; stuttering 580 *stammering*; tactless, indiscreet 464 *indiscriminating*; bumbling, bungling; lubberly, unhandy, maladroit, all thumbs, butter-fingered; left-handed, cack-h., one-h., heavy-h., ham-h., heavy-footed; ungainly, lumbering, hulking, gangling, stumbling, shambling; stiff, rusty 674 *unused*; unaccustomed, unpractised, out of practice, out of training, out of kilter, off form 611 *unhabituated*; losing one's touch, slipping; slovenly, slatternly, slapdash 458 *negligent*; fumbling, groping, tentative 461 *experimental*; ungraceful, graceless, clownish 576 *inelegant*; top-heavy, lop-sided 29 *unequal*; cumbersome, ponderous, clumsily built, ungainly, unmanageable, unsteerable 195 *unwieldy*; unadjusted 495 *inexact*.

*bungled*, badly done, botched, foozled, messed up, fouled up, screwed up, mismanaged, mishandled etc. vb.; faulty 647 *imperfect*; misguided, ill-advised, ill-considered, ill-judged; ill-prepared, unplanned 670 *unprepared*; ill-contrived, ill-devised, cobbled together; unhappy, infelicitous; crude, rough and ready, inartistic, amateurish, jerry-built, home-made, do-it-yourself 699 *artless*; slapdash, superficial, perfunctory 458 *neglected*; half-baked 726 *uncompleted*.

**Vb.** *be unskilful*, – inept, unqualified etc. adj.; not know how 491 *not know*; show one's ignorance, be handless, be clueless, go the wrong way about it, start at the wrong end; do things by halves, tinker, paper over the cracks 726 *not complete*; burn one's fingers, catch a Tartar, reckon without one's host 508 *not expect*; maladminister, mishandle, mismanage, misconduct, misrule, misgovern; misapply 675 *misuse*; misdirect 495 *blunder*; forget one's words, fluff one's lines, miss one's cue 506 *forget*; ham, overact, underact; lose one's cunning, lose one's skill, go rusty, get out of practice 611 *disaccustom*; come a cropper, come unstuck 728 *fail*; lose one's nerve, lose one's head 854 *be nervous*.

*act foolishly*, not know what one is about, act in one's own worst interests, stand in one's own light, cut one's own throat, cut off one's nose to spite one's face, throw out the baby with the bath water, make a fool of oneself, make an ass of oneself, lose face, be left with egg all over one's face 497 *be absurd*; become an object lesson, quarrel with one's bread and butter, bite the hand that feeds one, kill the goose that lays the golden eggs, spoil the ship for a ha'porth of tar, bring one's house about one's ears, knock one's head against a brick wall, put the cart before the horse, have too many eggs in one basket; bite off more than one can chew, have too many irons in the fire; spoil one's chances 138 *lose a chance*; put a square peg in a round hole, 'put new wine into old bottles' 495 *blunder*;

> No man putteth a piece of new cloth unto an old garment, for that which is put in to fill it up taketh from the garment, and the rent is made worse. Neither do men put new wine into old bottles: else the bottles break, and the wine runneth out, and the bottles perish: but they put new wine into new bottles, and both are preserved.
> Bible, Jesus in St Matthew's Gospel

labour in vain 470 *attempt the impossible*; go on a fool's errand 641 *waste effort*; 'strain at a gnat and swallow a camel'.

> Woe unto you, scribes and Pharisees, hypocrites! For ye pay tithe of mint and anise and cummin, and have omitted the weightier matters of the law, judgment, mercy and faith: these ought ye to have done, and not to leave the other undone. Ye blind guides, which strain at a gnat, and swallow a camel.
> Bible, Jesus in St Matthew's Gospel

*be clumsy*, lumber, bumble, galumph, hulk, get in the way, be de trop, stand in the light; trip, trip over, stumble, blunder, boob; not look where one is going 456 *be inattentive*; stutter 580 *stammer*; fumble, grope, flounder 461 *be tentative*; take two bites at a cherry, muff, fluff, foozle; pull, slice, mishit, misthrow; overthrow, overshoot 306 *overstep*; play into the hands of, give a catch, give a chance; spill, slop, drop, drop a catch, drop a sitter 311 *let fall*; catch a crab; let the cat out of the bag,

bungle, drop a brick, put one's foot in it, make a faux pas, get egg on one's face 495 *blunder*; botch, spoil, mar, blot 655 *impair*; fool with 678 *meddle*; make a mess of it, make a hash of it 728 *miscarry*; do a bad job, make a poor fist at 728 *fail*.

## 696 Proficient person

**N.** *proficient person*, sound player, expert, adept, dab hand, dabster; do-it-yourself type, all-rounder, Jack of all trades, handyman, admirable Crichton 646 *paragon*; Renaissance man, person of many parts; maître, master, past m., graduate, cordon bleu; intellectual, mastermind 500 *sage*; genius, wizard, gifted child 864 *prodigy*; magician 545 *conjuror*; maestro, virtuoso; bravura player 413 *musician*; prima donna, first fiddle, top sawyer, prizewinner, gold-medallist, champion, titleholder, cup-h., dan, black belt, sensei, ace 644 *exceller*; picked man, capped player, star p., seeded p., white hope; crack shot, dead s. 287 *shooter*; acrobat, gymnast 162 *athlete*.

*expert*, no novice, practitioner; professional, pro, specialist, authority, doyen, professor 537 *teacher*; pundit, guru, savant, polymath, walking encyclopaedia 492 *scholar*; veteran, old hand, old stager, old dog, old soldier, warhorse, sea dog, shellback; practised hand, practised eye; sophisticate, knowing person, smart customer, cunning fellow 698 *slyboots*; anorak, freak, geek 504 *enthusiast*; sharp, sharper 545 *trickster*; cosmopolitan, citizen of the world, man *or* woman about town, man *or* woman of the world, businessman *or* -woman, career woman, careerist; tactician, strategist, politician; diplomat, diplomatist; artist, craftsman *or* -woman; technician, skilled worker 686 *artisan*; experienced hand, right person for the job, key man *or* woman; consultant 691 *adviser*; boffin, backroom boy 623 *planner*; cognoscente, connoisseur, fancier.

## 697 Bungler

**N.** *bungler*, failure 728 *loser*; bad learner, the despair of –; incompetent, botcher, tinkerer; bumbler, blunderer, blunderhead, marplot, bungling idiot; mismanager, fumbler, muffer, muff, butterfingers; lump, lout, clumsy l., clumsy clot, hulk, lubber, looby, swab, bull in a china shop; duffer, stooge, clown, buffoon, booby, galoot, clot, clod, stick, hick, oaf, ass, plonker, big girl's blouse 501 *fool*; slob, sloven, slattern 61 *slut*; scribbler, hack, dauber, bad hand, poor h., bad shot, poor s., no marksman; amateur, cowboy, dabbler, ham, ladder gang; jack of all trades and master of none; novice, greenhorn, colt, raw recruit, sorcerer's appren-

tice 538 *beginner*; quack 545 *impostor*; landlubber, fair-weather sailor, freshwater s., horse
marine; ass in a lion's skin, jackdaw in peacock's feathers; fish out of water, square peg in
a round hole 25 *misfit*.

## 698 Cunning

**N.** *cunning*, craft 694 *skill*; know-how, lore 490
*knowledge*; resourcefulness, inventiveness,
ingenuity 513 *imagination*; guile, gamesmanship, cunningness, craftiness, artfulness,
subtlety, wiliness, slyness, foxiness; stealthiness, stealth 523 *latency*; cageyness 525 *concealment*; suppleness, slipperiness, shiftiness;
knavery, chicanery, chicane 930 *foul play*; finesse, jugglery 542 *sleight*; cheating, monkey
business, circumvention 542 *deception*; double-
dealing, imposture 541 *duplicity*; smoothness
925 *flattery*; disguise 525 *concealment*; wheeling
and dealing, manoeuvring, temporizing 688
*tactics*; policy, diplomacy, Machiavellism, realpolitik; jobbery, gerrymandering 930 *improbity*;
underhand dealing, under-the-counter
dealing, sharp practice; backdoor influence
178 *influence*; intrigue 623 *plot*.

*stratagem*, ruse, wile, art, artifice, resource,
resort, device, wrinkle, ploy, shift, dodge 623
*contrivance*; machination, game, little g. 623
*plot*; subterfuge, evasion; excuse 614 *pretext*;
white lie 543 *mental dishonesty*; cheat 542 *deception*; trick, old t., box of tricks, tricks of the
trade, rules of the game 542 *trickery*; feint,
catch, net, web, ambush, Greek gift, Trojan
horse, stalking h. 542 *trap*; ditch, pit 663 *pitfall*; Parthian shot; web of cunning, web of
deceit; blind, dust thrown in the eyes, red herring, flag of convenience 542 *sham*; thin end of
the wedge, manoeuvre, move 688 *tactics*.

*slyboots*, crafty fellow, artful dodger, wily
person, serpent, snake, fox, Reynard; lurker
527 *hider*; snake in the grass 663 *troublemaker*;
fraud, shammer, dissembler, wolf in sheep's
clothing, hypocrite, double-crosser 545
*deceiver*; cheat, sharper 545 *trickster*; juggler 545
*conjuror*; smoothie, glib tongue 925 *flatterer*;
diplomatist, Machiavelli, intriguer, plotter,
schemer 623 *planner*; strategist, tactician,
manoeuvrer, wheeler-dealer; wire-puller 612
*motivator*.

**Adj.** *cunning*, learned, knowledgeable 498
*wise*; crafty, disingenuous, artful, sly, wily,
subtle, serpentine, foxy, vulpine, feline; full of
ruses, tricky, tricksy; secret 525 *stealthy*;
scheming, contriving, practising, plotting,
intriguing, Machiavellian 623 *planning*;
knowing, fly, slick, smart, sophisticated,
urbane; canny, pawky, sharp, astute, shrewd,
acute; too clever for, too clever by half, too

smart for his *or* her own good, up to everything, not to be caught napping, no flies on,
not born yesterday 498 *intelligent*; not to be
drawn, cagey 525 *reticent*; experienced 694
*skilful*; resourceful, ingenious; tactical, strategical, deep-laid, well-planned; full of snares,
insidious 930 *perfidious*; shifty, slippery, time-
serving, temporizing 518 *equivocal*; deceitful,
flattering 542 *deceiving*; knavish 930 *rascally*;
crooked, devious 930 *dishonest*.

**Vb.** *be cunning*, – sly etc. adj.; play the fox,
try a ruse, finesse, shift, dodge, juggle,
manoeuvre, jockey, double-cross, twist, turn
251 *wriggle*; lie low 523 *lurk*; intrigue, scheme,
play a deep game, spin a web, weave a plot,
have an ulterior motive, have an axe to grind,
have an eye to the main chance 623 *plot*; contrive, wangle, devise 623 *plan*; monkey about
with, play tricks w., tinker, gerrymander; circumvent, overreach, pull a fast one, steal a
march on, trick, cheat 542 *deceive*; sweet-talk,
blarney 925 *flatter*; temporize, play for time; be
too clever for, be one up on, outsmart, outwit,
go one better, know a trick worth two of that
306 *outdo*; be too quick for, snatch from under
one's nose, pip at the post; waylay, dig a pit
for, undermine, bait the trap 527 *ambush*;
introduce the thin end of the wedge, create a
catch-22 situation (see quotation at 663 *pitfall*), get one's foot in the door; match in cunning, see the catch, avoid the trap; have a card
up one's sleeve, have a shot in one's locker;
know all the answers, live by one's wits.

**Adv.** *cunningly*, artfully, slily, on the sly.

## 699 Artlessness

**N.** *artlessness*, simplicity, simple-mindedness;
naivety, ingenuousness, guilelessness 935 *innocence*; inexperience, unworldliness; unaffectedness, unsophistication, naturalness,
freedom from artifice 573 *plainness*; sincerity,
candour, frankness; bluntness, matter-of-
factness, outspokenness 540 *veracity*; truth,
honesty 929 *probity*; uncivilized state, primitiveness, savagery; darkness, barbarism, no science, no art 491 *ignorance*; indifference to art,
Philistinism; no artistry 647 *imperfection*;
uncouthness, vulgarity, crudity 847 *bad taste*.

*ingenue*, ingenuous person,
unsophisticated p., Candide; child of nature,
savage, noble s.; enfant terrible; lamb, babe in
arms 935 *innocent*; simpleton 501 *ninny*; greenhorn, novice 538 *beginner*; rough diamond,
plain man, Philistine; simple soul, pure heart;
provincial, yokel, rustic, country cousin 869
*country dweller*.

**Adj.** *artless*, without art, without artifice,
without tricks; unstudied, unprepared; uncom-

plicated, uncontrived 44 *simple*; unadorned, unvarnished 573 *plain*; native, natural, unartificial, homespun, homemade; do-it-yourself 695 *unskilled*; in a state of nature, uncivilized, wild, savage, primitive, unguided, untutored, unlearned, unscientific, backward 491 *ignorant*; Arcadian, unsophisticated, ingenuous, naive, childlike 935 *innocent*; born yesterday, green, unworldly, simple-minded, callow, wet behind the ears; guileless, free from guile, unsuspicious, confiding; unaffected, unconstrained, unreserved, uninhibited 609 *spontaneous*; candid, frank, open, undissembling, straightforward 540 *veracious*; undesigning, single, single-hearted, true, honest, sincere 929 *honourable*; above-board, on the level; blunt, outspoken, free-spoken; transparent 522 *undisguised*; unpoetical, prosaic, no-nonsense, matter-of-fact, down-to-earth, literal, literal-minded 494 *accurate*; shy, inarticulate, unassuming, unpretentious, unpretending 874 *modest*; inartistic, Philistine; unmusical, tone-deaf 416 *deaf*; unrefined, unpolished, uncultured, uncouth 847 *vulgar*; hoydenish 847 *ill-bred*.

**Vb.** *be artless*, – natural etc. adj.; live in a state of nature, live in ignorance, know no better; have no guile, have no tricks 935 *be innocent*; have no affectations, eschew artifice; confide, wear one's heart upon one's sleeve; look one in the face, look one straight in the eyes, call a spade a spade, say what is in one's mind, speak one's mind 573 *speak plainly*; not mince one's words 540 *be truthful*.

**Adv.** *artlessly*, without art, without pretensions, without affectation; frankly, sincerely, openly, with an open heart.

SECTION FOUR

## Antagonism

### 700 Difficulty

**N.** *difficulty*, hardness, arduousness, laboriousness, the hard way 682 *exertion*; impracticability, no go, nonstarter 470 *impossibility*; intricacy, perplexity, inextricability, involvement 61 *complexity*; complication 832 *aggravation*; obscurity, impenetrability 517 *unintelligibility*; inconvenience, awkwardness, embarrassment 643 *inexpedience*; drag 333 *friction*; difficult terrain, rough ground, hard going, bad patch 259 *roughness*; quagmire, slough 347 *marsh*; knot, Gordian k. 251 *coil*; problem, thorny p., crux, hard nut to crack, poser, teaser, puzzle, the sixty-four-thousand-dollar question, headache 530 *enigma*; impediment, handicap, obstacle, snag, rub, where the shoe pinches 702 *hindrance*; teething troubles 702 *hitch*; maze, crooked path 251 *convolution*; cul-de-sac, dead end, impasse, no-go area, blank wall 264 *closure*; deadlock, standstill, logjam, stoppage, gridlock, 145 *stop*; stress, brunt, burden 684 *fatigue*; trial, ordeal, temptation, tribulation, vexation 825 *suffering*; trouble, sea of troubles 731 *adversity*; bad time, bad day, bad hair d., annus horribilis, mauvais quart d'heure; difficult person, handful, one's despair, kittle cattle; hot potato.

*hard task*, test, real t., trial of strength; labours of Hercules, Herculean task, superhuman t., thankless t., never-ending t., Sisyphean labour; task, job, bugger (inf), work cut out, hard row to hoe, hard furrow to plough, no picnic, a mountain to climb, a handful, tall order, tough assignment, stiff job, hard work, uphill struggle 682 *labour*.

*predicament*, embarrassment, false position, delicate situation; nonplus, quandary, dilemma, cleft stick; grey area, borderline case 474 *dubiety*; catch-22 situation (see quotation at 663 *pitfall*); fix, jam, hole, scrape, hot water, trouble, fine kettle of fish, pickle, shtook, stew, soup, imbroglio, mess, muddle; pinch, strait, straits, pass, pretty p.; slippery slope, sticky wicket, tight corner, painting oneself into a corner, diplomatic incident, ticklish situation, tricky s., hot seat 661 *danger*; critical situation, exigency, emergency 137 *crisis*.

**Adj.** *difficult*, hard, tough, formidable; steep, arduous, uphill; inconvenient, onerous, burdensome, irksome, toilsome, bothersome, plaguy 682 *laborious*; exacting, demanding, high maintenance 684 *fatiguing*; big, of Herculean *or* Sisyphean proportions, insuperable, impracticable 470 *impossible*; offering a problem, problematic, more easily said than done; delicate, ticklish, tricky; embarrassing, awkward, unwieldy, unmanageable, hard to cope with, not easily tackled; out of hand, intractable, refractory 738 *disobedient*; recalcitrant, stubborn, unyielding, perverse 602 *obstinate*; ill-behaved, naughty 934 *wicked*; perplexing, clueless, obscure 517 *unintelligible*; knotty, complex, complicated, inextricable, labyrinthine 251 *intricate*; impenetrable, impassable, trackless, pathless, unnavigable; thorny, rugged, craggy 259 *rough*; sticky, critical 661 *dangerous*.

*in difficulties*, hampered 702 *hindered*; labouring, labouring under difficulties; in a quandary, in a dilemma, in a cleft stick, between two stools, between Scylla and Charybdis, between the devil and the deep blue sea 474 *doubting*; baffled, clueless, nonplussed 517 *puzzled*; in a jam, in a fix, on the hook, up a gum tree, up the creek, up shit creek without a paddle (sl), in a spot, in a hole, in a scrape, in hot water, in the soup, in a pickle; in deep water, out of one's depth, under fire, not out of the wood, in danger, on the danger list, on a hit list, in the hot seat 661 *endangered*; worried, beset with difficulties, harassed with problems, tormented with anxiety 825 *suffering*; under pressure, up against it, in a catch-22 situation (see quotation at 663 *pitfall*), hard pressed, sore p., hard put to it, driven to extremities; in dire straits, in distressed circumstances; left holding the baby, left in the lurch; at one's wits' end, at the end of one's tether, cornered, at bay, with one's back against the wall; stuck, stuck fast, aground 728 *grounded*.

**Vb.** *be difficult*, – hard etc. adj.; make things difficult, make difficulties for; complicate, complicate matters 63 *bedevil*; put one on the spot, inconvenience, put to i., bother, be easier said than done, irk, plague, try one's patience, lead one a merry dance, be a thorn in one's flesh, be one's bête noire, go against the grain 827 *trouble*; present difficulties, set one a problem, pose, perplex, baffle, non-plus, stump 474 *puzzle*; encumber, clog, hamper, obstruct 702 *hinder*; make things worse 832 *aggravate*; lead to an impasse, create deadlock 470 *make impossible*; go hard with, run one hard, drive to the wall 661 *endanger*.

*be in difficulty*, have a problem; tread carefully, tread on eggs, walk among eggs, pick one's way 461 *be tentative*; have one's hands full, have more than one can cope with 678 *be busy*; not know which way to turn, be at a loss 474 *be uncertain*; have difficulties, have one's work cut out, be put to it, be hard put to it, be put to trouble, have trouble with; run into trouble, fall into difficulties, strike a bad patch; be asking for trouble, fish in troubled waters; let oneself in for, cop it, catch it, catch a packet, catch a Tartar, have a wolf by the ears, have a tiger by the tail, stir up a hornet's nest; have a hard time of it 731 *have trouble*; bear the brunt, feel the pinch 825 *suffer*; have more than enough, sink under the burden 684 *be fatigued*; invite difficulty, make it hard for oneself, bring it on oneself, make a problem of, make heavy weather of, flounder; stick, come unstuck 728 *miscarry*; do it the hard way, swim upstream, breast the current, struggle, fight 716 *contend*; have to face it, live dangerously 661 *face danger*; labour under difficulties, be disadvantaged, labour under a disadvantage, have one hand tied behind one's back, be handicapped by.

**Adv.** *with difficulty*, with much ado, hardly; the hard way, uphill, against the stream, against the wind, against the grain; despite, in spite of, in the teeth of; at a pinch; in difficulty.

## 701 Facility

**N.** *facility*, easiness, ease, convenience, comfort; flexibility, pliancy 327 *softness*; capability, capacity, feasibility 469 *possibility*; comprehensibility 516 *intelligibility*; facilitation, easing, making easy, simplification, dumbing down, smoothing, disencumbrance, disentanglement, disengagement, removal of difficulties 746 *liberation*; free hand, full play, full scope, blank cheque, clean slate 744 *scope*; facilities, provision for 703 *aid*; leave 756 *permission*; simplicity, no complication 44 *simpleness*; straightforwardness, no difficulty, no competition; an open-and-shut case; no friction, easy going, calm seas 258 *smoothness*; fair wind, clear coast, clear road 137 *opportunity*; straight road, royal r., highway, 'primrose path' (see quotation at 655 *deterioration*) 624 *road*; downhill 309 *descent*.

*easy thing*, no trouble, no sweat, a pleasure, child's play, kid's stuff, no-brainer; soft option, short work, light work, cushy number, sinecure 679 *inactivity*; picnic, doddle 837 *amusement*; chickenfeed, peanuts, piece of cake, money for jam *or* old rope; easy money, fast buck; smooth sailing, plain s., easy ride; nothing to it, sitter, easy target, sitting duck; easy meat, soft touch; pushover, walkover 727 *victory*; cinch, sure thing, dead cert 473 *certainty*.

**Adj.** *easy*, facile, undemanding, cushy; effortless, painless; light, short; frictionless 258 *smooth*; uncomplicated, user-friendly 44 *simple*; not hard, not difficult, foolproof; easy as pie, easily done, easily managed, no sooner said than done; as easy as falling off a log, as simple as ABC; feasible 469 *possible*; easing, facilitating, helpful 703 *aiding*; downhill, downstream, with the current, with the tide, with the crowd; convenient 376 *comfortable*; approachable, within reach, within easy reach 289 *accessible*; open to all 263 *open*; comprehensible, for the million 516 *intelligible*.

*tractable*, manageable, easy-going 597 *willing*; submissive 721 *submitting*; yielding, malleable, ductile, pliant 327 *flexible*; smooth-running, well-oiled, frictionless; handy, manoeuvrable, labour-saving.

*facilitated*, simplified, made easy; disembarrassed, disencumbered, disburdened, untrammelled, unloaded, light; disengaged, unimpeded, unobstructed, untrammelled, unfettered, unrestrained 744 *unconfined*; aided, given a chance, given a leg up, helped on one's way; in one's element, at home, quite at home, at ease 376 *comfortable.*

**Vb.** *be easy,* – simple etc. adj.; be trouble-free, require no effort, present no difficulties, give no trouble, make no demands; be open to all, be had for the asking; be one's for the asking, come out easily, be easily solved, have a simple answer 516 *be intelligible*; run well, go w., work w., go like clockwork 258 *go smoothly.*

*do easily,* have no trouble, see one's way to; make nothing of, make light of, make no bones about, make short work of, do it standing on one's head, do it with one hand tied behind one's back; have it all one's own way, carry all before one, have it in the bag, hold all the trumps, win hands down, win at a canter, have a walkover 727 *win*; sail home, coast h., freewheel; be at ease, be at home, be in one's element, take in one's stride, take to like a duck to water; take it easy 685 *be refreshed*; not strain oneself, drift with the tide, swim with the stream 721 *submit*; spare effort, save oneself trouble, take the easy way out, take the line of least resistance, look for a short cut.

*facilitate,* ease, make easy; iron out 258 *smooth*; grease, oil 334 *lubricate*; explain, gloss, simplify, vulgarize, popularize, dumb down 520 *interpret*; provide the means, enable 160 *empower*; make way for, not stand in the way, leave it open, allow 756 *permit*; give a chance to, put one in the way of 469 *make possible*; help, help on, speed, accelerate, expedite 703 *aid*; pioneer, open up, clear the way, blaze a trail, make a path for 64 *come before*; pave the way, bridge the gap; give full play to, make an opening for, leave open, leave a loophole 744 *give scope.*

*disencumber,* free, set free, liberate, unshackle, unfetter 668 *deliver*; clear, clear the ground, weed, clear away, unclog 648 *clean*; derestrict, deobstruct; cut through red tape; disengage, disentangle, extricate 62 *unravel*; unknot, untie 46 *disunite*; cut the knot, cut the Gordian k. 46 *cut*; ease, lighten, take off one's shoulders, unload, unhamper, unburden, disburden, ease the burden, alleviate, obviate 831 *relieve.*

**Adv.** *easily,* readily, smoothly, like clockwork; on wheels, swimmingly; effortlessly, with no effort, by the flick of a switch; without difficulty, with one's eyes closed, with one hand tied behind one's back, just like that; without a hitch, without let or hindrance, freely, without obstruction, on the nod; on easy terms.

## 702 Hindrance

**N.** *hindrance,* let or h., impediment, rub; inhibition, fixation, hang-up, block, emotional baggage; stalling, thwarting, obstruction, frustration; hampering, shackling, clogging etc. vb.; stopping up, blockage, logjam, blocking, bed-blocking, shutting 264 *closure*; blockade, siege 712 *attack*; limitation, restriction, control, squeeze 747 *restraint*; arrest 747 *detention*; check, retardation, retardment, deceleration 278 *slowness*; drag 333 *friction*; interference, meddling 678 *overactivity*; interruption, interception, interposition, intervention 231 *interjacency*; obtrusion 303 *insertion*; objection 762 *deprecation*; obstructiveness, picketing, secondary p., sabotage 704 *opposition*; countermeasure, strikebreaking, lockout 182 *counteraction*; defence 715 *resistance*; discouragement, active d., disincentive 613 *dissuasion*; hostility 924 *disapprobation*; blacking, boycott 620 *avoidance*; forestalling, prevention; prophylaxis, sanitation 652 *hygiene*; sterilization, birth control 172 *contraception*; dental dam; ban, embargo, no-no 757 *prohibition*; capacity for hindrance, nuisance value.

*obstacle,* impediment, hindrance, nuisance, drawback, inconvenience, handicap 700 *difficulty*; bunker, hazard; bottleneck, blockage, roadblock, rolling r., contraflow, traffic jam, logjam; a hindrance, wheel clamp, tie, tether 47 *bond*; previous engagement 138 *untimeliness*; red tape, regulations; snag, block, stop, stymie; stumbling block, tripwire, hurdle, hedge, ditch, moat; jump, water-j.; something in the way, lion in the path (see also *hinderer*); barrier, bulkhead, wall, brick w., stone w., sea w., groyne, boom, dam, weir, dike, embankment 662 *safeguard*; bulwark, breastplate, buffer, parapet, portcullis, barbed wire, razor w. 713 *defences*; fence, blockade 235 *enclosure*; curtain, 'Iron C.' (see quotation at 57 *exclusion*); Bamboo C. 231 *partition*; stile, gate, turnstile, tollgate; crosswind, headwind, crosscurrent; impasse, deadlock, stalemate, vicious circle, 'catch-22' (see quotation at 663 *pitfall*); cul-de-sac, blind alley, dead end, blank wall.

*hitch,* unexpected obstacle, snag, catch, lightning strike 145 *strike*; repulse, rebuff 760 *refusal*; contretemps, spot of trouble; teething troubles; technical hitch, operational difficulty, breakdown, failure, engine f., engine trouble; puncture, flat; leak, burst pipe; fuse, short circuit; stoppage, holdup, setback 145 *stop*; something wrong, computer malfunction, screw loose, spanner in the works, fly in the ointment.

*encumbrance,* handicap; drag, clog, shackle,

chain 748 *fetter*; trammels, meshes, toils; impedimenta, baggage, luggage, lumber; cross, millstone, albatross round one's neck, weight on one's shoulders, dead weight 322 *gravity*; pack, fardel, burden, load, overload, last straw; onus, incubus, Old Man of the Sea; family commitments, dependants; mortgage, debts 803 *debt*.

*hinderer*, hindrance; red herring 10 *irrelevance*; wet blanket, damper, spoilsport, killjoy; marplot 697 *bungler*; dog in the manger, thwarter, frustrator; interceptor, fielder; obstructor, staller; obstructionist, filibuster, saboteur; botherer, heckler, interrupter, interjector, barracker; intervener, interferer 678 *meddler*; interloper, intruder, gatecrasher, uninvited guest 59 *intruder*; mischief-maker, spoiler, poltergeist, gremlin 663 *troublemaker*; challenger 705 *opponent*; rival, competitor 716 *contender*.

**Adj.** *hindering*, impeding, obstructive, stalling, delaying, dragging; frustrating, thwarting etc. vb.; cross, contrary, unfavourable 731 *adverse*; restrictive, cramping, clogging 747 *restraining*; prohibitive, preventive 757 *prohibiting*; prophylactic, counteractive 182 *counteracting*; upsetting, disconcerting, offputting; intrusive, obtrusive, not wanted 59 *extraneous*; interloping, intercepting, interfering 678 *meddling*; blocking, in the way, in the light; inconvenient 643 *inexpedient*; hard, rough, snaggy 700 *difficult*; onerous, crushing, burdensome, cumbrous 322 *weighty*; tripping, entangling; choking, strangling, stifling; disincentive, discouraging; disheartening, damping 613 *dissuasive*; unhelpful, uncooperative, unaccommodating 598 *unwilling*; defensive, oppositional 704 *opposing*.

*hindered*, clogged, waterlogged, cramped, overgrown; handicapped, disadvantaged, encumbered, burdened with, lumbered w., saddled w., stuck w.; frustrated, thwarted, stymied etc. vb.; up against a brick wall; held up, delayed, held back, stuck, becalmed, windbound, fogbound, snowbound, snowed-up 747 *restrained*; stopped, prevented 757 *prohibited*; in check, hard-pressed, cornered, treed 700 *in difficulties*; heavy-laden, overburdened 684 *fatigued*; left in the lurch, unaided, singlehanded; marooned, stranded, left high and dry, up the creek.

**Vb.** *hinder*, hamper, obstruct, impede; delay, use Fabian tactics; bother, annoy, inconvenience 827 *trouble*; embarrass, disconcert, upset, disorder 63 *derange*; trip, trip up, get under one's feet; tangle, entangle, enmesh 542 *ensnare*; get in the way, stand in one's light, cross one's path; come between, intervene,

interpose 678 *meddle*; intercept, cut off, head off, undermine, stop one in the act, cut the ground from under one's feet, pull the rug from under one's f.; nip, nip in the bud, stifle, choke; gag, muzzle 578 *make mute*; suffocate, repress 165 *suppress*; quell, shoot down, kill stone dead 362 *kill*; hamper, burden, cumber, encumber; press, press down, hang like a millstone round one's neck 322 *weigh*; load with, saddle w. 193 *load*; cramp, handicap, shackle, trammel, tie one's hands, tie hand and foot 747 *fetter*; put under house arrest, put under curfew; restrict, circumscribe 236 *limit*; check, brake, be a drag on, hold back 747 *restrain*; hold up, slow down, set one back 278 *retard*; lame, cripple, hobble, hamstring, paralyse 161 *disable*; scotch, wing 655 *wound*; clip the wings, cramp the style of, take the wind out of one's sails; discountenance, put out of countenance 867 *shame*; intimidate, put off, deter 854 *frighten*; discourage, dishearten 613 *dissuade*; be the spectre at the feast, mar, spoil 655 *impair*; damp, damp down, throw cold water on; snub, rebuff 760 *refuse*.

*obstruct*, intervene, interpose, interfere 678 *meddle*; obtrude, interlope 297 *intrude*; stymie, snooker, stand in the way 231 *lie between*; buzz, jostle, crowd, elbow, squeeze; sit on one's tail 284 *follow*; stop, intercept, occlude, stop up, block, block up, wall up 264 *close*; jam, jam tight, foul up, cause a stoppage, bring to a standstill; bandage, bind 350 *staunch*; dam, dam up, earth up, embank; divert, draw off 495 *mislead*; fend off, stave off, stall off 713 *parry*; barricade 235 *enclose*; fence, hedge in, blockade 232 *circumscribe*; deny access, keep out 57 *exclude*; prevent, not allow, inhibit, ban, bar, debar 757 *prohibit*.

*be obstructive*, make it hard for, give trouble, play up 700 *be difficult*; put off, stall, stonewall; not play ball, noncooperate 598 *be unwilling*; baffle, foil, stymie, balk, be a dog in the manger; counter 182 *counteract*; check, countercheck, thwart, frustrate; object, raise objections 704 *oppose*; interrupt, interject, heckle, barrack; refuse a hearing, shout down 400 *be loud*; take evasive action 620 *avoid*; talk out time, filibuster 581 *be loquacious*; play for time, use Fabian tactics, protract, drag out 113 *spin out*; strike 145 *halt*; picket, molest; sabotage, throw a spanner in the works, gum up the works, spike the guns, put a spoke in one's wheel; cross one's bows, take the wind out of one's sails.

### 703 Aid

**N.** *aid*, assistance, help, helping hand, leg-up, lift, boost; succour, rescue 668 *deliverance*;

comfort, support, moral s., backing, seconding, abetment, encouragement; reinforcement 162 *strengthening*; helpfulness, willing help, cordial assistance, customer service 706 *cooperation*; service, ministry, ministration, subministration 897 *kind act*; interest, friendly i., kindly i., good offices; custom 792 *purchase*; patronage, auspices, sponsorship, countenance, suffrage, favour 660 *protection*, 178 *influence*; good will, charity, sympathy, tea and s. 897 *benevolence*; intercession 981 *prayers*; advocacy, championship; good advice, constructive criticism 691 *advice*; promotion, furtherance, advancement 654 *improvement*; nursing, spoonfeeding, featherbedding; first aid, medical assistance 658 *medical art*; relief, easing 685 *refreshment*; preferential treatment, most favoured nation t.; favourable conditions, favourable circumstances 730 *prosperity*; fair wind, following w., tail w. 287 *propulsion*; facilitation, facilities, magic carpet, magic wand, Aladdin's lamp 701 *facility*; self-help, DIY, do-it-yourself 744 *independence*.

*economic aid*, monetary help, pecuniary assistance, subvention; donation 781 *gift*; charity 901 *philanthropy*; social security, benefit, welfare b., welfare, unemployment benefit, job-seeker's allowance, the dole, broo (Scots), sickness benefit, supplementary b., child b.; loan, temporary accommodation 802 *credit*; subsidy, hand-out, bounty, grant, allowance, expense account; stipend, bursary, scholarship 962 *reward*; supplies, maintenance, alimony, aliment, support, child support, keep, upkeep, free board and lodging, dependency culture 633 *provision*; manna, 'manna in the wilderness' 301 *food*.

> Our fathers did eat manna in the desert; as it is written, He gave them bread from heaven to eat.
> Bible, St John's Gospel

*aider*, help, helper, assister, assistant, lieutenant, henchman, aide, right-hand man *or* woman, man Friday, girl F., backing group; stand-by, support, mainstay; tower of strength, rock 660 *protector*; district nurse, community n., Diana n., Macmillan n., Marie Curie n., palliative care n., social worker, Child Support Agency, CSA, helpline, helpdesk, counsellor, information bureau, information centre, information desk, call centre 691 *adviser*; good neighbour, Good Samaritan, friend in need; ally, brother-in-arms 707 *collaborator*; relieving force, reinforcements, recruits 707 *auxiliary*; deus ex machina, genie of the lamp, fairy godmother 903 *benefactor*; promoter, sponsor 707 *patron*; booster, friendly critic 923 *commender*; abettor, instigator 612 *motivator*; factor, useful

ingredient 58 *component*; springboard, jumping-off ground 628 *instrument*.

**Adj.** *aiding*, helpful, obliging 706 *cooperative*; kind, well-disposed, well-intentioned 897 *benevolent*; neighbourly 880 *friendly*; favourable, propitious; supporting, seconding, abetting; supportive, encouraging 612 *inducing*; of service, of help, of great assistance 640 *useful*; constructive, well-meant; morale-boosting; assistant, auxiliary, subsidiary, ancillary, accessory; in aid of, contributory, promoting; on call, at one's beck and call, subservient 742 *serving*; assisting 628 *instrumental*.

**Vb.** *aid*, help, assist, lend a hand, bear a h., give a helping hand 706 *cooperate*; lend one's aid, render assistance; be there for, hold out a hand to, take by the hand, take under one's wing, take in tow, give a lift to; hold one's hand, spoonfeed, featherbed; be kind to, do one a good turn, give a leg up, help a lame duck, help a lame dog over a stile 897 *be benevolent*; help one out, tide one over, see one through; oblige, accommodate, lend money to 784 *lend*; put up the money, finance, subsidize; pitch in, chip in, send the hat round; facilitate, speed, lend wings to, further, advance, boost 285 *promote*; abet, instigate, foment, nourish, feed the flame, fan the f. 612 *induce*; make for, contribute to, be accessory to, be a factor in 156 *conduce*; lend support to, boost one's morale, back up, stand by, bolster, prop up 218 *support*; comfort, sustain, hearten, give heart to, encourage, rally, embolden 855 *give courage*; succour, come to the help of, send help to, bail out, help o., relieve 668 *deliver*; step into the breach, reinforce, fortify 162 *strengthen*; ease 685 *refresh*; set one on his *or* her feet 656 *restore*.

*patronize*, favour, smile on, shine on 730 *be auspicious*; sponsor, back, guarantee, go bail for, stand surety for; recommend, put up for; propose, second; countenance, give countenance to, connive at, protect 660 *safeguard*; join, enlist under 78 *be included*; contribute to, subscribe to, lend one's name 488 *endorse*; take an interest in 880 *befriend*; espouse the cause of, take one's part, side with, champion, take up the cudgels for, stick up for, stand up f., stand by 713 *defend*; canvass for, root f., vote f. 605 *vote*; give moral support to, pray for, intercede; pay for, pay the piper 804 *defray*; entertain, keep, cherish, foster, spoonfeed, featherbed, nurse, wet-nurse, mother 889 *pet*; bestow one's custom, buy from 792 *purchase*.

*minister to*, wait on, do for, help, oblige 742 *serve*; give first aid to, nurse 658 *doctor*; squire, valet, mother; subserve, be of service to, make oneself useful to 640 *be useful*; anticipate the wishes of 597 *be willing*; pander to, toady, humour, be a cat's paw to, scratch one's back, suck up to 925 *flatter*; slave, do all one can for, wait hand and foot on, do everything for 682 *work*; be assistant to, make oneself the tool of 628 *be instrumental*.

**Adv.** *in aid of*, in the cause of, for the sake of, on behalf of; under the aegis *or* auspices of, by the aid of, thanks to; in the service of, in the name of.

## 704 Opposition

**N.** *opposition*, antagonism, hostility 881 *enmity*; clashing, conflict, friction, lack of harmony, office politics 709 *dissension*; dissociation, non-association, noncooperation, unhelpful attitude 598 *unwillingness*; repugnance 861 *dislike*; contrariness, cussedness, recalcitrance 602 *obstinacy*; impugnation, counterargument 479 *confutation*; contradiction, denial 533 *negation*; challenge 711 *defiance*; oppugnation, firm opposition, stout o., stand 715 *resistance*; contravention, infringement 738 *revolt*; going against, siding a., voting a., canvassing a. 924 *disapprobation*; withdrawal, walkout 489 *dissent*; physical opposition, headwind, crosscurrent 702 *obstacle*; mutual opposition, cross purposes, tug of war, tug of love, battle of wills; faction, rivalry, emulation, competition 716 *contention*; political opposition, the Opposition, Her Majesty's O., the other side, wrong s.; underground, alternative society 84 *nonconformity*.

*opposites*, contraries, extremes, opposite poles 14 *contrariety*; rivals, duellists, competitors 716 *contender*; opposite parties, factions, black and white, cat and dog 709 *quarreller*; town and gown, the right and the left, management and workers, Labour and Conservative, Democrat and Republican.

**Adj.** *opposing*, oppositional, opposed; in opposition, on the other side, on the wrong s.; anti, against, agin; antagonistic, hostile, unfriendly, antipathetic, unsympathetic, Eurosceptic 881 *inimical*; unfavourable, unpropitious 731 *adverse*; cross, thwarting 702 *hindering*; contradictory 14 *contrary*; cussed, bloody-minded, bolshie 602 *obstinate*; refractory, recalcitrant 738 *disobedient*; resistant 182 *counteracting*; clashing, conflicting, at variance, at odds with 709 *quarrelling*; militant, up in arms, at daggers drawn 716 *contending*; fronting, facing, face to face, eyeball to eyeball, man to man 237 *frontal*; polarized, at opposite extremes 240 *opposite*; mutually opposed, rival, competitive 911 *jealous*.

**Vb.** *oppose*, go against, militate a. 14 *be contrary*; side against, stand a., hold out a., fight a.,

dig one's heels in, refuse to budge, stand one's ground 715 *resist*; set one's face against, make a dead set a. 607 *reject*; object, kick, protest, protest against 762 *deprecate*; run one's head against, beat a. 279 *collide*; vote against, vote down 924 *disapprove*; not support, canvass against, dissociate oneself; contradict, belie 533 *negate*; counter 479 *confute*; work against 182 *counteract*; countermine, thwart, baffle, foil 702 *be obstructive*; be at cross purposes, play at c. p.; stand up to, challenge, dare 711 *defy*; set at naught 922 *hold cheap*; flout, fly in the face of 738 *disobey*; rebuff, spurn, slap in the face, slam the door in one's f. 760 *refuse*; emulate, rival, vie with, match oneself with, compete with, bid against 716 *contend*; set against, pit a., match a.

*withstand*, confront, face, look in the f., stand against, stand up to 661 *face danger*; rise against 738 *revolt*; take on, meet, encounter, cross swords with 716 *fight*; struggle against, breast, stem, breast the tide, stem the t., swim against the stream; cope with, grapple w., wrestle w. 678 *be active*; not be beaten 599 *stand firm*; hold one's own, bear the brunt 715 *resist*.

**Adv.** *in opposition*, against, versus, agin; in conflict with, against the crowd, against the tide, against the stream, against the wind, with the wind in one's teeth, against the grain, in the teeth of, in the face of, in defiance of, in spite of, despite.

## 705 Opponent

**N.** *opponent*, opposer, lion in the path; adversary, challenger, antagonist, foe, foeman 881 *enemy*; assailant 712 *attacker*; opposing party, opposition p., the opposition, opposite camp; factionist, partisan; obstructionist, filibusterer 702 *hinderer*; independent party, cross benches; diehard, bitter-ender, last-ditcher, irreconcilable; reactionary, counter-revolutionary, obscurantist; objector, conscientious o. 489 *dissentient*; resister, passive r.; dissident, noncooperator 829 *malcontent*, Eurosceptic; agitator, terrorist, bioterrorist, cyberterrorist, extremist 738 *revolter*; challenger, vier, rival, emulator, corrival, competitor, runner-up, fighter, combatant, contestant, duellist; entrant, the field, all comers 716 *contender*; bovver boy, boot boy, brawler, wrangler 709 *quarreller*; common enemy, public e., universal foe, outlaw 904 *offender*.

## 706 Cooperation

**N.** *cooperation*, helpfulness 597 *willingness*; contribution, coagency, interaction, synergy, symbiosis; duet, double harness, tandem; collaboration, joint effort, combined operation; team work, working together, concerted effort; relay, relay race, team r.; team spirit, esprit de corps; lack of friction, unanimity, agreement, concurrence, bipartisanship 710 *concord*; clanship, clannishness, party spirit, cliquishness, partisanship; connivance, collusion, abetment 612 *inducement*; conspiracy, complot 623 *plot*; complicity, participation, worker p.; sympathy 880 *friendliness*; fraternity, sorority, solidarity, fellowship, freemasonry, fellow feeling, comradeship, fellow-travelling; common cause, mutual assistance, helping one another, networking, backscratching, aiding and abetting, log-rolling; reciprocity, give and take, mutual concession 770 *compromise*; mutual advice, consultation 584 *conference*.

*association*, coming together; colleagueship, co-ownership, copartnership, partnership 775 *participation*; nationalization, internationalization 775 *joint possession*; pooling, pool, kitty; membership, affiliation 78 *inclusion*; connection, hook-up, tie-up 9 *relation*; consociation, ecosystem; combination, consolidation, centralization 45 *union*; integration, solidarity 52 *whole*; unification 88 *unity*; amalgamation, fusion, merger; voluntary association, coalition, cohabitation, alliance, league, federation, confederation, confederacy, umbrella organization; axis, united front, common f., people's f., popular f. 708 *political party*; association, fellowship, college, club, sodality, fraternity, sorority 708 *community*; set, clique, coterie, cell 708 *party*; workers' association, trade union, chapel; business association, company, joint-stock c., limited liability c., private c., public c., public limited c., PLC, Ltd, syndicate, combine, consortium, trust, cartel, ring 708 *corporation*; housing association, economic community, cooperative, workers' c., commune 708 *community*.

**Adj.** *cooperative*, helpful 703 *aiding*; en rapport 710 *concordant*; symbiotic, synergic; collaborating, in double harness, in tandem; married, associating, associated, leagued, in league, back-scratching, hand in glove with; bipartisan; federal 708 *corporate*.

**Vb.** *cooperate*, collaborate, work together, pull t., work as a team; hunt in pairs, run in double harness; team up, join forces, pool resources, go into partnership 775 *participate*; show willing, play ball, reciprocate, respond; lend oneself to, espouse 703 *patronize*; join in, take part, enter into, take a hand in, pitch in; rally round 703 *aid*; hang together, hold t., sail *or* row in the same boat, stand shoulder to

shoulder, stand by each other, sink or swim together; be in league with, be in cahoots with, make common cause with, take in each other's washing; network, band together, gang up, associate, league, confederate, federate, ally; coalesce, merge, unite 43 *be mixed*; combine, make common cause, club together; understand one another, think alike; conspire 623 *plot*; lay heads together, get into a huddle 691 *consult*; collude, connive, play another's game; work for an understanding, treat with, negotiate 766 *make terms*.

**Adv.** *cooperatively*, hand in hand, jointly, in cahoots with, unanimously, as one man, as one.

**Int.** All together now!, Harambee!

## 707 Auxiliary

**N.** *auxiliary*, relay, recruit, fresh troops, reinforcement; back-up, backroom boys; second line, paramilitary formation 722 *soldiery*; paramedic, auxiliary nurse; ally, brother-in-arms, confederate (see also *colleague*); coadjutor, adjuvant, assistant, helper, helpmate, helping hand 703 *aider*; right-hand man, second, tower of strength; adjutant, lieutenant, aide-de-camp; amanuensis, secretary, girl Friday, clerk; midwife, handmaid; dogsbody 742 *servant*; acolyte, server; best man, bridesmaid; friend in need 880 *friend*; hanger-on, satellite, henchman, sidekick, follower 742 *dependant*; disciple, adherent, votary 978 *sectarian*; loyalist, legitimist; flunkey, stooge, cat's-paw, puppet 628 *instrument*; shadow, familiar 89 *concomitant*; jackal, running dog, creature, âme damnée.

*collaborator*, cooperator, co-author, co-worker, fellow w.; team-mate, yoke-fellow; sympathizer, fellow traveller, fifth column, fifth columnist, quisling, traitor, mole, conspirator, conniver 603 *tergiversator*.

*colleague*, associate, confrère, fellow, fellow-worker, peer, brother, sister; co-director, partner, sharer 775 *participator*; comrade, companion, boon c., playmate; confidant(e), alter ego, second self, faithful companion, fidus Achates; mate, chum, pal, buddy, oppo, crony 880 *friend*; helpmate, better half 894 *spouse*; stand-by, stalwart; ally, confederate; accomplice, accessory, abettor, aider and abettor, fellow conspirator, partner in crime; co-religionist; one's fellows, one's own side.

*patron*, defender, guardian angel 660 *protector*; well-wisher, sympathizer; champion, advocate, friend at court; supporter, sponsor, backer, guarantor; proposer, seconder, voter; partisan, votary, aficionado, fan 887 *lover*; good friend, Jack at a pinch, friend in need, deus ex machina; fairy godmother, rich uncle, sugar daddy 903 *benefactor*; promoter, founder; patron of art, Maecenas 492 *collector*; customer, client 792 *purchaser*.

## 708 Party

**N.** *party*, movement; group, class 77 *classification*; subsect, confession, communion, denomination, church 978 *sect*; faction, groupuscule, cabal, cave, splinter group, breakaway movement 489 *dissentient*; circle, inner c., charmed c., kitchen cabinet; set, clique, incrowd, coterie, galère; caucus, junta, camarilla, politburo, committee, quango, club, cell, cadre; ring, closed shop; team, eight, eleven, fifteen; crew, team, complement 686 *personnel*; troupe, company 594 *actor*; gang, knot, bunch, outfit 74 *band*; horde 74 *crowd*; side, camp.

*political party*, left, centre, right; Conservatives, Tories, Unionists, Ulster Unionists, Democratic Unionists; British National Party, National Front; Liberals, Radicals, Whigs, Liberal Democrats; Socialists, Labour, New Labour, Social Democrats, Social Democratic and Labour Party; Nationalists, Mebyon Kernow, Mec Vannin, Plaid Cymru, Scottish National Party, Sinn Fein; United Kingdom Independence Party; Greens; Alliance Party; Fianna Fáil, Fine Gael; Democrats, Republicans, GOP; Militant Tendency, Scottish Socialist Party, Workers' Revolutionary Party, International Socialists, Trotskyists, Marxists, Communists, Bolsheviks, Mensheviks, Maoists; Fascists, Nazis, Falangists; Blackshirts, Brownshirts; Jacobins, Girondists; Monster Raving Loony Party; coalition, popular front, people's front, bloc; citoyen, comrade, tovarich, Red, commie, Trot; socialist, labourite, Fabian, syndicalist; anarchist 738 *revolter*; right-winger, rightist, true blue; left-winger, leftist, leftie (inf), pinko (inf), populist, democrat; moderate, centrist, wet; dry, extremist, fundamentalist; party worker, canvasser, party member, politician, politico; militant, activist 676 *doer*; Emily's list.

*society*, partnership, coalition, combination, combine 706 *association*; league, alliance, axis; federation, confederation, confederacy; economic association, cooperative, Bund, union, Benelux, EEC, Common Market, European Community, European Union, EU, Euroland, Eurozone, free trade area, single market; private society, club 76 *focus*; secret society, Ku Klux Klan, Freemasonry, lodge, cell; friendly society, trades union; chapel; group, division, branch, local b.; youth movement, Boy Scouts, Cubs, Rovers, Rangers, Girl Guides, Brownies; Pioneers, Komsomol; Women's Institute, Townswomen's Guild, Mother's Union; Daughters of the American Revolution, DAR; fellow, honorary f., associate, member, associate m.; party m., paid-up m., card-carrying m.; comrade, trade unionist; corresponding member, branch m., paired MP, affiliate 58 *component*.

*community*, fellowship, brotherhood, body, congregation, band of brothers, fraternity, confraternity, sorority, sisterhood; clique, coterie; guild, sodality; race, tribe, clan, sect 11 *family*; order 77 *classification*; social class 371 *social group*; state, nation s., multiracial s. 371 *nation*; planet, world, 'global village'.

> The new electronic interdependence re-creates the world in the image of a global village.
> Marshall McLuhan

*corporation*, body; incorporated society, body corporate, mayor and corporation 692 *council*; company, livery c., joint-stock c., limited liability c., public limited c., holding c.; private c.; multinational c., transnational corporation, dotcom 706 *association*; firm, concern, joint c., partnership; house, business h.; establishment, organization, institute; trust, combine, monopoly, cartel, syndicate, conglomerate 706 *association*; trade association, chamber of commerce, guild, cooperative society; consumers' association.

**Adj.** *corporate*, incorporate, corporative, joint-stock; joint, partnered, bonded, banded, leagued, federal, federative; allied, federate, confederate; social, clubbable 882 *sociable*; fraternal, comradely 880 *friendly*; cooperative, syndicalist; communal 775 *sharing*.

*sectional*, factional, denominational, Masonic 978 *sectarian*; partisan, clannish, cliquish, cliquey, exclusive; class-conscious; nationalistic 481 *biased*; rightist, right-wing, true-blue; right of centre, left of c.; leftist, left-wing, pink, red; Whiggish, Tory; radical, conservative; middle-of-the-road.

**Vb.** *join a party*, put one's name down, subscribe; join, swell the ranks, become one of, become a member, take out membership; sign on, enlist, enrol oneself, get elected; cut in, sneak in, creep in 297 *enter*; belong to, fit in, make one of 78 *be included*; align oneself, side with, take sides, range oneself with, team up w. 706 *cooperate*; club together, associate, ally, conspire, league, federate; cement a union, merge; found a party, lead a p.

**Adv.** *in league*, in partnership, in the same boat, in cahoots with, hand in glove w.; hand in hand, side by side, shoulder to shoulder, back to back; all together, en masse, jointly, collectively; unitedly, as one; with all the rest, in the swim.

## 709 Dissension

**N.** *dissension*, disagreement 489 *dissent*; noncooperation 704 *opposition*; disharmony, dissonance, disaccord, jar, jangle, jarring note, discordant n. 411 *discord*; recrimination 714 *retaliation*; wrangling, quarrelling, bickering, sniping, cat-and-dog life; differences, odds, variance, friction, tension, unpleasantness, scenes; soreness 891 *resentment*; no love lost, hostility, mutual h. 888 *hatred*; disunity, disunion, internal dissension, muttering in the ranks, house divided against itself 25 *disagreement*; office politics; rift, cleavage, cleavage of opinion, parting of the ways, separation 294 *divergence*; split, faction 978 *schism*; misunderstanding, cross purposes 481 *misjudgment*; breach, rupture, open r., severance of relations, recall of ambassadors; challenge 711 *defiance*; ultimatum, declaration of war, open war 718 *war*.

*quarrelsomeness*, factiousness, litigiousness; aggressiveness, combativeness, pugnacity, belligerence, warlike behaviour 718 *bellicosity*; provocativeness, inviting trouble, trailing one's coat 711 *defiance*; cantankerousness, awkwardness, prickliness, fieriness 892 *irascibility*; shrewishness, sharp tongue 899 *scurrility*; contentiousness 716 *contention*; rivalry 911 *jealousy*; thirst for revenge 910 *revengefulness*; mischievousness, mischief, spite 898 *malevolence*; apple of discord, spirit of mischief, Puck; Ate, Mars.

*quarrel*, open q.; feud, blood f., vendetta 910 *revenge*; blood on the carpet; war 718 *warfare*; strife 716 *contention*; conflict, clash 279 *collision*; legal battle 959 *litigation*; controversy, dispute, wrangle, argy-bargy; polemic, battle of arguments, paper war 475 *argument*; wordy warfare, words, war of w., high w., raised voices, stormy exchange, confrontation, altercation, set-to, abuse, slanging match 899 *scurrility*; jar, spat, tiff, squabble, jangle, wrangle, barney, hassle, squall, storm in a teacup; rumpus, dustup, disturbance, hubbub, racket, row, shindig, stramash, commotion, scrimmage, fracas, brawl, fisticuffs, breach of the peace 61 *turmoil*; gang warfare, street fighting, riot 716 *fight*.

*casus belli*, root of the trouble; flashpoint, breaking point; tender spot, sore point; apple of discord, bone of contention, bone to pick; disputed point, point at issue, disputed territory, area of disagreement, battleground.

*quarreller*, disputer, wrangler; controversialist 475 *reasoner*; duellist, rival, vier, emulator 716 *contender*; strange bedfellows, Kilkenny cats, cats and dogs, Montagues and Capulets; quarrelmonger, mischief-maker 663 *troublemaker*;

scold, bitter tongue 892 *shrew*; aggressor 712 *attacker*.

**Adj.** *quarrelling*, discordant, discrepant, clashing, conflicting 14 *contrary*; on bad terms, feuding, at odds, at sixes and sevens, at loggerheads, at variance, at daggers drawn, up in arms 881 *inimical*; divided, factious, schismatic 489 *dissenting*; mutinous, rebellious 738 *disobedient*; uncooperative, noncooperating 704 *opposing*; sore 891 *resentful*; awkward, cantankerous 892 *irascible*; sulky 893 *sullen*; implacable 910 *revengeful*; litigant, litigious 959 *litigating*; quarrelsome, nonpacific, bellicose 718 *warlike*; pugnacious, combative, spoiling for a fight, trailing one's coat, inviting trouble, asking for it, belligerent, aggressive, militant 712 *attacking*; abusive, shrewish, scolding, scurrilous 899 *cursing*; argumentative, contentious, disputatious, wrangling, polemical, controversial 475 *arguing*.

**Vb.** *quarrel*, disagree 489 *dissent*; clash, conflict 279 *collide*; cross, cross swords with, be at one another's throats; misunderstand, be at cross purposes, pull different ways, be at variance, have differences, have a bone to pick 15 *differ*; recriminate 714 *retaliate*; fall out, go one's separate ways, part company, split, break with; break away 978 *schismatize*; break off relations, break off diplomatic r., declare war 718 *go to war*; go to law, take it to court 959 *litigate*; dispute, try conclusions with 479 *confute*; have a feud with, carry on a vendetta 910 *be revengeful*; turn sulky, sulk 893 *be sullen*; noncooperate 704 *oppose*.

*make quarrels*, pick q., pick a fight, start it; look for trouble, ask for it, be spoiling for a fight, make something of it, trail one's coat, challenge 711 *defy*; irritate, rub up the wrong way, tread on one's toes, get up one's nose, provoke 891 *enrage*; have a bone to pick, have a crow to pluck; cherish a feud, enjoy a quarrel 881 *make enemies*; embroil, entangle, estrange, set at odds, set at variance, set by the ears 888 *excite hate*; create discord, sound a discordant note 411 *discord*; sow dissension, stir up strife, stir it, be a quarrelmonger, make mischief, make trouble, put the cat among the pigeons; divide, draw apart, disunite, come between, drive a wedge b. 46 *sunder*; widen the breach, fan the flame 832 *aggravate*; set against, pit a., match with; egg on, incite 612 *motivate*.

*bicker*, spat, tiff, squabble; nag, henpeck, jar, spar, spar with, live a cat-and-dog life; jangle, wrangle, dispute with, go at it hammer and tongs 475 *argue*; scold 899 *cuss*; have words with, altercate, pick a bone w., pluck a crow w., row, row with; brawl, kick up a shindy, disturb the peace, make the fur fly, raise the dust 61 *rampage*.

## 710 Concord

**N.** *concord*, harmony 410 *melody*; unison, unity, duet 24 *agreement*; unanimity, bipartisanship 488 *consensus*; lack of friction, understanding, good u., mutual u., rapport; solidarity, team spirit 706 *cooperation*; reciprocity 12 *correlation*; sympathy, fellow feeling 887 *love*; compatibility, coexistence, amity 880 *friendship*; rapprochement, détente, reunion, reconciliation, conciliation, conflict resolution, peacemaking 719 *pacification*; good offices, arbitration 720 *mediation*; entente cordiale, happy family, picture of content, the best of friends, sweetness and light, love and peace 717 *peace*; goodwill, goodwill amongst men, honeymoon period.

**Adj.** *concordant*, blended 410 *harmonious*; en rapport, eye to eye, unanimous, with one voice, of one mind, bipartisan 24 *agreeing*; coexistent, compatible, united, cemented, bonded, allied, leagued; fraternal, loving, amicable, on good terms 880 *friendly*; frictionless, happy, peaceable, pacific, at peace 717 *peaceful*; conciliatory 719 *pacificatory*.

**Vb.** *concord* 410 *harmonize*; bring into concord 719 *pacify*; agree 24 *accord*; hit it off, see eye to eye, play a duet, chime in with, pull together 706 *cooperate*; reciprocate, respond, run parallel 181 *concur*; fraternize 880 *be friendly*; keep the peace, remain at peace 717 *be at peace*.

## 711 Defiance

**N.** *defiance*, dare, daring, challenge, gage, gauntlet, hat in the ring; bold front, belling the cat, brave face 855 *courage*; war dance, war cry, war whoop, war song, battle cry, declaration of war 900 *threat*; brazenness 878 *insolence*; demonstration, display, bravura 875 *ostentation*.

**Adj.** *defiant*, defying, challenging, provocative, in-your-face (inf), belligerent, bellicose, militant 718 *warlike*; saucy, insulting 878 *insolent*; mutinous, rebellious 738 *disobedient*; greatly daring 855 *courageous*; stiff-necked 871 *proud*; reckless, trigger-happy 857 *rash*.

**Vb.** *defy*, challenge, take one up on 489 *dissent*; stand up to 704 *oppose*; caution 664 *warn*; throw in one's teeth, throw down the gauntlet, throw one's hat in the ring; demand satisfaction, call out, send one's seconds; dare, out-dare, beard; brave, run the gauntlet 661 *face danger*; laugh to scorn, laugh in one's face, laugh in one's beard, set at naught, snap one's fingers at 922 *hold cheap*; bid defiance to, set

at d., hurl d.; call one's bluff, double the bid; show fight, bare one's teeth, show one's fangs, double one's fist, clench one's f., shake one's f. 900 *threaten*; refuse to bow down to 871 *be proud*; look big, throw out one's chest, beat one's c., show a bold front; wave a banner 317 *brandish*; march, demonstrate, hold a demonstration, stage a sit-in, not be moved; cock a snook 878 *be insolent*; ask for trouble 709 *make quarrels*; crow over, shout 727 *triumph*; crow, bluster, brag 877 *boast*.

**Adv.** *defiantly*, challengingly, in defiance of, in one's teeth, to one's face, under the very nose of; in open rebellion.

**Int.** do your worst!, come on if you dare!

## 712 Attack

**N.** *attack*, hostile a., best method of defence; pugnacity, combativeness, aggressiveness 718 *bellicosity*; belligerence, aggression, unprovoked a. 914 *injustice*; blood on the carpet; stab in the back 930 *foul play*; assault, assault and battery, actual bodily harm, ABH, grievous bodily harm, GBH, mugging, -bashing (inf), -busting (inf) 176 *violence*; armed attack, offensive, charm o., drive, push, thrust, pincer movement 688 *tactics*; run at, dead set at; onslaught, onset, rush, shock, charge; sally, sortie, breakout, breakthrough; counterattack 714 *retaliation*; shock tactics, blitzkrieg, coup de main, surprise; encroachment, infringement 306 *overstepping*; invasion, incursion, irruption, overrunning 297 *ingress*; raid, ram r., foray 788 *brigandage*; blitz, air raid, air attack, land a., sea a.; night attack, camisado; storm, taking by s., escalade; boarding; investment, siege, blockade 230 *surroundings*; challenge, tilt.

*terror tactics*, guerrilla warfare, sniping, war of attrition, war of nerves 854 *intimidation*; 'war to the knife' 735 *severity*;

> **War to the knife.** A translation of Spanish 'Guerra a cuchillo'. The phrase was reputedly used by the Spanish general Palafox y Melzi in reply to the French demand for his capitulation at the siege of Saragossa. In fact what Palafox said was 'Guerra y cuchillo', 'war and the knife'.

whiff of grapeshot, shot across the bows; dragonnade, noyade, bloodbath 362 *slaughter*; devastation, laying waste 165 *havoc*.

*bombardment*, cannonade, barrage, strafe, blitz; broadside, volley, salvo; bomb-dropping, bombing, strategic b., tactical b., saturation b., carpet b.; firing, shooting, fire, gunfire, machine-gun f., rifle f., fusillade, burst of fire, rapid f., cross-f., plunging f.; raking f., enfilade; anti-aircraft fire, flak; sharpshooting, sniping; gunnery, musketry.

*lunge*, thrust, home-t., foin, pass, passado, quarte and tierce; cut, cut and thrust, stoccado, stab, jab; bayonet, cold steel; punch, swipe, kick 279 *knock*.

*attacker*, assailant, aggressor, mugger, -basher (inf), -buster (inf); hawk, militant; spearhead, storm troops, shock t., strike force; fighter pilot, air ace, bomber 722 *armed force*; sharpshooter, sniper; terrorist, guerrilla; invader, raider; besieger, blockader, stormer, escalader.

**Adj.** *attacking*, assailing, assaulting etc. vb.; vituperative, pugnacious, combative, aggressive, on the offensive 718 *warlike*; hawkish, militant, spoiling for a fight, hostile 881 *inimical*; up in arms, on the warpath 718 *warring*; storming, charging, boarding, going over the top.

**Vb.** *attack*, be spoiling for a fight; start a fight, declare war 718 *go to war*; strike the first blow, open fire on, fire the first shot; assault, assail, make a dead set at, go for, set on, pounce upon, fall u., pitch into, sail i., have at; attack tooth and nail, savage, maul, draw blood 655 *wound*; launch out at, let fly at, let one have it, lay into, tear into, lace into, round on; surprise, take by s., blitz, overwhelm; move in, invade 306 *encroach*; raid, foray, overrun, infest 297 *burst in*; show fight, take the offensive, assume the o., go over to the o., go over to the attack; counterattack 714 *retaliate*; thrust, push 279 *impel*; erupt, sally, make a sortie, break out, break through 298 *emerge*; board, lay aboard, grapple; escalade, storm, take by storm, carry, capture 727 *overmaster*; ravage, make havoc, scorch, burn 165 *lay waste*; harry, drive, beat, corner, bring to bay 619 *hunt*; challenge, enter the lists 711 *defy*; take on 704 *oppose*; take up the cudgels, draw the sword, couch one's lance, break a lance 716 *fight*.

*besiege*, lay siege to, beleaguer, invest, surround, beset, blockade 235 *enclose*; sap, mine, undermine, spring a mine.

*strike at*, raise one's hand against; lay about one, swipe, flail, hammer 279 *strike*; go berserk, run amok 176 *be violent*; have at, have a fling at, fetch a blow, have a cut at, lash out at; beat up, mug; clash, ram 279 *collide*; make a pass at, lunge; close with, grapple w., come to close quarters, fight hand to hand, cut and thrust; push, butt, thrust, poke at, thrust at; stab, spear, lance, bayonet, run through, cut down 263 *pierce*; strike home, lay low, bring down 311 *abase*; stab in the back 930 *be dishonest*.

*charge*, sound the c., advance against, march a., ride a., drive a., sail a., fly a.; go over the top; bear down on, come upon; rush, mob 61 *rampage*; make a rush, rush at, run at, dash

at, go full belt at, tilt at, ride full tilt at; ride down, run down, ram, shock 279 *collide*.

*fire at*, shoot at, fire upon; fire a shot at, take a potshot, pop at, snipe, pick off 287 *shoot*; shoot down, bring d.; torpedo, sink; soften up, strafe, bombard, blitz, cannonade, shell, fusillade, pepper; bomb, throw bombs, drop b., lay eggs, plaster, prang; open fire, let fly, volley; volley and thunder, rattle, blast, pour a broadside into, rake, straddle, enfilade; take aim, pull the trigger, level, draw a bead on 281 *aim*.

*lapidate*, stone, throw a stone, heave a brick; shy, sling, chuck, pelt; hurl at 287 *propel*.

**Adv.** *aggressively*, forcefully, assertively, offensively, on the offensive, on the attack, on the warpath.

## 713 Defence

**N.** *defence*, the defensive, self-defence 715 *resistance*; art of self-defence, boxing 716 *pugilism*; kick-boxing, Thai b., martial art, judo, jujitsu, karate 716 *martial arts*; counter, counterstroke, parry, warding off 182 *counteraction*; defensiveness 854 *nervousness*; posture of defence, guard; defensive alliance, balance of power; safekeeping 666 *preservation*; vigilance, self-protection 660 *protection*; a defence, rampart, bulwark, screen, buffer, fender, bumper, bull bars 662 *safeguard*; deterrent 723 *weapon*; munitions 723 *ammunition*.

*defences*, lines, entrenchment, fieldwork, redoubt, redan, lunette; breastwork, parados, contravallation; outwork, circumvallation; earthwork, embankment, mound; mole, boom; wall, barricade, fence 235 *barrier*; abatis, palisade, paling, stockade; moat, ditch, dike, fosse; trench, dugout; tripwire, booby trap 542 *trap*; barbed wire, barbed wire entanglements, razor wire; spike, caltrop, chevaux de frise; anti-tank obstacles, dragon's teeth; Maginot Line, Siegfried L., Hadrian's Wall, Antonine W., Great Wall of China; airraid shelter, fallout s., bunker 662 *shelter*; barrage, antiaircraft fire, flak; barrage balloon; wooden walls; minefield, mine, countermine; smokescreen 421 *screen*.

*fortification* (see also *fort*); circumvallation, bulwark, rampart, wall; parapet, battlement, machicolation, embrasure, casemate, merlon, loophole; banquette, barbette, emplacement, gun e.; vallum, scarp, escarp, counterscarp, glacis; curtain, bastion, ravelin, demilune, outwork, demibastion; buttress, abutment; gabion, gabionade.

*fort*, fortress, fortalice, stronghold, fastness; citadel, capitol, acropolis 662 *refuge*; castle, keep, ward, barbican, tower, turret, bartizan, donjon; portcullis, drawbridge; gate, postern, sally port; peel, Martello tower, pillbox; blockhouse, strong point; laager, zareba, encampment 235 *enclosure*; Roman camp, castrum; British camp 253 *earthwork*; broch.

*armour*, harness; full armour, panoply; mail, chain m.; scale armour, splint a., armour plate; breastplate, backplate; cuirass, lorica, plastron; hauberk, habergeon, brigandine, coat of mail; corslet; helmet, helm, casque, basinet, sallet, morion; visor, beaver; siege cap, steel helmet, tin hat; shako, bearskin, busby 228 *headgear*; greaves, gauntlet, vambrace; shield, buckler, scutum, target; pavis, mantelet, testudo; protective clothing, body armour, riot shield, gas mask 662 *safeguard*; exoskeleton.

*defender*, champion 927 *vindicator*; patron 703 *aider*; knight-errant, paladin; loyalist, legitimist, patriot; bodyguard, lifeguard, Praetorian Guard 722 *soldier*; watch, sentry, sentinel; vigilante; patrol, patrolman; security man *or* woman; garrison, picket, guard, escort, rearguard; Home Guard, Territorials, Territorial Army, militia, thin red line 722 *soldiery*; fireman, firefighter, firewatcher; Civil Defence; guardian, warden 660 *protector*; warder, custodian 749 *keeper*; deliverer, rescuer 668 *deliverance*; title-defender, titleholder.

**Adj.** *defending*, challenged, on the defensive 715 *resisting*; defensive, protective, antitank, anti-aircraft 660 *tutelary*; exculpatory, palliating, self-excusing 927 *vindicating*; pro-life.

*defended*, secured, armoured, armourplated; heavy-armed, mailed, mail-clad, armour-c., iron-c.; panoplied, accoutred, harnessed, armed to the teeth, armed at all points *or* cap-a-pie 669 *prepared*; moated, palisaded, barricaded, walled, fortified, machicolated, castellated, battlemented, loopholed; entrenched, dug in; defensible, proof, bomb-proof, bullet-proof 660 *invulnerable*.

**Vb.** *defend*, guard, protect, keep, watch, ward 660 *safeguard*; fence, hedge, moat 232 *circumscribe*; palisade, barricade 235 *enclose*; block 702 *obstruct*; cushion, pad, shield, curtain, cover 421 *screen*; cloak 525 *conceal*; provide with arms, munition, arm, accoutre 669 *make ready*; harness, armour, clothe in a., armour-plate; reinforce, fortify, crenellate, machicolate 162 *strengthen*; entrench, dig in 599 *stand firm*; stand in front, stand by; garrison, man, man the defences, man the breach, stop the gap; plead for, hold a brief for, argue for, take up the cause of, champion 927 *vindicate*; fight for, take up arms for, break a lance for, take up the cudgels for, cover up f. 703 *patronize*; rescue, come to the r. 668 *deliver*.

*parry*, counter, riposte, fence, fend, fend off, ward o., hold o., keep o., fight o., stave o., hold *or* keep at bay, keep at arm's length 620 *avoid*;

turn, avert 282 *deflect*; play, play with, keep in play; stall, beat about the bush, quibble, vacillate, blow hot and cold, stonewall, block 702 *obstruct*; act on the defensive, fight a defensive battle, play for a draw, stalemate; fight back, show fight, give a warm reception to 715 *resist*; butt away, repulse 292 *repel*; bear the brunt, hold one's own 704 *withstand*; fall back on 673 *avail oneself of*; beat a strategic retreat, get out while the going is good 286 *turn back*; survive, scrape through, live to fight another day 667 *escape*.

**Adv.** *defensively*, on the defensive, at bay; in defence, pro patria, in self-defence.

## 714 Retaliation

**N.** *retaliation*, reprisal, lex talionis 910 *revenge*; requital, recompense, quittance, comeuppance 962 *reward*; desert, deserts, just deserts 915 *dueness*; punitive action, poetic justice, retribution, Nemesis 963 *punishment*; reaction, boomerang, backlash 280 *recoil*; counter, counterstroke, counterblast, counterplot, countermine 182 *counteraction*; counterattack, sally, sortie 712 *attack*; recrimination, answering back, riposte, retort 460 *rejoinder*; 'returning good for evil', 'heaping coals of fire';

> Belinda: Ay, but you know we must return good for evil.
> Lady Brute: That may be a mistake in the translation.
>
> Sir John Vanbrugh, *The Provok'd Wife* (The reference is to the teaching of Jesus and the apostles.)

> If thine enemy be hungry, give him bread to eat; and if he be thirsty, give him water to drink: For thou shalt heap coals of fire upon his head, and the Lord shall reward thee.
>
> Bible, Proverbs (The words are also quoted by the apostle Paul in his letter to the Romans.)

reciprocation, like for like, tit for tat, quid pro quo, measure for measure, blow for blow, 'an eye for an eye and a tooth for a tooth', a taste of one's own medicine, a Roland for an Oliver, the biter bit, a game at which two can play;

> Ye have heard that it hath been said, An eye for an eye, and a tooth for a tooth:
> But I say unto you, That ye resist not evil: but whosoever shall smite thee on thy right cheek, turn to him the other also.
>
> Bible, Jesus in St Matthew's Gospel (The reference to 'an eye for an eye, a tooth for a tooth' is to the Jewish law as stated in Exodus, Leviticus and Deuteronomy.)

potential retaliation, what is coming to one; deterrent 854 *intimidation*.

**Adj.** *retaliatory*, in retaliation, in reprisal, in self-defence; retaliative, retributive, punitive, recriminatory; like for like, reciprocal; rightly served.

**Vb.** *retaliate*, exact compensation 31 *recoup*; take reprisals 963 *punish*; counter, riposte 713 *parry*; make a requital, pay one out, pay off old scores, wipe out a score, square the account, be quits, get even with, get upsides with, get one's own back, sort one out 910 *avenge*; requite, reward; serve rightly, teach one a lesson; 'return good for evil' (see quotation above), 'do unto others as you would be done by';

> Therefore all things whatsoever ye would that men should do to you, do ye even so to them: for this is the law and the prophets.
>
> Bible, Jesus in St Matthew's Gospel

reciprocate, give and take, return like for like; return the compliment, give as good as one gets, pay one in his own coin, give a quid pro quo, get one's pound of flesh; return, retort, cap, answer back 460 *answer*; recriminate 928 *accuse*; react, boomerang 280 *recoil*; round on, kick back, hit b., not take it lying down 715 *resist*; turn the tables on, hoist one with one's own petard (see quotation at 729 *defeated*), make one laugh on the other side of one's face, make one take back one's own words, have the last laugh.

*be rightly served*, serve one right, have had one's lesson; have to pay compensation 787 *restitute*; find one's match, meet one's match; catch a tiger by the tail; be hoist with one's own petard (see quotation at 729 *defeated*), get one's deserts, get what was coming to one, get a dose of one's own medicine 963 *be punished*.

**Adv.** *en revanche*, by way of return, in requital, tit for tat.

**Int.** it serves you right!, take that!, put that in your pipe and smoke it!, the laugh's on you!, now who's laughing?, you can laugh on the other side of your face!

## 715 Resistance

**N.** *resistance*, stand, firm s., brave front 704 *opposition*; intractability 602 *obstinacy*; reluctance, renitency 598 *unwillingness*; repugnance 861 *dislike*; objection, demur 468 *qualification*; recalcitrance, kicking, protest 762 *deprecation*; non-cooperation, passive resistance, civil disobedience, electronic civil disobedience, hacktivism; rising, insurrection, resistance movement, backlash 738 *revolt*; self-defence 713 *defence*; repulsion, repulse, rebuff, bloody nose 760 *refusal*; refusal to work, walk-out 145 *strike*.

**Adj.** *resisting*, standing firm against 704 *opposing*; protesting, unconsenting, reluctant 598 *unwilling*; recalcitrant, renitent, unsubmissive, mutinous 738 *disobedient*; stubborn 602 *obstinate*; holding out, unyielding, unconquerable, indomitable, unsubdued, undefeated 727 *unbeaten*; resistant, tough, proof, proofed,

bulletproof, waterproof, showerproof; repugnant, repelling 292 *repellent*.

**Vb.** *resist*, offer resistance, give a warm reception, stand against 704 *withstand*; obstruct 702 *hinder*; challenge, stand out against 711 *defy*; confront, out-face 661 *face danger*; struggle against, contend with, stem the tide 704 *oppose*; recalcitrate, kick, kick against the pricks, protest 762 *deprecate*; demur, object 468 *qualify*; down tools, vote with one's feet, walk out, come out 145 *cease*; engineer a strike, call out 145 *halt*; mutiny, rise, not take it lying down 738 *revolt*; make a stand, fight off, keep at arm's length, keep at bay, hold off 713 *parry*; make a fight of it 716 *contend*; hold out, not submit, stand one's ground, not give way 599 *stand firm*; bear up, bear the brunt, endure 825 *suffer*; be proof against, not admit, repel, rebuff 760 *refuse*; resist temptation, not be tempted; last 113 *outlast*.

**Int.** no surrender!, we shall not be moved!

## 716 Contention

**N.** *contention*, strife, tussle, conflict, clash, running battle 709 *dissension*; combat, fighting, war 718 *warfare*; debate, dispute, controversy, polemics, paper warfare, ink-slinging 475 *argument*; altercation, words, war of w. 709 *quarrel*; stakes, bone of contention 709 *casus belli*; competition, rivalry, emulation 911 *jealousy*; competitiveness, gamesmanship, price war, rat race, 'the survival of the fittest';

> It cannot but happen . . . that those will survive whose functions happen to be most nearly in equilibrium with the modified aggregate of external forces. . . . This survival of the fittest implies multiplication of the fittest.
>
> Herbert Spencer, *Principles of Biology*

> The expression often used by Mr Herbert Spencer of the Survival of the Fittest is more accurate, and is sometimes equally convenient.
>
> Charles Darwin, *The Origin of Species*

cut-throat competition, 'war to the knife' (see quotation at 712 *terror tactics*), no holds barred; sports, athletics 837 *sport*.

*contest*, trial, trial of strength, test of endurance, marathon, triathlon, pentathlon, decathlon, tug-of-war, tug of love 682 *exertion*; tussle, struggle 671 *attempt*; bitter struggle, needle match; equal contest, dingdong fight; nothing in it, close finish, photo f. 200 *short distance*; competition, open c., free-for-all; pro-am, knockout competition, tournament; tourney, joust, tilt; prize competition, stakes, Ashes; match, test m.; concours, rally; event, handicap, run-off; heat, final, semifinal, quarterfinal, Cup tie, Cup final; set, game, rubber; sporting event, wager, bet 837 *sport*; field day 837 *amusement*; Derby day (see also *racing*); athletics, gymnastics; gymkhana, horseshow, rodeo; games, Highland Games, Commonwealth G., Olympic G., Olympics, Winter O., Paralympics, Francophone Games, Maccabiah G.; Wimbledon, Wembley, Lord's 724 *arena.*

*racing,* speed contest 277 *speeding;* races, race, foot r., flat r., sprint, dash; racewalking, road race, marathon, fun run; long-distance race, cross-country r., orienteering; slalom, obstacle race; hare and hounds r., treasure hunt; sack race, egg and spoon r.; relay r., team r.; the Turf, horse racing, sport of kings; the Derby, the Oaks; point-to-point, steeple-chase, hurdles, sticks 312 *leap;* motor race, motor rally, dirt-track racing, stockcar r., speedway, motocross; cycle race, Tour de France, cyclocross; dog racing, the dogs; boat race, yacht r., America's Cup competition; regatta, eights, Henley; Epsom, Ascot, race-course, track, stadium 724 *arena.*

*pugilism,* noble art of self-defence, boxing, shadow b., sparring, milling, jabbing, socking, slugging, pummeling, lambasting, fisticuffs; kick-boxing, target b., Thai b.; fighting, prize f., boxing match, prizefight; mill, spar, clinch, infighting; round, bout; the ring, the fancy 837 *sport.*

*wrestling,* all-in wrestling, catch-as-catch-can, no holds barred, sumo, tag wrestling; catch, hold; wrestle, grapple, wrestling match; arm wrestling.

*martial arts,* budo, aikido, ba gua *or* pa kua, capoeira, iaido, jeet kune do, judo, jujitsu, karate, kendo, kung fu, ninjutsu, tae kwon do, tai ji quan *or* t'ai chi ch'uan, tang soo do, tukido, wu shu; kick-boxing 713 *defence.*

*duel,* triangular d.; affair of honour, pistols for two and coffee for one; seconds out; single combat, gladiatorial c.; jousting, tilting, tourney, tournament; fencing, swordplay, singlestick, quarterstaff; hand-to-hand fighting, close grips; bullfight, corrida, tauromachy; cockfight; bullring, cockpit, lists 724 *arena.*

*fight,* hostilities, blow-up, appeal to arms 718 *warfare;* battle royal, free fight, free-for-all, showdown, rough and tumble, roughhouse, horseplay, shindig, stramash, scuffle, scrum, scrimmage, scramble, dogfight, mêlée, fracas, uproar, rumpus, ruction 61 *turmoil;* gang warfare, street fight, riot, rumble; brawl, broil 709 *quarrel;* fisticuffs, blows, hard knocks; give and take, cut and thrust; affray, set-to, tussle; running fight, dingdong f., close fighting, hand-to-hand f.; close grips, close quarters; combat, fray, clash, conflict 279 *collision;* encounter, dustup, scrap, brush; skirmish, skirmishing;

engagement, action, pitched battle, stand-up fight, shoot-out 718 *battle;* deed of arms, feat of a., passage of a. 676 *deed;* campaign, struggle; death struggle, death grapple, 'war to the knife' (see quotation at 712 *terror tactics),* fight to the death; Armageddon, theomachy, gigantomachy; field of battle, battlefield 724 *battleground.*

*contender,* struggler, striver; tussler, fighter, battler, gamecock, fighting dog; gladiator, bull-fighter, matador, toreador 722 *combatant;* prize-fighter 722 *pugilist;* duellist 709 *quarreller;* fencer, swordsman; candidate, entrant, examinee; competitor, rival, corrival, emulator, vier; challenger, runner-up, finalist; front runner, favourite, top seed; starter, also-ran, the field, all comers; contestant, pot-hunter; racer, runner, marathoner 162 *athlete;* sprinter 277 *speeder.*

**Adj.** *contending,* struggling, grappling etc. vb.; rival, rivalling, vying, racing, outdoing 306 *surpassing;* competing, in the same business; agonistic, sporting; jogging; starting, running, in the running, in with a chance; athletic, palaestric, pugilistic, gladiatorial; contentious, quarrelsome 709 *quarrelling;* irritable 892 *irascible;* aggressive, combative, fight-hungry, spoiling for a fight, pugnacious, bellicose, war-mongering 718 *warlike;* at loggerheads, at odds, at war, belligerent 718 *warring;* competitive, keen, cutthroat; hand-to-hand, close, at close quarters; keenly contested, dingdong; close-run; well-fought, fought to the death, fought to the finish.

**Vb.** *contend,* combat, strive, struggle, battle, fight, tussle, wrestle, grapple 671 *attempt;* oppose, put up a fight 715 *resist;* argue for, stick out for, make a point of, insist 532 *emphasize;* contest, compete, challenge, stake, wager, bet; play, play against, match oneself, vie with, race, run a race; emulate, rival 911 *be jealous;* outrival 306 *outdo;* enter, enter for, take on, enter the lists, descend into the arena, take up the challenge, pick up the gauntlet; cross swords with, couch one's lance, tilt with, joust w., break a lance w.; take on, try a fall, try conclusions with, close w., grapple w., engage w., lock horns w. 712 *strike at;* have a hard fight, fight to a finish.

*fight,* break the peace, have a fight, scuffle, row, scrimmage, scrap, set to 176 *be violent;* pitch into, sail i. 712 *attack;* lay about one 712 *strike at;* mix it, join in the mêlée; square up to, come to blows, exchange b., put up one's fists, give hard knocks, give and take; box, spar, pummel, jostle, hit, kick, scratch, bite 279 *strike;* fall foul of, join issue with 709 *quarrel;* duel, call out, give satisfaction; encounter, have a brush with, scrap w., exchange shots, skirmish; take on, engage, fight a pitched battle 718 *give battle*; come to grips, come to close quarters, close with, grapple, lock horns; fence, cross swords, measure s.; fight hand to hand, use cold steel; appeal to arms 718 *go to war*; combat, campaign, 'fight the good fight' (see quotation at 933 *be virtuous*) 718 *wage war*; fight hard, fight like fiends, fight it out, fight to the last man 599 *be resolute*.

**717 Peace**

**N.** *peace*, state of p., peacefulness, peace and quiet, a quiet life, the line of least resistance 266 *quiescence*; harmony 710 *concord*; 'piping time of peace' (see quotation for 'grim-visaged war' at 718 *war*) 730 *palmy days*; peacetime, Civvy Street; universal peace, Pax Romana; law and order 60 *order*; end of hostilities, demobilization 145 *cessation*; truce, uneasy t., armistice 145 *lull*; freedom from war, cold w., coexistence, armed neutrality; neutrality, nonalignment; noninvolvement 860 *indifference*; nonintervention 620 *avoidance*; peaceableness, nonaggression 177 *moderation*; cordial relations 880 *friendship*; pacifism, peace at any price, peace in our time, nonviolence, ahimsa; disarmament, decommissioning, peacemaking, peace process, irenics 719 *pacification*; pipe of peace, calumet; league of peace, peace treaty, nonaggression pact 765 *treaty*; burial of the hatchet 506 *amnesty*; peace dividend.

*pacifist*, man *or* woman of peace, peace women, peace-lover, peacemonger, dove; peace camp, peace party, CND 177 *moderator*; neutral, civilian, noncombatant, nonbelligerent; passive resister, conscientious objector, conchie; peacemaker 720 *mediator*; Little Englander.

**Adj.** *peaceful*, quiet, halcyon 266 *tranquil*; piping 730 *palmy*; without war, without bloodshed, bloodless; harmless, dovelike 935 *innocent*; mild-mannered, easy-going 884 *amiable*; uncompetitive, uncontentious; peaceable, law-abiding, peace-loving, pacific, unmilitary, unwarlike, unmilitant, unaggressive, war-weary; pacifist, nonviolent; unarmed, noncombatant, civilian; unresisting, passive, submissive 721 *submitting*; peace-making, conciliatory, irenic 720 *mediatory*; without enemies, at peace; not at war, neutral; postwar, prewar, interwar; peacetime.

**Vb.** *be at peace*, enjoy p., stay at p., observe neutrality, keep out of war, keep out of trouble; mean no harm, forget one's differences, be pacific 935 *be innocent*; keep the peace, avoid bloodshed; work for peace, make p. 720 *mediate*; 'beat swords into plough-shares', 'make the lion lie down with the lamb', smoke the pipe of peace;

> . . . And they shall beat their swords into plowshares, and their spears into pruninghooks: nation shall not lift up sword against nation, neither shall they learn war any more. . . .
> . . . The wolf also shall dwell with the lamb, and the leopard shall lie down with the kid; and the calf and the young lion and the fatling together; and a little child shall lead them.
> Bible, Isaiah

civilianize, demilitarize.

**Adv.** *peacefully*, peaceably, pacifically; without violence, bloodlessly; quietly, tranquilly, in peace, at p.

**718 War**

**N.** *war*, arms, the sword; 'grim-visaged war', 'horrida bella', 'ultima ratio regum';

> Grim-visag'd war hath smooth'd his wrinkl'd front;
> And now, instead of mounting barbed steeds,
> To fright the souls of fearful adversaries, –
> He capers nimbly in a lady's chamber
> To the lascivious pleasing of a lute.
> But I . . .
> . . . I, in this weak piping time of peace,
> Have no delight to pass away the time.
> William Shakespeare, *Richard III*

> Bella, horrida bella,
> Et Thybrim multo spumantem sanguine cerno.
> (*I see wars, frightful wars, and the Tiber foaming with much blood.*)
> Virgil, *Aeneid*

> Ultima ratio regum
> (*The final argument of kings*)
> A saying that Louis XIV had engraved on his cannons.

appeal to arms, arbitrament of war, fortune of w.; undeclared war, cold w., armed neutrality; paper war, war of words, polemic 709 *quarrel*; war of nerves, sabre-rattling, gunboat diplomacy 854 *intimidation*; half-war, uneasy peace, doubtful war, phoney w.; disguised w., intervention, armed i., police action; real war, hot w.; ground war, air w.; internecine war, civil w., war of revolution, war of independence; wars of religion, holy war, crusade, jihad; aggressive war, war of expansion; limited war, localized w.; triphibious w., war on all fronts, all-out war; major w., general w., world w., global w.; total w., blitzkrieg, atomic war, nuclear w., push-button w.; war of attrition, truceless war, 'war to the knife' (see quotation at 712 *terror tactics*), war to the death, no holds barred; war to end all wars, Armageddon; price war, predatory pricing; war crimes, war criminals; pomp and circumstance of war, the panoply of w., chivalry, shining armour, rows of scarlet, nodding plumes; martial music, drums, bugle, trumpet; call to arms, bugle call 547 *call*; battle cry, rallying cry, slogan, war whoop, war song 711 *defiance*; god of war, Ares, Mars, Bellona. (See also *warfare*.)

*belligerency*, state of war, state of siege; resort to arms, declaration of war, outbreak of w., militancy, hostilities; wartime, wartime conditions, time of war.

*bellicosity*, war fever; love of war, warlike habits, military spirit, pugnacity, combativeness, aggressiveness, hawkishness, militancy 709 *quarrelsomeness*; militarism, expansionism; jingoism, chauvinism, gung-ho 481 *prejudice*.

*art of war*, warcraft, siegecraft, strategy, grand s. 688 *tactics*; castrametation 713 *fortification*; generalship, soldiership, seamanship, airmanship 694 *skill*; ballistics, gunnery, musketry practice; drill, training 534 *teaching*; staffwork, logistics, planning 623 *plan*; military evolutions, manoeuvres; military experience 490 *knowledge*.

*war measures*, war footing, war preparations, arming 669 *preparation*; call to arms, clarion call, fiery cross 547 *call*; war effort, war work, call-up, rally, mobilization, recruitment, conscription, national service, military duty; volunteering, doing one's duty, for king *or* queen and country, joining up, enlisting; rationing; blackout; censorship; internment.

*warfare*, war, open w., warpath, making war, waging w.; deeds of blood, bloodshed, battles, sieges 176 *violence*; fighting, campaigning, soldiering, active service; military s., naval s., air s.; bombing, saturation b. 712 *bombardment*; raiding, sea r.; besieging, blockading, investment 235 *enclosure*; aerial warfare, naval w., submarine w., undersea w., chemical w., gas w., germ w., bacteriological w., atomic w., nuclear w., theatre nuclear w., tactical n. w.; economic w., blockade, attrition, scorched earth policy; psychological warfare, propaganda; cyberwarfare, cyberwar, information w.; offensive warfare 712 *attack*; defensive warfare 713 *defence*; mobile warfare, static w., trench w., desert w., jungle w.; bush-fighting, guerrilla warfare, sniping; campaign, expedition; operations, land o., sea o., naval o., air o., combined o., joint o., amphibious o.; incursion, invasion, raid; order, word of command, orders 737 *command*; password, watchword; battle cry (see also *war*) 547 *call*; plan of campaign, strategy, battle orders 623 *plan*.

*battle*, pitched b., battle royal 716 *fight*; line of battle, order of b., array; line, firing l., first l., front l., front, battle f., battle station; armed conflict, action, scrap, skirmish, brush, collision, clash, shootout, gun battle, firefight; offensive, blitz 712 *attack*; defensive battle, stand 713 *defence*; engagement, naval e., sea fight, air f., dogfight; arena, battlefield, field of

battle, theatre of war, area of hostilities 724 *battleground*.

**Adj.** *warring*, on the warpath; campaigning, battling etc. vb.; at war, in a state of w.; belligerent, aggressive, bellicose, militant, engaged in war, mobilized, uniformed, under arms, in the army, at the front, on active service; militant, up in arms; armed, sword in hand 669 *prepared*; arrayed, embattled; engaged, at grips, at loggerheads 709 *quarrelling*; on the offensive 712 *attacking*.

*warlike*, militaristic, bellicose, hawkish, unpacific; militant, aggressive, belligerent, pugnacious, pugilistic, combative; war-loving, warmongering, fierce, untamed 898 *cruel*; bloodthirsty, battle-hungry, war-fevered; military, paramilitary, martial, exercised in arms, bearing a.; veteran, battle-scarred; knightly, chivalrous; soldierly, soldierlike; military, naval; operational, strategical, tactical.

**Vb.** *go to war*, resort to arms; declare war, open hostilities, 'let slip the dogs of war';

> Caesar's spirit, ranging for revenge,
> With Ate by his side, come hot from hell,
> Shall in these confines, with a monarch's voice
> Cry, 'Havoc!' and let slip the dogs of war,
> That this foul deed shall smell above the earth
> With carrion men, groaning for burial.
>
> William Shakespeare, *Julius Caesar*

appeal to arms, unsheathe the sword, throw away the scabbard, whet the sword, take up the cudgels 716 *fight*; take to arms, fly to a., rise, rebel 738 *revolt*; raise one's banner, set up one's standard, call to arms, send round the fiery cross; arm, militarize, mobilize, put on a war footing; rally, call up, call to the colours, recruit, conscript; join the army, join up, enlist, enrol, put on uniform, take a commission.

*wage war*, make w., go on the warpath; march to war, engage in hostilities, war, war against, war upon; campaign, open a c., take the field; go on active service, shoulder a musket, smell powder, flesh one's sword; soldier, be at the front; take the offensive, invade 712 *attack*; keep the field, hold one's ground 599 *stand firm*; act on the defensive 713 *defend*; manoeuvre, march, countermarch; blockade, beleaguer, besiege, invest 230 *surround*; shed blood, put to the sword 362 *slaughter*; ravage, burn, scorch 165 *lay waste*; press the button 165 *demolish, be destroyed*.

*give battle*, battle, offer b., accept b.; cross swords with, take issue with; join battle, meet on the battlefield; engage, provoke an engagement; stage a shootout, call for a showdown, combat, confront, fight it out 716 *fight*; take a position, choose one's ground, dig in; rally, close the ranks, stand, make a s. 715 *resist*; sound the charge, beat the drum, go over the top 712 *charge*; open fire 712 *fire at*; skirmish, brush with 716 *contend*.

**Adv.** *at war*, at the sword's point, at knife-point, at the point of the bayonet, in the thick of the fray, at the cannon's mouth.

## 719 Pacification

**N.** *pacification*, pacifying, peacemaking, conflict resolution; conciliation, appeasement, mollification 177 *moderation*; reconciliation, reconcilement, détente, improved relations, rapprochement; accommodation, adjustment 24 *agreement*; composition of differences 770 *compromise*; good offices 720 *mediation*; peace process, peace talks; convention, entente, understanding, peace treaty, nonaggression pact, SALT 765 *treaty*; suspension of hostilities, truce, armistice, cease-fire 145 *lull*; disarmament, decommissioning, CND, peace movement, demobilization, disbanding; nuclear-free zone, peace camp; peace dividend; imposed peace, forced reconciliation 740 *compulsion*.

*peace offering*, eirenicon, irenics 177 *moderator*; propitiation, appeasement 736 *leniency*; dove of peace, olive branch, overture, peaceful approach, hand of friendship, outstretched hand 880 *friendliness*; flag of truce, white flag, pipe of peace, calumet 717 *peace*; wergild, blood money, compensation 787 *restitution*; fair offer, easy terms 177 *moderation*; plea for peace 506 *amnesty*; mercy 909 *forgiveness*.

**Adj.** *pacificatory*, conciliatory, placatory, propitiatory, dove-like; irenic 880 *friendly*; disarming, soothing 177 *alleviative*; peacemaking, mediatory; pacified, happy 828 *content*.

**Vb.** *pacify*, make peace, impose p., give peace to; allay, tranquillize, mollify, soothe 177 *assuage*; smooth one's ruffled feathers, pour balm into one's wounds, heal 656 *cure*; hold out the olive branch, hold out one's hand, return a soft answer, coo like a dove 880 *be friendly*; conciliate, propitiate, disarm, reconcile, placate, appease, satisfy 828 *content*; pour oil on troubled waters 266 *bring to rest*; restore harmony 410 *harmonize*; win over, bring to terms, meet halfway 770 *compromise*; compose differences, settle d., accommodate 24 *adjust*; bridge over, bring together 720 *mediate*; show mercy 736 *be lenient*; grant a truce, grant an armistice, grant peace 766 *give terms*; keep the peace 717 *be at peace*.

*make peace*, stop fighting, cry quits, break it up 145 *cease*; bury the hatchet, let bygones be bygones, forgive and forget 506 *forget*; shake hands, make it up, make friends, kiss and make up, patch up a quarrel, come to an understanding, agree to differ; lay down one's arms, sheathe the sword, put up one's sword, 'beat swords into ploughshares' (see quotation at 717 *be at peace*); disarm, decommission, demilitarize, demobilize, make a truce, suspend hostilities; smoke the pipe of peace, 'close the gates of Janus'.

> It was the custom of the country [Latium], when war was to be undertaken, for the chief magistrate, clad in his robes of office, with solemn pomp to open the gates of the temple of Janus, which were kept shut as long as peace endured.
>
> Thomas Bulfinch, *Bulfinch's Mythology*

## 720 Mediation

**N.** *mediation*, good offices, mediatorship, intercession; umpirage, refereeship, arbitration; intervention, stepping-in, interposition 231 *interjacency*; intermeddling 678 *overactivity*; statesmanship, diplomacy; parley, negotiation, peace process, peace talks 584 *conference*.

*mediator*, common friend, go-between, middleman, negotiator 231 *intermediary*; matchmaker, marriage bureau, dating agency, introduction a., computer dating, lonely hearts column; pander, Pandarus; referee, assistant r., linesman *or* -woman, fourth official, umpire 480 *estimator*; arbitrator; diplomat, diplomatist, representative, attorney, agent, press a., spokesperson 754 *delegate*; intercessor, pleader, propitiator; moderating influence, peace party, peace movement, dove 177 *moderator*; peacemaker, peace-keeping force; pacifier, pacificator, troubleshooter, ombudsman, ACAS; marriage guidance counsellor, family conciliation service, Relate 691 *adviser*.

**Adj.** *mediatory*, mediatorial, intercessory, intercessorial, propitiatory 719 *pacificatory*.

**Vb.** *mediate*, intervene, intermeddle 678 *meddle*; step in, put oneself between, interpose 231 *put between*; proffer one's good offices, offer one's intercession, intercede for, beg off, propitiate; run messages for, be a go-between, act as a pander for; bring together, negotiate, act as agent; arbitrate, umpire 480 *judge*; compose differences 719 *pacify*.

## 721 Submission

**N.** *submission*, submissiveness 739 *obedience*; subservience, slavishness 745 *servitude*; acquiescence, compliance, consent 488 *assent*; supineness, peace at any price, line of least resistance, nonresistance, passiveness, resignation, fatalism 679 *inactivity*; yielding, giving way, giving in, white flag, capitulation, surrender, unconditional s., cession, abandonment 621 *relinquishment*; deference, humble submission 872 *humility*; act of submission, homage 739 *loyalty*; kneeling, genuflexion, kowtow, prostration 311 *obeisance*; defeatist, quitter; mouse, doormat 856 *coward*.

**Adj.** *submitting*, surrendering etc. vb.; quiet, meek, unresisting, nonresisting, law-abiding 717 *peaceful*; submissive 739 *obedient*; fatalistic, resigned, acquiescent 488 *assenting*; pliant, accommodating, malleable 327 *soft*; weak-kneed, bending; crouching, crawling, cringing, lying down, supine, prostrate, boot-licking, bowing and scraping; kneeling, on bended knees, sycophantic, Uriah Heepish, toadying 872 *humble*.

**Vb.** *submit*, yield, give in; not resist, not insist, defer to; bow to, make a virtue of necessity, yield with a good grace, admit defeat, yield the palm 728 *be defeated*; resign oneself, be resigned, bite the bullet 488 *acquiesce*; accept 488 *assent*; shrug one's shoulders 860 *be indifferent*; withdraw, make way for, draw in one's horns 286 *turn back*; not contest, let judgment go by default 679 *be inactive*; cease resistance, stop fighting, have no fight left, have all the fight knocked out of one, give up, cry quits, have had enough, throw up the sponge, throw in the towel, surrender, hold up one's hands, show the white flag, ask for terms; surrender on terms, capitulate; throw oneself on another's mercy; give oneself up, yield oneself, throw down one's arms, hand over one's sword, hang up one's sword, give one's parole; haul down the flag, strike one's colours; renounce authority, deliver the keys.

*knuckle under*, succumb, be out for the count, cave in, collapse; sag, wilt, faint, drop 684 *be fatigued*; show no fight, take the line of least resistance, bow before the inevitable, bow before the storm; be submissive, learn obedience, bow one's neck to the yoke, do homage 745 *be subject*; take one's medicine, swallow the pill 963 *be punished*; apologize, eat humble pie, eat dirt 872 *be humble*; take it, take it from one, take it lying down, pocket the insult, grin and bear it, suffer in patience, digest, stomach, put up with 825 *suffer*; bend, bow, kneel, kowtow, toady, crouch, cringe, crawl, bow and scrape 311 *stoop*; grovel, lick the dust, lick the boots of, kiss the rod; fall on one's knees, throw oneself at the feet of, clasp someone's knees, beg for mercy, cry *or* howl for m. 905 *ask mercy*.

**722 Combatant. Army. Navy. Air Force**
**N.** *combatant*, fighter, struggler 716 *contender*; aggressor, assailant, assaulter, mugger 712 *attacker*; besieger, stormer, escalader; storm-troops, shock troops; belligerent, fighting man,

man-at-arms, warrior, brave; bodyguard 713 *defender*; gunman, strongarm man, hitman 362 *killer*; bully, bravo, rough, rowdy, bovver boy, boot boy 904 *ruffian*; fire-eater, swashbuckler, swaggerer, miles gloriosus 877 *boaster*; duellist 709 *quarreller*; swordsman, sabreur, foilsman, fencer, sword, good s.; gladiator, laquearius, myrmillo, retiarius, Samnite, secutor, Thracian 162 *athlete*; fighting cock, gamecock; bull-fighter, matador, picador, toreador; grappler, wrestler, jujitsuist, judoist, karate expert 716 *wrestling*; competitor 716 *contender*; champion, champ 644 *exceller*; jouster, tilter; knight, knight-errant, paladin 707 *patron*; wrangler, disputer, controversialist 475 *reasoner*; barrister, advocate 959 *litigant*.

*pugilist*, pug, boxer, bruiser, champion, champ, sparring partner; flyweight, bantam-weight, featherweight, welterweight, middle-weight, cruiserweight, heavyweight; slogger, pummeler 716 *pugilism*.

*militarist*, jingoist, chauvinist, gungho, expansionist, militant, warmonger, hawk; crusader, Ghazi; kshatriya, Samurai, Mameluke; professional soldier, freelance, mercenary (see also *soldier*); soldier of fortune, adventurer, condottiere; freebooter, marauder, pirate, privateer, buccaneer 789 *robber*.

*soldier*, army man, pongo; military man, long-term soldier, regular; soldiery, troops (see also *armed force*); campaigner, old c., conquistador; old soldier, veteran, Chelsea pensioner; fighting man, warrior, brave; myrmidon; man-at-arms, redcoat, legionary, legionnaire, centurion; vexillary, standard-bearer, colour escort, colour sergeant, ensign, cornet; heavy-armed soldier, hoplite; light-armed soldier, peltast; velites, skirmishers; sharpshooter, sniper, franctireur 287 *shooter*; auxiliary, territorial, Home Guard, militiaman, fencible; yeomanry, yeoman; irregular, irregular troops, moss-trooper, cateran, kern, gallowglass, rapparee, bashi-bazouk; raider, tip-and-run r.; guerrilla, partisan, freedom fighter, fedayeen; resistance fighter, underground f., Maquis; picked troops 644 *elite*; guards, housecarls 660 *protector* (see also *armed force*); effective, enlisted man; reservist; volunteer; mercenary; pressed man; conscript, recruit, rookie; serviceman, Tommy, Tommy Atkins, Jock, GI, doughboy, Aussie, Anzac, poilu, sepoy, Gurkha, askari; woman soldier, female warrior, Amazon, Boadicea; battlemaid, valkyrie; Wren, WRAF, WRAC.

*soldiery*, cannon fodder, food for powder; gallant company, merry men, heroes; rank and file, the ranks, other r.; private, private soldier, common s., man-at-arms; slinger, archer, bowman, crossbowman, arbalester; spearman, pikeman, halberdier, lancer; arquebusier, matchlockman, musketeer, fusilier, rifleman, pistoleer, carabineer, bazookaman, grenadier, bombardier, gunner, machine-gunner, artilleryman; pioneer, sapper, miner, engineer; signalman; corporal, sergeant, lieutenant 741 *army officer*.

*army*, host, camp; phalanx, legion; cohorts, big battalions; horde, mass 104 *multitude*; warlike people, martial race; nation in arms, general levy, arrière-ban; National Guard, Home G.; militia, yeomanry; vigilantes; regular army, standing a., professional a., mercenary a., volunteer a., territorial a., conscript a., draft; the services, armed forces, air arm, fleet air arm, fleet.

*armed force*, forces, troops, contingents, effectives, men, personnel; armament, armada; ground forces, ground troops; corps d'élite, ceremonial troops, guards, household troops; Household Cavalry, Royal Horse Guards, The Blues and Royals, Life Guards, Foot Guards; Swiss G., Praetorian G., Varangian G., Immortals, janissaries; picked troops, crack t., shock t., storm t.; spearhead, reconnaissance party, expeditionary force, striking f., flying column; parachute troops, paratroops, commando, Commandoes, task force, raiding party, guerrilla force; combat troops, field army, line, thin red l., front l., front-line troops, first echelon; wing, van, vanguard, rear, rearguard, centre, main body; second echelon, base troops, reserves, recruits, reinforcements, draft, levy 707 *auxiliary*; base, staff; detachment, picket, party, detail; patrol, night patrol, night watch, sentry, sentinel, vedette 660 *protector*; garrison, occupying force, occupation troops, army of occupation.

*formation*, array, line; square, phalanx; legion, cohort, century, decury, maniple; column, file, rank; unit, group, detachment, corps, army c., division, armoured d., panzer d.; brigade, rifle b., light b., heavy b.; artillery brigade, battery; regiment, cavalry r., squadron, troop; battalion, company, platoon, section, squad, detail, party 74 *band*.

*infantry*, line i., bayonets, foot regiment, infantryman, foot soldier, foot, peon; footslogger, PBI; mountain infantry, light i.; chasseur, jaeger, Zouave.

*cavalry*, yeomanry; heavy cavalry, light c., sabres, horse, light h., cavalry regiment; horseman, cameleer, rider; mounted troops, mounted rifles, mounted police, mounted infantry, horse artillery; horse soldier, cavalryman, yeoman; trooper, sowar; chivalry, knight; man-at-arms, lancer, uhlan, hussar,

cuirassier, dragoon, light d., heavy d.; Ironsides, Cossack, spahi; rough-rider; armour, armoured car, armoured personnel carrier; tank, Panzer; charger, destrier 273 *warhorse*.

*navy*, sea power, admiralty; sail, wooden walls; fleet arm, naval armament, armada; fleet, flotilla, squadron; argosy; merchant marine.

*naval person*, naval service, navy, senior service; admiral, Sea Lord 741 *naval officer*; sailor 270 *mariner*; bluejacket, man-o'-war man, able seaman, rating, pressed man; foretopman; powder monkey; cabin boy; gobby, gob, swab, swabbie; marine, jolly, leatherneck, limey; submariner, naval airman 270 *nautical personnel*; Royal Navy, RN, WRNS; Royal Marines; Royal Naval Reserve, RNR, RNVR, Wavy Navy.

*warship*, war vessel, war galley, bireme, trireme, quinquereme, galleon, galleass 275 *ship*; raider, privateer, pirate ship; man-o'-war, ship of the line, armoured vessel, capital ship, battleship, dreadnought; monitor, ironclad; cruiser, light c., armoured c., battle c.; frigate, corvette; mosquito boat, fast patrol b., PT b.; gunboat, motor torpedo boat, E-boat; destroyer; fire ship, blockship; minelayer, minesweeper; submarine, nuclear s., U-boat; Q-ship, mystery s.; aircraft carrier, fleet c.; landing craft, duck, amphibian; transport, troopship; tender, store ship, depot s., parent s., guard s., hospital s.; flagship, flotilla leader.

*air force*, RAF, WRAF, USAF; Royal Air Force Volunteer Reserve; air arm, flying corps, air service, fleet air arm; squadron, flight, group, wing; warplane 276 *aircraft*; battle plane, bomber, fighter b., heavy b., light b., fighter, night f., interceptor, ground-attack aircraft, interdictor; flying boat, patrol plane, scout; transport plane, troop-carrier; Zeppelin, captive balloon, barrage b. 276 *airship*; air troops, airborne division; parachute troops, paratroopers; aircraftman, ground staff; fighter pilot, bomber p., navigator, observer, air crew.

### 723 Arms

**N.** *arms* (see also *weapon*); arming, armament, munitioning, munitions; armaments, arms race; nuclear deterrent, anti-missile defence system, Star Wars, Strategic Defence Initiative, SDI, Son of Star Wars 713 *defence*; arms traffic, gun-running; ballistics, rocketry, missilery, gunnery, musketry, archery, bowmanship.

*arsenal*, armoury, gun room, gun rack, ammunition chest; arms depot 632 *storage*; ammunition dump; magazine, powder m., powder barrel, powder keg, powder flask, powder horn; caisson, ammunition box; bullet-pouch, cartridge belt, bandolier; arrow-case, quiver; scabbard, sheath; holster 194 *receptacle*.

*weapon*, arm, deterrent; deadly weapon, defensive w.; armour, plate, mail 713 *defence*; offensive weapon 712 *attack*; conventional weapon, nuclear w., theatre n. w., tactical n. w. 718 *warfare*; secret weapon, death ray, laser, directed-energy weapon, kinetic energy w., particlebeam w.; germ warfare, chemical w.; biological weapon, aflatoxin; gas, war g., poison g., mustard g., nerve g., Sarin 659 *poison*; natural weapon, teeth, claws, nails 256 *sharp point*.

*missile weapon*, javelin, harpoon, dart, throwing star; bolas, lasso; boomerang, woomera, throwstick; arrow, barbed a., poisoned a., shaft, bolt, quarrel; arrowhead, barb; stone, brick, brickbat; slingstone, shot, ball, bullet, pellet, fléchette, shell, star s., gas s., shrapnel, whizzbang, rocket, MIRV (see also *ammunition*); bow, longbow, crossbow, arbalest, ballista, catapult, mangonel, sling; blowpipe; bazooka, rocket-thrower (see also *gun*); cruise missile, guided m., ballistic m., ICBM, intercontinental ballistic missile, surface-to-air m., Exocet (tdmk) 287 *missile*; anti-missile missile, ABM; Star Wars (see also *arms*).

*club*, mace, knobkerrie, knobstick, warhammer 279 *hammer*; bat, staff, stave, stick, switch, lathi, quarterstaff; life-preserver, bludgeon, truncheon, cudgel, shillelagh, blackjack, nunchaku, sandbag, knuckle-duster, brass knuckles, cosh, bicycle chain, blunt instrument; battering ram 279 *ram*.

*spear*, harpoon, gaff; lance, javelin, jerid, pike, assegai; partisan, bill, halberd 256 *sharp point*; throwing stick.

*axe*, battleaxe, tomahawk, hatchet, halberd, bill, gisarme; poleaxe, chopper 256 *sharp edge*.

*sidearms*, sword; cold steel, naked s.; broadsword, glaive, claymore, two-edged sword, two-handed s.; cutlass, hanger, short sword, swordstick; sabre, scimitar, yataghan, falchion, snickersnee; blade, fine b., trusty b., bilbo, Toledo; rapier, tuck; fencing sword, épée, foil; dagger, bayonet, dirk, skean, skean-dhu, poniard, dudgeon, miséricorde, stylet, stiletto 256 *sharp point*; matchet, machete, kukri, kris, parang, panga; knife, bowie k., flick k., switchblade 256 *sharp edge*.

*firearm*, small arms, hand gun, arquebus, hackbut; matchlock, wheel-lock, flintlock, fusil, musket, Brown Bess; blunderbuss, muzzleloader, smoothbore, carbine; breechloader, chassepot, needlegun; rifle, magazine r., repeating r., Winchester; fowling piece, sporting gun, shotgun, sawn-off s., single-

barrelled gun, double-barrelled g., elephant g.; Enfield rifle, Lee-Enfield, Lee-Metford, Martini-Henry, Mauser, Snider; bore, calibre; muzzle; trigger, lock; magazine; breech, butt, gunstock; sight, backsight; ramrod.

*pistol*, duelling p., horse p.; petronel, pistolet; six-shooter, colt, revolver, repeater, zipgun, rod, gat, shooting iron, automatic.

*gun*, guns, ordnance, cannonry, artillery, light a., heavy a., mountain a.; horse artillery, galloping guns; battery, broadside; artillery park, gun p.; cannon, brass c., bombard, falconet, swivel, jingal, basilisk, petard, carronade, culverin; mortar; piece, field piece, field gun, siege g.; great gun, heavy g., cannon royal, seventy-four, heavy metal, Big Bertha; howitzer, trench-mortar, minethrower, minenwerfer, Minnie, trench gun; anti-aircraft gun, antitank g., ack-ack, Bofors gun, bazooka; assault gun, quick-firing g., Gatling g., mitrailleuse, pom-pom, Maxim, Lewis gun, machine g., M 60 machine g., light machine g., Bren g., Sten g., submachine g., subgun, Thompson submachine gun, tommy g.; flame-thrower; guncarriage, limber, caisson; gun emplacement, rocket site, launching pad, silo.

*ammunition*, live a., ammo, live shot; round of ammunition, round; powder and shot; shot, round s., case s., grape s., chain s., small s., mitraille, buckshot; ball, cannonball, bullet, expanding b., soft-nosed b., dumdum b., rubber b., plastic b., baton round; projectile 287 *missile*; slug, stone, pellet; shell, shrapnel, flak, ack-ack; wad, cartouche, cartridge, live c.; spent cartridge, dud; blank cartridge, blank; cartridge belt, cartridge clip; cartridge case.

*explosive*, propellant; powder, gunpowder; saltpetre, high explosive, plastic e., lyddite, melinite, cordite, gun cotton, dynamite, gelignite, nitroglycerine, Semtex (tdmk), TNT; cap, detonator, fuse; priming, charge, warhead, atomic w.; fissionable material; fireworks.

*bomb*, explosive device, blast bomb, car b., letter b., nail b., parcel b., pipe b.; shell, bombshell, fuel-air bomb, fuel-air explosive, thermobaric weapon; grenade, hand g., pineapple, Molotov cocktail, petrol bomb, acid b.; megaton bomb, atom b., A-bomb, nuclear b., hydrogen b., H-bomb; neutron b., enhanced radiation b.; mushroom cloud, fallout; dirty bomb; smart bomb; blockbuster, daisy-cutter bomb; cluster bomb, fragmentation b.; bomblet; firebomb, incendiary b., napalm b.; carcass, Greek fire; mine, landmine, anti-personnel m., anti-tank m., magnetic m., acoustic m., limpet; minefield, minelaying; booby trap 542 *trap*; depth charge, torpedo, tin fish; flying bomb, V-1, doodlebug, V-2; rocket bomb; time bomb, infernal machine; unexploded bomb, UXB, unexploded ordnance, UXO; bomb disposal, mine detection, mine-clearing, demining, deminer.

### 724 Arena

**N.** *arena*, field, field of action; ground, terrain; centre, scene, stage, theatre; hustings, platform, floor; amphitheatre, coliseum, stadium, stand, grandstand; campus, Campus Martius, Champs de Mars, parade ground, training g.; forum, marketplace 76 *focus*; hippodrome, circus, course, racecourse, turf; racetrack, track, running t., cinder t., indoor t., dog t.; ring, bullring, boxing r., ropes; rink, skating r., ice r.; palaestra, gymnasium, gym, exercise room, work-out r.; range, shooting r., rifle r., butts; playground, beach, swimming complex, lido, marina, pier, fairground 837 *pleasure ground*; leisure centre, recreation ground, playing field, football f., football pitch, cricket p.; AstroTurf (tdmk); court, tennis c., badminton c., squash c.; putting green, bowling g., bowling alley, skittle a.; snooker club; lists, tiltyard; cockpit, beargarden; chessboard, checkerboard; bridge table; snooker t., pool t.; auction room; examination hall; courtroom 956 *lawcourt*.

*battleground*, battlefield, field of battle, field of conflict, scene of action; field of blood, Aceldama; theatre of war, combat zone, no-go area; front, front line, firing l., trenches, no-man's-land; sector, salient, bulge, pocket; beachhead, bridgehead; encampment, tented field; disputed territory 718 *battle*.

SECTION FIVE

## Results of action

### 725 Completion

**N.** *completion*, finish, termination, conclusion, end of the matter 69 *end*; terminus 295 *goal*; issue, upshot 154 *event*; result, end r., final r., end product 157 *effect*; fullness 54 *completeness*; fulfilment 635 *sufficiency*; maturity, maturation, fruition, readiness, perfect r. 669 *preparedness*; consummation, culmination, ne plus ultra 646 *perfection*; exhaustiveness, thoroughness 455 *attention*; elaboration, rounding off, finishing off, mopping up, winding up; roofing, topping out; top, crown, superstructure 213 *summit*; missing link 627 *requirement*; last touch, last stroke, crowning s., crowning glory, final stroke, finishing s., coup de grâce, clincher; the icing on the cake, achievement, fait accompli, work done, finished product (see also *effectuation*); boiling point, danger p., breaking p., last straw 236

*limit*; climax, payoff; resolution, solution, dénouement, catastrophe, last act, final curtain, swansong, finale, finis 69 *finality*.

*effectuation*, carrying through *or* out; execution, discharge, implementation; dispatch, performance 676 *action*; accomplishment, achievement, realization 727 *success*; elaboration, working out.

**Adj.** *completive*, completing, perfective; crowning, culminating 213 *topmost*; finishing, conclusive, final, last 69 *ending*; unanswerable, crushing; thorough, thoroughgoing, wholehogging 599 *resolute*.

*completed*, full, full-blown 54 *complete*; done, well d., achieved, accomplished etc. vb.; wrought out, highly wrought, elaborate 646 *perfect*; sewn up, buttoned up, done and dusted, in the can, in the bag, under one's belt, secured 727 *successful*.

**Vb.** *carry through*, follow t., follow up; drive home, clinch, seal, set the seal on, seal up; clear up, mop up, wipe up, finish off, polish off; dispose of, dispatch, give the coup de grâce; complete, consummate, put the finishing touch, put the icing on the cake, top out 54 *make complete*; elaborate, hammer out, work o. 646 *perfect*; ripen, bring to a head, bring to the boil 669 *mature*; sit out, see out, see it through (see also *carry out*); get through, get shot of, dispose of, bring to its close, drive a nail into the coffin 69 *terminate*; set at rest 266 *bring to rest*.

*carry out*, see through, effect, enact 676 *do*; dispatch, execute, discharge, implement, effectuate, realize, compass, bring about, accomplish, fulfil, consummate, achieve 727 *succeed*; make short work of, make no bones of; do thoroughly, leave no loose ends, leave no stone unturned, not do by halves, go the whole hog, be in at the death; deliver the goods, bring home the bacon, be as good as one's word, fill the bill.

*climax*, cap, crown all 213 *crown*; culminate, peak, reach its peak; reach the zenith, reach a climax, scale the heights, conquer Everest; have an orgasm, come; reach boiling point, come to a crisis; reach the limit, touch bottom; put the lid on, add the last straw; come to its end, attain one's e., come to fruition, achieve one's goal, touch the goal 295 *arrive*; have enough of, be through with 635 *have enough*.

### 726 Noncompletion

**N.** *noncompletion*, no success 728 *failure*; nonperformance, nonexecution, neglect 458 *negligence*; nonfulfilment 636 *insufficiency*; deficiency, deficit 307 *shortfall*; lack 55 *incompleteness*; unripeness, immaturity 670 *undevelopment*; never-ending task, painting the Forth Bridge, a woman's work, Penelope's web, Sisyphean labour, argument in a circle, going round in circles, recurring decimal 71 *continuity*; continuation 146 *continuance*; perfunctoriness, superficiality, a lick and a promise 456 *inattention*; tinkering, work undone, job half-done, loose ends; no decision, lack of finality, no result, drawn game, draw; stalemate, deadlock; semicompletion, launching stage.

**Adj.** *uncompleted*, partial, fragmentary 55 *incomplete*; not finalized 55 *unfinished*; undone, unperformed, unexecuted, unachieved, unaccomplished; unrealized, half-done, half-finished, half-begun, hardly b., scamped 458 *neglected*; half-baked, underdone, unripe 670 *immature*; unthorough, perfunctory, superficial; not cleared up, left hanging, left in the air; lacking finish, unelaborated, not worked out, not thought through, inchoate, sketchy, in outline 647 *imperfect*; unbleached, unprocessed, semiprocessed; never-ending 71 *continuous*.

**Vb.** *not complete*, hardly begin, leave undone, leave in the air, leave hanging 458 *neglect*; skip, skive, scamp, do by halves, tinker, paper over the cracks 636 *not suffice*; scotch the snake not kill it 655 *wound*; give up, not follow up, not follow through; fall out, drop o., not stay the course; fall short of one's goal, fall down on 728 *fail*; defer, postpone, put off till tomorrow 136 *put off*.

**Adv.** *on the stocks*, under construction, on the anvil, in the making, in preparation, in process of.

## 727 Success

**N.** *success*, sweet smell of s., coming up roses, glory 866 *famousness*; success all round, happy outcome, happy ending, favourable issue; success story, progress, steady advance, Godspeed, time well spent 285 *progression*; fresh advance, breakthrough, quantum leap; one's day, landing on one's feet, continued success, run of luck, good fortune 730 *prosperity*; advantage, lead, temporary l., first blood 34 *advantage*; momentary success, flash in the pan; exploit, feat, achievement 676 *deed*; accomplishment, goal, golden goal 725 *completion*; a success, feather in one's cap, triumph, hit, smash h., box-office h., top of the charts, chart-topper, best-seller, sell-out, triumphant success, howling s., succès fou, rave reviews; good hit, winning h., good shot 694 *skill*; beginner's luck, lucky stroke, fluke 618 *nondesign*; hat trick, stroke of genius, coup, tour de force, masterstroke 694 *masterpiece*; trump, trump

card, winning c., card up one's sleeve 623 *contrivance*; success in examination, dux, pass, qualification; match-winning 34 *superiority*.

*victory*, infliction of defeat, beating, whipping, licking, trouncing 728 *defeat*; conquest, subdual 745 *subjection*; successful attack, taking by storm, escalade 712 *attack*; honours of battle, the best of it; win, game and match; outright win, complete victory, checkmate; narrow win, Pyrrhic victory, well-fought field; easy win, runaway victory, love game, walkover, pushover, picnic 701 *easy thing*; crushing victory, quelling v., slam, grand s.; kill, knockout, KO; mastery, ascendancy, upper hand, whip h., advantage, edge, pole position, winning p., certain victory 34 *advantage*; no defeat, stalemate 28 *draw*; celebration of victory, triumph, ovation, standing o., bouquets, epinician ode 876 *celebration*.

*victor*, winner, champion, world-beater, medallist, prizewinner, dux, first, double f. 644 *exceller*, winning side, the winners; triumpher, conquering hero, Alexander, Tamburlaine; conqueror, conquistador; defeater, beater, vanquisher, overcomer, subjugator, subduer, queller; master, mistress, master or mistress of the field, master or mistress of the situation; a success, successful rival, successful person, self-made man or woman, man or woman to watch, whiz kid, rising star 730 *prosperous person*.

**Adj.** *successful*, effective, efficacious; crushing, quelling; efficient; sovereign 658 *remedial*; well-spent, fruitful 640 *profitable*; happy, lucky; felicitous, masterly 694 *skilful*; ever-victorious, unbeatable (see also *unbeaten*); never-failing, surefire, foolproof; unerring, infallible, surefooted 473 *certain*; home and dry 725 *completed*; prizewinning, victorious, world-beating, chart-topping 644 *excellent*; winning, leading, up, one up 34 *superior*; on top, on song, in the ascendant, rising, on the up and up, going places, sitting pretty 730 *prosperous*; triumphant, crowning; triumphal, epinician, victorious; crowned with success, flushed with victory; glorious 866 *renowned*.

*unbeaten*, undefeated, unbowed, unsubdued, unquelled, unvanquished 599 *resolute*; unbeatable, unconquerable, ever-victorious, invincible.

**Vb.** *succeed*, succeed in, effect, accomplish, achieve, compass 725 *carry through*; be successful, make out, win one's spurs; make a success of, make a go of, make short work of, rise to the occasion; make good, rise, do well, pull oneself up by one's bootstraps, become a self-made man or woman, get promotion, work one's way up the ladder, come to the top 730 *prosper*; pass, make the grade, qualify, graduate, come off well, land on one's feet, give a good account of oneself, come well out of it, come off with flying colours, come out on top, have the best of it 34 *be superior*; advance, break through, make a break-through 285 *progress*; strive to some purpose, gain one's end, reach one's goal, secure one's object, obtain one's objective, attain one's purpose; pull it off, bring it off, be as good as one's word, bring home the bacon; have a success, score a s., make the big time, make a hit, top the charts, make a kill, go over big; hit the jackpot, break the bank; score a point, win a p., carry a p.; arrive, be a success, get around, make one's mark, click.

*be successful*, – efficacious, effective, etc adj.; come off, come right in the end; answer, answer the purpose, do the trick, fill the bill, ring the bell, show results, turn out well; turn up trumps, rise to the occasion, do oneself proud; do the job, do wonders, do marvels, work miracles; compass, manage 676 *do*; work, act, work like magic, act like a charm 173 *operate*; take effect, tell, pull its weight 178 *influence*; pay off, pay dividends, bear fruit 171 *be fruitful*; get it, hit it, hit the nail on the head, find the mot juste; play one's hand well, not put a foot wrong, never go w., not be wrong-footed; be surefooted, keep on the right side of; have the ball at one's feet, hold all the trumps; have the world in his *or* her hand; be irresistible, not know the meaning of failure, brush obstacles aside 701 *do easily*; not know when one is beaten, land on one's feet, come up smiling, come up smelling of roses 599 *be resolute*; avoid defeat, hold one's own, maintain one's position 599 *stand firm*.

*triumph*, have one's day, be crowned with success, wear the laurels of victory 876 *celebrate*; crow, crow over 877 *boast*; score, score off, be one up on; triumph over difficulties, contrive a success, manage, make it, win through; surmount, overcome obstacles, get over a snag, sweep difficulties out of the way; find a loophole, find a way out, find a way round 667 *escape*; make headway against, stem the tide, weather the storm 715 *resist*; reap the fruits, reap the harvest 771 *gain*.

*overmaster*, be too much for, be more than a match for 34 *be superior*; master, overcome, overpower, overmatch, overthrow, overturn, override, overtrump 306 *outdo*; have the advantage, take the a., seize the a., hold the a., keep the a., prevail 34 *predominate*; have one on the hip, have someone where one wants him *or* her, have one by the short hairs *or* by the short

and curlies (inf); have at one's mercy; checkmate, trump, ruff; conquer, vanquish, quell, subdue, subject, suppress, put down, crush 745 *subjugate*; capture, carry, take, storm, take by s., escalade 712 *attack*.

*defeat* (see also *overmaster*); discomfit, dash, put another's nose out of joint, settle one's hash, cook one's goose; repulse, rebuff 292 *repel*; confound, dismay 854 *frighten*; best, be too good for, get the better of, get the upper hand, get the whip h. 34 *be superior*; worst, outplay, outpoint, outflank, outmanoeuvre, outclass, outwit, outshine 306 *outdo*; disconcert, cut the ground from under one's feet, trip, lay by the heels 702 *obstruct*; baffle, gravel, nonplus 474 *puzzle*; defeat easily, knock spots off, wipe the floor with; beat, lick, thrash, whip, trounce, swamp, overwhelm, crush, drub, give a drubbing, roll in the dust, trample underfoot, trample upon; beat hollow, rout, put to flight, scatter 75 *disperse*; silence, put the lid on, put hors de combat, put out of court 165 *suppress*; down one's opponent, flatten, knock the stuffing out of, put out for the count, knock out; knock for six, hit for s.; bowl out, skittle o.; run hard, corner, drive to the wall, check, put in check 661 *endanger*; put an end to, wipe out, do for, settle, fix, dish 165 *destroy*; sink, send to the bottom 313 *plunge*; break, bankrupt, beggar 801 *impoverish*.

*win*, win the battle, carry the day, achieve victory, defeat the enemy, down one's opponent (see also *defeat*); be victorious, remain in possession of the field, claim the victory; come off best, come off with flying colours; win hands down, carry all before one, have it all one's own way, romp home, have a walkover, walk off with, waltz away with, walk it 701 *do easily*; win on points, win by a short head, win by a whisker, scrape home, survive; win the last battle, win the last round; win the match, take the prize, take the cup, gain the palm, wear the crown, wear the laurel wreath; become champion, beat all comers, sweep the board, rule OK 34 *be superior*.

*be lucky*, – fortunate, jammy (inf), etc. adj.; luck out (US inf).

**Adv.** *successfully*, swimmingly, marvellously well; to some purpose, to good p., with good result, with good effect, with magical e.; to one's heart's content, beyond one's fondest dreams, beyond all expectation; with flying colours, in triumph.

## 728 Failure

**N.** *failure*, nonsuccess, lack of success, negative result; no luck, off day, close but no cigar 731 *misfortune*; nonfulfilment 726 *noncompletion*;

frustration 702 *hindrance*; inefficacy, ineffectiveness 161 *ineffectuality*; vain attempt, abortive a., wild-goose chase, futile effort, no result, no-win situation 641 *lost labour*; mess, muddle, bungle 695 *bungling*; disorder, dysfunction 651 *illness, disease*; abortion, miscarriage 172 *unproductiveness*; impotence, brewer's droop (inf), premature ejaculation; hopeless failure, sad f., damp squib, washout, fiasco, flop; no ball, bosh shot, misfire, slip, omission, faux pas, own goal, 495 *mistake*; no go, dead stop, halt 145 *stop*; engine failure, electrical fault, computer f., computer malfunction, machine malfunction, gremlin, bug, glitch, seizing up, breakdown 702 *hitch*; collapse, fall, stumble, trip 309 *descent*; incapacity 163 *weakness*; anticlimax 509 *disappointment*; losses 772 *loss*; bankruptcy 805 *insolvency*.

*defeat*, bafflement, bewilderment, puzzlement 474 *uncertainty*; nonplus, deadlock, stalemate 145 *stop*; lost battle, repulse, rebuff, bloody nose, check, reverse; no move left, checkmate, mate, fool's m.; the worst of it, discomfiture, stick, flak, beating, drubbing, hiding, licking, thrashing, trouncing; retreat; flight 290 *recession*; dispersal 75 *dispersion*; stampede, panic 854 *fear*; rout, landslide; fall, downfall, collapse, débâcle; wreck, perdition, graveyard 165 *ruin*; lost cause, losing game, losing battle; deathblow, nail in the coffin, quietus; utter defeat, total d., final d., Waterloo; conquest, subjugation 745 *subjection*.

*loser*, unsuccessful competitor, baffled enemy, defeated rival; also-ran, nonstarter; has-been, history, extinct volcano; defeatist, pessimist, misery 834 *moper*; fumbler 697 *bungler*; dud, failure, flop, no-hoper, lemon; sacrifice, victim, prey 544 *dupe*; born loser 731 *unlucky person*; underdog 35 *inferior*; underachiever, retardate, slow learner, early leaver; dropout 25 *misfit*; bankrupt, insolvent 805 *nonpayer*; the losers, losing side, the defeated, the conquered, the vanquished, the fallen.

**Adj.** *unsuccessful*, ineffective, pale; inglorious, obscure, unrewarded, emptyhanded; unlucky 731 *unfortunate*; vain, bootless, negative, fruitless, profitless; dud, misfired, hanging fire; miscarried, stillborn, aborted, abortive, premature; jilted, ditched; manqué, failed, bombed, ploughed, flunked; unplaced, losing, failing; vincible; stumbling, tripping, groping, wandering, out of one's depth, losing one's grip 474 *uncertain*.

*defeated*, beaten, bested, worsted, pipped, dished, done for; baffled, thwarted, foiled 702 *hindered*; disconcerted, dashed, discomfited, 'hoist with one's own petard';

> For 'tis the sport to have the enginer
> Hoist with his own petar; and it shall go hard
> But I will delve one yard below their mines
> And blow them at the moon.
> William Shakespeare, *Hamlet*

outmanoeuvred, outmatched, outplayed, outvoted; outwitted, outclassed, outshone 35 *inferior*; thrashed, licked, whacked; on the losing side, among the also-rans, unplaced, out of the running; in retreat, in flight 290 *receding*; routed, scattered, put to flight; swamped, overwhelmed, sunk; overborne, overthrown, struck down, had it, knocked out, kaput, brought low, fallen; captured, made a prey, victimized, sacrificed.

*grounded*, stranded, wrecked, washed up, left high and dry; on the rocks, on one's beamends 165 *destroyed*; unhorsed, dismounted, thrown, brought low; ruined, bankrupt 700 *in difficulties*.

**Vb.** *fail*, not succeed, have no success, get no results; be unsuccessful, – beaten etc. adj.; bomb, flop; flatline (sl); fall down on, foozle, muddle, botch, bungle 495 *blunder*; flunk, not make the grade, be found wanting 636 *not suffice*; fail one, let one down 509 *disappoint*; miss the boat 138 *lose a chance*; misdirect, miss one's aim, go wide, miss, hit the wrong target, fall between two stools, miss an opportunity 282 *deviate*; get nothing out of it, get no change out of it, draw a blank, back the wrong horse, return empty-handed, lose one's pains, labour in vain, have shot one's bolt 641 *waste effort*; kiss goodbye to 772 *lose*; overreach oneself, bite off more than one can chew, come a cropper, fall, collapse, slide 309 *tumble*; break down, malfunction, come to pieces, fall to bits, come unstuck; falter, stall, seize, seize up, crock up, pack up, conk out; stop, come to a dead stop, come up against a blank wall, come to a dead end; stick, stick in the mud, get bogged down 145 *cease*; come to a sticky end, come to a bad e. 655 *deteriorate*; go on the rocks, run aground, be left high and dry, ground, sink 313 *founder*; make a loss, crash, bust, go b., break, go bankrupt, go belly-up 805 *not pay*.

*miscarry*, be stillborn, abort; misfire, hang fire, flash in the pan, fizzle out; fall, fall to the ground, crash 309 *tumble*; not come off, come to naught, come to nothing, go by the board, end in futility 641 *be useless*; fail to succeed, fall flat, come to grief; burst, bust, explode, blow up, go up in smoke; flop, bomb, prove a fiasco; not go well, go wrong, go amiss, go awry, go pear-shaped (inf), gang agley, take a turn for the worse, take an ugly turn; do no good, make things worse 832 *aggravate*; dash one's hopes, frustrate one's expectations 509 *disappoint*.

*be defeated*, lose, lose out, suffer defeat, take a beating, lose the day, lose the battle, lose the match; lose the election, concede defeat, lose one's seat, lose the vote, be outvoted; just lose, lose by a whisker, just miss, get pipped at the post; 'be in a catch-22 situation' (see quotation at 663 *pitfall*); be on a hiding to nothing; get the worst of it, come off second best, go off with one's tail between one's legs, lick one's wounds; be taken to the cleaner's; lose hands down, come in last, not win a point; take the count, bite the dust; fall, succumb, be history 745 *be subject*; be captured, fall a prey to, be victimized; retreat, lose ground 290 *recede*; take to flight 620 *run away*; admit defeat, have had enough, cry quits 721 *submit*; have not a leg to stand on, have the ground cut from under one's feet; go downhill 655 *deteriorate*; go to the wall, go to the dogs 165 *be destroyed*.

**Adv.** *unsuccessfully*, to no purpose, to little or no p., in vain.

### 729 Trophy

**N.** *trophy*, sign of success; war trophy, spoils, spoils of war, spolia opima, capture, captives 790 *booty*; scalp, head; scars, wounds 655 *wound*; memorial, war m., memento 505 *reminder*; triumphal arch 548 *monument*; triumph, ovation, standing o. 876 *celebration*; plum, glittering prizes; benefit, benefit match; prize, first p., consolation p., booby p., wooden spoon 962 *reward*; sports trophy, Ashes, cup, pot, plate, shield; award, Academy Award., Oscar A. *or* Oscar, Tony A. *or* Tony, Emmy A. *or* Emmy, golden disc, Golden Rose; bays, laurels, the laurel and the rose, crown, laurel c., bay c., coronal, chaplet, garland, wreath, palm, palm of victory; epinician ode, pat on the back; bouquet; favour, feather in one's cap, love token 547 *badge*; flying colours 875 *ostentation*; glory 866 *repute*.

*decoration*, honour 870 *title*; blushing honours, battle h., spurs 866 *honours*; citation, mention in dispatches; rosette, ribbon, sash, cordon bleu; athletic honour, blue, oar, cap; medal, gong, star, cross, garter, order; service stripe, long-service medal, war m., campaign m.; Victoria Cross, VC, Military C., Croix de Guerre, Iron Cross; Distinguished Service Cross, Congressional Medal, Medal of Honour; George Cross, Medal for Merit, Legion of Honour, civic crown; honours list.

### 730 Prosperity

**N.** *prosperity*, thriving, health and wealth, having it good 727 *success*; wellbeing, welfare,

weal 824 *happiness*; social inclusion; economic prosperity, boom, booming economy, sunrise e.; roaring trade, seller's market, bullish m., favourable trade balance, no unemployment; luxury, affluence, Easy Street 800 *wealth*; golden touch, Midas t.; fleshpots, 'the fat of the land', 'land flowing with milk and honey', 'a chicken in every pot' 635 *plenty*;

> And Pharaoh said unto Joseph, Say unto thy brethren, This do ye; lade your beasts, and go, get you unto the land of Canaan;
> And take your father and your households, and come unto me: and I will give you the good of the land of Egypt, and ye shall eat the fat of the land.
> Bible, Genesis

> And I am come down to deliver them out of the hand of the Egyptians, and to bring them up out of that land unto a good land and a large, unto a land flowing with milk and honey; unto the place of the Canaanites, . . .
> Bible, Exodus

> A chicken in every pot and a car in every garage.
> Slogan used by the Republican Party during Herbert Hoover's presidential campaign in 1928.

auspiciousness, favour, smiles of fortune, good f., blessings, godsend, crowning mercy, goodness and mercy 615 *good*; bonanza, winning streak, luck, run of l., good l., break, lucky b., lucky gamble, lucky shot, luck of the draw 159 *chance*; glory, honour and g., renown 866 *prestige*.

*palmy days*, heyday, prime, peak, zenith, floruit; halcyon days, bright d., summer, sunshine, fair weather, Indian summer, Edwardian s.; 'piping times' (see quotation for 'grim-visaged war' at 718 *war*) 717 *peace*; easy times, life of Riley, 'place in the sun' (see quotation at 859 *desire*), clover, velvet, bed of roses, 'roses all the way' (see quotation at 824 *joy*) 376 *euphoria*; golden times, Golden Age, Saturnia Regna 824 *happiness*; expansive times, Periclean Age, Augustan A., Pax Romana, Elizabethan Age.

*prosperous person*, man *or* woman of substance, man *or* woman of property, fat cat 800 *rich person*; successful person, rising man *or* woman, whiz kid; favourite of the gods, child of fortune, lucky fellow, lucky dog, lucky devil; arriviste, upstart, parvenu, nouveau riche, profiteer; celebrity, hero 866 *person of repute*; lion 890 *favourite*.

**Adj.** *prosperous*, thriving, flourishing, booming 727 *successful*; rising, doing well, on a roll (inf), up and coming, on the up and up, in the ascendant, going up in the world; on the make, profiteering; well set-up, established, well-to-do, well-off, well-heeled, rolling in it, affluent, comfortable, comfortably off 800 *moneyed*; riding high on the hog's back, riding on the crest of a wave, buoyant, bullish; fortunate, lucky, born with a silver spoon in one's mouth, born under a lucky star; in clover, on velvet; on easy street, in the money, at ease, in bliss 824 *happy*; fat, sleek, euphoric.

*bringing prosperity*, get-rich-quick.

*palmy*, balmy, halcyon, golden, couleur de rose, rosy; piping, blissful, blessed; providential, favourable, promising, auspicious, propitious, cloudless, clear, fine, fair, set f.; glorious, expansive; euphoric, agreeable, cosy 376 *comfortable*.

**Vb.** *prosper*, thrive, flourish, have one's day; do well, fare w., be on a roll (inf), have a good time of it 376 *enjoy*; bask in sunshine, make hay, live in clover, lie on velvet, have it easy, live on easy street, have it made, live on milk and honey (see quotation at 730 *prosperity*), 'live on the fat of the land' (see quotation at 730 *prosperity*), 'have never had it so good';

> Let's be frank about it; most of our people have never had it so good.
> Harold Macmillan

be in the money, be rolling in it; be wellheeled, batten on, grow fat, feed well 301 *eat*; blossom, bloom, flower 171 *be fruitful*; win glory 866 *have a reputation*; boom, drive a roaring trade, enjoy a seller's market; profiteer 771 *gain*; get on, go far, rise in the world, work one's way up, make it, arrive 727 *succeed*; make money, make a fortune, strike it rich, make one's pile, feather one's nest, line one's pockets, 800 *get rich*; run smoothly, run on oiled wheels, run like clockwork 258 *go smoothly*; go on swimmingly, swim with the tide, go with the crowd, sail before the wind; keep afloat, keep one's head above water, not do badly.

*have luck*, have all the l., have a stroke of l., have a lucky break, have a run of luck; strike lucky, strike oil, strike a rich vein, be on to a good thing, get on the gravy train; fall on one's feet, enjoy the smiles of fortune, bear a charmed life, be born under a lucky star, be born with a silver spoon in one's mouth, have the ball at one's feet.

*be auspicious*, – propitious etc. adj.; promise, promise well, augur well, set fair; favour, prosper, profit 615 *benefit*; look kindly on, smile on, shine on, bless, shed blessings on; water, fertilize, make blossom like the rose; turn out well, take a good turn, take a favourable t., take a turn for the better, turn up trumps 644 *do good*; glorify 866 *honour*.

**Adv.** *prosperously*, swimmingly 727 *successfully*; beyond one's wildest dreams, in the swim, in clover, on velvet, on easy street; in luck's way.

**Int.** good luck!, all the best!, best of British!

## 731 Adversity

**N.** *adversity*, adverse circumstances, misfortune, frowns of fortune, mixed blessing (see also *misfortune*); continual struggle, weary way 700 *difficulty*; hardship, hard life, tough time, no bed of roses 825 *suffering*; groaning, travail 377 *pain*; bad times, hard t., iron age, ice a., dark a., hell upon earth, vale of sorrows 616 *evil*; burden, load, pressure, pressure of the times; ups and downs of life, vicissitude 154 *event*; troubles, 'sea of t.' (see quotation at 616 *evil*), peck of t., trials, cares, worries 825 *worry*; wretchedness, misery, despondency, 'the Slough of Despond' 834 *dejection*;

> Now I saw in my dream, that . . . they drew nigh to a very miry Slough that was in the midst of the plain; and they, being heedless, did both fall suddenly into the bog; the name of the Slough was Despond.
> John Bunyan, *The Pilgrim's Progress*

bitter cup, bitter pill 872 *humiliation*; cross, cup of sorrows 825 *sorrow*; curse, blight, blast, plague, scourge, infliction, visitation 659 *bane*; bleakness, cold wind, draught, chill, cold, winter 380 *coldness*; gloom 418 *darkness*; ill wind, cross w.; blow, hard b., blow between the eyes 704 *opposition*; setback, check, rebuff, reverse 728 *defeat*; rub, pinch, plight, funeral 700 *predicament*; poor lookout, trouble ahead; trough, bad patch, rainy day 655 *deterioration*; slump, crash, recession, depression 679 *inactivity*; dark clouds, storm c., gathering c. 900 *threat*; decline, fall, downfall 165 *ruin*; broken fortune, want, need, social exclusion, distress, extremity 801 *poverty*.

*misfortune*, bad fortune, ill f.; bad luck, hard l., ill l., a bad hair day, annus horribilis; no luck, no luck this time, no success 728 *failure*; evil dispensation, evil star, malign influence 645 *badness*; hard case, raw deal, rotten hand, chicane, yarborough; hard lot, hard fate, hard lines; ill hap, mishap, mischance, misadventure, contretemps, accident, casualty 159 *chance*; disaster, calamity, catastrophe, the worst, the pits.

*unlucky person*, poor unfortunate, constant loser, no-hoper, poor risk; starcrossed lover, sport of fortune, plaything of fate, plaything of the gods, Jonah; down-and-out 728 *loser*; underdog 35 *inferior*; new poor 801 *poor person*; lame dog, lame duck 163 *weakling*; scapegoat, victim, wretch, poor w. 825 *sufferer*; prey 544 *dupe*.

**Adj.** *adverse*, hostile, frowning, ominous, sinister, inauspicious, unfavourable; disadvantageous, antipathetic, bleak, cold, hard;

opposed, cross, thwart, contrary, untoward 704 *opposing*; malign 645 *harmful*; dire, dreadful, ruinous 165 *destructive*; disastrous, calamitous, catastrophic; too bad 645 *bad*.

*unprosperous*, unblest, inglorious 728 *unsuccessful*; unwell, in poor shape, out of kilter; not doing well, in low water, badly off, not well off 801 *poor*; in trouble, up against it, in adverse circumstances, with one's back to the wall, clouded, under a cloud 700 *in difficulties*; declining, on the wane, on the down grade, on the slippery slope, on one's last legs, on the road to ruin 655 *deteriorated*; in the wars, in a bad way, in an evil plight, in dire straits, in extremities.

*unfortunate*, ill-fated, unlucky, ill-starred, star-crossed, blasted; fraught, futureless; unblest, luckless, hapless, poor, wretched, forlorn, miserable, undone, unhappy; stricken, doomed, accursed; not lucky, out of luck, down on one's luck; out of favour, under a cloud 924 *disapproved*; born under an evil star; accident-prone.

**Vb.** *have trouble*, be in t., be born to t., be one's own worst enemy; stew in one's own juice; be fortune's sport, be the victim of fate, have no luck, get more kicks than ha'pence; get more bricks than bouquets; be in for it, go through it, be hard pressed, be up against it, fall foul of 700 *be in difficulty*; strike a bad patch 825 *suffer*; suffer humiliation 872 *be humbled*; come to grief 728 *miscarry*; feel the pinch, feel the draught, fall on evil days, have seen better d. 801 *be poor*; go downhill, go down in the world, fall from grace, decline 655 *deteriorate*; sink 313 *founder*; come to a bad end 728 *fail*; go to rack and ruin, go to the dogs 165 *be destroyed*; go hard with, be difficult for 700 *be difficult*.

**Adv.** *in adversity*, from bad to worse, from *or* out of the frying pan into the fire; sadly, sad to say, unfortunately, unhappily; as ill luck would have it, by mischance, by misadventure.

**732 Averageness**
**N.** *averageness*, mediocrity 30 *average*; golden mean, neither too much nor too little; common lot, ups and downs, mixed blessing; average circumstances, moderate c., a modest competence, enough to get by; modesty, plain living, no excess 177 *moderation*; respectability, middle class, bourgeoisie 869 *middle classes*; Main Street, suburbia, subtopia, villadom; common man, everyman, man in the street, Joe Bloggs, Joe Public, Joe Soap 869 *commoner*; hoi polloi.

**Adj.** *middling*, average, mediocre; neither good nor bad, betwixt and between, middle-brow; ordinary, commonplace 30 *median*; common, representative 83 *typical*; nonextreme, middle-of-the-road 177 *moderate*; decent, quiet 874 *modest*; not striking, undistinguished, inglorious, nothing to boast of, nothing to write home about; nothing special, minor, second-rate, second best 35 *inferior*; fair, fair to middling; so-so, comme ci comme ça, all right, OK, adequate; unobjectionable, tolerable, passable, fifty-fifty, much of a muchness; medium, middle, colourless, grey 625 *neutral*.

**Vb.** *be middling*, – mediocre etc. adj.; follow the mean 30 *average out*; pass muster 635 *suffice*; jog on, manage well enough, go on quietly, avoid excess, keep to the middle 625 *be halfway*; never *or* not set the Thames on fire, never *or* not set the heather on fire; leave something to be desired 647 *be imperfect*.

**5.2**
# Social volition

SECTION ONE

## *General social volition*

**733 Authority**
**N.** *authority*, power; powers that be, 'they', the Establishment, ruling classes, Big Brother, thought police 741 *master*; the Government, the Administration, Whitehall 690 *director*; right, divine r., divine right of kings, prerogative, royal p.; dynasticism, legitimacy; law, rightful power, legal p., lawful authority 953 *legality*; legislative assembly 692 *parliament*; delegated authority, regency, committee 751 *commission*; office of authority, office, place (see also *position of authority*); portfolio 955 *jurisdiction*; vicarious authority, power behind the throne 178 *influence*; indirect authority, patronage, prestige, credit; leadership, hegemony 689 *directorship*; ascendance, preponderance, predominance, supremacy 34 *superiority*; pride of place, seniority, priority 64 *precedence*; majesty, royalty, kingliness, crown, kingly c. 868 *nobility*; lordliness, authoritativeness, dignity; purse strings, financial control, treasury; sea power, admiralty, trident, Britannia; acquisition of power, succession, legitimate s., accession; seizure of power, usurpation.

*governance*, rule, sway, iron s., reins of government, direction, command 689 *directorship*; control, supreme c.; hold, grip, clutches 778 *retention*; domination, mastery, whip hand, effective control, reach, long arm;

ascendancy, dominion, joint d., condominium, sovereignty, suzerainty, raj, overlordship, presidency, supremacy 34 *superiority*; reign, regnancy, regency, dynasty; foreign rule, heteronomy, empery, empire, rod of e. 745 *subjection*; imperialism, colonialism, neocolonialism; white supremacy, black power; regime, regiment, regimen; state control, statism, dirigisme, paternalism; bureaucracy, apparat, civil service, officialism, beadledom, bumbledom, red tape, bumf; Parkinson's law 197 *expansion*.

*despotism*, benevolent d., paternalism, nanny state; one-man rule, monocracy, tyranny; dictatorship, Caesarism, tsarism, Stalinism; absolutism, autocracy, autarchy, absolute monarchy; statism, omnicompetent state, state socialism, state capitalism; 'dictatorship of the proletariat' (see quotation below); totalitarianism; police state, rule of terror 735 *brute force*.

*government*, direction 689 *management*; form of government, state system, polity; politics, politicking; constitutional government, constitutionalism, rule of law 953 *legality*; misgovernment 734 *anarchy*; theocracy, thearchy, priestly government, papal rule, hierocracy, clericalism 985 *ecclesiasticism*; monarchy, constitutional m., monarchical government, kingship; republicanism, federalism; tribal system, tribalism, clan system; patriarchy, matriarchate; feudalism, feudality; benevolent despotism, paternalism; squirearchy, aristocracy, meritocracy, oligarchy, minority rule, elitism; gynarchy, gynocracy, pornocracy 373 *womankind*; gerontocracy, senatorial government; duumvirate, triumvirate; rule of wealth, plutocracy; representative government, parliamentary g., government by the ballot box, party system 708 *political party*, 605 *vote*; democracy, egalitarianism, people's rule, 'government of the people, by the people, for the people';

It is rather for us to be here dedicated to the great task remaining before us – that from these honored dead we take increased devotion to that cause for which they gave the last full measure of devotion – that we here highly resolve that these dead shall not have died in vain – that this nation, under God, shall have a new birth of freedom – and that government of the people, by the people, for the people, shall not perish from the earth.
Abraham Lincoln

democracy unlimited, demagogy, demagoguery, popular will, vox populi, vox pop; majority rule, one man one vote, proportional representation; isocracy, pantisocracy, pluralism, collectivism, proletarianism, 'dictatorship of the proletariat';

. . . the class struggle necessarily leads to the dictatorship of the proletariat.
Karl Marx (Marx said that the phrase had been coined by Blanqui.)

communism, Leninism, Marxism-L., Castroism, Maoism, Titoism; party rule, Bolshevism, Fascism, Nazism, National Socialism; committee rule, sovietism; imperium in imperio, stratocracy, army rule, military government, martial law; ochlocracy, mobocracy, mob rule, mob law, anarchy; syndicalism, socialism, guild s., Fabianism, statism; bureaucracy, technocracy; self-government, autonomy, home rule 744 *independence*; puppet government 628 *instrument*; caretaker government, regency, interregnum; sphere of influence, mandate, mandated territory.

*position of authority*, post, place, office, high o., office of power, office of dignity; kingship, kinghood, tsardom, royalty, regality; regency, regentship, protectorship; rulership, chieftainship, sheikhdom, emirate, principate, lordship, seigniory; rajahship, sultanate, caliphate, governorship, viceroyalty; satrapy, ethnarchy; consulate, consulship, proconsulate, prefecture, tribunate, aedileship; magistrature, magistracy; mayoralty, aldermanship; headship, presidentship, presidency, premiership, chairmanship 689 *directorship*; overlordship, superintendency, inspectorship; masterdom, mastership; Big Brother; government post, Cabinet seat; seat of government, capital, metropolis, palace, White House, Kremlin, Number Ten, Whitehall; secretariat 687 *workshop*.

*political organization*, body politic; state, nation s., commonwealth; country, realm, kingdom, republic, city state, city, free c., polis; temple state; federation, confederation; principality, duchy, archduchy, dukedom, palatinate; empire, dominion, colony, dependency, protectorate, mandate, mandated territory 184 *territory*; free world, communist bloc, Third World, Fourth World 184 *region*; superpower 34 *superiority*; banana republic 35 *inferiority*; buffer state 231 *interjacency*; province, county 184 *district*; body politic, corporative state, social s., welfare s.; laws, constitution.

**Adj.** *authoritative*, empowered, sanctioned, approved, competent; in office, in authority, clothed with a., magisterial, official, ex officio; mandatory, binding, compulsory 740 *compelling*; magistral, masterful, domineering; commanding, lordly, dignified, majestic; overruling, imperious, bossy; peremptory, arbitrary, absolute, autocratic, tyrannical, dictatorial, totalitarian, paternalistic 735 *authoritarian*; powerful, puissant 162 *strong*; hegemonic, leading 178 *influential*; pre-eminent, preponderant, predominant, prepollent, dominant, paramount 34 *supreme*; Big Brotherish.

*ruling*, reigning, regnant, regnal; sovereign, holding the sceptre, holding the reins of government, on the throne; royal, regal, majestic, kinglike, kingly, queenly, princely, lordly; dynastic; imperial; magisterial; governing, controlling, dictating etc. vb.

*governmental*, gubernatorial, political, constitutional; administrative, ministerial, official, bureaucratic, centralized; technocratic; matriarchal, patriarchal; monarchical, feudal, aristocratic, oligarchic, plutocratic, democratic, popular, classless, republican; self-governing, autonomous, autarchic, autocephalous 744 *independent*; anarchy.

**Vb.** *rule*, hold sway, reign, reign supreme, sit on the throne, wear the crown, wield the sceptre; govern, control 737 *command*; manage, hold the reins, hold office 689 *direct*; have a place, occupy a post, fill a p.; be in power, have authority, wield a., exercise a., exert a., use one's a.; rule absolutely, tyrannize 735 *oppress*; dictate, lay down the law; plan, give laws to, legislate for; divide and rule, Balkanize; keep order, police.

*take authority*, mount the throne, ascend the t., accede to the t., succeed to the t., take office, take command, assume c., take over; take over the reins; assume authority, form a government; gain power, get a hold on, get the whip hand, take control; seize power, get the power into one's hands, usurp, usurp the throne.

*dominate*, have the power, have the prestige; preponderate, turn the scale, hold all the aces, hold all the cards 34 *predominate*; lord it over, boss, rule the roost, be queen bee, wear the trousers, be in the driving seat, be in the saddle 737 *command*; have the mastery, have the upper hand, have the whip h., call the tune, call the shots 727 *overmaster*; have in one's power, have over a barrel; lead by the nose, twist round one's little finger, have under one's thumb, have one by the short hairs *or* by the short and curlies (inf), bend to one's will, hold in the palm of one's hand 178 *influence*; regiment, discipline, drill, drive 735 *be severe*; dictate, coerce 740 *compel*; subject to one's influence, hold down, hold under, ride roughshod over 745 *subjugate*; override, overrule, overawe; have it all one's own way, do as one wishes 744 *be free*.

*be governed*, have laws, have a constitution; be ruled, be swayed by, be dictated to; be under authority, owe obedience, owe fealty, owe loyalty 745 *be subject*.

**Adv.** *by authority*, in the name of, de par le Roi; by warrant of, in virtue of one's authority.

## 734 Laxity: absence of authority

**N.** *laxity*, slackness, remissness, indifference 458 *negligence*; laissez-faire 744 *scope*; informality, lack of ceremony 769 *nonobservance*; looseness, loosening, relaxation, derestriction, loose cannon 746 *liberation*; loose organization, unbinding, decentralization 46 *disunion*; connivance 756 *permission*; indulgence, toleration, licence, overindulgence, permissiveness 736 *leniency*; line of least resistance 721 *submission*; weak will, feeble grasp, weak administration, crumbling power 163 *weakness*; no grip, no drive, no push, inertia 175 *inertness*; no control, no restrictions, noninterference, policy of nonintervention, abdication of authority, surrender of control 753 *resignation*; renunciation 621 *relinquishment*; concession 770 *compromise*; King Log.

*anarchy*, breakdown of law and order, no authority, writ not running; free-for-all, every man for himself, dog-eat-dog; disorder, disorganization, chaos 61 *turmoil*; licence, insubordination, indiscipline, cocking a snook 738 *disobedience*; anarchism, nihilism, antinomianism 769 *nonobservance*; interregnum, power vacuum, powerlessness 161 *impotence*; misrule, misgovernment; mob rule, mob law, lynch l., reign of terror 954 *lawlessness*; defiance of authority, unauthorized power, usurpation 916 *arrogation*; dethronement, deposition, uncrowning 752 *deposal*.

**Adj.** *lax*, loose, slack; devolved, decentralized; disorganized, unorganized 61 *orderless*; feeble, soft, wet, wimpish 163 *weak*; crippled 163 *weakened*; slipshod, remiss 458 *negligent*; uncaring 860 *indifferent*; relaxed, unstrict, informal, not standing on ceremony; free-and-easy, happy-go-lucky 744 *unconfined*; permissive, tolerant, undemanding, easy, gentle, indulgent, overindulgent 736 *lenient*; weak-willed, weak-kneed 601 *irresolute*; unassertive, unmasterful, lacking authority, uninfluential.

*anarchic*, anarchical; ungoverned, uncontrolled, unbridled, unsubmissive; insubordinate 878 *insolent*; rebellious 738 *disobedient*; disorderly, unruly 738 *riotous*; unauthorized 954 *illegal*; lawless, nihilistic, anarchistic, antinomian 769 *nonobservant*.

**Vb.** *be lax*, not enforce; hold a loose rein, give one his *or* her head, give rope enough 744 *give scope*; waive the rules, stretch a point, connive at; tolerate, put up with, suffer; laisser faire, laisser aller 756 *permit*; let one get away with, not say boo to a goose; spoonfeed, featherbed, indulge, spoil 736 *be lenient*; make concessions 770 *compromise*; relax, unbind 46 *disunite*; lose control 161 *be impotent*; renounce authority 621 *relinquish*; stand down, abdicate 753 *resign*; misrule, misgovern, mismanage, reduce to chaos 63 *derange*.

*please oneself*, let oneself go, indulge oneself 943 *be intemperate*; be a law unto oneself, stand in no awe of, defy authority, resist control 738 *disobey*; take on oneself, assume control, act without authority, act without instructions, act on one's own responsibility; arrogate, usurp authority 916 *be undue*.

*unthrone*, dethrone, uncrown, unseat, overthrow, cause to abdicate, force to resign 752 *depose*; usurp, snatch the sceptre, seize the crown.

### 735 Severity

**N.** *severity*, no weakness, rigorousness, strictness, stringency; formalism, pedantry; high standards 862 *fastidiousness*; rigidity, inflexibility 326 *hardness*; discipline, firm control, strong hand, iron h., tight h., tight grasp 733 *authority*; rod of iron, heavy hand, zero tolerance, Draconian laws; harshness, rigour, extremity, extremes; no concession, no compromise, letter of the law, pound of flesh; intolerance, rigorism, fanaticism, bigotry 602 *opinionatedness*; press laws, censorship, expurgation, suppression 747 *restraint*; blue laws, puritanism 950 *prudery*; infliction, visitation, inquisition, persecution, exploitation, sexploitation, harassment, oppression, Rachmanism; spite, victimization 910 *revenge*; callousness, lack of mercy, inclemency, inexorability, no appeal 906 *pitilessness*; harsh treatment, the hard way, 'tender mercies' (see quotation at 898 *cruel act*), cruelty 898 *inhumanity*; self-mortification, self-denial, austerity 945 *asceticism*.

*brute force*, naked f., show of f., rule of might, big battalions, gunboat diplomacy 160 *power*; coercion, bludgeoning 740 *compulsion*; bloodiness 176 *violence*; subjugation 745 *subjection*; arbitrary power, absolutism, autocracy, dictatorship 733 *despotism*; tyranny, liberticide; Fascism, Nazism, Hitlerism, Stalinism, totalitarianism; Prussianism, militarism; martial law, iron rule, iron hand, mailed fist, jackboot, bludgeon.

*tyrant*, rigorist, pedant, precisian, formalist, stickler, red-tapist, bureaucrat; petty tyrant, Jack-in-office; disciplinarian, martinet, sergeant major; militarist, jackboot; hanging judge; heavy father, Dutch uncle; Big Brother, authoritarian, despot, dictator 741 *autocrat*;

boss, commissar, gauleiter; inquisitor, persecutor; oppressor, bully, hard master, taskmaster, slave-driver; extortioner, grasper, bloodsucker, tax-gatherer, publican, predator, harpy; vulture, octopus; Moloch, ogre, brute 938 *monster*; hardliner; King Stork.

**Adj.** *severe*, austere, Spartan 945 *ascetic*; strict, rigorous, extreme; strait-laced, puritanical, prudish, old-maidish; donnish, pedagogic, hide-bound; formalistic, pedantic; bigoted, fanatical; hypercritical 862 *fastidious*; intolerant, censorious 924 *disapproving*; unbending, stiff-necked, rigid 326 *hard*; hard as nails, hard-headed, hard-boiled, flinty, dour; inflexible, obdurate, uncompromising 602 *obstinate*; inexorable, relentless, merciless, unsparing, implacable, unforgiving 906 *pitiless*; heavy, stern, stiff; punitive; stringent, Draconian, drastic, savage.

*authoritarian*, masterful, domineering, lordly, arrogant, haughty 878 *insolent*; despotic, absolute, unfettered, arbitrary; totalitarian, Fascist; dictatorial, Big Brotherish, autocratic; antidemocratic, undemocratic; coercive, imperative, compulsive 740 *compelling*; fussy, bossy, governessy, nannyish.

*oppressive*, hard on 914 *unjust*; tyrannical, despotic; tyrannous, harsh, overharsh; grinding, withering; exigent, exacting, grasping, griping, extortionate, exploitive, predatory; persecuting, inquisitorial, searching, unsparing; high-handed, overbearing, domineering; heavy-handed, ungentle, Draconian, rough, bloody 176 *violent*; brutal, ogreish 898 *cruel*.

**Vb.** *be severe*, – harsh, – strict etc. adj.; stand no nonsense, be cruel to be kind; exert authority, put one's foot down, discipline; bear hard on, deal hardly with, lay a heavy hand on; permit no liberties, keep a tight rein on 747 *restrain*; be down on, have a down on (see also *oppress*); come down on, come down like a ton of bricks, crack down on, stamp on, put a stop to, clamp down on 165 *suppress*; not tolerate, persecute, hunt down 619 *pursue*; illtreat, mishandle, abuse 675 *misuse*; treat rough, get tough with, pull no punches; take off the gloves, rule with an iron hand, inflict, visit on, visit with, chastise 963 *punish*; mete out stern punishment, wreak vengeance 910 *avenge*; exact reprisals 714 *retaliate*; strain one's authority 954 *be illegal*; be extreme, have one's pound of flesh; harden one's heart, show no mercy, take Draconian measures 906 *be pitiless*; give no quarter, put to the sword 362 *slaughter*.

*oppress*, tyrannize, play the tyrant, be despotic, take liberties, abuse one's authority 734 *please oneself*; assume, arrogate 916 *be undue*; domineer, lord it; overawe, intimidate, terrorize 854 *frighten*; bludgeon 740 *compel*; shove around, boss a., put upon; bully, bait, be always on one's back, harass, plague, annoy, hassle 827 *torment*; persecute, spite, victimize 898 *be malevolent*; break, break the spirit, crush the s., take the heart out of, tame 369 *break in*; task, tax, drive 684 *fatigue*; overtax, exploit, extort, suck, squeeze, grind, grind the faces of the poor; trample, tread down, tread underfoot, stamp on, hold down 165 *suppress*; enslave 745 *subjugate*; ride roughshod, injure, inflict injustice 914 *do wrong*; misgovern, misrule; rule with an iron hand, rule with a rod of iron; take Draconian measures; whip, scourge, rack, put the screws on 963 *torture*; shed blood, dye with b. 362 *murder*; be heavy, weigh on, burden, crush 322 *weigh*.

**Adv.** *severely*, sternly, strictly etc. adj.; tyrannically, despotically, arbitrarily; highhandedly, heavy-handedly; cruelly, mercilessly.

## 736 Leniency

**N.** *leniency*, lenience, softness 734 *laxity*; mildness, gentleness, tenderness; forbearance, easygoingness, long-suffering, soft answer 823 *patience*; pardon 909 *forgiveness*; quarter, mercy, lenity, clemency, mercifulness, compassion 905 *pity*; humanity, kindness 897 *benevolence*; favour, sop, concession; indulgence, toleration; sufferance, allowance, leave 756 *permission*; connivance, complaisance; justice with mercy 177 *moderation*; light rein, light hand, velvet glove, kid gloves; wet, liberal, soggy l.

**Adj.** *lenient*, soft, gentle, mild, mild as milk; indulgent, tolerant; conniving, complaisant; easy, easy-going, low-pressure, undemanding 734 *lax*; forbearing, longsuffering 823 *patient*; clement, merciful 909 *forgiving*; tender 905 *pitying*; too soft, overmerciful.

**Vb.** *be lenient*, show consideration, make no demands, make few d.; deal gently, handle tenderly, go easy, handle with kid gloves, pull one's punches, temper the wind to the shorn lamb 177 *moderate*; featherbed, spoonfeed, spoil, indulge, play the fond parent, humour 889 *pet*; gratify, favour 925 *flatter*; tolerate, allow, connive 756 *permit*; stretch a point 734 *be lax*; concede 758 *consent*; not press, refrain, forbear 823 *be patient*; pity, spare, give quarter 905 *show mercy*; pardon 909 *forgive*; amnesty, truce 506 *forget*; relax, humanize 897 *be benevolent*.

## 737 Command

**N.** *command*, royal c., invitation, summons; commandment, ordinance; injunction, imposition; dictation, bidding, behest, hest, will and pleasure; dictum, say-so 532 *affirmation*; charge, commission, appointment 751 *mandate*; instructions, manifesto, rules, regulations, code of practice, tablets of stone; brief 524 *information*; directive, order, order of the day, marching orders; word of command, word; beck, nod, sign 547 *gesture*; signal, bugle call, trumpet c. 547 *call*; whip, three-line w.; categorical imperative, dictate 740 *compulsion*; negative command, taboo, ban, embargo, proscription 757 *prohibition*; countermand, counterorder 752 *abrogation*.

*decree*, edict, fiat, ukase, firman, ipse dixit; law, canon, rescript, prescript 693 *precept*; bull, papal decree, decretal; circular, encyclical; ordinance, order in council; decree nisi, decree absolute; decision, placet, senatus consultum 480 *judgment*; enactment, act 953 *legislation*; plebiscite, manifesto, electoral mandate 605 *vote*; dictate, diktat, dictation.

*demand*, demand as of right, claim, revendication 915 *dueness*; requisition 761 *request*; notice, warning n., final n., final demand, ultimatum; blackmail 900 *threat*; imposition, exaction, levy, tax demand 809 *tax*.

*warrant*, search w., commission, brevet, authorization, written authority, letters patent, passport 756 *permit*; writ, summons, subpoena, citation, mandamus, mittimus, habeas corpus 959 *legal process*.

**Adj.** *commanding*, imperative, imperatival, categorical, dictatorial; jussive, mandatory, obligatory, peremptory, compulsive 740 *compelling*; decretory, decretal; exacting obedience 733 *authoritative*; decisive, conclusive, final, written on tablets of stone; demanding, insistent, hectoring, clamant, vocal.

**Vb.** *command*, bid, invite; order, tell, issue a command, give an order, send an o., lay down the law; signal, call, nod, beck, motion, sign, make a s. 547 *gesticulate*; wink, give a cue, tip the wink 524 *hint*; direct, give a directive, instruct, brief, circularize, send round instructions; rule, lay down, enjoin; give a mandate, charge, call upon 751 *commission*; impose, lay upon, set a task, make obligatory 917 *impose a duty*; detail, tell off; call together, rally, convene 74 *bring together*; send for, summon; cite, subpoena, issue a writ 959 *litigate*; send back, remand; dictate, enforce obedience, take a strong line, put one's foot down 740 *compel*; countermand 752 *abrogate*; lay an embargo, ban, impose a ban, taboo, declare t., proscribe 757 *prohibit*.

*decree*, pass a d., sign a d., pass an order in council, issue a ukase; promulgate 528 *proclaim*; declare, say, say so, lay down the law

532 *affirm*; signify one's will and pleasure, prescribe, ordain, appoint 608 *predetermine*; enact, make law, pass a l., legislate, decriminalize 953 *make legal*; pass judgment, give j., rule, give a ruling 480 *judge*.

*demand*, require, requisition 627 *require*; order, order up, indent 761 *request*; make demands on, send a final demand, issue a final warning, give final notice, present an ultimatum, demand with threats, blackmail 900 *threaten*; present one's claim, make claims upon, revendicate, reclaim 915 *claim*; demand payment, dun, sue, bill, invoice; charge 809 *price*; exact, levy 809 *tax*.

**Adv.** *commandingly*, imperatively, categorically, authoritatively; at the word of command.

## 738 Disobedience

**N.** *disobedience*, indiscipline, unbiddableness, recalcitrance, refractoriness 598 *unwillingness*; naughtiness, misbehaviour, mischief-making, monkey tricks; delinquency 934 *wickedness*; insubordination, mutinousness, mutineering; refusal to obey orders, defiance of o. 711 *defiance*; disregard of orders, non-compliance 769 *nonobservance*; disloyalty, defection, desertion 918 *undutifulness*; violation of orders, violation of the law, infraction, infringement, criminality, crime, sin 936 *guilty act*; noncooperation, civil disobedience, passive resistance, electronic civil disobedience, hacktivism 715 *resistance*; conscientious objection 704 *opposition*; obstructionism 702 *hindrance*; murmuring, restlessness 829 *discontent*; seditiousness, sansculottism (see also *sedition*); wildness 954 *lawlessness*; vandalism, banditry, mafia, guerrilla warfare 788 *brigandage*.

*revolt*, mutiny; direct action 145 *strike*; faction 709 *dissension*; breakaway, secession 978 *schism*; defection 603 *tergiversation*; explosive situation, restlessness, restiveness 318 *agitation*; sabotage, wrecking activities 165 *destruction*; breach of the peace, disturbance, disorder, riot, street r., rioting, gang warfare, street-fighting, émeute, tumult, barricades 61 *turmoil*; rebellion, insurrection, rising, uprising, intifada 176 *outbreak*; putsch, coup d'état; velvet revolution; resistance movement, insurgency 715 *resistance*; subversion 149 *revolution*; terrorism, bioterrorism, cyberterrorism, electronic civil disobedience, hacktivism 954 *lawlessness*; civil war 718 *war*; anarchy; regicide, tyrannicide 362 *homicide*.

*sedition*, seditiousness; agitation, cabal, intrigue 623 *plot*; agitprop, subversion, infiltration, fifth-columnism; spying, espionage, underground activities 523 *latency*; terrorism,

anarchism, nihilism; treasonable activities, disloyalty, treason, high t., lese-majesty 930 *perfidy*.

*revolter*, awkward person, difficult character, handful 700 *difficulty*; naughty child, scamp, pest, nuisance, scapegrace, little monkey 938 *bad person*; mutineer, rebel, frondeur; demonstrator, striker, picketer 705 *opponent*; secessionist, seceder, splinter group, rebel g. 978 *schismatic*; deviationist, dissident, Titoist 829 *malcontent*; blackleg, scab, nonstriker 84 *nonconformist*; independent, maverick, lone wolf; seditionary, seditionist; traitor, Quisling, fifth columnist, infiltrator, spy, industrial spy 603 *tergiversator*; tyrannicide, regicide; insurrectionist, insurgent; guerrilla, urban g., partisan; resistance, underground, Maquis; Black Panther, Black Muslim; Provisional, Provo; extremist, Jacobin, sansculotte, carbonaro, Bolshevist, Trotskyist, red, red republican 149 *revolutionist*; counter-revolutionary, reactionary, monarchist, White Russian, chouan; anarchist, nihilist, terrorist, cyberterrorist, hacktivist; mafia, bandit 789 *robber*; rebel against all laws, antinomian.

*agitator*, disruptive influence, agent provocateur; agitprop, protester, demonstrator, counterdemonstrator, marcher; soap-box orator, tub-thumper, ranter, rabble-rouser, fomenter, demagogue; fire-brand, mischief-maker 663 *troublemaker*; seditionist, sedition-monger; red, communist, commie, bolshie; suffragette, women's libber, bra-burner; Digger, Leveller; ringleader, Spartacus, Wat Tyler, Jack Cade, John Brown, Young Turk.

*rioter*, street r., urban guerrilla, bovver boy, boot boy, brawler, rowdy 904 *ruffian*; saboteur, wrecker, Luddite; secret society, Ku Klux Klan.

**Adj.** *disobedient*, undisciplined, badly disciplined; disobeying, naughty, mischievous, misbehaving; unfilial, undaughterly; unbiddable, awkward, difficult, self-willed, wayward, restive, impatient of control, vicious, unruly, unmanageable 176 *violent*; intractable, ungovernable 598 *unwilling*; insubordinate, mutinous, rebellious, bolshie, bloody-minded; contrary 704 *opposing*; nonconformist 84 *unconformable*; unsubmissive, recusant, uncomplying, uncompliant 769 *nonobservant*; recalcitrant 715 *resisting*; challenging 711 *defiant*; refractory, perverse, froward 602 *obstinate*; subversive, revolutionary, reactionary; seditious, troublemaking; traitorous, treasonous, disloyal 918 *undutiful*; antinomian 734 *anarchic*; gatecrashing, intrusive, uninvited, unbidden; wild, untamed, feral, savage.

*riotous*, rioting; anarchic, tumultuary,

rumbustious, rowdy, unruly, wild, rackety 61 *disorderly*; law-breaking 954 *lawless*; mutinous, insurrectionary, rebellious, in rebellion, up in arms 715 *resisting*.

**Vb.** *disobey*, not obey, not listen; be disobedient, misbehave, get into mischief; flout authority, not comply with 769 *not observe*; not do as one is told, disobey orders, show insubordination 711 *defy*; defy the whip, cross-vote; cock a snook, snap one's fingers, fly in the face of 704 *oppose*; set the law at defiance, break the law, commit a crime 954 *be illegal*; violate, infringe, transgress, trespass 306 *encroach*; turn restive, kick, chafe, fret, champ at the bit, play up; kick over the traces, take the bit between one's teeth, bolt, take French leave, go AWOL, go walkabout, take the law into one's own hands, be a law unto oneself 734 *please oneself*.

*revolt*, rebel, mutiny; down tools, strike, take industrial action, come out 145 *cease*; sabotage 702 *obstruct*; undermine, work underground; secede, break away 978 *schismatize*; betray 603 *change one's mind*; agitate, demonstrate, protest 762 *deprecate*; create, create a row, kick up a stink, raise Cain, start a riot, stage a revolt, lead a rebellion 715 *resist*; rise, rise up, rise in arms, throw off the yoke, throw off one's shackles, renounce allegiance, fight for independence 746 *achieve liberty*; overthrow, upset 149 *revolutionize*.

### 739 Obedience

**N.** *obedience*, compliance 768 *observance*; goodness, meekness, biddability, tractability, pliancy, malleability 327 *softness*; readiness 597 *willingness*; nonresistance, submissiveness, acquiescence 721 *submission*; passiveness, passivity 679 *inactivity*; dutifulness, morale, discipline 917 *duty*; deference, obsequiousness, slavishness 879 *servility*; tameness, docility; dumb driven cattle 742 *slave*.

*loyalty*, constancy, devotion, fidelity, faithfulness, good faith 929 *probity*; allegiance, fealty, homage, service, deference, submission; vote of confidence.

**Adj.** *obedient*, complying, compliant, cooperating, conforming 768 *observant*; loyal, leal, faithful, true-blue, steadfast, constant; devoted, dedicated, sworn; offering homage, submissive 721 *submitting*; law-abiding 717 *peaceful*; complaisant, amenable, docile; good, well-behaved; filial, daughterly; ready 597 *willing*; acquiescent, resigned, unresisting, nonresisting, passive 679 *inactive*; meek, sheep-like, biddable, like putty in one's hands, dutiful, under discipline; at one's beck and call, at one's orders, on a string, on a lead,

puppet-like, under one's thumb, under control; disciplined, regimented 917 *obliged*; trained, manageable, tame; respectful, deferential, subservient, obsequious, slavish 879 *servile*.

**Vb.** *obey*, comply, do to order, act upon 768 *observe*; do the needful, sign on the dotted line, toe the l., come to heel 83 *conform*; assent 758 *consent*; listen, hearken, heed, mind, obey orders, attend to instructions, do as one is told; observe discipline, wait for the word of command; hold oneself ready, put oneself at one's service 597 *be willing*; answer the helm, obey the rein; obey the whip, vote to order, follow the party line; do one's bidding, come at one's call, wait upon, follow, follow like a sheep, follow to the world's end 742 *serve*; be loyal, owe loyalty, bear allegiance, pay homage, offer h. 768 *keep faith*; be under, pay tribute 745 *be subject*; know one's duty 917 *do one's duty*; make oneself useful, do Trojan service, do sterling s. 703 *minister to*; yield, defer to, bow, bend, stoop, be submissive 721 *submit*; grovel, cringe, 879 *be servile*; play second fiddle 35 *be inferior*.

**Adv.** *obediently*, submissively etc. adj.; under orders, to order, as ordered, in obedience to; yours to command, at your service.

### 740 Compulsion

**N.** *compulsion*, spur of necessity, needs must 596 *necessity*; law of nature 953 *law*; act of God, force majeure; moral compulsion 917 *conscience*; Hobson's choice 606 *no choice*; carrot and stick; dictation, coercion, regimentation; arm-twisting, blackmail 900 *threat*; negative compulsion 747 *restraint*; sanction, sanctions 963 *penalty*; enforcement, constraint, duress, force, main force, physical f.; mailed fist, big stick, bludgeon, strong arm, strong-arm tactics 735 *brute force*; force-feeding; impressment, pressgang, conscription, call-up, draft 718 *war measures*; exaction, extortion 786 *taking*; slavery, corvée, forced labour, labour camp 745 *servitude*; command performance 737 *command*.

**Adj.** *compelling*, compulsive, involuntary, of necessity, unavoidable, inevitable 596 *necessary*; imperative, dictatorial, peremptory 737 *commanding*; compulsory, mandatory, binding 917 *obligatory*; urgent, pressing; overriding, constraining, coercive; omnipotent, irresistible, not to be trifled with 160 *powerful*; forcible, forceful, cogent; high-pressure, sledgehammer, strongarm, bludgeoning 735 *oppressive*.

**Vb.** *compel*, constrain, coerce 176 *force*; enforce, put into force; dictate, necessitate, oblige, bind; order 737 *command*; impose 917 *impose a duty*; make one, leave no option; leave no escape, pin down, tie d.; impress, draft, conscript; drive, dragoon, regiment, discipline; force one's hand, apply pressure, bulldoze, steamroller, railroad, stampede, pressgang, bully into, drag kicking and screaming 176 *force*; bludgeon 735 *oppress*; take by force, requisition, commandeer, extort, exact, wring from, drag f. 786 *take*; apply pressure, lean on, squeeze, take the gloves off, turn the heat on, put the screws on, twist one's arm 963 *torture*; blackmail, hijack, hold to ransom 900 *threaten*; be peremptory, insist, make a point of, press, urge 532 *emphasize*; brook no denial, not take no for an answer 532 *affirm*; compel to accept, force upon, ram down one's throat, inflict, foist, fob off on; force-feed; hold back 747 *restrain*.

**Adv.** *by force*, perforce, compulsorily, of necessity, on compulsion, under pressure, under protest, under duress, nolens volens; forcibly, willy-nilly, by force majeure, by main force; vi et armis; at the sword's point, at gunpoint, at knifepoint.

## 741 Master

**N.** *master*, mistress; master *or* mistress of, captor, possessor 776 *owner*; sire, lord, lady, dame; liege, lord, lord paramount, overlord, lord's lord, suzerain; protector 707 *patron*; seigneur, lord *or* lady of the manor, squire, laird 868 *aristocrat*; lord and master, man of the house 372 *male*; lady of the house, landlady 373 *lady*; senator, oligarch, plutocrat, technocrat; sir, madam 870 *title*; goodman, goodwife; patriarch, matriarch 169 *parentage*; senior, head, principal, provost 34 *superior*; schoolmaster *or* -mistress 537 *teacher*; president, chairman *or* -woman, chairperson, speaker 690 *director*; employer, captain of industry, capitalist, boss, governor, guvnor, guv 690 *manager*; leader, Caudillo, Duce, Führer (see also *autocrat*); cock of the walk, lord of creation 638 *bigwig*; ruling class, ruling party, dominant interest, vested i., the Establishment; the authorities, principalities and powers, the powers that be, 'them', Big Brother, Westminster, the Government, Whitehall, White House, Pentagon, Kremlin 733 *government*; staff, High Command 689 *directorship*.

*autocrat*, absolute ruler, absolute monarch; despot, dictator, tyrant, Caudillo, Duce, Führer, Big Brother; boss, tycoon, shogun, Great Cham, VIP, big gun, big shot 638 *notable*; petty tyrant, satrap, gauleiter, commissar, Jack-in-office, tin god, little Hitler 690 *official*.

*sovereign*, suzerain, crowned head, anointed king *or* queen; Majesty, Highness, Royal H., Excellence; dynasty, house, royal h., royal line, royal blood; royalty, monarch, king, queen, rex, regina; divine king, Pharaoh, Inca; imperator, emperor, empress; Caesar, Kaiser, Kaiserin, Tsar *or* Czar, Tsarina *or* Czarina, Tsarevitch *or* Czarevich; prince, princess, Infante, Infanta, Dauphin, Prince of Wales, Crown Prince *or* Princess, Great King, King of Kings, Padishah, Shah, Sophy; khan, Great Khan; Celestial Emperor; Mikado; Mogul, Sultan, Sultana; Negus, Prester John; pope, pontiff, Dalai Lama, Aga Khan; caliph, Commander of the Faithful.

*potentate*, dynast, ruler; chief, chieftain, headman, induna, cacique, sachem, sagamore, sheikh; prince, pendragon, princeling, rajah, rani, maharajah, maharani; emir, sirdar, sherif; nawab, begum; archduke, duke, duchess, burgrave, margrave, margravine, Palatine, Elector, Electress; regent, Prince Regent.

*governor*, military g., lieutenant-g., High Commissioner, Governor-General, Crown Representative, viceroy, vicereine, khedive; proconsul, satrap, hetman, stadholder, ethnarch; tetrarch; grand vizier, bey, pasha, bashaw; ecclesiastical governor, Prince Bishop; exarch, eparch, patriarch, metropolitan, archbishop, cardinal 986 *ecclesiarch*; imam, ayatollah 690 *leader*.

*officer*, person in office, p. in authority; functionary, mandarin, nabob, bureaucrat, apparatchik 690 *official*; civil servant, public s. 742 *servant*; gauleiter, commissar; chief officer, prime minister, premier, first minister, grand vizier, vizier, wazir, dewan, chancellor, vice-c., Pooh-bah; constable, marshal, seneschal, warden; burgomaster, mayor, lord m., lady m., mayoress, alderman, provost, bailie, city father, councillor; dignitary, local worthy 866 *person of repute*; sheriff, bailiff; justice, justice of the peace, alcalde, hakim 957 *judge*; magistrate, chief m., archon, podestà; president, doge; consul, proconsul, praetor, quaestor, aedile; prefect, intendant, district officer; commissioner, deputy c.; revenue officer, collector, headman; lictor, mace-bearer, beadle, bedel; process-server, pursuivant, tipstaff 955 *law officer*; sexton, verger 986 *church officer*; courier 529 *messenger*; party official, whip, chief whip; powers that be.

*naval officer*, Sea Lord; admiral of the fleet, admiral, vice-a., rear-a., commodore, captain, commander, lieutenant-c., lieutenant, flag-l., sub-l., petty officer, leading seaman 270 *nautical personnel*; trierarch, navarch; 722 *naval person*.

*army officer*, staff, High Command, staff officer, brass hat; commissioned officer, brevet o.; marshal, field m., commander-in-chief, seraskier, generalissimo, general, lieutenant-g., major-g.; brigadier, colonel, lieutenant-c., major, captain, lieutenant, second l., subaltern; ensign, cornet; warrant officer, noncommissioned o., NCO, sergeant major, company s. m., regimental s. m., sergeant, staff s., colour s., corporal, lance corporal; adjutant, aide-de-camp, quartermaster, orderly officer; imperator, military tribune, legate, centurion, decurion, vexillary; chiliarch, hipparch; subahdar 722 *soldiery*; war minister, warlord, commanding officer, commander, commandant; military rank 27 *degree*; other ranks, rank and file.

*air officer*, marshal of the air force, air marshal, air commodore, group captain, wing commander, squadron leader, flight lieutenant, flying officer, pilot o., warrant o., flight sergeant 722 *air force*.

## 742 Servant
**N.** *servant*, public s., civil s. 690 *official*; unpaid servant, fag, slave; general servant, factotum, skivvy, maid of all work, chief cook and bottle washer 678 *busy person*; humble servant, menial; orderly, attendant; verger 986 *church officer*, subordinate, underling, understrapper 35 *inferior*; subaltern, helper, assistant, secretary, right-hand man, girl Friday 703 *aider*; paid servant, mercenary, hireling, employee, hand, hired man; odd-job man, handyman, labourer, peon 686 *worker*; hewer of wood and drawer of water, hack, drudge, dogsbody, erk; farmhand 370 *farmer*; shepherd, cowherd, milkmaid 369 *herdsman*; shop assistant, salesperson 793 *seller*; steward, stewardess, air hostess, cabin personnel, cabin boy; waiter, waitress, waitperson, waitron, head waiter, wine w.; bartender, barman, barmaid, barista, mixologist (US), pot boy, tapster 192 *pub*; stableman, ostler, groom, stable boy *or* lad, postilion; errand boy, messenger, runner 529 *courier*; doorman, commissionaire, janitor, concierge 264 *doorkeeper*; porter, night p.; caddy 273 *bearer*; callboy, page boy, bellboy, bellhop, buttons; boots, sweeper 648 *cleaner*; caretaker, houseminder, house-sitter, home-sitter, housekeeper (see also *domestic*); occasional servant, help, daily, daily help, char, charwoman, cleaning lady; universal aunt; baby-sitter, baby-minder; nurse, nursemaid, nanny 749 *keeper*; companion, confidante.

*domestic*, staff; servant's hall 686 *personnel*; servitor, domestic servant, general s., manservant, man, serving m.; footman, flunkey,

lackey; servant girl, maid, maidservant, handmaid, parlour maid, housemaid, chambermaid, femme de chambre; domestic drudge, maid of all work, tweeny, skivvy, slavey; kitchen maid, scullery m., dairy m., laundry m.; kitchen boy, turnspit, scullion, washer-up, dishwasher, housekeeper, butler, cook; steward, chaplain, governess, tutor, nurse, nanny, nursemaid, doula; personal servant, body s., page, squire, valet, gentlemen's gentleman, batman; lady's maid, abigail, waiting woman; mother's help, ayah, amah, bonne, au pair; gyp, scout, bed-maker; outdoor staff, gardener, under-g., groom; coachman, chauffeur 268 *driver*.

*retainer*, follower, following, suite, train, cortege 67 *retinue*; court, courtier; attendant, usher, gillie; bodyguard, housecarl, henchman, squire, page, page of honour, donzel, armour-bearer, shield-b., train-b.; household staff, major-domo, chamberlain, equerry, steward, bailiff, castellan, chatelain, seneschal; chatelaine, housekeeper; cellarer, butler, cup-bearer; chaplain, beadsman; lady's maid, abigail, lady-in-waiting, companion, confidante; governess, nurse, nursemaid, mother's help, nanny 749 *keeper*.

*dependant*, clientèle, client; hanger-on, parasite, satellite, camp follower, groupie, creature, jackal, âme damnée 284 *follower*; stooge, puppet 628 *instrument*; subordinate 35 *inferior*; minion, myrmidon, lackey, flunkey (see also *domestic*); man, henchman, liegeman, vassal; pensioner, beadsman; apprentice, protégé(e), ward, charge, nursling, foster child; parasite, epizoon.

*subject*, state s., national, citizen, patrial 191 *native*; liege, vassal; people, citizenry 869 *commonalty*; subject population, dependency, colony, satellite.

*slave*, thrall, bondman, bondwoman, bondmaid, slave girl; helot, helotry, hewer of wood and drawer of water; serf, ascriptus glebae, villein; galley slave, wage s., sweated labour 686 *worker*; hierodule, temple prostitute; odalisque, eunuch; chattel, puppet, pawn; machine, robot 628 *instrument*; captive, chaingang 750 *prisoner*.

**Adj.** *serving*, ministering, fagging 703 *aiding*; in service, in domestic s., menial; working, in employment, on the payroll; on the staff, in the train of; at one's beck and call 739 *obedient*; unfree, unfranchised, unprivileged; in servitude, in slavery, in captivity, in bonds 745 *subject*.

**Vb.** *serve*, be in service, wait upon, wait on hand and foot 703 *minister to*; live in, be on hand 89 *accompany*; attend upon, follow 739 *obey*; tend, squire, valet, dress; char, do chores, do housework, clean for, do for, oblige; fag for, dogs-body for, do service, make oneself useful 640 *be useful*; be part of the workforce, work for 622 *function*.

## 743 Badge of rule

**N.** *regalia*, royal trappings, emblem of royalty, insignia of r.; crown, kingly c., orb, sceptre; coronet, tiara, diadem; rod of empire, sword of state 733 *authority*; robe of state, coronation robes, royal robe; ermine, royal purple; throne, Peacock t., royal seat, seat of kings; ensign 547 *flag*; royal standard, royal arms 547 *heraldry*; lion, eagle, fleur-de-lis; Prince of Wales's feathers; uraeus.

*badge of rule*, badge of office, chain of o.; emblem of authority, staff, wand, wand of office, verge, rod, Black Rod, baton, truncheon, gavel; herald's wand, caduceus; signet, seal, privy s., keys, ring; sword of state, sword of justice, mace, fasces, axes; pastoral staff, crosier; ankh, ansate cross; woolsack, chair, bench; sartorial insignia, triple crown, mitre, bishop's hat, cardinal's h., shovel h., biretta; bishop's apron, gaiters 989 *canonicals*; judge's cap, black c. 961 *condemnation*; peer's cap, cap of maintenance, cap of dignity; robe, mantle, toga.

*badge of rank*, sword, belt, sash, spurs, cocked hat, epaulette, tab 547 *badge*; uniform 547 *livery*; brass, star, pips, crown, crossed batons; gold braid, scrambled egg; chevron, stripe, anchor, curl, brassard, armlet; garter, order 729 *decoration*.

## 744 Freedom

**N.** *freedom*, liberty, being at large; freedom of action, initiative; free will 595 *will*; free thought, free speech, freedom of the press, academic f., the four freedoms; rights, civil rights, equal r. 915 *dueness*; privilege, prerogative, exemption, immunity, diplomatic i. 919 *nonliability*; liberalism, libertarianism, latitudinarianism; licence, artistic l., poetic l.; excess of freedom, indiscipline 738 *disobedience*; free love 951 *illicit love*; laisser faire, noninterference, nonintervention; noninvolvement, neutralism 860 *indifference*; nonalignment, cross benches; isolationism, isolation, splendid i. 883 *seclusion*; emancipation, setting free 746 *liberation*; women's liberation, women's lib; gay l.; enfranchisement, naturalization, citizenship, patriality; franchise, secret ballot 605 *vote*.

*independence*, freedom of action, unilaterality; freedom of choice 605 *choice*; no allegiance, floating vote, don't know; freedom of

thought, emancipation, bohemianism 84 *nonconformity*; unmarried state, bachelorhood 895 *celibacy*; individualism, self-expression, individuality 80 *speciality*; self-determination, statehood, nationhood, national status 371 *nation*; autonomy, autarchy, self-government, self-rule, home r.; autarky, self-regulation; self-sufficiency 635 *sufficiency*; freehold 777 *property*; independent means, private means, modest competence, competence 800 *wealth*.

*scope*, free s., full s., play, free p., full p. 183 *range*; swing, rope, long r.; manoeuvrability, leverage; field, room, living r., lebensraum, living space, elbowroom, room to swing a cat, searoom, wide berth, leeway, margin, clearance 183 *room*; latitude, liberty, Liberty Hall; permissive society; informality, unconstraint; fling, licence, excess 734 *laxity*; one's head, one's own way, nothing in one's way, one's own devices; a free hand, ball at one's feet 137 *opportunity*; facilities, the run of, free hand, blank cheque, carte blanche; free-for-all, free field, free enterprise, free trade, free port, free market, open m., free-trade area; open country, high seas.

*free person*, freeman, burgess, burgher, citizen, free c., patrial, voter; no slave, ex-slave, freedman, freedwoman; ex-convict, released prisoner; escapee 667 *escaper*; free agent, freelance, free spirit; independent, cross-bencher; isolationist, neutral 625 *moderate*; free-trader; free-thinker, latitudinarian, liberal; libertarian, bohemian, individualist, eccentric 84 *nonconformist*; loose cannon; loner, lone wolf 883 *solitary*.

**Adj.** *free*, freeborn, enfranchised; heart-whole, fancy-free, unattached; scot-free 960 *acquitted*; on the loose, at large 667 *escaped*; released, freed 746 *liberated*; free as air, free as the wind, free as a bird; footloose, go-as-you-please, ranging 267 *travelling*; ranging freely, having full play (see also *unconfined*); licensed, chartered, privileged 756 *permitted*; exempt, immune 919 *nonliable*; free-speaking, plain-spoken 573 *plain*; freethinking, emancipated, broad, broadminded, latitudinarian (see also *independent*); unbiased, unprejudiced, independent, uninfluenced 913 *just*; free and easy, all things to all men 882 *sociable*; loose, licentious, unbridled, incontinent, wanton 951 *impure*; at leisure, out of harness, retired; relaxed, unbuttoned, at home, at ease 681 *leisurely*; free of cost, gratis, freebie, on the house, for free, unpaid for 812 *uncharged*; unclaimed, going begging 860 *unwanted*; free for all, unreserved, vacant, unoccupied, up for grabs 289 *accessible*.

*unconfined*, uncribbed, uncabined, untrammelled, unshackled, unfettered, unbridled, uncurbed, unchained, unbound, unmuzzled; unchecked, unrestrained, unregulated, ungoverned; unprevented, unhindered, unimpeded, unobstructed; uninhibited, informal, dégagé(e), casual, freewheeling; free-range, wandering, random; left to one's own devices.

*independent*, unnecessitated, uncontrolled; uninduced, unilateral 609 *spontaneous*; unforced, uncompelled, uninfluenced; unattached, detached 860 *indifferent*; free to choose, uncommitted, neither one thing nor the other, uninvolved; nonpartisan, unaffiliated 625 *neutral*; isolationist 883 *unsociable*; unvanquished, unconquered, unconquerable, unbowed, irrepressible 727 *unbeaten*; enjoying liberty, unsubjected, unenslaved, not discriminated against; autonomous, autarchic, autocephalous, self-governing, self-ruling; autarkic, self-sufficient, self-supporting, self-contained, self-motivated, inner-directed; self-reliant, one's own master; ungoverned, masterless, owning no master, ungovernable 734 *anarchic*; self-employed, one's own boss, freelance; unofficial, cowboy, wildcat; free-minded, free-spirited, free-souled, maverick; single, bachelor 895 *unwedded*; individualistic, unconventional 84 *unconformable*; breakaway 489 *dissenting*.

*unconditional*, unconditioned, without strings, no strings attached, no catch; catch-as-catch-can, free-for-all, no holds barred, anything goes; unrestricted, unlimited, absolute; open, wide open; discretionary, arbitrary; freehold, allodial.

**Vb.** *be free*, enjoy liberty; go free, get f., save oneself 667 *escape*; take French leave 738 *disobey*; have the run of, be free of, have the freedom of, range, have scope, have room to swing a cat, have room to breathe, have play, have a free hand, have elbowroom; have plenty of rope, have one's head; feel at home, make oneself at home; feel free, be oneself, let oneself go, let it all hang out, let one's hair down 683 *repose*; have one's fling, have one's way, have it one's own w., cut loose, drop out, drift, do as one likes *or* chooses 734 *please oneself*; follow one's bent, do one's own thing; go as you please, drift, wander, roam 282 *stray*; go one's own way, go it alone, be one's own boss, shift for oneself, fend for oneself, paddle one's own canoe, stand alone; have a will of one's own 595 *will*; have a free mind, be independent, call no man master, be one's own man; stand up for one's rights, defy the whip, cross-vote 711 *defy*; stand on one's own feet, be self-sufficient, ask no favours 635 *suffice*; take liberties, make free with, go too far, presume,

presume on 878 *be insolent*; dare, venture, make bold to, permit oneself.

*give scope*, allow initiative, give one his head, allow full play, give free rein to, allow enough rope 734 *be lax*; give a free hand, not cramp one's style, give the run of 701 *facilitate*; release, set free, enfranchise 746 *liberate*; let, license, charter 756 *permit*; let alone, not interfere, live and let live, laissez aller, laissez faire; leave one to his own devices; leave it open, leave to one's own choice; keep the door open.

**Adv.** *freely*, liberally, ad libitum, without stinting, copiously, at will.

## 745 Subjection

**N.** *subjection*, subordination; subordinate position, inferior rank, cadetship, juniority, inferior status, satellite s. 35 *inferiority*; creaturehood; dependence, tutelage, guardianship, wardship, apron strings, leading s.; apprenticeship 536 *learning*; mutual dependence, symbiosis 12 *correlation*; subjecthood, allegiance, nationality, citizenship, patriality; subjugation, conquest, colonialism; loss of freedom, disfranchisement, bondage, thraldom, enslavement 721 *submission*; constraint, discipline 747 *restraint*; oppression 735 *severity*; yoke 748 *fetter*; slavishness 879 *servility*.

*service*, domestic s., government s., employ, employment; servitorship, flunkeydom, flunkeyism 739 *obedience*; tribute, suit and service; vassalage, feudality, feudalism 739 *loyalty*; compulsory service, corvée, forced labour 740 *compulsion*; conscription 718 *war measures*.

*servitude*, involuntary s., slavery, abject s.; enslavement, captivity, thraldom, bondage, yoke; helotry, helotism, serfdom, villeinage, peonage.

**Adj.** *subjected*, dominated etc. vb.; subjugated, overborne, overwhelmed 728 *defeated*; subdued, pacified; taken prisoner, deprived of freedom, in chains 747 *restrained*; discriminated against, underprivileged, disadvantaged, deprived, disfranchised; colonized, enslaved, reduced to slavery, sold into s.; in harness 742 *serving*; under the yoke, under the heel; oppressed, brought to one's knees, downtrodden, underfoot; treated like dirt, henpecked, browbeaten; the sport of, the plaything of, kicked around like a football; regimented, planned; brought to heel, quelled, domesticated 369 *tamed*; eating out of one's hand, like putty in one's hands, submissive 721 *submitting*; subservient, slavish 879 *servile*.

*subject*, unfree, not independent, unfranchised, unprivileged; satellite, satellitic; bond, bound, tributary, colonial; owing service, owing fealty, liege, vassal, feudal, feudatory

739 *obedient*; under, subordinate, of lower rank, junior, cadet 35 *inferior*; dependent, in chancery, in statu pupillari; tied to one's apron strings; subject to, liable to, exposed to 180 *liable*; a slave to 610 *habituated*; in the hands of, in the clutches of, under the control of, in the power of, at the mercy of, under the sway of, under one's thumb; not able to call one's soul one's own; puppet-like, like a puppet on a string; having no say in, voiceless; parasitical, hanging on 879 *servile*; paid, in the pay of; encumbranced, mortgaged 917 *obliged*.

**Vb.** *be subject*, live under, own the sway of, pay tribute, be under 739 *obey*; obey the whip, vote to order; depend on, lean on, hang on 35 *be inferior*; be a doormat, let oneself be trampled on, let oneself be kicked around, be the stooge of; serve, live in subjection, be a slave; lose one's independence 721 *submit*; pawn, mortgage 780 *assign*; sacrifice one's freedom, have no will of one's own, be unable to stand on one's own two feet, be cat's-paw, be a tool 628 *be instrumental*; cringe, fawn 879 *be servile*.

*subjugate*, subdue, reduce, subject 727 *overmaster*; colonize, annex, mediatize; take captive, lead in triumph, drag at one's chariot wheels 727 *triumph*; take, capture, lead captive, lay one's yoke upon, reduce to servitude, enslave, sell into slavery; fetter, bind, hold in bondage 747 *imprison*; rob of freedom, disfranchise; trample on, tread on, treat like dirt, treat like scum 735 *oppress*; keep under, keep down, hold d., repress, sit on, stamp out 165 *suppress*; enthral, captivate 821 *impress*; enchant 983 *bewitch*; dominate, lead by the nose 178 *influence*; discipline, regiment; tame, quell 369 *break in*; have eating out of one's hand, bring to heel, bring to his *or* her knees, have at one's beck and call; make one's plaything, make a stooge of, do what one likes with 673 *dispose of*.

## 746 Liberation

**N.** *liberation*, setting free, unchaining, unshackling, unbinding, release, discharge 960 *acquittal*; free expression, abreaction, catharsis 818 *feeling*; unravelling, disentanglement, extrication, disinvolvement 46 *separation*; riddance, good r. 831 *relief*; rescue, redemption, salvation, moksha 668 *deliverance*; manumission, emancipation, enfranchisement; parole, bail; liberalization, relaxation (of control) 734 *laxity*; decontrol, derationing, deregulation 752 *abrogation*; demobilization, disbandment 75 *dispersion*; forgiveness of sins, absolution 909 *forgiveness*; acquittance, deed of release, quittance, quitclaim.

**Adj.** *liberated*, rescued, delivered, saved 668 *extricable*; rid of, relieved; bailed, paroled, set free, freed, manumitted, unbound 744 *unconfined*; released, enlarged, discharged, acquitted; emancipated, enfranchised etc. vb.

**Vb.** *liberate*, rescue, save 668 *deliver*; dispense 919 *exempt*; pardon 909 *forgive*; discharge, absolve, let off the hook 960 *acquit*; make free, emancipate, manumit; enfranchise, give the vote; grant equal rights, end discrimination; introduce positive discrimination, adopt a policy of affirmative action, release, free, set free, set at liberty, let out; release conditionally, bail, parole 766 *give terms*; strike off the fetters, unfetter, unshackle, unchain; unbar, unbolt, unlock 263 *open*; loosen, unloose, loose, unbind, untie, disentangle, extricate, disengage, clear 62 *unravel*; unstop, unplug, uncork, ungag, unmuzzle; uncoop, uncage, unkennel; unleash, let off the lead; let loose, leave to wander, turn adrift; license, charter; give play to, give free rein 744 *give scope*; let out, vent, give vent to 300 *empty*; leave hold, unhand, let go 779 *not retain*; relax, liberalize 734 *be lax*; lift, lift off 831 *relieve*; lift controls, decontrol, deregulate, deration 752 *abrogate*; demobilize, disband, send home 75 *disperse*; unyoke, unharness, unload 701 *disencumber*; disentail, pay off the mortgage, clear the debt.

*achieve liberty*, gain one's freedom, breathe freely; get the bit between one's teeth, assert oneself, claim freedom of action; fight for independence 738 *revolt*; free oneself, shake oneself free; stand on one's own two feet; break loose, burst one's bonds, throw off the yoke, cast off one's shackles, throw off one's ball and chain, slip the collar, kick over the traces, get away 667 *escape*.

*lose control*, lose control of oneself, lose one's cool, lose it (inf), go berserk, go mad, go wild, go ape (inf), go ape-shit (US inf), spazz out (sl) 821 *get excited*.

## 747 Restraint

**N.** *restraint*, self-r., self-control 942 *temperance*; reserve, shyness, inhibitions; suppression, repression, coercion, constraint, straitjacket 740 *compulsion*; cramp, check, obstacle, stumbling-block 702 *hindrance*; brake, disc brake, anti-lock braking system, ABS; curb, drag, clamp, snaffle, bridle 748 *fetter*; arrest, retardation, deceleration 278 *slowness*; prevention, veto, ban, bar, embargo 757 *prohibition*; legal restraint, Official Secrets Act, D-notice, gagging order, public interest immunity certificate 953 *law*; control, strict c., discipline 733 *authority*; censorship 550 *obliteration*; press laws 735 *severity*; binding over 963 *penalty*.

*restriction*, limitation, limiting factor 236 *limit*; localization, keeping within limits 232 *circumscription*; speed limit, restricted area; restriction on movement, exclusion order, no-go area, curfew; constriction, squeeze 198 *compression*; duress, pressure 740 *compulsion*; control, food c., rationing; restrictive practice, restraint of trade, exclusive rights, exclusivity 57 *exclusion*; monopoly, price ring, cartel, closed shop; ring, circle, charmed c.; protection, protectionism, mercantilism, mercantile system, protective s., intervention, intervention price, interventionism, tariff, tariff wall; retrenchment, cuts 814 *economy*; economic pressure, freeze, price freeze, price control, credit squeeze; rate-capping; blockade, investment, starving out; monopolist, protectionist, interventionist, restrictionist, mercantilist, monetarist.

*detention*, preventive d., custody, protective c. 660 *protection*; arrest, house a., restriction on movement, curfew; custodianship, keeping, guarding, keep, care, charge, ward; quarantine, internment; remand, refusal of bail; lettre de cachet; captivity, duress, durance, durance vile; bondage, slavery 745 *servitude*; entombment, burial 364 *interment*; herding, impoundment, immurement, confinement, solitary c., incarceration, imprisonment; sentence, time, a stretch, bird, lag, lagging, porridge; penology, penologist.

**Adj.** *restraining*, checking etc. vb.; restrictive, conditional, with strings; limiting, limitary; custodial, keeping; cramping, hidebound; straitlaced, unbending, unyielding, strict 735 *severe*; stiff 326 *rigid*; tight 206 *narrow*; straitening, confining, close 198 *compressive*; confined, poky; coercive, coactive 740 *compelling*; repressive, inhibiting 757 *prohibiting*; monopolistic, protectionist, protective, mercantilist.

*restrained*, self-r., self-controlled 942 *temperate*; pent up, bottled up, choked back; reserved, shy; disciplined, controlled, under control 739 *obedient*; on a lead, kept on a leash, kept under restraint, under the thumb 232 *circumscribed*; pinned, pinned down, kept under 745 *subjected*; on parole 917 *obliged*; protected, rationed; limited, restricted, scant, tight; cramped, hampered, trammelled, shackled 702 *hindered*; tied, bound, gagged; held up, weatherbound, fogbound, snowbound, housebound, bedridden, confined to bed.

*imprisoned*, confined, detained, kept in; landlocked 232 *circumscribed*; entombed, confined 364 *buried*; quarantined, in quarantine; interned, in internment; under detention, under house arrest, kept close, incommunicado; under arrest, laid by the heels, in cus-tody; refused bail, on remand; behind bars, incarcerated, locked up 750 *captive*; inside, in jug, in clink, in quod, in the slammer, in stir, in the cooler, in a cell; gated, confined to barracks; herded, corralled, penned up, impounded; in irons, fettered, shackled; pilloried, in the stocks; serving a sentence, doing time, doing bird, doing porridge; caged, in captivity, trapped.

**Vb.** *restrain*, hold back, pull b.; arrest, check, curb, rein in, brake, put a brake on, put a drag on, put clamps on, act as a brake 278 *retard*; cramp, clog, hamper 702 *hinder*; swathe, bind, tie hand and foot 45 *tie*; call a halt, stop, put a stop to 145 *halt*; inhibit, veto, ban, bar, embargo 757 *prohibit*; bridle, discipline, control 735 *be severe*; subdue 745 *subjugate*; restrain oneself, keep one's cool, keep one's wool, keep one's hair *or* shirt on 823 *keep calm*; grip, hold, pin, keep a tight hold *or* rein on, hold in leash, hold in check 778 *retain*; hold in, keep in, fight down, fight back, bottle up, choke back; restrict, tighten, hem in, limit, keep within bounds, stop from spreading, localize, cordon off, declare a no-go area, draw the line 232 *circumscribe*; damp down, pour water on, assuage 177 *moderate*; hold down, slap d., clamp down on, crack down on, keep under, sit on, jump on, repress 165 *suppress*; muzzle, gag, silence 578 *make mute*; censor, black out 550 *obliterate*; restrict access, debar from, rope off, keep out 57 *exclude*; restrict imports, put on a tariff; restrict supplies, withhold, keep back, stint; restrict consumption, ration, dole out, be sparing, retrench 814 *economize*; try to stop, resist 704 *oppose*; police, patrol, keep order.

*arrest*, make an a., apprehend, lay by the heels, catch, cop, nab, collar, pinch, nick, pick up; haul in, run in; handcuff, put the handcuffs on, snap the bracelets on (see also *fetter*); take, make a prisoner, take prisoner, capture, lead captive; kidnap, seize, snatch, take hostage; put under arrest, run in, take into custody, take charge of, clap in jail, hold.

*fetter*, manacle, bind, pinion, tie up, handcuff, put in irons; pillory, put in the stocks, tether, picket 45 *tie*; shackle, trammel, hobble; enchain, chain, load with chains, put a ball and chain on; make conditions, attach strings.

*imprison*, confine, immure, quarantine, intern; hold, detain, keep in, gate; keep in detention, keep under arrest, keep close, hold incommunicado; cloister 883 *seclude*; entomb, bury 364 *inter*; wall up, seal up; coop up, cage, kennel, impound, corral, herd, pen, cabin, box up, shut up, shut in, trap 235 *enclose*; put in a straitjacket; incarcerate, throw into prison, send to p., commit to p., remand, give in charge, run in; jug, lock up; turn the key on, keep under lock and key, put in a cell, keep behind bars, clap in irons; keep prisoner, keep in captivity, keep in custody, refuse bail; hold hostage.

### 748 Prison

**N.** *prison*, prison-house, jail-house, jail, gaol, house of correction; quod, clink, jug, can, stir, slammer, cooler, big house; glasshouse, brig; panopticon; open prison, prison without bars, halfway house; penitentiary, reformatory, Borstal; boot camp; approved school, List D school, remand home, community h.; assessment centre, detention c.; sin bin; prison ship, hulk; dungeon, oubliette, black hole, limbo; Bastille, Tower; debtor's prison, Marshalsea, Fleet; Newgate, Wormwood Scrubs, Barlinnie, Holloway; Sing Sing, Alcatraz; Château d'If; criminal lunatic asylum, Broadmoor, Carstairs.

*lockup*, choky, calaboose, nick, police station; guardroom, guardhouse, roundhouse; cooler, slammer, peter, cell, prison c., condemned c., Death Row; dungeon cell, dungeon, oubliette, torture chamber; prison van, Black Maria, saladière; dock, bar; pound, pen, cage, coop, kennel 235 *enclosure*; ghetto, reserve; stocks, pillory; lock, padlock, bolt, bar, barred window.

*prison camp*, detention c., internment c., prisoner of war c., Stalag, Colditz; concentration camp, extermination camp, Auschwitz, Belsen, Buchenwald, Dachau, Treblinka; labour camp, Gulag, re-education camp; penal settlement *or* colony, Botany Bay, Devil's Island.

*fetter*, shackle, trammel, bond, chain, ball and c., ring-bolt, irons, gyves, bilboes, hobble; manacle, pinion, handcuff, bracelet, darbies; straitjacket, corset; muzzle, gag, bit, bridle, snaffle, headstall, halter; rein, bearing r., checkrein, leading rein, martingale; reins, ribbons, traces; yoke, collar, harness; curb, brake, clamp, skid, clog, drag 702 *hindrance*; lead, tether, rope, leading string, apron strings 47 *halter*.

### 749 Keeper

**N.** *keeper*, custodian, curator; archivist, record keeper 549 *recorder*; charge officer, officer in charge; caretaker, house-minder, janitor, concierge, housekeeper; castellan, seneschal, chatelaine, warden; ranger, gamekeeper; guard, escort, convoy; garrison 713 *defender*; watchdog, sentry, sentinel, lookout, watchman, night w., security man *or* woman, security officer, watch, house-minder, house-sitter, home-sitter, vigilante, coastguard, lighthouse keeper 660 *protector*; invigilator, tutor,

chaperon, duenna, governess, nurse, foster n., wet n., nanny, nursemaid, baby-sitter, baby-minder 742 *domestic*; foster parent, adoptive p.; guardian, legal g.; appropriate person, probation officer 901 *philanthropist*.

*gaoler*, jailer, turnkey, warder, wardress, prison guard, prison officer, screw; prison governor; Argus.

### 750 Prisoner

**N.** *prisoner*, captive, capture, prisoner of war, POW, battlefield detainee; parolee, ticket-of-leave man; close prisoner, person under arrest; political prisoner, prisoner of conscience; detainee, prisoner of state; prisoner at the bar, defendant, accused 928 *accused person*; first offender, Borstal boy; persistent offender, old lag, jailbird 904 *offender*; gaol inmate, prisoner behind bars, guest of Her Majesty; condemned prisoner, convict; lifer; trusty; chain gang, galley slave 742 *slave*; hostage, kidnap victim 767 *security*.

**Adj.** *captive*, imprisoned, chained, fettered, shackled, in chains, in irons, behind bars, under lock and key, cooling one's heels; jailed, in jail, in prison, in Dartmoor, in Borstal, inside 747 *imprisoned*; in the pillory, in the stocks, in the galleys; in custody, under arrest, without bail, remanded; detained, under detention, detained at her Majesty's pleasure; bound hand and foot, held hostage.

### 751 Commission: vicarious authority

**N.** *commission*, vicarious authority; committal, delegation; devolution, decentralization; deputation, legation, mission, embassy 754 *envoy*; regency, vice-r., regentship, vice-royalty 733 *authority*; representation, procuratory, proxy; card vote; agency, factorage, trusteeship, executorship 689 *management*; clerkship, public service, civil s., bureaucracy 733 *government*.

*mandate*, trust, charge 737 *command*; commission, assignment, appointment, office, task, errand, mission; enterprise 672 *undertaking*; nomination, return, election 605 *vote*; posting, translation, transfer 272 *transference*; investment, investiture, installation, induction, inauguration, ordination, enthronement, coronation; power of attorney, written authority, charter, writ 737 *warrant*; brevet, diploma 756 *permit*; terms of reference 766 *conditions*; responsibility, care, cure (of souls); ward, charge.

**Adj.** *commissioned*, empowered, entrusted etc. vb.; deputed, detailed, delegated, accredited, official; vicarious, representational, agential.

**Vb.** *commission*, put in c.; empower, authorize, charge, sanction, charter, license 756 *permit*; post, accredit, appoint, detail, collate, assign, name, nominate; engage, hire, staff 622 *employ*; invest, induct, install, ordain; raise to the throne, enthrone, crown, anoint; commit, put in one's hands, turn over to, leave it to; subcontract, contractorize, outsource; consign, entrust, trust with, grant powers of attorney; delegate, depute, send on a mission, send on an errand, send out, return, elect, give a mandate 605 *vote*.

**Adv.** *by proxy*, per procurationem, p.p., by delegated authority, in loco parentis.

## 752 Abrogation

**N.** *abrogation*, annulment, invalidation; voidance, nullification, disallowance, vacation, defeasance; cancelling, cancellation, cassation, suppression; recall, repeal, revocation, revoking, rescission, rescinding; abolition, abolishment, dissolution; neonomianism 126 *newness*; repudiation 533 *negation*; retractation 603 *recantation*; suspension, discontinuance, disuse, writing-off, dead letter 674 *nonuse*; reversal, undoing 148 *reversion*; counterorder, countermand, nolle prosequi; reprieve.

*deposal*, deposition, dethronement; demotion, degradation; disestablishment, disendowment; deconsecration, secularization; discharge, congé, dismissal, sack, redundancy, decruitment, downsizing, outplacement, removal, garden leave *or* gardening l. 300 *ejection*; unfrocking 963 *punishment*; ousting, deprivation, divestment 786 *expropriation*; replacement, supersession 150 *substitution*; recall, transfer, relief 272 *transference*.

**Adj.** *abrogated*, voided, vacated, set aside, quashed, cancelled etc. vb.; void, null and void; functus officio, dead; dormant, sleeping 674 *unused*; recalled, revoked.

**Vb.** *abrogate*, annul, disannul, cancel; scrub, scrub out, rub o., wipe o. 550 *obliterate*; invalidate, abolish, dissolve, nullify, void, vacate, render null and void, declare null and void; quash, set aside, reverse, overrule; repeal, revoke, recall; rescind, tear up; unmake, undo 148 *revert*; countermand, counterorder; disclaim, disown, deny 533 *negate*; repudiate, retract 603 *recant*; ignore 458 *disregard*; call off, call a halt 747 *restrain*; suspend, discontinue, write off, make a dead letter of 674 *stop using*; unwish, unwill, wish undone 830 *regret*; not proceed with 621 *relinquish*.

*depose*, discrown, uncrown, dethrone; unseat; divest 786 *deprive*; unfrock; disbench, disbar, strike off the roll, strike off the register, strike off 57 *exclude*; disaffiliate, disestablish, disendow; deconsecrate, secularize; suspend,

cashier 300 *dismiss*; ease out, edge out, elbow out, oust 300 *eject*; demote, degrade, reduce to the ranks, take down a peg or two, kick upstairs; recall, relieve, supersede, replace, remove 272 *transfer*.

## 753 Resignation

**N.** *resignation*, demission; retirement, retiral; leaving, withdrawal 296 *departure*; pension, compensation, golden handshake 962 *reward*; waiver, surrender, abandonment, abdication, renunciation 621 *relinquishment*; abjuration, disclaimer 533 *negation*; state of retirement 681 *leisure*; feeling of resignation, acquiescence 721 *submission*; abdicator, resigner, quitter; person in retirement, pensioner.

**Adj.** *resigning*, abdicating, renunciatory; outgoing, former, retired, ex-, quondam, onetime, ci-devant, late; emeritus.

**Vb.** *resign*, tender one's resignation, send in one's papers, hand in one's notice, give n., demit, lay down one's office, break one's staff; be relieved, hand over, vacate, vacate office; vacate one's seat, apply for the Chiltern Hundreds; stand down, stand aside, make way for, leave it to; sign off, declare (cricket); scratch, withdraw, back out, give a walkover, retire from the contest, throw in one's hand, surrender, give up 721 *submit*; quit, throw up, chuck it; ask for one's cards; sign away, give a. 780 *assign*; abdicate, abandon, renounce 621 *relinquish*; retire, go into retirement, take early retirement, accept redundancy, be superannuated, be put out to grass; be pensioned off; finish one's term, conclude one's term of office; decline to stand again, not renew the fight, refuse battle; waive, disclaim, abjure 533 *negate*; retract 603 *recant*.

## 754 Consignee

**N.** *consignee*, committee, steering c., panel, quango 692 *council*; counsellor, wise man *or* woman, team of experts, think tank, brains trust, working party 691 *adviser*; bailee, stakeholder; nominee, appointee, licensee; trustee, executor 686 *agent*; factor, one's man of business, bailiff, steward 690 *manager*; caretaker, curator 749 *keeper*; representative (see also *delegate*); legal representative, attorney, counsel, advocate 958 *law agent*; proxy, surrogate 755 *deputy*; negotiator, middleman, broker, stockbroker 231 *intermediary*; underwriter, insurer; purser, bursar 798 *treasurer*; rent collector, tax c., revenue c., income-tax officer; office-bearer, secretary of state 741 *officer*; functionary 690 *official*.

*delegate*, walking d., shop steward; nominee, representative, elected r., member; official representative, commissary, commissioner; man *or* woman on the spot, correspondent, war c., one's own c., special c. 588 *correspondent*; emissary, special messenger 529 *messenger*; plenipotentiary (see also *envoy*); delegation, trade d., mission.

*envoy*, emissary, legate, ablegate, nuncio, papal n., internuncio, permanent representative, resident, ambassador, ambassadress, High Commissioner, chargé d'affaires; ambassador at large; corps diplomatique, diplomatic corps; minister, diplomat; consul, vice-c.; first secretary, attaché; embassy, legation, mission, consulate, High Commission; diplomatist, negotiator, plenipotentiary.

## 755 Deputy

**N.** *deputy*, surrogate, alternate, proxy; scapegoat, substitute, locum tenens, locum, understudy, stand-in, temp 150 *substitution*; pro-, vice-, vice-gerent, vice-regent, viceroy, vice-president, vice-chairman, vice-chancellor, vice-admiral, vice-captain, vice-consul; pro-consul, propraetor; vicar, vicar-general; second-in-command, number two, deputy prime minister 741 *officer*; right-hand man, lieutenant, secretary 703 *aider*; alter ego, power behind the throne, éminence grise 612 *motivator*; caretaker government; heir, heir apparent, successor designate 776 *beneficiary*; spokesperson, spokesman *or* -woman, mouthpiece, herald 529 *messenger*; second, advocate, champion 707 *patron*; agent, factor, attorney 754 *consignee*.

**Adj.** *deputizing*, representing, acting for, agential; vice-, pro-; diplomatic, ambassadorial, plenipotentiary; standing-in for 150 *substituted*; negotiatory, intermediary 231 *interjacent*.

**Vb.** *deputize*, act for 622 *function*; act on behalf of, represent, hold a mandate for, hold a proxy f., appear f., sit f., speak f., answer f., hold a brief f., state the case f.; hold in trust, manage the business of, be executor 689 *manage*; negotiate, act as go-between for, be broker for, replace, stand for, stand in the stead of, stand in for, understudy, do duty for, stand in another's shoes 150 *substitute*; be the whipping boy, act as scapegoat.

**Adv.** *on behalf of*, for, pro; by proxy.

SECTION TWO

## Special social volition

## 756 Permission

**N.** *permission*, general p., liberty 744 *freedom*; leave, sanction, clearance; vouchsafement,

accordance, grant; licence, authorization, warrant; allowance, sufferance, tolerance, toleration, indulgence 736 *leniency*; acquiescence, passive consent, implied c. 758 *consent*; connivance 703 *aid*; blessing, approval 923 *approbation*; grace, grace and favour 897 *benevolence*; concession, dispensation, exemption 919 *nonliability*; release 746 *liberation*.

*permit*, express permission, written p.; authority, law 737 *warrant*; commission 751 *mandate*; brevet, grant, charter, patent, letters p.; pass, password; passport, pet p., animal p., passbook, visa, safe-conduct; ticket, chit; licence, driving l.; free hand, carte blanche, blank cheque 744 *scope*; leave, compassionate l., sick l., leave of absence, furlough, holiday, vacation, sabbatical; parole, ticket of leave; clearance, all clear, green light, go-ahead; nihil obstat, imprimatur.

**Adj.** *permitting*, permissive, indulgent, complaisant, laissez faire, easy-going, tolerant 736 *lenient*; conniving, with no questions asked 703 *aiding*.

*permitted*, allowed etc. vb.; licit, legalized, decriminalized 953 *legal*; licensed, chartered, patent; unforbidden, unprohibited, open, optional, discretional, without strings 744 *unconditional*; permissible, allowable; printable, sayable; passed.

**Vb.** *permit*, let 469 *make possible*; give permission, grant leave, grant, accord, vouchsafe 781 *give*; nod, say yes 758 *consent*; bless, give one's blessing; go out of one's way to 759 *offer*; sanction, pass 923 *approve*; entitle, authorize, warrant, charter, patent, license, enable 160 *empower*; ratify, legalize, decriminalize 953 *make legal*; restore permission, decontrol; lift, lift a ban, raise an embargo, dispense, release 919 *exempt*; clear, give clearance 746 *liberate*; give the go-ahead, give the all clear, give the green light, green-light, tip the wink, let off the hook; recognize, concede, allow 488 *assent*; give one a chance, let one try; make it easy for, favour, privilege, indulge 701 *facilitate*; leave the way open, open the door to, open the floodgates 263 *open*; foster, encourage 156 *conduce*; humour 823 *be patient*; suffer, tolerate, put up with, brook 736 *be lenient*; connive at, shut one's eyes to, turn a blind eye, wink at 734 *be lax*; laisser faire, laisser aller, allow a free hand, give carte blanche, issue a blank cheque 744 *give scope*; permit oneself, allow o., take the liberty 734 *please oneself*.

*ask leave*, beg l., beg permission, ask if one may, ask one's blessing; apply for leave, ask to be excused; seek a favour, petition 761 *request*; get leave, have permission; receive a charter, take out a patent.

**Adv.** *by leave*, with permission, by favour of, under licence; permissibly, allowably, legally, legitimately, licitly.

## 757 Prohibition

**N.** *prohibition*, inhibition, interdiction, disallowance, injunction; countermand, counterorder; intervention, interference; interdict, veto, ban, embargo, outlawry; restriction, curfew 747 *restraint*; proscription, taboo, index; rejection, red light, thumbs down 760 *refusal*; nonrecognition, intolerance 924 *disapprobation*; prohibition of drink, licensing laws 942 *temperance*; sumptuary law 814 *economy*; repressive legislation, censorship, press laws, repression, suppression 735 *severity*; abolition, cancellation, suspension 752 *abrogation*; blackout, news b. 550 *obliteration*; forbidden fruit, contraband article 859 *desired object*.

**Adj.** *prohibiting*, prohibitory, forbidding, prohibitive, excessive 470 *impossible*; repressive 747 *restraining*; penal 963 *punitive*; hostile 881 *inimical*; exclusive 57 *excluding*.

*prohibited*, forbidden, verboten, not allowed; barred, banned, under ban; censored, bluepencilled, blacked-out; contraband, illicit, unlawful, outlawed, against the law 954 *illegal*; verboten, taboo, untouchable, blacked; frowned on, not to be thought of, not done; not to be spoken, unmentionable, unsayable, unprintable; out of bounds; blackballed, ostracized 57 *excluded*.

**Vb.** *prohibit*, forbid; disallow, veto, refuse permission, withhold p., refuse leave, give the thumbs down, give the red light, forbid the banns 760 *refuse*; withdraw permission, cancel leave; countermand, counterorder, revoke, suspend 752 *abrogate*; inhibit, prevent 702 *hinder*; restrict, stop 747 *restrain*; ban, interdict, taboo, proscribe, outlaw; black, declare b.; impose a ban, place out of bounds; bar, debar, warn off, shut the door on, blackball, ostracize 57 *exclude*; excommunicate 300 *eject*; repress, stifle, kill 165 *suppress*; censor, blue-pencil, black out 550 *obliterate*; not tolerate, put one's foot down 735 *be severe*; frown on, not countenance, not brook 924 *disapprove*; discourage, crack down on 613 *dissuade*; clip, narrow, pinch, cramp 232 *circumscribe*; draw the line, block; intervene, interpose, interfere, dash the cup from one's lips.

## 758 Consent

**N.** *consent*, free c., full c., willing c. 597 *willingness*; implied consent, implicit c.; agreement 488 *assent*; compliance 768 *observance*; concession, grant, accord; acquiescence, acceptance, entertainment, allowance 756 *permission*; sanction, endorsement, ratification, confirmation; partial consent 770 *compromise*.

**Adj.** *consenting*, agreeable, compliant, ready, ready enough 597 *willing*; winking at, conniving 703 *aiding*; yielding 721 *submitting*.

**Vb.** *consent*, say yes, nod; give consent, give the go-ahead, give the green light, set one's seal on, ratify, confirm 488 *endorse*; sanction, pass 756 *permit*; give one's approval 923 *approve*; tolerate, recognize, allow, connive 736 *be lenient*; agree, fall in with, go along with, accede 488 *assent*; not say no, entertain the idea; have no objection 488 *acquiesce*; be persuaded, come over, come round 612 *be induced*; consent unwillingly, force oneself; yield, give way 721 *submit*; comply, grant a request, do as asked; grant, accord, concede, vouchsafe 781 *give*; deign, condescend 884 *be courteous*; listen, hearken 415 *hear*, turn a willing ear, go halfway to meet 597 *be willing*; meet one's wishes, do all that is required of one, do all one is asked 828 *content*; accept, take one at one's word, take up an offer, jump at; clinch a deal, seal a bargain, close with, settle 766 *make terms*.

## 759 Offer

**N.** *offer*, fair o., proffer; improper offer, bribery, bribe 612 *inducement*; tender, bid, takeover b., green mail, buy-out, merger, proposal; declaration, motion, proposition, proposal; approach, overture, advance, invitation; tentative approach, feeler; final offer; present, presentation, offering, gratuity, sacrifice 781 *gift*; dedication, consecration; candidature, application, solicitation 761 *request*.

**Adj.** *offering*, inviting; offered, advertised 522 *shown*; open, available; on offer, on special o., on the market, up for grabs; on hire, to let, for sale; open to bid, open to offers, up for auction.

**Vb.** *offer*, proffer, hold out, make an offer, bid, tender; set out one's stall; present, lay at one's feet, place in one's hands 781 *give*; dedicate, consecrate; sacrifice to; introduce, broach, move, propose, make a proposition, put forward, suggest 512 *propound*; not wait to be asked, need no invitation, approach, approach with, make overtures, make advances, hold out one's hand; keep the door ajar, leave the door open, keep one's offer open; induce 612 *bribe*; invite, send an invitation, ask one in 882 *be hospitable*; hawk, hawk about, invite tenders, put up for sale, offer for sale 793 *sell*; auction, declare the bidding open; cater, cater for 633 *provide*; make available, place at one's disposal, make a present of 469 *make possible*; pose, confront with.

*offer oneself*, sacrifice o.; stand, be a candidate, compete, run for, be in the running for, enter 716 *contend*; volunteer, come forward 597 *be willing*, apply, put in for 761 *request*; be on offer, look for takers, go begging.

## 760 Refusal

**N.** *refusal*, nonacceptance, declining, turning down, thumbs down, red light 607 *rejection*; denial, negative answer, no, nay 533 *negation*; disclaimer, uncompromising answer, flat refusal, point-blank r., peremptory r. 711 *defiance*; repulse, rebuff, slap in the face 292 *repulsion*; no facilities, denial policy 715 *resistance*; withholding 778 *retention*; recalcitrance 738 *disobedience*; noncompliance 769 *nonobservance*; recusancy 598 *unwillingness*; objection, protest 762 *deprecation*; self-denial 945 *asceticism*; restraint 942 *temperance*; renunciation, abnegation 621 *relinquishment*.

**Adj.** *refusing*, denying, withholding, rejecting etc. vb.; recusant, noncompliant, uncompliant 769 *nonobservant*; jibbing, objecting, demurring 762 *deprecatory*; deaf to, unhearing 598 *unwilling*.

*refused*, not granted, turned down, given the red light, given the thumbs down, disallowed, ungratified, rebuffed etc. vb.; inadmissible, not permitted 757 *prohibited*; out of the question 470 *impossible*; unoffered, withheld 778 *retained*.

**Vb.** *refuse*, say no, shake one's head; excuse oneself, send one's apologies; disagree 489 *dissent*; deny, negative, repudiate, disclaim 533 *negate*; decline, turn down, opt out, pass up, spurn 607 *reject*; deny firmly, repulse, rebuff, tell one where to get off 292 *repel*; turn away 300 *dismiss*; resist persuasion, dig in one's heels, be unmoved, harden one's heart 602 *be obstinate*; not hear, not listen, turn a deaf ear 416 *be deaf*; not give, close one's hand, close one's purse; turn one's back on; hang fire, hang back 598 *be unwilling*; beg off, back down; turn from, have nothing to do with, shy at, jib at 620 *avoid*; debar, keep out, shut the door 57 *exclude*; not want, not cater for; look askance at, frown on, dislike, disfavour, discountenance, not hear of 924 *disapprove*; refuse permission, not allow 757 *prohibit*; not consent, set one's face against 715 *resist*; oppose 704 *withstand*; kick, protest 762 *deprecate*; not comply 769 *not observe*; grudge, begrudge, withhold, keep from 778 *retain*; deny oneself, waive, renounce, give up 621 *relinquish*; deprive oneself, go without, do w. 945 *be ascetic*.

**Adv.** *denyingly*, with a refusal, without acceptance; no, never, on no account, nothing doing, not likely, no way, no chance, not on one's life, over one's dead body, not for all the tea in China.

## 761 Request

**N.** *request*, simple r., modest r., humble petition; negative request 762 *deprecation*; asking, first time of a.; canvass, canvassing, hawking 793 *sale*; strong request, forcible demand, requisition; last demand, final d., last time of asking, ultimatum 737 *demand*; demand with threats, blackmail 900 *threat*; assertion of one's rights, claim, counterclaim 915 *dueness*; consumer demand, steady d., seller's market 627 *requirement*; postulate 475 *premise*; proposition, proposal, motion, prompting, suggestion; overture, approach 759 *offer*; bid, application, suit; petition, memorial, round robin; prayer, appeal, plea. (see also *entreaty*); pressure, instance, insistence, urgency 740 *compulsion*; clamour, cry, cri de coeur; dunning, importunity; soliciting, accosting, solicitation, invitation, temptation; mendicancy, begging, street-b., aggressive begging, busking, bumming, panhandling; appeal for funds, begging letter, flag day, bazaar, charity performance, benefit match; advertising 528 *advertisement*; small ad, 'wanted' column; wish, want 859 *desire*.

*entreaty*, imploring, begging, beseeching; submission, humble s., clasped hands, bended knees; supplication, prayer 981 *prayers*; appeal, invocation, apostrophe 583 *allocution*; solemn entreaty, adjuration, conjuration, obsecration; incantation, imprecation.

**Adj.** *requesting*, asking, inviting, begging etc. vb.; mendicant, alms-seeking; invitatory 759 *offering*; claiming 627 *demanding*; insisting, insistent; clamorous, importunate, pressing, urgent, instant.

*supplicatory*, entreating, suppliant, praying, prayerful; on bended knees, with folded hands, cap in hand; precatory, precative; imploratory, imploring, beseeching, with tears in one's eyes; adjuratory, invocatory, imprecatory.

**Vb.** *request*, ask, invite, solicit; make overtures, approach, accost 759 *offer*; sue for, woo, pop the question 889 *court*; seek, look for 459 *search*; fish for, angle for; need, call for, clamour f. 627 *require*; crave, make a request, prefer an appeal, beg a favour, ask a f., ask a boon, have a request to make, make bold to ask, trouble one for 859 *desire*; apply, make application, put in for, bid, bid for, make a bid f.; apply to, call on, appeal to, run to, address oneself to, go cap in hand to; tout, hawk, doorstep, canvass, solicit orders 793 *sell*; petition, memorialize; press a suit, press a claim, expect 915 *claim*; make demands 737 *demand*; blackmail, put the bite on 900 *threaten*; be instant, insist 532 *emphasize*; urge, persuade 612 *induce*; coax, wheedle, cajole; importune, ply, press, dun, besiege, beset; knock at the door, demand entrance; touch, touch for 785 *borrow*; requisition 786 *take*; raise money, tax 786 *levy*; formulate one's demands, state one's terms, send an ultimatum 766 *give terms*.

*beg*, cadge, crave, sponge, freeload, lig, play the parasite; bum, scrounge, mooch, sorn; thumb a lift, hitchhike; panhandle, hold out one's hand, beg one's bread, go from door to door, doorstep, knock at doors; appeal for funds, pass the hat, make a collection, launch an appeal, raise subscriptions 786 *levy*; beg in vain, whistle for 627 *require*.

*entreat*, make entreaty, beg hard; supplicate, be a suppliant; pray, implore, beseech, appeal, conjure, adjure, obtest, obsecrate; invoke, imprecate; apostrophize, appeal to, call on 583 *speak to*; address one's prayers to, pray to 981 *offer worship*; kneel to, go down on one's knees, go down on bended knee, fall at one's feet; gain by entreaty, impetrate 771 *acquire*.

## 762 Deprecation: negative request
**N.** *deprecation*, negative request, contrary advice 613 *dissuasion*; begging off, plea for mercy, crossed fingers; intercession, mediation 981 *prayers*; counterpetition, counterclaim 761 *request*; murmur, cheep, squeak, complaint 829 *discontent*; exception, demur, expostulation, remonstrance, protest 704 *opposition*; reaction, backlash 182 *counteraction*; gesture of protest, tut-tut, raised eyebrows, groans, jeers, sniffs of disapproval 924 *disapprobation*; petition, open letter, round robin; demonstration, march, protest m., hunger m., hunger strike, industrial action, sit-in; protest meeting, indignation m.; noncompliance 760 *refusal*.

**Adj.** *deprecatory* 613 *dissuasive*; protesting, protestant, expostulatory; clamant, vocal; intercessory, mediatorial; averting, apotropaic.

**Vb.** *deprecate*, ask one not to, advise against, have a better idea, make a counterproposal 613 *dissuade*; avert the omen, touch wood, knock on w., cross one's fingers, keep one's fingers crossed 983 *practise sorcery*; beg off, plead for, intercede 720 *mediate*; pray, appeal 761 *entreat*; cry for mercy 905 *ask mercy*; show embarrassment, tut-tut, shake one's head, raise one's eyebrows, sniff 924 *disapprove*; remonstrate, expostulate 924 *reprove*; jeer, groan, stamp 926 *detract*; murmur, beef, complain 829 *be discon-*

*tented*; object, take exception to; demur, jib, kick, squeak, protest against, appeal a., petition a., lobby a., campaign a., raise one's voice a., cry out a., cry blue murder 704 *oppose*; demonstrate, organize a protest march, hold a protest meeting, go on hunger strike; strike, take industrial action, come out, walk o. 145 *cease*.

## 763 Petitioner
**N.** *petitioner*, humble p., suppliant, supplicant; appealer, appellant; claimant, pretender; postulant, aspirant, expectant; solicitor, asker, seeker, enquirer, advertiser; customer, bidder, tenderer; suitor, courter, wooer; canvasser, hawker, touter, tout, barker, spieler; dun, dunner; pressure group, ginger g., lobby, lobbyist; applicant, candidate, entrant; competitor, runner 716 *contender*; complainer, grouser 829 *malcontent*.

*beggar*, street b., professional b., schnorrer, busker, panhandler; mendicant, mendicant friar, fakir, sannyasi; tramp, bum 268 *wanderer*; cadger, borrower, moocher, bum, scrounger, sorner, hitch-hiker; sponger, freeloader, ligger, parasite 879 *toady*.

SECTION THREE

# Conditional social volition

## 764 Promise
**N.** *promise*, promise-making, pollicitation 759 *offer*; undertaking, pre-engagement, commitment; affiance, betrothal, engagement 894 *marriage*; troth, plight, plighted word, word, one's solemn w., parole, word of honour, sacred pledge, vow, marriage v. 532 *oath*; declaration, solemn d. 532 *affirmation*; declared intention 617 *intention*; profession, professions, fair words; assurance, pledge, credit, honour, warrant, warranty, guarantee, insurance 767 *security*; voluntary commitment, bargain, gentlemen's agreement, unwritten a., mutual a. 765 *compact*; covenant, bond, promise to pay 803 *debt*; obligation, debt of honour 917 *duty*; firm date, delivery d. 672 *undertaking*; promiser, promise-maker, votary; engager, party 765 *signatory*.

**Adj.** *promissory*, promising, votive; on oath, under o., under hand and seal; on credit, on parole.

*promised*, covenanted, guaranteed, secured 767 *pledged*; engaged, bespoke, reserved; betrothed, affianced; committed, in for it; bound, obligated 917 *obliged*.

**Vb.** *promise*, say one will 532 *affirm*; hold out, proffer 759 *offer*, make a promise, give one's word, pledge one's w.; vow, vow and protest, take one's oath on it 532 *swear*; vouch for, go bail for, warrant, guarantee, assure, confirm, secure, insure, underwrite 767 *give security*; pledge, stake; pledge one's honour, stake one's credit; engage, enter into an engagement, give a firm date 672 *undertake*; make a gentleman's agreement, strike a bargain, sign on the dotted line, shake on it, commit oneself, bind oneself, be bound, covenant 765 *contract*; accept an obligation, take on oneself, answer for, accept responsibility 917 *incur a duty*; accept a liability, promise to pay, incur a debt of honour 785 *borrow*; bespeak, pre-engage, reserve 617 *intend*; plight one's troth, exchange vows 894 *wed*.

*take a pledge*, demand security 473 *make certain*; put on oath, administer an o., adjure, swear, make one s. 466 *testify*; make one promise, exact a p.; take on credit, take one's word, accept one's parole, parole 485 *believe*; rely on, expect 473 *be certain*.

**Adv.** *as promised*, according to contract, as agreed, duly; professedly, truly 540 *truthfully*; upon one's word, upon one's honour, cross one's heart 532 *affirmatively*.

## 765 Compact

**N.** *compact*, contract, bargain, concordat, agreement, mutual a., mutual undertaking 672 *undertaking*; gentleman's agreement, unwritten a., a debt of honour 764 *promise*; mutual pledge, exchange of vows; engagement, betrothal 894 *marriage*; covenant, bond 767 *security*; league, alliance, cartel 706 *cooperation*; pact, convention, 24 *agreement*; understanding, private u., something between them; secret pact, conspiracy 623 *plot*; negotiation 766 *conditions*; deal, give and take 770 *compromise*; adjustment, composition, arrangement, settlement; completion, ratification, confirmation 488 *assent*; seal, sigil, signet, signature, countersignature; deed of agreement, indenture 767 *title deed*.

*treaty*, international agreement; Treaty of Rome, Warsaw Pact; peace treaty, nonaggression pact 719 *pacification*; convention, concordat, protocol; Geneva Convention.

*signatory*, signer, countersigner, subscriber, the undersigned; swearer, attestor, attestant 466 *witness*; endorser, ratifier; adherent, party, consenting p. 488 *assenter*; covenanter, contractor, contracting party; treaty-maker, negotiator 720 *mediator*.

**Adj.** *contractual*, conventional, consensual 488 *assenting*; bilateral, multilateral; agreed to, negotiated, signed, countersigned, sworn, ratified; covenanted, signed on the dotted line,

sealed and delivered; under one's hand and seal.

**Vb.** *contract*, enter into a contract, engage 672 *undertake*; precontract 764 *promise*; covenant, make a compact, strike a bargain, sign a pact, shake hands on, do a deal, clinch a d.; join in a compact, adhere; league, ally 706 *cooperate*; treat, negotiate 791 *bargain*; give and take 770 *compromise*; stipulate 766 *give terms*; agree, come to an agreement, arrive at a formula, come to terms 766 *make terms*; conclude, close, settle, indent, execute, sign, sign on the dotted line, subscribe, ratify, attest, confirm 488 *endorse*; insure, underwrite 767 *give security*.

## 766 Conditions

**N.** *conditions*, making terms, treaty-making, diplomacy, summitry, negotiation, bargaining, collective b.; hard bargaining, trade-off, horse-trading 791 *barter*; formula, terms, set t., written t., stated t., terms for agreement; final terms, ultimatum, time limit 900 *threat*; dictated terms 740 *compulsion*; part of the bargain, condition, set of terms, basis for negotiation, frame of reference; articles, articles of agreement; provision, clause, entrenched c., escape c., let-out c., saving c., proviso, limitation, strings, reservation, exception, small print 468 *qualification*; stipulation, sine qua non, essential clause 627 *requirement*; rule 693 *precept*; contractual terms, embodied t. 765 *treaty*; terms of reference 751 *mandate*.

**Adj.** *conditional*, with strings attached, stipulatory, qualificatory, provisory 468 *qualifying*; limiting, subject to terms, conditioned, contingent, provisional; guarded, safeguarded, entrenched; binding 917 *obligatory*.

**Vb.** *give terms*, propose conditions; condition, bind, tie down, attach strings; hold out for, insist on, make demands 737 *demand*; stipulate, make it a sine qua non 627 *require*; allow no exception 735 *be severe*; insert a proviso, leave a loop-hole 468 *qualify*; fix the terms, impose the conditions, write the articles, draft the clauses; add a clause, add a let-out c., write in; keep one's options open, hedge one's bets.

*make terms*, negotiate, treat, be in treaty, parley, powwow, hold conversations 584 *confer*; deal with, treat w., negotiate w.; make overtures, throw out a feeler 461 *be tentative*; haggle, higgle 791 *bargain*; proffer, make proposals, make a counterproposal 759 *offer*; give and take, yield a point, stretch a p. 770 *compromise*; negotiate a treaty, hammer out a formula, work something out, do a deal 765 *contract*; plea-bargain.

**Adv.** *on terms*, on one's own t.; conditionally, provisionally, subject to, with a reservation; strictly, to the letter.

## 767 Security

**N.** *security*, precaution 858 *caution*; guarantee, warranty, authorization, writ 737 *warrant*; word of honour 764 *promise*; sponsorship, sponsion, patronage 660 *protection*; suretyship, surety, bail, caution, replevin, recognizance, personal r., parole; gage, pledge, pawn, hostage; stake, stake money, deposit, earnest, handsel, token, instalment; colour of one's money, earnest m., caution m.; token payment, down p. 804 *payment*; indemnity, insurance, underwriting 660 *safety*; transfer of security, hypothecation, mortgage, bottomry 780 *transfer*; collateral, collateral security, real s., bailor, sponsor, underwriter 707 *patron*.

*title deed*, deed, instrument; unilateral deed, deed poll; bilateral deed, indenture; charter, covenant, bond, common money b., bearer b., junk b. 765 *compact*; receipt, IOU, voucher, counterfoil, acquittance, quittance; certificate, authentication, marriage lines; verification, seal, stamp, signature, endorsement, acceptance 466 *credential*; valuable security, banknote, treasury note, promissory n., note of hand, bill, treasury bill, bill of exchange; blue chip, gilt-edged security; portfolio, scrip, share, debenture; mortgage deed, policy, insurance p.; will, testament, last will and testament, living will, codicil, certificate of probate; muniments, archives 548 *record*.

**Adj.** *pledged*, pawned, popped, deposited; up the spout, in hock, in pawn, at one's uncle's, on deposit; on lease, on mortgage; on bail, on recognizance.

*secured*, covered, hedged, insured, mortgaged; gilt-edged, copper-bottomed; guaranteed, covenanted 764 *promised*.

**Vb.** *give bail*, go b., bail one out, go surety, give s.; take bail, take recognizance, release on bail; hold in pledge, keep in pawn 764 *take a pledge*.

*give security*, offer collateral, hypothecate, mortgage; pledge, pawn, pop, hock 785 *borrow*; guarantee, act as guarantor, stand surety for, warrant 473 *make certain*; authenticate, verify 466 *corroborate*; execute, endorse, seal, stamp, sign, sign on the dotted line, countersign, subscribe, give one's signature 488 *endorse*; accept, grant a receipt, write an IOU 782 *receive*; vouch for 764 *promise*; secure, indemnify, insure, assure, underwrite 660 *safeguard*.

## 768 Observance

**N.** *observance*, close o. 610 *practice*; full observance, fulfilment, satisfaction 635 *sufficiency*; diligence, conscientiousness; adherence to, attention to; paying respect to, acknowledgment; performance, discharge, acquittal 676 *action*; compliance 739 *obedience*; conformance 83 *conformity*; attachment, fidelity, faith, good f. 739 *loyalty*; sense of responsibility, dependability, reliability 929 *probity*.

**Adj.** *observant*, practising 676 *doing*; heedful, watchful, careful of, attentive to 455 *attentive*; conscientious, diligent, earnest, religious, happy-clappy (inf), punctilious; meticulous, overconscientious, perfectionist 862 *fastidious*; literal, pedantic, exact 494 *accurate*; responsible, reliable, dependable 929 *trustworthy*; loyal, true, compliant 739 *obedient*; adherent to, adhering to, sticking to 83 *conformable*; faithful 929 *honourable*.

**Vb.** *observe*, heed, respect, regard, have regard to, pay respect to, acknowledge, pay attention to, attend to 455 *be attentive*; keep, practise, adhere to, stick to, cling to, follow, hold by, abide by, be loyal to 83 *conform*; comply 739 *obey*; fulfil, discharge, perform, execute, carry out, carry out to the letter 676 *do*; satisfy 635 *suffice*.

*keep faith*, be faithful to, have loyalty; discharge one's functions 917 *do one's duty*; honour one's obligations, meet one's o., be as good as one's word, make good one's promise, keep one's p., fulfil one's engagement, be true to the spirit of, stand by 929 *be honourable*; come up to scratch, redeem one's pledge, pay one's debt, pay up 804 *pay*; give one his due 915 *grant claims*.

**Adv.** *with observance*, faithfully, religiously, loyally; literally, meticulously, punctiliously, according to the spirit of, to the full.

## 769 Nonobservance

**N.** *nonobservance*, inobservance; informality, indifference 734 *laxity*; inattention, omission, laches 458 *negligence*; nonadherence 84 *nonconformity*; abhorrence 607 *rejection*; anarchism 734 *anarchy*; nonperformance, nonfeasance 679 *inactivity*; nonfulfilment, shortcoming 726 *noncompletion*; infringement, violation, trespassing, transgression 306 *overstepping*; noncompliance, disloyalty 738 *disobedience*; protest 762 *deprecation*; disregard, discourtesy 921 *disrespect*; bad faith, breach of f., breach of promise 930 *perfidy*; retractation 603 *tergiversation*; repudiation, denial 533 *negation*; failure, bankruptcy 805 *insolvency*; forfeiture 963 *penalty*.

**Adj.** *nonobservant*, nonpractising, lapsed;

nonconforming, standing out, blacklegging, nonadhering, nonconformist 84 *unconformable*; inattentive to, disregarding, neglectful 458 *negligent*; unprofessional, uncanonical; maverick, cowboy; indifferent, informal 734 *lax*; noncompliant 738 *disobedient*; transgressive, infringing, unlawful 954 *lawbreaking*; disloyal 918 *undutiful*; unfaithful 930 *perfidious*; anarchical 734 *anarchic*.

**Vb.** *not observe*, not practise, abhor 607 *reject*; not conform, not adhere, not follow, stand out 84 *be unconformable*, discard 674 *stop using*; set aside 752 *abrogate*; omit, ignore, skip 458 *neglect*; disregard, slight, show no respect for, cock a snook, snap one's fingers at 921 *not respect*; stretch a point 734 *be lax*; violate, do violence to, drive a coach and horses through, ride roughshod over, trample underfoot 176 *force*; transgress 306 *overstep*; not comply with 738 *disobey*; desert 918 *fail in duty*; fail, not qualify, not come up to scratch 636 *not suffice*; perform less than one promised 726 *not complete*; break faith, break one's promise, break one's word, neglect one's vow, repudiate one's obligations, dishonour 533 *negate*; not fulfil one's engagement, renege on, go back on, back out, cancel 603 *change one's mind*; prove unreliable 930 *be dishonest*; give the go-by, cut, shirk, dodge, parry, evade, elude 620 *avoid*; shuffle, palter, quibble, fob off, equivocate 518 *be equivocal*; forfeit, incur a penalty 963 *be punished*.

**770 Compromise**
**N.** *compromise*, noninsistence, concession; mutual concession, give and take, trade-off, adjustment, formula 765 *compact*; composition, commutation; second best, pis aller, half a loaf 35 *inferiority*; modus vivendi, working arrangement 624 *way*; splitting the difference 30 *average*; halfway 625 *middle way*; balancing act, swings and roundabouts.

**Vb.** *compromise*, make a c., find a formula, find a basis; make mutual concessions, strike a balance, find a happy medium, steer a middle course, give and take, meet one halfway 625 *be halfway*; live and let live, not insist, stretch a point 734 *be lax*; strike an average, take the mean, go half and half, go Dutch, split the difference 30 *average out*; compound, commute 150 *substitute*; compose differences, adjust d., arbitrate, go to arbitration; patch up, bridge over 719 *pacify*; take the good with the bad, take what is offered, make a virtue of necessity, take the will for the deed; make the best of a bad job; sit on the fence.

SECTION FOUR

## Possessive relations

### 771 Acquisition
**N.** *acquisition*, getting, winning; breadwinning, earning; acquirement, obtainment, procurement; collection 74 *assemblage*; realization, profit-taking 793 *sale*; conversion, encashment 780 *transfer*; fund-raising; milking, exploitation, profiteering; money-grubbing 816 *avarice*; heap, stack, pile, mountain, pool, scoop, jackpot 74 *accumulation*; trover, finding, picking up 484 *discovery*; finding again, recovery, retrieval, revendication, recoupment 656 *restoration*; redemption 792 *purchase*; appropriation 786 *taking*; subreption, theft 788 *stealing*; inheritance, heirship, patrimony; thing acquired, acquest, find, trouvaille, windfall, treasure, treasure trove; something for nothing, free gift freebie, giveaway 781 *gift*; legacy, bequest; gratuity, baksheesh 962 *reward*; benefit match, prize, plum 729 *trophy*; gravy 615 *benefit*; easy money 701 *facility*; pelf, lucre 797 *money*; plunder 790 *booty*.

*earnings*, income, earned i., wage, minimum w., salary, screw, pay packet, take-home pay, productivity bonus, performance-related pay 804 *pay*; rate for the job, pay scale, differential; fee for service, honorarium; pension, superannuation, compensation, golden handshake; remuneration, emolument 962 *reward*; allowance, expense account; pickings, perquisite, perks, fringe benefits, extras; salvage, totting; commission, rake-off 810 *discount*; return, net r., gross r., receipts, proceeds, turnover, takings, revenue, taxes 807 *receipt*; reaping, harvest, vintage, crop, cash c., catch c., second c., aftermath, gleanings; output, produce 164 *product*.

*gain*, thrift, savings 814 *economy*; no loss, credit side, profit, net p., paper p., capital gain, winnings; dividend, share-out 775 *participation*; usury, interest, high i., compound i., simple i. 36 *increment*; paying transaction, profitable t., lucrative deal, successful speculation; pay increase, rise, raise 36 *increase*; advantage, benefit; selfish advantage, personal benefit 932 *selfishness*.

**Adj.** *acquiring*, acquisitive, accumulative; on the make, gold-digging, getting, winning 730 *prosperous*; hoarding, saving; greedy 816 *avaricious*.

*gainful*, paying, money-making, money-spinning, bankable, lucrative, remunerative 962 *rewarding*; advantageous 640 *profitable*; fruitful, fertile 164 *productive*; stipendiary, paid, remunerated, breadwinning.

*acquired*, had, got; ill-gotten; inherited, patri-monial; on the credit side.

**Vb.** *acquire*, get, come by; get by effort, earn, gain, obtain, procure, get at; find, strike, come across, come by, pick up, pitch upon, light u. 484 *discover*; get hold of, get possession of, lay one's hands on, make one's own, annex 786 *appropriate*; win, secure, capture, catch, land, net, bag 786 *take*; pick, tot, glean, fill one's pockets; gather, reap, crop, harvest; derive, draw, tap, milk, mine 304 *extract*; collect, accumulate, heap, pile up 74 *bring together*; scrape together, rake t.; collect funds, launch an appeal, raise, levy, raise the wind; save, save up, hoard 632 *store*; get by purchase, buy, pre-empt 792 *purchase*; get in advance, reserve, book, engage 135 *be early*; get somehow, beg, borrow or steal; get a living, earn a l., win one's bread, turn an honest penny, keep the wolf from the door 622 *busy oneself*; get money, make money, draw a salary, draw a pension, receive one's wages; have an income, be in receipt of, have a turnover, gross, take 782 *receive*; turn into money, convert, cash, encash, realize, clear, make; get back, come by one's own, recover, salvage, recycle, regain, redeem, recapture, reconquer 656 *retrieve*; take back, resume, reassume, reclaim; compensate one-self, recover one's losses 31 *recoup*; recover one's costs, break even, balance the books, practise creative accounting, balance accounts 28 *equalize*; attain, reach; come in for, catch, incur.

*inherit*, come into, be left, be willed, be bequeathed, fall heir to, come by, come in for, receive a legacy; succeed, succeed to, step into the shoes of, be the heir of.

*gain*, profit, make a p., reap a p., earn a divi-dend; make, win; make money, coin m., coin it, line one's pockets 730 *prosper*; make a for-tune, make a killing, make one's pile, rake in the shekels, rake it in, turn a pretty penny 800 *get rich*; scoop, make a s., win, win the jackpot, break the bank; see one's advantage, sell at a profit; draw one's interest, collect one's profit, credit to one's account.

*be profitable*, profit, repay, be worthwhile 640 *be useful*; pay, pay well; bring in, gross, yield 164 *produce*; be bankable, bring in a return, pay a dividend, show a profit 730 *prosper*; accrue, roll in, bring grist to the mill, stick to one's fingers.

## 772 Loss

**N.** *loss*, deprivation, privation, bereavement; dispossession, eviction 786 *expropriation*; sacri-fice, forfeiture, forfeit, lapse 963 *penalty*; hope-less loss, dead l., total l., utter l., irretrievable l.,

irreparable l., perdition 165 *ruin*; depreciation 655 *deterioration*; diminishing returns 42 *dec-rement*; setback, check, reverse; loss of profit, lack of p.; loss leader; overdraft, failure, bank-ruptcy 805 *insolvency*; consumption 806 *expen-diture*; nonrecovery, spilt milk, wastage, wear and tear, leakage 634 *waste*; dissipation, evapor-ation, drain 37 *decrease*; riddance, good r. 746 *liberation*; losing battle 728 *defeat*.

**Adj.** *losing*, unprofitable 641 *profitless*; squan-dering 815 *prodigal*; loss-leading; the worse for wear 655 *deteriorated*; forfeiting, sacrificing, sac-rificial; deprived, dispossessed, robbed; denuded, stripped of, shorn of, bereft, bereaved; minus, without, lacking; rid of, quit of; set back, out of pocket, down, in the red, overdrawn, broke, bankrupt, insolvent 805 *non-paying*; nonprofitmaking 931 *disinterested*.

*lost*, long l., gone, gone for ever; gone by the board, out of sight out of mind, consigned to oblivion 458 *neglected*; vanished, flown out of the window 446 *disappearing*; missing, astray, adrift, mislaid 188 *misplaced*; untraced, untrace-able, lost, stolen or strayed 190 *absent*; rid, off one's hands; wanting, lacking, short 307 *deficient*; irrecoverable, irreclaimable, irretriev-able, irredeemable, unsalvageable, nonreturn-able, nonrecyclable 634 *wasted*; spent, gone down the drain, squandered 806 *expended*; for-feit, forfeited, sacrificed.

**Vb.** *lose*, not find, be unable to f., look in vain for; mislay 188 *misplace*; miss, let slip, let slip through one's fingers, kiss *or* say good-bye to 138 *lose a chance*; meet one's Waterloo; have nothing to show for, squander, throw away 634 *waste*; deserve to lose, forfeit, sacrifice; spill, allow to leak, pour down the drain; fritter away, throw good money after bad, sink 806 *expend*; not improve matters, be the worse for 832 *aggravate*; be a loser, draw a blank, burn one's fingers 731 *have trouble*; lose one's stake, lose one's bet, pay out; make no profit, be down, be out of pocket; be set back, incur losses, meet with l., sell at a loss; be unable to pay, break, go broke, go bankrupt 805 *not pay*; overdraw, be overdrawn, be in the red, be minus.

*be lost*, be missing, be declared m. 190 *be absent*; lapse, go down the drain, go down the spout, go up in smoke, go to pot 165 *be destroyed*; melt away 446 *disappear*; be a good riddance 831 *relieve*.

## 773 Possession

**N.** *possession*, right of p., de jure p., ownership, proprietorship, rightful possession, lawful p., enjoyment, usufruct, uti possidetis; seisin, occupancy, nine points of the law, bird in the hand; mastery, hold, grasp, grip, de facto possession 778 *retention*; haves and have-nots 776 *possessor*, a possession 777 *property*; tenancy, holding 777 *estate*; tenure, fee, fief, feud, feudality, seigniory, socage, villeinage; long possession, prescription 610 *habit*; exclusive possession, sole p., monopoly, corner, ring; preoccupancy, pre-emption, squatting; future possession, expectations, heirship, heirdom, inheritance, heritage, patrimony, reversion, remaindership; taking possession, impropriation, appropriation, making one's own, claiming, laying claim to, hoisting one's flag over 786 *taking*.

**Adj.** *possessing*, seized of, having, holding, owning, enjoying etc. vb.; proprietorial, having possessions, propertied, landed; possessed of, in possession, occupying, squatting; endowed with, blest w., fraught w., instinct w.; exclusive, monopolistic, possessive.

*possessed*, enjoyed, had, held etc. vb.; in the possession of, in the ownership of, in one's hand, in one's grasp, in the bag; in the bank, in one's account, to one's name, to one's credit; at one's disposal, on hand, in store; proper, personal 80 *special*; belonging, one's own, one's very o., exclusive, unshared, private; monopolized by, engrossed by, taken up by, devoured by; booked, reserved, engaged, occupied; included in, inherent, appertaining, attaching; unsold, undisposed of, on one's hands.

**Vb.** *possess*, be possessed of, be the proud possessor of, number among one's possessions, own, have; die possessed of 780 *bequeath*; hold, have and hold, have a firm grip on, hold in one's grasp, grip 778 *retain*; have at one's command, have absolute disposal of, command 673 *dispose of*; call one's own, boast of 915 *claim*; contain, include 78 *comprise*; fill, occupy; squat, sit in, sit on, settle upon, inhabit; enjoy, have for one's own 673 *use*; have all to oneself, be a dog in the manger, monopolize, have exclusive rights to, hog, corner, corner the market; get, take possession, make one's own, impropriate 786 *take*; recover, reoccupy, re-enter 656 *retrieve*; preoccupy, preempt, reserve, book, engage 135 *be early*; come by, come into, come in for, succeed 771 *inherit*.

*belong*, be vested, be v. in, belong to; go with, be included in, inhere 78 *be included*; be subject to, owe service to 745 *be subject*.

**Adv.** *possessively*, exclusively, monopolistically; in one's own right, by right of possession.

## 774 Nonownership

**N.** *nonownership*, nonpossession, nonoccupancy, vacancy; tenancy, temporary lease; dependence 745 *subjection*; pauperism 801 *poverty*; loss of possession 786 *expropriation*; deprivation, disentitlement 772 *loss*; no-man's-land, debatable territory, Tom Tiddler's ground 190 *emptiness*.

**Adj.** *not owning*, not possessing, dependent 745 *subject*; dispossessed, disentitled; owning nothing, destitute, penniless, propertyless 801 *poor*; unblest with; lacking, minus, without 627 *required*.

*unpossessed*, unattached, not belonging; masterless, ownerless, nobody's, no man's; international, common; not owned, unowned, unappropriated; unclaimed, disowned; up for grabs, anybody's; unheld, unoccupied, untenanted, unleased; vacant 190 *empty*; derelict, abandoned 779 *not retained*; unobtained, unacquired, untaken, free, unoccupied, going begging 860 *unwanted*.

## 775 Joint possession

**N.** *joint possession*, possession in common; joint tenancy, tenancy in common; gavelkind; joint ownership, common o.; common land, common, global commons; public property, public domain 777 *property*; joint government, condominium 733 *political organization*; joint stock, common stock, pool, kitty 632 *store*; cooperative system, mutualism 706 *cooperation*; nationalization, public ownership, state o., socialism, communism, collectivism; community of possessions, community of women; collective farm, collective, commune, kolkhoz, kibbutz 370 *farm*; share-cropping, métayage; time-sharing.

*participation*, membership, affiliation 78 *inclusion*; sharing, co-sharing, partnership, co-p., profit-sharing, time-sharing 706 *association*; sharing facilities, hot-desking; Dutch treat, bottle party, byob p., dividend, share-out; share, fair s., lot, whack 783 *portion*; complicity, involvement, sympathy; fellow feeling, empathy, sympathetic strike, joint action.

*participator*, member, partner, co-p., sharer, partaker 707 *colleague*; parcener, coheir, joint h.; shareholder, stockholder 776 *possessor*; cotenant, joint t., flatmate, room-m., tenants in common, housing association; sharecropper, métayer 370 *farmer*; cooperator, mutualist; trade unionist; collectivist, socialist, communist; commune-dweller, communitarian, kolkhoznik, kibbutznik; sympathizer, contributor 707 *patron*.

**Adj.** *sharing*, joint, profit-sharing, time-sharing, cooperative; common, communal, international, global; collective, socialistic, communistic; partaking, participating, partici-patory, in on, involved, in the same boat 708 *corporate*; in the swim, in the thick of things; sympathetic, condoling.

**Vb.** *participate*, have a hand in, have a say in, join in, pitch in, sit in, be in on, have a finger in the pie 706 *cooperate*; partake of, share in, take a share, come in for a s.; share, go shares, go halves, go fifty-fifty, pull one's weight, share and share alike 783 *apportion*; share expenses, go Dutch 804 *defray*; job-share.

*communalize*, socialize, mutualize, nationalize, internationalize, communize; put in the kitty, pool, hold in common, have all in c.

**Adv.** *in common*, by shares, share and share alike; jointly, collectively, unitedly, communally.

## 776 Possessor

**N.** *possessor*, holder, person in possession; taker, captor, conqueror, hostage-taker; tres-passer, squatter; monopolizer, dog in the manger; occupant, lodger, occupier, incum-bent; mortgagee, bailee, trustee; renter, hirer, lessee, leaseholder, copyholder, rent-payer; tenantry, tenant, protected t., council t.; house-owner, owner-occupier, householder, freeholder, franklin, yeoman; feudatory, feoffee, feuar, tenant in fee, vassal 742 *dependant*; peasant, serf, villein, peon, kulak, moujik 370 *farmer*; subtenant, undertenant.

*owner*, monarch, 'monarch of all one surveys';

> I am monarch of all I survey,
>   My right there is none to dispute;
> From the centre all round to the sea
>   I am lord of the fowl and the brute.
> Oh, solitude! where are the charms
>   That sages have seen in thy face?
> Better dwell in the midst of alarms,
>   Than reign in this horrible place.
>
> William Cowper, *Verses Supposed to be Written by Alexander Selkirk*

master, mistress, proprietor, proprietress, pro-prietrix; purchaser, buyer 792 *purchaser*; lord, lord paramount, lord *or* lady of the manor, mesne lord, feoffer; landed gentry, landed interest; squire, laird 868 *aristocracy*; man *or* woman of property, property-owner, property-holder, shareholder, stockholder, landholder, zamindar, landowner, landlord, landlady; mortgagor; testator, testatrix, bequeather, devisor 781 *giver*.

*beneficiary*, feoffee, feuar, releasee, grantee; impropriator, lay i. 782 *recipient*; incumbent 986 *cleric*; devisee, legatee; inheritor, heritor, expectant, successor, successor apparent,

tanist; next of kin 11 *kinsman*; heir *or* heiress, expectant h., heir of the body, heir-at-law, heir in tail, heir apparent, heir presumptive; crown prince 741 *sovereign*; reversioner, remain-derman; coheir, joint heir 775 *participator*.

## 777 Property

**N.** *property*, meum et tuum, suum cuique; pos-session, possessions, one's all; stake, venture; personalty, personal property, public p., common p.; church property, temporalities; chose in possession, chattel, real property, immovables (see also *lands*); movables, per-sonal estate, goods and chattels, worldly goods, appurtenances, belongings, parapher-nalia, accoutrements, effects, personal e., impedimenta, baggage, bag and baggage, things, gear, what one stands up in; cargo, lading 193 *contents*; goods, wares, stock, stock-in-trade 795 *merchandise*; plant, fixtures, fur-niture.

*estate*, estate and effects, assets, frozen a., liquid a., assets and liabilities; circumstances, what one is worth, what one will cut up for; resources 629 *means*; substance, capital, one's money, one's fortune 800 *wealth*; revenue, income, rent-roll 807 *receipt*; valuables, securi-ties, stocks and shares, portfolio; stake, holding, investment, ethical investment; copy-right, patent, intellectual property; chose in action, claim, demand, debts; right, title, interest; living 985 *benefice*; lease, tenure, free-hold, copyhold, fee, fee simple, fee tail, feu; tenement, hereditament.

*lands*, land, acres, broad a., acreage, tract, grounds; estate, landed e., property, landed p.; real estate, real property, realty; hereditament, tenement, holding, tenure, allodium, freehold, copyhold, fief, feud, manor, honour, seigniory, lordship, domain, demesne; messuage, toft, plot 184 *territory*; farm, home f., manor f., homestead, plantation, ranch, hacienda; crown lands, common land, common 775 *joint possession*; dependency, dominion 733 *political organization*.

*dower*, dowry, dot, portion, marriage p., join-ture, marriage settlement; allotment, allow-ance, pin money; alimony, aliment, maintenance, palimony; patrimony, birthright 915 *dueness*; appanage, heritage; inheritance, legacy, bequest; heirloom; expectations, remainder, reversion; limitation, entail; mortmain.

**Adj.** *proprietary*, branded, patented; mov-able, immovable, real, personal; propertied, landed, predial, manorial, seigniorial, feudal, allodial, freehold, leasehold, commonhold, copyhold; patrimonial, hereditary, heritable, testamentary; entailed, limited; dowered, endowed, established.

**Vb.** *dower*, endow, possess with, bless w. 781 *give*; devise 780 *bequeath*; grant, allot 780 *assign*; possess, put in possession, instal 751 *commission*; establish, found.

## 778 Retention

**N.** *retention*, prehensility, tenacity; stickiness 354 *viscidity*; tenaciousness, retentiveness, holding on, hanging on, clinging to, prehension; handhold, foothold, toehold 218 *support*; bridgehead, beachhead 34 *advantage*; clutches, grip, iron g., vice-like g., gripe, grasp, hold, firm h., stranglehold, half-nelson; squeeze 198 *compression*; clinch, lock; hug, bear h., embrace, clasp, cuddle 889 *endearment*; keep, ward, keeping in 747 *detention*; finders keepers 760 *refusal*; containment, holding action, pincer movement 235 *enclosure*; plug, stop 264 *stopper*; ligament 47 *bond*.

*nippers*, pincers, tweezers, pliers, snub-nosed p., wrench, tongs, forceps, vice, clamp 47 *fastening*; talon, claw, nails 256 *sharp point*; tentacle, hook, tendril 378 *feeler*; teeth, fangs 256 *tooth*; paw, hand, fingers 378 *finger*; fist, clenched f., duke.

**Adj.** *retentive*, tenacious, prehensile; vice-like, retaining 747 *restraining*; clinging, adhesive, sticky, gummy, gluey, gooey 48 *cohesive*; firm, indissoluble, unshakable 45 *tied*; tight, strangling, throttling; tight-fisted 816 *parsimonious*; shut fast 264 *closed*.

*retained*, in the grip of, gripped, pinioned, pinned, clutched, strangled; fast, stuck f., bound, held; kept in, detained 747 *imprisoned*; penned, held in, contained 232 *circumscribed*; saved, kept 666 *preserved*; booked, reserved, engaged; not for sale, not for hire, not to let; unforfeited, kept back, withheld 760 *refused*; uncommunicated, esoteric, incommunicable 523 *occult*; nontransferable, inalienable; entailed, in mortmain.

**Vb.** *retain*, hold; grab, buttonhole, hold back 702 *obstruct*; hold up, catch, steady 218 *support*; hold on, hold fast, hold tight, keep a firm hold of, maintain one's hold, not let go; cling to, hang on to, freeze on to, stick to, adhere 48 *agglutinate*; fasten on, grip, gripe, grasp, grapple, clench, clinch, lock; hug, clasp, clutch, embrace; pin, pin down, hold d.; have by the throat, throttle, strangle, keep a stranglehold on, get a half-nelson on, tighten one's grip 747 *restrain*; fix one's teeth in, dig one's nails in, dig one's toes in, hang on like a bulldog, hang on with all one's might, hang on for dear life; keep in, detain 747 *imprison*; contain, keep within limits, draw the line 235

*enclose*; keep to oneself, keep in one's own hands, keep back, keep to one side, withhold 525 *keep secret*; keep in hand, have in hand, not dispose of 632 *store*; save, keep 666 *preserve*; not part with, keep back, withhold 760 *refuse*.

## 779 Nonretention

**N.** *nonretention*, parting with, disposal, alienation 780 *transfer*; selling off 793 *sale*; letting go, leaving hold of, release 746 *liberation*; unfreezing, decontrol; dispensation, exemption 919 *nonliability*; dissolution (of a marriage) 896 *divorce*; cession, abandonment, renunciation 621 *relinquishment*; cancellation 752 *abrogation*; disuse 611 *desuetude*; availability, salability, disposability; unsoundness, leaking, leak 298 *outflow*; incontinence 302 *excretion*.

*derelict*, deserted village, abandoned position; jetsam, flotsam 641 *rubbish*; cast-off, slough; waif, stray, foundling, orphan, maroon, outcast, pariah; down-and-out, vagrant.

**Adj.** *not retained*, not kept, under notice to quit; alienated, disposed of, sold off; left behind 41 *remaining*; dispensed with, abandoned 621 *relinquished*; released 746 *liberated*; fired, made redundant, given the sack *or* the chop, given the heave-ho; derelict, unclaimed, unappropriated; unowned 774 *unpossessed*; disowned, divorced, disinherited; heritable, inheritable, transferable; available, for hire, to let, for sale 793 *salable*; givable, bestowable.

**Vb.** *not retain*, part with, alienate, transfer 780 *assign*; sell off, dispose of 793 *sell*; be open-handed 815 *be prodigal*; free, let go, let slip, unhand, leave hold of, relax one's grip, release one's hold; unlock, unclinch, unclench 263 *open*; unbind, untie, disentangle 46 *disunite*; forego, dispense with, do without, spare, give up, waive, abandon, cede, yield 621 *relinquish*; renounce, abjure 603 *recant*; cancel, revoke 752 *abrogate*; lift, lift restrictions, derestrict, raise an embargo, decontrol, deregulate, deration 746 *liberate*; supersede, replace 150 *substitute*; wash one's hands of, turn one's back on, disown, disclaim 533 *negate*; dissolve (a marriage) 896 *divorce*; disinherit, cut off without a penny, cut off with a shilling 801 *impoverish*; marry off 894 *marry*; get rid of, cast off, ditch, jettison, throw overboard 300 *eject*; cast away, abandon, maroon; pension off, put out to grass, invalid out, retire; discharge, give notice to quit, declare redundant, give the heaveho, ease out, edge out, elbow out, kick o. 300 *dismiss*; lay off, stand o.; drop, discard 674 *stop using*; withdraw, abandon one's position 753 *resign*; lose friends, estrange 881 *make enemies*; sit loose to 860 *be indifferent*; let out, leak 300 *emit*.

**780 Transfer (of property)**

**N.** *transfer*, transmission, consignment, delivery, handover 272 *transference*; enfeoffment, feoffment, impropriation; settlement, limitation; conveyancing, conveyance; bequeathal; assignment; alienation 779 *nonretention*; demise, devise, bequest 781 *gift*; lease, let, rental, hire; buying, bargain and sale 793 *sale*; trade, trade-off 791 *barter*; conversion, exchange 151 *interchange*; nationalization, privatization; change of hands, changeover 150 *substitution*; devolution, delegation 751 *commission*; heritability, succession, reversion, inheritance; pledge, pawn, hostage.

**Adj.** *transferred*, made over; borrowed, lent, pawned, leased, rented, hired; transferable, conveyable, alienable, exchangeable, negotiable; heritable, reversional, reversionary; givable, bestowable; nationalized, privatized.

**Vb.** *assign*, convey, transfer by deed; transfer by will (see also *bequeath*); grant, sign away, give a. 781 *give*; let, rent, hire 784 *lease*; alienate 793 *sell*; negotiate, barter 791 *trade*; change over 150 *substitute*; exchange, convert 151 *interchange*; confer, confer ownership, put in possession, impropriate, invest with, enfeoff; commit, devolve, delegate, entrust 751 *commission*; give away, marry off 894 *marry*; deliver, give delivery, transmit, hand over, make o., unload on, pass to, pass the buck 272 *transfer*; pledge, pawn 784 *lend*; transfer ownership, withdraw a gift, give to another; disinherit, cut off, cut off without a penny, cut off with a shilling 801 *impoverish*; dispossess, expropriate, relieve of 786 *deprive*; transfer to the state, nationalize, municipalize 775 *communalize*; privatize.

*bequeath*, will, will and bequeath, devise, demise; grant, assign; leave, leave by will, make a bequest, leave a legacy; make a will, make one's last will and testament, put in one's will, add a codicil; leave a fortune, cut up well 800 *be rich*; have something to leave.

*change hands*, pass to another, be under new management, come into the hands of; change places, be transferred, pass, shift; revert to; devolve upon; pass from one to another, pass from hand to hand, circulate, go the rounds 314 *circle*; succeed, inherit 771 *acquire*.

**781 Giving**

**N.** *giving*, bestowal, donation; alms-giving, charity, welfare 901 *philanthropy*; generosity, generous giving 813 *liberality*; contribution, subscription to 703 *economic aid*; prize-giving,

presentation, award 962 *reward*; delivery, commitment, consignment, conveyance 780 *transfer*; endowment, settlement 777 *dower*; grant, accordance, presentment, conferment; investment, investiture, enfeoffment, infeudation; bequeathal, leaving, will-making.

*gift*, fairing, souvenir, memento, keep-sake, token; gift token, gift voucher; present, birthday p., Christmas p.; goodluck present, handsel; Christmas box, whip-round, tip, fee, honorarium, baksheesh, gratuity, pourboire, trinkgeld, drink money 962 *reward*; token, consideration; bribe, sweetener, douceur, slush fund 612 *inducement*; prize, award, presentation 729 *trophy*; benefit, benefit match, benefit performance; alms, maundy money, dole, benefaction, charity 901 *philanthropy*; food parcel, free meal; freebie, giveaway; bounty, manna; largesse, donation, donative, hand-out; bonus, bonanza; something extra, extras; perks, perquisites, expense account; grant, allowance, subsidy, aid 703 *subvention*; boon, grace, favour, service, labour of love 597 *voluntary work*; free gift, outright g., ex gratia payment; piece of luck, windfall 771 *acquisition*; repayment, unsolicited r., conscience money 804 *payment*; forced loan, benevolence, tribute 809 *tax*; bequest, legacy 780 *transfer*.

*offering*, dedication, consecration; votive offering 979 *piety*; peace offering, thank o., offertory, collection, sacrifice, self-s. 981 *oblation*; Easter offering, Peter's pence; widow's mite; contribution, subscription, flag day, tag day, appeal; ante, stake.

*giver*, donor, bestower; rewarder, tipper, briber; grantor, feoffer; presenter, awarder, prize-giver; settlor, testator, legator, devisor, bequeather; subscriber, contributor; sacrificer 981 *worshipper*; tributary, tribute-payer 742 *subject*; almoner, almsgiver, blood donor, kidney d., organ d. 903 *benefactor*; generous giver, distributor of largesse, Lady Bountiful, fairy godmother, rich uncle, sugar daddy, Santa Claus, Father Christmas 813 *good giver*; backer, angel.

**Adj.** *giving*, granting etc. vb.; tributary 745 *subject*; subscribing, contributory 703 *aiding*; alms-giving, charitable, eleemosynary, compassionate 897 *benevolent*; sacrificial, votive, sacrificing, oblatory 981 *worshipping*; generous, bountiful 813 *liberal*.

*given*, bestowed, gifted; given away, gratuitous, gratis, for nothing, free, freebie, giveaway 812 *uncharged*; givable, bestowable, allowed, allowable, concessional 756 *permitted*.

**Vb.** *give*, bestow, lend, render; afford, provide; vouchsafe, favour with, honour w., indulge w., show favour, grant a boon 736 *be lenient*; grant, accord 756 *permit*; gift, donate, make a present of; give by will, leave 780 *bequeath*; dower, endow, enrich; give a prize, present, award 962 *reward*; confer, bestow upon, vest, invest with; dedicate, consecrate, vow to 759 *offer*; devote, offer up, immolate, sacrifice 981 *offer worship*; spare for, make time for, have time for; give a present, gratify, tip, consider, remember, cross one's palm with silver; grease the palm 612 *bribe*; bestow alms, give to charity 897 *philanthropize*; give freely, open one's purse, put one's hand in one's pocket, lavish, pour out, shower upon 813 *be liberal*; spare, give free, give away, not charge; stand, treat, entertain 882 *be hospitable*; give out, dispense, dole out, mete o., share o., allot, deal out 783 *apportion*; contribute, subscribe, pay towards, subsidize, help, help with money 703 *aid*; have a whip-round, pass round the hat, launch an appeal; pay one's share *or* whack, chip in 775 *participate*; part with, fork out, dish o., shell o. 804 *pay*; share, share with, impart 524 *communicate*; render one's due, furnish one's quota 917 *do one's duty*; give one his due 915 *grant claims*; pay tribute; give up, cede, yield 621 *relinquish*; hand over, give o., make o., deliver 780 *assign*; commit, consign, entrust 751 *commission*; dispatch 272 *send*.

## 782 Receiving

**N.** *receiving*, admittance 299 *reception*; getting 771 *acquisition*; acceptance, recipience, assumption; inheritance, succession, heirship; collection, collectorship, receivership, receipt of custom; receipt, windfall 781 *gift*; toll, tribute, dues, receipts, proceeds, winnings, takings 771 *earnings*; receiving end.

*recipient*, acceptor, receiver, taker, biter; trustee 754 *consignee*; addressee 588 *correspondent*; buyer 792 *purchaser*; donee, grantee, assignee, allottee, licensee, patentee, concessionnaire, lessee, releasee; devisee, legatee, inheritor, heir, successor 776 *beneficiary*; payee, earner, stipendiary, wage-earner; pensioner, old-age p., pensionary, annuitant; remittance man 742 *dependant*; winner, prize w., scholar, exhibitioner; object of charity 763 *beggar*; one at the receiving end 825 *sufferer*.

*receiver*, official r., liquidator 798 *treasurer*; payee, collector, bill-c., debt-c., rent-c., tax-c., tax-farmer, publican; income-tax officer, excise o., excisemen, customs officer, douanier; booking clerk; shareholder, bondholder, rentier.

**Adj.** *receiving*, recipient; receptive, welcoming; impressionable 819 *sensitive*; paid, stipendiary, wage-earning; pensionary,

pensioned; awarded, given, donated, allotted, favoured.

**Vb.** *receive*, be given, have from; get 771 *acquire*; collect, take up, levy, toll 786 *take*; gross, net, clear, takehome, pocket, pouch; be in receipt of, have received; get one's share; accept, take in 299 *admit*; accept from, take f., draw, encash, be paid; have an income, draw a pension; inherit, succeed to, come into, come in for, be left; receipt, give a r., acknowledge, send an acknowledgment.

*be received*, be drawn, be receipted; be credited, be added unto 38 *accrue*; come to hand, come in, roll in; pass into one's hands, stick to one's fingers, fall to one's share, fall to one's lot.

## 783 Apportionment

**N.** *apportionment*, appointment, assignment, allotment, allocation, appropriation, earmarking; division, partition, repartition, jobsharing, job-splitting, sharing out, parcelling out, divvying up, doling out; shares, fair s., distribution, deal, new d.; stakeholder economy; dispensing, dispensation, administration; demarcation, delimitation 236 *limit*; place, assigned p., allotted sphere, seat, station 27 *degree*; public sector, private s.

*portion*, share, share-out, cut, split; dividend, interim d., final d., divvy, divi; allocation, allotment; lot, contingent; proportion, ratio; quantum, quota; halves, bigger half, moiety 53 *part*; deal, hand (at cards); dole, mess, modicum, pittance, allowance; ration, iron rations, ration book, coupon; dose, dosage, measure, dollop, whack, helping, slice, slice of the cake, piece of the action 53 *piece*; rake-off, cut, commission 810 *discount*; stake, ante; allotted task, taskwork, task, Herculean task, stint 682 *labour*.

**Vb.** *apportion*, allot, allocate, appropriate, earmark; appoint, assign; assign a part, cast, cast for a role; assign a place, detail, billet; partition, zone; demarcate, delimit 236 *limit*; divide, divide up, subdivide, carve up, split, cut; halve 92 *bisect*; go shares 775 *participate*; share, share out, divvy up, distribute, spread around; dispense, administer, serve, deal, deal out, portion o., dole o., parcel o., dish o. 781 *give*; mete out, measure, admeasure, ration, dose; divide proportionally, prorate; get a share, take one's cut, take one's whack; jobshare.

**Adv.** *pro rata*, to each according to his share; proportionately, respectively, each to each, per head, per capita

## 784 Lending

**N.** *lending*, hiring, leasing, farming out; letting, subletting, renting out, subinfeudation; lending at interest, on-lending, usury, giving credit 802 *credit*; investment; mortgage, bridging loan; advance, imprest, loan, accommodation, temporary a.; lending on security, lending on collateral, pawnbroking; lease, long l.; let, sublet.

*pawnshop*, pawnbroker's, one's uncle's, mont-de-piété, pop-shop, hock s.; bank, credit company, finance corporation, building society, International Monetary Fund, World Bank.

*lender*, creditor; harsh creditor, extortioner; investor, financier, banker; moneylender, usurer, loan shark, Shylock; pawnbroker, uncle; mortgagee, lessor, hirer, renter, letter; backer, angel; seller on credit, tallyman; hire-purchase dealer, HP d., tickshop-keeper.

**Adj.** *lending*, investing, laying out; usurious, extortionate; lent, loaned, on credit.

**Vb.** *lend*, loan, put out at interest, onlend; advance, accommodate, allow credit, give one a loan 802 *credit*; lend on security, lend on collateral; put up the money, back, finance; invest, sink; risk one's money, play the stockmarket 791 *speculate*.

*lease*, let, demise, let out, hire out, rent out, let out on hire, farm out; sublet, subinfeudate.

**Adv.** *on loan*, on credit, on advance; on security.

## 785 Borrowing

**N.** *borrowing*, touching; request for credit, loan application; loan transaction, mortgage 803 *debt*; credit account, credit card, plastic money, plastic; hire purchase, HP, tick, instalment plan, the never-never; pledging, pawning; temporary misappropriation, joyride 788 *stealing*; something borrowed, loan, bank loan, repayable amount 784 *lending*; forced loan, Morton's fork *or* crutch, benevolence 809 *tax*; unauthorized borrowing, infringement, plagiarism, piracy, copying 20 *imitation*; borrowed plumes 542 *deception*.

**Vb.** *borrow*, borrow from, cadge from, scrounge from, bum from, mooch from, touch, touch for 761 *request*; hypothecate, mortgage, pawn, pledge, pop, hock; provide collateral 767 *give security*; take a loan, exact a forced loan, exact a benevolence; use a credit card, use plastic money, use plastic, get credit, get accommodation, take on loan, take on credit, take on tick; buy in instalments, buy on hire purchase *or* the never-never 792 *purchase*; incur liabilities, run into debt 803 *be in debt*; promise to pay, ask for credit, apply for a loan, raise a loan, raise the wind, float a loan; invite investment, issue debentures, accept deposits; beg, borrow, or steal 771 *acquire*; cheat, crib, plagiarize, pirate, infringe 20 *copy*.

*hire*, charter, farm, lease, outsource, rent, take on lease.

## 786 Taking

**N.** *taking*, snatching; seizure, capture, rape; taking hold, grasp, prehension, apprehension 778 *retention*; taking possession, assuming ownership, appropriation, assumption 916 *arrogation*; requisition, earmarking, commandeering, compulsory purchase 771 *acquisition*; compulsory saving, postwar credit 785 *borrowing*; exaction, taxation, raising taxes, impost, levy, capital l. 809 *tax*; cash back, withdrawal 39 *subtraction*; taking back, recovery, retrieval, recoupment; taking away, removal 188 *displacement*; furtive removal 788 *stealing*; cadging, scrounging, mooching, bumming, touching one for money, totting; bodily removal, abduction, press gang, kidnapping, hijacking, slave-raiding, piracy; raid 788 *spoliation*; thing taken, hostage, take, haul, catch, bag, capture, prize, plum 790 *booty*; receipts, takings, winnings, pickings, ill-gotten gains, gleanings 771 *earnings*.

*expropriation*, dispossession, angary; forcible seizure, attachment, distraint, distress, foreclosure; eviction, expulsion 300 *ejection*; takeover, deprivation, divestment 752 *abrogation*; hiving off, asset-stripping; disinheritance 780 *transfer*; taking without compensation, confiscation, capital levy; exaction, extortion; swindle, rip-off; impounding, sequestration.

*rapacity*, rapaciousness, thirst for loot; avidity, thirst 859 *hunger*; greed, insatiable g., insatiability 816 *avarice*; vampirism, bloodsucking; extortion, blackmail.

*taker*, appropriator, remover; seizer, snatcher, grabber; spoiler, raider, pillager, marauder, ransacker, sacker, looter, despoiler 789 *robber*; kidnapper, hijacker, abductor, press gang; slave-raider, slaver; captor, capturer, hostage-taker 741 *master*; usurper, arrogator; extortioner, blackmailer; locust, devourer 168 *destroyer*; bloodsucker, leech, parasite, vampire, harpy, vulture, wolf, shark; beast *or* bird of prey, predator; confiscator, sequestrator 782 *receiver*; expropriator, disseisor; asset-stripper.

**Adj.** *taking*, abstractive, deductive; grasping, extortionate, rapacious, wolfish, vulturine; devouring, all-d., all-engulfing, voracious, ravening, ravenous 859 *hungry*; raptorial, predatory 788 *thieving*; privative, expropriatory, confiscatory; commandeering, requisitory; acquisitive, possessive 771 *acquiring*.

**Vb.** *take*, accept, be given 782 *receive*; take over, take back, claw back (see also *appropriate*); take in, let in 299 *admit*; take up, snatch up; take in advance, anticipate 135 *be early*; take hold, fasten on, stick to, clutch, grip, cling 778 *retain*; lay hands upon, seize, snatch, grab, pounce, pounce on, spring; snatch at, reach, reach out for, make a long arm; grasp at, clutch at, grab at, make a grab, scramble for, rush f.; capture, rape, storm, take by s. 727 *overmaster*; conquer, captive, lead c. 745 *subjugate*; catch, overtake, intercept 277 *outstrip*; apprehend, take into custody, make an arrest, run in, nab, nobble, collar, lay by the heels 747 *arrest*; make sure of, fasten, pinion 747 *fetter*; hook, trap, snare, lime 542 *ensnare*; net, land, bag, pocket, pouch; gross, have a turnover 771 *acquire*; gather, accumulate, amass, collect 74 *bring together*; cull, pick, pluck; reap, crop, harvest, glean 370 *cultivate*; scrounge, cadge, mooch, bum, tot, ransack 459 *search*; pick up, snap up, snaffle; knock off, help oneself 788 *steal*; pick clean, strip 229 *uncover*; remove, withdraw (see also *take away*); deduct 39 *subtract*; take out, unload, unlade, disburden 188 *displace*; draw, draw out, draw off, milk, tap, mine 304 *extract*; take the lot, sweep the board, scoop the pool, hit the jackpot.

*appropriate*, take to or for oneself, make one's own, annex; pirate, plagiarize 20 *copy*; take possession, lay claim to, stake one's claim; take over, assume, assume ownership, impropriate 773 *possess*; enter into, come i., succeed 771 *inherit*; instal oneself, seat o. 187 *place oneself*; overrun, swarm over, people, populate, occupy, settle, colonize; win, conquer; take back, get back one's own, recover, resume, repossess, recapture, reconquer 656 *retrieve*; reclaim 915 *claim*; earmark, commandeer, requisition 737 *demand*; nationalize, secularize 775 *communalize*; denationalize, privatize; usurp, arrogate, trespass, squat 916 *be undue*; dispossess (see also *deprive*); treat as one's own, make free with; monopolize, hog, be a dog in the manger; sweep everything into one's net, engulf, suck in, suck up, swallow, swallow up 299 *absorb*; devour, eat up. (See also *fleece*.)

*levy*, raise, extort, exact, wrest from, wring f., force f. 304 *extract*; compel to lend 785 *borrow*; exact tribute, extort protection money, make pay, collect a toll; raise taxes 809 *tax*; overtax, rackrent, suck dry (see also *fleece*); draw off, exhaust, drain 300 *empty*; wring, squeeze, squeeze dry, squeeze to the last drop, squeeze till the pips squeak 735 *oppress*; divert resources, sequestrate.

*take away*, remove, shift, unload, disburden 188 *displace*; send away 272 *send*; lighten 701

*disencumber*; hive off, abstract, relieve of 788 *steal*; remove bodily, escort 89 *accompany*; kidnap, crimp, shanghai, press, pressgang, impress, abduct, take hostage, hijack, ravish, carry off, bear off, bear away; hurry off with, run away w., run off w., elope w., clear off w. 296 *decamp*; raid, loot, plunder 788 *rob*.

*deprive*, bereave, orphan, widow; divest, denude, strip 229 *uncover*; unfrock, unthrone 752 *depose*; dispossess, usurp 916 *disentitle*; oust, elbow out, evict, expel 300 *eject*; expropriate, confiscate, sequester, sequestrate, distrain, foreclose; disinherit, cut out of one's will, cut off, cut off without a penny, cut off with a shilling.

*fleece*, pluck, skin, shear, clip, gut; strip, strip bare, denude 229 *uncover*; take to the cleaners, rip off; take one for a ride, swindle, bilk, welsh, con, cheat 542 *deceive*; blackmail, bleed, bleed white, sponge, suck, suck like a leech, suck dry; soak, sting; mulct 788 *defraud*; devour, eat up, eat out of house and home 301 *eat*; take one's all, rook, bankrupt, leave one without a penny *or* cent 801 *impoverish*.

**787 Restitution**

**N.** *restitution*, giving back, return, reversion; bringing back, repatriation; reinstatement, reenthronement, reinvestment; rehabilitation 656 *restoration*; redemption, ransom, rescue 668 *deliverance*; recuperation, replevin, recovery; compensation, indemnification; repayment, recoupment; refund, reimbursement; indemnity, damages 963 *penalty*; amends, reparation 941 *atonement*.

**Adj.** *restoring*, restitutory, refunding; indemnificatory, compensatory 941 *atoning*.

**Vb.** *restitute*, make restitution 656 *restore*; return, render, give back 779 *not retain*; pay up, cough up 804 *pay*; refund, repay, give one one's money back, recoup, reimburse; indemnify, pay an indemnity, pay damages, compensate, make it up to; pay compensation, make reparation, make redress, make amends 941 *atone*; bring back, repatriate; ransom, redeem 668 *deliver*; reinstate, reinvest, rehabilitate, set up again, raise one to his *or* her feet, restore one to favour; recover 656 *retrieve*.

**788 Stealing**

**N.** *stealing*, thieving, lifting, robbing etc. vb.; theft, larceny, petty l., grand l., compound l.; pilfering, snitching, swiping, nicking, filching, robbing the till, putting one's fingers in the till, pickpocketing, shoplifting, kleptomania; burglary, house-breaking, breaking and entering; safe-blowing, s.-breaking, s.-cracking; robbery, highway r., gang r., dacoity, thuggee;

robbery with violence, stickup, holdup, bag-snatching, mugging, smash and grab raid, ram r.; autocrime; poaching, lamping, cattle-raiding, c.-rustling; rape, abduction, kidnapping, dognapping, hijack, skyjack; slave-raiding; body-snatching; abstraction, removal 786 *taking*; literary theft, cribbing, plagiarism, lifting, pirating, copyright infringement 20 *imitation*; temporary misappropriation, joyride, autotheft, twoc (sl) 785 *borrowing*; thievery, act of theft; job, fiddle.

*brigandage*, banditry, outlawry, piracy, buccaneering, filibustering; privateering, letters of marque 718 *warfare*; raiding, raid, razzia, foray 712 *attack*.

*spoliation*, plundering, looting, pillage; cattle-rustling (see also *brigandage*); sack, sacking; depredations, rapine, ravaging 165 *havoc*.

*peculation*, embezzlement, misappropriation, malversation, breach of trust, fraudulent conversion; blackmail, extortion, protection racket; daylight robbery, rip-off; moonlighting, tax evasion, black economy, fraud, computer crime, white-collar c., fiddle, swindle, hustling, cheating; confidence trick, skin game 542 *deception*.

*thievishness*, thievery, light-fingeredness, light fingers, sticky fingers, kleptomania; predacity 786 *rapacity*; dishonesty, crookedness, unreliability 930 *improbity*; burglarious intent, intention to steal; den of thieves, thieves' kitchen.

**Adj.** *thieving*, in the act of theft; with intent to steal; thievish, light-fingered, sticky-fingered; kleptomaniac; furacious, larcenous, burglarious; predatory, predacious, raptorial; piratical, buccaneering, filibustering, privateering, raiding, marauding; scrounging, foraging; fraudulent, on the fiddle 930 *dishonest*.

**Vb.** *steal*, lift, thieve, pilfer, shoplift, help oneself; be light-fingered, be sticky-fingered, pick pockets, have a finger in the till; pick locks, blow a safe; burgle, burglarize, housebreak; rob, relieve of; rifle, sack, clean out; swipe, nobble, nick, pinch, half-inch, pocket, bone, prig, snaffle, snitch, knock off 786 *take*; forage, scrounge; lift cattle, rustle, drive off, make off with; abduct, kidnap, shanghai; abstract, purloin, liberate, souvenir, filch; sneak off with, walk off w., make away w., spirit away; crib, copy, lift, plagiarize, infringe copyright, pirate 20 *copy*; smuggle, run, bootleg, poach, hijack, skyjack.

*defraud*, embezzle, peculate, misappropriate, purloin, let stick to one's fingers; fiddle, cook the books, practise creative accounting, commit breach of trust, obtain money on false

pretences; commit a computer crime; con, swindle, cheat, diddle, chisel, do out of, bilk, shaft (sl) 542 *deceive*; rook, pigeon, gull, dupe; pluck, skin, rip off 786 *fleece*.

*rob*, rob with violence, mug; commit highway robbery, hold up, stick up; pirate, sail under the skull and crossbones, buccaneer, filibuster, maraud, reave *or* reive, raid; foray, forage, scrounge; strip, gut, ransack, rifle; plunder, pillage, loot, sack, put to the s., despoil, ravage, spoil 165 *lay waste*; make a prey of, victimize, blackmail, demand money with menaces; extort, extort protection money, screw, squeeze 735 *oppress*.

**789 Thief**
**N.** *thief*, thieving fraternity, swell mob, light-fingered gentry, den of thieves; crook, Artful Dodger; 'pickers and stealers' (see quotation at 379 *finger*), light fingers, sticky fingers; kleptomaniac, stealer, lifter, filcher, purloiner, pilferer, petty thief, larcenist; sneaker, sneak thief, shoplifter, pickpocket, dip, cutpurse, bag-snatcher; cattle thief, rustler; burglar, cat b., house-breaker, safe-b., safe-blower, cracksman, picklock, yegg, yeggman, peterman; poacher, bootlegger, smuggler, runner, night r., gun r.; abductor, kidnapper 786 *taker*; hijacker, skyjacker; slaver, slave-raider; body-snatcher, resurrectionist; fence, receiver of stolen property; plagiarist, infringer, pirate.

*robber*, robber band, forty thieves; brigand, bandit, outlaw, Robin Hood; footpad, highwayman, knight of the road, Dick Turpin, Jonathan Wild; mugger, thug, dacoit, gang-robber 904 *ruffian*; gangster, racketeer; gunman, hijacker, skyjacker, carjacker, yacht-j.; terrorist; sea rover, pirate, buccaneer, picaroon, corsair, filibuster, privateer; Captain Kidd, Long John Silver; reaver *or* reiver, marauder, raider, freebooter, moss-trooper, cateran, rapparee; plunderer, pillager, sacker, ravager, spoiler, despoiler, depredator; wrecker.

*defrauder*, embezzler, peculator, fiddler, creative accountant, diddler; defaulter, welsher; fraudster, fraudsman, swindler, sharper, cheat, computer criminal, shark, con man, chevalier d'industrie 545 *trickster*; forger, counterfeiter, coin-clipper.

**790 Booty**
**N.** *booty*, spoil, spoils; spoils of war, spolia opima 729 *trophy*; plunder, loot, pillage; prey, victim, quarry; find, strike, prize, purchase, haul, catch 771 *gain*; pickings, gleanings, tottings; stolen article, stolen goods, swag; moonshine, hooch, bootleg, contraband; illicit

gains, ill-gotten gains, graft, boodle, blackmail; pork barrel 703 *economic aid.*

## 791 Barter

**N.** *barter*, exchange, fair e., swap 151 *interchange*; exchange of goods, payment in kind, truck, truck system; traffic, trading, dealing, trade-off, buying and selling; factorage, factorship, brokerage, agiotage, arbitrage, jobbing, stock-jobbing, share-pushing; negotiation, bargaining, hard b., higgling, haggling, horse-trading.

*trade*, commercial intercourse; trading, exporting 272 *transference*; visible trade, invisible t.; foreign trade, home *or* domestic t.; protection, trade restrictions, intervention, interventionism 797 *restriction*; free trade, open market, single m., economic zone, EEC, OPEC 796 *market*; traffic, drug t., white slave t., slave trade; smuggling, black market; retail trade 793 *sale*; capitalism, free enterprise, laisser faire 744 *scope*; free-market economy, boom and bust 317 *fluctuation*; profit-making, mutual profit; tied aid, dollar diplomacy 612 *inducement*; commerce, business affairs 622 *business*; private enterprise, privatization, private sector, Private Finance Initiative, PFI, Public Private Partnership, PPP; state enterprise, nationalization; public sector; venture, business v. 672 *undertaking*; speculation 618 *gambling*; transaction, commercial t., deal, business d., bargain, trade-off, negotiation 765 *compact*; clientele, custom 792 *purchase.*

**Adj.** *trading*, trafficking, exchanging; swapping, au pair; commercial, commercialistic, mercantile; wholesale, retail; exchangeable, marketable, merchantable 793 *salable*; for profit 618 *speculative.*

**Vb.** *trade*, exchange 151 *interchange*; barter, haggle, truck, swap, do a s.; traffic in, merchandise in; vend, buy and sell, buy cheap and sell dear, sell short, export and import; open a trade, drive a t., peddle, merchant 622 *do business*; trade in, deal in, handle; deal in stolen property, fence; turn over, turn over one's stock 793 *sell*; commercialize, put on a business footing; trade with, do business w., deal w., have dealings w., open an account w.; finance, back, promote; look to one's profit, have an eye to business, go out for trade; be a thorough businessman *or* -woman, know the price of everything and the value of nothing.

*speculate*, venture, risk 618 *gamble*; invest, sink one's capital in, put one's money to work, make one's money work for one; rig the market, racketeer, profiteer; deal in the black market, sell under the counter; deal in futures, dabble in shares, play the market, go bust; go

on the Stock Exchange, operate, bull, bear, stag.

*bargain*, negotiate, chaffer; push up, beat down; huckster, haggle, higgle, dicker, argy-bargy 766 *make terms*; bid for, make a bid, make a takeover bid, propose a merger, act as white knight, pre-empt; raise the bid, outbid 759 *offer*; overbid 482 *overrate*; underbid 483 *underestimate*; stickle, stick out for, hold out for, state one's terms, ask for, charge 766 *give terms*; settle for, take; drive a bargain, drive a hard b., do a deal, shake hands on, sign on the dotted line 765 *contract*; plea-bargain.

**Adv.** *in trade*, in commerce, in business, in the marketplace, on Change; across the counter, under the counter.

## 792 Purchase

**N.** *purchase*, buying; buying up, takeover, buy-out, green mail, cornering, forestalling, pre-emption; redemption, ransom 668 *deliverance*; purchase on account, purchase on credit, hire purchase, HP, the never-never, tick 785 *borrowing*; shopping, window s., one-stop s., ethical s., spending, shopping spree, shop-aholic 806 *expenditure*; shopping by post, mail order, home shopping, tele-ordering, tele-shopping, electronic s., e-shopping, cyber-shopping, virtual s., virtual storefront, virtual mall; regular buying, custom, patronage; loyalty card, reward c.; consumer demand, consumerism 627 *requirement*; buying over, bribery 612 *inducement*; bid, takeover b. 759 *offer*; first refusal, right of purchase; a purchase, buy, good b., purchase on appro *or* on approval, bargain, real b., one's money's worth; purchases, shopping list, requirements; shop rage *or* shopping r., trolley r.; shopping therapy, retail t.

*purchaser*, buyer, emptor, pre-emptor; vendee, transferee, consignee; buyer of labour, employer; shopper, window-s.; customer, patron, client, clientele, consumer; offerer, bidder, highest b.; taker, acceptor; bargainer, haggler; ransomer, redeemer; share-buyer, bull, stag, corporate raider; user, end user.

**Adj.** *bought*, paid for, ransomed, redeemed; purchased, bribed; purchasable, bribable; worth buying 644 *valuable.*

*buying*, redemptive, purchasing, shopping, marketing, tele-ordering; cash and carry, cash on delivery, C.O.D., pre-emptive, bidding, bargaining, haggling; in the market for; bullish.

**Vb.** *purchase*, make a p., complete a p.; buy, acquire by purchase 771 *acquire*; shop, window-s., market, go shopping, purchase by mail order, purchase by tele-ordering, tele-shop; have a shopping list 627 *require*; make a good buy, get one's money's worth; buy out-right, buy over the counter, pay cash for, pay on the spot; buy on credit, buy on hire purchase; buy on the never-never, buy on an instalment plan, pay by instalment, buy on account, buy on tick 785 *borrow*; pay by cheque *or* by Giro, buy in 632 *store*; buy up, pre-empt, corner, make a corner in; buy out, make a takeover bid, propose a merger, act as a white knight for; buy over, square, suborn 612 *bribe*; buy back, redeem, repurchase, ransom 668 *deliver*, pay for, bear the cost of 804 *defray*; buy oneself in, invest in, sink one's money in 791 *speculate*; buy service, rent 785 *hire*; bid, bid for, bid up 759 *offer*; buy shares, bull, stag.

**793 Sale**
N. *sale*, selling, vendition; putting on sale, marketing, mass m., niche m., telemarketing, undercover m., viral m.; distribution; disposal 779 *nonretention*; disposal, sell-out; clearance sale, stock-taking s., closing-down s., white s.; jumble s., sale of work, charity sale, car boot s., garage s., bazaar; sale of office, simony 930 *improbity*; exclusive sale, monopoly, oligopoly 747 *restraint*; public sale, auctioneering, auction, sale by a., roup, Dutch auction, vendue; good market, market for; sales, good s., boom 730 *prosperity*; bad sales 731 *adversity*; salesmanship, service, sales talk, pitch, sales patter, spiel; hard sell, soft s. 528 *advertisement*; market research 459 *enquiry*; salability, vendibility, marketability; vendible, thing sold, seller, best-s., loss-leader, selling line 795 *merchandise*.

*seller*, vendor, consignor, transferor; share-seller, bear; auctioneer; market trader, barrow boy, costermonger, hawker 794 *pedlar*; shopkeeper, dealer 633 *caterer*; wholesaler, marketer, retailer 794 *tradespeople*; sales representative, rep, door-to-door salesman, doorstepper; traveller, commercial t., travelling salesman *or* -woman, knight of the road; agent, canvasser, tout; shop walker, shop assistant, shop girl, salesman, saleswoman, salesperson; clerk, booking c., ticket agent; roundsman, milkman.

Adj. *salable*, vendible, marketable, on sale, for sale; sold, sold out; in demand, sought after, called for; available, on the market, up for sale; bearish, up for grabs; on auction, under the hammer.

Vb. *sell*, make a sale; flog, dispose of; market, put on sale, offer for s., have for s., have on offer, vend; bring to market, unload on the market, dump; hawk, peddle, push; cross-sell, upsell; canvass, tout; cater for the market 633 *provide*; put up for sale, auction, auction off,

sell by a., bring under the hammer, sell to the highest bidder, knock down to; wholesale; retail, sell over the counter, sell under the counter, sell on the black market; turn over one's stock 791 *trade*; realize one's capital, encash; sell at a profit 771 *gain*; sell at a loss 772 *lose*; undercut 812 *cheapen*; sell off, remainder; sell up, sell out, wind up 145 *cease*; clear stock, hold a sale, hold a clearance s.; sell again, re-sell; sell forward.

*be sold*, be on sale, come under the hammer 780 *change hands*; sell, have a sale, have a market, meet a demand, be in d., sell well, sell like hot cakes, sell out, boom; be a selling line, be a best-seller, be a loss-leader; sell badly, stay on the shelf, gather dust.

**794 Merchant**
N. *merchant*, merchant prince, merchant venturer; liveryman, livery company, guild, chamber of commerce, concern, firm 708 *corporation*; business person, man *or* woman of business; entrepreneur, speculator, operator 618 *gambler*; trafficker, fence; slaver, slave trader; importer, exporter; wholesale merchant, wholesaler; retailer, merchandiser, dealer, chandler; middleman, broker, stockbroker; stock-jobber, share-pusher; estate agent, house a.; financier, company promoter; banker 784 *lender*; money-changer, cambist.

*tradespeople*, tradesfolk; tradesman, retailer, middleman, regrater, tallyman; shopkeeper, storekeeper 793 *seller*; monger, ironmonger, mercer, haberdasher, grocer, greengrocer, provision merchant, butcher, tobacconist, newsagent 633 *caterer*.

*pedlar*, peddler 793 *seller*; rag-and-bone man; itinerant tradesman, street seller, hawker, tinker, gipsy, huckster, colporteur, bagman, chapman, cheapjack; coster, costermonger, barrow boy; market trader, stall-keeper; sutler, vivandière 633 *caterer*.

**795 Merchandise**
N. *merchandise*, article of commerce, line, staple; article, commodity, salable c., vendible, stock, stock-in-trade, range, repertoire 632 *store*; freight, cargo 193 *contents*; stuff, things for sale, supplies, wares, goods, capital g., durables; shop goods, consumer g., consumer durables; perishable goods, canned g., dry g., white g., sundries.

**796 Market**
N. *market*, daily m., weekly m., mart; open market, free trade area, Common Market, EEC, OPEC, Comecon; free market, single m., economic zone, open-door policy 791 *trade*; black

market, underground economy, black e.; grey market, grey economy; seller's market, buyer's m.; marketplace, market cross, forum, agora 76 *focus*; street market, flea m., Petticoat Lane; auction room, Christie's, Sotheby's; fair, world f., international f., trade f., industries f., horse f., goose f., motor show; exhibition, exposition, shop window 522 *exhibit*; corn market, wheat pit, corn exchange; exchange, Stock E., Change, bourse, unlisted securities market, over-the-counter m., third m., kerb m., share shop, bucket shop 797 *finance*; Wall Street, Rialto; toll booth, custom house.

*emporium*, free port, entrepôt, depot, warehouse 632 *storage*; wharf, quay; trading centre, trading post; general market, bazaar, arcade, covered market, shopping mall, pedestrian precinct, shopping centre; virtual storefront, virtual mall 792 *purchase*.

*shop*, retailer's; store, multiple s., department s., chain s.; emporium, bazaar, boutique, bargain basement, supermarket, hypermarket, superstore, megastore, cash and carry, warehouse club; concern, firm, establishment, house, trading h.; corner shop, convenience store; stall, booth, stand, newsstand, kiosk, barrow, vending machine, slot m.; counter, shop window, window display; premises, place of business 687 *workshop*.

## 797 Money

**N.** *money*, Lsd, pounds, shillings and pence; pelf, Mammon 800 *wealth*; lucre, filthy l., 'the root of all evil';

> **For the love of money is the root of all evil.**
> Bible, St Paul, First Letter to Timothy

medium of exchange, circulating medium, cash nexus; currency, unit of c., decimal c., managed c., fluctuating c., hard c., soft c., single c.; sound currency, honest money, legal tender; money of account, sterling, pound s.; precious metal, gold, ringing g., clinking g.; silver, siller (see also *bullion*); ready money, the ready, the best, cash, spot c., hard c., petty c.; change, small c., coppers 33 *small coin*; pocket money, pin m., allowance; spending money; paltry sum, chickenfeed, peanuts.

*shekels*, dibs, shiners, spondulicks, brass, tin, rhino, poppy, dough, lolly, sugar, bread; boodle, swag, loot, gravy; soap, palm oil 612 *incentive*.

*funds*, money in the bank, account, bank a., current a., deposit a., savings a., bank annuities; PEP, ISA; liquid assets, temporary f., hot money; liquidity; the wherewithal, the needful 629 *means*; sinews of war, ready money, the ready, finances, exchequer, financial pro-

vision, Private Finance Initiative, PFI, Public Private Partnership, PPP, cash flow, cash supplies, monies, treasure 633 *provision*; remittance 804 *payment*; funds for investment, capital; funds in hand, reserves, balances, sterling b.; sum of money, amount, figure, sum, round s., lump s.; quid, smacker, oncer, buck, sov; fiver, tenner, pony, monkey, ton, century, grand; mint of money, wads, scads, pile, packet, stacks, heaps, mountains, million, millions, billions, crores, lakhs 32 *great quantity*, 104 *multitude*; moneybags, purse, bottomless p. 632 *store*.

*finance*, high f., world of finance, IMF; financial control, money power, purse strings, power of the purse, almighty dollar; money dealings, cash transaction; money market, Eurodollar m., exchange, stock e., LIFFE, Big Bang 796 *market*; share index, FT Index, FTSE, Footsie, Dow-Jones average, Nikkei average, EASDAQ, NASDAQ; exchange rate, bank r., minimum lending r., effective r., sterling effective r., valuta, parity, par 28 *equality*; agio, agiotage, snake; floating pound; devaluation, depreciation, falling exchange rate 655 *deterioration*; rising exchange rate, strong pound, rallying 654 *improvement*; bimetallism; gold standard; green pound; managed currency, equalization fund, sinking f., revolving f.; deficit finance, inflation, inflationary spiral; disinflation, deflation; stagflation; reflation.

*coinage*, minting, issue; metallic currency, stamped coinage, gold c., silver c., electrum c., copper c., nickel c., billon c., bronze c.; specie, minted coinage, coin, piece, coin of the realm; monetary unit, monetary denomination; guinea, sovereign, half s.; pound, quid, nicker; crown, half c., florin, shilling, bob, sixpence, tanner, threepenny bit, penny, bun p., copper, halfpenny, ship h.; farthing; decimal coinage, pound coin, fifty p, twenty p, ten p, five p, two p, one p, half p; dollar, buck, simoleon; half dollar, quarter, dime, nickel, jitney, cent; ten-dollar piece, eagle; napoleon, louis d'or; franc, new f.; mark, Deutschmark, Ostmark;; obol, talent, shekel, solidus, bezant, ducat, angel, noble, real, pistole, piece of eight; change, small c., groat, bawbee, obolus, centime, sou, pfennig, piastre, kopek, cash 33 *small coin*; Eurocurrency, ecu, euro, single currency, Euroland, Eurozone; shell money, cowrie, wampum; coin collecting, numismatics, numismatology, chrysology.

**Some Currency Units**
afghani (Afghanistan), baht (Thailand), balboa (Panama), birr (Ethiopia), bolívar (Venezuela), boliviano (Bolivia), cedi (Ghana), colón (Costa Rica, El Salvador), córdoba (Nicaragua), dalasi (The Gambia),

denar (Macedonia), dinar (Algeria, Bahrain, Iraq and other countries), dirham (Morocco, United Arab Emirates), dobra (São Tomé and Príncipe), dollar (Australia, Canada, New Zealand, United States and other countries), dong (Vietnam), dram (Armenia), escudo (Cape Verde), euro (Austria, Belgium, Finland, France, Germany, Greece, Ireland, Italy, Luxembourg, Netherlands, Portugal, Spain + Andorra, Monaco, San Marino), forint (Hungary), franc (Switzerland, Mali and other countries), gourde (Haiti), guaraní (Paraguay), guilder *or* gulden (Suriname), hryvnia *or* hryvna (Ukraine), kina (Papua New Guinea), kip (Laos), koruna (Czech Republic, Slovakia), krona (Sweden), króna (Iceland), krone (Denmark, Norway), kroon (Estonia), kuna (Croatia), kwacha (Malawi, Zambia), kyat (Myanmar), lari (Georgia), lat (Latvia), lek (Albania), lempira (Honduras), leone (Sierra Leone), leu (Romania), lev (Bulgaria), lilangeni (Swaziland), lira (Malta, Turkey), litas (Lithuania), loti (Lesotho), manat (Azerbaijan, Turkmenistan), marka (Bosnia-Hercegovina), metical (Mozambique), naira (Nigeria), nakfa (Eritrea), new kwanza (Angola), new sol (Peru), new zaire (Democratic Republic of Congo), ngultrum (Bhutan), ouguiya (Mauritania), pa'anga (Tonga), pataca (Macau), peso (Argentina, Chile, Colombia, Mexico and other countries), pound (Egypt, Lebanon, United Kingdom), pula (Botswana), quetzal (Guatemala), rand (South Africa), real (Brazil), rial (Iran), riel (Cambodia), ringgit (Malaysia), riyal (Oman, Qatar, Saudi Arabia, Yemen), rouble *or* ruble (Belarus, Russia), rufiyaa (Maldives), rupee (India, Nepal, Pakistan, Seychelles, Sri Lanka), rupiah (Indonesia), shekel (Israel), shilling (Kenya, Somalia, Tanzania, Uganda), som (Kyrgyzstan), somoni (Tajikistan), soum *or* sum (Uzbekistan), sucre (Ecuador), taka (Bangladesh), tala (Samoa), tenge (Kazakhstan), tolar (Slovenia), tugrik (Mongolia), vatu (Vanuatu), won (Korea), yen (Japan), yuan (China), zloty (Poland).

*paper money*, fiat m., fiduciary currency, assignat; bankroll, wad; note, banknote, treasury note, pound n., five-p. n., ten-p. n., bill, dollar b., greenback, buck, ten-dollar bill, sawbuck; bill of exchange, negotiable instrument; draft, order, money o., postal o., check, cheque, certified c., giro c., traveller's c., Eurocheque, letter of credit; promissory note, note of hand, IOU; standing order, direct debit; coupon, warrant, scrip, certificate, bond, premium b. 767 *security*.

*false money*, bad m., counterfeit m., base coin, snide; forged note, flash n., forgery; dud cheque 805 *nonpayment*; clipped coinage, depreciated currency, devalued c.; demonetized coinage, withdrawn c., obsolete c.

*bullion*, bar, gold b., ingot, nugget; solid gold, solid silver; precious metal, yellow m., platinum, gold, white g., electrum, silver, billon.

*minter*, moneyer, mint master; coiner, counterfeiter, forger; money-dealer, moneychanger, cambist 794 *merchant*; cashier 798 *treasurer*; financier, capitalist, profiteer, entrepreneur; moneyed man, moneybags 800 *rich person*.

**Adj.** *monetary*, numismatic, chrysological; pecuniary, financial, fiscal, budgetary, sumptuary; coined, stamped, minted, issued; numary, fiduciary; gold-based, sterling, sound, solvent 800 *rich*; inflationary, deflationary, floating; clipped, devalued, depreciated; withdrawn, demonetized.

**Vb.** *mint*, coin, stamp; monetize, issue, circulate; pass, utter; forge, counterfeit.

*demonetize*, withdraw, withdraw from circulation, call in an issue; clip, debase the coinage; devalue, depreciate, inflate 812 *cheapen*.

*draw money*, cash, encash, realize, turn into cash, liquidate, draw upon, cash a cheque, endorse a c., write a c. 804 *pay*.

## 798 Treasurer

**N.** *treasurer*, honorary t.; bursar, purser, quaestor; cashier, teller, croupier; depositary, stakeholder, trustee, steward 754 *consignee*; liquidator 782 *receiver*; bookkeeper 808 *accountant*; banker, financier; keeper of the purse, paymaster, almoner, controller, comptroller, Chancellor of the Exchequer, Secretary of the Treasury, Governor of the Bank of England; mint master 797 *minter*.

## 799 Treasury

**N.** *treasury*, treasure house, thesaurus; exchequer, fisc, public purse; reserves, fund 632 *store*; counting house, custom house; bursary, almonry; bank, Bank of England, Old Lady of Threadneedle Street; savings bank, Post Office savings b., penny b., building society; coffer, chest 194 *box*; treasure chest, depository 632 *storage*; strongroom, strongbox, safe, safe deposit, cash box, moneybox, piggy-bank, stocking, mattress; till, cash register, cash desk, slot machine; cash dispenser, cashpoint, automated teller machine, ATM, hole-in-the-wall (inf); personal identification number, PIN, PIN number; telebanking, receipt of custom, box office, gate, turnstile; moneybag, purse, purse strings 194 *pocket*; wallet, pocket book, billfold, wad, rouleau 194 *case*.

## 800 Wealth

**N.** *wealth* Mammon, lucre, pelf, brass, moneybags 797 *money*; moneymaking, golden touch, Midas t., philosopher's stone; riches, fleshpots, 'the fat of the land' (see quotation at 730 *prosperity*) 635 *plenty*; luxury 637 *superfluity*; opulence, affluence 730 *prosperity*; ease, comfort, easy circumstances, comfortable c., easy street 376 *euphoria*; solvency, soundness, credit-worthiness, white information 802 *credit*; solidity, substance 3 *substantiality*; independence, competence, self-sufficiency 635 *suf-*

*ficiency*; high income, surtax bracket 782 *receiving*; gains 771 *gain*; resources, substantial r., well-lined pockets, well-lined purse, capital 629 *means*; liquid assets, bank account, building society a., Post Office savings a., TESSA, Tax-Exempt Special Savings Account; limitless resources, bottomless purse, purse of Fortunatus, goose that lays golden eggs; nest egg 632 *store*; fortune, small f., tidy sum, power of money, mint of m., pots of m., pile, heap, mountain, scads, wads, megabucks (inf), packet, cool million, zillions 32 *great quantity*; fortune, handsome f., large inheritance, ample endowment; broad acres, estates, possessions 777 *property*; bonanza, mine, gold m.; El Dorado, Golconda, pot of gold, the end of the rainbow, riches of Solomon, king's ransom; sudden wealth syndrome.

*wealth-creation*, capitalism, plutocracy; fund management.

*rich person*, wealthy p., well-to-do p., man *or* woman of means; baron, tycoon, magnate, nabob, moneybags, millionaire, multi-m., millionairess; Croesus, Midas, Dives, Plutus, Loadsamoney; moneymaker, money-spinner, fat cat, capitalist, plutocrat, bloated p.; heir to riches, heiress, poor little rich girl 776 *beneficiary*; the haves, the privileged, moneyed class, propertied c., leisured c., the well-to-do, the well-off, the well-heeled, jeunesse dorée, jet set glitterati 848 *beau monde*; new rich, nouveau riche, parvenu, self-made man 730 *prosperous person*; plutocracy, timocracy.

**Adj.** *rich*, richly endowed, lush, fertile 171 *prolific*; abundant 635 *plenteous*; richly furnished, luxurious, upholstered, plush, plushy, ritzy, slap-up; diamond-studded, glittering, glitzy 875 *ostentatious*; wealthy, blest with this world's goods, well-endowed, well-provided for, born in the purple, born with a silver spoon in one's mouth; opulent, affluent 730 *prosperous*; well-off, well-to-do, well-situated, well-heeled, in easy circumstances, comfortably off, well-housed, well-paid, overpaid 376 *comfortable*.

*moneyed*, propertied, worth a lot, worth a packet, worth millions; made of money, lousy with m., rolling in m., rolling, rolling in it, dripping, loaded; stinking rich, filthy r., disgustingly r.; rich as Croesus, rich as Solomon; on easy street, in clover, in funds, in cash, in credit, in the black; well-heeled, flush, in the money, in the dough, quids in, doing nicely thank you; creditworthy, solvent, sound, able to pay; out of debt, all straight 804 *paying*.

**Vb.** *be rich*, be full to overflowing, turn all to gold 637 *superabound*; have money, have a power of m., have means, draw a large income; be rolling in money, stink of m., wallow in riches; be in clover, be on easy street, be on velvet, be born in the purple, be born with a silver spoon in one's mouth; be sitting on a goldmine, be raking it in; be flush, be in funds etc. adj.; have credit, command capital, have money to burn; die rich 780 *bequeath*.

*afford*, have the means, have the wherewithal, be able to pay, be able to meet the expense of, be solvent, make both ends meet, keep one's head above water, keep the wolf from the door, keep up with the Joneses 635 *have enough*.

*get rich*, come into money 771 *inherit*; do all right for oneself 730 *prosper*; enrich oneself, make a profit, make money, mint m., coin m., spin m., coin it, rake in the shekels, rake it in, laugh all the way to the bank; make a packet, make a pile, make a bomb, make a fortune, make a mint, make a killing, clean up, feather one's nest, line one's pocket, strike it rich, hit the jackpot, turn up trumps, win the pools, have one's ship come home, find one's Eldorado, find the pot of gold at the end of the rainbow 771 *gain*; seek riches, worship the golden calf, pay tribute to Mammon.

*make rich*, enrich, make one's fortune, put money in one's pocket, line one's p.; leave one a fortune 780 *bequeath*; enhance 36 *augment*; improve 654 *make better*.

## 801 Poverty

**N.** *poverty*, Lady Poverty 945 *asceticism*; renunciation of wealth, voluntary poverty 931 *disinterestedness*; impecuniosity, financial embarrassment, difficulties, Queer Street 805 *insolvency*; destitution, impoverishment, loss of fortune, social exclusion, beggary, mendicancy; pauperism, penury, pennilessness, utter poverty; privation, indigence, neediness, necessitousness, necessity, dire n., need, want, pinch 627 *requirement*; bare cupboard, empty larder 636 *scarcity*; wolf at the door, famine 946 *fasting*; light pocket, empty purse, insufficient income, slender means, meagre resources, reduced circumstances, straitened c., low water 636 *insufficiency*; straits, distress, belt-tightening 825 *suffering*; grinding poverty, subsistence level, breadline, poverty line, poverty trap, hand-to-mouth existence, mere e., bare e.; poorness, meanness, meagreness, shabbiness, seediness, beggarliness, raggedness, shreds and tatters; general poverty, recession, slump, depression 655 *deterioration*; squalor, public s., slum, substandard housing 655 *dilapidation*; workhouse, poorhouse; poor mouth.

*poor person*, broken man *or* woman, bankrupt, insolvent 805 *nonpayer*; hermit, sannyasi 945 *ascetic*; pauper, indigent, the socially excluded, poor beggar, rag-picker, starveling, vagrant, tramp, bum, down-and-out 763 *beggar*; slum-dweller, underdog: the poor, new poor, the have-nots, the disadvantaged, the underprivileged, underclass 869 *lower classes*; Cinderella 867 *object of scorn*; poor white, white trash; poor relation 35 *inferior*; Job, Lazarus.

**Adj.** *poor*, not well-off, badly o., poorly o., hard up, not blest with this world's goods; low-paid, low-income, underpaid, underprivileged; hard up, impecunious, short, short of funds, short of cash, out of pocket, in the red; skint, cleaned out, bust, broke, flat b., stony b., bankrupt, insolvent 805 *nonpaying*; reduced to poverty *or* beggary, on the breadline, below the poverty line, in the poverty trap, on the dole, in the dole queue; impoverished, pauperized, broken, beggared; dispossessed, deprived, stripped, fleeced, robbed; penurious, poverty-stricken; needy, indigent, in want, in need 627 *necessitous*; homeless, shelterless; hungry 636 *underfed*; in distress, straitened, pinched, hard put to it, put to one's shifts, on one's uppers, on one's beam ends, on the rocks, up against it, not knowing which way to turn 700 *in difficulties*; unable to make both ends meet, unable to pay one's way, unable to keep the wolf from the door; unprovided for, dowerless, portionless; penniless, moneyless, destitute; down to one's last penny, without a bean, without a cent, without a sou, without prospects, with nothing to hope for.

*beggarly*, starveling, shabby, seedy, down at heel, out at elbows, down and out, in rags, tattered, patched, barefoot, threadbare, tatty 655 *dilapidated*; scruffy, squalid, mean, slummy, back-street 649 *dirty*; poverty-stricken, pinched with poverty, poor as a church mouse, poor as Job.

**Vb.** *be poor*, earn little or nothing, live on a pittance, eke out a livelihood, scratch a living, scrape an existence, live from hand to mouth; feel the pinch, fall on hard times, be in dire straits, be on one's uppers, be on the breadline, be below the poverty line, be caught in the poverty trap, have to watch the pennies, be unable to afford; beg for one's bread, sing for one's supper; starve 859 *be hungry*; want, lack 627 *require*; not have a penny, not have two halfpennies to rub together; have no prospects, have no more shots in one's locker; become poor, go broke 805 *not pay*; decline in fortune, lose one's money, come down in the world 655 *deteriorate*; go on the parish, go on relief,

go to the workhouse; go on the dole, claim supplementary benefit.

*impoverish*, reduce to poverty, leave destitute, beggar, pauperize; ruin 165 *destroy*; rob, strip 786 *fleece*; dispossess, disinherit, cut off without a penny, cut off with a shilling 786 *deprive*.

## 802 Credit

**N.** *credit*, repute, reputation 866 *prestige*; credit-worthiness, white information, sound proposition; trust, confidence, reliability 929 *probity*; borrowing capacity, limit of credit; line of credit, tick; banker's credit, letter of c., credit card, charge card, plastic card, plastic money, plastic, affinity card, store card, phonecard, credit note, sum to one's account, credit a., the black; credits, balances, credit balance 807 *receipt*; postponed payment, unpaid bill, account, budget a., score, tally, bill 808 *accounts*; national credit, trading deficit, floating debt 803 *debt*; loan, mortgage 784 *lending*; sum entrusted, sum voted, vote.

*creditor*, importunate c., dun; mortgagee, pledgee, usurer 784 *lender*; depositor, investor.

**Vb.** *credit*, give *or* furnish c., extend c., forgo repayment, grant a loan 784 *lend*; place to one's credit, credit one's account; grant, vote; await payment, charge to one's account, charge to one's budget a., sell on credit; sell on tick, take credit, open an account, keep an account with, have a budget account with, run up an account, run up a bill 785 *borrow*.

## 803 Debt

**N.** *debt*, indebtedness, state of i. 785 *borrowing*; liability, obligation, commitment; encumbrance, mortgage 767 *security*; something owing, debit, charge; what one owes, debts, bills, hire-purchase debt; national debt, floating d., funded d.; promise to pay, debt of honour, unsecured debt 764 *promise*; gearing, leverage; bad debt, write-off 772 *loss*; good debt 771 *gain*; tally, account, account owing; deficit, overdraft, balance to pay, negative equity 307 *shortfall*; inability to pay 805 *insolvency*; overdraft, payment refused, frozen balance, blocked account, frozen assets, black information 805 *nonpayment*; deferred payment 802 *credit*; overdue payment, arrears, accumulated a., back pay, back rent; no more credit, foreclosure; debt counselling.

*interest*, simple i., compound i., high i., excessive i., usury, pound of flesh 784 *lending*; premium, rate of interest, minimum lending rate, discount rate, bank rate.

*debtor*, loanee, borrower, loan applicant; obligor, drawee; mortgagor, pledgor;

bad debtor, defaulter, insolvent 805 *non-payer*.

**Adj.** *indebted*, in debt, in hock, borrowing, indebted; pledged, liable, committed, responsible, answerable, bound 917 *obliged*; owing, overdrawn, in the red; encumbered, mortgaged; deep in debt, plunged in d., burdened with d., over head and ears in d., in Queer Street 700 *in difficulties*; defaulting, unable to pay, insolvent 805 *nonpaying*; at the mercy of one's creditors, in the hands of the receiver.

*owed*, unpaid, still u.; owing, due, overdue, in arrears; outstanding, unbalanced; on the debit side, chargeable, payable, debited, on credit, on deposit, on appro, on approval, repayable, returnable, bearing, payable on delivery, C.O.D.

**Vb.** *be in debt*, owe, have to repay; owe money, pay interest; accept a charge, be debited with, be liable; get credit, overdraw (one's account); get on tick, buy on hire purchase *or* the never-never 785 *borrow*; live on credit, buy on c., use a credit card, use a charge card, use plastic money, use plastic, keep an account with, have charged to one's account; charge to one's budget a., run up an a., run into debt; be in the red, be overdrawn; leave one's bills unpaid, cheat one's creditors, bilk, welsh, do a moonlight flit 805 *not pay*; back another's credit, make oneself responsible, stand surety for 917 *incur a duty*.

## 804 Payment

**N.** *payment*, paying for, bearing the cost, defrayment; defraying the cost, paying off, discharge, quittance, acquittance, release, satisfaction, full s., liquidation, clearance, settlement, settlement on account; receipted payment, receipt in full 807 *receipt*; cash payment, down p., ready money 797 *money*; EFTPOS, electronic funds transfer at point of sale, credit card, plastic card, plastic, smart card, store c., swipe c., Switch card 785 *borrowing*; first payment, earnest, earnest money, handsel, deposit; instalment; deferred payment, hire purchase 785 *borrowing*; due payment, subscription, tribute 809 *tax*; voluntary payment, contribution, whip-round, appeal, collection 781 *offering*; payment in lieu, composition 150 *substitution*; repayment, compensation, indemnity 787 *restitution*; disbursement, remittance 806 *expenditure*; bank draft, cash, cheque, direct debit, standing order.

*pay*, payout, payoff, pay packet, pay cheque, take-home pay, pay day, wages bill, wages, salary 771 *earnings*; bonus, overtime pay, performance-related pay 962 *reward*; grant, grant-in-aid, subsidy 703 *subvention*; salary, pension, annuity, remuneration, emolument, fee, honorarium, garnish, bribe 962 *reward*; cut, commission 810 *discount*; something paid, contribution, subscription, collection, tribute 809 *tax*; damages, indemnity 963 *penalty*; back pay, compensation, redundancy pay, severance pay, golden handshake, ex gratia payment; payer, paymaster, purser, cashier 798 *treasurer*.

**Adj.** *paying*, disbursing 806 *expending*; paying in full, paying cash, unindebted; out of debt, in the black, out of the red, owing nothing.

**Vb.** *pay*, disburse 806 *expend*; contribute 781 *give*; pay in kind, negotiate a trade-off, barter 791 *trade*; make payment, pay out, shell o., fork o., dole out, dish out, stump up, cough up; come across, do the needful, unloose the purse strings, put one's hand in one's pocket, open one's wallet, open one's purse; pay a high price, pay an exorbitant price, pay through the nose; pay back, repay, reimburse, compensate 787 *restitute*; tickle the palm, grease the palm, cross one's palm with silver 612 *bribe*; pay wages, remunerate, tip 962 *reward*; pay in advance, put money up front, ante up, pay on sight, pay on call, pay on delivery, C.O.D., pay on demand; pay by cheque *or* by giro; pay by banker's order, pay by standing o., pay by direct debit; pay on the nail, pay on the dot, pay cash, pay cash down, put d.; honour (a bill), pay up, pay in full, meet, satisfy, redeem, discharge, get a receipt; clear, liquidate, settle, settle an account, clear accounts with, balance accounts w., square accounts w. 808 *account*; settle accounts with, settle a score; pay off old scores, pay one out 714 *retaliate*.

*defray*, pay for, defray the cost, bear the c., stand the c., put up funds; pay one's way, pay one's share, pay one's shot; foot the bill, meet the b., pick up the b., pick up the tab, pay the piper; buy a round, stand a r., stand treat, treat 781 *give*; share expenses, go Dutch 775 *participate*.

**Adv.** *cash down*, money d.; cash on delivery, C.O.D.; with ready money, on the nail, on the dot, on demand; to the tune of.

## 805 Nonpayment

**N.** *nonpayment*, default, defalcation 930 *improbity*; reduced payment, stoppage, deduction 963 *penalty*; moratorium, embargo, freeze; dishonouring, refusal to pay, protest, repudiation 760 *refusal*; tax avoidance, tax evasion, creative accounting, black economy 620 *avoidance*; deferred payment, hire purchase 785 *borrowing*; cancellation of debts 752 *abrogation*; waste-paper bonds, protested bill, dishonoured cheque, bogus c., dud c., bouncing c.;

depreciation, devaluation, devalued currency 797 *false money*.

*insolvency*, inability to pay, failure to meet one's obligations; crash, failure; failure of credit, cash-flow crisis, run upon a bank; bankruptcy, bankruptcy court, bankruptcy proceedings; nothing to pay with, nothing in the kitty, overdrawn account, overdraft 636 *insufficiency*; unpayable debt 803 *debt*.

*nonpayer*, defaulter, defalcator, embezzler, tax dodger 789 *defrauder*; bilker, welsher, absconder; failure, lame duck; bankrupt, discharged b., undischarged b., insolvent debtor.

**Adj.** *nonpaying*, defaulting, behindhand, in arrears; unable to pay, insolvent, bankrupt; up to one's ears in debt, hopelessly in debt, always owing 803 *indebted*; beggared, ruined 801 *poor*.

**Vb.** *not pay*, default, embezzle, swindle 788 *defraud*; fall into arrears, get behindhand; stop payment, withhold p., freeze, block; refuse payment, protest a bill; disallow payment; fiddle one's income tax, practise tax evasion, moonlight, be part of the black economy 930 *be dishonest*; divert, sequester 786 *deprive*; bounce one's cheque, dishonour, repudiate; have a cash-flow crisis, become insolvent, go bankrupt, go through the bankruptcy court, go to the wall, get whitewashed; sink, fail, break, go bust, crash, wind up, go into liquidation; evade one's creditors, welsh, bilk 542 *deceive*; abscond 296 *decamp*; be unable to pay 801 *be poor*; go off the gold standard, devalue *or* depreciate the currency 797 *demonetize*; keep one's purse shut 816 *be parsimonious*; cancel a debt, wipe the slate clean, discharge a bankrupt 752 *abrogate*.

**806 Expenditure**
**N.** *expenditure*, spending, disbursement 804 *payment*; cost of living; outgoings, overheads, costs, cost incurred, expenses, out-of-pocket e., extras, expense account; expense, outlay, investment, ethical i.; dissaving, disinvestment, run on savings; fee, tax 804 *pay*; extravagance, spending spree 815 *prodigality*.

**Adj.** *expending*, spending, sumptuary; generous 813 *liberal*; extravagant, splashing out, spending money like water, throwing one's money around 815 *prodigal*; out of pocket, lighter in one's purse.

*expended*, spent, disbursed, paid, paid out; laid out, invested; costing, at one's expense.

**Vb.** *expend*, spend; buy 792 *purchase*; lay out, invest, sink money; be out of pocket, incur costs, incur expenses; afford, stand, bear the cost, defray the c., bankroll, meet charges, disburse, pay out 804 *pay*; run down one's

account, draw on one's savings, dissave, disinvest; untie the purse-strings, open one's purse, open one's wallet, put one's hand in one's pocket, empty one's pocket; give money, donate 781 *give*; spare no expense, go on a spree, do it proud, be lavish 813 *be liberal*; fling money around, splash out, blow, blow one's cash 815 *be prodigal*; use up, spend up, consume, run through, get t. 634 *waste*.

**807 Receipt**
**N.** *receipt*, voucher, counterfoil, acknowledgment of payment; money received, credits, revenue, royalty, rents, rent-roll, rates, dues; customs, taxes 809 *tax*; money coming in, turnover, takings, proceeds, returns, receipts, gross r., net r., box-office r., gate money, gate; income, national i., private i., privy purse; emolument, regular income, pay, half p., salary, wages 771 *earnings*; remuneration 962 *reward*; pension, annuity, tontine; allowance, personal a.; pin money, pocket money, spending m.; inadequate allowance, pittance; alimony, aliment, palimony, maintenance; bursary, scholarship 771 *acquisition*; interest, return, rake-off, cut; winnings, profits, gross p., net p., capital gain 771 *gain*; bonus, premium 40 *extra*; prize 729 *trophy*; draw, lucky d.; legacy, inheritance 777 *dower*.

**Adj.** *received*, paid, receipted, acknowledged, acknowledged with thanks.

**Vb.** see 771 *acquire*, 782 *receive*, *be received*, 786 *take*.

**808 Accounts**
**N.** *accounts*, accountancy, accounting, commercial arithmetic; book-keeping, entry, double e., single e.; audit, inspection of accounts; account, profit and loss a., balance sheet, debit and credit, receipts and expenditures; budgeting, budget, zero-based budgeting, budget estimates 633 *provision*; running account, current a., cash a., deposit a., savings a., suspense a., expense a.; statement of account, account rendered, compte rendu, statement, bill, waybill, invoice, manifest 87 *list*; account paid, account settled 804 *payment*; reckoning, computation, score, tally, facts and figures 86 *numeration*.

*account book*, pass b., cheque b.; cash b., day b., journal, ledger, register, books 548 *record*.

*accountant*, chartered a., certified public a.; cost accountant, bookkeeper, storekeeper; cashier, beancounter (inf) 798 *treasurer*; inspector of accounts, examiner of a., auditor; actuary, statistician.

**Adj.** *accounting*, bookkeeping, in charge of

accounts; actuarial, reckoning, computing, inventorial, budgetary; accountable.

**Vb.** *account*, keep the books, keep accounts; make up an account, cast an a.; budget, prepare a b.; cost, value, write up, write down 480 *estimate*; book, enter, journalize, post, carry over, debit, credit 548 *register*; prepare a cashflow forecast, prepare a balance sheet, balance accounts; settle accounts, square a., finalize a., wind up a.; prepare a statement, present an account, charge, bill, invoice; overcharge, surcharge, undercharge 809 *price*; practise creative accounting, cook the accounts *or* the books, falsify the a., fiddle, garble, doctor 788 *defraud*; audit, inspect accounts, examine the a., go through the books; take stock, check s., inventory, catalogue 87 *list*.

## 809 Price

**N.** *price*, selling p., world p., market p., standard p., retail p., wholesale p., factory-gate p., discount p., list p.; rate, going r., rate for the job, fee for service; piece rate, flat r.; high rate, ceiling 811 *dearness*; low rate, floor 812 *cheapness*; price control, fixed price, prix fixe 747 *restraint*; price-cutting, predatory pricing; value, face v., par v., fair v., worth, money's w., what it will fetch; premium, scarcity value, famine price; price list, tariff; quoted price, quotation, price charged; amount, figure, sum asked for; ransom, fine 963 *penalty*; demand, dues, charge; surcharge, supplement 40 *extra*; overcharge, excessive charge, rip-off, extortion, ransom; fare, flat f., hire, rental, rent, ground r., house r., quit r.; fee, entrance *or* admission fee; refresher, commission, cut, rake-off; charges, freight c., freightage, wharfage, lighterage; salvage; postage; cover charge, service c., corkage; bill, invoice, reckoning, shot.

*cost*, buying price, purchase p.; damage, costs, expenses 806 *expenditure*; business costs, running c., overheads; wages, wage bill, salary b.; legal costs, damages 963 *penalty*; cost of living, cost of living index.

*tax*, taxes, dues; taxation, Inland Revenue, tax return, tax form, self-assesment, tax demand 737 *demand*; rating, assessment, rateable value, appraisement, valorization 480 *estimate*; cess, rate, rates, council tax, community charge *or* tax, poll tax, capitation t., general rate, water r.; tartan tax; green taxes, windfall tax; levy, toll, duty; imposition, impost; charge, scot, scot and lot (see also *price*); exaction, forced loan, Morton's fork *or* crutch, aid, benevolence 740 *compulsion*; forced savings 785 *borrowing*; punitive tax 963 *penalty*; tribute, danegeld, blackmail, protection money,

ransom 804 *payment*; ecclesiastical tax, Peter's pence, tithe, tenths; national insurance; poll tax, capitation t.; estate duty, death duty, inheritance tax; direct taxation, income tax, PAYE, surtax, supertax, company tax, corporation t., excess profits t.; capital levy, capital gains tax, windfall t. 786 *expropriation*; indirect taxation, excise, customs, tariff, tonnage and poundage; local tax, octroi; purchase tax, sales t., value-added tax, VAT, zero-rated goods; road tax, vehicle excise duty; carbon tax; salt tax, gabelle; stealth tax; feudal tax, scutage; tax break, tax concession, tax credit, tax rebate.

**Adj.** *priced*, charged, fixed; chargeable, leviable, taxable, assessable, ratable, customable, dutiable, excisable; ad valorem; to the tune of, for the price of; taxed, rated, assessed; paid, stipendiary.

**Vb.** *price*, cost, assess, value, rate 480 *estimate*; put a price on, set a price on; place a value on, fix a price for; raise a price, lower a p.; control the p., fix the p.; ask a p., charge, require 737 *demand*; bill, invoice.

*cost*, be worth, fetch, bring in; amount to, come to, mount up to; be priced at, be valued at; bear a price, have a p., have its p.; sell for, go f., be going f., set one back, change hands for, realize.

*tax*, lay a tax on, impose a tax; fix a tariff, levy a rate, assess for tax, value, valorize; toll, excise, subject to duty, make dutiable; raise taxes, collect t., take a toll 786 *levy*; take a collection, launch an appeal, pass round the hat 761 *beg*; fine, punish by f., mulct 963 *punish*.

## 810 Discount

**N.** *discount*, something off, reduction, rebate, cut, markdown 42 *decrement*; stoppage, deduction; concession, allowance, margin, special price; tare, tare and tret; drawback, backwardation, contango; cut price, cut rate, special offer, loss leader 612 *incentive*; bargain price, knock-down p., bargain sale 812 *cheapness*; poundage, percentage; agio, brokerage; one's cut, commission, rake-off.

**Vb.** *discount*, deduct 39 *subtract*; allow a margin, tare; reduce, depreciate, abate, rebate 37 *abate*; offer a discount, allow a d.; mark down, take off, cut, slash 812 *cheapen*; let stick to one's fingers, rake off, take a discount, take one's cut, take one's percentage.

**Adv.** *at a discount*, below par, less than the market rate.

## 811 Dearness

**N.** *dearness*, costliness, expensiveness; value, high v., high worth, pricelessness; famine price, scarcity value, rarity, dearth 636 *scarcity*; exorbitance, extortion, rack rents, rip-off; over-charge, excessive charge, daylight robbery, unfair price, bad value, poor v.; bad bargain, high price, fancy p., luxury p.; cost, high c., heavy c., pretty penny; tax on one's pocket, ruinous charge; rising costs, rising prices, sel-lers' market, bull m., climbing prices, soaring p.; cheap money, inflation, inflationary pres-sure, bullish tendency.

**Adj.** *dear*, high-priced, pricy, expensive, exclusive, ritzy, upmarket; costly, multimil-lion; extravagant, dearly-bought; dear at the price, overrated, overcharged, overpriced, over-paid; exorbitant, excessive, extortionate, pre-posterous; steep, stiff, sky-high; beyond one's means, prohibitive, more than one can afford, more than one's pocket can stand; dear at any price 641 *useless*; rising in price, hardening, rising, soaring, climbing, mounting, going through the ceiling, inflationary; bullish.

*of price*, of value, of worth 644 *valuable*; price-less, beyond price, above p.; unpayable; invalu-able 640 *useful*; inestimable, worth a king's ransom, worth its weight in gold, worth a for-tune; precious, rare, scarce, like gold dust 140 *infrequent*; at a premium, not to be had for love or money.

**Vb.** *be dear*, cost a lot, cost a packet, cost a pretty penny, be high-priced, hurt one's pocket, make a hole in one's p.; gain in value, rise in price, harden; go up, appreciate, esca-late, soar, mount, climb, go through the ceiling; get too dear, be out of one's price range, price itself out of the market; prove expensive, cost one dear, cost a fortune, cost the earth.

*overcharge*, overprice, sell dear, oversell, ask too much; profiteer, soak, sting, bleed, skin, extort, charge rack rents, rip off, do, short-change, hold to ransom 786 *fleece*; put up prices, inflate p., mark up; bull, raise the price, raise the bid, bid up, auction 793 *sell*.

*pay too much*, pay through the nose, pay the devil, be stung, be ripped off, be had, be done; pay high, pay dear, buy a white elephant; achieve a Pyrrhic victory; pay beyond one's means, ruin oneself.

**Adv.** *dearly*, dear, at a price, at great cost, at heavy c., at huge expense; exorbitantly, extravagantly.

## 812 Cheapness

**N.** *cheapness*, inexpensiveness, affordability; good value, value for money, money's worth, snip, steal, bargain, good b., bon marché; sale goods, seconds, rejects; low price, reasonable charge, reasonableness; cheap rate, off-peak r.,

off-season r., concessional r., excursion fare, railcard 810 *discount*; nominal price, reduced p., knock-down p., cut p., bargain p., budget p., popular p., competitive p., sale p., sacrificial p., giveaway p., rockbottom p., loss leader; peppercorn rent, easy terms; buyers' market, sluggish m.; Dutch auction; falling prices, declining p., bearishness; depreciation, fall, slump; deflation; glut, drug on the market 635 *plenty*; superfluity 637 *redundance*; happy hour.

*no charge*, absence of c., nominal c. 781 *gift*; gratuitousness, labour of love 597 *voluntary work*; free trade, free port; free entry, free admis-sion, free seats, free pass, free ticket, freebie, complimentary ticket; free quarters, grace and favour; free board, free service, free delivery; everything for nothing.

**Adj.** *cheap*, inexpensive, uncostly, moderate, reasonable, fair; affordable, within one's means, easy on the pocket; cheap to make, low-budget; substandard, shop-soiled; econ-omical, economy, economy-size; not dear, worth its price, worth the money; low, low-priced, cheap-p., cheap at the price, cheap at half the p.; dirt-cheap, going cheap, going for a song, for peanuts; bargain-rate, bargain-basement, downmarket, cut-price, con-cessional, sale-price, reduced, r. to clear; marked down, half-price; tourist-class, off-season; easy to buy, two-a-penny; cheap and cheerful; worth nothing, cheap and nasty, cheapjack, jerry-built, catchpenny, Brum-magem 641 *useless*; cheapening, bearish, falling, declining, slumping; unsalable, unmar-ketable; unchargeable, valueless 860 *unwanted*; underpaid, underpriced.

*uncharged*, not charged for, gratuitous, com-plimentary, courtesy; gratis, for nothing, for love, for kicks, for nix, for the asking; costing nothing, free, scot-f., free of charge, for free, giveaway; zero-rated, untaxed, tax-free, rent-f., post-f., post-paid, carriage-p., f.o.b.; including extras; unpaid, unsalaried, honorary 597 *volun-tary*; given away, unbought, as a gift 781 *given*; costless, free, gratis and for nothing.

**Vb.** *be cheap*, – inexpensive etc. adj.; cost little, be economical, be easily afforded, be within anyone's reach, be easy on the pocket; be worth the money, be cheap at the price; be bought for a song, be picked up for nothing, go dirt-cheap; cost nothing, be without charge, be free, be had for the asking; cheapen, get cheaper, fall in price, depreciate, come down, decline, sag, fall, drift, slump, plunge, plummet.

*cheapen*, lower, lower the price, reduce the p.; put a low price on, keep cheap, lower one's charges, trim one's prices, mark down, cut, slash; undercharge, underrate, let go for a song, sacrifice, give away, make a present of 781 *give*; beat down, haggle, undercut, undersell, engage in cut-throat competition; dump, unload; flood the market, glut 637 *superabound*; depress the market, bear.

**Adv.** *cheaply*, on the cheap; at cost price, at prime cost, at wholesale prices, at a discount, for a song, for nothing, on the house.

## 813 Liberality

**N.** *liberality*, liberalness, bounteousness, bountifulness, munificence, generosity 931 *disinterestedness*; open-handedness, open heart, open hand, open purse, hospitality, open house 882 *sociability*; free hand, blank cheque, carte blanche 744 *scope*; cornucopia 635 *plenty*; lavishness 815 *prodigality*; bounty, largesse 781 *gift*; handsome offer, sporting o. 759 *offer*; benefaction, charity 897 *kind act*.

*good giver*, free g., princely g., generous g., cheerful g., donor, liberal d., unselfish d., blood d., organ d., kidney d.; good spender, good tipper; fairy godmother, Lady Bountiful, Father Christmas, Santa Claus, sugar daddy, rich uncle 903 *benefactor*.

**Adj.** *liberal*, free, free-spending, free-handed, open-h., lavish 815 *prodigal*; large-hearted, free-h. 931 *disinterested*; bountiful, charitable 897 *benevolent*; hospitable 882 *sociable*; handsome, generous, munificent, splendid, slap-up; lordly, princely, royal, right royal; ungrudging, unstinting, unsparing, unfailing; in liberal quantities, abundant, ample, overwhelming, bounteous, profuse, full, pressed down and running over 635 *plenteous*; overflowing 637 *redundant*.

**Vb.** *be liberal*, – generous etc. adj.; lavish, shower largesse, shower upon 781 *give*; unbelt, put one's hand in one's pocket, open one's wallet, open the purse strings; give generously, give with both hands, give one's last penny, give the shirt off one's back; give till it hurts 897 *philanthropize*; give more than asked, overpay, pay well, tip w.; keep open house 882 *be hospitable*; do one proud, not count the cost, spare no expense; give carte blanche, give a blank cheque 744 *give scope*; spend freely, not ask for the change, throw money about like water, throw one's money around 815 *be prodigal*.

**Adv.** *liberally*, ungrudgingly, with open hand, with both hands.

## 814 Economy

**N.** *economy*, frugality, thrift, thriftiness, stealth wealth; prudence, care, carefulness; hus-

bandry, good h., good housekeeping, good housewifery; sound stewardship, good management, careful m.; watchful eye on expense, terotechnology, avoidance of waste, sumptuary law, credit squeeze 747 *restriction*; economy drive, economy measures; time-saving, labour-s., time and motion study, management s.; husbanding of resources, economizing, saving, sparing, pinching, paring, cheese-p.; retrenchment, economies, cuts; savings, hoarded s. 632 *store*; conservation, energy-saving; economizer 816 *niggard*; economist, monetarist; conservationist, preservationist, green, ecologist; good housewife, careful steward; national economy.

**Adj.** *economical*, time-saving, labour-s., energy-s., money-s., cost-reducing, cost-cutting; money-conscious, chary of expense, counting every penny 816 *parsimonious*; thrifty, careful, prudent, canny, frugal, cheese-paring, saving, sparing, spare; unlavish, meagre, Spartan, sparse; marginal, with nothing to spare.

**Vb.** *economize*, be economical, – sparing etc. adj.; husband one's resources, avoid extravagance, keep costs down, waste nothing, find a use for everything, recycle, reuse; keep within one's budget, keep within compass, cut one's coat according to one's cloth, make both ends meet; watch expenses, pare e., cut costs, cut down expenditure, trim e., cut back, make economies, retrench, tighten one's belt; pinch, scrape, scrimp and save, look after the pennies 816 *be parsimonious*; save, spare, hoard 632 *store*; plough back, reinvest, get interest on one's money, not leave money idle, make one's money work for one, make every penny work 800 *get rich*.

**Adv.** *sparingly*, economically, frugally, nothing in excess.

## 815 Prodigality

**N.** *prodigality*, lavishness, profusion, profuseness 637 *redundance*; idle display, idle expenditure, 'conspicuous consumption', consumerism, potlatch 875 *ostentation*;

Conspicuous consumption of valuable goods is a means of reputability to the gentleman of leisure. . . .

. . . The basis on which good repute in any highly organized industrial community ultimately rests is pecuniary strength; and the means of showing pecuniary strength, and so of gaining or retaining a good name, are leisure and a conspicuous consumption of goods. . . .

. . . From the foregoing survey of the growth of conspicuous leisure and consumption, it appears that the utility of both alike for the purposes of reputability lies in the element of waste that is common to both. In the one case it is a waste of time and effort, in the other it is a waste of goods.

Thorstein Veblen, *The Theory of the Leisure Class*

extravagance, wasteful expenditure, spendthrift e., reckless e.; wastefulness, profligacy, dissipation, squandering, squandermania, orgy of spending, spending spree, splurge 634 *waste*; unthriftiness, improvidence, indifference to economy, no attempt at economy, uncontrolled expenditure, unregulated e., deficit finance; misapplication, misuse of funds 675 *misuse*; money burning a hole in one's pocket.

*prodigal*, prodigal son, spender, big s., free s., reckless s., waster, wastrel, profligate, spend-all, spendthrift, spendaholic, scattergood, squanderer; gas guzzler.

**Adj.** *prodigal*, lavish 813 *liberal*; profuse, overlavish, overliberal; extravagant, regardless of cost, wasteful, squandering, profligate; uneconomic, uneconomical, unthrifty, thriftless, spendthrift, improvident, dissipative, reckless, dissipated; penny wise and pound foolish.

**Vb.** be *prodigal*, prodigalize, go the pace, blow one's money, blue one's m.; overspend, pour out money, splash money around, throw one's money around, flash pound notes; splurge, go on a spending spree, spend money like water, pour one's money through a sieve; burn one's money, run through one's savings, exhaust one's resources, spend to the last farthing, spend up to the hilt, splurge out, lash out, blow everything, waste one's inheritance, consume one's substance, squander 634 *waste*; play ducks and drakes, burn the candle at both ends, fritter away, throw a., fling a., gamble a., dissipate, scatter to the winds, pour down the drain; not count the cost, keep no check on expenditure; have no money sense, think money grows on trees; misspend, fool one's money away, throw good money after bad, throw the helve after the hatchet; have no thought for the morrow, spend more than one has, overdraw; eat up one's capital, kill the goose that lays the golden eggs; save nothing, put nothing by, have no nest-egg, have nothing to fall back on, keep nothing for a rainy day.

**Adv.** *prodigally*, profusely, recklessly; like a prodigal, like a spendthrift.

**Int.** hang the expense!, a short life and a merry one!, easy come, easy go!, you can't take it with you!

## 816 Parsimony

**N.** *parsimony*, parsimoniousness; credit squeeze 814 *economy*; false economy, misplaced e., policy of penny wise and pound foolish; cheese-paring, scrimping, pinching, scraping, penny-pinching; tightfistedness, niggardliness, meanness, minginess, stinginess, miserliness; illiberality, ungenerosity, uncharitableness, shoestring, grudging hand, closed wallet, closed purse, moths in one's wallet 932 *selfishness*.

*avarice*, cupidity, acquisitiveness, covetousness, green-eyed monster, possessiveness; affluenza, money-grubbing, itching palm; rapacity, avidity, greed 859 *desire*; mercenariness, venality.

*niggard*, skinflint, screw, scrimp, scraper, pinchfist, penny pincher, pinchpenny, cheeseparer, tightwad, meanie; grudging giver, no tipper; miser, money-grubber, lickpenny, muckworm; cadger; saver, hoarder, squirrel, magpie; hunks, churl, codger, curmudgeon; usurer 784 *lender*; Harpagon, Scrooge.

**Adj.** *parsimonious*, careful 814 *economical*; too careful, overeconomical, overfrugal, frugal to excess; money-conscious, pennywise, miserly, mean, mingy, stingy, near, close, tight; tightfisted, close-f., hard-f. 778 *retentive*; grudging, curmudgeonly, churlish, cheeseparing, illiberal, ungenerous, uncharitable, empty-handed, giftless; penurious, chary, sparing, pinching, scraping, scrimping, shabby, small-minded.

*avaricious*, grasping, griping, monopolistic 932 *selfish*; possessive, acquisitive 771 *acquiring*; hoarding, saving; pinching; miserly; cadging; money-grubbing, money-conscious, money-mad, covetous 859 *greedy*; usurious, rapacious, extortionate; mercenary, venal, sordid.

**Vb.** *be parsimonious*, – niggardly etc. adj.; keep one's purse shut 778 *retain*; grudge, begrudge, withhold, keep back 760 *refuse*; dole out, stint, skimp, starve, spare 636 *make insufficient*; scrape, scrimp, scrimp and save, pinch 814 *economize*; screw, rack-rent, skin a flint 786 *fleece*; be penny-wise, spoil the ship for a ha'porth of tar; starve oneself, live on a shoestring, live like a pauper; hoard wealth, never spend a penny; grudge every farthing, beat down, haggle 791 *bargain*; cadge, beg, mooch, scrounge, bum, borrow; hoard, sit on, keep for oneself 932 *be selfish*.

**Adv.** *parsimoniously*, niggardly, sparingly, on a shoestring.

# Emotion, religion and morality

## General

### 817 Affections

**N.** *affections*, qualities, instincts; passions, feelings, inner f., emotions, emotional life; nature, disposition 5 *character*; spirit, temper, tone, grain, mettle 5 *temperament*; cast of mind, habit of m., trait 7 *state*; personality, psychology, psyche, mentality, outlook, mental and spiritual make-up, inherited characteristics 5 *heredity*; being, innermost b., breast, bosom, heart, soul, core, inmost soul, inner man, cockles of the heart, heart of hearts 5 *essential part*, 447 *spirit*; animus, attitude, frame of mind, state of m., vein, strain, humour, mood; predilection, predisposition, inclinations, turn, bent, bias 179 *tendency*; passion, ruling p., master p. 481 *prejudice*; heartstrings 818 *feeling*; fullness of heart; heyday of the blood; force of character, force of personality; anthropomorphism, pathetic fallacy.

**Adj.** *with affections*, affected, characterized, formed, moulded, shaped, cast, tempered, framed; instinct with, imbued w., penetrated w., permeated w., eaten up w., devoured w.; possessed w., obsessed w., hung up about, ingrained, inborn, inbred, congenital 5 *genetic*; deep-rooted, deep-set, ineffaceable 5 *intrinsic*; emotional, demonstrative 818 *feeling*.

### 818 Feeling

**N.** *feeling*, experience, emotional life, affect; sentience, sensation, sense of 374 *sense*; emotion, crystallized e., sentiment; true feeling, sincerity 540 *veracity*; impulse 609 *spontaneity*; intuition, instinct; responsiveness, response, reaction, fellow feeling, sympathy, involvement, personal i. 880 *friendliness*; vibrations, vibes, bad v., good v.; empathy, appreciation, realization, understanding 490 *knowledge*;

impression, deep feeling, deep sense of 819 *moral sensibility*; religious feeling, unction 979 *piety*; finer feelings 897 *benevolence*; tender feelings 887 *love*; hard feelings 891 *resentment*; stirred feeling, thrill, kick 318 *spasm*; shock, turn 508 *lack of expectation*; pathos 825 *suffering*; release of feeling, catharthis, abreaction; actuating feeling, animus, emotionality, emotionalism, affectivity 822 *excitability*; sentimentality, exaggerated emotion, romanticism; show of feeling, manifestation of feeling, demonstration, demonstrativeness; expression, facial e., play of features 547 *gesture*; blush, reddening, going pink, flush, hectic f., suffusion; tingling, gooseflesh, creeps, tremor, trembling, nervous tension, quiver, flutter, flurry, palpitation, pulsation, heaving, panting, throbbing 318 *agitation*; stew, ferment 318 *commotion*; swelling heart, lump in one's throat, tears in one's eyes; control of feeling, stoicism, endurance, stiff upper lip 823 *patience*.

*warm feeling*, glow; cordiality, empressement, effusiveness, heartiness, full heart, overflowing h.; hot head, impatience; unction, earnestness 834 *seriousness*; eagerness, keenness, fervour, ardour, vehemence, enthusiasm, dash, fire 174 *vigorousness*; vigour, zeal 678 *activity*; fanaticism, mania 481 *prejudice*; emotion, passion, ecstasy, inspiration, hwyl, elevation, transports, transports of delight 822 *excitable state*.

**Adj.** *feeling*, affective, sensible, sensorial, sensory 374 *sentient*; spirited, vivacious, lively 819 *sensitive*; sensuous 944 *sensual*; experiencing, living; enduring, bearing 825 *suffering*; intuitive, sensitive, vibrant, responsive, reacting; involved, sympathetic, empathetic, condoling 775 *sharing*; tenderhearted 819 *impressible*; emotional, passionate, red-blooded, full of feeling; touchy-feely (inf); unctuous, soulful; intense, tense 821 *excited*; cordial, hearty; gushing, effusive; sentimental, romantic; mawkish, maudlin, schmaltzy, cutesy, treacly, soppy, sloppy; thrilling, tingling, throbbing; blushing, flushing, reddening.

*impressed*, affected, influenced; stirred, aroused, moved, touched 821 *excited*; struck, awed, awestruck, overwhelmed, struck all of a heap; penetrated, imbued with, aflame w., consumed w., devoured by, inspired by; rapt, enraptured, enthralled, ecstatic; lyrical, raving 822 *excitable*.

*fervent*, fervid, perfervid, passionate, red-blooded, ardent, tense, intense; eager, breathless, panting, throbbing, pulsating; palpitating; impassioned, vehement, earnest, zealous; enthusiastic, exuberant, happy-clappy (inf) bubbling, bubbly; hot-headed, warm-blooded, impetuous, impatient 822 *excitable*; warm, fiery, glowing, burning, red-hot, flaming, white-hot, boiling 379 *hot*; hysterical, delirious, overwrought, feverish, hectic 503 *frenzied*; strong, uncontrollable, overwhelming, furious 176 *violent*.

*felt*, experienced, lived; heartfelt, cordial, hearty, warm, sincerely felt, sincere 540 *veracious*; deeply-felt, deep-seated, deep-rooted, visceral, profound 211 *deep*; stirring, soul-s., heart-warming, heart-swelling; emotive, strong, overwhelming 821 *impressive*; smart, acute, keen, poignant, piercing, trenchant, mordant 256 *sharp*; caustic, burning, smarting 388 *pungent*; penetrating, permeating, absorbing; thrilling, tingling, rapturous, ecstatic 826 *pleasurable*; pathetic, affecting 827 *distressing*.

**Vb.** *feel*, sense, receive an impression, get the feeling, have a funny feeling, feel in one's bones, have a hunch; entertain, entertain feelings, have f., cherish f., harbour f., feel deeply, take to heart 819 *be sensitive*; know the feeling, experience, live, live through, go t., pass t., taste; bear, endure, undergo, smart, smart under 825 *suffer*; suffer with, feel w., sympathize, empathize, condole, share 775 *participate*; respond, react, tingle, warm to, fire, kindle, catch, catch the infection, be infected by, be inspired 821 *be excited*; cause feeling 821 *impress*.

*show feeling*, exhibit f., show signs of emotion; demonstrate, be demonstrative, not hide one's feelings 522 *manifest*; enthuse, go into ecstasies, go into transports of delight 824 *be pleased*; fly into a passion, fly off the handle 891 *get angry*; turn colour, change c., colour up, look blue, look black; go livid, go black in the face, go purple 428 *blacken*; look pale, blench, turn pale, go white, look ashen 427 *whiten*; colour, blush, flush, go pink, glow, mantle, turn red, turn crimson, go red in the face 431 *redden*; quiver, tremble, shudder, wince; flutter, shake, quake 318 *be agitated*; tingle, thrill, vibrate, throb, pulsate, beat faster 317 *oscillate*; palpitate, pant, heave, draw a deep breath 352 *breathe*; reel, lurch, stagger; stutter 580 *stammer*.

**Adv.** *feelingly*, unctuously, earnestly, con amore, heart and soul; with a full heart, with a swelling h., with a bursting h., with a melting h., sympathetically; cordially, heartily, devoutly, sincerely, from the bottom of one's heart.

## 819 Sensibility

**N.** *moral sensibility*, sensitivity, sensitiveness, soul; over-sensitivity, touchiness, prickliness, irritability 892 *irascibility*; raw feelings, tender f., thin skin, soft spot, tender spot, Achilles heel; sore point, where the shoe pinches 891 *resentment*; impressibility, affectibility, susceptibility; plasticity, malleability 327 *softness*; finer feelings, sentiments; sentimentality, sentimentalism, mawkishness; tenderness, affection 887 *love*; spirit, spiritedness, vivacity, vivaciousness, liveliness, verve 571 *vigour*; emotionalism, over-emotionalism, ebullience, effervescence 822 *excitability*; fastidiousness, finickiness, fikiness, aestheticism 463 *discrimination*; temperament, mood, mobility, changeability 152 *changeableness*; physical sensitivity 374 *sensibility*; touchy person, moody p., over-sensitive p., sensitive plant, bundle of nerves.

**Adj.** *impressible*, malleable, plastic, putty-like 327 *soft*; sensible, aware, conscious of, mindful of, awake to, alive to, responsive 374 *sentient*; impressed with, touched, moved, moved to tears, touched to the quick 818 *impressed*; persuasible 612 *induced*; impressionable 822 *excitable*; susceptible, susceptive; romantic, sentimental; mawkish, maudlin, schmaltzy, soppy, wet, sentimentalizing; gushing; emotional, warm-hearted; soft, soft as butter, tender, tender-hearted, soft-h., compassionate 905 *pitying*.

*sensitive*, sensitized; tingling, sore, raw, tender 374 *sentient*; aesthetic, fastidious, particular, fiky 463 *discriminating*; oversensitive, hypersensitive, all feeling, all heart, with one's heart on one's sleeve 822 *excitable*; touchy, irritable, impatient, thin-skinned, easily stung, easily aroused 892 *irascible*.

*lively*, alive, tremblingly a.; vital, vivacious, animated, fun-loving; gamesome, skittish 833 *merry*; irrepressible, ebullient, effervescent, bubbly; mettlesome, spirited, high-s., lively-minded, spirituel(le); alert, aware, on one's toes 455 *attentive*; overquick, impatient; nervous, highly-strung, overstrung, temperamental; mobile, changeable; enthusiastic, impassioned, red-blooded 818 *fervent*; overenthusiastic, overzealous, fanatic; lively in style, expressive, racy 571 *forceful*.

**Vb.** *be sensitive*, – sentimental etc. adj.; be tender-hearted, have a soft heart, take it to heart, soften one's heart, let one's heart be touched, weep for, break one's heart for 905 *pity*; tingle 318 *be agitated*.

**Adv.** *on the raw*, to the quick, to the heart, where the shoe pinches, where it hurts most.

## 820 Insensibility

**N.** *moral insensibility*, lack of sensitivity, insensitiveness; insentience, lack of sensation, numbness, stupor 375 *insensibility*; inertia 175 *inertness*; lethargy 679 *inactivity*; quietism, stagnation, vegetation 266 *quiescence*; woodenness, blockishness, block of wood, obtuseness, stupidity, dullness, no imagination, no vision 499 *unintelligence*; slowness, delayed reaction 456 *inattention*; uninterest 454 *incuriosity*; nonchalance, insouciance, unconcern, lack of care, detachment, apathy 860 *indifference*; no nerves, imperturbation, imperturbability, ataraxy *or* ataraxia, phlegm, stolidness, calmness, steadiness, coolness, sangfroid 823 *inexcitability*; no feelings, aloofness, impassibility, impassivity, impassiveness; repression, repression of feeling, stoicism, stiff upper lip 823 *patience*; inscrutability, poker face, deadpan expression 834 *seriousness*; insensitivity, coarseness, Philistinism 699 *artlessness*; imperception, thick skin, rhinoceros hide, elephant h.; no pride, no honour; cold heart, frigidity; unsusceptibility, unimpressibility, dourness; unsentimentality, cynicism; callousness 326 *hardness*; lack of feeling, dry eyes, no heart, heart of stone, heart of marble, heart of ice, brutishness, brutality, brutalization 898 *inhumanity*; no joy, no humour, no life, no love of life, not a spark, no animation 838 *tedium*; no admiration for 865 *lack of wonder*.

*unfeeling person*, iceberg, icicle, cold fish, cold heart, cold-blooded animal; stoic, ascetic; vegetable, stock, stone, block, marble.

**Adj.** *impassive*, unconscious 375 *insensible*; unsusceptible, insensitive, unimaginative, uninspired; unresponsive, unimpressionable, unimpressible 823 *inexcitable*; phlegmatic, stolid, vegetable-like; wooden, blockish; bovine; dull, slow, slow-witted 499 *unintelligent*; unemotional, passionless, impassible; proof, proof against, steeled a., armed a.; stoical, with stiff upper lip, ascetic, controlled, undemonstrative; unconcerned, aloof, distant, detached 860 *indifferent*; unaffected, calm 266

*tranquil*; steady, unruffled, unshaken, unshocked, unshockable; imperturbable, without nerves, without a nerve in one's body, controlled, cool; inscrutable, blank, expressionless, deadpan, poker-faced; unseeing 439 *blind*; unhearing 416 *deaf*; unsentimental, cynical; impersonal, dispassionate, without warmth, reserved, unforthcoming, stony, frigid, frozen, icy, cold, cold-blooded, cold-hearted, cold as charity; unfeeling, heartless, soulless, inhuman; unsmitten, heart-free, fancy-f., heart-whole; unloving, unaffectionate, undemonstrative.

*apathetic*, unenthusiastic, unambitious; unimpassioned, uninspired, unexcited, unwarmed, unmoved, unstirred, untouched, unsmitten, unstruck, unaroused, unstung; half-hearted, lukewarm, Laodicean 860 *indifferent*; uninterested 454 *incurious*; nonchalant, insouciant, pococurante, careless, regardless, neglectful 458 *negligent*; unspirited, spiritless, lackadaisical, couldn't care less; lotus-eating, vegetative, stagnant, bovine, cow-like 266 *quiescent*; sluggish, supine 679 *inactive*; passive 175 *inert*; blunted 257 *unsharpened*; cloyed 863 *sated*; torpid, numb, benumbed, paralysed, comatose 375 *insensible*.

*thick-skinned*, pachydermatous; impenetrable, impervious, impermeable; blind to, deaf to, dead to, closed to; obtuse, unimaginative, insensitive, uninspired; callous, insensate, tough, toughened, hardened, case-h. 326 *hard*; hard-bitten, hard-boiled, inured 669 *matured*; shameless, brazen, unblushing, unmoral, amoral.

**Vb.** *be insensitive*, – impassive etc. adj.; have no sensation, have no feelings 375 *be insensible*; not see, miss the point of, be blind to 439 *be blind*; lack animation, lack spirit, lack verve *or* vivacity; harden oneself, steel o., harden one's heart against, own no pity 906 *be pitiless*; feel indifference 860 *be indifferent*; feel no emotion, despise e., have no finer feelings, be a Philistine, nil admirari 865 *not wonder*; show no regard for 922 *despise*; take no interest 454 *be incurious*; ignore 458 *disregard*; control one's feelings, keep a stiff upper lip, quell one's desires 942 *be temperate*; stagnate, vegetate 679 *be inactive*; not stir, not turn a hair, not bat an eyelid 599 *be resolute*.

*make insensitive*, benumb 375 *render insensible*; render callous, steel, toughen 326 *harden*; sear, dry up 342 *dry*; deafen, stop the ears 399 *silence*; shut the eyes of 439 *blind*; brutalize 655 *pervert*; stale, coarsen 847 *vulgarize*; satiate, cloy 863 *sate*; deaden, obtund, take the edge off 257 *blunt*.

**Adv.** *in cold blood*, with dry eyes, without

emotion, with steady pulse; without batting an eyelid; without enthusiasm.

## 821 Excitation

**N.** *excitation*, rousing, arousal, stirring up, waking up, working up, whipping up; igniting, galvanization, electrification 174 *stimulation*; possession, inspiration, muse, afflatus, exhilaration, intoxication, headiness; evocation, calling forth; encouragement, animation, incitement, invitation, appeal 612 *inducement*; provocation, irritation, casus belli; impression, image, impact 178 *influence*; fascination, bewitchment, enchantment 983 *sorcery*; rapture, ravishment 824 *joy*; emotional appeal, human interest, sentiment, sentimentalism, sob-stuff, pathos; sensationalism, thrill-seeking, melodrama; scandal-mongering, muck-raking 926 *detraction*; excitement, high pressure, tension 160 *energy*; state of excitement, perturbation, effervescence, ebullience 318 *agitation*; shock, thrill, kicks 318 *spasm*; stew, ferment, tizzy, flurry, furore 318 *commotion*; pitch of excitement, fever pitch, orgasm 503 *frenzy*; sexual arousal 376 *sexual pleasure*; climax 137 *crisis*, excited feeling, passion, emotion, enthusiasm, lyricism 818 *feeling*; fuss, hassle, drama 822 *excitable state*; temper, fury, rage 891 *anger*; interest 453 *curiosity*; amazement 864 *wonder*; awe 854 *fear*.

*excitant*, stimulator, agent provocateur, rabble-rouser, tub-thumper 738 *agitator*; sensationalist, sob sister, scandal-monger, muck-raker, chequebook journalist; headline, banner h. 528 *publicity*; fillip, ginger, tonic, pick-me-up 174 *stimulant*; upper, pep pill 949 *drug*; sting, prick, goad, spur, whip, lash, stick, carrot and stick 612 *incentive*; fan; irritant, gadfly.

**Adj.** *excited*, activated, stimulated, stung etc. vb.; busy, astir, bustling, rushing 678 *active*; ebullient, effervescent, boiling, seething 355 *bubbly*; tense, wrought up, uptight, strung up, keyed up, wound up; overheated, feverish, hectic; delirious, frantic 503 *frenzied*; glowing 818 *fervent*; heated, flushed 379 *hot*; red-hot with excitement, violent 176 *furious*; hot under the collar, hot and bothered; seeing red, wild, mad, livid, fuming, foaming at the mouth, frothing, ramping, stamping, roaring, raging 891 *angry*; avid, eager, itching, raring, agog, thrill-seeking, rubber-necking, watering at the mouth 859 *desiring*; tingling, atremble, aquiver 818 *feeling*; flurried, atwitter, all of a flutter, all of a doodah 318 *agitated*; restless, restive, overexcited, overwrought, distraught, distracted, distrait(e); freaked out, on a high, on a trip, on an ego-trip; beside oneself, hysterical,

out of control, uncontrollable, running amok, carried away, a prey to passion; turned on, hyped up; crazy about 887 *enamoured*; inspired, possessed, impassioned, enthusiastic, lyrical, raving 822 *excitable*.

*exciting*, stimulating, sparkling, intoxicating, heady, exhilarating, kicking (sl), sexy (inf); provocative, teasing, piquant, tantalizing; salty, spicy, appetizing; alluring 887 *lovable*; evocative, emotive, suggestive; suspenseful, cliff-hanging, hair-raising, spine-chilling; thrilling, agitating; moving, affecting, inspiring, possessing; heating, kindling, rousing, stirring, soul-s., heart-swelling, heart-thrilling; cheering, rousing, rabble-r.; sensational, dramatic, melodramatic, stunning, mind-boggling, mind-blowing; interesting, gripping, absorbing, enthralling.

*impressive*, imposing, grand, stately; dignified, august, lofty, majestic, regal, royal, kingly, queenly 868 *noble*; awe-inspiring, sublime, humbling; overwhelming, overpowering; picturesque, scenic; cool; striking, arresting, dramatic; telling, forceful 178 *influential*.

**Vb.** *excite*, affect, infect 178 *influence*; warm the heart 833 *cheer*; touch, move, draw tears, bring tears to one's eyes 834 *sadden*; impassion, touch the heartstrings, strike a chord, arouse the emotions, stir the feelings, play on one's f.; quicken the pulse, startle, electrify, galvanize; warm the blood, raise the temperature, raise to fever pitch, bring to the boil, make one's blood boil 381 *heat*; inflame, enkindle, kindle, draw a spark, set on fire, light the touchpaper 381 *burn*; sting, goad, pique, irritate 891 *enrage*; tantalize, tease 827 *torment*; touch on the raw, find one's Achilles heel, cut to the quick; rip up, open the wound, reopen old wounds 827 *hurt*; work on, work up, whip up, lash into a fury 612 *incite*; breathe into, enthuse, inspire, possess; stir, rouse, arouse, wake, awaken, kindle, turn on (see also *animate*); touch off, evoke, elicit, summon up, call forth; thrill, exhilarate, intoxicate; transport, send, send into ecstasies 826 *delight*.

*animate*, vivify, enliven, breathe life into, quicken 360 *vitalize*; revive, rekindle, resuscitate, breathe fresh life into, bring in new blood 656 *restore*; inspire, inspirit, put one on his mettle; infuse courage into, encourage, hearten, buoy up 855 *give courage*; give an edge, put teeth into, whet 256 *sharpen*; urge, nag, egg on, spur, goad, lash 277 *accelerate*; jolt, jog, shake up; buck up, pep up, fillip, give a fillip to, stimulate, ginger 174 *invigorate*; cherish, foster, foment 162 *strengthen*; fuel, intensify, fan, fan the flame, blow on the coals, add fuel to the fire, stir the embers.

*impress*, sink in, leave an impression; project *or* present an image; interest, hold, grip, absorb; intrigue, rouse curiosity, make one sit up; strike, claim attention, rivet the a. 455 *attract notice*; affect 178 *influence*; let sink in, bring home to, drive home 532 *emphasize*; come home to, make one realize, penetrate, pierce 516 *be intelligible*; arrest, shake, smite, stun, amaze, astound, stagger 508 *surprise*; stupefy, gorgonize, petrify 864 *be wonderful*; dazzle, fill with admiration; inspire with awe, humble; take one's breath away, overwhelm, overpower; oppress, perturb, disquiet, upset, unsettle, put in disarray, distress, worry 827 *trouble*.

*be excited*, lose one's cool, lose control of oneself; flare, flare up, flame, burn 379 *be hot*; sizzle, seethe, simmer, boil, explode 318 *effervesce*; be affected, catch the infection, thrill to 818 *feel*; tingle, tremble 822 *be excitable*; quiver, flutter, palpitate, pulsate 318 *be agitated*; mantle, flush 818 *show feeling*; squirm, writhe 251 *wriggle*; dance, stamp, ramp; jump, leap up and down with excitement 312 *leap*; toss and turn, be unable to sleep.

**Adv.** *excitedly*, uncontrollably, frenziedly; all agog, with one's heart in one's mouth, with beating heart, with hair on end; aquiver, atremble.

## 822 Excitability

**N.** *excitability*, excitableness, explosiveness, inflammability; instability, temperament, emotionalism; hot blood, hot temper, temper on a short rein, irritability, scratchiness, touchiness 892 *irascibility*; impatience, nonendurance; incontinence; intolerance, fanaticism 481 *bias*; passionateness, vehemence, impetuosity, recklessness, headstrong behaviour 857 *rashness*; hastiness 680 *haste*; effervescence, ebullition; turbulence, boisterousness; restlessness, fidgetiness, fidgets, nerves, butterflies in the stomach, collywobbles, flap, social phobia 318 *agitation*.

*excitable state*, exhilaration, elevation, elation, euphoria, intoxication, abandon, abandonment; thrill, transport, trip, high, ecstasy, inspiration, lyricism 818 *feeling*; fever, fever of excitement, fret, fume, perturbation, trepidation, bother, fuss, hassle, flurry, whirl 318 *agitation*; warmth 379 *heat*; ferment, pother, stew; gust, storm, tempest 352 *gale*; effervescence, ebullition, outburst, outbreak, explosion, scene, song and dance 318 *commotion*; brainstorm, hysterics, delirium, fit, apoplectic f., agony 503 *frenzy*; distraction, madness 503 *mental disorder*; mania, passion, master p., ruling p.; rage, towering r., fury 176

*violence*; temper, tantrums, rampage 891 *anger*.

**Adj.** *excitable*, sensitized, oversensitive, raw 819 *sensitive*; passionate, emotional; susceptible, romantic; out for thrills, thrill-loving, thrill-seeking, looking for kicks, rubbernecking; suggestible, inflammable, like tinder, like touch-paper; unstable, easily exhilarated, easily depressed; easily impressed, impressionable, impressible; variable, temperamental, moody, mercurial, volatile 152 *changeful*; fitful 604 *capricious*; restless, unquiet, nervy, fidgety, edgy, on edge, tense, wired (sl), wired-up (sl) ruffled 318 *agitated*; highly-strung, nervous, skittish, mettlesome 819 *lively*; easily provoked, irritable, fiery, hot-tempered, hot-headed 892 *irascible*; impatient, trigger-happy 680 *hasty*; impetuous, impulsive, madcap 857 *rash*; savage, fierce; vehement, boisterous, rumbustious, tempestuous, turbulent, stormy, uproarious, clamorous 176 *violent*; restive, uncontrollable 738 *riotous*; effervescent, simmering, seething, boiling; volcanic, explosive, ready to burst; fanatical, unbalanced, intolerant; rabid 176 *furious*; feverish, febrile, frantic, hysterical, delirious 503 *frenzied*; dancing, stamping; like a cat on hot bricks, like a hen on a hot girdle *or* griddle, like a cat on a hot tin roof; tense, electric; elated, inspired, raving, lyrical 821 *excited*.

**Vb.** *be excitable*, – impatient etc. adj.; show impatience, drum one's fingers, tap one's foot, fret, fume, stamp; shuffle, chafe, fidget, champ at the bit; show excitement, show temperament 818 *show feeling*; tingle with, be itching to, be dying to; be on edge, have nerves, be in a stew, be in a fuss, flap 318 *be agitated*; start, jump 854 *be nervous*; be under strain, be suffering from stress, break down, be on the verge of a breakdown; have a temper 892 *be irascible*; fume, foam, froth, throw fits, have hysterics 503 *go mad*; abandon oneself, let oneself go, throw a tantrum, go wild, run riot, run amok, go berserk, get out of control, see red; storm, rush about 61 *rampage*; ramp, rage, rant, roar 176 *be violent*; fly into a temper, fly off the handle, burst out, break o., explode, create 891 *get angry*; kindle, burn, smoulder, catch fire, flare up 821 *be excited*.

## 823 Inexcitability

**N.** *inexcitability*, imperturbability, good temper; calmness, steadiness, composure, ataraxy *or* ataraxia; coolness, cool, sangfroid, nonchalance; frigidity, coldness, impassibility 820 *moral insensibility*; unruffled state, tranquillity 266 *quietude*; serenity, placidity, peace of mind, calm of m. 828 *content*; equanimity, balance, poise, even temper, level t., philosophic t., philosophy, balanced mind 28 *equilibrium*; self-possession, self-command, self-control, self-restraint 942 *temperance*; repression, self-r., stoicism 945 *asceticism*; resignation, detachment, nonattachment, dispassion, dispassionateness 860 *indifference*; gravity, staidness, demureness, sobriety 834 *seriousness*; quietism, Quakerism; sweetness, gentleness 884 *courtesy*; tameness, meekness, lack of spirit, lack of mettle, lack of fire 734 *laxity*; tranquillization, soothing, calming 177 *moderation*.

*patience*, patience of Job; forbearance, endurance, longsuffering, longanimity; tolerance, toleration, refusal to be provoked; stoicism; resignation, acquiescence 721 *submission*.

**Adj.** *inexcitable*, impassible, dispassionate, cold, frigid, heavy, dull 820 *impassive*; stable 153 *unchangeable*; not given to worry, unworrying, unworried, cool, cool as a cucumber, imperturbable, unflappable; cool-headed, level-h.; steady, composed, controlled, grounded; self-controlled, moderate 942 *temperate*; inscrutable, deadpan, poker-faced; deliberate, unhurried, unhasty 278 *slow*; even, level, equable 16 *uniform*; not irritable, good-tempered, even-t., easy-going, sunny; staid, sedate, sober, sober-minded, demure, reserved, grave 834 *serious*; quiet, unemphatic 266 *quiescent*; placid, unruffled, calm, serene 266 *tranquil*; sweet, gentle, mild, lamblike, meek 935 *innocent*; mild as milk 177 *moderate*; unwarlike 717 *peaceful*; easy, easygoing, undemanding 736 *lenient*; comfortable, gemütlich 828 *content*; philosophic, unambitious 860 *indifferent*; acquiescent, resigned, submissive 739 *obedient*, spiritless, lackadaisical, torpid, passive, vegetable-like 175 *inert*; calmed down, in a reasonable frame of mind, tame 369 *tamed*; unmoved, unenthusiastic, unsentimental, unromantic, unpoetic, earthbound 593 *prosaic*.

*patient*, meek, like patience on a monument, armed with patience; tolerant, longsuffering, longanimous, forbearing, enduring; stoic, stoical, philosophic, philosophical, uncomplaining.

**Vb.** *keep calm*, be composed, be collected; compose oneself, collect o., keep cool, keep a cool head, remain unruffled; master one's feelings, swallow one's resentment, control one's temper, keep one's cool, not rise to the bait, keep one's hair *or* shirt on; not turn a hair, not bat an eyelid 820 *be insensitive*; relax, not excite oneself, not worry, stop worrying, take things easy, take things as they come 683 *repose*; resign oneself, take in good part, take philosophically, have patience, be resigned 721 *submit*.

*be patient*, show patience, show restraint, forbear; put up with, stand, tolerate, bear, endure, support, sustain, suffer, abide; resign oneself, grin and bear it, accept the situation with good grace, put a brave face on it; brook, take, take it from, swallow, digest, stomach, pocket 721 *knuckle under*; 'turn the other cheek' (see quotation for 'an eye for an eye' at 714 *retaliation*) 909 *forgive*; be tolerant, live and let live, condone 736 *be lenient*; turn a blind eye, overlook 734 *be lax*; allow 756 *permit*; ignore provocation, not rise to the bait, keep the peace 717 *be at peace*; find a modus vivendi, coexist 770 *compromise*.

*tranquillize*, steady, moderate, moderate one's transports, sober down 177 *assuage*; calm, rock, lull 266 *bring to rest*; cool down, compose 719 *pacify*; make one's mind easy, set one's mind at rest 831 *relieve*; control, repress 747 *restrain*.

SECTION TWO

## Personal emotion

### 824 Joy

**N.** *joy* 376 *pleasure*; great pleasure, keen p.; sensation of pleasure, enjoyment, thrill, kick, piquancy 826 *pleasurableness*; joyfulness, joyousness 835 *rejoicing*; delight, gladness, rapture, exaltation, exhilaration, transports of delight; abandonment, euphoria, ecstasy, enchantment, bewitchment, ravishment; unholy joy, gloating, schadenfreude, malice 898 *malevolence*; life of pleasure, hedonistic way of life, joys of life, 'rose-strewn path', 'roses all the way';

> Freude trinken alle Wesen
>   An den Brüsten der Natur,
> Alle Guten, alle Bösen,
>   Folgen ihrer Rosenspur.
> *(All the world's creatures / Draw joy from nature's breast; / Both the good and the evil / Follow her rose-strewn path.)*
> Friedrich von Schiller, *An die Freude (Ode to Joy)*

> It was roses, roses, all the way,
> With myrtle mixed in my path like mad.
> The house-roofs seemed to heave and sway,
> The church-spires flamed, such flags they had,
> A year ago on this very day!
> Robert Browning, *The Patriot*

halcyon days, holidays, honeymoon, 'days of wine and roses' 730 *palmy days*.

> They are not long, the days of wine and roses:
>   Out of a misty dream
> Our path emerges for a while, then closes
>   Within a dream.
> Ernest Dowson, *Vitae Summa Brevis*

*happiness*, felicity, good fortune, well-being, snugness, comfort, ease 376 *euphoria*;

unalloyed delight, rose without a thorn; flourishing time, Saturnia Regna, golden age, age of Aquarius, feel-good factor 730 *prosperity*; blessedness, bliss, beatitude, summum bonum; seventh heaven, cloud nine, nirvana, Paradise, Elysium, the happy hunting-ground in the sky, Garden of Eden, Fortunate Isles, Isles of the Blessed, Hesperides, Arcadia, Cockaigne 513 *fantasy*; happy valley, 'bower of bliss' (see quotation at 887 *love-nest*), home sweet home.

*enjoyment*, gratification, satisfaction, fulfilment 828 *content*; delectation, relish, lip-smacking, zest, gusto; indulgence, luxuriation, wallowing 943 *intemperance*; full life, eudaemonism, hedonism, Epicureanism 944 *sensualism*; glee, merry-making, lark, frolic, gambol 833 *merriment*; fun, treat, excursion, outing 837 *amusement*; feast, beanfeast, thrash; refreshment, good cheer, 'cakes and ale', 'beer and skittles', 'panem et circenses' 301 *eating*.

> Dost thou think, because thou art virtuous, there shall be no more cakes and ale?
> William Shakespeare, *Twelfth Night*

> Life isn't all beer and skittles.
> Thomas Hughes, *Tom Brown's Schooldays*

> Duas tantum res anxius optat,
> Panem et circenses.
> (The people are eager for just two things: bread and circuses.)
> Juvenal, *Satires*

**Adj.** *pleased*, well-p., glad, not sorry; welcoming, receiving with open arms; satisfied, happy 828 *content*; gratified, flattered, chuffed, pleased as Punch; over the moon, on top of the world; enjoying, loving it, tickled, tickled to death, tickled pink 837 *amused*; exhilarated 833 *merry*; euphoric, walking on air, with feet not touching the ground; exalted, elated, overjoyed 833 *jubilant*; cheering, shouting 835 *rejoicing*; delighted, transported, enraptured, ravished, rapturous, ecstatic, raving 923 *approving*; in raptures, in ecstasies, in transports, in seventh heaven, on cloud nine; captivated, charmed, enchanted, fascinated 818 *impressed*; maliciously pleased, gloating.

*happy*, happy as a king, happy as a sandboy, happy as a lark, happy as Larry, happy as the day is long, happy as a pig in muck, over the moon, blissed out (inf); blithe, joyful, joyous, gladsome 833 *merry*; beaming, smiling 835 *laughing*; radiant, radiating joy, sparkling, starry-eyed; felicitous, lucky, fortunate, to be congratulated 730 *prosperous*; blissful, blest, blessed, beatified; in felicity, in bliss, in paradise; at ease, made comfortable 376 *comfortable*; unduly happy, pronoid, starry-eyed, looking through rose-coloured *or* rose-tinted spectacles.

**Vb.** *be pleased*, – glad etc. adj.; have the pleasure; feel *or* experience pleasure, hug oneself, congratulate o., purr, purr with pleasure, dance with p., be like a cat with a dish of cream, be like a dog with two tails, jump for joy 833 *be cheerful*; laugh, smile 835 *rejoice*; get pleasure from, get a kick out of, take pleasure in, delight in, rejoice in; go into ecstasies, be in a state of euphoria, rave, rave about 818 *show feeling*; indulge in, have time for, luxuriate in, solace oneself with, refresh oneself w., bask in, wallow, spoil oneself 376 *enjoy*; have fun 837 *amuse oneself*; gloat, gloat over; savour, appreciate, relish, smack one's lips 386 *taste*; take a fancy to, like 887 *love*; think well of 923 *approve*; take in good part, take no offence.

## 825 Suffering

**N.** *suffering*, heartache, Weltschmerz, 'lacrimae rerum' 834 *melancholy*;

> . . . Sunt hic etiam sua praemia laudi,
> Sunt lacrimae rerum et mentem mortalia tangunt.
> (Even here merit has its due reward,
> Tears are shed over things and mortality touches people's hearts.)
> Virgil, *Aeneid*

longing, homesickness, nostalgia 859 *desire*; unsatisfied desire 829 *discontent*, weariness 684 *fatigue*; weight on the spirit, nightmare, waking nightmare, incubus; affliction, distress, dolour, anguish, angst, agony, torture, torment, mental t. 377 *pain*; twinge, stab, smart, sting, thorn 377 *pang*; bitter cup 827 *painfulness*; Passion, Crucifixion, Calvary, martyrdom; rack, the stake 963 *punishment*; purgatory, hell, pains of h., damnation, eternal d. 961 *condemnation*; bed of nails, bed of thorns, no bed of roses 700 *difficulty*; bad time, bad day, unpleasantness, mauvais quart d'heure, annus horribilis; setback, inconvenience, disagreeableness, discomfort, malaise; the hard way, trial, ordeal; shock, trauma, blow, infliction, visitation, tribulation 659 *bane*; extremity, death's door 651 *illness*; living death, death in life, fate worse than death 616 *evil*; dystopia; evil days, unhappy times, iron age 731 *adversity*.

*sorrow*, grief, sadness, mournfulness, gloom 834 *dejection*; dole, dolour, woe, wretchedness, misery, depths of m.; prostration, despair, despondency, desolation 853 *hopelessness*; unhappiness, infelicity, tale of woe 731 *adversity*; weariness of spirit, heavy heart, aching h., bleeding h., broken h.; displeasure, dissatisfaction 829 *discontent*; vexation, bitterness, mortification, chagrin, heart-burning, fretting, repining, remorse 830 *regret*.

*worry*, worrying, worriedness, unease, uneasiness, discomfort, disquiet, unquiet, inquietude, fret, fretting 318 *agitation*; discomposure, dismay, distress 63 *derangement*; phobia, hang-up, obsession, orthorexia; something on one's mind, weight on one's m., anxiety, concern, solicitude, thought, care; responsibility, weight of r., load, burden; strain, stress, tension, premenstrual t., PMT; a worry, worries, business w., cares, cares of the world; trouble, troubles 616 *evil*; bother, botheration, annoyance, irritation, bête noire, pest, thorn in the flesh, death of 659 *bane*; bothersome task 838 *bore*; something to worry about, lookout, hard cheese, funeral; headache, teaser, puzzle, problem 530 *enigma*.

*sufferer*, victim, scapegoat, sacrifice; prey, shorn lamb 544 *dupe*; willing sacrifice, martyr; object of compassion, wretch, poor w., misery 731 *unlucky person*; patient 651 *sick person*.

*worrier*, neurotic, obsessive, worryguts (inf); control freak.

**Adj.** *suffering*, ill, indisposed 651 *sick*; agonizing, writhing, aching, griped, in pain, on a bed of p., ravaged with p., in agony, bleeding, harrowed, on the rack, in torment, in hell 377 *pained*; inconvenienced, uncomfortable, ill at ease; anguished, distressed, anxious, unhappy about, worried, troubled, disquieted, apprehensive, dismayed 854 *nervous*; sick with worry, out of one's mind with w., cut up about, in a state 316 *agitated*; discomposed, disconcerted 63 *disarranged*; ill-used, maltreated, abused, severely handled, on the receiving end; long-suffering, downtrodden 745 *subjected*; martyred, victimized, made a prey, sacrificed; stricken, wounded; heavy-laden, crushed, prostrate 684 *fatigued*; care-worn, sad-looking, worried-l., harassed-l.; woeful, woebegone, haggard, wild-eyed.

*unhappy*, infelicitous, unlucky, accursed 731 *unfortunate*; despairing 853 *hopeless*; doomed 961 *condemned*; to be pitied, pitiable, poor, wretched, miserable; sad, melancholy, despondent, disconsolate; cut up, heart-broken, broken-hearted, heavy-h., sick at heart; sorrowful, sorrowing, grieved, grieving, grief-stricken, woebegone 834 *dejected*; plunged in grief, sunk in misery, weeping, weepy, wet-eyed, sobbing, tearful, in tears 836 *lamenting*, nostalgic, longing 859 *desiring*; displeased, dissatisfied, disappointed 829 *discontented*; offended, vexed, peeved, miffed, annoyed, pained 924 *disapproving*; piqued, chagrined, mortified, humiliated 891 *resentful*; sickened, disgusted, nauseated 861 *disliking*; sorry, remorseful, compunctious, regretful 830 *regretting*.

**Vb.** *suffer*, undergo, endure, go through,

experience 818 *feel*; bear, endure, put up with, grin and bear it; bear pain, suffer p., suffer torments, bleed; hurt oneself, be hurt, do harm to oneself, smart, chafe, ache 377 *feel pain*; wince, flinch, agonize, writhe, squirm 251 *wriggle*; take up one's cross, become a martyr, sacrifice oneself; take one's punishment, take it on the chin 599 *stand firm*; have a thin time, have a bad t., go through it, have trouble enough 731 *have trouble*; trouble oneself, distress o., fuss, hassle, worry, worry to death, fret, agonize, be on pins and needles, be on tenterhooks 318 *be agitated*; mind, be upset, let weigh upon one, take it badly, take it ill, take it to heart; sorrow, passion, grieve, weep, sigh, take on 836 *lament*; pity oneself, be despondent 834 *be dejected*; have regrets, kick oneself 830 *regret*.

## 826 Pleasurableness

**N.** *pleasurableness*, pleasures of, pleasantness, niceness, delectableness, delectability, delightfulness, amenity, sunny side, bright s.; invitingness, attractiveness, appeal, sex a., it, come-hither look 291 *attraction*; winning ways 925 *flattery*; amiability, winsomeness, charm, fascination, enchantment, witchery, loveliness, sight for sore eyes 841 *beauty*; joyfulness, honeymoon 824 *joy*; something nice, a real tonic, a little of what one fancies, a delight, a treat, a joy; novelty, pastime, fun 837 *amusement*; interest, human i.; melody, harmony 412 *music*; tastiness, deliciousness 390 *savouriness*; spice, zest, relish, je ne sais quoi; dainty, titbit, sweet 392 *sweetness*; 'manna in the wilderness' (see quotation at 703 *aid*), balm 685 *refreshment*; 'land flowing with milk and honey' (see quotation at 730 *prosperity*) 635 *plenty*; peace, perfect p., peace and quiet, tranquillity 266 *quietude*, 681 *leisure*; idyll; pipedream 513 *fantasy*.

**Adj.** *pleasurable*, pleasant, nice, good; pleasure-giving 837 *amusing*; pleasing, agreeable, grateful, gratifying, flattering; acceptable, welcome, welcome as the flowers in May; well-liked, to one's taste, to one's liking, just what the doctor ordered; wonderful, marvellous, fabulous, splendid 644 *excellent*; frictionless, painless 376 *comfortable*; easeful, refreshing 683 *reposeful*; peaceful, quiet 266 *tranquil*; bowery, luxurious, voluptuous 376 *sensuous*; genial, warm, sunny 833 *cheering*; delightful, delectable, delicious, exquisite, choice; luscious, juicy 356 *pulpy*; delicate, tasty 390 *savoury*; sugary 392 *sweet*; dulcet, musical, harmonious 410 *melodious*; picturesque, scenic, lovely 841 *beautiful*; amiable, dear, winning, disarming, endearing 887 *lovable*; attractive, fetching, appealing, alluring, interesting

291 *attracting*; seductive, enticing, inviting, captivating; charming, enchanting, bewitching, ravishing, Siren, Circean; haunting, thrilling, heart-melting, heart-warming 821 *exciting*; homely, cosy; pastoral, idyllic; Elysian, paradisal, heavenly, out of this world; beatific, blessed, blissful 824 *happy*.

**Vb.** *please*, give pleasure, afford p., yield p., agree with; make things pleasant 925 *flatter*; lull, soothe, calm 177 *assuage*; comfort 833 *cheer*; put at ease, make comfortable 831 *relieve*; give a golden hello to, give a sweetener to, sugar, gild *or* sugar the pill 392 *sweeten*; stroke, pat, pet, baby, coddle, nurse, cuddle 889 *caress*; indulge, pander to 734 *be lax*; charm, interest 837 *amuse*; rejoice, gladden, make happy; gratify, satisfy, crown one's wishes, leave one walking on air, leave nothing more to be desired 828 *content*; bless, crown one's bliss, raise to the seventh heaven, beatify.

*delight*, suprise with joy; rejoice, exhilarate, elate, elevate, uplift; rejoice one's heart, warm the cockles of one's h., do one's heart good, bring tears of joy *or* happiness; thrill, intoxicate, ravish; transport, turn on, send, send one into raptures *or* ecstasies 821 *excite*; make music in one's ears 925 *flatter*; take one's fancy, tickle one's f. 887 *excite love*; tickle one's palate 390 *make appetizing*; regale, refresh; tickle, tickle one to death, titillate, tease, tantalize; entrance, enrapture; enchant, charm, becharm 983 *bewitch*; take one's breath away 821 *impress*; allure, seduce 291 *attract*.

## 827 Painfulness

**N.** *painfulness*, painful treatment, harshness, roughness, abuse, child a., sexual a., harassment, sexual h., persecution 735 *severity*; hurtfulness, harmfulness 645 *badness*; disagreeableness, unpleasantness; loathsomeness, hatefulness, beastliness 616 *evil*; grimness 842 *ugliness*; hideosity 842 *eyesore*; friction, chafing, irritation, ulceration, inflammation, exacerbation 832 *aggravation*; soreness, tenderness 377 *pain*; irritability, inflammability 822 *excitability*; sore subject, sore point, rub, soft spot, tender s. 819 *moral sensibility*; sore, running s., ulcer, thorn in the flesh, pinprick, where the shoe pinches 659 *bane*; shock 508 *lack of expectation*; unpalatability, disgust, nausea, sickener 391 *unsavouriness*; sharpness, bitterness, bitter cup, bitter draught, bitter pill, 'gall and wormwood' (see quotation at 861 *dislike*), vinegar 393 *sourness*; bread of affliction 731 *adversity*; tribulation, trials and tribulations, ordeal, cross 825 *suffering*; trouble, care 825 *worry*; dreariness, cheerlessness; pitifulness, pathos; sorry sight,

pathetic s., painful s., sad spectacle, object of pity 731 *unlucky person*; heavy news 825 *sorrow*; disenchantment, disillusionment 509 *disappointment*; hornet's nest, hot water 700 *predicament*.

*annoyance*, vexation, the death of –, pest, bête noire, bugger (inf) curse, plague, pain in the neck 659 *bane*; botheration, hassle, embarrassment 825 *worry*; cause for annoyance, interference, nuisance, pinprick; burden, drag 702 *encumbrance*; grievance, complaint; hardship, troubles 616 *evil*; last straw, limit, the end; offence, affront, insult, provocation 921 *indignity*; molestation, infestation, persecution, malignity 898 *malevolence*; feeling of annoyance, displeasure, mortification 891 *resentment*.

*annoying person*, menace, troublemaker, enfant terrible; bugger (inf), fart (inf), fucker (offensive), pain, p. in the neck, p. in the arse (inf), arsehole (sl), tosser (sl), wanker (sl).

**Adj.** *paining*, hurting, aching, painful, sore, tender; dolorous, agonizing, racking, purgatorial 377 *painful*; scathing, searing, scalding, burning, sharp, shooting, biting, nipping, gnawing, throbbing; caustic, corrosive, vitriolic; harsh, hard, rough, cruel 735 *severe*; grinding, gruelling, punishing, searching, exquisite, excruciating, extreme; hurtful, harmful, poisonous 659 *baneful*.

*unpleasant*, unpleasing, disagreeable; uncomfortable, comfortless, joyless, dreary, dreich (Scots), dismal, depressing 834 *cheerless*; unattractive, uninviting, unappealing; hideous 842 *ugly*; unwelcome, undesired, unacceptable 860 *unwanted*; thankless, unpopular, displeasing 924 *disapproved*; disappointing, unsatisfactory 829 *discontenting*; distasteful, unpalatable, off 391 *unsavoury*; foul, nasty, beastly, horrible, ghastly, – from hell 645 *not nice*; malodorous, stinking 397 *fetid*; bitter, sharp 393 *sour*; invidious, obnoxious, offensive, objectionable, undesirable, odious, hateful, loathsome, nauseous, slimy, disgusting, revolting, repellent 861 *disliked*; execrable, accursed 645 *damnable*.

*annoying*, too bad; troublesome, embarrassing, discomfiting, worrying; bothersome, bothering, wearisome, irksome, tiresome, boring 838 *tedious*; burdensome, onerous, oppressive 322 *weighty*; disappointing, unlucky, unfortunate, untoward 731 *adverse*; awkward, unaccommodating, impossible, pesky, plaguy, harassing, hassling 702 *hindering*; importunate, pestering, plaguing; teasing, trying, irritating, vexatious, aggravating, provoking, maddening, infuriating; galling, stinging, biting, mortifying.

*distressing*, afflicting, crushing, prostrating,

grievous, traumatic; moving, affecting, touching, grieving; harrowing, heartbreaking, heart-rending, tear-jerking; pathetic, tragic, tragical, sad, woeful, rueful, mournful, pitiful, lamentable, deplorable 905 *pitiable*; ghastly, grim, dreadful, shocking, appalling, horrifying, horrific, nerve-racking 854 *frightening*.

*intolerable*, insufferable, impossible, – from hell, insupportable, unendurable, unbearable 32 *exorbitant*; past bearing, past enduring, not to be borne, not to be endured, not to be put up with; extreme, beyond the limits of tolerance, more than flesh and blood can stand, enough to make one mad, enough to make a parson swear, enough to try the patience of Job, enough to provoke a saint.

**Vb.** **hurt**, injure 645 *harm*; pain, cause p. 377 *give pain*; bite, cut, tear, rend 655 *wound*; wound the feelings, hurt the f., gall, pique, nettle, mortify 891 *huff*; rub up the wrong way, tread on one's corns; touch a soft spot, cut to the quick, pierce the heart, rend the heartstrings, bring tears to one's eyes, draw tears, grieve, afflict, cause trauma, distress 834 *sadden*; plunge into sorrow, bring grief to one's heart, plant an arrow in one's breast, plant a thorn in one's side; corrode, embitter, exacerbate, make matters worse, rub salt in the wound, gnaw, chafe, rankle, fester 832 *aggravate*; offend, aggrieve (see also *displease*); insult, affront 921 *not respect*.

*torment*, martyr; harrow, rack, put to the r., break on the wheel 963 *torture*; give one the third degree, give one the works; put one through it, put through the hoop, give one a bad time, maltreat, abuse, bait, bully, rag, bullyrag, persecute, assail 735 *oppress*; be offensive, snap at, bark at 885 *be rude*; importune, dun, doorstep, beset, besiege 737 *demand*; haunt, obsess; annoy, do it to a.; tease, pester, plague, nag, henpeck, badger, worry, try, chivvy, harass, hassle, harry, heckle; molest, bother, vex, provoke, peeve, miff, ruffle, irritate, needle, sting, chafe, fret, bug, gall, irk, rile, roil, wind up 891 *enrage*.

*trouble*, discomfort, disquiet, disturb, agitate, discompose, discombobulate, disconcert, discomfit, put one out, throw one out, upset, incommode 63 *derange*; worry, embarrass, perplex 474 *puzzle*; exercise, tire 684 *fatigue*; weary, bore 838 *be tedious*; obsess, haunt, bedevil; weigh upon one, prey on the mind, weigh on the spirits, act as a damper, deject 834 *depress*; infest, get in one's hair, dog one's footsteps, get under one's feet, get in one's way, thwart 702 *obstruct*.

*displease*, not please, not appeal, find no favour 924 *incur blame*; grate, jar, disagree

with, grate on, jar on, strike a jarring note, get on one's nerves, set the teeth on edge, go against the grain, give one the pip, give one a pain, get one's goat, get on one's wick, get up one's nose, get under one's skin; disenchant, disillusion, undeceive 509 *disappoint*; dissatisfy, give cause for complaint, aggrieve 829 *cause discontent*; offend, shock, horrify, scandalize, disgust, revolt, repel, put one off, turn one off, sicken, nauseate, fill one with loathing, stink in the nostrils, stick in the throat, stick in the gizzard, make one's gorge rise, turn one's stomach, make one sick, make one sick to one's stomach, make one vomit, make one throw up 861 *cause dislike*; make one's hair curl, make one's flesh creep, make one's blood run cold, curdle the blood, make one's hair stand on end, appal 854 *frighten*.

**Adv.** *horribile dictu.*

## 828 Content

**N.** *content*, contentment, contentedness, satisfaction, entire s., complacency; self-complacency, self-satisfaction, smugness 873 *vanity*; measure of content, half-smile, purr of content, feel-good factor, ray of comfort; serenity, quietism, tranquillity, resignation 266 *quietude*; ease of mind, trouble-free m., easy m., peace of m., heart's ease, nothing left to worry about 376 *euphoria*; conciliation, reconciliation 719 *pacification*; snugness, cosiness, comfort, sitting pretty; wish-fulfilment, dreams come true, desires fulfilled, ambition achieved, 'port after stormy seas' 730 *prosperity*;

> Sleep after toil, port after stormy seas,
> Ease after war, death after life does greatly please.
> Edmund Spenser, *The Faerie Queen*

acquiescence 758 *consent*; resignation 721 *submission*.

**Adj.** *content*, contented, satisfied, well-s. 824 *happy*; appeased, pacified 717 *peaceful*; cosy, snug 376 *comfortable*; at ease 683 *reposeful*; easy in mind, smiling 833 *cheerful*; flattered 824 *pleased*; with nothing left to wish for, with no desire unfulfilled, having nothing to grumble at 863 *sated*; unrepining, uncomplaining, with no regrets, without complaints; unenvious, unjealous 931 *disinterested*; philosophic, without desire, without passion 823 *inexcitable*; resigned, acquiescent 721 *submitting*; fairly content, better satisfied; easily pleased, easygoing, easy-osy 736 *lenient*; secure 660 *safe*; unmolested, unharassed, untroubled, unworried, unafflicted, unvexed, unplagued; blessed with contentment, thankful, gratified 907 *grateful*.

*contenting*, satisfying, satisfactory 635 *sufficient*; lulling, soothing, pacifying, appeasing

719 *pacificatory*; tolerable, bearable, endurable, survivable, livable; unobjectionable, passable, acceptable 923 *approvable*; desirable, wished for, much longed for, all that is wished for 859 *desired*.

**Vb.** *be content*, – satisfied etc. adj.; purr, purr with content 824 *be pleased*; rest and be thankful, rest satisfied, take the good that the gods provide, be glad of what one's got, count one's blessings; be thankful, have much to be thankful for 907 *be grateful*; have all one could ask for, have one's wish, make one's dreams come true, attain one's desire, fulfil one's ambition 730 *prosper*; congratulate oneself, hug o., give oneself a pat on the back 835 *rejoice*; be at ease, be at home, be in one's element, sit pat, sit pretty 376 *enjoy*; be reconciled 719 *make peace*; get over it, take comfort 831 *be relieved*; rest content, take in good part; take things as they come, make the best of, complain of nothing, have no complaints, have nothing to grouse about, have no regrets, not repine; put up with, acquiesce 721 *submit*.

*content*, make contented, satisfy, gratify, make one's day 826 *please*; meet with approval, go down well, go down a treat 923 *be praised*; make happy, bless with contentment; grant a boon 781 *give*; crown one's wishes, make one's dreams come true, leave no desire unfulfilled, quench one's thirst 863 *sate*; comfort 833 *cheer*; bring comfort to, speak peace to 831 *relieve*; be kind to 897 *philanthropize*; lull, set at ease, set at rest; propitiate, disarm, reconcile, conciliate, appease 719 *pacify*.

**Adv.** *contentedly*, complacently, with satisfaction, to one's heart's content, as one would wish.

## 829 Discontent

**N.** *discontent*, discontentment, disgruntlement, feel-bad factor; displeasure, pain, dissatisfaction, acute d. 924 *disapprobation*; cold comfort, not what one expected 509 *disappointment*; soreness, irritation, chagrin, pique, mortification, heart-burning, bitterness, bile, spleen 891 *resentment*; uneasiness, disquiet 825 *worry*; grief, vexation of spirit 825 *sorrow*; maladjustment, strain, stress, tension; restlessness, unrest, state of u., 'winter of discontent', restiveness 738 *disobedience*;

Now is the winter of our discontent
Made glorious summer by this sun of York.
William Shakespeare, *Richard III* ('Winter of discontent'
was used as a headline in the *Sun* to refer to 'the
long, cold months of industrial chaos' of the winter of
1978–79.)

agitation 318 *commotion*; finickiness, faddiness, fikiness, hypercriticism, perfectionism,

nit-picking 862 *fastidiousness*; querulousness 709 *quarrelsomeness*; ill will 912 *envy*; competition 911 *jealousy*; chip on one's shoulder, grievance, grudge, complaint 709 *quarrel*; weariness, world-w., Weltschmerz, melancholy, ennui 834 *dejection*; sulkiness, sulks, the hump, dirty look, grimace, scowl, frown 893 *sullenness*; groan, curse 899 *malediction*; cheep, squeak, murmur, murmuring, whispering campaign, smear c. 762 *deprecation*.

*malcontent*, grumbler, grouch, grouser, mutterer, sniper, croaker, complainer, whiner, bleater, bellyacher, Jonah 834 *moper*; plaintiff 763 *petitioner*; faultfinder, nit-picker, critic, censurer, envier 709 *quarreller*; person with a grievance, someone with a chip on their shoulder, angry young man; 'laudator temporis acti';

> Difficilis, querulus, laudator temporis acti
> Se puero, castigator censorque minorum.
> *(Tiresome, complaining, one who praises the time
> when he was a boy, a castigator and critic of the
> younger generation.)*
> Horace, *Ars Poetica*

dissident, dropout 738 *revolter*; murmurer, seditionist 738 *agitator*; indignation meeting, protest m., sit-in; the Opposition, Her Majesty's O., Government in Exile; conscientious objector; irreconcilable, bitter-ender, last-ditcher, diehard 705 *opponent*; hard taskmaster 735 *tyrant*.

**Adj.** *discontented*, displeased, not best pleased; dissatisfied 924 *disapproving*; unsatisfied, ungratified, frustrated 509 *disappointed*; defeated 728 *unsuccessful*; malcontent, dissident 489 *dissenting*; noncooperative, obstructive 702 *hindering*; restless, restive 738 *disobedient*; disgruntled, dischuffed, ill-content, weary, browned off, cheesed o., hacked off, gutted, fed up to the back teeth 838 *bored*, 825 *unhappy*; repining 830 *regretting*; sad, uncomforted, unconsoled, unrelieved, disconsolate 834 *dejected*; ill-disposed, grudging, jealous, envious; bileful, spleenful, bitter, embittered, soured 393 *sour*; peevish, testy, crabbed, crabbit, cross, sulky, sulking, pouting 893 *sullen*; grouchy, grumbling, grousing, whining, murmuring, swearing 899 *cursing*; protesting 762 *deprecatory*; unflattered, smarting, sore, mortified, insulted, affronted, piqued, vexed, miffed, put out, annoyed 891 *resentful*; fretful, querulous, petulant, complaining; difficult, hard to please, hard to satisfy, never satisfied, exigent, exacting 862 *fastidious*; fault-finding, critical, hypercritical, censorious 926 *detracting*; irreconcilable, hostile 881 *inimical*; resisting 704 *opposing*.

*discontenting*, unsatisfactory, unsatisfying

636 *insufficient*; sickening, nauseating 861 *disliked*; boring 838 *tedious*; displeasing, upsetting, mortifying 827 *annoying*; frustrating 509 *disappointing*; baffling, obstructive 702 *hindering*; discouraging, disheartening 613 *dissuasive*.

**Vb.** *be discontented*, – dissatisfied etc. adj.; be critical, crab, carp, criticize, give flak, find fault 862 *be fastidious*; lack, miss, feel something is missing 627 *require*; sneer, groan, jeer 924 *disapprove*; mind, take offence, take in bad part, take amiss, take ill, take to heart, take on, be offended, be miffed, smart under 891 *resent*; get out of bed the wrong side, get the hump, sulk 893 *be sullen*; look blue, look glum, make a wry face, pull a long f. 834 *be dejected*; moan, mutter, murmur, whine, whinge, winge, bleat, beef, protest, complain, object, cry blue murder 762 *deprecate*; bellyache, grumble, grouse, grouch, gripe, croak, snap; wail 836 *lament*; be aggrieved, have a grievance, cherish a g., nurse a grudge, have a chip on one's shoulder; join the opposition 704 *oppose*; rise up, be up in arms about 738 *revolt*; grudge 912 *envy*; quarrel with one's bread and butter 709 *quarrel*; not know when one is well off, look a gift horse in the mouth; make a meal of it 598 *be unwilling*; refuse to be satisfied, ask for one's money back, demand a refund, return 607 *reject*; repine 830 *regret*.

*cause discontent*, dissatisfy 636 *not suffice*; leave dissatisfied, leave room for complaint 509 *disappoint*; spoil for one, spoil one's pleasure, get one down 834 *depress*; dishearten, discourage 613 *dissuade*; sour, embitter, disgruntle, dischuff; upset, miff, chafe, fret, niggle, bite, put on edge, put out of humour, irritate 891 *huff*; put out of countenance, mortify 872 *humiliate*; offend, cause resentment 827 *displease*; shock, scandalize 924 *incur blame*; nauseate, sicken, disgust, gross out (US inf) 861 *cause dislike*; arouse discontent, sow the seeds of d., sow dragon's teeth, 'sow the wind' (see quotation at 915 *deserve*), make trouble, stir up t., mix it, agitate 738 *revolt*.

**Int.** *please!*

## 830 Regret

**N.** *regret*, regretfulness, regretting, repining; mortification, heart-burning 891 *resentment*; futile regret, vain r., harking back, crying over spilt milk; soul-searching, self-reproach, remorse, contrition, repentance, compunction, qualms, pangs of conscience, regrets, apologies 939 *penitence*; disillusion, second thoughts, better t. 67 *sequel*; longing, desiderium, homesickness, maladie du pays, nostalgia, 'nostalgie de la boue' (see quotation at 859 *desire*) 859 *desire*; sense of loss 737 *demand*; matter of regret, pity of it.

**Adj.** *regretting*, missing, homesick, nostalgic, wistful; harking back, looking over one's shoulder 125 *retrospective*; mortified, repining, bitter 891 *resentful*; irreconcilable, inconsolable 836 *lamenting*; compunctious, regretful, remorseful, rueful, conscience-stricken, sorry, full of regrets, apologetic, soul-searching, penitent, contrite 939 *repentant*; undeceived, disillusioned, sadder and wiser.

*regretted*, much r., sadly missed, badly wanted; regrettable, deplorable, much to be deplored, too bad, a shame, a crying s.

**Vb.** *regret*, rue, deplore, rue the day; curse one's folly, never forgive oneself, blame o., accuse o., reproach o., kick o., bite one's tongue; unwish, wish undone, repine, wring one's hands, cry over spilt milk, spend time in vain regrets 836 *lament*; want one's time over again, sigh for the good old days, fight one's battles over again, relive the past, reopen old wounds, hark back, evoke the past 505 *retrospect*; look back, look over one's shoulder; miss, sadly m., miss badly, regret the loss, want back; long for, pine for, hanker after, be homesick 859 *desire*; express regrets, apologize, feel compunction, be full of remorse, feel contrite, feel remorse, be sorry 939 *be penitent*; ask for another chance 905 *ask mercy*; deplore, deprecate, lament 924 *disapprove*; feel mortified, gnash one's teeth 891 *resent*; have cause for regret, have had one's lesson 963 *be punished*.

## 831 Relief

**N.** *relief*, welcome r., rest 685 *refreshment*; easing, alleviation, mitigation, palliation, abatement 177 *moderation*; good riddance; exemption 668 *deliverance*; solace, consolation, comfort, ray of c., crumb of c.; silver lining, break in the clouds 852 *hope*; load off one's mind, sigh of relief 656 *revival*; lulling, lullaby, cradle song, berceuse; soothing, salve 658 *balm*; painkiller, analgesic 375 *anaesthetic*; sedative, tranquillizer, sleeping pill 679 *soporific*; pillow 218 *cushion*; comforter, consoler, ray of sunshine.

**Adj.** *relieving*, soothing, smoothing, balsamic 685 *refreshing*; lulling, assuaging, painkilling, analgesic, anodyne 177 *alleviative*; curative, restorative 658 *remedial*; consoling, consolatory, comforting.

**Vb.** *relieve*, ease, soften, cushion; relax, lessen the strain; temper 177 *moderate*; lift, raise, take off, lighten, unburden, disburden, relieve the burden, take a load off one's mind 701 *disencumber*; spare, exempt from 919 *exempt*; save 668 *deliver*; console, dry the eyes, wipe the e., wipe away the tears, solace, comfort, bring c., offer a crumb of c., give hope; cheer up, buck up, encourage, hearten, pat on the back 833 *cheer*; shade, cool, fan, ventilate 685 *refresh*; restore, repair 656 *cure*; put a plaster on, bandage, bind up, apply a tourniquet, poultice, kiss it better 658 *doctor*; calm, soothe, nurse, pour balm, pour oil, palliate, mitigate, moderate, alleviate 177 *assuage*; smooth the brow, take out the wrinkles, iron out the difficulties 258 *smooth*; stroke, pat 889 *caress*; cradle, rock, lull, put to sleep 679 *sleep*; anaesthetize, kill the pain 375 *render insensible*; take pity on, put one out of one's misery, give the coup de grâce 905 *pity*.

*be relieved*, relieve oneself, ease o., obtain relief; feel relief, heave a sigh of r., draw a long breath, breathe again; console oneself, solace o.; take comfort, feel better, dry one's eyes, smile again 833 *be cheerful*; recover from the blow, get over it, come to, be oneself again, pick oneself up and dust oneself down, pull oneself together, regroup, snap out of it, buck up, perk up, sleep off 656 *be restored*; rest content 828 *be content*.

**Int.** thank God!, thank goodness!, thank heavens!, Heaven be praised!, Praise be!

## 832 Aggravation

**N.** *aggravation*, exacerbation, exasperation, irritation, embittering, embitterment; enhancement, augmentation 36 *increase*; intensification 162 *strengthening*; heightening, deepening, adding to 482 *overestimation*; making worse 655 *deterioration*; complication 700 *difficulty*; irritant 821 *excitant*.

**Adj.** *aggravated*, intensified; exacerbated, complicated; unrelieved, unmitigated, made worse, not improved 655 *deteriorated*; aggravable.

**Vb.** *aggravate*, intensify 162 *strengthen*; enhance, heighten, deepen; increase 36 *augment*; worsen, make worse, render w., make things w., disimprove, not improve matters 655 *deteriorate*, add insult to injury, rub salt in the wound, rub it in, rub one's nose in it, exacerbate, embitter, further embitter, sour, envenom, inflame 821 *excite*; exasperate, irritate 891 *enrage*; add fuel to the flame, fan the embers; complicate, make bad worse, escalate the war, go from bad to worse, jump from the frying pan into the fire.

**Adv.** *aggravatedly*, worse and worse, from bad to worse, out of the frying pan into the fire.

**Int.** so much the worse!, tant pis!

## 833 Cheerfulness

**N.** *cheerfulness*, alacrity 597 *willingness*; optimism, hopefulness 852 *hope*; cheeriness, happiness, blitheness 824 *joy*; geniality, sunniness, breeziness, smiles, good humour, bon naturel; vitality, spirits, animal s., high s., youthful h. s., joie de vivre 360 *life*; light-heartedness, sunshine in the soul, light heart, spring in one's step, optimistic outlook, carefree mind 828 *content*; liveliness, sparkle, vivacity, animation, elation, euphoria, exhilaration, elevation 822 *excitable state*; life and soul of the party, party spirit, conviviality 882 *sociability*; optimist, · perennial o., Pollyanna, Mr Micawber.

*merriment*, laughter and joy; cheer, good c.; exhilaration, high spirits, abandon, gay a.; jollity, joviality, jocularity, gaiety, glee, mirth, hilarity 835 *laughter*; levity, frivolity 499 *folly*; merry-making, fun, fun and games, sport, good s. 837 *amusement*; jubilation, jubilee 876 *celebration*.

**Adj.** *cheerful*, cheery, blithe, blithesome 824 *happy*; hearty, genial, convivial 882 *sociable*; sanguine, optimistic, pronoid, rose-coloured; smiling, sunny, bright, beaming, radiant 835 *laughing*; breezy, of good cheer, in high spirits, in good s., in a good humour; in good heart, unrepining, optimistic, upbeat, hopeful, buoyant, resilient, irrepressible; carefree, light-hearted, happy-go-lucky; debonair, bonny, buxom, bouncing; pert, jaunty, bright-eyed and bushy-tailed, perky, chirpy, chipper, spry, spirited, peppy, sprightly, vivacious, animated, vital, sparkling, all lit up, full of beans, full of pep, on the top of one's form 819 *lively*; alacritous 597 *willing*.

*merry*, joyous, joyful, merry as a cricket, happy as a sandboy, happy as a king, gay as a lark, happy as the day is long, happy as Larry; ebullient, effervescent, bubbly, sparkling, mirth-loving, laughter-l., waggish, jocular 839 *witty*; gay, light, frivolous 456 *light-minded*; playful, sportive, frisky, gamesome, frolicsome, kittenish 837 *amusing*; roguish, arch, sly, tricksy, full of tricks; merry-making, mirthful, jocund, jovial, jolly, joking, dancing, laughing, singing, drinking, Anacreontic; wild, rackety, rowdy, shouting, roaring with laughter, hilarious, uproarious, rip-roaring, rollicking, rattling, splitting one's sides, helpless with laughter, tickled pink 837 *amused*.

*jubilant*, jubilating, overjoyed, gleeful, gleesome, delighted 824 *pleased*; chuffed, elated, euphoric, flushed, exulting, exultant, triumphant, cock-a-hoop, dancing on air 727 *successful*; triumphing, celebrating, riotous, rioting 876 *celebratory*.

*cheering*, exhilarating, enlivening, encouraging etc. vb.; warming, heart-w., raising the spirits, exhilarating, animating, intoxicating 821 *exciting*; optimistic, tonic, uplifting, comforting, like a ray of sunshine, just what the doctor ordered; balmy, palmy, bracing, invigorating 652 *salubrious*.

**Vb.** *be cheerful*, be in good spirits, be in good humour, be in a good mood, be in good heart; keep cheerful, look on the bright side, keep one's spirits up 852 *hope*; keep one's pecker up, grin and bear it, make the best of it, put a good face upon it 599 *be resolute*; take heart, snap out of it, cheer up, perk up, buck up 831 *be relieved*; brighten, liven up, grow animated, let oneself go, let one's hair down, abandon oneself, drive dull care away; radiate good humour, smile, grin from ear to ear, beam, sparkle; dance, sing, carol, lilt, chirrup, chirp, whistle, laugh 835 *rejoice*; whoop, cheer 876 *celebrate*; have fun, frisk, frolic, rollick, romp, gambol, sport, disport oneself, enjoy o., have a good time, large it (inf) 837 *amuse oneself*; throw a party, make whoopee 882 *be sociable*.

*cheer*, gladden, warm, warm the heart, warm the cockles of the h. 828 *content*; comfort, console 831 *relieve*; rejoice the heart, put in a good humour 826 *please*; inspire, enliven 821 *animate*; exhilarate, elate 826 *delight*; encourage, inspirit, uplift, hearten, raise the spirits, buck up, perk up, jolly along, bolster, bolster up 855 *give courage*; act like a tonic, put new life into, energize 174 *invigorate*.

**Adv.** *cheerfully*, willingly, joyfully, gladly, gaily, joyously, light-heartedly, optimistically, without a care in the world; airily, breezily; allegro, con brio.

## 834 Dejection. Seriousness

**N.** *dejection*, joylessness, unhappiness, cheerlessness, dreariness, dejectedness, low spirits, blues, dumps, doldrums; droopiness, spiritlessness, dispiritedness, low spirits, feel-bad factor, sinking heart; disillusion 509 *disappointment*; defeatism, pessimism, cynicism, depression, despair, death wish, suicidal tendency 853 *hopelessness*; weariness, oppression, enervation, exhaustion 684 *fatigue*; oppression of spirit, heartache, heaviness, sadness, misery, wretchedness, disconsolateness, dolefulness 825 *sorrow*; despondency, prostration, languishment; 'the Slough of Despond' (see quotation at 731 *adversity*), grey dawn; gloominess, gloom, settled g.; glumness, dejected look, long face, face as long as a fiddle; haggardness, funereal aspect, downcast countenance, lacklustre eye; cause of dejection, sorry sight, memento mori, depressant 838 *bore*; gloom and doom, care, thought, trouble 825 *worry*.

*melancholy*, melancholia, depression, clinical d., endogenous d., exogenous d., SAD, seasonal affective disorder, cafard, black mood, blue devils, blues, horrors, mopes, moping, mopishness, sighing, sigh; dismals, vapours, megrims, spleen, bile 829 *discontent*; disgust of life, weariness of l., world-weariness, taedium vitae, Weltschmerz, angst, mal du siècle, nostalgia, homesickness 825 *suffering*.

*seriousness*, earnestness; gravity, solemnity, sobriety, demureness, staidness, grimness 893 *sullenness*; primness, humourlessness, heaviness, dullness; straight face, poker f., dead pan; sternness, heavy stuff; earnest, dead e.; no laughing matter, no cause for mirth, chastening thought.

*moper*, croaker, complainer, Jonah 829 *malcontent*; sourpuss, crosspatch, bear with a sore head, grouch; pessimist, damper, wet blanket, killjoy, spoilsport; Job's comforter; sad-sack, misery, sobersides, sourpuss; death's-head, skeleton at the feast, gloom and doom merchant, prophet of doom, doomwatcher, doomster, ecodoomster; hypochondriac, 'malade imaginaire', cyberchondriac;

> **Le Malade Imaginaire**
> *(The Hypochondriac)*
> Title of a play by Molière

seek-sorrow, self-tormentor.

**Adj.** *dejected*, joyless, dreary, dreich (Scots), cheerless, unhappy, sad (see also *melancholic*); gloomy, despondent, desponding, downbeat, unhopeful, pessimistic, defeatist, despairing 853 *hopeless*; beaten, overcome 728 *defeated*; discouraged, disheartened, dismayed; dispirited, unnerved, unmanned 854 *nervous*; troubled, worried 825 *suffering*; downcast, downhearted, droopy, low, down, down in the mouth, low-spirited, depressed; out of sorts, not oneself, out of spirits; sluggish, listless, spiritless, lackadaisical 679 *inactive*; lacklustre 419 *dim*; out of countenance, discountenanced, humbled, crushed, prostrate, chap-fallen, chop-f., crestfallen, ready to cry 509 *disappointed*; browned off, cheesed off, pissed off, hacked off, gutted, sick as a parrot 829 *discontented*; down in the dumps, in the doldrums, in low water, out of luck 731 *unprosperous*; chastened, sobered, sadder and wiser 830 *regretting*; vexed, chagrined, peeved, miffed, mortified, cut up; subdued, piano; cynical, disillusioned 509 *disappointed*.

*melancholic*, atrabilious, vapourish, hypochondriacal; blue, feeling blue, down in the dumps; jaundiced, sour, hipped, hippish; thoughtful, preoccupied, pensive, penseroso, full of thought, deep in t.; melancholy, sad, triste; saddened, cut up, heavy, heavy-hearted, full of heaviness, sick at heart, heart-sick, soul-s. 825 *unhappy*; sorry, rueful 830 *regretting*; mournful, doleful, woeful, tearful, lachrymose 836 *lamenting*; uncheerful, cheerless, joyless, dreary, comfortless; forlorn, miserable, broken up, wretched, unrelieved, refusing comfort, disconsolate; sorry for oneself, self-pitying, wallowing in self-pity; moody, sulky, sulking 893 *sullen*; mopish, dull, dismal, gloomy, morose, glum, sunk in gloom; long-faced, long in the face, down in the mouth, woebegone; wan, haggard, care-worn.

*serious*, sober, sober as a judge, sober-sided, solemn, sedate, stolid, staid, demure, muted, grave, stern, Puritanical 735 *severe*; sour, dour, Puritan, grim, grim-visaged, dark, frowning, wrinkle-browed, scowling, forbidding, saturnine 893 *sullen*; unlaughing, unsmiling; inscrutable, straight-faced, po-f., poker-f., deadpan; prim, unlively, humourless; unfunny, unwitty, without a laugh in it, heavy, heavy-going, dull, solid 838 *tedious*; chastening, sobering.

*cheerless*, comfortless, uncomforting, unconsoling; uncongenial, uninviting, unwelcoming; depressing, unrelieved, dreary, dreich (Scots), dull, flat 838 *tedious*; dismal, lugubrious, funereal, gloomy, dark, forbidding; drab, grey, sombre, sombrous, overcast, clouded, murky, louring; ungenial, cold.

**Vb.** *be dejected*, despond, become despondent, lose heart, admit defeat 853 *despair*; succumb, lie down 728 *be defeated*; languish, sink, droop, sag, wilt, flag, give up 684 *be fatigued*; look downcast, look down in the mouth, look blue, hang the head, pull a long face, laugh on the wrong side of one's mouth; mope, brood 449 *think*; lay to heart, take to h., sulk 893 *be sullen*; eat one's heart out, yearn, long 859 *desire*; sigh, grieve 829 *be discontented*; groan 825 *suffer*; weep 836 *lament*; repine 830 *regret*.

*be serious*, not smile, repress a s.; not laugh, keep a straight face, keep one's countenance, maintain one's gravity, recover one's g., sober up; look grave, look glum; lack sparkle, lack humour, not see the joke, have no sense of humour, take oneself seriously, be a bore 838 *be tedious*; sober, chasten.

*sadden*, grieve, grieve to the heart, bring grief, bring sorrow; turn one's hair grey, break one's heart, pluck at one's heartstrings, make one's heart bleed; draw tears, bring tears to one's eyes, bring t. to a glass eye, touch the heart, melt the h., leave not a dry eye 821 *impress*; annoy, pain, spoil one's pleasure 829 *cause discontent*; deny comfort, render disconsolate, drive to despair 853 *leave no hope*; crush, overcome, overwhelm, prostrate; orphan, bereave 786 *deprive*.

*depress*, deject, get one down; cause alarm and despondency, dismay, dishearten, discourage, dispirit, take the heart out of, unman, unnerve 854 *frighten*; spoil the fun, take the joy out of, cast a shadow, cast a gloom over 418 *darken*; damp, dampen, damp the spirits, put a damper on, be a wet blanket, throw cold water, frown upon 613 *dissuade*; dash one's hopes 509 *disappoint*; dull the spirits, prey on the mind, weigh heavy on one's heart, oppress the breast; make the heart sick, disgust 827 *displease*; strain, weary 684 *fatigue*; bore 838 *be tedious*; chasten, sober 534 *teach*.

**Adv.** *dejectedly*, disconsolately, dolefully, forlornly, gloomily, glumly, miserably, sadly, with a long face, like the last turkey in the shop.

## 835 Rejoicing

**N.** *rejoicing*, manifestation of joy 837 *festivity*; jubilation, jubilee, triumph, exultation 876 *celebration*; congratulations, felicitation, pat on the back, self-congratulation, mutual c. 886 *congratulation*; plaudits, clapping, shout, yell 923 *applause*; cheers, rousing c., three c., huzza, hurrah, high-five, hosanna, hallelujah 923 *praise*; thanksgiving 907 *thanks*; paean, psalm, Te Deum 981 *hymn*; raptures, elation, euphoria 824 *joy*; revelling, revels 837 *revel*; merrymaking, abandon, gay a., abandonment 833 *merriment*.

*laughter*, faculty of l., risibility; loud laughter, hearty l., rollicking l., Homeric l.; roar of laughter, shout of l., burst of l., peal of l., shrieks of l., hoots of l., gales of l., immoderate l., cachinnation; mocking laughter, derision 851 *ridicule*; laugh, belly l., horse l., guffaw, fou rire; chuckle, throaty c., chortle, gurgle, cackle, crow, coo; giggle, snigger, snicker, titter, tee-hee; fit of laughing, the giggles; forced laugh; smile, sweet s., simper, smirk, grin, broad g., sardonic g., grin from ear to ear, Cheshire cat grin; inclination to laughter, twinkle, half-smile; humour, sense of h. 839 *wit*; laughableness, laughing matter, comedy, farce 497 *absurdity*.

*laugher*, chuckler, smiler, grinner, smirker etc. vb.; Cheshire cat; mocker, derider 926 *detractor*; rejoicer, rollicker 837 *reveller*; god of ridicule, Momus; comic muse, Thalia.

**Adj.** *rejoicing*, revelling, rollicking, cheering, shouting, yelling etc. vb.; exultant, flushed, elated, euphoric 833 *jubilant*; lyrical, ecstatic 923 *approving*.

*laughing*, guffawing etc. vb.; splitting one's sides, laughing one's head off, creased, doubled up, convulsed with laughter, dying with l., shrieking with mirth, rolling in the aisles; humorous; mocking 851 *derisive*; laughable, risible, derisory 849 *ridiculous*; comic, comical, funny, farcical 497 *absurd*.

**Vb.** *rejoice*, be joyful, sing for joy, shout for j., leap for j., jump for j., dance for j., dance, skip 312 *leap*; clap, clap one's hands, throw one's cap in the air, whoop, cheer, slap high-fives, slap fives, huzza, hurrah 923 *applaud*; shout, yell oneself hoarse 408 *vociferate*; carol 413 *sing*; sing paeans, shout hosannahs, sound the trumpet 923 *praise*; exult, crow, jubilate 876 *celebrate*; felicitate 886 *congratulate*; bless, give thanks, thank one's lucky stars 907 *thank*; abandon oneself, let oneself go, loosen up, let one's hair down, paint the town red, riot, go mad for joy, dance in the streets, maffick 61 *rampage*; make merry 833 *be cheerful*; have a good time, frolic, frisk, rollick 837 *revel*; have a party, celebrate 882 *be sociable*; feel pleased, congratulate oneself, hug o., give oneself a pat on the back, rub one's hands, smack one's lips, gloat 824 *be pleased*; purr, coo, gurgle; sigh for pleasure, cry for joy.

*laugh*, laugh outright, start laughing, burst out l., crack up, break up, get the giggles, get a fit of the g., bubble with laughter; hoot, chuckle, chortle, crow, cackle; giggle, snigger, snicker, titter, tee-hee, ha-ha, haw-haw; make merry over, laugh at, laugh in one's sleeve *or* one's beard, mock, deride 851 *ridicule*; laugh loudly, cachinnate; shake, fall about, roll around, hold one's sides, split one's s., be in stitches, burst with laughter, split with l., double up, rock with l., roll with l., shriek with l., hoot with l., roar with l., choke with l., die with l., kill oneself laughing, laugh fit to burst, laugh one's head off.

*smile*, break into a s., grin, show one's teeth; grimace, curl one's lips, grin from ear to ear, grin like a Cheshire cat; give a half-smile, smirk, simper; twinkle, beam, flash a smile.

**Int.** cheers!, three c.!, hooray!, hurrah!, huzza!, hosannah!, hallelujah!, glory be!, hail the conquering hero!, vive –!, viva –!, vivat –!, long live –!

## 836 Lamentation

**N.** *lamentation*, lamenting, ululation, wail, wail of woe, groaning, weeping, wailing, keening; plangency, weeping and wailing, weeping and gnashing of teeth, beating the breast, tearing one's hair, wringing one's hands; mourning, deep m. 364 *obsequies*; rending one's garments, sackcloth and ashes; widow's weeds, weepers, crepe, black; cypress, willow; Wailing Wall; crying, sobbing, sighing, blubbering, whimpering, whining, greeting, grizzling, snivelling etc. vb.; tears, tearfulness, dolefulness 834 *dejec-*

*tion*; tenderness, melting mood, starting tears, tears of pity 905 *pity*; wet eyes, red e., swollen e.; eyes swimming *or* brimming with tears; falling tears, fit of t., flood of t., burst of t.; breakdown, hysterics; cry, good c.; tear, teardrop; heaving breast, sob, sigh, groan, moan, whimper, whine, grizzle, bawl, boo-hoo.

*lament*, plaint, complaint, jeremiad, dirge, knell, requiem, threnody, elegy, epicedium, death song, swansong, funeral oration 364 *obsequies*; keen, coronach, wake 905 *condolence*; howl, shriek, scream, outcry 409 *ululation*; tears of grief, tears of rage; sobstuff, sob-story, hard-luck s., tale of woe; cri de coeur, 'de profundis';

> **De profundis clamavi ad te, Domine.**
> *(Out of the depths have I cried unto thee, O Lord.)*
> Bible (Vulgate), Psalms

show of grief, crocodile tears 542 *sham*.

*weeper*, wailer, keener, lamenter, threnodist, elegist; banshee; mourner, professional m., mute 364 *funeral*; sobber, sigher, grizzler, sniveller, whimperer, whiner, blubberer, crybaby; complainer, grouser 829 *malcontent*; Jeremiah, Niobe; dying duck, dying swan.

**Adj.** *lamenting*, crying etc. vb.; lachrymatory, tear-shedding, tear-dropping; in tears, bathed in t., dissolved in t.; tearful, lachrymose; wet-eyed, red-e., with moist eyes; close to tears, on the verge of t., ready to cry; mourning, mournful, doleful, lugubrious 825 *unhappy*; woeful, woebegone, haggard, wild-eyed, wringing one's hands, beating one's breast 834 *dejected*; complaining, plangent, plaintive, singing the blues; elegiac, epecedial, threnodic, threnodial, dirgelike 364 *funereal*; condoling, in mourning, in black, in widow's weeds, in funeral garments, in sackcloth and ashes; half-masted, at half-mast; whining, fretful, querulous, with a hard-luck story, with a tale of woe; pathetic, pitiful, lamentable, fit for tears, tear-jerking 905 *pitiable*; lamented, deplorable 830 *regretted*.

**Vb.** *lament*, grieve, sorrow, sigh, heave a s. 825 *suffer*; deplore 830 *regret*; condole, commiserate 905 *pity*; grieve for, sigh for, weep over, cry o., bewail, bemoan, elegize, threnodize; bury with lamentation, sing the dirge, sing a requiem, toll the knell 364 *inter*; mourn, wail, weep and wail, keen; express grief, put on black, go into mourning, wear m., wear the willow, put on sackcloth and ashes, wring one's hands, beat the breast, tear one's hair, roll in the dust; take on, carry on, take it badly; complain, beef, bellyache, grouse, tell one's tale of woe 829 *be discontented*.

*weep*, wail, greet, pipe one's eye; shed tears, drop t., burst into t., melt in t., dissolve in t.;

hold back one's tears, be ready to cry; give way to tears, break down, cry, cry like a child, cry like a baby, boo-hoo, bawl, cry one's eyes out; howl, cry out, squall, yell, yammer, clamour, scream, shriek 409 *ululate*; sob, sigh, moan, groan 825 *suffer*; snivel, grizzle, blubber, pule, mewl, whine, whinge, whimper; get ready to cry, be on the verge of tears, weep without cause, cry for nothing, cry out before one is hurt.

**Adv.** *tearfully*, painfully, 'de profundis' (see quotation above).

## 837 Amusement

**N.** *amusement*, pleasure, interest, delight 826 *pleasurableness*; diversion, divertissement, entertainment, light e., popular e.; infotainment, edutainment; dramatic entertainment, happening 594 *drama*; radio, television 531 *broadcasting*; video, video game; pop music, personal stereo, ghetto blaster; karaoke; pastime, hobby, labour of love 597 *voluntary work*; solace, recreation 685 *refreshment*; relaxation 683 *repose*; holiday, Bank h. 681 *leisure*; April Fool's Day, rag day, gala day, red-letter d. 876 *special day*; play, sport, fun, good clean f., high jinks, good cheer, jollity, joviality, jocundity 833 *merriment*; occasion, do, show, junket, Gaudy night 876 *celebration*; outing, excursion, jaunt, day out, pleasure trip; treat, Sunday school t., wayzgoose, fête champêtre, picnic (see also *festivity*); social gathering, get-together, at-home, conversazione, garden party, bunfight, fête, flower show, gymkhana, jamboree 74 *assembly*; game, game of chance, game of skill; whist drive, bridge party (see also *card game*); round games, party g. (see also *indoor game*).

*festivity*, playtime, holiday-making, holidaying, vacationing; visiting 882 *social round*; fun 835 *laughter*; 'beer and skittles' (see quotation at 824 *enjoyment*) 824 *enjoyment*; social whirl, round of pleasure, round of gaiety; seeing life, high life, night l.; good time; living it up, painting the town red, burning the candle at both ends, a short life and a merry one 943 *intemperance*; festival, high f., fair, funfair, fun of the fair, kermesse, carnival, fiesta, Jahrmarkt, mi-carême, gala; masque, mummery; festivities, fun and games, merry-making, revels, Saturnalia, Mardi Gras 833 *merriment*; high day, feast d., May D., Derby D., Ascot 876 *special day*; carousal, wassail, wake 301 *feasting*; conviviality, house-warming, party, Dutch p., bottle p., byob (= bring your own bottle *or* booze) p. 882 *social gathering*; drinking party, drinking bout, bender, booze-up (inf) 301 *drinking*; orgy, carouse 949

*drunkenness*; bust, binge, beano, thrash, blowout; barbecue, ox-roasting, clambake (US), bump supper, harvest s., beanfeast, bunfight, dinner, annual d., banquet 301 *meal*.

*revel*, rout, rave-up, knees-up, jollification, whoopee, fun, great f., high old time; fun fast and furious, high jinks, spree, junket, junketing, horseplay; night out, night on the tiles; bonfire, pyrotechnics, Fifth of November 420 *fireworks*; play, game, romp, rollick, frolic, lark, skylarking, escapade, antic, prank, rag, trick, monkey t. 497 *foolery*.

*pleasure ground*, park, theme p., adventure p., deer p., wildlife p., safari p., national p., chase, grouse moor; green, village g., common; arbour, gardens, pleasure g., winter g. 192 *pleasance*; seaside, Riviera, lido, marina, bathing beach, holiday camp; playground, adventure p., recreation ground, playing field, links, golf course; rink, skating r., ice r.; tennis court, petanque c., bowling green, croquet lawn 724 *arena*; circus, fair, swing, swingboats, roundabout, merry-go-round, carousel, scenic railway, switchback, big wheel, big dipper, tunnel of love, ghost train; dodgems; seesaw, slide, helter-skelter.

*place of amusement*, fairground, funfair, amusement park, shooting gallery, amusement arcade; skittle alley, bowling a., covered court, billiard room, pool r., assembly r., pump r.; concert hall, music h., vaudeville, hippodrome; picture house, movie theatre 445 *cinema*; playhouse 594 *theatre*; ballroom, dance floor; dance hall, palais de danse, discothèque, disco; cabaret, night club, near beer c., strip joint, clip j.; bingo hall, casino, kursaal 618 *gaming-house*.

*sport*, outdoor life; sportsmanship, gamesmanship 694 *skill*; sports, field s., track events; games, gymnastics 162 *athletics*, 312 *leap*, 716 *contest, racing, pugilism, wrestling*; weight-lifting, weight-training, pumping iron, going for the burn; outdoor sports, cycling, hiking, rambling, orienteering, canyoning; camping, picnicking; running, jogging, trail-running, racewalking, speed-walking, marathon; riding, ponytrekking; archery, shooting, clay-pigeon s.; hunting shooting and fishing, paintball 619 *chase*; frisbee, ultimate frisbee, disc golf; water sports, swimming, bathing, surf-riding, surfing, body-s., wind-s., boardsailing; skin diving, subaqua, water skiing, aquaplaning, boating, rowing, rafting, yachting, sailing 269 *aquatics*; rock-climbing, mountaineering, Alpinism 308 *ascent*; exploring, caving, speleology, pot-holing 309 *descent*; winter sports, skiing, heli-skiing, snowboarding, Langlauf, ski-jumping, bobsleighing, tobogganning, luging, skeleton-bob, skating, ice s., ice hockey; curling; flying, microlighting, gliding, hang-g., paragliding, parasailing, parascending 271 *aeronautics*; extreme sports, base jumping, bungee-jumping, skydiving, whitewater rafting; tourism, touring, travelling, exploration 267 *land travel*; mind sports.

*ball game*, pat-ball, bat and ball game; King Willow, cricket, French c.; baseball, softball, rounders; tennis, lawn t., real t., table t., ping-pong; badminton, battledore and shuttlecock; squash, rackets; handball, volleyball, beach v.; fives, pelota; netball, basketball; football, Association f., soccer, fantasy football; rugby, Rugby football, R. Union, R. League, rugger, Australian Rules f.; lacrosse, hockey, ice h.; polo, water polo; croquet, putting, golf, clock g., crazy g.; skittles, ninepins, bowls, pet-anque, boule, curling; marbles, dibs; quoits, deck q., hoop-la; billiards, snooker, pool; baga-telle, pinball, bar billiards, shove ha'penny, shovelboard.

*indoor game*, nursery g., parlour g., panel g., round g., party g.; musical bumps, musical chairs, hunt the thimble, hunt the slipper, pass the parcel, postman's knock, kiss in the ring, oranges and lemons, nuts in May; sardines, rab-bits, murder; forfeits, guessing game; quiz, twenty questions; charades, dumb c., crambo, dumb c., parson's *or* minister's cat, I-spy; word game, spelling bee, riddles, crosswords, acros-tics, pangrams; paper game, consequences, noughts and crosses, ticktacktoe, battleships, boxes, hangman; darts, dominoes, mah-jong, tiddlywinks, jigsaw puzzle; computer game, video g.

*board game*, chess, three-dimensional c.; draughts, checkers, Chinese c., halma, fox and geese; backgammon; Scrabble (tdmk), ludo, snakes and ladders, crown and anchor, mah-jong, Monopoly (tdmk), Cluedo (tdmk), Trivial Pursuit (tdmk), go.

*children's games*, skipping, swinging, jumping, ring-a-ring-o'-roses; leapfrog, hop-scotch, peever 312 *leap*; touch, tag, tig, he, chain he, hide-and-seek, follow-my-leader, Simon says, blind man's buff, hares and hounds, cowboys and Indians, cops and rob-bers, prisoner's base, Tom Tiddler's ground.

*card game*, cards, game of cards, rubber of whist, rubber of bridge; boston, whist, solo w., auction w., German w., auction bridge, con-tract b.; nap, napoleon; skat; euchre, écarté, loo, picquet, cribbage, quadrille, bezique, pin-ochle; rummy, gin r., canasta, hearts, black Maria, casino, Newmarket, speculation, spite and malice, chase the ace, cheat; solo, solitaire, patience; snap, beggar-my-neighbour, draw-the-well-dry, old maid, racing demon, slap-jack, Happy Families, pelmanism; lotto, housey-housey, bingo; vingt-et-un, pontoon, black jack; brag, poker, strip p., stud p., seven-card stud p.; banker, baccarat, faro, fantan, chemin de fer, chemmy; monte, three-card m. (See also *gambling game*.)

*gambling game*, dice g., craps, dice, dicing; roulette, rouge et noir; coin-spinning, heads and tails, raffle, tombola, sweepstake, lottery, National Lottery, scratch card, football pool 618 *gambling*.

*dancing*, dance, ball, nautch; bal masqué, masquerade; bal costumé, fancy dress dance; thé dansant, tea dance, ceilidh, square dance, hoe-down; hop, jam session, disco, rave; disco dancing, breakdancing, body-popping; rock 'n' roll, slam dancing; ballet dancing, classical d. 594 *ballet*; tap dancing, clog d., folk d., country d., Scottish c. d., Highland d., Irish d., morris d., old-time d., sequence d.; ballroom d., line d., lap dancing, table d. ; chor-eography; eurhythmics, aerobics, step; muse of dancing, Terpsichore.

*dance*, war dance, sword d., corroboree; shuffle, soft-shoe s., cakewalk; solo dance, pas seul; clog dance, step d., tap d., toe d.; fan dance, dance of the seven veils, hula-hula; high kicks, cancan; belly dance, danse du ventre; gipsy dance, flamenco; country dance, morris d., barn d., square d., contredanse, hay; sailor's dance, hornpipe, keel row; folk dance, Russian d., Cossack d., polonaise, mazurka, czardas; jig, Irish j., Walls of Limerick, Waves of Torres; fling, Highland f.; reel, Virginia r., Scottish r., eightsome, foursome, strathspey, Gay Gordons, Petronella, Duke of Perth, Strip the Willow, Dashing White Sergeant, Sir Roger de Coverley; rigadoon, tarantella, bolero, fan-dango, farandole, galliard, écossaise, gavotte, quadrille, cotillion, minuet, pavane, saraband, allemande, galop, schottische, polka; valse, waltz, last w., Viennese w., hesitation w., St Ber-nard; valeta, Lancers; foxtrot, turkey trot, quickstep; Charleston, black bottom, blues, one-step, two-s., Boston t-s., military t-s.; bossa nova, beguine, cerok, cha-cha, habanera, lam-bada, macarena, mambo, paso-doble, rumba, salsa, samba, tango; conga, conga line; mosh, boomps-a-daisy, hokey-cokey, Lambeth Walk, Palais Glide; stomp, bop, bebop, shimmy, jive, Lindy-hopping, twist; excuse-me dance, Paul Jones, snowball; line-dancing; lap-dancing, table-dancing; dancer, tap d., clog d., ballet d., ballerina, corps de ballet 594 *actor*; high-kicker, cancan dancer, gogo d. 594 *entertainer*; waltzer, foxtrotter, shuffler, hoofer, jiver, jitterbug, bebopper, disco dancer 312 *jumper*.

*plaything*, bauble, knick-knack, souvenir, trinket, toy 639 *bauble*; children's toy, rattle, bricks, building b., Meccano (tdmk), Lego (tdmk); Jack-in-the-box, teddy bear, puppet, golliwog, doll, china d., rag d., Barbie (tdmk), Sindy (tdmk) d., Furby (tdmk), Action Man (tdmk), Power Ranger (tdmk), Teletubbies (tdmk); doll's house, doll's pram; Wendy house, bouncy castle; top, whipping t., tee-totum, yo-yo, diabolo; jacks, fivestones, marbles; ball, balloon 252 *sphere*; hoop, Hula-Hoop (tdmk), skipping rope, stilts, pogo stick, rocking horse, hobby h., bicycle, tricycle; scooter, microscooter; roller skates, Roller Blades (tdmk), blades (inf) skateboard, surf-board, snowboard; popgun, airgun, water pistol; toy soldier, tin s., lead s.; model, model yacht, model aeroplane, clockwork train, model railway; magic lantern, peep show, toy theatre 522 *exhibit*; puppet show, marionettes, Punch and Judy 551 *image*; pintable, billiard table; card, cards, pack, stack, deck; domino, tile; draught, counter, chip; tiddlywink; chess piece, pawn, knight, bishop, castle *or* rook, queen, king.

*player*, sportsman *or* -woman, sportsperson, sporting man *or* woman; competitor, comper (inf), pot-hunter 716 *contender*; gamesplayer, all-rounder; ball-player, footballer, forward, striker, winger, defence, libero, playmaker, sweeper, goalkeeper; cricketer, batsman, fielder, wicket-keeper, bowler; hockey-player, tennis-p.; marksman, archer 287 *shooter*; shot-putter 287 *thrower*; dicer, gamester 618 *gambler*; card-player, chess-p., chess tiger, chess rabbit; fellow sportsman *or* -woman, playmate 707 *colleague*.

*reveller*, merry-maker, rioter, roisterer, gam-boller, rollicker, frolicker; sky-larker, ragger; drinker, drunk 949 *drunkard*; feaster, diner-out 301 *eater*; party-goer 882 *sociable person*; plea-sure-seeker, thrill-s.; playboy, good-time girl; debauchee 952 *libertine*; holidaymaker, excur-sionist, day-tripper, tourist, rubber-necker 268 *traveller*; football supporter, pop fan; Lord of Misrule, master of the revels, master of cere-monies, MC, toastmaster *or* -mistress; symposi-arch, arbiter elegantiarum, 'elegantiae arbiter'.

> **Inter paucos familiarium Neroni adsumptus est, elegantiae arbiter.**
> (*He [Petronius] was chosen to be one of Nero's closest companions, as his authority on good taste and style.*)
> Tacitus, *Annals*

**Adj.** *amusing*, entertaining, diverting etc. vb.; fun-making, sportive, full of fun 833 *merry*; set-ting out to please, pleasant 826 *pleasurable*; laughable, ridiculous, clownish 849 *funny*; rec-reative, recreational 685 *refreshing*; festal, fes-tive, holiday.

*amused*, entertained, tickled 824 *pleased*; having fun, festive, sportive, rompish, rol-licking, roisterous, prankish, playful, kittenish, roguish, waggish, jolly, jovial; out to enjoy one-self, in festal mood, in festive m., in holiday spirit 835 *rejoicing*; horsy, sporty, sporting, gamesome, games-playing 162 *athletic*; dis-porting, playing, at play; working for pleasure, enjoying one's leisure time, following one's hobby; entertainable, easy to please, ready to be amused.

**Vb.** *amuse*, interest, entertain, beguile, divert, tickle, make one laugh, take one out of oneself; tickle the fancy, titillate, please 826 *delight*; recreate 685 *refresh*; solace, enliven 833 *cheer*; treat, regale, take out, take for an outing; raise a smile, wake laughter, stir l., convulse with l., set the table in a roar, have them rolling in the aisles, wow, slay, be the death of 849 *be ridiculous*; humour, keep amused, put in a good humour, put in a cheerful mood; give a party, have a get-together, play the host *or* hostess 882 *be hospitable*; be a sport, be a good s., be great fun.

*amuse oneself*, kill time, while away the t., pass the t. 681 *have leisure*; relax, hang out; pursue one's hobby, dabble in; play, play at, have fun, enjoy oneself, drown care, get one's jollies (inf), large it (inf) 833 *be cheerful*; make holiday, take a h., have a break, go on vaca-tion, go a-Maying, have an outing, have a field day, have a ball; sport, disport oneself; take one's pleasure, dally, toy, wanton; frisk, frolic, rollick, romp, gambol, caper; cut capers, play tricks, play pranks, lark around, skylark, fool about, play the fool 497 *be absurd*; jest, jape 839 *be witty*; play cards, take a hand; game, dice 618 *gamble*; play games, be devoted to sport, be a fitness freak; live the outdoor life, camp, caravan, take a holiday home, timeshare; picnic; sail, yacht, surf, windsurf, sailboard, fly; hunt, shoot, fish; play golf; ride, trek, hike, ramble; run, jog, race, jump; bathe, swim, dive; skate, roller-skate, ski, snowboard, toboggan; work out, pump iron.

*dance*, join the dance, go dancing; tap-dance, waltz, foxtrot, quickstep, Charleston, tango, rumba, jive, jitterbug, stomp, bop, twist, rock 'n' roll, disco-dance, breakdance, bodypop (see also *dance* vb); whirl 315 *rotate*; cavort, caper, jig about, bob up and down; shuffle, hoof, trip, tread a measure, trip the light fantastic 312 *leap*.

*revel*, make merry, make whoopee, have a ball, celebrate 835 *rejoice*; drive dull care away, make it a party, have a good time; let oneself go, let one's hair down, let off steam; go on the razzle, go on a bender, go on a spree, have a night out, have a night on the tiles, live it up, paint the town red; junket, roister, drown care; feast, banquet, quaff, carouse, wassail, make the rafters ring; go on a binge, go pub-crawling 301 *drink*; drown one's sorrows 949 *get drunk*; sow one's wild oats, burn the candle at both ends; stay up till all hours, never go home till morning, go home with the cows.

**Int.** carpe diem!, eat, drink and be merry!, on with the dance!, vogue la galère!, gaudeamus igitur!

## 838 Tedium

**N.** *tedium*, ennui, taedium vitae, world-weariness, Weltschmerz 834 *melancholy*; lack of interest, uninterest 860 *indifference*; weariness, languor 684 *fatigue*; wearisomeness, tediousness, irksomeness; dryness, stodginess, heaviness; too much of a good thing 863 *satiety*; disgust, loathing, nausea 861 *dislike*; flatness, staleness 387 *insipidity*; stuffiness 840 *dullness*; longueurs, prolixity 570 *diffuseness*; sameness 16 *uniformity*; monotony, dull m. 106 *repetition*; leaden hours, time to kill 679 *inactivity*; thumb-twiddling, devil's tattoo.

*bore*, utter b., no fun; boring thing, déjà vu; irk, drag, bind, chore; dull work, boring w.; beaten track, daily round, rut 610 *habit*; grindstone, treadmill 682 *labour*; boring person, bromide, anorak, train-spotter, saddo (sl) dweeb (sl), fart (offensive), geek (sl), pain in the neck, dryasdust, proser, buttonholer, pub bore; drip, wet blanket, killjoy, misery 834 *moper*; frump, Mrs Grundy; too much of a good thing; boring story, ancient history, old hat, old news, twice-told tale, Queen Anne's dead.

**Adj.** *tedious*, uninteresting, devoid of interest, strictly for the birds; unenjoyable, unexciting, uneventful, unentertaining, unamusing, unfunny; slow, dragging, leaden, heavy; dry, dryasdust, arid; flat, stale, insipid 387 *tasteless*; bald 573 *plain*; humdrum, soulless, suburban, depressing, dreary, dreich (Scots), stuffy, bourgeois 840 *dull*; stodgy, prosaic, uninspired, unreadable, unread; prosy, long, overlong, long-winded, drawn out 570 *prolix*; drowsy, somnific 679 *soporific*; boring, binding, wearisome, tiresome, irksome; wearing, chronic, mortal 684 *fatiguing*; repetitive, repetitious 106 *repeated*; same, unvarying, invariable, monotonous 16 *uniform*; too much, cloying, satiating; disgusting, nauseating, nauseous.

*bored*, unentertained, unamused, unexcited; afflicted with boredom, twiddling one's thumbs, kicking one's heels 679 *inactive*; fed

up to the back teeth, browned off, cheesed off, hacked off, had it up to here 829 *discontented*; stale, weary, jaded 684 *fatigued*; blue, world-weary, weary of life 834 *melancholic*; blasé, uninterested 860 *indifferent*; satiated, cloyed 863 *sated*; nauseated, sick of, sick and tired, fed up, loathing 861 *disliking*.

**Vb.** *be tedious*, pall, lose its novelty, cloy, glut, jade, satiate 863 *sate*; nauseate, sicken, disgust 861 *cause dislike*; bore, irk, try, weary 684 *fatigue*; bore to death, bore to tears, bore the pants off, bore stiff; weary to distraction, tire out, wear o.; get one down, get on one's nerves, try one's patience, outstay one's welcome, stay too long; fail to interest, make one yawn, send one to sleep; drag 278 *move slowly*; go on and on, never end; drone on, bang on, harp on, prove monotonous 106 *repeat oneself*; buttonhole, be prolix 570 *be diffuse*.

**Adv.** *boringly*, ad nauseam, to death.

## 839 Wit

**N.** *wit*, wittiness, pointedness, point, smartness, epigrammatism; esprit, ready wit, verbal readiness, badinage, repartee; esprit de l'escalier 67 *sequel*; saltiness, salt, Attic s., sal Atticum 575 *elegance*; sparkle, scintillation, brightness 498 *intelligence*; humour, sense of h., pleasant h.; wry humour, pawkiness, dryness, slyness; drollery, pleasantry, waggishness, waggery, facetiousness; jocularity, jocosity, jocoseness 833 *merriment*; comicalness, absurdity 849 *ridiculousness*; lack of seriousness, trifling, flippancy 456 *inattention*; fun, joking, practical j., jesting, tomfoolery, buffoonery, clowning, funny business 497 *foolery*; comic turn, laugh a minute; broad humour, low h., vulgarity 847 *bad taste*; farce, broad f., knockabout comedy, slapstick, custard-pie humour, ham, high camp 594 *dramaturgy*; whimsicality, fancy 604 *whim*; cartoon, comic strip, caricature; biting wit, cruel humour, satire, sarcasm 851 *ridicule*; irony, spoof 850 *affectation*; black comedy, black humour, sick h., gallows h.; word-fencing 477 *sophistry*; wordplay, play upon words, punning, equivocation 518 *equivocalness*.

*witticism*, witty remark, piece of humour, stroke of wit, jeu d'esprit, sally, mot, bon mot, aperçu; spoonerism; epigram, conceit; pun, play upon words, equivoque, calembour 518 *equivocalness*; point of the joke, cream of the jest; feed line, punch l., throwaway l.; banter, chaff, badinage, persiflage; retort, repartee, quid pro quo, backchat, backtalk 460 *answer*; sarcasm 851 *satire*; joke, standing j., private j., family j., in-joke; jest, dry j., good one, rib-tickler, side-splitter; quip, jape, quirk, crank, quips and cranks, gag, crack, wisecrack, one-liner; old joke, corny j., stale jest, chestnut, Joe Miller, bromide; practical joke, hoax, spoof, leg-pull; broad jest, dirty joke, blue j., sick j.; story, funny s., shaggy-dog s.; limerick, clerihew.

*humorist*, wit, bel esprit, epigrammatist, reparteeist; conversationalist; card, character, life and soul of the party, wag, wisecracker, japer, joker, Joe Miller, Sam Weller; jokesmith, funny man, gagsman, gagster, punster; banterer, persifleur, leg-puller, ragger, teaser; practical joker, hoaxer, spoof artist 545 *deceiver*; ironist 850 *affecter*; mocker, scoffer, satirist, lampooner 926 *detractor*; comedian, comedienne, comic, standup c., knockabout c., slapstick c. 594 *entertainer*; comic writer, cartoonist, caricaturist; burlesquer, impersonator, parodist 20 *imitator*; raconteur, raconteuse; jester, court j., wearer of the cap and bells, motley fool, clown, zany, farceur, buffoon, stooge 501 *fool*.

**Adj.** *witty*, spirituel(le), nimble-witted, quick; Attic 575 *elegant*; pointed, pithy, ben trovato, epigrammatic; brilliant, sparkling, smart, clever, too clever by half 498 *intelligent*; salty, racy, piquant; fruity, risqué; snappy, biting, pungent, keen, sharp, sarcastic; ironic, dry, sly, pawky; unserious, facetious, flippant 456 *light-minded*; jocular, jocose, joking, joshing, jokey, waggish, roguish; lively, pleasant, gay, merry and wise 833 *merry*; comic, 'funny ha-ha', rib-tickling 849 *funny*;

> **What do you mean, funny? Funny-peculiar, or funny ha-ha?**
> Ian Hay, *The Housemaster*

comical, humorous, droll; whimsical 604 *capricious*; playful, sportive, fooling 497 *absurd*.

**Vb.** *be witty*, scintillate, sparkle, flash; jest, joke, crack a j., quip, gag, wisecrack; tell a good story, raise a laugh, set the table in a roar, have the audience in stitches 837 *amuse*; pun, make a p., play upon words, equivocate 518 *be equivocal*; fool, jape 497 *be absurd*; play with, tease, chaff, rag, banter, twit, pull one's leg, have one on, put one on, make merry with, make fun of, poke fun at, get a rise out of, exercise one's wit upon 851 *ridicule*; ham up, camp up; mock, caricature, spoof, burlesque 851 *satirize*; retort, flash back, come back at 460 *answer*; have a sense of humour, enjoy a joke, see the point.

**Adv.** *in jest*, in joke, for a joke, in fun, in sport, in play; with tongue in cheek.

## 840 Dullness

**N.** *dullness*, heaviness 834 *dejection*; stuffiness, dreariness, dreichness (Scots), deadliness; monotony, boringness 838 *tedium*; colourlessness, drabness; lack of sparkle, lack of fire, lack of inspiration, lack of originality; stodginess, unreadability, turgidity, prosiness; staleness, flatness 387 *insipidity*; banality, triteness, superficiality; lack of humour, no sense of h., inability to see a joke, primness, impenetrable gravity, grimness 834 *seriousness*; prosaicness, prose, matter of fact 573 *plainness*.

**Adj.** *dull*, unamusing, uninteresting, unentertaining, unstimulating, uninspiring; unfunny, uncomical, straight; uncharming, uncaptivating; deadly dull, dull as ditchwater; stuffy, dreary, deadly; pointless, meaningless 838 *tedious*; unvivid, unlively, colourless, drab; flat, bland, vapid, insipid 387 *tasteless*; unimaginative, uninventive, unoriginal, derivative, superficial; stupid 499 *unintelligent*; without laughter, humourless, grave, prim, po-faced, poker-faced, frumpish 834 *serious*; unwitty, unsparkling, unscintillating; graceless, lacking wit 576 *inelegant*; heavy, heavy-footed, clod-hopping, ponderous, sluggish 278 *slow*; stodgy, turgid, prosaic, matter-of-fact, pedestrian, unreadable; stale, banal, commonplace, hackneyed, trite, platitudinous 610 *usual*.

**Vb.** *be dull*, drone on, bore 838 *be tedious*; platitudinize, prose; have no sense of humour, never see a joke, not see the point, miss the cream of the jest, miss the punch line.

## 841 Beauty

**N.** *beauty*, pulchritude, the beautiful; ripe perfection, highest p. 646 *perfection*; the sublime, sublimity, grandeur, magnificence, nobility; splendour, gorgeousness, brilliance, brightness, radiance 417 *light*; transfiguration 843 *beautification*; polish, gloss, ornament 844 *ornamentation*; scenic beauty, picturesqueness, scenery, view, landscape, seascape, snowscape, cloudscape 445 *spectacle*; form, fair proportions, regular features, classic f. 245 *symmetry*; physical beauty, loveliness, comeliness, fairness, handsomeness, bonniness, prettiness, chocolate-box p., picture-postcard p.; attraction, attractiveness, agreeableness, charm 826 *pleasurableness*; appeal, glamour, glitz, sex appeal, it, cuteness, kissability; attractions, physical a., charms, graces, perfections; good looks, handsome features, pretty face, beaux yeux; eyes of blue, cherry lips, ruby l., pearly teeth, schoolgirl complexion, peaches and cream c.; shapeliness, trim figure, curves, curvaceousness, vital statistics, the body beautiful; gracefulness, grace 575 *elegance*; chic, style, dress sense 848 *fashion*; delicacy, refinement 846 *good taste*; appreciation of beauty, aesthetics, aestheticism.

*a beauty*, thing of beauty, work of art; garden, beauty spot; masterpiece 644 *exceller*; bijou, jewel, jewel in the crown, pearl, treasure 646 *paragon*; peacock, swan, flower, rosebud, rose, lily; fair one, lady bright; belle, raving beauty, reigning b., toast, idol 890 *favourite*; beau idéal, dream girl; jolie laide; beauty queen, Miss World, Miss Universe, bathing belle, pin-up girl, cover girl, page-3 girl, centrefold, pin-up, cheesecake; beefcake, hunk, muscleman, Mr Universe; fine figure of a man *or* woman; blond(e), brunette, redhead; English rose; dream, a dream walking, vision, poem, picture, perfect p., sight for sore eyes; angel, charmer, dazzler; stunner, knockout, eyeful, good-looker, looker, babe; doll, dolly bird, cookie; glamour puss, glamour girl *or* boy, It girl; heartthrob, dreamboat; enchantress, femme fatale, vamp, seductress, siren, witch 983 *sorceress*; smasher, scorcher, stunner, lovely, cutie, honey, beaut, peach, dish; bimbo, arm candy, eye candy, über-babe, sex on a stick; fairy, peri, houri; Grace, the Graces, Venus, Aphrodite, Helen of Troy; Apollo, Hyperion, Endymion, Adonis, Narcissus.

**Adj.** *beautiful*, pulchritudinous, beauteous, of beauty; lovely, fair, bright, radiant; comely, goodly, bonny, pretty; sweet, sweetly pretty, picture-postcard, pretty-pretty, pretty in a chocolate box way, nice, good enough to eat; pretty as a picture, photogenic; handsome, good-looking, well-favoured, well-built, well-set-up, husky, manly; tall, dark and handsome; gracious, stately, majestic, statuesque, Junoesque; adorable, god-like, goddess-like, divine, 'divinely tall and most divinely fair';

> A daughter of the gods, divinely tall
> And most divinely fair.
>
> Alfred, Lord Tennyson, *A Dream of Fair Women*

pleasing to the eye, lovely to behold; picturesque, scenic, ornamental; landscaped, well laid-out; artistic, harmonious, well-grouped, well-composed, cunning, curious, quaint 694 *well-made*; aesthetic 846 *tasteful*; exquisite, choice 605 *chosen*; unspotted, unblemished 646 *perfect*.

*splendid*, sublime, heavenly, superb, fine 644 *excellent*; grand 868 *noble*; glorious, ravishing, rich, gorgeous, highly-coloured 425 *florid*; bright, resplendent, dazzling, beaming, radiant, sparkling, glowing 417 *radiating*; glossy, magnificent, specious 875 *showy*; ornate 844 *ornamented*.

*shapely*, well-proportioned, regular, classic, of classic proportions 245 *symmetrical*; formed, well-f., well-turned; rounded, well-r., well-stacked, well-endowed, buxom, bosomy, curvaceous 248 *curved*; slinky, callipygous;

clean-limbed, straight-l., straight, slender, slim, lissom, svelte, willowy 206 *lean*; lightsome, graceful, elegant, chic; petite, dainty, delicate; undeformed, undefaced, unwarped, untwisted 646 *perfect*.

*personable*, prepossessing, agreeable; comfortable, buxom, sonsy; attractive, dishy, phat (sl) fetching, appealing 826 *pleasurable*; sexy, cute, kissable; charming, entrancing, alluring, enchanting, glamorous; lovesome, winsome 887 *lovable*; fresh-faced, clean-cut, wholesome, lusty, blooming, in bloom, ruddy 431 *red*; rosy, rosy-cheeked, apple-c., cherry-lipped, fresh-complexioned, bright-eyed; sightly, becoming, fit to be seen, easy on the eye, passable, not amiss; presentable, proper, decent, neat, natty, tidy, trim; spruce, snappy, dapper, glossy, sleek; well-dressed, well turned out, smart, stylish, classy, chic, soigné(e) 848 *fashionable*; elegant, dainty, delicate, refined 846 *tasteful*.

**Vb.** *be beautiful*, – splendid etc. adj.; be entrancing 983 *bewitch*; take one's breath away, beggar all description; be photogenic, photograph well; have good looks, have bright eyes; bloom, glow, dazzle 417 *shine*; be dressed to kill; do one credit, win a beauty contest.

*beautify*, trim, neaten, improve; brighten 417 *make bright*; prettify, bejewel, tattoo, body-pierce 844 *decorate*; set (a jewel); set off, grace, suit, fit, become, go well, show one off, flatter; bring out the highlights, enhance one's looks, glamorize, transfigure; give a face-lift, smarten up; prink, prank, titivate, do oneself up, do one's face, powder, rouge 843 *primp*.

## 842 Ugliness

**N.** *ugliness*, unsightliness, hideousness, repulsiveness; lack of beauty, gracelessness, lumpishness, clumsiness 576 *inelegance*; lack of symmetry, asymmetry 246 *distortion*; unshapeliness, lack of form 246 *deformity*; mutilation, disfigurement 845 *blemish*; uglification, disfiguration, defacement; squalor, filth, grottiness, yuk 649 *uncleanness*; homeliness, plainness, plain features, ugly face; not much to look at, no beauty, no oil painting, a face to stop a clock; wry face, snarl, forbidding countenance, vinegarish expression, grim look, sour l. 893 *sullenness*; haggardness, haggard look; fading beauty, dim eyes, wrinkles, crowsfeet, hand of time, ravages of time 131 *age*.

*eyesore*, hideosity, blot, botch, patch 845 *blemish*; aesthetic crime, offence to the eyes; blot on the landscape, architectural monstrosity, satanic mills; ugly person, fright, sight, frump, not one's type; scarecrow, horror, death's-head, gargoyle, grotesque; monster, abortion; harridan, witch; toad, gorilla, baboon, crow; plain Jane, ugly duckling; satyr, Caliban; Gorgon, Medusa; Beast.

**Adj.** *ugly*, lacking beauty, unbeautiful, unlovely, uncomely, unhandsome; coarse-looking, blowzy, frowzy; ugly as sin, hideous, foul 649 *unclean*; frightful, shocking, monstrous; repulsive, repellent, odious, loathsome 861 *disliked*; beastly, nasty 645 *not nice*; not much to look at, short on looks, unprepossessing, unpretty, homely, plain, plain-featured, plain-looking, with no looks, without any looks; mousy, frumpish, frumpy; forbidding, ill-favoured, hard-featured, villainous, grim-visaged, grim, saturnine 893 *sullen*.

*unsightly*, faded, withered, worn, ravaged, wrinkled 131 *ageing*; not worth looking at, not fit to be seen, unseemly; imperfect, marred 845 *blemished*; unshapely, shapeless, formless, irregular, asymmetrical 244 *amorphous*; grotesque, twisted, deformed, disfigured 246 *distorted*; defaced, vandalized, litter-strewn; badly made, ill-proportioned, disproportionate, misshapen, misbegotten; dumpy, squat 196 *dwarfish*; bloated 195 *fleshy*; stained, discoloured, washed out 426 *colourless*; ghastly, wan, grisly, gruesome; tousled, in disarray, messy 61 *orderless*.

*graceless*, ungraced, ungraceful 576 *inelegant*; inartistic, unaesthetic; unbecoming, unattractive; squalid, dingy, poky, dreary, drab; lank, dull, mousy; dowdy, badly dressed, lacking clothes-sense; garish, gaudy, tawdry, gross, indelicate, coarse 847 *vulgar*; rude, crude, rough, rugged, uncouth 699 *artless*; clumsy, awkward, ungainly, cumbersome, hulky, hulking, slouching, clod-hopping 195 *unwieldy*.

**Vb.** *be ugly*, lack beauty, have no looks, be short on l., lose one's l.; fade, wither, age, show one's a. 131 *grow old*; look ill, look a wreck, look a mess, look a fright.

*make ugly*, uglify; fade, discolour 426 *decolorize*; wither 655 *deteriorate*; soil, sully 649 *make unclean*; spoil, deface, disfigure, mar, blemish, blot; misshape 244 *deform*; pull a face, grimace 893 *be sullen*; torture, twist 246 *distort*; mutilate, vandalize 655 *impair*.

### 843 Beautification

**N.** *beautification*, beautifying 844 *ornamentation*; make-over, transfiguration 143 *transformation*; scenic improvement, landscape gardening 844 *ornamental art*; beauty treatment, beauty therapy; eyebrow-pencilling, eyebrow-plucking; depilation, electrolysis, sugaring, waxing; face mask, face pack, mud p., oatmeal p., facial, facial scrub; plastic surgery, cosmetic s., bus-stop s. 658 *surgery*;

face lift, face-lifting, neck lift, nose-straightening, nose-job (inf), rhinoplasty, brow lift, ear tuck, eye lift, genoplasty, abdominoplasty, tummy tuck; breast enlargement, breast implant, breast lift; skin treatment, skin-grafting, mole-removing, skin peel, acid p., AHA p., chemical p., micro-dermabrasion, laser resurfacing; Botox (tdmk), gel-filler or filler-gel; liposuction, lipo (inf), microsuction, lipoplasty, lipectomy; body wrap; massage, face m., skin m., body m.; manicure, nail-polishing, buffing; pedicure, chiropody; tattooing 844 *ornamental art*; ear-piercing, eyebrow-p., navel-p., nose-p., tongue-p.; suntanning, browning; sun lamp, sun bed, ultra-violet rays; toilet, grooming, make-up, art of m., cosmetology; cleansing, moisturizing, toning, creaming, rouging, painting, dyeing, powdering, patching; scenting, soaping, shampooing; wash and brush up 648 *ablutions*.

*hairdressing*, trichology, hair-treatment, scalp massage; barbering, shaving, clipping, trimming, thinning, singeing; depilation, plucking; cutting, haircut, bobbing, shingling; shave, hair cut, wet c., razor c., clip, trim, singe, short back and sides; hair style, coiffure, crop, Eton c., bob, shingle, pageboy, crewcut, cut en brosse, urchin cut, baby doll c., bouffant c., coupe sauvage, spike; styling, hair-s., curling, frizzing, waving, setting, hair-straightening, defrizzing; hairdo, restyle, shampoo and set, set; blow-dry, fingerdry, scrunching; wave, blow w., marcel w., cold w.; permanent w., perm; curl 251 *coil*; bang, fringe, ponytail, bunches, pigtail, plaits, chignon, bun; pompadour, beehive, Afro 259 *hair*; false hair, hairpiece, toupee, switch, hair extension, hair weaving, hair implant 228 *wig*; curling iron, tongs, curl papers, curlers, rollers, heated r.; bandeau, Alice band; comb, hairpin, hairgrip, bobby pin, Kirbigrip (tdmk), slide; hairnet, snood 228 *headgear*.

*hairwash*, shampoo, conditioner, rinse, tinting, colour tone, highlights, lightening, bleach, tint, dye, henna, peroxide; hair mousse, hair gel, setting lotion, hair spray, lacquer, haircream, grease, brilliantine; hair-restorer.

*cosmetic*, beautifier, glamourizer, aid to beauty, beauty aid, patch, beauty spot; make-up, liquid m., stick m.; paint, greasepaint, warpaint, rouge, blusher, highlighter, concealer, pomade, cream, face c., cold c., cleansing c., vanishing c., moisturizing c., foundation c., night c., hormone c., lanolin 357 *unguent*; lipstick, lip gloss; nail polish, nail varnish, powder, face p., talcum p.; eye make-up, kohl, mascara, eye shadow, eyeliner, eyebrow pencil; hand lotion, astringent l., skin toner, aftershave lotion, suntan l.; scented soap, bath salts, bath oil, bath essence, bubble bath, foam b. 648 *cleanser*; antiperspirant, deodorant; scent, perfume, essence, cologne, eau de c., lavender water, toilet w., cologne stick; false eyelashes; powder puff, compact; vanity case, manicure set, nail file, nail scissors, clippers; shaver, razor, electric r., depilatory, strip wax; toiletry, toiletries.

*beauty parlour*, beauty salon, parfumerie; boudoir, dressing room, powder r.; health farm.

*beautician*, beauty specialist, beauty therapist; face-lifter, plastic surgeon; make-up artist, tattooer; cosmetician; barber, hairdresser, hair stylist, coiffeur, coiffeuse; trichologist; manicurist, pedicurist, chiropodist.

**Adj.** *beautified*, transfigured, transformed; prettified, glamorized, bedizened; made-up, rouged, farded, raddled, painted, powdered, scented; curled, bouffant; primped, dressed up, dolled up, tarted up, done up, done up to kill, done up like a dog's dinner, done up to the nines 841 *beautiful*.

**Vb.** *primp*, prettify, glamorize, doll up, do up, dress up, bedizen, bejewel; ornament 844 *decorate*; prink, prank, trick out; preen; titivate, make up, put on make-up, apply cosmetics, rouge, paint, shadow, highlight; powder; wear scent; shave, pluck one's eyebrows, wax one's e., varnish one's nails, dye *or* tint one's hair; curl, wave, perm; have a hairdo, have a facial, have a manicure 841 *beautify*.

## 844 Ornamentation

**N.** *ornamentation*, decoration, adornment, garnish; ornate style, ornateness 574 *ornament*; art deco, art nouveau, baroque, rococo; chinoiserie; richness, gilt, gaudiness 875 *ostentation*; enhancement, enrichment, embellishment; setting, background; table decoration, tablecloth, runner, centrepiece, epergne, silver, china, glass; floral decoration, flower arrangement, wreath, garland, bouquet, nosegay, posy, buttonhole; objet d'art, bric-à-brac, curio, bibelot.

*ornamental art*, gardening, landscape g., topiarism; architecture, landscape a., building; interior decoration, furnishing, draping, painting, decorating; statuary 554 *sculpture*; frieze, dado, cartouche, metope, triglyph; capital, acanthus; pilaster, caryatid, figurehead; boss, cornice, corbel, gargoyle; astragal, moulding, beading, fluting, reeding, chamfering, strapwork, linenfold; fretting, tracery; varnishing 226 *facing*; pargeting, veneering, panelling, graining; ormolu, gilding, gilt, gold

leaf; lettering, illumination, illustration, illustrating, sign-painting, graphic art 551 *art*; stained glass; tie-dyeing, batik; heraldic art 547 *heraldry*; tattooing, body-piercing, eyebrow-p., navel-p., tongue-p.; etching 555 *engraving*; work, handiwork, handicraft, fancywork, woodwork, fretwork, frostwork; pokerwork, pyrography; openwork, filigree; whittling, carving, scrimshaw; embossing, chasing, intaglio 254 *relievo*; inlay, inset, enamelling, cloisonné, champlevé, mosaic, marquetry 437 *variegation*; metalwork, toreutics; gemcutting, setting; cut glass, engraved g.; wrought iron.

*pattern*, motif, print, design, composition 331 *structure*; detail, elaborate d.; geometrical style, Decorated s., rose window, spandrel, cyma, ogee, fleuron, cusp, trefoil, fleur-de-lis; crocket, finial, tracery, scrollwork, fiddlehead, poppyhead, arabesque, flourish, curlicue 251 *coil*; swag, festoon; weave, diaper 331 *texture*; argyle, Arran, paisley 222 *textile*; chevron, key pattern; tartan, check 437 *chequer*; pin-stripe 437 *stripe*; spot, dot, polka d. 437 *mottling*; herringbone, zigzag, dogtooth, hound's tooth 220 *obliquity*; watermark, logo, marque 547 *identification*.

*needlework*, stitchery, tapestry, arras; cross-stitch, sampler; patchwork, appliqué; open work, drawn-thread w.; embroidery, smocking; crochet, lace, broderie anglaise; tatting, knitting 222 *network*; stitch, purl, plain, stocking stitch, garter s., moss s.; gros point, petit p., needle p.; chain stitch, cable s., hem s., stem s., blanket s., feather s., back s., satin s., herringbone s., French knot, lazy-daisy.

*trimming*, passementerie, piping, valance, border, fringe, frieze, frill, flounce, galloon, gimp 234 *edging*; binding 589 *bookbinding*; trappings; braid, frog, lapel, epaulette, star, rosette, cockade 547 *badge*; bow 47 *fastening*; bobble, pompom; tassel, dangler, bead, bugle; ermine, fur 259 *hair*; feather, ostrich f., osprey, aigrette, plume, panache 259 *plumage*; streamer, ribbon.

*finery*, togs, gear, glad rags, Sunday best, best bib and tucker 228 *clothing*; fal-de-lal, frippery, frills and furbelows, ribbons, chiffon, froufrou; gaudery, gaud, trinket, knick-knack, gewgaw, fandangle; tinsel, spangle, sequin, clinquant, diamante, costume jewellery, glass, paste, marcasite, rhinestone 639 *bauble*.

*jewellery*, bijouterie; crown jewels, diadem, tiara 743 *regalia*; costume jewellery; drop, pendant, locket 217 *hanging object*; crucifix; amulet, charm 983 *talisman*; rope, string, necklet, necklace, beads, pearls, choker, chain, watch c., albert 250 *loop*; torque, armlet, anklet, bracelet, wristlet, bangle; ring, earring, drop e., signet ring, wedding r., eternity r., engagement r., mourning r., dress r. 250 *circle*; eyebrow ring, navel r., nipple r., nose r., tongue r., labret, labret stud, nose s., tongue s.; cameo, brooch, clasp, fibula, badge, crest; stud, pin, gold p., tie p., collar stud, cufflinks 47 *fastening*; skin jewellery; medal, medallion.

*gem*, jewel, bijou; stone, precious s., semiprecious s.; uncut gem, cut g., cabochon; brilliant, sparkler, diamond, rock, ice; solitaire; pearl, cultured p., seed p., pink p.; carbuncle, ruby; opal, black o., fire o., girasol; aquamarine, sapphire, turquoise, emerald, beryl, chrysoberyl, chrysoprase, alexandrite; quartz, cairngorm, garnet, amethyst, topaz, chalcedony, cornelian *or* carnelian, sard, jasper, tiger's-eye, agate, onyx, sardonyx; heliotrope, bloodstone, moonstone, cat's-eye, zircon, jacinth, hyacinth, tourmaline, apatite, chrysolite, olivine, peridot, amazonite, malachite, rhodonite, haematite, obsidian; coral, ivory, mother of pearl, jet, amber, jade, lapis lazuli.

**Adj.** *ornamental*, arty-crafty, decorative, decorated, fancy, nonfunctional, patterned; intricate, elaborate, quaint, daedal; picturesque, pretty-pretty, chocolate box pretty; scenic, landscape, topiary; geometric; Doric, Ionic, Corinthian, Moresque, Romanesque, Decorated; baroque, rococo; gimmicky, with bells and whistles.

*ornamented*, richly o., luxuriant; adorned, decorated, embellished, tarted up, polished 574 *ornate*; picked out 437 *variegated*; patterned, inwrought, mosaic, inlaid, enamelled, chryselephantine; worked, embroidered, trimmed; wreathed, festooned, garlanded, crowned; overdone, chichi, overdecorated, overloaded, kitsch 847 *vulgar*; overcoloured 425 *florid*; luscious, plush, gilt, begilt, gilded 800 *rich*; gorgeous, garish, glittering, flashy, gaudy, meretricious 875 *showy*, gimmicky, with bells and whistles, all singing, all dancing.

*bedecked*, groomed, got up, togged up, wearing, sporting; decked, decked out, bedizened; looking one's best, in one's Sunday best, in one's best gear, in full fig, en grande toilette 228 *dressed*; tricked out, dolled up, dolled up to the nines, tarted up, dressed to kill 843 *beautified*; bejewelled, beribboned, festooned, studded, bemedalled.

**Vb.** *decorate*, adorn, embellish, enhance, enrich; grace, set, set off 574 *ornament*; paint, bejewel, tattoo, body-pierce; tart up, glamorize, prettify 841 *beautify*; garnish, trim, shape; array, deck, bedeck 228 *dress*; deck out, trick o., prank, preen, titivate 843 *primp*; add the finishing touches; freshen, smarten, spruce up, furbish, burnish 648 *clean*; bemedal,

beribbon, garland, crown 866 *honour*; stud, spangle, bespangle 437 *variegate*; colourwash, whitewash, varnish, grain, japan, lacquer 226 *coat*; enamel, gild, silver; blazon, emblazon, illuminate, illustrate 553 *paint*, 425 *colour*; border, trim 234 *hem*; work, pick out, broider, embroider, tapestry; pattern, inlay, engrave; enchase, encrust, emboss, bead, mould; fret, carve, foliate 262 *groove*, 260 *notch*; enlace, wreathe, festoon, trace, scroll 251 *twine*.

## 845 Blemish

**N.** *blemish*, no ornament; scar, cicatrice, weal, welt, mark, pockmark; injury, flaw, crack, defect 647 *imperfection*; disfigurement, deformity 246 *distortion*; stigma, blot, blot on the landscape 842 *eyesore*; scribbling, graffiti; blur, blotch, splotch, smudge 550 *obliteration*; smut, patch, smear, stain, tarnish, rust, patina 649 *dirt*; spot, speck, speckle, macula, spottiness 437 *mottling*; freckle, mole, birthmark, strawberry mark; excrescence, pimpliness, pimple, plook, zit, blackhead, whitehead, carbuncle, sebaceous cyst, wen, wart 253 *swelling*; blotchiness, acne, rosacea, eczema 651 *skin disease*; harelip, cleft palate; cast, squint; cut, scratch, scald, bruise, black eye, shiner, cauliflower ear, broken nose 655 *wound*.

**Adj.** *blemished*, defective, not in mint condition, flawed, cracked, damaged 647 *imperfect*; tarnished, stained, soiled, flyblown, fleabitten 649 *dirty*; shop-soiled, spoilt 655 *deteriorated*; marked, scarred, marred; foxed, spotted, pitted, pockmarked, maculate; spotty, freckled; squinting, bug-eyed 440 *dim-sighted*; club-footed, pigeon-toed, hammer-t.; knock-kneed, bandy, bandy-legged; hunch-backed, crooked 246 *deformed*.

**Vb.** *blemish*, flaw, crack, injure, damage 655 *impair*; blot, smudge, stain, smear, sully, soil 649 *make unclean*; stigmatize, brand 547 *mark*; scar, pit, pockmark; mar, spoil, spoil the look of 842 *make ugly*; deface, vandalize, disfigure, scratch, scribble on 244 *deform*.

## 846 Good Taste

**N.** *good taste*, tastefulness, taste, refined t., cultivated t.; restraint, simplicity 573 *plainness*; best of taste, choiceness, excellence 644 *goodness*; refinement, delicacy, euphemism 950 *purity*; fine feeling, nice appreciation, discernment, palate 463 *discrimination*; daintiness, finickiness, fikiness, kid gloves 862 *fastidiousness*; decency, seemliness 848 *etiquette*; tact, consideration, natural courtesy, dignity, manners, polished m., table m., breeding, civility, urbanity, social graces 884 *courtesy*; correctness, propriety, decorum; grace, polish, finish, sophistication, gracious living 575 *elegance*; cultivation, culture, virtu, connoisseurship, amateurship, dilettantism; epicureanism, epicurism; aestheticism, aesthetics, criticism, art c. 480 *judgment*; artistry, virtuosity, flair 694 *skill*.

*people of taste*, bon ton 848 *beau monde*; sophisticate, connoisseur, cognoscente, amateur, dilettante; epicurean, epicure, gourmet; aesthete, critic, art c. 480 *estimator*; arbiter of taste, arbiter elegantiarum, Beau Nash 848 *fop*; purist, precisian 602 *obstinate person*; euphemist 950 *prude*.

**Adj.** *tasteful*, gracious, dignified; in good taste, in the best of t.; choice, exquisite 644 *excellent*; simple, unmeretricious 573 *plain*; graceful, Attic, classical 575 *elegant*; chaste, refined, delicate, euphemistic 950 *pure*; aesthetic, artistic 819 *sensitive*; discerning, epicurean 463 *discriminating*; nice, dainty, choosy, finicky, fiky 862 *fastidious*; critical, appreciative 480 *judicial*; decent, seemly, becoming 24 *apt*; proper, correct, comme il faut 848 *fashionable*; mannerly 848 *well-bred*.

**Vb.** *have taste*, show good t., reveal fine feelings 463 *discriminate*; appreciate, value, criticize 480 *judge*; go in for the best, settle for nothing less than the best, take only the best, be a perfectionist 862 *be fastidious*.

**Adv.** *tastefully*, elegantly, in good taste, in the best t.; becomingly, fittingly, properly, agreeably 24 *pertinently*.

## 847 Bad Taste

**N.** *bad taste*, tastelessness, poor taste, excruciating t. 645 *badness*; no taste, lack of t.; bad art, kitsch; international airport plastic; commercialism, commercialization, commodification, prostitution of talent; yellow press, gutter p.; unrefinement, coarseness, barbarism, vulgarism, vandalism, philistinism, Babbittry 699 *artlessness*; vulgarity, gaudiness, garishness, loudness, blatancy, flagrancy; tawdriness, shoddiness; shoddy, frippery, tinsel, glitter, paste, ersatz, imitation 639 *bauble*; lack of feeling, insensitivity, crassness, grossness, coarseness; tactlessness, indelicacy, impropriety, unseemliness; bad joke, sick j., untimely jest, misplaced wit, mobile hangover; nastiness, obscenity 951 *impurity*; unfashionableness, dowdiness, frumpishness; frump, dowdy, square.

*ill-breeding*, vulgarity, commonness; loudness, heartiness, rusticity, provinciality, suburbanism, inurbanity, incivility, unfashionableness; bad form, incorrectness, lack of etiquette; bad manners, no manners, gaucherie, boorishness, rudeness, impoliteness

885 *discourtesy*; ungentlemanliness, caddishness; unladylikeness; brutishness, savagery; misbehaviour, indecorum, ribaldry; rough behaviour, rowdyism, ruffianism, yob culture 61 *disorder*.

*vulgarian*, snob, social climber, namedropper, cad, bounder; rough diamond, unlicked cub; arriviste, parvenu, nouveau arrivé, nouveau riche; proletarian, prole, pleb 869 *commoner*; Goth, Vandal, Philistine, Babbitt; barbarian, savage; yob, punk.

**Adj.** *vulgar*, undignified; unrefined, unpolished 576 *inelegant*; tasteless, in bad taste, in the worst possible t.; gross, crass, coarse, coarse-grained; unfastidious, not particular; knowing no better, philistine, yobbish, barbarian 699 *artless*; commercial, commercialized; tawdry, cheap, cheap and nasty, naff, catchpenny, gingerbread, kitschy, ersatz; flashy, meretricious, bedizened 875 *showy*; obtrusive, blatant, loud, screaming, gaudy, garish, raffish; flaunting, shameless, tarted up; fulsome, excessive; schmaltzy, novelettish; overdressed, underdressed; shabby genteel 850 *affected*; not respectable, ungenteel; common, common as muck, low, gutter, sordid 867 *disreputable*; improper, indelicate, indecorous; going too far, beyond the pale, scandalous, indecent, low-minded, ribald, obscene, risqué, pornographic 951 *impure*.

*ill-bred*, underbred, badly brought up; unpresentable, not to be taken anywhere; ungentlemanly, unladylike; unfeminine, hoydenish; ungenteel, non-U 869 *plebeian*; loud, hearty; tactless, insensitive, blunt; uncourtly, uncivil, impolite, mannerless, unmannerly, ill-mannered 885 *discourteous*; unfashionable, unsmart, frumpish, dowdy, rustic, provincial, countrified, gone native, suburban; crude, rude, boorish, churlish, yobbish, loutish, clodhopping, uncouth, uncultured, uncultivated, unpolished, unrefined 491 *ignorant*; unsophisticated, knowing no better 699 *artless*; unlettered, uncivilized, barbaric; awkward, gauche, lubberly 695 *clumsy*; misbehaving, rowdy, ruffianly, riotous 61 *disorderly*; snobbish, uppity, superior 850 *affected*.

**Vb.** *vulgarize*, cheapen, coarsen, debase, lower, lower the tone; commercialize, commodify, popularize; show bad taste, know no better 491 *not know*; be unfashionable, be out of date.

## 848 Fashion. Etiquette

**N.** *fashion*, style, mode, cut 243 *form*; method 624 *way*; vogue, cult 610 *habit*; prevailing taste, current fashion, trend 126 *modernism*; rage, fad, craze, cry, furore; the latest, latest fashion, what's new 126 *newness*; dernier cri, last word, ne plus ultra; extreme of fashion, height of f., pink of f.; changing world of fashion, New Look, sixties' look, seventies' l. etc., retro fashion, retro style; Gothic look, grunge; dash 875 *ostentation*; fashionableness, ton, bon t.; stylishness, flair, chic, retro chic; anti-chic; dress sense, fashion s.; fashion show, mannequin parade 522 *exhibit*; haute couture, nouvelle c., elegance, foppishness, dressiness; foppery 850 *affectation*; world of fashion, Vanity Fair, passing show, way of the world.

*etiquette*, point of e., punctilio 875 *formality*; protocol, convention, custom, conventionality 610 *practice*; snobbery, conventions of society, sanctions of s., done thing, good form, what is expected; convenances, proprieties, appearances, Mrs Grundy; bienséance, decency, decorum, propriety, right note, correctness, netiquette 846 *good taste*; civilized behaviour 884 *courtesy*; breeding, good b., polish; gentility, gentlemanliness, ladylike behaviour; manners, table m., good m., refined m., polished m., drawing-room m., court m., best behaviour; grand air, poise, dignity, savoir faire, savvy 688 *conduct*.

*beau monde*, society, good s., high s., civilized s., civilization; town, best end of town, Mayfair; St James's, court, drawing room, salon; high circles, top drawer, right people, best p., smart set, county s., upper ten 868 *nobility*; cream, upper crust, cream of society 644 *elite*; café society, jeunesse dorée, gilded youth, beautiful people, glitterati, jet set; fashionable person, glass of fashion; Sloane Ranger, Sloane; yuppy; man *or* woman about town, man *or* woman of fashion, high stepper, classy dame; follower of fashion, dedicated follower of f., slave to fashion, fashion victim; leader of f., fashionista, trendsetter, Beau Nash; man *or* woman of the world, mondain, mondaine, socialite, playboy, clubman, clubwoman, cosmopolitan 882 *sociable person*.

*fop*, fine gentleman, macaroni, buck, pearly king; fine lady, belle, pearly queen; debutante, deb; dandy, exquisite, beau, Beau Brummel; Teddy Boy; popinjay, peacock, clothes-horse, fashion plate; coxcomb, puppy, dandiprat, jackanapes; swell, toff, dude, nob, His Nibs, Lady Muck; Ted, mod; Corinthian, spark, blood, blade, buckeen, lad, gay dog; lounge lizard, gigolo, carpet knight, gallant; ladykiller, squire of dames.

**Adj.** *fashionable*, modish, stylish, voguish, bon ton; correct, comme il faut; in, in vogue, in fashion, in the latest f., à la mode, chichi; recherché, exquisite, chic, elegant, colour-supplement, well-dressed, well-groomed 846 *tasteful*; clothes-conscious, foppish, dressy; high-stepping, dashing, doggish, rakish, snazzy, flashy 875 *showy*; dandy, smart, classy, ritzy, swanky, swank, swell, swish, posh; up-to-the-minute, bang up-to-date, ultrafashionable, new-fangled, all the rage 126 *modern*; cool, groovy, hip, hep, trendy, with it; groomed, dandified, dressed up to the nines, dressed to kill, in full dress, en grande tenue 228 *dressed*; in society, in the best s., in the right set, from the top drawer, moving in the best circles, knowing the right people, belonging to the best clubs; in the swim 83 *conformable*; snobbish 850 *affected*; conventional, done 610 *usual*.

*well-bred*, thoroughbred, blue-blooded 868 *noble*; cosmopolitan, sophisticated, civilized, citified, urbane; polished, polite, well brought up, housetrained; U, gentlemanly, ladylike 868 *genteel*; civil, well-mannered, easy-m., good-m., well-spoken 884 *courteous*; courtly, stately, distingué(e), dignified 875 *formal*; poised, dégagé(e), easy, unembarrassed, smooth; correct, conventional, decorous, proper, convenable, decent; tactful, diplomatic; considerate 884 *amiable*; punctilious 929 *honourable*.

**Vb.** *be in fashion*, be done, catch on 610 *be wont*; be all the rage, be the latest, be the latest craze, be trendy 126 *modernize*; get with it, follow the fashion, jump on the band wagon, change with the times 83 *conform*; have the entrée, move in the best circles, be seen in the right places; savoir faire, savoir vivre 882 *be sociable*; entertain 882 *be hospitable*; keep up with the Jones's, keep up appearances; observe decorum, do the right thing; cut a dash, cut a figure, lead the fashion, set the f., be a trendsetter, set the tone, give a lead; look right, pass; have an air, have style; show flair, dress well, wear the right clothes, dandify 843 *primp*.

**Adv.** *fashionably*, in style, à la mode; for appearances, for fashion's sake.

## 849 Ridiculousness

**N.** *ridiculousness*, ludicrousness, risibility, laughability, height of nonsense, height of absurdity 497 *absurdity*; funniness, pricelessness, comicality, drollery, waggishness 839 *wit*; quaintness, oddness, queerness, eccentricity 84 *nonconformity*; bathos, anticlimax 509 *disappointment*; boasting 877 *boast*; extravagance, bombast 546 *exaggeration*; comic interlude, light relief, comic r.; light verse, comic v., nonsense v., doggerel, limerick 839 *witticism*; spoonerism, malapropism, bull; comic turn, comedy, farce, burlesque, slapstick, knockabout, clowning, buffoonery 594 *stage play*;

paradox, paradoxicality, Gilbertian situation 508 *lack of expectation*.

**Adj.** *ridiculous*, ludicrous, preposterous, monstrous, grotesque, fantastic, cock-eyed, inappropriate 497 *absurd*; awkward, clownish 695 *clumsy*; silly 499 *foolish*; derisory, contemptible 639 *unimportant*; laughable, risible; Pythonesque; bizarre, rum, quaint, odd, queer 84 *unusual*; strange, outlandish 59 *extraneous*; mannered, stilted 850 *affected*; inflated, bombastic, extravagant, outré 546 *exaggerated*; crazy, crackpot, fanciful 513 *imaginary*; whimsical 604 *capricious*; paradoxical.

*funny*, 'funny-peculiar' (see quotation at 839 *witty*) 84 *abnormal*; funny-ha-ha, laughter-inducing, good for a laugh 837 *amusing*; comical, droll, drollish, humorous, zany; waggish 839 *witty*; rich, priceless, side-splitting, wildly amusing, hilarious, a real hoot, a scream, too funny for words; light, comic, seriocomic, tragicomic; mocking, ironical, satirical 851 *derisive*; burlesque, mock-heroic; doggerel; farcical, slapstick, clownish, custard-pie, knockabout; Chaplinesque, Pickwickian, Malvolian, Shavian, Gilbertian.

**Vb.** *be ridiculous*, make one laugh, excite laughter, raise a laugh; tickle, shake *or* disturb one's gravity, make one fall about, give one the giggles; entertain 837 *amuse*; look silly, be a figure of fun, cut a ridiculous figure, be a laughingstock, fool, play the fool 497 *be absurd*; come down with a bump, descend to bathos, pass from the sublime to the ridiculous; make an exhibition of oneself, put oneself out of court 695 *act foolishly*; poke fun at, make one a laughingstock 851 *ridicule*.

## 850 Affectation

**N.** *affectation*, cult, fad 848 *fashion*; affectedness, pretentiousness 875 *ostentation*; assumption of airs, putting on a., grand a. 873 *airs*; posing, posturing, attitudinizing; striking attitude, high moral tone; pose, public image, façade; artificiality, mannerism, trick, literary affectation, esoteric vocabulary, grandiloquence 574 *rhetoric*; preciosity, euphuism 574 *ornament*; pout, moue, grimace 547 *gesture*; coquetry, minauderie 604 *caprice*; conceit, conceitedness, foppery, foppishness, dandyism, coxcombry 873 *vanity*; euphemism, mock modesty, false shame, mauvaise honte 874 *modesty*; irony, Socratic i., backhanded compliment 851 *ridicule*; insincerity, play-acting, tongue in cheek 541 *duplicity*; staginess, theatricality, camp, histrionics, breast-beating.

*pretension*, pretensions, false p.; artifice, sham, humbug, quackery, charlatanism, charlatanry, fraud 542 *deception*; superficiality, shallowness, shallow profundity 4 *insubstantiality*; stiffness, starchiness, buckram 875 *formality*; pedantry, purism, precisianism 735 *severity*; demureness, prunes and prisms 950 *prudery*; sanctimony, sanctimoniousness 979 *pietism*.

*affecter*, humbug, quack, charlatan, mountebank 545 *impostor*; play-actor 594 *actor*; hypocrite, flatterer 545 *deceiver*, bluffer 877 *boaster*; coquette, flirt; mass of affectation, attitudinizer, posturer, poser, poseur, poseuse 873 *vain person*; ironist 839 *humorist*; coxcomb, dandy 848 *fop*; grimacer, simperer; formalist, precisian, purist, pedant; know-all, smarty pants 500 *wise guy*; prig, puritan, pietist, goody-goody 950 *prude*; mannerist, euphuist, bluestocking; champagne socialist.

**Adj.** *affected*, full of affectation, self-conscious; studied, mannered, euphuistic, precious, chichi 574 *ornate*; artificial, unnatural, stilted, stiff, starchy 875 *formal*; prim, priggish, prudish, goody-goody, mealy-mouthed, euphemistic, sanctimonious, self-righteous, holier than thou, smug, demure 979 *pietistic*; arch, sly, nudging, winking 833 *merry*; coquettish, coy, cute, cutesy, twee, too-too, mock-modest, niminy-piminy, namby-pamby, mincing, simpering, grimacing, languishing; humbugging, canting, hypocritical, tongue-in-cheek, ironical 542 *deceiving*; bluffing 877 *boastful*; shallow, hollow, specious, pretentious, big-sounding, high-s.; big-mouthed, gushing, fulsome, stagy, theatrical, camp, over-dramatized 875 *ostentatious*; dandified, foppish, poncy, camp; conceited, la-di-da, giving oneself airs, putting on a., showing off, swanking, posturing, posing, striking poses, striking an attitude, attitudinizing 873 *vain*; stuck up 871 *prideful*; snobbish, social-climbing, name-dropping, keeping up appearances, all fur coat and nae knickers (Scots) 847 *ill-bred*; bogus 541 *false*; for effect, assumed, put on, insincere, phoney; overdone 546 *exaggerated*.

**Vb.** *be affected*, affect, put on, wear, assume; pretend, feign, go through the motions, make a show of, bluff 541 *dissemble*; make as if 20 *imitate*; affect zeal 678 *be busy*; perform, act a part, play-act, role-play 594 *act*; overact, ham, barnstorm 546 *exaggerate*; try for effect, seek an e., camp it up, play to the gallery; dramatize oneself, attitudinize, strike attitudes, posture, pose, strike a p., prance, mince, ponce about 875 *be ostentatious*; have pretensions, put on airs, give oneself a., put on side, swank, show off, make an exhibition of oneself 873 *be vain*; air one's knowledge 490 *know*; euphuize 575 *be elegant*; brag, vaunt, talk big 877 *boast*; pout, moue, simper, smirk 835 *smile*; coquette, flirt, languish 887 *excite love*; play the hypocrite 541 *cant*; save appearances, euphemize.

## 851 Ridicule

**N.** *ridicule*, derision, derisiveness, poking fun; mockery, mimicry, scoffing, flippancy 921 *disrespect*; sniggering, grinning 835 *laughter*; raillery, teasing, making fun of, ribbing, banter, persiflage, badinage, leg-pulling, chaff, leg-pull; buffoonery, horseplay, clowning, practical joke 497 *foolery*; grin, snigger, laugh, scoff, mock, fleer 926 *detraction*; irony, tongue in cheek, sarcasm, barbed shaft, backhanded compliment; catcall, hoot, hiss 924 *censure*; personalities, personal remarks, insult 921 *indignity*; ribaldry 839 *witticism*.

*satire*, denunciation 928 *accusation*; parody, burlesque, travesty, caricature, cartoon 552 *misrepresentation*; skit, spoof, send-up, take-off 20 *mimicry*; squib, lampoon, pasquinade 926 *detraction*.

*laughingstock*, object of ridicule, figure of fun, butt, universal b., common jest, by-word; sport, game, fair g.; cock-shy, Aunt Sally; April fool, silly f., buffoon, clown, zany 501 *fool*; stooge, foil, feed, straight man; guy, caricature, travesty, mockery of, apology for; eccentric 504 *crank*; original, card, caution, queer fish, odd f.; fogy, old f., geezer, museum piece, mossback, back number, square; fall guy, victim 728 *loser*.

**Adj.** *derisive*, ridiculing, mocking, chaffing, joshing etc. vb.; flippant 456 *light-minded*; sardonic, sarcastic; disparaging 926 *detracting*; ironical, quizzical; satirical, Hudibrastic 839 *witty*; ribald 847 *vulgar*; burlesque, mock-heroic.

**Vb.** *ridicule*, deride, pour scorn on, laugh at, grin at, smile at, smirk at; snigger, laugh in *or* up one's sleeve; banter, chaff, rally, twit, josh, rib, tease, roast, rag, pull one's leg, poke fun, make merry with, play w., exercise one's wit on, make fun of, make sport of, make game of, make a monkey of, take the mickey out of, have one on, kid, fool, make a fool of, make a butt of, make a laughingstock of, take the piss out of (vulg), make an April fool of, fool to the top of one's bent 542 *befool*; mock, scoff, fleer, jeer 926 *detract*; turn to a jest, make a joke of, turn to ridicule 922 *hold cheap*; take down, deflate, debunk, take the wind out of one's sails, make one look silly, make one laugh on the other side of his face 872 *humiliate*.

*satirize*, lampoon 921 *not respect*; mock, fleer, gibe; mimic, send up, take off 20 *imitate*; parody, travesty, spoof, burlesque, caricature, guy 552 *misrepresent*; expose, show up, denounce, pillory 928 *accuse*.

## 852 Hope

**N.** *hope*, hopes, expectations, assumption, presumption 507 *expectation*; good hopes, certain h., high h., sanguine expectation, hope and belief, conviction 485 *belief*; reliance, trust, confidence, faith, assurance 473 *certainty*; eager hope 471 *probability*; hope recovered, reassurance 831 *relief*; safe hope, security, anchor, sheet a., mainstay, staff 218 *support*; final hope, last h., last throw 618 *gambling*; ray of hope, beam of h., gleam of h., glimmer of h. 469 *possibility*; good omen, happy o., favourable auspices, promise, fair prospect, bright p. 511 *omen*; blue sky, silver lining, a break in the clouds; hopefulness, no cause for despair; buoyancy, airiness, breeziness, optimism, enthusiasm 833 *cheerfulness*; wishful thinking, self-deception; rose-coloured spectacles, rosy picture.

*aspiration*, ambition, purpose 617 *intention*; pious hope, fervent h., fond h., airy h.; vision, pipe dream, golden d., heart's desire, utopianism, chiliasm, millenarianism, Messianism; castles in the air, castles in Spain, El Dorado, fool's paradise 513 *fantasy*; the end of the rainbow, promised land, land of promise, utopia, millennium, the day, Der Tag 617 *objective*.

*hoper*, aspirant, candidate, waiting list; hopeful, young h., wannabe (inf); expectant, heir apparent 776 *beneficiary*; optimist, prisoner of hope; utopian, millenarian, chiliast 513 *visionary*; waiter on Providence, Micawber.

**Adj.** *hoping*, aspiring, soaring, starry-eyed; ambitious, go-getting, would-be 617 *intending*; dreaming, day-dreaming, dreaming of 513 *imaginative*; hopeful, in hopes 507 *expectant*; happy in the hope, next in succession, in sight of, on the verge of; in high hopes, sanguine, confident 473 *certain*; buoyant, optimistic, airy, uncritical; elated, euphoric, enthusiastic, flushed 833 *jubilant*; hoping for the best, ever-hoping, undespairing, undiscouraged 855 *unfearing*; Micawberish; not unhopeful, reasonably confident.

*promising*, full of promise, favourable, auspicious, propitious 730 *prosperous*; bright, fair, golden, roseate, rosy, rose-coloured, couleur de rose; affording hope, hopeful, encouraging, inspiriting; plausible, likely 471 *probable*; utopian, millennial, chiliastic; wishful, self-deluding 477 *illogical*; visionary 513 *imaginary*.

**Vb.** *hope*, trust, confide, have faith; rest assured, feel confident, hope in, put one's trust in, rely, lean on, bank on, count on, pin one's hopes on, hope and believe 485 *believe*; presume 471 *assume*; speculate, look forward 507 *expect*; hope for, dream of, aspire, be bent

upon, promise oneself, soar, aim high 617
*intend*; have a hope, be in hopes, have hopes,
have high h., have expectations, live in hopes,
keep one's fingers crossed; feel hope,
cherish h., nourish h., nurse h.; buck up, take
heart, take hope, pluck up h., recover h.,
renew h., see light at the end of the tunnel 831
*be relieved*; remain hopeful, refuse to give up
hope, not despair, see no cause for d., not
despond 599 *stand firm*; hope on, hope against
hope, cling to h., keep hope alive, never say
die; catch at a straw, keep one's spirits up, look
on the bright side, hope for the best 833 *be
cheerful*; keep smiling 600 *persevere*; be hopeful,
see life through rose-coloured spectacles;
flatter oneself, delude o. 477 *reason badly*;
anticipate, count one's chickens before they
are hatched 135 *be early*; indulge in wishful
thinking, dream 513 *imagine*.

   *give hope*, afford h., foster h., inspire h.,
raise h., inspirit, encourage, comfort 833 *cheer*;
show signs of, have the makings of, promise,
show p., promise well, shape up w., augur w.,
bid fair 471 *be likely*; raise expectations, paint a
rosy picture 511 *predict*.

   **Adv.** *hopefully*, expectantly, in all hopefulness, in all confidence; without discouragement, without despair; optimistically, airily,
lightly, gaily, uncritically.

   **Int.** nil desperandum!, never say die!,
while there's life, there's hope!, hope springs
eternal!

## 853 Hopelessness

**N.** *hopelessness*, no hope, loss of hope, discouragement, defeatism, despondency, dismay 834
*dejection*; pessimism, cynicism, despair, desperation, no way out, last hope gone; hopes overthrown, dashed hopes, hope deferred, hope
extinguished, cheated hope, frustrated h.,
deluded h. 509 *disappointment*; resignation 508
*lack of expectation*; not a hope 470 *impossibility*;
chimera, vain hope, forlorn h., futile h.,
impossible h. 513 *fantasy*; message of despair,
wan smile; poor lookout, no prospects; hopeless case, dead duck; hopeless situation,
'catch-22' (see quotation at 663 *pitfall*), bad
job, bad business 700 *predicament*; counsel of
despair, Job's comforter, misery, pessimist,
defeatist 834 *moper*.

   **Adj.** *hopeless*, bereft of hope, without h.,
devoid of h., desponding, despairing, in
despair, desperate, suicidal; unhopeful, pessimistic, cynical, looking on the black side;
defeatist, expecting the worst, fearing the w.,
resigned to the w.; sunk in despair, inconsolable, disconsolate, comfortless 834 *dejected*;
wringing one's hands 836 *lamenting*; cheated

of one's last hope 509 *disappointed*; desolate,
forlorn; ruined, undone, without resource 731
*unfortunate*.

   *unpromising*, holding out no hope, offering
no h., hopeless, comfortless, without comfort
834 *cheerless*; desperate 661 *dangerous*; unpropitious, inauspicious 731 *adverse*; ill-omened,
boding ill, threatening, ominous 511 *presageful*; inassuageable, immitigable, irremediable, remediless, incurable, cureless,
immedicable, inoperable, terminal; past cure,
beyond hope, past recall, despaired of; incorrigible, irreparable, irrecoverable, irrevocable,
irredeemable, irreclaimable; irreversible, inevitable; impracticable, out of the question 470
*impossible*.

   **Vb.** *despair*, lose heart, lose hope, have
no h., hope no more; despond, give way to
despair, wring one's hands 834 *be dejected*;
have shot one's last bolt, have no cards up
one's sleeves, give up hope, reject h.,
abandon h., relinquish h.; hope for nothing
more from, write off 674 *stop using*; give up,
turn one's face to the wall 721 *submit*.

   *leave no hope*, offer no h., deny h.; drive to
despair, bring to d.; shatter one's last hope 509
*disappoint*; be incurable, – inoperable etc. adj.

## 854 Fear

**N.** *fear*, healthy f., dread, awe 920 *respect*;
abject fear 856 *cowardice*; fright, stage f.; wind
up, funk, blue funk; phobia (see also *phobia*);
terror, mortal t., panic t.; state of terror, intimidation, trepidation, alarm, false a.; shock,
flutter, flap, flat spin 318 *agitation*; fit, fit of
terror, scare, stampede, panic, panic attack 318
*spasm*; flight, sauve qui peut; the creeps,
horror, horripilation, hair on end, cold
sweat, blood turning to water; consternation,
dismay 853 *hopelessness*; defence mechanism,
fight or flight, repression, escapism 620
*avoidance*.

   *nervousness*, lack of courage, lack of confidence, cowardliness 856 *cowardice*; self-
distrust, diffidence, shyness 874 *modesty*;
defensiveness, blustering, bluster 877 *boasting*;
timidity, timorousness, fearfulness, hesitation,
fighting shy, backing out 620 *avoidance*; loss of
nerve, cold feet, second thoughts, fears, suspicions, misgivings, qualms, mistrust, apprehension, apprehensiveness, uneasiness,
disquiet, disquietude, solicitude, anxiety,
angst, care 825 *worry*; depression, despondency
834 *dejection*; defeatism, pessimism 853 *hopelessness*; perturbation, trepidation, fear and
trembling, flutter, tremor, palpitation,
blushing, trembling, quaking, shaking, shuddering, shivering, stuttering; nerves, willies,

butterflies, collywobbles, creeps, shivers, jumps, jitters, heebie-jeebies 318 *agitation*; social phobia, performance anxiety; goose-flesh, hair on end, knees knocking, teeth chattering.

*phobia*, fear, hatred, prejudice, hang-up (inf), thing (inf); fear of death; technofear, fear of technology; anti-Semitism, racial prejudice, race hatred 888 *hatred*; McCarthyism, Reds under the beds, spy mania, witch-hunting.

### Some Common Phobias

acarophobia (mites and small insects), achluophobia (darkness), acrophobia (heights), aerophobia (draughts), agoraphobia (open spaces), aichmo-phobia (sharp or pointed objects), ailurophobia (cats), algophobia (pain), androphobia (men), Anglophobia (England or Britain, the English or British, English or British culture, etc.), anthophobia (flowers), anthropo-phobia (people), antlophobia (floods), apiphobia (bees), aquaphobia (water), arachnophobia (spiders), astraphobia (thunder and lightning), astrophobia (stars, space), autophobia (being alone, loneliness), bacillophobia (microbes), bacteriophobia (bacteria), bathophobia (depths), batophobia (heights, or being close to high buildings, mountains, etc), batracho-phobia (frogs, toads, etc), belonephobia (pins and needles), bibliophobia (books), brontophobia (thunder), canophobia (dogs), claustrophobia (enclosed places), cyberphobia (computers), cyno-phobia (dogs), dendrophobia (trees), doraphobia (fur or animal skins), entomophobia (insects), ergophobia (work), erythrophobia (blushing), Francophobia (France, the French, French culture, etc), frigophobia (cold or cold things), Gallophobia (= Francophobia), gynophobia (women), haemophobia *or* haemaphobia *or* haematophobia (blood), herpetophobia (reptiles), hippophobia (horses), homophobia (homosexuality or homosexual people), hydrophobia (water), iatro-phobia (doctors, or going to the doctor), ichthy-ophobia (fish), monophobia (being alone, loneliness), murophobia *or* musophobia (mice), myrmecophobia (ants), mysophobia (germs, dirt or contamination), necrophobia (death or corpses), nyctophobia (dark-ness, night), ochlophobia (crowds), ophiophobia *or* ophidiophobia (snakes), ornithophobia (birds), pan-phobia *or* pantophobia (everything), pathophobia (disease), phobophobia (fear), photophobia (light), pogonophobia (beards), pyrophobia (fire), sciophobia (shadows), siderophobia (stars), Sinophobia (China, the Chinese, Chinese culture, etc), technophobia (technology), thalassophobia (sea), thanatophobia (death), triskaidekaphobia (the number 13), xeno-phobia (foreigners, strangers), zoophobia (animals).

*intimidation*, deterrence, war of nerves, war cry, sabre-rattling, arms build up, fee, faw, fum; threatening 900 *threat*; caution 664 *warning*; terror, terrorization, terrorism, reign of terror 735 *severity*; alarmism, scare-mongering; sword of Damocles, suspended sen-tence 963 *punishment*; deterrent, weapon of retaliation 723 *weapon*; object of terror, goblin, hobgoblin 970 *demon*; spook, spectre 970 *ghost*; Gorgon, Medusa, scarecrow, tattie bogle, nightmare; bugbear, bugaboo, ogre 938

*monster*; skeleton, death's head, skull and crossbones.

*alarmist*, scaremonger, doom merchant, gloom and doom m., doom-watcher, doomster, ecodoomster, spreader of alarm and despondency, Cassandra, Calamity Jane; defeatist, pessimist; terrorist, terrorizer, intimi-dator, horrifier, frightener, nerve-shaker, sabre-rattler.

**Adj.** *fearing*, afeard, afraid, frightened, funky, panicky; overawed 920 *respectful*; intimi-dated, terrorized, demoralized; in fear, in mortal f., in trepidation, in a fright, in a cold sweat, in a flap, in a flat spin, in a panic, in a frenzy; terror-crazed, panic-stricken, panic-struck; stampeding, scared, alarmed, startled; hysterical, having fits, in hysterics, in the grip of a panic attack; dismayed, in consternation, consternated, flabbergasted; frozen, petrified, stunned; appalled, shocked, horrified, aghast, horror-struck, awestruck, unmanned, scared out of one's wits, trembling with fear, numbed with f., paralysed by f., rooted to the spot with f., frightened to death, fainting with fright, white as a sheet, pale as death, pale as a ghost, ashen-faced; more frightened than hurt, suffering from shock.

*nervous*, defensive, on the d., tense, uptight; waiting for the axe to fall, waiting for the bomb to drop; defeatist, pessimistic, despairing 853 *hopeless*; timid, timorous, shy, diffident, self-conscious, self-distrustful 874 *modest*; coy, wary, hesitating, shrinking, treading warily 858 *cautious*; doubtful, distrustful, mis-doubting, suspicious 474 *doubting*; windy, faint-hearted 601 *irresolute*; disturbed, dis-quieted, dismayed; apprehensive, uneasy, fearful, dreading, anxious, worried 825 *unhappy*; haunted, haunted by fears, a prey to f., terror-ridden, highly-strung, starting at a sound, afraid of one's own shadow, jittery, jumpy, nervy, on edge, uptight; tremulous, shaky, shaking, trembling, quaking, cowering, cringing 856 *cowardly*; with one's heart in one's mouth, shaking like a leaf *or* a jelly; on pins and needles, palpitating, breathless 318 *agitated*.

*frightening*, shocking, startling, alarming etc. vb.; formidable, redoubtable; hazardous, hairy 661 *dangerous*; tremendous, dreadful, fear-inspiring, awe-i., numinous, fearsome, awe-some 821 *impressive*; grim, grisly, hideous, ghastly, lurid, frightful, revolting, petrifying, horrifying, horrific, horrible, terrible, awful, appalling, mind-boggling, mind-blowing; hor-ripilant, hair-raising, flesh-creeping, blood-curdling; weird, eerie, creepy, scary, ghoulish, nightmarish, gruesome, macabre, sinister;

portentous, ominous, direful 511 *presageful*; intimidating, terroristic, sabre-rattling, bullying, hectoring 735 *oppressive*; minatory, menacing 900 *threatening*; bellowing, roaring 400 *loud*; nerve-racking 827 *distressing*.

**Vb.** *fear*, funk, be afraid, – frightened etc. adj.; stand in fear *or* awe, go in fear and trembling, dread 920 *respect*; flap, be in a f., – in a bit of a state, have the wind up, – the willies; get the wind up, take fright, – alarm; flap, panic, fall into p., have a panic attack, press the panic button, stampede, take to flight, fly 620 *run away*; start, jump, flutter 318 *be agitated*; faint, collapse, break down.

*quake*, shake, tremble, quiver, shiver, shudder, stutter, quaver; quake in one's shoes, shake like a jelly, fear for one's life, be frightened to death, be scared out of one's wits, faint for fear; change colour, blench, pale, go white as a sheet, turn ashen; wince, flinch, shrink, shy, jib 620 *avoid*; quail, cower, crouch, skulk, come to heel 721 *knuckle under*; stand aghast, be horrified, be petrified, be chilled with fear, freeze, freeze with horror, be rooted to the spot with terror, feel one's blood run cold, feel one's blood turn to water, feel one's hair stand on end.

*be nervous*, – apprehensive etc. adj.; feel shy, feel awkward 874 *be modest*; have misgivings, suspect, distrust, mistrust 486 *doubt*; shrink, shy, quail, funk it, not face it, put off the evil day; be anxious, dread, consult one's fears, have f., have qualms; hesitate, get cold feet, think twice, have second thoughts, think better of it, not dare 858 *be cautious*; get the wind up, start at one's own shadow, be on edge, sit on thorns, be all of a doodah 318 *be agitated*.

*frighten*, fright, affright, play the bogyman, make *or* pull faces, grimace; scare, panic, stampede; intimidate, put in fear, menace 900 *threaten*; stand over, hang o. 155 *impend*; alarm, cause a., raise the a., press the panic button, cry wolf; frighten to death, scare the living daylights out of, scare stiff, scare half to death; make one jump, give one a fright, give one a turn, startle, flutter, flurry, make one all of a doodah 318 *agitate*; start, flush 619 *hunt*; disquiet, disturb, perturb, prey on the mind, haunt, obsess, beset 827 *trouble*; raise apprehensions, put the wind up, make nervous, set on edge, rattle, shake, unnerve; play on one's nerves, wring one's n., unstring one's n., throw into a nervous state, 'frighten the horses';

> It doesn't matter what you do in the bedroom as long as you don't do it in the street and frighten the horses.
> Mrs Patrick Campbell

> I don't mind what Congress does, as long as they don't do it in the streets and frighten the horses.
> Victor Hugo

unman, make a coward of, cowardize, demoralize; strike with fear, put the fear of God into, awe, overawe 821 *impress*; quell, subdue, cow 727 *overmaster*; amaze, shock, stagger, flabbergast, stun 508 *surprise*; dismay, confound, abash, disconcert 63 *derange*; frighten off, daunt, deter, discourage 613 *dissuade*; terrorize, institute a reign of terror 735 *oppress*; browbeat, bully 827 *torment*; terrify, horrify, harrow, make aghast; chill, freeze, benumb, paralyse, petrify, rivet, turn to stone, Gorgonize, mesmerize 375 *render insensible*; appal, boggle the mind, chill the spine, freeze the blood, make one's blood run cold, turn one's blood to water; make one's hair stand on end *or* curl, make one's flesh creep, make one's knees knock, make one's teeth chatter, frighten out of one's wits, reduce one to a quivering jelly.

## 855 Courage

**N.** *courage*, bravery, valiance, valour, derring-do; moral courage, courage of one's convictions 929 *probity*; VC courage, courage in the face of the enemy, heroism, gallantry, chivalry; self-confidence, self-reliance; fearlessness, bottle (inf), daring, ignorance of fear, intrepidity, nerve; defiance of danger, boldness, hardihood, audacity 857 *rashness*; spirit, mettle, dash, go, élan, panache 174 *vigorousness*; enterprise 672 *undertaking*; tenacity, survivability, bulldog courage 600 *perseverance*; undauntedness, high morale, stoutness of heart, firmness, fortitude, determination, resoluteness 599 *resolution*; gameness, pluck, smeddum, spunk, cojones, guts, heart, great h., stout h., heart of oak, backbone, grit 600 *stamina*; sham courage, Dutch c., pot valour; desperate courage, courage of despair; brave face, bold front 711 *defiance*; fresh courage, new heart, encouragement, animation 612 *inducement*.

*manliness*, manhood, machismo 929 *probity*; virtue, chivalry; manly spirit, martial s., heroic qualities, soldierly q., morale, devotion to duty; militancy, aggressiveness, fierceness 718 *bellicosity*; endurance, stiff upper lip 599 *resolution*.

*prowess*, derring-do, deeds of d., chivalry, knightliness, knighthood, heroism, heroic achievement, knightly deed, gallant act, act of courage, soldierly conduct, courage in the face of the enemy; feat, feat of arms, emprise, exploit, stroke, bold s., coup de grâce 676 *deed*; desperate venture 857 *rashness*; heroics.

*brave person*, hero, heroine, VC, GC, Croix de Guerre; knight, paladin; good soldier, stout s., stout fellow, beau sabreur, brave, warrior 722 *soldier*; man, true m., man *or* woman of mettle, man *or* woman of spirit, plucky fellow, game dog, bulldog, braveheart; daredevil, risk-taker, stunt man *or* woman; fire-eater, bully, bravo 857 *desperado*; Galahad, Greatheart, Lionheart; Joan of Arc, Boadicea, Amazon; Don Quixote, Bayard, knight-errant, k. of the Round Table; gallant knight, preux chevalier; the brave, the bravest of the brave; band of heroes, gallant company, SAS; forlorn hope, picked troops 644 *elite*; lion, tiger, game-cock, fighting c., bulldog.

**Adj.** *courageous*, brave, valorous, valiant, gallant, heroic; chivalrous, knightly, knight-like; yeomanly, soldierly, soldier-like, martial, Amazonian 718 *warlike*; stout, doughty, tall, bonny, manful, manly, tough, macho, Ramboesque, redblooded; militant, bellicose, aggressive, fire-eating; fierce, bloody, savage 898 *cruel*; bold 711 *defiant*; dashing, hardy, audacious, daring, venturesome, bold as brass 857 *rash*; adventurous 672 *enterprising*; mettlesome, spirited, high-s., high-hearted, stout-h., brave-h., braveheart, lion-hearted, bold as a lion; firm-minded, strong-m., full of courage, full of fight, full of spirit, full of spunk, spunky; full of Dutch courage, pot-valiant; unbowed, unswayed, firm, steady, dogged, indomitable, never say die 600 *persevering*; desperate, determined 599 *resolute*; of high morale, game, plucky, sporting; ready for danger, ready for the fray, ready for anything, unflinching, unshrinking, leading the charge 597 *willing*.

*unfearing*, unafraid, intrepid, nerveless, without a nerve in one's body, with nerves of steel *or* of iron; despising danger, danger-loving; sure of oneself, confident, self-c., self-reliant; fearless, dauntless, dreadless, aweless; unshrinking, untrembling, unblenching; undismayed, undaunted, nothing daunted, undashed, unabashed, unawed, unalarmed, unconcerned, unapprehensive, unappalled, unshaken, unshakable.

**Vb.** *be courageous*, – bold etc. adj.; have what it takes, have guts, come up to scratch, show spirit, show one's mettle; fight with the best 716 *fight*; venture, adventure, bell the cat, take the plunge, take the bull by the horns 672 *undertake*; dare 661 *face danger*; show fight, brave, face, outface, outdare, beard, affront, snap one's fingers at 711 *defy*; confront, look in the face, look in the eyes, be eyeball to eyeball with, eyeball; speak out, speak one's mind, speak up, stand up and be counted 532 *affirm*; face the music, stick one's neck out, show a

bold front, stick to one's guns 599 *stand firm*; go over the top 712 *charge*; laugh at danger, mock at d. 857 *be rash*; show prowess, show valour, win one's spurs; keep one's head 823 *keep calm*; bear up, endure, grin and bear it, take one's medicine 825 *suffer*.

*take courage*, pluck up c., muster c., take heart of grace, nerve *or* steel oneself, take one's courage in both hands; put a brave face on it, show fight, cast away fear, screw up one's courage 599 *be resolute*; rally, stand 599 *stand firm*.

*give courage*, infuse c.; animate, put heart into, hearten, nerve, make a man of; embolden, encourage, inspirit, inspire 612 *incite*; buck up, rally 833 *cheer*; pat on the back, keep in countenance, keep in spirits, preserve morale, raise m., keep one's blood up; bolster up, reassure, take away fear, give confidence.

**Adv.** *bravely*, courageously, stoutly, doughtily, manfully; with one's blood up; with one's head held high.

## 856 Cowardice

**N.** *cowardice*, abject fear, funk, sheer f., blue f. 854 *fear*; cowardliness, lack of spirit, craven spirit, no grit, no guts 601 *irresolution*; pusillanimity, timidity, lack of courage, lack of daring; absence of morale, faint-heartedness, chicken-heartedness; unmanliness, poltroonery, dastardy, dastardliness; defeatism 853 *hopelessness*; leaving the sinking ship, desertion, quitting, shirking 918 *undutifulness*; white feather, yellow streak, low morale, faint heart, chicken liver; pot valiance, Dutch courage, braggadocio 877 *boasting*; cowering, skulking, leading from behind; discretion, better part of valour; safety first, overcaution 858 *caution*; moral cowardice, recantation 603 *tergiversation*.

*coward*, utter c., faintheart, no hero; funk, poltroon, craven, dastard, yellow-belly, lily-liver, chickenheart, wheyface; scaredycat, fraidycat, cowardy custard; sneak, rat, tell-tale, clype (Scots) 524 *informer*; runaway 603 *tergiversator*; coward at heart, bully, braggart 877 *boaster*; sissy, milksop, mummy's boy, baby, big b., cry-b., big girl's blouse 163 *weakling*; skulker, quitter, shirker, flincher, deserter, scuttler; cur, chicken, rabbit, mouse, jellyfish, invertebrate, doormat; scaremonger, defeatist, doomster 854 *alarmist*.

**Adj.** *cowardly*, coward, craven, poltroonish; not so brave, pusillanimous, timid, timorous, fearful, niddering, afraid of one's own shadow, unable to say boo to a goose, of a nervous disposition 854 *nervous*; soft, womanish, babyish, unmanly, sissy 163 *weak*; spiritless, spunkless, without grit, without guts, lacking smeddum, with no backbone, poor-spirited, weak-minded, faint-hearted, chicken-h., chicken-livered, white-l., yellow-l., milk-l., lily-l., yellow-bellied, chicken; sneaking, skulking, cowering, quailing; dastardly, yellow, abject, base, vile, mean-spirited, currish, recreant, caitiff; unsoldierly, unmilitary, unmartial, unwarlike, unaggressive; cowed, lacking morale, with no fight left 721 *submitting*; defeatist 853 *hopeless*; unheroic, unvaliant, uncourageous, prudent, discreet 858 *cautious*; bashful, shy, coy 874 *modest*; easily frightened, funky, shakable, unstable, unsteady, infirm of purpose 601 *irresolute*.

**Vb.** *be cowardly*, lack courage, have no fight, have no pluck, have no grit, have no guts, lack smeddum, have no backbone, have no heart *or* stomach for, not dare 601 *be irresolute*; lose one's nerve, get the jitters, have cold feet 854 *be nervous*; shrink, funk, shy from, back out, chicken o. 620 *avoid*; hide, slink, skulk, sneak; quail, cower, cringe 721 *knuckle under*; show a yellow streak, show the white feather, show fear, turn tail, cut and run, run for cover, panic, press the panic button, stampede, scuttle, show one's back, desert 620 *run away*; show discretion, live to fight another day, lead from behind, keep well to the rear 858 *be cautious*.

## 857 Rashness

**N.** *rashness*, lack of caution, lack of circumspection, incaution, incautiousness, unwariness, heedlessness 456 *inattention*; carelessness, neglect 458 *negligence*; imprudence, improvidence, indiscretion 499 *folly*; lack of consideration, inconsideration, irresponsibility, frivolity, flippancy, levity, light-mindedness; wildness, indiscipline, haughtiness 738 *disobedience*; scorn of the consequences, daredevilry, recklessness, foolhardiness, temerity, audacity, presumption, overconfidence, overdaring; hotheadedness, fieriness, impatience 822 *excitability*; rushing into things, impetuosity, precipitance, hastiness, overhastiness, overhaste 680 *haste*; overenthusiasm, quixotry, quixotism, knight-errantry; dangerous game, playing with fire, brinkmanship, game of chicken; desperation, courage of despair 855 *courage*; needless risk, leap in the dark 661 *danger*; too many eggs in one basket, under-insurance, counting one's chickens before they are hatched 661 *vulnerability*; reckless gamble, last throw 618 *gambling*; reckless expenditure 815 *prodigality*.

*desperado*, daredevil, madcap, hothead, Hotspur, fire-eater; stunt, adventurer, plunger,

inveterate gambler 618 *gambler*; harum-scarum, scapegrace, ne'er-do-well; one who sticks at nothing, gunman, terrorist, guerrilla; bully, bravo 904 *ruffian*.

**Adj.** *rash*, ill-considered, ill-conceived, ill-advised, harebrained, foolhardy, wildcat, injudicious, indiscreet, imprudent 499 *unwise*; careless, hit-and-miss, slapdash, free-and-easy, accident-prone 458 *negligent*; unforeseeing, not looking, uncircumspect, lemming-like, incautious, unwary, heedless, thoughtless, inconsiderate, uncalculating 456 *inattentive*; light, frivolous, airy, breezy, flippant, giddy, devil-may-care, harum-scarum, slaphappy, trigger-happy 456 *light-minded*; irresponsible, reckless, regardless, couldn't-care-less, don't-care, damning the consequences, lunatic, wanton, wild, cavalier; bold, daring, temerarious, audacious; overdaring, overbold, madcap, daredevil, do-or-die, neck or nothing, breakneck, suicidal; overambitious, over the top, oversanguine, oversure, overconfident 852 *hoping*; overweening, presumptuous, arrogant 878 *insolent*; precipitate, gadarene, headlong, hell-bent, desperate 680 *hasty*; unchecked, headstrong 602 *wilful*; untaught by experience 491 *ignorant*; impulsive, impatient, hot-blooded, hot-headed, fire-eating, furious 822 *excitable*; danger-loving 855 *unfearing*; venturesome 618 *speculative*; adventurous, thrill-seeking, risk-taking 672 *enterprising*; improvident, thriftless 815 *prodigal*.

**Vb.** *be rash*, – reckless etc. adj.; lack caution, want judgment, lean on a broken reed; expose oneself, drop one's guard, stick one's neck out, take unnecessary risks, put one's head in the lion's cage, ride the tiger; not look round, go bull-headed at, charge at, rush at, rush into, rush one's fences 680 *hasten*; take a leap in the dark, leap before one looks, buy a pig in a poke, take something on trust; ignore the consequences, damn the c.; plunge 618 *gamble*; put all one's eggs into one basket, not be insured, underinsure; not care 456 *be inattentive*; play fast and loose 634 *waste*; spend to the hilt 815 *be prodigal*; play the fool, play with edged tools, play with fire, burn one's fingers; venture to the brink, stand on the edge of a volcano, go out on a limb, risk one's neck, dice with death 661 *face danger*; play a desperate game, court disaster, ask for trouble, tempt providence, push one's luck, rush in where angels fear to tread; anticipate, reckon without one's host, count one's chickens before they are hatched, aim too high 695 *act foolishly*.

**Adv.** *rashly*, inconsiderately, carelessly, incautiously, lightly, gaily; headlong, recklessly, like Gadarene swine, like lemmings.

## 858 Caution

**N.** *caution*, cautiousness, wariness, heed-fulness, care, heed 457 *carefulness*; hesitation, doubt, second thoughts 854 *nervousness*; instinct of self-preservation 932 *selfishness*; looking before one leaps, looking twice, looking round, circumspection; guardedness, secretiveness, reticence 525 *secrecy*; calculation, careful reckoning, counting the risk, safety first; all possible precautions, nothing left to chance 669 *preparation*; deliberation, due d., mature consideration 480 *judgment*; sobriety, balance, level-headedness 834 *seriousness*; prudence, discretion, worldly wisdom 498 *wisdom*; insurance, precaution 662 *safeguard*; forethought 510 *foresight*; Fabianism, Fabian policy 823 *patience*; going slow, taking one's time, watching one's step, one step at a time, festina lente 278 *slowness*; wait-and-see policy, waiting game, cat-and-mouse 136 *delay*.

**Adj.** *cautious*, wary, watchful 455 *attentive*; heedful 457 *careful*; hesitating, doubtful, suspicious 854 *nervous*; taking no risks, insured, hedging; guarded, secret, secretive, incommunicative, cagey 525 *reticent*; experienced, taught by experience, once bitten, twice shy 669 *prepared*; on one's guard, circumspect, looking round, looking all ways, gingerly, stealthy, feeling one's way, taking one's time, watching one's step, tentative 461 *experimental*; conservative 660 *safe*; responsible 929 *trustworthy*; prudent, prudential, discreet 498 *wise*; noncommittal 625 *neutral*; frugal, counting the cost 814 *economical*; canny, counting the risk; timid, slow-moving, overcautious, unenterprising, unadventurous, overinsured; slow, unhasty, deliberate, Fabian 823 *patient*; sober, cool-headed, level-h., cool; cold-blooded, calm, self-possessed 823 *inexcitable*.

**Vb.** *be cautious*, beware, take good care 457 *be careful*; take no risks, go by the book, play it by the b., play safe, play for safety, play for a draw; play a waiting game, play a cat-and-mouse g. 498 *be wise*; ca' canny, go slow, festina lente 278 *move slowly*; cover up, cover one's tracks 525 *conceal*; not talk 525 *keep secret*; keep under cover, keep on the safe side, keep in the rear, keep in the background, keep out of the limelight, hide 523 *lurk*; look, look out, see how the land lies 438 *scan*; see how the wind blows, feel one's way, play it by ear, put a toe in the water 461 *be tentative*; be on one's guard, tread warily, watch one's step, pussyfoot 525 *be stealthy*; look twice, think t. 455 *be mindful*; calculate, reckon 480 *judge*; consider the risk factor, count the cost, cut one's coat according to one's cloth 814 *economize*;

know when to stop, take one's time, reculer pour mieux sauter; let well alone, let sleeping dogs lie, keep aloof, keep well out of 620 *avoid*; consider the consequences 511 *predict*; take precautions 124 *look ahead*; look a gift horse in the mouth 480 *estimate*; assure oneself, make sure 473 *make certain*; cover oneself, insure, take out a policy, reinsure, hedge, overinsure 660 *seek safety*; leave nothing to chance 669 *prepare*.

**Adv.** *cautiously*, with caution, gingerly, conservatively; softly softly.

## 859 Desire

**N.** *desire*, wish, will and pleasure 595 *will*; summons, call, cry 737 *command*; dun 737 *demand*; desideration, wanting, want, need, exigency 627 *requirement*; shopping list, wish list; claim 915 *dueness*; desiderium, homesickness, nostalgia, 'la nostalgie de la boue' 830 *regret*;

> Marquis: Mettez un canard sur un lac au milieu des cygnes, vous verrez qu'il regrettera sa mare et finira par y retourner.
> (*If you put a duck on a lake among swans, you will see that it will long for its pond and in the end will go back there.*)
> Montrichard: La nostalgie de la boue!
> (*A longing to be back in the mud!*)
> Émile Augier, *Le Mariage d'Olympe*

wistfulness, longing, hankering, yearning, sheep's eyes; wishing, thinking, daydreaming, daydream, castles in the air 513 *fantasy*; ambition, aspiration 852 *hope*; appetency, yen, urge 279 *impulse*; cacoethes, itch; thrill-seeking, rubber-necking, curiousness, thirst for knowledge, intellectual curiosity 453 *curiosity*; avidity, eagerness, zeal 597 *willingness*; passion, ardour, warmth, impetuosity, impatience 822 *excitability*; rage, fury 503 *frenzy*; monomania, mania 503 *personality disorder*; craving, lust for, appetite, hunger, thirst, hungry look (see also *hunger*); land-hunger, expansionism, 'a place in the sun';

> Wir wollen niemand in den Schatten stellen, aber wir verlangen auch unseren Platz an der Sonne.
> (*We do not want to put anyone in the shade, but we demand our place in the sun as well.*)
> Count von Bülow to the German Reichstag (A similar phrase was later used by Kaiser Wilhelm II.)

covetousness, cupidity, itching palm 816 *avarice*; graspingness, greediness, greed 786 *rapacity*; voracity, wolfishness, insatiability 947 *gluttony*; concupiscence, lust (see also *libido*); inordinate desire, incontinence 943 *intemperance*.

*hunger*, starvation, famine, famished condition, empty stomach, snack attack 946 *fasting*; appetite, good a., sharp a., keen a., voracious a., edge of a.; thirst, thirstiness 342 *dryness*; burning thirst, unquenchable t.; dipso-mania 949 *alcoholism*.

*liking*, fancy, fondness, infatuation 887 *love*; stomach, appetite, zest, craving; relish, tooth, sweet t. 386 *taste*; leaning, penchant, propensity, trend 179 *tendency*; weakness, partiality; affinity, mutual a.; sympathy, involvement 775 *participation*; inclination, mind 617 *intention*; predilection, favour 605 *choice*; whim, whimsy 604 *caprice*; hobby, craze, fad, mania 481 *bias*; fascination, allurement, attraction, temptation, titillation, seduction 612 *inducement*.

*libido*, Eros, life instinct, sexual urge; erotism, eroticism; erogenous zone, G-spot, Gräfenberg spot; concupiscence, sexual desire, carnal d., passion, rut, heat, oestrus; mating season; libidinousness, lickerishness, prurience, lust, lecherousness, letch, the hots 951 *unchastity*; nymphomania, priapism, satyriasis 84 *variance*.

*desired object*, one's desire, one's heart's d., wish, desire, desirable thing, desideratum 627 *requirement*; catch, prize, plum 729 *trophy*; lion, idol, cynosure 890 *favourite*; forbidden fruit, torment of Tantalus; envy, temptation; magnet, lure, draw 291 *attraction*; the unattainable, princesse lointaine 887 *loved one*; aim, goal, star, ambition, aspiration, dream 617 *objective*; ideal, dream team 646 *perfection*; height of one's ambition.

*desirer*, coveter, envier; wooer, suer, courter 887 *lover*; glutton, sucker for; fancier, amateur, dilettante 492 *collector*; devotee, votary, idolater 981 *worshipper*; well-wisher, favourer, sympathizer 707 *patron*; wisher, aspirant 852 *hoper*; claimant, pretender; candidate, parasite 763 *petitioner*; ambitious person, careerist; seducer 952 *libertine*.

**Adj.** *desiring*, appetent, desirous, wishing, wishful, tempted, unable to resist; oversexed, lustful, libidinous, concupiscent, hot for, letching for, rutting, on heat, ruttish, must, oestrous 951 *lecherous*; covetous (see also *greedy*); craving, needing, wanting 627 *demanding*; missing, nostalgic 830 *regretting*; fain, inclined, minded, set upon, bent upon, hell bent u. 617 *intending*; ambitious 852 *hoping*; aspiring, would-be, wistful, longing, yearning, hankering, hungry for; unsatisfied, demanding more, insatiable; curious, solicitous, sedulous, anxious; eager, keen, mad k., burning, ardent, agog, breathless, impatient, dying for; itching, spoiling for; clamant, vocal, avid, overeager, overinclined, mad for, wild about; liking, fond, partial to, with a weakness for.

*greedy*, acquisitive, possessive 932 *selfish*;

ambitious, status-seeking; voracious, omnivorous, open-mouthed 947 *gluttonous*; unsated, unsatisfied, unslaked, quenchless, unquenchable, inappeasable, insatiable, insatiate; rapacious, grasping, retentive 816 *avaricious*; exacting, extortionate 735 *oppressive*.

*hungry*, hungering; unfilled, empty, foodless, supperless, dinnerless 946 *fasting*; half-starved, starving, famished 636 *underfed*; peckish, ready for, ravenous, hungry as a hunter, pinched with hunger, ready to eat a horse; thirsty, thirsting, athirst, dry, drouthy, parched, parched with thirst, dehydrated.

*desired*, wanted, liked; likable, desirable, worth having, enviable, coveted, in demand, to die for, TDF; acceptable, welcome; appetizing 826 *pleasurable*; fetching, catchy, attractive, appealing 291 *attracting*; wished, self-sought, invited 597 *voluntary*.

**Vb.** *desire*, want, have a heart for; desiderate, miss, feel the lack of 627 *require*; ask for, cry out f., clamour f. 737 *demand*; desire the presence of, call, summon, send for, ring for 737 *command*; invite 882 *be hospitable*; wish, make a w., pray; wish otherwise, unwish 830 *regret*; wish for oneself, covet 912 *envy*; promise oneself, have a mind to, set one's heart on, set one's mind on, have designs on, set one's sights on, aim at, have at heart 617 *intend*; plan for, angle f., fish f. 623 *plan*; aspire, raise one's eyes to, dream of, dream, day-dream 852 *hope*; want a lot, aim high; look for, expect, think one deserves 915 *claim*; wish in vain, whistle for, cry for the moon 695 *act foolishly*; wish for another, pray for, intercede, invoke, wish on, call down on; wish ill 899 *curse*; wish one well 897 *be benevolent*; welcome, be glad of, jump at, catch at, grasp at, clutch at 786 *take*; lean towards 179 *tend*; favour, prefer, select 605 *choose*; crave, itch for, hanker after, have a yen for, long for; long, yearn, pine, languish; pant for, gasp f., burn f., die f., be dying f. 636 *be unsatisfied*; thirst for, hunger f., raven f. (see also *be hungry*); can't wait, must have; like, have a liking, affect, have a taste for, care for 887 *love*; take to, warm to, take a fancy to, fall in love with, dote, dote on, be infatuated with, moon after, sigh a., burn 887 *be in love*; ogle, make eyes at, make passes, solicit, woo 889 *court*; set one's cap at, make a dead set at, run after, chase 619 *pursue*; lust, lust for, lust after, letch after, have the hots for 951 *be impure*; rut, be on heat.

*be hungry*, hunger, famish, starve, be ravenous, have an empty stomach, have an aching void, be ready to eat a horse 636 *be unsatisfied*; have a good appetite, open one's mouth for, lick one's chops, salivate, water at the mouth 301 *eat*; thirst, be athirst, be dry, be dying for a drink, be parched, be dehydrated.

*cause desire*, incline 612 *motivate*; arouse desire, provoke d., arouse lust, fill with longing 887 *excite love*; stimulate 821 *excite*; smell good, whet the appetite, activate the taste buds, make the mouth water 390 *make appetizing*; parch, raise a thirst; dangle, tease, titillate, tantalize 612 *tempt*; allure, seduce, draw 291 *attract*; hold out hope 852 *give hope*.

**Adv.** *desirously*, wishfully, wistfully, eagerly, with appetite, hungrily, thirstily, greedily; by request, as desired.

## 860 Indifference

**N.** *indifference*, unconcern, uninterestedness 454 *incuriosity*; lack of interest, half-heartedness, lack of zeal, lukewarmness 598 *unwillingness*; coolness, coldness, faint praise, two cheers 823 *inexcitability*; unsurprise 865 *lack of wonder*; lovelessness, mutual indifference, nothing between them; anorexia, no appetite, loss of a.; inappetence, no desire for; inertia, apathy 679 *inactivity*; nonchalance, insouciance 458 *negligence*; perfunctoriness, carelessness 456 *inattention*; don't-care attitude 734 *laxity*; recklessness, heedlessness 857 *rashness*; promiscuousness 464 *indiscrimination*; amorality, indifferentism; open mind, unbiased attitude, impartiality, equity 913 *justice*; neutrality 625 *middle way*; nil admirari; nothing to choose between, six of one and half a dozen of the other; indifferentist, neutralist, neutral 625 *moderate*; Laodicean 598 *slacker*; object of indifference, wallflower.

**Adj.** *indifferent*, uncaring, unconcerned, insolicitous; uninterested 454 *incurious*; lukewarm, Laodicean, half-hearted 598 *unwilling*; impersonal, uninvolved, passionless, phlegmatic 820 *impassive*; unimpressed, unwondering, unsurprised, blasé 865 *unastonished*; calm, cool, cold 823 *inexcitable*; nonchalant, insouciant, careless, pococurante, perfunctory 458 *negligent*; supine, lackadaisical, listless 679 *inactive*; undesirous, unambitious, unaspiring; don't-care, easygoing 734 *lax*; unresponsive, unmoved, unallured, unattracted, untempted, insensible to 625 *undeviating*; loveless, heart-whole, fancy-free, uninvolved; disenchanted, disillusioned, out of love, cooling off; impartial, inflexible 913 *just*; noncommittal, moderate 625 *neutral*; promiscuous 464 *indiscriminating*; amoral, cynical.

*unwanted*, unwelcome, de trop, in the way; undesired, unwished for, unasked, uninvited, unbidden, unprovoked; loveless, unvalued, uncared for, unmissed 458 *neglected*;

unchosen, on the shelf; all one to 606 *choiceless*; insipid, tasteless 391 *unsavoury*; unattractive, unalluring, untempting, undesirable 861 *disliked*.

**Vb.** *be indifferent*, – unconcerned etc. adj.; see nothing wonderful 865 *not wonder*; not have one's heart in it, be uninvolved, take no interest 456 *be inattentive*; not mind, care little for, not lose any sleep over, damn with faint praise; care nothing for, not give a fig *or* a thankyou for, not care a straw about, have no taste for, have no relish f. 861 *dislike*; couldn't care less, take it or leave it; not think twice about, not care, not give a hoot, shrug, shrug off, dismiss, let go, make light of 922 *hold cheap*; not defend, hold no brief for, take neither side, sit on the fence 606 *be neutral*; grow indifferent, fall out of love, lose interest, cool off; not repine, have no regrets; fail to move, leave one cold 820 *make insensitive*.

**Int.** never mind!, what does it matter!, who cares?, so what?

## 861 Dislike

**N.** *dislike*, disinclination, no inclination for, no fancy for, no stomach for; reluctance, backwardness 598 *unwillingness*; displeasure 891 *resentment*; dissatisfaction 829 *discontent*; disagreement 489 *dissent*; shyness, aversion 620 *avoidance*; instinctive dislike, sudden *or* instant d., antipathy, allergy; rooted dislike, distaste, disrelish; repugnance, repulsion, disgust, abomination, abhorrence, detestation, loathing; shuddering, horror, mortal h. 854 *fear*; xenophobia 854 *phobia*; prejudice, sectarian p., odium theologicum 481 *bias*; animosity, bad blood, ill feeling, mutual hatred, common h. 888 *hatred*; Euroscepticism; nausea, queasiness, turn, heaving stomach, vomit 300 *voidance*; sickener, one's fill 863 *satiety*; 'gall and wormwood', bitterness 393 *sourness*;

> Remembering mine affliction and my misery, the wormwood and the gall.
>
> Bible, Lamentations of Jeremiah

object of dislike, not one's type, bête-noire, pet aversion, pet hate, a red rag to a bull, 'Dr Fell'.

> I do not love you, Dr Fell,
> But why, I cannot tell;
> But this I know full well,
> I do not love you, Dr Fell.
>
> Thomas Brown (Dr Fell was the dean of Christ Church, Oxford, who had threatened to expel Brown from the college. The lines are based on an epigram of the Roman poet Martial.)

**Adj.** *disliking*, not liking, displeased 829 *discontented*; undesirous, disinclined, loath 598 *unwilling*; squeamish, qualmish, queasy;

allergic, antipathetic; disagreeing 489 *dissenting*; averse, hostile 881 *inimical*; shy 620 *avoiding*; repelled, abhorring, loathing 888 *hating*; unfriendly, unloverlike, loveless; unsympathetic, out of sympathy; disenchanted, disillusioned, out of love 860 *indifferent*; sick of 863 *sated*; nauseated 300 *vomiting*.

*disliked*, unwished, undesired, undesirable, unwelcome 860 *unwanted*; unchosen 607 *rejected*; unpopular, out of favour, in one's bad books, avoided; disagreeing, not to one's taste, grating, jarring, unrelished, bitter, uncomforting, unconsoling; repugnant, antipathetic, rebarbative, repulsive 292 *repellent*; revolting, abhorrent, loathsome 888 *hateful*; abominable, disgusting 924 *disapproved*; nauseous, nauseating, sickening, fulsome, foul, stinking 391 *unsavoury*; disagreeable, insufferable 827 *intolerable*; loveless, unlovable, unsympathetic; unlovely 842 *ugly*.

**Vb.** *dislike*, mislike, disrelish, find not to one's taste; not care for, have no liking f., have no desire for; have no stomach for, have no heart for 598 *be unwilling*; not choose, prefer not to 607 *reject*; object 762 *deprecate*; mind 891 *resent*; take a dislike to, feel an aversion for, have a down on, have one's knife in, have it in for 481 *be biased*; react against 280 *recoil*; feel sick at, want to heave 300 *vomit*; shun, turn away, shrink from, have no time for 620 *avoid*; look askance at 924 *disapprove*; turn up the nose at, sniff at, sneer at 922 *despise*; make a face, grimace 893 *be sullen*; be unable to abide, not endure, can't stand, can't bear, detest, loathe, abominate, abhor 888 *hate*; not like the look of, shudder at 854 *fear*; unwish, wish undone 830 *regret*.

*cause dislike*, disincline, deter 854 *frighten*; go against the grain, rub the wrong way, antagonize, put one's back up 891 *enrage*; set against, set at odds, make bad blood 888 *excite hate*; satiate, pall, pall on, jade 863 *sate*; disagree with, upset 25 *disagree*; put off, revolt 292 repel; offend, grate, jar 827 *displease*; get one's goat, get up one's nose, get on one's nerves 827 *torment*; suck (US inf) disgust, stick in one's throat, nauseate, sicken, make one's gorge rise, turn one's stomach, make one sick; shock, scandalize, make a scandal 924 *incur blame*.

**Adv.** *ad nauseam*, disgustingly, to sickening lengths; horribile dictu.

**Int.** disgusting!, revolting!, ugh!, yuk!

## 862 Fastidiousness

**N.** *fastidiousness*, niceness, nicety, daintiness, finicalness, finicality, fikiness, pernicketiness, delicacy; discernment, perspicacity, sublety

463 *discrimination*; refinement 846 *good taste*; connoisseurship, epicurism; meticulousness, preciseness, particularity 457 *carefulness*; idealism, casuistry, artistic conscience, overdeveloped c. 917 *conscience*; perfectionism, fussiness, nit-picking, overnicety, over-refinement, hypercriticalness, donnishness, pedantry, hair-splitting; rigorism 735 *severity*; primness, prudishness, Puritanism 950 *prudery*.

*perfectionist*, idealist, purist, precisian, rigorist, fusspot, fussbudget, pedant, nit-picker, stickler, hard taskmaster; picker and chooser, gourmet, epicure.

**Adj.** *fastidious*, concerned with quality, quality-minded; nice, mincing, dainty, delicate, epicurean; perspicacious, discerning 463 *discriminating*; particular, demanding, choosy, finicky, finical, fiky; overnice, overparticular, scrupulous, meticulous, squeamish, qualmish 455 *attentive*; punctilious, painstaking, conscientious, overconscientious, critical, hypercritical, overcritical, fussy, pernickety, hard to please, fault-finding, censorious 924 *disapproving*; pedantic, donnish, precise, rigorous, exacting, difficult 735 *severe*; prim, puritanical 950 *prudish*.

**Vb.** *be fastidious*, – choosy etc. adj.; have only the best, settle for nothing less than the best; pick and choose 605 *choose*; refine, over-refine, split hairs, mince matters 475 *argue*; draw distinctions 463 *discriminate*; find fault 924 *dispraise*; fuss, turn up one's nose, wrinkle one's n., say ugh!; look a gift horse in the mouth, feel superior, disdain 922 *despise*; keep oneself to oneself 883 *be unsociable*.

## 863 Satiety

**N.** *satiety*, jadedness, fullness, repletion 54 *plenitude*; overfulness, plethora, overabundance, stuffing, engorgement, saturation, saturation point 637 *redundance*; glut, surfeit, too much of a good thing 838 *tedium*; overdose, excess 637 *superfluity*; spoiled child, spoilt brat, enfant gâté(e).

**Adj.** *sated*, satiated, satisfied, replete, saturated, brimming 635 *filled*; overfull, surfeited, gorged, glutted, cloyed, sick of; jaded, blasé 838 *bored*.

**Vb.** *sate*, satiate; satisfy, quench, slake 635 *suffice*; fill up, overfill, saturate 54 *fill*; soak 341 *drench*; stuff, gorge, glut, surfeit, cloy, jade, pall; overdose, overfeed; sicken 861 *cause dislike*; spoil, overindulge, kill with kindness; bore, weary 838 *be tedious*.

## 864 Wonder

**N.** *wonder*, state of wonder, wonderment, raptness; admiration, hero worship 887 *love*; awe, fascination; cry of wonder, gasp of admiration, whistle, wolf w., exclamation, exclamation mark; shocked silence 399 *silence*, open mouth, popping eyes, eyes on stalks; shock, surprise, surprisal 508 *lack of expectation*; astonishment, astoundment, amazement; stupor, stupefaction; bewilderment, bafflement 474 *uncertainty*; consternation 854 *fear*.

*miracle-working*, wonder-working, spellbinding, magic 983 *sorcery*; wonderful works, thaumatology, teratology; stroke of genius, feat, exploit 676 *deed*; transformation scene, coup de théâtre 594 *dramaturgy*.

*prodigy*, portent, sign, eye-opener 511 *omen*; something incredible, quite something, phenomenon, miracle, marvel, wonder; drama, sensation, cause célèbre, nine-days' wonder, annus mirabilis; object of wonder *or* admiration, wonderland, fairyland 513 *fantasy*; seven wonders of the world; sight 445 *spectacle*; infant prodigy, genius, man *or* woman of genius 696 *proficient person*; miracle-worker, thaumaturge, wizard, witch, fairy godmother 983 *sorcerer*; hero, heroine, wonder boy, superman, dream girl, superwoman, bionic man, whiz kid, Admirable Crichton 646 *paragon*; freak, sport, curiosity, oddity, guy, monster, monstrosity 84 *variance*; puzzle 530 *enigma*.

**Adj.** *marvelling* admiring, wondering, etc. vb.; awed, awestruck, fascinated, spellbound 818 *impressed*; surprised 508 *off guard*; astonished, amazed, astounded; in wonderment, rapt, lost in wonder, lost in amazement, unable to believe one's eyes *or* senses; wide-eyed, round-e., pop-e., with one's eyes starting out of one's head, with eyes on stalks; open-mouthed, agape, gaping; dazzled, blinded; dumbfounded, dumb, struck d., inarticulate, speechless, breathless, wordless, left without words, silenced 399 *silent*; bowled over, struck all of a heap, thunderstruck; transfixed, rooted to the spot; dazed, stupefied, bewildered 517 *puzzled*; aghast, flabbergasted; shocked, scandalized 924 *disapproving*.

*wonderful*, to wonder at, wondrous, marvellous, miraculous, monstrous, prodigious, phenomenal; stupendous, fearful 854 *frightening*; admirable, exquisite 644 *excellent*; record-breaking 644 *best*; striking, overwhelming, awesome, awe-inspiring, breathtaking 821 *impressive*; dramatic, sensational; shocking, scandalizing; rare, exceptional, extraordinary, unprecedented 84 *unusual*; remarkable, noteworthy; strange, passing s., odd, very odd, outré, weird, weird and wonderful, unaccountable, mysterious, enigmatic 517 *puzzling*; exotic, outlandish, unheard of 59

*extraneous*; fantastic 513 *imaginary*; impossible, hardly possible, too good *or* bad to be true 472 *improbable*; unbelievable, incredible, inconceivable, unimaginable, indescribable; unutterable, unspeakable, ineffable 517 *inexpressible*; surprising 508 *unexpected*; mind-boggling, mind-blowing, astounding, amazing, shattering, bewildering etc. vb.; wonder-working, thaumaturgic; magic, like m. 983 *magical*.

**Vb.** *wonder*, marvel, admire, whistle; hold one's breath, gasp, gasp with admiration; hero-worship 887 *love*; stare, gaze and gaze, goggle at, gawk, open one's eyes wide, rub one's e., not believe one's e.; gape, gawp, open one's mouth, stand in amazement, look aghast 508 *not expect*; be awestruck, be overwhelmed 854 *fear*; have no words to express, not know what to say, be reduced to silence, be struck dumb 399 *be silent*.

*be wonderful*, – marvellous etc. adj.; do wonders, work miracles, achieve marvels; surpass belief, stagger b., boggle the mind 486 *cause doubt*; beggar all description, baffle d., beat everything; spellbind, enchant 983 *bewitch*; dazzle, strike with admiration, turn one's head 887 *excite love*; strike dumb, awe, electrify 821 *impress*; make one's eyes open, make one sit up and take notice, take one's breath away; bowl over, stagger; blow one's mind, stun, daze, stupefy, petrify, dumbfound, confound, astound, astonish, amaze, flabbergast 508 *surprise*; baffle, bewilder 474 *puzzle*; startle 854 *frighten*; shock, scandalize 924 *incur blame*.

**Adv.** *wonderfully*, marvellously, remarkably, splendidly, fearfully; wondrous strange, strange to say, wonderful to relate, mirabile dictu, to the wonder of all.

**Int.** amazing!, incredible!, I don't believe it!, go on!, well I never!, blow me down!, did you ever!, gosh!, wow!, how about that!, bless my soul!, 'pon my word!, goodness gracious!, whatever next!, never!; please!

## 865 Lack of wonder

**N.** *lack of wonder*, lack of astonishment, unastonishment, unamazement, unsurprise; awelessness, irreverence, refusal to be impressed, nil admirari; blankness, stony indifference 860 *indifference*; quietism, composure, calmness, serenity, tranquillity 266 *quietude*; imperturbability, equability, impassiveness, cold blood 820 *moral insensibility*; taking for granted 610 *habituation*; lack of imagination, unimaginativeness; disbelief 486 *unbelief*; matter of course, just what one thought, nothing to wonder at, nothing to write home about, nothing in it.

**Adj.** *unastonished*, unamazed, unsurprised; unawed 855 *unfearing*; accustomed 610 *habituated*; calm, collected, composed; unimpressionable, phlegmatic, impassive 820 *apathetic*; blasé, undazzled, undazed, unimpressed, unadmiring, unmoved, unstirred, unaroused 860 *indifferent*; cold-blooded, unimaginative; blind to 439 *blind*; disbelieving 486 *unbelieving*; taking for granted, expecting 507 *expectant*.

*unastonishing*, unsurprising, foreseen, to be expected 507 *expected*; customary, common, ordinary, unimpressive, all in the day's work, nothing wonderful 610 *usual*.

**Vb.** *not wonder*, see nothing remarkable 820 *be insensitive*; be blind and deaf to; not believe 486 *disbelieve*; see through 516 *understand*; treat as a matter of course, not raise an eyebrow, take for granted, take as one's due; see it coming 507 *expect*; keep one's head 823 *keep calm*.

**Int.** no wonder; nothing to it; of course; why not?, as expected; quite so, naturally.

## 866 Repute

**N.** *repute*, good r., high r.; reputation, good r., special r.; report, good r.; title to fame, name, honoured n., great n., good n., fair n., character, known c., good c., high c., reputability, respectability 802 *credit*; regard, esteem 920 *respect*; opinion, good o., good odour, favour, high f., popular f., good books; popularity, vogue 848 *fashion*; acclaim, applause, approval, stamp of a., seal of a., cachet 923 *approbation*.

*prestige*, aura, mystique, magic; glamour, glitz, dazzle, éclat, lustre, splendour; brilliance, prowess; illustriousness, glory, honour, honour and glory, kudos, claim to fame, succès d'estime (see also *famousness*); esteem, estimation, account, high a., worship 638 *importance*; face, izzat, caste; degree, rank, ranking, standing, footing, status, honorary s., brevet rank 73 *serial place*; condition, position, position in society; top of the ladder *or* the tree, precedence 34 *superiority*; conspicuousness, prominence, eminence, supereminence 443 *visibility*; distinction, greatness, high rank, exaltedness, majesty 868 *nobility*; impressiveness, dignity, stateliness, solemnity, grandeur, sublimity, awesomeness; name to conjure with 178 *influence*; paramountcy, ascendancy, hegemony, primacy 733 *authority*; leadership, acknowledged l. 689 *directorship*; prestigiousness, snob value; status symbol, trophy wife.

*famousness*, title to fame, celebrity, notability, remarkability; illustriousness, renown, stardom, fame, name, note; household name,

synonym for; glory 727 *success*; notoriety 867 *disrepute*; talk of the town 528 *publicity*; claim to fame, place in history, posthumous fame 505 *memory*; undying name, immortal n., immortality, deathlessness; remembrance, commemoration, niche in the hall of fame.

*honours*, honour, blaze of glory, cloud of g., crown of g.; crown, martyr's c.; halo, aureole, nimbus, glory; blushing honours, battle h.; laurels, bays, wreath, garland, favour; feather, feather in one's cap 729 *trophy*; order, star, garter, ribbon, medal 729 *decoration*; spurs, sword, shield, arms 547 *heraldry*; an honour, signal h., distinction, accolade, award 962 *reward*; compliment, bouquet, flattery, incense, laud, eulogy 923 *praise*; memorial, statue, bust, picture, portrait, niche, plaque, temple, monument 505 *reminder*; title of honour, dignity, handle 870 *title*; patent of nobility, knighthood, baronetcy, peerage 868 *nobility*; academic honour, baccalaureate, doctorate, degree, academic d., honours d., pass d., ordinary d., aegrotat d., honorary d., diploma, certificate 870 *academic title*; sports trophy, cup, cap, blue; source of honour, fount of h., College of Arms; honours list, birthday honours, roll of honour 87 *list*.

*dignification*, glorification, lionization; honouring, complimenting; crowning, commemoration, coronation 876 *celebration*; sanctification, dedication, consecration, canonization, beatification; deification, apotheosis; enshrinement, enthronement; promotion, advancement, enhancement, aggrandizement 285 *progression*; exaltation 310 *elevation*; ennoblement, knighting; rehabilitation 656 *restoration*.

*person of repute*, honoured sir *or* madam, gentle reader; worthy, sound person, good citizen, loyal subject, pillar, pillar of society, pillar of the church, pillar of the state; man *or* woman of honour 929 *honourable person*; knight, dame, peer 868 *person of rank*; somebody, great man, great woman, big shot, big noise, big gun, big name, big wheel, VIP 638 *notable*; someone of mark, celebrity, notability, figure, public f.; champion 644 *exceller*; lion, star, rising star, luminary; man *or* woman of the hour, heroine of the hour, hero of the day, popular hero, icon; pop singer, idol 890 *favourite*; cynosure, model, mirror 646 *paragon*; cream, cream of society, crème de la crème 644 *elite*; choice spirit, master s., leading light 690 *leader*; grand old man, GOM 500 *sage*; noble army, great company, bevy, galaxy, constellation 74 *band*.

**Adj.** *reputable*, reputed, of repute, of good *or* sound reputation, of credit; creditworthy 929 *trustworthy*; gentlemanly 929 *honourable*; worthy, creditable, meritorious, prestigious 644 *excellent*; esteemed, respectable, regarded, well-r., well thought of 920 *respected*; edifying, moral 933 *virtuous*; in good odour, in the good books, in favour, in high f. 923 *approved*; popular, modish 848 *fashionable*; sanctioned, allowed, admitted 756 *permitted*.

*worshipful*, reverend, honourable; admirable 864 *wonderful*; heroic 855 *courageous*; imposing, dignified, august, stately, grand, sublime 821 *impressive*; lofty, high 310 *elevated*; high and mighty, mighty 32 *great*; lordly, princely, kingly, queenly, majestic, royal, regal 868 *noble*; aristocratic, well-born, high-caste, heaven-born; glorious, in glory, full of g., full of honours, honoured, titled, ennobled; time-honoured, ancient, age-old 127 *immemorial*; sacrosanct, sacred, holy 979 *sanctified*; honorific, dignifying.

*noteworthy*, notable, remarkable, extraordinary 84 *unusual*; fabulous 864 *wonderful*; of mark, of distinction, distinguished, distingué(e) 638 *important*; conspicuous, prominent, public, in the public eye, in the limelight, 'famous for fifteen minutes' 443 *obvious*;

> In the future everyone will be world-famous for fifteen minutes.
> Andy Warhol

eminent, pre-eminent, supereminent; peerless, nonpareil, foremost, in the forefront 34 *superior*; ranking, starring, leading, commanding; brilliant, bright, lustrous 417 *luminous*; illustrious, splendid, glorious 875 *ostentatious*.

*renowned*, celebrated, acclaimed, sung; of renown, of glorious name, of fame; famous, fabled, legendary, famed, far-f.; historic, illustrious, great, noble, glorious 644 *excellent*; notorious 867 *disreputable*; known as, well-known, on the map 490 *known*; of note, noted (see also *noteworthy*); talked of, resounding, on all lips, on every tongue, in the news 528 *published*; lasting, unfading, never-fading, evergreen, imperishable, deathless, immortal, eternal 115 *perpetual*.

**Vb.** *have a reputation*, enjoy a r., wear a halo; have a good name, have a name to lose; rank, stand high, have status *or* standing, have a position, enjoy consideration, be looked up to, have a name for, be praised f. 920 *command respect*; stand well with, earn golden opinions, do oneself credit, win honour, win renown, gain prestige, gain recognition, build a reputation, earn a name, acquire a character, improve one's credit 923 *be praised*; be somebody, make one's mark, set the heather on fire 730 *prosper*; win one's spurs, gain one's laurels,

take one's degree, graduate 727 *succeed*; cut a figure, cut a dash, cover oneself with glory 875 *be ostentatious*; rise to fame, get to the top of the ladder *or* tree, flash to stardom; shine, excel 644 *be good*; outshine, eclipse, steal the show, throw into the shade, overshadow 34 *be superior*; have precedence, play first fiddle, take the lead, play the l., star 64 *come before*; bask in glory, have fame, have a great name, hand down one's name to posterity; make history, live in h., be sure of immortality, carve a niche for oneself in the hall of fame 505 *be remembered*.

*seek repute*, thirst for honour, strive for glory, go for g., seek fame, wish to make one's mark, nurse one's ambition; be conscious of one's reputation, be status conscious, consider one's position, be mindful of one's prestige 871 *be proud*; wear one's honours, show off, flaunt 871 *feel pride*; lord it, queen it, prance, strut 875 *be ostentatious*; brag 877 *boast*.

*honour*, revere, regard, look up to, hold in respect, hold in reverence, hold in honour 920 *respect*; stand in awe of 854 *fear*; bow down to, recognize as superior 981 *worship*; know how to value, appreciate, prize, value, tender, treasure 887 *love*; show honour, pay respect, pay due regard, pay one's respects to 920 *show respect*; be polite to 884 *be courteous*; compliment 925 *flatter*; grace with, honour w., dedicate to, inscribe to; praise, sing the praises, laud, glorify, acclaim 923 *applaud*; crown, grant the palm, deck with laurels, make much of, eulogize, lionize, chair, ask for one's autograph; credit, give c., honour for 907 *thank*; glorify, immortalize, eternize, commemorate, memorialize 505 *remember*; celebrate, renown, blazon 528 *proclaim*; reflect honour, redound to one's honour *or* one's credit, lend distinction *or* lustre to, do credit to, be a credit to.

*dignify*, glorify, exalt; canonize, beatify, deify, consecrate, dedicate 979 *sanctify*; install, enthrone, crown 751 *commission*; signalize, mark out, distinguish 547 *indicate*; aggrandize, advance, upgrade 285 *promote*; honour, delight to h., confer an h.; bemedal, beribbon 844 *decorate*; bestow a title, create, elevate, raise to the peerage, ennoble; confer a knighthood, dub, knight, give the accolade; give one his *or* her title, sir, bemadam 561 *name*; take a title, take a handle to one's name, accept a knighthood.

## 867 Disrepute

**N.** *disrepute*, disreputableness, bad reputation, bad name, bad character, shady reputation, past; disesteem 921 *disrespect*; notoriety, infamy, ill repute, ill fame, succès de scandale; no reputation, no standing, ingloriousness, obscurity; bad odour, ill favour, disfavour, bad books, discredit, black books, bad light 888 *odium*; derogation, dishonour, disgrace, shame (see also *slur*), smear campaign 926 *detraction*; ignominy, loss of honour, loss of reputation, faded r., withered laurels, tarnished honour; departed glory, Ichabod; loss of face, loss of rank, demotion, degradation, reduction to the ranks, dishonourable discharge; debasement, abasement, comedown 872 *humiliation*; abjectness, baseness, vileness, turpitude 934 *wickedness*.

*slur*, reproach 924 *censure*; imputation, brick-bat, aspersion, reflection, slander, obloquy, opprobrium, abuse 926 *calumny*; slight, insult, put-down 921 *indignity*; scandal, shocking s., disgrace, shame, burning s., crying s.; defilement, pollution 649 *uncleanness*; stain, smear, smudge 649 *dirt*; stigma, brand, mark, black m., spot, blot, tarnish, taint 845 *blemish*; dirty linen; bar sinister, blot on one's scutcheon, badge of infamy, scarlet letter, mark of Cain.

*object of scorn*, scandalous person, reproach, byword, contempt, discredit 938 *bad person*; reject, sleazebag (sl), the dregs, the flotsam and jetsam 645 *badness*; Cinderella, poor relation 639 *nonentity*; failure 728 *loser*.

**Adj.** *disreputable*, not respectable, disrespectable, louche, shifty, shady 930 *rascally*; notorious, infamous, of ill fame, of ill repute, nefarious; arrant 645 *bad*; doubtful, dubious, questionable, objectionable 645 *not nice*; risqué, ribald, improper, indecent, obscene 951 *impure*; not thought much of, held in contempt, despised 922 *contemptible*; characterless, without references, of no repute *or* reputation; petty, pitiful 639 *unimportant*; outcast 607 *rejected*; down-and-out, degraded, base, abject, despicable, odious 888 *hateful*; mean, cheap, low 847 *vulgar*; shabby, squalid, dirty, scruffy 649 *unclean*; poor, down at heel, out at elbows 655 *dilapidated*; in a bad light, under a cloud, in one's bad *or* black books, in the doghouse, in Coventry, unable to show one's face; discredited, disgraced, in disgrace (see also *inglorious*); reproached 924 *disapproved*; unpopular 861 *disliked*.

*discreditable*, no credit to, bringing discredit, reflecting upon one, damaging, compromising; ignoble, unworthy; improper, unbecoming 643 *inexpedient*; dishonourable 930 *dishonest*; despicable 922 *contemptible*; censurable 924 *blameworthy*; shameful, shamemaking, disgraceful, infamous, unedifying, scandalous, shocking, outrageous, unmentionable, disgusting; too bad 645 *not nice*.

*degrading*, lowering, demeaning, ignom-

inious, opprobrious, mortifying, humiliating; derogatory, wounding one's honour, hurting one's dignity; beneath one, beneath one's dignity, infra dig.

*inglorious*, without repute, without prestige, without note; without a name, nameless 562 *anonymous*; grovelling, unheroic 879 *servile*; unaspiring, unambitious 874 *modest*; unnoted, unremarked, unnoticed, unmentioned 458 *neglected*; renownless, unrenowned, unknown to fame, unheard of, obscure 491 *unknown*; unseen, unheard 444 *invisible*; unhymned, unsung, unglorified, unhonoured, undecorated; titleless 869 *plebeian*; deflated, put down, cut down to size, debunked, humiliated, mortified 872 *humbled*; sunk low, shorn of glory, faded, withered, tarnished; stripped of reputation, discredited, creditless, disgraced, dishonoured, out of favour, in the bad *or* black books, in eclipse; degraded, demoted, reduced to the ranks.

**Vb.** *have no repute*, have no reputation, have no character, have no name to lose, have a past; have no credit, rank low, stand low in estimation, have no standing, have little status, be a nobody, cut no ice 639 *be unimportant*; be out of favour, be in the bad *or* black books, be in bad odour, be unpopular, be discredited, be in disgrace, stink in the nostrils; play second fiddle, take a back seat, stay in the background 35 *be inferior*; blush unseen, hide one's light 444 *be unseen*.

*lose repute*, fall *or* go out of fashion, pass from the public eye, fall out of favour; come down in the world, fall, sink 309 *descend*; fade, wither; fall into disrepute, incur discredit, incur dishonour, incur disgrace, achieve notoriety, get a bad name for oneself 924 *incur blame*; spoil one's record, blot one's copybook, disgrace oneself, compromise one's name, risk one's reputation, lose one's r., outlive one's r.; tarnish one's glory, forfeit one's honour, lose one's halo, lose one's good name, earn no credit, earn no honour, win no glory 728 *fail*; come down in the eyes of, forfeit one's good opinion, sink in estimation, suffer in reputation, lose prestige, lose face, lose rank; admit defeat, slink away, crawl, crouch 721 *knuckle under*; look silly, look foolish, be a laughing-stock, cut a sorry figure, blush for shame, laugh on the wrong side of one's mouth 497 *be absurd*; be exposed, be brought to book 963 *be punished*.

*demean oneself*, lower o., degrade o.; derogate, condescend, stoop, marry beneath one; compromise one's dignity, make oneself cheap, cheapen oneself, disgrace o., behave unworthily, have no sense of one's position;

sacrifice one's pride, forfeit self-respect; have no pride, feel no shame, think no s.

*shame*, put to s., hold up to s.; pillory, expose, show up, post; scorn, mock 851 *ridicule*; snub, put down, take down a peg or two 872 *humiliate*; discompose, disconcert, discomfit, put out of countenance, put one's nose out of joint, deflate, cut down to size, debunk; strip of one's honours, strip of rank, deplume, degrade, downgrade, demote, disrate, reduce to the ranks, cashier, disbar, defrock, deprive, strip 963 *punish*; blackball, ostracize 57 *exclude*; vilify, malign, disparage 926 *defame*; destroy one's reputation, take away one's good name, ruin one's credit; put in a bad light, reflect upon, taint; sully, mar, blacken, tarnish, stain, blot, besmear, smear, bespatter 649 *make unclean*; debase, defile, desecrate, profane 980 *be impious*; stigmatize, brand, cast a slur upon, tar 547 *mark*; dishonour, disgrace, discredit, give a bad name, bring into disrepute, bring shame upon, scandalize, be a public scandal 924 *incur blame*; heap shame upon, dump on, heap dirt u., drag through the mire *or* mud; trample, tread underfoot, ride roughshod over, outrage 735 *oppress*; contemn, disdain 922 *despise*; make one blush, outrage one's modesty 951 *debauch*; not spare one's blushes, eulogize, overpraise.

## 868 Nobility
**N.** *nobility*, nobleness, distinction, rank, high r., titled r., station, order 27 *degree*; royalty, kingliness, queenliness, princeliness, majesty, prerogative 733 *authority*; birth, high b., gentle b., gentility, noblesse; descent, high d., noble d., ancestry, long a., line, unbroken l., lineage, pedigree, ancient p. 169 *genealogy*; noble family, noble house, ancient h., royal h., dynasty, royal d. 11 *family*; blood, blue b., best b.; bloodstock, caste, high c.; badge of rank, patent of nobility, coat of arms, crest 547 *heraldry*.

*aristocracy*, patriciate, patrician order; nobility, hereditary n., lesser n., noblesse, ancien régime; lordship, lords, peerage, House of Lords, lords spiritual and temporal; dukedom, earldom, viscountcy, baronetcy; baronage, knightage; landed interest, squirearchy, squiredom; county family, county set, gentry, landed g., gentlefolk; the great, great folk, the high and the mighty, notables; life peerage.

*upper class*, upper classes, upper ten, upper crust, top layer, top drawer; first families, the quality, best people, better sort, chosen few 644 *elite*; high society, social register, high life, fashionable world 848 *beau monde*; ruling class, the twice-born, the Establishment 733 *auth-*

ority; high-ups, Olympians; the haves 800 *rich person*; salaried class, salariat.

*aristocrat*, patrician, nobleman *or* -woman, Olympian; person of high caste, Brahman, Rajput; descendant of the Prophet, sayyid; bloodstock, thoroughbred; senator, magnifico, magnate, dignitary; don, grandee, caballero, hidalgo; gentleman, gentlewoman, armiger; squire, squireen, buckeen, laird; boyar, Junker; emperor, king, queen, prince 741 *sovereign*; nob, swell, gent, toff 848 *fop*; panjandrum, superior person 638 *notable*.

*person of rank*, titled person, noble, nobleman *or* -woman, noble lord *or* lady, atheling, seigneur; princeling, lordling, aristo; lordship, milord; ladyship, milady; peer, hereditary p., life p.; peer of the realm, peeress; Prince of Wales, princess royal, duke, grand d., archduke, duchess; marquis, marquess, marquise, marchioness, margrave, margravine, count, countess, contessa; earl, belted e.; viscount, viscountess, baron, baroness, thane, baronet, knight, banneret, knight-bachelor, knight-banneret; rajah, bey, nawab, begum, emir, khan, sheikh 741 *potentate, governor*.

**Adj.** *noble*, chivalrous, knightly; gentlemanly, gentlemanlike, ladylike (see also *genteel*); majestic, royal, regal, every inch a king *or* queen; kingly, queenly, princely, lordly; ducal, baronial, seigneurial; of royal blood, of high birth, of gentle b., of good family, pedigreed, wellborn, high-b., born in the purple, born with a silver spoon in one's mouth; thoroughbred, pur sang, blue-blooded; of rank, ennobled, titled, in Debrett, in Burke's Peerage, in the Almanach de Gotha; haughty, high, exalted, high-up, grand 32 *great*.

*genteel*, patrician, senatorial; aristocratic, Olympian; superior, top-drawer, upper-crust, high-class, upper-c., cabin-c., classy, posh, 'U', highly respectable, comme il faut; of good breeding 848 *wellbred*.

U and Non-U. An Essay in Sociological Linguistics
Title of essay by Alan Ross

## 869 Commonalty
**N.** *commonalty*, commonality, commons, third estate, bourgeoisie, middle classes, lower c., plebs, plebeians, citizenry, demos, democracy; townsfolk, countryfolk; silent majority, grass roots; the public, general p., Joe Public; people at large, populace, the people, the common p., plain p.; vulgar herd, great unwashed; great unnumbered, the many, the many-headed, the multitude, the million, hoi polloi; the masses, mass of society, mass of the people, admass, lumpenproletariat, proletariat;

the general, rank and file, rag tag and bobtail, Tom Dick and Harry 79 *everyman*.

*rabble*, rabblement, mob, horde 74 *crowd*; clamjamphrie, rout, rabble r., rescal multitude, varletry; riffraff, scum, off-scourings, dregs of society, the flotsam and jetsam, canaille, cattle, vermin.

*lower classes*, lower orders, one's inferiors 35 *inferior*; common sort, small fry, humble folk; working class, servant c. workers, wage earners, blue-collar; steerage, steerage class, lower deck; second-class citizens, the have-nots, the under-privileged, the disadvantaged; proletariat, proles; underclass; sansculottes, submerged tenth, slum population; down-and-outs, depressed class, outcasts, outcasts of society, poor whites, white trash; demi-monde, under-world, low company, low life.

*middle classes*, bourgeoisie 732 *averageness*; professional classes, salaried c., white-collar workers; Brown, Jones and Robinson, Middle England, Middle America.

*commoner*, bourgeois(e), plebeian, pleb; untitled person, plain Mr *or* Mrs; citizen, mere citizen, John Citizen, Joe Bloggs, Joe Public, Joe Soap; one of the people, man *or* woman of the p., democrat, republican; proletarian, prole; working man *or* woman 686 *worker*; town-dweller, country-d. 191 *native*; little man, man *or* woman in the street, everyman, everywoman, common type, average t. 30 *common man*; common person, groundling, pittite, galleryite 35 *inferior*; backbencher, pri-vate; underling 742 *servant*; ranker, upstart, par-venu, social climber, arriviste, nouveau riche, Philistine 847 *vulgarian*; a nobody, nobody one knows, nobody knows who 639 *nonentity*; low-caste person, Sudra, outcaste; Untouchable, dalit, harijan; villein, serf 742 *slave*.

*country-dweller*, countryman *or* -woman, yeoman, rustic, Hodge, swain, gaffer, peasant, son *or* daughter of the soil, tiller of the soil, cul-tivator, ploughman, teuchter (Scots) 370 *farmer*; boor, churl, bog-trotter; yokel, hind, chawbacon, clod, clodhopper, rube, redneck, hayseed, hick, backwoodsman; bumpkin, country b., Tony Lumpkin, country cousin, provincial, hillbilly; village idiot 501 *ninny*.

*low fellow*, fellow, varlet 938 *cad*; slumdweller 801 *poor person*; guttersnipe, mud-lark, street arab, gamin, ragamuffin, tatter-demalion, sansculotte, down-and-out, tramp, bag lady, bum, vagabond 268 *wanderer*; gaber-lunzie (Scots), panhandler 763 *beggar*; low type, rough t., bully, ugly customer, plug ugly, ruffian, rowdy, rough, bit of rough (inf), boot boy, bovver boy, roughneck 904 *ruffian*; rascal 938 *knave*; gangster, hood, crook; criminal, delinquent, juvenile d. 904 *offender*; barbarian, savage, Goth, Vandal, Yahoo.

**Adj.** *plebeian*, common, simple, untitled, unennobled, without rank, titleless; ignoble, below the salt; below-stairs, servant-class; lower-deck, rank and file 732 *middling*; mean, low, low-down, street-corner 867 *disreputable*; lowly, base-born, low-born, low-caste, of low birth, of low origin, of mean parentage, of mean extraction; slave-born, servile; humble, of low estate, of humble condition 35 *inferior*, unaristocratic, middle-class, lower m.-c., working-c., cloth-cap, 'non-U' (see quotation at 868 *genteel*), proletarian; homely, homespun 573 *plain*; obscure 867 *inglorious*; coarse, brutish, uncouth, unpolished 847 *ill-bred*; unfashionable, cockney, bourgeois, Main Street, suburban, provincial, rustic; parvenu, risen from the ranks 847 *vulgar*; boorish, churlish, loutish, yobbish 885 *ungracious*.

*barbaric*, barbarous, barbarian, wild, savage, brutish, yobbish; uncivilized, uncultured, without arts, philistine, primitive, neolithic 699 *artless*.

## 870 Title

**N.** *title*, title to fame, entitlement, claim 915 *dueness*; title of honour, courtesy title, honor-ific, handle, handle to one's name; honour, dis-tinction, order, knighthood 866 *honours*; dignified style, royal we, editorial we 875 *for-mality*; mode of address, style of a., Royal High-ness, Serene H., Excellency, Grace, Lordship, Ladyship, noble, most n., my liege, my lord, my lady, dame; the Honourable, Right Honour-able; Reverend, Very R., Right R., Most R., Mon-signor, His Holiness; dom, padre; your reverence, your honour, your worship; sire, esquire, sir, dear s., madam, ma'am, master, mister, mistress, miss, Ms; monsieur, madame, mademoiselle; don, señor, señora, señorita; sig-nore, signora, signorina; Herr, Frau, Fräulein; meneer, mevrouw, mejuffrouw; babu, sahib, memsahib; bwana, effendi, mirza; citoyen, comrade, tovarich.

*academic title*, doctor, doctor honoris causa; doctor of divinity, DD; doctor of laws, LLD; doctor of letters *or* literature, DLitt, LittD; doctor of medicine, MD; doctor of music, MusD; doctor of philosophy, DPhil, PhD; doctor of science, DSc; master of arts, MA; master of education, MEd; master of letters *or* literature, MLitt, master of philosophy, MPhil; master of sacred theology, STM; master of sci-ence, MSc; bachelor of architecture, BArch; bachelor of arts, BA; bachelor of dental sur-gery, BDS; bachelor of divinity, BD; bachelor of education, BEd; bachelor of letters *or* literature,

BLitt; bachelor of medicine and surgery, MBChB, MBBS; bachelor of law, BL, bachelor of laws, LLB; bachelor of music, MusB, BMus; bachelor of science, BSc; bachelor of veterinary medicine and surgery, BVMS, BVM&S; diploma of art, DA; diploma in education, DipEd; diploma of higher education, DipHE; diploma in social work, DipSW; professor, professor emeritus; reader, lecturer; doctorate, baccalaureate.

## 871 Pride

**N.** *pride*, proud heart; proper pride, just p., modest p., natural p., justified p., innocent p.; self-esteem, amour propre; self-respect, self-confidence; self-admiration, conceit, self-c., swelled or swollen head, swank, side, puffed-out chest 873 *vanity*; snobbery, inverted s. 850 *affectation*; false pride, touchiness, prickliness 819 *moral sensibility*; dignity, reputation 866 *prestige*; stateliness, loftiness; condescension, hauteur, haughtiness, uppitiness, unapproachability, disdain 922 *contempt*; overweening pride, bumptiousness, arrogance, attitude, hubris 878 *insolence*; swelling pride, pomp, pomposity, grandiosity, show, display 875 *ostentation*; egoism, self-praise, vainglory 877 *boasting*; class-consciousness, race-prejudice, sexism 481 *prejudice*; object of pride, source of p., boast, joy, pride and j. 890 *favourite*; cynosure, pick, flower, jewel in the crown 646 *paragon*.

*proud person*, vain p., snob, parvenu; mass of pride, pride incarnate; swelled head, swank, swankpot; high muckamuck, lady muck, lord of creation 638 *notable*; fine gentleman, grande dame 848 *fop*; peacock, turkey cock, cock of the walk, swaggerer, bragger 877 *boaster*; purse-proud plutocrat 800 *rich person*; class-conscious person 868 *aristocrat*.

**Adj.** *proud*, elevated, haughty, lofty, sublime 209 *high*; plumed, crested 875 *showy*; fine, grand 848 *fashionable*; grandiose, dignified, stately, statuesque 821 *impressive*; majestic, royal, kingly, queenly, lordly, aristocratic 868 *noble*; self-respecting, self-confident, pronoid, proud-hearted, high-souled 855 *courageous*; high-stepping, high-spirited, high-mettled 819 *lively*; stiff-necked 602 *obstinate*; mighty, over-mighty 32 *great*; imperious, commanding 733 *authoritative*; high-handed 735 *oppressive*; overweening, overbearing, hubristic, arrogant, with attitude 878 *insolent*; brazen, unblushing, unabashed, flaunting, hardened 522 *undisguised*.

*prideful*, full of pride, blown-up with p., flushed with p., puffed-up, inflated, swelling, swollen, big-headed; over-proud, high and

mighty, stuck-up, toffee-nosed, snobbish, nose-in-the-air, snooty; upstage, uppish, uppity; on one's dignity, on one's high horse, on stilts; haughty, disdainful, superior, holier than thou, supercilious, hoity-toity, high-hat, patronizing, condescending 922 *despising*; standoffish, aloof, distant, unapproachable, stiff, starchy, unbending, undemocratic 885 *ungracious*; taking pride in, purse-proud, house-p; feeling pride, proud of, bursting with pride, inches taller; strutting, swaggering, vainglorious 877 *boastful*; pleased with oneself, pleased as Punch, pleased as a dog with two tails, like the cat that got the cream; cocky, bumptious, conceited 873 *vain*; pretentious 850 *affected*; swanky, swanking, pompous 875 *showy*; proud as Lucifer, proud as a peacock.

**Vb.** *be proud*, have one's pride, have one's self-respect, be jealous of one's honour, guard one's reputation, hold one's head high, stand erect, refuse to stoop, bow to no one, stand on one's dignity, mount one's high horse; give oneself airs, toss one's head, hold one's nose in the air, think it beneath one, be too proud to, be too grand to; be stuck-up, be snooty, swank, show off, swagger, strut 875 *be ostentatious*; condescend, patronize; look down on, disdain 922 *despise*; display hauteur 878 *be insolent*; lord it, queen it, come it over, throw one's weight about, pull rank, overween 735 *oppress*.

*feel pride*, swell with p., take pride in, glory in, boast of, not blush for 877 *boast*; hug oneself, congratulate o., pat o. on the back 824 *be pleased*; be flattered, flatter oneself, pride o., pique o., plume o., preen o., think a lot of oneself, think too much of o., be on an ego-trip 873 *be vain*.

## 872 Humility. Humiliation

**N.** *humility*, humbleness, humble spirit 874 *modesty*; abasement, lowness, lowliness; unpretentiousness, quietness; harmlessness, inoffensiveness 935 *innocence*; meekness, resignation, submissiveness, servility 721 *submission*; self-knowledge, self-deprecation, self-abnegation, self-effacement, self-abasement, mortification, kenosis 931 *disinterestedness*; condescension, stooping 884 *courtesy*; humble person, no boaster, mouse, violet, shrinking v.

*humiliation*, abasement, humbling, letdown, setdown, climbdown, comedown, slap in the face 921 *indignity*; crushing retort; rebuke 924 *reprimand*; disgrace, shame 867 *disrepute*; scandal, Watergate, -gate; sense of shame, sense of disgrace, blush, suffusion, confusion; shamefaced look, hangdog expression, tail between the legs; chastening thought, mortification, hurt pride, injured p., offended dignity 891 *resentment*.

**Adj.** *humble*, not proud, humble-minded, self-deprecating, poor in spirit, lowly; meek, submissive, resigned, unprotesting, servile 721 *submitting*; self-effacing, self-abnegating 931 *disinterested*; self-abasing, stooping, conde-scending 884 *courteous*; mouselike, harmless, inoffensive, unoffending 935 *innocent*; unassuming, unpretentious, without airs, without side 874 *modest*; mean, low 639 *unim-portant*; of lowly birth 869 *plebeian*.

*humbled*, broken-spirited, bowed down; chastened, crushed, dashed, abashed, crest-fallen, chapfallen, sheepish, disconcerted, out of countenance 834 *dejected*; humiliated, let down, set d., taken d., taken down a peg or two, cut down to size, put down, squashed, slapped in the face, deflated, debunked; not proud of, ashamed 939 *repentant*; mortified, shamed, blushing 867 *inglorious*; scorned, rebuked 924 *disapproved*; brought low, dis-comfited 728 *defeated*.

**Vb.** *be humble*, – lowly etc. adj.; have no sense of pride, have no self-conceit, be lacking self-confidence, humble oneself 867 *demean oneself*; play second fiddle, take a back seat 874 *be modest*; put others first, not think of oneself 931 *be disinterested*; condescend, unbend 884 *be courteous*; stoop, bow down, crawl, be a syco-phant, sing small, eat humble pie, eat crow 721 *knuckle under*; put up with insolence, 'turn the other cheek' (see quotation for 'an eye for an eye' at 714 *retaliation*), stomach, pocket 909 *forgive*.

*be humbled*, – humiliated etc. adj.; receive a snub, be cold-shouldered, get a slap in the face, be put in one's place, be taken down a peg; be ashamed, be ashamed of oneself, feel shame; blush, colour up 431 *redden*; feel small, hide one's face, hang one's head, avert one's eyes, have nothing to say for oneself, wish to sink through the floor, wish the earth would swallow one up; stop swanking, come off it.

*humiliate*, humble, chasten, abash, discon-cert, put to the blush; lower, take down a peg, put down, debunk, deflate; make one feel small, make one sing small, make one feel this high, teach one his place, make one crawl, rub one's nose in the dirt, rub one's nose in it; snub, cut, crush, squash, sit on, send away with a flea in their ear 885 *be rude*; slight 921 *not respect*; mortify, hurt one's pride, offend one's dignity, lower in all men's eyes, put to shame 867 *shame*; score off, put one's nose out of joint, make a fool of, make one look silly 542 *befool*; put in the shade 306 *outdo*; out-stare, outfrown, frown down, daunt 854

*frighten*; get the better of, gain the upper hand, triumph over, crow o. 727 *overmaster*.

## 873 Vanity

**N.** *vanity*, emptiness 4 *insubstantiality*; vain pride, empty p., idle p. 871 *pride*; immodesty, conceit, conceitedness, self-importance, mega-lomania; swank, side, puffed-up chest, swelled head; cockiness, bumptiousness, assurance, self-a.; good opinion of oneself, self-conceit, self-esteem, amour propre; self-satisfaction, smugness; self-love, self-admiration, nar-cissism; self-complacency, self-approbation, self-praise, self-applause, self-flattery, self-congratulation, self-glorification, vainglory 877 *boasting*; self-sufficiency, self-centredness, egotism, egocentrism, egocentricity, ego-mania, me-ism 932 *selfishness*; exhibitionism, showing off, self-display 875 *ostentation*; Vanity Fair 848 *beau monde*.

*airs*, fine a., airs and graces, mannerisms, pre-tensions, absurd p. 850 *affectation*; swank, side, pompousness 875 *ostentation*; coxcombry, prig-gishness, foppery.

*vain person*, self-admirer, Narcissus; self-centred person, me generation, egotist, cox-comb 848 *fop*; exhibitionist, peacock, turkey cock, show-off; know-all, bighead, God's gift to women; smartypants, smart alec, smart ass, cleverstick, clever dick, Mr Clever, Miss Clever 500 *wiseacre*; stuffed shirt, pompous twit 4 *insubstantial thing*.

**Adj.** *vain*, conceited, overweening, stuck-up, snooty, proud 871 *prideful*; egotistic, egocen-tric, self-centred, self-satisfied, self-complacent, full of oneself, self-important 932 *selfish*; smug, pleased with oneself; self-admiring, self-loving, narcissistic, stuck on oneself; wise in one's own conceit, dogmatic, opinionated, over-subtle, overclever, clever clever, too clever by half, too smart for one's own good 498 *intelli-gent*; swollen-headed, puffed-up, too big for one's boots, big-headed, bumptious, cocky, perky, smartalecky, smart-ass 878 *insolent*; immodest, blatant; showing off, swaggering, vainglorious, self-glorious 877 *boastful*; pompous 875 *ostentatious*; pretentious, soi-disant, so-called, self-styled; coxcombical, fan-tastical, putting on airs 850 *affected*.

**Vb.** *be vain*, – conceited etc. adj.; have a swelled head, have one's head turned; have a high opinion of oneself, set a high value on o., think a lot of o., think too much of o., think oneself the cat's pyjamas, think o. God Almighty, regard oneself as God's gift; exag-gerate one's own merits, blow one's own trumpet 877 *boast*; admire oneself, hug o., flatter o., give oneself a pat on the back; plume oneself, preen o., pride o. 871 *feel pride*; swank, strut, show off, put on airs, put on side, show one's paces, display one's talents, talk for effect, talk big, not hide one's light under a bushel, push oneself forward 875 *be ostentatious*; lap up flattery, fish for compliments; get above oneself, have pretensions, give oneself airs 850 *be affected*; play the fop, be overconcerned with one's appearance, dress up, doll oneself up, dandify 843 *primp*.

*make conceited*, fill with conceit, puff up, inflate, give a swelled head to, go to one's head, turn one's h. 925 *flatter*; take one at his own valuation.

**Adv.** *conceitedly*, vainly, vaingloriously, swankily.

### 874 Modesty

**N.** *modesty*, lack of ostentation, unboastfulness, shyness, retiring disposition; diffidence, constraint, self-distrust, timidness, timidity 854 *nervousness*; mauvaise honte, overmodesty, prudishness 950 *prudery*; bashfulness, blushing, blush; pudency, shamefacedness, shockability; chastity 950 *purity*; deprecation, self-deprecation, self-effacement, hiding one's light 872 *humility*; unobtrusiveness, unpretentiousness, unassuming nature; demureness, reserve; hidden merit; modest person, shy thing, shrinking violet, mouse.

**Adj.** *modest*, without vanity, free from pride; self-effacing, unobtrusive, unseen, unheard 872 *humble*; self-deprecating, unboastful; unassertive, unpushing, unthrustful, unambitious, quiet, unassuming, unpretentious, unpretending; unimposing, unimpressive, moderate, mediocre, underwhelming 639 *unimportant*; shy, retiring, shrinking, timid, mouse-like, diffident, unself-confident, unsure of oneself 854 *nervous*; overshy, awkward, constrained, embarrassed, inarticulate; deprecating, demurring; bashful, blushful, blushing, rosy; shamefaced, sheepish; reserved, demure, coy; shockable, overmodest, prudish 850 *affected*; chaste 950 *pure*.

**Vb.** *be modest*, show moderation, ration oneself 942 *be temperate*; not blow one's trumpet, have no ambition, shrink from notoriety; not push oneself forward, efface oneself, yield precedence 872 *be humble*; play second fiddle, keep in the background, merge into the background, take a back seat, be a back-room boy *or* girl, know one's place; blush unseen, shun the limelight, shrink from the public gaze, hide one's light under a bushel 456 *escape notice*; not look for praise, do good by stealth and blush to find it fame; retire, creep into one's shell, shrink, hang back, be coy 620 *avoid*;

show bashfulness, feel shame, stand blushing, blush, colour, go red, crimson, mantle 431 *redden*; preserve one's modesty 933 *be virtuous*.

**Adv.** *modestly*, quietly, soberly, demurely; unpretentiously, sans façon, without fuss, without ceremony, privately, without beat of drum.

### 875 Ostentation. Formality

**N.** *ostentation*, demonstration, display, parade, show 522 *manifestation*; unconcealment, blatancy, flagrancy, shamelessness, brazenness, exhibitionism 528 *publicity*; ostentatiousness, showiness, magnificence, ideas of m., delusions of grandeur, grandiosity; splendour, brilliance; self-consequence, self-importance 873 *vanity*; pomposity, fuss, swagger, showing off, pretension, pretensions, airs and graces 873 *airs*; swank, side, thrown-out chest, strut; machismo, bravado, heroics 877 *boast*; theatricality, camp, histrionics, dramatization, dramatics, sensationalism 546 *exaggeration*; demonstrativeness, back-slapping, bonhomie 882 *sociability*; showmanship, effect, window-dressing; solemnity (see also *formality*); grandeur, dignity, stateliness, impressiveness; declamation, rhetoric 574 *rhetoric*; flourish, flourish of trumpets, fanfaronade, big drum 528 *publication*; pageantry, pomp, circumstance, pomp and c., bravery, pride, panache, waving plumes, fine feathers, flying colours, dash, splash, splurge 844 *finery*; frippery, gaudiness, glitter, tinsel 844 *ornamentation*; idle pomp, idle how, false glitter, unsubstantial pageant, mummery, mockery, idle m., hollow m., solemn m. 4 *insubstantiality*; tomfoolery 497 *foolery*; travesty 20 *mimicry*; exterior, gloss, veneer, polish, varnish 223 *exteriority*; pretence, profession 614 *pretext*; insincerity, lip service, tokenism 542 *deception*.

*formality*, state, stateliness, dignity; ceremoniousness, stiffness, starchiness; royal we, editorial we 870 *title*; ceremony, ceremonial 988 *ritual*; drill, smartness, spit and polish, military bull; correctness, correctitude, protocol, form, good f., right f. 848 *etiquette*; punctilio, punctiliousness, preciseness 455 *attention*; routine, fixed r. 610 *practice*; solemnity, formal occasion, ceremonial o., state o., function, grand f., official f., red carpet 876 *celebration*; full dress, court d., robes, regalia, finery, black tie 228 *formal dress*; correct dress 228 *uniform*.

*pageant*, show 522 *exhibit*; fete, gala, gala performance, tournament, tattoo; field day, great doings 876 *celebration*; son et lumière 445 *spectacle*; set piece, tableau, scene, transformation s., stage effect 594 *stage set*; display, bravura, stunt; pyrotechnics 420 *fire-*

works; carnival, Lord Mayor's Show 837 *festivity, revel*; procession, promenade, march-past, flypast; changing the guard, trooping the colour; turnout, review, grand r., parade, array 74 *assembly.*

**Adj.** *ostentatious,* showy, pompous; aiming at effect, striving for e., done for e.; window-dressing, for show, for the sake of appearance; prestige, for p., for the look of the thing; spe-cious, seeming, hollow 542 *spurious;* conse-quential, self-important; pretentious, would-be 850 *affected;* showing off, swanking, swanky 873 *vain;* inflated, turgid, orotund, pontifi-cating, windy, magniloquent, declamatory, high-sounding, high-flown 574 *rhetorical;* grand, highfalutin, splendiferous, splendid, brilliant, magnificent, grandiose, posh; superb, royal 813 *liberal;* sumptuous, diamond-studded, luxurious, de luxe, plushy, ritzy, glitzy, costly, expensive, expense-account 811 *dear;* painted, glorified, tarted up.

*showy,* flashy, dressy, dressed to kill, all dolled up, foppish 848 *fashionable;* colourful, lurid, gaudy, gorgeous 425 *florid;* tinsel, glit-tering, garish, tawdry 847 *vulgar;* flaming, flaring, flaunting, flagrant, blatant, public; brave, dashing, gallant, gay, jaunty, rakish, sporty; spectacular, scenic, dramatic, histri-onic, theatrical, camp, stagy; sensational, daring; exhibitionist, stunting.

*formal,* dignified, solemn, stately, majestic, grand, fine; ceremonious, standing on cere-mony, punctilious, stickling, correct, precise, stiff, starchy; black-tie, white-tie, full-dress; of state, public, official; ceremonial, ritual 988 *ritualistic;* for a special occasion, for a gala o. 876 *celebratory.*

**Vb.** *be ostentatious,* – showy etc. adj.; observe the formalities, stand on ceremony; splurge, splash out, cut a dash, make a splash, make a figure; glitter, dazzle 417 *shine;* flaunt, sport 228 *wear;* dress up 843 *primp;* wave, flourish 317 *brandish;* blazon, trumpet, sound the t., beat the big drum 528 *proclaim;* stage a demon-stration, wave banners 711 *defy;* demonstrate, exhibit 522 *show;* act the showman, make a dis-play, put on a show; make the most of, put on a front, window-dress, stage-manage; see to the outside, paper the cracks, polish, veneer 226 *coat;* intend for effect, strive for e., sen-sationalize, camp up; talk for effect, shoot a line 877 *boast;* take the centre of the stage, grab *or* hog the limelight 455 *attract notice;* put one-self forward, advertise oneself, dramatize o.; play to the gallery, fish for compliments 850 *be affected;* show off, flaunt oneself, show one's paces, prance, promenade, swan around; parade, march, march past, fly past; peacock,

strut, swank, put on side 873 *be vain;* make an exhibition of oneself, make a public spectacle of oneself, make people stare.

## 876 Celebration

**N.** *celebration,* performance, solemnization 676 *action;* commemoration 505 *remembrance;* observance, solemn o. 988 *ritual;* ceremony, ceremonial, function, occasion, do; formal occasion, coronation, enthronement, inaugur-ation, installation, presentation 751 *com-mission;* debut, coming out 68 *beginning;* reception, welcome, hero's w., tickertape w., redcarpet treatment 875 *formality;* official reception 923 *applause;* festive occasion, fete, jubilee, diamond j. 837 *festivity;* jubilation, cheering, high-five, ovation, standing o., tri-umph, salute, salvo, tattoo, roll, roll of drums, fanfare, fanfaronade, flourish of trumpets, flying colours, flag waving, mafficking 835 *rejoicing;* flags, banners, bunting, streamers, dec-orations, Chinese lanterns, illuminations; firework display 420 *fireworks;* bonfire 379 *fire;* triumphal arch 729 *trophy;* harvest home, thanksgiving, Te Deum 907 *thanks;* paean, hosannah, hallelujah 886 *congratulation;* health, toast.

*special day,* day to remember, great day, red-letter d., gala d., flag d., field d.; Saint's day, feast d., fast d. 988 *holy day;* Armistice Day, D-Day, Remembrance Sunday; Fourth of July, Independence Day, Republic D., Bastille D.; birthday, name-day; wedding anniversary, silver wedding, golden w., diamond w., ruby w.; centenary, bicentenary, sesquicentenary 141 *anniversary.*

**Adj.** *celebratory,* celebrating, signalizing, observing, commemorative 505 *remembering;* occasional, anniversary, centennial, bicenten-nial, millennial 141 *seasonal;* festive, jubilant 835 *rejoicing;* triumphant, triumphal; wel-coming, honorific 886 *congratulatory.*

**Vb.** *celebrate,* solemnize, perform 676 *do;* hallow, keep holy, keep sacred 979 *sanctify;* commemorate 505 *remember;* honour, observe, keep, keep up, maintain; signalize, make it an occasion, mark the o.; make much of, wel-come, kill the fatted calf, do one proud 882 *be hospitable;* do honour to, fete; chair, carry shoulder-high 310 *elevate;* mob, rush 61 *ram-page;* garland, deck with flowers, wreathe, crown 962 *reward;* lionize, give a hero's wel-come, fling wide the gates, roll out the red carpet, hang out the flags, put out the bunting, beat a tattoo, blow the trumpets, clash the cym-bals, fire a salute, fire a salvo, fire a feu de joie 884 *pay one's respects;* cheer, slap high-fives, slap fives, jubilate, triumph, maffick 835 *rejoice*; make holiday 837 *revel*; instate, present, inaugurate, launch, install, induct 751 *commission*; make one's debut, come out *68 begin*.

*toast*, pledge, clink glasses; drink to, raise one's glass to, fill one's glass to, drain a bumper, drink a health 301 *drink*.

**Adv.** *in honour of*, in memory of, in celebration of, on the occasion of; to mark the occasion of.

## 877 Boasting

**N.** *boasting*, bragging, boastfulness, vainglory, braggadocio, braggartism, fanfaronade; jactation 875 *ostentation*; self-glorification, self-advertisement, swagger, swank, bounce 873 *vanity*; advertisement, hype 528 *publicity*; puffery 482 *overestimation*; grandiloquence, rodomontade, vapouring, gassing, fine talk 515 *empty talk*; swaggering, swashbuckling, heroics, bravado; flag-wagging or waving, chauvinism, jingoism, spreadeagleism 481 *bias*; defensiveness, blustering, bluster 854 *nervousness*; sabre-rattling, intimidation 900 *threat*.

*boast*, brag, vaunt; puff, hype 528 *advertisement*; gasconade, flourish, fanfaronade, bravado, bombast, rant, rodomontade, fustian, tall talk 546 *exaggeration*; hot air, gas, bunkum 515 *empty talk*; bluff, bounce 542 *deception*; presumptuous challenge 711 *defiance*; big talk, big drum, bluster, hectoring, idle threat 900 *threat*.

*boaster*, vaunter, swaggerer, braggart, braggadocio, macho; brag, big-mouth, loudmouth, shouter, prater, gasbag; blagueur, blusterer, charlatan, pretender 545 *impostor*; bouncer, bluffer 545 *liar*; swank, show-off 873 *vain person*; swashbuckler, gasconader, Gascon, Thraso, Matamore, Bobadil, Scaramouch, Pistol, miles gloriosus; advertiser, promotions manager, public relations officer, PR man *or* woman, puffer 528 *publicizer*; flourisher, fanfaron, trumpeter; ranter, hot air merchant; jingoist, chauvinist; sabre-rattler, intimidator.

**Adj.** *boastful*, boasting, bragging, vaunting, vaunty, crowing, big-mouthed; braggart, swaggering, high-hat 875 *ostentatious*; vainglorious, self-glorifying 873 *vain*; bellicose, sabre-rattling, jingoistic, chauvinistic 718 *warlike*; bluffing, hollow, pretentious, empty 542 *spurious*; bombastic, magniloquent, grandiloquent 546 *exaggerated*; flushed, exultant, triumphant, cock-a-hoop 727 *successful*.

**Vb.** *boast*, brag, crow, vaunt, gab, gasconade, talk big, have a big mouth, shoot one's mouth, shoot a line, bluff, huff and puff, bluster, hector, shout; bid defiance 711 *defy*; vapour, prate, rant, gas 515 *mean nothing*; enlarge, magnify, lay it on thick, draw the longbow 546

*exaggerate*; trumpet, parade, flaunt, show off 528 *publish*; puff, crack up, cry one's wares 528 *advertise*; sell oneself, advertise o., be a self-publicist, blow one's own trumpet, blow hard, sing one's own praises, bang the big drum 875 *be ostentatious*; flourish, wave 317 *brandish*; play the jingo, rattle the sabre 900 *threaten*; show off, strut, swagger, prance, swank, throw out one's chest 873 *be vain*; gloat, pat oneself on the back, hug oneself 824 *be pleased*; boast of, plume oneself on 871 *be proud*; glory in, crow over 727 *triumph*; jubilate, exult 835 *rejoice*.

## 878 Insolence

**N.** *insolence*, hubris, arrogance, haughtiness, attitude, loftiness 871 *pride*; domineering, tyranny 735 *severity*; bravado 711 *defiance*; bluster 900 *threat*; disdain 922 *contempt*; sneer, sneering 926 *detraction*; contumely, contumelious behaviour 899 *scurrility*; assurance, self-a., self-assertion, bumptiousness, cockiness, brashness; presumption 916 *arrogation*; audacity, hardihood, boldness, effrontery, chutzpah, shamelessness, brazenness, brass neck, blatancy, flagrancy; face, front, hardened f., brazen face.

*sauciness*, disrespect, impertinence, impudence, pertness, freshness, sassiness; flippancy, nerve, gall, brass, cheek, cool c., neck; lip, mouth, sauce, crust, sass, snook, V-sign 547 *gesture*; taunt, personality, insult, affront 921 *indignity*; rudeness, incivility, throwaway manner 885 *discourtesy*; petulance, defiance, answer, provocation, answering back, backtalk, backchat 460 *rejoinder*; raillery, banter 851 *ridicule*.

*insolent person*, saucebox, impertinent, jackanapes, cheeky devil; minx, hussy, baggage, madam; whippersnapper, pup, puppy; upstart, beggar on horseback, Jack-in-office, tin god 639 *nonentity*; blusterer, swaggerer, braggart 877 *boaster*; bantam-cock, cockalorum 871 *proud person*; bratpack; bully, hoodlum, roisterer, swashbuckler, fire-eater, desperado 904 *ruffian*.

**Adj.** *insolent*, bellicose 718 *warlike*; rebellious 711 *defiant*; sneering 926 *detracting*; insulting, calumnious 921 *disrespectful*; injurious, scurrilous 899 *cursing*; lofty, supercilious, disdainful, contemptuous 922 *despising*; undemocratic, snobbish, haughty, snooty, up-stage, high-hat, high and mighty 871 *proud*; hubristic, arrogant, presumptuous, assuming, with attitude; brash, bumptious, bouncing 873 *vain*; flagrant, blatant; shameless, lost to shame, unblushing, unabashed, brazen, brazen-faced, brass-necked, bold as brass; bold, hardy, audacious

857 *rash*; overweening, overbearing, domineering, imperious, magisterial, lordly, dictatorial, arbitrary, high-handed, harsh, tyrannical 735 *oppressive*; blustering, bullying, fire-eating, ruffianly 877 *boastful*.

*impertinent*, pert, malapert, forward, fresh; impudent, saucy, sassy, cheeky, smart-mouth, brassy, cool, jaunty, perky, cocky, cocksure, flippant, flip; cavalier, offhand, presumptuous, out of line, familiar, overfamiliar, free-and-easy, devil-may-care, breezy, airy 921 *disrespectful*; impolite, rude, uncivil, ill-mannered 885 *discourteous*; defiant, answering back, provocative, deliberately p., offensive; personal, ridiculing 851 *derisive*.

**Vb.** *be insolent*, – arrogant etc. adj.; forget one's manners, get personal 885 *be rude*; have a nerve, cheek, sauce, sass, give lip, taunt, provoke 891 *enrage*; have the audacity to, have the brass neck to, have the cheek to; retort, answer back 460 *answer*; shout down 479 *confute*; get above oneself, get above one's station, teach one's grandmother to suck eggs; not know one's place, presume, be out-of-line, arrogate, assume, take on oneself, make bold to, make free with, get fresh; put on airs, hold one's nose in the air, look one up and down 871 *be proud*; look down on, sneer at 922 *despise*; banter, rally 851 *ridicule*; express contempt, sniff, snort; not give a fig 860 *be indifferent*; cock a snook, put one's tongue out, give the V-sign, send to blazes 711 *defy*; outstare, outlook, outface, brazen it out, brave it o.; take a high tone, lord it, queen it, lord it over; lay down the law, throw one's weight around; hector, bully, browbeat, grind down, trample on, ride roughshod over, treat with a high hand 735 *oppress*; swank, swagger, swell, look big 873 *be vain*; brag, talk big 877 *boast*; brook no restraint, own no law, be a law unto oneself 738 *disobey*; defy nemesis, provoke the gods, tempt providence *or* fate.

**Adv.** *insolently*, impertinently, pertly; arrogantly, hubristically, outrageously.

## 879 Servility

**N.** *servility*, slavishness, abject spirit, no pride, lack of self-respect 856 *cowardice*; subservience 721 *submission*; submissiveness, obsequiousness, compliance, pliancy 739 *obedience*; time-serving 603 *tergiversation*; abasement 872 *humility*; prostration, genuflexion, stooping, bent back, bow, scrape, bowing and scraping, duck, bob 311 *obeisance*; truckling, cringing, crawling, fawning, bootlicking, bumsucking, toadyism, sycophancy, ingratiation, soft soap 925 *flattery*; flunkeyism 745 *service*; service condition, slavery 745 *servitude*.

*toady*, toad-eater; time-server, collaborator, Uncle Tom; yes-man, rubber stamp 488 *assenter*; lickspittle, bootlicker, backscratcher, bumsucker, apple-polisher, kow-tower, groveller, truckler, crawler, creep, brown-nose (US); hypocrite, creeping Jesus, Uriah Heep 850 *affecter*; spaniel, fawner, courtier, fortune-hunter, tuft-h., lion-h. 925 *flatterer*; sycophant, parasite, leech, sponger, freeloader; jackal, hanger-on, gigolo 742 *dependant*; flunkey, lackey 742 *retainer*; born slave, slave; doormat, footstool, lapdog, poodle; tool, creature, puppet, dupe, cat's-paw 628 *instrument*.

**Adj.** *servile*, not free, dependent 745 *subject*; slavish 856 *cowardly*; mean-spirited, mean, abject, base, tame 745 *subjected*; subservient, submissive, deferential 721 *submitting*; pliant, putty-like, compliant, supple 739 *obedient*; time-serving 603 *tergiversating*; bowed, stooping, prostrate, bootlicking, backscratching, bumsucking, grovelling, truckling, kowtowing, bowing, scraping, cringing, cowering, crawling, sneaking, fawning; begging, whining; toadying, toadyish, sycophantic, parasitical; creepy, obsequious, unctuous, soapy, oily, slimy, overcivil, overattentive, soft-soaping, ingratiating 925 *flattering*.

**Vb.** *be servile*, forfeit one's self-respect, stoop to anything 867 *demean oneself*; squirm, roll, sneak, cringe, crouch, creep, crawl, grovel, truckle, kiss the hands of, kiss the feet of, kiss the hem of one's garment, lick the boots of 721 *knuckle under*; bow, scrape, bow and scrape, bend, bob, duck, kowtow, touch the forelock, make obeisance, kneel 311 *stoop*; swallow insults 872 *be humble*; make up to, cosy up to (inf), toady to, suck up to, spaniel, fawn, ingratiate oneself, soft-soap, pay court to, curry favour, worm oneself into f. 925 *flatter*; squire, attend, dance attendance on, fetch and carry for 742 *serve*; comply 739 *obey*; be the tool of, do one's dirty work, pander to, stooge for 628 *be instrumental*; let oneself be walked all over, be a doormat, act as a footstool; whine, wheedle, beg for favours, beg for crumbs 761 *beg*; play the parasite, batten on, sponge, sponge on; jump on the band wagon, run with the hare and hunt with the hounds 83 *conform*; serve the times 603 *change one's mind*.

**Adv.** *servilely*, slavishly, with servility, with a bow and a scrape, cap in hand, touching one's forelock.

SECTION THREE

*Interpersonal emotion*

### 880 Friendship

**N.** *friendship*, bonds of f., amity 710 *concord*; compatibility, mateyness, chumminess, palliness; friendly relations, relations of friendship, friendly intercourse, social i., hobnobbing 882 *sociality*; companionship, belonging, togetherness; alignment, fellowship, comradeship, sodality, freemansonry, brotherhood, sisterhood 706 *association*; solidarity, support, mutual s. 706 *cooperation*; acquaintanceship, acquaintance, mutual a., familiarity, intimacy 490 *knowledge*; fast friendship, close f., warm f., cordial f., passionate f. 887 *love*; making friends, getting acquainted, shaking hands with, introduction, recommendation, commendation; overtures, rapprochement, bonding, male b. 289 *approach*; renewal of friendship, reconciliation 719 *pacification*.

*friendliness*, amicability, kindliness, kindness, neighbourliness 884 *courtesy*; heartiness, cordiality, warmth 897 *benevolence*; fraternization, camaraderie, palliness, mateyness; hospitality 882 *sociability*; greeting, welcome, open arms, handclasp, handshake, hand-kissing, kissing, peck on the cheek, hug, namaskar, namaste, rubbing noses 884 *courteous act*; regard, mutual r. 920 *respect*; goodwill, mutual g.; fellow feeling, sympathy, response 775 *participation*; understanding, friendly u., good u., same wavelength, entente, entente cordiale, hands across the sea, honeymoon 710 *concord*; partiality 481 *prejudice*; favouritism, partisanship 914 *injustice*; support, loyal s. 703 *aid*.

*friend*, girlfriend, boyfriend 887 *loved one*; one's friends and acquaintances, one's circle of friends, acquaintance, intimate a.; friend of the family, lifelong friend, mutual f., friend's f., friend of a friend; crony, old c. (see also *chum*); neighbour, good n., fellow townsman *or* -woman, fellow countryman *or* -woman; cousin, clansman 11 *kinsman*; wellwisher, favourer, partisan, backer, angel 707 *patron*; second 660 *protector*; fellow, sister, brother, confrère, partner, associate 707 *colleague*; ally, brother-in-arms 707 *auxiliary*; collaborator, helper, friend in need 703 *aider*; invitee, guest, welcome g., frequent visitor, persona grata; young friend, protégé(e); host, kind h. 882 *sociable person*; former friend, fairweather f. 603 *tergiversator*.

*close friend*, best f.; soul mate, kindred spirit; best man, bridesmaid 894 *bridal party*; dear friend, good f., close f., fast f., firm f., loyal f., f.

in need; intimate, bosom friend, bosom pal, confidant(e), fidus Achates; alter ego, other self, shadow; comrade, companion, boon c., drinking c.; good friends all, happy family; mutual friends, inseparables, band of brothers *or* sisters, Three Musketeers, David and Jonathan, Ruth and Naomi, Castor and Pollux; two minds with but a single thought, 'Arcades ambo' (see quotation at 18 *analogue*), birds of a feather.

*chum*, crony; pal, mate, amigo, cobber, copain, buddy, butty, marrow, sidekick, oppo; fellow, comrade, shipmate, messmate, roommate, stable companion 707 *colleague*; teammate, playmate, classmate, schoolmate, schoolfellow; pen friend, pen pal; hearties, my h.

*xenophile*, Anglophile, Francophile, Europhile, Russophile, Sinophile, friend of all the world 901 *philanthropist*.

**Adj.** *friendly*, nonhostile, amicable, wellaffected, devoted 887 *loving*; loyal, faithful, staunch, fast, firm, tested, tried, tried and true 929 *trustworthy*; fraternal, brotherly, sisterly, cousinly; natural, unstrained, easy, harmonious 710 *concordant*; compatible, congenial, sympathetic, understanding; well-wishing, well-meaning, well-intentioned, philanthropic 897 *benevolent*; hearty, cordial, warm, welcoming, hospitable 882 *sociable*; effusive, demonstrative, back-slapping, hailfellow-well-met; comradely, chummy, pally, matey, buddy-buddy, palsy-walsy; friendly with, good friends w., at home w.; acquainted 490 *knowing*; free and easy, on familiar terms, on visiting t., on intimate t., on the best of t., well in with, intimate, inseparable, thick, thick as thieves, hand in glove.

**Vb.** *be friendly*, be friends with, get on well w., be on friendly terms w.; have neighbourly relations, have dealings w., rub along w., be palsy-walsy w., be buddy-buddy w.; fraternize, hobnob, keep company with, keep up w., keep in w., cosy up to (inf), go about together, be inseparable 882 *be sociable*; have friends, make f., win f., have a wide circle of friends, have many friendships, have a large acquaintance; shake hands, clasp h., embrace 884 *greet*; welcome, entertain 882 *be hospitable*; sympathize 516 *understand*; like, warm to, become fond of 887 *love*; mean well, have the best intentions, have the friendliest feelings 897 *be benevolent*.

*befriend*, acknowledge, know, accept one's friendship; take up, take in tow, favour, protect 703 *patronize*; overcome hostility, gain one's friendship; extend the right hand of fellowship, make welcome; strike an acquaintance, scrape an a., knit friendship; break the ice, make overtures 289 *approach*; seek one's friendship, cultivate one's f., pay one's addresses to 889 *court*; take to, warm to, click with, hit it off; fraternize with, frat, hobnob, get pally with, get matey w., get chummy w., chum up w., make friends w.; make acquainted, make known to each other, introduce, present, commend; renew friendship, become reconciled, shake hands 719 *make peace*.

**Adv.** *amicably*, in a friendly spirit; as friends, arm in arm; heartily, cordially.

**881 Enmity**
**N.** *enmity*, inimicality, hostility, antagonism 704 *opposition*; no love lost, unfriendliness, incompatibility, antipathy 861 *dislike*; loathing 888 *hatred*; animosity, animus, spite, grudge, ill feeling, ill will, bad blood, intolerance, persecution 898 *malevolence*; jealousy 912 *envy*; coolness, coldness 380 *ice*; estrangement, alienation, strain, tension, no honeymoon 709 *dissension*; bitterness, bitter feelings, hard f., rancour, soreness 891 *resentment*; unfaithfulness, disloyalty 930 *perfidy*; breach, open b., breach of friendship 709 *quarrel*; hostile act 709 *casus belli*; conflict, hostilities, breaking off of diplomatic relations, state of war 718 *belligerency*; vendetta, feud, blood f.

*enemy*, no friend, bad f., unfriend; ex-friend 603 *tergiversator*; traitor, viper in one's bosom 663 *troublemaker*; bad neighbour, ill-wisher; antagonist, opposite side, other s., them 705 *opponent*; competitor, rival 716 *contender*; open enemy, foe, foeman, hostile force 722 *combatant*; aggressor 712 *attacker*; enemy within the gates, fifth column, Trojan Horse; public enemy, outlaw, pirate 789 *robber*; personal enemy, declared e., sworn e., bitter e., confirmed e., irreconcilable e., arch enemy; misanthropist, misogynist 902 *misanthrope*; xenophobe, Anglophobe, Francophobe, Europhobe, Eurosceptic, negrophobe, racialist, anti-Semite 481 *narrow mind*; persona non grata, pet aversion, bête-noire 888 *hateful object*.

**Adj.** *inimical*, unfriendly, not well-inclined, ill-disposed, disaffected; disloyal, unfaithful 930 *perfidious*; aloof, distant, unwelcoming 883 *unsociable*; cool, chilly, frigid, icy 380 *cold*; antipathetic, incompatible, unsympathetic 861 *disliking*; loathing 888 *hating*; hostile, antagonistic, warring, conflicting, actively opposed, Eurosceptic 704 *opposing*; antagonized, estranged, alienated, unreconciled, irreconcilable; bitter, embittered, rancorous 891 *resentful*; jealous, grudging 912 *envious*; spiteful 898 *malevolent*; bad friends with, on bad terms,

not on speaking t.; at feud, at enmity, at variance, at loggerheads, at daggers drawn 709 *quarrelling*; aggressive, militant, belligerent, at war with 718 *warring*; intolerant, persecuting 735 *oppressive*; dangerous, venomous, virulent, deadly, fell 659 *baneful*.

**Vb.** *be inimical*, – unfriendly etc. adj.; show hostility 883 *make unwelcome*; harden one's heart, bear ill will, bear malice 898 *be malevolent*; grudge, nurse a g. 912 *envy*; hound, persecute 735 *oppress*; chase, hunt down 619 *hunt*; battle 716 *fight*; make war 718 *wage war*; take offence, take something the wrong way, take umbrage 891 *resent*; fall out, come to blows 709 *quarrel*; be incompatible, have nothing in common, be on different wavelengths, conflict, collide, clash 14 *be contrary*; withstand 704 *oppose*.

*make enemies*, be unpopular, have no friends, be a social pariah 883 *be unsociable*; get across, cause offence, cause ill feeling, antagonize, irritate 891 *enrage*; estrange, alienate, make bad blood, set by the ears, set at odds, set at daggers drawn 709 *make quarrels*.

**882 Sociality**
**N.** *sociality*, membership, membership of society, intercommunity, consociation 706 *association*; making one of, being one of, belonging; team spirit, esprit de corps; fellowship, comradeship, companionship, society; camaraderie, fraternization, fratting, hobnobbing; social intercourse, familiarity, intimacy, palliness, mateyness, togetherness 880 *friendship*; social circle, home c., family c., one's friends and acquaintances 880 *friend*; social ambition, social climbing; society, claims of society, social demands, the world.

*sociability*, social activity, group a.; social adjustment, compatibility 83 *conformity*; sociableness, gregariousness, sociable disposition, fondness for company 880 *friendliness*; social success, popularity; street credibility, street cred (inf); social tact, common touch; social graces, savoir vivre, good manners, easy m. 884 *courtesy*; urbanity 846 *good taste*; ability to mix, clubbability, affability, readiness to chat 584 *interlocution*; acceptability, welcome, kind w., hearty w., cordial w., warm w., smiling reception, open door; greeting, glad hand, handshake, handclasp, embrace 884 *courteous act*; hospitality, entertaining, home from home, open house, Liberty Hall, pot luck 813 *liberality*; good company, good fellowship, geniality, cordiality, heartiness, back-slapping, bonhomie; conviviality, joviality, jollity, merrymaking 824 *enjoyment*; gaiety 837 *revel*; cheer, good c. 301 *food*; eating and drinking, social board, festive b., 'the cup that cheers', loving cup 301 *feasting*.

> Now stir the fire, and close the shutters fast,
> Let fall the curtains, wheel the sofa round,
> And, while the bubbling and loud-hissing urn
> Throws up a steamy column, and the cups,
> That cheer but not inebriate, wait on each,
> So let us welcome peaceful ev'ning in.

> William Cowper, *The Task* (Cowper is referring to tea. A similar phrase had earlier been applied by Berkeley to tar water, which is 'of a nature so mild and benign and proportioned to the human constitution, as to warm without heating, to cheer but not inebriate'.)

*social gathering*, forgathering, meeting 74 *assembly*; reunion, get-together, conversazione, social; reception, at home, soirée, levee; entertainment 837 *amusement*; singsong, camp fire; party, do, shindig, thrash, hen party, stag p., partie carrée, tête-à-tête; housewarming, house party, weekend p.; birthday p., coming-out p.; social meal, feast, banquet, orgy 301 *feasting*; communion, love feast, agape 988 *ritual* act; coffee morning, tea party, bun fight, drinks, cocktail party, dinner p., supper p., garden p., picnic, barbecue, bottle party, byob (= bring your own bottle *or* booze) p., booze-up (inf) 837 *festivity*; dance, ball, ceilidh, hop, disco, rave 837 *dancing*; pyjama party, sleepover.

*social round*, social activities, social whirl, season, social s., social entertainment; social calls, round of visits; seeing one's friends, visiting, calling, dropping in; weekending, stay, visit, formal v., call, courtesy c.; visiting terms, frequentation, haunting 880 *friendship*; social demands, engagement, something on; dating, trysting, rendezvous, assignation, date, blind d.; meeting place, club, pub, local 76 *focus*.

*sociable person*, active member, keen m.; caller, visitor, dropper-in, frequenter, haunter, habitué; convivial person, bon vivant, bon viveur, good fellow, charming companion; good mixer, good company, life and soul of the party; social success, catch, lion 890 *favourite*; jolly person, boon companion, hobnobber, clubman, club woman; active member of the community, good neighbour 880 *friend*; hostess, host, mine h.; guest, welcome g., one of the family; diner-out, parasite, freeloader, ligger, gatecrasher; gadabout, social butterfly; socialite, ornament of society, social climber 848 *beau monde*.

**Adj.** *sociable*, gregarious, social, sociably disposed, extrovert, outgoing, fond of company, party-minded; companionable, fraternizing, affable, conversable, chatty, gossipy, fond of talk, always ready for a chat; clubbable, clubby; couthie, cosy, folksy; neighbourly, matey, chummy, pally, palsy-walsy, buddy-buddy 880 *friendly*; hospitable, welcoming, smiling, cordial, warm, hearty, back-slapping, hail-fellow-well-met; convivial, festive, Christmassy, jolly, jovial 833 *merry*; lively, witty 837 *amusing*; urbane 884 *courteous*; easy, free-and-easy, easy-mannered; unbuttoned, post-prandial, after-dinner 683 *reposeful*.

*welcomed*, feted, entertained; welcome, ever-w., quite one of the family; popular, liked, sought-after, socially successful, invited, getting around, first on the invitation list.

**Vb.** *be sociable*, – gregarious etc. adj.; enjoy society, like company, love a party; have friends, make friends easily, hobnob, fraternize, socialize, mix with 880 *be friendly*; mix well, be a good mixer, get around, know how to live, mix in society, go out, dine o., go to parties, accept invitations, cadge i., freeload, lig, gate-crash; have fun, live it up, be the life and soul of the party 837 *amuse oneself*; join in, get together, make it a party, club together, go Dutch, share, go shares 775 *participate*; take pot luck, eat off the same platter 301 *eat*; join in a bottle, crack a b. 301 *drink*; pledge 876 *toast*; carouse 837 *revel*; make oneself welcome, make oneself at home, become one of the family; relax, unbend 683 *repose*; chat to 584 *converse*; make engagements, date, make a date; make friends, make friendly overtures 880 *befriend*; introduce oneself, exchange names, exchange telephone numbers; extend one's friendships, enlarge one's circle of acquaintances; keep up with, keep in touch w., keep in w., write to 588 *correspond*.

*visit*, see people, go visiting, go for a visit, pay a v., be one's guest, sojourn, stay, weekend; keep up with, keep in w., keep in touch, see one's friends; go and see, look one up, call, call in, look in, drop in; wait on, leave a card; exchange visits, be on visiting terms.

*be hospitable*, keep open house 813 *be liberal*; invite, have round, ask in, be at home to, receive, open one's home to, keep open house; welcome, make w., bid one w., welcome with open arms, hug, embrace 884 *greet*; act the host, do the honours, preside; do proud, kill the fatted calf 876 *celebrate*; send invitations, have company, entertain, regale 301 *feed*; give a party, throw a p. 837 *revel*; accept, take in, cater for, provide entertainment 633 *provide*.

**Adv.** *sociably*, hospitably, in friendly fashion, like friends, en famille; arm in arm, hand in hand.

## 883 Unsociability. Seclusion

**N.** *unsociability*, unsociableness, unsocial habits, shyness 620 *avoidance*; introversion, autism, schizothymia; refusal to mix, keeping one's own company, keeping oneself to oneself; staying at home, home life, domesticity; singledom, singleness 895 *celibacy*; inhospitality 816 *parsimony*; standoffishness, unapproachability, distance, aloofness, lonely pride 871 *pride*; unfriendliness, coolness, coldness, moroseness, savageness 893 *sullenness*; cut, dead c., cut direct 885 *discourtesy*; silence, lack of conversation 582 *taciturnity*; ostracism, boycott 57 *exclusion*; blacklist 607 *rejection*.

*seclusion*, privacy, private world, world of one's own; island universe 321 *star*; peace and quiet 266 *quietude*; home life, domesticity; loneliness, solitariness, solitude; retreat, retirement, withdrawal; hiddenness 523 *latency*; confinement, solitary c., purdah 525 *concealment*; isolation, splendid i. 744 *independence*; division, estrangement 46 *separation*; renunciation 621 *relinquishment*; renunciation of the world, coenobitism 985 *monasticism*; self-exile, expatriation; sequestration, segregation, ghettoization, rustication, excommunication, house arrest, quarantine, deportation, banishment, exile 57 *exclusion*; reserve, reservation, ghetto, native quarter, harem; gaol 748 *prison*; sequestered nook, godforsaken hole, back of beyond; island, desert, wilderness; hide-out, hideaway 527 *hiding-place*; den, study, sanctum, inner s., sanctum sanctorum, cloister, cell, hermitage 192 *retreat*; ivory tower, private quarters, shell; backwater, 'rus in urbe'.

**Rus in urbe.**
*(Countryside in the town.)*
Martial, *Epigrams*

*solitary*, unsocial person, iceberg; lonely person, lonely heart; loner, lone wolf, rogue elephant; isolationist, island; introvert; stay-at-home, home-body; ruralist, troglodyte, cave-dweller; recluse, coenobite, anchorite, anchoritess, hermit, eremite, marabout; stylite, pillar monk, Diogenes and his tub; maroon, castaway 779 *derelict*; Robinson Crusoe, Alexander Selkirk.

*outcast*, pariah, leper, outsider; outcaste, untouchable, harijan; expatriate, alien 59 *foreigner*; exile, expellee, evictee, deportee, evacuee, refugee, political r., asylum-seeker, displaced person, homeless p., the homeless, rough sleeper, skell (sl) 188 *displaced person*, 192 *homeless person*; stateless p.; nonperson, unperson; proscribed person, outlaw, bandit; Ishmael, vagabond 268 *wanderer*; waif, stray 779 *derelict*; reject, flotsam and jetsam, the dregs 641 *rubbish*.

**Adj.** *unsociable*, unsocial, antisocial, introverted, morose, not fit to live with; unassimi-

lated, foreign 59 *extraneous*; unclubbable, stay-at-home, home-keeping, quiet, domestic; inhospitable, unwelcoming, forbidding, hostile, unneighbourly, unfriendly, uncongenial, unaffable, misanthropic; distant, aloof, unbending, stiff; stand-offish, offish, haughty 871 *prideful*; unwelcoming, frosty, icy, cold 893 *sullen*; unforthcoming, in one's shell; unconversational, uncommunicative, close, silent 582 *taciturn*; cool, impersonal 860 *indifferent*; solitary, lonely, lone 88 *alone*; shy, reserved, retiring, withdrawn, afraid of company, avoiding society 620 *avoiding*; wild, feral, celibate, unmarried 895 *unwedded*; anchoretic, eremetic, the world forgetting, by the world forgot.

*friendless*, unfriended, lorn, forlorn, desolate, forsaken, without a friend in the world; companionless, lonely, lonesome, solitary; on one's own, without company, by oneself, all alone 88 *alone*; cold-shouldered, uninvited, without introductions; unpopular, avoided 860 *unwanted*; blacklisted, blackballed, ostracized, boycotted, sent to Coventry 57 *excluded*; expelled, evicted, disbarred, deported, exiled; under embargo, banned 757 *prohibited*.

*secluded*, private, sequestered, cloistered, shut away, hidden, buried, tucked away 523 *latent*; veiled, behind the veil, in purdah 421 *screened*; quiet, lonely, isolated, enisled, marooned; remote, out of the way; godforsaken, unvisited, unfrequented, unexplored, unseen, unfamiliar, off the beaten track, far from the madding crowd 491 *unknown*; uninhabited, deserted, desert, desolate 190 *empty*.

**Vb.** *be unsociable*, keep one's own company, keep oneself to oneself, shun company, see no one, talk to nobody; go it alone, play a lone hand, be a lone wolf; keep out, stay o., stew in one's own juice; stay in one's shell, shut oneself up, immure oneself, cloister o., remain private, maintain one's privacy, stand aloof 620 *avoid*; stay at home, cultivate one's garden, bury oneself, vegetate 266 *be quiescent*; retire, go into retirement, give up one's friends, leave the world, forsake the w., make a retreat, take the veil; live in seclusion, live in purdah.

*make unwelcome*, frown on 924 *disapprove*; repel, keep at arm's length, make one keep his distance, treat coolly, treat with frosty silence; not acknowledge, ignore, cut, cut dead 885 *be rude*; cold-shoulder, turn one's back on, shut the door on; rebuff, give one the brush-off; turn out, turf o., cast o., expel 300 *eject*; ostracize, boycott, send to Coventry, blacklist, blackball 57 *exclude*; have no time for, refuse to meet, refuse to mix with, refuse to associate w., have nothing to do with, treat as a leper, treat as an outsider 620 *avoid*; excommunicate, banish, exile, outlaw, ban 963 *punish*.

*seclude*, sequester, island, isolate, quarantine, segregate, ghettoize; keep in private, keep in purdah; confine, shut up 747 *imprison*.

## 884 Courtesy

**N.** *courtesy*, chivalry, knightliness, gallantry; common courtesy, deference 920 *respect*; consideration, condescension 872 *humility*; graciousness, politeness, civility, urbanity, mannerliness, manners, good m., noble m., good behaviour, best b.; good breeding, gentlemanliness, ladylikeness, gentility 846 *good taste*; tactfulness, diplomacy; courtliness, correctness, correctitude, etiquette 875 *formality*; comity, amenity, amiability, sweetness, niceness, obligingness, kindness, kindliness 897 *benevolence*; gentleness, mildness 736 *leniency*; easy temper, good humour, complaisance 734 *laxity*; agreeableness, affability, suavity, blandness, common touch, social tact 882 *sociability*; smooth tongue 925 *flattery*.

*courteous act*, act of courtesy, polite act, graceful gesture, courtesy, common c., civility, favour, charity, kindness 897 *kind act*; soft answer 736 *leniency*; compliment, bouquet 886 *congratulation*; kind words, fair w., sweet w. 889 *endearment*; introduction, presentation 880 *friendliness*; welcome, polite w., reception, invitation; acknowledgment, recognition, mark of r., nod, salutation, salute, greeting, affectionate g., welcoming gesture, smile, kiss, kiss on the cheek, air-kiss, air-kissing, hug, squeeze, handclasp, handshake 920 *respects*; bow, curtsy, kowtow, namaskar, namaste, salaam 311 *obeisance*; terms of courtesy, respects, regards, kind r., best r., duty, remembrances, love, best wishes; love and kisses, farewell 296 *valediction*.

**Adj.** *courteous*, chivalrous, knightly, generous 868 *noble*; courtly, gallant, old-world, correct 875 *formal*; polite, civil, urbane, gentle, gentlemanly, ladylike, dignified, well-mannered, fine-m. 848 *well-bred*; gracious, condescending 872 *humble*; deferential, mannerly 920 *respectful*; on one's best behaviour, minding one's P's and Q's, anxious to please 455 *attentive*; obliging, complaisant, kind 897 *benevolent*; conciliatory, sweet 719 *pacificatory*; agreeable, suave, bland, smooth, ingratiating, well-spoken, fair-s., honey-tongued 925 *flattering*; obsequious 879 *servile*.

*amiable*, nice, sweet, winning 887 *lovable*; affable, friendly, amicable 882 *sociable*; considerate, kind 897 *benevolent*; inoffensive, harmless 935 *innocent*; gentle, easy, mild, soft-spoken 736 *lenient*; good-tempered,

sweet-t., good-natured, unruffled 823 *inexcitable*; well-behaved, good 739 *obedient*; pacific, peaceable 717 *peaceful*.

**Vb.** *be courteous*, be on one's best behaviour, mind one's P's and Q's; mind one's manners, display good m.; show courtesy, treat with politeness, treat with deference 920 *respect*; give one his *or* her title, call sir, call madam; oblige, put oneself out 703 *aid*; condescend 872 *be humble*; notice, have time for, make time for 455 *be attentive*; conciliate, speak fair 719 *pacify*; not forget one's manners, keep a civil tongue in one's head, make oneself agreeable, be all things to all men; take no offence, take in good part, return a soft answer 823 *be patient*; become courteous, mend one's manners, express regrets 941 *atone*.

*pay one's respects*, give one's regards, send one's r., offer one's duty; send one's compliments, do one the honour; pay compliments 925 *flatter*; drink to, pledge 876 *toast*; homage, pay h., show one's respect, kneel, kiss hands 920 *show respect*; honour, crown, wreathe, garland, chair, give a hero's welcome 876 *celebrate*.

*greet*, send greetings (see also *pay one's respects*); flag 547 *signal*; accost, sidle up 289 *approach*; acknowledge, recognize, hold out one's hand 455 *notice*; shout *or* call out one's greeting, hail 408 *vociferate*; nod, wave, smile, kiss one's fingers, blow a kiss; say hallo, bid good morning 583 *speak to*; salute, make salutation, raise one's hat, uncap, uncover; touch one's cap, tug one's forelock; bend, bow, bob, duck, curtsy, salaam, make obeisance, kiss hands, prostrate oneself, kowtow 311 *stoop*; shake hands, clasp h., shake the hand, press *or* squeeze *or* wring *or* pump the hand, press the flesh; advance to meet 920 *show respect*; escort 89 *accompany*; make a salute, fire a s., present arms, parade, turn out 876 *celebrate*; receive, do the honours, be mother; welcome, welcome in, welcome home 882 *be sociable*; welcome with open arms 824 *be pleased*; open one's arms, embrace, hug, kiss, kiss on both cheeks 889 *caress*; usher, usher in, present, introduce 299 *admit*.

**Adv.** *courteously*, politely, with respect, with all due deference; condescendingly, graciously.

## 885 Discourtesy

**N.** *discourtesy*, impoliteness, bad manners, deplorable m., sheer bad m., shocking bad m., disgraceful table m.; no manners, mannerlessness, failure of courtesy, lack of chivalry, lack of politeness, lack of manners, scant courtesy, incivility, inurbanity; churlishness, uncouthness, boorishness, yobbishness, yob

culture 847 *ill-breeding*; unpleasantness, nastiness, beastliness; misbehaviour, misconduct,
unbecoming conduct; tactlessness, inconsiderateness, lack of consideration, stepping on
one's toes.

*rudeness*, ungraciousness, gruffness, bluntness; sharpness, tartness, acerbity, acrimony,
asperity; ungentleness, roughness, harshness
735 *severity*; offhandedness 456 *inattention*;
brusquerie, shortness, short answer, plain a.
569 *conciseness*; sarcasm 851 *ridicule*; excessive
frankness, unparliamentary language, bad l.,
rude words, virulence 899 *scurrility*; rebuff,
insult 921 *indignity*; personalities, impertinence, pertness, sauce, sassiness, lip, cheek,
truculence 878 *insolence*; impatience, interruption, shouting 822 *excitability*; black look,
sour l., scowl, frown, pulling faces, sticking out
the tongue 893 *sullenness*; a discourtesy, act
of d., piece of bad manners.

*rude person*, no true knight, no gentleman,
no lady; savage, barbarian, brute, lout, boor,
yob, loudmouth, mannerless brat, unlicked
cub 878 *insolent person*; bratpack; curmudgeon,
crab, bear; sourpuss, crosspatch, groucher,
grouser, fault-finder, bellyacher, beefer,
sulker 829 *malcontent*; bad driver, white van
man.

**Adj.** *discourteous*, unknightly, ungallant,
unchivalrous, unhandsome; uncourtly, unceremonious, ungentlemanly, unladylike; inur-
bane, impolite, uncivil, rude; mannerless,
unmannerly, ill-mannered, bad-m., boorish,
loutish, yobbish, uncouth, brutish, beastly,
savage, barbarian 847 *ill-bred*; insolent, impudent; cheeky, saucy, sassy, pert, forward 878
*impertinent*; unpleasant, disagreeable; cool, not
anxious to please, unaccommodating, uncom-
plaisant 860 *indifferent*; offhanded, cavalier,
airy, breezy, tactless, inconsiderate 456
*inattentive*.

*ungracious*, unsmiling, grim 834 *serious*;
gruff, grunting, growling, crabbed, crabbit,
bearish 893 *sullen*; peevish, testy 892 *irascible*;
difficult, surly, churlish, unfriendly, unneighbourly 883 *unsociable*; grousing, grouching,
grumbling, swearing 829 *discontented*;
ungentle, rough, rugged, harsh, brutal 735
*severe*; bluff, free, frank, overfrank, blunt, over-
blunt; brusque, short 569 *concise*; tart, sharp,
biting, acrimonious 388 *pungent*; sarcastic,
uncomplimentary, unflattering 926 *detracting*;
foul-mouthed, foul-spoken, abusive, vituperative 899 *cursing*; contumelious, offensive,
injurious, insulting, truculent 921 *disrespectful*.

**Vb.** *be rude,* – mannerless etc. adj.; want
manners, have no m., flout etiquette; know no
better 699 *be artless*; forget one's manners, dis-

play bad manners, show discourtesy 878 *be
insolent*; show no thought for others, show no
regard for one's feelings, step on everyone's
toes, ride roughshod over everyone 921 *not
respect*; have no time for 456 *be inattentive*;
treat rudely, be beastly to, snub, turn one's
back on, cold-shoulder, hand one the frozen
mitt, cut, ignore, look right through, cut dead
883 *make unwelcome*; show one the door, send
away with a flea in their ear 300 *eject*; cause
offence, miff, ruffle one's feelings 891 *huff*;
insult, abuse; take liberties, make free with,
make bold; stare, ogle 438 *gaze*; make one
blush 867 *shame*; lose one's temper, shout,
interrupt 891 *get angry*; curse, swear, damn 899
*cuss*; snarl, growl, frown, scowl, lour, pout, sulk
893 *be sullen*.

**Adv.** *impolitely*, discourteously, like a boor,
like an ill-mannered fellow, yobbishly.

## 886 Congratulation

**N.** *congratulation*, felicitation, gratulation, congratulations, felicitations, compliments,
best c., bouquets, compliments of the season;
good wishes, best w., happy returns; salute,
toast; welcome, hero's w., official reception
876 *celebration*; thanks 907 *gratitude*.

**Adj.** *congratulatory*, gratulatory, complimentary; honorific, triumphal, welcoming 876 *celebratory*.

**Vb.** *congratulate*, felicitate, compliment,
proffer bouquets; offer one's congratulations,
wish one joy, give one joy, wish many happy
returns, wish a merry Christmas and a happy
New Year, offer the season's greetings; send
one's congratulations, send one's compliments
884 *pay one's respects*; sanction a triumph,
accord an ovation, give one a hero's welcome,
give three cheers, clap 923 *applaud*; fete, mob,
rush, lionize 876 *celebrate*; congratulate oneself, give oneself a pat on the back, hug o.,
thank one's lucky stars 824 *be pleased*; thank
Heaven 907 *be grateful*.

**Int.** *bravo!*, congratulations!, mazel tov!,
way to go! (US inf), well done!

## 887 Love

**N.** *love*, affection, friendship, charity, Eros;
agape, brotherly love, sisterly l., Christian l.;
true love, real thing; natural affection,
parental a., paternal a., maternal a., mother-
love, protective l., protectiveness 931 *disinterestedness*; possessive love, possessiveness 911
*jealousy*; conjugal love, uxoriousness; closeness, intimacy; sentiment 818 *feeling*; kindness, tenderness 897 *benevolence*; Platonic love
880 *friendship*; two hearts that beat as one,
mutual love, mutual affection, mutual attrac-

tion, compatibility, sympathy, fellow feeling, understanding; fondness, liking, predilection, inclination 179 *tendency*; preference 605 *choice*; fancy 604 *caprice*; attachment, sentimental a., firm a.; devotion, loyal d., patriotism 739 *loyalty*; courtly love, gallantry; sentimentality, susceptibility, amorousness 819 *moral sensibility*; power of love, fascination, enchantment, bewitchment 983 *sorcery*; lovesickness, Cupid's sting, yearning, longing 859 *desire*; amativeness, amorism, eroticism, lust 859 *libido*; regard 920 *respect*; admiration, hero-worship, worship from afar 864 *wonder*; dawn of love, first l., calf l., puppy l., young l.; crush, pash, infatuation; worship 982 *idolatry*; romantic love, l. at first sight, coup de foudre, passion, tender p., fire of love, flames of l., enthusiasm, rapture, ecstasy, transport, transports of love 822 *excitable state*; erotomania, abnormal affection 84 *variance*; love psychology, narcissism, Oedipus complex, Electra c.; love-hate, 'odi et amo'.

> Odi et amo: quare id faciam, fortasse requiris.
> Nescio, sed fieri sentio et excrucior.
> *(I hate and I love: why I do, you may well ask.*
> *I don't know, but I feel it happening and am in*
> *torment.)*
> Catullus, *Poems*

*lovableness*, amiability, attractiveness, popularity, gift of pleasing; winsomeness, charm, fascination, appeal, sex a., it, attractions, charms, beauties; winning ways, pleasing qualities, endearing q.; coquetry, flirtatiousness; sentimental value.

*love affair*, romantic a., affair of the heart, affaire de coeur; romance, 'all for love and the world well lost';

> All for Love: or, The World Well Lost.
> Title of play by John Dryden

flirtation, amour, amourette, entanglement, relationship 604 *whim*; loves, amours; free love; liaison, intrigue, seduction, adultery 951 *illicit love*; falling in love, something between them; course of love, the old old story; betrothal, engagement, wedding bells 894 *marriage*; serial monogamy; broken engagement, broken romance, broken heart.

*lovemaking*, spooning, canoodling, necking, billing and cooing 889 *endearment*; sex 45 *sexual intercourse*, 376 *sexual pleasure*; courtship, courting, walking out, going with, going steady, sighing, suing, pressing one's suit, laying siege 889 *wooing*; pursuit of love, hoping for conquests, coquetting, coquetry, flirtation, flirting, cyberflirtation, philandering; gallantry, dalliance, dallying, toying, chambering and wantonness, libertinage 951 *unchastity*; bestowal of love, favours.

*love-nest*, abode of love, bower, 'Bower of Bliss';

> Nor e'er was to the bowers of bliss conveyed
> A fairer spirit or more welcome shade.
> Thomas Tickell, *On the Death of Mr. Addison*

honeymoon cottage, bridal suite, nuptial chamber, bridal bed; harem, seraglio.

*lover*, love, true l., sweetheart, squeeze; young man, boyfriend, Romeo; young woman, girlfriend, bird (inf), squeeze (inf); swain, beau, gallant, spark, cavalier, squire, escort, date; steady, fiancé(e); wooer, courter, suitor, follower, captive, admirer, hero-worshipper, adorer, votary, worshipper; aficionado, fan, devoted following, fan club; sugar daddy, dotard; cicisbeo, gigolo, squire of dames, ladies' man, lady-killer, seducer, Lothario, Don Juan, Casanova; toyboy; paramour, amorist 952 *libertine*; flirt, coquette, philanderer; gold-digger, vamp, cohabitee, common-law husband *or* wife, man, woman, live-in, bidie-in (Scots), POSSLQ (= person of opposite sex sharing living quarters).

*loved one*, beloved, love, true love, soul mate, heart's desire, light of one's life, one's own 890 *darling*; intimate 880 *close friend*; favoured suitor, lucky man, intended, betrothed, affianced, fiancé(e), bride-to-be 894 *spouse*; conquest, inamorata, lady-love, girlfriend, girl, bird (inf), bit (inf), honey, baby, sweetie, squeeze (inf); angel, princess, goddess; sweetheart, valentine, flame, old f.; idol, hero; heartthrob, maiden's prayer, dream man, Alpha man, dream girl, princesse lointaine 859 *desired object*; Phyllis, Dulcinea, Amaryllis; favourite, mistress, leman, concubine 952 *kept woman*; dangerous woman, femme fatale.

*lovers*, pair of lovers, loving couple, engaged c., turtledoves, lovebirds; POSSLQs, persons of opposite sex sharing living quarters; Daphnis and Chloe, Aucassin and Nicolette, Harlequin and Columbine; star-crossed lovers, tragic l., Pyramus and Thisbe, Romeo and Juliet, Hero and Leander, Tristan and Isolde, Lancelot and Guinevere, Troilus and Cressida; historic lovers, Héloïse and Abélard, Dante and Beatrice, Petrarch and Laura, Antony and Cleopatra.

*love god*, goddess of love, Venus, Aphrodite, Astarte, Freya; Amor, Eros, Kama, Cupid, blind boy; cupidon, amoretto.

*love emblem*, myrtle, turtledove; Cupid's bow, Cupid's arrows, Cupid's dart, Cupid's torch; golden arrow, leaden a.; pierced heart, bleeding h., broken h. 889 *love token*.

**Adj.** *loving*, brotherly, sisterly; loyal, patriotic 931 *disinterested*; wooing, courting, cuddling, making love 889 *caressing*; affectionate, cuddlesome, demonstrative; tender, motherly, wifely, conjugal; loverlike, loverly, gallant, romantic, sentimental, lovesick; mooning, moping, lovelorn, languishing 834 *dejected*; attached to, doting, fond, fond of, mad about, uxorious; possessive 911 *jealous*; admiring, adoring, devoted, enslaved (see also *enamoured*); flirtatious, coquettish 604 *capricious*; amatory, amorous, amative, ardent, passionate 818 *fervent*; yearning 859 *desiring*, lustful, concupiscent, libidinous 951 *lecherous*.

*enamoured*, in love, fallen in l., falling in l., inclined to, sweet on, soft on, keen on, set on, stuck on, gone on, sold on; struck with, taken w., smitten, bitten, caught, hooked; charmed, enchanted, fascinated 983 *bewitched*; mad on, infatuated, besotted, crazy about, wild a., head over heels in love 503 *crazy*; happily in love, blissfully in l. 824 *happy*; rapturous, ecstatic 821 *excited*; loved up (sl) 949 *drugged*.

*lovable*, likable, congenial, sympathetic, to one's liking, to one's taste, to one's fancy, after one's own heart 859 *desired*; lovesome, winsome, loveworthy 884 *amiable*; sweet, angelic, divine, adorable; lovely, graceful, good-looking 841 *beautiful*; interesting, intriguing, attractive, seductive, alluring 291 *attracting*; prepossessing, appealing, engaging, winning, endearing, captivating, irresistible; cuddly, desirable, kissable; charming, enchanting, bewitching 983 *sorcerous*; liked, beloved, endeared to, dear, darling, pet, fancy, favourite.

*erotic*, aphrodisiac, erotogenic, erogenous; sexy, page 3, pornographic 951 *impure*; amatory 821 *excited*.

**Vb.** love, like, care, rather care for, quite like, take pleasure in, be partial to, take an interest in; sympathize with, feel w., be fond of, have a soft spot for; be susceptible, have a heart, have a warm h.; bear love towards, hold in affection, hold dear, care for, cherish, cling to, embrace; appreciate, value, prize, treasure, think the world of, regard, admire, revere 920 *respect*; adore, worship, idolize, only have eyes for 982 *idolatrize*; live for, live only f.; burn with love, be on fire with passion (see also *be in love*); make love, bestow one's favours 45 *unite with*; make much of, spoil, indulge, pet, fondle, drool over, slobber o. 889 *caress*.

*be in love*, burn, sweat, faint, die of *or* for love 361 *die*; burn with love, glow with ardour, flame with passion, love to distraction, dote 503 *be insane*; take a fancy to, take a shine to, cotton on to, take to, warm to, be taken with, be sweet on, dig, have a crush on, have a pash for; carry a torch for, look with passion on 859 *desire*; form an attachment, fall for, fall in love,

get infatuated, get hooked on, have it bad; go crazy over, be nuts on 503 *go mad*; set one's heart on, lose one's heart, bestow one's affections; declare one's love, offer one's heart to, woo, sue, sigh, press one's suit, make one's addresses 889 *court*; set one's cap at, chase 619 *pursue*; enjoy one's favours; honeymoon 894 *wed*.

*excite love*, arouse desire 859 *cause desire*; warm, inflame 381 *heat*; rouse, stir, flutter, enrapture, enthral 821 *excite*; dazzle, bedazzle, charm, enchant, fascinate 983 *bewitch*; allure, draw 291 *attract*; make oneself attractive 843 *primp*; lure, bait, tantalize, seduce 612 *tempt*; lead on, flirt, coquette, philander, break hearts, be a prickteaser; toy, vamp 889 *caress*; smile, leer, make eyes, ogle, wink 889 *court*; catch one's eye 455 *attract notice*; enamour, take one's fancy, steal one's heart, gain one's affections, engage the a.; make a hit, bowl over, sweep off one's feet, turn one's head, infatuate 503 *make mad*; make a conquest, captivate 745 *subjugate*; catch, lead to the altar 894 *wed*; endear, endear oneself, ingratiate o., insinuate o., wind *or* worm oneself into the affections; be loved, be amiable, be lovable, make oneself a favourite, become a f., be the rage; steal every heart, set all hearts on fire, have a place in every heart; curry favour 925 *flatter*.

**Adv.** *affectionately*, kindly, lovingly, tenderly 457 *carefully*; fondly, dotingly, madly.

## 888 Hatred

**N.** *hatred*, hate, no love lost; love-hate, 'odi et amo' (see quotation at 887 *love*); revulsion of feeling, disillusion; aversion, antipathy, allergy, nausea 861 *dislike*; intense dislike, repugnance, detestation, loathing, abhorrence, abomination; disfavour, displeasure (see also *odium*); disaffection, estrangement, alienation 709 *dissension*; hostility, antagonism 881 *enmity*; animosity, ill feeling, bad blood, bitterness, acrimony, rancour 891 *resentment*; malice, ill will, evil eye, spite, grudge, ancient g. 898 *malevolence*; jealousy 912 *envy*; wrath 891 *anger*; execration, hymn of hate 899 *malediction*; scowl, black looks, snap, snarl, baring one's fangs 893 *sullenness*; xenophobia, Anglophobia, Gallophobia 854 *phobia*; anti-Semitism, racialism, racism, institutional r., race hatred, racial prejudice, colour prejudice, white supremacy 481 *prejudice*; misogyny 902 *misanthropy*.

*odium*, disfavour, unpopularity 924 *disapprobation*; discredit, bad odour, bad books, black books 867 *disrepute*; odiousness, hatefulness, loathsomeness, beastliness, obnoxiousness;

despicability, despisedness 922 *contemptibility*.

*hateful object*, anathema; unwelcome necessity, bitter pill; abomination, filth; object of
one's hate 881 *enemy*; not one's type, one's
aversion, pet a., bête-noire, bugbear, Dr Fell,
nobody's darling; pest, menace, public nuisance, good riddance 659 *bane*; rotter 938 *cad*;
heretic, blackleg, scab 603 *tergiversator*.

**Adj.** *hating*, loathing, envying etc. vb.; loveless; antipathetic, revolted, disgusted 861 *disliking*; set against 704 *opposing*; averse,
abhorrent, antagonistic, hostile, antagonized,
snarling 881 *inimical*; envious, spiteful, spleenful, malicious, full of malice, malignant 898
*malevolent*; bitter, rancorous 891 *resentful*; full
of hate, implacable; vindictive 910 *revengeful*;
virulent, execrative 899 *cursing*; out of love, disenchanted, disillusioned 509 *disappointed*.

*hateful*, odious, unlovable, unloved;
invidious, antagonizing, obnoxious, pestilential 659 *baneful*; beastly, nasty, horrid, – from
hell 645 *not nice*; abhorrent, loathsome, abominable; accursed, execrable, execrated 899
*cursed*; offensive, repulsive, repellent, nauseous, nauseating, revolting, disgusting 861 *disliked*; bitter, sharp 393 *sour*; unwelcome 860
*unwanted*.

*hated*, loathed etc. vb.; uncared for 458 *neglected*; out of favour, fallen from favour,
unpopular 861 *disliked*; in one's bad books, in
the black b., discredited, in the wilderness 924
*disapproved*; loveless, unloved; unvalued,
unmissed, unregretted, unlamented,
unmourned, unwept; unchosen, refused,
spurned, condemned, jilted, lovelorn, crossed
in love 607 *rejected*.

**Vb.** *hate*, bear hatred, have no love for; hate
one's guts; loathe, abominate, detest, abhor,
hold in horror; turn away from, shrink f. 620
*avoid*; revolt from, recoil at 280 *recoil*; can't
bear, can't stand, can't stomach 861 *dislike*;
find loathsome, find obnoxious; not choose,
refuse 607 *reject*; spurn, contemn 922 *despise*;
execrate, hold accursed, denounce 899 *curse*;
bear malice, have a down on 898 *be malevolent*;
feel envy 912 *envy*; bear a grudge, nurse resentment, have it in for 910 *be revengeful*, 891
*resent*; scowl, give black looks, growl, snap,
snarl, bare one's fangs 893 *be sullen*; insult 878
*be insolent*; conceive a hatred for, fall out of
love, become disenchanted with, turn to hate.

*excite hate*, grate, jar, go against the grain 292
*repel*; cause loathing, disgust, nauseate, stink in
the nostrils 861 *cause dislike*; shock, horrify 924
*incur blame*; turn one off, antagonize, destroy
goodwill, estrange, alienate, sow dissension,
set by the ears, set at each others' throats,
create bad blood, end friendship, turn all to

hate 881 *make enemies*; poison, envenom,
embitter, exacerbate 832 *aggravate*; exasperate,
incense 891 *enrage*.

## 889 Endearment

**N.** *endearment*, blandishments, compliments,
bouquets 925 *flattery*; loving words, affectionate speeches, pretty s., pretty names, pet
name; soft nothings, sweet n., lovers' vows;
affectionate behaviour, dalliance, billing and
cooing, holding hands, slap and tickle, footsie;
fondling, cuddling, canoodling, lovemaking,
petting, necking, smooching, snogging,
kissing, French k., tonsil hockey, osculation;
caress, embracement, embrace, clasp, hug,
bear h., cuddle, squeeze, pressure, fond p.;
salute, buss, kiss, butterfly k., French k.,
smacker; nibble, bite, love b., hickey; stroke,
tickle, slap, pat, pinch, nip 378 *touch*; familiarity, overfamiliarity, advances, pass.

*wooing*, courting, spooning, flirting; play,
love-p., lovemaking; wink, side-glance, glad
eye, come hither look, ogle, oeillade, amorous
glance, sheep's eyes, fond look, languishing l.,
sigh; flirtation, philandering, coquetry, gallantry, amorous intentions, honourable i.;
courtship, suit, love s., addresses, advances 887
*lovemaking*; serenade, aubade, love song, love
lyric, amorous ditty, caterwauling; love letter,
billet-doux; love poem, sonnet; proposal,
engagement, betrothal 894 *marriage*.

*love token*, true lover's knot, favour, ribbon,
glove; ring, engagement r., wedding r., eternity
r.; valentine, love letter, billet-doux; language
of flowers, posy, red roses; arrow, heart 887
*love emblem*; tattoo.

**Adj.** *caressing*, clinging, toying, fondling etc.
vb.; demonstrative, affectionate 887 *loving*;
soppy, spoony, lovey-dovey; cuddlesome, flirtatious, coquettish; wooing, sighing, suing.

**Vb.** *pet*, pamper, spoil, indulge, overindulge, spoonfeed, featherbed, mother,
smother, kill with kindness; cosset, cocker,
coddle; make much of, be all over one; treasure
887 *love*; cherish, foster 660 *safeguard*; nurse,
lap, rock, cradle, baby; sing to, croon over;
coax, wheedle 925 *flatter*.

*caress*, love, fondle, dandle, take in one's lap;
play with, stroke, smooth, pat, paw, pinch
one's cheek, pat one on the head, chuck under
the chin; osculate, kiss, buss, brush one's
cheek; embrace, enlace, enfold, lap, fold in
one's arms, press to one's bosom, hang on
one's neck, fly into the arms of; open one's
arms, clasp, hug, hold one tight, cling, not let
go 778 *retain*; squeeze, press, cuddle; snuggle,
nestle, nuzzle, nibble, give love bites; play,
romp, wanton, toy, trifle, dally, spark; make

dalliance, make love, carry on, canoodle, spoon, bill and coo, hold hands, slap and tickle, pet, neck, snog, smooch, play footsie; vamp 887 *excite love*; (of animals) lick, fawn, rub oneself against; (of a crowd) mob, rush, snatch at, be all over, swarm over.

*court*, make advances, give the glad eye; make eyes, make sheep's e., ogle, leer, eye 438 *gaze*; get off with, try to get off with, chat up, come on to, hit on, become familiar, get fresh, make a pass, make passes, pat one's bottom, goose; gallivant, philander, flirt, coquette 887 *excite love*; be sweet on 887 *be in love*; set one's cap at, run after, do all the running, chase 619 *pursue*; squire, escort, convoy 89 *accompany*; hang round, wait on 284 *follow*; date, make a date, take out; walk out with, go steady, go out with, go with; sue, woo, go a-wooing, go courting, pay court to, pay one's addresses to, pay attentions to, pay suit to, press one's suit; lay siege to one's affections, whisper sweet nothings, speak fondly to; serenade, caterwaul; sigh, sigh at the feet of, pine, languish 887 *love*; offer one's heart, offer one's hand, offer one's fortune; ask for the hand of, propose, propose marriage, pop the question, plight one's troth, become engaged, announce one's engagement, publish the banns, make a match 894 *wed*.

## 890 Darling. Favourite

**N.** *darling*, dear, my dear; dear friend; dearest, dear one, only one; one's own, one's all; truelove, love, beloved 887 *loved one*; heart, dear h.; sweetheart, fancy, valentine; sweeting, sweetling, sweetie, sugar, honey, honeybaby, honeybunch; flower, precious, jewel, treasure; chéri(e), chou, mavourneen; angel, angel child, cherub; pippin, poppet, popsy, moppet, mopsy; pet, petkins, lamb, precious l., chick, chicken, duck, ducks, ducky, hen, dearie, lovey.

*favourite*, darling, mignon; spoiled darling, spoiled child, enfant gâté, fondling, cosset, mother's darling, teacher's pet; jewel, jewel in the crown, heart's-blood, apple of one's eye, blue-eyed boy; persona grata, someone after one's own heart, one of the best, good man, good chap, fine fellow, diamond geezer (inf), marvellous woman, Mr *or* Miss Right; flavour of the month, the tops, salt of the earth; brick, sport, good s., real s.; first choice, front runner, top seed, only possible choice 644 *exceller*; someone to be proud of, boast, pride, p. and joy; national figure, favourite son, Grand Old Man, man *or* woman of the hour 866 *person of repute*; idol, pop i., hero, heroine, golden girl *or* boy, icon; screen goddess, media personality,

star, film s.; general favourite, universal f., cynosure, toast of the town; world's sweetheart, Queen of Hearts, pinup girl 841 *a beauty*; centre of attraction, honeypot 291 *attraction*; catch, lion 859 *desired object*.

## 891 Resentment. Anger

**N.** *resentment*, displeasure, dissatisfaction 829 *discontent*; huffiness, ill humour, the hump, sulks 893 *sullenness*; sternness 735 *severity*; heart-burning, heart-swelling, rankling, rancour, soreness, painful feelings; slow burn, growing impatience; indignation (see also *anger*); umbrage, offence, taking o., huff, tiff, pique; bile, spleen, gall; acerbity, acrimony, bitterness, bitter resentment, smouldering r., hard feelings, daggers drawn; virulence, hate 888 *hatred*; animosity, grudge, ancient g., bone to pick, crow to pluck 881 *enmity*; vindictiveness, revengefulness, spite 910 *revenge*; malice 898 *malevolence*; impatience, fierceness, hot blood 892 *irascibility*; cause of offence, red rag to a bull, sore point, dangerous subject; pinprick, irritation 827 *annoyance*; provocation, aggravation, insult, affront, last straw 921 *indignity*; wrong, injury 914 *injustice*.

*anger*, wrathfulness, irritation, exasperation, vexation, indignation; dudgeon, high d., wrath, ire, choler; rage, tearing r., air r., desk r., golf r., hedge r., office r., parking r., road r., shop r. *or* shopping r., trolley r., fury, raging f., passion, towering p. 822 *excitable state*; crossness, temper, tantrum, tizzy, paddy, paddywhack, fume, fret, pet, fit of temper, burst of anger, outburst, explosion, storm, stew, ferment, taking, paroxysm, tears of rage 318 *agitation*; rampage, fire and fury, gnashing the teeth, stamping the foot; shout, roar 400 *loudness*; fierceness, angry look, glare, frown, scowl, black look; growl, snarl, bark, bite, snap, snappishness, asperity 892 *irascibility*; warmth, heat, words, high words, angry w. 709 *quarrel*; box on the ear, rap on the knuckles, slap in the face 921 *indignity*; blows, fisticuffs 716 *fight*.

*Fury*, Erinys, Alecto, Megaera, Tisiphone, Furies, Eumenides 910 *avenger*.

**Adj.** *resentful*, piqued, stung, galled, huffed, miffed; hurt, sore, smarting 829 *discontented*; surprised, pained, hurt, offended; warm, indignant; unresigned, reproachful 924 *disapproving*; bitter, embittered, acrimonious, full of hate, rancorous, virulent 888 *hating*; full of spleen, spleenful, splenetic, spiteful 898 *malevolent*; full of revenge, vindictive 910 *revengeful*; jealous, green with envy 912 *envious*; grudging 598 *unwilling*.

*angry*, displeased, not amused, stern, frowning 834 *serious*; impatient, cross, crabbit, waxy, ratty, wild, mad, livid; wroth, wrathy, wrathful, ireful, irate; peeved, nettled, rattled, annoyed, irritated, vexed, provoked, stung; worked up, wrought up, het up, hot, hot under the collar; angry with, mad at; indignant, angered, incensed, infuriated, beside oneself with rage, leaping up and down in anger; shirty, in a temper, in a paddy, in a wax, in a huff, in a rage, in a boiling r., in a fury, in a taking, in a passion; warm, fuming, boiling, burning; speechless, stuttering, gnashing, spitting with fury, crying with rage, stamping one's foot in rage; raging, foaming, savage, violent 176 *furious*; apoplectic, rabid, foaming at the mouth, mad as a hornet, hopping m., dancing, rampaging, rampageous 503 *frenzied*; seeing red, berserk; roaring, ramping, rearing; snarling, snapping, glaring, glowering 893 *sullen*; red with anger, flushed with rage, purple with r., red-eyed, bloodshot 431 *red*; blue in the face; pale with anger; dangerous, fierce 892 *irascible*.

**Vb.** *resent*, be piqued, – offended etc. adj.; find intolerable, not bear, be unable to stomach 825 *suffer*; feel, mind, have a chip on one's shoulder, feel resentment, smart under 829 *be discontented*; take amiss, take ill, take the wrong way, not see the joke; feel insulted, take offence, take on the nose, take umbrage, take exception to 709 *quarrel*; jib, take in ill part, take in bad p., get sore, cut up rough; burn, smoulder, sizzle, simmer, boil with indignation; express resentment, vent one's spleen, indulge one's spite 898 *be malevolent*; take to heart, let it rankle, remember an injury, cherish a grudge, nurse resentment, bear malice 910 *be revengeful*; go green with envy 912 *envy*.

*get angry*, get cross, get wild, get mad; get peeved, get sore, get in a pet, go spare; kindle, grow warm, grow heated, colour, redden, go purple, flush with anger; take fire, flare up, start up, rear up, ramp; bridle, bristle, raise one's hackles, arch one's back; lose patience, lose one's temper, lose control of one's t., forget oneself; throw a tantrum, stamp, shout, throw things; get one's dander up, get one's monkey up, fall into a passion, fly into a temper, fly off the handle; let fly, burst out, let off steam, boil over, blow up, flip one's lid, blow one's top, explode; see red, go berserk, go mad, go ape-shit (US inf), foam at the mouth 822 *be excitable*.

*be angry*, – impatient etc. adj.; show impatience, interrupt, chafe, fret, fume, fuss, flounce, dance, ramp, stamp, champ, champ the bit, paw the ground; carry on, create, perform, make a scene, make an exhibition of one-self, make a row, go on the warpath 61 *rampage*; turn nasty, cut up rough, raise Cain; rage, rant, roar, bellow, bluster, storm, thunder, fulminate 400 *be loud*; look like thunder, look black, look daggers, glare, glower, frown, scowl, growl, snarl 893 *be sullen*; spit, snap, lash out; gnash one's teeth, grind one's t., weep with rage, boil with r., quiver with r., shake with passion, swell with fury, burst with indignation, stamp with rage, dance with fury, lash one's tail 821 *be excited*; breathe fire and fury, out-Lear Lear; let fly, express one's feelings, vent one's spleen 176 *be violent*.

*huff*, miff, pique, sting, nettle, rankle, smart; ruffle the dignity, ruffle one's feathers, wound, wound the feelings 827 *hurt*; antagonize, put one's back up, rub up the wrong way, get across, give umbrage, offend, cause offence, cause lasting o., put one's nose out of joint, embitter 888 *excite hate*; stick in the throat, raise one's gorge 861 *cause dislike*; affront, insult, outrage 921 *not respect*.

*enrage*, upset, discompose, ruffle, disturb one's equanimity, ruffle one's temper, irritate, rile, peeve, miff; annoy, vex, pester, bug, bother 827 *trouble*; get on one's nerves, get under one's skin, get up one's nose, get one's goat, give one the pip; do it to annoy, tease, bait, pinprick, needle, wind up 827 *torment*; bite, fret, nag, gnaw; put out of patience, put in an ill humour, try one's patience, exasperate; push too far, make one lose one's temper, put into a temper, work into a passion; anger, incense, infuriate, madden, drive mad; goad, sting, taunt, trail one's coat, invite a quarrel, throw down the gauntlet; drive into a fury, lash into f., whip up one's anger, rouse one's ire, rouse one's choler, kindle one's wrath, excite indignation, stir the blood, stir one's bile, make one's gorge rise, raise one's hackles, get one's dander up; make one's blood boil, make one see red; cause resentment, embitter, envenom, poison; exasperate, add fuel to the fire *or* flame, fan the flame 832 *aggravate*; embroil, set at loggerheads, set by the ears 709 *make quarrels*.

**Adv.** *angrily*, resentfully, bitterly; warmly, heatedly; with one's hackles up; in anger, in fury, in the heat of the moment, in the height of passion, with one's monkey up, with one's dander up.

**Int.** *blast!*, bollocks! (sl) bugger!, confound it!, damn!, damn it!, darn!, drat!, drat it!, fuck! (sl), hang it!, hell!, hell's bells!, hell's teeth!, knickers!, shit! (sl); please!

## 892 Irascibility

**N.** *irascibility*, choler, quick passions, irritability, impatience 822 *excitability*; grumpiness, gruffness 883 *unsociability*; sharpness, tartness, asperity, gall, bile, vinegar 393 *sourness*; sensitivity 819 *moral sensibility*; huffiness, touchiness, prickliness, readiness to take offence, pugnacity, bellicosity 709 *quarrelsomeness*; temperament, testiness, pepperiness, peevishness, petulance; captiousness, uncertain temper, doubtful t., sharp t., short t., quick t.; hot temper, fierce t., fiery t.; limited patience, snappishness, a word and a blow; fierceness, dangerousness, hot blood, fieriness, inflammable nature; bad temper, dangerous t., foul t., nasty t., evil t.

*shrew*, scold, fishwife; spitfire, termagant, virago, stramullion, vixen, battle-axe, harridan, fury, Xanthippe; Tartar, hornet; bear 902 *misanthrope*; crosspatch, mad dog; tigress, fiery person, redhead.

**Adj.** *irascible*, impatient, choleric, irritable, peppery, testy, crusty, peevish, crotchety, cranky, cross-grained; short-tempered, hot-t., sharp-t., uncertain-t.; prickly, touchy, tetchy, huffy, umbrageous, thin-skinned 819 *sensitive*; inflammable, like tinder; hot-blooded, fierce, fiery, passionate 822 *excitable*; quick, warm, hasty, overhasty, trigger-happy 857 *rash*; quick-tempered, easily roused 709 *quarrelling*; scolding, shrewish, vixenish; sharp-tongued 899 *cursing*; petulant, cantankerous, crabbed, crabbit, snarling, querulous; captious, bitter, vinegary 393 *sour*; splenetic, spleenful, bilious, liverish, gouty; scratchy, snuffy, snappy, snappish, waspish; tart, sharp, short; uptight, edgy; fractious, fretful, moody, temperamental, changeable; gruff, grumpy, pettish, ratty, like a bear with a sore head 829 *discontented*; ill-humoured, cross, stroppy 893 *sullen*.

**Vb.** *be irascible*, have a temper, have an uncontrollable t.; have a devil in one; snort, bark, snap, bite 893 *be sullen*; snap one's head off, bite one's head off, jump down one's throat 891 *get angry*.

## 893 Sullenness

**N.** *sullenness*, sternness, grimness 834 *seriousness*; sulkiness, ill humour, pettishness; morosity, surliness, churlishness, crabbedness, crustiness, unsociableness 883 *unsociability*; vinegar 393 *sourness*; grumpiness, grouchiness, pout, grimace 829 *discontent*; gruffness 885 *discourtesy*; crossness, peevishness, ill temper, bad t., savage t., shocking t. 892 *irascibility*; spleen, bile, liver; sulks, fit of the s., the hump, the pouts, mulligrubs, dumps, grouch, boud-

erie, moodiness, temperament; cafard, the blues, blue devils 834 *melancholy*; black look, hangdog l.; glare, glower, lour, frown, scowl; snort, growl, snarl, snap, bite; 'curses not loud but deep'.

> And that which should accompany old age,
> As honour, love, obedience, troops of friends,
> I must not look to have; but, in their stead,
> Curses, not loud but deep, mouth-honour, breath,
> Which the poor heart would fain deny, and dare not.
>
> William Shakespeare, *Macbeth*

**Adj.** *sullen*, forbidding, ugly; gloomy, saturnine, overcast, cloudy, sunless 418 *dark*; glowering, scowling; stern, frowning, unsmiling, grim 834 *serious*; sulky, sulking, cross, cross as two sticks, out of temper, out of humour, out of sorts, misanthropic 883 *unsociable*; surly, morose, dyspeptic, crabbed, crabbit, crusty, cross-grained, difficult; snarling, snapping, snappish, shrewish, vixenish, cantankerous, quarrelsome, stroppy 709 *quarrelling*; refractory, jibbing 738 *disobedient*; grouchy, grumbling, grousing, belly-aching, beefing, grumpy 829 *discontented*; acid, tart, vinegary 393 *sour*; gruff, rough, abrupt, brusque 885 *discourteous*; temperamental, moody, humoursome, up and down 152 *changeful*; bilious, jaundiced, dyspeptic; blue, down, down in the dumps, depressed, melancholy 834 *melancholic*; petulant, pettish, peevish, shirty, ill-tempered, bad-t. 892 *irascible*; smouldering, sultry.

**Vb.** *be sullen*, gloom, glower, glare, lour; look black, scowl, frown, knit one's brows; bare one's teeth, show one's fangs, spit; snap, snarl, growl, snort; make a face, grimace, pout, sulk 883 *be unsociable*; mope, have the blues 834 *be dejected*; get out of bed on the wrong side; grouch, grouse, bellyache, beef, carp, crab, complain, grumble, mutter, smoulder 829 *be discontented*.

**Adv.** *sullenly*, sulkily, gloomily, ill-humouredly, with a bad grace 598 *unwillingly*.

## 894 Marriage

**N.** *marriage*, matrimony, holy m., sacrament of m., one flesh; wedlock, wedded state, married s., state of matrimony, wedded bliss; match, union, alliance, partnership; conjugality, conjugal knot, nuptial bond, marriage tie, marriage bed, bed and board, cohabitation, living as man and wife, living together by habit and repute, living together, life together; husbandhood, husbandship; wifehood, wifeship; coverture, matronage, matronhood; banns, marriage certificate, marriage lines; marriage god, Hymen, Hera, Juno.

*type of marriage*, matrimonial arrangement, monogamy, serial monogamy, monandry, bigamy, polygamy, Mormonism, polygyny, polyandry; digamy, deuterogamy, second marriage, remarriage, levirate; endogamy, exogamy; arranged match, marriage of convenience, mariage de convenance, mariage blanc; love-match; mixed marriage, intermarriage, miscegenation 43 *mixture*; mismarriage, mésalliance, misalliance, morganatic marriage, left-handed m.; companionate marriage, temporary m., trial m., open m., common-law m., marriage by habit and repute; free union, free love, concubinage; compulsory marriage, forcible wedlock, shotgun wedding; abduction, Sabine rape.

*wedding*, getting married, match, matchmaking, betrothal, engagement, pre-nuptial agrement; nuptial vows, marriage v., ring, wedding r.; bridal, nuptials, spousals, hymenal rites; leading to the altar, tying the knot, getting spliced, getting hitched; marriage rites, marriage ceremony; wedding service, nuptial mass, nuptial benediction 988 *Christian rite*; church wedding, white w., civil marriage, registry-office m.; Gretna Green marriage, runaway match, elopement; solemn wedding, quiet w.; torch of Hymen, nuptial song, hymeneal, prothalamium, epithalamium; wedding day, wedding bells; marriage feast, wedding breakfast, reception; honeymoon; silver wedding, golden w., wedding anniversary 876 *special day*.

*bridal party*, groomsman, best man, paranymph, maid *or* matron of honour, bridesmaid, best maid, page, train-bearer; attendant, usher.

*spouse*, espouser, espoused; one's promised, one's betrothed 887 *loved one*; marriage partner, man, wife; spouses, man and wife, Mr and Mrs, Darby and Joan, Philemon and Baucis; married couple, young marrieds, bridal pair, newlyweds, honeymooners; bride, blushing b., young matron; bridegroom, benedick; consort, partner, mate, yoke-mate, helpmate, helpmeet, better half, soulmate, affinity; married man, husband, goodman, hubbie, man, old man, lord and master; much-married man, henpecked husband; new man; injured husband 952 *cuckold*; married woman, wedded wife, lawful w., lady, matron, feme covert, partner of one's bed and board; wife of one's bosom, woman, old w., missus, wifey, better half, old dutch, her indoors, rib, grey mare, trouble and strife, Duchess of Fife, joy of my life, she who must be obeyed; squaw, broadwife; faithful spouse, monogamist; digamist, second husband, second wife, bigamous

w.; common-law husband *or* wife, wife *or* husband in all but name 887 *lover*.

*polygamist*, polygynist, much-married man, owner of a harem, Turk, Mormon, Solomon; Bluebeard; bigamist.

*matchmaker*, matrimonial agent, marriage-broker, go-between; marriage bureau, dating agency, introduction a., lonely hearts club, lonely hearts column, personal column; computer dating.

*nubility*, marriageable age, fitness for marriage, marriageability; eligibility, suitability, good match, proper m., suitable m.; suitable party, eligible p., welcome suitor 887 *lover*.

**Adj.** *married*, partnered, paired, mated, matched; tied, spliced, hitched, in double harness; espoused, wedded, united, made man and wife, made one, joined in holy matrimony, 'bone of one's bones and flesh of one's flesh';

> And the rib, which the Lord God had taken from man, made he a woman, and brought her unto the man.
> And Adam said, This is now bone of my bones, and flesh of my flesh: she shall be called Woman, because she was taken out of Man.
> Bible, Genesis

monogamous; polygynous, polygamous, polyandrous; much-married, polygamistic; remarried, digamous, bigamous, serially monogamous; just married, newly m., newly-wed, honeymooning; mismarried, ill-matched.

*marriageable*, nubile, fit for marriage, ripe for m., of age, of marriageable a.; eligible, suitable; handfast, betrothed, promised, engaged, affianced, plighted, bespoke.

*matrimonial*, marital, connubial, concubinary; premarital, postmarital, extramarital; nuptial, bridal, spousal, hymeneal, epithalamic, epithalamial; conjugal, wifely, matronly, husbandly; digamous, bigamous; polygamous, polygynous, polyandrous; endogamous, exogamous; morganatic.

**Vb.** *marry*, marry off, find a husband *or* wife for, match, mate; matchmake, make a match, arrange a m., arrange a marriage; betroth, affiance, espouse, publish the banns, announce the engagement; bestow in marriage, give in marriage, give away; join in marriage, make fast in wedlock, declare man and wife; join, couple, splice, hitch, tie the knot.

*wed*, marry, espouse; take a wife, find a husband; ask for the hand of 889 *court*; quit the single state, give up one's freedom, renounce bachelorhood, take the plunge, get married, get hitched, get spliced, mate with, marry oneself to, unite oneself with, give oneself in marriage, bestow one's hand, accept a proposal, plight one's troth, become engaged, put up the banns; lead to the altar, walk down the aisle, say 'I do', take for better or worse, be made one 45 *unite with*; pair off, mate, couple; honeymoon, cohabit, live together, set up house together, share bed and board, live as man and wife; marry well, make a good match, make a marriage of convenience; mismarry, make a bad match, repent at leisure; make a love match 887 *be in love*; marry in haste, run away, elope; contract marriage, make an honest woman of, go through a form of marriage; marry again, remarry; commit bigamy; intermarry, miscegenate.

**Adv.** *matrimonially*, in the way of marriage; bigamously, polygamously, morganatically.

### 895 Celibacy
**N.** *celibacy*, singleness, singledom, single state, unmarried s., single blessedness 744 *independence*; bachelorhood, bachelorship, bachelordom; misogamy, misogyny 883 *unsociability*; spinsterhood, spinsterdom, the shelf; monkhood, the veil 985 *monasticism*; maidenhood, virginity 950 *purity*.

*celibate*, unmarried man, single m., bachelor, Benedick; confirmed bachelor, born b., old b., gay b., not the marrying kind; enemy of marriage, misogamist, misogynist 902 *misanthrope*; encratite, monastic 986 *monk*; hermit 883 *solitary*; monastic order, celibate o. 985 *holy orders*.

*spinster*, unmarried woman, feme sole, bachelor girl; maid unwed, debutante; maid, maiden, virgo intacta; maiden aunt, old maid; Vestal, Vestal Virgin 986 *nun*; Amazon, Diana, Artemis.

**Adj.** *unwedded*, unwed, unmarried; unpartnered, single, mateless, unmated; spouseless, wifeless, husbandless; unwooed, unasked, on the shelf; free, uncaught, heart-whole, fancy-free 744 *independent*; maidenly, virgin, virginal, vestal 950 *pure*; spinster, spinsterlike, spinsterish, old-maidish; bachelor, bachelorlike; celibate, monkish, nunnish 986 *monastic*.

**Vb.** *live single*, stay unmarried, live in single blessedness; refuse marriage, refuse all offers, keep heart-whole, remain fancy-free 744 *be free*; have no offers, receive no proposals; live like a hermit 883 *be unsociable*; take the veil 986 *take orders*.

### 896 Divorce. Widowhood
**N.** *divorce*, dissolution of marriage, divorcement, putting away, repudiation; bill of divorcement, divorce decree, decree nisi, decree absolute; separation, legal s., judicial s.; annulment, decree of nullity; no marriage, nonconsummation; nullity, impediment, diriment i.,

prohibited degree, consanguinity, affinity; desertion, living apart, separate maintenance, alimony, aliment, palimony; marriage on the rocks, breakup, split-up, broken marriage, broken engagement, forbidding the banns; divorce court, divorce case; divorced person, divorcee, divorcé(e), nor wife nor maid; corespondent; single parent.

*widowhood*, widowerhood, viduity, dowagerhood; grass widowhood; widows' weeds 228 *formal dress*; widower, widow, widow woman, relict; dowager, dowager duchess; war widow, grass w., grass widower, Merry Widow.

**Adj.** *divorced*, deserted, separated, living apart; dissolved.

*widowed*, husbandless, wifeless; vidual.

**Vb.** *divorce*, separate, split up, break up, go one's separate ways, live separately, live apart, desert 621 *relinquish*; unmarry, untie the knot 46 *disunite*; put away, sue for divorce, file a divorce suit; wear the horns, be cuckolded, bring a charge of adultery; get a divorce, revert to bachelorhood, revert to the single state, regain one's freedom; put asunder, dissolve marriage, annul a m., grant a decree of nullity, grant a divorce, pronounce a decree absolute.

*be widowed*, outlive one's spouse, survive one's s., lose one's wife, mourn one's husband, put on widow's weeds.

*widow*, bereave, make a widow *or* widower, leave one's wife a widow.

### 897 Benevolence
**N.** *benevolence*, good will, helpfulness 880 *friendliness*; ahimsa, harmlessness 935 *innocence*; benignity, kindly disposition, heart of gold; amiability, bonhomie 882 *sociability*; milk of human kindness, goodness of nature, warmth of heart, warm-heartedness, kind-heartedness, kindliness, kindness, loving-k., goodness and mercy, charity, Christian c. 887 *love*; godly love, brotherly l., brotherliness, fraternal feeling 880 *friendship*; tenderness, consideration 736 *leniency*; understanding, responsiveness, caring, concern, fellow feeling, empathy, sympathy, overflowing s. 818 *feeling*; condolence 905 *pity*; decent feeling, humanity, humaneness, humanitarianism 901 *philanthropy*; utilitarianism 901 *social care*; charitableness, hospitality, beneficence, unselfishness, generosity, magnanimity 813 *liberality*; gentleness, softness, mildness, tolerance, toleration 734 *laxity*; placability, mercy 909 *forgiveness*; God's love, grace of God; blessing, benediction.

*kind act*, kindness, act of goodwill, favour, service; good deed, charitable d.; charity, deed of c., relief, alms, almsgiving 781 *giving*;

prayers, good offices, kind o., good turn, helpful act 703 *aid*; labour of love 597 *voluntary work*.

*kind person*, bon enfant, Christian; motherly person, good sort, good neighbour, good Samaritan, well-wisher 880 *friend*; sympathizer 707 *patron*; altruist, idealist, do-gooder 901 *philanthropist*.

**Adj.** *benevolent*, well meant, well-intentioned, with the best intentions, for the best 880 *friendly*; out of kindness, to oblige; out of charity, eleemosynary; kind of one, good of one, so good of; sympathetic, wishing well, well-wishing, favouring, praying for; kindly disposed, benign, benignant, kindly, kind-hearted, overflowing with kindness, full of the milk of human k., warm-hearted, large-h., golden-h.; kind, good, human, decent, Christian; affectionate 887 *loving*; fatherly, paternal; motherly, maternal; brotherly, fraternal; sisterly, cousinly; good-humoured, good-natured, easy, sweet, gentle 884 *amiable*; placable, merciful 909 *forgiving*; tolerant, indulgent 734 *lax*; humane, considerate 736 *lenient*; soft-hearted, tender; pitiful, sympathizing, condolent 905 *pitying*; genial, hospitable 882 *sociable*; bounteous, bountiful 813 *liberal*; generous, magnanimous, unselfish, selfless, unenvious, unjealous, altruistic 931 *disinterested*; beneficent, charitable, humanitarian, doing good 901 *philanthropic*; obliging, accommodating, helpful 703 *aiding*; tactful, complaisant, gracious, gallant, chivalrous, chivalric 884 *courteous*.

**Vb.** *be benevolent*, – kind etc. adj.; feel the springs of charity, have one's heart in the right place, be of a caring disposition; show concern, care for, feel for; sympathize, understand, feel as for oneself, enter into another's feelings, empathize, put oneself in another's place, 'do as one would be done by' (see quotation at 714 *retaliation*), practise the golden rule; 'return good for evil' (see quotation at 714 *retaliation*), 'turn the other cheek' (see quotation for 'an eye for an eye' at 714 *retaliation*), 'love one's enemy' 909 *forgive*;

> But I say unto you which hear, Love your enemies, do good to them which hate you.
> Bless them that curse you, and pray for them which despitefully use you.
> Bible, Jesus in St Luke's Gospel

wish well, pray for, bless, give one's blessing, bestow a benediction; bear good will, wish the best for, have the right intentions, have the best i., mean well; look with a favourable eye, favour 703 *patronize*; benefit 644 *do good*; be a good Samaritan, do a good turn, do one a favour, render a service, oblige, put one under

an obligation 703 *aid*; humanize, reform 654 *make better*.

*philanthropize*, do good, go about doing good, do good works, be a caring person, have a social conscience, serve the community, show public spirit, care; get involved 678 *be active*; reform, improve; relieve the poor, go slumming; visit, nurse 703 *minister to*; mother 889 *pet*.

**Adv.** *benevolently*, kindly, tenderly, lovingly, charitably, generously; in kindness, in charity, in love and peace, out of kindness, to oblige; mercifully, by the grace of God.

## 898 Malevolence

**N.** *malevolence*, ill will 881 *enmity*; truculence, cussedness, bitchiness, beastliness, evil intent, bad intention, worst intentions, cloven hoof; spite, gall, spitefulness, viciousness, despite, malignity, malignancy, malice, deliberate m., malice prepense, malice aforethought; bad blood, hate 888 *hatred*; venom, virulence, deadliness, balefulness 659 *bane*; bitterness, acrimony, acerbity 393 *sourness*; mordacity 388 *pungency*; rancour, spleen 891 *resentment*; gloating, Schadenfreude, unholy joy 912 *envy*; evil eye 983 *spell*.

*inhumanity*, misanthropy, lack of humanity, inconsiderateness, lack of concern; lack of charity, uncharitableness; intolerance, persecution 735 *severity*; harshness, mercilessness, implacability, hardness of heart, obduracy, heart of marble, heart of stone 906 *pitilessness*; cold feelings, unkindness; callousness 326 *hardness*; cruelty, barbarity, blood-thirstiness, bloodiness, bloodlust; barbarism, savagery, ferocity, barbarousness, savageness, ferociousness; atrociousness, outrageousness; sadism, fiendishness, devilishness 934 *wickedness*; truculence, brutality, ruffianism; destructiveness, vandalism 165 *destruction*.

*cruel act*, cruel conduct, brutality; ill-treatment, bad t., ill usage 675 *misuse*; abuse, child a., sexual a., elder a., unkindness, disservice, ill turn; victimization, harassment, sexual h., stalking, e-stalking, bullying, 'tender mercies' 735 *severity*;

> A righteous man regardeth the life of his beast: but the tender mercies of the wicked are cruel.
> Bible, Proverbs

foul play, bloodshed 176 *violence*; excess, extremes; act of inhumanity, inhuman deed, atrocity, outrage, devilry; cruelty, cruelties, torture, tortures, barbarity, barbarities; cannibalism, murder 362 *homicide*; mass murder, genocide 362 *slaughter*.

**Adj.** *malevolent*, ill-wishing, ill-willed, evil-intentioned, ill-disposed, meaning harm 661 *dangerous*; ill-natured, churlish 893 *sullen*; nasty, bloody-minded, bitchy, cussed 602 *wilful*; malicious, catty, spiteful 926 *detracting*; mischievous, mischief-making (see also *maleficent*); baleful, squint-eyed, malign, malignant 645 *harmful*; vicious, viperous, venomous 362 *deadly*; black-hearted, full of spite 888 *hating*; jealous 912 *envious*; disloyal, treacherous 930 *perfidious*; bitter, rancorous 891 *resentful*; implacable, unforgiving, merciless 906 *pitiless*; vindictive, gloating 910 *revengeful*; hostile, fell 881 *inimical*; intolerant, persecuting 735 *oppressive*.

*maleficent*, malefic, hurtful, damaging 645 *harmful*; poisonous, venomous, virulent, caustic, mordacious 659 *baneful*; working evil, spreading evil, mischief-making, spreading mischief 645 *bad*.

*unkind*, unamiable, ill-natured 893 *sullen*; unkindly, unbenevolent, unloving, unaffectionate, untender, stepmotherly, unmaternal, unbrotherly, unfraternal, undaughterly, unfilial, unchristian; cold, unfriendly, hostile, misanthropic 881 *inimical*; unforthcoming, uncordial, inhospitable 883 *unsociable*; uncooperative, unhelpful, disobliging; ungenerous, uncharitable, unforgiving; mean, nasty; rude, harsh, gruff, beastly 885 *ungracious*; unsympathetic, unresponsive, uncaring, unfeeling, insensible, unmoved 820 *impassive*; stern 735 *severe*; unsqueamish, tough, hardboiled, hardbitten 326 *hard*; inhuman, unnatural.

*cruel*, grim, fell; steely, flinty, grim-faced, cold-eyed, steely-e., hard-hearted, flint-h., stony-h.; callous, cold-blooded; heartless, ruthless, merciless 906 *pitiless*; tyrannical 735 *oppressive*; gloating, sadistic; bloodthirsty, cannibalistic 362 *murderous*; bloody 176 *violent*; excessive, extreme; atrocious, outrageous; feral, tigerish, wolfish; unnatural, subhuman, dehumanized, brutalized, brutish; brutal, rough, truculent, fierce, ferocious; savage, barbarous, wild, untamed, untamable, tameless; inhuman, ghoulish, fiendish, devilish, diabolical, demoniacal, satanic, hellish, infernal.

**Vb.** *be malevolent*, bear malice, cherish a grudge, nurse resentment, have it in for 888 *hate*; show ill will, betray the cloven hoof; show envy 912 *envy*; disoblige, spite, do one a bad turn; go to extremes, do one's worst, wreak one's spite, break a butterfly on a wheel, have no mercy 906 *be pitiless*; take one's revenge, exact r., victimize, gloat 910 *be revengeful*; take it out of one, bully, maltreat, abuse 645 *illtreat*; molest, hurt, injure, annoy 645 *harm*; malign, run down, throw stones at 926 *detract*; tease, harass, sexually h., harry, hound, stalk,

persecute, tyrannize, torture 735 *oppress*; raven, thirst for blood 362 *slaughter*; rankle, fester, poison, be a thorn in the flesh; create havoc, blight, blast 165 *lay waste*; cast the evil eye 983 *bewitch*.

**Adv.** *malevolently*, with evil intent, with the worst intentions; unkindly, spitefully, out of spite.

## 899 Malediction

**N.** *malediction*, malison, curse, imprecation, anathema; evil eye 983 *spell*; no blessing, ill wishes, bad wishes, 'curses not loud but deep' (see quotation at 893 *sullenness*) 898 *malevolence*; execration, denunciation, commination 900 *threat*; onslaught 712 *attack*; fulmination, thunder, thunders of the Vatican; ban, proscription, excommunication; exorcism, ghostbusting (inf), bell, book and candle.

*scurrility*, ribaldry, vulgarity; profanity, swearing, profane s., cursing and swearing, blasting, effing and blinding, effing and ceeing; bad language, foul l., filthy l., blue l., shocking l., strong l., unparliamentary l., Limehouse, Billingsgate; naughty word, four-letter w., expletive, swearword, oath, swear, damn, curse, cuss, tinker's c.; invective, vituperation, abuse, volley of a.; mutual abuse, slanging match, stormy exchange; vain abuse, empty curse, more bark than bite 900 *threat*; no compliment, aspersion, reflection, vilification, slander 926 *calumny*; cheek, sauce 878 *sauciness*; personal remarks, epithet, insult 921 *indignity*; contumely, scorn 922 *contempt*; scolding, rough edge of one's tongue, lambasting, tongue-lashing 924 *reproach*.

**Adj.** *maledictory*, cursing, maledictive, imprecatory, anathematizing, comminatory, fulminatory, denunciatory, damnatory.

*cursing*, evil-speaking, swearing, damning, blasting; profane, foul-mouthed, foul-tongued, foul-spoken, effing and ceeing, unparliamentary, scurrilous, scurrile, ribald 847 *vulgar*; sulphurous, blue; viperish, vituperative, abusive, vitriolic, injurious, vilipendious, reproachful 924 *disapproving*; contumelious, scornful 922 *despising*.

*cursed*, wished, wished on one; accursed, unblest, execrable; anathematized, under a ban, excommunicated, damned 961 *condemned*; under a spell 983 *bewitched*.

**Vb.** *curse*, cast the evil eye 983 *bewitch*; accurse, wish ill 898 *be malevolent*; wish on, call down on; wish one joy of; curse with bell, book and candle, curse up hill and down dale; anathematize, imprecate, invoke curses on, execrate, hold up to execration; fulminate, thunder against, rant and rail against, inveigh 924 *reprove*; denounce 928 *accuse*; excommunicate, damn 961 *condemn*; round upon, confound, send to the devil, send to blazes; abuse, vituperate, revile, rail, chide, heap abuse, pour vitriol 924 *reprobate*; bespatter, throw mud 926 *detract*.

*cuss*, curse, swear, damn, blast; blaspheme 980 *be impious*; swear like a trooper, use expletives, use Billingsgate, curse and swear, use four-letter words, eff and blind, eff and cee, turn the air blue; slang, slangwhang, abuse, blackguard 924 *reprobate*; rail at, scold, lash out at, give the rough edge of one's tongue, slag off.

**Int.** blast –!, bugger –!, curse –!, damn –!, darn –!, drat –!, fuck –! (sl), hang –!; a curse on –!, a plague on –!, woe to –!, woe betide –!, ill b. –!, confusion seize –!, confound –!, devil take –!, God damn –!, bad cess to –!; the deuce!, the dickens!

## 900 Threat

**N.** *threat*, menace; commination, fulmination 899 *malediction*; minacity, threatfulness, ominousness; challenge, dare 711 *defiance*; blackmail 737 *demand*; battle cry, war c., war whoop, sabre-rattling, war of nerves 854 *intimidation*; deterrent, big stick 723 *weapon*; black cloud, gathering clouds 511 *omen*; hidden fires, secret weapon 663 *pitfall*; impending danger, sword of Damocles 661 *danger*; danger signal, fair warning, writing on the wall 664 *warning*; bluster, idle threat, hollow t. 877 *boast*; bark, growl, snarl, bared teeth 893 *sullenness*; aggressive begging.

**Adj.** *threatening*, menacing, minatory, minatorial, minacious; sabre-rattling 711 *defiant*; blustering, bullying, hectoring 877 *boastful*; muttering, grumbling 893 *sullen*; bodeful, portentous, ominous, foreboding 511 *presageful*; hovering, louring, hanging over 155 *impending*; ready to spring, growling, snarling 891 *angry*; abusive 899 *cursing*; comminatory 899 *maledictory*; deterrent 854 *frightening*; nasty, unpleasant 661 *dangerous*.

**Vb.** *threaten*, menace, use threats, hold out t., utter t.; demand with menaces, blackmail 737 *demand*; hijack, hold to ransom, take hostage; frighten, deter, intimidate, bully, wave the big stick 854 *frighten*; roar, bellow 408 *vociferate*; fulminate, thunder 899 *curse*; bark, talk big, bluster, hector 877 *boast*; shake, wave, flaunt 317 *brandish*; rattle the sabre, clench the fist, draw one's sword, make a pass 711 *defy*; bare the fangs, snarl, growl, mutter 893 *be sullen*; bristle, spit, look daggers, grow nasty 891 *get angry*; pull a gun on, hold at gunpoint;

draw a bead on, cover, have one covered, keep one c. 281 *aim*; gather, mass, lour, hang over, hover 155 *impend*; bode ill, presage, disaster, mean no good, promise trouble, spell danger 511 *predict*; serve notice, caution, forewarn 664 *warn*; breathe revenge, promise r., threaten reprisals 910 *be revengeful*.

**Adv.** *threateningly*, menacingly, on pain of death.

**Int.** banzai!

## 901 Philanthropy

**N.** *philanthropy*, humanitarianism, humanity, humaneness, the golden rule 897 *benevolence*; humanism, cosmopolitanism, internationalism; altruism 931 *disinterestedness*; idealism, ideals 933 *virtue*; universal benevolence, the greatest happiness of the greatest number, utilitarianism, Benthamism; common good, socialism, communism; passion for improvement, urge to set the world to rights 654 *reformism*; chivalry, knight-errantry; dedication, crusading spirit, missionary s., nonconformist conscience, social c; ethical investment, ethical shopping; good works, mission, civilizing m., 'white man's burden';

> Take up the White Man's burden –
>   Send forth the best ye breed –
> Go, bind your sons to exile
>   To serve your captives' need;
> To wait in heavy harness
>   On fluttered folk and wild –
> Your new-caught, sullen peoples,
>   Half-devil and half-child. . . .
>
> Take up the White Man's burden –
>   And reap his old reward:
> The blame of those ye better,
>   The hate of those ye guard.

Rudyard Kipling, *The White Man's Burden*

Holy War, jihad, crusade, campaign, cause, good c.; voluntary agency, charitable foundation, charity, affinity card 703 *aid*.

*social care*, social science, sociology, social issues, social engineering, social planning, social inclusion, social chapter; poor relief, social security, benefit, dole, welfare 703 *economic aid*; social services, Welfare State; dependency culture; social service, social work, slumming, good works; care in the community, community care.

*patriotism*, civic ideals, good citizenship, public spirit, concern for the community, love of one's country; local patriotism, parochialism; nationalism, chauvinism, 'my country right or wrong' (see quotation at 481 *prejudice*); irredentism, Zionism; Euroscepticism.

*philanthropist*, friend of the human race 903 *benefactor*; humanitarian, do-gooder, social

worker, slummer 897 *kind person*; community
service worker, VSO, Peace Corps 597 *volunteer*;
paladin, champion, crusader, knight, knight
errant; Messiah 690 *leader*; missionary, person
with a mission, dedicated soul, bodhissatva;
ideologist, idealist, altruist, flower people 513
*visionary*; reformist 654 *reformer*; utilitarian,
Benthamite; Utopian, millenarian, chiliast;
humanist, cosmopolite, cosmopolitan, citizen
of the world, internationalist.

*patriot*, lover of one's country, fighter for
one's c.; father *or* mother of the people; nation-
alist, chauvinist, irredentist, Zionist; Eurosceptic.

**Adj.** *philanthropic*, humanitarian, humane,
human 897 *benevolent*; charitable, aid-giving
703 *aiding*; enlightened, humanistic, liberal;
cosmopolitan, international, internationally
minded; idealistic, altruistic 931 *disinterested*;
visionary, dedicated; sociological, socialistic,
communistic; utilitarian.

*patriotic*, civically minded, public-spirited,
community-minded; irredentist, nationalistic,
chauvinistic; loyal, true, true-blue.

**Vb.** *be charitable*, 897 *philanthropize*.

**Adv.** *pro bono publico*.

## 902 Misanthropy

**N.** *misanthropy*, hatred of mankind, distrust of
one's fellows, disillusionment with society,
cynicism 883 *unsociability*; misandry, misogyny; moroseness 893 *sullenness*; inhumanity, incivism; egotism.

*misanthrope*, misanthropist, hater of the
human race, man-hater, woman-h., misandrist, misogynist; cynic, Diogenes, Alceste;
egotist; no patriot, defeatist; world-hater,
unsocial animal 883 *solitary*; bear, crosspatch,
sulker 829 *malcontent*.

**Adj.** *misanthropic*, inhuman, antisocial 883
*unsociable*; cynical; uncivic, unpatriotic,
defeatist.

**Vb.** *misanthropize*, become a misanthrope,
lose faith in humankind.

**Adv.** *misanthropically*, cynically.

## 903 Benefactor

**N.** *benefactor*, benefactress 901 *philanthropist*;
Lady Bountiful, Father Christmas, Santa Claus
781 *giver*; fairy godmother, guardian angel,
tutelary saint, good genius 660 *protector*;
founder, foundress, supporter, angel, backer
707 *patron*; tyrannicide, pater patriae, protector of the people 901 *patriot*; saviour, ransomer, redeemer, deliverer, rescuer 668
*deliverance*; champion 713 *defender*; Lady
Godiva, Good Samaritan 897 *kind person*; good
neighbour 880 *friend*; helper, present help in

time of trouble 703 *aider*; salt of the earth,
saint 937 *good person*.

## 904 Evildoer

**N.** *evildoer*, malefactor, wrongdoer, sinner 934
*wickedness*; villain, blackguard, bad lot, baddy;
one up to no good, mischief-maker 663 *troublemaker*; scamp, monkey, imp of mischief, little
devil, holy terror; gossip, slanderer, calumniator 926 *detractor*; snake in the grass, viper in
the bosom, traitor 545 *deceiver*; obstructionist,
saboteur 702 *hinderer*; spoiler, despoiler,
wrecker, defacer, vandal, Hun, iconoclast 168
*destroyer*; terrorist, nihilist, anarchist 738
*revolter*; incendiary, arsonist 381 *incendiarism*;
disturber of the peace 738 *rioter*.

*ruffian*, blackguard, rogue, scoundrel 938
*knave*; lout, lager l., hooligan, football h.,
hoodlum, boot boy, bovver boy, larrikin 869
*low fellow*; Hell's Angel, skinhead, yob, yobbo,
punk; bully, terror, terror of the neighbourhood; rough, tough, rowdy, ugly customer,
hard man, plug-ugly, bruiser, thug, apache;
bravo, desperado, assassin, hired a.; cutthroat,
hatchet man, gunman, contract man, killer,
butcher 362 *murderer*; genocide, mass murderer; plague, scourge, scourge of the human
race, Attila 659 *bane*; petty tyrant, gauleiter
735 *tyrant*; molester, brute, savage b., beast,
savage, barbarian, ape-man, caveman; cannibal, head-hunter; homicidal maniac 504
*madman*; white van man.

*offender*, sinner, black sheep 938 *bad person*;
suspect; culprit, guilty person, law-breaker;
criminal, villain, crook, malefactor, mal-
feasant, wrongdoer, misdemeanant, felon;
archcriminal, master c., 'the Napoleon of
crime';

> **He is the Napoleon of crime.**
> Sir Arthur Conan Doyle, *The Final Problem* (Sherlock
> Holmes referring to Dr Moriarty.)

delinquent, juvenile d., first offender; recidivist, backslider, old offender, hardened o., lag,
old l., convict, ex-c., jailbird; lifer, gallowsbird,
'quare fellow'; parolee, probationer, ticket-of-
leave man; mafioso, mobster, gangster, racketeer; housebreaker 789 *thief, robber*; forger 789
*defrauder*; blackmailer, bloodsucker; poisoner
362 *murderer*; outlaw, public enemy 881 *enemy*;
intruder, trespasser; criminal world, underworld, Mafia 934 *wickedness*.

*hellhag*, hellhound, fiend, devil incarnate;
hellcat, bitch, virago, stramullion 892 *shrew*;
tigress, she-devil, fury, harpy, siren; ogre,
ogress, witch, vampire, werewolf 938 *monster*,
970 *demon*.

*noxious animal*, brute, beast, wild b.; beast of

prey, predator; tiger, man-eater, wolf, hyena, jackal, fox; kite, vulture 365 *bird*; snake, serpent, viper 365 *reptile*; cockatrice, basilisk, salamander 365 *mythical beast*; scorpion, wasp, hornet; pest, locust, Colorado beetle, deathwatch b. 365 *insect*; rat 659 *bane*; wild cat, mad dog, rogue elephant.

## 905 Pity

**N.** *pity*, springs of p., ruth; remorse, compunction 830 *regret*; charity, compassion, bowels of c., compassionateness, humanity 897 *benevolence*; soft heart, tender h., bleeding h.; gentleness, softness 736 *leniency*; commiseration, touched feelings, melting mood, tears of sympathy 825 *sorrow*; Weltschmerz, 'lacrimae rerum' (see quotation at 825 *suffering*) 834 *dejection*; sympathy, empathy, understanding, deep u., fellow feeling (see also *condolence*); self-pity, self-compassion, self-commiseration, tears for oneself.

*condolence*, commiseration, sympathetic grief, sympathy, fellow feeling, fellowship in sorrow 775 *participation*; consolation, comfort 831 *relief*; professional condolence, keen, coronach, wake 836 *lament*.

*mercy*, 'tender mercies' (see quotation at 898 *cruel act*), quarter, grace; second chance; mercifulness, clemency, lenity, placability, forbearance, longsuffering 909 *forgiveness*; light sentence 963 *penalty*; let-off, pardon 960 *acquittal*.

**Adj.** *pitying*, compassionate, sympathetic, understanding, condolent, commiserating; sorry for, feeling for; merciful, clement, full of mercy 736 *lenient*; melting, tender, tenderhearted, soft, soft-hearted 819 *impressible*; weak 734 *lax*; unhardened, easily touched, easily moved; placable, disposed to mercy 909 *forgiving*; remorseful, compunctious; humane, charitable 897 *benevolent*; forbearing 823 *patient*.

*pitiable*, pitiful, piteous, pathetic, heartrending, tear-jerking; deserving pity, demanding p., claiming p., challenging sympathy; arousing compassion.

**Vb.** *pity*, feel p., weep for p.; show compassion, show pity, take pity on; sympathize, sympathize with, enter into one's feelings, empathize, feel for, feel with, share the grief of 775 *participate*; sorrow, grieve, bleed for, feel sorry for, weep f., lament f., commiserate, condole, condole with, express one's condolences, send one's c.; yearn over 836 *lament*; console, comfort, offer consolation, afford c., wipe away one's tears 833 *cheer*; have pity, have compassion, melt, thaw, relent 909 *forgive*.

*show mercy*, have m., offer m., spare, spare

the life of, give quarter; commute (a sentence), pardon, grant a p., amnesty; forget one's anger 909 *forgive*; be slow to anger, forbear; give one a break, give one a second chance 736 *be lenient*; relent, unbend, not proceed to extremes, relax one's rigour, show consideration, not be too hard upon, go easy on, let one down gently; put out of their misery, give the coup de grâce, be cruel to be kind.

*ask mercy*, plead for m., appeal for m., pray for m., beg for m., throw oneself upon another's mercy, fall at one's feet, cry mercy, ask for quarter, plead for one's life; excite pity, move to compassion, propitiate, disarm, melt, thaw, soften 719 *pacify*.

**Int.** alas!, poor thing!, for pity's sake!, for mercy's s.!, for the love of God!, have mercy!, have a heart!

## 906 Pitilessness

**N.** *pitilessness*, lack of pity, heartlessness, ruthlessness, mercilessness, unmercifulness; inclemency, intolerance, rigour, zero tolerance 735 *severity*; callousness, hardness of heart, compassion fatigue, disaster f. 898 *inhumanity*; inflexibility 326 *hardness*; inexorability, relentlessness, remorselessness, unforgivingness 910 *revengefulness*; letter of the law, pound of flesh; no pity, no heart, no feelings, short shrift, no quarter.

**Adj.** *pitiless*, unpitying, uncompassionate, uncondoling, uncomforting, unconsoling, unfeeling, unresponsive 820 *impassive*; unsympathizing, unsympathetic; unmelting, unmoved, tearless, dry-eyed; hard-hearted, stony-h.; unsqueamish, callous, tough, hardened 326 *hard*; harsh, rigorous, intolerant, persecuting 735 *severe*; brutal, sadistic 898 *cruel*; merciless, ruthless, heartless; indisposed to mercy, inclement, unmerciful, unrelenting, relentless, remorseless, inflexible, inexorable, implacable; unforgiving, unpardoning, vindictive 910 *revengeful*.

**Vb.** *be pitiless*, – ruthless etc. adj.; have no heart, have no feelings, have no compassion, have no pity, know no p.; not be moved, turn a deaf ear; show no pity, show no mercy, give no quarter, spare none; harden one's heart, be deaf to appeal, admit no excuse; not tolerate, persecute 735 *be severe*; stand on the letter of the law, insist on one's pound of flesh 735 *be severe*; take one's revenge 910 *avenge*.

## 907 Gratitude

**N.** *gratitude*, gratefulness, thankfulness, grateful heart, feeling of obligation, sense of o.; grateful acceptance, appreciativeness, appreciation, lively sense of favours received.

thanks, hearty t., grateful t.; giving thanks, vote of t., thankyou; thanksgiving, eucharist, benediction, blessing; praises, Te Deum 876 *celebration*; grace, bismillah, grace before meals; thankyou letter, bread-and-butter l., Collins; credit, credit title, acknowledgment, due a., grateful a., recognition, grateful r., ungrudging r., full praise; tribute 923 *praise*; thank-offering, parting present, leaving p., recognition of one's services, token of one's gratitude, tip 962 *reward*; requital, return, favour returned 714 *retaliation*.

**Adj.** *grateful*, thankful, appreciative; showing appreciation, thanking, blessing, praising; acknowledging favours, crediting, giving credit; obliged, much o., under obligation, in one's debt, owing a favour, beholden, indebted.

**Vb.** *be grateful*, have a grateful heart, overflow with gratitude; thank one's lucky stars, praise Heaven; feel an obligation, cherish a favour, never forget; accept gratefully, pocket thankfully, receive with open arms, not look a gift horse in the mouth; be privileged, have the honour to.

*thank*, give thanks, render t., return t., express t., pour out one's t., praise, bless; acknowledge, express acknowledgments, credit, give c., give due c., give full c. 158 *attribute*; appreciate, show appreciation, tip 962 *reward*; return a favour, requite, repay, repay with interest; return with thanks 787 *restitute*.

**Adv.** *gratefully*, thankfully, with gratitude, with thanks, with interest.

**Int.** thanks!, many t.!, much obliged!, thank you!, ta!, cheers!, thank goodness!, thank Heaven!, Heaven be praised!

## 908 Ingratitude

**N.** *ingratitude*, lack of gratitude, lack of appreciation, ungratefulness, unthankfulness, thanklessness; grudging thanks, cold t., more kicks than ha'pence; no sense of obligation, indifference to favours, taking everything as one's due, 'benefits forgot' 506 *oblivion*;

> Blow, blow, thou winter wind,
> Thou art not so unkind
> As man's ingratitude: . . .
>
> Freeze, freeze, thou bitter sky,
> That dost not bite so nigh
> As benefits forgot.
> William Shakespeare, *As You Like It*

no reward, unrewardingness, thankless task, thankless office; thankless person, ingrate, ungrateful wretch.

**Adj.** *ungrateful*, unthankful 885 *discourteous*; unobliged, not obliged, unbeholden; unmindful 506 *forgetful*; unmindful of favours, insensible of benefits, incapable of gratitude 820 *apathetic*.

*unthanked*, unappreciated, thankless, without credit, without acknowledgment, unacknowledged, forgotten; rewardless, bootless, unrewarding, unrewarded, unrequited, ill-r., untipped.

**Vb.** *be ungrateful*, show ingratitude, admit no obligation, acknowledge no favour; take for granted, take as one's due; not thank, omit to t., forget to t.; see no reason to thank, grudge thanks, not give a thankyou for, look a gift horse in the mouth; forget a kindness, return evil for good.

**Int.** thank you for nothing!, no thanks to.

## 909 Forgiveness

**N.** *forgiveness*, pardon, free p., full p., reprieve 506 *amnesty*; indemnity, grace, indulgence, plenary i. 905 *mercy*; cancellation, remission, absolution 960 *acquittal*; condonation; justification, exculpation, exoneration, excuse 927 *vindication*; conciliation, mutual forgiveness, reconciliation 719 *pacification*; forgiving nature, mercifulness, placability, lenity 905 *pity*; longsuffering, forbearance 823 *patience*; forgiver, pardoner.

**Adj.** *forgiving*, merciful, placable, condoning, admitting excuses, conciliatory; willing to forgive 736 *lenient*; magnanimous 897 *benevolent*; unreproachful, unresentful, forbearing, longsuffering 823 *patient*; reluctant to punish, more in sorrow than in anger.

*forgiven*, pardoned, forgiven and forgotten, amnestied, reprieved; remitted, cancelled, blotted out; condoned, excused, exonerated, let off 960 *acquitted*; absolved, shriven; unresented, unavenged, unrevenged, unpunished, unchastened; pardonable, forgivable, venial, excusable.

**Vb.** *forgive*, pardon, reprieve, amnesty, forgive and forget, think no more of, not give another thought 506 *forget*; remit, absolve, assoil, shrive; cancel, blot out, wipe the slate clean 550 *obliterate*; relent, unbend, accept an apology 736 *be lenient*; be merciful, not be too hard upon, let one down gently, let one off the hook 905 *show mercy*; bear with, put up w., forbear, tolerate, make allowances 823 *be patient*; take no offence, bear no malice, take in good part, pocket, stomach, not hold it against one; forget an injury, ignore a wrong, overlook, pass over, not punish, leave unavenged, 'turn the other cheek' (see quotation for 'an eye for an eye' at 714 *retaliation*); 'return good for evil' (see quotation at 714 *retaliation*) 897 *be benevolent*; connive, wink at, condone, not make an issue of, turn a blind eye 458 *disregard*; excuse, find excuses for 927 *justify*; recommend for pardon, intercede 720 *mediate*; exculpate, exonerate 960 *acquit*; be ready to forgive, make the first move, bury the hatchet, let bygones be bygones, make it up, extend the hand of forgiveness, shake hands, kiss and be friends, kiss and make up, be reconciled 880 *be friendly*; restore to favour, kill the fatted calf 876 *celebrate*.

*beg pardon*, plead for forgiveness, offer apologies, ask for absolution 905 *ask mercy*; propitiate, placate 941 *atone*.

**Adv.** *forgivingly*, without resentment, without bearing a grudge, more in sorrow than in anger.

### 910 Revenge

**N.** *revengefulness*, thirst for revenge; vengefulness, vindictiveness, spitefulness, spite 898 *malevolence*; ruthlessness 906 *pitilessness*; remorselessness, relentlessness, implacability, irreconcilability, unappeasability; unappeasable resentment, deadly rancour 891 *resentment*.

*revenge*, sweet r.; crime passionel 911 *jealousy*; vengeance, avengement, day of reckoning 963 *punishment*; victimization, reprisal, reprisals, punitive expedition 714 *retaliation*; tit for tat, a Roland for an Oliver, measure for measure, lex talionis, 'an eye for an eye and a tooth for a tooth' (see quotation at 714 *retaliation*); vendetta, feud, blood f. 881 *enmity*.

*avenger*, vindicator, punisher, revanchist; Nemesis, Eumenides, avenging furies.

**Adj.** *revengeful*, vengeful, breathing vengeance, thirsting for revenge; avenging, taking vengeance, retaliative 714 *retaliatory*; at feud 881 *inimical*; unforgiving, unforgetting, implacable, unappeasable, unrelenting, relentless, remorseless 906 *pitiless*; vindictive, spiteful 898 *malevolent*; rancorous 891 *resentful*; enjoying revenge, gloating.

**Vb.** *avenge*, avenge oneself, revenge o., take one's revenge, exact r., take vengeance, wreak v., take the law into one's own hands; exact retribution, get one's own back, repay, pay out, pay off *or* settle old scores, square an account, give someone what was coming to them, give someone his *or* her come-uppance; get back at, give tit for tat 714 *retaliate*; sate one's vengeance, have one's fill of revenge, enjoy one's r., gloat.

*be revengeful*, – vindictive etc. adj.; get one's knife into 898 *be malevolent*; bear malice, cry out for revenge, breathe r., promise vengeance 888 *hate*; nurse one's revenge, harbour a grudge, carry on a feud, conduct a blood feud, have a rod in pickle, have a crow to pluck, have a bone to pick, have a score *or* accounts to settle 881 *be inimical*; let it rankle, remember an injury, brood on one's wrongs, refuse to forget 891 *resent*.

### 911 Jealousy

**N.** *jealousy*, pangs of j., jealousness; jaundiced eye, green-eyed monster; distrust, mistrust 486 *doubt*; heart-burning 891 *resentment*; enviousness 912 *envy*; hate 888 *hatred*; inferiority complex, emulation, competitiveness, competitive spirit, competition, rivalry, jealous r. 716 *contention*; possessiveness 887 *love*; sexual jealousy, eternal triangle, crime passionel 910 *revenge*; object of jealousy, competitor, rival, hated r., the other man, the other woman; Othello.

**Adj.** *jealous*, green-eyed, yellow-e., jaundiced, envying 912 *envious*; devoured with jealousy, consumed with j., eaten up with j.; possessive 887 *loving*; suspicious, mistrusting, distrustful 474 *doubting*; emulative, competitive, rival, competing.

**Vb.** *be jealous*, scent a rival, suspect, mistrust, distrust 486 *doubt*; view with jealousy, view with a jaundiced eye 912 *envy*; resent another's superiority, nurse an inferiority complex; brook no rival, resent competition; strive to keep for oneself, not allow out of one's sight.

### 912 Envy

**N.** *envy*, envious eye, enviousness, covetousness 859 *desire*; rivalry 716 *contention*; envious rivalry 911 *jealousy*; ill will, spite, spleen, bile 898 *malevolence*; mortification, unwilling admiration, grudging praise.

**Adj.** *envious*, envying, envious-eyed, green with envy 911 *jealous*; greedy, unsated, unsatisfied 829 *discontented*; covetous, longing 859 *desiring*; grudging; mortified 891 *resentful*.

**Vb.** *envy*, view with e., cast envious looks, cast covetous l., turn green with e., resent; covet, crave, lust after, must have for oneself, long to change places with 859 *desire*.

SECTION FOUR

## Morality

### 913 Right

**N.** *right*, rightfulness, rightness, fitness, what is fitting, what ought to be, what should be; obligation 917 *duty*; fittingness, seemliness, propriety, decency 848 *etiquette*; normality 83 *conformity*; rules, rules and regulations 693 *precept*; ethicalness, ethical investment, ethical shopping, morality, moral code, good morals

917 *morals*; righteousness 933 *virtue*; rectitude, uprightness, honour 929 *probity*; one's right, one's due, one's prerogative, deserts, merits, claim 915 *dueness.*

*justice*, freedom from wrong, justifiability; righting wrong, redress; reform 654 *reformism*; tardy justice, overdue reform; even-handed justice, impartial j.; scales of justice, justice under the law, process of l., McNaghten rules 953 *legality*; retribution, retributive justice, poetic j. 962 *reward*; give and take, lex talionis 714 *retaliation*; fair-mindedness, objectivity, lack of bias, disinterestedness, detachment, impartiality, equalness 28 *equality*; equity, equitableness, reasonableness, fairness; fair deal, square d., fair treatment, fair play; no discrimination, equal opportunity; fair society; good law, Queensberry rules; Astraea, Themis, Nemesis.

**Adj.** *right*, rightful, proper, right and p., meet and right; fitting, suitable, appropriate 24 *fit*; good 917 *ethical*; put right, redressed, reformed 654 *improved*; normal, standard, classical 83 *conformable.*

*just*, upright, righteous, right-minded, high-principled, 'on the side of the angels' 933 *virtuous*;

> What is the question now placed before society with a glib assurance the most astounding? The question is this – Is man an ape or an angel? My lord, I am on the side of the angels.
> Benjamin Disraeli

fair-minded, disinterested, unprejudiced, unbiased, unswerving, undeflected 625 *neutral*; detached, impersonal, dispassionate, objective, open-minded; equal, egalitarian, impartial, even-handed; fair, square, fair and s., equitable, reasonable, fair enough; in the right, justifiable, justified, unchallengeable, unchallenged, unimpeachable; above-board, legitimate, according to law 953 *legal*; sporting, sportsmanlike 929 *honourable*; deserved, well-d., earned, merited, well-m., 915 *due*; overdue, demanded, claimed, rightly c., claimable 627 *required.*

**Vb.** *be right*, behove 915 *be due*; have justice, have good cause, be justified, be in the right, have right on one's side.

*be just*, – impartial etc. adj.; play the game 929 *be honourable*; do justice, give the devil his due, give full marks to, hand it to 915 *grant claims*; see justice done, see fair play, hold the scales even, hear both sides, go by merit, consider on its merits 480 *judge*; temper justice with mercy 905 *show mercy*; see one righted, right a wrong, redress, remedy, mend, reform, put right 654 *rectify*; serve one right 714 *retaliate*; try to be fair, lean over backwards,

overcompensate; hide nothing, declare one's interest.

**Adv.** *rightly*, justly, justifiably, with justice; in the right, within one's rights; like a judge, impartially, without bias, indifferently, equally, without distinction, without respect of persons, without fear or favour, fairly, without favouritism; on its merits.

## 914 Wrong

**N.** *wrong*, wrongness, something wrong, something amiss, oddness, queerness 84 *variance*; something rotten, curse, bane, scandal 645 *badness*; disgrace, shame, crying s., dishonour 867 *slur*; impropriety, indecorum 847 *bad taste*; wrongheadedness, unreasonableness 481 *misjudgment*; unjustifiability, what ought not to be, what must not be 916 *undueness*; inexcusability, culpability, guiltiness 936 *guilt*; immorality, vice, sin 934 *wickedness*; dishonesty, unrighteousness 930 *improbity*; irregularity, illegitimacy, criminality, crime, lawlessness 954 *illegality*; wrongfulness, misdoing, misfeasance, transgression, trespass, encroachment; delict, misdeed, offence, arrestable o. 936 *guilty act*; a wrong, injustice, tort, mischief, outrage, foul 930 *foul play*; sense of wrong, complaint, charge 928 *accusation*; grievance, just g. 891 *resentment*; wrongdoer, immoralist, unjust judge 938 *bad person.*

*injustice*, no justice; miscarriage of justice, wrong verdict 481 *misjudgment*; corrupt justice, uneven scales, warped judgment, packed jury 481 *bias*; one-sidedness, inequity, unfairness; discrimination, race d., sex d., racism, institutional r., sexism, heterosexism, ageism, greylisting, classism, ableism, handicappism; partiality, leaning, favouritism, favour, nepotism; preferential treatment, positive discrimination, affirmative action; partisanship, party spirit, old school tie 481 *prejudice*; unlawfulness, no law 954 *illegality*; justice denied, right withheld, privilege curtailed 916 *undueness*; unfair advantage, 'heads I win, tails you lose'; no equality, wolf and the lamb 29 *inequality*; not cricket 930 *foul play*; imposition, robbing Peter to pay Paul.

**Adj.** *wrong*, not right 645 *bad*; odd, queer, suspect 84 *abnormal*; unfitting, inappropriate, unseemly, improper 847 *vulgar*; wrongheaded, unreasonable 481 *misjudging*; wrong from the start, out of court, inadmissible; irregular, against the rules, foul, unauthorized, unwarranted 757 *prohibited*; wrongful, illegitimate, illicit, tortious, felonious, criminal 954 *illegal*; condemnable, culpable, in the wrong, offside 936 *guilty*; unwarrantable, inexcusable, unpardonable, unforgivable, unjustifiable (see also unjust); open to objection, objectionable, reprehensible, scandalous 861 *disliked*; injurious, mischievous 645 *harmful*; unrighteous 930 *dishonest*; iniquitous, sinful, vicious, immoral 934 *wicked*.

*unjust*, unjustifiable; uneven, weighted 29 *unequal*; inequitable, iniquitous, unfair; hard, hard on 735 *severe*; foul, not playing the game, not keeping to the rules, below the belt, unsportsmanlike; discriminatory, favouring, one-sided, leaning to one side, partial, partisan, prejudiced 481 *biased*; selling justice 930 *venal*; wresting the law 954 *illegal*.

**Vb.** *be wrong*, – unjust etc. adj.; be in the wrong, go wrong, err, stray 655 *deteriorate*.

*do wrong*, wrong, hurt, injure, do an injury 645 *harm*; be hard on, have a down on 735 *be severe*; not play the game, not play cricket, hit below the belt; break the rules, commit a foul; commit a tort, commit a crime, break the law, wrest the l., pervert the l. 954 *be illegal*; transgress, infringe, trespass 306 *encroach*; wink at, connive at, turn a blind eye; leave unrighted, leave unremedied; do less than justice, withhold justice, deny j., deny one's rights; weight, load the scales, pack the jury, rig the jury; lean, lean to one side, discriminate against, show partiality, show favouritism, discriminate 481 *be biased*; favour 703 *patronize*; go too far, overcompensate, lean over backwards; commit, perpetrate.

**Adv.** *wrongly*, unrightfully, unjustly, wrongfully, illegally; criminally, with criminal intent.

## 915 Dueness

**N.** *dueness*, what is due, what is owing; accountability, responsibility, obligation 917 *duty*; 'from each according to his ability and to each according to his need';

> From each according to his abilities, to each according to his needs.
> Karl Marx, *Criticism of the Gotha Programme* (A similar slogan had been used by other radicals of the time.)

the least one can do, bare minimum; what one looks for, expectations; payability, dues 804 *payment*; something owed, indebtedness 803 *debt*; tribute, credit 158 *attribution*; recognition, acknowledgment 907 *thanks*; something to be said for, something in favour of, case for; qualification, merits, deserts, just d. 913 *right*; justification 927 *vindication*; entitlement, claim, title 913 *right*; birthright, patriality, patrimony 777 *dower*; interest, vested i., vested right, prescriptive r., absolute r., indefeasible r., inalienable r.; legal right, easement, prescription, ancient lights; human rights, social justice, women's rights, equal opportunity, gay

rights, animal r. 744 *freedom*; constitutional right, civil rights, bill of r., Magna Carta; privilege, exemption, immunity 919 *non-liability*; prerogative, privilege; charter, warrant, licence 756 *permit*; liberty, franchise; bond, security 767 *title deed*; patent, copyright, intellectual property; recovery of rights, restoration, revendication, compensation 787 *restitution*; owner, title-holder 776 *possessor*; heir 776 *beneficiary*; claimant, plaintiff, pursuer, appellant; person with a grievance 763 *petitioner*.

**Adj.** *due*, owing, payable 803 *owed*; ascribable, attributable, assignable; merited, well-m., deserved, well-d., richly-d., condign, earned, well-e., coming to one; admitted, allowed, sanctioned, warranted, licit, lawful 756 *permitted*; constitutional, entrenched, untouchable, uninfringeable, unchallengeable, unimpeachable, inviolable; privileged, sacrosanct; confirmed, vested, prescriptive, inalienable, imprescriptible; secured by law, legalized, legitimate, rightful, of right, de jure, by habit and repute 953 *legal*; claimable, heritable, inheritable, earmarked, reserved, set aside; expected, fit, fitting, befitting 913 *right*; proper, en règle 642 *advisable*.

*deserving*, meriting, worthy of, worthy, meritorious, emeritus, honoris causa; grant-worthy, credit-w.; justifiable, justified; entitled, having the right, having the title, claiming the right, asserting one's privilege, standing up for one's rights.

**Vb.** *be due*, – owing etc. adj.; ought, ought to be, should be, should have been; be one's due, be due to, have it coming; be the least one can offer, be the least one can do, be the bare minimum; behove, befit, beseem 917 *be one's duty*.

*claim*, claim as a right, lay claim to, stake a c., take possession 786 *appropriate*; claim unduly, arrogate; demand one's rights, assert one's r., stand up for one's r., vindicate one's r., insist on one's r., stand on one's r.; draw on, come down on for, take one's toll 786 *levy*; call in (debts), reclaim 656 *retrieve*; publish one's claims, declare one's right; sue, demand redress 761 *request*; enforce a claim, exercise a right; establish a right, patent, copyright.

*have a right*, expect, have a right to e., claim; be entitled, be privileged, have the right to, have a claim to, make out a case for 478 *demonstrate*; justify, substantiate 927 *vindicate*; be justified, have the law on one's side, have the court in one's favour, get a favourable verdict.

*deserve*, merit, be worthy, be found w., have a claim on; earn, receive one's due, meet with one's deserts, get one's d.; have it coming to one, get one's come-uppance, have only oneself to thank; 'sow the wind and reap the whirlwind'.

> **For they have sown the wind, and they shall reap the whirlwind.**
> Bible, Hosea

*grant claims*, give every man his due 913 *be just*; ascribe, assign, credit 158 *attribute*; hand it to, acknowledge, recognize 907 *thank*; allow a claim, sanction a c., warrant, authorize 756 *permit*; admit a right, acknowledge a claim, satisfy a c., pay one's dues, honour, meet an obligation, honour a bill 804 *pay*; privilege, give a right, confer a r., give one a title; allot, prescribe 783 *apportion*; legalize, legitimize, decriminalize 953 *make legal*; confirm, validate 488 *endorse*.

**Adv.** *duly*, by right, in one's own right, by law, de jure, ex officio, virtute officii, by divine right; as expected of one, as required of one.

## 916 Undueness

**N.** *undueness*, not what one expects *or* would expect 508 *lack of expectation*; not the thing, not quite the t., impropriety, unseemliness, indecorum 847 *bad taste*; inappropriateness, unfittingness 643 *inexpedience*; unworthiness, demerit 934 *vice*; illicitness, illegitimacy, bastardy 954 *illegality*; no thanks to 908 *ingratitude*; absence of right, lack of title, failure of t., nonentitlement; no claim, no right, no title, false t., weak t., empty t., courtesy t.; gratuitousness, gratuity, bonus, grace marks, unearned increment; inordinacy, excessiveness, too much, overpayment 637 *redundance*; imposition, exaction 735 *severity*; unfair share, lion's s. 32 *main part*; violation, breach, infraction, infringement, encroachment 306 *overstepping*; profanation, desecration 980 *impiety*.

*arrogation*, assumption, unjustified a., presumption, unwarranted p., swollen claims; pretendership, usurpation, tyranny; misappropriation 786 *expropriation*; encroachment, inroad, trespass 306 *overstepping*.

*loss of right*, disentitlement, disfranchisement, disqualification; denaturalization, detribalization 147 *conversion*; forfeiture 772 *loss*; deportation, dismissal, deprivation, dethronement 752 *deposal*; ouster, dispossession 786 *expropriation*; seizure, forcible s., robbery 788 *stealing*; cancellation 752 *abrogation*; waiver, abdication 621 *relinquishment*.

*usurper*, arrogator 735 *tyrant*; pretender 545 *impostor*; desecrator; violator, infringer, encroacher, trespasser, squatter, cuckoo in the nest.

**Adj.** *undue*, not owing, unattributable; unowed, gratuitous, by favour; not expected, unlooked for, uncalled for 508 *unexpected*; inappropriate, improper, unseemly, unfitting, unbefitting 643 *inexpedient*; preposterous, not to be countenanced, not to be thought of, out of the question 497 *absurd*.

*unwarranted*, unwarrantable; unauthorized, unsanctioned, unlicensed, unchartered, unconstitutional; unrightful, unlegalized, illicit, illegitimate, ultra vires 954 *illegal*; arrogated, usurped, stolen, borrowed; excessive, presumptuous, assuming 878 *insolent*; unjustified, unjustifiable 914 *wrong*; undeserved, unmerited, unearned; overpaid, underpaid; invalid, weak; forfeited, forfeit; false, bastard 542 *spurious*; fictitious, would-be, self-styled 850 *affected*.

*unentitled*, without title, uncrowned; unqualified, without qualifications, unempowered, incompetent; unworthy, undeserving, meritless, unmeritorious; underprivileged, unprivileged, without rights, unchartered, unfranchised, voteless; disentitled, discrowned; dethroned, deposed; disqualified, invalidated, disfranchised, defrocked; deprived, bereft, dispossessed.

**Vb.** *be undue*, – undeserved etc. adj.; not be due, be unclaimed, be unclaimable; show bad taste, misbecome, ill beseem 847 *vulgarize*; presume, arrogate 878 *be insolent*; usurp, borrow 788 *steal*; take advantage, be given an inch and take an ell; trespass, squat 306 *encroach*; infringe, break, violate 954 *be illegal*; desecrate, profane 980 *be impious*.

*disentitle*, uncrown, dethrone 752 *depose*; disqualify, unfrock, disfranchise, alienize, denaturalize, detribalize, denationalize; invalidate 752 *abrogate*; disallow 757 *prohibit*; dispossess, expropriate 786 *deprive*; forfeit, declare f.; defeat a claim, mock the claims of; make illegitimate, illegalize, criminalize 954 *make illegal*; bastardize, debase 655 *impair*.

**Adv.** *unduly*, improperly; undeservedly, without desert, no thanks to.

## 917 Duty

**N.** *duty*, what ought to be done, what is up to one, the right thing, the proper t., the decent t.; one's duty, bounden d., imperative d., inescapable d.; obligation, liability, onus, responsibility, accountability 915 *dueness*; fealty, allegiance, loyalty 739 *obedience*; sense of duty, dutifulness, duteousness 597 *willingness*; discharge of duty, performance, acquittal, discharge 768 *observance*; call of duty, 'stern daughter of the voice of God', claims of conscience, case of c.;

> **Stern daughter of the voice of God!**
> **O Duty! If that name thou love**

bond, tie, engagement, commitment, word, pledge 764 *promise*; task, office, charge 751 *commission*; walk of life, station, profession 622 *vocation*.

*conscience*, professional c., tender c., nonconformist c., exacting c., peremptory c.; categorical imperative, inner voice, 'a still, small voice'.

*code of duty*, code of honour, unwritten code, professional c., bushido; Decalogue, Ten Commandments, Hippocratic oath 693 *precept*.

*morals*, morality 933 *virtue*; honour 929 *probity*; moral principles, high p., the moral high ground, 'the Protestant work ethic' (see quotation at 682 *labour*), ideals, high i., standards, high s., professional s.; ethics, religious e., humanist e., professional e.; ethology, deontology, casuistry, ethical philosophy, moral p., moral science, idealism, humanism, utilitarianism, behaviourism 449 *philosophy*; ethical investment, ethical shopping; the moral majority.

**Adj.** *obliged*, duty-bound, on duty, bound by duty, called by d.; under duty, in duty bound, in the line of duty; obligated, beholden, under obligation; tied, bound, sworn, pledged, committed, engaged; unexempted, liable, chargeable, answerable, responsible, accountable; in honour bound, bound in conscience, answerable to God; plagued by conscience, conscience-stricken 939 *repentant*; conscientious, punctilious 768 *observant*; duteous, dutiful 739 *obedient*; vowed, under a vow.

*obligatory*, incumbent, imposed, behoving, up to one; binding, de rigueur, compulsory, mandatory, peremptory, operative 740 *compelling*; inescapable, unavoidable; strict, unconditional, categorical.

*ethical*, moral, principled 933 *virtuous*; honest, decent 929 *honourable*; moralistic, ethological, casuistical; moralizing; humanistic, idealistic; utilitarian.

**Vb.** *be one's duty*, be incumbent, behove, become, befit 915 *be due*; devolve on, belong to, be up to, pertain to, fall to, arise from one's functions, be part of the job; lie with, lie at one's door, rest with, rest on one's shoulders.

*incur a duty*, make it one's d., take on oneself, accept responsibility, shoulder one's r.; make oneself liable, commit oneself, pledge o., engage for 764 *promise*; assume one's functions, enter upon one's office, receive a posting; have the office, have the function, have the charge, have the duty; owe it to oneself, feel it up to one, feel it incumbent upon one; feel duty's call, accept the c., answer the c., submit to one's vocation.

*do one's duty*, fulfil one's d. 739 *obey*; discharge, acquit, perform, do the needful 676 *do*; do one's bit, play one's part; perform one's office, discharge one's functions 768 *observe*; be on duty, stay at one's post, go down with one's ship; come up to what is expected of one, come up to expectation, not be found wanting; keep faith with one's conscience, meet one's obligations, discharge an obligation, make good one's promise, redeem a pledge, be as good as one's word; honour, meet, pay up 804 *pay*.

*impose a duty*, require, oblige, look to, call upon; devolve, call to office, swear one in, offer a post, post 751 *commission*; assign a duty, saddle with, detail, order, enjoin, decree 737 *command*; tax, overtax, task, overtask 684 *fatigue*; exact 735 *be severe*; demand obedience, expect it of one, expect too much of one 507 *expect*; bind, condition 766 *give terms*; bind over, take security 764 *take a pledge*.

**Adv.** *on duty*, at one's post; under an obligation; in the line of duty, as in duty bound; with a clear conscience; for conscience' sake.

## 918 Undutifulness

**N.** *undutifulness*, default, want of duty, dereliction of d.; neglect, wilful n., laches, culpable negligence 458 *negligence*; undutifulness, unduteousness 921 *disrespect*; malingering, evasion of duty, cop-out 620 *avoidance*; nonpractice, nonperformance 769 *nonobservance*; idleness, laziness 679 *sluggishness*; forgetfulness 506 *oblivion*; noncooperation, lack of alacrity 598 *unwillingness*; truancy, absenteeism 190 *absence*; absconding 667 *escape*; infraction, violation, breach of orders, indiscipline, mutiny, rebellion 738 *disobedience*; incompetence, mismanagement 695 *bungling*; obstruction, sabotage 702 *hindrance*; desertion, defection 603 *tergiversation*; disloyalty, treachery, treason 930 *perfidy*; secession, breakaway 978 *schism*; irresponsibility, escapism; truant, absentee, malingerer, defaulter 620 *avoider*; slacker 679 *idler*; deserter, absconder 667 *escaper*; betrayer, traitor 603 *tergiversator*; saboteur 702 *hinderer*; mutineer, rebel 738 *revolter*; seceder, splinter group 978 *schismatic*.

**Adj.** *undutiful*, wanting in duty, uncooperative 598 *unwilling*; unduteous, unfilial, undaughterly 921 *disrespectful*; mutinous, rebellious, seceding, breakaway 738 *disobedient*; disloyal, treacherous, treasonous 930 *perfidious*; irresponsible, unreliable; truant, absentee 190 *absent*; absconding 667 *escaped*.

**Vb.** *fail in duty*, neglect one's d., be wilfully negligent 458 *neglect*; ignore one's obligations 458 *disregard*; oversleep, sleep in 679 *sleep*; default, let one down, leave one in the lurch 509 *disappoint*; mismanage, bungle 495 *blunder*; not remember 506 *forget*; shirk, evade, wriggle out of, malinger, dodge the column 620 *avoid*; wash one's hands of, pass the buck 919 *be exempt*; play truant, overstay leave 190 *be absent*; abscond 667 *escape*; quit, scuttle, scarper 296 *decamp*; abandon, abandon one's post, desert, desert the colours 621 *relinquish*; break orders, disobey o., violate o., exceed one's instructions 738 *disobey*; mutiny, rebel 738 *revolt*; be disloyal, prove treacherous, betray, commit treason 603 *change one's mind*; sabotage 702 *obstruct*; noncooperate, withdraw, walk out, break away, form a splinter group, secede 978 *schismatize*.

## 919 Nonliability

**N.** *nonliability*, nonresponsibility, exemption, dispensation; conscience clause, escape c., let-out c., force majeure 468 *qualification*; immunity, impunity, privilege, special treatment, special case, benefit of clergy; extraterritoriality, diplomatic immunity; franchise, charter 915 *dueness*; independence, liberty, the four freedoms 744 *freedom*; licence, leave 756 *permission*; compassionate leave, aegrotat, certificate of exemption 756 *permit*; excuse, exoneration, exculpation 960 *acquittal*; absolution, pardon, amnesty 909 *forgiveness*; discharge, release 746 *liberation*; renunciation 621 *relinquishment*; evasion of responsibility, escapism, self-exemption, washing one's hands, passing the buck 753 *resignation*.

**Adj.** *nonliable*, not responsible, not answerable, unaccountable, unpunishable; excused, exonerated, freed from blame, scot-free 960 *acquitted*; dispensed, exempted, privileged, prerogatived; shielded, protected; untouched, exempt, immune; unaffected, well out of; independent, free-born 744 *free*; tax-free, post-f., duty-f. 812 *uncharged*.

**Vb.** *exempt*, set apart, set aside; eliminate, count out, rule o. 57 *exclude*; excuse, exonerate, exculpate 960 *acquit*; grant absolution, absolve, pardon 909 *forgive*; spare 905 *show mercy*; grant immunity, privilege, charter 756 *permit*; license, dispense, give dispensation, grant impunity; amnesty, declare an amnesty

506 *forget*; enfranchise, manumit, set free, set at liberty, release 746 *liberate*; pass over, stretch a point 736 *be lenient*.

*be exempt*, – exempted etc. adj.; owe no responsibility, be free from r., have no liability, not come within the scope of; enjoy immunity, enjoy diplomatic i., enjoy impunity, enjoy a privileged position, enjoy independence 744 *be free*; spare oneself the necessity, exempt oneself, excuse oneself, absent oneself, take leave, go on leave 190 *go away*; transfer the responsibility, pass the buck, shift the blame 272 *transfer*; evade or escape liability, get away with 667 *escape*; own or admit no responsibility, wash one's hands of 918 *fail in duty*.

## 920 Respect

**N.** *respect*, regard, consideration, esteem 923 *approbation*; high standing, honour, favour 866 *repute*; polite regard, attention, attentions, flattering a. 884 *courtesy*; due respect, respectfulness, deference, humbleness 872 *humility*; obsequiousness 879 *servility*; humble service, devotion 739 *loyalty*; admiration, awe 864 *wonder*; terror 854 *fear*; reverence, veneration, adoration 981 *worship*.

*respects*, regards, duty, kind regards, kindest r., greetings 884 *courteous act*; red carpet, guard of honour, address of welcome, illuminated address, salutation, salaam; nod, bob, duck, bow, scrape, curtsy, genuflexion, prostration, kowtow 311 *obeisance*; reverence, homage; salute, presenting arms; honours of war, flags flying.

**Adj.** *respectful*, deferential, knowing one's place 872 *humble*; obsequious, bootlicking, kowtowing 879 *servile*; submissive 721 *submitting*; reverent, reverential 981 *worshipping*; admiring, awestruck 864 *wondering*; polite 884 *courteous*; ceremonious, at the salute, saluting, cap in hand, bare-headed, forelock-tugging; kneeling, on one's knees, prostrate; bobbing, bowing, scraping, bowing and s., bending; obeisant, showing respect, rising, standing, on one's feet, all standing.

*respected*, admired, much-a., honoured, esteemed, revered 866 *reputable*; respectable, reverend, venerable; time-honoured 866 *worshipful*; imposing 821 *impressive*.

**Vb.** *respect*, entertain r. for, hold in r., hold in honour, hold in high regard, hold in high esteem, think well of, rank high, place h., look up to, esteem, regard, value; admire 864 *wonder*; reverence, venerate, exalt, magnify 866 *honour*; adore 981 *worship*; idolize 982 *idolatrize*; revere, stand in awe of, have a wholesome respect for 854 *fear*; know one's place, defer to, take a back seat to 721 *submit*; pay tribute to, take one's hat off to 923 *praise*; do homage to, make much of, lionize, chair, carry shoulder-high 876 *celebrate*.

*show respect*, render honour, pay homage, do the honours 884 *pay one's respects*; make way for, leave room for, keep one's distance, take a back seat to, know one's place; welcome, hail, salute, present arms, turn out the guard, roll out the red carpet, put out the bunting 884 *greet*; cheer, drink to 876 *toast*; bob, duck, bow, bow and scrape, curtsy, kneel, kowtow, prostrate oneself 311 *stoop*; observe decorum, stand on ceremony, stand, rise, rise to one's feet, rise from one's seat, uncover, remove one's hat *or* cap, stand bareheaded; humble oneself, condescend 872 *be humble*.

*command respect*, inspire r., awe, strike with a., overawe, impose 821 *impress*; enjoy a reputation, rank high, stand h., stand well in the eyes of all 866 *have a reputation*; compel respect, demand r., command admiration 864 *be wonderful*; dazzle, bedazzle 875 *be ostentatious*; receive respect, gain honour, gain a reputation, receive bouquets 923 *be praised*.

**Adv.** *respectfully*, humbly, with all respect, with due r.; obsequiously, deferentially, reverentially, reverently; saving your grace, saving your presence.

## 921 Disrespect

**N.** *disrespect*, lack of respect, scant r., disrespectfulness, irreverence, impoliteness, incivility, discourtesy 885 *rudeness*; dishonour, disfavour 924 *disapprobation*; neglect, undervaluation 483 *underestimation*; low esteem 867 *disrepute*; depreciation, disparagement 926 *detraction*; contumely 899 *scurrility*; scorn 922 *contempt*; mockery 851 *ridicule*; desecration 980 *impiety*.

*indignity*, humiliation, mortification, affront, insult, slight, snub, slap in the face, outrage 878 *insolence*; snook, V-sign, Harvey Smith salute 878 *sauciness*; gibe, taunt, jeer 922 *contempt*; quip, sarcasm, mock, flout 851 *ridicule*; hiss, hoot, boo, catcall, brickbat, rotten eggs 924 *disapprobation*.

**Adj.** *disrespectful*, wanting in respect, slighting, neglectful 458 *negligent*; insubordinate 738 *disobedient*; irreverent, irreverential, aweless 865 *unastonished*; sacrilegious 980 *profane*; outspoken, overcandid 573 *plain*; rude, impolite 885 *discourteous*; airy, breezy, offhand, offhanded, cavalier, familiar, cheeky, saucy 878 *impertinent*; insulting, outrageous 878 *insolent*; flouting, jeering, gibing, scoffing, mocking, satirical, cynical, sarcastic 851 *derisive*; injurious, contumelious, scurrilous 899 *cursing*; denigratory, depreciative, pejor-

ative 483 *deprecating*; snobbish, supercilious, disdainful, scornful 922 *despising*; unflattering, uncomplimentary 924 *disapproving*.

*unrespected*, disrespected, held in low esteem, of no account 867 *disreputable*; ignored, disregarded, disobeyed, unregarded, unsaluted, ungreeted 458 *neglected*; unenvied, unadmired, unflattered, unreverenced, unrevered, unworshipped; underrated, denigrated, disparaged 483 *undervalued*; despised, looked down on, spat on 922 *contemptible*.

**Vb.** *not respect*, deny r., be disrespectful; be unable to respect, have no respect for, have no regard f., have no use f. 924 *disapprove*; misprize, undervalue, underrate 483 *underestimate*; disdain, have a low opinion of, look down on, scorn 922 *despise*; run down, denigrate, disparage 926 *defame*; marginalize, spit on, toss aside 607 *reject*; show disrespect, show no respect, lack courtesy, remain seated, remain covered, keep one's hat on, push aside, shove a., elbow a., crowd, jostle 885 *be rude*; ignore, turn one's back 458 *disregard*; snub, slight, insult, affront, outrage 872 *humiliate*; dishonour, disgrace, put to shame, drag in the mud 867 *shame*; trifle with, treat lightly 922 *hold cheap*; cheapen, lower, degrade 847 *vulgarize*; have no awe, not reverence, desecrate, profane 980 *be impious*; call names, abuse 899 *curse*; taunt, twit, cock a snook 878 *be insolent*; laugh at, guy, scoff, mock, flout, deride 851 *ridicule*; make mouths at, make faces at, jeer, hiss, hoot, heckle, boo, point at, spit at 924 *reprobate*; mob, hound, chase 619 *pursue*; pelt, stone, heave a brick 712 *lapidate*.

**Adv.** *disrespectfully*, irreverently, profanely, sacrilegiously; mockingly, derisively.

## 922 Contempt

**N.** *contempt*, sovereign c., supreme c., utter c., unutterable c.; scorn, disdain, disdainfulness, superiority, loftiness 871 *pride*; contemptuousness, sniffiness; snootiness, superciliousness, snobbishness 850 *affectation*; superior airs, side, scornful eye, smile of contempt, curl of the lip, snort, sniff; slight, humiliation 921 *indignity*; sneer, dig at 926 *detraction*; derision, scoffing 851 *ridicule*; snub, rebuff 885 *discourtesy*.

*contemptibility*, unworthiness, despisedness, insignificance, puerility, pitiability, futility 639 *unimportance*; pettiness, meanness, littleness, paltriness 33 *smallness*; cause for shame, byword of reproach 867 *object of scorn*.

**Adj.** *despising*, full of contempt, contemptuous, disdainful, holier than thou, snooty, snuffy, sniffy, snobbish; haughty, lofty, airy, supercilious 871 *proud*; scornful, withering, jeering, sneering, booing 924 *disapproving*; disrespectful, impertinent 878 *insolent*; slighting, pooh-poohing 483 *deprecating*, denigrating.

*contemptible*, despicable, beneath contempt; abject, worthless 645 *bad*; petty, paltry, little, mean 33 *small*; spurned, spat on 607 *rejected*; scorned, despised, contemned, low in one's estimation 921 *unrespected*; trifling, pitiable, futile, of no account 639 *unimportant*.

**Vb.** *despise*, contemn, hold in contempt, feel utter contempt for, have no use for 921 *not respect*; look down on, consider beneath one, be too good for, be too grand for 871 *be proud*; disdain, spurn, sniff at, snort at 607 *reject*; come it over, turn up one's nose, wrinkle the n., curl one's lips, toss one's head, snort; snub, turn one's back on 885 *be rude*; scorn, whistle, hiss, boo, give a slow handclap, point at, point the finger of scorn 924 *reprobate*; laugh at, have a dig at, laugh to scorn, scoff, scout, flout, gibe, jeer, mock, deride 851 *ridicule*; trample on, ride roughshod over 735 *oppress*; disgrace, roll in the mire 867 *shame*.

*hold cheap*, misprize, have a low opinion of 921 *not respect*; ignore, dismiss, discount, marginalize, take no account of 458 *disregard*; belittle, disparage, fail to appreciate, underrate, undervalue 483 *underestimate*; decry 926 *detract*; set no value on, set no store by, think nothing of, think small beer of, not care a rap for, not care a straw, not give a hoot *or* a damn, not give that for, laugh at, treat as a laughing matter, snap one's fingers at, shrug away, pooh-pooh; slight, trifle with, treat lightly, treat like dirt, denigrate, lower, degrade 872 *humiliate*.

**Adv.** *contemptuously*, disdainfully, scornfully, with contempt, with disdain.

*contemptibly*, pitiably, miserably; to one's utter contempt.

**Int.** get lost!, get stuffed! (sl), in your face! (sl), get a life!

## 923 Approbation

**N.** *approbation*, approval, sober a., modified rapture; satisfaction 828 *content*; appreciation, recognition, acknowledgment 907 *gratitude*; good opinion, golden opinions, kudos, credit 866 *prestige*; regard, admiration, esteem 920 *respect*; good books, good graces, grace, favour, popularity, affection 887 *love*; adoption, acceptance, welcome, favourable reception 299 *reception*; sanction 756 *permission*; nod of approval, seal of a., blessing; nod, wink, thumbs up, consent 488 *assent*; countenance, patronage, championship, advocacy, backing 703 *aid*; friendly notice, favourable review, rave r. 480 *estimate*;

good word, kind w., testimonial, written t., reference, commendation, recommendation 466 *credential*.

*praise*, loud p., lyrical p., praise and glory, laud, laudation, benediction, blessing; compliment, high c., encomium, eulogy, panegyric, glorification, adulation, idolatry 925 *flattery*; hero worship 864 *wonder*; overpraise 482 *overestimation*; faint praise, two cheers; shout of praise, hosanna, alleluia; praises, song of praise, hymn of p., paean of p., dithyramb, doxology, Gloria, Te Deum; tribute, credit, due credit 907 *thanks*; complimentary reference, bouquet, accolade, citation, honourable mention, commendation, glowing terms; official biography, hagiography; self-praise, self-glorification 877 *boasting*; name in lights, letters of gold; puff, blurb 528 *advertisement*.

*applause*, clamorous a., acclaim, universal a.; enthusiasm, excitement 821 *excitation*; warm reception, hero's welcome 876 *celebration*; acclamation, plaudits, clapping, stamping, whistling, cheering; clap, three cheers, paean, hosannah; thunderous applause, peal of a., shout of a., chorus of a., round of a., salvo of a., storm of a., ovation, standing o., shouts of 'encore', shouts of 'more, more'; encore, curtain call; bouquet, pat on the back.

*commender*, praiser, laudator, encomiast, eulogist, panegyrist; clapper, applauder, shouter, claqueur, claque; approver, friendly critic, admirer, devoted a., hero-worshipper, fan club, supporters' c.; advocate, recommender, supporter, speaker for the motion 707 *patron*; Europhile; inscriber, dedicator; advertiser, blurb-writer, puffer, promotions manager, booster; agent, tout, touter, barker 528 *publicizer*; canvasser, electioneer, election agent.

**Adj.** *approving*, uncensorious, uncomplaining, satisfied 828 *content*; favouring, supporting, advocating, Europhile 703 *aiding*; appreciative 907 *grateful*; approbatory, favourable, friendly, well-inclined; complimentary, commendatory, laudatory, eulogistic, encomiastic, panegyrical, lyrical; admiring, hero-worshipping, idolatrous; lavish, generous; fulsome, overpraising, uncritical, undiscriminating; acclamatory, clapping, applauding, thunderous 400 *loud*; dithyrambic, ecstatic, rapturous, in raptures 821 *excited*.

*approvable*, admissible, permissible, acceptable; worthwhile 640 *useful*; deserving, meritorious, commendable, laudable, estimable, worthy, praiseworthy, creditable, admirable, uncensurable, unimpeachable, beyond all praise 646 *perfect*; enviable, desirable 859 *desired*.

*approved*, passed, tested, tried; uncensured, free from blame, stamped with approval, blessed; popular, in favour, in high f., in one's good books, in the good graces of, in good odour, in high esteem, thought well of 866 *reputable*; praised etc. vb.; commended, highly c.; favoured, backed, odds on 605 *chosen*.

**Vb.** *approve*, see nothing wrong with, sound pleased, have no fault to find, be unable to fault, have nothing but praise for, think highly of 920 *respect*; like well 887 *love*; think well of, admire, esteem, value, prize, treasure, cherish, set store by 866 *honour*; appreciate, give credit, give full c., give credit where credit is due, salute, take one's hat off to, hand it to, give full marks; think no worse of, think the better of; count it to one's credit, see the good points, see the good in one, think good, think perfect; think desirable 912 *envy*; think the best, award the palm; see to be good, find g., pronounce g., mark with approbation, give the seal *or* stamp of approval; accept, pass, tick, give marks for, give points for; nod, wink, nod one's approval, give one's assent 488 *assent*; sanction, bless, give one's blessing 756 *permit*; ratify 488 *endorse*; commend, recommend, advocate, support, back, favour, countenance, stand up for, speak up f., put in a good word for, give one a reference *or* a testimonial, act as referee for 703 *patronize*.

*praise*, compliment, pay compliments 925 *flatter*; speak well of, speak highly, swear by; bless 907 *thank*; salute, pay tribute to, hand it to, take one's hat off to; commend, give praise, hand out bouquets to, laud, eulogize, panegyrize, praise to the skies, sound the praises, sing the p., hymn the p., swell the p., doxologize, exalt, extol, glorify, magnify; wax lyrical, get carried away; not spare one's blushes 546 *exaggerate*; puff, inflate, overpraise, overestimate 482 *overrate*; lionize, hero-worship, idolize 982 *idolatrize*; trumpet, write up, cry up, puff up, hype up, crack up, boost 528 *advertise*; praise oneself, glorify o. 877 *boast*.

*applaud*, receive with applause, welcome, hail, hail with satisfaction; acclaim, receive with acclamation, clap, clap one's hands, give a big hand, stamp, whistle, bring the house down, raise the roof; give a standing ovation; cheer, raise a c., give three cheers, give three times three; cheer to the echo, shout for, root for; clap on the back, pat on the back, hand out bouquets to; welcome, congratulate, garland, chair 876 *celebrate*; drink to 876 *toast*.

*be praised*, – praiseworthy etc. adj.; get a citation, be mentioned in dispatches, receive an accolade; recommend oneself 866 *seek*

*repute*; find favour, win praise, gain credit, earn golden opinions 866 *have a reputation*; get a compliment, receive a tribute, be handed a bouquet, get a hand, get a clap, get a cheer; receive an ovation, take the house by storm 727 *triumph*; deserve praise, be to one's credit, redound to the honour; pass, do, pass muster, pass the test.

**Adv.** *approvingly*, admiringly, with admiration, with praises, with compliments; ungrudgingly, without demur; enviously.

*commendably*, admirably, wonderfully, unimpeachably; acceptably, satisfactorily, to satisfaction, to approval.

**Int.** bravo!, well done!, hear hear!, encore!, more, more!, bis!, three cheers!, hurrah!, hosannah!, olé!, way to go! (inf).

## 924 Disapprobation

**N.** *disapprobation*, disapproval, dissatisfaction 829 *discontent*; nonapproval, return 607 *rejection*; no permission 760 *refusal*; disfavour, displeasure, unpopularity 861 *dislike*; low opinion 921 *disrespect*; bad books, black b. 867 *disrepute*; disparagement, decrial, crabbing, carping, niggling 926 *detraction*; censoriousness, fault-finding 862 *fastidiousness*; hostility, Euroscepticism 881 *enmity*; objection, exception, cavil 468 *qualification*; complaint, clamour, outcry, protest, tut-tut, sniffing 762 *deprecation*; indignation 891 *anger*; sibilation, hissing, hiss, boo, slow handclap, whistle, cat-call; brickbats 851 *ridicule*; ostracism, boycott, bar, colour b., ban, nonadmission 57 *exclusion*; blackball, blacklist, index.

*censure*, dispraise, discommendation, blame, reprehension, impeachment, inculpation 928 *accusation*; home truth, no compliment, left-handed c., back-handed c.; criticism, hostile c., stricture; lambasting, hypercriticism, fault-finding; hostile attack, slashing a., onslaught 712 *attack*; brickbats, bad press, critical review, hostile r., slashing r., slating, panning; open letter, tirade, jeremiad, philippic, diatribe 704 *opposition*; conviction 961 *condemnation*; false accusation 928 *false charge*; slur, slander, aspersions, insinuation, innuendo 926 *calumny*; brand, stigma.

*reproach*, reproaches; recriminations 709 *quarrel*; home truths, invective, vituperation, calling names, bawling out, shouting down 899 *scurrility*; execration 899 *malediction*; personal remarks, aspersion, reflection 921 *indignity*; taunt, sneer 878 *insolence*; sarcasm, irony, satire, biting wit, biting tongue, dig, cut, hit, brickbat 851 *ridicule*; rough side of one's tongue, tongue-lashing, lambasting, hard words, cutting w., bitter w. (see also *reprimand*);

silent reproach, disapproving look, dirty l., black l. 893 *sullenness*.

*reprimand*, remonstrance 762 *deprecation*; stricture, animadversion, reprehension, reprobation; censure, rebuke, flea in one's ear, reproof, snub; rocket, raspberry; piece of one's mind, expression of displeasure, mark of d., black mark; castigation, correction, rap over the knuckles, smack *or* slap on the wrist, box on the ears 963 *punishment*; inculpation, admonition, admonishment, objurgation, tongue-lashing, chiding, talking-to, upbraiding, scolding, rating, slating, strafing, trouncing, lambasting, dressing down, blowing up, roasting, wigging, carpeting, mauvais quart d'heure; talking to, lecture, curtain l., jobation.

*disapprover*, no friend, no admirer, no fan; nonsupporter, nonvoter; damper, wet blanket, spoilsport, misery 834 *moper*; pussyfoot, puritan, rigorist 950 *prude*; attacker, opposer 705 *opponent*; critic, hostile c., captious c., knocker, fault-finder, carper, caviller; reprover, castigator, censurer, censor; satirist, lampooner, mocker 926 *detractor*; brander, stigmatizer; misogynist, misandrist 902 *misanthrope*; grouser, groucher 829 *malcontent*; Eurosceptic.

**Adj.** *disapproving*, unapproving, unable to approve, not amused, unamused; shocked, scandalized; unadmiring, unimpressed; disillusioned 509 *disappointed*; sparing of praise, grudging; silent 582 *taciturn*; disapprobatory, unfavourable, hostile 881 *inimical*; objecting, protesting, clamorous 762 *deprecatory*; reproachful, chiding, scolding, upbraiding, vituperative, lambasting 899 *maledictory*; critical, unflattering, uncomplimentary; withering, hard-hitting, pulling no punches, strongly worded; overcritical, hypercritical, captious, fault-finding, niggling, carping, cavilling; disparaging, defamatory, damaging 926 *detracting*; caustic, sharp, bitter, venomous, trenchant, mordant; sarcastic, sardonic, cynical 851 *derisive*; censorious, holier than thou; blaming, faulting, censuring, reprimanding, recriminative, denunciatory, accusatory, condemning, damning, damnatory 928 *accusing*.

*disapproved*, unapproved, blacklisted, blackballed 607 *rejected*; unsatisfactory, found wanting 636 *insufficient*; ploughed, plucked, failed 728 *unsuccessful*; cancelled 752 *abrogated*; deleted, censored 550 *obliterated*; fallen foul of, out of favour, fallen from f., in one's bad books, under a cloud, in the wilderness; unpraised, dispraised, criticized, decried, run down, slandered, calumniated, denigrated; lectured, henpecked, nagged, reprimanded,

scolded, chidden; before the beak, on the mat, on the carpet; unregretted, unlamented, unbewailed, unpitied 861 *disliked*; hooted, booed, hissed, hissed off the stage; discredited, disowned, out; in bad odour, in one's bad books 867 *disreputable*.

*blameworthy*, not good enough, too bad; blamable, exceptionable, open to criticism, blameworthy, censurable, condemnable 645 *bad*; reprehensible, dishonourable, unjustifiable 867 *discreditable*; unpraiseworthy, uncommendable, not to be recommended, not to be thought of; reprobate, culpable, to blame 928 *accusable*.

**Vb.** *disapprove*, not admire, hold no brief for, fail to appreciate, have no regard for, have no praise for, not think much of, think little of, take a dim view of; think the worse of, think ill of 922 *despise*; not pass, fail, plough; return 607 *reject*; disallow 757 *prohibit*; cancel 752 *abrogate*; censor 550 *obliterate*; withhold approval, look grave, shake one's head, not hold with 489 *dissent*; disfavour, reprehend, lament, deplore 830 *regret*; abhor, reprobate 861 *dislike*; wash one's hands of, turn one's back on, disown, look askance, avoid, ignore; keep at a distance, draw the line, ostracize, ban, bar, blacklist 57 *exclude*; protest, tut-tut, sniff, remonstrate, object, take exception to, demur 762 *deprecate*; discountenance, show disapproval, exclaim, shout down, bawl d., hoot, boo, bay, heckle, hiss, whistle, give a slow handclap, give the bird, drive off the stage; hand out brickbats, throw mud, throw rotten eggs, throw bricks *or* stones 712 *lapidate*; hound, chase, mob, lynch; make a face, grimace, make a moue, make mouths at, spit; look black 893 *be sullen*; look daggers 891 *be angry*.

*not recommend*, discommend, give no marks *or* points to, damn with faint praise, damn, dispraise 961 *condemn*; criticize, fault, find f., pick holes, niggle, crab, cavil, carp, nitpick, depreciate, run down, belittle 926 *detract*; oppose, tilt at, shoot at, throw the book at 712 *attack*; weigh in, pitch into, hit out at, let fly, lay into, lam into, savage, maul, slash, slate, lambast, scourge, flay, put the boot in; inveigh, thunder, fulminate, storm against, rage a. 61 *rampage*; shout down, cry shame, slang, call names; gird, rail, revile, abuse, heap abuse, pour vitriol, objurgate, anathematize, execrate 899 *curse*; vilify, blacken, denigrate 926 *defame*; stigmatize, brand, pillory; expose, denounce, recriminate 928 *accuse*; sneer, twit, taunt 921 *not respect*.

*reprove*, reprehend, reproach, rebuke, administer a r., snub, rebuff, send away with a flea in the ear; call to order, caution, wag one's finger, read the Riot Act 664 *warn*; book, give one a black mark; censure, reprimand, take to task, rap over the knuckles, smack *or* slap the wrist, box the ears; tick off, tell off, have one's head for, carpet, have on the carpet, haul over the coals, send before the beak; remonstrate, expostulate, admonish, castigate, chide, correct; lecture, read one a lecture, give one a talking to, give one a wigging, give one a dressing-down, lambast, trounce, roast, browbeat, blow up, tear strips off, come down hard on, come down on like a ton of bricks, chastise 963 *punish*.

*blame*, find fault, carp, cavil, nitpick, pick holes in; get at, henpeck 709 *bicker*; reprehend, hold to blame, pick on, put the blame on, hold responsible; throw the first stone, inculpate, incriminate, complain against, impute, impeach, charge, criminate 928 *accuse*; round on, return the charge, recriminate 714 *retaliate*; think the worst of 961 *condemn*.

*reprobate*, reproach, heap reproaches on; upbraid, slate, rate, berate, rail, slag, strafe, shend, lambast, revile, abuse, denigrate, blackguard 899 *curse*; go for, inveigh against, bawl out, scold, tonguelash, lash, give the rough edge of one's tongue, rail in good set terms against, give one a piece of one's mind, give one what for, give it to one straight from the shoulder, give to one straight, not mince matters, not pull one's punches, let it rip.

*incur blame*, take the blame, take the rap, carry the can, catch it; be held responsible, have to answer for; be open to criticism, blot one's copy book, get a bad name 867 *lose repute*; be up on a charge, be carpeted, be up before the beak, be court-martialled, stand accused; stand corrected; be an example, be a scandal, scandalize, shock, revolt 861 *cause dislike*.

**Adv.** *disapprovingly*, reluctantly, unwillingly, against one's better judgment, under protest; reproachfully, complainingly.

## 925 Flattery

**N.** *flattery*, cajolery, wheedling, getting round, taffy, blarney, blandiloquence, blandishments, sweet talk; flannel, soft soap, soft sawder, salve, lip-salve, rosewater, incense, adulation; voice of the charmer, honeyed words, sweet nothings 889 *endearment*; compliment, pretty speeches, bouquets; coquetry, winning ways; fawning, backscratching; assentation, obsequiousness, flunkeyism, sycophancy, toadying 879 *servility*; unctuousness, smarminess, euphemism, insincerity, hypocrisy, tongue in cheek, lip-homage 542 *sham*.

*flatterer*, adulator, cajoler, wheedler; coquette, charmer; tout, puffer, hyper, promoter, booster, claqueur, claque 923 *commender*; courtier, yes-man 488 *assenter*; creep, fawner, backscratcher, sycophant, parasite, minion, hanger-on 879 *toady*; fair-weather friend, hypocrite 545 *deceiver*.

**Adj.** *flattering*, overpraising, overdone 546 *exaggerated*; boosting, puffing, hyping, overpromoting; complimentary, overcomplimentary, full of compliments; fulsome, adulatory; sugary, saccharine; cajoling, wheedling, coaxing, blarneying, blandandering, blandiloquent; mealymouthed, glozing, canting; smooth-tongued, honey-t., bland; smooth, oily, unctuous, soapy, slimy, smarmy; obsequious, all over one, courtly, fawning, crawling, back-scratching, sycophantic 879 *servile*; specious, plausible, beguiling, ingratiating, insinuating; lulling, soothing; vote-catching, vote-snatching; false, insincere, tongue-in-cheek, unreliable 541 *hypocritical*.

**Vb.** *flatter*, deal in flattery, have kissed the Blarney Stone; compliment, hand out bouquets 923 *praise*; overpraise, overdo it, lard it on, lay it on thick, lay it on with a trowel, not spare one's blushes; puff, hype, promote, boost, cry up 482 *overrate*; adulate, burn incense to, assail with flattery, turn one's head 873 *make conceited*; butter up, soften up, sawder, soft-soap; blarney, blandander, flannel; sweet-talk, sugar; wheedle, coax, cajole, coo; lull, soothe, beguile 542 *deceive*; humour, jolly along, pander to; gild the pill, sugar the p., make things pleasant, tell people what they want to hear; blandish, smooth, smarm; press the flesh, make much of, be all over one 889 *caress*; fawn, fawn on, cultivate, court, pay court to, play the courtier, massage one's ego; smirk 835 *smile*; scratch one's back, backscratch, curry favour, make up to, suck up to; truckle to, toady to, pander to 879 *be servile*; insinuate oneself, worm oneself into favour, get on the right side of, creep into one's good graces; flatter oneself, have a swelled head 873 *be vain*.

**Adv.** *flatteringly*, speciously; ad captandum.

## 926 Detraction

**N.** *detraction*, faint praise, two cheers, understatement 483 *underestimation*; criticism, hostile c., destructive c., flak, bad review, slating r., bad press 924 *disapprobation*; onslaught 712 *attack*; vivisection, hatchet job; impeachment 928 *accusation*; exposure, bad light 867 *disrepute*; decrial, disparagement, depreciation, running down; lowering, derogation; slighting language, scorn 922 *contempt*;

envenomed tongue 899 *malediction*; contumely, obloquy, vilification, abuse, invective 899 *scurrility*; calumniation, defamation, traducement 543 *untruth*; backbiting, cattiness, spite 898 *malevolence*; aspersion, reflection, snide remark (see also *calumny*); whisper, innuendo, insinuation, imputation, whispering campaign; smear campaign, mud-slinging, smirching, denigration, character assassination; brand, stigma; muck-raking, scandalmongering; nil admirari, disillusionment, cynicism 865 *lack of wonder*.

*calumny*, slander, libel, aspersion, false report, roorback 543 *untruth*; a defamation, defamatory remark, damaging report; smear, smear-word, dirty word 867 *slur*; offensive remark, personal r., personality, insult, taunt, dig at, brick-bat 921 *indignity*; scoff, sarcasm 851 *ridicule*; sneer, sniff; caricature 552 *misrepresentation*; skit, lampoon, pasquinade, squib 851 *satire*; scandal, scandalous talk, malicious gossip, bad mouth.

*detractor*, decrier, disparager, depreciator, slighter, despiser; nonadmirer, debunker, deflater, cynic; mocker, scoffer, satirizer, satirist, lampooner; castigator, denouncer, reprover, censurer, censor 924 *disapprover*; no respecter of persons, no flatterer, candid friend, candid critic; critic, hostile c., destructive c., attacker; arch-critic, chief accuser, impeacher 928 *accuser*; captious critic, knocker, Zoilus; fault-finder, carper, caviller, niggler, nitpicker, hair-splitter; heckler, barracker 702 *hinderer*; Philistine 847 *vulgarian*.

*defamer*, calumniator, traducer, destroyer of reputations, hatchet man; smircher, smearer, slanderer, libeller; backbiter, gossiper, scandalmonger, muck-raker; gossip columnist, gutter press, chequebook journalist; denigrator, mudslinger; brander, stigmatizer; vituperator, reviler; scold, Thersites 892 *shrew*; poison pen.

**Adj.** *detracting*, derogatory, pejorative; disparaging, deprecatory, decrying, crying down, slighting, contemptuous 922 *despising*; whispering, insinuating, blackening, denigratory, mud-slinging, smearing; compromising, damaging; scandalous, calumnious, calumniatory, defamatory, slanderous, libellous; insulting 921 *disrespectful*; contumelious, injurious, abusive, scurrilous 899 *cursing*; shrewish, scolding, caustic, bitter, venomous, denunciatory, castigatory, accusatory, blaming 924 *disapproving*; sarcastic, mocking, scoffing, sneering, cynical, snide 851 *derisive*; catty, bitchy, spiteful 898 *malevolent*; unflattering, candid 573 *plain*.

**Vb.** *detract*, derogate, deprecate, disparage, run down, sell short; debunk, deflate, punc-

ture, cut down to size 921 *not respect*; minimize 483 *underestimate*; belittle, slight, dis *or* diss (sl) 922 *hold cheap*; sneer at, sniff at 922 *despise*; decry, cry down, rubbish, damn with faint praise, fail to appreciate 924 *disapprove*; find nothing to praise, criticize, knock, badmouth, slam, rip (sl), slaughter (sl), fault, find f., pick holes in, slash, slate, pull to pieces, tear to ribbons 924 *dispraise*; caricature, guy 552 *misrepresent*; lampoon, dip one's pen in gall 851 *satirize*; scoff, mock 851 *ridicule*; make catty remarks, get in a dig at; whisper, insinuate, cast aspersions.

*defame*, dishonour, damage, compromise, scandalize, degrade, lower, put to shame 867 *shame*; give a dog a bad name, lower *or* lessen one's reputation, destroy one's good name; denounce, expose, pillory, stigmatize, brand 928 *accuse*; calumniate, libel, slander, traduce, malign; vilify, denigrate, blacken, tarnish, sully; reflect upon, put in a bad light; speak ill of, speak evil, gossip, badmouth, make scandal, talk about, backbite, talk behind one's back; discredit 486 *cause doubt*; smear, start a smear campaign, besmear, smirch, besmirch, spatter, bespatter, throw mud, fling dirt, drag in the gutter 649 *make unclean*; hound, witchhunt 619 *hunt*; look for scandal, smell evil, muck-rake, rake about in the gutter 619 *pursue*.

### 927 Vindication

**N.** *vindication*, restoration, rehabilitation 787 *restitution*; triumph of justice, right triumphant, wrong righted, right asserted, truth established; exoneration, exculpation, clearance 960 *acquittal*; justification, good grounds, just cause, every excuse; compurgation, apologetics, self-defence, apologia, defence, legal d., good d., successful d.; alibi, plea, excuse, whitewash, gloss 614 *pretext*; fair excuse, good e., just e. 494 *truth*; partial excuse, extenuation, palliation, mitigation, mitigating circumstance, extenuating c., palliative 468 *qualification*; counterargument 479 *confutation*; reply, reply for the defence, rebuttal 460 *rejoinder*; recrimination, tu quoque, countercharge, charge retorted; justifiable charge, true bill 928 *accusation*; bringing to book, poetic justice, just punishment 963 *punishment*.

*vindicator*, punisher 910 *avenger*; apologist, advocate, defender, champion; justifier, excuser, whitewasher; compurgator, oathhelper, character witness 466 *witness*; self-defender, defendant 928 *accused person*.

**Adj.** *vindicating*, vindicatory, vindicative, avenging; apologetic, exculpatory, justifying, defending; extenuatory, mitigating, palliative.

*vindicable*, justifiable, maintainable, defensible, arguable; specious, plausible; allowable, warrantable, unobjectionable 756 *permitted*; excusable, having some excuse, pardonable, forgivable, venial, expiable; vindicated, justified, within one's rights, not guilty 935 *innocent*; justified by the event 494 *true*.

**Vb.** *vindicate*, revenge 910 *avenge*; do justice to, give the devil his due 915 *grant claims*; set right, restore, rehabilitate 787 *restitute*; maintain, speak up for, argue f., contend f., advocate 475 *argue*; undertake to prove, bear out, confirm, make good, prove the truth of, prove 478 *demonstrate*; champion, stand up for, stick up for 713 *defend*; support, offer moral support 703 *patronize*.

*justify*, warrant, justify by the event, give grounds for, provide justification, furnish an excuse, give a handle, give one cause; put one in the right, put one in the clear, clear, clear one's name, free from blame, exonerate, exculpate 960 *acquit*; give colour to, colour, whitewash, varnish, gloss; salve one's conscience, justify oneself, defend o. 614 *plead*; plead one's own cause, say in defence, rebut the charge, plead ignorance.

*extenuate*, excuse, make excuses for, make allowances; palliate, mitigate, soften, mince one's words, soft-pedal, slur, slur over, play down, downplay, gloss, gloss over, varnish, whitewash; take the will for the deed 736 *be lenient*.

## 928 Accusation

**N.** *accusation*, complaint, charge, home truth; censure, blame, stricture 924 *reproach*; challenge 711 *defiance*; inculpation, crimination; countercharge, recrimination, tu quoque argument 460 *rejoinder*; twit, taunt 921 *indignity*; imputation, allegation, information, delation, denunciation; plaint, suit, action 959 *litigation*; prosecution, impeachment, arraignment, indictment, citation, summons; bill of indictment, true bill; gravamen, substance of a charge, main c.; case, case to answer, case for the prosecution 475 *reasons*; items in the indictment, particular charge, count 466 *evidence*.

*false charge*, faked c., cooked-up c., trumped-up c., put-up job, frame-up; false information, perjured testimony, hostile evidence, suspect e., false e.; counterfeit evidence, plant; illegal prosecution, vexatious p.; lie, libel, slander, scandal, stigma 926 *calumny*.

*accuser*, complainant, plaintiff, pursuer, petitioner, appellant, libellant, litigant; challenger, denouncer, charger; grass, supergrass, nark, copper's n. 524 *informer*; common informer, delator, relator; impeacher, indicter, prosecutor, public p., procurator fiscal; libeller,

slanderer, calumniator, stigmatizer 926 *defamer*; hostile witness 881 *enemy*; the finger of suspicion.

*accused person*, the accused, prisoner, prisoner at the bar; defendant, respondent, corespondent; culprit; suspect, victim of suspicion, marked man; slandered person, libellee, victim.

**Adj.** *accusing*, alleging, accusatory, denunciatory, criminatory, recriminatory; incriminating, pointing to; imputative, stigmatizing, damnatory, condemnatory; tale-bearing, clyping, sycophantic, calumnious, defamatory 926 *detracting*; suspicious 924 *disapproving*.

*accused*, informed against, reported a., complained a., suspect; in the frame, under suspicion, under a cloud; denounced, impeached etc. vb.; charged, up on a charge, up before the beak, prosecuted, hauled up, had up, booked, summoned; awaiting trial, on bail, on remand, remanded; slandered, libelled, calumniated 924 *disapproved*.

*accusable*, imputable; actionable, suable, chargeable, justiciable, liable to prosecution; inexcusable, unpardonable, unforgivable, indefensible, unjustifiable 924 *blameworthy*; without excuse, without defence, condemnable 934 *heinous*; undefended 661 *vulnerable*.

**Vb.** *accuse*, challenge 711 *defy*; taunt, twit 878 *be insolent*; point, point a finger at, finger, cast the first stone, throw in one's teeth, reproach 924 *reprove*; stigmatize, brand, pillory, gibbet, cast a slur on, cast aspersions, calumniate 926 *defame*; impute, charge with, saddle w., tax w., hold against, lay to one's charge, lay at one's door, hold responsible, make r.; pick on, fix on, hold to blame, put the blame on, pin on, stick on, bring home to 924 *blame*; point at, expose, show up, name, name names 526 *divulge*; denounce, inform against, tell, tell on, clype, peach on, blab, squeal, sing, rat on, split on, turn Queen's evidence 524 *inform*; involve, implicate, inculpate, incriminate, name and shame; recriminate, countercharge, rebut the charge, retort the c., turn the tables upon 479 *confute*; make one a scapegoat, shift the blame; accuse oneself, admit the charge, plead guilty 526 *confess*; involve oneself, implicate o., lay oneself open, put oneself out of court.

*indict*, impeach, arraign, inform against, complain a., lodge a complaint, lay information against; complain, charge, bring a charge, file charges, swear an indictment 959 *litigate*; book, cite, summon, serve with a writ, prosecute, sue; bring an action, bring a suit, bring a case: haul up, send before the beak, have up, put on trial, put in the dock; throw the book at 712 *attack*; charge falsely, lie against 541 *be false*; frame, trump up a charge, cook the evidence, use false e., fake the e., plant the e. 541 *fake*.

**Adv.** *accusingly*, censoriously.

## 929 Probity

**N.** *probity*, rectitude, uprightness, goodness, sanctity 933 *virtue*; stainlessness 950 *purity*; good character, moral fibre, honesty, soundness, incorruptibility, integrity; high character, nobleness, nobility; honourableness, decent feelings, finer f., tender conscience; honour, personal h., sense of h., honour among thieves, omertà, principles, high p.; conscientiousness 768 *observance*; scrupulousness, scrupulosity, punctiliousness, meticulousness 457 *carefulness*; ingenuousness, single-heartedness; trustworthiness, reliability, sense of responsibility; truthfulness 540 *veracity*; candour, plainspeaking 573 *plainness*; sincerity, good faith, bona fides 494 *truth*; fidelity, faith, troth, faithfulness, constancy 739 *loyalty*; clean hands, clear conscience 935 *innocence*; impartiality, fairness, sportsmanship 913 *justice*; respectability 866 *repute*; gentlemanliness, ladylikeness, chivalry; principle, point of honour, punctilio, code, code of honour, bushido 913 *right*; court of justice, court of honour, field of h.

*honourable person*, honest p., man *or* woman of honour, man *or* woman of his/her word, sound character, trusty soul 937 *good person*; true lady, perfect gentleman, true knight, preux chevalier, galant homme; Galahad, Parsifal; fair fighter, clean f., fair player, good loser, sportsman, sportswoman, sport, good sport, trump, brick, good sort, true Brit.

**Adj.** *honourable*, upright, erect, of integrity, of honour 933 *virtuous*; correct, strict; law-abiding, honest, strictly h., on the level; principled, high-p., above-board, on the up-and-up; scrupulous, conscientious, soul-searching; incorruptible, unbribable, not to be bought off; incorrupt, immaculate 935 *innocent*; stainless, unstained, untarnished, unsullied 648 *clean*; noble, high-minded, pure-m. 950 *pure*; ingenuous, unsuspicious, guileless, unworldly 699 *artless*; good, straight, straight as a die, square, on the square, one hundred per cent; fair, fair-dealing, equitable, impartial 913 *just*; sporting, sportsmanlike, playing the game; gentlemanly, chivalrous, knightly, sans peur et sans reproche; jealous of one's honour, careful of one's reputation, respectable 866 *reputable*; saintly 979 *pious*.

*trustworthy*, creditworthy, reliable, dependable, tried, tested, proven; trusty, true-hearted, true-blue, true to the core, sure, staunch, single-hearted, constant, unchanging, faithful, loyal 739 *obedient*; responsible, duteous, dutiful 768 *observant*; conscientious, religious, scrupulous, meticulous, punctilious 457 *careful*; candid, frank, open, open and above-board, open-hearted, transparent, ingenuous, without guile, guileless 494 *true*; straightforward, truthful, truth-speaking, as good as one's word 540 *veracious*; unperjured, unperfidious, untreacherous.

**Vb.** *be honourable*, – chivalrous etc. adj.; behave well, behave like a gentleman 933 *be virtuous*; deal honourably, play fair, play the game, stick to the rules, go by the book, shoot straight 913 *be just*; be a sport, be a good s., be a brick, turn up trumps; preserve one's honour, fear God 979 *be pious*; keep faith, keep one's promise, be as good as one's word; hate a lie, stick to the truth, speak the truth and shame the devil 540 *be truthful*; go straight, reform, turn over a new leaf 654 *get better*.

## 930 Improbity

**N.** *improbity*, dishonesty; lack of probity, lack of conscience, lack of principle; suppleness, flexibility, laxity; unconscientiousness 456 *inattention*; unscrupulousness, opportunism; insincerity, disingenuousness, unstraightforwardness, untrustworthiness, unreliability, undependability, untruthfulness 541 *falsehood*; unfairness, partiality, bias 914 *injustice*; shuffling, slipperiness, snakiness, artfulness; fishiness, suspiciousness, shadiness, obliquity, twistiness, deviousness, crookedness, crooked paths; corruption, sleaze, sleaze factor, corruptibility, venality, bribability, graft, palm-greasing, jobbery, nepotism, simony, barratry; Tammanyism; baseness, shabbiness, abjectness, abjection, debasement, shamefulness, disgrace, dishonour, shame 867 *disrepute*; worthlessness, good-for-nothingness, villainousness, villainy, knavery, roguery, rascality, spivvery, skulduggery, racketeering, black market, under-the-counter dealings; criminality, crime, complicity, aiding and abetting 954 *lawbreaking*; turpitude, moral t. 934 *wickedness*.

*perfidy*, perfidiousness, faithlessness, unfaithfulness, infidelity, unfaith 543 *untruth*; bad faith, Punic f., questionable f.; divided allegiance, wavering loyalty, sitting on the fence, disloyalty 738 *disobedience*; running with the hare and hunting with the hounds, double-dealing, double-crossing, Judas kiss 541 *duplicity*; volte face, U-turn 603 *tergiversation*; defection, desertion 918 *undutifulness*; betrayal, treachery, stab in the back, sell-out; treason, high t. 738 *sedition*; fifth column, Trojan horse; breach of faith, broken word, broken faith, broken promise, breach of p., oath forsworn, scrap of paper; cry of treason, Perfide Albion!

*foul play*, dirty trick, stab in the back; not playing the game, foul, hitting below the belt 914 *wrong*; professional foul 623 *contrivance*; trick, shuffle, chicane, chicanery 542 *trickery*; practice, sharp p., heads I win tails you lose; fishy transaction, dirty work, job, deal, ramp, racket; under-the-counter dealing, fiddle, wangle, manipulation, gerrymandering, hanky-panky, monkey business; tax evasion 620 *avoidance*; malversation 788 *peculation*; crime, felony 954 *lawbreaking*.

**Adj.** *dishonest*, not on the level 914 *wrong*; 'economical with the truth' (see quotation at 542 *deceiving*), lying 542 *deceiving*; not particular, unfastidious, unsqueamish; unprincipled, unscrupulous, conscienceless; shameless, dead to honour, lost to shame; unethical, immoral 934 *wicked*; shaky, untrustworthy, unreliable, undependable, not to be trusted; supple, flexible 603 *tergiversating*; disingenuous, unstraightforward, untruthful, uncandid 543 *untrue*; two-faced, insincere 541 *hypocritical*; creeping, crawling; tricky, artful, dodging, opportunist, slippery, snaky, foxy 698 *cunning*; shifty, shuffling, prevaricating 518 *equivocal*; designing, scheming; sneaking, underhand 523 *latent*; up to something, on the fiddle, wangling; not straight, unstraight, indirect, bent, crooked, devious, oblique, tortuous, winding 251 *labyrinthine*; insidious, dark, sinister; shady, fishy, suspicious, doubtful, questionable; fraudulent 542 *spurious*; illicit 954 *illegal*; foul 645 *bad*; unclean 649 *dirty*; mean, shabby, dishonourable, infamous 867 *disreputable*; derogatory, unworthy, undignified; inglorious, ignominious 867 *degrading*; ignoble, unchivalrous, ungentlemanly; unsporting, unsportsmanlike, unfair.

*rascally*, criminal, felonious 954 *lawless*; knavish, picaresque, spivvish; infamous, blackguard, villainous; scurvy, scabby, arrant, low, low-down, base, vile, rotten, currish; mean, shabby, paltry, pettifogging, abject, wretched, contemptible 639 *unimportant*; time-serving, crawling 925 *flattering*.

*venal*, corruptible, purchasable, bribable, hireling, mercenary 792 *bought*; palm-greasing, corrupt, jobbing, grafting, simoniacal, nepotistic; barratrous, selling justice.

*perfidious*, treacherous, unfaithful, inconstant, faithless 541 *false*; double-dealing, double-crossing, time-serving 541 *hypocritical*; disloyal 603 *tergiversating*; false-hearted,

guileful, traitorous, treasonous, treasonable, disloyal, untrue 738 *disobedient*; plotting, scheming, intriguing 623 *planning*; insidious, dark, Machiavellian; cheating 542 *deceiving*; fraudulent 542 *spurious*.

**Vb.** *be dishonest*, – dishonourable etc. adj.; have no morals, forget one's principles, yield to temptation, be lost to shame; lack honesty, live dishonestly, live by one's wits, lead a picaresque existence, lead a life of crime 954 *be illegal*; fiddle, finagle, wangle, gerrymander, start a racket, racketeer; defalcate, peculate 788 *defraud*; cheat, swindle 542 *deceive*; betray, play false, do the dirty on, stab in the back; play double, run with the hare and hunt with the hounds, double-cross 541 *dissemble*; fawn 925 *flatter*; break faith, break one's word, go back on one's promises, tell lies 541 *be false*; shuffle, dodge, prevaricate 518 *be equivocal*; sell out, sell down the river 603 *change one's allegiance*; sink into crime, sell one's honour 867 *lose repute*; smack of dishonesty, smell fishy.

**Adv.** *dishonestly*; shamelessly, by fair means or foul; treacherously, mala fide; knavishly, villainously, without regard for honesty.

## 931 Disinterestedness

**N.** *disinterestedness*, impartiality, lack of bias 913 *justice*; unselfishness, unpossessiveness, selflessness, no thought for self, self-effacement 872 *humility*; self-control, self-abnegation, self-denial, self-surrender, self-sacrifice, self-immolation, self-devotion, martyrdom; rising above oneself, heroism, stoicism, keeping a stiff upper lip 855 *courage*; loftiness of purpose, elevation of soul, high principles, idealism, ideals, high i.; sublimity, elevation, loftiness, nobility, magnanimity; knightliness, chivalry, knight-errantry, quixotry; generosity, munificence, liberality, liberalism 897 *benevolence*; purity of motive, dedication, consecration, labour of love; loyalty, faith, faithfulness 929 *probity*; patriotism 901 *philanthropy*; selflessness, altruism, thought for others, consideration, considerateness, kindness 884 *courtesy*; compassion 905 *pity*; charity 887 *love*; lack of interest 454 *incuriosity*.

**Adj.** *disinterested*, impartial, without self-interest, without bias 913 *just*; selfcontrolled, stoical 942 *temperate*; incorruptible, uncorrupted, unbought, unbribed, honest 929 *honourable*; self-effacing, modest 872 *humble*; unjealous, unpossessive, unenvious, ungrudging; unselfish, selfless, self-forgetful; self-denying, self-sacrificing, ready to die for, martyr-like; devoted, dedicated, consecrated; loyal, faithful; heroic 855 *courageous*;

thoughtful, considerate, kind 884 *courteous*; altruistic, philanthropic, patriotic 897 *benevolent*; pure, unmixed; undesigning; sacrificial, unmercenary, for love, non-profitmaking; idealistic, quixotic, high-minded, lofty, elevated, sublime, noble, great-hearted, magnanimous, chivalrous, knightly; generous, liberal, unsparing 781 *giving*; uninterested 45 *incurious*.

**Vb.** *be disinterested*, – unselfish etc. adj.; sacrifice, make a s., sacrifice oneself, devote o., live for, die f.; do as one would be done by, think of others, put oneself last, take a back seat 872 *be humble*; rise above petty considerations, rise above oneself, surrender personal considerations; have no axe to grind, have nothing to gain, have no ulterior motive, do for its own sake.

## 932 Selfishness

**N.** *selfishness*, self-consideration, self-love, self-admiration, narcissism, self-worship, self-approbation, self-praise 873 *vanity*; self-pity, self-indulgence, ego trip 943 *intemperance*; self-absorption, egocentrism, egocentricity, egomania; egoism, egotism, individualism, particularism; self-preservation, everyone for themselves; axe to grind, personal considerations, personal motives, private ends, personal advantage, selfish benefit; self-seeking, self-serving, self-aggrandizement, self-interest, concern for number one, looking after number one; no thought for others, 'I'm all right, Jack'; charity that begins at home, cupboard love; illiberality, no magnanimity, mean-mindedness, pettiness, paltriness; meanness, miserliness, niggardliness 816 *parsimony*; greed, acquisitiveness, affluenza 816 *avarice*; possessiveness 911 *jealousy*; worldliness, wordly wisdom; 'heads I win tails you lose' 914 *injustice*; careerism, career-mindedness, selfish ambition, naked a., ruthless a.; power politics.

*egotist*, egoist, self-centred person, narcissist 873 *vain person*; particularist, individualist, mass of selfishness; self-seeker, careerist, arriviste, go-getter, adventurer, gold-digger, fortune-hunter; money-grubber, miser 816 *niggard*; monopolist, dog in the manger, hog, road h.; opportunist, time-server, worldling.

**Adj.** *selfish*, egocentric, self-centred, self-absorbed, wrapped up in oneself; egoistic, egotistic, egotistical; personal, individualistic, concerned with number one; self-interested, self-regarding, self-considering, self-seeking; self-indulgent 943 *intemperate*; self-loving, self-admiring, narcissistic 873 *vain*; not altruistic, with an interest; unphilanthropic, unneighbourly; unpatriotic; uncharitable, unsympathetic, cold-hearted 898 *unkind*; unhandsome, mean, mean-minded, petty, paltry; illiberal, ungenerous, niggardly 816 *parsimonious*; acquisitive, money-grubbing, mercenary 816 *avaricious*; venal 930 *dishonest*; covetous 912 *envious*; hoggish, hogging, monopolistic 859 *greedy*; possessive, dog-in-the-manger; competitive 911 *jealous*; self-serving, designing, axe-grinding; go-getting, on the make, on the gravy train, gold-digging, opportunist, time-serving, careerist; unidealistic, materialistic, mundane, worldly, earthly, worldly-minded, worldly-wise.

**Vb.** *be selfish*, – egoistic etc. adj.; put oneself first, think only of oneself, take care of number one; love oneself, indulge o., spoil o., look after o., coddle o., cosset o., have only oneself to please; feather one's nest, look out for oneself, have an eye to the main chance, know on which side one's bread is buttered; keep for oneself, hang onto, hog, monopolize, be a dog in the manger 778 *retain*; have personal motives, have private ends, have an axe to grind, have one's own game to play; pursue one's interests, advance one's own i., sacrifice the interests of others.

**Adv.** *selfishly*, self-regardingly, only for oneself; on the make, for profit; ungenerously, illiberally; for one's own sake, from personal motives, for private ends; jealously, possessively.

## 933 Virtue

**N.** *virtue*, virtuousness, moral strength, moral tone; goodness, sheer g.; saintliness, holiness, spirituality, odour of sanctity 979 *sanctity*; righteousness 913 *justice*; uprightness, rectitude, moral r., character, integrity, principles, high principle, honour, personal h., honour among thieves, omertà 929 *probity*; perfect honour, stainlessness, irreproachability; avoidance of guilt, guiltlessness 935 *innocence*; morality, ethics 917 *morals*; sexual morality, temperance, chastity 950 *purity*; straight and narrow path, virtuous conduct, christian c., good behaviour, well-spent life, duty done; good conscience, clear c., conscious rectitude; self-improvement, moral rearmament.

*virtues*, cardinal v., moral v., moral laws; theological virtues, faith, hope, charity; natural virtues, prudence, justice, temperance, fortitude; qualities, fine q., saving quality, saving grace; a virtue, good fault, fault on the right side; worth, merit, desert; excellence, perfections 646 *perfection*; nobleness, magnanimity, altruism, unselfishness 931 *disinterestedness*; idealism, ideals; self-control 942 *temperance*.

**Adj.** *virtuous*, moral 917 *ethical*; good, good

as gold 644 *excellent*; stainless, blemish-free, without a spot on one's character 950 *pure*; guiltless 935 *innocent*; irreproachable, above reproach, impeccable, above temptation 646 *perfect*; saint-like, seraphic, angelic, saintly, holy 979 *sanctified*; principled, high-p., well-p., right-minded, 'on the side of the angels' (see quotation at 913 *just*) 913 *right*; righteous 913 *just*; upright, sterling, honest 929 *honourable*; duteous, dutiful 739 *obedient*; unselfish 931 *disinterested*; generous, magnanimous, idealistic, well-intentioned, philanthropic 897 *benevolent*; sober 942 *temperate*; chaste, virginal; proper, edifying, improving, exemplary; elevated, sublimated; meritorious, worthy, praiseworthy, commendable 923 *approved*.

**Vb.** *be virtuous*, – good etc. adj.; have all the virtues, be a shining light, qualify for sainthood 644 *be good*; behave, be on one's good *or* best behaviour; practise virtue, resist temptation, command one's passions 942 *be temperate*; rise superior to, have a soul above; keep to the straight and narrow path, follow one's conscience, 'walk humbly with one's God', 'fight the good fight';

> He hath shewed thee, O man, what is good; and what doth the Lord require of thee, but to do justly, and to love mercy, and to walk humbly with thy God?
> Bible, Micah

> Fight the good fight of faith, lay hold on eternal life, whereunto thou art also called, . . .
> Bible, St Paul, First Letter to Timothy

> I have fought a good fight, I have finished my course, I have kept the faith.
> Bible, St Paul, Second Letter to Timothy

discharge one's obligations 917 *do one's duty*; go straight, keep s. 929 *be honourable*; love good, hate wrong 913 *be just*; hear no evil, see no evil, speak no evil; edify, set a good example, be a shining e., shame the devil 644 *do good*.

**Adv.** *virtuously*, well, with merit; righteously, purely, innocently; holily.

## 934 Wickedness

**N.** *wickedness*, principle of evil 645 *badness*; Devil, cloven hoof 969 *Satan*; fallen nature, Old Adam; unrighteousness, iniquity, sinfulness, sin 914 *wrong*; peccability, loss of innocence 936 *guilt*; ungodliness 980 *impiety*; ignorance of good, no morals; amorality, amoralism 860 *indifference*; hardness of heart 898 *malevolence*; wilfulness, stubbornness, obduracy, obdurateness 602 *obstinacy*; waywardness, naughtiness, bad behaviour 738 *disobedience*; immorality, turpitude, moral t.; loose morals, carnality, profligacy 951 *impurity*;

demoralization, degeneration, degeneracy, vitiation, degradation 655 *deterioration*; recidivism, backsliding 603 *tergiversation*; vice, corruption, depravity 645 *badness*; flagitiousness, heinousness, shamelessness, flagrancy; bad character, viciousness, unworthiness, baseness, vileness; villainy, knavery, roguery 930 *foul play*; laxity, lack of principle, dishonesty 930 *improbity*; crime, criminality 954 *law-breaking*; devilry, hellishness 898 *inhumanity*; devil worship, diabolism 982 *idolatry*; shame, scandal, abomination, enormity, infamy 867 *disrepute*; infamous conduct, misbehaviour, delinquency, wrongdoing, evil-doing, transgression, evil courses, wicked ways, career of crime; 'primrose path' (see quotation at 655 *deterioration*), slippery slope; low life, criminal world, underworld, demi-monde; den of vice, sink of iniquity 649 *sink*.

*vice*, fault, demerit, unworthiness; human weakness, moral w., infirmity, frailty, human f., foible 163 *weakness*; imperfection, shortcoming, defect, deficiency, limitation, failing, flaw, fatal f., weak point, weak side, weakness of the flesh; transgression, trespass, injury, outrage, enormity 914 *wrong*; sin, besetting s., capital s., deadly s.; seven deadly sins, pride, covetousness, lust, anger, gluttony, envy, sloth; venial sin, small fault, slight transgression, peccadillo, scrape; impropriety, indecorum 847 *bad taste* offence 936 *guilty act*; crime, felony, deadly crime, capital c., hanging matter 954 *illegality*.

**Adj.** *wicked*, virtueless, unvirtuous, immoral; amoral, amoralistic 860 *indifferent*; lax, unprincipled, unscrupulous, conscienceless 930 *dishonest*; unblushing, hardened, callous, shameless, brazen, brass-necked, flaunting; ungodly, irreligious, profane 980 *impious*; iniquitous, unrighteous 914 *unjust*; evil 645 *bad*; evil-minded, bad-hearted, black-hearted 898 *malevolent*; evil-doing 898 *maleficent*; misbehaving, bad, naughty 738 *disobedient*; weak (see also *frail*); peccant, erring, sinning, transgressing; sinful, full of sin 936 *guilty*; unworthy, undeserving, unmeritorious; graceless, not in a state of grace, reprobate; hopeless, incorrigible, irreclaimable, unredeemed, irredeemable; accursed, godforsaken; hellish, infernal, devilish, fiendish, Mephistophelian, satanic 969 *diabolic*.

*vicious*, steeped in vice, sunk in iniquity; good-for-nothing, ne'er-do-well; hopeless, past praying for; punk, worthless, unworthy, meritless, graceless 924 *disapproved*; villainous, knavish, miscreant, double-dyed 930 *rascally*; improper, unseemly, indecent, unedifying 847 *vulgar*; without morals, immoral; unvirtuous, intemperate 951 *unchaste*; profligate, dissolute, abandoned, characterless, lost to virtue, lost to shame 867 *disreputable*; vitiated, corrupt, degraded, demoralized, debauched, ruined, depraved, perverted, degenerate, sick, rotten, rotten to the core 655 *deteriorated*; brutalized, brutal 898 *cruel*.

*frail*, infirm, feeble 163 *weak*; having a weaker side, having one's foibles, having a touch of human frailty, human, only h., too h. 734 *lax*; suggestible, easily tempted 661 *vulnerable*; not above temptation, not impeccable, not perfect, fallen 647 *imperfect*; slipping, sliding, recidivous 603 *tergiversating*.

*heinous*, heavy, grave, serious, deadly; black, scarlet, of deepest dye; abysmal, hellish, infernal; sinful, immoral, wicked 914 *wrong*; demoralizing, unedifying, contra bonos mores; criminal, nefarious, felonious 954 *lawbreaking*; flagitious, monstrous, flagrant, scandalous, scandalizing, infamous, shameful, disgraceful, shocking, outrageous, obscene; gross, foul, rank; base, vile, abominable, accursed; mean, shabby, despicable 645 *bad*; blameworthy, culpable 928 *accusable*; reprehensible, indefensible, unjustifiable 916 *unwarranted*; atrocious, brutal 898 *cruel*; unforgivable, unpardonable, inexcusable, irremissible, inexpiable, unatonable.

**Vb.** *be wicked*, – vicious, – sinful etc. adj.; not be in a state of grace, scoff at virtue; fall from grace, spoil one's record, blot one's copybook, lapse, relapse, backslide 603 *change one's mind*; fall into evil ways, go to the bad or to the dogs 655 *deteriorate*; do wrong, transgress, misbehave, misdemean oneself, carry on, be naughty, sow one's wild oats, kick over the traces; trespass, offend, sin, commit s.; leave or stray from the straight and narrow, deviate from the paths of virtue, err, stray, slip, trip, stumble, fall; have one's foibles, have one's weak side 163 *be weak*.

*make wicked*, render evil, corrupt, demoralize, deform one's character, brutalize 655 *pervert*; mislead, lead astray, seduce 612 *tempt*; set a bad example, teach wickedness, dehumanize, brutalize, diabolize.

**Adv.** *wickedly*, wrongly, sinfully; viciously, vilely, devilishly; unforgivably, unpardonably, irredeemably, inexpiably; to one's discredit.

## 935 Innocence

**N.** *innocence*, blessed i., freedom from guilt, guiltlessness, clean hands; conscious innocence, clear conscience, irreproachability; nothing to declare, nothing to confess; inculpability, blamelessness, freedom from blame, every excuse; declared innocence 960 *acquittal*; ignorance of evil 491 *ignorance*; inexperience, unworldliness 699 *artlessness*; playfulness, harmlessness, inoffensiveness, innocent intentions, pure motives; freedom from sin, unfallen state, saintliness, purity of heart, state of grace 933 *virtue*; undefilement, stainlessness 950 *purity*; incorruption, incorruptibility 929 *probity*; impeccability 646 *perfection*; days of innocence, golden age 824 *happiness*.

*innocent*, Holy Innocents, babe, newborn babe, babe unborn, babes and sucklings; child, ingénue; lamb, dove; angel, pure soul; milksop, goody-goody; one in the right, innocent party, injured p., not the culprit.

**Adj.** *innocent*, pure, unspotted, stainless, unblemished, spotless, immaculate 648 *clean*; incorrupt, uncorrupted, undefiled; unfallen, sinless, free from sin, unerring, impeccable 646 *perfect*; green, inexperienced, callow, naive, knowing no better, unhardened, unversed in crime 491 *ignorant*; unworldly, guileless 699 *artless*; well-meaning, well-intentioned 897 *benevolent*; innocuous, harmless, inoffensive, playful, gentle, lamb-like, dove-like, child-like, angelic, saintly; wide-eyed, looking as if butter would not melt in one's mouth; innocent as a lamb or a dove, innocent as a babe unborn, innocent as a child; shockable, goody-goody, holier than thou; Arcadian.

*guiltless*, free from guilt, not guilty, not responsible, squeaky-clean 960 *acquitted*; 'more sinned against than sinning';

> I am a man more sinned against than sinning.
> William Shakespeare, *King Lear*

falsely accused, wrongly a., misunderstood; clean-handed, bloodless; blameless, faultless, unblameworthy, not culpable; irreproachable, above reproach, above suspicion; unobjectionable, unexceptionable, unimpeachable, entirely defensible, with every excuse 923 *approvable*; pardonable, forgivable, excusable, venial, exculpable, expiable.

**Vb.** *be innocent*, know no wrong, wrong no one, have no guile 929 *be honourable*; live in a state of grace, not fall from g. 933 *be virtuous*; have every excuse, have no need to blush, have clean hands, have a clear conscience, have nothing to be ashamed of, have nothing to confess or declare; have the best intentions, mean no harm; know no better 699 *be artless*; stand free of blame, stand above suspicion; acquit oneself, salve one's conscience.

**Adv.** *innocently*, blamelessly, harmlessly; with the best intentions; with clean hands, with a clear conscience, with an easy c.

## 936 Guilt

**N.** *guilt*, guiltiness, blood g., red-handedness; culpability; criminality, delinquency 954 *illegality*; sinfulness, original sin 934 *wickedness*; involvement, complicity, aiding and abetting; liability, one's fault; burden of guilt 702 *encumbrance*; blame, censure 924 *reproach*; guilt complex 503 *eccentricity*; guilty feelings, conscious guilt, guilty conscience, bad c.; guilty behaviour, suspicious conduct, blush, stammer, embarrassment; admitted guilt, confessed g., confession 526 *disclosure*; twinge of conscience, remorse, shame 939 *penitence*.

*guilty act*, sin, deadly s., venial s. 934 *vice*; misdeed, wicked deed, misdoing, sinning, transgression, trespass, offence, arrestable o., crime, corpus delicti 954 *illegality*; misdemeanour, felony; misconduct, misbehaviour, malpractice, malversation; infamous conduct, unprofessional c.; indiscretion, impropriety, peccadillo; naughtiness, scrape; lapse, slip, faux pas, blunder 495 *mistake*; omission, sin of o. 458 *negligence*; culpable omission, laches; fault, failure, dereliction of duty 918 *undutifulness*; injustice, delict, tort, injury 914 *wrong*; enormity, atrocity, outrage 898 *cruel act*.

**Adj.** *guilty*, found g., convicted 961 *condemned*; thought guilty, suspected, blamed, censured, made responsible 924 *disapproved*; responsible 180 *liable*; in the wrong, at fault, to blame, culpable, chargeable 928 *accusable*; blameful, shameful, reprehensible, censurable 924 *blameworthy*; unjustifiable, without excuse, inexcusable, unpardonable; inexpiable, mortal, deadly 934 *heinous*; trespassing, transgressing, peccant, sinful 934 *wicked*; criminal 954 *illegal*; blood-guilty 362 *murderous*; red-handed, caught in the act, flagrante delicto, surprised in the attempt, caught with one's pants *or* trousers down, caught with one's hand in the till, caught bang to rights (inf); hangdog, sheepish, shamefaced, blushing, ashamed.

**Vb.** *be guilty*, be at fault, be in the wrong, be to blame, bear the blame; have sins upon one's conscience, have crimes to answer for, have blood on one's hands; be caught in the act, be caught red-handed, be caught with one's hand in the till, be caught bang to rights (inf); acknowledge one's guilt, have nothing to say for oneself, plead guilty 526 *confess*; have no excuse, stand condemned; trespass, transgress, sin 934 *be wicked*.

*find guilty*, blame 924 *blame*, 928 *accuse*; condemn, convict, judge, sentence, pass judgment on, pronounce judgment on 961 *condemn*; catch one in the act, catch one red-handed, catch one with one's hand in the till, catch *or* have one bang to rights (inf).

**Adv.** *guiltily*, criminally; inexcusably, without excuse; red-handed, in the very act, bang to rights (inf), flagrante delicto.

## 937 Good person

**N.** *good person*, fine human being, sterling character, exemplary c. 929 *honourable person*; pillar of society, model of virtue, salt of the earth, shining light, perfection 646 *paragon*; Christian, true C.; saint 979 *pietist*; mahatma, maharishi, great saint; seraph, angel 935 *innocent*; heart of gold 897 *kind person*; good neighbour, Good Samaritan 903 *benefactor*; idealist 901 *philanthropist*; the best, one of the b., one in a million, the tops 890 *favourite*; hero, heroine 855 *brave person*; goody, good guy, good sort, good old boy, stout fellow, brick, trump, sport; rough diamond, ugly duckling.

## 938 Bad person

**N.** *bad person*, evil p., no saint, sinner, hardened s., limb of Satan, Antichrist 904 *evildoer*; fallen angel, backslider, recidivist, lost sheep, lost soul, âme damnée, one without morals, immoralist; reprobate, slubberdegullion, scapegrace, good-for-nothing, ne'er-do-well, black sheep, the despair of; scallywag, scamp; rake, roué, profligate 952 *libertine*; wanton, hussy 952 *loose woman*; wastrel, waster, prodigal son 815 *prodigal*; scandalous person, reproach, outcast, dregs, riffraff, trash, scum 867 *object of scorn*; nasty type, ugly customer, undesirable, bad 'un, wrong 'un, badmash, thug, bully, boot boy, bovver boy, hitman, terrorist, roughneck 904 *ruffian*; bad lot, bad egg, bad hat, bad character, bad guy, baddy, villain; rotten apple; bad influence, bad example; bad child, naughty c., terror, holy t., enfant terrible, whelp, monkey, little m., little devil 663 *troublemaker*.

*knave*, scurvy k., varlet, vagabond, varmint, caitiff, wretch, rascal, rapscallion 869 *low fellow*; rogue, prince of rogues; criminal 904 *offender*; thief, pirate, freebooter 789 *robber*; villain, blackguard, scoundrel, miscreant; cheat, liar, crook; impostor, twister, con-man 545 *trickster*; sneak, grass, supergrass, squealer, canary, rat 524 *informer*; renegade, recreant 603 *tergiversator*; betrayer, traitor, archtraitor, Quisling, Judas; animal, dog, hound, swine, snake, serpent, viper, viper in the bosom, reptile, vermin 904 *noxious animal*.

*cad*, utter cad, nasty bit of work, scoundrel, blackguard; rotter, out-and-out r., blighter, bastard, dastard, bounder, jerk, heel, shit (offensive), cunt (offensive), slob, scab, son of a bitch; stinker, skunk, dirty dog, filthy beast; pimp, pander, pervert, degenerate; cur, hound, swine, rat, worm; louse, insect, vermin; pig, beast, horrid b., cat, bitch; the end, absolute e.

*monster*, shocker, horror, unspeakable villain; monster of cruelty, brute, savage, sadist; ogre 735 *tyrant*; Juggernaut, Moloch; public enemy number one; monster of wickedness, monster of iniquity *or* depravity, fiend, demon, ghoul 969 *devil*; hellhound, fury 904 *hellhag*; devil in human shape, devil incarnate, fiend i., ape-man, gorilla, King Kong, Franken-stein's monster, Frankenstein, bogy *or* bogey, terror, nightmare.

## 939 Penitence

**N.** *penitence*, repentance, contrition, attrition, compunction, remorse, self-reproach 830 *regret*; self-accusation, self-condemnation, humble confession 526 *disclosure*; confession 988 *Christian rite*; self-humiliation 872 *humility*; guilt-feeling, weight on one's mind, voice of conscience, uneasy c., unquiet c., guilty c., bad c., twinge of c., qualms of c., pangs of c., stings of c., pricks of c. 936 *guilt*; awakened conscience 603 *recantation*; last-minute repentance, deathbed r.; sackcloth and ashes, white sheet, stool of repentance 941 *penance*; apology 941 *atonement*; half-repentance, grudging apology.

*penitent*, confessor; flagellant 945 *ascetic*; magdalen, prodigal son, returned prodigal, a sadder and a wiser man; reformed character, 'a brand plucked from the burning'.

> I have overthrown some of you, as God overthrew Sodom and Gomorrah, and ye were as a firebrand plucked out of the burning: yet have ye not returned unto me, saith the Lord.
> Bible, Amos

**Adj.** *repentant*, contrite, remorseful, regretful, sorry, apologetic, full of regrets 830 *regretting*; ashamed 872 *humbled*; unhardened, softened, melted, weeping 836 *lamenting*; compunctious, relenting, conscience-stricken, conscience-smitten, pricked by conscience, plagued by c.; self-reproachful, self-accusing, self-convicted, self-condemned; confessing, in the con-fessional; penitent, penitential, penitentiary, doing penance 941 *atoning*; chastened, sob-ered, awakened; reclaimed, reformed, con-verted, regenerate, born again.

**Vb.** *be penitent*, repent, show compunction, feel remorse, feel shame, blush for s., feel sorry, say one is s., express regrets, apologize; reproach oneself, blame o., reprove o., accuse o., convict o., condemn o.; go to con-fession, acknowledge one's faults 526 *confess*; do penance, wear a white sheet, repent in sack-

cloth and ashes 941 *atone*; bewail one's sins, sing Miserere, sing De Profundis 836 *lament*; beat one's breast, scourge oneself, prostrate o.; eat humble pie 721 *knuckle under*; rue, have regrets, wish undone 830 *regret*; think again, have second thoughts, think better of, stop in time; learn one's lesson, learn from experience, find out from bitter e. 536 *learn*; reform, be reformed, be a reformed character, be reclaimed, turn over a new leaf 654 *get better*; see the light, see the error of one's ways, be converted, put on the new man, turn from sin, return to the straight and narrow 147 *be turned to*; recant one's error 603 *recant*.

**Adv.** *penitently*, like a penitent, on the stool of repentance, in sackcloth and ashes; repent-antly, regretfully.

**Int.** sorry!, mea culpa!, repent!, for pity!

## 940 Impenitence

**N.** *impenitence*, lack of contrition; contumacy, recusance, refusal to recant, obduracy, stub-bornness 602 *obstinacy*; hardness of heart, indu-ration 326 *hardness*; no apologies, no regrets, no remorse, no compunction 906 *pitilessness*; incorrigibility, seared conscience, unawakened c., sleeping c.; hardened sinner, despair of 938 *bad person*.

**Adj.** *impenitent*, unregretting, unapolo-gizing, unrecanting, recusant; contumacious, obdurate, inveterate, stubborn 602 *obstinate*; unconfessing, unrepentant, uncontrite; unre-gretful, without regrets; unrelenting, relentless 600 *persevering*; without compunction, without remorse, remorseless, without a pang, heartless 898 *cruel*; unsoftened, unmoved; hard, hard-ened, case-h.; conscienceless, unashamed, unblushing, brazen; incorrigible, irreclaimable, irredeemable, hopeless, despaired of, lost 934 *wicked*; unconfessed, unshriven; unchastened, unreformed, unregenerate, unreconciled; unre-claimed, unconverted, unreconstructed.

*unrepented*, unregretted, unapologized for, unatoned.

**Vb.** *be impenitent*, make no excuses, offer no apologies, have no regrets, not wish things otherwise, would do it again; not see the light, not see the error of one's ways, refuse to recant 602 *be obstinate*; make no confession, die and make no sign, die in one's sins, die in contu-macy; stay unreconciled, want no forgiveness; feel no compunction, feel no remorse, harden one's heart, steel one's h. 906 *be pitiless*.

**Adv.** *impenitently*, unashamedly, unblush-ingly; without compunction, with no regrets.

## 941 Atonement

**N.** *atonement*, making amends, amends,

amende honorable, apology, full a., satisfaction; reparation, compensation, indemnity,
indemnification, blood money, wergild, conscience money 787 *restitution*; repayment, quittance, quits; composition 770 *compromise*.

*propitiation*, expiation, satisfaction, reconciliation, conciliation 719 *pacification*; reclamation, redemption 965 *divine function*;
sacrifice, offering, burnt o., peace o., sin o. 981
*oblation*; sin-eater, scapegoat, whipping boy,
chopping block 150 *substitute*.

*penance*, shrift, confession, acknowledgment
939 *penitence*; sacrament of penance, penitential exercise, austerities, fasting, flagellation
945 *asceticism*; lustration, purgation 648
*cleansing*; purgatorial torments, purgatory;
penitent form, anxious seat, stool of repentance, cutty stool, corner 964 *pillory*; white
sheet, sanbenito; sackcloth and ashes, breast-
beating 836 *lamentation*.

**Adj.** *atoning*, making amends 939 *repentant*;
reparatory, compensatory, indemnificatory
787 *restoring*; conciliatory, apologetic; pro-
piatory, expiatory, piacular, purgatorial, lustral
648 *cleansing*; sacrificial 759 *offering*; penitential, penitentiary, doing penance,
undergoing p. 963 *punitive*.

**Vb.** *atone*, salve one's conscience, make
amends, make reparation, offer r., indemnify,
compensate, pay compensation, make it up to;
apologize, make apologies, offer one's a. 909
*beg pardon*; propitiate, conciliate 719 *pacify*;
give satisfaction, offer s. 787 *restitute*; redeem
one's error, repair one's fault, make up for,
make *or* put matters right, be restored to
favour; sacrifice to, offer sacrifice; expiate, pay
the penalty, pay the forfeit, pay the cost, smart
for it 963 *be punished*; become the whipping
boy, make oneself the scapegoat 931 *be disinterested*; reclaim, redeem.

*do penance*, undergo p., perform penitential
exercises; pray, fast, flagellate oneself, deny o.,
scourge o.; purge one's contempt *or* one's
offences, suffer purgatory; put on sackcloth
and ashes, don a hair-shirt, rend one's garments, stand in the corner, sit on the stool of
repentance; take one's punishment, swallow
one's medicine 963 *be punished*; salve one's
conscience, go to confession 526 *confess*.

**942 Temperance**
**N.** *temperance*, temperateness, nothing in
excess 177 *moderation*; self-denial 931 *disinterestedness*; self-restraint, self-control, self-
discipline, keeping a stiff upper lip, stoicism
747 *restraint*; continence, chastity 950 *purity*;
soberness 948 *sobriety*; forbearance 620 *avoidance*; renunciation 621 *relinquishment*; abstemi-

ousness, abstinence, abstention, total
abstinence, teetotalism; enforced abstention,
prohibition, prohibitionism 747 *restriction*; vegetarianism, veganism 942 *abstainer*; dieting
946 *fasting*; frugality 814 *economy*; plain living,
simple life, self-sufficiency, getting away from
it all; frugal diet 945 *asceticism*.

*abstainer*, total a., teetotaller, non-drinker
948 *sober person*; prohibitionist, pussyfoot;
non-smoker; vegetarian, demi-v., lacto-v.,
lacto-ovo-v., vegan, veggie (inf), fruitarian;
dropout, advocate of the simple life, self-
sufficiency freak; dieter, faster; enemy of
excess, Spartan 945 *ascetic*.

**Adj.** *temperate*, not excessive, within
bounds, within reasonable limits; measured,
tempered, understated 177 *moderate*; plain,
Spartan, sparing 814 *economical*; frugal 816 *parsimonious*; forbearing, abstemious, abstinent
620 *avoiding*; dry, teetotal 948 *sober*; vegan, vegetarian 942 *abstainer*; ungreedy, not self-
indulgent, self-controlled, self-disciplined,
continent 747 *restrained*; chaste 950 *pure*; self-
denying 945 *ascetic*.

**Vb.** *be temperate*, – moderate etc. adj.; moderate, temper, keep within bounds, observe a
limit, avoid excess, know when one has had
enough, know when to stop 177 *be moderate*;
keep sober 948 *be sober*; forbear, refrain,
abstain 620 *avoid*; control oneself, contain o.
747 *restrain*; deny oneself 945 *be ascetic*; go dry,
take the pledge, sign the p., go on the wagon;
give up, swear off; ration oneself, restrict o.,
tighten one's belt, draw in one's b. 946 *starve*;
diet, go on a d. 206 *make thin*.

**943 Intemperance**
**N.** *intemperance*, lack of moderation, immoderation, unrestraint, abandon; excess, excessiveness, luxury 637 *redundance*; too much 637
*superfluity*; wastefulness, extravagance, profligacy, waste, consumerism, consumer society
815 *prodigality*; lack of self-control, indiscipline, incontinence 734 *laxity*; indulgence,
self-i., overindulgence; addiction, bad habit
610 *habit*; drug habit 949 *drug-taking*; high
living, dissipation, licentiousness, debauchery
944 *sensualism*; overeating 947 *gluttony*;
excessive drinking, binge-drinking, intoxication, hangover 949 *drunkenness*.

**Adj.** *intemperate*, immoderate, exceeding,
excessive 637 *redundant*; untempered,
unmeasured, unlimited 635 *plenteous*;
unfrugal, wasteful, extravagant, profligate,
spendthrift 815 *prodigal*; luxurious 637
*superfluous*; unascetic, unspartan, hedonistic,
indulgent, self-i., overindulgent, denying oneself nothing; unrestrained, uncontrolled,

lacking self-control, undisciplined 738 *riotous*; incontinent 951 *unchaste*; unsober, nonteetotal 949 *drunk*; animal 944 *sensual*.

**Vb.** *be intemperate*, – immoderate etc. adj.; roll in, luxuriate, plunge, wallow; lack self-control, want discipline, lose control 734 *be lax*; deny oneself nothing, indulge oneself, give oneself up to 734 *please oneself*; kick over the traces, have one's fling, sow one's wild oats 815 *be prodigal*; run to excess, run riot, exceed 306 *overstep*; observe no limits, go to any lengths, stick at nothing, not know when to stop, overindulge, burn the candle at both ends 634 *waste*; live it up, go on a spree, go on a binge, go on a bender 837 *revel*; overdrink, drink like a fish, drink to excess, be a heavy drinker 949 *get drunk*; eat to excess, gorge, overeat, binge, pig it, make oneself sick 947 *gluttonize*; be incontinent, grow dissipated 951 *be impure*; addict oneself, become a slave to habit 610 *be wont*.

**Adv.** *intemperately*, immoderately, excessively, with abandon; without moderation, without control; incontinently, licentiously; not wisely but too well.

**944 Sensualism**

**N.** *sensualism*, life of the senses, unspirituality, earthiness, materialism 319 *materiality*; cultivation of the senses, sensuality, carnality, sexuality, the flesh; grossness, beastliness, bestiality, animalism, hoggishness, wallowing; craze for excitement 822 *excitability*; love of pleasure, search for p., hedonism, epicurism, epicureanism, eudaemonism 376 *pleasure*; sybaritism, voluptuousness, voluptuosity, softness, luxuriousness, dolce vita; luxury, lap of l. 637 *superfluity*; full life, wine of l., life of pleasure, high living, fast l., wine, women and song 824 *enjoyment*; dissipation, abandon 943 *intemperance*; licentiousness, dissoluteness, debauchery 951 *impurity*; indulgence, self-i., overindulgence, greediness, gourmandise 947 *gluttony*; eating and drinking, Lucullan banquet 301 *feasting*; bingeing, orgy, debauch, saturnalia, Bacchanalia 837 *revel*.

*sensualist*, animal, pig, swine, hog, wallower; no ascetic, hedonist, playboy *or* -girl, pleasure-lover, thrill-seeker; luxury-lover, sybarite, voluptuary; eudaemonist, epicurean, free-liver, bon vivant, bon viveur; epicure, gourmet, foodie (inf), gourmand 947 *glutton*; hard drinker 949 *drunkard*; loose liver, profligate, rake 952 *libertine*; drug addict 949 *drug-taking*; degenerate, decadent; sadist, masochist.

**Adj.** *sensual*, earthy, gross, unspiritual 319 *material*; fleshly, carnal, bodily; sexual, venereal 887 *erotic*; animal, bestial, beastly,

brutish, swinish, hoggish, wallowing; Circean, pleasure-giving 826 *pleasurable*; sybaritic, voluptuous, pleasure-loving, thrill-seeking, living for kicks; hedonistic, eudaemonistic, epicurean, Lucullan, luxury-loving, luxurious; pampered, spoilt, indulged, self-i., overindulged, featherbedded; overfed 947 *gluttonous*; high-living, fast-l., incontinent 943 *intemperate*; licentious, dissipated, debauched 951 *impure*; riotous, orgiastic, bingeing, Bacchanalian 949 *drunken*.

**Vb.** *be sensual*, – voluptuous etc. adj.; cultivate one's senses, be the slave of one's desires, live for pleasure, wallow in luxury, live well, 'live off the fat of the land' (see quotation at 730 *prosperity*) 730 *prosper*; indulge oneself, pamper o., spoil o., do oneself proud; run riot, go the pace, live in the fast lane, burn the candle at both ends 943 *be intemperate*.

**Adv.** *sensually*, voluptuously, bestially, hoggishly, swinishly.

**945 Asceticism**

**N.** *asceticism*, austerity, mortification, self-m., self-chastisement, self-torture, self-mutilation; maceration, flagellation 941 *penance*; ascetic practice, encratism, yoga; anchoritism, eremitism 883 *seclusion*; Cynicism, Diogenes and his tub 883 *unsociability*; holy poverty 801 *poverty*; plain living, simple fare, dinner of herbs, Spartan fare, Lenten f. 946 *fasting*; fast day 946 *fast*; self-denial 942 *temperance*; frugality 814 *economy*; Puritanism, Sabbatarianism; sackcloth, hair shirt, cilice.

*ascetic*, spiritual athlete, gymnosophist, yogi, sannyasi, fakir, dervish, firewalker; hermit, eremite, anchoret, anchorite, anchoritess, recluse 883 *solitary*; Cynic, Diogenes; flagellant 939 *penitent*; water-drinker 948 *sober person*; faster, Encratite 942 *abstainer*; Puritan, Plymouth Brethren, Sabbatarian; spoilsport, killjoy, pussyfoot 702 *hinderer*.

**Adj.** *ascetic*, yogic, self-mortifying, fasting, flagellating; hermit-like, eremitical, anchoretic; puritanical; Sabbatarian; austere, rigorous 735 *severe*; Spartan, unpampered 942 *temperate*; water-drinking 948 *sober*; plain, wholesome 652 *salubrious*.

**Vb.** *be ascetic*, live like a Spartan, live the simple life; fast, live on air 946 *starve*; live like a hermit, wear a hair shirt, put on sackcloth; control one's senses, lie on nails, walk through fire.

**Adv.** *ascetically*, austerely, abstinently, simply, plainly, frugally, painfully.

**946 Fasting**

**N.** *fasting*, abstinence from food; no appetite, anorexia, a. nervosa 651 *ill health*; cutting down 301 *dieting*; keeping fast, strict fast, xerophagy, hunger strike; lenten fare, bread and water, spare diet, meagre d., starvation d., soupe maigre, potatoes and point 945 *asceticism*; iron rations, short commons 636 *scarcity*; no food, starvation, utter s., famishment, inanition 859 *hunger*.

*fast*, fast day, Friday, Good Friday, Lent, Ramadan; day of abstinence, meatless day, fish d., jour maigre 945 *asceticism*; hunger strike 145 *strike*.

**Adj.** *fasting*, not eating, off one's food; abstinent 942 *temperate*; keeping fast, keeping Lent, on hunger strike; without food, unfed, empty, with an empty stomach, dinnerless, supperless; poorly fed, half-starved 636 *underfed*; starved, starving, clemmed, famished, famishing, ravenous, dying for food, wasting away 206 *lean*; wanting food 859 *hungry*; sparing, frugal 814 *economical*; scanty 636 *scarce*; meagre, thin, poor, Spartan; Lenten.

**Vb.** *starve*, famish, clem 859 *be hungry*; macerate, waste with hunger, show one's bones, be a bag of bones; have no food, have nothing to eat, live on water, live on air, dine with Duke Humphrey 801 *be poor*; fast, go without food, abstain from f., eat no meat; keep Lent, keep Ramadan; lay off food, give up eating, eat nothing, refuse one's food, go on hunger strike; eat less, diet, go on a d., go on a crash d., reduce, take off weight 37 *abate*; tighten one's belt, go on short commons, live on iron rations; eat sparingly, make a little go a long way, control one's appetite 942 *be temperate*; keep a poor table 816 *be parsimonious*.

## 947 Gluttony

**N.** *gluttony*, greediness, greed, rapacity, insatiability, gulosity, voracity, voraciousness, wolfishness, hoggishness, piggishness; edacity, polyphagia, insatiable appetite 859 *hunger*; good living, high l., indulgence, overeating, overfeeding 943 *intemperance*; guzzling, gorging, bingeing, gormandizing, gluttonizing, pampered appetite, belly worship, gourmandise, epicureanism, epicurism, foodism, pleasures of the table 301 *gastronomy*; bust, binge, blowout, masses of food, groaning table 301 *feasting*.

*glutton*, glutton for food, guzzler, gormandizer, bolter, gorger, crammer, stuffer, binger; locust, wolf, vulture, cormorant, pig, hog; vampire, blood-sucker; trencherman *or* -woman, good eater, hearty e. 301 *eater*; coarse feeder, greedy-guts, greedy pig; gourmand, gastronome, gourmet, epicure, bon vivant, bon viveur, Lucullus.

**Adj.** *gluttonous*, rapacious, ventripotent 859

*greedy*; devouring, voracious, edacious, wolfish; omnivorous, all-swallowing, all-engulfing 464 *indiscriminating*; starving, insatiable, never full 859 *hungry*; pampered, full-fed, overfed, eating one's fill 301 *feeding*; guzzling, gormandizing, gorging, bingeing, stuffing, cramming, belly-worshipping, licking one's lips, licking one's chops, drooling, watering at the mouth; gastronomic, epicurean.

**Vb.** *gluttonize*, gormandize; guzzle, bolt, wolf, gobble, gobble up, devour, gulp down; fill oneself, gorge, cram, stuff, binge; glut oneself, overeat 301 *eat*; have the run of one's teeth, eat one's head off, eat out of house and home; have a good appetite, be a good trencherman *or* -woman, ply a good knife and fork; eat like a trooper, eat like a horse, eat like a pig, have two feet in the trough, make a beast of oneself, have eyes bigger than one's stomach; make oneself sick; indulge one's appetite, pamper one's a., tickle one's palate; savour one's food, lick one's lips, lick one's chops, water at the mouth, drool at the sight of food; keep a good table, have the best cook; like one's food, worship one's belly, live to eat, not eat to live, live only for eating.

**Adv.** *gluttonously*, ravenously, wolfishly, hungrily; at a gulp, with one bite; gastronomically.

## 948 Sobriety

**N.** *sobriety*, soberness 942 *temperance*; water-drinking, tea-d., teetotalism, pussyfootism; state of sobriety, unintoxicated state, clear head, unfuddled brain, no hangover; dry area.

*sober person*, moderate drinker, no toper; non-addict, nonalcoholic; water-drinker, tea-d., non-d., teetotaller, total abstainer 942 *abstainer*; Rechabite, Band of Hope, temperance society, Alcoholics Anonymous; prohibitionist, pussyfoot.

**Adj.** *sober*, abstinent, abstemious 620 *avoiding*; water-drinking, tea-d. 942 *temperate*; not drinking, off drink, on soft drinks, drying out, on the water-wagon, on the wagon; teetotal, strictly TT, pussyfoot, prohibitionist, dry; unintoxicated, unfuddled, clear-headed, with a clear head, sober as a judge, stone-cold sober; sobered, come to one's senses, sobered up, without a hangover; dried out, off the bottle; unfermented, nonalcoholic, soft.

**Vb.** *be sober*, – abstemious, etc. adj.; drink water, prefer soft drinks; not drink, not imbibe, keep off liquor, never touch drink, drink moderately 942 *be temperate*; give up drinking, dry out, come off (drugs), go on the water-wagon, go on the wagon, give up alcohol, become teetotal, sign the pledge, join the Band of Hope; go dry, turn prohibitionist; carry one's liquor, hold one's l., keep a clear head, be sober as a judge; sober up, clear one's head, get the fumes out of one's brain, get rid of a hangover, sleep it off.

**Adv.** *soberly*, with sobriety, abstemiously.

## 949 Drunkenness. Drug-taking

**N.** *drunkenness*, excessive drinking, binge-drinking 943 *intemperance*; ebriosity, insobriety, inebriety, temulency; bibulousness, winebibbing, weakness for liquor, fondness for the bottle; sottishness, beeriness, vinousness; influence of liquor, inspiration, exhilaration 821 *excitation*; Dutch courage 855 *courage*; intoxication, inebriation, befuddlement, fuddledness, blackout; hiccoughing, hiccup, thick speech, slurred s. 580 *speech defect*; tipsiness, wooziness, staggering, titubancy 317 *oscillation*; getting drunk, one for the road, one over the eight, drop too much, hard drinking, swilling, soaking 301 *drinking*; compotation, potation, deep potations, libations, libation to Bacchus; hair of the dog that bit one; flowing bowl, booze, liquor, John Barleycorn 301 *alcoholic drink*, *wine*; drinking bout, jag, lush, blind, binge, spree, bender, pub-crawl, orgy of drinking, Bacchanalia 837 *revel*; Bacchus, Dionysus.

*crapulence*, crapulousness; morning after the night before, morning after, hangover, thick head, sick headache.

*drunkard*, habitual d., inebriate, drunk, sot, lush; slave to drink, wino, alcoholic, dipsomaniac, dipso, pathological drunk; drinker, social d., hard d., secret d.; bibber, wine-b., tippler, toper, boozer, swiller, soaker, old soak, souse, sponge, wineskin; lovepot, tosspot, barfly, froth-blower, thirsty soul; devotee of Bacchus, Bacchanal, Bacchant(e), maenad, Silenus; carouser, pub-crawler 837 *reveller*; recovering alcoholic.

*alcoholism*, alcohol addiction, alcohol abuse, dipsomania; delirium tremens, dt's, the horrors, heebiejeebies, jimjams, pink elephants; grog-blossom, red nose.

*drug*, hard drug, soft d., controlled d., designer d., recreational d., drugs, substance, illegal s.; joint, reefer, spliff, roach; shot, fix (sl); narcotic, dope; nicotine 388 *tobacco*; cannabis, marijuana, ganja, hemp, hashish, hash, bhang, kef, pot (sl), grass (sl), Acapulco gold, sinsemilla; cocaine, coke, basuco, basuko, snow, crack, rock, free-base; heroin, horse (sl), junk (sl), smack (sl), scag, black tar, candy (sl), nose candy (sl), dogfood (sl), gumball, Mexican mud, peanut butter (sl), tootsie roll (sl); methadone; downers, barbiturates, barbs

(sl), morphia, morphine, opium 658 *drug*; stimulant, pep pill, amphetamine, speed, purple hearts, dexies, uppers 821 *excitant*; performance-enhancing drug; intoxicant, hallucinogen, LSD, lysergic acid diethylamide, acid (sl), Ecstasy, MDMA, phencyclidine, PCP, angel dust, STP, mescalin, peyote, magic mushroom; drug addiction (see also *drug-taking*), habit 943 *intemperance*; trip (see also *drug experience*), drug-selling, drug-pushing (see also *drug-peddler*); gateway substance; lifestyle drug, Viagra (tdmk); date rape drug, Rohypnol.

*drug-taker*, drug-user, user, drug addict, dope fiend, freak (sl); head (sl), acidhead (sl), coke-head (sl), basehead (sl), junkie (inf), mainliner, acid-scorer (sl), drug-s.

*drug-taking*, drug abuse, drug addiction, drug dependence, drug habit, habit, substance abuse 943 *intemperance*; smoking, snorting (sl), freebasing (sl), hitting up (sl), shooting up (sl), injecting, skin-popping (sl), mainlining; pill-popping (inf), cocktailing; chasing the dragon (sl); glue-sniffing, sniffing, inhalant abuse, solvent a., volatile substance a., VSA.

*drug-peddler*, drug-dealer, drug-pusher, pusher, dope-peddlar, drug baron, drug trafficker; drug-carrier, mule (sl), stuffer (sl); narco-terrorist; drug-peddling, etc, narco-terrorism.

*drug experience*, trip (sl), acid t. (sl), bad t. (sl), freak-out (sl); withdrawal symptoms, drying-out, cold turkey (sl), bogue (sl).

*action against drugs*, drug rehabilitation, rehab (inf); drug tsar.

**Adj.** *drunk*, inebriated, intoxicated, under the influence, having had a drop too much; in one's cups, in liquor, the worse for l.; half-seas over, three sheets in the wind, one over the eight; boozed up (sl), ginned up (sl), liquored up, lit up, flushed, merry, happy, high, elevated, exhilarated 821 *excited*; comfortably drunk, feeling no pain, mellow, full, fou (Scots), primed, well-p., tanked up (sl), bevvied up (sl); gloriously drunk, roaring d., fighting d., pot-valiant, drunk and disorderly 61 *disorderly*.

*tipsy*, tiddly, squiffy, tight, half-cut, pissed, Brahms and Liszt; well-oiled, pickled, canned, bottled, stewed, fried, well-lubricated; pixilated, fuddled, muddled, flustered; maudlin, tearful, tired and emotional; drunken, boozy, muzzy, woozy; glazed, glassy-eyed, pie-e., seeing double; dizzy, giddy, reeling, staggering 317 *oscillating*; hiccupping 580 *stammering*.

*dead drunk*, (all sl) smashed, sloshed, sozzled, soaked, soused, plastered; stinking drunk, stinko, stoned; blind drunk, blind, blotto; legless, paralytic, stocious (Scots); gone, shot, stiff, out, in a drunken stupor; under the table, dead to the world; drunk as a lord, drunk as a fiddler's bitch; drunk as an owl, drunk as David's sow; pissed as a newt (sl), fou as a coot (Scots), fou as a wulk, etc. (Scots).

*hungover*, crapulent, crapulous, with a hangover, with a thick head; dizzy, giddy, sick.

*drugged*, doped, freaked o. (sl), high, in a trance, incapacitated, spaced out (sl), stoned (sl), zonked (sl) 375 *insensible*; loved up (sl), turned on (sl); addicted, hooked on drugs.

*drunken*, inebriate 943 *intemperate*; habitually drunk, always tight, never sober; scottish, sodden, gin-s., boozy (sl), beery, vinous, smelling of drink, stinking of liquor; thirsty, bibulous, fond of a drink, having a drink problem; tippling, boozing, toping, swilling, swigging, hard-drinking; pub-crawling, carousing, wassailing; red-nosed, bloodshot, gouty, liverish; given to drink, a slave to d., addicted to d., on the bottle, alcoholic, dipsomaniac.

*intoxicating*, poisonous, inebriating, inebriative, temulent; exhilarating, going to the head, heady, winy, like wine 821 *exciting*; stimulant, intoxicant; opiate, narcotic; hallucinatory, psychedelic, psychotropic, mind-bending, mind-blowing; addictive, habit-forming; alcoholic, spirituous, vinous, beery; not soft, hard, potent, double-strength, overproof 162 *strong*; neat 44 *unmixed*.

**Vb.** *be drunk*, – tipsy etc. adj.; be under the influence of liquor, be under the influence, have had too much, have had one too many; have a weak head, not hold one's liquor, succumb, be overcome, pass out; hiccup, stutter 580 *stammer*; see double, not walk straight, lurch, stagger, reel 317 *oscillate*.

*get drunk*, have too much, have one over the eight, drink deep, drink hard, drink like a fish, drink to get tight (inf); liquor up, tank up (sl); crack a bottle, knock back a few, bend one's elbow, lush, bib, tipple, fuddle, booze (sl), tope, guzzle, swig, swill, souse, hit the bottle 301 *drink*; go on the spree, go on a blind *or* a bender, go on the fuddle, go pub-crawling, pub-crawl; drown one's sorrows, commune with the spirits; quaff, carouse, wassail, sacrifice to Bacchus 837 *revel*.

*take drugs*, smoke, sniff, snort (sl), inject oneself, mainline, shoot, shoot up; turn on, trip out (sl), take a trip (sl), blow one's mind; freak out (sl). (See also *drug-taking*.)

*inebriate*, be intoxicating, – heady etc. adj.; exhilarate, elevate 821 *excite*; go to one's head, make one's head swim, fuddle, befuddle, stupefy; make drunk, tipsify; drink one under the table.

**950 Purity**
**N.** *purity*, faultlessness 646 *perfection*; sinlessness, immaculacy 935 *innocence*; moral purity, morals, good m., morality 933 *virtue*; decency, propriety, delicacy 846 *good taste*; pudency, shame, bashfulness 874 *modesty*; chastity, continence, encratism 942 *temperance*; coldness, frigidity 820 *moral insensibility*; honour, one's h.; virginity, maidenhood, maidenhead 895 *celibacy*.

*prudery*, prudishness, squeamishness, shockability; overmodesty, false modesty, false shame, mauvaise honte 874 *modesty*; demureness, gravity 834 *seriousness*; priggishness, primness, coyness 850 *affectation*; sanctimony, sanctimoniousness 979 *pietism*; Puritanism, blue laws 735 *severity*; euphemism, Grundyism, genteelism, mealy-mouthedness; censorship, expurgation, bowdlerization 550 *obliteration*.

*virgin*, maiden, vestal, vestal virgin, virgo intacta, maid, old maid, spinster 895 *celibate*; Encratite, religious celibate 986 *monk, nun*; Joseph, Galahad; virtuous woman, Procne, Lucretia; Diana, Artemis.

*prude*, prig, Victorian, euphemist 850 *affecter*; Puritan, wowser; guardian of morality, censor, Watch Committee, Mrs Grundy.

**Adj.** *pure*, faultless 646 *perfect*; undefiled, unfallen, sinless 935 *innocent*; maidenly, virgin, virginal, vestal, untouched 895 *unwedded*; blushful, blushing, rosy 874 *modest*; coy, shy 620 *avoiding*; chaste, continent 942 *temperate*; unmovable, unassailable, impregnable, incorruptible 929 *honourable*; unfeeling 820 *impassive*; frigid 380 *cold*; immaculate, spotless, snowy 427 *white*; good, moral 933 *virtuous*; Platonic, sublimated, elevated, purified; decent, decorous, delicate, refined 846 *tasteful*; edifying, printable, quotable, repeatable, mentionable, 'virginibus puerisque' 648 *clean*;

> Favete linguis; carmina non prius
> Audita Musarum sacerdos
> Virginibus puerisque canto.
> *(Be quiet; as a priest of the Muses, I sing songs to girls and boys that have never been heard before.)*
> Horace, *Odes*

censored, bowdlerized, expurgated, edited, in usum Delphini.

*prudish*, squeamish, shockable, Victorian; prim 850 *affected*; overdelicate, overmodest; old-maidish, straitlaced, narrow-minded, puritan, priggish; holy, sanctimonious 979 *pietistic*.

**951 Impurity**
**N.** *impurity*, impure thoughts, filthiness, defilement 649 *uncleanness*; indelicacy 847 *bad*

*taste*; indecency, immodesty, impudicity, shamelessness, exhibitionism; coarseness, grossness, nastiness; ribaldry, bawdry, bawdiness, salaciousness; loose talk, filthy t., blue joke, blue story, smoking-room s., double entendre, equivoque; smut, dirt, filth, obscenity, obscene literature, adult l., curious l., erotic l., erotica, facetiae; pornography, hard-core p., porn, soft porn, page 3, girlie magazine; banned book; blue film, skin flick, video nasty; hentai, H-anime; prurience, voyeurism, scopophilia.

*unchastity*, lightness, promiscuity, wantonness; incontinence, easy virtue, no morals, amorality; permissive society 734 *laxity*; vice, immorality, sexual delinquency; sex consciousness, roving eye; lickerishness, prurience, concupiscence, lust 859 *libido*; carnality, sexuality, eroticism, erotism, fleshliness, the flesh 944 *sensualism*; sex-indulgence, sexiness, lasciviousness, lewdness, salacity, lubricity; dissoluteness, dissipation, debauchery, licentiousness, licence, libertinism, libertinage, gallantry; seduction, defloration; venery, lechery, priapism, fornication, wenching, womanizing, whoring, screwing around, sleeping a.; harlotry, whorishness.

*illicit love*, guilty l., unlawful desires, forbidden fruit; extramarital relations, criminal conversation, unlawful carnal knowledge; incestuous affection, incest; perversion, pederasty, anal intercourse, buggery, sodomy, bestiality; satyriasis, priapism, nymphomania; paedophilia; masturbation, onanism 376 *sexual pleasure*; adultery, infidelity, marital i., unfaithfulness, cuckolding, cuckoldry; amour, amourette, eternal triangle, intrigue, liaison, seduction 887 *love affair*; free love, living together, irregular union, concubinage, companionate marriage, unwedded cohabitation 894 *type of marriage*; wife-swapping.

*rape*, ravishment, violation, indecent assault, sexual a., grope; acquaintance rape, date r., drug r., stranger r.; date rape drug, Rohypnol; gang rape, gang bang; sexual abuse, sex crime, sex murder.

*social evil*, prostitution, open p., hooking, sex industry, soliciting, streetwalking, survival sex, harlot's trade, harlotry, whoredom, the oldest profession, 'Mrs Warren's p.';

**Mrs Warren's Profession**
Title of a play by George Bernard Shaw

pimping, pandering, brothel-keeping, living on immoral earnings, white slave traffic; sex tourism; public indecency, indecent exposure, exposing oneself, flashing; vice squad.

*brothel*, bordello, bagnio; whorehouse, bawdy-house, cathouse, disorderly h., house of ill fame, house of ill repute; knocking-shop; red-light district.

**Adj.** *impure*, defiling, defiled, unclean, nasty 649 *dirty*; unwholesome 653 *insalubrious*; indelicate, not for the squeamish; vulgar, coarse, gross; ribald, broad, free, loose; strong, racy, bawdy, Fescennine, Rabelaisian; uncensored, unexpurgated, unbowdlerized; suggestive, Freudian, provocative, piquant, titillating, near the knuckle, near the bone; spicy, juicy, fruity; immoral, risqué, equivocal, nudge-nudge wink-wink; naughty, wicked, blue; unmentionable, unquotable, unprintable; smutty, filthy, scrofulous, scabrous, scatological, stinking, rank, offensive; indecent, obscene, lewd, salacious, lubricious; licentious, pornographic; prurient, erotic, phallic, ithyphallic, priapic; sexual, sexy, hot.

*unchaste*, unvirtuous 934 *vicious*; susceptible, not impregnable 934 *frail*; fallen, seduced, prostituted, taken advantage of; of easy virtue, of loose morals, amoral, immoral; incontinent, light, wanton, loose, fast, naughty; wild, rackety; immodest, daring, revealing; unblushing, shameless, brazen, flaunting, scarlet, meretricious, whorish, tarty; promiscuous, sleeping around, screwing a.; streetwalking, on the game; Paphian, Aphrodisian.

*lecherous*, carnal, fleshly, carnal-minded, voluptuous 944 *sensual*; libidinous, lustful, lickerish, goatish; prurient, concupiscent 859 *desiring*; rampant, on *or* in heat, rutting, ruttish; turned-on, hot, sexed-up, randy; sex-conscious, man-c., woman-c.; oversexed, sex-mad, sex-crazy, priapic, nymphomaniac; perverted, bestial; lewd, licentious, libertine, free, loose, rakish; depraved, debauched, dissolute, dissipated, profligate 934 *vicious*; whore-mongering, brothel-haunting.

*extramarital*, irregular, concubinary, on the side; unlawful, incestuous; homosexual, lesbian 84 *abnormal*; adulterous, unfaithful; committing adultery, anticipating marriage; bed-hopping, wife-swapping.

**Vb.** *be impure*, – unchaste etc. adj.; be immoral, have no morals; be unfaithful, deceive one's spouse, break the marriage vow, commit adultery, cuckold; be dissipated 943 *be intemperate*; fornicate, womanize, whore, wench, haunt brothels; keep a mistress, have a lover; lech, lust, rut, be on heat, be hot, have the hots 859 *desire*; be promiscuous, sleep around, screw a.; become a prostitute, become a hooker, become a rent-boy, street-walk, be on the streets; pimp, pander, procure, keep a brothel.

*debauch*, defile, smirch 649 *make unclean*;

proposition, seduce, lead astray; take advantage of, have one's way with, take one's pleasure with; dishonour, deflower, wreck, ruin, disgrace 867 *shame*; prostitute, make a whore of; lay, screw, knock off, bed, go to bed with, lie with, sleep w. 45 *have sexual intercourse with*; rape, commit r., ravish, violate, molest, abuse, outrage, interfere with, assault, indecently a., sexually abuse.

**Adv.** *impurely*, immodestly, shamelessly; loosely, bawdily, sexily, erotically; lewdly, salaciously, suggestively; carnally, sexually 944 *sensually*; lustfully, pruriently, concupiscently.

**Int.** nudge nudge wink wink.

## 952 Libertine

**N.** *libertine*, no Joseph; gay bachelor, not the marrying kind; philanderer, flirt; free-lover, loose fellow, fast man *or* woman, gay dog, rip, rake, rakehell, roué, debauchee, profligate 944 *sensualist*; lady-killer, gallant, squire of dames; fancy-man, gigolo, gig, sugar daddy; seducer, deceiver, gay d., false lover, Lothario 887 *lover*; corespondent, adulterer, cuckolder, bedhopper, wife-swapper; immoralist, amorist, Don Juan, Casanova; wolf, woman-hunter, woman-chaser, skirt-c., kerb-crawler; womanizer, fornicator, stud; whoremonger, whoremaster; voyeur, lecher, flasher, satyr, goat, dirty old man; sex maniac; raper, rapist, ravisher; catamite, male prostitute, rent-boy 45 *sexual partner*; paedophile, pederast, sodomite, pervert 84 *nonconformist*.

*cuckold*, deceived husband, injured h., complaisant h.; wearer of horns.

*loose woman*, light w., light o' love, wanton, easy lay, anybody's; fast woman, sexpot, hot stuff; woman of easy virtue, w. of doubtful reputation, demi-rep, one no better than she should be; flirt, piece, bit, bint, wench, floozy, jade, hussy, minx, miss, nymphet, sex kitten, Lolita, groupie; baggage, trash, trollop, trull, drab, slut; tart, chippy (sl), scrubber, slapper (sl), pick-up; vamp, adventuress, temptress, seductress, femme fatale, scarlet woman, painted w., Jezebel, Delilah; adultress, other woman; nymphomaniac, nympho, Messalina.

*kept woman*, fancy w., mistress, paramour, leman, hetaera, concubine, unofficial wife 887 *loved one*; bit of fluff, bit on the side, floozie, doxy, moll.

*prostitute*, common p., pro 45 *sexual partner*; white slave, fallen woman, erring sister; frail sisterhood, demi-monde; harlot, trollop, whore, strumpet; streetwalker, woman of the streets, broad, hustler, hooker (sl), scrubber, slapper (sl); pick-up, casual conquest, call-girl; fille de joie, f. de nuit, poule, cocotte, courtesan;

demi-mondaine, demi-rep; Aspasia, Thais; Cyprian, Paphian; odalisque, temple prostitute 742 *slave*; male prostitute 45 *sexual partner* (see also *libertine*).

*bawd*, go-between, pimp, ponce, pander, procurer, procuress, mack, brothelkeeper, madam; white slaver.

## 953 Legality

**N.** *legality*, formality, form, formula, rite, due process 959 *litigation*; form of law, letter of the l., four corners of the l. (see also *law*); respect for law, constitutionality, constitutionalism; good law, judgment according to the l. 480 *judgment*; justice under the law 913 *justice*; keeping within the law, lawfulness, legitimateness, legitimacy, validity.

*legislation*, legislature, legislatorship, lawgiving, law-making, constitution-m.; codification; legalization, legitimization, validation, ratification, confirmation 532 *affirmation*; passing into law, enacting, enactment, regulation, regulation by law, regulation by statute; plebiscite 605 *vote*; plebiscitum, psephism, popular decree; law, statute, ordinance, order, standing o., bylaw 737 *decree*; canon, rule, edict, rescript 693 *precept*; legislator, lawgiver, lawmaker.

*law*, law and equity, the law; body of law, corpus juris, constitution, written c., unwritten c.; charter, institution; codification, codified law, statute book, legal code, pandect, Twelve Tables, Ten Commandments, Pentateuch; penal code, civil c., Napoleonic c.; written law, statute l., common l., unwritten l., natural l.; personal law, private l., canon l., ecclesiastical l.; international law, jus gentium, law of nations, law of the sea, law of the air; law of commerce, commercial law, lex mercatoria, law of contract, law of crime, criminal law, civil l., constitutional l., law of the land; cyberlaw; arm of the law, legal process 955 *jurisdiction*; writ, summons, lawsuit 959 *legal trial*.

*jurisprudence*, nomology, science of law, knowledge of l., legal learning; law consultancy, legal advice.

**Adj.** *legal*, lawful 913 *just*; law-abiding 739 *obedient*; legitimate, competent; licit, licensed, permissible, allowable 756 *permitted*; within the law, sanctioned by law, according to l., de jure, legally sound, good in law; statutable, statutory, constitutional; nomothetic, lawgiving, legislatorial, legislational, legislative, decretal; legislated, enacted, passed, voted, made law, ordained, decreed, ordered, by order; legalized, legitimized, decriminalized, brought within the law; liable *or* amenable to law, actionable, justiciable, triable, cognizable

928 *accusable*; fit for legislation, suitable for enactment; pertaining to law, jurisprudential, nomological, learned in the law.

**Vb.** *be legal*, – legitimate etc. adj.; stand up in law *or* court; come within the law, respect the l., abide by the l., keep within the l., stay the right side of the l.

*make legal*, legalize, legitimize, decriminalize, validate, confirm, ratify, formalize 488 *endorse*; vest, establish 153 *stabilize*; legislate, make laws, give l.; pass, enact, ordain, enforce 737 *decree*.

**Adv.** *legally*, by law, by order; legitimately, de jure, in the eye of the law.

## 954 Illegality

**N.** *illegality*, bad law, legal flaw, loophole, let-out, irregularity, error of law, mistake of l.; wrong verdict, bad judgment 481 *misjudgment*; contradictory law, antinomy; miscarriage of justice 914 *injustice*; wrong side of the law, unlawfulness; unauthorization, incompetence, illicitness, illegitimacy, impermissibility 757 *prohibition*.

*lawbreaking*, breach of law, violation of l., transgression, contravention, infringement, encroachment 306 *overstepping*; trespass, offence, offence against the law, tort, civil wrong; champerty, malpractice 930 *foul play*; shadiness, dishonesty 930 *improbity*; criminality 936 *guilt*; criminal activity, criminal offence, indictable o., crime, capital c., misdemeanour, felony; misprision, misfeasance, malfeasance, wrongdoing 914 *wrong*; criminology, criminal statistics; criminal 904 *offender*.

*lawlessness*, antinomianism; outlawry, disfranchisement; no law, absence of l., paralysis of authority, breakdown of law and order, crime wave 734 *anarchy*; summary justice, vigilantism; kangaroo court, gang rule, mob law, lynch l.; riot, race r., rioting, hooliganism, ruffianism, rebellion 738 *revolt*; coup d'état, usurpation 916 *arrogation*; arbitrary rule, arbitrariness, negation of law, abolition of l.; martial law; mailed fist, jackboot 735 *brute force*.

*bastardy*, bar *or* bend *or* baton sinister; bastardization, illegitimacy; bastard, illegitimate child, natural c., love c., by-blow, spurious offspring, offspring of adultery, fruit of a.

**Adj.** *illegal*, illegitimate, illicit; contraband, black-market, hot; impermissible, verboten 757 *prohibited*; unauthorized, incompetent, without authority, unwarrantable, informal, unofficial; unlawful, wrongous, wrongful 914 *wrong*; unlegislated, not covered by law, exceeding the l., bad in law; unchartered, unconstitutional, unstatutory; no longer law,

superseded, suspended, null and void, nullified, annulled 752 *abrogated*; irregular, contrary to law, not according to l., unknown to l.; injudicial, extrajudicial; on the wrong side of the law, against the l.; outside the law, outwith the l., outlawed, out of bounds; tortious, actionable, cognizable, justiciable, triable, punishable 928 *accusable*.

*lawbreaking*, trespassing, transgressing, infringing, encroaching; sinning 934 *wicked*; offending 936 *guilty*; criminal, felonious; fraudulent, shady 930 *dishonest*.

*lawless*, antinomian, without law, chaotic 734 *anarchic*, ungovernable, licentious 738 *riotous*; violent, summary; arbitrary, irresponsible, unanswerable, unaccountable; without legal backing, unofficial, cowboy; above the law, overmighty; despotic, tyrannical 735 *oppressive*.

*bastard*, illegitimate, spurious; misbegotten, adulterine, baseborn; born out of wedlock, born on the wrong side of the blanket; without a father, without a name, without benefit of clergy; bastardized.

**Vb.** *be illegal*, be against the law, be bad in law, break the law, violate the l., offend against the l., circumvent the l., disregard the statute; wrest the law, twist *or* strain the l., torture the l.; be lawless, defy the law, drive a coach and horses through the l. 914 *do wrong*; take the law into one's own hands, exceed one's authority, encroach 734 *please oneself*; have no law, know no l., stand above the law; stand outside the law, suffer outlawry.

*make illegal*, – unlawful etc. adj.; put outside the law, outlaw; illegalize, criminalize 757 *prohibit*, forbid by law, penalize 963 *punish*; bastardize, illegitimize; suspend, annul, cancel, make the law a dead letter 752 *abrogate*.

**Adv.** *illegally*, illicitly, illegitimately, unlawfully, criminally, against the law; on the black market, under the counter.

## 955 Jurisdiction

**N.** *jurisdiction*, portfolio 622 *function*; judicature, magistracy, commission of the peace; mayoralty, shrievalty, bumbledom; competence, legal c., legal authority, arm of the law 733 *authority*; administration of justice, legal administration, Home Office; local jurisdiction, local authority, corporation, municipality, county council, regional c., district c., parish c., community c., bailiwick 692 *council*; vigilance committee, watch c. 956 *tribunal*; office, bureau, secretariat 687 *workshop*; legal authority, competence, cognizance 751 *mandate*.

*law officer*, legal administrator, Lord Chancellor, Attorney General, Lord Advocate, Solicitor General, Queen's Proctor; Crown Counsel, public prosecutor; judge advocate, procurator fiscal, district attorney 957 *judge*; mayor, lord m., provost, lord p., sheriff 733 *position of authority*; court officer, clerk of the court, tipstaff, bailiff; summoner, process-server, catchpoll, Bow-street runner; apparitor, beadle, mace-bearer 690 *official*.

*police*, forces of law and order, long arm of the law; police force, the force, the fuzz, Old Bill, the boys in blue; Scotland Yard; constabulary, gendarmerie, military police, transport p.; police officer, limb of the law, policeman *or* -woman, constable, special c., community policeman, copper, cop, traffic c., patrolman *or* -woman; bobby, flatfoot, rozzer, pig, smokey bear, flic; sergeant, police sergeant, inspector, police inspector, superintendent, police superintendent, chief inspector, chief superintendent, commissioner of police, commander, chief constable, provost marshal; watch, posse comitatus; special patrol group, SPG; plain-clothes man, dick 459 *detective*.

**Adj.** *jurisdictional*, jurisdictive, competent; executive, administrative, administrational, directive 689 *directing*, justiciary, judiciary, juridical; justiciable, subject to jurisdiction, liable to the law.

**Vb.** *hold court*, administer justice, sit on the bench, sit in judgment 480 *judge*; hear complaints, hear causes 959 *try a case*; be seized of, take cognizance, take judicial notice.

### 956 Tribunal
**N.** *tribunal*, seat of justice, woolsack, throne; judgment seat, bar, bar of justice; court of conscience, tribunal of penance, confessional, Judgment Day; forum, ecclesia, wardmote 692 *council*; public opinion, vox populi, electorate; judicatory, bench, board, bench of judges, panel of j., judge and jury; judicial assembly, Areopagus; commission of the peace; Justices of the Peace.

*lawcourt*, court, open c.; court of law, court of justice, criminal court, civil c.; Federal Court, High Court, Court of Justiciary; Sheriff Court, District Court, County Court; Supreme Court, appellate court, Court of Appeal; C. of Cassation; Court of Exchequer, Star Chamber; House of Lords 692 *parliament*; High Court of Justice, Queen's Bench, Queen's Bench Division, Court of Criminal Appeal; Admiralty Division; Probate Court, Divorce C.; Court of Chancery, court of equity, c. of arbitration; Court of Common Pleas; Eyre of Justice, court of oyer and terminer, circuit court; assizes; Court of Session, sessions, quarter s., petty s.;

Central Criminal Court, Old Bailey; magistrate's court, juvenile c., police c.; coroner's court; court of piepowder *or* pie poudre; court of record, feudal c., manorial c., Stannary C., court baron, court leet; guild court, hustings; court-martial, drumhead court, summary c.

*ecclesiastical court*, C. of Arches, Papal C., Curia; Inquisition, Holy Office.

*courtroom*, courthouse, lawcourts, bench, woolsack, jury box; judgment seat, mercy s.; dock, bar; witness box.

**Adj.** *judicatory*, judicial, justiciary, curial, inquisitional, Rhadamanthine; original, appellate 955 *jurisdictional*.

### 957 Judge
**N.** *judge*, justice, justiceship, your Lordship, my lud, m'lud; justiciary, podestà; verderer; Lord Chancellor, Lord Chief Justice, Master of the Rolls, Lords of Appeal; military judge, Judge Advocate General; chief justice, puisné judge, county court j., recorder, Common Serjeant; sessions judge, assize j., circuit j.; district judge, subordinate j.; sheriff, sheriff substitute; magistrate, district m., city m., police m., stipendiary m.; coroner; honorary magistrate, justice of the peace, JP; bench, judiciary; hanging judge, Judge Jeffreys.

*magistracy*, the beak, his *or* her Worship, his *or* her Honour, his nibs, her nibs; arbiter, umpire, referee, assessor, arbitrator, Ombudsman 480 *estimator*; Recording Angel 549 *recorder*; Solomon, Rhadamanthus, 'a Daniel come to judgment'.

> A Daniel come to judgment! yea, a Daniel!
> O wise young judge, how I do honour thee!
> William Shakespeare, *The Merchant of Venice*

*jury*, twelve good men and true, twelve just men, twelve men in a box; grand jury, special j., common j., petty j., trial j., coroner's j.; vetted j., rigged j.; hung j.; juror's panel, jury list; juror, juryman *or* -woman, jurat; foreman *or* forewoman of the jury.

### 958 Lawyer
**N.** *lawyer*, practising l., legal practitioner, solicitor, member of the legal profession, man *or* woman of law; common lawyer, canon l., civil l., criminal l., cyber l.; one called to the bar, barrister, barrister-at-law, devil, advocate, counsel, learned c.; junior barrister, stuff gown, junior counsel; senior barrister, bencher, bencher of the Inns of Court; silk gown, silk, leading counsel, King's C., K.C., Queen's C., Q.C.; serjeant, serjeant-at-law; circuit barrister, circuiteer; Philadelphia lawyer 696 *expert*; ambulance chaser; shyster, pettifogger, crooked lawyer.

*law agent*, attorney, public a., attorney at law, proctor, procurator; Writer to the Signet, solicitor before the Supreme Court; solicitor, legal adviser; legal representative, legal agent, pleader, advocate; equity draftsman; conveyancer.

*notary*, notary public, commissioner for oaths; scrivener, petition-writer; clerk of the court 955 *law officer*; solicitor's clerk, barrister's c., barrister's devil.

*jurist*, jurisconsult, legal adviser, legal expert, legal light, master of jurisprudence, pundit, legist, legalist, canonist; student of law, law student.

*bar*, civil b., criminal b., English bar, Scottish b., junior b., senior b.; Inns of Chancery, Inns of Court, Gray's I., Lincoln's I., Inner Temple, Middle T.; profession of law, legal profession, the Robe; barristership, advocacy, pleading; solicitorship, attorneyship; legal consultancy.

**Adj.** *jurisprudential*, learned in the law, called to the bar, at the b., practising at the b., barristerial, forensic; notarial.

**Vb.** *do law*, study l., go in for l., take up l.; eat one's dinners, be called to the bar; take silk, be called within the bar; practise at the bar, accept a brief, take a case, advocate, plead; practise law; devil.

**959 Litigation**

**N.** *litigation*, going to law, litigiousness 709 *quarrelsomeness*; legal dispute 709 *quarrel*; issue, legal i., matter for judgment, case for decision; lawsuit, suit at law, suit, case, cause, action; prosecution, arraignment, impeachment, charge 928 *accusation*; test case 461 *experiment*; claim, counter c. 915 *dueness*; plea, petition 761 *request*; affidavit, written statement, averment, pleading, demurrer 532 *affirmation*.

*legal process*, proceedings, legal procedure, course of law, arm of the l. 955 *jurisdiction*; citation, subpoena, summons, search warrant 737 *warrant*; arrest, apprehension, detention, committal 747 *restraint*; habeas corpus, bail, surety, security, recognizance, personal r.; injunction, stay order; writ, certiorari, nisi prius.

*legal trial*, trial, fair t., justice seen to be done; trial by law, trial by jury, trial at the bar, trial in court, assize, sessions 956 *lawcourt*; inquest, inquisition, examination 459 *enquiry*; hearing, prosecution, defence; hearing of evidence, taking of e. 466 *evidence*; examination, cross-e., re-e., objection sustained, objection overruled 466 *testimony*; pleadings, arguments 475 *reasoning*; counter-argument, rebutter, rebuttal 460 *rejoinder*; proof 478 *dem-*

*onstration*; disproof 479 *confutation*; summing-up, charge to the jury; ruling, finding, decision, verdict 480 *judgment*; majority verdict, hung jury; favourable verdict 960 *acquittal*; unfavourable verdict 961 *condemnation*; execution of judgment 963 *punishment*; appeal, motion of a.; successful appeal, reversal of judgment, retrial; precedent, case law; law reports; cause list; case record, dossier 548 *record*.

*litigant*, litigator, libellant, party, party to a suit, suitor 763 *petitioner*; claimant, plaintiff, pursuer, defendant, appellant, respondent, objector, intervener; accused, prisoner at the bar 928 *accused person*; litigious person, common informer 524 *informer*; prosecutor 928 *accuser*.

**Adj.** *litigating*, at law with, litigant, suing 928 *accusing*; going to law, appearing in court; contesting, objecting, disputing 475 *arguing*; litigious 709 *quarrelling*.

*litigated*, on trial, coram judice; argued, disputed, contested; up for trial, brought before the court, up before the beak, had up, submitted for judgment, offered for arbitration; sub judice, on the cause list, down for hearing, ready for h.; litigable, disputable, arguable, suable, actionable, justiciable 928 *accusable*.

**Vb.** *litigate*, go to law, appeal to l., set the law in motion, institute legal proceedings, start an action, bring a suit, file a s., petition 761 *request*; prepare a case, prepare a brief, brief counsel; file a claim, contest at law 915 *claim*; have the law on one, take one to court, haul before the c., have one up, make one a party, sue, implead, arraign, impeach, accuse, charge, prefer charges, press c. 928 *indict*; cite, summon, serve notice on; prosecute, put on trial, bring to justice, bring to trial, bring to the bar; argue one's case, advocate, plead, call evidence 475 *argue*.

*try a case*, take cognizance, put down for hearing, empanel a jury, hear a cause; call witnesses, examine, cross-examine, take statements; sit in judgment, rule, find, decide, adjudicate 480 *judge*; close the pleadings, sum up, charge the jury; bring in a verdict, pronounce sentence; commit for trial.

*stand trial*, come before, come up for trial, be put on t., stand in the dock; plead guilty, plead not guilty; plead to the charge, ask to be tried, submit to judgment, hear sentence; defend an action, put in one's defence, make one's d.

**Adv.** *in litigation*, at law, in court, before the judge; sub judice, pendente lite; litigiously.

**960 Acquittal**

**N.** *acquittal*, favourable verdict, verdict of not

guilty, verdict of not proven, benefit of the doubt; clearance, exculpation, exoneration 935 *innocence*; absolution, discharge; let-off, thumbs up 746 *liberation*; whitewashing, justification, compurgation 927 *vindication*; successful defence, defeat of the prosecution; nonsuit, case dismissed; no case, withdrawal of the charge, quashing, quietus; reprieve, pardon 909 *forgiveness*; nonprosecution, exemption, impunity 919 *nonliability*.

**Adj.** *acquitted*, not guilty, not proven 935 *guiltless*; clear, cleared, in the clear, exonerated, exculpated, vindicated; uncondemned, unpunished, unchastised, immune, exempted, exempt 919 *nonliable*; let off, let off the hook, discharged, without a stain on one's character 746 *liberated*; reprieved 909 *forgiven*; recommended for mercy.

**Vb.** *acquit*, find *or* pronounce not guilty, prove innocent, find that the case is not proven, justify, whitewash, get one off 927 *vindicate*; clear, absolve, exonerate, exculpate; find there is no case to answer, not press charges, not prosecute 919 *exempt*; discharge, let go, let off 746 *liberate*; reprieve, respite, pardon, remit the penalty 909 *forgive*; quash, quash the conviction, set aside the sentence, allow an appeal 752 *abrogate*.

## 961 Condemnation

**N.** *condemnation*, unfavourable verdict, hostile v.; finding of guilty, conviction; successful prosecution, unsuccessful defence; final condemnation, damnation, perdition; blacklist, index 924 *disapprobation*; excommunication 899 *malediction*; doom, judgment, sentence 963 *punishment*; writing on the wall 511 *omen*; outlawry, price on one's head, proscription, attainder; death warrant, condemned cell, execution chamber, electric chair, Death Row; black cap, thumbs down.

**Adj.** *condemned*, found guilty, made liable; convicted, sentenced; sentenced to death; proscribed, outlawed, with a price on one's head; self-convicted, confessing; without a case, having no case, without a leg to stand on; nonsuited 924 *disapproved*; lost, damned, in hell, burning, frying.

**Vb.** *condemn*, prove guilty, bring home the charge; find liable, find against, nonsuit; find guilty, pronounce g., convict, sentence; sentence to death, put on the black cap, sign one's death warrant; reject one's defence, reject one's appeal 607 *reject*; proscribe, attaint, outlaw, bar, put a price on one's head 954 *make illegal*; blacklist 924 *disapprove*; damn, excommunicate 899 *curse*; convict oneself, stand condemned out of one's own mouth 936

*be guilty*; plead guilty, sign a confession, be verballed 526 *confess*.

## 962 Reward

**N.** *reward*, guerdon, remuneration, recompense; meed, deserts, just d. 913 *justice*; recognition, due r., acknowledgment, thanks 907 *gratitude*; tribute, deserved t., proof of regard, bouquets, brownie points (inf) 923 *praise*; prize-giving, award, presentation, prize, Nobel P.; crown, cup, pot, shield, certificate, medal 729 *trophy*; consolation prize, booby p.; honour 729 *decoration*; birthday honours 866 *honours*; letters after one's name, peerdom 870 *title*; prize money, cash prize, jackpot; prize fellowship, scholarship, bursary, stipend, exhibition 703 *economic aid*; reward for service, fee, retainer, refresher, honorarium, payment, payment in kind, remuneration, emolument, pension, salary, wage, wages, increment 804 *pay*; overtime pay, performance-related pay, productivity bonus 612 *incentive*; perquisite, perks, expense account, fringe benefits; income, turnover 771 *earnings*; return, profitable r., profit, margin of p., bottom line 771 *gain*; compensation, indemnification, satisfaction; consideration, quid pro quo 31 *offset*; comeuppance 714 *retaliation*; reparation 787 *restitution*; bounty, gratuity, golden handshake, golden parachute, redundancy money; commission, dastur, rake-off, kickback; golden handcuffs; tip, solatium, douceur, sweetener, pourboire, trinkgeld, baksheesh 781 *gift*; tempting offer 759 *offer*; golden hello, bait, lure, bribe, backhander, brown envelope 612 *incentive*; slush fund, hush money, smart m., protection m., blackmail.

**Adj.** *rewarding*, prize-giving; generous, open-handed 813 *liberal*; paying, profitable, remunerative, bankable 771 *gainful*; promising 759 *offering*; compensatory, indemnificatory, reparatory 787 *restoring*; retributive 714 *retaliatory*.

**Vb.** *reward*, recompense; award, present, give a prize, offer a reward; bestow a medal, honour with a title 866 *honour*; recognize, acknowledge, pay tribute, hand out bouquets, thank, show one's gratitude 907 *be grateful*; remunerate 804 *pay*; satisfy, tip 781 *give*; tip well 813 *be liberal*; repay, requite 714 *retaliate*; compensate, indemnify, make reparation 787 *restitute*; offer a bribe, grease the palm, win over 612 *bribe*.

*be rewarded*, gain a reward, win a prize, get a medal, receive a title; be given an honorarium, get paid, draw a salary, earn an income, have a gainful occupation 771 *acquire*; accept payment, accept a gratification 782 *receive*; take a bribe, have one's palm greased; have one's reward, get one's deserts, receive one's due 915 *deserve*; get one's comeuppance 714 *be rightly served*; reap, reap a profit 771 *gain*; reap the fruits, 'reap the whirlwind' (see quotation at 915 *deserve*).

**Adv.** *rewardingly*, profitably; for a consideration, as a reward, in compensation, for one's pains.

## 963 Punishment

**N.** *punishment*, sentence 961 *condemnation*; execution of sentence, exaction of penalty, penalization, victimization; chastisement, heads rolling, zero tolerance; chastening, castigation, carpeting 924 *reprimand*; disciplinary action, discipline; dose, pill, bitter p., hard lines, infliction, trial, visitation, punishing experience, carrying the can 731 *adversity*; just deserts, meet reward, comeuppance 915 *dueness*; doom, judgment, day of j., day of reckoning, divine justice 913 *justice*; poetic justice, retributive j., retribution, Nemesis; reckoning, repayment 787 *restitution*; requital, reprisal 714 *retaliation*; avengement 910 *revenge*; penance, self-punishment 941 *atonement*; self-mortification, self-discipline 945 *asceticism*; seppuku, hara-kiri 362 *suicide*; penology, penologist.

*corporal punishment*, bodily chastisement, smacking, slapping, trouncing, hiding, dusting, beating, punishment b., thrashing, t. of a lifetime, kicking; caning, whipping, flogging, birching; scourging, flagellation, running the gauntlet; ducking, keel-hauling; slap, smack, rap, rap over the knuckles, box on the ear; drubbing, blow, buffet, cuff, clout, stroke, stripe 279 *knock*; kick; third degree, torture, peine forte et dure, racking, strappado 377 *pain*.

*capital punishment*, extreme penalty 361 *death*; death sentence, death warrant; execution 362 *killing*; decapitation, beheading, guillotining, decollation; traitor's death, hanging, drawing and quartering; strangulation, garrotte, bow-stringing; hanging, long drop; electrocution, hot seat, electric chair; lethal injection; stoning, lapidation; crucifixion, impalement, flaying alive; burning, burning at the stake, auto da fé; drowning, noyade; breaking on the wheel; death by a thousand cuts; massacre, mass murder, mass execution, purge, genocide 362 *slaughter*; martyrdom, martyrization, persecution to the death; illegal execution, lynching, lynch law, contract; judicial murder.

*penalty*, injury, damage 772 *loss*; infliction, imposition, task, lines, punishment exercise;

prescribed punishment, sentence, tariff, three strikes and you're out, penalization, pains and penalties, penal code, penology; community service, community service order, community penalties; devil to pay, liability, legal l. 915 *dueness*; damages, costs, compensation, restoration 787 *restitution*; amercement, fining, mulct, fine, deodand, compulsory payment 804 *payment*; ransom 809 *price*; forfeit, forfeiture, sequestration, escheat, confiscation, deprivation 786 *expropriation*; keeping in, gating, imprisonment 747 *detention*; suspension, rustication; binding over 747 *restraint*; penal servitude, hard labour, galley service, galleys; transportation; expulsion, deportation 300 *ejection*; ostracism, sending to Coventry, banishment, exile, proscription, ban, outlawing, blackballing 57 *exclusion*; reprisal 714 *retaliation*.

*punisher*, vindicator, retaliator 910 *avenger*; inflicter, chastiser, castigator, corrector, chastener, discipliner; persecutor 735 *tyrant*; sentencer, justiciary, magistrate, court, law 957 *judge*; whipper, caner, flogger, flagellator; torturer, inquisitor; executioner, headsman, hangman, Jack Ketch; garrotter, bow-stringer; firing squad; lyncher 362 *murderer*.

**Adj.** *punitive*, penological, penal, punitory; castigatory, disciplinary, corrective; vindictive, retributive 910 *revengeful*; in reprisal 714 *retaliatory*; penalizing, fining; confiscatory, expropriatory 786 *taking*; scourging, flagellatory, torturing 377 *painful*.

*punishable*, liable, amerceable, mulctable; indictable 928 *accusable*; deserving punishment, asking for it.

**Vb.** *punish*, visit, afflict 827 *hurt*; persecute, victimize, make an example of 735 *be severe*; inflict, impose, inflict punishment, administer correction, take disciplinary action; give *or* teach one a lesson, chasten, discipline, correct, chastise, castigate; reprimand, strafe, rebuke, tell off, rap across the knuckles, smack on the wrist, have one's head for 924 *reprove*; throw the book at, come down hard on, come down on like a ton of bricks, give one what for; penalize, impose a penalty, sentence 961 *condemn*; execute justice, execute judgment, execute a sentence, carry out a s.; exact a penalty, exact retribution, settle with, get even w., pay one out *or* back 714 *retaliate*; settle, fix, bring to book, give one what was coming to him, give one his/her comeuppance, revenge oneself 910 *avenge*; amerce, mulct, fine, forfeit, deprive, sequestrate, confiscate 786 *take away*; unfrock, demote, degrade, downgrade, reduce to the ranks, suspend 867 *shame*; stand in a corner, send out of the room; tar and feather, toss in a blanket; pillory, set in the stocks; masthead; duck, keelhaul; picket, spread-eagle; lock up 747 *imprison*; transport; condemn to the galleys.

*spank*, paddle, slap, smack, slipper; cuff, clout, box on the ears, rap over the knuckles, smack on the wrist; drub, trounce, beat, belt, strap, leather, lather, larrup, wallop, welt, tan, cane, birch, switch, whack, dust, tan one's hide, give one a hiding, beat black and blue 279 *strike*.

*flog*, whip, horsewhip, thrash, hide, give a hiding, belabour, cudgel, fustigate 279 *strike*; scourge, give stripes, give strokes, give one the cat; lash, lay on the l., birch, give one the birch, flay, flay one's back, lay one's back open; flail, flagellate, bastinado.

*torture*, give the third degree; give one the works 377 *give pain*; put one to torture, thumbscrew, rack, put on the r., break on the wheel, mutilate, kneecap, persecute, martyrize 827 *torment*.

*execute*, punish with death, put to death 362 *kill*; lynch 362 *murder*; dismember, tear limb from limb; crucify, impale; flay, flay alive; stone, stone to death 712 *lapidate*; shoot, fusillade, stand against a wall; burn, burn alive, burn at the stake, send to the s.; necklace, give one a n.; bow-string, garrotte, strangle; gibbet, hang, hang by the neck, string up, bring to the gallows; hang, draw and quarter; send to the scaffold, bring to the block, strike off one's head, behead, decapitate, decollate, guillotine; electrocute, send to the chair, send to the hot seat; gas, put in the gas chamber; commit genocide, hold mass executions, purge, massacre, decimate 362 *slaughter*.

*be punished*, suffer punishment, take the consequences, be for the high jump, have it coming to one, get one's come-uppance, catch it, catch *or* get it in the neck; take the rap, stand the racket, face the music; take one's medicine, take one's gruel, hold one's hand out; get what one was asking for, get one's deserts; kiss the gunner's daughter; regret it, smart for it; pay the ultimate price, come to execution, lay one's head on the block; come to the gallows, take a ride to Tyburn, dance upon nothing, swing; pay for it with one's head, die the death.

**Int.** off with his head!, à la lanterne!

**964 Means of punishment**
**N.** *scourge*, birch, birch-rod, cat, cat-o'-nine-tails, rope's end, knout, cowhide, sjambok, chabouk, kourbash; whip, horsewhip, switch, quirt; lash, strap, tawse, thong, belt; cane, rattan; stick, big s., paddle, rod, ferule, ruler;

cudgel, cosh 723 *club*; rubber hose, bicycle chain, sandbag.

*pillory*, stocks, whipping post, ducking stool, cucking stool; corner, dunce's cap; stool of repentance, cutty stool; chain, irons, bilboes 748 *fetter*; prison house 748 *prison*.

*instrument of torture*, rack, thumbscrew, iron boot, pilliwinks; Iron Maiden, scavenger's daughter, triangle, wheel, treadmill; torture chamber.

*means of execution*, scaffold, block, gallows, gibbet, Tyburn tree; cross; stake; Tarpeian rock; hemlock 659 *poison*; bullet, wall; axe, headsman's a., guillotine, maiden, widow-maker; hempen collar, halter, rope, noose, drop; garrotte, bowstring; necklace; electric chair, hot seat; death chamber, lethal c., gas c., lethal injection; condemned cell, Death Row 961 *condemnation*.

SECTION FIVE

## Religion

### 965 Divineness
**N.** *divineness*, divinity, deity; godhood, godhead, godship; divine principle, Brahma; numen, numinousness, mana; being of God, divine essence, perfection, the Good the True and the Beautiful; love, Fatherhood; Brahmahood, nirvana; impersonal God, Atman, Paramatman, oversoul, world soul; Ens Entium, First Cause, primum mobile 156 *source*; divine nature, God's ways, Providence.

*divine attribute*, being 1 *existence*; perfect being 646 *perfection*; oneness 88 *unity*; infinitude 107 *infinity*; immanence, omnipresence 189 *presence*; omniscience, wisdom 490 *knowledge*; omnipotence, almightiness 160 *power*; timelessness, eternity 115 *perpetuity*; immutability, changelessness 153 *stability*; truth, sanctity, holiness, goodness, justice, mercy; transcendence, sublimity, supremacy, sovereignty, majesty, glory, light; glory of the Lord, Shekinah.

*the Deity*, God, personal god, Supreme Being, Divine B., 'Alpha and Omega' (see quotation at 52 *all*); the Infinite, the Eternal, the All-wise, the Almighty, the Most High; the All-holy, the All-merciful; Ruler of Heaven and Earth, Judge of all men, Maker of all things, Creator, Preserver; Allah; Elohim, Yahweh, Jehovah, Adonai, ineffable name, I AM; name of God, Tetragrammaton; God of Abraham, God of Moses, Lord of Hosts, God of our fathers; our Father; Demiurge; All-Father, Great Spirit, Manitou; Ahura Mazda, Ormuzd; Krishna.

*Trinity*, triad, Hindu Triad, Brahma, Siva,

Vishnu; Holy Trinity, Hypostatic Union; Triune God, Three Persons in one God, Three in One and One in Three; God the Father, God the Son, God the Holy Ghost.

*Holy Ghost*, third person of the Trinity; Holy Spirit, Spirit of Truth; Paraclete, Comforter, Consoler; Dove.

*God the Son*, second person of the Trinity, Word, Logos, Son of God, the Only Begotten, 'the Word made flesh' (see quotation at 975 *revelation*), Incarnate Son; Messiah, Son of David, rod of Jesse, the Lord's Anointed, Christ; Immanuel; Lamb of God, Son of Man, Man of Sorrows; Son of Mary, Jesus, Jesu, Jesus Christ; Holy Infant, Christ Child, Child of Bethlehem; Jesus of Nazareth, the Nazarene, the Galilean; the Good Shepherd, Saviour, Redeemer, Friend; Lord, Master; Rock of Ages, Bread of Life, True Vine; the Way the Truth and the Life; Light of the World, Sun of Righteousness; King of Kings, King of Heaven, King of Glory, Prince of Peace.

*divine function*, creation, preservation, judgment; mercy, compassion, forgiveness; inspiration, unction, regeneration, comfort, strengthening, consolation, grace, prevenient g.; propitiation, atonement, redemption, justification, salvation, mediation, intercession.

*theophany*, divine manifestation, divine emanation, descent, descent to earth, divine intervention, incarnation; transfiguration; Shekinah, Glory of the Lord; avatar, avatar of Vishnu, Krishna.

*theocracy*, divine government, divine dispensation, God's law, Kingdom of God; God's ways, God's dealings, providence, special p., deus ex machina.

*Saviour*, Redeemer, Jesus (see also *God the Son*), bodhisattva, Amitabha, Amida.

**Adj.** *divine*, holy, hallowed, sanctified, sacred, sacrosanct, heavenly, celestial; transcendental, sublime, ineffable; numinous, mystical, religious, spiritual, superhuman, supernatural, transcendent; unearthly, supramundane, extramundane, not of this world; providential; theophanic; theocratic.

*godlike*, divine, superhuman; transcendent, immanent; omnipresent 189 *ubiquitous*; immeasurable 107 *infinite*; absolute, undefined, self-existent, living 1 *existing*; timeless, eternal, everlasting, immortal 115 *perpetual*; immutable, unchanging, changeless 144 *permanent*; almighty, all-powerful, omnipotent 160 *powerful*; creative 160 *dynamic*; prescient, providential 510 *foreseeing*; all-wise, all-seeing, all-knowing, omniscient 490 *knowing*; oracular 511 *predicting*; all-merciful, merciful 909 *forgiving*; compassionate 905 *pitying*; parent-like

887 *loving*; holy, all-h., worshipped 979 *sanctified*; sovereign 34 *supreme*; majestic 733 *authoritative*; transfigured, glorious, all-g. 866 *worshipful*; theomorphic, incarnate, in the image of God, deified; messianic, anointed; Christly, Christlike.

*deistic*, theistic, Yahwistic, Elohistic.

*redemptive*, intercessional, mediatory, propitiatory; incarnational; soteriological, messianic.

**Adv.** *divinely*, as God; under God, by God's will, deo volente, D.V.; by divine right, jure divino; redemptively, as a saviour.

## 966 Deities in general

**N.** *deity*, god, goddess, deva, devi; the gods, the immortals; Olympian 967 *Olympian deity*; the unknown god, pagan g., false g., idol; godling, petty god, inferior g., subordinate g. 967 *lesser deity*; demi-god, half-god, divine hero, deified person, divine king; object of worship, fetish, totem 982 *idol*; mumbo jumbo; theogony; pantheon.

*mythic deity*, nature god *or* goddess, Pan, Flora; earth goddess, Gaia; mother earth, mother goddess, earth mother, Great Mother, Magna Mater, Cybele, Ishtar, Astarte, Isis; fertility god, Adonis, Tammuz, Marduk, Atys; god of the underworld, Pluto, Dis 967 *Chthonian deity*; sky god, Zeus, Jupiter; storm god, Indra, wind god, Aeolus; sun god, Apollo, Hyperion, Helios, Ra, Mithras; river god, sea g., Poseidon, Neptune, Varuna; war god *or* goddess, Ares, Mars, Bellona; god *or* goddess of love, Cupid, Eros, Venus, Aphrodite; household gods, Teraphim, Lares, Penates; the Fates, the Norns 596 *fate*.

**Adj.** *mythological*, mythical; theogonic; deiform, theomorphic, deific, deified.

## 967 Pantheon: classical and non-classical deities

**N.** *classical deities*, gods and goddesses of Greece and Rome, Graeco-Roman pantheon; Homeric deities, Hesiodic theogony; primeval deities, Erebus, Nox; Ge, Gaia, Tellus, Uranus, Cronus, Saturn, Rhea, Ops; Pontus, Oceanus, Tethys; Helios, Sol, Hyperion, Phaëthon; Titan, Atlas, Prometheus; Giant, Enceladus; the Fates, Parcae, Clotho, Lachesis, Atropos.

*Olympian deity*, Olympian, Zeus, Jupiter, Jove, president of the immortals; Pluto, Hades; Poseidon, Neptune; Apollo, Phoebus; Hermes, Mercury; Ares, Mars; Hephaestus, Vulcan; Dionysus, Bacchus; Hera, Juno; Demeter, Ceres; Persephone, Proserpina; Athena, Minerva; Aphrodite, Venus; Artemis, Diana; Eros, Cupid; Iris; Hebe.

*Chthonian deity*, Ge, Gaia, Dis Pater, Orcus, Hades, Pluto, Persephone; Erectheus, Trophonius, Pytho; Eumenides, Erinyes, Furies.

*lesser deity*, Pan, Silvanus, Flora, Faunus, Silenus; Aurora, Eos; Luna, Selene; Aeolus, Boreas 352 *wind*; Triton, Nereus, Proteus, Glaucus; Ate, Eris, Bellona, Nike; Astraea, Themis, Nemesis; Muses, tuneful Nine, Erato, Euterpe, Terpsichore, Polyhymnia, Clio, Calliope, Melpomene, Thalia, Urania; Asclepius, Aesculapius; Hypnos, Somnus, Morpheus; Hymen; Hestia, Vesta; Lares, Penates; local god, genius loci.

*nymph*, wood n., tree n., dryad, hamadryad; mountain nymph, oread; water nymph, naiad; sea nymph, nereid, Oceanid; Thetis, Calypso, Callisto; Pleiades, Maia; Latona, Leto; siren 970 *mythical being*.

*demigod*, divine offspring, divine hero; Heracles, Hercules; Dioscuri, Castor and Pollux, Castor and Polydeuces; Perseus, Achilles, Aeneas, Memnon.

*Hindu deities*, Brahmanic d., Vedic d.; Dyaus Pitar, Prithivi; Varuna (sky), Mitra (light), Indra (thunder), Agni (fire), Surya (sun); Trimurti, Brahma, Siva, Vishnu; Sakti, Uma *or* Parvat, Kali *or* Durga; Ganesha (luck-bringer), Karttikeya (fertility), Sarasvati (learning), Hanuman (monkey-god), Sitala (smallpox), Manasa (snakes), Lakshmi (wealth and fortune).

*Egyptian deities*, Nun, Atum; Shu (air), Tefnut (moisture), Nut (sky), Geb (earth), Osiris, Isis, Set, Nephthys; Ra *or* Re, Amon- *or* Amun-Ra, Atum-ra, Aton; Horus, elder Horus, Ra-Harakhte, Khepera; Amon, Min (all-father), Hathor (all-mother), Neith, Anata; Ptah (creator), Ma'at (truth), Imhotep (peace), Bes (dancing), Serapis (underworld); theriomorphic deity, theriocephalous d.; Apis (sacred bull), Thoth (ibis), Anubis (jackal), Sekhmet (lioness), Sebek (crocodile), Bast (cat), Setekh (hound), Uadjit (cobra), Taurt (hippopotamus).

*Semitic deities*, Nammu, Anu, Enlil, Enki *or* Ea; Shamash, Sin, Adad; Bel, Marduk; El, Baal, Aleyan-Baal; Moloch, Rimmon, Asshur; great mother, Ishtar, Ashtoreth, Astarte, Asherah, Inanna, Anat; fertility god, Tammuz, Atys; Mot, Allatu.

*Nordic deities*, Aesir, Vanir; Odin *or* Wotan, Frigg his wife; Thor (thunder god), his wife Sif, his son Ull; Tiu *or* Tyr (war), Heimdall, Balder the beautiful, Vidar the silent, Hoder the blind, Bragi (god of poetry), Hermoder (messenger), Vali (youngest son of Odin); Frey *or* Freyr (peace, fertility), Freya *or* Freyja (goddess of

love), Njord *or* Nerthus (wealth and ships), Hoenir, Odmir; Skadi; Loki (evil and strife), Hel (goddess of the dead); Aegir (ocean), his wife Ran, Mimir (guardian of the spring of wisdom), Ymir (father of the Giants).

*Celtic deities*, Dagda, Math, Magog, Oengus *or* Dwyn; Ogma, Belinus, Esos, Teutates, Taranis; Mabon, Borvo *or* Bormo; Epona; Bilé *or* Beli, Govannon or Goibniu (smith), Diancecht (medicine); Lludd *or* Nudd *or* Nuada (sun); Gwydion, Amaethon; Lleu *or* Lug (light), Dylan (darkness); sea gods, Ler or Llyr, Bran *or* Branwen, Manannan *or* Manawydan; Dana *or* Don, Morrigan (war), Brigit, Blathnat, Arianrod, Blodeuwedd, Creirwy (love), Keridwen (poetry), Rhiannon (underworld).

*Aztec deities*, Nahuan d.; Cipactli (earth dragon); Coatlicue (ancient earth goddess); Red Tezcatlipoca, Black T., White T., Blue T., Xipe Topec (spring), Quetzalcoatl (culture), Huitzilopochtli (warrior); god and goddess of creation, Tonacatecuhtli, Tonicacihuatl; deities of fertility, Cihuacoatl, Chicomecoatl, Centeotl, Tlazolteotl, Xochipilli; Tlaloc (rain), Chalcihuitlicue (water); Xiuhtecuhtli (fire), Tonatiuh (sun), Teccuiztecutl, Metztli (moon), Mixcoatl (sky), Mictlantecuhtli (death).

## 968 Angel. Saint. Madonna

**N.** *angel*, archangel, heavenly host, angelic h., choir invisible; heavenly hierarchy, thrones, principalities and powers; seraph, seraphim, cherub, cherubim; ministering spirit, Michael, Gabriel, Raphael, Uriel, Zadkiel; Israfel, Azrael, angel of death; guardian angel, tutelary spirit; angelhood, archangelship; angelophany; angelolatry; angelology.

*saint*, patron s., s. and martyr, the blessed . . . ; glorified soul, soul in bliss, Church Triumphant.

*Madonna*, Our Lady, Blessed Virgin Mary, Mother of God, Mater Dolorosa; Queen of Heaven, Queen of Angels, Stella Maris, Star of the Sea; Mariolatry.

**Adj.** *angelic*, angelical, archangelic, seraphic, cherubic; saintly, glorified, celestial.

**Vb.** *angelize*, angelify; beatify 979 *sanctify*.

## 969 Devil

**N.** *Satan*, Lucifer, fallen angel, rebel a.; Archfiend, Prince of Darkness, Prince of this world; serpent, Old S., Tempter, Adversary, Antichrist, Common Enemy, Enemy of mankind; Diabolus, Father of Lies; evil genie, Shaitan, Eblis; King of Hell, angel of the bottomless pit, Apollyon, Abaddon; the foul fiend, the Devil, the Evil One, Wicked O., Auld Nick, cloven hoof; spirit of evil, principle of e., Ahriman, Angra Mainyu.

*Mephisto*, Mephistopheles, His Satanic Majesty, the old one, the Old Gentleman, Old Nick, Auld N., Old Harry, Old Scratch, Auld Hornie, Clootie.

*devil*, fiend; devilkin, deviling, devilet, familiar, imp, imp of Satan, devil's spawn 938 *bad person*; Tutivillus, Asmodeus, Azazel 970 *demon*; malevolent spirit, unclean s., dybbuk; powers of darkness, diabolic hierarchy; damned spirit, fallen angel, lost soul, sinner, dweller in Pandemonium, denizen of Hell; Mammon, Belial, Beelzebub, Lord of the Flies; devildom, devilship, devilhood, demonship; horns, cloven hoof.

*diabolism*, devilry, demonry, diablerie 898 *inhumanity*; Satanism, devilism; devil worship, demonism, polydaemonism, demonolatry; demonomania, demoniac possession; witchcraft, black magic, Black Mass 983 *sorcery*; Satanology, demonology; demonization.

*diabolist*, Satanist, devil-worshipper, demonolater, demonist; demonologist, demonologer.

**Adj.** *diabolic*, diabolical, devil-like, satanic, Mephistophelean, fiendish, demonic, demoniacal, devilish 898 *malevolent*; infernal, hellish, hell-born; devil-worshipping, demonolatrous; demoniac, possessed; demonological.

**Vb.** *diabolize*, demonize; possess, bedevil 983 *bewitch*.

## 970 Fairy

**N.** *fairy*, fairy world, magic w., elfland, fairyland, faerie; fairy folk, good f., little people; fairy being, fay, peri; good fairy, fairy godmother 903 *benefactor*; bad fairy, witch 983 *sorceress*; fairy queen, Mab, Queen M., Titania; fairy king, Oberon, Erl King; Puck, Robin Goodfellow; spirit of air, Ariel; elemental spirit, sylph, sylphid; genius; fairy ring, pixie r.; fairyism, fairy lore, fairy tales, folklore; A Midsummer Night's Dream, The Faerie Queene.

*elf*, elves, elfin folk, alfar, hidden folk, pixie, piskie, brownie, kobold; gnome, dwarf, Nibelung; troll, trow; orc, goblin, flibbertigibbet; imp, sprite, hobgoblin; changeling; leprechaun, cluricaune, pigwidgin; poltergeist, gremlin, dybbuk; Puck, Hob, Robin Goodfellow; elvishness, goblinry.

*ghost*, spirit, departed s.; shades, souls of the dead, Manes, lemures; revived corpse, zombie; visitant, revenant, haunter, walker, poltergeist, duppy; spook, spectre, apparition, phantom, phantasm, shape, shade, wraith, presence, doppelganger, fetch 440 *visual fallacy*; control

984 *spiritualism*; White Lady, Grey L., Herne the Hunter, the Wild Huntsman, Black Shuck.

*demon*, cacodemon, flibbertigibbet, Friar Rush; imp, familiar, familiar spirit 969 *devil*; afreet *or* afrit, rakshasa; daeva, asura; shedemon, lamia, banshee; kelpie, troll, troll woman; ogre, ogress, giant, giantess, Baba Yaga; bugbear, bugaboo, bogle, bogy, bogyman, bunyip 938 *monster*; ghoul, vampire, lycanthrope, loup garou, werewolf, werefolk; incubus, succubus, succuba, nightmare; fury, harpy; Gorgon; ogreishness, ghoulishness.

*mythical being* 968 *angel*, 969 *devil*; demon, genie, jinn; houri; Valkyrie, battlemaid; centaur, cyclops, faun, gorgon, satyr; sea nymph, river n., water n., Oceanid, Naiad, water elf, kelpie, water horse, nix, nixie; merfolk, merman, mermaid; Lorelei, Siren; water spirit, Undine 967 *nymph*; the Lady of the Lake, the Old Man of the Sea; Merlin, Morgan le Fay 983 *sorcerer*; Wayland Smith, the Green Man, Wodwose; hobbit; the Abominable Snowman, Yeti, leviathan, phoenix 365 *mythical beast*.

**Adj.** *fairylike*, fairy, nymphean; sylphlike 206 *lean*; dwarf-like 196 *dwarfish*; gigantic 195 *huge*; monstrous, ogreish, devilish, demonic 969 *diabolic*; vampirish, lycanthropic; gorgonian; elf-like, elfin, elvish, impish, Puckish 898 *maleficent*; magic 983 *magical*; mythical, mythic, folklorish 513 *imaginary*.

*spooky*, spookish, ghostly, ghoulish; haunted, hagridden; nightmarish, macabre 854 *frightening*; weird, uncanny, unearthly, eldritch 84 *abnormal*; eerie, numinous, supernatural, supernormal; spectral, apparitional, wraith-like; disembodied, discarnate 320 *immaterial*; ectoplasmic, astral, spiritualistic, mediumistic 984 *psychical*.

**Vb.** *haunt*, visit, walk; ghost, gibber, mop and mow.

**Adv.** *spookishly*, spectrally, uncannily, nightmarishly; elfishly, puckishly; with its head tucked underneath its arm.

## 971 Heaven

**N.** *heaven*, presence of God, abode of G., throne of G., kingdom of G., kingdom of heaven, heavenly kingdom, kingdom come; Paradise, abode of the blest, abode of the saints, land of the leal, gates of St Peter; Abraham's bosom, eternal home, happy h.; eternal rest, celestial bliss, blessed state; nirvana, seventh heaven; the Millennium, earthly Paradise, heaven on earth, Zion, Land of Beulah, New Jerusalem, Holy City, Celestial C.; afterlife, the hereafter, eternal life, eternity 124 *future state*; Pure Land; resurrection; assumption, translation, glorification; deification, apotheosis.

*mythic heaven*, Olympus; Valhalla, Asgard; Elysium, Elysian fields, happy hunting grounds, happy hunting grounds in the skies; Earthly Paradise, Eden, Garden of E., garden of the Hesperides, Islands of the Blest, the Happy Isles, Isle of Avalon, Tir nan Og 513 *fantasy*.

**Adj.** *paradisiac*, paradisiacal, paradisal; heavenly, celestial, supernal, eternal; beatific, blessed, blissful 824 *happy*; resurrectional, glorified; Elysian, Olympian; millennial.

## 972 Hell

**N.** *hell*, place of the dead, lower world, nether w., nether regions, infernal r., underworld; grave, limbo, Sheol, Hades; purgatory; perdition, place of the damned, abode of evil spirits, inferno, Satan's palace, Pandemonium; abyss, bottomless pit, Abaddon; place of torment, Tophet, Gehenna, lake of fire and brimstone; hellfire, everlasting fire, unquenchable f.

*mythic hell*, Hel, Niflheim; realm of Pluto, Hades, Tartarus, Avernus, Erebus; river of hell, Acheron, Styx, Cocytus, Phlegethon, Lethe; Stygian Ferryman, Charon; infernal watchdog, Cerberus; infernal judge, Minos, Rhadamanthus; nether gods, Chthonians, Pluto, Osiris 967 *Chthonian deity*.

**Adj.** *infernal*, bottomless 211 *deep*; chthonian, subterranean 210 *low*; hellish, Plutonian, Avernal, Tartarean; Acherontic, Stygian, Lethean; Cerberian; Rhadamanthine; damned, devilish 969 *diabolic*.

## 973 Religion

**N.** *religion*, religious instinct 872 *humility*; religious conviction, religious belief, creed, dogma; religious feeling 979 *piety*; Messianism 507 *expectation*; search for truth, religious quest; natural religion, deism; primitive religion, early faith; paganism 982 *idolatry*; neo-paganism, Wicca; nature religion, orgiastic r., mystery r., mysteries, Eleusinian m., Orphism; dharma, revealed religion, historical r., incarnational r., sacramental r.; mysticism, Sufism; yoga 981 *worship*; Eightfold Path; theosophy 449 *philosophy*; theolatry 981 *worship*; religious cult, state religion, official r. 981 *cult*; untheological religion, creedless r., personal r.; no religion, atheism 974 *irreligion*.

*deism*, belief in a god, theism; animism, pantheism, panentheism, polytheism, henotheism, monotheism, dualism; gnosticism.

*religious faith*, faith 485 *belief*; Christianity, the Cross; Judaism; Islam, Muhammadanism *or* Mohammedanism, the Crescent; Baha'ism

*or* Baha'i; Ahmaddiya; Zoroastrianism, Mazdaism; Vedic religion, Dharma; Hinduism, Brahmanism, Vedantism, Tantrism; Vaishnavism 978 *sectarianism*; Sikhism; Jainism; Buddhism, Theravada, Hinayana, Mahayana, Jodo, Pure Land, Zen; Shintoism; Taoism, Confucianism; Theosophy; Scientology.

*theology*, study of religion; natural theology, revealed t.; religious knowledge, religious learning, divinity; scholastic theology, scholasticism, Scotism, Thomism; Rabbinism; isagogics, theological exegesis; typology; demythologization; Christology; soteriology, theodicy; pneumatology; hamartiology; eschatology; hagiology, hagiography, iconology; dogmatics, dogmatic theology; symbolics, credal theology; liberation theology; tradition, deposit of faith; teaching, doctrine, religious d., received d., defined d.; definition, canon; doxy, dogma, tenet; articles of faith, credo 485 *creed*; confession, Thirty-nine Articles, Westminster Confession of Faith, Augsburg Confession, Apostles' Creed, Nicene C., Athanasian C.; fundamentalism 976 *orthodoxism*; Bibliology, higher criticism; comparative religion.

*theologian*, theologue; divinity student, divine; doctor, doctor of the Church; doctor of the Law, rabbi, scribe, mufti, mullah; schoolman, scholastic, scholastic theologian, Thomist, Talmudist, canonist; theogonist, hagiologist, hagiographer, iconologist; psalmist, hymnographer, hymnwriter; textualist, Masorete; Bible critic, higher c.; scripturalist, fundamentalist, rabbinist.

*religious teacher*, prophet, rishi, inspired writer; guru, maharishi 500 *sage*; evangelist, apostle, missionary; reformer, religious r.; expected leader, Messiah, Mahdi, Invisible Imam, twelfth avatar of Vishnu, future Buddha, Maitreya; founder of Christianity, Christ, Jesus Christ; Prophet of God, Muhammad, Mohammed *or* Mahomet; Zoroaster *or* Zarathustra; Ramakrishna, Baha'ullah; Buddha, Gautama; Confucius, Lao-tzu; Joseph Smith, Mary Baker Eddy, Madame Blavatsky; expounder, hierophant, gospeller, catechist 520 *interpreter*.

*religionist*, deist, theist; monotheist, henotheist, polytheist, pantheist; animist, fetishist 982 *idolater*; pagan, gentile 974 *heathen*; people of the book; adherent, believer, true b., orthodoxist 976 *the orthodox*; militant, believer 979 *zealot*; Christian, Nazarene; Jew; Muslim *or* Moslem, Islamite, Mussulman, Muhammedan *or* Mohammedan; Sunnite, Shi'ite 978 *non-Christian sect*; Sufi, dervish; Druze, Mandaean *or* Mandean, Manichaean *or* Manichean,

Yezidi; Baha'i; Parsee, Zoroastrian; Hindu, gymnosophist, Brahmanist; Sikh; Jain; Buddhist, Zen B.; Tantrist; Taoist; Confucianist; Shintoist; Theosophist; Mormon 978 *sect*; Rosicrucian 984 *occultist*; gnostic 977 *heretic*.

**Adj.** *religious*, divine, holy, sacred, spiritual, sacramental; deistic, theistic, animistic, pantheistic, henotheistic, monotheistic, dualistic; Christian; Islamic, Muslim *or* Moslem, Muhammadan *or* Mohammedan; Jewish, Judaistic, Mosaic; Baha'i; Zoroastrian, Avestan; Confucian, Taoistic; Buddhistic, Hinduistic, Vedic, Brahminical, Upanishadic, Vedantic; yogic, mystic, Sufic; devotional, devout, practising 981 *worshipping*.

*theological*, theosophical, scholastic, rabbinic, rabbinical; doctrinal, dogmatic, credal, canonical; Christological, soteriological; doxological 988 *ritualistic*; hagiological, iconological.

## 974 Irreligion

**N.** *irreligion*, unreligiousness, unspirituality; nothing sacred, profaneness, ungodliness, godlessness 980 *impiety*; false religion, heathenism 982 *idolatry*; no religion, atheism, nullifidianism, dissent from all creeds, disbelief 486 *unbelief*; humanism; agnosticism, scepticism, Pyrrhonism 486 *doubt*; probabilism, euhemerism 449 *philosophy*; lack of faith, infidelity; lapse, lapse from faith, recidivism, backsliding 603 *tergiversation*; paganization, dechristianization, post-Christian state; amoralism, apathy, indifferentism 860 *indifference*.

*antichristianity*, antichristianism 704 *opposition*; paganism, heathenism, heathendom; Satanism 969 *diabolism*; free thinking, free thought, rationalism, positivism, nihilism 449 *philosophy*; hylotheism, materialism; secularism, worldliness, fleshliness 944 *sensualism*; Mammonism 816 *avarice*.

*irreligionist*, Antichrist; nullifidian, dissenter, dissenter from all creeds, no believer, atheist 486 *unbeliever*; humanist; rationalist, euhemerist, freethinker; agnostic, sceptic, Pyrrhonist; nihilist, materialist, positivist; secularist, Mammonist, Mammonite, worldling, amoralist, indifferentist.

*heathen*, non-Christian, pagan, paynim; misbeliever, infidel, giaour; gentile, the uncircumcised, the unbaptized, the unconverted; apostate, backslider, lapsed Christian 603 *tergiversator*.

**Adj.** *irreligious*, having no religion, without r., without a god, godless, altarless, profane 980 *impious*; nihilistic, atheistic, atheistical; humanistic; creedless, nullifidian, agnostic, doubting, sceptical, Pyrrhonian, Pyrrhonic 486 *unbelieving*; free-thinking,

rationalizing, rationalistic, euhemeristic; nonreligious, nonworshipping, nonpractising, nontheological, noncredal 769 *nonobservant*; undevout, unreligious, unspiritual, ungodly 934 *wicked*; amoral, morally neutral 860 *indifferent*; secular, mundane, of this world, worldly, materialistic, Mammonistic 944 *sensual*; lacking faith, faithless, backsliding, recidivous, lapsed, paganized, post-Christian 603 *tergiversating*; unchristian, non-Christian; anti-religious, anti-Christian, anti-Church, anti-clerical.

*heathenish*, unholy, unhallowed, unsanctified, unblest, unconsecrated 980 *profane*; unchristian, unbaptized, unconfirmed; gentile, uncircumcised; heathen, pagan, infidel; pre-Christian, unconverted, in darkness 491 *uninstructed*.

**Vb.** *be irreligious*, – atheistic etc. adj.; have no religion, lack faith; remain unconverted 486 *disbelieve*; shut one's eyes to the light, love darkness, serve Mammon; lose one's faith, suffer a lapse of faith, give up the Church 603 *change one's allegiance*; have no use for religion, scoff at r.; euhemerize, demythologize, rationalize; persecute the faith, deny God, blaspheme 980 *be impious*.

*paganize*, heathenize, de-Christianize; desanctify, deconsecrate, undedicate, secularize.

## 975 Revelation

**N.** *revelation*, divine r., apocalypse 526 *disclosure*; illumination 417 *light*; afflatus, divine a., inspiration, divine i.; prophecy, prophetic inspiration, word of knowledge; intuition, mystical i., mysticism; direct communication, the Law, Mosaic L., Ten Commandments; divine message, God's word, gospel, gospel message; God revealed, theophany, burning bush, epiphany; incarnation, avatar, 'the Word made flesh';

> In the beginning was the Word, and the Word was with God, and the Word was God. . . .
> . . . And the Word was made flesh, and dwelt among us, . . .
> Bible, St John's Gospel

emanation, divine e.

*scripture*, word of God, inspired text, sacred t., sacred writings; Bible, Holy B., Holy Scripture, Holy Writ, the Book, the Good Book, the Word; Wyclif's Bible, Geneva *or* Breeches B., King James's Bible, Authorized Version, Revised V., Revised Standard V., Jerusalem Bible, New English B., Good News B., New International Version; Itala, Italic Version, Vulgate, Douai Version; Greek version, Septuagint; canonical writings, canonical books, canon; Old Testament, Pentateuch,

Hexateuch, Octateuch, Major Prophets, Minor P.; Torah, the Law and the Prophets, Hagiographa; New Testament, Gospels, Synoptic G., Epistles, Pastoral E., Pauline E., Johannine E., Petrine E.; Acts of the Apostles, Revelation, Apocalypse; noncanonical writings, Apocrypha, agrapha, logia, sayings, noncanonical gospel; patristic writings; psalter, psalmbook, breviary, missal; prayer book, Book of Common Prayer 981 *prayers*; hymn book, hymnal 981 *hymn*; textual commentary, Masorah, Higher Criticism; fundamentalism, scripturalism.

---

**Scriptures**

*Christian scriptures:* Bible, Old Testament, New Testament; Apocrypha; Book of Mormon, Science and Health with Key to the Scriptures.

*Jewish scriptures:* Torah, Targum, Talmud, Mishnah, Gemara.

*Muslim scriptures:* Koran *or* Qur'an, the Glorious Koran; Hadith, Sunna *or* Sunnah.

*Baha'i scriptures:* Kitab-i-Aqdas (Most Holy Book), Kitab-i-Iqan (Book of Certitude), Kalimat-i-Maknunih (The Hidden Words), Haft Vadi (Seven Valleys), Epistle to the Son of the Wolf.

*Hindu scriptures:* Veda, the Four Vedas, Rigveda, Yajurveda, Samaveda, Atharvaveda; Brahmana, Upanishad, Purana; Bhagavad Gita.

*Buddhist scriptures:* Pitaka, Tripitaka *or* Tipitaka, Dhammapada, Lotus Sutra, Nikaya.

*Sikh scriptures:* Granth, Adi Granth, Guru Granth Sahib, Dasam Granth, Japji.

*Taoist scriptures:* Tao Te Ching *or* Lao-tzu, Chuang-tzu, Lieh-tzu.

*Zoroastrian scriptures:* Avesta, Zend-Avesta.

---

*non-Biblical scripture*, sruti, smriti, shastra, sutra, tantra; Book of the Dead (Egyptian).

**Adj.** *revelational*, inspirational, mystic; inspired, prophetic, revealed, epiphanous; visional; apocalyptic; prophetic, evangelical; mystagogic.

*scriptural*, sacred, holy; hierographic, hieratic; revealed, inspired, prophetic; canonical 733 *authoritative*; biblical, Mosaic, pre-exilic, exilic, postexilic; gospel, evangelistic, apostolic; subapostolic, patristic, homiletic; Talmudic, Mishnaic; Koranic, uncreated; Vedic, Upanishadic, Puranic; textuary, textual, Masoretic.

## 976 Orthodoxy

**N.** *orthodoxy*, orthodoxness, correct opinion, right belief; sound theology, Trinitarianism; religious truth, gospel t., pure Gospel 494 *truth*; scripturality, canonicity; the Faith, the true faith, the whole f., deposit of f., 'the faith once delivered unto the saints';

> Beloved, when I gave all diligence to write unto you of the common salvation, it was needful for me to write unto you, and exhort you that ye

> should earnestly contend for the faith which was once delivered unto the saints.
>
> Bible, Epistle of Jude

primitive faith, early Church, Apostolic age; ecumenicalism, catholicity, Catholicism; formulated faith, credo 485 *creed*; Apostles' Creed, Nicene C., Athanasian C.; Thirty-nine Articles, Westminster Confession of Faith, Augsburg Confession, Tridentine decrees; textuary, catechism, Church Catechism.

*orthodoxism*, strictness, strict interpretation; scripturalism, textualism, fundamentalism, literalism, precisianism; Karaism (Jewish); traditionalism, institutionalism, ecclesiasticism, churchianity 985 *the church*; sound churchmanship 83 *conformity*; Christian practice 768 *observance*; intolerance, heresy-hunting, persecution; suppression of heresy, extermination of error, Counter-Reformation; religious censorship, Holy Office 956 *tribunal*; Inquisition 459 *interrogation*; Index, Index Expurgatorius, Index Librorum Prohibitorum 924 *disapprobation*; guaranteed orthodoxy, imprimatur 923 *approbation*.

*Christendom*, Christian world, the Church; undivided Church; Christian fellowship, communion of saints; Holy Church, Mother C.; Bride of Christ; Body of Christ, universal Church; Church Militant, Church on earth, visible Church; invisible Church, Church Triumphant; established Church, recognized C., denominational C.; Orthodox C., Eastern Orthodox C., Armenian C., Coptic C.; Church of Rome, Roman Catholic and Apostolic C.; Church of England, Episcopalian C.; Church of Scotland; United Free Church, Free Church; Church of South India; Reformed Church, Protestant C., Lutheran C., Calvinist C.; Ecumenical Council, World Council of Churches.

*Catholicism*, Orthodoxy, Eastern O.; Roman Catholicism, Romanism, popery, papistry, ultramontanism, Scarlet Woman; Counter-Reformation; Old Catholicism; Anglicanism, Episcopalianism, prelacy; Anglo-Catholicism, High Church; Tractarianism, Oxford Movement.

*Protestantism*, the Reformation, Anglicanism, Lutheranism, Zwinglianism, Calvinism; Presbyterianism, Congregationalism, United Reformed Church, Baptists; Quakerism, Society of Friends; Wesleyanism, Methodism, Primitive M. 978 *sect*.

*Catholic*, Orthodox, Eastern O.; Greek O., Russian O., Coptic; Roman Catholic, Romanist, papist, ultramontanist; Old Catholic, Anglo-C., Anglican, Episcopalian, High-Churchman, Tractarian.

*Protestant*, reformer, Anglican, Lutheran,

Zwinglian, Calvinist, Huguenot, Anabaptist; Presbyterian, Wee Free, Congregationalist, United Reformist, Baptist, Wesleyan, Methodist, Wesleyan M., Primitive M.; Quaker, Friend; Plymouth Brother.

*church member*, churchman *or* -woman, churchgoer, regular churchgoer, pillar of the church; Christian, disciple of Christ, follower of C.; the baptized, the confirmed; practising Christian, communicant 981 *worshipper*; the saints, the faithful, the body of the f., church people, chapel p.; congregation, coreligionist, fellow-worshipper.

*the orthodox*, the believing, the faithful, the converted; born-again Christian, evangelical; believer, true b.; pillar of orthodoxy, conformer 83 *conformist*; traditionalist, scripturalist, textualist, literalist, fundamentalist, fundie (inf), inerrantist 973 *theologian*.

**Adj.** *orthodox*, holding the faith, reciting the creed 485 *believing*; right-minded, sound, balanced 480 *judicial*; nonheretical, unschismatical 488 *assenting*; undivided 52 *whole*; unswerving, undeviating, loyal, devout 739 *obedient*; practising, conforming, conventional 83 *conformable*; churchy 979 *pietistic*; precise, strict, pedantic; hyperorthodox, overreligious, holier than thou, bible-thumping *or* bashing; intolerant, witch-hunting, heresy-h., inquisitional 459 *enquiring*; correct 494 *accurate*; of faith, to be believed, doctrinal 485 *creedal*; authoritative, defined, canonical, biblical, scriptural, evangelical, gospel 494 *genuine*; textual, literal, fundamentalist, fundamentalistic, fundie (inf); Trinitarian; Athanasian; catholic, ecumenical, universal; accepted, held, widely h., believed, generally b. 485 *credible*; traditional, customary 610 *usual*.

*Roman Catholic*, Catholic, Roman, Romish, Romanist, Romanizing, ultramontanist; popish, papistic.

*Anglican*, episcopalian; tractarian, Anglo-Catholic, High-Church, high, spiky; Low-Church; Broad-C., Latitudinarian.

*Protestant*, reformed; denominational 978 *sectarian*; Lutheran, Zwinglian, Calvinist, Calvinistic; Presbyterian, Congregational, United Reformed, Baptist, Methodist, Wesleyan, Quaker; bishopless, nonepiscopal.

**Vb.** *be orthodox*, – catholic etc. adj.; hold the faith, recite the creeds 485 *believe*; support the church, go to c., be a regular churchgoer 83 *conform*; catholicize, Romanize; Protestantize; Anglicanize; Lutheranize; Calvinize; Presbyterianize.

**Adv.** *orthodoxly*, catholicly, ecumenically.

## 977 Heterodoxy

**N.** *heterodoxy*, other men's doxy; unorthodoxy, unauthorized belief, unauthorized doubts, personal judgment; erroneous opinion, wrong belief, misbelief, false creed, superstition 495 *error*; strange doctrine, new teaching, bad t.; perversion of the truth 535 *misteaching*; doubtful orthodoxy, heretical tendency, latitudinarianism, modernism, Higher Criticism; unscripturality, noncatholicity, partial truth; heresy, rank h.

*heresy*, heathen theology, Gnosticism; Monarchianism, Arianism; Socinianism; Unitarianism; Apollinarianism, Nestorianism; Monophysitism, Monothelitism; Pelagianism, Semi-Pelagianism; Montanism, Donatism, Manichaeism, Albigensianism, antinomianism; Lollardy; Erastianism, antipapalism.

*heretic*, arch-h., heresiarch; Ebionite; Monarchian, Unitarian; Sabellius, Sabellian; Arius, Arian; Nestorius, Nestorian; Eutyches, Eutychian; Apollinaris, Apollinarian; Monophysite, Monothelite; Pelagius, Pelagian, Semi-Pelagian; Montanus, Montanist, millenarian; Donatus, Donatist; Gnostic, Basilidian, Marcionist *or* Marcionite, Ophite, Valentinian; Mani, Manichaean *or* Manichean *or* Manichee, Paulician, Bogomil, Albigensian, Cathar; antinomian; Wycliffite, Lollard, Hussite; Socinus, Socinian; Waldenses.

**Adj.** *heterodox*, differing, unconventional 15 *different*; dissentient 489 *dissenting*; nondoctrinaire, nonconformist 84 *unconformable*; uncatholic, antipapal; less than orthodox, erroneous 495 *mistaken*; unorthodox, unbiblical, unscriptural, unauthorized, unsanctioned, proscribed 757 *prohibited*; heretical, anathematized, damnable 961 *condemned*.

*heretical*, heretic; heathen, Gnostic, Manichean, Monarchian, Unitarian, Socinian; Arian, Eutychian, Apollinarian, Nestorian, Monophysitic, Monothelite; Pelagian; Montanist; Manichaean, Albigensian; Antinomian, Waldensian, Wycliffite, Lollard, Hussite.

**Vb.** *declare heretical*, anathematize 961 *condemn*.

*be heretical*, – unorthodox etc. adj.

**Adv.** *heretically*, unorthodoxly.

## 978 Sectarianism

**N.** *sectarianism*, particularism, exclusiveness, clannishness, cliquishness, sectionalism 481 *prejudice*; bigotry 481 *bias*; party-mindedness, party spirit, factiousness 709 *quarrelsomeness*; independence, separatism, schismaticalness, schismatical tendency 738 *disobedience*; denominationalism, nonconformism, nonconformity 489 *dissent*; Lutheranism, Calvinism, Anabaptism, Pietism, Moravianism, Puritanism 976 *Protestantism*; Puseyism, Tractarianism 976 *Catholicism*.

*schism*, division, divisions, differences 709 *quarrel*; dissociation, breakaway, splintering, secession, withdrawal 46 *separation*; nonrecognition, mutual excommunication 883 *seclusion*; recusancy 769 *nonobservance*; religious schism, Great Schism.

*church party*, Judaizers, Ebionites; Homoousians, Homoiousians; ultramontanists, papalists; Gallicans; Erastians; High-Church party, Episcopalians, Puseyites, Tractarians 976 *Catholic*; Low-Church party, Evangelicals, Puritans 976 *Protestant*; Broad Church party, Latitudinarians, Modernists; Universalists.

*sect*, division, off-shoot, branch, group, faction, splinter group 708 *party*; order, religious o., brotherhood, sisterhood 708 *community*; nonconformist sect, chapel, conventicle 976 *Protestantism*; Society of Friends, Friends, Quakers; Unitarians; Moravians; Plymouth Brethren; Churches of Christ; Sabbatarians, Seventh-day Adventists; Church of Christ Scientist; Church of Jesus Christ of the Latter-Day Saints, Mormons; Jehovah's Witnesses; Salvation Army, Salvationists; Oxford Group, Moral Rearmament.

*non-Christian sect*, Jewish s.; Orthodox Jews, Reform J.; Pharisees, Sadducees; Hasidim, Rabbinists; Karaites; Nazarites, Essenes; pagano-christian sect, Gnostics, Mandaeans *or* Mandeans, Manichaeans *or* Manicheans, Euchites; Islamic sect, Sunnis, Shi'ites, Sufis, Wahhabis; Druze, Yezidis; Black Muslims; Rastafarians, Rastas; Hindu sect, Vedantists, Vaishnavas, Saivas, Shaktas; Brahmoists, Hare Krishna sect; Tantrists, Pure Land sect, Jodo s. 973 *religious faith*.

*sectarian*, particularist; follower, adherent, devotee; Sectary, Nonconformist, Independent; Puritan, Shaker; Quaker, Friend; Pentecostalist; Presbyterian, Wee Free, Covenanter 976 *Protestant*; Salvationist; Christian Scientist; Jehovah's Witness; Unitarian; Seventh-day Adventist, Mennonite; Mormon; Moonie; Christadelphian, Scientologist, Gnostic 977 *heretic*.

*schismatic*, separated brother; schismatics, separated brethren; separatist, separationist; seceder, secessionist; splinter group; factionary, factionist 709 *quarreller*; rebel, mutineer 738 *revolter*; recusant, nonjuror; dissident, dissenter, nonconformist 489 *dissentient*; wrong believer 977 *heretic*; apostate 603 *tergiversator*.

**Adj.** *sectarian*, particularist; party-minded, partisan 481 *biased*; clannish, exclusive 708 *sectional*; Judaizer, Ebionite; Gallican; Erastian; High-Church, episcopalian 976 *Anglican*; Low-Church, evangelical 976 *Protestant*; Puritan, Independent, Presbyterian, Covenanting; revivalist, Pentecostalist; Vaishnavite, Saiva, Shakta, Tantrist; Ramakrishna; Rastafarian; Sunni, Shi'ite, Sufic; Essene, Pharisaic, Sadducean, Hasidic; Gnostic.

*schismatical*, schismatic, secessionist, seceding, breakaway; divided, separated 46 *separate*; excommunicated, excommunicable 977 *heretical*; dissentient, non-conformist 489 *dissenting*; recusant 769 *nonobservant*; rebellious, rebel, contumacious 738 *disobedient*; apostate 603 *change one's allegiance*.

**Vb.** *sectarianize*, follow a sect 708 *join a party*.

*schismatize*, commit schism, separate, divide, withdraw, secede, break away, form a splinter group, hive off 603 *apostatize*; be in a state of schism, be contumacious 738 *disobey*.

## 979 Piety

**N.** *piety*, piousness, goodness 933 *virtue*; reverence, veneration, honour, decent respect 920 *respect*; affection, kind feeling, friendly f. 897 *benevolence*; dutifulness, loyalty, conformity, attendance at worship, regular churchgoing 768 *observance*; churchmanship, sound c. 976 *orthodoxy*; religiousness, religion, theism 973 *deism*; religious feeling, pious sentiment, theopathy; fear of God, godly fear 854 *fear*; submissiveness, humbleness 872 *humility*; pious belief, faith, trust, trust in God 485 *belief*; devotion, dedication, self-surrender 931 *disinterestedness*; devoutness, sincerity, earnestness, unction; enthusiasm, fervour, zeal, muscular Christianity; exaltation, inspiration, word of knowledge, charisma, speaking in tongues, glossolalia, xenoglossia, charismatic movement 821 *excitation*; adoration, prostration 981 *worship*; prayerfulness, meditation, retreat; contemplation, mysticism, communion with God, mystic communion 973 *religion*; faith healing 656 *restoration*; act of piety, pious duty, charity 901 *philanthropy*; pious fiction, edifying reading, tract, sermon; good works, Christian behaviour, Christian life; pilgrimage, hajj.

*sanctity*, sanctitude, holiness, hallowedness, sacredness, sacrosanctity; goodness, cardinal virtues, theological v. 933 *virtue*; cooperation with grace, synergism; state of grace, odour of sanctity 950 *purity*; godliness, saintliness, holy character; spirituality, unworldliness, otherworldliness; spiritual life, life in God; sainthood, blessedness, blessed state; enlightenment, Buddhahood, satori 981 *wor-*

*ship*; conversion, regeneration, rebirth, new birth 656 *revival*; sanctification, justification, adoption 965 *divine function*; canonization, beatification, consecration, dedication 866 *dignification*.

*pietism*, show of piety, sanctimony; sanctimoniousness, unction, cant 542 *sham*; religionism, religiosity, religious mania; bible-thumping *or* bashing, overpiety, overorthodoxy 976 *orthodoxism*; scrupulosity, tender conscience; austerity 945 *asceticism*; formalism, precisianism, Puritanism 481 *narrow mind*; literalness, fundamentalism, Bible-worship, bibliolatry 494 *accuracy*; sabbatarianism 978 *sectarianism*; churchianity, churchiness, sacerdotalism, ritualism 985 *ecclesiasticism*; preachiness, unctuousness; odium theologicum 888 *hatred*; bigotry, fanaticism 481 *prejudice*; persecution, witch-hunting, heresy-h. 735 *severity*; crusading spirit, missionary s., salvationism 901 *philanthropy*.

*pietist*, pious person, real saint 937 *good person*; children of God, c. of light; the good, the righteous, the just; conformist 488 *assenter*; professing Christian, practising C., communicant 981 *worshipper*; confessor, martyr; beatified person, saint, bodhissattva, marabout; man *or* woman of prayer, contemplative, mystic, sufi; holy man, sadhu, sannyasi, bhikshu, fakir, dervish 945 *ascetic*; hermit, anchorite 883 *solitary*; monk, nun, religious 986 *clergy*; devotee, dedicated soul; convert, neophyte, catechumen, ordinand 538 *learner*; believer, true b., the faithful 976 *church member*; the chosen people, the elect, children of delight; pilgrim, palmer, hajji; votary.

*zealot*, religionist, enthusiast, wowser, fanatic, bigot, image-breaker, iconoclast; formalist, precisian, Puritan; Pharisee, scribe, scribes and Pharisees; the unco guid (Scots), goody-goody; fundamentalist, fundie (inf), inerrantist, Bible-worshipper, bibliolater, Sabbatarian 978 *sectarian*; bible-puncher *or* -thumper *or* -basher; sermonizer, pulpiteer 537 *preacher*; evangelical, salvationist, hot-gospeller; missionary 901 *philanthropist*; revivalist, speaker in tongues, faith healer; champion of the faith, crusader, militant Christian; militant Islamite, ghazi; persecutor 735 *tyrant*.

**Adj.** *pious*, good, kind 897 *benevolent*, 933 *virtuous*; decent, reverent 920 *respectful*; faithful, true, loyal, devoted 739 *obedient*; conforming, traditional 768 *observant*; believing, holding the faith 976 *orthodox*; sincere, practising, professing, confessing 540 *veracious*; pure, pure in heart, holy-minded, heavenly-m.; unworldly, otherworldly, spiritual; godly, God-fearing,

religious, devout; praying, prayerful, psalm-singing, happy-clappy (inf) 981 *worshipping*; in retreat, meditative, contemplative, mystic; holy, saintly, saintlike, sainted; Christian, Christ-like, full of grace.

*pietistic*, ardent, fervent, seraphic; enthusiastic, inspired; austere 945 *ascetic*; hermit-like, anchoretic 883 *unsociable*; earnest, pi, religiose, overreligious, overpious, overdevout, overrighteous, self-righteous, holier than thou; overstrict, precise, Puritan 678 *meddling*; formalistic, Pharisaic, ritualistic 978 *sectarian*; priest-ridden, churchy; psalm-singing, hymn-s.; preachy, bible-thumping *or* -bashing, sanctimonious, canting 850 *affected*; goody-goody, too good to be true 933 *virtuous*; crusading, evangelical, missionary-minded.

*sanctified*, made holy, consecrated, dedicated, enshrined; reverend, holy, sacred, solemn, sacrosanct 866 *worshipful*; haloed, sainted, canonized, beatified; adopted, justified; chosen; saved, redeemed, ransomed 746 *liberated*; regenerate, renewed, reborn, born again 656 *restored*.

**Vb.** *be pious*, – religious etc. adj.; be holy, wear a halo; have one's mind on higher things, mind heavenly things, think of God; fear God 854 *fear*; have faith 485 *believe*; keep the faith, 'fight the good fight' (see quotations at 933 *be virtuous*) 162 *be strong*; walk humbly with one's God (see quotation at 933 *be virtuous*), humble oneself 872 *be humble*; go to church, be a regular churchgoer, attend divine worship; pray, say one's prayers 981 *worship*; kneel, genuflect, bow 311 *stoop*; cross oneself, make the sign of the cross; make offering, sacrifice, devote 759 *offer*; give alms and oblations, lend to God 781 *give*; give to the poor, give to charity 897 *be benevolent*; glorify God 923 *praise*; give God the glory 907 *thank*; revere, show reverence 920 *show respect*; hearken, listen 739 *obey*; sermonize, preachify, preach at 534 *teach*; let one's light shine, set a good example.

*become pious*, be converted, experience religion, get religion; change one's religion, go over, turn 603 *change one's mind*; see the light, see the error of one's ways 603 *recant*; mend one's ways, reform, repent, repent of one's evil ways, receive Christ 939 *be penitent*; enter the church, become ordained, take holy orders, take vows, take the veil 986 *take orders*; be a pilgrim, go on a pilgrimage, perform the hajj.

*make pious*, bring religion to, bring to God, proselytize, convert 485 *convince*; Christianize, win for Christ, baptize, receive into the church 299 *admit*; Islamize, Judaize; depaganize, spiritualize 648 *purify*; edify, confirm, strengthen one's faith, confirm in the f. 162 *strengthen*; inspire, fill with grace, uplift 654 *make better*; redeem, regenerate 656 *restore*.

*sanctify*, hallow, make holy, keep h. 866 *honour*; spiritualize, consecrate, dedicate, enshrine 866 *dignify*; make a saint of, saint, canonize, beatify, invest with a halo; bless, pronounce a blessing, make the sign of the cross.

## 980 Impiety

**N.** *impiety*, impiousness; irreverence, disregard 921 *disrespect*; nonworship, lack of piety, lack of reverence; godlessness 974 *irreligion*; scoffing, mockery, derision 851 *ridicule*; scorn, pride 922 *contempt*; sacrilegiousness, profanity; blasphemy, cursing, swearing 899 *malediction*; sacrilege, desecration, violation, profanation, perversion, abuse 675 *misuse*; unrighteousness, consciencelessness, immorality, sin, pervertedness 934 *wickedness*; hardening, stubbornness 940 impenitence; regression 655 *deterioration*; lapse of faith, backsliding, apostasy 603 *tergiversation*; profaneness, unholiness, worldliness, materialism 319 *materiality*; amoralism, indifferentism 464 *indiscrimination*; misdirected devotion 982 *idolatry*; paganism, heathenism; rejection, reprobation 924 *disapprobation*.

*false piety*, sham p. 541 *falsehood*; solemn mockery, mummery 542 *sham*; sanctimony, sanctimoniousness, Pharisaism 979 *pietism*; hypocrisy, religious h., lip service 541 *duplicity*; cant 850 *affectation*.

*impious person*, blasphemer, curser, swearer 899 *malediction*; mocker, scorner, contemner, defamer, calumniator 926 *detractor*; sacrilegious person, desecrator, violator, profaner 904 *offender*; profane person, nonworshipper, gentile, pagan, infidel, unbeliever 974 *heathen*; misbeliever 982 *idolater*; disbeliever, atheist, sceptic 974 *irreligionist*; indifferentist, amoralist; worldling, materialist, immoralist 944 *sensualist*; sinner, reprobate, the wicked, the unrighteous, sons of Belial, children of darkness 938 *bad person*; recidivist, backslider, apostate, adulterous generation 603 *tergiversator*; fallen angel, Tempter, Wicked One 969 *Satan*; hypocrite, religious h., Tartuffe 545 *deceiver*; canter, lip-worshipper 850 *affecter*.

**Adj.** *impious*, ungodly, antireligious, anti-Christian, antichurch, anticlerical 704 *opposing*; recusant, dissenting 977 *heretical*; unbelieving, nonbelieving, atheistical, godless 974 *irreligious*; nonworshipping, undevout, nonpractising 769 *nonobservant*; misbelieving 982 *idolatrous*; scoffing, mocking, deriding 851 *derisive*; blaspheming, blasphemous, swearing 899 *cursing*; irreligious, irreverent, without reverence 921 *disrespectful*; sacrilegious, profaning, desecrating, violating, iconoclastic 954 *lawless*; unawed, brazen, bold 855 *unfearing*; hard, unmoved, unfeeling 898 *cruel*; sinning, sinful, impure, hardened, perverted, reprobate, unregenerate 934 *wicked*; lapsing, backsliding, apostate 603 *tergiversating*; canting, sanctimonious, bible-thumping *or* bashing 850 *affected*; pharisaical 541 *hypocritical*.

*profane*, unholy, unhallowed, unsanctified, unblest; forsaken by God, accursed; undedicated, unconsecrated, deconsecrated, secularized; infidel, pagan, gentile; paganized, dechristianized 974 *heathenish*.

**Vb.** *be impious*, – sacrilegious etc. adj.; rebel against God 871 *be proud*; sin 934 *be wicked*; swear, blaspheme, take the name of the Lord in vain 899 *curse*; have no reverence, show no respect 921 *not respect*; profane, desecrate, violate 675 *misuse*; commit sacrilege, lay profane hands on, defile, sully 649 *make unclean*; misbelieve, worship false gods; cant, beat one's breast 850 *be affected*; play the hypocrite, play false 541 *dissemble*; lapse, backslide 603 *change one's allegiance*; sin against the light, grow hardened, harden one's heart 655 *deteriorate*.

## 981 Worship

**N.** *worship*, honour, reverence, homage 920 *respect*; holy fear, awe 854 *fear*; veneration, adoration, prostration of the soul; humbling oneself, humbleness 872 *humility*; devotion, devotedness, bhakti 979 *piety*; prayer, one's devotions, one's prayers; retreat, quiet time, meditation, contemplation, communion, communion with God, yoga;

---

**Words associated with Yoga and Meditation**
bhakti yoga, jnana yoga, karma yoga; dharma yoga; astanga yoga, dru yoga, hatha yoga, Iyengar yoga, raja yoga, tantric yoga; asana, dhyana, mantra; chakra, kundalini; zen, zazen, koan; enlightenment, bodhi, moksha, samadhi, satori.

---

*cult*, mystique; type of worship, service 917 *duty*; service of God, supreme worship, latria; inferior worship, dulia, hyperdulia; Christolatry, Mariolatry; iconolatry, image-worship; false worship 982 *idolatry*.

*act of worship*, rites, mysteries 988 *rite*; laud, laudation, praises, doxology 923 *praise*; glorification, giving glory, extolment 866 *dignification*; hymning, hymn-singing, psalm-s., psalmody, plainsong, chanting 412 *vocal music*; thanksgiving, blessing, benediction 907 *thanks*; offering, oblation, almsgiving, sacrifice, making s., sacrificing, offering (see also *oblation*); praying, saying one's prayers, reciting the rosary; self-examination 939 *penitence*; self-denial, self-discipline 945 *asceticism*; keeping fast 946 *fasting*; hajj, pilgrimage 267 *wandering*.

*prayers*, orisons, devotions; private devotion, retreat, contemplation 449 *meditation*; prayer, bidding prayer; impetration, petition, petitionary prayer 761 *request*; invocation, invocatory prayer 583 *allocution*; intercession, intercessory prayer, arrow p. 762 *deprecation*; suffrage, prayers for the dead, vigils; special prayer, intention; rogation, supplication, solemn s., litany, solemn l.; comminatory prayer, commination, denunciation 900 *threat*; imprecation, imprecatory prayer 899 *malediction*; excommunication, ban 883 *seclusion*; exorcism, ghost-busting (inf) 300 *ejection*; benediction, benedicite, benison, grace 907 *thanks*; prayer for the day, collect; liturgical prayer, the Lord's Prayer, Paternoster, Our Father; Ave, Ave Maria, Hail Mary; Kyrie Eleison, Sursum Corda, Sanctus; Nunc Dimittis; dismissal, blessing; rosary, beads, beadroll; prayer-wheel; prayer book, missal, breviary, book of hours; call to prayer, muezzin's cry 547 *call*.

*hymn*, song, psalm, metrical p.; religious song, spiritual; processional hymn, recessional; introit; plainsong, Gregorian chant, Ambrosian c., descant 412 *vocal music*; anthem, cantata, motet; antiphon, response; canticle, Te Deum, Benedicite; song of praise, paean, Magnificat; doxology, Gloria; greater doxology, Gloria in Excelsis; lesser doxology, Gloria Patri; paean, Hallelujah, Hosanna; Homeric hymn; Vedic hymn; hymn-singing, hymnody; psalm-singing, psalmody; hymn-book, hymnal, hymnary, psalter; Vedic hymns, Rigveda, Samaveda; hymnology, hymnography.

*oblation*, offertory, collection, alms and oblations 781 *offering*; pew rent, pewage; libation, incense, censing 988 *rite*; dedication, consecration 866 *dignification*; votive offering, de voto o.; thank-offering 907 *gratitude*; sin-offering, victim, scapegoat 150 *substitute*; burnt offering, holocaust; sacrifice, devotion; immolation, hecatomb 362 *slaughter*; human sacrifice 362 *homicide*; self-sacrifice, self-devotion 931 *disinterestedness*; self-immolation, suttee 362 *suicide*; expiation, propitiation 941 *atonement*; a humble and a contrite heart 939 *penitence*.

*public worship*, common prayer, intercommunion; agape, love-feast; service, divine service, divine office, mass, matins, evensong, benediction 988 *church service*; psalm-singing, psalmody, hymn-singing 412 *vocal music*; church, church-going, chapel-g. 979 *piety*; meeting for prayer, gathering for worship 74

*assembly*; prayer meeting, revival m.; open-air service, mission s., street evangelism, revivalism; temple worship, state religion 973 *religion*.

*worshipper*, fellow w., coreligionist 976 *church member*; adorer, venerator; votary, devotee, oblate 979 *pietist*; glorifier, hymner, praiser, idolizer, admirer, ardent a., humble a. 923 *commender*; follower, server 742 *servant*; image-worshipper, iconolater 982 *idolater*; sacrificer, offerer 781 *giver*; invocator, invoker, caller 583 *allocution*; supplicator, supplicant, suppliant 763 *petitioner*; man *or* woman of prayer, beadsman, intercessor; contemplative, mystic, sufi, visionary; dervish, marabout, enthusiast, revivalist, prophet 973 *religious teacher*; celebrant, officiant 986 *clergy*; communicant, churchgoer, chapelgoer, temple worshipper; congregation, the faithful 976 *church member*; psalm-singer, hymn-s., psalmodist, chanter, cantor; psalmist, hymn-writer, hymnologist 988 *ritualist*; pilgrim, palmer, hajji 268 *traveller*.

**Adj.** *worshipping*, – adoring etc. vb.; worshipping falsely 982 *idolatrous*; devout, devoted 979 *pious*; reverent, reverential 920 *respectful*; prayerful, fervent 761 *supplicatory*; meditating, praying, interceding; in the act of worship, communicating; kneeling, on one's knees; at one's prayers, at one's devotions, in retreat; regular in worship, church-going, chapel-g., communicant 976 *orthodox*; participating in worship, hymn-singing, psalm-s.; celebrating, officiating, ministering 988 *ritualistic*; mystic, mystical.

*devotional*, appertaining to worship 988 *ritualistic*; worshipful, solemn, sacred, holy 979 *sanctified*; revered, worshipped 920 *respected*; sacramental, mystic, mystical; invocatory; precatory, intercessory, petitionary 761 *supplicatory*; imprecatory 899 *maledictory*; sacrificial; oblationary, votive, ex voto 759 *offering*; doxological, giving glory, praising 923 *approving*.

**Vb.** *worship*, honour, revere, venerate, adore 920 *respect*; honour and obey 854 *fear*; do worship to, pay homage to, acknowledge 917 *do one's duty*; pay divine honours to, make a god of one, deify, apotheosize 982 *idolatrize*; bow down before, kneel to, genuflect, humble oneself, prostrate o. 872 *be humbled*; lift up one's heart, bless, give thanks 907 *thank*; extol, laud, magnify, glorify, give glory to, doxologize 923 *praise*; hymn, anthem, celebrate 413 *sing*; light candles to, burn incense before, offer sacrifice to; call on, invoke, address 583 *speak to*; petition, beseech, supplicate, intercede, make intercession, pray over 761 *entreat*; pray, say a prayer, say one's prayers, recite the rosary, tell one's beads; meditate, contemplate, commune with God, be slain in the Spirit 979 *be pious*.

*offer worship*, celebrate, officiate, minister, administer the sacraments 988 *perform ritual*; lead the congregation, lead in prayer; sacrifice, make s., offer up 781 *give*; sacrifice to, propitiate, appease 719 *pacify*; vow, make vows 764 *promise*; praise not only with one's lips, live a life of praise; dedicate, consecrate 979 *sanctify*; take vows, enter holy orders 986 *take orders*; go on a pilgrimage 267 *travel*; go to church, go to chapel, go to meeting, meet for prayer 979 *be pious*; go to service, hear Mass, take the sacraments, receive the Eucharist, communicate, take Holy Communion, share in the Lord's Supper; fast, observe Lent 946 *starve*; deny oneself, practise asceticism 945 *be ascetic*; go into retreat 449 *meditate*; chant psalms, sing hymns, sing praises, carol 413 *sing*; shout hallelujah, doxologize 923 *praise*.

**Int.** Alleluia!, Hallelujah!, Hosanna!, Glory be to God!, Holy, Holy, Holy!, Lift up your hearts, Sursum Corda!, Lord, have mercy, Kyrie Eleison!, Our Father; Lord, bless us!, God save!

## 982 Idolatry

**N.** *idolatry*, idolatrousness, false worship, superstition 981 *worship*; heathenism, paganism 973 *religion*; fetishism, anthropomorphism, zoomorphism; iconolatry, image worship; idolism, idol worship, idolomania; idolomancy, mumbo jumbo, hocus-pocus 983 *sorcery*; cult, cargo c.; sacrifice, human s. 981 *oblation*; heliolatry, sun worship; star worship, Sabaism; pyrolatry, fire worship; zoolatry, animal worship; ophiolatry, snake worship; necrolatry, worship of the dead, demonolatry, devil worship 969 *diabolism*; Mammonism, worship of wealth; bibliolatry, ecclesiolatry.

*deification*, god-making, apotheosis; idolization, hero worship 920 *respect*; king worship, emperor w. 981 *worship*.

*idol*, statue 554 *sculpture*; image, graven i., molten i.; cult image, fetish, totem pole; lingam, yoni; golden calf 966 *deity*; godling, joss; teraphim, lares et penates, totem; Mumbo-Jumbo; Juggernaut, Baal, Moloch.

*idolater*, idolatress; idol-worshipper, idolatrizer; anthropomorphite; fetishist, totemist; iconolater, image-worshipper 981 *worshipper*; heliolater, sun-worshipper; pyrolater, fire-worshipper; bibliolater, ecclesiolater 979 *pietist*; Mammonist, Mammon-worshipper; demonolater, demonist, devil-worshipper 969 *diabolist*; pagan, heathendom 974 *heathen*; idolizer, deifier 923 *commender*; idol-maker, image-m., maker of graven images.

**Adj.** *idolatrous*, pagan, heathen 974 *hea-*

*thenish*; fetishistic; anthropomorphic, theriomorphic; fire-worshipping, sun-w., star-w.; devil-worshipping 969 *diabolic*.

**Vb.** *idolatrize*, worship idols, worship false gods, worship the golden calf, bow down to a graven image; anthropomorphize, make God in one's own image; deify, apotheosize 979 *sanctify*; idealize, idolize, put on a pedestal 923 *praise*; heathenize 974 *paganize*.

**Adv.** *idolatrously*, heathenishly.

## 983 Sorcery

**N.** *sorcery*, spellbinding, witchery, magic arts, enchantments; witchcraft, sortilege; Magianism, gramarye, magic lore 490 *knowledge*; wizardry, magic skill 694 *skill*; wonderworking, miracle-mongering, thaumaturgy 864 *miracle-working*; magic, jugglery, illusionism 542 *sleight*; sympathetic magic, influence 612 *inducement*; white magic, theurgy; black magic, black art, necromancy, diablerie 969 *diabolism*; priestcraft, superstition, witch doctoring, shamanism; obeah, obi, voodooism, voodoo, hoodoo, macumba, muti; psychomancy, spirit-raising 511 *divination*, 984 *occultism*; spirit-laying, ghost-l., exorcism 988 *rite*; magic rite, conjuration, invocation, incantation; ghost dance; coven, witches' sabbath, witches' coven; Walpurgisnacht, Hallowe'en; witching hour.

*spell*, charm, enchantment, cantrip, hoodoo, curse; evil eye, jinx, hex, influence; bewitchment, fascination 291 *attraction*; obsession, possession, demoniacal p., bedevilment, nympholepsy; Dionysiac frenzy 503 *frenzy*; incantation, rune; magic sign, pass; magic word, magic formula, abraxas, open sesame, abracadabra; hocus pocus, mumbo jumbo, fee faw fum 515 *lack of meaning*; philtre, love potion (see also *magic instrument*).

*talisman*, charm, countercharm; cross, phylactery; St Christopher medal 662 *safeguard*; juju, obeah, mojo, fetish 982 *idol*; periapt, amulet, mascot, lucky charm; luck-bringer, rabbit's foot, four-leaf clover, horseshoe, black cat; pentacle, pentagram 547 *indication*; swastika, fylfot, gammadion; scarab; birthstone; emblem, flag, national f.; relic, holy r.; palladium 662 *refuge*.

*magic instrument*, bell, book and candle, wizard's cap, witches' broomstick; magic recipe, witches' brew, hell-broth, witches' cauldron; philtre, potion, moly; wand, magic w., fairy w.; magic ring, wishing cap; Aladdin's lamp, purse of Fortunatus, peau de chagrin; magic mirror, magic sword, flying carpet, magic c.; seven-league boots; Excalibur; cap of darkness, cloak of invisibility; wish-fulfiller, wishing well, wishbone, merry-thought; divining rod 484 *detector*.

*sorcerer*, wise man, seer, soothsayer, Chaldean, sortileger 511 *diviner*, astrologer, alchemist 984 *occultist*; Druid; magus, mage, Magian, the Magi; thaumaturgist, wonderworker, miracle-w. 864 *miracle-working*; shaman, witch doctor, medicine man, fetishist, angekok 982 *idolater*; obi-man, voodooist, hoodooist, spirit-raiser 984 *occultist*; exorcist, ghost-buster (inf); charmer, snake-c.; juggler, illusionist 545 *conjuror*; spellbinder, enchanter, wizard, warlock; magician, theurgist; necromancer 969 *diabolist*; familiar, imp, evil spirit 969 *devil*; sorcerer's apprentice; Merlin, Prospero, Gandalf; Faust, Pied Piper.

*sorceress*, wise woman, Sibyl 511 *diviner*; enchantress, witch, weird sister; hag, hellcat; Druidess; succubus, succuba; lamia; fairy godmother, wicked fairy, Morgan le Fay 970 *fairy*; Witch of Endor, Hecate, Circe, Medea; three witches in 'Macbeth'.

**Adj.** *sorcerous*, sortilegious; wizardly, witchlike; Circean; magician, Chaldean; thaumaturgic 864 *wonderful*; theurgic, theurgical; necromantic 969 *diabolic*; shamanistic, voodooistic; spell-like, incantatory, runic; conjuring, spirit-raising; witching, spellbinding, enchanting, fascinating 291 *attracting*; malignant, blighting, blasting, withering, casting the evil eye, overlooking 898 *maleficent*; occult, esoteric 984 *cabbalistic*.

*magical*, witching; otherworldly, supernatural, uncanny, eldritch, weird 970 *fairylike*; talismanic, phylacteric 660 *tutelary*; having magic power, having supernatural powers, magic, charmed, enchanted 178 *influential*.

*bewitched*, witched, ensorcelled, tranced, enchanted, charmed, becharmed, fey; hypnotized, fascinated, spellbound, under a spell, under a charm; overlooked, under the evil eye; under a curse, cursed; blighted, blasted, withered; hag-ridden, haunted, beghosted.

**Vb.** *practise sorcery*, – witchcraft etc. n.; cast horoscopes, cast a nativity 511 *divine*; do magic, weave spells; make wax effigies; speak mystically, recite a spell, recite an incantation, say the magic word, make passes; conjure, invoke, call up; raise spirits, command s.; exorcize, lay ghosts; wave a wand, rub the magic ring; put on seven-league boots; ride a broomstick.

*bewitch*, witch, charm, becharm, enchant, fascinate 291 *attract*; hypnotize; magic, magic away; spellbind, cast a spell on, weave a spell over, lay under a spell; hoodoo, voodoo, put a voodoo on; overlook, cast the evil eye, blight, blast 898 *be malevolent*; put a curse on, lay

under a curse 899 *curse*; lay under a ban, taboo, make t. 757 *prohibit*; hag-ride, walk, ghost 970 *haunt*.

**Adv.** *sorcerously*, by means of enchantment; as under a spell.

## 984 Occultism

**N.** *occultism*, esotericism, hermeticism, mysticism, transcendentalism 973 *religion*; mystical interpretation, cabbalism, cabbala, gematria; theosophy, reincarnationism; yogism; sciosophy, hyperphysics, metapsychics; supernaturalism, psychicism, pseudopsychology; secret art, esoteric science, occult lore, alchemy, astrology, psychomancy, spiritualism, magic 983 *sorcery*; sortilege 511 *divination*; fortune-telling, crystal-gazing, palmistry, chiromancy, tea-leaf reading 511 *prediction*; clairvoyance, feyness, second sight 438 *vision*; sixth sense 476 *intuition*; animal magnetism, mesmerism, hypnotism; hypnosis, hypnotic trance 375 *insensibility*.

*psychics*, parapsychology, psychism 447 *psychology*; psychic science, psychical research; paranormal perception, extrasensory p., ESP; telaesthesia, clairaudience, clairvoyance, feyness, second sight 476 *intuition*; psychokinesis, fork-bending; telepathy, telergy; thought reading, mind-r., thought transference; precognition, psi faculty; déjà vu.

*spiritualism*, spiritism; spirit communication, psychomancy 983 *sorcery*; sciomancy 511 *divination*; mediumism, mediumship; séance, sitting; astral body, spirit b., ethereal b. 320 *immateriality*; spirit manifestation, materialization, ectoplasm 319 *materiality*; apport, telekinesis; poltergeists; spirit-rapping, table-tapping, table-turning; automatism, automatic writing, spirit w., psychography 586 *writing*; spirit message, psychogram; spiritualistic apparatus, psychograph, planchette, ouija board; control 970 *ghost*; ghost-hunting; psychical research; exorcism.

*occultist*, mystic, transcendentalist, supernaturalist; esoteric, cabbalist; reincarnationist; theosophist, yogi; spiritualist, believer in spiritualism; Rosicrucian; alchemist 983 *sorcerer*; astrologer, fortune-teller, spaewife *or* man, crystal-gazer, palmist 511 *diviner*; Cagliostro, Dr Dee, Friar Bungay, Mesmer.

*psychic*, clairvoyant, clairaudient; telepath, telepathist; mind reader, thought r.; mesmerist, hypnotist; medium, spirit-rapper, automatist, psychographer, spirit-writer; seer, prophet 511 *oracle*, dowser, water diviner 484 *detector*.

*psychist*, parapsychologist, metapsychologist, psychophysicist, psychical researcher.

**Adj.** *cabbalistic*, esoteric, hermetic, cryptic, hidden 523 *occult*; dark, mysterious 491 *unknown*; mystic, transcendental, supernatural 973 *religious*; theosophic, theosophical, reincarnational; Rosicrucian; astrological, alchemic, necromantic 983 *sorcerous*; ghosty, poltergeistish 970 *spooky*.

*psychical*, psychic, fey, second-sighted; prophetic 511 *predicting*; telepathic, clairvoyant, clairaudient; thought-reading, mind-r.; spiritualistic, mediumistic; ectoplasmic, telekinetic, spirit-rapping; mesmeric, hypnotic.

*paranormal*, parapsychological, metapsychological, supernatural, preternatural, hyperphysical, supranormal, supranatural.

**Vb.** *practise occultism*, mysticize, theosophize; cabbalize; alchemize 147 *transform*; astrologize 511 *divine*; hypnotize, mesmerize; practise spiritualism, dabble in s.; hold a séance; practise mediumship, have a control, go into a trance, rap tables, write spirit messages; materialize, dematerialize; study spiritualism, engage in psychical research.

## 985 The Church

**N.** *the church*, churchdom, pale of the church 976 *Christendom*; priestly government, hierocracy, theocracy 733 *authority*; the elect, priestly nation, kingdom of priests; church government, Canterbury, Vatican 733 *government*; ecclesiastical order, hierarchy 60 *order*; papalism, papacy, popedom; popishness, ultramontanism; prelatism, prelacy; archiepiscopacy, episcopacy, episcopalianism; presbytery, presbyterianism, congregationalism, independence 978 *sectarianism*; ecclesiology, ecclesiologist.

*ecclesiasticism*, clericalism, sacerdotalism; priestliness, priesthood, brahminhood; priestdom, priestcraft; Brahminism; ecclesiastical privilege, benefit of clergy 919 *nonliability*; ecclesiastical censorship, Holy Office, Index Expurgatorious 757 *prohibition*.

*monasticism*, monastic life, monachism 895 *celibacy*; cenobitism 883 *seclusion*; monkhood, monkishness 945 *asceticism*.

*church ministry*, ecclesiastical vocation, call, call to the ministry 622 *vocation*; apostleship, apostolate, mission, overseas m., inner-city m. 147 *conversion*; working priesthood, industrial p. 775 *participation*; pastorate, pastorship, cure, cure of souls; spiritual comfort, spiritual leadership 901 *philanthropy*; spiritual guidance, confession, absolution 988 *ministration*; preaching, homiletics 534 *teaching*.

*holy orders*, orders, minor o. 986 *cleric*; apostolic succession, ordination, consecration; induction, reading in; installation, enthronement; nomination, presentation, appointment 751 *commission*; preferment, translation, elevation 285 *progression*.

*church office* 689 *management*; ecclesiastical rank; priesthood; apostolate, apostleship; pontificate, papacy, Holy See, Vatican; cardinalate, cardinalship; patriarchate, exarchate, metropolitanate; primacy, primateship; archiepiscopate, archbishopric; see, bishopric, episcopate, episcopacy, prelacy, prelature; abbotship, abbacy, abbotric; priorate, priorship; archdeaconry, archdeaconate, archdeaconship; deanery, deanship; canonry, canonicate; prebendaryship; deaconate, deaconship; diaconate, subdiaconate; presbyterate, presbytership, eldership, moderatorship, ministership, pastorship, pastorate; rectorship, vicarship, vicariate; curacy, cure of souls; chaplainship, chaplaincy, chaplainry; incumbency, tenure, benefice 773 *possession*.

*parish*, deanery; presbytery; diocese, bishopric, see, archbishopric; metropolitanate, patriarchate, province 184 *district*.

*benefice*, incumbency, tenure; living, rectorship, parsonage; glebe, tithe; prebend, prebendal stall, canonry; temporalities, church lands, church endowments 777 *property*; patronage, advowson, right of presentation.

*synod*, provincial s., convocation, general council, ecumenical c. 692 *council*; college of cardinals, consistory, conclave; bench of bishops, episcopal bench; chapter, vestry; kirk session, presbytery, synod, Sanhedrim 956 *tribunal*; consistorial court, Court of Arches 956 *ecclesiastical court*.

**Adj.** *ecclesiastical*, ecclestiastic, churchly, ecclesiological, theocratic; infallible 733 *authoritative*; hierocratic, priest-ridden, ultramontane 976 *orthodox*; apostolic; hierarchical, pontifical, papal 976 *Roman Catholic*; patriarchal, metropolitan; archiepiscopal, episcopal, prelatic, prelatical 986 *clerical*; episcopalian, presbyterian, Wee Free 978 *sectarian*; prioral, abbatial; conciliar, synodic, presbyteral, capitular; sanhedral, consistorial; provincial, diocesan, parochial.

*priestly*, sacerdotal, hieratic, Aaronic, Levitical; brahminic; sacramental, spiritual; ministering, apostolic, pastoral.

**Vb.** *be ecclesiastical*, be churchly, – priestly etc. adj.; episcopize, prelatize; frock, ordain, order, consecrate, enthrone; cowl, tonsure, make a monk of; call, confer, nominate, present; benefice, prefer, bestow a living 781 *give*; translate 272 *transfer*; elevate 285 *promote*; beatify, canonize, saint 979 *sanctify*; enter the church, become a priest etc. 986 *take orders*.

**Adv.** *ecclesiastically*, church-wise.

## 986 Clergy

**N.** *clergy*, hierarchy; clerical order, parsondom, the cloth, the pulpit, the ministry; sacerdotal order, priesthood, secular clergy, regular clergy, religious.

*cleric*, clerical; clerk in holy orders, priest, deacon, subdeacon, acolyte, exorcist, lector, ostiary; churchman *or* -woman, ecclesiastic, divine; Doctor of Divinity; clergyman, clergywoman, clergyperson, man *or* woman of the cloth, minister of the Gospel, servant of God; reverend, father, father in God; padre, sky pilot, Holy Joe; beneficed clergyman, beneficiary, pluralist, parson, minister, rector, incumbent, residentiary 776 *possessor*; hedgepriest, priestling 639 *nonentity*; ordinand, seminarist 538 *learner*.

*pastor*, shepherd, father in God, minister, woman m., parish priest, rector, vicar, perpetual curate, curate, 'episcopal curate', abbé;

> ... the absence of so many good protestants, who have chosen rather to leave their country than stay at home and pay tithes against their conscience to an episcopal curate.
>
> Jonathan Swift, *A Modest Proposal For Preventing The Children of Poor People in Ireland From Being A Burden to Their Parents or Country, and For Making Them Beneficial to The Public*

chaplain; confessor, father c., penitentiary; spiritual director, spiritual adviser; pardoner; friar; preaching order, predicant; pulpiteer, lay preacher 537 *preacher*; field preacher, missioner, missionary 901 *philanthropist*; evangelist, revivalist, salvationist, hot-gospeller.

*ecclesiarch*, ecclesiastical potentate, hierarch, dignitary 741 *governor*; pope, Supreme Pontiff, Holy Father, Vicar of Christ, Bishop of Rome, servant of the servants of God, servus servorum Dei; cardinal, prince of the church; patriarch, exarch, metropolitan, primate, archbishop; prelate, diocesan, bishop; suffragan, assistant bishop; bench of bishops, episcopate, Lords Spiritual; episcopi vagantes; archpriest, archpresbyter; archdeacon, deacon, subdeacon; dean, subdeacon, rural dean; canon, canon regular, canon secular, residentiary; prebendary, capitular; archimandrite; Superior, Mother S.; abbot, abbess; prior, prioress, Grand Prior; elder, presbyter, moderator.

*monk*, monastic 895 *celibate*; hermit, cenobite, Desert Father 883 *solitary*; Orthodox monk, caloyer; Islamic monk, santon, marabout; sufi 979 *pietist*; dervish, fakir 945 *ascetic*; Buddhist monk, pongye, bonze; brother, regular, conventual; superior, archimandrite, abbot, prior; novice, lay brother; friar, begging f., mendicant f., discalced f., barefoot f.; monks, religious; fraternity, brotherhood, lay b., friary; order, religious o. 708 *community*; Black Monk, Benedictine, Cistercian, Bernardine, Trappist; Carthusian; Cluniac; Gilbertine; Premonstratensian, Mathurin, Trinitarian; Dominicans, Friars Majors, Black Friars; Franciscans, Poverelli, Grey Friars, Friars Minors, Capuchins; Augustines, Austin Friars; Carmelites, White Friars; Crutched Friars; Beghards; teaching order, missionary o., Society of Jesus, Jesuits; crusading order, Templars, Knights Templars; Hospitallers, Knights Hospitallers, Knights of the Hospital of St John of Jerusalem, Knights of Malta.

*nun*, clergywoman; anchoress, recluse; religious, bride of Christ; sister, mother; novice, postulant; lay sister; Superioress, Mother Superior, abbess, prioress, canoness, deaconess; sisterhood, lay s., beguinage, Beguine; Carmelites, Ursulines, Poor Clares, Little Sisters of the Poor, Sisters of Mercy.

*church officer*, elder, presbyter, deacon 741 *officer*; priest, chantry p., chaplain; curate in charge, minister; lay preacher, lay reader; acolyte, server, altar boy; crucifer, thurifer 988 *ritualist*; chorister, choirboy, precentor, succentor, cantor 413 *choir*; sidesman *or* -woman; churchwarden; clerk, vestry c., parish c.; beadle, verger, pew-opener; sacristan, sexton; grave digger, bellringer.

*priest*, chief p., high p., archpriest, hierophant; priestess, Vestal, Pythia, Pythoness, prophetess, prophet 511 *oracle*; Levite; rabbi; imam, mufti; Brahmin; bonze, lama, Dalai L., Panchen L., Karmapa L.; pontifex, pontiff, flamen, archflamen; Druid, Druidess; shaman, witch doctor.

*church title*, Holy Father (see also *ecclesiarch*); Eminence; Monsignor, Monseigneur; Lordship, Lord Spiritual; Most Reverend, Right R., Very R.; the Reverend; parson, rector, vicar; father, brother, Dom; mother, sister.

*monastery*, monkery, bonzery, lamasery; friary; priory, abbey; cloister, convent, nunnery, beguinage; ashram, hermitage 192 *retreat*; community house 192 *abode*; theological college, seminary 539 *training school*; cell 194 *chamber*.

*parsonage*, presbytery, rectory, vicarage; manse; deanery, archdeaconry 192 *abode*; palace, bishop's p., patriarchate; Lambeth, Vatican; close, cathedral c., precincts 235 *enclosure*.

**Adj.** *clerical*, in orders, in holy o.; regular; secular; ordained, consecrated; gaitered, aproned, mitred 989 *vestured*; prebendal, beneficed, pluralistic; unbeneficed, glebeless, lay; parsonical, rectorial, vicarial; pastoral, ministerial, presbyteral, sacerdotal 985 *priestly*; diaconal, subdiaconal, archidiaconal, prelatical, episcopal 985 *ecclesiastical*.

*monastic*, monasterial, cloistral, cloisterly; cloistered, conventual, enclosed 232 *circumscribed*; monkish, monachic, celibate 895 *unwedded*; contemplative, in retreat; cowled, veiled 989 *vestured*; tonsured, shaven and shorn.

**Vb.** *take orders*, take holy orders, be ordained, enter the church, enter the ministry, become a minister *or* vicar, wear the cloth; take vows, take the tonsure, take the cowl; take the veil, become a nun; enter a monastery *or* a nunnery, renounce the world.

**Adv.** *clerically*, parsonically.

## 987 Laity

**N.** *laity*, temporalty, lay people, people, civilians 869 *commonalty*; cure, charge, parish; flock, sheep, fold; diocesans, parishioners; brethren, congregation, society 976 *church member*; lay brethren, lay sisterhood, lay community 708 *community*; the profane, the worldly.

*secularity*, laicity; laicization, secularization, deconsecration.

*lay person*, laic; lay rector, lay deacon; lay brother, lay sister; catechumen, ordinand, seminarist, novice, postulant 538 *learner*; lay preacher, lay reader; elder, deacon, deaconess 986 *church officer*; parishioner, diocesan, member of the flock 976 *church member*; laicizer, secularizer.

**Adj.** *laical*, congregational, parochial; laic, lay, nonclerical, nonpriestly, unordained, not in orders; nonecclesiastical, unclerical, unpriestly, secular; temporal, in the world, of the w., nonreligious 974 *irreligious*; profane, unholy, unconsecrated; laicized, secularized, deconsecrated.

**Vb.** *laicize*, secularize, undedicate, deconsecrate.

## 988 Ritual

**N.** *ritual*, procedure, way of doing things, method, routine 624 *way*; prescribed procedure, due order 60 *order*; form, order, liturgy 610 *practice*; symbolization, symbolism 519 *metaphor*; ceremonial, ceremony 875 *formality*.

*ritualism*, ceremonialism, ceremony, formalism; liturgics.

*rite*, mode of worship 981 *cult*; institution, observance, ritual practice 610 *practice*; form, order, ordinance, rubric, formula, formulary 693 *precept*; ceremony, solemnity, sacrament, mystery 876 *celebration*; rites, mysteries 551 *representation*; initiatory rite, rite of passage, circumcision, initiation, initiation rites, baptism

299 *reception*; christening (see also *Christian rite*); non-Christian rites, salat, puja.

*ministration*, functioning, officiation, performance 676 *action*; administration, celebration, solemnization; the pulpit, sermon, address, preaching 534 *teaching*; homily 534 *lecture*; sacred rhetoric, homiletics 579 *oratory*; pastorship, pastoral care, cure of souls; pastoral epistle, pastoral letter; confession, auricular c.; shrift, absolution, penance.

*Christian rite*, rites of the Church; sacrament, the seven sacraments; baptism, christening, adult b., believer's b., infant b., paedobaptism 299 *reception*; immersion, total i. 303 *immersion*; affusion 341 *moistening*; laying on of hands, confirmation, chrism, First Communion; Holy Communion, Eucharist, mass, reservation of the sacraments; penitential rites 941 *penance*; absolution 960 *acquittal*; Holy Matrimony 894 *marriage*; Holy Orders 985 *the church*; Holy Unction, chrism; visitation of the sick, extreme unction, last rites, viaticum; burial of the dead; requiem mass; liturgy, order of service, order of baptism, marriage service, solemnization of matrimony, nuptial mass; churching of women; ordination, ordering of deacons, ordering of priests; consecration, consecration of bishops; exorcism 300 *ejection*; excommunication, ban, bell book and candle; canonization, beatification 866 *dignification*; dedication, undedication.

*Holy Communion*, Eucharist, Blessed E.; mass, high m., missa solemnis; sung m., missa cantata; low mass; public mass, private m.; communion, the Lord's Supper; preparation, confession, asperges; service of the book, introit, the Kyries, the Gloria, the Lesson, the Gradual, the Collects, the Gospel, the creed; service of the Altar, the offertory, offertory sentence, offertory prayers, the biddings; the blessing, the thanksgiving, Sursum Corda, Preface, Sanctus, Great Amen; the breaking of the bread, the commixture; the Pax; consecration; elevation of the Host; Agnus Dei; the Communion; kiss of peace; prayers of thanksgiving, the dismissal; the blessing.

*the sacrament*, the Holy Sacrament, the Blessed Eucharist; Corpus Christi, body and blood of Christ; real presence, transubstantiation, consubstantiation, impanation; the elements, bread and wine, altar bread; consecrated bread, host; reserved sacrament; viaticum.

*church service*, office, duty, service 981 *act of worship*; liturgy, celebration, concelebration; canonical hours, matins, lauds, prime, terce, sext, none, vespers, compline; the little hours; morning prayer, matins; evening prayer, evensong, benediction; Tenebrae; vigil, midnight mass, watchnight service; devotional service, three-hour s.; novena.

*ritual act*, symbolical act, sacramental, symbolism 551 *representation*; lustration, purification 648 *cleansing*; thurification, incense-burning 338 *vaporization*; sprinkling, aspersion, asperges 341 *moistening*; circumambulation 314 *circuition*; procession 285 *progression*; stations of the cross 981 *act of worship*; obeisance, bowing, kneeling, genuflexion, prostration, homage 920 *respects*; crossing oneself, signation, sign of the cross 547 *gesture*; eucharistic rite, breaking the bread; intinction; elevating of the Host; kiss of peace; sacrifice.

*ritual object*, cross, rood, Holy Rood, crucifix; altar, Lord's table, communion t.; altar furniture, altar cloth, candle, candlestick; communion wine, communion bread; cup, chalice, grail, Holy Grail, Sangrail; cruet; paten, ciborium, pyx, pyx chest, tabernacle; monstrance, chrism, chrismatory; collection plate, salver; incense, incensory, censer, thurible; holy water; aspergillum; aspersorium; piscina; sacring bell, Sanctus bell; font, baptismal f., baptistery; baptismal garment, chrisom, christening gown; wedding garment, wedding dress, bridal veil, wedding ring; devotional object, relics, sacred relics; reliquary, shrine, aedicule, casket 194 *box*; icon, Pietà, Holy Sepulchre, stations of the cross 551 *image*; osculatory, pax; Agnus Dei, rosary, beads, bead-roll 981 *prayers*; votive candle; non-Christian objects, Ark of the Covenant, Mercy-seat; seven-branched candlestick; shewbread; laver; hyssop; sackcloth and ashes; libation dish, patina; joss stick; prayer wheel; altar of incense; urim, thummim; temple veil.

*ritualist*, ceremonialist, sabbatarian, formalist; liturgist, litanist; sacramentarian, sacramentalist; celebrant, minister 986 *priest*; server, acolyte; thurifer; crucifer, processionist.

*office-book*, service-b., ordinal, lectionary; liturgy, litany; formulary, rubric, canon 693 *precept*; book of hours, breviary; missal, mass-book; prayer book, Book of Common Prayer, Alternative Service Book 981 *prayers*; beads, rosary.

*hymnal*, hymn book, hymnary, choir book; psalter, psalm-book, book of psalms 981 *hymn*.

*holy day*, feast, feast day, festival 837 *festivity*; fast day, meatless d. 946 *fast*; high day, day of observance, day of obligation 876 *celebration*; sabbath, sabbath-day, day of rest 681 *leisure*; Lord's Day, Sunday; saint's day 141 *anniversary*

---

**Religious Festivals and Holy Days**

*Christian:* Advent; Christmas, Christmastide, Yuletide, Noel, Nativity; Epiphany, Twelfth Night; Lent, Shrove Tuesday, Ash Wednesday, Passion Sunday; Easter, Eastertide, Holy Week, Passion Week, Palm Sunday, Maundy Thursday, Good Friday, Easter Sunday; Ascension Day; Whitsuntide, Whitsun, Pentecost; Corpus Christi; Trinity Sunday; All Hallows, All Saints, All Souls, Lady Day, Feast of the Annunciation; Candlemas, Feast of the Purification; Feast of the Assumption; Lammas, Martinmas, Michaelmas.

*Jewish:* Hanukkah *or* Chanukkah *or* Chanukah, Feast of Dedication, Feast of Lights; Pesach *or* Pesah, Passover; Purim, Feast of Lots; Rosh Hashanah, New Year, Feast of Trumpets; Shavuot *or* Shavuoth *or* Shabuoth, Feast of Weeks, Pentecost; Sukkot *or* Sukkoth *or* Succoth, Feast of Tabernacles, Feast of Ingathering; Yom Kippur, Day of Atonement.

*Muslim:* Ashura; Bairam, Lesser Bairam, Greater Bairam; Eid *or* Id al-Adha, Feast of Sacrifice; Eid *or* Id al-Fitr, Feast of the Breaking of the Fast; Mawlid an-Nabi, the Birthday of the Prophet Muhammad; Moharram *or* Muharram, New Year; Ramadan.

*Hindu:* Diwali *or* Divali *or* Dewali, Festival of Lights; Durga Puja; Holi, Festival of Fire; Maha Shivaratri; Mela, Kumbh Mela, Maha Kumbh Mela; Navaratri; Ramnavami.

*Buddhist:* Bodhi Day; Dharma Day; Sangha Day; Paranirvana Day; Wesak *or* Vesak, Buddha Day.

*Sikh:* Baisakhi, Diwali *or* Divali *or* Dewali, Festival of Lights; gurpurb; Hola Mohalla; Maghi.

*Wiccan:* Beltane, Imbolc, Lughnasadh, Samhain.

---

**Adj.** *ritual*, procedural; formal, solemn, ceremonial, liturgical; processional, recessional; symbolic, symbolical, representational 551 *representing*; sacramental, eucharistic; chrismal; baptismal; sacrificial, paschal; festal, pentecostal; fasting, lenten; prescribed, ordained; unleavened; kosher; consecrated, blessed.

*ritualistic*, ceremonious, ceremonial, formulistic; sabbatarian; observant of ritual, addicted to r.

**Vb.** *perform ritual*, perform the rites, say office, celebrate, concelebrate, officiate; take the service, lead worship 981 *offer worship*; baptize, christen, confirm, ordain, lay on hands; minister, administer the sacraments, give communion; sacrifice, offer s., make s.; offer prayers, bless, give benediction; anathematize, ban, ban with bell, book and candle; excommunicate, unchurch, unfrock; dedicate, consecrate, deconsecrate; purify, lustrate, asperge; cense, burn incense; anoint, give extreme unction; confess, absolve, pronounce absolution, shrive; take communion, partake of Holy Communion, receive the sacraments; bow, kneel, genuflect, prostrate oneself; sign oneself, cross o., make the sign of the cross; take holy water; tell one's beads, say one's rosary; make one's stations; process, go in procession; circumambulate; fast, flagellate oneself, do penance.

*ritualize*, ceremonialize, institute a rite, organize a cult; sabbatize, sacramentalize, observe, keep, keep holy.

**Adv.** *ritually*, ceremonially; symbolically, sacramentally; liturgically.

## 989 Canonicals

**N.** *canonicals*, clericals, clerical dress, cloth, clerical black 228 *dress*; frock, soutane, cassock, scapular; cloak, gown, Geneva g. 228 *cloak*; robe, cowl, hood, capuche; lappet, bands, Geneva b.; clerical collar, dog c.; chimere, lawn sleeves; apron, gaiters, shovel hat; cardinal's hat; priests' cap, biretta, black b., purple b., red b.; skullcap, calotte, zucchetto; Salvation Army bonnet 228 *headgear*; tonsure, shaven crown 229 *bareness*; prayer-cap; tallith.

*vestments*, ephod, priestly vesture, canonical robes; pontificalia, pontificals; cassock, surplice, rochet; cope, tunicle, dalmatic, alb 228 *robe*; amice, chasuble; stole, deacon's s.; scarf, tippet, pallium; cingulum 47 *girdle*; maniple, fanon; mitre, tiara, triple crown 743 *regalia*; papal vestment, orale; crosier, crook, staff, pastoral s. 743 *badge of rank*; pectoral 222 *cross*; episcopal ring; orphrey *or* orfray, ecclesiastical embroidery 844 *ornamentation*.

**Adj.** *vestmental*, vestmentary, vestiary; canonical, pontifical.

*vestured*, robed 228 *dressed*; surpliced, stoled etc. n.; cowled, hooded, veiled 986 *monastic*; gaitered, aproned 986 *clerical*; mitred, crosiered; wearing the triple crown, tiara'd.

## 990 Temple

**N.** *temple*, fane, pantheon; shrine, aedicule, sacellum; joss house, teocalli 982 *idolatry*; house of God, tabernacle, the Temple, House of the Lord; place of worship 981 *worship*; masjid, mosque; house of prayer, oratory; sacred edifice, pagoda, stupa, tope, dagoba, ziggurat 164 *building*; torii, toran, gopuram 263 *doorway*.

*holy place*, holy ground, sacred g., sacred precinct, temenos; sacrarium, sanctuary, adytum, cella, naos; Ark of the Covenant, Mercy-seat, Sanctum, Holy of Holies, oracle; martyry, sacred tomb, marabout, sepulchre, Holy Sepulchre; graveyard, God's Acre 364 *cemetery*; place of pilgrimage; Holy City, Zion, Jerusalem; Mecca, Benares.

*church*, God's house; parish church, daughter c., chapel of ease; cathedral, minster, procathedral; basilica; abbey; kirk, chapel, tabernacle, temple, bethel, ebenezer; conventicle, meeting house, prayer h.; house of prayer, oratory, chantry, chantry chapel; synagogue, mosque.

*altar*, high a., sacrarium, sanctuary, bema; altar stone, altar slab; altar table, Lord's t., communion t.; altar bread 988 *the sacrament*; altar pyx; prothesis, credence, credence table 988 *ritual object*; canopy, baldachin, altarpiece, diptych, triptych, altar screen, reredos; altar cloth, altar frontal, antependium; predella, altar rails.

*church utensil*, font, baptistry; ambry, stoup, piscina; chalice, paten 988 *ritual object*; pulpit, lectern; bible, chained b., hymnal, hymnary, prayer book 981 *prayers*; hassock, kneeler; salver, collection plate, offertory bag; organ, harmonium; bell, church b., carillon 412 *campanology*.

*church interior*, nave, aisle, apse, ambulatory, transept; chancel, chevet, choir, sanctuary; hagioscope, squint; chancel screen, rood screen, jube, rood loft, gallery, organ loft; stall, choir s., sedile, sedilia, misericorde; pew, box pew; pulpit, ambo; lectern; chapel, side c., Lady c., feretory; confessional; clerestory, triforium; spandrel; stained glass, stained-glass window, rose w., jesse w.; calvary, stations of the cross, Easter sepulchre; baptistry, font; aumbry, sacristy, vestry; undercroft, crypt, vault; rood, cross, crucifix.

*church exterior*, porch, narthex, galilee; tympanum 263 *doorway*; tower, steeple, spire 209 *high structure*; bell tower, bellcote, belfry, campanile; buttress, flying b. 218 *prop*; cloister, ambulatory; chapterhouse, presbytery 692 *council*; churchyard, kirkyard, lychgate; close 235 *enclosure*.

**Adj.** *churchlike*, basilican, cathedral-like, cathedralesque; cruciform 222 *crossed*; apsidal 248 *curved*; Romanesque, Norman, Gothic, Early English, Decorated, Perpendicular, baroque, Puginesque, Gothic revival.

*Index*

# A

**a**
  *one* 88 adj.
**A1**
  *supreme* 34 adj.
  *notable* 638 adj.
  *best* 644 adj.
  *perfect* 646 adj.
  *healthy* 650 adj.
**aback**
  *rearward* 238 adv.
**abacus**
  *counting instrument*
    86 n.
**abaft**
  *rearward* 238 adv.
**abandon**
  *exclude* 57 vb.
  *depart* 296 vb.
  *disregard* 458 vb.
  *tergiversate* 603 vb.
  *relinquish* 621 vb.
  *resign* 753 vb.
  *not retain* 779 vb.
  *excitable state* 822 n.
  *merriment* 833 n.
  *rejoicing* 835 n.
  *intemperance* 943 n.
  *sensualism* 944 n.
  – hope
    *despair* 853 vb.
  – one's post
    *fail in duty* 918 vb.
**abandoned**
  *remaining* 41 adj.
  *separate* 46 adj.
  *alone* 88 adj.
  *unpossessed* 774 adj.
  *not retained* 779 adj.
  *vicious* 934 adj.
**abandonment**
  *tergiversation* 603 n.
  *relinquishment* 621 n.
  *submission* 721 n.
  *resignation* 753 n.
  *nonretention* 779 n.
  *excitable state* 822 n.
  *joy* 824 n.
  *rejoicing* 835 n.
**abase**
  *abase* 311 vb.
  *pervert* 655 vb.
**abasement**
  *disrepute* 867 n.
  *humiliation* 872 n.
  *humility* 872 n.
  *servility* 879 n.
**abash**
  *frighten* 854 vb.
  *humiliate* 872 vb.
**abate**
  *abate* 37 vb.
  *decrease* 37 vb.
  *weaken* 163 vb.
  *moderate* 177 vb.

*blow* 352 vb.
  *qualify* 468 vb.
  *discount* 810 vb.
**abatement**
  *diminution* 37 n.
  *contraction* 198 n.
  *relief* 831 n.
**abattoir**
  *place of slaughter* 362 n.
**abbess**
  *ecclesiarch* 986 n.
  *nun* 986 n.
**abbey**
  *house* 192 n.
  *monastery* 986 n.
  *church* 990 n.
**abbot**
  *ecclesiarch* 986 n.
  *monk* 986 n.
**abbotship**
  *church office* 985 n.
**abbreviate**
  *subtract* 39 vb.
  *shorten* 204 vb.
  *be concise* 569 vb.
  *abstract* 592 vb.
**abbreviation**
  *smallness* 33 n.
  *diminution* 37 n.
  *contraction* 198 n.
  *word* 559 n.
  *compendium* 592 n.
**ABC**
  *beginning* 68 n.
  *directory* 87 n.
  *guidebook* 524 n.
  *curriculum* 534 n.
  *letter* 558 n.
**abdicate**
  *relinquish* 621 vb.
  *be lax* 734 vb.
  *resign* 753 vb.
**abdication**
  *relinquishment* 621 n.
  *resignation* 753 n.
  *loss of right* 916 n.
**abdomen**
  *maw* 194 n.
  *insides* 224 n.
**abdomen, cutting
  into**
  *surgery* 658 n. box
**abdomen, inflam-
  mation in**
  *inflammation* 651 n.
    box
**abdominal**
  *ligature* 47 n.
  *cellular* 194 adj.
**abduct**
  *take away* 786 vb.
  *steal* 788 vb.
**abduction**
  *type of marriage* 894 n.
**abductor**
  *taker* 786 n.
  *thief* 789 n.

**abeam**
  *sideways* 239 adv.
**abed**
  *supine* 216 adj.
**aberrant**
  *nonuniform* 17 adj.
  *unconformable* 84 adj.
  *erroneous* 495 adj.
**aberration**
  *variance* 84 n.
  *displacement* 188 n.
  *deviation* 282 n.
  *divergence* 294 n.
  *inattention* 456 n.
  *mental disorder* 503 n.
**abet**
  *conduce* 156 vb.
  *concur* 181 vb.
  *incite* 612 vb.
  *aid* 703 vb.
**abetment**
  *inducement* 612 n.
  *cooperation* 706 n.
**abettor**
  *cause* 156 n.
  *assenter* 488 n.
  *motivator* 612 n.
  *aider* 703 n.
  *colleague* 707 n.
**abeyance**
  *extinction* 2 n.
  *lull* 145 n.
  *nonuse* 674 n.
  *inaction* 677 n.
**ABH**
  *attack* 712 n.
**abhor**
  *not observe* 769 vb.
  *dislike* 861 vb.
  *hate* 888 vb.
  *disapprove* 924 vb.
**abide**
  *be 1* vb.
  *continue* 108 vb.
  *last* 113 vb.
  *stay* 144 vb.
  *go on* 146 vb.
  *dwell* 192 vb.
  *be quiescent* 266 vb.
  *be patient* 823 vb.
  – by
    *acquiesce* 488 vb.
    *affirm* 532 vb.
    *observe* 768 vb.
**ability**
  *intrinsicality* 5 n.
  *ability* 160 n.
  *influence* 178 n.
  *possibility* 469 n.
  *intelligence* 498 n.
  *means* 629 n.
  *utility* 640 n.
  *skill* 694 n.
**ab initio**
  *initially* 68 adv.
**abject**
  *cowardly* 856 adj.

*disreputable* 867 adj.
  *servile* 879 adj.
  *contemptible* 922 adj.
  *rascally* 930 adj.
**abjure**
  *negate* 533 vb.
  *recant* 603 vb.
  *resign* 753 vb.
  *not retain* 779 vb.
**ablaze**
  *fiery* 379 adj.
  *luminous* 417 adj.
**able**
  *powerful* 160 adj.
  *possible* 469 adj.
  *intelligent* 498 adj.
  *useful* 640 adj.
  *active* 678 adj.
  *skilful* 694 adj.
  *See also* **ability**
**able-bodied**
  *stalwart* 162 adj.
  *active* 678 adj.
**abled**
  *stalwart* 162 adj.
  *active* 678 adj.
**ablegate**
  *envoy* 754 n.
**ableism**
  *prejudice* 481 n.
  *injustice* 914 n.
**able seaman**
  *mariner* 270 n.
  *naval person* 722 n.
**ablutions**
  *ablutions* 648 n.
**abnegate**
  *negate* 533 vb.
  *reject* 607 vb.
  *relinquish* 621 vb.
**abnegation**
  *relinquishment* 621 n.
**abnormal**
  *nonuniform* 17 adj.
  *abnormal* 84 adj.
  *misplaced* 188 adj.
  *deviating* 282 adj.
  *crazy* 503 adj.
  *mentally disordered*
    503 adj.
  *unexpected* 508 adj.
  *puzzling* 517 adj.
  *funny* 849 adj.
  *wrong* 914 adj.
  *spooky* 970 adj.
**abnormality**
  *misfit* 25 n.
  *variance* 84 n.
  *deformity* 246 n.
  *eccentricity* 503 n.
  *illicit love* 951 n.
**abnormal psychology**
  *psychology* 447 n.
  *mental disorder* 503 n.
**aboard**
  *here* 189 adv.
  *afloat* 275 adv.

**abode**
*district* 184 n.
*station* 187 n.
*abode* 192 n.
**abolish**
*nullify* 2 vb.
*destroy* 165 vb.
*abrogate* 752 vb.
**abolition**
*revolution* 149 n.
*destruction* 165 n.
*abrogation* 752 n.
*prohibition* 757 n.
**abolitionist**
*revolutionist* 149 n.
**abominable**
*not nice* 645 adj.
*unclean* 649 adj.
*disliked* 861 adj.
*hateful* 888 adj.
*heinous* 934 adj.
**Abominable Snowman**
*mythical beast* 365 n.
*mythical being* 970 n.
**abominably**
*extremely* 32 adv.
**abomination**
*badness* 645 n.
*uncleanness* 649 n.
*dislike* 861 n.
*hateful object* 888 n.
*hatred* 888 n.
*wickedness* 934 n.
**aboriginal**
*beginning* 68 adj.
*primal* 127 adj.
*native* 191 n., adj.
**aborigine**
*earliness* 135 n.
*humankind* 371 n.
**abort**
*suppress* 165 vb.
*be unproductive* 172 vb.
*miscarry* 728 vb.
**aborticide**
*contraception* 172 n.
*homicide* 362 n. box
**abortifacient**
*contraception* 172 n.
**abortion**
*variance* 84 n.
*destruction* 165 n.
*deformity* 246 n.
*homicide* 362 n.
*killing* 362 n.
*undevelopment* 670 n.
*failure* 728 n.
*eyesore* 842 n.
**abortionist**
*killer* 362 n.
**abortion pill**
*contraception* 172 n.
**abortive**
*unproductive* 172 adj.
*disappointing* 509 adj.
*profitless* 641 adj.

*unsuccessful* 728 adj.
**ABO system**
*blood* 335 n.
**abound**
*abound* 635 vb.
*superabound* 637 vb.
*See also* **abundance**
**about**
*concerning* 9 adv.
*about* 33 adv.
*nearly* 200 adv.
*around* 230 adv.
**about, be**
*be near* 200 vb.
**about to**
*prospectively* 124 adv.
*tending* 179 adj.
**about to be**
*impending* 155 adj.
**about-turn**
*reversion* 148 n.
*turn round* 282 vb.
*return* 286 n.
*tergiversation* 603 n.
**above**
*before* 64 adv.
*aloft* 209 adv.
**above all**
*eminently* 34 adv.
*importantly* 638 adv.
**above average**
*superior* 34 adj.
**above-board**
*veracious* 540 adj.
*artless* 699 adj.
*just* 913 adj.
*honourable* 929 adj.
**above-mentioned**
*preceding* 64 adj.
*repeated* 106 adj.
*prior* 119 adj.
**above par**
*beyond* 34 adv.
*excellent* 644 adj.
**above price**
*valuable* 644 adj.
*of price* 811 adj.
**above reproach**
*virtuous* 933 adj.
*guiltless* 935 adj.
**above suspicion**
*guiltless* 935 adj.
**above temptation**
*virtuous* 933 adj.
**above the law**
*lawless* 954 adj.
**ab ovo**
*initially* 68 adv.
**abracadabra**
*lack of meaning* 515 n.
*spell* 983 n.
**abrade**
*abate* 37 vb.
*subtract* 39 vb.
*uncover* 229 vb.
*pulverize* 332 vb.
*rub* 333 vb.

*obliterate* 550 vb.
**abrasion**
*wound* 655 n.
**abrasive**
*pulverizer* 332 n.
*rubbing* 333 adj.
*obliteration* 550 n.
**abreaction**
*recuperation* 656 n.
*liberation* 746 n.
*feeling* 818 n.
**abreast**
*equal* 28 adj.
*in parallel* 219 adv.
*sideways* 239 adv.
**abreast of the times**
*progressive* 285 adj.
**abridge**
*abate* 37 vb.
*subtract* 39 vb.
*make smaller* 198 vb.
*shorten* 204 vb.
*translate* 520 vb.
*be concise* 569 vb.
*abstract* 592 vb.
**abridgement**
*edition* 589 n.
*compendium* 592 n.
**abroad**
*existing* 1 adj.
*abroad* 59 adv.
*afar* 199 adv.
**abrogate**
*nullify* 2 vb.
*disable* 161 vb.
*suppress* 165 vb.
*negate* 533 vb.
*recant* 603 vb.
*reject* 607 vb.
*relinquish* 621 vb.
*make useless* 641 vb.
*stop using* 674 vb.
*liberate* 746 vb.
*abrogate* 752 vb.
*prohibit* 757 vb.
*not observe* 769 vb.
*not retain* 779 vb.
*disentitle* 916 vb.
*make illegal* 954 vb.
**abrogation**
*revolution* 149 n.
*obliteration* 550 n.
*abrogation* 752 n.
**abrupt**
*instantaneous* 116 adj.
*violent* 176 adj.
*vertical* 215 adj.
*sloping* 220 adj.
*inelegant* 576 adj.
*sullen* 893 adj.
**abruptly**
*unexpectedly* 508 adv.
**abscess**
*ulcer* 651 n.
**abscission**
*subtraction* 39 n.
*scission* 46 n.

*uncovering* 229 n.
**abscond**
*decamp* 296 vb.
*run away* 620 vb.
*escape* 667 vb.
*not pay* 805 vb.
*fail in duty* 918 vb.
**abseil**
*descend* 309 vb.
**absence**
*nonexistence* 2 n.
*absence* 190 n.
*farness* 199 n.
*invisibility* 444 n.
*avoidance* 620 n.
*requirement* 627 n.
*undutifulness* 918 n.
**absence of mind**
*abstractedness* 456 n.
**absent**
*nonexistent* 2 adj.
*incomplete* 55 adj.
*misplaced* 188 adj.
*absent* 190 adj.
*disappearing* 446 adj.
*abstracted* 456 adj.
*required* 627 adj.
*unprovided* 636 adj.
*unused* 674 adj.
*inactive* 679 adj.
*lost* 772 adj.
*undutiful* 918 adj.
**absenteeism**
*absence* 190 n.
*inactivity* 679 n.
*undutifulness* 918 n.
**absent-minded**
*abstracted* 456 adj.
*forgetful* 506 adj.
**absent oneself**
*be absent* 190 vb.
*depart* 296 vb.
*disappear* 446 vb.
*run away* 620 vb.
*be exempt* 919 vb.
**absinth, absinthe**
*alcoholic drink* 301 n.
*sourness* 393 n.
**absolute**
*existing* 1 adj.
*unrelated* 10 adj.
*absolute* 32 adj.
*complete* 54 adj.
*one* 88 adj.
*positive* 473 adj.
*credal* 485 adj.
*assertive* 532 adj.
*authoritative* 733 adj.
*authoritarian* 735 adj.
*unconditional* 744 adj.
*godlike* 965 adj.
**absolute end**
*exceller* 644 n.
*cad* 938 n.
**absolutely**
*positively* 32 adv.
*unanimously* 488 int.

*association* 706 n.
*participation* 775 n.
**affinity**
*relation* 9 n.
*consanguinity* 11 n.
*similarity* 18 n.
*tendency* 179 n.
*attraction* 291 n.
*liking* 859 n.
*spouse* 894 n.
**affirm**
*testify* 466 vb.
*dogmatize* 473 vb.
*confute* 479 vb.
*believe* 485 vb.
*opine* 485 vb.
*suppose* 512 vb.
*mean* 514 vb.
*proclaim* 528 vb.
*affirm* 532 vb.
*indicate* 547 vb.
*speak* 579 vb.
*plead* 614 vb.
*decree* 737 vb.
*promise* 764 vb.
**affirmation**
*testimony* 466 n.
*assent* 488 n.
*affirmation* 532 n.
*promise* 764 n.
**affirmative**
*positive* 473 adj.
*demonstrating* 478 adj.
*affirmative* 532 adj.
*forceful* 571 adj.
**affirmative action**
*equalization* 28 n.
*injustice* 914 n.
**affix**
*add* 38 vb.
*adjunct* 40 n.
*affix* 45 vb.
*agglutinate* 48 vb.
*sequel* 67 n.
*part of speech* 564 n.
**afflatus**
*imagination* 513 n.
*poetry* 593 n.
*excitation* 821 n.
*revelation* 975 n.
**afflict**
*hurt* 827 vb.
*punish* 963 vb.
**affliction**
*evil* 616 n.
*illness* 651 n.
*bane* 659 n.
*suffering* 825 n.
**affluence**
*plenty* 635 n.
*prosperity* 730 n.
*wealth* 800 n.
**afford**
*provide* 633 vb.
*have enough* 635 vb.
*give* 781 vb.
*afford* 800 vb.

*expend* 806 vb.
**affordable**
*cheap* 812 adj.
**afforestation**
*forestry* 366 n.
*agriculture* 370 n.
**affray**
*turmoil* 61 n.
*fight* 716 n.
**affront**
*annoyance* 827 n.
*hurt* 827 vb.
*be courageous* 855 vb.
*sauciness* 878 n.
*resentment* 891 n.
*huff* 891 vb.
*indignity* 921 n.
*not respect* 921 vb.
**affronted**
*discontented* 829 adj.
**aficionado**
*enthusiast* 504 n.
*patron* 707 n.
*lover* 887 n.
**afield**
*afar* 199 adv.
**afire**
*fiery* 379 adj.
*luminous* 417 adj.
**aflame**
*fiery* 379 adj.
*luminous* 417 adj.
**aflame with**
*impressed* 818 adj.
**aflatoxin**
*weapon* 723 n.
**afloat**
*existing* 1 adj.
*happening* 154 adj.
*seafaring* 269 adj.
*swimming* 269 adj.
*afloat* 275 adv.
*at sea* 343 adv.
*rumoured* 529 adj.
**afoot**
*existing* 1 adj.
*happening* 154 adj.
*operative* 173 adj.
*in question* 452 adv.
*busy* 678 adj.
**aforesaid**
*preceding* 64 adj.
*repeated* 106 adj.
*prior* 119 adj.
**aforethought**
*predetermined* 608 adj.
*intended* 617 adj.
**aforetime**
*before* 119 adv.
*formerly* 125 adv.
**a fortiori**
*eminently* 34 adv.
*reasonably* 475 adv.
**afraid**
*fearing* 854 adj.
**afraid of one's own
   shadow**

*nervous* 854 adj.
*cowardly* 856 adj.
**afraid to touch**
*careful* 457 adj.
**afresh**
*again* 106 adv.
*newly* 126 adv.
**Africanize, Africanise**
*transform* 147 vb.
**Afrocentric**
*biased* 361 adj.
**aft**
*rearward* 238 adv.
**after**
*similar* 18 adj.
*after* 65 adv.
*subsequent* 120 adj.
*subsequently* 120 adv.
*back* 238 adj.
*rearward* 238 adv.
*behind* 284 adv.
*pursuant to* 619 adv.
**after a fashion**
*partially* 33 adv.
**after all**
*in return* 31 adv.
*nevertheless* 468 adv.
**after, be**
*aim at* 617 vb.
*pursue* 619 vb.
**afterbirth**
*obstetrics* 167 n.
**aftercare**
*therapy* 658 n.
**afterclap**
*sequel* 67 n.
*lack of expectation*
   508 n.
**after-dinner**
*subsequent* 120 adj.
*culinary* 301 adj.
*reposeful* 683 adj.
*sociable* 882 adj.
**after due thought**
*in minds* 449 adv.
**aftereffect**
*sequel* 67 n.
**afterglow**
*remainder* 41 n.
*sequel* 67 n.
*glow* 417 n.
**afterimage**
*appearance* 445 n.
*image* 551 n.
**afterlife**
*sequel* 67 n.
*future state* 124 n.
*heaven* 971 n.
**aftermath**
*sequel* 67 n.
*posteriority* 120 n.
*effect* 157 n.
**afternoon**
*evening* 129 n.
*vespertine* 129 adj.
**afternoon tea**
*meal* 301 n.

**after one's own heart**
*lovable* 887 adj.
**afterpart**
*sequel* 67 n.
*poop* 238 n.
*rear* 238 n.
**afters**
*sequel* 67 n.
**aftertaste**
*sequel* 67 n.
*taste* 386 n.
**after the fashion of**
*similar* 18 adj.
**afterthought**
*sequel* 67 n.
*lateness* 136 n.
*thought* 449 n.
*remembrance* 505 n.
*tergiversation* 603 n.
**after time**
*late* 136 adj., adv.
**afterwards**
*after* 65 adv.
*subsequently* 120 adv.
**afterworld**
*sequel* 67 n.
*destiny* 155 n.
**again**
*twice* 91 adv.
*again* 106 adv.
**again and again**
*repeatedly* 106 adv.
*often* 139 adv.
**against**
*although* 182 adv.
*against* 240 adv.
*opposing* 704 adj.
*in opposition* 704 adv.
**against nature**
*impossible* 470 adj.
**against one's better
   judgment**
*disapprovingly* 924 adv.
**against one's will**
*unwillingly* 598 adv.
**against the clock**
*hastily* 680 adv.
**against the grain**
*disagreeing* 25 adj.
*on edge* 259 adv.
*unwillingly* 598 adv.
*with difficulty* 700 adv.
*in opposition* 704 adv.
**against the law**
*prohibited* 757 adj.
*illegal* 954 adj.
*illegally* 954 adv.
**against the rules**
*unconformable* 84 adj.
*impossible* 470 adj.
*wrong* 914 adj.
**against the stream**
*with difficulty* 700 adv.
*in opposition* 704 adv.
**agape**
*open* 263 adj.
*wondering* 864 adj.

territorial 344 adj.
agrarian 370 adj.
**agree**
accord 24 vb.
concur 181 vb.
believe 485 vb.
be willing 597 vb.
concord 710 vb.
consent 758 vb.
contract 765 vb.
– to differ
dissent 489 vb.
make peace 719 vb.
– with one
be salubrious 652 vb.
**agreeable**
agreeing 24 adj.
conformable 83 adj.
pleasant 376 adj.
willing 597 adj.
palmy 730 adj.
consenting 758 adj.
pleasurable 826 adj.
personable 841 adj.
courteous 884 adj.
**agreeably**
tastefully 846 adv.
**agreement**
identity 13 n.
uniformity 16 n.
similarity 18 n.
agreement 24 n.
equality 28 n.
conformity 83 n.
concurrence 181 n.
symmetry 245 n.
melody 410 n.
assent 488 n.
consensus 488 n.
cooperation 706 n.
concord 710 n.
pacification 719 n.
consent 758 n.
compact 765 n.
**agribusiness**
agriculture 370 n.
business 622 n.
**agricultural**
territorial 344 adj.
agrarian 370 adj.
**agriculturalist, agric-
ulturist**
producer 164 n.
farmer 370 n.
preparer 669 n.
**agricultural worker**
farmer 370 n.
**agriculture**
production 164 n.
agriculture 370 n.
maturation 669 n.
**agrochemical**
agriculture 370 n.
**agro-industry**
agriculture 370 n.
**agronomics**
agriculture 370 n.

**agronomist**
farmer 370 n.
**aground**
in difficulties 700 adj.
**ague**
spasm 318 n.
illness 651 n.
tropical disease 651 n.
**ahead**
superior 34 adj.
before 64 adv.
future 124 adj.
beyond 199 adv.
in front 237 adv.
ahead 283 adv.
forward 285 adv.
**ahead of its time**
early 135 adj.
**ahead of one's time**
in front 237 adv.
**ahimsa**
peace 717 n.
benevolence 897 n.
**Ahriman**
Satan 969 n.
**Ahura Mazda**
the Diety 965 n.
**AI**
computing 86 n.
**aid**
strengthening 162 n.
support 218 n., vb.
incite 612 vb.
instrumentality 628 n.
utility 640 n.
be expedient 642 vb.
remedy 658 n.
facility 701 n.
facilitate 701 vb.
aid 703 n., vb.
cooperate 706 vb.
gift 781 n.
kind act 897 n.
philanthropy 901 n.
– and abet
concur 181 vb.
incite 612 vb.
**aide-de-camp**
auxiliary 707 n.
army officer 741 n.
**aide-mémoire**
reminder 505 n.
**aider**
cause 156 n.
motivator 612 n.
instrument 628 n.
aider 703 n.
auxiliary 707 n.
defender 713 n.
servant 742 n.
friend 880 n.
benefactor 903 n.
**aid-giving**
philanthropic 901 adj.
**AIDS**
blood 335 n.
blood disease 651 n.

venereal disease 651 n.
**aiguillette**
livery 547 n.
**aikido**
martial arts 716 n.
**aileron**
equilibrium 28 n.
wing 271 n.
aircraft 276 n.
**ailing**
sick 651 adj.
**ailment**
illness 651 n.
**aim**
place 187 vb.
direction 281 n.
aim 281 vb.
objective 617 n.
attempt 671 n., vb.
fire at 712 vb.
desired object 859 n.
– at
aim 281 vb.
aim at 617 vb.
pursue 619 vb.
desire 859 vb.
– high
hope 852 vb.
– too high
overstep 306 vb.
be rash 857 vb.
**aimless**
orderless 61 adj.
designless 618 adj.
**aimless activity**
restlessness 678 n.
**aimlessness**
inattention 456 n.
**ain folk**
kinsman 11 n.
**air**
insubstantial thing 4 n.
initiate 68 vb.
element 319 n.
lightness 323 n.
rarity 325 n.
gas 336 n.
air 340 n.
aerate 340 vb.
dry 342 vb.
ventilation 352 n.
wind 352 n.
tune 412 n.
mien 445 n.
enquire 459 vb.
divulge 526 vb.
salubrity 652 n.
refresh 685 vb.
conduct 688 n.
– one's knowledge
be affected 850 vb.
– one's views
dissertate 591 vb.
**air-bag**
safeguard 662 n.
**air base**
station 187 n.

air travel 271 n.
**airbed**
bed 218 n.
**airborne**
high 209 adj.
flying 271 adj.
ascending 308 adj.
**airbus**
aircraft 276 n.
**air commodore**
air officer 741 n.
**air-conditioned**
airy 340 adj.
cooled 382 adj.
salubrious 652 adj.
**air-conditioner**
ventilation 352 n.
**air-conditioning**
ventilation 352 n.
**aircraft**
aircraft 276 n.
air force 722 n.
**aircraft carrier**
ship 275 n.
warship 722 n.
**air crew**
aeronaut 271 n.
air force 722 n.
**air current**
wind 352 n.
**airdrop**
transference 272 n.
**airer**
hanger 217 n.
dryer 342 n.
**airfield**
air travel 271 n.
**air force**
aeronaut 271 n.
aircraft 276 n.
air force 722 n.
air officer 741 n.
**air freight**
transport 272 n.
**airgun**
propellant 287 n.
plaything 837 n.
**air-hole**
orifice 263 n.
air pipe 353 n.
**air hostess**
aeronaut 271 n.
**airily**
cheerfully 833 adv.
hopefully 852 adv.
**airiness**
rarity 325 n.
hope 852 n.
**airing**
enquiry 459 n.
**air-kissing**
endearment 884 n.
**airlane**
air travel 271 n.
route 624 n.
**airless**
tranquil 266 adj.

*cooperate* 706 vb.
*auxiliary* 707 n.
*colleague* 707 n.
*join a party* 708 vb.
*contract* 765 vb.
*friend* 880 n.

**almagest**
*dissertation* 591 n.

**alma mater**
*academy* 539 n.

**almanac**
*directory* 87 n.
*chronology* 117 n.

**almighty**
*powerful* 160 adj.
*godlike* 965 adj.

**Almighty, the**
*the Deity* 965 n.

**almond**
*fruit* 301 n.

**almond oil**
*oil* 357 n.

**almoner**
*nurse* 658 n.
*giver* 781 n.
*treasurer* 798 n.

**almost**
*almost* 33 adv.
*on the whole* 52 adv.
*nearly* 200 adv.
*imperfectly* 647 adv.

**almost all**
*main part* 32 n.
*chief part* 52 n.

**alms**
*gift* 781 n.
*kind act* 897 n.

**alms-giving**
*giving* 781 n.
*kind act* 897 n.
*act of worship* 981 n.

**almshouse**
*retreat* 192 n.
*shelter* 662 n.

**aloes**
*unsavouriness* 391 n.

**aloft**
*overhanging* 209 adj.
*aloft* 209 adv.
*up* 308 adv.

**alone**
*unrelated* 10 adj.
*separate* 46 adj.
*alone* 88 adj.
*singly* 88 adv.
*friendless* 883 adj.
*unsociable* 883 adj.

**alone, fear of being**
*phobia* 854 n. box

**along**
*longwise* 203 adv.

**alongside**
*near* 200 adv.
*in parallel* 219 adv.
*sideways* 239 adv.

**along with**
*in addition* 38 adv.

*with* 89 adv.
*synchronously* 123 adv.

**aloof**
*distant* 199 adj.
*incurious* 454 adj.
*impassive* 820 adj.
*prideful* 871 adj.
*inimical* 881 adj.
*unsociable* 883 adj.

**aloofness**
*noncoherence* 49 n.
*inattention* 456 n.
*unsociability* 883 n.

**aloud**
*loudly* 400 adv.
*vocal* 577 adj.

**alpaca**
*fibre* 208 n.
*textile* 222 n.

**alpenglow**
*glow* 417 n.

**alpha**
*beginning* 68 n.

**Alpha and Omega**
*all* 52 n.
*the Deity* 965 n.

**alphabet**
*beginning* 68 n.
*list* 87 n.
*letter* 558 n.
*lettering* 586 n.

**alphabetical order**
*order* 60 n.

**alpha-fetoprotein test**
*obstetrics* 167 n.
*diagnosis* 658 n.

**alphanumeric**
*computerized* 86 adj.

**alpha plus**
*excellent* 644 adj.

**alpha ray**
*radiation* 417 n.

**alpha waves**
*intellect* 447 n.

**alpine**
*alpine* 209 adj.

**alpinism**
*ascent* 308 n.

**Alps**
*high land* 209 n.

**already**
*before* 119 adv.
*at present* 121 adv.
*retrospectively* 125 adv.

**also**
*in addition* 38 adv.

**also-ran**
*inferior* 35 n.
*contender* 716 n.
*loser* 728 n.

**altar**
*ritual object* 988 n.
*altar* 990 n.

**altar bread**
*the sacrament* 988 n.

**altazimuth**
*astronomy* 321 n.

**alter**
*change* 143 vb.
*modify* 143 vb.
*qualify* 468 vb.

– course
*deviate* 282 vb.

– the case
*tell against* 467 vb.
*qualify* 468 vb.

**alterable**
*changeful* 152 adj.
*unstable* 152 adj.

**alteration**
*difference* 15 n.
*change* 143 n.
*transition* 147 n.

**alteration of plan**
*tergiversation* 603 n.

**altercation**
*quarrel* 709 n.
*contention* 716 n.

**alter ego**
*identity* 13 n.
*analogue* 18 n.
*colleague* 707 n.
*deputy* 755 n.
*close friend* 880 n.

**alternate**
*correlative* 12 adj.
*correlate* 12 vb.
*sequential* 65 adj.
*come after* 65 vb.
*discontinuous* 72 adj.
*be discontinuous* 72 vb.
*periodical* 141 adj.
*be periodic* 141 vb.
*substitute* 150 n.
*vary* 152 vb.
*fluctuate* 317 vb.
*deputy* 755 n.

**alternating current**
*electricity* 160 n.

**alternative**
*changeable* 143 adj.
*substitute* 150 n.
*choice* 605 n.
*contrivance* 623 n.
*means* 629 n.

**alternative birth**
*obstetrics* 167 n.
*dissent* 489 n.

**alternative comedy**
*dissent* 489 n.
*stage show* 594 n.

**alternative energy**
*sources of energy* 160 n.
*choice* 605 n.

**alternative fuel**
*sources of energy* 160 n.
*fuel* 385 n.

**alternative life style**
*dissent* 489 n.

**alternatively**
*instead* 150 adv.
*optionally* 605 adv.

**alternative medicine**
*dissent* 489 n.

*medical art* 658 n.

**alternative reading**
*speciality* 80 n.
*interpretation* 520 n.

**alternative therapy**
*alternative therapy* 658 n.

**alternative voting**
*vote* 605 n.

**alternator**
*electronics* 160 n.

**although**
*in return* 31 adv.
*although* 182 adv.
*provided* 468 adv.

**altimetry**
*altimetry* 209 n.
*angular measure* 247 n.
*geometry* 465 n.
*meter* 465 n.

**altitude**
*degree* 27 n.
*superiority* 34 n.
*height* 209 n.

**alto**
*vocalist* 413 n.

**altogether**
*on the whole* 52 adv.
*completely* 54 adv.

**altruism**
*philanthropy* 901 n.
*disinterestedness* 931 n.
*virtues* 933 n.

**altruist**
*kind person* 897 n.
*philanthropist* 901 n.

**altruistic**
*benevolent* 897 adj.
*philanthropic* 901 adj.
*disinterested* 931 adj.

**alum**
*sourness* 393 n.

**alumnus, alumna**
*student* 538 n.

**alveolus**
*cavity* 255 n.

**always**
*generally* 79 adv.
*while* 108 adv.

**Alzheimer's disease**
*helplessness* 161 n.
*mental disorder* 503 n.

**a.m.**
*o'clock* 117 adv.
*morning* 128 n.
*at sunrise* 128 adv.

**amalgam**
*a mixture* 43 n.
*compound* 50 n.

**amalgamate**
*mix* 43 vb.
*combine* 50 vb.

**amalgamation**
*association* 706 n.

**amanuensis**
*recorder* 549 n.
*instrument* 628 n.

**angry**
*furious* 176 adj.
*frenzied* 503 adj.
*excited* 821 adj.
*angry* 891 adj.
*threatening* 900 adj.
**angry young man**
*nonconformist* 84 n.
*malcontent* 829 n.
**angst**
*evil* 616 n.
*badness* 645 n.
*bane* 659 n.
*suffering* 825 n.
*melancholy* 834 n.
*nervousness* 854 n.
**anguine**
*snaky* 251 adj.
**anguish**
*pain* 377 n.
*badness* 645 n.
*suffering* 825 n.
**angular**
*oblique* 220 adj.
*crossed* 222 adj.
*angular* 247 adj.
*curved* 248 adj.
**angularity**
*joint* 45 n.
*nonconformity* 84 n.
*obliquity* 220 n.
*angularity* 247 n.
*curvature* 248 n.
*camber* 253 n.
*leg* 267 n.
*divergence* 294 n.
**anhydrous**
*dry* 342 adj.
**aniline dye**
*pigment* 425 n.
**anility**
*old age* 131 n.
*folly* 499 n.
**anima**
*spirit* 447 n.
**animadversion**
*reprimand* 924 n.
**animal**
*young creature* 132 n.
*animal* 365 n., adj.
*mindless* 448 adj.
*unthinking* 450 adj.
*knave* 938 n.
*intemperate* 943 adj.
*sensualist* 944 n.
*sensual* 944 adj.
**animal and vegetable kingdom**
*organism* 358 n.
**animal behaviour**
*zoology* 367 n.
**animal companion**
*animality* n.
**animal cry**
*cry* 408 n.
**animalcule**
*microorganism* 196 n.

**animal disease**
*animal disease* 651 n.
**animal doctor**
*animal husbandry* 369 n.
**animal food**
*provender* 301 n.
**animal groups, names of**
*group* 74 n. box
**animal husbandry**
*production* 164 n.
*propagation* 167 n.
*animal husbandry* 369 n.
*agriculture* 370 n.
**animalism**
*animality* 365 n.
*sensualism* 944 n.
**animalist**
*animality* 365 n.
**animality**
*life* 360 n.
*animality* 365 n.
*absence of intellect* 448 n.
**animal life**
*life* 360 n.
*animality* 365 n.
**animal management**
*animal husbandry* 369 n.
**animal rights movement**
*animality* 365 n.
**animals, fear of**
*phobia* 854 n. box
**animal skins, fear of**
*phobia* 854 n. box
**animal spirits**
*vitality* 162 n.
*life* 360 n.
*cheerfulness* 833 n.
**animal trainer**
*trainer* 537 n.
**animal worship**
*idolatry* 982 n.
**animate**
*strengthen* 162 vb.
*invigorate* 174 vb.
*incite* 612 vb.
*animate* 821 vb.
*cheer* 833 vb.
*give courage* 855 vb.
**animated**
*alive* 360 adj.
*active* 678 adj.
*lively* 819 adj.
*cheerful* 833 adj.
**animated cartoon**
*film* 445 n.
**animate existence**
*life* 360 n.
**animate matter**
*organism* 358 n.
**animation**
*life* 360 n.
*cinema* 445 n.
*restlessness* 678 n.
*excitation* 821 n.

*cheerfulness* 833 n.
*courage* 855 n.
**animator**
*director* 690 n.
**anime**
*cinema* 445 n.
*film* 445 n.
**animism**
*immateriality* 320 n.
*deism* 973 n.
**animosity**
*dislike* 861 n.
*enmity* 881 n.
*hatred* 888 n.
*resentment* 891 n.
**animus**
*spirit* 447 n.
*willingness* 597 n.
*intention* 617 n.
*affections* 817 n.
*feeling* 818 n.
*enmity* 881 n.
**ankh**
*cross* 222 n.
*badge of rule* 743 n.
**ankle**
*joint* 45 n.
*foot* 214 n.
*angularity* 247 n.
**ankle-deep**
*deep* 211 adj.
*shallow* 212 adj.
**ankle-length**
*long* 203 adj.
**anklet**
*jewellery* 844 n.
**ankus**
*sharp point* 256 n.
**annalist**
*chronologist* 117 n.
*chronicler* 549 n.
*narrator* 590 n.
**annals**
*chronology* 117 n.
*record* 548 n.
*narrative* 590 n.
**anneal**
*be tough* 329 vb.
**annex**
*add* 38 vb.
*connect* 45 vb.
*subjugate* 745 vb.
*acquire* 771 vb.
*appropriate* 786 vb.
**annexation**
*addition* 38 n.
*joining together* 45 n.
**annexe**
*adjunct* 40 n.
**annihilate**
*nullify* 2 vb.
*abate* 37 vb.
*destroy* 165 vb.
*slaughter* 362 vb.
**anniversary**
*date* 108 n.
*period* 110 n.

*anniversary* 141 n.
*seasonal* 141 adj.
*special day* 876 n.
*celebratory* 876 adj.
*holy day* 988 n.
**anno domini**
*anno domini* 108 adv.
*old age* 131 n.
**annotate**
*interpret* 520 vb.
*mark* 547 vb.
*dissertate* 591 vb.
**annotated edition**
*edition* 589 n.
**annotated text**
*textbook* 589 n.
**annotation**
*commentary* 520 n.
*record* 548 n.
**announce**
*predict* 511 vb.
*communicate* 524 vb.
*proclaim* 528 vb.
*name* 561 vb.
– *itself*
*happen* 154 vb.
**announcement**
*prediction* 511 n.
*information* 524 n.
*publication* 528 n.
**announcer**
*precursor* 66 n.
*informant* 524 n.
*publicizer* 528 n.
*messenger* 529 n.
*broadcaster* 531 n.
*nomenclator* 561 n.
*speaker* 579 n.
**annoy**
*give pain* 377 vb.
*meddle* 678 vb.
*hinder* 702 vb.
*oppress* 735 vb.
*torment* 827 vb.
*sadden* 834 vb.
*enrage* 891 vb.
*be malevolent* 898 vb.
**annoyance**
*evil* 616 n.
*badness* 645 n.
*bane* 659 n.
*worry* 825 n.
*annoyance* 827 n.
*resentment* 891 n.
**annoyed**
*unhappy* 825 adj.
*discontented* 829 adj.
*angry* 891 adj.
**annoying**
*bad* 645 adj.
*not nice* 645 adj.
*annoying* 827 adj.
*discontenting* 829 adj.
**annual**
*periodic* 110 adj.
*ephemeral* 114 adj.
*seasonal* 141 adj.

contrary 14 adj.
opposing 704 adj.
**antiaircraft**
defending 713 adj.
**antiaircraft gun**
gun 723 n.
**antibiotic**
antidote 658 n.
drug 658 n.
**antibody**
antidote 658 n.
**anti-chic**
inelegance 576 n.
fashion 848 n.
**Antichrist**
bad person 938 n.
Satan 969 n.
irreligionist 974 n.
**anti-Christian**
irreligious 974 adj.
impious 980 adj.
**antichristianism**
antichristianity
974 n.
**anticipate**
misdate 118 vb.
do before 119 vb.
look ahead 124 vb.
be early 135 vb.
expect 507 vb.
foresee 510 vb.
be willing 597 vb.
prepare 669 vb.
be active 678 vb.
take 786 vb.
hope 852 vb.
be rash 857 vb.
**anticipation**
precursor 66 n.
anticipation 135 n.
expectation 507 n.
foresight 510 n.
preparation 669 n.
**anticipatory**
expectant 507 adj.
foreseeing 510 adj.
**anticlerical**
irreligious 974 adj.
impious 980 adj.
**anticlimax**
decrease 37 n.
absurdity 497 n.
lack of expectation
508 n.
disappointment 509 n.
feebleness 572 n.
failure 728 n.
ridiculousness 849 n.
**anticlinal**
sloping 220 adj.
arched 253 adj.
**anticline**
dome 253 n.
fold 261 n.
**anticlockwise**
towards 281 adv.
regressive 286 adj.

round and round
315 adv.
**anticoagulant**
liquefaction 337 n.
antidote 658 n.
**anticonvulsant**
antidote 658 n.
**antics**
foolery 497 n.
bungling 695 n.
revel 837 n.
**anticyclone**
weather 340 n.
**antidepressant**
drug 658 n.
**antidote**
contrariety 14 n.
moderator 177 n.
counteraction 182 n.
liquefaction 337 n.
antidote 658 n.
**antifreeze**
heating 381 adj.
**antigen**
antidote 658 n.
**antihero**
acting 594 n.
**antihistamine**
antidote 658 n.
**antilogarithm**
numerical element 85 n.
**antilogy**
contrariety 14 n.
sophism 477 n.
**antimalarial pill**
prophylactic 658 n.
**anti-missile defence
system**
rocket 276 n.
safeguard 662 n.
arms 723 n.
**anti-missile missile**
missile weapon 723 n.
**antinomian**
anarchic 734 adj.
revolter 738 n.
disobedient 738 adj.
lawless 954 adj.
heretic 977 n.
**antinomy**
contrariety 14 n.
illegality 954 n.
**antinovel**
novel 590 n.
**antiparticle**
element 319 n. box
**antipasto**
hors-d'oeuvres 301 n.
**antipathetic**
contrary 14 adj.
disagreeing 25 adj.
unconformable 84 adj.
counteracting 182 adj.
repellent 292 adj.
opposing 704 adj.
disliked 861 adj.
disliking 861 adj.

inimical 881 adj.
hating 888 adj.
**antipathy**
contrariety 14 n.
difference 15 n.
counteraction 182 n.
dislike 861 n.
enmity 881 n.
hatred 888 n.
**antiperspirant**
cosmetic 843 n.
**antiphon**
answer 460 n.
hymn 981 n.
**antipodal, anti-
podean**
contrary 14 adj.
distant 199 adj.
inverted 221 adj.
opposite 240 adj.
**antipodes**
extremity 69 n.
farness 199 n.
contraposition 240 n.
**antipyretic**
antidote 658 n.
remedial 658 adj.
**antiquarian**
antiquarian 125 n.
olden 127 adj.
collector 492 n.
chronicler 549 n.
bibliographical 589 adj.
**antiquary**
antiquarian 125 n.
collector 492 n.
**antiquated**
anachronistic 118 adj.
not contemporary
122 adj.
past 125 adj.
antiquated 127 adj.
ageing 131 adj.
useless 641 adj.
disused 674 adj.
**antique**
archaism 127 n.
olden 127 adj.
**antiquity**
time 108 n.
era 110 n.
long duration 113 n.
antiquity 125 n.
past time 125 n.
oldness 127 n.
monument 548 n.
collection 632 n.
**antireligious**
irreligious 974 adj.
impious 980 adj.
**anti-Semite**
enemy 881 n.
**anti-Semitism**
prejudice 481 n.
phobia 854 n.
hatred 888 n.
**antiseptic**

clean 648 adj.
salubrious 652 adj.
prophylactic 658 n.
remedial 658 adj.
tutelary 660 adj.
**antisepticize, antisep-
ticise**
purify 648 vb.
sanitate 652 vb.
doctor 658 vb.
**antisocial**
unsociable 883 adj.
misanthropic 902 adj.
**antispasmodic**
antidote 658 n.
**antithesis**
contrariety 14 n.
difference 15 n.
contraposition 240 n.
comparison 462 n.
trope 519 n.
ornament 574 n.
**antithetic, anti-
thetical**
contrary 14 adj.
rhetorical 574 adj.
**antitoxin**
antidote 658 n.
**antitype**
prototype 23 n.
**antivivisectionist**
animality 365 n.
**antler**
protuberance 254 n.
sharp point 256 n.
**antonomasia**
trope 519 n.
nomenclature 561 n.
**antonym**
contrariety 14 n.
connotation 514 n.
word 559 n.
**antrum**
cavity 255 n.
**ants, fear of**
phobia 854 n. box
**anus**
buttocks 238 n.
orifice 263 n.
**anvil**
stand 218 n.
hammer 279 n.
**anxiety**
carefulness 457 n.
expectation 507 n.
worry 825 n.
nervousness 854 n.
**anxiety neurosis**
neurosis 503 n.
**anxious**
careful 457 adj.
expectant 507 adj.
suffering 825 adj.
nervous 854 adj.
desiring 859 adj.
**anxious to please**
courteous 884 adj.

*farm* 370 n.
**arachnid**
  *animal* 365 n.
**arachnology**
  *zoology* 367 n.
  *study* 536 n. box
**arbiter**
  *adviser* 691 n.
  *magistracy* 957 n.
**arbiter elegantiarum**
  *reveller* 837 n.
  *people of taste* 846 n.
**arbitrage**
  *gamble* 618 n.
  *barter* 791 n.
**arbitrageur**
  *gambler* 618 n.
**arbitral**
  *judicial* 480 adj.
**arbitrament**
  *judgment* 480 n.
**arbitrarily**
  *severely* 735 adv.
**arbitrary**
  *unrelated* 10 adj.
  *unconformable* 84 adj.
  *illogical* 477 adj.
  *volitional* 595 adj.
  *wilful* 602 adj.
  *capricious* 604 adj.
  *authoritative* 733 adj.
  *authoritarian* 735 adj.
  *unconditional* 744 adj.
  *insolent* 878 adj.
  *lawless* 954 adj.
**arbitrary power**
  *brute force* 735 n.
**arbitrate**
  *judge* 480 vb.
  *mediate* 720 vb.
  *compromise* 770 vb.
**arbitrator**
  *estimator* 480 n.
  *adviser* 691 n.
  *mediator* 720 n.
  *magistracy* 957 n.
**arboreal**
  *arboreal* 366 adj.
**arborescence**
  *symmetry* 245 n.
**arboretum**
  *wood* 366 n.
  *garden* 370 n.
**arbour**
  *pavilion* 192 n.
  *arbour* 194 n.
  *screen* 421 n.
  *pleasure ground* 837 n.
**Arbroath smoky**
  *fish food* 301 n.
**arc**
  *part* 53 n.
  *curve* 248 n.
  *arc* 250 n.
  *fire* 379 n.
**arcade**
  *pavilion* 192 n.

*curve* 248 n.
  *path* 624 n.
  *emporium* 796 n.
**Arcadia**
  *happiness* 824 n.
**Arcadian**
  *artless* 699 adj.
  *innocent* 935 adj.
**arcane**
  *unintelligible* 517 adj.
  *latent* 523 adj.
  *concealed* 525 adj.
**arch**
  *consummate* 32 adj.
  *supreme* 34 adj.
  *bond* 47 n.
  *foot* 214 n.
  *prop* 218 n.
  *curve* 248 n.
  *be curved* 248 vb.
  *make curved* 248 vb.
  *camber* 253 n.
  *be convex* 253 vb.
  *merry* 833 adj.
  *affected* 850 adj.
**archaeological ex-**
  **cavation**
  *search* 459 n.
**archaeologist**
  *antiquarian* 125 n.
  *excavator* 255 n.
  *detector* 484 n.
  *chronicler* 549 n.
**archaeology**
  *antiquity* 125 n.
  *palaeology* 125 n.
  *discovery* 484 n.
  *study* 536 n. box
**archaic**
  *antiquated* 127 adj.
  *olden* 127 adj.
**archaism**
  *antiquity* 125 n.
  *archaism* 127 n.
  *reversion* 148 n.
  *neology* 560 n.
**archangel**
  *angel* 968 n.
**archbishop**
  *governor* 741 n.
  *ecclesiarch* 986 n.
**archbishopric**
  *district* 184 n.
  *church office* 985 n.
  *parish* 985 n.
**archdeacon**
  *ecclesiarch* 986 n.
**archduchy**
  *political organization*
    *733 n.
**archduke**
  *potentate* 741 n.
  *person of rank* 868 n.
**arched**
  *curved* 248 adj.
  *arched* 253 adj.
  *concave* 255 adj.

**arch enemy**
  *enemy* 881 n.
**archer**
  *shooter* 287 n.
  *soldiery* 722 n.
  *player* 837 n.
**archery**
  *sport* 837 n.
**archetypal**
  *original* 21 adj.
**archetype**
  *prototype* 23 n.
  *idea* 451 n.
**archimandrite**
  *ecclesiarch* 986 n.
  *monk* 986 n.
**Archimedes' screw**
  *extractor* 304 n.
  *irrigator* 341 n.
**archipelago**
  *island* 349 n.
**architect**
  *producer* 164 n.
  *artist* 556 n.
  *planner* 623 n.
  *artisan* 686 n.
**architect-designed**
  *produced* 164 adj.
  *architectural* 192 adj.
**architectonics**
  *structure* 331 n.
**architectural**
  *architectural* 192 adj.
  *formative* 243 adj.
  *structural* 331 adj.
**architectural mon-**
  **strosity**
  *eyesore* 842 n.
**architecture**
  *composition* 56 n.
  *arrangement* 62 n.
  *production* 164 n.
  *form* 243 n.
  *structure* 331 n.
  *art* 551 n.
  *ornamental art* 844
**architrave**
  *summit* 213 n.
  *beam* 218 n.
**archives**
  *record* 548 n.
  *collection* 632 n.
  *title deed* 767 n.
**archivist**
  *recorder* 549 n.
  *keeper* 749 n.
**archpriest**
  *ecclesiarch* 986 n.
  *priest* 986 n.
**archway**
  *doorway* 263 n.
**arc light**
  *lamp* 420 n.
**arctic**
  *opposite* 240 adj.
  *cold* 380 adj.
**Arctic**

*coldness* 380 n.
**arcuate**
  *make curved* 248 vb.
  *arched* 253 adj.
**ardent**
  *fiery* 379 adj.
  *forceful* 571 adj.
  *active* 678 adj.
  *hasty* 680 adj.
  *fervent* 818 adj.
  *desiring* 859 adj.
  *loving* 887 adj.
  *pietistic* 979 adj.
**ardent admirer**
  *worshipper* 981 n.
**ardour**
  *heat* 379 n.
  *vigour* 571 n.
  *willingness* 597 n.
  *resolution* 599 n.
  *restlessness* 678 n.
  *warm feeling* 818 n.
  *desire* 859 n.
**arduous**
  *laborious* 682 adj.
  *difficult* 700 adj.
**area**
  *quantity* 26 n.
  *greatness* 32 n.
  *measure* 183 n.
  *space* 183 n.
  *region* 184 n.
  *place* 185 n.
  *size* 195 n.
  *function* 622 n.
**arena**
  *athletics* 162 n.
  *range* 183 n.
  *region* 184 n.
  *contest* 716 n.
  *battle* 718 n.
  *arena* 724 n.
  *pleasure ground* 837 n.
**arenaceous**
  *powdery* 332 adj.
**areola**
  *circle* 250 n.
**Ares**
  *war* 718 n.
  *Olympian Deity* 967 n.
**arête**
  *sharp point* 256 n.
**argent**
  *white* 427 adj.
  *heraldry* 547 n.
  *heraldic* 547 adj.
**argil**
  *soil* 344 n.
**argilaceous**
  *soft* 327 adj.
**argon**
  *element* 319 n. box
  *air* 340 n.
**argosy**
  *merchant ship* 275 n.
  *shipping* 275 n.
  *navy* 722 n.

**argot**
*slang* 560 n.
**arguable**
*possible* 469 adj.
*uncertain* 474 adj.
**argue**
*disagree* 25 vb.
*testify* 466 vb.
*argue* 475 vb.
*sophisticate* 477 vb.
*dissent* 489 vb.
*propound* 512 vb.
*publish* 528 vb.
*affirm* 532 vb.
*indicate* 547 vb.
*confer* 584 vb.
*dissertate* 591 vb.
*plead* 614 vb.
*bicker* 709 vb.
*vindicate* 927 vb.
*litigate* 959 vb.
– against
*cause doubt* 486 vb.
*dissuade* 613 vb.
– for
*contend* 716 vb.
– in a circle
*reason badly* 477 vb.
**argufy**
*argue* 475 vb.
**argument**
*disagreement* 25 n.
*topic* 452 n.
*question* 459 n.
*argument* 475 n.
*demonstration* 478 n.
*supposition* 512 n.
*conference* 584 n.
*dissertation* 591 n.
*quarrel* 709 n.
*contention* 716 n.
**argumentation**
*argumentation* 475 n.
**argumentative**
*arguing* 475 adj.
*quarrelling* 709 adj.
**Argus**
*doorkeeper* 264 n.
*eye* 438 n.
*protector* 660 n.
*gaoler* 749 n.
**Argus-eyed**
*seeing* 438 adj.
*vigilant* 457 adj.
**argy-bargy**
*argue* 475 vb.
*quarrel* 709 n.
*bargain* 791 n.
**aria**
*tune* 412 n.
**Arian**
*heretic* 977 n.
*heretical* 977 adj.
**Aricept**
*drug* 658 n.
**arid**
*unproductive* 172 adj.

*dry* 342 adj.
*tedious* 838 adj.
**aridity**
*unproductiveness* 172 n.
*desert* 172 n.
*dryness* 342 n.
**Ariel**
*speeder* 277 n.
*courier* 529 n.
*fairy* 970 n.
**Aries**
*zodiac* 321 n. box
**aright**
*well* 615 adv.
*aright* 644 adv.
**arioso**
*musical* 412 adj.
**arise**
*become* 1 vb.
*begin* 68 vb.
*happen* 154 vb.
*lift oneself* 310 vb.
*be visible* 443 vb.
*appear* 445 vb.
– from
*result* 157 vb.
– from the dead
*be restored* 656 vb.
**aristocracy**
*superior* 34 n.
*superiority* 34 n.
*social group* 371 n.
*elite* 644 n.
*government* 733 n.
*owner* 776 n.
*aristocracy* 868 n.
**aristocrat**
*notable* 638 n.
*master* 741 n.
*aristocrat* 868 n.
*proud person* 871 n.
**Aristotelianism**
*philosophy* 449 n.
**arithmetic**
*mathematics* 86 n.
*curriculum* 534 n.
**arithmetical**
*numerical* 85 adj.
*statistical* 86 adj.
**arithmetical pro-
   gression**
*series* 71 n.
*ratio* 85 n.
**arithmetician**
*enumerator* 86 n.
**ark**
*retreat* 192 n.
*box* 194 n.
*refuge* 662 n.
**Ark of the Covenant**
*ritual object* 988 n.
*holy place* 990 n.
**arm**
*adjunct* 40 n.
*limb* 53 n.
*extremity* 69 n.
*empower* 160 vb.

*prop* 218 n.
*sleeve* 228 n.
*laterality* 239 n.
*indicator* 547 n.
*tool* 630 n.
*provide* 633 vb.
*safeguard* 660 vb.
*make ready* 669 vb.
*defend* 713 vb.
*go to war* 718 vb.
*weapon* 723 n.
**armada**
*shipping* 275 n.
*armed force* 722 n.
*navy* 722 n.
**Armageddon**
*fight* 716 n.
*war* 718 n.
**armagnac**
*alcoholic drink* 301 n.
**armament**
*fitting out* 669 n.
*armed force* 722 n.
*arms* 723 n.
**arm and a leg**
*greatness* 32 n.
**armature**
*sculpture* 554 n.
**armband**
*belt* 228 n.
**armchair**
*seat* 218 n.
*softness* 327 n.
*suppositional* 512 adj.
**armchair critic**
*theorist* 512 n.
**armchair travel**
*quietude* 266 n.
**armed**
*strong* 162 adj.
*prepared* 669 adj.
*warring* 718 adj.
**armed conflict**
*battle* 718 n.
**armed force(s)**
*band* 74 n.
*protection* 660 n.
*attacker* 712 n.
*armed force* 722 n.
*army* 722 n.
**armed intervention**
*war* 718 n.
**Armenian Church**
*Christendom* 976 n.
**armhole**
*sleeve* 228 n.
*orifice* 263 n.
**armiger**
*aristocrat* 868 n.
**arm in arm**
*joined* 45 adj.
*with* 89 adv.
*near* 200 adv.
*contiguously* 202 adv.
*across* 222 adv.
*amicably* 880 adv.
*sociably* 882 adv.

**armistice**
*lull* 145 n.
*peace* 717 n.
*pacification* 719 n.
**Armistice Day**
*special day* 876 n.
**armless**
*fragmentary* 53 adj.
*incomplete* 55 adj.
*disabled* 163 adj.
*imperfect* 647 adj.
**armlet**
*belt* 228 n.
*loop* 250 n.
*badge of rank* 743 n.
*jewellery* 844 n.
**arm of the law**
*law* 953 n.
*jurisdiction* 955 n.
*legal process* 959 n.
**arm of the sea**
*gulf* 345 n.
**armorial**
*heraldic* 547 adj.
**armour**
*covering* 226 n.
*headgear* 228 n.
*legwear* 228 n.
*protection* 660 n.
*safeguard* 660 vb.
*safeguard* 662 n.
*armour* 713 n.
*defend* 713 vb.
*cavalry* 722 n.
*weapon* 723 n.
**armour-bearer**
*retainer* 742 n.
**armoured**
*hard* 326 adj.
*resolute* 599 adj.
*invulnerable* 660 adj.
*defended* 713 adj.
**armoured car**
*war chariot* 274 n.
*cavalry* 722 n.
**armoured cruiser**
*warship* 722 n.
**armoured division**
*formation* 722 n.
**armour plate**
*covering* 226 n.
*protection* 660 n.
*safeguard* 660 vb.
*armour* 713 n.
*defend* 713 vb.
**armoury**
*accumulation* 74 n.
*storage* 632 n.
*workshop* 687 n.
*arsenal* 723 n.
**armpit**
*cavity* 255 n.
**arms**
*garment* 228 n.
*vocation* 622 n.
*tool* 630 n.
*safeguard* 662 n.

**baksheesh**
*acquisition* 771 n.
*gift* 781 n.
*reward* 962 n.
**balalaika**
*stringed instrument*
414 n.
**balance**
*relate* 9 vb.
*correlate* 12 vb.
*adjust* 24 vb.
*equilibrium* 28 n.
*equalize* 28 vb.
*average* 30 n.
*set off* 31 vb.
*remainder* 41 n.
*part* 53 n.
*completeness* 54 n.
*stability* 153 n.
*stabilize* 153 vb.
*symmetry* 245 n.
*scales* 322 n.
*compare* 462 vb.
*measure* 465 vb.
*sagacity* 498 n.
*sanity* 502 n.
*elegance* 575 n.
*be irresolute* 601 vb.
*middle way* 625 n.
*superfluity* 637 n.
*inexcitability* 823 n.
*caution* 858 n.
– accounts with
*pay* 804 vb.
*account* 808 vb.
– the books
*be careful* 457 vb.
**balance due**
*requirement* 627 n.
**balance of power**
*defence* 713 n.
**balance of the mind**
*sanity* 502 n.
**balances**
*funds* 797 n.
*credit* 802 n.
**balance sheet**
*accounts* 808 n.
**balance to pay**
*debt* 803 n.
**balancing act**
*equivocalness* 518 n.
*compromise* 770 n.
**balcony**
*lobby* 194 n.
*projection* 254 n.
*theatre* 594 n.
**bald**
*hairless* 229 adj.
*smooth* 258 adj.
*veracious* 540 adj.
*feeble* 572 adj.
*plain* 573 adj.
*inelegant* 576 adj.
*tedious* 838 adj.
**baldachin**
*canopy* 226 n.

*altar* 990 n.
**balderdash**
*silly talk* 515 n.
**baldric**
*belt* 228 n.
*loop* 250 n.
**bale**
*bunch* 74 n.
*stow* 187 vb.
*cultivate* 370 vb.
*evil* 616 n.
– out
*fly* 271 vb.
*emerge* 298 vb.
**bale fire**
*fire* 379 n.
*signal light* 420 n.
*signal* 547 n.
**baleful**
*harmful* 645 adj.
*malevolent* 898 adj.
**baler**
*ladle* 194 n.
*farm tool* 370 n.
**balk, baulk**
*beam* 218 n.
*partition* 231 n.
*disappointment* 509 n.
*disappoint* 509 vb.
*be obstructive* 702 vb.
– at
*avoid* 620 vb.
**Balkanize**
*rule* 733 vb.
**ball**
*sphere* 252 n.
*round* 252 vb.
*missile* 287 n.
*ammunition* 723 n.
*missile weapon* 723 n.
*dancing* 837 n.
*plaything* 837 n.
*social gathering* 882 n.
**ballad**
*vocal music* 412 n.
*narrative* 590 n.
*poem* 593 n.
**balladist**
*poet* 593 n.
**balladry**
*doggerel* 593 n.
*poetry* 593 n.
**ballad singer**
*vocalist* 413 n.
**ball and chain**
*fetter* 748 n.
**ballast**
*offset* 31 n.
*compensate* 31 vb.
*stabilizer* 153 n.
*gravity* 322 n.
*railway* 624 n.
*safeguard* 662 n.
**ball at one's feet**
*scope* 744 n.
**ballerina**
*actor* 594 n.

*dance* 837 n.
**ballet**
*composition* 56 n.
*ballet* 594 n.
*dancing* 837 n.
**ballet dancer**
*jumper* 312 n.
*actor* 594 n.
*dance* 837 n.
**balletomane**
*enthusiast* 504 n.
*playgoer* 594 n.
**ballet school**
*academy* 539 n.
**ball game**
*ball game* 837 n.
**ballgown**
*dress* 228 n.
**ballistic missile**
*missile weapon* 723 n.
**ballistics**
*propulsion* 287 n.
*study* 536 n. box
*art of war* 718 n.
*arms* 723 n.
**ballon d'essai**
*empiricism* 461 n.
**balloon**
*bladder* 194 n.
*expand* 197 vb.
*circumscription* 232 n.
*outline* 233 n.
*sphere* 252 n.
*round* 252 vb.
*be convex* 253 vb.
*airship* 276 n.
*lightness* 323 n.
*gas* 336 n.
*plaything* 837 n.
**balloonist**
*aeronaut* 271 n.
**ballot**
*affirmation* 532 n.
*vote* 605 n.
**ballot box**
*electorate* 605 n.
**ball-player**
*player* 837 n.
**ballpoint pen**
*stationery* 586 n.
**ballroom**
*place of amusement*
837 n.
**ballroom dancing**
*dancing* 837 n.
**balls-up**
*mistake* 495 n.
*bungling* 695 n.
**ballyhoo**
*loudness* 400 n.
*overestimation* 482 n.
*advertisement* 528 n.
*publicity* 528 n.
*exaggeration* 546 n.
**balm**
*moderator* 177 n.
*herb* 301 n.

*lubricant* 334 n.
*scent* 396 n.
*balm* 658 n.
*medicine* 658 n.
*pleasurableness* 826 n.
*relief* 831 n.
**bal masqué**
*concealment* 525 n.
*dancing* 837 n.
**balmy**
*warm* 379 adj.
*fragrant* 396 adj.
*palmy* 730 adj.
*cheering* 833 adj.
**balsa**
*raft* 275 n.
**balsam**
*balm* 658 n.
*medicine* 658 n.
**balsamic vinegar**
*cookery* 301 n.
*condiment* 389 n.
*sourness* 393 n.
**balthazar**
*vessel* 194 n.
**Baltic**
*ocean* 343 n.
**baluster**
*pillar* 218 n.
**balustrade**
*handle* 218 n.
*barrier* 235 n.
*fence* 235 n.
**bambino**
*child* 132 n.
**bamboo**
*grass* 366 n.
**bamboo curtain**
*partition* 231 n.
*obstacle* 702 n.
**bamboozle**
*puzzle* 474 vb.
*keep secret* 525 vb.
*befool* 542 vb.
*deceive* 542 vb.
**bamboozler**
*trickster* 545 n.
**ban**
*exclusion* 57 n.
*exclude* 57 vb.
*publication* 528 n.
*proclaim* 528 vb.
*call* 547 n.
*hindrance* 702 n.
*obstruct* 702 vb.
*command* 737 n., vb.
*restraint* 747 n.
*restrain* 747 vb.
*prohibition* 757 n.
*prohibit* 757 vb.
*make unwelcome* 883 vb.
*malediction* 899 n.
*disapprobation* 924 n.
*disapprove* 924 vb.
*penalty* 963 n.
– with bell, book and
candle

*strike* 279 vb.
*waste effort* 641 vb.
– the big drum
  *proclaim* 528 vb.
  *be ostentatious* 875 vb.
– the bounds
  *limit* 236 vb.
  *traverse* 267 vb.
  *measure* 465 vb.
  *circuit* 626 vb.
– the breast
  *lament* 836 vb.
– the drum
  *play music* 413 vb.
  *signal* 547 vb.
– the record
  *be superior* 34 vb.
– time
  *time* 117 vb.
  *play music* 413 vb.
– up
  *strike* 279 vb.
  *thicken* 354 vb.
  *strike at* 712 vb.
**beaten track**
  *habit* 610 n.
  *route* 624 n.
  *bore* 838 n.
**beatific**
  *good* 615 adj.
  *pleasurable* 826 adj.
  *paradisiac* 971 adj.
**beatify**
  *please* 826 vb.
  *dignify* 866 vb.
  *angelize* 968 vb.
  *sanctify* 979 vb.
  *be ecclesiastical* 985 vb.
**beating**
  *corporal punishment*
    963 n.
**beatitude**
  *happiness* 824 n.
**beatnik**
  *nonconformist* 84 n.
  *unconformable* 84 adj.
**beau**
  *male* 372 n.
  *fop* 848 n.
  *lover* 887 n.
**Beaufort scale**
  *anemometry* 352 n.
**beau geste**
  *deed* 676 n.
**beau idéal**
  *prototype* 23 n.
  *paragon* 646 n.
  *a beauty* 841 n.
**Beaujolais**
  *wine* 301 n.
**beau monde**
  *rich person* 800 n.
  *people of taste* 846 n.
  *beau monde* 848 n.
  *upper class* 868 n.
**beauteous**
  *beautiful* 841 adj.

**beautiful**
  *pleasant* 376 adj.
  *elegant* 575 adj.
  *excellent* 644 adj.
  *pleasurable* 826 adj.
  *beautiful* 841 adj.
  *beautified* 843 adj.
  *lovable* 887 adj.
**beautify**
  *ornament* 574 vb.
  *make better* 654 vb.
  *beautify* 841 vb.
  *primp* 843 vb.
  *decorate* 844 vb.
**beauty**
  *symmetry* 245 n.
  *elegance* 575 n.
  *pleasurableness* 826 n.
  *beauty* 841 n.
**beauty, a**
  *exceller* 644 n.
  *paragon* 646 n.
  *masterpiece* 694 n.
  *a beauty* 841 n.
  *favourite* 890 n.
**beauty spot**
  *a beauty* 841 n.
  *cosmetic* 843 n.
**beaux arts**
  *art* 551 n.
**beaux yeux**
  *beauty* 841 n.
**beaver**
  *headgear* 228 n.
  *hair* 259 n.
  *mammal* 365 n.
  *busy person* 678 n.
  *worker* 686 n.
  *armour* 713 n.
**beaver away**
  *be active* 678 vb.
  *work* 682 vb.
**bebop**
  *music* 412 n.
  *dance* 837 n.
**becalmed**
  *quiescent* 266 adj.
  *hindered* 702 adj.
**because (of)**
  *causally* 156 adv.
  *consequently* 157 adv.
  *hence* 158 adv.
**beck**
  *stream* 350 n.
  *gesture* 547 n.
  *gesticulate* 547 vb.
  *command* 737 n., vb.
**beckon**
  *gesticulate* 547 vb.
**become**
  *become* 1 vb.
  *be turned to* 147 vb.
  *happen* 154 vb.
  *evolve* 316 vb.
**becoming**
  *agreeing* 24 adj.
  *personable* 841 adj.

  *tasteful* 846 adj.
**becquerel**
  *radiation* 417 n.
**bed**
  *have sexual intercourse*
    *with* 45 vb.
  *place* 187 vb.
  *layer* 207 n.
  *base* 214 n.
  *basis* 218 n.
  *bed* 218 n.
  *resting place* 266 n.
  *garden* 370 n.
  *sleep* 679 n.
  *debauch* 951 vb.
– down
  *place* 187 vb.
  *groom* 369 vb.
  *sleep* 679 vb.
– out
  *cultivate* 370 vb.
**BEd**
  *academic title* 870 n.
**bed and breakfast**
  *inn* 192 n.
  *provision* 633 n.
**bedaub**
  *coat* 226 vb.
**bedazzle**
  *shine* 417 vb.
  *blur* 440 vb.
  *excite love* 887 vb.
  *command respect* 920 vb.
**bed-blocking**
  *hospital* 658 n.
  *hindrance* 702 n.
**bed bug**
  *insect* 365 n.
**bedclothes**
  *coverlet* 226 n.
**bedding**
  *stratification* 207 n.
  *bed* 218 n.
  *coverlet* 226 n.
**bedeck**
  *decorate* 844 vb.
**bedevil**
  *bedevil* 63 vb.
  *destroy* 165 vb.
  *be difficult* 700 vb.
  *trouble* 827 vb.
  *diabolize* 969 vb.
**bedevilment**
  *impairment* 655 n.
  *spell* 983 n.
**bedew**
  *moisten* 341 vb.
**bedim**
  *darken* 418 vb.
  *bedim* 419 vb.
  *blur* 440 vb.
  *conceal* 525 vb.
  *make unclean* 649 vb.
**bedizen**
  *dress* 228 vb.
  *primp* 843 vb.
**bedlam**

  *disorder* 61 n.
  *confusion* 61 n.
  *turmoil* 61 n.
  *loudness* 400 n.
  *discord* 411 n.
  *mental hospital* 503 n.
**bed of nails**
  *suffering* 825 n.
**bed of Procrustes**
  *equalization* 28 n.
**bed of roses**
  *euphoria* 376 n.
  *fragrance* 396 n.
  *palmy days* 730 n.
**bedouin**
  *dweller* 191 n.
  *wanderer* 268 n.
**bedpan**
  *vessel* 194 n.
  *latrine* 649 n.
**bedraggled**
  *orderless* 61 adj.
  *dirty* 649 adj.
**bedridden**
  *sick* 651 adj.
  *restrained* 747 adj.
**bedrock**
  *reality* 1 n.
  *simpleness* 44 n.
  *permanence* 144 n.
  *fixture* 153 n.
  *source* 156 n.
  *base* 214 n.
  *basis* 218 n.
  *chief thing* 638 n.
  *important* 638 adj.
**bedroom**
  *room* 194 n.
**bedside manner**
  *therapy* 658 n.
**bedside reading**
  *novel* 590 n.
**bed-sitter**
  *flat* 192 n.
**bedtime**
  *clock time* 117 n.
  *evening* 129 n.
  *vespertine* 129 adj.
**bee**
  *insect* 365 n.
  *busy person* 678 n.
  *See also* **bees**
**beech**
  *tree* 366 n.
**beef**
  *meat* 301 n.
  *deprecate* 762 vb.
  *be discontented* 829 vb.
  *lament* 836 vb.
  *be sullen* 893 vb.
– up
  *strengthen* 162 vb.
**beefcake**
  *a beauty* 841 n.
**beefy**
  *stalwart* 162 adj.
  *fleshy* 195 adj.

*large* 195 adj.
*important* 638 adj.
*difficult* 700 adj.
*finance* 797 n.
**bigamist**
*polygamist* 894 n.
**Big Bang**
*bourse* 618 n.
*market* 796 n.
**big battalions**
*notable* 638 n.
*army* 722 n.
*brute force* 735 n.
**Big Brother**
*influence* 178 n.
*authority* 733 n.
*position of authority* 733 n.
*tyrant* 735 n.
*master* 741 n.
*autocrat* 741 n.
**big business**
*business* 622 n.
**big Daddy**
*notable* 638 n.
**big drum**
*drum* 414 n.
*ostentation* 875 n.
*boast* 877 n.
**Bigfoot**
*mythical beast* 365 n.
**big game**
*animal* 365 n.
**big-game hunter**
*hunter* 619 n.
**bigger**
*expanded* 197 adj.
**biggest slice of the cake**
*chief part* 52 n.
**big girl's blouse**
*fool* 501 n.
*bungler* 697 n.
*coward* 856 n.
**big gun**
*autocrat* 741 n.
*person of repute* 866 n.
**bighead**
*vain person* 873 n.
**bight**
*curve* 248 n.
*cavity* 255 n.
*gulf* 345 n.
**bigmouth**
*informant* 524 n.
*boaster* 877 n.
**big name**
*person of repute* 866 n.
**big noise**
*influence* 178 n.
*notable* 638 n.
*person of repute* 866 n.
**bigot**
*doctrinaire* 473 n.
*narrow mind* 481 n.
*ignoramus* 493 n.
*obstinate person* 602 n.

*zealot* 979 n.
**bigotry**
*narrow mind* 481 n.
*credulity* 487 n.
*opinionatedness* 602 n.
*severity* 735 n.
*sectarianism* 978 n.
*pietism* 979 n.
**big shot**
*influence* 178 n.
*notable* 638 n.
*autocrat* 741 n.
*person of repute* 866 n.
**big spender**
*prodigal* 815 n.
**big stick**
*incentive* 612 n.
*compulsion* 740 n.
*threat* 900 n.
*scourge* 964 n.
**big talk**
*exaggeration* 546 n.
*boast* 877 n.
**big top**
*canopy* 226 n.
*theatre* 594 n.
**big white chief**
*notable* 638 n.
**bigwig**
*superior* 34 n.
*notable* 638 n.
*elite* 644 n.
*manager* 690 n.
*master* 741 n.
*person of repute* 866 n.
*aristocrat* 868 n.
*proud person* 871 n.
**big with fate**
*presageful* 511 adj.
**bijou**
*little* 196 adj.
*a beauty* 841 n.
*gem* 844 n.
**bijouterie**
*jewellery* 844 n.
**bike**
*ride* 267 vb.
*bicycle* 274 n.
**bikini**
*beachwear* 228 n.
**bilabial**
*speech sound* 398 n.
**bilateral**
*correlative* 12 adj.
*dual* 90 adj.
*lateral* 239 adj.
*contractual* 765 adj.
**bilboes**
*fetter* 748 n.
*pillory* 964 n.
**bildungsroman**
*novel* 590 n.
**bile**
*discontent* 829 n.
*melancholy* 834 n.
*resentment* 891 n.
*irascibility* 892 n.

*sullenness* 893 n.
*envy* 912 n.
**bilge**
*leavings* 41 n.
*base* 214 n.
*silly talk* 515 n.
*rubbish* 641 n.
*swill* 649 n.
**bilharzia**
*infection* 651 n.
*tropical disease* 651 n.
**bilingual**
*linguist* 557 n.
*linguistic* 557 adj.
*speaking* 579 adj.
**bilious**
*yellow* 433 adj.
*unhealthy* 651 adj.
*irascible* 892 adj.
*sullen* 893 adj.
**bilk**
*disappoint* 509 vb.
*deceive* 542 vb.
*defraud* 788 vb.
*be in debt* 803 vb.
*not pay* 805 vb.
**bilker**
*trickster* 545 n.
*avoider* 620 n.
*nonpayer* 805 n.
**bill**
*numerical result* 85 n.
*list* 87 n.
*protuberance* 254 n.
*advertisement* 528 n.
*advertise* 528 vb.
*label* 547 n.
*correspondence* 588 n.
*dramatize* 594 vb.
*axe* 723 n.
*spear* 723 n.
*demand* 737 vb.
*title deed* 767 n.
*paper money* 797 n.
*credit* 802 n.
*accounts* 808 n.
*account* 808 vb.
*price* 809 n., v.
**bill and coo**
*caress* 889 vb.
**billboard**
*advertisement* 528 n.
**bill-collector**
*receiver* 782 n.
**billet**
*stopping place* 145 n.
*place* 185 n.
*quarters* 192 n.
*goal* 295 n.
*apportion* 783 vb.
**billfold**
*case* 194 n.
**billiards**
*ball game* 837 n.
**Billingsgate**
*slang* 560 n.
*scurrility* 899 n.

**billion**
*over one hundred* 99 n.
**billions**
*great quantity* 32 n.
*multitude* 104 n.
*funds* 797 n.
**bill of exchange**
*title deed* 767 n.
*paper money* 797 n.
**bill of fare**
*list* 87 n.
*meal* 301 n.
**bill of indictment**
*accusation* 928 n.
**bill of lading**
*list* 87 n.
**bill of mortality**
*death roll* 361 n.
**bill of rights**
*dueness* 915 n.
**billon**
*a mixture* 43 n.
*bullion* 797 n.
**billow**
*high water* 209 n.
*swelling* 253 n.
*be convex* 253 vb.
*wave* 350 n.
**billows**
*ocean* 343 n.
**billowy**
*curved* 248 adj.
*convex* 253 adj.
**bills**
*debt* 803 n.
**billycan**
*cooking pot* 194 n.
**billy goat**
*cattle* 365 n.
*male animal* 372 n.
**bimbo**
*ignoramus* 493 n.
*dunce* 501 n.
**bimetallism**
*finance* 797 n.
**bin**
*vessel* 194 n.
**binary**
*computerized* 86 adj.
*dual* 90 adj.
*star* 321 n.
**binaural**
*sounding* 398 adj.
**bind**
*tie* 45 vb.
*combine* 50 vb.
*bring together* 74 vb.
*stabilize* 153 vb.
*make smaller* 198 vb.
*cover* 226 vb.
*close* 264 vb.
*be dense* 324 vb.
*cultivate* 370 vb.
*repair* 656 vb.
*doctor* 658 vb.
*obstruct* 702 vb.
*compel* 740 vb.

*redness* 431 n.
*fop* 848 n.
*nobility* 868 n.
**blood, fear of**
*phobia* 854 n. box
**blood-and-thunder**
*exaggerated* 546 adj.
*stage play* 594 n.
*dramatic* 594 adj.
**bloodbath**
*slaughter* 362 n.
*terror tactics* 712 n.
**blood-curdling**
*frightening* 854 adj.
**blood disease**
*blood disease* 651 n.
**blood donor**
*giver* 781 n.
*good giver* 813 n.
**blood feud**
*quarrel* 709 n.
*enmity* 881 n.
*revenge* 910 n.
**blood group**
*classification* 77 n.
*blood* 335 n.
**blood heat**
*heat* 379 n.
**bloodhound**
*dog* 365 n.
*detective* 459 n.
*hunter* 619 n.
**bloodiness**
*brute force* 735 n.
*inhumanity* 898 n.
**bloodless**
*insubstantial* 4 adj.
*weak* 163 adj.
*colourless* 426 adj.
*diseased* 651 adj.
*peaceful* 717 adj.
*guiltless* 935 adj.
**blood-letting**
*killing* 362 n.
*surgery* 658 n.
**blood lust**
*violence* 176 n.
*inhumanity* 898 n.
**blood money**
*peace offering* 719 n.
*atonement* 941 n.
**blood on one's hands**
*be guilty* 936 vb.
**blood-poisoning**
*infection* 651 n.
*poisoning* 659 n.
**blood pressure**
*cardiovascular disease*
  651 n.
**blood-red**
*bloodstained* 431 adj.
**blood relation**
*kinsman* 11 n.
**bloodshed**
*slaughter* 362 n.
*warfare* 718 n.
*cruel act* 898 n.

**bloodshot**
*bloodstained* 431 adj.
*angry* 891 adj.
*drunken* 949 adj.
**blood sports**
*killing* 362 n.
*chase* 619 n.
**bloodstained**
*sanguineous* 335 adj.
*murderous* 362 adj.
*bloodstained* 431 adj.
**bloodstock**
*thoroughbred* 273 n.
*aristocrat* 868 n.
*nobility* 868 n.
**bloodstone**
*gem* 844 n.
**bloodsucker**
*tyrant* 735 n.
*taker* 786 n.
*offender* 904 n.
*glutton* 947 n.
**blood test**
*diagnosis* 658 n.
**bloodthirsty**
*furious* 176 adj.
*murderous* 362 adj.
*harmful* 645 adj.
*warlike* 718 adj.
*cruel* 898 adj.
**blood transfusion**
*blood* 335 n.
**bloodwagon**
*vehicle* 274 n.
**bloody**
*violent* 176 adj.
*sanguineous* 335 adj.
*humid* 341 adj.
*murderous* 362 adj.
*bloodstained* 431 adj.
*harmful* 645 adj.
*oppressive* 735 adj.
*courageous* 855 adj.
*cruel* 898 adj.
**bloody-minded**
*obstinate* 602 adj.
*opposing* 704 adj.
*disobedient* 738 adj.
*malevolent* 898 adj.
**bloody nose**
*wound* 655 n.
*resistance* 715 n.
*defeat* 728 n.
**bloom**
*salad days* 130 n.
*adultness* 134 n.
*reproduce itself* 167 vb.
*be fruitful* 171 vb.
*expand* 197 vb.
*layer* 207 n.
*open* 263 vb.
*flower* 366 n.
*redness* 431 n.
*health* 650 n.
*healthy* 650 adj.
*maturation* 669 n.
*prosper* 730 vb.

*be beautiful* 841 vb.
**bloomer**
*mistake* 495 n.
**bloomers**
*trousers* 228 n.
*underwear* 228 n.
**blooming**
*young* 130 adj.
*grown-up* 134 adj.
*vigorous* 174 adj.
*open* 263 adj.
*vegetable life* 366 n.
*vegetal* 366 adj.
*healthy* 650 adj.
*personable* 841 adj.
**blossom**
*grow* 36 vb.
*growth* 157 n.
*product* 164 n.
*be fruitful* 171 vb.
*expand* 197 vb.
*flower* 366 n.
*prosper* 730 vb.
**blossom-time**
*spring* 128 n.
**blot**
*tincture* 43 n.
*sphere* 252 n.
*absorb* 299 vb.
*dry* 342 vb.
*blacken* 428 vb.
*variegate* 437 vb.
*mistake* 495 n.
*blunder* 495 vb.
*mark* 547 vb.
*obliteration* 550 n.
*obliterate* 550 vb.
*write* 586 vb.
*defect* 647 n.
*dirt* 649 n.
*make unclean* 649 vb.
*impair* 655 vb.
*be clumsy* 695 vb.
*eyesore* 842 n.
*make ugly* 842 vb.
*blemish* 845 n., vb.
*slur* 867 n.
*shame* 867 vb.
– one's copybook
*blunder* 495 vb.
*lose repute* 867 vb.
*incur blame* 924 vb.
*be wicked* 934 vb.
– out
*destroy* 165 vb.
*conceal* 525 vb.
*obliterate* 550 vb.
*forgive* 909 vb.
**blotch**
*maculation* 437 n.
*blemish* 845 n.
**blot on the landscape.**
*eyesore* 842 n.
**blotter**
*dryer* 342 n.
*stationery* 586 n.
*cleaning utensil* 648 n.

**blotto**
*dead drunk* 949 adj.
**blouse**
*shirt* 228 n.
**blouson**
*jacket* 228 n.
**blow**
*be violent* 176 vb.
*expand* 197 vb.
*form* 243 vb.
*knock* 279 n.
*aerate* 340 vb.
*gale* 352 n.
*wind* 352 n.
*blow* 352 vb.
*play music* 413 vb.
*lack of expectation*
  508 n.
*disappointment* 509 n.
*evil* 616 n.
*deed* 676 n.
*be fatigued* 684 vb.
*adversity* 731 n.
*expend* 806 vb.
*suffering* 825 n.
*corporal punishment*
  963 n.
– down
*demolish* 165 vb.
*fell* 311 vb.
– hard
*boast* 877 vb.
– hot and cold
*change* 143 vb.
*vary* 152 vb.
*be irresolute* 601 vb.
*be capricious* 604 vb.
– in
*arrive* 295 vb.
*enter* 297 vb.
– it
*blunder* 495 vb.
– off
*belch* 300 vb.
*stink* 397 vb.
– one's cover
*disclose* 526 vb.
– one's mind
*make mad* 503 vb.
*be wonderful* 864 vb.
*take drugs* 949 vb.
– one's money
*be prodigal* 815 vb.
– one's own trumpet
*be vain* 873 vb.
*boast* 877 vb.
– one's top
*get angry* 891 vb.
– open
*force* 176 vb.
– out
*nullify* 2 vb.
*suppress* 165 vb.
*extinguish* 382 vb.
*snuff out* 418 vb.
– over
*be past* 125 vb.

*wood* 366 n.
*safeguard* 662 n.
*hinder* 702 vb.
*restraint* 747 n.
*restrain* 747 vb.
*fetter* 748 n.
**brake light**
*lamp* 420 n.
**bramble**
*prickle* 256 n.
*plant* 366 n.
**bran**
*leavings* 41 n.
*cereals* 301 n.
*powder* 332 n.
**branch**
*adjunct* 40 n.
*branch* 53 n.
*be dispersed* 75 vb.
*classification* 77 n.
*descendant* 170 n.
*extend* 183 vb.
*filament* 208 n.
*make angular* 247 vb.
*stream* 350 n.
*foliage* 366 n.
*tree* 366 n.
*society* 708 n.
*sect* 978 n.
– off
*bifurcate* 92 vb.
*diverge* 294 vb.
– out
*be dispersed* 75 vb.
*deviate* 282 vb.
*diverge* 294 vb.
**branched**
*brachial* 53 adj.
**branching**
*symmetry* 245 n.
**branch line**
*railway* 624 n.
**brand**
*sort* 77 n.
*burning* 381 n.
*burn* 381 vb.
*furnace* 383 n.
*lighter* 385 n.
*torch* 420 n.
*identification* 547 n.
*label* 547 n.
*mark* 547 vb.
*blemish* 845 vb.
*slur* 867 n.
*shame* 867 vb.
*censure* 924 n.
*dispraise* 924 vb.
*detraction* 926 n.
*defame* 926 vb.
*accuse* 928 vb.
**branded**
*marked* 547 adj.
*proprietary* 777 adj.
**brandish**
*brandish* 317 vb.
*agitate* 318 vb.
*show* 522 vb.

*use* 673 vb.
*defy* 711 vb.
*be ostentatious* 875 vb.
*boast* 877 vb.
*threaten* 900 vb.
**brand-new**
*new* 126 adj.
**brandy**
*alcoholic drink* 301 n.
**brashness**
*insolence* 878 n.
**brashy**
*fragmentary* 53 adj.
**brass**
*a mixture* 43 n.
*blowing* 352 n.
*resonance* 404 n.
*stridor* 407 n.
*orchestra* 413 n.
*horn* 414 n.
*yellowness* 433 n.
*monument* 548 n.
*director* 690 n.
*badge of rank* 743 n.
*shekels* 797 n.
*wealth* 800 n.
*sauciness* 878 n.
**brassard**
*livery* 547 n.
*badge of rank* 743 n.
**brasserie**
*restaurant* 192 n.
**brass farthing**
*trifle* 639 n.
**brass hat**
*notable* 638 n.
*army officer* 741 n.
**brassiere**
*underwear* 228 n.
**brass knuckles**
*club* 723 n.
**brass neck**
*insolence* 878 n.
**brass plate**
*label* 547 n.
**brass rubbing**
*picture* 553 n.
**brass tacks**
*reality* 1 n.
**brassy**
*loud* 400 adj.
*strident* 407 adj.
*orange* 432 adj.
*ornate* 574 adj.
*impertinent* 878 adj.
**brat**
*child* 132 n.
**brattice**
*lining* 227 n.
*partition* 231 n.
**bravado**
*ostentation* 875 n.
*boast* 877 n.
*boasting* 877 n.
*insolence* 878 n.
**brave**
*be in front* 237 vb.

*defy* 711 vb.
*combatant* 722 n.
*brave person* 855 n.
*courageous* 855 adj.
*showy* 875 adj.
– it out
*be courageous* 855 vb.
**braveheart**
*brave person* 855 n.
*courageous* 855 adj.
**bravo**
*violent creature* 176 n.
*murderer* 362 n.
*combatant* 722 n.
*brave person* 855 n.
*desperado* 857 n.
*ruffian* 904 n.
– 886 int.
– 923 int.
**bravura**
*musical skill* 413 n.
*masterpiece* 694 n.
*defiance* 711 n.
**bravura player**
*proficient person* 696 n.
**braw**
*excellent* 644 adj.
**brawl**
*turmoil* 61 n.
*quarrel* 709 n.
*bicker* 709 vb.
*fight* 716 n.
**brawler**
*rioter* 738 n.
**brawn**
*vitality* 162 n.
*meat* 301 n.
**brawny**
*stalwart* 162 adj.
*fleshy* 195 adj.
**bray**
*pulverize* 332 vb.
*be loud* 400 vb.
*resound* 404 vb.
*rasp* 407 vb.
*ululate* 409 vb.
**braze**
*join* 45 vb.
*agglutinate* 48 vb.
**brazen**
*strident* 407 adj.
*undisguised* 522 adj.
*proud* 871 adj.
*insolent* 878 adj.
*wicked* 934 adj.
*impenitent* 940 adj.
*impious* 980 adj.
– it out
*be obstinate* 602 vb.
*be insolent* 878 vb.
**brazier**
*furnace* 383 n.
**breach**
*disagreement* 25 n.
*disunion* 46 n.
*gap* 201 n.
*dissension* 709 n.

*enmity* 881 n.
*undueness* 916 n.
**breach of promise**
*untruth* 543 n.
*nonobservance* 769 n.
*perfidy* 930 n.
**breach of the peace**
*turmoil* 61 n.
*quarrel* 709 n.
*revolt* 738 n.
**bread**
*cereals* 301 n.
*food* 301 n.
*shekels* 797 n.
**bread-and-butter,**
**one's**
*vocation* 622 n.
**bread and water**
*unsavouriness* 391 n.
*insufficiency* 636 n.
*fasting* 946 n.
**bread and wine**
*the sacrament* 988 n.
**breadline**
*needfulness* 627 n.
*insufficiency* 636 n.
*poverty* 801 n.
**breadth**
*greatness* 32 n.
*measure* 183 n.
*size* 195 n.
*breadth* 205 n.
*metrology* 465 n.
**breadth of mind**
*wisdom* 498 n.
**breadwinner**
*worker* 686 n.
**breadwinning**
*gainful* 771 adj.
**break**
*disunion* 46 n.
*break* 46 vb.
*separate* 46 vb.
*incompleteness* 55 n.
*series* 71 n.
*discontinuity* 72 n.
*discontinue* 72 vb.
*interim* 108 n.
*opportunity* 137 n.
*change* 143 n.
*lull* 145 n.
*continuance* 146 n.
*disable* 161 vb.
*weakness* 163 n.
*demolish* 165 vb.
*force* 176 n.
*gap* 201 n.
*interval* 201 n.
*deviate* 282 vb.
*be brittle* 330 vb.
*pulverize* 332 vb.
*flow* 350 vb.
*pain* 377 n.
*rasp* 407 vb.
*be disclosed* 526 vb.
*wound* 655 vb.
*leisure* 681 n.

**steal** 788 vb.
**burgomaster**
  *officer* 741 n.
**burgundy**
  *wine* 301 n. box
  *redness* 431 n.
**burial**
  *immersion* 303 n.
  *interment* 364 n.
  *concealment* 525 n.
  *obliteration* 550 n.
  *detention* 747 n.
**burial chamber**
  *tomb* 364 n.
**burial of the dead**
  *Christian rite* 998 n.
**burial of the hatchet**
  *amnesty* 506 n.
  *peace* 717 n.
**burial place**
  *cemetery* 364 n.
**burial service**
  *obsequies* 364 n.
**buried**
  *deep* 211 adj.
  *inserted* 303 adj.
  *dead* 361 adj.
  *buried* 364 adj.
  *neglected* 458 adj.
  *forgotton* 506 adj.
  *concealed* 525 adj.
  *imprisoned* 747 adj.
  *secluded* 883 adj.
**burin**
  *engraving* 555 n.
**burka**
  *robe* 228 n.
**Burke's Peerage**
  *directory* 87 n.
**burl**
  *solid body* 324 n.
**burlesque**
  *imitate* 20 vb.
  *uncovering* 229 n.
  *foolery* 497 n.
  *exaggeration* 546 n.
  *misrepresentation* 552 n.
  *doggerel* 593 n.
  *stage play* 594 n.
  *be witty* 839 vb.
  *funny* 849 adj.
  *satire* 851 n.
  *satirize* 851 vb.
**burly**
  *stalwart* 162 adj.
  *fleshy* 195 adj.
**burn**
  *destroy* 165 vb.
  *lay waste* 165 vb.
  *dry* 342 vb.
  *stream* 350 n.
  *inter* 364 vb.
  *be hot* 379 vb.
  *burning* 381 n.
  *burn* 381 vb.
  *shine* 417 vb.
  *blacken* 428 vb.

*brown* 430 vb.
*waste* 634 vb.
*wound* 655 n.
*attack* 712 vb.
*be excited* 821 vb.
*desire* 859 vb.
*be in love* 887 vb.
*resent* 891 vb.
– alive
  *kill* 362 vb.
  *execute* 963 vb.
– in
  *mark* 547 vb.
– incense
  *worship* 981 vb.
  *perform ritual* 988 vb.
– one's boats/bridges
  *initiate* 68 vb.
  *overstep* 306 vb.
  *be resolute* 599 vb.
  *choose* 605 vb.
– one's fingers
  *be foolish* 499 vb.
  *be unskilful* 695 vb.
  *lose* 772 vb.
  *be rash* 857 vb.
– out
  *burn* 381 vb.
  *extinguish* 382 vb.
  *waste* 634 vb.
  *fatigue* 684 vb.
– the candle at both ends
  *waste* 634 vb.
  *be prodigal* 815 vb.
  *revel* 837 vb.
  *be intemperate* 943 vb.
– the midnight oil
  *be late* 136 vb.
  *study* 536 vb.
  *be busy* 678 vb.
  *work* 682 vb.
– up
  *destroy* 165 vb.
  *burn* 381 vb.
**burnable**
  *combustible* 385 adj.
**burner**
  *burning* 381 n.
  *furnace* 383 n.
  *torch* 420 n.
**burning**
  *painful* 377 adj.
  *fiery* 379 adj.
  *burning* 381 n.
  *pungent* 388 adj.
  *fervent* 818 adj.
**burnish**
  *smooth* 258 vb.
  *rub* 333 vb.
  *make bright* 417 vb.
  *decorate* 844 vb.
**burnous**
  *cloak* 228 n.
**burnt**
  *culinary* 301 adj.
  *dry* 342 adj.
  *heated* 381 adj.

*unsavoury* 391 adj.
**burnt offering**
  *propitiation* 941 n.
  *oblation* 981 n.
**burnt out**
  *weakened* 163 adj.
**burn-up**
  *speeding* 277 n.
**burp**
  *belch* 300 vb.
  *breathe* 352 vb.
**burr**
  *roughness* 259 n.
  *perforator* 263 n.
  *rasp* 407 vb.
  *engraving* 555 n.
  *dialect* 560 n.
  *neologize* 560 vb.
  *pronunciation* 577 n.
  *voice* 577 vb.
  *speech defect* 580 n.
**burro**
  *beast of burden* 273 n.
**burrow**
  *place oneself* 187 vb.
  *dwelling* 192 n.
  *dwell* 192 vb.
  *cavity* 255 n.
  *excavation* 255 n.
  *make concave* 255 vb.
  *pierce* 263 vb.
  *descend* 309 vb.
  *lurk* 523 vb.
  *refuge* 662 n.
**bursar**
  *consignee* 754 n.
  *treasurer* 798 n.
**bursary**
  *economic aid* 703 n.
  *receipt* 807 n.
  *reward* 962 n.
**burst**
  *break* 46 vb.
  *rend* 46 vb.
  *be dispersed* 75 vb.
  *instant* 116 n.
  *outbreak* 176 n.
  *be violent* 176 vb.
  *open* 263 vb.
  *spurt* 277 n.
  *be brittle* 330 vb.
  *be loud* 400 vb.
  *bang* 402 vb.
  *activity* 678 n.
  *miscarry* 728 vb.
– forth
  *begin* 68 vb.
  *expand* 197 vb.
– in
  *burst in* 297 vb.
– into flame
  *be hot* 379 vb.
– into tears
  *weep* 836 vb.
– in upon
  *intrude* 297 vb.
– out

*be violent* 176 vb.
*be excitable* 822 vb.
*get angry* 891 vb.
– upon
  *meet* 295 vb.
  *surprise* 508 vb.
– with
  *superabound* 637 vb.
**bursting at the seams**
  *full* 54 adj.
  *redundant* 637 adj.
**bury**
  *implant* 303 vb.
  *insert* 303 vb.
  *inter* 364 vb.
  *conceal* 525 vb.
  *obliterate* 550 vb.
  *store* 632 vb.
  *imprison* 747 vb.
– one's head in the sand
  *avoid* 620 vb.
– the hatchet
  *forget* 506 vb.
  *make peace* 719 vb.
  *forgive* 909 vb.
**bus**
  *conveyance* 267 n.
  *car* 274 n.
  *bus* 274 n.
**busby**
  *headgear* 228 n.
  *armour* 713 n.
**bus driver**
  *driver* 268 n.
  *carrier* 273 n.
**bush**
  *desert* 172 n.
  *district* 184 n.
  *lining* 227 n.
  *plain* 348 n.
  *tree* 366 n.
  *wood* 366 n.
**bushel**
  *great quantity* 32 n.
  *certain quantity* 104 n.
  *metrology* 465 n.
**bush-fighting**
  *warfare* 718 n.
**bush fire**
  *fire* 379 n.
**bush hat**
  *headgear* 228 n.
**bushido**
  *code of duty* 917 n.
  *probity* 929 n.
**bushmeat**
  *meat* 301 n.
**bushmen**
  *humankind* 371 n.
**bush telegraph**
  *rumour* 529 n.
  *telecommunication*
    531 n.
**bushy**
  *dense* 324 adj.
  *arboreal* 366 adj.
**business**

*instrumentalist* 413 n.
**cello**
*viol* 414 n.
**Cellophane (tdmk)**
*wrapping* 226 n.
*transparency* 422 n.
*paper* 631 n.
**cellphone**
*telecommunication*
531 n.
**cellular**
*cellular* 194 adj.
*concave* 255 adj.
*organic* 358 adj.
**cellular radio**
*broadcasting* 531 n.
**cellular telephone**
*sound* 398 n.
*hearing instrument*
415 n.
*telecommunication*
531 n.
**celluloid**
*film* 445 n.
*materials* 631 n.
**Celt**
*native* 191 n.
**Celtic deities**
*Celtic deities* 967 n.
**Celtic fringe**
*foreigner* 59 n.
**cement**
*join* 45 vb.
*adhesive* 47 n.
*bond* 47 n.
*agglutinate* 48 vb.
*overlay* 226 vb.
*solid body* 324 n.
*hardness* 326 n.
*building material* 631 n.
**cemetery**
*death* 361 n.
*cemetery* 364 n.
*holy place* 990 n.
**cenobite**
*monk* 986 n.
**cenotaph**
*obsequies* 364 n.
*tomb* 364 n.
**censer**
*scent* 396 n.
*ritual object* 988 n.
**censor**
*exclude* 57 vb.
*alterer* 143 n.
*enquirer* 459 n.
*estimator* 480 n.
*obliterate* 550 vb.
*restrain* 747 vb.
*prohibit* 757 vb.
*disapprover* 924 n.
*disapprove* 924 vb.
*detractor* 926 n.
*prude* 950 n.
**censored**
*prohibited* 757 adj.
*disapproved* 924 adj.

*pure* 950 adj.
**censorious**
*judicial* 480 adj.
*severe* 735 adj.
*discontented* 829 adj.
*fastidious* 862 adj.
*disapproving* 924 adj.
**censorship**
*obliteration* 550 n.
*severity* 735 n.
**censurable**
*discreditable* 867 adj.
*blameworthy* 924 adj.
*guilty* 936 adj.
**censure**
*estimate* 480 n., vb.
*slur* 867 n.
*censure* 924 n.
*reprimand* 924 n.
*reprove* 924 vb.
*accusation* 928 n.
*guilt* 936 n.
**census**
*numeration* 86 n.
*statistics* 86 n.
*list* 87 n.
*enquiry* 459 n.
**census-taker**
*enumerator* 86 n.
**cent**
*small coin* 33 n.
*trifle* 639 n.
*coinage* 797 n.
**centaur**
*mythical beast* 365 n.
*mythical being* 970 n.
**centenarian**
*hundred* 99 n.
*old person* 133 n.
**centenary**
*hundred* 99 n.
*anniversary* 141 n.
*special day* 876 n.
**centennial**
*fifth and over* 99 adj.
*periodic* 110 adj.
*seasonal* 141 adj.
*celebratory* 876 adj.
**centime**
*small coin* 33 n.
*coinage* 797 n.
**centimetre**
*long measure* 203 n.
*shortness* 204 n.
**centipede**
*creepy-crawly* 365 n.
**cento**
*a mixture* 43 n.
*anthology* 592 n.
*doggerel* 593 n.
**central**
*intrinsic* 5 adj.
*middle* 70 adj.
*fundamental* 156 adj.
*interior* 224 adj.
*central* 225 adj.
*inland* 344 adj.

*neutral* 625 adj.
*undeviating* 625 adj.
*important* 638 adj.
**central heating**
*heating* 381 n.
**centralization, cen-
tralisation**
*uniformity* 16 n.
*combination* 50 n.
*arrangement* 62 n.
*accumulation* 74 n.
*centrality* 225 n.
*plan* 623 n.
*association* 706 n.
**centralized**
*governmental* 733 adj.
**centre**
*essence* 1 n.
*essential part* 5 n.
*middle point* 30 n.
*middle* 70 n.
*bring together* 74 vb.
*focus* 76 n.
*interiority* 224 n.
*centre* 225 n.
*centralize* 225 vb.
*converge* 293 vb.
*political party* 708 n.
*armed force* 722 n.
*arena* 724 n.
– on
*focus* 76 vb.
*converge* 293 vb.
**centreboard**
*stabilizer* 153 n.
*pivot* 218 n.
**centre forward**
*front* 237 n.
*leader* 690 n.
**centre of attraction**
*focus* 76 n.
*attraction* 291 n.
*favourite* 890 n.
**centrepiece**
*ornamentation* 844 n.
**centrifugal**
*unassembled* 75 adj.
*exterior* 223 adj.
*repellent* 292 adj.
*divergent* 294 adj.
*avoiding* 620 adj.
**centripetal**
*central* 225 adj.
*attracting* 291 adj.
*convergent* 293 adj.
**centrist**
*political party* 708 n.
**centurion**
*hundred* 99 n.
*army officer* 741 n.
**century**
*hundred* 99 n.
*period* 110 n.
**cephalic**
*topmost* 213 adj.
**cepheid**
*star* 321 n.

**ceramics**
*pottery* 381 n.
*sculpture* 554 n.
**Cerberus**
*three* 93 n.
*doorkeeper* 264 n.
*protector* 660 n.
*mythic hell* 972 n.
**cereal farming**
*agriculture* 370 n.
**cereals**
*cereals* 301 n.
*grass* 366 n.
**cerebral**
*mental* 447 adj.
**cerebral haem-
orrhage**
*nervous disorders* 651 n.
**cerebral thrombosis**
*cardiovascular disease*
651 n.
**cerebrate**
*think* 449 vb.
**cerecloth**
*grave clothes* 364 n.
**ceremonial**
*formality* 875 n.
*formal* 875 adj.
*ritual* 988 n., adj.
*ritualistic* 988 adj.
**ceremonial occasion**
*formality* 875 n.
**ceremonious**
*formal* 875 adj.
*respectful* 920 adj.
*ritualistic* 988 adj.
**ceremony**
*formality* 875 n.
*celebration* 876 n.
*rite* 988 n.
**Ceres**
*fertilizer* 171 n.
*Olympian deity* 967 n.
**cerise**
*red* 431 adj.
**cerography**
*engraving* 555 n.
*writing* 586 n.
**ceroplastic**
*glyptic* 554 adj.
**cert**
*certainty* 473 n.
**certain**
*quantitative* 26 adj.
*definite* 80 adj.
*unchangeable* 153 adj.
*impending* 155 adj.
*certain* 473 adj.
*demonstrated* 478 adj.
*known* 490 adj.
*true* 494 adj.
*expectant* 507 adj.
*manifest* 522 adj.
*necessary* 596 adj.
*hoping* 852 adj.
**certain, a**
*one* 88 adj.

detraction 926 n.
**characteristic**
characteristic 5 adj.
intrinsic 5 adj.
distinctive 15 adj.
speciality 80 n.
special 80 adj.
tendency 179 n.
identification 547 n.
indicating 547 adj.
**characterization,**
**characterisation**
representation 551 n.
description 590 n.
dramaturgy 594 n.
**characterized**
marked 547 adj.
with affections 817 adj.
**characterless**
insubstantial 4 adj.
uniform 16 adj.
irresolute 601 adj.
**character sketch**
description 590 n.
**character witness**
vindicator 927 n.
**charade(s)**
sham 542 n.
representation 551 n.
indoor game 837 n.
**charcoal**
ash 381 n.
fuel 385 n.
black thing 428 n.
art equipment 553 n.
**charge**
fill 54 vb.
empower 160 vb.
be violent 176 vb.
load 193 vb.
move fast 277 vb.
collide 279 vb.
make heavy 322 vb.
call 547 n.
heraldry 547 n.
mark 547 vb.
job 622 n.
protection 650 n.
management 689 n.
advise 691 vb.
precept 693 n.
attack 712 n.
charge 712 vb.
give battle 718 vb.
explosive 723 n.
command 737 n., vb.
demand 737 vb.
dependant 742 n.
detention 747 n.
mandate 751 n.
commission 751 vb.
account 808 vb.
price 809 n., vb.
duty 917 n.
blame 924 vb.
accusation 928 n.
litigate 959 vb.

– at
pursue 619 vb.
be rash 857 vb.
– in
burst in 297 vb.
– to one's account
credit 802 vb.
– with
attribute 158 vb.
accuse 928 vb.
**charge card**
credit 802 n.
**chargé d'affaires**
envoy 754 n.
**charge nurse**
nurse 658 n.
**charger**
plate 194 n.
warhorse 273 n.
cavalry 722 n.
accuser 928 n.
**chariot**
carriage 274 n.
**charioteer**
driver 268 n.
**charisma**
power 160 n.
influence 178 n.
piety 979 n.
**charismatic**
influential 178 adj.
**charismatic leader**
leader 690 n.
**charismatic**
**movement**
piety 979 n.
**charitable**
giving 781 adj.
liberal 813 adj.
benevolent 897 adj.
philanthropic 901 adj.
pitying 905 adj.
**charity**
aid 703 n.
economic aid 703 n.
gift 781 n.
giving 781 n.
liberality 813 n.
courteous act 884 n.
love 887 n.
benevolence 897 n.
kind act 897 n.
philanthropy 901 n.
pity 905 n.
disinterestedness 931 n.
virtues 933 n.
piety 979 n.
**charity that begins at**
**home**
selfishness 932 n.
**charlady**
cleaner 648 n.
**charlatan**
dabbler 493 n.
impostor 545 n.
doctor 658 n.
unskilled 695 adj.

affecter 850 n.
boaster 877 n.
**Charleston**
dance 837 n.
**charlie**
ninny 501 n.
**charlotte**
dessert 301 n.
**charm**
attraction 291 n.
attract 291 vb.
inducement 612 n.
motivate 612 vb.
preserver 666 n.
delight 826 vb.
please 826 vb.
beauty 841 n.
jewellery 844 n.
lovableness 887 n.
excite love 887 vb.
spell 983 n.
talisman 983 n.
bewitch 983 vb.
**charmed circle**
elite 644 n.
party 708 n.
**charmed life**
safety 660 n.
**charmer**
a beauty 841 n.
flatterer 925 n.
sorcerer 983 n.
**charming**
attracting 291 adj.
pleasurable 826 adj.
personable 841 adj.
lovable 887 adj.
**charm offensive**
inducement 612 n.
attack 712 n.
**charms**
beauty 841 n.
lovableness 887 n.
**charnel house**
death 361 n.
interment 364 n.
**Charon**
boatman 270 n.
mythic hell 972 n.
**chart**
list 87 n.
sailing aid 269 n.
guidebook 524 n.
map 551 n.
represent 551 vb.
**charter**
record 548 n.
give scope 744 vb.
liberate 746 vb.
mandate 751 n.
commission 751 vb.
permit 756 n., vb.
title deed 767 n.
hire 785 vb.
dueness 915 n.
nonliability 919 n.
law 953 n.

**chartered accountant**
accountant 808 n.
**charter flight**
air travel 271 n.
**chartreuse**
yellow 433 adj.
green 434 adj.
**charts**
vocal music 412 n.
**charwoman**
cleaner 648 n.
**chary**
parsimonious 816 adj.
cautious 858 adj.
**chase**
groove 262 vb.
move fast 277 vb.
follow 284 vb.
killing 362 n.
cry 408 n.
sculpt 554 vb.
press 587 n.
chase 619 n.
pursue 619 vb.
pleasure ground 837 n.
sport 837 n.
desire 859 vb.
court 889 vb.
– away
repel 292 vb.
– one's own tail
rotate 315 vb.
be busy 678 vb.
**chaser**
draught 301 n.
**chasm**
disunion 46 n.
gap 201 n.
depth 211 n.
cavity 255 n.
pitfall 663 n.
**chassis**
base 214 n.
frame 218 n.
prop 218 n.
structure 331 n.
**chaste**
plain 573 adj.
elegant 575 adj.
tasteful 846 adj.
modest 874 adj.
virtuous 933 adj.
temperate 942 adj.
pure 950 adj.
**chasten**
moderate 177 vb.
educate 534 vb.
be serious 834 vb.
depress 834 vb.
humiliate 872 vb.
punish 963 vb.
**chastened**
repentant 939 adj.
**chastise**
be severe 735 vb.
reprove 924 vb.
punish 963 vb.

**chastisement**
  *punishment* 963 n.
**chastity**
  *contraception* 172 n.
  *modesty* 874 n.
  *virtue* 933 n.
  *temperance* 942 n.
  *purity* 950 n.
**chasuble**
  *vestments* 989 n.
**chat**
  *rumour* 529 n.
  *chat* 584 n.
  *converse* 584 vb.
**château**
  *house* 192 n.
**chatelaine**
  *keeper* 749 n.
**chatoyant**
  *iridescent* 437 adj.
**chatroom**
  *Internet* 531 n.
**chat show**
  *broadcast* 531 n.
**chattel**
  *slave* 742 n.
  *property* 777 n.
**chatter**
  *be cold* 380 vb.
  *roll* 403 n.
  *ululate* 409 vb.
  *empty talk* 515 n.
  *speak* 579 vb.
  *chatter* 581 n.
  *be loquacious* 581 vb.
  *chat* 584 n.
**chatterbox**
  *chatterer* 581 n.
**chattering**
  *spasm* 318 n.
  *chilly* 380 adj.
**chatty**
  *informative* 524 adj.
  *loquacious* 581 adj.
  *conversing* 584 adj.
  *sociable* 882 adj.
**chauffeur**
  *driver* 268 n.
  *domestic* 742 n.
**chauvinism**
  *nation* 371 n.
  *prejudice* 481 n.
  *bellicosity* 718 n.
  *boasting* 877 n.
  *patriotism* 901 n.
**chauvinist**
  *narrow mind* 481 n.
  *militarist* 722 n.
  *patriot* 901 n.
**cheap**
  *inferior* 35 adj.
  *spurious* 542 adj.
  *cheap* 812 adj.
  *vulgar* 847 adj.
  *disreputable* 867 adj.
**cheapen**
  *underestimate* 483 vb.

*impair* 655 vb.
  *demonetize* 797 vb.
  *discount* 810 vb.
  *cheapen* 812 vb.
  *vulgarize* 847 vb.
  *not respect* 921 vb.
– oneself
  *demean oneself* 867 vb.
**cheap-jack**
  *bad* 645 adj.
  *cheap* 812 adj.
**cheapness**
  *inferiority* 35 n.
  *cheapness* 812 n.
**cheat**
  *duplicity* 541 n.
  *deception* 542 n.
  *trickery* 542 n.
  *deceive* 542 vb.
  *trickster* 545 n.
  *slyboots* 698 n.
  *stratagem* 698 n.
  *be cunning* 698 vb.
  *fleece* 786 vb.
  *defraud* 788 vb.
  *defrauder* 789 n.
  *be dishonest* 930 vb.
  *knave* 938 n.
**check**
  *number* 86 vb.
  *delay* 136 n.
  *stop* 145 n.
  *halt* 145 vb.
  *moderation* 177 n.
  *moderate* 177 vb.
  *counteraction* 182 n.
  *retard* 278 vb.
  *chequer* 437 n.
  *pied* 437 adj.
  *variegate* 437 vb.
  *be careful* 457 vb.
  *enquiry* 459 n.
  *enquire* 459 vb.
  *experiment* 461 n., vb.
  *comparison* 462 n.
  *measurement* 465 n.
  *make certain* 473 vb.
  *label* 547 n.
  *hindrance* 702 n.
  *be obstructive* 702 vb.
  *hinder* 702 vb.
  *defeat* 727 vb.
  *defeat* 728 n.
  *adversity* 731 n.
  *restraint* 747 n.
  *restrain* 747 vb.
  *paper money* 797 n.
  *pattern* 844 n.
– on
  *enquire* 459 vb.
  *experiment* 461 vb.
– oneself
  *be mute* 578 vb.
**check-in desk**
  *air travel* 271 n.
**checklist**
  *list* 87 n.

*comparison* 462 n.
**checkmate**
  *halt* 145 vb.
  *overmaster* 727 vb.
  *defeat* 728 n.
**checkout**
  *recording instrument*
    549 n.
**checkup**
  *attention* 455 n.
  *enquiry* 459 n.
**Cheddar**
  *dairy product* 301 n. box
**cheek**
  *laterality* 239 n.
  *sauciness* 878 n.
  *be insolent* 878 vb.
  *rudeness* 885 n.
  *scurrility* 899 n.
**cheek by jowl**
  *with* 89 adv.
  *near* 200 adv.
  *contiguously* 202 adv.
  *sideways* 239 adv.
**cheeky**
  *impertinent* 878 adj.
  *discourteous* 885 adj.
  *disrespectful* 921 adj.
**cheep**
  *ululation* 409 n.
  *ululate* 409 vb.
**cheer**
  *invigorate* 174 vb.
  *food* 301 n.
  *cry* 408 n., vb.
  *vociferate* 408 vb.
  *gesture* 547 n.
  *please* 826 vb.
  *relieve* 831 vb.
  *merriment* 833 n.
  *be cheerful* 833 vb.
  *cheer* 833 vb.
  *rejoice* 835 vb.
  *give hope* 852 vb.
  *give courage* 855 vb.
  *celebrate* 876 vb.
  *sociability* 882 n.
  *show respect* 920 vb.
  *applaud* 923 vb.
– on
  *incite* 612 vb.
– up
  *relieve* 831 vb.
  *be cheerful* 833 vb.
**cheerful**
  *content* 828 adj.
  *cheerful* 833 adj.
**cheerfulness**
  *vitality* 162 n.
  *expectation* 507 n.
  *cheerfulness* 833 n.
  *hope* 852 n.
**cheerio!**
– 296 int.
**cheerleader**
  *living model* 23 n.
  *cry* 408 n.

**cheerless**
  *unpleasant* 827 adj.
  *cheerless* 834 adj.
  *dejected* 834 adj.
  *melancholic* 834 adj.
  *unpromising* 853 adj.
**cheers!**
– 301 int.
– 835 int.
**cheery**
  *cheerful* 833 adj.
**cheese**
  *dairy product* 301 n.
**cheese board**
  *dessert* 301 n.
**cheesecake**
  *pastries* 301 n.
  *a beauty* 841 n.
**cheesecloth**
  *textile* 222 n.
**cheesed off**
  *discontented* 829 adj.
  *dejected* 834 adj.
  *bored* 838 adj.
**cheese-paring**
  *economy* 814 n.
  *economical* 814 adj.
  *parsimony* 816 n.
  *parsimonious* 816 adj.
**cheeses**
  *dairy product* 301 n. box
**cheetah**
  *speeder* 277 n.
  *cat* 365 n.
**chef**
  *cookery* 301 n.
  *caterer* 633 n.
**chef d'oeuvre**
  *product* 164 n.
  *exceller* 644 n.
  *perfection* 646 n.
  *deed* 676 n.
  *masterpiece* 694 n.
**chemical**
  *compound* 50 n.
  *element* 319 n.
  *physical* 319 adj.
**chemical elements**
  *element* 319 n. box
**chemical peel**
  *beautification* 843 n.
**chemical warfare**
  *poisoning* 659 n.
  *warfare* 718 n.
  *weapon* 723 n.
**chemise**
  *dress* 228 n.
  *underwear* 228 n.
**chemist**
  *alterer* 143 n.
  *physics* 319 n.
  *experimenter* 461 n.
  *druggist* 658 n.
**chemistry**
  *physics* 319 n.
  *study* 536 n. box
**chemoprevention**

*prophylactic* 658 n.

**chemotherapy**
*therapy* 658 n.

**chenille**
*textile* 222 n.

**cheque**
*paper money* 797 n.
See also **cheques**

**chequebook**
*record* 548 n.
*account book* 808 n.

**chequebook jour-
nalist**
*inquisitive person* 453 n.
*informant* 524 n.
*publicizer* 528 n.

**chequer**
*chequer* 437 n.
*variegate* 437 vb.
*pattern* 844 n.

**chequered**
*changeable* 143 adj.
*pied* 437 adj.

**cheques, collector of**
*collector* 492 n. box

**cherish**
*look after* 457 vb.
*safeguard* 660 vb.
*preserve* 666 vb.
*patronize* 703 vb.
*love* 887 vb.
*pet* 889 vb.
*approve* 923 vb.
– the memory
*remember* 505 vb.

**cheroot**
*tobacco* 388 n.

**cherry**
*fruit* 301 n.
*redness* 431 n.

**cherry-pick**
*select* 605 vb.

**cherub**
*child* 132 n.
*image* 551 n.
*darling* 890 n.
*angel* 968 n.

**cherubic**
*angelic* 968 adj.

**cherubim**
*angel* 968 n.

**chervil**
*herb* 301 n.

**Cheshire Cat**
*cat* 365 n.
*laughter* 835 n.

**chess**
*board game* 837 n.

**chessboard**
*chequer* 437 n.
*arena* 724 n.

**chess piece**
*plaything* 837 n.

**chess-player**
*player* 837 n.

**chest**
*box* 194 n.

*insides* 224 n.
*bosom* 253 n.
*treasury* 799 n.

**chest, surgery of**
*surgery* 658 n. box

**chesterfield**
*seat* 218 n.

**chestnut**
*repetition* 106 n.
*horse* 273 n.
*fruit* 301 n.
*brown* 430 adj.
*witticism* 839 n.

**chest of drawers**
*cabinet* 194 n.

**chesty**
*puffing* 352 adj.

**cheval glass**
*mirror* 442 n.

**chevalier d'industrie**
*defrauder* 789 n.

**chevaux-de-frise**
*sharp point* 256 n.
*defences* 713 n.

**chevet**
*church interior* 990 n.

**chevron**
*obliquity* 220 n.
*angularity* 247 n.
*heraldry* 547 n.
*livery* 547 n.
*badge of rank* 743 n.
*pattern* 844 n.

**chew**
*rend* 46 vb.
*chew* 301 vb.
*pulverize* 332 vb.
– a quid
*smoke* 388 vb.
– over
*meditate* 449 vb.
– the fat
*converse* 584 vb.

**chewing gum**
*sweets* 301 n.
*elasticity* 328 n.

**ch'i**
*energy* 160 n.
*strength* 162 n.
*life* 360 n.

**Chianti**
*wine* 301 n.

**chiaroscuro**
*light contrast* 417 n.
*painting* 553 n.

**chiasmus**
*inversion* 221 n.
*ornament* 574 n.

**chic**
*beauty* 841 n.
*shapely* 841 adj.
*fashion* 848 n.
*fashionable* 848 adj.

**chicanery**
*sophistry* 477 n.
*trickery* 542 n.
*cunning* 698 n.

*foul play* 930 n.

**chichi**
*ornamented* 844 adj.
*fashionable* 848 adj.
*affected* 850 adj.

**chick**
*young creature* 132 n.
*youngster* 132 n.
*woman* 373 n.
*darling* 890 n.

**chicken**
*young creature* 132 n.
*meat* 301 n.
*poultry* 365 n.
*coward* 856 n.
*cowardly* 856 adj.

**chickenfeed**
*small quantity* 33 n.
*provender* 301 n.
*trifle* 639 n.
*easy thing* 701 n.
*money* 797 n.

**chicken out**
*be cowardly* 856 vb.

**chickenpox**
*infection* 651 n.

**chicken run**
*stock farm* 369 n.

**chicken wire**
*network* 222 n.

**chick peas**
*vegetable* 301 n.

**chicory**
*vegetable* 301 n.

**chide**
*curse* 899 vb.
*reprove* 924 vb.

**chief**
*superior* 34 n.
*supreme* 34 adj.
*first* 68 adj.
*central* 225 adj.
*heraldry* 547 n.
*notable* 638 n.
*important* 638 adj.
*director* 690 n.
*potentate* 741 n.

**chieftain**
*potentate* 741 n.

**chieftainship**
*position of authority*
733 n.

**chiffon**
*textile* 222 n.
*transparency* 422 n.
*finery* 844 n.

**chiffonier**
*cabinet* 194 n.

**chignon**
*hair* 259 n.
*hairdressing* 843 n.

**chilblain(s)**
*coldness* 380 n.
*ulcer* 651 n.

**child**
*child* 132 n.
*descendant* 170 n.

*posterity* 170 n.
*dwarf* 196 n.
*ninny* 501 n.
*innocent* 935 n.

**child abuse**
*painfulness* 827 n.
*cruel act* 898 n.

**childbirth**
*obstetrics* 167 n.

**childhood**
*youth* 130 n.

**childish**
*young* 130 adj.
*infantine* 132 adj.
*foolish* 499 adj.
*feeble* 572 adj.
*trivial* 639 adj.

**childless**
*unproductive* 172 adj.

**childlike**
*infantine* 132 adj.
*artless* 699 adj.
*innocent* 935 adj.

**childminder**
*carer* 457 n.

**child of fortune**
*prosperous person* 730 n.

**child of nature**
*ingenue* 699 n.

**children's home**
*shelter* 662 n.

**child's play**
*trifle* 639 n.
*easy thing* 701 n.

**Child Support Agency**
*economic aid* 703 n.

**chiliad**
*over one hundred* 99 n.

**chiliasm**
*aspiration* 852 n.

**chill**
*moderate* 177 vb.
*coldness* 380 n.
*cold* 380 adj.
*be cold* 380 vb.
*refrigerate* 382 vb.
*dissuade* 613 vb.
*adversity* 731 n.
*frighten* 854 vb.

**chiller**
*refrigerator* 384 n.

**chill factor**
*coldness* 380 n.

**chilli**
*vegetable* 301 n.
*spice* 301 n.
*condiment* 389 n.

**chilly**
*chilly* 380 adj.
*cold* 380 adj.
*inimical* 881 adj.

**chime**
*sound faint* 401 vb.
*resound* 404 vb.
*melody* 410 n.
*harmonize* 410 vb.
*campanology* 412 n.

**finger** 378 n.
  wound 655 vb.
  weapon 723 n.
  nippers 778 n.
**clawback**
  decrement 42 n.
**clay**
  adhesive 47 n.
  changeable thing 152 n.
  solid body 324 n.
  softness 327 n.
  soil 344 n.
  corpse 363 n.
  sculpture 554 n.
  materials 631 n.
**claymore**
  sidearms 723 n.
**clay-pigeon shooting**
  sport 837 n.
**clay pipe**
  tobacco 388 n.
**clean**
  unmixed 44 adj.
  completely 54 adv.
  new 126 adj.
  empty 190 adj.
  empty 300 vb.
  make bright 417 vb.
  whiten 427 vb.
  careful 457 adj.
  plain 573 adj.
  cleansing 648 n.
  clean 648 adj., vb.
  salubrious 652 adj.
  sanitate 652 vb.
  make better 654 vb.
  honourable 929 adj.
  pure 950 adj.
– out
  empty 300 vb.
  search 459 vb.
  clean 648 vb.
  purify 648 vb.
  steal 788 vb.
– up
  unravel 62 vb.
  empty 300 vb.
  clean 648 vb.
  purify 648 vb.
  get rich 800 vb.
**clean breast**
  assent 488 n.
  disclosure 526 n.
  veracity 540 n.
**clean-cut**
  definite 80 adj.
  positive 473 adj.
**cleaned**
  clean 648 adj.
**cleaner**
  cleaner 648 n.
**clean hands**
  probity 929 n.
  innocence 935 n.
**clean-limbed**
  shapely 841 adj.
**cleanliness**

cleanness 648 n.
  hygiene 652 n.
**clean pair of heels**
  speeding 277 n.
**cleanse**
  eliminate 44 vb.
  purify 648 vb.
  sanitate 652 vb.
**cleanser**
  cleanser 648 n.
**clean-shaven**
  hairless 229 adj.
  smooth 258 adj.
**cleansing**
  beautification 843 n.
  ritual act 988 n.
**cleansing cream**
  cleanser 648 n.
  cosmetic 843 n.
**clean slate**
  newness 126 n.
  obliteration 550 n.
  facility 701 n.
**clean sweep**
  revolution 149 n.
  ejection 300 n.
**clear**
  unmixed 44 adj.
  eliminate 44 vb.
  orderly 60 adj.
  space 201 vb.
  be high 209 vb.
  fly 271 vb.
  empty 300 vb.
  leap 312 vb.
  fluid 335 adj.
  make flow 350 vb.
  striking 374 adj.
  melodious 410 adj.
  undimmed 417 adj.
  make bright 417 vb.
  transparent 422 adj.
  obvious 443 adj.
  certain 473 adj.
  semantic 514 adj.
  intelligible 516 adj.
  manifest 522 adj.
  perspicuous 567 adj.
  elegant 575 adj.
  vocal 577 adj.
  clean 648 vb.
  safe 660 adj.
  disencumber 701 vb.
  liberate 746 vb.
  permit 756 vb.
  acquire 771 vb.
  pay 804 vb.
  justify 927 vb.
  acquitted 960 adj.
  acquit 960 vb.
– away
  displace 188 vb.
  empty 300 vb.
  disencumber 701 vb.
– off (with)
  decamp 296 vb.
  take away 786 vb.

– out
  decamp 296 vb.
  emerge 298 vb.
  empty 300 vb.
  clean 648 vb.
– stock
  sell 793 vb.
– the decks
  make ready 669 vb.
  disencumber 701 vb.
– the throat
  eruct 300 vb.
  rasp 407 vb.
– the way/path
  come before 64 vb.
  precede 283 vb.
  make possible 469 vb.
  facilitate 701 vb.
– up
  cease 145 vb.
  make bright 417 vb.
  be intelligible 516 vb.
  carry through 725 vb.
**clearance**
  elimination 44 n.
  room 183 n.
  interval 201 n.
  voidance 300 n.
  preparation 669 n.
  scope 744 n.
  permission 756 n.
  permit 756 n.
  sale 793 n.
**clear as ditch water**
  puzzling 517 adj.
**clear blue water**
  difference 15 n.
  divergence 294 n.
**clear coast**
  facility 701 n.
**clear conscience**
  probity 929 n.
  virtue 933 n.
  innocence 935 n.
**clear-cut**
  definite 80 adj.
  obvious 443 adj.
  positive 473 adj.
  intelligible 516 adj.
  perspicuous 567 adj.
**clear field**
  opportunity 137 n.
**clear-headed**
  rational 475 adj.
  intelligent 498 adj.
  sane 502 adj.
  sober 948 adj.
**clearing**
  open space 263 n.
  wood 366 n.
**clearness**
  transparency 422 n.
  visibility 443 n.
  intelligibility 516 n.
  perspicuity 567 n.
**clear of**
  beyond 199 adv.

**clear-sighted**
  seeing 438 adj.
  intelligent 498 adj.
**clear thinking**
  sagacity 498 n.
**clearway**
  traffic control 305 n.
  road 624 n.
**cleat**
  fastening 47 n.
**cleavage**
  disunion 46 n.
  scission 46 n.
  structure 331 n.
  dissension 709 n.
**cleave**
  sunder 46 vb.
  bisect 92 vb.
– to
  cohere 48 vb.
**cleaver**
  sharp edge 256 n.
**clef**
  key 410 n.
  notation 410 n.
**cleft**
  disunion 46 n.
  disunited 46 adj.
  bisected 92 adj.
  gap 201 n.
**cleft palate**
  speech defect 580 n.
  blemish 845 n.
**cleft stick**
  dubiety 474 n.
  predicament 700 n.
**clemency**
  leniency 736 n.
  mercy 905 n.
**clementine**
  fruit 301 n.
**clench**
  make smaller 198 vb.
  close 264 vb.
  retain 778 vb.
– one's fist
  defy 711 vb.
  threaten 900 vb.
– one's teeth
  gesticulate 547 vb.
  be resolute 599 vb.
**clenched fist**
  gesture 547 n.
  nippers 778 n.
**clerestory**
  church interior 990 n.
**clergy**
  clergy 986 n.
**clergyman, clergy-
   woman, clergy-
   person**
  cleric 986 n.
**clerical**
  recording 548 adj.
  ecclesiastical 985 adj.
  clerical 986 adj.
**clerical collar**

*moral insensibility*
820 n.
*bad taste* 847 n.
*impurity* 951 n.
**coarsening**
*deterioration* 655 n.
**coast**
*edge* 234 n.
*laterality* 239 n.
*flank* 239 vb.
*go smoothly* 258 vb.
*be in motion* 265 vb.
*travel* 267 vb.
*ride* 267 vb.
*voyage* 269 vb.
*pass* 305 vb.
*shore* 344 n.
*be neglectful* 458 vb.
*not act* 677 vb.
*do easily* 701 vb.
– *down*
*descend* 309 vb.
**coastal**
*marginal* 234 adj.
*coastal* 344 adj.
**coast clear**
*safety* 660 n.
**coaster**
*stand* 218 n.
*sledge* 274 n.
*merchant ship* 275 n.
**coastguard**
*nautical personnel* 270 n.
*protector* 660 n.
*keeper* 749 n.
**coastline**
*outline* 233 n.
*edge* 234 n.
*shore* 344 n.
**coat**
*layer* 207 n.
*laminate* 207 vb.
*skin* 226 n.
*wrapping* 226 n.
*coat* 226 vb.
*line* 227 vb.
*jacket* 228 n.
*overcoat* 228 n.
*colour* 425 vb.
*paint* 553 vb.
*decorate* 844 vb.
– *the pill*
*sweeten* 392 vb.
**coating**
*layer* 207 n.
*covering* 226 n.
*facing* 226 n.
*lining* 227 n.
**coat of arms**
*heraldry* 547 n.
*nobility* 868 n.
**coat of mail**
*armour* 713 n.
**coat of paint**
*facing* 226 n.
**coat tails**
*hanging object* 217 n.

*garment* 228 n.
**coax**
*tempt* 612 vb.
*request* 761 vb.
*pet* 889 vb.
*flatter* 925 vb.
**cob**
*architectural* 192 adj.
*pony* 273 n.
*fruit* 301 n.
*bird* 365 n.
*building material* 631 n.
**cobalt**
*blue pigment* 435 n.
**cobber**
*chum* 880 n.
**cobble(s)**
*paving* 226 n.
*road* 624 n.
*building material* 631 n.
*repair* 656 vb.
**cobbled together**
*produced* 164 adj.
*bungled* 695 adj.
**cobbler**
*clothier* 228 n.
*mender* 656 n.
**coble**
*fishing boat* 275 n.
**Cobol**
*computing* 86 n.
**cobra**
*reptile* 365 n.
**cobweb**
*weak thing* 163 n.
*filament* 208 n.
*network* 222 n.
*lightness* 323 n.
*trifle* 639 n.
*dirt* 649 n.
**cobwebs of antiquity**
*oldness* 127 n.
**cocaine**
*anaesthetic* 375 n.
*drug* 658 n.
*drug* 949 n.
**coccyx**
*buttocks* 238 n.
**cochineal**
*red pigment* 431 n.
**cochlea**
*ear* 415 n.
**cock**
*genitalia* 167 n.
*poultry* 365 n.
*male animal* 372 n.
*make ready* 669 vb.
– *a snook*
*gesticulate* 547 vb.
*defy* 711 vb.
*disobey* 738 vb.
*not observe* 769 vb.
*be insolent* 878 vb.
*not respect* 921 vb.
– *up*
*make vertical* 215 vb.
*jut* 254 vb.

*impair* 655 vb.
**cockade**
*livery* 547 n.
*trimming* 844 n.
**cock-a-hoop**
*jubilant* 833 adj.
*boastful* 877 adj.
**Cockaigne**
*city* 184 n.
*happiness* 824 n.
**cock and bull story**
*insubstantial thing* 4 n.
*fable* 543 n.
**cockatrice**
*mythical beast* 365 n.
*eye* 438 n.
*heraldry* 547 n.
*noxious animal* 904 n.
**cockcrow**
*morning* 128 n.
**cocked hat**
*headgear* 228 n.
*badge of rank* 743 n.
**cock-eyed**
*oblique* 220 adj.
*distorted* 246 adj.
*dim-sighted* 440 adj.
*erroneous* 495 adj.
*absurd* 497 adj.
*ridiculous* 849 adj.
**cockiness**
*vanity* 873 n.
*insolence* 878 n.
**cockle**
*fish food* 301 n.
*marine life* 365 n.
**cockleshell**
*ship* 275 n.
**cockles of the heart**
*affections* 817 n.
**cockney**
*native* 191 n.
*dialect* 560 n.
*plebeian* 869 adj.
**cock of the walk**
*exceller* 644 n.
*master* 741 n.
*proud person* 871 n.
**cockpit**
*room* 194 n.
*aircraft* 276 n.
*arena* 724 n.
**cockroach**
*insect* 365 n.
**cock-shy**
*propulsion* 287 n.
*laughingstock* 851 n.
**cocksure**
*believing* 485 adj.
*impertinent* 878 adj.
**cocktail**
*a mixture* 43 n.
*alcoholic drink* 301 n.
*box*
*draught* 301 n.
**cocktail party**
*social gathering* 882 n.

**cocky**
*prideful* 871 adj.
*vain* 873 adj.
*impertinent* 878 adj.
**cocoa**
*milk* 301 n.
*soft drink* 301 n.
**coconut**
*fruit* 301 n.
**coconut matting**
*floor-cover* 226 n.
**cocoon**
*young creature* 132 n.
*source* 156 n.
*receptacle* 194 n.
*wrapping* 226 n.
*safeguard* 660 vb.
**cod**
*fish food* 301 n.
**C.O.D.**
*buying* 792 adj.
*owed* 803 adj.
*cash down* 804 adv.
*pay* 804 vb.
**coda**
*adjunct* 40 n.
*sequel* 67 n.
*end* 69 n.
*rear* 238 n.
*melody* 410 n.
*musical piece* 412 n.
**coddle**
*cook* 301 vb.
*please* 826 vb.
*pet* 889 vb.
**code**
*arrangement* 62 n.
*rule* 81 n.
*latency* 523 n.
*secrecy* 525 n.
*conceal* 525 vb.
*enigma* 530 n.
*symbology* 547 n.
*writing* 586 n.
*precept* 693 n.
*probity* 929 n.
**code-breaker**
*interpreter* 520 n.
**codeine**
*drug* 658 n.
**code of honour**
*code of duty* 917 n.
*probity* 929 n.
**codex**
*script* 586 n.
*book* 589 n.
**codicil**
*adjunct* 40 n.
*sequel* 67 n.
*title deed* 767 n.
**codification**
*law* 953 n.
*legislation* 953 n.
**codify**
*class* 62 vb.
**coeducation**
*education* 534 n.

*relief* 831 n.
**Comforter, the**
*Holy Ghost* 965 n.
**comforting**
*alleviative* 177 adj.
*comfortable* 376 adj.
*refreshing* 685 adj.
*relieving* 831 adj.
*cheering* 833 adj.
**comfortless**
*unpleasant* 827 adj.
*cheerless* 834 adj.
*melancholic* 834 adj.
*hopeless* 853 adj.
*unpromising* 853 adj.
**comic**
*fool* 501 n.
*the press* 528 n.
*entertainer* 594 n.
*dramatic* 594 adj.
*laughing* 835 adj.
*humorist* 839 n.
*witty* 839 adj.
*funny* 849 adj.
**comical**
*absurd* 497 adj.
*witty* 839 adj.
*funny* 849 adj.
**comic verse**
*poem* 593 n.
*doggerel* 593 n.
**coming**
*future* 124 adj.
*See also* **come**
**coming out**
*debut* 68 n.
**coming to one**
*due* 915 adj.
**comity**
*courtesy* 884 n.
**comity of nations**
*social group* 371 n.
**comma**
*punctuation* 547 n.
**command**
*advantage* 34 n.
*be superior* 34 vb.
*be high* 209 vb.
*will* 595 n., vb.
*dispose of* 673 vb.
*directorship* 689 n.
*direct* 689 vb.
*warfare* 718 n.
*governance* 733 n.
*dominate* 733 vb.
*rule* 733 vb.
*command* 737 n., vb.
*mandate* 751 n.
*possess* 773 vb.
*desire* 859 vb.
*impose a duty* 917 vb.
– one's passions
*be virtuous* 933 vb.
– respect
*be important* 638 vb.
*have a reputation*
*866 vb.*

*command respect* 920 vb.
**commandant**
*army officer* 741 n.
**commandeer**
*compel* 740 vb.
*appropriate* 786 vb.
**commander**
*superior* 34 n.
*army officer* 741 n.
*naval officer* 741 n.
**commanding**
*superior* 34 adj.
*influential* 178 adj.
*notable* 638 adj.
*authoritative* 733 adj.
*commanding* 737 adj.
*noteworthy* 866 adj.
*proud* 871 adj.
**commandment**
*precept* 693 n.
*command* 737 n.
**commando**
*armed force* 722 n.
**command of**
**language**
*style* 566 n.
*eloquence* 579 n.
**command per-**
**formance**
*dramaturgy* 594 n.
**commedia dell'arte**
*stage play* 594 n.
**comme il faut**
*tasteful* 846 adj.
*fashionable* 848 adj.
*genteel* 868 adj.
**commemorate**
*remind* 505 vb.
*honour* 866 vb.
*celebrate* 876 vb.
**commemoration**
*remembrance* 505 n.
**commemorative**
*remembering* 505 adj.
*celebratory* 876 adj.
**commence**
*begin* 68 vb.
**commencement**
*beginning* 68 n.
**commend**
*advise* 691 vb.
*befriend* 880 vb.
*approve* 923 vb.
*praise* 923 vb.
**commendable**
*good* 615 adj.
*advisable* 642 adj.
*approvable* 923 adj.
*virtuous* 933 adj.
**commendation**
*friendship* 880 n.
*approbation* 923 n.
*praise* 923 n.
**commensurable**
*numerical* 85 adj.
*numerable* 86 adj.
**commensurate**

*relative* 9 adj.
*agreeing* 24 adj.
*numerable* 86 adj.
*sufficient* 635 adj.
**comment**
*estimate* 480 n., vb.
*commentary* 520 n.
*affirmation* 532 n.
*affirm* 532 vb.
*speech* 579 n.
*article* 591 n.
– on
*interpret* 520 vb.
**commentary**
*commentary* 520 n.
*oration* 579 n.
**commentator**
*estimator* 480 n.
*interpreter* 520 n.
*informant* 524 n.
*broadcaster* 531 n.
*dissertator* 591 n.
**commerce**
*business* 622 n.
*vocation* 622 n.
*trade* 791 n.
**commercial**
*advertisement* 528 n.
*broadcast* 531 n.
*businesslike* 622 adj.
*trading* 791 adj.
*vulgar* 847 adj.
**commercial break**
*broadcast* 531 n.
**commercialism**
*bad taste* 847 n.
**commercialize, com-**
**mercialise**
*trade* 791 vb.
*vulgarize* 847 vb.
**commercial traveller**
*traveller* 268 n.
*seller* 793 n.
**commination**
*malediction* 899 n.
*threat* 900 n.
*prayers* 981 n.
**comminute**
*break* 46 vb.
*pulverize* 332 vb.
**commiserate**
*lament* 836 vb.
*pity* 905 vb.
**commissar**
*tyrant* 735 n.
*autocrat* 741 n.
*officer* 741 n.
**commissariat**
*provision* 633 n.
**commissary**
*provider* 633 n.
*delegate* 754 n.
**commission**
*auspicate* 68 vb.
*band* 74 n.
*message* 529 n.
*select* 605 vb.

*job* 622 n.
*employ* 622 vb.
*fitting out* 669 n.
*make ready* 669 vb.
*action* 676 n.
*authority* 733 n.
*command* 737 n., vb.
*warrant* 737 n.
*commission* 751 n., vb.
*mandate* 751 n.
*permit* 756 n.
*earnings* 771 n.
*transfer* 780 n.
*assign* 780 vb.
*pay* 804 n.
*dignify* 866 vb.
*duty* 917 n.
*impose a duty* 917 vb.
**commissionaire**
*doorkeeper* 264 n.
*courier* 529 n.
**commissioned officer**
*army officer* 741 n.
**commissioner**
*official* 690 n.
*officer* 741 n.
*delegate* 754 n.
**commissioner for**
**oaths**
*notary* 958 n.
**commission of**
**enquiry**
*enquiry* 459 n.
**commit**
*transfer* 272 vb.
*do* 676 vb.
*commission* 751 vb.
*assign* 780 vb.
*give* 781 vb.
*do wrong* 914 vb.
– for trial
*try a case* 959 vb.
– oneself
*affirm* 532 vb.
*be resolute* 599 vb.
*choose* 605 vb.
*undertake* 672 vb.
*promise* 764 vb.
*incur a duty* 917 vb.
– to memory
*memorize* 505 vb.
– to writing
*record* 548 vb.
*write* 586 vb.
**commitment**
*resolution* 599 n.
*perseverance* 600 n.
*promise* 764 n.
*giving* 781 n.
*debt* 803 n.
*duty* 917 n.
**committal**
*transference* 272 n.
*commission* 751 n.
*legal process* 959 n.
**committed**
*resolute* 599 adj.

promised 764 adj.
indebted 803 adj.
obliged 917 adj.
**committee**
band 74 n.
party 708 n.
authority 733 n.
consignee 754 n.
**commode**
cabinet 194 n.
latrine 649 n.
**commodification**
misuse 675 n.
bad taste 847 n.
**commodify**
misuse 675 vb.
vulgarize 847 n.
**commodious**
spacious 183 adj.
useful 640 adj.
**commodity**
object 319 n.
utility 640 n.
merchandise 795 n.
**commodore**
nautical personnel 270 n.
naval officer 741 n.
**common**
inferior 35 adj.
general 79 adj.
typical 83 adj.
frequent 139 adj.
plain 348 n.
usual 610 adj.
middling 732 adj.
unpossessed 774 adj.
sharing 775 adj.
lands 777 n.
pleasure ground 837 n.
vulgar 847 adj.
unastonishing 865 adj.
plebeian 869 adj.
**commonalty**
everyman 79 n.
social group 371 n.
commonalty 869 n.
**common cause**
cooperation 706 n.
**common cold**
excretion 302 n.
coldness 380 n.
**common core**
curriculum 534 n.
**common denominator**
relation 9 n.
numerical element 85 n.
**commoner**
common man 30 n.
student 538 n.
commoner 869 n.
**commonhold**
proprietary 777 adj.
**common good**
good 615 n.
philanthropy 901 n.
**common knowledge**

knowledge 490 n.
information 524 n.
publicity 528 n.
**common land**
joint possession 775 n.
lands 777 n.
**common law**
tradition 127 n.
precept 693 n.
law 953 n.
**common-law husband/wife**
lover 887 n.
spouse 894 n.
**commonly**
often 139 adv.
**common man**
common man 30 n.
everyman 79 n.
averageness 732 n.
commoner 869 n.
**Common Market**
society 708 n.
market 796 n.
**commonness**
inferiority 35 n.
generality 79 n.
ill-breeding 847 n.
**common noun**
part of speech 564 n.
**common or garden**
typical 83 adj.
**common ownership**
joint possession 775 n.
**commonplace**
median 30 adj.
general 79 adj.
typical 83 adj.
topic 452 n.
known 490 adj.
maxim 496 n.
aphoristic 496 adj.
phrase 563 n.
plain 573 adj.
usual 610 adj.
trivial 639 adj.
middling 732 adj.
dull 840 adj.
**Common Prayer**
public worship 981 n.
**commons**
provisions 301 n.
commonalty 869 n.
**commonsense**
intelligence 498 n.
sanity 502 n.
**common touch**
conduct 688 n.
sociability 882 n.
courtesy 884 n.
**commonwealth**
territory 184 n.
nation 371 n.
political organization 733 n.
**commotion**
turmoil 61 n.

violence 176 n.
commotion 318 n.
overactivity 678 n.
excitable state 822 n.
discontent 829 n.
**communal**
national 371 adj.
corporate 708 adj.
sharing 775 adj.
**communalize, communalise**
communalize 775 vb.
**communally**
in common 775 adv.
**commune**
district 184 n.
inhabitants 191 n.
association 706 n.
joint possession 775 n.
**commune with**
communicate 524 vb.
converse 584 vb.
**communicable**
transferable 272 adj.
infectious 653 adj.
**communicant**
church member 976 n.
pietist 979 n.
worshipper 981 n.
**communicate**
connect 45 vb.
communicate 524 vb.
divulge 526 vb.
publish 528 vb.
signal 547 vb.
correspond 588 vb.
describe 590 vb.
offer worship 981 vb.
**communicating**
accessible 289 adj.
communicating 624 adj.
**communication**
message 529 n.
interlocution 584 n.
**communications**
access 624 n.
**communications satellite**
satellite 321 n.
broadcasting 531 n.
**communicative**
informative 524 adj.
disclosing 526 adj.
loquacious 581 adj.
conversing 584 adj.
**communion**
interlocution 584 n.
party 708 n.
Holy Communion 988 n.
**communion of saints**
Christendom 976 n.
**communiqué**
report 524 n.
news 529 n.
**communism**
government 733 n.
joint possession 775 n.

**communist**
reformer 654 n.
agitator 738 n.
participator 775 n.
**Communist bloc**
political organization 733 n.
**communistic**
sharing 775 adj.
philanthropic 901 adj.
**Communists**
political party 708 n.
**community**
subdivision 53 n.
district 184 n.
inhabitants 191 n.
housing 192 n.
social group 371 n.
association 706 n.
community 708 n.
sect 978 n.
monk 986 n.
**community care**
protection 660 n.
social care 901 n.
**community centre**
focus 76 n.
meeting place 192 n.
**community chest**
store 632 n.
**community council**
council 692 n.
jurisdiction 955 n.
**community home**
school 539 n.
prison 748 n.
**community of possessions**
joint possession 775 n.
**community relations**
sociality 882 n.
**community service**
sociology 901 n.
**commutation**
compensation 31 n.
substitution 150 n.
interchange 151 n.
**commute**
substitute 150 vb.
interchange 151 vb.
travel 267 vb.
compromise 770 vb.
show mercy 905 vb.
**commuter**
dweller 191 n.
traveller 268 n.
**compact**
small 33 adj.
little 196 adj.
make smaller 198 vb.
short 204 adj.
dense 324 adj.
be dense 324 vb.
consensus 488 n.
concise 569 adj.
promise 764 n.
compact 765 n.

*regularity* 81 n.
*density* 324 n.
*truth* 494 n.
**consistent**
*rational* 475 adj.
**consistent with**
*agreeing* 24 adj.
*comformable* 83 adj.
**consist in**
*be* 1 vb.
**consist of**
*contain* 56 vb.
*comprise* 78 vb.
**consistorial**
*ecclesiastical* 985 adj.
**consistory**
*council* 692 n.
*synod* 985 n.
**consolation**
*relief* 831 n.
*condolence* 905 n.
**consolation prize**
*imperfection* 647 n.
*trophy* 729 n.
*reward* 962 n.
**console**
*cabinet* 194 n.
*shelf* 218 n.
*relieve* 831 vb.
*cheer* 833 vb.
*pity* 905 vb.
– *oneself*
*be relieved* 831 vb.
**consolidate**
*join* 45 vb.
*cohere* 48 vb.
*bring together* 74 vb.
*centralize* 225 vb.
*be dense* 324 vb.
*abstract* 592 vb.
**consolidation**
*contraction* 198 n.
*association* 706 n.
**consommé**
*hors-d'oeuvres* 301 n.
**consonance**
*agreement* 24 n.
*melody* 410 n.
**consonant**
*agreeing* 24 adj.
*speech sound* 398 n.
*harmonious* 410 adj.
*spoken letter* 558 n.
**consort**
*concomitant* 89 n.
*spouse* 894 n.
**consortium**
*agreement* 24 n.
*association* 706 n.
**consort with**
*accompany* 89 vb.
**conspectus**
*combination* 50 n.
*whole* 52 n.
*generality* 79 n.
*compendium* 592 n.
**conspicuous**

*obvious* 443 adj.
*manifest* 522 adj.
*notable* 638 adj.
*noteworthy* 866 adj.
**conspicuous by one's absence, be**
*be absent* 190 vb.
**conspicuous consumption**
*prodigality* 815 n.
**conspicuously**
*remarkably* 32 adv.
**conspicuousness**
*prominence* 254 n.
*visibility* 443 n.
*manifestation* 522 n.
*prestige* 866 n.
**conspiracy**
*assemblage* 74 n.
*concurrence* 181 n.
*secrecy* 525 n.
*plot* 623 n.
*cooperation* 706 n.
*compact* 765 n.
**conspirator**
*deceiver* 545 n.
*planner* 623 n.
*collaborator* 707 n.
**conspiratorial**
*stealthy* 525 adj.
*planning* 623 adj.
**conspire**
*plot* 623 vb.
*See also* **conspiracy**
**constable**
*officer* 741 n.
*police* 955 n.
**constabulary**
*police* 955 n.
**constancy**
*uniformity* 16 n.
*regularity* 81 n.
*stability* 153 n.
*resolution* 599 n.
*perseverance* 600 n.
*obstinacy* 602 n.
*loyalty* 739 n.
*probity* 929 n.
**constant**
*characteristic* 5 adj.
*identity* 13 n.
*identical* 13 adj.
*uniform* 16 adj.
*continuous* 71 adj.
*regular* 81 adj.
*number* 85 n.
*lasting* 113 adj.
*perpetual* 115 adj.
*frequent* 139 adj.
*periodical* 141 adj.
*fixture* 153 n.
*unchangeable* 153 adj.
*accurate* 494 adj.
*resolute* 599 adj.
*persevering* 600 adj.
*obedient* 739 adj.
*trustworthy* 929 adj.

**constantly**
*for ever* 115 adv.
*perpetually* 139 adv.
**constellation**
*group* 74 n.
*star* 321 n.
*person of repute* 866 n.
**consternation**
*fear* 854 n.
*wonder* 864 n.
**constipating**
*compressive* 198 adj.
*solidifying* 324 adj.
**constipation**
*closure* 264 n.
*defecation* 302 n.
*condensation* 324 n.
*digestive disorders* 651 n.
**constituency**
*district* 184 n.
*electorate* 605 n.
**constituent(s)**
*part* 53 n.
*component* 58 n., adj.
*included* 78 adj.
*contents* 193 n.
*electorate* 605 n.
**constitute**
*constitute* 56 vb.
*be one of* 58 vb.
*be included* 78 vb.
*produce* 164 vb.
**constitution**
*character* 5 n.
*composition* 56 n.
*beginning* 68 n.
*inclusion* 78 n.
*structure* 331 n.
*precept* 693 n.
*political organization* 733 n.
*law* 953 n.
**constitutional**
*intrinsic* 5 adj.
*walking* 267 n.
*habit* 610 n.
*hygiene* 652 n.
*exercise* 682 n.
*governmental* 733 adj.
*due* 915 adj.
*legal* 953 adj.
**constitutionalism**
*government* 733 n.
*legality* 953 n.
**constitutive principle**
*essence* 1 n.
**constraint**
*limit* 236 n.
*compulsion* 740 n.
*subjection* 745 n.
*restraint* 747 n.
*modesty* 874 n.
**constrict**
*tighten* 45 vb.
*make smaller* 198 vb.
**constriction**
*compression* 198 n.

*narrowing* 206 n.
*restriction* 747 n.
**constrictor**
*compressor* 198 n.
**construct**
*make complete* 54 vb.
*compose* 56 vb.
*produce* 164 vb.
*form* 243 vb.
– *a figure*
*outline* 233 vb.
*represent* 551 vb.
**construction**
*composition* 56 n.
*arrangement* 62 n.
*production* 164 n.
*structure* 331 n.
*conjecture* 512 n.
*connotation* 514 n.
*interpretation* 520 n.
*sculpture* 554 n.
**constructional**
*structural* 331 adj.
**constructive**
*productive* 164 adj.
*semantic* 514 adj.
*interpretive* 520 adj.
*aiding* 703 adj.
**constructive criticism**
*estimate* 480 n.
*advice* 691 n.
**constructivism**
*sculpture* 554 n.
**constructor**
*producer* 164 n.
**construe**
*interpretation* 520 n.
*translation* 520 n.
*interpret* 520 vb.
*parse* 564 vb.
**consubstantiality**
*identity* 13 n.
*unity* 88 n.
**consubstantiation**
*the sacrament* 988 n.
**consuetude**
*habit* 610 n.
**consul**
*official* 690 n.
*officer* 741 n.
*envoy* 754 n.
**consulate**
*position of authority* 733 n.
*envoy* 754 n.
**consult**
*confer* 584 vb.
*consult* 691 vb.
– *one's pillow*
*wait* 136 vb.
*meditate* 449 vb.
**consultant**
*sage* 500 n.
*oracle* 511 n.
*teacher* 537 n.
*doctor* 658 n.
*adviser* 691 n.

**continent**
*region* 184 n.
*land* 344 n.
*temperate* 942 adj.
*pure* 950 adj.
**continental**
*foreigner* 59 n.
*extraneous* 59 adj.
*regional* 184 adj.
*dweller* 191 n.
*land* 344 n.
*inland* 344 adj.
**continental drift**
*transference* 272 n.
*world* 321 n.
**continental quilt**
*coverlet* 226 n.
**continental shelf**
*territory* 184 n.
*shore* 344 n.
**contingency**
*juncture* 8 n.
*event* 154 n.
*chance* 159 n.
**contingent**
*extrinsic* 6 adj.
*circumstantial* 8 adj.
*part* 53 n.
*eventual* 154 adj.
*caused* 157 adj.
*casual* 159 adj.
*liable* 180 adj.
*qualifying* 468 adj.
*possible* 469 adj.
*uncertain* 474 adj.
*conditional* 766 adj.
**contingents**
*armed force* 722 n.
**continual**
*continuous* 71 adj.
*perpetual* 115 adj.
*frequent* 139 adj.
*unceasing* 146 adj.
**continuance**
*uniformity* 16 n.
*sequence* 65 n.
*continuity* 71 n.
*course of time* 111 n.
*durability* 113 n.
*perpetuity* 115 n.
*present time* 121 n.
*permanence* 144 n.
*continuance* 146 n.
*perseverance* 600 n.
*habit* 610 n.
**continuation**
*adjunct* 40 n.
*sequel* 67 n.
*continuity* 71 n.
*continuance* 146 n.
*noncompletion* 726 n.
**continue**
*be* 1 vb.
*continue* 71 vb.
*run on* 71 vb.
*perpetuate* 115 vb.
*lengthen* 203 vb.

**continuity**
*uniformity* 16 n.
*order* 60 n.
*sequence* 65 n.
*continuity* 71 n.
*recurrence* 106 n.
*perpetuity* 115 n.
*frequency* 139 n.
*periodicity* 141 n.
*continuance* 146 n.
*contiguity* 202 n.
*motion* 265 n.
*progression* 285 n.
*cinema* 445 n.
*dramaturgy* 594 n.
**continuity girl**
*stagehand* 594 n.
**continuo**
*melody* 410 n.
**continuous**
*continuous* 71 adj.
*See also* **continuity**
**continuum**
*continuity* 71 n.
*space* 183 n.
**contort**
*distort* 246 vb.
**contorted**
*convoluted* 251 adj.
**contortionist**
*athlete* 162 n.
**contour**
*outline* 233 n.
*form* 243 n.
*feature* 445 n.
**contour lines**
*indication* 547 n.
**contour ploughing**
*agriculture* 370 n.
**contra-**
*contrary* 14 adj.
**contraband**
*prohibited* 757 adj.
*booty* 790 n.
*illegal* 954 adj.
**contraception**
*impotence* 161 n.
*contraception* 172 n.
*drug* 658 n.
*hindrance* 702 n.
**contraceptive**
*contraception* 172 n.
**contract**
*abate* 37 vb.
*decrease* 37 vb.
*be little* 196 vb.
*become small* 198 vb.
*make smaller* 198 vb.
*shorten* 204 vb.
*make thin* 206 vb.
*be dense* 324 vb.
*be concise* 569 vb.
*undertaking* 672 n.
*promise* 764 vb.
*compact* 765 n.
*contract* 765 vb.
*make terms* 766 vb.

*bargain* 791 vb.
*capital punishment*
  963 n.
– a disease
*be ill* 651 vb.
– marriage
*wed* 894 vb.
**contract bridge**
*card game* 837 n.
**contractibility**
*compression* 198 n.
**contractility**
*compression* 198 n.
**contraction**
*joining together* 45 n.
*contraction* 198 n.
*closure* 264 n.
*word* 559 n.
*conciseness* 569 n.
*compendium* 592 n.
*See also* **contract**
**contractions**
*obstetrics* 167 n.
**contractor**
*trier* 671 n.
*doer* 676 n.
*signatory* 765 n.
**contractorization**
*job* 622 n.
**contractorize**
*commission* 751 vb.
**contractual**
*agreeing* 24 adj.
*contractual* 765 adj.
**contradict**
*be contrary* 14 vb.
*disagree* 25 vb.
*answer* 460 vb.
*tell against* 467 vb.
*confute* 479 vb.
*dissent* 489 vb.
*negate* 533 vb.
*oppose* 704 vb.
– oneself
*tell against* 467 vb.
**contradiction**
*contrariety* 14 n.
*disagreement* 25 n.
*divergence* 294 n.
*rejoinder* 460 n.
*confutation* 479 n.
*dissent* 489 n.
*negation* 533 n.
*opposition* 704 n.
**contradiction in terms**
*sophism* 477 n.
**contradictory**
*illogical* 477 adj.
*See also* **contradiction**
**contradistinction**
*contrariety* 14 n.
*differentiation* 15 n.
**contradistinguish**
*discriminate* 463 vb.
**contraflow**

*contrariety* 14 n.
*traffic control* 305 n.
*obstacle* 702 n.
**contraindicate**
*be contrary* 14 vb.
*tell against* 467 vb.
**contralto**
*resonance* 404 n.
*vocalist* 413 n.
**contraposition**
*contraposition* 240 n.
**contraption**
*contrivance* 623 n.
*tool* 630 n.
**contrapuntal**
*musical* 412 adj.
**contrarian**
*nonconformist* 84 n.
**contraries**
*polarity* 14 n.
*opposites* 704 n.
**contrariety**
*word* 559 n.
*See also* **contrary**
**contrariwise**
*correlatively* 12 adv.
*contrarily* 14 adv.
*inversely* 221 adv.
*against* 240 adv.
**contrary**
*contrary* 14 adj.
*different* 15 adj.
*nonuniform* 17 adj.
*disagreeing* 25 adj.
*unconformable* 84 adj.
*counteracting* 182 adj.
*inverted* 221 adj.
*opposite* 240 adj.,
*discordant* 411 adj.
*countervailing* 467 adj.
*semantic* 514 adj.
*negative* 533 adj.
*capricious* 604 adj.
*hindering* 702 adj.
*opposing* 704 adj.
*adverse* 731 adj.
*disobedient* 738 adj.
**contrary to**
*although* 182 adv.
**contrast**
*contrariety* 14 n.
*be contrary* 14 vb.
*difference* 15 n.
*differ* 15 vb.
*dissimilarity* 19 n.
*nonconformity* 84 n.
*comparison* 462 n.
*compare* 462 vb.
*trope* 519 n.
*figure* 519 vb.
*painting* 553 n.
**contravene**
*be contrary* 14 vb.
*tell against* 467 vb.
*negate* 533 vb.
**contravention**
*lawbreaking* 954 n.

refrigeration 382 n.
**crypt**
cellar 194 n.
depth 211 n.
tomb 364 n.
church interior 990 n.
**cryptanalysis**
hermeneutics 520 n.
**cryptic**
uncertain 474 adj.
unintelligible 517 adj.
occult 523 adj.
concealed 525 adj.
cabbalistic 984 adj.
**crypto-**
latent 523 adj.
concealed 525 adj.
**cryptogram**
secrecy 525 n.
enigma 530 n.
**cryptographer**
interpreter 520 n.
**crystal**
minuteness 196 n.
solid body 324 n.
transparency 422 n.
transparent 422 adj.
optical device 442 n.
**crystal ball**
sphere 252 n.
oracle 511 n.
**crystal-clear**
transparent 422 adj.
obvious 443 adj.
**crystal clear**
intelligible 516 adj.
**crystal-gazer**
diviner 511 n.
occultist 984 n.
**crystal healing**
alternative therapy
658 n.
**crystalline**
symmetrical 245 adj.
dense 324 adj.
hard 326 adj.
transparent 422 adj.
**crystallization**
conversion 147 n.
condensation 324 n.
hardening 326 n.
**crystallize, crystallise**
harden 326 vb.
sweeten 392 vb.
**crystal set**
broadcasting 531 n.
**crystal therapy**
alternative therapy
658 n.
**CSE**
exam 459 n.
**CS gas**
poison 659 n.
**cub**
young creature 132 n.
youngster 132 n.
reproduce itself 167 vb.

**cubbyhole**
retreat 192 n.
compartment 194 n.
**cube**
do sums 86 vb.
treble 94 vb.
angular figure 247 n.
**cube root**
numerical element 85 n.
**cubic**
spatial 183 adj.
metrical 465 adj.
**cubicle**
room 194 n.
compartment 194 n.
**Cubism**
school of painting 553 n.
**cub reporter**
news reporter 529 n.
**cucking stool**
pillory 964 n.
**cuckold**
be impure 951 vb.
cuckold 952 n.
**cuckoo**
repetition 106 n.
resident 191 n.
bird 365 n.
ululation 409 n.
fool 501 n.
crazy 503 adj.
**cuckoo in the nest**
intruder 59 n.
impostor 545 n.
usurper 916 n.
**cucumber**
vegetable 301 n.
**cud**
mouthful 301 n.
**cuddle**
be near 200 vb.
surround 230 vb.
circumscribe 232 vb.
enclose 235 vb.
retention 778 n.
endearment 889 n.
caress 889 vb.
**cuddly**
fleshy 195 adj.
lovable 887 adj.
**cudgel**
hammer 279 n.
strike 279 vb.
club 723 n.
flog 963 vb.
scourge 964 n.
**cudgel one's brains**
think 449 vb.
**cue**
ram 279 n.
reminder 505 n.
hint 524 n.
dramaturgy 594 n.
**cuff**
garment 228 n.
sleeve 228 n.
fold 261 n.

knock 279 n.
corporal punishment
963 n.
spank 963 vb.
**cufflink**
fastening 47 n.
jewellery 844 n.
**cui bono**
why 158 adv.
in search of 459 adv.
usefully 640 adv.
**cuirass**
armour 713 n.
**cuirassier**
cavalry 722 n.
**Cuisenaire rods**
counting instrument
86 n.
**cuisine**
cookery 301 n.
**cuisine minceur**
dieting 301 n.
**cul-de-sac**
closure 264 n.
road 624 n.
obstacle 702 n.
**culinary**
culinary 301 adj.
**culinary herb**
herb 301 n.
plant 366 n.
**cull**
killing 362 n.
select 605 n.
take 786 vb.
**culm**
coal 385 n.
**culminate**
culminate 34 vb.
be complete 54 vb.
be high 209 vb.
crown 213 vb.
ascend 308 vb.
climax 725 vb.
**culottes**
skirt 228 n.
**culpable**
wrong 914 adj.
blameworthy 924 adj.
heinous 934 adj.
guilty 936 adj.
**culpable negligence**
negligence 458 n.
undutifulness 918 n.
**culprit**
offender 904 n.
accused person 928 n.
**cult**
fashion 848 n.
affectation 850 n.
religion 973 n.
cult 981 n.
idolatry 982 n.
**cult image**
idol 982 n.
**cultivate**
produce 164 vb.

make fruitful 171 vb.
cultivate 370 vb.
cause feeling 374 vb.
train 534 vb.
make better 654 vb.
mature 669 vb.
prepare 669 vb.
flatter 925 vb.
**cultivated**
instructed 490 adj.
**cultivation**
agriculture 370 n.
culture 490 n.
learning 536 n.
civilization 654 n.
maturation 669 n.
good taste 846 n.
**cultivator**
farmer 370 n.
farm tool 370 n.
country-dweller 869 n.
**cultural**
educational 534 adj.
improving 654 adj.
**culture**
culture 490 n.
education 534 n.
learning 536 n.
civilization 654 n.
good taste 846 n.
**cultured**
horticultural 370 adj.
instructed 490 adj.
spurious 542 adj.
**cultured pearl**
gem 844 n.
**culture shock**
lack of expectation
508 n.
**culvert**
drain 351 n.
**cum**
in addition 38 adv.
with 89 adv.
and 90 adv.
**cumber**
weigh 322 vb.
hinder 702 vb.
**cumbersome**
unwieldy 195 adj.
weighty 322 adj.
clumsy 695 adj.
graceless 842 adj.
**cumin**
spice 301 n.
**cummerbund**
girdle 47 n.
belt 228 n.
loop 250 n.
**cumulative**
increasing 36 adj.
evidential 466 adj.
**cumulativeness**
increase 36 n.
continuity 71 n.
**cumulative vote**
vote 605 n.

**dactyl**
  *prosody* 593 n.
**dactylology**
  *deafness* 416 n.
  *gesture* 547 n.
  *symbology* 547 n.
**dad, daddy**
  *paternity* 169 n.
**Dada**
  *school of painting* 553 n.
**daddy longlegs**
  *insect* 365 n.
**dado**
  *base* 214 n.
  *ornamental art* 844 n.
**daedal**
  *variegated* 437 adj.
  *well-made* 694 adj.
  *ornamental* 844 adj.
**Daedalian**
  *labyrinthine* 251 adj.
**daffodil**
  *plant* 366 n.
  *yellowness* 433 n.
  *heraldry* 547 n.
**daft**
  *foolish* 499 adj.
  *crazy* 503 adj.
**dagger**
  *sharp point* 256 n.
  *punctuation* 547 n.
  *sidearms* 723 n.
**daggers drawn**
  *resentment* 891 n.
**daguerrotype**
  *photography* 551 n.
**dahlia**
  *plant* 366 n.
**Dail**
  *parliament* 692 n. box
**daily**
  *often* 139 adv.
  *seasonal* 141 adj.
  *periodically* 141 adv.
  *journal* 528 n.
  *the press* 528 n.
  *usual* 610 adj.
  *cleaner* 648 n.
  *servant* 742 n.
**daily bread**
  *food* 301 n.
  *vocation* 622 n.
**daily dozen**
  *exercise* 682 n.
**daily help**
  *cleaner* 648 n.
  *servant* 742 n.
**daily round**
  *uniformity* 16 n.
  *continuity* 71 n.
  *regular return* 141 n.
  *habit* 610 n.
  *business* 622 n.
**dainties**
  *food* 301 n.
**daintiness**
  *cleanness* 648 n.

  *good taste* 846 n.
  *fastidiousness* 862 n.
**dainty**
  *small* 33 adj.
  *flimsy* 163 adj.
  *little* 196 adj.
  *edible* 301 adj.
  *savoury* 390 adj.
  *clean* 648 adj.
  *pleasurableness* 826 n.
  *personable* 841 adj.
  *shapely* 841 adj.
  *tasteful* 846 adj.
  *fastidious* 862 adj.
**daiquiri**
  *alcoholic drink* 301 n.
**dairy**
  *room* 194 n.
  *workshop* 687 n.
**dairy farming**
  *animal husbandry* 369 n.
  *agriculture* 370 n.
**dairymaid**
  *herdsman* 369 n.
  *domestic* 742 n.
**dairy product**
  *dairy product* 301 n.
**dais**
  *stand* 218 n.
  *rostrum* 539 n.
**daisy**
  *plant* 366 n.
**daisy-cutter**
  *lowness* 210 n.
**daisy wheel**
  *stationery* 586 n.
**dak bungalow**
  *inn* 192 n.
**Dalai Lama**
  *sovereign* 741 n.
**dale**
  *valley* 255 n.
**Dalek**
  *image* 551 n.
**dalesman,
    daleswoman**
  *dweller* 191 n.
**dalliance**
  *lovemaking* 887 n.
  *endearment* 889 n.
**dally**
  *be late* 136 vb.
  *be irresolute* 601 vb.
  *be inactive* 679 vb.
  *amuse oneself* 837 vb.
  *caress* 889 vb.
**Dalmatian**
  *dog* 365 n.
  *mottling* 437 n.
**dalmatic**
  *vestments* 989 n.
**daltonism**
  *dim sight* 440 n.
**dam**
  *exclusion* 57 n.
  *maternity* 169 n.
  *irrigator* 341 n.

  *lake* 346 n.
**dam (up)**
  *close* 264 vb.
  *staunch* 350 vb.
  *obstruct* 702 vb.
**damage**
  *break* 46 vb.
  *derange* 63 vb.
  *weaken* 163 vb.
  *lay waste* 165 vb.
  *tell against* 467 vb.
  *evil* 616 n.
  *waste* 634 n., vb.
  *inutility* 641 n.
  *badness* 645 n.
  *harm* 645 vb.
  *impairment* 655 n.
  *impair* 655 vb.
  *cost* 809 n.
  *blemish* 845 vb.
  *defame* 926 vb.
**damages**
  *restitution* 787 n.
  *cost* 809 n.
  *penalty* 963 n.
**damaging**
  *harmful* 645 adj.
  *discreditable* 867 adj.
  *maleficent* 898 adj.
**damascene**
  *variegate* 437 vb.
**damask**
  *textile* 222 n.
  *red* 431 adj.
**dame**
  *lady* 373 n.
  *master* 741 n.
  *person of repute* 866 n.
  *title* 870 n.
**damn**
  *trifle* 639 n.
– 891 int.
  *scurrility* 899 n.
  *curse* 899 vb.
  *cuss* 899 vb.
– 899 int.
  *dispraise* 924 vb.
  *condemn* 961 vb.
– all
  *zero* 103 n.
– the consequences
  *be obstinate* 602 vb.
  *be rash* 857 vb.
– with faint praise
  *be indifferent* 860 vb.
  *dispraise* 924 vb.
  *detract* 926 vb.
**damnable**
  *evil* 616 adj.
  *damnable* 645 adj.
  *unpleasant* 827 adj.
**damnably**
  *extremely* 32 adv.
**damnation**
  *future state* 124 n.
  *suffering* 825 n.
  *condemnation* 961 n.

**damnatory**
  *maledictory* 899 adj.
  *disapproving* 924 adj.
  *accusing* 928 adj.
**damned**
  *damnable* 645 adj.
  *cursed* 899 adj.
  *condemned* 961 adj.
  *infernal* 972 adj.
**damning**
  *evidential* 466 adj.
**damp**
  *gas* 336 n.
  *water* 339 n.
  *moisture* 341 n.
  *humid* 341 adj.
  *extinguish* 382 vb.
  *sound dead* 405 vb.
  *See also* **dampen**
– down
  *abate* 37 vb.
  *hinder* 702 vb.
  *restrain* 747 vb.
**damp course**
  *base* 214 n.
**dampen**
  *moderate* 177 vb.
  *moisten* 341 vb.
  *mute* 401 vb.
  *dissuade* 613 vb.
  *depress* 834 vb.
**damper**
  *moderator* 177 n.
  *stopper* 264 n.
  *heater* 383 n.
  *silencer* 401 n.
  *nonresonance* 405 n.
  *mute* 414 n.
  *moper* 834 n.
  *disapprover* 924 n.
**dampness**
  *moisture* 341 n.
**damp-proof**
  *unyielding* 162 adj.
  *coat* 226 vb.
  *sealed off* 264 adj.
  *dry* 342 adj.
**damp squib**
  *disappointment* 509 n.
  *failure* 728 n.
**damsel**
  *youngster* 132 n.
  *woman* 373 n.
**damson**
  *fruit* 301 n.
  *purpleness* 436 n.
**dance**
  *composition* 56 n.
  *be in motion* 265 vb.
  *leap* 312 vb.
  *rotation* 315 n.
  *oscillate* 317 vb.
  *be agitated* 318 vb.
  *musical piece* 412 n.
  *shine* 417 vb.
  *ballet* 594 n.
  *be excited* 821 vb.

*premise* 475 n.
*supposition* 512 n.
**data bank**
*computing* 86 n.
*mnemonics* 505 n.
*storage* 632 n.
**data base**
*computing* 86 n.
*information* 524 n.
**data processing**
*computing* 86 n.
*electronics* 160 n.
*microelectronics* 196 n.
*optical device* 442 n.
*information* 524 n.
*record* 548 n.
*language* 557 n.
**date**
*date* 108 n.
*fix the time* 108 vb.
*chronology* 117 n.
*fruit* 301 n.
*social round* 882 n.
*be sociable* 882 n., vb.
*lover* 887 n.
**dated**
*dated* 108 adj.
*antiquated* 127 adj.
**dateless**
*perpetual* 115 adj.
**date line**
*dividing line* 92 n.
*clock time* 117 n.
**date rape**
*rape* 951 n.
**dating agency**
*mediator* 720 n.
*matchmaker* 894 n.
**datum**
*premise* 475 n.
See also **data**
**daub**
*coat* 226 vb.
*colour* 425 vb.
*lack of meaning* 515 n.
*misrepresentation* 552 n.
*picture* 553 n.
*paint* 553 vb.
*make unclean* 649 vb.
**dauber**
*artist* 556 n.
*bungler* 697 n.
**daughter**
*descendant* 170 n.
*woman* 373 n.
**daughterly**
*filial* 170 adj.
*obedient* 739 adj.
**daunt**
*dissuade* 613 vb.
*frighten* 854 vb.
*humiliate* 872 vb.
**dauntless**
*unfearing* 855 adj.
**Dauphin**
*sovereign* 741 n.
**davit**

*hanger* 217 n.
**Davy Jones's locker**
*ocean* 343 n.
*the dead* 361 n.
**Davy lamp**
*lamp* 420 n.
**dawdle**
*drag on* 113 vb.
*be late* 136 vb.
*walk* 267 vb.
*wander* 267 vb.
*slowness* 278 n.
*move slowly* 278 vb.
*be inactive* 679 vb.
**dawdler**
*slowcoach* 278 n.
*idler* 679 n.
**dawn**
*precursor* 66 n.
*beginning* 68 n.
*begin* 68 vb.
*primal* 127 adj.
*morning* 128 n.
*glow* 417 n.
*make bright* 417 vb.
*redness* 431 n.
*appear* 445 vb.
– on/upon
*be visible* 443 vb.
*dawn upon* 449 vb.
*be intelligible* 516 vb.
**dawn chorus**
*morning* 128 n.
*vocal music* 412 n.
**day**
*date* 108 n.
*period* 110 n.
**day after day**
*repeatedly* 106 adv.
*perpetually* 139 adv.
**day and night**
*polarity* 14 n.
*perpetually* 139 adv.
**day book**
*account book* 808 n.
**daybreak**
*morning* 128 n.
*half-light* 419 n.
**day by day**
*repeatedly* 106 adv.
*while* 108 adv.
*all along* 113 adv.
**day centre**
*meeting place* 192 n.
**daydream**
*fantasy* 513 n.
*imagine* 513 vb.
*desire* 859 n., vb.
**daydreaming**
*abstractedness* 456 n.
*desire* 859 n.
**day in, day out**
*repeatedly* 106 adv.
*all along* 113 adv.
*perpetually* 139 adv.
**daylight**
*morning* 128 n.

*interval* 201 n.
*light* 417 n.
*manifestation* 522 n.
*disclosure* 526 n.
**daylight robbery**
*dearness* 811 n.
**daylight saving**
*clock time* 117 n.
**day of abstinence**
*fast* 946 n.
**day off**
*lull* 145 n.
*leisure* 681 n.
*repose* 683 n.
**Day of Judgment**
*finality* 69 n.
*punishment* 963 n.
**day of obligation**
*holy day* 988 n.
**day of reckoning**
*revenge* 910 n.
*punishment* 963 n.
**day of rest**
*repose* 683 n.
*holy day* 988 n.
**day of the week**
*date* 108 n.
*regular return* 141 n.
**day out**
*amusement* 837 n.
**day pupil**
*learner* 538 n.
**day release**
*education* 534 n.
**days**
*time* 108 n.
*era* 110 n.
**days of grace**
*delay* 136 n.
**days of old**
*past time* 125 n.
**daystar**
*morning* 128 n.
*sun* 321 n.
**daytime**
*morning* 128 n.
*matinal* 128 adj.
**day to remember**
*special day* 876 n.
**day trip**
*land travel* 267 n.
**day-tripper**
*traveller* 268 n.
*reveller* 837 n.
**daze**
*blur* 440 vb.
*distract* 456 vb.
*puzzle* 474 vb.
**dazed**
*insensible* 375 adj.
*dim-sighted* 440 adj.
*distracted* 456 adj.
*doubting* 474 adj.
*foolish* 499 adj.
*off guard* 508 adj.
*wondering* 864 adj.
**dazzle**

*light* 417 n.
*reflection* 417 n.
*shine* 417 vb.
*blind* 439 vb.
*blur* 440 vb.
*distract* 456 vb.
*deceive* 542 vb.
*impress* 821 vb.
*be beautiful* 841 vb.
*be wonderful* 864 vb.
*prestige* 866 n.
*be ostentatious* 875 vb.
*excite love* 887 vb.
*command respect* 920 vb.
**dazzler**
*a beauty* 841 n.
**dazzling**
*excellent* 644 adj.
*splendid* 841 adj.
**DD**
*academic title* 870 n.
**D-day**
*start* 68 n.
*date* 108 n.
*special day* 876 n.
**DDT**
*poison* 659 n.
**deacon, deaconess**
*church officer* 986 n.
*lay person* 987 n.
**deaconship**
*church office* 985 n.
**deactivate**
*weaken* 163 vb.
*assuage* 177 vb.
*counteract* 182 vb.
*impair* 655 vb.
**deactivated**
*inert* 175 adj.
**dead**
*extinct* 2 adj.
*past* 125 adj.
*inert* 175 adj.
*quiescent* 266 adj.
*dead* 361 adj.
*buried* 364 adj.
*insensible* 375 adj.
*muted* 401 adj.
*nonresonant* 405 adj.
*soft-hued* 425 adj.
*colourless* 426 adj.
*nonactive* 677 adj.
*abrogated* 752 adj.
**dead, the**
*death roll* 361 n.
**dead and buried**
*past* 125 adj.
*forgotten* 506 adj.
**dead as the dodo**
*extinct* 2 adj.
*past* 125 adj.
**dead beat**
*fatigued* 684 adj.
**dead body**
*corpse* 363 n.
**dead centre**
*centre* 225 n.

*derisive* 851 adj.
*disrespectful* 921 adj.
*detracting* 926 adj.
**derisory**
*ridiculous* 849 adj.
**derivation**
*origin* 68 n.
*reversion* 148 n.
*source* 156 n.
*effect* 157 n.
*attribution* 158 n.
*connotation* 514 n.
*etymology* 559 n.
**derivative**
*imitative* 20 adj.
*numerical element* 85 n.
*caused* 157 adj.
*word* 559 n.
*dull* 840 adj.
**derive (from)**
*result* 157 vb.
*attribute* 158 vb.
*acquire* 771 vb.
**dermatitis**
*skin disease* 651 n.
*inflammation* 651 n.
  box
**dermatology**
*medical art* 658 n.
*study* 536 n. box
**dermis**
*skin* 226 n.
**dernier cri**
*modernism* 126 n.
*fashion* 848 n.
**derogate**
*demean oneself* 867 vb.
*detract* 926 vb.
**derogatory**
*depreciating* 483 adj.
*degrading* 867 adj.
*detracting* 926 adj.
**derrick**
*lifter* 310 n.
**derrière**
*buttocks* 238 n.
**derring-do**
*courage* 855 n.
*prowess* 855 n.
**derris**
*poison* 659 n.
**Der Tag**
*aspiration* 852 n.
**derv**
*fuel* 385 n.
**dervish**
*ascetic* 945 n.
*religionist* 973 n.
*pietist* 979 n.
*worshipper* 981 n.
**desalinate**
*purify* 648 vb.
**desanctify**
*paganize* 974 vb.
**descant**
*tune* 412 n.
*sing* 413 vb.

*be diffuse* 570 vb.
*dissertate* 591 vb.
*hymn* 981 n.
**descend**
*land* 295 vb.
*descend* 309 vb.
*lower* 311 vb.
*plunge* 313 vb.
– from
*result* 157 vb.
**descendant**
*survivor* 41 n.
*successor* 67 n.
*descendant* 170 n.
**descendants**
*posteriority* 120 n.
*futurity* 124 n.
**descending order**
*decrease* 37 n.
*series* 71 n.
*contraction* 198 n.
**descent**
*consanguinity* 11 n.
*decrease* 37 n.
*sequence* 65 n.
*continuity* 71 n.
*posteriority* 120 n.
*source* 156 n.
*genealogy* 169 n.
*sonship* 170 n.
*presence* 189 n.
*depth* 211 n.
*incline* 220 n.
*motion* 265 n.
*descent* 309 n.
*plunge* 313 n.
*deterioration* 655 n.
*nobility* 868 n.
*theophany* 965 n.
**describe**
*communicate* 524 vb.
*represent* 551 vb.
*write* 586 vb.
*describe* 590 vb.
– a circle
*circle* 314 vb.
**description**
*assimilation* 18 n.
*indication* 547 n.
*representation* 551 n.
*literature* 557 n.
*name* 561 n.
*writing* 586 n.
*description* 590 n.
**descriptive**
*expressive* 516 adj.
*representing* 551 adj.
*descriptive* 590 adj.
**descry**
*see* 438 vb.
*detect* 484 vb.
*understand* 516 vb.
**desecrate**
*make unclean* 649 vb.
*impair* 655 vb.
*misuse* 675 vb.
*shame* 867 vb.

*be undue* 916 vb.
*not respect* 921 vb.
*be impious* 980 vb.
**desecrator**
*impious person* 980 n.
**deselect**
*vote* 605 vb.
*reject* 607 vb.
**desert**
*havoc* 165 n.
*desert* 172 n.
*unproductive* 172 adj.
*emptiness* 190 n.
*dryness* 342 n.
*plain* 348 n.
*change one's mind*
  603 vb.
*run away* 620 vb.
*relinquish* 621 vb.
*not observe* 769 vb.
*be cowardly* 856 vb.
*seclusion* 883 n.
*fail in duty* 918 vb.
**deserted**
*alone* 88 adj.
*empty* 190 adj.
*neglected* 458 adj.
*secluded* 883 adj.
**deserter**
*tergiversator* 603 n.
*avoider* 620 n.
*coward* 856 n.
*undutifulness* 918 n.
**desert fever**
*disease* 651 n.
**desertification**
*dryness* 342 n.
**desertion**
*disobedience* 738 n.
*divorce* 896 n.
*perfidy* 930 n.
*See also* **desert**
**desertization,**
  **desertisation**
*unproductiveness* 172 n.
*dryness* 342 n.
**deserts**
*conduct* 688 n.
*retaliation* 714 n.
*dueness* 915 n.
*reward* 962 n.
**deserve**
*be good* 644 vb.
*behave* 688 vb.
*deserve* 915 vb.
*be rewarded* 962 vb.
**deserved**
*just* 913 adj.
*due* 915 adj.
**deserving**
*excellent* 644 adj.
*approvable* 923 adj.
**déshabillé**
*informal dress* 228 n.
*uncovering* 229 n.
**desiccation**
*desiccation* 342 n.

*preservation* 666 n.
**desideratum**
*requirement* 627 n.
*desired object* 859 n.
**design**
*prototype* 23 n.
*composition* 56 n.
*production* 164 n.
*form* 243 n.
*representation* 551 n.
*picture* 553 n.
*intend* 617 vb.
*plan* 623 n., vb.
*undertaking* 672 n.
*pattern* 844 n.
**designate**
*specify* 80 vb.
*subsequent* 120 adj.
*future* 124 adj.
*mark* 547 vb.
*chosen* 605 adj.
*select* 605 vb.
**designation**
*classification* 77 n.
*name* 561 n.
*nomenclature* 561 n.
**designed**
*architectural* 192 adj.
*predetermined* 608 adj.
*intended* 617 adj.
**designer**
*producer* 164 n.
*architectural* 192 adj.
*tailored* 228 adj.
*formed* 243 adj.
*artist* 556 n.
*stage manager* 594 n.
*planner* 623 n.
**designer drug**
*drug* 949 n.
**designing**
*hypocritical* 541 adj.
*dishonest* 930 adj.
**designless**
*casual* 159 adj.
*designless* 618 adj.
**desirability**
*choice* 605 n.
*needfulness* 627 n.
*good policy* 642 n.
**desirable**
*advisable* 642 adj.
*contenting* 828 adj.
*desired* 859 adj.
*lovable* 887 adj.
*approvable* 923 adj.
**desire**
*attraction* 291 n.
*fantasy* 513 n.
*will* 595 n., vb.
*motive* 612 n.
*intention* 617 n.
*require* 627 vb.
*request* 761 n., vb.
*suffering* 825 n.
*desire* 859 n.
*desired object* 859 n.

dilation 197 n.
**diathermic**
*heating* 381 adj.
**diathesis**
*ill health* 651 n.
**diatonic scale**
*key* 410 n.
**diatribe**
*oration* 579 n.
*censure* 924 n.
**diazepam**
*drug* 658 n.
**dibber**
*farm tool* 370 n.
**dibble**
*perforator* 263 n.
*implant* 303 vb.
*farm tool* 370 n.
*cultivate* 370 vb.
**dice**
*cut* 46 vb.
*oracle* 511 n.
*gamble* 618 vb.
*gambling game* 837 n.
– with death
*face danger* 661 vb.
*be rash* 857 vb.
**dicer**
*gambler* 618 n.
*player* 837 n.
**dicer's oath**
*unreliability* 474 n.
*untruth* 543 n.
**dicey**
*casual* 159 adj.
*speculative* 618 adj.
*dangerous* 661 adj.
**dichotomy**
*disunion* 46 n.
*bisection* 92 n.
**dichromatic**
*variegated* 437 adj.
*dim-sighted* 440 adj.
**dick**
*detective* 459 n.
**dicker**
*bargain* 791 vb.
**Dick Turpin**
*robber* 789 n.
**dicky, dickey**
*seat* 218 n.
*garment* 228 n.
*unsafe* 661 adj.
**Dictaphone**
*hearing instrument*
415 n.
*recording instrument*
549 n.
**dictate**
*speak* 579 vb.
*necessitate* 596 vb.
*direct* 689 vb.
*advise* 691 vb.
*dominate* 733 vb.
*rule* 733 vb.
*decree* 737 n.
*compel* 740 vb.

**dictation**
*teaching* 534 n.
*no choice* 606 n.
*command* 737 n.
**dictator**
*tyrant* 735 n.
*autocrat* 741 n.
**dictatorial**
*narrow-minded* 481 adj.
*volitional* 595 adj.
*directing* 689 adj.
*authoritative* 733 adj.
*authoritarian* 735 adj.
*commanding* 737 adj.
*compelling* 740 adj.
*insolent* 878 adj.
**dictatorship**
*directorship* 689 n.
*despotism* 733 n.
*brute force* 735 n.
**diction**
*meaning* 514 n.
*phrase* 563 n.
*style* 566 n.
**dictionary**
*word list* 87 n.
*dictionary* 559 n.
*reference book* 589 n.
*collection* 632 n.
**Dictograph (tdmk)**
*hearing instrument*
415 n.
**dictum**
*maxim* 496 n.
*affirmation* 532 n.
*speech* 579 n.
**didactic**
*educational* 534 adj.
*advising* 691 adj.
**diddle**
*deceive* 542 vb.
*defraud* 788 vb.
**diddled**
*gullible* 544 adj.
**diddler**
*trickster* 545 n.
*defrauder* 789 n.
**didicoi**
*wanderer* 268 n.
**die**
*mould* 23 n.
*end* 69 vb.
*die* 361 vb.
*printing* 555 n.
*gambling* 618 n.
– away
*shade off* 27 vb.
*decrease* 37 vb.
*cease* 145 vb.
*sound faint* 401 vb.
– down
*be quiescent* 266 vb.
*extinguish* 382 vb.
– fighting
*perish* 361 vb.
*stand firm* 599 vb.
– for

*desire* 859 vb.
*be in love* 887 vb.
*be disinterested* 931 vb.
– in harness
*perish* 361 vb.
*persevere* 600 vb.
– in one's sins
*be impenitent* 940 vb.
– out
*pass away* 2 vb.
*end* 69 vb.
*perish* 361 vb.
– the death
*perish* 361 vb.
*be punished* 963 vb.
**dieback**
*blight* 659 n.
**died out**
*extinct* 2 adj.
*past* 125 adj.
**diehard**
*stamina* 600 n.
*obstinate person* 602 n.
*malcontent* 829 n.
**diesel engine**
*locomotive* 274 n.
*machine* 630 n.
**diesel oil**
*propellant* 287 n.
*fuel* 385 n.
**Dies irae**
*obsequies* 364 n.
**dies non**
*neverness* 109 n.
**diet**
*make smaller* 198 vb.
*make thin* 206 vb.
*dieting* 301 n.
*therapy* 658 n.
*council* 692 n.
*be temperate* 942 vb.
*starve* 946 vb.
**dieter**
*abstainer* 942 n.
**dietician, dietitian**
*dieting* 301 n.
*doctor* 658 n.
**differ**
*differ* 15 vb.
*quarrel* 709 vb.
**difference**
*unrelatedness* 10 n.
*contrariety* 14 n.
*difference* 15 n.
*dissimilarity* 19 n.
*disagreement* 25 n.
*inequality* 29 n.
*remainder* 41 n.
*change* 143 n.
*divergence* 294 n.
*discrimination* 463 n.
*dissent* 489 n.
*dissension* 709 n.
*schism* 978 n.
**different**
*different* 15 adj.
*nonuniform* 17 adj.

*superior* 34 adj.
*extraneous* 59 adj.
*special* 80 adj.
*multiform* 82 adj.
*converted* 147 adj.
*changeful* 152 adj.
**different ball game**
*variant* 15 n.
**differentiae**
*speciality* 80 n.
**differential**
*difference* 15 n.
*degree* 27 n.
*numerical element* 85 n.
*earnings* 771 n.
**differential calculus**
*mathematics* 86 n.
**differentiate**
*differentiate* 15 vb.
*set apart* 46 vb.
*specify* 80 vb.
*discriminate* 463 vb.
**differently abled**
*disabled* 163 n.
**difficult**
*impracticable* 470 adj.
*puzzling* 517 adj.
*unclear* 568 adj.
*laborious* 682 adj.
*difficult* 700 adj.
*hindering* 702 adj.
*disobedient* 738 adj.
*fastidious* 862 adj.
*ungracious* 885 adj.
*sullen* 893 adj.
**difficulty**
*complexity* 61 n.
*unintelligibility* 517 n.
*enigma* 530 n.
*imperspicuity* 568 n.
*difficulty* 700 n.
*obstacle* 702 n.
*adversity* 731 n.
*suffering* 825 n.
**diffidence**
*nervousness* 854 n.
*modesty* 874 n.
**diffident**
*doubting* 474 adj.
**diffraction**
*dispersion* 75 n.
*reflection* 417 n.
**diffuse**
*disperse* 75 vb.
*generalize* 79 vb.
*publish* 528 vb.
*diffuse* 570 adj.
**diffuseness**
*diffuseness* 570 n.
*loquacity* 581 n.
**diffusion**
*dispersion* 75 n.
*presence* 189 n.
*transference* 272 n.
*ingress* 297 n.
*information* 524 n.
**diffusive**

*prolix* 570 adj.
**dig**
 *antiquity* 125 n.
 *excavation* 255 n.
 *make concave* 255 vb.
 *knock* 279 n.
 *cultivate* 370 vb.
 *search* 459 n., vb.
 *understand* 516 vb.
 *work* 682 vb.
 *reproach* 924 n.
 – a pit for
 *plot* 623 vb.
 *be cunning* 698 vb.
 – for
 *search* 459 vb.
 *pursue* 619 vb.
 – in
 *place oneself* 187 vb.
 *stand firm* 599 vb.
 *seek safety* 660 vb.
 *defend* 713 vb.
 *give battle* 718 vb.
 – one's nails in
 *retain* 778 vb.
 – one's toes/heels in
 *stay* 144 vb.
 *stand firm* 599 vb.
 *oppose* 704 vb.
 – out
 *make concave* 255 vb.
 *extract* 304 vb.
 – up
 *extract* 304 vb.
 *exhume* 364 vb.
 *be curious* 453 vb.
 *discover* 484 vb.
 – up the past
 *look back* 125 vb.
 *retrospect* 505 vb.
**dig at**
 *contempt* 922 n.
 *calumny* 926 n.
**digest**
 *arrangement* 62 n.
 *class* 62 vb.
 *modify* 143 vb.
 *absorb* 299 vb.
 *eat* 301 vb.
 *meditate* 449 vb.
 *be attentive* 455 vb.
 *literature* 557 n.
 *compendium* 592 n.
 *knuckle under* 721 vb.
 *be patient* 823 vb.
**digestible**
 *edible* 301 adj.
**digestion**
 *reception* 299 n.
 *eating* 301 n.
**digestive**
 *remedial* 658 adj.
**digger**
 *excavator* 255 n.
 *gardener* 370 n.
**Digger**
 *agitator* 738 n.

**dig in the ribs**
 *gesture* 547 n.
**digit**
 *number* 85 n.
 *feeler* 378 n.
**digital**
 *numerical* 85 adj.
 *computerized* 86 adj.
 *handed* 378 adj.
**digital clock**
 *timekeeper* 117 n.
**digital computer**
 *computer* 86 n.
**digital music player**
 *record player* 414 n.
**digital video disc**
 *computing* 86 n.
 *recording instrument*
  549 n.
**dignification**
 *dignification* 866 n.
**dignified**
 *elegant* 575 adj.
 *authoritative* 733 adj.
 *impressive* 821 adj.
 *tasteful* 846 adj.
 *well-bred* 848 adj.
 *worshipful* 866 adj.
 *proud* 871 adj.
 *formal* 875 adj.
 *courteous* 884 adj.
**dignify**
 *dignify* 866 vb.
**dignitary**
 *officer* 741 n.
 *aristocrat* 868 n.
 *ecclesiarch* 986 n.
**dignity**
 *elegance* 575 n.
 *conduct* 688 n.
 *authority* 733 n.
 *good taste* 846 n.
 *etiquette* 848 n.
 *honours* 866 n.
 *prestige* 866 n.
 *pride* 871 n.
 *formality* 875 n.
 *ostentation* 875 n.
**digraph**
 *spoken letter* 558 n.
**digress**
 *deviate* 282 vb.
 *be inattentive* 456 vb.
 *be diffuse* 570 vb.
**digression**
 *deviation* 282 n.
 *pleonasm* 570 n.
 *circuit* 626 n.
**digressive**
 *unrelated* 10 adj.
**digs**
 *quarters* 192 n.
**dike, dyke**
 *gap* 201 n.
 *fence* 235 n.
 *furrow* 262 n.
 *rock* 344 n.

*lake* 346 n.
 *conduit* 351 n.
 *obstacle* 702 n.
 *defences* 713 n.
 See also **dyke**
**diktat**
 *decree* 737 n.
**dilapidated**
 *antiquated* 127 adj.
 *weakened* 163 adj.
 *dirty* 649 adj.
 *unsafe* 661 adj.
 *used* 673 adj.
 *beggarly* 801 adj.
**dilapidation**
 *decay* 51 n.
 *destruction* 165 n.
 *dilapidation* 655 n.
**dilatation and cur-
   ettage**
 *surgery* 658 n.
**dilate**
 *grow* 36 vb.
 *expand* 197 vb.
 *be diffuse* 570 vb.
**dilation**
 *increase* 36 n.
 *dilation* 197 n.
 *convexity* 253 n.
 *diffuseness* 570 n.
**dilatory**
 *late* 136 adj.
 *slow* 278 adj.
 *lazy* 679 adj.
**dildo**
 *sexual intercourse* 45 n.
 *sexual pleasure* 376 n.
**dilemma**
 *circumstance* 8 n.
 *dubiety* 974 n.
 *argumentation* 475 n.
 *choice* 605 n.
 *predicament* 700 n.
**dilettante**
 *dabbling* 491 adj.
 *collector* 492 n.
 *dabbler* 493 n.
 *people of taste* 846 n.
 *desirer* 859 n.
**diligence**
 *stagecoach* 274 n.
 *attention* 455 n.
 *carefulness* 457 n.
 *assiduity* 678 n.
 *observance* 768 n.
**diligent**
 *studious* 536 adj.
**dill**
 *herb* 301 n.
**dill water**
 *purgative* 658 n.
**dilly-dally**
 *be late* 136 vb.
 *be irresolute* 601 vb.
 *be inactive* 679 vb.
**dilute**
 *weaken* 163 vb.

*rarefy* 325 vb.
 *add water* 339 vb.
 *moisten* 341 vb.
**dim**
 *darken* 418 vb.
 *dim* 419 adj.
 *bedim* 419 vb.
 *decolorize* 426 vb.
 *blur* 440 vb.
 *indistinct* 444 adj.
 *unintelligent* 499 adj.
 *puzzling* 517 adj.
**dime**
 *small coin* 33 n.
 *coinage* 797 n.
**dimension**
 *quantity* 26 n.
 *measure* 183 n.
 *appearance* 445 n.
**dimensional**
 *formed* 243 adj.
 *metrical* 465 adj.
**dimensions**
 *size* 195 n.
 *metrology* 465 n.
**diminish**
 *abate* 37 vb.
 *render few* 105 vb.
 *moderate* 177 vb.
**diminishing returns**
 *decrease* 37 n.
 *loss* 772 n.
**diminuendo**
 *diminuendo* 37 adv.
**diminution**
 *smallness* 33 n.
 *diminution* 37 n.
 *subtraction* 39 n.
 *decrement* 42 n.
 *contraction* 198 n.
**diminutive**
 *small* 33 adj.
 *little* 196 adj.
 *word* 559 n.
 *name* 561 n.
**dimity**
 *textile* 222 n.
**dimness**
 *darkness* 418 n.
 *dimness* 419 n.
 *invisibility* 444 n.
 *latency* 523 n.
**dimple**
 *cavity* 255 n.
 *notch* 260 n.
 *lowering* 311 n.
**dimpled**
 *fleshy* 195 adj.
**dim sight**
 *dim sight* 440 n.
**dimwit**
 *dunce* 501 n.
**dim-witted**
 *unintelligent* 499 adj.
**din**
 *commotion* 318 n.
 *loudness* 400 n.

*dishonest* 930 adj.
**dishwasher**
  *cleaner* 648 n.
  *cleaning utensil* 648 n.
  *domestic* 742 n.
**dishwater**
  *weak thing* 163 n.
  *swill* 649 n.
**dishy**
  *personable* 841 adj.
**disillusion**
  *disappoint* 509 vb.
  *disclose* 526 vb.
  *dissuade* 613 vb.
  *displease* 827 vb.
  *dejection* 834 n.
  *hatred* 888 n.
**disillusioned**
  *regretting* 830 adj.
  *indifferent* 860 adj.
  *disliking* 861 adj.
**disimprove**
  *harm* 645 vb.
  *deteriorate* 655 vb.
  *impair* 655 vb.
  *aggravate* 832 vb.
**disincentive**
  *dissuasion* 613 n.
  *hindrance* 702 n.
**disinclination**
  *unwillingness* 598 n.
  *dislike* 861 n.
**disincline**
  *dissuade* 613 vb.
  *cause dislike* 861 vb.
**disinfect**
  *make sterile* 172 vb.
  *purify* 648 vb.
  *sanitate* 652 vb.
  *doctor* 658 vb.
  *safeguard* 660 vb.
**disinfectant**
  *cleanser* 648 n.
  *prophylactic* 658 n.
**disinfection**
  *hygiene* 652 n.
**disinfestation**
  *cleansing* 648 n.
**disinflation**
  *finance* 797 n.
**disinformation**
  *information* 524 n.
  *concealment* 525 n.
  *misteaching* 535 n.
  *untruth* 543 n.
  *misrepresentation* 552 n.
**disingenuous**
  *false* 541 adj.
  *dishonest* 930 adj.
**disinherit**
  *not retain* 779 vb.
  *deprive* 786 vb.
  *impoverish* 801 vb.
**disintegrate**
  *break* 46 vb.
  *disunite* 46 vb.
  *separate* 46 vb.

*decompose* 51 vb.
  *be dispersed* 75 vb.
  *pulverize* 332 vb.
  *deteriorate* 655 vb.
**disintegration**
  *decomposition* 51 n.
**disinter**
  *exhume* 364 vb.
  *discover* 484 vb.
**disinterested**
  *benevolent* 897 adj.
  *philanthropic* 901 adj.
  *just* 913 adj.
  *disinterested* 931 adj.
**disinterment**
  *inquest* 364 n.
**disjecta membra**
  *piece* 53 n.
  *dispersion* 75 n.
**disjoin**
  *disunite* 46 vb.
**disjointed**
  *feeble* 572 adj.
**disjunctive**
  *separate* 46 adj.
**disk**
  *See* **disc**
**disk drive**
  *computing* 86 n.
**dislike**
  *unwillingness* 598 n.
  *be unwilling* 598 vb.
  *resistance* 715 n.
  *refuse* 760 vb.
  *dislike* 861 n., vb.
  *enmity* 881 n.
  *hatred* 888 n.
  *hate* 888 vb.
  *disapprobation* 924 n.
  *disapprove* 924 vb.
**disliked**
  *disagreeing* 25 adj.
  *repellent* 292 adj.
  *unsavoury* 391 adj.
  *not nice* 645 adj.
  *unpleasant* 827 adj.
  *unwanted* 860 adj.
  *disliked* 861 adj.
  *hated* 888 adj.
  *wrong* 914 adj.
  *disapproved* 924 adj.
**dislocate**
  *disunite* 46 vb.
  *derange* 63 vb.
  *disable* 161 vb.
  *force* 176 vb.
  *displace* 188 vb.
**dislocation**
  *impairment* 655 n.
**dislodge**
  *derange* 63 vb.
  *displace* 188 vb.
  *eject* 300 vb.
**disloyal**
  *changeful* 152 adj.
  *tergiversating* 603 adj.
  *disobedient* 738 adj.

*nonobservant* 769 adj.
  *inimical* 881 adj.
  *malevolent* 898 adj.
  *undutiful* 918 adj.
  *perfidious* 930 adj.
**dismal**
  *dark* 418 adj.
  *unpleasant* 827 adj.
  *cheerless* 834 adj.
  *melancholic* 834 adj.
**dismantle**
  *break* 46 vb.
  *weaken* 163 vb.
  *demolish* 165 vb.
  *make useless* 641 vb.
  *impair* 655 vb.
  *stop using* 674 vb.
  *make inactive* 679 vb.
**dismantled**
  *unequipped* 670 adj.
**dismay**
  *defeat* 727 vb.
  *worry* 825 n.
  *depress* 834 vb.
  *hopelessness* 853 n.
  *fear* 854 n.
  *frighten* 854 vb.
**dismember**
  *rend* 46 vb.
  *sunder* 46 vb.
  *execute* 963 vb.
**dismemberment**
  *decomposition* 51 n.
**dismiss**
  *exclude* 57 vb.
  *disperse* 75 vb.
  *dismiss* 300 vb.
  *disregard* 458 vb.
  *confute* 479 vb.
  *depose* 752 vb.
  *refuse* 760 vb.
  *not retain* 779 vb.
  *be indifferent* 860 vb.
  *hold cheap* 922 vb.
  – out of hand
  *reject* 607 vb.
**dismissal**
  *valediction* 296 n.
  *ejection* 300 n.
  *loss of right* 916 n.
**dismount**
  *unstick* 49 vb.
  *descend* 309 vb.
**disobedience**
  *disorder* 61 n.
  *disobedience* 738 n.
  *refusal* 760 n.
**disobedient**
  *revolutionary* 149 adj.
  *unwilling* 598 adj.
  *wilful* 602 adj.
  *difficult* 700 adj.
  *opposing* 704 adj.
  *defiant* 711 adj.
  *resisting* 715 adj.
  *anarchic* 734 adj.
  *disobedient* 738 adj.

*nonobservant* 769 adj.
  *sullen* 893 adj.
  *undutiful* 918 adj.
  *disrespectful* 921 adj.
**disobey**
  *be contrary* 14 vb.
  *please oneself* 734 vb.
  *disobey* 738 vb.
  *be insolent* 878 vb.
**disoblige**
  *be malevolent* 898 vb.
**disorder**
  *decompose* 51 vb.
  *disorder* 61 n.
  *derangement* 63 n.
  *derange* 63 vb.
  *discontinuity* 72 n.
  *disperse* 75 vb.
  *amorphism* 244 n.
  *deform* 244 vb.
  *badness* 645 n.
  *uncleanness* 649 n.
  *disease* 651 n.
  *hinder* 702 vb.
  *failure* 728 n.
  *anarchy* 734 n.
  *revolt* 738 n.
**disordered reason**
  *insanity* 503 n.
**disorderly**
  *disorderly* 61 adj.
  *violent* 176 adj.
  *anarchic* 734 adj.
  *riotous* 738 adj.
  *ill-bred* 847 adj.
  *drunk* 949 adj.
**disorderly house**
  *brothel* 951 n.
**disorganize, disor-**
  **ganise**
  *derange* 63 vb.
  *impair* 655 vb.
**disorganized**
  *orderless* 61 adj.
  *lax* 734 adj.
**disorientate**
  *derange* 63 vb.
  *displace* 188 vb.
**disorientated**
  *deviating* 282 adj.
  *doubting* 474 adj.
**disown**
  *negate* 533 vb.
  *avoid* 620 vb.
  *abrogate* 752 vb.
  *not retain* 779 vb.
  *disapprove* 924 vb.
**disparage**
  *underestimate* 483 vb.
  *shame* 867 vb.
  *not respect* 921 vb.
  *hold cheap* 922 vb.
  *detract* 926 vb.
**disparaging**
  *derisive* 851 adj.
  *disapproving* 924 adj.
  *detracting* 926 adj.

*selfish* 932 adj.
**dog-in-the-manger policy**
 *exclusion* 57 n.
**dogma**
 *certainty* 473 n.
 *creed* 485 n.
 *theology* 973 n.
**dogmatic**
 *certain* 473 adj.
 *positive* 473 adj.
 *narrow-minded* 481 adj.
 *credal* 485 adj.
 *assertive* 532 adj.
 *obstinate* 602 adj.
 *theological* 973 adj.
**dogmatist**
 *doctrinaire* 473 n.
 *obstinate person* 602 n.
**do-gooder**
 *volunteer* 597 n.
 *kind person* 897 n.
 *philanthropist* 901 n.
**dogs, fear of**
 *phobia* 854 n. box
**dogsbody**
 *busy person* 678 n.
 *worker* 686 n.
 *auxiliary* 707 n.
 *servant* 742 n.
**dog's breakfast**
 *bungling* 695 n.
**dog-tired**
 *fatigued* 684 adj.
**dogtooth**
 *notch* 260 n.
 *pattern* 844 n.
**dog track**
 *meeting place* 192 n.
 *arena* 724 n.
**dog trot**
 *gait* 265 n.
 *slowness* 278 n.
**dogwatch**
 *period* 110 n.
**doing**
 *production* 164 n.
 *agency* 173 n.
 *representation* 551 n.
 *action* 676 n.
 *doing* 676 adj.
**doings**
 *affairs* 154 n.
 *deed* 676 n.
**doing time**
 *imprisoned* 747 adj.
**doing well**
 *prosperous* 730 adj.
**do-it-yourself**
 *bungled* 695 adj.
 *artless* 699 adj.
**dolce far niente**
 *inaction* 677 n.
 *leisure* 681 n.
**dolce vita**
 *sensualism* 944 n.
**doldrums**

*weather* 340 n.
 *inaction* 677 n.
 *inactivity* 679 n.
 *dejection* 834 n.
**dole**
 *small quantity* 33 n.
 *insufficiency* 636 n.
 *gift* 781 n.
 *portion* 783 n.
 *social care* 901 n.
**doleful**
 *melancholic* 834 adj.
 *lamenting* 836 adj.
**dole out**
 *mete out* 465 vb.
 *give* 781 vb.
 *apportion* 783 vb.
 *pay* 804 vb.
 *be parsimonious* 816 vb.
**doll**
 *dwarf* 196 n.
 *woman* 373 n.
 *image* 551 n.
 *plaything* 837 n.
 *a beauty* 841 n.
**dollar**
 *coinage* 797 n.
**dollar bill**
 *paper money* 797 n.
**dollar diplomacy**
 *trade* 791 n.
**dolled up**
 *beautified* 843 adj.
 *bedecked* 844 adj.
**doll oneself up**
 *be vain* 873 vb.
**dollop**
 *piece* 53 n.
 *portion* 783 n.
**doll's house**
 *plaything* 837 n.
**dolly bird**
 *a beauty* 841 n.
**dolmen**
 *tomb* 364 n.
 *monument* 548 n.
**dolorous**
 *paining* 827 adj.
**dolour**
 *sorrow* 825 n.
 *suffering* 825 n.
**dolphin**
 *mammal* 365 n.
**dolt**
 *dunce* 501 n.
**doltish**
 *unintelligent* 499 adj.
**Dom**
 *church title* 986 n.
**domain**
 *classification* 77 n.
 *territory* 184 n.
 *Internet* 531 n.
 *function* 622 n.
 *lands* 777 n.
**dome**
 *building* 164 n.

*house* 192 n.
 *high structure* 209 n.
 *head* 213 n.
 *roof* 226 n.
 *sphere* 252 n.
 *dome* 253 n.
**Domesday Book**
 *list* 87 n.
**domestic**
 *native* 191 adj.
 *provincial* 192 adj.
 *interior* 224 adj.
 *animal* 365 adj.
 *tamed* 369 adj.
 *domestic* 742 n.
 *unsociable* 883 adj.
**domesticate**
 *break in* 369 vb.
 *habituate* 610 vb.
**domesticated**
 *located* 187 adj.
 *native* 191 adj.
 *tamed* 369 adj.
**domesticity**
 *unsociability* 883 n.
**domestic science**
 *cookery* 301 n.
**domestic service**
 *service* 745 n.
**domestic violence**
 *violence* 176 n.
 *misuse* 675 n.
**domicile**
 *abode* 192 n.
**domiciled**
 *residing* 192 adj.
**domiciliary**
 *native* 191 adj.
**dominance**
 *influence* 178 n.
**dominant**
 *supreme* 34 adj.
 *influential* 178 adj.
 *musical note* 410 n.
 *authoritative* 733 adj.
**dominant charac-
 teristic**
 *speciality* 80 n.
**dominate**
 *be able* 160 vb.
 *influence* 178 vb.
 *prevail* 178 vb.
 *be high* 209 vb.
 *dominate* 733 vb.
 *subjugate* 745 vb.
**domination**
 *superiority* 34 n.
 *influence* 178 n.
 *governance* 733 n.
**domineering**
 *authoritarian* 735 adj.
 *oppressive* 735 adj.
 *insolent* 878 adj.
**Dominican**
 *monk* 986 n.
**dominie**
 *teacher* 537 n.

**dominion**
 *territory* 184 n.
 *governance* 733 n.
 *political organization* 733 n.
 *lands* 777 n.
**domino**
 *cloak* 228 n.
 *disguise* 527 n.
**domino effect**
 *continuity* 71 n.
**dominoes**
 *indoor game* 837 n.
**domino theory**
 *continuity* 71 n.
**don**
 *wear* 228 vb.
 *male* 372 n.
 *scholar* 492 n.
 *teacher* 537 n.
 *aristocrat* 868 n.
 *title* 870 n.
**donate**
 *give* 781 vb.
 *expend* 806 vb.
**donation**
 *transference* 272 n.
 *economic aid* 703 n.
 *gift* 781 n.
**Donatist**
 *heretic* 977 n.
**done**
 *past* 125 adj.
 *usual* 610 adj.
 *completed* 725 adj.
 *fashionable* 848 adj.
**done, be**
 *pay too much* 811 vb.
**done for**
 *destroyed* 165 adj.
 *dying* 361 adj.
 *defeated* 728 adj.
**done in/up**
 *deteriorated* 655 adj.
 *fatigued* 684 adj.
**done thing**
 *practice* 610 n.
 *etiquette* 848 n.
**done to a turn**
 *culinary* 301 adj.
 *savoury* 390 adj.
**done up to the nines**
 *beautified* 843 adj.
**done with**
 *disused* 674 adj.
**donjon**
 *fort* 713 n.
**Don Juan**
 *lover* 887 n.
 *libertine* 952 n.
**donkey**
 *beast of burden* 273 n.
 *fool* 501 n.
**donkey's years**
 *long duration* 113 n.
**donkeywork**
 *labour* 682 n.

**donna**
  *lady* 373 n.
**donnish**
  *narrow-minded* 481 adj.
  *instructed* 490 adj.
  *severe* 735 adj.
  *fastidious* 862 adj.
**Donnybrook**
  *turmoil* 61 n.
**donor**
  *propagation* 167 n.
  *provider* 633 n.
  *giver* 781 n.
  *good giver* 813 n.
**do-nothing**
  *nonactive* 677 adj.
  *lazy* 679 adj.
**Don Quixote**
  *crank* 504 n.
  *visionary* 513 n.
  *brave person* 855 n.
**don't-care**
  *rash* 857 adj.
  *indifferent* 860 adj.
**don't know**
  *changeable thing* 152 n.
  *uncertainty* 474 n.
  *no choice* 606 n.
  *choiceless* 606 adj.
  *moderate* 625 n.
  *neutral* 625 adj.
  *independence* 744 n.
**doodad**
  *bauble* 639 n.
**doodah**
  *tool* 630 n.
**doodle**
  *be inattentive* 456 vb.
  *picture* 553 n.
**doodlebug**
  *bomb* 723 n.
**doohickey**
  *tool* 630 n.
**doom**
  *finality* 69 n.
  *predestine* 155 vb.
  *ruin* 165 n.
  *death* 361 n.
  *fate* 596 n.
  *condemnation* 961 n.
  *punishment* 963 n.
**doomed**
  *ephemeral* 114 adj.
  *destroyed* 165 adj.
  *dying* 361 adj.
  *fated* 596 adj.
  *unfortunate* 731 adj.
  *unhappy* 825 adj.
**doom merchant**
  *overestimation* 482 n.
  *oracle* 511 n.
  *alarmist* 854 n.
**doomsday**
  *future state* 124 n.
**doomster**
  *overestimation* 482 n.
  *oracle* 511 n.

*moper* 834 n.
  *alarmist* 854 n.
**doomwatch**
  *surveillance* 457 n.
**doomwatcher**
  *oracle* 511 n.
  *moper* 834 n.
  *alarmist* 854 n.
**door**
  *threshold* 234 n.
  *barrier* 235 n.
  *doorway* 263 n.
  *stopper* 264 n.
  *way in* 297 n.
  *access* 624 n.
**doorbell**
  *signal* 547 n.
**do-or-die**
  *rash* 857 adj.
**door in one's face**
  *closure* 264 n.
**door jamb**
  *pillar* 218 n.
  *doorway* 263 n.
**doorkeeper**
  *doorkeeper* 264 n.
**doorknob**
  *opener* 263 n.
**door knocker**
  *hammer* 279 n.
  *signal* 547 n.
**doorman**
  *doorkeeper* 264 n.
**doormat**
  *weakling* 163 n.
  *floor-cover* 226 n.
  *cleaning utensil* 648 n.
  *submission* 721 n.
  *coward* 856 n.
  *toady* 879 n.
**doorstep**
  *doorway* 263 n.
  *beg* 761 vb.
  *torment* 827 vb.
**doorway**
  *entrance* 68 n.
  *doorway* 263 n.
  *way in* 297 n.
  *access* 624 n.
**doo-wop**
  *music* 412 n.
  *musical* 412 adj.
**dope**
  *anaesthetic* 375 n.
  *render insensible* 375 vb.
  *ninny* 501 n.
  *information* 524 n.
  *drug* 658 n.
  *doctor* 658 vb.
  *poison* 659 n.
  *make inactive* 679 vb.
  *drug* 949 n.
**doped**
  *insensible* 375 adj.
  *drugged* 949 adj.
**dope fiend**
  *maladjusted* 504 n.

*habitué* 610 n.
  *drug-taker* 949 n.
**dope-peddler**
  *drug-taking* 949 n.
**dopey, dopy**
  *foolish* 499 adj.
  *inactive* 679 adj.
  *sleepy* 679 adj.
**doppelgänger**
  *analogue* 18 n.
  *ghost* 970 n.
**Doppler effect**
  *displacement* 188 n.
**Doric**
  *dialectal* 560 adj.
  *ornamental* 844 adj.
**dormancy**
  *inaction* 677 n.
**dormant**
  *inert* 175 adj.
  *quiescent* 266 adj.
  *latent* 523 adj.
  *abrogated* 752 adj.
**dormitory**
  *quarters* 192 n.
  *room* 194 n.
**dormitory suburb**
  *district* 184 n.
**dormitory town**
  *housing* 192 n.
**Dormobile (tdmk)**
  *small house* 192 n.
  *car* 274 n.
**dormouse**
  *mammal* 365 n.
  *idler* 679 n.
**dorp**
  *housing* 192 n.
**dorsal**
  *back* 238 adj.
**dose**
  *finite quantity* 26 n.
  *measurement* 465 n.
  *medicine* 658 n.
  *portion* 783 n.
  *punishment* 963 n.
**doss down**
  *dwell* 192 vb.
  *sleep* 679 vb.
**dosshouse**
  *inn* 192 n.
**dossier**
  *information* 524 n.
  *record* 548 n.
**dot**
  *small thing* 33 n.
  *place* 185 n.
  *mottling* 437 n.
  *punctuation* 547 n.
  *mark* 547 vb.
  *lettering* 586 n.
  *dower* 777 n.
  *pattern* 844 n.
- the i's and cross the t's
  *be careful* 457 vb.
  *emphasize* 532 vb.
**dotage**

*old age* 131 n.
  *folly* 499 n.
  *mental disorder* 503 n.
**dotard**
  *old man* 133 n.
**dotcom**
  *Internet* 531 n.
  *business* 622 n.
  *corporation* 708 n.
**dote**
  *be credulous* 487 vb.
  *be foolish* 499 vb.
  *be insane* 503 vb.
  *be in love* 887 vb.
- on
  *desire* 859 vb.
**dottle**
  *leavings* 41 n.
  *tobacco* 388 n.
**dotty**
  *foolish* 499 adj.
  *crazy* 503 adj.
**double**
  *identity* 13 n.
  *analogue* 18 n.
  *augment* 36 vb.
  *dual* 90 adj.
  *double* 91 vb.
  *substitute* 150 n.
  *invigorate* 174 vb.
  *enlarge* 197 vb.
  *fold* 261 vb.
  *gait* 265 n.
  *speeding* 277 n.
  *turn back* 286 vb.
  *spirit* 447 n.
  *equivocal* 518 adj.
  *hypocritical* 541 adj.
  *representation* 551 n.
- up
  *disable* 161 vb.
  *fatigue* 684 vb.
  *laugh* 835 vb.
**double agent**
  *secret service* 459 n.
  *deceiver* 545 n.
**double-barrelled**
  *dual* 90 adj.
**double bass**
  *viol* 414 n.
**double-blind test**
  *experiment* 461 n.
**double-breasted**
  *tailored* 228 adj.
**double-check**
  *make certain* 473 vb.
**double chin**
  *bulk* 195 n.
**double-cross**
  *deceive* 542 vb.
  *be cunning* 698 vb.
  *be dishonest* 930 vb.
**double-crosser**
  *deceiver* 545 n.
  *slyboots* 698 n.
  *perfidy* 930 n.
**double-dealing**

*ignorant* 491 adj.
*unintelligent* 499 adj.
*voiceless* 578 adj.
*wondering* 864 adj.
**dumbfound**
*surprise* 508 vb.
*disappoint* 509 vb.
*make mute* 578 vb.
*be wonderful* 864 vb.
**dumbing down**
*change* 143 n.
*regression* 286 n.
*facility* 701 n.
**dumb show**
*gesture* 547 n.
*representation* 551 n.
*drama* 594 n.
**dumbwaiter**
*cabinet* 194 n.
*lifter* 310 n.
**dummy**
*copy* 22 n.
*prototype* 23 n.
*substituted* 150 adj.
*ineffectuality* 161 n.
*stopper* 264 n.
*sham* 542 n.
*image* 551 n.
**dump**
*accumulation* 74 n.
*computerize* 86 vb.
*small house* 192 n.
*storage* 632 n.
*rubbish* 641 n.
*stop using* 674 vb.
*sell* 793 vb.
*cheapen* 812 vb.
**dumpling**
*bulk* 195 n.
*pastries* 301 n.
**dumps**
*dejection* 834 n.
*sullenness* 893 n.
**dumpy**
*fleshy* 195 adj.
*dwarfish* 196 adj.
*short* 204 adj.
*thick* 205 adj.
**dun**
*horse* 273 n.
*dim* 419 adj.
*grey* 429 adj.
*brown* 430 adj.
*demand* 737 vb.
*petitioner* 763 n.
*creditor* 802 n.
*torment* 827 vb.
**dunce**
*ignoramus* 493 n.
*dunce* 501 n.
**dunderhead**
*dunce* 501 n.
**dune**
*small hill* 209 n.
**dung**
*fertilizer* 171 n.
*excrement* 302 n.

*agriculture* 370 n.
*cultivate* 370 vb.
*stench* 397 n.
*dirt* 649 n.
**dungarees**
*trousers* 228 n.
**dungeon**
*cellar* 194 n.
*depth* 211 n.
*darkness* 418 n.
*refuge* 662 n.
*lockup* 748 n.
*prison* 748 n.
**dunghill**
*sink* 649 n.
**dunk**
*drench* 341 vb.
**duo**
*duality* 90 n.
*duet* 412 n.
**duodecimal**
*fifth and over* 99 adj.
**duodecimo**
*miniature* 196 n.
*little* 196 adj.
*edition* 589 n.
**duologue**
*interlocution* 584 n.
*stage play* 594 n.
**dupe**
*credulity* 487 n.
*befool* 542 vb.
*deceive* 542 vb.
*dupe* 544 n.
*loser* 728 n.
*defraud* 788 vb.
*toady* 879 n.
**duped**
*gullible* 544 adj.
**duplex**
*dual* 90 adj.
*double* 91 adj.
*flat* 192 n.
**duplicate**
*identity* 13 n.
*copy* 20 vb.
*duplicate* 22 n.
*double* 91 adj., vb.
*repeat* 106 vb.
*reproduce* 166 vb.
*label* 547 n.
*record* 548 n.
*representation* 551 n.
*be superfluous* 637 vb.
**duplicator**
*imitator* 20 n.
**duplicity**
*concealment* 525 n.
*duplicity* 541 n.
*deception* 542 n.
*sham* 542 n.
*mental dishonesty* 543 n.
*cunning* 698 n.
*affectation* 850 n.
*perfidy* 930 n.
*false piety* 980 n.
**duppy**

*ghost* 970 n.
**durable**
*lasting* 113 adj.
*perpetual* 115 adj.
*permanent* 144 adj.
*unchangeable* 153 adj.
*tough* 329 adj.
**durables**
*merchandise* 795 n.
**duration**
*time* 108 n.
*course of time* 111 n.
*permanence* 144 n.
**durbar**
*council* 692 n.
**duress**
*compulsion* 740 n.
*detention* 747 n.
*restriction* 747 n.
**during**
*while* 108 adv.
**dusk**
*evening* 129 n.
*darkness* 418 n.
*half-light* 419 n.
*dim* 419 adj.
**dusky**
*vespertine* 129 adj.
*dark* 418 adj.
*dim* 419 adj.
*blackish* 428 adj.
**dust**
*minuteness* 196 n.
*overlay* 226 vb.
*let fall* 311 vb.
*lightness* 323 n.
*powder* 332 n.
*soil* 344 n.
*corpse* 363 n.
*obfuscation* 421 n.
*variegate* 437 vb.
*trifle* 639 n.
*rubbish* 641 n.
*clean* 648 vb.
*dirt* 649 n.
**dustbin**
*cleaning utensil* 648 n.
*sink* 649 n.
**dustbowl**
*desert* 172 n.
**dust devil**
*gale* 352 n.
**duster**
*overcoat* 228 n.
*obliteration* 550 n.
*cleaning cloth* 648 n.
**dusting**
*corporal punishment* 963 n.
**dust jacket/cover**
*wrapping* 226 n.
*bookbinding* 589 n.
**dustman**
*cleaner* 648 n.
*worker* 686 n.
**dustpan and brush**
*cleaning utensil* 648 n.

**dustsheet**
*cleaning cloth* 648 n.
**dust thrown in the eyes**
*pretext* 614 n.
*stratagem* 698 n.
**dustup**
*turmoil* 61 n.
*quarrel* 709 n.
*fight* 716 n.
**dusty**
*travelling* 267 adj.
*powdery* 332 adj.
*dry* 342 adj.
*whitish* 427 adj.
*mottled* 437 adj.
*dirty* 649 adj.
**Dutch auction**
*sale* 793 n.
*cheapness* 812 n.
**Dutch cap**
*contraception* 172 n.
**Dutch courage**
*drunkenness* 949 n.
**Dutch oven**
*cauldron* 194 n.
**Dutch treat**
*participation* 775 n.
**Dutch uncle**
*adviser* 691 n.
*tyrant* 735 n.
**dutiable**
*priced* 809 adj.
**dutiful**
*obedient* 739 adj.
*obliged* 917 adj.
*trustworthy* 929 adj.
*virtuous* 933 adj.
**dutifulness**
*obedience* 739 n.
**duty**
*necessity* 596 n.
*motive* 612 n.
*job* 622 n.
*needfulness* 627 n.
*labour* 682 n.
*obedience* 739 n.
*tax* 809 n.
*right* 913 n.
*dueness* 915 n.
*duty* 917 n.
*respects* 920 n.
**duty-bound**
*obliged* 917 adj.
**duty-free**
*nonliable* 919 adj.
**duvet**
*bed* 218 n.
*coverlet* 226 n.
**DVD**
*computing* 86 n.
*recording instrument* 549 n.
**DVT**
*cardiovascular disease* 651 n.
**dwarf**

*land* 344 n.
*mineralogy* 359 n.
**earth-shaking**
*revolutionary* 149 adj.
*influential* 178 adj.
*oscillating* 317 adj.
*important* 638 adj.
*notable* 638 adj.
**earthshine**
*glimmer* 419 n.
**earthwork**
*antiquity* 125 n.
*earthwork* 253 n.
*monument* 548 n.
*defences* 713 n.
**earthworm**
*creepy-crawly* 365 n.
**earthy**
*territorial* 344 adj.
*sensual* 944 adj.
**ear trumpet**
*megaphone* 400 n.
*hearing instrument* 415 n.
**ear tuck**
*beautification* 843 n.
**earwig**
*creepy-crawly* 365 n.
**EASDAQ**
*finance* 797 n.
**ease**
*abate* 37 vb.
*assuage* 177 vb.
*lighten* 323 vb.
*euphoria* 575 n.
*elegance* 575 n.
*leisure* 681 n.
*repose* 683 vb.
*refresh* 685 vb.
*skill* 694 n.
*facility* 701 n.
*disencumber* 701 vb.
*facilitate* 701 vb.
*aid* 703 vb.
*wealth* 800 n.
*happiness* 824 n.
*relieve* 831 vb.
– along
*move slowly* 278 vb.
*propel* 287 vb.
– into place
*insert* 303 vb.
– off/up
*be moderate* 177 vb.
*decelerate* 278 vb.
– oneself
*excrete* 302 vb.
*be relieved* 831 vb.
– out
*depose* 752 vb.
*not retain* 779 vb.
**easel**
*frame* 218 n.
*art equipment* 553 n.
**ease of mind**
*content* 828 n.
**easily aroused**

*sensitive* 819 adj.
**easily deceived**
*credulous* 487 adj.
**easily depressed**
*excitable* 822 adj.
**easily done**
*easy* 701 adj.
**easily pleased**
*content* 828 adj.
**easily provoked**
*excitable* 822 adj.
*irascible* 892 adj.
**easiness**
*possibility* 469 n.
*facility* 701 n.
**east**
*laterality* 239 n.
*compass point* 281 n.
**east and west**
*polarity* 14 n.
*region* 184 n.
**Easter**
*holy day* 988 n. box
**Easter bonnet**
*headgear* 228 n.
**easterly**
*lateral* 239 adj.
**eastern**
*lateral* 239 adj.
*directed* 281 adj.
**Easterner**
*foreigner* 59 n.
**Eastertide**
*spring* 128 n.
*holy day* 988 n. box
**eastward**
*lateral* 239 adj.
**easy**
*sloping* 220 adj.
*comfortable* 376 adj.
*intelligible* 516 adj.
*elegant* 575 adj.
*easy* 701 adj.
*lax* 734 adj.
*lenient* 736 adj.
*inexcitable* 823 adj.
*well-bred* 848 adj.
*friendly* 880 adj.
*sociable* 882 adj.
*amiable* 884 adj.
**easy circumstances**
*wealth* 800 n.
**easy come, easy go**
*transiently* 114 adv.
– 815 int.
**easy-going**
*tranquil* 266 adj.
*willing* 597 adj.
*irresolute* 601 adj.
*tractable* 701 adj.
*lenient* 736 adj.
*permitting* 756 adj.
*inexcitable* 823 adj.
*content* 828 adj.
*indifferent* 860 adj.
**easy-mannered**
*well-bred* 848 adj.

*sociable* 882 adj.
**easy money**
*easy thing* 701 n.
*acquisition* 771 n.
**easy on the eye**
*personable* 841 adj.
**easy on the pocket**
*cheap* 812 adj.
**easy-osy**
*content* 828 adj.
**easy prey**
*dupe* 544 n.
**easy stages**
*slowness* 278 n.
**Easy Street**
*prosperity* 730 n.
**easy terms**
*peace offering* 719 n.
*cheapness* 812 n.
**easy virtue**
*unchastity* 951 n.
**eat**
*absorb* 299 vb.
*eat* 301 vb.
*taste* 386 vb.
*waste* 634 vb.
*gluttonize* 947 vb.
– away
*abate* 37 vb.
*encroach* 306 vb.
*impair* 655 vb.
– crow
*be humble* 872 vb.
– dirt
*knuckle under* 721 vb.
– humble pie
*recant* 603 vb.
*knuckle under* 721 vb.
*be humble* 872 vb.
*be penitent* 939 vb.
– in
*engrave* 555 vb.
– one's fill
*be complete* 54 vb.
*have enough* 635 vb.
– one's hat if
*make impossible* 470 vb.
*negate* 533 vb.
– one's heart out
*be dejected* 834 vb.
– one's words
*recant* 603 vb.
– out of house and home
*fleece* 786 vb.
*gluttonize* 947 vb.
– up
*consume* 165 vb.
*eat* 301 vb.
*appropriate* 786 vb.
**eatable**
*edible* 301 adj.
**eatables**
*food* 301 n.
**eaten up with**
*misjudging* 481 adj.
*crazy* 503 adj.
*with affections* 817 adj.

*sociable* 882 adj.
**eater**
*eater* 301 n.
*reveller* 837 n.
*glutton* 947 n.
**eatery**
*restaurant* 192 n.
**eating and drinking**
*feasting* 301 n.
*sociability* 882 n.
*sensualism* 944 n.
**eating disorder**
*eating* 301 n.
*disease* 651 n.
**eating-house**
*restaurant* 192 n.
**eau de cologne**
*scent* 396 n.
*cosmetic* 843 n.
**eau de toilette**
*scent* 396 n.
**eaves**
*roof* 226 n.
*edge* 234 n.
*projection* 254 n.
**eavesdrop**
*hear* 415 vb.
*be curious* 453 vb.
**eavesdropper**
*listener* 415 n.
*inquisitive person* 453 n.
*informer* 524 n.
**ebb**
*decrease* 37 n., vb.
*revert* 148 vb.
*regress* 286 vb.
*recede* 290 vb.
*flow* 350 vb.
*scarcity* 636 n.
*deterioration* 655 n.
– away
*decrease* 37 vb.
*waste* 634 vb.
**ebb and flow**
*periodicity* 141 n.
*fluctuation* 317 n.
*current* 350 n.
**ebb tide**
*decrease* 37 n.
*lowness* 210 n.
**Ebionite**
*heretic* 977 n.
**ebony**
*tree* 366 n.
*black thing* 428 n.
**e-book**
*Internet* 531 n.
**ebullience**
*stimulation* 174 n.
*moral sensibility* 819 n.
*excitation* 821 n.
**ebullient**
*merry* 833 adj.
**ebullition**
*outbreak* 176 n.
*bubble* 355 n.
*excitable state* 822 n.
**e-business**

*science of forces* 162 n.
**electrotherapy**
  *therapy* 658 n.
**electrotype**
  *copy* 22 n.
  *print* 587 n.
**electrum**
  *a mixture* 43 n.
  *bullion* 797 n.
**electuary**
  *medicine* 658 n.
**eleemosynary**
  *giving* 781 adj.
  *benevolent* 897 adj.
**elegance**
  *elegance* 575 n.
**elegant**
  *apt* 24 adj.
  *stylistic* 566 adj.
  *elegant* 575 adj.
  *well-made* 694 adj.
  *witty* 839 adj.
  *personable* 841 adj.
  *shapely* 841 adj.
  *tasteful* 846 adj.
  *fashionable* 848 adj.
**elegiac**
  *funereal* 364 adj.
  *poetic* 593 adj.
  *lamenting* 836 adj.
**elegy**
  *obsequies* 364 n.
  *poem* 593 n.
  *lament* 836 n.
**element**
  *tincture* 43 n.
  *part* 53 n.
  *component* 58 n.
  *source* 156 n.
  *filament* 208 n.
  *element* 319 n.
  *person* 371 n.
**elemental**
  *intrinsic* 5 adj.
  *simple* 44 adj.
  *beginning* 68 adj.
  *fundamental* 156 adj.
**elementary**
  *simple* 44 adj.
  *beginning* 68 adj.
**elementary particle**
  *element* 319 n. box
**elements, the**
  *weather* 340 n.
  *the sacrament* 988 n.
**elenchus**
  *confutation* 479 n.
**elephant**
  *giant* 195 n.
  *beast of burden* 273 n.
  *mammal* 365 n.
**elephantine**
  *large* 195 adj.
  *unwieldy* 195 adj.
**elevate**
  *make higher* 209 vb.
  *make vertical* 215 vb.

*promote* 285 vb.
*elevate* 310 vb.
*make better* 654 vb.
*delight* 826 vb.
*dignify* 866 vb.
*See also* **elevation**
**elevated**
  *elevated* 310 adj.
  *worshipful* 866 adj.
  *disinterested* 931 adj.
  *virtuous* 933 adj.
  *drunk* 949 adj.
**elevation**
  *height* 209 n.
  *elevation* 310 n.
  *feature* 445 n.
  *map* 551 n.
  *vigour* 571 n.
  *improvement* 654 n.
  *warm feeling* 818 n.
  *excitable state* 822 n.
  *cheerfulness* 833 n.
  *dignification* 866 n.
  *disinterestedness* 931 n.
  *holy orders* 985 n.
**elevation of the Host**
  *Holy Communion* 988 n.
**elevator**
  *conveyance* 267 n.
  *ascent* 308 n.
  *lifter* 310 n.
  *farm tool* 370 n.
**eleven**
  *band* 74 n.
  *over five* 99 n.
  *party* 708 n.
**eleven plus**
  *exam* 459 n.
**elevenses**
  *meal* 301 n.
**eleventh hour**
  *lateness* 136 n.
  *crisis* 137 n.
**elf**
  *dwarf* 196 n.
  *elf* 970 n.
**elfin**
  *little* 196 adj.
  *fairylike* 970 adj.
**elfland**
  *fairy* 970 n.
**elflock**
  *hair* 259 n.
**elicit**
  *cause* 156 vb.
  *extract* 304 vb.
  *discover* 484 vb.
  *manifest* 522 vb.
**eligible**
  *included* 78 adj.
  *marriageable* 894 adj.
**Elijah's mantle**
  *sequence* 65 n.
**eliminate**
  *eliminate* 44 vb.
  *exclude* 57 vb.
  *class* 62 vb.

*render few* 105 vb.
*eject* 300 vb.
*empty* 300 vb.
*extract* 304 vb.
*obliterate* 550 vb.
*reject* 607 vb.
*purify* 648 vb.
*exempt* 919 vb.
**elimination**
  *elimination* 44 n.
  *destruction* 165 n.
**elision**
  *contraction* 198 n.
  *prosody* 593 n.
**elite**
  *superior* 34 n.
  *group* 74 n.
  *type size* 587 n.
  *elite* 644 n.
  *beau monde* 848 n.
  *person of repute* 866 n.
  *upper class* 868 n.
**elitism**
  *government* 733 n.
**elixir**
  *medicine* 658 n.
  *remedy* 658 n.
**Elizabethan Age**
  *past time* 125 n.
  *palmy days* 730 n.
**elk**
  *mammal* 365 n.
**elk, group of**
  *group* 74 n. box
**ellipse**
  *arc* 250 n.
**ellipsis**
  *punctuation* 547 n.
  *grammar* 564 n.
  *imperspicuity* 568 n.
  *conciseness* 569 n.
**elliptic, elliptical**
  *short* 204 adj.
  *round* 250 adj.
  *concise* 569 adj.
**elm**
  *tree* 366 n.
**elocution**
  *pronunciation* 577 n.
  *eloquence* 579 n.
  *oratory* 579 n.
**elocutionist**
  *speaker* 579 n.
**Elohistic**
  *deistic* 965 adj.
**elongate**
  *lengthen* 203 vb.
**elongation**
  *distance* 199 n.
**elope**
  *decamp* 296 vb.
  *run away* 620 vb.
  *escape* 667 vb.
  *wed* 894 vb.
– with
  *take away* 786 vb.
**eloquence**

*vigour* 571 n.
*rhetoric* 574 n.
*eloquence* 579 n.
*loquacity* 581 n.
*inducement* 612 n.
**eloquent**
  *stylistic* 566 adj.
  *forceful* 571 adj.
  *rhetorical* 574 adj.
  *eloquent* 579 adj.
**else**
  *in addition* 38 adv.
**elsewhere**
  *not here* 190 adv.
**elucidate**
  *be intelligible* 516 vb.
  *interpret* 520 vb.
  *manifest* 522 vb.
  *teach* 534 vb.
**elude**
  *mislead* 477 vb.
  *avoid* 620 vb.
  *elude* 667 vb.
  *not observe* 769 vb.
**elusive**
  *impracticable* 470 adj.
  *puzzling* 517 adj.
  *avoiding* 620 adj.
  *escaped* 667 adj.
**elvish**
  *fairylike* 970 adj.
**Elysian fields**
  *the dead* 361 n.
  *mythic heaven* 971 n.
**Elysium**
  *happiness* 824 n.
**em**
  *print-type* 587 n.
**emaciated**
  *lean* 206 adj.
  *underfed* 636 adj.
  *unhealthy* 651 adj.
**emaciation**
  *contraction* 198 n.
**e-magazine**
  *Internet* 531 n.
**e-mail**
  *news* 529 n.
  *telecommunication*
    531 n.
  *Internet* 531 n.
**emanate**
  *result* 157 vb.
  *emerge* 298 vb.
  *be visible* 443 vb.
**emancipation**
  *deliverance* 668 n.
  *freedom* 744 n.
  *independence* 744 n.
  *liberation* 746 n.
**emasculate**
  *abate* 37 vb.
  *subtract* 39 vb.
  *unman* 161 vb.
  *make useless* 641 vb.
**emasculated**
  *impotent* 161 adj.

*feeble* 572 adj.
**embalm**
  *inter* 364 vb.
  *be fragrant* 396 vb.
  *preserve* 666 vb.
**embankment**
  *prop* 218 n.
  *earthwork* 253 n.
  *safeguard* 662 n.
  *obstacle* 702 n.
  *defences* 713 n.
**embargo**
  *quiescence* 266 n.
  *hindrance* 702 n.
  *restraint* 747 n.
  *restrain* 747 vb.
  *prohibition* 757 n.
**embarkation**
  *start* 68 n.
  *departure* 296 n.
**embark on**
  *begin* 68 vb.
  *undertake* 672 vb.
**embarras de choix**
  *choice* 605 n.
  *plenty* 635 n.
**embarras de richesses**
  *greatness* 32 n.
  *productiveness* 171 n.
  *plenty* 635 n.
  *redundance* 637 n.
  *superfluity* 637 n.
**embarrass**
  *be inexpedient* 643 vb.
  *hinder* 702 vb.
  *trouble* 827 vb.
**embarrassed**
  *modest* 874 adj.
**embarrassing**
  *uncertain* 474 adj.
  *difficult* 700 adj.
  *annoying* 827 adj.
**embarrassment**
  *predicament* 700 n.
**embassy**
  *message* 529 n.
  *commission* 751 n.
  *envoy* 754 n.
**embattled**
  *warring* 718 adj.
**embed**
  *place* 187 vb.
  *support* 218 vb.
  *hold within* 224 vb.
  *implant* 303 vb.
**embellish**
  *add* 38 vb.
  *make better* 654 vb.
  *decorate* 844 vb.
**embellishment**
  *ornament* 574 n.
  *ornamentation* 844 n.
**ember**
  *ash* 381 n.
  *lighter* 385 n.
  *glimmer* 419 n.
  *torch* 420 n.

**embezzlement**
  *peculation* 788 n.
**embezzler**
  *defrauder* 789 n.
  *nonpayer* 805 n.
**embitter**
  *impair* 655 vb.
  *hurt* 827 vb.
  *cause discontent* 829 vb.
  *aggravate* 832 vb.
  *excite hate* 888 vb.
  *enrage* 891 vb.
  *huff* 891 vb.
**embittered**
  *biased* 481 adj.
  *discontented* 829 adj.
  *inimical* 881 adj.
  *resentful* 891 adj.
**emblazon**
  *colour* 425 vb.
  *mark* 547 vb.
  *represent* 551 vb.
  *decorate* 844 vb.
**emblazoned**
  *heraldic* 547 adj.
**emblem**
  *insubstantial thing* 4 n.
  *badge* 547 n.
  *indication* 547 n.
  *talisman* 983 n.
**emblematic**
  *representing* 551 adj.
**emblem of authority**
  *badge of rule* 743 n.
**emblem of royalty**
  *regalia* 743 n.
**embodiment**
  *essential part* 5 n.
**embody**
  *combine* 50 vb.
  *contain* 56 vb.
  *comprise* 78 vb.
  *materialize* 319 vb.
  *figure* 519 vb.
  *represent* 551 vb.
**embolden**
  *aid* 703 vb.
  *give courage* 855 vb.
**embolism**
  *closure* 264 n.
  *cardiovascular disease* 651 n.
**embonpoint**
  *bulk* 195 n.
**emboss**
  *be convex* 253 vb.
  *mark* 547 vb.
  *sculpt* 554 vb.
  *decorate* 844 vb.
**embossed**
  *projecting* 254 adj.
**embouchure**
  *orifice* 263 n.
  *flute* 414 n.
**embrace**
  *unite with* 45 vb.
  *contain* 56 vb.

*comprise* 78 vb.
  *surround* 230 vb.
  *circumscribe* 232 vb.
  *enclose* 235 vb.
  *choose* 605 vb.
  *protection* 660 n.
  *retention* 778 n.
  *sociability* 882 n.
  *greet* 884 vb.
  *love* 887 vb.
  *endearment* 889 n.
  *caress* 889 vb.
**embrasure**
  *notch* 260 n.
  *window* 263 n.
  *fortification* 713 n.
**embrocation**
  *unguent* 357 n.
  *balm* 658 n.
**embroider**
  *variegate* 437 vb.
  *cant* 541 vb.
  *exaggerate* 546 vb.
  *decorate* 844 vb.
**embroidery**
  *adjunct* 40 n.
  *art* 551 n.
  *ornament* 574 n.
  *needlework* 844 n.
**embroil**
  *bedevil* 63 vb.
  *make quarrels* 709 vb.
**embroilment**
  *complexity* 61 n.
  *confusion* 61 n.
**embryo**
  *child* 132 n.
  *source* 156 n.
  *undevelopment* 670 n.
**embryology**
  *biology* 358 n.
  *zoology* 367 n.
  *study* 536 n. box
**embryonic**
  *beginning* 68 adj.
  *causal* 156 adj.
  *amorphous* 244 adj.
  *immature* 670 adj.
**emendation**
  *interpretation* 520 n.
  *amendment* 654 n.
  *repair* 656 n.
**emerald**
  *greenness* 434 n.
  *gem* 844 n.
**emerge**
  *begin* 68 vb.
  *result* 157 vb.
  *start out* 296 vb.
  *emerge* 298 vb.
  *flow* 350 vb.
  *be visible* 443 vb.
  *be proved* 478 vb.
  *be disclosed* 526 vb.
**emergence**
  *beginning* 68 n.
  *egress* 298 n.

**emergency**
  *juncture* 8 n.
  *crisis* 137 n.
  *event* 154 n.
  *needfulness* 627 n.
  *danger* 661 n.
  *predicament* 700 n.
**emergency exit**
  *means of escape* 667 n.
**emergency rations**
  *provision* 633 n.
**emeritus**
  *prior* 119 adj.
  *former* 125 adj.
  *resigning* 753 adj.
  *deserving* 915 adj.
**emery paper**
  *sharpener* 256 n.
  *smoother* 258 n.
  *pulverizer* 332 n.
**emetic**
  *ejector* 300 n.
  *expulsive* 300 adj.
  *excretory* 302 adj.
  *unsavoury* 391 adj.
  *purgative* 658 n.
  *remedial* 658 adj.
  *bane* 659 n.
**émeute**
  *revolt* 738 n.
**emigrant**
  *foreigner* 59 n.
  *wanderer* 268 n.
  *egress* 298 n.
**emigration**
  *wandering* 267 n.
  *departure* 296 n.
  *egress* 298 n.
**Emily's list**
  *woman* 373 n.
  *political party* 708 n.
**eminence**
  *greatness* 32 n.
  *superiority* 34 n.
  *height* 209 n.
  *high land* 209 n.
  *prominence* 254 n.
  *elevation* 310 n.
  *importance* 638 n.
  *goodness* 644 n.
  *prestige* 866 n.
**Eminence**
  *church title* 986 n.
**éminence grise**
  *latency* 523 n.
  *deputy* 755 n.
**eminent**
  *remarkable* 32 adj.
  *notable* 638 adj.
  *noteworthy* 866 adj.
**emir**
  *potentate* 741 n.
  *person of rank* 868 n.
**emirate**
  *position of authority* 733 n.
**emissary**

equilibrium 28 n.
**equilibrium**
equilibrium 28 n.
quiescence 266 n.
inexcitability 823 n.
**equine**
equine 273 adj.
animal 365 adj.
**equinoctial**
vernal 128 adj.
autumnal 129 adj.
celestial 321 adj.
**equinox**
uranometry 321 n.
**equip**
dress 228 vb.
find means 629 vb.
provide 633 vb.
make ready 669 vb.
**equipage**
carriage 274 n.
**equipment**
adjunct 40 n.
contents 193 n.
means 629 n.
equipment 630 n.
provision 633 n.
fitting out 669 n.
**equipoise**
equilibrium 28 n.
weighing 322 n.
**equitable**
equal 28 adj.
just 913 adj.
honourable 929 adj.
**equitation**
gait 265 n.
equitation 267 n.
**equity**
indifference 860 n.
justice 913 n.
**equivalence**
identity 13 n.
equivalence 28 n.
connotation 514 n.
**equivalent**
analogue 18 n.
compeer 28 n.
equivalent 28 adj.
offset 31 n.
quid pro quo 150 n.
interpretive 520 adj.
**equivocal**
double 91 adj.
uncertain 474 adj.
puzzling 517 adj.
equivocal 518 adj.
unclear 568 adj.
cunning 698 adj.
dishonest 930 adj.
impure 951 adj.
**equivocalness**
equivocalness 518 n.
concealment 525 n.
mental dishonesty 543 n.
word 559 n.
imperspicuity 568 n.

**equivocation**
sophistry 477 n.
equivocalness 518 n.
falsehood 541 n.
pretext 614 n.
wit 839 n.
**equivocator**
sophist 477 n.
liar 545 n.
**equivoque**
absurdity 497 n.
equivocalness 518 n.
witticism 839 n.
impurity 951 n.
**era**
date 108 n.
era 110 n.
chronology 117 n.
past time 125 n.
**eradicate**
revolutionize 149 vb.
destroy 165 vb.
displace 188 vb.
eject 300 vb.
extract 304 vb.
**erase**
destroy 165 vb.
rub 333 vb.
disappear 446 vb.
obliterate 550 vb.
clean 648 vb.
**Erebus**
darkness 418 n.
classical deities 967 n.
mythic hell 972 n.
**erect**
produce 164 vb.
place 187 vb.
vertical 215 adj.
make vertical 215 vb.
elevated 310 adj.
elevate 310 vb.
honourable 929 adj.
**erection**
building 164 n.
genitalia 167 n.
**eremite**
solitary 883 n.
ascetic 945 n.
**erg**
energy 160 n.
**ergo**
hence 158 adv.
**ergonomics**
exertion 682 n.
**Erinys**
Fury 891 n.
**eristic**
reasoner 475 n.
arguing 475 adj.
**Erl King**
fairy 970 n.
**ermine**
skin 226 n.
heraldry 547 n.
regalia 743 n.
trimming 844 n.

**erode**
abate 37 vb.
decompose 51 vb.
encroach 306 vb.
pulverize 332 vb.
rub 333 vb.
waste 634 vb.
impair 655 vb.
**eroded**
unproductive 172 adj.
**erogenous**
erotic 887 adj.
**Eros**
libido 859 n.
love 887 n.
love god 887 n.
**erosion**
destroyer 168 n.
See also **erode**
**erotic**
erotic 887 adj.
sensual 944 adj.
impure 951 adj.
**eroticism**
libido 859 n.
love 887 n.
unchastity 951 n.
**err**
stray 282 vb.
err 495 vb.
be wicked 934 vb.
**errand**
message 529 n.
job 622 n.
mandate 751 n.
**errandboy**
traveller 268 n.
courier 529 n.
servant 742 n.
**errant**
travelling 267 adj.
deviating 282 adj.
**errata**
edition 589 n.
**erratic**
nonuniform 17 adj.
fitful 142 adj.
unstable 152 adj.
moving 265 adj.
deviating 282 adj.
inexact 495 adj.
crazy 503 adj.
capricious 604 adj.
**erratum**
mistake 495 n.
**erroneous**
unreal 2 adj.
illogical 477 adj.
erroneous 495 adj.
imaginary 513 adj.
heterodox 977 adj.
**error**
deviation 282 n.
misjudgment 481 n.
ignorance 491 n.
error 495 n.
deception 542 n.

inexpedience 643 n.
defect 647 n.
imperfection 647 n.
**ersatz**
simulating 18 adj.
imitative 20 adj.
substituted 150 adj.
spurious 542 adj.
vulgar 847 adj.
**erstwhile**
prior 119 adj.
**eruct**
belch 300 vb.
**eructation**
voidance 300 n.
respiration 352 n.
**erudite**
instructed 490 adj.
studious 536 adj.
**erudite person**
scholar 492 n.
**erudition**
erudition 490 n.
learning 536 n.
**erupt**
be violent 176 vb.
emerge 298 vb.
attack 712 vb.
**eruption**
revolution 149 n.
outbreak 176 n.
egress 298 n.
voidance 300 n.
fire 379 n.
skin disease 651 n.
**escalade**
ascent 308 n.
attack 712 n.
**escalate**
grow 36 vb.
be dear 811 vb.
**escalator**
conveyance 267 n.
carrier 273 n.
conveyor 274 n.
ascent 308 n.
lifter 310 n.
**escalator clause**
qualification 468 n.
**escalope**
meat 301 n.
**escapade**
foolery 497 n.
whim 604 n.
revel 837 n.
**escape**
departure 296 n.
decamp 296 vb.
outflow 298 n.
outlet 298 n.
flow out 298 vb.
disappear 446 vb.
avoidance 620 n.
run away 620 vb.
be safe 660 vb.
seek safety 660 vb.
escape 667 n., vb.

engraving 555 n.
ornamental art 844 n.
**eternal**
existing 1 adj.
infinite 107 adj.
lasting 113 adj.
perpetual 115 adj.
renowned 866 adj.
godlike 965 adj.
paradisiac 971 adj.
**Eternal, the**
the Deity 965 n.
**eternal, be**
be eternal 115 vb.
go on 146 vb.
be remembered 505 vb.
**eternal life**
heaven 971 n.
**eternally**
uniformly 16 adv.
See also **eternal**
**eternal rest**
quietude 266 n.
death 361 n.
heaven 971 n.
**eternal triangle**
jealousy 911 n.
illicit love 951 n.
**eternity**
existence 1 n.
infinity 107 n.
time 108 n.
neverness 109 n.
perpetuity 115 n.
immateriality 320 n.
divine attribute 965 n.
heaven 971 n.
**Etesian winds**
wind 352 n.
**ether, aether**
heavens 321 n.
lightness 323 n.
rarity 325 n.
gas 336 n.
air 340 n.
anaesthetic 375 n.
**ethereal**
immaterial 320 adj.
celestial 321 adj.
**ethereal body**
spiritualism 984 n.
**ethical**
right 913 adj.
ethical 917 adj.
virtuous 933 adj.
**ethical drug**
medicine 658 n.
**ethical investment**
estate 777 n.
expenditure 806 n.
philanthropist 901 n.
right 913 n.
morals 917 n.
**ethical shopping**
purchase 792 n.
philanthropy 901 n.
right 913 n.

morals 917 n.
**ethics**
philosophy 449 n.
study 536 n. box
morals 917 n.
virtue 933 n.
**ethnarch**
governor 741 n.
**ethnic**
ethnic 11 adj.
native 191 adj.
human 371 adj.
**ethnic cleansing**
race 11 n.
slaughter 362 n.
**ethnic group**
race 11 n.
social group 371 n.
**ethnic type**
humankind 371 n.
**ethnography**
anthropology 371 n.
**ethnology**
anthropology 371 n.
study 536 n. box
**ethology**
biology 358 n.
zoology 367 n.
study 536 n. box
morals 917 n.
**ethos**
character 5 n.
conduct 688 n.
**etiolate**
decolorize 426 vb.
**etiolation**
achromatism 426 n.
whiteness 427 n.
**etiquette**
conformity 83 n.
practice 610 n.
etiquette 848 n.
formality 875 n.
courtesy 884 n.
**étourderie**
inattention 456 n.
**étude**
musical piece 412 n.
**etymological**
semantic 514 adj.
linguistic 557 adj.
verbal 559 adj.
**etymology**
source 156 n.
attribution 158 n.
formation 243 n.
connotation 514 n.
study 536 n. box
linguistics 557 n.
etymology 559 n.
**Eucharist**
Holy Communion 988 n.
**eucharistic**
ritual 988 adj.
**eudaemonism**
philosophy 449 n.
enjoyment 824 n.

sensualism 944 n.
**eugenics**
propagation 167 n.
biology 358 n.
**euhemerism**
interpretation 520 n.
irreligion 974 n.
**euhemeristic**
rational 475 adj.
irreligious 974 adj.
**eulogist**
commender 923 n.
**eulogize, eulogise**
honour 866 vb.
shame 867 vb.
praise 923 vb.
**eulogy**
oration 579 n.
description 590 n.
honours 866 n.
praise 923 n.
**Eumenides**
Fury 891 n.
avenger 910 n.
Chthonian deity 967 n.
**eunuch**
eunuch 161 n.
male 372 n.
slave 742 n.
**eupepsia**
health 650 n.
**euphemism**
underestimation
483 n.
trope 519 n.
falsehood 541 n.
ornament 574 n.
good taste 846 n.
affectation 850 n.
flattery 925 n.
prudery 950 n.
**euphemize,**
**euphemise**
moderate 177 vb.
**euphonium**
horn 414 n.
**euphony**
melody 410 n.
elegance 575 n.
**euphoria**
euphoria 376 n.
health 650 n.
repose 683 n.
palmy days 730 n.
excitable state 822 n.
happiness 824 n.
content 828 n.
rejoicing 835 n.
**euphoric**
comfortable 376 adj.
pleased 824 adj.
jubilant 833 adj.
rejoicing 835 adj.
**euphuism**
trope 519 n.
ornament 574 n.
affectation 850 n.

**euphuist**
phrasemonger 574 n.
affecter 850 n.
**Eurasian**
hybrid 43 n.
**eureka!**
– 484 int.
**eurhythmic**
symmetrical 245 adj.
**eurhythmics**
education 534 n.
exercise 682 n.
dancing 837 n.
**euro**
coinage 797 n.
**Eurocentric**
biased 361 adj.
**Eurocheque**
paper money 797 n.
**Eurocrat**
official 690 n.
**Euroland**
society 708 n.
coinage 797 n.
**Euro-MP**
official 690 n.
councillor 692 n.
**European Com-**
**munity**
society 708 n.
**Europeanize, Euro-**
**peanise**
transform 147 vb.
**European Union**
society 708 n.
**Europhile**
enthusiast 504 n.
xenophile 880 n.
commender 923 n.
approving 923 adj.
**Eurosceptic**
opposing 704 adj.
opponent 705 n.
enemy 881 n.
inimical 881 adj.
patriot 901 n.
disapprover 924 n.
**Euroscepticism**
dislike 861 n.
patriotism 901 n.
disapprobation 924 n.
**Eurostar**
train 274 n.
**Eurozone**
society 708 n.
coinage 797 n.
**euthanasia**
decease 361 n.
killing 362 n.
euphoria 376 n.
**Eutychian**
heretic 977 n.
**evacuate**
be absent 190 vb.
decamp 296 vb.
emerge 298 vb.
empty 300 vb.

**evident**
visible 443 adj.
certain 473 adj.
demonstrated 478 adj.
manifest 522 adj.
**evidential**
evidential 466 adj.
**evil**
evil 616 n., adj.
badness 645 n.
harmful 645 adj.
bane 659 n.
misuse 675 n.
adversity 731 n.
suffering 825 n.
wicked 934 adj.
**evildoer**
evildoer 904 n.
bad person 938 n.
**evil-doing**
wickedness 934 n.
**evil eye**
malevolence 898 n.
malediction 899 n.
spell 983 n.
**evil hour**
untimeliness 138 n.
**evil intent**
malevolence 898 n.
**evil omen**
danger signal 665 n.
**Evil One, the**
Satan 969 n.
**evil spirit**
sorcerer 983 n.
**evil star**
misfortune 731 n.
**evince**
evidence 466 vb.
demonstrate 478 vb.
manifest 522 vb.
indicate 547 vb.
**eviscerate**
weaken 163 vb.
empty 300 vb.
extract 304 vb.
impair 655 vb.
**evocation**
causation 156 n.
remembrance 505 n.
representation 551 n.
description 590 n.
**evocative**
meaningful 514 adj.
descriptive 590 adj.
**evoke**
incite 612 vb.
excite 821 vb.
**evolution**
existence 1 n.
numerical operation
    86 n.
conversion 147 n.
event 154 n.
motion 265 n.
progression 285 n.
evolution 316 n.

biology 358 n.
improvement 654 n.
action 676 n.
**evolve**
become 1 vb.
unravel 62 vb.
be turned to 147 vb.
result 157 vb.
produce 164 vb.
generate 167 vb.
extract 304 vb.
evolve 316 vb.
get better 654 vb.
**ewe**
sheep 365 n.
female animal 373 n.
**ewer**
vessel 194 n.
water 339 n.
**ex-**
preceding 64 adj.
prior 119 adj.
former 125 adj.
resigning 753 adj.
**exacerbate**
augment 36 vb.
make violent 176 vb.
impair 655 vb.
hurt 827 vb.
aggravate 832 vb.
excite hate 888 vb.
**exacerbation**
increase 36 n.
exaggeration 546 n.
impairment 655 n.
painfulness 827 n.
**exact**
lifelike 18 adj.
definite 80 adj.
careful 457 adj.
accurate 494 adj.
veracious 540 adj.
perspicuous 567 adj.
concise 569 adj.
demand 737 vb.
compel 740 vb.
observant 768 adj.
levy 786 vb.
impose a duty 917 vb.
**exacting**
fatiguing 684 adj.
difficult 700 adj.
oppressive 735 adj.
discontented 829 adj.
greedy 859 adj.
fastidious 862 adj.
**exaction**
demand 737 n.
compulsion 740 n.
taking 786 n.
tax 809 n.
undueness 916 n.
**exactitude**
carefulness 457 n.
accuracy 494 n.
veracity 540 n.
**exaggerate**

augment 36 vb.
enlarge 197 vb.
overstep 306 vb.
overrate 482 vb.
be absurd 497 vb.
imagine 513 vb.
misinterpret 521 vb.
be untrue 543 vb.
exaggerate 546 vb.
misrepresent 552 vb.
make important 638 vb.
be affected 850 vb.
boast 877 vb.
**exaggerated**
exorbitant 32 adj.
unusual 84 adj.
exaggerated 546 adj.
flattering 925 adj.
**exaggeration**
trope 519 n.
publicity 528 n.
falsehood 541 n.
liar 545 n.
exaggeration 546 n.
rhetoric 574 n.
redundance 637 n.
ostentation 875 n.
**exalt**
elevate 310 vb.
make important 638 vb.
dignify 866 vb.
respect 920 vb.
praise 923 vb.
**exaltation**
joy 824 n.
piety 979 n.
**exalted**
great 32 adj.
noble 868 adj.
**examination, exam**
inspection 438 n.
meditation 449 n.
attention 455 n.
enquiry 459 n.
exam 459 n.
experiment 461 n.
dissertation 591 n.
legal trial 959 n.
**examination paper**
question 459 n.
**examine**
scan 438 vb.
interrogate 459 vb.
estimate 480 vb.
know 490 vb.
try a case 959 vb.
**examinee**
respondent 460 n.
testee 461 n.
beginner 538 n.
contender 716 n.
**examiner**
listener 415 n.
spectator 441 n.
inquisitive person 453 n.
enquirer 459 n.
estimator 480 n.

interlocutor 584 n.
**example**
relevance 9 n.
analogue 18 n.
originality 21 n.
duplicate 22 n.
prototype 23 n.
precursor 66 n.
rule 81 n.
example 83 n.
exhibit 522 n.
warning 664 n.
precept 693 n.
**exasperate**
make violent 176 vb.
aggravate 832 vb.
excite hate 888 vb.
enrage 891 vb.
**ex cathedra**
credal 485 adj.
assertive 532 adj.
affirmatively 532 adv.
**excavation**
antiquity 125 n.
cavity 255 n.
excavation 255 n.
tunnel 263 n.
extraction 304 n.
descent 309 n.
search 459 n.
discovery 484 n.
**exceed**
be great 32 vb.
be superior 34 vb.
grow 36 vb.
outdo 306 vb.
overstep 306 vb.
be intemperate 943 vb.
– requirements
be superfluous 637 vb.
**exceedingly**
extremely 32 adv.
**excel**
be superior 34 vb.
be good 644 vb.
be skilful 694 vb.
have a reputation
    866 vb.
**excellence**
superiority 34 n.
See also **excellent**
**Excellency**
sovereign 741 n.
title 870 n.
**excellent**
great 32 adj.
supreme 34 adj.
notable 638 adj.
excellent 644 adj.
perfect 646 adj.
skilful 694 adj.
pleasurable 826 adj.
splendid 841 adj.
tasteful 846 adj.
wonderful 864 adj.
renowned 866 adj.
virtuous 933 adj.

touch 378 n.
intuition 476 n.
opinion 485 n.
interpretation 520 n.
vigour 571 n.
liberation 746 n.
with affections 817 adj.
feeling 818 n., adj.
excited 821 adj.
love 887 n.
benevolence 897 n.
**feeling for words**
style 566 n.
**feeling no pain**
drunk 949 adj.
**feelings**
affections 817 n.
**feet**
foot 214 n.
conveyance 267 n.
**feet of clay**
weakness 163 n.
defect 647 n.
vulnerability 661 n.
**feign**
dissemble 541 vb.
be affected 850 vb.
**feint**
trickery 542 n.
stratagem 698 n.
**felicitate**
rejoice 835 vb.
congratulate 886 vb.
**felicitous**
apt 24 adj.
elegant 575 adj.
well-made 694 adj.
successful 727 adj.
**felicity**
elegance 575 n.
happiness 824 n.
**feline**
cat 365 n.
animal 365 adj.
cunning one 698 adj.
**fell**
cut 46 vb.
demolish 165 vb.
high land 209 n.
flatten 216 vb.
skin 226 n.
strike 279 vb.
fell 311 vb.
plain 348 n.
deadly 362 adj.
evil 616 adj.
inimical 881 adj.
cruel 898 adj.
**fellatio**
sexual intercourse 45 n.
sexual pleasure 376 n.
**felloe**
edge 234 n.
wheel 250 n.
**fellow**
analogue 18 n.
compeer 28 n.

concomitant 89 n.
male 372 n.
teacher 537 n.
student 538 n.
colleague 707 n.
society 708 n.
low fellow 869 n.
chum 880 n.
**fellow citizen**
native 191 n.
**fellow creature**
person 371 n.
**fellow feeling**
bond 47 n.
cooperation 706 n.
concord 710 n.
participation 775 n.
feeling 818 n.
friendliness 880 n.
love 887 n.
benevolence 897 n.
condolence 905 n.
pity 905 n.
**fellowship**
group 74 n.
association 706 n.
cooperation 706 n.
community 708 n.
friendship 880 n.
sociality 882 n.
**fellow traveller**
assenter 488 n.
collaborator 707 n.
**fellow worker**
personnel 686 n.
colleague 707 n.
collaborator 707 n.
**fell walker**
climber 308 n.
**felly**
edge 234 n.
wheel 250 n.
**felon**
offender 904 n.
**felony**
foul play 930 n.
vice 934 n.
guilty act 936 n.
lawbreaking 954 n.
**felt**
textile 222 n.
weave 222 vb.
felt 818 adj.
**felucca**
sailing ship 275 n.
**female**
female 373 n., adj.
**female animals,**
  **names of**
female animal 373 n.
**female impersonator**
entertainer 594 n.
**feminine**
generic 77 adj.
female 373 adj.
grammatical 564 adj.
**feminine logic**

intuition 476 n.
**femininity**
female 373 n.
**feminism**
female 373 n.
reformism 654 n.
**feminist**
woman 373 n.
reformist 654 n.
**femme fatale**
motivator 612 n.
a beauty 841 n.
**fen**
moisture 341 n.
marsh 347 n.
**fence**
separation 46 n.
partition 231 n.
fence 235 n.
stopper 264 n.
mislead 477 vb.
avoid 620 vb.
protection 660 n.
shelter 662 n.
obstacle 702 n.
defences 713 n.
parry 713 vb.
fight 716 vb.
thief 789 n.
trade 791 vb.
– off
exclude 57 vb.
**fencing**
duel 716 n.
**fender**
furnace 383 n.
shelter 662 n.
**fend for oneself**
come of age 134 vb.
be free 744 vb.
– off
repel 292 vb.
parry 713 vb.
**fenestration**
window 263 n.
**feng shui**
production 164 n.
situation 186 n.
plan 623 n.
**fennel**
herb 301 n.
**feral**
animal 365 adj.
disobedient 738 adj.
unsociable 883 adj.
cruel 898 adj.
**ferment**
turmoil 61 n.
alterer 143 n.
conversion 147 n.
be turned to 147 vb.
stimulation 174 n.
violence 176 n.
commotion 318 n.
effervesce 318 vb.
leaven 323 n.
bubble 355 vb.

be sour 393 vb.
feeling 818 n.
excitation 821 n.
excitable state 822 n.
anger 891 n.
**fermented liquor**
alcoholic drink 301 n.
**fermion**
element 319 n. box
**fern**
plant 366 n.
**ferocious**
furious 176 adj.
cruel 898 adj.
**ferret**
mammal 365 n.
**ferreting**
chase 619 n.
**ferret out**
enquire 459 vb.
discover 484 vb.
**ferrets, group of**
group 74 n. box
**ferroconcrete**
hardness 326 n.
building material 631 n.
**ferrule**
covering 226 n.
**ferry**
voyage 269 vb.
transfer 272 vb.
carry 273 vb.
boat 275 n.
**fertile**
imaginative 513 adj.
profitable 640 adj.
gainful 771 adj.
rich 800 adj.
**fertile soil**
seedbed 156 n.
**fertility**
propagation 167 n.
productiveness 171 n.
plenty 635 n.
**fertility drug**
propagation 167 n.
fertilizer 171 n.
**fertility god**
mythic deity 966 n.
**fertility symbol**
fertilizer 171 n.
**fertilize, fertilise**
make fruitful 171 vb.
invigorate 174 vb.
cultivate 370 vb.
be auspicious 730 vb.
**fertilizer, fertiliser**
propagation 167 n.
fertilizer 171 n.
agriculture 370 n.
**fervent**
hot 379 adj.
forceful 571 adj.
active 678 adj.
hasty 680 adj.
fervent 818 adj.
lively 819 adj.

*excited* 821 adj.
*loving* 887 adj.
*pietistic* 979 adj.
*worshipping* 981 adj.
**fervid**
*hot* 379 adj.
*fervent* 818 adj.
**fervour**
*vigorousness* 174 n.
*warm feeling* 818 n.
**fess, fesse**
*heraldry* 547 n.
**fester**
*be unclean* 649 vb.
*deteriorate* 655 vb.
*hurt* 827 vb.
*be malevolent* 898 vb.
**festering**
*diseased* 651 adj.
*toxic* 653 adj.
**festina lente**
*slowness* 278 n.
*caution* 858 n.
**festival**
*assembly* 74 n.
*festivity* 837 n.
*holy day* 988 n.
**festivals, religious**
*holy day* 988 n. box
**festive**
*amusing* 837 adj.
*celebratory* 876 adj.
*sociable* 882 adj.
**festivity**
*meal* 301 n.
*rejoicing* 835 n.
*festivity* 837 n.
*celebration* 876 n.
*social gathering* 882 n.
**festoon**
*curve* 248 n.
*pattern* 844 n.
*decorate* 844 vb.
**Festschrift**
*reading matter* 589 n.
**fetch**
*analogue* 18 n.
*carry* 273 vb.
*trickery* 542 n.
*cost* 809 vb.
*ghost* 970 n.
– up at
*arrive* 295 vb.
**fetching**
*pleasurable* 826 adj.
*personable* 841 adj.
*desired* 859 adj.
**fete, fête**
*feed* 301 n.
*amusement* 837 n.
*pageant* 875 n.
*celebration* 876 n.
*congratulate* 886 vb.
**feted**
*welcomed* 882 adj.
**fetid**
*unsavoury* 391 adj.

*fetid* 397 adj.
*bad* 645 adj.
*unclean* 649 adj.
**fetish**
*idol* 982 n.
*talisman* 983 n.
**fetishism**
*variance* 84 n.
*idolatry* 982 n.
**fetlock**
*foot* 214 n.
**fetter**
*tie* 45 vb.
*fastening* 47 n.
*make inactive* 679 vb.
*hinder* 702 vb.
*subjugate* 745 vb.
*fetter* 747 vb.
*fetter* 748 n.
**fettered**
*imprisoned* 747 adj.
*captive* 750 adj.
**fettle**
*state* 7 n.
**fettuccine**
*dish* 301 n.
**feu**
*estate* 777 n.
**feud**
*quarrel* 709 n.
*enmity* 881 n.
*revenge* 910 n.
**feudal**
*olden* 127 adj.
*governmental* 733 adj.
*subject* 745 adj.
*proprietary* 777 adj.
**feudalism**
*government* 733 n.
*service* 745 n.
**feuilleton**
*the press* 528 n.
*article* 591 n.
**fever**
*agitation* 318 n.
*beat* 379 n.
*illness* 651 n.
*tropical disease* 651 n.
*restlessness* 678 n.
*excitable state* 822 n.
**fevered**
*frenzied* 503 adj.
**feverish**
*sick* 651 adj.
*hasty* 680 adj.
*fervent* 818 adj.
*excited* 821 adj.
**few**
*inconsiderable* 33 adj.
*few* 105 adj.
*infrequent* 140 adj.
*scarce* 636 adj.
**few, a**
*plurality* 101 n.
*fewness* 105 n.
**few and far between**
*discontinuous* 72 adj.

*unassembled* 75 adj.
*few* 105 adj.
*infrequent* 140 adj.
*seldom* 140 adv.
**few words**
*conciseness* 569 n.
*taciturnity* 582 n.
**fey**
*dying* 361 adj.
*bewitched* 983 adj.
*psychical* 984 adj.
**fez**
*headgear* 228 n.
**fiancé(e)**
*loved one* 887 n.
*lover* 887 n.
**fiasco**
*failure* 728 n.
**fiat**
*decree* 737 n.
**fib**
*be false* 541 vb.
*untruth* 543 n.
**fibber**
*liar* 545 n.
**fibre**
*essential part* 5 n.
*fibre* 208 n.
*textile* 222 n.
*food content* 301 n.
*texture* 331 n.
**fibreglass**
*textile* 222 n.
*materials* 631 n.
**fibrositis**
*pang* 377 n.
*rheumatism* 651 n.
*inflammation* 651 n.
box
**fibrous**
*fibrous* 208 adj.
*tough* 329 adj.
*See also* **fibre**
**fichu**
*neckwear* 228 n.
**fickle**
*transient* 114 adj.
*changeable* 143 adj.
*changeful* 152 adj.
*unreliable* 474 adj.
*tergiversating* 603 adj.
*capricious* 604 adj.
**fickleness**
*irresolution* 601 n.
**fiction**
*product* 164 n.
*idea* 451 n.
*ideality* 513 n.
*falsehood* 541 n.
*untruth* 543 n.
*literature* 557 n.
*novel* 590 n.
**fictional**
*imaginative* 513 adj.
*descriptive* 590 adj.
**fiction-writer**
*author* 589 n.

*narrator* 590 n.
**fictitious**
*unreal* 2 adj.
*insubstantial* 4 adj.
*imaginary* 513 adj.
*untrue* 543 adj.
*descriptive* 590 adj.
*unwarranted* 916 adj.
**fiddle**
*play music* 413 vb.
*viol* 414 n.
*deceive* 542 vb.
*contrivance* 623 n.
*defraud* 788 vb.
*foul play* 930 n.
*be dishonest* 930 vb.
– one's income tax
*not pay* 805 vb.
– with
*modify* 143 vb.
*touch* 378 vb.
**fiddle-faddle**
*silly talk* 515 n.
*trifle* 639 n.
*be inactive* 679 vb.
**fiddlehead**
*coil* 251 n.
*pattern* 844 n.
**fiddler**
*instrumentalist* 413 n.
*trickster* 545 n.
*defrauder* 789 n.
**fiddling**
*trivial* 639 adj.
*laborious* 682 adj.
**fidelity**
*accuracy* 494 n.
*veracity* 540 n.
*loyalty* 739 n.
*observance* 768 n.
*probity* 929 n.
**fidget**
*haste* 680 n.
*be excitable* 822 vb.
**fidgets**
*agitation* 318 n.
*restlessness* 678 n.
*excitability* 822 n.
**fidgety**
*unstable* 152 adj.
*irresolute* 601 adj.
*active* 678 adj.
*excitable* 822 adj.
**fief**
*lands* 777 n.
**field**
*classification* 77 n.
*opportunity* 137 n.
*range* 183 n.
*enclosure* 235 n.
*grassland* 348 n.
*farm* 370 n.
*topic* 452 n.
*heraldry* 547 n.
*hunter* 619 n.
*function* 622 n.
*arena* 724 n.

*be early* 135 vb.
*growth* 157 n.
*product* 164 n.
*progression* 285 n.
*arrive* 295 vb.
*benefit* 615 n.
*utility* 640 n.
*triumph* 727 vb.
*gain* 771 n., vb.
*acquire* 771 vb.
*booty* 790 n.
*get rich* 800 vb.
*receipt* 807 n.
*be rewarded* 962 vb.
– a footing
*prevail* 178 vb.
*place oneself* 187 vb.
– a hearing
*influence* 178 vb.
*be heard* 415 vb.
– ground
*grow* 36 vb.
*progress* 285 vb.
– on/upon
*outstrip* 277 vb.
*progress* 285 vb.
*approach* 289 vb.
*outdo* 306 vb.
– one's affections
*excite love* 887 vb.
– one's confidence
*convince* 485 vb.
– one's end
*succeed* 727 vb.
– power
*be able* 160 vb.
*take authority* 733 vb.
– recognition
*have a reputation*
  866 vb.
– the upper hand
*prevail* 178 vb.
– time
*spin out* 113 vb.
*be early* 135 vb.
*put off* 136 vb.
– weight
*make heavy* 322 vb.
**gainful**
*good* 615 adj.
*profitable* 640 adj.
*gainful* 771 adj.
*rewarding* 962 adj.
**gaining**
*anachronistic* 118 adj.
*inexact* 495 adj.
**gains**
*wealth* 800 n.
**gainsay**
*negate* 533 vb.
**gait**
*gait* 265 n.
*equitation* 267 n.
*way* 624 n.
**gaitered**
*clerical* 986 adj.
**gaiters**

*legwear* 228 n.
*badge of rule* 743 n.
*canonicals* 989 n.
**gala**
*festivity* 837 n.
*pageant* 875 n.
**galactic**
*cosmic* 321 adj.
**Galahad**
*brave person* 855 n.
*honourable person* 929 n.
*virgin* 950 n.
**gala night**
*dramaturgy* 594 n.
**galantine**
*hors-d'oeuvres* 301 n.
**galaxy**
*group* 74 n.
*certain quantity* 104 n.
*star* 321 n.
*island* 349 n.
*luminary* 420 n.
*person of repute* 866 n.
**gale**
*storm* 176 n.
*commotion* 318 n.
*gale* 352 n.
*excitable state* 822 n.
**gale force**
*violent* 176 adj.
*windy* 352 adj.
**Galenic**
*medical* 658 adj.
**galenical**
*medicine* 658 n.
**galère**
*party* 708 n.
**galette**
*pastries and cakes* 301 n.
**galilee**
*church exterior* 990 n.
**galimatias**
*lack of meaning* 515 n.
**gall**
*swelling* 253 n.
*rub* 333 vb.
*give pain* 377 vb.
*sourness* 393 n.
*bane* 659 n.
*torment* 827 vb.
*sauciness* 878 n.
*resentment* 891 n.
*irascibility* 892 n.
*malevolence* 898 n.
**gall and wormwood**
*unsavouriness* 391 n.
*painfulness* 827 n.
*dislike* 861 n.
**gallant**
*fop* 848 n.
*courageous* 855 adj.
*showy* 875 adj.
*courteous* 884 adj.
*lover* 887 n.
*benevolent* 897 adj.
*libertine* 952 n.
**gallantry**

*courage* 855 n.
*wooing* 889 n.
**gall bladder, surgical
  operation on or
  removal of**
*surgery* 658 n. box
**galleon**
*merchant ship* 275 n.
*warship* 722 n.
**gallery**
*lobby* 194 n.
*excavation* 255 n.
*tunnel* 263 n.
*listener* 415 n.
*onlookers* 441 n.
*exhibit* 522 n.
*playgoer* 594 n.
*theatre* 594 n.
*collection* 632 n.
*church interior* 990 n.
**galley**
*room* 194 n.
*galley* 275 n.
*cookery* 301 n.
*press* 587 n.
**galley proof**
*letterpress* 587 n.
**galleys**
*penalty* 963 n.
**galley slave**
*boatman* 270 n.
*busy person* 678 n.
*slave* 742 n.
*prisoner* 750 n.
**galliard**
*dance* 837 n.
**Gallican**
*sectarian* 978 adj.
**Gallicism**
*dialect* 560 n.
**galligaskins**
*trousers* 228 n.
**gallimaufry**
*medley* 43 n.
**gallinaceous**
*animal* 365 adj.
**gallipot**
*vessel* 194 n.
**gallivant**
*wander* 267 vb.
*court* 889 vb.
**gallon**
*metrology* 465 n.
**gallons**
*great quantity* 32 n.
**galloon**
*trimming* 844 n.
**gallop**
*be transient* 114 vb.
*gait* 265 n.
*ride* 267 vb.
*move fast* 277 vb.
**gallop rhythm**
*cardiovascular disease*
  651 n.
**gallows**
*hanger* 217 n.

*means of execution*
  964 n.
**gallowsbird**
*offender* 904 n.
**gallows humour**
*wit* 839 n.
**gallstones**
*digestive disorders* 651 n.
**Gallup poll**
*statistics* 86 n.
*enquiry* 459 n.
*vote* 605 n.
**galoot**
*ninny* 501 n.
*bungler* 697 n.
**galop**
*dance* 837 n.
**galore**
*great quantity* 32 n.
*many* 104 adj.
*plenty* 635 n.
**galumph**
*be clumsy* 695 vb.
**galvanize, galvanise**
*invigorate* 174 vb.
*move* 265 vb.
*incite* 612 vb.
*excite* 821 vb.
**gambade**
*leap* 312 n.
**gambit**
*debut* 68 n.
*attempt* 671 n.
*tactics* 688 n.
**gamble**
*chance* 159 vb.
*be tentative* 461 vb.
*uncertainty* 474 n.
*suppose* 512 vb.
*gamble* 618 vb.
*face danger* 661 vb.
*speculate* 791 vb.
*be rash* 857 vb.
– away
*be prodigal* 815 vb.
– on
*be certain* 473 vb.
**gambler**
*experimenter* 461 n.
*diviner* 511 n.
*gambler* 618 n.
*player* 837 n.
*desperado* 857 n.
**gambling**
*equal chance* 159 n.
*gambling* 618 n.
*gambling game* 837 n.
**gambling den**
*gaming-house* 618 n.
**gamboge**
*yellow pigment* 433 n.
**gambol**
*leap* 312 n., vb.
*enjoyment* 824 n.
*be cheerful* 833 vb.
*amuse oneself* 837 vb.
**gamboller**

*reveller* 837 n.

**game**
*disabled* 163 adj.
*meat* 301 n.
*animal* 365 n.
*savouriness* 390 n.
*trickery* 542 n.
*resolute* 599 adj.
*persevering* 600 adj.
*objective* 617 n.
*gamble* 618 vb.
*chase* 619 n.
*plot* 623 n.
*attempting* 671 adj.
*tactics* 688 n.
*stratagem* 698 n.
*contest* 716 n.
*amusement* 837 n.
*laughingstock* 851 n.
*courageous* 855 adj.

**game at which two
    can play, a**
*retaliation* 714 n.

**game bird**
*table bird* 365 n.

**gamecock**
*contender* 716 n.
*combatant* 722 n.
*brave person* 855 n.

**game for**
*willing* 597 adj.

**gamekeeper**
*animal husbandry* 369 n.
*keeper* 749 n.

**game not worth the
    candle**
*lost labour* 641 n.

**game of cards**
*card game* 837 n.

**game of chance**
*gambling* 618 n.
*amusement* 837 n.

**game park**
*zoo* 369 n.

**game preserve**
*wood* 366 n.
*stock farm* 369 n.

**game reserve**
*zoo* 369 n.
*preservation* 666 n.

**games**
*exercise* 682 n.
*contest* 716 n.
*sport* 837 n.

**gamesmanship**
*sagacity* 498 n.
*tactics* 688 n.
*cunning* 698 n.

**gamesome**
*lively* 819 adj.
*merry* 833 adj.

**gamester**
*gambler* 618 n.

**game warden**
*animal husbandry* 369 n.

**gamin**
*low fellow* 869 n.

**gaming-house**
*gaming-house* 618 n.
*place of amusement*
    837 n.

**gaming machine**
*gambling* 618 n.

**gammadion**
*cross* 222 n.
*talisman* 983 n.

**gamma ray**
*radiation* 417 n.

**gammon**
*meat* 301 n.

**gammy**
*disabled* 163 adj.

**gamp**
*shade* 226 n.

**gamut**
*series* 71 n.
*musical note* 410 n.

**gamy**
*pungent* 388 adj.
*savoury* 390 adj.
*fetid* 397 adj.

**gander**
*bird* 365 n.
*male animal* 372 n.

**gang**
*band* 74 n.
*be in motion* 265 vb.
*party* 708 n.

– agley
*miscarry* 728 vb.

– up
*congregate* 74 vb.
*cooperate* 706 vb.

– up with
*accompany* 89 vb.

**ganger**
*worker* 686 n.
*manager* 690 n.

**gangling**
*unwieldy* 195 adj.
*narrow* 206 adj.
*clumsy* 695 adj.

**ganglion**
*centre* 225 n.

**gangplank**
*bridge* 624 n.

**gangrene**
*decay* 51 n.
*infection* 651 n.
*deteriorate* 655 vb.

**gang rule**
*lawlessness* 954 n.

**gangsta**
*vocal music* 412 n.

**gangster**
*murderer* 362 n.
*robber* 789 n.
*low fellow* 869 n.
*offender* 904 n.

**gang warfare**
*turmoil* 61 n.
*quarrel* 709 n.
*fight* 716 n.

**gangway**

*doorway* 263 n.
*open space* 263 n.
*access* 624 n.
*bridge* 624 n.

**ganja**
*drug* 949 n.

**gannet**
*eater* 301 n.
*bird* 365 n.

**gantry**
*stand* 218 n.
*railway* 624 n.

**gaol, jail**
*prison* 748 n.
*seclusion* 883 n.

**gaoler, jailer**
*doorkeeper* 264 n.
*gaoler* 749 n.

**gap**
*disunion* 46 n.
*incompleteness* 55 n.
*discontinuity* 72 n.
*gap* 201 n.
*concavity* 255 n.
*valley* 255 n.
*opening* 263 n.
*requirement* 627 n.
*defect* 647 n.

**gape**
*space* 201 vb.
*be deep* 211 vb.
*open* 263 vb.
*gaze* 438 vb.
*watch* 441 vb.
*be curious* 453 vb.
*wonder* 864 vb.

**gaping**
*expanded* 197 adj.

**gap year**
*lull* 145 n.
*interval* 201 n.
*leisure* 681 n.

**garage**
*shed* 192 n.
*room* 194 n.
*music* 412 n.
*storage* 632 n.
*store* 632 vb.
*safeguard* 660 vb.

**garage sale**
*sale* 793 n.

**garb**
*dressing* 228 n.
*appearance* 445 n.

**garbage**
*dirt* 649 n.

**garble**
*mislead* 495 vb.
*misinterpret* 521 vb.
*be false* 541 vb.

**garbled**
*incomplete* 55 adj.
*inexact* 495 adj.

**garden**
*seedbed* 156 n.
*arbour* 194 n.
*enclosure* 235 n.

*garden* 370 n.
*cultivate* 370 vb.
*a beauty* 841 n.
See also **gardens**

**Garden**
*philosopher* 449 n.

**garden city**
*district* 184 n.
*housing* 192 n.

**gardener**
*producer* 164 n.
*gardener* 370 n.
*domestic* 742 n.

**garden flat**
*cellar* 194 n.

**gardening**
*agriculture* 370 n.
*ornamental art* 844 n.

**Garden of Eden**
*happiness* 824 n.
*mythic heaven* 971 n.

**garden of remem-
    brance**
*cemetery* 364 n.

**garden of rest**
*cemetery* 364 n.

**garden party**
*amusement* 837 n.
*social gathering* 882 n.

**gardens**
*pleasance* 192 n.
*pleasure ground* 837 n.

**gargantuan**
*huge* 195 adj.

**gargle**
*cleanser* 648 n.
*prophylactic* 658 n.

**gargoyle**
*outlet* 298 n.
*drain* 351 n.
*image* 551 n.
*eyesore* 842 n.
*ornamental art* 844 n.

**garish**
*luminous* 417 adj.
*florid* 425 adj.
*graceless* 842 adj.
*ornamented* 844 adj.
*vulgar* 847 adj.
*showy* 875 adj.

**garland**
*loop* 250 n.
*badge* 547 n.
*anthology* 592 n.
*trophy* 729 n.
*ornamentation* 844 n.
*honours* 866 n.
*celebrate* 876 vb.
*pay one's respects*
    884 vb.

**garlic**
*vegetable* 301 n.
*condiment* 389 n.
*stench* 397 n.

**garment(s)**
*garment* 228 n.
*clothing* 228 n.

**garner**
 *bring together* 74 vb.
 *store* 632 vb.
**garnet**
 *redness* 431 vb.
 *gem* 844 n.
**garnish**
 *adjunct* 40 n.
 *food* 301 n.
 *condiment* 389 n.
 *make appetizing* 390 vb.
 *decorate* 844 vb.
**garniture**
 *dressing* 228 n.
**garret**
 *attic* 194 n.
 *vertex* 213 n.
**garrison**
 *resident* 191 n.
 *protector* 660 n.
 *defender* 713 n.
 *defend* 713 vb.
 *armed force* 722 n.
 *keeper* 749 n.
**garrotte**
 *kill* 362 vb.
 *execute* 963 vb.
 *means of execution*
  964 n.
**garrotter**
 *murderer* 362 n.
 *punisher* 963 n.
**garrulous**
 *disclosing* 526 adj.
 *loquacious* 581 adj.
**garter**
 *fastening* 47 n.
 *compressor* 198 n.
 *legwear* 228 n.
 *badge* 547 n.
 *decoration* 729 n.
 *badge of rank* 743 n.
 *honours* 866 n.
**garter stitch**
 *needlework* 844 n.
**garth**
 *enclosure* 235 n.
**gas**
 *sources of energy* 160 n.
 *lifter* 310 n.
 *rarity* 325 n.
 *gas* 336 n.
 *air* 340 n.
 *murder* 362 vb.
 *anaesthetic* 375 n.
 *render insensible* 375 vb.
 *heater* 383 n.
 *fuel* 385 n.
 *stench* 397 n.
 *empty talk* 515 n.
 *chatter* 581 n.
 *weapon* 723 n.
 *boast* 877 n., vb.
 *execute* 963 vb.
**gasbag**
 *bladder* 194 n.
 *chatterer* 581 n.

 *boaster* 877 n.
**gas chamber**
 *place of slaughter* 362 n.
 *means of execution*
  964 n.
**Gascon**
 *boaster* 877 n.
**gasconade**
 *boast* 877 n.
**gaseous**
 *insubstantial* 4 adj.
 *gaseous* 336 adj.
 *windy* 352 adj.
 *bubbly* 355 adj.
**gas guzzler**
 *car* 274 n.
 *prodigal* 815 n.
**gash**
 *cut* 46 vb.
 *gap* 201 n.
 *notch* 260 n.
 *pain* 377 n.
 *wound* 655 n., vb.
**gasholder**
 *storage* 632 n.
**gasification**
 *vaporization* 338 n.
**gaslight**
 *gas* 336 n.
 *light* 417 n.
 *lighting* 420 n.
**gas main**
 *air pipe* 353 n.
**gas mantle**
 *lamp* 420 n.
**gas mask**
 *safeguard* 662 n.
 *preserver* 666 n.
 *armour* 713 n.
**gasoline**
 *oil* 357 n.
 *fuel* 385 n.
**gasometer**
 *gas* 336 n.
 *storage* 632 n.
**gas oven**
 *furnace* 383 n.
**gasp**
 *breathe* 352 vb.
 *rasp* 407 vb.
 *cry* 408 n., vb.
 *voice* 577 n.
 *be fatigued* 684 vb.
 *wonder* 864 vb.
**gasproof**
 *sealed off* 264 adj.
 *invulnerable* 660 adj.
**gasser**
 *chatterer* 581 n.
**gas shell**
 *missile weapon* 723 n.
**gassy**
 *gaseous* 336 adj.
 *vaporific* 338 adj.
 *windy* 352 adj.
**Gastarbeiter**
 *foreigner* 59 n.

**gastroenteritis**
 *digestive disorders* 651 n.
 *infection* 651 n.
 *inflammation* 651 n.
 box
**gastronomic**
 *culinary* 301 adj.
 *gluttonous* 947 n.
**gastronomy**
 *gastronomy* 301 n.
 *gluttony* 947 n.
**gastroscopy**
 *diagnosis* 658 n.
**gasworks**
 *gas* 336 n.
 *workshop* 687 n.
**gat**
 *pistol* 723 n.
**gate**
 *barrier* 235 n.
 *doorway* 263 n.
 *onlookers* 441 n.
 *obstacle* 702 n.
 *fort* 713 n.
 *imprison* 747 vb.
 *receipt* 807 n.
**-gate**
 *humiliation* 872 n.
**gateau**
 *pastries* 301 n.
**gatecrash**
 *intrude* 297 vb.
 *be sociable* 882 vb.
**gatecrasher**
 *intruder* 59 n.
 *resident* 191 n.
**gatekeeper**
 *doorkeeper* 264 n.
**gate money**
 *receipt* 807 n.
**gate of horn**
 *veracity* 540 n.
 *sleep* 679 n.
**gate of ivory**
 *untruth* 543 n.
 *sleep* 679 n.
**gatepost**
 *doorway* 263 n.
**gates of St Peter**
 *heaven* 971 n.
**gateway**
 *entrance* 68 n.
 *doorway* 263 n.
**gather**
 *join* 45 vb.
 *congregate* 74 vb.
 *expand* 197 vb.
 *fold* 261 n., vb.
 *meet* 295 vb.
 *cultivate* 370 vb.
 *be dark* 418 vb.
 *assume* 471 vb.
 *be informed* 524 vb.
 *store* 632 vb.
 *acquire* 771 vb.
 *take* 786 vb.
 – grapes from thorns

 *attempt the impossible*
  470 vb.
 – momentum
 *accelerate* 277 vb.
 – round
 *congregate* 74 vb.
 – together
 *converge* 293 vb.
 – way
 *be in motion* 265 vb.
 *navigate* 269 vb.
**gathered**
 *tailored* 228 adj.
**gathered to one's
 fathers**
 *dead* 361 adj.
**gatherer**
 *accumulator* 74 n.
**gathering**
 *assembly* 74 n.
 *conference* 584 n.
 *edition* 589 n.
 *ulcer* 651 n.
 *toxic* 653 adj.
**gathering clouds**
 *omen* 511 n.
 *warning* 664 n.
 *adversity* 731 n.
 *threat* 900 n.
 – storm
 *danger* 661 n.
**gating**
 *penalty* 963 n.
**Gatling gun**
 *gun* 723 n.
**gauche**
 *ignorant* 491 adj.
 *foolish* 499 adj.
 *inelegant* 576 adj.
 *clumsy* 695 adj.
 *ill-bred* 847 adj.
**gaucherie**
 *unskilfulness* 695 n.
**gaucho**
 *rider* 268 n.
 *herdsman* 369 n.
**gaudery**
 *finery* 844 n.
**gaudy**
 *florid* 425 adj.
 *graceless* 842 adj.
 *ornamented* 844 adj.
 *vulgar* 847 adj.
 *showy* 875 adj.
**gauge**
 *prototype* 23 n.
 *breadth* 205 n.
 *testing agent* 461 n.
 *gauge* 465 n., vb.
 *estimate* 480 vb.
 *indicator* 547 n.
**gauleiter**
 *tyrant* 735 n.
 *autocrat* 741 n.
**gaunt**
 *unproductive* 172 adj.
 *lean* 206 adj.

*theology* 973 n.

**hagioscope**
*window* 263 n.
*view* 438 n.
*church interior* 990 n.

**hagridden**
*spooky* 970 adj.
*bewitched* 983 adj.

**ha-ha**
*separation* 46 n.
*gap* 201 n.
*fence* 235 n.
*laugh* 835 vb.

**haiku**
*conciseness* 569 n.
*verse form* 593 n.

**hail**
*crowd* 74 n.
*rain* 350 n.
*wintriness* 380 n.
*cry* 408 n., vb.
*assent* 488 vb.
*call* 547 n.
*speak to* 583 vb.
*greet* 884 vb.
*applaud* 923 vb.

**hail-fellow-well-met**
*friendly* 880 adj.
*sociable* 882 adj.

**Hail Mary**
*prayers* 981 n.

**hailstone**
*ice* 380 n.

**hailstorm**
*storm* 176 n.
*wintriness* 380 n.

**hair**
*small thing* 33 n.
*fibre* 208 n.
*filament* 208 n.
*hair* 259 n.
*hairdressing* 843 n.

**hairband**
*girdle* 47 n.

**hairbrush**
*smoother* 258 n.
*cleaning utensil* 648 n.

**haircut, hairdo**
*hairdressing* 843 n.

**hairdresser**
*cleaner* 648 n.
*beautician* 843 n.

**hairless**
*hairless* 229 adj.
*smooth* 258 adj.

**hair of the dog that bit one**
*drunkenness* 949 n.

**hair on end**
*danger signal* 665 n.
*fear* 854 n.

**hairpiece**
*wig* 228 n.
*hair* 259 n.
*hairdressing* 843 n.

**hairpin**
*fastening* 47 n.

**hairdressing** 843 n.

**hairpin bend**
*curve* 248 n.

**hair-raising**
*exciting* 821 adj.
*frightening* 854 adj.

**hair-restorer**
*hairwash* 843 n.

**hair's breadth**
*short distance* 200 n.
*narrowness* 206 n.

**hair shirt**
*asceticism* 945 n.

**hairspace**
*interval* 201 n.
*print-type* 587 n.

**hair-splitting**
*discrimination* 463 n.
*argument* 475 n.
*sophistry* 477 n.
*fastidiousness* 862 n.

**hair spray**
*adhesive* 47 n.
*hairwash* 843 n.

**hairspring**
*machine* 630 n.

**hair style**
*hairdressing* 843 n.

**hairy**
*fibrous* 208 adj.
*hairy* 259 adj.
*textural* 331 adj.
*frightening* 854 adj.

**hajj, hadj**
*land travel* 267 n.
*act of worship* 981 n.

**hajji**
*traveller* 268 n.
*pietist* 979 n.
*worshipper* 981 n.

**hake**
*fish food* 301 n.

**hakim**
*doctor* 658 n.
*officer* 741 n.

**halberd**
*axe* 723 n.
*spear* 723 n.

**halcyon**
*tranquil* 266 adj.
*peaceful* 717 adj.
*palmy* 730 adj.

**halcyon days**
*palmy days* 730 n.
*joy* 824 n.

**hale**
*draw* 288 vb.
*healthy* 650 adj.

**half**
*part* 53 n.
*incompleteness* 55 n.
*bisection* 92 n.

**half-a-dozen**
*over five* 99 n.
*fewness* 105 n.

**half a loaf**
*compromise* 770 n.

**half-and-half**
*equal* 28 adj.
*mixed* 43 adj.
*neutral* 625 adj.

**half-asleep**
*inattentive* 456 adj.
*sleepy* 679 adj.

**half-baked**
*ignorant* 491 adj.
*dabbling* 491 adj.
*immature* 670 adj.
*bungled* 695 adj.
*uncompleted* 726 adj.

**half-breed**
*hybrid* 43 n.
*nonconformist* 84 n.

**half-caste**
*hybrid* 43 n.
*mixed* 43 adj.

**half cock, at**
*immature* 670 adj.

**half crown**
*coinage* 797 n.

**half-cut**
*tipsy* 949 adj.

**half-dead**
*dying* 361 adj.

**half-done**
*incomplete* 55 adj.
*deficient* 307 adj.
*neglected* 458 adj.
*uncompleted* 726 adj.

**half-face**
*laterality* 239 n.
*sideways* 239 adv.

**half-frozen**
*semiliquid* 354 adj.

**half glimpse**
*not known* 491 vb.

**half-grown**
*infantine* 132 adj.
*immature* 670 adj.

**half-hardy**
*vegetal* 366 adj.

**half-hearted**
*weak* 163 adj.
*unwilling* 598 adj.
*irresolute* 601 adj.
*apathetic* 820 adj.
*indifferent* 860 adj.

**half-hidden**
*shadowy* 419 adj.

**half hitch**
*ligature* 47 n.

**half-inch**
*steal* 788 vb.

**half-knowledge**
*dabbling* 491 n.

**half-life**
*radiation* 417 n.

**half-light**
*evening* 129 n.
*half-light* 419 n.

**halfling**
*dwarf* 196 n.

**half-mast**
*lower* 311 vb.

*signal* 547 vb.

**half mast, at**
*lamenting* 836 adj.

**half measures**
*incompleteness* 55 n.
*shortfall* 307 n.
*irresolution* 601 n.
*middle way* 625 n.
*insufficiency* 636 n.
*lost labour* 641 n.
*bungling* 695 n.

**half-melted**
*semiliquid* 354 adj.

**half-moon**
*curve* 248 n.
*arc* 250 n.
*moon* 321 n.

**half-nelson**
*retention* 778 n.

**halfpenny**
*small coin* 33 n.
*coinage* 797 n.

**half-price**
*cheap* 812 adj.

**half-ripe**
*immature* 670 adj.

**half-seas over**
*drunk* 949 adj.

**half-seen**
*shadowy* 419 adj.
*indistinct* 444 adj.

**half-smile**
*content* 828 n.
*laughter* 835 n.

**half sovereign**
*coinage* 797 n.

**half-spoken**
*tacit* 523 adj.

**half-starved**
*underfed* 636 adj.
*hungry* 859 adj.
*fasting* 946 adj.

**half the battle**
*chief thing* 638 n.

**half-timbered**
*architectural* 192 adj.

**half-title**
*edition* 589 n.

**half-tone**
*light contrast* 417 n.
*hue* 425 n.
*picture* 553 n.
*edition* 589 n.

**half-truth**
*mental dishonesty* 543 n.

**halfway**
*midway* 70 adv.
*undeviating* 625 adj.
*compromise* 770 n.

**halfway house**
*middle* 70 n.
*retreat* 192 n.
*intermediary* 231 n.
*middle way* 625 n.
*shelter* 662 n.

**half-wit**
*fool* 501 n.

**half-witted**
 *unintelligent* 499 adj.
**halibut**
 *fish food* 301 n.
**halitosis**
 *stench* 397 n.
**hall**
 *building* 164 n.
 *house* 192 n.
 *chamber* 194 n.
 *lobby* 194 n.
 *front* 237 n.
 *access* 624 n.
**halleluja, hallelujah**
 *rejoicing* 835 n.
 *celebration* 876 n.
 *hymn* 981 n.
**halliard**
 *tackling* 47 n.
**hallmark**
 *label* 547 n.
**hallmarked**
 *genuine* 494 adj.
**hall of mirrors**
 *visual fallacy* 440 n.
**hall of residence**
 *quarters* 192 n.
**halloo**
 *cry* 408 n.
 *pursue* 619 vb.
**hallow**
 *sanctify* 979 vb.
**hallowed**
 *divine* 965 adj.
**hallowed by custom**
 *usual* 610 adj.
**Hallowe'en**
 *sorcery* 983 n.
**hallucination(s)**
 *insubstantiality* 4 n.
 *insubstantial thing* 4 n.
 *appearance* 445 n.
 *error* 495 n.
 *psychosis* 503 n.
 *fantasy* 513 n.
 *deception* 542 n.
**hallucinatory**
 *untrue* 543 adj.
 *intoxicating* 949 adj.
**hallucinogen**
 *drug* 949 n.
**hallux**
 *foot* 214 n.
 *finger* 378 n.
**hallway**
 *access* 624 n.
**halma**
 *board game* 837 n.
**halo**
 *loop* 250 n.
 *light* 417 n.
 *honours* 866 n.
**haloed**
 *sanctified* 979 adj.
**halt**
 *end* 69 n.
 *be discontinuous* 72 vb.

 *stop* 145 n.
 *stopping place* 145 n.
 *halt* 145 vb.
 – 145 int.
 *quiescence* 266 n.
 *come to rest* 266 vb.
 *goal* 295 n.
 *railway* 624 n.
 *be obstructive* 702 vb.
 *failure* 728 n.
 *restrain* 747 vb.
**halter**
 *halter* 47 n.
 *fetter* 748 n.
 *means of execution*
  964 n.
**halter neck**
 *neckline* 228 n.
**halting**
 *fitful* 142 adj.
 *slow* 278 adj.
 *inelegant* 576 adj.
**halve**
 *sunder* 46 vb.
 *bisect* 92 vb.
 *apportion* 783 vb.
**ham**
 *leg* 267 n.
 *meat* 301 n.
 *actor* 594 n.
 *act* 594 vb.
 *unskilled* 695 adj.
 *bungler* 697 n.
 *be affected* 850 vb.
 – up
 *be witty* 839 vb.
**hamadryad**
 *reptile* 365 n.
 *nymph* 967 n.
**hamartiology**
 *theology* 973 n.
**hamburger**
 *meal* 301 n.
 *dish* 301 n.
 *meat* 301 n.
**ham-handed**
 *clumsy* 695 adj.
**hamlet**
 *district* 184 n.
 *housing* 192 n.
**Hamlet without the**
  **Prince, like**
 *incomplete* 55 adj.
**hammam**
 *ablutions* 648 n.
**hammer**
 *be vigorous* 174 vb.
 *hammer* 279 n.
 *strike* 279 vb.
 *missile* 287 n.
 *pulverizer* 332 n.
 *be loud* 400 vb.
 *tool* 630 n.
 *strike at* 712 vb.
 *club* 723 n.
 – at
 *repeat oneself* 106 vb.

 *exert oneself* 682 vb.
 – away at
 *persevere* 600 vb.
 – in/into
 *affix* 45 vb.
 *pierce* 263 vb.
 *insert* 303 vb.
 – into one's head
 *memorize* 505 vb.
 – out
 *form* 243 vb.
 *think* 449 vb.
 *carry through* 725 vb.
**hammer and sickle**
 *heraldry* 547 n.
**hammer and tongs**
 *violently* 176 adv.
**hammerbeam roof**
 *roof* 226 n.
**hammer-toed**
 *footed* 214 adj.
 *blemished* 845 adj.
**hammock**
 *hanging object* 217 n.
 *bed* 218 n.
**hamper**
 *basket* 194 n.
 *impair* 655 vb.
 *be difficult* 700 vb.
 *hinder* 702 vb.
 *restrain* 747 vb.
**hams**
 *buttocks* 238 n.
**hamster**
 *animal* 365 n.
**hamstring**
 *disable* 161 vb.
 *hinder* 702 vb.
**hamstrings**
 *leg* 267 n.
**hand**
 *limb* 53 n.
 *bunch* 74 n.
 *group* 74 n.
 *timekeeper* 117 n.
 *long measure* 203 n.
 *laterality* 239 n.
 *pass* 305 vb.
 *person* 371 n.
 *feeler* 378 n.
 *finger* 378 n.
 *indicator* 547 n.
 *lettering* 586 n.
 *instrument* 628 n.
 *doer* 676 n.
 *worker* 686 n.
 *servant* 742 n.
 *nippers* 778 n.
 *portion* 783 n.
 – back
 *restore* 656 vb.
 – down
 *transfer* 272 vb.
 – it to
 *be inferior* 35 vb.
 *be just* 913 vb.
 *grant claims* 915 vb.

 *praise* 923 vb.
 – on
 *transfer* 272 vb.
 – out
 *provide* 633 vb.
 – over
 *transfer* 272 vb.
 *pass* 305 vb.
 *relinquish* 621 vb.
 *resign* 753 vb.
 *give* 781 vb.
**handbag**
 *bag* 194 n.
**handball**
 *ball game* 837 n.
**handbill**
 *advertisement* 528 n.
 *the press* 528 n.
**handbook**
 *guidebook* 524 n.
 *textbook* 589 n.
**handcart**
 *pushcart* 274 n.
**hand-clapping**
 *gesture* 547 n.
**handclasp**
 *friendliness* 880 n.
 *sociability* 882 n.
 *courteous act* 884 n.
**handcuff**
 *tie* 45 vb.
 *bond* 47 n.
 *arrest* 747 n.
 *fetter* 747 vb.
**handcuffs**
 *fastening* 47 n.
 *fetter* 748 n.
**handful**
 *small quantity* 33 n.
 *bunch* 74 n.
 *nonconformist* 84 n.
 *fewness* 105 n.
 *contents* 193 n.
 *difficulty* 700 n.
 *hard task* 700 n.
 *revolter* 738 n.
**hand grenade**
 *bomb* 723 n.
**handhold**
 *support* 218 n.
 *retention* 778 n.
**hand-holder**
 *aider* 703 n.
**handicap**
 *equalize* 28 vb.
 *advantage* 34 n.
 *inferiority* 35 n.
 *retard* 278 vb.
 *inexpedience* 643 n.
 *illness* 651 n.
 *encumbrance* 702 n.
 *hinder* 702 vb.
 *contest* 716 n.
**handicapped**
 *disabled* 163 adj.
 *deformed* 246 adj.
**handicraft**

**heirs**
*futurity* 124 n.
*posterity* 170 n.
**heirship**
*sonship* 170 n.
*acquisition* 771 n.
*possession* 773 n.
**held**
*credible* 485 adj.
*retained* 778 adj.
**held up**
*late* 136 adj.
*hindered* 702 adj.
**heliacal**
*celestial* 321 adj.
**helical**
*coiled* 251 adj.
**Helicon**
*poetry* 593 n.
**helicopter**
*aircraft* 276 n.
**heliobacter pylorus**
*infection* 651 n.
**heliocentric**
*central* 225 adj.
*celestial* 321 adj.
**heliograph**
*signal* 547 n., vb.
**Helios**
*sun* 321 n.
*classical deities* 967 n.
**helioscope**
*optical device* 442 n.
**heliotrope**
*purple* 436 adj.
*gem* 844 n.
**heliotype**
*photography* 551 n.
*printing* 555 n.
**heliport**
*air travel* 271 n.
*goal* 295 n.
**helium**
*lifter* 310 n.
*element* 319 n. box
*lightness* 323 n.
**helix**
*coil* 251 n.
*circuition* 314 n.
**hell**
*future state* 124 n.
*depth* 211 n.
*pain* 377 n.
*gaming-house* 618 n.
*bane* 659 n.
*suffering* 825 n.
– 891 int.
*hell* 972 n.
**hell-bent**
*intending* 617 adj.
*rash* 857 adj.
**hell-born**
*diabolic* 969 adj.
**hellcat**
*violent creature* 176 n.
*hellhag* 904 n.
*sorceress* 983 n.

**hellebore**
*poisonous plant* 659 n.
**Hellenic**
*olden* 127 adj.
**Hellenist**
*linguist* 557 n.
**hellfire**
*fire* 379 n.
*hell* 972 n.
**hell for leather**
*swiftly* 277 adv.
**hellhag**
*hellhag* 904 n.
*monster* 938 n.
**hellish**
*damnable* 645 adj.
*cruel* 898 adj.
*heinous* 934 adj.
*wicked* 934 adj.
*diabolic* 969 adj.
*infernal* 972 adj.
**Hell's Angel**
*ruffian* 904 n.
**hell to pay**
*turmoil* 61 n.
**helm**
*sailing aid* 269 n.
*directorship* 689 n.
**helmet**
*headgear* 228 n.
*heraldry* 547 n.
*armour* 713 n.
**helminthology**
*zoology* 367 n.
*study* 536 n. box
**helmsman**
*navigator* 270 n.
*director* 690 n.
**helot**
*slave* 742 n.
**helotry**
*servitude* 745 n.
**help**
*concur* 181 vb.
*benefit* 615 vb.
*instrumentality* 628 n.
*be instrumental* 628 vb.
*utility* 640 n.
*be expedient* 642 vb.
*do good* 644 vb.
*cleaner* 648 n.
*remedy* 658 n., vb.
*facilitate* 701 vb.
*aid* 703 n., vb.
*aider* 703 n.
*servant* 742 n.
*give* 781 vb.
– oneself
*take* 786 vb.
*steal* 788 vb.
**help desk**
*informant* 524 n.
*adviser* 691 n.
*aider* 703 n.
**helper**
*prop* 218 n.
*aider* 703 n.

*auxiliary* 707 n.
*servant* 742 n.
*friend* 880 n.
*benefactor* 903 n.
**helpful**
*willing* 597 adj.
*cooperative* 706 adj.
*benevolent* 897 adj.
**helping**
*meal* 301 n.
*provision* 633 n.
*portion* 783 n.
**helpless**
*defenceless* 161 adj.
*impotent* 161 adj.
*weak* 163 adj.
*vulnerable* 661 adj.
**helplessly**
*uselessly* 641 adv.
**helpline**
*informant* 524 n.
*adviser* 691 n.
*aider* 703 n.
**helpmate**
*auxiliary* 707 n.
*colleague* 707 n.
*spouse* 894 n.
**helter-skelter**
*confusedly* 61 adv.
*descent* 309 n.
*hastily* 680 adv.
*pleasure ground* 837 n.
**hem**
*edging* 234 n.
*hem* 234 vb.
*limit* 236 vb.
*flank* 239 vb.
*fold* 261 n., vb.
*rasp* 407 vb.
*decorate* 844 vb.
– in
*surround* 230 vb.
*circumscribe* 232 vb.
*restrain* 747 vb.
**he-man**
*athlete* 162 n.
*violent creature* 176 n.
*male* 372 n.
**hemi-**
*fragmentary* 53 adj.
*bisected* 92 adj.
**hemiplegia**
*helplessness* 161 n.
*nervous disorders* 651 n.
**hemisphere**
*part* 53 n.
*bisection* 92 n.
*region* 184 n.
*sphere* 252 n.
*dome* 253 n.
**hemistich**
*verse form* 593 n.
**hemline**
*garment* 228 n.
*edging* 234 n.
**hemlock**
*poisonous plant* 659 n.

*means of execution*
964 n.
**hemp**
*fibre* 208 n.
*pungency* 388 n.
*drug-taking* 949 n.
**hen**
*poultry* 365 n.
*female animal* 373 n.
*darling* 890 n.
**hence**
*hence* 158 adv.
**henceforth**
*henceforth* 124 adv.
**henchman**
*aider* 703 n.
*auxiliary* 707 n.
*retainer* 742 n.
**hencoop, henhouse**
*shed* 192 n.
*cattle pen* 369 n.
**hendecasyllabic**
*poetic* 593 adj.
**henna**
*orange* 432 n.
*hairwash* 843 n.
**henotheism**
*deism* 973 n.
**hen party**
*womankind* 373 n.
*social gathering* 882 n.
**henpecked**
*subjected* 745 adj.
**hen run**
*stock farm* 369 n.
**hentai**
*cinema* 445 n.
*film* 445 n.
*picture* 553 n.
*impurity* 951 n.
**hepatitis**
*digestive disorders*
651 n.
*inflammation* 651 n.
box
**heptad**
*over five* 99 n.
**heptameter**
*prosody* 593 n.
**her**
*female* 373 n.
**Hera**
*marriage* 894 n.
*Olympian deity* 967 n.
**herald**
*come before* 64 vb.
*precursor* 66 n.
*initiate* 68 vb.
*precede* 283 vb.
*omen* 511 n.
*predict* 511 vb.
*informant* 524 n.
*proclaim* 528 vb.
*messenger* 529 n.
*heraldry* 547 n.
*indicate* 547 vb.
*deputy* 755 n.

**homage**
  *submission* 721 n.
  *loyalty* 739 n.
  *respects* 920 n.
**Homburg**
  *headgear* 228 n.
**home**
  *focus* 76 n.
  *source* 156 n.
  *place* 185 n.
  *native* 191 adj.
  *home* 192 n.
  *house* 192 n.
  *retreat* 192 n.
  *near* 200 adj.
  *interior* 224 adj.
  *resting place* 266 n.
  *arrive* 295 vb.
  *refuge* 662 n.
**home and dry**
  *safe* 660 adj.
  *successful* 727 adj.
**home-body**
  *solitary* 883 n.
**home alone**
  *neglected* 458 adj.
**home circle**
  *family* 11 n.
  *sociality* 882 n.
**homecoming**
  *return* 286 n.
  *arrival* 295 n.
**Home Counties**
  *district* 184 n.
**home economics**
  *cookery* 301 n.
**home from home**
  *abode* 192 n.
  *sociability* 882 n.
**home ground**
  *focus* 76 n.
  *home* 192 n.
**Home Guard**
  *defender* 713 n.
  *soldier* 722 n.
**home help**
  *cleaner* 648 n.
**homeknit**
  *jersey* 228 n.
**homeland**
  *territory* 184 n.
  *home* 192 n.
**homeless**
  *unrelated* 10 adj.
  *alone* 88 adj.
  *unstable* 152 adj.
  *displaced* 188 adj.
  *travelling* 267 adj.
  *poor* 801 adj.
**homeless person**
  *wanderer* 268 n.
  *outcast* 883 n.
**home life**
  *seclusion* 883 n.
**home-loving**
  *quiescent* 266 adj.
**homely**

  *comfortable* 376 adj.
  *dialectal* 560 adj.
  *plain* 573 adj.
  *pleasurable* 826 adj.
  *ugly* 842 adj.
  *plebeian* 869 adj.
**homemade**
  *produced* 164 adj.
  *native* 191 adj.
  *artless* 699 adj.
**Home Office**
  *jurisdiction* 955 n.
**home page**
  *Internet* 531 n.
**Homeric**
  *poetic* 593 adj.
**Homeric deities**
  *classical deities* 967 n.
**home rule**
  *government* 733 n.
  *independence* 744 n.
**home shopping**
  *purchase* 792 n.
**homesickness**
  *suffering* 825 n.
  *regret* 830 n.
  *melancholy* 834 n.
  *desire* 859 n.
**homesitting**
  *surveillance* 457 n.
**homespun**
  *simple* 44 adj.
  *produced* 164 adj.
  *textile* 222 n.
  *roughness* 259 n.
  *textural* 331 adj.
  *plain* 573 adj.
  *artless* 699 adj.
  *plebeian* 869 adj.
**homestead**
  *home* 192 n.
  *lands* 777 n.
**home stretch**
  *end* 69 n.
  *arrival* 295 n.
**home-sweet-home**
  *home* 192 n.
  *happiness* 824 n.
**home-thrust**
  *lunge* 712 n.
**home town**
  *home* 192 n.
**home truth**
  *truth* 494 n.
  *veracity* 540 n.
  *plainness* 573 n.
  *censure* 924 n.
  *accusation* 928 n.
**homeward bound**
  *regressive* 286 adj.
  *arriving* 295 adj.
**homework**
  *curriculum* 534 n.
  *study* 536 n.
  *preparation* 669 n.
  *labour* 682 n.
**homey, homy**

  *plain* 573 adj.
**homicidal maniac**
  *violent creature* 176 n.
  *killer* 362 n.
  *ruffian* 904 n.
**homicide**
  *homicide* 362 n. box
  *murderer* 362 n.
**homiletics**
  *teaching* 534 n.
  *church ministry* 985 n.
**homily**
  *lecture* 534 n.
  *oration* 579 n.
  *dissertation* 591 n.
  *ministration* 988 n.
**homing**
  *regressive* 286 adj.
  *arriving* 295 adj.
  *incoming* 297 adj.
**hominid**
  *humankind* 371 n.
**hominoid**
  *human* 371 adj.
**homo**
  *non-heterosexual* 84 n.
  *male* 372 n.
**homoeopath,**
  **homeopath**
  *doctor* 658 n.
**homoeopathic, hom-**
  **eopathic**
  *small* 33 adj.
  *exiguous* 196 adj.
  *medical* 658 adj.
**homoeopathy, hom-**
  **eopathy**
  *medical art* 658 n.
  *alternative therapy*
    658 n.
**homoeostatis,**
  **homeostasis**
  *equilibrium* 28 n.
  *stability* 153 n.
**homogeneous**
  *identical* 13 adj.
  *uniform* 16 adj.
  *similar* 18 adj.
  *simple* 44 adj.
**homogenize, hom-**
  **ogenise**
  *make uniform* 16 vb.
**homograph**
  *identity* 13 n.
  *word* 559 n.
**Homoiousians**
  *church party* 978 n.
**homologate**
  *endorse* 488 vb.
**homologous**
  *relative* 9 adj.
  *equal* 28 adj.
**homology**
  *relativeness* 9 n.
  *similarity* 18 n.
**homomorphism**
  *similarity* 18 n.

**homonym**
  *identity* 13 n.
  *equivocalness* 518 n.
  *word* 559 n.
**Homoousians**
  *church party* 978 n.
**homophobia**
  *prejudice* 481 n.
  *phobia* 854 n. box
**homophone**
  *identity* 13 n.
  *equivocalness* 518 n.
  *word* 559 n.
**homophonic**
  *identical* 13 adj.
  *harmonious* 410 adj.
**homo sapiens**
  *humankind* 371 n.
**homosexual**
  *non-heterosexual* 84 n.
  *male* 372 n.
**homosexuality**
  *variance* 84 n.
**homosexuality, hos-**
  **tility to**
  *phobia* 854 n. box
**homunculus**
  *small animal* 33 n.
  *dwarf* 196 n.
**hone**
  *sharpen* 256 vb.
**honest**
  *genuine* 494 adj.
  *true* 494 adj.
  *veracious* 540 adj.
  *plain* 573 adj.
  *artless* 699 adj.
  *ethical* 917 adj.
  *honourable* 929 adj.
  *disinterested* 931 adj.
  *virtuous* 933 adj.
**honest to God**
  *undisguised* 522 adj.
  *veracious* 540 adj.
**honesty**
  *straightness* 249 n.
**honey**
  *viscidity* 354 n.
  *woman* 373 n.
  *sweet thing* 392 n.
  *yellowness* 433 n.
  *a beauty* 841 n.
  *darling* 890 n.
**honeycomb**
  *network* 222 n.
  *cavity* 255 n.
  *porosity* 263 n.
  *pierce* 263 vb.
  *sweet thing* 392 n.
  *storage* 632 n.
  *impair* 655 vb.
**honeycombed**
  *cellular* 194 adj.
**honeydew**
  *fruit* 301 n.
  *sweet thing* 392 n.
**honeyed words**

dissension 709 n.
*See also* **hostile**
**host in oneself, a**
  influence 178 n.
**hosts**
  great quantity 32 n.
**hot**
  violent 176 adj.
  dry 342 adj.
  hot 379 adj.
  pungent 388 adj.
  musical 412 adj.
  radiating 417 adj.
  red 431 adj.
  fervent 818 adj.
  excited 821 adj.
  angry 891 adj.
  impure 951 adj.
  lecherous 951 adj.
  illegal 954 adj.
**hot air**
  insubstantial thing 4 n.
  overestimation 482 n.
  empty talk 515 n.
  boast 877 n.
**hot-air balloon**
  airship 276 n.
**hot-air duct**
  heater 383 n.
**hotbed**
  seedbed 156 n.
  abundance 171 n.
  heater 383 n.
  badness 645 n.
  infection 651 n.
  pitfall 663 n.
**hot blood**
  excitability 822 n.
**hot-blooded**
  violent 176 adj.
  rash 857 adj.
  irascible 892 adj.
**hotching with**
  full 54 adj.
  assembled 74 adj.
  multitudinous 104 adj.
**hotchpotch,**
  **hodgepodge**
  nonuniformity 17 n.
  medley 43 n.
  confusion 61 n.
**hot composition**
  print 587 n.
**hot dog**
  meal 301 n.
**hotel**
  inn 192 n.
**hotelier**
  caterer 633 n.
**hot flush**
  heat 379 n.
**hotfoot**
  hastily 680 adv.
**hot from the press**
  new 126 adj.
**hot gospeller**
  preacher 537 n.

zealot 979 n.
  pastor 986 n.
**hothead**
  desperado 857 n.
**hot-headed**
  hasty 680 adj.
  fervent 818 adj.
  excitable 822 adj.
  rash 857 adj.
**hothouse**
  extraneous 59 adj.
  seedbed 156 n.
  invigorate 174 vb.
  arbour 194 n.
  promote 285 vb.
  garden 370 n.
  heater 383 n.
**hot line**
  telecommunication
    531 n.
**hot-metal**
  printed 587 adj.
**hot money**
  funds 797 n.
**hot on the trail**
  pursuant to 619 adv.
**hotplate**
  heater 383 n.
**hotpot**
  dish 301 n.
**hot potato**
  difficulty 700 n.
**hot rod**
  car 274 n.
**hots, the**
  libido 859 n.
**hot seat**
  predicament 700 n.
  means of execution
    964 n.
**hot springs**
  stream 350 n.
  heat 379 n.
  hospital 658 n.
**hotspur**
  violent creature 176 n.
  desperado 857 n.
**hot stuff**
  loose woman 952 n.
**hot-tempered**
  excitable 822 adj.
  irascible 892 adj.
**hot toddy**
  alcoholic drink 301 n.
  pungency 388 n.
**hot tub**
  ablutions 648 n.
**hot under the collar**
  excited 821 adj.
  angry 891 adj.
**hot up**
  heat 381 vb.
  endanger 661 vb.
**hot water**
  cleanser 648 n.
  predicament 700 n.
  painfulness 827 n.

**hot-water bottle**
  cooking pot 194 n.
  heater 383 n.
**Houdini**
  escaper 667 n.
**hound**
  dog 365 n.
  hunter 619 n.
  be malevolent 898 vb.
  defame 926 vb.
  cad 938 n.
  knave 938 n.
**hounding**
  pursuit 619 n.
**hounds, group of**
  group 74 n. box
**hound's-tooth**
  chequer 437 n.
  pattern 844 n.
**hour**
  juncture 8 n.
  period 110 n.
  clock time 117 n.
**hourglass**
  timekeeper 117 n.
  contraction 198 n.
  narrowing 206 n.
**hour hand**
  indicator 547 n.
**houri**
  a beauty 841 n.
  mythical being 970 n.
**hourly**
  while 108 adv.
  periodic 110 adj.
  frequent 139 adj.
  often 139 adv.
  seasonal 141 adj.
  periodically 141 adv.
**house**
  race 11 n.
  edifice 164 n.
  genealogy 169 n.
  place 187 n.
  abode 192 n.
  house 192 n.
  zodiac 321 n.
  music 412 n.
  onlookers 441 n.
  class 538 n.
  playgoer 594 n.
  safeguard 660 vb.
  corporation 708 n.
  sovereign 741 n.
  shop 796 n.
**house arrest**
  detention 747 n.
**houseboat**
  small house 192 n.
  boat 275 n.
**housebound**
  quiescent 266 adj.
  restrained 747 adj.
**house-breaker**
  thief 789 n.
  offender 904 n.
**housecarl**

soldier 722 n.
  retainer 742 n.
**housecoat**
  informal dress 228 n.
**house divided against**
  **itself**
  dissension 709 n.
**houseful**
  crowd 74 n.
  inhabitants 919 n.
**household**
  family 11 n.
  group 74 n.
  inhabitants 191 n.
  home 192 n.
  known 490 adj.
  usual 610 adj.
**householder**
  resident 191 n.
  possessor 776 n.
**household gods**
  home 192 n.
  mythic deity 966 n.
**household name**
  famousness 866 n.
**household pet**
  animal 365 n.
**household staff**
  retainer 742 n.
**household troops**
  armed force 722 n.
**household words**
  plainness 573 n.
**househusband**
  male 372 n.
  manager 690 n.
**housekeeper**
  resident 191 n.
  caterer 633 n.
  manager 690 n.
  domestic 742 n.
  keeper 749 n.
**housekeeping**
  management 689 n.
**houselights**
  lighting 420 n.
  theatre 594 n.
**housemaid**
  domestic 742 n.
**housemaid's knee**
  rheumatism 651 n.
**houseman**
  doctor 658 n.
**housemaster, house-**
  **mistress**
  teacher 537 n.
  manager 690 n.
**houseminding**
  surveillance 457 n.
**house of cards**
  weak thing 163 n.
  brittleness 330 n.
**House of Commons**
  parliament 692 n.
**house officer**
  doctor 658 n.
**house of God**

**iconoclast**
*destroyer* 168 n.
*violent creature* 176 n.
*evildoer* 904 n.
*zealot* 979 n.
**iconoclastic**
*impious* 980 adj.
**iconography**
*representation* 551 n.
*art style* 553 n.
**iconolatry**
*cult* 981 n.
*idolatry* 982 n.
**iconology**
*theology* 973 n.
**icosahedron**
*angular figure* 247 n.
**ictus**
*pronunciation* 577 n.
*prosody* 593 n.
**icy**
*hard* 326 adj.
*cold* 380 adj.
*impassive* 820 adj.
*inimical* 881 adj.
*unsociable* 883 adj.
**id**
*self* 80 n.
*subjectivity* 320 n.
*spirit* 447 n.
**Id al-Adha, Id al-Fitr**
*holy day* 988 n. box
**idea**
*reason why* 156 n.
*form* 243 n.
*thought* 449 n.
*idea* 451 n.
*opinion* 485 n.
*intelligence* 498 n.
*supposition* 512 n.
*ideality* 513 n.
*meaning* 514 n.
*contrivance* 623 n.
**idea'd**
*imaginative* 513 adj.
**ideal**
*insubstantial* 4 adj.
*prototype* 23 n.
*ideational* 451 adj.
*imaginary* 513 adj.
*motive* 612 n.
*perfect* 646 adj.
*perfection* 646 n.
*desired object* 859 n.
**idealess**
*unthinking* 450 adj.
**idealism**
*immateriality* 320 n.
*philosophy* 449 n.
*fantasy* 513 n.
*literature* 557 n.
*reformism* 654 n.
*fastidiousness* 862 n.
*philanthropy* 901 n.
*morals* 917 n.
*disinterestedness* 931 n.
*virtues* 933 n.

**idealist**
*revolutionist* 149 n.
*visionary* 513 n.
*reformer* 654 n.
*trier* 671 n.
*perfectionist* 862 n.
*kind person* 897 n.
*philanthropist* 901 n.
*good person* 937 n.
**idealistic**
*impossible* 470 adj.
*See also* **idealism**
**ideality**
*thought* 449 n.
*supposition* 512 n.
*ideality* 513 n.
**idealize, idealise**
*overrate* 482 vb.
*imagine* 513 vb.
*idolatrize* 982 vb.
**ideals**
*conduct* 688 n.
*philanthropy* 901 n.
*morals* 917 n.
*disinterestedness* 931 n.
*virtues* 933 n.
**ideate**
*cognize* 447 vb.
*think* 449 vb.
*imagine* 513 vb.
**idée fixe**
*positiveness* 473 n.
*prejudgment* 481 n.
*opinionatedness* 602 n.
**identical**
*identical* 13 adj.
*one* 88 adj.
**identical twin**
*kinsman* 11 n.
*duality* 90 n.
**identifiable**
*manifest* 522 adj.
**identification**
*identity* 13 n.
*assimilation* 18 n.
*comparison* 462 n.
*identification* 547 n.
**identification papers**
*label* 547 n.
**identify**
*discover* 484 vb.
*See also* **identification**
**identikit**
*representation* 551 n.
**identity**
*identity* 13 n.
*equivalence* 28 n.
*self* 80 n.
*unity* 88 n.
*authenticity* 494 n.
**identity card**
*label* 547 n.
**identity crisis**
*personality disorder* 503 n.
**ideogram, ideograph**
*letter* 558 n.

*lettering* 586 n.
**ideological**
*philosophic* 449 adj.
**ideologist**
*philanthropist* 901 n.
**ideology**
*philosophy* 449 n.
*creed* 485 n.
**ides**
*date* 108 n.
**idiocy**
*folly* 499 n.
*unintelligence* 499 n.
*learning disability* 503 n.
**idiolect**
*speciality* 80 n.
*unintelligibility* 517 n.
*identification* 547 n.
*language* 557 n.
*dialect* 560 n.
*style* 566 n.
**idiom**
*speciality* 80 n.
*connotation* 514 n.
*language* 557 n.
*dialect* 560 n.
*phrase* 563 n.
*style* 566 n.
**idiomatic**
*apt* 24 adj.
*special* 80 adj.
*semantic* 514 adj.
*linguistic* 557 adj.
*phraseological* 563 adj.
*stylistic* 566 adj.
*forceful* 571 adj.
*elegant* 575 adj.
**idiosyncrasy**
*temperament* 5 n.
*originality* 21 n.
*speciality* 80 n.
*nonconformity* 84 n.
*tendency* 179 n.
*style* 566 n.
*whim* 604 n.
*habit* 610 n.
**idiot**
*fool* 501 n.
*person with a learning disability* 503 n.
**idiotic**
*absurd* 497 adj.
*foolish* 499 adj.
*crazy* 503 adj.
**idle**
*operate* 173 vb.
*move slowly* 278 vb.
*be inattentive* 456 vb.
*profitless* 641 adj.
*unused* 674 adj.
*nonactive* 677 adj.
*lazy* 679 adj.
**idle gossip**
*chatter* 581 n.
**idleness**
*unproductiveness* 172 n.
*inaction* 677 n.

*inactivity* 679 n.
*leisure* 681 n.
*undutifulness* 918 n.
**idler**
*slowcoach* 278 n.
*negligence* 458 n.
*slacker* 598 n.
*avoider* 620 n.
*idler* 679 n.
**idol**
*image* 551 n.
*exceller* 644 n.
*desired object* 859 n.
*person of repute* 866 n.
*loved one* 887 n.
*favourite* 890 n.
*deity* 966 n.
*idol* 982 n.
**idolater, idolatress**
*worshipper* 981 n.
*idolater* 982 n.
**idolatrous**
*ignorant* 491 adj.
*approving* 923 adj.
*idolatrous* 982 adj.
**idolatry**
*love* 887 n.
*praise* 923 n.
*religion* 973 n.
*cult* 981 n.
*idolatry* 982 n.
**idolization, idol-
isation**
*deification* 982 n.
**idolize, idolise**
*love* 887 vb.
*respect* 920 vb.
*praise* 923 vb.
*idolatrize* 982 vb.
**idol-maker**
*sculptor* 556 n.
*idolater* 982 n.
**idol worship**
*idolatry* 982 n.
**idyll**
*description* 590 n.
*poem* 593 n.
*pleasurableness* 826 n.
**idyllic**
*pleasurable* 826 adj.
**i.e.**
*namely* 80 adv.
*in plain words* 520 adv.
**if**
*if* 8 adv.
*provided* 468 adv.
**if push comes to
shove**
*necessarily* 596 adv.
**igloo**
*dwelling* 192 n.
**igneous**
*fiery* 379 adj.
**igneous rock**
*rock* 344 n.
**ignis fatuus**
*glow* 417 n.

glow-worm 420 n.
visual fallacy 440 n.

**ignite**
kindle 381 vb.
make bright 417 vb.

**igniter**
lighter 385 n.

**ignition**
burning 381 n.

**ignoble**
discreditable 867 adj.
plebeian 869 adj.
dishonest 930 adj.

**ignominious**
degrading 867 adj.
dishonesty 930 adj.

**ignominy**
disrepute 867 n.

**ignoramus**
ignoramus 493 n.
dunce 501 n.

**ignorance**
blindness 439 n.
ignorance 491 n.
error 495 n.
unskilfulness 695 n.
artlessness 699 n.
innocence 935 n.

**ignorant**
ignorant 491 adj.
foolish 499 adj.
off guard 508 adj.
ill-bred 847 adj.

**ignore**
be blind 439 vb.
be inattentive 456 vb.
disregard 458 vb.
disbelieve 486 vb.
not know 491 vb.
reject 607 vb.
not observe 769 vb.
be insensitive 820 vb.
make unwelcome 883 vb.
be rude 885 vb.
not respect 921 vb.

**ilk**
sort 77 n.

**ill**
evil 616 n.
badness 645 n.
badly 645 adv.
sick 651 adj.
suffering 825 adj.

**ill-advised**
ill-timed 138 adj.
unwise 499 adj.
inexpedient 643 adj.
bungled 695 adj.
rash 857 adj.

**ill-assorted**
disagreeing 25 adj.

**ill at ease**
suffering 825 adj.

**ill-behaved**
difficult 700 adj.

**ill-bred**
ill-bred 847 adj.

discourteous 885 adj.

**ill-conceived**
rash 857 adj.

**ill-considered**
unwise 499 adj.
See also **ill-advised**

**ill-defined**
amorphous 244 adj.
shadowy 419 adj.
indistinct 444 adj.

**ill-disposed**
harmful 645 adj.
discontented 829 adj.
malevolent 898 adj.

**illegal**
anarchic 734 adj.
prohibited 757 adj.
unjust 914 adj.
unwarranted 916 adj.
dishonest 930 adj.
illegal 954 adj.

**illegality**
guilty act 936 n.
illegality 954 n.

**illegal substance**
drug 949 n.

**illegible**
unintelligible 517 adj.

**illegible writing**
lettering 586 n.

**illegitimacy**
sonship 170 n.
wrong 914 n.
undueness 916 n.
bastardy 954 n.
illegality 954 n.

**ill-equipped**
unprovided 636 adj.

**ill fame**
disrepute 867 n.

**ill-fated**
unfortunate 731 adj.

**ill-favoured**
ugly 842 adj.

**ill feeling**
dislike 861 n.
enmity 881 n.
hatred 888 n.

**ill-gotten**
acquired 771 adj.

**ill health**
ill health 651 n.

**ill humour**
resentment 891 n.
sullenness 893 n.

**ill-humoured**
irascible 892 adj.

**illiberal**
biased 481 adj.
parsimonious 816 adj.
selfish 932 adj.

**illiberality**
opinionatedness 602 n.

**illicit**
illegal 954 adj.

**illicit gains**
booty 790 n.

**illicit love**
love affair 887 n.
illicit love 951 n.

**illimitable**
infinite 107 adj.

**ill-informed**
uninstructed 491 adj.
mistaken 495 adj.

**illiterate**
uninstructed 491 adj.
ignoramus 493 n.

**ill-judged**
ill-timed 138 adj.
indiscriminating 464 adj.
unwise 499 adj.
bungled 695 adj.

**ill-kept**
neglected 458 adj.

**ill-mannered**
ill-bred 847 adj.
impertinent 878 adj.
discourteous 885 adj.

**ill-matched**
disagreeing 25 adj.
married 894 adj.

**ill-natured**
malevolent 898 adj.
unkind 898 adj.

**illness**
illness 651 n.

**illogical**
irrelevant 10 adj.
discontinuous 72 adj.
unthinking 450 adj.
intuitive 476 adj.
illogical 477 adj.
erroneous 495 adj.
absurd 497 adj.
unwise 499 adj.

**illogicality**
lack of meaning 515 n.

**ill-omened**
inopportune 138 adj.
cautionary 664 adj.
unpromising 853 adj.

**ill-prepared**
bungled 695 adj.

**ill-provided**
unequipped 670 adj.

**ill-spent**
wasted 634 adj.
profitless 641 adj.

**ill-starred**
inopportune 138 adj.
unfortunate 731 adj.

**ill-tempered**
sullen 893 adj.

**ill-timed**
ill-timed 138 adj.
inexpedient 643 adj.

**ill-treat**
force 176 vb.
ill-treat 645 vb.
misuse 675 vb.
be severe 735 vb.

**ill turn**
cruel act 898 n.

**illuminant**
lighter 385 n.
luminary 420 n.

**illuminate**
make bright 417 vb.
illuminate 420 vb.
colour 425 vb.
interpret 520 vb.
manifest 522 vb.
paint 553 vb.
decorate 844 vb.

**illuminati**
intellectual 492 n.

**illumination**
progression 285 n.
light 417 n.
lighting 420 n.
discovery 484 n.
knowledge 490 n.
ornamental art 844 n.
revelation 975 n.

**illuminations**
fireworks 420 n.
spectacle 445 n.
celebration 876 n.

**illuminator**
artist 556 n.

**illumine**
educate 534 vb.

**ill-use**
ill-treat 645 vb.

**illusion**
visual fallacy 440 n.
appearance 445 n.
error 495 n.
deception 542 n.
sleight 542 n.

**illusionism**
mimicry 20 n.
sorcery 983 n.

**illusionist**
imitator 20 n.
conjuror 545 n.
sorcerer 983 n.

**illusory**
immaterial 320 adj.
sophistical 477 adj.
erroneous 495 adj.
imaginary 513 adj.
deceiving 542 adj.

**illustrate**
exemplify 83 vb.
interpret 520 vb.
represent 551 vb.
decorate 844 vb.

**illustration**
example 83 n.
interpretation 520 n.
representation 551 n.
picture 553 n.
edition 589 n.
ornamental art 844 n.

**illustrative**
typical 83 adj.
expressive 516 adj.

**illustrator**
artist 556 n.

**illustrious**
  *renowned* 866 adj.
**ill will**
  *discontent* 829 n.
  *enmity* 881 n.
  *hatred* 888 n.
  *malevolence* 898 n.
  *envy* 912 n.
**ill wind**
  *badness* 645 n.
  *adversity* 731 n.
**ill-wisher**
  *troublemaker* 663 n.
  *enemy* 881 n.
**ill wishes**
  *malediction* 899 n.
**image**
  *analogue* 18 n.
  *copy* 22 n.
  *reflection* 417 n.
  *appearance* 445 n.
  *idea* 451 n.
  *ideality* 513 n.
  *trope* 519 n.
  *figure* 519 vb.
  *exhibit* 522 n.
  *monument* 548 n.
  *image* 551 n.
  *sculpture* 554 n.
  *idol* 982 n.
**imagery**
  *imagination* 513 n.
  *metaphor* 519 n.
**image-maker**
  *publicizer* 528 n.
  *sculptor* 556 n.
**image-worship**
  *cult* 981 n.
  *idolatry* 982 n.
**imaginable**
  *possible* 469 adj.
  *supposed* 512 adj.
**imaginary**
  *unreal* 2 adj.
  *insubstantial* 4 adj.
  *ideational* 451 adj.
  *erroneous* 495 adj.
  *supposed* 512 adj.
  *imaginary* 513 adj.
  *descriptive* 590 adj.
  *fairylike* 970 adj.
**imagination**
  *vision* 438 n.
  *thought* 449 n.
  *idea* 451 n.
  *imagination* 513 n.
  *falsehood* 541 n.
**imaginative**
  *original* 21 adj.
  *imaginative* 513 adj.
  *descriptive* 590 adj.
**imagine**
  *be inattentive* 456 vb.
  *suppose* 512 vb.
  *imagine* 513 vb.
  *describe* 590 vb.
  *plan* 623 vb.

  *hope* 852 vb.
  *See also* **imagination**
**imagined**
  *imaginary* 513 adj.
  *untrue* 543 adj.
**imago**
  *insect* 365 n.
**I'm all right Jack**
  *selfishness* 932 n.
**imam**
  *governor* 741 n.
  *priest* 986 n.
**imbalance**
  *inequality* 29 n.
  *distortion* 246 n.
**imbecile**
  *weak* 163 adj.
  *foolish* 499 adj.
  *unintelligent* 499 adj.
  *fool* 501 n.
  *person with a learning disability* 503 n.
**imbecility**
  *helplessness* 161 n.
  *learning disability* 503 n.
**imbibe**
  *absorb* 299 vb.
  *drink* 301 vb.
  *learn* 536 vb.
**Imbolc**
  *holy day* 988 n. box
**imbrication**
  *covering* 226 n.
**imbroglio**
  *medley* 43 n.
  *complexity* 61 n.
  *confusion* 61 n.
  *predicament* 700 n.
**imbrue**
  *infuse* 303 vb.
  *drench* 341 vb.
  *colour* 425 vb.
**imbue**
  *mix* 43 vb.
  *pervade* 189 vb.
  *infuse* 303 vb.
  *drench* 341 vb.
  *colour* 425 vb.
  *educate* 534 vb.
  *habituate* 610 vb.
**imbued with**
  *believing* 485 adj.
  *with affections* 817 adj.
  *impressed* 818 adj.
**imitable**
  *imitative* 20 adj.
**imitate**
  *liken* 18 vb.
  *resemble* 18 vb.
  *imitate* 20 vb.
  *conform* 83 vb.
  *fake* 541 vb.
  *represent* 551 vb.
  *act* 594 vb.
  *satirize* 851 vb.
**imitation**
  *imitation* 20 n.

  *copy* 22 n.
  *substituted* 150 adj.
  *false* 541 adj.
  *sham* 542 n.
  *spurious* 542 adj.
  *representation* 551 n.
  *bad taste* 847 n.
**imitative**
  *simulating* 18 adj.
  *imitative* 20 adj.
  *conformable* 83 adj.
  *repeated* 106 adj.
  *mindless* 448 adj.
  *unthinking* 450 adj.
**imitator**
  *imitator* 20 n.
  *actor* 594 n.
  *humorist* 839 n.
**immaculate**
  *perfect* 646 adj.
  *clean* 648 adj.
  *honourable* 929 adj.
  *innocent* 935 adj.
  *pure* 950 adj.
**immanent**
  *intrinsic* 5 adj.
  *godlike* 965 adj.
**immaterial**
  *insubstantial* 4 adj.
  *irrelevant* 10 adj.
  *immaterial* 320 adj.
  *psychic* 447 adj.
  *spiritualism* 984 n.
  *spooky* 970 adj.
**immateriality**
  *immateriality* 320 n.
  *rarity* 325 n.
  *spiritualism* 984 n.
**immature**
  *incomplete* 55 adj.
  *beginning* 68 adj.
  *new* 126 adj.
  *young* 130 adj.
  *unintelligent* 499 adj.
  *unhabituated* 611 adj.
  *imperfect* 647 adj.
  *immature* 670 adj.
  *unskilled* 695 adj.
  *uncompleted* 726 adj.
**immaturity**
  *nonage* 130 n.
**immeasurable**
  *infinite* 107 adj.
**immediate**
  *continuous* 71 adj.
  *instantaneous* 116 adj.
  *early* 135 adj.
  *impending* 155 adj.
  *speedy* 277 adj.
  *hasty* 680 adj.
**immemorial**
  *perpetual* 115 adj.
  *former* 125 adj.
  *immemorial* 127 adj.
  *permanent* 144 adj.
  *worshipful* 866 adj.
**immense**

  *enormous* 32 adj.
  *infinite* 107 adj.
  *huge* 195 adj.
**immensity**
  *space* 183 n.
**immerse**
  *immerse* 303 vb.
  *plunge* 313 vb.
  *drench* 341 vb.
**immersed**
  *deep* 211 adj.
**immersion**
  *ingress* 297 n.
  *immersion* 303 n.
  *plunge* 313 n.
  *moistening* 341 n.
  *Christian rite* 988 n.
**immersion heater**
  *heater* 383 n.
**immersion method**
  *teaching* 534 n.
**immigrant**
  *foreigner* 59 n.
  *settler* 191 n.
  *incomer* 297 n.
**immigrate**
  *travel* 267 vb.
  *enter* 297 vb.
**imminent**
  *future* 124 adj.
  *early* 135 adj.
  *impending* 155 adj.
  *approaching* 289 adj.
**immiscible**
  *separate* 46 adj.
  *nonadhesive* 49 adj.
**immitigable**
  *unpromising* 853 adj.
**immixture**
  *mixture* 43 n.
**immobile**
  *permanent* 144 adj.
  *fixed* 153 adj.
  *still* 266 adj.
  *nonactive* 677 adj.
**immobility**
  *permanence* 144 n.
  *stability* 153 n.
  *inertness* 175 n.
  *quiescence* 266 n.
  *inaction* 677 n.
**immobilize,**
    **immobilise**
  *bring to rest* 266 vb.
  *make inactive* 679 vb.
**immoderate**
  *violent* 176 adj.
  *exaggerated* 546 adj.
  *inelegant* 576 adj.
  *redundant* 637 adj.
  *intemperate* 943 adj.
**immoderately**
  *extremely* 32 adv.
**immodest**
  *undisguised* 522 adj.
  *vain* 873 adj.
  *unchaste* 951 adj.

**immolate**
 *kill* 362 vb.
 *give* 781 vb.
**immoral**
 *dishonest* 930 adj.
 *wicked* 934 adj.
**immorality**
 *wrong* 914 n.
 *wickedness* 934 n.
 *unchastity* 951 n.
 *impiety* 980 n.
**immortal**
 *existing* 1 adj.
 *perpetual* 115 adj.
 *renowned* 866 adj.
 *godlike* 965 adj.
**immortal(s)**
 *intellectual* 492 n.
 *armed force* 722 n.
 *deity* 966 n.
**immortality**
 *perpetuity* 115 n.
 *famousness* 866 n.
**immortalize, immor-
 talise**
 *perpetuate* 115 vb.
 *honour* 866 vb.
**immovable,
 immoveable**
 *firm* 45 adj.
 *fixed* 153 adj.
 *still* 266 adj.
 *resolute* 599 adj.
 *obstinate* 602 adj.
**immovables, im-
 moveables**
 *property* 777 n.
**immune**
 *salubrious* 652 adj.
 *invulnerable* 660 adj.
 *nonliable* 919 adj.
**immunity**
 *freedom* 744 n.
 *nonliability* 919 n.
**immunization,
 immunisation**
 *hygiene* 652 n.
 *prophylactic* 658 n.
 *protection* 660 n.
**immunology**
 *medical art* 658 n.
 *study* 536 n.
**immunotherapy**
 *therapy* 658 n.
**immure**
 *circumscribe* 232 vb.
 *enclose* 235 vb.
 *imprison* 747 vb.
– **oneself**
 *be unsociable* 883 vb.
**immutable**
 *perpetual* 115 adj.
 *permanent* 144 adj.
 *unchangeable* 153 adj.
 *godlike* 965 adj.
**imp**
 *child* 132 n.

 *devil* 969 n.
 *demon* 970 n.
 *elf* 970 n.
 *sorcerer* 983 n.
**impact**
 *affix* 45 vb.
 *tighten* 45 vb.
 *influence* 178 n.
 *collision* 279 n.
 *implant* 303 vb.
 *excitation* 821 n.
**impair**
 *derange* 63 vb.
 *disable* 161 vb.
 *weaken* 163 vb.
 *deform* 244 vb.
 *retard* 278 vb.
 *waste* 634 vb.
 *make useless* 641 vb.
 *harm* 645 vb.
 *impair* 655 vb.
 *misuse* 675 vb.
 *hinder* 702 vb.
 *blemish* 845 vb.
**impairment**
 *incompleteness* 55 n.
 *impairment* 655 n.
**impale**
 *pierce* 263 vb.
 *mark* 547 vb.
 *execute* 963 vb.
**impalpable**
 *minute* 196 adj.
**imparity**
 *inequality* 29 n.
**impart**
 *inform* 524 vb.
 *give* 781 vb.
**impartial**
 *equal* 28 adj.
 *wise* 498 adj.
 *choiceless* 606 adj.
 *neutral* 625 adj.
 *indifferent* 860 adj.
 *just* 913 adj.
 *honourable* 929 adj.
 *disinterested* 931 adj.
**impartiality**
 *moderation* 177 n.
**impartible**
 *indivisible* 52 adj.
**impassable**
 *closed* 264 adj.
 *impracticable* 470 adj.
 *difficult* 700 adj.
**impasse**
 *stop* 145 n.
 *closure* 264 n.
 *impossibility* 470 n.
 *difficulty* 700 n.
 *obstacle* 702 n.
**impassible**
 *unfeeling* 375 adj.
 *impassive* 820 adj.
 *inexcitable* 823 adj.
**impassioned**
 *forceful* 571 adj.

 *fervent* 818 adj.
 *lively* 819 adj.
 *excited* 821 adj.
**impassive**
 *inert* 175 adj.
 *still* 266 adj.
 *unfeeling* 375 adj.
 *incurious* 454 adj.
 *inattentive* 456 adj.
 *indiscriminating* 464 adj.
 *nonactive* 677 adj.
 *inactive* 679 adj.
 *impassive* 820 adj.
 *inexcitable* 823 adj.
 *indifferent* 860 adj.
 *unastonished* 865 adj.
 *pitiless* 906 adj.
**impasto**
 *art style* 553 n.
**impatience**
 *willingness* 597 n.
 *haste* 680 n.
 *warm feeling* 818 n.
 *excitability* 822 n.
 *rashness* 857 n.
 *desire* 859 n.
 *rudeness* 885 n.
 *resentment* 891 n.
 *irascibility* 892 n.
**impatient**
 *unwise* 499 adj.
 *lively* 819 adj.
**impeach**
 *blame* 924 vb.
 *indict* 928 vb.
 *litigate* 959 vb.
**impeachment**
 *accusation* 928 n.
**impeccable**
 *perfect* 646 adj.
 *virtuous* 933 adj.
 *innocent* 935 adj.
**impecunious**
 *poor* 801 adj.
**impede**
 *hinder* 702 vb.
**impediment**
 *difficulty* 700 n.
 *hindrance* 702 n.
 *obstacle* 702 n.
**impedimenta**
 *box* 194 n.
 *thing transferred* 272 n.
 *equipment* 630 n.
 *encumbrance* 702 n.
 *property* 777 n.
**impel**
 *be vigorous* 174 vb.
 *move* 265 vb.
 *impel* 279 vb.
 *propel* 287 vb.
 *insert* 303 vb.
 *motivate* 612 vb.
**impelling**
 *causal* 156 adj.
 *dynamic* 160 adj.
**impend**

 *be to come* 124 vb.
 *impend* 155 vb.
 *frighten* 854 vb.
 *threaten* 900 vb.
**impending**
 *early* 135 adj.
 *impending* 155 adj.
 *approaching* 289 adj.
 *arriving* 295 adj.
 *expected* 507 adj.
**impenetrable**
 *closed* 264 adj.
 *dense* 324 adj.
 *unintelligent* 499 adj.
 *unintelligible* 517 adj.
 *latent* 523 adj.
 *difficult* 700 adj.
 *thick-skinned* 820 adj.
**impenitence**
 *obstinacy* 602 n.
 *impenitence* 940 n.
 *impiety* 980 n.
**imperative**
 *necessary* 596 adj.
 *demanding* 627 adj.
 *important* 638 adj.
 *authoritarian* 735 adj.
 *commanding* 737 adj.
 *compelling* 740 adj.
**imperative duty**
 *duty* 917 n.
**imperator**
 *army officer* 741 n.
 *sovereign* 741 n.
**imperceptible**
 *minute* 196 adj.
 *slow* 278 adj.
 *dim* 419 adj.
 *invisible* 444 adj.
**imperceptibly**
 *slightly* 33 adv.
**imperceptive**
 *insensible* 375 adj.
 *indiscriminating* 464 adj.
**impercipient**
 *unintelligent* 499 adj.
**imperfect**
 *inferior* 35 adj.
 *fragmentary* 53 adj.
 *incomplete* 55 adj.
 *preterite* 125 adj.
 *crippled* 163 adj.
 *deformed* 246 adj.
 *deficient* 307 adj.
 *inelegant* 576 adj.
 *bad* 645 adj.
 *imperfect* 647 adj.
 *immature* 670 adj.
 *bungled* 695 adj.
 *uncompleted* 726 adj.
 *unsightly* 842 adj.
 *blemished* 845 adj.
 *frail* 934 adj.
**imperfection**
 *insufficiency* 636 n.
 *imperfection* 647 n.
 *nonpreparation* 670 n.

*turmoil* 61 n.
*hell* 972 n.
**inferred**
*attributed* 158 adj.
*tacit* 523 adj.
**infertile**
*impotent* 161 adj.
*unproductive* 172 adj.
**infest**
*congregate* 74 vb.
*be many* 104 vb.
*encroach* 306 vb.
*attack* 712 vb.
*trouble* 827 vb.
**infestation**
*bane* 659 n.
**infibulation**
*joining together* 45 n.
**infidel**
*unbeliever* 486 n.
*heathen* 974 n.
*impious person* 980 n.
**infidelity**
*unbelief* 486 n.
*perfidy* 930 n.
*illicit love* 951 n.
*irreligion* 974 n.
**in-fighting**
*pugilism* 716 n.
*dissension* 709 n.
**infiltrate**
*pervade* 189 vb.
*introduce* 231 vb.
*infiltrate* 297 vb.
*admit* 299 vb.
*infuse* 303 vb.
*pass* 305 vb.
**infiltration**
*mixture* 43 n.
*sedition* 738 n.
**infinite**
*absolute* 32 adj.
*multitudinous* 104 adj.
*infinite* 107 adj.
**Infinite, the**
*the Deity* 965 n.
**infinitesimal**
*small* 33 adj.
*minute* 196 adj.
**infinitesimal calculus**
*mathematics* 86 n.
**infinity**
*infinity* 107 n.
*perpetuity* 115 n.
*space* 183 n.
*divine attribute* 965 n.
**infirm**
*weakly* 163 adj.
*irresolute* 601 adj.
*unhealthy* 651 adj.
*cowardly* 856 adj.
*frail* 934 adj.
**infirmary**
*hospital* 658 n.
**infirmity**
*old age* 131 n.
*weakness* 163 n.

*ill health* 651 n.
*vice* 934 n.
**infirmity of purpose**
*weakness* 163 n.
*irresolution* 601 n.
**in fits and starts**
*discontinuously* 72 adv.
*jerkily* 318 adv.
**infix**
*add* 38 vb.
*implant* 303 vb.
*educate* 534 vb.
*part of speech* 564 n.
**in flagrante delicto**
*in the act* 676 adv.
**inflame**
*invigorate* 174 vb.
*make violent* 176 vb.
*itch* 378 vb.
*heat* 381 vb.
*excite* 821 vb.
*aggravate* 832 vb.
*excite love* 887 vb.
**inflammable**
*combustible* 385 adj.
*dangerous* 661 adj.
*excitable* 822 adj.
*irascible* 892 adj.
**inflammation**
*heat* 379 n.
*burning* 381 n.
*inflammation* 651 n.
*painfulness* 827 n.
**inflammatory**
*violent* 176 adj.
**inflatable**
*bladder* 194 n.
**inflate**
*enlarge* 197 vb.
*blow up* 352 vb.
*overrate* 482 vb.
*demonetize* 797 vb.
*make conceited* 873 vb.
*praise* 923 vb.
**inflated**
*airy* 340 adj.
*exaggerated* 546 adj.
*rhetorical* 574 adj.
*ridiculous* 849 adj.
*prideful* 871 adj.
*ostentatious* 875 adj.
**inflation**
*increase* 36 n.
*dilation* 197 n.
*superfluity* 637 n.
*finance* 797 n.
**inflationary**
*monetary* 797 adj.
*dear* 811 adj.
**inflect**
*make curved* 248 vb.
*parse* 564 vb.
*voice* 577 vb.
**inflected**
*linguistic* 557 adj.
**inflection, inflexion**
*curvature* 248 n.

*grammar* 564 n.
*pronunciation* 577 n.
**inflexible**
*unchangeable* 153 adj.
*straight* 249 adj.
*rigid* 326 adj.
*resolute* 599 adj.
*obstinate* 602 adj.
*severe* 735 adj.
*indifferent* 860 adj.
*pitiless* 906 adj.
**inflict**
*be severe* 735 vb.
*compel* 740 vb.
*punish* 963 vb.
**infliction**
*adversity* 731 n.
*severity* 735 n.
*suffering* 825 n.
*punishment* 963 n.
**in-flight**
*flying* 271 adj.
**inflorescence**
*flower* 366 n.
**inflow**
*ingress* 297 n.
*current* 350 n.
**influence**
*component* 58 n.
*modify* 143 vb.
*convert* 147 vb.
*causation* 156 n.
*cause* 156 n., vb.
*effect* 157 n.
*power* 160 n.
*agency* 173 n.
*influence* 178 n., vb.
*tend* 179 vb.
*bias* 481 vb.
*convince* 485 vb.
*teach* 534 vb.
*inducement* 612 n.
*motivate* 612 vb.
*instrumentality* 628 n.
*be important* 638 vb.
*make better* 654 vb.
*troublemaker* 663 n.
*action* 676 n.
*authority* 733 n.
*impress* 821 vb.
*prestige* 866 n.
*sorcery* 983 n.
**influential**
*great* 32 adj.
*influential* 178 adj.
**influenza**
*infection* 651 n.
**influx**
*ingress* 297 n.
**infomercial**
*advertisement* 528 n.
*broadcast* 531 n.
**in force**
*operative* 173 adj.
**in for it, be**
*have trouble* 731 vb.
**inform**

*inform* 524 vb.
*divulge* 526 vb.
*publish* 528 vb.
*educate* 534 vb.
*warn* 664 vb.
– against
*inform* 524 vb.
*indicate* 547 vb.
*accuse* 928 vb.
**informal**
*unconformable* 84 adj.
*lax* 734 adj.
*unconfined* 744 adj.
*nonobservant* 769 adj.
**informal dress**
*informal dress* 228 n.
*uncovering* 229 n.
**informant**
*witness* 466 n.
*interpreter* 520 n.
*informant* 524 n.
*news reporter* 529 n.
*correspondent* 588 n.
**informatics**
*computing* 86 n.
*information* 524 n.
*study* 536 n. box
**information**
*enquiry* 459 n.
*testimony* 466 n.
*knowledge* 490 n.
*information* 524 n.
*message* 529 n.
*news* 529 n.
*broadcasting* 531 n.
*indication* 547 n.
*warning* 664 n.
*advice* 691 n.
*accusation* 928 n.
**information desk**
*informant* 524 n.
*adviser* 691 n.
*aider* 703 n.
**information highway**
*information* 524 n.
*Internet* 531 n.
**information science**
*computing* 86 n.
**information super-**
**highway**
*information* 524 n.
*Internet* 531 n.
**information tech-**
**nology**
*computing* 86 n.
*information* 524 n.
**information warfare**
*Internet* 531 n.
*warfare* 718 n.
**informative**
*informative* 524 adj.
*disclosing* 526 adj.
*educational* 534 adj.
*loquacious* 581 adj.
*conversing* 584 adj.
**informed**
*instructed* 490 adj.

safeguard 660 vb.
**insulation**
  *lining* 227 n.
  *preservation* 666 n.
**insulator**
  *electricity* 160 n.
**insulin**
  *drug* 658 n.
**insult**
  *hurt* 827 vb.
  *ridicule* 851 n.
  *slur* 867 n.
  *sauciness* 878 n.
  *rudeness* 885 n.
  *hate* 888 vb.
  *scurrility* 899 n.
  *indignity* 921 n.
  *not respect* 921 vb.
  *calumny* 926 n.
**insuperable**
  *impracticable* 470 adj.
  *difficult* 700 adj.
**insupportable**
  *intolerable* 827 adj.
**insurance**
  *calculation of chance* 159 n.
  *protection* 660 n.
  *promise* 764 n.
  *security* 767 n.
  *caution* 858 n.
**insurance policy**
  *title deed* 767 n.
**insure**
  *prepare* 669 vb.
  *give security* 767 vb.
**insurer**
  *consignee* 754 n.
**insurgent**
  *revolter* 738 n.
**insurmountable**
  *impracticable* 470 adj.
**insurrection**
  *resistance* 715 n.
  *revolt* 738 n.
**in suspense**
  *inactively* 175 adv.
  *in suspense* 474 adv.
  *expectant* 507 adj.
**intact**
  *intact* 52 adj.
  *complete* 54 adj.
  *perfect* 646 adj.
  *undamaged* 646 adj.
  *safe* 660 adj.
  *preserved* 666 adj.
**intaglio**
  *mould* 23 n.
  *concavity* 255 n.
  *sculpture* 554 n.
  *ornamental art* 844 n.
**intake**
  *size* 195 n.
  *ingress* 297 n.
  *way in* 297 n.
  *reception* 299 n.
  *requirement* 627 n.

waste 634 n.
**in tandem**
  *longwise* 203 adv.
  *rearward* 238 adv.
  *cooperative* 706 adj.
**intangible**
  *unreal* 2 adj.
  *minute* 196 adj.
  *immaterial* 320 adj.
**integer**
  *whole* 52 n.
  *number* 85 n.
  *unit* 88 n.
**integral**
  *intrinsic* 5 adj.
  *whole* 52 adj.
  *complete* 54 adj.
  *numerical* 85 adj.
**integral calculus**
  *mathematics* 86 n.
**integral part**
  *component* 58 n.
**integrate**
  *combine* 50 vb.
  *make complete* 54 vb.
**integrated care**
  *medical art* 658 n.
**integrated circuit**
  *electronics* 160 n.
  *microelectronics* 196 n.
**integration**
  *combination* 50 n.
  *completeness* 54 n.
  *inclusion* 78 n.
  *unity* 88 n.
  *association* 706 n.
**integrity**
  *whole* 52 n.
  *probity* 929 n.
  *virtue* 933 n.
**integument**
  *layer* 207 n.
  *exteriority* 223 n.
  *skin* 226 n.
**intellect**
  *intellect* 447 n.
  *thought* 449 n.
  *knowledge* 490 n.
  *intelligence* 498 n.
**intellectual**
  *mental* 447 adj.
  *philosopher* 449 n.
  *reasoner* 475 n.
  *instructed* 490 adj.
  *intellectual* 492 n.
  *wise* 498 adj.
  *sage* 500 n.
  *proficient person* 696 n.
**intellectual property**
  *estate* 777 n.
  *dueness* 915 n.
**intelligence**
  *head* 213 n.
  *intellect* 447 n.
  *secret service* 459 n.
  *intelligence* 498 n.
  *information* 524 n.

news 529 n.
wit 839 n.
**intelligence officer**
  *secret service* 459 n.
**intelligence test**
  *exam* 459 n.
**intelligent**
  *knowing* 490 adj.
  *intelligent* 498 adj.
  *skilful* 694 adj.
  *cunning* 698 adj.
**intelligentsia**
  *intellectual* 492 n.
**intelligent wear**
  *Internet* 531 n.
**intelligibility**
  *plainness* 573 n.
  *facility* 701 n.
**intelligible**
  *sane* 502 adj.
  *semantic* 514 adj.
  *intelligible* 516 adj.
  *manifest* 522 adj.
  *perspicuous* 567 adj.
**intemperance**
  *overstepping* 306 n.
  *festivity* 837 n.
  *desire* 859 n.
  *intemperance* 943 n.
  *sensualism* 944 n.
  *gluttony* 947 n.
  *drug-taking* 949 n.
  *drunkenness* 949 n.
**intemperate**
  *violent* 176 adj.
  *selfish* 932 adj.
  *vicious* 934 adj.
**intend**
  *predestine* 155 vb.
  *be mindful* 455 vb.
  *expect* 507 vb.
  *mean* 514 vb.
  *will* 595 vb.
  *be willing* 597 vb.
  *be resolute* 599 vb.
  *predetermine* 608 vb.
  *intend* 617 vb.
  *pursue* 619 vb.
  *plan* 623 vb.
  *attempt* 671 vb.
  *promise* 764 vb.
  *hope* 852 vb.
  *desire* 859 vb.
**intendant**
  *official* 690 n.
  *officer* 741 n.
**intended**
  *veracious* 540 adj.
  *volitional* 595 adj.
  *loved one* 887 n.
**intense**
  *great* 32 adj.
  *vigorous* 174 adj.
  *florid* 425 adj.
  *fervent* 818 adj.
**intensification**
  *stimulation* 174 n.

aggravation 832 n.
**intensify**
  *augment* 36 vb.
  *invigorate* 174 vb.
  *exaggerate* 546 vb.
  *animate* 821 vb.
  *aggravate* 832 vb.
**intensity**
  *degree* 27 n.
  *greatness* 32 n.
  *vigorousness* 174 n.
  *light* 417 n.
  *hue* 425 n.
**intensive**
  *increasing* 36 adj.
  *part of speech* 564 n.
**intensive care unit**
  *hospital* 658 n.
**intent**
  *attentive* 455 adj.
  *will* 595 n.
  *intention* 617 n.
**intention**
  *relation* 9 n.
  *expectation* 507 n.
  *connotation* 514 n.
  *will* 595 n.
  *predetermination* 608 n.
  *motive* 612 n.
  *intention* 617 n.
  *plan* 623 n.
  *aspiration* 852 n.
  *prayers* 981 n.
**intentional**
  *volitional* 595 adj.
  *intended* 617 adj.
**intentness**
  *attention* 455 n.
  *assiduity* 678 n.
**inter-**
  *correlative* 12 adj.
  *interchanged* 151 adj.
  *interjacent* 231 adj.
**inter**
  *inter* 364 vb.
  *conceal* 525 vb.
**interaction**
  *correlation* 12 n.
  *agency* 173 n.
  *action* 676 n.
  *cooperation* 706 n.
**inter alia**
  *among* 43 adv.
**interbred**
  *ethnic* 11 adj.
  *mixed* 43 adj.
**intercalary**
  *intermediate* 108 adj.
  *interjacent* 231 adj.
**intercede**
  *interfere* 231 vb.
  *patronize* 703 vb.
  *mediate* 720 vb.
  *worship* 981 vb.
**intercept**
  *interfere* 231 vb.
  *converge* 293 vb.

malcontent 829 n.
moper 834 n.
**jongleur**
  musician 413 n.
  poet 593 n.
**jorum**
  bowl 194 n.
**Joseph**
  virgin 950 n.
**Joseph's coat**
  variegation 437 n.
**josh**
  ridicule 851 vb.
**joss**
  idol 982 n.
**joss house**
  temple 990 n.
**joss stick**
  fumigator 385 n.
  scent 396 n.
  ritual object 988 n.
**jostle**
  be near 200 vb.
  be contiguous 202 vb.
  impel 279 vb.
  obstruct 702 vb.
  fight 716 vb.
  not respect 921 vb.
**jot**
  small quantity 33 n.
  trifle 639 n.
**jot down**
  record 548 vb.
  write 586 vb.
**jotter**
  stationery 586 n.
**jottings**
  record 548 n.
  reading matter 589 n.
**joule**
  energy 160 n.
**jounce**
  agitate 318 vb.
**jour maigre**
  fast 946 n.
**journal**
  chronology 117 n.
  journal 528 n.
  the press 528 n.
  record 548 n.
  biography 590 n.
  account book 808 n.
**journalese**
  neology 560 n.
**journalism**
  publicity 528 n.
  writing 586 n.
**journalist**
  enquirer 459 n.
  publicizer 528 n.
  news reporter 529 n.
  chronicler 549 n.
  author 589 n.
**journey**
  travel 267 vb.
  passage 305 n.
**journeyman**

artisan 686 n.
**journey's end**
  resting place 266 n.
  goal 295 n.
**journeywork**
  labour 682 n.
**joust**
  contest 716 n.
**jouster**
  combatant 722 n.
**Jove**
  Olympian deity 967 n.
**jovial**
  merry 833 adj.
  amused 837 adj.
  sociable 882 adj.
**jowl**
  laterality 239 n.
**joy**
  pleasure 376 n.
  excitation 821 n.
  joy 824 n.
  pleasurableness 826 n.
  cheerfulness 833 n.
  rejoicing 835 n.
**joyful**
  happy 824 adj.
  merry 833 adj.
**joyless**
  unpleasant 827 adj.
  dejected 834 adj.
  melancholic 834 adj.
**joyous**
  happy 824 adj.
  merry 833 adj.
**joy ride**
  land travel 267 n.
  borrowing 785 n.
  stealing 788 n.
**joystick**
  aircraft 276 n.
  directorship 689 n.
**JP**
  judge 957 n.
**jubbah**
  robe 228 n.
**jubilant**
  pleased 824 adj.
  jubilant 833 adj.
  rejoicing 835 adj.
  celebratory 876 adj.
**jubilation**
  merriment 833 n.
  rejoicing 835 n.
  celebration 876 n.
**jubilee**
  twenty and over 99 n.
  period 110 n.
  anniversary 141 n.
  merriment 833 n.
  rejoicing 835 n.
  celebration 876 n.
**Judaism**
  religious faith 973 n.
**Judaize, Judaise**
  make pious 979 vb.
**Judas**

deceiver 545 n.
tergiversator 603 n.
knave 938 n.
**Judas kiss**
  duplicity 541 n.
  perfidy 930 n.
**judder**
  be agitated 318 vb.
**judge**
  discriminate 463 vb.
  appraise 465 vb.
  estimator 480 n.
  judge 480 vb.
  choose 605 vb.
  leader 690 n.
  have taste 846 vb.
  find guilty 936 vb.
  judge 957 n.
  try a case 959 vb.
  punisher 963 n.
– beforehand
  prejudge 481 vb.
– for oneself
  will 595 vb.
**judge and jury**
  tribunal 956 n.
**judgment**
  intellect 447 n.
  discrimination 463 n.
  judgment 480 n.
  opinion 485 n.
  sagacity 498 n.
  decree 737 n.
  good taste 846 n.
  legality 953 n.
  legal trial 959 n.
  condemnation 961 n.
  punishment 963 n.
  divine function 965 n.
**judgment seat**
  courtroom 956 n.
  tribunal 956 n.
**judicatory**
  judicatory 956 adj.
**judicature**
  jurisdiction 955 n.
**judicial**
  judicial 480 adj.
  judicatory 956 adj.
**judicial murder**
  capital punishment
    963 n.
**judicial separation**
  divorce 896 n.
**judiciary**
  judge 957 n.
**judicious**
  moderate 177 adj.
  discriminating 463 adj.
  judicial 480 adj.
  wise 498 adj.
  advisable 642 adj.
**judo**
  defence 713 n.
  martial arts 716 n.
**judoist**
  combatant 722 n.

**jug**
  vessel 194 n.
  prison 748 n.
**juggernaut**
  destroyer 168 n.
  flattener 216 n.
  carrier 273 n.
  lorry 274 n.
**Juggernaut**
  monster 938 n.
  idol 982 n.
**juggins**
  ninny 501 n.
**juggle**
  modify 143 vb.
  deceive 542 vb.
  be cunning 698 vb.
**juggler**
  conjuror 545 n.
  entertainer 594 n.
  slyboots 698 n.
  sorcerer 983 n.
**jugular vein**
  essential part 5 n.
  conduit 351 n.
**juice**
  fluid 335 n.
  moisture 341 n.
  semiliquidity 354 n.
  fuel 385 n.
**juice box**
  soft drink 301 n.
**juiceless**
  dry 342 adj.
**juicy**
  new 126 adj.
  vernal 128 adj.
  soft 327 adj.
  fluid 335 adj.
  humid 341 adj.
  semiliquid 354 adj.
  pulpy 356 adj.
  savoury 390 adj.
  super 644 adj.
  pleasurable 826 adj.
  impure 951 adj.
**jujitsu**
  defence 713 n.
  martial arts 716 n.
**juju**
  talisman 983 n.
**jujube**
  sweet thing 392 n.
**jukebox**
  record player 414 n.
**julep**
  soft drink 301 n.
  sweet thing 392 n.
**Julian calendar**
  chronology 117 n.
**julienne**
  hors-d'oeuvres 301 n.
**jumble**
  medley 43 n.
  confusion 61 n.
  jumble 63 vb.
  deform 244 vb.

sort 77 n.
form 243 n.
beneficial 644 adj.
aiding 703 adj.
amiable 884 adj.
benevolent 897 adj.
disinterested 931 adj.
**kindergarten**
nonage 130 n.
school 539 n.
**kindest regards**
respects 920 n.
**kind-hearted**
benevolent 897 adj.
**kindle**
cause 156 vb.
invigorate 174 vb.
make violent 176 vb.
be hot 379 vb.
kindle 381 vb.
make bright 417 vb.
incite 612 vb.
feel 818 vb.
excite 821 vb.
be excitable 822 vb.
get angry 891 vb.
**kindling**
fuel 385 n.
**kindly**
affectionately 887 adv.
benevolent 897 adj.
**kindness**
leniency 736 n.
friendliness 880 n.
courtesy 884 n.
love 887 n.
benevolence 897 n.
kind act 897 n.
disinterestedness 931 n.
**kindred**
relative 9 adj.
consanguinity 11 n.
kinsman 11 n.
**kindred spirit**
close friend 880 n.
**kind regards**
courteous act 884 n.
respects 920 n.
**kind word**
approbation 923 n.
**kinematics**
motion 265 n.
**kinesiology**
alternative therapy
658 n.
**kinetics**
gesture 547 n.
**kinetic**
dynamic 160 adj.
moving 265 adj.
**kinetic art**
sculpture 554 n.
**kinetic energy**
energy 160 n.
**kinetics**
motion 265 n.
**king**

sovereign 741 n.
aristocrat 868 n.
**kingdom**
territory 184 n.
political organization
733 n.
**kingdom come**
future state 124 n.
heaven 971 n.
**Kingdom of God**
theocracy 965 n.
heaven 971 n.
**kingfisher**
bird 365 n.
**King Kong**
giant 195 n.
monster 938 n.
**King Log**
laxity 734 n.
**kingly**
ruling 733 adj.
impressive 821 adj.
worshipful 866 adj.
noble 868 adj.
proud 871 adj.
**kingly crown**
authority 733 n.
regalia 743 n.
**king maker**
influence 178 n.
director 690 n.
**kingpin**
fastening 47 n.
notable 638 n.
manager 690 n.
**king post**
pillar 218 n.
**king's** or **queen's
evidence**
information 524 n.
**kingship**
government 733 n.
position of authority
733 n.
**king size**
great 32 adj.
large 195 adj.
**King's** or **Queen's
messenger**
bearer 273 n.
**king's ransom**
wealth 800 n.
**King Stork**
tyrant 735 n.
**King Willow**
ball game 837 n.
**kink**
complexity 61 n.
coil 251 n.
eccentricity 503 n.
whim 604 n.
defect 647 n.
**kinky**
abnormal 84 adj.
undulatory 251 adj.
**kinsfolk**
kinsman 11 n.

**kinship**
relation 9 n.
consanguinity 11 n.
similarity 18 n.
parentage 169 n.
**kinship group**
social group 371 n.
**kinsman, kinswoman**
kinsman 11 n.
**kiosk**
pavilion 192 n.
small house 192 n.
shop 796 n.
**kip**
inn 192 n.
sleep 679 n.
**kipper**
dry 342 vb.
season 388 vb.
preserve 666 vb.
**kippers**
fish food 301 n.
**Kirbigrip (tdmk)**
hairdressing 843 n.
**kirk**
church 990 n.
**kirk session**
synod 985 n.
**kirkyard**
church exterior 990 n.
**kirsch**
alcoholic drink 301 n.
**kirtle**
skirt 228 n.
**kismet**
fate 596 n.
**kiss**
be contiguous 202 vb.
touch 378 vb.
courteous act 884 n.
endearment 889 n.
caress 889 vb.
– goodbye to
fail 728 vb.
lose 772 vb.
– hands
stoop 311 vb.
pay one's respects
884 vb.
– the rod
knuckle under 721 vb.
be servile 879 vb.
**kissable**
personable 841 adj.
lovable 887 adj.
**kiss curl**
hair 259 n.
**kisser**
face 237 n.
orifice 263 n.
**kissing cousin**
kinsman 11 n.
**kiss of life**
revival 656 n.
**kiss of peace**
ritual act 988 n.
**kit**

accumulation 74 n.
sort 77 n.
unit 88 n.
young creature 132 n.
clothing 228 n.
equipment 630 n.
**kitbag**
bag 194 n.
**kitchen**
room 194 n.
cookery 301 n.
heater 383 n.
workshop 687 n.
**kitchen cabinet**
council 692 n.
party 708 n.
**kitchenette**
room 194 n.
**kitchen garden**
farm 370 n.
garden 370 n.
**kitchen maid**
domestic 742 n.
**kitchen scales**
scales 322 n.
**kitchen sink**
descriptive 590 adj.
sink 649 n.
**kitchenette**
chamber 194 n.
**kite**
airship 276 n.
bird 365 n.
noxious animal 904 n.
**kite-flying**
empiricism 461 n.
publication 528 n.
rumour 529 n.
indication 547 n.
**kith and kin**
kinsman 11 n.
**kit out**
provide 633 vb.
make ready 669 vb.
**kitsch**
inferiority 35 n.
art 551 n.
ornamented 844 adj.
bad taste 847 n.
**kitten**
young creature 132 n.
weakling 163 n.
cat 365 n.
**kittenish**
infantine 132 adj.
merry 833 adj.
amused 837 adj.
**kittens, group of**
group 74 n. box
**kitty**
store 632 n.
association 706 n.
joint possession 775 n.
**Kiwi**
foreigner 59 n.
**kiwi fruit**
food 301 n.

**knockout blow**
*ruin* 165 n.
**knockout drops**
*anaesthetic* 375 n.
**knoll**
*small hill* 209 n.
**knot**
*tie* 45 vb.
*ligature* 47 n.
*complexity* 61 n.
*crowd* 74 n.
*long measure* 203 n.
*cross* 222 vb.
*distort* 246 vb.
*loop* 250 n.
*swelling* 253 n.
*solid body* 324 n.
*difficulty* 700 n.
*party* 708 n.
**knots**
*velocity* 277 n.
**knotted hand-**
 **kerchief**
*reminder* 505 n.
**knotty**
*dense* 324 adj.
*moot* 459 adj.
*difficult* 700 adj.
**knotty point**
*question* 459 n.
*unintelligibility* 517 n.
*enigma* 530 n.
**know**
*have sexual intercourse*
*with* 45 vb.
*cognize* 447 vb.
*be certain* 473 vb.
*believe* 485 vb.
*know* 490 vb.
*be wise* 498 vb.
*memorize* 505 vb.
*understand* 516 vb.
*be informed* 524 vb.
*be expert* 694 vb.
*befriend* 880 vb.
– a hawk from a handsaw
*discriminate* 463 vb.
– a little
*not know* 491 vb.
– all the answers
*dogmatize* 473 vb.
*know* 490 vb.
*be skilful* 694 vb.
*be cunning* 698 vb.
– a thing or two
*be wise* 498 vb.
*be expert* 694 vb.
– a trick worth two of
 that
*be cunning* 698 vb.
– backwards
*know* 490 vb.
*be expert* 694 vb.
– by instinct
*intuit* 476 vb.
– for certain
*believe* 485 vb.

– how many beans make
 five
*discriminate* 463 vb.
– no better
*not know* 491 vb.
*be artless* 699 vb.
*vulgarize* 847 vb.
– no bounds
*be great* 32 vb.
*superabound* 637 vb.
– one's own mind
*will* 595 vb.
*be resolute* 599 vb.
– one's place
*conform* 83 vb.
*be modest* 874 vb.
*show respect* 920 vb.
– one's stuff
*discriminate* 463 vb.
*know* 490 vb.
*be expert* 694 vb.
– the right people
*influence* 178 vb.
– what's what
*discriminate* 463 vb.
*know* 490 vb.
*be wise* 498 vb.
*be skilful* 694 vb.
– when to stop
*be cautious* 858 vb.
*be temperate* 942 vb.
**knowall**
*doctrinaire* 473 n.
*intellectual* 492 n.
*wiseacre* 500 n.
*affecter* 850 n.
*vain person* 873 n.
**know-how**
*knowledge* 490 n.
*way* 624 n.
*means* 629 n.
*skill* 694 n.
*cunning* 698 n.
**knowing**
*knowing* 490 adj.
*cunning* 698 adj.
**knowingly**
*knowingly* 490 adv.
*purposely* 617 adv.
**knowledge**
*knowledge* 490 n.
*wisdom* 498 n.
*information* 524 n.
*skill* 694 n.
**knowledgeable**
*instructed* 490 adj.
*wise* 498 adj.
*cunning* 698 adj.
**knowledge engineer**
*enumerator* 86 n.
**known**
*known* 490 adj.
*remembered* 505 adj.
*published* 528 adj.
*habitual* 610 adj.
*usual* 610 adj.
*renowned* 866 adj.

**known as**
*named* 561 adj.
**known by**
*marked* 547 adj.
**know-nothing**
*ignoramus* 493 n.
**knuckle**
*joint* 45 n.
*angularity* 247 n.
*swelling* 253 n.
**knuckle-duster**
*hammer* 279 n.
*club* 723 n.
**knucklehead**
*dunce* 501 n.
**knuckle under**
*knuckle under* 721 vb.
**knurled**
*rough* 259 adj.
**KO**
*ruin* 165 n.
*victory* 727 n.
**koan**
*unintelligibility* 517 n.
*worship* 981 n. box
**kobold**
*elf* 970 n.
**kohl**
*cosmetic* 843 n.
**kohlrabi**
*vegetable* 301 n.
**koine**
*language* 557 n.
**kolkhoz**
*farm* 370 n.
*joint possession* 775 n.
**kolkhoznik**
*participator* 775 n.
**Komsomol**
*society* 708 n.
**kook**
*madman* 504 n.
**kopek, kopeck**
*coinage* 797 n.
**kopje**
*small hill* 209 n.
**Koran**
*scripture* 975 n. box
**koruna**
*coinage* 797 n. box
**kosher**
*edible* 301 adj.
*clean* 648 adj.
*ritual* 988 adj.
**koumiss**
*milk* 301 n.
**kowtow, kotow**
*obeisance* 311 n.
*submission* 721 n.
*be servile* 879 vb.
*courteous act* 884 n.
*show respect* 920 vb.
**kraal**
*dwelling* 192 n.
*enclosure* 235 n.
**kraken**
*mythical beast* 365 n.

**Kremlin**
*position of authority*
 733 n.
*master* 741 n.
**kris**
*sharp edge* 256 n.
*sidearms* 723 n.
**Krishna**
*the Deity* 965 n.
*theophany* 965 n.
**krona, krone**
*coinage* 797 n. box
**kudos**
*prestige* 866 n.
*approbation* 923 n.
**Ku Klux Klan**
*society* 708 n.
*rioter* 738 n.
**kukri**
*sidearms* 723 n.
**kulak**
*farmer* 370 n.
*possessor* 776 n.
**kultur**
*civilization* 654 n.
**Kumbh Mela**
*holy day* 988 n. box
**kung fu**
*martial arts* 716 n.
**kursaal**
*place of amusement*
 837 n.
**kuru**
*mental disorder* 503 n.
**kwashiorkor**
*tropical disease* 651 n.
**kyle**
*gulf* 345 n.
**kyphosis**
*deformity* 246 n.
**Kyrie Eleison**
*prayers* 981 n.

# L

**laager**
*site* 187 n.
*fort* 713 n.
**lab**
*classroom* 539 n.
**labdanum**
*resin* 357 n.
**label**
*class* 62 vb.
*label* 547 n.
*mark* 547 vb.
**labial**
*marginal* 234 adj.
*speech sound* 398 n.
**labile**
*unstable* 152 adj.
**laboratory**
*crucible* 147 n.
*testing agent* 461 n.
*workshop* 687 n.
**laborious**

**enjoyment** 824 n.
 revel 837 n.
**lark about/around**
 be absurd 497 vb.
 amuse oneself 837 vb.
**larks, group of**
 group 74 n. box
**larrikin**
 ruffian 904 vb.
**larrup**
 spank 963 vb.
**larva**
 young creature 132 n.
 insect 365 n.
**laryngitis**
 respiratory disease 651 n.
 inflammation 651 n.
  box
**larynx**
 air pipe 353 n.
 voice 577 n.
**larynx, inflammation of**
 inflammation 651 n.
  box
**larynx, surgical operation on or removal of**
 surgery 658 n. box
**lasagne**
 dish 301 n.
**lascivious**
 lecherous 951 adj.
**laser**
 electronics 160 n.
 weapon 723 n.
**laser disc**
 recording instrument 549 n.
**laser printing**
 printing 555 n.
 print 587 n.
**laser resurfacing**
 beautification 843 n.
**lash**
 tie 45 vb.
 stimulant 174 n.
 make violent 176 vb.
 filament 208 n.
 strike 279 vb.
 incentive 612 n.
 animate 821 vb.
 reprobate 924 vb.
 flog 963 vb.
 scourge 964 n.
 – out
 be violent 176 vb.
 be prodigal 815 vb.
 be angry 891 vb.
 – out at
 strike at 712 vb.
 cuss 899 vb.
**lashes**
 eye 438 n.
**lashings**
 great quantity 32 n.
 plenty 635 n.

**lass**
 youngster 132 n.
 woman 373 n.
**Lassa fever**
 tropical disease 651 n.
**lassie**
 woman 373 n.
**lassitude**
 sleepiness 679 n.
 fatigue 684 n.
**lasso**
 halter 47 n.
 loop 250 n.
**last**
 mould 23 n.
 ending 69 adj.
 continue 108 vb.
 last 113 vb.
 foregoing 125 adj.
 stay 144 vb.
 completive 725 adj.
**last arrival**
 lateness 136 n.
**last breath**
 end 69 n.
 decease 361 n.
**last ditcher**
 stamina 600 n.
 obstinate person 602 n.
 opponent 705 n.
 malcontent 829 n.
**last gasp**
 end 69 n.
 decease 361 n.
 means 629 n.
**lasting**
 lasting 113 adj.
 perpetual 115 adj.
 permanent 144 adj.
 unchangeable 153 adj.
 unyielding 162 adj.
**last lap**
 end 69 n.
 arrival 295 n.
**last minute**
 lateness 136 n.
 crisis 137 n.
 hasty 680 adj.
**last place**
 sequence 65 n.
 rear 238 n.
 following 284 n.
**last post**
 evening 129 n.
 valediction 296 n.
 obsequies 364 n.
 call 547 n.
**last resort**
 necessity 596 n.
 contrivance 623 n.
 means 629 n.
 refuge 662 n.
**last rites**
 obsequies 364 n.
 Christian rite 988 n.
**last straw**
 instrument 156 n.

**encumbrance** 702 n.
 completion 725 n.
 annoyance 827 n.
 resentment 891 n.
**last things**
 finality 69 n.
**last throw**
 gambling 618 n.
 means 629 n.
 attempt 671 n.
 hope 852 n.
 rashness 857 n.
**last will and testament**
 title deed 767 n.
**last word**
 answer 460 n.
 certainty 473 n.
 confutation 479 n.
**last word in**
 modernism 126 n.
 exceller 644 n.
 fashion 848 n.
**last words**
 sequel 67 n.
 end 69 n.
 valediction 296 n.
**latch**
 join 45 vb.
 fastening 47 n.
 – on to
 understand 516 vb.
**late**
 anachronistic 118 adj.
 former 125 adj.
 modern 126 adj.
 vespertine 129 adj.
 late 136 adj., adv.
 ill-timed 138 adj.
 slow 278 adj.
 dead 361 adj.
 negligent 458 adj.
 immature 670 adj.
 unprepared 670 adj.
**latecomer**
 successor 67 n.
 posteriority 120 n.
 lateness 136 n.
**late developer**
 learner 538 n.
 undevelopment 670 n.
**lately**
 formerly 125 adv.
 newly 126 adv.
**latency**
 influence 178 n.
 connotation 514 n.
 latency 523 n.
 intention 617 n.
 See also **latent**
**lateness**
 evening 129 n.
 lateness 136 n.
**latent**
 inert 175 adj.
 invisible 444 adj.
 latent 523 adj.

**concealed** 525 adj.
 deceiving 542 adj.
 unclear 568 adj.
**later**
 after 65 adv.
 subsequent 120 adj.
 not now 122 adv.
 future 124 adj.
 behind 284 adv.
**lateral**
 lateral 239 adj.
**lateral thinking**
 meditation 449 n.
 reasoning 475 n.
**latest**
 present 121 adj.
**latest, the**
 modernism 126 n.
 fashion 848 n.
**latex**
 fluid 335 n.
 materials 631 n.
**lath**
 lamina 207 n.
 strip 208 n.
 materials 631 n.
**lathe**
 rotator 315 n.
**lather**
 excrement 302 n.
 lubricant 334 n.
 bubble 355 n.
 clean 648 vb.
 spank 963 vb.
**lathi**
 club 723 n.
**Latin**
 language 557 n.
**latitude**
 range 183 n.
 room 183 n.
 region 184 n.
 breadth 205 n.
 scope 744 n.
**latitude and longitude**
 bearings 186 n.
 coordinate 465 n.
**latitudinarian**
 wise 498 adj.
 free 744 adj.
**latitudinarianism**
 heterodoxy 977 n.
**latria**
 cult 981 n.
**latrine**
 latrine 649 n.
**latte**
 soft drink 301 n.
**latten**
 lamina 207 n.
**latter**
 sequential 65 adj.
 foregoing 125 adj.
**latter-day**
 present 121 adj.
 modern 126 adj.

be parsimonious 816 vb.
– out of a suitcase
travel 267 vb.
– through
continue 108 vb.
be restored 656 vb.
feel 818 vb.
– to fight another day
outlast 113 vb.
seek safety 660 vb.
parry 713 vb.
– together
wed 894 vb.
– under
be subject 745 vb.
– well
be sensual 944 vb.
– with
have sexual intercourse
with 45 vb.
accompany 89 vb.
wed 894 vb.
**lived in**
occupied 191 adj.
**live-in**
male 372 n.
woman 373 n.
lover 887 n.
**livelihood**
vocation 622 n.
**liveliness**
energy 160 n.
vitality 162 n.
vigorousness 174 n.
vigour 571 n.
restlessness 678 n.
moral sensibility 819 n.
cheerfulness 833 n.
**livelong**
lasting 113 adj.
**lively**
vigorous 174 adj.
speedy 277 adj.
agitated 318 adj.
alive 360 adj.
striking 374 adj.
imaginative 513 adj.
forceful 571 adj.
active 678 adj.
feeling 818 adj.
lively 819 adj.
excitable 822 adj.
cheerful 833 adj.
sociable 882 adj.
**live music**
music 412 n.
**liven up**
vitalize 360 vb.
be cheerful 833 vb.
**liver**
insides 224 n.
meat 301 n.
sullenness 893 n.
**liver, inflammation
of**
inflammation 651 n.
box

**liver-coloured**
brown 430 adj.
**live relay**
broadcast 531 n.
**liveried**
uniform 16 adj.
dressed 228 adj.
**liverish**
irascible 892 adj.
drunken 949 adj.
**liverishness**
digestive disorders 651 n.
**liverwort**
plant 366 n.
**livery**
uniform 228 n.
livery 547 n.
**livery company**
corporation 708 n.
**livestock**
animal 365 n.
cattle 365 n.
**live theatre**
drama 594 n.
**live wire**
electricity 160 n.
vigorousness 174 n.
busy person 678 n.
**livid**
blackish 428 adj.
grey 429 adj.
blue 435 adj.
purple 436 adj.
excited 821 adj.
angry 891 adj.
**living**
vocation 622 n.
benefice 985 n.
**living, the**
life 360 n.
humankind 371 n.
**living death**
suffering 825 n.
**living image**
analogue 18 n.
duplication 91 n.
**living matter**
organism 358 n.
life 360 n.
**living quarters**
quarters 192 n.
**living room**
room 194 n.
**living soul**
person 371 n.
**living space**
room 183 n.
scope 744 n.
**living wage**
sufficiency 635 n.
**living will**
credential 767 n.
**lixiviate**
purify 648 vb.
**lizard**
reptile 365 n.
**llama**

beast of burden 273 n.
**LLB, LLD**
academic title 870 n.
**llyn**
lake 346 n.
**load**
fill 54 vb.
bunch 74 n.
stow 187 vb.
contents 193 n.
load 193 vb.
thing transferred 272 n.
gravity 322 n.
redundance 637 n.
encumbrance 702 n.
adversity 731 n.
worry 825 n.
– the dice
deceive 542 vb.
– with
add 38 vb.
hinder 702 vb.
**loaded**
hearing 273 adj.
weighty 322 adj.
moneyed 800 adj.
**loaded table**
feasting 301 n.
plenty 635 n.
**load off one's mind**
relief 831 n.
**loads**
great quantity 32 n.
multitude 104 n.
**loaf**
head 213 n.
cereals 301 n.
intelligence 498 n.
be inactive 679 vb.
**loafer**
wanderer 268 n.
idler 679 n.
**loam**
soil 344 n.
**loan**
economic aid 703 n.
lending 784 n.
borrowing 785 n.
credit 802 n.
**loan shark**
lender 784 n.
**loanword**
neology 560 n.
**loath, loth**
unwilling 598 adj.
disliking 861 adj.
**loathe**
dislike 861 vb.
hate 888 vb.
**loathing**
dislike 861 n.
enmity 881 n.
hatred 888 n.
**loathsome**
unsavoury 391 adj.
not nice 645
uu

ugly 842 adj.
disliked 861 adj.
hateful 888 adj.
**lob**
strike 279 vb.
propel 287 vb.
elevate 310 vb.
**lobby**
influence 178 n., vb.
lobby 194 n.
motivator 612 n.
incite 612 vb.
access 624 n.
petitioner 763 n.
– against
deprecate 762 vb.
**lobe**
hanging object 217 n.
ear 415 n.
**lobotomy**
surgery 658 n. box
**lobster**
fish food 301 n.
marine life 365 n.
**local**
focus 76 n.
regional 184 adj.
situated 186 adj.
native 191 n.
pub 192 n.
provincial 192 adj.
near 200 adj.
**local area network**
Internet 531 n.
**local authority**
jurisdiction 955 n.
**local colour**
accuracy 494 n.
painting 553 n.
description 590 n.
**locale**
region 184 n.
situation 186 n.
**locality**
district 184 n.
region 184 n.
place 185 n.
locality 187 n.
**localize, localise**
place 187 vb.
restrain 747 vb.
**locally**
somewhere 185 adv.
near 200 adv.
**locate**
specify 80 vb.
place 187 vb.
orientate 281 vb.
discover 484 vb.
**located**
remaining 41 adj.
situated 186 adj.
located 187 ~~
di~~

**lore**
*tradition* 127 n.
*erudition* 490 n.
*knowledge* 490 n.
*learning* 536 n.
*cunning* 698 n.
**Lorelei**
*vocalist* 413 n.
*motivator* 612 n.
*mythical being* 970 n.
**lorgnette**
*eyeglass* 442 n.
**loricate**
*covered* 226 adj.
**lorn**
*friendless* 883 adj.
**lorry**
*lorry* 274 n.
**lose**
*decrease* 37 vb.
*misdate* 118 vb.
*be late* 136 vb.
*misplace* 188 vb.
*outstrip* 277 vb.
*relinquish* 621 vb.
*be defeated* 728 vb.
*lose* 772 vb.
– a chance
*be late* 136 vb.
*lose a chance* 138 vb.
– colour
*be dim* 419 vb.
*lose colour* 426 vb.
– consciousness
*be impotent* 161 vb.
*be insensible* 375 vb.
– control
*be lax* 734 vb.
*be intemperate* 943 vb.
– control of oneself
*be excited* 821 vb.
– face
*be inferior* 35 vb.
*act foolishly* 695 vb.
*lose repute* 867 vb.
– ground
*decelerate* 278 vb.
*regress* 286 vb.
*fall short* 307 vb.
*relapse* 657 vb.
*be defeated* 728 vb.
– heart
*be dejected* 834 vb.
*despair* 853 vb.
– no time
*be early* 135 vb.
*hasten* 680 vb.
– one's bearings
*stray* 282 vb.
– one's cool
*be excited* 821 vb.
– one's head
*go mad* 503 vb.
*be unskilful* 695 vb.
– one's heart
*be in love* 887 vb.
– one's life

*die* 361 vb.
– one's nerve
*be unskilful* 695 vb.
*be cowardly* 856 vb.
– one's temper
*be rude* 885 vb.
*get angry* 891 vb.
– one's tongue
*be mute* 578 vb.
*be taciturn* 582 vb.
– out
*be defeated* 728 vb.
– patience
*get angry* 891 vb.
– repute
*lose repute* 867 vb.
– sight of
*be blind* 439 vb.
*be inattentive* 456 vb.
*neglect* 458 vb.
*forget* 506 vb.
– the scent
*have no smell* 395 vb.
*be uncertain* 474 vb.
– the thread
*be unrelated* 10 vb.
*stray* 282 vb.
*be inattentive* 456 vb.
*be uncertain* 474 vb.
– the way
*wander* 267 vb.
*stray* 282 vb.
– track of
*misplace* 188 vb.
*stray* 282 vb.
*be inattentive* 456 vb.
*be uncertain* 474 vb.
– weight
*decrease* 37 vb.
*make thin* 206 vb.
*lighten* 323 vb.
**loser**
*bungler* 697 n.
*loser* 728 n.
*unlucky person* 731 n.
*laughingstock* 851 n.
**losing**
*inexact* 495 adj.
*profitless* 641 adj.
*unsuccessful* 728 adj.
*losing* 772 adj.
**losing business**
*unproductiveness* 172 n.
**losing game**
*defeat* 728 n.
**losing ground**
*deterioration* 655 n.
**losing height**
*flying* 271 adj.
**losing one's touch**
*clumsy* 695 adj.
**losing side**
*loser* 728 n.
**losing weight**
*dieting* 301 n.
**loss**
*decrease* 37 n.

*decrement* 42 n.
*deficit* 55 n.
*ruin* 165 n.
*unproductiveness* 172 n.
*absence* 190 n.
*outflow* 298 n.
*shortfall* 307 n.
*disappearance* 446 n.
*waste* 634 n.
*inutility* 641 n.
*impairment* 655 n.
*loss* 772 n.
**losses**
*failure* 728 n.
**loss leader**
*incentive* 612 n.
*discount* 810 n.
**loss-making**
*profitless* 641 adj.
**loss of right**
*loss of right* 916 n.
**lost**
*past* 125 adj.
*destroyed* 165 adj.
*misplaced* 188 adj.
*absent* 190 adj.
*deviating* 282 adj.
*disappearing* 446 adj.
*doubting* 474 adj.
*unknown* 491 adj.
*concealed* 525 adj.
*lost* 772 adj.
*impenitent* 940 adj.
*condemned* 961 adj.
**lost cause**
*rejection* 607 n.
*defeat* 728 n.
**lost in thought**
*thoughtful* 449 adj.
*abstracted* 456 adj.
**lost in wonder**
*wondering* 864 adj.
**lost labour**
*unproductiveness* 172 n.
*lost labour* 641 n.
*failure* 728 n.
**lost leader**
*tergiversator* 603 n.
**lost sheep**
*bad person* 938 n.
**lost soul**
*bad person* 938 n.
*devil* 969 n.
**lost to shame**
*vicious* 934 adj.
**lost to sight**
*distant* 199 adj.
*disappearing* 446 adj.
**lot**
*state* 7 n.
*finite quantity* 26 n.
*all* 52 n.
*bunch* 74 n.
*chance* 159 n.
*territory* 184 n.
*enclosure* 23⁵
*or⸱*

*fate* 596 n.
*nondesign* 618 n.
*participation* 775
*portion* 783 n.
**Lothario**
*lover* 887 n.
*libertine* 952 n.
**lotion**
*water* 339 n.
*cleanser* 648 n.
*balm* 658 n.
**lots**
*great quantity* 32 n.
*multitude* 104 n.
*plenty* 635 n.
**lottery**
*equal chance* 159 n.
*gambling* 618 n.
*gambling game* 837 n.
**lotus-eater**
*idler* 679 n.
**louche**
*disreputable* 867 adj.
**loud**
*loud* 400 adj.
*resonant* 404 adj.
*strident* 407 adj.
*crying* 408 adj.
*florid* 425 adj.
*manifest* 522 adj.
*ornate* 574 adj.
*rhetorical* 574 adj.
*vulgar* 847 adj.
**loudhailer**
*megaphone* 400 n.
*publicity* 528 n.
**loudmouth**
*boaster* 877 n.
*rude person* 885 n.
**loud pedal**
*piano* 414 n.
**loudspeaker**
*megaphone* 400 n.
*hearing instrument* 415 n.
*publicity* 528 n.
**lough**
*lake* 346 n.
**lounge**
*room* 194 n.
*be inactive* 679 vb.
*repose* 683 vb.
**lounge bar**
*pub* 192 n.
**lounge lizard**
*fop* 848 n.
**lounger**
*seat* 218 n.
*idler* 679 n.
**loupe**
*eyeglass* 442 n.
**lour, lower**
*impend* 155 v⸱
*ha⸱*

*be sullen* 893 vb.
*threaten* 900 vb.
**louse**
*insect* 365 n.
*cad* 938 n.
**lousy**
*not nice* 645 adj.
*unclean* 649 adj.
**lousy with**
*full* 54 adj.
*assembled* 74 adj.
*multitudinous* 104 adj.
**lout**
*dunce* 501 n.
*bungler* 697 n.
*rude person* 885 n.
*ruffian* 904 n.
**loutish**
*ill-bred* 847 adj.
*plebeian* 869 adj.
*discourteous* 885 adj.
**louvre**
*air pipe* 353 n.
**lovable, loveable**
*personable* 841 adj.
*amiable* 884 adj.
*lovable* 887 adj.
**love**
*zero* 103 n.
*enjoy* 376 vb.
*moral sensibility* 819 n.
*be pleased* 824 vb.
*liking* 859 n.
*desire* 859 vb.
*be friendly* 880 vb.
*love* 887 n., vb.
*loved one* 887 n.
*lover* 887 n.
*caress* 889 vb.
*pet* 889 vb.
*darling* 890 n.
*benevolence* 897 n.
*jealousy* 911 n.
*disinterestedness* 931 n.
*divineness* 965 n.
– to
*be wont* 610 vb.
**love affair**
*love affair* 887 n.
**love all**
*draw* 28 n.
**love and kisses**
*courteous act* 884 n.
**love and peace**
*concord* 710 n.
**lovebirds**
*lovers* 887 n.
**love bite**
*endearment* 889 n.
**love child**
*descendant* 170 n.
*bastardy* 954 n.
**loved one**
*desired object* 859 n.
*loved one* 887 n.
*darling* 890 n.
**love emblem**

*love emblem* 887 n.
*love token* 889 n.
**love feast**
*social gathering* 882 n.
*public worship* 981 n.
**love god**
*love god* 887 n.
**love-hate**
*contrary* 14 adj.
**love knot**
*badge* 547 n.
**loveless**
*indifferent* 860 adj.
*unwanted* 860 adj.
*disliked* 861 adj.
*disliking* 861 adj.
*hated* 888 adj.
*hating* 888 adj.
**love letter**
*love token* 889 n.
*wooing* 889 n.
**lovelock**
*coil* 251 n.
*hair* 259 n.
**lovelorn**
*loving* 887 adj.
*hated* 888 adj.
**lovely**
*pleasant* 376 adj.
*super* 644 adj.
*pleasurable* 826 adj.
*a beauty* 841 n.
*beautiful* 841 adj.
*lovable* 887 adj.
**lovemaking**
*sexual intercourse* 45 n.
*sexual pleasure* 376 n.
*lovemaking* 887 n.
*endearment* 889 n.
*wooing* 889 n.
**love-match**
*type of marriage* 894 n.
**love-nest**
*love-nest* 887 n.
**love of one's country**
*patriotism* 901 n.
**love of pleasure**
*sensualism* 944 n.
**love philtre**
*stimulant* 174 n.
**love potion**
*stimulant* 174 n.
**lover**
*sexual partner* 45 n.
*concomitant* 89 n.
*patron* 707 n.
*desirer* 859 n.
*lover* 887 n.
*spouse* 894 n.
*libertine* 952 n.
**lovers**
*lovers* 887 n.
**lovesick**
*loving* 887 adj.
**love song**
*vocal music* 412 n.
*poem* 593 n.

*wooing* 889 n.
**love story**
*novel* 590 n.
**love token**
*love token* 889 n.
**lovey**
*darling* 890 n.
**lovey-dovey**
*caressing* 889 adj.
**loving care**
*carefulness* 457 n.
**loving cup**
*draught* 301 n.
*sociability* 882 n.
**loving it**
*pleased* 824 adj.
**loving-kindness**
*benevolence* 897 n.
**lovingly**
*carefully* 457 adv.
*affectionately* 887 adv.
*benevolently* 897 adv.
**loving words**
*endearment* 889 n.
**low**
*small* 33 adj.
*inferior* 35 adj.
*weak* 163 adj.
*low* 210 adj.
*muted* 401 adj.
*ululate* 409 vb.
*not nice* 645 adj.
*cheap* 812 adj.
*dejected* 834 adj.
*vulgar* 847 adj.
*disreputable* 867 adj.
*plebeian* 869 adj.
*humble* 872 adj.
*rascally* 930 adj.
**lowborn**
*plebeian* 869 adj.
**lowbrow**
*uninstructed* 491 adj.
*ignoramus* 493 n.
*unintelligent* 499 adj.
**low-budget**
*cheap* 812 adj.
**low-caste**
*inferior* 35 adj.
*plebeian* 869 adj.
**Low-Church**
*Anglican* 976 adj.
*sectarian* 978 adj.
**low-density**
*few* 105 adj.
**lowdown**
*truth* 494 n.
*information* 524 n.
**lower**
*inferior* 35 adj.
*abate* 37 vb.
*low* 210 adj.
*lower* 311 vb.
*impair* 655 vb.
*pervert* 655 vb.
*cheapen* 812 vb.
*vulgarize* 847 vb.

*humiliate* 872 vb.
*not respect* 921 vb.
*hold cheap* 922 vb.
*defame* 926 vb.
– oneself
*descend* 309 vb.
*sit down* 311 vb.
*demean oneself* 867 vb.
– one's sights
*relinquish* 621 vb.
– one's voice
*sound faint* 401 vb.
**lower case**
*print-type* 587 n.
**lower classes**
*lower classes* 869 n.
**lower deck**
*layer* 207 n.
*plebeian* 869 adj.
**Lower House**
*parliament* 692 n.
**lowermost**
*undermost* 214 adj.
**lower orders**
*nonentity* 639 n.
*lower classes* 869 n.
**lowest**
*lesser* 35 adj.
**low-fat**
*salubrious* 652 adj.
**low fellow**
*low fellow* 869 n.
**low gear**
*slowness* 278 n.
**low-grade**
*inferior* 35 adj.
*bad* 645 adj.
**low-key**
*moderate* 177 adj.
**lowlander**
*dweller* 191 n.
**lowlands**
*lowness* 210 n.
*plain* 348 n.
**Lowlands**
*district* 184 n.
**low-level**
*inferior* 35 adj.
*low* 210 adj.
*unimportant* 639 adj.
**low-life**
*descriptive* 590 adj.
*lower classes* 869 n.
*wickedness* 934 n.
**lowly**
*inferior* 35 adj.
*plebeian* 869 adj.
*humble* 872 adj.
**low-lying**
*low* 210 adj.
**low-minded**
*vulgar* 847 adj.
**low neck**
*neckline* 228 n.
*bareness* 229 n.
**low on**
*insufficient* 636 adj.

occultism 984 n.
– away
  bewitch 983 vb.
**magical**
  *magical* 983 adj.
**magic arts**
  *sorcery* 983 n.
**magic carpet**
  *airship* 276 n.
  *speeder* 277 n.
  *aid* 703 n.
  *magic instrument* 983 n.
**magic eye**
  *representation* 551 n.
**magician**
  *alterer* 143 n.
  *conjuror* 545 n.
  *proficient person* 696 n.
  *sorcerer* 983 n.
**magic instrument**
  *magic instrument* 983 n.
**magic lantern**
  *lamp* 420 n.
  *optical device* 442 n.
  *plaything* 837 n.
**magic lore**
  *sorcery* 983 n.
**magic mushroom**
  *drug* 949 n.
**magic rite**
  *sorcery* 983 n.
**magic symbol**
  *indication* 547 n.
**magic wand**
  *magic instrument* 983 n.
**magic word**
  *spell* 983 n.
**magic world**
  *fairy* 970 n.
**Maginot Line**
  *defences* 713 n.
**magisterial**
  *skilful* 694 adj.
  *authoritative* 733 adj.
  *ruling* 733 adj.
  *insolent* 878 adj.
**magistracy**
  *position of authority* 733 n.
  *magistracy* 957 n.
**magistrate**
  *official* 690 n.
  *officer* 741 n.
  *judge* 957 n.
  *punisher* 963 n.
**magistrate's court**
  *lawcourt* 956 n.
**magistrature**
  *position of authority* 733 n.
**magma**
  *a mixture* 43 n.
  *rock* 344 n.
**Magna Carta**
  *dueness* 915 n.
**magnanimity**
  *benevolence* 897 n.

*disinterestedness* 931 n.
*virtues* 933 n.
**magnanimous**
  *forgiving* 909 adj.
  *disinterested* 931 adj.
  *virtuous* 933 adj.
**magnate**
  *notable* 638 n.
  *aristocrat* 868 n.
**magnet**
  *traction* 288 n.
  *magnet* 291 n.
  *incentive* 612 n.
  *desired object* 859 n.
**magnetic**
  *dynamic* 160 adj.
  *drawing* 288 adj.
  *attracting* 291 adj.
  *inducing* 612 adj.
**magnetic field**
  *energy* 160 n.
  *attraction* 291 n.
**magnetic needle**
  *sailing aid* 269 n.
  *indicator* 547 n.
  *directorship* 689 n.
**magnetic north**
  *compass point* 281 n.
**magnetic tape**
  *computing* 86 n.
  *rotator* 315 n.
  *hearing instrument* 415 n.
  *record* 548 n.
**magnetism**
  *energy* 160 n.
  *influence* 178 n.
  *traction* 288 n.
  *attraction* 291 n.
  *inducement* 612 n.
**magnetize, magnetise**
  *empower* 160 vb.
  *attract* 291 vb.
**magneto**
  *electronics* 160 n.
**Magnificat**
  *hymn* 981 n.
**magnification**
  *greatness* 32 n.
  *optics* 417 n.
  *vision* 438 n.
  *See also* **magnify**
**magnificent**
  *large* 195 adj.
  *excellent* 644 adj.
  *splendid* 841 adj.
  *ostentatious* 875 adj.
**magnifico**
  *aristocrat* 868 n.
**magnify**
  *augment* 36 vb.
  *enlarge* 197 vb.
  *overrate* 482 vb.
  *exaggerate* 546 vb.
  *make important* 638 vb.
  *boast* 877 vb.
  *respect* 920 vb.

*praise* 923 vb.
*worship* 981 vb.
**magnifying glass**
  *eyeglass* 442 n.
**magniloquence**
  *exaggeration* 546 n.
  *vigour* 571 n.
  *magniloquence* 574 n.
  *affectation* 850 n.
  *ostentation* 875 n.
**magniloquent**
  *boastful* 877 adj.
**magnitude**
  *quantity* 26 n.
  *degree* 27 n.
  *greatness* 32 n.
  *size* 195 n.
  *light* 417 n.
  *importance* 638 n.
**magnolia**
  *tree* 366 n.
  *whitish* 427 adj.
**Magnox reactor**
  *nucleonics* 160 n.
**magnum**
  *vessel* 194 n.
  *size* 195 n.
**magnum opus**
  *product* 164 n.
  *book* 589 n.
  *masterpiece* 694 n.
**magpie**
  *bird* 365 n.
  *chatterer* 581 n.
  *niggard* 816 n.
**magus**
  *sage* 500 n.
  *sorcerer* 983 n.
**maharaja, maharajah**
  *potentate* 741 n.
**maharani,**
  **maharanee**
  *potentate* 741 n.
**maharishi**
  *good person* 937 n.
  *religious teacher* 973 n.
**mahatma**
  *sage* 500 n.
  *good person* 937 n.
**Mahayana**
  *religious faith* 973 n.
**Mahdi**
  *leader* 690 n.
  *religious teacher* 973 n.
**mah-jong**
  *indoor game* 837 n.
**mahogany**
  *smoothness* 258 n.
  *tree* 366 n.
  *brownness* 430 n.
**Mahomet**
  *religious teacher* 973 n.
**mahout**
  *rider* 268 n.
**maiasaur**
  *animal* 365 n.
**maid**

*youngster* 132 n.
*domestic* 742 n.
*spinster* 895 n.
*virgin* 950 n.
**maiden**
  *first* 68 adj.
  *new* 126 adj.
  *youngster* 132 n.
  *woman* 373 n.
  *spinster* 895 n.
  *virgin* 950 n.
**maidenhood**
  *celibacy* 895 n.
  *purity* 950 n.
**maiden name**
  *name* 561 n.
**maiden speech**
  *debut* 68 n.
**maid-of-all work**
  *busy person* 678 n.
  *worker* 686 n.
  *domestic* 742 n.
**maid/matron of**
  **honour**
  *bridal party* 894 n.
**maieutic**
  *enquiring* 459 adj.
  *rational* 475 adj.
  *instrumental* 628 adj.
**mail**
  *covering* 226 n.
  *send* 272 vb.
  *postal communications* 531 n.
  *correspondence* 588 n.
  *safeguard* 662 n.
  *armour* 713 n.
**mailbag**
  *postal communications* 531 n.
**mail-clad**
  *defended* 713 adj.
**mailed fist**
  *brute force* 735 n.
  *compulsion* 740 n.
  *lawlessness* 954 n.
**mailing list**
  *information* 524 n.
  *correspondence* 588 n.
**mail order**
  *purchase* 792 n.
**maim**
  *disable* 161 vb.
  *impair* 655 vb.
**maimed**
  *incomplete* 55 adj.
  *imperfect* 647 adj.
**main**
  *great* 32 adj.
  *supreme* 34 adj.
  *conduit* 351 n.
  *communicating* 624 adj.
  *important* 638 adj.
  *sink* 649 n.
**main chance**
  *fair chance* 159 n.
  *chief thing* 638 n.

*gain* 771 n.
**main force**
   *strength* 162 n.
   *compulsion* 740 n.
**mainframe**
   *computer* 86 n.
**mainland**
   *land* 344 n.
   *inland* 344 adj.
**mainline**
   *take drugs* 949 vb.
**mainly**
   *substantially* 3 adv.
   *greatly* 32 adv.
   *on the whole* 52 adv.
   *generally* 79 adv.
**mainmast**
   *sail* 275 n.
**main part**
   *main part* 32 n.
   *chief thing* 638 n.
**main point**
   *chief thing* 638 n.
**mainsail**
   *sail* 275 n.
**mainspring**
   *cause* 156 n.
   *motive* 612 n.
   *machine* 630 n.
**mainstay**
   *prop* 218 n.
   *chief thing* 638 n.
   *aider* 703 n.
**mainstream**
   *greater number* 104 n.
   *tendency* 179 n.
**mainstream jazz**
   *music* 412 n.
**Main Street**
   *averageness* 732 n.
   *irreligious* 974 adj.
**maintain**
   *stay* 144 vb.
   *sustain* 146 vb.
   *operate* 173 vb.
   *support* 218 vb.
   *believe* 485 vb.
   *affirm* 532 vb.
   *persevere* 600 vb.
   *provide* 633 vb.
   *preserve* 666 vb.
   *celebrate* 876 vb.
   *vindicate* 927 vb.
**maintenance**
   *economic aid* 703 n.
   *receipt* 807 n.
**main thing**
   *chief thing* 638 n.
**maisonette**
   *flat* 192 n.
**maître**
   *proficient person* 696 n.
**maître d'hôtel**
   *caterer* 633 n.
**maize**
   *cereals* 301 n.
   *food* 301 n.

**majestic**
   *elegant* 575 adj.
   *authoritative* 733 adj.
   *impressive* 821 adj.
   *beautiful* 841 adj.
   *worshipful* 866 adj.
   *proud* 871 adj.
   *formal* 875 adj.
   *godlike* 965 adj.
**majesty**
   *greatness* 32 n.
   *superiority* 34 n.
   *authority* 733 n.
   *sovereign* 741 n.
   *prestige* 866 n.
   *nobility* 868 n.
**Majlis**
   *parliament* 692 n. box
**major**
   *great* 32 adj.
   *superior* 34 adj.
   *first* 68 adj.
   *older* 131 adj.
   *grown-up* 134 adj.
   *harmonic* 410 adj.
   *important* 638 adj.
   *army officer* 741 n.
**majordomo**
   *retainer* 742 n.
**major in**
   *study* 536 vb.
**majority**
   *main part* 32 n.
   *chief part* 52 n.
   *greater number* 104 n.
   *adultness* 134 n.
**majority rule**
   *government* 733 n.
**make**
   *character* 5 n.
   *have sexual intercourse*
     *with* 45 vb.
   *composition* 56 n.
   *compose* 56 vb.
   *constitute* 56 vb.
   *sort* 77 n.
   *convert* 147 vb.
   *cause* 156 vb.
   *produce* 164 vb.
   *influence* 178 vb.
   *form* 243 vb.
   *arrive* 295 vb.
   *structure* 331 n.
   *estimate* 480 vb.
   *make better* 654 vb.
   *compel* 740 vb.
   *gain* 771 vb.
– a balls-up of
   *impair* 655 vb.
– a clean breast of it
   *confess* 526 vb.
   *be truthful* 540 vb.
– a clean sweep (of)
   *revolutionize* 149 vb.
   *empty* 300 vb.
   *clean* 648 vb.
– a comeback

   *be restored* 656 vb.
– acquainted
   *befriend* 880 vb.
– a dead set at
   *attack* 712 vb.
   *desire* 859 vb.
– a dent in
   *waste* 634 vb.
– advances
   *offer* 759 vb.
   *court* 889 vb.
– a face
   *distort* 246 vb.
   *dislike* 861 vb.
   *be sullen* 893 vb.
   *disapprove* 924 vb.
– a fight of it
   *resist* 715 vb.
– a fool of
   *be absurd* 497 vb.
   *befool* 542 vb.
   *ridicule* 851 vb.
   *humiliate* 872 vb.
– a fool of oneself
   *be foolish* 499 vb.
   *act foolishly* 695 vb.
– a fortune
   *prosper* 730 vb.
   *gain* 771 vb.
   *get rich* 800 vb.
– a go of
   *succeed* 727 vb.
– a hash of it
   *blunder* 495 vb.
   *be clumsy* 695 vb.
– a hit
   *succeed* 727 vb.
   *excite love* 887 vb.
– a killing
   *succeed* 727 vb.
   *gain* 771 vb.
   *get rich* 800 vb.
– a laughing-stock of
   *ridicule* 851 vb.
– a man of
   *do good* 644 vb.
   *give courage* 855 vb.
– amends
   *compensate* 31 vb.
   *restitute* 787 vb.
   *atone* 941 vb.
– a mess of it
   *be clumsy* 695 vb.
– a mint
   *get rich* 800 vb.
– a monkey of
   *ridicule* 851 vb.
– a moue
   *distort* 246 vb.
– an entrance
   *be visible* 443 vb.
– an example of
   *punish* 963 vb.
– an exception
   *be unconformable* 84 vb.
– an exhibition of oneself
   *be ridiculous* 849 vb.

   *be ostentatious* 875 vb.
– an impression
   *be vigorous* 174 vb.
   *cause thought* 449 vb.
– a pass at
   *court* 889 vb.
– a point of
   *make important* 638 vb.
   *compel* 740 vb.
– a profit
   *flourish* 615 vb.
   *be useful* 640 vb.
   *gain* 771 vb.
– a scapegoat
   *attribute* 158 vb.
– a scene
   *be angry* 891 vb.
– a show of
   *imitate* 20 vb.
   *dissemble* 541 vb.
   *be affected* 850 vb.
– a silk purse out of a
     sow's ear
   *attempt the impossible*
     470 vb.
– a splash
   *superabound* 637 vb.
   *be ostentatious* 875 vb.
– a stand
   *resist* 715 vb.
   *give battle* 718 vb.
– available
   *offer* 759 vb.
– a virtue of necessity
   *have no choice* 606 vb.
   *submit* 721 vb.
   *compromise* 770 vb.
– away with
   *destroy* 165 vb.
   *kill* 362 vb.
   *murder* 362 vb.
   *steal* 788 vb.
– better
   *transform* 147 vb.
   *benefit* 615 vb.
   *make better* 654 vb.
– bold to
   *be free* 744 vb.
   *be insolent* 878 vb.
– both ends meet
   *afford* 800 vb.
   *economize* 814 vb.
– bright
   *make bright* 417 vb.
   *illuminate* 420 vb.
   *clean* 648 vb.
   *beautify* 841 vb.
– capital out of
   *plead* 614 vb.
   *find useful* 640 vb.
   *use* 673 vb.
– certain
   *corroborate* 466 vb.
   *make certain* 473 vb.
   *demonstrate* 478 vb.
   *give security* 767 vb.
   *be cautious* 858 vb.

**martyrology**
list 87 n.
death roll 361 n.
biography 590 n.
**martyr's crown**
honours 866 n.
**martyr to ill health**
sick person 651 n.
**marvel**
prodigy 864 n.
wonder 864 vb.
**marvellous**
prodigious 32 adj.
excellent 644 adj.
pleasurable 826 adj.
wonderful 864 adj.
**Marxism**
philosophy 449 n.
**Marxism-Leninism**
government 733 n.
**Marxist**
revolutionist 149 n.
revolutionary 149 adj.
reformer 654 n.
**Marxists**
political party 708 n.
**marzipan**
sweet thing 392 n.
**mascara**
cosmetic 843 n.
**mascot**
preserver 666 n.
talisman 983 n.
**masculine**
generic 77 adj.
manly 162 adj.
male 372 adj.
grammatical 564 adj.
**masculinism**
reformism 654 n.
**masculinist**
reformer 654 n.
**masculinity**
male 372 n.
**mash**
mix 43 vb.
soften 327 vb.
pulverize 332 vb.
thicken 354 vb.
pulpiness 356 n.
**mask**
covering 226 n.
screen 421 n., vb.
conceal 525 vb.
disguise 527 n.
duplicity 541 n.
sham 542 n.
mental dishonesty 543 n.
**masochism**
variance 84 n.
**masochist**
nonconformist 84 n.
sensualist 944 n.
**mason**
form 243 vb.
artisan 686 n.
**Masonic**

sectional 708 adj.
**masonry**
building material 631 n.
**Masorah**
scripture 975 n.
**Masorete**
theologian 973 n.
**masque**
stage play 594 n.
**masquerade**
clothing 228 n.
concealment 525 n.
disguise 527 n.
sham 542 n.
dancing 837 n.
**masquerader**
hider 527 n.
impostor 545 n.
**mass**
quantity 26 n.
great quantity 32 n.
main part 32 n.
extensive 32 adj.
chief part 52 n.
accumulation 74 n.
crowd 74 n.
congregate 74 vb.
general 79 adj.
greater number 104 n.
bulk 195 n.
size 195 n.
matter 319 n.
gravity 322 n.
solid body 324 n.
army 722 n.
public worship 981 n.
**massacre**
slaughter 362 n., vb.
execute 963 vb.
**massage**
soften 327 vb.
friction 333 n.
touch 378 n., vb.
surgery 658 n.
beautification 843 n.
**massed**
multitudinous 104 adj.
dense 324 adj.
**masses, the**
everyman 79 n.
social group 371 n.
commonalty 869 n.
**masseur, masseuse**
friction 333 n.
doctor 658 n.
**mass grave**
tomb 364 n.
**mass hysteria**
crowd 74 n.
**massif**
high land 209 n.
**massive**
great 32 adj.
large 195 adj.
weighty 322 adj.
dense 324 adj.
**mass media**

information 524 n.
**mass meeting**
assembly 74 n.
**mass murder**
destruction 165 n.
**mass-produce**
produce 164 vb.
reproduce 166 vb.
**mass production**
uniformity 16 n.
production 164 n.
productiveness 171 n.
**mast**
high structure 209 n.
hanger 217 n.
prop 218 n.
sail 275 n.
**mastaba**
tomb 364 n.
**mastectomy**
surgery 658 n. box
**master**
superior 34 n.
prevail 178 vb.
mariner 270 n.
male 372 n.
know 490 vb.
sage 500 n.
understand 516 vb.
learn 536 vb.
teacher 537 n.
artisan 686 n.
director 690 n.
proficient person 696 n.
victor 727 n.
overmaster 727 vb.
master 741 n.
owner 776 n.
title 870 n.
academic title 870 n.
– one's feelings
keep calm 823 vb.
**master copy**
duplicate 22 n.
**masterful**
skilful 694 adj.
authoritative 733 adj.
authoritarian 735 adj.
**master key**
opener 263 n.
instrument 628 n.
**masterless**
independent 744 adj.
unpossessed 774 adj.
**masterly**
perfect 646 adj.
skilful 694 adj.
successful 727 adj.
**mastermind**
superior 34 n.
intellectual 492 n.
planner 623 n.
direct 689 vb.
proficient person 696 n.
**master of arts, master of education, etc**
academic title 870 n.

**master of ceremonies**
leader 690 n.
reveller 837 n.
**master of hounds**
manager 690 n.
**master/mistress of one's profession, be**
be expert 694 vb.
**master/mistress of one's time, be**
have leisure 681 vb.
**master of science**
academic title 870 n.
**Master of the Rolls**
recorder 549 n.
judge 957 n.
**masterpiece**
product 164 n.
picture 553 n.
exceller 644 n.
perfection 646 n.
masterpiece 694 n.
success 727 n.
a beauty 841 n.
**master plan**
prototype 23 n.
plan 623 n.
**master spirit**
sage 500 n.
notable 638 n.
person of repute 866 n.
**masterstroke**
contrivance 623 n.
masterpiece 694 n.
success 727 n.
**masterwork**
masterpiece 694 n.
**mastery**
knowledge 490 n.
skill 694 n.
victory 727 n.
governance 733 n.
possession 773 n.
**masthead**
vertex 213 n.
label 547 n.
punish 963 n.
**mastic**
viscidity 354 n.
resin 357 n.
**masticate**
chew 301 vb.
**mastiff**
dog 365 n.
**mastodon**
animal 365 n.
**masturbate**
have or give sexual pleasure 376 vb.
**masturbation**
sexual pleasure 376 n.
illicit love 951 n.
**mat**
seat 218 n.
enlace 222 vb.
floor-covering 226 n.

*do sums* 86 vb.
moderation 177 n.
*measure* 183 n.
size 195 n.
tempo 410 n.
tune 412 n.
gauge 465 n.
metrology 465 n.
measure 465 vb.
estimate 480 vb.
prosody 593 n.
deed 676 n.
portion 783 n.
apportion 783 vb.
– one's length
be horizontal 216 vb.
tumble 309 vb.
– up to
be equal 28 vb.
be able 160 vb.
suffice 635 vb.
**measured**
uniform 16 adj.
periodical 141 adj.
moderate 177 adj.
measured 465 adj.
sufficient 635 adj.
temperate 942 adj.
**measured against**
compared 462 adj.
**measured by**
comparative 27 adj.
**measure for measure**
compensation 31 n.
interchange 151 n.
retaliation 714 n.
revenge 910 n.
**measureless**
infinite 107 adj.
**measurement**
size 195 n.
measurement 465 n.
See also **measure**
**measures**
policy 623 n.
means 629 n.
actions 676 n.
**measuring**
   **instrument**
meter 465 n.
**measuring tape**
line 203 n.
gauge 465 n.
**meat**
substance 3 n.
food 301 n.
meat 301 n.
materials 631 n.
**meat and two veg**
dish 301 n.
**meat-eater**
eater 301 n.
**meatless day**
fast 946 n.
holy day 988 n.
**meat loaf**
dish 301 n.

**meaty**
substantial 3 adj.
fleshy 195 adj.
meaningful 514 adj.
forceful 571 adj.
**Mecca**
focus 76 n.
objective 617 n.
holy place 990 n.
**mechanic**
machinist 630 n.
artisan 686 n.
**mechanical**
dynamic 160 adj.
involuntary 596 adj.
instrumental 628 adj.
mechanical 630 adj.
**mechanical device**
machine 630 n.
tool 630 n.
**mechanical drawing**
representation 551 n.
**mechanical energy**
energy 160 n.
**mechanically**
habitually 610 adv.
**mechanician**
machinist 630 n.
**mechanics**
physics 319 n.
study 536 n. box
mechanics 630 n.
**mechanism**
biology 358 n.
philosophy 449 n.
machine 630 n.
**mechanistic**
involuntary 596 adj.
**mechanization, mech-**
   **anisation**
instrumentality 628 n.
**mechanize,**
   **mechanise**
produce 164 vb.
**mechanized, mech-**
   **anised**
productive 164 adj.
mechanical 630 adj.
**MEd**
academic title 870 n.
**medal**
badge 547 n.
decoration 729 n.
jewellery 844 n.
honours 866 n.
reward 962 n.
See also **medals**
**medallion**
sculpture 554 n.
jewellery 844 n.
**medalist**
victor 727 n.
**medals, collector of**
collector 492 n. box
**meddle**
derange 63 vb.
interfere 231 vb.

be curious 453 vb.
busy oneself 622 vb.
impair 655 vb.
meddle 678 vb.
be clumsy 695 vb.
obstruct 702 vb.
mediate 720 vb.
**meddler**
inquisitive person 453 n.
meddler 678 n.
adviser 691 n.
hinderer 702 n.
**media, the**
publication 528 n.
broadcasting 531 n.
**medial**
middle 70 adj.
**median**
average 30 n.
median 30 adj.
middle 70 adj.
interjacent 231 adj.
**mediant**
musical note 410 n.
**media personality**
broadcaster 531 n.
favourite 890 n.
**mediate**
be instrumental 628 vb.
pacify 719 vb.
mediate 720 vb.
**mediation**
mediation 720 n.
deprecation 762 n.
**mediator**
moderator 177 n.
intermediary 231 n.
mediator 720 n.
**medic**
doctor 658 n.
**medicable**
restored 656 adj.
medical 658 adj.
**medical**
enquiry 459 n.
medical 658 adj.
**medical care**
therapy 658 n.
**medical officer**
sanitorian 652 n.
doctor 658 n.
**medical practitioner**
doctor 658 n.
**medical school**
training school 539 n.
**medicament**
medicine 658 n.
**medicate**
cure 656 vb.
doctor 658 vb.
**medication**
medicine 658 n.
**medicinal**
restorative 656 adj.
remedial 658 adj.
**medicine**
draught 301 n.

medical art 658 n.
medicine 658 n.
**medicine cabinet**
medicine 658 n.
**medicine man**
doctor 658 n.
sorcerer 983 n.
**medieval, mediaeval**
olden 127 adj.
**medieval times**
antiquity 125 n.
**medievalist, medi-**
   **aevalist**
antiquarian 125 n.
**mediocre**
inferior 35 adj.
not bad 644 adj.
middling 732 adj.
**mediocrity**
nonentity 639 n.
**meditate**
meditate 449 vb.
enquire 459 vb.
intend 617 vb.
**meditation**
meditation 449 n.
attention 455 n.
alternative therapy
   658 n.
piety 979 n.
prayers 981 n.
**meditative**
thoughtful 449 adj.
pious 979 adj.
**mediterranean**
middle 70 adj.
interjacent 231 adj.
**Mediterranean**
ocean 343 n.
**medium**
average 30 n.
middle 70 n.
surroundings 230 n.
intermediary 231 n.
oracle 511 n.
interpreter 520 n.
instrument 628 n.
instrumentality 628 n.
middling 732 adj.
psychic 984 n.
**mediumistic**
psychic 447 adj.
psychical 984 adj.
**medium wave**
radiation 417 n.
**medley**
nonuniformity 17 n.
medley 43 n.
confusion 61 n.
accumulation 74 n.
musical piece 412 n.
**medley of colour**
variegation 437 n.
**medullary**
soft 327 adj.
**Medusa**
eyesore 842 n.

record 548 n.
plan 623 n.
important matter 638 n.
**memorial**
perpetuity 115 n.
reminder 505 n.
report 524 n.
monument 548 n.
trophy 729 n.
request 761 n.
honours 866 n.
**memorialist**
chronicler 549 n.
**memorial service**
obsequies 364 n.
**memorize, memorise**
know 490 vb.
memorize 505 vb.
learn 536 vb.
**memory**
computing 86 n.
memory 505 n.
storage 632 n.
famousness 866 n.
**memory like a sieve**
oblivion 506 n.
**memsahib**
lady 373 n.
title 870 n.
**men**
mariner 270 n.
personnel 686 n.
armed force 722 n.
**men, fear of**
phobia 854 n. box
**menace**
danger 661 n.
endanger 661 vb.
warn 664 vb.
annoyance 827 n.
frighten 854 vb.
hateful object 888 n.
threat 900 n.
threaten 900 vb.
**ménage**
inhabitants 191 n.
management 689 n.
**ménage à trois**
type of marriage 894 n.
**menagerie**
medley 43 n.
accumulation 74 n.
zoo 369 n.
collection 632 n.
**menarche**
productiveness 171 n.
haemorrhage 302 n.
**mend**
join 45 vb.
get healthy 650 vb.
get better 654 vb.
make better 654 vb.
repair 656 vb.
– one's ways
change one's mind 603 n.
get better 654 vb.

become pious 979 vb.
**mendacious**
false 541 adj.
untrue 543 adj.
**mendacity**
falsehood 541 n.
**Mendelian**
inherited 157 adj.
filial 170 adj.
**Mendelism**
heredity 5 n.
**mendicant**
idler 679 n.
beggar 763 n.
**menfolk**
male 372 n.
**menial**
inferior 35 adj.
servant 742 n.
serving 742 adj.
**meningitis**
infection 651 n.
inflammation 651 n. box
**men in grey suits**
uniformity 16 n.
**meniscus**
curve 248 n.
optical device 442 n.
**Mennonite**
sectarian 978 n.
**menology**
chronology 117 n.
**menopause**
middle age 131 n.
unproductiveness 172 n.
**menorrhagia**
haemorrhage 302 n.
**Mensa**
intelligence 498 n.
**menses**
regular return 141 n.
haermorrhage 302 n.
**Menshevik**
moderate 625 n.
political party 708 n.
**Men's Movement**
male 372 n.
**mens sana in corpore sano**
health 650 n.
**menstrual**
seasonal 141 adj.
excretory 302 adj.
**mensurable**
numerable 86 adj.
measured 465 adj.
**mensuration**
measurement 465 n.
**mental**
immaterial 320 adj.
mental 447 adj.
mentally disordered 503 adj.
**mental and spiritual make-up**
affections 817 n.

**mental attitude**
conduct 688 n.
**mental block**
oblivion 506 n.
**mental capacity**
intellect 447 n.
intelligence 498 n.
**mental case**
madman 504 n.
sick person 651 n.
**mental deficiency**
unintelligence 499 n.
mental handicap 503 n.
**mental dishonesty**
concealment 525 n.
learning disability 543 n.
stratagem 698 n.
**mental disorder**
absence of intellect 448 n.
unintelligence 499 n.
mental disorder 503 n.
excitable state 822 n.
**mental handicap**
unintelligence 499 n.
learning disability 503 n.
**mental health**
sanity 502 n.
**mental hospital**
mental hospital 503 n.
hospital 658 n.
shelter 662 n.
**mental illness**
mental disorder 503 n.
**mental image**
idea 451 n.
ideality 513 n.
image 551 n.
**mentality**
intellect 447 n.
affections 817 n.
**mentally disordered**
mentally disordered 503 n.
**mentally handicapped**
unintelligent 499 adj.
mentally handicapped 504 n.
**mentally ill**
mentally disturbed 503 adj.
**mental process**
thought 449 n.
**mental reservation**
sophistry 477 n.
equivocalness 518 n.
mental dishonesty 543 n.
**mental torment**
suffering 825 n.
**mention**
referral 9 n.
specify 80 vb.
notice 455 vb.
information 524 n.
hint 524 vb.
inform 524 vb.

speak 579 vb.
**mentionable**
pure 950 adj.
**mentioned in dispatches, be**
be praised 923 vb.
**mentor**
sage 500 n.
teacher 537 n.
adviser 691 n.
**menu**
computing 86n.
list 87 n.
meal 301 n.
**Mephistophelean**
wicked 934 adj.
diabolic 969 adj.
**Mephistopheles**
Mephisto 969 n.
**mephitis**
stench 397 n.
insalubrity 653 n.
poison 659 n.
**mercantile**
businesslike 622 adj.
trading 791 adj.
**mercantile marine**
shipping 275 n.
**Mercator's projection**
distortion 246 n.
map 551 n.
**mercenary**
militarist 722 n.
avaricious 816 adj.
venal 930 adj.
selfish 932 adj.
**mercer**
tradespeople 794 n.
**mercerize, mercerise**
be tough 329 vb.
**merchandise**
product 164 n.
equipment 630 n.
store 632 n.
sale 793 n.
merchandise 795 n.
**merchandise in**
trade 791 vb.
**merchant**
transferrer 272 n.
agent 686 n.
merchant 794 n.
**merchantman**
merchant ship 275 n.
**merchant marine**
navy 722 n.
**merchant navy**
shipping 275 n.
**merchant venturer**
gambler 618 n.
merchant 794 n.
**merciful**
lenient 736 adj.
benevolent 897 adj.
pitying 905 adj.
forgiving 909 adj.
godlike 965 adj.

**microminiaturiz-
   ation, microminia-
   turisation**
  *microelectronics* 196 n.
**micron**
  *small quantity* 33 n.
  *long measure* 203 n.
**microorganism**
  *microorganism* 196 n.
  *animal* 365 n.
  *insalubrity* 653 n.
**microphone**
  *megaphone* 400 n.
  *hearing instrument*
     415 n.
  *telecommunication*
     531 n.
  *rostrum* 539 n.
**microphotography**
  *microscopy* 196 n.
  *photography* 551 n.
**microphyte**
  *microorganism* 196 n.
**microprocessor**
  *counting instrument* 86 n.
  *electronics* 160 n.
  *microelectronics* 196 n.
**microscooter**
  *conveyance* 267 n.
  *plaything* 837 n.
**microscope**
  *microscopy* 196 n.
  *microscope* 442 n.
**microscopic**
  *small* 33 adj.
  *minute* 196 adj.
  *indistinct* 444 adj.
**microtechnique**
  *microscopy* 196 n.
**microwave**
  *cook* 301 vb.
  *radiation* 417 n.
**microwave oven**
  *furnace* 383 n.
**mid**
  *middle* 70 adj.
  *between* 231 adv.
**Midas**
  *rich person* 800 n.
**Midas touch**
  *prosperity* 730 n.
  *wealth* 800 n.
**midday**
  *noon* 128 n.
  *heat* 379 n.
**midden**
  *rubbish* 641 n.
**middle**
  *median* 30 adj.
  *middle* 70 n., adj.
  *interim* 108 n.
  *centre* 225 n.
  *interjacency* 231 n.
  *interjacent* 231 adj.
  *middling* 732 adj.
**middle age**
  *middle age* 131 n.

  *adultness* 134 n.
**Middle Ages**
  *era* 110 n.
  *antiquity* 125 n.
**middlebrow**
  *median* 30 adj.
  *middling* 732 adj.
**middle classes**
  *social group* 371 n.
  *averageness* 732 n.
  *middle classes* 869 n.
**middle course**
  *middle way* 625 n.
**middle distance**
  *middle point* 30 n.
  *middle* 70 n.
**Middle America**
  *middle classes* 869 n.
**Middle England**
  *middle classes* 869 n.
**middle ground**
  *middle point* 30 n.
**middleman**
  *intermediary* 231 n.
  *provider* 633 n.
  *agent* 686 n.
  *consignee* 754 n.
  *merchant* 794 n.
**middle-of-the-road**
  *moderate* 177 adj.
  *neutral* 625 adj.
  *not bad* 644 adj.
  *imperfect* 647 adj.
  *sectional* 708 adj.
  *middling* 732 adj.
**middle-of-the-roader**
  *moderate* 625 n.
**middle way**
  *middle way* 625 n.
  *compromise* 770 n.
**middleweight**
  *pugilist* 722 n.
**middle youth**
  *youth* 130 n.
  *middle age* 131 n.
**middling**
  *inconsiderable* 33 adj.
  *not bad* 644 adj.
  *middling* 732 adj.
**midge**
  *insect* 365 n.
**midget**
  *small animal* 33 n.
  *dwarf* 196 n.
**midi skirt**
  *skirt* 228 n.
**Midlands**
  *interiority* 224 n.
  *inland* 344 adj.
**midmost**
  *middle* 70 adj.
  *interior* 224 adj.
  *central* 225 adj.
**midnight**
  *midnight* 129 n.
  *darkness* 418 n.
**midpoint**

  *middle* 70 n.
  *centre* 225 n.
**midrib**
  *middle* 70 n.
  *centre* 225 n.
**midriff**
  *partition* 231 n.
**midshipman**
  *nautical personnel* 270 n.
**midships**
  *midway* 70 adv.
**midst**
  *middle* 70 n.
  *centrally* 225 adv.
  *between* 231 adv.
**midstream**
  *midway* 70 adv.
  *middle way* 625 n.
**midsummer**
  *summer* 128 n.
**midway**
  *midway* 70 adv.
**midweek**
  *intermediate* 108 adj.
**midwife**
  *obstetrics* 167 n.
  *instrument* 628 n.
  *doctor* 658 n.
  *auxiliary* 707 n.
**midwinter**
  *winter* 129 n.
**mien**
  *mien* 445 n.
  *gesture* 547 n.
  *conduct* 688 n.
**miff**
  *torment* 827 vb.
  *cause discontent* 829 vb.
  *be rude* 885 vb.
  *enrage* 891 vb.
**miffed**
  *unhappy* 825 adj.
  *discontented* 829 adj.
  *dejected* 834 adj.
  *resentful* 891 adj.
**might**
  *greatness* 32 n.
  *power* 160 n.
  *strength* 162 n.
  *be possible* 469 vb.
**might and main**
  *exertions* 682 n.
**might-have-been, the**
  *possibility* 469 n.
**mighty**
  *great* 32 adj.
  *powerful* 160 adj.
  *strong* 162 adj.
  *influential* 178 adj.
  *huge* 195 adj.
  *worshipful* 866 adj.
  *proud* 871 adj.
**mignon**
  *favourite* 890 n.
**migraine**
  *pang* 377 n.
  *illness* 651 n.

**migrant**
  *foreigner* 59 n.
  *wanderer* 268 n.
  *incomer* 297 n.
  *bird* 365 n.
**migration**
  *wandering* 267 n.
  *departure* 296 n.
**migratory**
  *travelling* 267 adj.
**Mikado**
  *sovereign* 741 n.
**mike**
  *megaphone* 400 n.
  *hearing instrument*
     415 n.
**milady**
  *lady* 373 n.
  *person of rank* 868 n.
**milch cow**
  *abundance* 171 n.
  *cattle* 365 n.
  *store* 632 n.
**mild**
  *moderate* 177 adj.
  *alcoholic drink* 301 n.
  *warm* 379 adj.
  *tasteless* 387 adj.
  *lenient* 736 adj.
  *inexcitable* 823 adj.
  *amiable* 884 adj.
**mildew**
  *dirt* 649 n.
  *dilapidation* 655 n.
  *impair* 655 vb.
  *blight* 659 n.
**mildewed**
  *antiquated* 127 adj.
  *dim* 419 adj.
**mild-mannered**
  *peaceful* 717 adj.
**mildness**
  *moderation* 177 n.
  *leniency* 736 n.
  *courtesy* 884 n.
  *benevolence* 897 n.
**mile**
  *long measure* 203 n.
**mileage**
  *distance* 199 n.
  *length* 203 n.
  *utility* 640 n.
**milepost**
  *signpost* 547 n.
**miles away**
  *abstracted* 456 adj.
**miles gloriosus**
  *combatant* 722 n.
  *boaster* 877 n.
**miles per hour**
  *velocity* 277 n.
**milestone**
  *degree* 27 n.
  *serial place* 73 n.
  *event* 154 n.
  *situation* 186 n.
  *itinerary* 267 n.

*opacity* 423 n.
*blur* 440 vb.
*invisibility* 444 n.
*uncertainty* 474 n.
**mistake**
*mistake* 495 n.
*misinterpretation* 521 n.
*solecism* 565 n.
*bungling* 695 n.
*failure* 728 n.
**mistaken**
*misjudging* 481 adj.
*mistaken* 495 adj.
*unwise* 499 adj.
**misteach**
*mislead* 495 vb.
*misinterpret* 521 vb.
*misteach* 535 vb.
*misrepresent* 552 vb.
**mister**
*male* 372 n.
*title* 870 n.
**misthrow**
*bungling* 695 n.
**mistime**
*mistime* 138 vb.
**mistletoe**
*plant* 366 n.
**mistral**
*wind* 352 n.
**mistranslate**
*misinterpret* 521 vb.
**mistreatment**
*misuse* 675 n.
**mistress**
*sexual partner* 45 n.
*lady* 373 n.
*teacher* 537 n.
*victor* 727 n.
*master* 741 n.
*owner* 776 n.
*title* 870 n.
*loved one* 887 n.
*kept woman* 952 n.
**mistress of the**
**wardrobe**
*clothier* 228 n.
**mistrust**
*doubt* 486 n., vb.
*nervousness* 854 n.
*be jealous* 911 vb.
**misty**
*insubstantial* 4 adj.
*cloudy* 355 adj.
*dim* 419 adj.
*opaque* 423 adj.
*semitransparent* 424 adj.
*indistinct* 444 adj.
*uncertain* 474 adj.
*puzzling* 517 adj.
**misunderstand**
*not know* 491 vb.
*err* 495 vb.
*not understand* 517 vb.
*misinterpret* 521 vb.
**misunderstanding**
*error* 495 n.

*misinterpretation* 521 n.
*dissension* 709 n.
**misusage**
*solecism* 565 n.
*misuse* 675 n.
**misuse**
*force* 176 vb.
*waste* 634 n., vb.
*ill-treat* 645 vb.
*impairment* 655 n.
*misuse* 675 n., vb.
*be unskilful* 695 vb.
*be severe* 735 vb.
*cruel act* 898 n.
**misuse of funds**
*prodigality* 815 n.
**misuse of language**
*inexactness* 495 n.
**mite**
*small coin* 33 n.
*small quantity* 33 n.
*child* 132 n.
*dwarf* 196 n.
*insect* 365 n.
*insufficiency* 636 n.
**Mithras**
*mythic deity* 966 n.
**mithridate**
*antidote* 658 n.
**mitigate**
*abate* 37 vb.
*moderate* 177 vb.
*qualify* 468 vb.
*make better* 654 vb.
*relieve* 831 vb.
*extenuate* 927 vb.
**mitigating circum-**
**stance**
*vindication* 927 n.
**mitrailleuse**
*gun* 723 n.
**mitre**
*joint* 45 n.
*join* 45 vb.
*badge of rule* 743 n.
*vestments* 989 n.
**mitt**
*glove* 228 n.
*feeler* 378 n.
**mittimus**
*warrant* 737 n.
**mix**
*mix* 43 vb.
*combine* 50 vb.
*jumble* 63 vb.
*modify* 143 vb.
*agitate* 318 vb.
– in
*add* 38 vb.
*infiltrate* 297 vb.
– in society
*be sociable* 882 vb.
– it
*fight* 716 vb.
*cause discontent* 829 vb.
– up
*mix* 43 vb.

*jumble* 63 vb.
– with
*be sociable* 882 vb.
**mixed-ability**
*educational* 534 adj.
**mixed bag**
*nonuniformity* 17 n.
*medley* 43 n.
*accumulation* 74 n.
**mixed blessing**
*inexpedience* 643 n.
*adversity* 731 n.
**mixed economy**
*middle* 70 n.
**mixed grill**
*dish* 301 n.
**mixed metaphor**
*metaphor* 519 n.
**mixed number**
*numerical element* 85 n.
**mixed up in**
*component* 58 adj.
**mixer**
*mixture* 43 n.
*soft drink* 301 n.
**mixture**
*mixture* 43 n.
*combination* 50 n.
*composition* 56 n.
*confusion* 61 n.
*draught* 301 n.
*imperfection* 647 n.
*medicine* 658 n.
**mixture as before**
*uniformity* 16 n.
*recurrence* 106 n.
**mixture of colour**
*variegation* 437 n.
**mix-up**
*confusion* 61 n.
**mizzenmast**
*poop* 238 n.
*sail* 275 n.
**mizzle**
*rain* 350 vb.
**MLitt**
*academic title* 870 n.
**MMR**
*prophylactic* 658 n.
**mnemonic**
*reminder* 505 n.
**mnemonics**
*mnemonics* 505 n.
**moan**
*blow* 352 vb.
*faintness* 401 n.
*cry* 408 n.
*be discontented* 829 vb.
*lamentation* 836 n.
*weep* 836 vb.
**moat**
*fence* 235 n.
*cavity* 255 n.
*furrow* 262 n.
*conduit* 351 n.
*protection* 660 n.
*obstacle* 702 n.

*defences* 713 n.
**mob**
*rampage* 61 vb.
*crowd* 74 n.
*multitude* 104 n.
*be violent* 176 vb.
*pursue* 619 vb.
*charge* 712 vb.
*rabble* 869 n.
*celebrate* 876 vb.
*congratulate* 886 vb.
*caress* 889 n.
*not respect* 921 vb.
*disapprove* 924 vb.
**mob cap**
*headgear* 228 n.
**mobile**
*changeable thing* 152 n.
*hanging object* 217 n.
*moving* 265 adj.
*telecommunication*
531 n.
*sculpture* 554 n.
*lively* 819 adj.
**mobile home**
*small house* 192 n.
*cart* 274 n.
**mobile phone**
*hearing instrument*
415 n.
*telecommunication*
531 n.
**mobility**
*changeableness* 152 n.
**mobilization, mobil-**
**isation**
*war measures* 718 n.
**mobilize, mobilise**
*bring together* 74 vb.
*make ready* 669 vb.
**Möbius strip**
*continuity* 71 n.
**mob law**
*anarchy* 734 n.
*lawlessness* 954 n.
**mobster**
*offender* 904 n.
**moccasins**
*footwear* 228 n.
**mocha**
*brown* 430 adj.
**mock**
*simulating* 18 adj.
*substituted* 150 adj.
*disbelieve* 486 vb.
*spurious* 542 adj.
*befool* 542 vb.
*laugh* 835 vb.
*ridicule* 851 n., vb.
*shame* 867 vb.
*not respect* 921 vb.
*despise* 922 vb.
*detract* 926 vb.
**mock epic**
*doggerel* 593 n.
**mocker**
*imitator* 20 n.

*harmonious* 410 adj.
**Monophysite**
  *heretic* 977 n.
**monoplane**
  *aircraft* 276 n.
**monopolist**
  *restriction* 747 n.
  *egotist* 932 n.
**monopolistic**
  *restraining* 747 adj.
  *avaricious* 816 adj.
**monopolize, mon-**
  **opolise**
  *prevail* 178 vb.
  *engross* 449 vb.
  *attract notice* 455 vb.
  *possess* 773 vb.
  *appropriate* 786 vb.
  *be selfish* 932 vb.
**monopoly**
  *exclusion* 57 n.
  *corporation* 708 n.
  *restriction* 747 n.
  *possession* 773 n.
  *sale* 793 n.
**Monopoly (tdmk)**
  *board game* 837 n.
**monorail**
  *railway* 624 n.
**monosyllabic**
  *linguistic* 557 adj.
  *concise* 569 adj.
  *taciturn* 582 adj.
**monosyllable**
  *word* 559 n.
**monotheism**
  *unity* 88 n.
  *deism* 973 n.
**monotheistic**
  *religious* 973 adj.
**Monothelite**
  *heretic* 977 n.
**monotone**
  *uniformity* 16 n.
  *musical note* 410 n.
**monotonous**
  *uniform* 16 adj.
  *equal* 28 adj.
  *continuous* 71 adj.
  *repeated* 106 adj.
  *rolling* 403 adj.
  *feeble* 572 adj.
**monotony**
  *uniformity* 16 n.
  *recurrence* 106 n.
  *tedium* 838 n.
  *dullness* 840 n.
**monotype**
  *breed* 77 n.
  *print* 587 n.
**Monsieur**
  *title* 870 n.
**Monsignor**
  *church title* 986 n.
**monsoon**
  *rain* 350 n.
  *wind* 352 n.

**monster**
  *violent creature* 176 n.
  *giant* 195 n.
  *eyesore* 842 n.
  *intimidation* 854 n.
  *prodigy* 864 n.
  *monster* 938 n.
  *demon* 970 n.
**monstrance**
  *ritual object* 988 n.
**monstrosity**
  *variance* 84 n.
  *hugeness* 195 n.
  *deformity* 246 n.
  *prodigy* 864 n.
**monstrous**
  *exorbitant* 32 adj.
  *unusual* 84 adj.
  *huge* 195 adj.
  *not nice* 645 adj.
  *ugly* 842 adj.
  *ridiculous* 849 adj.
  *wonderful* 864 adj.
  *heinous* 934 adj.
  *fairylike* 970 adj.
**montage**
  *cinema* 445 n.
  *picture* 553 n.
**Montanist**
  *heretic* 977 n.
**monte**
  *card game* 837 n.
**Montessori system**
  *education* 534 n.
**month**
  *period* 110 n.
**monthly**
  *seasonal* 141 adj.
  *journal* 528 n.
  *usual* 610 adj.
**month of Sundays, a**
  *long duration* 113 n.
**months of the year**
  *regular return* 141 n.
**monticle**
  *small hill* 209 n.
**monument**
  *antiquity* 125 n.
  *edifice* 164 n.
  *reminder* 505 n.
  *monument* 548 n.
  *trophy* 729 n.
  *honours* 866 n.
**monumental**
  *enormous* 32 adj.
  *large* 195 adj.
  *tall* 209 adj.
**monumental mason**
  *obsequies* 364 n.
  *sculptor* 556 n.
**moo**
  *ululate* 409 vb.
**mooch**
  *beg* 761 vb.
  *take* 786 vb.
  *be parsimonious* 816 vb.
**mooch about**

*move slowly* 278 vb.
*be inactive* 679 vb.
**mood**
  *temperament* 5 n.
  *state* 7 n.
  *tendency* 179 n.
  *grammar* 564 n.
  *whim* 604 n.
  *conduct* 688 n.
  *affections* 817 n.
  *moral sensibility* 819 n.
**moody**
  *fitful* 142 adj.
  *changeful* 152 adj.
  *capricious* 604 adj.
  *excitable* 822 adj.
  *melancholic* 834 adj.
  *irascible* 892 adj.
  *sullen* 893 adj.
**moody person**
  *moral sensibility* 819 n.
**moon**
  *period* 110 n.
  *changeable thing* 152 n.
  *moon* 321 n.
  *satellite* 321 n.
  *luminary* 420 n.
  *be inattentive* 456 vb.
  – about
  *be inactive* 679 vb.
  – after
  *desire* 859 vb.
**moon, the**
  *impossibility* 470 n.
**moonbeam**
  *glimmer* 419 n.
**moon buggy**
  *vehicle* 274 n.
**mooncalf**
  *fool* 501 n.
**Moonie**
  *sectarian* 978 n.
**moonless**
  *unlit* 418 adj.
**moonlight**
  *moon* 321 n.
  *light* 417 n.
  *glimmer* 419 n.
  *work* 682 vb.
  *not pay* 805 vb.
**moonlight flit**
  *departure* 296 n.
  *escape* 667 n.
**moonlit**
  *undimmed* 417 adj.
**moonraker**
  *ninny* 501 n.
**moonrise**
  *evening* 129 n.
**moonscape**
  *moon* 321 n.
**moonshine**
  *insubstantial thing* 4 n.
  *alcoholic drink* 301 n.
  *moon* 321 n.
  *light* 417 n.
  *empty talk* 515 n.

*fable* 543 n.
*booty* 790 n.
**moonstone**
  *gem* 844 n.
**moon-struck**
  *mentally disordered*
  503 adj.
**moor**
  *tie* 45 vb.
  *desert* 172 n.
  *place* 187 vb.
  *high land* 209 n.
  *arrive* 295 vb.
  *marsh* 347 n.
  *plain* 348 n.
**moored**
  *quiescent* 266 adj.
**moorhen**
  *bird* 365 n.
**mooring(s)**
  *cable* 47 n.
  *site* 187 n.
**moorland**
  *space* 183 n.
  *high land* 209 n.
  *See also* **moor**
**moose**
  *mammal* 365 n.
**moot**
  *moot* 459 adj.
  *interrogate* 459 adj.
  *uncertain* 474 adj.
  *argue* 475 vb.
  *propound* 512 vb.
  *council* 692 n.
**moot point**
  *topic* 452 n.
  *question* 459 n.
**mop**
  *hair* 259 n.
  *dry* 342 vb.
  *cleaning utensil*
  648 n.
  *clean* 648 vb.
  – and mow
  *distort* 246 vb.
  *haunt* 970 vb.
  – up
  *destroy* 165 vb.
  *absorb* 299 vb.
  *dry* 342 vb.
  *clean* 648 vb.
  *carry through* 725 vb.
**mope**
  *be dejected* 834 vb.
  *be sullen* 893 vb.
**moped**
  *conveyance* 267 n.
  *bicycle* 274 n.
**moper**
  *idler* 679 n.
  *malcontent* 829 n.
  *moper* 834 n.
  *hopelessness* 853 n.
  *disapprover* 924 n.
**mopes**
  *melancholy* 834 n.

**moppet**
child 132 n.
darling 890 n.
**moraine**
leavings 41 n.
thing transferred 272 n.
soil 344 n.
**moral**
judgment 480 n.
maxim 496 n.
commentary 520 n.
phrase 563 n.
good 615 adj.
advising 691 adj.
precept 693 n.
reputable 866 adj.
ethical 917 adj.
virtuous 933 adj.
pure 950 adj.
**moral certainty**
positiveness 473 n.
**moral code**
right 913 n.
**morale**
state 7 n.
obedience 739 n.
manliness 855 n.
**morale-boosting**
aiding 703 adj.
**moral fibre**
resolution 599 n.
probity 929 n.
**moral high ground**
morals 917 n.
**moral insensibility**
indiscrimination 464 n.
moral insensibility
820 n.
**moralistic**
judicial 480 adj.
ethical 917 adj.
**morality**
right 913 n.
morals 917 n.
virtue 933 n.
purity 950 n.
**morality play**
stage play 594 n.
**moralize, moralise**
judge 480 vb.
teach 534 vb.
**moralizing,**
**moralising**
educational 534 adj.
advising 691 adj.
preceptive 693 adj.
**moral philosophy**
morals 917 n.
**Moral Re-Armament**
reformism 654 n.
sect 978 n.
**morals**
conduct 688 n.
right 913 n.
morals 917 n.
virtue 933 n.
purity 950 n.

**moral sensibility**
discrimination 463 n.
moral sensibility 819 n.
**moral support**
aid 703 n.
**moral training**
education 534 n.
**moral turpitude**
improbity 930 n.
wickedness 934 n.
**morass**
marsh 347 n.
**moratorium**
delay 136 n.
lull 145 n.
nonpayment 805 n.
**Moravians**
sect 978 n.
**morbid**
abnormal 84 adj.
diseased 651 adj.
**morbidity**
badness 645 n.
ill health 651 n.
**morbific**
infectious 653 adj.
**mordacious**
maleficent 898 adj.
**mordant**
keen 174 adj.
pungent 388 adj.
pigment 425 n.
forceful 571 adj.
disapproving 924 adj.
**mordent**
musical note 410 n.
**more**
beyond 34 adv.
in addition 38 adv.
plural 101 adj.
**more and more**
crescendo 36 adv.
**more bark than bite**
scurrility 899 n.
**more dead than**
**alive**
fatigued 684 adj.
**more easily said than**
**done**
difficult 700 adj.
**more in sorrow than**
**in anger**
forgiving 909 adj.
**moreish**
savoury 390 adj.
**more kicks than**
**ha'pence**
rejection 607 n.
ingratitude 908 n.
**more often than not**
often 139 adv.
**more or less**
quantitative 26 adj.
about 33 adv.
nearly 200 adv.
**moreover**
in addition 38 adv.

**mores**
practice 610 n.
conduct 688 n.
**more sinned against**
**than sinning**
guiltless 935 adj.
**more so**
superior 34 adj.
crescendo 36 adv.
**Moresque**
ornamental 844 adj.
**more than a match**
**for**
powerful 160 adj.
**more than enough**
plenty 635 n.
redundance 637 n.
**more than ever**
greatly 32 adv.
**more than flesh and**
**blood can stand**
intolerable 827 adj.
**more than meets the**
**eye**
latency 523 n.
**more than one**
plural 101 adj.
**morganatic**
matrimonial
894 adj.
**morgue**
death 361 n.
interment 364 n.
inactivity 679 n.
**moribund**
sick 651 adj.
dying 361 adj.
**Mormon**
sectarian 978 n.
**morn**
morning 128 n.
**morning**
beginning 68 n.
period 110 n.
morning 128 n.
earliness 135 n.
**morning after**
sequel 67 n.
crapulence 949 n.
**morning dress**
formal dress 228 n.
**morning noon and**
**night**
repeatedly 106 adv.
perpetually 139 adv.
**morning star**
planet 321 n.
luminary 420 n.
**morocco**
skin 226 n.
bookbinding 589 n.
**moron**
fool 501 n.
person with learning dis-
ability 504 n.
**moronic**
mindless 448 adj.

unintelligent 499 adj.
mentally handicapped
503 adj.
**morose**
melancholic 834 adj.
sullen 893 adj.
**moroseness**
unsociability 883 n.
misanthropy 902 n.
**morpheme**
word 559 n.
part of speech 564 n.
**Morpheus**
sleep 679 n.
lesser deity 967 n.
**morphine, morphia**
anaesthetic 375 n.
drug 658 n.
soporific 679 n.
drug 949 n.
**morphological**
territorial 344 adj.
linguistic 557 adj.
**morphology**
form 243 n.
biology 358 n.
zoology 367 n.
study 536 n. box
linguistics 557 n.
etymology 559 n.
**morris dance**
dance 837 n.
**morris dancer**
jumper 312 n.
**morrow**
futurity 124 n.
**morse**
fastening 47 n.
telecommunication
531 n.
signal 547 n.
**morsel**
small quantity 33 n.
piece 53 n.
mouthful 301 n.
**mortal**
ephemeral 114 adj.
destructive 165 adj.
deadly 362 adj.
person 371 n.
human 371 adj.
tedious 838 adj.
guilty 936 adj.
**mortal illness**
decease 361 n.
**mortality**
transience 114 n.
death 361 n.
death roll 361 n.
humankind 371 n.
**mortally**
extremely 32 adv.
painfully 32 adv.
**mortally ill**
sick 651 adj.
**mortal remains**
corpse 363 n.

**mushroom cloud**
*high structure* 209 n.
*radiation* 417 n.
*poison* 659 n.
*bomb* 723 n.

**mushy**
*soft* 327 adj.
*semiliquid* 354 adj.
*pulpy* 356 adj.

**music**
*melody* 410 n.
*music* 412 n.
*pleasurableness* 826 n.

**musical**
*melodious* 410 adj.
*musical* 412 adj.
*musicianly* 413 adj.
*film* 445 n.
*stage play* 594 n.
*pleasurable* 826 adj.

**musical appreciation**
*musical skill* 413 n.

**musical box**
*gramophone* 414 n.

**musical chairs**
*indoor game* 837 n.

**musical comedy**
*vocal music* 412 n.
*stage play* 594 n.

**musical glasses**
*gong* 414 n.

**musical instrument**
*musical instrument*
    414 n.

**musical note**
*musical note* 410 n.

**musical piece**
*composition* 56 n.
*musical piece* 412 n.

**musical quality**
*melody* 410 n.

**musical saw**
*viol* 414 n.

**musical skill**
*music* 412 n.
*musical skill* 413 n.

**music centre**
*gramophone* 414 n.

**music critic**
*musician* 413 n.

**music hall**
*stage show* 594 n.
*theatre* 594 n.
*place of amusement*
    837 n.

**musician**
*musician* 413 n.
*interpreter* 520 n.
*proficient person* 696 n.

**musicianship**
*music* 412 n.
*musical skill* 413 n.

**music lover**
*musician* 413 n.

**music-making**
*music* 412 n.

**music of the spheres**

*order* 60 n.
*heavens* 321 n.

**musique concrète**
*music* 412 n.

**musk**
*scent* 396 n.

**musket**
*firearm* 723 n.

**musketeer**
*shooter* 287 n.
*soldiery* 722 n.

**Muslim**
*religionist* 973 n.
*religious* 973 adj.

**Muslim festivals**
*holy day* 988 n. box

**Muslim scriptures**
*scripture* 975 n. box

**muslin**
*textile* 222 n.
*semitransparency* 424 n.

**mussel**
*fish food* 301 n.
*marine life* 365 n.

**must**
*desiring* 859 adj.

**must, a**
*necessity* 596 n.
*requirement* 627 n.

**mustang**
*saddle horse* 273 n.

**mustard**
*condiment* 389 n.
*yellowness* 433 n.

**mustard and cress**
*vegetable* 301 n.

**mustard gas**
*poison* 659 n.
*weapon* 723 n.

**mustard seed**
*minuteness* 196 n.

**muster**
*assemblage* 74 n.
*bring together* 74 vb.
*number* 86 vb.
– courage
*take courage* 855 vb.

**muster roll**
*list* 87 n.

**must have**
*require* 627 vb.
*desire* 859 vb.

**musty**
*fetid* 397 adj.
*dirty* 649 adj.

**mutable**
*transient* 114 adj.
*changeable* 143 adj.
*changeful* 152 adj.

**mutant**
*nonconformist* 84 n.

**mutation**
*variant* 15 n.
*misfit* 25 n.
*variance* 84 n.
*change* 143 n.
*conversion* 147 n.

*deformity* 246 n.

**mutatis mutandis**
*mutatis mutandis*
    143 adv.
*in exchange* 151 adv.

**mute**
*speech sound* 398 n.
*silent* 399 adj.
*silencer* 401 n.
*mute* 401 vb.
*mute* 414 n.
*voiceless* 578 adj.
*taciturn* 582 adj.
*weeper* 836 n.

**muted**
*weak* 163 adj.
*muted* 401 adj.
*nonresonant* 405 adj.
*melodious* 410 adj.
*soft-hued* 425 adj.

**mutilate**
*deform* 244 vb.
*impair* 655 vb.
*make ugly* 842 vb.
*torture* 963 vb.

**mutilated**
*incomplete* 55 adj.
*imperfect* 647 adj.

**mutineer**
*revolter* 738 n.

**mutinous**
*quarrelling* 709 adj.
*defiant* 711 adj.
*resisting* 715 adj.
*disobedient* 738 adj.
*riotous* 738 adj.
*undutiful* 918 adj.

**mutiny**
*strike* 145 n.
*resist* 715 vb.
*revolt* 738 n., vb.
*fail in duty* 918 vb.

**mutt**
*dog* 365 n.
*dunce* 501 n.

**mutter**
*sound faint* 401 vb.
*roll* 403 n.
*stammer* 580 vb.
*be discontented* 829 vb.
*be sullen* 893 vb.
*threaten* 900 vb.

**mutton**
*meat* 301 n.

**muttonchops**
*hair* 259 n.

**mutton dressed up as
    lamb**
*misfit* 25 n.
*old woman* 133 n.

**muttonhead**
*dunce* 501 n.

**mutual**
*correlative* 12 adj.
*interchanged* 151 adj.

**mutual affection**
*love* 887 n.

**mutual agreement**
*promise* 764 n.
*compact* 765 n.

**mutual assistance**
*cooperation* 706 n.

**mutual hostility**
*dissension* 709 n.

**mutualist**
*participator* 775 n.

**mutualization, mutu-
    alisation**
*change* 143 n.
*means* 629 n.

**mutual support**
*friendship* 880 n.

**mutual under-
    standing**
*agreement* 24 n.
*concord* 710 n.

**muzak**
*music* 412 n.

**muzzle**
*protuberance* 254 n.
*orifice* 263 n.
*stopper* 264 n.
*silence* 399 vb.
*make mute* 578 vb.
*hinder* 702 vb.
*firearm* 723 n.
*restrain* 747 vb.
*fetter* 748 n.

**muzzy**
*tipsy* 949 adj.

**M-way**
*road* 624 n.

**mycology**
*botany* 368 n.
*study* 536 n. box

**my country right or
    wrong**
*prejudice* 481 n.
*patriotism* 901 n.

**my lady**
*title* 870 n.

**my lord**
*title* 870 n.

**my lud**
*judge* 957 n.

**myna bird**
*imitator* 20 n.

**myopic**
*dim-sighted* 440 adj.
*misjudging* 481 adj.

**myriad**
*over one hundred* 99 n.
*many* 104 adj.

**myrmidon**
*soldier* 722 n.
*dependant* 742 n.

**myrrh**
*resin* 357 n.
*interment* 364 n.
*scent* 396 n.

**myrtle**
*love emblem* 887 n.

**myself**
*self* 80 n.

**physics** 319 n.
science 490 n.
**natural resources**
means 629 n.
store 632 n.
**natural science**
physics 319 n.
science 490 n.
**natural selection**
biology 358 n.
**nature**
essence 1 n.
character 5 n.
composition 56 n.
sort 77 n.
tendency 179 n.
truth 494 n.
affections 817 n.
**Nature**
producer 164 n.
matter 319 n.
**nature cure**
medical art 658 n.
therapy 658 n.
**nature god/goddess**
mythic deity 966 n.
**nature reserve**
preservation 666 n.
**nature study**
biology 358 n.
**naturist**
stripper 229 n.
sanitarian 652 n.
**naturopath**
doctor 658 n.
**naturopathy**
medical art 658 n.
**naught**
insubstantiality 4 n.
See also **nought**
**naughty**
difficult 700 adj.
disobedient 738 adj.
wicked 934 adj.
impure 951 adj.
**naughty word**
scurrility 899 n.
**nausea**
voidance 300 n.
digestive disorders 651 n.
dislike 861 n.
**nauseate**
be unpalatable 391 vb.
displease 827 vb.
cause discontent 829 vb.
be tedious 838 vb.
cause dislike 861 vb.
excite hate 888 vb.
**nauseated**
vomiting 300 adj.
sick 651 adj.
unhappy 825 adj.
bored 838 adj.
disliking 861 adj.
**nauseous**
unsavoury 391 adj.
not nice 645 adj.

unclean 649 adj.
unpleasant 827 adj.
**nautch girl**
entertainer 594 n.
**nautical**
seafaring 269 adj.
seamanlike 270 adj.
marine 275 adj.
**nautical almanac**
sailing aid 269 n.
guidebook 524 n.
**nautical mile**
long measure 203 n.
**nautical personnel**
nautical personnel 270 n.
naval person 722 n.
**naval**
seafaring 269 adj.
seamanlike 270 adj.
marine 275 adj.
warlike 718 adj.
**naval man**
naval person 722 n.
**naval officer**
naval officer 741 n.
**Navaratri**
holy day 988 n. box
**nave**
middle 70 n.
church interior 990 n.
**navel**
middle 70 n.
centre 225 n.
**navel-gazing**
meditation 449 n.
enquiry 459 n.
knowledge 490 n.
**navigable**
deep 211 adj.
seafaring 269 adj.
**navigate**
navigate 269 vb.
orientate 281 vb.
direct 689 vb.
**navigation**
navigation 269 n.
water travel 269 n.
**navigational instrument**
sailing aid 269 n.
**navigator**
navigator 270 n.
aeronaut 271 n.
director 690 n.
**navvy**
worker 686 n.
**navy**
shipping 275 n.
blue 435 adj.
navy 722 n.
**Navy List**
directory 87 n.
list 87 n.
**nawab**
potentate 741 n.
person of rank 868 n.
**nay**

negation 533 n.
refusal 760 n.
**Nazarene**
religionist 973 n.
**Nazarites**
non-Christian sect 978 n.
**naze**
projection 254 n.
**Nazis**
political party 708 n.
**Nazism**
government 733 n.
brute force 735 n.
**NB**
– 455 int.
**NCO**
army officer 741 n.
**Neanderthal man**
antiquity 125 n.
fossil 125 n.
humankind 371 n.
**neap**
decrease 37 n.
**neap tide**
lowness 210 n.
current 350 n.
**near**
akin 11 adj.
similar 18 adj.
future 124 adj.
early 135 adj.
impending 155 adj.
near 200 adj., adv.
approach 289 vb.
parsimonious 816 adj.
**nearby**
near 200 adj.
accessible 289 adj.
**near-death experience**
astral projection 272 n.
death 361 n.
**near enough**
about 33 adv.
nearly 200 adv.
**nearly**
almost 33 adv.
on the whole 52 adv.
nearly 200 adv.
**near miss**
collision 279 n.
**nearness**
nearness 200 n.
**near relative**
kinsman 11 n.
**near side**
laterality 239 n.
sinistrality 242 n.
**near-sighted**
dim-sighted 440 adj.
**near the bone**
impure 951 adj.
**near the knuckle**
impure 951 adj.
**near the surface**
shallow 212 adj.
**near the truth, be**

detect 484 vb.
**near thing**
draw 28 n.
danger 661 n.
escape 667 n.
**neat**
unmixed 44 adj.
orderly 60 adj.
strong 162 adj.
careful 457 adj.
concise 569 adj.
plain 573 adj.
elegant 575 adj.
clean 648 adj.
skilful 694 adj.
personable 841 adj.
intoxicating 949 adj.
**neaten**
arrange 62 vb.
unravel 62 vb.
make better 654 vb.
beautify 841 vb.
**neatly**
skilfully 694 adv.
**nebula**
nebula 321 n.
**nebular hypothesis**
universe 321 n.
**nebulous**
amorphous 244 adj.
celestial 321 adj.
cloudy 355 adj.
dim 419 adj.
puzzling 517 adj.
**necessarily**
consequently 157 adv.
necessarily 596 adv.
**necessary**
necessary 596 adj.
choiceless 606 adj.
required 627 adj.
important 638 adj.
compelling 740 adj.
**necessary, a**
necessity 596 n.
requirement 627 n.
**necessitarian**
fatalist 596 n.
**necessitate**
predestine 155 vb.
make certain 473 vb.
necessitate 596 vb.
require 627 vb.
compel 740 vb.
**necessitous**
poor 801 adj.
**necessitude**
necessity 596 n.
**necessity**
destiny 155 n.
cause 156 n.
certainty 473 n.
necessity 596 n.
no choice 606 n.
predetermination 608 n.
requirement 627 n.
inexpedience 643 n.

**neigh**
 *ululate* 409 vb.
**neighbour**
 *be near* 200 vb.
 *friend* 880 n.
**neighbourhood**
 *district* 184 n.
 *locality* 187 n.
 *inhabitants* 191 n.
 *near place* 200 n.
 *surroundings* 230 n.
**neighbourly**
 *aiding* 703 adj.
 *sociable* 882 adj.
**neither**
 *neither* 606 adv.
**neither here nor**
 **there**
 *irrelevant* 10 adj.
**neither . . . nor**
 *neither* 606 adv.
**neither one thing nor**
 **the other**
 *nonconformist* 84 n.
 *neutral* 625 adj.
 *independent* 744 adj.
**neither too much nor**
 **too little**
 *averageness* 732 n.
**nekton**
 *marine life* 365 n.
**nem. con.**
 *unanimously* 488 adv.
**Nemesis**
 *retaliation* 714 n.
 *avenger* 910 n.
 *justice* 913 n.
 *punishment* 963 n.
**neoclassical**
 *architectural* 192 adj.
**neocolonialism**
 *governance* 733 n.
**neo-Gothic**
 *architectural* 192 adj.
**neolith**
 *antiquity* 125 n.
**neolithic**
 *secular* 110 adj.
 *primal* 127 adj.
 *barbaric* 869 adj.
**neologian**
 *modernist* 126 n.
**neological**
 *modern* 126 adj.
 *neological* 560 adj.
**neologism**
 *word* 559 n.
 *neology* 560 n.
**neologize, neologise**
 *neologize* 560 vb.
**neology**
 *neology* 560 n.
**neon light**
 *gas* 336 n.
 *lamp* 420 n.
**neophiliac**
 *modernist* 126 n.

**neophyte**
 *changed person* 147 n.
 *beginner* 538 n.
 *pietist* 979 n.
**neoplasm**
 *swelling* 253 n.
 *cancer* 651 n.
**Neo-Platonism**
 *philosophy* 449 n.
**neoteric**
 *modern* 126 adj.
**nepenthe**
 *oblivion* 506 n.
 *drug* 658 n.
**nephew**
 *kinsman* 11 n.
**nephology**
 *cloud* 355 n.
**nephritis**
 *digestive disorders* 651 n.
 *inflammation* 651 n.
 box
**ne plus ultra**
 *superiority* 34 n.
 *completeness* 54 n.
 *extremity* 69 n.
 *farness* 199 n.
 *summit* 213 n.
 *limit* 236 n.
 *exceller* 644 n.
 *perfection* 646 n.
 *completion* 725 n.
 *fashion* 848 n.
**nepotism**
 *injustice* 914 n.
 *improbity* 930 n.
**Neptune**
 *planet* 321 n.
 *sea god* 343 n.
 *Olympian deity* 967 n.
**nerd**
 *weakling* 163 n.
**nereid**
 *sea nymph* 343 n.
 *nymph* 967 n.
**nerve**
 *vitality* 162 n.
 *strengthen* 162 vb.
 *courage* 855 n.
 *sauciness* 878 n.
 – oneself
 *take courage* 855 vb.
**nerve, inflammation**
 **of**
 *inflammation* 651 n.
 box
**nerve centre**
 *focus* 76 n.
 *centre* 225 n.
**nerve gas**
 *poison* 659 n.
 *weapon* 723 n.
**nerveless**
 *impotent* 161 adj.
 *weak* 163 adj.
 *feeble* 572 adj.
 *irresolute* 601 adj.

 *unfearing* 855 adj.
**nerve-racking**
 *distressing* 827 adj.
 *frightening* 854 adj.
**nerve, removal of**
 *surgery* 658 n. box
**nerves**
 *neurosis* 503 n.
 *ill health* 651 n.
 *excitability* 822 n.
 *nervousness* 854 n.
**nervous**
 *impotent* 161 adj.
 *agitated* 318 adj.
 *distracted* 456 adj.
 *expectant* 507 adj.
 *irresolute* 601 adj.
 *avoiding* 620 adj.
 *lively* 819 adj.
 *excitable* 822 adj.
 *nervous* 854 adj.
 *cowardly* 856 adj.
 *cautious* 858 adj.
**nervous breakdown**
 *psychopathy* 503 n.
 *nervous disorders* 651 n.
**nervous system**
 *sense* 374 n.
**nervous tic**
 *spasm* 318 n.
**nervy**
 *active* 678 adj.
 *excitable* 822 adj.
 *nervous* 854 adj.
**nescient**
 *ignorant* 491 adj.
**ness**
 *projection* 254 n.
**Nessie**
 *mythical beast* 365 n.
**Nessie-hunter**
 *zoologist* 367 n.
**nest**
 *origin* 68 n.
 *group* 74 n.
 *focus* 76 n.
 *seedbed* 156 n.
 *nest* 192 n.
 *dwell* 192 vb.
 *sit down* 311 vb.
 *refuge* 662 n.
**nest egg**
 *store* 632 n.
 *preparation* 669 n.
 *wealth* 800 n.
**nestle**
 *dwell* 192 vb.
 *seek refuge* 662 vb.
 *caress* 889 vb.
**nestled**
 *located* 187 adj.
**nestling**
 *young creature* 132 n.
**Nestor**
 *old man* 133 n.
 *sage* 500 n.
 *adviser* 691 n.

**Nestorian**
 *heretic* 977 n.
**Net, the**
 *information* 524 n.
 *Internet* 531 n.
**net**
 *remaining* 41 adj.
 *bring together* 74 vb.
 *receptacle* 194 n.
 *network* 222 n.
 *textile* 222 n.
 *enclosure* 235 n.
 *semitransparency* 424 n.
 *trap* 542 n.
 *hunt* 619 vb.
 *stratagem* 698 n.
 *acquire* 771 vb.
 *receive* 782 vb.
 *take* 786 vb.
**netball**
 *ball game* 837 n.
**nether**
 *low* 210 adj.
**nethermost**
 *undermost* 214 adj.
**nether regions**
 *lowness* 210 n.
**netherworld**
 *the dead* 361 n.
 *hell* 972 n.
**netiquette**
 *Internet* 531 n.
 *practice* 610 n.
 *etiquette* 848 n.
**net profit**
 *gain* 771 n.
 *receipt* 807 n.
**net-surfing**
 *Internet* 531 n.
**netting**
 *network* 222 n.
**nettle**
 *prickle* 256 n.
 *bane* 659 n.
 *hurt* 827 vb.
 *huff* 891 vb.
**nettlerash**
 *formication* 378 n.
 *skin disease* 651 n.
**net-top box**
 *Internet* 531 n.
**network**
 *correlation* 12 n.
 *union* 45 n.
 *connect* 45 vb.
 *bond* 47 n.
 *complexity* 61 n.
 *gap* 201 n.
 *network* 222 n.
 *texture* 331 n.
 *broadcasting* 531 n.
 *cooperate* 706 vb.
**networking**
 *cooperation* 706 n.
**neuralgia**
 *pang* 377 n.
**neurasthenia**

*ninny* 501 n.
**nine**
  *over five* 99 n.
**nine days' wonder**
  *insubstantial thing* 4 n.
  *brief span* 114 n.
  *prodigy* 864 n.
**ninepins**
  *ball game* 837 n.
**nine points of the law**
  *possession* 773 n.
**nineteenth hole**
  *refreshment* 685 n.
**nineteen to the dozen**
  *swiftly* 277 adv.
**ninety**
  *twenty and over* 99 n.
**ninety-nine per cent**
  *chief part* 52 n.
**ninny**
  *ninny* 501 n.
**ninth**
  *fifth and over* 99 adj.
  *musical note* 410 n.
**Niobe**
  *weeper* 836 n.
**nip**
  *make smaller* 198 vb.
  *shorten* 204 vb.
  *make thin* 206 vb.
  *move fast* 277 vb.
  *draught* 301 n.
  *pang* 377 n.
  *give pain* 377 vb.
  *blight* 659 n.
 – *in the bud*
  *be early* 135 vb.
  *destroy* 165 vb.
  *suppress* 165 vb.
  *hinder* 702 vb.
**nip and tuck**
  *equal* 28 adj.
  *synchronism* 123 n.
  *near* 200 adj.
**nip in the air**
  *wintriness* 380 n.
**nipper**
  *youngster* 132 n.
**nippers**
  *extractor* 304 n.
  *finger* 378 n.
  *tool* 630 n.
  *nippers* 778 n.
**nipple**
  *bosom* 253 n.
**nippy**
  *vigorous* 174 adj.
  *cold* 380 adj.
  *active* 678 adj.
**nirvana**
  *extinction* 2 n.
  *happiness* 824 n.
  *divineness* 965 n.
  *heaven* 971 n.
**nisi prius**
  *legal process* 959 n.
**Nissen hut**

*small house* 192 n.
**nit**
  *insect* 365 n.
  *dirt* 649 n.
**nitid**
  *luminous* 417 adj.
**nitpick**
  *blame* 924 vb.
  *dispraise* 924 vb.
**nit-picker**
  *malcontent* 829 n.
  *detractor* 926 n.
**nit-picking**
  *trivial* 639 adj.
  *fastidiousness* 862 n.
**nitrates**
  *fertilizer* 171 n.
**nitrogen**
  *element* 319 n. box
  *air* 340 n.
**nitroglycerine**
  *explosive* 723 n.
**nitrous oxide**
  *anaesthetic* 375 n.
**nitty-gritty**
  *reality* 1 n.
  *substance* 3 n.
  *essential part* 5 n.
  *chief part* 52 n.
  *element* 319 n.
  *meaning* 514 n.
  *chief thing* 638 n.
**nitwit**
  *dunce* 501 n.
**nix**
  *zero* 103 n.
  *mythical being* 970 n.
**no**
  *no* 489 adv.
  *negation* 533 n.
  *nay* 533 adv.
  *refusal* 760 n.
**No**
  *stage play* 594 n.
**no-account**
  *unimportant* 639 adj.
**no admission**
  *exclusion* 57 n.
**Noah's Ark**
  *ship* 275 n.
  *zoo* 369 n.
**no alternative**
  *necessity* 596 n.
  *no choice* 606 n.
**no appeal**
  *severity* 735 n.
**no appetite**
  *indifference* 860 n.
  *fasting* 946 n.
**nob**
  *head* 213 n.
  *fop* 848 n.
  *aristocrat* 868 n.
**no ball**
  *failure* 728 n.
**nobble**
  *disable* 161 vb.

*take* 786 vb.
  *steal* 788 vb.
**nobbly**
  *projecting* 254 adj.
**no bed of roses**
  *adversity* 731 n.
  *suffering* 825 n.
**Nobel Prize**
  *reward* 962 n.
**no better**
  *equivalent* 28 adj.
  *deteriorated* 655 adj.
**no bigger than**
  *little* 196 adj.
**nobility**
  *greatness* 32 n.
  *superiority* 34 n.
  *beau monde* 848 n.
  *aristocracy* 868 n.
  *nobility* 868 n.
  *probity* 929 n.
  *disinterestedness* 931 n.
**noble**
  *great* 32 adj.
  *important* 638 adj.
  *coinage* 797 n.
  *impressive* 821 adj.
  *splendid* 841 adj.
  *well-bred* 848 adj.
  *renowned* 866 adj.
  *worshipful* 866 adj.
  *person of rank* 868 n.
  *noble* 868 adj.
  *title* 870 n.
  *proud* 871 adj.
  *honourable* 929 adj.
  *disinterested* 931 adj.
**noble descent**
  *nobility* 868 n.
**nobleman,**
    **noblewoman**
  *aristocrat* 868 n.
  *person of rank* 868 n.
**noble savage**
  *ingenue* 699 n.
**noblesse**
  *aristocracy* 868 n.
**nobody**
  *nonexistence* 2 n.
  *insubstantiality* 4 n.
  *zero* 103 n.
  *nobody* 190 n.
  *nonentity* 639 n.
  *commoner* 869 n.
**nobody's business**
  *unrelatedness* 10 n.
**nobody's fool**
  *unbeliever* 486 n.
  *sage* 500 n.
**no business of**
  *unrelatedness* 10 n.
**no case to answer**
  *certainty* 473 n.
  *acquittal* 960 n.
**no chance**
  *impossibility* 470 n.
  *denyingly* 760 adv.

**no change**
  *identity* 13 n.
  *permanence* 144 n.
**no charge**
  *no charge* 812 n.
**no chicken**
  *ageing* 131 adj.
**no choice**
  *necessity* 596 n.
  *no choice* 606 n.
**no competition**
  *facility* 701 n.
**no concern of**
  *unrelatedness* 10 n.
**no connection**
  *unrelatedness* 10 n.
  *disunion* 46 n.
**noctiluca**
  *glimmer* 419 n.
  *glowing thing* 420 n.
**nocturnal**
  *vespertine* 129 adj.
  *dark* 418 adj.
  *black* 428 adj.
**nocturnal mammal**
  *mammal* 365 n.
**nocturne**
  *musical piece* 412 n.
  *art subject* 553 n.
**nod**
  *hang* 217 vb.
  *obeisance* 311 n.
  *oscillate* 317 vb.
  *be inattentive* 456 vb.
  *be neglectful* 458 vb.
  *assent* 488 n., vb.
  *hint* 524 n.
  *gesture* 547 n.
  *gesticulate* 547 vb.
  *sleep* 679 vb.
  *be fatigued* 684 vb.
  *command* 737 n.
  *permit* 756 vb.
  *consent* 758 vb.
  *greet* 884 vb.
  *respects* 920 n.
  *approve* 923 vb.
**nodding**
    **acquaintance**
  *knowledge* 490 n.
**noddle**
  *head* 213 n.
  *intelligence* 498 n.
**noddy**
  *ninny* 501 n.
**node**
  *joint* 45 n.
  *swelling* 253 n.
  *uranometry* 321 n.
  *foliage* 366 n.
**no desire for**
  *indifference* 860 n.
**no distance**
  *short distance* 200 n.
**nodose**
  *rough* 259 adj.
**no doubt**

*loser* 728 n.
**nonstop**
  *continuous* 71 adj.
  *perpetual* 115 adj.
  *unceasing* 146 adj.
  *vehicular* 274 adj.
  *loquacious* 581 adj.
**nonstriker**
  *nonconformist* 84 n.
  *revolter* 738 n.
**nonsuit**
  *acquittal* 960 n.
**nontransferable**
  *retained* 778 adj.
**non-U**
  *unwonted* 611 adj.
  *ill-bred* 847 adj.
  *plebeian* 869 adj.
**nonuniform**
  *nonuniform* 17 adj.
  *disagreeing* 25 adj.
  *multiform* 82 adj.
  *changeful* 152 adj.
**nonuse**
  *rejection* 607 n.
  *desuetude* 611 n.
  *relinquishment* 621 n.
  *nonuse* 674 n.
**nonviolence**
  *moderation* 177 n.
  *peace* 717 n.
**nonvoter**
  *absence* 190 n.
  *disapprover* 924 n.
**nonvoting**
  *choiceless* 606 adj.
**nonworshipper**
  *impious person* 980 n.
**noodles**
  *dish* 301 n.
**nook**
  *place* 185 n.
  *compartment* 194 n.
  *angularity* 247 n.
  *hiding-place* 527 n.
**noon**
  *noon* 128 n.
  *light* 417 n.
**noon and night**
  *repeatedly* 106 adv.
  *perpetually* 139 adv.
**no one**
  *nonexistence* 2 n.
  *nobody* 190 n.
**no option**
  *necessity* 596 n.
**noose**
  *halter* 47 n.
  *trap* 542 n.
  *means of execution* 964 n.
**no other**
  *identity* 13 n.
**no picnic**
  *hard task* 700 n.
**no preference**
  *no choice* 606 n.

**no pride**
  *moral insensibility* 820 n.
  *servility* 879 n.
**no progress**
  *inactivity* 679 n.
**no prospects**
  *hopelessness* 853 n.
**no purpose**
  *inutility* 641 n.
**no quarter**
  *pitilessness* 906 n.
  – 362 int.
**no question**
  *certainly* 473 adv.
**no quorum**
  *fewness* 105 n.
  *insufficiency* 636 n.
**Nordic deities**
  *Nordic deities* 967 n.
**no recollection**
  *oblivion* 506 n.
**no regrets**
  *impenitence* 940 n.
**no restrictions**
  *laxity* 734 n.
**no reward**
  *ingratitude* 908 n.
**no right**
  *undueness* 916 n.
**norm**
  *prototype* 23 n.
  *average* 30 n.
  *rule* 81 n.
  *gauge* 465 n.
  *paragon* 646 n.
  *precept* 693 n.
**N or M**
  *everyman* 79 n.
  *no name* 562 n.
**normal**
  *average* 30 n.
  *median* 30 adj.
  *general* 79 adj.
  *regular* 81 adj.
  *typical* 83 adj.
  *sane* 502 adj.
  *right* 913 adj.
**normality**
  *regularity* 81 n.
  *sanity* 502 n.
  *right* 913 n.
**normalize, normalise**
  *regularize* 62 vb.
  *make conform* 83 vb.
**Norman**
  *olden* 127 adj.
  *architectural* 192 adj.
  *churchlike* 990 adj.
**normative**
  *regular* 81 adj.
  *educational* 534 adj.
**Norns, the**
  *fate* 596 n.
  *mythic deity* 966 n.
**north**
  *compass point* 281 n.

**north and south**
  *polarity* 14 n.
  *region* 184 n.
**northbound**
  *directed* 281 adj.
**northern**
  *opposite* 240 adj.
  *directed* 281 adj.
**Northerner**
  *native* 191 n.
**northern lights**
  *heavens* 321 n.
  *glow* 417 n.
  *luminary* 420 n.
**northing**
  *bearings* 186 n.
**north of Potters Bar**
  *district* 184 n.
**North Pole**
  *summit* 213 n.
  *coldness* 380 n.
**North Sea**
  *ocean* 343 n.
**north wind**
  *wind* 352 n.
**nor'wester**
  *gale* 352 n.
**no saint**
  *bad person* 938 n.
**no score**
  *zero* 103 n.
**nose**
  *face* 237 n.
  *prow* 237 n.
  *angularity* 247 n.
  *protuberance* 254 n.
  *person* 371 n.
  *odour* 394 n.
  *detective* 459 n.
  *detect* 484 vb.
  *informer* 524 n.
  – around
  *enquire* 459 vb.
  – into
  *be curious* 453 vb.
  – out
  *enquire* 459 vb.
  *discover* 484 vb.
**nose, inflammation in**
  *inflammation* 651 n. box
**nosebag**
  *bag* 194 n.
**nose cone**
  *rocket* 276 n.
**no secret**
  *known* 490 adj.
**nose dive**
  *aeronautics* 271 n.
  *descent* 309 n.
  *plunge* 313 n.
**nosegay**
  *bunch* 74 n.
  *fragrance* 396 n.
  *ornamentation* 844 n.
**nosehole**

**orifice** 263 n.
**nose-in-the-air**
  *prideful* 871 adj.
**nose job**
  *beautification* 843 n.
**noseless**
  *odourless* 395 adj.
**nose to tail**
  *continuously* 71 adv.
**nosh**
  *food* 301 n.
**no signs of**
  *latency* 523 n.
**no sinecure**
  *activity* 678 n.
**no slouch**
  *busy person* 678 n.
**nosology**
  *study* 536 n. box
  *pathology* 651 n.
**no sooner said than done**
  *instantaneously* 116 adv.
  *easy* 701 adj.
**no spring chicken**
  *old woman* 133 n.
**nostalgia**
  *remembrance* 505 n.
  *regret* 830 n.
  *melancholy* 834 n.
  *desire* 859 n.
**nostalgic**
  *unhappy* 825 adj.
**nostalgie de la boue**
  *desire* 859 n.
**no standing**
  *disrepute* 867 n.
**no stomach for**
  *unwillingness* 598 n.
  *dislike* 861 n.
**Nostradamus**
  *oracle* 511 n.
**no stranger to**
  *knowing* 490 adj.
**nostril**
  *orifice* 263 n.
  *air pipe* 353 n.
  *odour* 394 n.
**no strings attached**
  *unconditional* 744 adj.
**nostrum**
  *contrivance* 623 n.
  *remedy* 658 n.
**no such thing**
  *nonexistence* 2 n.
**no surrender**
  – 715 int.
**nosy, nosey**
  *inquisitive* 453 adj.
  *enquiring* 459 adj.
**nosy parker**
  *inquisitive person* 453 n.
  *meddler* 678 n.
**not a bit**
  *in no way* 33 adv.
**notable**
  *remarkable* 32 adj.

*reason badly* 477 vb.
**not have an inkling**
  *not know* 491 vb.
**not have long to go**
  *be weak* 163 vb.
**not have one's heart**
  **in it**
  *be indifferent* 860 vb.
**not have the heart to**
  *be unwilling* 598 vb.
**not have a word**
  **against**
  *be credulous* 487 vb.
**not hear of**
  *refuse* 760 vb.
**not help**
  *be useless* 641 vb.
  *be inexpedient* 643 vb.
**not hesitate**
  *be willing* 597 vb.
**not hide one's**
  **feelings**
  *show feeling* 818 vb.
**nothing**
  *nonexistence* 2 n.
  *insubstantiality* 4 n.
  *zero* 103 n.
  *trifle* 639 n.
**nothing but**
  *simple* 44 adj.
**nothing daunted**
  *resolute* 599 adj.
  *persevering* 600 adj.
  *unfearing* 855 adj.
**nothing doing**
  *inaction* 677 n.
  *denyingly* 760 adv.
**nothing for it**
  *necessarily* 596 adv.
**nothing in common**
  *dissimilarity* 19 n.
**nothing in it**
  *equivalence* 28 n.
  *contest* 716 n.
  *lack of wonder* 865 n.
**nothing like it**
  *best* 644 adj.
**nothing loath**
  *willingly* 597 adv.
**nothingness**
  *See* **nothing**
**nothing sacred**
  *irreligion* 974 n.
**nothing special**
  *inferior* 35 adj.
  *middling* 732 adj.
**nothing to add**
  *completeness* 54 n.
**nothing to boast of**
  *trifle* 639 n.
  *imperfect* 647 adj.
  *middling* 732 adj.
**nothing to choose**
  **between**
  *similar* 18 adj.
  *equivalence* 28 n.
  *indifference* 860 n.

**nothing to do with**
  *unrelated* 10 adj.
**nothing to go on**
  *uncertainty* 474 n.
  *ignorance* 491 n.
**nothing to it**
  *trifle* 639 n.
  *easy thing* 701 n.
  – 865 int.
**nothing to show for**
  *profitless* 641 adj.
**nothing to spare**
  *insufficiency* 636 n.
**nothing to worry**
  **about**
  *trifle* 639 n.
**nothing to write**
  **home about**
  *inferior* 35 adj.
  *trifle* 639 n.
  *imperfect* 647 adj.
  *middling* 732 adj.
  *lack of wonder* 865 n.
**nothing wrong with**
  *perfection* 646 n.
**not hold it against**
  **one**
  *forgive* 909 vb.
**not hold water**
  *be untrue* 543 vb.
**not hold with**
  *dissent* 489 vb.
  *disapprove* 924 vb.
**no thought for others**
  *selfishness* 932 n.
**no thought for self**
  *disinterestedness* 931 n.
**notice**
  *period* 110 n.
  *see* 438 vb.
  *cognize* 447 vb.
  *attention* 455 vb.
  *notice* 455 vb.
  *estimate* 480 vb.
  *detect* 484 vb.
  *prediction* 511 n.
  *interpretation* 520 n.
  *information* 524 n.
  *advertisement* 528 n.
  *article* 591 n.
  *warning* 664 n.
  *demand* 737 n.
  *greet* 884 vb.
**noticeable**
  *remarkable* 32 adj.
  *visible* 443 adj.
  *manifest* 522 adj.
**notice board**
  *advertisement* 528 n.
**not ideal**
  *imperfect* 647 adj.
**notifiable disease**
  *disease* 651 n.
**notification**
  *information* 524 n.
  *publication* 528 n.
  *indication* 547 n.

**notify**
  *predict* 511 vb.
  *communicate* 524 vb.
  *proclaim* 528 vb.
  *warn* 664 vb.
**not imagined**
  *real* 1 adj.
**no time to lose**
  *haste* 680 n.
**not immune**
  *vulnerable* 661 adj.
**not in one's right**
  **mind**
  *mentally disordered*
    503 adj.
**not in the habit of**
  *unhabituated* 611 adj.
**not in the least**
  *in no way* 33 adv.
**not in the mood**
  *unwilling* 598 adj.
**not in the slightest**
  *in no way* 33 adv.
**not in use**
  *inactive* 679 adj.
**notion**
  *idea* 451 n.
  *supposition* 512 n.
  *ideality* 513 n.
  *contrivance* 623 n.
**notional**
  *ideational* 451 adj.
  *suppositional* 512 adj.
  *imaginary* 513 adj.
**not know**
  *be neutral* 606 vb.
**not know from Adam**
  *not know* 491 vb.
**not know how**
  *be unskilful* 695 vb.
**not know one's own**
  **mind**
  *be irresolute* 601 vb.
**not know one's place**
  *be insolent* 878 vb.
**not know what to**
  **make of**
  *be uncertain* 474 vb.
  *not know* 491 vb.
  *not understand* 517 vb.
**not know what to**
  **say**
  *wonder* 864 vb.
**not know when one is**
  **beaten**
  *be successful* 727 vb.
**not know when one is**
  **well off**
  *be discontented* 829 vb.
**not know when to**
  **stop**
  *exaggerate* 546 vb.
  *be intemperate* 943 vb.
**not know which way**
  **to turn**
  *be uncertain* 474 vb.
  *be busy* 678 vb.

*be in difficulty* 700 vb.
**not last**
  *be transient* 114 vb.
**not let go**
  *persevere* 600 vb.
  *retain* 778 vb.
**not let one get a word**
  **in edgeways**
  *be loquacious* 581 vb.
**not let the grass grow**
  **under one's feet**
  *be active* 678 vb.
**not lift a finger**
  *not act* 677 vb.
**not likely**
  *denyingly* 760 adv.
  – 472 int.
  – 533 int.
**not like the look of**
  *dislike* 861 vb.
**not listen**
  *be deaf* 416 vb.
  *be inattentive* 456 vb.
  *be obstinate* 602 vb.
  *disobey* 738 vb.
  *refuse* 760 vb.
**not long ago**
  *newly* 126 adv.
**not long to go**
  *dying* 361 adj.
**not look**
  *be blind* 439 vb.
  *be clumsy* 695 vb.
**not look a gift horse**
  **in the mouth**
  *be grateful* 907 vb.
**not look for**
  *not expect* 508 vb.
**not looking**
  *negligent* 458 adj.
  *rash* 857 adj.
**not lose any sleep**
  **over**
  *be indifferent* 860 vb.
**not lose sight of**
  *be mindful* 455 vb.
**not make an issue of**
  *forgive* 909 vb.
**not make the grade**
  *be inferior* 35 vb.
  *be impotent* 161 vb.
  *fall short* 307 vb.
  *be imperfect* 647 vb.
  *fail* 728 vb.
**not many**
  *inconsiderable* 33 adj.
  *few* 105 adj.
**not matter**
  *be unimportant* 639 vb.
**not meant**
  *unintentional* 618 adj.
**not mean what one**
  **says**
  *mean nothing* 515 vb.
**not meet**
  **requirements**
  *not suffice* 636 vb.

**not with it**
  *antiquated* 127 adj.
  *abstracted* 456 adj.
**notwithstanding**
  *in return* 31 adv.
  *although* 182 adv.
**not wonder**
  *be insensitive* 820 vb.
  *be indifferent* 860 vb.
  *not wonder* 865 vb.
**not work**
  *be impotent* 161 vb.
  *be useless* 641 vb.
  *be inactive* 679 vb.
**not working**
  *orderless* 61 adj.
**not worry**
  *keep calm* 823 vb.
**not worth a thought**
  *trivial* 639 adj.
**not worthwhile**
  *trivial* 639 adj.
  *profitless* 641 adj.
**no two ways about it**
  *certainly* 473 adv.
  *necessarily* 596 adv.
**nougat**
  *sweets* 301 n.
**nought**
  *zero* 103 n.
**noughts and crosses**
  *indoor games* 837 n.
**noumenal**
  *insubstantial* 4 adj.
  *intuitive* 476 adj.
**noumenon**
  *idea* 451 n.
**noun**
  *name* 561 n.
  *part of speech* 564 n.
**nourish**
  *feed* 301 vb.
  *aid* 703 vb.
**nourishing**
  *nourishing* 301 adj.
  *salubrious* 652 adj.
**nous**
  *intelligence* 498 n.
  *skill* 694 n.
**nouveau arrivé**
  *intruder* 59 n.
  *successor* 67 n.
  *new* 126 adj.
  *upstart* 126 n.
  *arrival* 295 n.
  *incomer* 297 n.
  *vulgarian* 847 n.
**nouveau riche**
  *upstart* 126 n.
  *prosperous person* 730 n.
  *rich person* 800 n.
  *vulgarian* 847 n.
  *commoner* 869 n.
**nouvelle cuisine**
  *dieting* 301 n.
**nouvelle vague**
  *film* 445 n.

**nova**
  *star* 321 n.
**novel**
  *dissimilar* 19 adj.
  *original* 21 adj.
  *new* 126 adj.
  *unknown* 491 adj.
  *reading matter* 589 n.
  *novel* 590 n.
**novelese**
  *neology* 560 n.
**novelette**
  *novel* 590 n.
**novelettish**
  *feeble* 572 adj.
  *vulgar* 847 adj.
**novelist**
  *author* 589 n.
  *narrator* 590 n.
**novelization, novel-**
  **isation**
  *novel* 590 n.
**novelty**
  *bauble* 639 n.
  *pleasurableness* 826 n.
  *See also* **novel**
**novena**
  *period* 110 n.
  *church service* 988 n.
**novice**
  *ignoramus* 493 n.
  *beginner* 538 n.
  *bungle* 697 n.
  *ingenue* 699 n.
  *monk* 986 n.
  *nun* 986 n.
  *lay person* 987 n.
**novitiate**
  *learning* 536 n.
  *preparation* 669 n.
**no voice**
  *voicelessness* 578 n.
  *no choice* 606 n.
**no vote**
  *no choice* 606 n.
**now**
  *at present* 121 adv.
**now, be**
  *be* 1 vb.
  *be now* 121 vb.
**nowadays**
  *present time* 121 n.
**now and again/then**
  *discontinuously* 72 adv.
  *sometimes* 139 adv.
  *fitfully* 142 adv.
  *at intervals* 201 adv.
**no way**
  *in no way* 33 adv.
  *impossibility* 470 n.
  *impossibly* 470 adv.
  – 472 int.
  *no* 489 adv.
  – 533 int.
  *denyingly* 760 adv.
**no way out**
  *hopelessness* 853 n.

**nowhere**
  *nonexistent* 2 adj.
  *not here* 190 adv.
**no will of one's own**
  *irresolution* 601 n.
**no-win situation**
  *lost labour* 641 n.
  *failure* 728 n.
**no wiser**
  *uninstructed* 491 adj.
**no wonder**
  – 865 int.
**no word of**
  *ignorance* 491 n.
  *concealment* 525 n.
**no words wasted**
  *conciseness* 569 n.
**no work**
  *inaction* 677 n.
  *leisure* 681 n.
**now or never**
  *at present* 121 adv.
  *opportunely* 137 adv.
**no worse**
  *equivalent* 28 adj.
  *healthy* 650 adj.
**now this now that**
  *changeably* 152 adv.
  *capriciously* 604 adv.
**noxious**
  *fetid* 397 adj.
  *harmful* 645 adj.
  *insalubrious* 653 adj.
**noxious animal**
  *creepy-crawly* 365 n.
  *bane* 659 n.
  *noxious animal* 904 n.
  *knave* 938 n.
**noyade**
  *slaughter* 362 n.
**nozzle**
  *projection* 254 n.
  *orifice* 263 n.
  *outlet* 298 n.
  *air pipe* 353 n.
**nuance**
  *differentiation* 15 n.
  *degree* 27 n.
  *small quantity* 33 n.
  *hue* 425 n.
  *discrimination* 463 n.
**nub**
  *substance* 3 n.
  *essential part* 5 n.
  *focus* 76 n.
  *centre* 225 n.
  *swelling* 253 n.
  *chief thing* 638 n.
**nubbly**
  *convex* 253 adj.
  *rough* 259 adj.
**nubile**
  *grown-up* 134 adj.
  *marriageable* 894 adj.
**nuclear**
  *dynamic* 160 adj.
  *central* 225 adj.

**nuclear blast**
  *havoc* 165 n.
**nuclear bomb**
  *bomb* 723 n.
**nuclear deterrent**
  *arms* 723 n.
**nuclear disarmament**
  *pacification* 719 n.
**nuclear fallout**
  *radiation* 417 n.
  *poison* 659 n.
**nuclear family**
  *family* 11 n.
**nuclear fission**
  *separation* 46 n.
**nuclear-free zone**
  *pacification* 719 n.
**nuclear fuel**
  *fuel* 385 n.
**nuclear medicine**
  *medical art* 658 n.
**nuclear missile**
  *nucleonics* 160 n.
  *rocket* 276 n.
**nuclear physics**
  *nucleonics* 160 n.
  *physics* 319 n.
**nuclear power**
  *sources of energy* 160 n.
**nuclear reactor**
  *nucleonics* 160 n.
**nuclear submarine**
  *warship* 722 n.
**nuclear war**
  *war* 718 n.
**nuclear warhead**
  *nucleonics* 160 n.
  *destroyer* 168 n.
**nuclear winter**
  *havoc* 165 n.
  *blight* 659 n.
**nucleate**
  *make smaller* 198 vb.
  *centralize* 225 vb.
  *be dense* 324 vb.
**nucleic acid**
  *organism* 358 n.
**nucleolus**
  *organism* 358 n.
**nucleon**
  *element* 319 n. box
**nucleonics**
  *separation* 46 n.
  *decomposition* 51 n.
  *nucleonics* 160 n.
  *physics* 319 n.
  *fuel* 385 n.
  *radiation* 417 n.
**nucleus**
  *essential part* 5 n.
  *middle* 70 n.
  *source* 156 n.
  *minuteness* 196 n.
  *centre* 225 n.
  *element* 319 n.
  *solid body* 324 n.
  *organism* 358 n.

be in love 887 vb.
**nutter**
crank 504 n.
**nutty**
pungent 388 adj.
crazy 503 adj.
**nuzzle**
touch 378 vb.
caress 889 vb.
**nyctalopia**
dim sight 440 n.
**nylon**
fibre 208 n.
textile 222 n.
**nylons**
legwear 228 n.
**nymph**
young creature 132 n.
youngster 132 n.
woman 373 n.
nymph 967 n.
mythical being 970 n.
**nymphet**
youngster 132 n.
loose woman 952 n.
**nympholepsy**
frenzy 503 n.
spell 983 n.
**nympholept**
crank 504 n.
**nymphomania**
personality disorder
503 n.
psychosis 503 n. box
libido 859 n.
illicit love 951 n.
**nymphomaniac,**
**nympho**
neurotic 503 adj.
libertine 952 n.
loose woman 952 n.
**nystagmus**
dim sight 440 n.

*O*

**oaf**
dunce 501 n.
bungler 697 n.
**oafish**
unintelligent 499 adj.
**oak**
strength 162 n.
hardness 326 n.
tree 366 n.
**oakum**
fibre 208 n.
**OAP**
old person 133 n.
**oar**
propeller 269 n.
propellant 287 n.
**oarsman**
boatman 270 n.
**oasis**
nonconformity 84 n.

land 344 n.
**oasthouse**
furnace 383 n.
**oath**
testimony 466 n.
oath 532 n.
word 559 n.
promise 764 n.
scurrility 899 n.
**oatmeal**
cereals 301 n.
brown 430 adj.
**oats**
cereals 301 n.
provender 301 n.
grass 366 n.
**obbligato**
concomitant 89 n.
musical piece 412 n.
**obdurate**
obstinate 602 adj.
severe 735 adj.
impenitent 940 adj.
**obeah, obi**
sorcery 983 n.
**obedience**
obedience 739 n.
service 745 n.
**obedient**
willing 597 adj.
submitting 721 adj.
obedient 739 adj.
observant 768 adj.
servile 879 adj.
See also **obey**
**obeisance**
obeisance 311 n.
submission 721 n.
courteous act 884 n.
respects 920 n.
**obelisk**
high structure 209 n.
monument 548 n.
**Oberon**
fairy 970 n.
**obese**
fleshy 195 adj.
expanded 197 adj.
**obesity**
eating 301 n.
disease 651 n.
**obey**
be inferior 35 vb.
conform 83 vb.
acquiesce 488 vb.
obey 739 vb.
serve 742 vb.
be subject 745 vb.
do one's duty 917 vb.
**obeyed**
influential 178 adj.
**obfuscate**
darken 418 vb.
make opaque 423 vb.
conceal 525 vb.
**obfuscation**
obfuscation 421 n.

concealment 525 n.
misteaching 535 n.
**obit**
death roll 361 n.
biography 590 n.
**obiter dictum**
interjection 231 n.
**obituary**
obsequies 364 n.
biography 590 n.
**object**
substance 3 n.
product 164 n.
object 319 n.
dissent 489 vb.
part of speech 564 n.
be unwilling 598 vb.
objective 617 n.
oppose 704 vb.
resist 715 vb.
deprecate 762 vb.
be discontented 829 vb.
disapprove 924 vb.
**objectify**
make extrinsic 6 vb.
materialize 319 vb.
cognize 447 vb.
imagine 513 vb.
**objection**
qualification 468 n.
doubt 486 n.
dissent 489 n.
unwillingness 598 n.
dissuasion 613 n.
hindrance 702 n.
resistance 715 n.
refusal 760 n.
**objectionable**
inexpedient 643 adj.
unpleasant 827 adj.
disreputable 867 adj.
wrong 914 adj.
**objective**
substantial 3 adj.
goal 295 n.
material 319 adj.
optical device 442 n.
true 494 adj.
objective 617 n.
attempt 671 n.
aspiration 852 n.
**object lesson**
example 83 n.
warning 664 n.
**object of scorn**
nonentity 639 vb.
object of scorn 867 n.
contemptibility 922 n.
**objector**
dissentient 489 n.
opponent 705 n.
litigant 959 n.
**objet d'art**
masterpiece 694 n.
ornamentation 844 n.
**objet trouvé**
sculpture 554 n.

**objurgate**
dispraise 924 vb.
**oblate**
worshipper 981 n.
**oblation**
offering 781 n.
propitiation 941 n.
oblation 981 n.
**obligated**
obliged 917 adj.
**obligation**
necessity 596 n.
needfulness 627 n.
undertaking 672 n.
promise 764 n.
debt 803 n.
dueness 915 n.
duty 917 n.
**obligatory**
necessary 596 adj.
commanding 737 adj.
compelling 740 adj.
conditional 766 adj.
obligatory 917 adj.
**oblige**
necessitate 596 vb.
require 627 vb.
compel 740 vb.
be courteous 884 vb.
impose a duty 917 vb.
**obliged**
indebted 803 adj.
grateful 907 adj.
obliged 917 adj.
**obliging**
aiding 703 adj.
courteous 884 adj.
benevolent 897 adj.
**oblique**
oblique 220 adj.
distorted 246 adj.
angular 247 adj.
curved 248 adj.
directed 281 adj.
deviating 282 adj.
occult 523 adj.
**obliquely**
obliquely 220 adv.
sideways 239 adv.
**obliterate**
destroy 165 vb.
conceal 525 vb.
obliterate 550 vb.
clean 648 vb.
**obliteration**
extinction 2 n.
oblivion 506 n.
obliteration 550 n.
**oblivion**
extinction 2 n.
oblivion 506 n.
obliteration 550 n.
desuetude 611 n.
**oblivious**
insensible 375 adj.
inattentive 456 adj.
negligent 458 adj.

**occult**
unknown 491 adj.
unintelligible 517 adj.
occult 523 adj.
concealed 525 adj.
cabbalistic 984 adj.
**occultation**
obscuration 418 n.
disappearance 446 n.
**occultism**
spirit 447 n.
latency 523 n.
occultism 984 n.
**occultist**
oracle 511 n.
sorcerer 983 n.
occultist 984 n.
**occupant**
resident 191 n.
**occupation**
presence 189 n.
habit 610 n.
business 622 n.
job 622 n.
undertaking 672 n.
action 676 n.
**occupational**
habitual 610 adj.
businesslike 622 adj.
doing 676 adj.
**occupational disease**
disease 651 n.
**occupational therapy**
therapy 658 n.
**occupied**
occupied 191 adj.
busy 678 adj.
**occupied, be**
be engaged 138 vb.
**occupier**
resident 191 n.
possessor 776 n.
**occupy**
fill 54 vb.
dwell 192 vb.
attract notice 455 vb.
employ 622 vb.
possess 773 vb.
appropriate 786 vb.
**occur**
be 1 vb.
happen 154 vb.
be present 189 vb.
– to
dawn upon 449 vb.
**occurrence**
event 154 n.
**ocean**
region 184 n.
depth 211 n.
water 339 n.
ocean 343 n.
**ocean-going**
seafaring 269 adj.
marine 275 adj.
oceanic 343 adj.
**oceanic**

oceanic 343 adj.
**Oceanid**
sea nymph 343 n.
mythical being 970 n.
**oceanographer**
surveyor 465 n.
**oceanography**
earth sciences 321 n.
oceanography 343 n.
**oceans**
great quantity 32 n.
**Oceanus**
sea god 343 n.
classical deities 967 n.
**ocelot**
cat 365 n.
**ochlocracy**
government 733 n.
**ochre**
brown pigment 430 n.
orange 432 n.
**o'clock**
o'clock 117 adv.
**octad**
over five 99 n.
**octagon**
angular figure 247 n.
**octaroon**
hybrid 43 n.
**Octateuch**
scripture 975 n.
**octave**
period 110 n.
musical note 410 n.
**octavo**
edition 589 n.
**octet**
over five 99 n.
duet 412 n.
**octogenarian**
old person 133 n.
**octopus**
marine life 365 n.
tyrant 735 n.
**octosyllabic**
poetic 593 adj.
**octroi**
tax 809 n.
**ocular**
seeing 438 adj.
optical device 442 n.
**ocular proof**
visibility 443 n.
**oculist**
doctor 658 n.
**odalisque**
slave 742 n.
**odd**
disagreeing 25 adj.
unequal 29 adj.
remaining 41 adj.
unusual 84 adj.
numerical 85 adj.
crazy 503 adj.
puzzling 517 adj.
ridiculous 849 adj.
wonderful 864 adj.

**odd fish, oddball**
nonconformist 84 n.
crank 504 n.
laughingstock 851 n.
**oddity**
misfit 25 n.
nonconformist 84 n.
nonconformity 84 n.
crank 504 n.
prodigy 864 n.
**odd-job man**
servant 742 n.
**oddly**
remarkably 32 adv.
**odd man out**
dissimilarity 19 n.
misfit 25 n.
nonconformist 84 n.
dissentient 489 n.
**oddment(s)**
extra 40 n.
medley 43 n.
**odd moments**
leisure 681 n.
**odds**
difference 15 n.
advantage 34 n.
fair chance 159 n.
dissension 709 n.
**odds and ends**
extra 40 n.
leavings 41 n.
medley 43 n.
rubbish 641 n.
**odds on**
fair chance 159 n.
approved 923 adj.
**ode**
poem 593 n.
**odi et amo**
love 887 n.
hatred 888 n.
**Odin**
Nordic deities 967 n.
**odious**
unpleasant 827 adj.
ugly 842 adj.
disreputable 867 adj.
hateful 888 adj.
**odium**
odium 888 n.
**odium theologicum**
pietism 979 n.
**odorous**
odorous 394 adj.
fragrant 396 adj.
**odour**
odour 394 n.
fragrance 396 n.
**odourless**
odourless 395 adj.
**odour of sanctity**
virtue 933 n.
sanctity 979 n.
**Odysseus**
traveller 268 n.
**odyssey**

land travel 267 n.
**oedema**
swelling 253 n.
**oedematous**
diseased 651 adj.
**Oedipus complex**
eccentricity 503 n.
love 887 n.
**oeillade**
wooing 889 n.
**oesophagus**
maw 194 n.
air pipe 353 n.
**oestrogen**
drug 658 n.
**oestrus**
libido 859 n.
**oeuvre**
product 164 n.
**of age**
grown-up 134 adj.
marriageable 894 adj.
**of all sorts**
different 15 adj.
nonuniform 17 adj.
multiform 82 adj.
**of all things**
eminently 34 adv.
**of a piece**
uniform 16 adj.
similar 18 adj.
agreeing 24 adj.
**of course**
conformably 83 adv.
consequently 157 adv.
certainly 473 adv.
of course 478 adv.
necessarily 596 adv.
habitually 610 adv.
– 865 int.
**off**
decomposed 51 adj.
ending 69 adj.
absent 190 adj.
pungent 388 adj.
unprovided 636 adj.
unpleasant 827 adj.
**off, be**
go away 190 vb.
– 292 int.
decamp 296 vb.
run away 620 vb.
**offal**
insides 224 n.
meat 301 n.
rubbish 641 n.
**off balance**
unequal 29 adj.
**off-beam**
deviating 282 adj.
mistaken 495 adj.
**offbeat**
unconformable 84 adj.
**off-chance**
possibility 469 n.
improbability 472 n.
**off colour**

*travelling* 267 adj.
**of old**
  *formerly* 125 adv.
**of one mind**
  *concurrent* 181 adj.
  *concordant* 710 adj.
**of one's own accord**
  *at will* 595 adv.
  *voluntary* 597 adj.
**of right**
  *established* 153 adj.
  *due* 915 adj.
**of service**
  *useful* 640 adj.
  *aiding* 703 adj.
**often**
  *repeatedly* 106 adv.
  *often* 139 adv.
**of the first water**
  *excellent* 644 adj.
**ogee**
  *curve* 248 n.
  *convolution* 251 n.
  *pattern* 844 n.
**ogham alphabet**
  *letter* 558 n.
**ogive**
  *prop* 218 n.
**ogle**
  *look* 438 n.
  *watch* 441 vb.
  *gesture* 547 n.
  *desire* 859 vb.
  *court* 889 vb.
**ogre**
  *giant* 195 n.
  *tyrant* 735 n.
  *intimidation* 854 n.
  *monster* 938 n.
  *demon* 970 n.
**ogress**
  *hellhag* 904 n.
  *demon* 970 n.
**Ogygian**
  *immemorial* 127 adj.
**ohm**
  *electronics* 160 n.
  *metrology* 465 n.
**oil**
  *sources of energy*
    160 n.
  *smoother* 258 n.
  *cookery* 301 n.
  *soften* 327 vb.
  *lubricant* 334 n.
  *oil* 357 n.
  *grease* 357 vb.
  *fuel* 385 n.
  *silencer* 401 n.
  *bribe* 612 vb.
  *materials* 631 n.
  *balm* 658 n.
  *facilitate* 701 vb.
**oilfield**
  *store* 632 n.
**oil-fired**
  *heating* 381 adj.

**oil on troubled**
  **waters**
  *moderator* 177 n.
  *remedy* 658 n.
**oil painting**
  *picture* 553 n.
**oils**
  *art equipment* 553 n.
**oilskins**
  *overcoat* 228 n.
  *shelter* 662 n.
**oil slick**
  *semiliquidity* 354 n.
**oilstone**
  *sharpener* 256 n.
**oil tanker**
  *merchant ship* 275 n.
**oil well**
  *store* 632 n.
**oily**
  *smooth* 258 adj.
  *unctuous* 357 adj.
  *hypocritical* 541 adj.
  *dirty* 649 adj.
  *servile* 879 adj.
  *flattering* 925 adj.
**ointment**
  *lubricant* 334 n.
  *unguent* 357 n.
  *balm* 658 n.
**OK, okay**
  *in order* 60 adv.
  *assent* 488 n.
  *not bad* 644 adj.
  *middling* 732 adj.
**okra**
  *vegetable* 301 n.
**old**
  *antiquated* 127 adj.
  *olden* 127 adj.
  *ageing* 131 adj.
  *weak* 163 adj.
**old age**
  *old age* 131 n.
**old-age pensioner**
  *old person* 133 n.
  *recipient* 782 n.
**old as the hills**
  *immemorial* 127 adj.
  *ageing* 131 adj.
**Old Bailey**
  *lawcourt* 956 n.
**Old Bill**
  *police* 955 n.
**old boy**
  *old man* 133 n.
  *learner* 538 n.
**old-boy network**
  *latency* 523 n.
**Old Country, the**
  *home* 192 n.
**old couple**
  *old couple* 133 n.
**old crock**
  *car* 274 n.
  *sick person* 651 n.
**old dutch**

*old woman* 133 n.
  *spouse* 894 n.
**olden**
  *past* 125 adj.
  *olden* 127 adj.
  *architectural* 192 adj.
**olden days**
  *past time* 125 n.
**olden times**
  *oldness* 127 n.
**older**
  *older* 131 adj.
**old-fashioned**
  *anachronistic* 118 adj.
  *antiquated* 127 adj.
  *alcoholic drink* 301 n.
  *unwonted* 611 adj.
  *unwonted* 611 adj.
**old flame**
  *loved one* 887 n.
**old fogy, old fogey**
  *archaism* 127 n.
  *old man* 133 n.
  *fool* 501 n.
  *obstinate person* 602 n.
  *laughingstock* 851 n.
**old folks, the**
  *family* 11 n.
  *old couple* 133 n.
**old girl**
  *old woman* 133 n.
  *learner* 538 n.
**Old Glory**
  *flag* 547 n.
**old gold**
  *orange* 432 n.
**old guard**
  *stamina* 600 n.
**old hand**
  *expert* 696 n.
**old hat**
  *antiquated* 127 adj.
  *unwonted* 611 adj.
**oldie**
  *archaism* 127 n.
**old lag**
  *prisoner* 750 n.
  *offender* 904 n.
**old maid**
  *card game* 837 n.
  *spinster* 895 n.
**old-maidish**
  *prudish* 950 adj.
**old man**
  *old man* 133 n.
  *paternity* 169 n.
  *spouse* 894 n.
**Old Man of the Sea**
  *encumbrance* 702 n.
  *mythical being* 970 n.
**old master**
  *picture* 553 n.
  *artist* 556 n.
**Old Moore**
  *oracle* 511 n.
**oldness**
  *beginning* 68 n.

*time* 108 n.
  *durability* 113 n.
  *past time* 125 n.
  *oldness* 127 n.
  *permanence* 144 n.
**old news**
  *repetition* 106 n.
  *news* 529 n.
  *bore* 838 n.
**Old Nick**
  *Mephisto* 969 n.
**old people's home**
  *gerontology* 131 n.
  *retreat* 192 n.
  *shelter* 662 n.
**old salt**
  *mariner* 270 n.
**old-school**
  *antiquated* 127 adj.
  *opinionatedness* 602 n.
  *habit* 610 n.
**old school tie**
  *livery* 547 n.
  *cooperative* 706 n.
**old-stager**
  *old man* 133 n.
  *expert* 696 n.
**old story**
  *repetition* 106 n.
  *news* 529 n.
**old style**
  *chronology* 117 n.
**Old Testament**
  *scripture* 975 n. box
**old-time**
  *antiquated* 127 adj.
**old-timer**
  *archaism* 127 n.
  *old man* 133 n.
**old wives' tales**
  *error* 495 n.
  *fable* 543 n.
**old woman**
  *old woman* 133 n.
  *maternity* 169 n.
  *spouse* 894 n.
**old-world**
  *antiquated* 127 adj.
  *courteous* 884 adj.
**Old World**
  *region* 184 n.
  *world* 321 n.
**oleaginous**
  *unctuous* 357 adj.
**Olestra**
  *cookery* 301 n.
**O level**
  *exam* 459 n.
**olfactory**
  *odorous* 394 adj.
**oligarchy**
  *government* 733 n.
**olive**
  *green* 434 adj.
**olive branch**
  *peace offering* 719 n.
**olive oil**

*pleasurable* 826 adj.
*paradisiac* 971 adj.
**Paradise**
*happiness* 824 n.
*heaven* 971 n.
**parados**
*defences* 713 n.
**paradox**
*contrariety* 14 n.
*misfit* 25 n.
*argumentation* 475 n.
*absurdity* 497 n.
*lack of expectation*
　508 n.
*unintelligibility* 517 n.
*trope* 519 n.
*ridiculousness* 849 n.
**paradoxical**
*uncertain* 474 adj.
**paraffin**
*oil* 357 n.
*fuel* 385 n.
**paragon**
*prototype* 23 n.
*exceller* 644 n.
*paragon* 646 n.
*prodigy* 864 n.
*person of repute* 866 n.
*good person* 937 n.
**paragraph**
*subdivision* 53 n.
*punctuation* 547 n.
*phrase* 563 n.
*edition* 589 n.
**paralipsis**
*ornament* 574 n.
**parallax**
*displacement* 188 n.
**parallel**
*correlative* 12 adj.
*analogue* 18 n.
*equal* 28 adj.
*concurrent* 181 adj.
*region* 184 n.
*parallelism* 219 n.
*parallel* 219 adj.
*compare* 462 vb.
**parallel lines**
*parallelism* 219 n.
**parallelogram**
*angular figure* 247 n.
**paralogism**
*sophism* 477 n.
**paralyse**
*disable* 161 vb.
*render insensible* 375 vb.
*make inactive* 679 vb.
*hinder* 702 vb.
*frighten* 854 vb.
**paralysed**
*still* 266 adj.
*diseased* 651 adj.
*nonactive* 677 adj.
**paralysis**
*helplessness* 161 n.
*inertness* 175 n.
*insensibility* 375 n.

*inaction* 677 n.
**paralytic**
*sick person* 651 n.
*dead drunk* 949 adj.
**paramedic**
*doctor* 658 n.
*auxiliary* 707 n.
**parameter**
*numerical element* 85 n.
*limit* 236 n.
**paramilitary**
*warlike* 718 adj.
**paramilitary for-
　mation**
*auxiliary* 707 n.
**paramount**
*supreme* 34 adj.
*important* 638 adj.
*authoritative* 733 adj.
**paramountcy**
*prestige* 866 n.
**paramour**
*lover* 887 n.
*kept woman* 952 n.
**parang**
*sharp edge* 256 n.
**paranoia**
*psychosis* 503 n.
**paranoiac**
*psychotic* 504 n.
**paranoid**
*psychotic* 503 adj.
**paranormal**
*paranormal* 984 adj.
**parapet**
*summit* 213 n.
*fortification* 713 n.
**paraph**
*label* 547 n.
**paraphernalia**
*medley* 43 n.
*equipment* 630 n.
*property* 777 n.
**paraphrase**
*imitation* 20 n.
*copy* 20 vb.
*copy* 22 n.
*intelligibility* 516 n.
*translation* 520 n.
*phrase* 563 n.
**paraphrastic**
*semantic* 514 adj.
*interpretive* 520 adj.
**paraplegia**
*helplessness* 161 n.
*nervous disorders* 651 n.
**paraplegic**
*sick person* 651 n.
**parapsychology**
*psychology* 447 n.
*study* 536 n. box
*psychics* 984 n.
**paraquat**
*poison* 659 n.
**paraselene**
*moon* 321 n.
**parasite**

*concomitant* 89 n.
*resident* 191 n.
*insect* 365 n.
*plant* 366 n.
*superfluity* 637 n.
*bane* 659 n.
*idler* 679 n.
*dependant* 742 n.
*beggar* 763 n.
*desirer* 859 n.
*toady* 879 n.
*sociable person* 882 n.
*flatterer* 925 n.
**parasitical**
*inferior* 35 adj.
*residing* 192 adj.
*lazy* 679 adj.
**parasitology**
*study* 536 n. box
*pathology* 651 n.
**parasol**
*shade* 226 n.
*screen* 421 n.
**parasuicide**
*suicide* 362 n.
**parataxis**
*grammar* 564 n.
**paratha**
*cereals* 301 n.
**paratrooper**
*aeronaut* 271 n.
*descent* 309 n.
**paratroops**
*armed force* 722 n.
**paratyphoid**
*infection* 651 n.
**parboil**
*cook* 301 vb.
**parbuckle**
*lifter* 310 n.
**parcel**
*piece* 53 n.
*bunch* 74 n.
*bring together* 74 vb.
– out
*sunder* 46 vb.
*apportion* 783 vb.
**parcel post**
*postal communications*
　531 n.
**parcener**
*participator* 775 n.
**parched**
*dry* 342 adj.
*hot* 379 adj.
*hungry* 859 adj.
**parchment**
*stationery* 586 n.
*bookbinding* 589 n.
**pardon**
*amnesty* 506 n.
*leniency* 736 n.
*liberate* 746 vb.
*show mercy* 905 vb.
*forgive* 909 vb.
*nonliability* 919 n.
*acquit* 960 vb.

**pardonable**
*vindicable* 927 adj.
*guiltless* 935 adj.
**pare**
*shade off* 27 vb.
*abate* 37 vb.
*subtract* 39 vb.
*cut* 46 vb.
*render few* 105 vb.
*laminate* 207 vb.
– expenses
*economize* 814 vb.
**paregoric**
*remedial* 658 adj.
**parent**
*source* 156 n.
*parentage* 169 n.
**parentage**
*consanguinity* 11 n.
*precursor* 66 n.
*attribution* 158 n.
*producer* 164 n.
*propagation* 167 n.
*parentage* 169 n.
**parental**
*parental* 169 adj.
**parenthesis**
*irrelevance* 10 n.
*discontinuity* 72 n.
*interjection* 231 n.
*insertion* 303 n.
*punctuation* 547 n.
**parenthood**
*parentage* 169 n.
*life* 360 n.
**paresis**
*nervous disorders* 651 n.
**par excellence**
*eminently* 34 adv.
*importantly* 638 adv.
**parfumerie**
*beauty parlour* 843 n.
**pargeting**
*facing* 226 n.
*ornamental art* 844 n.
**parhelion**
*sun* 321 n.
**pariah**
*nonconformist* 84 n.
*dog* 365 n.
*derelict* 779 n.
*outcast* 883 n.
**parietal**
*lateral* 239 adj.
**pari mutuel**
*gaming-house* 618 n.
**paring**
*small thing* 33 n.
*piece* 53 n.
*economy* 814 n.
**pari passu**
*equally* 28 adv.
*synchronously* 123 adv.
**parish**
*district* 184 n.
*parish* 985 n.
*laity* 987 n.

- oneself on the back
  *feel pride* 871 vb.
  *boast* 877 vb.
- on the back
  *give courage* 855 vb.
  *applaud* 923 vb.
**pat-ball**
  *ball game* 837 n.
**patch**
  *adjunct* 40 n.
  *join* 45 vb.
  *piece* 53 n.
  *modify* 143 vb.
  *garden* 370 n.
  *mottling* 437 n.
  *variegate* 437 vb.
  *dirt* 649 n.
  *repair* 656 n., vb.
  *surgical dressing* 658 n.
  *eyesore* 842 n.
  *cosmetic* 843 n.
  *blemish* 845 n.
- up
  *repair* 656 vb.
  *make peace* 719 vb.
  *compromise* 770 vb.
**patcher**
  *mender* 656 n.
**patchouli**
  *scent* 396 n.
**patchwork**
  *nonuniformity* 17 n.
  *medley* 43 n.
  *variegation* 437 n.
  *needlework* 844 n.
**patchy**
  *nonuniform* 17 adj.
  *inferior* 35 adj.
  *mixed* 43 adj.
  *discontinuous* 72 adj.
  *mottled* 437 adj.
  *imperfect* 647 adj.
**pate**
  *head* 213 n.
**pâté**
  *hors-d'oeuvres* 301 n.
**paten**
  *plate* 194 n.
  *ritual object* 988 n.
  *church utensil* 990 n.
**patent**
  *open* 263 adj.
  *manifest* 522 adj.
  *permit* 756 n., vb.
  *dueness* 915 n.
**patented**
  *proprietary* 777 adj.
**patent leather**
  *skin* 226 n.
**patent medicine**
  *medicine* 658 n.
  *remedy* 658 n.
**paterfamilias**
  *paternity* 169 n.
**paternal**
  *akin* 11 adj.
  *parental* 169 adj.

*benevolent* 897 adj.
**paternalism**
  *despotism* 733 n.
  *governance* 733 n.
**paternity**
  *propagation* 167 n.
  *paternity* 169 n.
**Paternoster**
  *prayers* 981 n.
**path**
  *direction* 281 n.
  *way in* 297 n.
  *outlet* 298 n.
  *passage* 305 n.
  *trace* 548 n.
  *path* 624 n.
**pathetic**
  *unimportant* 639 adj.
  *bad* 645 adj.
  *felt* 818 adj.
  *distressing* 827 adj.
  *lamenting* 836 adj.
  *pitiable* 905 adj.
**pathetic fallacy**
  *anthropology* 371 n.
  *affections* 817 n.
**pathfinder**
  *precursor* 66 n.
  *traveller* 268 n.
**pathless**
  *spacious* 183 adj.
  *difficult* 700 adj.
**pathogen**
  *infection* 651 n.
**pathogenic**
  *diseased* 651 adj.
  *infectious* 653 adj.
**pathological**
  *diseased* 651 adj.
  *medical* 658 adj.
**pathologist**
  *doctor* 658 n.
**pathology**
  *study* 536 n. box
  *pathology* 651 n.
  *medical art* 658 n.
**pathos**
  *feeling* 818 n.
  *excitation* 821 n.
  *painfulness* 827 n.
**pathway**
  *path* 624 n.
**patience**
  *perseverance* 600 n.
  *leniency* 736 n.
  *patience* 823 n.
  *card game* 837 n.
  *caution* 858 n.
  *forgiveness* 909 n.
**patient**
  *slow* 278 adj.
  *testee* 461 n.
  *sick person* 651 n.
  *patient* 823 adj.
  *sufferer* 825 n.
**patina**
  *layer* 207 n.

*hue* 425 n.
  *greenness* 434 n.
  *impairment* 655 n.
  *blemish* 845 n.
**patio**
  *lobby* 194 n.
**patisserie**
  *pastries* 301 n.
**patois**
  *speciality* 80 n.
  *dialect* 560 n.
**patrial**
  *native* 191 n.
  *subject* 742 n.
  *free person* 744 n.
**patriality**
  *freedom* 744 n.
  *subjection* 745 n.
  *dueness* 915 n.
**patriarch**
  *precursor* 66 n.
  *old man* 133 n.
  *paternity* 169 n.
  *governor* 741 n.
  *master* 741 n.
  *ecclesiarch* 986 n.
**patriarchal**
  *olden* 127 adj.
**patriarchate**
  *church office* 985 n.
**patriarchy**
  *family* 11 n.
  *male* 372 n.
  *government* 733 n.
**patrician**
  *aristocrat* 868 n.
  *genteel* 868 adj.
**patricide**
  *homicide* 362 n. box
**patrilineal**
  *akin* 11 adj.
  *parental* 169 adj.
**patrimony**
  *acquisition* 771 n.
  *possession* 773 n.
  *dower* 777 n.
  *dueness* 915 n.
**patriot**
  *defender* 713 n.
  *patriot* 901 n.
  *benefactor* 903 n.
**patriotism**
  *love* 887 n.
  *patriotism* 901 n.
  *disinterestedness* 931 n.
**patristic**
  *scriptural* 975 adj.
**patrol**
  *land travel* 267 n.
  *traverse* 267 vb.
  *pass* 305 vb.
  *circler* 314 n.
  *spectator* 441 n.
  *safeguard* 660 vb.
  *defender* 713 n.
  *armed force* 722 n.
  *restrain* 747 vb.

**patrolman,
  patrolwoman**
  *police* 955 n.
**patron, patroness**
  *prop* 218 n.
  *onlookers* 441 n.
  *enthusiast* 504 n.
  *protector* 660 n.
  *aider* 703 n.
  *patron* 707 n.
  *defender* 713 n.
  *master* 741 n.
  *security* 767 n.
  *participator* 775 n.
  *purchaser* 792 n.
  *friend* 880 n.
  *kind person* 897 n.
  *benefactor* 903 n.
  *commender* 923 n.
**patronage**
  *influence* 178 n.
  *protection* 660 n.
  *management* 689 n.
  *aid* 703 n.
  *authority* 733 n.
  *security* 767 n.
  *purchase* 792 n.
  *approbation* 923 n.
  *benefice* 985 n.
**patronize, patronise**
  *endorse* 488 vb.
  *choose* 605 vb.
  *patronize* 703 vb.
  *defend* 713 vb.
  *be proud* 871 vb.
  *befriend* 880 vb.
  *be benevolent* 897 vb.
**patronizing**
  *prideful* 871 adj.
**patron saint**
  *saint* 968 n.
**patronymic**
  *name* 561 n.
**patsy**
  *dupe* 544 n.
**patten**
  *footwear* 228 n.
**patter**
  *be in motion* 265 vb.
  *walk* 267 vb.
  *strike* 279 vb.
  *rain* 350 vb.
  *faintness* 401 n.
  *roll* 403 vb.
  *empty talk* 515 n.
  *language* 557 n.
  *slang* 560 n.
  *speech* 579 n.
  *loquacity* 581 n.
  *inducement* 612 n.
**pattern**
  *correlation* 12 n.
  *uniformity* 16 n.
  *prototype* 23 n.
  *composition* 56 n.
  *arrangement* 62 n.
  *rule* 81 n.

*example* 83 n.
*form* 243 n., vb.
*structure* 331 n.
*variegate* 437 vb.
*comparison* 462 n.
*picture* 553 n.
*plan* 623 n.
*paragon* 646 n.
*pattern* 844 n.
*decorate* 844 vb.
– oneself on
*do likewise* 20 vb.
**patty**
*pastries* 301 n.
**patulous**
*expanded* 197 adj.
*broad* 205 adj.
**paucity**
*smallness* 33 n.
*fewness* 105 n.
*scarcity* 636 n.
**Paulician**
*heretic* 977 n.
**Paul Jones**
*dance* 837 n.
**paunch**
*maw* 194 n.
*swelling* 253 n.
*enter* 301 n.
**paunchy**
*fleshy* 195 adj.
**pauper**
*poor person* 801 n.
**pauperize, pauperise**
*impoverish* 801 vb.
**pause**
*discontinuity* 72 n.
*interim* 108 n.
*period* 110 n.
*delay* 136 n.
*lull* 145 n.
*pause* 145 vb.
*interval* 201 n.
*quiescence* 266 n.
*notation* 410 n.
*be uncertain* 474 vb.
*doubt* 486 vb.
*not act* 677 vb.
*repose* 683 n.
**pavane**
*dance* 837 n.
**pave**
*overlay* 226 vb.
*smooth* 258 vb.
– the way
*prepare* 669 vb.
*facilitate* 701 vb.
**pavement**
*paving* 226 n.
*path* 624 n.
*road* 624 n.
**pavilion**
*pavilion* 192 n.
*arbour* 194 n.
*canopy* 226 n.
**paving**
*base* 214 n.

*basis* 218 n.
*paving* 226 n.
*building material* 631 n.
**paving stone**
*paving* 226 n.
**pavis**
*armour* 713 n.
**Pavlovian response**
*intuition* 476 n.
**pavonine**
*iridescent* 437 adj.
**paw**
*foot* 214 n.
*strike* 279 vb.
*feeler* 378 n.
*touch* 378 vb.
*nippers* 778 n.
*caress* 889 vb.
– the ground
*leap* 312 vb.
*gesticulate* 547 vb.
*be angry* 891 vb.
**pawky**
*cunning* 698 adj.
*witty* 839 adj.
**pawl**
*fastening* 47 n.
**pawn**
*inferior* 35 n.
*dupe* 544 n.
*fatalist* 596 n.
*instrument* 628 n.
*nonentity* 639 n.
*slave* 742 n.
*security* 767 n.
*give security* 767 vb.
*transfer* 780 n.
*borrow* 785 vb.
*plaything* 837 n.
**pawnbroker**
*lender* 784 n.
**pax**
*ritual object* 988 n.
**Pax Romana**
*peace* 717 n.
*palmy days* 730 n.
**pay**
*coat* 226 vb.
*incentive* 612 n.
*benefit* 615 vb.
*employ* 622 vb.
*be useful* 640 vb.
*earnings* 771 n.
*be profitable* 771 vb.
*restitute* 787 vb.
*pay* 804 n vb
*expend* 806 vb.
*receipt* 807 n.
*reward* 962 n vb
– attention (to)
*be attentive* 455 vb.
*observe* 768 vb.
– back
*compensate* 31 vb.
– compensation
*restitute* 787 vb.
*atone* 941 vb.

– court to
*be servile* 879 vb.
*court* 889 vb.
*flatter* 925 vb.
– dividends
*be successful* 727 vb.
– for
*patronize* 703 vb.
*purchase* 792 vb.
*defray* 804 vb.
*be punished* 963 vb.
– heed
*be attentive* 455 vb.
– no attention
*be inattentive* 456 vb.
– no regard to
*disregard* 458 vb.
– off
*be useful* 640 vb.
*stop using* 674 vb.
*make inactive* 679 vb.
*be successful* 727 vb.
– off old scores
*retaliate* 714 vb.
*avenge* 910 vb.
– one out
*retaliate* 714 vb.
*punish* 963 vb.
– one's respects to
*honour* 866 vb.
*pay one's respects* 884 vb.
– one's way
*defray* 804 vb.
– out
*lengthen* 203 vb.
*expend* 806 vb.
*avenge* 910 vb.
– the penalty
*atone* 941 vb.
– the piper
*patronize* 703 vb.
*defray* 804 vb.
– through the nose
*pay too much* 811 vb.
– tribute to
*respect* 920 vb.
*praise* 923 vb.
*reward* 962 vb.
– up
*keep faith* 768 vb.
*restitute* 787 vb.
*pay* 804 vb.
**payable**
*owed* 803 adj.
*due* 915 adj.
**PAYE**
*tax* 809 n.
**payee**
*recipient* 164 adj.
**paying**
*productive* 164 adj.
*profitable* 640 adj.
*gainful* 771 adj.
*rewarding* 962 adj.
**paying guest**
*resident* 191 n.

**payload**
*contents* 193 n.
*thing transferred* 272 n.
**paymaster**
*treasurer* 798 n.
*pay* 804 n.
**payment**
*incentive* 612 n.
*payment* 804 n.
*expenditure* 806 n.
**payment in kind**
*barter* 791 n.
*reward* 962 n.
**payoff**
*end* 69 n.
*completion* 725 n.
*pay* 804 n.
**payola**
*offset* 31 n.
**pay packet**
*earnings* 771 n.
**pay rise**
*increment* 36 n.
**payroll**
*personnel* 686 n.
**PC**
*conformity* 83 n.
*regulated* 83 adj.
*computing* 86 n.
**p.d.q.**
*swiftly* 277 adv.
**PE**
*education* 534 n.
*exercise* 682 n.
**pea**
*sphere* 252 n.
*vegetable* 301 n.
**peace**
*quietude* 266 n.
*euphoria* 376 n.
*silence* 399 n.
*concord* 710 n.
*peace* 717 n.
*pleasurableness* 826 n.
**peaceable**
*moderate* 177 adj.
*amiable* 884 adj.
**peace and quiet**
*repose* 683 n.
*seclusion* 883 n.
**peace at any price**
*submission* 721 n.
**Peace Corps**
*philanthropist* 901 n.
**peace dividend**
*peace* 717 n.
**peaceful**
*inert* 175 adj.
*moderate* 177 adj.
*tranquil* 266 adj.
*comfortable* 376 adj.
*silent* 399 adj.
*reposeful* 683 adj.
*peaceful* 717 adj.
*submitting* 721 adj.
*obedient* 739 adj.
*inexcitable* 823 adj.

**peeing**
  *excretion* 302 n.
**peek**
  *look* 438 n.
  *be curious* 453 vb.
  *enquire* 459 vb.
**peel**
  *leavings* 41 n.
  *disunite* 46 vb.
  *layer* 207 n.
  *skin* 226 n.
  *uncover* 229 vb.
  *rubbish* 641 n.
– off
  *come unstuck* 49 vb.
  *unstick* 49 vb.
  *doff* 229 vb.
**peen**
  *hammer* 279
**peep**
  *ululate* 409 vb.
  *look* 438 n.
  *gaze* 438 vb.
  *scan* 438 vb.
  *be curious* 453 vb.
  *enquire* 459 vb.
– out
  *emerge* 298 vb.
  *be disclosed* 526 vb.
**peepers**
  *eye* 438 n.
**peephole**
  *window* 263 n.
  *view* 438 n.
**peeping Tom**
  *spectator* 441 n.
  *inquisitive person* 453 n.
**peep show**
  *spectacle* 445 n.
  *plaything* 837 n.
**peer**
  *compeer* 28 n.
  *gaze* 438 vb.
  *scan* 438 vb.
  *be dim-sighted* 440 vb.
  *enquire* 459 vb.
  *councillor* 692 n.
  *person of repute* 866 n.
  *person of rank* 868 n.
**peerage**
  *honours* 866 n.
  *aristocracy* 868 n.
**peeress**
  *person of rank* 868 n.
**peer group**
  *contemporary* 123 n.
**peerless**
  *dissimilar* 19 adj.
  *supreme* 34 adj.
  *best* 644 adj.
  *noteworthy* 866 adj.
**peeve**
  *torment* 827 vb.
  *enrage* 891 vb.
**peever**
  *children's games* 837 n.
**peevish**

*discontented* 829 adj.
  *ungracious* 885 adj.
  *irascible* 892 adj.
  *sullen* 893 adj.
**peewit**
  *bird* 365 n.
**peg**
  *degree* 27 n.
  *fastening* 47 n.
  *hanger* 217 n.
  *stopper* 264 n.
  *draught* 301 n.
  *tool* 630 n.
  *See also* **pegs**
– away
  *go on* 146 vb.
  *persevere* 600 vb.
– out
  *dry* 342 vb.
  *die* 361 vb.
– to hang something on
  *pretext* 614
**Pegasus**
  *aeronaut* 271 n.
  *horse* 273 n.
**pegs**
  *leg* 267 n.
**peignoir**
  *informal dress* 228 n.
**pejorative**
  *depreciating* 483 adj.
  *word* 559 n.
  *disrespectful* 921 adj.
  *detracting* 926 adj.
**pekinese, pekingese**
  *dog* 365 n.
**pekoe**
  *soft drink* 301 n.
**pelagian**
  *oceanic* 343 adj.
**Pelagian**
  *heretic* 977 n.
**pelagic**
  *oceanic* 343 adj.
**pelerine**
  *cloak* 228 n.
**pelf**
  *money* 797 n.
  *wealth* 800 n.
**pelican**
  *bird* 365 n.
**pelican crossing**
  *traffic control* 305 n.
  *road* 624 n.
  *access* 624 n.
  *refuge* 662 n.
**pelisse**
  *cloak* 228 n.
**pellagra**
  *disease* 651 n.
**pellet**
  *sphere* 252 n.
  *missile* 287 n.
  *excrement* 302 n.
  *ammunition* 723 n.
**pellicle**
  *layer* 207 n.

*skin* 226 n.
**pell-mell**
  *confusedly* 61 adv.
  *hastily* 680 adv.
**pellucid**
  *undimmed* 417 adj.
  *transparent* 422 adj.
  *intelligible* 516 adj.
**Pelmanism**
  *mnemonics* 505 n.
  *card game* 837 n.
**pelorus**
  *direction* 281 n.
**pelota**
  *ball game* 837 n.
**pelt**
  *skin* 226 n.
  *move fast* 277 vb.
  *strike* 279 vb.
  *propel* 287 vb.
  *rain* 350 vb.
  *lapidate* 712 vb.
  *not respect* 921 vb.
**pemmican**
  *food* 301 n.
**pen**
  *enclosure* 235 n.
  *bird* 365 n.
  *female animal* 373 n.
  *recording instrument*
  549 n.
  *art equipment* 553 n.
  *stationery* 586 n.
  *write* 586 vb.
  *imprison* 747 vb.
  *lockup* 748 n.
**PEN**
  *literature* 557 n.
**penal**
  *prohibiting* 757 adj.
  *punitive* 963 adj.
**penal code**
  *precept* 693 n.
  *law* 953 n.
  *penalty* 963 n.
**penalize, penalise**
  *be inexpedient* 643 vb.
  *make illegal* 954 vb.
  *punish* 963 vb.
**penal servitude**
  *penalty* 963 n.
**penal settlement**
  *prison camp* 748 n.
**penalty**
  *loss* 772 n.
  *cost* 809 n.
  *penalty* 963 n.
**penalty clause**
  *qualification* 468 n.
**penance**
  *offset* 31 n.
  *penitence* 939 n.
  *penance* 941 n.
  *asceticism* 945 n.
  *punishment* 963 n.
  *Christian rite* 988 n.
**Penates**

*mythic deity* 966 n.
  *lesser deity* 967 n.
**penchant**
  *tendency* 179 n.
  *bias* 481 n.
  *willingness* 597 n.
  *liking* 859 n.
**pencil**
  *flash* 417 n.
  *recording instrument*
  549 n.
  *art equipment* 553 n.
  *paint* 553 vb.
  *stationery* 586 n.
  *write* 586 vb.
**pencil box**
  *small box* 194 n.
**pendant, pendent**
  *analogue* 18 n.
  *adjunct* 40 n.
  *hanging object* 217 n.
  *flag* 547 n.
  *jewellery* 844 n.
**pendent**
  *hanging* 217 adj.
**pending**
  *continuing* 108 adj.
  *while* 108 adv.
**pendragon**
  *potentate* 741 n.
**pendulous**
  *nonadhesive* 49 adj.
  *hanging* 217 adj.
  *oscillating* 317 adj.
**pendulum**
  *timekeeper* 117 n.
  *hanging object* 217 n.
  *oscillation* 317 n.
**Penelope's web**
  *lost labour* 641 n.
  *noncompletion* 726 n.
**peneplain**
  *plain* 348 n.
**penetrable**
  *intelligible* 516 adj.
**penetralia**
  *interiority* 224 n.
**penetrate**
  *be general* 79 vb.
  *pierce* 263 vb.
  *infiltrate* 297 vb.
  *pass* 305 vb.
  *cause thought* 449 vb.
  *be wise* 498 vb.
  *understand* 516 vb.
  *impress* 821 vb.
**penetrating**
  *strident* 407 adj.
  *intelligent* 498 adj.
  *felt* 818 adj.
**penetration**
  *interjacency* 231 n.
  *ingress* 297 n.
  *passage* 305 n.
  *sagacity* 498 n.
**penfriend**
  *correspondent* 588 n.

**pessimist**
*underestimation* 483 n.
*loser* 728 n.
*moper* 834 n.
*alarmist* 854 n.
**pest**
*evil* 616 n.
*plague* 651 n.
*bane* 659 n.
*worry* 825 n.
*annoyance* 827 n.
*hateful object* 888 n.
*noxious animal* 904 n.
**pester**
*recur* 139 vb.
*meddle* 678 vb.
*torment* 827 vb.
*enrage* 891 vb.
**pester power**
*inducement* 612 n.
**pesticide**
*killer* 362 n.
*poison* 659 n.
**pestilence**
*badness* 645 n.
*plague* 651 n.
**pestilent, pastilential**
*infectious* 653 adj.
*toxic* 653 adj.
*baneful* 659 adj.
*hateful* 888 adj.
**pestle**
*pulverizer* 332 n.
**pesto**
*sauce* 389 n.
**pet**
*animal* 365 n.
*look after* 457 vb.
*chosen* 605 adj.
*be lenient* 736 vb.
*please* 826 vb.
*love* 887 vb.
*caress* 889 vb.
*pet* 889 vb.
*darling* 890 n.
*anger* 891 n.
*philanthropize* 897 vb.
**petal**
*flower* 366 n.
**petanque**
*ball game* 837 n.
**pet aversion**
*dislike* 861 n.
*enemy* 881 n.
*hateful object* 888 n.
**peter**
*lockup* 748 n.
**peter out**
*decrease* 37 vb.
*end* 69 vb.
*cease* 145 vb.
**Peter Pan**
*youth* 130 n.
**Peter's pence**
*offering* 781 n.
**Peter principle**
*unskilfulness* 695 n.

**pethidine**
*anaesthetic* 375 n.
**pétillant**
*light* 323 adj.
*gaseous* 336 adj.
*bubbly* 355 adj.
**petiole**
*foliage* 366 n.
**petite**
*little* 196 adj.
*shapely* 841 adj.
**petit four**
*mouthful* 301 n.
**petition**
*report* 524 n.
*ask leave* 756 vb.
*request* 761 n., vb.
*deprecation* 762 n.
*litigation* 959 n.
*prayers* 981 n.
– against
*deprecate* 762 vb.
**petitioner**
*petitioner* 763 n.
*malcontent* 829 n.
*litigant* 959 n.
*worshipper* 981 n.
**petitio principii**
*sophism* 477 n.
**petit mal**
*nervous disorders* 651 n.
**petit point**
*needlework* 844 n.
**petits pois**
*vegetable* 301 n.
**pet name**
*name* 561 n.
*misnomer* 562 n.
*endearment* 889 n.
**Petrarchan**
*poetic* 593 adj.
**petrel**
*bird* 365 n.
**petrified**
*still* 266 adj.
*fearing* 854 adj.
**petrified forest**
*fossil* 125 n.
**petrify**
*be dense* 324 vb.
*harden* 326 vb.
*frighten* 854 vb.
*be wonderful* 864 vb.
**petroglyph**
*sculpture* 554 n.
**petrography**
*mineralogy* 359 n.
**petrol**
*propellant* 287 n.
**petroleum**
*oil* 357 n.
*fuel* 385 n.
**petrology**
*mineralogy* 359 n.
**petrol pump**
*storage* 632 n.
**pet-sitter**

*carer* 457 n.
**petticoat**
*underwear* 228 n.
*female* 373 adj.
**pettifogger**
*trickster* 545 n.
*lawyer* 958 n.
**pettifogging**
*sophistical* 477 adj.
*trivial* 639 adj.
*rascally* 930 adj.
**petting**
*endearment* 889 n.
**pettish**
*irascible* 892 adj.
*sullen* 893 adj.
**petty**
*inconsiderable* 33 adj.
*little* 196 adj.
*narrow-minded* 481 adj.
*unimportant* 639 adj.
*contemptible* 922 adj.
*selfish* 932 adj.
**petty cash**
*money* 797 n.
**petty officer**
*naval officer* 741 n.
**petty sessions**
*lawcourt* 956 n.
**petty tyrant**
*tyrant* 735 n.
*autocrat* 741 n.
**petulant**
*discontented* 829 adj.
*irascible* 892 adj.
*sullen* 893 adj.
**pew**
*compartment* 194 n.
*seat* 218 n.
*church interior* 990 n.
**pewter**
*a mixture* 43 n.
*greyness* 429 n.
**peyote**
*drug* 949 n.
**pfennig**
*coinage* 797 n.
**PG**
*film* 445 n.
**Phaëthon**
*classical deities* 967 n.
**phaeton**
*carriage* 274 n.
**phalanx**
*coherence* 48 n.
*solid body* 324 n.
*formation* 722 n.
**phaleristics**
*study* 536 n. box
**phallic**
*generative* 167 adj.
*impure* 951 adj.
**phallus**
*genitalia* 167 n.
*fertilizer* 171 n.
**phantasm**
*visual fallacy* 440 n.

*appearance* 445 n.
*ghost* 970 n.
**phantasmagoria**
*medley* 43 n.
*visual fallacy* 440 n.
*spectacle* 445 n.
**phantom**
*insubstantial thing* 4 n.
*the dead* 361 n.
*visual fallacy* 440 n.
*fantasy* 513 n.
*ghost* 970 n.
**Pharaoh**
*sovereign* 741 n.
**pharisaic, pharisaical**
*hypocritical* 541 adj.
*pietistic* 979 adj.
**pharisaism**
*duplicity* 541 n.
*false piety* 980 n.
**Pharisee**
*non-Christian sect* 978 n.
*zealot* 979 n.
**pharmacology**
*study* 536 n. box
*medical art* 658 n.
**pharmacopoeia**
*medicine* 658 n.
**pharmacy**
*druggist* 658 n.
**pharyngitis**
*respiratory disease* 651 n.
*inflammation* 651 n.
box
**pharynx, inflam-
mation of**
*inflammation* 651 n.
box
**pharynx, operation
on**
*surgery* 658 n. box
**phase**
*modality* 7 n.
*be identical* 13 vb.
*regularize* 62 vb.
*time* 117 vb.
*synchronize* 123 vb.
*appearance* 445 n.
*plan* 623 vb.
**phased**
*synchronous* 123 adj.
*changeful* 152 adj.
**phat**
*personable* 841 adj.
*excellent* 644 adj.
**PhD**
*excellent* 644 adj.
*academic title* 870 n.
**pheasant**
*meat* 301 n.
*table bird* 365 n.
**pheasant, group of**
*group* 74 n. box
**phencyclidine**
*drug* 949 n.
**phenomenal**
*substantial* 3 adj.

photon
 *element* 319 n. box
 *radiation* 417 n.
photoplay
 *cinema* 445 n.
 *stage play* 594 n.
photosensitive
 *luminous* 417 adj.
photosetting
 *print* 587 n.
photosphere
 *sun* 321 n.
photostat
 *copy* 20 vb.
phrase
 *subdivision* 53 n.
 *tune* 412 n.
 *word* 559 n.
 *phrase* 563 n., vb.
 *style* 566 n.
phrasemonger
 *phrasemonger* 574 n.
 *stylist* 575 n.
phraseology
 *phrase* 563 n.
 *style* 566 n.
phrasing
 *musical skill* 413 n.
 *style* 566 n.
phratry
 *race* 11 n.
phrenology
 *head* 213 n.
 *hermeneutics* 520 n.
 *study* 536 n. box
Phrygian mode
 *key* 410 n.
phthisis
 *respiratory disease* 651 n.
phylactery
 *maxim* 496 n.
 *talisman* 983 n.
phyletic
 *parental* 169 adj.
phylogeny
 *biology* 358 n.
phylum
 *breed* 77 n.
physic
 *medicine* 658 n.
 *doctor* 658 vb.
physical
 *real* 1 adj.
 *substantial* 3 adj.
 *material* 319 adj.
 *sensuous* 376 adj.
physical being
 *materiality* 319 n.
physical chemistry
 *physics* 319 n.
physical condition
 *state* 7 n.
 *materiality* 319 n.
physical education
 *education* 534 n.
 *exercise* 682 n.
physical features

*land* 344 n.
physical insensibility
 *insensibility* 375 n.
physical jerks
 *education* 534 n.
physically challenged
 *disabled* 163 adj.
physical pain
 *pain* 377 n.
physical pleasure
 *pleasure* 376 n.
physical presence
 *presence* 189 n.
 *object* 319 n.
physical science
 *physics* 319 n.
physical sensibility
 *sensibility* 374 n.
physical well-being
 *euphoria* 376 n.
 *health* 650 n.
physical wreck
 *dilapidation* 655 n.
physician
 *doctor* 658 n.
physicist
 *physics* 319 n.
physics
 *physics* 319 n.
 *study* 536 n. box
physiognomy
 *face* 237 n.
 *form* 243 n.
 *feature* 445 n.
physiography
 *earth sciences* 321 n.
physiological
 *biological* 358 adj.
physiology
 *structure* 331 n.
 *biology* 358 n.
 *study* 536 n. box
physiotherapist
 *doctor* 658 n.
physiotherapy
 *therapy* 658 n.
physique
 *vitality* 162 n.
 *structure* 331 n.
 *animality* 365 n.
phytography
 *biology* 358 n.
 *botany* 368 n.
pi
 *ratio* 85 n.
 *pietistic* 979 adj.
piacular
 *atoning* 941 adj.
piaffer
 *equitation* 267 n.
pianissimo
 *faintly* 401 adv.
 *adagio* 412 adv.
pianist
 *instrumentalist* 413 n.
piano
 *muted* 401 adj.

*adagio* 412 adv.
 *piano* 414 n.
 *dejected* 834 adj.
piano accordion
 *organ* 414 n.
pianola
 *piano* 414 n.
piastre
 *coinage* 797 n.
piazza
 *meeting place* 192 n.
 *lobby* 194 n.
pibroch
 *musical piece* 412 n.
pica
 *type size* 587 n.
picador
 *athlete* 162 n.
 *killer* 362 n.
 *combatant* 722 n.
picaresque
 *descriptive* 590 adj.
 *rascally* 930 adj.
picaroon
 *robber* 789 n.
piccalilli
 *sauce* 389 n.
piccolo
 *stridor* 407 n.
 *flute* 414 n.
pick
 *sharp point* 256 n.
 *perforator* 263 n.
 *extractor* 304 n.
 *cultivate* 370 vb.
 *play music* 413 vb.
 *choice* 605 n.
 *select* 605 vb.
 *store* 632 vb.
 *chief thing* 638 n.
 *elite* 644 n.
 *clean* 648 vb.
 *acquire* 771 vb.
 *take* 786 vb.
 *pride* 871 n.
– a bone with
 *dissent* 489 vb.
– a fight
 *make quarrels* 709 vb.
– and choose
 *be capricious* 604 vb.
 *select* 605 vb.
 *be fastidious* 862 vb.
– clean
 *clean* 648 vb.
 *take* 786 vb.
– holes
 *dispraise* 924 vb.
 *detract* 926 vb.
– locks
 *steal* 788 vb.
– off
 *kill* 362 vb.
 *fire at* 712 vb.
– on
 *blame* 924 vb.
 *accuse* 928 vb.

– one's brains
 *interrogate* 459 vb.
– oneself up
 *lift oneself* 310 vb.
 *be restored* 656 vb.
– one's steps
 *be careful* 457 vb.
– one's way
 *travel* 267 vb.
 *be in difficulty* 700 vb.
– out
 *set apart* 46 vb.
 *extract* 304 vb.
 *see* 438 vb.
 *discriminate* 463 vb.
 *select* 605 vb.
 *decorate* 844 vb.
– out a tune
 *play music* 413 vb.
– over
 *search* 459 vb.
– to pieces
 *demolish* 165 vb.
– up
 *elevate* 310 vb.
 *hear* 415 vb.
 *detect* 484 vb.
 *get better* 654 vb.
 *be restored* 656 vb.
 *arrest* 747 vb.
 *acquire* 771 vb.
 *take* 786 vb.
– up speed
 *accelerate* 277 vb.
– up the bill
 *defray* 804 vb.
– up the gauntlet
 *contend* 716 vb.
– up the pieces
 *repair* 656 vb.
– up the tab
 *defray* 804 vb.
pick-a-back
 *astride* 218 adv.
 *bearing* 273 adj.
pickaxe
 *perforator* 263 n.
 *extractor* 304 n.
picked
 *chosen* 605 adj.
 *excellent* 644 adj.
picked out
 *separate* 46 adj.
 *ornamented* 844 adj.
picked troops
 *armed force* 722 n.
 *brave person* 855 n.
picker
 *accumulator* 74 n.
 *farmer* 370 n.
pickers and stealers
 *finger* 378 n.
 *thief* 789 n.
picket
 *tie* 45 vb.
 *place* 187 vb.
 *circumscribe* 232 vb.

warner 664 n.
*be obstructive* 702 vb.
*defender* 713 n.
*armed force* 722 n.
*fetter* 747 vb.
**picket fence**
*fence* 235 n.
**picket line**
*exclusion* 57 n.
**pickings**
*choice* 605 n.
*earnings* 771 n.
*booty* 790 n.
**pickle**
*state* 7 n.
*circumstance* 8 n.
*drench* 341 vb.
*pungency* 388 n.
*season* 388 vb.
*preserve* 666 vb.
*predicament* 700 n.
**pickled**
*tipsy* 949 adj.
**pickles**
*sauce* 389 n.
**pick-me-up**
*stimulant* 174 n.
*pungency* 388 n.
*tonic* 658 n.
*excitant* 821 n.
**pick of the bunch**
*elite* 644 n.
**pickpocket**
*thief* 789 n.
**pick-up**
*record player* 414 n.
*loose woman* 952 n.
**pickup truck**
*lorry* 274 n.
**Pickwickian**
*meaningless* 515 adj.
*funny* 849 adj.
**picky**
*choosing* 605 adj.
**picnic**
*meal* 301 n.
*easy thing* 701 n.
*victory* 727 n.
*amusement* 837 n.
*social gathering* 882 n.
**picot**
*edging* 234 n.
**pictogram**
*letter* 558 n.
*lettering* 586 n.
**pictorial**
*representing* 551 adj.
*painted* 553 adj.
**picture**
*composition* 56 n.
*miniature* 196 n.
*spectacle* 445 n.
*photography* 551 n.
*represent* 551 vb.
*picture* 553 n.
*description* 590 n.
*a beauty* 841 n.

– *to oneself*
*imagine* 513 vb.
**picture frame**
*frame* 218 vb.
*enclosure* 235 n.
*art equipment* 553 n.
**picture house**
*cinema* 445 n.
*place of amusement*
837 n.
**picture of, the**
*analogue* 18 n.
**picture palace**
*cinema* 445 n.
*theatre* 594 n.
**picture paper**
*the press* 528 n.
**picture postcard**
*correspondence* 588 n.
*beautiful* 841 adj.
**pictures**
*film* 445 n.
**picture show**
*spectacle* 445 n.
**picturesque**
*descriptive* 590 adj.
*impressive* 821 adj.
*pleasurable* 826 adj.
*beautiful* 841 adj.
*ornamental* 844 adj.
**picture writing**
*symbology* 547 n.
*representation* 551 n.
*writing* 586 n.
**piddle**
*excrete* 302 vb.
**piddling**
*trivial* 639 adj.
**pidgin**
*language* 557 n.
*dialect* 560 n.
**pie**
*dish* 301 n.
*pastries* 301 n.
*bird* 365 n.
*print-type* 587 n.
**piebald**
*horse* 273 n.
*pied* 437 adj.
**piece**
*small thing* 33 n.
*piece* 53 n.
*incompleteness* 55 n.
*component* 58 n.
*unit* 88 n.
*product* 164 n.
*textile* 222 n.
*meal* 301 n.
*musical piece* 412 n.
*reading matter* 589 n.
*stage play* 594 n.
*gun* 723 n.
*portion* 783 n.
*coinage* 797 n.
*loose woman* 952 n.
**pièce de résistance**
*dish* 301 n.

*exceller* 644 n.
*masterpiece* 694 n.
**piece goods**
*textile* 222 n.
**piecemeal**
*separately* 46 adv.
*piecemeal* 53 adv.
**piece of cake**
*easy thing* 701 n.
**piece of eight**
*coinage* 797 n.
**piece of one's mind**
*reprimand* 924 n.
**piece of the action**
*deed* 676 n.
*portion* 783 n.
**piece on the board**
*instrument* 628 n.
*nonentity* 639 n.
**piece rate**
*price* 809 n.
**piece together**
*join* 45 vb.
*make complete* 54 vb.
*decipher* 520 vb.
*repair* 656 vb.
**piecework**
*labour* 682 n.
**pie chart**
*statistics* 86 n.
**piecrust**
*pastries* 301 n.
*brittleness* 330 n.
**pied**
*pied* 437 adj.
**pied-à-terre**
*abode* 192 n.
**Pied piper**
*sorcerer* 983 n.
**pie-eyed**
*tipsy* 949 adj.
**pie in the sky**
*fantasy* 513 n.
**pier**
*shed* 192 n.
*pillar* 218 n.
*prop* 218 n.
*projection* 254 n.
*theatre* 594 n.
**pierce**
*cut* 46 vb.
*pierce* 263 vb.
*insert* 303 vb.
*pass* 305 vb.
*give pain* 377 vb.
*wound* 655 vb.
*impress* 821 vb.
– *the heart*
*hurt* 827 vb.
**piercing**
*cold* 380 adj.
*loud* 400 adj.
*strident* 407 adj.
*felt* 818 adj.
**Pierian spring**
*poetry* 593 n.
**pierrot, pierrette**

*entertainer* 594 n.
**pietà**
*art subject* 553 n.
*ritual object* 988 n.
**pietism**
*sectarianism* 978 n.
*pietism* 979 n.
*false piety* 980 n.
**pietist**
*affecter* 850 n.
*pietist* 979 n.
**piety**
*religion* 973 n.
*piety* 979 n.
*worship* 981 n.
**piezoelectricity**
*electricity* 160 n.
**piffle**
*silly talk* 515 n.
**piffling**
*trivial* 639 adj.
**pig**
*pig* 365 n.
*dirty person* 649 n.
*cad* 938 n.
*sensualist* 944 n.
*glutton* 947 n.
*See also* **pigs**
**pigeon**
*bird* 365 n.
*dupe* 544 n.
*function* 622 n.
**pigeon-chested**
*deformed* 246 adj.
**pigeon-fancier**
*breeder* 369 n.
**pigeonhole**
*class* 62 vb.
*classification* 77 n.
*put off* 136 vb.
*place* 185 n.
*compartment* 194 n.
**pigeonholed**
*neglected* 458 adj.
*unused* 674 adj.
**pigeon loft**
*shed* 192 n.
**pigeon post**
*postal communications*
531 n.
**pigeon's neck**
*variegation* 437 n.
**pigeon-toed**
*deformed* 246 adj.
*blemished* 845 adj.
**pig farm, piggery**
*stock farm* 369 n.
**piggin**
*vessel* 194 n.
**piggishness**
*gluttony* 947 n.
**piggyback**
*astride* 218 adv.
**piggybank**
*treasury* 799 n.
**pig-headed**
*obstinate* 602 adj.

*trace* 548 n.
**pistil**
  *flower* 366 n.
**pistol**
  *kill* 362 vb.
  *pistol* 723 n.
**pistolshot**
  *short distance* 200 n.
  *bang* 402 n.
**piston**
  *stopper* 264 n.
**piston movement**
  *periodicity* 141 n.
**pit**
  *depth* 211 n.
  *interiority* 224 n.
  *cavity* 255 n.
  *excavation* 255 n.
  *tunnel* 263 n.
  *onlookers* 441 n.
  *trap* 542 n.
  *playgoer* 594 n.
  *theatre* 594 n.
  *pitfall* 663 n.
  *workshop* 687 n.
  *stratagem* 698 n.
  *blemish* 845 vb.
– against
  *oppose* 704 vb.
  *make quarrels* 709 vb.
**pit-a-pat**
  *agitation* 318 n.
  *faintness* 401 n.
  *roll* 403 n.
**pitch**
  *adjust* 24 vb.
  *degree* 27 n.
  *serial place* 73 n.
  *territory* 184 n.
  *place* 185 n.
  *summit* 213 n.
  *make vertical* 215 vb.
  *obliquity* 220 n.
  *coat* 226 vb.
  *voyage* 269 vb.
  *propel* 287 vb.
  *tumble* 309 vb.
  *let fall* 311 vb.
  *oscillate* 317 vb.
  *be agitated* 318 vb.
  *resin* 357 n.
  *sound* 398 n.
  *musical note* 410 n.
  *black thing* 428 n.
  *voice* 577 n.
  *arena* 724 n.
  *sale* 793 n.
– and toss
  *plunge* 313 vb.
– in
  *aid* 703 vb.
  *cooperate* 706 vb.
  *participate* 775 vb.
– into
  *attack* 712 vb.
  *fight* 716 vb.
  *dispraise* 924 vb.

– one's tent
  *place oneself* 187 vb.
  *dwell* 192 vb.
– upon/on
  *meet* 295 vb.
  *acquire* 771 vb.
**pitched battle**
  *fight* 716 n.
  *battle* 718 n.
**pitcher**
  *vessel* 194 n.
**pitchfork**
  *propel* 287 vb.
  *farm tool* 370 n.
**pitch-pipe**
  *flute* 414 n.
**pitchy**
  *resinous* 357 adj.
  *dark* 418 adj.
**piteous**
  *pitiable* 905 adj.
**pitfall**
  *invisibility* 444 n.
  *latency* 523 n.
  *ambush* 527 n.
  *trap* 542 n.
  *danger* 661 n.
  *pitfall* 663 n.
  *stratagem* 698 n.
**pith**
  *substance* 3 n.
  *essential part* 5 n.
  *interiority* 224 n.
  *centre* 225 n.
  *pulpiness* 356 n.
  *topic* 452 n.
  *meaning* 514 n.
  *importance* 638 n.
**Pithecanthropus**
  *humankind* 371 n.
**pith helmet**
  *headgear* 228 n.
**pithy**
  *substantial* 3 adj.
  *aphoristic* 496 adj.
  *meaningful* 514 adj.
  *concise* 569 adj.
  *compendious* 592 adj.
  *witty* 839 adj.
**pitiable**
  *unimportant* 639 adj.
  *bad* 645 adj.
  *unhappy* 825 adj.
  *distressing* 827 adj.
  *pitiable* 905 adj.
  *contemptible* 922 adj.
**pitiful**
  *unimportant* 639 adj.
  *bad* 645 adj.
  *distressing* 827 adj.
  *disreputable* 867 adj.
  *pitiable* 905 adj.
**pitiless**
  *resolute* 599 adj.
  *severe* 735 adj.
  *cruel* 898 adj.
  *pitiless* 906 adj.

**pit pony**
  *draught horse* 273 n.
**pits, the**
  *lowness* 210 n.
  *misfortune* 731 n.
**pittance**
  *small quantity* 33 n.
  *insufficiency* 636 n.
  *portion* 783 n.
  *receipt* 807 n.
**pitted**
  *rough* 259 adj.
  *blemished* 845 adj.
**pitter-patter**
  *oscillation* 317 n.
  *faintness* 401 n.
**pity**
  *leniency* 736 n.
  *be sensitive* 819 vb.
  *lamentation* 836 n.
  *benevolence* 897 n.
  *pity* 905 n., vb.
**pity of it**
  *regret* 830 n.
**pivot**
  *joint* 45 n.
  *instrument* 156 n.
  *influence* 178 n.
  *pivot* 218 n.
  *centre* 225 n.
  *chief thing* 638 n.
**pivot on**
  *depend* 157 vb.
**pivotal**
  *crucial* 137 ad.
**pixel**
  *image* 551 n.
**pixie, pixy**
  *elf* 970 n.
**pixilated**
  *crazy* 503 adj.
  *tipsy* 949 adj.
**pizza**
  *dish* 301 n.
**pizzazz**
  *vigorousness* 174 n.
  *vigour* 571 n.
**pizzeria**
  *restaurant* 192 n.
**pizzicato**
  *adagio* 412 adv.
**placable**
  *benevolent* 897 adj.
  *forgiving* 909 adj.
**placard**
  *exhibit* 522 n.
  *advertisement* 528 n.
**placate**
  *pacify* 719 vb.
  *beg pardon* 909 vb.
**placatory**
  *pacificatory* 719 adj.
**place**
  *order* 60 n.
  *arrange* 62 vb.
  *serial place* 73 n.
  *specify* 80 vb.

  *region* 184 n.
  *place* 185 n.
  *situation* 186 n.
  *locality* 187 n.
  *place* 187 vb.
  *house* 192 n.
  *aim* 281 vb.
  *meal* 301 n.
  *discover* 484 vb.
  *authority* 733 n.
  *apportionment* 783 n.
– after
  *place after* 65 vb.
– at one' disposal
  *offer* 759 vb.
– high
  *respect* 920 vb.
– side by side
  *bring near* 200 vb.
– under
  *number with* 78 vb.
**placebo**
  *balm* 658 n.
  *medicine* 658 n.
**placed**
  *circumstantial* 8 adj.
**place in the sun**
  *palmy days* 730 n.
**placement**
  *location* 187 n.
**placenta**
  *sequel* 67 n.
  *obstetrics* 167 n.
**place of amusement**
  *meeting place* 192 n.
  *place of amusement* 837 n.
**place of pilgrimage**
  *focus* 76 n.
  *objective* 617 n.
  *holy place* 990 n.
**place of residence**
  *abode* 192 n.
**place of worship**
  *temple* 990 n.
**placet**
  *decree* 737 n.
**placid**
  *inexcitable* 823 adj.
**placidity**
  *quietude* 266 n.
**placket**
  *garment* 228 n.
  *opening* 263 n.
**plage**
  *shore* 344 n.
**plagiarism**
  *imitation* 20 n.
  *repetition* 106 n.
  *stealing* 788 n.
**plagiarist**
  *imitator* 20 n.
**plagiarize, plagiarise**
  *copy* 20 vb.
  *fake* 541 vb.
  *borrow* 785 vb.
  *steal* 788 vb.

*wine* 301 n.
*crackle* 402 vb.
*nonresonance* 405 n.

**plop**
*descend* 309 vb.
*plunge* 313 vb.
*sound faint* 401 vb.
*nonresonance* 405 n.

**plosive**
*speech sound* 398 n.

**plot**
*combination* 50 n.
*territory* 184 n.
*place* 185 n.
*garden* 370 n.
*topic* 452 n.
*secrecy* 525 n.
*deceive* 542 vb.
*narrative* 590 n.
*dramaturgy* 594 n.
*plot* 623 n., vb.
*prepare* 669 vb.
*stratagem* 698 n.
*cooperate* 706 vb.
*compact* 765 n.

**plotted**
*measured* 465 adj.
*planned* 623 adj.

**plotter**
*deceiver* 545 n.
*planner* 623 n.
*slyboots* 698 n.

**plotting**
*perfidious* 930 adj.

**plough**
*cut* 46 vb.
*groove* 262 vb.
*farm tool* 370 n.
*cultivate* 370 vb.
*disapprove* 924 vb.
– back
*economize* 814 vb.
– through
*travel* 267 vb.

**ploughed**
*unsuccessful* 728 adj.

**ploughman**
*farmer* 370 n.
*country-dweller* 869 n.

**ploughman's lunch**
*meal* 301 n.

**ploughshare**
*sharp edge* 256 n.
*farm tool* 370 n.

**plover**
*bird* 365 n.

**plovers, group of**
*group* 74 n. box

**ploy**
*contrivance* 623 n.
*stratagem* 698 n.

**pluck**
*insides* 224 n.
*uncover* 229 vb.
*draw* 288 vb.
*extract* 304 vb.
*agitate* 318 vb.

*cultivate* 370 vb.
*play music* 413 vb.
*resolution* 599 n.
*stamina* 600 n.
*fleece* 786 vb.
*take* 786 vb.
*defraud* 788 vb.
*courage* 855 n.
– to pieces
*rend* 46 vb.
*demolish* 165 vb.
– up courage
*take courage* 855 vb.

**plucking**
*hairdressing* 843 n.

**plucky**
*persevering* 600 adj.
*courageous* 855 adj.

**plug**
*repeat oneself* 106 vb.
*covering* 226 n.
*stopper* 264 n.
*staunch* 350 vb.
*tobacco* 388 n.
*advertise* 528 vb.
*emphasize* 532 vb.
– away at
*persevere* 600 vb.
– in
*connect* 45 vb.
*empower* 160 vb.

**plug-ugly**
*low fellow* 869 n.
*ruffian* 904 n.

**plum**
*fruit* 301 n.
*purpleness* 436 n.
*elite* 644 n.
*trophy* 729 n.
*desired object* 859 n.

**plumage**
*plumage* 259 n.

**plumb**
*positively* 32 adv.
*complete* 54 adj.
*be deep* 211 vb.
*vertical* 215 adj.
*straight on* 249 adv.
*measure* 465 vb.
*truly* 494 adv.

**plumbago**
*lubricant* 334 n.

**plumber**
*mender* 656 n.
*artisan* 686 n.

**plumbing**
*conduit* 351 n.
*cleansing* 648 n.

**plumbline**
*verticality* 215 n.

**plume**
*plumage* 259 n.
*trimming* 844 n.

**plume oneself (on)**
*feel pride* 871 vb.
*be vain* 873 vb.
*boast* 877 vb.

**plum in one's mouth**
*speech defect* 580 n.

**plummet**
*depth* 211 n.
*verticality* 215 n.
*be in motion* 265 vb.
*sailing aid* 269 n.
*tumble* 309 vb.
*descend* 309 vb.
*founder* 313 vb.
*plunge* 313 vb.
*gravity* 322 n.

**plummy**
*speaking* 579 adj.
*super* 644 adj.

**plumose**
*downy* 259 adj.

**plump**
*instantaneously* 116 adv.
*fleshy* 195 adj.
*tumble* 309 vb.
*nonresonance* 405 n.
– for
*choose* 605 vb.
– up
*enlarge* 197 vb.

**plum pudding**
*dessert* 301 n.

**plunder**
*acquisition* 771 n.
*take away* 786 vb.
*rob* 788 vb.
*booty* 790 n.

**plunge**
*decrease* 37 n., vb.
*revolution* 149 n.
*be destroyed* 165 vb.
*be deep* 211 vb.
*be in motion* 265 vb.
*aquatics* 269 n.
*swim* 269 vb.
*move fast* 277 vb.
*enter* 297 vb.
*immersion* 303 n.
*immerse* 303 vb.
*descend* 309 vb.
*lower* 311 vb.
*leap* 312 vb.
*plunge* 313 n., vb.
*be agitated* 318 vb.
*drench* 341 vb.
*gambling* 618 n.
*ablutions* 648 n.
*be cheap* 812 vb.
*be rash* 857 vb.
*be intemperate* 943 vb.
– into
*enter* 297 vb.
*undertake* 672 vb.

**plunger**
*diver* 313 n.
*gambler* 618 n.
*desperado* 857 n.

**plunging neckline**
*bareness* 229 n.

**plunk**
*bang* 402 n.

*nonresonance* 405 n.

**pluperfect**
*past time* 125 n.

**plural**
*plural* 101 adj.
*grammatical* 564 adj.

**pluralism**
*philosophy* 449 n.
*government* 733

**pluralist**
*cleric* 986 n.

**plurality**
*plurality* 101 n.
*greater number* 104 n.

**plus**
*in addition* 38 adv.

**plus fours**
*trousers* 228 n.

**plush**
*hair* 259 n.
*softness* 327 n.
*rich* 800 adj.
*ornamented* 844 adj.

**plushy**
*rich* 800 adj.
*ostentatious* 875 adj.

**Pluto**
*planet* 321 n.
*Chthonian deity* 967 n.
*mythic hell* 972 n.

**plutocracy**
*government* 733 n.
*wealth* 800 n.

**plutocrat**
*master* 741 n.
*rich person* 800 n.

**plutonic**
*fiery* 379 adj.

**plutonic rock**
*rock* 344 n.

**plutonium**
*element* 319 n. box
*fuel* 385 n.
*poison* 659 n.

**pluvial**
*humid* 341 adj.

**pluviometer**
*hygrometry* 341 n.

**ply**
*be periodic* 141 vb.
*layer* 207 n.
*fold* 261 n.
*voyage* 269 vb.
*busy oneself* 622 vb.
*use* 673 vb.
*do* 676 vb.
*request* 761 vb.

**Plymouth Brethren**
*ascetic* 945 n.
*sect* 978 n.

**plywood**
*lamina* 207 n.
*materials* 631 n.

**p.m.**
*o'clock* 117 adv.
*evening* 129 n.

**pneumatic**

**defamer** 926 n.
**poke**
pierce 263 vb.
touch 378 vb.
gesticulate 547 vb.
– at
strike 279 vb.
strike at 712 vb.
– fun at
be witty 839 vb.
ridicule 851 vb.
– into
insert 303 vb.
– one's nose in
interfere 231 vb.
be curious 453 vb.
meddle 678 vb.
– out
jut 254 vb.
**poke bonnet**
headgear 228 n.
**poker**
furnace 383 n.
card game 837 n.
**poker-faced**
still 266 adj.
unintelligible 517 adj.
reticent 525 adj.
impassive 820 adj.
serious 834 adj.
**pokerwork**
ornamental art 844 n.
**poky**
little 196 adj.
restraining 747 adj.
graceless 842 adj.
**polacre**
merchant ship 275 n.
**polar**
ending 69 adj.
topmost 213 adj.
opposite 240 adj.
telluric 321 adj.
cold 380 adj.
**polariscope**
optical device 442 n.
**polarity**
polarity 14 n.
duality 90 n.
tendency 179 n.
counteraction 182 n.
contraposition 240 n.
**polarization**
reflection 417 n.
**Polaroid (tdmk)**
camera 442 n.
picture 553 n.
**polder**
land 344 n.
**pole**
extremity 69 n.
farness 199 n.
long measure 203 n.
high structure 209 n.
summit 213 n.
verticality 215 n.
pillar 218 n.

pivot 218 n.
limit 236 n.
impel 279 vb.
gauge 465 n.
**poleaxe**
slaughter 362 vb.
axe 723 n.
**polecat**
mammal 365 n.
stench 397 n.
**polemic**
argument 475 n.
reasoner 475 n.
quarrel 709 n.
**polemics**
argument 475 n.
conference 584 n.
contention 716 n.
**polenta**
cereals 301 n.
**pole position**
advantage 34 n.
**poles apart**
contrariety 14 n.
contrary 14 adj.
different 15 adj.
contraposition 240 n.
against 240 adv.
**pole star**
star 321 n.
signpost 547 n.
directorship 689 n.
**pole vault**
ascent 308 n.
leap 312 vb.
**pole-vaulter**
jumper 312 n.
**police**
order 60 vb.
protector 660 n.
safeguard 660 vb.
manage 689 vb.
rule 733 n.
restrain 747 vb.
police 955 n.
**police court**
lawcourt 956 n.
**police enquiry**
police enquiry 459 n.
**police force**
police 955 n.
**policeman,**
   **policewoman**
protector 660 n.
police 955 n.
**police state**
despotism 733 n.
**police station**
lockup 748 n.
**police whistle**
signal 547 n.
danger signal 665 n.
**policy**
topic 452 n.
sagacity 498 n.
policy 623 n.
action 676 n.

tactics 688 n.
management 689 n.
cunning 698 n.
title deed 767 n.
**poliomyelitis, polio**
infection 651 n.
nervous disorders 651 n.
inflammation 651 n.
box
**polish**
facing 226 n.
smoothness 258 n.
friction 333 n.
reflection 417 n.
make bright 417 vb.
elegance 575 n.
cleanser 648 n.
civilization 654 n.
make better 654 vb.
beauty 841 n.
good taste 846 n.
etiquette 848 n.
– off
be active 678 vb.
carry through 725 vb.
**politburo**
party 708 n.
**polite**
literary 557 adj.
elegant 575 adj.
well-bred 848 adj.
courteous 884 adj.
respectful 920 adj.
**politic**
wise 498 adj.
advisable 642 adj.
skilful 694 adj.
**political**
directing 689 adj.
governmental 733 adj.
**political correctness**
conformity 83 n.
**political economy**
management 689 n.
**political favours**
incentive 612 n.
**politically correct**
regulated 83 adj.
**political organ-**
   **ization**
territory 184 n.
nation 371 n.
political organization
   733 n.
**political party**
association 706 n.
political party 708 n.
government 733 n.
**political prisoner**
prisoner 750 n.
**political refugee**
outcast 883 n.
**political science**
tactics 688 n.
**politician**
planner 623 n.
manager 690 n.

expert 696 n.
political party 708 n.
**politicking**
government 733 n.
**politico**
political party 708 n.
**politics**
tactics 688 n.
government 733 n.
**polity**
government 733 n.
**polka**
musical piece 412 n.
dance 837 n.
**polka dot**
mottling 437 n.
pattern 844 n.
**poll**
numeration 86 n.
statistics 86 n.
enquiry 459 n.
judgment 480 n.
vote 605 n vb
**pollard**
make smaller 198 vb.
tree 366 n.
**pollen**
powder 332 n.
flower 366 n.
**pollex**
finger 378 n.
**pollicitation**
promise 764 n.
**pollination**
propagation 167 n.
productiveness 171 n.
**pollster**
enumerator 86 n.
enquirer 459 n.
**poll tax**
tax 809 n.
**pollute**
make useless 641 vb.
harm 645 vb.
make unclean 649 vb.
impair 655 vb.
misuse 675 vb.
**pollution**
uncleanness 649 n.
infection 651 n.
insalubrity 653 n.
impairment 655 n.
poison 659 n.
misuse 675 n.
slur 867 n.
**Pollyanna**
cheerfulness 833 n.
**polo**
ball game 837 n.
**polonaise**
musical piece 412 n.
dance 837 n.
**polo-neck**
jersey 228 n.
neckline 228 n.
**poltergeist**
hinderer 702 n.

**postman's knock**
indoor game 837 n.
**postmarital**
matrimonial 894 adj.
**post meridiem**
post meridiem
129 adv.
**postmortem**
inquest 364 n.
enquiry 459 n.
**post-obit**
post-obit 361 adv.
**post office**
postal communications
531 n.
**post-paid**
uncharged 812 adj.
**postpone**
put off 136 vb.
avoid 620 vb.
relinquish 621 vb.
not complete 726 vb.
**postponement**
unwillingness 598 n.
**postposition**
sequence 65 n.
**postprandial**
culinary 301 adj.
reposeful 683 adj.
sociable 882 adj.
**postscript**
adjunct 40 n.
sequel 67 n.
extremity 69 n.
**postulant**
petitioner 763 n.
nun 986 n.
lay person 987 n.
**postulate**
premise 475 n., vb.
axiom 496 n.
supposition 512 n.
request 761 n.
**posture**
circumstance 8 n.
situation 186 n.
form 243 n.
mien 445 n.
conduct 688 n.
behave 688 vb.
be affected 850 vb.
**postwar**
dated 108 adj.
peaceful 717 adj.
**posy**
bunch 74 n.
ornamentation 844 n.
love token 889 n.
**pot**
vessel 194 n.
shorten 204 vb.
propulsion 287 n.
insert 303 vb.
pottery 381 n.
abstract 592 vb.
preserve 666 vb.
trophy 729 n.

drug 949 n.
reward 962 n.
– at
shoot 287 vb.
**potable**
edible 301 adj.
**potash**
fertilizer 171 n.
**potation(s)**
drinking 301 n.
drunkenness 949 n.
**potato**
vegetable 301 n.
**pot-bellied**
fleshy 195 adj.
expanded 197 adj.
convex 253 adj.
**pot belly**
maw 194 n.
**potboiler**
author 589 n.
novel 590 n.
**pot calling the kettle
    black**
equivalent 28 adj.
**poteen**
alcoholic drink 301 n.
**potency**
power 160 n.
strength 162 n.
utility 640 n.
**potent**
powerful 160 adj.
strong 162 adj.
generative 167 adj.
operative 173 adj.
vigorous 174 adj.
influential 178 adj.
heraldry 547 n.
intoxicating 949 adj.
**potentate**
potentate 741 n.
person of rank 868 n.
**potential**
unreal 2 adj.
intrinsic 5 adj.
quantity 26 n.
future 124 adj.
energy 160 n.
possible 469 adj.
latent 523 adj.
**potentiality**
existence 1 n.
ability 160 n.
influence 178 n.
liability 180 n.
**pother**
turmoil 61 n.
excitable state 822 n.
**potherb**
herb 301 n.
condiment 389 n.
**pothole**
depth 211 n.
interiority 224 n.
cavity 255 n.
orifice 263 n.

**potholed**
rough 259 adj.
**pot-holing**
depth 211 n.
descent 309 n.
search 459 n.
discovery 484 n.
sport 837 n.
**pothook**
lettering 586 n.
**pothouse**
pub 192 n.
**pot-hunter**
contender 716 n.
player 837 n.
**potion**
draught 301 n.
medicine 658 n.
magic instrument 983 n.
**potluck**
chance 159 n.
meal 301 n.
gambling 618 n.
nonpreparation 670 n.
sociability 882 n.
**pot of gold**
wealth 800 n.
**potpourri**
medley 43 n.
scent 396 n.
musical piece 412 n.
**pot-roast**
cook 301 vb.
**pots**
great quantity 32 n.
**potsherd**
piece 53 n.
**pot shot**
propulsion 287 n.
**pots of money**
wealth 800 n.
**potted**
short 204 adj.
compendious 592 adj.
preserved 666 adj.
**potter**
wander 267 vb.
be inactive 679 vb.
artisan 686 n.
**pottering**
restlessness 678 n.
**potter's clay**
soil 344 n.
materials 631 n.
**pottery**
product 164 n.
receptacle 194 n.
brittleness 330 n.
pottery 381 n.
art 551 n.
**pottle**
basket 194 n.
**potty**
crazy 593 adj.
trivial 639 adj.
unimportant 639 adj.
latrine 649 n.

**pot-valiant**
courageous 855 adj.
drunk 949 adj.
**pouch**
stow 187 vb.
pocket 194 n.
receive 782 vb.
**pouchy**
expanded 197 adj.
**pouffe**
seat 218 n.
**poulterer**
provider 633 n.
**poultice**
pulpiness 356 n.
heat 381 vb.
surgical dressing 658 n.
relieve 831 vb.
**poultry**
meat 301 n.
poultry 365 n.
**poultry farming**
animal husbandry 369 n.
**pounce**
move fast 277 vb.
descent 309 n.
leap 312 vb.
– on
surprise 508 vb.
attack 712 vb.
take 786 vb.
**pound**
enclosure 235 n.
strike 279 vb.
weighing 322 n.
pulverize 332 vb.
sound dead 405 vb.
lockup 748 n.
coinage 797 n.
**poundage**
discount 810 n.
**poundal**
energy 160 n.
**pound note**
paper money 797 n.
**pound of flesh**
severity 735 n.
interest 803 n.
pitilessness 906 n.
**pour**
emit 300 vb.
let fall 311 vb.
be wet 341 vb.
flow 350 vb.
rain 350 vb.
abound 635 vb.
– down the drain
waste 634 vb.
lose 772 vb.
be prodigal 815 vb.
– in
converge 293 vb.
burst in 297 vb.
– oil on troubled waters
assuage 177 vb.
pacify 719 vb.
relieve 831 vb.

preservation 666 n.
**preview**
priority 119 n.
inspection 438 n.
film 445 n.
manifestation 522 n.
**previous**
preceding 64 adj.
anachronistic 118 adj.
prior 119 adj.
early 135 adj.
**prevision**
foresight 510 n.
**prewar**
prior 119 adj.
antiquated 127 adj.
peaceful 717 adj.
**prey**
animal 365 n.
objective 617 n.
chase 619 n.
loser 728 n.
unlucky person 731 n.
booty 790 n.
sufferer 825 n.
– on/upon
eat 301 vb.
ill-treat 645 vb.
– on one's mind
engross 449 vb.
trouble 827 vb.
**prey to**
liable 180 adj.
**priapism**
libido 859 n.
**price**
equivalence 28 n.
quid pro quo 150 n.
appraise 465 vb.
goodness 644 n.
price 809 n vb
penalty 963 n.
**price-cutting**
price 889 n.
**price freeze**
restriction 747 n.
**price index**
statistics 86 n.
**priceless**
valuable 644 adj.
of price 811 adj.
funny 849 adj.
**price on one's head**
condemnation 961 n.
**price ring**
restriction 747 n.
**price war**
war 718 n.
price 889 n.
**prick**
small thing 33 n.
cut 46 vb.
stimulant 174 n.
sharp point 256 n.
pierce 263 vb.
give pain 377 vb.
itch 378 vb.

indication 547 n.
mark 547 vb.
incite 612 vb.
wound 655 n.
excitant 821 n.
– out
cultivate 370 vb.
– up
jut 254 vb.
elevate 310 vb.
– up one's ears
hear 415 vb.
be curious 453 vb.
be attentive 455 vb.
**prickle**
prickle 256 n.
roughness 259 n.
foliage 366 n.
itch 378 vb.
**prickliness**
sharpness 256 n.
quarrelsomeness 709 n.
moral sensibility 819 n.
pride 871 n.
irascibility 892 n.
**prickly**
unconformable 84 adj.
**prickly heat**
skin disease 651 n.
**pricks of conscience**
penitence 939 n.
**pricy**
dear 811 adj.
**pride**
group 74 n. box
pride 871 n.
vanity 873 n.
ostentation 875 n.
insolence 878 n.
unsociability 883 n.
vice 934 n.
impiety 980 n.
**pride and joy**
pride 871 n.
favourite 890 n.
**pride of place**
superiority 34 n.
precedence 64 n.
**pride oneself**
feel pride 871 vb.
be vain 873 vb.
**prie-dieu**
seat 218 n.
**priest, priestess**
priest 986 n.
**priesthole**
retreat 192 n.
hiding-place 527 n.
**priesthood**
church office 985 n.
clergy 986 n.
**priest-ridden**
pietistic 979 adj.
ecclesiastical 985 adj.
**prig**
affecter 850 n.
prude 950 n.

**priggishness**
airs 873 n.
**prim**
serious 834 adj.
dull 840 adj.
affected 850 adj.
fastidious 862 adj.
prudish 950 adj.
**prima ballerina**
actor 594 n.
**primacy**
superiority 34 n.
importance 638 n.
prestige 866 n.
church office 985 n.
**prima donna**
superior 34 n.
vocalist 413 n.
actor 594 n.
notable 638 n.
proficient person 696 n.
proud person 871 n.
**prima facie**
at sight 438 adv.
evidential 466 adj.
probably 471 adv.
manifestly 522 adv.
**primal**
beginning 68 adj.
primal 127 adj.
fundamental 156 adj.
**primary**
intrinsic 5 adj.
original 21 adj.
simple 44 adj.
first 68 adj.
fundamental 156 adj.
educational 534 adj.
vote 605 n.
important 638 adj.
**primary care**
medical art 658 n.
**primary colour**
colour 425 n.
**primate**
mammal 365 n.
ecclesiarch 986 n.
**primateship**
church office 985 n.
**prime**
numerical 85 adj.
morning 128 n.
adultness 134 n.
earliness 135 n.
educate 534 vb.
important 638 adj.
elite 644 n.
excellent 644 adj.
make ready 669 vb.
palmy days 730 n.
church service 988 n.
**prime constituent**
essence 1 n.
essential part 5 n.
**primed**
instructed 490 adj.
informed 524 adj.

prepared 669 adj.
drunk 949 adj.
**prime minister**
director 690 n.
officer 741 n.
**prime mover**
cause 156 n.
motivator 612 n.
**prime number**
number 85 n.
**prime of life**
salad days 130 n.
middle age 131 n.
adultness 134 n.
**primer**
beginning 68 n.
textbook 589 n.
**primeval, primaeval**
beginning 68 adj.
primal 127 adj.
**priming**
preparation 669 n.
explosive 723 n.
**primitive**
past 125 adj.
primal 127 adj.
earliness 135 n.
fundamental 156 adj.
violent 176 adj.
representing 551 adj.
artist 556 adj.
artless 699 adj.
barbaric 869 adj.
**primitive form**
prototype 23 n.
**Primitive Methodist**
Protestant 976 n.
**primo**
initially 68 adv.
**primogeniture**
priority 119 n.
seniority 131 n.
sonship 170 n.
**primordial**
original 21 adj.
beginning 68 adj.
primal 127 adj.
fundamental 156 adj.
**primp**
beautify 841 vb.
primp 843 vb.
be vain 873 vb.
**primrose**
plant 366 n.
yellowness 433 n.
**primrose path**
deterioration 655 n.
facility 701 n.
wickedness 934 n.
**primula**
plant 366 n.
**primum mobile**
cause 156 n.
heavens 321 n.
divineness 965 n.
**primus inter pares**
superior 34 n.

missile 287 n.
ammunition 723 n.
**projecting**
overhanging 209 adj.
projecting 254 adj.
**projection**
extrinsicality 6 n.
high land 209 n.
distortion 246 n.
convexity 253 n.
projection 254 n.
propulsion 287 n.
cinema 445 n.
ideality 513 n.
manifestation 522 n.
image 551 n.
map 551 n.
representation 551 n.
**projector**
optical device 442 n.
cinema 445 n.
**prolapse**
descend 309 vb.
**prole**
vulgarian 847 n.
commoner 869 n.
**prolegomena**
prelude 66 n.
dissertation 591 n.
**prolepsis**
anachronism 118 n.
**proletarian**
vulgarian 847 n.
commoner 869 n.
**proletariat**
personnel 686 n.
lower classes 869 n.
**pro-life**
choosing 605 adj.
**proliferate**
grow 36 vb.
be fruitful 171 vb.
abound 635 vb.
**proliferation**
propagation 167 n.
**prolific**
increasing 36 adj.
multitudinous 104 adj.
productive 164 adj.
prolific 171 adj.
diffuse 570 adj.
plenteous 635 adj.
profitable 640 adj.
**prolix**
protracted 113 adj.
prolix 570 adj.
tedious 838 adj.
**prologue**
prelude 66 n.
oration 579 n.
speaker 579 n.
actor 594 n.
dramaturgy 594 n.
**prolong**
augment 36 vb.
continue 71 vb.
spin out 113 vb.

sustain 146 vb.
preserve 666 vb.
**prolongation**
adjunct 40 n.
sequence 65 n.
lengthening 203 n.
**prolusion**
prelude 66 n.
**prom**
music 412 n.
**promenade**
pleasance 192 n.
land travel 267 n.
walking 267 n.
path 624 n.
be ostentatious 875 vb.
**promenader**
wanderer 268 n.
**Promethean**
alive 360 adj.
**Prometheus**
classical deities 967 n.
**prominence**
superiority 34 n.
convexity 253 n.
prominence 254 n.
elevation 310 n.
visibility 443 n.
importance 638 n.
prestige 866 n.
**prominent**
overhanging 209 adj.
projecting 254 adj.
obvious 443 adj.
manifest 522 adj.
notable 638 adj.
noteworthy 866 adj.
**promiscuity**
indiscrimination 464 n.
unchastity 951 n.
**promiscuous**
indifferent 860 adj.
**promise**
predict 511 vb.
oath 532 n.
affirm 532 vb.
intention 617 n.
undertake 672 vb.
be auspicious 730 vb.
promise 764 n., vb.
compact 765 n.
hope 852 n.
give hope 852 vb.
incur a duty 917 vb.
– oneself
expect 507 vb.
desire 859 vb.
– well
progress 285 vb.
**promised**
future 124 adj.
expected 507 adj.
promised 764 adj.
**promised land**
fantasy 513 n.
objective 617 n.
aspiration 852 n.

**promising**
probable 471 adj.
presageful 511 adj.
palmy 730 adj.
promising 852 adj.
**promissory**
promissory 764 adj.
**promissory note**
title deed 767 n.
paper money 797 n.
**promontory**
projection 254 n.
land 344 n.
**promote**
augment 36 vb.
initiate 68 vb.
conduce 156 vb.
tend 179 vb.
concur 181 vb.
promote 285 vb.
make likely 471 vb.
advertise 528 vb.
be instrumental 628 vb.
find means 629 vb.
be useful 640 vb.
be expedient 642 vb.
make better 654 vb.
aid 703 vb.
trade 791 vb.
dignify 866 vb.
**promoter**
publicizer 528 n.
planner 623 n.
aider 703 n.
patron 707 n.
**promotion**
progression 285 n.
publicity 528 n.
See also **promote**
**prompt**
initiate 68 vb.
early 135 adj.
influence 178 vb.
speedy 277 adj.
remind 505 vb.
hint 524 n., vb.
willing 597 adj.
incite 612 vb.
active 678 adj.
hasty 680 adj.
advise 691 vb.
**prompt book**
stage play 594 n.
**prompt box**
stage set 594 n.
**prompter**
reminder 505 n.
stagehand 594 n.
motivator 612 n.
adviser 691 n.
**promptly**
instantaneously 116 adv.
**promulgate**
proclaim 528 vb.
decree 737 vb.
**prone**
supine 216 adj.

inverted 221 adj.
**prone to**
tending 179 adj.
**prong**
bifurcation 92 n.
sharp point 256 n.
**pronoun**
part of speech 564 n.
**pronounce**
judge 480 vb.
proclaim 528 vb.
affirm 532 vb.
voice 577 vb.
speak 579 vb.
**pronounced**
obvious 443 adj.
manifest 522 adj.
vocal 577 adj.
**pronouncement**
judgment 480 n.
publication 528 n.
**pronto**
instantaneously 116 adv.
swiftly 277 adv.
**pronunciamento**
publication 528 n.
**pronunciation**
dialect 560 n.
pronunciation 577 n.
speech 579 n.
speech defect 580 n.
**proof**
unyielding 162 adj.
sealed off 264 adj.
hard 326 adj.
dry 342 adj.
unfeeling 375 adj.
experiment 461 n.
evidence 466 n.
certainty 473 n.
demonstration 478 n.
manifestation 522 n.
letterpress 587 n.
reading matter 589 n.
resolute 599 adj.
plan 623 n.
amendment 654 n.
invulnerable 660 adj.
defended 713 adj.
resisting 715 adj.
impassive 820 adj.
**proofread**
print 587 n.
rectify 654 vb.
**proofreader**
printer 587 n.
**prop**
bond 47 n.
stabilizer 153 n.
strengthen 162 vb.
prop 218 n.
support 218 vb.
elevate 310 vb.
stage set 594 n.
refuge 662 n.
aider 703 n.
– up

*passing along* 305 n.
**queue-jumping**
 *precedence* 64 n.
 *preceding* 283 n.
**queue up**
 *run on* 71 vb.
 *await* 507 vb.
**quibble**
 *argue* 475 vb.
 *mislead* 477 vb.
 *absurdity* 497 n.
 *equivocalness* 518 n.
 *pretext* 614 n.
 *parry* 713 vb.
**quiche**
 *dish* 301 n.
**quick**
 *brief* 114 adj.
 *speedy* 277 adj.
 *alive* 360 adj.
 *intelligent* 498 adj.
 *willing* 597 adj.
 *active* 678 adj.
 *skilful* 694 adj.
 *witty* 839 adj.
 *irascible* 892 adj.
**quick and the dead,**
 **the**
 *all* 52 n.
**quick as lightning**
 *instantaneous* 116 adj.
**quick-change artist**
 *conjuror* 545 n.
 *entertainer* 594 n.
**quick ear**
 *hearing* 415 n.
**quicken**
 *strengthen* 162 vb.
 *invigorate* 174 vb.
 *make violent* 176 vb.
 *accelerate* 277 vb.
 *live* 360 vb.
 *animate* 821 vb.
**quickie**
 *draught* 301 n.
**quick march**
 *gait* 265 n.
 *marching* 267 n.
 *speeding* 277 n.
**quick one**
 *draught* 301 n.
**quick on the uptake**
 *intelligent* 498 adj.
**quick passions**
 *irascibility* 892 n.
**quicksand**
 *marsh* 347 n.
 *pitfall* 663 n.
**quickset hedge**
 *fence* 235 n.
**quicksilver**
 *changeable thing* 152 n.
**quickstep**
 *dance* 837 n.
**quick-tempered**
 *irascible* 892 adj.
**quick-witted**

*intelligent* 498 adj.
**quid**
 *mouthful* 301 n.
 *tobacco* 388 n.
 *coinage* 797 n.
 *funds* 797 n.
**quiddity**
 *essence* 1 n.
 *essential part* 5 n.
**quidnunc**
 *news reporter* 529 n.
**quid pro quo**
 *offset* 31 n.
 *quid pro quo* 150 n.
 *retaliation* 714 n.
 *reward* 962 n.
**quids in**
 *moneyed* 800 adj.
**quiescence**
 *quiescence* 266 n.
 *repose* 683 n.
 *peace* 717 n.
**quiescent**
 *inert* 175 adj.
 *quiescent* 266 adj.
 *silent* 399 adj.
 *latent* 523 adj.
 *inactive* 679 adj.
 *inexcitable* 823 adj.
**quiet**
 *inert* 175 adj.
 *moderation* 177 n.
 *assuage* 177 vb.
 *smooth* 258 adj.
 *quietude* 266 n.
 *still* 266 adj.
 *euphoria* 376 n.
 *silent* 399 adj.
 *soft-hued* 425 adj.
 *grey* 429 adj.
 *dissuade* 613 vb.
 *inaction* 677 adj.
 *reposeful* 683 adj.
 *peaceful* 717 adj.
 *submitting* 721 adj.
 *middling* 732 adj.
 *inexcitable* 823 adj.
 *pleasurable* 826 adj.
 *modest* 874 adj.
 *secluded* 883 adj.
**quieten**
 *bring to rest* 266 vb.
 *silence* 399 vb.
**quietism**
 *quietude* 266 n.
 *moral insensibility*
  820 n.
 *inexcitability* 823 n.
 *content* 828 n.
**quietude**
 *quietude* 266 n.
 See also **quiet**
**quietus**
 *end* 69 n.
 *death* 361 n.
 *killing* 362 n.
**quiff**

*hair* 259 n.
**quill**
 *prickle* 256 n.
 *plumage* 259 n.
 *stationery* 586 n.
**quill-driving**
 *writing* 586 n.
**quilt**
 *coverlet* 226 n.
 *variegate* 437 vb.
**quilting**
 *lining* 227 n.
**quin**
 *five* 99 n.
**quincentenary**
 *anniversary* 141 n.
**quincunx**
 *five* 99 n.
 *crossing* 222 n.
**quinine**
 *antidote* 658 n.
 *prophylactic* 658 n.
**quinquennial**
 *periodic* 110 adj.
 *seasonal* 141 adj.
**quinquepartite**
 *multifid* 100 adj.
**quinquereme**
 *galley* 275 n.
**quint**
 *five* 99 n.
**quintain**
 *objective* 617 n.
**quintal**
 *weighing* 322 n.
**quintessence**
 *essential part* 5 n.
 *goodness* 644 n.
 *perfection* 646 n.
**quintet**
 *five* 99 n.
 *duet* 412 n.
 *orchestra* 413 n.
**quintuple**
 *fifth and over* 99 adj.
**quintuplet**
 *five* 99 n.
**quip**
 *witticism* 839 n.
 *indignity* 921 n.
**quipu**
 *counting instrument*
  86 n.
**quire**
 *edition* 589 n.
 *paper* 631 n.
**quirk**
 *speciality* 80 n.
 *nonconformity* 84 n.
 *eccentricity* 503 n.
 *interpretation* 520 n.
 *misinterpretation* 521 n.
 *whim* 604 n.
 *witticism* 839 n.
**quisling**
 *tergiversator* 603 n.
 *collaborator* 707 n.

*knave* 938 n.
**quit**
 *depart* 296 vb.
 *relinquish* 621 vb.
 *resign* 753 vb.
 *fail in duty* 918 vb.
**quite**
 *greatly* 32 adv.
 *slightly* 33 adv.
 *completely* 54 adv.
**quite a few**
 *great quantity* 32 n.
 *many* 104 adj.
**quite another matter**
 *variant* 15 n.
**quite so**
 – 865 int.
**quite something**
 *prodigy* 864 n.
**quite the reverse**
 *contrariety* 14 n.
**quit of**
 *losing* 772 adj.
**quit rent**
 *price* 809 n.
**quits**
 *equivalence* 28 n.
 *atonement* 941 n.
**quits, be**
 *retaliate* 714 vb.
**quittance**
 *liberation* 746 n.
 *payment* 804 n.
**quitter**
 *tergiversator* 603 n.
 *avoider* 620 n.
 *submission* 721 n.
 *resignation* 753 n.
 *coward* 856 n.
**quiver**
 *accumulation* 74 n.
 *oscillate* 317 vb.
 *be agitated* 318 vb.
 *feel pain* 377 vb.
 *be cold* 380 vb.
 *arsenal* 723 n.
 *show feeling* 818 vb.
 *be excited* 821 vb.
 *quake* 854 vb.
**quixotic**
 *imaginative* 513 adj.
 *disinterested* 931 adj.
**quixotry**
 *ideality* 513 n.
 *rashness* 857 n.
 *disinterestedness* 931 n.
**quiz**
 *be curious* 453 vb.
 *interrogate* 459 vb.
 *broadcast* 531 n.
 *indoor game* 837 n.
**quizzer**
 *questioner* 459 n.
**quizzical**
 *enquiring* 459 adj.
 *derisive* 851 adj.
**quod**

*prison* 748 n.
**quodlibet**
  *question* 459 n.
  *argumentation* 475 n.
**quoin**
  *angularity* 247 n.
  *press* 587 n.
**quoit(s)**
  *circle* 250 n.
  *missile* 287 n.
  *ball game* 837 n.
**quondam**
  *former* 125 adj.
**Quorn (tdmk)**
  *vegetable* 301 n.
**quorum**
  *finite quantity* 26 n.
  *eletorate* 605 n.
  *sufficiency* 635 n.
**quota**
  *finite quantity* 26 n.
  *portion* 783 n.
**quotation**
  *referral* 9 n.
  *part* 53 n.
  *repetition* 106 n.
  *evidence* 466 n.
  *exhibit* 522 n.
  *price* 809 n.
**quotation marks**
  *punctuation* 547 n.
**quote**
  *exemplify* 83 vb.
  *repeat* 106 vb.
  *manifest* 522 vb.
**quotes**
  *punctuation* 547 n.
**quotidian**
  *seasonal* 141 adj.
**quotient**
  *quantity* 26 n.
  *numerical element* 85 n.
**Qur'an**
  *scripture* 975 n. box

---

**R**

**Ra, Re**
  *Egyptian deities* 967 n.
**RA**
  *artist* 556 n.
**rabbet**
  *join* 45 vb.
  *furrow* 262 n.
**rabbi**
  *theologian* 973 n.
  *priest* 986 n.
**rabbinical**
  *theological* 973 adj.
**rabbit**
  *mammal* 365 n.
  *bungler* 697 n.
  *coward* 856 n.
**rabbiting**
  *chase* 619 n.
**rabbit on**

*be loquacious* 581 vb.
**rabbit punch**
  *knock* 279 n.
**rabbit warren**
  *abundance* 171 n.
**rabble**
  *crowd* 74 n.
  *rabble* 869 n.
**rabble-rouser**
  *motivator* 612 n.
  *leader* 690 n.
  *agitator* 738 n.
  *excitant* 821 n.
**Rabelaisian**
  *impure* 951 adj.
**rabid**
  *furious* 176 adj.
  *frenzied* 503 adj.
  *excitable* 822 adj.
  *angry* 891 adj.
**rabies**
  *animal disease* 651 n.
  *infection* 651 n.
**raccoon**
  *mammal* 365 n.
**race**
  *race* 11 n.
  *breed* 77 n.
  *genealogy* 169 n.
  *speeding* 277 n.
  *outdo* 306 vb.
  *current* 350 n.
  *humankind* 371 n.
  *hasten* 680 vb.
  *community* 708 n.
  *racing* 716 n.
**racecourse**
  *meeting place* 192 n.
  *gaming-house* 618 n.
  *racing* 716 n.
  *arena* 724 n.
**race discrimination**
  *injustice* 914 n.
**race hatred**
  *phobia* 854 n.
  *hatred* 888 n.
**racehorse**
  *thoroughbred* 273 n.
  *speeder* 277 n.
**racer**
  *bicycle* 274 n.
  *speeder* 277 n.
  *contender* 716 n.
**race relations**
  *sociality* 882 n.
**race riot**
  *lawlessness* 954 n.
**racetrack**
  *arena* 724 n.
**race walking**
  *walking* 267 n.
  *racing* 716 n.
  *sport* 837 n.
**Rachmanism**
  *severity* 735 n.
**racial**
  *ethnic* 11 adj.

*parental* 169 adj.
  *human* 371 adj.
**racialism**
  *prejudice* 481 n.
  *hatred* 888 n.
**racial prejudice**
  *prejudice* 481 n.
  *phobia* 854 n.
**racing**
  *speeding* 277 n.
  *racing* 716 n.
  *sport* 837 n.
**racism**
  *prejudice* 481 n.
  *hatred* 888 n.
  *injustice* 914 n.
**racist**
  *narrow mind* 481 n.
**rack**
  *compartment* 194 n.
  *shelf* 218 n.
  *distort* 246 vb.
  *cloud* 355 n.
  *pain* 377 n.
  *ill-treat* 645 vb.
  *purify* 648 vb.
  *oppress* 735 vb.
  *torment* 827 vb.
  *torture* 963 vb.
  *instrument of torture* 964 n.
– *one's brains*
  *think* 449 vb.
  *retrospect* 505 vb.
**rack and pinion**
  *railway* 624 n.
**rack and ruin**
  *ruin* 165 n.
**racket**
  *turmoil* 61 n.
  *commotion* 318 n.
  *loudness* 400 n.
  *roll* 403 n.
  *discord* 411 n.
  *trickery* 542 n.
  *plot* 623 n.
  *foul play* 930 n.
**racketeer**
  *robber* 789 n.
  *offender* 904 n.
  *be dishonest* 930 vb.
**racketing**
  *activity* 678 n.
**rackets**
  *ball game* 837 n.
**rackety**
  *riotous* 738 adj.
  *merry* 833 adj.
**racking**
  *painful* 377 adj.
  *paining* 827 adj.
  *corporal punishment* 963 n.
**rack-rent**
  *levy* 786 vb.
  *be parsimonious* 816 vb.
**rack rents**

*dearness* 811 n.
**raconteur, raconteuse**
  *narrator* 590 n.
  *humorist* 839 n.
**racy**
  *vigorous* 174 adj.
  *tasty* 386 adj.
  *savoury* 390 adj.
  *stylistic* 566 adj.
  *forceful* 571 adj.
  *lively* 819 adj.
  *witty* 839 adj.
  *impure* 951 adj.
**rad**
  *radiation* 417 n.
**radar**
  *location* 187 n.
  *sailing aid* 269 n.
  *detector* 484 n.
  *telecommunication* 531 n.
  *indicator* 547 n.
  *directorship* 689 n.
**radar trap**
  *velocity* 277 n.
  *traffic control* 305 n.
**raddle**
  *redden* 431 vb.
**radial**
  *divergent* 294 adj.
**radially**
  *longwise* 203 adv.
**radial velocity**
  *star* 321 n.
**radian**
  *angular measure* 247 n.
**radiance**
  *glow* 417 n.
  *light* 417 n.
  *beauty* 841 n.
**radiant**
  *luminous* 417 adj.
  *radiating* 417 adj.
  *luminescent* 420 adj.
  *happy* 824 adj.
  *cheerful* 833 adj.
  *beautiful* 841 adj.
  *splendid* 841 adj.
**radiate**
  *separate* 46 vb.
  *be dispersed* 75 vb.
  *diverge* 294 vb.
  *emit* 300 vb.
  *radiate* 417 vb.
**radiation**
  *nucleonics* 160 n.
  *oscillation* 317 n.
  *radiation* 417 n.
  *poison* 659 n.
**radiation sickness**
  *illness* 651 n.
**radiator**
  *heater* 383 n.
**radical**
  *intrinsic* 5 adj.
  *complete* 54 adj.
  *numerical* 85 adj.

– a laugh
*be witty* 839 vb.
*be ridiculous* 849 vb.
– Cain
*be loud* 400 vb.
*revolt* 738 vb.
*be angry* 891 vb.
– one's eyebrows
*gesticulate* 547 vb.
*deprecate* 762 vb.
– one's glass (to)
*drink* 301 vb.
*toast* 876 vb.
– one's hackles
*enrage* 891 vb.
*get angry* 891 vb.
– one's hand
*gesticulate* 547 vb.
*vote* 605 vb.
*strike at* 712 vb.
– one's hat
*doff* 229 vb.
*greet* 884 vb.
– one's sights
*progress* 285 n.
*aim at* 617 vb.
– one's voice
*emphasize* 532 vb.
*speak* 579 vb.
– one's voice against
*dissent* 489 vb.
*deprecate* 762 vb.
– spirits
*practise sorcery* 983 vb.
– the alarm
*signal* 547 vb.
*warn* 664 vb.
*raise the alarm* 665 vb.
*frighten* 854 vb.
– the dust
*be violent* 176 vb.
*be active* 678 vb.
– the money
*find means* 629 vb.
– the rafters
*be loud* 400 vb.
– the roof
*be loud* 400 vb.
*applaud* 923 vb.
– the spirits
*cheer* 833 vb.
– the subject
*initiate* 68 vb.
– the temperature
*heat* 381 vb.
*excite* 821 vb.
– the wind
*acquire* 771 vb.
**raised**
*projecting* 254 adj.
**raised eyebrows**
*deprecation* 762 n.
**raised voice(s)**
*cry* 408 n.
*quarrel* 709 n.
**raisin**
*fruit* 301 n.

**raising agent**
*leaven* 323 n.
**raison d'être**
*reason why* 156 n.
*intention* 617 n.
**raj**
*governance* 733 n.
**rajah, raja**
*potentate* 741 n.
*person of rank* 868 n.
**rajahship**
*position of authority* 733 n.
**Rajput**
*aristocrat* 868 n.
**rake**
*thinness* 206 n.
*obliquity* 220 n.
*projection* 254 n.
*smoother* 258 n.
*draw* 288 vb.
*extractor* 304 n.
*farm tool* 370 n.
*cultivate* 370 vb.
*cleaning utensil* 648 n.
*fire at* 712 vb.
*bad person* 938 n.
*sensualist* 944 n.
*libertine* 952 n.
– in
*bring together* 74 vb.
– in the shekels
*gain* 771 vb.
*get rich* 800 vb.
– out
*extinguish* 382 vb.
*clean* 648 vb.
– over
*search* 459 vb.
– together
*acquire* 771 vb.
– up
*bring together* 74 vb.
*extract* 304 vb.
*retrospect* 505 vb.
**rake-off**
*earnings* 771 n.
*discount* 810 n.
*reward* 962 n.
**rakish**
*oblique* 220 adj.
*fashionable* 848 adj.
*showy* 875 adj.
*lecherous* 951 adj.
**rallentando**
*tempo* 410 n.
*adagio* 412 adv.
**rally**
*arrange* 62 vb.
*assemblage* 74 n.
*congregate* 74 vb.
*continuance* 146 n.
*interchange* 151 n.
*be strong* 162 vb.
*propulsion* 287 n.
*call* 547 n.
*persevere* 600 vb.

*incite* 612 vb.
*get better* 654 vb.
*be restored* 656 vb.
*aid* 703 vb.
*contest* 716 n.
*give battle* 718 vb.
*ridicule* 851 vb.
*give courage* 855 vb.
– round
*cooperate* 706 vb.
**rallying cry**
*call* 547 n.
*inducement* 612 n.
**rallying point**
*focus* 76 n.
**ram**
*demolish* 165 vb.
*ram* 279 n.
*collide* 279 vb.
*sheep* 365 n.
*male animal* 372 n.
*tool* 630 n.
*charge* 712 vb.
*strike at* 712 vb.
– down
*fill* 54 vb.
*close* 264 vb.
*be dense* 324 vb.
– down one's throat
*compel* 740 vb.
**Ramadan**
*fast* 946 n.
*holy day* 988 n. box
**Ramakrishna**
*religious teacher* 973 n.
*sectarian* 978 adj.
**Ramapithecus**
*humankind* 371 n.
**ramble**
*walking* 267 n.
*wander* 267 vb.
*be insane* 503 vb.
*be diffuse* 570 vb.
*amuse oneself* 837 vb.
**rambler**
*traveller* 268 n.
*wanderer* 268 n.
**rambling**
*irrelevant* 10 adj.
*orderless* 61 adj.
*wandering* 267 n.
*deviating* 282 adj.
*feeble* 572 adj.
*sport* 837 n.
**ramekin**
*bowl* 194 n.
**ramification**
*bond* 47 n.
*branch* 53 n.
*range* 183 n.
*filament* 208 n.
*divergence* 294 n.
**ramify**
*bifurcate* 92 vb.
*diverge* 294 vb.
**ramose**
*symmetrical* 245 adj.

**ramp**
*be vertical* 215 vb.
*obliquity* 220 n.
*ascent* 308 n.
*be agitated* 318 vb.
*trickery* 542 n.
*be excited* 821 vb.
*be angry* 891 vb.
*get angry* 891 vb.
*foul play* 930 n.
**rampage**
*rampage* 61 vb.
*be violent* 176 vb.
*be agitated* 318 vb.
*be loud* 400 vb.
*be active* 678 vb.
*excitable state* 822 n.
*anger* 891 n.
**rampant**
*universal* 79 adj.
*furious* 176 adj.
*violent* 176 adj.
*vertical* 215 adj.
*heraldic* 547 adj.
*plenteous* 635 adj.
**rampart**
*refuge* 662 n.
*fortification* 713 n.
**ram raid**
*attack* 712 n.
*stealing* 788 n.
**ramrod**
*ram* 279 n.
*firearm* 723 n.
**ramshackle**
*flimsy* 163 adj.
*dilapidated* 655 adj.
*unsafe* 661 adj.
**ranch**
*stock farm* 369 n.
*lands* 777 n.
**rancher**
*herdsman* 369 n.
**rancid**
*decomposed* 51 adj.
*unsavoury* 391 adj.
*fetid* 397 adj.
**rancour**
*enmity* 881 n.
*hatred* 888 n.
*resentment* 891 n.
*malevolence* 898 n.
**rand**
*coinage* 797 n. box
**randem**
*bicycle* 274 n.
**random**
*orderless* 61 adj.
*casual* 159 adj.
*deviating* 282 adj.
*indiscriminate* 464 adj.
*designless* 618 adj.
**random sample**
*example* 83 n.
*equal chance* 159 n.
*empiricism* 461 n.
**randy**

*lecherous* 951 adj.
**range**
  *medley* 43 n.
  *arrange* 62 vb.
  *series* 71 n.
  *accumulation* 74 n.
  *classification* 77 n.
  *ability* 160 n.
  *range* 183 n.
  *distance* 199 n.
  *breadth* 205 n.
  *layer* 207 n.
  *traverse* 267 vb.
  *plain* 348 n.
  *furnace* 383 n.
  *hearing* 415 n.
  *visibility* 443 n.
  *choice* 605 n.
  *function* 622 n.
  *arena* 724 n.
  *scope* 744 n.
  *be free* 744 vb.
  *merchandise* 795 n.
 – oneself with
  *choose* 605 vb.
  *join a party* 708 vb.
**range finder**
  *direction* 281 n.
  *telescope* 442 n.
**ranger**
  *wanderer* 268 n.
  *keeper* 749 n.
**rangy**
  *narrow* 206 adj.
  *tall* 209 adj.
**rani, ranee**
  *potentate* 741 n.
**rank**
  *relativeness* 9 n.
  *degree* 27 n.
  *graduate* 27 vb.
  *consummate* 32 adj.
  *order* 60 n.
  *class* 62 vb.
  *serial place* 73 n.
  *classification* 77 n.
  *vegetal* 366 adj.
  *unsavoury* 391 adj.
  *fetid* 397 adj.
  *estimate* 480 vb.
  *plenteous* 635 adj.
  *importance* 638 n.
  *bad* 645 adj.
  *formation* 722 n.
  *prestige* 866 n.
  *nobility* 868 n.
  *heinous* 934 adj.
  *impure* 951 adj.
**rank and file**
  *commonalty* 869 n.
**ranker**
  *commoner* 869 n.
**rankle**
  *hurt* 827 vb.
  *huff* 891 vb.
**rank, person of**
  *person of repute* 866 n.

*person of rank* 868 n.
**ranks, the**
  *soldiery* 722 n.
**ransack**
  *lay waste* 165 vb.
  *search* 459 vb.
  *take* 786 vb.
  *rob* 788 vb.
**ransom**
  *restoration* 656 n.
  *deliverance* 668 n.
  *restitution* 787 n.
  *purchase* 792 n., vb.
  *price* 809 n.
  *penalty* 963 n.
**ransomed**
  *sanctified* 979 adj.
**rant**
  *be absurd* 497 vb.
  *empty talk* 515 n.
  *exaggerate* 546 vb.
  *rhetoric* 574 n.
  *orate* 579 vb.
  *act* 594 vb.
  *boast* 877 vb.
**ranter**
  *speaker* 579 n.
  *chatterer* 581 n.
  *agitator* 738 n.
  *boaster* 877 n.
**rantipole**
  *disorderly* 61 adj.
  *light-minded* 456 adj.
**rap**
  *knock* 279 n.
  *bang* 402 n.
  *vocal music* 412 n.
  *speech* 579 n.
  *speak* 579 vb.
  *chatter* 581 n.
  *interlocution* 584 n.
  *converse* 584 vb.
  *chat* 584 n.
  *corporal punishment*
   963 n.
 – out
  *voice* 577 vb.
 – over the knuckles
  *reprove* 924 vb.
  *spank* 963 vb.
**rapacious**
  *taking* 786 adj.
  *avaricious* 816 adj.
  *greedy* 859 adj.
**rapacity**
  *rapacity* 786 n.
  *thievishness* 788 n.
**rape**
  *force* 176 vb.
  *taking* 786 n.
  *rape* 951 n.
  *debauch* 951 vb.
**raper**
  *libertine* 952 n.
**rapid**
  *speedy* 277 adj.
**rapid-fire**

*speedy* 277 adj.
  *bombardment* 712 n.
**rapids**
  *waterfall* 350 n.
  *pitfall* 663 n.
**rapid succession**
  *frequency* 139 n.
**rapier**
  *sharp point* 256 n.
  *sidearms* 723 n.
**rapine**
  *spoliation* 788 n.
**rapist**
  *libertine* 952 n.
**rap on the knuckles**
  *anger* 891 n.
  *reprimand* 924 n.
**rapparee**
  *robber* 789 n.
**rapport**
  *relation* 9 n.
  *concord* 710 n.
**rapprochement**
  *concord* 710 n.
  *pacification* 719 n.
  *friendship* 880 n.
**rapscallion**
  *knave* 938 n.
**rapt**
  *attentive* 455 adj.
  *obsessed* 455 adj.
  *abstracted* 456 adj.
  *impressed* 818 adj.
  *wondering* 864 adj.
**raptor**
  *bird* 365 n.
  *animal* 365n. box
**raptorial**
  *liking* 786 adj.
**rapture(s)**
  *excitation* 821 n.
  *joy* 824 n.
  *rejoicing* 835 n.
  *love* 887 n.
**rapturous**
  *felt* 818 adj.
  *pleased* 824 adj.
**rara avis**
  *mythical beast* 365 n.
  *infrequency* 140 n.
  *paragon* 646 n.
  *prodigy* 864 n.
  *mythical being* 970 n.
**rare**
  *superior* 34 adj.
  *unusual* 84 adj.
  *few* 105 adj.
  *infrequent* 140 adj.
  *culinary* 301 adj.
  *rare* 325 adj.
  *airy* 340 adj.
  *improbable* 472 adj.
  *scarce* 636 adj.
  *excellent* 644 adj.
  *valuable* 644 adj.
  *uncooked* 670 adj.
  *of price* 811 adj.

*wonderful* 864 adj.
**rarefy**
  *enlarge* 197 vb.
  *make smaller* 198 vb.
  *make thin* 206 vb.
  *rarefy* 325 vb.
**rarely**
  *here and there* 105 adv.
  *seldom* 140 adv.
**raring to go**
  *willing* 597 adj.
  *prepared* 669 adj.
**rarity**
  *nonconformist* 84 n.
  *nonconformity* 84 n.
  *infrequency* 140 n.
  *rarity* 325 n.
  *improbability* 472 n.
  *paragon* 646 n.
  *See also* **rare**
**rascal**
  *low fellow* 869 n.
  *knave* 938 n.
**rascally**
  *cunning* 698 adj.
  *disreputable* 867 adj.
  *rascally* 930 adj.
  *vicious* 934 adj.
**rash**
  *formication* 378 n.
  *inattentive* 456 adj.
  *negligent* 458 adj.
  *indiscriminating* 464 adj.
  *absurd* 497 adj.
  *unwise* 499 adj.
  *spontaneous* 609 adj.
  *skin disease* 651 n.
  *unprepared* 670 adj.
  *hasty* 680 adj.
  *defiant* 711 adj.
  *excitable* 822 adj.
  *rash* 857 adj.
**rasher**
  *piece* 53 n.
**rasp**
  *rub* 333 vb.
  *breathe* 352 vb.
  *rasp* 407 vb.
  *discord* 411 vb.
**raspberry**
  *fruit* 301 n.
  *gesture* 547 n.
  *reprimand* 924 n.
**Rastafarian, Rasta**
  *sectarian* 978 adj.
**rat**
  *mammal* 365 n.
  *testee* 461 n.
  *inform* 524 vb.
  *divulge* 526 vb.
  *deceiver* 545 n.
  *tergiversator* 603 n.
  *apostatize* 603 vb.
  *relinquish* 621 vb.
  *coward* 856 n.
  *noxious animal* 904 n.
  *knave* 938 n.

*undevelopment* 670 n.
**raw recruit**
  *ignoramus* 493 n.
  *beginner* 538 n.
  *bungler* 697 n.
**ray**
  *small quantity* 33 n.
  *divergence* 294 n.
  *flash* 417 n.
**ray of comfort**
  *content* 828 n.
  *relief* 831 n.
**ray of hope**
  *hope* 852 n.
**rayon**
  *fibre* 208 n.
  *textile* 222 n.
**raze**
  *demolish* 165 vb.
  *fell* 311 vb.
  *obliterate* 550 vb.
**razor**
  *sharp edge* 256 n.
  *cosmetic* 843 n.
**razor's edge**
  *narrowness* 206 n.
  *danger* 661 n.
**razor wire**
  *defences* 713 n.
**razzia**
  *brigandage* 788 n.
**re**
  *concerning* 9 adv.
**re-**
  *again* 106 adv.
**reach**
  *degree* 27 n.
  *ability* 160 n.
  *range* 183 n.
  *distance* 199 n.
  *be long* 203 vb.
  *straightness* 249 n.
  *arrive* 295 vb.
  *pass* 305 vb.
  *gulf* 345 n.
  *hearing* 415 n.
  *suffice* 635 vb.
  *governance* 733 n.
  – out for
  *take* 786 vb.
  – to
  *fill* 54 vb.
  *extend* 183 vb.
  *be distant* 199 vb.
**reach-me-downs**
  *clothing* 228 n.
**react**
  *correlate* 12 vb.
  *be active* 678 vb.
  – against
  *dislike* 861 vb.
  – instinctively
  *intuit* 476 vb.
**reaction**
  *compensation* 31 n.
  *reversion* 148 n.
  *effect* 157 n.

*counteraction* 182 n.
  *recoil* 280 n.
  *sense* 374 n.
  *answer* 460 n.
  *restoration* 656 n.
  *retaliation* 714 n.
  *deprecation* 762 n.
  *feeling* 818 n.
**reactionary**
  *regressive* 286 adj.
  *tergiversating* 603 adj.
  *opponent* 705 n.
  *revolter* 738 n.
  *disobedient* 738 adj.
**reactivation**
  *revival* 656 n.
**read**
  *be attentive* 455 vb.
  *gauge* 465 vb.
  *decipher* 520 vb.
  *learn* 536 vb.
  *study* 536 vb.
  *speak* 579 vb.
  – aloud
  *vocal* 577 adj.
  *speak* 579 vb.
  – between the lines
  *decipher* 520 vb.
  – into
  *misinterpret* 521 vb.
  – off
  *gauge* 465 vb.
  – one like a book
  *know* 490 vb.
  – one's palm
  *foresee* 510 vb.
  *divine* 511 vb.
  – the future
  *foresee* 510 vb.
  *divine* 511 vb.
  – the Riot Act
  *reprove* 924 vb.
  – through
  *scan* 438 vb.
**readable**
  *intelligible* 516 adj.
**reader**
  *scholar* 492 n.
  *teacher* 537 n.
  *literature* 557 n.
  *bookperson* 589 n.
  *textbook* 589 n.
  *academic title* 870 n.
**readership**
  *publicity* 528 n.
  *lecture* 534 n.
**readily**
  *instantaneously* 116 adv.
  *willingly* 597 Adv.
  *easily* 701 adv.
**readiness**
  *tendency* 179 n.
  *attention* 455 n.
  *intelligence* 498 n.
  *foresight* 510 n.
  *willingness* 597 n.
  *utility* 640 n.

*preparedness* 669 n.
  *completion* 725 n.
  *obedience* 739 n.
**reading**
  *measurement* 465 n.
  *erudition* 490 n.
  *interpretation* 520 n.
  *lecture* 534 n.
  *study* 536 n.
  *oration* 579 n.
**reading glasses**
  *eyeglass* 442 n.
**reading lamp**
  *lamp* 420 n.
**reading list**
  *reference book* 589 n.
**reading matter**
  *journal* 528 n.
  *literature* 557 n.
  *reading matter* 589 n.
**readjust**
  *adjust* 24 vb.
  *equalize* 28 vb.
**readjustment**
  *restoration* 656 n.
**ready**
  *impending* 155 adj.
  *on the spot* 189 adj.
  *formed* 243 adj.
  *attentive* 455 adj.
  *vigilant* 457 adj.
  *intelligent* 498 adj.
  *expectant* 507 adj.
  *elegant* 575 adj.
  *loquacious* 581 adj.
  *willing* 597 adj.
  *useful* 640 adj.
  *prepared* 669 adj.
  *active* 678 adj.
  *skilful* 694 adj.
  *obedient* 739 adj.
  *consenting* 758 adj.
**ready for**
  *hungry* 859 adj.
**ready for anything**
  *skilful* 694 adj.
  *courageous* 855 adj.
**ready for more**
  *refreshed* 685 adj.
**ready for use**
  *useful* 640 adj.
  *prepared* 669 adj.
**ready-made**
  *produced* 164 adj.
  *formed* 243 adj.
  *ready-made* 669 adj.
**ready money**
  *funds* 797 n.
**ready reckoner**
  *counting instrument* 86 n.
**ready to**
  *future* 124 adj.
  *tending* 179 adj.
**ready to drop**
  *fatigued* 684 adj.
**ready to hand**

*prepared* 669 adj.
**ready-to-serve**
  *culinary* 301 adj.
**ready-to-wear**
  *tailored* 228 adj.
  *ready-made* 669 adj.
**reaffirm**
  *emphasize* 532 vb.
**reafforestation**
  *restoration* 656 n.
**reagent**
  *testing agent* 461 n.
**real**
  *real* 1 adj.
  *substantial* 3 adj.
  *inimitable* 21 adj.
  *material* 319 adj.
  *true* 494 adj.
**real estate**
  *lands* 777 n.
**realism**
  *existence* 1 n.
  *mimicry* 20 n.
  *philosophy* 449 n.
  *accuracy* 494 n.
  *veracity* 540 n.
  *representation* 551 n.
  *description* 590 n.
**Realism**
  *school of painting* 553 n.
  *literature* 557 n.
**realist**
  *materiality* 319 n.
**realistic**
  *lifelike* 18 adj.
  *true* 494 adj.
  *wise* 498 adj.
  *representing* 551 adj.
  *descriptive* 590 adj.
**reality**
  *reality* 1 n.
  *substantiality* 3 n.
  *event* 154 n.
  *truth* 494 n.
  *chief thing* 638 n.
**realizable, realisable**
  *possible* 469 adj.
**realization,**
  **realisation**
  *existence* 1 n.
  *event* 154 n.
  *materiality* 319 n.
  *appearance* 445 n.
  *discovery* 484 n.
  *knowledge* 490 n.
  *representation* 551 n.
  *effectuation* 725 n.
  *feeling* 818 n.
**realize, realise**
  *make extrinsic* 6 vb.
  *cognize* 447 vb.
  *imagine* 513 vb.
  *understand* 516 vb.
  *be informed* 524 vb.
  *acquire* 771 vb.
  *draw money* 797 vb.
**real-life**

receiving 782 n.
receipt 807 n.
**receive**
meet 295 vb.
admit 299 vb.
believe 485 vb.
receive 782 vb.
take 786 vb.
be hospitable 882 vb.
greet 884 vb.
**received**
usual 610 adj.
**Received Pronunciation**
language 557 n.
**received wisdom**
opinion 485 n.
consensus 488 n.
**receiver**
hearing instrument
415 n.
receiver 782 n.
recipient 782 n.
taker 786 n.
thief 789 n.
treasurer 798 n.
**recension**
amendment 654 n.
**recent**
foregoing 125 adj.
new 126 adj.
**receptacle**
receptable 194 n.
**reception**
inclusion 78 n.
arrival 295 n.
ingress 297 n.
reception 299 n.
sound 398 n.
hearing 415 n.
conference 584 n.
receiving 782 n.
celebration 876 n.
social gathering 882 n.
courteous act 884 n.
**receptionist**
recorder 549 n.
**reception room**
room 194 n.
**receptive**
admitting 299 adj.
intelligent 498 adj.
studious 536 adj.
willing 597 adj.
induced 612 adj.
receiving 782 adj.
**recess**
compartment 194 n.
angularity 247 n.
cavity 255 n.
hiding-place 527 n.
repose 683 n.
refreshment 685 n.
**recesses**
interiority 224 n.
**recession**
decrease 37 n.

contraction 198 n.
regression 286 n.
recession 290 n.
departure 296 n.
deterioration 655 n.
inactivity 679 n.
adversity 731 n.
**recessional**
hymn 981 n.
**recessive**
reverted 148 adj.
**recessive characteristic**
speciality 80 n.
**Rechabite**
sober person 948 n.
**recherché**
unusual 84 adj.
chosen 605 adj.
excellent 644 adj.
fashionable 848 adj.
**recidivism**
reversion 148 n.
relapse 657 n.
**recidivist**
tergiversator 603 n.
deteriorated 655 adj.
offender 904 n.
**recipe**
cookery 301 n.
contrivance 623 n.
remedy 658 n.
precept 693 n.
**recipient**
recipient 194 adj.
correspondent 588 n.
beneficiary 776 n.
recipient 782 n.
**reciprocal**
correlative 12 adj.
equivalent 28 adj.
numerical element 85 n.
interchanged 151 adj.
retaliatory 714 adj.
**reciprocate**
correlate 12 vb.
be periodic 141 vb.
cooperate 706 vb.
concord 710 vb.
**reciprocation**
equivalence 28 n.
interchange 151 n.
fluctuation 317 n.
**reciprocity**
correlation 12 n.
interchange 151 n.
cooperation 706 n.
**recital**
repetition 106 n.
music 412 n.
oration 579 n.
**recitation**
oration 579 n.
**recitative**
vocal music 412 n.
**recite**
repeat 106 vb.

speak 579 vb.
describe 590 vb.
**reck**
be careful 457 vb.
**reckless**
negligent 458 adj.
unwise 499 adj.
defiant 711 adj.
prodigal 815 adj.
rash 857 adj.
**reckon**
do sums 86 vb.
measure 465 vb.
expect 507 vb.
– among
number with 78 vb.
– on
believe 485 vb.
intend 617 vb.
– without
misjudge 481 vb.
– without one's host
be unskilful 695 vb.
be rash 857 vb.
**reckoning**
numeration 86 n.
measurement 465 n.
expectation 507 n.
accounts 808 n.
price 809 n.
punishment 963 n.
**reclaim**
cultivate 370 vb.
make better 654 vb.
restore 656 vb.
retrieve 656 vb.
demand 737 vb.
acquire 771 vb.
appropriate 786 vb.
claim 915 vb.
atone 941 vb.
**recline**
be horizontal 216 vb.
be supported 218 vb.
sit down 311 vb.
repose 683 vb.
**recluse**
solitary 883 n.
ascetic 945 n.
**recognition**
vision 438 n.
assent 488 n.
knowledge 490 n.
courteous act 884 n.
thanks 907 n.
dueness 915 n.
approbation 923 n.
reward 962 n.
**recognizable, recognisable**
visible 443 adj.
intelligible 516 adj.
manifest 522 adj.
**recognizance, recognisance**
security 767 n.
legal process 959 n.

**recognize, recognise**
see 438 vb.
notice 455 vb.
discover 484 vb.
know 490 vb.
remember 505 vb.
understand 516 vb.
permit 756 vb.
consent 758 vb.
greet 884 vb.
grant claims 915 vb.
**recognized, recognised**
influential 178 adj.
usual 610 adj.
**recoil**
counteraction 182 n.
recoil 280 n., vb.
recede 290 vb.
repulsion 292 n.
elasticity 328 n.
be unwilling 598 vb.
avoidance 620 n.
dislike 861 vb.
**recollect**
remember 505 vb.
retrospect 505 vb.
**recollection**
remembrance 505 n.
imagination 513 n.
**recommencement**
reversion 148 n.
**recommend**
select 605 vb.
incite 612 vb.
patronize 703 vb.
– oneself
be praised 923 vb.
**recommendation**
credential 466 n.
advice 691 n.
friendship 880 n.
approbation 923 n.
**recompense**
compensation 31 n.
retaliation 714 n.
reward 962 n., vb.
**reconcilable**
agreeing 24 adj.
**reconcile**
pacify 719 vb.
content 828 vb.
**reconciliation**
adaptation 24 n.
conformity 83 n.
concord 710 n.
friendship 880 n.
forgiveness 909 n.
propitiation 941 n.
**recondite**
puzzling 517 adj.
concealed 525 adj.
**recondition**
repair 656 vb.
**reconnaissance**
inspection 438 n.
enquiry 459 n.

**safety net**
  *receptacle* 194 n.
  *safeguard* 662 n.
**safety pin**
  *fastening* 47 n.
**safety valve**
  *safeguard* 662 n.
  *means of escape* 667 n.
**saffron**
  *yellowness* 433 n.
**sag**
  *be weak* 163 vb.
  *hang* 217 vb.
  *be oblique* 220 vb.
  *be curved* 248 vb.
  *descend* 309 vb.
  *knuckle under* 721 vb.
  *be dejected* 834 vb.
**saga**
  *narrative* 590 n.
**sagacious**
  *intelligent* 498 adj.
  *foreseeing* 510 adj.
**sagacity**
  *sagacity* 498 n.
  *foresight* 510 n.
  *skill* 694 n.
**sage**
  *old man* 133 n.
  *herb* 301 n.
  *intellectual* 492 n.
  *wise* 498 adj.
  *sage* 500 n.
  *teacher* 537 n.
  *notable* 638 n.
  *person of repute* 866 n.
  *religious teacher* 973 n.
**sage-green**
  *green* 434 adj.
**Sagittarius**
  *zodiac* 321 n. box
**Sahara**
  *desert* 172 n.
**Saharan**
  *dry* 342 adj.
**sahib**
  *male* 372 n.
  *title* 870 n.
**said**
  *preceding* 64 adj.
  *prior* 119 adj.
**sail**
  *propeller* 269 n.
  *water travel* 269 n.
  *voyage* 269 vb.
  *sail* 275 n.
  *ship* 275 n.
  *navy* 722 n.
– home
  *do easily* 701 vb.
– into
  *attack* 712 vb.
  *fight* 716 vb.
– too near the wind
  *be in danger* 661 vb.
– under false colours
  *dissemble* 541 vb.

**sailcloth**
  *textile* 222 n.
  *sail* 275 n.
**sailing**
  *aquatics* 269 n.
  *seafaring* 269 adj.
  *sport* 837 n.
**sailing dinghy**
  *boat* 275 n.
**sailing master**
  *navigator* 270 n.
**sailing ship**
  *sailing ship* 275 n.
**sailor**
  *mariner* 270 n.
  *naval person* 722 n.
**sailplane**
  *aircraft* 276 n.
**saint**
  *paragon* 646 n.
  *benefactor* 903 n.
  *good person* 937 n.
  *saint* 968 n.
  *pietist* 979 n.
**sainted**
  *dead* 361 adj.
  *sanctified* 979 adj.
**sainthood**
  *sanctity* 979 n.
**saintly**
  *honourable* 929 adj.
  *virtuous* 933 adj.
  *angelic* 968 adj.
  *pious* 979 adj.
**saints, the**
  *the dead* 361 n.
  *elite* 644 n.
  *church member* 976 n.
**saint's day**
  *anniversary* 141 n.
  *special day* 876 n.
  *holy day* 988 n.
**Saivas**
  *non-Christian sect* 978 n.
**sake, saki**
  *alcoholic drink* 301 n.
**salaam**
– 295 int.
  *obeisance* 311 n.
  *courteous act* 884 n.
  *respects* 920 n.
**salable, saleable**
  *not retained* 779 adj.
  *trading* 791 adj.
  *salable* 793 adj.
**salable commodity**
  *merchandise* 795 n.
**salacious**
  *impure* 951 adj.
**salad**
  *dish* 301 n.
  *hors d'oeuvres* 301 n.
  *vegetable* 301 n.
**salad days**
  *salad days* 130 n.
**salad dressing**
  *sauce* 389 n.

**salamander**
  *mythical beast* 365 n.
  *amphibian* 365 n.
  *fire* 379 n.
  *noxious animal* 904 n.
**salami**
  *hors-d'oeuvres* 301 n.
**salaried classes**
  *middle classes* 869 n.
**salary**
  *incentive* 612 n.
  *earnings* 771 n.
  *pay* 804 n.
  *receipt* 807 n.
  *reward* 962 n.
**salary earner**
  *worker* 686 n.
**salary increase**
  *increment* 36 n.
**salat**
  *rite* 988 n.
**sal Atticum**
  *wit* 839 n.
**sale**
  *transfer* 780 n.
  *sale* 793 n.
**salebrosity**
  *roughness* 259 n.
**sale-price**
  *cheap* 812 adj.
**salesman,**
    **saleswoman**
  *motivator* 612 n.
  *seller* 793 n.
**salesmanship**
  *publicity* 528 n.
  *inducement* 612 n.
  *sale* 793 n.
**sales patter**
  *empty talk* 515 n.
**salesperson**
  *seller* 793 n.
**sales promotion**
  *publicity* 528 n.
  *inducement* 612 n.
**sales representative**
  *seller* 793 n.
**sales talk**
  *inducement* 612 n.
**salient**
  *region* 184 n.
  *projecting* 254 adj.
  *obvious* 443 adj.
  *battleground* 724 n.
**salientian**
  *animal* 365 adj.
**salina**
  *marsh* 347 n.
**saline**
  *salty* 388 adj.
**saliva**
  *excrement* 302 n.
  *lubricant* 334 n.
  *fluid* 335 n.
  *moisture* 341 n.
**salivate**
  *exude* 298 vb.

  *excrete* 302 vb.
  *be wet* 341 vb.
  *be hungry* 859 vb.
**sallow**
  *weakly* 163 adj.
  *tree* 366 n.
  *colourless* 426 adj.
  *whitish* 427 adj.
  *yellow* 433 adj.
  *unhealthy* 651 adj.
**sally**
  *attack* 712 n.
  *retaliation* 714 n.
  *witticism* 839 n.
**sally forth**
  *start out* 296 vb.
  *emerge* 298 vb.
**sallyport**
  *outlet* 298 n.
  *fort* 713 n.
**salmagundi**
  *a mixture* 43 n.
**salmon**
  *fish food* 301 n.
  *fish* 365 n.
**salmonella**
  *poison* 659 n.
**salmon-pink**
  *red* 431 adj.
**salon**
  *room* 194 n.
  *beau monde* 848 n.
**saloon**
  *pub* 192 n.
  *car* 274 n.
**salt**
  *mariner* 270 n.
  *salty* 388 adj.
  *condiment* 389 n.
  *white thing* 427 n.
  *chief thing* 638 n.
  *preserve* 666 vb.
  *wit* 839 n.
– away
  *store* 632 vb.
**SALT**
  *pacification* 719 n.
**saltatory**
  *leaping* 312 adj.
  *agitated* 318 adj.
**salt cellar**
  *small box* 194 n.
  *cavity* 255 n.
**salted**
  *preserved* 666 adj.
**salt flat**
  *desert* 172 n.
  *marsh* 347 n.
**saltimbanco**
  *imposter* 545 n.
**saltire**
  *cross* 222 n.
  *heraldry* 547 n.
**saltlick**
  *provender* 301 n.
**salt of the earth**
  *elite* 644 n.

**scald**
  *burn* 381 vb.
  *wound* 655 n.
**scalding**
  *hot* 379 adj.
  *paining* 827 adj.
**scale**
  *relativeness* 9 n.
  *degree* 27 n.
  *series* 71 n.
  *plate* 194 n.
  *layer* 207 n.
  *skin* 226 n.
  *doff* 229 vb.
  *climb* 308 vb.
  *scales* 322 n.
  *key* 410 n.
  *musical note* 410 n.
  *obfuscation* 421 n.
  *opacity* 423 n.
  *gauge* 465 n.
  – down
  *abate* 37 vb.
  *render few* 105 vb.
**scale drawing**
  *plan* 623 n.
**scalene**
  *unequal* 29 adj.
  *distorted* 246 adj.
**scales**
  *scales* 322 n.
**scallion**
  *vegetable* 301 n.
**scallop**
  *edging* 234 n.
  *convolution* 251 n.
  *crinkle* 251 vb.
  *notch* 260 n., vb.
  *fish food* 301 n.
**scallywag**
  *bad person* 938 n.
**scalp**
  *head* 213 n.
  *skin* 226 n.
  *uncover* 229 vb.
  *trophy* 729 n.
**scalpel**
  *sharp edge* 256 n.
**scalplock**
  *hair* 259 n.
**scaly**
  *layered* 207 adj.
  *dermal* 226 adj.
  *rough* 259 adj.
**scamp**
  *neglect* 458 vb.
  *be unwilling* 598 vb.
  *not complete* 726 vb.
  *revolter* 738 n.
  *evildoer* 904 n.
  *bad person* 938 n.
**scamped**
  *hasty* 680 adj.
**scamper**
  *move fast* 277 vb.
  *run away* 620 vb.
**scampi**

*fish food* 301 n.
**scan**
  *look along* 203 vb.
  *scan* 438 vb.
  *be attentive* 455 vb.
  *enquire* 459 vb.
  *know* 490 vb.
  *photography* 551 n.
  *photograph* 551 vb.
  *poetize* 593 vb.
**scandal**
  *rumour* 529 n.
  *badness* 645 n.
  *slur* 867 n.
  *humiliation* 872 n.
  *wrong* 914 n.
  *calumny* 926 n.
  *false charge* 928 n.
  *wickedness* 934 n.
**scandalize, scandalise**
  *displease* 827 vb.
  *cause dislike* 861 vb.
  *shame* 867 vb.
  *incur blame* 924 vb.
**scandalized, scan-
    dalised**
  *wondering* 864 adj.
  *disapproving* 924 adj.
**scandalizing, scan-
    dalising**
  *unusual* 84 adj.
  *heinous* 934 adj.
**scandalmonger**
  *news reporter* 529 n.
  *defamer* 926 n.
**scandalous**
  *vulgar* 847 adj.
  See also **scandal**
**scanner**
  *computing* 86 n.
  *hospital* 658 n.
**scanning**
  *photography* 551 n.
  *diagnosis* 658 n.
**scansion**
  *prosody* 593 n.
**scant**
  *incomplete* 55 adj.
  *few* 105 adj.
  *exiguous* 196 adj.
  *insufficient* 636 adj.
  *restrained* 747 adj.
**scantling**
  *size* 195 n.
**scanty**
  *small* 33 adj.
  *few* 105 adj.
  *exiguous* 196 adj.
  *short* 204 adj.
  *insufficient* 636 adj.
**scapegoat**
  *substitute* 150 n.
  *unlucky person* 731 n.
  *deputy* 755 n.
  *sufferer* 825 n.
  *propitiation* 941 n.
  *oblation* 981 n.

**scapegrace**
  *revolter* 738 n.
  *desperado* 857 n.
  *bad person* 938 n.
**scapular**
  *canonicals* 989 n.
**scar**
  *high land* 209 n.
  *rock* 344 n.
  *identification* 547 n.
  *mark* 547 vb.
  *trace* 548 n.
  *wound* 655 n.
  *blemish* 845 n., vb.
**scarab**
  *talisman* 983 n.
**scarce**
  *few* 105 adj.
  *infrequent* 140 adj.
  *unproductive* 172 adj.
  *deficient* 307 adj.
  *scarce* 636 adj.
  *of price* 811 adj.
**scarcely**
  *slightly* 33 adv.
  *seldom* 140 adv.
**scarcity**
  *fewness* 105 n.
  *absence* 190 n.
  *scarcity* 636 n.
  *poverty* 801 n.
  See also **scarce**
**scare**
  *false alarm* 665 n.
  *fear* 854 n.
  *frighten* 854 vb.
**scarecrow**
  *thinness* 206 n.
  *sham* 542 n.
  *image* 551 n.
  *eyesore* 842 n.
  *intimidation* 854 n.
**scaremonger**
  *false alarm* 665 n.
  *alarmist* 854 n.
**scarf**
  *wrapping* 226 n.
  *neckwear* 228 n.
  *warm clothes* 381 n.
**scarify**
  *cut* 46 vb.
  *notch* 260 vb.
  *wound* 655 vb.
**scarlet**
  *redness* 431 n.
  *heinous* 934 adj.
**scarlet fever**
  *infection* 651 n.
**scarlet woman**
  *loose woman* 952 n.
**scarp**
  *verticality* 215 n.
  *incline* 220 n.
  *fortification* 713 n.
**scarper**
  *fail in duty* 918 vb.
**scarred**

*marked* 547 adj.
  *blemished* 845 adj.
**scathe**
  *harm* 645 vb.
  *impair* 655 vb.
**scatheless**
  *undamaged* 646 adj.
**scathing**
  *paining* 827 adj.
**scatological**
  *unclean* 649 adj.
  *impure* 951 adj.
**scat singing**
  *vocal music* 412 n.
**scatter**
  *disunite* 46 vb.
  *be disordered* 61 vb.
  *jumble* 63 vb.
  *dispersion* 75 n.
  *be dispersed* 75 vb.
  *destroy* 165 vb.
  *displace* 188 vb.
  *diverge* 294 vb.
  *let fall* 311 vb.
  *disappear* 446 vb.
  *waste* 634 vb.
  *defeat* 727 vb.
**scatterbrain**
  *inattention* 456 n.
  *fool* 501 n.
**scatterbrained**
  *disorderly* 61 adj.
  *light-minded* 456 adj.
  *foolish* 499 adj.
**scatter diagram**
  *statistics* 86 n.
**scattered**
  *few* 105 adj.
**scattering**
  *noncoherence* 49 n.
  *disorder* 61 n.
  *dispersion* 75 n.
**scatty**
  *light-minded* 456 adj.
  *foolish* 499 adj.
  *crazy* 503 adj.
**scavenger**
  *cleaner* 648 n.
  *dirty person* 649 n.
**scenario**
  *cinema* 445 n.
  *reading matter* 589 n.
  *narrative* 590 n.
  *stage play* 594 n.
  *policy* 623 n.
**scenario writer**
  *dramatist* 594 n.
**scene**
  *situation* 186 n.
  *surroundings* 230 n.
  *view* 438 n.
  *visibility* 443 n.
  *spectacle* 445 n.
  *exhibit* 522 n.
  *art subject* 553 n.
  *dramaturgy* 594 n.
  *stage set* 594 n.

**scrutator**
 *spectator* 441 n.
**scrutineer**
 *enquirer* 459 n.
**scrutinize, scrutinise**
 *scan* 438 vb.
**scrutiny**
 *attention* 455 n.
 *enquiry* 459 n.
**scuba diver**
 *diver* 313 n.
**scud**
 *navigate* 269 vb.
 *move fast* 277 vb.
 *cloud* 355 n.
**scuff**
 *move slowly* 278 vb.
 *rub* 333 vb.
**scuffle**
 *fight* 716 n.
**scuffmark**
 *trace* 548 n.
**scull**
 *propeller* 269 n.
 *row* 269 vb.
**sculler**
 *boatman* 270 n.
**scullery**
 *room* 194 n.
**scullion**
 *cleaner* 648 n.
 *domestic* 742 n.
**sculp**
 *sculpt* 554 vb.
**sculpt**
 *form* 243 vb.
 *sculpt* 554 vb.
**sculptor, sculptress**
 *producer* 164 n.
 *sculptor* 556 n.
**sculpture**
 *art* 551 n.
 *sculpture* 554 n.
 *sculpt* 554 vb.
**scum**
 *leavings* 41 n.
 *layer* 207 n.
 *bubble* 355 n.
 *rubbish* 641 n.
 *dirt* 649 n.
 *rabble* 869 n.
 *bad person* 938 n.
**scumble**
 *coat* 226 vb.
 *make opaque* 423 vb.
 *paint* 553 vb.
**scupper**
 *suppress* 165 vb.
 *drain* 351 n.
 *slaughter* 362 vb.
**scurf**
 *powder* 332 n.
 *dirt* 649 n.
**scurrility**
 *scurrility* 899 n.
**scurrilous**
 *insolent* 878 adj.

 *cursing* 899 adj.
 *disrespectful* 921 adj.
 *detracting* 926 adj.
**scurry**
 *move fast* 277 vb.
 *be busy* 678 vb.
 *hasten* 680 vb.
**scurvy**
 *disease* 651 n.
 *rascally* 930 adj.
**scut**
 *rear* 238 n.
**scutage**
 *tax* 809 n.
**scuttle**
 *suppress* 165 vb.
 *vessel* 194 n.
 *pierce* 263 vb.
 *move fast* 277 vb.
 *decamp* 296 vb.
 *plunge* 313 vb.
 *run away* 620 vb.
 *be cowardly* 856 vb.
 *fail in duty* 918 vb.
**scutum**
 *armour* 713 n.
**Scylla and Charybdis**
 *danger* 661 n.
**scyphate**
 *concave* 255 adj.
**scythe**
 *cut* 46 vb.
 *sharp edge* 256 n.
 *farm tool* 370 n.
**SDI**
 *rocket* 276 n.
 *safeguard* 662 n.
 *arms* 723 n.
**sea**
 *great quantity* 32 n.
 *ocean* 343 n.
 *wave* 350 n.
**sea, fear of**
 *phobia* 854 n. box
**sea air**
 *air* 340 n.
 *salubrity* 652 n.
**seaboard**
 *shore* 344 n.
**seaborne**
 *seafaring* 269 adj.
**sea breeze**
 *alcoholic drink* 301 n.
 *breeze* 352 n.
**sea change**
 *change* 143 n.
 *revolution* 149 n.
**sea dog**
 *mariner* 270 n.
 *expert* 696 n.
**seafarer**
 *mariner* 270 n.
**seafaring**
 *water travel* 269 n.
 *seafaring* 269 adj.
 *marine* 275 adj.
**seafood**

 *fish food* 301 n.
**sea front**
 *path* 624 n.
**sea-girt**
 *insular* 349 adj.
**sea god**
 *sea god* 343 n.
 *mythic deity* 966 n.
**sea-going**
 *seafaring* 269 adj.
**sea-green**
 *green* 434 adj.
**sea horse**
 *fish* 365 n.
**sea king**
 *mariner* 270 n.
**seal**
 *mould* 23 n.
 *close* 264 vb.
 *mammal* 365 n.
 *credential* 466 n.
 *make certain* 473 vb.
 *endorse* 488 vb.
 *label* 547 n.
 *repair* 656 vb.
 *carry through* 725 vb.
 *badge of rule* 743 n.
 *compact* 765 n.
 *give security* 767 vb.
 – up
 *join* 45 vb.
 *conceal* 525 vb.
 *imprison* 747 vb.
 See also **seals**
**sea lane**
 *water travel* 269 n.
 *route* 624 n.
**sea lawyer**
 *reasoner* 475 n.
**sealed book**
 *unknown thing* 491 n.
 *unintelligibility* 517 n.
 *secret* 530 n.
**sealed lips**
 *latency* 523 n.
**sealed off**
 *sealed off* 264 adj.
**sealed orders**
 *secret* 530 n.
**sea legs**
 *equilibrium* 28 n.
 *navigation* 269 n.
**sea level**
 *lowness* 210 n.
 *horizontality* 216 n.
**sea line**
 *limit* 236 n.
**sealing wax**
 *adhesive* 47 n.
**sea lion**
 *mammal* 365 n.
**sea loch**
 *gulf* 345 n.
**seal of approval**
 *approbation* 923 n.
**Sea Lord**
 *naval officer* 741 n.

**seals, group of**
 *group* 74 n. box
**sealskin**
 *skin* 226 n.
**seam**
 *joint* 45 n.
 *dividing line* 92 n.
 *gap* 201 n.
 *layer* 207 n.
 *store* 632 n.
**seaman**
 *mariner* 270 n.
**seamanlike**
 *seamanlike* 270 adj.
**seamanship**
 *navigation* 269 n.
 *skill* 694 n.
 *art of war* 718 n.
**sea mark**
 *sailing aid* 269 n.
 *signpost* 547 n.
**seamless**
 *whole* 52 adj.
**seamstress**
 *clothier* 228 n.
**séance**
 *manifestation* 522 n.
 *spiritualism* 984 n.
**sea nymph**
 *sea nymph* 343 n.
 *mythical being* 970 n.
**sea of, a**
 *multitude* 104 n.
**sea of faces**
 *onlookers* 441 n.
**sea of troubles**
 *adversity* 731 n.
**seaplane**
 *aircraft* 276 n.
**sea power**
 *navy* 722 n.
 *authority* 733 n.
**sear**
 *dry* 342 vb.
 *heat* 381 vb.
 *make insensitive* 820 vb.
**search**
 *be curious* 453 vb.
 *search* 459 n., vb.
 *pursuit* 619 n.
 *undertaking* 672 n.
**search engine**
 *Internet* 531 n.
**searcher**
 *inquisitive person* 453 n.
 *enquirer* 459 n.
 *hunter* 619 n.
 *trier* 671 n.
**searching**
 *inquisitive* 453 adj.
 *oppressive* 735 adj.
 *paining* 827 adj.
**searchlight**
 *flash* 417 n.
 *lamp* 420 n.
**search party**
 *search* 459 n.

secluded 883 adj.
**sequestrate**
  deprive 786 vb.
**sequestration**
  expropriation 786 n.
  seclusion 883 n.
  penalty 963 n.
**sequin**
  circle 250 n.
  finery 844 n.
**sequoia**
  tall creature 209 n.
**seraglio**
  womankind 373 n.
**seraph**
  good person 937 n.
  angel 968 n.
**seraphic**
  virtuous 933 adj.
  angelic 968 adj.
  pietistic 979 adj.
**Serapis**
  Egyptian deities 967 n.
**sere**
  continuity 71 n.
**sere, sear**
  dry 342 adj.
  deteriorated 655 adj.
**serenade**
  musical piece 412 n.
  sing 412 vb.
  wooing 889 n.
**serenader**
  vocalist 413 n.
**serendipitous**
  casual 159 adj.
**serendipity**
  chance 159 n.
  discovery 484 n.
**serene**
  tranquil 266 adj.
  transparent 422 adj.
  inexcitable 823 adj.
**Serene Highness**
  title 870 n.
**serenity**
  inexcitability 823 n.
  content 828 n.
  lack of wonder 865 n.
**serf**
  farmer 370 n.
  slave 742 n.
  possessor 776 n.
  commoner 869 n.
**serfdom**
  servitude 745 n.
**serge**
  textile 222 n.
**sergeant**
  soldiery 722 n.
  army officer 741 n.
**sergeant major**
  uniformist 16 n.
  tyrant 735 n.
  army officer 741 n.
**serial**
  relative 9 adj.

continuous 71 adj.
  recurrence 106 n.
  periodical 141 adj.
  reading matter 589 n.
  narrative 590 n.
**serialization,
  serialisation**
  sequence 65 n.
  continuity 71 n.
  periodicity 141 n.
**serialize, serialise**
  publish 528 vb.
**serial killing**
  recurrence 106 n.
  killing 362 n.
**serial monogamy**
  recurrence 106 n.
  type of marriage 894 n.
**serial place**
  degree 27 n.
  serial place 73 n.
**seriatim**
  in order 60 adv.
  severally 80 adv.
**sericulture**
  animal husbandry 369 n.
**series**
  all 52 n.
  order 60 n.
  sequence 65 n.
  series 71 n.
  accumulation 74 n.
  number 85 n.
  recurrence 106 n.
  continuance 146 n.
  following 284 n.
  broadcast 531 n.
  edition 589 n.
**serif**
  print-type 587 n.
**serigraphy**
  printing 555 n.
**seriocomic**
  funny 849 adj.
**serious**
  great 32 adj.
  attentive 455 adj.
  wise 498 adj.
  resolute 599 adj.
  intending 617 adj.
  important 638 adj.
  dangerous 661 adj.
  serious 834 adj.
  dull 840 adj.
  heinous 934 adj.
**seriously**
  painfully 32 adv.
  positively 32 adv.
  affirmatively 532 adv.
  resolutely 599 adv.
**seriousness**
  vigour 571 n.
  warm feeling 818 n.
  seriousness 834 n.
  See also **serious**
**serjeant-at-law**
  lawyer 958 n.

**sermon**
  lecture 534 n.
  diffuseness 570 n.
  oration 579 n.
  dissertation 591 n.
**sermonize, sermonise**
  orate 579 vb.
  be pious 979 vb.
**serotonin**
  organism 358 n.
**serpent**
  serpent 251 n.
  reptile 365 n.
  sibilation 406 n.
  horn 414 n.
  deceiver 545 n.
  bane 659 n.
  slyboots 698 n.
  noxious animal 904 n.
  knave 938 n.
  Satan 969 n.
**serpentine**
  snaky 251 adj.
  animal 365 adj.
  cunning 698 adj.
**serrated**
  angular 247 adj.
  sharp 256 adj.
  toothed 256 adj.
**serration**
  sharpness 256 n.
  roughness 259 n.
  notch 260 n.
**serried**
  cohesive 48 adj.
  assembled 74 adj.
  dense 324 adj.
**serulate**
  notched 260 adj.
**serum**
  blood 335 n.
  fluid 335 n.
**servant**
  instrument 628 n.
  worker 686 n.
  auxiliary 707 n.
  servant 742 n.
**serve**
  be inferior 35 vb.
  have sexual intercourse
    with 45 vb.
  operate 173 vb.
  follow 284 vb.
  propel 287 vb.
  look after 457 vb.
  benefit 615 vb.
  function 622 vb.
  be instrumental 628 vb.
  suffice 635 vb.
  be useful 640 vb.
  be expedient 642 vb.
  work 692 vb.
  minister to 703 vb.
  obey 739 vb.
  serve 742 vb.
  be subject 745 vb.
  apportion 783 vb.

– one right
  be rightly served 714 vb.
  be just 913 vb.
– one's turn
  be useful 640 vb.
– up
  provide 633 vb.
**server**
  auxiliary 707 n.
  church officer 986 n.
  ritualist 988 n.
**service**
  agency 173 n.
  benefit 615 n.
  job 622 n.
  instrumentality 628 n.
  provision 633 n.
  utility 640 n.
  restore 656 vb.
  repair 656 vb.
  preserve 666 vb.
  use 673 n.
  aid 703 n.
  loyalty 739 n.
  service 745 n.
  sale 793 n.
  kind act 897 n.
  cult 961 n.
  church service 988 n.
**serviceable**
  operative 173 adj.
  instrumental 628 adj.
  useful 640 adj.
**service book**
  office-book 988 n.
**service charge**
  price 809 n.
**serviceman, ser-
  vicewoman**
  soldier 722 n.
**services, the**
  army 722 n.
**servile**
  conformable 83 adj.
  subject 745 adj.
  inglorious 867 adj.
  humble 872 adj.
  servile 879 adj.
  respectful 920 adj.
  flattering 925 adj.
**servility**
  servility 879 n.
**serving**
  meal 301 n.
**serving a sentence**
  imprisoned 747 adj.
**servitor**
  domestic 742 n.
**servitude**
  submission 721 n.
  servitude 745 n.
**servomechanism**
  machine 630 n.
**servomotor**
  machine 630 n.
**sesquicentenary**
  fifth and over 99 adj.

shortness 204 n.
shortfall 307 n.
requirement 627 n.
insufficiency 636 n.
**slipped disc**
rheumatism 651 n.
**slipper(s)**
footwear 228 n.
informal dress 228 n.
spank 963 vb.
**slippered**
comfortable 376 adj.
reposeful 683 adj.
**slipperiness**
changeableness 152 n.
unreliability 474 n.
**slippery**
nonadhesive 49 adj.
smooth 258 adj.
unctuous 357 adj.
deceiving 542 adj.
tergiversating 603 adj.
avoiding 620 adj.
unsafe 661 adj.
escaped 667 adj.
cunning 698 adj.
dishonest 930 adj.
**slippery slope**
ruin 165 n.
danger 661 n.
wickedness 934 n.
**slips**
workshop 687 n.
**slipshod**
orderless 61 adj.
negligent 458 adj.
feeble 572 adj.
lax 734 adj.
**slip stream**
wind 352 n.
**slip-up**
mistake 495 n.
**slipway**
smoothness 258 n.
**slit**
rend 46 vb.
sunder 46 vb.
gap 201 n.
furrow 262 n.
wound 655 vb.
**slither**
be in motion 265 vb.
**slithery**
smooth 258 adj.
**sliver**
small thing 33 n.
piece 53 n.
**slivovitz**
alcoholic drink 301 n.
**Sloane Ranger**
idler 679 n.
beau monde 848 n.
**slob**
bungler 697 n.
cad 938 n.
**slobber**
exude 298 vb.

emit 300 vb.
excrement 302 n.
moisture 341 n.
make unclean 649 vb.
**sloe**
sourness 393 n.
black thing 428 n.
**slog**
strike 279 vb.
propel 287 vb.
be busy 678 vb.
work 682 vb.
– away
persevere 600 vb.
– on
progress 286 vb.
**slogan**
maxim 496 n.
advertisement 528 n.
call 547 n.
warfare 718 n.
**slogger**
busy person 678 n.
pugilist 722 n.
**sloop**
sailing ship 275 n.
**slop**
let fall 311 vb.
moisten 341 vb.
waste 634 vb.
be clumsy 695 vb.
– about
fluctuate 317 vb.
– over
be complete 54 vb.
flow out 298 vb.
**slope**
high land 209 n.
be oblique 220 vb.
ascent 308 n.
descent 309 n.
– off
travel 267 vb.
decamp 296 vb.
run away 620 vb.
**sloping**
sloping 220 adj.
written 586 adj.
**sloppiness**
inexactness 495 n.
**sloppy**
orderless 61 adj.
semiliquid 354 adj.
tasteless 387 adj.
negligent 458 adj.
feeble 572 adj.
feeling 818 adj.
**sloppy joe**
jersey 228 n.
**sloppy thinking**
sophism 477 n.
**slops**
weak thing 163 n.
clothing 228 n.
insipidity 387 n.
swill 649 n.
**slosh**

strike 279 vb.
drench 341 vb.
flow 350 vb.
– about
fluctuate 317 vb.
**sloshed**
tipsy 949 adj.
**slot**
sorting 62 n.
serial place 73 n.
classification 77 n.
place 185 n.
receptacle 194 n.
gap 201 n.
furrow 262 n.
orifice 263 n.
trace 548 n.
**sloth**
inertness 175 n.
sluggishness 679 n.
vice 934 n.
**slothful**
lazy 679 adj.
**slot in**
place 187 vb.
**slot machine**
shop 796 n.
treasury 799 n.
**slouch**
be low 210 vb.
slowcoach 278 n.
move slowly 278 vb.
stoop 311 vb.
be inactive 679 vb.
**sloucher**
slowcoach 278 n.
slacker 598 n.
avoider 620 n.
idler 679 n.
**slouching**
graceless 842 adj.
**slough**
leavings 41 n.
doff 229 vb.
marsh 347 n.
disaccustom 611 vb.
**Slough of Despond**
adversity 731 n.
dejection 834 n.
**sloven**
slut 61 n.
dirty person 649 n.
**slovenly**
orderless 61 adj.
negligent 458 adj.
feeble 572 adj.
dirty 649 adj.
**slow**
protracted 113 adj.
anachronistic 118 adj.
late 136 adj.
inert 175 adj.
slow 278 adj.
inexact 495 adj.
unintelligent 499 adj.
unwilling 598 adj.
lazy 679 adj.

leisurely 681 adj.
inexcitable 823 adj.
tedious 838 adj.
dull 840 adj.
cautious 858 adj.
– down
come to rest 266 vb.
decelerate 278 vb.
be inactive 679 vb.
repose 683 vb.
hinder 702 vb.
– up
decelerate 278 vb.
**slowcoach**
slowcoach 278 n.
idler 679 n.
**slow-down**
strike 145 n.
slowness 278 n.
**slow handclap**
disapprobation 924 n.
**slowly but surely**
by degrees 27 adv.
**slowness**
slowness 278 n.
See also **slow**
**slow-witted**
unintelligent 499 adj.
**slowworm**
reptile 365 n.
**slub**
weave 222 vb.
**slubbed**
rough 259 adj.
**slubberdegullion**
idler 679 n.
bad person 938 n.
**sludge**
leavings 41 n.
semiliquidity 354 n.
dirt 649 n.
**slug**
strike 279 vb.
draught 301 n.
creepy-crawly 365 n.
print-type 587 n.
ammunition 723 n.
**sluggard**
slowcoach 278 n.
idler 679 n.
**sluggish**
inert 175 adj.
slow 278 adj.
flowing 350 adj.
nonactive 677 adj.
inactive 679 adj.
apathetic 820 adj.
dull 840 adj.
**sluice**
outlet 298 n.
irrigator 341 n.
drench 341 vb.
waterfall 350 n.
conduit 351 n.
clean 648 vb.
**slum**
housing 192 n.

*lose control* 746 vb.
**speak**
  *communicate* 524 vb.
  *inform* 524 vb.
  *divulge* 526 vb.
  *signal* 547 vb.
  *voice* 577 vb.
  *speak* 579 vb.
 – for
  *deputize* 755 vb.
 – for itself
  *be visible* 443 vb.
  *evidence* 466 vb.
  *be intelligible* 516 vb.
  *be plain* 522 vb.
 – one's mind
  *be truthful* 540 vb.
  *speak* 579 vb.
  *be artless* 699 vb.
  *be courageous* 855 vb.
 – out
  *be plain* 522 vb.
  *affirm* 532 vb.
  *be courageous* 855 vb.
 – plainly
  *speak plainly* 573 vb.
 – to
  *testify* 466 vb.
  *speak to* 583 vb.
 – up
  *be loud* 400 vb.
  *emphasize* 532 vb.
  *be courageous* 855 vb.
 – up for
  *approve* 923 vb.
  *vindicate* 927 vb.
 – volumes
  *evidence* 466 vb.
  *mean* 514 vb.
**speakeasy**
  *pub* 192 n.
**speaker**
  *megaphone* 400 n.
  *record player* 416 n.
  *speaker* 579 n.
  *director* 690 n.
**speaking clock**
  *timekeeper* 117 n.
**speaking of**
  *concerning* 9 adv.
**speaking part**
  *acting* 594 n.
**speaking tube**
  *hearing instrument*
   415 n.
**spear**
  *sharp point* 256 n.
  *pierce* 263 vb.
  *spear* 723 n.
**spearhead**
  *front* 237 n.
  *precede* 283 vb.
  *chief thing* 638 n.
  *leader* 690 n.
  *attacker* 712 n.
**spear side**
  *race* 11 n.

*male* 372 n.
**special**
  *characteristic* 5 adj.
  *different* 21 adj.
  *special* 80 adj.
  *original* 80 adj.
  *unconformable* 84 adj.
  *chosen* 605 adj.
**special case**
  *variant* 15 n.
  *nonuniformity* 17 n.
  *speciality* 80 n.
**special constable**
  *police* 955 n.
**special correspondent**
  *informant* 524 n.
  *author* 589 n.
  *delegate* 754 n.
**special day**
  *anniversary* 141 n.
  *festivity* 837 n.
  *special day* 876 n.
**specialism**
  *knowledge* 490 n.
  *skill* 694 n.
**specialist**
  *scholar* 492 n.
  *student* 538 n.
  *doctor* 658 n.
  *expert* 696 n.
**speciality**
  *unrelatedness* 10 n.
  *speciality* 80 n.
  *tendency* 179 n.
  *dish* 301 n.
  *qualification* 468 n.
  *See also* **special**
**specialize, specialise**
  *study* 536 vb.
**specialized,**
  **specialised**
  *instructed* 490 adj.
  *expert* 694 adj.
**specially**
  *greatly* 32 adv.
  *specially* 80 adv.
**special messenger**
  *bearer* 273 n.
  *delegate* 754 n.
**special needs**
  *learning disability* 503 n.
**special offer**
  *incentive* 612 n.
  *discount* 810 n.
**special pleading**
  *argument* 475 n.
  *sophistry* 477 n.
  *pretext* 614 n.
**specialty**
  *speciality* 80 n.
**specie**
  *coinage* 797 n.
**species**
  *subdivision* 53 n.
  *group* 74 n.
  *breed* 77 n.
**specific**

*special* 80 adj.
  *means* 629 n.
  *remedy* 658 n.
**specifically**
  *positively* 32 adv.
  *specially* 80 adv.
**specification**
  *classification* 77 n.
  *particulars* 80 n.
  *report* 524 n.
  *description* 590 n.
  *See also* **specify**
**specific gravity**
  *gravity* 322 n.
  *density* 324 n.
**specify**
  *class* 62 vb.
  *specify* 80 vb.
  *indicate* 547 vb.
  *name* 561 vb.
**specimen**
  *duplicate* 22 n.
  *prototype* 23 n.
  *example* 83 n.
  *exhibit* 522 n.
**specious**
  *appearing* 445 adj.
  *plausible* 471 adj.
  *sophistical* 477 adj.
  *ostensible* 614 adj.
  *splendid* 841 adj.
  *affected* 850 adj.
  *ostentatious* 875 adj.
  *flattering* 925 adj.
**speck**
  *small thing* 33 n.
  *mottling* 437 n.
  *blemish* 845 n.
**speckle**
  *mottling* 437 n.
  *variegate* 437 vb.
**speckled**
  *mottled* 437 adj.
**speckless**
  *clean* 648 adj.
**spectacle**
  *spectacle* 445 n.
  *exhibit* 522 n.
  *stage show* 594 n.
  *beauty* 841 n.
  *prodigy* 864 n.
  *pageant* 875 n.
**spectacles**
  *eyeglass* 442 n.
**spectacular**
  *obvious* 443 adj.
  *appearing* 445 adj.
  *showy* 875 adj.
**spectate**
  *watch* 441 vb.
**spectator**
  *presence* 189 n.
  *spectator* 441 n.
  *witness* 466 n.
**spectral**
  *insubstantial* 4 adj.
  *variegated* 437 adj.

*spooky* 970 adj.
**spectre**
  *insubstantial thing* 4 n.
  *visual fallacy* 440 n.
  *appearance* 445 n.
  *intimidation* 854 n.
  *ghost* 970 n.
**spectre at the feast,**
  **be the**
  *hinder* 702 vb.
**spectrogram**
  *photography* 551 n.
**spectrohelioscope**
  *astronomy* 321 n.
**spectroscope**
  *astronomy* 321 n.
  *chromatics* 425 n.
  *optical device* 442 n.
**spectroscopy**
  *optics* 417 n.
**spectrum**
  *series* 71 n.
  *light* 417 n.
  *colour* 425 n.
  *variegation* 437 n.
**spectrum analysis**
  *chromatics* 425 n.
**speculate**
  *meditate* 449 vb.
  *suppose* 512 vb.
  *speculate* 791 vb.
**speculation**
  *calculation of chance*
   159 n.
  *meditation* 449 n.
  *empiricism* 461 n.
  *conjecture* 512 n.
  *gambling* 618 n.
  *attempt* 671 n.
  *undertaking* 672 n.
  *trade* 791 n.
  *card game* 837 n.
**speculative**
  *uncertain* 474 adj.
  *speculative* 618 adj.
  *dangerous* 661 adj.
  *rash* 857 adj.
**speculator**
  *experimenter* 461 n.
  *theorist* 512 n.
  *gambler* 618 n.
**speculum**
  *mirror* 442 n.
**speech**
  *language* 557 n.
  *diffuseness* 570 n.
  *voice* 577 n.
  *oration* 579 n.
  *speech* 579 n.
  *allocution* 583 n.
**speech defect**
  *speech defect* 580 n.
**speechify**
  *orate* 579 vb.
**speech impediment**
  *speech defect* 580 n.
**speechless**

*land travel* 267 n.
*aeronautics* 271 n.
*rotation* 315 n.
*rotate* 315 vb.
*mislead* 495 vb.
*misteaching* 535 n.
*falsehood* 541 n.
*fake* 541 vb.
– a yarn
*be untrue* 543 vb.
*exaggerate* 546 vb.
*describe* 590 vb.
– out
*continue* 71 vb.
*spin out* 113 vb.
*lengthen* 203 vb.
*be diffuse* 570 vb.
*be loquacious* 581 vb.
*be obstructive* 702 vb.
– the wheel
*modify* 143 vb.
*gamble* 618 vb.
– words
*show style* 566 vb.
**spina bifida**
*nervous disorders* 651 n.
**spinach**
*vegetable* 301 n.
**spinach beet**
*vegetable* 301 n.
**spinal**
*supporting* 218 adj.
*central* 225 adj.
*back* 238 adj.
**spinal cord, inflam-
   mation of**
*inflammation* 651 n.
   box
**spindle**
*pivot* 218 n.
*rotator* 315 n.
*tree* 366 n.
**spindle-shaped**
*tapering* 256 adj.
**spindly**
*lean* 206 adj.
*legged* 267 adj.
**spin-doctor**
*interpreter* 520 n.
*interpret* 520 vb.
**spindrift**
*moisture* 341 n.
*bubble* 355 n.
**spin-dry**
*dry* 342 vb.
**spine**
*pillar* 218 n.
*centre* 225 n.
*rear* 238 n.
*prickle* 256 n.
*bookbinding* 589 n.
**spine-chilling**
*exciting* 821 adj.
**spineless**
*impotent* 161 adj.
*weak* 163 adj.
*irresolute* 601 adj.

**spinet**
*piano* 414 n.
**spinnaker**
*sail* 275 n.
**spinner**
*weaving* 222 n.
*planner* 623 n.
**spinney**
*wood* 366 n.
**spinning wheel**
*weaving* 222 n.
*rotator* 315 n.
**spin-off**
*sequel* 67 n.
*effect* 157 n.
**spin of the coin**
*equal chance* 159 n.
**Spinozism**
*philosophy* 449 n.
**spinster**
*woman* 373 n.
*spinster* 895 n.
**spiny**
*sharp* 256 adj.
**spiracle**
*orifice* 263 n.
*outlet* 298 n.
*air pipe* 353 n.
**spiral**
*increase* 36 n.
*coil* 251 n.
*twine* 251 vb.
*fly* 271 vb.
*ascend* 308 vb.
*tumble* 309 vb.
*rotation* 315 n.
**spiral staircase**
*ascent* 308 n.
**spirant**
*speech sound* 398 n.
*spoken letter* 558 n.
**spire**
*high structure* 209 n.
*vertex* 213 n.
*ascend* 308 vb.
*church exterior* 990 n.
**spired**
*tapering* 256 adj.
**spirit**
*insubstantial thing* 4 n.
*essential part* 5 n.
*temperament* 5 n.
*self* 80 n.
*vigorousness* 174 n.
*subjectivity* 320 n.
*life* 360 n.
*fuel* 385 n.
*spirit* 447 n.
*meaning* 514 n.
*vigour* 571 n.
*resolution* 599 n.
*restlessness* 678 n.
*affections* 817 n.
*moral sensibility* 819 n.
*courage* 855 n.
*ghost* 970 n.
– away

*steal* 788 vb.
**Spirit, the**
*Holy Ghost* 965 n.
**spirit duplicator**
*imitator* 20 n.
**spirited**
*forceful* 571 adj.
*active* 678 adj.
*lively* 819 adj.
*cheerful* 833 adj.
*courageous* 855 adj.
**spiritless**
*apathetic* 820 adj.
*inexcitable* 823 adj.
*dejected* 834 adj.
*cowardly* 856 adj.
**spirit level**
*horizontality* 216 n.
**spirit message**
*spiritualism* 984 n.
**spirit of place**
*locality* 187 n.
**spirit of the age**
*tendency* 179 n.
**spirit-rapping**
*spiritualism* 984 n.
**spirits**
*state* 7 n.
*alcoholic drink* 301 n.
*tonic* 658 n.
*cheerfulness* 833 n.
**spirits, the**
*the dead* 361 n.
**spiritual**
*immaterial* 320 adj.
*vocal music* 412 n.
*psychic* 447 adj.
*divine* 965 adj.
*religious* 973 adj.
*pious* 979 adj.
*priestly* 985 adj.
**spiritual adviser**
*pastor* 986 n.
**spiritualism**
*occultism* 984 n.
*spiritualism* 984 n.
**spiritualist**
*occultist* 984 n.
**spiritualistic**
*psychic* 447 adj.
*spooky* 970 adj.
*psychical* 984 adj.
**spirituality**
*immateriality* 320 n.
*virtue* 933 n.
*sanctity* 979 n.
**spiritualize, spiri-
   tualise**
*disembody* 320 vb.
*make pious* 979 vb.
*sanctify* 979 vb.
**spirituel(le)**
*lively* 819 adj.
*witty* 839 adj.
**spirituous**
*edible* 301 adj.
*intoxicating* 949 adj.

**spiry**
*high* 209 adj.
*tapering* 256 adj.
**spit**
*projection* 254 n.
*sharp point* 256 n.
*perforator* 263 n.
*pierce* 263 vb.
*belch* 300 vb.
*excrement* 302 n.
*rotator* 315 n.
*effervesce* 318 vb.
*rain* 350 vb.
*hiss* 406 vb.
*be angry* 891 vb.
*be sullen* 893 vb.
*threaten* 900 vb.
*disapprove* 924 vb.
– at/on
*not respect* 921 vb.
– it out
*divulge* 526 vb.
– out
*eject* 300 vb.
**spit and polish**
*cleanness* 648 n.
*formality* 875 n.
**spit-and-sawdust bar**
*pub* 192 n.
**spite**
*ill-treat* 645 vb.
*quarrelsomeness* 709 n.
*severity* 735 n.
*oppress* 735 vb.
*enmity* 881 n.
*hatred* 888 n.
*resentment* 891 n.
*malevolence* 898 n.
*revengefulness* 910 n.
*envy* 912 n.
*detraction* 926 n.
**spiteful**
*malevolent* 898 adj.
*See also* **spite**
**spitfire**
*violent creature* 176 n.
*shrew* 892 n.
**spit-roast**
*cook* 301 vb.
**spitting image**
*identity* 13 n.
*analogue* 18 n.
*representation* 551 n.
*image* 551 n.
**spittle**
*excrement* 302 n.
*moisture* 341 n.
**spittoon**
*sink* 649 n.
**spiv**
*idler* 679 n.
**spivvish**
*rascally* 930 adj.
**splash**
*small quantity* 33 n.
*disperse* 75 vb.
*water* 339 n.

**stand**
*be* 1 vb.
*be in a state of* 7 vb.
*last* 113 vb.
*be pending* 136 vb.
*cease* 145 vb.
*be stable* 153 vb.
*be situated* 186 vb.
*place* 187 vb.
*be present* 189 vb.
*meeting place* 192 n.
*pavilion* 192 n.
*be vertical* 215 vb.
*stand* 218 n.
*support* 218 vb.
*be quiescent* 266 vb.
*view* 438 n.
*be proved* 478 vb.
*opinion* 485 n.
*be true* 494 vb.
*supposition* 512 n.
*suffice* 635 vb.
*opposition* 704 n.
*resistance* 715 n.
*battle* 718 n.
*arena* 724 n.
*offer oneself* 759 vb.
*give* 781 vb.
*shop* 796 n.
*expend* 806 vb.
*be patient* 823 vb.
*show respect* 920 vb.
– about
*wait* 136 vb.
– a chance
*be possible* 469 vb.
*be likely* 471 vb.
– against
*withstand* 704 vb.
– aside
*recede* 290 vb.
*be neutral* 606 vb.
*resign* 753 vb.
– by
*be present* 189 vb.
*await* 507 vb.
*prepare oneself* 669 vb.
*not act* 677 vb.
*aid* 703 vb.
*defend* 713 vb.
*keep faith* 768 vb.
– comparison
*be good* 644 vb.
– corrected
*incur blame* 924 vb.
– down
*resign* 753 vb.
– firm
*stand firm* 599 vb.
*persevere* 600 vb.
*withstand* 704 vb.
*resist* 715 vb.
*be courageous* 855 vb.
– for
*be* 1 vb.
*steer for* 281 vb.
*mean* 514 vb.

*indicate* 547 vb.
*represent* 551 vb.
*be patient* 823 vb.
– in for
*substitute* 150 vb.
*function* 622 vb.
*deputize* 755 vb.
– in one's light
*hinder* 702 vb.
– in the corner
*do penance* 941 vb.
– in the way
*obstruct* 702 vb.
– no nonsense
*be severe* 735 vb.
– off
*be distant* 199 vb.
*recede* 290 vb.
*make inactive* 679 vb.
*not retain* 779 vb.
– on ceremony
*be ostentatious* 875 vb.
*show respect* 920 vb.
– one in good stead
*be useful* 640 vb.
– one's ground
*stand firm* 599 vb.
*resist* 715 vb.
– on one's dignity
*be proud* 871 vb.
– on one's head
*be inverted* 221 vb.
– on one's own feet
*be free* 744 vb.
– on one's rights
*claim* 915 vb.
– out
*be contrary* 14 vb.
*be unlike* 19 vb.
*jut* 254 vb.
*be visible* 443 vb.
*be plain* 522 vb.
*be obstinate* 602 vb.
*not observe* 769 vb.
– out against
*resist* 715 vb.
– over
*be pending* 136 vb.
– pat
*stay* 144 vb.
*be quiescent* 266 vb.
– still
*stay* 144 vb.
*be quiescent* 266 vb.
– surety for
*safeguard* 660 vb.
*patronize* 703 vb.
*give security* 767 vb.
– the test
*be true* 494 vb.
*be good* 644 vb.
– to
*be quiescent* 266 vb.
*invigilate* 457 vb.
– together
*concur* 181 vb.
– to reason

*be certain* 473 vb.
*be reasonable* 475 vb.
*be proved* 478 vb.
*be plain* 522 vb.
– trial
*stand trial* 959 vb.
– up
*be vertical* 215 vb.
*lift oneself* 310 vb.
– up and be counted
*be courageous* 855 vb.
– up for
*safeguard* 660 vb.
*patronize* 703 vb.
*approve* 923 vb.
*vindicate* 927 vb.
– up for one's rights
*be free* 744 vb.
*claim* 915 vb.
– up in law
*be legal* 953 vb.
– up to
*support* 218 vb.
*suffice* 635 vb.
*withstand* 704 vb.
*defy* 711 vb.
– well with
*have a reputation*
866 vb.
**standard**
*uniform* 16 adj.
*prototype* 23 n.
*degree* 27 n.
*median* 30 adj.
*general* 79 adj.
*rule* 81 n.
*typical* 83 adj.
*high structure* 209 n.
*lamp* 420 n.
*testing agent* 461 n.
*gauge* 465 n.
*flag* 547 n.
*linguistic* 557 adj.
*paragon* 646 n.
*right* 913 adj.
**standard-bearer**
*soldier* 722 n.
**standard deviation**
*statistics* 86 n.
**Standard Grade**
*exam* 459 n.
**standardize, stan-
dardise**
*make uniform* 16 vb.
*regularize* 62 vb.
*make conform* 83 vb.
**standards**
*morals* 917 n.
**standby**
*means* 629 n.
*aider* 703 n.
*colleague* 707 n.
**stand-in**
*substitute* 150 n.
*actor* 594 n.
*deputy* 755 n.
**standing**

*existing* 1 adj.
*state* 7 n.
*circumstance* 8 n.
*degree* 27 n.
*serial place* 73 n.
*permanent* 144 adj.
*unceasing* 146 adj.
*fixed* 153 adj.
*vertical* 215 adj.
*prestige* 866 n.
**standing order**
*rule* 81 n.
*practice* 610 n.
*payment* 804 n.
*legislation* 953 n.
**standing ovation**
*victory* 727 n.
*trophy* 729 n.
*celebration* 876 n.
**standing rigging**
*tackling* 47 n.
**standing room**
*room* 183 n.
**standing room only**
*full* 54 adj.
**standing water**
*lake* 346 n.
**standoffish**
*unconformable* 84 adj.
*prideful* 871 adj.
*unsociable* 883 adj.
**standpipe**
*current* 350 n.
*conduit* 351 n.
**standpoint**
*situation* 186 n.
*view* 438 n.
*supposition* 512 n.
**standstill**
*lull* 145 n.
*stop* 145 n.
*quiescence* 266 n.
*deliverance* 668 n.
*difficulty* 700 n.
**Stanley (tdmk) knife**
*tool* 630 n.
**stannary**
*workshop* 687 n.
**stanza**
*verse form* 593 n.
**staple**
*fastening* 47 n.
*chief part* 52 n.
*fibre* 208 n.
*sharp point* 256 n.
*texture* 331 n.
*materials* 631 n.
*important* 638 adj.
*merchandise* 795 n.
**stapler**
*perforator* 263 n.
**star**
*supreme* 34 adj.
*divergence* 294 n.
*star* 321 n.
*luminary* 420 n.
*guide* 520 n.

be patient 823 vb.
liking 859 n.
be humble 872 vb.
forgive 909 vb.

**stomach, inflam-
    mation of**
inflammation 651 n.
box

**stomach ache**
pang 377 n.
digestive disorders 651 n.

**stomacher**
garment 228 n.

**stomach, removal of**
surgery 658 n. box

**stomata**
orifice 263 n.

**stomp**
dance 837 n., vb.

**stone**
architectural 192 adj.
uncover 229 vb.
strike 279 vb.
missile 287 n.
weighing 322 n.
solid body 324 n.
hardness 326 n.
rock 344 n.
kill 362 vb.
dunce 501 n.
sculpture 554 n.
engraving 555 n.
building material 631 n.
lapidate 712 vb.
missile weapon 723 n.
unfeeling person 820 n.
gem 844 n.
execute 963 vb.

**Stone Age**
era 110 n.
antiquity 125 n.

**stoned**
insensible 375 adj.
dead drunk 949 adj.
drugged 949 adj.

**stone's throw**
short distance 200 n.

**stonewall**
repel 292 vb.
be obstructive 702 vb.
parry 713 vb.

**stonewalling**
protraction 113 n.
delay 136 n.

**stoneware**
hardness 326 n.
pottery 381 n.

**stonework**
building 164 n.
structure 331 n.

**stonking**
huge 195 adj.

**stony**
unproductive 172 adj.
rough 259 adj.
hard 326 adj.
territorial 344 adj.

unfeeling 375 adj.
impassive 820 adj.

**stony-hearted**
cruel 898 adj.
pitiless 906 adj.

**stooge**
fool 501 n.
dupe 544 n.
instrument 628 n.
nonentity 639 n.
bungler 697 n.
auxiliary 707 n.
dependant 742 n.
humorist 839 n.
laughingstock 851 n.

**stooge for**
be servile 879 vb.

**stook**
bunch 74 n.

**stool**
seat 218 n.
excrement 302 n.

**stoolpigeon**
informer 524 n.
ambush 527 n.
trickster 545 n.

**stoop**
lobby 194 n.
be low 210 vb.
descend 309 vb.
stoop 311 vb.
plunge 313 vb.
obey 739 vb.
be humble 872 vb.
be servile 879 vb.
show respect 920 vb.
– to
demean oneself 867 vb.
be dishonest 930 vb.

**stop**
end 69 n., vb.
stop 145 n.
halt 145 vb.
come to rest 266 vb.
– 266 int.
arrive 295 vb.
speech sound 398 n.
silence 399 vb.
punctuation 547 n.
repair 656 vb.
doctor 658 vb.
inaction 677 n.
obstruct 702 vb.
restrain 747 vb.
prohibit 757 vb.
retention 778 n.
– a leak
staunch 350 vb.
– for breath
pause 145 vb.
– off
arrive 295 vb.
– one's ears
be deaf 416 vb.
be inattentive 456 vb.
be obstinate 602 vb.
– short

fall short 307 vb.
– up
obstruct 702 vb.
– using
reject 607 vb.
relinquish 621 vb.
stop using 674 vb.
make inactive 679 vb.
abrogate 752 vb.
not retain 779 vb.

**stopcock**
stopper 264 n.
tool 630 n.

**stopgap**
substitute 150 n.
preparatory 669 adj.

**stop-go**
discontinuous 72 adj.
fitful 142 adj.

**stopover**
itinerary 267 n.
goal 295 n.

**stoppage**
strike 145 n.
closure 264 n.
hitch 702 n.
nonpayment 805 n.

**stopper**
covering 226 n.
stopper 264 n.
retention 778 n.

**stopping**
discontinuous 72 adj.
vehicular 274 adj.

**stopping at nothing**
resolute 599 adj.

**stopping place**
stopping place 145 n.

**stop-press news**
news 529 n.

**stopwatch**
timekeeper 117 n.
recording instrument
    549 n.

**storage**
assemblage 74 n.
computing 86 n.
room 183 n.
storage 632 n.
preservation 666 n.

**storage battery**
electronics 160 n.

**store**
great quantity 32 n.
accumulation 74 n.
stow 187 vb.
store 632 n., vb.
provide 633 vb.
plenty 635 n.
preserve 666 vb.
make ready 669 vb.
not use 674 vb.
acquire 771 vb.
retain 778 vb.
shop 796 vb.
treasury 799 n.
wealth 800 n.

**store card**
credit 802 n.
payment 804 n.

**storehouse**
storage 632 n.

**storekeeper**
provider 633 n.
tradespeople 794 n.

**storeroom**
room 194 n.
storage 632 n.

**stores**
provisions 301 n.
provision 633 n.

**storey**
compartment 194 n.
layer 207 n.

**storied**
descriptive 590 adj.

**stork**
obstetrics 167 n.
bird 365 n.

**storm**
turmoil 61 n.
crowd 74 n.
havoc 165 n.
storm 176 n.
be violent 176 vb.
burst in 297 vb.
commotion 318 n.
rain 350 n.
gale 352 n.
be loud 400 vb.
attack 712 vb.
overmaster 727 vb.
take 786 vb.
be angry 891 vb.
– against
dispraise 924 vb.

**storm brewing**
danger 661 n.

**storm in a teacup**
overestimation 482 n.
exaggeration 546 n.
trifle 639 n.
quarrel 709 n.

**storm signal**
warning 664 n.

**storm-tossed**
rough 259 adj.

**storm troops**
attacker 712 n.
armed force 722 n.

**stormy**
violent 176 adj.
windy 352 adj.
excitable 822 adj.

**stormy exchange**
quarrel 709 n.
scurrility 899 n.

**stormy petrel**
bird 365 n.
warning 664 n.

**story**
ideality 513 n.
news 529 n.
fable 543 n.

**telecommuter**
*Internet* 531 n.
**teleconferencing**
*telecommunication*
531 n.
**telegony**
*heredity* 5 n.
*influence* 178 n.
**telegram**
*message* 529 n.
*telecommunication*
531 n.
**telegraph**
*velocity* 277 n.
*communicate* 524 vb.
*signal* 547 n.
**telegrapher**
*telecommunication*
531 n.
**telegraphese**
*neology* 560 n.
*conciseness* 569 n.
**telegraphic**
*speedy* 277 adj.
*concise* 569 adj.
**telegraphy**
*telecommunication*
531 n.
**telekinesis**
*spiritualism* 984 n.
**telemarketing**
*sale* 793 n.
**telematics**
*computing* 86 n.
*information* 524 n.
**telemedicine**
*medical art* 658 n.
**telemessage**
*information* 524 n.
*message* 529 n.
*telecommunication*
531 n.
**teleology**
*philosophy* 449 n.
*intention* 617 n.
**tele-ordering**
*purchase* 792 n.
*buying* 792 adj.
**telepath**
*psychic* 984 n.
**telepathic**
*intuitive* 476 adj.
*psychical* 984 adj.
**telepathy**
*thought* 449 n.
*intuition* 476 n.
*psychics* 984 n.
**telephone**
*hearing instrument*
415 n.
*communicate* 524 vb.
*telecommunication*
531 n.
**telephone directory**
*directory* 87 n.
*guidebook* 524 n.
**telephone receiver**

*reception* 299 n.
**telephonist**
*telecommunication*
531 n.
**telephotography**
*photography* 551 n.
**telephoto lens**
*optical device* 442 n.
**teleprinter**
*telecommunication*
531 n.
*recording instrument*
549 n.
**telerecord**
*record* 548 vb.
**telergy**
*psychics* 984 n.
**telescope**
*shorten* 204 vb.
*astronomy* 321 n.
*telescope* 442 n.
*be concise* 569 vb.
**telescopic**
*distant* 199 adj.
*astronomic* 321 adj.
*visible* 443 adj.
**teleshopping**
*purchase* 792 n.
**telesurgery**
*surgery* 658 n.
**teletext**
*computing* 86 n.
*broadcasting* 531 n.
**telethon**
*broadcast* 531 n.
**Teletubbies (tdmk)**
*plaything* 837 n.
**televiewer**
*spectator* 441 n.
**televise**
*show* 522 vb.
*communicate* 524 vb.
*publish* 528 vb.
**television**
*spectacle* 445 n.
*broadcasting* 531 n.
*stage play* 594 n.
*amusement* 837 n.
**teleworker**
*worker* 686 n.
**telex**
*information* 524 n.
*communicate* 524 vb.
*telecommunication*
531 n.
**tell**
*number* 86 vb.
*influence* 178 vb.
*earthwork* 253 n.
*inform* 524 vb.
*divulge* 526 vb.
*describe* 590 vb.
*be important* 638 vb.
*be successful* 727 vb.
*command* 737 vb.
*accuse* 928 vb.
– against

*tell against* 467 vb.
– all
*divulge* 526 vb.
*confess* 526 vb.
*speak* 579 vb.
– another story
*tell against* 467 vb.
– fortunes
*divine* 511 vb.
– it like it is
*speak plainly* 573 vb.
– its own story
*evidence* 466 vb.
*be plain* 522 vb.
– lies
*be false* 541 vb.
*be dishonest* 930 vb.
– of
*evidence* 466 vb.
*mean* 514 vb.
– off
*reprove* 924 vb.
– on
*inform* 524 vb.
– one straight
*speak plainly* 573 vb.
– one where to get off
*refuse* 760 vb.
– the truth
*be truthful* 540 vb.
– the world
*advertise* 528 vb.
– upon
*influence* 178 vb.
**teller**
*enumerator* 86 n.
*informant* 524 n.
*treasurer* 798 n.
**teller of tales**
*narrator* 590 n.
**telling**
*influential* 178 adj.
*evidential* 466 adj.
*meaningful* 514 adj.
*expressive* 516 adj.
*assertive* 532 adj.
*instrumental* 628 adj.
*important* 638 adj.
*impressive* 821 adj.
**telling against**
*countervailing* 467 adj.
**telling the truth**
*veracious* 540 adj.
**telltale**
*informer* 524 n.
*disclosing* 526 adj.
*indicating* 547 adj.
*tergiversator* 603 n.
**tellurian**
*native* 191 n.
*humankind* 371 n.
**telluric**
*telluric* 321 adj.
*territorial* 344 adj.
**telpher line**
*railway* 624 n.
**temazepan**

*drug* 658 n.
**temerity**
*rashness* 857 n.
**temp**
*deputy* 755 n.
**temper**
*temperament* 5 n.
*state* 7 n.
*mix* 43 vb.
*composition* 56 n.
*strength* 162 n.
*strengthen* 162 vb.
*moderate* 177 vb.
*hardness* 326 n.
*harden* 326 vb.
*be tough* 329 vb.
*qualify* 468 vb.
*mature* 669 vb.
*affections* 817 n.
*excitable state* 822 n.
*anger* 891 n.
**tempera**
*art equipment* 553 n.
*art style* 553 n.
**temperament**
*temperament* 5 n.
*state* 7 n.
*composition* 56 n.
*affections* 817 n.
*moral sensibility* 819 n.
*excitability* 822 n.
*irascibility* 892 n.
*sullenness* 893 n.
**temperamental**
*capricious* 604 adj.
*lively* 819 adj.
*excitable* 822 adj.
**temperance**
*moderation* 177 n.
*avoidance* 620 n.
*restraint* 747 n.
*virtues* 933 n.
*temperance* 942 n.
*asceticism* 945 n.
*sobriety* 948 n.
**temperate**
*moderate* 177 adj.
*warm* 379 adj.
*cold* 380 adj.
*restrained* 747 adj.
*temperate* 942 adj.
**temperature**
*illness* 651 n.
**tempered**
*strong* 162 adj.
*moderate* 177 adj.
*hard* 326 adj.
**tempest**
*storm* 176 n.
*commotion* 318 n.
**tempestuous**
*disorderly* 61 adj.
*violent* 176 adj.
*speedy* 277 adj.
*windy* 352 adj.
*excitable* 822 adj.
**Templars**

*prodigal* 815 adj.
*rash* 857 adj.
**thrifty**
*careful* 457 adj.
*economical* 814 adj.
**thrill**
*be agitated* 318 vb.
*sexual pleasure* 376 n.
*pang* 377 n.
*itch* 378 vb.
*feeling* 818 n.
*excitation* 821 n.
*excite* 821 vb.
*excitable state* 822 n.
*joy* 824 n.
*delight* 826 vb.
**thriller**
*film* 445 n.
*novel* 590 n.
**thrilling**
*descriptive* 590 adj.
*felt* 818 adj.
*exciting* 821 adj.
*pleasurable* 826 adj.
**thrill-seeker**
*reveller* 837 n.
*sensualist* 944 n.
**thrive**
*grow* 36 vb.
*be vigorous* 174 vb.
*flourish* 615 vb.
*be healthy* 650 vb.
*be active* 678 vb.
*prosper* 730 vb.
**throat**
*orifice* 263 n.
*conduit* 351 n.
*air pipe* 353 n.
**throat, inflammation of**
*inflammation* 651 n.
box
**throaty**
*hoarse* 407 adj.
**throb**
*be periodic* 141 vb.
*oscillation* 317 n.
*spasm* 318 n.
*be agitated* 318 vb.
*give pain* 377 vb.
*show feeling* 818 vb.
**throes**
*violence* 176 n.
*spasm* 318 n.
*pang* 377 n.
**thrombosis**
*cardiovascular disease* 651 n.
**throne**
*seat* 218 n.
*regalia* 743 n.
*tribunal* 956 n.
**throng**
*crowd* 74 n.
*congregate* 74 vb.
*multitude* 104 n.
– in

*burst in* 297 vb.
**throttle**
*disable* 161 vb.
*close* 264 vb.
*retain* 778 vb.
– down
*retard* 278 vb.
**through**
*until now* 121 adv.
*vehicular* 274 adj.
*towards* 281 adv.
*communicating* 624 adj.
*through* 628 adv.
*by means of* 629 adv.
**through and through**
*completely* 54 adv.
**throughout**
*throughout* 54 adv.
*while* 108 adv.
*widely* 183 adv.
**throughput**
*computing* 86 n.
*production* 164 n.
*transference* 272 n.
**through road**
*road* 624 n.
**through thick and thin**
*completely* 54 adv.
*persistently* 600 adv.
**through with, be**
*climax* 725 vb.
**throw**
*form* 243 vb.
*move* 265 vb.
*impulse* 279 n.
*propel* 287 vb.
*gambling* 618 n.
*exertion* 682 n.
– a fit
*be agitated* 318 vb.
*be excitable* 822 vb.
– a spanner in the works
*disable* 161 vb.
*make useless* 641 vb.
*be obstructive* 702 vb.
– a tantrum
*be excitable* 822 vb.
– away
*eject* 300 vb.
*act* 594 vb.
*reject* 607 vb.
*waste* 634 vb.
*stop using* 674 vb.
*lose* 772 vb.
*be prodigal* 815 vb.
– cold water on
*moderate* 177 vb.
*dissuade* 613 vb.
– down
*demolish* 165 vb.
*fell* 311 vb.
– down the gauntlet
*be resolute* 599 vb.
*defy* 711 vb.
*enrage* 891 vb.
– dust in one's eyes

*be unrelated* 10 vb.
*deflect* 282 vb.
*blind* 439 vb.
*deceive* 542 vb.
– good money after bad
*lose* 772 vb.
*be prodigal* 815 vb.
– in one's hand
*relinquish* 621 vb.
*resign* 753 vb.
– in one's teeth
*defy* 711 vb.
*accuse* 928 vb.
– in the sponge/the towel
*relinquish* 621 vb.
*submit* 721 vb.
– into the shade
*be superior* 34 vb.
*have a reputation* 866 vb.
– light on
*make bright* 417 vb.
*interpret* 520 vb.
*manifest* 522 vb.
– mud
*disapprove* 924 vb.
*defame* 926 vb.
– off
*disaccustom* 611 vb.
– off balance
*derange* 63 vb.
– off the mask
*disclose* 526 vb.
– off the scent
*distract* 456 vb.
*puzzle* 474 vb.
*elude* 667 vb.
– off the yoke
*revolt* 738 vb.
*achieve liberty* 746 vb.
– one out
*trouble* 827 vb.
– oneself at
*pursue* 619 vb.
– one's hat in the ring
*defy* 711 vb.
– one's money around
*be liberal* 813 vb.
*be prodigal* 815 vb.
– one's weight about
*be vigorous* 174 vb.
*be insolent* 878 vb.
– open
*open* 263 vb.
*admit* 299 vb.
*manifest* 522 vb.
– out
*eject* 300 vb.
*reject* 607 vb.
– out the baby with the bathwater
*overstep* 306 vb.
*act foolishly* 695 vb.
– over
*change one's mind* 603 vb.
*relinquish* 621 vb.

– overboard
*eject* 300 vb.
*stop using* 674 vb.
*not retain* 779 vb.
– stones at
*lapidate* 712 vb.
*be malevolent* 898 vb.
*disapprove* 924 vb.
– the book at
*dispraise* 924 vb.
*indict* 928 vb.
*punish* 963 vb.
– up
*eject* 300 vb.
*vomit* 300 vb.
*elevate* 310 vb.
*submit* 721 vb.
*resign* 753 vb.
**throwaway**
*ephemeral* 114 adj.
*wasteful* 634 adj.
**throwaway manner**
*sauciness* 878 n.
**throwback**
*recurrence* 106 n.
*reversion* 148 n.
*deterioration* 655 n.
*relapse* 657 n.
**thrower**
*thrower* 287 n.
*player* 837 n.
**throwing overboard**
*ejection* 300 n.
**thrown**
*formed* 243 adj.
*grounded* 728 adj.
**thrown, be**
*tumble* 309 vb.
**throwstick**
*missile weapon* 723 n.
**thrum**
*edging* 234 n.
*resound* 404 vb.
*play music* 413 vb.
**thrush**
*bird* 365 n.
*vocalist* 413 n.
*animal disease* 651 n.
**thrust**
*energy* 160 n.
*vigorousness* 174 n.
*influence* 178 n.
*distortion* 246 n.
*spurt* 277 n.
*impulse* 279 n.
*propellant* 287 n.
*lunge* 712 n.
**thruster**
*propellant* 287 n.
*busy person* 678 n.
**thrustful**
*vigorous* 174 adj.
*assertive* 532 adj.
*active* 678 adj.
**thud**
*impulse* 279 n.
*sound faint* 401 vb.

**compressor** 198 n.
*stopper* 264 n.
*surgical dressing* 658 n.
**tousle**
*jumble* 63 vb.
*roughen* 259 vb.
**tout**
*request* 761 vb.
*petitioner* 763 n.
*seller* 793 n.
*commender* 923 n.
**tout à fait**
*truly* 494 adv.
**tovarich, tovarish**
*title* 870 n.
**tow**
*fibre* 208 n.
*navigate* 269 vb.
*draw* 288 vb.
**towards**
*straight on* 249 adv.
*towards* 281 adv.
**towel**
*rub* 333 vb.
*dryer* 342 n.
*cleaning cloth* 648 n.
**towelling**
*textile* 222 n.
**tower**
*be great* 32 vb.
*building* 164 n.
*dwelling* 192 n.
*be large* 195 vb.
*high structure* 209 n.
*be high* 209 vb.
*ascend* 308 vb.
*refuge* 662 n.
*fort* 713 n.
*church exterior* 990 n.
– over
*be superior* 34 vb.
*influence* 178 vb.
**Tower, the**
*prison* 748 n.
**tower block**
*flat* 192 n.
*high structure* 209 n.
**towering**
*furious* 176 adj.
*high* 209 adj.
**tower of silence**
*cemetery* 364 n.
**tower of strength**
*refuge* 662 n.
*aider* 703 n.
**tow-headed**
*whitish* 427 adj.
**to wit**
*namely* 80 adv.
*in plain words* 520 adv.
**towline**
*cable* 47 n.
*traction* 288 n.
**town**
*district* 184 n.
*abode* 192 n.
*housing* 192 n.

**town centre**
*focus* 76 n.
**town crier**
*publicizer* 528 n.
**townee**
*native* 191 n.
**town plan**
*map* 551 n.
**township**
*district* 184 n.
**townspeople**
*inhabitants* 191 n.
*commonalty* 869 n.
**towny**
*urban* 192 adj.
**towpath**
*path* 624 n.
**toxaemia**
*infection* 651 n.
*poisoning* 659 n.
**toxic**
*harmful* 645 adj.
*unclean* 649 adj.
*toxic* 653 adj.
*baneful* 659 adj.
*dangerous* 661 adj.
**toxicology**
*study* 536 n. box
**toxin**
*poison* 659 n.
**toxophilite**
*shooter* 287 n.
**toy**
*little* 196 adj.
*bauble* 639 n.
*plaything* 837 n.
*caress* 889 vb.
– with
*be inattentive* 456 vb.
*neglect* 458 vb.
**toyboy**
*youngster* 132 n.
*male* 372 n.
*lover* 887 n.
**trace**
*copy* 20 vb.
*small quantity* 33 n.
*remainder* 41 n.
*effect* 157 n.
*outline* 233 n., vb.
*detect* 484 vb.
*indication* 547 n.
*identification* 547 n.
*trace* 548 n.
*decorate* 844 vb.
– back
*look back* 125 vb.
*retrospect* 505 vb.
**traceable**
*attributed* 158 adj.
*recorded* 548 adj.
**tracery**
*network* 222 n.
*curve* 248 n.
*ornamental art* 844 n.
*pattern* 844 n.
**traces**

*coupling* 47 n.
*fetter* 748 n.
**trachea**
*air pipe* 353 n.
**trachea, inflam-**
**mation of**
*inflammation* 651 n.
box
**trachoma**
*tropical disease* 651 n.
**track**
*continuity* 71 n.
*accompany* 89 vb.
*water travel* 269 n.
*direction* 281 n.
*follow* 284 vb.
*passage* 305 n.
*recording* 414 n.
*identification* 547 n.
*trace* 548 n.
*pursue* 619 vb.
*path* 624 n.
*railway* 624 n.
*racing* 716 n.
*arena* 724 n.
– down
*detect* 484 vb.
**tracker**
*hunter* 619 n.
**track events**
*sport* 837 n.
**tracking station**
*astronomy* 321 n.
**trackless**
*spacious* 183 adj.
*difficult* 700 adj.
**track record**
*conduct* 688 n.
**tracksuit**
*suit* 228 n.
**tract**
*region* 184 n.
*land* 344 n.
*reading matter* 589 n.
*dissertation* 591 n.
*lands* 777 n.
*piety* 979 n.
**tractability**
*willingness* 597 n.
*persuadability* 612 n.
*obedience* 739 n.
**tractable**
*flexible* 327 adj.
*tractable* 701 adj.
**Tractarian**
*Anglican* 976 adj.
*church party* 978 n.
**traction**
*transport* 272 n.
*traction* 288 n.
**traction engine**
*locomotive* 274 n.
**tractor**
*vehicle* 274 n.
*farm tool* 370 n.
**trad**
*music* 412 n.

**trade**
*interchange* 151 vb.
*transference* 272 n.
*business* 622 n.
*vocation* 622 n.
*transfer* 780 n.
*assign* 780 vb.
*trade* 791 n., vb.
*sell* 793 vb.
– on
*use* 673 vb.
**trade fair**
*market* 796 n.
**trademark**
*speciality* 80 n.
*identification* 547 n.
*label* 547 n.
**trade-off**
*interchange* 151 n.
*compromise* 770 n.
*transfer* 780 n.
*barter* 791 n.
*trade* 791 n.
**trader**
*merchant ship* 275 n.
**tradesman**
*artisan* 686 n.
*tradespeople* 794 n.
**tradesmen's entrance**
*rear* 238 n.
**trade union, trades**
**union**
*association* 706 n.
**trade unionist**
*worker* 686 n.
*participator* 775 n.
**trade wind**
*wind* 352 n.
**trading centre**
*emporium* 796 n.
**tradition**
*tradition* 127 n.
*permanence* 144 n.
*information* 524 n.
*narrative* 590 n.
*habit* 610 n.
*theology* 973 n.
**traditional**
*conformable* 83 adj.
*immemorial* 127 adj.
*descriptive* 590 adj.
*habitual* 610 adj.
*orthodox* 976 adj.
**traditional Chinese**
**medicine**
*alternative therapy*
658 n.
**traditionalist**
*conformist* 83 n.
*the orthodox* 976 n.
**traduce**
*misinterpret* 521 vb.
*defame* 926 vb.
**traffic**
*motion* 265 n.
*conveyance* 267 n.
*passing along* 305 n.

*calligrapher* 586 n.
**transcript**
*copy* 22 n.
*script* 586 n.
**transcription**
*transformation* 143 n.
*transference* 272 n.
*musical piece* 412 n.
*writing* 586 n.
**transect**
*bisect* 92 vb.
*be oblique* 220 vb.
**transection**
*crossing* 222 n.
**transept**
*church interior* 990 n.
**transfatty acid**
*food content* 301 n.
*food* 357 n.
**transfer**
*duplicate* 22 n.
*disunite* 46 vb.
*transition* 147 n.
*substitution* 150 n.
*displace* 188 vb.
*move* 265 vb.
*transference* 272 n.
*transfer* 272 vb.
*carry* 273 vb.
*picture* 553 n.
*deposal* 752 n.
*acquisition* 771 n.
*nonretention* 779 n.
*transfer* 780 n.
*assign* 780 vb.
*giving* 781 n.
**transferable**
*transferable* 272 adj.
**transferable vote**
*vote* 605 n.
**transference**
*change* 143 n.
*interchange* 151 n.
*transference* 272 n.
*passage* 305 n.
*metaphor* 519 n.
*See also* **transfer**
**Transfiguration**
*theophany* 965 n.
**transfigure**
*modify* 143 vb.
*transform* 147 vb.
*make better* 654 vb.
*beautify* 841 vb.
**transfix**
*pierce* 263 vb.
**transfixed**
*fixed* 153 adj.
*still* 266 adj.
*wondering* 864 adj.
**transform**
*modify* 143 vb.
*transform* 147 vb.
*revolutionize* 149 vb.
*influence* 178 vb.
*make better* 654 vb.
*pervert* 655 vb.

*practise occultism*
  984 vb.
**transformation**
*transformation* 143 n.
*beautification* 843 n.
**transformation scene**
*spectacle* 445 n.
*stage show* 594 n.
*thaumaturgy* 864 n.
**transformer**
*electronics* 160 n.
**transfuse**
*infuse* 303 vb.
*make flow* 350 vb.
**transfusion**
*mixture* 43 n.
*transference* 272 n.
*surgery* 658 n.
**transgenic**
*different* 15 adj.
*converted* 147 adj.
**transgress**
*encroach* 306 vb.
*disobey* 738 vb.
*not observe* 769 vb.
*do wrong* 914 vb.
**transgression**
*wickedness* 934 n.
*guilty act* 936 n.
*lawbreaking* 954 n.
**tranship, transship**
*displace* 188 vb.
*transpose* 272 vb.
**transience**
*transience* 114 n.
**transient**
*elapsing* 111 adj.
*transient* 114 adj.
*unstable* 152 adj.
*dweller* 191 n.
*travelling* 267 adj.
*dying* 361 adj.
*disappearing* 446 adj.
*uncertain* 474 adj.
**transilluminate**
*make bright* 417 vb.
*be transparent* 422 vb.
**transistor**
*electronics* 160 n.
*broadcasting* 531 n.
**transistorize, transis-**
  **torise**
*empower* 160 vb.
**transit**
*transition* 147 n.
*motion* 265 n.
*travelling* 267 adj.
*passage* 305 n.
**transit instrument**
*astronomy* 321 n.
**transition**
*change* 143 n.
*transition* 147 n.
*transference* 272 n.
*passage* 305 n.
**transitive verb**
*part of speech* 564 n.

**transitory**
*transient* 114 adj.
**transit stop**
*goal* 295 n.
**translate**
*transform* 147 vb.
*transpose* 272 vb.
*translate* 520 vb.
**translation**
*imitation* 20 n.
*copy* 22 n.
*change* 143 n.
*transference* 272 n.
*translation* 520 n.
**translator**
*interpreter* 520 n.
**transliterate**
*copy* 20 vb.
*transpose* 272 vb.
*translate* 520 vb.
*spell* 558 vb.
**translocation**
*displacement* 188 n.
*transference* 272 n.
**translucent**
*undimmed* 417 adj.
*semitransparent* 424 adj.
**transmigration**
*wandering* 267 n.
*transformation* 143 n.
**transmission**
*broadcast* 531 n.
**transmit**
*send* 272 vb.
*transfer* 272 vb.
*pass* 305 vb.
*communicate* 524 vb.
*assign* 780 vb.
**transmitter**
*broadcasting* 531 n.
**transmute**
*modify* 143 vb.
*convert* 147 vb.
**transoceanic**
*removed* 199 adj.
**transom**
*beam* 218 n.
*prop* 218 n.
*cross* 222 n.
*window* 263 n.
**transonic**
*speedy* 277 adj.
**trans-Pacific**
*removed* 199 adj.
**transparency**
*transparency* 422 n.
*photography* 551 n.
**transparent**
*insubstantial* 4 adj.
*undimmed* 417 adj.
*transparent* 422 adj.
*intelligible* 516 adj.
*disclosing* 526 adj.
*perspicuous* 567 adj.
*artless* 699 adj.
*trustworthy* 929 adj.
**transpire**

*happen* 154 vb.
*emerge* 298 vb.
*exude* 298 vb.
*vaporize* 338 vb.
*be plain* 522 vb.
*be disclosed* 526 vb.
**transplant**
*substitute* 150 n.
*implant* 303 vb.
*cultivate* 370 vb.
*surgery* 658 n.
**transplantation**
*transference* 272 n.
**transplant surgery**
*surgery* 658 n.
**transport**
*displace* 188 vb.
*move* 265 vb.
*transport* 272 n.
*carry* 273 vb.
*vehicle* 274 n.
*ship* 275 n.
*aircraft* 276 n.
*excitable state* 822 n.
*delight* 826 vb.
*punish* 963 vb.
**transportation**
*penalty* 963 n.
**transport café**
*restaurant* 192 n.
**transporter**
*carrier* 273 n.
**transports**
*warm feeling* 818 n.
*joy* 824 n.
**transpose**
*jumble* 63 vb.
*interchange* 151 vb.
*invert* 221 vb.
*move* 265 vb.
*transpose* 272 vb.
*compose music* 413 vb.
**transposition**
*change* 143 n.
**transputer**
*microelectronics* 196 n.
**transsexual**
*non-heterosexual* 84 n.
**transubstantiation**
*transformation* 143 n.
*the sacrament* 988 n.
**transude**
*exude* 298 vb.
**transverse**
*oblique* 220 adj.
*crossed* 222 adj.
**transvestite**
*non-heterosexual* 84 n.
**tranter**
*carrier* 273 n.
**trap**
*receptacle* 194 n.
*orifice* 263 n.
*close* 264 vb.
*carriage* 274 n.
*detect* 484 vb.
*surprise* 508 vb.

*preservation* 666 n.
**treeless**
  *unproductive* 172 adj.
**treelike**
  *arboreal* 366 adj.
**treen**
  *wooden* 366 adj.
**trees, fear of**
  *phobia* 854 n. box
**treetop**
  *vertex* 213 n.
  *foliage* 366 n.
**trefoil**
  *three* 93 n.
  *heraldry* 547 n.
  *pattern* 844 n.
**trek**
  *land travel* 267 n.
  *travel* 267 vb.
**trekker**
  *traveller* 268 n.
**trellis**
  *frame* 218 n.
  *network* 222 n.
**tremble**
  *vary* 152 vb.
  *be weak* 163 vb.
  *be agitated* 318 vb.
  *be cold* 380 vb.
  *sound faint* 401 vb.
  *show feeling* 818 vb.
  *be excited* 821 vb.
  *quake* 854 vb.
– *in the balance*
  *be pending* 136 vb.
  *be uncertain* 474 vb.
  *be in danger* 661 vb.
**tremendous**
  *prodigious* 32 adj.
  *frightening* 854 adj.
**tremolo**
  *roll* 403 n.
  *musical note* 410 n.
  *adagio* 412 adv.
**tremor**
  *outbreak* 176 n.
  *oscillation* 317 n.
  *agitation* 318 n.
  *nervous disorders* 651 n.
  *danger signal* 665 n.
  *feeling* 818 n.
  *nervousness* 854 n.
**tremulous**
  *agitated* 318 adj.
  *irresolute* 601 adj.
  *nervous* 854 adj.
**trench**
  *gap* 201 n.
  *fence* 235 n.
  *excavation* 255 n.
  *furrow* 262 n.
  *conduit* 351 n.
  *cultivate* 370 vb.
  *refuge* 662 n.
  *defences* 713 n.
**trenchant**
  *keen* 174 adj.

*assertive* 532 adj.
  *concise* 569 adj.
  *forceful* 571 adj.
  *disapproving* 924 adj.
**trench coat**
  *overcoat* 228 n.
**trencher**
  *plate* 194 n.
**trencherman,**
  **trencherwoman**
  *eater* 301 n.
  *glutton* 947 n.
**trenches**
  *battleground* 724 n.
**trench on/upon**
  *be near* 200 vb.
  *encroach* 306 vb.
**trend**
  *modality* 7 n.
  *similarity* 18 n.
  *continuity* 71 n.
  *go on* 146 vb.
  *ability* 160 n.
  *tendency* 179 n.
  *form* 243 n.
  *direction* 281 n.
  *point to* 281 vb.
  *approach* 289 vb.
  *intention* 617 n.
  *fashion* 848 n.
  *liking* 859 n.
**trend-setter**
  *precursor* 66 n.
  *beau monde* 848 n.
**trendy**
  *modernist* 126 n.
  *modern* 126 adj.
  *fashionable* 848 adj.
**trephine, trepan**
  *pierce* 263 vb.
  *doctor* 658 vb.
**trepidation**
  *agitation* 318 n.
  *excitable state* 822 n.
  *fear* 854 n.
**trespass**
  *interfere* 231 vb.
  *intrude* 297 vb.
  *encroach* 306 vb.
  *disobey* 738 vb.
  *wrong* 914 n.
  *be undue* 916 vb.
  *be wicked* 934 vb.
  *guilty act* 936 n.
  *lawbreaking* 954 n.
**trespasser**
  *intruder* 59 n.
**tresses**
  *hair* 259 n.
**trestle**
  *frame* 218 n.
**trews**
  *trousers* 228 n.
**tri-**
  *three* 93 adj.
**triable**
  *legal* 953 adj.

*illegal* 954 adj.
**triad**
  *three* 93 n.
  *musical note* 410 n.
  *Trinity* 965 n.
**triage**
  *medical art* 658 n.
**trial**
  *enquiry* 459 n.
  *experiment* 461 n., vb.
  *bane* 659 n.
  *preparation* 669 n.
  *attempt* 671 n.
  *difficulty* 700 n.
  *adversity* 731 n.
  *suffering* 825 n.
  *legal trial* 959 n.
**trial and error**
  *empiricism* 461 n.
**trial marriage**
  *type of marriage* 894 n.
**trial of strength**
  *contest* 716 n.
**trial run**
  *experiment* 461 n.
  *preparation* 669 n.
**trials and tribulation**
  *painfulness* 827 n.
**triangle**
  *three* 93 n.
  *angular figure* 247 n.
  *gong* 414 n.
**triangle of forces**
  *science of forces* 162 n.
**triangular**
  *angulated* 247 adj.
**triangulate**
  *measure* 465 vb.
**triathlon**
  *contest* 716 n.
**tribadism**
  *sexual pleasure* 376 n.
**tribal**
  *ethnic* 11 adj.
  *national* 371 adj.
**tribalism**
  *social group* 371 n.
  *government* 733 n.
**tribal memory**
  *memory* 505 n.
**tribe**
  *family* 11 n.
  *race* 11 n.
  *group* 74 n.
  *breed* 77 n.
  *multitude* 104 n.
  *genealogy* 169 n.
  *native* 191 n.
  *community* 708 n.
**tribulation**
  *difficulty* 700 n.
  *suffering* 825 n.
  *painfulness* 827 n.
**tribunal**
  *council* 692 n.
  *jurisdiction* 955 n.
  *tribunal* 956 n.

**tribunate**
  *position of authority*
    733 n.
**tribune**
  *rostrum* 539 n.
  *leader* 690 n.
  *official* 690 n.
**tributary**
  *stream* 350 n.
  *subject* 745 adj.
  *giving* 781 adj.
**tribute**
  *service* 745 n.
  *gift* 781 n.
  *receiving* 782 n.
  *payment* 804 n.
  *tax* 809 n.
  *thanks* 907 n.
  *dueness* 915 n.
  *praise* 923 n.
  *reward* 962 n.
**trice**
  *instant* 116 n.
**trice up**
  *tighten* 45 vb.
  *draw* 288 vb.
  *elevate* 310 vb.
**trichology**
  *study* 536 n. box
  *hairdressing* 843 n.
**trichotomy**
  *trisection* 95 n.
**trichroism**
  *variegation* 437 n.
**trick**
  *trickery* 542 n.
  *befool* 542 vb.
  *habit* 610 n.
  *contrivance* 623 n.
  *labour* 682 n.
  *skill* 694 n.
  *stratagem* 698 n.
  *revel* 837 n.
  *affectation* 850 n.
  *foul play* 930 n.
– *out*
  *primp* 843 vb.
  *decorate* 844 vb.
**trick cyclist**
  *psychologist* 447 n.
**trickery**
  *duplicity* 541 n.
  *trickery* 542 n.
  *foul play* 930 n.
**trickle**
  *small quantity* 33 n.
  *fewness* 105 n.
  *move slowly* 278 vb.
  *flow out* 298 vb.
  *be wet* 341 vb.
  *flow* 350 vb.
  *trifle* 639 n.
**trick of light**
  *visual fallacy* 440 n.
**trick of speech**
  *identification* 547 n.
**tricks of the trade**

secluded 883 adj.
**tucker**
food 301 n.
**tuckered out**
fatigued 684 adj.
**tucket**
resonance 404 n.
tune 412 n.
**tuck in/into**
eat 301 vb.
insert 303 vb.
**tuck up**
place 187 vb.
shorten 204 vb.
**Tudor**
olden 127 adj.
architectural
192 adj.
**Tudor rose**
heraldry 547 n.
**tuff**
rock 344 n.
ash 381 n.
**tuft**
bunch 74 n.
fewness 105 n.
hair 259 n.
**tug**
move 265 vb.
boat 275 n.
traction 288 n.
draw 288 vb.
attraction 291 n.
extraction 304 n.
exertion 682 n.
work 682 vb.
– one's forelock
greet 884 vb.
**tug of love**
opposition 704 n.
contest 716 n.
**tug of war**
opposition 704 n.
contest 716 n.
**tuition**
teaching 534 n.
**tulle**
textile 222 n.
**tumble**
jumble 63 vb.
be inverted 221 vb.
descent 309 n.
tumble 309 vb.
fell 311 vb.
oscillate 317 vb.
– to
discover 484 vb.
understand 516 vb.
**tumbledown**
dilapidated 655 adj.
**tumble-dry**
dry 342 vb.
**tumbler**
athlete 162 n.
cup 194 n.
**tumbril**
vehicle 274 n.

**tumescent**
expanded 197 adj.
convex 253 adj.
**tumid**
expanded 197 adj.
convex 253 adj.
rhetorical 574 adj.
**tummelberry**
druit 301 n.
**tummy**
maw 194 n.
insides 224 n.
**tummy ache**
digestive disorders 651 n.
**tummy tuck**
beautification 843 n.
**tummy upset**
digestive disorders 651 n.
**tumour**
dilation 197 n.
swelling 253 n.
cancer 651 n.
**tumult**
turmoil 61 n.
commotion 318 n.
loudness 400 n.
discord 411 n.
activity 678 n.
revolt 738 n.
**tumultuous**
disorderly 61 adj.
violent 176 adj.
**tumulus**
earthwork 253 n.
**tun**
vat 194 n.
**tuna**
fish food 301 n.
fish 365 n.
**tundra**
plain 348 n.
**tune**
adjust 24 vb.
synchronize 123 vb.
sound 398 n.
harmonize 410 vb.
tune 412 n.
play music 413 vb.
make ready 669 vb.
– in
hear 415 vb.
– up
harmonize 410 vb.
make ready 669 vb.
**tuneful**
pleasant 376 adj.
melodious 410 adj.
poetic 593 adj.
**tuneless**
discordant 411 adj.
**tunic**
wrapping 226 n.
jacket 228 n.
**tuning fork**
prototype 23 n.
gong 414 n.
**tunnel**

excavation 255 n.
tunnel 263 n.
pierce 263 vb.
descend 309 vb.
bridge 624 n.
railway 624 n.
**tunneller**
excavator 255 n.
**tunnel vision**
blindness 439 n.
dim sight 440 n.
inattention 456 n.
prejudice 481 n.
narrow mind 481 n.
**tunny, tunny fish**
fish food 301 n.
fish 365 n.
**tup**
sheep 365 n.
male animal 372 n.
**tuppence**
trifle 639 n.
**tu quoque**
rejoinder 460 n.
**turban**
headgear 228 n.
coil 251 n.
**turbid**
opaque 423 adj.
dirty 649 adj.
**turbine**
instrument 156 n.
sources of energy 160 n.
rotator 315 n.
machine 630 n.
**turbofan**
aircraft 276 n.
**turbojet**
aircraft 276 n.
**turboprop**
aircraft 276 n.
**turbot**
fish food 301 n.
fish 365 n.
**turbulence, tur-
bulency**
storm 176 n.
roughness 259 n.
commotion 318 n.
**turbulent**
disorderly 61 adj.
violent 176 adj.
excitable 822 adj.
**tureen**
bowl 194 n.
**turf**
piece 53 n.
soil 344 n.
grassland 348 n.
grass 366 n.
fuel 385 n.
arena 724 n.
**Turf, the**
racing 716 n.
gambling 618 n.
**turf accountant**
gambler 618 n.

**turf out**
eject 300 vb.
make unwelcome 883 vb.
**turgid**
expanded 197 adj.
convex 253 adj.
diffuse 570 adj.
rhetorical 574 adj.
inelegant 576 adj.
ostentatious 875 adj.
**turkey**
table bird 365 n.
**turkey cock**
proud person 871 n.
**Turkish bath**
heater 383 n.
ablutions 648 n.
**Turkish coffee**
soft drink 301 n.
**Turkish delight**
sweets 301 n.
**Turk's head**
ligature 47 n.
coil 251 n.
**turmeric**
spice 301 n.
condiment 389 n.
**turmoil**
turmoil 61 n.
havoc 165 n.
violence 176 n.
commotion 318 n.
activity 678 n.
anarchy 734 n.
revolt 738 n.
**turn**
period 110 n.
periodicity 141 n.
change 143 n., vb.
reversion 148 n.
tendency 179 n.
form 243 vb.
curve 248 n.
make round 250 vb.
blunt 257 vb.
land travel 267 n.
deviate 282 vb.
circuition 314 n.
rotation 315 n.
rotate 315 vb.
be sour 393 vb.
lack of expectation
508 n.
interpretation 520 n.
stage show 594 n.
circuit 626 vb.
aptitude 694 n.
parry 713 vb.
feeling 818 n.
– a blind eye
be inattentive 456 vb.
disregard 458 vb.
avoid 620 vb.
not act 677 vb.
permit 756 vb.
forgive 909 vb.
– about

access 624 n.
obstacle 702 n.
treasury 799 n.
**turntable**
rotator 315 n.
record player 414 n.
railway 624 n.
**turn-up**
fold 261 n.
**turnup for the book**
benefit 615 n.
**turpitude**
disrepute 867 n.
improbity 930 n.
wickedness 934 n.
**turquoise**
blueness 435 n.
gem 844 n.
**turret**
high structure 209 n.
fort 713 n.
**turtle**
reptile 365 n.
**turtle dove**
bird 365 n.
love emblem 887 n.
**turtle neck**
jersey 228 n.
**tusk**
tooth 256 n.
**tusker**
pig 365 n.
mammal 365 n.
**tussle**
contention 716 n.
contend 716 vb.
**tussock**
bunch 74 n.
small hill 209 n.
**tussore, tussah**
fibre 208 n.
textile 222 n.
**tutelage**
teaching 534 n.
learning 536 n.
protection 660 n.
subjection 745 n.
**tutelary**
tutelary 660 adj.
defending 713 adj.
**tutelary saint**
benefactor 903 n.
**tutor**
teach 534 vb.
teacher 537 n.
protector 660 n.
manager 690 n.
domestic 742 n.
keeper 749 n.
**tutorial**
teaching 534 n.
**tutti**
loudness 400 n.
duet 412 n.
**tut-tut**
deprecate 762 vb.
disapprove 924 vb.

**tutu**
skirt 228 n.
**tuxedo**
formal dress 228 n.
jacket 228 n.
**TV**
broadcasting 531 n.
See also **television**
**TVP**
meat 301 n.
**twaddle**
absurdity 497 n.
silly talk 515 n.
**twain**
duality 90 n.
**twang**
resonance 404 n.
play music 413 vb.
pronunciation 577 n.
speech defect 580 n.
**tweak**
draw 288 vb.
give pain 377 vb.
**twee**
affected 850 adj.
**tweed**
textile 222 n.
roughness 259 n.
**Tweedledum and Tweedledee**
identity 13 n.
duality 90 n.
**tweeds**
suit 228 n.
**tweedy**
textural 331 adj.
**tweeny**
domestic 742 n.
**tweet**
ululate 409 vb.
**tweezers**
extractor 304 n.
tool 630 n.
nippers 778 n.
**twelfth**
fifth and over 99 adj.
**twelfth man**
substitute 150 n.
**Twelfth Night**
holy day 988 n. box
**twelve**
over five 99 n.
**twelvemonth**
period 110 n.
**twelve noon**
noon 128 n.
**twelve o'clock**
noon 128 n.
**Twelve Tables**
fixture 153 n.
**twelve-tone scale**
key 410 n.
discord 411 n.
**twenty**
twenty and over 99 n.
**twerp**
fool 501 n.

nonentity 639 n.
**twice**
double 91 adj.
twice 91 adv.
**twice the man/ woman one was**
refreshed 685 adj.
**twice-told tale**
repetition 106 n.
bore 838 n.
**twiddle**
rotate 315 vb.
touch 378 vb.
– one's thumbs
be inactive 679 vb.
**twig**
branch 53 n.
foliage 366 n.
know 490 vb.
understand 516 vb.
**twiggy**
lean 206 adj.
**twigloo**
preservation 666 n.
**twilight**
evening 129 n.
vespertine 129 adj.
darkness 418 n.
half-light 419 n.
deterioration 655 n.
**twilight sleep**
insensibility 375 n.
**twill**
crossed 222 adj.
**twilled**
textural 331 adj.
**twin**
kinsman 11 n.
identity 13 n.
analogue 18 n.
compeer 28 n.
join 45 vb.
concomitant 89 n.
dual 90 adj.
double 91 adj., vb.
contemporary 123 n.
**twine**
tie 45 vb.
fibre 208 n.
enlace 222 vb.
distort 246 vb.
make curved 248 vb.
twine 251 vb.
deviate 282 vb.
decorate 844 vb.
**twiner**
plant 366 n.
**twinge**
pang 377 n.
suffering 825 n.
**twinge of conscience**
guilt 936 n.
penitence 939 n.
**twinkle**
vary 152 vb.
agitation 318 n.
flash 417 n.

shine 417 vb.
gesticulate 547 vb.
laughter 835 n.
**twinkling**
instant 116 n.
**twin set**
jersey 228 n.
**twin tub**
ablutions 648 n.
**twirl**
coil 251 n.
twine 251 vb.
rotate 315 vb.
**twist**
tie 45 vb.
complexity 61 n.
derange 63 vb.
modify 143 vb.
force 176 vb.
fibre 208 n.
obliquity 220 n.
enlace 222 vb.
deform 244 vb.
distortion 246 n.
coil 251 n.
twine 251 vb.
be in motion 265 vb.
deviate 282 vb.
circle 314 vb.
tobacco 388 n.
bias 481 vb.
eccentricity 503 n.
misinterpret 521 vb.
pervert 655 vb.
be cunning 698 vb.
dance 837 n., vb.
make ugly 842 vb.
– and turn
meander 251 vb.
– one's arm
induce 612 vb.
compel 740 vb.
– round one's little finger
befool 542 vb.
dominate 733 vb.
**twisted**
distorted 246 adj.
convoluted 251 adj.
biased 481 adj.
imperfect 647 adj.
unsightly 842 adj.
**twister**
jumper 312 n.
gale 352 n.
trickster 545 n.
knave 938 n.
**twit**
fool 501 n.
ridicule 851 vb.
not respect 921 vb.
dispraise 924 vb.
**twitch**
move 265 vb.
draw 288 vb.
spasm 318 n.
be agitated 318 vb.
feel pain 377 vb.

sociable 882 adj.
**uncage**
liberate 746 vb.
**uncalculated**
spontaneous 609 vb.
**uncalculating**
unwise 499 adj.
rash 857 adj.
**uncalled for**
superfluous 637 adj.
undue 916 adj.
**uncandid**
false 541 adj.
dishonest 930 adj.
**uncanny**
spooky 970 adj.
magical 983 adj.
**uncanonical**
uncertified 474 adj.
nonobservant 769 adj.
**uncap**
open 263 vb.
**uncared for**
neglected 458 adj.
unwanted 860 adj.
**uncaring**
negligent 458 adj.
lax 734 adj.
indifferent 860 adj.
unkind 898 adj.
**uncatered for**
unexpected 508 adj.
**unceasing**
continuing 108 adj.
perpetual 115 adj.
frequent 139 adj.
permanent 144 adj.
unceasing 146 adj.
persevering 600 adj.
active 678 adj.
**uncensored**
intact 52 adj.
impure 951 adj.
**unceremonious**
discourteous 885 adj.
**uncertain**
fitful 142 adj.
changeful 152 adj.
casual 159 adj.
moot 459 adj.
unattested 467 adj.
improbable 472 adj.
uncertain 474 adj.
puzzled 517 adj.
irresolute 601 adj.
capricious 604 adj.
speculative 618 adj.
**uncertain temper**
irascibility 892 n.
**uncertainty**
uncertainty 474 n.
doubt 486 n.
ignorance 491 n.
equivocalness 518 n.
gambling 618 n.
**uncertified**
uncertified 474 adj.

**unchain**
disunite 46 vb.
liberate 746 vb.
**unchallengeable**
undisputed 473 adj.
invulnerable 660 adj.
just 913 adj.
due 915 adj.
**unchangeable**
lasting 113 adj.
unchangeable 153 adj.
obstinate 602 adj.
**unchanging**
characteristic 5 adj.
identical 13 adj.
uniform 16 adj.
perpetual 115 adj.
permanent 144 adj.
unchangeable 153 adj.
trustworthy 929 adj.
godlike 965 adj.
**unchaperoned**
alone 88 adj.
**uncharacteristic**
abnormal 84 adj.
**uncharged**
free 744 adj.
given 781 adj.
uncharged 812 adj.
**uncharitable**
parsimonious 816 adj.
unkind 898 adj.
selfish 932 adj.
**uncharted**
unknown 491 adj.
**unchartered**
unentitled 916 adj.
unwarranted 916 adj.
illegal 954 adj.
**unchaste**
unchaste 951 adj.
**unchastened**
impenitent 940 adj.
**unchastity**
unchastity 951 n.
**unchecked**
uncertified 474 adj.
unconfined 744 adj.
rash 857 adj.
**unchivalrous**
discourteous 885 adj.
dishonest 930 adj.
**unchosen**
rejected 607 adj.
unwanted 860 adj.
**unchristian**
unkind 898 adj.
heathenish 974 adj.
**unchurch**
perform ritual 988 vb.
**uncial**
letter 558 n.
written 586 adj.
**uncinate**
angular 247 adj.
**uncircumcised**
heathenish 974 adj.

**uncircumscribed**
spacious 183 adj.
**uncivil**
ill-bred 847 adj.
impertinent 878 adj.
discourteous 885 adj.
**uncivilized,**
    **uncivilised**
ignorant 491 adj.
immature 670 adj.
artless 699 adj.
ill-bred 847 adj.
barbaric 869 adj.
**unclad**
uncovered 229 adj.
**unclaimed**
free 744 adj.
unpossessed 774 adj.
not retained 779 adj.
**unclarified**
semiliquid 354 adj.
opaque 423 adj.
**unclasp**
disunite 46 vb.
**unclassical**
inelegant 576 adj.
**unclassifiable**
unrelated 10 adj.
unconformable 84 adj.
**unclassified**
mixed 43 adj.
orderless 61 adj.
uncertain 474 adj.
unknown 491 adj.
**uncle**
kinsman 11 n.
male 372 n.
lender 784 n.
**unclean**
unclean 649 adj.
insalubrious 653 adj.
impure 951 adj.
**unclean spirit**
devil 969 n.
**unclear**
indistinct 444 adj.
puzzling 517 adj.
unclear 568 adj.
inelegant 576 adj.
**unclench**
open 263 vb.
relinquish 621 vb.
not retain 779 vb.
**Uncle Sam**
native 191 n.
**Uncle Tom**
toady 879 n.
**Uncle Tom Cobbley**
    **and all**
everyman 79 n.
**unclinch**
separate 46 vb.
not retain 779 vb.
**unclipped**
intact 52 adj.
**uncloak**
uncover 229 vb.

disclose 526 vb.
**unclog**
disencumber 701 vb.
**unclose**
open 263 vb.
**unclothed**
uncovered 229 adj.
**unclotted**
fluid 335 adj.
**unclouded**
undimmed 417 adj.
obvious 443 adj.
**unclubbable**
unsociable 883 adj.
**uncluttered**
orderly 60 adj.
**unco**
remarkably 32 adv.
foreigner 59 n.
unusual 84 adj.
**unco guid, the**
zealot 979 n.
**uncoil**
unravel 62 vb.
lengthen 203 vb.
straighten 249 vb.
recoil 280 vb.
evolve 316 vb.
**uncollected**
disunited 46 adj.
**uncolonized, uncol-**
    **onised**
empty 190 adj.
**uncoloured**
unmixed 44 adj.
colourless 426 adj.
genuine 494 adj.
plain 573 adj.
**uncombed**
orderless 61 adj.
**uncombined**
unmixed 44 adj.
nonadhesive 49 adj.
decomposed 51 adj.
**uncomely**
ugly 842 adj.
**uncomfortable**
painful 377 adj.
suffering 825 adj.
unpleasant 827 adj.
**uncomforted**
discontented 829 adj.
**uncomforting**
cheerless 834 adj.
**uncommendable**
inexpedient 643 adj.
blameworthy 924 adj.
**uncommitted**
irresolute 601 adj.
avoiding 620 adj.
neutral 625 adj.
independent 744 adj.
**uncommon**
remarkable 32 adj.
special 80 adj.
infrequent 140 adj.
**uncommunicated**

*undutiful* 918 adj.
**undaunted**
  *resolute* 599 adj.
  *persevering* 600 adj.
  *unfearing* 855 adj.
**undazzled**
  *unastonished* 865 adj.
**undecayed**
  *preserved* 666 adj.
**undeceive**
  *inform* 524 vb.
  *disclose* 526 vb.
**undeceived**
  *regretting* 830 adj.
**undecided**
  *moot* 459 adj.
  *uncertain* 474 adj.
  *unbelieving* 486 adj.
  *irresolute* 601 adj.
  *choiceless* 606 adj.
**undecipherable**
  *unintelligible* 517 adj.
**undeclared**
  *tacit* 523 adj.
**undecorated**
  *inglorious* 867 adj.
**undecorousness**
  *inaptitude* 25 n.
**undedicated**
  *profane* 980 adj.
**undefeated**
  *resisting* 715 adj.
  *unbeaten* 727 adj.
**undefended**
  *vulnerable* 661 adj.
  *accusable* 928 adj.
**undefiled**
  *unmixed* 44 adj.
  *innocent* 935 adj.
  *pure* 950 adj.
**undefined**
  *amorphous* 244 adj.
  *shadowy* 419 adj.
  *indistinct* 444 adj.
  *indiscriminate* 464 adj.
  *uncertain* 474 adj.
**undeflected**
  *straight* 249 adj.
  *just* 913 adj.
**undeformed**
  *symmetrical* 245 adj.
  *shapely* 841 adj.
**undemanding**
  *easy* 701 adj.
  *lax* 734 adj.
  *lenient* 736 adj.
  *inexcitable* 823 adj.
**undemocratic**
  *unequal* 29 adj.
  *authoritarian* 735 adj.
  *prideful* 871 adj.
  *insolent* 878 adj.
**undemonstrated**
  *uncertified* 474 adj.
**undemonstrative**
  *impassive* 820 adj.
**undeniable**

*undisputed* 473 adj.
  *demonstrated* 478 adj.
  *credal* 485 adj.
**undenominational**
  *general* 79 adj.
**undependable**
  *unreliable* 474 adj.
  *dishonest* 930 adj.
**under**
  *concerning* 9 adv.
  *inferior* 35 adj.
  *in place* 186 adv.
  *low* 210 adj.
  *under* 210 adv.
  *subject* 745 adj.
**underachieve**
  *fall short* 307 vb.
**underachiever**
  *learner* 538 n.
  *loser* 728 n.
**under a cloud**
  *disreputable* 867 adj.
  *disapproved* 924 adj.
  *accused* 928 adj.
**underact**
  *act* 594 vb.
  *be unskilful* 695 vb.
**under age**
  *young* 130 adj.
**under an obligation**
  *on duty* 917 adv.
**under arms**
  *warring* 718 adj.
**under arrest**
  *imprisoned* 747 adj.
  *captive* 750 adj.
**under a spell**
  *involuntary* 596 adj.
  *cursed* 899 adj.
  *bewitched* 983 adj.
**under ban**
  *prohibited* 757 adj.
**underbelly**
  *lowness* 210 n.
  *insides* 224 n.
  *vulnerability* 661 n.
**under canvas**
  *covered* 226 adj.
  *under way* 269 adv.
**undercapitalized,
  undercapitalised**
  *unprovided* 636 adj.
**undercarriage**
  *prop* 218 n.
  *frame* 218 n.
  *carrier* 273 n.
  *aircraft* 276 n.
**undercharge**
  *account* 808 vb.
  *cheapen* 812 vb.
**underclass**
  *lower classes* 869 n.
**underclothes**
  *underwear* 228 n.
**undercoat**
  *layer* 207 n.
  *pigment* 425 n.

**under consideration**
  *in mind* 449 adv.
  *in question* 452 adv.
  *planned* 623 adj.
**under construction**
  *in preparation* 669 adv.
  *on the stocks* 726 adv.
**under control**
  *orderly* 60 adj.
  *obedient* 739 adj.
  *restrained* 747 adj.
**under cover**
  *covered* 226 adj.
  *concealed* 525 adj.
  *under shelter* 660 adv.
**undercover agent**
  *secret service* 459 n.
**under cover of**
  *deceptively* 542 adv.
  *epistolary* 588 adj.
**undercroft**
  *church interior* 990 n.
**undercurrent**
  *cause* 156 n.
  *current* 350 n.
  *latency* 523 n.
**undercut**
  *engrave* 555 vb.
  *sell* 793 vb.
  *cheapen* 812 vb.
**underdeveloped**
  *incomplete* 55 adj.
  *immature* 670 adj.
**underdevelopment**
  *imperfection* 647 n.
**under discussion**
  *in question* 452 adv.
**underdog**
  *inferior* 35 n.
  *loser* 728 n.
  *unlucky person* 731 n.
  *poor person* 801 n.
**underdone**
  *culinary* 301 adj.
  *uncooked* 670 adj.
**underdressed**
  *vulgar* 847 adj.
**underemployment**
  *superfluity* 637 n.
  *inaction* 677 n.
**under establishment**
  *unprovided* 636 adj.
**underestimate**
  *misjudge* 481 vb.
  *underestimate* 483 vb.
  *err* 495 vb.
  *misinterpret* 521 vb.
  *not respect* 921 vb.
  *detract* 926 vb.
**underestimation**
  *untruth* 543 n.
**underexpose**
  *darken* 418 vb.
**under false pretences**
  *falsely* 541 adv.
**underfed**
  *lean* 206 adj.

*underfed* 636 adj.
  *unhealthy* 651 adj.
  *poor* 801 adj.
  *hungry* 859 adj.
**under fire**
  *endangered* 661 adj.
  *in difficulties* 700 adj.
**underfoot**
  *low* 210 adj.
  *subjected* 745 adj.
**undergo**
  *meet with* 154 vb.
  *feel* 818 vb.
  *suffer* 825 vb.
**undergraduate**
  *student* 538 n.
  *immature* 670 adj.
**underground**
  *low* 210 adj.
  *deep* 211 adj.
  *tunnel* 263 n.
  *buried* 364 adj.
  *concealed* 525 adj.
  *hiding-place* 527 n.
  *opposition* 704 n.
  *revolter* 738 n.
**underground railway**
  *tunnel* 263 n.
  *railway* 624 n.
**undergrowth**
  *roughness* 259 n.
  *wood* 366 n.
**underhand**
  *occult* 523 adj.
  *stealthy* 525 adj.
  *dishonest* 930 adj.
**underhung**
  *projecting* 254 adj.
**under investigation**
  *on trial* 459 adv.
  *sub judice* 480 adv.
**underived**
  *original* 21 adj.
**underlay**
  *layer* 207 n.
  *base* 214 n.
**under licence**
  *by leave* 756 adv.
**underlie**
  *cause* 156 vb.
  *be low* 210 vb.
  *lurk* 523 vb.
**underline**
  *attract notice* 455 vb.
  *emphasize* 532 vb.
  *mark* 547 vb.
  *make important* 638 vb.
**underling**
  *inferior* 35 n.
  *nonentity* 639 n.
  *servant* 742 n.
  *commoner* 869 n.
**under lock and key**
  *safe* 660 adj.
  *captive* 750 adj.
**underlying**
  *undermost* 214 adj.

*unexpected* 508 adj.
*undue* 916 adj.
**unloose**
*disunite* 46 vb.
*deliver* 668 vb.
*liberate* 746 vb.
**unlovable,**
**unloveable**
*disliked* 861 adj.
*hateful* 888 adj.
**unloved**
*hated* 888 adj.
**unlovely**
*ugly* 842 adj.
*disliked* 861 adj.
**unloving**
*impassive* 820 adj.
*unkind* 898 adj.
**unluckily**
*by chance* 159 adv.
*amiss* 616 adv.
**unlucky**
*inopportune* 138 adj.
*evil* 616 adj.
*unsuccessful* 728 adj.
*unfortunate* 731 adj.
*unhappy* 825 adj.
*annoying* 827 adj.
**unlucky person**
*loser* 728 n.
*unlucky person* 731 n.
**unmade**
*unborn* 2 adj.
*amorphous* 244 adj.
**unmake**
*revert* 148 vb.
*destroy* 165 vb.
*abrogate* 752 vb.
**unmalleable**
*unconformable* 84 adj.
*rigid* 326 adj.
**unman**
*unman* 161 vb.
*make sterile* 172 vb.
*frighten* 854 vb.
**unmanageable**
*wilful* 602 adj.
*clumsy* 695 adj.
*difficult* 700 adj.
*disobedient* 738 adj.
**unmanifested**
*latent* 523 adj.
**unmanly**
*female* 373 adj.
*cowardly* 856 adj.
**unmannerly**
*ill-bred* 847 adj.
*discourteous* 885 adj.
**unmarked**
*undamaged* 646 adj.
**unmarketable**
*cheap* 812 adj.
**unmarried**
*unsociable* 883 adj.
*unwedded* 895 adj.
**unmarried mother**
*maternity* 169 n.

**unmarry**
*divorce* 896 vb.
**unmartial**
*cowardly* 856 adj.
**unmask**
*disclose* 526 vb.
**unmasterful**
*lax* 734 adj.
**unmatched**
*dissimilar* 19 adj.
*inimitable* 21 adj.
*best* 644 adj.
**unmated**
*unwedded* 895 adj.
**unmeaning**
*meaningless* 515 adj.
**unmeant**
*unmeant* 515 adj.
*unintentional* 618 adj.
**unmeasured**
*infinite* 107 adj.
*indiscriminate* 464 adj.
*plenteous* 635 adj.
*intemperate* 943 adj.
**unmediated**
*simple* 44 adj.
*continuous* 71 adj.
*intuitive* 476 adj.
**unmeditated**
*spontaneous* 609 adj.
**unmelodious**
*discordant* 411 adj.
**unmelting**
*pitiless* 906 adj.
**unmentionable**
*prohibited* 757 adj.
*discreditable* 867 adj.
*impure* 951 adj.
**unmentioned**
*tacit* 523 adj.
*inglorious* 867 adj.
**unmerciful**
*pitiless* 906 adj.
**unmerited**
*unwarranted* 916 adj.
**unmethodical**
*orderless* 61 adj.
**unmilitary**
*peaceful* 717 adj.
*cowardly* 856 adj.
**unmindful**
*inattentive* 456 adj.
*negligent* 458 adj.
*forgetful* 506 adj.
*ungrateful* 908 adj.
**unmissed**
*neglected* 458 adj.
*unwanted* 860 adj.
*hated* 888 adj.
**unmistakable, unmis-**
**takeable**
*visible* 443 adj.
*certain* 473 adj.
*intelligible* 516 adj.
*manifest* 522 adj.
**unmitigated**
*consummate* 32 adj.

*complete* 54 adj.
*violent* 176 adj.
*aggravated* 832 adj.
**unmixed**
*absolute* 32 adj.
*unmixed* 44 adj.
*whole* 52 adj.
*disinterested* 931 adj.
**unmodified**
*unmixed* 44 adj.
**unmolested**
*safe* 660 adj.
*content* 828 adj.
**unmoor**
*separate* 46 vb.
*navigate* 269 vb.
*start out* 296 vb.
**unmotivated**
*causeless* 159 adj.
*spontaneous* 609 adj.
**unmourned**
*hated* 888 adj.
**unmoved**
*quiescent* 266 adj.
*obstinate* 602 adj.
*apathetic* 820 adj.
*indifferent* 860 adj.
*unastonished* 865 adj.
*unkind* 898 adj.
*pitiless* 906 adj.
*impenitent* 940 adj.
**unmoving**
*still* 266 adj.
**unmusical**
*discordant* 411 adj.
*deaf* 416 adj.
*artless* 699 adj.
**unmuzzle**
*liberate* 746 vb.
**unnamed**
*unknown* 491 adj.
*concealed* 525 adj.
*anonymous* 562 adj.
**unnatural**
*disagreeing* 25 adj.
*extraneous* 59 adj.
*abnormal* 84 adj.
*impossible* 470 adj.
*inelegant* 576 adj.
*affected* 850 adj.
*cruel* 898 adj.
*unkind* 898 adj.
**unnavigable**
*shallow* 212 adj.
*impracticable* 470 adj.
*difficult* 700 adj.
**unnecessary**
*wasteful* 634 adj.
*superfluous* 637 adj.
*unimportant* 639 adj.
*useless* 641 adj.
*unused* 674 adj.
**unneeded**
*useless* 641 adj.
**unneighbourly**
*unsociable* 883 adj.
*ungracious* 885 adj.

*selfish* 932 adj.
**unnerve**
*unman* 161 vb.
*weaken* 163 vb.
*frighten* 854 vb.
**unnoticeable**
*inconsiderable* 33 adj.
*slow* 278 adj.
*invisible* 444 adj.
**unnoticed**
*invisible* 444 adj.
*neglected* 458 adj.
*inglorious* 867 adj.
**unnoticing**
*blind* 439 adj.
*inattentive* 456 adj.
**unnourishing**
*insufficient* 636 adj.
**unnumbered**
*many* 104 adj.
*infinite* 107 adj.
**unobjectionable**
*not bad* 644 adj.
*middling* 732 adj.
*contenting* 828 adj.
*vindicable* 927 adj.
*guiltless* 935 adj.
**unobliged**
*ungrateful* 908 adj.
**unobservant**
*blind* 439 adj.
*inattentive* 456 adj.
**unobserved**
*neglected* 458 adj.
**unobstructed**
*open* 263 adj.
*facilitated* 701 adj.
*unconfined* 744 adj.
**unobtainable**
*impracticable* 470 adj.
*scarce* 636 adj.
**unobtrusive**
*modest* 874 adj.
**unoccupied**
*empty* 190 adj.
*unthinking* 450 adj.
*nonactive* 677 adj.
*inactive* 679 adj.
*leisurely* 681 adj.
*free* 744 adj.
*unpossessed* 774 adj.
**unoffending**
*humble* 872 adj.
**unofficial**
*uncertified* 474 adj.
*independent* 744 adj.
*illegal* 954 adj.
**unoiled**
*strident* 407 adj.
**unopened**
*closed* 264 adj.
*unused* 674 adj.
**unopposed**
*assented* 488 adj.
**unordained**
*laical* 987 adj.
**unorganized**

*unceasing* 146 adj.
**unrevised**
  *inexact* 495 adj.
**unrevoked**
  *unceasing* 146 adj.
**unrewarded**
  *profitless* 641 adj.
  *unsuccessful* 728 adj.
  *unthanked* 908 adj.
**unrhythmical**
  *fitful* 142 adj.
**unriddle**
  *decipher* 520 vb.
**unrighteous**
  *wrong* 914 adj.
  *wicked* 934 adj.
**unrighteousness**
  *impiety* 980 n.
**unrightful**
  *unwarranted* 916 adj.
**unrigorous**
  *poorly reasoned* 477 adj.
  *inexact* 495 adj.
**unrip**
  *open* 263 vb.
**unripe**
  *incomplete* 55 adj.
  *young* 130 adj.
  *sour* 393 adj.
  *immature* 670 adj.
  *unskilled* 695 adj.
  *uncompleted* 726 adj.
**unrivalled**
  *supreme* 34 adj.
**unrobe**
  *uncover* 229 vb.
**unroll**
  *lengthen* 203 vb.
  *straighten* 249 vb.
  *evolve* 316 vb.
  *manifest* 522 vb.
  *disclose* 526 vb.
**unromantic**
  *true* 494 adj.
  *inexcitable* 823 adj.
**unroof**
  *uncover* 229 vb.
**unruffled**
  *orderly* 60 adj.
  *smooth* 258 adj.
  *tranquil* 266 adj.
  *impassive* 820 adj.
  *inexcitable* 823 adj.
  *amiable* 884 adj.
**unruly**
  *disorderly* 61 adj.
  *violent* 176 adj.
  *wilful* 602 adj.
  *anarchic* 734 adj.
  *disobedient* 738 adj.
  *riotous* 738 adj.
**unrumpled**
  *orderly* 60 adj.
**unsafe**
  *uncertain* 474 adj.
  *harmful* 645 adj.
  *unsafe* 661 adj.

**unsaid**
  *unknown* 491 adj.
  *tacit* 523 adj.
**unsalable, unsaleable**
  *profitless* 641 adj.
  *cheap* 812 adj.
**unsalaried**
  *uncharged* 812 adj.
**unsaluted**
  *unrespected* 921 adj.
**unsalvageable**
  *lost* 772 adj.
**unsanctified**
  *heathenish* 974 adj.
  *profane* 980 adj.
**unsanctioned**
  *unwarranted* 916 adj.
  *heterodox* 977 adj.
**unsatisfactory**
  *incomplete* 55 adj.
  *disappointing* 509 adj.
  *insufficient* 636 adj.
  *inexpedient* 643 adj.
  *bad* 645 adj.
  *unpleasant* 827 adj.
  *discontenting* 829 adj.
  *disapproved* 924 adj.
**unsatisfied**
  *unprovided* 636 adj.
  *discontented* 829 adj.
  *desiring* 859 adj.
  *greedy* 859 adj.
  *envious* 912 adj.
**unsavoury**
  *tasteless* 387 adj.
  *unsavoury* 391 adj.
  *unpleasant* 827 adj.
  *disliked* 861 adj.
**unsay**
  *recant* 603 adj.
**unscalable, unsca-**
  **leable**
  *impracticable* 470 adj.
**unscarred**
  *undamaged* 646 adj.
**unscathed**
  *undamaged* 646 adj.
**unscented**
  *odourless* 395 adj.
**unscholarly**
  *uninstructed* 491 adj.
**unschooled**
  *uninstructed* 491 adj.
**unscientific**
  *impossible* 470 adj.
  *illogical* 477 adj.
  *ignorant* 491 adj.
  *erroneous* 495 adj.
  *unskilled* 695 adj.
**unscramble**
  *simplify* 44 vb.
  *decompose* 51 vb.
  *unravel* 62 vb.
**unscratched**
  *undamaged* 646 adj.
**unscriptural**
  *erroneous* 495 adj.

  *heterodox* 977 adj.
**unscrupulous**
  *dishonest* 930 adj.
  *wicked* 934 adj.
**unseal**
  *disclose* 526 vb.
**unsearchable**
  *unintelligible* 517 adj.
**unseasonable**
  *unapt* 25 adj.
  *ill-timed* 138 adj.
  *inexpedient* 643 adj.
**unseasoned**
  *unmixed* 44 adj.
  *tasteless* 387 adj.
  *unhabituated* 611 adj.
  *immature* 670 adj.
**unseat**
  *unstick* 49 vb.
  *derange* 63 vb.
  *displace* 188 vb.
  *unthrone* 734 vb.
  *depose* 752 vb.
**unseeing**
  *insensible* 375 adj.
  *blind* 439 adj.
  *inattentive* 456 adj.
  *misjudging* 481 adj.
  *ignorant* 491 adj.
  *unwise* 499 adj.
  *impassive* 820 adj.
**unseemly**
  *unwise* 499 adj.
  *inexpedient* 643 adj.
  *unsightly* 842 adj.
  *wrong* 914 adj.
  *undue* 916 adj.
**unseen**
  *invisible* 444 adj.
  *unknown* 491 adj.
  *latent* 523 adj.
  *inglorious* 867 adj.
  *modest* 874 adj.
  *secluded* 883 adj.
**unsegregated**
  *indiscriminating* 464 adj.
  *designless* 618 adj.
**unselfish**
  *benevolent* 897 adj.
  *disinterested* 931 adj.
  *virtuous* 933 adj.
**unsensational**
  *plain* 573 adj.
**unsentimental**
  *impassive* 820 adj.
  *inexcitable* 823 adj.
**unserious**
  *witty* 839 adj.
**unserviceable**
  *useless* 641 adj.
**unsettle**
  *decompose* 51 vb.
  *derange* 63 vb.
  *impress* 821 vb.
**unsettled**
  *unstable* 152 adj.
  *displaced* 188 adj.

*empty* 190 adj.
  *travelling* 267 adj.
**unsevered**
  *intact* 52 adj.
**unsex**
  *unman* 161 vb.
**unsexed**
  *impotent* 161 adj.
**unshackle**
  *disencumber* 701 vb.
  *liberate* 746 vb.
**unshaded**
  *undimmed* 417 adj.
**unshakable,**
  **unshakeable**
  *firm* 45 adj.
  *fixed* 153 adj.
  *certain* 473 adj.
  *credal* 485 adj.
  *resolute* 599 adj.
  *retentive* 778 adj.
  *unfearing* 855 adj.
**unshapely**
  *amorphous* 244 adj.
  *unsightly* 842 adj.
**unshared**
  *possessed* 773 adj.
**unsharpened**
  *unsharpened* 257 adj.
**unshaven**
  *hairy* 259 adj.
**unsheathe**
  *uncover* 229 vb.
  *manifest* 522 vb.
**unshielded**
  *vulnerable* 661 adj.
**unshifting**
  *unceasing* 146 adj.
**unship**
  *displace* 188 vb.
  *empty* 300 vb.
**unshockable**
  *impassive* 820 adj.
**unshod**
  *uncovered* 229 adj.
**unshorn**
  *intact* 52 adj.
  *hairy* 259 adj.
**unshortened**
  *long* 203 adj.
**unshrinkable**
  *unchangeable* 153 adj.
**unshrinking**
  *resolute* 599 adj.
  *courageous* 855 adj.
  *unfearing* 855 adj.
**unshriven**
  *impenitent* 940 adj.
**unshut**
  *open* 263 adj.
**unsightly**
  *amorphous* 244 adj.
  *deformed* 246 adj.
  *unsightly* 842 adj.
**unsigned**
  *uncertified* 474 adj.
  *anonymous* 562 adj.

*water travel* 269 n.
*follower* 284 n.
*eddy* 350 n.
*obsequies* 364 n.
*trace* 548 n.
*be active* 678 vb.
*excite* 821 vb.
*lament* 836 n.
*festivity* 837 n.
*condolence* 905 n.
– up
*have feeling* 374 vb.
*be active* 678 vb.
**wakeboarding**
*aquatics* 269 n.
**wakeful**
*attentive* 455 adj.
*vigilant* 457 adj.
*active* 678 adj.
**wake-up call**
*warning* 664 n.
**Waldenses**
*heretic* 977 n.
**walk**
*state* 7 n.
*pleasance* 192 n.
*gait* 265 n.
*walking* 267 n.
*walk* 267 n.
*move slowly* 278 vb.
*appear* 445 vb.
*path* 624 n.
*conduct* 688 n.
*haunt* 970 vb.
– into the trap
*not expect* 508 vb.
*be duped* 544 vb.
– it
*win* 727 vb.
– off
*emerge* 298 vb.
– off with
*win* 727 vb.
*steal* 788 vb.
– off with all the prizes
*be good* 644 vb.
– out
*cease* 145 vb.
*decamp* 296 vb.
*relinquish* 621 vb.
*resist* 715 vb.
*deprecate* 762 vb.
*fail in duty* 918 vb.
– out on
*change one's mind*
603 vb.
– out with
*accompany* 89 vb.
*court* 889 vb.
– the plank
*plunge* 313 vb.
*perish* 361 vb.
**walkabout**
*walking* 267 n.
*wandering* 267 n.
**walked off one's feet**
*fatigued* 684 adj.

**walker**
*pedestrian* 268 n.
*traveller* 268 n.
**walkie-talkie**
*hearing instrument*
415 n.
*telecommunication*
531 n.
**walking encyclo-**
**paedia**
*scholar* 492 n.
*expert* 696 n.
**walking on air**
*pleased* 824 adj.
**walking stick**
*prop* 218 n.
**Walkman (tdmk)**
*record player* 414 n.
**walk of life**
*state* 7 n.
*vocation* 622 n.
*conduct* 688 n.
**walk-on part**
*acting* 594 n.
**walkout**
*strike* 145 n.
*departure* 296 n.
*dissent* 489 n.
*opposition* 704 n.
**walkover**
*easy thing* 701 n.
*victory* 727 n.
**walkthrough**
*dramaturgy* 594 n.
**walkup**
*flat* 192 n.
**wall**
*separation* 46 n.
*exclusion* 57 n.
*prop* 218 n.
*surroundings* 230 n.
*partition* 231 n.
*barrier* 235 n.
*solid body* 324 n.
*screen* 421 n.
*fortification* 713 n.
**wallaby**
*mammal* 365 n.
**wallah**
*worker* 686 n.
**wallet**
*case* 194 n.
*treasury* 799 n.
**wall-eyed**
*dim-sighted* 440 adj.
**wallflower**
*rejection* 607 n.
*indifference* 860 n.
**wallop**
*strike* 279 vb.
*alcoholic drink* 301 n.
*spank* 963 vb.
**walloping**
*whopping* 32 adj.
**wallow**
*be low* 210 vb.
*voyage* 269 vb.

*plunge* 313 vb.
*be agitated* 318 vb.
*weigh* 322 vb.
*be wet* 341 vb.
*marsh* 347 n.
*swill* 649 n.
*be unclean* 649 vb.
– in
*enjoy* 376 vb.
*abound* 635 vb.
*be pleased* 824 vb.
*be intemperate* 943 vb.
**wallower**
*dirty person* 649 n.
*sensualist* 944 n.
**wallpaper**
*covering* 226 n.
*lining* 227 n.
**wall plate**
*beam* 218 n.
**walls have ears**
*inquisitive person* 453 n.
**Wall Street**
*city* 184 n.
*market* 796 n.
**wall up**
*enclose* 235 vb.
*obstruct* 702 vb.
*imprison* 747 vb.
**wally**
*fool* 501 n.
**walnut**
*fruit* 301 n.
*tree* 366 n.
*brownness* 430 n.
**Walpurgisnacht**
*sorcery* 983 n.
**walrus**
*mammal* 365 n.
**Walter Mitty**
*inattention* 456 n.
**waltz**
*rotate* 315 vb.
*musical piece* 412 n.
*dance* 837 n., vb.
– away with
*win* 727 vb.
**wamble**
*oscillate* 317 vb.
**wampum**
*coinage* 797 n.
**wan**
*dim* 419 adj.
*colourless* 426 adj.
*melancholic* 834 adj.
*unsightly* 842 adj.
**wand**
*badge of rule* 743 n.
*magic instrument* 983 n.
**wander**
*be unrelated* 10 vb.
*be dispersed* 75 vb.
*wander* 267 vb.
*stray* 282 vb.
*be inattentive* 456 vb.
*be insane* 503 vb.
*be diffuse* 570 vb.

*be free* 744 vb.
**wanderer**
*displacement* 188 n.
*wanderer* 268 n.
*idler* 679 n.
**wandering**
*unstable* 152 adj.
*wandering* 267 n.
*designless* 618 adj.
*See also* **wander**
**wanderlust**
*wandering* 267 n.
**wane**
*decrease* 37 n., vb.
*become small* 198 vb.
*be dim* 419 vb.
*deteriorate* 655 vb.
**wangle**
*trickery* 542 n.
*contrivance* 623 n.
*be cunning* 698 vb.
*foul play* 930 n.
**wank**
*sexual pleasure* 376 n.
*have or give sexual plea-*
*sure* 376 vb.
**wannabe**
*hoper* 852 n.
*new* 126 adj.
**want**
*deficit* 55 n.
*shortfall* 307 n.
*require* 627 vb.
*scarcity* 636 n.
*be unsatisfied* 636 vb.
*imperfection* 647 n.
*adversity* 731 n.
*request* 761 n.
*poverty* 801 n.
*desire* 859 n., vb.
– one's own way
*be obstinate* 602 vb.
– to know
*be curious* 453 vb.
*enquire* 459 vb.
**wanted**
*absent* 190 adj.
*required* 627 adj.
**wanting**
*incomplete* 55 adj.
*absent* 190 adj.
*deficient* 307 adj.
*unintelligent* 499 adj.
*crazy* 503 adj.
*lost* 772 adj.
**wanton**
*changeful* 152 adj.
*capricious* 604 adj.
*free* 744 adj.
*amuse oneself* 837 vb.
*rash* 857 adj.
*unchaste* 951 adj.
*loose woman* 952 n.
**war**
*destroyer* 168 n.
*slaughter* 362 n.
*dissension* 709 n.

*missile weapon* 723 n.
**whoa!**
– 145 int.
– 266 int.
**whodunit**
*novel* 590 n.
**whole**
*finite quantity* 26 n.
*quantity* 26 n.
*simple* 44 adj.
*whole* 52 n.adj.
*completeness* 54 n.
*generality* 79 n.
*universal* 79 adj.
*numerical* 85 adj.
*unity* 88 n.
*undamaged* 646 adj.
*preserved* 666 adj.
**wholefood**
*food* 301 n.
*salubrity* 652 n.
**whole-hearted**
*simple* 44 adj.
*resolute* 599 adj.
**whole hog**
*completeness* 54 n.
*actively* 678 adv.
**wholemeal**
*cereals* 301 n.
**whole mind**
*attention* 455 n.
**wholesale**
*extensive* 32 adj.
*comprehensive* 52 adj.
*complete* 54 adj.
*inclusive* 78 adj.
*indiscriminate* 464 adj.
*plenteous* 635 adj.
*trading* 791 adj.
*sell* 793 vb.
**wholesale price**
*price* 809 n.
**wholesaler**
*seller* 793 n.
*merchant* 794 n.
**whole skin**
*health* 650 n.
**wholesome**
*nourishing* 301 adj.
*beneficial* 644 adj.
*healthy* 650 adj.
*salubrious* 652 adj.
*personable* 841 adj.
*ascetic* 945 adj.
**whole time, the**
*time* 108 n.
*while* 108 adv.
**whole truth**
*truth* 494 n.
*disclosure* 526 n.
**whole world over, the**
*widely* 183 adv.
**wholly**
*wholly* 52 adv.
*completely* 54 adv.
**whoop**
*loudness* 400 n.

*cry* 408 n., vb.
*be cheerful* 833 vb.
*rejoice* 835 vb.
**whoopee**
*revel* 837 n.
**whooping cough**
*respiration* 352 n.
*infection* 651 n.
*respiratory disease* 651 n.
**whopper**
*whopper* 195 n.
*untruth* 543 n.
**whore**
*prostitute* 952 n.
**whorehouse**
*brothel* 951 n.
**whoremonger**
*libertine* 952 n.
**whorl**
*weaving* 222 n.
*coil* 251 n.
**whosoever**
*everyman* 79 n.
**Who's Who**
*directory* 87 n.
**why?**
*why* 158 adv.
– 435 int.
**why and wherefore,**
**the**
*reason why* 156 n.
**whydunit**
*novel* 590 n.
**Wicca**
*religion* 973 n.
**Wiccan festivals**
*holy day* 988 n. box
**wick**
*filament* 208 n.
*lighter* 385 n.
*torch* 420 n.
**wicked**
*great* 32adj
*evil* 616 adj.
*excellent* 644adj
*bad* 645 adj.
*difficult* 700 adj.
*wrong* 914 adj.
*dishonest* 930 adj.
*wicked* 934 adj.
*guilty* 936 adj.
*impenitent* 940 adj.
*lawbreaking* 954 adj.
*irreligious* 974 adj.
*impious* 980 adj.
**wicked fairy**
*sorceress* 983 n.
**wickedness**
*deterioration* 655 n.
*disobedience* 738 n.
*disrepute* 867 n.
*inhumanity* 898 n.
*evildoer* 904 n.
*offender* 904 n.
*wickedness* 934 n.
*See also* **wicked**
**wickerwork**

*basket* 194 n.
*network* 222 n.
**wicket**
*doorway* 263 n.
**wicket-keeper**
*player* 837 n.
**widdershins**
*towards* 281 adv.
*round and round*
315 adv.
**wide**
*great* 32 adj.
*spacious* 183 adj.
*distant* 199 adj.
*broad* 205 adj.
*deviating* 282 adj.
*mistaken* 495 adj.
**wide-angle lens**
*optical device* 442 n.
**wide apart**
*different* 15 adj.
**wide-awake**
*attentive* 455 adj.
*vigilant* 457 adj.
**wide berth**
*avoidance* 620 n.
*safety* 660 n.
*scope* 744 n.
**wide-bodied**
*broad* 205 adj.
**wide circulation**
*publicity* 528 n.
**wide-eyed**
*wondering* 864 adj.
*innocent* 935 adj.
**wide horizons**
*space* 183 n.
**widely**
*greatly* 32 adv.
*throughout* 54 adv.
*widely* 183 adv.
*afar* 199 adv.
**widely held**
*orthodox* 976 adj.
**widen**
*augment* 36 vb.
*generalize* 79 vb.
*enlarge* 197 vb.
*expand* 197 vb.
*be broad* 205 vb.
– *the breach*
*make quarrels* 709 vb.
**wide of**
*beyond* 199 adv.
**wide of the mark**
*deviating* 282 adj.
*astray* 282 adv.
*erroneous* 495 adj.
**wide open**
*expanded* 197 adj.
*open* 263 adj.
*vulnerable* 661 adj.
*unconditional* 744 adj.
**wide-ranging**
*extensive* 32 adj.
*broad* 205 adj.
**wide reading**

*erudition* 490 n.
*learning* 536 n.
**widespread**
*extensive* 32 adj.
*comprehensive* 52 adj.
*unassembled* 75 adj.
*universal* 79 adj.
*spacious* 183 adj.
*expanded* 197 adj.
*usual* 610 adj.
**widgeon, wigeon**
*bird* 365 n.
**widow**
*survivor* 41 n.
*deprive* 786 vb.
*widowhood* 896 n.
*widow* 896 vb.
**widower**
*survivor* 41 n.
*widowhood* 896 n.
**widow-maker**
*means of execution*
964 n.
**widow's mite**
*small coin* 33 n.
*offering* 781 n.
**widow's peak**
*hair* 259 n.
**widow's weeds**
*formal dress* 228 n.
*badge* 547 n.
*lamentation* 836 n.
*widowhood* 896 n.
**width**
*quantity* 26 n.
*size* 195 n.
*breadth* 205 n.
**wield**
*operate* 173 vb.
*touch* 378 vb.
*use* 673 vb.
**wife**
*woman* 373 n.
*spouse* 894 n.
**wifehood**
*marriage* 894 n.
**wifeless**
*unwedded* 895 adj.
*widowed* 896 adj.
**wifely**
*loving* 887 adj.
*matrimonial* 894 adj.
**wife-swapping**
*illicit love* 951 n.
**wig**
*wig* 228 n.
*hair* 259 n.
*hairdressing* 843 n.
**wigeon, group of**
*group* 74 n. box
**wigging**
*reprimand* 924 n.
**wiggle**
*oscillate* 317 vb.
**wigwam**
*dwelling* 192 n.
**wild**

*debt* 803 n.
**writer**
  *recorder* 549 n.
  *calligrapher* 586 n.
  *author* 589 n.
  *dissertator* 591 n.
**write-up**
  *publicity* 528 n.
  *article* 591 n.
**writhe**
  *distort* 246 vb.
  *wriggle* 251 vb.
  *leap* 312 vb.
  *be agitated* 318 vb.
  *feel pain* 377 vb.
  *be excited* 821 vb.
  *suffer* 825 vb.
**writing**
  *composition* 56 n.
  *production* 164 n.
  *writing* 586 n.
  *reading matter* 589 n.
**writing on the wall**
  *omen* 511 n.
  *warning* 664 n.
  *danger signal* 665 n.
  *threat* 900 n.
**writing paper**
  *stationery* 586 n.
**written**
  *recorded* 548 adj.
  *literary* 557 adj.
  *written* 586 adj.
**written all over one**
  *manifest* 522 adj.
**written character**
  *letter* 558 n.
**written testimonial**
  *approbation* 923 n.
**WRNS**
  *naval man* 722 n.
**wrong**
  *unapt* 25 adj.
  *misjudging* 481 adj.
  *erroneous* 495 adj.
  *evil* 616 n adj
  *amiss* 616 adv.
  *inexpedient* 643 adj.
  *ill-treat* 645 vb.
  *wrong* 914 n.adj.
  *do wrong* 914 vb.
  *unwarranted* 916 adj.
  *foul play* 930 n.
  *dishonest* 930 adj.
  *wickedness* 934 n.
  *heinous* 934 adj.
  *lawbreaking* 954 n.
**wrongdoer**
  *evildoer* 904 n.
  *offender* 904 n.
  *wrong* 914 n.
**wrongdoing**
  *wickedness* 934 n.
  *lawbreaking* 954 n.
**wrong end of the stick**
  *misinterpretation* 521 n.

**wrongful**
  *bad* 645 adj.
  *wrong* 914 adj.
  *illegal* 954 adj.
**wrong-headed**
  *misjudging* 481 adj.
  *erroneous* 495 adj.
  *unintelligent* 499 adj.
  *wrong* 914 adj.
**wrongheadedness**
  *obstinacy* 602 n.
**wrong idea**
  *error* 495 n.
**wrong impression**
  *misjudgment* 481 n.
  *mistake* 495 n.
**wrong side**
  *contrariety* 14 n.
  *rear* 238 n.
  *opposition* 704 n.
**wrong side of the law**
  *illegality* 954 n.
**wrong side out**
  *reversibly* 148 adv.
  *inverted* 221 adj.
**wrong 'un**
  *bad person* 938 n.
**wrong verdict**
  *misjudgment* 481 n.
  *injustice* 914 n.
**wrought**
  *elegant* 575 adj.
  *matured* 669 adj.
**wrought iron**
  *hardness* 326 n.
  *ornamental art* 844 n.
**wrought up**
  *excited* 821 adj.
  *angry* 891 adj.
**wry**
  *oblique* 220 adj.
  *distorted* 246 adj.
**Wycliffite**
  *heretic* 977 n.
**wynd**
  *road* 624 n.
**wyvern**
  *mythical beast* 365 n.

# X

**x**
  *number* 85 n.
  *indication* 547 n.
**Xanthippe**
  *shrew* 892 n.
**X certificate**
  *film* 445 n.
**xebec**
  *sailing ship* 275 n.
**xenophile**
  *xenophile* 880 n.
**xenophobe**
  *enemy* 881 n.
**xenophobia**
  *prejudice* 481 n.

*phobia* 854 n. box
  *dislike* 861 n.
  *hatred* 888 n.
**xenotransplant**
  *substitute* 150 n.
  *surgery* 658 n.
**xerox**
  *copy* 20 vb.
  *double* 91 vb.
**Xerox (tdmk)**
  *copy* 22 n.
  *duplication* 91 n.
  *reproduction* 166 n.
  *recording instrument* 549 n.
**X-rated**
  *grown-up* 134 adj.
**X-ray**
  *radiation* 417 n.
  *enquire* 459 vb.
  *photography* 551 n.
**X-shape**
  *crossing* 222 n.
**xylography**
  *engraving* 555 n.
**xylophone**
  *gong* 414 n.

---

# Y

**yacht**
  *sailing ship* 275 n.
  *boat* 275 n.
**yachting**
  *aquatics* 269 n.
  *water travel* 269 n.
  *sport* 837 n.
**yachtsman, yachtswoman**
  *boatman* 270 n.
**yackety-yack**
  *empty talk* 515 n.
  *loquacity* 581 n.
**yahoo**
  *low fellow* 869 n.
**Yahweh**
  *the Deity* 965 n.
**yak**
  *cattle* 365 n.
  *mean nothing* 515 vb.
  *be loquacious* 581 vb.
**Yale (tdmk) lock**
  *stopper* 264 n.
**yam**
  *vegetable* 301 n.
**yammer**
  *cry* 408 vb.
  *weep* 836 vb.
**yammering**
  *empty talk* 515 n.
**yank**
  *draw* 288 vb.
**Yank, Yankee**
  *foreigner* 59 n.
**yap**
  *cry* 408 vb.

*ululate* 409 vb.
**yarborough**
  *misfortune* 731 n.
**yard**
  *place* 185 n.
  *long measure* 203 n.
  *prop* 218 n.
  *enclosure* 235 n.
  *open space* 263 n.
  *workshop* 687 n.
**yardarm**
  *prop* 218 n.
**yardstick**
  *prototype* 23 n.
  *counting instrument* 86 n.
  *testing agent* 461 n.
  *gauge* 465 n.
**yarn**
  *fibre* 208 n.
  *news* 529 n.
  *fable* 543 n.
  *exaggeration* 546 n.
  *be diffuse* 570 vb.
  *narrative* 590 n.
  *materials* 631 n.
**yarn spinner**
  *liar* 545 n.
  *narrator* 590 n.
**yashmak**
  *headgear* 228 n.
**yaw**
  *vary* 152 vb.
  *navigate* 269 vb.
  *deviation* 282 n.
**yawl**
  *sailing ship* 275 n.
  *cry* 408 n., vb.
  *ululate* 409 vb.
**yawn**
  *open* 263 vb.
  *respiration* 352 n.
  *sleep* 679 vb.
  *be fatigued* 684 vb.
**yawning**
  *deep* 211 adj.
  *opening* 263 n.
  *sleepy* 679 adj.
**yawning gulf**
  *gap* 201 n.
**yawp**
  *stridor* 407 n.
  *ululation* 409 n.
**yaws**
  *skin disease* 651 n.
  *tropical disease* 651 n.
**yea**
  *assent* 488 n.
**year**
  *date* 108 n.
  *period* 110 n.
  *contemporary* 123 n.
**yearbook**
  *reference book* 589 n.
**year in year out**
  *repeatedly* 106 adv.
  *all along* 113 adv.

**yowl**
  *cry* 408 vb.
  *ululate* 409 vb.
**yoyo**
  *oscillation* 317 n.
  *plaything* 837 n.
**yoyo, like a**
  *to and fro* 317 adv.
**Y-shape**
  *divergence* 294 n.
**Yuga**
  *era* 110 n.
**yuk**
  *dirt* 649 n.
**yuk!**
  – 391 int.
  – 861 int.
**Yule, Yuletide**
  *winter* 129 n.
  *holy day* 988 n. box
**yummy**
  *savoury* 390 adj.
**yuppy**
  *modernist* 126 n.

---

## Z

**zany**
  *fool* 501 n.
  *humorist* 839 n.
  *funny* 849 adj.
  *laughingstock* 851 n.
**zap**
  *spurt* 277 n.
  *move fast* 277 vb.
  *cook* 301vb.
**zareba**
  *enclosure* 235 n.
  *fort* 713 n.
**Z-bend**
  *obliquity* 220 n.
  *curve* 248 n.
**zeal**
  *keenness* 174 n.
  *willingness* 597 n.
  *resolution* 599 n.
  *warm feeling* 818 n.
  *desire* 859 n.
  *piety* 979 n.
**zealot**
  *doctrinaire* 473 n.
  *narrow mind* 481 n.
  *enthusiast* 504 n.
  *obstinate person*
    602 n.
  *busy person* 678 n.
  *religionist* 973 n.
  *zealot* 979 n.
**zealous**
  *willing* 597 adj.
  *resolute* 599 adj.
  *active* 678 adj.
  *fervent* 818 adj.
**zebra**
  *mammal* 365 n.
  *stripe* 437 n.

**zebra crossing**
  *traffic control* 305 n.
  *access* 624 n.
**zebu**
  *cattle* 365 n.
**Zeitgeist**
  *tendency* 179 n.
**zemstvo**
  *council* 692 n.
**Zen**
  *philosophy* 449 n.
  *religious faith* 973 n.
**zenana**
  *womankind* 373 n.
**Zen Buddhist**
  *religionist* 973 n.
**Zend-Avesta**
  *scripture* 975 n. box
**zenith**
  *superiority* 34 n.
  *serial place* 73 n.
  *height* 209 n.
  *summit* 213 n.
  *perfection* 646 n.
**zenith distance**
  *angular measure*
    247 n.
**zephyr**
  *breeze* 352 n.
**Zeppelin**
  *airship* 276 n.
**zero**
  *insubstantiality* 4 n.
  *quantity* 26 n.
  *smallness* 33 n.
  *zero* 103 n.
  *not one* 103 adj.
  *coldness* 380 n.
  – in on
  *focus* 76 vb.
  *centralize* 225 vb.
  *converge* 293 vb.
  *aim at* 617 vb.
**zero-based budgeting**
  *accounts* 808 n.
**zero-emission vehicle**
  *car* 274 n.
  *cleanness* 648 n.
**zero hour**
  *start* 68 n.
  *date* 108 n.
  *departure* 296 n.
**zero option**
  *necessity* 596 n.
  *no choice* 606 n.
**zero-rated**
  *uncharged* 812 adj.
**zero-rated goods**
  *tax* 809 n.
**zero tolerance**
  *severity* 735 n.
  *pitilessness* 906 n.
  *punishment* 963 n.
**zest**
  *vigorousness* 174 n.
  *pleasure* 376 n.
  *taste* 386 n.

*enjoyment* 824 n.
  *pleasurableness* 826 n.
  *liking* 859 n.
**zestful**
  *vigorous* 174 adj.
  *savoury* 390 adj.
**zesty**
  *pungent* 388 adj.
**zetetic**
  *enquiring* 459 adj.
**zeugma**
  *trope* 519 n.
  *ornament* 574 n.
**Zeus**
  *Olympian deity* 967 n.
**ziggurat**
  *temple* 990 n.
**zigzag**
  *obliquity* 220 n.
  *be oblique* 220 vb.
  *angularity* 247 n.
  *angular* 247 adj.
  *meander* 251 vb.
  *deviating* 282 adj.
  *deviate* 282 vb.
  *to and fro* 317 adv.
  *pattern* 844 n.
**zilch**
  *nonexistence* 2 n.
  *insubstantiality* 4 n.
  *zero* 103 n.
**zillion(s)**
  *over one hundred* 99 n.
  *multitude* 104 n.
  *funds* 797 n.
  *wealth* 800 n.
**zincography**
  *engraving* 555 n.
**zing**
  *vigorousness* 174 n.
  *spurt* 277 n.
  *move fast* 277 vb.
**zingy**
  *vigorous* 174 adj.
  *forceful* 571 adj.
**Zion**
  *focus* 76 n.
  *heaven* 971 n.
  *holy place* 990 n.
**Zionist**
  *patriot* 901 n.
**zip**
  *fastening* 47 n.
  *energy* 160 n.
  *vigorousness* 174 n.
  *move fast* 277 vb.
  – up
  *join* 45 vb.
  *wear* 228 vb.
  *close* 264 vb.
**zippy**
  *vigorous* 174 adj.
**zircon**
  *gem* 844 n.
**zither**
  *stringed instrument*
    414 n.

**zloty**
  *coinage* 797 n. box
**zodiac**
  *circle* 250 n.
  *zodiac* 321 n.
**zodiacal**
  *celestial* 321 adj.
**zodiacal light**
  *heavens* 321 n.
  *glow* 417 n.
**zombie**
  *alcoholic drink* 301 n.
  *corpse* 363 n.
  *fool* 501 n.
  *ghost* 970 n.
**zone**
  *disunion* 46 n.
  *set apart* 46 vb.
  *region* 184 n.
  *territory* 184 n.
  *layer* 207 n.
  *land* 344 n.
  *apportion* 783 vb.
**zone parking**
  *passing along* 305 n.
**zonked**
  *drugged* 949 adj.
**zoo**
  *medley* 43 n.
  *zoo* 369 n.
  *collection* 632 n.
**zoological**
  *biological* 358 adj.
  *animal* 365 adj.
  *zoological* 367 adj.
**zoologist**
  *zoologist* 367 n.
**zoology**
  *biology* 358 n.
  *study* 536 n. box
**zoom**
  *spurt* 277 n.
  *ascent* 308 n.
  *ascend* 308 vb.
  *photography* 551 n.
**zoom lens**
  *optical device* 442 n.
**zoomorphism**
  *animality* 365 n.
  *idolatry* 982 n.
**zoophyte**
  *microorganism* 196 n.
  *animal* 365 n.
**zoot suit**
  *suit* 228 n.
**Zoroaster/
    Zarathustra**
  *religious teacher* 973 n.
**Zoroastrianism**
  *religious faith* 973 n.
**Zoroastrian
    scriptures**
  *scripture* 975 n. box
**Zouave**
  *infantry* 722 n.
**zucchetto**
  *canonicals* 989 n.